www.wadsworth.com

wadsworth.com is the World Wide Web site for Wadsworth and is your direct source to dozens of online resources.

At *wadsworth.com* you can find out about supplements, demonstration software, and student resources. You can also send email to many of our authors and preview new publications and exciting new technologies.

wadsworth.com
Changing the way the world learns®

*The Gateway Arch on the Missis-
sippi River in St. Louis, Missouri,
designed by architect: Eero Saarinen.
This tallest man-made monument in
the nation was visited by more than
4 million people in 1999.*

DENNIS COON

INTRODUCTION TO

PSYCHOLOGY

GATEWAYS TO MIND

AND BEHAVIOR

NINTH EDITION

WADSWORTH

THOMSON LEARNING

Australia • Canada • Mexico • Singapore Spain • United Kingdom • United States

WADSWORTH

THOMSON LEARNING

Executive Editor: Lisa Gebo
Development Editor: Jim Strandberg
Assistant Editor: Jennifer Wilkinson
Editorial Assistants: JoAnne von Zastrow, Sheila Walsh
Marketing Manager: Jenna Opp
Project Editor: Tanya Nigh
Print Buyer: Karen Hunt
Permissions Editor: Robert Kauser
Production Service: Graphic World Publishing Services

Text Designer: Norman Baugher
Art Editor: Bruce Siebert
Photo Researcher: Sue C. Howard
Copy Editor: Joy Matkowski
Cover Designer: Norman Baugher
Cover Printer: Phoenix Color
Compositor: Graphic World Inc.
Printer: RR Donnelley & Sons, Willard

Wadsworth/Thomson Learning
10 Davis Drive
Belmont, CA 94002-3098
USA

For more information about our products, contact us:
Thomson Learning Academic Resource Center
1-800-423-0563
http://www.wadsworth.com

International Headquarters
Thomson Learning
International Division
290 Harbor Drive, 2nd Floor
Stamford, CT 06902-7477
USA

UK/Europe/Middle East/South Africa
Thomson Learning
Berkshire House
168-173 High Holborn
London WC1V 7AA
United Kingdom

Asia
Thomson Learning
60 Albert Street, #15-01
Albert Complex
Singapore 189969

Canada
Nelson Thomson Learning
1120 Birchmount Road
Toronto, Ontario M1K 5G4
Canada

FOR MY PARENTS

After earning a doctorate in psychology from the University of Arizona, Dennis Coon taught for 22 years at Santa Barbara City College, California. Throughout his career, Dr. Coon has especially enjoyed the challenge of teaching introductory psychology. He and his wife Sevren recently returned to Tucson, where he continues to teach, write, edit, and consult.

Dr. Coon is the author of **Introduction to Psychology,** as well as **Essentials of Psychology.** Together, these texts have been used by over 2 million students. Dr. Coon frequently serves as a reviewer and consultant to publishers, and he edited the best-selling trade book, **Choices.** He also helped design modules for **PsychNow!,** Wadsworth's interactive CD-ROM.

In his leisure hours, Dr. Coon enjoys hiking, photography, painting, woodworking, and music. He also designs, builds, and plays classical and steel string acoustic guitars. He has published articles on guitar design and occasionally offers lectures on this topic, in addition to his more frequent presentations on psychology. His recent return to Arizona has made it possible for him to fulfill a lifelong dream of using operant conditioning to teach scorpions to tap dance.

My first psychology course was taught by a woman whose intellect, warmth, and wisdom had a lot to do with my decision to major in psychology. In the years that followed, I was inspired and challenged by other gifted teachers. Their voices, as well as my own, can be heard throughout this book.

Brief Contents

Contents

CHAPTER 4 · CHILD DEVELOPMENT   83

CHAPTER 9 · CONDITIONING AND LEARNING 274

Preview: What Did You Learn in School Today? 275

CHAPTER 10 · MEMORY 310

Preview: "What the Hell's Going on Here?" 311

CHAPTER 11 · COGNITION, LANGUAGE, AND CREATIVITY   343

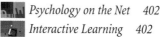

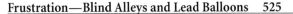

CHAPTER 16 · HEALTH, STRESS, AND COPING   517

CHAPTER 18 · THERAPIES 596

Preface to the Ninth Edition

TO THE STUDENT

Psychology is an exciting field. It is at once familiar, exotic, surprising, and challenging. Most of all, psychology is changing. Indeed, this book can be no more than a "snapshot" of a colorful passing scene. And yet, change makes psychology especially fascinating: What, really, could be more intriguing than our evolving understanding of human behavior?

Psychology is about each of us. Psychology asks, "How can we step outside of ourselves for a more objective look at how we live, think, and act?" Psychologists believe the answer is through careful thought, observation, and inquiry. As simple as that may seem, it is the guiding light for everything that follows in this book.

Gateways to Psychology

I sincerely hope that you will find human behavior as fascinating as I do. In this text, I have done all that I could imagine to make your first encounter with psychology enjoyable and worthwhile. At the beginning of every chapter, you will find a list of *Gateways to Psychology.* These "big ideas" and enduring principles are the very heart of psychology.

The first time you read a chapter, you shouldn't feel obligated to memorize the Gateway concepts. However, you should take a moment to think about each one before you continue reading. Doing so will provide an overview to help you keep your bearings as you read. Most likely, you'll find it easier to remember the details of psychology if you can relate them to a framework of major concepts. Later, you can use the Gateways to review the most important points in each chapter. Eventually, the Gateways will provide a good summary of what you have learned in this course. The Gateway concepts can forever transform the way you see yourself and the behavior of others. If you make them a part of your knowledge, you will gain something of lasting value: You will learn how to view human behavior as a psychologist would.

GETTING STARTED   To help you get off to a good start, a short Introduction precedes Chapter 1. The Introduction describes study skills you can use to get the most out of this text and your psychology course. It also tells how you can use the Internet, electronic databases, and interactive CDs to further explore the realm of psychology.

In the chapters that follow, I hope the delight I have found in my own students' curiosity, insights, imagination, and interests will be apparent. Please view this book as a long letter from me to you. It is, in a very real sense, written about you, for you, and to you.

TO THE INSTRUCTOR

This book is designed to promote an interest in human behavior, to foster an appreciation for human diversity, to facilitate learning, and to encourage critical thinking. If you are already familiar with its format, a brief summary of ninth edition changes follow shortly. If the text is unfamiliar, a brief sketch of its design and underlying philosophy appears here.

A Book for Students

Selecting a textbook is half the battle in teaching a successful course. A good text does much of the work of imparting information to students. This frees class time for discussion or media presentations, and it leaves students asking for more. When a book overwhelms students or cools their interest, teaching and learning become uphill battles. For this reason, I have worked hard to make this a clear, readable, and interesting text.

I believe an important question to ask about the introductory course is, "What will students remember next year? Or in 10 years?" Consequently, *Introduction to Psychology* gives students a clear grasp of major concepts, without burying them in details. At the same time, it provides a broad overview that reflects psychology's diversity. I think students will find this book informative and intellectually challenging. In addition, I have made a special effort to relate psychology to the practical problems of daily life.

A major feature of this book is the *Psychology in Action* section found in each chapter. These high-interest features bridge the gap between theory and practical applications. I believe students are justified in asking, "Does this mean anything to me? Can I use it? Why should I learn it if I can't?" The Psychology in Action feature spells out how students can use the principles of psychology. By doing so, they breathe life into its concepts.

At the end of each chapter, students will also find a section called *A Step Beyond.* These short discussions cover controversies, current issues, cutting-edge topics, or subjects likely to promote critical thinking. In essence, they serve as brief, high-interest articles within the text. My goal in the A Step Beyond features is to provide a taste of changing issues and ideas in psychology.

To encourage broader explorations, inquiring readers will find a section called *Psychology on the Net* at the end of each chapter. The URLs listed there will take students to interesting sites on the Internet. Each list also directs students to relevant articles in *InfoTrac® College Edition,* Wadsworth's exclusive on-line college library. InfoTrac® College Edition is available at no extra charge with new copies of the text for North America-based adoptions. Finally, all chapters conclude with a list of relevant modules in *Psyk.trek* and *PsychNow!*. *PsychNow!* is a text-specific CD-ROM from Wadsworth Publishing which offers an exciting assortment of interactive learning experiences.

A Format for Learning

Before this book first appeared, psychology texts made surprisingly little use of cognitive principles to teach psychology. I have employed many learning aids in this text because I believe that students can be guided into more effective study and reading habits while learning psychology. Each chapter in *Introduction to Psychology* includes the following elements:

Chapter Survey	**A Step Beyond**
Theme	Guide Questions
Key Questions	**Bridges**
Key Topics	Figures
Preview	Tables
Gateways	Integrated Glossary
Major Topics	Running Glossary
Guide Questions	**Knowledge Builder**
Bridges	Relate
Figures	Learning Check
Tables	Critical Thinking
Integrated Glossary	Answers
Running Glossary	**Chapter in Review**
Highlights	Key Questions
Knowledge Builders	Point-by-Point Summary
Relate	**Psychology on the Net**
Learning Check	Web Site URLs
Critical Thinking	InfoTrac® College Edition
Answers	**Interactive Learning**
Psychology in Action	*PsychNow!* Modules
Guide Questions	*Psyk.trek* Modules
Bridges	
Figures	
Tables	
Integrated Glossary	
Running Glossary	
Knowledge Builder	
Relate	
Learning Check	
Critical Thinking	
Answers	

How the Chapter Design Supports the SQ4R Method

Each chapter of this text is built around the SQ4R study-reading formula. In addition to helping students learn psychology, this format promotes valuable study skills. Notice how the steps of the SQ4R method—*survey, question, read, recite, relate,* and *review*—are incorporated into the chapter design.

SURVEY   To begin, a full-page Chapter Survey provides an overview of upcoming topics. The Chapter Survey states the Theme, or main message, of the chapter. It also relates Key Questions to Key Topics that will appear in the chapter. Next, a short, high-interest Preview focuses attention on the task at hand so that students will read with a purpose. To complete the initial survey, a list of Gateway concepts summarizes the most important ideas covered in the chapter. These are the "take home" ideas every student should be able to remember 10 years after reading this text.

QUESTION   Throughout each chapter, italicized Guide Questions serve as advance organizers. That is, Guide Questions prompt students to look for important ideas as they read. In doing so, they promote active learning. They also establish a dialogue in which the questions and reactions of students are anticipated. This clarifies difficult points—in a lively give-and-take between questions and responses.

READ   I've made every effort to make this a clear, readable text. To further aid comprehension, I've used a full array of traditional learning aids. These include boldface terms (with phonetic pronunciations), bullet summaries, a robust illustration program, summary tables, a name index, a subject index, and a detailed glossary. As an additional aid, figure and table references in the text are marked with small geometric shapes. These "place-holders" make it easier for students to return to reading after they have paused to view a table or figure.

An Integrated Glossary aids reading comprehension by providing precise definitions directly in context. When important terms first appear, they are immediately defined. In this way, students get clear definitions when and where they need them—in the general text itself. In addition, a parallel Running Glossary defines key terms in the lower margin of right-hand pages. The Running Glossary makes it easier for students to find, study, and review important terms.

Several times per chapter, boxed highlights discuss recent research, interesting topics, original viewpoints, and human diversity. Highlights are stimulating but nonintrusive supplements to the main text. They enrich the presentation and encourage critical thinking.

RECITE   Every few pages, a Knowledge Builder provides opportunities for students to test their understanding and recall of preceding topics. The Knowledge Builders are practically a built-in study guide. Each includes a Learning Check, which is a short, noncomprehensive quiz. Learning Checks help students actively process information and assess their progress. Students who miss any questions are encouraged to backtrack and clarify their understanding before reading more. Completing Learning Checks serves as a form of recitation to enhance learning.

RELATE   Cognitive psychology tells us that elaborative rehearsal is one of the best ways to form lasting memories. Elaborative rehearsal increases the meaningfulness of new information by relating it to existing, familiar knowledge. To help students practice elaborative rehearsal, each Knowledge Builder includes a series of "Relate" questions. These questions encourage students to associate new concepts with meaningful personal experiences and prior knowledge.

By necessity, topics tend to be compartmentalized in textbooks. The new Bridges featured in this edition are designed to help students make connections between widely separated topics. Again, interrelating information gives it greater meaning and helps students deepen their knowledge of psychology.

A course in psychology naturally contributes to the development of critical thinking abilities. To further facilitate critical thinking, each Knowledge Builder also includes one or more Critical Thinking questions. These stimulating questions challenge students to think critically and analytically about psychology. Each is followed by a brief answer with which students can compare their own thoughts. Many of these answers are based on research and are informative in their own right.

REVIEW   As noted previously, all important terms appear in a Running Glossary throughout the book, which aids review. As also noted, a Psychology in Action section completes each chapter. Each Psychology in Action feature shows students how psychological concepts relate to practical problems, including problems in their own lives. The information found in Psychology in Action sections helps reinforce learning by illustrating psychology's practicality. The chapter-ending A Step Beyond articles also encourage students to review and extend the ideas they have learned.

Next, a point-by-point summary provides a concise synopsis of all major concepts. The Chapter in Review summary is organized around the same Key Questions found in the Chapter Survey. This brings the SQ4R process full-circle and provides closure with respect to the learning objectives of each chapter.

Critical Thinking

The active, questioning nature of the SQ4R method is, in itself, an inducement to think critically. Many of the Guide Questions that introduce topics in the text act as models of critical thinking. More important, Chapter 1 contains a brief discussion of critical thinking skills and a rational appraisal of pseudo-psychologies. The presentation of research methods in Chapter 2 is actually a short course on how to think clearly about behavior. It is supplemented by suggestions about how to critically evaluate claims in the popular media. Chapter 11, "Cognition, Intelligence, and Creativity," discusses many topics that focus on thinking skills. Throughout the text, many boxed highlights promote critical thinking about topics that students should approach with healthy skepticism. In addition, many A Step Beyond articles critically evaluate controversial topics. As mentioned earlier, every Knowledge Builder includes Critical Thinking questions. Taken together, these features will help students gain thinking skills of lasting value.

Human Diversity

Student populations increasingly reflect the multicultural, multifaceted nature of contemporary society. In the ninth edition of *Introduction to Psychology* students will find numerous discussions of human diversity, including differences in race, ethnicity, culture, gender, abilities, sexual orientation, and age. Too often, such differences needlessly divide people into opposing groups. My aim throughout the text is to discourage stereotyping, prejudice, discrimination, and intolerance. Many topics and examples in this edition encourage students to appreciate social, physical, and cultural differences and to accept them as a natural part of being human. The topics listed in ◆Table 1 illustrate the diversity content to be found in this edition (page numbers are shown in parentheses).

Positive Psychology

In January 2000, Martin E. P. Seligman and Mihaly Csikszentmihalyi co-edited a special issue of *American Psychologist* devoted to optimal functioning, happiness, and "positive psychology." Over the past 100 years, psychologists have paid ample attention to the negative side of human behavior. This is easy to understand because of the need to find remedies for human problems. However, Seligman and Csikszentmihalyi have urged us to also study positive psychology. What do we know, for instance, about love, happiness, creativity, well-being, self-confidence, and achievement? Throughout this edition, I have attempted to answer such questions for students. ◆Table 2 identifies some of the topics in positive psychology found in this text (page numbers are in parentheses). My hope is that students who read this book will gain an appreciation for the potential we all have for optimal functioning. Also, of course, I hope that they will leave introductory psychology with emotional and intellectual tools they can use to enhance their lives.

What's New in the Ninth Edition?

The publication of this book marks the twenty-third anniversary of *Introduction to Psychology*. Thanks to the vitality of the field, and suggestions from professors, this edition has improved in many ways, as described next.

- An improved Chapter Survey launches each chapter. The Chapter Survey combines elements of "In This Chapter" and "Survey Questions" from the previous edition. My goal in the Chapter Survey is to help students form a cognitive map of upcoming topics before they begin reading.
- A new list of Gateway statements precedes the main contents of each chapter. Students are encouraged to read these statements and to think about them before they read the rest of the chapter. Doing so will help them organize the detailed information they will encounter as they progress through the text.
- The chapter pedagogy in this edition has evolved from an SQ3R design to one based on the SQ4R method. That is, I have incorporated a fourth R, for "relate," into the study-reading format of the text. The *relate* step of SQ4R prompts students to engage in elaborative rehearsal and actively process new information.
- Knowledge Builders, which are designed to further enhance learning, are a major new feature of the ninth edition. In addition to Learning Check questions and Critical Thinking questions, which appeared in previous editions, Knowledge Builders

◆ TABLE 2 Positive Psychology in the Ninth Edition

Altruism and helping behavior (686–688)	High achievers (421–422)	Positive childbirth practices (130–131)
Androgyny and adaptability (452–454)	Hope (533–534)	Positive models on television (684)
Appreciating human diversity (15–16)	Hospice movement (159)	Promoting secure attachment (96)
Characteristics of the gifted (386–387)	Humanistic psychology and self-actualization (13–14)	Promoting self-esteem in children (103)
Constructive child discipline (116–118)	Improving memory (333–338)	Prosocial behavior (685–688)
Designing for optimum human use (204)	Intrinsic motivation and creativity (423–424)	Psychology of creativity (361–366)
Dreams and creativity (267–268)	Jigsaw classrooms (679–680)	Psychology of love (440–442)
Elements of positive mental health (598)	Job enrichment (A-8)	Psychology of well-being and happiness (156–158)
Emotional intelligence (437)	Job satisfaction (A-7)	Quality day care (97)
Enhancing creativity (368–370)	Jung and self-actualization (493–494)	Repair of brain damage (78–80)
Enriching early development (113–115)	Loving, liking, and attachment (645–647)	Self-confidence (422)
Ethical research (46–48)	Maslow and self-actualization (499–500)	Self-esteem (103)
Exceptional memory (323–324)	Meditation (548–550)	Self-regulated learning (304–305)
Facilitating cognitive development in children (110)	Meta-needs and self-actualization (422–423)	Striving for superiority (419–422)
Friendship and interpersonal attraction (642–645)	Moral behavior (141–143)	Successful aging (150)
Fully functioning person (500)	Multiculturalism (688–690)	Superordinate goals (678–679)
Hardiness and happiness (541)	Multiple intelligences (394–395)	Teaching intelligence (392)
Health-promoting behaviors (519–521)	Optimal caregiving (100)	Traits of master therapists (618)
Health-promoting conditions in therapy (602)	Peak performance (499–500)	Well-being at midlife (147)
Helping behaviors (687–688)	Perceptual awareness (226)	Wellness (521–522)

now include a series of "Relate" questions. Knowledge Builders, which support the SQ4R method, represent a significant improvement in the pedagogical design of this text.

- Blending an Integrated Glossary into the Eighth Edition of the text added greatly to its precision. Now, for convenience, all important terms also appear in a separate Running Glossary.
- Guide Questions, which are a key element of the SQ4R format, are retained in this edition. However, I have made them more subtle by blending them into the general narrative. This format still cues students to actively search for information, but it allows reading to flow more smoothly.
- A new feature called *Bridges* helps students link information that appears in different chapters. In this way, students can build a more coherent view of psychology, rather than learning isolated bits of information.
- Each chapter now ends with Psychology on the Net and Interactive Learning sections. These features direct students to appropriate software and online resources, including *InfoTrac® College Edition,* a text-specific Web site with interactive practice quizzes, and two powerful, interactive CD-ROMs: *PsychNow!* and *Psyk.trek.*
- More than ever, I've tried to make this edition gender neutral and sensitive to diversity issues. All pronouns and examples involving females and males are equally divided by gender. In artwork, photographs, and examples, I have tried to portray the rich diversity of humanity.
- The text's contribution to critical thinking skills continues to grow stronger. For example, several new and revised highlights challenge students to think critically about topics that have been presented noncritically in the news.
- All chapters benefit from new and/or improved art and photographs, as well as several new cartoons. Several new or improved tables also complement the text.
- This edition features 11 new highlights, plus updates and revisions of several more.

- Each chapter has fewer highlights so that reading flows more smoothly and pages are less cluttered.
- A revised Introduction, "The Psychology of Studying," features a new section on using electronic media, including the Internet, electronic databases, and interactive CD-ROMs.
- Chapters 4, 5, and 17 have been significantly reorganized. Chapter 4 gathers much of the coverage of child development into one chapter. Chapter 5 now offers a more balanced overview of life-span development. By reviewer request, I have combined former Chapters 17 and 18 into one streamlined Psychological Disorders chapter. The Health, Stress, and Coping chapter now precedes the discussion of psychological disorders. In another change requested by reviewers, Applied Psychology has become an appendix.
- Although the book contains more information than before, the actual text is shorter. Tighter editing has made it possible to include new features such as the improved Chapter Survey, Gateways, Bridges, Knowledge Builders, Psychology on the Net, and Interactive Learning without adding to the number of pages in the book.
- I have deleted the appendix on careers in psychology, which is replaced by an excellent booklet titled *Psychology: Careers for the 21st Century.* Through an exclusive agreement with the American Psychological Association, Wadsworth is able to offer the booklet shrink-wrapped with this text at no additional cost to students.
- By popular request, I have added Knowledge Builders and other standard features to the Behavioral Statistics appendix.
- A new Name Index now supplements the Subject Index.

In sum, the new subtitle of this text reflects not only the importance of the Gateways feature, but also the fact that the book has been extensively redesigned to give students even better access to psychology. The comments that follow provide more details about some of the changes listed here.

New Topics and Updated Coverage

In addition to the changes and improvements already noted, my general goal in this edition has been to present psychology's latest ideas, findings, and insights. I have drawn on hundreds of new references (some as recent as 2000 and some in press) for this revision. I think it is fair to say that every chapter contains fascinating new information.

NEW PREVIEWS   The chapter Previews are designed to arouse interest and draw students into reading. The following Previews are new to this edition (chapters are shown in parentheses):

- The Story of a Lifetime (5)
- Gizmos and Doohickeys (11)
- Taylor's (Not So Very) Fine Adventure (16)
- Beware the Helicopters (17)

NEW OR REVISED HIGHLIGHTS   Over the years, I have used highlights to report recent research, controversies, issues, and findings. My review of the literature this year prompted me to update many existing highlights and to create 11 that are entirely new or significantly revised, including the following (chapters are shown in parentheses):

- Psychologists: Perceptions and Realities (1)
- Child's Play—Learning about Others (4)
- Ethnic Differences in Child-Rearing—Three Flavors of Parenting (4)
- A Child's Theory of Mind—Other People, Other Minds (4)
- The Mozart Effect—Smart Music? (4)
- Why Most People Can't Draw What They See (7)
- College Students—They're all Alike (10)
- Memories of a Lifetime (10)
- Bilingualism—*Si o No, Oui ou Non,* Yes or No? (11)
- Self-Esteem and Culture (15)
- Running Amok with Cultural Maladies (17)

NEW OR REVISED PSYCHOLOGY IN ACTION FEATURES   The Psychology in Action sections (formerly called "Applications") are a hallmark of this text. In these brief discussions, I strive to give students information that they can apply to practical problems in their lives. The first example below is entirely new, and the second is substantially revised.

- Well-Being and Happiness—What Makes a Good Life? (5)
- Enhancing Creativity—Brainstorms (11)

NEW OR REVISED A STEP BEYOND FEATURES   These short articles discuss controversies, issues, emerging ideas, and other topics that take students beyond the core content of each chapter. The following articles are new or heavily revised in this edition:

- Neurogenesis and Plasticity—The Plastic, Fantastic Brain (3)
- The Recovered Memory–False Memory Debate (10)
- Who Is "Crazy"? What Should Be Done about It (17)

NEW DIVERSITY   As noted earlier, I have tried to encourage students to accept, appreciate, and celebrate the wonderful diversity of humanity. To further enhance the coverage of diversity

in this book, I have added the following features and topics to the ninth edition:

- Human Diversity: Appreciating Social and Cultural Differences (1)
- Ethnic Differences in Child-Rearing—Three Flavors of Parenting (4)
- Vygotsky's Sociocultural Theory (4)
- Diversity and Identity (5)
- Human Diversity: College Students—They're All Alike (10)
- Bilingualism—*Si o No, Oui ou Non,* Yes or No? (11)
- Culture, Ethnicity, and Dieting (13)
- Cultural Differences in Emotion (13)
- Gender Differences in Emotion (13)
- Human Diversity: Self-Esteem and Culture (15)
- Running Amok with Cultural Maladies (17)
- Ethnic Group Membership (17)

Chapter Notes

With respect to more detailed updates, I am pleased to report that every chapter of *Introduction to Psychology—Gateways to Mind and Behavior* has been improved. The following annotations spotlight some of the new topics that appear in this edition.

INTRODUCTION: THE PSYCHOLOGY OF STUDYING   The Introduction has been rewritten for clarity and brevity. It also includes new information on note taking, mnemonics, test-taking skills, and procrastination. A new section shows students how to use the Internet and electronic databases to find additional information about psychology. A discussion of the PsycINFO database includes a sample journal abstract, plus directions for using PsycINFO and conducting searches.

CHAPTER 1: PSYCHOLOGY: THE SEARCH FOR UNDERSTANDING   A recent empirical analysis of trends in psychology by Richard Robins, Samuel Gosling, and Kenneth Craik (1999) makes it clear that cognitive psychology has become a dominant school of thought. In view of this, I have revised the definition of psychology in this chapter to give more prominence to cognition and cognitive processes. Likewise, the growing importance of cognitive science is reflected in the discussion of major perspectives in psychology. My initial description of the profession of psychology now specifically notes the contribution that teachers make to the field. A new section, "Human Diversity—Appreciating Social and Cultural Differences," discusses the impact that human diversity has had on contemporary psychology. The highlight titled "Psychologists: Perceptions and Realities" now includes information about media stereotypes and inaccurate portrayals of psychologists. A revised and enlarged table lists various types of psychologists and what they do. Updated charts show specialties in psychology, where psychologists work, and their principal activities at work.

CHAPTER 2: RESEARCH METHODS AND CRITICAL THINKING   A brief new section introduces students to the concept of meta-analysis. Meta-analytic studies have become common in the literature. Students interested in reading journal articles need to have at least a basic idea of what a meta-analysis is and how the technique is used to combine and synthesize research. The case of Eve White-Eve Black has become highly suspect. To illustrate the clinical method, I have replaced it with a contemporary case study about the effects of amnesia. The discussion of survey research has been reorganized and updated. This chapter also includes brief updates on naturalistic observation, correlation, the observer effect, placebo effects, gender bias in the psychological literature, research ethics, and misinformation in the popular media.

CHAPTER 3: THE BRAIN, BIOLOGY, AND BEHAVIOR   This chapter has been rewritten for greater interest, brevity, and clarity. Information on biopsychological research methods now appears earlier in the chapter. This allows students to better understand subsequent discussions of brain structure and function. The discussion of hemispheric specialization has been significantly updated. Chapter 3 concludes with a new A Step Beyond feature about brain plasticity, neurogenesis, and the repair of brain damage. Additional research updates also appear throughout the chapter.

CHAPTER 4: CHILD DEVELOPMENT   While this chapter retains its topical structure, the first third has been reorganized to offer a more chronological flow of topics. In addition, I have moved some topics into this chapter from Chapter 5 and some have migrated from here to Chapter 5. The result is a more coherent focus on early childhood in Chapter 4. Another benefit of this reorganization is that it makes clearer links between related topics. For the sake of interest, discussions throughout the chapter have been personalized in ways that will make them more relevant to students. A new highlight, "Child's Play— Learning about Others," briefly discusses the role of play in social development. Another new highlight, "Ethnic Differences in Child-Rearing," describes how cultural values and social customs affect child-rearing. A new section explores the origins of the "terrible twos" and reassures parents. A third new highlight, "A Child's Theory of Mind—Other People, Other Minds," provides a brief glimpse into theory-of-mind research. A new table summarizes Piaget's stages of cognitive development and provides guidelines for parents. A new section explains the core concepts of Vygotsky's sociocultural theory of cognitive development. A fourth new highlight, "The Mozart Effect—Smart Music?," critically evaluates research concerning the Mozart effect. This chapter also presents new information on the following topics: environment and temperament, motor development, infant emotions, attachment and day care, language development, parentese and baby talk, self-esteem, and the effects of deprivation and enrichment.

CHAPTER 5: FROM BIRTH TO DEATH: LIFE-SPAN DEVELOPMENT   I have reorganized this chapter to provide a better overview of challenges, tasks, and problems that occur across the life-span. For example, the psychological aspects of birth, which were previously covered in Chapter 4, now appear here. As a result, Chapter 5 really does include topics "from birth to death." Moral development, which begins in childhood and proceeds into adulthood, has also moved here from Chapter 4. A new Pre-

view provides a better introduction to life-span development. A new section explores the impact of ethnic group membership on identity formation. A major new Psychology in Action section discusses happiness and well-being, and answers the question "What makes a good life?" Research updates and new information enhance discussions of childbirth, ADHD, adolescence, moral development, mid-life transitions, life expectancy, successful aging, and living wills.

CHAPTER 6: SENSATION AND REALITY   This chapter includes updates on artificial vision, simultaneous color contrast, olfaction, pheromones, taste, pain management, and motion sickness. Improved art illustrates the firing rates of the three types of cones. The discussion of taste has been updated to include *umami,* an increasingly well-documented fifth taste quality. Art depicting the distribution of taste receptors on the tongue has been revised to correct erroneous information that has appeared in textbooks for more than 80 years.

CHAPTER 7: PERCEIVING THE WORLD   A new highlight, "Why Most People Can't Draw What They See," explains how perception affects drawing ability. It also notes parallels to perception (and misperception) in general. The discussion of perceptual learning begins with a better overview of mechanisms underlying changes in perceptual habits. Updated coverage of the moon illusion reports the strongest evidence yet for the accuracy of the apparent-distance hypothesis. This chapter contains updates on pictorial depth, habituation, eyewitness credibility, and the reconstructive nature of perception. It also includes some new and/or improved art. The A Step Beyond article reports recent data that cast serious doubt on Charles Honorton's claim that he has demonstrated ESP with the Ganzfeld technique.

CHAPTER 8: STATES OF CONSCIOUSNESS   A new "Sleep Quiz" arouses interest in the sleep phenomena discussed in this chapter. New information details the effects of chronic sleep deprivation and explains how to estimate personal sleep needs. A brief new section alerts students to the prevalence and dangers of binge drinking. New findings enhance discussions of microsleeps and highway accidents, REM sleep, insomnia, SIDS, the soporific effects of tryptophan and serotonin, the activation-synthesis theory of dreaming, sensory deprivation, drug dependence, the health risks of caffeine and marijuana, and why people abuse drugs.

CHAPTER 9: CONDITIONING AND LEARNING   This chapter needed very few changes. Nevertheless, I have found ways to make some of the discussions shorter and clearer. In addition, small but worthwhile research updates appear throughout the chapter.

CHAPTER 10: MEMORY   A new highlight, "Human Diversity: College Students—They're All Alike!" illustrates how shallow encoding of memories contributes to the tendency of eyewitnesses to think that members of other social groups "all look alike." A new highlight, "Memories of a Lifetime," reveals an interesting bias in the coding of autobiographical memories. The list of techniques for improving memory now includes the expanding retrieval-interval mnemonic. I have shortened and updated the discussion of recovered memories of sexual abuse. Also, brief research updates provide new information on repression, flashbulb memories, rehearsal, eyewitness memories, hypnosis and memory, aging and memory, hunger and memory, spaced practice, the hippocampus, consolidation, and mnemonics.

CHAPTER 11: COGNITION, LANGUAGE, AND CREATIVITY A new Preview, "Gizmos and Doohickeys," reports on the National Rube Goldberg Machine Contest to pique students' interest in problem solving and creativity. A new highlight, "Bilingualism— *Si o No, Oui ou Non,* Yes or No?," examines some of the benefits and pitfalls of bilingual education. New art clarifies the encoding function of language and the role of phonemes. I have updated discussions of mental rotation, kinesthetic imagery, conceptual features, gestural languages, heuristics, and creativity. The Psychology in Action section presents a revised and updated discussion of techniques for promoting creative problem solving.

CHAPTER 12: INTELLIGENCE Portions of this chapter have been rewritten for improved readability and greater clarity. I have moved a discussion of the drawbacks of forced teaching (previously in Chapter 4) to this chapter. Brief research updates and new information enhance discussions of giftedness, organic causes of retardation, heredity and IQ, the Flynn effect, instrumental enrichment, culture-fair tests, and Gardner's theory of multiple intelligences.

CHAPTER 13: MOTIVATION AND EMOTION A brief new section, "Culture, Ethnicity, and Dieting," discusses cultural values and body image. Another brief new section, "Cultural Differences in Emotion," examines cultural influences on emotional expression. A short section under the heading "Gender Differences in Emotion" describes how differences in socialization affect the expression of emotion by males and females. Research updates improve discussions of external eating cues, eating disorders, behavioral weight management, test anxiety, intrinsic motivation, hemispheric differences in emotion, and the "chameleon effect" in social interactions.

CHAPTER 14: GENDER AND SEXUALITY The terms *sex* and *gender* are now clearly distinguished throughout the chapter, in keeping with the usage that has emerged in the literature. For example, sex roles are now referred to as gender roles. A new table details the most common excuses given for not practicing safer sex. I have revised the discussion of atypical sexual behavior (previously in the Psychological Disorders chapter) and moved it here. I also updated the section on rape from the Psychological Disorders chapter and moved it into this chapter, where it is combined with information about date rape. The coverage of STDs and HIV has been updated. The Psychology in Action section contains some new information on the causes and treatments of sexual dysfunctions.

CHAPTER 15: PERSONALITY A new highlight, "Human Diversity: Self-Esteem and Culture," describes some interesting differ-

ences in the self-esteem of people from individualistic cultures, such as North America, and collectivistic cultures, such as Japan. I have restored a brief discussion of Alfred Adler's ideas to the section on neo-Freudian theories. Recent research updates enhance discussions of traits, self-concept, self-esteem, self-appraisals of competence, the stability of personality traits, situational determinants of behavior, the incongruent person, unconditional positive regard, the ideal self, honesty tests, and the TAT.

CHAPTER 16: HEALTH, STRESS, AND COPING This chapter begins with a new Preview, "Taylor's (Not So Very) Fine Adventure," which provides a more student-oriented introduction to stress and health. A new illustrated table summarizes major health-promoting behaviors. In an important update, new LCU values are provided for the *Social Readjustment Rating Scale.* These are the correct values to use when rating the impact of contemporary life events. A brief new section relates hardiness and happiness to stress resistance. This chapter also includes updates on behavioral risk factors, eustress, pressure, frustration and aggression, the college blues, biofeedback, Type A personality, acculturative stress, the hardy personality, and psychoneuroimmunology. In the Psychology in Action section, students will find a new *College Life Stress Inventory* that they can use to estimate their own stress levels. Also included are brief new discussions of writing as a means of stress reduction and the use of humor as a coping mechanism.

CHAPTER 17: PSYCHOLOGICAL DISORDERS This retitled chapter combines information from former Chapters 17 and 18 into a more concise and integrated discussion of psychological disorders. By popular request, medical therapies are now covered in Chapter 18 (Therapies). Likewise, paraphilias have moved to Chapter 14 (Gender and Sexuality). An updated definition of psychopathology places more emphasis on cultural factors and loss of ability to control one's thoughts, behaviors, and feelings. David Rosenhan's famous pseudo-patient study is now discussed earlier in the chapter and integrated into the general discussion of abnormal behavior. A brief new discussion illustrates how social stigma affects the mentally ill. A revised table provides additional information to help students recognize and differentiate major psychological disorders. A new highlight, "Running Amok with Cultural Maladies," provides examples of various culture-specific "disorders." This highlight also emphasizes the value of empirically based classification systems, such as the DSM. A brief new section illustrates how cultural factors can influence vulnerability to various psychological disorders. A reorganized discussion, along with an enlarged and improved table, clarifies distinctions among various mood disorders, especially Bipolar I and Bipolar II. The A Step Beyond section ("Who Is "Crazy"? What Should Be Done about It?") combines, condenses, and updates information from two "Explorations" in the prior edition. This chapter also benefits from updates on risk factors, anxiety disorders, social phobia, PTSD, dissociative disorders, conversion reactions, lead poisoning, the causes of schizophrenia, SAD, and suicide.

CHAPTER 18: THERAPIES   This chapter is more concise and features a variety of updates. Medical therapies, which were formerly discussed in Chapter 17, are now presented here. This allows students to gain a better perspective on the range of therapies available and the differences between psychological and somatic approaches. A brief new discussion of telehealth (therapy conducted by videoconferencing) adds balance to the coverage of distance therapy. It also alerts students to an emerging method for delivering mental health services. The discussion of virtual reality exposure therapy reports additional studies that show the value of this technique for treating phobias. The highlight on eye movement desensitization and reprocessing presents recent evidence for and against the effectiveness of this new technique. A new discussion briefly summarizes the characteristics of peer-nominated master therapists.

CHAPTER 19: SOCIAL BEHAVIOR   I have rewritten the discussion of attribution theory in this chapter to make it clearer and more accessible to students. Also, this section makes a better distinction between the fundamental attributional error and actor-observer bias. This chapter has also been improved by small, but valuable, updates on role conflicts, group cohesion, self-handicapping, interpersonal attraction, the halo effect, homogamy, mate selection, romantic love, groupthink, conformity, and compliance.

CHAPTER 20: ATTITUDES, CULTURE, AND HUMAN RELATIONS   The discussion of discrimination in this chapter now includes a brief discussion of racial profiling by police officers. (That is, detaining people for "driving while black.") A brief new section summarizes conditions that tend to reduce intergroup conflict and prejudice. New information in the Psychology in Action feature shows students that "race" is a matter of social labeling, not a biological reality. This chapter also includes brief research updates on attitudes, authoritarianism, prejudice, status inequalities, and stereotypes.

APPENDIX A: APPLIED PSYCHOLOGY   Research updates in this chapter enhance discussions of work analysis, work efficiency, flextime, job interviewing, crowding, noise pollution, pro-environmental behavior, death-qualified juries, jury selection, and space psychology.

APPENDIX B: BEHAVIORAL STATISTICS   This appendix now includes all features of the pedagogy used throughout the text, including Chapter Survey, Preview, Gateways, Knowledge Builders, In Review, and Psychology on the Net.

TEACHING AND LEARNING SUPPLEMENTS

A rich array of supplements accompanies the ninth edition of *Introduction to Psychology,* including several that make use of the latest information technologies. These supplements are designed to make teaching and learning more effective. Many are available free to professors or students. Others can be packaged with this text at a discount. For more information on any of the listed resources, please call the Thomson Learning™ Academic Resource Center at 800-423-0563.

Student Support Materials

Introductory students must learn a multitude of abstract concepts, which can make a first course in psychology difficult. The materials listed here are designed to greatly improve students' chances for success.

GATEWAYS TO PSYCHOLOGY BROCHURE   The ninth edition's new, chapter-opening Gateways are designed to help students identify key concepts in psychology, especially those that will change the way they view human behavior. The *Gateways to Psychology* brochure is a compilation of all the "transformative" concepts from the text. As such, the brochure serves as a valuable reference to core ideas in psychology. By reading *Gateways to Psychology,* students can gain an overview of their entire introductory course—before, during, or after taking it. The brochure lists Web sites related to each chapter's major topic, as well as suggested key search terms for InfoTrac® College Edition, so students can continue to learn more about psychology. Because Web site addresses frequently change, these links will be updated periodically on the book's own Web site (visit http://psychology.wadsworth.com/ and then proceed to the book-specific Web page). The *Gateways to Psychology* brochure can be packaged with new copies of this text at no cost (for North American Adoptions) to your students (use bundle ISBN: 0-534-57674-5).

STUDY GUIDE   To facilitate learning, the *Study Guide* provides abundant opportunities for practice, self-testing, and rehearsal. The *Study Guide,* which is structured around the SQ4R method, is closely coordinated with this text. Each chapter includes the following sections: Chapter Overview (a concise chapter summary), Learning Objectives (a detailed list of what students need to know), Recite and Review (a survey of major terms and concepts), Connections (matching items), Check Your Memory (true-false items), Final Survey and Review (fill-in-the-blank questions), and a Mastery Test (multiple-choice questions similar to in-class test items). All *Study Guide* chapters conclude with a brief Language Development Guide that "translates" idiomatic phrases, cultural and historic references, and other difficult language for students. (*Study Guide,* by Dennis Coon, ISBN: 0-534-57674-5)

LANGUAGE DEVELOPMENT GUIDE   For some students, language and culture can be major barriers to comprehension. The *Language Development Guide,* prepared by Janice Hartgrove-Freile, and available as a customized addition to the text, helps clarify idioms and special phrases, cultural and historic allusions, and difficult vocabulary. Much of this information would be difficult or impossible to look up in a dictionary. All terms and phrases in the guide are page-referenced to the text and followed by concise definitions. Like a helpful tutor, the *Language Development Guide* can answer questions about the meaning of unfamiliar terms and expressions. The same material is included in the *Study Guide;* however, if you would like to order the LDG with the text, please contact your Wadsworth/Thomson Learning™ Representative for ordering information.

CHAPTER QUIZZES This collection of self-administered quizzes (ISBN: 0-534-57680-X) is available packaged free with new copies of this text. Each 30-item multiple-choice quiz provides questions that students can use to evaluate their understanding and prepare for tests.

PSYCHOLOGY/CAREERS FOR THE TWENTY-FIRST CENTURY
Wadsworth is able to offer this informative booklet to students through an exclusive agreement with the American Psychological Association. This 30-page pamphlet describes the field of psychology, as well as how to prepare for a career in psychology. It can be packaged with this text at no additional cost to students. Career options and resources are also discussed. (Available only packaged with the text. Contact your local Wadsworth/Thomson Learning™ Representative for ordering information.)

Multimedia CD-ROMs

Interactive CD-ROMs make it possible for students to directly experience some of the phenomena they are studying. The following CDs from Wadsworth provide a wealth of engaging modules and exercises.

PSYCHNOW!™ INTERACTIVE EXPERIENCES IN PSYCHOLOGY This exciting CD-ROM was created by Joel Morgovsky, Lonnie Yandell, Elizabeth Lynch, and project consultant Dennis Coon. *PsychNow!* (ISBN: 0-314-07220-9) was specifically designed to accompany *Introduction to Psychology: Gateways to Mind and Behavior*. At the end of each chapter of this text, students will find a list of *PsychNow!* modules they can access for additional, "hands-on" learning experiences.

PsychNow! provides a dynamic, multimedia experience that goes beyond the boundaries of the classroom, allowing students to explore psychology like never before. Stunning graphics and animations, interesting video clips, and interactive exercises bring psychology to life. With *PsychNow!*, students can do more than just read about a topic—they can read, watch, listen, react, and reflect on the meaning of their own responses. *PsychNow!*, which is available for Macintosh and Windows, contains 39 fully interactive modules that will pique students' curiosity and enhance their understanding. While *PsychNow!* can be used alone, it is also available in a discount bundle for students when packaged with this textbook (Bundle ISBN: 0-534-36212-5).

INTEGRATOR™ ONLINE FOR INTRODUCTORY PSYCHOLOGY Arthur Kohn and Wendy Kohn created this CD-ROM for Windows and Macintosh to provide new ways for instructors to teach and students to learn. *Integrator ONLINE* (ISBN: 0-534-35746-6) is designed for use with any of Wadsworth's introductory psychology titles.

The faculty version of *Integrator ONLINE* includes *CourseWeaver ONLINE™*, which allows you to deliver course materials via local lecture, individual computers, or the Internet. With *CourseWeaver ONLINE* you can also export static images from the *Integrator ONLINE* into *PowerPoint* or word-processing documents. Using the *LecturePresenter* program, you can deliver individual lessons or an entire course with embedded Internet links, interactive activities, study sessions, and simulations. Alternatively, students can use the *Integrator* on their own to explore activities, complete homework, or practice for quizzes.

PSYK.TREK™ FOR INTRODUCTORY PSYCHOLOGY: A MULTIMEDIA INTRODUCTION TO PSYCHOLOGY, GENERAL VERSION, 1.0 This CD-ROM for Windows and Macintosh (ISBN: 0-534-36226-5) covers the core topics of introductory psychology and can be used with any introductory text. Students using *Psyk.trek* will find studying fun, as they create illusions, run simulated experiments, view videos, and quiz themselves on the content of the introductory psychology course.

SNIFFY™ THE VIRTUAL RAT, LITE VERSION There's no better way to master the basic principles of learning than working with a real laboratory rat. However, this is usually impractical in introductory psychology courses. *Sniffy the Virtual Rat* offers a fun, interactive alternative to working with lab animals. This innovative and entertaining software teaches students about operant and classical conditioning by allowing them to condition a virtual rat. Users begin by training Sniffy to press a bar to obtain food. Then they progress to studying the effects of reinforcement schedules and simple classical conditioning. In addition, special "Mind Windows" enable students to visualize how Sniffy's experiences in the Skinner Box produce learning. The Sniffy CD-ROM includes a Lab Manual that shows students how to set up various operant and classical conditioning experiments. *Sniffy™ the Virtual Rat, Lite Version* may be packaged with this text for a discount (dual-platform CD-ROM, ISBN: 0-534-35869-1).

Internet Resources

The Internet is providing new ways to exchange information and enhance education. In psychology, Wadsworth is at the forefront in making use of this exciting technology.

INFOTRAC® COLLEGE EDITION *InfoTrac* is a powerful online learning resource, consisting of thousands of full-text articles from hundreds of journals and periodicals. Students using *Introduction to Psychology: Gateways to Mind and Behavior* may receive four months of free access to the *InfoTrac College Edition* database. By doing a simple keyword search, students can quickly generate a list of relevant articles from thousands of possibilities. Then they can select articles to read, explore, and print for reference or further study. *InfoTrac's* continuously updated collection of articles can be useful for doing reading and writing assignments that reach beyond the pages of this text. Packaged free with every new copy of the text, *InfoTrac College Edition* is available to North American colleges and universities only.

THE ONLINE WADSWORTH PSYCHOLOGY RESOURCE CENTER As users of this text, you and your students will have access to the *Introduction to Psychology: Gateways to Mind and Behavior* section of the Wadsworth Psychology Resource Center (http://

psychology.wadsworth.com). This Internet site includes the following features for instructors and students:

- *Online Quizzes.* These chapter-by-chapter multiple-choice quizzes help students practice for tests and check their understanding.
- *Interactive Activities.* Demonstrations and mini-experiments allow students to directly experience some of the phenomena they are studying.
- *Internet Resources.* This area is a "launching pad" that links to other psychology-related sites on the Internet. If a site sounds interesting, a click of the mouse will take students to it.
- *Gateways to the Net and InfoTrac College Edition.* These links guide students directly to relevant Internet sites correlated chapter-by-chapter. Links to suggested key terms for InfoTrac® College Edition are also provided.
- *Online Flashcards.* These chapter-by-chapter interactive glossary terms allow students to test their psychology vocabulary.
- *Hot Topics.* This section features a news item or current event that is explored from a psychological perspective. After students have thought about a topic, they can share their opinions with others in an online discussion.
- *Discussion Forum.* In the Discussion Forum, students have a chance to share ideas with those of psychology students all over the country.
- *Research and Teaching Showcase.* The showcase features regularly updated summaries of presentations, articles, or other teaching and research materials.
- *Archives.* Using the archives, students can quickly search for current and past articles from Hot Topics and the Research and Teaching Showcase.
- *Meet the Author.* Students can meet Dennis Coon in an interactive, multimedia presentation.

THOMSON LEARNING *WEB TUTOR 2.0+* ™ This online supplement helps students succeed by taking them into an environment rich with study and mastery tools, communication aids, and additional course content. Professors can use *Web Tutor 2.0+* to offer virtual office hours, to post syllabi, to set up threaded discussions, to track student progress on quizzes, and more. For students, *Web Tutor 2.0+* offers real-time access to a full array of study tools, including flashcards (with audio), practice quizzes and tests, online tutorials, exercises, discussion questions, Web links, and a full glossary. In the new enhanced 2.0+ version, simulations and activities have been added to augment students' learning opportunities. Professors can customize the content of *Web Tutor 2.0+* in any way they choose, including uploading images and other resources, adding Web links, and creating course-specific practice materials (*Web Tutor 2.0+* on *WebCT*: 0-534-57676-1; *Web Tutor 2.0+* on *Blackboard*: 0-534-57685-0).

Essential Teaching Resources

As every professor knows, teaching an introductory psychology course is a tremendous amount of work. The supplements listed here not only should make life easier for you, but also should make it possible for you to concentrate on the more creative and rewarding facets of teaching.

INSTRUCTOR'S RESOURCE MANUAL   The *Instructor's Resource Manual* (ISBN: 0-534-57677-X) for this edition was revised by psychologist and master teacher Saundra K. Ciccarelli. This manual contains Learning Objectives, Discussion Questions, Lecture Enhancements, Role-Playing Scenarios, Value Clarification Statements, Supplemental Activities, Journal Questions, Suggestions for Further Reading, and Media Suggestions. Special sections called "Broadening Our Cultural Horizons" are designed to help students examine and role-play diverse cultural values. In addition, the *Instructor's Resource Manual* includes general teaching strategies, references, and other helpful materials. This manual also includes notes on *PsychNow!* and *Psyk.trek, General Version,* and tips for using *InfoTrac® College Edition.* Finally, the *Instructor's Resource Manual* also includes a chapter-by-chapter *Supplement Correlation Guide* as well as a *Conversion Guide* to help new users of this text adapt existing class outlines and lecture notes.

PSYCHLINK 2001™ FOR INTRODUCTORY PSYCHOLOGY   Free to adopters of this text, this *PowerPoint*-based CD-ROM presentation tool will help you create engaging lectures that include art, graphics, CNN video clips, and animations. Using a displayed table of contents from this book, you can simply click on a chapter to access a prepared lecture that includes text, art, video clips, and animations. You can also create customized lectures that include your own selection of materials. In addition, *PsychLink 2001* includes links to a text-specific Web site (ISBN: 0-534-57690-7).

TEST BANK   The *Test Bank* (ISBN: 0-534-57678-8) includes approximately 5,600 multiple-choice questions organized by chapter and by Learning Objectives. All items include correct answers and page references to this text. These test items, which were meticulously updated by Karen Wolford, SUNY Oswego, are classified by question type (factual, conceptual, or applied). Owing to Karen's efforts, this is one of the best test banks available, with an abundance of high-quality questions.

EXAMVIEW™ COMPUTERIZED TESTING   This software helps you create, deliver, and customize tests and study guides (both in print and online). In just minutes, this easy-to-use system can generate the assessment and tutorial materials your students need. *ExamView* offers both a Quick Test Wizard and an Online Test Wizard that guide you step-by-step through the process of creating tests. *ExamView* shows the test you are creating on the screen exactly as it will print or display online. You can build tests of up to 250 questions using up to 12 question types. Using *ExamView's* complete word-processing capabilities, you can also enter an unlimited number of new questions or edit existing questions (ISBN: 0-534-57682-6).

TRANSPARENCY ACETATES   A revised set of transparencies (ISBN: 0-534-57682-6) will again be available to illustrate and enliven lectures. These text-specific transparencies contain approximately

140 tables, graphs, charts, and drawings—most of them in color. All of the acetates are reproduced from figures and tables in this text.

Videotapes and Films

Wadsworth offers a variety of videotapes and films to enhance classroom presentations. Many video segments in the Wadsworth collection pertain directly to major topics in this text, making them excellent lecture supplements.

WADSWORTH FILM AND VIDEO LIBRARY FOR INTRODUCTORY PSYCHOLOGY   Adopters can select from a variety of continually updated film and video options, including the exclusive CNN offerings described below. Contact your local Wadsworth/ Thomson Learning™ sales representative or Wadsworth Marketing at 877-999-2350 for details.

CNN TODAY VIDEOS FOR INTRODUCTORY PSYCHOLOGY   These one-to four-minute video clips, a Wadsworth exclusive, allow you to integrate the newsgathering and programming power of CNN into the classroom to show students the relevance of psychology to daily life. Organized by course topics, these compelling clips are ideal for launching lectures and encouraging discussion. Adopters receive one new, updated video each year. A Wadsworth/Thomson Learning™ Exclusive!

CNN Today: Introductory Psychology, Volume I (ISBN: 0-534-36634-1)
Section 1: Mental Health and Stress
Section 2: The Brain
Section 3: The Mind and Therapy
Section 4: Genetic Mapping
Section 5: Health
Section 6: Gender and Sexuality
Section 7: Learning

CNN Today: Introductory Psychology, Volume 2 (ISBN: 0-534-50420-5)
Section 1: The Brain
Section 2: The Mind and Therapy
Section 3: Health
Section 4: Mental Health
Section 5: Gender and Sexuality
Section 6: Learning
Section 7: Diversity

THE BRAIN VIDEO, SECOND EDITION   Newly updated and expanded teaching modules from *The Brain* series offer your students extensive new footage of research into the inner workings of the brain. Segments cover the latest findings on Alzheimer's disease, schizophrenia, autism, Parkinson's disease, and many other topics. These modules can enhance classroom lectures on topics found throughout the introductory course, not just in the realm of biopsychology. *The Brain* video series was produced by Colorado State University (1997).

GRADE IMPROVEMENT: TAKING CHARGE OF YOUR LEARNING VIDEO   This 20-minute video uses an upbeat and entertaining delivery to show first-year and re-entry students strategies they can use to enjoy greater success in college. Students will learn proven techniques for choosing an approach to learning, time management, class preparation, effective test taking, and more. Above all, the video presentation stresses that students must be actively involved in their learning. Contact Wadsworth Marketing for more information.

PSYCHOLOGY/CAREERS FOR THE TWENTY-FIRST CENTURY VIDEO   Wadsworth has an exclusive agreement with the American Psychological Association to offer this dynamic 13-minute video free to adopters of *Introduction to Psychology: Gateways to Mind and Behavior*. The video, which was produced by the APA, gives students an overview of the emerging growth opportunities in the field of psychology and advice about how to choose a career path (ISBN: 0-534-34293-0).

Supplementary Books

No text can cover all of the topics that might be included in an introductory psychology course. If you would like to enrich your course, or make it more challenging, the titles listed here may be of interest.

CHALLENGING YOUR PRECONCEPTIONS: THINKING CRITICALLY ABOUT PSYCHOLOGY   A newly revised edition of this popular paperbound book (ISBN: 0-534-26739-4), written by Randolph Smith, helps students strengthen their critical thinking skills. Psychological issues such as hypnosis and repressed memory, statistical seduction, the validity of pop psychology, and other topics arc used to illustrate the principles of critical thinking.

WRITING PAPERS IN PSYCHOLOGY: A STUDENT GUIDE   The Fifth Edition of *Writing Papers in Psychology* (ISBN: 0-534-52975-5), by Ralph L. Rosnow and Mimi Rosnow, is a valuable "how to" manual for writing term papers and research reports. This new edition has been updated to reflect the latest APA guidelines. The book covers each task with examples, hints, and two complete writing samples. Citation ethics, how to locate information, and new research technologies are also covered.

COLLEGE SURVIVAL GUIDE: HINTS AND REFERENCES TO AID COLLEGE STUDENTS   This Fourth Edition of Bruce Rowe's *College Survival Guide* (ISBN: 0-534-35569-2) is designed to help students succeed. Rowe provides valuable tips on how to finance an education, how to manage time, how to study for and take exams, and more. Other sections focus on maintaining concentration, credit by examination, use of the credit/no credit option, cooperative education programs, and the importance of a liberal arts education.

CROSS-CULTURAL PERSPECTIVES IN PSYCHOLOGY   How well do the concepts of psychology apply to various cultures? What can we learn about human behavior from cultures different from our own? These questions lie behind a collection of original articles written by William F. Price and Rich Crapo. The Third Edition of *Cross-Cultural Perspectives in Psychology* (ISBN: 0-534-35570-6) contains articles on North American ethnic groups as well as cultures from around the world.

UNDERSTANDING DIVERSITY: A LEARNING-AS-PRACTICE PRIMER Barbara Okun, Jane Fried, and Marcia Okun turn the field of multicultural studies inside out, using readers' own personal development as a framework for appreciating others. "Learning-as-practice" methods—role-plays, self-awareness exercises, communication techniques—help readers first identify their own beliefs and behaviors, then turn that understanding outward. Ultimately, readers learn that diversity is not about borders and groups, but about people and perspectives (ISBN: 0-534-34810-6).

THE 'NET, THE WEB, AND YOU This paperback by Daniel Kurland offers a brief, comprehensive, easy-to-understand introduction to the Internet. It is useful for any course that requires students to use the Internet for research or inquiry (ISBN: 0-534-51281-X).

Summary

I sincerely hope that teachers and students will consider this book and its supporting materials a refreshing change from the ordinary. Writing and revising it has been quite an adventure. In the pages that follow, I think students will find an attractive blend of the theoretical and the practical, plus many of the most exciting ideas in psychology.

Acknowledgments

Psychology is a cooperative effort requiring the talents and energies of a large community of scholars, teachers, researchers, and students. As with earlier versions of this text, this edition reflects the efforts of a large number of people.

I would first like to thank the many students who sent comments, suggestions, and letters of encouragement.

To the professional reviewers who gave their time and expertise I extend my sincere thanks. I deeply appreciate the contributions of all those who have, over the years, supported this text's evolution, including:

Faren R. Akins
University of Arizona

Clark E. Alexander
Arapahoe Community College

Lynn Anderson
Wayne State University

Frank Barbehenn
Bucks County Community College

Michael Bardo
University of Kentucky

Brian R. Bate
Cuyahoga Community College

Hugh E. Bateman
Jones Junior College

Galen V. Bodenhausen
Michigan State University

Tom Bond
Thomas Nelson Community College

John Boswell
University of Missouri, St. Louis

Anne Bright
Jackson State Community College

Derek Cadman
El Camino Community College

Lorry Cology
Owens College

William N. Colson
Norfolk State College

Chris Cozby
California State University, Fullerton

Corinne Crandell
Broome County Community College

Thomas L. Crandell
Broome County Community College

Charles Croll
Broome Community College

Daniel B. Cruse
University of Miami

Diane DeArmond
University of Missouri, Kansas City

Patrick T. DeBoll
St. John's University

Lorraine P. Dieudonne
Foothill College

Wendy Domjan
University of Texas at Austin

John Dworetzky
Glendale Community College

Bill Dwyer
Memphis State University

Thomas Eckle
Modesto Community College

David Edwards
Iowa State University

Raymond Elish
Cuyahoga Community College

Paul W. Fenton
University of Wisconsin, Stout

Linda E. Flickinger
Saint Clair County Community College

William F. Ford
Bucks County Community College

Marie Fox
Metropolitan State College of Denver

Chris Fraser
Gippsland Institute of Advanced Education

Christopher Frost
Southwest Texas State University

Eugenio J. Galindro
El Paso Community College

Irby J. Gaudet
University of Southwestern Louisiana

David A. Gershaw
Arizona Western College

Carolyn A. Gingrich
South Dakota State University

Michael E. Gorman
Michigan Technological University

Peter Gram
Pensacola Junior College

David A. Griesé
State University of New York, Farmingdale

John Grivas
Monash University

Anne Groves
Montgomery College

Michael B. Guyer
John Carroll University

Janice Hartgrove-Freile
North Harris County College

Raquel Henry
Kingwood College

Don Hockenbury
Tulsa Junior College

Barbara Honhart
Lansing Community College

James A. Johnson
Sam Houston State University

Myles E. Johnson
Normandale Community College

Pat Jones
Brevard Community College

Charles Karis
Northeastern University

John P. Keating
University of Washington

Cindy Kennedy
Sinclair Community College

Richard R. Klene
University of Cincinnati

Ronald J. Kopcho
Mercer Community College

Mary Kulish
Thomas Nelson Community College

Billie Laney
Central Texas College

Phil Lau
DeAnza College

Walter Leach
College of San Mateo

Elizabeth Levin
Laurentian University

Philip Lom
West Connecticut State University

Salvador Macias, III
University of South Carolina, Sumter

Al Mayer
Portland Community College

Edward R. McCrary III
El Camino College

Yancy B. McDougal
University of South Carolina,
Spartanburg

Mark McGee
Texas A & M University

Mark McKinley
Lorain County Community College

John Mitterer
Brock University

Edward Mosley
Pasiac County Community College

Andrew Neher
Cabrillo College

Don Nelson
Indiana State University

Steve Nida
Franklin University

James P. B. O'Brien
Tidewater Community College

Frances O'Keefe
Tidewater Community College

Steve G. Ornelas
Central Arizona College

Darlene Pacheco
Moorpark College

Debra Parish
Tomball College

Cora F. Patterson
University of Southwestern
Louisiana

Leon Peek
North Texas State University

Steven J. Pollock
Moorpark College

Robin Raygor
Anoka-Ramsey Community
College

Jeffrey Rudski
Mulhenberg College

James J, Ryan
University of Wisconsin, La Crosse

Michael Schuller
Fresno City College

Carol F. Shoptaugh
Southwest Missouri State University

Steven M. Smith
Texas A&M University

Francine Smolucha
Moraine Valley Community College

Michael C. Sosulski
College of DuPage

Donald M. Stanley
North Harris County College

Harvey Taub
Staten Island Community College

Christopher Taylor
University of Arizona

Bruce Trotter
Santa Barbara City College

Pat Tuntland
Pima College

Paul E. Turner
David Lipscomb University

Mark Vernoy
Palomar College

Paul J. Wellman
Texas A&M University

Sharon Whelan
University of Kentucky

Robert Wiley
Montgomery College

Thomas Wilke
University of Wisconsin, Parkside

Carl D. Williams
University of Miami

Kaye D. Young
North Iowa Area Community
College

Michael Zeller
Mankato State University

Otto Zinser
East Tennessee State College

I especially wish to thank the
following professors, whose sage
advice helped make this ninth
edition a reality:

Dennis Cogan, Texas Tech
University

Jack Demick, Suffolk University

Dave Filak, Joliet Junior College

David Gersh, Houston Community
College

Andrew Getzfeld, New Jersey City
University

David Griesé, SUNY-Farmingdale

Sidney Hockman, Nassau
Community College

Christopher Legrow, Marshall
University

Linda Lockwood, Metropolitan
State College of Denver

Angela McGlynn, Mercer County
Community College

Chelley Merrill, Tidewater
Community College

James Murray, San Jacinto
University

Peggy Norwood, Tidewater
Community College

Laura Overstreet, Tarrant County
College

Jack Powell, University of Hartford

Ravi Prasad, Texas Tech University

Marcia Rossi, Tuskegee University

Richard Siegel, University of
Massachusetts-Lowell

Glenda Smith, North Harris
Community College

Don Stanley, North Harris College

Laura Thompson, New Mexico
State University

Susan Troy, Northeast Iowa
Community College

Frank Vitro, Texas Women's
University

The complexity of revising
Introduction to Psychology and its
supplements continues to be a
formidable challenge. The ninth
edition reflects the work of many
talented people. I am especially
indebted to each of the following
people, who are the architects of
this edition:

Susan Badger

Lisa Gebo

Stephen Rapley

Sean Wakely

I also wish to thank the many
people who so generously shared
their knowledge and skills over the
past year. These are the people who
made it happen:

Edith Beard Brady

Saundra Ciccarelli

Christine Davis

Janice Hartgrove-Freile

Sue Howard

Bob Kauser

Vicki Knight,

Leslie Krongold

Jessica McFadden

Felicia Moore-Davis

Tanya Nigh

Jenna Opp

Margaret Parks

Robert Pred

Glenda Smith

Jim Strandberg

Joanne Terhaar

JoAnne von Zastrow

Sheila Walsh

Joy Westberg

Jennifer Wilkinson

Susan Wilson

Karen Wolford

It has been a pleasure and an
inspiration to work with such a
gifted group of people.

I also want to give special
recognition to Jim Strandberg,
whose analysis and insightful
comments have greatly improved
this text.

Likewise, I want to express my
sincere gratitude to Lisa Gebo for
her dedication to making the ninth
edition the best ever, and for her
creativity, energy, and vision.

Last of all, I would like to thank
my wife Sevren, for again bringing
love and light to an arduous
journey.

DENNIS COON

Introduction

THE PSYCHOLOGY OF STUDYING

EVEN IF YOU'RE DOING WELL IN SCHOOL, *you might be able to improve your study skills. Research has shown that students who get good grades tend to work* smarter, *not just longer or harder (Dickinson & O'Connell, 1990; Hill, 1990). To help you get a good start, let's look at several ways to improve studying.*

THE SQ4R METHOD—HOW TO TAME A TEXTBOOK

How much do you typically remember after you've read a textbook chapter? If the answer is "Nada," "Zip minus 1," or simply "Not enough," it may be time to try the **SQ4R method.** SQ4R stands for survey, question, read, recite, relate, and review. These six steps can help you grasp ideas quickly, learn as you read, remember more, and review effectively:

S = *Survey.* Skim through a chapter before you begin reading it. Start by looking only at topic headings, captions, and the chapter summary. Try to get an overall picture of what lies ahead.

Q = *Question.* As you read, turn each topic heading into one or more questions. For example, the heading "Stages of Sleep" might lead you to ask: "Is there more than one stage of sleep?" "What are the stages of sleep?" "How do they differ?" Asking questions helps you read with a purpose.

R1 = *Read.* The first R in SQ4R stands for *read.* As you read, look for answers to the questions you asked. Read in short "bites," from *one topic heading* to the next, then stop. For difficult material, you may want to read only a paragraph or two at a time.

R2 = *Recite.* After reading a small amount, you should pause and *recite* or *rehearse.* That is, try to mentally answer your questions and summarize what you read. Or better yet, summarize by making brief notes (Lahtinen, Lonka, & Lindbloom-Ylaenne, 1997).

If you can't summarize the main ideas, skim over each section again. Until you can remember what you just read, there's little point in reading more.

After you've studied a short "bite" of text, turn the next topic heading into questions. Then read to the following heading. Remember to look for answers as you read and to recite or take notes before moving on. Repeat the question-read-recite cycle until you've finished an entire chapter.

R3 = *Relate.* You've probably noticed that it is easier to remember ideas that are personally meaningful. When you study a chapter, try to link new facts, terms, and concepts with information you already know well.

Effective studying is planned and systematic. The number of hours you spend studying is less important than the quality and efficiency of your learning strategies (Woehr & Cavell, 1993).

R4 = *Review.* When you're done reading, skim back over the chapter, or read your notes. Then check your memory by reciting and quizzing yourself again. Try to make frequent, active review a key part of your study habits. (See ❖ Figure I.1.)

Does this method really work? Yes. The SQ4R method improves reading comprehension and course grades. Simply reading straight through a chapter can give you "intellectual indigestion." That's why it's better to stop often to think, question, recite, relate, review, and thoroughly "digest" information as you read (Chastain & Thurber, 1989; Martin, 1985).

How To Use This Text

You can apply the SQ4R method to any text. However, this book is specifically designed to help you practice active learning.

SURVEY Each chapter opens with a *Chapter Survey,* a short *Preview,* and a list of "*Gateway*" concepts. All three features will help you identify important information to look for as you read.

SQ4R method *An active study-reading technique based on these steps: survey, question, read, recite, relate, and review.*

◆ **FIGURE I.1** *The SQ4R method promotes active learning and information processing. You should begin with a survey of the chapter, proceed through cycles of questioning, reading, reciting, and relating, and conclude with a review of the chapter.*

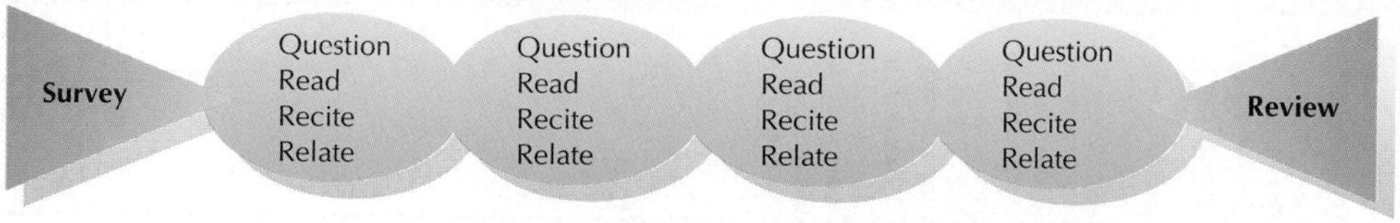

- The Chapter Survey lists *Key Questions* addressed in the chapter, plus *Key Topics* to watch for as you read.
- The Preview introduces the chapter and helps arouse your interest in upcoming topics.
- The Gateways section summarizes the most important concepts or "big ideas" of the chapter. Keeping these ideas in mind as you read will deepen your understanding of psychology.

After you've studied all three of these sections, take a few minutes to do your own survey of the chapter. That way, you can build your own "mental map" of upcoming topics.

QUESTION   *How can I use the SQ4R method to make reading more interesting and effective?*   One of the key steps is to ask yourself lots of questions while you read. *Guide Questions*, like the one you just read, appear throughout this text. They are designed to help you focus your attention and actively process information as you read. However, be sure to ask your own questions, too. Try to actively interact with your textbooks as you read them.

READ   As an aid to reading, new terms are printed in **boldface type** and defined where they first appear. (Some are followed by pronunciations—capital letters show which syllables are accented.) You'll also find a *running glossary* on each page, so you never need to guess about the meaning of technical terms. If you need to look up a term from a lecture or another chapter, check the main *glossary*. This "mini-dictionary" is located near the end of the book. Perhaps you should take a moment to find it now.

RECITE AND RELATE   Every few pages, a learning guide called a *Knowledge Builder* provides chances to think, rehearse, relate, and test your memory. (Don't forget to also take notes or recite on your own.) If you would like to study chapters in smaller "bites," these "study breaks" make good stopping points.

Bridges are another feature you'll see occasionally in this text. Each "bridge" links ideas from one chapter to ideas in another. Crossing some of these bridges will help you discover connections that interrelate various topics in psychology.

Near the end of each chapter, you'll find a section called *Psychology in Action*. These discussions are filled with practical ideas you can put to use in your own life. Then, a feature called *A Step Beyond* will extend your knowledge.

REVIEW   Each chapter of this book concludes with a final summary, called *Chapter in Review*, that will help you identify key

◆ **TABLE I.1**   Using the SQ4R Method

SURVEY

Chapter Survey
Preview
Gateways
Figure Captions
Chapter in Review

QUESTION

Topic Headings
Survey Questions
Guide Questions

READ

Topic Headings
Boldface Terms
Margin Glossary
Figures and Tables

RECITE

Learning Check Questions
Practice Quizzes

RELATE

Relate Questions
Critical Thinking Questions
Bridges

REVIEW

Chapter in Review
Boldface Terms
Running Glossary
Tables
Practice Quizzes
Study Guide

ideas to remember. These chapters are organized around the same questions you read in the Chapter Survey. You can also return to the glossary items throughout each chapter for further review.

◆Table I.1 summarizes how this text helps you apply the SQ4R method. Even with all this help, there is still much more you can do on your own.

EFFECTIVE NOTE-TAKING—GOOD STUDENTS, TAKE NOTE!

The SQ4R method may be good for study-reading, but what about taking notes in class? Sometimes it's hard to know what's important. Good notes are based on active listening. An **active listener** avoids distractions and skillfully gathers information from lectures. Here's a listening and note-taking plan that works for many students. The letters LISAN, pronounced like the word *listen,* will help you remember the steps (Carman & Adams, 1985).

L = *Lead. Don't follow.* Try to anticipate what your teacher will say by asking yourself questions. Questions can come from study guides, reading assignments, or your own curiosity.

I = *Ideas.* Every lecture is based on a core of ideas. Usually, an idea is followed by examples or explanations. Ask yourself often, "What is the main idea now? What ideas support it?"

S = *Signal words.* Listen for words that tell you the direction the instructor is taking. For instance, here are some groups of signal words:

There are three reasons why . . .	Here come ideas
Most important is . . .	Main idea
On the contrary . . .	Opposite idea
As an example . . .	Support for main idea
Therefore . . .	Conclusion

A = *Actively listen.* Sit where you can hear and where you can ask questions. Look at the teacher while he or she talks. Bring questions you want answered from the last lecture or from your text. Raise your hand at the beginning of class or approach your professor before the lecture. Do anything that helps you stay active and alert.

N = *Note-taking.* As you listen, write down only key points. Listen to everything, but be selective. If you are too busy writing, you may not grasp what your professor is saying.

Actually, most students take reasonably good notes—and then don't use them! Most students wait until just before exams to review (Palkovitz & Lore, 1980). By then, their notes have lost much of their meaning. If you don't want your notes to seem like hieroglyphics or "chicken scratches," it pays to review them *on a regular basis*—daily, if possible (Luckie & Smethurst, 1998).

Using and Reviewing Your Notes

When you review, you will learn more if you take the extra steps listed here (Kiewra et al., 1991; King, 1992, 1995; Luckie & Smethurst, 1998).

- As soon as you can, improve your notes by filling in gaps and completing thoughts.
- Look for connections among ideas. How do concepts in your notes relate to one another?
- Remember to link new ideas to what you already know.
- Summarize your notes. Boil them down and *organize* them.
- After each class session, write down at least seven major ideas, definitions, or details that are likely to become test questions.
- Make up questions from your notes and be sure you can answer them.

SUMMARY The letters LISAN are a guide to active listening, but listening and good note-taking are not enough. You must also review, organize, relate, extend, and think about new ideas. Teachers nearly always know the names of the best listeners in their classes. Get involved and you will undoubtedly learn more (Luckie & Smethurst, 1998).

STUDY HABITS—AVOIDING THE LAST-MINUTE BLUES

Virtually every topic is interesting to someone, somewhere. I'm not particularly interested in the sex life of South American tree frogs. However, a biologist might be fascinated. (Another tree frog might be, too.) If you wait for teachers to "make" their courses interesting, you are missing the point. Interest is a matter of *your attitude.* It's a mistake to blame poor grades on events "beyond your control." Students who believe that success is based on effort tend to do better in the long run (Noel et al., 1987).

Let's consider a few more things you can do to improve your study habits.

STUDY IN A SPECIFIC PLACE Ideally, you should study in a quiet, well-lighted area free of distractions. If possible, you should also have at least one place where you *only study.* Do nothing else at that spot: Keep magazines, CD players, friends, pets, posters, video games, puzzles, food, lovers, sports cars, elephants, pianos, televisions, hang gliders, kazoos, and other distractions out of the area. In this way, the habit of studying will become strongly linked with one specific place (Beneke & Harris, 1972). Then, rather than trying to force yourself to study, all you have to do is go to your study area. Once there, you'll find it is relatively easy to get started.

USE SPACED STUDY SESSIONS It is reasonable to review intensely before an exam. However, you're taking a big risk if you are only "cramming" (learning new information at the last minute). Research suggests that spaced practice is much more efficient (Naveh-Benjamin, 1990). **Spaced practice** consists of a large number of relatively short study sessions. Long, uninterrupted study sessions are called **massed practice.** (If you "massed up" your studying, you probably messed it up, too.)

Cramming places a big burden on memory. Usually, you shouldn't try to learn anything new about a subject during the last day before a test. It is far better to learn small amounts every day and review frequently (Luckie & Smethurst, 1998).

TRY MNEMONICS Learning has to start somewhere, and memorizing is often the first step. Many of the best ways to improve memory are covered in Chapter 10. Let's consider just one technique here.

Active listener *A person who knows how to maintain attention, avoid distractions, and actively gather information from lectures.*
Spaced practice *Practice spread over many relatively short study sessions.*
Massed practice *Practice done in a long, uninterrupted study session.*

Mnemonics make new information more familiar and memorable. Forming an image of a duck wearing a pot for a hat might help you remember that *pato* is the Spanish word for duck.

A **mnemonic** (nee-MON-ik) is a memory aid. Most mnemonics link new information to ideas or images that are easy to remember. For example, what if you want to remember that the Spanish word for duck is *pato* (pronounced POT-oh)? To use a mnemonic, you could picture a duck in a pot or a duck wearing a pot for a hat (Pressley, 1987). Likewise, to remember that the cerebellum controls coordination, you might picture someone named Sarah Bellum who is very co-ordinated. For best results, make your mnemonic images exaggerated or bizarre, vivid, and interactive (Campos & Perez, 1997).

TEST YOURSELF   A great way to improve grades is to take several practice tests before the real one in class. In other words, studying should include **self-testing,** in which you pose questions to yourself. You can use flash cards, "Learning Check" questions, a study guide, or other means. As you study, ask many questions and be sure you can answer them. Studying without self-testing is like practicing for a basketball game without shooting any baskets.

To make self-testing more convenient, your professor may make a *Study Guide* or a separate booklet of *Practice Quizzes* available. You can use either to review for tests. Practice quizzes are also available on the Internet, as described later in this Introduction.

OVERLEARN   Many students *underprepare* for exams, and most *overestimate* how well they will do (Murray, 1980). A solution to both problems is **overlearning,** in which you continue studying beyond initial mastery of a topic. In other words, plan to do extra study and review *after* you think you are prepared for a test.

Here's another reason for overlearning: Students who expect to take an essay test (usually the hardest kind) do better on essay, multiple-choice, and short-answer tests (Foos & Clark, 1984). Before tests, students always ask, "Will it be essay or multiple choice?" But as you can see, *it is best to approach all tests as if they will be essays.* That way, you will learn more completely, so you really "know your stuff."

BRIDGES

There are many ways to create mnemonics.

If you would like to learn more about memory strategies, see Chapter 10, pages 336–338.

Procrastination

All of these study techniques are fine. But what can I do about procrastination?   A tendency to procrastinate is almost universal. (When campus workshops on procrastination are offered, many students never get around to signing up!) Even when procrastination doesn't lead to failure, it can cause much suffering. Procrastinators work only under pressure, skip classes, give false reasons for late work, and feel ashamed of their last-minute efforts (Burka & Yuen, 1990). They also experience higher stress and more frequent illness (Tice & Baumeister, 1997).

Why do so many students procrastinate?   Many students equate grades with their *personal worth.* That is, they act like grades tell if they are good, smart people who will succeed in life. By procrastinating, they can blame poor work on a late start, rather than a lack of ability (Ferrari, 1991). After all, it wasn't their best effort, was it?

Perfectionism is a related problem. If you expect the impossible, it's hard to start an assignment. Students with high standards often end up with all-or-nothing work habits (Burka & Yuen, 1990). This is especially true if you are sensitive about how other people rate you (Clark & Hill, 1994; Ferrari, 1992).

TIME MANAGEMENT   Most procrastinators must eventually face the self-worth issue. Nevertheless, most can improve by learning better study skills and good time management. Because we have already discussed study skills, let's consider time management.

A **weekly time schedule** is a written plan that allocates time for study, work, and leisure activities. To prepare your schedule, make a chart showing all of the hours in each day of the week. Then fill in times that are already committed: sleep, meals, classes, work, team practices, lessons, appointments, and so forth. Next, fill in times when you will study for various classes. Finally, label the remaining hours as open or free times.

Each day, you can use your schedule as a checklist. That way you'll know at a glance which tasks are done and which still need attention (Luckie & Smethurst, 1998).

You may also find it valuable to make a **term schedule** that lists the dates of all quizzes, tests, reports, papers, and other major assignments for each class.

The beauty of sticking to a schedule is that you know you are making an honest effort. It will also help you avoid feeling bored while you are working or guilty when you play.

Be sure to treat your study times as serious commitments, but respect your free times, too. And remember, students who study hard and practice good time management *do* get better grades (Britton & Tesser, 1991; Leeming, 1997).

GOAL SETTING   Many students find it helpful to set **specific goals** for studying. Such goals should be clear-cut and measurable (Schunk, 1990). If you find it hard to stay motivated, try setting goals for the semester, the week, the day, and even for single study sessions. Also, be aware that more effort early in a

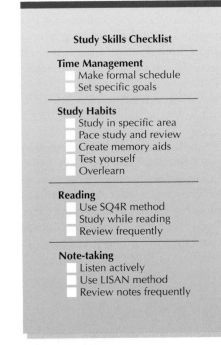

❖ **FIGURE I.2** *Study skills checklist.*

course can greatly reduce the "pain" and stress you will experience later (Brown, 1991). If your professors don't give frequent assignments, set your own day-by-day goals. An example would be reading, studying, and reviewing 8 pages a day to complete a 40-page chapter in 5 days. Remember, many small steps can add up to an impressive journey.

QUALITY TIME   Grades depend nearly as much on effort as they do on "intelligence." However, don't forget that good students work more *efficiently*, not just harder. Many study practices are notoriously poor, such as re-copying lecture notes, studying class notes but not the textbook (or the textbook but not class notes), outlining chapters, answering study questions with the book open, and "group study" (which often becomes a party). The best students emphasize *quality*: They study their books and notes in depth and attend classes regularly (Woehr & Cavell, 1993). (See ❖Figure I.2 for a summary of study skills.)

TAKING TESTS—ARE YOU "TEST WISE"?

If I read and study effectively, is there anything else I can do to improve my grades?   You must also be able to show what you know on tests. Here are some suggestions for improving your test-taking skills.

General Test-Taking Skills

You'll do better on all types of tests if you observe the following guidelines (Wood & Willoughby, 1995).

1. Read all directions and questions carefully. They may give you good advice or clues.

2. Quickly survey the test before you begin.
3. Answer easy questions before spending time on more difficult ones.
4. Be sure to answer all questions.
5. Use your time wisely.
6. Ask for clarification when necessary.

Several additional strategies can help you do better on objective tests.

OBJECTIVE TESTS   Objective tests (multiple-choice and true-false items) require you to recognize a correct answer among wrong ones or a true statement versus a false one. Here are some strategies for taking objective tests.

1. First, relate the question to what you know about the topic. Then, read the alternatives. Does one match the answer you expected to find? If none matches, reexamine the choices and look for a *partial* match.
2. Read *all* the choices for each question before you make a decision. Here's why: If you immediately think that *a* is correct and stop reading, you might miss seeing a better answer like "both *a* and *d*."
3. Read rapidly and skip items you are unsure about. You may find "free information" in later questions that will help you answer difficult items.
4. Eliminate certain alternatives. With a four-choice multiple-choice test, you have one chance in four of guessing right. If you can eliminate two alternatives, your guessing odds improve to 50-50.
5. Unless there is a penalty for guessing, be sure to answer any skipped items. Even if you are not sure of the answer, you may be right. If you leave a question blank, it is automatically wrong.

   When you are forced to guess, don't choose the longest answer or the letter you've used the least. Both strategies lower scores more than random guessing does (Shatz, 1986).
6. There is a bit of folk wisdom that says "Don't change your answers on a multiple-choice test. Your first choice is usually right." Careful study of this idea has shown it is *false* (Harvil & Davis, 1997).

   If you change answers, you are three times more likely to gain points than to lose them (Geiger, 1991). This is especially true if you feel *very* uncertain of your first answer. ("When in doubt, scratch it out!") When you have doubts, your second answer is more likely to be correct (Ramsey et al., 1987).

7. Remember, you are searching for the one *best* answer to each question. Some answers may be partly true, yet flawed in some way. If you are uncertain, try rating each multiple-choice alternative on a 1-to-10 scale. The answer with the highest rating is the one you are looking for.
8. Few circumstances are *always* or *never* present. Answers that include superlatives such as *most, least, best, worst, largest,* or *smallest* are often false (Luckie & Smethurst, 1998).

ESSAY TESTS   Essay questions are a weak spot for students who lack organization, don't support their ideas, or don't directly answer the question. When you take an essay exam, try the following:

1. Read the question carefully. Be sure to note key words, such as *compare, contrast, discuss, evaluate, analyze,* and *describe.* These words all demand a certain emphasis in your answer.
2. Think about your answer for a few minutes, and list the main points you want to make. Just write them as they come to mind. Then rearrange the ideas in a logical order and begin writing. Elaborate plans or outlines are not necessary (Torrance, Thomas, & Robinson, 1991).
3. Don't beat around the bush or pad your answer. Be direct. Make a point and support it. Get your list of ideas into words.
4. Look over your essay for errors in spelling and grammar. Save this for last. Your *ideas* are of first importance. You can work on spelling and grammar separately if they affect your grades.

SHORT-ANSWER TESTS   Tests that ask you to fill in a blank, define a term, or list specific items can be difficult. Usually, the questions themselves contain little information. If you don't know the answer, you won't get much help from the questions.

The best way to prepare for short-answer tests is to overlearn the details of the course. As you study, pay special attention to lists of related terms.

Again, it is best to start with the questions you're sure you know. Follow that by completing items you think you probably know. Questions you have no idea about can be left blank (Luckie & Smethurst, 1998).

Again, for your convenience, ❖Figure I.2 provides a checklist summary of the main study skills we have covered.

USING ELECTRONIC MEDIA—NETTING NEW KNOWLEDGE

The Internet and electronic media are providing exciting new ways to explore topics ranging from affection to zoophobia. Let's see how you can use these technologies to learn more about psychology.

Electronic Gateways

The **Internet** is a network of computers that communicate through the phone system and other electronic links. An important subpart of the Internet is the **World Wide Web,** an interlinked system of information "sites" or "pages." A Web site is just a collection of information stored on a computer. Through the Internet, you can retrieve Web pages from other computers and display them on your own screen. Thus, if you know the electronic "address" of a Web site, you can view the information it contains.

Many Web pages also have links to other Web sites. These **links** let you "jump" from one site to the next to find more information. In seconds, you can connect with university computers, services that search the Internet for specific topics, electronic journals, and even virtual libraries, where all the books are electronic.

USING THE "NET"   To find psychological information on the Internet, you'll need a computer and a modem. If you don't own a computer, you can usually use one on campus.

Various software browsers make it easier to navigate around the Internet and receive information over the telephone. A **browser** allows you to see text, images, sounds, video, and other information stored in formats used on the Internet. Browsers also keep lists of your favorite Internet addresses so you can return to them.

The Psychology Resource Center

Once I have access to the Internet, how would I find information about psychology?   Your first stop on the Internet should be the Psychology Resource Center. This specialized site is designed to support students who are using Wadsworth textbooks to learn psychology. Here's what you'll find there:

- **On-line Quizzes.** You can use these chapter-by-chapter multiple-choice quizzes to practice for tests and check your understanding.
- **Interactive Activities.** The demonstrations and mini-experiments in this feature allow you to directly experience various psychological principles.
- **Internet Resources.** This area is a "launching pad" that will take you to other psychology-related sites on the Internet. If a site sounds interesting, a click of the mouse will link you to it.
- **On-line Flashcards.** These on-line flashcards allow you to practice terms and concepts interactively.
- **Hot Topics.** This section features a news item or current event that is explored from a psychological perspective. After you've thought about a topic, you can share your opinions with others in an on-line discussion.
- **Discussion Forum.** In the Discussion Forum, you'll have a chance to share your ideas with those of psychology students from all over the country.
- **Research and Teaching Showcase.** Here you'll find regularly updated summaries of presentations, articles, or other teaching and research materials.
- **Archives.** Using the Archives, you can quickly search for current and past articles from Hot Topics and the Research and Teaching Showcase.
- **Meet the Author.** Meet the author of your text in an interactive, multimedia presentation.

The Psychology Resource Center is located at **http://psychology.wadsworth.com.** Be sure to visit this site for valuable information about how to improve your grades and enhance your appreciation of psychology.

Wadsworth's Psychology Resource Center gives you online access to a variety of valuable learning aids and interesting materials.

Combat exposure and adult psychosocial adjustment among U.S. Army veterans serving in Vietnam, 1965–1971.
  Antisocial Behavior, Combat Experience, Military Veterans
This study investigated the relationship between combat exposure and adult antisocial behavior in a sample of 2,490 male Army veterans of the Vietnam War who completed questionnaires about their psychological functioning. After adjustment for history of childhood behavior problems, posttraumatic stress disorder diagnosis, and demographic and military characteristics, it was found that veterans who experienced high and very high levels of combat were twice as likely to report adult antisocial behavior as veterans with no or low levels of combat and were also more likely to meet criteria for antisocial personality disorder. The results indicate that exposure to traumatic events during late adolescence or early adulthood is associated with multiple adult adjustment problems in vocational, interpersonal, and societal functioning. Treatment focusing on the effects of the trauma is likely to be necessary but not sufficient for improving affected veterans' behavior.
Barrett, Drue H.; Resnick, Heidi S.; Foy, David W.; Dansky, Bonnie S. et al. (Ctrs for Disease Control & Prevention, National Ctr for Environmental Health, Atlanta, GA). Journal of Abnormal Psychology, 1996(Nov), Vol 105(4), 575–581.

❖ **FIGURE I.3** *This is a sample abstract from the PsycINFO database. Notice the key words listed after the title. Searching for any of these terms would produce this abstract and others on similar topics. The PsycLIT CD-ROM database contains similar abstracts of journal articles, books, and book chapters.*

Psych Sites

As mentioned earlier, you can use links in the Psychology Resource Center to jump to other Internet sites. To explore the Internet more directly, try visiting any of the psychology-related sites listed at the end of each chapter in this book. The sites I've listed are generally of high quality. However, be aware that information on the Internet is not always accurate. It is wise to approach all Web sites with a healthy dose of skepticism. Also, because of the fluid nature of the Internet, some of these sites may be inactive or out of date by the time you try them. Nevertheless, most will lead you to interesting materials.

INFOTRAC *InfoTrac College Edition* is an on-line university library of articles from more than 700 publications. These articles cover a multitude of topics in psychology. You can read them on-line or print complete articles right from InfoTrac. InfoTrac is great for writing reports, doing research, or just reading more about psychology.

  InfoTrac is located at **http://www.infotrac-college.com/ wadsworth.** Again, you will need a password to use this service. If InfoTrac was included with this textbook, you already have a password. Otherwise, you can buy a subscription to InfoTrac at the campus bookstore.

PsycINFO Psychological knowledge can also be found in specialized on-line databases. One of the best is PsycINFO, offered by the American Psychological Association. **PsycINFO** provides summaries of the scientific and scholarly literature in psychology. Each record in PsycINFO consists of an abstract (short summary), plus notes about the author, title, source, and other details (❖ Fig. I.3). All entries are indexed by key terms. Thus, you can search for various topics by entering words such as *drug abuse, postpartum depression,* or *creativity.*

  You can gain access to PsycINFO in several ways. Many colleges and universities subscribe to PsycINFO or to a related CD-ROM version called PsycLIT. (PsycLIT is described in a moment.) If this is the case, you can usually search PsycINFO from a terminal in the college library or computer center—for free. PsycINFO can also be accessed through the Internet, either directly, through APA's PsycDIRECT service, or through a "gateway" such as CompuServe or other Internet providers.

  If you would like to search PsycINFO by using your own computer, you can reach it through an online vendor or PsycDIRECT. For more information on how to gain access to PsycINFO, check this Web site: **http://www.apa.org/psycinfo/.**

CD-ROM Databases

CD-ROM databases are another valuable way to do research in psychology. In the previous section, we discussed how to retrieve information from computers at remote locations, via the Internet. With **CD-ROM databases,** all of the information is stored on a compact disk.

Internet *An electronic network that enables computers to communicate with one another, usually through the telephone system.*
World Wide Web *A system of information "sites" accessible through the Internet.*
Links *Connections built into Internet sites that let you "jump" from one site to the next.*
Browser *Software that facilitates access to text, images, sounds, video, and other information stored in formats used on the Internet.*
PsycINFO *A searchable, on-line database that provides brief summaries of the scientific and scholarly literature in psychology.*
CD-ROM database *A searchable database of information stored on a compact disk.*

To use a CD database, you would typically go to a college library or computer center. There, you would check out a CD and place it in a computer for viewing and searching. Using a "database on a disk" is fast and free. In fact, it may be the easiest way of all to explore the psychological literature.

PsycLIT AND ClinPSYC **PsycLIT** and **ClinPSYC** are CD-ROM databases produced by the American Psychological Association. PsycLIT is stored on two disks. The first contains references to journal articles from 1974 through 1989. The second lists articles from 1990 to the present. Disk two also contains a database of book chapters and books published from 1987 to the present. ClinPSYC is a collection of information related to abnormal and clinical psychology.

As with the PsycINFO database, PsycLIT provides references to the scientific literature in psychology and related fields. PsycLIT is most likely to be found at a college or university library. It is far too expensive for individual purchase.

Please do try some of the "electronic gateways" described here. You might be surprised by the fascinating information that awaits you. Investigating psychology on your own is one of the best ways to enrich an already valuable course.

Multimedia CD-ROMs

Multimedia CD-ROMs are an exciting recent development in education. A single compact disk can store reams of text and thousands of pieces of art. All of the information contained in traditional print textbooks can easily fit on a CD for display on a computer screen. In addition, CDs are capable of presenting animations, audio clips, film clips, and interactive exercises. A CD you may be interested in trying is *PsychNow!* offered by Wadsworth to complement this textbook.

PSYCHNOW! Using this dynamic multimedia CD allows you to actively explore the world of psychology. Full audio and video presentations will help you discover interesting principles—frequently by observing your own behavior (❖Fig. I.4). *Psych-Now!* includes many interactive demonstrations, experiments, games, and activities, all designed to expand your understanding. Rather than just reading about concepts, *PsychNow!* makes it possible to experience them directly. With the click of a mouse, you can call up a large variety of helpful materials that make learning psychology more exciting than ever.

USING MULTIMEDIA CD-ROMS *PsychNow!* and similar CD-ROMs can be used alone or in conjunction with a textbook. At the end of each chapter in this book, you'll find a list of *PsychNow!* modules. Using these materials will allow you to see psychology come to life in ways that are not possible in a printed text. If you would like to be part of the electronic revolution in psychology, give *PsychNow!* a try.

A Final Word

There is a distinction in Zen between "live words" and "dead words." Live words come from personal experience; dead words are "about" a subject. This book can be only a collection of

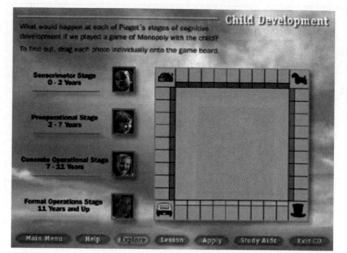

❖ **FIGURE I.4** *A sample screen from PsychNow!*

dead words unless you accept the challenge of making an intellectual journey. You will find many helpful, useful, and exciting ideas in the pages that follow. To make them yours, you must set out to *actively* learn as much as you can. The ideas presented here should get you off to a good start. Good luck!

For more information, consult any of the following books.

- Burka, J. B., & Yuen, L. M. (1990). *Procrastination: Why you do it; what to do about it.* Cambridge, MA: Perseus Books.
- Campanelli, J. F., & Price, J. L. (1991). *Write in time: Essay exam strategies.* Ft. Worth, TX: Holt, Rinehart & Winston.
- Hettich, P. I. (1998). *Learning skills for college and career.* Belmont, CA: Wadsworth-Brooks/Cole.
- Luckie, W., & Smethurst, W. (1998). *Study power.* Cambridge, MA: Brookline.
- Rosnow, R. L., & Rosnow, M. (1998). *Writing papers in psychology: A student guide.* Belmont, CA: Wadsworth-Brooks/Cole.
- Rowe, B. (1998). *College survival guide: Hints and references to aid college students.* Belmont, CA: Wadsworth-Brooks/Cole.

K N O W L E D G E   B U I L D E R
STUDY SKILLS

RELATE

Which study skills do you think would help you the most? Which techniques do you already use? Which do you think you should try? How else could you improve your performance as a student?

LEARNING CHECK

1. The four Rs in SQ4R stand for "read, recite, relate, and review." T or F?

2. When using the LISAN method, students try to write down as much of a lecture as possible so that their notes are complete. T or F?

3. Spaced study sessions are usually superior to massed practice. T or F?

4. According to recent research, you should almost always stick with your first answer on multiple-choice tests. T or F?

5. To use the technique known as overlearning, you should continue to study after you feel you have begun to master a topic. T or F?

6. Procrastination is related to seeking perfection and equating self-worth with grades. T or F?

7. An Internet browser is typically used to search CD-ROM databases for articles on various topics. T or F?

CRITICAL THINKING

8. How are the SQ4R method and the LISAN method related?

Answers:
1. T 2. F 3. T 4. F 5. T 6. T 7. F 8. Both encourage people to actively seek information as a way of learning more effectively.

PSYCHOLOGY ON THE NET

- **The Psychology Resource Center** From the publishers of this book, this site offers a study center for this text, on-line activities, links to multimedia brochures, catalogues, software demos, and more. http://psychology.wadsworth.com
- **How to Succeed as a Student** Advice on how to be a college student. Topics from studying to housing to preparation for

work are included. http://www.gu.edu.au/gwis/stubod/stuadv/stu_advice_con.html
- **Library Research in Psychology** Hints on how to do library research in psychology. http://www.apa.org/science/lib.html
- **Psychology Glossary** You can use this glossary to get additional definitions for common psychological terms. http://ucnet.canberra.edu.au/~packrat/Psychology.101/glossary.html
- **Study Skills** More information on SQ4R, taking tests, note-taking, and time management. http://www.gac.peachnet.edu/student_affairs/study_skills/stskills.html
- **InfoTrac® College Edition** For recent articles on studying, use Subject Guide search for STUDY SKILLS.

INTERACTIVE LEARNING

- *PsychNow!* 1a. Study skills.

PsycLIT *A searchable CD-ROM database that contains brief summaries of journal articles and other publications in all areas of psychology.*
ClinPSYC *A searchable CD-ROM database that contains brief summaries of journal articles and other publications concerning abnormal and clinical psychology.*

CHAPTER 1

Psychology: The Search for Understanding

Chapter Survey

Theme: Psychology is both a profession and a natural science.

▼ KEY QUESTIONS
● KEY TOPICS

▼ What is psychology? What are its goals?

- A definition of psychology
- Psychology's scientific basis
- Major areas of psychological research
- Psychology's four basic goals

▼ How did psychology emerge as a field of knowledge?

- Important persons in psychology's history
- Ideas that shaped modern psychology

▼ KEY QUESTIONS
● KEY TOPICS

▼ What are the major trends and specialties in psychology?

- Five ways to view behavior
- How human diversity has affected psychology
- Education and licensing of psychologists
- Kinds of psychologists and what they do

▼ What is critical thinking?

- Basic principles of critical thinking

▼ How does psychology differ from false explanations of behavior?

- A critique of pseudo-psychologies

1

WHY STUDY PSYCHOLOGY?

YOU ARE A UNIVERSE, *a collection of worlds within worlds. Your brain is possibly the most complicated device in existence. Through its action, you are capable of art, music, science, war, philosophy, love, hatred, and charity. You are the most challenging riddle ever written, a mystery even to yourself at times. Your thoughts, emotions, and actions—your behavior and conscious experience—are the subject of this book.*

Look around you. Newspapers, radio, magazines, television, and the Internet are loaded with psychological information. Psychology is an ever-changing panorama of people and ideas. You can hardly call yourself educated without knowing something about it.

There is another reason for studying psychology. Socrates said, "Know thyself," and while we must envy those who have walked on the moon or cruised the ocean's dreamlike depths, the ultimate frontier still lies close to home. What, really, could be more fascinating than a journey of self-discovery?

In a sense, this book is a travel guide. Psychologists can't claim to have "the answers" to all your questions. But they can show you some of the landscape already explored. More important, you may gain skills that will aid your own search for answers. Ultimately, the answers must be your own, but psychology is a rich starting point.

Before we begin, take a few moments to think about each of the "gateways to psychology" listed next. These core ideas will help you better understand and appreciate the topics we are about to cover.

Gateways to Psychology

PSYCHOLOGY is the science of behavior and mental processes. Psychology provides objective answers to questions about human behavior.

PSYCHOLOGISTS GATHER SCIENTIFIC DATA to describe, understand, predict, and control behavior.

PSYCHOLOGICAL THEORIES furnish valuable insights into our behavior and reveal its deeper meanings.

PSYCHOLOGISTS ARE HIGHLY TRAINED PROFESSIONALS who specialize in creating, teaching, and applying psychological knowledge.

CRITICAL THINKING is central to the scientific method, to psychology, and to effective behavior in general.

TESTING has shown that astrology and similar unscientific systems that claim to explain behavior are false.

PSYCHOLOGY—DISCOVERING HUMAN BEHAVIOR

Psychology is a rich and complex field, as shown by the following:

- *Snapshot:* A clinical psychologist finds new ways to help people eliminate terrifying nightmares.
- *Snapshot:* A biopsychologist uses computerized brain scans to study how we see colors.
- *Snapshot:* An educational psychologist helps a child overcome reading disabilities that could handicap her for life.
- *Snapshot:* A personnel psychologist uses personality tests to select future police officers.
- *Snapshot:* A cognitive psychologist provides dramatic new insights into how memory works.

As these images imply, psychology touches many areas of our lives. Psychology is about memory, stress, therapy, love, persuasion, hypnosis, perception, death, conformity, creativity, learning, personality, aging, intelligence, sexuality, emotion, happiness, and many more topics.

A SCIENCE AND A PROFESSION   As our "snapshots" also suggest, psychology is both a *science* and a *profession*. Some psychologists are scientists who do research to create new knowledge. Others are teachers who pass this knowledge on to students.

Still others apply psychology to solve problems in mental health, education, business, sports, law, and medicine. In short, some psychologists generate knowledge, some transmit it to others, and some apply it. Many, of course, do more than one of these activities (Meltzoff, 1998).

Later we will return to the profession of psychology. For now, let's focus on how knowledge is created. Whether they work in a lab, a classroom, or a clinic, all psychologists rely on information gained from scientific research.

Defining Psychology

The word *psychology* comes from the roots *psyche,* which means "mind" and *logos,* meaning "knowledge or study." However, the "mind," which cannot be seen or touched, is notoriously difficult to study. That's why **psychology** is defined as the scientific study of behavior and mental processes.

BEHAVIOR   *What does behavior refer to in the definition of psychology?*   Anything you do—eating, sleeping, talking, or sneezing—is a behavior. So are dreaming, gambling, watching television, learning Spanish, basket weaving, and reading this book. Naturally, we are interested in **overt behaviors** (observable actions and responses). But psychologists also study **covert behaviors**. These are private, internal activities, such as

Psychologists are highly trained professionals. In addition to the psychological knowledge they possess, psychologists learn specialized skills in counseling and therapy, measurement and testing, research and experimentation, statistics, diagnosis, treatment, and many other areas.

thinking, remembering, and other mental events (Kelly & Saklofske, 1994).

Empiricism

At various times in the last 100 years, world-renowned experts have made statements such as these: "Heavier-than-air flying machines are impossible," "Radio has no future," "X-rays are a hoax," "Computers will never serve any practical purpose," and "Space travel is utter bilge." Obviously, all of these statements eventually proved to be false.

In the realm of human behavior, the opinions of "authorities" are also often wrong. As a result, psychologists have a special respect for **empirical evidence** (information gained from direct observation and measurement). When possible, psychologists study behavior directly, by collecting **data** (observed facts) (Kimble, 1989). Gathering data allows us to compare observations and draw valid conclusions. Would you say it's true, for instance, that "You can't teach an old dog new tricks"? Why argue about it? A psychologist would get 10 "new" dogs, 10 "used" dogs, and 10 "old" dogs and then try to teach them all new tricks to find out!

In essence, the empirical approach says, "Let's take a look" (Stanovich, 1998). For example, have you ever wondered if drivers become more hostile when it's blazing hot outside? Psychologists Douglas Kenrick and Steven MacFarlane (1986) decided to find out. Kenrick and MacFarlane parked a car at a green light in a one-lane intersection, in Phoenix, Arizona, in temperatures ranging from 88° to 116°. Then they recorded the number of times other drivers honked at the stalled car and how long they honked. The results are shown in ❖Figure 1.1. As you can see, higher temperatures were closely related to an increase in the amount of time spent leaning on the horn (which may be why cars have horns and not cannons).

Isn't the outcome of this study fairly predictable? In many studies, the results are surprising or unexpected. In this instance, you may have guessed how drivers would react. However, it's possible that drivers tend to become lethargic in hot

weather, rather than more aggressive. Thus, the study does tell us something interesting about frustration, discomfort, and aggression.

Now, let's see if you can tell, from your own experience or common sense, which of the items in a brief psychology quiz

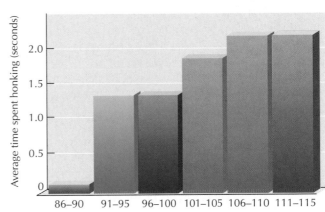

❖ **FIGURE 1.1** *Results of an empirical study. The graph shows that horn honking by frustrated motorists becomes more likely as air temperature increases. This suggests that physical discomfort is associated with interpersonal hostility. Riots and assaults also increase during hot weather. Here we see a steady rise in aggression as temperatures go higher. However, research done by other psychologists has shown that hostile actions that require physical exertion, such as a fist fight, may become less likely at very high temperatures. (Data from Kenrick & MacFarlane, 1986.)*

Psychology *The scientific study of behavior and mental processes.*
Overt behaviors *Actions or responses that are directly observable.*
Covert behaviors *Responses that are internal or hidden from view.*
Empirical evidence *Facts or information based on direct observation or experience.*
Data *Observed facts or evidence (data: plural; datum: singular).*

are true. After you've completed the quiz, we will compare your answers with those arrived at empirically.

Scoring this quiz is easy. Empirical studies have shown that all the statements are *false*. (To find out why, you can look at the listed chapters.) If you missed some questions, don't despair. The point is simply this: Psychology became a science when researchers began to make careful, systematic observations. You'll become a better observer of human behavior if you do the same.

Psychological Research

Many fields, such as history, law, art, and business, are interested in human behavior. How is psychology different? The great strength of psychology is that it uses the scientific method to study behavior. True **scientific observation** is structured so that it answers questions about the world (Stanovich, 1998). This is also what separates real psychology from the "pop" psychology found in trendy books and magazines. For instance, is it true that playing the music of Mozart for babies increases their intelligence? Many popular magazines and books say yes. Scientific testing says no. (See "The Mozart Effect" in Chapter 4 for more information.)

Sometimes it is impossible to study a topic because of ethical or practical concerns. More often, questions go unanswered for lack of a suitable **research method** (a systematic procedure for answering scientific questions). For example, at one time we had to accept the reports of people who say they never dream. Then the EEG (electroencephalograph, or brain-wave machine) was developed. The EEG can reveal when a person is dreaming. People who "never dream," it turns out, dream frequently. If they are awakened during a dream, they vividly remember it. Thus, the EEG helped make the study of dreaming more scientific.

What kinds of topics would a research psychologist study? Here's a sample of what various research psychologists might say about their work.

DEVELOPMENTAL PSYCHOLOGY "In general, **developmental psychologists** study the course of human growth and development, from conception until death. I'm especially interested in how young children develop the ability to think, speak, perceive, and act. Currently, I am studying how parents contribute to language development in young children."

LEARNING "I'm also interested in how people get to be the way they are, but in a more abstract sense. I believe that most human behavior is learned. Like other **learning theorists,** I study

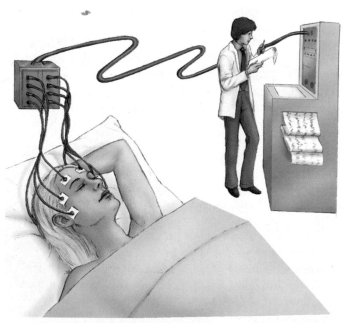

The scientific study of dreaming was made possible by use of the EEG, a device that records the tiny electrical potentials generated by the brain as a person sleeps. The EEG converts these electrical potentials to a written record of brain activity. Certain shifts in brain activity, coupled with the presence of rapid eye movements, are strongly related to dreaming. (See Chapter 8 for more information.)

The variety and complexity of human behavior make psychological investigation challenging. How would you explain the behaviors shown here?

how and why learning occurs in humans and animals. Right now, I'm investigating how different patterns of reward affect learning."

PERSONALITY "In many ways my area is one of the most challenging. **Personality theorists** study personality traits, dynamics, and theories. We draw on other areas, as well as our own work, to understand personality structure, motivation, and individual differences. I am especially interested in the personality profiles of highly creative college students."

Scientific observation *An empirical investigation that is structured so that it answers questions about the world.*
Research method *A systematic approach to answering scientific questions.*
Developmental psychologist *A psychologist interested in the course of human growth and development from birth until death.*
Learning theorist *A psychologist interested in variables affecting learning and in theories of learning.*
Personality theorist *A psychologist who studies personality traits, dynamics, and theories.*

COGNITIVE PSYCHOLOGY "I regard myself as part of a new wave of psychological inquiry. Like other **cognitive psychologists**, I am primarily interested in thinking. My colleagues and I want to know how reasoning, problem solving, memory, and other mental processes contribute to behavior. I'm working on a computer model of problem solving. If my program responds like a human does, it may be a good model of how people think."

SENSATION AND PERCEPTION "How do we become aware of the world? How does information 'get into' our nervous systems? How is it processed into meaningful patterns? These are my interests. **Sensation and perception psychologists** study the sense organs and the process of perception. I am using a perceptual theory to study how we are able to recognize faces."

COMPARATIVE PSYCHOLOGY "**Comparative psychologists** study and compare the behavior of different species, especially animals. Personally, I am fascinated by the echolocation abilities of porpoises. In a typical study, we ask porpoises to select different shapes while they are underwater and blindfolded. If they choose the right target, we reward them with food. Their ability to discriminate in this way is superb."

BIOPSYCHOLOGY "The brain and nervous system are my meat . . . so to speak. **Biopsychologists** study the relationship between behavior and biological processes, especially activities in the nervous system. I've been doing some exciting research on hunger. Altering different parts of the brain can cause a rat to eat uncontrollably or to entirely lose its appetite. I believe that ultimately all behavior will be explained by the actions of nerve cells and brain chemicals."

THE PSYCHOLOGY OF GENDER "**Gender psychologists** study differences between the sexes and how they develop. I want to understand how gender differences are influenced by biology, child development, culture, and stereotypes. Much of my research is on how we learn basic 'male' and 'female' identities. For example, I've observed that girls are praised for playing with 'nurturing,' or 'female,' toys, whereas boys are ignored or scolded for doing the same thing."

SOCIAL PSYCHOLOGY "**Social psychologists** are interested in human social behavior. We study attitudes, persuasion, riots, conformity, leadership, racism, friendship, and many other topics. My own interest is interpersonal attraction. I investigate factors that influence how strongly two people are attracted to each other."

CULTURAL PSYCHOLOGY "**Cultural psychologists** study how culture affects human behavior. The language you speak, the foods you eat, how your parents disciplined you, what laws you obey, whom you regard as 'family,' whether you eat with a spoon or your fingers—these and countless other details of behavior are strongly influenced by culture. For the last 5 years I have been comparing early child development in Canada, Mexico, India, and Central Africa."

This small sample should give you an idea of the variety of psychological research. It also hints at some of the topics covered later in this book.

Some of the most interesting research with animals has focused on attempts to teach primates to communicate by using sign language. Such research has led to better methods for teaching language to aphasic children (children with serious language impairment). (See Chapter 11 for more information.)

Animals and Psychology

Research involving animals was mentioned in some of the preceding examples. Why is that? Most psychologists are primarily interested in human behavior. However, psychologists seek the natural laws governing the behavior of any living creature—from flatworms to humans. Indeed, some psychologists spend their entire careers studying rats, cats, dogs, turtles, or chimpanzees. Overall, about 8 percent of all psychological research involves animals (McCarty, 1998).

In many instances, **animal models** are used to discover principles that apply to humans. Studying animals has added greatly to our understanding of obesity, memory, stress, learning, psychosis, therapy, aging, and many other topics. Psychology also benefits animals. The care of endangered species in zoos, for example, relies on behavioral studies.

Psychology's Goals

What do psychologists hope to achieve? In general, the goals of psychology as a science are to describe, understand, predict, and control behavior. Beyond that, psychology's ultimate goal is to gather knowledge to benefit humanity (Kimble, 1989).

DESCRIPTION *What do psychology's goals mean in practice?* Assume that we would like to answer the following questions: What happens when the right side of the brain is injured? Is there more than one type of memory? Do autistic children react abnormally to their parents? The answer to each question requires a careful description of behavior. Description, or naming and classifying, is typically based on making a detailed record of behavioral observations.

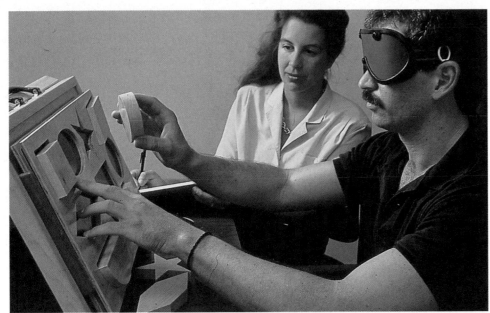

Some psychologists specialize in administering, scoring, and interpreting psychological tests, such as tests of intelligence, creativity, personality, or aptitude.

But a description doesn't explain anything, does it? Right. Useful knowledge begins with accurate description, but descriptions fail to answer the important "why" questions. *Why* do more women attempt suicide, and *why* do more men complete it? *Why* are people more aggressive when they are uncomfortable? *Why* are bystanders often unwilling to help in an emergency?

③ UNDERSTANDING   Psychology's second goal is met when we can explain an event. That is, **understanding** usually means we can state the causes of a behavior. Take our last "why" question as an example: Research on "bystander apathy" has shown that people often fail to help when *other* possible helpers are nearby. Why? Because a "diffusion of responsibility" occurs, so no one feels required to pitch in. Generally, the more potential helpers present, the less likely it is that help will be given (Darley & Latané, 1968). Now we can explain a perplexing problem.

② PREDICTION   Psychology's third goal, **prediction**, is the ability to forecast behavior accurately. Notice that our explanation of bystander apathy makes a prediction about the chances of getting help. Anyone who has been stranded by car trouble on a busy freeway will recognize the accuracy of this prediction: Having many potential helpers nearby is no guarantee that anyone will stop to help.

Behavioral predictions are quite useful. For instance, research predicts that you will suffer less jet lag if you fly east early in the day and west late in the day (see Chapter 8 to learn why). Prediction is especially important in **psychometrics** (mental measurement). Experts in this area use tests to predict success in school, work, or a career.

④ CONTROL   *Description, explanation, and prediction seem reasonable, but is control a valid goal for psychology?*   Psychology's

BRIDGES

Bystander apathy and conditions that influence whether people will help in an emergency interest social psychologists.

See Chapter 20, pages 685–688, for details.

most misunderstood goal is control, which may seem like a threat to personal freedom. However, **control** simply means altering conditions that influence behavior in predictable ways. If a psychologist suggests changes in a classroom that help children learn better, she has exerted control. If she helps a person overcome a crippling fear of heights, control is involved. Control is also an element of designing airplanes to reduce pilot errors. Clearly, psychology can change behavior. But, as is true of other types of knowledge, psychology must be used wisely and humanely (Kipnis, 1987).

Cognitive psychologist *A psychologist who studies thinking, knowing, understanding, and information processing.*
Sensation and perception psychologist *A psychologist who studies the sense organs and the process of perception.*
Comparative psychologist *A psychologist primarily interested in studying and comparing the behavior of different species, especially animals.*
Biopsychologist *A psychologist who studies the relationship between behavior and biological processes, especially activity in the nervous system.*
Gender psychologist *A psychologist who investigates differences between females and males and how they develop.*
Social psychologist *A psychologist particularly interested in human social behavior.*
Cultural psychologist *A psychologist who studies the ways in which culture affects human behavior.*
Animal model *In research, an animal whose behavior is used to derive principles that may apply to human behavior.*
Description *In scientific research, the process of naming and classifying.*
Understanding *In psychology, understanding is achieved when the causes of a behavior can be stated.*
Prediction *An ability to accurately forecast behavior.*
Psychometrics *A specialty that focuses on mental measurement or testing, such as personality and intelligence testing.*
Control *Altering conditions that influence behavior.*

In summary, psychology's goals are a natural outgrowth of our desire to understand behavior. Basically, they boil down to asking the following questions:

- What is the nature of this behavior? (description)
- Why does it occur? (understanding and explanation)
- Can we predict when it will occur? (prediction)
- What conditions affect it? (control)

Wilhelm Wundt, 1832–1920. Wundt is credited with making psychology an independent science, separate from philosophy. Wundt's original training was in medicine, but he became deeply interested in psychology. In his laboratory, Wundt investigated how sensations, images, and feelings combine to make up personal experience.

A BRIEF HISTORY OF PSYCHOLOGY—PSYCHOLOGY'S FAMILY ALBUM

Psychology has a long past but a short history. Psychology's past is centuries old because it includes **philosophy**, the study of knowledge, reality, and human nature. In contrast, psychology's history is short, beginning only about 100 years ago. Of course, to some students any history is "not short enough!" Nevertheless, to understand psychology now, we need to consider its past.

INTO THE LAB Psychology's history as a science began in 1879 in Leipzig, Germany. There, the "father of psychology," **Wilhelm Wundt** (VILL-helm Voont), set up the first psychological laboratory to study conscious experience. How, he wondered, are sensations, images, and feelings formed? To find out, Wundt observed and measured stimuli of various kinds (lights, sounds, weights). A **stimulus** is any physical energy that affects a person and evokes a response (stimulus: singular; stimuli [STIM-you-lie]: plural). Wundt then used **introspection**, or "looking inward," to probe his reactions to various stimuli. If you stop reading right now and carefully examine your thoughts, feelings, and sensations, you will have done some introspecting.

Wundt called his approach **experimental self-observation** because he used both trained introspection and objective measurement. Over the years, he studied vision, hearing, taste, touch, memory, time perception, and many other subjects. By insisting on careful observation and measurement, Wundt got psychology off to a good start.

Structuralism

Wundt's ideas were carried to the United States by one of his students, a man named Edward B. Titchener (TICH-in-er). In America, Wundt's ideas were called **structuralism** because they dealt with the structure of mental life. Essentially, the structuralists hoped to analyze private experiences into basic "elements" or "building blocks."

How could they do that? You can't analyze experience like a chemical compound, can you? Perhaps not, but the structuralists tried, mostly by using introspection. For instance, an observer might heft an apple and decide that she or he had experienced the elements "hue" (color), "roundness," and "weight." Likewise, a structuralist would have been fascinated by a question like this: What basic tastes mix together to create complex flavors as different as liver, lime, bacon, and burnt-almond fudge?

It soon became clear that introspection was a poor way to answer many questions. Why? Because the structuralists often *disagreed*. And when they did, there was no way to settle differences. If two people came up with different lists of basic taste sensations, for example, who could say which was right? Despite such limitations, "looking inward" still has a role in studies of hypnosis, meditation, problem solving, moods, and many other topics (e.g., Mayer & Hanson, 1995).

Functionalism

William James, an American scholar, broadened psychology to include animal behavior, religious experience, abnormal behavior, and other interesting topics. James's brilliant first book, *Principles of Psychology* (1890), helped establish the field as a serious discipline (Simon, 1998).

The term **functionalism** comes from an interest in how the mind functions to adapt us to our environment. James regarded consciousness as an ever-changing stream or flow of images and sensations—not a set of lifeless building blocks, as the structuralists claimed.

The functionalists admired Charles Darwin, who deduced that creatures evolve in ways that favor their survival. According to Darwin's principle of **natural selection**, physical features that help animals adapt to their environments are retained in evolution. Similarly, the functionalists wanted to find out how the mind, perception, habits, emotions, and other psychological processes aid survival.

What effect did functionalism have on modern psychology? Functionalism brought the study of animals into psychology. It also promoted **educational psychology** (the study of learning, teaching, classroom dynamics, and related topics). Learning makes us more adaptable, so the functionalists tried to find ways to improve education. For similar reasons, functionalism spurred the rise of **industrial psychology**, the study of people at work.

BRIDGES

Educational psychology and industrial psychology are two major applied specialties.

See Appendix A for more information.

William James, 1842–1910. William James was the son of philosopher Henry James, Sr., and the brother of novelist Henry James. During his long academic career, he taught anatomy, physiology, psychology, and philosophy at Harvard University. James believed strongly that ideas should be judged in terms of their practical consequences for human conduct.

Philosophy *The formal study of knowledge, reality, and human nature.*
Wilhelm Wundt *The "father of psychology"; set up the first psychological laboratory to study conscious experience.*
Stimulus *Any physical energy that has some effect on an organism and that evokes a response.*
Introspection *To look within; to examine one's own thoughts, feelings, or sensations.*
Experimental self-observation *Wilhelm Wundt's technique of combining trained introspection with objective measurement.*
Structuralism *The school of thought concerned with analyzing sensations and personal experience into basic elements.*
Functionalism *The school of psychology concerned with how behavior and mental abilities help people adapt to their environments.*
Natural selection *Darwin's theory that evolution favors those plants and animals best suited to their living conditions.*
Educational psychology *The psychological study of learning, teaching, and related topics.*
Industrial psychology *The application of psychology to work, especially to personnel selection, human relations, and machine design.*

John B. Watson, 1878–1958. Watson's intense interest in observable behavior began with his doctoral studies in biology and neurology. Watson became a psychology professor at Johns Hopkins University in 1908 and advanced his theory of behaviorism. He remained at Johns Hopkins until 1920, when he left for a career in advertising!

Behaviorism

Functionalism was soon challenged by **behaviorism**, the study of overt, observable behavior. Behaviorist John B. Watson objected strongly to the study of the "mind" or "conscious experience." "Introspection," he said, "is unscientific." Watson realized that he could study animals even though he couldn't ask them questions or know what they were thinking. He simply observed the relationship between stimuli (events in the environment) and an animal's **responses** (any muscular action, glandular activity, or other identifiable behavior). Why not, he asked, apply the same objectivity to studying humans (Watson, 1994)?

Watson soon adopted Russian physiologist Ivan Pavlov's (ee-VAHN PAV-lahv) concept of conditioning to explain most behavior. (A **conditioned response** is a learned reaction to a particular stimulus.) Watson enthusiastically proclaimed, "Give me a dozen healthy infants, well-formed, and my own special world to bring them up in and I'll guarantee to take any one at

B. F. SKINNER, AMERICAN BEHAVIORIST

A CLOSER LOOK

Burrhus Frederic Skinner was fascinating and controversial. Skinner believed that our behavior is controlled by rewards, or positive reinforcers.

To study learning, Skinner created his famous conditioning chamber or "Skinner box." With it, he could present stimuli to animals and record their responses (see Chapter 9, "Operant Conditioning"). Many of Skinner's ideas about learning grew out of work with rats and pigeons. Nevertheless, he believed that the same laws of behavior apply to all organisms, including humans.

Skinner was convinced that a "designed culture" based on positive reinforcement could encourage desirable behavior. (Contrary to common belief, Skinner disliked the use of punishment.) It is essential, he said, to change our behavior before overpopulation, pollution, or nuclear war shatters humanity. Too often, misguided rewards lead us into destructive actions.

Among the general public, B. F. Skinner was perhaps best known as the man who taught pigeons to play table tennis (see Chapter 9), as the inventor of a "teaching machine," and as the creator of a mechanical "baby tender" that looked suspiciously like a big Skinner box. Skinner's own daughter Deborah lived for two and a half years in the baby tender—a crib-sized chamber with warm filtered air, sound-absorbing walls, special toys, and a large window on one side. "How dehumanizing!" said the critics. But contrary to news reports, Deborah was frequently taken out of the box for cuddling and play. As an adult, she said, "I think I was a very happy baby. Most of the criticisms of the box are by people who don't understand what it was." The same is true of many criticisms of Skinner, which are often based on a misunderstanding of his ideas (DeBell & Harless, 1992).

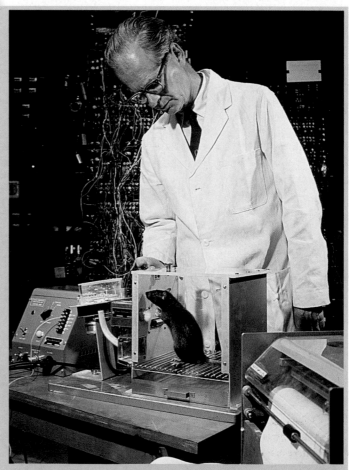

B. F. Skinner, 1904–1990. Skinner studied simple behaviors under carefully controlled conditions. The "Skinner box" you see here has been widely used to study learning in simplified animal experiments. In addition to advancing psychology, Skinner hoped that his radical brand of behaviorism would improve human life.

random and train him to become any type of specialist I might select—doctor, lawyer, artist, merchant-chief, and yes, beggar-man and thief" (Watson, 1913).

Would most psychologists agree with Watson's claim? Today, most would consider it an overstatement. Just the same, behaviorism helped make psychology a natural science, rather than a branch of philosophy (Richelle, 1995).

One of the best-known modern behaviorists, B. F. Skinner (1904–1990), said, "In order to understand human behavior we must take into account what the environment does to an organism before and after it responds. Behavior is shaped and maintained by its consequences" (Skinner, 1971). As a "radical behaviorist," Skinner also believed that mental events are not needed to explain behavior (Richelle, 1995). (See "B. F. Skinner, American Behaviorist" for a glimpse into his view.)

Strict behaviorists have been criticized for ignoring the role that thinking and other mental processes play in our lives. One critic even charged that Skinnerian psychology had "lost consciousness!" However, many criticisms have been answered by **cognitive behaviorism**, a view that combines thinking and conditioning to explain behavior (Sperry, 1995). For example, let's say you frequently visit a particular Website because it offers free music you can download. A behaviorist would say that you visit the site because you are rewarded with music each time you go there. A cognitive behaviorist would add that, in addition, you *expect* to find free music at the site. This is the cognitive component of your behavior.

Behaviorists deserve credit for much of what we know about learning, conditioning, and the proper use of reward and punishment. Behaviorism is also the source of **behavior modification**. In this type of therapy, learning principles are used to change problem behaviors such as overeating, unrealistic fears, or temper tantrums (see Chapter 18).

Gestalt Psychology

Imagine that you just played "Happy Birthday" on a tuba. Next, you play it on a high-pitched violin. None of the tuba's sounds are duplicated by the violin. Yet, we notice something interesting: The melody is still completely recognizable—as long as the *relationship* between notes remains the same.

Now, what would happen if you played the notes of "Happy Birthday" in the correct order, but at a rate of one per hour? What would we have? Nothing! The separate notes would no longer be a melody. Perceptually, the melody is somehow more than the individual notes that define it.

Observations like these launched the Gestalt school of thought. **Gestalt psychology** emphasizes the study of thinking, learning, and perception in whole units, not by analyzing experiences into parts. Its slogan is "The whole is greater than the sum of its parts" (see ❖Figure 1.2).

Max Wertheimer (VERT-hi-mer), a German psychologist, was the first person to advance the Gestalt viewpoint. It is a mistake, he said, to analyze psychological events into pieces, or "elements," as the structuralists did. Like a melody, many experiences resist being broken into smaller units. For this reason, studies of perception and personality have been especially in-

fluenced by the Gestalt viewpoint. Gestalt psychology also inspired a type of psychotherapy. If you are curious about what Gestalt therapy is like, look ahead to Chapter 18.

Were all the early psychologists men? So far, no women have been mentioned. For the most part, men dominated science and education at the beginning of the twentieth century. Nevertheless, women have contributed to psychology from the beginning. Take a moment and read "Women in Psychology" for more information.

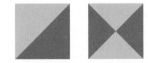

❖ **FIGURE 1.2** *The design you see here is entirely made up of the two elements shown below it. If you stare at the design for a moment, you should quickly see that as a whole it contains patterns and complexities that greatly exceed the sum of its parts.*

Behaviorism *The school of psychology that emphasizes the study of overt, observable behavior.*

Response *Any muscular action, glandular activity, or other identifiable aspect of behavior.*

Conditioned response *A reflex response that has become associated with a new stimulus.*

Cognitive behaviorism *An approach that combines behavioral principles with cognition (perception, thinking, anticipation) to explain behavior.*

Behavior modification *The application of learning principles to change human behavior, especially maladaptive behavior.*

Gestalt psychology *A school of psychology emphasizing the study of thinking, learning, and perception in whole units, not by analysis into parts.*

Max Wertheimer, 1880–1941. Wertheimer first proposed the Gestalt viewpoint to help explain perceptual illusions. He later promoted Gestalt psychology as a way to understand not only perception, problem solving, thinking, and social behavior but also art, logic, philosophy, and politics.

Psychoanalytic Psychology

As mainstream psychology grew more scientific, an Austrian physician named Sigmund Freud was developing his own theories. Freud believed that mental life is like an iceberg: Only a small part is exposed to view. He called the area of the mind that lies outside personal awareness the **unconscious**. According to Freud, our behavior is deeply influenced by unconscious thoughts, impulses, and desires—especially those concerning sex and aggression. Freud's ideas opened new horizons in art, literature, and history, as well as psychology (Westen, 1998).

Freud theorized that many unconscious thoughts are threatening, which causes them to be **repressed** (actively held out of awareness). But sometimes, Freud said, hidden thoughts and wishes are revealed by dreams, emotions, or slips of the tongue. ("Freudian slips" are often humorous, as when a student who is tardy for class says, "I'm sorry I couldn't get here any later.")

Freud believed that all thoughts, emotions, and actions are determined. In other words, if we probe deeply enough, we will find the causes of everything we think, feel, or do. Freud was also among the first to appreciate that early childhood experiences affect adult personality ("The child is father to the man"). Most of all, perhaps, Freud is known for creating **psychoanalysis**, a method of psychotherapy that explores unconscious conflicts and emotional problems.

WOMEN IN PSYCHOLOGY

Women were actively discouraged from seeking advanced degrees in the late 1800s (Bohan, 1990). Even so, by 1906 in America, about 1 psychologist in every 10 was a woman. Who were these "foremothers" of psychology? Three who became well known are Mary Calkins, Christine Ladd-Franklin, and Margaret Washburn.

Mary Calkins did valuable research on memory. She was also the first woman president of the American Psychological Association, in 1905. Christine Ladd-Franklin studied color vision. In 1906, she was ranked among the 50 most important psychologists in America. In 1908, Margaret Washburn published an influential textbook on animal behavior, titled *The Animal Mind*.

The first woman to be awarded a Ph.D. in psychology was Margaret Washburn, in 1894. Over the next 15 years, many more women followed her pioneering lead. Today, two of three graduate students in psychology are women. And, in recent years, nearly 75 percent of all college graduates with a major in psychology have been women. Clearly, psychology has become fully open to both men and women (sources: Furumoto & Scarborough, 1986; Howard et al., 1986; Madigan & O'Hara, 1992; Martin, 1995).

Mary Calkins, 1863–1930

Christine Ladd-Franklin, 1847–1930

Margaret Washburn, 1871–1939

Sigmund Freud, 1856–1939. For more than 50 years, Freud probed the unconscious mind. In doing so, he altered modern views of human nature. His early experimentation with a "talking cure" for hysteria is regarded as the beginning of psychoanalysis. Through psychoanalysis, Freud added psychological treatment methods to psychiatry.

◆ **TABLE 1.1** The Early Development of Psychology

APPROXIMATE ORIGIN	DATE	NOTABLE EVENTS
Experimental psychology	1875	• First psychology course offered by William James
	1878	• First American Ph.D. in psychology awarded
	1879	• Wilhelm Wundt establishes first pyschology laboratory in Germany
	1883	• First American psychology lab founded at Johns Hopkins University
	1886	• First American psychology textbook published by John Dewey
Structuralism	1898	• Edward Titchener advances pyschology based on introspection
Functionalism	1890	• James publishes *Principles of Psychology*
	1892	• American Psychological Association founded
Psychoanalytic psychology	1895	• Sigmund Freud publishes first studies
	1900	• Freud publishes *The Interpretation of Dreams*
Behaviorism	1906	• Ivan Pavlov reports his research on conditioning
	1913	• John Watson presents behavioristic view
Gestalt psychology	1912	• Max Wertheimer and others advance Gestalt viewpoint
Neo-Freudianism	1914	• Carl Jung breaks with Freud

It wasn't very long before some of Freud's students began to break away to promote their own theories. Several who modified Freud's ideas became known as **neo-Freudians** (*neo* means "new" or "recent"). Neo-Freudians accept the broad features of Freud's theory but revise parts of it. For instance, many placed less emphasis on sex and aggression and more on social motives and relationships. Some well-known neo-Freudians are Alfred Adler, Anna Freud (Sigmund's daughter), Karen Horney (HORN-eye), Carl Jung (yoong), Otto Rank (rahnk), and Erik Erikson.

Today, Freud's ideas have been altered so much that few strictly psychoanalytic psychologists are left. However, Freud's legacy is still evident in various **psychodynamic theories**, which emphasize internal motives, conflicts, and unconscious forces (Westen, 1998). (See Table 1.1.)

Humanistic Psychology

Humanism is a view that focuses on understanding subjective human experience. As a group, humanistic psychologists are interested in human problems, potentials, and ideals.

How is the humanistic approach different from others? Carl Rogers, Abraham Maslow, and other humanists rejected the Freudian idea that personality is ruled by unconscious forces. They were also uncomfortable with the behaviorist emphasis on environmental control. Both views have a strong undercurrent of **determinism** (the idea that behavior is determined by forces beyond our control). In contrast, the humanists stress **free will**, the ability to make voluntary choices. Of course, past experiences affect us. Nevertheless, humanists believe that people can freely *choose* to live more creative, meaningful, and satisfying lives.

Humanists helped stimulate interest in psychological needs for love, self-esteem, belonging, self-expression, creativity, and spirituality. Such needs, they believe, are as important as our biological urges for food and water. For example, newborn infants deprived of human love may die just as surely as they would if deprived of food.

How scientific is the humanistic approach? Humanists collect data and seek evidence to support their ideas. However,

Unconscious *Contents of the mind that are beyond awareness, especially impulses and desires not directly known to a person.*
Repression *The unconscious process by which memories, thoughts, or impulses are held out of awareness.*
Psychoanalysis *A Freudian approach to psychotherapy emphasizing the exploration of unconscious conflicts.*
Neo-Freudian *A psychologist who accepts the broad features of Freud's theory but has revised the theory to fit his or her own concepts.*
Psychodynamic theory *Any theory of behavior that emphasizes internal conflicts, motives, and unconscious forces.*
Humanism *An approach to psychology that focuses on human experience, problems, potentials, and ideals.*
Determinism *The doctrine that all behavior has prior causes that would completely explain one's choices and actions if all such causes were known.*
Free will *The doctrine that human beings are capable of freely making choices or decisions.*

Abraham Maslow, 1908–1970. As a founder of humanistic psychology, Maslow was interested in studying people of exceptional mental health. Such self-actualized people, he believed, make full use of their talents and abilities. Maslow offered his positive view of human potential as an alternative to the schools of behaviorism and psychoanalysis.

they tend to be less interested in treating psychology as an objective, behavioral science. Instead, they stress subjective factors, such as one's self-image, self-evaluation, and frame of reference. **Self-image** is your perception of your own body, personality, and capabilities. **Self-evaluation** refers to the positive and negative feelings you have about yourself. A **frame of reference** is a mental or emotional perspective used for evaluating events. Thus, humanists seek to understand how people perceive themselves and experience the world.

Maslow's concept of self-actualization is a special feature of humanism. **Self-actualization** refers to developing one's potential fully and becoming the best person possible. According to humanists, everyone has this potential. Humanists seek ways to help it emerge. (Return to ◆Table 1.1 for a summary of psychology's early development.)

PSYCHOLOGY TODAY—FIVE VIEWS OF BEHAVIOR

At one time, the schools of thought were almost like political parties. Loyalty to each view was fierce, and clashes were common. Today, viewpoints such as functionalism and Gestalt psychology have blended into newer, broader perspectives. Also, some early systems, such as structuralism, have disappeared entirely. Certainly, loyalties and specialties still exist. But today,

many psychologists are **eclectic** (ek-LEK-tik: they draw from many sources and embrace a variety of theories). Even so, five major perspectives shape modern psychology. These are the *psychodynamic, behavioristic,* and *humanistic* views, plus the increasingly important *cognitive* and *biopsychological* perspectives (◆Table 1.2) (Robins, Gosling, & Craik, 1999).

Biopsychology is a fast-growing area of knowledge. As noted earlier, biopsychologists expect to eventually explain all behavior in terms of physical mechanisms, such as brain activity and genetics. Their optimism is based on exciting new insights about how the brain relates to thinking, feelings, perception, abnormal behavior, and other important topics (Robins, Gosling, & Craik, 1998).

Cognitive science is another rapidly expanding area. In fact, over the last 10 years, a "cognitive revolution" has taken place in psychology. *Cognition* means "thinking" or "knowing." As stated earlier, **cognitive psychologists** study thoughts, expectations, memory, language, perception, problem solving, consciousness, creativity, and other mental processes. With all this renewed interest in thinking, it could be said that psychology recently "regained consciousness" (Robins, Gosling, & Craik, 1999).

Behavior in Perspective

Each of the five major perspectives adds to our understanding of human behavior. For example, Marcia has become deeply depressed during her first year at college. In the last month, her grades have fallen, she has been sleeping all the time, and she barely speaks to other students. What would each viewpoint say about Marcia's depression?

Psychodynamic psychologist: "It's interesting that Marcia broke up with her boyfriend shortly before she became depressed. Depression is often related to loss. Marcia may be unconsciously turning feelings of loss, anger, or rejection into self-blame and self-hate."

Behaviorist: "I've noticed that Marcia's grades were mediocre before her depression began and that they have dropped further. When rewards such as grades, affection, friendship, or approval are withdrawn, studying and other activities can grind to a halt. As Marcia became depressed, her behavior may have changed in ways that made it even less likely that she would be rewarded with successes, praise, and affection."

Humanistic psychologist: "Because Marcia got good grades in high school, she may have been unprepared for the difficulty of college. If being intelligent and competent is important to her self-image, she may be threatened by her poor performance. The breakup with her boyfriend could be a similar threat. I believe that she may be feeling depressed, vulnerable, and confused because of such threats to her self-image and self-esteem."

Biopsychologist: "Heredity can influence whether a person is prone to depression. I would like to know if there is a history of depression in Marcia's family. Also, depression can be caused by changes in brain chemistry, regardless of a person's life circumstances. Marcia might have a medical problem that needs treatment."

BRIDGES

Behaviorism, Gestalt psychology, psychoanalytic theory, and humanism have given rise to various forms of psychotherapy.

See Chapter 18 for more information about how psychological disorders are treated.

PSYCHODYNAMIC VIEW
Key Idea: *Behavior is directed by forces within one's personality that are often hidden or unconscious.*
Emphasizes internal impulses, desires, and conflicts—especially those that are unconscious; views behavior as the result of clashing forces within personality; somewhat negative, pessimistic view of human nature.

BEHAVIORISTIC VIEW
Key Idea: *Behavior is shaped and controlled by one's environment.*
Emphasizes the study of observable behavior and the effects of learning; stresses the influence of external rewards and punishments; neutral, scientific, somewhat mechanistic view of human nature.

HUMANISTIC VIEW
Key Idea: *Behavior is guided by one's self-image, by subjective perceptions of the world, and by needs for personal growth.*
Focuses on subjective, conscious experience, human problems, potentials, and ideals; emphasizes self-image and self-actualization to explain behavior; positive, philosophical view of human nature.

BIOPSYCHOLOGICAL VIEW
Key Idea: *Human and animal behavior is the result of internal physical, chemical, and biological processes.*
Seeks to explain behavior through activity of the brain and nervous system, physiology, genetics, the endocrine system, biochemistry, and evolution; neutral, reductionistic, mechanistic view of human nature.

COGNITIVE VIEW
Key Idea: *Much human behavior can be understood in terms of the mental processing of information.*
Concerned with thinking, knowing, perception, understanding, memory, decision making, and judgment; explains behavior in terms of information processing; neutral, somewhat computer-like view of human nature.

Cognitive psychologist: "Marcia's depression might be explained by her thinking patterns. For example, she could be magnifying the importance of bad things that have happened to her recently. She may also have unrealistic beliefs that lead to depression, such as 'I must be completely competent and achieving to be a worthwhile person' or 'I must always be loved and approved by every significant person in my life.'"

SUMMARY   As you can see, it is helpful to view human behavior from more than one perspective. This is also true in another sense. We are rapidly becoming a multicultural society, made up of people from many different nations. How has this affected psychology? The next section explains why it is important for all of us to be aware of cultural differences.

HUMAN DIVERSITY—APPRECIATING SOCIAL AND CULTURAL DIFFERENCES

Jerry, who is Japanese American, is married to an Irish Catholic American. Here is what Jerry, his wife, and their children did on New Year's Day:

> We woke up in the morning and went to Mass at St. Brigid's, which has a black gospel choir. . . . Then we went to the Japanese-American Com-

munity Center for the Oshogatsu New Year's program and saw Buddhist archers shoot arrows to ward off evil spirits for the year. Next, we ate traditional rice cakes as part of the New Year's service and listened to a young Japanese-American storyteller. On the way home, we stopped in Chinatown and after that we ate Mexican food at a taco stand (Njeri, 1991).

Jerry and his family reflect a new social reality: Cultural diversity is becoming the norm. About one third of the population in the United States is now African American, Hispanic, Asian American, Native American, or Pacific Islander. In some large cities, "minority" groups are already the majority. By 2056, the "average" U.S. resident will no longer trace his or her roots to Europe. Similar trends can be found in Canada and other Western nations.

The Impact of Culture

In the past, psychology was based mostly on the cultures of North America and Europe. Now, we must ask, Do the principles of Western psychology apply to people in all cultures? Are some psychological concepts invalid in other cultures? Are any universal? As psychologists have addressed such questions, one thing has become clear: Most of what we think, feel, and do is influenced in one way or another by the social and cultural worlds in which we live (Segall, Lonner, & Berry, 1998).

CULTURAL RELATIVITY   Imagine that you are a psychologist. Your client, Linda, who is a Native American, tells you that spirits live in the trees near her home. Is Linda suffering from a delusion? Is she abnormal? Obviously, you will misjudge Linda's mental health if you fail to take her cultural beliefs into account. **Cultural relativity** (the idea that behavior must be judged relative to the values of the culture in which it occurs) can greatly affect the diagnosis of mental disorders (Alarcon, 1995). Cases like Linda's teach us to be wary of using inappropriate standards when judging others or comparing groups. Here's another example: Let's say an observer notes that child-rearing practices in Culture A are "indulgent." What does that tell us? Is parenting *inferior* in Culture A? Actually, it probably means that the observer used his or her own culture as a standard. Child care that is more lenient than the North American, Eurocentric standard is not neces-

Self-image   *Total subjective perception of oneself, including images of one's body, personality, and capabilities.*
Self-evaluation   *Positive and negative feelings held toward oneself.*
Frame of reference   *A mental or emotional perspective used for judging and evaluating events.*
Self-actualization   *The ongoing process of fully developing one's personal potential.*
Eclectic   *Selected or chosen from many sources.*
Cognitive psychology   *The area of psychology concerned with human thinking, knowing, understanding, and information processing.*
Cultural relativity   *The idea that behavior must be judged relative to the values of the culture in which it occurs.*

To fully understand human behavior, we must take into account personal differences in age, culture, ethnicity, disabilities, gender, and sexual orientation.

sarily bad for children. Such parenting might actually be more accurately described as tolerant or affectionate, rather than "indulgent."

A BROADER VIEW OF DIVERSITY   In addition to cultural differences, age, ethnicity, gender, religion, disability, and sexual orientation all affect the **norms** that guide behavior. (Norms are rules that define acceptable and expected behavior for members of various groups.) All too often, the unstated standard for judging what is "average," "normal," or "correct" is the behavior of white, middle-class males. To fully understand human behavior, psychologists need to know how people differ, as well as the ways in which we are all alike. For the same reason, an appreciation of human diversity can enrich your life, as well as your understanding of psychology (additional sources for this section: Denmark, 1994; Graham, 1992; Sampson, 1993; Shweder, 1999; Tomes, 1998).

In a moment, we will further explore what psychologists do. First, here are some questions to enhance your learning.

K N O W L E D G E   B U I L D E R
HISTORY AND MAJOR PERSPECTIVES

RELATE

Which school of thought most closely matches your own view of behavior? Do you think any of the early schools offers a complete explanation of why we behave as we do? What about the five contemporary perspectives? Can you explain why so many psychologists are eclectic?

A group of psychologists were asked to answer this question: "Why did the chicken cross the road?" Their answers are listed next. Can you identify their theoretical orientations?

The chicken had been rewarded for crossing road in the past.
The chicken had an unconscious wish to become a trivet.
The chicken was trying to solve the problem of how to reach the other side of the road.
The chicken felt a need to explore new possibilities as a way to actualize its potentials.
The chicken's motor cortex was activated by messages from its hypothalamus.

LEARNING CHECK

Match the following.

1. _H_ Philosophy
2. _J_ Wundt
3. _B_ Structuralism
4. _E_ Functionalism
5. _G_ Behaviorism
6. _A_ Gestalt
7. _D_ Psychodynamic
8. _C_ Humanistic
9. _I_ Cognitive
10. _F_ Washburn
11. _K_ Biopsychology

A. Against analysis; studied whole experiences
B. "Mental chemistry" and introspection
C. Emphasizes self-actualization and personal growth
D. Interested in unconscious causes of behavior
E. Gave rise to educational and industrial psychology
F. First woman Ph.D. in psychology
G. Studied stimuli and responses, conditioning
H. Part of psychology's "long past"
I. Concerned with thinking, language, problem solving
J. Used "experimental self-observation"
K. Relates behavior to the brain, physiology, and genetics
L. Also known as engineering psychology

12. Cultural relativity refers to the fact that some universal behavior patterns are not related to culture. T or F?

13. Universal norms exist for judging the behavior of people in various cultural and social groups. T or F?

CRITICAL THINKING

14. Modern sciences like psychology are built on observations that can be verified by two or more independent observers. Did structuralism meet this standard?

Answers:

1. H 2. J 3. B 4. E 5. G 6. A 7. D 8. C 9. I 10. F 11. K 12. F 13. F 14. No, it did not. The downfall of structuralism was that each observer examined the contents of his or her own mind—which is something that no other person can observe.

PSYCHOLOGISTS—GUARANTEED NOT TO SHRINK

Question: What is the difference between a psychologist and a psychiatrist?
Answer: About $30 an hour. (And going up.)

What are the differences among psychologists, psychiatrists, psychoanalysts, counselors, and other mental health professionals? Certainly, they're not all "shrinks." Each title reflects a specific blend of training and skills.

PSYCHOLOGISTS: PERCEPTIONS AND REALITIES

Public impressions of psychologists are often inaccurate. Perhaps this occurs because so many stereotyped images appear in movies and on television. For example, in the film *Good Will Hunting*, a psychologist angrily chokes his rebellious young patient. No ethical therapist would ever engage in such behavior, yet it is not unusual in the movies. Other films have featured psychologists who are more disturbed than their patients or psychologists who are bumbling buffoons. Evil, mind-controlling therapists who victimize or seduce patients are another popular Hollywood stereotype. Such characters may be dramatic and entertaining, but they seriously distort public perceptions of responsible and hardworking psychologists (Sleek, 1998).

Even without media distortions, misconceptions about psychologists are common, as revealed by the results of a public survey.

- **Public perception:** Most psychologists work in private practice.
- **Reality:** Only one psychologist in three works in private practice. Most psychologists are employed by schools, businesses, social agencies, and other organizations.
- **Public perception:** Most psychologists work in clinics or hospitals.
- **Reality:** Only 16 percent of psychologists work in clinics or hospitals. The specialties of psychologists are extremely varied. They are not all therapists.
- **Public perception:** Most practicing psychologists do not hold doctoral degrees.

- **Reality:** Doctoral-level training is required to obtain a license to practice psychology. Most professional psychologists hold doctoral degrees.
- **Public perception:** A psychologist's job is to help people.
- **Reality:** In this instance, the public view is mostly correct. About 75 percent of all psychologists do help people directly. In addition, nearly all psychologists aid people in one way or another (Peterson, 1995).

In the film *Good Will Hunting*, Robin Williams plays a psychologist who physically assaults a defiant patient, played by Matt Damon. Such dramatic scenes are typical of the way psychologists and psychotherapy are misrepresented in the media.

A **psychologist** is a person highly trained in the methods, factual knowledge, and theories of psychology. Psychologists usually have a master's degree or a doctorate. These degrees typically require from 3 to 8 years of postgraduate training. (See "Psychologists: Perceptions and Realities.") Psychologists may teach, do research, give psychological tests, or serve as consultants to business, industry, government, or the military. In most industrialized nations, the number of professional psychologists continues to grow (Rosenzweig, 1999).

Psychologists interested in emotional problems specialize in clinical or counseling psychology (see ◆Table 1.3). **Clinical psychologists** treat psychological problems or do research on psychotherapy and mental disorders. **Counseling psychologists** treat milder emotional and behavioral disturbances. Counseling psychology used to be limited to problems such as poor adjustment at work or school. Now, many counseling psychologists are mainly doing psychotherapy. As a result, differences between counseling and clinical psychology are beginning to fade (Tyler, 1992).

BRIDGES

Psychotherapy can be less effective if a therapist and client come from different cultures.

See Chapter 18, pages 629–630, for a discussion of the impact of culture on therapy

To enter the profession of psychology, it is best to have a doctorate (Ph.D., Psy.D., or Ed.D.). Most clinical psychologists hold a Ph.D. degree and follow a **scientist-practitioner model**, in which they are trained to do either scientific research or therapy (O'Sullivan & Quevillon, 1992). Many do both. Other clinicians earn the Psy.D. (Doctor of Psychology) degree, which emphasizes therapy skills, rather than research (Hershey, Kopplin, & Cornell, 1991).

Norms *Rules that define acceptable and expected behavior for members of a group.*
Psychologist *A person highly trained in the methods, factual knowledge, and theories of psychology.*
Clinical psychologist *A psychologist who specializes in the treatment of psychological and behavioral disturbances or who does research on such disturbances.*
Counseling psychologist *A psychologist who specializes in the treatment of milder emotional and behavioral disturbances.*
Scientist-practitioner model *The view that clinical psychologists should be skilled both as scientists and as therapists.*

◆ **TABLE 1.3** Kinds of Psychologists and What They Do

SPECIALTY		TYPICAL ACTIVITIES
Biopsychology	B*	Does research on the brain, nervous system, and other physical origins of behavior
Clinical	A	Does psychotherapy; investigates clinical problems; develops methods of treatment
Cognitive	B	Studies human thinking and information processing abilities
Community	A	Promotes community-wide mental health through research, prevention, education, and consultation
Comparative	B	Studies and compares the behavior of different species, especially animals
Consumer	A	Researches packaging, advertising, marketing methods, and characteristics of consumers
Counseling	A	Does psychotherapy and personal counseling; researches emotional disturbances and counseling methods
Cultural	B	Studies the ways in which culture, subculture, and ethnic group membership affect behavior
Developmental	A, B	Conducts research on infant, child, adolescent, and adult development; does clinical work with disturbed children; acts as consultant to parents and schools
Educational	A	Investigates classroom dynamics, teaching styles, and learning; develops educational tests, evaluates educational programs
Engineering	A	Does applied research on the design of machinery, computers, airplanes, automobiles, and so on, for business, industry, and the military
Environmental	A, B	Studies the effects of urban noise, crowding, attitudes toward the environment, and human use of space; acts as a consultant on environmental issues
Forensic	A	Studies problems of crime and crime prevention, rehabilitation programs, prisons, courtroom dynamics; selects candidates for police work
Gender	B	Does research on differences between males and females, the acquisition of gender identity, and the role of gender throughout life
Health	A, B	Studies the relationship between behavior and health; uses psychological principles to promote health and prevent illness
Industrial-organizational	A	Selects job applicants, does skills analysis, evaluates on-the-job training, improves work environments and human relations in organizations and work settings
Learning	B	Studies how and why learning occurs; develops theories of learning
Medical	A	Applies psychology to manage medical problems, such as the emotional impact of illness, self-screening for cancer, compliance in taking medicine
Personality	B	Studies personality traits and dynamics; develops theories of personality and tests for assessing personality traits
School	A	Does psychological testing, referrals, emotional and vocational counseling of students; detects and treats learning disabilities; improves classroom learning
Sensation and perception	B	Studies the sense organs and the process of perception; investigates the mechanisms of sensation and develops theories about how perception occurs
Social	B	Investigates human social behavior, including attitudes, conformity, persuasion, prejudice, friendship, aggression, helping, and so forth

*Research in this area is typically applied (A), basic (B), or both (A, B).

Other Mental Health Professionals

A **psychiatrist** is a medical doctor who specializes in treating mental disorders. Most psychiatrists are "talking doctors" who primarily do psychotherapy. However, they may also prescribe drugs, which is something a psychologist cannot do. This distinction may disappear, however. Some psychologists in the military are already prescribing drugs (Rabasca, 1999). Others in civilian settings are seeking similar prescription privileges. It will be interesting to see whether lawmakers agree they should have them. Several U.S. states may soon allow psychologists to write prescriptions, but many medical doctors are opposed (Foxhall, 1999).

To be a psychoanalyst, you must have a mustache and goatee, spectacles, a German accent, and a well-padded couch—or so the TV and movie stereotype goes. Actually, to become a **psychoanalyst**, you must have an M.D. or Ph.D. degree plus further specialized training in the theory and practice of Freudian psychoanalysis. In other words, either a physician or a psychologist may become an analyst by completing more training in a specific type of therapy. Analysts typically undergo psychoanalysis themselves before applying the method to others.

Is psychoanalysis widely used? Traditional Freudian analysis is expensive and time-consuming. As a result, psychoanalysts are becoming a rare breed, and few clients seek analysis today. Modern clinicians tend to be eclectic, rather than applying only a single method of therapy.

In many states, counselors also do mental health work. A **counselor** is an adviser who helps solve problems with marriage, career, school, work, or the like. To be a licensed counselor (such as a marriage and family counselor, a child counselor, or a school counselor) typically requires a master's degree plus 1 or 2 years of full-time supervised counseling experience. Almost all of a counselor's training is related to practical helping skills. Counselors are not as highly skilled as clinical or counseling psychologists, and they do not treat serious mental disorders.

Psychiatric social workers apply social science principles to help patients in clinics, hospitals, and mental health programs. Most hold an M.S.W. (Master of Social Work) degree. Often, they assist psychologists and psychiatrists as part of a team. Their typical duties include evaluating patients and families, conducting group psychotherapy, or visiting a patient's home, school, or job to alleviate problems.

The Profession of Psychology

Does a person have to have a license to practice psychology? Before the American Psychological Association (APA) began a push for licensing and certification, it was possible in many states for anyone to "hang out a shingle" as a "psychologist." Now a person must meet rigorous educational requirements to be legally called a psychologist. To work as a clinical or counseling psychologist, she or he must have a license issued by a state examining board. However, the law does not prevent you from calling yourself anything else you choose—psychotherapist, rebirther, primal feeling facilitator, cosmic aura balancer, or Rolfer—or from selling your "services" to anyone willing to pay. Beware of people advertising under such self-proclaimed titles. Even if their intentions are honorable, their training may be limited or nonexistent. A fully trained, certified psychologist who chooses to use a particular type of therapy is not the same as someone "trained" solely in that technique.

ETHICS Most psychologists take pride in following a professional code that stresses (1) high levels of competence, integrity, and responsibility; (2) respect for people's rights to privacy, dignity, confidentiality, and personal freedom; and above all, (3) protection of the client's welfare. Psychologists are also expected to use their knowledge to contribute to society. Many do volunteer work in the communities in which they live ("Ethical," 1992; Sullivan et al., 1998).

BRIDGES

Ethical standards are an important part of conducting psychological research with humans or animals.

See Chapter 2, pages 46–48.

Specialties in Psychology

Do all psychologists do therapy and treat abnormal behavior? No. Only about 58 percent are clinical and counseling psychologists. The rest are found in other specialties. At present, the APA consists of more than 50 divisions, each reflecting special skills or areas of interest. Some of the major specialties are listed in ◆Table 1.3 (also see ❖Figure 1.3). Nearly 30 percent of all psychologists are employed full-time at colleges or universities, where they teach and do research, consulting, or therapy. Some do **basic research**, in which they seek knowledge for the sake of knowledge. For example, a psychologist might study memory purely out of a desire to understand how it works. Others do **applied research** to solve immediate practical problems, such as finding ways to improve the memory of eyewitnesses to crimes. Some do research of both types.

In addition to the specialties listed in ◆Table 1.3, it shouldn't be long before job titles such as the following become more common: shyness counselor, thanatologist, retirement counselor, jury selection specialist, weight-control counselor, stress-reduction counselor, executive recruiter, and sleep disorders therapist. In short, psychology should remain a stimulating and innovative field for years to come.

Psychiatrist *A medical doctor with additional training in the diagnosis and treatment of mental and emotional disorders.*
Psychoanalyst *A mental health professional (usually a medical doctor) trained to practice psychoanalysis.*
Counselor *A mental health professional who specializes in helping people with problems not involving serious mental disorder; for example, marriage counselors, career counselors, or school counselors.*
Psychiatric social worker *A mental health professional trained to apply social science principles to help patients in clinics and hospitals.*
Basic (or "pure") research *Scientific study undertaken without concern for immediate practical application.*
Applied research *Scientific study undertaken to solve immediate practical problems.*

A good summary of our discussion so far is provided by psychologists Gary VandenBos and Brenda Bryant:

Psychologists are explorers and discoverers. They explore the reactions of human beings to small frustrations and great successes, to pleas-ing colors and the aftermath of disaster, always looking for answers to how and why people think, feel, and behave as they do. . . . The psychologist, regardless of where she or he may work, is always applying what is known in an effort to resolve the unknown. The psychologist, no matter how small the question being asked may appear to be, is looking for the larger answer (VandenBos & Bryant, 1987).

A Look Ahead

To help you get the most out of psychology, each chapter of this text includes a "Psychology in Action" section like the one that follows. These sections discuss ideas you can actually use, now or in the future. Our first discussion explains how to think more analytically about human behavior. After that, a final section called "A Step Beyond" provides a critical look at some decidedly unscientific explanations of behavior.

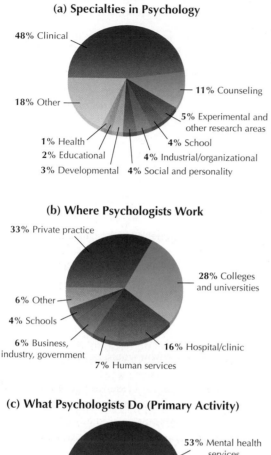

(a) Specialties in Psychology

48% Clinical
11% Counseling
18% Other
5% Experimental and other research areas
1% Health
4% School
2% Educational
4% Industrial/organizational
3% Developmental
4% Social and personality

(b) Where Psychologists Work

33% Private practice
28% Colleges and universities
6% Other
4% Schools
6% Business, industry, government
16% Hospital/clinic
7% Human services

(c) What Psychologists Do (Primary Activity)

53% Mental health services
4% Other
4% Applied psychology
10% Research
19% Education and educational services
10% Management/administration

❖ **FIGURE 1.3** (a) Specialties in psychology. Percentages are approximate. (b) *Where psychologists work.* (c) *This chart shows the main activities psychologists do at work. Any particular psychologist might do several of these activities during a work week (APA, 1998). The percentages shown here are based on membership in the American Psychological Association (APA). The APA welcomes both scientists and practitioners. However, some psychological researchers belong to other organizations, such as the American Psychological Society. As a result, the percentage of clinical and counseling psychologists working in the United States may be a little lower than shown in chart a. Nevertheless, it is accurate to say that most psychologists specialize in applied areas and work in applied settings.*

KNOWLEDGE BUILDER
PSYCHOLOGISTS AND THEIR SPECIALTIES

RELATE

You're going to meet four psychologists at a social gathering. How many would you expect to be therapists in private practice? Odds are that only two will be clinical (or counseling) psychologists and only one of these will work in private practice. On the other hand, at least one out of the four (and probably two) will work at a college or university.

LEARNING CHECK

See if you can answer these questions before continuing.

1. Which of the following can typically prescribe drugs?
   a. a psychologist *b.* a psychiatrist *c.* a psychotherapist *d.* a counselor

2. A psychologist who specializes in treating human emotional difficulties is called a _____ psychologist.

3. Roughly 40 percent of psychologists specialize in counseling psychology. T or F?

4. Who among the following would most likely be involved in the detection of learning disabilities?
   a. a consumer psychologist *b.* a forensic psychologist *c.* an experimental psychologist *d.* a school psychologist

CRITICAL THINKING

5. If most psychologists work in applied settings, why is basic research still of great importance?

Answers:

1. *b* 2. clinical or counseling 3. F 4. *d* 5. Because practitioners benefit from basic psychological research in the same way that physicians benefit from basic research in biology. Discoveries in basic science form the knowledge base that leads to useful applications.

psychology in action

Most of us would be skeptical when buying a used car. But all too often, we may be tempted to "buy" outrageous claims about topics such as "channeling," dowsing, the occult, the Bermuda Triangle, hypnosis, UFOs, numerology, and "psychic" advisers. Likewise, most of us easily accept our ignorance of subatomic physics. But because we deal with human behavior every day, we tend to think that we already know what is true and what is false in psychology.

For these and many more reasons, learning to think critically is one of the lasting benefits of getting an education. Facts and theories may change. Thinking and problem-solving skills last a lifetime.

In the broadest terms, **critical thinking** refers to an ability to evaluate, compare, analyze, critique, and synthesize information. Critical thinkers are willing to ask hard questions and challenge conventional wisdom. For example, many people believe that punishment (a spanking) is a good way to reinforce learning in children. A critical thinker would immediately ask: "Does punishment work? If so, when? Under what conditions does it not work? What are its drawbacks? Are there better ways to guide learning?" (Halonen, 1986). (Punishment is actually a poor way to discipline children; see Chapter 4 for details.)

THINKING ABOUT BEHAVIOR

The core of critical thinking is a willingness to actively evaluate ideas. It is, in a sense, the ability to stand outside yourself and reflect on the quality of your own thoughts. Critical thinkers analyze the evidence supporting their beliefs and probe for weaknesses in their reasoning. They question assumptions and look for alternate conclusions. True knowledge, they recognize, comes from constantly revising and enlarging our understanding of the world.

Critical thinking is built upon these four basic principles (Gill, 1991; Shore, 1990):

1. *Few "truths" transcend the need for empirical testing.* It is true that religious beliefs and personal values may be held without supporting evidence. But most other ideas can be evaluated by applying the rules of logic and evidence.
2. *Evidence varies in quality.* Judging the quality of evidence is crucial. Imagine that you are a juror in a courtroom, judging claims made by two battling lawyers. To judge correctly, you can't just weigh the evidence. You must also critically evaluate the *quality* of the evidence. Then you can give greater weight to the most credible facts.
3. *Authority or claimed expertise does not automatically make an idea true.* Just because a teacher, guru, celebrity, or authority is convinced or sincere doesn't mean you should au-

tomatically believe him or her. It is unscientific and self-demeaning to just take the word of an "expert" without asking, "What evidence convinced her or him? How good is it? Is there a better explanation?"

4. *Critical thinking requires an open mind.* Be prepared to consider daring departures and go wherever the evidence leads. However, it is possible to be so "open-minded" that you simply become gullible. Critical thinkers try to strike a balance between open-mindedness and healthy skepticism. Being open-minded means that you consider all possibilities before drawing a conclusion. It is the ability to change your views under the impact of new and more convincing evidence.

EVALUATING CLAIMS AND EVIDENCE

An anxious mother watches her son eat a candy bar and says, "Watch, it's like lighting a fuse on a skyrocket. He'll be bouncing off the walls in a few minutes." Is she right? Will a "sugar buzz" make her son "hyper"? How would you evaluate the claim that sugar adversely affects behavior? Here are some basic steps.

1. *State the claim clearly. What are its implications?* It's important to spell out what you would expect to see if the claim is true.
2. *Gather evidence.* Look for evidence relevant to the claim. Also, be sure to collect evidence both for and against the claim. Evidence may come from many sources, such as casual observations, opinions of authorities, published studies, or direct scientific observation.
3. *Evaluate the evidence.* Is the evidence you found consistent with the claim? If the information is conflicting, what conclusion does the strongest evidence support? (In general, scientific observations provide the highest quality of evidence.)
4. *Draw a conclusion.* If you have carefully evaluated the arguments and evidence bearing on a claim, you should have little trouble drawing a valid conclusion.

A CASE STUDY OF CRITICAL THINKING

To see how the preceding steps apply, let's return to the question about sugar. What we want to know is, Does eating excessive amounts of sugar adversely affect children's behavior?

Critical thinking *An ability to evaluate, compare, analyze, critique, and synthesize information.*

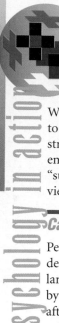
What are the implications of this claim? If it is true, children who eat sugar should display measurable changes in behavior.

Anecdotal Evidence

What evidence is there to support the claim? It should be easy to find parents who will attest that their children become high-strung, inattentive, or unruly after eating sugar. However, parents are not likely to be objective observers. Beliefs about "sugar highs" are common and could easily color parents' views.

Casual Observation

Perhaps it would help to observe children directly. Let's say you decide to watch children at a birthday party, where you know large amounts of sugary foods will be consumed. As predicted by the claim, children at the party become loud and boisterous after eating cake, ice cream, and candy. How persuasive is this evidence? Actually, it is seriously flawed. Birthday parties expose children to bright lights, loud noises, and unfamiliar situations. Any of these conditions, and others as well, could easily explain the children's "hyper" activity.

Authority

For nearly 50 years, many doctors, teachers, nutritionists, and other "experts" have emphatically stated that sugar causes childhood misbehavior. Should you believe them? Unfortunately, most of these "expert" opinions are based on anecdotes and casual observations that are little better than those we have already reviewed.

Formal Evidence

The truth is, parents, casual observers, and many authorities have been wrong. Dr. Mark Wolraich and his colleagues recently reviewed 23 scientific studies on sugar and children. In each study, children consumed known amounts of sugar and were then observed or tested. The clear-cut conclusion in all of the studies was that sugar does not affect aggression, mood, motor skills, or cognitive skills (Wolraich, Wilson, & White, 1995).

Studies like those we just reviewed tend to be convincing because they are based on systematic, controlled observation. To evaluate psychological questions, you will often have to rely on similar published evidence. But don't just accept the investigators' conclusions. It is important to review the evidence yourself and decide if it is convincing. (The Introduction to this book explains how you can use the Internet and other electronic resources to locate studies on various topics.)

SUMMARY

How do the principles of critical thinking apply to everyday questions about behavior? To apply critical thinking on a day-to-

day basis, you should be prepared to ask the following questions over and over again (Bartz, 1990):

1. What claims are being made?
2. What test of these claims (if any) has been made?
3. Who did the test? How good is the evidence?
4. What was the nature and quality of the tests? Are they credible? Can they be repeated?
5. How reliable and trustworthy were the investigators? Do they have conflicts of interest? Do their findings appear to be objective? Has any other independent researcher duplicated the findings?
6. Finally, how much credence can the claim be given? High, medium, low, provisional?

A course in psychology naturally enriches thinking skills. To add to the process, all upcoming Knowledge Builders include Critical Thinking questions like the ones you have already seen here. Tackling these exercises will sharpen your thinking skills and make learning livelier. For an immediate thinking challenge, the next section offers a critical look at several nonscientific systems that claim to explain behavior.

KNOWLEDGE BUILDER

CRITICAL THINKING

RELATE

Choose a dubious claim that you have encountered recently. (The "psychic hotline" commercials on TV might be a good example.) What claims are being made? What are their implications? What evidence is offered to support the claims? What is the quality of the evidence? Do you need more information to draw a conclusion?

LEARNING CHECK

1. An important aspect of _____ _____ is to seek evidence for and against an idea and to also evaluate the _____ of that evidence.

2. Most truths transcend the need for empirical testing. T or F?

3. To effectively evaluate a claim you must be able to clearly state its _____.

4. Evidence derived from _____ _____ is usually of the highest quality because it is based on systematic investigation.

CRITICAL THINKING

5. In studies of the effects of sugar, some children are fed diets that are low in sugar. Typically, aspartame is used to artificially sweeten the foods in these diets. Why is it important for the low-sugar diet to include sweet flavors?

Answers:

1. critical thinking, quality 2. F 3. implications 4. scientific observation 5. So that the children being tested won't know their food is low in sugar. Otherwise, they might be affected by their own expectations concerning the effects of eating sugar.

a step beyond

Focus: What are false psychologies? Why do they sometimes seem to work?

A **pseudo-psychology** (SUE-doe-psychology) is any unfounded system that resembles psychology. Many pseudo-psychologies give the appearance of science but are actually false. (*Pseudo* means "false.") Pseudo-psychologies change little over time because their followers avoid evidence that contradicts their beliefs (Kelly & Saklofske, 1994). Scientists, in contrast, actively look for contradictions as a way to advance knowledge (see ◆Table 1.4). They are skeptical critics of their own theories (Woodward & Goodstein, 1996).

Unlike the real thing, pseudo-psychologies are not based on scientific testing. For instance, **palmistry** is a false system that claims lines on the hand reveal personality and predict the future. Despite the overwhelming evidence against this, palmists can still be found separating the gullible from their money in many cities. A similar false system is **phrenology**, which claims that personality traits are revealed by the shape of the skull. Phrenology was popularized in the nineteenth century by Franz Gall, a German anatomy teacher. Modern research has long since shown that bumps on the head have nothing to do with talents or abilities. In fact, the phrenologists were so far off that they listed the brain area for hearing as a center for "combativeness"!

At first glance, a pseudo-psychology called **graphology** might seem more reasonable. Graphologists claim that personality traits are revealed by handwriting. Based on such claims, some companies use graphologists to select job candidates. This is troubling because graphologists score close to zero on tests of accuracy in rating personality (Ben-Shakhar et al., 1986). In fact, graphologists do no better than untrained

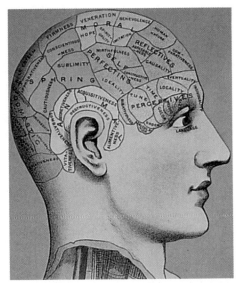

Phrenology was an attempt to assess personality characteristics by examining various areas of the skull. Phrenologists used charts such as the one shown here as guides. Like other pseudo-psychologists, phrenologists made no attempt to empirically verify their concepts.

◆ **TABLE 1.4** Some Key Differences Between Scientists and Pseudo-Scientists

	SCIENTIST	PSEUDO-SCIENTIST
Admits own ignorance; accepts need for more research	Yes	No
Advances knowledge by posing and solving new problems	Yes	No
Welcomes new hypotheses and methods	Yes	No
Theories and hypotheses are testable	Yes	Sometimes
Systematically tests concepts by gathering data	Yes	No
Looks for examples that contradict his or her beliefs	Yes	No
Applies objective checking procedures	Yes	No
Settles disputes by experimentation or systematic data collection	Yes	No
Suppresses or distorts unfavorable data	No	Yes
Seeks criticism from others	Yes	No

(Adapted from Bunge, 1984.)

Pseudo-psychology *Any false and unscientific system of beliefs and practices that is offered as an explanation of behavior.*
Palmistry *False system that claims to reveal personality traits and to predict the future by "reading" lines on the palms of the hands.*
Phrenology *False and antiquated system based on the belief that personality traits are revealed by the shape of the skull.*
Graphology *False system based on the belief that handwriting can reveal personality traits.*

college students in rating personality and job performance (Neter & Ben-Shakhar, 1989; Rafaeli & Klimoski, 1983). (By the way, graphology's failure at revealing personality should be separated from its proven value for detecting forgeries.)

Graphology might seem harmless enough. However, this false system has been used to determine who is hired, given bank credit, or selected for juries. In these and similar situations, pseudo-psychologies do, in fact, harm people (Barker, 1993; Beyerstein & Beyerstein, 1992).

If pseudo-psychologies have no scientific basis, how do they survive and why are they popular? There are several reasons, all of which can be demonstrated by a critique of astrology.

PROBLEMS IN THE STARS

Astrology is probably the most popular pseudo-psychology. **Astrology** holds that the positions of the stars and planets at the time of one's birth determine personality traits and affect behavior. Like other pseudo-psychologies, astrology has repeatedly been shown to have no scientific validity (Kelly, 1998, 1999; Stewart, 1996).

The objections to astrology are numerous and devastating:

1. The zodiac has shifted in the sky by one full constellation since astrology was first set up. However, most astrologers simply ignore this shift. (In other words, if astrology calls you a Scorpio you are really a Libra, and so forth.)
2. There is no connection between the "compatibility" of couples' astrological signs and their marriage and divorce rates.
3. Studies have found no connection between astrological signs and leadership, physical characteristics, career choices, or personality traits.
4. The force of gravity exerted by the obstetrician's body at the moment of birth is greater than that exerted by the stars. Also, astrologers have failed to explain why the moment of birth should be more important than the moment of conception.

Would you hire this man? Here's a sample of your author's handwriting. What do you think it reveals? Your interpretations are likely to be as accurate (or inaccurate) as those of a graphologist.

5. A study of more than 3,000 predictions by famous astrologers found that only a small percentage were fulfilled. These "successful" predictions tended to be vague ("There will be a tragedy somewhere in the east in the spring") or easily guessed from current events.
6. If astrologers are asked to match people with their horoscopes, they do not perform better than would be expected by chance (Kelly, 1999).
7. A few astrologers have tried to test astrology. Their results have been just as negative as those obtained by critics (sources: Kelly, 1998, 1999; Martens & Trachet, 1998; Stewart, 1996).

In short, astrology doesn't work.

Then why does astrology often seem to work? The following discussion tells why.

Uncritical Acceptance

If you have ever had your astrological chart done, you may have been impressed with its apparent accuracy. However, such perceptions are typically based on **uncritical acceptance** (the tendency to believe positive or flattering descriptions of yourself). Many astrological charts are made up of mostly flattering traits. Naturally, when your personality is described in *desirable* terms, it is hard to deny that the description has the "ring of truth." How much acceptance would astrology receive if a birth sign read like this?

> Virgo: You are the logical type and hate disorder. Your nitpicking is unbearable to your friends. You are cold, unemotional, and usually fall asleep while making love. Virgos make good doorstops.

Positive Instances

Even when an astrological description contains a mixture of good and bad traits, it may seem accurate. To find out why, read the following personality description:

Your Personality Profile

You have a strong need for other people to like you and for them to admire you. You have a tendency to be critical of yourself. You have a great deal of unused energy which you have not turned to your advantage. While you have some personality weaknesses, you are generally able to compensate for them. Your sexual adjustment has presented some problems for you. Disciplined and controlled on the outside, you tend to be worrisome and insecure inside. At times you have serious doubts as to whether you have made the right decision or done the right thing. You prefer a certain amount of change and variety and become dissatisfied when hemmed in by restrictions and limitations. You pride yourself on being an independent thinker and do not accept other opinions without satisfactory proof. You have found it unwise to be too frank in revealing yourself to others. At times you are extroverted, affable, sociable, while at other times you are introverted, wary, and reserved. Some of your aspirations tend to be pretty unrealistic.*

*Reprinted with permission of author and publisher from: R. E. Ulrich, T. J. Stachnik, and N. R. Stainton, "Student acceptance of generalized personality interpretations," *Psychological Reports*, 13, 1963, 831–834.

Does this describe your personality? A psychologist read this summary individually to college students who had taken a personality test. Only 5 students of 79 felt that the description was inaccurate. Another study found that people rated this "personality profile" as more accurate than their actual horoscopes (French et al., 1991).

Reread the description and you will see that it contains both sides of several personality dimensions ("At times you are extroverted . . . while at other times you are introverted"). Its apparent accuracy is an illusion based on the **fallacy of positive instances,** in which we remember or notice things that confirm our expectations and forget the rest. The pseudo-psychologies thrive on this effect. For example, you can always find "Leo characteristics" in a Leo. If you looked, however, you could also find "Gemini characteristics," "Scorpio characteristics," or whatever.

The Barnum Effect

Pseudo-psychologies also take advantage of the **Barnum effect,** which is a tendency to consider personal descriptions accurate if they are stated in general terms. P. T. Barnum, the famed circus showman, had a formula for success: "Always have a little something for everybody." Like the all-purpose personality profile, palm readings, fortunes, horoscopes, and other products of pseudo-psychology are stated in such general terms that they can hardly miss. There is always "a little something for everybody." To observe the Barnum effect, read *all 12* of the daily horoscopes found in newspapers for several days. You will find that predictions for other signs fit events as well as those for your own sign do.

Astrology's popularity shows that many people have difficulty separating valid psychology from systems that seem valid but are not. The goal of this discussion, then, has been to make you a more critical observer of human behavior and to clarify what is, and what is not, psychology. Here is what the "stars" say about your future:

> Emphasis now on education and personal improvement. A learning experience of lasting value awaits you. Take care of scholastic responsibilities before engaging in recreation. The word *psychology* figures prominently in your future.

Pseudo-psychologies may seem like no more than a nuisance, but they can do harm. For instance, people seeking treatment for psychological disorders may become the victims of self-appointed "experts" who offer ineffective, pseudo-scientific "therapies" (Kalal, 1999). Valid psychological principles are based on observation and evidence, not fads, opinions, or wishful thinking.

CONCLUSION: Pseudo-psychologies are not supported by scientific evidence. Belief in pseudo-psychologies is based on thinking errors such as uncritical acceptance, the fallacy of positive instances, and the Barnum effect.

KNOWLEDGE BUILDER
PSEUDO-PSYCHOLOGIES

RELATE

It is nearly impossible to get through a day without encountering people who believe in pseudo-psychologies or who make unscientific or unfounded statements. How stringently do you evaluate your own beliefs and the claims made by others?

LEARNING CHECK

1. _____ is the outdated theory that personality is revealed by the skull. It was popularized by Franz _____.

2. The fallacy of positive instances refers to graphology's accepted value for the detection of forgeries. T or F?

3. Personality descriptions provided by pseudo-psychologies are stated in general terms, which provide "a little something for everybody." This fact is the basis of the
   a. palmist's fallacy b. uncritical acceptance pattern c. fallacy of positive instances d. Barnum effect

4. So-called "psychics" typically dispense lots of flattering information to callers. Obviously they are relying on _____ to create an illusion of accuracy.
   a. graphology b. uncritical acceptance c. analysis of the zodiac d. the Barnum effect

CRITICAL THINKING

5. Each New Year's Day, phony "psychics" make predictions about events that will occur during the coming year. The vast majority of these predictions are wrong, but the practice continues each year. Can you explain why?

Answers:
1. Phrenology, Gall 2. F 3. *d* 4. *b* 5. Because of the fallacy of positive instances, people remember only the predictions that seemed to come true and forget all of the errors. Incidentally, "predictions" that appear to be accurate are usually deduced from current events or are stated in very general terms to take advantage of the Barnum effect.

Non Sequitur

YOU WILL BE TOLD WHAT YOU WANT TO HEAR. IT WILL BE SO GENERALIZED THAT IT COULD FIT ANYONE. YOU WILL PAY A RIDICULOUS AMOUNT OF MONEY FOR IT...

THE MOST ACCURATE FORTUNE EVER TOLD

Astrology *False system based on the belief that human behavior is influenced by the position of stars and planets.*
Uncritical acceptance *The tendency to believe generally positive or flattering descriptions of oneself.*
Fallacy of positive instances *The tendency to remember or notice information that fits one's expectations, while forgetting discrepancies.*
Barnum effect *The tendency to consider a personal description accurate if it is stated in general terms.*

CHAPTER IN REVIEW

What is psychology?

- Psychology is the scientific study of behavior and mental processes.
- Whenever possible, psychologists seek empirical (objective and observable) evidence based on scientific observation.

What do psychologists hope to achieve?

- Some major areas of research in psychology are comparative, learning, sensation, perception, personality, biopsychology, social, cognitive, developmental, the psychology of gender, and cultural psychology.
- Psychologists study animals as well as people.
- Psychologists may be directly interested in animal behavior, or they may study animals as models of human behavior.
- As a science, psychology's goals are to describe, understand, predict, and control behavior.

How did psychology emerge as a field of knowledge?

- Historically, psychology is an outgrowth of philosophy, an "armchair" approach to understanding human behavior.
- The first psychological laboratory was established in Germany by Wilhelm Wundt, who tried to apply scientific methods to the study of conscious experience.
- The first school of thought in psychology was structuralism, a kind of "mental chemistry" based on Wundt's ideas and the method of introspection.
- Structuralism was followed by functionalism, behaviorism, and Gestalt psychology.
- The psychodynamic approach emphasizes unconscious determinants of behavior. Freud's psychoanalytic psychology is an early example of a psychodynamic approach.
- A more recent development is humanistic psychology, which emphasizes subjective experience, human potentials, and personal growth.

What are the major perspectives in psychology?

- Five main streams of thought in modern psychology are behaviorism, humanism, the psychodynamic approach, biopsychology, and cognitive psychology.
- Today, there is a strong trend toward an eclectic blending of the best features of many viewpoints within psychology.
- Human diversity presents a challenge to anyone trying to fully understand human behavior. The cultural relativity of most judgments and the differing norms found in various cultural and social groups require us to be aware of human differences, as well as universals.

What roles and specialties are found in psychology and related fields?

- Although psychologists, psychiatrists, psychoanalysts, and counselors all work in the field of mental health, their training and methods differ considerably.
- Clinical and counseling psychologists, who do psychotherapy, represent only two of dozens of specialties in psychology.
- Other representative areas of specialization are industrial, educational, consumer, school, developmental, engineering, medical, environmental, forensic, community, psychometric, and experimental psychology.
- Psychological research may be basic or applied.

What is critical thinking?

- Critical thinking is the ability to evaluate, compare, analyze, critique, and synthesize information.
- To judge the validity of a claim, it is important to gather evidence for and against the claim and to evaluate the *quality* of the evidence.

How does psychology differ from false explanations of behavior?

- Numerous pseudo-psychologies exist. These false systems are often confused with valid psychology.
- Belief in pseudo-psychologies is based in part on uncritical acceptance, the fallacy of positive instances, and the Barnum effect.

PSYCHOLOGY ON THE NET

- **American Psychological Association** Home page of the APA, with links to PsychNET, student information, member information, and more. http://www.apa.org/
- **American Psychological Society** Home page of the APS, with links to information, services, and Internet resources. http://psychologicalresearch.org
- **Psychweb** This award-winning page provides a multitude of services and links. http://www.psychweb.com/
- **Psycoloquy** An on-line journal with short articles on all areas of psychology. http://www.princeton.edu/~harnad/psyc.html
- **PsycPORT** This site is a large database of psychological information, including daily updates on news related to psychology. http://www.psycport.com
- **The Psychology Study Center** From the publishers of this book, this site offers a study center for this text, on-line activities, links to multimedia brochures, catalogues, software demos, and more. http://psychstudy.wadsworth.com
- **Today in the History of Psychology** Events in the history of psychology by the date. http://www.cwu.edu/~warren/today.html
- **InfoTrac® College Edition** For recent articles related to the pseudo-psychologies discussed in this chapter, use Key Words search for PHRENOLOGY and ASTROLOGY.

INTERACTIVE LEARNING

- *PsychNow!* 1b. Psychology and its history. 1c. Research methods. 1d. Critical thinking in psychology.
- *Psyk.trek* 1a. Psychology's timeline. 1e. How to do library research.

CHAPTER 2

Research Methods and Critical Thinking

Theme: Scientific observation is the most powerful way to answer questions about behavior.

▼ **KEY QUESTIONS**

● *KEY TOPICS*

▼ Why is the scientific method important to psychologists?

- *Six elements of the scientific method*

▼ How do psychologists collect information?

- *Five major research methods*
- *Naturalistic observation*
- *Correlational studies and types of relationships*

▼ How is an experiment performed?

- *Types of variables and the logic of experiments*
- *Placebo effects and double-blind studies*
- *Statistical significance and meta-analysis*

▼ **KEY QUESTIONS**

● *KEY TOPICS*

▼ What other research methods do psychologists use?

- *The clinical method*
- *The survey method*

▼ How dependable is psychological information found in the popular media?

- *Tips on how to critically evaluate information in the news*

▼ What ethical questions does psychological research raise?

- *The effects of deception, loss of privacy, and potential harm*
- *The ethics of animal research*

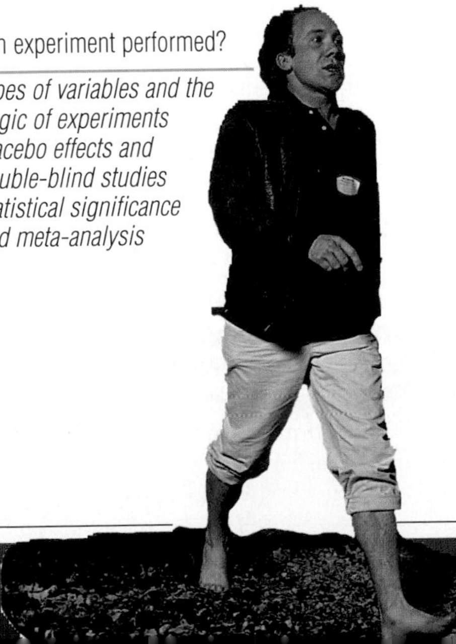

27

FROM COMMON SENSE TO CONTROLLED OBSERVATION

COMMENT OVERHEARD ON CAMPUS: *"I don't know why he bothers taking psychology. It's just common sense."* Is psychology common sense? Is common sense a good source of information?

Consider some commonsense statements. Let's say that your grandfather has gone back to college. What do people say? "Ah . . . never too old to learn." And what do they say when he loses interest and quits? "Well, you can't teach an old dog new tricks." Let's examine another commonsense statement. It is frequently said that "absence makes the heart grow fonder." Those of us separated from friends and lovers can take comfort in this knowledge—until we remember "out of sight, out of mind!" Much of what passes for common sense is equally vague and inconsistent. Notice also that most of these B.S. statements work best after the fact. (B.S., of course, stands for Before Science.)

Common sense is not without value. Without it, many of us would be dead. Yet, common sense can prevent us from seeking better information or seeing the truth. Albert Einstein said, "Common sense is the layer of prejudice laid down in our minds before we are 18." During the scientific revolution, people laughed at the idea that the world is round. (Anyone with eyes could see it wasn't.) They laughed at Pasteur when he proposed that microbes cause disease. (How could creatures too small to be seen kill a human?) Scientific ideas such as these directly contradicted the common sense of their times. Now, few people argue with the findings of sciences such as chemistry, physics, and biology. But many still write off psychology as "just common sense."

Jab a hat pin into your finger. The sensation of pain seems instantaneous. We can go no further with personal observation. However, by using electrical recorders, psychologists have found that nerve impulses travel at a maximum of 120 meters per second. That's fast, but certainly not instantaneous. Pain messages from the finger take at least a hundredth of a second to reach the brain.

As you can see, psychologists use careful measurement and specialized research techniques to avoid the pitfalls of "common sense." Their techniques are the topic of this chapter.

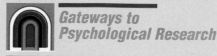
Gateways to Psychological Research

THE SCIENTIFIC METHOD consists of highly refined procedures for observing the natural world, testing hypotheses, and drawing valid conclusions.

PSYCHOLOGICAL RESEARCH is an ongoing search for truth. It begins with observations, questions, and hypotheses. Next, evidence is gathered, hypotheses are tested, and results are published. Scientific debate and theory building suggest new hypotheses, which lead to further research.

PSYCHOLOGISTS USE SEVERAL SPECIALIZED RESEARCH METHODS. Each has strengths and weaknesses, so all are needed to fully investigate human behavior.

EXPERIMENTATION is the most powerful way to identify cause-and-effect relationships in psychology and other sciences.

THE POPULAR MEDIA are rife with inaccurate information. It is essential to critically evaluate information from popular sources—or from any source for that matter.

PSYCHOLOGICAL RESEARCHERS make every effort to maintain high ethical standards in their work.

SCIENTIFIC RESEARCH—HOW TO THINK LIKE A PSYCHOLOGIST

It is a strange medical fact that if you ate Frosted Flakes cereal as a child your current chance of having cancer is half that of adults who never ate the cereal as children. Does this mean that doctors should prescribe Frosted Flakes to growing children? Only a scientifically naive person would think so. The apparent link between diet and cancer is actually related to an age bias. Older people naturally have higher cancer rates. They also never ate Frosted Flakes. That's because Frosted Flakes *weren't available* when they were young. Thus, Frosted Flakes *appear* to be related to cancer, but age is the real connection (Tierny, 1987).

In many ways, psychologists must avoid similar traps of faulty observation. To do so, they use the **scientific method,** which is based on solid evidence, accurate description and measurement, precise definition, controlled observation, and repeatable results (Schick & Vaughn, 1995).

The Scientific Method

Observation, or carefully recording facts and events, is the heart of all sciences. In its ideal form the scientific method has six elements:

1. Observation
2. Defining a problem
3. Proposing a hypothesis
4. Gathering evidence/testing the hypothesis
5. Publishing results
6. Theory building

HYPOTHESIS TESTING   *What exactly is a hypothesis?*   A **hypothesis** (hi-POTH-eh-sis) is a tentative explanation of an event or relationship. In common terms, a hypothesis is a *testable* hunch or educated guess about behavior. For example, you might hypothesize that "Frustration encourages aggression." How would you test this hypothesis? First you would have to decide how

Applying the scientific method to the study of behavior requires careful observation. Here, a psychologist videotapes a session in which a child's thinking abilities are being tested.

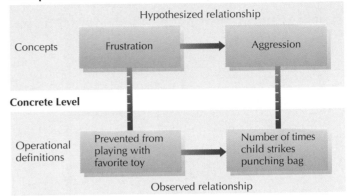

❖ **FIGURE 2.1** *Operational definitions are used to link concepts with concrete observations. Do you think the examples given are reasonable operational definitions of frustration and aggression? Operational definitions vary in how well they represent concepts. For this reason, many different experiments may be necessary to draw clear conclusions about hypothesized relationships in psychology.*

you are going to frustrate people. (This part might be fun.) Then you would need to find a way to measure whether they become more aggressive. (Not so much fun if you plan to be nearby.) Your observations would then provide evidence to confirm or disconfirm the hypothesis.

OPERATIONAL DEFINITIONS   Because we cannot see or touch frustration, it must be defined *operationally*. An **operational definition** states the exact procedures used to represent a concept. Operational definitions allow abstract ideas to be tested in real-world terms. (See ❖Figure 2.1.) For example, you might define frustration as "interrupting an adult before he or she can finish a puzzle and win a $100 prize." And aggression might be defined as "the number of times a frustrated individual insults the person who prevented work on the puzzle."

CLEVER HANS   Several steps of the scientific method can be illustrated with the story of Clever Hans, a "wonder horse" (Rosenthal, 1965). Clever Hans seemed to solve difficult math problems, which he answered by tapping his foot. If you asked Hans, "What is 12 times 2, minus 18," Hans would tap his foot six times. Hans was so astonishing that an inquiring scientist decided to discover if Hans actually did arithmetic. Assume that you are the scientist and that you are just itching to find out how Hans *really* does his trick.

Can a Horse Add?

Your investigation of Hans's math skills would probably begin with careful *observation* of both the horse and his owner. Assume that these observations fail to reveal any obvious cheating. Then the *problem* becomes more clearly *defined*: What signals Hans to start and stop tapping his foot? Your first *hypothesis* might be that the owner is giving Hans a signal. Your proposed *test* would be to make the owner

BRIDGES

IQ tests serve as operational definitions of intelligence. Without such tests, it would be difficult to study intelligence.

See Chapter 12, pages 379–386.

leave the room. Then someone else could ask Hans questions. Your test would either confirm or deny the owner's role. This *evidence* would support or eliminate the cheating hypothesis. By changing the conditions under which you observe Hans, you have *controlled* the situation to gain more information from your observations.

Incidentally, Hans could still answer when his owner was out of the room. But a brilliant series of controlled observations revealed Hans's secret. If Hans couldn't see the questioner, he couldn't answer. It seems that questioners always *lowered their heads* (to look at Hans's foot) after asking a question. This was Hans's cue to start tapping. When Hans had tapped the correct number, a questioner would always *look up* to see if Hans was going to stop. This was Hans's cue to stop tapping!

THEORIES   *What about theory formulation?*   Because Clever Hans's ability to do math was an isolated problem, no theorizing was involved. However, in actual research, theory building is quite important. A **theory** interrelates concepts and facts in a way that summarizes a large number of observations. Good theories explain existing data, predict new observations, and

---

Scientific method *Testing a proposition by systematic observation.*
Observation *Directly gathering data by recording facts or events.*
Hypothesis *An educated guess about relationships or the causes of behavior.*
Operational definition *The specific procedures used to define a scientific concept.*
Theory *A system of ideas that interrelates facts and concepts, summarizes existing data, and predicts future observations.*

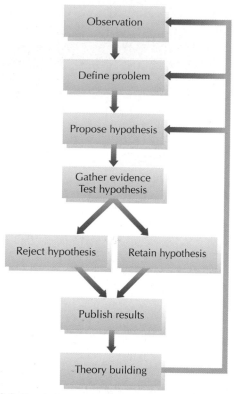

❖ **FIGURE 2.2** *Psychologists use the logic of science to answer questions about behavior. Specific hypotheses can be tested in a variety of ways, including naturalistic observation, correlational studies, controlled experiments, clinical studies, and the survey method. Psychologists revise their theories to reflect the evidence they gather. New or revised theories then lead to new observations, problems, and hypotheses.*

◆ **TABLE 2.1**   Outline of a Research Report

- **Abstract**   Research reports begin with a very brief summary of the study and its findings. The abstract allows you to get an overview without reading the entire article.
- **Introduction**   The introduction describes the question to be investigated. It also provides background information by reviewing prior studies on the same or related topics.
- **Method**   This section tells how and why observations were made. It also describes the specific procedures used to gather data so that other researchers can duplicate the study.
- **Results**   The outcome of the investigation is presented. Data may be graphed, summarized in tables, or statistically analyzed.
- **Discussion**   The results of the study are discussed in relation to the original question. Implications of the study are explored, and further studies may be proposed.

guide further research (❖Fig. 2.2). Think of it this way: A theory is like a map of an area of knowledge. It shows how a large number of concepts relate to one another (Meltzoff, 1998). Without theories of forgetting, personality, stress, mental illness, and the like, psychologists would drown in a sea of disconnected facts.

A good scientific theory, like a good hypothesis, must be *falsifiable* (defined so that it can be disconfirmed). For instance, if you hypothesize that "All dreams occur during rapid-eye-movement sleep," then recording even one dream at any other time will disconfirm the hypothesis. True science focuses on solvable problems. It avoids pie-in-the-sky theories that cannot be tested (Stanovich, 1998).

PUBLICATION   Scientific information must always be *publicly available.* The results of scientific studies are usually published in professional journals. (See ◆Table 2.1.) That way, anyone willing to make appropriate observations can see whether a claim is true (Schick & Vaughn, 1995).

SUMMARY   Now let's summarize more realistically. All the basic elements of the scientific method are found in the example that follows.

BRIDGES

One of the major limitations of Freudian personality theory is that many of its concepts are not testable or falsifiable.

See Chapter 15, page 492.

- **Observation:** Suzanne, a psychologist, observes that some business managers seem to experience less work-related stress than others do.
- **Defining a Problem:** Suzanne's problem is to identify the ways in which high-stress and low-stress managers are different.
- **Observation:** Suzanne carefully questions managers about how much stress they experience. These additional observations suggest that managers with low stress levels feel they have more control over their work.
- **Proposing a Hypothesis:** Suzanne hypothesizes that having control over difficult tasks reduces stress.
- **Gathering Evidence/Testing the Hypothesis:** Suzanne designs an experiment in which people must solve a series of very difficult problems. In one group, people solve the problems at a forced pace, dictated by Suzanne. In another group, they are allowed to set the pace themselves. While working, the second group reports lower stress levels than the first did. This suggests that Suzanne's hypothesis is correct.
- **Publishing Results:** In a scholarly article, Suzanne carefully describes the question she investigated, the methods she used, and the results of her experiment. The article is published in the *Journal of Clinical Psychology.*
- **Theory Building:** Drawing on the results of similar experiments, Suzanne and other psychologists create a theory to explain why having control over a task helps reduce stress.

Research Methods

In their search for accurate information and useful theories, psychologists gather evidence and test hypotheses in many ways: They observe behavior as it unfolds in natural settings (naturalistic observation); they make measurements to discover relationships between events (correlational method); they use the powerful technique of controlled experimentation (experimental method); they study psychological problems and therapies in clinical settings (clinical method); and they use questionnaires and surveys to poll large groups of people (survey method). Let's see how each of these is used to advance psychological knowledge.

NATURALISTIC OBSERVATION—PSYCHOLOGY STEPS OUT!

Instead of waiting for a chance encounter, psychologists may actively observe behavior in a **natural setting** (the typical environment in which a person or animal lives). The work of Jane Goodall provides a good example. She and her staff have been observing chimpanzees in Tanzania since 1960. A quote from her book, *In the Shadow of Man*, captures the excitement of a scientific discovery:

> Quickly focusing my binoculars, I saw that it was a single chimpanzee, and just then he turned my direction. . . . He was squatting beside the red earth mound of a termite nest, and as I watched I saw him carefully push a long grass stem into a hole in the mound. After a moment he withdrew it and picked something from the end with his mouth. I was too far away to make out what he was eating, but it was obvious that he was actually using a grass stem as a tool (❖Fig. 2.3) (Van Lawick-Goodall, 1971).

❖ **FIGURE 2.3** *A special moment in Jane Goodall's naturalistic study of chimpanzees. A chimp uses a grass stem to extract a meal from a termite nest. Goodall's work also documented the importance of long-term emotional bonds between chimpanzee mothers and their offspring, as well as fascinating differences in the behavior and "personalities" of individual chimps (Goodall, 1990). (Photo by Baron Hugo van Lawick. © National Geographic Society.)*

Notice that naturalistic observation provides only *descriptions* of behavior. To *explain* observations, we may need information from other research methods. Just the same, Goodall's discovery forced scientists to recognize that humans are not the only tool-making animals (Lavallee, 1999).

Chimpanzees in zoos use objects as tools. Doesn't that demonstrate the same thing? Not necessarily. Naturalistic observation allows us to study behavior that hasn't been tampered with by outside influences. Only by observing chimps in their natural environment can we tell if they use tools without human interference.

Limitations

Doesn't the presence of human observers in an animal colony affect the animals' behavior? Yes. A major problem is the **observer effect,** which refers to changes in a subject's behavior caused by an awareness of being observed. Naturalists must be careful to keep their distance and avoid "making friends" with the animals they are observing. Likewise, if you were interested in the differences between aggressive and nonaggressive schoolchildren, you couldn't simply stroll onto a playground and start taking notes. As a stranger, your presence would probably change students' behavior. When possible, this problem is minimized by concealing the observer. Another solution is to use hidden recorders. For example, a recent naturalistic study of playground aggression was done with video cameras and remote microphones (Pepler, Craig, & Roberts, 1998).

Observer bias is a related problem in which observers see what they expect to see or record only selected details. Teachers in one study were told to watch elementary school children (all normal) who had been labeled as either learning disabled, mentally retarded, emotionally disturbed, or normal. The results were troubling: Teachers gave the children very different ratings, depending on the labels used (Foster & Ysseldyke, 1976). In some situations, observer bias can have serious consequences. An example is studies of psychotherapy, where therapists tend to get better results with the type of therapy they favor (Lambert, 1999).

THE ANTHROPOMORPHIC ERROR A special trap that must be avoided while observing animals is the **anthropomorphic fallacy** (AN-thro-po-MORE-fik). This is the error of attributing human thoughts, feelings, or motives to animals—especially as a way of explaining their behavior (Blumberg & Wasserman, 1995).

Why is it risky to attribute motives or emotions to animals? The temptation to assume that an animal is "angry," "jealous,"

Natural setting *The typical environment in which a person or animal lives.*
Observer effect *Changes in behavior caused by an awareness of being observed.*
Observer bias *The tendency of observers to distort their perceptions to match their expectations.*
Anthropomorphic fallacy *The error of attributing human thoughts, feelings, or motives to animals, especially as a way of explaining their behavior.*

"bored," or "guilty" can be strong, but it can lead to false conclusions. For instance, let's say I observe gorillas in the wild (where food is plentiful) and conclude that by nature gorillas are not very "greedy." You, on the other hand, place two hungry gorillas in a cage with a banana, stand back to watch the action, and conclude that gorillas are in fact *very* "greedy." Actually, all we have observed is that competition for food is related to the amount of food available. Allowing the human concept of greed into the picture just clouds our understanding of gorilla behavior. If you have pets at home, you probably already know how difficult it is to avoid anthropomorphizing.

Recording Observations

Psychologists doing naturalistic studies make a special effort to minimize bias by keeping a formal log of data and observations, called an **observational record**. As suggested in the study of playground aggression, videotaping often provides the best record of all (Pepler & Craig, 1995).

Despite its problems, naturalistic observation can supply a wealth of information and raise many interesting questions. In most scientific research, it is an excellent starting point.

CORRELATIONAL STUDIES—IN SEARCH OF THE PERFECT RELATIONSHIP

Let's say a psychologist notes an association between the IQs of parents and their children, or between beauty and social popularity, or between anxiety and test performance, or even between crime and the weather. In each instance, two observations or events are **correlated** (linked together in an orderly way).

A **correlational study** finds the degree of relationship, or correlation, between two existing traits, behaviors, or events. Unlike naturalistic observation, correlational studies can be done either in the lab or in the natural environment. First, two factors of interest are measured. Then a statistical technique is used to find their degree of correlation. (See Appendix B for more information.) For example, we could find the correlation between the number of hours slept at night and afternoon sleepiness. If the correlation is large, knowing how long a person sleeps at night would allow us to predict his or her degree of afternoon sleepiness. Likewise, afternoon sleepiness could be used to predict the duration of nighttime sleep.

Correlation Coefficients

How is the degree of correlation expressed? The strength and direction of a relationship can be expressed as a **coefficient of correlation**. This is simply a number falling somewhere between $+1.00$ and -1.00 (see Appendix B). If the number is zero or close to zero, the association between two measures is weak or nonexistent. For example, the correlation between shoe size and intelligence is zero. (Sorry, size 12 readers.) If the correlation is $+1.00$, a perfect positive relationship exists; if it is -1.00, a perfect negative relationship has been discovered.

Correlations in psychology are rarely perfect. But the closer the coefficient is to $+1.00$ or -1.00, the stronger the relationship. For example, identical twins tend to have almost identical IQs. In contrast, the IQs of parents and their children are only generally similar. The correlation between the IQs of parents and children is .35; between identical twins it's .86.

What do the terms "positive" and "negative" correlation mean? A **positive correlation** shows that increases in one measure are matched by increases in the other (or decreases correspond with decreases). For example, there is a positive correlation between high school grades and college grades; students who do better in high school tend to do better in college (and the reverse). In a **negative correlation**, increases in the first measure are associated with decreases in the second (❖Fig. 2.4). We might observe, for instance, that the higher the air temperature, the lower the activity level of animals in a zoo.

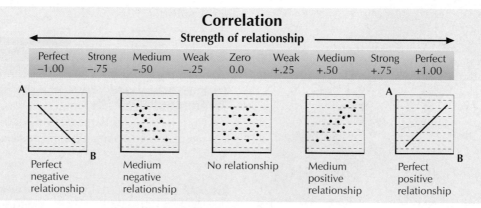

Correlation

Strength of relationship

Perfect	Strong	Medium	Weak	Zero	Weak	Medium	Strong	Perfect
-1.00	$-.75$	$-.50$	$-.25$	0.0	$+.25$	$+.50$	$+.75$	$+1.00$

Perfect negative relationship

Medium negative relationship

No relationship

Medium positive relationship

Perfect positive relationship

❖ **FIGURE 2.4** *The correlation coefficient tells how strongly two measures are related. These graphs show a range of relationships between two measures, A and B. If a correlation is negative, increases in one measure are associated with decreases in the other. (As B gets larger, A gets smaller.) In a positive correlation, increases in one measure are associated with increases in the other. (As B gets larger, A gets larger.) The center-left graph ("medium negative relationship") might result from comparing anxiety level (B) with test scores (A): Higher anxiety is associated with lower scores. The center graph ("no relationship") would result from plotting a person's shoe size (B) and IQ (A). The center-right graph ("medium positive relationship") could be a plot of the number of hours pilots went without sleep (B) and the number of errors each made when tested on a flight simulator (A). In this case, longer periods without sleep are associated with a greater number of errors.*

Would that show that air temperature causes changes in activity level? It might seem so, but we cannot be sure without performing an experiment.

CORRELATION AND CAUSATION   Correlational studies help us discover relationships and make predictions. However, correlation *does not demonstrate causation.* Just because two things *appear* to be related does not mean that **causation** (a cause-and-effect connection) exists (Meltzoff, 1998). The animals' activity might be affected by seasonal changes in weight, hormone levels, or even the feeding schedule at the zoo.

Here is another example of mistaking correlation for causation: What if a psychologist discovers that the blood of schizophrenic patients contains a certain chemical not found in normal people? Does this show that the chemical *causes* schizophrenia? It may seem so, but schizophrenia could cause the chemical to form. Or, both schizophrenia and the chemical might be caused by some unknown third factor, such as the typical diet in mental hospitals.

Just because one thing *appears* to cause another does not *confirm* that it does. This fact can be seen clearly in the case of obviously noncausal relationships. For example, there is a correlation between the number of churches in American cities and the number of bars; the more churches, the more bars. Does this mean that drinking makes you religious? Does it mean that religion makes you thirsty? No one, of course, would leap to such conclusions about cause and effect. But in less obvious situations, it's tempting. (The real connection is that both the number of churches and the number of bars are related to the population size of cities.)

Relationships in Psychology

Do students who study more get better grades? To answer this question, we could record how long a number of students study each week. Then we could match hours studied with grades earned. Suppose we find that low study times correspond to low grades. Likewise, large amounts of studying are associated with high grades. If this were the case, there would be a positive relationship between studying and grades. Similarly, we might discover that students who watch many hours of television tend to get lower grades than those who watch few hours. (This is the well-known TV zombie effect.) This time, a negative relationship would exist. That is, low viewing times go with high grades, and high viewing times go with low grades. Obviously, these examples are only hypothetical. However, when real patterns can be identified, they have great value. Relationships summarize large amounts of data and allow us to make accurate predictions.

GRAPHICAL DATA   Drawing graphs of relationships can help clarify their nature. For instance, ❖Figure 2.5 shows the results of a memory experiment. Before being tested, subjects learned from 1 to 20 word lists. The question was, How well would they remember the last list? The graph shows that when participants learned only 1 list, they remembered 80 percent of it. When they learned 4 lists, their scores on the last list dropped to 43 percent (blue arrows). When they memorized 10 other lists, their recall fell even

more, to 22 percent (red arrows). Overall, there was a negative relationship between the number of lists memorized and recall of the last list. (The meaning of this finding is discussed in Chapter 10. For now, let's just say that you shouldn't memorize the telephone book before studying for a test.)

Some graphs reveal **linear (straight-line) relationships**. Others are **curvilinear** (kur-vih-LIN-ee-er) and consist of a curved line, like the one shown in ❖Figure 2.5. In either case, relationships need not be perfect to be useful. Suppose, for instance, that we randomly select 10 people. We then compare the years of college completed with each person's income at age 25. Results like those shown in ❖Figure 2.6 would make it clear that there is a strong positive relationship between education and earnings. Remember that such correlations do not prove that education increases earnings. Nevertheless, a pattern like this might be of great interest to a high school student thinking about whether to attend college.

The shaded area and the colored line in ❖Figure 2.6 show that the relationship is approximately linear, but not perfect. (If it were perfect, all the dots would lie on the black line.) The correlation coefficient (r) also shows that the relationship is strong, and positive, but not perfect. (How often do you find a perfect relationship?) If the relationship *was* perfect, the coefficient would be 1.00.

For comparison, ❖Figure 2.7 plots more hypothetical data. Assume that the manager of a college cafeteria has recorded the amount of coffee sold on 10 different days, as well as the air temperature on each day. Notice again that the relationship appears to be linear. However, this time it is negative. Also note how the shaded area and the correlation coefficient both indicate a weaker relationship. Even so, knowing the correlation between temperature and how much coffee people drink would help the manager plan how much "mud" to brew each morning.

On a higher plane, psychologists seek to identify relationships concerning memory, perception, stress, aging, therapy,

BRIDGES

Correlations between the IQs of family members are used to estimate the degree to which intelligence is affected by heredity and environment.

See Chapter 12, pages 390–392.

Observational record *A detailed summary of observed events or a videotape of observed behavior.*
Correlation *The existence of a consistent, systematic relationship between two events, measures, or variables.*
Correlational study *A nonexperimental study designed to measure the degree of relationship (if any) between two or more events, measures, or variables.*
Coefficient of correlation *A statistical index ranging from −1.00 to +1.00 that indicates the direction and degree of correlation.*
Positive correlation *A statistical relationship in which increases in one measure are matched by increases in the other (or decreases correspond with decreases).*
Negative correlation *A statistical relationship in which increases in one measure are matched by decreases in the other.*
Causation *The act of causing some effect.*
Linear relationships *Relationships that form a straight line when graphed.*
Curvilinear relationship *A relationship that forms a curved line when graphed.*

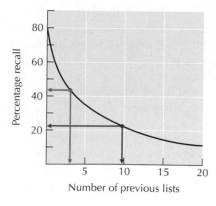

❖ **FIGURE 2.5** *Effects of interference on memory. A graph of the approximate relationship between percentage recalled and number of different word lists memorized. (Adapted from Underwood, 1957.)*

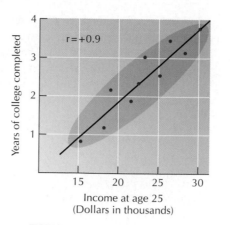

❖ **FIGURE 2.6** *The relationship between years of college completed and personal income (hypothetical data).*

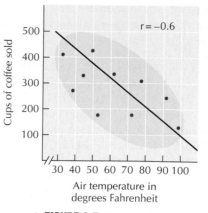

❖ **FIGURE 2.7** *The relationship between air temperature and amount of coffee consumed (hypothetical data).*

and a host of similar topics. Much of this book is a summary of such relationships.

The best way to be confident that a cause-and-effect relationship exists is to perform a controlled experiment. You'll learn how in the next section. But before you read more, check your progress by answering the questions that follow.

THE PSYCHOLOGY EXPERIMENT—WHERE CAUSE MEETS EFFECT

The most powerful research tool is an **experiment** (a formal trial undertaken to confirm or disconfirm a hypothesis). Psychologists carefully control experimental conditions to identify cause-and-effect relationships. To perform an experiment, you would do the following:

1. Directly vary a condition you think might affect behavior.
2. Create two or more groups of subjects. These groups should be alike in all ways *except* the condition you are varying.
3. Record whether varying the condition has any effect on behavior.

Assume that you want to find out if hunger affects memory. First, you would form two groups of people. Then you could give the members of one group a memory test while they are hungry. The second group would take the same test after eating a meal. By comparing average memory scores for the two groups, you could tell if hunger affects memory.

As you can see, the simplest psychological experiment is based on two groups of **subjects** (animals or people whose behavior is investigated). One group is called the *experimental group;* the other becomes the *control group.* The control group and the experimental group are treated exactly alike except for the condition you intentionally vary. This condition is called the *independent variable.*

Variables and Groups

A **variable** is any condition that can change and that might affect the outcome of the experiment. Identifying causes and effects in an experiment involves three types of variables:

1. **Independent variables** are conditions altered or varied by the experimenter, who sets their size, amount, or value. Independent variables are suspected *causes* for differences in behavior.
2. **Dependent variables** measure the results of the experiment. Dependent variables reveal the *effects* that independent variables have on *behavior.* Such effects are often revealed by measures of performance, such as test scores.
3. **Extraneous variables** are conditions that a researcher wishes to prevent from affecting the outcome of the experiment.

We can apply these terms to our hunger/memory experiment in this way: Hunger is the independent variable—we want to know if hunger affects memory. Memory (defined by scores on the memory test) is the dependent variable—we want to know if the ability to memorize depends on how hungry a person is. All other conditions that could affect memory scores are extraneous. Examples are the number of hours slept the night before the test, intelligence, or the difficulty of the questions.

As you can see, an **experimental group** consists of subjects exposed to the independent variable (hunger in the preceding example). Members of the **control group** are exposed to all conditions except the independent variable.

Let's examine another simple experiment. Suppose you notice that you seem to study better while listening to music. This suggests the hypothesis that music improves learning. We could test this idea by forming an experimental group that studies with music. A control group would study without music. Then we could compare their scores on a test.

Is a control group really needed? Can't people just study with music on to see if they do better?   Without a control group, it would be impossible to tell if music had any effect on learning. The control group provides a *point of reference*

CONTROL GROUP   OUT OF CONTROL GROUP

COURTESY OF PETER S. MUELLER

for comparison with scores of the experimental group. If the average test score of the experimental group is higher than that of the control group, we can conclude that music improves learning. If the average is lower than the control group's average, we will know that music slows learning. If there is no difference, we know that the independent variable has no effect on learning.

In the experiment described, the amount learned (indicated by scores on the test) is the *dependent variable.* We are asking, Does the independent variable *affect* the dependent variable? (Does music affect or influence learning?)

Experimental Control

How do we know that the people in one group aren't more intelligent than those in the other group?   It's true that personal differences among subjects might influence the outcome of an experiment. However, these can be controlled by randomly assigning subjects to groups. **Random assignment** means that a subject has an equal chance of being in either the experimental group or the control group. Randomization evenly balances personal differences in the two groups. In our musical

Experiment *A formal trial undertaken to confirm or disconfirm a fact or principle.*
Experimental subjects *Humans or animals whose behavior is investigated in an experiment.*
Variable *Any condition that changes or can be made to change; a measure, event, or state that may vary.*
Independent variable *In an experiment, the condition being investigated as a possible cause of some change in behavior. The values that this variable takes do not depend on any other condition; they are chosen by the experimenter.*
Dependent variable *In an experiment, the condition (usually a behavior) that is affected by the independent variable.*
Extraneous variables *In an experiment, those conditions or factors to be excluded from possible influence on the outcome.*
Experimental group *In a controlled experiment, the group of subjects exposed to the independent variable or experimental condition.*
Control group *In a controlled experiment, the group of subjects exposed to all experimental conditions or variables except the independent variable.*
Random assignment *The use of chance (for example, flipping a coin) to assign subjects to experimental and control groups.*

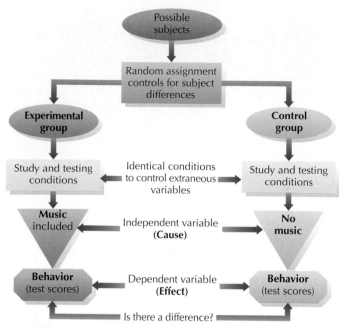

❖ **FIGURE 2.8** *Elements of a simple psychological experiment to assess the effects of music during study on test scores.*

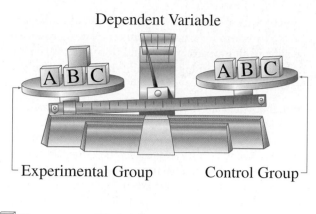

☐ Extraneous Variables

▨ Independant Variable

❖ **FIGURE 2.9** *Experimental control is achieved by balancing or equalizing extraneous variables for the experimental group and the control group. Then, when the independent variable is applied to the experimental group, any change in the dependent variable must be caused by the independent variable.*

experiment, this could be done by simply flipping a coin for each subject: Heads, and the subject is in the experimental group; tails, it's the control group. This would result in few differences in the number of people in each group who are geniuses or dunces, hungry, hung over, tall, music lovers, or whatever.

Other *extraneous,* or outside, variables—such as the amount of study time, the sex of subjects, the temperature in the room, the time of day, or the amount of light—must also be prevented from affecting the outcome of an experiment. But how? Usually this is done by making all conditions except the independent variable *exactly* alike for both groups. When all conditions are the same for both groups—*except* the presence or absence of music—then a difference in the amount learned *must* be caused by the music (❖Fig. 2.8).

CAUSE AND EFFECT   Now let's summarize more formally. In an experiment, two or more groups of subjects are treated differently with respect to the independent variable. In all other ways they are treated the same. That is, extraneous variables are equalized for all groups in the experiment. The effect of the independent variable (or variables) on some behavior (the dependent variable) is then measured. In a carefully controlled experiment, the independent variable is the only possible *cause* for any *effect* noted in the dependent variable. This allows clear cause-and-effect connections to be identified (❖Fig. 2.9).

Field Experiments

Experiments seem to set up artificial situations. Do experimental findings have anything to do with the real world?   Being able to "custom design" conditions in a laboratory experi-

ment has many advantages. But there is also a degree of artificiality. An alternative is the **field experiment**, which uses natural settings in the "real world" as a laboratory. Here is an illustration:

One Good Flat Deserves Another

James Bryan and Mary Test (1967) wanted to know, Are people more likely to help someone in distress if they have just seen someone else receiving help? To find out, they parked a Ford Mustang with a flat tire on a busy street. An inflated tire leaned against the car, and a young woman stood nearby. Of the 2,000 cars that passed, only 35 stopped in this control condition. In the experimental condition, a second car was parked a quarter of a mile back from the test car. A woman stood watching as a man changed a tire on the second car. Of the 2,000 vehicles that first passed this staged helping scene, 58 stopped to help the woman in the test car.

Such "real-life" experiments are popular among psychologists as a way to bridge the gap between laboratory studies and everyday life. You may have even taken part in an experiment without knowing it!

Evaluating Results

Is the difference between 35 helpers and 58 helpers really enough to draw a conclusion?   How can we tell if the independent variable made a difference? The problem is handled statistically. Reports in psychology journals almost always include the statement "Results were **statistically significant**." What this means is that the obtained results would occur very rarely by chance alone. To be statistically significant, a difference must be large enough so that it would occur by chance in fewer than 5 experiments out of 100. (See Appendix B for more information.) Of course, research findings also become more convincing when they can be duplicated or repeated. See "Replication and Parascience" to learn why.

REPLICATION AND PARASCIENCE

The question "Could you repeat that, please?" takes on special meaning in psychology. A key element in any science is the ability to **replicate** (repeat) observations or experiments to confirm prior conclusions. In contrast, a failure to replicate observations is a major flaw of **parascience** (that which resembles science but is not truly scientific). A good example is the idea that plants have feelings. This claim, which received wide media coverage, was largely based on "experiments" performed by Cleve Backster, a polygraph expert. (The polygraph is commonly referred to as a lie detector; see Chapter 13.)

Backster claimed that plants wired to a lie detector responded to music, threats (such as a lighted match), and other stimuli. However, when scientists tried to repeat the experiments, using either identical or improved methods, the results were completely negative (Galston & Slayman, 1983).

A long list of other purported wonders—from subliminal persuasion to "pyramid power" to dowsing to moon madness—have likewise disappeared in the light of careful scrutiny. Psychology, too, has admittedly had its share of unrepeatable results. However, what separates psychology and other sciences from parascience is that they are self-correcting.

When a finding cannot be repeated, the scientific response is, "We don't believe the result." Maintaining such high standards can be frustrating at times. Among other things, it requires a willingness to change one's beliefs as new or better evidence comes along. Yet, the result is highly satisfying. High standards of evidence and a demand for repeatability ensure that science moves slowly, but surely, toward the truth (Lett, 1990).

META-ANALYSIS As you might guess, numerous studies are done on important topics in psychology. Although each study adds to our understanding, the results of various studies don't always agree. Let's say we are interested in whether males or females tend to be greater risk takers. A computer search would reveal that more than 100 studies have investigated various types of risk taking (for example, smoking, driving fast, or having unprotected sex).

Is there a way to combine the results of the studies? Yes, a statistical technique called **meta-analysis** can be used to combine the results of many studies, as if they were all part of one big study (Schafer, 1999). In other words, a meta-analysis is a study of the results of other studies. In recent years, meta-analysis has been used to summarize and synthesize mountains of psychological research. This allows us to see the big picture and draw conclusions that might be missed in a single, small-scale study. Oh, and about that risk-taking question: A recent meta-analysis showed that males do tend to take more risks than females (Byrnes, Miller, & Schafer, 1999). (The most frequent last words uttered by deceased young males are rumored to be, "Hey, watch this!")

PLACEBO EFFECTS—SUGAR PILLS AND SALTWATER

Let's do an experiment to see whether the drug amphetamine (a stimulant) affects learning: Before studying, members of our experimental group take an amphetamine pill. Control group members get nothing. Later, we assess how much each subject learned. Does this experiment seem valid? Actually, it is seriously flawed.

Why? The experimental group took the drug and the control group didn't. Differences in the amount they learned must have been caused by the drug, right? No, because the drug wasn't the only difference between the groups. People in the experimental group swallowed a pill, and control subjects did not. Without using a *placebo* (plah-SEE-bo), it is impossible to tell whether the drug affects learning. It could be that those who swallowed a pill *expected* to do better. This alone might have affected their performance, even if the pill didn't.

What is a placebo? Why would it make a difference? A **placebo** is a fake pill or injection. Inert substances such as sugar pills and saline (saltwater) injections are common placebos. Thus, if a placebo has any effect, it must be based on suggestion, rather than chemistry (Quitkin, 1999).

The **placebo effect** (changes in behavior caused by the belief that one has taken a drug) can be powerful. For instance, a saline injection is 70 percent as effective as morphine in reducing pain. That's why doctors sometimes prescribe placebos—especially for complaints that seem to have no physical basis. Placebos have been shown to affect pain, anxiety, depression, alertness, tension, sexual arousal, cravings for alcohol, and many other processes (Kirsch & Lynn, 1999).

How could an inert substance have any effect? Placebos alter people's expectations about their own emotional and physical reactions. These expectancies, in turn, influence bodily activities. For example, placebos that relieve pain do so by causing the pituitary gland to release **endorphins**. These powerful chemicals are similar to painkilling opiate drugs such as morphine (ter Riet et al., 1998).

Field experiment *An experiment conducted in a natural setting.*

Statistical significance *Experimental results that would rarely occur by chance alone.*

Replication *Repeating observations or experiments to confirm prior conclusions.*

Parascience *A system that resembles science but is not truly scientific.*

Meta-analysis *A statistical technique for combining the results of many studies on the same subject.*

Placebo *An inactive substance given in the place of a drug in psychological research or by physicians who wish to treat a complaint by suggestion.*

Placebo effect *Changes in behavior resulting from expectations that a drug (or other treatment) will have some effect.*

Endorphins *A class of chemicals produced by the pituitary gland that are similar in structure and pain-killing effect to opiate drugs such as morphine.*

The placebo effect is a major factor in medical treatments. Would you also expect the placebo effect to occur in psychotherapy? It does, which complicates studies on the effectiveness of new therapies (Quitkin, 1999).

Controlling Placebo Effects

To control for placebo effects, we could use a **single-blind experiment**. In this case, subjects do not know if they are receiving a real drug or a placebo. All subjects get a pill or injection. People in the experimental group get a real drug and the control group gets a placebo. Because subjects are *blind* as to whether they received the drug, their expectations are the same. Any difference in their behavior must be caused by the drug.

Keeping subjects "blind" is not necessarily enough, however. In a **double-blind experiment**, neither subjects nor experimenters know who has received a drug and who has taken a placebo. This keeps researchers from unconsciously influencing subjects. Typically, someone else prepares the pills or injections so that experimenters don't know until after testing who got what. Testing of this type has shown that about 50 percent of the effectiveness of antidepressant drugs, such as the "wonder drug" Prozac, are the result of the placebo effect (Kirsch & Sapirstein, 1998).

The Experimenter Effect

How could a researcher influence subjects? The **experimenter effect** (changes in behavior caused by the unintended influence of an experimenter) is a common problem in psychological research. In essence, experimenters run the risk of finding what they expect to find. This occurs because humans are very sensitive to hints about what is expected of them (Rosenthal, 1994).

The experimenter effect even applies outside the laboratory. Psychologist Robert Rosenthal (1973) reports an example of how expectations can influence people: At the U.S. Air Force Academy Preparatory School, 100 airmen were randomly assigned to five different math classes. Their teachers did not know about this random placement. Instead, each teacher was told that his or her students had unusually high or low ability. Students in the classes labeled "high ability" improved much more in math scores than those in "low-ability" classes. Yet, initially, all of the classes had students of equal ability.

Apparently, the teachers subtly communicated their expectations to students. Most likely, they did this through tone of voice and body language and by giving encouragement or criticism. Their "hints," in turn, created a self-fulfilling prophecy that affected the students. A **self-fulfilling prophecy** is a prediction that prompts people to act in ways that make the prediction come true. In short, people sometimes become what we prophesy for them. It is wise to remember that others tend to live *up* or *down* to our expectations for them (Jussim & Eccles, 1992; Madon, Jussim, & Eccles, 1997).

4. A researcher performs an experiment to learn if room temperature affects the amount of aggression displayed by college students under crowded conditions in a simulated prison environment. In this experiment, the independent variable is
   a. room temperature *b.* the amount of aggression
   c. crowding *d.* the simulated prison environment

5. A procedure used to control both the placebo effect and the experimenter effect in drug experiments is the
   a. correlation method *b.* extraneous prophecy
   c. double-blind technique *d.* random assignment of subjects

CRITICAL THINKING

6. There is a loophole in the statement "I've been taking vitamin C tablets, and I haven't had a cold all year. Vitamin C is great!" What is the loophole?

7. People who believe strongly in astrology have personality characteristics that actually match, to a degree, those predicted by their astrological signs. Can you explain why this occurs?

Answers:

1. variable 2. experimental, control 3. independent, dependent, extraneous 4. *a* 5. *c* 6. The statement implies that vitamin C prevented colds. However, not getting a cold could just be a coincidence. A controlled experiment with a group given vitamin C and a control group not taking vitamin C would be needed to learn if vitamin C actually has any effect on susceptibility to colds. 7. A study showed that belief in astrology can create a self-fulfilling prophecy in which people alter their behaviors and self-concepts to match their astrological signs (van Rooij, 1994).

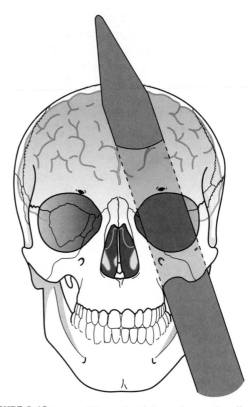

❖ **FIGURE 2.10** *Some of the earliest information on the effects of damage to frontal areas of the brain came from a case study of the accidental injury of Phineas Gage.*

THE CLINICAL METHOD—DATA BY THE CASE

Many experiments that might be revealing are impractical, unethical, or impossible to perform. In instances such as these, information may be gained from a **case study** (an in-depth focus on all aspects of a single subject). Clinical psychologists rely heavily on case studies.

Case studies may sometimes be thought of as **natural clinical tests** (accidents or other natural events that provide psychological data). Gunshot wounds, brain tumors, accidental poisonings, and similar disasters provide much information about the human brain. One remarkable case from the history of psychology is reported by Dr. J. M. Harlow (1868). Phineas Gage, a young foreman on a work crew, had a 13-pound steel rod blown through the front of his brain by an excavating charge (❖Fig. 2.10). Amazingly, he survived the accident. Within 2 months, Gage could walk, talk, and move normally. But the injury forever changed his personality. Instead of the honest and dependable worker he had been before, Gage became a surly, foul-mouthed liar. Dr. Harlow carefully recorded all details of what was perhaps the first in-depth case study of an accidental frontal lobotomy (the destruction of front brain matter).

When a Los Angeles carpenter named Michael Melnick suffered a similar injury 120 years later, he recovered completely, with no sign of lasting ill effects ("Man tells," 1981). Melnick's very different reaction to a similar injury shows why psychologists prefer controlled experiments and often use lab animals for studies of the brain. Case studies lack formal control groups. This, of course, limits the conclusions that can be drawn from clinical observations. Nonetheless, when a purely psychological problem is under study, the clinical method may be the *only* source of information.

Case studies can provide special opportunities to answer interesting questions. For instance, how do you know what kind of person you are? Would your self-image change if you lost your memory for past events? To answer these questions, psychologists recently did a case study of W. J., an 18-year-old

Single-blind experiment *An arrangement in which subjects remain unaware of whether they are in the experimental group or the control group.*
Double-blind experiment *An arrangement in which both subjects and experimenters are unaware of whether subjects are in the experimental group or the control group.*
Experimenter effect *Changes in subjects' behavior caused by the unintended influence of an experimenter's actions.*
Self-fulfilling prophecy *A prediction that prompts people to act in ways that make the prediction come true.*
Case study *An in-depth focus on all aspects of a single person.*
Natural clinical tests *Accidents or other natural events that provide psychological data.*

female college student. After she suffered a head injury, W. J. had amnesia for about a month. During that time, W. J. could recall little of what had occurred during the previous 6 months. Nevertheless, her ratings of her own personality appeared to be unaffected by her memory loss. This suggests that an awareness of one's own personal characteristics is based on memories that are more lasting than those for everyday events (Klein, Loftus, & Kihlstrom, 1996).

The careful recording of cases like W. J.'s is essential to psychology. Case studies often provide insights into human behavior that couldn't be obtained by any other method (Edwards, 1998).

SURVEY METHOD—HERE, HAVE A SAMPLE

Sometimes psychologists would like to ask everyone in the world a few well-chosen questions: "Do you drink alcoholic beverages? How often per week?" "What form of discipline did your parents use when you were a child?" "What is the most creative thing you've done?" The answers to such questions can reveal much about people's behavior. But because it is impossible to question everyone, doing a survey is often more practical.

In the **survey method**, public polling techniques are used to answer psychological questions. Typically, a group of people are asked a series of carefully worded questions. These questions must be carefully phrased because wording can greatly affect how people answer. In a survey conducted in 1991 during the Persian Gulf War, people were asked if they were concerned about the "collateral damage" caused by bombing in Iraq. When this military euphemism for civilian deaths was used, 55 percent of those polled said they were concerned. In contrast, when people were asked if they were concerned about "the number of civilian casualties and other unintended damage," 82 percent said yes (Rosenstiel, 1991).

Pretesting of survey questions can usually remove those that are bad, confusing, or easily misunderstood. Also, new computerized surveys can ask a different series of questions, depending on the answers to the first few items. This helps avoid asking unnecessary questions and it brings a person's responses into sharper focus (Krosnick, 1999).

Sampling

To be valid, a survey must be based on a **representative sample**. This is a small group that accurately reflects a larger population. In other words, a good sample must include the same proportion of men, women, young, old, professionals, blue-collar workers, Republicans, Democrats, whites, African Americans, Latinos, Asians, and so on, as found in the population as a whole.

A **population** is an entire group of animals or people belonging to a particular category (for example, all college students or all married women). Ultimately, we are interested in entire populations. But by selecting a smaller sample, we can draw conclusions about the larger group without polling each and every person. Representative samples are typically obtained by *randomly* selecting who will be included (❖Fig. 2.11). (Notice that this is similar to randomly assigning subjects to groups in an experiment.)

In recent years, 93 percent of human subjects in psychology experiments were recruited from introductory psychology courses (Sieber & Saks, 1989). Most of these subjects were white members of the middle class (Graham, 1992). This doesn't automatically invalidate the results of psychology experiments, but it may place some limitations on their meanings. (See "Is There a Gender Bias in Psychological Research?") The distinguished psychologist Edward Tolman once noted that much of psychology is based on two sets of subjects: rats and college sophomores. Tolman urged scientists to remember that rats are certainly not people and that college sophomores may not be!

Limitations

How accurate is the survey method? Modern surveys like the Gallup and Harris polls are quite accurate. The Gallup poll has erred in its election predictions by only 1.5 percent since 1954. However, if a survey is based on a biased sample, the picture it paints may be completely inaccurate. A **biased sample** does not accurately reflect the population from which it was drawn. Surveys done by magazines, Websites, and on-line

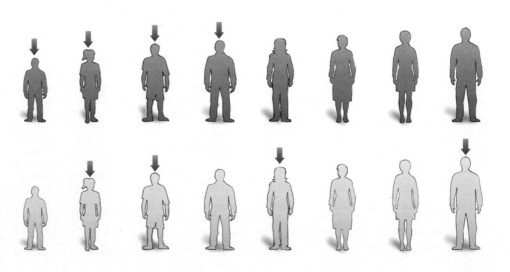

❖ **FIGURE 2.11** *If you were conducting a survey in which a person's height might be an important variable, the upper, nonrandom sample would be very unrepresentative. The lower sample, selected using a table of random numbers, better represents the group as a whole.*

IS THERE A GENDER BIAS IN PSYCHOLOGICAL RESEARCH?

Many doctors recommend that adults take an aspirin a day to help prevent heart attack. Both men and women are given this advice. The problem? Not a single woman was included in the sample on which the advice is based. Although females make up more than half the population, they continue to be neglected in psychological and medical research (Denmark, 1994).

Gender bias is a tendency for researchers to base conclusions solely on subjects of one gender, usually males. Owing to a gender bias, researchers must often *assume* that conclusions based on men also apply to women. But without directly studying women, it is impossible to know how often this assumption is wrong. A related problem occurs when researchers combine results from men and women. Doing so can hide important male-female differences. An additional problem is that unequal numbers of men and women may volunteer for some kinds of research. For example, in studies of sexuality, more male college students volunteer to participate than females (Wiederman, 1999). (What a surprise!)

Similar biases exist concerning the race, ethnicity, age, and sexual orientation of participants in psychological research (Denmark, 1994). Far too many conclusions are based on small groups of people who do not represent the rich tapestry of humanity. However, the solution to such problems is straightforward: When possible, researchers need to include a wider array of people in their studies. In recognition of human diversity, many researchers are doing just that.

---

information services can be quite biased. Surveys on the use of illicit drugs done by *Cosmopolitan* and *Rolling Stone* would probably produce very different results—neither of which would represent the general population. That's why psychologists using the survey method go to great lengths to ensure that their samples are representative. Fortunately, people can often be polled by telephone, which makes it easier to obtain large samples. Also, recent studies have shown that even if 30 percent of the people approached refuse to answer survey questions, the results are still likely to be valid (Krosnick, 1999).

SOCIAL DESIRABILITY   Even well-designed surveys may be limited by another problem. If a psychologist were to ask you detailed questions about your sexual history and current sexual behavior, how accurate would your replies be? Would you exaggerate? Would you be embarrassed?

Replies to survey questions are not always accurate or truthful. Many people show a distinct **courtesy bias** (a tendency to give "polite" or socially desirable answers). For example, pollsters working on an election found that African-American persons talking to white interviewers were less likely

to admit support for an African-American candidate. Similarly, white persons talking to African-American interviewers were more likely to claim support for the African-American candidate (McKean, 1984). For similar reasons, answers to questions concerning sex, alcohol or drug use, income, and church attendance may be less than truthful. The week after an election, more people say they voted than actually did (Krosnick, 1999). When asked if they are interested in the latest celebrity marriage or scandal, people say they have little interest in such stories. However, they can answer more factual questions about those stories than about other, more important, issues in the news.

SUMMARY   Despite their limitations, surveys often produce valuable information. For instance, in recent years working women have complained of sexual harassment at their jobs. How widespread is this problem? In 1981, psychologist Barbara Gutek found that 53 percent of women had experienced some form of sexual harassment at work (Gutek, 1981). A more recent survey obtained a figure of 45 percent (Janus & Janus, 1993). These results suggest that sexual harassment has declined slightly, perhaps because of greater public awareness of the problem. Although such information does not solve the problem of sexual harassment, it is a first step toward understanding it and remedying it.

To sum up, the survey method can be a powerful research tool. Like other methods, it has limitations, but new techniques and strategies are providing valuable information about our behavior (Krosnick, 1999).

SUMMARY—SCIENCE AND CRITICAL THINKING

Is so much emphasis on research really necessary in psychology? In a word, yes. As we have seen, science is a powerful way of asking questions about the world and getting trustworthy answers. More important, we might ask, What is the alternative to using the scientific method? In most areas of knowledge, wiping out scientific advances would mean a return to the Dark Ages. Your awareness of this fact, along with your understanding of research methods, should help make you a more critical observer of human behavior. ◆Table 2.2 summarizes many of the important ideas we have covered.

Survey method   *The use of public polling techniques to answer psychological questions.*
Representative sample   *A small, randomly selected part of a larger population that accurately reflects characteristics of the whole population.*
Population   *An entire group of animals or people belonging to a particular category (for example, all college students or all married women).*
Biased sample   *A subpart of a larger population that does not accurately reflect characteristics of the whole population.*
Gender bias   *The tendency to base conclusions solely on subjects of one gender, usually males.*
Courtesy bias   *The tendency to give "polite" or socially desirable answers to survey questions.*

◆ **TABLE 2.2** Comparison of Psychological Research Methods

	ADVANTAGES	DISADVANTAGES
Naturalistic observation	Behavior is observed in a natural setting; much information is obtained, and hypotheses and questions for additional research are formed	Little or no control is possible; observed behavior may be altered by the presence of the observer; observations may be biased; causes cannot be conclusively identified
Correlational method	Demonstrates the existence of relationships; allows prediction; can be used in lab, clinic, or natural setting	Little or no control is possible; relationships may be coincidental; cause-and-effect relationships cannot be confirmed
Experimental method	Clear cause-and-effect relationships can be identified; powerful controlled observations can be staged; no need to wait for natural event	May be somewhat artificial; some natural behavior not easily studied in laboratory (field experiments may avoid these objections)
Clinical method	Takes advantage of "natural clinical trials" and allows investigation of rare or unusual problems or events	Little or no control is possible; does not provide a control group for comparison, subjective interpretation is often necessary, a single case may be misleading or unrepresentative
Survey method	Allows information about large numbers of people to be gathered; can address questions not answered by other approaches	Obtaining a representative sample is critical and can be difficult to do; answers may be inaccurate; people may not do what they say or say what they do

In many ways, scientific thinking is a refinement of the critical thinking skills described in Chapter 1. Of course, thinking critically about behavior is not easy. A special trap to watch for is called the **my-side bias**, which is the tendency to pay more attention to evidence that supports your existing beliefs and to avoid contradictory evidence. To minimize the my-side bias, critical thinkers actively look for reasons why their ideas might be wrong or incomplete (Baron, 1993).

As you seek to understand your own behavior and that of others, it is valuable to ask yourself frequently: How might my initial conclusions be wrong? What counterarguments can I identify? What contradictory evidence might cause me to draw a new conclusion? Remember, too, that critical thinking can help you resist persuasion based on faulty logic, irrational thinking, or invalid conclusions. Searching for contradictory evidence and arguments is a wonderful antidote to misguided persuasion by advertisers, gurus, pundits, politicians, "experts," medical quacks, and sometimes even psychologists and educators!

A LOOK AHEAD   To complete our discussion, this chapter's "Psychology in Action" section offers a critical look at information reported in the popular press. Unfortunately, these reports abound with sloppy thinking, misinformation, and pie-in-the-sky theories. The first words to spring to your lips when you read outlandish claims should be, "Prove it." "Psychology in Action" gives some pointers on what to look for. After that, we'll explore the ethics of psychological research. You should find these topics an interesting way to conclude our survey of research in psychology.

KNOWLEDGE BUILDER
CASE STUDIES AND THE SURVEY METHOD

RELATE

If you were going to do a case study of a celebrity or other public figure, whom would you choose? What aspect of the person's behavior would you investigate?

Have you ever known someone who suffered a brain injury or disease? How did his or her behavior change? Was the change clear-cut enough to serve as a natural clinical test?

If you could ask only three questions in a psychological survey, what would they be? What population would you be interested in studying? How would you obtain a valid sample? Is it likely that any of your questions would be affected by a courtesy bias?

LEARNING CHECK

1. Case studies can often be thought of as natural tests and are frequently used by clinical psychologists. T or F?

2. For the survey method to be valid, a representative sample of people must be polled. T or F?

3. The phenomenon of multiple personality would most likely be investigated by use of
   a. a representative sample b. field experiments c. the double-blind procedure d. case studies

4. A problem with the survey method is that answers to questions may not always be _____ or _____.

5. People who abuse certain "designer drugs" develop neurological symptoms similar to Parkinson's disease. Studying damage to the brains of these people would provide a _____ test of theories about the causes of Parkinson's.

psychology in action

PSYCHOLOGY IN THE NEWS—SEPARATING FACT FROM FICTION

Psychology is discussed extensively on television, radio, and the Internet, and in magazines and newspapers. Unfortunately, much of what you'll find in the media is based on wishful thinking rather than science. Here are some suggestions for separating high-quality information from misleading fiction.

SUGGESTION 1: BE SKEPTICAL

Reports in the popular media tend to be made uncritically and with a definite bias toward reporting "astonishing" findings. Remember, saying "That's incredible" means "That's not believable"—which is often true.

Example 1

Some years ago, numerous articles appeared concerning "dermo-optical perception." According to these reports, people had been found who could use their fingertips to identify colors and read print (even under glass) while blindfolded. Many articles referred to the existence of a "sixth sense" or "X-ray eyes."

In reality, such "abilities" are based on what stage magicians call a "nose peek." It is impossible to prepare a blindfold (without damaging the eyes) that does not leave a tiny space on each side of the nose through which a person can peek. In accordance with this criticism, the phenomenal abilities reported in the first dermo-optical perception experiments disappeared each time the opportunity to peek was controlled.

Example 2

In 1994, the National Enquirer *reported that "Top University Researchers Reveal . . . 8 Million Americans may have been abducted by UFOs." However, one of the researchers cited in the article actually concluded "the public can rest assured that there is no evidence that millions of Americans are being abducted." In other words, the* Enquirer *story completely reversed the real findings. You'll find similar misinformation and sensationalism throughout the popular media. Be on guard.*

SUGGESTION 2: CONSIDER THE SOURCE OF INFORMATION

It should come as no surprise that information used to sell a product often reflects a desire for profit rather than the objective truth. Here is a typical advertising claim: "Government tests prove that no pain reliever is stronger or more effective than Brand X aspirin." A statement like this usually means that there was *no difference* between the product and others tested. No other pain reliever was stronger or more effective. But none was weaker either.

Keep the source in mind when reading the claims of makers of home biofeedback machines, sleep-learning devices, subliminal tapes, and the like. Remember that psychological services may be merchandised as well. Be wary of expensive courses that promise instant mental health and happiness, increased efficiency, memory, ESP or psychic ability, control of the uncon-

My-side bias *The tendency to pay attention to evidence and arguments that support one's existing beliefs.*

scious mind, an end to smoking, and so on. Usually they are promoted with a few testimonials and many unsupported claims (Lilienfeld, 1998).

Psychic claims should be viewed with special caution. Stage mentalists make a living by deceiving the public. Understandably, they are highly interested in promoting belief in their nonexistent powers. Psychic phenomena, when (and if) they do occur, are quite unpredictable. It would be impossible for a mentalist to do three shows a night, six nights a week without consistently using deception. The same is true of the so-called psychic advisers promoted in TV commercials. These charlatans make use of the Barnum effect (described in Chapter 1) to create an illusion that they know private information about people who call them.

I've seen some amazing things on TV. Could you give an example of how I may have been fooled? Here is a typical stage mentalist's routine. The mentalist picks an audience member "at random" and begins telling him personal things that "the mentalist could not possibly know." How does the mentalist do it? Easy! One of the mentalist's assistants stood in line outside the theater and eavesdropped on conversations before the show. The assistant then made careful note of where the audience member was seated. The seating location and the overheard information were then passed to the mentalist. The mentalist then announces, "You have an aunt . . . Aunt Bessy . . . she has been very ill . . . you were thinking about her earlier this evening . . . you had a flat tire on the way here this evening."

Firewalking is based on simple physics, not on any form of supernatural psychological control. The temperature of the coals may be as high as 1200°F. However, coals are like the air in a hot oven: They are very inefficient at transferring heat during brief contact.

SUGGESTION 3: ASK YOURSELF IF THERE WAS A CONTROL GROUP

The key importance of a control group in any experiment is often overlooked by the unsophisticated—an error to which you are no longer susceptible! The popular press is full of reports of "experiments" performed without control groups: "Talking to Plants Speeds Growth"; "Special Diet Controls Hyperactivity in Children"; "Food Shows Less Spoilage in Pyramid Chamber"; "Graduates of Firewalking Seminar Risk Their Soles."

Consider the last example for a moment. In recent years, expensive commercial courses have been promoted to teach people to walk barefoot on hot coals. (Why anyone would want to do this is itself an interesting question.) Firewalkers supposedly protect their feet with a technique called "neurolinguistic programming." Many people have paid good money to learn the technique, and most do manage a quick walk on the coals. But is the technique necessary? And is anything remarkable happening? We need a comparison group!

Fortunately, physicist Bernard Leikind has provided one. Leikind showed with volunteers that anyone (with reasonably callused feet) can walk over a bed of coals without being burned. The reason is that the coals, which are light, fluffy carbon, transmit little heat when touched. The principle involved is similar to briefly putting your

hand in a hot oven. If you touch a pan, you will be burned because metal transfers heat efficiently. But if your hand stays in the heated air, you'll be fine because air transmits little heat (Mitchell, 1987). Mystery solved.

BRIDGES

The question of whether ESP and other psychic phenomena exist has been thoroughly investigated.

To review the evidence, see Chapter 7, pages 228–231.

SUGGESTION 4: LOOK FOR ERRORS IN DISTINGUISHING BETWEEN CORRELATION AND CAUSATION

As you now know, it is dangerous to presume that one thing *caused* another just because they are correlated. Despite this, you will see many claims based on questionable correlations. Recently, a nutritionist was quoted in the news as saying that drinking excessive amounts of milk may cause juvenile delinquency. (This must have been a real hit with the National Dairy Association.) On what did he base this conclusion? Adolescent males who are often in trouble, he said, drink greater than average amounts of milk.

In no way does this correlation demonstrate that milk causes delinquency. It could easily be, for instance, that young males who mature early are more likely to be aggressive or get into trouble. Maturing early involves rapid growth. And rapid growth promotes hunger. It is entirely possible that this is the only link between milk and delinquency. Or perhaps some other unknown factor is involved.

Here's another example of mistaking correlation for causation. Jeanne Dixon, an astrologer, once answered a group of prominent scientists—who had declared that there is no scientific foundation for astrology—by saying, "They would do well to check the records at their local police stations, where they will learn that the rate of violent crime rises and falls with lunar cycles." Dixon, of course, believes that the moon affects human behavior.

If it is true that violent crime is more frequent at certain times of the month, doesn't that prove her point? Far from it. Increased crime could be due to darker nights, the fact that bills fall due at the first of the month, or any number of similar factors. More important, direct studies of the alleged "lunar effect" have shown that it doesn't occur (Simon, 1998; Wilkinson et al., 1997). Moonstruck criminals, along with "moon madness," are a fiction (Raison, Klein, & Steckler, 1999).

SUGGESTION 5: BE SURE TO DISTINGUISH BETWEEN OBSERVATION AND INFERENCE

If you see a person *crying,* is it correct to assume that she or he is *sad?* Although it seems reasonable to make this assumption, it is actually quite risky. We can observe objectively that the person is crying, but to *infer* sadness may be in error. It could be that the individual has just peeled five pounds of onions. Or maybe he or she just won a million-dollar lottery or is trying contact lenses for the first time.

Psychologists, politicians, physicians, scientists, and other experts often go far beyond the available facts in their claims. This does not mean that their inferences, opinions, and interpretations have no value; the opinion of an expert on the causes of mental illness, criminal behavior, learning problems, or whatever can be revealing. But be careful to distinguish between fact and opinion.

SUGGESTION 6: BEWARE OF OVERSIMPLIFICATIONS, ESPECIALLY THOSE MOTIVATED BY MONETARY GAIN

Courses or programs that offer a "new personality in three sessions," "six steps to love and fulfillment in marriage," or newly discovered "secrets of unlocking the powers of the mind" should be immediately suspect.

An excellent example of oversimplification is provided by a brochure entitled "Dr. Joyce Brothers Asks: How Do You Rate

as a 'Superwoman'?" Brothers, a "media" psychologist who has no private practice and is not known for research, wrote the brochure as a consultant for the Aerosol Packaging Council of the Chemical Specialties Manufacturers Association. A typical suggestion in this brochure tells how to enhance a marriage: "Sweep him off to a weekend hideaway. Tip: When he's not looking spray a touch of your favorite *aerosol* cologne mist on the bedsheets and pillows" (italics added). Sure, Joyce.

SUGGESTION 7: REMEMBER, "FOR EXAMPLE" IS NO PROOF

After reading this chapter, you should be sensitive to the danger of selecting single examples. If you read, "Law student passes state bar exam using sleep-learning device," don't rush out to buy one. Systematic research has shown that these devices are of little or no value (Druckman & Bjork, 1994; Wood et al., 1992). A corollary to this suggestion is to ask, Are the reported observations important or widely applicable?

Examples, anecdotes, single cases, and testimonials are all potentially deceptive. Unfortunately, *individual cases* tell nothing about what is true *in general* (Stanovich, 1998). For instance, studies of large groups of people show that smoking increases the likelihood of lung cancer. It doesn't matter if you know a lifelong heavy smoker who is 94 years old. The general finding is the one to remember.

SUMMARY

We are all bombarded daily with such a mass of new information that it is difficult to absorb it. The available knowledge, even in a limited area like psychology, biology, medicine, or contemporary rock music, is so vast that no single person can completely know and comprehend it. With this situation in mind, it becomes increasingly important that you become a critical, selective, and informed consumer of information.

KNOWLEDGE BUILDER

PSYCHOLOGY IN THE MEDIA

RELATE

Do you tend to assume that a statement must be true if it is in print, on television, or stated by an authority? How actively do you evaluate and question claims found in the media? Could you be a more critical consumer of information? *Should* you be a more critical consumer of information?

LEARNING CHECK

1. Newspaper accounts of dermo-optical perception have generally reported only the results of carefully designed psychological experiments. T or F?

2. Stage mentalists and psychics often use deception in their acts. T or F?

3. Blaming the lunar cycle for variations in the rate of violent crime is an example of mistaking correlation for causation. T or F?

4. To investigate possible links between drinking milk and delinquent behavior, it would be desirable to create an experimental group that consumes large amounts of milk and a control group that drinks none. T or F?

CRITICAL THINKING

5. In what way is reading the popular press like being a jury member in a courtroom trial?

6. Many parents believe that children become "hyperactive" when they eat too much sugar, and some early studies seemed to confirm this connection. However, as you may remember from Chapter 1, we now know that eating sugar rarely has any effect on children. Why do you think that sugar appears to cause hyperactivity?

7. Mystics have shown that fresh eggs can be balanced on their large ends during the vernal equinox when the sun is directly over the equator, day and night are equal in length, and the world is in perfect balance. What is wrong with their observation?

Answers:

1. F 2. T 3. T 4. T 5. In both instances it is important to not only study the evidence supporting various claims but also to evaluate the *quality* of that evidence. 6. This is another case of mistaking correlation for causation. Children who are hyperactive may eat more sugar (and other foods) to fuel their frenetic activity levels. 7. The mystics have neglected to ask if eggs can be balanced at other times. They can. The lack of a control group gives the illusion that something amazing is happening, but the equinox has nothing to do with egg balancing (Meltzoff, 1998).

a step beyond

RESEARCH ETHICS—SMILE, YOU'RE ON CANDID CAMERA!

Focus: Is it ethical to use humans or animals as subjects in psychology experiments?

Some years ago, social psychologist Philip Zimbardo and his associates set up a simulated prison at Stanford University. Their goal was to probe the effects of imprisonment on healthy individuals. Students were recruited to play the roles of prisoners and guards. Much to everyone's surprise, the 2-week experiment had to be called off after just 6 days. The "guards" had become so sadistic that 4 of the 10 "prisoners" suffered severe emotional reactions, including crying, depression, anxiety, and rage (Zimbardo et al., 1973). (This experiment is discussed further in Chapter 19.)

The Stanford prison experiment is only one of several to raise serious ethical questions. Were the participants harmed? Did the information gained justify the emotional costs? Are such experiments dehumanizing? Questions like these raise three issues to which researchers must be sensitive: *deception, invasion of privacy,* and *lasting harm.* Each issue is illustrated by the following experiments. See if you think they are ethical.

DECEPTION

To obtain genuine reactions, the true purpose of many experiments is hidden by deception. For example, a researcher interested in guilt once led subjects to believe they had broken an expensive piece of machinery. During the experiment, a machine suddenly popped loudly, released a plume of smoke, and sputtered to a stop. As embarrassed subjects were about to leave, the experimenter asked them to sign a petition he was

circulating. The petition called for doubling tuition fees at the school. Almost all control subjects had refused to sign the same petition. However, because of their guilt, more than 50 percent of the experimental subjects signed (Rubin, 1970a). Perhaps guilt could have been studied in some other way. Nevertheless, some questions simply can't be answered without using deception. When this is the case, researchers must deceive subjects as little as possible. They must also take extra steps to make sure they are treating people ethically (Kimmel, 1998).

INVASION OF PRIVACY

To what extent should invasions of privacy be allowed in psychological research? One study that has been both criticized and defended involved secret observation of men in a rest room. Psychologist Eric Knowles was interested in the stress caused by "personal space" invasions. An observer concealed himself in a toilet stall in a public rest room and used a hidden periscope to monitor activity at the urinals. As predicted, urination took longer to begin when an assistant occupied a urinal next to the unsuspecting subject (Koocher, 1977; Middlemist et al., 1976). This finding is interesting, but does it justify the invasion of privacy used to obtain it?

LASTING HARM

Do psychological experiments ever do lasting harm to participants? This is perhaps the most serious ethical question of all. A classic experiment on obedience to authority illustrates the problem. In the study, subjects thought they were giving painful and dangerous electrical shocks to another person

(Milgram, 1974). (No shocks were actually given; see Chapter 19.) Belief that they were hurting someone proved extremely stressful for most subjects. Many left the experiment shaken and upset. Some presumably suffered guilt and distress for some time afterward.

This experiment may sound clearly unethical, but the researcher, Stanley Milgram, did follow-up studies on the participants. Most felt positive about their experience and claimed they were glad they had taken part. Many added that they had learned something of value about themselves. But what about the few who felt otherwise? As in medical research, there are no easy answers to the ethical questions raised by psychology.

Most students find the studies just described interesting and informative. How can the search for knowledge be properly balanced with human rights? As a reply to this question, ethical guidelines of the American Psychological Association state: "Psychologists must carry out investigations with respect for the people who participate and with concern for their dignity and welfare." To ensure that this is the case, most college psychology departments have ethics committees that oversee proposed research. Nevertheless, no easy answers exist for the ethical questions raised by some research. How do *you* think a psychologist should decide whether his or her research is ethical?

◆ **TABLE 2.3** Basic Ethical Guidelines for Psychological Researchers
Do no harm.
Accurately describe risks to potential subjects.
Ensure that participation is voluntary.
Minimize any discomfort to participants.
Maintain confidentiality.
Do not unnecessarily invade privacy.
Use deception only when absolutely necessary.
Remove any misconceptions caused by deception (debrief).
Provide results and interpretations to participants.
Treat participants with dignity and respect.

BECOMING A SUBJECT

The ethics of research may turn out to be highly pertinent for many students. As mentioned earlier, college students often serve as subjects in psychology experiments. If you become a subject, what should you expect? First of all, count on having an interesting educational experience. There is no better way to learn how research is done than to observe it firsthand. Beyond that, you have a right to expect that your reactions will remain confidential, that you will be debriefed about the purpose of the research, that you will receive an interpretation of your responses or test results, and finally, that the results of the research project will be made available to you (Blanck et al., 1992; Fisher & Fyrberg, 1994). (See ◆Table 2.3.)

Psychological research can be truly fascinating. If you do participate as a subject, you may be inspired to try experiments or answer questions of your own. Many careers in psychology were launched in just this way.

THE ETHICS OF ANIMAL RESEARCH

Research with animals can also raise difficult ethical questions. In recognition of this fact, Principle 10 of the *Ethical Principles of Psychologists* states:

An investigator of animal behavior strives to advance understanding of basic behavioral principles and/or to contribute to the improvement of human health and welfare. In seeking these ends, the investigator ensures the welfare of animals and treats them humanely. Laws and reg-

BRIDGES

Many important experiments in social psychology have involved deception.

You can read about Milgram's classic study of obedience in Chapter 19, pages 652–654.

ulations notwithstanding, an animal's immediate protection depends upon the scientist's own conscience ("Ethical," 1992).

Behind this statement lies a storm of controversy. Opinions about the ethics of animal research range widely—from medical researchers who routinely conduct animal experiments to vegetarian animal rights activists who raid labs to "liberate" animals. It is not possible here to discuss all of the arguments for and against animal research. However, a brief sketch of the debate may serve as a starting point for further thought.

At one extreme, members of the animal liberation movement believe that animals have a right to live without human interference. Animal liberators oppose animal research of all kinds, the raising of animals for food, hunting, rodeos, zoos, and circuses. They regard behavioral research as worthless and cruel and want to abolish it entirely (Herzog, 1990). At the other extreme are scientists who believe human welfare always takes precedence over animal welfare. These individuals believe that they have a moral imperative to improve the human condition and save human lives. Doing so, they believe, inescapably involves animal research.

Is there a middle ground? Most scientists, 80 percent of the general public, and many animal welfare advocates take a more moderate position. These individuals accept the necessity for scientific experiments. They note, for instance, that creating vaccines to end crippling polio epidemics would have been impossible without animal research. They also recognize that animals, as well as humans, benefit from knowledge gained from scientific research. Moderates primarily seek to ensure humane treatment of animals and to minimize the use of animals when possible. As animal activist Phyllis Macy (1990) says:

What is called for here is not the cessation of research with animals, but a different attitude toward their use. . . . Research with animals should above all be humane. This means respecting another creature's aspirations for life and capacity for pain. On this variable, all animals, including humans, are equal. We earn respect for ourselves by respecting life around us.

It is probably fair to say that the animal rights movement has called needed attention to the abuse of animals for such purposes as testing cosmetics and other products. It has also encouraged development of alternatives to animal research. Part of the middle ground in this debate, if indeed one exists, is the agreed-upon value of finding alternatives that minimize the use of animals. For example, it may be possible to use computer simulations of animal behavior for teaching and preliminary research. Also, use of animals could be limited to critical studies. But, again questions arise: Who is to say what research is worthwhile? Is it possible to guess where new knowledge will lead? Might a seemingly minor finding eventually unleash a breakthrough?

Think about It

No easy answers exist for the ethical questions raised by animal research. However, a government report on behavioral research concluded, "The chance that alternatives will completely replace animals in the future is nil" ("Research," 1989).

Perhaps the most important lesson to be learned from animal research is that anyone working with vulnerable subjects, be they animals, children, or the mentally ill, must maintain the highest ethical standards. Psychological studies are vital for advancing knowledge, but research cannot continue unless researchers are able to retain the public's trust (Hyman, 1999).

CONCLUSION: Most psychological studies are harmless. However, some behavioral research does raise ethical concerns. When there is a risk of possible harm, investigators must ensure that subjects are protected and that strict ethical standards are upheld.

RESEARCH ETHICS

RELATE

If you were participating in an experiment, would you object to being deceived? How concerned would you be about invasions of privacy?

Under what circumstances, if any, would you regard it as ethical to use animals in medical experiments? Veterinary experiments? Psychology experiments? Teaching labs? Product testing? Entertainment?

LEARNING CHECK

1. Deception is regarded as a necessary part of almost all psychology experiments. T or F?

2. Most of the subjects who participated in Milgram's obedience experiment felt that they had not been harmed. T or F?

3. The major ethical question raised by the Stanford prison experiment concerned an invasion of privacy. T or F?

4. In the United States, the American Psychological Association must rule on whether an experiment is ethical before it is performed. T or F?

5. Principle 10 of the *Ethical Principles of Psychologists* states that humane treatment of animals ultimately depends on each scientist's own conscience. T or F?

CRITICAL THINKING

6. Perhaps the most basic of all ethical requirements in psychological research involves the accurate reporting of results. Can you explain why?

7. Studies designed to test the effectiveness of psychiatric drugs often involve control groups in which subjects receive placebos. In what way might this practice be unethical?

Answers:

1. F 2. T 3. F 4. F 5. T 6. To advance scientific knowledge and human welfare, psychologists must report the results of their studies honestly—even when the results contradict the researcher's beliefs or expectations. It takes a high level of integrity to do psychological research and follow the evidence wherever it leads (Melzoff, 1998). 7. If the drugs are effective, it may be unethical to deprive people in the control group from being helped by them.

CHAPTER IN REVIEW

Why is the scientific method important to psychologists?

- The scientific method is used to improve on common sense and avoid the pitfalls of informal observation.
- Important elements in a scientific investigation include observing, defining a problem, proposing a hypothesis, gathering evidence/testing the hypothesis, publishing the results, and forming a theory.
- Before they can be investigated, psychological concepts must be given operational definitions.

How do psychologists collect information?

- Naturalistic observation is a starting place in many investigations. Three problems with this approach are the effects of the observer on the observed, observer bias, and an inability to explain observed behavior.
- In animal studies, the anthropomorphic fallacy can lead to false conclusions. This error is the tendency to treat animals as if they had human characteristics.
- In the correlational method, relationships between two traits, responses, or events are measured.
- A correlation coefficient is computed to gauge the strength of the relationship. Correlations allow prediction, but they are usually insufficient to demonstrate cause-and-effect connections.
- Relationships in psychology may be positive or negative, linear or curvilinear. Relationships are often clarified by graphing.
- Cause-and-effect relationships are best identified by controlled experiments.

How is an experiment performed?

- In an experiment, two or more groups of subjects are formed. These groups differ only with regard to the independent variable (condition of interest as a cause in the experiment).
- Effects on the dependent variable are then measured. All other conditions (extraneous variables) are held constant.
- It must be possible to replicate (repeat) observations or experiments for them to be meaningful.
- In experiments testing drugs, a placebo (fake pill or injection) must be used to control for the effects of expectations.
- Drug research also frequently uses a double-blind procedure so that neither subjects nor experimenters know who is receiving a drug.
- A related problem is the experimenter effect. This is the tendency for experimenters to subtly and unconsciously influence the outcome of an experiment.
- Expectations can create a self-fulfilling prophecy, in which a person changes in the direction of the expectation.

What other research methods do psychologists use?

- The clinical method uses case studies, which are in-depth records of a single subject. Case studies provide important information on topics that would not be studied any other way.
- In the survey method, people in a representative sample are asked a series of carefully worded questions. Responses to these questions provide information on the attitudes and psychological functioning of large groups of people.

How dependable is psychological information found in the popular media?

- Information in the media varies greatly in quality and accuracy.
- It is wise to approach such information with skepticism and caution. This is especially true with regard to the source of information, uncontrolled observation, correlation and causation, inferences, oversimplification, and single examples. Critical thinking will help you cut through the misinformation.

What ethical questions does psychological research raise?

- Psychological research raises a number of ethical questions. Three ethical issues of particular importance in human research are deception, invasion of privacy, and lasting harm.
- Animal research also poses ethical dilemmas. Debates concerning animal welfare are based on personal values and morals and are therefore not easily resolved. The American Psychological Association strongly endorses the humane treatment of research animals.

PSYCHOLOGY ON THE NET

- **American Psychological Association** Home page of the APA, with links to PsychNET, student information, member information, and more. http://www.apa.org/
- **American Psychological Society** Home page of the APS, with links to information, services, and Internet resources. http://psych.psychologicalscience.org
- **Ethical Principles of Psychologists and Code of Conduct** The full text of the ethical principles that guide professional psychologists. http://www.apa.org/ethics/code.html
- **Psychweb** This award-winning page provides a multitude of services and links. http://www.psychweb.com/
- **Psycoloquy** An on-line journal with short articles on all areas of psychology. http://www.princeton.edu/~harnad/psyc.html
- **InfoTrac® College Edition** For recent articles related to topics discussed in this chapter, use Key Words search for PSYCHOLOGICAL RESEARCH.

INTERACTIVE LEARNING

- *PsychNow!* 1c. Research methods. 1d. Critical thinking in psychology.
- *Psyk.trek* 1b. The experimental method. 1c. Statistics: Central tendency and variability. 1d. Statistics: Correlation.

CHAPTER 3

The Brain, Biology, and Behavior

Chapter Survey

Theme: *Brain activity is the source of human consciousness, intelligence, and behavior.*

▼ **KEY QUESTIONS**

● *KEY TOPICS*

▼ How do nerve cells operate and communicate?

   ● *Neurons, nerve impulses, and neurotransmitters*

▼ What are the functions of major parts of the nervous system?

   ● *Divisions of the nervous system*

▼ How do we know how the brain works?

   ● *Research methods in biopsychology*

▼ How is the brain organized, and what do its higher structures do?

   ● *The cerebral cortex*
   ● *Right and left brain hemispheres*
   ● *Lobes of the cortex*

▼ **KEY QUESTIONS**

● *KEY TOPICS*

▼ Why are the brain's association areas important? What happens when they are injured?

   ● *Association areas*
   ● *Aphasias and agnosias*

▼ What kinds of behaviors are controlled by the subcortex?

   ● *The medulla, cerebellum, and reticular formation*
   ● *The thalamus and hypothalamus*
   ● *The limbic system and emotion*

▼ Does the glandular system affect behavior?

   ● *Endocrine glands and hormones*

▼ How do right- and left-handed individuals differ?

   ● *Handedness, brain dominance, and laterality*

▼ Is brain damage always permanent?

   ● *Brain plasticity and neurogenesis*

WORLDS WITHIN WORLDS WITHIN WORLDS

*I*MAGINE YOURSELF SMALLER *than the period at the end of this sentence. Then join me as we enter a bizarre microscopic world. A tangle of spidery branches, delicate fibers, and transparent globes surrounds us. As we watch, pulsing waves of electrical energy flash by, scattering everywhere. Meanwhile, all is bathed in a swirling sea of exotic chemicals. We are indeed in a strange realm. Yet there is beauty here, and mind-bending complexity—for we have just entered that most amazing of all computers, the human brain.*

The brain is about the size of a large grapefruit. Weighing a little over 3 pounds, it consists of some 100 billion **neurons** *(NEW-rons: individual nerve cells). Neurons carry and process information. They also activate muscles and glands. Thus, everything you do, think, or feel can be traced back to these tiny cells. The mass of neurons we call the brain allows humans to make music of exquisite beauty, seek a cure for cancer, fall in love, or read a book like this one.*

Each neuron in the brain's "enchanted loom" is linked to as many as 15,000 others. This network makes it possible to combine and store immense amounts of information. In fact, there may be more possible pathways between the neurons in your brain than there are atoms in the entire universe!

***Biopsychology** is the study of how biological processes, especially activity in the brain and nervous system, relate to behavior. It is clear that answers to many age-old questions concerning the mind, consciousness, and knowledge lie buried within the brain. Let us enter this fascinating realm.*

Gateways to Brain and Behavior

BIOPSYCHOLOGISTS study how processes in the body, brain, and nervous system relate to behavior.

ULTIMATELY, ALL BEHAVIOR CAN BE TRACED to the activity of nerve cells.

TO MAP THE BRAIN, researchers activate or disable specific areas and observe changes in behavior.

BIOELECTRICAL RECORDINGS AND COMPUTER-GENERATED IMAGES of brain activity provide additional insights into how the brain works.

SENSATIONS, THOUGHTS, FEELINGS, MOTIVES, ACTIONS, MEMORIES, AND ALL OTHER HUMAN CAPACITIES are associated with brain activities and structures.

ENDOCRINE GLANDS serve as a chemical communication system within the body. Behavior is greatly influenced by the ebb and flow of hormones in the bloodstream.

BRAIN DOMINANCE AND BRAIN ACTIVITY determine whether you are right-handed, left-handed, or ambidextrous.

THE BRAIN'S CIRCUITRY is not static. The brain grows new nerve cells and it can "rewire" itself in response to changing environmental conditions.

NEURONS—BUILDING A "BIOCOMPUTER"

Unraveling the brain's mysteries begins with neurons. A single neuron is not very smart—it couldn't even make you blink. Yet, when neurons form vast networks, they produce intelligence and consciousness. Neurons link to one another in tight clusters and long "chains." Each neuron receives messages from others, processes the messages, and sends its own message on. Millions of neurons must send messages at the same time to produce even the most fleeting thought (Carter, 1998).

Parts of a Neuron

What does a neuron look like? What are its main parts? No two neurons are exactly alike in size or shape, but most have four basic parts (❖Fig. 3.1). The **dendrites** (DEN-drytes), which look like the roots of a tree, receive messages from other neurons. The **soma** (SOH-mah: cell body) also accepts incoming information. Every so often, arriving messages cause

the soma to send a nerve impulse down a thin fiber called the **axon** (AK-sahn). The axon carries information away from the cell body.

Most axons end in **axon terminals** (branches) that link with the dendrites and somas of other neurons. These links allow information to pass from neuron to neuron. Some axons are only 0.1 millimeter long. (That's about the width of a pencil line.) Others stretch up to a meter—from the base of your spine to your big toe, for instance—through the nervous system. Like miniature cables, axons carry messages throughout

Neuron *An individual nerve cell.*
Biopsychology *The study of how biological processes, especially activity in the brain and nervous system, relate to behavior.*
Dendrites *Neuron fibers that receive incoming messages.*
Soma *The main body of a neuron or other cell.*
Axon *Fiber that carries information away from the cell body of a neuron.*
Axon terminals *Branching fibers at the ends of axons.*

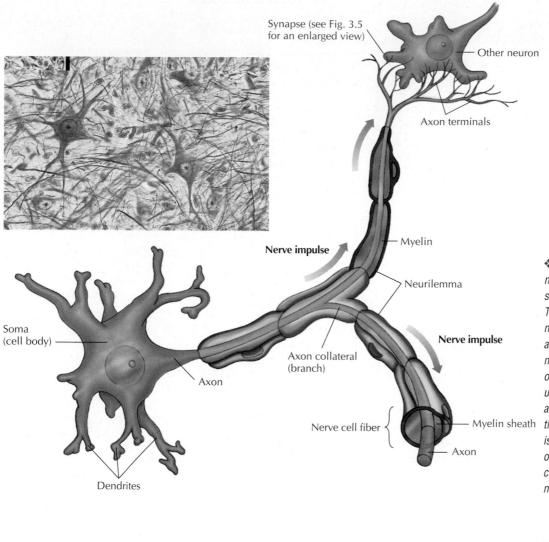

Synapse (see Fig. 3.5 for an enlarged view)

Other neuron

Axon terminals

Nerve impulse

Myelin

Neurilemma

Nerve impulse

Soma (cell body)

Axon collateral (branch)

Axon

Nerve cell fiber {

Myelin sheath

Axon

Dendrites

❖ **FIGURE 3.1** *An example of a neuron, or nerve cell, showing several of its important features. The right foreground shows a nerve cell fiber in cross section, and the upper left inset gives a more realistic picture of the shape of neurons. The nerve impulse usually travels from the dendrites and soma to the branching ends of the axon. The neuron shown here is a motor neuron. Motor neurons originate in the brain or spinal cord and send their axons to the muscles or glands of the body.*

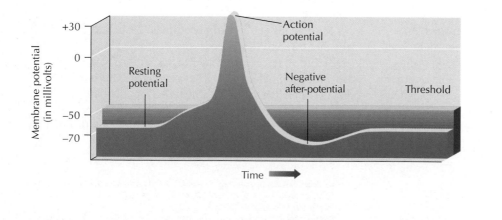

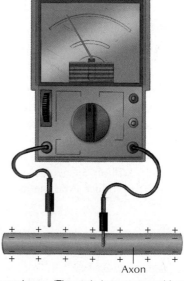

Action potential

Resting potential

Negative after-potential

Threshold

Membrane potential (in millivolts)

+30

0

−50

−70

Time

Axon

❖ **FIGURE 3.2** *Activity in an axon can be measured by placing electrical probes inside and outside the axonal membrane. (The scale is exaggerated here. Such measurements require ultra-small electrodes, as described later in this chapter.) At rest, the inside of an axon is about minus 60 to 70 millivolts, compared with the outside. Electrochemical changes in a nerve cell generate an action potential. When positively charged sodium ions (Na+) rush into the cell, its interior briefly becomes positive. This is the action potential. After the action potential, an outward flow of positive potassium ions (K+) restores the negative charge inside the axon. (See ❖Figure 3.3 for further explanation.)*

the brain and nervous system. Altogether, your brain has about 3 million miles of axons (Hyman, 1999).

Now let's summarize with a metaphor. Imagine that you are standing in a long line of people who are holding hands. A person on the far right end of the line wants to silently send a message to the person on the left end. She does this by pressing the hand of the person to her left, who presses the hand of the person to his left, and so on. The message arrives at your right hand (your dendrites). You decide whether to pass it on (you are the soma). The message goes out through your left arm (the axon). With your left hand (the axon terminals), you squeeze the hand of the person to your left, and the message moves on.

The Nerve Impulse

Each neuron is like a tiny biological battery. Electrically charged chemical molecules called **ions** (EYE-ons) are found in and around nerve cells (❖Fig. 3.2). Some ions have a positive charge. Others have a negative charge. Also, different numbers of "plus" and "minus" charges can be found inside and outside of nerve cells. As a result, the inside of a human neuron has an electrical charge of about minus 70 millivolts, compared to outside the cell. (A millivolt is one thousandth of a volt.)

The electrical charge of a neuron at rest is called its **resting potential**. But neurons seldom get much rest: Messages arriving from other neurons constantly alter the resting potential. If it changes enough, the cell reaches a **threshold**, or trigger point for firing. The threshold for human neurons is about minus 50 millivolts (see ❖Fig. 3.2). When a neuron reaches 50 millivolts, an **action potential**, or nerve impulse, sweeps down the axon at up to 200 miles per hour (❖Fig. 3.3). At this very instant, millions of these action potentials are firing in your brain.

What happens during an action potential? The axon membrane is pierced by tiny molecular tunnels called **ion channels**. Normally, these channels are blocked by molecules that act like gates or doors. During an action potential, the gates pop open. This allows sodium ions (Na⁺) to rush into the axon (Carlson,

1998). The channels open up first near the soma. Then, gate after gate opens down the axon, as the action potential zips along (❖Fig. 3.4).

The action potential is an **all-or-nothing event** (an impulse occurs completely or not at all). You might find it helpful to picture the axon as a row of dominoes set on end. Tipping over the dominoes is an all-or-nothing act. Once the first domino drops, a wave of falling blocks zips rapidly to the end of the line. Similarly, when a nerve impulse is triggered near the soma, a wave of activity (the action potential) travels down the length of the axon.

Synapses and Neurotransmitters

How does information move from one neuron to another? The nerve impulse is primarily electrical. That's why electrically stimulating the brain affects behavior. To prove the point, researcher José Delgado once entered a bullring with a cape and a radio transmitter. The bull charged. Delgado retreated. At the last instant, the speeding bull stopped short. Why? Because

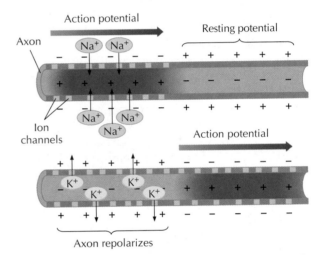

❖ **FIGURE 3.4** *Cross-sectional views of an axon. The right end of the top axon is at rest, with a negatively charged interior. An action potential begins when the ion channels open and sodium ions (Na⁺) enter the axon. In this drawing, the action potential would travel rapidly along the axon, from left to right. In the lower axon, the action potential has moved to the right. After it passes, potassium ions (K⁺) flow out of the axon. This quickly renews the negative charge inside the axon, so it can fire again. Sodium ions that enter the axon during an action potential are pumped back out more slowly. Their removal restores the original resting potential.*

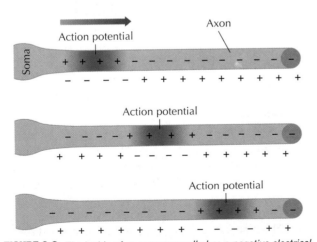

❖ **FIGURE 3.3** *The inside of an axon normally has a negative electrical charge. The fluid surrounding an axon is normally positive. As an action potential passes along the axon, these charges reverse, so that the interior of the axon briefly becomes positive.*

Ion *An electrically charged molecule.*
Resting potential *The electrical charge of a neuron at rest.*
Threshold *The point at which a nerve impulse is triggered.*
Action potential *The nerve impulse.*
Ion channels *Channels through the axon membrane.*
All-or-nothing event *An event that happens completely, or not at all.*

Delgado's radio activated electrodes (metal wires) implanted deep within the bull's brain. These, in turn, stimulated "control centers" that brought the bull to a halt.

In contrast to the nerve impulse, communication between neurons is chemical. The microscopic space between two neurons, over which messages pass, is called a **synapse** (SIN-aps) (❖Fig. 3.5). When an action potential reaches the tips of the axon terminals, **neurotransmitters** (NUE-roh-TRANS-mit-ers) are released into the synaptic gap. Neurotransmitters are chemicals that alter activity in neurons.

Let's return to the metaphor of people standing in a line. To be more realistic, you and the others shouldn't be holding hands. Instead, each of you should have a toy squirt gun in your left hand. To pass along a message, you would squirt the right hand of the person to your left. When that person notices this "message," he or she would squirt the right hand of the person to the left, and so on.

Neurotransmitter molecules cross the synaptic gap and attach to special receptor sites on the receiving neuron (❖Fig. 3.5). **Receptor sites** are tiny areas on the cell membrane that are sensitive to neurotransmitters. These sites are found in large numbers on nerve cell bodies and dendrites. Muscles and glands have receptor sites, too.

Does the release of a neurotransmitter immediately trigger an action potential in the next neuron? Not always. Transmitters may *excite* the next neuron (move it closer to firing) or *inhibit* it (make an impulse less likely). At any instant, a neuron may receive hundreds or thousands of messages. Does it fire an impulse? It depends: If several "exciting" messages arrive close in time, the neuron fires—but only if it hasn't been pushed *away* from its trigger point by also getting "inhibiting" messages. In this way,

messages are *combined* before a neuron "decides" to fire its all-or-nothing action potential. Multiply these events by 100 billion neurons and 100 trillion synapses and you have an amazing computer—one that fits into a space smaller than a shoe box.

There are more than 100 neurotransmitters in the brain. Some important "chemical messengers" are acetylcholine, epinephrine, norepinephrine, serotonin, dopamine, histamine, and various amino acids. Many drugs operate by imitating, duplicating, or blocking these substances. For example, **acetylcholine** (ah-SEET-ul-KOH-leen) normally activates muscles. However, the drug **curare** (cue-RAH-ree) competes with acetylcholine. It does this by attaching to receptor sites on muscles, which prevents acetylcholine from affecting the muscle. As a result, a person or animal given curare will be paralyzed—a fact known to South American Indians of the Amazon River Basin, who use curare as an arrow poison.

BRIDGES

Under some circumstances, pain can produce feelings of relaxation or euphoria.

Endorphins underlie this effect. See Chapter 6, pages 189–190.

NEURAL REGULATORS More subtle brain activities are affected by chemicals called neuropeptides (NEW-row-PEP-tides) (Agnati et al., 1992). **Neuropeptides** do not carry messages directly. Instead, these chemicals seem to *regulate* the activity of other neurons. In doing so, they affect memory, pain, emotion, pleasure, moods, hunger, sexual behavior, and other basic processes. For example, when you touch something hot, you jerk your hand away. The messages for this action are carried by neurotransmitters. At the same time, pain may cause the brain to release **enkephalins** (en-KEF-ah-lins). These opiate-like neural regulators relieve pain and stress. Related chemicals called **endorphins** (en-DORF-ins) are released by the pituitary gland. Together, these chemical regulators reduce the pain so that it is not too disabling.

Ultimately, brain regulators may help explain depression, schizophrenia, drug addiction, the placebo effect, acupuncture, and other puzzling topics.

THE NERVOUS SYSTEM—WIRED FOR ACTION

Jamal and Vicki are playing catch with a Frisbee. To toss the Frisbee or catch it, a huge amount of information must be sensed, interpreted, and then directed to countless muscle fibers. Jamal and Vicki's neural circuits are ablaze with activity. Let's explore the "wiring diagram" that makes their Frisbee game possible.

Neurons and Nerves

Are neurons the same as nerves? No. Neurons are tiny individual cells. You would need a microscope to see one. **Nerves** are large bundles of axons and dendrites. You can easily see nerves without magnification.

Many nerves have a whitish color because they contain axons coated with a fatty layer of tissue called **myelin** (MY-eh-lin). Small gaps in the myelin help nerve impulses move faster. Instead of passing down the entire length of the axon, the action potential leaps from gap to gap. When the myelin layer is damaged, a person may suffer from numbness, weakness, or

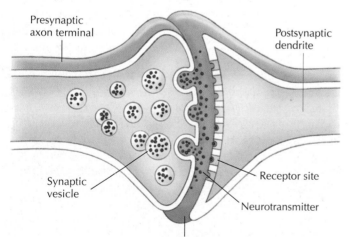

❖ **FIGURE 3.5** *A highly magnified view of the synapse shown in* ❖*Fig. 3.1. Neurotransmitters are stored in tiny sacs called synaptic vesicles. When a nerve impulse arrives at an axon terminal, the vesicles move to the surface and release neurotransmitters. These transmitter molecules cross the synaptic gap to affect the next neuron. The size of the gap is exaggerated here; it is actually only about one millionth of an inch. Transmitter molecules vary in their effects: Some excite the next neuron, and some inhibit its activity.*

Labels in figure: Presynaptic axon terminal; Postsynaptic dendrite; Synaptic vesicle; Receptor site; Neurotransmitter; Synaptic gap

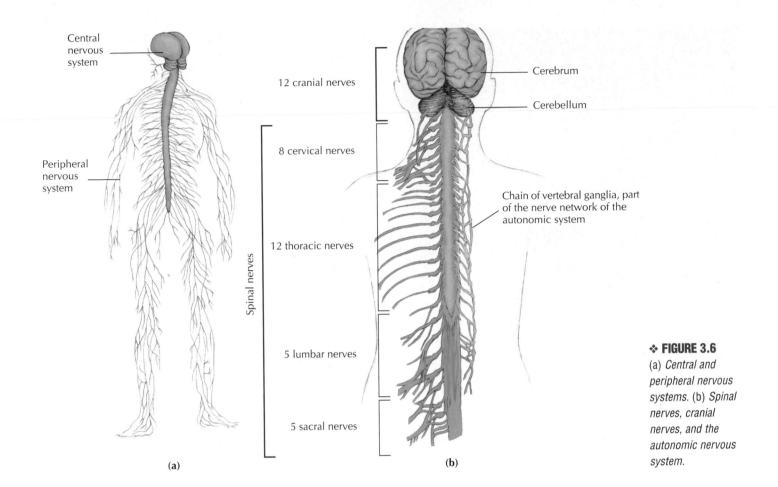

Central nervous system

Peripheral nervous system

12 cranial nerves

8 cervical nerves

Spinal nerves

12 thoracic nerves

5 lumbar nerves

5 sacral nerves

(a)

Cerebrum

Cerebellum

Chain of vertebral ganglia, part of the nerve network of the autonomic system

(b)

❖ FIGURE 3.6
(a) *Central and peripheral nervous systems.* (b) *Spinal nerves, cranial nerves, and the autonomic nervous system.*

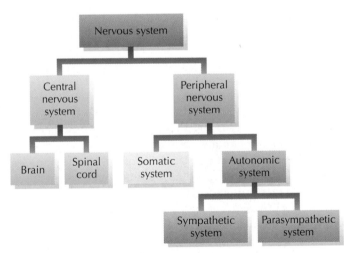

❖ FIGURE 3.7 *Subparts of the nervous system.*

paralysis. That, in fact, is what happens in multiple sclerosis, a disease that occurs when a person's immune system attacks and destroys myelin.

A thin layer of cells called the **neurilemma** (NEW-rih-LEM-ah) is also wrapped around most axons outside the brain and spinal cord. (Return to ❖Fig. 3.1.) The neurilemma forms a "tunnel" that damaged fibers can follow as they repair themselves. However, this generally does not

apply to the brain and spinal cord. There, most axons must last a lifetime.

Neural Networks

As you can see in ❖Figures 3.6 and 3.7, the **central nervous system (CNS)** consists of the brain and spinal cord. The brain is the central "computer" of the nervous system. Jamal must

Synapse *The microscopic space between two neurons, over which messages pass.*
Neurotransmitter *Any chemical released by a neuron that alters activity in other neurons.*
Receptor sites *Areas on the surface of neurons and other cells that are sensitive to neurotransmitters or hormones.*
Acetylcholine *The neurotransmitter released by neurons to activate muscles.*
Curare *A drug that competes with acetylcholine, causing paralysis.*
Neuropeptides *Brain chemicals that regulate the activity of neurons.*
Enkephalins *Opiate-like brain chemicals that regulate reactions to pain and stress.*
Endorphins *Chemicals that are similar in structure and pain-killing effect to opiate drugs such as morphine.*
Nerve *A bundle of neuron fibers.*
Myelin *A fatty layer coating some axons.*
Neurilemma *A layer of cells that encases many axons.*
Central nervous system (CNS) *The brain and spinal cord.*

Each year spinal cord injuries rob many thousands of people, like actor Christopher Reeve, of the ability to move. Yet, there is growing hope that nerve-grafting techniques may someday make it possible for some of these people to walk again.

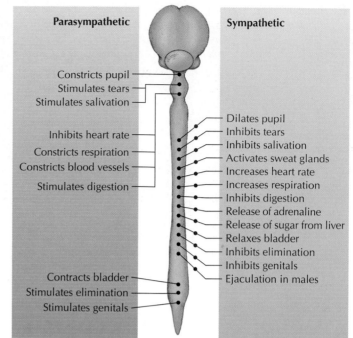

❖ **FIGURE 3.8** *Sympathetic and parasympathetic branches of the autonomic nervous system. Both branches control involuntary actions. The sympathetic system generally activates the body. The parasympathetic system generally quiets it. The sympathetic branch relays through a chain of ganglia (clusters of cell bodies) outside the spinal cord.*

use this "computer" to anticipate when and where the Frisbee will arrive. Jamal's brain communicates with the rest of his body through a large "cable" called the spinal cord. From there, messages flow through the **peripheral nervous system (PNS)**. This intricate network of nerves carries information to and from the CNS.

A serious injury to the brain or spinal cord is usually permanent. However, scientists are starting to make progress in repairing damaged neurons in the CNS. For instance, they were recently able to partially repair cut spinal cords in rats. First, they closed the gap with nerve fibers from outside the spinal cord. Then, they biochemically coaxed the severed spinal nerve fibers to grow through the "tunnels" provided by the implanted fibers. Within 2 months, the rats had regained some use of their hind legs (Cheng, Cao, & Olson, 1996). Imagine what that could mean to a person confined to a wheelchair. Although it is unwise to raise false hopes, solutions to such problems are beginning to emerge (Baisden, 1995). For instance, medical researchers recently began the first human trials in which nerve grafts will be used to repair damaged spinal cords (Levesque & Neuman, 1999). (Also, be sure to read "A Step Beyond" at the end of this chapter.)

THE PERIPHERAL NERVOUS SYSTEM   The peripheral system can be divided into two major parts. The **somatic system** carries messages to and from the sense organs and skeletal muscles. In general, it controls voluntary behavior, such as when Vicki tosses the Frisbee. In contrast, the **autonomic system** serves the internal organs and glands of the body. The word *autonomic* means "self-governing." Activities governed by the autonomic nervous system (ANS) are mostly "vegetative" or automatic, such as heart rate, digestion, or perspiration. Thus, messages carried by the somatic system can make your hand move, but they cannot cause your eyes to dilate. Likewise, messages car-

ried by the ANS can stimulate digestion, but they cannot help you write a letter. If Jamal feels a flash of anger when he misses a catch, a brief burst of activity will spread through his autonomic system.

The autonomic nervous system can be subdivided into the sympathetic and parasympathetic branches. Both branches are related to emotional responses, such as crying, sweating, heart rate, and other involuntary behavior (❖Fig. 3.8). The ANS and the somatic system work together to coordinate the inner world of the body with the world outside. If a snarling dog lunges at you, the somatic system will control your leg muscles so you can run. At the same time, the autonomic system raises your blood pressure, quickens your heart, and so forth.

How do the branches of the autonomic system differ?   The **sympathetic branch** is an "emergency" system. It prepares the body for "fight or flight" during times of danger or high emotion. In essence, it arouses the body for action.

The **parasympathetic branch** quiets the body and returns it to a lower level of arousal. It is most active soon after an emotional event. The parasympathetic branch also helps keep vital functions such as heart rate, breathing, and digestion at moderate levels.

Of course, both branches of the ANS are always active. At any given moment, their combined activity determines if your body is relaxed or aroused.

THE SPINAL CORD   As mentioned earlier, the spinal cord acts like a cable connecting the brain to other parts of the body. If you were to cut through this "cable," you would see columns of **white mat-**

ter in areas where myelin is present. This tissue is made up of axons that leave the spinal cord. Outside the cord, they are bundled together into nerves. Return to ❖Figure 3.6b and you will see that 30 pairs of spinal nerves leave the sides of the spinal cord. Another pair (not shown) leaves the tip. The 31 **spinal nerves** carry sensory and motor messages to and from the spinal cord. In addition, 12 pairs of **cranial nerves** leave the brain directly. Together, these nerves keep your entire body in communication with your brain.

How is the spinal cord related to behavior? The simplest behavior pattern is a **reflex arc**, which occurs when a stimulus provokes an automatic response. Such reflexes occur within the spinal cord, without any help from the brain (❖Fig. 3.9). Imagine that Vicki steps on a thorn. (Yes, they're still playing catch.) Pain is detected in her foot by a **sensory neuron** (a nerve cell that carries messages from the senses toward the CNS). Instantly, the sensory neuron fires off a message to Vicki's spinal cord.

Inside the spinal cord, the sensory neuron synapses with a **connector neuron** (a nerve cell that links two others). The connector neuron activates a **motor neuron** (a cell that carries commands from the CNS to muscles and glands). The muscle fibers are made up of **effector cells** (cells capable of producing a response). The muscle cells contract and cause Vicki's foot to withdraw. Note that no brain activity is re-

quired for a reflex arc to occur. Vicki's body will react automatically to protect itself.

In reality, even a simple reflex usually triggers more complex activity. For example, muscles of Vicki's other leg must contract to support her as she shifts her weight. Even this can be done by the spinal cord, but it involves many more cells and several spinal nerves. Also, the spinal cord normally informs the brain of the actions it has taken. As her foot pulls away from the thorn, Vicki will feel the pain and think, "Ouch, what was that?"

Perhaps you have realized how adaptive it is to have a spinal cord capable of responding on its own. Such automatic responses leave the brains of our Frisbee aces free to deal with more important information—such as the location of trees, lampposts, and attractive onlookers—as they take turns making grandstand catches.

In a few moments, we will probe more deeply into the brain. Before we do, it might be wise to explore some of the research tools biopsychologists use. Uncovering the brain's mysteries has not been easy. Usually a combination of methods is required. Let's consider some of the basics.

BRIDGES

The ANS plays a central role in our emotional lives. In fact, without the ANS a person would feel little emotion.

See Chapter 13, pages 427–430.

RESEARCH METHODS—CHARTING THE BRAIN'S INNER REALMS

Many of the functions of the brain have been identified by **clinical studies**. Such studies examine changes in personality, behavior, or sensory capacity caused by brain diseases or injuries. A related experimental technique is based on **ablation**

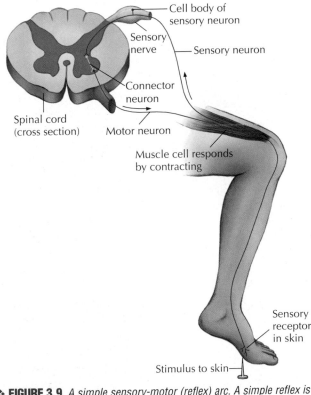

- Cell body of sensory neuron
- Sensory nerve
- Sensory neuron
- Connector neuron
- Spinal cord (cross section)
- Motor neuron
- Muscle cell responds by contracting
- Sensory receptor in skin
- Stimulus to skin

❖ **FIGURE 3.9** *A simple sensory-motor (reflex) arc. A simple reflex is set in motion by a stimulus to the skin (or other part of the body). The nerve impulse travels to the spinal cord and then back out to a muscle, which contracts. Reflexes provide an "automatic" protective device for the body.*

Peripheral nervous system (PNS) *All parts of the nervous system outside the brain and spinal cord.*
Somatic system *The system of nerves linking the spinal cord with the body and sense organs.*
Autonomic system *The system of nerves carrying information to and from the internal organs and glands.*
Sympathetic branch *A branch of the ANS that arouses the body.*
Parasympathetic branch *A branch of the ANS that quiets the body.*
White matter *Areas that appear white because of the presence of myelin.*
Spinal nerves *Major nerves that carry sensory and motor messages in and out of the spinal cord.*
Cranial nerves *Major nerves that leave the brain without passing through the spinal cord.*
Reflex arc *The simplest behavior, in which a stimulus provokes an automatic response.*
Sensory neuron *A nerve cell that carries information from the senses toward the CNS.*
Connector neuron *A nerve cell that serves as a link between two others.*
Motor neuron *A nerve cell that carries motor commands from the CNS to muscles and glands.*
Effector cells *Cells in muscles and glands that are capable of producing some type of response.*
Clinical study *An intensive investigation of the behavior of a single person, especially one suffering from some injury, disease, or disorder.*
Ablation *Surgical removal of tissue.*

(ab-LAY-shun: surgical removal) of parts of the brain (❖Fig. 3.10). When ablation is followed by a change in behavior or sensory capacity, we gain insight into the purpose of the missing "part." An alternate approach is to use electrical stimulation to "turn on" brain structures. For example, the surface of the brain can be activated by touching it with a small, electrified wire called an **electrode**. When this is done during brain surgery, the patient can tell what effect the stimulation had. (The brain has no pain receptors so surgery can be done while a patient is awake. Only local painkillers are used for the scalp and skull.) (Any volunteers?)

Even if a structure lies below the surface of the brain, it can be activated or removed. In **deep lesioning** (LEE-zhun-ing), a thin wire electrode, insulated except at the tip, is lowered into a target area inside the brain (❖Fig. 3.10). An electric current is then used to destroy a small amount of brain tissue. Again, changes in behavior give clues about the function of the lesioned area. Using a weaker current, it is also possible to *activate* target areas, rather than remove them. This is called ESB, for **electrical stimulation of the brain**. ESB can call forth behavior with astonishing power. Instantly, it can bring about aggression, alertness, escape, eating, drinking, sleeping, movement, euphoria, memories, speech, tears, and more. By using ESB, researchers are creating a three-dimensional brain map or "atlas." This atlas shows the sensory, motor, and emotional responses that can be elicited from various parts of the brain. It promises to be a valuable guide for medical treatment, as well as for exploring the brain (Carter, 1998; Yoshida, 1993).

Could ESB be used to control a person against his or her will? It might seem that ESB could be used to control a person in a robot-like way. But the details of emotions and behaviors elicited by ESB are modified by personality and immediate surroundings. SciFi movies to the contrary, it would be impossible for a ruthless dictator to enslave people by "radio controlling" their brains.

If we are interested in large brain structures or groups of neurons, wire electrodes can be used to record their activity.

Observing a single neuron requires a micro-electrode recording. A **micro-electrode** is an extremely thin glass tube filled with a salty, electrically conducting fluid. The tip of a micro-electrode is small enough to detect the electrical activity of a *single* neuron. Watching the action potentials of just one neuron provides a fascinating glimpse into the origins of behavior. (The action potential shown in ❖Fig. 3.2 would have been recorded with a micro-electrode.)

What about the bigger picture? Is it possible to record what the brain is doing as a whole? Yes, it is, with **electroencephalography** (ee-LEK-tro-in-SEF-ah-LOG-ruh-fee). This technique measures the waves of electrical activity produced by the brain. Small disk-shaped metal plates are placed on a person's scalp. Electrical impulses from the brain are detected by these electrodes and sent to an **electroencephalograph (EEG)**. The EEG amplifies these very weak signals (brain waves) and records them on a moving sheet of paper or a computer screen (❖Fig. 3.11). Various brain-wave patterns can identify the presence of tumors, epilepsy, and other diseases. The EEG also reveals changes in brain activity during sleep, daydreaming, hypnosis, and other mental states.

BRIDGES

The EEG has been valuable in studies of sleep and dreaming because brain waves help define various stages of sleep.

Chapter 8, pages 238–240.

New Images of the Living Brain

Many of the brain's riddles have been solved with the methods just described, plus others based on drugs and brain chemistry. Yet, each technique lets us see only a part of the whole picture. What if we could peek inside an intact brain while a person is

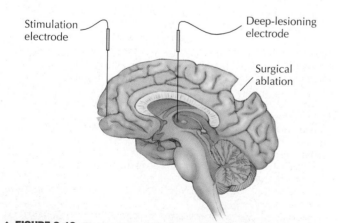

❖ **FIGURE 3.10** *The functions of brain structures are explored by selectively activating or removing them. Brain research is often based on electrical stimulation, but chemical stimulation is also used at times.*

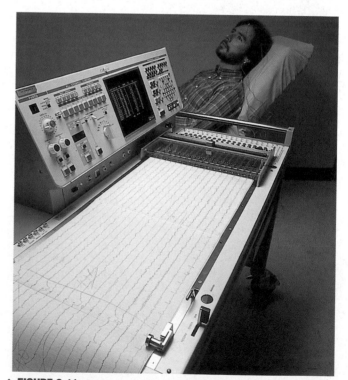

❖ **FIGURE 3.11** *By using an EEG, scientists can record activity in the brain without invading the skull. Brain-wave patterns correspond to various psychological states, such as sleep, waking, and coma.*

thinking, perceiving, and reacting? Computer-enhanced images are now making this age-old dream possible. Let's look through some of these newly opened "windows" into the human biocomputer.

CT SCAN   Computerized scanning equipment has virtually revolutionized the study of brain diseases and injuries. At best, conventional X-rays produce only shadowy images of the brain. **Computed tomographic (CT) scanning** is a specialized type of X-ray that does a much better job of making the brain visible. In a CT scan, X-ray information is collected by a computer and formed into an image of the brain. A CT scan can reveal the effects of strokes, injuries, tumors, and other brain disorders. These, in turn, can be related to a person's behavior.

MRI SCAN   **Magnetic resonance imaging** (MRI) uses a very strong magnetic field, rather than X-rays, to produce an image of the body's interior. During an MRI scan, the body is placed inside a magnetic field. Processing by a computer then creates a three-dimensional representation of the brain or body. Any two-dimensional plane, or slice, of the body can be selected from the MRI data and displayed as an image on a computer screen. This allows scientists to peer into the living brain almost as if it were transparent (❖Fig. 3.12).

A **functional MRI** (fMRI) goes one step further by making brain activity visible. For example, the motor cortex will be highlighted in an fMRI image when a person taps her fingers. Such images are allowing scientists to pinpoint areas in the brain responsible for thoughts, feelings, and actions.

Is it true that most people use only 10 percent of their brain capacity?   This is one of the enduring myths about the brain. Brain scans show that all parts of the brain are active during waking hours. Obviously, some people make better use of their innate brainpower than others do. Nevertheless, there are no great hidden or untapped reserves of mental capacity in a normally functioning brain.

BRIDGES

PET scans suggest that different patterns of brain activity accompany major psychological disorders, such as depression or schizophrenia.

See Chapter 17, pages 580–581.

PET SCAN   Positron emission tomography (PET) images of the brain are perhaps the most remarkable of all. A **PET scan** detects positrons (subatomic particles) emitted by weakly radioactive glucose (sugar) as it is consumed by the brain. Because the brain runs on glucose, a PET scan shows which areas are using more energy. Higher energy use corresponds with higher activity. Thus, by placing positron detectors around the head and sending data to a computer, it is possible to create a moving, color picture of changes in brain activity. As you can see in ❖Figure 3.13, PET scans re-

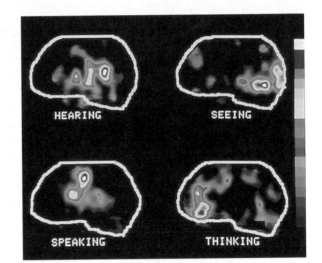

❖ **FIGURE 3.13** *These PET images show scans of the left side of the brain made while a person heard a word, saw a word, repeated a word aloud, and said a word related to the one that was seen (Petersen et al., 1988).*

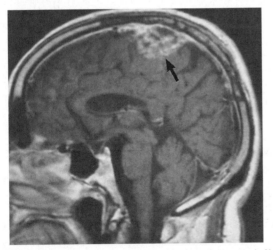

❖ **FIGURE 3.12** *An MRI scan reveals a brain tumor (see arrow). Notice how it is possible to display a precise "slice" from the middle of the three-dimensional MRI data.*

Electrode *Any device (such as a wire, needle, or metal plate) used to electrically stimulate nerve tissue or to record its activity.*
Deep lesioning *Removal of tissue within the brain by use of an electrode.*
Electrical stimulation of the brain *Direct electrical stimulation and activation of brain tissue.*
Micro-electrode *An electrode small enough to record the activity of a single neuron.*
Electroencephalography *Technique to measure waves of electrical activity produced by the brain.*
Electroencephalograph (EEG) *A device that detects, amplifies, and records electrical activity in the brain.*
Computed tomographic (CT) scanning *A computer-enhanced X-ray image of the brain or body.*
Magnetic resonance imaging *A computer-enhanced three-dimensional representation of the brain or body, based on the body's response to a magnetic field.*
Functional MRI *Magnetic resonance imaging that records brain activity.*
PET scan *Positron emission tomography; a computer-generated image of brain activity, based on glucose consumption in the brain.*

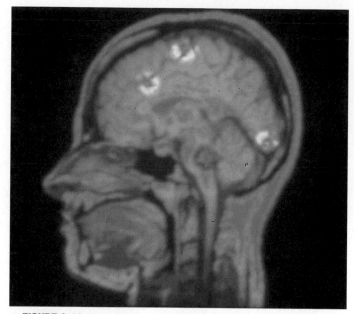

❖ **FIGURE 3.14** *The bright spots you see here were created by a PET scan. They are similar to the spots in Figure 3.13. However, here they have been placed over an MRI scan so that the brain's anatomy is visible. The three bright spots are areas in the left brain related to language. The spot on the right is active during reading. The top-middle area is connected with speech. The area to the left, in the frontal lobe is linked with thinking about a word's meaning (Montgomery, 1989).*

veal that very specific brain areas are active when you are reading a word, hearing a word, saying a word, or thinking about the meaning of a word.

Today, still more exotic brain scanning methods are being developed. For example, a new "diffusion weighted" MRI technique makes it possible to record changes in the connections between parts of the cortex. This should be valuable for studying learning, memory, and the progress of brain diseases such as schizophrenia (Rye, 1999). It is just a matter of time until even brighter beacons are flashed into the shadowy inner world of thought (❖Fig. 3.14).

K N O W L E D G E   B U I L D E R

NEURONS, THE NERVOUS SYSTEM, AND BRAIN RESEARCH

RELATE

To cope with all of the technical terms in this chapter, it might help to think of neurons as strange little creatures. How do they act? What excites them? How do they communicate? To remember the functions of major branches of the nervous system, think about what you *couldn't* do if each part were missing.

You suspect that a certain part of the brain is related to memory. How could you use clinical studies, ablation, deep lesioning, and ESB to study the structure? You are interested in finding out how single neurons in the optic nerve respond when the eye is exposed to light. What technique will you use? You want to know which areas of the brain's surface are most active when a person sees a face. What methods will you use?

LEARNING CHECK

1. The _____ and _____ are receiving areas where information from other neurons is accepted.

2. Nerve impulses are carried down the _____ to the _____ _____.

3. The point of interchange between two neurons is called a myelin. T or F?

4. The _____ potential becomes an _____ potential when a neuron passes the threshold for firing.

5. Neuropeptides are transmitter substances that help regulate the activity of neurons. T or F?

6. The somatic and autonomic systems are part of the _____ nervous system.

7. Sodium and potassium ions flow through ion channels in the synapse to trigger a nerve impulse in the receiving neuron. T or F?

8. The simplest behavior sequence is a _____ _____.

9. The parasympathetic nervous system is most active during times of high emotion. T or F?

10. Which of the following research techniques has the most in common with clinical studies of the effects of brain injuries? *a.* EEG recording *b.* deep lesioning *c.* micro-electrode recording *d.* PET scan

CRITICAL THINKING

11. What effect would you expect a drug to have if it blocked passage of neurotransmitters across the synapse?

12. Deep lesioning is used to ablate an area in the hypothalamus of a rat. After the operation, the rat seems to lose interest in food and eating. Why would it be a mistake to conclude that the ablated area is a "hunger center"?

Answers:

1. dendrites, soma 2. axon, axon terminals 3. F 4. resting, action 5. T 6. peripheral 7. F 8. reflex arc 9. F 10. *b* 11. Such a drug could have wide-ranging effects. If the drug blocked excitatory synapses, it would depress brain activity. If it blocked inhibitory messages, it would act as a powerful stimulant. 12. Because other factors might explain the apparent loss of appetite. For example, the taste or smell of food might be affected, or the rat might simply have difficulty swallowing. It is also possible that hunger originates elsewhere in the brain and the ablated area merely relays messages that cause the rat to eat.

THE CEREBRAL CORTEX—MY, WHAT A BIG BRAIN YOU HAVE!

In many ways we are pretty unimpressive creatures. Animals surpass humans in almost every category of strength, speed, and sensory sensitivity. The one area in which we excel is intelligence.

Do humans have the largest brains? Surprisingly, no. Elephant brains weigh 13 pounds, and whale brains, 19 pounds.

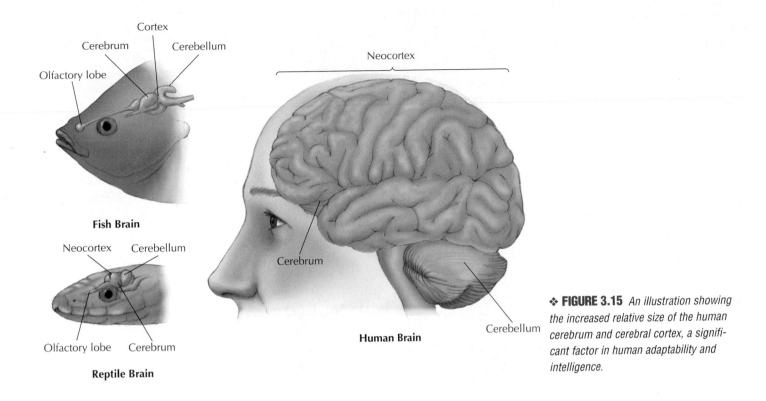

Fish Brain

Cortex
Cerebrum
Cerebellum
Olfactory lobe

Neocortex

Neocortex   Cerebellum

Olfactory lobe   Cerebrum

Reptile Brain

Cerebrum

Cerebellum

Human Brain

❖ **FIGURE 3.15** *An illustration showing the increased relative size of the human cerebrum and cerebral cortex, a significant factor in human adaptability and intelligence.*

At 3 pounds, the human brain seems puny—until we compare brain weight to body weight. We then find that an elephant's brain is 1/1,000 of its weight; the ratio for sperm whales is 1 to 10,000. The ratio for humans is 1 to 60. If someone tells you that you have a "whale of a brain," be sure to find out if they mean size or ratio!

So, relatively speaking, humans have highly developed brains. More important, as we move from lower to higher animals, an ever-increasing proportion of the brain is devoted to the **cerebrum** (SER-eh-brum or ser-REE-brum: two large hemispheres that cover the upper part of the brain) (see ❖Fig. 3.15). The cerebrum is the highest brain area in humans. Its outer layer, or "bark," is known as the **cerebral cortex** (seh-REE-brel or ser-EH-brel). Although the cortex is only 3 millimeters thick (one tenth of an inch), it contains 70 percent of the neurons in the central nervous system. Without the cortex, humans wouldn't be much brighter than lizards.

CORTICALIZATION   The cerebral cortex looks a little like a giant, wrinkled walnut. It covers most of the brain with a mantle of **gray matter** (spongy tissue made up mostly of cell bodies). The cortex in lower animals is small and smooth. In humans, it is highly convoluted and the largest brain structure. The fact that humans are more intelligent than other animals is related to this **corticalization** (KORE-tih-kal-ih-ZAY-shun), or increase in the size and wrinkling of the cortex.

Does having a larger brain make a person smarter? A small positive correlation exists between intelligence and brain size (Flashman et al., 1997; Rushton, 1995; Wickett, Vernon, & Lee, 1995). However, it is a mistake to think that size *alone* determines human intelligence. A person with an average size brain could be extremely intelligent, and someone with a very large brain could have average intelligence. Smart behavior is based on what you know and how efficiently you use your mental capacities, not just the size of your "biocomputer." See "The Brain at Work" for more information.

Cerebral Hemispheres

The cortex is composed of two sides, or **cerebral hemispheres** (half-globes). The two hemispheres are connected by a thick band of fibers called the **corpus callosum** (KORE-pus kah-LOH-sum) (❖Fig. 3.17). The left side of the brain mainly controls the right side of the body. Likewise, the right brain mainly controls left body areas. When my friend Marge had a stroke, her right hemisphere suffered damage. (A stroke occurs when an artery carrying blood to the brain becomes blocked, causing some brain tissue to die.) In Marge's case, the stroke caused some paralysis and loss of sensation on the left side of her

Cerebrum *The two large hemispheres that cover the upper part of the brain.*
Cerebral cortex *The outer layer of the cerebrum.*
Gray matter *Areas in the nervous system made up mostly of nerve cell bodies.*
Corticalization *An increase in the relative size of the cerebral cortex.*
Cerebral hemispheres *The right and left halves of the cerebrum.*
Corpus callosum *The bundle of fibers connecting the cerebral hemispheres.*

THE BRAIN AT WORK

According to folklore, a person with a large head and a high forehead is likely to be intelligent. But brain efficiency has as much to do with intelligence as brain size does (Gazzaniga, 1995).

Psychologist Richard J. Haier and his colleagues found that the brains of people who perform well on mental tests consume less energy than those of poor performers (Haier et al., 1988). Haier measured brain activity with a PET scan. Recall that a PET scan records the amount of glucose (sugar) used by brain cells. The harder neurons work, the more sugar they use. By using harmless, radioactively labeled glu-

cose, it is possible to record an image of how hard the brain is working (❖Fig. 3.16).

What did PET scans reveal when subjects took a difficult reasoning test? Surprisingly, the brains of those who scored lowest on the test used the most glucose. Although we might assume that smart brains are hardworking brains, the reverse appears to be true. Brighter subjects actually used less energy than poor performers did. Haier believes this shows that intelligence is related to brain efficiency: Less efficient brains work harder and still accomplish less. We've all had days like that!

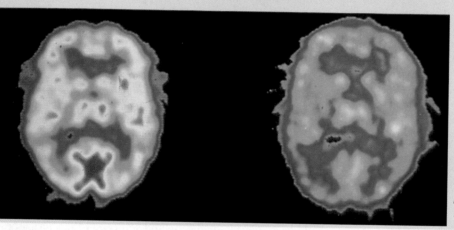

❖ **FIGURE 3.16** *In the images you see here, red, orange, and yellow indicate high consumption of glucose; green, blue, and pink show areas of low glucose use. The PET scan of the brain on the left shows that a man who solved 11 of 36 reasoning problems burned more glucose than the man on the right, who solved 33.*

Corpus callosum Cerebral cortex

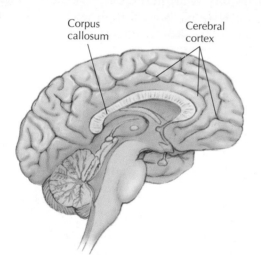

❖ **FIGURE 3.17** *The corpus callosum is the major "cable system" through which the right and left cerebral hemispheres communicate. A recent study found that the corpus callosum is larger in classically trained musicians than it is in nonmusicians. When a person plays a violin or piano, the two hemispheres must communicate rapidly as they coordinate the movements of both hands. Presumably, the size of the corpus callosum can be altered by early experience, such as musical training.*

body. Damage to the right hemisphere may also cause a curious problem called **spatial neglect**. Affected patients pay no attention to the left side of visual space. (See ❖Figure 3.18.) Often, the patient will not eat food on the left side of a plate.

Some even refuse to acknowledge a paralyzed left arm as their own (Springer & Deutsch, 1998). If you point to the "alien" arm, the patient is likely to say, "Oh, that's not my arm. It must belong to someone else."

Hemispheric Specialization

We turn now to some remarkable findings. In 1981, biopsychologist Roger Sperry (1914–1994) won a Nobel prize for his work on the special abilities of the cerebral hemispheres. Sperry and other scientists have shown that the right and left brain perform differently on tests of language, perception, music, and other capabilities.

How is it possible to test only one side of the brain? One way is to work with people who've had a **"split-brain" operation**. This is a rare type of surgery in which the corpus callosum is cut to control severe epilepsy. The result is essentially a person with two brains in one body. After the surgery, it is a simple matter to route information to one hemisphere or the other (❖Fig. 3.19).

"SPLIT BRAINS" Separating the right and left brain doubles consciousness. As Sperry said, "In other words, each hemisphere seems to have its own separate and private sensations; its own perceptions; its own concepts; and its own impulses to act."

How does a split-brain person function after the operation? Having two "brains" in one body can create quite a dilemma. When one split-brain patient dressed himself, he sometimes

Model   Patient's copy

❖ **FIGURE 3.18** *Spatial neglect. A patient with right-hemisphere damage was asked to copy three model drawings. Notice the obvious neglect of the left side in his drawings. Similar instances of neglect occur in many patients with right-hemisphere damage. (From* Left Brain, Right Brain, *Revised Edition by S. P. Springer and G. Deutsch, copyright 1981, 1985, 1989, 1993, 1998. Reprinted with the permission of W. H. Freeman and Company.)*

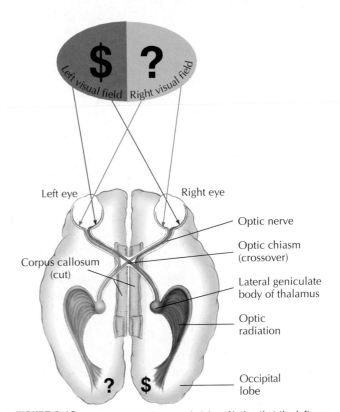

❖ **FIGURE 3.19** *Basic nerve pathways of vision. Notice that the left portion of each eye connects only to the left half of the brain; likewise, the right portion of each eye connects to the right brain. When the corpus callosum is cut, a "split brain" results. Then visual information can be directed to one hemisphere or the other by flashing it in the right or left visual field as the person stares straight ahead.*

pulled his pants down with one hand and up with the other. Once, the patient grabbed his wife with his left hand and shook her violently. Gallantly, his right hand came to her aid and grabbed the belligerent left hand (Gazzaniga, 1970). Although such conflicts do occur, it is far more typical for split-brain patients to act completely normal. The reason is that both halves of the brain have about the same experience at the same time. Also, if a conflict arises, one hemisphere usually overrides the other.

Split-brain effects are easiest to see in specialized testing. For example, we could flash a dollar sign to the right brain and a question mark to the left brain of a patient named Tom. (❖Figure 3.19 shows how this is possible.) Next, Tom is asked to draw what he saw, using his left hand, out of sight. Tom's left hand draws a dollar sign. If Tom is then asked to point with his right hand to a picture of what his hidden left hand drew, he will point to a question mark (Sperry, 1968). In short, for the split-brain person, one hemisphere may not know what is happening in the other. This has to be the ultimate case of the "right hand not knowing what the left hand is doing"! ❖Figure 3.20 provides another example of split-brain testing.

RIGHT BRAIN, LEFT BRAIN   *Earlier it was stated that the hemispheres differ in abilities; in what ways are they different?*   The

brain divides its work in interesting ways. Roughly 95 percent of all adults use the left brain for language (speaking, writing, and understanding). In addition, the left hemisphere is superior at math, judging time and rhythm, and coordinating the order of complex movements, such as those needed for speech.

In contrast, the right hemisphere can produce only the simplest language and numbers. Working with the right brain is like talking to a child who can say only a dozen words or so. To answer questions, the right hemisphere must use nonverbal responses, such as pointing at objects (see ❖Fig. 3.20).

Although it is poor at producing language, the right brain has it own talents. The right brain is especially good at perceptual skills, such as recognizing patterns, faces, and melodies, putting together a puzzle, or drawing a picture. It is also involved in detecting and expressing emotion (Borod et al., 1998; Christianson et al., 1995).

Spatial neglect   *Ignoring one side of vision or of the body after damage to a brain hemisphere.*
"Split-brain" operation   *Cutting the corpus callosum.*

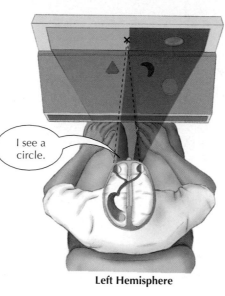
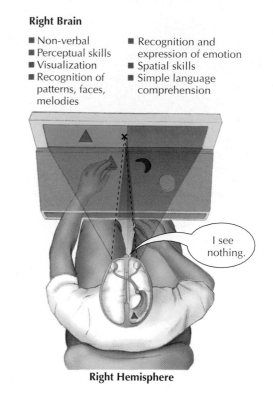

Left Brain

- Language
- Speech
- Writing
- Calculation
- Time sense
- Rhythm
- Ordering of complex movements

Right Brain

- Non-verbal
- Perceptual skills
- Visualization
- Recognition of patterns, faces, melodies
- Recognition and expression of emotion
- Spatial skills
- Simple language comprehension

I see a circle.

I see nothing.

Left Hemisphere

Right Hemisphere

❖ **FIGURE 3.20** *If a circle is flashed to the left brain and a split-brain patient is asked to say what she or he saw, the circle is easily named. The person can also pick out the circle by touching shapes with the right hand, out of sight under a tabletop (shown semitransparent in the drawing). However, the left hand will be unable to identify the shape. If a triangle is flashed to the right brain, the person cannot say what was seen (speech is controlled by the left hemisphere). The person will also be unable to identify the correct shape by touch with the right hand. Now, however, the left hand will have no difficulty picking out the hidden triangle. Separate testing of each hemisphere reveals distinct specializations, as listed above. (Figure adapted from an illustration by Edward Kasper in McKean, 1985.)*

Even though the right hemisphere is nearly "speechless," it is superior at some aspects of understanding language. If the right brain is damaged, people lose their ability to understand jokes, irony, sarcasm, implications, and other nuances of language. Basically, the right hemisphere helps us see the overall context in which something is said (Beeman & Chiarello, 1998). For instance, let's say you tell a patient with right-brain damage the following joke:

"Dad," said Jason, "I'm late for soccer practice. Would you do my math homework for me?"
The boy's father answered, "Son, it just wouldn't be right."
"That's okay," replied Jason. "You could at least try, right?"

When asked what this story means, the patient might say, "The father doesn't want to do it, but the son is persistent." Without the right brain's ability to perceive context, the patient doesn't get the joke about the father's math abilities. The left hemisphere understands the words, one at a time, but it can't grasp the bigger picture.

ONE BRAIN, TWO STYLES In general, the left hemisphere is mainly involved with *analysis* (breaking information into parts). It also processes information *sequentially* (in order, one item after the next). The right hemisphere appears to process information *simultaneously* and *holistically* (all at once) (Springer & Deutsch, 1998).

To summarize further, you could say that the right hemisphere is better at assembling pieces of the world into a coherent picture; it sees overall patterns and general connections. The left brain focuses on small details. (See ❖Fig. 3.21.) The right brain sees the wide-angle view; the left zooms in on specifics. The focus of the left brain is local; the right is global (Heinze et al., 1998; Hellige, 1993; Huebner, 1998).

Do people normally do puzzles or draw pictures with just the right hemisphere? Do they do other things with only the left? Numerous books have been written about how to use the right brain to manage, teach, draw, ride horses, learn, cook, and even make love (Carter, 1998). But such books drastically oversimplify right- and left-brain differences. People normally use both sides of the brain at all times. It's true that some tasks may make *more* use of one hemisphere or the other. But in most "real-world" activities, the hemispheres share the work. Each does the parts it does best and shares information with the other side. Popular books and courses that claim to teach "right-brain thinking" ignore the fact that everyone already uses the right brain for thinking (Hellige, 1990; Ornstein, 1997).

It is possible, of course, to prefer right- or left-brain styles of thought. For example, students who prefer right-brain thinking tend to major in subjects such as music, journalism, art, oral communication, and architecture. A left-brain preference is associated with majors in subjects such as management, computer science, mathematics, nursing, criminal justice, and education (Monfort et al., 1990). Nevertheless, to do anything well requires the talents and processing abilities of both hemispheres. A smart brain is one that grasps both the details and the overall picture at the same time (Ornstein, 1997).

Lobes of the Cerebral Cortex

In addition to the hemispheres, the cerebral cortex can be divided into several **lobes** (areas bordered by major fissures or defined by their functions) (see ❖Fig. 3.22).

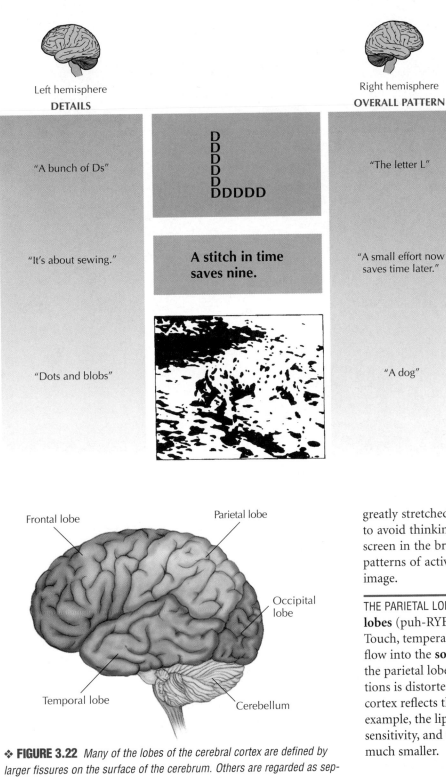

Left hemisphere
DETAILS

"A bunch of Ds"

"It's about sewing."

"Dots and blobs"

DDDD
DDDDD

A stitch in time saves nine.

Right hemisphere
OVERALL PATTERN

"The letter L"

"A small effort now saves time later."

"A dog"

❖ **FIGURE 3.21** *The left and right brain have different information-processing styles. The right brain gets the big pattern; the left focuses on small details. (Photograph by R. C. James.)*

greatly stretched and distorted (Carlson, 1998). It is important to avoid thinking of the visual area as being like a little TV screen in the brain. Visual information creates complex patterns of activity in nerve cells; it does *not* make a TV-like image.

THE PARIETAL LOBES   Bodily sensations register in the **parietal lobes** (puh-RYE-ih-tal), located just above the occipital lobes. Touch, temperature, pressure, and other somatic sensations flow into the **somatosensory area** (SO-mat-oh-SEN-so-ree) on the parietal lobes. Again, we find that the map of bodily sensations is distorted. The drawing in ❖Figure 3.23 shows that the cortex reflects the *sensitivity* of body areas, not their size. For example, the lips are large in the drawing because of their great sensitivity, and the back and trunk, which are less sensitive, are much smaller.

Frontal lobe

Parietal lobe

Occipital lobe

Temporal lobe

Cerebellum

❖ **FIGURE 3.22** *Many of the lobes of the cerebral cortex are defined by larger fissures on the surface of the cerebrum. Others are regarded as separate areas because their functions are quite different.*

THE OCCIPITAL LOBES   At the back of the brain, we find the **occipital lobes** (awk-SIP-ih-tal), the primary visual area of the cortex. Patients with **tumors** (cell growths that interfere with brain activity) in the occipital lobes experience blind spots in their vision.

Do the visual areas of the cortex correspond directly to what is seen?   Images are mapped onto the cortex, but the map is

Lobes of the cerebral cortex *Areas on the cortex bordered by major fissures or defined by their functions.*
Occipital lobes *Portion of the cerebral cortex where vision registers in the brain.*
Tumor *A mass of abnormal cells.*
Parietal lobes *Area of the brain where bodily sensations register.*
Somatosensory area *A receiving area for bodily sensations.*

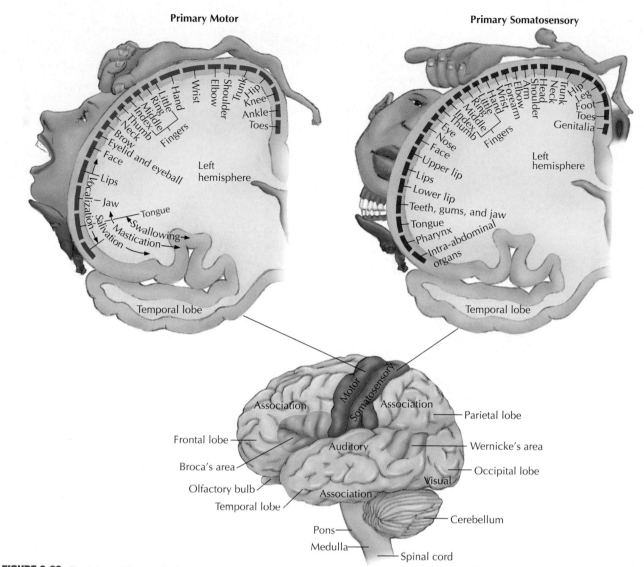

Primary Motor

Primary Somatosensory

❖ **FIGURE 3.23** *The lobes of the cerebral cortex and the primary sensory, motor, and association areas on each. The top diagrams show (in cross section) the relative amounts of cortex "assigned" to the sensory and motor control of various parts of the body. (Each cross section, or "slice," of the cortex has been turned 90 degrees so that you see it as it would appear from the back of the brain.)*

THE TEMPORAL LOBES   The temporal lobes are located on each side of the brain. Auditory information projects directly to the **temporal lobes**, making them the main site where hearing registers. If we were to stimulate the auditory area of a temporal lobe, our subject would "hear" a series of sound sensations.

For most people, the left temporal lobe also contains a language "center." (For 5 percent of all people, the area is on the right temporal lobe.) Damage to the temporal lobe can severely limit ability to use language. (More on this later.)

THE FRONTAL LOBES   The **frontal lobes** are associated with higher mental abilities. This area is also responsible for the control of movement. Specifically, an arch of tissue over the top of the brain, called the **motor cortex**, directs the body's muscles. If this area is stimulated with an electrical current, various parts of the body twitch or move. Like the somatosensory area, the motor cortex corresponds to the importance of

bodily areas, not to their size. The hands, for example, get more area than the feet (see ❖Fig. 3.23). If you've ever wondered why your hands are more dexterous than your feet, it's partly because more motor cortex is devoted to the hands.

The frontal lobes are also related to more complex behaviors. If the frontal lobes are damaged, a patient's personality and emotional life may change dramatically. (Remember Phineas Gage, the railroad foreman described in Chapter 2?) Reasoning or planning may also be affected. Patients with frontal lobe damage often get "stuck" on mental tasks and repeat the same wrong answers over and over (Goel & Grafman, 1995). Sadly, drug abuse is one way in which this important area of the brain may be damaged (Liu et al., 1998).

ASSOCIATION AREAS   In the human brain, primary sensory and motor areas make up only a small part of the cerebral cortex. All the surrounding areas are called the **association cortex**. The

HIS AND HER BRAINS?

A patient has had a stroke. It looks like Broca's area was damaged. As expected, the patient's speech is impaired. Will the patient recover any language skills? It may depend on his or her sex.

When Broca's area is damaged, women typically regain more of their lost abilities than men do. Why should this be so? Let's look at some male and female brains for an answer.

Researchers used brain imaging to observe brain activity while people did language tasks. As they worked, both men and women showed increased activity in Broca's area, on the left side of the brain. This is exactly what we would expect. However, to the scientists' surprise, both the left *and the right* brain were activated in more than half the women tested. Apparently, male and female brains tend to differ in ways that can affect speech and language (Jaeger et al., 1998; Shaywitz & Gore, 1995; Skrandies, Reik, & Kunze, 1999). (See ❖Fig. 3.24.)

Using both sides of the brain for language may be a big advantage. When Broca's area is damaged, some women can use the right side of their brains to compensate for the loss (Hochstenbach et al., 1998). Men with similar damage have little chance of improving. Thus, when a man says, "I have half a mind to tell you what I think," he may be stating a curious truth.

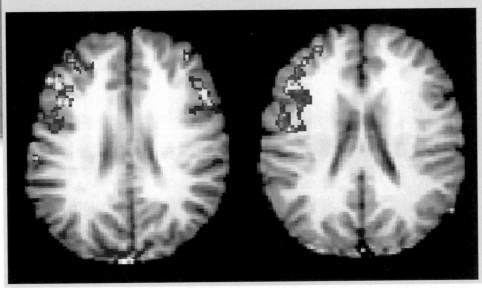

❖ **FIGURE 3.24** *Language tasks activate the left side of the brain in men and both sides in many women.*

---

higher an animal is on the evolutionary scale, the more association cortex it has.

The association cortex combines and processes information from the senses. If you see a rose, the association areas help you recognize it and name it. The association cortex also contributes to higher mental abilities. For example, a person with damage to association areas on the left hemisphere may suffer an **aphasia** (ah-FAZE-yah: impaired ability to use language).

One type of aphasia is related to **Broca's area** (BRO-cahs), a "speech center" on the left frontal lobe (Leonard, 1997). Damage to Broca's area causes great difficulty in speaking or writing. Typically, a patient's grammar and pronunciation are poor, and speech is slow and labored. For example, the person may say "bife" for bike, "seep" for sleep, or "zokaid" for zodiac. Generally, the person knows what she or he wants to say but can't seem to utter the words (Geschwind, 1979).

If Broca's area is damaged, the amount of language loss a person suffers may relate to his or her sex. "His and Her Brains?" explains why.

A second language site, called **Wernicke's area** (VER-nick-ees; see ❖Fig. 3.23), lies on the left temporal lobe. If it is damaged, the person has problems with the *meaning* of words, not their pronunciation. Someone with Broca's aphasia might say "tssair" when shown a picture of a chair. In contrast, a Wernicke's patient might say "stool" (Leonard, 1997).

One of the most fascinating results of brain injury is **agnosia** (ag-KNOW-zyah: an inability to identify seen objects). This condition is sometimes referred to as "mindblindness."

Temporal lobes *Areas that include the sites where hearing registers in the brain.*
Frontal lobes *A brain area associated with movement, the sense of smell, and higher mental functions.*
Motor cortex *A brain area associated with control of movement.*
Association cortex *All areas of the cerebral cortex that are not primarily sensory or motor in function.*
Aphasia *A speech disturbance resulting from brain damage.*
Broca's area *A language area related to grammar and pronunciation.*
Wernicke's area *An area related to language comprehension.*
Agnosia *An inability to grasp the meaning of stimuli, such as words, objects, or pictures.*

Here's an example: If we show an agnosia patient named Alice a candle, she will describe it as "a long narrow object that tapers at the top." Alice can even draw the candle accurately, but she cannot name it. However, if she is allowed to *feel* the candle, she will name it immediately (Warrington & McCarthy, 1995). In short, Alice can still see color, size, and shape. She just can't perceive the meanings of objects (De Haan et al., 1995).

Are agnosias limited to objects? No. A fascinating form of mindblindness is **facial agnosia**, an inability to perceive familiar faces. One patient with facial agnosia couldn't recognize her husband or mother when they visited her in the hospital, and she was unable to identify pictures of her children. However, as soon as a visitor spoke, she knew them immediately from their voices (Benton, 1980).

Areas devoted to recognizing faces lie on the underside of the occipital lobes. These areas appear to have no other function. Why would part of the brain be set aside solely for identifying faces? From an evolutionary standpoint, it is not really so surprising. After all, we are social animals, for whom facial recognition is very important. This specialization is just one example of what a marvelous organ of consciousness we possess.

In summary, the bulk of our daily experience and all of our understanding of the world can be traced to the sensory, motor, and association areas of the cortex. The human brain is among the most advanced and sophisticated of the brain-bearing species on earth. This, of course, is no guarantee that this marvelous "biocomputer" will be put to full use. Still, we must stand in awe of the potential it represents.

KNOWLEDGE BUILDER
CEREBRAL CORTEX AND LOBES OF THE BRAIN

RELATE

Learning the functions of the brain lobes is like learning areas on a map. Try drawing a map of the cortex. Can you label all of the different "countries" (lobes)? Can you name their functions? Where is the motor cortex? The somatosensory area? Broca's area? Keep redrawing the map until it becomes more detailed and you can do it easily.

LEARNING CHECK

See if you can match the following.

1. _____ Corpus callosum	A.	Visual area
2. _____ Occipital lobes	B.	Language, speech, writing
3. _____ Parietal lobes	C.	Motor cortex and abstract thinking
4. _____ Temporal lobes	D.	Spatial skills, visualization, pattern recognition
5. _____ Frontal lobes		
6. _____ Association cortex	E.	Speech disturbances
7. _____ Aphasias	F.	Causes sleep
8. _____ Corticalization	G.	Increased ratio of cortex in brain
9. _____ Left hemisphere	H.	Bodily sensations
10. _____ Right hemisphere	I.	Treatment for severe epilepsy
11. _____ "Split brain"	J.	Inability to identify seen objects
12. _____ Agnosia	K.	Fibers connecting the cerebral hemispheres
	L.	Cortex that is not sensory or motor in function
	M.	Hearing

CRITICAL THINKING

13. If you wanted to increase the surface area of the cerebrum so that more cerebral cortex would fit within the skull, how would you do it?

14. What would be some of the possible advantages and disadvantages to having a "split brain"?

15. If your brain were removed, replaced by another, and moved to a new body, which would you consider to be yourself, your old body with the new brain, or your new body with the old brain?

Answers:

1. K 2. A 3. H 4. M 5. C 6. L 7. E 8. G 9. B 10. D 11. I 12. J 13. One solution would be to gather the surface of the cortex into folds, just as you might if you were trying to fit a large piece of cloth into a small box. This, in fact, is probably why the cortex is more convoluted (folded or wrinkled) in higher animals. 14. If information were properly routed to each brain hemisphere, it would be possible to have both hands working simultaneously on conflicting tasks. However, such possible benefits would apply only under highly controlled conditions. 15. Although there is no "correct" answer to this question, your personality, knowledge, personal memories, and self-concept all derive from brain activity—which makes a strong case for your old brain in a new body being more nearly the "real you."

THE SUBCORTEX—AT THE CORE OF THE (BRAIN) MATTER

A person can lose large portions of the cerebrum and still survive. Not so with the brain areas below the cortex. Most are so indispensable that any damage at all could endanger a person's life.

Why are the lower brain areas so important? The **subcortex** lies immediately below the cerebral hemispheres. This area can be divided into the brainstem (or hindbrain), the midbrain, and the forebrain. (The forebrain also includes the cerebral cortex, which we have already discussed because of its size and importance.) For our purposes, the midbrain can be viewed as a link between the forebrain and the brainstem. Therefore, let us focus on the rest of the subcortex (❖Fig. 3.25).

The Hindbrain

As the spinal cord joins the brain, it widens into the brainstem. The **brainstem** consists mainly of the medulla (meh-DUL-ah) and the cerebellum (ser-ah-BEL-uhm). The **medulla** contains centers important for the reflex control of vital life functions, including heart rate, breathing, swallowing, and the like. Various drugs, diseases, or injuries can disrupt the medulla and end or endanger life. That's why a karate chop to the back of the neck can be extremely dangerous.

The **pons**, which looks like a small bump on the brainstem, acts as a bridge between the medulla and other brain areas. (The word *pons* means bridge.) In addition to connecting with many other locations, including the cerebellum, the pons influences sleep and arousal.

The cerebellum, which looks like a miniature cerebral cortex, lies at the base of the brain. The **cerebellum** primarily reg-

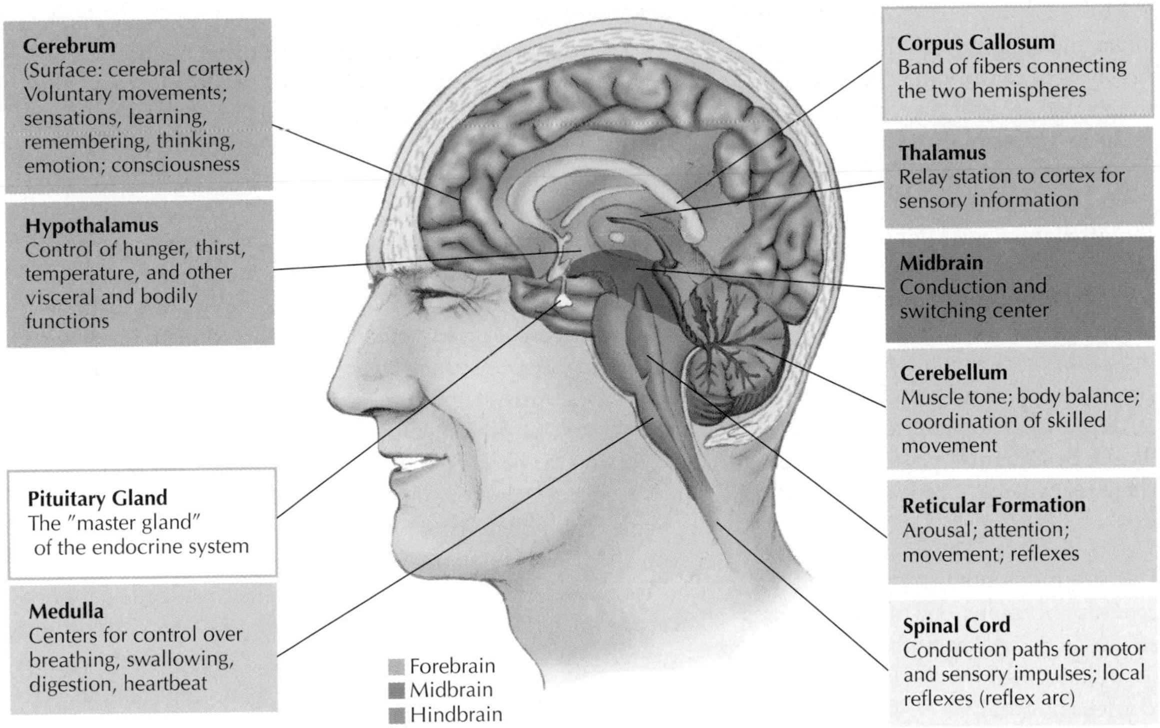

Cerebrum
(Surface: cerebral cortex)
Voluntary movements;
sensations, learning,
remembering, thinking,
emotion; consciousness

Hypothalamus
Control of hunger, thirst,
temperature, and other
visceral and bodily
functions

Pituitary Gland
The "master gland"
of the endocrine system

Medulla
Centers for control over
breathing, swallowing,
digestion, heartbeat

Corpus Callosum
Band of fibers connecting
the two hemispheres

Thalamus
Relay station to cortex for
sensory information

Midbrain
Conduction and
switching center

Cerebellum
Muscle tone; body balance;
coordination of skilled
movement

Reticular Formation
Arousal; attention;
movement; reflexes

Spinal Cord
Conduction paths for motor
and sensory impulses; local
reflexes (reflex arc)

Forebrain
Midbrain
Hindbrain

❖ **FIGURE 3.25** *This simplified drawing shows the main structures of the human brain and describes some of their most important features. (You can use the color code in the foreground to identify which areas are part of the forebrain, midbrain, and hindbrain.)*

ulates posture, muscle tone, and muscular coordination. The cerebellum also stores memories related to skills and habits (Thompson, 1991).

What happens if the cerebellum is injured? Without the cerebellum, tasks like walking, running, or playing catch would be impossible. The first symptoms of a crippling disease called *spinocerebellar degeneration* are tremor, dizziness, and muscular weakness. Eventually, victims have difficulty merely standing, walking, or feeding themselves.

RETICULAR FORMATION A network of fibers and cell bodies called the **reticular (reh-TICK-you-ler) formation** (RF) lies inside the medulla and brainstem. As nerve impulses flow into the brain, the RF gives priority to some messages, while turning others aside. By doing so, the RF influences *attention*. The reticular formation also modifies outgoing commands to the body. In this way, the RF affects muscle tone, posture, and movements of the eyes, face, head, body, and limbs. At the same time, the RF controls reflexes involved in breathing, sneezing, coughing, and vomiting (Stalheim-Smith & Fitch, 1993).

Keeping us vigilant, alert, and awake is another important task of the reticular formation. Incoming messages from the sense organs branch into a part of the RF called the **reticular activating system (RAS)**. The RAS bombards the cortex with stimulation, keeping it active and alert. For instance, let's say a sleepy driver rounds a bend and sees a deer standing in the road. The driver snaps to attention and applies the brakes. She can thank her RAS for arousing the rest of her brain and avert-

BRIDGES

The cerebellum stores "know how" or "skill memories." "Know what" memories are stored elsewhere in the brain.

See Chapter 10, pages 331–332.

ing an accident. If you're getting sleepy while reading this chapter, try pinching your ear—a little pain will cause the RAS to momentarily arouse your cortex.

The Forebrain

Like gemstones of nerve tissue, two of the most important parts of your body lie buried deep within the brain. The thalamus (THAL-uh-mus) and an area just below it called the hypothalamus (HI-po-THAL-uh-mus) are key parts of the forebrain (see ❖Fig. 3.25).

How could these be any more important than other areas already described? The **thalamus** acts as a final "switching sta-

Facial agnosia *An inability to recognize familiar faces.*
Subcortex *All brain structures below the cerebral cortex.*
Brainstem *The lowest portions of the brain, including the cerebellum, medulla, pons, and reticular formation.*
Medulla *The structure that connects the brain with the spinal cord and controls vital life functions.*
Pons *An area on the brainstem that acts as a bridge between the medulla and other structures.*
Cerebellum *A brain structure that controls posture and coordination.*
Reticular formation *A network within the medulla and brainstem; associated with attention, alertness, and some reflexes.*
Reticular activating system (RAS) *A part of the reticular formation that activates the cerebral cortex.*
Thalamus *A brain structure that relays sensory information to the cerebral cortex.*

tion" for sensory messages on their way to the cortex. Vision, hearing, taste, and touch pass through this small, football-shaped structure. Some analysis of sensory messages occurs there as well. Injury to even small areas of the thalamus can cause deafness, blindness, or loss of any other sense, except smell.

The human hypothalamus is about the size of a small grape. Small as it may be, the **hypothalamus** is a kind of master control center for emotion and many basic motives (Carlson, 1998). The hypothalamus affects behaviors as diverse as sex, rage, temperature control, hormone release, eating and drinking, sleep, waking, and emotion. The hypothalamus is basically a crossroads area that connects with many parts of the cortex and subcortex. As such, it acts as a "final path" for many kinds of behavior leaving the brain. You might think of the hypothalamus as the last place where many behaviors are organized or "decided on."

THE LIMBIC SYSTEM   As a group, the hypothalamus, parts of the thalamus, the amygdala, the hippocampus, and other structures make up the limbic system (❖Fig. 3.26). The **limbic system** has a major role in producing emotion and motivated behavior. Rage, fear, sexual response, and intense arousal can be obtained from various points in the limbic system. For example, cats can be made to behave aggressively by electrically stimulating the limbic system. Typically, they crouch, hiss, expose their claws, lean forward, and tense their muscles—all characteristic of defense or attack. In humans, damage to the limbic system often leads to aggressive and self-destructive behavior (Garza-Trevino, 1994).

During evolution, the limbic system was the earliest layer of the forebrain to develop. In lower animals, the limbic system helps organize basic survival responses: feeding, fleeing, fighting, and reproduction. In humans, a clear link to emotion

BRIDGES

Unconscious fear produced by the amygdala seems to explain why people who survive horrible experiences can have debilitating fears years later.

See Chapter 17, pages 567–568.

remains. The **amygdala** (ah-MIG-dah-luh), in particular, is strongly related to fear. For example, during medical testing one woman reacted with a sudden outburst of fear and anger when the amygdala was stimulated, saying, "I feel like I want to get up from this chair! Please don't let me do it! I don't want to be mean! I want to get something and just tear it up!" (King, 1961).

The amygdala provides a primitive, "quick pathway" to the cortex. Like lower animals, we are able to react to dangerous stimuli before we fully know what is going on. In situations where true danger exists, such as military combat, the amygdala's rapid response may aid survival. However, disorders of the brain's fear system can be very disruptive. An example is the war veteran who involuntarily dives into the bushes when he hears a car backfire (LeDoux, 1996, 1999).

Some parts of the limbic system have taken on additional, higher level functions. A part called the **hippocampus** (HIP-oh-CAMP-us) is important for forming lasting memories (Bigler et al., 1996). The hippocampus lies inside the temporal lobes, which is why stimulating the temporal lobes can produce memory-like or dreamlike experiences. The hippocampus also helps us navigate through space. Your right hippocampus will become more active, for instance, if you mentally plan a drive across town (Maguire et al., 1997).

Psychologists have discovered that animals will learn to press a lever to deliver a rewarding dose of electrical stimulation to the limbic system. The animals act as if the stimulation is satisfying or pleasurable. Indeed, several areas of the limbic system act as reward, or "pleasure," pathways. Many are found in the hypothalamus, where they overlap with areas that control thirst, sex, and hunger. Commonly abused drugs, such as cocaine, amphetamine, heroin, nicotine, marijuana, and alcohol, activate many of the same pleasure pathways. This appears to explain, in part, why these drugs are so powerfully rewarding (Wise & Rompre, 1989).

Punishment, or "aversive," areas have also been found in the limbic system. When these locations are activated, animals show discomfort and will work hard to turn off the stimulation. Because much of our behavior is based on seeking pleasure and avoiding pain, these discoveries continue to fascinate psychologists.

The Magnificent Brain

Given the amount of information covered in our journey through the brain, a short review is in order. We have seen that the human brain is an impressive assembly of billions of sensitive cells and nerve fibers. The brain controls vital bodily functions, keeps track of the external world, issues commands to the muscles and glands, responds to current needs, creates the magic of consciousness, and regulates its own behavior—*all* at the same time.

A final note of caution: For the sake of simplicity, we have assigned functions to each "part" of the brain as if it were a

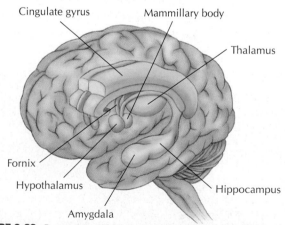

Cingulate gyrus   Mammillary body

Thalamus

Fornix

Hypothalamus

Hippocampus

Amygdala

❖ **FIGURE 3.26** *Parts of the limbic system are shown in this highly simplified drawing. Although only one side is shown, the hippocampus and the amygdala extend out into the temporal lobes at each side of the brain. The limbic system is a sort of "primitive core" of the brain strongly associated with emotion.*

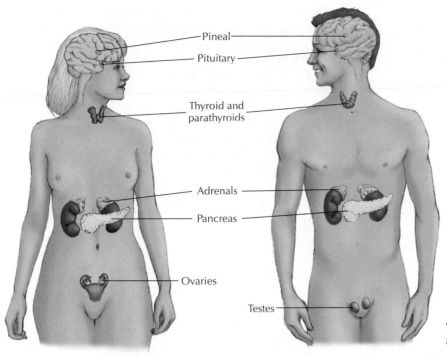

Pineal

Pituitary

Thyroid and parathyroids

Adrenals

Pancreas

Ovaries

Testes

❖ **FIGURE 3.27** *Locations of the endocrine glands in the male and female.*

computer. This is only a half-truth. In reality, the brain is a vast information-processing system. Incoming information scatters all over the brain and converges again as it goes out through the spinal cord, to muscles and glands. The overall system is much, much more complicated than our discussion of separate "parts" implies. In addition, the brain revises its circuits in response to changing life experiences (Conlan, 1999). The last part of this chapter explains how such "rewiring" takes place.

THE ENDOCRINE SYSTEM—HORMONES AND BEHAVIOR

Our behavior is not solely a product of the nervous system. The endocrine glands (EN-duh-krin) serve as a second great communication system in the body. The **endocrine system** is made up of glands that pour chemicals directly into the bloodstream or lymph system (see ❖Fig. 3.27). These chemicals, called **hormones**, are carried throughout the body, where they affect both internal activities and visible behavior. Hormones are related to neurotransmitters. Like other transmitter chemicals, hormones activate cells in the body. To respond, the cells must have receptor sites for the hormone.

How do hormones affect behavior? Although we are seldom aware of them, hormones affect us in many ways. Here is a brief sample: Hormone output from the adrenal glands rises during stressful situations; androgens ("male" hormones) are related to the sex drive in both males and females; hormones secreted during times of high emotion intensify memory formation; at least some of the emotional turmoil of adolescence is due to elevated hormone levels; different hormones prevail when you are angry, rather than fearful. Since this is just a sam-

ple, let's consider some additional effects hormones have on the body and behavior.

The pituitary is a pea-sized globe hanging from the base of the brain (return to ❖Fig. 3.27). One of the pituitary's more important roles is to regulate growth. During childhood, the pituitary secretes a hormone that speeds body development. If too little **growth hormone** is released, a person may remain far smaller than average. (See "A Tall Question.") Too much growth hormone produces **giantism** (excessive bodily growth). Secretion of too much growth hormone late in the growth period causes **acromegaly** (AK-row-MEG-uh-lee), a condition in which the arms, hands, feet, and facial bones become enlarged. Acromegaly produces prominent facial features, which some people have used as a basis for careers as character actors, wrestlers, and the like.

Hypothalamus *A small area of the brain that regulates emotional behaviors and motives.*
Limbic system *A system in the forebrain that is closely linked with emotional response.*
Amygdala *A part of the limbic system associated with fear responses.*
Hippocampus *A part of the limbic system associated with storing memories.*
Endocrine system *Glands whose secretions pass directly into the bloodstream or lymph system.*
Hormone *A glandular secretion that affects bodily functions or behavior.*
Growth hormone *A hormone, secreted by the pituitary gland, that promotes bodily growth.*
Giantism *Excessive bodily growth caused by too much growth hormone.*
Acromegaly *Enlargement of the arms, hands, feet, and face caused by excess growth hormone production late in the human growth period.*

A TALL QUESTION

Children who lag far behind in growth may suffer lasting emotional scars from rejection by peers or adults. One common cause of limited growth is insufficient growth hormone. If this condition is not treated, a child may be 6 to 12 inches shorter than age-mates. As adults, some will be **hypopituitary dwarfs** (HI-po-pih-TU-ih-ter-ee). Such individuals are perfectly proportioned, but tiny. Should they receive medical treatment?

For many years, dwarfism could be treated only with injections of human growth hormone. Supplies were extracted from the pituitary glands of human cadavers—a painstaking and expensive process. Now, a cheaper synthetic growth hormone is available. (Treatment still costs about $15,000 per child per year.) Regular injections of growth hormone can raise a hypopituitary child's height by several inches, usually to the short side of average. Treatment, however, can last from 3 to 7 years and cost from $45,000 to $105,000.

Growth hormone therapy is usually safe. However, it does raise ethical concerns. Some experts believe that it is wrong to treat shortness as a medical problem. Also, some parents and children are bitterly disappointed when the child fails to grow as much as expected. Surprisingly, some short children adjust poorly to becoming more "ordinary." Many go from playing with younger children to being ignored by age-mates.

The greatest risk comes from parents who pressure physicians to increase the growth of "normal short" children. If a child's body produces normal amounts of growth hormone, drugs typically will not make the child taller as an adult. Such children grow *faster* when given growth hormone, but not taller. Nevertheless, thousands of "normal short" children are being given growth hormone injections.

With all this in mind, perhaps it is fair to say that the success of growth hormone therapy should be measured by increased emotional well-being—not merely by an increase in stature (Adler, 1992; Roan, 1993).

Underactivity of the pituitary gland may produce a dwarf, overactivity a giant.

The pituitary also governs the functioning of other glands (especially the thyroid, adrenal glands, and ovaries or testes). These glands, in turn, regulate such bodily processes as metabolism, responses to stress, and reproduction. In women, the pituitary controls milk production during pregnancy.

The **pituitary gland** is often called the "master gland" because its hormones influence other endocrine glands. But the master has a master: The pituitary is directed by the hypothalamus, which lies directly above it. In this way, the hypothalamus affects glands throughout the body. This, then, is the major link between the brain and the glandular system (Carlson, 1998).

The pineal gland (pin-EE-ul) was once considered a useless remnant of evolution. In certain fishes, frogs, and lizards, the

gland is associated with a well-developed light-sensitive organ, or so-called "third eye." In humans, the function of the pineal gland is just now coming to light (so to speak). The **pineal gland** releases a hormone called **melatonin** (mel-ah-TONE-in) in response to daily variations in light. Melatonin levels in the bloodstream rise at dusk and peak around midnight. They fall again as morning approaches. This light-driven cycle helps control body rhythms and sleep cycles.

The **thyroid gland**, located in the neck, regulates metabolism. As you may remember from a biology course, **metabo-**

lism is the rate at which energy is produced and expended in the body. By altering metabolism, the thyroid can have a sizable effect on personality. A person suffering from **hyperthyroidism** (an overactive thyroid) tends to be thin, tense, excitable, and nervous. An underactive thyroid (**hypothyroidism**) in an adult can cause inactivity, sleepiness, slowness, and obesity. In infancy, hypothyroidism limits development of the nervous system, leading to severe mental retardation (see Chapter 12).

When you are frightened or angry, some important reactions prepare your body for action: Your heart rate and blood pressure rise, stored sugar is released into the bloodstream for quick energy, the muscles tense and receive more blood, and blood is prepared to clot more quickly in case of injury. As we discussed earlier, these changes are controlled by the autonomic nervous system. Specifically, the sympathetic branch of the ANS causes the adrenal glands to release the hormones *epinephrine* and *norepinephrine*. (Epinephrine is also known as adrenaline, which may be a more familiar term.) **Epinephrine** (ep-eh-NEF-rin), which is associated with fear, tends to arouse the body. **Norepinephrine** also tends to arouse the body, but it is associated with anger. (As mentioned earlier, both substances also act as neurotransmitters.)

The **adrenal glands** are located just under the back of the rib cage, atop the kidneys. The **adrenal medulla**, or inner core of the adrenal glands, is the source of epinephrine and norepinephrine. The **adrenal cortex**, or outer "bark" of the adrenal glands, produces a set of hormones called corticoids (KOR-tih-coids). One of their jobs is to regulate salt balance in the body. A deficiency of certain corticoids can evoke a powerful craving for the taste of salt in humans. The corticoids also help the body adjust to stress, and they are a secondary source of sex hormones. (For a full discussion of the role of sex glands in development, see Chapter 16.)

An oversecretion of the adrenal sex hormones can cause **virilism** (exaggerated male characteristics). For instance, a woman may grow a beard or a man's voice may become so low it is difficult to understand. Oversecretion early in life can cause **premature puberty** (full sexual development during childhood). One of the most remarkable cases on record is that of a 5-year-old Peruvian girl who gave birth to a son (Strange, 1965).

While we are on the topic of sex hormones, there is a related issue worth mentioning. One of the principal androgens or "male" hormones is testosterone, which is supplied in small amounts by the adrenal glands. (The testes are the main source of testosterone in males.) Perhaps you have heard about the use of anabolic steroids by athletes who want to "bulk up" or promote muscle growth. Most of these drugs are synthetic versions of testosterone.

Although many athletes believe otherwise, there is no evidence that steroids improve performance, and they may cause serious side effects. Problems include voice deepening or baldness in women and shrinkage of the testicles, sexual impotence, or breast enlargement in men. Also common are an increased risk of

BRIDGES

Melatonin can be used to reset the body's "clock" and minimize jet lag for long-distance pilots, air crews, and travelers.

See Chapter 13, pages 418–419.

heart attack and stroke, liver damage, and stunted growth when younger adolescents use steroids (Bahrke, Yesalis, & Brower, 1998). For some users, steroids may cause mania or suicidal depression, antisocial behavior ("roid rage"), and near-psychotic reactions (Harrison & Katz, 1987). Understandably, all major sports organizations ban the use of anabolic steroids.

In this brief discussion of the endocrine system, we have considered only a few of the more important glands. Nevertheless, this should give you an appre-

Professional football player Lyle Alzado used anabolic steroids throughout his athletic career. Alzado died of brain cancer, which he attributed to his abuse of steroids.

Hypopituitary dwarfism *Shortness and smallness caused by too little growth hormone.*
Pituitary gland *The "master gland" whose hormones influence other endocrine glands.*
Pineal gland *Gland in the brain that helps regulate body rhythms and sleep cycles.*
Melatonin *Hormone released by the pineal gland in response to daily cycles of light and dark.*
Thyroid gland *Endocrine gland that helps regulate the rate of metabolism.*
Metabolism *The rate at which energy is produced and used by the body.*
Hyperthyroidism *Faster metabolism and excitability caused by an overactive thyroid gland.*
Hypothyroidism *Slower metabolism and sluggishness caused by an underactive thyroid gland.*
Epinephrine *An adrenal hormone that tends to arouse the body; epinephrine is associated with fear (also known as adrenaline).*
Norepinephrine *An adrenal hormone that tends to arouse the body; norepinephrine is associated with anger (also known as noradrenaline).*
Adrenal glands *Endocrine glands that arouse the body, regulate salt balance, adjust the body to stress, and affect sexual functioning.*
Adrenal medulla *The inner core of the adrenal glands; a source of epinephrine and norepinephrine.*
Adrenal cortex *The outer layer of the adrenal glands; produces hormones that affect salt intake, reactions to stress, and sexual development.*
Virilism *The development of male sexual characteristics in a female.*
Premature puberty *The development of sexual maturity in childhood.*

ciation of how completely behavior and personality are tied to the ebb and flow of hormones in the body.

A LOOK AHEAD In the upcoming "Psychology in Action" section, we will return to the brain to see how hand preference relates to brain organization. You'll also find out if being right- or left-handed affects your chances of living to a ripe old age. After that, "A Step Beyond" explores some startling recent findings about the brain.

KNOWLEDGE BUILDER
SUBCORTEX AND ENDOCRINE SYSTEM

RELATE

If Mr. Medulla met Ms. Cerebellum at a party, what would they say their roles are in the brain? Would a marching band in a "reticular formation" look like a network? Would it get your attention? If you were standing in the final path for behavior leaving the brain, would you be in the thalamus? Or in the hy-path-ala-mus (please forgive the misspelling)? When you are emotional, do you wave your limbs around (and does your limbic system become more active)?

Name as many of the endocrine glands as you can. Which did you leave out? Can you summarize the functions of each of the glands?

LEARNING CHECK

1. Three major divisions of the brain are the brainstem or _____, the _____, and the _____.

2. Reflex centers for heartbeat and respiration are found in the
   a. cerebellum b. thalamus c. medulla d. RF

3. A portion of the reticular formation, known as the RAS, serves as an _____ system in the brain.
   a. activating b. adrenal c. adjustment d. aversive

4. The _____ is a final relay, or "switching station," for sensory information on its way to the cortex.

5. "Reward" and "punishment" areas are found throughout the _____ system, which is also related to emotion.

6. Undersecretion from the thyroid can cause
   a. dwarfism b. giantism c. overweight d. mental retardation

7. The body's ability to resist stress is related to the action of the adrenal _____.

CRITICAL THINKING

8. Subcortical structures in humans are quite similar to corresponding lower brain areas in animals. Why would knowing this allow you to predict, in general terms, what functions are controlled by the subcortex?

9. Where in all the brain's "hardware" do you think the mind is found? What is the relationship between mind and brain?

Answers:

1. hindbrain, midbrain, forebrain 2. c 3. a 4. thalamus 5. limbic 6. c, d (in infancy) 7. cortex 8. Because the subcortex must be related to basic functions common to all higher animals: motives, emotions, sleep, attention, and vegetative functions, such as heartbeat, breathing, and temperature regulation. The subcortex also routes and processes incoming information from the senses and outgoing commands to the muscles. 9. This question, known as the mind-body problem, has challenged thinkers for centuries. One recent view is that mental states are "emergent properties" of brain activity. That is, brain activity forms complex patterns that are, in a sense, more than the sum of their parts. Or, to use a rough analogy, if the brain were a musical instrument, then mental life would be like music played on that instrument.

---

psychology in action

HANDEDNESS—IF YOUR BRAIN IS RIGHT, WHAT'S LEFT?

In the English language, "what's right is right," but what's left may be wrong. We have left-handed compliments, people with "two left feet," those who are left out, and the left-handed. On the other hand (so to speak), we have the right way, the right angle, the "right-hand man" (or woman), righteousness, and the right-handed.

The Sinister Hand

Left-handedness has a long and undeserved bad reputation. Southpaws have been accused of being clumsy, stubborn (for refusing to use their right hand), and maladjusted. But as any

lefty will tell you, and psychology has confirmed, none of this is true. The supposed clumsiness of lefties is merely a result of living in a right-handed world: If it can be gripped, turned, folded, held, or pulled, it's probably designed for the right hand. Even toilet handles are on the right side.

What causes **handedness** (a preference for the right or left hand)? Why are there more right-handed than left-handed people? How do left-handed and right-handed people differ? Does being left-handed create any problems—or benefits? The answers to these questions lead us back to the brain, where handedness begins. Let's see what research has revealed about handedness, the brain, and you.

HAND DOMINANCE

Take a moment and write your name on a sheet of paper, first using your right hand and then your left. You were probably much more comfortable writing with your dominant hand. This is interesting because there's no real difference in the strength or dexterity of the hands themselves. The agility of your dominant hand is an outward expression of superior motor control on one side of the brain. If you are right-handed, there is literally more area on the left side of your brain devoted to controlling your right hand. If you are left-handed, the reverse applies (Volkman et al., 1998).

The preceding exercise implies that you are either entirely right- or left-handed. But handedness is a matter of degree (Coren, 1992). To better assess your handedness, circle an answer for each of the questions that follow.

Are You Right- or Left-Handed?

1. Which hand do you normally use to write? Right Left Either
2. Which hand would you use to throw a ball at a target? Right Left Either
3. Which hand do you use to hold your toothbrush? Right Left Either
4. Which hand do you use to hold a knife when cutting food? Right Left Either
5. With which hand do you hold a hammer when hitting a nail? Right Left Either
6. When you thread a needle, which hand holds the thread? Right Left Either

To find your score, count the number of "Rights" you circled and multiply by 3. Then multiply the number of "Eithers" by 2. Next count the number of "Lefts" you circled. Now add all three totals and compare the result with the following scale (adapted from Coren, 1992).

17–18: Strongly right-handed
15–16: Moderately right-handed (mixed)
13–14: Mildly right-handed (mixed)
    12: Ambidextrous
10–11: Mildly left-handed (mixed)
  8–9: Moderately left-handed (mixed)
  6–7: Strongly left-handed

A majority of people (about 77 percent) are strongly right- or left-handed. The rest show some inconsistency in hand preference. As ◆Table 3.1 indicates, such differences can affect performance in some sports.

If a person is strongly left-handed, does that mean the right hemisphere is dominant? Not necessarily. It's true that the right hemisphere controls the left hand, but a left-handed person's language-producing, **dominant hemisphere** may be on the opposite side of the brain.

BRAIN DOMINANCE

About 97 percent of right-handers process speech in the left hemisphere and are left-brain dominant (❖Fig. 3.28). A good 68 percent of left-handers produce speech from the left hemi-

◆ **TABLE 3.1** Sports and Handedness

SPORT	HANDEDNESS ADVANTAGE
Boxing	Left
Fencing	Left
Basketball	Mixed and ambidextrous
Ice hockey	Mixed and ambidextrous
Field hockey	Mixed and ambidextrous
Tennis	Strong left or strong right
Squash	Strong left or strong right
Badminton	Strong left or strong right

Coren, 1992.

Left-handers have an advantage in sports such as fencing and boxing. Most likely, their movements are less familiar to opponents, who usually face right-handers (Coren, 1992).

Handedness *A preference for the right or left hand in most activities.*
Dominant hemisphere *A term usually applied to the side of a person's brain that produces language.*

sphere, just as right-handed people do. About 19 percent of all lefties and 3 percent of righties use their right brain for language. Some left-handers (approximately 12 percent) use both sides of the brain for language processing. All totaled, 94 percent of the population uses the left brain for language (Coren, 1992).

Is there any way for a person to tell which of his or her hemispheres is dominant? One interesting clue is based on the way you write. Right-handed individuals who write with a straight hand, and lefties who write with a hooked hand, are usually left-brain dominant for language. Left-handed people who write with their hand below the line, and righties who use a hooked position, are usually right-brain dominant (Levy & Reid, 1976). Another hint is provided by hand gestures. If you gesture mostly with your right hand as you talk, you probably process language in your left hemisphere. Gesturing with your left hand is associated with right-brain language processing (Hellige, 1993). Are your friends right brained or left brained? (See ❖Fig. 3.29.)

Before you leap to any conclusions, be aware that writing position is not foolproof. The only sure way to check brain dominance is to do a medical test that involves briefly anesthetizing one cerebral hemisphere at a time (Springer & Deutsch, 1998).

Handedness

How common is left-handedness, and what causes it? Ninety percent of all humans are right-handed; 10 percent are left-handed. The prevalence of right-handedness probably reflects the left brain's specialization for producing language (Coren, 1992).

In the past, many left-handed children were forced to use their right hand for writing, eating, and other skills. But as fetal ultrasound images show, clear hand preferences are apparent even before birth (Hepper, McCartney, & Shannon, 1998). (See ❖Fig. 3.30.) This suggests that handedness cannot be dictated. Parents should never try to force a left-handed child to use the right hand. To do so may create speech or reading problems.

Is handedness inherited from parents? Studies of twins show that hand preferences are not directly inherited like eye color or skin color (Reiss et al., 1999; Ross et al., 1999). What is inherited is the *degree* of handedness. If your parents are strongly handed, you probably have a strong hand preference, too—even though your dominant hand may not match theirs. If your parents are ambidextrous or mixed handed, you probably are, too (Coren, 1992).

Are there any drawbacks to being left-handed? A minority of lefties owe their hand preference to birth traumas (such as prematurity, low birth weight, and breech birth). These individuals have a higher incidence of allergies, learning disorders, and other problems (Betancur et al., 1990). But in most instances, left-handedness is unrelated to intelligence or the overall rate of illness and accidental injury (McManus et al., 1988; Porac et al., 1998).

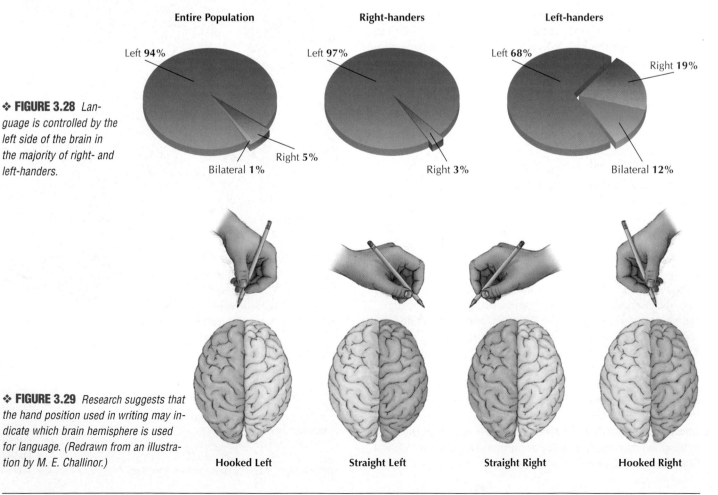

Entire Population   **Right-handers**   **Left-handers**

Left **94%**   Left **97%**   Left **68%**   Right **19%**

Right **5%**   Right **3%**   Bilateral **12%**

Bilateral **1%**

❖ **FIGURE 3.28** *Language is controlled by the left side of the brain in the majority of right- and left-handers.*

❖ **FIGURE 3.29** *Research suggests that the hand position used in writing may indicate which brain hemisphere is used for language. (Redrawn from an illustration by M. E. Challinor.)*

Hooked Left   **Straight Left**   **Straight Right**   **Hooked Right**

Many people have been alarmed by news reports that lefties tend to die younger than right-handed persons (Coren & Halpern, 1991). However, three rather decisive studies found that there is no difference in the age at which left- and right-handed persons die (Harris, 1993a, 1993b; Salive et al., 1993). More important, there are some clear advantages to being left-handed.

ADVANTAGE LEFT   Throughout history, a notable number of artists have been lefties, from Leonardo da Vinci and Michelangelo to Pablo Picasso and M. C. Escher. Conceivably, because the right hemisphere is superior at imagery and visual abilities, there is some advantage to using the left hand for drawing or painting (Springer & Deutsch, 1998). At the least, lefties are definitely better at visualizing three-dimensional objects. This may be why there are more left-handed architects, artists, and chess players than would be expected (Coren, 1992).

Lateralization refers to specialization in the abilities of the brain hemispheres. One striking feature of lefties is that they are generally less lateralized than the right-handed (Hellige, 1990). In fact, even the physical size and shape of their cerebral hemispheres are more alike. If you are a lefty, you can take pride in the fact that your brain is less lopsided than most! In general, left-handers are more symmetrical on almost everything, including eye dominance, fingerprints—even foot size.

In some situations, less lateralization may be a real advantage. For instance, individuals who are moderately left-handed or ambidextrous seem to have better than average pitch memory, which is a basic musical skill. Correspondingly, more musicians are ambidextrous than would normally be expected (Springer & Deutsch, 1998).

Math abilities may also benefit from fuller use of the right hemisphere. Students who are extremely gifted in math are much more likely to be left-handed or ambidextrous (Benbow, 1986). Even in ordinary arithmetic skills, lefties seem to excel (Annett & Manning, 1990).

The clearest advantage of being left-handed shows up when there is a brain injury. Because of their milder lateralization, left-handed individuals typically experience less language loss after damage to either brain hemisphere, and they recover more easily (Geschwind, 1979). Maybe having "two left feet" isn't so bad after all.

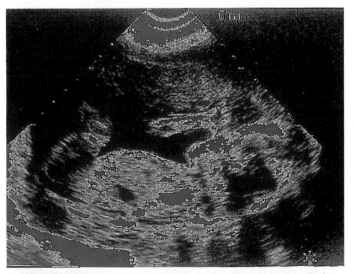

❖ **FIGURE 3.30** In this ultrasound image, a 4-month-old fetus sucks her right thumb. A study by psychologist Peter Hepper suggests that she will continue to prefer her right hand after she is born and that she will be right-handed as an adult.

Lateralization Differences between the two sides of the body, especially differences in the abilities of the brain hemispheres.

Focus: Is brain damage always permanent?

The brain is both highly vulnerable and amazingly resilient. In one astounding case, a child had the entire left hemisphere of his brain removed at age 5. As an adult, he was paralyzed on the right side and blind in his right visual field. But he was able to speak, read, write, and comprehend so well that he had a double major in college and an above-average IQ (Smith & Sugar, 1975). How did he manage such a miraculous recovery after losing half his brain? How did his brain rewire itself? The answers can be found in the concept of brain plasticity.

PLASTICITY

To the touch, the human brain feels like tofu or grandma's Jell-O salad. However, squishiness is not what psychologists have in mind when they talk about the brain's "plasticity." **Plasticity** refers to the brain's ability to change its structure and functions. Remarkably, the brain can "rewire" itself after some types of damage. It also forms new connections in response to changing environmental conditions (Hyman, 1999; Kolb & Whishaw, 1998).

Aren't connections within the brain pretty much the same for everyone? They are for major brain structures—otherwise, neurosurgeons wouldn't know where to begin when operating on the brain. However, the brain is also wonderfully adaptable. Throughout life, it modifies its circuits in various ways. This is what makes our behavior flexible and efficient (Conlan, 1999; Posner & Levitin, 1999).

How does the "rewiring" occur? Learning a new skill, such as playing the piano, requires many changes in the brain. Some dendrites grow longer and sprout new branches. Others are "pruned" away. New synapses form. Others disappear. Activity levels change in groups of neurons. Through such processes, parts of the cortex are "rewired" and "tuned" to carry out tasks more efficiently (Johnson, 1999). For example, as a result of cortical tuning, distinct areas of your brain are especially good at recognizing faces, animals, furniture, and other specific types of objects. Likewise, the brain of an adult violinist will be different if she began practicing as a child, rather than later in life (Posner & Levitin, 1999). Over the course of a lifetime, our experiences literally shape, mold, and remodel details of the brain.

Brain Injuries

Plasticity can help adults recover some lost abilities following brain injuries. For example, let's say that an older man suffers a stroke. Immediately after his cerebral accident, the man suffers

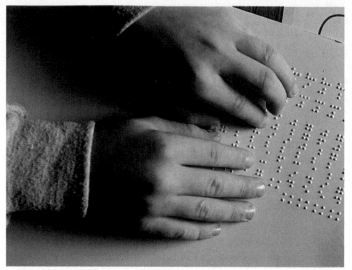

A study of blind people found that they show a high level of activity in the visual area of the brain when reading Braille, a remarkable example of brain plasticity and reorganization (Sadato, Pascual-Leone, & Hallett, 1996).

from paralysis and cannot speak. Will he be able to regain any of his lost abilities? Fortunately, many people do improve in the months following a stroke. Because of the brain's plasticity, healthy areas in the brain can sometimes take over for damaged areas (Kolb, 1999; Posner & Levitin, 1999).

Does it make any difference at what age a person experiences a brain injury? Yes, children have far more plasticity than adults. For example, if the left hemisphere is severely damaged, children under age 2 can shift language processing to the right side of the brain. If damage occurs between ages 2 and 6, new language areas tend to develop in both hemispheres. For an adult, such drastic shifts in language processing would be impossible (Mueller et al., 1999).

Implications

Psychologists used to think that you can't "exercise" the brain in any general sense. However, studies of neural plasticity suggest that for the brain it's a case of "use it or lose it." Using your brain in novel or stimulating ways actually increases its size and the number of dendritic branches it contains (Kempermann & Gage, 1999). The more you challenge and engage your brain—especially by learning new skills—the healthier it will be and the better it will function.

NEUROGENESIS

Perhaps the most dazzling recent advance in brain science involves **neurogenesis** (nue-roh-JEN-uh-sis: the production of

new brain cells). Until only a few years ago, it was widely believed that we are born with all the neurons we will ever have. This led to the depressing idea that we all slowly go downhill, as the brain loses thousands of neurons each day. However, we now know that a healthy 75-year-old brain has just as many neurons as it did when it was careening through life in the body of a 25-year-old. Although it is true that the brain loses cells every day, it simultaneously grows new neurons to replace them.

New brain cells were first found in the hippocampus, where they probably play a role in storing memories (Gould et al., 1999). More recent studies with monkeys have shown that new cells grow in other parts of the brain, too. Each day, thousands of new cells originate deep within the brain and then migrate to the cerebral cortex. Once there, they link up with other neurons to become part of the brain's circuitry (Gould, Reeves, & Gross, 1999). In other words, the cortex, which is the seat of intelligence, receives a steady stream of new brain cells. This is stunning news to brain scientists, who must now figure out what the new cells do.

Brain Repair

The discovery of neurogenesis in adult brains has raised new hopes that some types of brain damage can be repaired. For example, doctors are testing a new method to treat strokes. Rather than relying on plasticity to provide gradual improvement, they are injecting millions of immature nerve

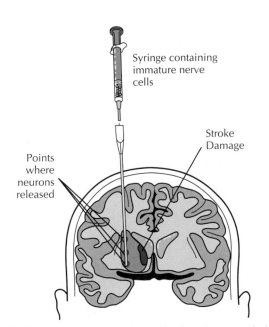

Syringe containing immature nerve cells

Stroke Damage

Points where neurons released

❖ **FIGURE 3.31** *Neuroscientists are searching for ways to repair damage caused by strokes and other brain injuries. One promising technique involves growing neurons in the laboratory and injecting them into the brain. These immature cells are placed near damaged areas, where they can link up with healthy neurons. The technique has proved successful in animals and is now under study in humans.*

cells into damaged areas. (See ❖Fig. 3.31.) This technique works remarkably well with rats. If it is successful in humans, the new cells will link up with existing neurons and repair some of the stroke damage (Borlongan, Sanberg, & Freeman, 1999).

Researchers are also working on nudging immature brain cells to develop into particular types of neurons. For instance, blindness might be treated by guiding them into becoming the type of cells found in the brain's visual areas. Or, if immature cells could be nurtured into supplying dopamine, they might provide a cure for Parkinson's disease, which is caused by a loss of dopamine-producing neurons (Kolb & Whishaw, 1998).

The Future

Imagine being completely paralyzed and unable to speak. Even though you would remain alert and intelligent, you would be unable to communicate your simplest thoughts and feelings to others. Each year, this is the fate of thousands of people who are paralyzed by stroke, disease, or injury. Unable to move or speak, they suffer from "locked-in syndrome." In a very real sense, these people become prisoners in their own bodies. What if they could "will" a computer to speak for them? Although that possibility is years away, neuroscientists have taken a first step toward freeing victims of total paralysis (Christensen, 1999).

In pioneering studies, doctors Roy Bakay and Philip Kennedy have inserted "neurotrophic electrodes" into the motor cortex of paralyzed patients. (The term *neurotrophic* refers to anything that has growth-enhancing properties in the nervous system.) The device consists of two thin gold wires inside a small, hollow glass cone. Natural substances released near the tip of the cone promote nerve growth. As brain cells grow into the tip of the cone, they link up with the recording wires. Then, when the patient thinks certain thoughts, bursts of activity in the brain are detected by the wires. Instantly, these signals are amplified and transmitted to a computer, where they control the movements of a cursor on the screen (Kennedy & Bakay, 1998). (See ❖Fig. 3.32.)

How does thinking cause the cursor to move? Patients discover through trial and error what will move the cursor. For instance, thinking about lifting a cup might activate the motor cortex and make the cursor move in a particular way. By repeating the same thought, patients can learn to select icons on the screen that direct the computer to say phrases such as "Please turn the light on" or "See you later, nice talking to you."

Neuroscientists realize that they have taken only baby steps toward freeing locked-in patients. Nevertheless, what was merely science fiction a few years ago is starting to become

Plasticity *The brain's capacity to change its structure and functions.*
Neurogenesis *The production of new brain cells.*

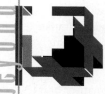

reality. The human brain is just beginning to understand itself. What an adventure the next decade of brain research will be.

CONCLUSION: Most brain injuries are permanent. However, brain plasticity, neurogenesis, and new medical techniques offer some hope of recovering lost abilities following brain damage.

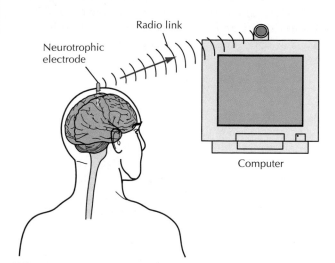

Radio link

Neurotrophic electrode

Computer

❖ **FIGURE 3.32** *A direct brain-computer link may provide a way of communicating for people who are paralyzed and unable to speak. Activity in the patient's motor cortex is detected by an implanted electrode. The signal is then amplified and transmitted to a nearby computer. By thinking in certain ways, patients can move an on-screen cursor. This allows them to spell out words or select from a list of messages, such as "I am thirsty."*

KNOWLEDGE BUILDER
NEUROGENESIS AND BRAIN PLASTICITY

RELATE

How flexible did you think brain organization was before you read about neural plasticity? Has attending college changed your brain structure? (The answer is yes. College graduates have denser dendrites in the language areas of the cortex.) What is the most challenging new skill you have learned? Did it change you as a person?

New rows of neurons in the hippocampus are helping you form new memories about neurogenesis. Will you be able to remember that?

An older friend of yours quips, "I guess I can't remember that because of all the brain cells I've lost." What can you tell him about neurogenesis?

LEARNING CHECK

1. The function of virtually any structure in the brain can be revised through neural plasticity. T or F?

2. Major structural and functional changes in the brain are much more likely to occur during adolescence, when the body is growing rapidly. T or F?

3. Healthy areas of the brain can sometimes take over the duties of areas that have been damaged by disease or injury. T or F?

4. Learning novel or challenging new skills can change the way neurons function and interconnect within the brain. T or F?

5. Except for some minor replacements of neurons in the hippocampus, we are born with all of the brain cells we will ever have. T or F?

6. The most successful attempts to use thoughts to control a computer have made use of neuroplastic electrodes implanted in the hippocampus. T or F?

CRITICAL THINKING

7. Why do you think it is best to learn a second language before age 10?

Answers:
1. F 2. F 3. T 4. T 5. F 6. F 7. Because of greater brain plasticity in childhood, a person who learns a second language early in life can usually attain a native accent. Later, there will always be hints that the person is not a native speaker, even if the person can speak the language fluently. When a second language is learned in childhood, the brain literally develops a second language area on the cortex for that language.

CHAPTER IN REVIEW

How do nerve cells operate and communicate?

- The brain and nervous system are made up of linked nerve cells called neurons. Neurons pass information from one to another through synapses.
- The basic conducting fibers of neurons are axons, but dendrites, the soma, and axon terminals are also involved in communication.
- The firing of an action potential (nerve impulse) is basically electrical. Communication between neurons is chemical.
- Neurons release neurotransmitters at synapses. These chemicals cross to receptor sites on the receiving cell, causing it to be excited or inhibited.
- Transmitters called neuropeptides appear to regulate activity in the brain.
- Nerves are made of axons and associated tissues. Neurons and nerves in the peripheral nervous system can often regenerate. At present, damage in the central nervous system is permanent, although scientists are working on ways to repair damaged neural tissue.

What are the functions of major parts of the nervous system?

- The nervous system can be divided into the central nervous system (the brain and spinal cord) and the peripheral nervous system, which includes the somatic (bodily) and autonomic (involuntary) nervous systems.
- The autonomic system has two divisions: the sympathetic (emergency, activating) branch and the parasympathetic (sustaining, conserving) branch.

How do we know how the brain works?

- Brain research relies on clinical studies, electrical stimulation, ablation, deep lesioning, electrical recording, micro-electrode recording, and EEG recording.
- Computer-enhanced images are providing three-dimensional pictures of the living human brain and its activity. Examples of such techniques are CT scans, MRI scans, and PET scans.

How is the brain organized, and what do its various areas do?

- The human brain is marked by advanced corticalization, or enlargement of the cerebral cortex.
- The left cerebral hemisphere contains speech or language "centers" in most people. It also specializes in writing, calculating, judging time and rhythm, and ordering complex movements.
- The right hemisphere is largely nonverbal. It excels at spatial and perceptual skills, visualization, and recognition of patterns, faces, and melodies.
- "Split brains" have been created in animals and humans by cutting the corpus callosum. The split-brain individual shows a remarkable degree of independence between the right and left hemispheres.
- The most basic functions of the lobes of the cerebral cortex are as follows: occipital lobes—vision; parietal lobes—bodily sensation; temporal lobes—hearing and language; frontal lobes—motor control, speech, and abstract thought. Damage to any of these areas impairs the named functions.

Why are the brain's association areas important? What happens when they are injured?

- Association areas on the cortex are neither sensory nor motor in function. They are related to more complex skills such as language, memory, recognition, and problem solving.
- Damage to either Broca's area or Wernicke's area causes speech and language problems known as aphasias.
- Damage in other areas may cause agnosia, the inability to identify objects by sight.

What kinds of behaviors are controlled by the subcortex?

- The brain can be subdivided into the forebrain, midbrain, and hindbrain. The subcortex includes several crucial brain structures found at all three levels, below the cortex.
- The medulla contains centers essential for reflex control of heart rate, breathing, and other "vegetative" functions.
- The cerebellum maintains coordination, posture, and muscle tone.
- The reticular formation directs sensory and motor messages, and part of it, known as the RAS, acts as an activating system for the cerebral cortex.
- The thalamus carries sensory information to the cortex. The hypothalamus exerts powerful control over eating, drinking, sleep cycles, body temperature, and other basic motives and behaviors.
- The limbic system is strongly related to emotion. It also contains distinct reward and punishment areas and an area known as the hippocampus that is important for forming memories.

Is behavior affected by the glandular system?

- The endocrine system provides chemical communication in the body by releasing hormones into the bloodstream. Endocrine glands influence moods, behavior, and even personality.
- Many of the endocrine glands are influenced by the pituitary (the "master gland"), which is, in turn, influenced by the hypothalamus. Thus, the brain controls the body through the fast nervous system and the slower endocrine system.

In what ways do right- and left-handed individuals differ?

- Hand dominance ranges from strongly left- to strongly right-handed, with mixed handedness and ambidexterity in between. Ninety percent of the population is basically right-handed, 10 percent left-handed.
- The vast majority of people are right-handed and therefore left-brain dominant for motor skills. Ninety-seven percent of right-handed persons and 68 percent of the left-handed also produce speech from the left hemisphere.
- In general, the left-handed are less strongly lateralized in brain function than are right-handed people.

Is brain damage always permanent?

- Plasticity refers to the brain's ability to change its structure and functions following damage and in response to changing environmental conditions.
- The brain shows the greatest plasticity in infancy and early childhood and can partially recover from some injuries.
- Recent studies have demonstrated that neurogenesis (the production of new neurons) occurs in adult brains.

- Neuroscientists are working on various ways to use brain plasticity and neurogenesis to repair damaged brains.

PSYCHOLOGY ON THE NET

- **Brain Briefings** Articles on a variety of topics in neuroscience. http://www.sfn.org/briefings/
- **Probe the Brain** Explore the motor homunculus of the brain interactively. http://www.pbs.org/wgbh/aso/tryit/brain/
- **The Human Brain: Dissections of the Real Brain** Detailed photographs and drawings of the human brain. http://www.vh.org/Providers/Textbooks/BrainAnatomy/BrainAnatomy.html

● • **InfoTrac® College Edition** For recent articles related to brain mapping, use Key Words search for MAGNETIC RESONANCE IMAGING and ELECTROENCEPHALOGRAPHY.

INTERACTIVE LEARNING

- **PsychNow!** 2a. Neurons and synaptic transmission. 2b. Brain and behavior.
- **Psyk.trek** 2a. The neuron and the neural impulse. 2b. Synaptic transmission. 2c. Looking inside the brain. 2d. The hindbrain and the midbrain. 2e. The forebrain: Subcortical structures. 2f. The cerebral cortex. 2g. Right brain/left brain.

CHAPTER 4

Child Development

Chapter Survey

Theme: *The principles of development help us better understand not only children but our own behavior as well.*

ALIEN MINDS

STUDYING CHILD DEVELOPMENT *helps answer the question, How did I become the person I am today? This makes children fascinating, but there is another reason for interest: A child's understanding of the world can be delightfully different from yours and mine. Entering a child's awareness can be as intriguing as meeting a person from another culture—or another planet! In short, children are extremely interesting creatures. A tremendous amount of psychological research has focused on them.*

What branch of psychology studies children? *Children lie at the heart of* **developmental psychology** *(the study of progressive changes in behavior and abilities). However, you should be aware that human development reaches beyond childhood to include every stage of life from conception to death (or "the womb to the tomb").*

An entire lifetime of development includes so many topics that some appear in other chapters. In this chapter, we will discuss important events in early childhood. The next chapter provides an overview of an entire life span. It also spotlights interesting problems and challenges that occur at various points in life.

Human development is a story of growth and transformation. Perhaps learning about development will contribute to your own development. Find out by reading more!

Gateways to Child Development

YOU ARE A PRODUCT of both your genetic heritage and the environments in which you have lived.

INFANT DEVELOPMENT is strongly influenced by heredity. However, environmental factors such as nutrition, parenting, and learning are also important.

FORMING AN EMOTIONAL BOND with a caregiver is a crucial event during infancy.

LEARNING TO USE LANGUAGE is a cornerstone of early intellectual development.

PIAGET'S STAGE THEORY provides a valuable map of how thinking abilities unfold.

VYGOTSKY'S THEORY reminds us that a child's mind is shaped by human relationships.

ALL AREAS OF DEVELOPMENT are affected by deprivation and enrichment.

EFFECTIVE CHILD DISCIPLINE is consistent, humane, encouraging, and based on respectful communication.

GENETIC RESEARCH is making it possible to control some hereditary aspects of human reproduction, development, and behavior.

HEREDITY AND ENVIRONMENT—THE NURTURE OF NATURE

Olivia has just given birth to her first child, Amy. As Olivia and her husband, Tom, look at Amy, they wonder, "How will her life unfold? What kind of a person will she be?" The answers will depend on the combined effects of heredity and environment.

Some events in a person's life, such as achieving sexual maturity, are mostly governed by heredity. Others, such as learning to swim or use a computer, are primarily a matter of environment. But which is more important, heredity or environment? Let's consider some arguments on both sides of the nature-nurture debate.

Heredity

Heredity ("nature") refers to the genetic transmission of physical and psychological characteristics from parents to their children. An incredible number of personal features are set at **conception**, when a sperm and an ovum (egg) unite.

How does heredity operate? The nucleus of every human cell contains 46 **chromosomes**. (The word *chromosome* means "colored body.") These thread-like structures hold the coded instructions of heredity (❖Fig. 4.1). A notable exception is

sperm cells and ova, which contain only 23 chromosomes. Thus, Amy received 23 chromosomes from Olivia and 23 from Tom. This is her genetic heritage. Chromosomes are made up of **DNA**, deoxyribonucleic acid (dee-OX-see-RYE-bo-new-KLEE-ik). DNA is a long, ladder-like chain of chemical molecules (❖Fig. 4.2). The order of these molecules, or organic bases, acts as a code for genetic information.

The DNA in each cell contains 3 billion base pairs. That's enough to record all the instructions needed to make a human—with room left over to spare. Amazingly, the DNA of everyone who has ever lived is 99.9 percent the same. Geneti-

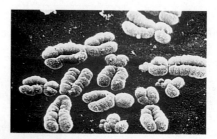

❖ **FIGURE 4.1** *This image, made with a scanning electron microscope, shows several pairs of human chromosomes. (Colors are artificial.)*

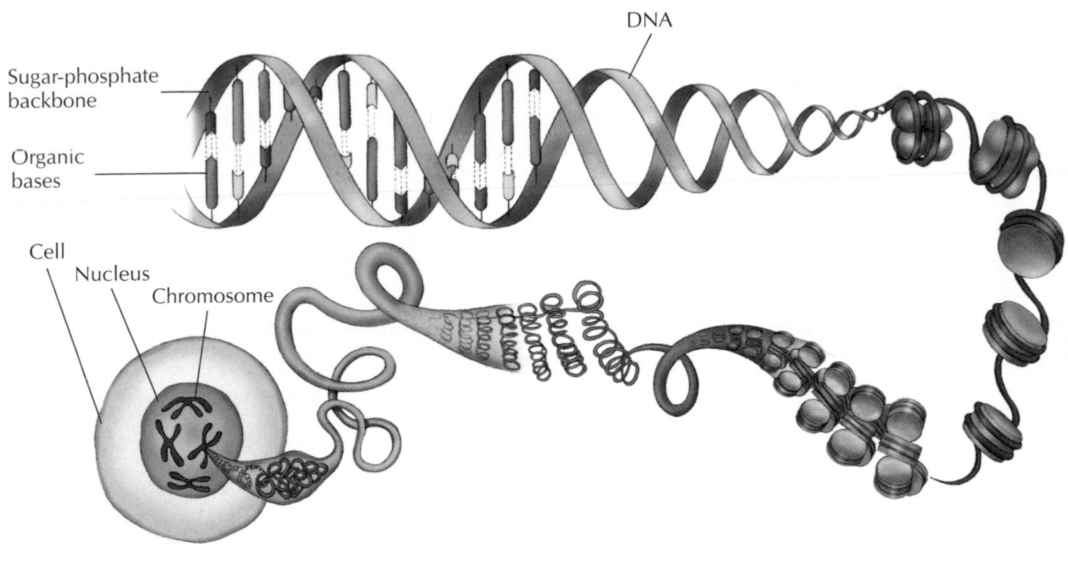

Sugar-phosphate backbone

Organic bases

DNA

Cell
Nucleus
Chromosome

❖ **FIGURE 4.2** (Top left) *Linked molecules (organic bases) make up the "rungs" on DNA's twisted "molecular ladder." The order of these molecules serves as a code for genetic information. The code provides a genetic blueprint that is unique for each individual (except identical twins). The drawing shows only a small section of a DNA strand. An entire strand of DNA is composed of billions of smaller molecules. (Bottom left) The nucleus of each cell in the body contains chromosomes made up of tightly wound coils of DNA. (Don't be misled by the drawing: Chromosomes are microscopic in size and the chemical molecules that make up DNA are even smaller.)*

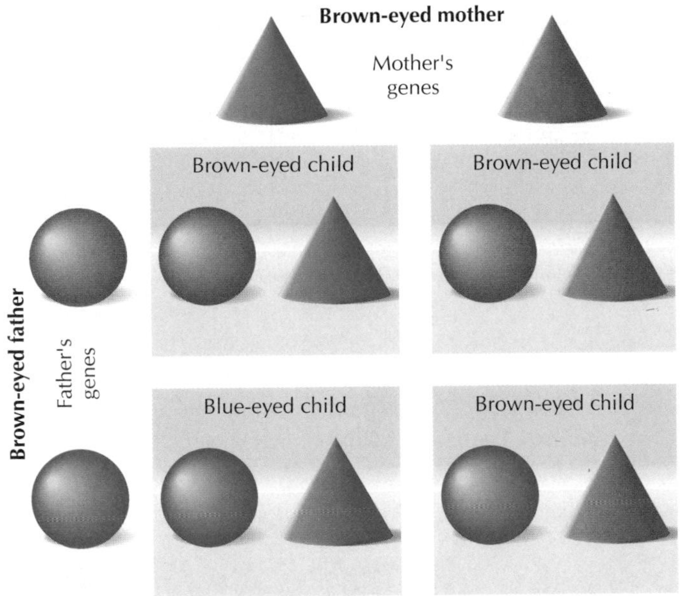

Brown-eyed mother

Mother's genes

Brown-eyed father

Father's genes

Brown-eyed child

Brown-eyed child

Blue-eyed child

Brown-eyed child

❖ **FIGURE 4.3** *Gene patterns for children of brown-eyed parents, where each parent has one brown-eye gene and one blue-eye gene. Because the brown-eye gene is dominant, one child in four will be blue-eyed. Thus, there is a significant chance that two brown-eyed parents will have a blue-eyed child.*

ited feature, such as Amy's eye color. Most characteristics, however, are **polygenic** (pol-ih-JEN-ik), or controlled by many genes working in combination.

Genes may be dominant or recessive. When a gene is **dominant**, the feature it controls will appear every time the gene is present. When a gene is **recessive**, it must be paired with a second recessive gene before its effect will be expressed. For example, if Amy got a blue-eye gene from Tom and a brown-eye gene from Olivia, Amy will be brown-eyed, because brown-eye genes are dominant.

If brown-eye genes are dominant, why do two brown-eyed parents sometimes have a blue-eyed child? If each parent has two brown-eye genes, the couple's children can only be brown-eyed. But what if each parent has one brown-eye gene and one blue-eye gene? In that case, the parents would both have brown eyes. Yet, there is 1 chance in 4 that their children will get two blue-eye genes and have blue eyes (❖Fig. 4.3).

cally, the difference between you and Michael Jordan, Albert Einstein, Rosa Parks, Princess Diana, or Charles Manson is based on only about one of every 1,000 base pairs. However, the crucial pairs can occur in endless combinations, which explains the rich diversity of humanity (Hamer & Copeland, 1998).

Genes are small areas of the DNA code. Each of the 100,000 genes in your cells affects a particular process or personal characteristic. Sometimes, a single gene is responsible for an inher-

Developmental psychology *The study of progressive changes in behavior and abilities from conception to death.*
Heredity ("nature") *The transmission of physical and psychological characteristics from parents to offspring through genes.*
Conception *The union of an ovum and a sperm cell.*
Chromosomes *Thread-like "colored bodies" in the nucleus of each cell that are made up of DNA.*
DNA *Deoxyribonucleic acid, a molecular structure that contains coded genetic information.*
Genes *Specific areas on a strand of DNA that carry hereditary information.*
Polygenic characteristics *Personal traits or physical properties that are influenced by many genes working in combination.*
Dominant gene *A gene whose influence will be expressed each time the gene is present.*
Recessive gene *A gene whose influence will be expressed only when it is paired with a second recessive gene.*

Genetic Programming

Heredity influences events from conception to **senescence** (seh-NESS-ens: aging) and death (see ◆Table 4.1). That's why the **human growth sequence**, or overall pattern of physical development, is universal. Heredity also determines eye color, skin color, and susceptibility to some diseases. To a degree, genetic instructions affect body size and shape, height, intelligence, athletic potential, personality traits, sexual orientation, and a host of other details (Hamer & Copeland, 1998). Score 1 for those who favor heredity as the more important factor in development!

◆**TABLE 4.1** Human Growth Sequence

PERIOD	DURATION	DESCRIPTIVE NAME
Prenatal period	From conception to birth	
Germinal period	First 2 weeks after conception	Zygote
Embryonic period	2–8 weeks after conception	Embryo
Fetal period	From 8 weeks after conception to birth	Fetus
Neonatal period	From birth to a few weeks after birth	Neonate
Infancy	From a few weeks after birth until child is walking securely; some children walk securely at less than a year, while others may not be able to until age 17–18 months	Infant
Early childhood	From about 15–18 months until about 2–2½ years	Toddler
	From age 2–3 to about age 6	Preschool child
Middle childhood	From about age 6 to age 12	School-age child
Pubescence	Period of about 2 years before puberty	
Puberty	Point of development at which biological changes of pubescence reach a climax marked by sexual maturity	
Adolescence	From the beginning of pubescence until full social maturity is reached (difficult to fix duration of this period)	Adolescent
Adulthood	From adolescence to death; sometimes subdivided into other periods as shown at left	Adult
Young adulthood (19–25)		
Adulthood (26–40)		
Maturity (41 plus)		
Senescence	No defined limit that would apply to all people; extremely variable; characterized by marked physiological and psychological deterioration	Adult (senile), "old age"

*Note: There is no exact beginning or ending point for various growth periods. The ages are approximate, and each period may be thought of as blending into the next. (Table courtesy of Tom Bond.)

Identical twins. Twins who share identical genes (identical twins) demonstrate the powerful influence of heredity. Even when they are reared apart, identical twins are strikingly alike in motor skills, physical development, and appearance. At the same time, twins are less alike as adults than they were as children, which shows environmental influences are at work (McCartney, Bernieri, & Harris, 1990).

TEMPERAMENT *How soon do hereditary differences appear?* Some appear right away. For instance, newborn babies differ noticeably in **temperament**. This is the physical core of personality. It includes sensitivity, irritability, distractibility, and typical mood (Braungart et al., 1992). About 40 percent of all newborns are **easy children**, who are relaxed and agreeable. Ten percent are **difficult children**, who are moody, intense, and easily angered. **Slow-to-warm-up children** (about 15 percent) are restrained, unexpressive, or shy. The remaining children do not fit neatly into a single category (Chess & Thomas, 1986). (Perhaps we should call them "generic" children?)

Imagine that we start with two groups of infants, some who are temperamentally very shy and some very bold. By the time they are 4 to 5 years old, most of these children will be only moderately shy or bold. This suggests that inherited temperaments are modified by learning (Kagan, 1999). In other words, nurture immediately enters the picture.

Environment

Environment ("nurture") refers to the sum of all external conditions that affect a person. The environments in which a child grows up can have a powerful impact on development. Humans today are genetically very similar to cave dwellers who lived 30,000 years ago. Nevertheless, a bright baby born today could learn to become almost anything—a ballet dancer, an engineer, a gangsta rapper, or a biochemist who likes to paint in watercolors. But an Upper Paleolithic baby could have become only a hunter or food gatherer. Score 1 for the environmentalists!

Early experiences can have very lasting effects. For example, children who are abused may suffer lifelong emotional problems (Rutter, 1995). At the same time, extra care can sometimes reverse the effects of a poor start in life (Bornstein, 1995). In short, environmental forces guide human development, for better or worse, throughout life.

CRITICAL PERIODS *Why do some experiences have more lasting effects than others?* Part of the answer lies in the concept of **critical periods**. These are times of increased sensitivity to environmental influences. Events that occur during a critical period can permanently alter the course of development (Bornstein, 1989). For instance, if a woman has German measles during early pregnancy, her child may be born with heart defects, cataracts, or hearing loss. Later in pregnancy, the child would escape without damage.

Often, certain events must occur during a critical period for a person to develop normally. As we will see later, for instance, forming a loving bond with a caregiver early in life seems to be crucial for optimal development.

Prenatal Influences

The impact of nurture actually starts before birth. Although the **intrauterine environment** (interior of the womb) is highly

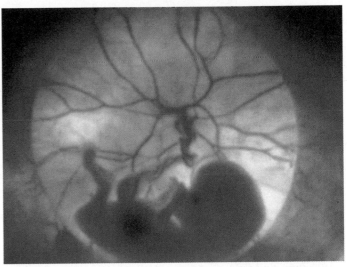

Because of the rapid growth of basic structures, the developing fetus is sensitive to a variety of diseases, drugs, and sources of radiation. This is especially true during the first trimester (3 months) of gestation (pregnancy).

protected, environmental conditions can affect the developing child. For example, fetal heart rate and movements increase when sounds or vibrations penetrate the womb (Kisilevsky & Low, 1998).

If a mother's health or nutrition is poor, if she contracts diseases such as German measles, syphilis, or HIV, uses drugs, or is exposed to X-rays or atomic radiation, the fetus may be harmed. The result is a **congenital problem** or "birth defect." These problems affect the developing fetus and become apparent at birth. In contrast, **genetic problems** are inherited from parents who carry defective genes. (See "A Step Beyond" at the end of this chapter for more information.)

BRIDGES

Child abuse is a serious problem, but steps can be taken to prevent it.

See Chapter 5, pages 136–137, for more information.

Senescence *Aging; the latter years of life.*
Human growth sequence *The pattern of physical development from conception to death.*
Temperament *The physical foundation of personality, including emotional and perceptual sensitivity, energy levels, typical mood, and so forth.*
Easy child *A child who is temperamentally relaxed and agreeable.*
Difficult child *A child who is temperamentally moody, intense, and easily angered.*
Slow-to-warm-up child *A child who is temperamentally restrained and unexpressive.*
Environment ("nurture") *The sum of all external conditions affecting development, including especially the effects of learning.*
Critical period *During development, a period of increased sensitivity to environmental influences. Also, a time during which certain events must take place for normal development to occur.*
Intrauterine environment *The physical and chemical environment within the uterus during prenatal development.*
Congenital problem *Problem or defect that originates during prenatal development in the womb.*
Genetic problem *Problem caused by defects in the genes or by inherited characteristics.*

How is it possible for the embryo or the fetus to be harmed?
No direct intermixing of blood takes place between a mother and her unborn child. Yet some substances—especially drugs—do reach the fetus. If the mother is addicted to morphine, heroin, or methadone, the baby may be born with an addiction.

TERATOGENS   Anything capable of causing birth defects is called a **teratogen** (teh-RAT-uh-jen). Sometimes women are exposed to powerful teratogens, such as radiation, lead, pesticides, or PCBs, without knowing it (Eliot, 1999). But pregnant women do have direct control over many teratogens. For example, a woman who takes cocaine runs a serious risk of injuring her fetus. Cocaine-exposed children tend to have deficits in language, attention, memory, sensorimotor abilities, and self-control. Many will never be completely normal (Arendt et al., 1998; Espy, Kaufmann, & Glisky, 1999; Singer et al., 1999; Swanson et al., 1999).

Most common prescription drugs also reach the fetus. Damage can be done by general anesthetics, cortisone, tetracycline, excessive amounts of vitamins A, D, B_6, and K, some barbiturates, opiates, tranquilizers, steroids, and synthetic sex hormones (Rosenblith, 1992). Even aspirin, a seemingly safe drug, has been linked with lowered infant IQs when taken during pregnancy (Streissguth et al., 1987). In short, when a pregnant woman takes drugs, her unborn child does, too.

What about alcohol and tobacco?   Repeated heavy drinking during pregnancy causes **fetal alcohol syndrome (FAS)**. Affected infants have low birth weight, a small head, bodily defects, and facial malformations. Many are also mentally retarded. Later, FAS children suffer from emotional, behavioral, and mental handicaps (Mattson et al., 1998; Steinhausen & Spohr, 1998).

Some of the typical features of children suffering from fetal alcohol syndrome include a small nonsymmetrical head, a short nose, a flattened area between the eyes, oddly shaped eyes, and a thin upper lip. Many of these features become less noticeable by adolescence. However, mental retardation and other problems commonly follow the FAS child into adulthood. The child shown here represents a moderate example of FAS.

During pregnancy, frequent drinking of even small amounts of alcohol, or a single "binge" of five or more drinks, can cause fetal brain damage. Considering the risks, the best advice for pregnant women is to entirely avoid drinking alcohol. The tragedy of FAS is that it is completely preventable (Short & Hess, 1995).

Tobacco is also harmful. A pregnant woman who smokes two packs of cigarettes a day blocks off about 25 percent of the oxygen supply to the fetus. Heavy smokers risk miscarrying or having premature, underweight babies (Slotkin, 1998). The infant death rate is 27 percent higher if a woman smokes during pregnancy. Children of smoking mothers score lower on tests of language and mental ability (Fried et al., 1992). Clearly, pregnancy is a compelling reason for not smoking. An unborn child's future can literally go "up in smoke."

Nature-Nurture Interactions

As we pass through life, we must learn countless bits of information: how to eat with a fork, the names of animals, proper etiquette at a wedding, how to reboot a computer. This knowledge reflects billions of connections in the brain. No conceivable amount of genetic programming could make all the right connections. With this fact in mind, the outcome of the nature-nurture debate is clear: Heredity and environment are equally important. Heredity gives us a variety of potentials, and it imposes various limitations. These, in turn, are affected by environmental events, such as learning, nutrition, disease, and culture. Each of us is the product of a constant *interaction*, or interplay, between the forces of nature and nurture (Gopnik, Meltzoff, & Kuhl, 1999).

Because of differences in temperament, some babies are more likely than others to smile, cry, vocalize, reach out, or pay attention. This means that babies rapidly become active participants in their own development. Growing infants alter their parents' behavior at the same time they are changed by it. For example, Amy is an easy baby who smiles frequently and is easily fed. This encourages Olivia to touch, feed, and sing to Amy. Olivia's affection rewards Amy, causing her to smile more. Soon, a dynamic relationship blossoms between mother and child.

A person's **developmental level** is his or her current state of physical, emotional, and intellectual development. To summarize, three factors combine to determine your developmental level at any stage of life. These are *heredity, environment,* and your *own behavior,* each tightly interwoven with the others.

K N O W L E D G E   B U I L D E R
HEREDITY AND ENVIRONMENT

RELATE

Do you think that heredity or environment best explains who you are today? Can you think of clear examples of the ways in which heredity and environmental forces have affected your development?

What kind of temperament did you have as an infant? How did it affect your relationship with your parents or caregivers?

What advice would you give a friend who has just become pregnant? Be sure to consider the prenatal environment and critical periods.

Newborn babies display a special interest in the human face. A preference for seeing the mother's face develops rapidly and encourages social interactions between mother and baby.

THE NEWBORN BABY—THE BASIC MODEL COMES WITH OPTIONS

At birth, the human **neonate** (NEE-oh-NATE: newborn infant) must depend on others and will die if not given care. Newborn babies cannot lift their heads, turn over, or feed themselves. Does this mean they are inert and unfeeling? Definitely not! Neonates like Amy can see, hear, smell, taste, and respond to pain and touch. Although their senses are less acute, babies are immediately responsive. Amy will follow a moving object with her eyes and will turn in the direction of sounds.

INFANT REFLEXES   Neonates also have a number of adaptive reflexes. To elicit the **grasping reflex**, press an object in the neonate's palm, and she will grasp it with surprising strength. Many infants, in fact, can hang from a raised bar, like little trapeze artists. The grasping reflex aids survival by helping infants avoid falling. You can observe the **rooting reflex** (reflexive head turning and nursing) by touching Amy's cheek. Immediately, she will turn toward your finger, as if searching for something.

How is such turning adaptive?   The rooting reflex helps infants find a bottle or a breast. Then, when a nipple touches the infant's mouth, the **sucking reflex** (rhythmic nursing) helps her obtain needed food. Like other reflexes, this is a genetically programmed action (Koepke & Bigelow, 1997). But at the same time, food rewards nursing. As a result, nursing rapidly increases in vigor during the first days after birth. Again, we see how nature-nurture interactions alter a baby's behavior.

Teratogen *Radiation, a drug, or other substance capable of altering fetal development in ways that cause birth defects.*
Fetal alcohol syndrome (FAS) *A pattern of birth complications and bodily defects in infants caused by excessive consumption of alcohol by the mother during pregnancy.*
Developmental level *An individual's current state of physical, emotional, and intellectual development.*
Neonate *A term used for newborn infants during the first weeks following birth.*
Grasping reflex *A neonatal reflex consisting of grasping objects placed in the palms.*
Rooting reflex *Neonatal reflex elicited by a light touch to the cheek, causing the infant to turn toward the object and attempt to nurse.*
Sucking reflex *Neonatal reflex elicited by touching the mouth, whereupon the infant makes rhythmic sucking movements.*

The **Moro reflex** is also interesting. If Amy's position is changed abruptly or if she is startled by a loud noise, she will make movements similar to an embrace. This reaction has been compared to the movements baby monkeys use to cling to their mothers. (It is left to the reader's imagination to decide if there is any connection.)

The World of the Neonate

Thirty years ago, many people thought of newborn babies as mere bundles of reflexes, like the ones just described. But infants can respond in ways that are subtler than once imagined. For example, Andrew Meltzoff and Keith Moore (1983) found that babies are born mimics. ❖Figure 4.4 shows Meltzoff as he sticks out his tongue, opens his mouth, and purses his lips at a 20-day-old girl. Will she imitate him? Videotapes of babies confirm that they imitate adult facial gestures. As early as 9 months of age, infants can imitate actions a full day after seeing them (Heimann & Meltzoff, 1996). Such mimicry is obviously an aid to rapid learning in infancy.

How much intelligence does a newborn have? Babies are smarter than many people think. From the earliest days of life, babies seem to be trying to learn how the world works. They immediately begin to look, touch, taste, and otherwise explore their surroundings. From an evolutionary perspective, a baby's mind is designed to soak up information, which it does at an amazing pace (Gopnik, Meltzoff, & Kuhl, 1999).

In the first weeks and months of life, babies are increasingly able to think, learn from what they see, make predictions, and search for explanations. For example, psychologist Jerome Bruner (1983) observed that 3- to 8-week-old babies seem to understand that a person's voice and body should be con-

nected. If a baby hears his mother's voice coming from where she is standing, the baby will remain calm. If her voice comes from a loudspeaker several feet away, the baby will become agitated and begin to cry.

Another look into the private world of infants can be drawn from testing their vision. However, such testing is a challenge because infants cannot talk.

How is it possible to test a baby's vision? Robert Fantz invented a device called a **looking chamber** to find out what infants can see and what holds their attention (❖Fig. 4.5a). Imagine that Amy is placed on her back inside the chamber, facing a lighted area above. Next, two objects are placed in the chamber. By observing the movements of Amy's eyes and the images they reflect, we can tell what she is looking at. Such tests show that adult vision is about 30 times sharper, but babies can see large patterns, shapes, and edges.

Fantz found that 3-day-old babies prefer complex patterns, such as checkerboards and bull's-eyes, to simpler colored rectangles. Other researchers have learned that infants are excited by circles, curves, and bright lights (❖Fig. 4.5b) (Brown, 1990). Immediately after birth, babies are aware of changes in the position of objects (Slater et al., 1991). Before they are 6 months old, babies can recognize categories of objects that differ in shape or color. By 9 months of age, they can tell the difference between dogs and birds or other groups of animals (Mandler & McDonough, 1998). Infants also appear to be aware of differences in the number of objects they see, such as being able to tell that three dots is different from two dots (Eliot, 1999). So, there really is a person inside that little body!

Neonates can most clearly see objects about a foot away from them. It is as if they are best prepared to see the people who love and care for them (Gopnik, Meltzoff, & Kuhl, 1999).

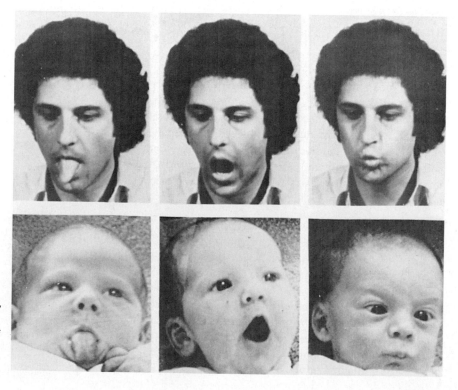

❖ **FIGURE 4.4** *Infant imitation. In the top row of photos, Andrew Meltzoff makes facial gestures at an infant. The bottom row records the infant's responses. Videotapes of Meltzoff and of tested infants helped ensure objectivity. (Photos courtesy of Andrew N. Meltzoff.)*

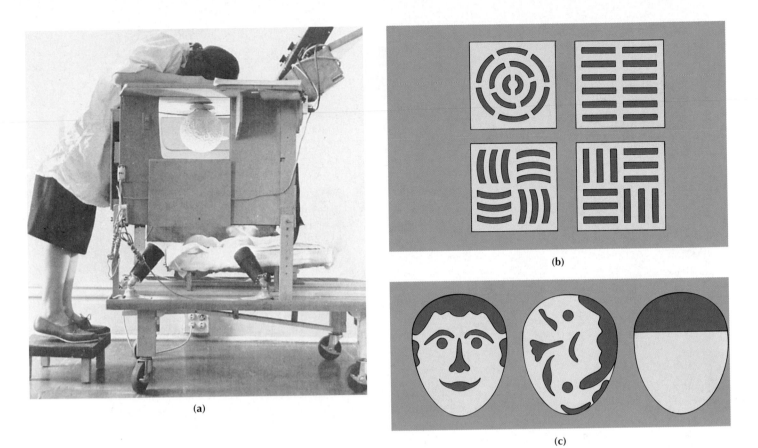

(a)

(b)

(c)

❖ **FIGURE 4.5** (a) *Eye movements and fixation points of infants are observed in Fantz's "looking chamber."* (b) *Thirteen-week-old infants prefer concentric and curved patterns like those on the left to nonconcentric and straight-line patterns like those on the right.* (c) *Infants tested in a looking chamber look at the normal face longer than at the scrambled face and at both faces longer than at the design on the right. (Photo courtesy of David Linton. Drawing from "The Origin of Form Perception" by Robert L. Fantz, Copyright © 1961 by Scientific American, Inc. All rights reserved.)*

Perhaps that's why babies have a special fascination with human faces. Just *hours* after birth, a baby begins to prefer seeing his or her mother's face, rather than a stranger's (Walton, Bower, & Bower, 1992).

In a looking chamber, most infants will spend more time looking at a human face pattern than a scrambled face or a colored oval (❖Fig. 4.5c). When real human faces are used, infants prefer familiar faces to unfamiliar faces. However, this preference reverses at about age 2. At that time, unusual objects begin to interest the child. For instance, Jerome Kagan (1971) showed face masks to 2-year-olds. Kagan found that the toddlers were fascinated by a face with eyes on the chin and a nose in the middle of the forehead. He believes the babies' interest came from a need to understand why the scrambled face differed from what they had come to expect. Such behavior is further evidence that babies actively try to make sense of their surroundings (Gopnik, Meltzoff, & Kuhl, 1999).

Maturation

The emergence of many basic abilities is closely tied to **maturation** (physical growth and development of the body, brain, and nervous system). Maturation will be especially evident as Amy learns motor skills, such as crawling and walking. Of course, the *rate* of maturation varies from child to child. Nevertheless, the

order of maturation is almost universal. For instance, the strength and coordination Amy will need to sit without support will appear before she has matured enough to crawl. Therefore, infants around the world typically sit before they crawl, crawl before they stand, and stand before they walk (❖Fig. 4.6).

What about my weird cousin Emo, who never crawled? Like cousin Emo, a few children substitute rolling, creeping, or shuffling for crawling. A very few move directly from sitting to standing and walking (Robson, 1984). Even so, an orderly sequence of motor development remains evident. In general, increased muscular control spreads in a pattern that is **cephalocaudal** (SEF-eh-lo-KOD-ul: from head to toe) and **proximodistal** (PROK-seh-moe-DIS-tul: from the center of

Moro reflex *Neonatal reflex evoked by sudden loss of support or the sounding of a loud noise; in response, the arms are extended and then brought toward each other.*
Looking chamber *An experimental apparatus used to test infant perception by presenting visual stimuli and observing infant responses.*
Maturation *The physical growth and development of the body and nervous system.*
Cephalocaudal *From head to toe.*
Proximodistal *From the center of the body to the extremities.*

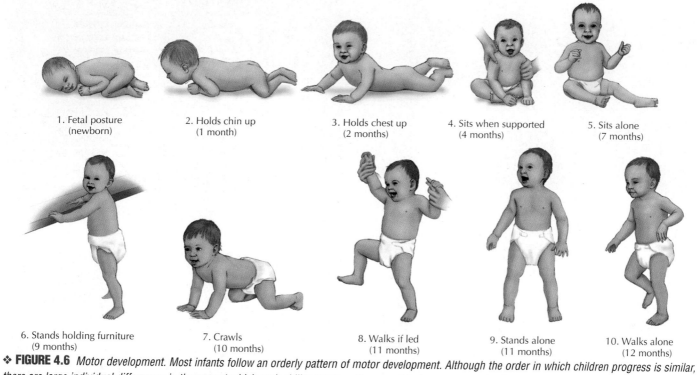

1. Fetal posture (newborn)
2. Holds chin up (1 month)
3. Holds chest up (2 months)
4. Sits when supported (4 months)
5. Sits alone (7 months)
6. Stands holding furniture (9 months)
7. Crawls (10 months)
8. Walks if led (11 months)
9. Stands alone (11 months)
10. Walks alone (12 months)

❖ **FIGURE 4.6** *Motor development. Most infants follow an orderly pattern of motor development. Although the order in which children progress is similar, there are large individual differences in the ages at which each ability appears. The ages listed are averages for American children. It is not unusual for many of the skills to appear 1 or 2 months earlier than average or several months later (Frankenberg & Dodds, 1967; Harris & Liebert, 1991). Parents should not be alarmed if a child's behavior differs some from the average.*

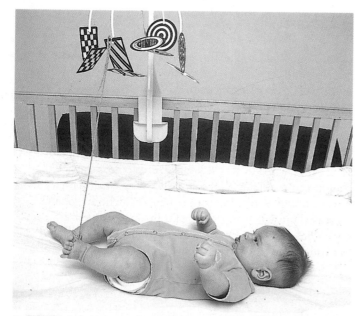

❖ **FIGURE 4.7** *Psychologist Carolyn Rovee-Collier has shown that babies as young as 3 months old can learn to control their movements. In her experiments, babies lie on their backs under a colorful crib mobile. A ribbon is tied around the baby's ankle and connected to the mobile. Whenever babies spontaneously kick their legs, the mobile jiggles and rattles. Within a few minutes, infants learn to kick faster. Their reward for kicking is a chance to see the mobile move (Hayne & Rovee-Collier, 1995).*

the body to the extremities). Even if cousin Emo flunked Elementary Crawling, his motor development followed the standard top-down, center-outward pattern.

Motor Development

Although maturation has a big impact, motor skills don't simply "emerge." Amy must learn to control her actions. Babies who are trying to crawl or walk actively explore new movements and select those that work. Amy's first efforts may be approximate—a wobbly crawl or some shaky first steps. However, with practice, babies "tune" their movements to be smoother and more effective. Such learning is evident from the very first months of life (Adolph, 1997; Thelen, 1995). (See ❖Fig. 4.7.)

READINESS   At what ages will Amy be ready to feed herself, walk alone, or say goodbye to diapers? Such milestones tend to be governed by a child's **readiness** for rapid learning. That is, minimum levels of maturation must occur before some skills can be learned. It is impossible, for instance, to teach children to walk or use a toilet before they have matured enough to control their bodies. Parents are asking for failure when they try to force a child to learn skills too early. Doing so just frustrates children (Luxem & Christophersen, 1994).

Then are there definite ages at which children become ready to learn particular skills? No. Readiness usually emerges over a

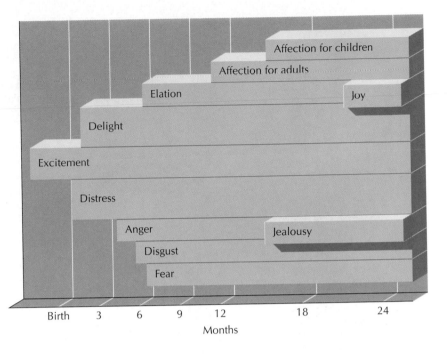

❖ **FIGURE 4.8** *The traditional view of infancy holds that emotions are rapidly differentiated from an initial capacity for excitement. (After K. M. B. Bridges, 1932. Reprinted by permission of the Society for Research in Child Development, Inc.)*

period of weeks or months. Training that begins much too soon will fail; training that begins a little early will proceed slowly; and training when a child is maturationally ready will produce rapid learning.

Much needless grief can be avoided by respecting a child's personal rate of growth. Consider the eager parents who toilet trained an 18-month-old child in 10 trying weeks of false alarms and "accidents." If they had waited until the child was 24 months old, they might have succeeded in just 3 weeks. Parents may control when toilet training starts, but maturation tends to dictate when it will be completed (Luxem & Christophersen, 1994). Around 30 months is average for completion. So why fight nature? (The wet look is in.)

Emotional Development

Early emotional development also follows a pattern closely tied to maturation. Even the **basic emotions** of *anger, fear,* and *joy*—which appear to be unlearned—take time to develop. General **excitement** is the only emotion newborn infants clearly express. However, as Tom and Olivia can tell you, a baby's emotional life blossoms rapidly. One researcher (Bridges, 1932) observed that all the basic human emotions appear before age 2. Bridges found that emotions appear in a consistent order and that the first basic split is between pleasant and unpleasant emotions (❖Fig. 4.8).

Many experts continue to believe that emotions unfold slowly, as the nervous system matures (Camras, Sullivan, & Michel, 1993; Matias & Cohen, 1993). However, psychologist Carroll Izard thinks that infants can express several basic emotions as early as 10 weeks of age. When Izard looks carefully at the faces of babies, he sees abundant signs of emotion. (See ❖Fig. 4.9.) The most common infant expression, he found, is

not excitement, but *interest*—followed by *joy, anger,* and *sadness* (Izard et al., 1995).

If Izard is right, then emotions are "hard-wired" by heredity and related to evolution. Perhaps that's why smiling is one of a baby's most common reactions. Smiling probably helps babies survive by inviting parents to care for them (Izard et al., 1995).

At first, a baby's smiling is haphazard. By the age of 10 months, however, infants smile more frequently when another person is nearby (Jones, Collins, & Hong, 1991). This **social smile** is especially rewarding to parents. On the other hand, when new parents see and hear a crying baby, they feel annoyed, irritated, disturbed, or unhappy. Babies the world over, it seems, rapidly become capable of letting others know what they like and dislike. (Prove this to yourself sometime by driving a baby buggy.)

Human infants are transformed from helpless babies to independent persons with dazzling speed. Early growth is extremely rapid. By her third year, Amy will have a unique personality, and she will be able to stand, walk, talk, and explore. At no other time after birth does development proceed more rapidly. During the same period, Amy's relationships with other people will expand as well. Before we explore that topic, here's a chance to rehearse what you've learned.

Readiness *A condition that exists when maturation has advanced enough to allow the rapid acquisition of a particular skill.*
Basic emotions *The first distinct emotions to emerge in infancy.*
Excitement *General emotional arousal.*
Social smile *Smiling elicited by social stimuli, such as seeing a parent's face.*

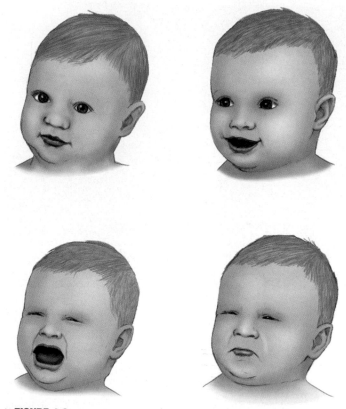

❖ **FIGURE 4.9** *Infants display many of the same emotional expressions as adults do. Carroll Izard believes such expressions show that distinct emotions appear within the first months of life. Other theorists argue that specific emotions come into focus more gradually, as an infant's nervous system matures. Either way, parents can expect to see a full range of basic emotions by the end of a baby's first year. Over the first 2 years, children become increasingly active in initiating emotional exchanges with parents (Grolnick, Cosgrove, & Bridges, 1996).*

KNOWLEDGE BUILDER
THE NEONATE AND MATURATION

RELATE

What infant reflexes have you observed? How would maturation affect the chances of teaching an infant to eat with a spoon? Can you give an example of how heredity and environment interact during motor development?

To know what a baby is feeling, would it be more helpful to be able to detect delight and distress (Bridges) or joy, anger, and sadness (Izard)?

LEARNING CHECK

1. An infant who is startled will make movements similar to an embrace. This is known as the
   a. grasping reflex *b.* rooting reflex *c.* Moro reflex *d.* adaptive reflex

2. During infancy, a capacity for imitating others first becomes evident at about 9 months of age. T or F?

3. After age 2, infants tested in a looking chamber show a marked preference for familiar faces and simpler designs. T or F?

4. The orderly sequence observed in the unfolding of many basic responses can be attributed to _____.

5. The principle of _____ states that minimum levels of physical maturation must precede the learning of certain skills.

6. General excitement or interest is the clearest emotional response present in newborn infants, but meaningful expressions of delight and distress appear soon after. T or F?

7. Neonates display a social smile as early as 10 days after birth. T or F?

CRITICAL THINKING

8. If you were going to test newborn infants to see if they prefer their own mothers' faces to a stranger's face, what precautions would you take?

Answers:

1. c 2. F 3. F 4. maturation 5. readiness 6. T 7. F 8. In one study of the preferences of newborns, the hair color and complexion of strangers was matched to that of the mothers. Also, only the mother's or stranger's face was visible during testing. And finally, a scent was used to mask olfactory (smell) cues so that an infant's preference could not be based on the mother's familiar odor (Bushnell, Sai, & Mullin, 1989).

SOCIAL DEVELOPMENT—BABY, I'M STUCK ON YOU

Like all humans, babies are social creatures. Let's explore the origins of infant social life. Early **social development** lays a foundation for relationships with parents, siblings, friends, and relatives. Two basic steps into the social world are gaining self-awareness and becoming aware of others.

SELF-AWARENESS   When you look in a mirror, you recognize the image staring back as your own—except, perhaps, early on Monday mornings. At what age did this sense of recognition first emerge? Like many such events, initial **self-awareness** depends on maturation of the nervous system.

How is self-awareness demonstrated in a baby?   In one test of self-recognition, infants are shown images of themselves on a TV. Most infants have to be 15 months old before they recognize themselves (Lewis & Brooks-Gunn, 1979).

SOCIAL AWARENESS   Once self-awareness develops, an infant's social relationships expand rapidly (Asendorpf, 1996; Kagan, 1991). At about the same time, infants become more aware of others. Have you noticed how adults sometimes glance at the facial expressions of others to decide how to respond to them? Babies also engage in **social referencing** (observing others to obtain information or guidance). For example, imagine that Amy is 14 months old and that Olivia is going to show her two boxes. Olivia looks inside the first box and makes a joyous facial ex-

A sense of self, or self-awareness, develops at about age 18 months. Before children develop self-awareness, they do not recognize their own image in a mirror. Typically, they think they are looking at another child. Some children hug the child in the mirror or go behind it looking for the child they see there (Lewis, 1995).

pression. (There must be something really good inside!) She then peers into the second box and appears to be disgusted. (Yuck, what is that?) Now its Amy's turn. If the boxes are pushed toward her, Amy will try to open the "joy box" but not the "disgust box" (Repacholi, 1998). Thus, early in their second year of life, infants are aware of the facial expressions of others and seek guidance from them—especially from their mothers (Hirshberg & Svejda, 1990; Stenberg & Hagekull, 1997).

The real core of social development is found in the emotional attachments that human babies form with their caregivers. Before we consider that topic, let's see what we can learn from some baby animals.

Imprinting

Konrad Lorenz (1903–1989) was a German **ethologist** who studied animal behavior. Lorenz was curious why baby geese follow their mothers. The obvious explanation seemed to be "It's instinctive," but Lorenz showed otherwise.

Mother Lorenz

Normally the first large moving object a baby goose sees is its mother. Lorenz hatched geese in an incubator, so the first moving object they saw was Lorenz. From then on, these baby geese followed Lorenz. They even reacted to his call as if he were their mother. (Lorenz, 1937)

As you can see, baby geese aren't born knowing that they should follow a mother goose. Instead, they are born with a tendency to follow large moving objects. Normally that would be their mother. But it need not be. Mother-goose following is acquired during a critical period by exposure to an adult goose (or whatever else happens to be around). The rapid and early learning of permanent behavior patterns of this type is called **imprinting**.

If newly hatched ducklings don't imprint on their mother (or some other object) within 30 hours, they never will (Hess,

"Mother" Lorenz leads his charges. The goslings have imprinted on Lorenz because he was the first moving object they saw after they hatched.

Social development *The development of self-awareness, attachment to parents or caregivers, and relationships with other children and adults.*
Self-awareness *Consciousness of oneself as a person.*
Social referencing *Observing others in social situations to obtain information or guidance.*
Ethologist *A person who studies the natural behavior patterns of animals.*
Imprinting *A rapid and relatively permanent type of learning that occurs during a limited time period early in life.*

1959). (Ducklings have been imprinted on decoys, rubber balls, wooden blocks, and other unlikely objects.) In many animals, imprinting has lifelong consequences (Lorenz, 1962).

Revenge of the Jackdaw

Imprinting normally serves to attach a young animal to its mother. It also guides the selection of a mate of the same species at sexual maturity. In another of Lorenz's experiments, a jackdaw (European starling) imprinted on him. When the bird reached sexual maturity, Lorenz became the target of its mating ritual. Part of this ritual involves stuffing worms into the mouth of the intended mate—as a surprised Lorenz learned while asleep on the lawn one day. When Lorenz refused its gift, the jackdaw stuffed a worm in Lorenz's ear. (Showing, perhaps, that it's not nice to fool Mother Nature!)

Attachment

Does imprinting occur in humans? True imprinting is limited to birds and a few other animals. However, human infants do form an **emotional attachment**, or close emotional bond, to their **primary caregivers**. There is a critical period (roughly the first year of life) during which this must occur for optimal development. Returning to Amy's story, we find that attach-

ment keeps her close to Olivia, who provides safety, stimulation, and a secure "home base" from which Amy can go exploring.

Mothers usually begin to cultivate a parent-child bond within hours of giving birth. For example, they touch their own infants more and hold them closer than they do other babies (Kaitz et al., 1995). A direct sign that an emotional bond has formed appears around 8 to 12 months of age. At that time, Amy will display **separation anxiety** (crying and signs of fear) when she is left alone or left with a stranger.

ATTACHMENT QUALITY   Psychologist Mary Ainsworth believes the quality of attachment is revealed by how babies act when their mothers return after a brief separation. Infants who are **securely attached** have a stable and positive emotional bond. They are upset by the mother's absence and seek to be near her when she returns. **Insecure-avoidant** infants have an anxious emotional bond. They tend to turn away from the mother when she returns. **Insecure-ambivalent** attachment is also an anxious emotional bond. In this case, babies are ambivalent: They both seek to be near the returning mother and angrily resist contact with her. Studies of several cultures suggest that these are universal patterns. However, the percentage of children falling into each category differs from culture to culture (Sagi, 1990). (See ❖Fig. 4.10.)

Attachment can have lasting effects. Infants who are securely attached at the age of 1 year show more resiliency, curiosity, problem-solving ability, and social competence in preschool (Collins & Gunnar, 1990). The key to secure attachment is a mother who is accepting and sensitive to her baby's signals and rhythms (Isabella, 1993; Susman-Stillman et al., 1996). Poor attachment occurs when a mother's actions are inappropriate, inadequate, intrusive, overstimulating, or rejecting. An example is the mother who tries to play with a drowsy infant or who ignores a baby who is looking at her and vocalizing (Isabella & Belsky, 1991).

What about attachment to fathers? Fathers of securely attached infants tend to be outgoing, agreeable, and happy in their marriage. In general, a warm family atmosphere tends to produce secure children (Belsky, 1996).

BRIDGES

Your first emotional attachments can establish patterns that influence adult love relationships many years later.

See Chapter 19, pages 646–647, for information on this connection.

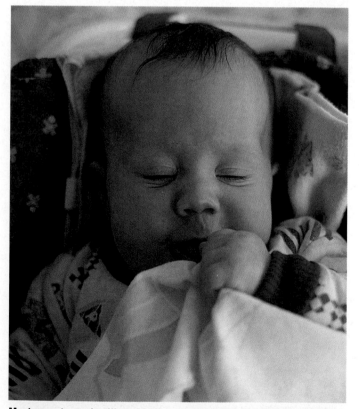

Most parents are familiar with the storm of crying that sometimes occurs when babies are left alone at bedtime. Bedtime distress can be a mild form of separation anxiety. As many parents know, it is often eased by the presence of "security objects," such as a stuffed animal or favorite blanket (Morelli et al., 1992).

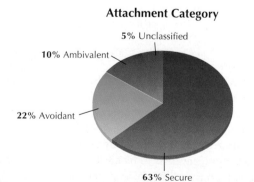

Attachment Category

5% Unclassified
10% Ambivalent
22% Avoidant
63% Secure

❖ **FIGURE 4.10** *In the United States, about two thirds of all children from middle-class families are securely attached. About one child in three is insecurely attached. (Percentages are approximate. From Kaplan, 1998.)*

A chance to play with other children is one of the benefits of day care. For instance, in one corner, a 2-year-old stacks colored blocks, pounds on them with a toy truck, and then chews on the truck. On the other side of the room, some 5-year-olds have built a "store" out of cardboard boxes. For the next half hour, one child is the "owner" and the others are "customers." With just 3 years' difference in age, we see a dramatic change in how children play.

Naturally, **play** is fun for children. However, it's also serious business. Children use play to explore the world and to practice skills—especially social skills. By the time children are 4 or 5, they will have progressed from **solitary play** (playing alone) to **cooperative play** (in which two or more children must coordinate their actions). Children engaged in cooperative play take parts or play roles, follow rules, and lead or follow others. Playing this way helps them learn to handle cooperation and competition, conflicts, power, role taking, and communication.

Cooperative play is a big step toward participating in social life. It's easy for adults to dismiss play as silly or trivial. In fact, play is one of the most important activities of childhood (Kaplan, 1998).

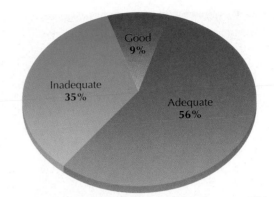

❖ **FIGURE 4.11** *This graph shows the results of a study of child care in homes other than the child's. In most cases, parents paid for this care, although many of the caregivers were unlicensed. As you can see, child care was "good" in only 9 percent of the homes. In 35 percent of the homes, it was rated as inadequate (Mehren, 1994).*

What effect does the arrival of a second child have on attachment? Attachment security often drops for a firstborn child when a second baby arrives. The former "star" of the family is temporarily demoted to second fiddle! Aware parents, therefore, make a special effort to involve their firstborn child in the excitement of the new arrival. They also give the firstborn extra attention and affection (Teti, 1996).

DAY CARE *Does commercial child care interfere with the quality of attachment?* A study done by the National Institute of Child Health and Human Development (1999) has finally answered some major questions about day care. Overall, high-quality day care does not adversely affect children's attachment to parents. This finding offers some reassurance to working parents, but the quality of day care remains extremely important. High-quality day care is related to better mother-child relationships and fewer child behavior problems. If a mother is not very sensitive to her child's needs at home, day care can promote more secure attachment. Children receiving high-quality day care also have better cognitive skills and language abilities (Peisner-Feinberg & Burchinal, in press).

Thus, high-quality day care can actually improve children's social and mental skills (Scarr, 1998). (See "Child's Play.") However, all of the positive effects just noted are *reversed* for low-quality day care (❖Fig. 4.11). Parents are wise to carefully evaluate and monitor the quality of day care their children are receiving (Barnet & Barnet, 1998).

What should parents look for when they evaluate the quality of child care? Low-quality day care *is* risky, and it *may* weaken

attachment. Parents seeking quality should insist on *at least* the following (Howes, 1997):

- A small number of children per caregiver
- Small overall group size (12–15)
- Trained caregivers
- Minimal staff turnover
- A stable day care experience

(Also, avoid any child-care center with the words *zoo, menagerie,* or *stockade* in its name.) Now let's return to some animal research to explore another dimension of attachment.

Motherless Monkeys

To investigate mother-infant relationships, Harry Harlow separated baby rhesus monkeys from their mothers at birth. The real mothers were replaced with **surrogate (substitute) mothers.** Some were made of cold, unyielding wire. Others were

Emotional attachment *An especially close emotional bond that infants form with their parents, caregivers, or others.*
Primary caregiver *A person primarily responsible for the care of an infant; usually the infant's mother or father.*
Separation anxiety *Distress displayed by infants when they are separated from their parents or principal caregivers.*
Secure attachment *A stable and positive emotional bond.*
Insecure-avoidant attachment *An anxious emotional bond marked by a tendency to avoid reunion with a parent or caregiver.*
Insecure-ambivalent attachment *An anxious emotional bond marked by both a desire to be with a parent or caregiver and some resistance to being reunited.*
Play *Any activity done for sheer enjoyment.*
Solitary play *Playing alone.*
Cooperative play *Play in which two or more children must coordinate their actions; if children don't cooperate, the game ends.*
Surrogate mother *A substitute mother (often an inanimate dummy in animal research).*

❖ **FIGURE 4.12** *An infant monkey clings to a cloth-covered surrogate mother. Baby monkeys become attached to the cloth "contact-comfort" mother but not to a similar wire mother. This is true even when the wire mother provides food. Contact comfort may also underlie the tendency of children to become attached to inanimate objects, such as blankets or stuffed toys. However, a study of 2- to 3-year-old "blanket-attached" children found that they were no more insecure than others (Passman, 1987). (So, maybe Linus is okay after all.) (Photo courtesy of Harry Harlow, University of Wisconsin Primate Laboratory.)*

covered with soft terry cloth (❖Fig. 4.12). When the infants were given a choice between the two mothers, they spent most of their time clinging to the cuddly terry cloth mother. This was true even when the wire mother held a bottle, making her the source of food.

CONTACT COMFORT   The "love" and attachment displayed toward the cloth replicas were identical to those shown toward natural mothers. For example, when frightened by rubber snakes, wind-up toys, and other "fear stimuli," the infant monkeys ran to their cloth mothers and clung to them for security. These classic studies suggest that "contact comfort" is an important part of attachment. **Contact comfort** refers to the pleasant, reassuring feeling infants get from touching something soft and warm, especially their mothers.

The emotional well-being of human infants is also related to contact comfort (Eliot, 1999). Touching helps shape "body maps" in a baby's brain that affect tactile sensitivity and motor skills. Premature babies, in particular, benefit greatly from affectionate touching and massage (Field, 1998).

BREAST-FEEDING   Contact comfort is one reason why breast-feeding infants for the first 6 to 12 months of life is beneficial. Breast-fed babies are touched more, and they make more eye contact with their mothers. This extra contact seems to strengthen the mother-infant bond and produces more capable children (Golding, Rogers, & Emmett, 1997; Lavelli & Poli, 1998).

In addition to the psychological benefits, breast-feeding has another advantage. For the first few days after giving birth, mothers produce **colostrum** (kuh-LOSS-trum: a fluid rich in proteins). Colostrum carries antibodies from the mother to the newborn. This helps prevent certain infectious diseases. Colostrum is also easier for the newborn to digest than cow's milk and infant formulas.

What about the mother who can't breast-feed or who prefers not to?   If a mother is aware of the importance of touching, bottle feeding can be perfectly fine. A mother's warmth or

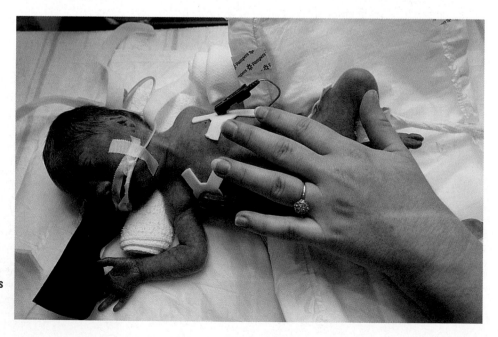

Extra touching, massage, and human contact is especially beneficial for premature and low-birth-weight infants.

Worldwide, the number of women who breast-feed their babies is declining. This is mostly due to the efforts of large businesses to promote sales of infant formulas in developing countries. Many companies give free samples of their products to new mothers, a practice that discourages many mothers from trying breast-feeding (Dermer, 1998).

coldness, relaxation or tension, and acceptance or rejection can be more important than the choice of breast or bottle. Being sensitive to a baby's feeding rhythms is the real key to healthy infant attachment.

Affectional Needs

A baby's **affectional needs** (needs for love and affection) are every bit as important as more obvious needs for food, water, and physical care. Parents are sometimes afraid of "spoiling" babies with too much attention or affection. However, for the first year or two this is nearly impossible (Konner, 1991). As a matter of fact, a later capacity to experience warm and loving relationships may depend on it.

KNOWLEDGE BUILDER
SOCIAL DEVELOPMENT

RELATE

Have you ever seen ducklings or goslings that have imprinted on their mothers? What does the purpose of imprinting appear to be? In what ways is attachment similar to imprinting? How is it different?

Think of a child you know who seems to be securely attached and a child who seems to be insecurely attached. How do the children differ? Do their parents treat them differently?

Do you think you were securely or insecurely attached as a child? Are there any parallels in your relationships today?

LEARNING CHECK

1. Clear signs of self-awareness or self-recognition are evident in most infants by the time they reach 8 months of age. T or F?

2. Social _____ of parents' facial expressions is evident in infants by the time they are 1 year old.

3. A duckling can be imprinted after the critical period has passed if special attention is given to its affectional needs. T or F?

4. The development of separation anxiety in an infant corresponds to the formation of an attachment to parents. T or F?

5. In Mary Ainsworth's system for rating the quality of attachment, secure attachment is revealed by a lack of distress when an infant is left alone with a stranger. T or F?

6. Harlow's research with surrogate mothers showed that baby rhesus monkeys became emotionally attached to the mother that provided food. T or F?

CRITICAL THINKING

7. Can you think of another way to tell if infants have self-awareness?

8. Can emotional bonding begin before birth?

9. Attachment quality is usually attributed to the behavior of parents or caregivers. How might infants contribute to the quality of attachment?

Answers:

1. F 2. referencing 3. F 4. T 5. F 6. F 7. Another successful method is to secretly rub a spot of rouge on an infant's nose. The child is then placed in front of a mirror. The question is, Will the child touch the red spot, showing recognition of the mirror image as his or her own? The probability that a child will do so jumps dramatically during the second year. 8. It certainly can for parents. When a pregnant woman begins to feel fetal movements, she becomes aware that a baby is coming to life inside her. Likewise, prospective parents who hear a fetal heartbeat at the doctor's office or see an ultrasound image of the fetus begin to become emotionally attached to the unborn child (Konner, 1991). 9. An infant's behavior patterns, temperament, and emotional style may greatly influence parents' behavior. As a result, infants can affect attachment as much as parents do (Oatley & Jenkins, 1992).

MATERNAL AND PATERNAL INFLUENCES—LIFE WITH MOM AND DAD

For the first few years of life, caregivers are the center of a child's world. This makes the quality of mothering and fathering very important. For example, one classic study focused on

Contact comfort *A pleasant and reassuring feeling human and animal infants get from touching or clinging to something soft and warm, usually their mother.*
Colostrum *The first milk produced by a woman for a few days after giving birth. Colostrum is rich in antibodies to disease.*
Affectional needs *Emotional needs for love and affection.*

maternal influences (all the effects a mother has on her child).

Researchers began by selecting children who were very competent (A children) or low in competence (C children). As they observed increasingly younger children, it soon became apparent that A and C patterns were already set by age 3. To learn how this was possible, psychologists visited homes and observed children under age 3 (White & Watts, 1973). The **caregiving styles** they saw ranged from the "supermother" to the "zookeeper mother." Supermothers went out of their way to provide educational experiences for children and let them initiate activities. This caregiving style produced A children, who were competent in most areas of development. At the other end of the scale, zookeeper mothers gave their children good physical care but interacted with them very little. Their childcare routines were rigid and highly structured. The result was C children who approached problems inflexibly.

Optimal Caregiving

More recent studies mirror the earlier findings: Optimal caregiving is marked by **proactive maternal involvement** (warm, educational interactions with a child) (Olson, Bates, & Kaskie, 1992). For example, Olivia is a proactive mother who talks to Amy often and helps her explore her surroundings. This speeds Amy's mental growth, and it minimizes behavior problems.

Optimal caregiving also depends on the **goodness of fit**, or compatibility, of parent and child temperaments (Chess & Thomas, 1986). For instance, Damion is a slow-to-warm-up child who has impatient parents. Damion will probably have more problems than he would with easygoing parents.

A third ingredient of caregiving is **parental responsiveness** to a child's feelings, needs, rhythms, and signals. When Amy is a month old, Olivia should focus on touching, holding, feeding, and stimulating her. When Amy is a year old, give-and-take interactions that promote Amy's social skills will be more important. Thus, effective mothers alter their behavior to meet children's changing needs (Heermann, Jones, & Wikoff, 1994).

Aren't you overlooking the effects of fathering? Yes. In fact, fathers make a unique contribution to parenting. Studies of **paternal influences** (the sum of all effects a father has on his child) reveal that fathers typically act as playmates for infants (Parke, 1995). In many homes, fathers spend four or five times more hours playing with infants than they do in caregiving. It's true that fathers are beginning to get more involved in child care. Just the same, mothers spend much more time feeding, dressing, grooming, disciplining, teaching, and caring for children (de Luccie & Davis, 1991).

It might seem that the father's role as a playmate makes him less important. Not so. From birth onward, fathers pay more visual attention to children than mothers do. Fathers are much more tactile (lifting, tickling, and handling the baby), more physically arousing (engaging in rough-and-tumble play), and more likely to engage in unusual play (imitating the baby, for example) (Crawley & Sherrod, 1984). In comparison, mothers speak to infants more, play more conventional games (such as peekaboo), and, as noted, spend much more time in caregiving (❖Fig 4.13).

Fathering typically makes a contribution to early development that differs in emphasis from mothering.

Amy's playtime with Tom is actually very valuable. Young children who spend a lot of time playing with their fathers tend to be more competent in many ways (Pettit et al., 1998).

Overall, fathers can be as affectionate, sensitive, and responsive as mothers are. Nevertheless, infants tend to get very different views of males and females. Females, who offer comfort, nurturance, and verbal stimulation, tend to be close at hand. Males come and go, and when they are present, action, exploration, and risk taking prevail. It's no wonder, then, that the caregiving styles of mothers and fathers have a major impact on children's gender role development (Lindsay, Mize, & Pettit, 1997).

As children mature and become more independent, parents must find ways to control the child's behavior. ("No, you may not smear pudding on daddy's face.") Such attempts can have a variety of effects, as described next.

Parenting Styles

Psychologist Diana Baumrind (1991) has studied the effects of three major styles of parenting. See if you recognize the styles she describes.

Authoritarian parents enforce rigid rules and demand strict obedience to authority. Typically, they view children as having few rights but adult-like responsibilities. The child is expected to stay out of trouble and to accept, without question, what parents regard as right or wrong. ("Do it because I say so.") The children of authoritarian parents are usually obedient and self-controlled. But they also tend to be emotionally stiff, withdrawn, apprehensive, and lacking in curiosity. One 22-year-

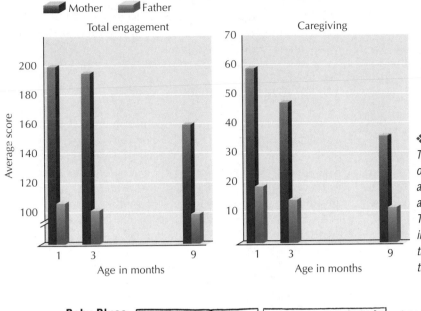

Total engagement

Caregiving

❖ **FIGURE 4.13** *Mother-infant and father-infant interactions. These graphs show what occurred on routine days in a sample of 72 American homes. The graph on the left records the total amount of contact parents had with their babies, including such actions as talking to, touching, hugging, or smiling at the infant. The graph on the right shows the amount of caregiving (diapering, washing, feeding, and so forth) done by each parent. Note that in both cases mother-infant interactions greatly exceed father-infant interactions. (Adapted from Belsky et al., 1984.)*

long study found that children whose parents are critical, harsh, or authoritarian often become self-absorbed adults. They also have higher rates of violence and drug abuse (Dubow et al., 1987; Weiss et al., 1992).

Overly permissive parents give little guidance, allow too much freedom, or don't hold children accountable for their actions. Typically, the child has rights similar to an adult's but few responsibilities. Rules are not enforced, and the child usually gets his or her way. ("Do whatever you want.") Permissive parents tend to produce dependent, immature children who misbehave frequently. Such children are aimless and likely to "run amok."

Baumrind describes **authoritative parents** as those who supply firm and consistent guidance, combined with love and affection. Such parents balance their own rights with those of their children. They control their children's behavior in a caring, responsive, nonauthoritarian way. ("Do it for this reason.") Effective parents are firm and consistent, not harsh or rigid. In general, they encourage the child to act responsibly, to think, and to make good decisions. This style produces children who are competent, self-controlled, independent, assertive, and inquiring (Baumrind, 1991).

CULTURE Diana Baumrind's work provides a good overall summary of the effects of parenting. However, her conclusions are probably most valid for families of European descent. Child-rearing in other ethnic groups often reflects different

customs and belief systems. This is especially true with respect to the meaning attached to a child's behavior. Is a particular behavior "good" or "bad"? Should it be encouraged or discouraged? The answer will depend greatly on parents' cultural values and beliefs (Rubin, 1998). (See "Ethnic Differences in Child-Rearing.")

Maternal influences *The aggregate of all psychological effects mothers have on their children.*

Caregiving styles *Identifiable patterns of parental caretaking and interaction with children.*

Proactive maternal involvement *Sensitive caregiving in which the mother actively seeks to interact with her child and to provide educational experiences.*

Goodness of fit *With respect to caregiving, the degree to which parents and children have compatible temperaments.*

Parental responsiveness *Caregiving that is based on sensitivity to a child's feelings, needs, rhythms, and signals.*

Paternal influences *The aggregate of all psychological effects fathers have on their children.*

Authoritarian parents *Parents who enforce rigid rules and demand strict obedience to authority.*

Overly permissive parents *Parents who give little guidance, allow too much freedom, or do not require the child to take responsibility.*

Authoritative parents *Parents who supply firm and consistent guidance combined with love and affection.*

ETHNIC DIFFERENCES IN CHILD-REARING—THREE FLAVORS OF PARENTING

Making generalizations about groups of people is always risky. Nevertheless, some typical differences in child-rearing patterns have been observed in North American ethnic communities (Kaplan, 1998).

AFRICAN-AMERICAN FAMILIES

Traditional African-American values emphasize loyalty and interdependence among family members, security, developing a positive identity, and not giving up in the face of adversity. African-American parents typically stress obedience and respect for elders. Child discipline tends to be fairly strict, but many African-American parents see this as a necessity, especially if they live in urban areas where safety is a concern. Self-reliance, resourcefulness, and an ability to take care of themselves in difficult situations are also qualities that African-American parents seek to promote in their children.

HISPANIC FAMILIES

Like African-American parents, Hispanic parents tend to have relatively strict standards of discipline. They also stress family values, family pride, and loyalty. Hispanic families are typically affectionate and indulgent toward younger children. However, as children grow older, they are expected to learn social skills and to be calm, obedient, courteous, and respectful. In fact, such social skills may be valued more than cognitive skills (Delgado & Ford, 1998). In addition, Hispanic par-

ents tend to stress cooperation more than competition. Such values can put Hispanic children at a disadvantage in highly competitive, Anglo-American culture.

ASIAN-AMERICAN FAMILIES

Asian cultures tend to be group-oriented, and they emphasize interdependence among individuals. In contrast, Western cultures value individual effort and independence (Markus & Kitayama, 1991). This difference is often reflected in Asian-American child-rearing practices. Asian-American children are taught that their behavior can bring either pride or shame to the family. Therefore, they are obliged to set aside their own desires when the greater good of the family is at stake. Parents tend to act as teachers who encourage hard work, moral behavior, and achievement. For the first few years, parenting is lenient and permissive. However, after about age 5, Asian-American parents begin to expect respect, obedience, self-control, and self-discipline from their children.

CONCLUSION

Child-rearing is done in a remarkable variety of ways around the world. In fact, many of the things we do in North America, such as forcing young children to sleep alone, would be considered odd or wrong in other cultures. In the final analysis, parenting can only be judged if we know what culture or ethnic community a child is being prepared to enter (Bornstein et al., 1998).

Close to Home

"All right now, give Mommy the super-glue."

Effects of Child Discipline

When parents fail to provide **discipline** (guidance regarding acceptable behavior), children become antisocial, aggressive, and insecure. Effective discipline is fair but loving, authoritative yet sensitive. It socializes a child without destroying the bond of love and trust between parent and child.

TYPES OF DISCIPLINE Parents typically discipline children in one of three ways. **Power assertion** refers to physical punishment or a show of force, such as taking away toys or privileges. As an alternative, some parents use **withdrawal of love** (withholding affection) by refusing to speak to a child, by threatening to leave, by rejecting the child, or by otherwise acting as if the child is temporarily unlovable. **Management techniques** combine praise, recognition, approval, rules, reasoning, and the like to encourage desirable behavior. Each of these approaches can control a child's behavior, but their side effects differ considerably.

What are the side effects? Power-oriented techniques—particularly harsh or severe physical punishment—are associated with fear, hatred of parents, and a lack of spontaneity and warmth. Severely punished children also tend to be defiant, rebellious, and aggressive (Patterson, 1982). Despite its drawbacks, power assertion is the most popular mode of discipline (Papps et al., 1995).

Withdrawal of love produces children who tend to be self-disciplined. You could say that such children have developed a good conscience. Often, they are described as "model" children or as unusually "good." But as a side effect, they are also frequently anxious, insecure, and dependent on adults for approval.

Management techniques also have limitations. Most important is the need to carefully adjust to a child's level of understanding. Younger children don't always see the connection between rules, explanations, and their own behavior. Nevertheless, management techniques receive a big plus in another area. Psychologist Stanley Coopersmith (1968) found a direct connection between discipline and a child's self-esteem.

SELF-ESTEEM   If you regard yourself as a worthwhile person, you have **self-esteem**. High self-esteem is essential for emotional health. Individuals with low self-esteem don't think much of themselves as people. In elementary school, children with high self-esteem tend to be more popular, cooperative, and successful in class. Children with low self-esteem are more withdrawn and tend to perform below average (Hay, Ashman, & Van Kraayenoord, 1998).

How does discipline affect self-esteem?   Coopersmith found that low self-esteem is related to physical punishment and the withholding of love. And why not? What message do children receive if a parent beats them or tells them they are not worthy of love?

High self-esteem is promoted by management techniques. Thus, it is best to minimize physical punishment and avoid unnecessary withdrawal of love. Children who feel that their parents support them emotionally tend to have high self-esteem (Hay, Ashman, & Van Kraayenoord, 1998; Nielsen & Metha, 1994).

KNOWLEDGE BUILDER
PARENTAL INFLUENCES

RELATE

Picture a mother you know who seems to be a good caregiver. Which of the optimal caregiving behaviors does she engage in?

Do you know any parents with young children who are authoritarian, permissive, or authoritative? What are their children like?

What do you think are the best ways to discipline children? How would your approach be classified? What are its advantages and disadvantages?

LEARNING CHECK

1. Three important elements of effective mothering are _____ maternal involvement, parental _____ to a child's feelings, needs, rhythms, and signals, and compatibility between parent and child _____.

---

2. Fathers are more likely to act as playmates for their children, rather than caregivers. T or F?

3. According to Diana Baumrind's research, effective parents are authoritarian in their approach to their children's behavior. T or F?

4. Authoritarian parents view children as having few rights but many responsibilities. T or F?

5. Coopersmith found that high self-esteem in childhood is related to discipline based on either management techniques or withdrawal of love. T or F?

CRITICAL THINKING

6. Why is it risky to make generalizations about child-rearing differences for various ethnic groups?

7. If power assertion is a poor way to discipline children, why do so many parents use it?

Answers:

1. proactive, responsiveness, temperaments 2. T 3. F 4. T 5. F 6. Because there may be as much variation within ethnic groups as there is between them. For example, there are sizable differences in the child-rearing styles of Hispanic parents from Puerto Rico, Argentina, and Guatemala. 7. Most parents discipline their children in the same ways that they themselves were disciplined. Parenting is a responsibility of tremendous importance, for which most people receive almost no training.

BRIDGES

Punishment has important effects on learning.

For more tips on how to use punishment wisely, see Chapter 9, pages 294–297.

LANGUAGE DEVELOPMENT—FAST-TALKING BABIES

There's something almost miraculous about a baby's first words. As infants, how did we manage to leap into the world of language? As will soon be apparent, social development provides a foundation for language learning. But before we probe that connection, let's begin with a quick survey of language development.

Language Acquisition

Language development is closely tied to maturation. As every parent knows, babies can cry from birth on. By 1 month of age, they use crying to gain attention. Typically, parents can tell if an infant is hungry, angry, or in pain from the tone of the cry-

---

Discipline *A framework of guidelines for acceptable behavior.*
Power assertion *The use of physical punishment or coercion to enforce child discipline.*
Withdrawal of love *Withholding affection to enforce child discipline.*
Management techniques *Combining praise, recognition, approval, rules, and reasoning to enforce child discipline.*
Self-esteem *Regarding oneself as a worthwhile person; a positive evaluation of oneself.*

Baby Blues

ing (Kaplan, 1998). Around 6 to 8 weeks of age, babies begin **cooing** (the repetition of vowel sounds like "oo" and "ah").

By 7 months of age, Amy's nervous system had matured enough to allow her to grasp objects, smile, laugh, sit up, and **babble**. In the babbling stage, the consonants *b, d, m,* and *g* are combined with the vowel sounds to produce meaningless language sounds: *dadadadada* or *bababa*. At first, babbling is the same around the world. But soon, the language spoken by parents begins to have an influence. That is, Chinese babies start to babble in a way that sounds like Chinese, Mexican babies babble in Spanish-like sounds, and so forth (Gopnik, Meltzoff, & Kuhl, 1999).

At about 1 year of age, children can stand alone for a short time and respond to real words such as *no* or *hi*. Soon afterward, the first connection between words and objects forms, and children may address their parents as "Mama" or "Dada." By age 18 months to 2 years, children have learned to stand and walk alone. By then, their vocabulary may include from 24 to 200 words. At first there is a **single-word stage**, during which the child says one word at a time such as "go," "juice," or "up." Soon after, words are arranged in simple two-word sentences called **telegraphic speech**: "Want-Teddy," "Mama-gone." (The word *telegraphic* refers to messages sent by telegraph, which were usually very short.)

LANGUAGE AND THE TERRIBLE TWOS   At about the same time that children begin to put two or three words together, they become much more independent. Two-year-olds understand some of the commands parents make, but they are not always willing to carry them out. A child like Amy may assert her independence by saying "No drink," "Me do it," "My cup, my cup," and the like. It can be worse, of course. A 2-year-old may look at you intently, make eye contact, listen as you shout "No, no," and still pour her juice on the cat.

During their second year, children become increasingly mobile—and capable of mischief. It's not surprising, perhaps, that temper tantrums peak during this period. So do conflicts between mother and child (Kaplan, 1998). Thus, as many parents will attest, calling this time "the terrible twos" is not entirely inappropriate. One-year-olds can do plenty of things parents don't want them to do. However, it's usually 2-year-olds who do things *because* you don't want them to (Gopnik, Meltzoff, & Kuhl, 1999).

Of course, there may be a hidden danger in expecting oppositional behavior from 2-year-olds. It's possible that such ex-

pectations will just lead to a self-fulfilling prophecy. On the other hand, it may be comforting to know that a stubborn, negative 2-year-old is simply becoming more independent. Parents of active 2-year-olds, repeat after me: "This, too, shall pass."

After age 2, the child's comprehension and use of words takes a dramatic leap forward (Reznick & Goldfield, 1992). From this point on, vocabulary and language skills grow at a phenomenal rate. By first grade, Amy will be able to understand around 8,000 words and use about 4,000. She will have truly entered the world of language.

The Roots of Language

In a fascinating study, researchers William Condon and Louis Sander (1974) filmed newborn infants as the babies listened to various sounds. A frame-by-frame analysis of the films showed something astonishing: Infants move their arms and legs to the rhythms of human speech. Random noise, rhythmic tapping, or disconnected vowel sounds will not produce a "language dance." Only natural speech has this effect.

Why do day-old infants "dance" to speech but not other sounds? One possibility is that language recognition is innate. Linguist Noam Chomsky (1975, 1986) has long claimed that humans have a **biological predisposition** or hereditary readiness to develop language. According to Chomsky, language patterns are inborn, much like a child's ability to coordinate walking. If such inborn language recognition does exist, it may explain why children around the world use a limited number of patterns in their first sentences. Typical patterns include (Mussen et al., 1979):

IDENTIFICATION:	"See kitty."
NONEXISTENCE:	"Allgone milk."
POSSESSION:	"My doll."
AGENT-ACTION:	"Mama give."
NEGATION:	"Not ball."
QUESTION:	"Where doggie?"

Does Chomsky's theory explain why language develops so rapidly?   Perhaps. But many psychologists feel that Chomsky underestimates the importance of learning. **Psycholinguists** (specialists in the psychology of language) have shown that language is not magically "switched on" by adult speech. Imitation of adults and rewards for correctly using words (as when a child asks for a cookie) are important parts of language learn-

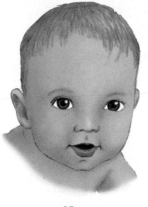

85
Medium high positive

50
Neutral attention

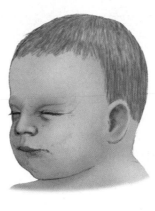

20
Avert

❖ **FIGURE 4.14** *Infant engagement scale. These samples from a 90-point scale show various levels of infant engagement, or attention. Babies participate in prelanguage "conversations" with parents by giving and withholding attention and by smiling, gazing, or vocalizing. (From Beebe et al., 1982.)*

ing. Also, babies actively participate in language learning by asking questions, such as "What dis?" (Domingo & Goldstein-Alpern, 1999).

When a child makes a language error, parents typically repeat the child's sentence, with needed corrections (Bohannon & Stanowicz, 1988). More important, still, is the fact that parents and children begin to communicate long before the child can speak. Months of shared effort precede a child's first word. From this point of view, an infant's "language dance" reflects a readiness to interact *socially* with parents, not innate language recognition. The next section explains why.

EARLY COMMUNICATION *How do parents communicate with infants before they can talk?* Parents go to a great deal of trouble to get babies to smile and vocalize (❖Fig. 4.14). In doing so, they quickly learn to change their actions to keep the infant's attention, arousal, and activity at optimal levels. A familiar example is the "I'm-Going-to-Get-You" game. In it, the adult says, "I'm gonna getcha . . . I'm gonna getcha . . . I'm gonna getcha . . . Gotcha!" Through such games, adults and babies come to share similar rhythms and expectations (Stern, 1982). Soon a system of shared **signals** is created, such as touching, vocalizing, gazing, and smiling. These help lay a foundation for later language use. Specifically, signals establish a pattern of "conversational" **turn-taking** (alternate sending and receiving of messages).

OLIVIA	AMY
	(smiles)
"Oh what a nice little smile!"	
"Yes, isn't that nice?"	
"There."	
"There's a nice little smile."	(burps)
"Well, pardon you!"	
"Yes, that's better, isn't it?"	
"Yes."	(vocalizes)
"Yes."	(smiles)
"What's so funny? "	

From the outside, such exchanges may look meaningless. In reality, they represent real communication. Amy's vocalizations and attention provide a way of interacting emotionally with Olivia and Tom. Even infants as young as 3 months make more

speech-like sounds when an adult engages them in turn-taking (see ❖Fig. 4.15) (Bloom et al., 1987). The more children interact with parents, the faster they learn to talk (Tamis-LeMonvda & Bornstein, 1994). Unmistakably, social relationships contribute to early language learning.

Psychologists Betty Hart and Todd Risley found that, on average, children hear the following number of words per hour during the first two and a half years of life:

- Children of professional parents—2,100 words per hour
- Children of working-class parents—1,200 words per hour
- Children of welfare parents—600 words per hour

By age 3, the children of professional parents score higher in mental abilities than children in the other two groups. Hart and Risley believe that a richer language environment in professional homes explains much of the gap (Hart & Risley, 1999).

PARENTESE When talking to infants, parents use an exaggerated pattern of speaking called **motherese** or **parentese**. Typically, they raise their tone of voice, use short, simple sentences,

Cooing *Spontaneous repetition of vowel sounds by infants.*
Babbling *The repetition by infants of meaningless language sounds (including both vowel and consonant sounds).*
Single-word stage *In language development, the period during which a child first begins to use single words.*
Telegraphic speech *In language development, the formation of simple two-word sentences that "telegraph" (communicate) a simple idea.*
Biological predisposition *The presumed hereditary readiness of humans to learn certain skills, such as how to use language, or a readiness to behave in particular ways.*
Psycholinguist *A specialist in the psychology of language and language development.*
Signal *In early language development, any behavior, such as touching, vocalizing, gazing, or smiling, that allows nonverbal interaction and turn-taking between parent and child.*
Turn-taking *In early language development, the tendency of parent and child to alternate in the sending and receiving of signals or messages.*
Motherese (or parentese) *A pattern of speech used when talking to infants, marked by a higher-pitched voice, short, simple sentences, repetition, slower speech, and exaggerated voice inflections.*

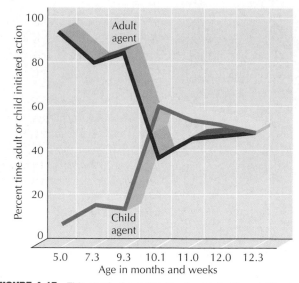

❖ **FIGURE 4.15** *This graph shows the development of turn-taking in games played by an infant and his mother. For several months, Richard responded to games such as peekaboo and "hand-the-toy-back" only when his mother initiated action. At about 9 months, however, he rapidly began to initiate action in the games. Soon, he was the one to take the lead about half of the time. Learning to take turns and to direct actions toward another person underlies basic language skills. (From Bruner, 1983.)*

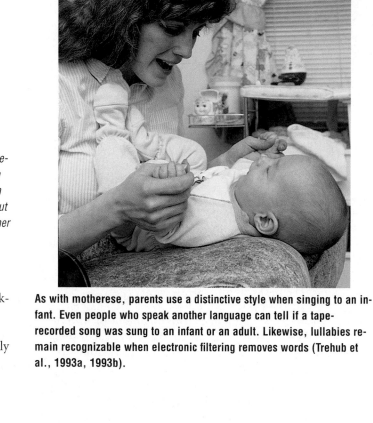

As with motherese, parents use a distinctive style when singing to an infant. Even people who speak another language can tell if a tape-recorded song was sung to an infant or an adult. Likewise, lullabies remain recognizable when electronic filtering removes words (Trehub et al., 1993a, 1993b).

and repeat themselves more. They also slow their rate of speaking and use exaggerated voice inflections: "Did Amy eat it A-L-L UP?"

What is the purpose of such changes? Parents are apparently trying to help their children learn language. When a baby is still babbling, parents tend to use long, adult-style sentences. But as soon as the baby says its first word, they switch to parentese. By the time babies are 4 months old, they prefer parentese over normal speech (Cooper et al., 1997).

In addition to being simpler, parentese has a distinct "musical" quality (Fernald & Mazzie, 1991). No matter what language mothers speak, the melodies, pauses, and inflections they use to comfort, praise, or give warning are universal. Psychologist Anne Fernald has found that mothers of all nations talk to their babies with similar changes in pitch. For instance, we praise babies with a rising, then falling pitch ("BRA-vo!" "GOOD girl!"). Warnings are delivered in a short, sharp rhythm ("Nein! Nein!" "Basta! Basta!" "Not! Dude!"). To give comfort, parents use low, smooth, drawn-out tones ("Oooh poor baaa-by." "Oooh pobrecito.") A high-pitched, rising melody is used to call attention to objects ("See the pretty BIRDIE?") (Fernald, 1989).

Note that parentese is not literally "baby talk." Many parents can't seem to resist imitating a baby's "cute" mispronunciations of words, like "wa-wa" (water) or "pah-getty" (spaghetti). This is harmless enough for a short time. However, parents who continue to use baby talk may slow a child's language learning. Unless parents help their children pronounce words correctly, a child can easily reach school age still using baby talk. ("Teacher, can I go wee-wee?")

Motherese helps parents get babies' attention, communicate with them, and teach them language (Kaplan et al., 1995). Later, as a child's speaking improves, parents tend to adjust their speech to the child's language ability. Especially when the child is 18 months to 4 years of age, parents seek to clarify what a child says and prompt the child to say more. Two typical strategies are (Newman & Newman, 1978):

EXPANSION:	*Child:*	Doggie bite.
	Parent:	Yes, the dog bit *the toy.*
PROMPTING:	*Child:*	Doggie briggle.
	Parent:	What did the doggie do?

In summary, some elements of language are innate: All normal children learn language, unless they grow up in an extremely abnormal environment. Nevertheless, our inherited tendency to learn language does not determine if we will speak English or Vietnamese, Spanish or Russian. Environmental forces also influence whether a person develops simple or sophisticated language skills. The first 7 years of life are a critical period in language learning (Eliot, 1999). Clearly, a full flowering of speech requires careful cultivation.

RELATE

In order, see if you can name and imitate the language abilities you had as you progressed from birth to age 2 years. Now see if you can label and imitate some basic elements of parentese.

In your own words, state at least one argument for and against Chomsky's view of language acquisition.

You are going to spend a day with a person who speaks a different language than you do. Do you think you would be able to communicate with the other person? How does this relate to language acquisition?

LEARNING CHECK

1. The development of speech and language usually occurs in which order?
   a. crying, cooing, babbling, telegraphic speech
   b. cooing, crying, babbling, telegraphic speech
   c. babbling, crying, cooing, telegraphic speech
   d. crying, babbling, cooing, identification

2. Simple two-word sentences are characteristic of _____ speech.

3. Noam _____ has advanced the idea that language acquisition is built upon innate patterns.

4. Prelanguage turn-taking and social interactions would be of special interest to a psycholinguist. T or F?

5. The style of speaking known as _____ is higher in pitch and has a musical quality.

CRITICAL THINKING

6. The children of professional parents hear more words per hour than the children of welfare parents, and they also tend to score higher on tests of mental abilities. How else could their higher scores be explained?

Answers:

1. a 2. telegraphic 3. Chomsky 4. T 5. parentese 6. Children in professional homes receive many educational benefits that are less common in welfare homes. Yet, even when such differences are taken into account, brighter children tend to come from richer language environments (Hart & Risley, 1999).

❖ **FIGURE 4.16** *Children under age 7 intuitively assume that a volume of liquid increases when it is poured from a short, wide container into a taller, thinner one. This boy thinks the tall container holds more than the short one. Actually each holds the same amount of liquid. Children make such judgments based on the height of the liquid, not its volume.*

mentally change the shape or form of a substance (such as clay or water). Let's visit Amy at age 5: If you show her a short, wide glass full of milk and a tall, narrow glass (also full), she will tell you that the taller glass contains more milk. Amy will tell you this even if she watches you pour milk from the short glass into an empty tall glass. She is not bothered by the fact that the milk appears to be transformed from a smaller to a larger amount. Instead, she responds only to the fact that *taller* seems to mean *more.* (See ❖Fig. 4.16.) After about age 7, children are no longer fooled by this situation. Perhaps that's why 7 has been called the "age of reason." From age 7 on, we see a definite trend toward more logical, adult-like thought (Flavell, 1992).

Is there any pattern to the growth of intellect in childhood? According to the Swiss psychologist and philosopher Jean Piaget (1951, 1952), there is.

Piaget's Theory of Cognitive Development

Jean Piaget (Jahn pea-ah-JAY) believed that all children pass through a series of distinct stages in intellectual development. Many of his ideas came from observing his own children as they solved various thought problems. (It is tempting to imag-

Transformation *The mental ability to change the shape or form of a substance (such as clay or water) and to perceive that its volume remains the same.*

COGNITIVE DEVELOPMENT—HOW DO CHILDREN LEARN TO THINK?

Now that we have our subjects (babies) talking, let's move on to a broader view of intellectual development.

How different is a child's understanding of the world from that of an adult? Generally speaking, their thinking is less abstract. Children use fewer generalizations, categories, and principles. They also tend to base their understanding on particular examples and objects they can see or touch.

Before the age of 6 or 7, thinking is very concrete. Younger children cannot make **transformations** in which they must

Jean Piaget—philosopher, psychologist, and keen observer of children.

Crossing a busy street can be dangerous for the preoperational child. Because their thinking is still egocentric, younger children cannot understand why the driver of a car can't see them if they can see the car. Children under the age of 7 also cannot consistently judge speeds and distances of oncoming cars. Adults can easily overestimate the "street smarts" of younger children. It is advisable to teach children to cross with a light, in crosswalks, or with assistance.

ine that Piaget's illustrious career was launched one day when his wife said to him, "Watch the children for a while, will you, Jean?")

MENTAL ADAPTATIONS   Piaget was convinced that intellect grows through processes he called *assimilation* and *accommodation*. **Assimilation** is the use of existing mental patterns in new situations. Let's say that a plastic hammer is the favorite toy of a boy named Benjamin. Benjamin holds the hammer properly and loves to pound on blocks with it. For his birthday, Benjamin gets an oversized toy wrench. If he uses the wrench for pounding, it has been assimilated to an existing knowledge structure.

In **accommodation**, existing ideas are modified to fit new requirements. For instance, a younger child might think that a dime is worth less than a (larger) nickel. As the child begins to spend money, she or he will be forced to alter ideas about what *more* and *less* mean. Thus, new situations are assimilated to existing ideas, and new ideas are created to accommodate new experiences.

Piaget's theories have had a profound effect on our thinking about children (Beilin, 1992). The following is a brief summary of what he found.

THE SENSORIMOTOR STAGE (0–2 YEARS)   In the first 2 years of life, a child's intellectual development is largely nonverbal. During the sensorimotor stage, children are mainly concerned with learning to coordinate purposeful movements with information from the senses. Also, **object permanence** (an understanding that objects continue to exist when they are out of sight) emerges at this time. By about 18 months of age, children begin to actively pursue disappearing objects. By age 2, they can anticipate the movement of an object behind a screen. For ex-

ample, when watching an electric train, Amy looks ahead to the end of a tunnel, rather than staring at the spot where the train disappeared.

In general, developments in this stage indicate that the child's conceptions are becoming more *stable*. Objects cease to appear and disappear magically, and a more orderly and predictable world replaces the confusing and disconnected sensations of infancy.

THE PREOPERATIONAL STAGE (2–7 YEARS)   During the **preoperational stage**, children begin to think *symbolically* and use language. But the child's thinking is still very **intuitive** (it makes little use of reasoning and logic). (Do you remember thinking as a child that the sun and the moon followed you when you took a walk?) In addition, the child's use of language is not as sophisticated as it might seem. Children have a tendency to confuse words with the objects they represent. If Benjamin calls a toy block a "car" and you use it to make a "train," he may be upset. To children, the name of an object is as much a part of the object as its size, shape, and color. This seems to underlie a preoccupation with name-calling. To the preoperational child, an insulting name may hurt as much as "sticks and stones." Consider, for instance, one rather protected youngster who was angered by her older brother. Searching for a way to retaliate against her larger and stronger foe, she settled on "You panty-girdle!" It was the worst thing she could think of saying.

A CHILD'S THEORY OF MIND—OTHER PEOPLE, OTHER MINDS

Why are young children so egocentric? In many instances, it's because they have a limited understanding of mental states, such as desires, beliefs, thoughts, intentions, and feelings. In other words, it could be said that they have a very simplified **theory of mind** (Flavell, 1999).

The following example is based on theory-of-mind research. Imagine that you show 5-year-old Nicky a candy box. "What do you think is inside?" you ask. "Candy," Nicky replies. Then you let Nicky look inside, where he finds a surprise: The box contains crayons, not candy. "Nicky," you ask, "what will your friend Max think is inside the box if I show it to him?" Nicky replies, "Candy!" amused at the thought that Max is going to get fooled, too.

Now imagine that we try the procedure again, this time with Sheila, who is only 3 years old. Like Nicky, Sheila thinks she will find candy in the box. She opens the box and sees the crayons. Now we ask Sheila what she thinks Max will expect to find in the box. "Crayons," she replies. Because Sheila knows that there are crayons in the box, she assumes that everyone else does, too. It's as if only one reality exists for Sheila. She doesn't seem to understand that the minds of other people contain different information, beliefs, thoughts, and so forth (Gopnik, Meltzoff, & Kuhl, 1999).

Between the ages of 3 and 4, children normally gain a richer understanding of mental life. As their "theory of mind" becomes more accurate, they are able to participate more fully in the complex psychological world in which we all live.

During the preoperational stage, the child is also quite **egocentric** (unable to take the viewpoint of other people). The child's ego seems to stand at the center of his or her world. To illustrate, show Amy a two-sided mirror. Then hold it between the two of you so she can see herself in it. If you ask her what she thinks *you* can see, she imagines that you see *her* reflected image instead of your own. The concept of egocentrism helps us to understand why children can seem exasperatingly selfish or uncooperative at times. If Benjamin blocks your view by standing in front of the TV, he assumes that you can see it if he can. If you ask him to move so you can see better, he may move so that he can see better! Benjamin is not being selfish, in the ordinary sense. He just doesn't realize that your view differs from his. (See "A Child's Theory of Mind.")

THE CONCRETE OPERATIONAL STAGE (7–11 YEARS)   An important development during the concrete operational stage is mastery of **conservation** (the concept that mass, weight, and volume remain unchanged when the shape of objects changes). Children have learned conservation when they understand that rolling a ball of clay into a "snake" does not increase the amount of clay. Likewise, pouring liquid from a tall, narrow

glass into a shallow dish does not reduce the amount of liquid. In each case, the volume remains the same, despite changes in shape or appearance. The original amount is *conserved* (see ❖Fig. 4.16).

During the concrete operational stage, children begin to use concepts of time, space, and number. The child can think logically about very concrete objects or situations, categories, and principles. Such abilities explain why children stop believing in Santa Claus when they reach this stage. Because they can conserve volume, they realize that Santa's sack couldn't possibly hold enough toys for millions of girls and boys.

Another important development at this time is the ability to *reverse* thoughts or mental operations. A conversation with a 4-year-old boy in the preoperational stage shows what happens when a child's thinking *lacks* reversibility (Phillips, 1969).

"Do you have a brother?"
"Yes."
"What's his name?"
"Jim."
"Does Jim have a brother?"
"No."

Reversibility of thought allows children in the concrete operational stage to recognize that if $4 \times 2 = 8$, then 2×4 does, too. Younger children must memorize each relationship separately. Thus, a preoperational child may know that $4 \times 9 = 36$, without being able to tell you what 9×4 equals.

THE FORMAL OPERATIONS STAGE (11 YEARS AND UP)   Sometime after about the age of 11, children begin to break away from con-

Assimilation *In Piaget's theory, the application of existing mental patterns to new situations (that is, the new situation is assimilated to existing mental schemes).*

Accommodation *In Piaget's theory, the modification of existing mental patterns to fit new demands (that is, mental schemes are changed to accommodate new information or experiences).*

Sensorimotor stage *Stage of intellectual development during which sensory input and motor responses become coordinated.*

Object permanence *Concept, gained in infancy, that objects continue to exist even when they are hidden from view.*

Preoperational stage *Period of intellectual development during which children begin to use language and think symbolically, yet remain intuitive and egocentric in their thought.*

Intuitive thought *Thinking that makes little or no use of reasoning and logic.*

Theory of mind *A child's current state of knowledge about the mind, including his or her understanding of desires, beliefs, thoughts, intentions, and feelings.*

Egocentric thought *Thought that is self-centered and fails to consider the viewpoints of others.*

Concrete operational stage *Period of intellectual development during which children become able to use the concepts of time, space, volume, and number, but in ways that remain simplified and concrete, rather than abstract.*

Conservation *In Piaget's theory, mastery of the concept that the weight, mass, and volume of matter remain unchanged (are conserved) even when the shape or appearance of objects changes.*

Reversibility of thought *Recognition that relationships involving equality or identity can be reversed (for example, if A = B, then B = A).*

crete objects and specific examples. Thinking is based more on **abstract principles**, such as "democracy," "honor," or "correlation." Children who reach the formal operations stage can think about their thoughts, and they become less egocentric. Older children and young adolescents also gradually become able to consider **hypothetical possibilities** (suppositions, guesses, or projections). For example, if you ask a younger child, "What do you think would happen if it suddenly became possible for people to fly?" the child might respond, "People can't fly." Older children are able to consider the possibilities and discuss their implications.

Full adult intellectual ability is attained during the stage of formal operations. Older adolescents are capable of inductive and deductive reasoning, and they can comprehend math, physics, philosophy, psychology, and other abstract systems. They can learn to test hypotheses in a scientific manner. Of course, not everyone reaches this level of thinking. Also, many adults can think formally about some topics, but their thinking becomes concrete when the topic is unfamiliar. This implies that formal thinking may be more a result of culture and learning than maturation. In any case, after late adolescence, improvements in intellect are based on gaining knowledge, experience, and wisdom, rather than on any leaps in basic thinking capacity.

PRACTICAL IMPLICATIONS   *How can parents apply Piaget's ideas?* Piaget's theory suggests that the ideal way to guide intellectual development is to provide experiences that are only slightly novel, unusual, or challenging. Remember, a child's intellect develops mainly through accommodation. It is usually best to follow a *one-step-ahead strategy,* in which your teaching efforts are aimed just beyond a child's current level of comprehension (Heckhausen, 1987).

In addition, Piaget's work shows the importance of relating to a child on the right level. If you give a physical explanation when a very young child asks, "Why does the sun come up in the morning?" you may have missed the point. Answering in terms of the child's egocentric viewpoint is often more meaningful. An answer such as "So you will know it's time to get up" is completely satisfactory for a young child. Later, explanations can be made increasingly abstract and accurate.

For your convenience, ◆Table 4.2 briefly summarizes each Piagetian stage. To help you remember Piaget's theory, the table describes what would happen at each stage if we played a game of Monopoly with the child. You'll also find brief suggestions about how to relate to children in each stage.

Piaget Today

Piaget's theory is a valuable "road map" for understanding how children think. But some research suggests that intellectual growth is not as age and stage related as Piaget claimed. Today, many psychologists are convinced that Piaget gave too little credit to the effects of learning. For example, children of pottery-making parents can correctly answer questions about the conservation of clay at an earlier age than Piaget would have predicted (Bransford et al., 1986). According to learning theorists, children continuously gain specific knowledge; they do not undergo stage-like leaps in general mental ability.

Numerous studies do show that children make swift mental gains at about the ages Piaget stated. In fact, cycles of brain growth occur at times that correspond with Piaget's stages

◆ **TABLE 4.2** Piaget—A Guide for Parents

PIAGET	MONOPOLY GAME	GUIDELINES FOR PARENTS
Sensorimotor stage The stage during which sensory input and motor responses become coordinated.	The child puts houses, hotels, and dice in her mouth and plays with "Chance" cards.	Active play with a child is most effective at this stage. Encourage explorations in touching, smelling, and manipulating objects. Peekaboo is a good way to establish the permanence of objects.
Preoperational stage The period of cognitive development when children begin to use language and think symbolically, yet remain intuitive and egocentric.	The child plays Monopoly but makes up her own rules and cannot understand instructions.	Specific examples and touching or seeing things continue to be more useful than verbal explanations. Learning the concept of conservation may be aided by demonstrations with liquids, beads, clay, and other substances.
Concrete operational stage The period of cognitive development during which children begin to use concepts of time, space, volume, and number, but in ways that remain simplified and concrete.	The child understands basic instructions and will play by the rules but is not capable of hypothetical transactions dealing with mortgages, loans, and special pacts with other players.	Children are beginning to use generalizations, but they still require specific examples to grasp many ideas. Expect a degree of inconsistency in the child's ability to apply concepts of time, space, quantity, and volume to new situations.
Formal operations stage The period of intellectual development marked by a capacity for abstract, theoretical, and hypothetical thinking.	The child no longer plays the game mechanically; complex and hypothetical transactions unique to each game are now possible.	It is now more effective to explain things verbally or symbolically and to help children master general rules and principles. Encourage the child to create hypotheses and to imagine how things could be.

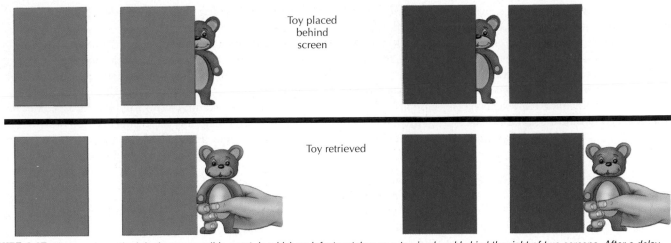

Toy placed behind screen

Toy retrieved

❖ **FIGURE 4.17** *The panels on the left show a possible event, in which an infant watches as a toy is placed behind the right of two screens. After a delay of 70 seconds, the toy is brought into view from behind the right screen. In the two panels on the right, an impossible event occurs. The toy is placed behind the left screen and retrieved from behind the right. (A duplicate toy was hidden there before testing.) Eight-month-old infants react with surprise when they see the impossible event staged for them. Their reaction implies that they remember where the toy was hidden. Infants appear to have a capacity for memory and thinking that greatly exceeds what Piaget claimed is possible during the sensorimotor period. (Adapted from Baillargeon et al., 1989.)*

(Thatcher et al., 1987). Thus, the truth may lie somewhere between Piaget's stage theory and modern learning theory. On a broad scale, many of Piaget's *observations* have held up well. However, his *explanations* for the growth of thinking abilities in childhood continue to be debated.

Where early infancy is concerned, even Piaget's observations may need revision. It looks like Piaget greatly underestimated the thinking abilities of infants during the sensorimotor stage.

INFANT COGNITION   *What evidence is there that Piaget underestimated infant abilities?*   Piaget believed that infants under the age of 1 year cannot think. Babies, he said, have no memory of people and objects that are out of sight. Yet, research described earlier in this chapter suggests that infants begin forming representations of the world very early in life. For example, babies as young as 3 months appear to know that objects are solid and do not disappear when out of view (Baillargeon & DeVos, 1992; Johnson & Nanez, 1995). Others have found that babies have memories at age 6 to 8 months that Piaget didn't see until 18 months (Hayne & Rovee-Collier, 1995; Raymond, 1991; Shields & Rovee-Collier, 1992).

Why did Piaget fail to detect the thinking skills of infants? Most likely, he mistook babies' limited *physical* skills for *mental* incompetence. Piaget's tests required babies to search for objects or reach out and touch them. Newer, more sensitive methods are uncovering abilities Piaget could not have detected. One such method takes advantage of the fact that babies, like adults, act surprised when they see something "impossible" or unexpected occur. To make use of this effect, psychologist Renee Baillargeon (1991) puts on little "magic shows" for infants. In her "theater," babies watch as possible and impossible events occur with toys or other objects. Some 3-month-old infants act surprised and gaze longer at impossible events. An example is seeing two solid objects appear to pass through each other. By the time they are 8 months old, babies can remember where objects are (or should be) for at least 1 minute

(❖Fig. 4.17). Children as young as 11 months old can remember and imitate simple two-step actions, such as setting up a small ramp and then placing a toy car at the top (Bauer, 1996).

Piaget believed that abilities like those described in ❖Figure 4.17 emerge only after a long sensorimotor period of development. However, evidence continues to mount that babies are born with the capacity to form concepts about the world, or acquire this ability early in life (Eimas, Quinn, & Cowan, 1994). It looks as if further study is likely to refine and amend the ideas that grew from Piaget's fateful decision to "watch the children for a while."

Another criticism of Piaget is that he underestimated the impact of culture on mental development. The next section provides some insight into how children master the intellectual tools valued by their culture.

Vygotsky's Sociocultural Theory

In recent years, psychologists have become interested in the **sociocultural theory** of Russian scholar Lev Vygotsky (1896-1934). Vygotsky developed his ideas during the 1920s and 1930s, which is when Piaget was creating his theory. Vygotsky's key insight is that children's thinking develops through dialogues with more capable persons (Vygotsky, 1962; 1978).

How does that relate to intellectual growth? So far, no one has ever published *A child's guide to life on Earth.* Instead, children must learn about life from various "tutors," such as par-

Formal operations stage *Period of intellectual development characterized by thinking that includes abstract, theoretical, and hypothetical ideas.*
Abstract principles *Concepts and ideas removed from specific examples and concrete situations.*
Hypothetical possibilities *Suppositions, guesses, or projections.*
Sociocultural theory *Vygotsky's theory of child development that emphasizes social and cultural influences on cognitive growth.*

ents, teachers, and older siblings. Even if *A child's guide to life on Earth* did exist, we would need a separate version for every culture, subculture, and ethnic group. It is not enough for children to learn how to think; they must also learn specific intellectual skills valued by their culture.

Like Piaget, Vygotsky believed that children actively seek to discover new principles. However, Vygotsky emphasized that many of a child's most important "discoveries" are guided by skillful tutors. Developmental psychologist David Shaffer (1999) offers the following example:

> Annie, a 4-year-old, has just received her first jigsaw puzzle as a birthday present. She attempts to work the puzzle but gets nowhere until her father comes along, sits down beside her, and gives her some tips. He suggests that it would be a good idea to put together the corners first, points to the pink area at the edge of one corner piece and says, "Let's look for another pink piece." When Annie seems frustrated, he places two interlocking pieces near each other so that she will notice them, and when Annie succeeds, he offers words of encouragement. As Annie gradually gets the hang of it, he steps back and lets her work more and more independently. (p. 260)

Interactions of this sort are most helpful when they take place within a child's **zone of proximal development**.

What did Vygotsky mean by that?   The word *proximal* means close or nearby. Vygotsky realized that, at any given time, some tasks are just beyond a child's reach. The child is close to having the mental skills needed to do the task, but it is a little too complex for the child to master it alone. However, children working within this zone can make rapid progress if they receive sensitive guidance from a skillful partner.

Vygotsky also emphasized a process he called **scaffolding**. A scaffold is a framework or temporary support. Vygotsky believed that adults help children learn how to think by "scaffolding," or supporting, their attempts to solve problems or discover principles. To be most effective, scaffolding must be responsive to a child's needs. For example, as Annie's father helped her with the puzzle, he tailored his hints and guidance to match her evolving abilities. The two of them worked together, step by step, so that Annie could better understand how to assemble a puzzle. In a sense, Annie's father set up a series of temporary bridges that helped her move into new mental territory.

During their collaborations with others, children learn important cultural beliefs and values. For example, imagine that a boy wants to know how many Pokemon cards he has. His mother helps him stack and count the cards, moving each card to a new stack as they count it. She then shows him how to write the number on a slip of paper so he can remember it. This sequence of events teaches the child not only about counting but also that writing is valued in our culture. In other parts of the world, a child learning to count might be shown how to make notches on a stick or tie knots in a cord.

SUMMARY   Vygotsky saw that grown-ups play a crucial role in what children know. As they try to decipher the world, children

BRIDGES

"Brain Plasticity and Neurogenesis" in Chapter 3 presents more information about how learning experiences can "rewire" the brain.

See pages 78–80.

rely on adults to help them understand how things work. Vygotsky further noticed that adults unconsciously adjust their behavior to give children the information they need to solve problems that interest the child. In this way, children use adults to learn about their culture and society (Gopnik, Meltzoff, & Kuhl, 1999).

We have now examined some interesting aspects of development in several major areas. The next section describes the effects of *deprivation* and *enrichment*. These are conditions that can affect nearly all aspects of a child's early years.

DEPRIVATION AND ENRICHMENT—IN SEARCH OF TENDER LOVING CARE

The brain of a newborn baby has fewer **dendrites** (nerve cell branches) and **synapses** (connections between nerve cells) than an adult brain. (See ❖Fig. 4.18.) However, during the first 3 years of life, the brain dramatically increases in density. Millions of new connections form every day. But at the same time, unused connections disappear. As a result, early learning environments literally shape the developing brain (Nelson, 1999). This is especially true of environments that can be described as enriched or deprived.

Early Deprivation

What happens when children suffer severe **deprivation** (a lack of normal stimulation, nutrition, comfort, or love)? Tragically, a few mistreated children have spent their first years in closets, attics, and other restricted environments. When first discovered, these children are usually mute, retarded, and emotionally damaged. Some suffer from **deprivation dwarfism**— stunted growth associated with stress, isolation, or general deprivation (see "Closet Child"). Efforts to teach such severely deprived children to speak and behave normally rarely succeed.

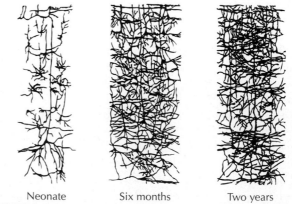

Neonate   Six months   Two years

❖ **FIGURE 4.18** *A rapid increase in brain synapses continues until about age 4. At that point, children actually have more brain synapses than adults do. Then, after age 10, the number slowly declines, reaching adult levels at about age 16. (From Conel, 1939–1963.)*

Children who grow up in poverty run a high risk of experiencing many forms of deprivation. There is evidence that lasting damage to social, emotional, and cognitive development occurs when children must cope with severe early deprivation.

Fortunately, such extreme deprivation is unusual. Nevertheless, milder levels of perceptual, intellectual, or emotional deprivation occur in many families, especially those that must cope with poverty. By the age of 5, children who grow up in poor homes tend to have lower IQs. They are also more fearful, unhappy, and prone to hostile or aggressive behavior (Carnegie Corporation, 1994; McLoyd, 1998).

What aspects of deprivation are responsible for doing damage? In infancy, attachment failures are a major element of deprivation. Consider, for example, the plight of children raised in severely overcrowded Romanian orphanages. These children received almost no attention from adults for the first year or more of their lives. Some have been adopted by Canadian families, where they are making progress toward normalcy. However, many of the children have remained poorly attached to adoptive parents. Some, for instance, will readily wander off with strangers (Chisholm et al., 1995).

A lack of perceptual stimulation (varied, patterned, and meaningful sensory input) is a second major element of early deprivation. For instance, one early study focused on infants placed in foundling homes and orphanages. The babies received good physical care, but they were kept in shrouded cribs that allowed them to see only a blank ceiling. The babies' only contact with adults occurred when they were quickly fed or changed. To put it mildly, there was *nothing happening* for these children: no variety, no input, no cuddling, no attention, and very little stimulation. In view of this, it's not surprising that many of the babies were retarded and showed little interest in other humans. They also died at an alarmingly high rate (Spitz, 1945).

Later in childhood, damage may result from a lack of intellectual stimulation or parents who are cold, neglectful, or rejecting. In light of this, it is wise to view all of childhood as a *relatively critical period* (Barnet & Barnet, 1998; Nelson, 1999). Prolonged deprivation at any time in childhood can seriously limit development (Joseph, 1999).

BRIDGES

Adults experience a number of disruptive effects when they are deprived of perceptual stimulation.

See Chapter 8, pages 249–251, for details.

Enrichment

If too little stimulation impairs development, can abundant stimulation enhance it? To answer this question, psychologists have created various **enriched environments**. These are surroundings that have been made especially novel, complex, and stimulating. Enriched environments may be the "soil" from which brighter children grow. To illustrate, let us begin with an experiment in which rats were raised in an enriched environment.

Building Bigger and Better Brains
One group of infant rats was raised in *stimulus-poor* conditions inside adequate but unstimulating cages. These gray-walled cages contained nothing to explore or investigate. The second group was housed in a sort of "rat wonderland." The walls of this *stimulus-enriched* environment were decorated with colored patterns and each cage was filled with platforms, ladders, and cubbyholes. When the rats reached adulthood, their ability to learn mazes was tested. The stimulated rats dramatically outperformed their deprived relatives. In addition, rats living in enriched environments typically have larger, heavier brains, with a thicker cortex (Benloucif, Bennett, & Rosenzweig, 1995).

"Closet Child" Now with Loving Parents
LONG BEACH (AP)—Becky's story began to unfold when the Sheriff's Department responded to a tip like hundreds of others. They found Becky in urine-soaked clothes, asleep on a hard cot in her parents' bedroom.

"She was almost like an animal," one of the deputies reported.

Her world then was the bedroom and its closet, in which she was kept for untold hours. Now Becky lives in a spacious foster home.

Since Becky's rescue, she has gained 12 pounds and grown 6 inches. But she is still a mite, for she weighed only 24 pounds and stood only 32 inches tall last April.

When she was found, Becky couldn't even crawl; now she walks. Then, she knew only a few words—now she speaks in sentences. She is, except for the hurt in her eyes, like almost any toddler.

But Rebecca is no toddler. She is 9 years old, and her pediatrician says she may never catch up.

Zone of proximal development *Refers to the range of tasks a child cannot yet master alone, but that she or he can accomplish with the guidance of a more capable partner.*
Scaffolding *The process of adjusting instruction so that it is responsive to a beginner's behavior and supports the beginner's efforts to understand a problem or gain a mental skill.*
Dendrites *Nerve cell fibers that receive incoming messages from other nerve cells.*
Synapse *A connection point between two nerve cells, over which messages pass.*
Deprivation *In development, the loss or withholding of normal stimulation, nutrition, comfort, love, and so forth; a condition of lacking.*
Deprivation dwarfism *A stunting of early growth caused by isolation, rejection, or general deprivation.*
Enriched environment *An environment deliberately made more novel, complex, and perceptually stimulating.*

THE MOZART EFFECT—SMART MUSIC?

CRITICAL THINKING

Frances Rauscher and Gordon Shaw have reported that after college students listen to a Mozart piano sonata they score higher on a spatial reasoning test (Rauscher & Shaw, 1998; Shaw, 1999). Soon after this observation made the news, doting parents were playing Mozart for their babies around the clock. Obviously, they hoped that, like the college students, their babies would become smarter. However, parents should be suspicious of *any* practice that claims to offer such "magical" benefits.

A major problem with the "Mozart effect" is that the original experiment was done with adults; it tells us nothing about infants. Also, the study didn't test other styles of music. Why not use the music of Bach, Schubert, or MTV, for that matter? An even more important question is, Does the Mozart effect actually exist?

What does the evidence suggest? A few studies have found small increases in spatial intelligence following exposure to Mozart's music (Rideout, Dougherty, & Wernert, 1998; Rideout & Taylor, 1997). However, most researchers have been unable to duplicate the effect (Chabris et al., 1999; Steele, Bass, & Crook, 1999; Steele, Brown, & Stoecker, 1999; Wilson & Brown, 1997).

Why do some studies support the effect and others disconfirm it? Most studies have compared students who heard music to students who rested in silence. However, Canadian psychologists Kristin Nantais and Glenn Schellenberg found that listening to a narrated story also improves test scores. This is especially true for students who like listening to stories. Thus, students who scored higher after listening to Mozart might have just been more alert or in a better mood (Nantais & Schellenberg, 1999).

As wonderful as Mozart's music may be, it appears that there is nothing magical about it, at least where infant intelligence is concerned.

enter school. Follow-up studies have confirmed that Head Start children show real improvements in their abilities and school performance (Barnett, 1995; Campbell & Ramey, 1994). This is especially true for the neediest children.

Programs like Head Start can't work miracles, but they can prepare children for school. They also teach children social and emotional skills that may help them cope better with life (Zigler & Styfco, 1994). As teens, former Head Start participants are less likely to drop out of school, get arrested, or get pregnant, among other things (Zigler & Muenchow, 1992). High-quality enrichment programs can be expensive. But if such programs can prevent children from falling behind or dropping out of school, they are a bargain (Barnet & Barnet, 1998).

What can parents do to enrich a child's environment? The examples we have reviewed emphasize that it is important to nourish the mind. However, it is equally important for parents to avoid overstimulating or "pushing" a child. The next section explains why.

Parents and Enrichment

Every morning, Derek's mother drills him with flash cards in hopes that he will learn to read before any of the neighbor children. In the afternoon, Derek watches educational videotapes about premath skills. Every evening, a Mozart sonata fills Derek's room, repeating over and over. Derek is taking dancing lessons and learning sign language. His favorite toy is a fake cell phone.

Is this enrichment? It depends. Derek is two and a half. His parents obviously mean well. But by the time he is 5, if Derek's parents ask him to change a light bulb, he will hold it in the socket and wait for the world to revolve around him. As Derek's example suggests, "enrichment" that does not match a child's needs is of little value.

BENEFICIAL STIMULATION Parents can encourage exploration of the world by paying attention to a baby's signals, likes, and dislikes. What actually holds a baby's interest is far more important than what parents think is interesting. Parental attitudes toward *investigation* also affect intellectual growth. Children who repeatedly hear, "Don't touch that" (chair, handle, trash, radio, pencil, flower) or "I told you not to" (go up there, play with that, leave this spot, get dirty) may become passive and intellectually dulled. Placing virtually all common objects off-limits is a serious mistake. It is better to "childproof" a house than to strictly list what a child can and cannot touch.

There is also value in actively enriching sensory experiences. Babies should be surrounded by colors, music, people, and things to see, taste, smell, and touch. Infants are not vegetables. It makes perfect sense to take them outside, to hang mobiles over their cribs, to place mirrors nearby, to play music for them, or to rearrange their rooms now and then. (However, see "The Mozart Effect" for a caution.) The presence of stimulating play materials in the home, together with responsive parents, is strongly related to how quickly children progress (Bradley et al., 1989; Luster & Dubow, 1992).

STIMULATING ENVIRONMENTS It's a long leap from rats to people, but an actual increase in brain size is impressive. If stimulation can enhance the "intelligence" of a lowly rat, it seems reasonable to assume that human infants also benefit from enrichment.

Is there any evidence that this is actually the case? Yes, many studies have shown that enriched environments improve abilities or enhance development (Dieter & Emory, 1997). In Chapter 12, you will find a full discussion of the effects of environment on intelligence. For now, let's consider one example of enrichment applied to humans.

EARLY CHILDHOOD EDUCATION An encouraging example of enrichment can be found in **early childhood education programs**, which provide stimulating intellectual experiences for disadvantaged children. In the United States, for example, the Head Start program helps children "learn to learn" before they

It also makes sense to talk to infants, from birth onward. Try to talk about present events, such as what you are doing, objects the baby is looking at, and parts of the baby's body you are touching. Remember, the more time babies spend interacting with parents, the faster they develop language and thinking abilities (Hart & Risley, 1999). Remember, too, that TV is no substitute for real conversations (Golinkoff & Hirsh-Pasek, 1999).

Summary

Psychologists are highly critical of misguided attempts to produce "superbabies" by pushing the pace of development. Overloading a toddler with a barrage of stimuli, flash cards, and exercises is not enriching. True enrichment does not make the child feel pressured to perform. Instead, it fosters interest, enthusiasm, and motivation to learn (Eliot, 1999). Many of the things Derek's parents did (in the earlier vignette) would be perfectly appropriate for an older child—especially when the child's own interests are taken into account.

Most people recognize that babies need lots of tender loving care for their physical needs. But as our discussion has shown, adequate nurturing should also include perceptual and intellectual stimulation. Here is a final summary of many of the points we have discussed in this chapter, in the words of child experts Ann Barnet and Richard Barnet (1998):

Babies need closeness, nurture, communication, play, and engagement; they need quiet, stability, and predictability. They need challenge, the stimulation of new experiences, and the opportunity to explore their surroundings in safety. All children need to feel that they are treasured, that their developmental accomplishments are celebrated, and that their parents' devotion is rock solid.

A LOOK AHEAD   In the upcoming section, we will return to the topics of parenting and discipline. These are key processes that deeply link the lives of adults and children.

KNOWLEDGE BUILDER
COGNITIVE DEVELOPMENT, DEPRIVATION AND ENRICHMENT

RELATE

You are going to make cookies with children of various ages. See if you can name each of Piaget's stages and give an example of what a child in that stage might be expected to do.

You have been asked to help a child learn to use a pocket calculator to do simple addition. How would you go about identifying the child's zone of proximal development for this task? How would you scaffold the child's learning?

If you were designing a preschool classroom, what would you do to make it an enriched environment?

LEARNING CHECK

Match each item with one of the following stages.
A. Sensorimotor B. Preoperational C. Concrete operational D. Formal operations

1. _____ egocentric thought
2. _____ abstract or hypothetical
3. _____ purposeful movement
4. _____ intuitive thought
5. _____ conservation
6. _____ reversibility of thought
7. _____ object permanence
8. _____ nonverbal development

9. Assimilation refers to applying existing thought patterns or knowledge to new situations. T or F?

10. Newer methods for testing infant thinking abilities frequently make note of whether an infant is _____ by seemingly _____ events.

11. Vygotsky called the process of providing a temporary framework of supports for learning new mental abilities _____.

12. During the first 2 years of life, the number of synapses in an infant's brain increases, while the number of dendrites decreases. T or F?

13. Early childhood education programs can be characterized as attempts to enrich the environments of deprived children. T or F?

CRITICAL THINKING

14. Using Piaget's theory as a guide, at what age would you expect a child to recognize that a Styrofoam cup has weight?

Answers:
1. B 2. D 3. A 4. B 5. C 6. C 7. A 8. A 9. T 10. surprised, impossible 11. scaffolding 12. F 13. T 14. Seventy-five percent of 4- to 6-year-olds say that a Styrofoam cup has no weight after lifting it! Most children judge weight intuitively (by the way an object feels) until they begin to move into the concrete operational stage (Smith, Carey, & Wiser, 1985).

Early childhood education programs *Programs that provide stimulating intellectual experiences, typically for disadvantaged preschoolers.*

When parents fail to give children a good start in life, everybody suffers—the child, the parents, and society as a whole. Children need to reach adulthood with a capacity for love, joy, fulfillment, responsibility, and self-control. Most people discipline their children in the same way they were disciplined. Unfortunately, this means that many parents make the same mistakes their parents did (Covell, Grusec, & King, 1995).

Two key ingredients of effective parenting are communication and discipline. In each area, parents must strike a balance between freedom and guidance.

CONSISTENCY

How can parents strike a healthy balance? Children should feel free to express their deepest feelings through speech and actions. However, this does not mean they can do whatever they please. Rather, the child is able to move freely within well-defined guidelines for acceptable behavior. Of course, individual parents may choose limits that are more or less "strict." But this choice is less important than **consistency** (maintaining stable rules of conduct). Consistent discipline gives a child a sense of security and stability. Inconsistency makes the child's world seem insecure and unpredictable.

What does consistency in child management mean in practice? To illustrate the errors parents often make, let's consider some examples of *inconsistency* (Fontenelle, 1989). The following are mistakes to avoid.

- Saying one thing and doing something else. You tell the child, "Bart, if you don't eat your brussels sprouts, you can't have any dessert." Then you feel guilty and offer him some dessert.
- Making statements you don't mean. "If you don't quiet down, I'm going to stop the car and make you walk home."

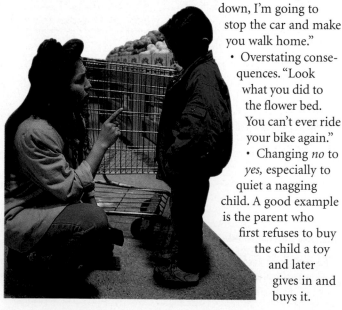

- Overstating consequences. "Look what you did to the flower bed. You can't ever ride your bike again."
- Changing *no* to *yes,* especially to quiet a nagging child. A good example is the parent who first refuses to buy the child a toy and later gives in and buys it.

- Not checking to see if the child has actually done something you requested, such as picking up clothes or making a bed.
- Contradicting the rules your spouse has set for the child. Parents need to agree on child discipline and not undermine each other's efforts.
- Not meaning what you say the first time. Children quickly learn how many times they can be warned before they are actually about to be punished.
- Responding differently to the same misbehavior. One day a child is sent to his room for fighting with his sister. The next day the fighting is overlooked.

Random discipline makes children feel angry and confused because they cannot control the consequences of their own behavior. Inconsistency also gives children the message: "Don't believe what I say because I usually don't mean it."

Constructive Discipline

At one time or another, most parents use power assertion, withdrawal of love, or management techniques to control their children. Each mode of discipline has its place. However, physical punishment and withdrawal of love should always be used with caution. Here are some guidelines:

1. Parents should separate disapproval of the act from disapproval of the child. Instead of saying, "I'm going to punish you because *you are bad,*" say, "I'm upset about *what you did.*"
2. State specifically what misbehavior you are punishing. Explain why you have set limits on this kind of conduct.
3. Punishment should never be harsh or injurious to a child. Don't physically punish a child while you are angry. Also remember that giving a child the message "I don't love you right now" can be more painful and damaging than any spanking.
4. Punishment is most effective when it is administered immediately. This statement is especially true for younger children.
5. Spanking and other forms of physical punishment are not particularly effective for children under age 2. The child will only be confused and frightened. Spankings also become less effective after age 5 because they tend to humiliate the child and breed resentment.
6. Many psychologists believe that children should never be physically punished. If you do use physical punishment, reserve it for situations that pose an immediate danger to younger children, for example, when a child runs into the street.
7. Remember, too, that it is usually more effective to reward children when they are being good than it is to punish them for misbehavior.

After age 5, management techniques are the most effective form of discipline, especially techniques that emphasize communication and the relationship between parent and child.

Calvin and Hobbes

WHAT ASSURANCE DO I HAVE THAT YOUR PARENTING ISN'T SCREWING ME UP?

© 1993 Watterson/Distributed by Universal Press Syndicate

THE PARENT-CHILD RELATIONSHIP

The heart of child management is the relationship between parents and their children. Parenting experts Don Dinkmeyer and Gary McKay (1997) believe that there are four basic ingredients of positive parent-child interactions.

- **Mutual respect** Effective parents try to avoid nagging, hitting, debating, and talking down to their children. They also avoid doing things for their children that children can do for themselves. (Constantly stripping children of opportunities to learn and take responsibility prevents them from becoming independent and developing self-esteem.)
- **Shared enjoyment** Some time each day, effective parents spend time with their children, doing something that both the parent and child enjoy.
- **Love** This goes almost without saying, but many parents assume their children know that they are loved. It is important to communicate your caring by words and by actions such as hugging.
- **Encouragement** Children who get frequent encouragement come to believe in themselves. Effective parents don't just praise their children for success, winning, or good behavior. They also recognize a child's *progress and attempts to improve.* Show you have faith in children by letting them try things on their own and by encouraging their efforts.

EFFECTIVE COMMUNICATION

Creative communication is another important ingredient of successful child management (Bath, 1996). Child expert Haim Ginott (1965) believed that making a distinction between feelings and behavior is the key to clear communication. Because children (and parents, too) do not choose how they feel, it is important to allow free expression of feelings.

Accepting Feelings

The child who learns to regard some feelings as "bad," or unacceptable, is being asked to deny a very real part of his or her experience. Ginott encouraged parents to teach their children that all feelings are appropriate; it is only actions that are subject to disapproval. Many parents are unaware of just how often they block communication and the expression of feelings

in their children. Consider this typical conversation excerpted from Ginott's book (1965):

> *Son:* I am stupid, and I know it. Look at my grades in school.
> *Father:* You just have to work harder.
> *Son:* I already work harder and it doesn't help. I have no brains.
> *Father:* You are smart, I know.
> *Son:* I am stupid, I know.
> *Father:* (loudly) You are not stupid!
> *Son:* Yes, I am!
> *Father:* You are not stupid. Stupid!

By debating with the child, the father misses the point that his son *feels* stupid. It would be far more helpful for the father to encourage the boy to talk about his feelings.

How could he do that? He might say, "You really feel that you are not as smart as others, don't you? Do you feel this way often? Are you feeling bad at school?" In this way, the child is given a chance to express his emotions and to feel understood. The father might conclude the conversation by saying, "Look, son, in my eyes you are a fine person. But I understand how you feel. Everyone feels stupid at times."

Encouragement

Again, it is valuable to remember that supportive parents encourage their children. In terms of communication, encouragement sounds like this (Dinkmeyer, McKay, & Dinkmeyer, 1997):

> "It looks like you enjoyed that."
> "I have confidence in you; you'll make it."
> "It was thoughtful of you to _____."
> "Thanks. That helped a lot."
> "You really worked hard on that."
> "You're improving. Look at the progress you've made."

I-Messages

Communication with a child can also be the basis of effective discipline. Thomas Gordon (1970), a child psychologist who devel-

---

Consistency *With respect to child discipline, the maintenance of stable rules of conduct.*

---

oped a program called Parent Effectiveness Training (PET), offers a useful suggestion. Gordon believes that parents should send *I-messages* to their children, rather than *you-messages*.

What's the difference? A **you-message** takes the form of threats, name-calling, accusing, bossing, lecturing, or criticizing. Generally, you-messages tell children what's "wrong" with them. An **I-message** tells children what effect their behavior had on you. To illustrate the difference, consider this example. After a hard day's work, Susan wants to sit down and rest a while. She begins to relax with a newspaper when her 5-year-old daughter starts banging loudly on a toy drum. Most parents would respond with a you-message:

"You go play outside this instant." (bossing)
"Don't ever make such a racket when someone is reading." (lecturing)
"You're really pushing it today, aren't you?" (accusing)
"You're a spoiled brat." (name-calling)
"You're going to get a spanking!" (threatening)

Gordon suggests sending an I-message such as "I am very tired, and I would like to read. I feel upset and can't read with so much noise." This forces the child to accept responsibility for the effects of her actions.

To summarize, an I-message states the behavior to which you object. It then clearly tells the child the consequence of his or her behavior and how that makes you feel. Here's a "fill-in-the-blanks" I-message: "When you (state the child's behavior), I feel (state your feelings) because (state the consequences of the child's behavior)." For example, "When you go to Jenny's without telling me, I worry that something might have happened to you because I don't know where you are" (Dinkmeyer, McKay, & Dinkmeyer, 1997).

NATURAL AND LOGICAL CONSEQUENCES

Sometimes events automatically discourage misbehavior. For example, the child who refuses to eat dinner will get uncomfortably hungry. A child who throws a temper tantrum may gain nothing but a sore throat and a headache if the tantrum is ignored (Fontenelle, 1989). In such instances, a child's actions have **natural consequences** (intrinsic effects). In situations that don't produce natural consequences, parents can set up **logical consequences** (rational and reasonable effects). For example, a parent might say, "We'll go to the zoo when you've picked up all these toys," or "You can play with your dolls as soon as you've taken your bath," or "You two can stop arguing or leave the table until you're ready to join us."

The concept of logical, parent-defined consequences can be combined with I-messages to handle many day-to-day instances of misbehavior. The key idea is to use an I-message to set up consequences and then give the child a choice to make: "Michelle, we're trying to watch TV. You may settle down and watch with us or go play elsewhere. You decide which you'd rather do" (Dinkmeyer, McKay, & Dinkmeyer, 1997).

How could Susan have dealt with her 5-year-old—the one who was banging on a drum? A response that combines an I-message with logical consequences would be "I would like

for you to stop banging on that drum; otherwise, please take it outside." If the child continues to bang on the drum inside the house, then she has caused the toy to be put away. If she takes it outside, she has made a decision to play with the drum in a way that respects her mother's wishes. In this way, both parent and child have been allowed to maintain a sense of self-respect, and a needless clash has been averted.

After you have stated consequences and let the child decide, be sure to respect the child's choice. If the child repeats the misbehavior, you can let the consequences remain in effect longer. But later, give the child another chance to cooperate.

With all child management techniques, remember to be firm, kind, consistent, respectful, and encouraging. And most of all, try every day to live the message you wish to communicate.

KNOWLEDGE BUILDER
PARENTING AND CHILD DISCIPLINE

RELATE

What do you think are the best ways to balance freedom and restraint in child discipline?

Parents can probably never be completely consistent. Think of a time when your parents were inconsistent in disciplining you. How did it affect you?

To what extent do the four basic ingredients of positive parent-child interactions apply to any healthy relationship?

Think of a you-message you have recently given a child, family member, roommate, or spouse. Can you change it into an I-message?

LEARNING CHECK

1. Effective discipline gives children freedom within a structure of consistent and well-defined limits. T or F?

2. One good way to maintain consistency in child management is to overstate the consequences for misbehavior. T or F?

3. Spankings and other physical punishments are most effective for children under the age of 2. T or F?

4. Giving recognition for progress and attempts to improve is an example of parental _____.

5. I-messages are a gentle way of accusing a child of misbehavior. T or F?

6. In situations where natural consequences are unavailable or do not discourage misbehavior, parents should define logical consequences for a child. T or F?

CRITICAL THINKING

7. Several Scandinavian countries have made it illegal for parents to spank their own children. Does this infringe on the rights of parents?

Answers:

1. T 2. F 3. T 4. encouragement 5. F 6. T 7. Such laws are based on the view that it should be illegal to physically assault any person, regardless of age. Although parents may believe they have a "right" to spank their children, it can be argued that children need special protection because they are small, powerless, and dependent.

Focus: How has new knowledge about genetics affected parenthood?

In his famous novel, *Brave New World,* Aldous Huxley described a futuristic society in which "baby factories" produce thousands of duplicate humans to do society's labor. Huxley, writing in the 1930s, envisioned a future in which biological engineering would be used for sinister and totalitarian ends. Now that the future has arrived, we find instead that some of the advances Huxley anticipated have made it possible for previously infertile couples to have children. And yet, as is often true, new solutions create new problems. Let's explore some recent developments in medicine and genetics that raise interesting social, psychological, and ethical questions.

ASSISTED CONCEPTION

In the recent past, adoption was the only alternative for infertile couples. Now, couples have an array of new options, from fertility drugs to surrogate mothers. Two techniques of special interest are artificial insemination and in vitro fertilization.

Artificial Insemination

If her husband is sterile, a woman can undergo **artificial insemination** (medically engineered conception). In this procedure, sperm cells from an anonymous donor are used to impregnate the woman. Donors are selected so that their eye and hair color, height, and so on, match the husband's as closely as possible. For emotional reasons, some of the husband's sperm cells are sometimes mixed with the donor sperm so that it is impossible to tell who was actually the father. (Men who are sterile often produce sperm, but their sperm count is too low for them to father a child.)

Test Tube Babies

In vitro fertilization (fertilization of an ovum outside a woman's body) has made it possible for some infertile couples to bear children who share both the mother's and father's genes. To produce a "test tube" baby, egg cells are surgically collected from the mother's ovary. The egg cells are placed in a petri dish of nutrients, and the father's sperm cells are added (❖Fig. 4-19). (A womb with a view!) After an egg cell is fertilized and begins dividing, it is implanted in the mother's womb, where it develops normally. In a variation on in vitro fertilization, an unrelated woman may donate an egg cell to the infertile couple. The egg cell is then fertilized with the husband's sperm and implanted in the wife's uterus. Infertile couples who are considering this technique should be warned, however. Even using the

latest methods, only 15 percent of in vitro attempts are successful, and the cost ranges from $10,000 to $20,000.

Questions and Controversies

The procedures outlined here raise a number of practical, emotional, moral, and even religious issues. Many will no doubt occur to you. A few that may not are listed here.

Many donors for artificial insemination are used repeatedly. One clinic reported that a single donor fathered 50 babies.

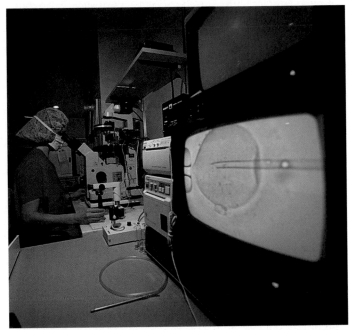

❖ **FIGURE 4.19** *During in vitro fertilization, ova from the woman or a donor are mixed with sperm from the man or a donor. In the advanced techniques shown here, a sperm cell is placed inside an ovum. If both the egg and sperm are donated, both nominal parents are genetically unrelated to the "test tube" baby.*

You-message *Threatening, accusing, bossing, lecturing, or criticizing another person.*
I-message *A message that states the effect someone else's behavior had on you.*
Natural consequences *The effects that naturally tend to follow a particular behavior.*
Logical consequences *Reasonable consequences that are defined by parents.*
Artificial insemination *Medically engineered impregnation.*
In vitro fertilization *Fertilization of an ovum outside a woman's body.*

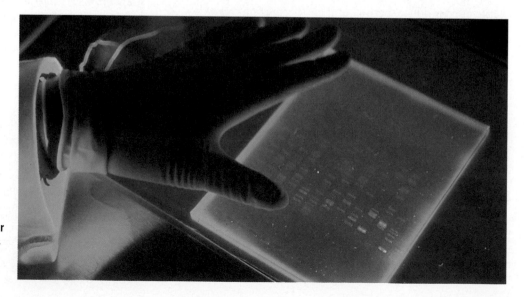 *sidebar:* a step beyond

What if this donor harbored a genetic disease or defect? What if children fathered by the same donor were to meet and marry? Because they would be half-siblings, their offspring would run a high risk of genetic defects. What rules of testing and record keeping should apply to artificial insemination by a donor?

Many scientists believe that handling egg cells for in vitro fertilization may increase the risk of deformities in babies. If a child is born with a defect, is the physician responsible? Frequently, more than one egg is fertilized. Should they be donated to another infertile couple? Is letting them die an abortion? Should in vitro fertilization be allowed if the man and woman are not married? If they divorce, who should get "custody" of the ova? Should single women or women over 50 be allowed to undergo artificial insemination?

In two very important ways, assisted conception has not been a problem. A revealing study found that the quality of parenting in families with assisted conception was *superior* to that of families with naturally conceived or adopted children. Also, assisted conception had no effect on children's emotions, behavior, or relationships with parents (Golombok et al., 1995).

Sex Selection

Another recent development that may have an impact on parenthood is the possibility of selecting an infant's sex prior to conception. The procedure involves separating *X*- and *Y*-bearing sperm and then artificially fertilizing the egg cell with all male-producing or all female-producing sperm.

Currently, sex selection techniques cannot *guarantee* to produce a child of the desired sex. Sex selection is also relatively expensive (about $500), and some couples may be discouraged by the need for artificial insemination. A further worry is that two thirds of all childless couples say they would prefer to have a boy as a first child.

If large numbers of couples select their children's sex, would there be an excess of male births? Seventy-three percent of all potential parents who would be willing to use sex-selection technology say they would choose sons (Steinbacher & Gilroy, 1990). If many couples were to make this choice, the male-female population balance would be upset. Birth rate and population growth would slow dramatically once 70 percent of the population became male. (Also, of course, beer sales would skyrocket.)

GENETICS AND PARENTHOOD

In recent years, having children has been influenced by an improved understanding of human genetics and problems that "run in the family." Increasingly, it has become possible to identify genetic disorders such as sickle-cell anemia, hemophilia, cystic fibrosis, muscular dystrophy, albinism, and some forms of mental retardation.

Scientists are currently hard at work on a giant project to identify, in order, every gene on every human chromosome. The result will be a map of the **human genome** (JEEN-ome), or entire set of human genes. Having, in essence, a "full set of instructions for making a human" will allow advanced identification of genetic diseases and new tests to detect them. In 1999, scientists for the first time mapped an entire human chromosome. You could say that this is the first time that we've had a complete chapter in the human instruction book (Dunham, Shimizu, & Chissoe, 1999). By sometime in the year 2000, or soon after, the entire human genome should be mapped. At that point, doctors, biologists, and you and I will face a host of new ethical and practical dilemmas.

Genetic Counseling

Today, prospective parents who suspect that they may be carriers of genetic disorders may seek **genetic counseling**. By examining the family history of each future parent, and in some cases by directly mapping chromosomes, geneticists can calculate the risk of a genetic disorder.

What can a couple do if the risk of a genetic defect is high? Knowing the risks, parents can choose not to have a child; or, if

Strands of DNA can be chemically broken into shorter segments, which (after further manipulation) can be displayed for analysis. The pink-glowing pieces of DNA you see here are enlarged many times.

the odds are in their favor, they may elect to take the chance. Even when there is a reasonable likelihood of a genetic disorder, some couples elect to have children. If pregnancy occurs, however, they can then have a test performed to detect the genetic defect. Such prenatal testing is done by **amniocentesis** (AM-nee-oh-SEN-tee-sis: taking a sample of amniotic fluid from the mother's womb). This procedure allows determination of fetal sex, as well as detection of many genetic defects.

Amniocentesis is usually done at about the 15th week of pregnancy. An alternate procedure, called **chorionic villus sampling**, can be done between 6 and 8 weeks of pregnancy. This technique takes a small piece of the placenta for analysis. Either method allows couples who do not object to abortion to terminate the pregnancy when a serious genetic defect is detected. Parents who consider abortion unacceptable still have the advantage of forewarning so that they may prepare the best possible care for the child.

One of the challenges of genetic counseling today is that new tests are making it possible to identify genetic problems long before any cures will be available (Kenen & Smith, 1995).

Bree Walker Lampley, a TV celebrity in Los Angeles, has a genetic condition that causes deformity of the hands and feet. Before she became pregnant, she knew she had a 50 percent chance of giving birth to a baby with the same trait. Despite public criticism, she had a baby (who did, in fact, inherit her genetic condition). The social pressures she faced illustrate the dilemmas people who carry genetic defects often face (Rennie, 1994).

THE FUTURE

Recent advances in genetics, the exploding knowledge about how DNA controls heredity, and mapping of the human genome will bring profound changes to the human condition. Let's sample some of the possibilities.

Eugenics

Domestic plants and animals have been improved more in the past 50 years than in the previous 5,000. This improvement has been accomplished primarily through **eugenics** (you-JEN-iks: selective breeding for desirable characteristics). Some extremists have already proposed that eugenics be applied to humans. But the very idea is loaded with ethical problems. How would we decide what characteristics are desirable? And who would decide who can have children and who cannot? Typically, eugenic arguments are applied to the least powerful individuals in any society (Smith, 1995).

In practice, it is unlikely that widespread human eugenics will ever be practiced. On the other hand, some genetic diseases will almost certainly be "cured." Even without such direct efforts, the steady use of genetic counseling could have a eugenic effect on future generations.

Genetic Engineering

It is now becoming possible to remove defective genes and replace them with normal ones. Could such genetic engineering also be used to produce beauty, intelligence, resistance to aging, or superhuman athletic potential? In theory, yes, but practically speaking, probably not. Literally thousands of genes affect such qualities, not to mention the effects of environment. For this reason, limited genetic engineering involving one or two genes may soon be used to combat specific diseases such as diabetes or cancer, as well as inherited disorders.

Tampering with genes on a major scale is not likely in the near future. **Cloning**, the production of an entire organism from a single cell, is also likely to remain science fiction (where humans are concerned) for the immediate future. Athough it's true that sheep and other farm animals have been cloned, there is no medical reason why anyone would attempt to clone a human. In addition, a cloned individual would not be genetically identical to the donor, and his or her life experiences would be

Human genome *The entire set of human genes.*
Genetic counseling *Providing guidance and testing to prospective parents regarding the risks of bearing a child with a genetic disorder.*
Amniocentesis *Testing of the amniotic fluid from a pregnant woman's womb to identify fetal sex and to detect genetic defects in the fetus.*
Chorionic villus sampling *Testing of a small piece of the placenta early in pregnancy to detect genetic defects in the fetus.*
Eugenics *Selective breeding for desirable characteristics.*
Cloning *The production of an entire organism by using the DNA from a single cell.*

totally different. Thus, the specter of humankind being besieged by hundreds of cloned Hitlers, or Saddams, or textbook authors is pure fantasy (Pence, 1998).

Gene Therapy

Genetic researchers and medical specialists are in the first stages of trying gene therapies with humans. In the future, some genetic diseases will be treated by inserting corrective genes into the cells of a patient's body. Typically, beneficial genes are carried into a patient's body by viruses that have been genetically engineered to be harmless. Recently, researchers succeeded in creating artificial human chromosomes, an advance that should expand the possibilities for directly correcting genetic defects (Higgins, Schueler, & Willard, 1999).

Gene Cards

One authority on genetic engineering and genetic defects predicts that people will one day carry a "gene identity card" based on blood tests made during childhood. These would show what hereditary diseases a person is predisposed to, or which problems may be passed on in childbearing when combined with the gene pattern of a mate (Milunsky, 1992).

Rapid advances in techniques that affect heredity and conception have an important place in the understanding of behavior. And as we have seen, such changes raise a number of important psychological and ethical questions. Brace yourself, the brave new world of genetics is here.

CONCLUSION: Greater biological knowledge has created new opportunities to control conception and to avoid or cure genetic diseases. However, increased genetic control also raises medical and moral issues that have no easy solutions.

KNOWLEDGE BUILDER
GENETICS AND REPRODUCTION

RELATE

In your opinion, what are the pros and cons of assisted conception? What advice would you give a couple if they were considering artificial insemination? What about in vitro fertilization?

Why do you think more parents want to have boys than girls?

Decoding the human genome has been described as perhaps the greatest scientific accomplishment of the century. Do you agree?

Who do you think should receive genetic counseling? Everyone? Couples who plan to have children? Individuals with known risks in their families?

Under what circumstances, if any, do you think it would be ethical to practice eugenics, genetic engineering, or cloning?

LEARNING CHECK

1. The procedure known as in vitro fertilization involves fertilizing a woman with donor sperm. T or F?

2. Test tube babies are produced by fertilizing an egg cell outside the body. T or F?

3. Current sex selection procedures can consistently produce male offspring, but they cannot guarantee female babies. T or F?

4. Amniocentesis is primarily used to select sex before birth. T or F?

5. The term *eugenics* refers to the production of an entire organism from a single cell. T or F?

CRITICAL THINKING

6. Many people who should seek genetic screening choose not to be tested. Why do you think people resist testing?

Answers:

1. F 2. T 3. F 4. F 5. F 6. The most typical reasons given are that people would rather not know they carry a defect because it would mean their children might be at risk, too; they fear being stigmatized; they worry that their health insurance may be affected; and they are concerned that they may be turned down for future employment.

CHAPTER IN REVIEW

How do heredity and environment affect development?

- The nature-nurture controversy concerns the relative contributions to development of heredity (nature) and environment (nurture).
- Hereditary instructions are carried by the chromosomes and genes in each cell of the body. Most characteristics are polygenic and reflect the combined effects of dominant and recessive genes.
- Heredity affects a large number of personal characteristics, and it organizes the human growth sequence.
- Heredity is also involved in differences in temperament. Most infants fall into one of three temperament categories: easy children, difficult children, and slow-to-warm-up children.
- During critical periods in development, infants experience an increased sensitivity to specific environmental influences.
- Prenatal development is subject to environmental influences in the form of diseases, drugs, radiation, and the mother's diet, health, and emotions. Various teratogens can cause prenatal damage to the fetus, resulting in congenital problems.
- Heredity and environment are inseparable and interacting forces. A child's developmental level therefore reflects heredity, environment, and the effects of the child's own behavior.

What can newborn babies do?

- The human neonate has a number of adaptive reflexes, including the grasping, rooting, sucking, and Moro reflexes. Neonates show immediate evidence of learning and of appreciating the consequences of their actions.
- Tests in a looking chamber reveal a number of visual preferences in the newborn. The neonate is drawn to bright lights and circular or curved designs.
- Infants prefer human face patterns, especially familiar faces. In later infancy, interest in the unfamiliar emerges.

What influence does maturation have on early development?

- Maturation of the body and nervous system underlies the orderly sequence of motor, cognitive, emotional, and language development.
- The rate of maturation, however, varies from person to person. Also, learning contributes greatly to the development of basic motor skills.
- Emotions develop in a consistent order from the generalized excitement observed in newborn babies. Three of the basic emotions—fear, anger, and joy—may be innate.
- Many early skills are subject to the principle of readiness.

Of what significance is a child's emotional attachment to parents?

- Self-awareness and social referencing are elements of early social development.
- Imprinting in animals has some similarities to the emotional bonding that occurs between human infants and their caregivers.
- Emotional attachment of human infants is a critical early event.
- Infant attachment is reflected by separation anxiety. The quality of attachment can be classified as secure, insecure-avoidant, or insecure-ambivalent.
- High-quality day care does not appear to harm children. Low-quality care can be risky.
- Work with subhuman primates (monkeys) has pointed to contact comfort as a source of infant stimulation and attachment.
- Meeting a baby's affectional needs is as important as meeting needs for physical care.

How important are parenting styles?

- Studies suggest that caregiving styles have a substantial impact on emotional and intellectual development.
- Whereas mothers typically emphasize caregiving, fathers tend to function as playmates for infants.
- Optimal caregiving includes proactive maternal involvement, responsiveness to a child's needs and signals, and a good fit between the temperaments of parents and their children.
- Three major parental styles are authoritarian, permissive, and authoritative (effective). When judged by its effects on children, authoritative parenting appears to benefit children the most.
- Effective parental discipline tends to emphasize child management techniques (especially communication), rather than power assertion or withdrawal of love.

How do children acquire language?

- Language development proceeds from control of crying, to cooing, then babbling, the use of single words, and then to telegraphic speech.
- The underlying patterns of telegraphic speech suggest a biological predisposition to acquire language. This innate predisposition is augmented by learning.
- Prelanguage communication between parent and child involves shared rhythms, nonverbal signals, and turn-taking.
- Motherese or parentese is a simplified, musical style of speaking used by parents to help their children learn language.

How do children learn to think?

- The intellect of a child is less abstract than that of an adult. Jean Piaget theorized that intellectual growth occurs through a combination of assimilation and accommodation.
- Piaget also held that children go through a fixed series of cognitive stages. The stages and their approximate age ranges are: sensorimotor (0–2), preoperational (2–7), concrete operational (7–11), and formal operations (11–adult).
- Learning principles provide an alternate explanation, which assumes that cognitive development is continuous; it does not occur in stages.
- Recent studies of infants under the age of 1 year suggest that they are capable of thought well beyond that observed by Piaget.
- Lev Vygotsky's sociocultural theory emphasizes that a child's mental abilities are advanced by interactions with more competent partners. Mental growth takes place in a child's zone of proximal development, where a more skillful person may scaffold the child's progress.

What are the effects of a poor early environment?

- During the first few years of life, rapid changes in connections between brain cells tend to amplify the impact of early learning environments.
- Early perceptual, intellectual, and emotional deprivation seriously retards development. Even physical growth may be affected, as is the case in deprivation dwarfism.
- Research on deprivation suggests that secure attachment and perceptual stimulation are essential for normal development.
- Deliberate enrichment of the environment has a beneficial effect on development in infancy.

How do effective parents discipline their children?

- Responsibility, mutual respect, consistency, love, encouragement, and clear communication are features of effective parenting.
- Much misbehavior can be managed by use of I-messages and the application of natural and logical consequences.

How has new knowledge about genetics affected parenthood?

- Many recent developments in genetics and reproduction raise ethical and social questions. Examples of such developments are artificial insemination, in vitro fertilization, sex selection techniques, amniocentesis, chorionic villus testing, eugenics, cloning, and genetic counseling.

PSYCHOLOGY ON THE NET

- **Choosing Quality Child Care** Provides information on issues related to quality child care. http://www.nncc.org/Choose.Quality.Care/qual.care.page/html
- **Diving into the Gene Pool** From the Exploratorium, teaches about modern genetics. http://www.exploratorium.edu/genepool/genepool_home.html

- **Human Relations Publications** Covers more than 50 topics, spanning the entire range of human development. http://muextension.missouri.edu/xplor/hesguide/humanrel/
- **I Am Your Child** Information for parents of children up to 3 years of age. http://www.iamyourchild.org
- **Jean Piaget Archives: Biography** The life of Jean Piaget, plus five photos from birth to old age. http://www.unige.ch/piaget/biog.html
- **Parenthood Web** A comprehensive site for parents. http://www.parenthoodweb.com/
- **Sesame Street Parents** General advice for parents on dozens of topics. http://www.ctw.org/parents/
- **The NICHD Study of Early Child Care** A summary of the findings of a major study on the effects of day care. http://www.nichd.nih.gov/publications/pubs/early_child_care.htm
- **The Parent's Page** Comprehensive site full of links for expectant couples and new parents. http://www.efn.org/~djz/birth/babylist.html
- **InfoTrac® College Edition** For recent articles related to early thinking processes, use subject guide search for COGNITION IN INFANTS.

INTERACTIVE LEARNING

- *PsychNow!* 6a. Infant development. 6b. Child development.
- *Psyk.trek.* 9a. Parental development. 9c. Piaget's theory of cognitive development.

CHAPTER 5

From Birth to Death: Life-Span Development

Chapter Survey

Theme: Development over a lifetime reflects a delicate balance between stability and change.

▼ **Key Questions**
● **KEY TOPICS**

▼ What are the typical tasks and dilemmas through the life span?
- Erikson's stages of life

▼ What are the psychological implications of childbirth?
- Conventional and prepared childbirth
- Postpartum depression
- The bonding controversy

▼ What are some of the more serious childhood problems?
- Normal and serious problems of childhood
- The tragedy of child abuse

▼ Why is adolescent development especially challenging?
- Adolescence and puberty
- Early versus late maturation
- The search for identity

▼ How do we develop morals and values?
- Moral reasoning
- Stages of moral development

▼ **Key Questions**
● **KEY TOPICS**

▼ How do people select careers for themselves?
- Stages and phases of career development

▼ What happens psychologically during adulthood?
- Typical patterns of adult development

▼ What are the psychological challenges of aging?
- Biological aging
- Successful aging, ageism

▼ How do people typically react to death and bereavement?
- Reactions to impending death
- Bereavement and grief

▼ What factors contribute most to a happy and fulfilling life?
- Subjective well-being, meaning, and integrity

▼ In what ways are attitudes toward death changing?
- The hospice movement
- Living wills, euthanasia, and cryonics

THE STORY OF A LIFETIME

EVERYONE IS BORN. *Everyone will die. This is the short summary of a human life. Although it's accurate, the story certainly leaves out a lot, doesn't it? How might we develop a fuller picture of what happens during a lifetime?*

Perhaps we could begin by studying interesting lives. For example, what do Mick Jagger, Hillary Clinton, Bill Gates, Whoopi Goldberg, John Glenn, and Maya Angelou have in common? Of course, they've all been uncommonly successful. Yet beyond that, their lives appear to be quite different. However, if we consider many people, and look beyond surface differences, all lives follow at least some general patterns. Why should this be so? What do you and I have in common with someone like John Glenn or Maya Angelou? The answer is that we all face similar challenges in growing up, becoming an adult, and aging. Also, we are all affected by the same universal principles that guide human development.

In the following pages, we will examine development from a **life-span perspective***. Life-span psychologists study both continuity and change in behavior during a lifetime (Kaplan, 1998). Every life is marked by a number of* **developmental milestones***. These are notable events, markers, or turning points in personal development. Some examples include graduating from school, voting for the first time, getting married, watching a child leave home (or move back!), the death of a parent, becoming a grandparent, retirement, and one's own death (Kimmel, 1990).*

It is not practical here to describe all of the significant events of a lifetime. We will, nevertheless, touch on several major milestones you are likely to encounter. Each of us also faces problems on the path to healthy development. Some obstacles, such as toilet training or finding a personal identity, are universal. Others are unusual or specialized. In either case, the challenges of development extend far beyond childhood and into old age. Let's scan a selection of interesting topics, challenges, and potential problems from across the life span.

Gateways to Life-Span Development

DEVELOPMENT over a lifetime is marked by both continuity and changes in behavior.

LIFE-SPAN PSYCHOLOGISTS seek to identify general patterns that provide an approximate map of human development.

ERIK ERIKSON identified a series of challenges that occur across the life span. These range from a need to gain trust in infancy to the need to live with integrity in old age.

CAREFUL MANAGEMENT of the psychological dimensions of childbirth benefits parents and babies.

PARENTS must be able to distinguish normal childhood problems from more serious ones.

THE INCIDENCE OF CHILD ABUSE could be reduced with appropriate social and psychological efforts.

FORMING AN IDENTITY is a major task of adolescence. Developing moral standards and choosing a vocation are also important during this period.

PERSONAL DEVELOPMENT does not end after adolescence. Periods of stability and transition occur throughout adulthood.

PHYSICAL AGING STARTS early in adulthood. Every adult must find ways to successfully cope with aging.

DEATH is a natural part of life. There is value in understanding it and accepting it.

SUCCESSFUL LIVES are based on happiness, purpose, meaning, and integrity.

THE CYCLE OF LIFE—ROCKY ROAD OR GARDEN PATH?

Each of us can take pride in being "one of a kind." There really is no such thing as a "typical person" or a "typical life." Nevertheless, broad similarities can be found in the **life stages** of infancy, childhood, adolescence, young adulthood, middle adulthood, and old age. Each stage confronts a person with new **developmental tasks** that must be mastered for optimal development. Examples are learning to read in childhood, adjusting to sexual maturity in adolescence, and establishing a vocation as an adult.

In an influential book entitled *Childhood and Society* (1963), personality theorist Erik Erikson (1903–1994) suggests that we face a specific *psychosocial dilemma,* or "crisis," at each stage of life. A **psychosocial dilemma** is a conflict between personal impulses and the social world. Resolving each dilemma creates a new balance between a person and society. A string of "successes" produces healthy development and a satisfying life. Unfavorable outcomes throw us off balance, making it harder to deal with later crises. Life becomes a "rocky road," and personal growth is stunted. ◆Table 5.1 lists Erikson's dilemmas.

What are the major developmental tasks and life crises? A brief description of each psychosocial dilemma follows.

STAGE ONE, FIRST YEAR OF LIFE: TRUST VERSUS MISTRUST   During the first year of life, children are completely dependent on others. Erikson believes that a basic attitude of trust or mistrust is formed at this time. **Trust** is established when babies are given adequate warmth, touching, love, and physical care. **Mistrust** is caused by inadequate or unpredictable care and by parents who are cold, indifferent, or rejecting. Basic mistrust may later cause

◆ TABLE 5.1 Erikson's Psychosocial Dilemmas

AGE	CHARACTERISTIC DILEMMA
Birth to 1 year	Trust versus mistrust
1 to 3 years	Autonomy versus shame and doubt
3 to 5 years	Initiative versus guilt
6 to 12 years	Industry versus inferiority
Adolescence	Identity versus role confusion
Young adulthood	Intimacy versus isolation
Middle adulthood	Generativity versus stagnation
Late adulthood	Integrity versus despair

Personality theorist Erik Erikson (1903–1994) is best known for his life-stage theory of human development. His last book, *Vital Involvement in Old Age,* published in 1986, described his ideas about successful aging.

insecurity, suspiciousness, or an inability to relate to others. Notice that trust comes from the same conditions that help babies become securely attached to their parents (see Chapter 4).

STAGE TWO, 1–3 YEARS: AUTONOMY VERSUS SHAME AND DOUBT   In stage two, children express their growing self-control by climbing, touching, exploring, and trying to do things for themselves. Parents can foster a sense of **autonomy** by encouraging children to try new skills. However, the child's first efforts can be crude. Often, they result in spilling, falling, wetting, and other "accidents." Thus, parents who ridicule or overprotect their children may cause them to **doubt** their abilities and feel **shameful** about their actions.

STAGE THREE, 3–5 YEARS: INITIATIVE VERSUS GUILT   In stage three, children move beyond simple self-control and begin to take initiative. Through play, children learn to make plans and carry out tasks. Parents reinforce **initiative** by giving children freedom to play, ask questions, use imagination, and choose activities. Feelings of **guilt** about initiating activities are formed if parents criticize severely, prevent play, or discourage a child's questions.

STAGE FOUR, 6–12 YEARS: INDUSTRY VERSUS INFERIORITY   Many events of middle childhood are symbolized by that fateful day when you first entered school. With dizzying speed, your world expanded beyond your family, and you faced a whole series of new challenges.

Erikson describes the elementary school years as the child's "entrance into life." In school, children begin to learn skills valued by society, and success or failure can affect a child's feelings of adequacy. Children learn a sense of **industry** if they win praise for productive activities, such as building, painting, cooking, reading, and studying. If a child's efforts are regarded as messy, childish, or inadequate, feelings of **inferiority** result. For the first time, teachers, classmates, and adults outside the home become as important as parents in shaping attitudes toward oneself.

According to Erikson, children aged 3 to 5 learn to plan and initiate activities through play.

Life-span perspective *The study of continuity and change in behavior over a lifetime.*
Developmental milestones *Significant turning points or markers in personal development.*
Life stages *Widely recognized periods of life corresponding to broad phases of development.*
Developmental task *Any skill that must be mastered, or personal change that must take place, for optimal development.*
Psychosocial dilemma *A conflict between personal impulses and the social world that affects development.*
Trust versus mistrust *A conflict early in life centered on learning to trust others and the world.*
Autonomy versus shame and doubt *A conflict created when growing self-control (autonomy) is pitted against feelings of shame or doubt.*
Initiative versus guilt *A conflict centered around learning to take initiative while at the same time overcoming feelings of guilt about doing so.*
Industry versus inferiority *A conflict in middle childhood centered around lack of support for industrious behavior, which can result in feelings of inferiority.*

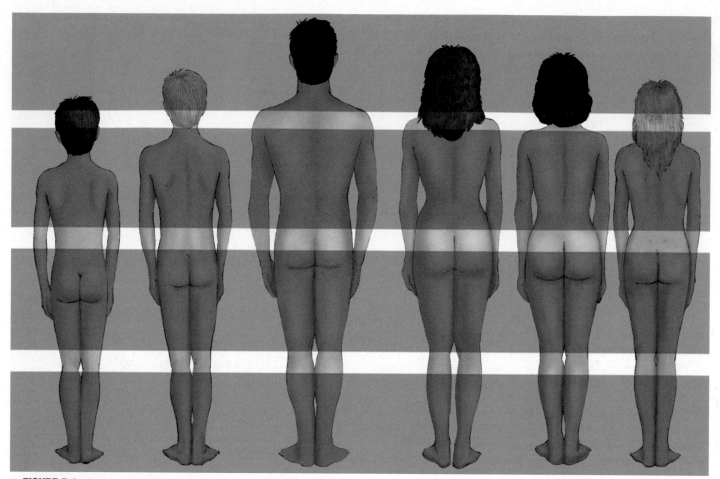

❖ **FIGURE 5.1** *Dramatic differences in physical size and maturity are found in adolescents of the same age. The girls pictured are all 13, the boys 16. Maturation that occurs earlier or later than average can affect the "search for identity." (Adapted from "Growing Up" by J. M. Tanner. Copyright © September 1973 by Scientific American, Inc. All rights reserved.)*

STAGE FIVE, ADOLESCENCE: IDENTITY VERSUS ROLE CONFUSION
Adolescence is often a turbulent time. Caught between childhood and adulthood, the adolescent faces some unique problems. Erikson considers a need to answer the question "Who am I?" the primary task during this stage of life. Mental and physical maturation brings new feelings, a new body, and new attitudes (❖Fig. 5.1). Adolescents must build a consistent **identity** out of their talents, values, life history, relationships, and the demands of their culture (Douvan, 1997). Conflicting experiences as a student, friend, athlete, worker, son or daughter, lover, and so forth must be integrated into a unified sense of self (more on this later). People who fail to develop a sense of identity suffer from **role confusion**, an uncertainty about who they are and where they are going.

STAGE SIX, YOUNG ADULTHOOD: INTIMACY VERSUS ISOLATION
What does Erikson believe is the major conflict in early adulthood?   In stage six, the individual feels a need for *intimacy* in his or her life. After establishing a stable identity, a person is prepared to share meaningful love or deep friendship with others. By **intimacy**, Erikson means an ability to care about

others and to share experiences with them. In line with Erikson's view, 75 percent of college-age men and women rank a good marriage and family life as important adult goals (Bachman & Johnson, 1979). And yet, marriage or sexual involvement is no guarantee of intimacy: Many adult relationships remain superficial and unfulfilling. Failure to establish intimacy with others leads to a deep sense of **isolation** (feeling alone and uncared for in life). This often sets the stage for later difficulties.

STAGE SEVEN, MIDDLE ADULTHOOD: GENERATIVITY VERSUS STAGNATION   According to Erikson, an interest in guiding the next generation is the main source of balance in mature adulthood. Erikson called this quality **generativity**. It is expressed by caring about oneself, one's children, and future generations. Generativity may be achieved by guiding one's own children or by helping other children (as a teacher, pastor, or coach, for example). Productive or creative work can also express generativity. In any case, a person's concerns and energies must broaden to include the welfare of others and society as a whole. Failure to do this is marked by a **stagnant** concern with one's own needs and comforts. Life loses meaning, and the person feels bitter, dreary, and trapped (Peterson & Klohnen, 1995).

STAGE EIGHT, LATE ADULTHOOD: INTEGRITY VERSUS DESPAIR *What does Erikson see as the conflicts of old age?* Old age is a time of reflection. According to Erikson, a person must be able to look back over life with acceptance and satisfaction. The person who has lived richly and responsibly develops a sense of **integrity** (self-respect). This allows the person to face aging and death with dignity. If previous life events are viewed with regret, the elderly person experiences **despair** (heartache and remorse). In this case, life seems like a series of missed opportunities. The person feels like a failure and knows it's too late to reverse what has been done. Aging and the threat of death then become sources of fear and depression.

To squeeze a lifetime into a few pages, we must ignore countless details. Although much is lost, the net effect is a clearer picture of an entire life cycle. Is Erikson's description, then, an exact map of your future? Probably not. Still, the dilemmas we have discussed reflect major psychological events in the lives of many people. Knowing about them may allow you to anticipate typical trouble spots in life. You may also be better prepared to understand the problems and feelings of friends and relatives at various stages in the life cycle.

Now that we've completed a whirlwind birth-to-death tour, we will revisit several points in life for a closer look at a variety of challenges, tasks, and problems. Before we begin, it might be a good idea to complete the Knowledge Builder that follows.

According to Erikson, an interest in future generations characterizes optimal adult development.

PSYCHOSOCIAL DILEMMAS

RELATE

See if you can think of a person you know who is facing one of Erikson's psychosocial dilemmas. Now see if you can think of specific people who seem to be coping with each of the other dilemmas.

LEARNING CHECK

As a way to improve your memory, you might find it helpful to summarize Erikson's eight life stages. Complete this do-it-yourself summary and compare your answers to those given below.

STAGE	CRISIS	FAVORABLE OUTCOME
First year of life	1. _____ vs. 2. _____	Faith in the environment and in others
Ages 1–3	Autonomy vs. 3. _____	Feelings of self-control and adequacy
Ages 3–5	4. _____ vs. guilt	Ability to begin one's own activities
Ages 6–12	Industry vs. 5. _____	Confidence in productive skills, learning how to work
Adolescence	6. _____ vs. role confusion	An integrated image of oneself as a unique person
Young adulthood	Intimacy vs. 7. _____	Ability to form bonds of love and friendship with others
Middle adulthood	Generativity vs. 8. _____	Concern for family, society, and future generations
Late adulthood	9. _____ vs. 10. _____	Sense of dignity and fulfillment, willingness to face death

CRITICAL THINKING

11. Trying to make generalizations about development throughout life is complicated by at least one major factor. What do you think it is?

Identity versus role confusion *A major conflict of adolescence, involving the need to establish a consistent personal identity.*
Intimacy versus isolation *The challenge in early adulthood of establishing intimacy with friends, family, a lover, or a spouse, versus experiencing a sense of isolation.*
Generativity versus stagnation *A conflict of middle adulthood in which stagnant concern for oneself is countered by interest in guiding the next generation.*
Integrity versus despair *A conflict in old age between feelings of personal integrity and the despair that occurs when previous life events are viewed with regret.*

CHILDBIRTH—THE FIRST JOURNEY

Birth is an emotionally complex event. In various parts of the world, it occurs in high-tech medical facilities, at home, or outside, in fields. The father may be present, or he may be strictly forbidden from witnessing the birth. New mothers and fathers may be calm, joyous, depressed, relieved, anxious, or bewildered.

More than ever before, parents can now choose how their children will be born. Do their choices make a difference? What are the psychological implications of birth? In recent years, researchers have probed these questions. Let's explore what they have learned.

Conventional Delivery

In a traditional **medicated birth**, the mother is assisted by a physician and given drugs to relieve pain. Until recently, this was the rule for hospital births. The drugs used range from local analgesics (painkillers) to general anesthetics, which cause a loss of consciousness.

Increasingly, doctors and parents have come to realize that general anesthesia has major drawbacks. For one thing, drugs dull or block the mother's awareness of birth, one of life's most wondrous events. They also reduce oxygen flow to the fetus. Often, a forceps delivery is necessary (in which the baby is pulled through the birth canal). In many cases, infants are born partially anesthetized. For such reasons, babies tend to lag in muscular and neural development if their mothers were heavily anesthetized.

In the last two decades, there has been a marked move away from medicated births. Nevertheless, 95 percent of all deliveries in the United States and Canada use at least some painkillers. Certainly, mothers should not feel guilty if they need pain relief. Drugs injected near the spinal cord (an epidural block) can greatly reduce pain without affecting the child or the mother's alertness. However, it appears wise to use general anesthetics as little as possible.

The medical profession has also been criticized for treating pregnancy and birth as health problems rather than natural processes. Understandably, giving birth is likely to be a negative experience for women who feel a lot of pain or anxiety. However, common medical procedures, such as induced labor, cesarean section, a forceps delivery, or anesthesia, also tend to produce negative birth experiences (Waldenstroem, 1999).

Prepared Childbirth

What can parents do to give babies the best possible start in life, while avoiding overmedicated births? In **prepared childbirth** classes, parents learn specific techniques to manage discomfort and facilitate labor. The most popular approach is the Lamaze method (la-MAHZ), developed by French physician Ferdinand Lamaze.

Early in pregnancy, Lamaze instructors explain the entire birth process to couples. Women who understand what is happening in their bodies tend to have fewer fears and less anxiety.

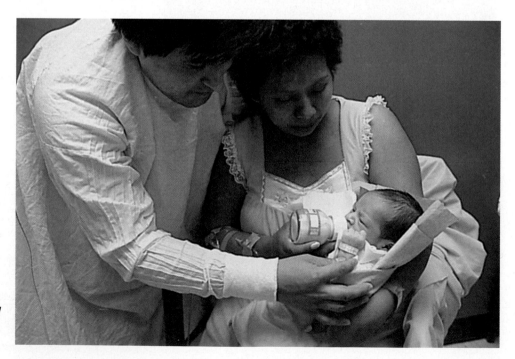

Changing attitudes toward childbirth have encouraged mothers and fathers to actively prepare for birth and to participate more fully in caring for the newborn.

Expectant mothers then learn methods of breathing and muscular control to reduce pain. Another important element is training the father or a friend to give emotional support to the mother during childbirth.

Prepared childbirth typically shortens labor and reduces pain. It makes birth a celebration of life, rather than a medical problem. Accordingly, prepared parents are more likely to experience birth as a time of great joy (Mackey, 1995).

How important is it for fathers to participate in the birth process? Men generally make a better transition to parenthood when they help prepare for childbirth. During birth, a father may form life-long memories that will affect his willingness to love and care for his child. Fortunately, fathers are now commonly allowed to be present during birth, either as observers or to coach the mother

through labor. Many hospitals also have home-like birthing rooms so that fathers can sleep at the hospital.

In many hospitals, babies spend their first night with parents in a birthing room. Even in ordinary wards, mothers are usually allowed to spend more time with their newborns. Initially, some of these practices were thought to promote stronger mother-infant bonds. We now know that extra contact is not absolutely necessary (see "Mother-Infant Bonding"). Nevertheless, caring for emotional needs can make birth more satisfying for mothers, fathers, and babies.

Pregnancy and childbirth require many challenging adjustments. In fact, giving birth has been described as a "developmental crisis" for many women. New mothers assume a new identity, and they may suffer loss of independence, power, or employment. One particularly difficult time comes soon after new mothers return home. Instead of savoring the joy they anticipated, many are surprised to find they are seriously depressed (Mauthner, 1999).

MOTHER-INFANT BONDING—A TOUCHING DEBATE

CRITICAL THINKING

In one hospital ward, mothers get a brief glimpse of their newborns shortly after birth, followed by 30-minute visits every 4 hours. In a second ward, "extended-contact" mothers are given their babies for 1 hour during the first 3 hours after birth and for an extra 5 hours of contact each afternoon for the first 3 days after delivery. Does the extra contact have any effect?

An initial series of studies reported by Marshall Klaus and John Kennell (1984) seemed to suggest that close early contact between a mother and her infant has lasting benefits. According to Klaus and Kennell, the first few hours after birth are a sensitive period. Therefore, mother-child pairs who spend extra time together, especially if they make skin-to-skin contact, form a stronger emotional bond.

Were they right? Probably not. More careful studies have generally failed to support a "superglue" version of the bonding concept. Although long-term infant attachments are a reality, "instant bonding" appears to be a myth (Eyer, 1994).

Skeptics point out that adopted children, premature babies, and babies born by cesarean section (surgical birth) all develop normal, affectionate bonds with their mothers. Even Klaus and Kennell now acknowledge that it is unlikely that something as important as emotional attachment would depend *solely* on the first few hours of life (Klaus, Kennell, & Klaus, 1995). Humans are highly adaptable, and there are many opportunities for babies to form an attachment to parents during the first year of life.

Even if early contact is unnecessary, allowing mother, father, and infant to be together during the first few hours following birth is humane and natural (Feldman et al., 1999). So, although most evidence suggests that early contact is *not* necessary, it is undoubtedly a positive, emotionally satisfying experience. Ultimately, it is less important *when* secure attachment occurs than *if* it occurs.

Understanding Postpartum Depression

Two weeks after her child was born, Cheryl realized something was wrong. She could no longer ignore that she was extremely irritable, fatigued, tearful, and depressed. "Shouldn't I be happy?" she wondered. "What's wrong with me?"

The two most common emotional problems following birth are maternity blues and postpartum depression. (The term *postpartum* refers to the time following childbirth.) An estimated 50 to 80 percent of all women experience **maternity blues**, a mild depression that usually lasts from 1 to 2 days after childbirth. These "third-day blues" are marked by crying, fitful sleep, tension, anger, and irritability. For most women, such reactions are a normal part of adjusting to childbirth. The depression is usually brief and not too severe.

For some women, maternity blues can be the beginning of a serious depression. Roughly 13 percent of all women who give birth develop **postpartum depression**, a moderately severe depression that begins within 3 months following childbirth. Typical signs of postpartum depression are mood swings, despondency, feelings of inadequacy, and an inability to cope with the new baby. Depression of this kind may last from 2 months to about a year.

Stress and anxiety before birth and negative attitudes toward child-rearing increase the risk of postpartum depression. A poor marital relationship and lack of support from the father

Medicated birth *The common practice in Western medicine of giving painkilling drugs during labor and birth.*
Prepared childbirth *A collection of techniques designed to manage discomfort and facilitate birth so that the use of painkilling drugs can be avoided or minimized.*
Maternity blues *A brief and relatively mild state of depression often experienced by mothers 2 or 3 days after giving birth.*
Postpartum depression *A mild to moderately severe depression that begins within 3 months following childbirth.*

are also danger signs. Part of the problem may be hormonal: After a woman gives birth, her estrogen levels can drop, altering her mood (Harris, 1996). However, about 10 percent of new *fathers* also become depressed after the birth of a child, which suggests that psychological factors play a major role in such depressions (Ballard & Davies, 1996).

Women who become depressed tend to see their husbands as unsupportive. Therefore, educating new parents about the importance of mutual support may reduce the risk of depression. Groups where new mothers can discuss their feelings are also helpful. If depression is severe or long-lasting, new mothers should seek professional help. (Additional sources for this section include Demyttenaere et al., 1995; Gilbert, 1996; Hyde et al., 1995; Zelkowitz & Milet, 1995.)

SUMMARY   To sum up, birth is a psychologically important event for mother, father, and baby alike. Women tend to cope best with birth when they actively prepare for motherhood and have some control over the birth process. Many medical procedures tend to make women feel alienated from their bodies and less in control of pregnancy and childbirth (Williams & Umberson, 1999). Participation in prepared childbirth classes can help address these issues. Immediately following birth, it is desirable to cultivate mother-infant bonding. However, this is not a now-or-never process. Real emotional attachments develop over a matter of months, not hours or days. Finally, a woman's adjustment to birth and motherhood tends to be superior if she receives emotional support from her partner before, during, and after the birth (Lidderdale & Walsh, 1998).

PROBLEMS OF CHILDHOOD—WHY PARENTS GET GRAY HAIR

Can you remember a time in childhood when your actions led to a disaster or a near disaster? It shouldn't be hard. It's a wonder that many of us survive childhood at all. Where I grew up, digging underground tunnels, wiggling down chimneys, hopping on trains, jumping off houses, crawling through storm drains—and worse—were common childhood adventures.

Stress is a normal part of life—even in childhood. Certainly, this does not mean that parents should go out of their way to stress a child. However, it does suggest that children need not be completely sheltered from distress. Overprotection, or "smother love," can be as damaging as overstressing a child. (**Overprotection** refers to excessively shielding a child from ordinary stresses.)

Most children do a good job of keeping stress at comfortable levels when *they* initiate an activity (Murphy & Moriarty, 1976). At a public swimming pool, for instance, some children can be observed making death-defying leaps from the high dive, while others stick close to the wading area. If there's no immediate danger, it is reasonable to let children get stuck in trees, make themselves dizzy, squabble with neighborhood chil-

BRIDGES

Women experience higher rates of depression than men do.

See Chapter 17, page 584, to learn why.

dren, and so forth. Getting into a few scrapes can help prepare a child to cope with later challenges. (Just think, if your author hadn't crawled through a few storm pipes, his adult interest in plumbing the depths of the psyche might have gone down the drain.)

Normal Childhood Problems

How can you tell if a child is being subjected to too much stress?   Child specialist Stella Chess has identified difficulties experienced at times by almost every child. These can be considered normal reactions to the unavoidable stresses of growing up.

1. All children experience occasional *sleep disturbances*, including wakefulness, frightening dreams, or a desire to get into their parents' bed.
2. *Specific fears* of the dark, dogs, school, or a particular room or person are also common.

Childhood can be a challenging period of life. However, most children do a good job of keeping stress at comfortable levels when they initiate an activity.

3. Most children will be *overly timid* at times and allow themselves to be bullied by other children.
4. Temporary periods of *general dissatisfaction* may occur, when nothing pleases the child.
5. Children also normally display periods of *general negativism*. Repeatedly saying "no" or refusing to do anything requested is typical of such times.
6. Another normal problem is *clinging*. Children who "cling" refuse to leave the sides of their mothers or do anything on their own.
7. Development does not always advance smoothly. *Reversals* or *regressions* to more infantile behavior occur with almost all children (Chess, Thomas, & Birch, 1976).

An added problem in the elementary school years is **sibling rivalry** (competition among brothers and sisters). It is normal for a certain amount of jealousy, rivalry, and even hostility to develop between siblings. In fact, some sibling conflict may even be constructive. A limited amount of aggressive give-and-take between siblings provides an opportunity to learn emotional control, self-assertion, and good sportsmanship (Bank & Kahn, 1982). Parents can help keep such conflicts within bounds by not "playing favorites" and by not comparing one child with another. Supportive and affectionate fathering, in particular, seems to minimize conflicts and jealousy among siblings (Rolling & Belsky, 1992).

Parents should also expect to see some **childhood rebellion** (open defiance of adult authority). Most school-age children rebel at times against the rules and limitations imposed by parents. Being with other children offers a chance to "let off steam" by doing some of the things the adult world forbids. It is normal for children to be messy, noisy, hostile, or destructive to a moderate degree.

Keep in mind that "normal problems" that intensify or last for long periods may become serious disturbances. Some examples of more serious problems are identified in the following discussion.

Serious Childhood Problems

By the time he was 5, Billy had not learned to talk. He threw wild temper tantrums and never seemed to sleep. He got into closets and tore up his mother's dresses and urinated on her clothes. He smashed furniture and spread soap powder and breakfast food all over the floors. He attacked his mother at every opportunity, sometimes going for her throat with his teeth. Billy once tried to stuff his baby brother in a toy box.

Billy refused to eat anything but cold, greasy hamburgers from a local fast-food business. To get through a week, his parents had to buy hamburgers by the sack. Then, they hid them around the house, so Billy wouldn't eat them all at once. When his parents went out driving, they had to detour around fast-food restaurants to prevent Billy from frothing at the mouth and trying to jump out the window (Moser, 1965). Billy, you may note, was not an average 5-year-old.

What was his problem?   Billy was an *autistic* child. His problem is rare. Few children get off to as bad a start in life as Billy. However, severe emotional disturbances affect more children than many people realize. Let's consider some of the more serious problems that many parents face.

Toilet-Training Disturbances

Difficulty sometimes centers on toilet training or bowel and bladder habits. The two most common problems are **enuresis** (EN-you-REE-sis: lack of bladder control) and **encopresis** (EN-coh-PREE-sis: lack of bowel control). Enuresis is more common than encopresis and many times more common among males than females.

Both wetting and soiling are sometimes an expression of frustration or pent-up hostility. But parents should not be overly alarmed by some delays in toilet training or by a few "accidents." As mentioned in Chapter 4, 30 months is the average age for completing toilet training. It is not unusual, however, for some children to take 6 months longer (age 3).

Even when problems persist, they may be purely physical. For example, some bed-wetters simply do not wake up when they need to go to the bathroom. These children can be helped by limiting the amount they drink during the evening. They should also use the toilet before going to bed, and they can be rewarded for "dry" nights. For older children, learning various self-control strategies can be effective (Ronen & Wozner, 1995). In all cases, understanding, tact, and sympathy help. When serious problems exist, parents should seek professional help (Goin, 1998).

Feeding Disturbances

Feeding disturbances take a variety of forms. The disturbed child may vomit or refuse food for no reason or may drastically overeat or undereat. **Overeating** (eating in excess of daily caloric needs) can be a serious problem. Some parents overfeed simply because they consider a fat baby healthy or "cute." Others, who feel unloved, may compensate by showering the child with "love" in the form of food. Whatever the case, overfed children develop eating habits and conflicts that have lifelong consequences.

Serious cases of undereating, or self-starvation, are called **anorexia nervosa** (AN-or-REX-yah ner-VOH-sah: nervous loss of appetite). The victims of anorexia nervosa are mostly adolescent females. Many seem to have conflicts about maturing sexually. By starving themselves, girls can limit figure development and prevent menstruation. This delays the time when

Overprotection *Excessively guarding and shielding a child from possible stresses.*
Sibling rivalry *Competition among brothers and sisters for attention, dominance, status within the family, and so forth.*
Childhood rebellion *Open resistance to, or defiance of, adult authority.*
Enuresis *An inability to control urination, particularly with regard to bed-wetting.*
Encopresis *A lack of bowel control; "soiling."*
Overeating *Eating in excess of one's daily caloric needs.*
Anorexia nervosa *Active self-starvation or a sustained loss of appetite that has psychological origins.*

they must face adulthood. As we will discuss in Chapter 13, pressures to conform to unrealistic standards of beauty also contribute to self-starvation (Nagel & Jones, 1992a).

Pica (PIE-ka: a craving for unnatural foods) is another childhood eating difficulty. Some children go through a period of intense appetite, when they eat or chew on all sorts of inedible substances, such as plaster and chalk. Some children try to eat things like buttons, rubber bands, mud, or paint flakes. Old paint can be quite dangerous because it may contain lead, which is highly poisonous. Persistent pica can be a serious problem. However, it can be treated with various behavioral techniques (Woods, Miltenberger, & Lumley, 1996).

Speech Disturbances

Delayed speech (learning to talk after the normal age for language development) is another serious handicap. An example is Tommy, who at age 5 was still using telegraphic speech: "Me go. Outdoor. Mama in car now. Dink Tommy cup." Delayed speech is sometimes caused by a lack of intellectual stimulation in the home. Other possible causes are parents who discourage the child's attempts to grow up, childhood stresses, mental retardation, and emotional disturbances.

Stuttering (chronic stumbling in speech) is a second major language problem. In the past, many parents were blamed for "causing" stuttering. Now, researchers believe the problem involves speech-timing mechanisms in the brain (Wieneke, Janssen, & Brutten, 1995). Stuttering is four times more common in males and seems to be partially inherited (Felsenfeld, 1996).

Although parents don't cause stuttering, they can certainly make it worse. Children who fear that they are about to stutter are, in fact, more likely to stutter. That's why parents should avoid criticizing speech difficulties. With support from parents and formal speech therapy, many children do overcome stuttering (Wagaman et al., 1995).

Learning Disorders

Soon after Gary entered school, he became shy and difficult. Gary's teacher suspected a learning disorder, and a specialist confirmed it. **Learning disorders** include problems with reading, math, or writing. A learning disorder may exist when school achievement is much lower than we would expect for a child's age and intelligence (DSM-IV, 1994). Gary's specific problem was **dyslexia** (dis-LEX-yah), an inability to read with understanding. Because of it, he often felt confused and "stupid" in class, although his intelligence was normal.

Approximately 10 to 15 percent of school-age children have some dyslexia, or "word blindness." When dyslexic children try to read, they often reverse letters (such as seeing *b* for *d*) and words (*was* and *saw,* for example). Dyslexia appears to be caused by a malfunction of language-processing areas on the left side of the brain. It is typically treated with exercises in hearing, touch, and vision that improve reading comprehension.

BRIDGES

Early language development is greatly affected by the number of words young children hear daily.

See Chapter 4, page 105.

Attention-Deficit Hyperactivity Disorder

One of the most serious childhood problems is **attention-deficit hyperactivity disorder (ADHD)** (Erk, 1995). The ADHD child is constantly in motion and cannot concentrate. The child talks rapidly, rarely finishes work, acts on impulse, and cannot pay attention. ADHD afflicts 4 to 6 percent of all children and some adults. Five times as many boys as girls have the problem. Unless it is carefully managed, ADHD can lead to school dropouts and lifelong problems with antisocial behavior (Faigel et al., 1995).

What causes ADHD? Specific areas of the brain associated with language, motor control, and attention suffer from chemical imbalances (Sagvolden & Sergeant, 1998). ADHD tends to run in families, which suggests it may be hereditary. In one striking example, doctors found that an 8-year-old boy, his father, and his grandfather all suffered from the problem (Zametkin, 1995).

Many parents believe that hyperactive behavior is triggered by eating sugar. However, sugary diets have no effect at all on the behavior of either normal or hyperactive children. "Sugar highs" are a myth (Wolraich, Wilson, & White, 1995).

How is ADHD treated? Treatment for ADHD includes drugs, behavioral management approaches, and family counseling. Physicians typically use the stimulant drug Ritalin (methylphenidate) to control ADHD. It might seem that stimulants would make hyperactivity worse, but the drugs are actually calming. Most likely, this is because they lengthen the ADHD child's attention span and reduce impulsiveness (Diller, 1998; Faigel et al., 1995).

Ritalin is a potent, amphetamine-like drug that can cause withdrawal symptoms. In view of this, it is remarkable that 5 percent (1 in 20) of all school-age boys in the United States take Ritalin for ADHD. The drug's possible side effects include insomnia, weight loss, irritability, depression, and a slowing of physical growth.

Many experts are concerned that Ritalin is overused. Drugs, they suspect, are sometimes being prescribed for ordinary misbehavior, not because a child actually suffers from ADHD. Ritalin does seem to be effective when the diagnosis of ADHD is accurate. The problem is that doctors, parents, and teachers may be tempted to use drugs to control children who are merely disobedient (Diller, 1998; Hancock, 1996; Leutwyler, 1996).

Few specialists today would recommend treating ADHD with drugs unless a child also receives therapy for behavioral and emotional problems. For many children, behavior modification is as effective as drug treatment (Carlson et al., 1992). **Behavior modification** is the application of learning principles to change or eliminate maladaptive or abnormal behavior. (See Chapter 18 for more information.) The basic idea is to reward the ADHD child for being calm and for paying attention. Children are also taught how to monitor their own behavior and how to ignore distractions (Hoff & DuPaul, 1998).

The ADHD child's inability to hold still and pay attention can seriously disrupt learning.

Autism

Children who suffer from **autism** (AW-tiz'm) display an extreme preoccupation with their own thoughts, fantasies, and private impulses. Autism is one of the most severe childhood problems. It affects 1 in 2,500 children, boys four times more often than girls. Autistic children are locked into private worlds and appear to have no need for affection or contact with others (Sigman, 1995).

In addition to being extremely isolated, the autistic child may throw gigantic temper tantrums—sometimes including self-destructive behavior such as head banging. Many autistic children are mute. If they speak at all, they may infuriatingly parrot back everything said, a response known as **echolalia** (EK-oh-LAY-li-ah). Some autistic children also engage in repetitive actions such as rocking, flapping their arms, or waving their fingers in front of their eyes. Additionally, they may show no response to an extremely loud noise (sensory blocking), or they may spend hours watching a water faucet drip (sensory "spin-out"). Finally, the autistic don't seem to understand what other people are thinking—or even that they do think. This makes autistic people very inept in social situations (Firth, 1993).

Do parents cause autism? At one time, experts blamed parents for autism. It is now recognized that autism is caused by congenital defects in the nervous system. Although they can be subtle, the symptoms of autism appear before a child is 1 year old (Baranek, 1999). That's why even as babies autistic children are aloof and do not cuddle or mold to their parents' arms. Medical scans reveal that the brains of autistic adults are larger than normal. This suggests that something goes wrong during development of the autistic brain (Piven, Arndt, & Palmer, 1995).

BRIDGES

Psychologists suspect that autistic children fail to develop a normal "theory of mind" concerning the thoughts, feelings, and intentions of other people.

See Chapter 4, page 109

Can anything be done for an autistic child? Even with help, only about 25 percent of all autistic children approach normalcy, and only 2 percent are able to live independently. Nevertheless, almost all autistic children can make progress with proper care. When treatment is begun early, behavior modification has been particularly successful.

Do you remember Billy, the autistic child described earlier? Billy was one of the first patients in a pioneering program designed by psychologist Ivar Lovaas. Billy was selected because of his unusual appetite for hamburgers. Teaching Billy to talk illustrates one aspect of his treatment. It began with his learning to blow out a match—making a sound like "who." Each time he made the "who" sound, Billy was rewarded with a bite of his beloved hamburgers. Next, he was rewarded for babbling meaningless sounds. If he accidentally said a word, he was rewarded. After several weeks, he was able to say words such as *ball, milk, mama,* and *me.* By this painstaking process, Billy was eventually taught to talk. (This process, which is called *operant shaping,* is discussed further in Chapter 9.)

In a behavior modification program, each of an autistic child's maladaptive behaviors is altered by using reward and punishment. In addition to food, therapists have found that sensory stimulation, such as tickling or music, is often very reinforcing for autistic children. And strangely enough, following actions such as head banging and hand biting with punishment can bring a swift end to self-destructive behavior. When such efforts are combined with home treatment by parents, considerable progress is possible. A few children, in fact, approach near-normal functioning (McEachen, Smith, & Lovaas, 1993).

Autism and other severe childhood problems are a monumental challenge to the ingenuity of psychologists, educators, and parents. However, great strides have been made. There is reason to believe that in the future even more help will be available to children who get a bad start in life.

Pica *Eating or chewing on inedible objects or substances such as chalk, ashes, and the like.*

Delayed speech *Speech that begins well after the normal age for language development has passed.*

Stuttering *Chronic hesitation or stumbling in speech.*

Learning disorder *Any problem with thinking, perception, language, attention, or activity levels that tends to impair learning ability.*

Dyslexia *An inability to read with understanding, often caused by a tendency to misread letters (by seeing their mirror images, for instance).*

Attention-deficit hyperactivity disorder (ADHD) *A behavioral problem characterized by short attention span, restless movement, and impaired learning capacity.*

Behavior modification *Application of principles of learning to change or eliminate maladaptive or abnormal behavior.*

Autism *A severe disorder involving mutism, sensory spin-outs, sensory blocking, tantrums, unresponsiveness to others, and other difficulties.*

Echolalia *A compulsion, sometimes observed in autistic children, to repeat everything that is said.*

CHILD ABUSE—CYCLES OF VIOLENCE

Sadly, no account of problems in development would be complete without a brief discussion of **child abuse** (physical or emotional harm caused by violence, mistreatment, or neglect). Much as we might like to believe otherwise, child abuse is widespread (Barnet & Barnet, 1998). From 3.5 to 14 percent of all children are physically abused by parents. Even if the lower figure is right, that would mean 2 million children are physically battered each year in the United States and Canada alone. In about one third of all cases of physical abuse, the child is seriously injured. Every year, thousands of children are killed by their own parents (Finkelhor & Dziuba-Leatherman, 1994).

Characteristics of Abusive Parents

What are abusive parents like?   Typically, they have a high level of stress and frustration in their lives. Common problems include depression, loneliness, marital discord, unemployment, drug abuse, divorce, family violence, heavy drinking, and work anxieties ("A Nation's," 1995; Famularo et al., 1992).

Some parents are aware they are mistreating a child but are unable to stop. Other abusive parents literally hate their children or are disgusted by them. The child's sloppiness, diapers, crying, or needs are unbearable to the parent. Abusive mothers tend to believe their children are *intentionally* annoying them (Bauer & Twentyman, 1985). In many cases, troubled parents expect the child to love them and make them happy. When the child (who is usually under 3 years old) cannot meet such unrealistic demands, the parent reacts with lethal anger.

CYCLES OF VIOLENCE   The core of much child abuse is a cycle of violence that flows from one generation to the next. Roughly one third of all parents who were abused as children mistreat their own children (Knutson, 1995). A second third do not routinely abuse their children. However, they are likely to do so when they are stressed (Oliver, 1993). Such parents simply never learned to love, communicate with, or discipline a child. In short, many abused children later become abusive adults (Oliver, 1993).

How do caring parents who were abused as children differ from abusive parents who continue the cycle of violence?   Those who break the abusive cycle are more likely to have received emotional support from a nonabusive adult during childhood, to have received therapy, or to have had an emotionally supportive relationship with a mate (Egeland, Jacobvitz, & Sroufe, 1988). Without such support, childhood abuse greatly increases the lifetime risk of emotional problems, substance abuse, and violence (Malinosky-Rummell & Hansen, 1993; Mullen et al., 1996).

Preventing Child Abuse

What can be done about child abuse?   Many public agencies now have teams to identify battered or neglected children.

CHILD ABUSE IS PREVENTABLE

If you need help or know someone who does, call the
CHILD ABUSE HOTLINE
ask the operator for
1-800-4-A-CHILD
Child Help U.S.A. 1-800-422-4453

Los Angeles County, Department of Children's Services

Widespread acceptance of physical punishment creates an atmosphere in which angry parents can easily lose control and abuse their children. Even parents who would never strike a child may fall prey to the "shaken baby syndrome." In such cases, an angry parent violently shakes an infant (often one that won't stop crying). The result can be brain injuries that cause mental retardation, blindness, or even death.

However, legal "cures" leave a lot to be desired. The courts can take custody of a child, or the parents may voluntarily agree to place the child in a foster home. Foster care can be an improvement, but it may also further traumatize the child. In some cases, the child is allowed to remain with the parents but under court supervision. Even then, there is a chance of further injury unless the parents get help. Some of the most effective programs teach parents child-care skills, how to manage stress, anger control, and how to avoid using corporal punishment (Fetsch, Schultz, & Wahler,1999; Reppucci, Woolard, & Fried, 1999). It would be best if such skills were taught in high school, before potential abusers become parents.

Self-help groups staffed by former child abusers and concerned volunteers are a major aid to parents. One such group is Parents Anonymous, a national organization of parents who want to help each other stop abusing children. Local groups set up networks of members that parents can call in an abuse crisis or when they feel one coming on. Parents also learn how to curb violent impulses and how to cope with their children. Experts recommend that a parent who is tempted to shake or strike a crying infant should try any of the following (Evans, 1993):

- Leave the room and call a friend.
- Put on some soothing music.
- Take 10 deep breaths and calm yourself; then take 10 more.
- Move to another room and do some exercise.
- Take a shower.
- Sit down, close your eyes, and vividly imagine yourself in a pleasant place.
- If none of the preceding strategies work, seek professional help. (Telephone numbers are listed at the end of this chapter.)

DANGEROUS ATTITUDES Another way of preventing child abuse is by changing attitudes. Despite newspaper and TV coverage of the problem, many parents believe it is their "right" to slap or hit their children. A survey of parents found that physical punishment is widely accepted. In a 1994 *USA Today* poll, 67 percent of adults agreed that "a good, hard spanking" is sometimes necessary to discipline a child. For many parents, "sometimes" occurs quite often: Parents report spanking their children an average of 2.5 times a week (Holden, Coleman, & Schmidt, 1995).

As a society we seem to say, "Violence is okay if the child isn't injured; if the child is injured, then it's child abuse." Of course, when the child is injured, it's too late to take back the violence. By condoning punishment that borders on abuse, we greatly raise the chances of injury. The best solution to physical abuse, then, may lie in rethinking our attitudes toward physical punishment and toward the rights of children. It is also important to remember that emotional abuse can be just as damaging as physical abuse. Parents inflict long-lasting emotional scars when they persistently neglect, humiliate, intimidate, or terrorize their children.

To face the problem squarely, we must realize that the line between acceptable discipline and child abuse is easily blurred. Fortunately, public opinion regarding spanking is starting to shift. Several states have banned spanking in schools. However, child victimization will continue as long as we as a society tolerate it (Finkelhor & Dziuba-Leatherman, 1994).

KNOWLEDGE BUILDER
BIRTH AND PROBLEMS OF CHILDHOOD

RELATE
What would you say are the pros and cons of prepared childbirth compared with conventional birth practices?

What normal problems could first-time parents expect their children to have? Can you also describe some of the more serious problems that occur?

You have been hired as director of a nonprofit agency that is concerned with child abuse. What would you have your staff do to reduce the incidence of child abuse in your community?

LEARNING CHECK
1. The Lamaze method is a type of epidural block that is used to control pain during childbirth. T or F?

2. Roughly 13 percent of all new mothers experience the maternity blues, which is the first stage of postpartum depression. T or F?

3. Occasional reversals and regressions to more infantile behavior are sure signs that a significant childhood problem exists. T or F?

4. Sleep disturbances and specific fears can be a sign of significant childhood problems when they are prolonged or exaggerated. T or F?

5. A moderate amount of sibling rivalry is considered normal. T or F?

6. Encopresis is the formal term for lack of bladder control. T or F?

7. The ADHD child is lost in his or her own private world. T or F?

8. Approximately 30 percent of all parents who were abused as children mistreat their own children. T or F?

CRITICAL THINKING
9. Regarding so-called anorexia nervosa, is it really possible to be too thin in today's fashion-conscious society?

Answers:
1. F 2. F 3. F 4. T 5. T 6. F 7. F 8. T 9. Anorexia nervosa is certainly is! It is best described as pathological self-starvation. Often it leads to serious health problems and, sometimes, even to death. See Chapter 13 for details.

ADOLESCENCE—THE BEST OF TIMES, THE WORST OF TIMES

Adolescence is a time of change, exploration, exuberance, and youthful searching. It can also be a time of worry and problems, especially in today's world. It might even be fair to describe adolescence as "the best of times, the worst of times." Just in case you weren't taking notes in junior high, let's survey the challenges of this colorful chapter of life.

Adolescence and Puberty

Adolescence is the culturally defined period between childhood and adulthood. Socially, the adolescent is no longer a child, yet not quite an adult. Almost all cultures recognize this transitional status. However, the length of adolescence varies greatly from culture to culture. For example, most 14-year-old girls in North America live at home and go to school. In contrast, many 14-year-old girls in rural villages of the Near East are married and have children. In our culture, 14-year-olds are adolescents. In others, they may be adults.

Child abuse *Physical or emotional harm caused by violence, mistreatment, or neglect.*
Adolescence *The culturally defined period between childhood and adulthood.*

Is marriage the primary criterion for adult status in North America? No, it's not even one of the top three criteria. Today, the most widely accepted standards are taking responsibility for oneself, making independent decisions, and becoming financially independent. In practice, this typically means breaking away from parents by taking a job and setting up a separate residence (Arnett, 1998).

PUBERTY   Many people confuse adolescence with puberty. However, puberty is a *biological* event, not a social status. During **puberty**, hormonal changes promote rapid physical growth and sexual maturity. Interestingly, the peak **growth spurt** (accelerated growth rate) during puberty occurs earlier for girls than for boys (❖Fig. 5.2). This difference accounts for the 1- to 2-year period when girls tend to be taller than boys. (Remember going to dances where the girls towered over the boys?) For girls, the onset of puberty typically occurs between 9 and 12 years of age. For most boys, the age range is 11 to 14 years.

Biologically, most people reach reproductive maturity in the early teens. Social and intellectual maturity, however, may still lie years ahead. Young adolescents often make fateful decisions that affect their entire lives, even though they are immature in cognitive development, knowledge, and social experience. The tragically high rates of teenage pregnancy and drug abuse in many Western nations are prime examples. The younger an adolescent becomes sexually active, delinquent, or involved with drugs, the greater the resulting damage (White & DeBlassie,

1992). Other major risks during adolescence include alcohol abuse, learning to smoke, eating disorders, suicide, risk taking, violence, sexually transmitted diseases, and school failure (Johnson & Roberts, 1999).

EARLY AND LATE MATURATION   When you were going through puberty, did you ever spend *hours* preparing to attend a party, dance, or other social event? If you did, you weren't alone. Puberty tends to dramatically increase body awareness and concerns about physical appearance. About half of all boys and one third of all girls report being dissatisfied with their appearance during early adolescence (Rosenbaum, 1979). In many instances, such feelings are related to the *timing* of puberty. Girls who are temporarily "too tall," boys who are "too small," and both boys and girls who lag in sexual development are likely to be upset about their bodies (Petersen et al., 1991).

How much difference does the timing of puberty make? Because puberty involves so many rapid changes, it can be stressful for just about anyone. When puberty comes unusually early or late, its impact may be magnified—for both good and bad.

For boys, maturing early is generally beneficial. Typically, it enhances their self-image and gives them an advantage socially and athletically. For such reasons, early-maturing boys tend to be more poised, relaxed, dominant, self-assured, and popular with their peers. Many late-maturing boys are anxious about being behind in development. However, after they catch up, they tend to be more eager, talkative, self-assertive, and tolerant of themselves than average maturers (Dusek, 1996).

For girls, the advantages of early maturation are less clearcut. In elementary school, developmentally advanced girls tend to have *less* prestige among peers. They also have poorer self-images (Alsaker, 1992). This may be because they are larger and heavier than their classmates. By junior high, however, early development includes sexual features. This leads to a more positive body image, *greater* peer prestige, and adult approval (Brooks-Gunn & Warren, 1988). In contrast, later-maturing girls have the possible advantage of usually growing taller and thinner than early-maturing girls. Other relevant findings are that early-maturing girls date sooner and are more independent and more active in school; they are also more often in trouble at school and at greater risk for engaging in early sex (Flannery et al., 1993). For all girls, changes in self-confidence, body image, sexual maturity, and relationships with friends and family tend to be prominent issues during adolescence (Kaplan, 1997).

As you can see, there are costs and benefits associated with both early and late puberty. One added cost of early maturation is that it may force premature identity formation. When a teenager begins to look like an adult, she or he may be treated like an adult. Ideally, this change can encourage greater maturity and independence. But what happens when a person is treated as an adult before he or she is emotionally ready? Then the search for identity may end too soon, leaving the person with a distorted, poorly formed sense of self. (See "Hurried into Adulthood?")

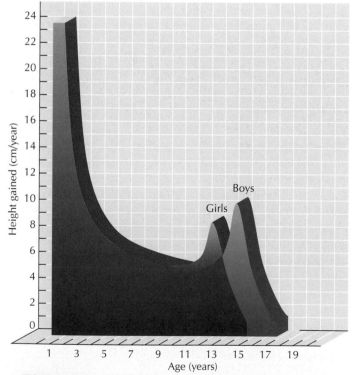

❖ **FIGURE 5.2** *The typical rate of growth for boys and girls. Notice that growth in early adolescence equals that for ages 1 to 3. Note, too, the earlier growth spurt for girls.*

HURRIED INTO ADULTHOOD?

Psychologist David Elkind (1981) believes that many parents are hurrying their children's development. Elkind is concerned about parents who try to raise their babies' IQs, force them to "read" flash cards, or have them swimming and doing gymnastics before they are 3 months old. Such pushing, he believes, partly explains why more children have recently begun to show serious stress symptoms. Moreover, hurried children are turning into hurried teenagers—urged by parents and the media alike to grow up fast. Elkind believes that too many teenagers are left without the guidance, direction, and support they need to become healthy adults (Elkind, 1984). In part, this occurs because many parents are too busy dealing with demands outside the family and expect their children to "take care of themselves" (Elkind, 1995).

Elkind's main point is that today's teenagers have adulthood thrust on them too soon. Violence, drug abuse, X-rated movies, youth crime, teenage pregnancy, divorce and single-parent families, date rape, aimless schools—all this, and more, strikes Elkind as evidence that there is no place for teenagers in today's society.

According to Elkind, the traditional **social markers** of adolescence have all but disappeared. (Social markers are visible or tangible signs that indicate a person's social status or role—such as a driver's license or a wedding ring.) As an example, Elkind notes that clothing for children and teenagers

is increasingly adult-like. Girls especially are urged to wear seductive clothing and revealing swimsuits.

Clearly, Elkind is stating a clinical opinion. It's possible that his view exaggerates the problem somewhat. Indeed, much of what he says is debatable. Nevertheless, his portrayal of hurried adolescents as "all grown up with no place to go" is highly thought provoking.

Typical clothing worn by young adolescents 60 years ago and today.

The Search for Identity

As discussed earlier, identity formation is a key task of adolescence. To be sure, problems of identity occur at other times, too. But in a very real sense, puberty signals that it's time to begin forming a new, more mature self-image (Douvan, 1997). Many problems stem from unclear standards about the role adolescents should play within society. Are they adults or children? Should they be autonomous or dependent? Should they work or play? Such ambiguities make it difficult for young people to form clear images of themselves and of how they should act (Alsaker, 1995).

Answering the question "Who am I?" is also spurred by cognitive development. After adolescents have attained the stage of formal operations, they are better able to ask questions about their place in the world and about morals, values, politics, and social relationships. Then, too, being able to think about hypothetical possibilities allows the adolescent to contemplate the future and ask more realistically, "Who will I be?" (Suls, 1989).

DIVERSITY AND IDENTITY   Ethnic heritage can have a powerful influence on personal identity. Yet, at a time when teens are

trying to find their place in society, they may feel rejected or excluded because of their ethnic heritage. Despite their numbers, adolescents of color are often portrayed in negative terms in the media. For example, popular culture is loaded with images that dismiss anyone who doesn't look like a Barbie or Ken doll. Also, ethnic adolescents often face degrading stereotypes concerning their intelligence, sexuality, social status, manners, and so forth. Such stereotypes can lead adolescents of color to feel that they are never quite good enough, attractive enough, smart enough, or "white" enough. The result can be lowered self-esteem and confusion about roles, values, and personal identity (de las Fuentes & Vasquez, 1999).

Puberty *The biologically defined period during which a person matures sexually and becomes capable of reproduction.*
Growth spurt *An often dramatic acceleration in physical growth that coincides with puberty.*
Social markers *Visible or tangible signs that indicate a person's social status or role.*

In forming an identity, adolescents of ethnic descent face the question of how they should think of themselves. Is Lori an American or a Chinese American? Is Jaime a Chicano, a Mexicano, or a Mexican American? The answer typically depends on how strongly adolescents identify with their family and ethnic community. Teens who take pride in their ethnic heritage have higher self-esteem, a better self-image, and a stronger sense of personal identity (Roberts et al., 1999; Tse, 1999; Verkuyten & Lay, 1998). Incidentally, the same can be said of anyone who is "different." Sexual orientation and disabilities, for instance, create many of the same conflicts as ethnicity does. Enhanced group pride, positive models, and a more tolerant society could do much to keep a broad range of options open to *all* adolescents (Vasquez & de las Fuentes, 1999).

PARENTS AND TEENS *What effects do parents have on identity formation?* The adolescent search for identity frequently leads to conflict with parents, especially in early adolescence (Laursen et al., 1998). However, some disagreement with parents is probably necessary for growth of a separate identity. A complete lack of conflict may mean that the adolescent is afraid to seek independence.

Actually, adolescents and parents usually agree to a large degree about basic topics such as religion, marriage, and morals. Even though teens disagree with parents more than they did as children, less conflict occurs than might be expected (Fuligni, 1998). (This may be because teens spend so little time at home!) The conflicts that do occur tend to be over superficial differences regarding styles of dress, manners, social behavior, and the like. However, superficial disputes sometimes mask struggles about more basic issues, such as substance use, dangerous driving, and sex. For instance, parents who resist a 13-year-old's request to begin dating may actually be concerned about sex, not dating (Arnett, 1999).

Adolescents naturally desire more freedom, but they do not want their parents to abruptly abandon them. Teenagers do best when they are given gradual increases in personal freedom and more opportunities to make decisions. In the majority of cases, adolescents who ask their parents for emotional or practical support actually receive it (Valery, O'Conner, & Jennings, 1997). Problems occur when parents crack down too hard or

throw their hands up and surrender control over the adolescent's behavior (Eccles et al., 1993).

IMAGINARY AUDIENCES David Elkind has noted an interesting pattern in adolescent thought. According to Elkind (1984), many teenagers are preoccupied with **imaginary audiences** (people they imagine are watching them). In other words, teenagers may act like others are aware of their thoughts and feelings. Sometimes this leads to painful self-consciousness—as in thinking that *everyone* is staring at a bad haircut you just received. The imaginary audience also seems to underlie attention-seeking "performances" involving outlandish dress or behavior. In any case, adolescents become very concerned with controlling the impressions they make on others. For many, being "on stage" in this way helps define and shape an emerging identity.

PEER GROUPS In high school, were you a jock, preppy, brain, hacker, surfer, cowboy, punk, mod, rapper, druggy, warthog, dervish, zork, or aardvark? (Well, okay, I made up the last four—the rest are real.) Increased identification with peer groups is quite common during adolescence. A **peer group** consists of people who share similar social status. To an extent, membership in such groups gives a measure of security and a sense of identity apart from the family. Beyond this, group membership provides practice in belonging to a social network. Children tend to see themselves more as members of families and small friendship groups, not as members of society as a whole. Therefore, gaining a broader, member-of-society perspective can be a major step toward adulthood (Hill, 1993).

Aren't groups also limiting? Yes, they are. Conformity to peer values peaks in early adolescence, but it remains strong at least through high school (Newman, 1982). Throughout this period, there is always a danger of allowing group pressure to **foreclose** (shut down) personal growth (Newman & Newman, 1987). Cliques, in particular, can be very confining because members typically don't socialize with people outside the clique (Degirmencioglu et al., 1998).

Peer groups can also encourage problem behaviors. For example, groups that value having fun and seeking pleasure (a

Membership in friendship groups, cliques, "posses," or "crews" helps adolescents build an identity apart from their relationship to parents. However, overidentification with a clannish group that rejects anyone who looks or acts differently can limit personal growth.

"Let's party" attitude) are associated with delinquency and substance use. Groups that value self-respect, being respected, achievement, warm relationships with others, and a sense of belonging have low rates of delinquent behavior and substance use (Goff & Goddard, 1999).

THE TRANSITION TO ADULTHOOD By the end of high school, many adolescents have not yet sufficiently explored various interests, values, vocations, skills, or ideologies on their own. Perhaps that is why many students view moving on to work or college as a chance to break out of earlier roles—to expand or reshape personal identity. For many who choose college, the effect may be more a matter of placing further changes in identity on hold. By doing so, college students keep open the possibility of changing majors, career plans, personal style, and so on. Typically, commitment to an emerging adult identity grows stronger in later college years (Santrock, 1995).

By the time a person reaches adolescence, his or her moral values begin to come into sharper focus (Fabes et al., 1999). This is a significant development that has an impact on behavior throughout life. Like many important processes, moral development starts in childhood and continues into adulthood. In the next section, we will take a brief look at this interesting aspect of personal growth.

MORAL DEVELOPMENT—GROWING A CONSCIENCE

A person with a terminal illness is in great pain. She is pleading for death. Should extraordinary medical efforts be made to keep her alive? If a friend of yours desperately needed to pass a test and asked you to help him cheat, would you do it? These are *moral* questions, or questions of conscience. How are moral values acquired? Psychologist Lawrence Kohlberg (1981a) held

that they are learned, in part, as children develop the ability to think and reason.

Moral Dilemmas

Through **moral development**, we acquire values, beliefs, and thinking abilities that guide responsible behavior. To study moral development, Kohlberg posed dilemmas to children of different ages. The following is one of the moral dilemmas he used (Kohlberg, 1969, adapted).

> A woman was near death from cancer, and there was only one drug that might save her. It was discovered by a druggist who was charging 10 times what it cost to make the drug. The sick woman's husband could only pay $1,000, but the druggist wanted $2,000. He asked the druggist to sell it cheaper or to let him pay later. The druggist said no. So the husband became desperate and broke into the store to steal the drug for his wife. Should he have done that? Was it wrong or right? Why?

Each child was asked what action the husband should take. Kohlberg classified the reasons given for each choice and identified three levels of moral development. Each is based not so much on the choices made but on the reasoning used to arrive at a choice.

At the **preconventional level**, moral thinking is guided by the consequences of actions (punishment, reward, or an exchange of favors). In the **conventional level**, reasoning is based on a desire to please others or to follow accepted rules and values. The advanced moral reasoning of the **postconventional level** follows self-accepted moral principles. In addition to the three major levels, Kohlberg identified six stages of moral reasoning (◆Table 5.2). In time, Kohlberg found it necessary to combine stages 5 and 6 because it proved difficult, in practice, to separate them (Kohlberg, 1981b). He was firm in his belief, however, that morality develops in preconventional, conventional, and postconventional phases.

Does everyone eventually reach the highest level? People advance through the stages at different rates, and many fail to reach the postconventional stage. In fact, many do not even reach the conventional level. For instance, a survey in England revealed that 11 percent of men and 3 percent of women would commit murder for $1 million if they could be sure of getting away with the crime ("They'd kill," 1991).

Imaginary audience *The group of people a person imagines is watching (or will watch) his or her actions.*
Peer group *A group of people who share similar social status.*
Foreclosed identity formation *A premature end to the search for identity.*
Moral development *The development of values, beliefs, and thinking abilities that act as a guide regarding what is acceptable behavior.*
Preconventional moral reasoning *Moral thinking based on the consequences of one's choices or actions (punishment, reward, or an exchange of favors).*
Conventional moral reasoning *Moral thinking based on a desire to please others or to follow accepted rules and values.*
Postconventional moral reasoning *Moral thinking based on carefully examined and self-chosen moral principles.*

PRECONVENTIONAL	CONVENTIONAL	POSTCONVENTIONAL
Stage 1: Punishment orientation. Actions are evaluated in terms of possible punishment, not goodness or badness; obedience to power is emphasized. *Example:* "He shouldn't steal the drug because he could get caught and sent to jail" (avoiding punishment).	**Stage 3: Good boy/good girl orientation.** Good behavior is that which pleases others in the immediate group or which brings approval; the emphasis is on being "nice." *Example:* "He shouldn't steal the drug because others will think he is a thief. His wife would not want to be saved by thievery" (avoiding disapproval).	**Stage 5: Social-contract orientation.** Support of laws and rules is based on rational analysis and mutual agreement; rules are recognized as open to question but are upheld for the good of the community and in the name of democratic values. *Example:* "He should not steal the drug. The druggist's decision is reprehensible, but mutual respect for the rights of others must be maintained" (social contract).
Stage 2: Pleasure-seeking orientation. Proper action is determined by one's own needs; concern for the needs of others is largely a matter of "You scratch my back and I'll scratch yours," not of loyalty, gratitude, or justice. *Example:* "It won't do him any good to steal the drug because his wife will probably die before he gets out of jail" (self-interest).	**Stage 4: Authority orientation.** In this stage, the emphasis is on upholding law, order, and authority, doing one's duty, and following social rules. *Example:* "Although his wife needs the drug, he should not break the law to get it. Everyone is equal in the eyes of the law, and his wife's condition does not justify stealing" (traditional morality of authority).	**Stage 6: Morality of individual principles.** Behavior is directed by self-chosen ethical principles that tend to be general, comprehensive, or universal; high value is placed on justice, dignity, and equality. *Example:* "He should steal the drug and then inform the authorities that he has done so. He will have to face a penalty, but he will have saved a human life" (self-chosen ethical principles).

Each of us faces moral dilemmas, both large and small, every day. Dishonesty on taxes, sexual faithfulness, abortion, speeding, found valuables, temptations to lie, honesty in business—these and many other situations raise moral questions. A moral dilemma familiar to most students involves being unprepared for an exam. Sadly, the majority of American children function at the preconventional level of moral development at school: A 1990 poll found that two thirds would cheat to pass an important exam.

The preconventional stages (1 and 2) are most characteristic of young children and delinquents (Nelson, Smith, & Dodd, 1990). Conventional, group-oriented morals of stages 3 and 4 are typical of older children and most adults. Kohlberg estimated that only about 20 percent of the adult population achieves postconventional morality, representing self-direction and higher principles. (It would appear that few of these people enter politics!)

Moral development is a promising topic for further study. As an example, consider the work of psychologist Carol Gilligan.

Justice or Caring?

Gilligan (1982) pointed out that Kohlberg's system is concerned mainly with *justice*. Based on studies of women who faced real-

life dilemmas, Gilligan argued that there is also an ethic of *caring* about others. As one illustration, Gilligan presented the following story to 11- to 15-year-old American children.

The Porcupine and the Moles

Seeking refuge from the cold, a porcupine asked to share a cave for the winter with a family of moles. The moles agreed. But because the cave was small, they soon found they were being scratched each time the porcupine moved about. Finally, they asked the porcupine to leave. But the porcupine refused, saying, "If you moles are not satisfied, I suggest that you leave."

Boys who read this story tended to opt for justice in resolving the dilemma: "It's the moles' house. It's a deal. The porcupine leaves." In contrast, girls tended to look for solutions that would keep all parties happy and comfortable, such as "Cover the porcupine with a blanket."

Gilligan's point is that male psychologists have, for the most part, defined moral maturity in terms of justice and autonomy. From this perspective, women's concern with relationships can look like a weakness rather than a strength. (A woman who is concerned about what pleases or helps others would be placed at stage 3 in Kohlberg's system.) But Gilligan believes that caring is also a major element of moral development, and she suggests that males may lag in achieving it (Gilligan & Attanucci, 1988).

Does the evidence support Gilligan's position? Several studies have found little or no difference in men's and women's overall moral reasoning abilities (Mednick, 1989; Wilson, 1995). Indeed, both men and women may use caring *and* justice to make moral decisions. The moral yardstick they use appears to depend on the situation they face (Wark & Krebs, 1996). Just the same, Gilligan deserves credit for identifying a second major way in which moral choices are made.

Although gender may not affect moral reasoning, culture does. People from Eastern cultures, such as China, Japan, or India, are more likely to make moral choices with group welfare in mind. That is, they place a high value on interpersonal harmony and concern for others. In Western cultures, justice is given a higher priority (Turiel, in press). So, again we see that understanding moral behavior requires an appreciation of both justice and caring.

Like the development of moral values, the process of selecting a career often starts in childhood and continues into adolescence. Setting a course in the world of work is part of the process of defining personal identity during adolescence and gaining adult social status. How do people choose their vocations?

VOCATIONAL CHOICE—CHARTING A COURSE IN THE WORLD OF WORK

John was always an excellent student, but his real love was sports. Being on the track team was, in fact, the high point of his college career. (About 7 feet high, to be exact. John was a high-jumper.) After he graduated, John was hired by a large accounting firm at an enviable starting salary. Yet within 2 years, John knew he had made a mistake. Accounting left him dissatisfied, restless, and often bored.

In college, John's career choice had seemed highly practical. Now he was miserable. What could he do about it? John decided to take a chance. He quit his job, and after several years of additional education, financial hardship, and personal sacrifice, he accepted his first college coaching position.

Vocational Choice

As John's story illustrates, vocational decisions are neither permanent nor easily undone. Usually, by the time a person has selected a career path, it takes a big effort to change course. Moreover, changing careers can be a major risk. (What if John had discovered that he also disliked coaching?) The reality that

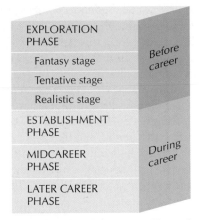

❖ **FIGURE 5.3** *A model of career development. The exploration phase can be divided into three substages of vocational choice.*

John faced is illustrated by a survey in which 44 percent of those polled said that, for better or worse, they felt locked into their current jobs (Renwick & Lawler, 1979). Clearly, there is value in making good vocational choices, and in making them early, if possible.

Career Development

Career development refers an entire career path, from choosing an initial occupation through retirement. John's abrupt change is somewhat unusual. For people who enter professions, career development tends to flow through four broad phases (❖Fig. 5.3). These are (1) the **exploration phase**, during which an initial search for a career is made; (2) the **establishment phase**, during which the person finds a job, enters a career, develops competence, and gains status; (3) the **midcareer phase**, which is a stable period of high productivity and acceptance by coworkers; and (4) the **later career phase**, a time before retirement when the individual serves as a respected expert and often as a mentor (role model and guide) for younger workers (Van Maanen & Schein, 1977).

STAGES OF EXPLORATION Of the four phases, the one most likely to be of immediate relevance to you is exploration. During the exploration phase, most people go through a recognizable series of stages as they choose an occupation (Ginzberg, 1984).

Career development *One's entire career path, from choosing an initial vocation through retirement.*
Exploration phase *The period during which career alternatives are explored.*
Establishment phase *The period during which a person enters a career and builds competence in it.*
Midcareer phase *A stable central career phase marked by high competence and full status.*
Later career phase *The concluding career phase prior to retirement; marked by high status and respect arising from long experience.*

In the **fantasy stage**, children under age 10 simply imagine what they want to be when they grow up. The roles they fantasize—such as president, pilot, rock star, rodeo rider, or TV announcer—may be unrealistic, but they do show that children realize that they will need to work someday.

During the **tentative stage** (roughly, ages 10 to 18), adolescents begin to form more realistic, if somewhat general, ideas about what they want to do. However, their plans may shift several times during this period, and they typically remain tentative. Toward the end of high school, many students begin to more fully appreciate the importance of choosing a vocation. They also become aware that there are limits to their options and barriers to certain careers.

After high school, various social and practical pressures lead most people to narrow their range of vocational options. During this **realistic stage**, the first steps are taken to find out what specific jobs are like and to prepare for one. At this time, many college students use course work to discover what they are good at and what holds their interest.

By the early 20s, most people begin to carry out their vocational plans. This involves completing necessary training and landing that important first job.

The preceding description implies that most people carefully choose a vocation or career. Actually, vocational choice is frequently rather haphazard. For example, it is not unusual for students to allow a "temporary" major to determine which courses they take. Soon, they find themselves channeled into a career path—without really having made a clear decision.

VOCATIONAL ASPIRATION *How would a person go about improving the quality of his or her vocational choice?* To begin with, it helps to recognize that our attraction to certain jobs or careers is influenced by many factors. Some of the more important influences are socioeconomic status, intelligence, school achievement, family background, gender, and personal interests (Kaplan & Stein, 1984). As much as these factors may influence your own choice, it is also important to realize that you have the potential to succeed in a variety of occupations. In fact, the best single predictor of what job category you will enter is your **vocational aspiration**, which is simply what you tell yourself you would like to do.

The world of work is complex and rapidly changing. In the face of such changes, it is becoming more important to make careful, informed decisions about what kind of work to pursue. To make sure your vocational choice will be realistic and personally rewarding, you must (1) gain an accurate understanding of various occupations and (2) get a clear picture of your own interests, needs, and goals. *That seems obvious. But how?*

VOCATIONAL COUNSELING A good way to improve occupational choice is to consult a **vocational counselor**. These professionals are counseling psychologists who specialize in matching people with jobs. A vocational counselor can help you clarify your career goals, and she or he can administer vocational interest and aptitude tests to guide your choice. Many colleges now have **career centers**, which offer testing and career guidance. These centers also typically hold a wealth of information about various jobs and careers. Many offer computerized programs that

guide students through the initial steps of career decision making (Katz, 1993).

If formal guidance is unavailable, you will have to serve as your own "vocational counselor." A good way to start is to consult the *Occupational Outlook Handbook,* available in most libraries. This book provides objective information about the outlook for various occupations. The *Handbook* includes job descriptions, information on training requirements, average earnings, and the number of jobs likely to be available in coming years. A simple look at such facts could prevent many students from pursuing overpopulated careers (law, for instance).

Finding out what a particular job is really like may require more initiative. In many occupations, the nature of the work is not what it seems from the outside. For instance, medical students are often dismayed when they first begin to realize that disease is ugly and that many medical procedures are distasteful. To find out beforehand what an occupation is like, it is advisable to talk to several people in that line of work. Be sure to ask your informants what they dislike about their jobs, as well as what they like. If possible, you might even spend a day observing people in an occupation that interests you.

Beginning a career is only one of the challenges of adulthood. We'll explore others in a moment. Before you read more, here's a chance to check your progress.

KNOWLEDGE BUILDER
ADOLESCENCE, MORAL DEVELOPMENT, AND VOCATIONAL CHOICE

RELATE

To what extent does the concept of identity formation apply to your own experience during adolescence? Did you mature early, average, or late? How do you think the timing of puberty affected you? In what ways did peer group membership affect your personal identity?

At what stage of moral development was U.S. President Bill Clinton functioning in his well-publicized affair with Monica Lewinsky?

What stage of career development do you think you are in?

LEARNING CHECK

1. In most societies, adolescence begins with the onset of puberty and ends with its completion. T or F?

2. Early-maturing boys tend to experience more clear-cut advantages than do early-maturing girls. T or F?

3. According to David Elkind, the traditional markers of adolescence and adulthood have been blurred. T or F?

4. The imaginary audience refers to conformity pressures that adolescents believe adults apply to them. T or F?

5. According to Kohlberg, the conventional level of moral development is marked by a reliance on outside authority. T or F?

6. Self-interest and avoiding punishment are elements of postconventional morality. T or F?

7. About 80 percent of all adults function at the postconventional level of moral reasoning. T or F?

◆ TABLE 5.3 Typical Life Goals and Concerns

	TYPICAL GOALS ARE RELATED TO:	TYPICAL CONCERNS ARE RELATED TO:
Young adults	Education and family	Relationships and friends
Middle-aged	Children's lives and personal property	Occupational worries
Elderly	Good health, retirement, leisure, community	Health fears

Nurmi, 1992.

CHALLENGES OF ADULTHOOD—CHARTING LIFE'S UPS AND DOWNS

After a "settling down" period somewhere in the 20s, adult development is uniform and uninteresting, right? Wrong! A fairly predictable series of challenges is associated with development from adolescence to old age.

What personality changes and psychological developments can a person look forward to in adulthood? Further study has added important detail to the events discussed by Erikson. One informative account is based on clinical work by Roger Gould, a psychiatrist interested in adult personality. Gould's research (1975) reveals that common patterns for North American adults are as follows.

AGES 16–18: ESCAPE FROM DOMINANCE   Ages 16 to 18 are marked by a struggle to escape from parental dominance. Efforts to do so cause considerable anxiety about the future and conflicts about continuing dependence on parents.

AGES 18–22: LEAVING THE FAMILY   The majority of people break away from their families in their early 20s. Leaving home is usually associated with building new friendships with other adults. These friends serve as substitutes for the family and as allies in the process of breaking ties.

AGES 22–28: BUILDING A WORKABLE LIFE   The trend in the mid-20s is to seek mastery of the real world. Two dominant activities are striving for accomplishment (seeking competence) and reaching out to others. Note that the second activity corresponds to Erikson's emphasis on seeking intimacy at this time. Married couples in this age group tend to place a high value on "togetherness."

AGES 29–34: CRISIS OF QUESTIONS   Around the age of 30, many people experience a minor life crisis. The heart of this crisis is a serious questioning of what life is all about. People tend to ask themselves, "Is this it?" and confidence in previous choices and values can waver. Unsettled by these developments, the person actively searches for a style of living that will bring more meaning to life. Marriages are particularly vulnerable during this time of dissatisfaction. Extramarital affairs and divorces are common symptoms of the "crisis of questions."

AGES 35–43: CRISIS OF URGENCY   People ages 35 to 43 are typically beginning to become more aware of the reality of death. Having a limited number of years to live begins to exert pressure on the individual. Intensified attempts are made to succeed at a career or to achieve one's life goals. Generativity, in the form of nurturing, teaching, or serving others, helps alleviate many of the anxieties of this stage.

AGES 43–50: ATTAINING STABILITY   The urgency of the previous stage gives way to a calmer acceptance of one's fate in the late 40s. The predominant feeling is that the die is cast and that former decisions can be lived with. Those who have families begin to appreciate their children as individuals and ease up on their tendency to extend their own goals to their children's behavior.

AGE 50 AND UP: MELLOWING   After age 50, a noticeable mellowing occurs. Emphasis is placed on sharing day-to-day joys and sorrows. There is less concern with glamor, wealth, accomplishment, and abstract goals. Many of the tensions of earlier years give way to a desire to savor life and its small pleasures. (A study of typical life goals and concerns at various ages parallels many of the points made by Gould. See Table ◆5.3.)

Fantasy stage *Stage of career exploration in which people imagine themselves filling unlikely roles.*
Tentative stage *Stage of career exploration in which planning becomes more realistic, although still broad.*
Realistic stage *Stage of career exploration in which career options are narrowed and more specific plans are made.*
Vocational aspiration *The line of work a person hopes to enter as an adult.*
Vocational counselor *A counseling psychologist who helps people match their interests, talents, and goals with available careers.*
Career center *A counseling facility that offers testing, career guidance, and information on various careers.*

Psychologists aim for universal accounts of development. It should be clear, however, that Gould's summary is highly idealized. Each person's path through life is unique. Also, adult development varies greatly in different cultures and at different times in history (Stewart & Ostrove, 1998). Accordingly, Gould's description is merely a starting point for understanding typical patterns in adult development. Let's see what we can learn from other investigations.

A Midlife Crisis?

Gould describes two "crisis" points in adult development. How common is it to have a "midlife crisis"? Serious difficulties at the midpoint of life are certainly not universal. A recent study of more than 8,000 Americans found that only 23 percent (about 1 in 4) believed they had experienced a midlife crisis. In other words, most people thrive during middle adulthood and have no special problems (Brim et al., 1999).

If a midlife crisis does occur, what does it look like? Psychologist Daniel Levinson carried out an in-depth study of adulthood and identified five periods when people typically make major transitions (◆Table 5.4). A **transition period** ends one life pattern and opens the door to new possibilities (Levinson, 1978, 1986). At such times, people address concerns about their identity, work, and relationships to others.

Levinson's first study focused on the lives of men. As they approached the midlife transition (between the ages of 37 and 41), most men went through a period of instability, anxiety, and change. (Notice that this corresponds closely to Gould's crisis-of-urgency period.) In a later study, Levinson found that most of what he learned about men also applies to women (Levinson & Levinson, 1996).

Of the men Levinson studied, roughly half defined the midlife period as a "last chance" to achieve their goals. Such goals were often stated as a key event, such as reaching a certain income or becoming a supervisor, a full professor, or a shop steward. For these men, the midlife period was stressful but manageable.

A smaller percentage of men experienced a serious midlife decline. Many of these men had to face the fact that they had chosen a dead-end job or lifestyle. Others had achieved financial success but felt that what they were doing was pointless.

In a third pattern, a few hardy individuals appeared to break out of a seriously flawed life structure. For them, a decision to start over was typically followed by 8 to 10 years of rebuilding.

In what ways does the midlife transition differ for women? Compared with men, women were less likely to enter adulthood with clearly formulated "goals." As a result, they were less likely to define success in terms of some key event. Rather than focusing on external goals, women tended to seek changes in personal identity at midlife. For example, a woman might become more self-reliant and independent—qualities she may have regarded as "masculine" earlier in life (Levinson & Levinson, 1996). But make no mistake, midlife can be challenging for women, too. Of women surveyed in a recent study, two thirds had made major changes in their lives between ages 37 and 43 (Stewart & Vandewater, 1999).

In summary, most people repeatedly move through cycles of stability and transition in their adult lives (Ornstein & Isabella, 1990). If a midlife crisis takes place at all, it can be both a danger and an opportunity. In fact, the term *crisis* may be too strong a word. Most people make "midcourse corrections" in their lives, rather than survive a crisis. Ideally, midlife transitions involve reworking old identities, achieving long-sought goals, finding one's own truths, and preparing for later maturity and aging. Midlife can be challenging, but it is not inevitably a crisis (Stewart & Ostrove, 1998).

◆**TABLE 5.4** Three Views of Developmental Challenges

	ERIKSON	GOULD	LEVINSON
Childhood	Trust/mistrust (1) Autonomy/shame, doubt (1–3) Initiative/guilt (3–5) Industry/inferiority (6–12)		
Adolescence	Identity/confusion (12–18)	Escape from dominance (16–18)	Early adulthood transition (17–22)
Early Adulthood	Intimacy/isolation	Leaving the family (18–22) Building a workable life (22–28) Crisis of questions (29–34)	Early adulthood transition (17–22) Age 30 transition (28–33)
Middle Adulthood	Generativity/self-absorption	Crisis of urgency (35–43) Attaining stability (43–50) Mellowing (50+)	Midlife transition (40–45) Age 50 transition (50–55)
Late Adulthood			Late adult transition (60–65)
Old Age	Integrity/despair		

Middle Age

When individuals reach their 40s and 50s, declining vigor, strength, and youthfulness make it clear that more than half their years are gone. At the same time, greater stability comes from letting go of the "impossible dream." That is, there is an increased attempt to be satisfied with the direction one's life has taken and to accept that hoped-for life goals may no longer be possible.

For most women during this era, menopause represents the first real encounter with growing "old" (Kirk, 1995). At **menopause**, which occurs at an average age of 51, monthly menstruation ends, and a woman is no longer able to bear children. At the same time, the level of the hormone estrogen drops—sometimes causing changes in mood or appearance. Menopause also can cause physical symptoms, such as "hot flashes" (a sudden uncomfortable sensation of heat) or night sweats. Many of the small discomforts of menopause appear to be related to a disruption of bodily rhythms. They are, in other words, a little like suffering from jet lag (Gannon, 1993). Women who are bothered by such problems can benefit from hormonal replacement therapy, in which estrogen is taken to reduce the symptoms of menopause (Bech et al., 1998).

A few women find menopause as difficult to adjust to as adolescence, and some experience anxiety, irritability, or depression at this time. Most women, however, are neutral about the loss of reproductive ability. Many, in fact, express relief at being freed from concerns about pregnancy, birth control, and menstruation. All considered, the vast majority of women easily take "the pause" in stride, with no major emotional problems (Stewart & Ostrove, 1998).

Do men go through similar changes? Males do not undergo any physical change that is directly comparable to menopause. With aging, the production of the male hormone testosterone gradually lessens. However, men remain fertile at this time. On the other hand, aging males may be affected by changes in appearance and physical vigor. Some 40- to 60-year-old men do appear to pass through a **climacteric** (kly-MAK-ter-ik: "change of life"). For some men, testosterone levels drop enough to cause symptoms such as depression, anxiety, irritability, and insomnia (Sternbach, 1998). However, for most men, such symptoms are probably psychological in origin.

WELL-BEING AT MIDLIFE   The pitfalls of adulthood are all too familiar: marital discord, divorce, career difficulties, unemployment, health problems, financial pressures, legal conflicts, and personal tragedies—to name but a few. How do people maintain a state of well-being as they run the gauntlet of modern life?

Psychologist Carol Ryff (1995) believes that well-being during adulthood consists of six elements:

- Self-acceptance
- Positive relations with others
- Autonomy (personal freedom)
- Environmental mastery
- A purpose in life
- Continued personal growth

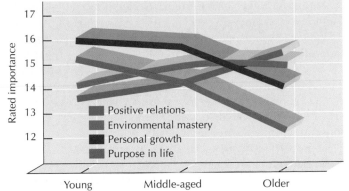

❖ **FIGURE 5.4** *Feelings of personal growth and of having a purpose in life tend to decline with increasing age. However, positive relations with other people and mastery of the environment tend to increase. Thus, the basis for a continued sense of well-being makes an interesting shift between young adulthood and old age. (Graph courtesy of Dr. Carol Ryff.)*

Based on a national survey, Ryff found that personal growth and having a sense of purpose in life tend to decline with increasing age. However, these declines are offset by increases in two other areas (❖Fig. 5.4). As people age, positive relations with others tend to increase, as does mastery of the complex demands of life (Ryff & Keyes, 1995).

Thus, sharing life's joys and sorrows with others, coupled with a better understanding of how the world works, can help carry people through the midlife period and into their later years.

As author Gail Sheehy (1995) has pointed out, signs of aging may be unmistakable in middle age, but people are also at their peak in many respects. Instead of emphasizing decline, many of today's adults seek active, healthy lifestyles. This can make the middle-age years a positive experience, not something to be dreaded or endured (Sheehy, 1995).

After the late 50s, the problems an individual faces in maintaining a healthy and meaningful life are complicated by the inevitable process of aging. How unique are the problems of older people, and how severely do they challenge the need to maintain integrity and personal comfort? We will look at some answers in the next section.

AGING—WILL YOU STILL NEED ME WHEN I'M 64?

Some years ago, students at Long Beach City College in California elected Pearl Taylor their spring festival queen. Ms. Taylor had everything necessary to win: looks, intelligence, personality, and campus-wide popularity. At about the same time,

Transition period *Time span during which a person leaves an existing life pattern behind and moves into a new pattern.*
Menopause *The female "change of life" signaled by the end of regular monthly menstrual periods.*
Climacteric *A point during late middle age when males experience a significant change in health, vigor, or appearance.*

citizens of Raleigh, North Carolina, elected Isabella Cannon as their mayor.

What's so remarkable about these events? Not too much really, except that Pearl was 90 years old when elected, and Isabella was 73. Both are part of the graying of North America. Currently, some 35 million North Americans are over the age of 65. By the year 2020, some 60 million persons in the United States and Canada, or 1 of every 5, will be 65 years of age or older (❖Fig. 5.5). These figures make the elderly the fastest-growing segment of society. Understandably, psychologists have become increasingly interested in aging. You should be, too. If you are

BRIDGES

The most common cause of dementia in old age is Alzheimer's disease.

See page 574 in Chapter 17 for a discussion of this devastating illness.

now in your 20s, you will be part of the "grandparent boom" in 2050.

What is life like for the aged? There are large variations in aging. Most of us have known elderly persons at both extremes: those who are active, healthy, satisfied, lucid, and alert and those who are confused, child-like, or dependent. Despite such variations, some generalizations can be made.

The Course of Aging

Biological aging refers to age-related changes in physiological functioning. Aging is a gradual process that begins quite early in life. Peak functioning in most physical capacities reaches a maximum by about 25 to 30 years of age (❖Fig. 5.6). Thereafter, gradual declines occur in muscular strength, flexibility, circulatory efficiency, speed of response, sensory acuity, and other functions (Birren & Fisher, 1995b). Given the natural course of aging, it is extremely unlikely that a 50-year-old, or even a 40-year-old, will ever hold the world record for the 100-meter dash (Schulz & Heckhausen, 1996). (See "Biological Aging.")

So people are "over the hill" by 30? Hardly! Prime abilities come at different ages for different activities. Peak performances for professional football and baseball players usually occur in the mid-20s; for professional bowlers, the mid-30s; for artists and musicians, the 50s; and for politicians, philosophers, business or industrial leaders, and others, the early 60s (❖Fig. 5.7).

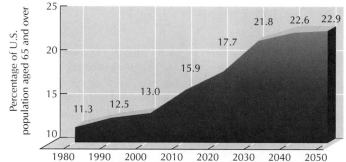

❖ **FIGURE 5.5** *Longer life expectancy will produce an unprecedented increase in the percentage of the population over age 65. The "boom" is expected to start now and peak by about 2030 to 2050 (Taeuber, 1993).*

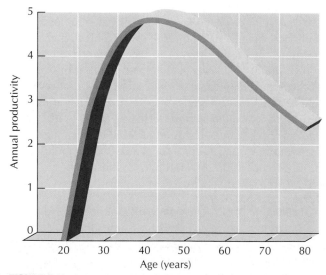

❖ **FIGURE 5.7** *At what point during life are people most productive? On average, when do people make their greatest contributions to fields such as science, literature, philosophy, music, and the visual arts? No matter how achievement is tallied, productivity tends to rise rapidly to a single peak that is followed by a slow decline. The graph you see here is typical of contributions to the field of psychology. Fields such as poetry, pure math, and theoretical physics have earlier peaks, around the early 30s or even the late 20s. Other fields, such as novel writing, history, philosophy, medicine, and scholarship, are marked by peaks in the late 40s, 50s, or even 60s. (After Simonton, 1988.)*

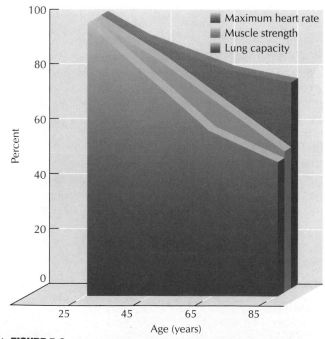

❖ **FIGURE 5.6** *Physical aging, which is biologically programmed, progresses steadily from early adulthood onward. Regular exercise, good health practices, and a positive attitude can help minimize the impact of physical aging.*

A CLOSER LOOK

BIOLOGICAL AGING—HOW LONG IS A LIFETIME?

Whatever the biological causes of aging, humans seem to grow, mature, age, and die within a set time. The length of our lives is limited by a biological boundary called the **maximum life span** (the maximum age humans can attain under optimal conditions). Estimates of the maximum human life span place it around 110 to 120 years. The oldest documented age ever achieved is 122 years by Jeanne Calment, a French woman who died in 1997. Among the more than 5 billion persons currently living, only two or three are likely to reach the age of 115.

For most people, **life expectancy** (the actual number of years the average person lives) is shorter than the maximum

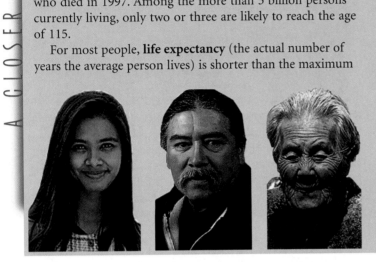

life span. In the 1800s, the average life expectancy was 36 years. Now, average life expectancy at birth for American males is 73 years, and for females it is 81 years. With improved health care, life expectancy should move even closer to the maximum life span.

At present, there is no known way to extend the maximum human life span. On the other hand, there is every reason to believe that life expectancy can be increased. If you would personally like to add to a new, higher average, here are some deceptively simple rules for delaying aging and living a long life (Coni et al., 1984; Roizen, 1999).

1. Do not smoke.
2. Use alcohol in moderation (one or two drinks per day, maximum).
3. Avoid becoming overweight.
4. Maintain a healthy diet, including taking any necessary dietary supplements.
5. If you suffer from high blood pressure, have it treated.
6. Remain socially and economically active in retirement.
7. Exercise regularly throughout life.

To this we can add: Get married (*happily* married persons live longer), learn to manage stress, and choose long-lived parents!

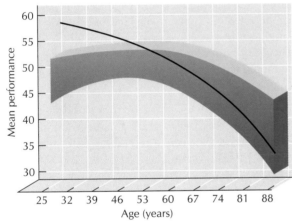

❖ **FIGURE 5.8** *Average performance at various ages for verbal, numeric, spatial, and reasoning abilities all fall within the blue area of this graph. Notice that, in general, mental abilities show modest gains from young adulthood to early middle age. After that, they begin a slow decline. Notice, too, that most abilities at age 70 return to about the same levels found at age 25. Only after age 80 do declines become large enough to make a practical difference in mental abilities. One exception is perceptual speed (black line). This fluid ability declines steadily after age 25. (Adapted from Schaie, 1994.)*

For those who are still young, physical aging may be the greatest threat of old age. However, it is wrong to believe that most elderly people are sickly, infirm, or senile. Only about 5 percent of those over 65 years old are in nursing homes. In fact, the percentage of elderly who are chronically disabled has declined significantly in the last 10 years (Rowe & Kanh, 1998).

As for the possibility of a mental slide, physician Alex Comfort comments, "The human brain does not shrink, wilt, perish, or deteriorate with age. It normally continues to function well through as many as 9 decades."

MENTAL ABILITIES **Gerontologists** (jer-on-TOL-o-jists: those who study aging) estimate that only 25 percent of the disability of old people is medical. The remaining 75 percent is social, political, and cultural. This view is backed up by intelligence test scores, which decline little with aging. Although it is true that **fluid abilities** (those requiring speed or rapid learning) may diminish, many **crystallized abilities** (learned knowledge and skills), such as vocabulary and stored-up facts, actually improve—at least into the 60s (Baltes, Staudinger, & Lindenberger, 1999; Schaie, 1994). (See ❖Fig. 5.8.)

Biological aging *Physiological changes that accompany growing older.*
Maximum life span *The biologically defined maximum number of years humans can live under optimal conditions.*
Life expectancy *The average number of years a person of a given sex, race, and nationality can expect to live.*
Maximum life span *The biologically defined maximum number of years humans can live under optimal conditions.*
Life expectancy *The average number of years a person of a given sex, race, and nationality can expect to live.*
Gerontologist *One who scientifically studies aging and its effects.*
Fluid abilities *Innate, nonlearned abilities based on perceptual, motor, or intellectual speed and flexibility.*
Crystallized abilities *Abilities that a person has intentionally learned; accumulated knowledge and skills.*

Many elderly people are at least as mentally able as the average young adult. On intellectual tests, top scorers over the age of 65 match the average for men under 35. What sets these silver-haired stars apart? Typically, they are people who have continued to work and remain intellectually active (Weintraub et al., 1994). Gerontologist Warner Schaie (1994) found that you are most likely to stay mentally sharp in old age if:

1. You remain healthy.
2. You live in a favorable environment (you are educated and have a stimulating occupation, above-average income, and an intact family).
3. You are involved in intellectually stimulating activities (reading, travel, cultural events, continuing education, clubs, professional associations).
4. You have a flexible personality.
5. You are married to a smart spouse.
6. You maintain your perceptual processing speed.
7. You were satisfied with your accomplishments in midlife.

A shorter summary of the preceding is "Those who live by their wits die with their wits."

Successful Aging

In general, what kind of person adjusts most successfully to aging? Two theories have been proposed to explain successful adjustment to aging. **Disengagement theory** assumes that it is normal and desirable for people to withdraw from society as they age (Cumming & Henry, 1961). According to this theory, the elderly welcome disengagement because it relieves them of roles and responsibilities they are less able to fulfill. Likewise, society benefits from disengagement, as younger persons with new energy and skills fill positions vacated by aging individuals.

Certainly, we have all known people who disengaged from society as they grew older. Nevertheless, disengagement theory seems to describe successful aging as a retreat. Although disengagement may be common, it is not necessarily ideal (Clair, Karp, & Yoels, 1994).

What does the second theory say? The second theory of optimal aging is a sort of "use-it-or-lose-it" view. **Activity theory** assumes that activity is the essence of life for people of all ages. Activity theory predicts that people who remain physically, mentally, and socially active will adjust better to aging (Havighurst, 1961).

Proponents of activity theory believe that aging persons should maintain the activities of their earlier years for as long as possible. If a person is forced to give up particular roles or activities, they should be replaced with others. That way, the aging person is able to maintain a better self-image, greater satisfaction, and more social support—resulting in more successful aging.

Which theory is correct? The majority of studies support the activity theory (Clair, Karp, & Yoels, 1994). At the same time, some people do seek disengagement, so neither theory is absolutely "correct." Actually, successful aging probably requires a combination of continued activity and selective disengagement. The best mix appears to include productive pursuits as well as leisure activities (Herzog et al., 1998).

At age 77, John Glenn became the oldest person to fly into space, in October 1998. Glenn was also the first American astronaut to orbit the Earth, in 1962. As Glenn's space adventure shows, aging does not inevitably bring an end to engaging in challenging activities. The same is true of productive and creative work. Many artists, writers, composers, poets, and scientists have continued to make contributions to society during the seventh, eighth, and even ninth decades of their lives.

COMPENSATION AND OPTIMIZATION Learning to compensate for age-related changes is one of the real keys to remaining active and happy in old age. In fact, the challenge at any age is to make good use of one's potentials (Schroots, 1996). Gerontologist Paul Baltes believes this occurs when people use a strategy of "selective optimization with compensation." That is, older people should focus on what they can still do, find ways to perform well, and compensate for any age-related losses. Baltes offers the following as an example:

> When the concert pianist Arthur Rubinstein, as an 80-year-old, was asked in a television interview how he managed to maintain such a high level of expert piano playing, he hinted at the coordination of three strategies. First, he played fewer pieces (selection); he practiced these pieces more often (optimization); and to counteract his loss in mechanical speed he now used a kind of impression management, such as playing more slowly before fast segments to make the latter appear faster (compensation). (Baltes, Staudinger, & Lindenberger, 1999)

Another key to successful aging is spending as much time as possible doing the things one finds meaningful. Activities done just "to pass the time" tend to lower happiness in old age (Everard, 1999). Finally, people age best when they are able to maintain *control* of their lives (Schulz & Heckhausen, 1996).

Ageism

You have almost certainly encountered ageism in one way or another. **Ageism**, which refers to discrimination or prejudice based on age, can oppress the young as well as the old. For instance, a person applying for a job may just as well be told "You're too young" as "You're too old." In some societies, ageism is based on respect for the elderly. In Japan, for instance, aging is seen as posi-

Social centers and exercise programs for senior citizens are a direct expression of the benefits predicted by activity theory. Remaining active may also give older persons a feeling of *control* over their lives. As we will discuss further in Chapter 16, feelings of control contribute to mental and physical well-being.

In the United States, commercial airline pilots are required to retire at age 60. However, in the 35 years since this age limit was set, many changes have taken place in life expectancy and the nature of flying. There is no reason why a person who is physically healthy cannot continue flying beyond age 60. Actual job performance is probably the best measure of a pilot's ability to continue working (Birren & Fisher, 1995b). The same is true of most jobs.

expel people from useful work: Too often, retirement is just another name for dismissal and unemployment.

Stereotyping is a major facet of ageism. Popular stereotypes of the "dirty old man," "meddling old woman," "senile old fool," and the like help perpetuate the myths underlying ageism. Contrast such images to those associated with youthfulness: The young are perceived as fresh, whole, attractive, energetic, active, emerging, and appealing. Yet, even positive stereotypes can be a problem. For example, if older people are perceived as financially well off, wise, or experienced, it can blind others to the real problems of the elderly (Gatz & Pearson, 1988). The important point is that age-based stereotypes are often wrong. A tremendous diversity exists among the elderly—ranging from the infirm and demented to aerobic-dancing grandmothers.

Countering Myths about Aging

What can be done about ageism? One of the best ways to combat ageism is to counter stereotypes with facts. For example, studies show that in many occupations older workers perform better at jobs requiring *both* speed and skill (Giniger et al., 1983). Gradual slowing with age is a reality, but often, it can be countered by experience, skill, or expertise (Schaie, 1988). Overall, very little loss of job performance occurs as workers grow older. In the professions, wisdom and expertise can usually more than offset any loss of mental quickness. Basing retirement solely on a person's age makes little sense (Baltes, Staudinger, & Lindenberger, 1999; Salthouse & Maurer, 1996).

Disengagement theory of aging *Theory stating that it is normal for older people to withdraw from society and from roles they held earlier.*
Activity theory *Theory stating that the best adjustment to aging occurs when people remain active mentally, socially, and physically.*
Ageism *Discrimination or prejudice based on a person's age.*

tive, and greater age brings more status and respect (Kimmel, 1988). In most Western nations, however, ageism tends to have a negative impact on older individuals. Usually, it is expressed as a rejection of the elderly. The concept of "oldness" is often used to

Taking a broader view, Bernice Neugarten (1971) examined the lives of 200 people between the ages of 70 and 79. Neugarten found that 75 percent of these people were satisfied with their lives after retirement. Similarly, another study found that only 30 percent of retirees find retirement stressful (Bosse et al., 1991). Neugarten's findings also refuted other myths about aging.

1. Old persons generally do not become isolated and neglected by their families. Most *prefer* to live apart from their children.
2. Old persons are rarely placed in mental hospitals by uncaring children.
3. Old persons who live alone are not necessarily lonely or desolate.
4. Few elderly persons ever show signs of senility or mental decay, and few ever become mentally ill.

In short, most of the elderly studied by Neugarten were integrated, active, and psychologically healthy.

Enlightened views of aging call for an end to the forced obsolescence of the elderly. As a group, older people represent a valuable source of skill, knowledge, and energy that we can't afford to cast aside. As we face the challenges of this planet's uncertain future, we need all the help we can get!

KNOWLEDGE BUILDER
ADULTHOOD AND AGING

RELATE

Do any of the patterns of adult development described by Gould match your own experience? Using Gould's summary as a guide, what do you expect to be major issues during the next 5, 10, and 15 years of your life?

Do you know anyone who seems to be making a difficult life transition? How well are they handling it?

See if you can describe three instances of ageism you have witnessed.

LEARNING CHECK

1. According to Gould, building a workable life tends to be the dominant activity during which age range?
   a. 18–22 *b.* 22–28 *c.* 29–34 *d.* 35–43

2. Levinson's description of a "midlife crisis" corresponds roughly to Gould's
   a. escape from dominance *b.* crisis of questions *c.* crisis of urgency *d.* settling down period

3. Nearly everyone experiences a midlife crisis sometime around age 40. T or F?

4. The average male experiences menopause between the ages of 45 and 50. T or F?

5. Many indications of biological aging start to become evident as early as the mid-20s. T or F?

6. An expert on the problems of aging is called a _____ .

7. The activity theory of optimal aging holds that aging individuals should restrict their activities and withdraw from former community activities. T or F?

8. After age 65, a large proportion of older people show significant signs of mental disability, and most require special care. T or F?

CRITICAL THINKING

9. Why might you reasonably question Gould's and Levinson's accounts of adult development?

10. In Japan, aging is seen as positive, and growing older brings increased status and respect. Is this an example of ageism?

Answers:

1. b 2. c 3. F 4. F 5. T 6. gerontologist 7. F 8. F 9. Both Gould and Levinson may be describing typical patterns of adult development *in Western societies.* It is doubtful that these patterns apply equally well to all cultures. 10. Yes, it is. Even when the elderly are revered, they are being *prejudged* on the basis of age (Kimmel, 1988). Also, giving higher status to the elderly relegates the young to lower status—another instance of ageism.

■■■■

DEATH AND DYING—THE CURTAIN FALLS

DEAR ABBY:
Do you think about dying much?

(SIGNED) *CURIOUS*

DEAR CURIOUS:
No, it's the last thing I want to do.

"I'm not afraid of dying. I just don't want to be there when it happens."

WOODY ALLEN

"Why not? Why not?"

LSD GURU TIMOTHY LEARY (HIS LAST WORDS BEFORE DYING)

"To die well is no less an accomplishment than to live well."

SOGYAL RINPOCHE

The statistics on death are very convincing: One out of one dies. In spite of this, there tends to be a conspiracy of silence surrounding death. As a result, most of us are poorly informed about a process that is as basic as birth.

We have seen in this chapter that it is valuable to understand major trends and problem areas in development. With this in mind, let us now explore emotional responses to death, the inevitable conclusion of every life.

Fears of Death

Fears of death are not as common as you might think. In a poll of adults, only about 4 percent directly feared dying (Kastenbaum & Aisenberg, 1972). It might also seem that older people would fear death more. However, older persons actually have fewer death fears than younger people. Older people more often fear the *circumstances* of dying, such as pain or helplessness, rather than death itself (Thorson & Powell, 1990). These findings may actually reflect a widespread denial of death. Notice how denial is apparent in the language used to talk about death: Often we speak of a dead person as having "passed away," "expired," "gone to God," or "gone to rest" (Morgan, 1995).

Death may be inevitable, but it can be faced with dignity and, sometimes, even humor. Mel Blanc's famous sign-off, "That's all folks," is engraved on a marble headstone over his grave. Blanc was the voice of Bugs Bunny, Porky Pig, and many other cartoon characters.

Many people have little direct experience with death until they, themselves, are fairly old (Morgan, 1995). The average person's exposure to death consists of the artificial and unrealistic portrayals of death on TV. By the time the average person is 17 years old, she or he will have witnessed roughly 18,000 TV deaths. With few exceptions, these are *homicides*, not deaths due to illness or aging.

Reactions to Impending Death

A more direct account of emotional responses to death comes from the work of Elizabeth Kübler-Ross (1975). Kübler-Ross is a **thanatologist** (THAN-ah-TOL-oh-jist: one who studies death). Over the years, she spent hundreds of hours at the bedsides of the terminally ill, where she observed emotional reactions to impending death. Five basic reactions are described here.

1. **Denial and isolation.** A typical first reaction is to deny death's reality and isolate oneself from information confirming that death is really going to occur. Initially, the person may be sure that "It's all a mistake." "Surely," he or she thinks, "the lab reports have been mixed up or the doctor made an error." This sort of denial may proceed to attempts to avoid any reminder of the situation.
2. **Anger.** Many dying individuals feel anger and ask, "Why me?" As they face the ultimate threat of having life torn away, their anger may spill over into rage toward the living. Even good friends may temporarily evoke anger because their health is envied.
3. **Bargaining.** In another common reaction, the terminally ill bargain with themselves or with God. The dying person

thinks, "Just let me live a little longer and I'll do anything to earn it." Individuals may bargain for time by trying to be "good" ("I'll never smoke again"), by righting past wrongs, or by praying that if they are granted more time they will dedicate themselves to their religion.
4. **Depression.** As death draws near and the person begins to recognize it cannot be prevented, feelings of futility, exhaustion, and deep depression may set in. The person realizes she or he will be separated from friends, loved ones, and the familiar routines of life, and this knowledge causes a profound sadness.
5. **Acceptance.** If death is not sudden, many people manage to come to terms with dying and accept it calmly. The person who accepts death is neither happy nor sad, but at peace with the inevitable. Acceptance usually signals that the struggle with death has been resolved. The need to talk about death ends, and silent companionship from others is frequently all the person desires.

Not all terminally ill persons display all these reactions, nor do they always occur in this order. Individual styles of dying vary greatly, according to emotional maturity, religious beliefs, age, education, the attitudes of relatives, and other factors. Generally, there does tend to be a movement from initial shock, denial, and anger toward eventual acceptance of the situation. However, some people who seem to have accepted death may die angry and raging against the inevitable. Conversely, the angry fighter may let go of the struggle and die peacefully. In general, one's approach to dying will mirror his or her style of living (DeSpelder & Strickland, 1995).

It is best not to think of Kübler-Ross's list as a fixed series of stages to go through in order. It is an even bigger mistake to assume that someone who does not show all the listed emotional reactions is somehow deviant or immature. Rather, the list describes typical reactions to impending death. Note, as well, that many of the same reactions accompany any major loss, be it divorce, loss of a home due to fire, death of a pet, or loss of a job.

How can I make use of this information? First, it can help both the dying and survivors to recognize and cope with periods of depression, anger, denial, and bargaining. Second, it helps to realize that close friends or relatives may feel many of the same emotions before or after a person's death because they, too, are facing a loss.

Perhaps the most important thing to recognize is that the dying person needs to share feelings with others and to discuss death openly. Too often, dying persons feel isolated and separated from others by the wall of silence erected by doctors, nurses, and family members. Adults tend to "freeze up" with someone who is dying, saying such things as "I don't know how to deal with this."

Understanding what the dying person is going through may make it easier for you to offer support at this important time.

Thanatologist *A specialist who studies emotional and behavioral reactions to death and dying.*

A CLOSER LOOK

The emergency room doctors work feverishly over a heart attack victim. "I think we've lost him," says one of the doctors. The patient, who appears to have died, hears the doctor's words, then a buzzing sound. From somewhere above, he sees his own lifeless body on the table. Then he enters a dark tunnel and passes into an area of bright light. There, he is met by a "being of light" who shows him a rapid playback of his entire life. At some point, he reaches a barrier. He is completely at peace and feels engulfed by love, but he knows he must go back. Suddenly, he is in his body again. One of the doctors exclaims, "Look, his heart's beating!" The patient recovers. For the rest of his life, he is profoundly affected by his journey to the threshold of death and back.

The preceding description contains all the core elements of a **near-death experience** (NDE) (a pattern of experiences that may occur when a person is clinically dead and then re-suscitated). During an NDE, people typically experience all or most of the following: a feeling of separation from the body, entering darkness or a tunnel, seeing a light, entering the light, a life review, feeling at peace.

Many people regard NDEs as spiritual experiences that seem to verify the existence of an afterlife. In contrast, medical explanations attribute NDEs to the physiological reactions of an oxygen-starved brain (❖Fig. 5.9). Indeed, many elements of NDEs can be produced by other conditions, such as hallucinogenic drugs, migraine headaches, general anesthetics, extreme fatigue, high fever, or just falling asleep.

Although debate about the meaning of NDEs continues, one thing is certain: Near-death experiences can profoundly change personality and life goals. Many near-death survivors claim that they are no longer motivated by greed, competition, or material success. Instead, they become more concerned about the needs of other people.

There is a degree of comfort in knowing that people who have "died" and lived to tell about it were not frightened or in pain. Beyond that, perhaps we can learn something from such close encounters with death. As many near-death survivors have learned, death can be an excellent yardstick for measuring what is really important in life. (Sources: Blackmore, 1991b, 1993; Kellehear, 1993; MacHovec, 1994; Moody, 1975; Ring, 1980.)

❖ **FIGURE 5.9** *Visual sensations in the form of a tunnel of light or a spiral can be induced by many conditions other than near-death experiences. Such patterns appear to be related to activity in the visual cortex of the brain—especially activities that occur when the brain is deprived of oxygen (Blackmore, 1993).*

A simple willingness to be with the person and to honestly share his or her feelings can help bring dignity, acceptance, and meaning to death.

Emotional reactions to impending death tell us little about what it is actually like to die. As you will soon discover, however, many people have "died" and then lived to tell about it. See "Near-Death Experiences" for information about some very close encounters with death.

Bereavement and Grief

Typically, a period of grief follows **bereavement** (the loss of a friend or relative to death). **Grief** (intense sorrow and distress) is a natural and normal reaction as survivors adjust to their loss. Bereavement can make a person feel vulnerable or worthless. It typically changes one's views of the world and the future. Understandably, there's a lot to work through emotionally when you lose someone you love (Gluhoski, 1995).

Grief tends to follow a predictable pattern (Parkes, 1979; Schulz, 1978). Usually, grief begins with a period of **shock** or emotional numbness. For a brief time, the bereaved remain in a dazed state in which they may show little emotion. Most find it extremely difficult to accept the reality of their loss. This phase usually ends by the time of the funeral, which unleashes tears and bottled-up feelings of despair.

Initial shock is followed by sharp **pangs of grief**. These are episodes of painful yearning for the dead person and, sometimes, anguished outbursts of anger. During this period, the wish to have the dead person back is intense. Often, mourners continue to think of the dead person as alive. They may hear his or her voice and see the deceased vividly in dreams. For some time, agitated distress alternates with silent despair, and suffering is acute.

The first powerful reactions of grief gradually give way to weeks or months of **apathy** (listlessness), **dejection** (demoralization), and **depression** (deep despondency). The person faces

As cultural rituals, funerals and memorial services are rites of separation and leave-taking. Funerals encourage a release of emotion and provide a sense of closure for survivors, who must come to terms with the death of a loved one (Morgan, 1995).

a new emotional landscape with a large gap that cannot be filled. Life seems to lose much of its meaning, and a sense of futility dominates. The mourner is usually able to resume work or other activities after 2 or 3 weeks. However, insomnia, loss of energy and appetite, and similar signs of depression may continue.

Little by little, the bereaved person accepts what cannot be changed and makes a new beginning. Pangs of grief may still occur, but they are less severe and less frequent. Memories of the dead person, though still painful, now include positive images and nostalgic pleasure. At this point, the person can be said to be moving toward **resolution** (acceptance and re-building). For many people, the pain of grieving will have eased considerably by the end of about 1 year (Lindstrom, 1995). However, it is not unusual for 2 to 3 years to pass before grief is fully resolved. At a lower level of intensity, mourning the loss of someone you love can continue indefinitely (Rando, 1995).

As was true of approaching death, individual reactions to grief vary considerably. The amount of pain a person feels depends on his or her personality, relationship to the deceased, the nature of the death (Was it natural, a homicide, suicide, peaceful, agonized?), and the bereaved person's social situation—especially the amount of support she or he receives from others (Rando, 1995).

Is it true that suppressing grief causes more problems later? It has long been assumed that suppressing grief may lead to more severe and lasting depression. However, there is little evidence to support this idea. A lack of intense grief does not usually predict later problems (Bonanno et al., 1995). Bereaved persons should work through their grief at their own pace and in their own way—without worrying about whether they are grieving too much or too little. Time doesn't heal all wounds, but with the passage of time the pain of loss does lessen (Reif, Patton, & Gold, 1995).

Grief allows survivors to discharge their anguish, but it may not prepare them to go on living. Typically, they must also do **grief work**, in which they actively adapt to their loss and integrate changes into their lives (Rando, 1995). Some suggestions for coping with grief follow.

Coping with Grief
- Acknowledge and accept that the person is gone.
- Face the loss directly and do not isolate yourself.
- Discuss your feelings with relatives and friends.
- Do not block out your feelings with drugs or alcohol.
- Allow grief to progress naturally; neither hurry nor suppress it.
- Honor the memory of the deceased, but accept the need to rebuild your life.

(CONI ET AL., 1984; RANDO, 1995)

Near-death experience *A pattern of subjective experiences that may occur when a person is clinically dead and then resuscitated.*
Bereavement *Period of emotional adjustment that follows the death of a loved one.*
Grief *An intense emotional state that follows the death of a lover, friend, or relative.*
Shock *During grief, a period during which a person seems dazed or numb and shows little emotion.*
Pangs of grief *Episodes of intense and anguished yearning for a person who has died.*
Apathy *Indifference, listlessness, and a loss of motivation.*
Dejection *Demoralization and discouragement.*
Depression *A state of deep despondency marked by emotional negativity and behavioral inhibition.*
Resolution *With respect to grief, an acceptance of loss and the need for building a new life.*
Grief work *The process of adapting to the loss of a loved one.*

A LOOK AHEAD   The subject of death brings us full circle in the cycle of life. In the upcoming Psychology in Action section, we will probe the question, What makes a good life? But first, it's time for a study break.

psychology in action

WELL-BEING AND HAPPINESS—WHAT MAKES A GOOD LIFE?

What makes you happy? Love? Money? Music? Sports? Partying? Religion? Clearly, there is no simple, universal formula for happiness. And what does it mean to have a good life? Is it a matter of health? Achievement? Friendship? Leisure? Personal growth? Again, there are no simple answers. Both happiness and living a "good life" depend greatly on individual needs and cultural values. Nevertheless, psychologists are beginning to understand some aspects of what it means to be happy and live well. Their findings provide valuable hints about how to live a successful life.

HAPPINESS

Most people want to be happy. But what does that mean? To study happiness, psychologist Ed Diener and his associates have focused on what they call **subjective well-being** (SWB). According to them, feelings of well-being, or happiness, occur when people are satisfied with their lives, have frequent positive emotions, and have relatively few negative emotions (Diener et al., 1999).

Life Satisfaction

What does life satisfaction refer to?   You are high in life satisfaction if you strongly agree with the following statements (from the "Satisfaction with Life Scale," Pavot & Diener, 1993):

- In most ways my life is close to my ideal.
- The conditions of my life are excellent.
- I am satisfied with my life.
- So far I have gotten the important things I want in life.
- If I could live my life over, I would change almost nothing.

These statements seem to cover a lot of what it means to be happy. However, Diener and his colleagues believe day-to-day emotional experiences are also important.

Emotions

Imagine that several pleasant or rewarding events have occurred today. These events caused you to experience moments of laughter, joy, delight, and satisfaction. As a result, you feel happy, and life seems good. In contrast, imagine that your day was marred by a series of unpleasant or punishing events, which left you feeling sad. In reality, of course, we rarely have entirely good or bad days. Life is a mixture of rewarding and punishing events, so everyone feels both positive and negative emotions. It's possible for the same person to have lots of positive feelings *and* lots of negative feelings. That's why happiness is not just a matter of having good feelings. The happiest people are those who have many positive emotional experiences and relatively few negative experiences (Diener et al., 1999).

LIFE EVENTS

Then do good and bad events in life dictate if a person is happy? Happiness is related to good and bad life events, but the impact is smaller than you might imagine. The reason for this is that happiness tends to come from within a person. Subjective well-being is affected by our goals, choices, emotions, values, and personality. The way you perceive, interpret, and manage events is as important as the nature of the events themselves. People who are good at dodging life's hard knocks tend to create their own "luck." As a result, they are happier and seem to negotiate life's demands more smoothly (Eronen & Nurmi, 1999).

PERSONAL FACTORS

What about factors such as income, age, or marital status? Are they related to happiness? Personal characteristics have only a small connection with overall happiness. Let's see why.

Wealth

It is tempting to think that wealth brings happiness. But does it? To a small degree, wealthier people are happier than poorer people. However, the overall association between money and happiness is weak. In fact, people who win lotteries are often *less* happy than they were before. Instant riches usually bring new stresses into a person's life that tend to cancel out any positive effects of wealth. In short, money may make it possible to buy the good things in life, but money can't buy a good life. Happiness usually must come from other sources (King & Napa, 1998).

Education

More educated people tend to be a little happier than the less educated. However, this is most likely just another way of saying that there is a small connection between wealth and happiness. Higher education generally results in higher income and more social status.

Marriage

Married people report greater happiness than people who are divorced, separated, or single. It could be that happier people are simply more likely to get married. But a better explanation for this association is that marriage partners can act as emotional and economic buffers against the hardships of life.

Religion

There is a small but positive association between happiness and holding spiritual beliefs. Religious beliefs may add to feelings of purpose and meaning in life, resulting in greater happiness. Another possibility is that church membership may simply provide social support that softens the impact of life's negative events.

Age

The stereotype of the crotchety old person who is dissatisfied with everything is inaccurate. Life satisfaction and happiness generally *do not* decline with age. People are living longer and staying healthier, which has greatly delayed age-related declines. When declines do occur, older people today seem better able to cope with them.

Sex

Overall, men and women do not differ in happiness. However, women do have a tendency to experience higher emotional highs and lower lows than men do. Thus, more women are found among those rare individuals who are extremely happy or extremely unhappy.

Work

People who are satisfied with their jobs tend to be happier, but the association is weak. In fact, it probably just reflects the fact that job satisfaction is a large part of greater life satisfaction.

Personality

With respect to happiness and personality, it may be fair to paraphrase the movie character Forrest Gump and say, "Happy is as happy does." To a degree, some people are more temperamentally disposed to be happy, regardless of life events. In general, happier people also tend to be extraverted (outgoing), optimistic, and worry-free. This combination probably influences the balance of positive and negative emotions a person feels (Diener et al., 1999).

GOALS AND HAPPINESS

The preceding account gives some insight into who is happy, but we can learn more by examining people's goals. To know if someone is happy, it is helpful to ask, "What is this person trying to do in life? How well is she or he succeeding at it?"

Do you want to be healthy and physically fit? To do well in school? To be liked by friends? To own a shopping mall? A Ferrari? The goals people choose vary widely. Nevertheless, one generalization we can make is that people tend to be happy if they are meeting their personal goals. This is especially true if you feel you are making progress, on a day-to-day basis, on smaller goals that relate to long-term, life goals (King, Richards, & Stemmerich, 1998; McGregor & Little, 1998).

The importance of personal goals helps explain why life-specific circumstances tell us so little about happiness. It is often difficult to know if an event is good or bad without know-

Subjective well-being *A person's private sense of happiness and satisfaction with life.*

ing what a person is trying to achieve in life (Diener et al., 1999).

It seems that people who attain their goals are sometimes no happier than before. If making progress toward one's goals brings happiness, how could that be?

Meaning and Integrity

Canadian psychologists Ian McGregor and Brian Little believe they can explain why achieving one's goals doesn't always lead to happiness. Consider the highly successful person who is absorbed in his or her accomplishments. All it may take is a crisis, like a child's illness or the death of a friend, to make life feel meaningless. But meaning can be restored and the crisis resolved if the person begins to act with integrity. Thus, McGregor and Little believe that optimal human functioning involves integrity as well as an ability to accomplish goals. "Doing well," they say, is associated with happiness. In contrast, "being yourself" is associated with leading a meaningful life. In short, the goals we pursue must express our core interests and values if we are to live with integrity (McGregor & Little, 1998).

McGregor and Little give examples of the kinds of "personal projects" (short-term goals) and long-term goals that occupy us: "finish my calculus assignment," "help the poor," "take a trip to Florida," "lose weight," "earn an M.A. in psych," "play professional hockey," "become a police officer with investments in property and live comfortably." Among a wealth of possibilities such as these, the question becomes "To what extent does this project feel distinctly like me—like a personal trademark, as opposed to something alien or imposed?" Such goals are crucial, because overall well-being is a combination of happiness and meaning. Pursuing goals that are inconsistent with personal interests and values can leave a person feeling uneasy, bothered, and uncomfortable (McGregor & Little, 1998).

Conclusion

In summary, happier persons tend to be married, comfortable with their work, extraverted, religious, optimistic, and generally satisfied with their lives. They also are making progress toward

their goals (Diener et al., 1999). However, attaining goals that do not express our deeper interests and values may add little to happiness (Sheldon & Elliot, 1999).

What, then, makes a good life? Earlier in this chapter, we noted that purpose and meaning are important sources of well-being at midlife (Ryff, 1995). Actually, this appears to be true at any point in life. As we have seen, a good life is one that is happy *and* meaningful (McGregor & Little, 1998).

We are most likely to experience life as meaningful when we act with integrity. It's interesting that this agrees with Erikson's analysis at the beginning of this chapter. Although achievement and external goals may preoccupy younger people, integrity becomes increasingly important later in life (McGregor & Little, 1998).

"To thine own self be true" may seem like a cliché, but it's actually not a bad place to begin a search for a happy and satisfying life.

Focus: In what ways are attitudes toward death changing?

When Mr. Bedford, a psychology professor from Glendale, California, died at the age of 73, his body was immediately frozen—submerged in liquid nitrogen. This made him the first person in the United States to try to cheat death by cryonic suspension. Mr. Bedford's story is only one indication of changing attitudes toward dying.

For some, death is a sudden tragedy. For others, it is a long-wished-for release. Whatever the case, death—the last phase of life—is something we all must face. It therefore behooves each of us to know something about death. In this section, we will add to our earlier discussion by considering four departures from traditional approaches to dying: the hospice movement, passive euthanasia, active euthanasia, and cryonics.

HOSPICE

At the beginning of this century, most people died at home. Today, more than 70 percent of all deaths in the United States and Canada take place outside the home, most often in a hospital or nursing home. Just as some people have begun to question traditional funeral practices (embalming, viewing, elaborate and expensive caskets and ceremonies), many now question the treatment of the terminally ill. Too often, dying people are isolated, frightened, in pain, and stripped of control over their final days of life. The hospice concept was created to counter this situation.

A **hospice** provides supportive care for the terminally ill. Hospices may be housed in medical centers, or they may combine temporary inpatient care with care at home. Hospice care neither hastens nor postpones death. The goal is to improve the quality of life in the person's final days. The first hospice was created in recognition of dying individuals' needs to be included, to know that someone still cares, to maintain control over their lives, and to have a say in their own deaths. In operation, the first hospices presented a striking contrast to the grim wards for the terminally ill in many hospitals (Lattanzi-Licht & Connor, 1995).

How is a hospice different? First, there are lots of people present. A hospice offers support, counseling, guidance, and companionship from volunteers, other patients, staff, clergy, and visitors. Friendship and kindness are expressed toward patients so that when the time comes to die, they know they will be remembered with respect and love. This support from others is a major factor in how well people cope with dying (Dobratz, 1995).

Second, the atmosphere differs markedly from that of a traditional hospital. A hospice attempts to provide pleasant sur-

roundings, an atmosphere of intentional informality, and a sense of continued living for patients. Relatives, friends, children, and even pets are permitted unlimited around-the-clock visits. Patients receive constant attention, play games, make day trips, have cocktails before dinner if they choose, enjoy entertainment, and visit with volunteers. In short, life goes on for them.

A third aspect of hospice care is the freedom of choice allowed to patients. Patients decide about their own diets, activities, and whether they want to continue medical care. Patients can also choose freedom from intolerable pain. This is usually achieved by giving drugs, such as morphine, in dosages that relieve pain without making the person groggy (Larson, 1990).

Many communities in the United States now have hospice programs or freestanding hospice facilities. In either case, treatment for the terminally ill has drastically improved. Even traditional hospitals are doing a better job—largely as a result of pioneering efforts in the hospice movement.

A RIGHT TO DIE?

The "right to die" concept might be better stated as a right to live in peace and comfort until death. Much of the interest in this issue began with the Karen Ann Quinlan case. In 1975, Karen lapsed into a coma after suffering an overdose of drugs and alcohol. After doctors said she would never recover, Karen's parents began a legal fight to turn off the respirator and other devices being used to prolong her life. In 1976, the New Jersey Supreme Court issued a landmark decision, giving permission to the parents to order removal of Karen's life-support equipment. Despite the doctors' prediction, Karen continued to live for another 10 years. She died in 1985 at the age of 31.

Is there a right to die? Doctors and other medical personnel are legally and morally bound to prolong and preserve life. Likewise, in most states, relatives and guardians cannot legally give permission to remove life-supporting equipment. One way out of this dilemma that is gaining support is the **living will** (a declaration that a person's life should not be artificially prolonged). The intent of a living will is to free the terminally ill from a slow and cruel death, allowing death with dignity. The will is made out when the person is still healthy and states that, in the event of terminal illness (as diagnosed by two or

---

Hospice *A medical facility or program dedicated to providing optimal care for people who are dying.*
Living will *A written declaration stating that a person prefers not to have his or her life artificially prolonged in the event of a terminal illness.*

more doctors), the person does not want to have life sustained by medical machines or heroic measures.

A living will is not yet binding in most states, but it does make clear the wishes of terminally ill persons who can't speak for themselves. The following excerpt is from one widely used living will.

A Living Will

If at such a time the situation should arise in which there is no reasonable expectation of my recovery from extreme physical or mental disability, I direct that I be allowed to die and not be kept alive by medications, artificial means or "heroic measures." I do, however, ask that medication be mercifully administered to me to alleviate suffering even though this may shorten my remaining life. (Reprinted with permission from Concern for Dying, 250 West 57th Street, New York, NY 10017.)

In addition, it would be wise for each person to record his or her wishes concerning the following questions (Aging with Dignity, 1998).

Five Wishes

- Who do I want to make decisions about my medical care when I cannot make them for myself?
- What kind of medical treatment do I want or not want?
- How much discomfort am I willing to accept?
- How do I want people to treat me?
- What do I want my loved ones to know if I am unable to speak for myself?

To make sure your living will is effective, you should do the following: Use a form that is recognized by your state's laws. Obtain signatures of the required number of witnesses, preferably nonrelatives. Ask your doctor whether she or he will honor your wishes. If so, give your physician a copy of your living will. Give copies of your living will to several close friends and relatives. Periodically review your living will and revise it if necessary.

EUTHANASIA

The right to die won for Karen Quinlan by her parents may be thought of as **passive euthanasia** (YOU-tha-NAY-zyah), in which death is allowed to occur but is not actively caused. In **active euthanasia**, or "physician-assisted suicide," steps would be taken at a patient's request to deliberately hasten death, perhaps by administering drugs that induce death painlessly. Both forms of euthanasia present ethical dilemmas for physicians, who are trained to keep patients alive. On the other hand, doctors are sworn to *humane* treatment. With the second point in mind, proponents of euthanasia believe that it is a basic human right to die with dignity and a minimum of discomfort (Markson, 1995).

To a degree, passive euthanasia is already practiced in North America. However, it is done quietly here, without legal protection for doctors. In the Netherlands and parts of Australia, doctors are allowed to help patients die, as long as certain safeguards are followed. The patient has to be terminally ill, in pain, and mentally competent and must repeatedly express a

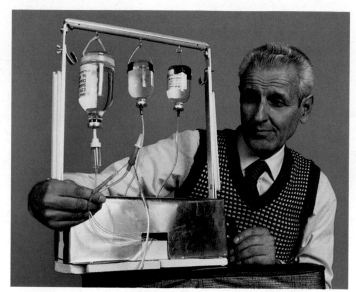

In the United States, public debate about euthanasia has focused on Dr. Jack Kevorkian, a retired pathologist. In 1999, Dr. Kevorkian was convicted of murder for assisting a suicide. It is perhaps unfortunate that Dr. Kevorkian has been in the spotlight because some of the people he "helped die" were not terminally ill. In the Netherlands, euthanasia is not permitted in such cases. Only hopelessly terminal patients, who are suffering dire physical and emotional pain, are candidates for legal, doctor-assisted euthanasia. Despite Kevorkian's excesses, a large percentage of people in the United States favor making some form of euthanasia legal. Nevertheless, the debate about euthanasia continues.

wish to die (Shapiro & Bowermaster, 1994). Should active euthanasia ever become legal in other countries (many people find the idea totally unacceptable), it might also become possible for next of kin to request euthanasia for an incapacitated individual.

There are several arguments against euthanasia. The case of Karen Delahanty of Avon, Connecticut, provides a good starting point. After a head-on automobile accident, Karen entered a coma from which doctors predicted she would never recover. One year later, she miraculously regained consciousness. What if euthanasia had been carried out?

Other questions arise, in addition to unexpected recovery. What guarantee is there that the choice of euthanasia would be made freely and without pressure (Hendin, 1995)? Would the infirm feel that it is their "duty" to die, to avoid being a burden to their families? Can family members be trusted to make a correct decision? Would they feel guilt afterward? What about the medical personnel involved; how would they respond emotionally to "mercy killing"? (Shapiro & Bowermaster, 1994). No doubt you can think of other objections.

CRYONICS

To complete our brief sampling of new approaches to death, let's return to cryonics. **Cryonic suspension** involves freezing a person's body (or head) immediately after death. The idea is to

keep the person frozen until medical science perfects ways to thaw, restore, and revive the person. Those who have been placed in cryonic suspension obviously are gambling that if they are revived, a cure will exist for whatever killed them.

Does freezing actually work?   Cryonic suspension must be viewed as a symbolic attempt to cheat death or perhaps as an emotional hedge against the finality of death. At this point, cryonic suspension is impractical because freezing does serious damage to the body. The ice crystals formed by freezing and unfreezing the human brain would almost surely turn it to mush—wiping out most or all of the memories stored there. If persons frozen at death were ever successfully revived, they would have no identity, and perhaps no understanding of where they were or why they were there. Such persons would, in most cases, be quite old. (To date, most frozen individuals have been middle-aged or older.) Even the most optimistic supporters of cryonic suspension admit that there is currently no way to preserve bodies so that their organs will resume functioning when they are thawed (Darwin & Wowk, 1992).

Another problem is the great expense of maintaining cryonic capsules for many years. (LSD guru Tim Leary arranged to have his head frozen—he couldn't afford the whole-body treatment.) And in California (where else?), a case has already surfaced where careless operators of a cryonics service allowed a number of bodies to defrost.

Whereas it is true that for a few pioneering souls there is clearly "ice after death," immortality, it would seem, does not yet fall within the province of technology (Shermer, 1992).

CONCLUSION: Attitudes toward death and the ways in which death is managed are slowly changing. In many ways, western societies have much to learn about how to provide comfort and support to dying persons.

KNOWLEDGE BUILDER
NEW APPROACHES TO DEATH

RELATE

If you had a choice, where would you prefer to die? At home, in a hospital, or in a hospice?

If you were to make out a living will today, what would it say?

What arguments can you supply for and against passive euthanasia? What about active euthanasia?

In your opinion, are people who arrange for cryonic suspension pioneers, gamblers, dreamers, or fools?

LEARNING CHECK

1. The goal of a hospice is to freeze people who have died of diseases that might one day become curable. T or F?

2. In passive euthanasia, death is allowed to occur but is not actively induced. T or F?

3. Cryonic suspension is a type of passive euthanasia. T or F?

4. Active euthanasia is now legal in most countries, provided that the terminally ill patient has signed a living will. T or F?

CRITICAL THINKING

5. Which of the emotional reactions to impending death (described earlier) relates most directly to cryonic suspension?

Answers:

1. F 2. T 3. F 4. F 5. A good case can be made for the idea that people seeking cryonic suspension are still *bargaining:* "Just let me live a little longer, and I'll do anything to earn it."

Passive euthanasia *Allowing death to occur without trying to prevent it or encourage it.*
Active euthanasia *Deliberately inducing death.*
Cryonic suspension *Freezing the body or head at death in hopes that future revival will become possible.*

CHAPTER IN REVIEW

What are the typical tasks and dilemmas through the life span?

- Life-span psychologists study continuity and change in behavior from birth to death.
- According to Erikson, each life stage provokes a specific psychosocial dilemma.
- In addition to the dilemmas identified by Erikson, we recognize that each life stage requires successful mastery of certain developmental tasks.

What are the psychological implications of childbirth?

- Healthy children are produced by both conventional birth and by prepared childbirth. However, prepared births have the advantage of minimizing the use of anesthetics and giving mothers a sense of control.
- The father's presence at birth appears to be desirable, although his attitude toward birth may be of more basic importance.
- In the days immediately following birth, ample mother-infant contact is desirable, but rapid and permanent emotional bonding is a myth.
- Many women experience a brief period of depression, called the *maternity blues*, shortly after giving birth. Some women suffer from a more serious and lasting condition called *postpartum depression*.

What are some of the more serious childhood problems?

- Few children grow up without experiencing some of the normal problems of childhood, including negativism, clinging, specific fears, sleep disturbances, general dissatisfaction, regression, sibling rivalry, and rebellion.
- Major areas of difficulty in childhood include toilet training (including enuresis and encopresis); feeding disturbances, such as overeating, anorexia nervosa (self-starvation), and pica (eating nonfood substances); speech disturbances (delayed speech, stuttering); learning disorders, including dyslexia; and attention-deficit hyperactivity disorder.
- Childhood autism is representative of some of the more severe problems that can occur. Some cases of autism are being treated successfully with behavior modification.
- Child abuse is a major problem for which few solutions currently exist. Roughly 30 percent of all abused children become abusive adults. Emotional support and therapy appear to help break the cycle of abuse.

Why is adolescent development especially challenging?

- Adolescence is a culturally defined social status. Puberty is a biological event.
- Early maturation is beneficial mostly for boys; its effects are mixed for girls. One danger of early maturation is premature identity formation.
- Adolescent identity formation is accelerated by cognitive development and influenced by parents and peer groups.

How do we develop morals and values?

- Lawrence Kohlberg theorized that moral development passes through a series of stages revealed by moral reasoning.
- Kohlberg identified preconventional, conventional, and post-conventional levels of morality.
- Kohlberg emphasized a morality of justice. Adults appear to base moral choices on either justice or caring, depending on the situation.
- People in some cultures may prefer to use justice as the primary standard for making moral choices; in other cultures, a morality of caring is preferred.

How do people select careers for themselves?

- Four broad periods in career development are the exploration phase, the establishment phase, the midcareer phase, and the later career phase.
- The exploration phase can be further divided into a fantasy stage, a tentative stage, and a realistic stage.
- Vocational counseling can greatly aid career decision making.

What happens psychologically during adulthood?

- Certain relatively consistent events mark adult development in Western societies. These range from escaping parental dominance in the late teens to a noticeable acceptance of one's lot in life during the 50s.
- A midlife crisis affects some people in the 37–41 age range, but this is by no means universal. Even if no crisis occurs, people tend to move through repeated cycles of stability and transition throughout adulthood.
- Women's adjustment to later middle age can be complicated by menopause. To a lesser degree, some men may experience a psychologically based climacteric.
- Well-being during adulthood consists of six elements: self-acceptance, positive relations with others, autonomy, environmental mastery, having a purpose in life, and continued personal growth.

What are the psychological challenges of aging?

- Both the number and proportion of older people in the population has grown.
- Biological aging begins between 25 and 30, but peak performance in specific pursuits may come at various points throughout life.
- Intellectual declines associated with aging are limited, at least through one's 70s. This is especially true of individuals who remain mentally active.
- Gerontologists have proposed two major theories of successful aging. The disengagement theory holds that withdrawal from society is necessary and desirable in old age. The activity theory counters that optimal adjustment to aging is tied to continuing activity and involvement. There is an element of truth to each, but the activity theory applies to more people.
- The best adaptation to aging is based on selection, optimization, and compensation, which together allow people to continue to perform tasks well.
- Ageism refers to prejudice, discrimination, and stereotyping on the basis of age. It affects people of all ages, but is especially damaging to older people. Most ageism is based on stereotypes, myths, and misinformation.

How do people typically react to death and bereavement?

- Typical emotional reactions to impending death are denial, anger, bargaining, depression, and acceptance.

- Near-death experiences frequently result in significant changes in personality, values, and life goals.
- Bereavement also brings forth a typical series of grief reactions, ranging from shock to final acceptance.

What factors contribute most to a happy and fulfilling life?

- Subjective well-being (happiness) combines general life satisfaction with more positive emotions than negative emotions.
- Life events and various demographic factors have relatively little influence on happiness.
- People with extraverted (outgoing), optimistic, and worry-free personalities tend to be happier.
- Making progress toward one's goals is associated with happiness.
- Overall well-being is a combination of happiness and meaning in life, which comes from pursuing goals that have integrity (they express one's deeper interests and values).

In what ways are attitudes toward death changing?

- New approaches to death include the hospice movement, living wills, and cryonic suspension.
- A continuing controversy concerns the ethics of passive euthanasia and active euthanasia.

Where to Write for Information

- **Anorexia Nervosa** National Association of Anorexia Nervosa and Associated Disorders, Box 271, Highland Park, IL 60035.
- **Autism** The National Society for Autistic Children, 101 Richmond St., Huntington, West Virginia 25701; or Autism Society of America, Suite C1017, 1234 Massachusetts Ave., NW, Washington, DC 20005.
- **Child Abuse** Parents Anonymous, call toll-free (800) 421-0353 to find local chapters or call the National Child Abuse Hot Line toll-free (800) 422-4453.
- **Hospice** The National Hospice Organization, 1901 North Ft. Meyer Drive, Arlington, VA 22180.
- **Hyperactivity** Department of Health, Education, and Welfare, Office of the Secretary, Secretary's Committee on Mental Retardation, Washington, DC 20201.

- **Learning Disorders** National Association for Children with Learning Disabilities, 5225 Grace St., Pittsburgh, PA 15236.
- **Living Will** Society for the Right to Die, 250 West 57th St., New York, NY 10107.

PSYCHOLOGY ON THE NET

- **Alzheimer's Association** Has many links to material on Alzheimer's disease. http://www.alz.org/
- **Mental Health Risk Factors for Adolescents** Links to resources concerning eating disorders, drug abuse, suicide, and other topics. http://education.indiana.edu/cas/adol/mental.html
- **MIDMAC** Reports on a major study of middle age. http://midmac.med.harvard.edu/midmac.html
- **The AARP Webplace** Home page of the American Association of Retired Persons. http://www.aarp.org/
- **What Works for Girls** A summary of research about what contributes positively to healthy development. http://www.aauw.org/4000/lessonslearned.html
  - •**InfoTrac® College Edition** For recent articles on the maltreatment of children, use Key Words search for CHILD ABUSE.

INTERACTIVE LEARNING

- *PsychNow!* 6c. Adolescent development. 6d. Adult development, aging, and death.
- *Psyk.trek.* 9b. Erikson's theory of personality development. 9d. Kohlberg's theory of moral development.

Sensation
and Reality

Chapter Survey

Theme: *Sensory systems link us to the external world and shape the flow of information to the brain.*

preview
SENSATION—A WINDOW ON THE WORLD

AT THIS VERY MOMENT, *you are bathed in a swirling kaleidoscope of light, heat, pressure, vibrations, molecules, radiation, and mechanical forces. Without the senses, all of this would seem like a void of darkness and silence. The next time you drink in the beauty of a sunset, a flower, or a friend, remember this: Sensation makes it all possible.*

What would the world be like if new senses could be added—if we could "see" gamma rays, "hear" changes in barometric pressure, or "taste" light? We can only guess. It is far easier to imagine losing or regaining a sensory system. Consider the words of Bob Edens, who had his sight restored at age 51 after being blind since birth:

Yellow Is Amazing, but Red Is Best

I never would have dreamed that yellow is so . . . so yellow. I don't have the words, I'm amazed by yellow. But red is my favorite color. I just can't believe red. I can't wait to get up each day to see what I can see. I saw some bees the other day, and they were magnificent. I saw a truck drive by in the rain and throw a spray in the air. It was marvelous. And did I mention, I saw a falling leaf just drifting through the air?

If you are ever tempted to take sensory impressions for granted, remember Bob Edens. As his words show, sensation is our window on the world. All our meaningful behavior, our awareness of physical reality, and our ideas about the universe ultimately spring from the senses. It may be no exaggeration, then, to claim that this chapter is quite . . . "sensational."

Gateways to Sensation

SENSORY SYSTEMS select, analyze, and transduce information from the surrounding world and send it to the brain.

PRIVATE SENSATIONS do not correspond perfectly to external stimuli. Studies in psychophysics relate physical energies to the sensations we experience.

THE EYES AND THE BRAIN form a complex system for sensing light. Vision is based on an active, computer-like analysis of light patterns.

ALL OF THE SENSES rely on a complex series of mechanical, chemical, and neural events to convert stimuli into messages understood by the brain.

SENSORY ADAPTATION, SELECTIVE ATTENTION, AND SENSORY GATING significantly modify sensory experiences. Only a small part of the sensory information surrounding us actually reaches the brain or registers there.

PAIN can be reduced or controlled by altering factors that affect pain intensity.

MOTION SICKNESS is based on sensory conflict and neural mechanisms for expelling poison from the body. Motion sickness can be reduced with various psychological strategies.

GENERAL PROPERTIES OF SENSORY SYSTEMS—WHAT YOU SEE IS WHAT YOU GET

We begin with a paradox. On one hand, we have the magnificent power of the senses. In one instant, you can view a star light-years away, and in the next, you can peer into the microscopic universe of a dewdrop. Yet, vision is also narrowly limited in sensitivity. Like all senses, vision acts as a **data reduction system** (a system that selects, analyzes, and condenses incoming information). As you will see, each of our senses routinely "boils down" floods of information into a stream of useful data.

Sensory selection is illustrated by visible light, which is actually just a small slice of a broad range of energies. The **electromagnetic spectrum** (entire spread of electromagnetic wavelengths) includes visible light, infrared and ultraviolet light, radio waves, television broadcasts, gamma rays, and other energies (see ❖Fig. 6.3). If our eyes weren't limited to light sensitivity, "seeing" would be like getting hundreds of different "channels" at once. The confusion would be disorienting.

How are selection and data reduction accomplished? Some selection occurs simply because all sensory receptors are biological transducers. A **transducer** is a device that converts one kind of energy into another. For example, an electric guitar converts string vibrations into electrical signals, which are amplified and fed to a speaker. Pluck a string, and the speaker will blast out sound. However, if you shine a light on the string, or pour cold water on it, the speaker will remain silent. (The owner of the guitar, however, may get quite loud at this point!) Similarly, each sensory organ is most sensitive to a select type and range of energy.

Data reduction system *Any system that selects, analyzes, or condenses information.*
Electromagnetic spectrum *The full range of electrical and magnetic wavelengths, including X-rays, radio waves, light waves, and other frequencies.*
Transducer *A device that converts energy from one system into energy in another.*

As they transduce information, many senses *analyze* the environment before sending messages to the brain. **Sensory analysis** is the separation of sensory information into important *features*. **Perceptual features,** in turn, are basic elements of a stimulus pattern, such as lines, shapes, edges, spots, or colors (❖Fig. 6.1). The neural circuits of many sensory systems act as **feature detectors** (the system is highly attuned to specific stimulus patterns). Frog eyes, for example, are especially sensitive to small, dark, moving spots. Researcher Jerome Lettvin (1961) calls this sensitivity a "bug detector." It seems that the frog's eyes are "wired" to detect bugs flying nearby. But the insect (spot) must be moving. A frog may starve to death surrounded by dead flies.

After they have selected and analyzed information, sensory systems must *code* it. **Sensory coding** refers to converting important features of the world into neural messages understood by the brain (Hubel & Wiesel, 1979). To see coding at work, try this simple demonstration:

> Close your eyes for a moment. Then take your fingertips and press firmly on your eyelids. Apply enough pressure to "squash" your eyes slightly. Do this for about 30 seconds and observe what happens. (Readers with eye problems or contact lenses should not try this.)

Did you "see" stars, checkerboards, and flashes of color? These are called **phosphenes** (FOSS-feens: visual sensations caused by mechanical excitation of the retina). They occur because the eye's receptor cells, which normally respond to light, are also somewhat sensitive to pressure. Notice though, that the eye is only prepared to code stimulation—including pressure— into visual features. As a result, you experience light sensations, not pressure. Also important in producing this effect is localization of function in the brain.

What does localization of function mean? **Localization of function** means that the type of sensation you experience depends on the area of the brain that is activated. Some brain areas receive visual information; others receive auditory information; still others receive taste, touch, and so forth. Knowing which brain areas are active would tell us, in general, what kinds of sensations you are feeling.

Sensory localization may someday make it possible to artificially stimulate the brain to restore sight, hearing, or other senses. Researchers have already used a miniature television camera to send electrical signals to the visual cortex of the brain (Dobelle, 2000; Normann et al., 1999). (See ❖Fig. 6.2.) Unfortunately, artificial vision of this type still faces major hurdles. However, artificial hearing is proving more workable—as we will see later.

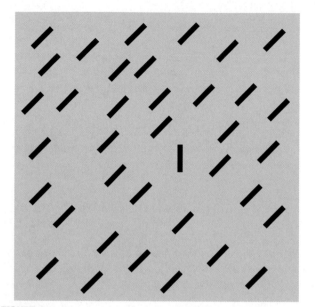

❖ **FIGURE 6.1** *Notice how eye-catching the single vertical line is among a group of slanted lines. This visual effect is known as pop-out. Pop-out occurs because the visual system is highly sensitive to elementary visual features, such as colors, shapes, and lines. Identification of such features appears to take place very early in the processing of visual information. (Adapted from Ramachandran, 1992b.) Pop-out is so basic that babies as young as 3 months respond to it (Quinn & Bhatt, 1998).*

❖ **FIGURE 6.2** *In this artificial visual system, TV cameras mounted on a pair of glasses transmit electrical signals to a grid of tiny electrodes placed in the visual areas of the brain (shown in cutaway view). One man who has an experimental implant of this type can "see" 100 dots of light. Like a sports scoreboard, these lights can be used to form crude letters. Researchers are also working on software that alters the TV image so that the edges of objects are accentuated (Dobelle, 2000). This, plus a larger number of dots, could make reading and the perception of large objects, such as furniture and doorways, possible (Normann et al., 1999). A major barrier to such systems is the brain's tendency to reject implanted electrodes.*

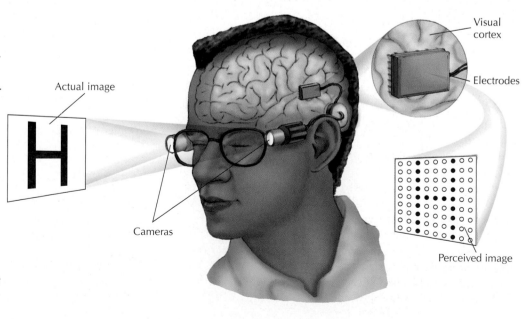

It is fascinating to realize that experiences such as "seeing" and "hearing" take place in the brain, not in the eye or ear. Each sense organ is merely the first link in a long chain of events that ends in the brain. Much as we may be tempted to think so, sensory systems do not operate like cameras or tape recorders, sending back "pictures" of the world. Rather, they collect, transduce, analyze, code, and transmit an unending flow of data to an active, information-hungry "biocomputer." This incoming flow of information is what we refer to as **sensation.** (When the brain organizes sensations into meaningful patterns, we speak of perception, which is the topic of Chapter 7.) In a moment, you will learn how each of the senses operates. But first, let's explore a little more. How sensitive are we to our "sensational" world?

PSYCHOPHYSICS—LIFE AT THE LIMIT

What is the quietest sound that can be heard? The weakest light that can be seen? The lightest touch that can be felt? The sense organs are our link to reality. What are their limits? An approach called *psychophysics* provides some answers. In **psychophysics,** physical changes in stimuli are measured and related to psychological sensations, such as loudness, brightness, or taste. A basic question psychophysics asks is, What is the absolute minimum amount of energy necessary for a sensation to occur? The answer defines the **absolute threshold** for a sensory system.

Testing for absolute thresholds shows just how sensitive we are. For example, it takes only 3 photons of light striking the retina of the eye to produce a sensation. A **photon** (FOE-tahn: one quantum of energy) is the smallest possible "package" of light. Responding to 3 photons is like seeing a candle flame 30 miles away! ◆Table 6.1 gives the approximate absolute thresholds for the five major senses.

Some sensory systems have upper limits as well as lower ones. For example, when the ears are tested for pitch (higher and lower tones), we find that humans can hear sounds down to 20 **hertz** (vibrations per second) and up to about 20,000 hertz. This is an impressive range—from the lowest rumble of a pipe organ to the highest squeak of a stereo "tweeter." On the lower end, the threshold is as low as practical. If the ears could respond to tones below 20 hertz, you would hear the movements of your own muscles. Imagine how disturbing it would be to hear your body creak and groan like an old wooden ship each time you moved.

The 20,000-hertz upper threshold for human hearing, on the other hand, could easily be higher. Dogs, bats, cats, and other animals can hear sounds well above this limit. That's why a "silent" dog whistle (which may make sounds as high as 50,000 hertz) can be heard by dogs, but not by humans. For dogs, the sound exists. For humans, it is beyond awareness. It's easy to see how thresholds define the limits of the sensory world in which we live. (If you want to buy a stereo system for your dog, you will have a hard time finding one that reproduces sounds above 20,000 hertz!)

Difference Thresholds

Psychophysics also involves the study of **difference thresholds.** Here we are asking, How much must a stimulus change (increase or decrease) before it becomes just noticeably different? The study of **just noticeable differences** (JNDs) led to one of psychology's first natural "laws." **Weber's law** (VAY-bears) can be roughly stated as follows: The amount of change needed to produce a JND is a constant proportion of the original stimulus intensity. ◆Table 6.2 lists some Weber's proportions.

Notice how much more sensitive hearing is than taste. Very small changes in pitch and loudness are easy to detect. A voice or a musical instrument that is off pitch 1/3 of 1 percent will be noticeable. For taste, we find that a 20 percent change is necessary to produce a JND. If a cup of coffee has 5 teaspoons of sugar in it, 1 more (1/5 of 5) must be added before you would notice an increase in sweetness. It takes a lot of cooks to spoil the broth.

◆ **TABLE 6.1** Absolute Thresholds

SENSORY MODALITY	ABSOLUTE THRESHOLD
Vision	Candle flame seen at 30 miles on a clear, dark night
Hearing	Tick of a watch under quiet conditions at 20 feet
Taste	1 teaspoon of sugar in 2 gallons of water
Smell	1 drop of perfume diffused into a three-room apartment
Touch	A bee's wing falling on your cheek from 1 centimeter above

(From Galanter, 1962.)

Sensory analysis *Separation of sensory information into important elements.*
Perceptual features *Basic elements of a stimulus, such as lines, shapes, edges, or colors.*
Feature detector *A sensory system highly attuned to a specific stimulus pattern.*
Sensory coding *Codes used by the sense organs to transmit information to the brain.*
Phosphene *A visual sensation caused by mechanical excitation of the retina.*
Localization of function *The principle that the type of sensation experienced is related to the area of the brain activated.*
Sensation *The immediate response in the brain caused by excitation of a sensory organ.*
Psychophysics *Study of the relationship between physical stimuli and the sensations they evoke in a human observer.*
Absolute threshold *The minimum amount of physical energy necessary to produce a sensation.*
Photon *One quantum (the smallest unit) of light energy.*
Hertz *One cycle (or vibration) per second.*
Difference threshold *A change in stimulus intensity that is detectable to an observer.*
Just noticeable difference *Any noticeable difference in a stimulus.*
Weber's law *The just noticeable difference is a constant proportion of the original stimulus intensity.*

◆ TABLE 6.2 Weber's Proportions for Common Judgments

Pitch	1/333 (1/3 of 1 percent)
Weight	1/50
Loudness	1/10
Taste	1/5

Perceptual Defense and Subliminal Perception

Wouldn't the absolute threshold be different for different people? Not only do absolute thresholds vary for different people, they also vary from time to time for a single person. The type of stimulus, the state of one's nervous system, and the costs of false "detections" all make a difference. Emotional factors are also important. Unpleasant stimuli, for example, may *raise* the threshold for recognition. This resistance to perceiving threatening or disturbing stimuli is called **perceptual defense.** It was first revealed in experiments on the perception of "dirty" and "clean" words (McGinnies, 1949). So-called dirty words such as *whore, rape, bitch,* and *penis* were briefly flashed on a screen. Such words took longer to recognize than did "clean" words such as *wharf, rope, batch,* and *pencil.*

ROCK MUSIC—SUBLIMINAL MESSAGES OR SUBLIMINAL MYTHS?

In another uproar over subliminal perception, critics heatedly charged that spoken messages recorded backward ("backmasking") in rock music are perceived unconsciously by listeners.

Psychologists John Vokey and Don Read (1985) point out that religious leaders, journalists, and lawmakers merely *assumed* that if subliminal messages exist in records, they must affect listeners. But do they? Vokey and Read decided to find out.

Vokey and Read recorded a variety of sentences backward, including selections from Lewis Carroll's *Jabberwocky* and the 23rd Psalm of the Bible. In tests using the backward sentences, Vokey and Read found no evidence that listeners consciously or unconsciously recognized their meaning. Other studies have shown that backward messages have no influence whatsoever on behavior (Begg et al., 1993; Swart & Morgan, 1992).

Undoubtedly, a few misguided musicians have placed backward messages in their recordings—some of which are highly offensive. However, Vokey and Read's research shows that subliminal messages in music offer no threat to listeners. Musicians who have played this game are just fooling themselves.

Couldn't it be that people wanted to be really sure they had seen a word like penis *before saying it?* Yes, especially in 1949! For years, psychologists worried about this and other flaws in the original experiment. But researchers continue to find that perceptual defense occurs. For example, new mothers who are emotionally depressed take longer than nondepressed women to recognize pictures related to pregnancy, birth, and babies (David et al., 1990). Apparently, we process stimuli on more than one level. This allows us to resist information that causes anxiety, discomfort, or embarrassment (Mogg et al., 1993).

Is that "subliminal" perception? Basically, yes. Any time information is processed below the normal **limen** (LIE-men: threshold or limit) for awareness, it is *subliminal.* **Subliminal perception** was demonstrated by a study in which college students saw photographs of a person flashed on a screen. Each time before the face appeared, it was preceded by a subliminal image. Some were images (such as cute kittens) that made viewers feel good. Others (a face on fire) made them feel bad. All of the emotional images were flashed too briefly to be recognized. Nevertheless, they altered the impressions students formed of the target person (Krosnick et al., 1992).

SUBLIMINAL PERSUASION? *Could such effects be applied to advertising?* The urge to manipulate shoppers must be strong, because many businesses have tried subliminal advertising over the years. But do subliminal sales pitches actually work? Let's see.

In a famous early attempt at subliminal advertising, a New Jersey theater flashed the words *Eat popcorn* and *Drink Coca-Cola* on the screen. The words appeared for 1/3,000 of a second every 5 seconds during movies. At that speed, they were below the normal threshold for awareness. During the 6 weeks the messages ran, the firm claimed increases in popcorn and Coca-Cola sales.

Soon, politicians were rushing to pass laws against the "invisible sell." However, they really had nothing to fear. We now know that the "experiment" was seriously flawed. Among other things, it failed to control other conditions that might increase sales. These include temperature, the time of year, the films shown, the type of audience, snack bar displays, and so forth. Some years later, subliminal persuasion suffered an even bigger blow: The advertising expert who supposedly performed the "Eat popcorn, drink Coke" experiment admitted that he faked the whole thing. By lying about his ability to control audiences, he had hoped to gain customers for his marketing business (Pratkanis, 1992). Today, after many careful experiments, we can conclude that subliminal advertising is largely ineffective (Moore, 1992; Pratkanis, 1992; Smith & Rogers, 1994; Trappey, 1996).

To summarize, there is evidence that subliminal perception occurs. However, well-controlled experiments have shown that subliminal stimuli are basically *weak* stimuli. There is little evidence that subliminal messages can persuade us or greatly influence our behavior (Trappey, 1996). Advertisers are better off using the loudest, clearest, most attention-demanding stimuli available—as most do (Smith & Rogers, 1994).

Despite the evidence, some advertisers still use subliminal messages. Maybe *they* haven't gotten the message. Similar conclusions apply to the so-called subliminal tapes and computer software offered by mail-order promoters: There is no scientific evidence that they work (Merikle & Skanes, 1992; Mitchell, 1995; Moore, 1995). (See "Rock Music.")

It's now time to examine each of the senses in more detail. In the next section, we will begin with vision, which is perhaps the most magnificent sensory system of all. Before you read more, it might be a good idea to stop and review some of the ideas we have covered.

KNOWLEDGE BUILDER

SENSATION AND PSYCHOPHYSICS

RELATE

How does sensation affect what you are experiencing right now? What if data reduction didn't occur? What if you could transduce other energies? What if your senses were tuned to detect different perceptual features? What if your absolute thresholds were higher or lower for each sense? How would the sensory world you live in change?

LEARNING CHECK

1. Sensory receptors are biological _______________, or devices for converting one type of energy to another.
2. Lettvin found that a frog's eyes are especially sensitive to phosphenes. T or F?
3. Important features of the environment are transmitted to the brain through a process known as
a. phosphenation *b.* coding *c.* detection *d.* programming
4. The minimum amount of stimulation necessary for a sensation to occur defines the _____________ _____________.
5. A stimulus that causes discomfort or embarrassment may have to be viewed longer before it is perceived because of _____________ _____________.
6. Subliminal stimuli have been shown to have a powerful effect on the behavior of viewers, especially when embedded in movies. T or F?

CRITICAL THINKING

7. Is a doorbell a transducer?
8. If the human ear were more sensitive than it is now, our hearing would be impaired. How could this be true?
9. Can you think of another way in which McGinnies's original experiment on perceptual defense was flawed?
10. When promoters of self-help "subliminal tapes" are challenged to provide evidence that their products work, what study do you think they most often cite?

Answers:

1. transducers 2. F 3. *b* 4. absolute threshold 5. perceptual defense 6. F 7. In a broad sense, it is. The button converts mechanical energy from your finger into an electrical signal that is converted again into mechanical energy in order to strike a bell; the physical vibrations of the bell then produce sound waves that are transduced into nerve impulses by the ears of the person in the house. 8. Under ideal conditions, vibrations of the eardrum as small as one billionth of a centimeter (one tenth the diameter of a hydrogen atom) can be heard. Therefore, if your ears were more sensitive, they would convert the random movement of air molecules into a constant roaring or hissing noise. 9. So-called clean words occur more frequently in everyday speech and writing. This alone could make them easier to recognize than "dirty" words. 10. Good guess! That's right, it's the faked "Eat popcorn, drink Coke" study (Pratkanis, 1992).

VISION—CATCHING SOME RAYS

For most people, loss of vision is the single most devastating sensory disability. Because of its great importance, we will explore vision in more detail than the other senses. Let's begin with the basic dimensions of light and vision.

DIMENSIONS OF VISION Recall that the room in which you are sitting is filled with electromagnetic radiation, including light and other energies. Light of various wavelengths makes up the **visible spectrum** (electromagnetic energies to which the eyes respond). The spectrum starts at "short" wavelengths of 400 **nanometers** (nan-OM-et-er: one billionth of a meter). Wavelengths at this end of the spectrum produce sensations of purple or violet. Longer wavelengths produce blue, green, yellow, and orange, until we reach red, with a wavelength of 700 nanometers (❖Fig. 6.3).

The formal term for color is **hue,** which refers to the basic color categories of red, orange, yellow, green, blue, indigo, and violet. As we have seen, various hues (or color sensations) correspond to light's wavelength. White light, in contrast, is a mixture of many wavelengths. Hues (colors) produced by a narrow band of wavelengths are said to be very **saturated,** or "pure." (An intense fire-engine red is more saturated than a muddy brick red.) A third dimension of vision, **brightness,** corresponds roughly to the physical amplitude of light waves. Waves of greater amplitude are "taller," carry more energy, and cause colors to appear brighter or more intense. For example, the same brick red would look bright under intense, high-energy illumination and drab under dim light.

Structure of the Eye

Is it true that the eye is like a camera? By pushing the issue a bit, the eye could be used as a camera. If you bathe the light-sensitive back surface of the eye in alum solution, the last image to strike it will appear like a tiny photograph. This fact might make for a great murder mystery, but it's not much of a way to take a photograph. In any case, several basic elements of eyes and cameras are similar. Both have a transparent structure called a **lens** that focuses images on a light-sensitive layer at the

Perceptual defense *Resistance to perceiving threatening or disturbing stimuli.*
Limen *A threshold or limit.*
Subliminal perception *Perception of a stimulus below the threshold for conscious recognition.*
Visible spectrum *That part of the electromagnetic spectrum to which the eyes are sensitive.*
Nanometer *One billionth of a meter.*
Hue *Classification of colors into basic categories of red, orange, yellow, green, blue, indigo, and violet.*
Saturation *The degree of a color's purity.*
Brightness *The intensity of lights or colors.*
Lens *Structure in the eye that focuses light rays.*

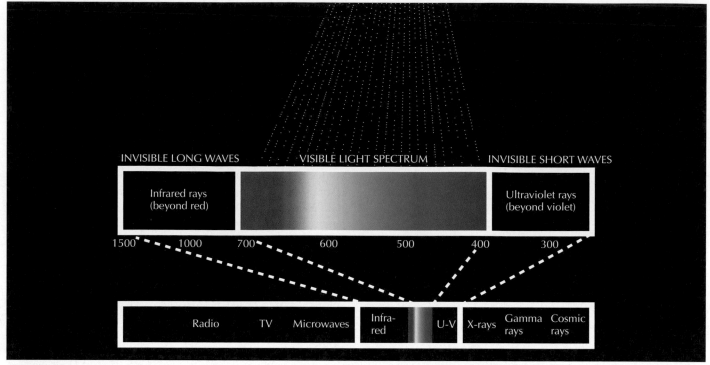

❖ **FIGURE 6.3** *The visible spectrum.*

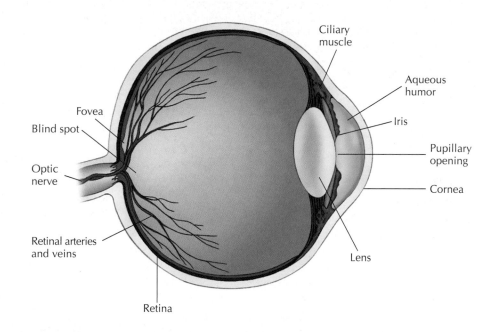

❖ **FIGURE 6.4** *The human eye, a simplified view.*

back of a closed space. In a camera, this layer is the film. In the eye, it is a layer of **photoreceptors** (light-sensitive cells). These cells are part of the **retina,** a receiving area for images that is about the size and thickness of a postage stamp (❖Fig. 6.4).

FOCUSING   *How does the eye focus?*   The front of the eye is covered by a clear membrane called the **cornea.** The curvature of this transparent "window" bends light rays inward. It is responsible for most of the focusing in the eye. Smaller adjustments in focusing

occur as the shape of the lens is altered by a series of muscles, a process called **accommodation.** In cameras, focusing is done more simply—by changing the distance between the lens and the film.

VISUAL PROBLEMS   The shape of the eye also affects focusing. If the eye is too short, nearby objects cannot be focused, but distant objects are clear. This is called **hyperopia** (HI-per-OPE-ee-ah: farsightedness). If the eyeball is too long, the image falls short of the retina, and distant objects cannot be focused. This results in

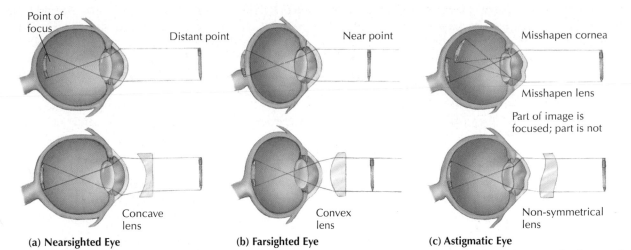

FIGURE 6.5 *Visual defects and corrective lenses:* (a) *A myopic (longer than usual) eye. The concave lens spreads light rays just enough to increase the eye's focal length.* (b) *A hyperopic (shorter than usual) eye. The convex lens increases refraction (bending), returning the point of focus to the retina.* (c) *An astigmatic (lens or cornea not symmetrical) eye. In astigmatism, parts of vision are sharp, and parts are unfocused. Lenses to correct astigmatism are asymmetrical.*

myopia (my-OPE-ee-ah: nearsightedness). When the cornea or the lens is misshapen, part of the visual field will be focused and part will be fuzzy. In this case, the eye has more than one focal point, a problem called **astigmatism** (ah-STIG-mah-tiz-em). All three visual defects can be corrected by placing glasses or contact lenses in front of the eye. These added lenses change the path of incoming light to restore crisp focusing (❖Fig. 6.5).

As people age, the lens becomes less flexible and less able to accommodate. Because the lens must do its greatest bending to focus nearby objects, the result is **presbyopia** (prez-bee-OPE-ee-ah: old vision, or farsightedness due to aging). Perhaps you have seen a grandparent or older friend reading a newspaper at arm's length because of presbyopia. If you now wear glasses for nearsightedness, you may need bifocals as you age (unless your arms grow longer in the meantime). Bifocal lenses correct near vision *and* distance vision.

LIGHT CONTROL There is one more major similarity between the eye and a camera. In front of the lens in both is a mechanism to control the amount of light entering. This mechanism in a camera is the diaphragm; in the eye, it is the iris (❖Fig. 6.6). The **iris** is a colored circular muscle that expands and contracts. As it does so, it changes the size of the **pupil** (the opening at the center of the eye).

The retina can adapt to changing light conditions, but only slowly. By making rapid adjustments, the iris allows us to move quickly from darkness to bright sunlight, or the reverse. In dim light, the pupils dilate (enlarge), and in bright light they constrict (narrow). At the largest opening of the iris, the pupil is 17 times larger than at the smallest. Were it not for this, you would be blinded for quite some time upon walking into a darkened room.

RODS AND CONES At this point, our eye-camera comparison breaks down. From the retina on, vision becomes a complex system for analyzing patterns of light. (See "How the Brain Sees the World.") Besides, the eye would make a very strange camera. First of all, the eye has two types of "film," consisting of re-

❖ **FIGURE 6.6** *The iris and diaphragm.*

ceptor cells called *rods* and *cones.* The **cones,** numbering about 6.5 million in each eye, work best in bright light. They also produce color sensations and pick up fine details. In contrast, the **rods,** numbering about 100 million, are unable to detect colors. Pure rod vision is black and white. However, the rods are much more sensitive to light than the cones are. The rods therefore allow us to see in very dim light.

Compared with the film in a camera, the visual receptors are backward. The rods and cones point toward the *back* of the eye, away from incoming light (❖Fig. 6.7). In addition, the eye is constantly in motion. This would be disastrous for a camera,

Photoreceptor *A sensory receptor for light.*
Retina *The light-sensitive layer of cells at the back of the eye.*
Cornea *Transparent membrane covering the front of the eye.*
Accommodation *Changes in the shape of the lens of the eye.*
Hyperopia *Difficulty focusing nearby objects (farsightedness).*
Myopia *Difficulty focusing distant objects (nearsightedness).*
Astigmatism *Defects in the cornea, lens, or eye that cause some areas of vision to be out of focus.*
Presbyopia *Farsightedness caused by aging.*
Iris *Circular muscle that controls the amount of light entering the eye.*
Pupil *The opening at the front of the eye through which light passes.*
Cones *Visual receptors for colors and daylight visual acuity.*
Rods *Visual receptors for dim light that produce only black and white sensations.*

but as we shall see later, it is essential for normal vision. Finally, the "film" (retina) has a hole in it: Each eye has a **blind spot** because there are no receptors where the optic nerve leaves the eye (❖Fig. 6.8a).

The blind spot shows again that vision depends greatly on the brain. If you close one eye, part of the scene ahead will fall on the blind spot of your open eye. Why isn't there a gap in your vision? The answer is that the visual cortex of the brain actively extends patterns into the gap from surrounding areas (❖Fig. 6.8b). According to folklore, King Charles II of England used this feature of the blind spot to amuse himself. Whenever he became bored, Charles II closed one eye and visually "beheaded" members of his court (Ramachandran, 1992a, 1992b).

VISUAL ACUITY The rods and cones also affect **visual acuity,** or sharpness. The cones lie mainly at the center of the eye. In fact,

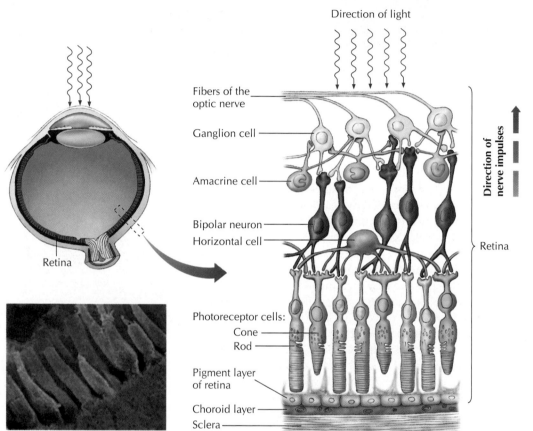

❖ **FIGURE 6.7** *Anatomy of the retina, the light-sensitive element of the eye. The retina lies behind the vitreous humor, which is the jelly-like substance that fills the eyeball. Note that light does not fall directly on the rods and cones. It must first pass through the outer layers of the retina, made up of additional nerve cells. Only about half of the light falling on the front of the eye reaches the rods and cones—testimony to the eye's amazing light sensitivity. The rods and cones are much smaller than implied here. The smallest receptors are 1 micron (one millionth of a meter) wide. The lower left photograph shows rods and cones as seen through an electron microscope. In the photograph, the cones are colored green and the rods blue.*

❖ **FIGURE 6.8** *Experiencing the blind spot. (a) With your right eye closed, stare at the upper right cross. Hold the book about 1 foot from your eye and slowly move it back and forth. You should be able to locate a position that causes the black spot to disappear. When it does, it has fallen on the blind spot. With a little practice, you can learn to make people or objects you dislike disappear, too! (b) Repeat the procedure described, but stare at the lower cross. When the white space falls on the blind spot, the black lines will appear to be continuous. This may help you understand why you do not usually experience a blind spot in your visual field.*

HOW THE BRAIN SEES THE WORLD

Early ideas of vision often assumed an almost movie-like projection of pictures to the brain. But this mistaken notion immediately raises the question, Who's watching the movie? Thanks to the Nobel Prize–winning work of biopsychologists David Hubel and Torsten Wiesel, we now know that vision acts more like a computer than like a television or movie camera.

Hubel and Wiesel directly recorded the activities of single cells in the visual cortex of the brain in cats and monkeys. As they did, they noted the area of the retina to which each cell responded. Then they shone lights of various sizes and shapes on the retina and recorded how often the corresponding brain cell fired nerve impulses (❖Fig. 6.9).

The results were fascinating. Many brain cells responded only to lines of a certain width or orientation. These same cells didn't get the least bit "excited" over a dot of light or overall illumination. Other cells responded only to lines at certain angles, lines of certain lengths, or lines moving in a particular direction (Hubel, 1979b; Hubel & Wiesel, 1979).

The upshot of such findings is that cells in the brain, like the frog's retina described earlier, act as feature detectors. The brain seems to first analyze incoming information into lines, angles, shading, movement, and other basic features. Then, other brain areas combine these features into meaningful visual experiences. (This concept is discussed further in Chapter 7.) Reading the letters on this page is a direct result of such feature analysis. Given the size of the task, it's little wonder that as much as 30 percent of the human brain may be involved in vision.

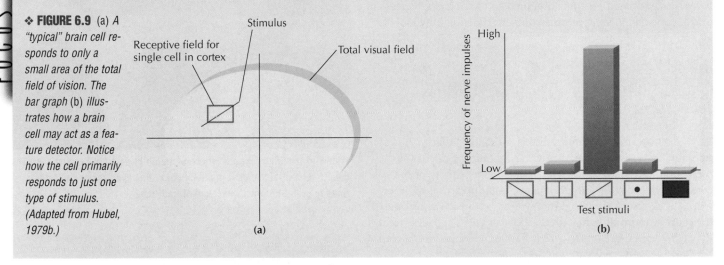

❖ **FIGURE 6.9** (a) A "typical" brain cell responds to only a small area of the total field of vision. The bar graph (b) illustrates how a brain cell may act as a feature detector. Notice how the cell primarily responds to just one type of stimulus. (Adapted from Hubel, 1979b.)

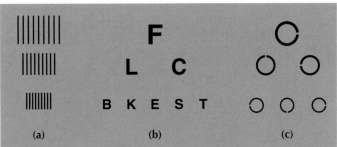

❖ **FIGURE 6.10** Tests of visual acuity. Here are some common tests of visual acuity. In (a), sharpness is indicated by the smallest grating still seen as individual lines. The Snellen chart (b) requires that you read rows of letters of diminishing size until you can no longer distinguish them. The Landolt rings (c) require no familiarity with letters. All that is required is a report of which side has a break in it. Normal acuity is designated as 20/20 vision: At 20 feet in distance, you can distinguish what the average person can see at 20 feet. If your vision is 20/40, you can only see at 20 feet what the average person can see at 40 feet. If your vision is 20/200, you need glasses! Vision that is 20/12 would mean that you can see at 20 feet what the average person must be 8 feet nearer to see, indicating better than average acuity. American astronaut Gordon Cooper, who claimed to see railroad lines in northern India from 100 miles above, had 20/12 acuity.

the **fovea** (FOE-vee-ah: a small, cup-shaped area in the middle of the retina) contains only cones—about 50,000 of them. If you look at your thumbnail at arm's length, its image just about covers the fovea. Like a newspaper photograph made of many small dots, the tightly packed cones in the fovea produce the greatest visual acuity. In other words, vision is sharpest when an image falls on the fovea. Acuity steadily decreases toward the edge of the retina. Note that visual acuity is based on the optics of the eye. Sharpness cannot be improved by eye exercises or commercial "vision training" courses (Long, 1994).

❖Figure 6.10 describes a widely used rating system for acuity. If vision can be corrected to no better than 20/200 acuity, a person is considered legally blind. With 20/200 vision, the world is seen as nothing but a blur.

PERIPHERAL VISION *What is the purpose of the rest of the retina?* Areas outside the fovea also get light, creating a large region of

Blind spot An area of the retina lacking visual receptors.
Visual acuity The sharpness of visual perception.
Fovea An area at the center of the retina containing only cones.

peripheral (side) **vision.** The rods are most numerous about 20 degrees from the center of the retina, so much peripheral vision is rod vision. Although rod vision is not very sharp, the rods are quite sensitive to *movement.* Thus, the eye maintains a radar-like scan for movement in side vision. Seeing "out of the corner of the eye" is important for sports, driving, and walking down dark alleys. People who suffer from **tunnel vision** (a loss of peripheral vision) feel as if they are wearing blinders. Tunnel vision can also occur temporarily when we are overloaded by a task. For example, if you were playing a demanding video game, you might be excused for not noticing that a friend had walked up beside you (Williams, 1995).

Sailors, pilots, astronomers, and military spotters have long made use of an interesting fact. Although the rods give poor acuity, they are many times more responsive to light than the cones are. Because most rods are 20 degrees to each side of the fovea, the best night vision is obtained by looking *next to* an object you wish to see. Test this yourself some night by looking at, and next to, a very dim star.

COLOR VISION—THERE'S MORE TO IT THAN MEETS THE EYE

What would you say is the brightest color? Red? Yellow? Blue? Actually, there are two answers to this question, one for the rods and one for the cones. Maximal color sensitivity of the cones lies in the *yellowish green* part of the spectrum. In other words, if all colors are tested in daylight (with each reflecting the same amount of light), then yellowish green appears *brightest.* Yellow-green fire trucks and the Day-Glo yellow vests worn by roadside work crews are a reflection of this fact.

To what color are the rods most sensitive? Remember that the rods do not produce color sensations. If very dim colored lights are used, no color will be seen. Even so, one light will appear brighter than the others. When tested this way, the rods are most sensitive to *blue-green* lights. Thus, at night or in dim light, when rod vision prevails, the brightest-colored light will be one that is blue or blue-green. For this reason, police and highway patrol cars in many states now have blue emergency lights for night work. Also, you may have wondered why the taxiway lights at airports are blue. It seems to be a poor choice, but blue is actually highly visible to pilots.

Color Theories

How do the cones produce color sensations? No short answer can do justice to the complexities of color vision, but briefly, here is the best current explanation. The **trichromatic theory** (TRY-kro-MAT-ik) of color vision holds that there are three types of cones, each most sensitive to either red, green, or blue. Other colors are assumed to result from combinations of these three, whereas black and white sensations are produced by the rods.

A basic problem with the trichromatic theory is that four colors—red, green, blue, and yellow—seem to be primary (they cannot be obtained by mixing other colors). Also, why is it im-

Yellow-green fire trucks are far more visible in daylight because their color matches the cones' sensitivity peak. However, many cities continue to prefer red trucks because of tradition.

possible to have a reddish green or a yellowish blue? A second view, known as the **opponent-process theory,** states that vision analyzes colors into "either-or" messages. It is assumed that the visual system can produce messages for either red or green, yellow or blue, black or white. Coding one color in a pair (red, for instance) seems to block the opposite message (green), so a reddish green is impossible, but a yellowish red (orange) can occur.

According to opponent-process theory, fatigue caused by making one response produces an afterimage of the opposite color as the system recovers. **Afterimages** are visual sensations that persist after a stimulus is removed. To see an afterimage of the type predicted by opponent-process theory, look at ❖Figure 6.11 and follow the instructions given there.

Which color theory is correct? Both! The three-color theory applies to the retina, where three types of **visual pigments** (light-sensitive chemicals) have been found. As predicted, each pigment is most sensitive to light in roughly the red, green, or blue region. As a result, the three types of cones fire nerve impulses at different rates when various colors are viewed (❖Fig. 6.12).

In contrast, the opponent-process theory seems to explain events recorded in optic pathways and the brain *after* information leaves the eye. For example, nerve cells can be found in the brain that are excited by the color red and inhibited by the color green. So both theories are "correct." One explains what

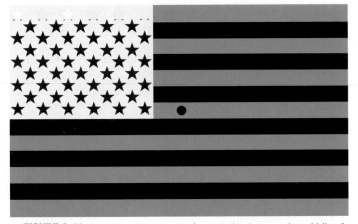

❖ FIGURE 6.11 *Negative afterimages. Stare at the dot near the middle of the flag for at least 30 seconds. Then look immediately at a plain sheet of white paper or a white wall. You will see the American flag in its normal colors. Reduced sensitivity to yellow, green, and black in the visual system, caused by prolonged staring, results in the appearance of complementary colors. Project the afterimage of the flag on other colored surfaces to get additional effects.*

❖ FIGURE 6.13 *Notice how different the gray-blue color looks when it is placed on different backgrounds. Unless you are looking at a large, solid block of color, simultaneous contrast is constantly affecting your color experiences.*

apparent color of an object is influenced by the colors of other nearby objects. This effect is called **simultaneous color contrast.** It occurs because brain cell activity in one area of the cortex can be altered by activity in nearby areas. Simultaneous contrast can make it difficult to paint a picture or decorate a room. If you add a new color to a canvas or a room, all of the existing colors will suddenly look different. Typically, each time a new color is added, all the other colors must be adjusted (see ❖Fig. 6.13).

More striking than simultaneous contrast is the fact that color experiences are *actively constructed* in the brain. The brain does not simply receive prepackaged color messages. It must generate color from the data it receives. As a result, it is possible to experience color where none exists. (See ❖Fig. 6.14 for an example.) Indeed, all of our experiences

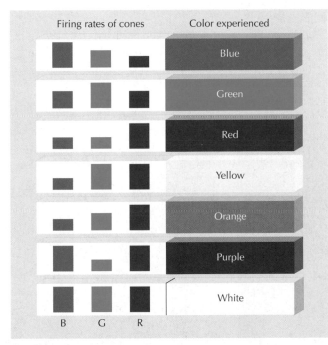

❖ FIGURE 6.12 *Firing rates of blue, green, and red cones in response to different colors. The taller the colored bar, the higher the firing rates for that type of cone. As you can see, colors are coded by differences in the activity of all three types of cones in the normal eye. (Adapted from Goldstein, 1999.)*

happens in the eye itself. The other explains how visual information is analyzed after it leaves the eye.

CONSTRUCTING COLORS   The preceding explanations present a fairly mechanical view of how color is analyzed and sensed. In reality, color experiences are more complex. For example, the

Peripheral vision   *Vision at the edges of the visual field.*
Tunnel vision   *Vision restricted to the center of the visual field.*
Trichromatic theory   *Theory of color vision based on three cone types: red, green, and blue.*
Opponent-process theory   *Theory of color vision based on three coding systems (red or green, yellow or blue, black or white).*
Afterimage   *Visual sensation that persists after a stimulus is removed.*
Visual pigments   *Light-sensitive chemicals found in the rods and cones.*
Simultaneous color contrast   *Changes in perceived hue that occur when a colored stimulus is displayed on backgrounds of various colors.*

Color Blindness and Color Weakness

Do you know anyone who regularly draws hoots of laughter by wearing clothes of wildly clashing colors? Or someone who sheepishly tries to avoid saying what color an object is? If so, you probably know someone who is color-blind.

What is it like to be color-blind? What causes color blindness? A person who is **color-blind** cannot perceive colors. It is as if the world is a black-and-white movie. How do we know? In a few rare cases, people have been color-blind in only one eye and can compare. Two colors of equal brightness look exactly

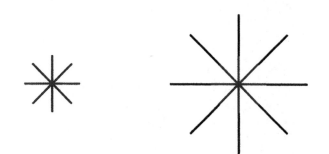

❖ **FIGURE 6.14** *On the left is a "star" made of red lines. On the right, the red lines are placed on top of longer black lines. Now, in addition to the red lines, you will see a glowing red disk, with a clear border. Of course, no red disk is printed on this page. No ink can be found between the red lines. The glowing red disk exists only in your mind. (After Hoffman, 1999, p.111.)*

alike to the color-blind individual. The color-blind person either lacks cones or has cones that do not function normally (Hsia & Graham, 1997).

Total color blindness is rare. In **color weakness,** the person is unable to distinguish some colors. Partial color blindness of this type is more common. Approximately 8 percent of the male population (but less than 1 percent of women) are red-green color-blind. Another form of color weakness, involving yellow and blue, is extremely rare (Hsia & Graham, 1997).

Color blindness is caused by changes in the genes that control red, green, and blue pigments in the cones (Nathans et al., 1986). Red-green color blindness is a recessive, sex-linked trait. That means it is carried on the *X*, or female, chromosome. Women have two *X* chromosomes, so if they receive only one defective color gene, they still have normal vision. Color-blind men, however, have only one *X* chromosome, so they can inherit the defect from their mothers (who are usually not color-blind themselves). The red-green color-blind individual sees both reds and greens as the same color, usually a yellowish brown (see ❖Fig. 6.15).

Then how can color-blind individuals drive? Don't they have trouble with traffic lights? Red-green color-blind individuals have normal vision for yellow and blue, so their main problem is telling red lights from green. In practice, this is not difficult. In the United States and Canada, the red light is always on top, and the green light is brighter than the red. Also, to help remedy this problem, traffic signals have a "red" light that has a background of yellow light mixed with it and a "green" light that is really blue-green.

(a)   (b)   (c)

❖ **FIGURE 6.15** *Color blindness and color weakness. (a) Photograph illustrates normal color vision. (b) Photograph is printed in blue and yellow and gives an impression of what a red-green color-blind person sees. (c) Photograph simulates total color blindness. If you are totally color-blind, all three photos will look nearly identical.*

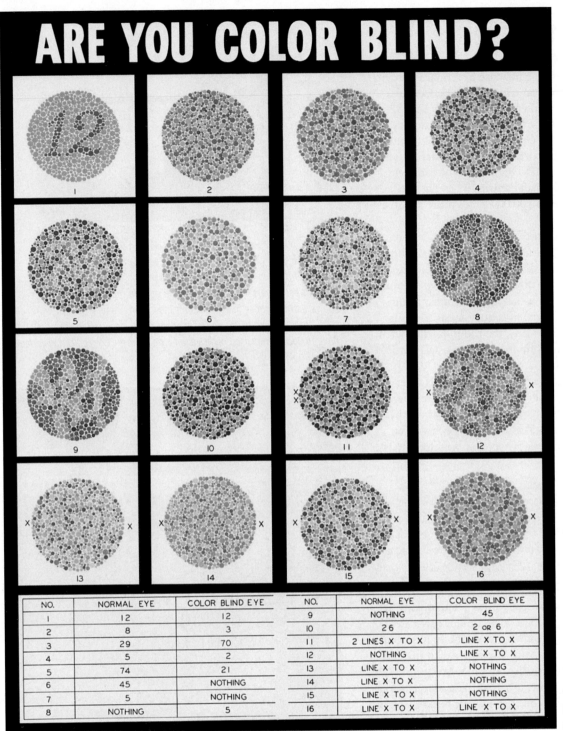

ARE YOU COLOR BLIND?

NO.	NORMAL EYE	COLOR BLIND EYE	NO.	NORMAL EYE	COLOR BLIND EYE
1	12	12	9	NOTHING	45
2	8	3	10	26	2 OR 6
3	29	70	11	2 LINES X TO X	LINE X TO X
4	5	2	12	NOTHING	LINE X TO X
5	74	21	13	LINE X TO X	NOTHING
6	45	NOTHING	14	LINE X TO X	NOTHING
7	5	NOTHING	15	LINE X TO X	NOTHING
8	NOTHING	5	16	LINE X TO X	LINE X TO X

❖ **FIGURE 6.16** *A replica of the Ishihara test for color blindness.*

How can a person tell if she or he is color-blind? The **Ishihara test** is a common measure of color blindness and weakness. In the test, numbers and other designs made of dots are placed on a background also made of dots. The background and the numbers are of different colors (red and green, for example). A person who is color-blind sees only a jumble of dots. The person with normal color vision can detect the presence of the numbers or designs. ❖Figure 6.16 is a replica of the Ishihara test. You should not consider ❖Figure 6.16 a true test of color vision, but it may give you some idea of whether you are color-blind. The real test is highly accurate (Birch & McKeever, 1993).

Color blindness *A total inability to perceive colors.*
Color weakness *An inability to distinguish some colors.*
Ishihara test *A test for color blindness and color weakness.*

DARK ADAPTATION—LET THERE BE LIGHT!

What happens to the eyes when they adapt to a dark room?
Dark adaptation is the dramatic increase in retinal sensitivity to light that occurs after a person enters the dark. Consider walking into a theater. If you enter from a brightly lighted lobby, you practically need to be led to your seat. After a short time, however, you can see the entire room in detail (including the couple kissing over in the corner). Studies of dark adaptation show that it takes about 30 to 35 minutes of complete darkness to reach maximum visual sensitivity (❖Fig. 6.17). A completely dark-adapted eye is 100,000 times more sensitive to light (Goldstein, 1999).

What causes dark adaptation? Like the cones, the rods contain a light-sensitive visual pigment. When struck by light, visual pigments *bleach,* or break down chemically. (The afterimages caused by flashbulbs are a direct result of this bleaching.) To restore light sensitivity, the visual pigments must recombine, which takes time. Night vision is due mainly to an increase in **rhodopsin** (row-DOP-sin), the rod pigment. When completely dark adapted, the human eye is almost as sensitive to light as the eye of an owl.

Before artificial lighting, gradual adaptation at sunset posed few problems. Now we are often caught in temporary semi-blindness. Usually this isn't dangerous, but it can be. Even though dark adaptation takes a long time, it can be wiped out by just a few seconds of viewing bright light. Try this demonstration:

See (and Don't See) for Yourself

Spend 15 or 20 minutes in a darkened room. At the end of this time, you should be able to see clearly. Now, close your left eye and cover it tightly with your hand. Turn on a bright light for 1 or 2 seconds and look at it with your right eye. With the light off again, compare the vision in your two eyes, first opening one and then the other. You will be completely blinded in your right eye.

This experience should convince you to avoid looking at the headlights of approaching cars during night driving. Under normal conditions, glare recovery takes about 20 seconds, plenty of time for an accident. After a few drinks, it may take 30 to 50 percent longer, because alcohol dilates the pupils, allowing more light to enter. Note, too, that dark adaptation occurs more slowly as we grow older. This is one reason why injuries caused by falling in the dark become more common among the elderly (McMurdo & Gaskell, 1991).

Is there any way to speed up dark adaptation? The rods are *insensitive* to extremely red light. To take advantage of this lack of sensitivity, submarines and airplane cockpits are illuminated with red light. So are the ready rooms for fighter pilots and ground crews. In each case, this allows people to move quickly into the dark without having to adapt. Because the red light doesn't stimulate the rods, it is as if they had already spent time in the dark.

Can eating carrots really improve vision? One chemical "ingredient" of rhodopsin is **retinal,** which the body makes from vitamin A. (Retinal is also called **retinene.**) When too little vit-

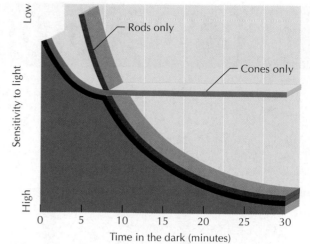

❖ **FIGURE 6.17** *Typical course of dark adaptation. The black line shows how the threshold for vision lowers as a person spends time in the dark. (A lower threshold means that less light is needed for vision.) The green line shows that the cones adapt first, but they soon cease adding to light sensitivity. Rods, shown by the red line, adapt more slowly. However, they continue to add to improved night vision long after the cones are fully adapted.*

Red light allows dark adaptation to occur because it provides little or no stimulation to the rods.

amin A is available, less rhodopsin is produced. Thus, a person lacking vitamin A may develop night blindness. In **night blindness,** the person can see normally in bright light while using the cones but becomes blind at night, when the rods must function. Carrots are an excellent source of vitamin A, so they could improve night vision for someone suffering a deficiency, but not the vision of anyone with an adequate diet (Carlson, 1994).

HEARING—GOOD VIBRATIONS

Rock, classical, jazz, rap, country, hip-hop—whatever your musical taste, you have probably been moved or soothed by the riches of sound. Hearing also provides the brain with a wealth of information not available through the other senses, such as the approach of an unseen car. Hearing collects information from all around the body. Vision, in all its glory, is limited to stimuli in front of the eyes (unless, of course, your "shades" have rearview mirrors attached).

What is the stimulus for hearing? If you throw a stone into a quiet pond, a circle of waves will spread in all directions. In much the same way, sound travels as a series of invisible waves of **compression** (peaks) and **rarefaction** (RARE-eh-fak-shun: valleys) in the air. Any vibrating object—a tuning fork, the string of a musical instrument, or the vocal cords—will produce **sound waves** (rhythmic movement of air molecules). Other materials, such as fluids or solids, can also carry sound. But sound does not travel in a vacuum. Movies that show characters reacting to the "roar" of alien starships or titanic battles in deep space are in error.

The *frequency* of sound waves (the number of waves per second) corresponds to the perceived **pitch** (higher or lower tone) of a sound. The *amplitude*, or physical "height," of a sound wave tells how much energy it contains. Psychologically, amplitude corresponds to sensed **loudness** (sound intensity) (❖Fig. 6.18).

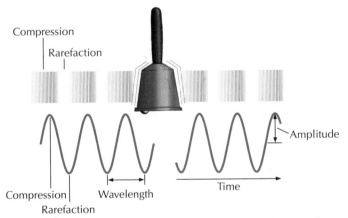

❖ **FIGURE 6.18** *Waves of compression in the air, or vibrations, are the stimulus for hearing. The frequency of sound waves determines their pitch. The amplitude determines loudness.*

Dark adaptation *Increased retinal sensitivity to light.*
Rhodopsin *The light-sensitive pigment in the rods.*
Retinal *Part of the chemical compound that makes up rhodopsin (also known as retinene).*
Night blindness *Blindness under conditions of low illumination.*
Compression *Higher sound pressure; the peaks of sound waves.*
Rarefaction *Lower sound pressure; the valleys of sound waves.*
Sound wave *Cyclic, wave-like movement of air molecules.*
Pitch *Higher or lower tones; related to the frequency of sound waves.*
Loudness *The intensity of a sound; determined by the amplitude of sound waves.*

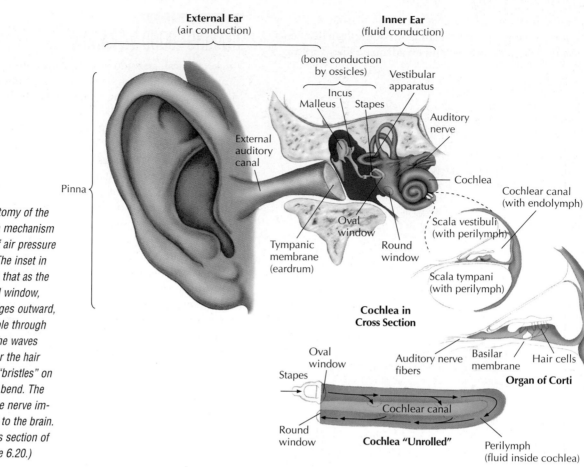

External Ear (air conduction) | **Inner Ear** (fluid conduction)

(bone conduction by ossicles)

Vestibular apparatus

Incus

Malleus | Stapes

Auditory nerve

External auditory canal

Cochlea

Cochlear canal (with endolymph)

Pinna

Scala vestibuli (with perilymph)

Oval window

Tympanic membrane (eardrum) | Round window

Scala tympani (with perilymph)

Cochlea in Cross Section

Oval window

Auditory nerve fibers | Basilar membrane | Hair cells

Stapes

Organ of Corti

Round window

Cochlear canal

Cochlea "Unrolled"

Perilymph (fluid inside cochlea)

❖ **FIGURE 6.19** *Anatomy of the ear. The entire ear is a mechanism for changing waves of air pressure into nerve impulses. The inset in the foreground shows that as the stapes moves the oval window, the round window bulges outward, allowing waves to ripple through fluid in the cochlea. The waves move membranes near the hair cells, causing cilia or "bristles" on the tips of the cells to bend. The hair cells then generate nerve impulses that are carried to the brain. (See an enlarged cross section of the cochlea in ❖ Figure 6.20.)*

How are sounds converted to nerve impulses? What we call the "ear" is only the **pinna** (PIN-ah: the visible, external part of the ear). In addition to being a good place to hang earrings or balance pencils, the pinna acts like a funnel to concentrate sounds. After they are guided into the ear, sound waves collide with the **tympanic membrane** (eardrum), which is like a tight drumhead within the ear canal. The sound waves set the eardrum in motion. This, in turn, causes three small bones (the **auditory ossicles**) (OSS-ih-kuls) to vibrate (❖ Fig. 6.19). The

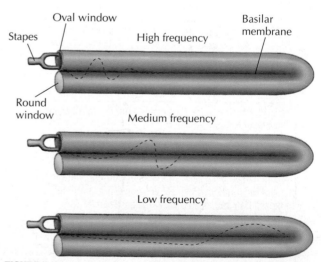

Oval window

Basilar membrane

Stapes

High frequency

Round window

Medium frequency

Low frequency

❖ **FIGURE 6.21** *Here we see a simplified side view of the cochlea "unrolled." Remember that the basilar membrane is the elastic "roof" of the lower chamber of the cochlea. The organ of Corti, with its sensitive hair cells, rests atop the basilar membrane. The colored line shows where waves in the cochlear fluid cause the greatest deflection of the basilar membrane. (The amount of movement is exaggerated in the drawing.) Hair cells respond most in the area of greatest movement, which helps identify sound frequency.*

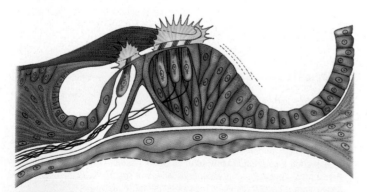

❖ **FIGURE 6.20** *A closer view of the hair cells shows how movement of fluid in the cochlea causes the bristling "hairs" or cilia to bend, generating a nerve impulse.*

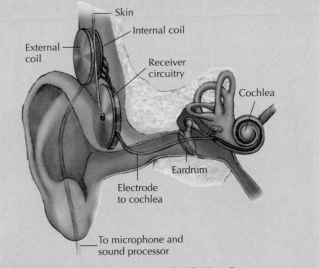

ARTIFICIAL HEARING

USING PSYCHOLOGY

In many cases of "nerve" deafness, the nerve is actually intact. This finding has spurred development of **cochlear implants** that bypass hair cells and stimulate the auditory nerve directly (❖Fig. 6.22).

As you can see, wires from a microphone carry electrical signals to an external coil. A matching coil under the skin picks up the signals and carries them to one or more areas of the cochlea. Early implants allowed patients to hear only low-frequency sounds, such as a dog's bark or the horn of a speeding car. Newer multichannel models make use of place theory to separate higher and lower tones. This has allowed some formerly deaf people to hear human voices and other higher frequency sounds. About 60 percent of all multichannel implant patients can understand some spoken words, and some children learn to speak (Cohen et al, 1993; Tye-Murray et al., 1995).

At present, artificial hearing remains crude. All but the most successful implant patients describe the sound as "like a radio that isn't quite tuned in." In fact, 30 percent of all adults who have tried implants have given up on them. But the implants are improving, and even now it is hard to argue with enthusiasts like Kristen Cloud. Shortly after Kristen re-

ceived an implant, she was able to hear a siren and avoid being struck by a speeding car (Williams, 1984). She says simply, "The implant saved my life."

❖ **FIGURE 6.22** *A cochlear implant, or "artificial ear."*

ossicles are the malleus (MAL-ee-us), incus, and stapes (STAY-peas). Their common names are the hammer, anvil, and stirrup. The ossicles link the eardrum with the **cochlea** (KOCK-lee-ah: a snail-shaped organ that makes up the inner ear). The stapes is attached to a membrane on the cochlea called the **oval window.** As the oval window moves back and forth, it makes waves in a fluid inside the cochlea.

The cochlea is really the organ of hearing. It is here that tiny **hair cells** detect waves in the fluid. The hair cells are part of a structure called the **organ of Corti** (KOR-tee), which makes up the center part of the cochlea (❖Fig. 6.20). A set of **stereocilia** (STER-ee-oh-SIL-ih-ah) or bristles atop each hair cell brush against the tectorial membrane when waves ripple through the fluid surrounding the organ of Corti. As the stereocilia are bent, nerve impulses are triggered, which then flow to the brain.

How are higher and lower sounds detected? The **frequency theory** of hearing states that as pitch rises, nerve impulses of the same frequency are fed into the auditory nerve. That is, an 800-hertz tone produces 800 nerve impulses per second. This explains how sounds up to about 4,000 hertz reach the brain. But higher tones require a different explanation. **Place theory** states that higher and lower tones excite specific areas of the cochlea. High tones register most strongly at the base of the cochlea (near the oval window). Lower tones, on the other hand, mostly move hair cells near the outer tip of the cochlea (❖Fig. 6.21). Pitch is therefore signaled by the area of the cochlea most strongly activated. Place theory also explains why hunters sometimes lose hearing in a narrow pitch range. *Hunter's notch,* as it is called, occurs when hair cells are damaged in the area activated by the pitch of gunfire.

DEAFNESS *What causes other types of deafness?* There are two main types of deafness. **Conduction deafness** occurs when there is poor transfer of sounds from the eardrum to the inner ear. For example, the eardrums or ossicles may be damaged or immobilized by disease or injury. In many cases, conduction deafness can be overcome by a hearing aid, which makes sounds louder and clearer.

Nerve deafness results from damage to the hair cells or auditory nerve. Hearing aids are of no help in this case, because auditory messages are blocked from reaching the brain. However, a new artificial hearing system is making it possible for some people with nerve deafness to break through the wall of silence. (See "Artificial Hearing.")

Pinna *The visible, external part of the ear.*
Tympanic membrane *The eardrum.*
Auditory ossicles *The three small bones that link the eardrum to the cochlea.*
Cochlear implant *An electronic device that stimulates the auditory nerve.*
Cochlea *The snail-shaped organ that makes up the inner ear.*
Oval window *A membrane on the cochlea connected to the third auditory ossicle.*
Hair cells *Receptor cells within the cochlea that transduce vibrations into nerve impulses.*
Organ of Corti *Center part of the cochlea, containing hair cells, canals, and membranes.*
Stereocilia *Bristle-like structures on hair cells.*
Frequency theory *Holds that tones up to 4,000 hertz are converted to nerve impulses that match the frequency of each tone.*
Place theory *Theory that higher and lower tones excite specific areas of the cochlea.*
Conduction deafness *Poor transfer of sounds from the eardrum to the inner ear.*
Nerve deafness *Deafness caused by damage to the hair cells or auditory nerve.*

A particular type of nerve deafness is of special interest, because many jobs, hobbies, and pastimes can cause it. **Stimulation deafness** occurs when very loud sounds damage hair cells in the cochlea (as in hunter's notch). Each of us starts life with about 32,000 hair cells (❖Fig. 6.23). However, we begin losing them the moment we are born. By age 65, more than 40 percent are gone.

If you work in a noisy environment or enjoy loud music, motorcycling, snowmobiling, hunting, or similar pursuits, you may be risking stimulation deafness. The hair cells, which are about as thick as a cobweb, are very fragile and easily damaged. Once dead, they are never replaced: When you abuse them, you lose them.

How loud must a sound be to be hazardous? The danger of hearing loss depends on both the loudness of sound and how long you are exposed to it. Daily exposure to 85 decibels or more may cause permanent hearing loss. Even short periods at 120 decibels (a rock concert) may cause a **temporary threshold shift** (a partial, transitory loss of hearing). Brief exposure to 150 decibels (a jet airplane nearby) can cause permanent deafness.

You might find it interesting to check the decibel ratings of some of your activities in ❖Figure 6.24. Don't be fooled by the numbers, though. Decibels are plotted on a logarithmic scale (like earthquake intensity!). Every 20 decibels increases the sound pressure by a factor of 10. In other words, a rock concert at 120 decibels is not just twice as powerful as a normal voice at 60 decibels. It is actually 1,000 times stronger.

Music, as well as noise, can do damage. People who sit directly in front of the speaker columns at highly amplified musical concerts run considerable risk of hearing loss. Dancing or aerobic exercise heightens the risk by diverting blood flow from the inner ear to the extremities. Walkman-style stereo headphones also present a danger. Many can reach 115 decibels or more. If you can hear the sound from the headset on the person standing next to you, the volume is probably damaging the user's ears. "Boom box" car stereos present similar dangers.

If **tinnitus** (tin-NYE-tus: a ringing or buzzing sensation) follows exposure to loud sounds, chances are that hair cells

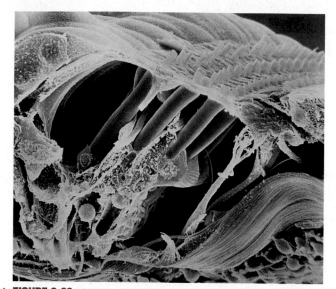

❖ **FIGURE 6.23** *A highly magnified electron microscope photo of the cilia (orange bristles) on the top of human hair cells. (Colors are artificial.)*

❖ **FIGURE 6.24** *The loudness of sound is measured in decibels. Zero decibels is the faintest sound most people can hear. Sound in the range of 110 decibels is uncomfortably loud. Prolonged exposure to sounds above 85 decibels may damage the inner ear. Rock music, which may rate 120 decibels, is known to have caused hearing loss in musicians and may affect audiences as well. Sounds of 130 decibels pose an immediate danger to hearing.*

Typical Decibel Level		Dangerous Time Exposure	Examples
	180		Space Shuttle launch
	170		
	160	Hearing loss certain	Shotgun blast
	150		Jet airplane
	140	Any exposure dangerous	Siren at 50 feet / Stereo headset (full volume)
Extremely loud	130		Threshold of pain
	120	Immediate danger	Thunder, rock concert / Basketball or hockey crowd
	110		Riveter
	100		Factory noise, chain saw / Subway, tractor, power mower
Very loud	90	Less than 8 hours	Screaming child / Bus, motorcycle, snowmobile
	80	More than 8 hours	Loud home stereo, food blender / Heavy traffic
	70		Average automobile
	60		Normal conversation
Quiet	50		Quiet auto
	40		Quiet office
Very quiet	30		Whisper at 5 feet
	20		Broadcast studio when quiet
	10		Studio for making sound pictures
Just audible	0		

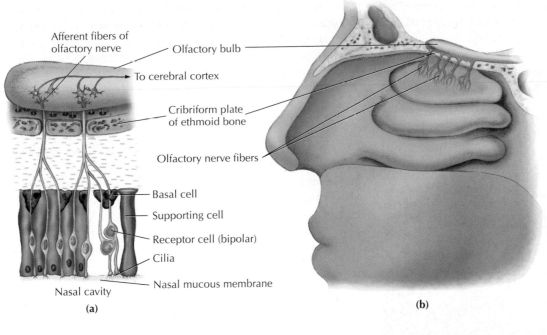

Afferent fibers of
olfactory nerve

Olfactory bulb

To cerebral cortex

Cribriform plate
of ethmoid bone

Olfactory nerve fibers

Basal cell

Supporting cell

Receptor cell (bipolar)

Cilia

Nasal mucous membrane

Nasal cavity

(a)

(b)

❖ **FIGURE 6.25** *Receptors for the sense of smell (olfaction). Olfactory nerve fibers respond to gaseous molecules. Receptor cells are shown in cross section at right of part* (a).

have been damaged. Almost everyone has tinnitus at times, especially with increasing age. But after repeated sounds that produce this warning, you can expect to become permanently hard-of-hearing. A study of people who regularly go to amplified concerts found that 44 percent had tinnitus and most had some hearing loss (Meyer-Bisch, 1996).

The next time you are exposed to a very loud sound, remember ❖Figure 6.24 and take precautions against damage. (Remember, too, that for temporary ear protection, fingers are always handy.)

SMELL AND TASTE—THE NOSE KNOWS WHEN THE TONGUE CAN'T TELL

Unless you are a wine taster, a perfume blender, a chef, or a gourmet, you may think of **olfaction** (smell) and **gustation** (taste) as minor senses. Certainly, a person could survive without these two **chemical senses** (receptors that respond to chemical molecules). Just the same, smell and taste occasionally prevent poisonings, and they add pleasure to our lives. Let's see how they operate.

The Sense of Smell

The receptors for smell respond primarily to gaseous molecules. As air enters the nose, it passes over roughly 5 million nerve fibers embedded in the lining of the upper nasal passages. Airborne molecules passing over the exposed fibers trigger nerve signals that are sent to the brain (❖Fig. 6.25).

How are different odors produced? This is still an unfolding mystery. One hint comes from a problem called **anosmia** (an-OZE-me-ah: defective smell), a sort of "smell blindness" for a single odor. Anosmia suggests that olfactory nerve fibers have receptors for specific odors. Indeed, molecules with a particular

odor are quite similar in shape. Specific shapes produce the following odors: floral (flower-like), camphoric (camphor-like), musky (Have you ever smelled a sweaty musk ox?), minty (mint-like), and etherish (like ether or cleaning fluid). This does not mean, however, that there are five different olfactory receptors, like the three types of cones in vision. At least 1,000 types of receptors for smell exist.

Does the existence of 1,000 different types of receptors mean that we can sense only 1,000 different odors? No, researchers recently discovered that various molecules trigger activity in different *combinations* of odor receptors. Thus, humans can detect at least 10,000 different odors. Just as many thousands of words can be made from the 26 letters of the alphabet, many combinations of receptors are possible, resulting in many different odors. The brain uses the distinctive patterns of messages it gets from the olfactory receptors to recognize particular scents (Malnic, Hirono, & Buck, 1999; Mombaerts, 1999). (See ❖Fig. 6.26.)

It appears that different-shaped "holes," or "pockets," exist on the surface of olfactory receptors. Like a piece fits in a puzzle, chemicals produce odors when part of a molecule matches a hole of the same shape. This is called the **lock and key theory.** Scents are also identified, in part, by the *location* of receptors in

Stimulation deafness *Damage caused by exposing the hair cells to excessively loud sounds.*
Temporary threshold shift *A temporary, partial loss of hearing.*
Tinnitus *A ringing or buzzing sensation in the ears.*
Olfaction *The sense of smell.*
Gustation *The sense of taste.*
Chemical senses *Senses, such as smell and taste, that respond to chemical molecules.*
Anosmia *Loss or impairment of the sense of smell.*
Lock and key theory *Holds that odors are related to the shapes of chemical molecules.*

the nose activated by an odor. And finally, the *number of activated receptors* tells the brain how strong an odor is (Freeman, 1991).

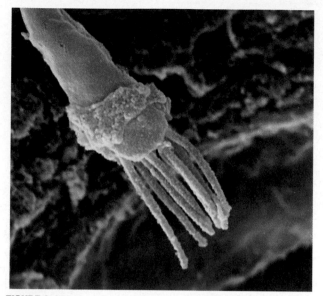

❖ **FIGURE 6.26** *This extreme close-up of an olfactory receptor cell shows the thread-like fibers that project into the airflow inside the nose. Receptor proteins on the surface of the fibers are sensitive to different airborne molecules. Nerve impulses are triggered when gaseous molecules match the structure of specific proteins in a lock-and-key fashion.*

A large-scale test found that 1 person out of 100 cannot smell at all (Gilbert & Wysocki, 1987). People with total anosmia typically find that olfaction is not such a minor sense after all. One anosmic individual, for instance, failed to notice that his apartment building was on fire. He was awakened just in time by neighbors, not by the smell of smoke (Monmaney, 1987). Even in everyday terms, anosmia can be a real loss. Many anosmics are unable to cook, and they may be poisoned by spoiled food.

What causes anosmia? Risks include infections, allergies, and blows to the head (which may tear the olfactory nerves). Exposure to chemicals such as ammonia, photo-developing chemicals, and hairdressing potions can also cause anosmia. If you value your sense of smell, be careful what you breathe.

Could the nose be the home of another, poorly understood chemical sense? Read "Pheromones—A Sixth Sense?" to find out.

Taste

There are at least four basic taste sensations: *sweet, salt, sour,* and *bitter.* We are most sensitive to bitter, less sensitive to sour, even less sensitive to salt, and least sensitive to sweet. This order may have helped prevent poisonings when most humans foraged for food, because bitter and sour foods are more likely to be inedible (McLaughlin & Margolskee, 1994).

An increasing number of experts believe that a fifth taste quality exists. The Japanese word *umami* describes a pleasant "brothy" taste associated with certain amino acids in chicken

FOCUS ON RESEARCH

PHEROMONES—A SIXTH SENSE?

Among animals, **pheromones** (FAIR-oh-monz: airborne chemical signals) greatly affect mating, sexual behavior, recognition of family members, and territorial marking. For example, when a female pig is exposed to the pheromones in a male pig's breath, she immediately becomes sexually receptive.

The **vomeronasal organ** (VNO) (voh-MARE-oh-NAZE-ul) is the sense organ for pheromones. Until recently, humans were assumed to have only a vestigial VNO or none at all. Now, however, scientists believe they have located the VNO in humans.

The suspected human vomeronasal organ looks like a small pit inside the nose (one on each side of the septum).

These pits are lined with nerve cells and respond to chemicals that are suspected pheromones.

What would a pheromone smell like? Pheromones are not smelled, felt, seen, tasted, or heard. In humans, pheromones would most likely produce vague feelings, such as well-being, attraction, aversion, unease, or anxiety. When people say that their relationships are influenced by good or bad "chemistry," there may be some truth to it. Pheromones could add to the intoxicating feelings of romantic attraction or the sourness of instant dislike. In fact, one group of researchers believe that adding a pheromone to aftershave lotion can make men more sexually attractive (Cutler, 1999; Cutler, Friedmann, & McCoy, 1998).

Evidence for the existence of human pheromones remains preliminary and controversial. (Men shouldn't expect Boar's Breath cologne to be offered anytime soon!) Nevertheless, the possibilities are intriguing. For instance, human pheromones appear to explain why the menstrual cycles of women who live together tend to become synchronized. It's also possible that pheromones may one day be used to decrease anxiety, curb hunger, relieve premenstrual discomforts, or aid sex therapy. Only further study will tell if searching for a sixth sense makes sense. (Additional sources: Monti-Bloch et al., 1994; Ryba, 1999; Weller & Weller, 1995.)

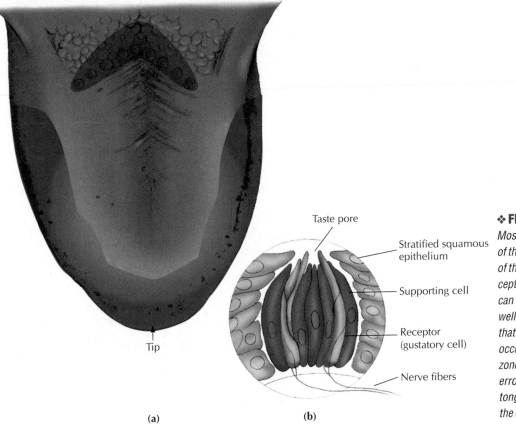

Taste pore

Stratified squamous epithelium

Supporting cell

Receptor (gustatory cell)

Nerve fibers

Tip

(a)   (b)

❖ **FIGURE 6.27** *Receptors for taste:* (a) *Most taste buds are found around the edges of the tongue. Stimulation of the central part of the tongue causes no taste sensations. Receptors for the four primary taste sensations can be found in all of the shaded areas, as well as under the tongue. That is, anywhere that taste buds are found, all taste sensations occur. Textbooks that show specific "taste zones" for sweet, salt, sour, and bitter are in error.* (b) *Detail of a taste bud within the tongue. The buds also occur in other parts of the digestive system.*

soup, some meat extracts, kelp, tuna, human milk, cheese, and soy products (Lindemann, 1996). The receptors for *umami* are sensitive to glutamate. This substance is found in MSG (monosodium glutamate), which is added to an increasing number of foods. Perhaps MSG's reputation as a "flavor enhancer" is based on the pleasant *umami* taste (Bellisle, 1999). At the very least, we at last know why chicken soup is such a "comfort food."

If there are only four or five tastes, how can there be so many different flavors? Flavors seem more varied than the four taste qualities suggest because we tend to include sensations of texture, temperature, smell, and even pain ("hot" chili peppers) along with taste. Smell is particularly important in determining flavor. Small bits of apple, potato, and onion "taste" almost exactly alike when the nose is plugged. So do gourmet jelly beans! It is probably no exaggeration to say that subjective flavor is half smell. This is why food loses its "taste" when you have a cold.

Taste buds (taste-receptor cells) are mainly located on the top side of the tongue, especially around the edges. However, a few are found elsewhere inside the mouth (❖Fig. 6.27). As food is chewed, it dissolves and enters the taste buds, where it sets off nerve impulses to the brain. Much like smell, sweet and bitter tastes appear to be based on a lock-and-key match between molecules and intricately shaped receptors. Saltiness and sourness, however, are triggered by a direct flow of charged atoms into the tips of taste cells.

People seem to have very different tastes. Why is that? Some differences are genetic. The chemical phenylthiocarbamide (FEEN-il-thi-oh-CAR-bah-mide), or PTC, tastes bitter to about 70 percent of those tested and has no taste for the other 30 percent. More generally, taste sensitivity is related to how many taste buds you have on your tongue. Some people have as few as 500 taste buds; others have as many as 10,000. Those with many taste buds are "supertasters" who need only half as much sugar in their coffee to make it sweet (Pennisi, 1992). (See "Are You a Supertaster?")

The sense of taste also varies with age. Taste cells have a life of only several days. With aging, cell replacement slows down, so the sense of taste diminishes. That's why many foods you disliked in childhood may seem appetizing now. Children who will not eat broccoli, spinach, and liver may be having a very different taste experience than an adult. Aside from this fact, however, most taste preferences are acquired. Would you eat the coagulated secretion of the modified skin glands of a cow after it had undergone bacterial decomposition? If you would, you are a *cheese* fancier!

Pheromone *An airborne chemical signal.*
Vomeronasal organ *A sensory organ sensitive to pheromones.*
Taste bud *The receptor organ for taste.*

ARE YOU A SUPERTASTER?

Spicy foods? Some like it hot. Others breathe fire if a dish contains a tiny bit too much pepper. And what about sweets? One person's sumptuous delight is another's cloying goo. Clearly, all tongues are not created equal. To learn a little more about taste sensitivity, try the following tests, devised by Linda Bartoshuk and Laurie Lucchina of Yale University.

SWEET Place one-half cup of sugar in a measuring cup and add enough water to make one cup of solution. Rinse your mouth with plain water. Use a cotton swab dipped in the sugar solution to coat the front half of your tongue, including the tip. Wait a few seconds and rate the sensation of sweetness according to the taste scale.

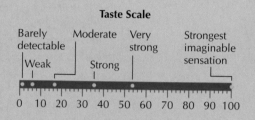

Taste Scale

SPICY Add one teaspoon of Tabasco sauce to one cup of water. Coat one-half inch of your tongue, starting at the tip. Keep your tongue outside your mouth until the burning sensation peaks. Rate the sensation of "heat" you feel on the scale.

RESULTS ◆Table 6.3 shows typical ratings for nontasters and supertasters. Most people, of course, fall in between these extremes. About 1 in 4 is a supertaster.

Supertasters tend to have stronger tastes for sweet, bitter, and irritants such as alcohol and capsaicin (the chemical that makes chilies hot). Women are more often supertasters. Nontasters tend to prefer sweets and fatty foods, which may be why supertasters tend to be slimmer than nontasters. (Sources: Bartoshuk, Duffy, & Miller, 1994; Brownlee, 1997.)

◆ **TABLE 6.3** Average Taste Test Ratings

	NONTASTER	SUPERTASTER
Sweet	32	56
Spicy	31	64

KNOWLEDGE BUILDER
HEARING, SMELL, AND TASTE

RELATE

Close your eyes and listen to the sounds around you. As you do, try to mentally trace the events necessary to convert vibrations in the air into the sounds you are hearing. Review the discussion of hearing if you leave out any steps.

What is your favorite food odor? What is your favorite taste? Can you explain how you are able to sense the aroma and taste of foods?

LEARNING CHECK

1. The frequency of a sound wave corresponds to how loud it is. T or F?

2. Which of the following is not a part of the cochlea?
   a. ossicles b. pinna c. tympanic membrane d. all of the above

3. Which of the following is *not* important for the transduction of sound?
   a. pinna b. ossicles c. phosphenes d. oval window e. hair cells

4. According to the place theory of hearing, higher tones register most strongly near the base of the cochlea. T or F?

5. Nerve deafness occurs when the auditory ossicles are damaged. T or F?

6. Daily exposure to sounds with a loudness of _____ decibels may cause permanent hearing loss.

7. Cochlear implants have been used primarily to overcome
   a. conduction deafness b. stimulation deafness c. nerve deafness d. tinnitus

8. Olfaction appears to be at least partially explained by the _____ _____ _____ theory of molecule shapes and receptor sites.

9. From the standpoint of survival, we are fortunate that we are least sensitive to bitter tastes. T or F?

CRITICAL THINKING

10. Why do you think your voice sounds so different when you hear a tape recording of your speech?

11. Smell and hearing differ from vision in a way that may aid survival. What is it?

Answers:

1. F 2. d 3. c 4. T 5. F 6. 85 7. c 8. lock and key 9. F 10. The answer lies in another question: How else might vibrations from the voice reach the cochlea? Other people hear your voice only as it is carried through the air. You hear not only that sound but also vibrations conducted by the bones of your skull. 11. Both smell and hearing can detect stimuli (including signals of approaching danger) around corners, behind objects, and behind the head.

THE SOMESTHETIC SENSES—FLYING BY THE SEAT OF YOUR PANTS

A gymnast "flying" through a routine on the uneven bars may rely as much on the **somesthetic senses** as on vision (*soma* means

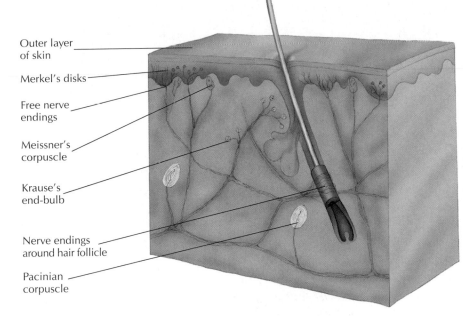

Outer layer of skin

Merkel's disks

Free nerve endings

Meissner's corpuscle

Krause's end-bulb

Nerve endings around hair follicle

Pacinian corpuscle

❖ **FIGURE 6.28** *The skin senses include touch, pressure, pain, cold, and warmth. This drawing shows different forms the skin receptors can take. Other shapes were once recognized, but most turned out to be variations of the shapes shown here. The only clearly specialized receptor is the Pacinian corpuscle, which is highly sensitive to pressure. Free nerve endings are receptors for pain and any of the other sensations. For reasons that are not clear, cold is sensed near the surface of the skin, and warmth is sensed deeper (Carlson, 1994).*

"body," *esthetic* means "feel"). Even the most routine activities, such as walking, running, or passing a sobriety test, would be impossible without somesthetic information from the body.

What are the somesthetic senses? Somesthetic sensitivity includes the **skin senses** (touch), the **kinesthetic senses** (receptors in muscles and joints that detect body position and movement), and the **vestibular senses** (receptors in the inner ear for balance, gravity, and acceleration). (The vestibular senses also contribute to motion sickness, as discussed in this chapter's "A Step Beyond" section.) Because of their importance, let us focus on the skin senses.

Skin Senses

It's difficult to imagine what life would be like without the sense of touch, but the plight of Ian Waterman gives a hint. After an illness, Waterman permanently lost all feeling below his neck. Now, in order to know what position his body is in, he has to be able to see it. If he closes his eyes, he can't move. If the lights go out in a room, he's in big trouble (Cole, 1995).

Skin receptors produce at least five different sensations: *light touch, pressure, pain, cold,* and *warmth.* Receptors with particular shapes appear to specialize somewhat in various sensations (❖Fig. 6.28). However, the surface of the eye, which has only free nerve endings, can produce all five sensations (Carlson, 1994). Altogether, the skin has about 200,000 nerve endings for temperature, 500,000 for touch and pressure, and 3 million for pain.

Does the number of receptors in an area of skin relate to its sensitivity? Yes. Your skin could be "mapped" by applying heat, cold, touch, pressure, or pain to points all over your body. Such testing would show that the number of skin receptors varies and that sensitivity generally matches the number of receptors in a given area. As a rough-and-ready illustration, try this two-point touch test:

The density of touch receptors on various body areas can be checked by having a friend apply two pencil points to the skin with varying distances between them. Without looking, you should respond "one" or "two" each time. Record the distance between the pencils each time you feel two points.

You should find that two points are recognizable when they are 1/10 inch apart on the fingertips, 1/4 inch on the nose, and 3 inches at the middle of the back. Generally speaking, important areas such as the lips, tongue, face, hands, and genitals have a higher density of receptors.

PAIN *There are many more pain receptors than other kinds. Why is pain so heavily represented, and does the concentration of pain receptors also vary?* Like the other skin senses, pain receptors vary in their distribution. An average of about 232 pain points per square centimeter are found behind the knee, 184 per centimeter on the buttocks (an area preferred by many parents for spankings), 60 on the pad of the thumb, and 44 on the tip of the nose. (Is it better, then, to be pinched on the nose than behind the knee? It depends on what you like!)

Pain fibers are also found in the internal organs. Stimulation of these fibers causes **visceral pain.** Curiously, visceral pain is often felt on the surface of the body, at a site some distance

Somesthetic sense *Sensations produced by the skin, muscles, joints, viscera, and organs of balance.*
Skin senses *The senses of touch, pressure, pain, heat, and cold.*
Kinesthetic senses *The senses of body movement and positioning.*
Vestibular senses *The senses of balance, position in space, and acceleration.*
Skin receptors *Sensory organs for touch, pressure, pain, cold, and warmth.*
Visceral pain *Pain originating in the internal organs.*

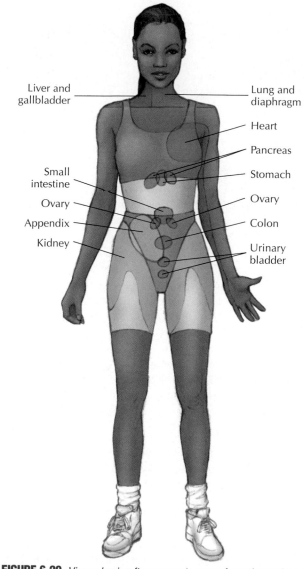

Liver and gallbladder

Lung and diaphragm

Heart

Pancreas

Small intestine

Stomach

Ovary

Ovary

Appendix

Colon

Kidney

Urinary bladder

❖ **FIGURE 6.29** *Visceral pain often seems to come from the surface of the body, even though its true origin is internal. Referred pain is believed to result from the fact that pain fibers from internal organs enter the spinal cord at the same location as sensory fibers from the skin. Apparently, the brain misinterprets the visceral pain messages as impulses from the body's surface (Chiras, 1991).*

from the point of origin (Chiras, 1991). Experiences of this type are called **referred pain** (❖Fig. 6.29). For example, a person having a heart attack may feel pain in the left shoulder, arm, or even the little finger.

Pain from the skin, muscles, joints, and tendons is known as **somatic** (bodily) **pain.** Somatic pain carried by *large nerve fibers* is sharp, bright, and fast and seems to come from specific body areas. This is the body's **warning system.** Give yourself a small jab with a pin, and you will feel this type of pain. As you do this, notice that warning pain quickly disappears. Much as we may dislike warning pain, it is usually a signal that the body has been, or is about to be, damaged. Without warning pain, we would be unable to detect or prevent injury. Children who are born with a rare inherited in-

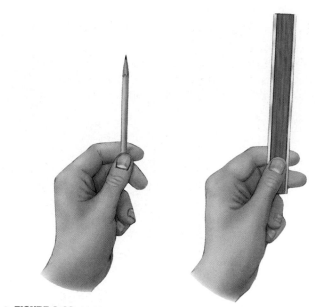

❖ **FIGURE 6.30** *Hold a variety of elongated objects upright between your fingertips. Close your eyes and move each object about. Your ability to estimate the size, length, shape, and orientation of each object will be quite accurate. (After Turvey, 1996.)*

sensitivity to pain repeatedly burn themselves, break bones, bite their tongues, and become ill without knowing it (Larner et al., 1994).

A second type of somatic pain is carried by *small nerve fibers.* This type is slower, nagging, aching, widespread, and very unpleasant. It gets worse if the pain stimulus is repeated. This is the body's **reminding system.** It reminds the brain that the body has been injured. A sad thing about the reminding system is that it often causes agony even when the reminder is useless, as in terminal cancer, or when pain continues after an injury has healed. Later in the chapter, we will return to pain to learn how it can be controlled. If you got carried away with the pin demonstration, maybe you should read ahead now!

DYNAMIC TOUCH   A carpenter swings a hammer with practiced precision. A juggler fluidly tosses and catches five balls. An ice hockey player embeds his stick in an opposing player's helmet. In sports and everyday life, touch is rarely static. Most skilled performances rely on **dynamic touch,** which combines sensations from skin receptors with kinesthetic information from the muscles and tendons.

Recent studies have shown that dynamic touch provides surprisingly detailed information about objects, such as their size and shape. (See ❖Figure 6.30.) How are we able to make such judgments? Psychologist M. T. Turvey has found that most bodily motions form an arc or a combination of arcs. Dynamic touch is largely a matter of sensing the *inertia* of objects as they move through these arcs.

The fact that dynamic touch is a reliable source of information is what makes it possible for us to use a wide range of tools, utensils, and objects as if they were extensions of our bodies (Turvey, 1996).

ADAPTATION, ATTENTION, AND GATING—TUNING IN AND TUNING OUT

Each of the senses we have described is continuously active. Even so, many sensory events never reach awareness. One reason for this is *sensory adaptation*, a second is *selective attention*, and a third is *sensory gating*. Let's see how these processes filter information.

SENSORY ADAPTATION   Think about walking into a house where fried fish, sauerkraut, and head cheese were prepared for dinner. (Some dinner!) You would probably pass out at the door, yet people who had been in the house for some time would be unaware of the food odors. Why? Because **sensory adaptation** (decreased response to a constant or unchanging stimulus) would occur.

Fortunately, the olfactory (smell) receptors are among the most quickly adapting. When exposed to a constant odor, they send fewer and fewer nerve impulses to the brain until the odor is no longer noticed. Adaptation to sensations of pressure from a wristwatch, waistband, ring, or glasses is based on the same principle. Sensory receptors generally respond best to *changes* in stimulation. As David Hubel says, "We need above all to know about changes; no one wants or needs to be reminded 16 hours a day that his shoes are on" (Hubel, 1979a).

If change is necessary to prevent sensory adaptation, why doesn't vision undergo adaptation like the sense of smell does? If you stare at something, it certainly doesn't go away.   The rods and cones, like other receptor cells, would respond less to a constant stimulus were it not for the fact that the eye normally makes thousands of tiny movements every minute. These movements are caused by **physiological nystagmus** (nis-TAG-mus: involuntary tremors of the eye muscles). Although they are too small to be seen, these movements shift visual images from one receptor cell to another.

Constant eye movement ensures that images always fall on fresh, unfatigued rods and cones. Evidence for this comes from fitting people with a contact lens that has a miniature slide projector attached to it (❖Fig. 6.31a). Because the projector follows the exact movements of the eye, an image can be stabilized on the retina. When this is done, projected geometric designs fade from view within a few seconds (Pritchard, 1961). You can get a similar effect by staring at ❖Figure 6.31b. The lighter circle does not form a distinct edge, so the retina adapts to the brightness difference. As it does, the circle gradually disappears.

SELECTIVE ATTENTION   The so-called seat-of-your-pants phenomenon provides another glimpse into how sensory systems work. As you sit reading this chapter, receptors for touch and pressure in the seat of your pants are sending nerve impulses to your brain. Although these sensations have been present all along, you were probably not aware of them until just now. The seat-of-your-pants phenomenon is an example of **selective attention** (voluntarily focusing on a specific sensory input). We are able to "tune in on" a single sensory message while excluding others. Another familiar example of this is the "cocktail

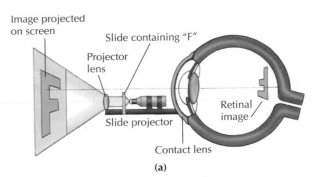

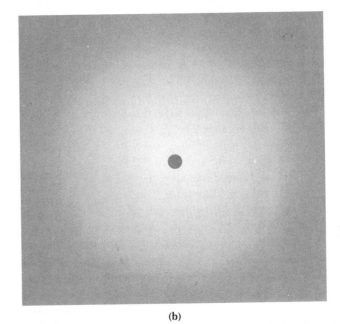

(b)

❖ **FIGURE 6.31** *Stabilized images. (a) Miniature slide projector attached to a contact lens moves each time the eye moves. As a result, the projected image disappears in a few seconds because it does not move on the retina. (b) A similar effect occurs when changes in brightness do not define a distinct edge. In this case, eye movements cannot prevent adaptation. Therefore, if you stare at the dot, the lighter area will disappear. (After Cornsweet, 1970.)*

party effect." When you are in a group of people, surrounded by voices, you can still select and attend to the voice of the person you are facing. Or if that person gets dull, you can eavesdrop on conversations all over the room. (Be sure to smile and

Referred pain *Pain felt in one part of the body that comes from another.*
Somatic pain *Pain from the skin, muscles, joints, and tendons.*
Warning system *Pain based on large nerve fibers; warns that bodily damage may be occurring.*
Reminding system *Pain based on small nerve fibers; reminds the brain that the body has been injured.*
Dynamic touch *Touch experienced when the body is in motion; a combination of sensations from skin receptors, muscles, and joints.*
Sensory adaptation *A decrease in sensory response to an unchanging stimulus.*
Physiological nystagmus *An involuntary tremor of the eye.*
Selective attention *Voluntarily focusing on a specific sensory input.*

nod your head occasionally!) The cocktail party effect is quite powerful. If you are listening to one person, another person nearby can talk *backward,* and you will not notice the strange speech (Wood & Cowan, 1995).

What makes that possible? Selective attention appears to be based on the ability of various brain structures to select and divert incoming sensory messages (Mangun, 1995). But what about messages that haven't reached the brain? Is it possible that some are blocked while others are allowed to pass? Evidence suggests that *sensory gates* control the flow of incoming nerve impulses in just this way. In particular, **sensory gating** refers to facilitating or blocking sensory messages in the spinal cord (Melzack, 1993; Melzack & Wall, 1996).

SENSORY GATING OF PAIN   A fascinating example of sensory gating is provided by Ronald Melzack and Patrick Wall, who study "pain gates" in the spinal cord (Melzack & Wall, 1996). Melzack and Wall noticed, as you may have, that one type of pain will sometimes cancel another. Their **gate control theory** suggests that pain messages from different nerve fibers pass through the same neural "gate" in the spinal cord. If the gate is "closed" by one pain message, other messages may not be able to pass through (Humphries, Johnson, & Long, 1996).

How is the gate closed? Messages carried by large, fast nerve fibers seem to close the spinal pain gate directly. Doing so can prevent slower, "reminding system" pain from reaching the brain. Pain clinics use this effect by applying a mild electrical current to the skin. Such stimulation, felt only as a mild tingling, can greatly reduce more agonizing pain (Long, 1991).

Messages from small, slow fibers seem to take a different route. After going through the pain gate, they pass on to a "central biasing system" in the brain. Under some circumstances, the brain then sends a message back down the spinal cord, closing the pain gates. (See ❖Figure 6.32.) Melzack and Wall believe that gate control theory explains the painkilling effects of acupuncture.

Acupuncture is the Chinese medical art of relieving pain and illness by inserting thin needles into the body. As the acupuncturist's needles are twirled, heated, or electrified, they activate small pain fibers. These relay through the biasing system to close the gates to intense or chronic pain (Melzack & Wall, 1996). Studies have shown that acupuncture produces short-term pain relief for 50 to 80 percent of patients tested (Ernst, 1994; Murray, 1995).

Acupuncture has an interesting side effect not predicted by sensory gating. People given acupuncture often report feelings of light-headedness, relaxation, or euphoria. How are these feelings explained? The answer seems to lie in the body's ability to produce opiate-like chemicals. To combat pain, the brain causes the pituitary gland to release a painkilling chemical called **beta-endorphin** (BAY-tah-en-DOR-fin: from *endo,* "within," and *orphin,* "opiate"). Chemically, beta-endorphin is quite similar to morphine.

Receptor sites for endorphins are found in large numbers in the limbic system and other brain areas associated with pleasure, pain, and emotion. Both acupuncture and electrical stimulation cause a buildup of endorphins in the brain. In other words, the nervous system makes its own "drugs" to block pain.

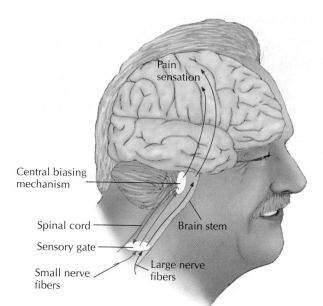

❖ **FIGURE 6.32** *Diagram of a sensory gate for pain. A series of pain impulses going through the gate may prevent other pain messages from passing through. Or pain messages may relay through a "central biasing mechanism" that exerts control over the gate, closing it to other impulses.*

Actually, this ties in nicely with the idea of pain gates. The central biasing system, which closes pain gates in the spinal cord, is highly sensitive to morphine and other opiate painkillers (Melzack & Wall, 1996).

The discovery of endorphins may make it possible to explain some puzzling phenomena. For example, the painkilling effect of placebos (fake pills or injections) appears to be based on a rise in beta-endorphin levels (Lipman et al., 1990). A release of endorphins also seems to underlie "runner's high," masochism, acupuncture, and the euphoria sometimes associated with childbirth and painful initiation rites. In each case, pain and stress cause the release of endorphins. These, in turn, induce feelings of pleasure or euphoria similar to morphine intoxication (Kruger & Liebeskind, 1984; Ulett, 1992).

The "high" often felt by long-distance runners serves as a good example of the endorphin effect. In one experiment, subjects were tested for pain tolerance. After running 1 mile, each was tested again. In the second test, all could withstand pain about 70 percent longer than before. The runners were then given naloxone, a drug that blocks the effects of endorphins. Following another 1-mile run, the subjects were tested again. This time they had lost their earlier protection from pain (Haier et al., 1988). A similar effect occurs with athletes, who temporarily become less sensitive to pain during competition (Sternberg et al., 1998). People who say they are "addicted" to running or other sports may be closer to the truth than they realize. More important, we may at last have an explanation for those hardy souls who take hot saunas followed by cold showers!

CONCLUSION AND A LOOK AHEAD   The senses supply raw data to the brain, but the information remains mostly meaningless until it is interpreted. It's as if the senses provide only the jumbled

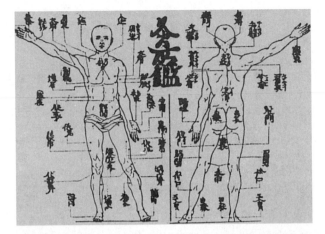

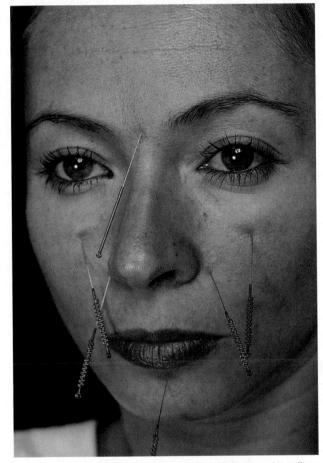

(Top) An acupuncturist's chart. **(Bottom)** Thin stainless steel needles are inserted into areas defined by the chart. Modern research has begun to explain the painkilling effects of acupuncture (see text). Acupuncture's claimed ability to cure diseases is more debatable.

RELATE

Stand on one foot with your eyes closed. Now touch the tip of your nose with your index finger. Which of the somesthetic senses did you use to perform this feat?

As you sit reading this book, which sensory inputs have undergone adaptation? What new inputs can you become aware of by shifting your focus of attention?

LEARNING CHECK

1. Which of the following is a somesthetic sense?
   a. gustation *b.* olfaction *c.* rarefaction *d.* kinesthesis

2. An ability to sense the inertia of objects as we move them through space is the basis for _____ _____.

3. Pain that originates in the internal organs is sometimes felt on the surface of the body as "referred pain." T or F?

4. Warning pain is carried by _____ nerve fibers.

5. Sensory adaptation refers to an increase in sensory response that accompanies a constant or unchanging stimulus. T or F?

6. The brain-centered ability to influence what sensations we will receive is called
   a. sensory gating *b.* central adaptation *c.* selective attention *d.* sensory biasing

7. The painkilling effects of acupuncture appear to result from _____ _____ and the release of beta-endorphin.

CRITICAL THINKING

8. What special precautions would you have to take to test the ability of acupuncture to reduce pain?

9. In a very real sense, we all live slightly in the past. How could that be true?

Answers:

1. *d* 2. dynamic touch 3. T 4. large 5. F 6. *c* 7. sensory gating 8. At the very least, you would have to control for the placebo effect by giving fake acupuncture to control group members. However, a true double-blind study would be difficult to do. Acupuncturists would always know if they were giving a placebo treatment or the real thing, which means they might unconsciously influence subjects. 9. For all of the senses, it takes a split second for sensory receptors to sense a change in external stimuli and for a neural message to arrive at the brain. Therefore, by the time we are aware of an event, such as a very brief flash of light, it is already over.

---

pieces of a complex puzzle. In the next chapter, we will explore some perceptual processes that help us put the puzzle together.

A variety of psychological factors affect the severity of pain. Because you may not want to try acupuncture or electrical stimulation to control everyday pain, the following "Psychology in Action" section describes several practical ways to reduce pain. Before we turn to this useful topic, here's a chance to rehearse what you've learned.

Sensory gating *Alteration of sensory messages in the spinal cord.*
Gate control theory *Proposes that pain messages pass through neural "gates" in the spinal cord.*
Acupuncture *Chinese medical art of relieving pain and illness by inserting thin needles into the body.*
Beta-endorphin *A natural, painkilling brain chemical similar to morphine.*

psychology in action

CONTROLLING PAIN—THIS WON'T HURT A BIT

There are many indications that pain may be controlled psychologically. In India, fakirs pierce their cheeks with needles or sit on beds of spikes. In other cultures, people endure tattooing, stretching, cutting, burning, and the like, with little apparent pain. How is such insensitivity achieved? There is no evidence that these people lack normal pain responses. Very likely the answer lies in four factors that anyone can use to alter the amount of pain felt in a particular situation: (1) anxiety, (2) control, (3) attention, and (4) interpretation.

ANXIETY The basic sensory message of pain can be separated from emotional reactions to it. Fear or high levels of anxiety almost always increase pain. (**Anxiety** is a feeling of apprehension or uneasiness similar to fear but based on an unclear threat.) A dramatic reversal of this effect is the surprising lack of pain displayed by soldiers wounded in battle. Being excused from further combat apparently produces a flood of relief. This emotional state leaves many soldiers insensitive to wounds that would agonize a civilian (Melzack & Wall, 1996).

CONTROL If you can regulate a painful stimulus, you have **control** over it. A moment's reflection should convince you that the most upsetting pain is that over which you have no control. Loss of control seems to increase pain by increasing anxiety and emotional distress. People who are allowed to regulate,

avoid, or control a painful stimulus suffer less. In general, the more control one *feels* over a painful stimulus, the less pain experienced (Kruger & Liebeskind, 1984; Wells, 1994).

ATTENTION Distraction can also radically reduce pain. As you'll recall, **attention** refers to voluntarily focusing on a specific sensory input. Pain, even though it is highly persistent, can be selectively "tuned out" (at least partially), just like any other sensation. Subjects in one experiment who were exposed to intense pain experienced the greatest relief when they were distracted by the task of watching for signal lights to come on (Johnson et al., 1998).

In another experiment, pain was lessened when subjects concentrated on trying to name all their high school courses and teachers (Ahles et al., 1983). For the same reason, you may have temporarily forgotten about a toothache or similar pain while absorbed in a movie or book. Concentrating on pleasant, soothing images can be especially helpful (Fernandez & Turk, 1989). Instead of listening to the whir of a dentist's drill, for example, you might imagine that you are lying in the sun at a beach, listening to the roar of the surf. At home, music can be a good distracter from chronic pain (Good, 1995; Michel & Chesky, 1995).

INTERPRETATION The meaning or **interpretation** given a painful stimulus also affects pain (Keefe, 1982). For example, if you give a child a swat on the behind while playing, you'll probably get a burst of laughter. Yet the same swat given as punishment may bring tears (Bresler & Trubo, 1979). The effects of interpretation have also been demonstrated in the lab (Devine & Spanos, 1990). For example, in one experiment it was found that thinking of pain as pleasurable (denying the pain) greatly increased pain tolerance (Neufeld, 1970). Another found that people who believed a painful procedure had health benefits felt less pain during the procedure (Staats et al., 1998).

Coping with Pain

How can these facts be applied? In a sense, they have already been applied to childbirth. **Prepared childbirth training,** which promotes birth with a minimum of drugs or painkillers, uses all four factors. To prepare for natural childbirth, the expectant mother learns in great detail what to anticipate at each stage of labor. This greatly relieves her fears and anxieties. During labor, she attends to sensations that mark her progress, and she adjusts her breathing accordingly. Her attention is shifted to sensations other than pain, resulting in less discomfort (Leventhal et al., 1989). Also, her positive attitude is maintained by use of the term *contractions* rather than *labor pains*. Finally, because of her months of preparation and her active participation, she feels *in control* of the situation.

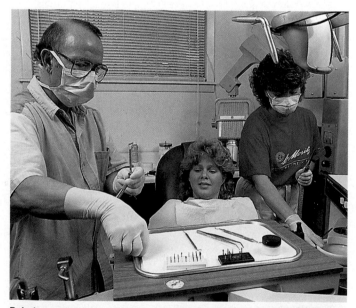

Pain is a complex experience. In addition to producing a physical sensation, pain messages activate areas of the brain associated with emotion. If you are fearful or anxious, the emotional part of pain will be magnified, and you will feel more intense pain. Reducing fear and anxiety is one of several things you can do to diminish pain.

Natural childbirth techniques reduce pain by an average of about 30 percent. Many women find this reduction quite helpful. However, it is important to remember that labor can produce very severe pain. A woman should not feel guilty if she needs painkillers during labor. Many women who have had prepared childbirth training still end up asking for an epidural block (Melzack, 1984).

With moderate pain, reduced anxiety, redirected attention, and added control can make quite a difference. In any situation where pain can be anticipated (a trip to the doctor, dentist, and so on), lowered anxiety may be achieved by making sure that you are *fully informed*. Be sure that everything that will happen or could happen to you is explained. Also, be sure to fully discuss any fears you have. If you are physically tense, the use of relaxation exercises can help lower your level of arousal. Relaxation methods involve tensing and then releasing muscles in various parts of the body. A typical technique is described in detail in the "Psychology in Action" section of Chapter 18. (The desensitization procedure described there may also help reduce anxiety.)

DISTRACTION AND REINTERPRETATION Some dentists are now equipped to help you shift attention away from pain. Patients are actively distracted with video games and headphones carrying music. In other situations, focusing on some external object may help you shift attention away from pain. Pick a tree outside a window, a design on the wall, or some other stimulus, and examine it in great detail. Prior practice in meditation can be a tremendous aid to such attention shifts. (Meditation techniques are described in Chapter 16.) Research suggests that distraction of this type works best for mild or brief pain. For chronic or strong pain, reinterpretation is more effective (McCaul & Malott, 1984).

COUNTERIRRITATION *Is there any way to increase control over a painful stimulus?* Practically speaking, the choices may be limited. You may be able to arrange a signal with a doctor or dentist that will give you control over whether a painful procedure will continue. A second possibility is more unusual. Ronald Melzack's gate control theory of pain suggests that sending *mild* pain messages to the spinal cord and brain may effectively close the neurological gates to more severe or unpredictable pain. Medical texts have long recognized this effect. Physicians have found that intense surface stimulation of the skin can control pain from other parts of the body. Likewise, a brief, mildly painful stimulus can relieve more severe pain. Such procedures, known as **counterirritation,** are evident in some of the oldest techniques used to control pain: applying ice packs, hot-water bottles, mustard packs, vibration, or massage to other parts of the body (Kakigi et al., 1993; Melzack, 1974).

These facts suggest a way to minimize pain that is based on increased control, counterirritation, and the release of endorphins. If you pinch yourself, you can easily *create and endure* pain equal to that produced by many medical procedures (re-

BRIDGES

In addition to reducing pain, prepared childbirth has other benefits.

See Chapter 5, pages 130–131.

ceiving an injection, having a tooth drilled, and so on). The pain doesn't seem too bad because you have control over it, and it is predictable.

This fact can be used to *mask* one pain with a second painful stimulus that is under your control. For instance, if you are having a tooth filled, try pinching yourself or digging a fingernail into a knuckle while the dentist is working. Focus your attention on the pain you are creating, and increase its intensity whenever the dentist's work becomes more painful. This suggestion may not work for you, but casual observation suggests that it can be a useful technique for controlling pain in some circumstances. Generations of children have used it to take the edge off a spanking.

KNOWLEDGE BUILDER

PAIN CONTROL

RELATE

Think about a strategy you have used for reducing pain at the doctor's office, dentist's, or some other painful situation. Did you alter anxiety, control, attention, or interpretation? Can you think of any ways in which you have used counterirritation to lessen pain?

LEARNING CHECK

1. Like heightened anxiety, increased control tends to increase subjective pain. T or F?

2. In one experiment, subjects given the task of watching signal lights experienced less pain than subjects who paid attention to the pain stimulus. T or F?

3. Imagining a pleasant experience can be an effective way of reducing pain in some situations. T or F?

4. The concept of counterirritation holds that relaxation and desensitization are key elements of pain control. T or F?

CRITICAL THINKING

5. What measures would you take to ensure that an experiment involving pain is ethical?

Answers:

1. F 2. T 3. T 4. F 5. Experiments that cause pain must be handled with care and sensitivity. Participation must be voluntary, the source of pain must be noninjurious, and subjects must be allowed to quit at any time.

Anxiety *Apprehension or uneasiness similar to fear but based on an unclear threat.*
Control *Where pain is concerned, control refers to an ability to regulate the pain stimulus.*
Attention *Voluntarily focusing on a specific sensory input.*
Interpretation *Where pain is concerned, the meaning given to a stimulus.*
Prepared childbirth training *System for preparing women and their partners for childbirth.*
Counterirritation *Using mild pain to block more intense or long-lasting pain.*

a step beyond

Focus: How is the sense of balance related to motion sickness?

During space flights, astronauts are often shown playfully enjoying the acrobatics made possible by weightlessness. But adapting to life in space is not as easy or pleasant as such images imply. Indeed, if you were to ride into space, it is about 70 percent likely that your first experience in orbit would be throwing up (Davis et al., 1988). More than half of all astronauts have suffered from **space adaptation syndrome,** or "space sickness."

SPACE SICKNESS *Is space sickness like seasickness?* Space sickness is a type of motion sickness. Like seasickness, car sickness, and airsickness, its first signs are dizziness and mild disorientation. However, space sickness usually does not produce the pallor, "cold sweating," and nausea so common on earth. In most types of motion sickness, these signs warn that vomiting is about to occur. But in space, vomiting is usually sudden and unexpected. Seeing another astronaut drift by upside down or viewing the earth at an odd angle is often all it takes to trigger repeated vomiting. Space sickness is especially intense because weightlessness drastically alters sensations the brain receives from the head, muscles, and joints (Lackner & DiZio, 1993).

The Vestibular System

What causes motion sickness? Motion sickness is directly related to the vestibular system (❖Fig. 6.33). Fluid-filled sacs called **otolith organs** (OH-toe-lith) are sensitive to movement, acceleration, and gravity. The otolith organs contain tiny crystals in a soft, gelatin-like mass. The tug of gravity or rapid head movements can cause the mass to shift. This, in turn, stimulates hair-like receptor cells, allowing us to sense gravity and movement through space.

Three fluid-filled tubes called the **semicircular canals** are the sensory organs for balance. If you could climb inside these tubes, you would find that head movements cause the fluid to swirl about. As the fluid moves, it bends a small "flap," or "float," called the **crista,** that detects movement in the semicircular canals. A crista can be found within each **ampulla** (am-PULL-ah), a wider part of the canal. The bending of each crista again stimulates hair cells and signals head rotation.

MOTION SICKNESS The most widely accepted explanation of motion sickness is the **sensory conflict theory.** According to this theory, dizziness and nausea occur when sensations from the vestibular system fail to match information received from the eyes and body (Warwick-Evans et al., 1998).

You can create an example of sensory conflict by turning around repeatedly until you become dizzy. Doing so sets the fluid spinning in the semicircular canals. When you stop, the fluid continues to swirl about, so the brain thinks your head

Weightlessness presents astronauts with a real challenge in sensory adaptation.

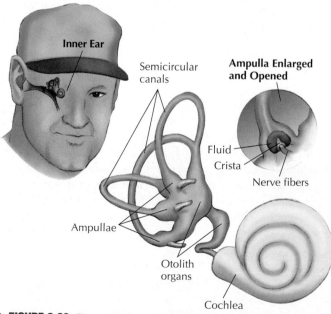

❖ **FIGURE 6.33** *The vestibular system. (See text for explanation.)*

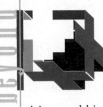
is still moving. This causes the eyes to move involuntarily and makes the world seem like it is still spinning.

On solid ground, information from the vestibular system, vision, and kinesthesis usually matches. However, in a heaving, pitching boat, car, or airplane, a serious mismatch can occur—causing disorientation and heaving of another kind.

Why would sensory conflict cause nausea? According to the most popular theory, you can blame (or thank) evolution. Many poisons disturb the coordination of messages from the vestibular system, vision, and the body. Therefore, we may have evolved so that we react to sensory conflict by vomiting to expel poison. The value of this reaction, however, may be of little comfort to anyone who has ever been "green" and miserable with motion sickness.

In space, sensory conflict can be especially intense. During weightlessness, merely pulling on one's shoes can result in a backward somersault. Under such conditions, the otolith organs send unexpected signals to the brain, and head movements are no longer confirmed by the semicircular canals. Few of the messages the brain receives from the vestibular system and kinesthetic receptors agree with a lifetime of past experience (Yardley, 1992).

How long does it take to adapt to weightlessness? Space sickness usually disappears in 2 or 3 days. Recent research suggests

BRIDGES

Space habitats are difficult living environments in ways that go far beyond weightlessness.

See Appendix A, pages A-26–A-28, for more information about life in space.

that this adaptation occurs because astronauts shift to using visual cues instead of vestibular information. Later, this same shift can cause "earth sickness." Immediately after returning to earth (especially after very long missions), some astronauts have experienced dizziness and nausea. All had considerable difficulty in standing with their eyes closed for the first day or two (Von Baumgarten et al., 1984).

How to Minimize Motion Sickness

Researchers trying to prevent space sickness have learned a great deal about what helps and what doesn't. The following points may be of some aid to you here on earth (Jackson, 1994).

- Medical treatment for space sickness has concentrated on drugs. The most successful so far is scopolamine, which is available by prescription. Nonprescription "seasickness" pills also offer some protection. Alcohol and other intoxicating drugs usually make motion sickness worse.
- Russian cosmonauts have had some success with a system that limits head movements for the first 2 days in space. In a boat, car, or airplane, it helps to move your head as little as possible (Jackson, 1994). You may even want to place a towel around your neck to restrict head movement. (If it doesn't help, you may soon find another use for it.)
- To minimize sensory conflict, stay out of the cabin on boats. In cars and airplanes, try closing your eyes. Or as an alternative, fixate your eyes on an unmoving point (such as the horizon) or look above the horizon at the unmoving sky (Harm et al., 1998; Stern et al., 1990).
- If possible, you should lie down. The otoliths are less sensitive to vertical movements when you are horizontal, and your head will move less.
- Anxiety intensifies motion sickness. Some of the astronauts have had success at learning to focus their attention on pleasant, distracting thoughts or calming images.
- If you're beginning to feel queasy, be sure to breathe slowly and deeply. Slow, deep breathing can greatly reduce nausea and motion sickness (Jokerst et al., 1999).
- Relaxation helps minimize motion sickness. You may find it valuable to learn relaxation exercises that you can use when needed (Jackson, 1994). (Relaxation methods are described in Chapter 18 of this book.)

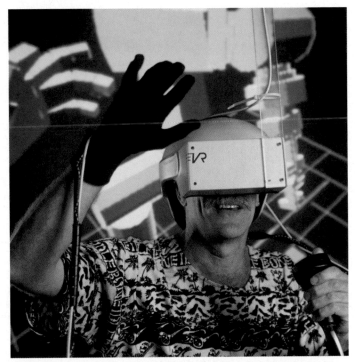

Many people become nauseated the first time they experience virtual reality. Why? Because virtual reality also creates a sensory conflict: Computer-generated visual images change as if the viewer's body is in motion, but the vestibular system tells viewers that they are standing still. The result? The scenery may not be real, but the nausea is.

Space adaptation syndrome *Motion sickness caused by weightlessness.*
Otolith organs *Vestibular structures sensitive to movement, acceleration, and gravity.*
Semicircular canals *Fluid-filled canals containing the sensory organs for balance.*
Crista *A floating structure that responds to fluid movement within the semicircular canals.*
Ampulla *An enlarged area in a semicircular canal containing a crista.*
Sensory conflict theory *Explains motion sickness as the result of a mismatch between information from vision, the vestibular system, and kinesthesis.*

Space sickness is only one of the behavioral challenges of space travel. In fact, the long-term effects of space flight are still largely unknown. Although space missions seem relatively routine, astronauts remain true pioneers in a strange and alien sensory environment.

CONCLUSION: Like other types of motion sickness, space sickness occurs because sensations from the vestibular system conflict with information from the eyes and body. Minimizing such conflicts can reduce susceptibility to motion sickness.

KNOWLEDGE BUILDER
THE VESTIBULAR SYSTEM AND MOTION SICKNESS

RELATE

Imagine you are on a boat ride with a friend who starts to feel queasy. Can you explain to your friend what causes motion sickness and what she or he can do to prevent it?

LEARNING CHECK

1. At least 170 of every 200 astronauts have suffered from space sickness. T or F?

2. Head movements are detected primarily in the semicircular canals, and gravity by the otolith organs. T or F?

3. Sensory conflict theory appears to explain space sickness, but it does not seem to apply to other types of motion sickness. T or F?

4. The drug amphetamine has been used successfully to prevent motion sickness. T or F?

CRITICAL THINKING

5. Drivers are less likely to become carsick than passengers are. Why do you think drivers and passengers differ in susceptibility to motion sickness?

Answers:

1. F 2. T 3. F 4. F 5. Drivers experience less sensory conflict because they control the car's motion. This allows them to anticipate the car's movements and to coordinate their head and eye movements with those of the car.

CHAPTER IN REVIEW

In general, how do sensory systems function?

- Sensory organs transduce physical energies into nerve impulses.
- Because of selectivity, limited sensitivity, feature detection, and coding patterns, the senses act as data reduction systems.
- Sensory response can be partially understood in terms of localization of function in the brain.

What are the limits of our sensory sensitivity?

- The minimum amount of physical energy necessary to produce a sensation defines the absolute threshold. The amount of change necessary to produce a just noticeable difference in a stimulus defines a difference threshold. The study of thresholds and related topics is called *psychophysics*.
- Threatening or anxiety-provoking stimuli may raise the threshold for recognition, an effect called *perceptual defense*.
- Any stimulus below the level of conscious awareness is said to be subliminal. There is evidence that subliminal perception occurs, but subliminal advertising is largely ineffective.

How is vision accomplished?

- The visible spectrum consists of electromagnetic radiation in a narrow range.
- The eye is a visual system, not a photographic one. Individual cells in the visual cortex of the brain act as feature detectors to analyze visual information.
- Four common visual defects are myopia (nearsightedness), hyperopia (farsightedness), presbyopia (loss of accommodation), and astigmatism.
- The rods and cones are photoreceptors making up the retina of the eye.
- The rods specialize in night vision, seeing black and white, and motion detection.
- The cones, found exclusively in the fovea and otherwise toward the middle of the eye, specialize in color vision, acuity, and daylight vision.
- Much peripheral vision is supplied by the rods.

How do we perceive colors?

- The rods and cones differ in color sensitivity. *Yellowish green* is brightest for cones, and *blue-green* for the rods (although they will see it as colorless). Color vision is explained by the trichromatic theory in the retina and by the opponent-process theory in the visual system beyond the eyes.
- Total color blindness is rare, but 8 percent of males and 1 percent of females are red-green color-blind or color-weak. Color blindness is a sex-linked trait carried on the X chromosome. The Ishihara test is used to detect color blindness.
- Dark adaptation, an increase in sensitivity to light, is caused by increased concentration of visual pigments in both the rods and the cones, but mainly by rhodopsin recombining in the rods. Vitamin A deficiencies may cause night blindness.

What are the mechanisms of hearing?

- Sound waves are the stimulus for hearing. They are transduced by the eardrum, auditory ossicles, oval window, cochlea, and ultimately, the hair cells.
- The frequency theory and place theory of hearing together explain how pitch is sensed.
- Three basic types of deafness are nerve deafness, conduction deafness, and stimulation deafness.

How do the chemical senses operate?

- Olfaction (smell) and gustation (taste) are chemical senses responsive to airborne or liquefied molecules. It is also suspected that humans are sensitive to pheromones, although the evidence for this sense remains preliminary.
- The lock and key theory partially explains smell. In addition, the location of the olfactory receptors in the nose helps identify various scents.
- Sweet and bitter tastes are based on a lock-and-key coding of molecule shapes. Salty and sour tastes are triggered by a direct flow of ions into taste receptors.

What are the somesthetic senses, and why are they important?

- The somesthetic senses include the skin senses, vestibular senses, and kinesthetic senses (receptors that detect muscle and joint positioning).
- The skin senses include touch, pressure, pain, cold, and warmth. Sensitivity to each is related to the number of receptors found in an area of skin.
- Distinctions can be made among various types of pain, including visceral pain, somatic pain, referred pain, warning system pain, and reminding system pain.

Why are we more aware of some sensations than others?

- Incoming sensations are affected by sensory adaptation (a reduction in the number of nerve impulses sent), by selective attention (selection and diversion of messages in the brain), and by sensory gating (blocking or alteration of messages flowing toward the brain).
- Selective gating of pain messages apparently takes place in the spinal cord. Gate control theory proposes an explanation for many pain phenomena.

How can pain be reduced in everyday situations?

- Pain is greatly affected by anxiety, attention, control over the stimulus, the interpretation placed on an experience, and counterirritation. Pain can therefore be reduced by controlling these factors.

How is the sense of balance related to motion sickness?

- Various forms of motion sickness are related to messages received from the vestibular system, which senses gravity and movement.
- According to sensory conflict theory, motion sickness is caused by a mismatch of visual, kinesthetic, and vestibular sensations. Motion sickness can be avoided by minimizing sensory conflict.

PSYCHOLOGY ON THE NET

- **HEARNET** A page that promotes ear protection for rock musicians. http://www.hearnet.com/text/mainframe.html
- **How We See** A tutorial on the basic processes of vision. http://www.gene.com/ae/AE/AEC/CC/vision_background.html
- **Smell and Taste Disorders FAQ** Questions and answers about smell and taste disorders. http://www.nih.gov/nidcd/health/st.htm
- **Vestibular Disorders Association** Provides links to sites concerned with vestibular problems. http://www.teleport.com/~veda/index.shtml

• • **InfoTrac® College Edition** For recent articles related to pain control, use Key Words search for ANXIETY and COUNTERIRRITATION.

INTERACTIVE LEARNING

- ***PsychNow!*** 3a. Vision and hearing. 3b. Chemical and somesthetic senses.
- ***Psyk.trek*** 3a. Light and the eye. 3b. The retina. 3c. Vision and the brain. 3d. Perception of color. 3h. The sense of hearing.

CHAPTER 7

Perceiving the World

Chapter Survey

Theme: Perception is an active process; perceptual impressions are not always accurate representations of events.

▼ KEY QUESTIONS
● KEY TOPICS

▼ What are perceptual constancies, and what is their role in perception?

  ● Shape, size, and brightness constancy

▼ What basic principles do we use to group sensations into meaningful patterns?

  ● Gestalt principles of perceptual organization

▼ How is it possible to see depth and judge distance?

  ● Stereoscopic vision
  ● Physical and pictorial depth cues

▼ What effect does learning have on perception?

  ● Perceptual habits
  ● Adaptation level
  ● Perceptual illusions

▼ KEY QUESTIONS
● KEY TOPICS

▼ How is perception altered by attention, motives, values, and expectations?

  ● Selective attention and divided attention
  ● Habituation and the orientation response
  ● Perceptual expectancies

▼ How reliable are eyewitness reports?

  ● Perception and objectivity
  ● Enhancing perceptual accuracy

▼ Is extrasensory perception possible?

  ● Parapsychology
  ● A critique of psi research
  ● Stage ESP

MURDER!

THE FOLLOWING IS a true account. Only the degree of exaggeration has been changed for educational purposes.

I was in a supermarket when an 8-year-old girl suddenly came running around a corner. She looked back and screamed, "Stop! Stop! You're killing him! You're killing my father!" Naturally, I was interested! As I quickly retraced her path, I was greeted by a grisly scene. A man was stretched out on the floor with another man on top of him. The guy on top was huge and looked only half-human. He had his victim by the throat and was beating his head against the floor. There was blood everywhere. I decided to do the right thing. I ran.

By the time the store manager and I returned to the "scene of the crime," the police were just arriving. It took quite a while to sort things out, but here is what happened: The "guy on the bottom" had passed out and hit his head. That caused the cut (actually quite minor), which explained the "blood everywhere." The "guy on top" saw the first man fall and was trying to prevent him from further injuring himself. He was also loosening the man's collar.

If I had never returned, I would have sworn in court that I had seen a murder. The girl's description completely shaped my own perceptions. This perhaps is understandable. But I'll never forget the shock I felt when I met the "murderer"—the man I had seen a few moments before as huge, vicious, and horrible-looking. The man was not a stranger. He was a neighbor of mine. I had seen him dozens of times before. I know him by name. He is a rather small man.

In the last chapter, we discussed sensation, the process of bringing information into the nervous system. This chapter is about **perception,** or how we assemble sensations into meaningful patterns. As we perceive events, the brain actively selects, organizes, and integrates sensory information to construct a "picture" or model of the world. This process is so automatic that it can take a drastic misperception like mine to call attention to it.

Perception creates faces, melodies, works of art, illusions, and, on occasion, "murders" out of the raw material of sensation. Let's see how this takes place.

Gateways to Perception

PERCEPTION is an active process of assembling sensations into meaningful patterns that represent external events.

SIZE, SHAPE, AND BRIGHTNESS CONSTANCIES bring stability to our visual perceptions, which would otherwise seem distorted and erratic.

WE UNCONSCIOUSLY USE GESTALT PRINCIPLES to help us organize sensations into meaningful patterns.

OUR WONDROUS ABILITY TO PERCEIVE THREE-DIMENSIONAL SPACE is largely based on retinal disparity (differences between what the right and left eyes see).

DEPTH PERCEPTION also depends on a combination of bodily cues and pictorial cues that provide information about depth and distance.

PERCEPTION is greatly affected by learning, motives, values, attention, and expectations. Private perceptual experiences don't always accurately represent external events.

EYEWITNESSES frequently misperceive events—even important events such as crimes or accidents.

PERCEPTUAL ACCURACY AND OBJECTIVITY can be improved by conscious effort and an awareness of factors that contribute to erroneous perceptions.

SCIENTIFIC EVIDENCE CONCERNING THE EXISTENCE OF EXTRASENSORY PERCEPTION is mostly negative or inconclusive.

PERCEPTUAL CONSTANCIES—TAMING AN UNRULY WORLD

What would it be like to have your vision restored after a lifetime of blindness? In reality, a first look at the world can be disappointing. Newly sighted persons must *learn* to identify objects, to read clocks, numbers, and letters, and to judge sizes and distances (Senden, 1960). Indeed, learning to "see" can be quite frustrating.

Richard Gregory (1990) describes a cataract patient named Mr. S. B. who had been blind since birth. After an operation restored his sight at age 52, Mr. S. B. struggled to use his vision. At first, he could only judge distance in familiar situations. One day he was found crawling out of a hospital window to get a closer look at traffic on the street. It's easy to understand his curiosity, but he had to be restrained. His room was on the fourth floor!

Why would Mr. S. B. try to crawl out of a fourth-story window? Couldn't he at least tell distance from the size of the cars? No, because using size to judge distance requires familiarity with the appearance of objects. Try holding your left hand a few inches in front of your eyes and your right hand at arm's length. Your right hand should appear to be about half the size of your left hand. Still, you know your right hand did not suddenly shrink, because you have seen it at various distances countless times. We call this **size constancy:** The perceived size of an object remains the same, despite changes in the size of the image it casts on the retina. Even newborn ba-

Visual perception involves finding meaningful patterns in complex stimuli. If you look closely at this painting by the artist Yvaral, you will see that it is entirely made up of small, featureless squares. An infant or newly sighted person would see only a jumble of meaningless colors. But because the squares form a familiar pattern, you should easily see Marilyn Monroe's face. (Or is that Madonna?) ("Marilyn Numerisée," 1990, courtesy Circle Gallery.)

Almost everyone's family album has at least one photo like this. Extreme viewing angles can make maintaining size constancy difficult, even for familiar objects.

bies show some evidence of size constancy (Slater, Mattock, & Brown, 1990).

To perceive your hand accurately, you had to draw on past experience. Some perceptions are so basic they seem to be **native** (inborn). An example is the ability to see a line on a piece of paper. However, much perception is **empirical** (based on prior experience). For instance, Colin Turnbull (1961) tells of the time he took a Pygmy from the dense rain forests of Africa to the vast African plains. The Pygmy had never before seen objects at a great distance. Hence, the first time he saw a herd of buffalo in the distance, he thought it was a swarm of insects. Imagine his confusion when he was driven toward the animals. He concluded that he was being fooled by witchcraft because the "insects" seemed to grow into buffalo before his eyes.

Perhaps you, too, have also experienced the failure of size constancy in unfamiliar situations. When viewed from an airplane or the top of a skyscraper, cars, houses, and people no longer seem normal in size; instead, they begin to look like toys. Thus, we can summarize that size constancy, although innate, is also molded by experience.

In **shape constancy,** the perceived shape of an object is unaffected by changes in the shape of its retinal image. You can demonstrate shape constancy by looking at this page from directly overhead and then from an angle. Obviously, the page is rectangular, but most of the time the image that reaches your eye is distorted. Even though the book's image changes, your perception of its shape remains constant. (For additional examples, see ❖Figure 7.1.) In a movie theater, preserving shape con-

stancy is difficult if you sit in the front row or near the front and to the side. Nevertheless, most people are able to tolerate a fair amount of shape distortion, as long as all objects on the screen are similarly deformed (Cutting, 1987). On the highway, alcohol intoxication impairs size and shape constancy, adding to the accident rate among drunk drivers (Farrimond, 1990).

Let's say that you are outside in bright sunlight. Beside you is a friend who is wearing a gray skirt and a white blouse. Sud-

---

Perception *The mental process of organizing sensations into meaningful patterns.*
Size constancy *The perceived size of an object remains constant, despite changes in its retinal image.*
Native perception *A perceptual experience based on innate processes.*
Empirical perception *A perception strongly influenced by prior experience.*
Shape constancy *The perceived shape of an object is unaffected by changes in its retinal image.*

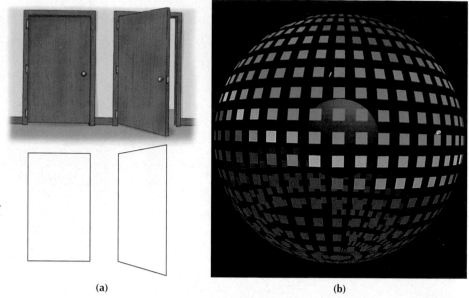

❖ **FIGURE 7.1** *Shape constancy. (a) When a door is open, its image actually forms a trapezoid. Shape constancy is indicated by the fact that it is still perceived as a rectangle. (b) With great effort, you may be able to see this design as a collection of flat shapes. However, if you maintain shape constancy, the distorted squares strongly suggest the surface of a sphere. (From "Spherescapes-1" by Scott Walter and Kevin McMahon, 1983.)*

(a)　　　　　　**(b)**

denly a cloud shades the sun. It might seem that the blouse would grow dimmer, but it still appears to be bright white. This happens because the blouse continues to reflect a larger *proportion* of light than nearby objects. **Brightness constancy** refers to the fact that the apparent brightness of an object stays the same under changing light conditions. However, this holds true only if the blouse and surrounding objects are all illuminated by the same amount of light. You could make an area on your friend's gray skirt look whiter than the shaded blouse by shining a bright spotlight on the skirt.

To summarize, the energy patterns reaching our senses are constantly changing, even when they come from the same object. Size, shape, and brightness constancy rescue us from a confusing world in which objects would seem to shrink and grow, change shape as if made of rubber, and light up or fade like neon lamps. Gaining these constancies was only one of the hurdles Mr. S. B. faced in learning to see. In the next section, we will consider some others.

PERCEPTUAL GROUPING—GETTING IT ALL TOGETHER

William James said, "To the infant the world is just a big, blooming, buzzing confusion." Like an infant, Mr. S. B. had to find meaning in his visual sensations. He was soon able to tell time from a large wall clock and to read block letters he had known only from touch. At a zoo, he recognized an elephant from descriptions he had heard. However, handwriting meant nothing to him for more than a year after he regained sight, and many objects were meaningless until he touched them. Thus, while Mr. S. B. had visual *sensations,* his ability to *perceive* remained limited.

FIGURE AND GROUND　*How are sensations organized into meaningful perceptions?*　The simplest organization involves grouping some sensations into an object, or figure, that stands out on

❖ **FIGURE 7.2** *A reversible figure-ground design. Do you see two faces in profile or a wineglass?*

a plainer background. **Figure-ground organization** is probably inborn, because it is the first perceptual ability to appear after cataract patients regain sight. In the brain, cells that process visual information respond more actively to figures than to backgrounds (Lamme, 1995).

In normal figure-ground perception, only one figure is seen. In **reversible figures,** however, figure and ground can be switched. In ❖Figure 7.2 it is equally possible to see either a wineglass figure on a dark background or two face profiles on a light background. As you shift from one pattern to the other, you should get a clear sense of what figure-ground organization means.

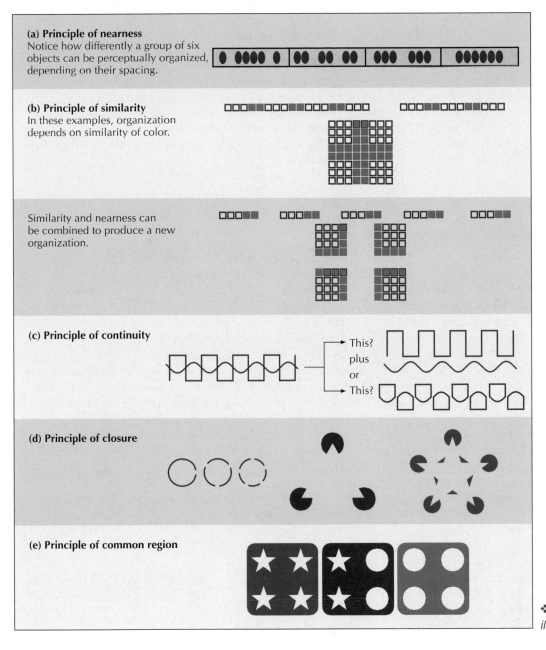

(a) Principle of nearness
Notice how differently a group of six objects can be perceptually organized, depending on their spacing.

(b) Principle of similarity
In these examples, organization depends on similarity of color.

Similarity and nearness can be combined to produce a new organization.

(c) Principle of continuity

This?
plus
or
This?

(d) Principle of closure

(e) Principle of common region

❖ **FIGURE 7.3** *Perceptual grouping illustrations.*

Gestalt Principles

What causes the formation of a figure? The Gestalt psychologists (see Chapter 1) studied this question in detail. Even if you were seeing for the first time, they concluded, a number of factors would bring some order to your perceptions (❖Fig. 7.3).

1. **Nearness.** All other things being equal, stimuli that are near each other tend to be grouped together (Kubovy & Holcombe, 1998). Thus, if three people stand near each other and a fourth person stands 10 feet away, the adjacent three will be seen as a group and the distant person as an outsider (see ❖Fig. 7.3a).
2. **Similarity.** "Birds of a feather flock together," and stimuli that are similar in size, shape, color, or form tend to be grouped together (see ❖Fig. 7.3b). Picture two bands marching side by side. If their uniforms are different colors,

the bands will be seen as two separate groups, not as one large group.
3. **Continuation, or continuity.** Perceptions tend toward simplicity and continuity. In ❖Figure 7.3c it is easier to visualize a wavy line on a squared-off line than it is to see a complex row of shapes.

Brightness constancy *The apparent (or relative) brightness of objects remains the same as long as they are illuminated by the same amount of light.*
Figure-ground organization *Part of a stimulus appears to stand out as an object (figure) against a less prominent background (ground).*
Reversible figure *A stimulus pattern in which figure-ground organization can be reversed.*

4. **Closure.** Closure refers to the tendency to *complete* a figure, so that it has a consistent overall form. Each of the drawings in ❖Figure 7.3d has one or more gaps, yet each is perceived as a recognizable figure. The "shapes" that appear in the two right drawings in ❖Figure 7.3d are **illusory figures** (implied shapes that are not actually bounded by an edge or an outline). Even young children see these shapes, despite knowing that they are "not really there." Illusory figures reveal that our tendency to form shapes—even with minimal cues—is powerful.

5. **Contiguity.** A principle that can't be shown in ❖Figure 7.3 is contiguity, or nearness in time *and* space. Contiguity is often responsible for the perception that one thing has *caused* another (Michotte, 1963). A psychologist friend of the author's demonstrates this principle in class by knocking on his head with one hand while knocking on a wooden table (out of sight) with the other. The knocking sound is perfectly timed with the movements of his visible hand. This leads to the irresistible perception that his head is made of wood.

USING PSYCHOLOGY

DESIGNING FOR HUMAN USE

Machines are of little value unless humans can operate them. A pocket calculator that is difficult to handle might just as well be a paperweight. An automobile design that blocks large areas of the driver's vision could be deadly. To adapt machines for human use, the **engineering psychologist** (human factors engineer) must make them *compatible* with our sensory and motor capacities (Howell, 1993). For example, *displays* must be easy to perceive, *controls* must be easy to use, and the tendency to make errors must be minimized (❖Fig. 7.4). (A **display** is any dial, screen, light, or other device used to provide information about a machine's activity to a human operator. A **control** is any knob, handle, button, lever, or other device used to alter the activity of a machine.)

Many of the machines we rely on each day were designed, in part, by human factors engineers. Some familiar examples include push-button telephones, "user-friendly" computers, home appliances, cameras, airplane controls, and traffic signals.

Psychologist Donald Norman (1994) refers to successful human factors engineering as **natural design.** Effective design makes use of perceptual signals that people understand naturally, without needing to learn them. An example is the row of vertical buttons in elevators. The buttons mimic the layout of the floors. This is simple, natural, and clear. Effective design also provides **feedback** (information about the effect of making a response). The audible click designed into many computer keyboards is a good example. As Norman points out, the cause of many accidents is not just "human error." The real culprit is poor design.

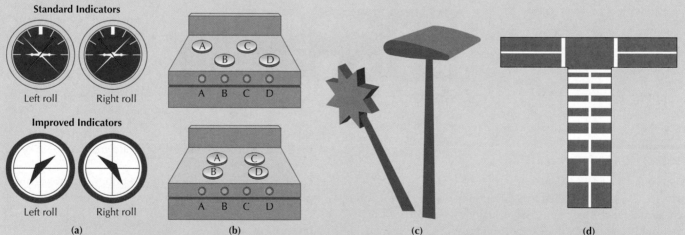

❖ **FIGURE 7.4** *Human factors engineering. (a) Early roll indicators in airplanes were perceptually confusing and difficult to read (top). Improved displays are clear even to nonpilots. Which would you prefer if you were flying an airplane in heavy fog? (b) Even on a stove, the placement of controls is important. During simulated emergencies, people made no errors in reaching for the controls on the top stove. In contrast, they erred 38 percent of the time with the bottom arrangement (Chapanis & Lindenbaum, 1959). (c) Sometimes the shape of a control is used to indicate its function, so as to discourage errors. For example, the left control might be used to engage and disengage the gears of an industrial machine, whereas the right control might operate the landing flaps on an airplane. (d) This design depicts a street intersection viewed from above. Psychologists have found that painting white lines across the road makes drivers feel they are traveling faster. This effect is even stronger if the lines get progressively closer together. Placing lines near dangerous intersections or sections of highway has dramatically lowered accident rates.*

6. **Common region.** As you can see in ❖Figure 7.3e, stimuli that are found within a common region or area tend to be seen as a group (Palmer, 1992). On the basis of similarity and nearness, the stars in ❖Figure 7.3e should be one group and the dots another. However, the colored backgrounds define regions that create three groups of objects (four stars, two stars plus two dots, and four dots). Perhaps the principle of common region explains why we tend to mentally group together people from a particular country, state, province, or geographic region.

To learn about how the principles that guide perceptual organization can be applied to practical problems, see "Designing for Human Use."

Clearly, the Gestalt principles shape our day-to-day perceptions, but so do learning and past experience. Take a moment and look for the camouflaged animal pictured in ❖Figure 7.5. (**Camouflage** patterns break up figure-ground organization.) If you had never seen similar animals before, could you have located this one? Mr. S. B. would have been at a total loss to find meaning in such a picture.

In a way, we are all detectives, seeking patterns in what we see. In this sense, a meaningful pattern represents a **perceptual hypothesis,** or initial guess about how to organize sensations. Have you ever seen a "friend" in the distance, only to have the person turn into a stranger as you drew closer? Preexisting ideas and expectations *actively* guide our interpretation of sensations (Coren, Ward, & Enns, 1994).

The active nature of perception is perhaps most apparent for **ambiguous stimuli** (patterns allowing more than one interpretation). If you look at a cloud, you may discover dozens of ways to organize its contours into fanciful shapes and scenes. Even clearly defined stimuli may permit more than one interpretation. Stare at the design in ❖Figure 7.6 if you doubt that perception is an active process. In short, we *construct* meaningful perceptions; we do not simply record the events and stimuli around us (Hoffman, 1999).

In some instances, a stimulus may offer such conflicting information that perceptual organization becomes impossible. For example, the tendency to make a three-dimensional object out of a drawing is frustrated by the "three-pronged widget" (❖Fig. 7.7), an **impossible figure.** Such patterns cannot be organized into stable, consistent, or meaningful perceptions.

Is the ability to understand drawings learned? Humans almost always appear to understand lines that represent the *edges of surfaces.* We also have no problem with a single line used to depict the *parallel edges* of a narrow object, such as a rope. One thing that we *do not* easily recognize is lines showing color boundaries on the surface of an object (Kennedy, 1983).

The last point is illustrated by the Songe, a small tribe in Papua New Guinea that does not make or use line drawings. As a test, the Songe were shown drawings like that in ❖Figure 7.8.

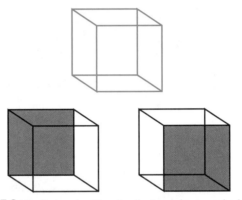

❖ **FIGURE 7.6** *Necker's cube. Visualize the top cube as a wire box. If you stare at the cube, its organization will change. Sometimes it will seem to project upward, like the lower left cube; other times it will project downward. The difference lies in how the brain interprets the same information.*

❖ **FIGURE 7.5** *A challenging example of perceptual organization. Once the camouflaged insect (known as a giant walking-stick) becomes visible, it is almost impossible to view the picture again without seeing the insect.*

Illusory figure *An implied shape that is not actually bounded by an edge or an outline.*

Engineering psychology (human factors engineering) *A specialty concerned with making machines and work environments compatible with human perceptual and physical capacities.*

Display *Any dial, screen, light, or other device used to provide information about a machine's activity.*

Control *Any knob, handle, button, lever, or other device used to alter the activity of a machine.*

Natural design *Human factors engineering that makes use of naturally understood perceptual signals.*

Feedback *Information on the effects of a response; feedback is returned to the person performing the response.*

Camouflage *Designs that break up figure-ground organization.*

Perceptual hypothesis *An initial guess regarding how to organize (perceive) a stimulus pattern.*

Ambiguous stimuli *Patterns that allow more than one perceptual organization.*

Impossible figure *A stimulus pattern that cannot be organized into a stable perception.*

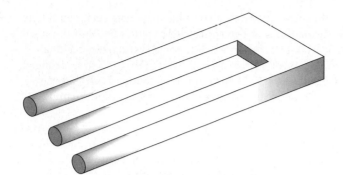

They easily recognized the parrot from its outlines. But lines showing color boundaries confused them. Most thought that the parrot had been cut repeatedly, even though the lines matched the colors of parrots they saw in daily life (Kennedy, 1983).

One of the most amazing perceptual feats is our capacity to create three-dimensional space from flat retinal images. We'll explore that topic in a moment, but first here's a chance to rehearse what you've learned.

❖ **FIGURE 7.7** (Above) *An impossible figure—the "three-pronged widget." If you cover either end of the drawing, it makes sense perceptually. However, a problem arises when you try to organize the entire drawing. Then, the conflicting information it contains prevents you from forming a stable perception. (Below) It might seem that including more information in a drawing would make perceptual conflicts impossible. However, Japanese artist Shigeo Fukuda has shown otherwise. ("Disappearing Column" © Shigeo Fukuda, 1985.)*

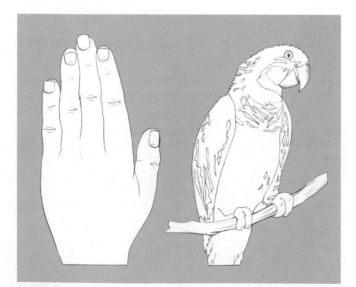

❖ **FIGURE 7.8** *Stimuli similar to those used by Kennedy (1983) to study the kinds of information universally recognized in drawings. (See text for explanation.)*

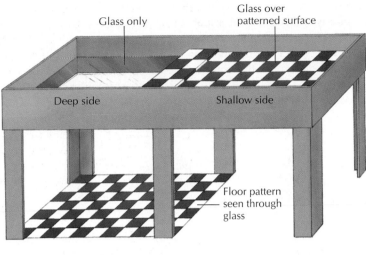

Glass only

Glass over patterned surface

Deep side

Shallow side

Floor pattern seen through glass

❖ **FIGURE 7.9** *Human infants and newborn animals refuse to go over the edge of the visual cliff.*

DEPTH PERCEPTION—WHAT IF THE WORLD WERE FLAT?

Depth perception is the ability to see three-dimensional space and to accurately judge distances. Without depth perception, you would be unable to drive a car or ride a bicycle, play catch, shoot baskets, thread a needle, or simply navigate around a room. The world would look like a flat surface.

Mr. S. B. had trouble with depth perception after his sight was restored. Is depth perception learned? Some psychologists (nativists) hold that depth perception is inborn. Others (the empiricists) view it as learned. Most likely, depth perception is partly learned and partly innate. Some evidence on the issue comes from work with the **visual cliff,** an apparatus that looks like the edge of an elevated platform. Basically, a visual cliff is a glass-topped table (❖Fig. 7.9). On one side, a checkered surface lies directly beneath the glass. On the other side, the checkered surface is 4 feet below. This makes the glass look like a tabletop on one side and a cliff, or drop-off, on the other.

To test for depth perception, 6- to 14-month-old infants were placed in the middle of the visual cliff. This gave them a choice of crawling to the shallow side or the deep side. (The glass prevented them from doing any "skydiving" if they chose the deep side.) Most infants chose the shallow side. In fact, most refused the deep side even when their mothers tried to call them toward it (Gibson & Walk, 1960).

If the infants were at least 6 months old when they were tested, isn't it possible that they learned to perceive depth? Yes, it is. However, other tests have shown that human depth perception consistently emerges at about 4 months of age (Aslin & Smith, 1988). For example, psychologist Jane Gwiazda fitted infants with goggles that make some designs stand out three-dimensionally while others remain flat. By watching head movements, Gwiazda could tell when babies first became aware of

"3-D" designs. As in other tests, this occurred at age 4 months. The nearly universal emergence of depth perception at this time suggests that it depends more on brain development than on individual learning. It is very likely that at least a basic level of depth perception is innate.

Then why do some babies crawl off tables or beds? As soon as infants become active crawlers, they refuse to cross the deep side of the visual cliff (Campos et al., 1978). But even babies who perceive depth may not be able to catch themselves if they slip. A lack of coordination—not an inability to see depth—probably explains most "crash landings" after about 4 months of age.

How do adults perceive depth? A number of depth cues combine to produce our experience of three-dimensional space. **Depth cues** are features of the environment and messages from the body that supply information about distance and space. Some cues work with just one eye (**monocular cues**); others require two eyes (**binocular cues**).

MUSCULAR CUES As their name implies, muscular cues come from within the body. One such cue is **accommodation,** the bending of the lens that occurs when the eye focuses on nearby objects. Sensations from muscles attached to each lens are channeled back to the brain. Changes in these sensations help

Depth perception *The ability to see three-dimensional space and to accurately judge distances.*
Visual cliff *An apparatus that looks like the edge of an elevated platform or cliff.*
Depth cues *Perceptual features that impart information about distance and three-dimensional space.*
Monocular depth cue *A depth cue that can be sensed with one eye.*
Binocular depth cue *A depth cue that requires two eyes.*
Accommodation *Changes in the shape of the lens of the eye.*

us judge distances within about 4 feet of the eyes. This information is available even if you are using just one eye, so accommodation is a monocular cue.

Beyond 4 feet, accommodation has limited value. Obviously, accommodation is more important to a watchmaker or a person trying to thread a needle than it is to a basketball player or someone driving an automobile.

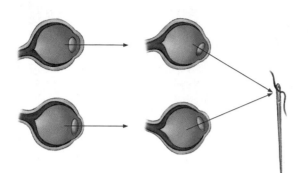

❖ **FIGURE 7.10** *The eyes must converge, or turn in toward the nose, to focus close objects.*

A second bodily source of information about depth is **convergence,** a binocular cue. When you look at a distant object, the lines of vision from your eyes are parallel. However, when you look at something 50 feet or less in distance, your eyes must converge (turn in) to focus the object (❖Fig. 7.10).

You are probably not aware of it, but whenever you estimate a distance under 50 feet (as when you approach a stop sign, play catch, or zap flies with your personal laser), you are using convergence. How? Again, there is a relationship between muscle sensations and distance. Convergence is controlled by a group of muscles attached to the eyeball. These muscles feed information on eye position to the brain to help it judge distance. You can feel convergence by exaggerating it: Focus on your fingertip and bring it toward your eyes until they almost cross. At that point, you can feel the sensations from the muscles that control eye movement.

STEREOSCOPIC VISION The most basic source of depth perception is **retinal disparity** (a discrepancy in the images that reach the right and left eyes). Retinal disparity, which is a binocular cue, is based on the fact that the eyes are about 2.5 inches apart. Because of this, each eye receives a slightly different view

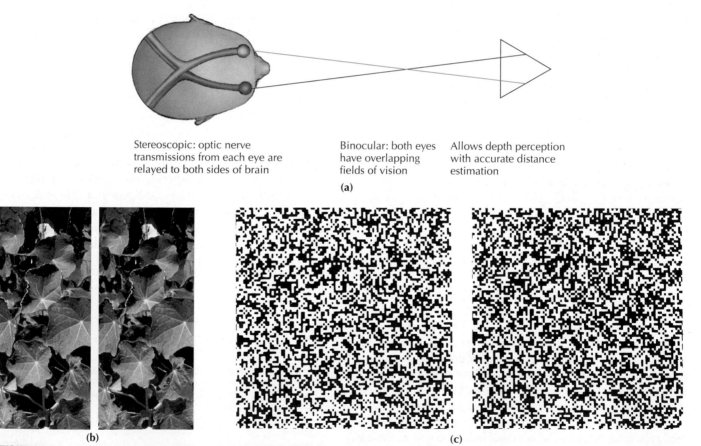

Stereoscopic: optic nerve transmissions from each eye are relayed to both sides of brain

Binocular: both eyes have overlapping fields of vision

Allows depth perception with accurate distance estimation

(a)

(b)

(c)

❖ **FIGURE 7.11** (a) *Stereoscopic vision.* (b) *The photographs show what the right and left eyes would see when viewing a plant. Hold the page about 6 to 8 inches from your eyes. Allow your eyes to cross and focus on the overlapping image between the two photos. Then try to fuse the leaves into one image. If you are successful, the third dimension will appear like magic.* (c) *Now do the same with the random dot stereogram, but with your eyes 10 inches from the page. With luck, you will see a diamond shape hovering over the background. (See text for explanation.) (Julesz, 1971; reprinted by permission of the University of Chicago Press.)*

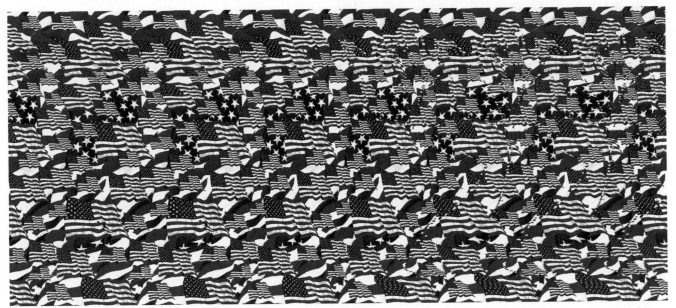

❖ **FIGURE 7.12** *This popular style of computer-generated art creates a 3-D illusion by superimposing two patterns. There are mismatches between some areas of the two patterns. This simulates retinal disparity and creates a sensation of depth. To get the 3-D effect, hold the stereogram about 8 inches from the end of your nose. Relax your eyes and look* through *the art, as if you were focusing on something in the distance. If you're patient, you may see a 3-D globe. (Stereogram © Anything Enterprises, 1994.)*

of the world. When the two images are fused into one overall image, **stereoscopic vision** (three-dimensional sight) occurs. The result is a powerful sensation of depth (❖Fig. 7.11).

Retinal disparity can be used to produce 3-D movies by filming with two cameras separated by several inches. Later, both images are simultaneously projected on a screen. Audience members wear glasses that filter out one of the images to each eye. Because each eye gets a separate image, normal stereoscopic vision is duplicated. Try the following demonstration of retinal disparity and fusion.

Totally Tubular

Roll a piece of paper into a tube. Close your left eye. Hold the tube to your right eye like a telescope. Look through the tube at some object in the distance. Place your left hand against the tube halfway down its length and in front of your left eye. Now open your left eye. You should see a "hole" in your hand. You couldn't expect a professional photographer to do a better job of blending the two images than your visual system does automatically.

How does retinal disparity produce depth? Perceiving depth is more than a simple blending of two "pictures" of the world. In ❖Figure 7.11c, you will find two **random dot stereograms** (patterns of dots that produce an illusion of depth). Notice that they contain no objects, lines, or edges. Just the same, when the stereograms are properly viewed (one to each eye), a center area seems to float above the background. Such designs show that the brain is very sensitive to any mismatch of information from the eyes. In ❖Figure 7.11c, depth comes from shifting dots in the center of one square so they do not match dots in the other square (Julcsz, 1971; Ross, 1976). (Also see ❖Figure 7.12.)

To a large extent, three-dimensional space is woven from countless tiny differences between what the right and left eyes

see. Direct studies of the brain have shown that visual areas do, in fact, contain cells that detect disparities (Ohzawa, DeAngelis, & Freeman, 1990).

If disparity is so important, can a person with one eye perceive depth? A one-eyed person lacks convergence and retinal disparity, and accommodation is helpful mainly for judging short distances. That means a person with only one eye will have limited depth perception. Try driving a car or riding a bicycle with one eye closed. You will find yourself braking too soon or too late, and you will have difficulty estimating your speed. ("But officer, my psychology text said to. . . .") Despite this, you will be able to drive, although it will be more difficult than usual. A person with one eye can even successfully land an airplane—a task that depends strongly on depth perception. Overall, testing shows that stereoscopic vision is 10 times better for judging depth than perception based on just one eye (Rosenberg, 1994).

It is tempting to assume that higher animals perceive depth much as we do. Although this is sometimes true, there are many exceptions. Let's explore some examples of how a "bird's-eye" view of the world might differ from our own.

Convergence *The simultaneous turning inward of the two eyes.*
Retinal disparity *Small discrepancies in images on the right and left retinas.*
Stereoscopic vision *Perception of space and depth caused chiefly by the fact that the eyes receive different images.*
Random dot stereogram *Two designs made up of dots. The dots are identical in each design, except for small areas that contain mismatched dots. The offset areas create an illusion of depth.*

STEREOSCOPIC VISION—A BIRD'S-EYE VIEW

Harness yourself to a hang glider, step off a cliff, and soar. No matter how exhilarating, your flight still wouldn't provide a true "bird's-eye" view.

Many birds see the world in ways that would seem strange to us. For example, pigeons, ducks, and hummingbirds can see ultraviolet light, which adds an extra color to their visual palette.

It might seem that birds would have acute stereoscopic vision, and some do. But most birds are prey for other animals. When you spend life as a potential meal, it's important to detect approaching predators. That's why many birds have an unusually wide field of view (❖Fig. 7.13a and ❖Fig. 7.13b). An extreme case is the American woodcock, a bird that can survey a 360-degree panorama without moving its eyes or head. The trade-off for this wideangle view is a very limited area of binocular vision

(❖Fig. 7.13c). But to the woodcock, an ability to spot hungry predators is probably more valuable than depth perception.

What does the world look like to a woodcock? Computer scientist Ping-Kang Hsiung (1990) used optical ray-tracing to simulate the woodcock's view (❖Fig. 7.13e, 7.13f). As you can see in ❖Figure 7.13, even a pretty foxy predator would have trouble sneaking up on a woodcock.

Most variations in vision have a purpose. Scientists theorize that human depth perception is an evolutionary holdover—from life in the treetops. The superb depth perception that helped our distant ancestors swing from branch to branch now helps us swing at a softball or avoid erratic drivers in traffic. Perhaps it's too bad that a little of the woodcock's wide-angle vision didn't get thrown in as well. (Source: Waldvogel, 1990.)

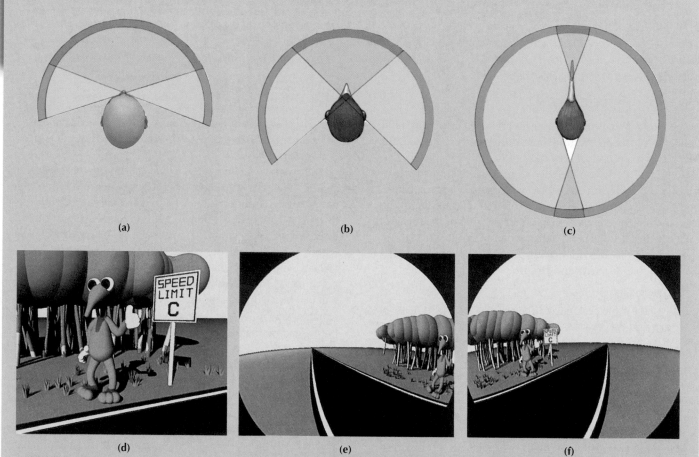

❖ **FIGURE 7.13** (a) *When viewed from above the head, a human's field of view for the right and left eyes contains a large area of overlapping, stereoscopic vision (darker shading).* (b) *The barn swallow's vision, like that of many birds, covers a much wider field of view than ours. Although the swallow's area of binocular vision is smaller than a human's, the swallow has sharper peripheral vision.* (c) *A bird called the American woodcock can see all the way around its head. Binocular vision is limited to a narrow band, but an extremely wide field of view helps the woodcock detect predators. (Adapted from Waldvogel, 1990.)* (d) *This image, created by Ping-Kang Hsiung (1990), shows how an imaginary scene would look to a person standing across the road from a rather strange hitchhiker.* (e) (f) *This is what a woodcock's left and right eyes would see if the bird were at the same point as the human in view* d. *(Computer graphics courtesy of Dr. Hsiung.)*

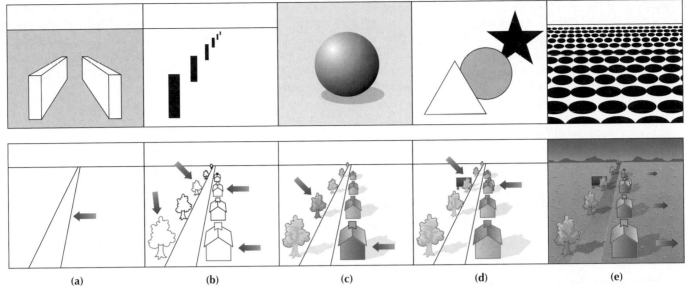

❖ **FIGURE 7.14** (a) *Linear perspective.* (b) *Relative size.* (c) *Light and shadow.* (d) *Overlap.* (e) *Texture gradients. Drawings in the top row show fairly "pure" examples of each of the pictorial depth cues. In the bottom row, the pictorial depth cues are used to assemble a more realistic scene.*

PICTORIAL CUES FOR DEPTH—A DEEP TOPIC

A good movie, painting, or photograph can create a convincing sense of depth where none exists. And, as noted, a one-eyed person can learn to gauge depth.

How is the illusion of depth created on a two-dimensional surface, and how is it possible to judge depth with one eye? The answers lie in the pictorial depth cues, all of which are monocular (they will work with just one eye). **Pictorial depth cues** are features found in paintings, drawings, and photographs that impart information about space, depth, and distance. To understand how these cues work, imagine that you are looking outdoors through a window. If you trace everything you see onto the glass, you will have an excellent drawing, with convincing depth. If you then analyze what is on the glass you will find the following features.

Pictorial Depth Cues

1. **Linear perspective.** This cue is based on the apparent convergence of parallel lines in the environment. If you stand between two railroad tracks, they appear to meet near the horizon. Because you know they are parallel, their convergence implies great distance (❖Fig. 7.14a).
2. **Relative size.** If an artist wishes to depict two objects of the same size at different distances, the artist makes the more distant object smaller (❖Fig. 7.14b). Films in the *Star Wars* series create sensational illusions of depth by rapidly changing the image size of planets, space stations, and starships. (Also see ❖Figure 7.15.)
3. **Height in the picture plane.** Objects that are placed higher (closer to the horizon line) in a drawing tend to be perceived as more distant. In the upper frame of ❖Figure 7.14b, the black columns look like they are receding into the

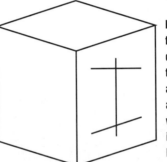

Linear perspective is a very powerful cue for depth. Because of the depth cues implied in this drawing, the upper cross on the vertical line appears to be diagonal. It is actually a right angle. The lower cross, which appears to be a right angle, is actually diagonal to the vertical line. (After Enns & Coren, 1995.)

❖ **FIGURE 7.15** *On a dry lake bed, relative size is just about the only depth cue available for judging the camera's distance from this vintage aircraft. What do you estimate the distance to be? For the answer, look ahead to ❖Figure 7.20.*

Pictorial depth cues *Features found in paintings, drawings, and photographs that impart information about space, depth, and distance.*

distance partly because they become smaller but also because they move higher in the drawing.

4. **Light and shadow.** Most objects are lighted in ways that create clear patterns of light and shadow. Copying such patterns of light and shadow can give a two-dimensional design a three-dimensional appearance (❖Fig. 7.14c). (Also, ❖Figure 7.16 provides more information on light and shadow.)

5. **Overlap.** Overlap (also known as *interposition*) is a depth cue that occurs when one object partially blocks another object. Hold up your hands and have a friend try to tell from across the room which is nearer. Relative size will give the answer if one hand is much nearer to your friend than the other. But if one hand is only slightly closer than the other, your friend may have difficulty—until you slide one hand in front of the other. Overlap then removes any doubt (❖Fig. 7.14d).

6. **Texture gradients.** Changes in texture also contribute to depth perception. If you stand in the middle of a cobblestone street, the street will look coarse near your feet. However, its texture will get smaller and finer if you look into the distance (❖Fig. 7.14e).

7. **Aerial perspective.** Smog, fog, dust, and haze add to the apparent distance of an object. Because of aerial perspective, distant objects tend to be hazy, washed out in color, and lacking in detail. Aerial haze is often most noticeable when it is missing. If you have traveled the wide-open spaces of the United States or Canada, you may have seen mountain ranges that seemed to be only a few miles away. In reality, you could have been viewing them through 50 miles of crystal-clear air.

8. **Relative motion.** Relative motion, also known as *motion parallax* (PAIR-ah-lax), can be seen by looking out a window and moving your head from side to side. Notice that nearby objects appear to move a sizable distance as your head moves. In comparison, trees, houses, and telephone poles at a greater distance appear to move slightly in relation to the background. Distant objects like hills, mountains, or clouds don't seem to move at all.

When combined, pictorial cues can create a powerful illusion of depth. (See ◆Table 7.1 for a summary of all the depth cues we have discussed.)

Is motion parallax really a pictorial cue? Strictly speaking, it is not, except in movies, television, or animated cartoons. However, when parallax is present, depth is almost always perceived. Much of the apparent depth of a good movie comes from relative motion captured by the camera. People who can see with only one eye depend heavily on motion parallax. Typically, they make frequent head movements to exaggerate parallax and improve depth perception. In fact, we all use head movements at times to more accurately judge the distance of objects (Enright, 1996).

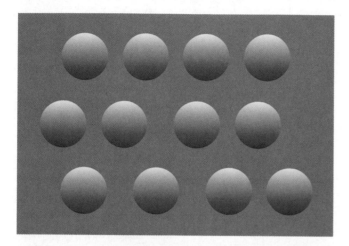

❖ **FIGURE 7.16** (Above) *We typically make two assumptions when using light and shadow to judge depth in a picture or drawing. First, we usually assume that light comes mainly from one direction. Second, we tend to assume that the source of light is above pictured objects. Squint a little to blur the image you see here. You should perceive a collection of globes projecting outward. If you turn this page upside down, the globes should become cavities. (After Ramachandran, 1995.) (Below) The famed Dutch artist M. C. Escher violated both assumptions about light to create the dramatic illusions of depth found in his 1955 lithograph "Convex and Concave." In this print, light appears to come from all sides of the scene. (Courtesy of the Collection Haags Gemeente Museum, The Hague. © 1994 M. C. Escher/Cordon Art, Baarn, The Netherlands. All rights reserved.)*

◆ **TABLE 7.1** Summary of Visual Depth Cues

BINOCULAR CUES
    Convergence
    Retinal disparity

MONOCULAR CUES
    Accommodation
    Pictorial depth cues (listed below)
        Linear perspective
        Relative size
        Height in the picture plane
        Light and shadow
        Overlap
        Texture gradients
        Aerial perspective
        Relative motion (motion parallax)

❖Figure 7.17 illustrates an interesting feature of motion parallax. Imagine that you are in a bus and watching the passing scenery with your gaze at a right angle to the road. Under these conditions, nearby objects will appear to rush *backward*. Those farther away, such as distant mountains, will seem to move very little or not at all. Objects that are more remote, such as the sun or moon, will appear to move in the *same* direction you are traveling. (That's why the moon appears to "follow" you when you take a stroll at night.) To re-create motion parallax in cartoons, animators draw scenes in several layers, each of which is moved during filming.

Are pictorial depth cues universal, like the understanding of basic drawings noted earlier? Not entirely. Some cultures use only selected pictorial cues to represent depth. People in these cultures may not easily recognize other cues (Deregowski, 1972). For example, researcher William Hudson tested members of remote tribes who do not use relative size to show depth in drawings. These people perceive simplified drawings as flat designs. As you can see in ❖Figure 7.18, they do not assume, as we do, that a larger image means that an object is closer. Of course, members of non-Western cultures can learn to interpret drawings of depth if they are given a chance to practice (Mshelia & Lapidus, 1990).

THE MOON ILLUSION   *How do the depth perception cues relate to daily experience?*   We constantly use both pictorial cues and bodily cues to sense depth and judge distances. Depth cues also produce an intriguing perceptual effect called the **moon illusion** (perceiving the moon as larger when it is low in the sky). When the moon is on the horizon, it tends to look as large as a silver dollar. When it is directly overhead, it looks like a dime, very much smaller than it did earlier the same evening. Contrary to what some people believe, the moon is not magnified by the atmosphere. If you take a photograph of the moon and

measure its image, you will find that it is not larger when it is near the horizon. But the moon *looks* nearly twice as large when it's low in the sky (Plug & Ross, 1994). This occurs, in part, because the moon's *apparent distance* is greater when it is near the horizon than when it is overhead (Kaufman & Kaufman, 2000).

But if it seems farther away, shouldn't it look smaller?   No. When the moon is overhead, few depth cues surround it. In contrast, when you see the moon on the horizon, it is behind houses, trees, telephone poles, and mountains. These objects add numerous depth cues, which cause the horizon to seem more distant than the sky overhead. The moon illusion is so powerful that it can occur in photographs if they contain depth cues (Coren & Aks, 1990).

To better understand the moon illusion, picture two balloons, one 10 feet away and the second 20 feet away. Suppose the more distant balloon is inflated until its image matches the image of the nearer balloon. How do we know the more distant balloon is larger? Because its image is the same size as a balloon that is closer. Similarly, the moon makes the same-size image on the horizon as it does overhead. However, the horizon seems more distant because more depth cues are present. As a result, the horizon moon must be perceived as larger. (See ❖Figure 7.19.)

This explanation is known as the **apparent-distance hypothesis** (the horizon seems more distant than the night sky). You can test it by removing depth cues while looking at a horizon moon. Try looking at the moon through a rolled-up paper tube, or make your hands into a "telescope" and look at the next large moon you see. It will immediately appear to shrink when viewed without depth cues (Plug & Ross, 1994).

❖ **FIGURE 7.18** *A Hudson test picture. Two-dimensional perceivers assume the hunter is trying to spear the distant elephant rather than the nearby antelope. Some acquaintance with conventions for representing depth in pictures and photographs seems necessary. (From "Pictorial Perception and Culture" by J. B. Deregowski. © 1972 by Scientific American, Inc. All rights reserved.)*

◄ Direction of travel

❖ **FIGURE 7.17** *The apparent motion of objects viewed during travel depends on their distance from the observer. Apparent motion can also be influenced by an observer's point of fixation. At middle distances, objects closer than the point of fixation appear to move backward; those beyond the point of fixation appear to move forward. Objects at great distances, such as the sun or moon, always appear to move forward.*

Moon illusion *The apparent change in size that occurs as the moon moves from the horizon (large moon) to overhead (small moon).*
Apparent-distance hypothesis *An explanation of the moon illusion stating that the horizon seems more distant than the night sky.*

❖ **FIGURE 7.19** *The Ponzo illusion may help you understand the moon illusion. Picture the two white bars as resting on the railroad tracks. In the drawing, the upper bar is the same length as the lower bar. However, because the upper bar appears to be farther away than the lower bar, we perceive it as longer. The same logic applies to the moon illusion.*

❖ **FIGURE 7.20** *Before you can use familiar size to judge distance, objects must actually be the size you assume they are. Either these men are giants, or the model airplane was closer than you may have thought when you looked at ❖Figure 7.15.*

To what extent has the apparent-distance hypothesis been confirmed? The father-and-son team of Lloyd and James Kaufman recently used a computer to project images of the moon on a mirror. This allowed them to superimpose an artificial moon on the sky. In addition, the mirrors were movable. Volunteer observers reported that as the moon moved closer, it

appeared to get smaller. This effect was most dramatic when the moon was near the horizon, where more depth cues are found. This is the most powerful confirmation yet of the apparent-distance theory (Kaufman & Kaufman, 2000).

PERCEPTUAL LEARNING—WHAT IF THE WORLD WERE UPSIDE DOWN?

England is one of the few countries in the world where people drive on the left side of the road. In view of this reversal, it is not unusual for visitors to step off curbs in front of cars—after carefully looking for traffic in the *wrong* direction. As this example suggests, learning has a powerful impact on our perceptions.

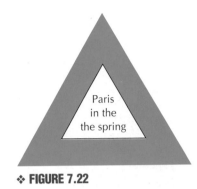

❖ **FIGURE 7.21** *The effects of prior experience on perception. The doctored face looks far worse when viewed right side up because it can be related to past experience.*

Paris
in the
the spring

❖ **FIGURE 7.22**

The term **perceptual learning** refers to any change in perception that is based on past experience. Perceptual learning is associated with lasting changes in the brain that alter the ways in which we process sensory information (Ahissar, 1999).

How does learning affect perception? One way is by changing the amount of attention given to various stimuli. For example, to use a computer program, you must learn where to look for icons, commands, and signals.

We also learn to distinguish between stimuli that may have seemed identical at first. An example is discovering how to tell the difference between dried basil, oregano, and tarragon when you are cooking.

In some situations, we learn to focus on just one part of a group of related stimuli. This saves us from having to process all of the stimuli in the group. For instance, a linebacker in football may be able to tell if the next play will be a run or a pass by watching one or two key players, rather than the entire opposing team (Goldstone, 1998).

PERCEPTUAL HABITS   When combined, the changes we have noted create **perceptual habits** (ingrained patterns of organization and attention) that affect our daily experience. Stop for a moment and look at ❖Figure 7.21. The left face looks somewhat unusual, to be sure. But the distortion seems mild—until the page is turned upside down. Viewed normally, the face looks quite grotesque. Why is there a difference? Apparently, most people have little experience with upside-down faces. Perceptual learning, therefore, has less impact on our perceptions of an upside-down face. With a face in the normal position, you know what to expect and where to look. Also, you tend to see the entire face as a recognizable pattern. When a face is inverted, we are forced to perceive its individual features separately (Bartlett & Searcy, 1993).

Before we continue, read aloud the short phrase in ❖Figure 7.22. Did you read "Paris in the spring"? If so, look again. The word *the* appears twice in the phrase. Because of past experi-

ence with the English language, good readers often overlook the repeated word. Again, the effects of perceptual learning are apparent.

Magicians rely on perceptual habits when they use sleight of hand to distract observers while performing tricks. Another kind of "magic" is related to consistency in the environment. It is usually safe to assume that a room is shaped roughly like a box. This need not be true, however. An **Ames room** (named for the man who designed it) is a lopsided space that appears square when viewed from a certain point (❖Fig. 7.23). This illusion is achieved by carefully distorting the proportions of the walls, floor, ceiling, and windows.

Because the left corner of the Ames room is farther from a viewer than the right, a person standing in that corner looks very small; one standing in the nearer, shorter right corner looks very large. If a person walks from the left corner of the room to the right, observers are faced with a conflict. They can maintain shape constancy by perceiving the room as square, or they can maintain size constancy by refusing to see the person "grow." Most people choose shape constancy and see people "shrink" and "grow" before their eyes.

As mentioned in the previous chapter, the brain is especially sensitive to **perceptual features** such as lines, shapes, edges, spots, and colors. At least some of this sensitivity appears to be learned. Colin Blakemore and Graham Cooper of Cambridge

Perceptual learning *Changes in perception that can be attributed to prior experience.*
Perceptual habits *Well-established patterns of perceptual organization and attention.*
Ames room *A distorted room that appears normal when viewed from a specific location.*
Perceptual features *Important elements of a stimulus pattern, such as lines, shapes, edges, spots, and colors.*

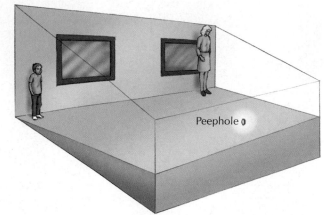

University raised kittens in a room with only vertical stripes on the walls. Another set of kittens saw only horizontal stripes. When returned to normal environments, the "horizontal" cats could easily jump onto a chair, but when walking on the floor, they bumped into chair legs. "Vertical" cats, on the other hand, easily avoided chair legs, but they missed when trying to jump to horizontal surfaces. The cats raised with vertical stripes were "blind" to horizontal lines, and the "horizontal" cats acted as if vertical lines were invisible. Other experiments show that there is an actual decrease in brain cells tuned to the missing features (Grobstein & Chow, 1975).

INVERTED VISION *Would it be possible for an adult to adapt to a completely new perceptual world?* An answer comes from an experiment in which a person wore goggles that turned the world upside down and reversed objects from right to left. At first, even the simplest tasks—walking, eating, and so forth—were incredibly difficult. Imagine trying to reach for a door handle and watching your hand shoot off in the wrong direction.

Participants in the experiment also reported that head movements made the world swing violently through space, causing severe headaches and nausea. Yet, after several days they began to adapt to inverted vision. Their success, while not complete, was impressive.

Did everything turn upright again for the humans? No. While they wore the goggles, their visual images remained upside down. But in time they learned to perform most routine activities, and their inverted world began to seem relatively normal. In later experiments, some people wearing inverting lenses were able to successfully drive cars. One person even flew an airplane (Kohler, 1962). These feats are like driving or flying upside down, with right and left reversed. Some ride!

Interacting with a new visual world through **active movement** (self-generated action) seems to be a key to rapid adaptation. In one experiment, people wore glasses that grossly distorted vision. Those who walked on their own adapted more quickly than persons pushed around in a wheeled cart (Held, 1971). Why does movement help? Probably because commands sent to the muscles can be related to sensory feedback. Remaining immobile would be like watching a weird movie over which you have no control. There would be little reason for any perceptual learning to occur.

ADAPTATION LEVEL The external context in which a stimulus is judged is an important factor affecting perception. **Context** refers to information surrounding a stimulus. For example, a man 6 feet in height will look "tall" when surrounded by others of average height and "short" among a group of professional basketball players. In ❖Figure 7.24, the center circle is the same

Inverted vision. Adaptation to complete inversion of the visual world is possible, but challenging.

Even small distortions of the visual world may necessitate perceptual learning. For example, the size, distance, and curvature of objects appear distorted underwater. Experiments confirm that professional divers gradually correct for these distortions as they gain experience with them (Vernoy, 1989).

size in both designs. But like the man in different company, context alters the circle's apparent size. The importance of context is also shown by ❖Figure 7.25. What do you see in the middle? If you read across, context causes it to be organized as a *13*. Reading down makes it a *B*.

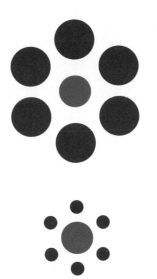

❖ **FIGURE 7.24** *Are the center dots in both figures the same size?*

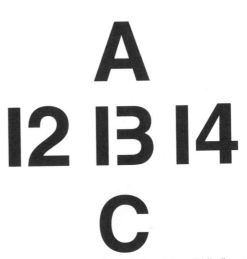

❖ **FIGURE 7.25** *Context alters the meaning of the middle figure.*

In addition to external contexts, we all have personal **frames of reference** (internal standards for judging stimuli). If you were asked to lift a 10-pound weight, would you label it light, medium, or heavy? The answer to this question depends on your **adaptation level** (the "medium point" of your personal frame of reference). Each person's adaptation level is constantly modified by experience (Helson, 1964). If most of the weights you lift in day-to-day life *average* around 10 pounds, you will call a 10-pound weight medium. If you are a watchmaker and spend your days lifting tiny watch parts, you will probably call

Active movement *Self-generated action (a factor that accelerates perceptual adaptation).*
Context *Information surrounding a stimulus.*
Frame of reference *An internal perspective relative to which events are perceived and evaluated.*
Adaptation level *An internal or mental "average" or "medium" point that is used to judge amounts.*

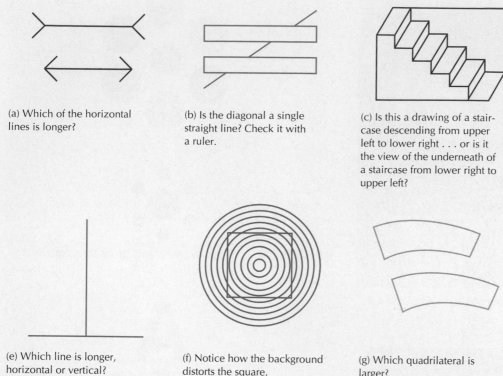

(a) Which of the horizontal lines is longer?

(b) Is the diagonal a single straight line? Check it with a ruler.

(c) Is this a drawing of a staircase descending from upper left to lower right . . . or is it the view of the underneath of a staircase from lower right to upper left?

(d) Are these lines parallel? Cover some of the slash marks to see.

(e) Which line is longer, horizontal or vertical?

(f) Notice how the background distorts the square.

(g) Which quadrilateral is larger?

(h) Which column is shortest? Which is longest?

❖ **FIGURE 7.26** *Some interesting perceptual illusions.*

a 10-pound weight heavy. If you work as a furniture mover, your adaptation level will exceed 10 pounds, and you will call a 10-pound weight light. (If you are an aging rock star, you will no doubt call everything "heavy," man.)

ILLUSIONS Perceptual learning is responsible for a number of illusions. In an **illusion,** length, position, motion, curvature, or direction is consistently misjudged (Gillam, 1980). Note that illusions distort stimuli that actually exist. In a **hallucination,** people perceive objects or events that have no external reality. For example, they hear voices that are not there. If you think you see a 3-foot-tall butterfly, you can confirm you are hallucinating by trying to touch its wings. To detect an illusion, it is often necessary to measure a drawing or apply a straightedge to it.

Illusions are a fascinating challenge to our understanding of perception. On occasion, they also have practical uses. An illusion called *stroboscopic movement* (strobe-oh-SKOP-ik) puts the "motion" in motion pictures. **Stroboscopic movement** refers to the illusory movement perceived when an object is shown in rapidly changing positions. The strobe lights sometimes used on dance floors reverse this illusion. Each time the strobe flashes, it "freezes" dancers in particular positions. However, if the light flashes fast enough, normal motion is seen. In a similar way, movies project a rapid series of "snapshots," so the gaps in motion are imperceptible.

Can other illusions be explained? Not in all cases, or to everyone's satisfaction. Generally speaking, size and shape constancy, habitual eye movements, continuity, and perceptual habits combine in various ways to produce the illusions in ❖Figure 7.26. Rather than attempt to explain all of the pictured illusions, let's focus on one deceptively simple example.

Consider the drawing in ❖Figure 7.26a. This is the familiar **Müller-Lyer illusion** (MUE-ler-LIE-er) in which the horizontal line with arrowheads appears shorter than the line with **V**s. A

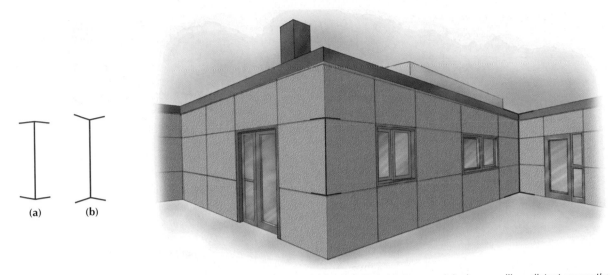

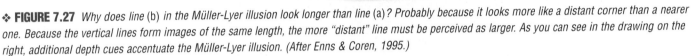

❖ **FIGURE 7.27** *Why does line (b) in the Müller-Lyer illusion look longer than line (a)? Probably because it looks more like a distant corner than a nearer one. Because the vertical lines form images of the same length, the more "distant" line must be perceived as larger. As you can see in the drawing on the right, additional depth cues accentuate the Müller-Lyer illusion. (After Enns & Coren, 1995.)*

quick measurement will show that they are the same length. How can we explain this illusion? Evidence suggests it is based on a lifetime of experience with the edges and corners of rooms and buildings. Richard Gregory (1990) believes you see the horizontal line with the **V**s as if it were the corner of a room viewed from inside (❖Fig. 7.27). The line with arrowheads, on the other hand, suggests the corner of a room or building seen from outside. In other words, cues that suggest a 3-D space alter our perception of a two-dimensional design (Enns & Coren, 1995).

Earlier, to explain the moon illusion, we said that if two objects make images of the same size, the more distant object must be larger. This is known formally as **size-distance invariance** (the size of an object's image is precisely related to its distance from the eyes). Gregory believes the same concept explains the Müller-Lyer illusion. If the **V**-tipped line looks farther away than the arrowhead-tipped line, then you must compensate by seeing the **V**-tipped line as longer. This explanation presumes that you have had years of experience with straight lines, sharp edges, and corners—a pretty safe assumption in our culture.

Is there any way to show that past experience causes the illusion? If we could test someone who saw only curves and wavy lines as a child, we would know if experience with a "square" culture is important. Fortunately, a group of people in South Africa, the Zulus, live in a "round" culture. In their daily lives, Zulus rarely encounter a straight line: Their homes are shaped like rounded mounds and arranged in a circle, tools and toys are curved, and there are no straight roads or square buildings.

What happens if a Zulu looks at the Müller-Lyer design? The typical Zulu villager does not experience the illusion. At most, she or he sees the **V**-shaped line as *slightly* longer than the other (Gregory, 1990). This seems to confirm the importance of past experience and perceptual habits in determining

our view of the world. But, like many topics in psychology, room for debate remains. The Müller-Lyer illusion also seems to be partly based on directly misperceiving the location of the ends of the lines (Morgan, Hole, & Glennerster, 1990). Thus, it could be that both apparent size and misperception cause the illusion.

KNOWLEDGE BUILDER
PERCEPTUAL LEARNING

RELATE

How has perceptual learning affected your ability to safely drive a car? For example, what do you pay attention to at intersections? Where do you habitually look as you are driving?

What do you regard as a "medium-priced" meal at a restaurant? Does your adaptation level affect what you are comfortable paying?

If you spent a year hiking the Amazon River basin, what effect might it have on your perception of the Müller-Lyer illusion?

LEARNING CHECK

1. Perceptual habits may become so ingrained that they lead us to misperceive a stimulus. T or F?

Illusion *A misleading or distorted perception.*
Hallucination *An imaginary sensation—such as seeing, hearing, or smelling something that does not exist in the external world.*
Stroboscopic movement *Illusion of movement in which an object is shown in a rapidly changing series of positions.*
Müller-Lyer illusion *Two equal-length lines tipped with inward or outward pointing Vs appear to be of different lengths.*
Size-distance invariance *The strict relationship between the distance an object lies from the eyes and the size of its image.*

2. Perceptual learning seems to program the brain for sensitivity to important _____ of the environment.

3. The Ames room is used to test for adaptation to inverted vision. T or F?

4. An important factor in adaptation to inverted vision is
   a. learning new categories *b.* active movement *c.* overcoming illusions *d.* the horizontal-vertical invariance

5. Size-distance relationships appear to underlie which two illusions? _____ and _____

6. An adaptation level represents a personal "medium point," or internal _____ ___ _____.

CRITICAL THINKING

7. What size object do you think you would have to hold at arm's length to cover up a full moon?

Answers:

1. T 2. features 3. F 4. b 5. moon illusion, Müller-Lyer illusion 6. frame of reference 7. The most popular answers range from a quarter to a softball. Actually, a pea held in the outstretched hand will cover a full moon (Kunkel, 1993). If you listed an object larger than a pea, be aware that perceptions, no matter how accurate they seem, may distort reality.

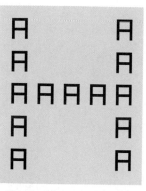

❖ **FIGURE 7.28** *The attentional "spotlight" can be widened or narrowed. If you focus on local details in this drawing, you will see the letter* A *repeated 13 times. If you broaden your field of attention to encompass the overall pattern, you will see the letter* H. *(After Lamb & Yund, 1996.)*

MOTIVES AND PERCEPTION—MAY I HAVE YOUR . . . ATTENTION!

You are surrounded by sights, sounds, odors, tastes, and touch sensations. Which are you aware of? The first stage of perception is attention, the selection of incoming messages. There is little doubt about the importance of attention. Think, for instance, about an airline pilot who fails to notice that the flaps are not down before a landing. This error caused a major air disaster at Detroit's airport in 1987.

ATTENTION   As you may recall from Chapter 6, **selective attention** refers to the fact that we give some messages priority and put others on hold (Johnston & Dark, 1986). Psychologists have found it helpful to think of selective attention as a sort of *bottleneck,* or narrowing in the information channel linking the senses to perception. When one message enters the bottleneck, it seems to prevent others from passing through. This may be why it is very difficult to listen to two people speaking at once. Typically, you can "tune in" one person or the other, but not both (Reed, 1996). (See ❖Figure 7.28.)

Have you ever felt overloaded while trying to do several things at once? **Divided attention** arises when you must divide your mental effort among tasks, each of which requires more or less attention ("multitasking"). Divided attention is related to our limited *capacity* for storing and thinking about information. For example, when people first learn to drive, almost all of their attention is needed to steer, brake, shift, and so forth. However, as a skill becomes more

In many sports, experts are much better than beginners at paying attention to key information. Compared with novices, experts scan actions and events more quickly, and they focus on only the most meaningful information. This allows experts to make decisions and react more quickly (Bard, Fleury, & Goulet, 1994).

automatic, it requires less attention. In driving, greater skill frees mental capacity for other things, such as tuning the car's radio or carrying on a conversation (Desimone & Duncan, 1995).

Are some stimuli more attention getting than others?   Yes. Very *intense* stimuli usually command attention. Stimuli that are brighter, louder, or larger tend to capture attention: A gun-

❖ **FIGURE 7.29** *One of the drawings used by Mackworth and Loftus (1978) to investigate attention. Observers attend to unexpected objects longer than they do to expected objects. In this drawing, observers looked longer at the octopus than they did at a tractor placed in the same spot. What do you think would happen if a tractor were shown upside down or on the roof of the barn?*

THE "BOILED FROG SYNDROME"

As we have noted, the perceptual system is impressed most by dramatic changes. Humans evolved to detect sharp changes and distinctive events, such as the sudden appearance of a lion, a potential mate, or sources of food. We are far less able to detect gradual changes.

Robert Ornstein, a biopsychologist, and Paul Ehrlich, a population biologist, believe perceptual capacities that aided survival when humans were hunters and gatherers can now be a handicap. Many of the threats facing civilization develop very slowly. Examples include the stockpiling of nuclear warheads, degradation of the environment, global deforestation, global warming, erosion of the ozone layer, and runaway human population growth.

Ornstein and Ehrlich relate the large-scale threats we face to what they call the "boiled frog syndrome." Frogs placed in a pan of water that is slowly heated cannot detect the gradual rise in temperature. They will sit still until they die.

Like the doomed frogs, many people seem unable to detect gradual but deadly trends in modern civilization. To avoid disasters, it may take a conscious effort by large numbers of people to see the "big picture" and reverse lethal but easily overlooked patterns (Ornstein & Ehrlich, 1989).

shot in a library would be hard to ignore. Big, bright cars probably get more tickets than small, dull ones.

Repetitious stimuli, repetitious stimuli, repetitious stimuli, repetitious stimuli, repetitious stimuli, repetitious stimuli are also attention getting. A dripping faucet at night makes little noise by normal standards, but because of repetition, it may get as much attention as a single sound many times louder. This effect is used repeatedly, so to speak, in television and radio commercials.

ATTENTION IS ALSO **FREQUENTLY** RELATED TO contrast OR *change* IN STIMULATION. The contrasting type styles in the preceding sentence draw attention because they are *unexpected*. Norman Mackworth and Geoffrey Loftus (1978) found that people who look at drawings like ❖Figure 7.29 focus first and longest on unexpected objects (the octopus, in this case).

HABITUATION   Change, contrast, and incongruity are perhaps the most basic sources of attention. We quickly **habituate** (respond less) to predictable and unchanging stimuli. Notice that repetition without variation leads to habituation. Repetition is attention getting when it is irritating or annoying. A dripping faucet varies in timing just enough to gain attention. In contrast, we quickly habituate to the steady tick of a clock.

How does habituation differ from sensory adaptation?   As described in Chapter 6, *adaptation* decreases the actual number of sensory messages sent to the brain. When messages do reach the brain, the body makes a sort of "What is it?" reaction, known as an *orientation response*. An **orientation response** (**OR**) prepares us to receive information from a stimulus: The pupils enlarge, brain wave patterns shift, breathing stops briefly, blood flow to the head increases, and we turn toward the stimulus. Have you ever seen someone do a double take? If so, you have observed an orientation response.

Now, think about what happens when you buy a new CD. At first, the music holds your attention all the way through. But when the CD becomes "old," all the songs may play without your really attending to them. When a stimulus is repeated *without change*, the OR habituates, or decreases. (Also, see "The 'Boiled Frog Syndrome.'")

Interestingly, creative people habituate *more slowly* than average. We might expect that they would rapidly become bored with a repeated stimulus. Instead, it seems that creative people actively attend to stimuli, even those that are repeated (Colin, Moore, & West, 1996).

MOTIVES   Motives also play a role in attention. For example, if you are hungry, food-related words are more likely to gain your attention than other words (Mogg et al., 1998). Thus, if you get hungry while driving a car, you will notice restaurants and billboards picturing food. If you are running low on gas, your attention will shift to gas stations. Advertisers, of course, know that their pitch will be more effective if it gets your attention. Ads are therefore loud, repetitious, and often intentionally irri-

Selective attention *Giving priority to a particular incoming sensory message.*
Divided attention *Allotting mental space or effort to various tasks or parts of a task.*
Habituation *A decrease in perceptual response to a repeated stimulus.*
Orientation response *Bodily changes that prepare an organism to receive information from a particular stimulus.*

tating. They are also designed to take advantage of two motives that are widespread in our society: *anxiety* and *sex.*

Everything from mouthwash to automobile tires is merchandised by using sex to gain attention. For instance, an ad for Triple Sec liqueur ran under the heading "Sec's Appeal." Another liquor ad shows a woman in a seductive velvet dress and says, "Feel the velvet." And what could be more obvious than ads for designer jeans that feature a shapely posterior pointed at the camera? Other ads combine sex with anxiety. Mouthwash, deodorant, soaps, toothpaste, and countless other articles are pushed in ads that play on desires to be attractive, to have "sex appeal," or to avoid embarrassment. Is it really so terrible to have "morning breath" or a poor shave or to perspire at times?

In addition to directing attention, motives may alter what is perceived:

> As part of a supposed study of "the dating practices of college students," male volunteers were shown a picture of a female student and asked to give a first impression of how attractive she was. Before making these ratings, each person read one of two short written passages: One was sexually arousing and the other was not. The important finding was that men who read the more arousing passage rated the female as more attractive (Stephan et al., 1971).

This result may come as no surprise if you have ever been infatuated with someone and then fallen out of love. A person who once seemed highly attractive may look quite different when your feelings change.

An emotional stimulus can shift attention away from other information. In an experiment, members of a Jewish organization watched as pictures like ❖Figure 7.30 were flashed on a screen for a split second. People were less likely to recognize symbols around the drawing's edge when the center item was an emotional symbol like the swastika (Erdelyi & Appelbaum, 1973). This effect probably explains why fans of opposing sports teams often act as if they had seen two completely different games.

PERCEPTUAL EXPECTANCIES—ON YOUR MARK, GET SET

On a piece of paper, draw a circle about 3 inches in diameter. Inside the circle, above and to the left of center, make a large black dot, about one-half inch in diameter. Make another dot inside the circle above and to the right of center. Now, still inside the circle, draw an arc, curved upward and about 2 inches long just below the center of the circle. If you followed these instructions, your reaction might now be "Oh! Why didn't you just say to draw a happy face?"

Like the happy face drawing, perception seems to proceed in two major ways. In **bottom-up processing,** we analyze information starting at the "bottom" with small sensory units (features) and build upward to a complete perception. The reverse also seems to occur. In **top-down processing,** preexisting knowledge is used to rapidly organize features into a meaningful whole. Bottom-up processing is like putting together a picture puzzle you've never seen before: You must assemble small pieces until a recognizable pattern appears. Top-down processing is like putting together a puzzle you have solved many times: After only a few pieces are in place, you begin to see outlines of the final picture.

Both types of processing are illustrated by ❖Figure 7.31. Also, return to ❖Figure 7.5, the giant walking-stick. The first time you saw the photo, you probably processed it bottom-up, picking out features until the insect was recognizable. This time, because of top-down processing, you should see the insect instantly. Another good example of top-down processing is found in perceptual expectancies.

❖ **FIGURE 7.30** *Emotionally significant stimuli influence attention.* *(Erdelyi & Appelbaum, 1973, p. 50. Reprinted by permission.)*

❖ **FIGURE 7.31** *This painting by abstract artist Al Held is 9 feet by 9 feet. If you process the painting "bottom-up," all you will see is two small dark geometric shapes. Would you like to try some top-down processing? Knowing the painting's title will allow you to apply your knowledge and see the painting in an entirely different way. The title? It's "The Big N." Can you see it now? (Courtesy The Museum of Modern Art, New York.)*

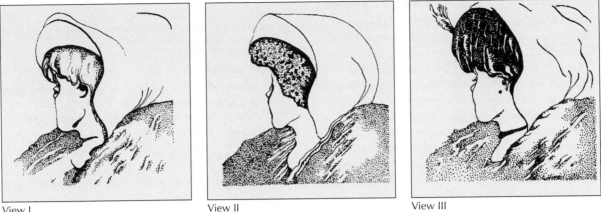

View I   View II   View III

❖ **FIGURE 7.32** *"Young woman, old woman" illustrations. As an interesting demonstration of perceptual expectancy, show some of your friends view I and some view II (cover all other views). Next show your friends view III and ask them what they see. Those who saw view I should see the old woman in view III; those who saw view II should see the young woman in view III. Can you see both? (After Leeper, 1935.)*

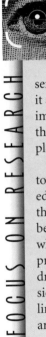

FOCUS ON RESEARCH

WHY MOST PEOPLE CAN'T DRAW WHAT THEY SEE

Why is drawing so difficult for most people? Are they just clumsy with a pencil? Do they make bad decisions about how to use lines to represent objects? Do they misperceive their own drawing—see it as more accurate than it really is? A recent series of experiments by Dale Cohen and Susan Bennett eliminated all of these possibilities. The problem, it seems, is that most people misperceive the objects they are trying to draw.

The perceptions of beginning artists tend to be distorted by labels, categories, assumptions, and prior knowledge. The person sees what she or he expects to see, rather than what's there. For example, in trying to draw a face, beginners think, "nose, mouth, eyes, ears" and try to draw what they *think* each of these features looks like. That's probably why beginning artists can more accurately copy a drawing of a face turned upside down than one that's right side up. When the face is upside down, they just copy the lines and shapes they see. When it's upright, their drawings are affected by what they *think* eyes, noses, mouths, and ears should look like (Cohen & Bennett, 1997).

It is worth remembering that all perceptions, to a degree, are affected by similar processes of labeling, categorizing, and expectation.

Perceptual Set

What is a perceptual expectancy? A runner in the starting blocks at a track meet is *set* to respond in a certain way. Likewise, past experience, motives, context, or suggestions may create a **perceptual expectancy** (or **set**) that prepares you to perceive in a certain way. If a car backfires, runners at a track meet may jump the gun. As a matter of fact, we all frequently jump the gun when perceiving. In essence, an expectancy is a percep-

tual hypothesis we are *very likely* to apply to a stimulus—even if applying it is inappropriate. (For another angle on this idea, read "Why Most People Can't Draw What They See.")

Perceptual sets often lead us to see what we *expect* to see. For example, let's say you are driving across the desert. You are very low on gas. Finally, you see a sign approaching. On it are the words FUEL AHEAD. You relax, knowing you will not be stranded. But as you draw nearer, the words on the sign become FOOD AHEAD. Most people have had similar experiences in which expectations altered their perceptions. To observe perceptual expectancies firsthand, perform the demonstration described in ❖Figure 7.32.

Perceptual expectancies are frequently created by *suggestion.* This is especially true of perceiving other people. For example, a psychology professor once arranged for a guest lecturer to teach his class. Half the students in the class were given a page of notes that described the lecturer as a "rather *cold* person, industrious, critical, practical, and determined." The other students got notes describing him as a "rather *warm* person, industrious, critical, practical, and determined" (Kelley, 1950; italics added). Students who received the "cold" description perceived the lecturer as unhappy and irritable and didn't volunteer in class discussion. Those who got the "warm" description saw the lecturer as happy and good-natured, and they actively took part in discussion with him.

CATEGORIES   Have you ever seen playing cards with a *red* ace of spades or a *black* four of hearts? Psychologist Jerome Bruner used a tachistoscope (tack-ISS-toh-scope: a device for displaying images for very brief periods) to flash pictures of cards on a screen.

Bottom-up processing *Organizing perceptions by beginning with low-level features.*
Top-down processing *Applying higher-level knowledge to rapidly organize sensory information into a meaningful perception.*
Perceptual expectancy (or set) *A readiness to perceive in a particular manner, induced by strong expectations.*

He found that observers misperceived cards that did not fit their knowledge and expectations. For instance, a *red* six of spades would be misperceived as a normal six of hearts (Bruner & Postman, 1949). Bruner believes that learning builds up **perceptual categories** (classes, types, or groups). Experiences are then "sorted" into these categories. Because observers had no category for a red six of spades, they saw it as a six of hearts. Categories such as "punk," "mental patient," "queer," "illegal immigrant," and "bitch" are particularly likely to distort perceptions.

Those are extremes. Does it really make that much difference what you call someone or something? Perceptual categories, especially those defined by labels, do make a difference. This is especially true in perceiving people, when even trained observers may be influenced. For example, in one study, psychotherapists were shown a videotaped interview. Half of the therapists were told that the man being interviewed was applying for a job. The rest were told that the man was a mental patient. Therapists who thought the man was a job applicant perceived him as "realistic," "sincere," and "pleasant." Those who thought he was a patient perceived him as "defensive," "dependent," and "impulsive" (Langer & Abelson, 1974).

A LOOK AHEAD In this chapter, we have moved from basic perceptions to the complexities of perceiving people and events. In the "Psychology in Action" section, we will continue this progression with a look at objectivity and eyewitness testimony. After that, the "A Step Beyond" feature addresses an interesting question: Does extrasensory perception exist?

K N O W L E D G E   B U I L D E R

ATTENTION AND PERCEPTUAL EXPECTANCIES

RELATE

Have you ever tried to listen to two people who were talking to you at the same time? What happens to your ability to process information when there's a conflict in selective attention?

You have almost certainly misperceived a situation at some time because of a perceptual expectancy or the influence of motives. How were your perceptions influenced?

LEARNING CHECK

1. Selective attention is promoted by all but one of the following. Which does not fit?
   a. habituation *b.* contrast *c.* change *d.* intensity

2. The occurrence of an orientation response shows that habituation is complete. T or F?

3. Changes in brain waves and increased blood flow to the head are part of an OR. T or F?

4. Research shows that heightened sexual arousal can cause a person to perceive members of the opposite sex as more physically attractive. T or F?

5. In top-down processing of information, individual features are analyzed and assembled into a meaningful whole. T or F?

6. When a person is prepared to perceive events in a particular way, it is said that a perceptual expectancy or _____ exists.

7. Perceptual expectancies are greatly influenced by the existence of mental categories and labels. T or F?

CRITICAL THINKING

8. Cigarette advertisements in the United States are required to carry a warning label about the health risks of smoking. How have tobacco companies made these labels less visible?

Answers:

1. a 2. F 3. T 4. T 5. F 6. set 7. T 8. Advertisers place health warnings in the corners of ads, where they attract the least possible attention. Also, the labels are often placed on "busy" backgrounds so that they are partially camouflaged. Finally, the main images in ads are designed to strongly attract attention. This further distracts readers from seeing the warnings.

psychology in action

PERCEPTION AND OBJECTIVITY—BELIEVING IS SEEING

Have you ever seen the sun set? You may think you have. Yet, in reality, we know the sun does not "set." Instead, our viewing angle changes as the earth turns, until the sun is obscured by the horizon. Want to try the alternative? This evening, stand facing the west. With practice, you can learn to feel yourself being swept backward on the rotating surface of the earth as you watch an unmoving sun recede in the distance (Fuller, 1969).

This radical shift in perspective illustrates the limitations of "objective" observation. Like most experiences, seeing a "sunset" is a **perceptual reconstruction** (mental model) of an external event. Another way of appreciating this is to real-

ize that it takes about 50 milliseconds for a visual signal to move from the retina to the brain. Therefore, the images we see are always slightly in the past. An event that happens quickly, like the pop of a flashbulb, may be over by the time we perceive it.

As we have seen, perception reflects the needs, expectations, attitudes, values, and beliefs of the perceiver. In this light, the phrase "seeing is believing" must be modified. Clearly, we see what we believe, as well as believe what we see (❖Fig. 7.33).

In some cases, subjective perception nurtures the personal vision valued in art, music, poetry, and scientific innovation. Often, however, it is a real liability.

EYEWITNESS In the courtroom, eyewitness testimony can be a key to proving guilt or innocence. The claim "I saw it with my own eyes" carries a lot of weight with a jury. Most jurors (unless they have taken a psychology course) tend to assume that eyewitness testimony is nearly infallible (Durham & Dane, 1999). Even police officers, who are presumably more familiar with witnesses, generally believe that eyewitnesses are rarely incorrect (Kebbell & Milne, 1998). But, to put it bluntly, eyewitness testimony is frequently wrong.

Juries are most swayed by witnesses who are certain that their testimony is accurate. Yet, in fact, a person's confidence in his or her testimony has almost no bearing on its accuracy (Wells, 1993)! In addition, being questioned tends to make witnesses more confident about what they saw, even if they are wrong. Thus, police questioning can actually degrade the value of the testimony witnesses give later, in court (Shaw, 1996).

Psychologists are gradually convincing lawyers, judges, and police officers of the fallibility of eyewitness testimony. Even so, thousands of people have been wrongfully convicted (Loftus, 1993). In one typical court case, a police officer testified that he saw the defendant shoot the victim as both stood in a doorway 120 feet away. Measurements made by a psychologist showed that, at that distance, light from the dimly lit doorway was extremely weak—less than a fifth of that from a candle. To further show that identification was improbable, a juror stood in the doorway under identical lighting conditions. None of the other jurors could identify him. The defendant was acquitted (Buckhout, 1974).

Unfortunately, perception rarely provides an "instant replay" of events. Even in broad daylight, eyewitness testimony is untrustworthy. After a horrible DC-10 airliner crash in Chicago, 84 pilots who saw the accident were interviewed. Forty-two said the DC-10's landing gear was up, and 42 said it was down! As one investigator commented, the best witness may be a "kid under 12 years old who doesn't have his parents around." Adults, it seems, are easily swayed by their expectations.

Impressions formed when a person is surprised, threatened, or under stress are especially prone to distortion. That's why witnesses to crimes so often disagree. As a dramatic demonstration of this problem, a college professor was attacked by an actor in a staged assault. Immediately after the event, 141 witnesses were questioned in detail. Their descriptions were then compared to a videotape made of the staged "crime." The total accuracy score for the group (on features such as appearance, age, weight, and height of the assailant) was only *25 percent* of the maximum possible (Buckhout, 1974). Similarly, a study of real eyewitness cases found that the *wrong person* was chosen from police lineups 25 percent of the time (Levi, 1998).

Wouldn't the victim of a crime remember more than a mere witness? A revealing study found that eyewitness accuracy is virtually the same for witnessing a crime (seeing a pocket calculator stolen) as it is for being a victim (seeing one's own watch stolen) (Hosch & Cooper, 1982). Jurors who place more weight on the testimony of victims may be making a serious mistake. Also, it is worth repeating that witnesses who are confident in their testimony are no more likely to be accurate than those who have doubts (Smith, Kassin, & Ellsworth, 1989).

In many crimes, victims fall prey to the phenomenon of **weapon focus.** Understandably, victims often fix their entire attention on the knife, gun, or other weapon used by an attacker. In doing so, they fail to perceive details of appearance, dress, or other clues to identity (Steblay, 1992).

Additional factors affecting eyewitnesses are summarized in ◆Table 7.2.

In summary, jurors who place more weight on the testimony of victims may be making a serious mistake. Also, it is worth repeating that witnesses who are confident in their testimony are no more likely to be accurate than those who have doubts (Smith, Kassin, & Ellsworth, 1989). Now that DNA testing is available, more than 60 people who were convicted of murder, rape, and other crimes have been exonerated. In each instance, these innocent people were convicted mainly on the basis of eyewitness testimony. Each of them spent *years* in prison before being cleared (Foxhall, 2000).

IMPLICATIONS How often are everyday perceptions as inaccurate or distorted as those of an emotional eyewitness? The an-

---

BRIDGES

Distortions in memory also affect the accuracy of eyewitness testimony.

See Chapter 10, pages 316–317.

❖ **FIGURE 7.33** *It is difficult to look at this simple drawing without perceiving depth. Yet, the drawing is nothing more than a collection of flat shapes. Turn this page counterclockwise 90° and you will see 3 Cs, one within another. When the drawing is turned sideways, it seems nearly flat. However, if you turn the page upright again, a sense of depth will reappear. Clearly, you have used your knowledge and expectations to construct an illusion of depth. The drawing itself would be only a flat design if you didn't invest it with meaning.*

Perceptual category *A preexisting class, type, or grouping.*
Perceptual reconstruction *A mental model of external events.*
Weapon focus *The tendency of crime victims to fix their attention on an attacker's weapon.*

---

swer we have been moving toward is, very frequently. Bearing this in mind may help you be more tolerant of the views of others and more cautious about your own objectivity. It may also encourage more frequent *reality testing* on your part.

REALITY TESTING   *What do you mean by reality testing?*   In any situation with an element of doubt or uncertainty, **reality testing** involves obtaining additional information to check your perceptions. Even simple designs like those in ❖Figure 7.34 are easily misperceived. One of the designs in the drawing is a continuous line; the other is not. Most people cannot see this difference spontaneously. Instead, they must carefully trace and compare the two designs as a check on pure perception (Julesz, 1975).

Psychologist Sidney Jourard once offered a more pertinent example of reality testing. One of Jourard's students believed her roommate was stealing from her. The student gradually became convinced of her roommate's guilt but said nothing. As her distrust and anger grew, their relationship turned cold and distant. Finally, at Jourard's urging, she confronted her roommate. The roommate cleared herself immediately and expressed relief when the puzzling change in their relationship was explained (Jourard, 1974). With their friendship reestablished, the true culprit was soon caught. (The cleaning woman did it!)

If you have ever concluded that someone was angry, upset, or unfriendly without checking the accuracy of your perceptions, you have fallen into a subtle trap. Personal objectivity is an elusive quality, requiring frequent reality testing to maintain. At the very least, it pays to ask a person what she or he is feeling when you are in doubt. Clearly, most of us could learn to be better "eyewitnesses" to daily events.

PERCEPTUAL AWARENESS   *Do some people perceive things more accurately than others?*   Humanistic psychologist Abraham Maslow (1969) believed that some people perceive themselves and others with unusual accuracy. Maslow characterized these people as especially alive, open, aware, and mentally healthy. He found that their perceptual styles were marked by immersion in the present, a lack of self-consciousness, freedom from selecting, criticizing, or evaluating, and a general "surrender" to experience. The kind of perception Maslow described is like that of a mother with her newborn infant, a child at Christmas, or two people in love.

Seeking enlightenment through meditation is a core religious practice in Zen Buddhism. Does the remarkable mental clarity attained by Zen masters affect their perceptions? For example, how do Zen masters respond to repeated stimuli? Amazingly, they fail to show the expected habituation (Kasamatsu & Hirai, 1966). This finding lends some credibility to claims that Zen masters perceive a tree as vividly after seeing it 500 times as they did the first time.

ATTENTION   Whereas the average person has not reached perceptual restriction of the "if you've seen one tree, you've seen

❖ **TABLE 7.2** Factors Affecting the Accuracy of Eyewitness Perceptions

SOURCES OF ERROR	SUMMARY OF FINDINGS
1. Stress	Very high levels of stress impair the accuracy of eyewitness perceptions.
2. Weapon focus	The presence of a weapon impairs an eyewitness's ability to accurately identify the culprit's face.
3. Exposure time	The less time an eyewitness has to observe an event, the less well she or he will perceive and remember it.
4. Accuracy-confidence	An eyewitness's confidence is not a good predictor of his or her accuracy.
5. Cross-racial perceptions	Eyewitnesses are better at identifying members of their own race than they are at identifying people of other races.
6. Post-event information	Eyewitness testimony about an event often reflects not only what was actually seen but also information obtained later on.
7. Color perception	Judgments of color made under monochromatic light (such as an orange street light) are highly unreliable.
8. Wording of questions	An eyewitness's testimony about an event can be affected by how the questions put to that witness are worded.
9. Unconscious transference	Eyewitnesses sometimes identify as a culprit someone they have seen in another situation or context.
10. Trained observers	Police officers and other trained observers are no more accurate as eyewitnesses than the average person.
11. Time estimation	Eyewitnesses tend to overestimate the duration of events.
12. Attitudes, expectations	An eyewitness's perception and memory for an event may be affected by his or her attitudes and expectations.

(Adapted from Kassin, Ellsworth, & Smith, 1989.)

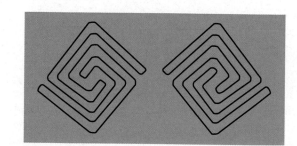

❖ **FIGURE 7.34** *The limits of pure perception. Even simple designs are easily misperceived. The drawing on the left is a continuous line; the one on the right is not. Most people cannot see this difference without carefully tracing the lines. (Adapted from patterns devised by Marvin Minsky and Seymour Papert.)*

them all" variety, the fact remains that most of us tend to look at a tree and classify it into the perceptual category of "trees in general" without really appreciating the miracle standing before us. How, then, can we bring about **dishabituation** (a reversal of habituation) on a day-to-day basis? Does perceptual clarity require years of meditative discipline, like that of a Zen master? Fortunately, a more immediate avenue is available. The deceptively simple key to dishabituation is: Pay attention.

The following quote summarizes the importance of attention:

> One day a man of the people said to Zen Master Ikkyu: "Master, will you please write for me some maxims of the highest wisdom?"
>
> Ikkyu immediately took his brush and wrote the word "Attention."
>
> "Is that all?" asked the man. "Will you not add something more?"
>
> Ikkyu then wrote twice running: "Attention. Attention."
>
> "Well," remarked the man rather irritably, "I really don't see much depth or subtlety in what you have just written."
>
> Then Ikkyu wrote the same word three times running: "Attention. Attention. Attention." Half angered, the man demanded, "What does that word 'Attention' mean anyway?"
>
> And Ikkyu answered gently: "Attention means attention" (Kapleau, 1966).

To this we can add only one thought, provided by the words of poet William Blake: "If the doors of perception were cleansed, man would see everything as it is, infinite."

Becoming a Better "Eyewitness" to Life

Here's a summary of ideas from this chapter to help you maintain and enhance perceptual accuracy.

1. *Remember that perceptions are reconstructions of reality.* Learn to regularly question your own perceptions. Are they accurate? Could another interpretation fit the facts? What assumptions are you making? Could they be false? How might your assumptions be distorting your perceptions?
2. *Break perceptual habits and interrupt habituation.* Each day, try to do some activities in new ways. For example, take different routes when you travel to work or school. Do routines, such as brushing your teeth or combing your hair, with your nonpreferred hand. Try to look at friends and family members as if they are people you just met for the first time.
3. *Shift adaptation levels and broaden frames of reference by seeking out-of-the-ordinary experiences.* The possibilities here range from trying foods you don't normally eat to reading opinions very different from your own. Experiences ranging from a quiet walk in the woods to a trip to an amusement park may be perceptually refreshing.
4. *Beware of perceptual sets.* Anytime you pigeonhole people, objects, or events, there is a danger that your perceptions will be distorted by expectations or preexisting categories. Be especially wary of labels and stereotypes. Try to see people as individuals and events as unique, one-time occurrences.
5. *Be aware of the ways in which motives and emotions influence perceptions.* It is difficult to avoid being swayed by your own interests, needs, desires, and emotions. But be aware of this trap and actively try to see the world through the eyes of others. Taking the other person's perspective is especially

valuable in disputes or arguments. Ask yourself, "How does this look to her or him?"

6. *Make a habit of engaging in reality testing.* Actively look for additional evidence to check the accuracy of your perceptions. Ask questions, seek clarifications, and find alternate channels of information. Remember that perception is not automatically accurate. You could be wrong—we all are, frequently.
7. *Pay attention.* Make a conscious effort to pay attention to other people and your surroundings. Don't drift through life in a haze. Listen to others with full concentration. Watch their facial expressions. Make eye contact. Try to get in the habit of approaching perception as if you are going to have to testify later about what you saw and heard.

KNOWLEDGE BUILDER
PERCEPTUAL AWARENESS AND OBJECTIVITY

RELATE

Because perceptions are reconstructions or models of external events, we should all engage in more frequent reality testing. Can you think of a recent event when a little reality testing would have saved you from misjudging a situation?

In order to improve your own perceptual awareness and accuracy, which strategies would you emphasize first?

LEARNING CHECK

1. Most perceptions can be described as active reconstructions of external reality. T or F?

2. Inaccuracies in eyewitness perceptions obviously occur in real life, but they cannot be reproduced in psychology experiments. T or F?

3. Accuracy scores for facts provided by witnesses to staged crimes may be as low as 25 percent correct. T or F?

4. Victims of crimes are more accurate eyewitnesses than are impartial observers. T or F?

5. *Reality testing* is another term for dishabituation. T or F?

CRITICAL THINKING

6. Return for a moment to the incident described in the chapter Preview. What perceptual factors were involved in the first version of the "murder"? How did the girl affect what was seen?

Answers:

1. T 2. F 3. T 4. F 5. F 6. The girl's misperception, communicated so forcefully to other eyewitnesses, created a powerful expectancy that influenced what they perceived. Also, the stressful or emotional nature of the incident encouraged misperception.

Reality testing *Obtaining additional information to check the accuracy of perceptions.*

Dishabituation *A reversal of habituation.*

Focus: Has the existence of ESP been demonstrated?

In a quiet laboratory, Uri Geller, a self-proclaimed "psychic," has agreed to demonstrate his claimed paranormal abilities. In the course of testing, Geller was supposedly able to select, from a row of 10 film canisters, the one that contained an object, correctly guess the number that would come up on a die shaken in a closed box 8 out of 8 times, and reproduce drawings sealed in opaque envelopes.

Was Geller cheating, or was he using some ability beyond normal perception? There is little doubt that Geller was cheating (Randi, 1980). But how? The answer lies in a discussion of **extrasensory perception (ESP)**—the purported ability to perceive events in ways that cannot be explained by known sensory capacities.

Parapsychology

Parapsychology is the study of ESP and other psi phenomena (events that seem to defy accepted scientific laws). (*Psi* is pronounced like *sigh*.) Parapsychologists seek answers to the questions raised by three basic forms that ESP could take.

1. **Clairvoyance.** The purported ability to perceive events or gain information in ways that appear unaffected by distance or normal physical barriers.
2. **Telepathy.** Extrasensory perception of another person's thoughts or, more simply, the purported ability to read someone else's mind.
3. **Precognition.** The purported ability to perceive or accurately predict future events. Precognition may take the form of *prophetic dreams* that foretell the future.

While we are at it, we might as well toss in another purported psi ability:

4. **Psychokinesis.** The purported ability to exert influence over inanimate objects by willpower ("mind over matter"). (Psychokinesis cannot be classed as a type of ESP, but it is frequently studied by parapsychologists.)

Have parapsychologists confirmed the existence of ESP and other psi abilities? Psychologists as a group are highly skeptical about psi abilities. But the general public remains split on the issue. A national poll found that 49 percent of all American adults believe in ESP (Gallup & Newport, 1991). If you doubt ESP, then you should know that some experiments seem to hint that it may exist. If you are among those who believe in ESP, then you should know why the scientific community doubts many of these experiments!

COINCIDENCE   Anyone who has ever had an apparent clairvoyant or telepathic experience may find it hard to question the existence of ESP. Yet, the difficulty of excluding *coincidence* makes natural ESP occurrences less conclusive than they might seem. Consider a typical psychic experience: During the middle of the night, a woman away for a weekend visit suddenly had a strong impulse to return home. When she arrived, she found the house on fire with her husband asleep inside (Rhine, 1953).

An experience like this is striking, but it does not confirm the existence of ESP. If, by coincidence, a hunch turns out to be correct, it may be *reinterpreted* as precognition or clairvoyance (Marks & Kammann, 1979). If it is not confirmed, it will simply be forgotten. Most people don't realize it, but such coincidences occur quite often. In fact, we should *expect* them, not consider them strange or mysterious (Alcock, 1990). Believers

Most so-called psychics are simply keen observers. The "psychic" begins a "reading" by making general statements about a person. The "psychic" then plays "hot and cold" by attending to the person's facial expressions, body language, or tone of voice. When the "psychic" is "hot" (on the right track), the "psychic" continues to make similar statements about the person. If the person's reactions signal that the "psychic" is "cold," the psychic drops that topic or line of thought and tries another (Schouten, 1994).

a step beyond

in ESP are especially prone to misjudge seemingly unusual events. That's because believers tend to falsely see cause-and-effect links in everyday coincidences (Brugger, Landis, & Regard, 1990).

The formal study of psi events owes much to the late J. B. Rhine. Rhine established the first parapsychological laboratory at Duke University and spent the rest of his life trying to document ESP. To avoid the problems of "natural" psi events, Rhine tried to study ESP more objectively. Many of his experiments made use of the **Zener cards** (a deck of 25 cards, each bearing one of five symbols) (❖Fig. 7.35). In a typical clairvoyance test, people tried to guess the symbols on the cards as they were turned up from a shuffled deck. Pure guessing in this test will produce an average score of 5 "hits" out of 25 cards.

FRAUD Unfortunately, some of Rhine's most dramatic early experiments used badly printed Zener cards that allowed the symbols to show faintly on the back. It is also very easy to cheat, by marking cards with a fingernail or by noting marks on the cards caused by normal use. Even if this were not the case, there is evidence that early experimenters sometimes unconsciously gave people cues about the cards with their eyes, facial gestures, or lip movements. In short, none of the early studies in parapsychology was done in a way that eliminated the possibility of fraud or "leakage" of helpful information (Alcock, 1990).

Modern parapsychologists are now well aware of the need for double-blind experiments, security and accuracy in record keeping, meticulous control, and repeatability of experiments (Milton & Wiseman, 1997). In the last 10 years, hundreds of experiments have been reported in parapsychological journals. Many of them seem to support the existence of psi abilities.

SKEPTICISM *Then why do most psychologists remain skeptical about psi abilities?* For one thing, fraud continues to plague the field. Walter J. Levy, who was the former director of Rhine's laboratory, was caught faking records. So have some others who got positive results. Even honest scientists have been fooled by various frauds and cheats, so there is reason to remain skeptical and on guard. The greatest danger may lie in errors by sincere, but self-deceiving, investigators (Hyman, 1989). It is remarkable, for instance, that many parapsychologists chose to ignore a famous "psychic's" habit of peeking at ESP cards during testing (Cox, 1994). As one critic put it, positive ESP results usually mean "Error Some Place" (Marks, 1990). The more closely psi experiments are examined, the more likely it is that claimed successes will evaporate (Alcock, 1990; Hyman, 1996b).

❖ **FIGURE 7.35** *ESP cards used by J. B. Rhine, an early experimenter in parapsychology.*

STATISTICS AND CHANCE A major criticism of psi research has to do with inconsistency. For every study with positive results, there are others that fail (Hansel, 1980; Hyman, 1996b). It is rare—in fact, almost unheard of—for a person to maintain psi ability over any sustained period of time (Jahn, 1982). ESP researchers consider this "decline effect" an indication that parapsychological skills are very fragile and unpredictable. But critics argue that a person who only temporarily scores above chance has just received credit for a **run of luck** (a statistically unusual outcome that could occur by chance alone). When the run is over, it is not fair to assume that ESP is temporarily gone. We must count *all* attempts.

To understand the run-of-luck criticism, consider an example. Say that you flip a coin 100 times and record the results. You then flip another coin 100 times, again recording the results. The two lists are compared. For any 10 pairs of flips, we would expect heads or tails to match 5 times. Let's say that you go through the list and find a set of 10 pairs where 9 out of 10 matched. This is far above chance expectation. But does it mean that the first coin "knew" what was going to come up on the second coin? The idea is obviously silly.

Now, what if a person guesses 100 times what will come up on a coin. Again, we might find a set of 10 guesses that matches the results of flipping the coin. Does this mean that the person, for a time, had precognition—then lost it? Parapsychologists tend to believe the answer is yes. Skeptics assume that nothing more than random matching occurred, as in the two-coin example.

Research Methods

Unfortunately, many of the most spectacular findings in parapsychology simply cannot be **replicated** (reproduced or repeated) (Hyman, 1996a). Even the same researchers using the same experimental subjects typically can't get similar results every time (Schick & Vaughn, 1995). More important, improved research methods usually result in fewer positive results (Hyman, 1996b).

Extrasensory perception *The purported ability to perceive events in ways that cannot be explained by known capacities of the sensory organs.*
Parapsychology *The study of extranormal psychological events, such as extrasensory perception.*
Psi phenomena *Events that seem to lie outside the realm of accepted scientific laws.*
Clairvoyance *The purported ability to perceive events at a distance or through physical barriers.*
Telepathy *The purported ability to directly know another person's thoughts.*
Precognition *The purported ability to accurately predict future events.*
Psychokinesis *The purported ability to mentally alter or influence objects or events.*
Zener cards *A deck of 25 cards bearing various symbols and used in early parapsychological research.*
Run of luck *A statistically unusual outcome (such as getting five heads in a row when flipping a coin) that could still occur by chance alone.*
Replicate *To reproduce or repeat.*

A few years ago, parapsychologist Charles Honorton conducted some interesting studies of ESP. Participants in Honorton's experiments had Ping-Pong balls (cut in half) taped over their eyes and they heard "white noise" (a hissing sound) played through headphones. The intent of these measures was to create a **ganzfeld,** or perceptual "blank screen." After about 15 minutes, Honorton's subjects began to have vivid mental images. At that time, a "sender" in another room tried to mentally transmit images to the subject. Honorton claims that some of his participants received impressions of the images and thereby demonstrated ESP (Honorton & Bem, 1994).

Honorton's study raised a flurry of renewed interest in ESP. However, it now looks like the ganzfeld experiments must be added to parapsychology's long history of unrepeatable results. Thirty studies done since Honorton claimed to have observed ESP all failed to replicate his findings (Milton & Wiseman, 1999a).

Believers in ESP, such as ex-astronaut Edgar Mitchell, claim that failures to find ESP may occur for another reason. According to Mitchell, "The scientist has to recognize that his own mental processes may influence the phenomenon he's observing. If he's really a total skeptic, the scientist may well turn off the psychic subject." This may sound convincing, but skeptics consider it unfair. With Mitchell's argument in effect, anyone attempting an objective experiment can get only two results: He or she may find evidence of ESP or be accused of having suppressed it. This makes it impossible to disprove ESP to believers, even if it truly does not exist.

Reinterpretation is also a problem in psi experiments. For example, Mitchell claimed he did a successful telepathy experiment from space. Yet news accounts never mentioned that on some trials Mitchell's "receivers" scored above chance, and on others they scored *below* chance. The second outcome, Mitchell decided, was also a "success" because it represented intentional "psi missing." But, as skeptics have noted, if both high scores and low scores count as successes, how can you lose?

Of course, in many ESP tests the outcome is beyond debate. For instance, English "psychic" Chris Robinson, who claims to have precognitive dreams, was tested recently. The result? His performance did not exceed what would be expected on the basis of chance (Blackmore, 1995). It's interesting that Mr. Robinson didn't foresee his own impending failure and refuse to be tested! Even more telling, perhaps, is a recent analysis of ESP experiments done through newspapers, radio, and television. In mass media studies, people attempt to identify ESP targets from a distance. (This is similar to trying to guess what lottery numbers will come up.) Such studies allow large numbers of people to be tested. The results of over 1.5 million ESP trials recently done through the mass media are easy to summarize: There was no significant ESP effect. Zero. Zip. Nada. Clearly, state lottery organizers have nothing to fear (Milton & Wiseman, 1999b).

Stage ESP

Skeptics and serious researchers in ESP both agree on one point. If psychic phenomena do occur, they cannot be controlled well enough to be used by entertainers. **Stage ESP** simulates ESP for the purpose of entertainment. Like stage magic, it is based on a combination of sleight of hand, deception, and patented gadgets (❖Fig. 7.36). A case in point is Uri Geller, a former nightclub magician who "astounded" audiences—and some scientists—with apparent telepathy, psychokinesis, and precognition.

Geller's performance on tests was described earlier. Not mentioned is what psychologist Ray Hyman calls the "incredible sloppiness" of these tests. One example is Geller's reproductions of sealed drawings. These, it turns out, were done in a room next to the one where the drawings were made. Original reports of Geller's alleged "ability" failed to mention that there was a hole in the wall between the two rooms, through which Geller might have heard discussions of the pictures being drawn. Also unreported was the fact that Geller's friend Shipi

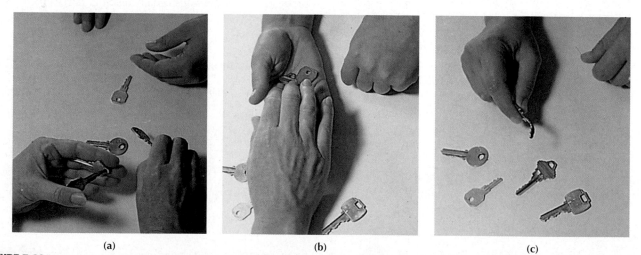

| (a) | (b) | (c) |

❖ **FIGURE 7.36** *Fake psychokinesis. (a) The performer shows an observer several straight keys. While doing so, he bends one of the keys by placing its tip in the slot of another key. Normally, this is done out of sight, behind the "psychic's" hand. It is clearly shown here so you can see how the deception occurs. (b) Next, the "psychic" places the two keys in the observer's hand and closes it. By skillful manipulation, the observer has been kept from seeing the bent key. The performer then "concentrates" on the keys to "bend them with psychic energy." (c) The bent key is revealed to the observer. "Miracle" accomplished! (Adapted from Randi, 1983.)*

Stang was present at every test. Geller's manager has since testified that Stang frequently acted as Geller's accomplice in trickery (Alcock, 1990). Is it a coincidence that when a picture of a rocket ship was drawn, Stang hummed the theme music from the motion picture *2001: A Space Odyssey?* A similar lack of control pervaded every other test. In the "die in the box" tests, for instance, Geller was allowed to hold the box, shake it, and have the honor of opening it (Randi, 1980; Wilhelm, 1976). Why weren't such pertinent details reported?

Sensational and uncritical reporting of apparent paranormal events is widespread. Hundreds of books, articles, and television programs are produced each year by people who have become wealthy promoting unsupported claims. A person who did have psychic powers would not have to make a living by entertaining, giving demonstrations, or making personal appearances. A quick trip to a casino would allow the person to retire for life.

IMPLICATIONS After close to 130 years of investigation, it is still impossible to say conclusively whether psi events occur. As we have seen, a close look at psi experiments often reveals serious problems of evidence, procedure, and scientific rigor (Alcock, 1990; Hyman, 1996b; Marks & Kammann, 1979; Swets et al., 1988). It is also interesting to note that a survey of leading parapsychologists and skeptics found that almost all in both camps said their belief in psi had decreased (Blackmore, 1989). Yet, being a skeptic does not mean a person is against something. It means that you are unconvinced. The purpose of this discussion, then, has been to counter the *uncritical* acceptance of psi events that is rampant in the media.

What would it take to scientifically demonstrate the existence of ESP? Quite simply, a set of instructions that would allow any competent, unbiased observer to produce a psi event under standardized conditions that rule out any possibility of fraud (Schick & Vaughn, 1995). Undoubtedly, some intrepid researchers will continue their attempts to supply just that. Others remain skeptics and consider 130 years of inconclusive efforts reason enough to abandon the concept of ESP (Marks, 1990; Swets et al., 1988). At the least, it seems essential to be carefully skeptical of evidence reported in the popular press or by researchers who are uncritical "true believers." (But then, you already knew I was going to say that, didn't you!)

CONCLUSION: The existence of ESP has not been scientifically demonstrated. The most careful studies report negative results, and positive results are typically inconclusive and open to criticism.

KNOWLEDGE BUILDER

EXTRASENSORY PERCEPTION

RELATE

Let's say that a friend of yours is an avid fan of TV shows that feature paranormal themes. See if you can summarize for her or him what is known about ESP. Be sure to include evidence for and against the existence of ESP and some of the thinking errors associated with nonskeptical belief in the paranormal.

LEARNING CHECK

1. Four purported psi events investigated by parapsychologists are clairvoyance, telepathy, precognition, and _____.

2. The _____ cards were used by J. B. Rhine in early tests of ESP.

3. Natural, or "real life," occurrences are regarded as the best evidence for the existence of ESP. T or F?

4. Skeptics attribute positive results in psi experiments to statistical runs of luck. T or F?

5. Replication rates are very high for ESP experiments. T or F?

CRITICAL THINKING

6. What would you estimate is the chance that two people will have the same birthday (day and month, but not year) in a group of 30 people?

7. A "psychic" on television offers to fix broken watches for viewers. Moments later, dozens of viewers call the station to say that their watches miraculously started running again. What have they overlooked?

Answers:

1. psychokinesis 2. Zener 3. F 4. T 5. F 6. Most people assume that this would be a relatively rare event. Actually there is a 71 percent chance that two people in a group of 30 will share a birthday. Most people probably underestimate the natural rate of occurrence of many seemingly mysterious coincidences (Alcock, 1990). 7. When psychologists handled watches awaiting repair at a store, 57 percent began running again, with no help from a "psychic." Believing the "psychic's" claim also overlooks the impact of big numbers: If the show reached a large audience, at least a few "broken" watches would start working merely by chance.

Ziggy

...FROM THE VOLUMES OF COMMERCIALS I'VE SEEN LATELY, i FIGURE THAT 40% OF THE NATIONAL POPULATION ARE "GiFTED PSYCHiCS."

www.uexpress.com

Ganzfeld *A perceptual "blank screen"; usually achieved by creating a uniform white visual field and a neutral auditory tone.*
Stage ESP *The simulation of ESP for the purpose of entertainment.*

CHAPTER IN REVIEW

What are perceptual constancies, and what is their role in perception?

- Perception is the process of assembling sensations into a usable mental representation of the world.
- In vision, the image projected on the retina is constantly changing, but the external world appears stable and undistorted because of size, shape, and brightness constancy.

What basic principles do we use to group sensations into meaningful patterns?

- The most basic organization of sensations is a division into figure and ground (object and background).
- A number of factors contribute to the organization of sensations. These are nearness, similarity, continuity, closure, contiguity, common region, and combinations of the preceding. Basic elements of line drawings appear to be universally recognized.
- A perceptual organization may be thought of as a hypothesis held until evidence contradicts it. Perceptual organization shifts for ambiguous stimuli. Impossible figures resist stable organization altogether.

How is it possible to see depth and judge distance?

- Depth perception (the ability to perceive three-dimensional space and judge distances) is present in basic form soon after birth (as shown by testing with the visual cliff and other methods).
- Depth perception depends on the muscular cues of accommodation (bending of the lens) and convergence (inward movement of the eyes). Stereoscopic vision is created mainly by retinal disparity and the resulting overlap and mismatch of visual sensations.
- Various pictorial cues also underlie depth perception. They are linear perspective, relative size, height in the picture plane, light and shadow, overlap, texture gradients, aerial haze, and relative motion (motion parallax). All are monocular depth cues (only one eye is needed to make use of them).
- The moon illusion appears to be best explained by the apparent distance hypothesis, which emphasizes the greater number of depth cues present when the moon is on the horizon.

What effect does learning have on perception?

- Perceptual habits influence the ways in which we organize and interpret sensations. Studies of inverted vision show that even the most basic organization is subject to a degree of change. Active movement speeds adaptation to a new perceptual environment.
- Perceptual judgments are not made in a vacuum. They are almost always related to context or to an internal frame of reference called the *adaptation level*.
- One of the most familiar of all illusions, the Müller-Lyer illusion, seems to be related to perceptual learning, linear perspective, size-distance invariance relationships, and mislocation of the end-points of the figure.

How is perception altered by attention, motives, values, and expectations?

- Attention is selective, and it may be divided among various activities. Attention is closely related to stimulus intensity, repetition, contrast, change, and incongruity.
- Attention is accompanied by an orientation response. When a stimulus is repeated without change, the orientation response undergoes habituation.
- Personal motives and values often alter perceptions by changing the evaluation of what is seen or by altering attention to specific details.
- Perceptions may be based on top-down or bottom-up processing of information.
- Attention, prior experience, suggestion, and motives combine in various ways to create perceptual sets, or expectancies. These prepare a person to perceive or misperceive in a particular way.

How reliable are eyewitness reports?

- Perception is an active reconstruction of events. This is one reason why eyewitness testimony is surprisingly unreliable. Eyewitness accuracy is further damaged by weapon focus and a number of similar factors.
- Perceptual accuracy is enhanced by reality testing, dishabituation, and conscious efforts to pay attention. It is also valuable to break perceptual habits, to broaden frames of reference, to beware of perceptual sets, and to be aware of the ways in which motives and emotions influence perceptions.

Is extrasensory perception possible?

- Parapsychology is the study of purported psi phenomena, including clairvoyance, telepathy, precognition, and psychokinesis.
- Research in parapsychology remains controversial, owing to a variety of problems and shortcomings. The bulk of the evidence to date is against the existence of ESP. Stage ESP is based on deception and tricks.

PSYCHOLOGY ON THE NET

- **IllusionWorks** A large collection of visual illusions. http://www.illusionworks.com/
- **Perceptual Processes** A wide-ranging tutorial on perception. http://onesun.cc.geneseo.edu/~intd225/prcptn.html
- **Stereogram Links** Provides links to stereograms and information about stereograms, including how to create your own. http://icdweb.cc.purdue.edu/~sexton/
- **The Joy of Visual Perception** An on-line book about visual perception. http://www.yorku.ca/eye/
- **Vision Test** An on-screen vision test. http://www.milfordeye.com/vtest.htm#chart
- **InfoTrac® College Edition** For recent articles related to the "A Step Beyond" feature, use Key Words search for EXTRASENSORY PERCEPTION.

INTERACTIVE LEARNING

- *PsychNow!* 3c. Perception.
- *Psyk.trek* 3e. Gestalt psychology. 3f. Depth perception. 3g. Visual illusions.

CHAPTER 8

States of Consciousness

Chapter Survey

Theme: *Understanding states of consciousness can promote self-awareness and enhance personal effectiveness.*

▼ **KEY QUESTIONS**

● *KEY TOPICS*

▼ What is an altered state of consciousness?

● *Normal and altered states of consciousness*

▼ What are the effects of sleep loss or changes in sleep patterns?

● *Sleep needs, sleep deprivation, and sleep patterns*

▼ Are there different stages of sleep?

● *Stages and types of sleep*

▼ How does dream sleep differ from dreamless sleep?

● *REM sleep and NREM sleep*

▼ What are the causes of sleep disorders and unusual sleep events?

● *Sleep disturbances, types and causes of insomnia*
● *How to get to sleep*

▼ Do dreams have meaning?

● *Dream theories*

▼ **KEY QUESTIONS**

● *KEY TOPICS*

▼ How is hypnosis done, and what are its limitations?

● *Hypnotic induction, susceptibility, and phenomena*
● *Stage hypnosis*

▼ How does sensory deprivation affect consciousness?

● *Sensory deprivation*
● *REST*

▼ What are the effects of the more commonly used psychoactive drugs?

● *Effects of psychoactive drugs*
● *Dependence and abuse*

▼ How are dreams used to promote personal understanding?

● *Dream interpretation*
● *Lucid dreaming*

▼ Why is drug abuse so widespread?

● *Perspectives on drug abuse*

LIVING NIGHTMARES

I N NEW YORK'S TIMES SQUARE, a strange spectacle unfolds: To raise money for charity, disc jockey Peter Tripp has agreed to forgo sleep for 200 hours. All too soon, Tripp's fight to stay awake turns brutal. After 100 hours, he begins to have hallucinations: He sees cobwebs in his shoes, and he watches in terror as a tweed coat becomes a suit of "furry worms." When Tripp goes to a hotel to change clothes, a dresser drawer seems to burst into flames.

After 170 hours, Tripp is in agony. He struggles with simple thought, reasoning, and memory problems. His brain wave patterns look like those of sleep, and he is no longer sure who he is. By the end of 200 hours, Tripp is unable to distinguish between his waking nightmares, hallucinations, and reality (Luce, 1965).

THE WOMB TANK   We shift now to a scene far removed from Peter Tripp's ordeal. Some years ago, physician John Lilly pioneered the use of an unusual sensory deprivation environment. Subjects in Lilly's experiments wore dark goggles and floated naked in a tank of body-temperature water (Lilly, 1972). As they drifted weightlessly in this "womb-like" environment, participants were cut off from smell, touch, vision, hearing, and taste sensations.

What effect does sensory deprivation have?   Under such conditions, people often lose track of time and find it hard to concentrate. Some also undergo strange changes in consciousness. For example, one person screamed in panic, "There is an animal having a long slender body with many legs. It's on the screen, crawling in back of me!"

As you can see, consciousness can be dramatically altered by conditions such as sleep loss and sensory deprivation. In the discussion that follows, we will begin with the familiar realms of sleep and dreaming and then move to more exotic states of consciousness.

Gateways to Consciousness

CONSCIOUSNESS AND ALTERED STATES OF AWARENESS are core features of mental life.

SLEEP is necessary for survival. It occurs in four stages, from shallow to deep, and two basic states, REM sleep and non-REM sleep.

SLEEP LOSS AND SLEEP DISORDERS are serious health problems that should be corrected when they persist.

REM SLEEP helps us form memories, and it contributes to general mental effectiveness.

DREAMS are at least as meaningful as waking thoughts. Whether they have deeper, symbolic meaning is still debated.

HYPNOSIS is useful but not "magical." Hypnosis can change private experiences more readily than behaviors or habits.

PSYCHOACTIVE DRUGS, which alter consciousness, are highly prone to abuse.

COLLECTING AND INTERPRETING YOUR DREAMS can promote self-awareness.

DRUG ABUSE is related to personal maladjustment, the reinforcing qualities of drugs, peer group influences, and expectations about drug effects.

STATES OF CONSCIOUSNESS—THE MANY FACES OF AWARENESS

To be conscious means to be aware. **Consciousness** consists of all the sensations, perceptions, memories, and feelings you are aware of at any instant (Farthing, 1992). We spend most of our lives in **waking consciousness,** a state of clear, organized alertness. In waking consciousness, we perceive times, places, and events as real, meaningful, and familiar. But states of consciousness related to fatigue, delirium, hypnosis, drugs, and ecstasy may differ markedly from "normal" awareness.

Everyone experiences at least some altered states, such as sleep, dreaming, and daydreaming. In everyday life, changes in consciousness may also accompany long-distance running, listening to music, making love, or other circumstances.

ALTERED STATES OF CONSCIOUSNESS   *It's clear that there are many altered states of consciousness. How are they distinguished from* normal awareness?   During an **altered state of consciousness** (**ASC**), changes occur in the quality and pattern of mental activity. Typically, there are shifts in perceptions, emotions, memory, time sense, thinking, feelings of self-control, and suggestibility (Tart, 1986). Definitions aside, most people know when they have experienced an ASC.

Are there other causes of ASCs?   In addition to those already mentioned, we could add sensory overload (for example, a light show, Mardi Gras crowd, rave, or mosh pit), monotonous stimulation (such as "highway hypnotism" on long drives), unusual physical conditions (high fever, hyperventilation, dehydration, sleep loss, near-death experiences), sensory deprivation, and many other possibilities. In some instances, altered states of awareness have important cultural significance. (See "Consciousness and Culture" for more information.)

In this chapter we will focus on sleep, dreaming, hypnosis, sensory deprivation, and the effects of drugs. To get right to the questions raised by the Preview, let's begin with sleep, the most familiar ASC.

CONSCIOUSNESS AND CULTURE

Throughout history, people have found ways to alter consciousness. A dramatic example is the sweat lodge ceremony of the Sioux Indians. During the ritual, several men sit in total darkness inside a small chamber heated by coals. Cedar smoke, bursts of steam, and sage fill the air. The men chant rhythmically. The heat builds. At last they can stand it no more. The door is thrown open. Cooling night breezes rush in. And then? The cycle begins again—often to be repeated four or five times more.

The ritual "sweats" of the Sioux are meant to cleanse the mind and body. When they are especially intense, they bring altered awareness and personal revelation.

People seek some altered states for pleasure, as is often true of drug intoxication. Yet, as the Sioux illustrate, many cultures regard altered consciousness as a pathway to personal enlightenment. Indeed, all cultures and most religions recognize and accept some alterations of consciousness. However, the meanings given to these states vary greatly—from signs of "madness" and "possession" by spirits, to life-enhancing breakthroughs. Thus, cultural conditioning greatly affects what altered states each of us recognizes, seeks, considers normal, and attains (Metzner, 1998; Ward, 1989).

In many cultures, rituals of healing, prayer, purification, or personal transformation are accompanied by altered states of consciousness.

SLEEP QUIZ

1. People can learn to sleep for just a few hours a night and still function well. T or F?
2. Everyone dreams every night. T or F?
3. The brain rests during sleep. T or F?
4. Resting during the day can replace lost sleep. T or F?
5. As people get older, they sleep more. T or F?
6. Alcohol may help a person get to sleep, but it disturbs sleep later during the night. T or F?
7. If a person goes without sleep long enough, death will occur. T or F?
8. Dreams mostly occur during deep sleep. T or F?
9. A person prevented from dreaming would soon go crazy. T or F?
10. Sleepwalking occurs when a person acts out a dream. T or F?

Answers:

1. F 2. T 3. F 4. F 5. F 6. T 7. T 8. F 9. F 10. F

ing sleep. For instance, you are more likely to awaken if you hear your own name spoken, instead of another. Likewise, a sleeping mother may ignore a jet thundering overhead but wake at the slightest whimper of her child. Some people can even do simple tasks while asleep. In one experiment, people learned to avoid an electric shock by touching a switch after a tone sounded. Eventually, they could do it without waking. (This is much like the basic survival skill of turning off your alarm clock without waking.) Of course, sleep does impose limitations. There is no evidence, for instance, that you can learn math, a foreign language, or other complex skills while asleep—especially when the snooze takes place in class (Druckman & Bjork, 1994; Wood et al., 1992).

Because sleep is familiar, many people think they know all about it. Before reading more, test your knowledge with the Sleep Quiz you see here. Were you surprised by any of the answers? Let's see what we know about our "daily retreat from the world."

Consciousness *Mental awareness of sensations, perceptions, memories, and feelings.*
Waking consciousness *A state of normal, alert awareness.*
Altered state of consciousness *A condition of awareness distinctly different in quality or pattern from waking consciousness.*

SLEEP—A NICE PLACE TO VISIT

Each of us will spend some 25 years of life asleep. Contrary to common belief, people are not totally unresponsive dur-

The Need for Sleep

How strong is the need for sleep? Sleep is an innate **biological rhythm** that can never be entirely sidestepped (Webb, 1994). Of course, sleep will give way temporarily, especially at times of great danger. As one comic put it, "The lion and the lamb shall lie down together, but the lamb will not be very sleepy." However, there are limits to how long humans can go without sleeping. A rare disease that prevents sleep always ends the same way: The patient falls into a stupor, followed by coma, followed by death (Oliwenstein, 1993). (See ❖Fig. 8.1.)

In various studies, animals have been placed on moving treadmills over pools of water. This is not a good way to sleep. Even so, sleep always wins. The animals soon begin to drift into repeated microsleeps (Goleman, 1982). A **microsleep** is a brief shift in brain activity to patterns normally recorded during sleep. When you drive, remember that a microsleep can lead to a macro-accident. Even a driver whose eyes are open can be asleep for a few seconds. Roughly 2 out of every 100 highway crashes are caused by sleepiness (Lyznicki et al., 1998). By the way, if you are struggling to stay awake while driving, you should stop, quit fighting it, and take a short nap. Coffee helps, too, but briefly giving in to sleep helps the most (Horne & Reyner, 1996).

SLEEP DEPRIVATION   *How long could a person go without sleep?* With few exceptions, 4 days or more without sleep becomes

❖ **FIGURE 8.1** *Not all animals sleep, but, like humans, those that do have powerful sleep needs. For example, dolphins must voluntarily breathe air, which means they face the choice of staying awake or drowning. The dolphin solves this problem by sleeping on just one side of its brain at a time! The other half of the brain, which remains awake, controls breathing (Jouvet, 1999).*

hell for everyone. Nevertheless, longer sleepless periods are possible. The world record is held by Randy Gardner—who at age 17 went 268 hours (11 days) without sleep. Surprisingly, Randy needed only 14 hours of sleep to recover. It is not necessary to completely replace lost sleep. As Randy found, most symptoms of **sleep deprivation** (sleep loss) are reversed by a single night's rest.

What are the costs of sleep loss? Age and personality make a big difference. Recall that disc jockey Peter Tripp's behavior became quite bizarre. Randy Gardner was less seriously impaired by sleep loss. However, make no mistake: Sleep is a necessity, not an option. At various times, Randy experienced irritability, memory lapses, difficulty in concentrating, slurred speech, and difficulty in naming common objects (Coren, 1996).

In general, people who have not slept for 2 or 3 days show little impairment on relatively interesting or complex mental tasks (Binks, Waters, & Hurry, 1999). But most do have problems with paying attention. Staying alert and following simple routines is very difficult for the sleep deprived. For a driver, pilot, or machine operator, this may be enough to spell disaster (Fairclough & Graham, 1999). If a task is monotonous (such as factory work or air traffic control), no amount of sleep loss is safe (Gillberg & Akerstedt, 1998).

It's not necessary to go completely without sleep to feel the effects of sleep loss. One third of all adults and most college students get too little sleep every night. Such partial sleep deprivation leaves many people exhausted, groggy, and unproductive by midday. Just 1 hour a night of lost sleep can affect your mood, memory, ability to pay attention, and even your health (Everson, 1998; Maas, 1999).

How can I tell how much sleep I really need? Pick a day when you feel well rested. Then sleep that night until you wake the next morning without an alarm clock. If you feel rested when you wake up, that's your natural sleep need. If you're sleeping fewer hours than you need, you're building up a sleep debt every day (Maas, 1999).

Severe sleep loss can cause a temporary **sleep-deprivation psychosis** like the problems Peter Tripp suffered. Confusion, disorientation, delusions, and hallucinations are typical of this reaction. Hallucinations may be visual, like Tripp's "coat of furry worms," or tactile, like feeling cobwebs on the face. Fortunately, such "crazy" behavior is not common. Hallucinations and delusions rarely appear before 60 hours of wakefulness. The most typical reactions to sleep loss are trembling hands, drooping eyelids, inattention, staring, increased pain sensitivity, and general discomfort (Naitoh et al., 1989).

Calvin and Hobbes

Time of Day

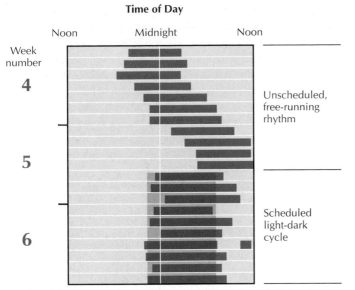

❖ **FIGURE 8.2** *Sleep rhythms. Bars show periods of sleep during the fourth, fifth, and sixth weeks of an experiment with a human subject. During unscheduled periods, the subject was allowed to select times of sleep and lighting. The result was a sleep rhythm of about 25 hours. Notice how this free-running rhythm began to advance around the clock. When periods of darkness were scheduled (colored area), the rhythm quickly resynchronized with 24-hour days. (Adapted from Czeisler, 1981.)*

Sleep Patterns

Sleep was described as an innate biological rhythm. What does that mean? Daily sleep and waking periods create a variety of **sleep patterns.** These rhythms of sleep and waking are so steady that they continue for many days, even when clocks and light-dark cycles are removed (Palinkas, Suedfeld, & Steel, 1995). However, under such conditions, humans eventually shift to a sleep-waking cycle that averages *25 hours,* not 24. This finding suggests that external time markers, especially light and dark, help tie our sleep rhythms to a normal 24-hour day (❖Fig. 8.2). Otherwise, many of us would drift into our own unusual sleep cycles.

What is the normal range of sleep? A few individuals can get by on only an hour or so of sleep a night—and feel perfectly fine. However, this is rare. Only 8 percent of the population are **short sleepers,** averaging 5 hours of sleep or less per night. On the other end of the scale we find **long sleepers,** who doze 9 hours or more (and tend to be daytime worriers) (McCann & Stewin, 1988). The majority of us sleep on a familiar 7- to 8-hour-per-night schedule. For a few people, however, it is quite normal to sleep as little as 5 hours per night or as much as 11. Urging everyone to sleep 8 hours would be like advising everyone to wear medium-size shoes.

Do elderly people need more sleep? Sleep needs actually remain fairly constant as people age. However, older people rarely get the sleep they need. Total sleep time declines throughout life. Those over the age of 50 average only 6 hours

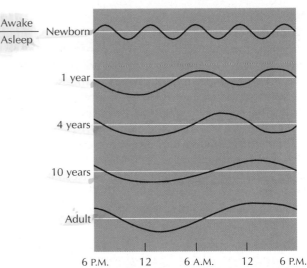

❖ **FIGURE 8.3** *Development of sleep patterns. Short cycles of sleep and waking gradually become the night-day cycle of an adult. Although most adults don't take naps, midafternoon sleepiness is a natural part of the sleep cycle. (After Williams et al., 1964.)*

of sleep a night. In contrast, infants spend up to 20 hours a day sleeping, usually in 2- to 4-hour cycles.

As they mature, most children go through a "nap" stage and eventually settle into a steady cycle of sleeping once a day (❖Fig. 8.3). Some people, of course, maintain the afternoon "siesta" as an adult pattern. Perhaps we all should: Midafternoon sleepiness is a natural part of the sleep cycle. Brief, well-timed naps can help maintain alertness in people like truck drivers and hospital interns, who often must fight drowsiness (Batejat & Lagarde, 1999).

It is very tempting to try to reduce sleep time. However, people on *shortened* cycles—for example, 3 hours of sleep to 6 hours awake—often can't get to sleep when the cycle calls for it. The underlying sleep rhythm simply won't cooperate. That's why astronauts continue to sleep on their normal earth schedule while in space. Adapting to *longer* than normal days is more promising. Such days can be tailored to match natural sleep patterns, which have a ratio of 2 to 1 between time awake and time asleep. For instance, one study showed that 28-hour "days" work for some people. Overall, however, sleep is a "gentle tyrant." Sleep patterns may be bent and stretched, but they rarely yield entirely to human whims (Akerstedt et al., 1993).

BRIDGES

Daily sleep cycles can be disrupted by rapid travel across time zones (jet lag) and by shift work.

See Chapter 13, pages 418–419, for more information.

Biological rhythm *Any repeating cycle of biological activity, such as sleep and waking cycles or changes in body temperature.*
Microsleep *A brief shift in brain wave patterns to those of sleep.*
Sleep deprivation *Being deprived of desired or needed amounts of sleep.*
Sleep-deprivation psychosis *A major disruption of mental and emotional functioning brought about by sleep loss.*
Sleep patterns *The order and timing of daily sleep and waking periods.*
Short sleeper *A person averaging 5 hours of sleep or less per night.*
Long sleeper *A person who averages 9 hours of sleep or more per night.*

STAGES OF SLEEP—THE NIGHTLY ROLLER-COASTER RIDE

What causes sleep? Early sleep experts thought that some substance in the bloodstream must cause sleep. But studies of Siamese twins (individuals whose bodies are joined at birth) show that this is false. One twin can frequently be observed sleeping while the second is awake (❖Fig. 8.4). During waking hours, a **sleep hormone** (sleep-promoting chemical) collects in the brain and spinal cord, *not* in the blood. If this sleep hormone is extracted from one animal and injected into another, the second animal will sleep deeply for many hours (Cravatt et al., 1995). Notice, however, that this explanation is incomplete.

For example, how do we explain why well-rested students may have to fight to stay awake during a boring lecture?

Whether you are awake or asleep right now depends on the *balance* between separate sleep and waking systems. Brain circuits and chemicals in one system promote sleep. A network of brain cells in the other system responds to chemicals that inhibit sleep. The two systems seesaw back and forth, switching the brain between sleep and wakefulness. Note that the brain does not "shut down" during sleep. Rather, the *pattern* of activity changes. The total *amount* of activity remains fairly constant (Steriade & McCarley, 1990).

Stages of Sleep

What happens when you fall asleep? The changes that come with sleep can be measured with an **electroencephalograph** (eh-LEK-tro-en-SEF-uh-lo-graf), or brain wave machine, commonly called an **EEG.** The brain gives off tiny electrical signals that can be amplified and recorded. When you are awake and alert, the EEG reveals a pattern of small, fast waves called **beta** (❖Fig. 8.5). Immediately before sleep, the pattern shifts to larger and slower waves called **alpha.** (Alpha waves also occur when you are relaxed and allow your thoughts to drift.) As your eyes close, your breathing becomes slow and regular, your pulse rate slows, and your body temperature drops. Soon after, four separate **sleep stages** can be identified, based on brain wave patterns and behavioral changes.

STAGE 1   As you lose consciousness and enter light sleep (stage 1 sleep), your heart rate slows even more. Breathing becomes more irregular. The muscles of your body relax. This may trigger a reflex muscle contraction throughout the body called a **hypnic jerk** (HIP-nik: sleep). (This is quite normal, so have no fear about admitting to your friends that you fell asleep with a hypnic jerk.)

In stage 1 sleep, the EEG is made up mainly of small, irregular waves with some alpha. People awakened at this time may or may not say they were asleep.

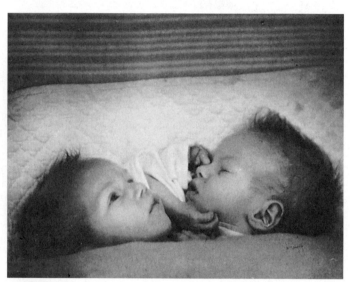

❖ **FIGURE 8.4** *These Siamese twins share the same blood supply, yet one sleeps while the other is awake. (Photo by Yale Joel, Life Magazine. © 1954 Time, Inc.)*

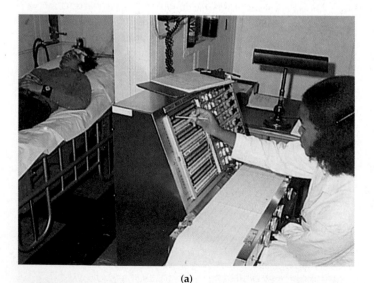

Awake	Beta waves
Eyes closed, relaxed	Alpha waves
Stage 1	Small, irregular waves
Stage 2	Sleep spindles
Stage 3	Delta waves appear
Stage 4	Mostly delta

(a)   **(b)**

❖ **FIGURE 8.5** (a) *Photograph of an EEG recording session. The man in the background is asleep.* (b) *Changes in brain wave patterns associated with various stages of sleep. Actually, most wave types are present at all times, but they occur more or less frequently in various sleep stages.*

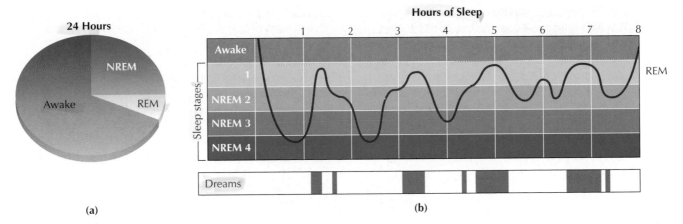

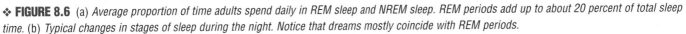

(a)   (b)

❖ **FIGURE 8.6** (a) *Average proportion of time adults spend daily in REM sleep and NREM sleep. REM periods add up to about 20 percent of total sleep time.* (b) *Typical changes in stages of sleep during the night. Notice that dreams mostly coincide with REM periods.*

STAGE 2   As sleep deepens, body temperature drops further. Also, the EEG begins to include **sleep spindles,** which are short bursts of distinctive brain wave activity. Spindles seem to mark the true boundary of sleep. Within 4 minutes after spindles appear, most people who are awakened say they were asleep.

STAGE 3   In stage 3, a new brain wave called *delta* begins to appear. **Delta waves** are very large and slow. Their presence signals deeper sleep and a further loss of consciousness. In fact, delta waves closely resemble the EEG pattern of a person in a coma (Shafton, 1995).

STAGE 4   **Deep sleep** (the deepest level of normal sleep) is reached after about an hour. In stage 4, brain waves become almost pure delta, and the sleeper is in a state of oblivion. If you make a loud noise during stage 4, the sleeper will awaken in confusion and may not remember the noise.

After spending some time in stage 4, the sleeper returns (through stages 3 and 2) to stage 1. Further shifts between deeper and lighter sleep occur throughout the night (❖Fig. 8.6).

Two Basic States of Sleep

If you watch a person who is asleep, you will soon notice that the sleeper's eyes occasionally move under the eyelids. These **rapid eye movements** (or **REMs**) are strongly associated with dreaming (❖Fig. 8.6). Roughly 85 percent of the time, people awakened during REMs report vivid dreams. In addition to rapid eye movements, **REM sleep** is marked by a return to fast, irregular EEG patterns similar to stage 1 sleep. In fact, the brain is so active during REM sleep that it looks as if the person is awake (Hobson et al., 1998). REM sleep is easy to observe in pets, such as dogs and cats. Watch for eye and facial movements and for irregular breathing. (You can forget about your pet iguana, though. Reptiles show no signs of REM sleep.)

REM AND NREM SLEEP   The two most basic states of sleep are REM sleep with its associated dreaming and **non-REM**

BRIDGES

The EEG is also used to study brain activity and to detect abnormal conditions caused by diseases.

See Chapter 3, page 58, for more information.

(NREM) sleep, which occurs during stages 1, 2, 3, and 4 (Jouvet, 1999). NREM sleep is dream-free about 90 percent of the time. Your first period of stage 1 sleep is usually free of REMs and dreams. Later returns to stage 1 are usually accompanied by rapid eye movements. Dreams during REM sleep tend to be longer, clearer, more detailed, more bizarre, and more "dream-like" than thoughts and images that occur in NREM sleep (Shafton, 1995). Recent studies have shown that brain areas associated with imagery and emotion become more active during REM sleep. This may explain why REM dreams tend to be more vivid than those that occur during NREM sleep (Braun, Balkin, & Herscovitch, 1998). For example, here's a typical description of a REM dream:

Sleep hormone *A sleep-promoting substance found in the brain and spinal cord.*
Electroencephalograph (EEG) *A device designed to detect, amplify, and record electrical activity in the brain.*
Beta waves *Small, fast brain waves associated with being awake and alert.*
Alpha waves *Large, slow brain waves associated with relaxation and falling asleep.*
Sleep stages *Levels of sleep identified by brain wave patterns and behavioral changes.*
Light sleep *Stage 1 sleep, marked by small, irregular brain waves and some alpha waves.*
Hypnic jerk *A reflex muscle twitch throughout the body that often occurs as one is falling asleep.*
Sleep spindles *Distinctive bursts of brain wave activity that indicate a person is asleep.*
Delta waves *Large, slow brain waves that occur in deeper sleep (stages 3 and 4).*
Deep sleep *Stage 4 sleep; the deepest form of normal sleep.*
Rapid eye movements (REMs) *Swift eye movements during sleep.*
REM sleep *Sleep marked by rapid eye movements and a return to stage 1 EEG patterns.*
NREM sleep *Non–rapid eye movement sleep characteristic of stages 2, 3, and 4.*

I was snowboarding down a mountain that looked like a huge pile of diamonds. Then I was flying over the treetops. I could go up or down just by thinking about where I wanted to go. I looked down and saw a friend of mine below and suddenly I was walking next to her. She said, "You're supposed to be at school. Why are you here?" Then I was in class and the professor was handing out a quiz I wasn't ready for.

In comparison, NREM dream reports look more like this:

I was thinking about snowboarding and wondering if I should try it sometime.

What is the function of NREM sleep? NREM sleep increases after physical exertion. This suggests that it helps us recover from fatigue built up during the day. In comparison, daytime stress tends to increase REM sleep. REM sleep totals only about 90 minutes per night (about the same as a feature movie). Yet, its link with dreaming makes it as important as NREM sleep. REM sleep may rise dramatically when there is a death in the family, trouble at work, a marital conflict, or other emotionally charged events.

REM SLEEP AND DREAMING \ *What happens to the body when a person dreams?* REM sleep is a time of high emotion. The heart beats irregularly. Blood pressure and breathing waver. Both males and females appear to be sexually aroused: Males usually have an erection, and genital blood flow increases in women. This occurs for all REM sleep, so it is not strictly related to erotic dreams (Jouvet, 1999).

During REM sleep, your body becomes quite still, as if you were paralyzed. Imagine for a moment the results of acting out some of your recent dreams. Very likely, REM-sleep paralysis prevents some hilarious—and dangerous—nighttime escapades. When it fails, some people thrash violently, leap out of bed, and may attack their bed partners. A lack of muscle paralysis during REM sleep is called **REM behavior disorder.** One patient suffering from the disorder tied himself to his bed every night. That way, he couldn't jump up and crash into furniture or walls (Shafton, 1995).

In a moment, we will survey some additional sleep problems—if you are still awake. First, here are a few questions to check your memory of our discussion so far.

KNOWLEDGE BUILDER
ALTERED STATES AND SLEEP

RELATE

Make a quick list of some altered states of consciousness you have experienced. What do they have in common? How are they different? What conditions caused them?

Imagine that you are a counselor at a sleep clinic. You must explain the basics of sleep and dreaming to a new client who knows little about these topics. Can you do it?

LEARNING CHECK

1. Altered states of consciousness are defined mainly by changes in patterns of alertness. T or F?

2. A momentary shift in brain activity to a pattern characteristic of sleep is referred to as
   a. delta sleep *b.* light sleep *c.* microsleep *d.* deprivation sleep

3. Delusions and hallucinations typically continue for several days after a sleep-deprived individual returns to normal sleep. T or F?

4. Older adults, and particularly the elderly, sleep more than children do because the elderly are more easily fatigued. T or F?

5. Most studies of sleep patterns show a consistent ratio of 2 to 1 between time awake and time asleep. T or F?

6. Rapid eye movements (REMs) indicate that a person is in deep sleep. T or F?

7. Alpha waves are to presleep drowsiness as _____ _____ are to stage 4 sleep.

CRITICAL THINKING

8. Why might it be better for the unscheduled human sleep-waking cycle to average more than 24 hours, instead of less?

9. Biologically, what advantages might sleeping provide?

Answers:

1. F 2. c 3. F 4. F 5. T 6. F 7. delta waves 8. Sleep experts theorize that the 25-hour average leaves a little "slack" in the cycle. External time markers can then retard the bodily cycle slightly to synchronize it with light-dark cycles. If the bodily cycle were shorter than 24 hours, we all might have to "stretch" every day to adjust. 9. Lowering bodily activity and metabolism during sleep may help conserve energy and lengthen life. Also, natural selection may have favored sleep because animals that remained active at night probably had a higher chance of being killed. (I'll bet they had more fun, though.)

SLEEP DISTURBANCES—SHOWING NIGHTLY: SLEEP WARS!

Sleep clinics treat thousands of people each year who suffer from sleep disorders or complaints. (See ◆Table 8.1.) Let's explore some of the more interesting problems these people face.

Insomnia

Staring at the ceiling at 2 A.M. is pretty low on most people's list of favorite pastimes. Yet, about 30 percent of all adults report some degree of insomnia. Roughly 9 percent have a serious or chronic problem. **Insomnia** includes difficulty in going to sleep, frequent nighttime awakenings, waking too early, or a combination of these problems (Bond & Wooten, 1996). Insomnia is more than just a nuisance; it is very costly in terms of lowered productivity, poor health, and damaged relationships (Walsh & Uestuen, 1999).

The citizens of North America will spend well over half a billion dollars this year on sleeping pills. There is real irony in this expense. Nonprescription sleeping pills such as Sominex, Nytol, and Sleep-eze have little or no sleep-inducing effect. Even worse are barbiturates. These prescription sedatives decrease both stage 4 sleep and REM sleep, drastically lowering sleep quality. In addition, a drug tolerance builds rapidly. Many users become "sleeping pill junkies," who need an ever greater number of pills to get to sleep. The end result is **drug-dependency insomnia** (sleeplessness caused by withdrawal from sleeping pills). Victims must be painstakingly weaned from their sleep medicines. Otherwise, terrible nightmares and "rebound insomnia" may drive them back to drug use.

If sleeping pills are a poor way to treat insomnia, what can be done? Actually, triazolam (try-AS-o-lam) and several related drugs are fairly effective at inducing sleep. However, even these drugs have drawbacks, and they, too, can cause rebound insomnia. Rather than prescribing drugs, many sleep specialists now prefer to treat insomnia with lifestyle changes and behavioral techniques (Walsh & Scweitzer, 1999).

TYPES AND CAUSES OF INSOMNIA Worry, stress, and excitement often cause **temporary insomnia** (a brief period of sleeplessness) and a self-defeating cycle. First, heightened arousal blocks sleep. Then, frustration and anger cause more arousal, which further delays sleep. Delayed sleep causes more frustration, and so on. A good way to beat this cycle is to avoid fighting it. It is usually best to get up and do something useful or satisfying when you have difficulty sleeping. (Reading a textbook might be a good choice of useful activities.) Return to bed only when you begin to feel that you are struggling to stay awake.

What you eat can also affect how easily you get to sleep. Eating starchy foods increases the amount of **tryptophan** (TRIP-tuh-fan: an amino acid) reaching the brain. More tryptophan, in turn, increases the amount of serotonin in the brain. Serotonin is associated with relaxation, a positive mood, and sleepiness. Thus, to promote sleep, try eating a snack that is nearly all starch. Good sleep-inducing snacks are cookies, bread, pasta, oatmeal, pretzels, bagels, and dry cereal. If you really want to drop the bomb on insomnia, try eating a baked potato (which may be the world's largest sleeping pill!) (Sahelian, 1998).

What about more serious cases of insomnia? **Chronic insomnia** exists if sleeping problems last for more than 3 weeks. Treatment for chronic insomnia usually begins with a careful analysis of a patient's sleep history. Possible reasons for insomnia, such as depression, anxiety, medical problems, lifestyle, stress, and sleep habits, are carefully assessed (Bond & Wooten, 1996).

The first thing anyone suffering from insomnia should do is to consume less caffeine, alcohol, and tobacco. Some insomniacs benefit from relaxation training to lower arousal before sleep. Stimulus control strategies also help. **Stimulus control** refers to linking a response with specific stimuli. For example, patients are told to strictly avoid doing anything but sleeping when they are in bed. They are not to study, eat, watch TV, read, pay the bills, or even think in bed. In this way, only sleeping becomes associated with retiring (Hauri & Linde, 1990).

One of the best ways to combat insomnia is also the simplest. Many insomniacs have scattered sleep habits. For these people, adopting a regular schedule helps establish a firm body rhythm, greatly improving sleep. Patients are told to get up and go to sleep at the same time each day, including weekends. (Many people disturb their sleep rhythms by staying up late on weekends.) These, and other ways of combating insomnia, are summarized in "Behavioral Remedies for Insomnia."

BRIDGES

Learning how to achieve deep relaxation is a highly useful skill.

See Chapter 18, pages 624–625, for more information.

◆ **TABLE 8.1** Sleep Disturbances—Things That Go Wrong in the Night

Hypersomnia Excessive daytime sleepiness. This can result from depression, insomnia, narcolepsy, sleep apnea, sleep drunkenness, periodic limb movements, drug abuse, and other problems.

Insomnia Difficulty in getting to sleep or staying asleep; also, not feeling rested after sleeping.

Narcolepsy Sudden, irresistible, daytime sleep attacks that may last anywhere from a few minutes to a half hour. Victims may fall asleep while standing, talking, or even driving.

Nightmare disorder Vivid, recurrent nightmares that significantly disturb sleep.

Periodic limb movement syndrome Muscle twitches (primarily affecting the legs) that occur every 20 to 40 seconds and severely disturb sleep.

REM behavior disorder A failure of normal muscle paralysis, leading to violent actions during REM sleep.

Restless legs syndrome An irresistible urge to move the legs in order to relieve sensations of creeping, tingling, prickling, aching, or tension.

Sleep apnea During sleep, breathing stops for 20 seconds or more until the person wakes a little, gulps in air, and settles back to sleep; this cycle may be repeated hundreds of times per night.

Sleep drunkenness A slow transition to clear consciousness after awakening; sometimes associated with irritable or aggressive behavior.

Sleep terror disorder The repeated occurrence of night terrors that significantly disturb sleep.

Sleep-wake schedule disorder A mismatch between the sleep-wake schedule demanded by a person's bodily rhythm and that demanded by the environment.

Sleepwalking disorder Repeated incidents of leaving the bed and walking about while asleep.

(Bond & Wooten, 1996; DSM-IV, 1994; Hauri & Linde, 1990.)

REM behavior disorder *A failure of normal muscle paralysis, leading to violent actions during REM sleep.*
Insomnia *Difficulty in getting to sleep or staying asleep.*
Drug-dependency insomnia *Insomnia that follows withdrawal from sleeping pills.*
Temporary insomnia *A brief episode of insomnia.*
Tryptophan *A sleep-promoting amino acid.*
Chronic insomnia *Insomnia that persists for more than 3 weeks.*
Stimulus control *Linking a particular response with specific stimuli.*

BEHAVIORAL REMEDIES FOR INSOMNIA

All of the approaches listed here are helpful for treating insomnia (Hopson, 1986). Experiment a little and find out what works for you. Of the methods listed, sleep restriction and stimulus control are the most effective (Lacks & Morin, 1992).

STIMULANTS Avoid stimulants such as coffee and cigarettes. Remember, too, that alcohol, while not a stimulant, impairs sleep quality.

WORRIES Schedule time in the early evening to write down worries or concerns. Plan what you will do about them the next day. Then put them out of mind until morning.

RELAXATION Learn a physical or mental strategy for relaxing, such as progressive muscle relaxation (see Chapter 18), meditation (see Chapter 16), or blotting out worries with calming images. Strenuous exercise during the day promotes sleep. It is best if done about 6 hours before bedtime (Maas, 1999). Exercise in the evening is helpful only if it is very light.

SLEEP RESTRICTION Even if you miss an entire night's sleep, do not sleep late in the morning, nap more than an hour, sleep during the evening, or go to bed early the following night. Try to restrict sleep to your normal bedtime hours. That way, you will avoid fragmenting your sleep rhythms (Lacks & Morin, 1992).

STIMULUS CONTROL Link only sleep with your bedroom so that it does not trigger worrying: (1) Go to bed only when you are feeling sleepy. (2) Awaken at the same time each morning. (3) Avoid nonsleep activities in bed. (4) Always leave the bedroom if sleep has not occurred within 10 minutes. (5) Do something else when you are upset about not being able to sleep (Lacks & Morin, 1992).

PARADOXICAL INTENTION To remove the pressures of trying to get to sleep, try instead to keep your eyes open (in the dark) and stay awake as long as possible (Horvath & Goheen, 1990). This allows sleep to overtake you unexpectedly and lowers performance anxiety. Never try to go to sleep. Arrange to let it happen.

◆ **TABLE 8.2** Was It a Nightmare or a Night Terror?

	NIGHTMARE	NIGHT TERROR
Stage of sleep	REM	NREM
Activity	Slight or no movement	Violent body movement, sits up, cries out, may run
Emotion	Fear or anxiety	Terror and disorganizing panic
Mental state when awakened	Coherent, can be calmed	Incoherent, disoriented, cannot be calmed, may be hallucinating
Physiological changes	No perspiration	Perspires heavily
Recall	Dream activity usually remembered	Amnesia for episode

(Adapted from Woods & Greenhouse, 1974.)

Sleepwalking and Sleeptalking

Sleepwalking is eerie and fascinating. **Somnambulists** (som-NAM-bue-lists: those who sleepwalk) avoid obstacles, descend stairways, climb trees, and on rare occasions may step out of windows or in front of automobiles. The sleepwalker's eyes are usually open, but a blank face and shuffling feet reveal that the person is still asleep. Parents who are sleepwalkers or sleeptalkers tend to have children with the same problems. This suggests that these disturbances are partially hereditary (Abe et al., 1984). A parent who finds a child sleepwalking should gently guide the child back to bed. Awakening a sleepwalker does no harm, but it is not necessary.

Does sleepwalking occur during dreaming? It might seem that sleepwalkers are acting out dreams. But remember that people are normally immobilized during REM sleep. EEG studies have shown that somnambulism occurs during NREM stages 3 and 4. **Sleeptalking** also occurs mostly in NREM stages of sleep. The link with deep sleep probably explains why sleeptalking makes little sense and why sleepwalkers are confused and remember little when awakened (DSM-IV, 1994).

Nightmares and Night Terrors

Stage 4 sleep is also the realm of night terrors. These frightening episodes are quite different from ordinary nightmares (◆Table 8.2). A **nightmare** is simply a bad dream that takes place during REM sleep. Nightmares, which occur about twice a month, are usually brief and easily remembered (Wood & Bootzin, 1990).

During stage 4 **night terrors,** a person suffers total panic and may hallucinate frightening dream images into the bedroom. An attack may last 15 or 20 minutes. When it is over, the person awakens drenched in sweat but only vaguely remembers the terror. Because night terrors occur during NREM sleep (when the body is not immobilized), victims may sit up, scream, get out of bed, or run around the room. Victims remember little afterward. (Other family members, however, may have a story to tell.) Night terrors are most common in childhood, but they continue to plague about 2 out of every 100 adults (Ohayon et al., 1999).

HOW TO ELIMINATE A NIGHTMARE   *Is there any way to stop a recurring nightmare?*   A bad nightmare can be worse than any horror movie. You can leave a theater, but often we remain trapped in our most terrifying dreams. Yet bad as they may be, most nightmares can be banished by following three simple steps. First, write down your nightmare, describing it in detail. Next, change the dream any way you wish, but be sure to spell out the details of the new dream. The third step is **imagery rehearsal,** in which you mentally rehearse the changed dream before you fall asleep again (Krakow & Neidhardt, 1992).

Imagery rehearsal may work because it makes upsetting dreams familiar while a person is awake and feeling safe. Or perhaps it mentally "reprograms" future dream content. In any case, the technique has proved helpful for many people (Krakow et al., 1996).

Narcolepsy

One of the most dramatic sleep problems is **narcolepsy** (NAR-koe-lep-see), or sudden, irresistible sleep attacks. These last anywhere from a few minutes to a half hour. Victims may fall asleep while standing, talking, or even driving. Emotional excitement, especially laughter, commonly triggers narcolepsy. (Tell an especially good joke, and a narcoleptic may fall asleep.) More than half of all victims also suffer from **cataplexy** (CAT-uh-plex-see), a sudden temporary paralysis of the muscles, leading to complete body collapse. It's easy to understand why narcolepsy can devastate careers and relationships (Broughton & Broughton, 1994).

Sudden paralysis sounds like what happens during dreaming. Does that suggest a connection between narcolepsy and REM sleep?   Yes. When monitored on an EEG, narcoleptics tend to fall directly into REM sleep. Thus, the narcoleptic's sleep attacks and paralysis appear to occur when REM sleep intrudes into the waking state (Siegel et al., 1991).

Fortunately, narcolepsy is rare. It tends to run in families, which suggests that it is hereditary. In fact, this has been confirmed by breeding several generations of narcoleptic dogs. (These dogs, by the way, are simply outstanding at learning the trick "Roll over and play dead.") There is no known cure for narcolepsy, but stimulant drugs may cut down the frequency of attacks. Scheduling a long nap each day also helps narcoleptics manage their sleep attacks (Mullington & Broughton, 1993).

Sleep Apnea

Some sage once said, "Laugh and the whole world laughs with you; snore and you sleep alone." Nightly "wood sawing" is often harmless, but it can signal a serious problem. A person who snores loudly, with short silences and loud gasps or snorts, may suffer from apnea (AP-nee-ah: interrupted breathing). In **sleep apnea,** breathing stops for periods of 20 seconds to 2 minutes. As the need for oxygen becomes intense, the person wakes a little and gulps in air. She or he then settles back to sleep. But soon, breathing stops again. This cycle is repeated hundreds of times a night. As you might guess, apnea victims complain of **hypersomnia** (hi-per-SOM-nee-ah: excessive daytime sleepiness) (DSM-IV, 1994).

What causes sleep apnea?   Some cases occur because the brain stops sending signals to the diaphragm to maintain breathing. Another cause is blockage of the upper air passages. Apnea should be suspected any time a person snores loudly. In addition to the misery it causes, apnea seriously endangers health. People who suspect they are apneic should seek treatment at a sleep clinic. The most effective treatments are weight loss, surgery for breathing obstructions, and use of a CPAP (continuous positive airway pressure) mask to aid breathing during sleep (Koenig, 1996).

SIDS   Sleep apnea is suspected as one cause of **sudden infant death syndrome (SIDS),** or "crib death." SIDS is the most frequent cause of death for infants under 1 year of age. Each year, 1 out of every 500 babies is a victim of SIDS. In the "typical" crib death, a slightly premature or small baby with some signs of a cold or cough is bundled up and put to bed. A short time later, parents return and find the child is dead.

Some cases of SIDS are caused by apnea due to immature breathing centers in the brainstem (Thoman et al., 1988). In other instances, it appears that direct blockage of the nose is responsible. A few babies remain passive when breathing is blocked, raising the risk of crib death. Secondhand smoke may pose an even higher risk. Babies are three times more likely to die of SIDS if they are in the same house with adults who smoke (Klonoff-Cohen et al., 1995).

Babies at risk for SIDS must be carefully watched for the first 6 months of life. To aid parents in this task, a special monitor may be used that sounds an alarm when a baby's breathing or pulse becomes weak (❖Fig. 8.7). The list that follows gives some danger signals for SIDS (Einspieler et al., 1988). Be aware, however, that SIDS can also strike babies who show none of these signs.

Somnambulism *Sleepwalking; occurs during NREM sleep.*
Sleeptalking *Speaking that occurs during NREM sleep.*
Nightmare *A bad dream that occurs during REM sleep.*
Night terror *A state of panic during NREM sleep.*
Imagery rehearsal *Mentally rehearsing and changing a nightmare in order to prevent it from recurring.*
Narcolepsy *A sudden, irresistible sleep attack.*
Cataplexy *A sudden temporary paralysis of the muscles.*
Sleep apnea *Repeated interruption of breathing during sleep.*
Hypersomnia *Extreme daytime sleepiness.*
Sudden infant death syndrome (SIDS) *The sudden, unexplained death of an apparently healthy infant.*

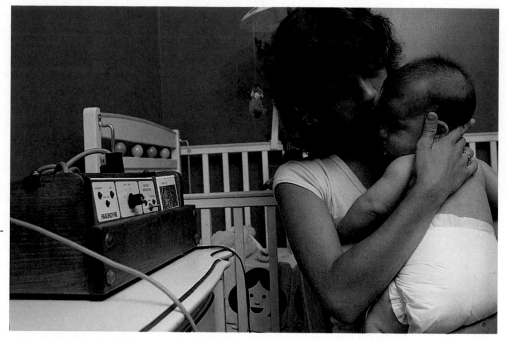

❖ **FIGURE 8.7** *Infants at risk for SIDS are often attached to devices that monitor breathing and heart rate during sleep. An alarm sounds to alert parents if either pulse or respiration falters. SIDS rarely occurs after an infant is 1 year old. Babies at risk for SIDS should be placed on their sides or on their backs. (Photo courtesy of Healthdyne, Inc.)*

SOME WARNING SIGNS FOR SIDS

- The mother is a teenager.
- The baby is premature.
- The baby has a shrill, high-pitched cry.
- The baby engages in "snoring," breath-holding, or frequent awakening at night.
- The baby breathes mainly through an open mouth.
- The baby moves little during sleep and remains passive when its face rolls into a pillow or blanket.
- Parents or other adults in the home are smokers.

"BACK TO SLEEP"   Pop quiz: Should babies be placed face down or face up in bed? Another major risk factor for SIDS is the position in which babies sleep. In the past, doctors advised parents to place infants face down in bed. Now, experts believe that healthy infants are better off sleeping on their backs or sides (Meyers et al., 1998). (Premature babies, those with respiratory problems, and those who often vomit may still need to sleep face down. Ask a pediatrician for guidance.) Since this advice was first publicized, there has been a 50 percent drop in SIDS deaths. Remember, "*back* to sleep" is the safest position for most infants (Willinger et al., 1994).

DREAMS—A SEPARATE REALITY?

When REM sleep was first discovered, it ushered in a "golden era" of dream inquiry. To conclude our discussion of sleep, let's consider some age-old questions about dreaming.

Does everyone dream? Do dreams occur in an instant?   Most people dream four or five times a night, but not all people remember their dreams. "Nondreamers" are often surprised by their dreams when first awakened during REM sleep. Dreams are usually spaced about 90 minutes apart. The first dream lasts only about 10 minutes; the last averages 30 minutes and may run as long as 50. Dreams, therefore, occur in real time, not as a "flash" (Shafton, 1995).

REM SLEEP DEPRIVATION   *How important is dream sleep? Is it essential for normal functioning?*   To answer these questions, sleep expert William Dement awakened volunteers each time they entered REM sleep. Soon, their attempts to dream grew more urgent. By the fifth night, many had to be awakened 20 or 30 times to prevent REM sleep. When the volunteers were finally allowed to sleep undisturbed, they dreamed extra amounts. This effect, called a **REM rebound,** explains why alcoholics have horrible nightmares after they quit drinking. Alcohol suppresses REM sleep and sets up a powerful rebound when it is withdrawn. It's worth remembering that although alcohol and other depressant drugs may help a person get to sleep, they greatly reduce sleep quality (Lobo & Tufik, 1997).

Dement's volunteers complained of memory lapses, poor concentration, and daytime anxiety. For a while, it was thought that people deprived of REM sleep might go crazy. But this is now known as the "REM myth." Later experiments showed that missing *any* sleep stage can cause a rebound for that stage. In general, daytime disturbances are related to the *total amount* of sleep lost, not to the *type* of sleep lost (Devoto et al., 1999).

FUNCTIONS OF REM SLEEP   What, then, is the purpose of REM sleep? Early in life, REM sleep may stimulate the developing brain. Newborn babies spend a hearty 8 or 9 hours a day in

REM sleep. That's about 50 percent of their total sleep time. In adulthood, REM sleep may prevent sensory deprivation during sleep, and it may help us process emotional events. REM sleep also seems to help us sort and integrate memories formed during the day. (See "REM Sleep and Memory.") Although we have much to learn, it's clear that REM sleep and dreaming are valuable for keeping the brain in good working order (Hobson, 1999; Shafton, 1995).

Dream Worlds

Calvin Hall, a noted dream expert, collected and analyzed more than 10,000 dreams (Hall, 1966; Hall et al., 1982). Hall found that most dreams reflect everyday events. The favorite dream setting is a familiar room in a house. Action usually takes place between the dreamer and two or three other emotionally important people—friends, enemies, parents, or employers. Dream actions are also mostly familiar: running, jumping, riding, sitting, talking, and watching. About half of all dreams have sexual elements. Dreams of flying, floating, and falling occur less frequently. Hall also found that if you're dreaming more now, you may be enjoying it less. Unpleasant emotions such as fear, anger, and sadness are more common in dreams than pleasant emotions (Merritt et al., 1994).

FOCUS ON RESEARCH

REM SLEEP AND MEMORY

No one has to remember to dream. But do we dream to remember? In one study, college students did two mental tasks, one easy and the other difficult. For the easy task, students merely memorized a list of paired words. The difficult task was a logic game that required some tricky mental gymnastics. Later, students spent the night in a sleep lab. Some were awakened each time they entered REM sleep. Others were awakened only during NREM periods. A third group was kept awake all night. The lucky fourth group was allowed to sleep undisturbed.

The following day, all four groups performed equally well on the easy memory task. But on the hard task, those who lost REM sleep did much worse than the other groups (Chollar, 1989). To succeed at the logic game, students had to create new *mental strategies* and remember what worked.

In summary, REM sleep seems to aid the development of memories and strategies that help us cope with the world (Hennevin et al., 1995; Smith, 1995). Dreaming may also help *remove* useless memories before they are stored (Crick & Mitchison, 1995). Speaking very loosely, it's as if the dreaming brain were reviewing messages left on a telephone-answering machine, in order to decide which are worth keeping. During the day, when information continues to stream in, the brain may be too busy to efficiently sort and consolidate memories.

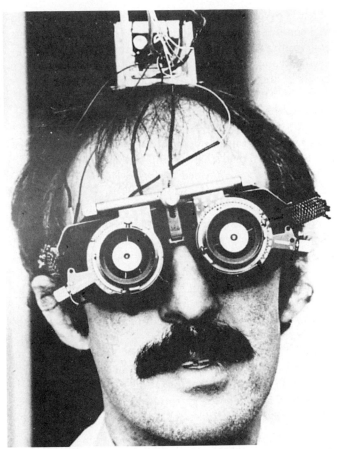

John Herman of the University of Texas may look like he just stepped out of the movie *Star Wars,* but he is actually involved in dream research. Herman is wearing goggles that electronically monitor eye movements during sleep. Use of such devices has greatly extended our understanding of dreaming.

Dream Theories

How meaningful are dreams? Most theorists agree that dreams reflect our waking thoughts, fantasies, and emotions (Cartwright & Lamberg, 1992; Domhoff, 1999). Thus, the real question might be, How deep should we dig in interpreting dreams? Some theorists believe that dreams have deeply hidden meanings. Others regard dreams as no more meaningful than ordinary thinking. Let's examine both views.

PSYCHODYNAMIC DREAM THEORY Sigmund Freud's landmark book on the topic, *The Interpretation of Dreams* (1900), first advanced the idea that many dreams are based on **wish fulfillment** (an expression of unconscious desires). Thus, a student who is angry at a teacher might dream of embarrassing the teacher in class, a lonely person may dream of romance, or a hungry child may dream of food.

REM rebound *The occurrence of extra rapid eye movement sleep following REM sleep deprivation.*
Wish fulfillment *Freudian belief that many dreams express unconscious desires.*

Freud's **psychodynamic theory** of dreaming emphasizes internal conflicts and unconscious forces. Although many of his ideas are attractive, there is evidence against them. For example, volunteers in a study of starvation showed no particular increase in dreams about food and eating. In general, dreams show few signs of directly expressing hidden wishes (Fischer & Greenberg, 1996).

Freud's response to critics, no doubt, would have been that dreams rarely express needs so directly. One of Freud's key insights is that ideas in dreams are expressed as *images* or pictures, rather than in words (Globus, 1987). Freud believed that dreams express unconscious desires and conflicts as disguised **dream symbols** (images that have deeper symbolic meaning). For instance, death might be symbolized by a journey, children by small animals, or sexual intercourse by horseback riding or dancing. Similarly, a woman sexually attracted to her best friend's husband might dream of stealing her friend's wedding ring and placing it on her own hand, an indirect symbol of her true desires.

Do all dreams have hidden meanings? Probably not. Even Freud realized that some dreams are trivial "day residues" or carryovers from ordinary waking events. On the other hand, dreams do tend to reflect a person's current concerns, so Freud wasn't entirely wrong (Nikles et al., 1998).

THE ACTIVATION-SYNTHESIS HYPOTHESIS Psychiatrists Allan Hobson and Robert McCarley have a radically different view of dreaming. Hobson and McCarley believe that dreams are made in this way: During REM sleep, brain cells are activated that normally control eye movements, balance, and actions. However, messages from the cells are blocked from reaching the body, so no movement occurs. Nevertheless, the cells continue to tell higher brain areas of their activities. Struggling to interpret this information, the brain searches through stored memories and manufactures a dream (Hobson, 1999).

How does that help explain dream content? Let's use the classic chase dream as an example. In such dreams, we feel we are running but not going anywhere. This occurs because the brain is told the body is running, but it gets no feedback from the motionless legs. To make sense of this information, the brain creates a chase drama. A similar process probably explains dreams of floating or flying.

Hobson and McCarley call their view of dreaming the **activation-synthesis hypothesis.** Hobson explains that several parts of the brain are "turned on" (activated) during REM sleep. This triggers sensations, motor commands, and memories. The cortex of the brain, which also becomes more active during REM sleep, synthesizes this activity into stories and visual images. However, frontal areas of the cortex, which control higher mental abilities, are mostly shut down during REM sleep. This explains why dreams are more primitive and more bizarre than daytime thoughts (Hobson, 1999). Viewed this way, dreams are merely a different type of thinking that occurs during sleep (McCarley, 1998).

BRIDGES

Interpreting dreams is an important part of Freudian psychoanalysis, a psychodermic therapy.

See Chapter 18, page 600.

Then, does the activation-synthesis hypothesis rule out the idea that dreams have meaning? No. Because dreams are created from memories and past experiences, they can tell us quite a lot about each person's mental life, emotions, and concerns (Hobson, 1999). However, many psychologists continue to believe that dreams have deeper meaning (Cartwright & Lamberg, 1992; Globus, 1987; Shafton, 1995).

There seems to be little doubt that dreams can make a difference in our lives: Veteran sleep researcher William Dement once dreamed that he had lung cancer. In the dream, a doctor told Dement he would die soon. At the time, Dement was smoking two packs of cigarettes a day. He says, "I will never forget the surprise, joy, and exquisite relief of waking up. I felt reborn." Dement quit smoking the following day.

It was once assumed that dreams can be interpreted only by trained professionals. Now, there is greater acceptance of the personal nature of dream meanings. As a result, many people collect and interpret their dreams. If you're interested in joining them, you'll find some suggestions later about how to "catch" and explore your own dreams.

KNOWLEDGE BUILDER
SLEEP DISTURBANCES AND DREAMING

RELATE

Almost everyone suffers from insomnia at least occasionally. Are any of the techniques for combating insomnia similar to strategies you have discovered on your own?

How many sleep disturbances can you name (including those listed in ◆Table 8.1)? Are there any that you have experienced? Which do you think would be most disruptive?

Do you think the activation-synthesis theory provides an adequate explanation of your own dreams? Have you had dreams that seem to reflect Freudian wish fulfillment? Do you think your dreams have symbolic meaning?

LEARNING CHECK

1. Night terrors, sleepwalking, and sleeptalking all occur during stage 1, NREM sleep. T or F?

2. Narcolepsy and cataplexy are both associated with _____ sleep.

3. Sleep _____ is suspected as one cause of SIDS.

4. Which of the following is *not* a behavioral remedy for insomnia?
   a. daily hypersomnia *b.* stimulus control *c.* progressive relaxation *d.* paradoxical intention

5. The favored setting for dreams is
   a. work *b.* school *c.* outdoors or unfamiliar places *d.* familiar rooms

6. Unpleasant emotions such as fear, anger, and sadness are more frequent in dreams than pleasant emotions. T or F?

7. According to the activation-synthesis model of dreaming, dreams are constructed from _____ to explain messages received from nerve cells controlling eye movement, balance, and bodily activity.

8. REM sleep seems to contribute to learning, especially to the formation of memories associated with _____ that aid survival or coping.

CRITICAL THINKING

9. Even without being told that somnambulism is a NREM event, you could have predicted that sleepwalking doesn't occur during dreaming. Why?

Answers:

1. F 2. REM 3. apnea 4. a 5. d 6. T 7. memories 8. strategies 9. Because people are immobilized during REM sleep and REM sleep is strongly associated with dreaming. This makes it unlikely that sleepwalkers are acting out dreams.

HYPNOSIS—LOOK INTO MY EYES

"Your body is becoming heavy. You can barely keep your eyes open. You are so tired you can't move. Relax. Let go. Relax. Close your eyes and relax." These are the last words a textbook should ever say to you, and the first a hypnotist might say.

Hypnosis, like dreaming, has an aura of mystery surrounding it. Actually, hypnosis is not nearly so mysterious as it might seem. **Hypnosis** is an altered state of consciousness, characterized by narrowed attention and an increased openness to suggestion. Not all psychologists accept this definition. To them, hypnosis is merely a blend of conformity, relaxation, imagination, obedience, suggestion, and role playing (Braffman & Kirsch, 1999; Sapp, 1997). Either way, the point is that hypnosis can be explained by normal psychological principles. It is not "magical."

Interest in hypnosis began in the 1700s with Franz Mesmer, whose name is the basis for the term **mesmerize** (to hypnotize). Mesmer, an Austrian physician, believed he could cure diseases by passing magnets over the body. Mesmer's strange "treatments" were related to hypnosis because he relied heavily on the power of suggestion. For a time, mesmerism enjoyed quite a following. In the end, however, Mesmer's theories of "animal magnetism" were rejected, and he was branded as a fraud.

The term *hypnosis* was coined by an English surgeon named James Braid. The Greek word *hypnos* means "sleep," and Braid used it to describe the hypnotic state. Today we know that hypnosis is *not* sleep. Confusion about this point remains because some hypnotists give the suggestion, "Sleep, sleep." However, EEG records made during hypnosis differ from those made when a person is asleep (Graffin, Ray, & Lundy, 1995).

HYPNOTIC SUSCEPTIBILITY   *Can everyone be hypnotized?*   About 8 people out of 10 can be hypnotized, but only 4 out of 10 will be good hypnotic subjects. People who are imaginative and prone to fantasy are often highly responsive to hypnosis (Silva & Kirsch, 1992). But people who lack these traits may also be hypnotized. If

◆ **TABLE 8.3** Stanford Hypnotic Susceptibility Scale

SUGGESTED BEHAVIOR	CRITERION OF PASSING
1. Postural sway	Falls without forcing
2. Eye closure	Closes eyes without forcing
3. Hand lowering (left)	Lowers at least 6 inches by end of 10 seconds
4. Immobilization (right arm)	Arm rises less than 1 inch in 10 seconds
5. Finger lock	Incomplete separation of fingers at end of 10 seconds
6. Arm rigidity (left arm)	Less than 2 inches of arm bending in 10 seconds
7. Hands moving together	Hands at least as close as 6 inches after 10 seconds
8. Verbal inhibition (name)	Name unspoken in 10 seconds
9. Hallucination (fly)	Any movement, grimacing, acknowlegment of effect
10. Eye catalepsy	Eyes remain closed at end of 10 seconds
11. Posthypnotic (changes chairs)	Any partial movement response
12. Amnesia test	Three or fewer items recalled

Adapted from Weitzenhoffer & Hilgard, 1959.

you are willing to be hypnotized, chances are good that you could be. Hypnosis depends more on the efforts and abilities of the hypnotized person than on the skills of the hypnotist (Kirsch & Lynn, 1995). But make no mistake: People who are hypnotized are not merely faking their responses (Perugini et al., 1998).

Hypnotic susceptibility refers to how easily a person can become hypnotized. It can be measured by giving suggestions and counting the number to which a person responds. A typical hypnotic test is the *Stanford Hypnotic Susceptibility Scale* shown in ◆Table 8.3. (Also see ❖Fig. 8.8.) Notice that the scale ranges

Psychodynamic theory *Any theory of behavior that emphasizes internal conflicts, motives, and unconscious forces.*
Dream symbols *Images in dreams that serve as visible signs of hidden ideas, desires, impulses, emotions, relationships, and so forth.*
Activation-synthesis hypothesis *An attempt to explain how dream content is affected by motor commands in the brain that occur during sleep, but are not carried out.*
Hypnosis *An altered state of consciousness characterized by narrowed attention and increased suggestibility.*
Mesmerize *To hypnotize.*
Hypnotic susceptibility *One's capacity for becoming hypnotized.*

❖ **FIGURE 8.8** *In one test of hypnotizability, subjects attempt to pull their hands apart after hearing suggestions that their fingers are "locked" together.*

moral or repulsive (such as disrobing in public or harming someone) (Kirsch & Lynn, 1995).

A key element in hypnosis is the **basic suggestion effect** (a tendency of hypnotized persons to carry out suggested actions as if they were involuntary). Hypnotized persons feel like their actions and experiences are *automatic*—they seem to happen without effort (Kihlstrom, 1985). Here is how one person described his hypnotic session:

> I felt lethargic, my eyes going out of focus and wanting to close. My hands felt real light.... I felt I was sinking deeper into the chair.... I felt like I wanted to relax more and more.... My responses were more automatic. I didn't have to *wish* to do things so much or *want* to do them.... I just did them.... I felt floating... very close to sleep (Hilgard, 1968).

Hypnosis may also cause a *dissociation* or "split" in awareness. To illustrate, researcher Ernest Hilgard asked hypnotized subjects to plunge one hand into a painful bath of ice water. Subjects told to feel no pain said they felt none. The same subjects were then asked if there was any part of their mind that did feel pain. With their free hand, many wrote, "It hurts," or "Stop it, you're hurting me," while they continued to act pain-free (Hilgard, 1977, 1978). Thus, one part of the hypnotized person says there is no pain and acts as if there is none. Another part, which Hilgard calls the *hidden observer*, is aware of the pain but remains in the background. The **hidden observer** is a detached part of the hypnotized person's awareness that silently observes events.

from easy to more difficult tasks. If you were to score high on the scale today, you probably would do the same years from now. Hypnotizability is very stable over time (Piccione et al., 1989).

INDUCING HYPNOSIS *How is hypnosis done? Could I be hypnotized against my will?* There are as many different hypnotic routines as there are hypnotists. Still, all techniques encourage a person (1) to focus attention on what is being said, (2) to relax and feel tired, (3) to "let go" and accept suggestions easily, and (4) to use vivid imagination (Druckman & Bjork, 1994).

You must cooperate to become hypnotized. Many theorists believe that all hypnosis is really **self-hypnosis** (autosuggestion). From this perspective, hypnotists act as guides. They basically help another person follow a series of suggestions. These suggestions, in turn, alter sensations, perceptions, thoughts, feelings, and behaviors (Druckman & Bjork, 1994; Kirsch & Lynn, 1995).

What does it feel like to be hypnotized? You might be surprised at some of your actions during hypnosis. You also might have mild feelings of floating, sinking, anesthesia, or separation from your body. Personal experiences vary widely. However, hypnotized people generally remain in control of their behavior and aware of what is going on. A person who is deeply hypnotized may relax "reality testing" so that normal "willpower," or self-control, is reduced. Nevertheless, most people will not act out hypnotic suggestions that they consider im-

EFFECTS OF HYPNOSIS *What can (and cannot) be achieved with hypnosis?* Many abilities have been tested during hypnosis, leading to the following conclusions (Burgess & Kirsch, 1999; Kihlstrom, 1985; Kirsch & Lynn, 1995):

1. **Superhuman acts of strength.** Hypnosis has no more effect on physical strength than instructions that encourage a person to make his or her best effort.
2. **Memory.** There is some evidence that hypnosis can enhance memory. However, it frequently increases the number of false memories as well. For this reason, many states now bar persons who have been hypnotized from testifying in court.
3. **Amnesia.** A person told not to remember something heard during hypnosis may claim not to remember. In some instances, this may be nothing more than a deliberate attempt to avoid thinking about specific ideas. However, brief memory loss of this type actually does seem to occur (Bowers & Woody, 1996).
4. **Pain relief.** Hypnosis can relieve pain (Mauer et al., 1999). Therefore, it can be especially useful in situations where chemical painkillers cannot be used or are ineffective. One such situation is control of phantom limb pain. (Phantom limb pains are recurring pains that amputees sometimes feel coming from the missing limb.)
5. **Age regression.** Given the proper suggestions, some hypnotized people appear to "regress" to childhood. However, most theorists now believe that "age-regressed" subjects are only acting out a suggested role.

BRIDGES

Should the police use hypnosis to enhance the memories of witnesses? The evidence generally says no.

See Chapter 10, page 316.

6. **Sensory changes.** Hypnotic suggestions concerning sensations are among the most effective. Given the proper instructions, a person can be made to smell a small bottle of ammonia and respond as if it were a wonderful perfume. It is also possible to alter color vision, hearing sensitivity, time sense, perception of illusions, and many other sensory responses.

Hypnosis is a valuable tool. It can help people relax, feel less pain, and make better progress in therapy (Kirsch, Montgomery, & Sapirstein, 1995). In general, hypnosis is more successful at changing subjective experience than it is at modifying behaviors such as smoking or overeating. In short, hypnotic effects are useful but seldom amazing (Druckman & Bjork, 1994; Gibson & Heap, 1991).

Stage Hypnosis

On stage, the hypnotist intones, "When I count to three, you will imagine that you are on a train to Disneyland and growing younger and younger as the train approaches." Responding to these suggestions, grown men and women begin to giggle and squirm like children on their way to a circus.

How do stage entertainers use hypnosis to get people to do strange things? They don't. Little or no hypnosis is needed to do a good hypnosis act. **Stage hypnosis** is often merely a simulation of hypnotic effects. T. X. Barber, an authority on hypnosis, says that stage hypnotists make use of several features of the stage setting to perform their act (Barber, 1970).

1. **Waking suggestibility.** We are all more or less open to suggestion, but on stage people are unusually cooperative because they don't want to "spoil the act." As a result, they readily follow almost any instruction given by the entertainer.

2. **Selection of responsive subjects.** Participants in stage hypnotism (all *volunteers*) are first "hypnotized" as a group. Thus, anyone who doesn't yield to instructions is eliminated.

3. **The hypnosis label disinhibits.** Once a person has been labeled "hypnotized," she or he can sing, dance, act silly, or whatever, without fear or embarrassment. On stage, being "hypnotized" takes away personal responsibility for one's actions.

4. **The hypnotist as a "director."** After volunteers loosen up and respond to a few suggestions, they find that they are suddenly the stars of the show. Audience response to the antics on stage brings out the "ham" in many people. All the "hypnotist" needs to do is direct the action.

5. **The stage hypnotist uses tricks.** Stage hypnosis is about 50 percent taking advantage of the situation and 50 percent deception. Here is a common deception: One of the more impressive stage tricks is to rigidly suspend a person between two chairs. This is astounding only because the audience does not question it. Anyone can do it, as is shown in the photographs and instructions in ❖Figure 8.9. Try it!

To summarize, hypnosis is real, and it can significantly alter private experience. Hypnosis is a useful tool that has been applied in a variety of settings. The TV or nightclub stage, however, is not one of these settings. Stage "hypnotists" entertain; they rarely hypnotize.

❖ **FIGURE 8.9** *Arrange three chairs as shown. Have someone recline as shown. Ask him to lift slightly while you remove the middle chair. Accept the applause gracefully! (Concerning hypnosis and similar phenomena, the moral, of course, is "Suspend judgment until you have something solid to stand on.")*

SENSORY DEPRIVATION—LIFE ON A SENSORY DIET

Throughout history, sensory deprivation has been one of the most widely used means of altering consciousness. **Sensory deprivation** (**SD**) refers to any major reduction in the amount or variety of sensory stimulation.

What happens when stimulation is greatly reduced? A hint comes from reports by prisoners in solitary confinement, Arctic explorers, high-altitude pilots, long-distance truck drivers, and radar operators. When faced with limited or monotonous stimulation, people sometimes have bizarre sensations, dangerous lapses in attention, and wildly distorted perceptions. To find out why, D. O. Hebb paid volunteers to undergo sensory deprivation under controlled conditions.

In Hebb's classic experiments, subjects spent several days lying on their backs in a small cubicle. To prevent vision, they wore darkened goggles. Gloves and cardboard cuffs restricted

Self-hypnosis *A state of hypnosis attained without the aid of a hypnotist; autosuggestion.*
Basic suggestion effect *The tendency of hypnotized persons to carry out suggested actions as if they were involuntary.*
Hidden observer *A detached part of the hypnotized person's awareness that silently observes events.*
Stage hypnosis *Use of hypnosis to entertain; often, merely a simulation of hypnosis for that purpose.*
Sensory deprivation *Any major reduction in the amount or variety of sensory stimulation.*

French artist René Magritte drew on hypnogogic imagery as an inspiration for his work (McKellar, 1995). Vivid hypnogogic images that occur during sensory deprivation can contribute to other creative pursuits as well.

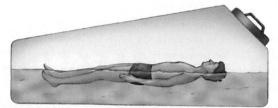

❖ **FIGURE 8.10** *A sensory isolation chamber. Small flotation tanks like the one pictured have been used by psychologists to study the effects of mild sensory deprivation. Subjects float in darkness and silence. The shallow, body-temperature water contains hundreds of pounds of Epsom salts, so that subjects float near the surface. Mild sensory deprivation produces deep relaxation.*

touch. In the background, a constant hissing noise masked all other sounds. Do these conditions sound interesting? If you were placed in similar circumstances, you might be in for a surprise. Few subjects could take more than 2 or 3 days of sensory deprivation without "pushing the panic button."

Disruptive Effects

What sort of changes take place during sensory deprivation? As mentioned in the Preview, a person may misjudge time and have trouble concentrating. After emerging from sensory deprivation, some people experience color distortions, heightened visual illusions, slower reactions, and a brief warping of visual lines and spaces. Volunteers in some early studies also reported strange and vivid images.

Spurred by such reports, researchers soon created an ingenious array of sensory deprivation environments, and volunteers seeking a drugless high flocked to experiments. Most were disappointed, however. We now know that true hallucinations are rare during sensory deprivation. The fanciful, dreamlike visions that sometimes occur are more likely to be **hypnogogic images** (hip-no-GAH-jik) (images like those that occur just before sleep). These images may be vivid and surprising, but they are rarely mistaken for real objects. Hypnogogic images are linked to an increase in the number of *theta waves* produced by the brain. These brain waves, in the 4- to 7-cycles-per-second range, are usually recorded just before sleep. Sensory deprivation also increases their occurrence (Taylor, 1983).

Benefits of Sensory Restriction

In recent years, psychologists have begun to explore the possible benefits of sensory deprivation. Much of this work has involved sensory restriction in small isolation tanks like the one pictured in ❖Figure 8.10.

SENSORY ENHANCEMENT   *How could sensory deprivation be beneficial?* One of the most consistent aftereffects of sensory deprivation is increased sensory acuity. That is, vision, hearing, touch, and taste are temporarily more sensitive. This effect could be used to reawaken the dulled senses of someone who is listless or overworked. At the very least, wearing earplugs for a day might be an interesting prelude to hearing a musical concert!

RELAXATION   As we already noted, prolonged sensory deprivation is stressful and uncomfortable. Yet, oddly, brief periods of restricted sensation can be very relaxing. An hour or two spent in a flotation tank, for instance, causes a large drop in blood pressure, muscle tension, and other signs of stress. Of course, it could be argued that a warm bath has the same effect. But evidence suggests that brief sensory deprivation is one of the surest ways to induce deep relaxation (Suedfeld & Borrie, 1999).

CHANGING HABITS   Psychologists have also found that mild sensory deprivation can help people quit smoking, lose weight, and reduce their use of alcohol and drugs (Borrie, 1990–91; Cooper, Adams, & Scott, 1988; Suedfeld, 1990). Canadian researcher Peter Suedfeld calls such benefits *restricted environmental stimulation therapy,* or **REST.** In one study, Suedfeld tested the effects of standard anti-smoking messages. These were then compared to the effects of the same messages combined with sensory deprivation. He found that roughly equal numbers of people succeeded in stopping smoking with either treatment. But 3 months later, members of the REST group were smoking 40 percent less than the others (Suedfeld, 1980). Another study found similar benefits for people in a weight-loss program based on sensory deprivation (Borrie & Suedfeld, 1980).

How does sensory deprivation help? Tape-recorded suggestions to eat less or stop smoking are played for clients in a flotation tank. It may be that deep relaxation makes a person less likely to argue against suggestions or otherwise resist them. In addition, REST temporarily increases mental and behavioral flexibility. Perhaps this is because spending time in a restricted environment completely interrupts a person's routines and behavior patterns. In any case, REST can "loosen" belief systems and behavior patterns in ways that make it easier to change bad habits (Suedfeld & Borrie, 1999).

PROSPECTS   After years of being viewed only as a disruptive state, sensory deprivation may yet prove to have additional benefits. For example, REST shows promise as a way to stimulate creative thinking (Norlander et al., 1998). REST sessions also enhance performance in skilled sports, such as gymnastics, tennis, basketball, darts, archery, and marksmanship (Druckman & Bjork, 1994; Norlander et al., 1999). There is also evidence that REST can improve memory, relieve pain, and reduce stress. Clearly, there is much yet to be learned from studying "nothingness" (Suedfeld & Borrie, 1999).

DRUG-ALTERED CONSCIOUSNESS—THE HIGH AND LOW OF IT

Alcohol, heroin, amphetamines, barbiturates, marijuana, cocaine, LSD, caffeine, nicotine. . . . The list of mind-altering drugs—legal and illegal—is extensive. The surest way to alter human consciousness is to administer a **psychoactive drug** (a substance capable of altering attention, judgment, memory, time sense, self-control, emotion, or perception) (Julien, 1998).

Facts about Drugs

Most psychoactive drugs can be placed on a scale ranging from stimulation to depression. A **stimulant** is a substance that increases activity in the body and nervous system. A **depressant** does the reverse. ❖Figure 8.11 shows various drugs and their approximate effects. A more complete summary of frequently abused psychoactive drugs is given in ◆Table 8.4.

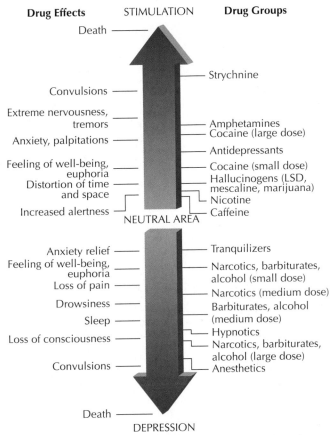

❖ **FIGURE 8.11** *Spectrum and continuum of drug action. Many drugs can be rated on a stimulation-depression scale according to their effects on the central nervous system. Although LSD, mescaline, and marijuana are listed here, the stimulation-depression scale is less relevant to these drugs. The principal characteristic of such hallucinogens is their mind-altering quality.*

Hypnogogic images *Vivid mental images that may occur just as one enters stage 1 sleep.*
REST *Restricted environmental stimulation therapy; the use of sensory restriction to change habits or to improve performance.*
Psychoactive drug *A substance capable of altering attention, memory, judgment, time sense, self-control, mood, or perception.*
Stimulant *A substance that increases activity in the body and nervous system.*
Depressant *A substance that decreases activity in the body and nervous system.*

◆ **TABLE 8.4** Comparison of Psychoactive Drugs

NAME	CLASSIFICATION	MEDICAL USE	USUAL DOSE	DURATION OF EFFECT
Alcohol	Sedative-hypnotic	Solvent, antiseptic	Varies	1–4 hours
Amphetamines	Stimulant	Relief of mild depression, control of appetite and narcolepsy	2.5–5 milligrams	4 hours
Barbiturates	Sedative-hypnotic	Sedation, relief of high blood pressure, hyperthyroidism	50–100 milligrams	4 hours
Benzodiazepines	Anxiolytic	Tranquilizer	2–100 milligrams	1–8 hours
Caffeine	Stimulant	Counteract depressant drugs, treatment of migraine headaches	Varies	Varies
Cocaine	Stimulant, local anesthetic	Local anesthesia	Varies	Varied, brief periods
Codeine	Narcotic	Ease pain and coughing	30 milligrams	4 hours
Heroin	Narcotic	Pain relief	Varies	4 hours
LSD	Hallucinogen	Experimental study of mental function, alcoholism	100–500 milligrams	10 hours
Marijuana (THC)	Relaxant, euphoriant; in high doses, hallucinogen	Treatment of glaucoma and side effects of chemotherapy	1–2 cigarettes	4 hours
Mescaline	Hallucinogen	None	350 micrograms	12 hours
Methadone	Narcotic	Pain relief	10 milligrams	4–6 hours
Morphine	Narcotic	Pain relief	15 milligrams	6 hours
PCP	Anesthetic	None	2–10 milligrams	4–6 hours, plus 12-hour recovery
Psilocybin	Hallucinogen	None	25 milligrams	6–8 hours
Tobacco (nicotine)	Stimulant	Emetic (nicotine)	Varies	Varies

Question marks indicate conflict of opinion. It should be noted that illicit drugs are frequently adulterated and thus pose unknown hazards to the user.

EFFECTS SOUGHT	LONG-TERM SYMPTOMS	PHYSICAL DEPENDENCE POTENTIAL	PSYCHOLOGICAL DEPENDENCE POTENTIAL	ORGANIC DAMAGE POTENTIAL
Sense alteration, anxiety reduction, sociability	Cirrhosis, toxic psychosis, neurologic damage, addiction	Yes	Yes	Yes
Alertness, activeness	Loss of appetite, delusions, hallucinations, toxic psychosis	Yes	Yes	Yes
Anxiety reduction, euphoria	Addiction with severe withdrawal symptoms, possible convulsions, toxic psychosis	Yes	Yes	Yes
Anxiety relief	Irritability, confusion, depression, sleep disorders	Probably	Yes	No
Wakefulness, alertness	Insomnia, heart arrhythmias, high blood pressure	No?	Yes	Yes
Excitation, talkativeness	Depression, convulsions	Yes	Yes	Yes
Euphoria, prevent withdrawal discomfort	Addiction, constipation, loss of appetite	Yes	Yes	No
Euphoria, prevent withdrawal discomfort	Addiction, constipation, loss of appetite	Yes	Yes	No*
Insightful experiences, exhilaration, distortion of senses	May intensify existing psychosis, panic reactions	No	No?	No?
Relaxation; increased euphoria, perceptions, sociability	Possible lung cancer, other health risks	No	Yes	Yes
Insightful experiences, exhiliration, distortion of senses	May intensify existing psychosis, panic reactions	No	No?	No?
Prevent withdrawal discomfort	Addiction, constipation, loss of appetite	Yes	Yes	No
Euphoria, prevent withdrawal discomfort	Addiction, constipation, loss of appetite	Yes	Yes	No*
Euphoria	Unpredictable behavior, suspicion, hostility, psychosis	Debated	Yes	Yes
Insightful experiences, exhilaration, distortion of senses	May intensify existing psychosis, panic reactions	No	No?	No?
Alertness, calmness, sociability	Emphysema, lung cancer, mouth and throat cancer, cardiovascular damage, loss of appetite	Yes	Yes	Yes

*Persons who inject drugs under nonsterile conditions run a high risk of contracting AIDS, hepatitis, abscesses, or circulatory disorders.

DEPENDENCE Drug dependence falls into two broad categories. When a person compulsively uses a drug to maintain bodily comfort, a **physical dependence** (addiction) exists. Physical dependence occurs most often with drugs that cause **withdrawal symptoms** (physical illness that follows removal of a drug) (Julien, 1998). Withdrawal from drugs such as alcohol, barbiturates, and opiates can be extremely unpleasant. Quitting opiates, for example, causes violent flu-like symptoms of nausea, vomiting, diarrhea, chills, sweating, and cramps (Feldman & Meyer, 1996). Addiction is often accompanied by a **drug tolerance** (reduced response to a drug). This leads users to take larger and larger doses to get the desired effect.

It's fascinating to note that withdrawal from alcohol, nicotine, caffeine, food, gambling, and even a love relationship can all produce similar symptoms. This may occur because a variety of reinforcers activate the same pleasure pathways in the brain. In this sense, a person may be "addicted" to food, sex, or love, as well as to drugs (Gilbert, Gilbert, & Schultz, 1998).

When a person develops a **psychological dependence**, he or she feels that a drug is necessary to maintain emotional or psychological well-being. Usually, the person intensely craves the drug and its rewarding qualities (Feldman & Meyer, 1996). Psychological dependence can be just as powerful as physical addiction. That's why some psychologists define *addiction* as any compulsive habit pattern. By this definition, a person who has lost control over his or her drug use, for whatever reason, is addicted (Marlatt et al., 1988).

Here are some typical signs of drug dependence (DSM-IV, 1994):

- The person has a strong desire to use the drug or can't stop using it.
- The person tends to use more of the drug than he or she intends to.
- The person has withdrawal symptoms if drug taking stops.
- The person uses the drug even though he or she knows it is doing harm.
- The person has developed a tolerance for the drug.

Actually, the answers to just two questions can identify most people with alcohol and drug problems. People who answer yes to both of the following questions should seriously consider seeking professional help (Brown et al., 1997):

- In the last year, did you ever drink or use drugs more than you meant to?
- Have you felt you wanted or needed to cut down on your drinking or drug use in the last year?

PATTERNS OF ABUSE Some drugs, of course, have a higher potential for abuse than others. Heroin is certainly more dangerous than caffeine. However, this is only one side of the picture. It can be as useful to classify drug-taking *behavior* as it is to rate drugs. For example, some people remain social drinkers for life, whereas others become alcoholics within weeks of taking their first drink. In this sense,

drug use can be classified as **experimental** (short-term use based on curiosity), **social-recreational** (occasional social use for pleasure or relaxation), **situational** (use to cope with a specific problem, such as needing to stay awake), **intensive** (daily use with elements of dependence), or **compulsive** (intense use and extreme dependence). The last three categories of drug taking tend to be damaging no matter what drug is used.

DRUGS OF ABUSE Note in ◆Table 8.4 that the drugs most likely to lead to physical dependence are alcohol, amphetamines, barbiturates, cocaine, codeine, heroin, methadone, morphine, and tobacco (nicotine). Using *any* of the drugs listed in ◆Table 8.4 can result in psychological dependence. Note, too, that people who take drugs intravenously are at high risk for developing hepatitis and AIDS (see Chapter 14). The discussion that follows focuses on the drugs most often abused by students.

UPPERS—AMPHETAMINES, COCAINE, CAFFEINE, NICOTINE

Amphetamines are a large group of synthetic stimulants, such as Dexedrine and Methamphetamine. Amphetamines were once widely prescribed for weight loss or depression. Both practices are now frowned on because too many patients became dependent on their legal amphetamines. The only fully legitimate medical uses of amphetamines are to treat narcolepsy, childhood hyperactivity, and overdoses of depressant drugs. Illicit use of amphetamines is widespread, especially by people seeking to stay awake and by those who think drugs can improve mental or physical performance.

Amphetamines rapidly produce a drug tolerance. Most abusers who begin with one or two pills a day progress to taking dozens to get the same effect. Eventually, some users switch to injecting "Meth" ("speed") directly into the bloodstream. True speed freaks typically go on binges lasting several days, after which they "crash" from lack of sleep and food.

ABUSE *How dangerous are amphetamines?* Amphetamines pose many dangers. To stay high, the abuser must take more and more of the drug as the body's tolerance grows. Higher doses can cause nausea, vomiting, high blood pressure, fatal heart arrhythmias, and crippling strokes. Also, it is important to realize that amphetamines speed up the use of bodily resources; they do not magically supply energy. Hence, the aftereffects of an amphetamine binge can include overwhelming fatigue, depression, terrifying nightmares, confusion, uncontrolled irritability, and aggression. Repeatedly overextending the body with stimulants may lead to self-starvation, sores and nonhealing ulcers, chronic chest infections, liver disease, high blood pressure, and brain hemorrhage.

Amphetamines can also cause a loss of contact with reality known as **amphetamine psychosis.** Affected users suffer from paranoid delusions that someone is out to get them. Acting on these delusions, the speed freak may become violent and cause self-injury or injury to others (Kratofil, Baberg, & Dimsdale, 1996).

BRIDGES

The symptoms of amphetamine psychosis and paranoid schizophrenia are nearly identical, suggesting that both are based on similar changes in brain chemistry.

See Chapter 17, pages 577–582.

DESIGNER DRUGS—AGONY OR ECSTASY?

Small variations in the structure of a drug can change its effects. For example, the drug MDMA ("ecstasy") is chemically similar to amphetamine. But in addition to producing a rush of energy, users say it makes them feel closer to others and heightens their sensory experiences.

MDMA is a "designer drug," a chemically engineered variation of an existing drug. Many designer drugs were first created in clandestine labs to circumvent drug laws. Because designer drugs are not tested for safety, some have extremely toxic effects. One notorious drug damaged the brain in a way that left hundreds of users suffering from severe Parkinson's disease.

The risk posed by MDMA remains unclear. In England, a number of deaths have been traced to the use of MDMA at "rave" parties. However, these deaths were caused by heat exhaustion, not by drug poisoning. MDMA raises body temperature, which can be fatal when combined with all-night dancing in an overheated club.

MDMA sometimes causes severe liver damage, which can also be fatal. Aside from these documented risks, the long-term effects of MDMA are unknown. It may take another 10 to 20 years before MDMA's impact on the health of users emerges. Of more immediate concern is the fact that many of the street drugs sold as "ecstasy" are impure and adulterated with other substances. Like other designer drugs, MDMA may ultimately prove to be a costly trip into the unknown (Abbott & Concar, 1992; McKim, 1997).

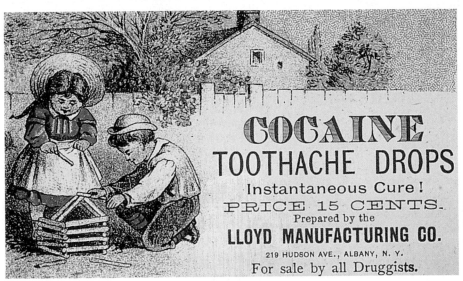

Cocaine was the main ingredient in many nonprescription elixirs before the turn of the twentieth century. Today cocaine is recognized as a powerful and dangerous drug. Its high potential for abuse has damaged the lives of countless users.

A potent new smokable form of crystal methamphetamine has recently added to the risks of stimulant abuse. This drug, known as "ice" on the street, is highly addictive. Like "crack," the smokable form of cocaine, it produces an intense high. But also like crack (discussed in a moment), crystal methamphetamine leads very rapidly to compulsive abuse and severe drug dependence. (For information on a related problem, see "Designer Drugs.")

Cocaine

Cocaine is a powerful central nervous system stimulant extracted from the leaves of the coca plant. Cocaine produces feelings of alertness, euphoria, well-being, power, boundless energy, and pleasure (Julien, 1998).

Cocaine has a long history of use and misuse. At the turn of the twentieth century, dozens of nonprescription potions and cure-alls contained cocaine. It was during this time that Coca-Cola was, indeed, the "real thing." From 1886 until 1906, when

Physical dependence *Physical addiction, as indicated by the presence of drug tolerance and withdrawal symptoms.*
Withdrawal symptoms *Physical illness and discomfort following the withdrawal of a drug.*
Drug tolerance *A reduction in the body's response to a drug.*
Psychological dependence *Drug dependence that is based primarily on emotional or psychological needs.*
Experimental drug use *Short-term use based on curiosity.*
Social-recreational drug use *Occasional social use for pleasure or relaxation.*
Situational drug use *Use to cope with a specific problem, such as needing to stay awake.*
Intensive drug use *Daily use with elements of dependence.*
Compulsive drug use *Intense use and extreme dependence.*
Amphetamines *A class of synthetic drugs having stimulant effects on the nervous system.*
Amphetamine psychosis *A severe disruption of psychological functioning caused by abuse of amphetamines.*
Cocaine *A crystalline drug derived from coca leaves; used as a central nervous system stimulant and local anesthetic.*

The future looked bright when college basketball star Len Bias was chosen to play for the Boston Celtics. Thrilled by his hard-earned achievement, and perhaps feeling invincible, Bias tried cocaine, probably for the first time. Hours later, his dream perished. Bias was dead from cardiac arrest at age 22.

the U.S. Pure Food and Drug Act was passed, Coca-Cola contained cocaine (which has since been replaced with caffeine). An estimated 4 to 5 million Americans use cocaine at least once a month, and half of all Americans between the ages of 25 and 30 have tried cocaine.

How does cocaine differ from amphetamines? The two are very much alike in their effects on the central nervous system. The main difference is that amphetamine lasts several hours; cocaine is quickly metabolized, so its effects last only about 15 to 30 minutes.

ABUSE *How dangerous is cocaine?* Cocaine is one of the most dangerous drugs of abuse. Even casual or first-time users run a risk because cocaine can cause convulsions, a heart attack, or a stroke (Cregler & Mark, 1985; Lacayo, 1995). The highly publicized death of all-American basketball star Len Bias is a case in point. The most tragic cocaine victims are children who were exposed to the drug before birth. As discussed in Chapter 4, some "cocaine babies" suffer subtle damage that can affect them for life.

When rats and monkeys are given free access to cocaine, they find it irresistible. Many, in fact, end up dying of convulsions from self-administered overdoses of the drug. Cocaine increases activity in brain pathways sensitive to the chemical messengers dopamine (DOPE-ah-meen) and noradrenaline (nor-ah-DREN-ah-lin). Noradrenaline arouses the brain, and added dopamine produces a "rush" of pleasure. This combination is so powerfully rewarding that cocaine users run a high risk of becoming compulsive abusers (Aston-Jones & Druhan, 1999).

A person who stops using cocaine does not experience heroin-like withdrawal symptoms. But cocaine can be highly addictive. The brain adapts to cocaine abuse in ways that upset its chemical balance, causing depression when cocaine is withdrawn. First, there is a jarring "crash" of mood and energy. Within a few days, the person enters a long period of fatigue, anxiety, paranoia, boredom, and **anhedonia** (an-he-DAWN-ee-ah: an inability to feel pleasure). Before long, the urge to use cocaine grows overwhelming.

So, although cocaine does not fit the classic pattern of physical addiction, there is little doubt about its potential for compulsive abuse. Even a person who gets through withdrawal may crave cocaine months or years later (Withers et al., 1995).

Many authorities estimate that if cocaine were cheaper, 9 out of 10 users would progress to compulsive abuse. In fact, rock cocaine (or "crack"), which is cheaper, produces very high abuse rates among those who try it. Here are some increasingly serious signs of cocaine abuse (Pursch, 1983).

- **Compulsive use.** If cocaine is available—say, at a party—you will undoubtedly use it. You can't say no to it.
- **Loss of control.** Once you have had some cocaine, you will keep using it until you are exhausted or the cocaine is gone.
- **Disregarding consequences.** You don't care if the rent gets paid, your job is endangered, your lover disapproves, or your health is affected; you'll use cocaine anyway.

Clearly, cocaine's capacity for abuse and social damage rivals that of heroin. Anyone who thinks she or he has a cocaine problem should seek advice at a drug clinic or a Cocaine Anonymous meeting. Quitting cocaine use is extremely difficult. Nevertheless, three out of four cocaine abusers who remain in treatment programs succeed in breaking their coke dependence (Simpson et al., 1999).

Caffeine

Caffeine is the most frequently used psychoactive drug in North America. (And that's not counting Seattle!) **Caffeine** stimulates the brain by blocking chemicals that normally inhibit or slow nerve activity (Julien, 1998). Its effects become apparent with doses as small as 50 milligrams, the amount found in about one-half cup of brewed coffee. Physically, caffeine causes sweating, talkativeness, tinnitus (ringing in the ears), and hand tremors. Psychologically, caffeine suppresses fatigue or drowsiness and increases feelings of alertness (Smith et al., 1999). Some people have a hard time starting a day without it.

How much caffeine did you consume today? It is common to think of coffee as the major source of caffeine, but there are many others. Caffeine is found in tea, many soft drinks (especially colas), chocolate, and cocoa (◆Table 8.5). More than 2,000 nonprescription drugs also contain caffeine, including stay-awake pills, cold remedies, and many name-brand aspirin products.

ABUSE *Are there any serious drawbacks to using caffeine?* Serious abuse may result in an unhealthy dependence on caffeine known as **caffeinism.** Insomnia, irritability, loss of appetite, chills, racing heart, and elevated body temperature are all signs

◆ TABLE 8.5 Average Caffeine Content of Various Foods
Instant coffee (5 ounces), 64 milligrams
Percolated coffee (5 ounces), 108 milligrams
Drip coffee (5 ounces), 145 milligrams
Decaf coffee (5 ounces), 3 milligrams
Black tea (5 ounces), 42 milligrams
Canned ice tea (17 ounces), 30 milligrams
Cocoa drink (6 ounces), 8 milligrams
Chocolate drink (8 ounces), 14 milligrams
Sweet chocolate (1 ounce), 20 milligrams
Colas (12 ounces), 50 milligrams
Soft drinks (12 ounces), 0–52 milligrams

The Far Side

The real reason dinosaurs became extinct

Chronicle Features, 1982 Larson 12-15

of caffeinism. It is not uncommon to find that individuals with these symptoms are drinking 15 or 20 cups of coffee a day. Even at lower doses, caffeine can intensify anxiety and other psychological problems (Larson & Carey, 1998).

Caffeine has a variety of health risks. Caffeine encourages the growth of breast cysts in women, and it may contribute to bladder cancer, heart problems, and high blood pressure. Pregnant women should consider giving up caffeine entirely because of a suspected link between caffeine and birth defects. Pregnant women who consume 6 or more cups of coffee a day double their risk of having a miscarriage (Klebanoff et al., 1999).

It is customary to think of caffeine as a nondrug. But as few as 2.5 cups of coffee a day (or the equivalent) can be a problem. People who consume even such modest amounts may experience anxiety, depression, fatigue, headaches, and flu-like symptoms during withdrawal (Silverman et al., 1992). About half of all caffeine users show some signs of dependence (Hughes, et al., 1998). It is wise to remember that caffeine *is* a drug and use it in moderation.

Nicotine

Nicotine is a natural stimulant found mainly in tobacco. Next to caffeine, it is the most widely used psychoactive drug (Julien, 1998).

How does nicotine compare with other stimulants? Nicotine is a potent drug. It is so toxic that it is sometimes used as an insecticide! In large doses, it causes stomach pain, vomiting and diarrhea, cold sweats, dizziness, confusion, and muscle tremors. In very large doses, nicotine may cause convulsions, respiratory failure, and death. For a nonsmoker, 50 to 75 milligrams of nicotine taken in a single dose could be lethal.

(Chain-smoking about 17 to 25 cigarettes will produce this dosage.)

Most first-time smokers get sick on one or two cigarettes. In contrast, a heavy smoker may inhale 40 cigarettes a day without feeling ill. This indicates that regular smokers build a tolerance for nicotine (Perkins, 1995; Stolerman & Jarvis, 1995).

ABUSE *Is it true that nicotine can be addicting?* A vast array of evidence confirms that nicotine is addictive (Henningfield & Heishman, 1995). For many smokers, withdrawal from nicotine causes headaches, sweating, cramps, insomnia, digestive upset, irritability, and a sharp craving for cigarettes (Killen & Fortmann, 1997). These symptoms may last from 2 to 6 weeks and may be worse than heroin withdrawal. Indeed, relapse patterns are nearly identical for alcoholics, heroin addicts, cocaine abusers, and smokers who try to quit (Stolerman & Jarvis, 1995). A staggering 8 out of 10 people who quit smoking relapse within 1 year (Jarvik, 1995).

Anhedonia *An inability to feel pleasure.*
Caffeine *A natural drug with stimulant properties; found in coffee and tea and added to artificial beverages and medicines.*
Caffeinism *Excessive consumption of caffeine, leading to dependence and a variety of physical and psychological complaints.*
Nicotine *A potent stimulant drug found primarily in tobacco; nicotine is a known carcinogen.*

IMPACT ON HEALTH   *How serious are the health risks of smoking?*
A burning cigarette releases more than 6,800 different chemicals. Many of these are potent **carcinogens** (car-SIN-oh-jins: cancer-causing substances). Lung cancer and other cancers caused by smoking are now considered the single most preventable cause of death in the United States and Canada. Among men, 97 percent of lung cancer deaths are caused by smoking. For women, 74 percent of all lung cancers are due to smoking. Skeptics take note: Wayne McLaren, who portrayed the rugged "Marlboro Man" in cigarette ads, died of lung cancer at age 51.

Smoking Facts

Here are some sobering facts about smoking:

- Every cigarette reduces a smoker's life expectancy by 7 minutes.
- Smoking is the number one cause of deaths in the United States and Canada—more than the number of deaths from alcohol, drugs, car accidents, and AIDS combined.
- In the United States alone, smoking-related costs total $50 billion a year. Taxpayers pick up the bill for 43 percent of this total.
- Forty percent of all smokers who develop throat cancer try smoking again.
- Each year, only one out of five smokers who tries to quit smoking succeeds.
- Some tobacco companies manipulate nicotine levels in their cigarettes to keep smokers addicted.
- Daily exposure to secondhand smoke at home or work causes a 24 to 39 percent increase in cancer risk to nonsmokers.

If you think smoking is harmless, or that there's no connection between smoking and cancer, you're kidding yourself. The scientific link between tobacco smoking and cancer is undeniable. By the way, urban cowboys and Skol bandits, the same applies to chewing tobacco and snuff. Users of smokeless tobacco run a four to six times higher risk of developing oral cancer. Smokeless tobacco also causes shrinkage of the gums, contributes to heart disease, and is as addicting as cigarettes (Christian & McDonald, 1987; Foreyt, 1987b).

Smokers don't just risk their own health; they also endanger those who live and work nearby. Secondary smoke causes 20 percent of all lung cancers. Nonsmoking women who are married to smokers suffer a 30 percent increase in their risk of developing lung cancer. It is particularly irresponsible of smokers to expose young children to secondhand smoke (Abramson, 1993).

DYNAMICS OF SMOKING   Smokers, unless they have a death wish, must be getting something out of their habit. Most claim that smoking helps them concentrate, feel sociable, or calm down. But heavy smokers get nothing positive out of smoking. They smoke only to prevent withdrawal. Studies have shown that smoking does not improve the mood or performance of heavy smokers. On the other hand, heavy smokers who are deprived of nicotine feel worse and perform worse than nonsmokers (Foulds et al., 1996). In other words, smokers need nicotine to feel normal (Parrott, 1999).

Heavy smokers adjust their smoking to keep bodily levels of nicotine constant. Thus, when smokers are given lighter cigarettes, they smoke more. This can do extra damage because light cigarettes have as much tar as regular cigarettes do (Kozlowski et al., 1998). If smokers are under stress (which speeds the removal of nicotine from the body), they smoke more. This relationship probably explains why students smoke more during stressful periods, such as final exams, or at parties, which are also stressful.

QUITTING SMOKING   *Is it better for a person to quit smoking abruptly or taper down gradually?*   For many years, smokers were advised to quit cold turkey. The current view is that quitting all at once isn't as effective as tapering off. Going cold turkey makes

Actress Lily Tomlin took up smoking for a role in the movie *Shadows and Fog* and developed a four-pack-a-day habit. As Tomlin's experience shows, the best way to avoid developing a nicotine addiction is to not begin smoking in the first place.

A study of 5th through 12th graders found that those who smoke are less likely than nonsmokers to believe the health warning labels on cigarette packs (Cecil, Evans, & Stanley, 1996). Smokers in general are less likely to believe that smoking poses a serious risk to health.

NEW STRATEGIES TO STOP SMOKING

If you smoke and would like to quit, here are some basic steps you can take: (1) Delay having a first cigarette in the morning. Then try to delay a little longer each day. (2) Gradually reduce the total number of cigarettes you smoke each day. (3) Quit completely, but for just 1 week. Then quit again, a week at a time, for as many times as necessary to make it stick (Pierce, 1991).

You will probably be most successful at strategy number 2 if you *schedule* a gradual reduction in smoking. To begin, count the number of cigarettes you smoke per day. For the first week, your goal will be to smoke only two thirds of that baseline number each day. In addition, you should divide the 16 waking hours in each day by the number of cigarettes you will smoke that day. For example, if you plan to smoke 16 cigarettes per day, then you get to smoke only one per hour. When a scheduled "smoking time" arrives, smoke for

only 5 minutes, whether you finish the cigarette or not. Don't smoke any "missed" cigarettes later.

During the second week, you should smoke only one third as many cigarettes as you did during your baseline. Again, divide each 16-hour day by the number of cigarettes, so you can plan how much time to allow between smoking periods.

During week 3, reduce your cigarette allowance to 20 percent of the original baseline number.

In the fourth week, stop smoking entirely.

Gradually stretching the time periods between cigarettes is a key part of this program. Scheduled smoking apparently helps people learn to cope with the urge to smoke. As a result, people using this method are more likely to succeed. Also, they more often remain permanent nonsmokers than people using other approaches (Cincirpini et al., 1997).

---

quitting an all-or-nothing proposition. Smokers who smoke even one cigarette after "quitting forever" tend to feel they've failed. Many figure they might just as well resume smoking. Those who quit gradually accept that success may take many attempts, spread over several months. The box titled "New Strategies to Stop Smoking" summarizes several ways to quit smoking.

Whatever approach is taken, quitting smoking is not easy. It does help, though, if you get a spouse or partner to support your efforts (Cohen & Lichtenstein, 1990). Also, as we have noted, anyone trying to quit should be prepared to make several attempts before succeeding. But the good news is that tens of millions of people have quit.

BRIDGES

Behavioral self-management techniques can be very useful for breaking habits such as smoking.

See Chapter 9, pages 303–305, and Chapter 18, page 606.

DOWNERS—SEDATIVES, TRANQUILIZERS, AND ALCOHOL

How do downers differ from the stimulant drugs? The most widely used downers, or depressant drugs, are alcohol, barbiturates, and benzodiazepine (ben-zoe-die-AZ-eh-peen) tranquilizers. These drugs are much alike in their effects. In fact, barbiturates and tranquilizers are sometimes referred to as "solid alcohol." Let's examine the properties of each.

Barbiturates

Barbiturates are sedative drugs that depress brain activity. Medically, they are used to calm patients or to induce sleep. In mild doses, barbiturates have an effect similar to alcohol intoxication. Higher doses can cause severe mental confusion or even psychotic symptoms (a loss of contact with reality). Overdoses can easily cause coma or death. Barbiturates are often taken in excess amounts because a first dose may be followed by others, as the user becomes uninhibited or forgetful. Overdoses first cause unconsciousness. Then they severely depress

brain centers that control heartbeat and breathing. The result is death (McKim, 1997).

Tranquilizers

A **tranquilizer** is a drug that lowers anxiety and reduces tension. Doctors prescribe benzodiazepine tranquilizers to alleviate nervousness and stress. Valium is the best-known drug in this family; others are Xanax, Halcion, and Librium. Even at normal doses, these drugs can cause drowsiness, shakiness, and confusion. When used at too high a dose or for too long a time, benzodiazepines have strong addictive potential (McKim, 1997).

Recently, a drug sold under the trade name Rohypnol (ro-HIP-nol) has added to the problem of tranquilizer abuse. This drug, which is related to Valium, is cheap and potent. It lowers inhibitions and produces relaxation or intoxication. Large doses induce short-term amnesia and sleep. "Roofies," as they are known on the street, are odorless and tasteless. They have been used to spike drinks, which are given to the unwary. Drugged victims are then sexually assaulted or raped while they are unconscious (Navarro, 1995). (Be aware, however, that drinking too much alcohol is by far the most common prelude to rape.)

ABUSE   The most frequently abused barbiturates are Seconal and Amytal. These drugs act quickly, and the rush of intoxication lasts only from 2 to 4 hours. Repeated use of any barbitu-

---

Carcinogen *A substance capable of causing cancer.*
Barbiturate *One of a large group of sedative drugs that depress activity in the nervous system.*
Tranquilizer *A drug that lowers anxiety and reduces tension.*

rate can cause physical dependence. Some abusers suffer severe emotional depression that may end in suicide. Similarly, when tranquilizers are used at too high a dose or for too long a time, addiction may occur. Many people have learned the hard way that their legally prescribed tranquilizers are as dangerous as many illicit drugs (McKim, 1997).

Combining barbiturates or tranquilizers with alcohol is extremely risky. When mixed, the effects of both drugs are multiplied by a **drug interaction** (one drug enhances the effect of another). This combination is responsible for many hundreds of fatal drug overdoses every year. All too often, depressants are gulped down with alcohol or added to a spiked punch bowl. This is the combination that left a young woman named Karen Ann Quinlan in a coma that lasted 10 years, ending with her

death. It is no exaggeration to restate that mixing depressants with alcohol can be fatal.

Alcohol

Alcohol is the common name for ethyl alcohol, the intoxicating element in fermented and distilled liquors. Contrary to popular belief, alcohol is not a stimulant. The apparent gaiety at drinking parties is due to alcohol's effect as a *depressant*. As ❖Figure 8.12 shows, small amounts of alcohol reduce inhibitions and produce feelings of relaxation and euphoria. Larger amounts cause ever greater impairment of the brain until the drinker loses consciousness. Alcohol is also not an aphrodisiac. It usually impairs sexual perfor-

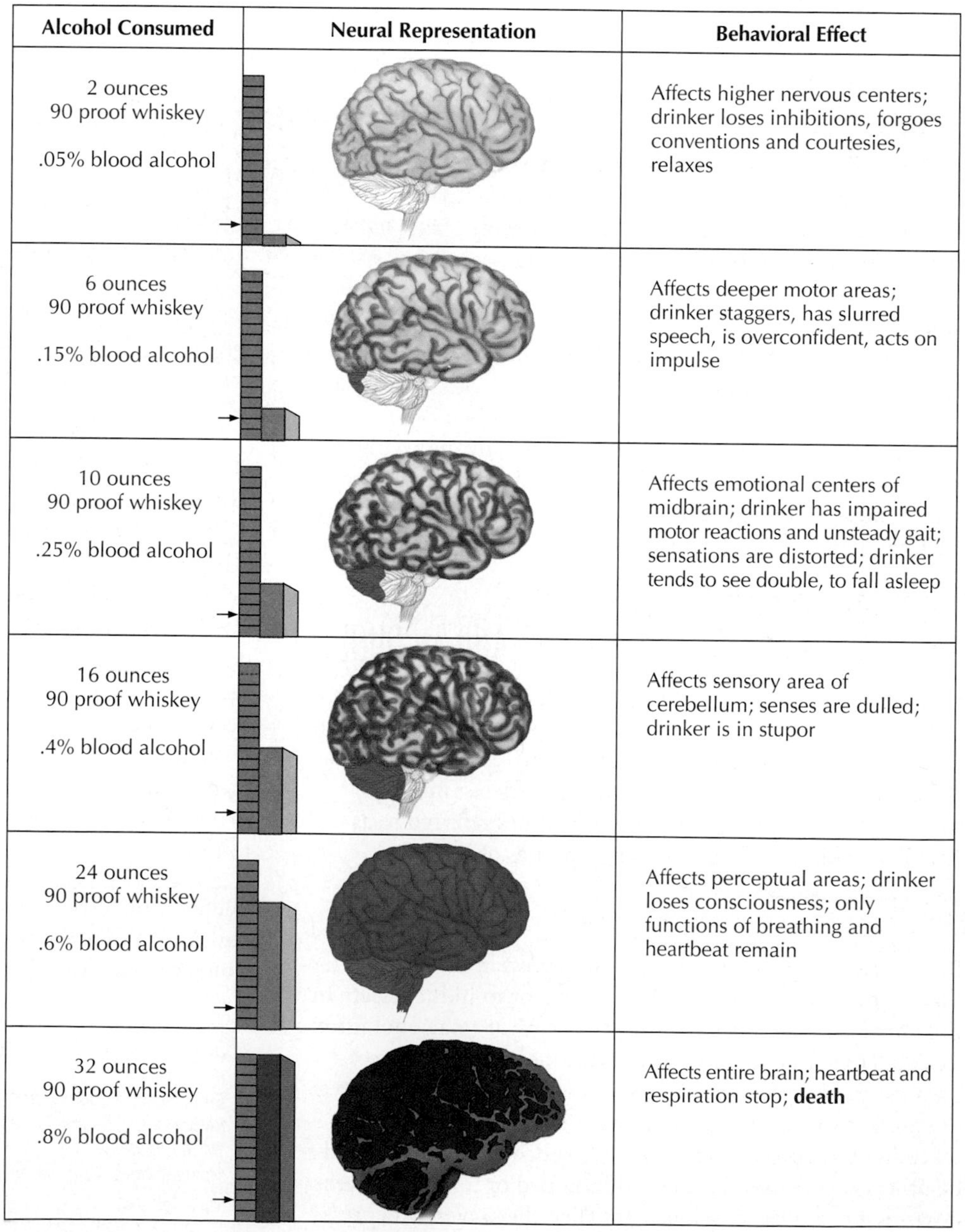

Alcohol Consumed	Neural Representation	Behavioral Effect
2 ounces 90 proof whiskey .05% blood alcohol		Affects higher nervous centers; drinker loses inhibitions, forgoes conventions and courtesies, relaxes
6 ounces 90 proof whiskey .15% blood alcohol		Affects deeper motor areas; drinker staggers, has slurred speech, is overconfident, acts on impulse
10 ounces 90 proof whiskey .25% blood alcohol		Affects emotional centers of midbrain; drinker has impaired motor reactions and unsteady gait; sensations are distorted; drinker tends to see double, to fall asleep
16 ounces 90 proof whiskey .4% blood alcohol		Affects sensory area of cerebellum; senses are dulled; drinker is in stupor
24 ounces 90 proof whiskey .6% blood alcohol		Affects perceptual areas; drinker loses consciousness; only functions of breathing and heartbeat remain
32 ounces 90 proof whiskey .8% blood alcohol		Affects entire brain; heartbeat and respiration stop; **death**

❖ **FIGURE 8.12** *The behavioral effects of alcohol are related to blood alcohol content and the resulting suppression of higher mental function. Arrows indicate the typical threshold for legal intoxication in the United States. (From Jozef Cohen,* Eyewitness Series in Psychology, *p. 44. Copyright © by Rand McNally and Company. Reprinted by permission.)*

mance, particularly in males. As William Shakespeare observed long ago, drink "provokes the desire, but it takes away the performance."

Some people become aggressive and want to argue or fight when they are drunk. Others become relaxed and friendly. How can the same drug have such different effects? When a person is drunk, thinking and perception become dulled or shortsighted, a condition that has been called **alcohol myopia** (my-OH-pea-ah). Only the most obvious and immediate stimuli catch a drinker's attention. Worries and "second thoughts" that would normally restrain behavior are banished from the drinker's mind. That's why many behaviors become more extreme when a person is drunk. Alcohol also reduces anxiety and temporarily makes people feel better about themselves (Steele & Josephs, 1990). It's easy to see why it is such a seductive drug.

ABUSE Alcohol, the world's favorite depressant, breeds our biggest drug problem. More than 200 million people in the United States and Canada use alcohol. An estimated 25 million have serious drinking problems. An alarming trend is the high level of alcohol abuse among adolescents and young adults. Fifty percent of male college students and 40 percent of college women have engaged in binge drinking. For fraternity and sorority members, the figure jumps to 84 percent. **Binge drinking** is defined as downing five or more drinks in a short time. Apparently, many students think it's entertaining to get completely wasted and throw up on their friends. However, binge drinking is a serious sign of alcohol abuse (Wechsler, 1999). It is responsible for an estimated 50 deaths of U.S. college students a year and thousands of trips to the ER (McCormick, & Kalb, 1998).

Children of alcoholics and those who have other relatives who abuse alcohol are at greater risk for becoming alcohol abusers themselves (Blane, 1988). So are youths who begin drinking before the age of 15 (Grant & Dawson, 1997). Women also face some special risks. For one thing, alcohol is absorbed faster and metabolized more slowly by women's bodies. As a result, women get intoxicated from less alcohol than men do. Women who drink are also more prone to liver disease, osteo-

porosis, and depression. As few as three drinks a week may increase a woman's risk of breast cancer by 50 percent. In addition, women who abuse alcohol are more likely to face social rejection and stigma than men who drink similar amounts (Gomberg, 1993).

Positive reinforcement—drinking for pleasure—motivates most people who consume alcohol. What sets alcohol abusers apart is that they also drink to cope with negative emotions, such as anxiety and depression. That's why alcohol abuse increases with the level of stress in people's lives. People who drink to relieve bad feelings are at great risk of becoming alcoholics (Kenneth, Carpenter, & Hasin, 1998).

RECOGNIZING PROBLEM DRINKING *What are the signs of alcohol abuse?* Because alcohol abuse is such a common problem, it is important to recognize the danger signals of growing dependency. The path from a social drinker to an alcohol abuser to an alcoholic is often subtle. Jellinek (1960) gives these typical steps in the development of a drinking problem.

1. **Initial phase.** At first, the social drinker begins to turn more often to alcohol to relieve tension or to feel good. Four danger signals in this period that signal excessive dependence on alcohol are:
   - **Increasing consumption.** The individual drinks more and more and may begin to worry about his or her drinking.
   - **Morning drinking.** Morning drinking is a dangerous sign, particularly when it is used to combat a hangover or to "get through the day."
   - **Regretted behavior.** The person engages in extreme behavior while drunk that leaves her or him feeling guilty or embarrassed.
   - **Blackouts.** Abusive drinking may be revealed by an inability to remember what happened during intoxication.
2. **Crucial phase.** A crucial turning point comes as the person begins to lose control over drinking. At this stage, there is still some control over when and where a first drink is taken. But one drink starts a chain reaction leading to a second, a third, and so on.
3. **Chronic phase.** At this point, the person is alcohol dependent. Victims drink compulsively and continuously. They rarely eat, they become intoxicated from far less alcohol than before, and they crave alcohol when deprived of it. Work, family ties, and social life all deteriorate. The person's self-drugging is usually so compulsive that, when given a choice, the bottle comes before friends, relatives, employment, and self-esteem. The person is an addict.

Binge drinking and alcohol abuse have become serious problems among college students. Many alcohol abusers regard themselves as "moderate" drinkers, which suggests that they are in denial about how much they actually drink (Grant & Dawson, 1997).

Drug interaction *A combined effect of two drugs that exceeds the addition of one drug's effects to the other.*
Alcohol *Common name for ethyl alcohol, the intoxicating element in fermented and distilled liquors.*
Alcohol myopia *Shortsighted thinking and perception that occurs during alcohol intoxication.*
Binge drinking *Consuming five or more drinks in a short time.*

THE DEVELOPMENT OF A DRINKING PROBLEM   To add to this summary, the following lists will help you form a more detailed picture of how alcohol abuse develops.

Early Warnings
- You are beginning to feel guilty about your drinking.
- You drink more than you used to and tend to gulp your drinks.
- You try to have a few extra drinks before or after drinking with others.
- You have begun to drink at certain times or to get through certain situations.
- You drink to relieve feelings of boredom, depression, anxiety, or inadequacy.
- You are sensitive when others mention your drinking.
- You have had memory blackouts or have passed out while drinking.

Signals Not to Be Ignored
- There are times when you need a drink.
- You drink in the morning to overcome a hangover.
- You promise to drink less and are lying about your drinking.
- You often regret what you have said or done while drinking.
- You have begun to drink alone.
- You have weekend drinking bouts and Monday hangovers.
- You have lost time at work or school because of drinking.
- You are noticeably drunk on important occasions.
- Your relationship to family and friends has changed because of your drinking.

MODERATED DRINKING   Many social-recreational drinkers could do a far better job of managing their use of alcohol. Almost everyone has been to a party spoiled by someone who drank too much too fast. Those who avoid overdrinking have a better time, and so do their friends. But how do you avoid drinking too much? After all, as one wit once observed, "The conscience dissolves in alcohol." Psychologists Roger Vogler and Wayne Bartz (1982, 1992) provide a partial answer.

Vogler and Bartz observe that drinking makes you feel good while blood alcohol is rising and remains below a level of about 0.05. In this range, people feel relaxed, euphoric, and sociable. At higher levels, they go from moderately intoxicated to thoroughly drunk. Later, as blood alcohol begins to fall, those who overdrink become sick and miserable. ◆Table 8.6 shows the approximate amount per hour that can be consumed without exceeding the 0.05 blood alcohol level. (Even at this level, driving may be impaired.) By pacing themselves, those who

choose to drink can remain comfortable, pleasant, and coherent during a long party or other social event. In short, if you drink, it might be wise to learn your "magic" number from ◆Table 8.6.

It takes skill to regulate drinking in social situations, where the temptation to drink can be strong. If you choose to drink, here are some guidelines that may be helpful. (Adapted from Vogler & Bartz, 1992.)

Paced Drinking
1. Think about your drinking beforehand and plan how you will manage it.
2. Drink slowly, eat while drinking, and make every other drink (or more) a nonalcoholic beverage.
3. Limit drinking primarily to the first hour of a social event or party. Pace your drinking by using the information from ◆Table 8.6.
4. Practice how you will politely but firmly refuse drinks.
5. Learn how to relax, meet people, and socialize without relying on alcohol.

TREATMENT   Treatment for alcohol dependence begins with sobering up the person and cutting off the supply. This phase is referred to as **detoxification** (literally, "to remove poison"). It frequently produces all the symptoms of drug withdrawal and can be extremely unpleasant. The next step is to try to restore the person's health. Heavy abuse of alcohol usually causes severe damage to body organs and the nervous system. After al-

◆ **TABLE 8.6** Drinking in Moderation

YOUR WEIGHT (POUNDS)	APPROXIMATE NUMBER OF DRINKS PER HOUR TO STAY BELOW 0.05 BLOOD ALCOHOL*	
	Male	Female
100	0.75	0.60
120	1.00	0.75
140	1.25	0.90
160	1.30	1.00
180	1.50	1.10
200	1.60	1.20
220	1.80	1.35

One drink = 12 ounces beer, 4 ounces wine, 2.5 ounces brandy, or 1.25 ounces 80 proof liquor.
*Table entries are approximate, owing to individual differences in metabolism, recency of meals, and other factors. Estimates are from tables prepared by Vogler and Bartz (1982, 1992).

coholics have "dried out," and some degree of health has been restored, they may be treated with tranquilizers, antidepressants, or psychotherapy. Unfortunately, the success of these procedures has been limited.

One mutual-help approach that has been fairly successful is Alcoholics Anonymous (AA). AA acts on the premise that it takes a former alcoholic to understand and help a current alcoholic. Participants at AA meetings admit that they have a problem, share feelings, and resolve to stay "dry" 1 day at a time. Other group members provide support for those struggling to end dependency. (Cocaine Anonymous and Narcotics Anonymous use the same approach.)

Eighty-one percent of those who remain in AA for more than 1 year get through the following year without a drink. However, AA's success rate may simply reflect the fact that members join voluntarily, meaning they have admitted they have a serious problem (Morgenstern et al., 1997). Sadly, it seems that alcohol abusers often will not face their problems until they have "hit rock bottom." If they are willing, though, AA presents a practical approach to the problem.

Two newer groups offer a rational, nonspiritual approach to alcohol abuse that better fits the needs of some people. These are Rational Recovery and Secular Organizations for Sobriety (SOS). Other alternatives to AA include medical treatment, group therapy, and individual psychotherapy (Institute of Medicine, 1990). There is a strong tendency for abusive drinkers to deny they have a problem. The sooner they seek help, the better.

MARIJUANA—WHAT'S IN THE POT?

If you pick any three citizens at random, one will have tried marijuana at least once. More than 20 million people in Canada and the United States may be regular users, which puts marijuana in a league with tobacco and alcohol. Marijuana and hashish are derived from the hemp plant *Cannabis sativa*. **Marijuana** consists of the leaves and flowers of the hemp plant. **Hashish** is a resinous material scraped from *Cannabis* leaves. The main active chemical in marijuana is **tetrahydrocannabinol** (tet-rah-hydro-cah-NAB-ih-nol), or **THC,** for short. THC is a mild **hallucinogen** (hal-LU-sin-oh-jin: a substance that alters sensory impressions).

HALLUCINOGENS   The drug LSD (lysergic acid diethylamide) is perhaps the best-known hallucinogen. Even when taken in tiny amounts, LSD can produce hallucinations and psychotic-like disturbances in thinking and perception. Two other common hallucinogens are mescaline (peyote) and psilocybin ("magic mushrooms"). Incidentally, the drug PCP (phencyclidine) can have hallucinogenic effects. However, PCP, which is an anesthetic, also has stimulant and depressant effects. This potent combination can cause extreme agitation, disorientation, violence—and, too often, tragedy. All of the hallucinogens, including marijuana, typically affect neurotransmitter systems that carry messages between brain cells (Julien, 1998).

Artists have tried at times to capture the effects of hallucinogens. Here, the artist depicts visual experiences he had while under the influence of LSD.

MARIJUANA   Marijuana's psychological effects include a sense of euphoria or well-being, relaxation, altered time sense, and perceptual distortions. At high dosages, however, paranoia, hallucinations, and delusions can occur (Palfai & Jankiewicz, 1991). All considered, marijuana intoxication is relatively subtle by comparison with drugs such as LSD or alcohol (Kelly et al., 1990). Despite this, driving a car while high on marijuana can be extremely hazardous. As a matter of fact, driving under the influence of any intoxicating drug is dangerous.

No overdose deaths have been reported from marijuana. However, marijuana cannot be considered harmless. Particularly worrisome is the fact that THC accumulates in the body's fatty tissues, especially in the brain and reproductive organs. Even if a person smokes marijuana just once a week, the body is never entirely free of THC. Scientists have located a specific receptor site on the surface of brain cells where THC binds to produce its effects (❖Fig. 8.13). These receptor sites are found in large numbers in the cerebral cortex, which is the seat of human consciousness (Matsuda et al., 1990).

Does marijuana produce physical dependence?   Studies of long-term heavy users of marijuana in Jamaica, Greece, and

Detoxification *In the treatment of alcoholism, the withdrawal of the patient from alcohol.*
Marijuana *The leaves and flowers of the hemp plant,* Cannabis sativa.
Hashish *Resinous material scraped from the leaves of the hemp plant; hashish has a high concentration of THC.*
THC *Tetrahydrocannabinol, the main active chemical in marijuana.*
Hallucinogen *A substance that alters or distorts sensory impressions.*

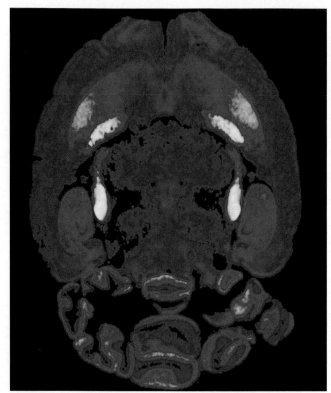

❖ **FIGURE 8.13** *This thin slice of a rat's brain has been washed with a radioactive THC-like drug. Yellowish areas show where the brain is rich in THC receptors. In addition to the cortex, or outer layer of the brain, THC receptors are found in abundance in areas involved in the control of coordinated movement. Naturally occurring chemicals similar to THC may help the brain cope with pain and stress. However, when THC is used as a drug, high doses can cause paranoia, hallucinations, and dizziness (Julien, 1998).*

Costa Rica failed to find any physical dependence (Carter, 1980; Rubin & Comitas, 1975; Stefanis et al., 1977). Marijuana's potential for abuse lies primarily in the realm of psychological dependence, not addiction. Nevertheless, frequent users of marijuana find it very difficult to quit, so dependence is a risk (Budney et al., 1999; Haney et al., 1999).

Dangers of Marijuana Use

There have been very alarming reports in the press about the dangers of marijuana. Are they accurate? As one pharmacologist put it, "Those reading only *Good Housekeeping* would have to believe that marijuana is considerably more dangerous than the black plague." Unfortunately, the evaluation of marijuana's risks has been clouded by emotional debate. Let's see if we can make a realistic appraisal.

In the past, it was widely reported that marijuana causes brain damage, genetic damage, and a loss of motivation. Each of these charges can be criticized for being based on poorly done or inconclusive research. However, that doesn't mean that marijuana gets a clean bill of health. For about a day after a person smokes marijuana, his or her attention, coordination, and short-term memory are affected (Pope, Gruber, & Yurgelun-Todd, 1995). Long-term marijuana users tend to show small but persistent impairments of learning, memory, attention, and thinking abilities. These changes, although subtle, can be a serious problem for frequent users (Pope & Yurgelun-Todd, 1996; Solowij, Michie, & Fox, 1995).

HEALTH RISKS After many years of conflicting information, some of marijuana's health hazards are also being clarified.

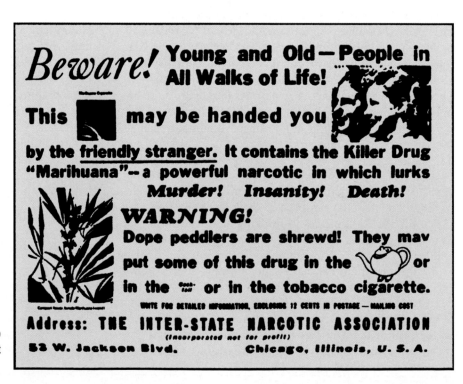

An outdated anti-marijuana poster demonstrates the kind of misinformation that has long been attached to this drug. Research has finally begun to sort out what risks are associated with use of marijuana.

Marijuana's long-term effects include the following health risks.

1. In regular users, marijuana causes pre-cancerous changes in lung cells. At present, no direct link between marijuana and lung cancer has been proved, but it is suspected. Marijuana smoke contains 50 percent more cancer-causing hydrocarbons than tobacco smoke does. One marijuana cigarette has 16 times more tar than one tobacco cigarette. Thus, smoking several "joints" a week may be the equivalent of smoking a dozen cigarettes a day (Barsky et al., 1998).

2. Marijuana temporarily lowers sperm production in males, and users produce more abnormal sperm. This could be a problem for a man who is marginally fertile and wants to have a family (Palfai & Jankiewicz, 1991).

3. In experiments with female monkeys, THC causes abnormal menstrual cycles and disrupts ovulation. Other animal studies show that THC causes a higher rate of miscarriages and that it can reach the developing fetus. As is true for so many other drugs, it appears that marijuana should be avoided during pregnancy.

4. THC can suppress the body's immune system, possibly increasing the risk of disease (Turkington, 1986).

5. In animals, marijuana causes genetic damage within cells of the body. It is not known to what extent this happens in humans, but it does suggest that marijuana can be detrimental to health (Zimmerman & Zimmerman, 1990).

6. Activity levels in the cerebellum are lower than normal in marijuana abusers. This may explain why chronic marijuana users tend to show some loss of coordination (Volkow et al., 1996).

7. There is some evidence that THC damages parts of the brain important for memory (Chan et al., 1998).

When the preceding findings are compared with the studies of veteran marijuana users, it is clear that no one can say with certainty that marijuana is extremely harmful or completely safe. Although much is still unknown, marijuana appears to be in a class with two other potent drugs—tobacco and alcohol. Only future research will tell for sure "what's in the pot."

A LOOK AHEAD   Of the many states of consciousness we have discussed, dreaming remains one of the most familiar—and the most surprising. Are there lessons to be learned from dreams? What personal insights lie hidden in the ebb and flow of dream images? The "Psychology in Action" section probes such questions. After that, we will conclude by wrestling with the questions, Why do people abuse drugs? and What can be done about it?

psychology in action

At one time or another, almost everyone has had a dream that seemed to have deep meaning. What strategies do psychologists use to interpret dreams? Let's start with Sigmund Freud's approach.

Interpreting Your Dreams

To unlock dreams, Freud identified four **dream processes,** or mental filters, that disguise the meanings of dreams. The first is **condensation,** in which several people, objects, or events are combined into a single dream image. A dream character that looks like a teacher, acts like your father, talks like your mother, and is dressed like your employer might be a condensation of authority figures in your life.

Displacement is a second way of disguising dream content. Displacement may cause important emotions or actions of a dream to be redirected toward safe or seemingly unimportant images. Thus, a student angry at his parents might dream of accidentally wrecking their car instead of directly attacking them.

Dream images may contain symbolic messages, as well as literal meanings. If you find yourself wearing a mask in a dream, for instance, it could relate to important roles that you play at school, work, or home. It could also mean that you want to hide or that you are looking forward to a costume party. To accurately interpret a dream, it is important to learn your own "vocabulary" of dream images and meanings. Keeping a dream diary is the first step toward gaining valuable insights.

A third dream process is **symbolization.** As mentioned earlier, Freud believed that dreams are often expressed in images that are symbolic rather than literal. That's why it helps to ask what feelings or ideas a dream image might symbolize. Let's say, for example, that a student dreams of coming to class naked. A literal interpretation would be that the student is an exhibitionist! A more likely symbolic meaning is that the student feels vulnerable or unprepared in the class.

Secondary elaboration is the fourth method by which dream meanings are disguised. **Secondary elaboration** is the tendency to make a dream more logical and to add details when remembering it. The fresher a dream memory is, the more useful it is likely to be.

Looking for condensation, displacement, symbolization, and secondary elaboration may help you unlock your dreams. But there are other ways to proceed that may be more effective. Dream theorist Calvin Hall (1974) preferred to think of dreams as plays and the dreamer as a playwright. Hall admitted that dream images and ideas tend to be more primitive than waking thoughts. Nevertheless, much can be learned by simply considering the *setting, cast of characters, plot,* and *emotions* portrayed in a dream.

Another dream theorist, Rosalind Cartwright, suggests that dreams are primarily "feeling statements." According to her, the overall *emotional tone* (underlying mood) of a dream is a major clue to its meaning. Is the dream comical, threatening, joyous, or depressing? Were you lonely, jealous, frightened, in love, or angry? Cartwright believes that exploring everyday dream life can be a source of personal enrichment and personal growth (Cartwright & Lamberg, 1992).

In many ways, dreams can be thought of as messages *from* you *to* yourself. Thus, the way to understand dreams is to remember them, write them down, look for the messages they contain, and become deeply acquainted with *your own* symbol system. Here's how.

How to Catch a Dream

1. Before retiring, plan to remember your dreams. Keep a pen and paper or a tape recorder beside your bed.
2. If possible, arrange to awaken gradually without an alarm. Natural awakening almost always follows soon after a REM period.
3. If you rarely remember your dreams, you may want to set an alarm clock to go off an hour before you usually awaken. Although less desirable than awakening naturally, this may let you catch a dream.
4. Upon awakening, lie still and review the dream images with your eyes closed. Try to recall as many details as possible.
5. If you can, make your first dream record (whether by writing or by tape) with your eyes closed. Opening your eyes will disrupt dream recall.
6. Review the dream again, and record as many additional details as you can remember. Dream memories disappear quickly. Be sure to describe feelings as well as the plot, characters, and actions of the dream.

7. Put your dreams into a permanent dream diary. Keep dreams in chronological order and review them periodically. This procedure will reveal recurrent themes, conflicts, and emotions. It almost always produces valuable insights.

8. Remember, a number of drugs suppress dreaming (see ◆Table 8.7).

DREAM WORK Because each dream has several possible meanings or levels of meaning, there is no fixed way to work with it. Telling the dream to others and discussing its meaning can be a good start. Describing it may help you relive some of the feelings in the dream. Also, family members or friends may be able to offer interpretations to which you would be blind. Watch for verbal or visual puns and other playful elements in dreams. For example, if you dream that you are in a wrestling match and your arm is pinned behind your back, it may mean that you feel someone is "twisting your arm" in real life.

The meaning of most dreams will yield to a little detective work. Rosalind Cartwright suggests asking a series of questions about dreams you would like to understand (Cartwright & Lamberg, 1992).

Probing Dreams

1. Who was in the dream? Do you recognize any of the characters?
2. What was happening? Were you active in the dream or watching it transpire? Did someone else do something to you?
3. Where did the action of the dream take place? Have you seen the setting or any part of it in real life, or was it a fantasy scene?
4. What was the time frame? What was your age in the dream?
5. Who is responsible for what happened in the dream?
6. Who are you in your dreams? Are you someone you would like to be or someone you'd rather not be?

If you still have trouble seeing the meaning of a dream, you may find it helpful to use a technique developed by Fritz Perls.

◆ **TABLE 8.7** Effects of Selected Drugs on Dreaming

DRUG	EFFECT ON REM SLEEP
Alcohol	Decrease
Amphetamines	Decrease
Barbiturates	Decrease
Caffeine	None
Cocaine	Decrease
LSD	Slight increase
Marijuana	Slight decrease or no effect
Opiates	Decrease
Valium	Decrease

Perls, the originator of Gestalt therapy, considered most dreams a special message about what's missing in our lives, what we avoid doing, or feelings that need to be "re-owned." Perls felt that dreams are a way of filling in gaps in personal experience (Perls, 1969).

An approach that Perls found helpful is to "take the part of" or "speak for" each of the characters and objects in the dream. In other words, if you dream about a strange man standing behind a doorway, you would speak aloud to the man, then answer for him. To use Perls's method, you would even speak for the door, perhaps saying something like "I am a barrier. I keep you safe, but I also keep you locked inside. The stranger has something to tell you. You must risk opening me to learn it."

A particularly interesting dream exercise is to continue a dream as waking fantasy so that it may be concluded or carried on to a more meaningful ending. As the world of dreams and your personal dream language become more familiar, you will doubtless find many answers, paradoxes, intuitions, and insights into your own behavior.

Using Your Dreams

Creative people tend to remember more dreams (Schredl, 1995). It could be that such people just pay more attention to their dreams. But dream theorist Gordon Globus (1987) believes that dreams make a major contribution to creativity. Globus points out that some of our most creative moments take place during dreaming. Even unimaginative people may create amazing worlds each night in their dreams. For many of us, this rich ability to create is lost in the daily rush of sensory input. How might we tap the creative power of dreams that is so easily lost during waking?

DREAMS AND CREATIVITY History is full of cases when dreams have been a pathway to creativity and discovery. A striking example is provided by Otto Loewi, a pharmacologist and winner of a Nobel Prize. Loewi had spent years studying the chemical transmission of nerve impulses. A tremendous breakthrough in his research came when he dreamed of an experiment 3 nights in a row. The first 2 nights he woke up and scribbled the experiment on a pad. But the next morning, he couldn't tell what the notes meant. On the third night, he got up after having the dream. This time, instead of making notes, he went straight to his laboratory and performed the crucial experiment. Loewi later said that, if the experiment had occurred to him while he was awake, he would have rejected it.

Dream processes *Mental filters that hide the true meanings of dreams.*
Condensation *Combining several people, objects, or events into a single dream image.*
Displacement *Directing emotions or actions toward safe or unimportant dream images.*
Symbolization *The nonliteral expression of dream content.*
Secondary elaboration *Making a dream more logical and complete while remembering it.*

Loewi's experience gives some insight into using dreams to produce creative solutions. Inhibitions are reduced during dreaming, which may be especially useful in solving problems that require a fresh point of view.

Being able to take advantage of dreams for problem solving is improved if you "set" yourself before retiring. Before you go to bed, try to think intently about a problem you wish to solve. Steep yourself in the problem by stating it clearly and reviewing all relevant information. Then use the suggestions listed in the previous section to catch your dreams. Although this method is not guaranteed to produce a novel solution or a new insight, it is certain to be an adventure. About half of a group of college students who used the method for 1 week recalled a dream that helped them solve a personal problem (Barrett, 1993).

LUCID DREAMING   If you would like to press further into the territory of dreams, you may want to learn lucid dreaming, a relatively rare but fascinating experience. During a **lucid dream,** a person feels fully awake within the dream world and capable of normal thought and action. If you ask yourself, "Could this be a dream?" and answer, "Yes," you are having a lucid dream (Blackmore, 1991a).

Stephen La Berge and his colleagues at the Stanford University Sleep Research Center have used a unique approach to show that lucid dreams are real and that they occur during REM sleep. In the sleep lab, lucid dreamers agree to make prearranged signals when they become aware they are dreaming. One such signal is to look up abruptly in a dream, causing a distinct upward eye movement. Another signal is to clench the right and left fists (in the dream) in a prearranged pattern. Such signals show very clearly that lucid dreaming and voluntary action in dreams is possible (La Berge, 1981, 1985; La Berge et al., 1981; Moss, 1989).

How would a person go about learning to have lucid dreams? La Berge found he could greatly increase lucid dreaming by following this simple routine: When you awaken spontaneously from a dream, take a few minutes to try to memorize it. Next, engage in 10 to 15 minutes of reading or any other activity requiring full wakefulness. Then, while lying in bed and returning to sleep, say to yourself, "Next time I'm dreaming, I want to remember I'm dreaming." Finally, visualize yourself lying in bed asleep while in the dream you just rehearsed. At the same time, picture yourself realizing that you are dreaming. Follow this routine each time you awaken (substitute a dream memory from another occasion if you don't awaken from a dream). Researchers have also found that stimulation from the vestibular system tends to increase lucidity. Thus, sleeping in a hammock or a boat or on a waterbed might increase the number of lucid dreams you have (Leslie & Ogilvie, 1996).

Why would anyone want to have more lucid dreams?   Researchers are interested in lucid dreams because they provide a tool for understanding dreaming. Using subjects who can signal while they are dreaming makes it possible to explore dreams with firsthand data from the dreamer's world itself.

On a more personal level, lucid dreaming can convert dreams into a nightly "workshop" for emotional growth. Consider, for example, a recently divorced woman who kept dreaming that she was being swallowed by a giant wave. Rosalind Cartwright asked the woman to try swimming the next time the wave engulfed her. She did, with great determination, and the nightmare lost its terror. More important, her revised dream made her feel that she could cope with life again. For reasons such as this, people who have lucid dreams tend to feel a sense of emotional well-being (Wolpin et al., 1992). So, day or night, don't be afraid to dream a little.

KNOWLEDGE BUILDER
EXPLORING AND USING DREAMS

RELATE

Some people are very interested in remembering and interpreting their dreams. Others pay little attention to dreaming. What importance do you place on dreams? Do you think dreams and dream interpretation can increase self-awareness?

LEARNING CHECK

1. In secondary elaboration, one dream character stands for several others. T or F?

2. Calvin Hall's approach to dream interpretation emphasizes the setting, cast, plot, and emotions portrayed in a dream. T or F?

3. Rosalind Cartwright stresses that dreaming is a relatively mechanical process having little personal meaning. T or F?

4. Both alcohol and LSD cause a slight increase in dreaming. T or F?

5. "Taking the part of" or "speaking for" dream elements is a dream interpretation technique originated by Fritz Perls. T or F?

6. Recent research shows that lucid dreaming occurs primarily during NREM sleep or micro-awakenings. T or F?

CRITICAL THINKING

7. The possibility of having a lucid dream raises an interesting question: If you were dreaming right now, how could you prove it?

Answers:

1. F 2. T 3. F 4. F 5. T 6. F 7. In waking consciousness, our actions have consequences that produce immediate sensory feedback. Dreams lack such external feedback. Thus, trying to walk through a wall or doing similar tests would reveal if you were dreaming.

Focus: Why do people abuse drugs? What can be done about it?

People take drugs for reasons such as curiosity, wanting to belong to a group, or to escape from feelings of inadequacy. The best predictors of adolescent drug use and abuse are having friends who use drugs, parental drug use, delinquency, troubled family life, poor self-esteem, social nonconformity, and stressful life changes (Marlatt et al., 1988).

How early do danger signs for drug use appear? A recent study followed 1,000 boys in French-Canadian schools for more than a decade, starting in kindergarten. Investigators found that 5 to 10 percent of the kindergartners tended to act without thinking, showed little caution, and were anxious to experiment. Years later, in childhood and early adolescence, these boys were significantly more likely to begin smoking, get drunk, and use drugs (Masse & Tremblay, 1997).

For many young people, drug abuse is just one part of a general pattern of problem behavior. Another study found that adolescents who abuse drugs tend to be maladjusted, alienated, impulsive, and emotionally distressed. Antisocial behavior, school failure, and risky sexual behavior are also commonly associated with drug abuse (Ary et al., 1999). Such patterns make it clear that taking drugs is a symptom, rather than a cause, of personal and social maladjustment (Derzon & Lipsey, 1999; Welte et al., 1999).

The Dynamics of Drug Abuse

Many abusers turn to drugs in a self-defeating attempt to cope with life. All of the frequently abused drugs produce immediate feelings of pleasure. The negative consequences follow much later. This combination of immediate pleasure and delayed punishment allows abusers to feel good on demand. In time, of course, most of the pleasure goes out of drug abuse, and the abuser's problems get worse. But if an abuser merely feels *better* (however briefly) after taking a drug, drug taking can become compulsive (Barrett, 1985). In contrast, people who stop using drugs often say that they quit because the drawbacks had come to exceed the benefits (Toneatto et al., 1999).

DRUG EXPECTANCIES   Closely related to a drug's actual effects are users' beliefs and expectations about drugs (Stacy et al., 1996). Patterns of drinking alcohol offer a good example of how expectations promote abuse. In one study, drinkers were asked about alcohol's effects on good feelings, sexual performance, social and physical pleasure, self-assertion, relaxation, and feelings of power. Heavy drinkers expect far more positive effects and fewer negative consequences from drinking alcohol than light drinkers do (Brown, Goldman, & Christiansen, 1985). Children who learn such expectancies are likely to be-

come problem drinkers (Christiansen et al., 1989). The three most dangerous beliefs are:

- Alcohol makes experiences more positive.
- Alcohol facilitates social behavior.
- Alcohol improves thinking and physical performance.

CULTURAL VALUES   There is a widespread tendency to think of drugs as a magic way to produce good feelings by avoiding, minimizing, or escaping negative situations. Some observers believe that drug use is so deeply ingrained that "we are addicted to addiction. This is to say that, with few exceptions we subscribe to the premise that life cannot be lived without drugs." We are so used to having our own way that we have come to believe "we should be able to will ourselves to be calm, cheerful, thin, industrious, creative—and moreover, to have a good night's sleep." Some critics believe that the medical profession, well meaning but misguided, unnecessarily encourages legal drug use. Indeed, one psychologist observed: "Depression, social inadequacy, anxiety, apathy, marital discord, children's misbehavior, and other psychological and social problems of living are now being redefined as medical problems, to be solved by physicians with prescription pads" (Rogers, 1971).

Perhaps we all can be partially excused for placing undue faith in drugs. Doctors and the general public are the target of multimillion-dollar advertising campaigns aimed at encouraging drug use. Even the lowly aspirin is pushed as a means of relieving "nervous tension." Advertisements directed at physicians encourage overuse of drugs even more blatantly. An ad pictures a distraught mother with a child and asks, "Her kind of pressures last all day . . . shouldn't her tranquilizer?" Another reads:

> School, the dark, separation, dental visits, monsters. The everyday anxiety of children sometimes gets out of hand. A child can usually deal with his anxieties. But sometimes the anxieties overpower the child. Then he needs your help. Your help may include Vistaril.

Drugs have legitimate uses and have alleviated much suffering. The problem is that drugs strong enough to ease pain, induce sleep, end depression, or otherwise alter consciousness have a high potential for abuse. Rather than sounding the alarm about illicit drug use, politicians and public health officials need to pay more attention to the far more widespread abuse of legally prescribed drugs (MacCoun, 1993).

Drug abuse in Western nations has reached epidemic proportions in recent years. Problems once restricted to drug-related

Lucid dream *A dream in which the dreamer feels awake and capable of normal thought and action.*

subcultures and the urban poor are now seen regularly among high school and college students and among the vast middle classes.

Prevention

What, if anything, should be done about drug abuse? Traditional approaches have emphasized limiting drug supplies, strict law enforcement, and legal penalties. Limiting supplies has been relatively successful in the case of some drugs. For example, many communities have had at least partial success in discouraging teenagers from smoking by fining businesses that sell tobacco to minors (Reppucci et al., 1999). But drug abuse and legality are actually two separate issues. This distinction becomes clear when one recognizes that two of the most potent, destructive, and potentially dangerous drugs available are nicotine and alcohol. By the government's own standards, nicotine and alcohol should be at the top of the list of controlled substances. Yet they are legal.

Facts such as these have led some observers to conclude that anyone who seeks drug-induced consciousness alteration will find a drug, legal or illegal, to achieve it. Psychiatrist Thomas Szasz (1983) believes that it is futile for the government to attempt to "legislate morality" by regulating what drugs a person chooses to take. Szasz suggests that current drug regulations have an effect similar to the prohibition of alcohol in the United States in the 1920s. That is, they encourage a black market, organized crime, disrespect for the law, and occasional poisonings from adulterated drugs.

As Szasz points out, "tobacco is not legally considered a drug, marijuana is, gin is not, but Valium is. . . ." To this we could add that marijuana is equated with heroin and cocaine is still listed as a narcotic when it is clearly a stimulant. The list could go on, but it is clear that a scientifically based legal system should replace the current politically based one.

THINK ABOUT IT   Whereas it is true that drug *use* is essentially a "victimless crime," the fact remains that *abuse* of drugs—legal or illegal—represents a serious loss to society.

The point of view expressed earlier by Szasz is obviously controversial. Many, in fact, believe that the answer to drug problems is to be found in stricter penalties and law enforcement. And yet, a sober look at drug abuse makes it clear that some psychoactive drugs are almost always available. In general, we tend to overlook the frequent abuse of legal drugs such as tranquilizers or alcohol and overestimate the misuse of illegal drugs (MacCoun, 1993).

Although billions of dollars have been spent on drug enforcement, there has been an increase in the overall level of drug use. On the other hand, there was no increase in marijuana use in states that relaxed penalties for its possession to a fine (Thies & Register, 1993).

In the Dutch city of Amsterdam, drug addiction is treated as a medical problem rather than a criminal offense. Methadone is freely available to heroin addicts, and little effort is made to prevent the use of "soft drugs" such as marijuana. Contrary to what critics predicted, the proportion of younger addicts in Amsterdam has fallen during the last decade. The overall addict population has dropped by a third. The rate in other European countries is twice as high; in the United States, it is six times higher.

Given such facts, many experts believe that prevention through education and early intervention—rather than tougher enforcement—is the answer to drug problems (MacCoun, 1993). Drug expert Robert Julien (1998) suggests that a rational approach to reducing drug abuse should include at least the following elements:

- Drug education to discourage experimentation with drugs.
- A scientifically based legal system for classifying psychoactive drugs.
- A definition of "responsible use" that takes into account risk factors such as the drug used and the time and place it is used. (For instance, we currently make a distinction between drinking at a party and drinking while driving.)
- Limits on pro-drug advertising, including ads for tobacco and alcohol and sponsorship of sporting events.
- Taxes to discourage the purchase of legal drugs and to pay for the damage they cause.
- Adults willing to set an example by using drugs responsibly or not at all.

Well-crafted information and education can discourage drug use. This billboard is part of California's anti-smoking campaign. It emphasizes the dangers of secondhand smoke. Research has shown that this is one of several issues that motivate children and adolescents to resist pressures to begin smoking.

Such efforts might be a reasonable start in any effort to curb drug abuse. What do you think should be done?

CONCLUSION: Drug abuse is a complex problem with multiple causes. Unfortunately, many attempts to curb drug use have been ineffective and politically motivated, rather than scientifically based.

KNOWLEDGE BUILDER

DRUG ABUSE

RELATE

What information would you use to persuade a group of skeptical parents that drug abuse is a symptom of maladjustment, rather than its cause?

What expectancies do you have about the following drugs: alcohol, marijuana, cocaine, nicotine? Have your expectations influenced your behavior?

If you were given the authority and resources to solve the problem of drug abuse, what steps would you take?

LEARNING CHECK

1. Advertising campaigns directed at physicians tend to overstate the need for treating behavioral problems with drugs. T or F?

2. Heavy drinkers of alcohol learn from experience to expect more negative consequences from alcohol's effects. T or F?

3. Thomas Szasz believes that it is time for the government to take a lead in "legislating morality" with regard to drug use. T or F?

4. Current laws in the United States have been accused of misclassifying some drugs. T or F?

5. The immediate reinforcing effects of drugs and the delayed negative consequences are believed to play a major role in drug abuse. T or F?

CRITICAL THINKING

6. Why do you think there is such a contrast between the laws regulating marijuana and those regulating alcohol and tobacco?

Answers:

1. T 2. F 3. F 4. T 5. T 6. Drug laws in Western societies reflect cultural values and historical patterns of use. Inconsistencies in the law often cannot be justified on the basis of pharmacology, health risks, or abuse potential.

CHAPTER IN REVIEW

What is an altered state of consciousness?

- States of awareness that differ from normal, alert, waking consciousness are called *altered states of consciousness* (ASCs). Altered states are especially associated with sleep and dreaming, hypnosis, sensory deprivation, and psychoactive drugs.
- Cultural conditioning greatly affects what altered states a person recognizes, seeks, considers normal, and attains.

What are the effects of sleep loss and changes in sleep patterns?

- Sleep is an innate biological rhythm essential for survival. Higher animals and people deprived of sleep experience involuntary microsleeps.
- Moderate sleep loss mainly affects vigilance and performance on routine or boring tasks. Extended sleep loss can (somewhat rarely) produce a temporary sleep-deprivation psychosis.
- Sleep patterns show some flexibility, but 7 to 8 hours remains average. The amount of daily sleep decreases steadily from birth to old age. Once-a-day sleep patterns, with a 2-to-1 ratio of waking and sleep, are most efficient for most people.

Are there different stages of sleep?

- Sleep occurs in four stages. Stage 1 is light sleep, and stage 4 is deep sleep. The sleeper alternates between stages 1 and 4 (passing through stages 2 and 3) several times each night.

How does dream sleep differ from dreamless sleep?

- There are two basic sleep states, rapid eye movement (REM) sleep and non-REM (NREM) sleep. REM sleep is much more strongly associated with dreaming than non-REM sleep is.
- Dreaming and REMs occur mainly during light sleep, similar to stage 1. Dreaming is accompanied by emotional arousal but relaxation of the skeletal muscles.
- People deprived of dream sleep show a REM rebound when allowed to sleep without interruption. However, total sleep loss seems to be more important than loss of a single stage.
- In addition to several other possible functions, REM sleep appears to aid the processing of memories.

What are the causes of sleep disorders and unusual sleep events?

- Sleepwalking and sleeptalking occur during NREM sleep. Night terrors occur in NREM sleep, whereas nightmares occur in REM sleep. Narcolepsy (sleep attacks) and cataplexy are caused by a sudden shift to stage 1 REM patterns during normal waking hours.
- Sleep apnea (interrupted breathing) is one source of insomnia and daytime hypersomnia (sleepiness).
- Apnea is suspected as one cause of sudden infant death syndrome (SIDS). Exposure to secondhand smoke is a major risk factor for SIDS. With only a few exceptions, healthy infants should sleep face up or on their sides.
- Insomnia may be temporary or chronic. When it is treated through the use of drugs, sleep quality is often lowered, and drug-dependency insomnia may develop.
- Behavioral approaches to managing insomnia, such as sleep restriction and stimulus control, are quite effective.

Do dreams have meaning?

- Most dream content is about familiar settings, people, and actions. Dreams more often involve negative emotions than positive emotions.
- The Freudian, or psychodynamic, view is that dreams express unconscious wishes, frequently hidden by dream symbols.
- Many theorists have questioned Freud's view of dreams. For example, the activation-synthesis model portrays dreaming as a physiological process.

How is hypnosis done, and what are its limitations?

- Hypnosis is an altered state characterized by narrowed attention and increased suggestibility. (Not all psychologists agree that hypnotic effects require an alteration of consciousness.)
- Hypnosis appears capable of producing relaxation, controlling pain, and altering perceptions. Stage hypnotism takes advantage of typical stage behavior and uses deception to simulate hypnosis.

How does sensory deprivation affect consciousness?

- Extreme or unusual stimulus conditions often induce altered states of consciousness. A prime example is sensory deprivation.
- Prolonged sensory deprivation is stressful and disruptive. However, brief sensory deprivation can enhance sensitivity and promote relaxation. Sensory deprivation also appears to aid the breaking of long-standing habits, and it facilitates creative thinking.

What are the effects of the more commonly used psychoactive drugs?

- A psychoactive drug is a substance that affects the brain in ways that alter consciousness. Most psychoactive drugs can be placed on a scale ranging from stimulation to depression.
- Drugs may cause a physical dependence (addiction), a psychological dependence, or both. The physically addicting drugs are heroin, morphine, codeine, methadone, barbiturates, alcohol, amphetamines, tobacco, and cocaine. All psychoactive drugs can lead to psychological dependence.
- Drug use can be classified as experimental, recreational, situational, intensive, and compulsive. Drug abuse is most often associated with the last three.
- Stimulant drugs are readily abused because of the period of depression that often follows stimulation. The greatest risks are associated with amphetamines, cocaine, and nicotine, but even caffeine can be a problem. Nicotine includes the added risk of lung cancer, heart disease, and other health problems.
- Barbiturates and tranquilizers are depressant drugs whose action is similar to that of alcohol. The overdose level for barbiturates is close to the intoxication dosage, making them dangerous drugs. Mixing barbiturates or tranquilizers and alcohol may result in a fatal drug interaction.
- Alcohol is the most heavily abused drug in common use today. The development of a drinking problem is usually marked by an initial phase of increasing consumption; a crucial phase, in which a single drink can set off a chain reaction; and a chronic phase, in which a person lives to drink and drinks to live.

- Marijuana is subject to an abuse pattern similar to alcohol. Studies have linked chronic marijuana use with lung cancer, various mental impairments, and other health problems.

How are dreams used to promote personal understanding?

- Dreams may be used to promote self-understanding. Freud held that the meaning of dreams is hidden by condensation, displacement, symbolization, and secondary elaboration.
- Hall emphasizes the setting, cast, plot, and emotions of a dream. Cartwright's view of dreams as feeling statements and Perls's technique of speaking for dream elements are also helpful. Dreams may be used for creative problem solving, especially when dream control is achieved through lucid dreaming.

Why is drug abuse so widespread?

- Drug abuse is related to a variety of factors, especially personal and social maladjustment, attempts to cope, the immediate reinforcing qualities of psychoactive drugs, peer group influences, and expectations about the value and effects of drugs.
- Proposed remedies for drug abuse have ranged from severe punishment to legalization. The search for a solution continues.

- **Drugs and Behavior Links** Comprehensive links to topics in drugs and behavior. http://www.uwsp.edu/acad/psych/tdrugs.htm
- **Marijuana Anonymous** Offers advice and information on how to quit smoking marijuana. http://www.marijuana-anonymous.org/
- **Self-scoring Alcohol Checkup** A short quiz for identifying drinking problems. http://www.cts.com/crash/habtsmrt/chkup.html
- **SleepNet** Information about sleep and sleep disorders, with many links to other sites. http://www.sleepnet.com/index.shtml
- **Sudden Infant Death and Other Infant Death** Information about SIDS, with links to related topics. http://sids-network.org/
- **The Antidrug.com** Advice to parents and other adults about how to help children resist drug use. http://theantidrug.com
- **The Reality of Hypnosis** An extended discussion of hypnosis. http://goinside.com/97/4/barber.html

- **InfoTrac® College Edition** For recent articles related to the "Psychology in Action" feature, use subject guide search for DREAM ANALYSIS.

PSYCHOLOGY ON THE NET

- **Alcoholics Anonymous (AA)** Home page of Alcoholics Anonymous. http://www.alcoholics-anonymous.org/index.html
- **Circadian Rhythms** Basic information about circadian rhythms and jet lag. http://www.sfu.ca/~mcantle/rhythms.html
- **Cocaine Anonymous** Offers advice and information on how to quit cocaine addiction. http://www.ca.org/

INTERACTIVE LEARNING

- *PsychNow!* 2c. Sleep and dreaming. 2d. Psychoactive drugs.
- *Psyk.trek* 4a. Biological rhythms. 4b. Sleep. 4c. Abused drugs and their effects. 4d. Drugs and synaptic transmissions.

Conditioning and Learning

WHAT DID YOU LEARN IN SCHOOL TODAY?

WHEN YOUR AGING AUTHOR WAS IN COLLEGE WE discovered an intriguing flaw in the dorm plumbing: Flush a toilet while someone was taking a shower and the cold water pressure would suddenly drop. This caused the shower to become scalding hot. Naturally, the shower victim screamed in terror as his reflexes caused him to leap backward in pain. Soon we discovered that if we flushed all the toilets at once, the effects were multiplied many times over!

A toilet has to be one of the world's most uninspiring stimuli. But for a time, a whole flock of college students twitched involuntarily whenever they heard a toilet flush. Their reactions were the result of classical conditioning, *a basic type of learning*. Details about classical conditioning are explored in this chapter.

Now, let's say that you are at school and you feel like you are "starving to death." Locating a vending machine, you deposit your last two quarters to buy a candy bar. You press the button, and . . . nothing happens. Being civilized and in complete control, you press the other buttons, try the coin return, and look for an attendant. Still nothing. Your stomach growls. Impulsively, you give the machine a little kick (just to let it know how you feel). Then, as you turn away, out pops a candy bar plus 25 cents change. Once this happens, chances are good that you will repeat the "kicking response" in the future. If it pays off several times more, kicking vending machines may become a regular feature of your behavior. In this case, learning is based on operant conditioning *(also called* instrumental learning).

Classical and operant conditioning underlie much human learning. In fact, conditioning reaches into every corner of our lives. Are you ready to learn more about learning? If so, read on! This chapter explores conditioning and other forms of learning.

 **Gateways to Learning**

CONDITIONING is a fundamental type of learning that affects many aspects of daily life.

IN CLASSICAL CONDITIONING, a neutral stimulus is repeatedly paired with a stimulus that reliably provokes a response. By association, the neutral stimulus also begins to elicit a response.

IN OPERANT CONDITIONING, responses that are followed by reinforcement occur more frequently.

COGNITIVE LEARNING involves acquiring higher level information, rather than just linking stimuli and responses.

WE ALSO LEARN BY OBSERVING AND IMITATING the actions of others.

BEHAVIORAL PRINCIPLES can be used to manage one's own behavior.

EFFECTIVE PERFORMANCE IN SCHOOL is based on self-regulated learning, an active, self-guided approach to studying.

BIOLOGICAL BEHAVIOR PATTERNS facilitate the learning of some responses while making others more difficult to learn.

WHAT IS LEARNING—DOES PRACTICE MAKE PERFECT?

Most behavior is learned. Imagine if you suddenly lost all you had ever learned. What could you do? You would be unable to read, write, or speak. You couldn't feed yourself, find your way home, drive a car, play the bassoon, or "party." Needless to say, you would be totally incapacitated. (Dull, too!)

Learning is obviously important. What's a formal definition of learning? **Learning** is a relatively permanent change in behavior due to experience. Notice that this definition excludes temporary changes caused by motivation, fatigue, maturation, disease, injury, or drugs. Each of these can alter behavior, but none qualifies as learning.

Isn't learning the result of practice? It depends on what you mean by practice. Merely repeating a response will not necessarily produce learning. You could close your eyes and swing a tennis racket hundreds of times without learning anything about tennis.

Reinforcement is the key to learning. **Reinforcement** refers to any event that increases the probability that a response will occur again. A **response** is any identifiable behavior. Responses may be observable actions, such as blinking, eating a piece of candy, or turning a doorknob. They can also be internal, such as having a faster heartbeat.

To teach a dog a trick, I could reinforce correct responses by giving the dog some food each time it sits up. Similarly, you could teach a child to be neat by praising her for picking up her toys. Learning can also occur in other ways. For instance, if a girl gets stung by a bee, she may learn to fear bees. In this case, the girl's fear is reinforced by the pain she feels immediately after seeing the bee. Later, we will see how such varied experiences lead to learning.

ANTECEDENTS AND CONSEQUENCES Unlocking the secrets of learning begins with noting what happens before and after a response. Events that precede a response are called **antecedents.**

Learning *Any relatively permanent change in behavior that can be attributed to experience.*
Reinforcement *Any event that increases the probability that a particular response will occur.*
Response *Any identifiable behavior.*
Antecedents *Events that precede a response.*

Effects that follow a response are **consequences**. Paying careful attention to the "before and after" of learning is a key to understanding it.

Classical Conditioning

Classical conditioning is based on what happens before a response. We begin with a stimulus that reliably triggers a response. Imagine, for example, that a puff of air (the stimulus) is aimed at your eye. The air-puff will make you blink (a response) every time. The eye-blink is a **reflex** (automatic, non-learned response).

Now, assume that we sound a horn (another stimulus) just before each puff of air hits your eye. If the horn and the air-puff occur together many times, what happens? Soon, the horn alone will make you blink. What happened? Clearly, you've learned something. Before, the horn didn't make you blink. Now it does. Similarly, if your mouth waters each time you eat a cookie, you may learn to salivate when you merely *see* a cookie, a picture of cookies, a cookie jar, or other stimuli that preceded salivation.

In **classical conditioning,** antecedent events become associated with one another: A stimulus that does not produce a response is linked with one that does (a horn is associated with a puff of air to the eye, for example). Learning is evident when the new stimulus will also elicit (bring forth) responses (❖Fig. 9.1).

Operant Conditioning

In **operant conditioning,** learning is based on the consequences of responding. A response may be followed by a rein-

forcer (such as food). Or by punishment. Or by nothing. These results determine whether a response is likely to be made again (❖Fig. 9.1). For example, if you wear a particular hat and get lots of compliments (reinforcement), you are likely to wear it more often. If people snicker, insult you, call the police, or scream (punishment), you will probably wear it less often.

Now that you have an idea of what happens in the two basic kinds of learning, let's look at classical conditioning in more detail.

CLASSICAL CONDITIONING–DOES THE NAME PAVLOV RING A BELL?

How was classical conditioning discovered?   At the beginning of the twentieth century, something happened in the lab of Russian physiologist Ivan Pavlov that brought him lasting fame. The event seems so trivial that a lesser man might have ignored it: Pavlov's subjects drooled at him.

Actually, Pavlov was studying digestion. To observe salivation, he placed meat powder or some tidbit on a dog's tongue. After doing this many times, Pavlov noticed that his dogs were salivating *before* the food reached their mouths. Later, the dogs even began to salivate when they saw Pavlov enter the room. Was this misplaced affection? Pavlov knew better. Salivation is normally a reflex. For the animals to salivate at the mere sight of food, some type of learning had to have occurred. Pavlov called it conditioning (❖Fig. 9.2). Because of its importance in psychology's history, it is now called classical conditioning (also known as **Pavlovian conditioning** or **respondent conditioning**).

PAVLOV'S EXPERIMENT   *How did Pavlov study conditioning?*   After Pavlov observed that meat powder made his dogs salivate, he began his classic experiments (see ❖Fig. 9.2). To begin, he rang a bell. At first, the bell was a neutral stimulus (it did not evoke a response). Immediately after Pavlov rang the bell, he

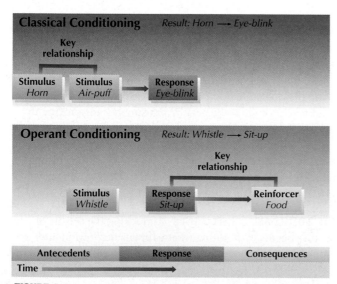

❖ **FIGURE 9.1** *In classical conditioning, a stimulus that does not produce a response is paired with a stimulus that does elicit a response. After many such pairings, the stimulus that previously had no effect begins to produce a response. In the example shown, a horn precedes a puff of air to the eye. Eventually, the horn alone will produce an eye-blink. In operant conditioning, a response that is followed by a reinforcing consequence becomes more likely to occur on future occasions. In the example shown, a dog learns to sit up when it hears a whistle.*

❖ **FIGURE 9.2** *An apparatus for Pavlovian conditioning. A tube carries saliva from the dog's mouth to a lever that activates a recording device (far left). During conditioning, various stimuli can be paired with a dish of food placed in front of the dog. The device pictured here is more elaborate than the one Pavlov used in his early experiments.*

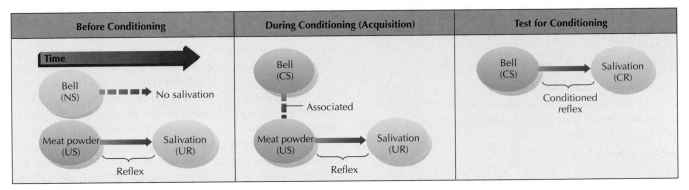

❖ **FIGURE 9.3** *The classical conditioning procedure.*

◆ **TABLE 9.1** Elements of Classical Conditioning

ELEMENT	SYMBOL	DESCRIPTION	EXAMPLE
Neutral stimulus	NS	A stimulus that does not evoke a response	Bell
Unconditioned stimulus	US	A stimulus innately capable of eliciting a response	Meat powder
Conditioned stimulus	CS	A stimulus that evokes a response because it has been repeatedly paired with an unconditioned stimulus	Bell
Unconditioned response	UR	An innate reflex response elicited by an unconditioned stimulus	Reflex salivation
Conditioned response	CR	A learned response elicited by a conditioned stimulus	Salivation

placed meat powder on the dog's tongue, which caused reflex salivation. This sequence was repeated many times: bell, meat powder, salivation; bell, meat powder, salivation. Eventually (as conditioning took place), the dogs began to salivate when they heard the bell (❖Fig. 9.3). By association, the bell, which before had no effect, began to evoke the same response as food. This was shown by sometimes ringing the bell alone. Pavlov then observed that the dog salivated, even when no food was present.

Psychologists use several terms to describe these events. The bell in Pavlov's experiment starts out as a **neutral stimulus (NS).** In time, the bell becomes a **conditioned stimulus (CS)** (a stimulus that, because of learning, will evoke a response). The meat powder is an **unconditioned stimulus (US)** (a stimulus innately capable of eliciting a response). Notice that the dog did not have to learn to respond to the US. Such stimuli naturally elicit reflexes or emotional reactions.

Since a reflex is innate, or built in, it is called an **unconditioned** (nonlearned) **response (UR).** Reflex salivation was the UR in Pavlov's experiment. When Pavlov's bell also produced salivation, the dog was making a new response. Thus, salivation had become a **conditioned** (learned) **response (CR)** (❖Fig. 9.3). ◆Table 9.1 summarizes the important elements of classical conditioning.

Are all these terms really necessary? Yes, because they help us recognize similarities in various instances of learning. Let's summarize the terms using an earlier example:

Before Conditioning	Example	
US → UR	Puff of air	→ eye-blink
NS → no effect	Horn	→ no effect

After Conditioning	Example	
CS → CR	Horn	→ eye-blink

Now let's see if we can explain the shower and flushing toilet example described earlier. The unconditioned, or non-learned, response was a reflex jump from the hot water. The unconditioned stimulus was the hot water (or the pain it caused). The conditioned stimulus was the sound of a flushing toilet. That is, the flushing sound was at first neutral. But as a result of conditioning, it became capable of eliciting a reflex.

Consequences *Effects that follow a response.*
Reflex *An innate, automatic response to a stimulus; for example, an eye-blink.*
Classical conditioning *A form of learning in which reflex responses are associated with new stimuli.*
Operant conditioning *Learning based on the consequences of responding.*
Neutral stimulus *A stimulus that does not evoke a response.*
Conditioned stimulus *A stimulus that evokes a response because it has been repeatedly paired with an unconditioned stimulus.*
Unconditioned stimulus *A stimulus innately capable of eliciting a response.*
Unconditioned response *An innate reflex response elicited by an unconditioned stimulus.*
Conditioned response *A learned response elicited by a conditioned stimulus.*

PRINCIPLES OF CLASSICAL CONDITIONING—TEACH YOUR LITTLE BROTHER TO SALIVATE

To observe conditioning, you could ring a bell, squirt lemon juice into a boy's mouth, and condition salivation to the bell. The boy's reactions might then be used to explore other aspects of classical conditioning.

Acquisition

During **acquisition,** or training, a conditioned response must be reinforced (strengthened) (❖Fig. 9.4). Classical conditioning is **reinforced** when the CS is followed by, or paired with, an unconditioned stimulus. For our boy, the bell is the CS; salivating is the UR; and the sour lemon juice is an unconditioned stimulus. To reinforce salivating to the bell, we must link the bell with the lemon juice. Conditioning will be most rapid if the US (lemon juice) follows *immediately* after the CS (the bell). With most reflexes, the optimal delay between CS and US is from half a second to about 5 seconds (Schwartz & Robbins, 1995).

HIGHER ORDER CONDITIONING   Once a response is learned, it can bring about **higher order conditioning.** In this case, a well-learned CS is used to reinforce further learning. That is, the CS has become strong enough to be used like an unconditioned stimulus. Let's illustrate again with our salivating boy.

As a result of earlier learning, the bell now makes the boy salivate. (No lemon juice is needed.) To go a step further, you could clap your hands and then ring the bell. (Again, no lemon juice would be used.) Through higher order conditioning, the boy would soon learn to salivate when you clapped your hands (❖Fig. 9.5). (This little trick could be a real hit with friends and neighbors.)

Higher order conditioning extends learning one or more steps beyond the original conditioned stimulus. Many advertisers use this effect by pairing images that evoke good feelings (such as people smiling and having fun) with pictures of their products. Obviously, they hope that you will learn, by association, to feel good when you see their products (Johnsrude et al., 1999).

Expectancies

How does classical conditioning occur? Many psychologists believe it takes place as we process information that might aid survival. According to this **informational view,** classical conditioning occurs as we detect associations among events. Doing so creates new mental **expectancies,** or expectations about how events are related.

How does classical conditioning alter expectancies?   Notice that the conditioned stimulus reliably precedes the unconditioned stimulus. Because it does, the CS *predicts* the US (Rescorla, 1987). During conditioning, the brain learns to *expect* that the US will follow the CS. As a result, the brain prepares the body to respond to the US. Here's an example: When you are about to get a shot with a hypodermic needle, your muscles tighten and there is a catch in your breathing. Why? Because your body is preparing for pain. You have learned to expect that getting poked with a needle will hurt. This expectancy, which was acquired during classical conditioning, changes your behavior.

Extinction and Spontaneous Recovery

After conditioning has occurred, what would happen if the US no longer followed the CS?   If the US never again follows the CS, conditioning will extinguish. Let's return to the boy and the bell. If you ring the bell many times and do not follow it with lemon juice, the boy's expectancy that "bell precedes lemon juice" will weaken. As it does, he will lose his tendency to salivate when he hears the bell. Thus, we see that classical condi-

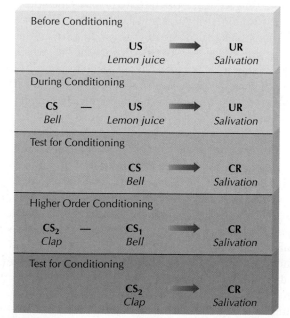

❖ **FIGURE 9.5** *Higher order conditioning takes place when a well-learned conditioned stimulus is used as if it were an unconditioned stimulus. In this example, a child is first conditioned to salivate to the sound of a bell. In time, the bell will elicit salivation. At that point, you could clap your hands and then ring the bell. Soon, after repeating the procedure, the child would learn to salivate when you clapped your hands.*

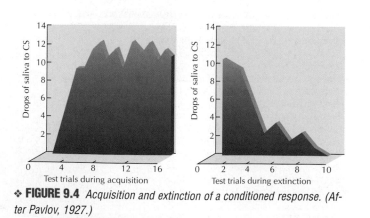

❖ **FIGURE 9.4** *Acquisition and extinction of a conditioned response. (After Pavlov, 1927.)*

tioning can be weakened by removing reinforcement (see ❖Fig. 9.4). This process is called **extinction.**

If conditioning takes a while to build up, shouldn't it take time to reverse? Yes. In fact, several extinction sessions may be necessary to completely reverse conditioning. If the bell is rung until the boy quits responding, it might seem that extinction is complete. However, the boy will probably respond to the bell again on the following day, at least at first. The reappearance of a response following apparent extinction is called **spontaneous recovery.** It explains why people who have had terrifying automobile accidents may need many slow, calm rides before their fears extinguish.

Generalization

After conditioning, other stimuli similar to the CS may also trigger a response. This is called **stimulus generalization.** For example, we might find that our boy salivates to the sound of a ringing telephone or doorbell, even though they were never used as conditioning stimuli.

It is easy to see the value of stimulus generalization. Consider the child who burns her finger while playing with matches. Most likely, lighted matches will become conditioned fear stimuli for her. But will she fear only matches? Because of stimulus generalization, she should also have a healthy fear of flames from lighters, fireplaces, and stoves. It's fortunate that generalization extends learning to related situations. Otherwise, we would all be far less adaptable.

As you may have guessed, stimulus generalization has limits. As stimuli become less like the original CS, responding decreases. If you condition a person to blink each time you play a particular note on a piano, blinking will decline as you play higher or lower notes. If the notes are *much* higher or lower, the person will not respond at all (❖Fig. 9.6). Stimulus generalization explains why many stores carry imitations of nationally known products. For many customers, positive attitudes conditioned to the real products tend to generalize to the cheaper knockoffs (Till & Priluck, 2000).

Discrimination

Let's consider one more idea with our salivating boy (who by now must be ready to hide in the closet). Suppose the boy is again conditioned with a bell as the CS. As an experiment, we occasionally sound a buzzer instead of the bell but never follow it with the US (lemon juice). At first, the buzzer produces salivation (because of generalization). But after hearing the buzzer several times more, the child will stop responding to it. The child has now learned to *discriminate*, or respond differently, to the bell and the buzzer. In essence, the child's generalized response to the buzzer has extinguished.

Stimulus discrimination is the ability to respond differently to various stimuli. As an example, you might remember the feelings of anxiety or fear you had as a child when your mother's or father's voice changed to its you're-about-to-get-swatted tone. (Or the dreaded give-me-that-Game-Boy tone.) Most children quickly learn to discriminate voice tones associated with pain from those associated with praise or affection.

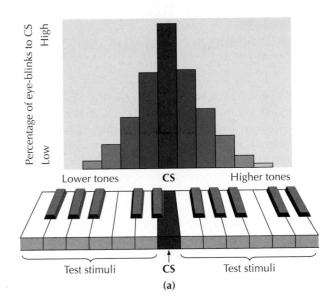

❖ **FIGURE 9.6** (a) *Stimulus generalization. Stimuli similar to the CS also elicit a response.* (b) *This cat has learned to salivate when it sees a cat food box. Because of stimulus generalization, it also salivates when shown a similar-looking detergent box of bleach.*

Acquisition *The period in conditioning during which a response is reinforced.*
Respondent reinforcement *Reinforcement that occurs when an unconditioned stimulus closely follows a conditioned stimulus.*
Higher order conditioning *Classical conditioning in which a conditioned stimulus is used to reinforce further learning; that is, a CS is used as if it were a US.*
Informational view *Perspective that explains learning in terms of information imparted by events in the environment.*
Expectancy *An anticipation concerning future events or relationships.*
Extinction *The weakening of a conditioned response through removal of reinforcement.*
Spontaneous recovery *The reappearance of a learned response after its apparent extinction.*
Stimulus generalization *The tendency to respond to stimuli similar to, but not identical to, a conditioned stimulus.*
Stimulus discrimination *The learned ability to respond differently to similar stimuli.*

CLASSICAL CONDITIONING IN HUMANS—AN EMOTIONAL TOPIC

How much human learning is based on classical conditioning? At its simplest, classical conditioning depends on reflex responses. As mentioned earlier, a reflex is a dependable, inborn, stimulus-and-response connection. For example, your hand reflexively draws back from pain. Bright light causes the pupil of the eye to narrow. Various foods elicit salivation. Any of these reflexes, and others as well, can be associated with a new stimulus. At the very least, you have probably noticed how your mouth waters when you see or smell a bakery. Even pictures of food may make you salivate (a photo of a sliced lemon is great for this).

Conditioned Emotional Responses

Of larger importance, perhaps, are the subtler ways that conditioning affects us. In addition to simple reflexes, more complex *emotional,* or "gut," responses may be linked to new stimuli. For instance, if your face reddened when you were punished as a child, you may blush now when you are embarrassed or ashamed. Or think about the effects of associating pain with a dentist's office during your first visit. On later visits, did your heart pound and your palms sweat *before* the dentist began?

Many *involuntary,* autonomic nervous system responses (fight-or-flight reflexes) are linked with new stimuli and situations by classical conditioning. For example, learned reactions aggravate many cases of hypertension (high blood pressure). Traffic jams, arguments with a spouse, and similar situations can become conditioned stimuli that trigger a dangerous rise in blood pressure (Reiff, Katkin, & Friedman, 1999).

Of course, emotional conditioning also applies to animals. One of the most common mistakes people make with pets (especially dogs) is hitting them if they do not come when called. Calling the animal then becomes a conditioned stimulus for fear and withdrawal. No wonder the pet disobeys when called on future occasions. Parents who belittle, scream at, or physically abuse their children make the same mistake.

BRIDGES

Desensitization is a type of behavior therapy. (Behavior therapists apply the principles of learning to change human behavior patterns.)

See Chapter 18, pages 605–613, for details.

LEARNED FEARS   Some phobias (FOE-bee-ahs) are also based on emotional conditioning. A **phobia** is a fear that persists even when no realistic danger exists. Fears of animals, water, heights, thunder, fire, bugs, and elevators are common. Psychologists believe that many phobias begin as **conditioned emotional responses (CERs).** (A CER is a learned emotional reaction to a previously neutral stimulus.) People who have phobias can often trace their fears to a time when they were frightened, injured, or upset by a particular stimulus. Many spider phobias, for example,

(a)

(b)

❖ **FIGURE 9.7** *Hypothetical example of a CER becoming a phobia. Child approaches dog (a) and is frightened by it (b). Fear generalizes to other household pets (c) and later to virtually all furry animals (d).*

(c)

(d)

start in childhood. Just one bad experience with a spider may condition fears that last for years (Merckelbach & Muris, 1997).

Stimulus generalization and higher order conditioning can broaden CERs to other stimuli (Gewirtz & Davis, 1998). As a result, what began as a limited fear may become a disabling phobia (❖Fig. 9.7). However, a therapy called **desensitization** is now widely used to extinguish fears, anxieties, and phobias. It is done by gradually exposing phobic people to feared stimuli while they remain calm and relaxed. Incidentally, desensitization works on animals, too. For example, dogs have been desensitized to fears of fireworks, thunder, airplanes, bees, hot air balloons, and other frightening stimuli (Rogerson, 1997).

Undoubtedly, we acquire many of our likes, dislikes, and fears as conditioned emotional responses. For example, in one study, college students developed CERs when colored geometric shapes were paired with the theme music from the movie *Star Wars*. The colored shapes were the CS and the music, which made the students feel good, was the US. When tested later, the students gave higher ratings to shapes paired with the pleasant music than to shapes associated with silence (Bierly et al., 1985). As noted before, advertisers try to achieve the same effect by pairing products with pleasant images and music. So do many students on a first date.

Vicarious, or Secondhand, Conditioning

Conditioning also occurs indirectly, which adds to its impact on us. Let's say, for example, that you watch another person get an electric shock. Each time, a signal light comes on before the shock is delivered. Even if you don't receive a shock yourself, you will soon develop a CER to the light (Bandura & Rosenthal, 1966). Children who learn to fear thunder by watching their parents react to it have undergone similar conditioning.

Vicarious classical conditioning occurs when we learn to respond emotionally to a stimulus by observing another person's emotional reactions. Such secondhand learning affects feelings in many situations. For example, horror movies filled with screaming actors probably add to fears of snakes, caves, spiders, heights, and other terrors. If movies can affect us, we might expect the emotions of parents, friends, and relatives to have even more impact. How, for instance, does a city child learn to fear snakes and respond emotionally to mere pictures of them? Being told that "snakes are dangerous" may not explain the child's *emotional* response. More likely, the child has observed others react fearfully to the word *snake* or to snake images on television (Ollendick & King, 1991).

The emotional attitudes we develop toward foods, political parties, ethnic groups, escalators—whatever—are probably conditioned not only by direct experiences but also vicariously. No one is born prejudiced—all attitudes are learned. Parents may do well to look in a mirror if they wonder how or where a child "picked up" a particular fear or emotional attitude (Mineka & Hamida, 1998).

Phobia *An intense and unrealistic fear of some specific object or situation.*
Conditioned emotional response *An emotional response that has been linked to a previously non-emotional stimulus by classical conditioning.*
Desensitization *Reducing fear or anxiety by repeatedly exposing a person to emotional stimuli while the person is deeply relaxed.*
Vicarious classical conditioning *Classical conditioning brought about by observing another person react to a particular stimulus.*

OPERANT CONDITIONING—CAN PIGEONS PLAY PING-PONG?

As stated earlier, in **operant conditioning** (or instrumental learning), we associate responses with their consequences. The basic principle is simple: Acts that are reinforced tend to be repeated. Pioneer learning theorist Edward L. Thorndike called this the **law of effect** (the probability of a response is altered by the effect it has). Learning is strengthened each time a response is followed by a satisfying state of affairs. Think of the earlier example of the vending machine. Because kicking the machine had the effect of producing food and money, the likelihood of repeating the "kicking response" increased.

Classical conditioning is passive. It simply "happens to" the learner when a US follows a CS. In operant conditioning, the learner actively "operates on" the environment. Thus, operant conditioning refers mainly to learning *voluntary* responses. For example, waving your hand in class to get a teacher's attention is a learned operant response. It is reinforced by gaining the teacher's attention. (See ◆Table 9.2 for a further comparison of classical and operant conditioning.)

The idea that reward affects learning is certainly nothing new to parents (and other trainers of small animals). However, parents, as well as teachers, politicians, supervisors, and even you, may use reward in ways that are inexact or misguided. A case in point is the term *reward*. To be correct, it is better to say *reinforcer*. Why? Because rewards do not always increase responding. If you try to give licorice candy to a child as a "reward" for good behavior, it will work only if the child likes licorice. What is reinforcing for one person may not be for another. As a practical rule of thumb, psychologists define an **operant reinforcer** as any event that follows a response and increases its probability (❖Fig. 9.8).

Acquiring an Operant Response

Most studies of instrumental learning take place in a **conditioning chamber,** an apparatus designed for the study of operant conditioning in animals. This device is also sometimes called a Skinner box, after B. F. Skinner, who invented it (❖Fig. 9.9). A look into a typical Skinner box will clarify the process of operant conditioning.

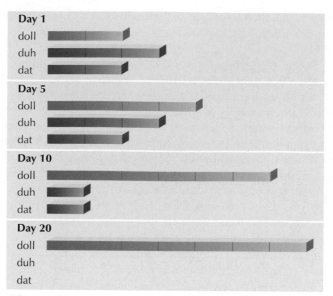

❖ FIGURE 9.8 *Assume that a child who is learning to talk points to her favorite doll and says either "doll," "duh," or "dat" when she wants it. Day 1 shows the number of times the child uses each word to ask for the doll (each block represents one request). At first, she uses all three words interchangeably. To hasten learning, her parents decide to give her the doll only when she names it correctly. Notice how the child's behavior shifts as operant reinforcement is applied. By Day 20, saying "doll" has become the most probable response.*

The Adventures of Mickey Rat

A hungry rat is placed in a small cage-like chamber. The walls are bare, except for a metal lever and a tray into which food pellets can be dispensed (see ❖Fig. 9.9).

Frankly, there's not much to do in a Skinner box. This increases the chances that our subject will make the response we want to reinforce, which is pressing the bar. Also, hunger keeps the animal motivated to seek food and actively *emit*, or freely give off, a variety of responses. Now let's take another look at our subject.

Further Adventures of Mickey Rat

For a while our subject walks around, grooms, sniffs at the corners, or stands on his hind legs—all typical rat behaviors. Then it happens. He places his paw on the lever to get a better view of the top of the cage.

◆ **TABLE 9.2** Comparison of Classical and Operant Conditioning

	CLASSICAL CONDITIONING	OPERANT CONDITIONING
Nature of response	Involuntary, reflex	Spontaneous, voluntary
Reinforcement	Occurs *before* response (conditioned stimulus paired with unconditioned stimulus)	Occurs *after* response (response is followed by reinforcing stimulus or event)
Role of learner	Passive (response is *elicited* by US)	Active (response is *emitted*)
Nature of learning	Neutral stimulus becomes a CS through association with a US	Probability of making a response is altered by consequences that follow it
Learned expectancy	US will follow CS	Response will have a specific effect

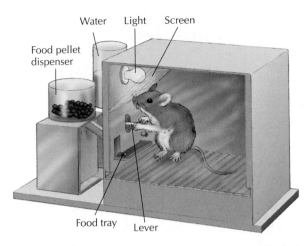

FIGURE 9.9 *The Skinner box. This simple device, invented by B. F. Skinner, allows careful study of operant conditioning. When the rat presses the bar, a pellet of food or a drop of water is automatically released. (A photograph of a Skinner box appears in Chapter 2.)*

Click! The lever depresses, and a food pellet drops into the tray. The rat walks to the tray, eats the pellet, and then grooms himself. Up and exploring the cage again, he leans on the lever. *Click!* After a trip to the food tray, he returns to the bar and sniffs it, then puts his foot on it. *Click!* Soon the rat settles into a smooth pattern of frequent bar pressing.

Notice that the rat did not acquire a new skill in this situation. He was already able to depress the bar. Reward alters only how *frequently* he presses the bar. In operant conditioning, reinforcement is used to alter the frequency of responses, or to mold them into new patterns.

INFORMATION   Like classical conditioning, operant learning is based on information and expectancies. In operant conditioning, we learn to expect that a certain response will have a certain effect at certain times (Bolles, 1979). That is, we learn that a particular stimulus is associated with a particular response, which is associated with reinforcement (Dragoi & Staddon, 1999). From this point of view, a reinforcer tells a person or an animal that a response was "right" and worth repeating.

❖Figure 9.10 shows how operant reinforcement can change behavior. The results are from an effort to teach a severely disturbed 9-year-old child to say, "Please," "Thank you," and "You're welcome." As you can see, during the initial, baseline period, the child rarely used the word *please*. Typically, he just grabbed objects and became angry if he couldn't have them. However, when he was reinforced for saying "Please," he soon learned to use the word nearly every time he wanted something. When the child said, "Please," he was reinforced in three ways: He received the object he asked for (a crayon, for example); he was given a small food treat, such as a piece of candy, popcorn, or a grape; and he was praised for his good behavior (Matson et al., 1990).

CONTINGENT REINFORCEMENT   Operant reinforcement works best when it is **response contingent** (kon-TIN-jent). That is, it must be given only after a desired response has occurred. If the disturbed child received reinforcers haphazardly, his behavior wouldn't have changed at all. In situations ranging from study-

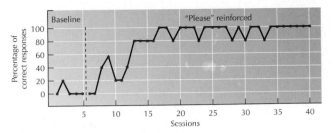

FIGURE 9.10 *Reinforcement and human behavior. The percentage of times that a severely disturbed child said "Please" when he wanted an object was increased dramatically by reinforcing him for making a polite request. Reinforcement produced similar improvements in saying "Thank you" and "You're welcome," and the boy applied these terms in new situations as well. (Adapted from Matson et al., 1990.)*

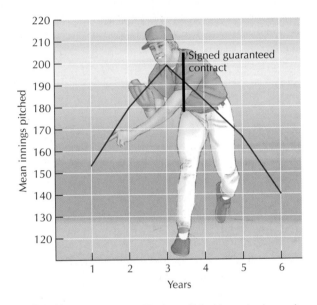

FIGURE 9.11 *Mean number of innings pitched by major league baseball players before and after signing long-term guaranteed contracts. The performance of 38 pitchers who signed multiyear contracts for large salaries is shown. When salary was no longer contingent on good performance, there was a rapid decline in innings pitched and in the number of wins. During the same 6-year period, the performance of pitchers on 1-year contracts remained fairly steady. (Data from O'Brien et al., 1981.)*

ing to working hard on the job, contingent reinforcement also affects the *performance* of responses (❖Fig. 9.11). "Life in an Operant Community" discusses an interesting application of this principle.

Operant conditioning *Learning based on the consequences of responding.*
Law of effect *Responses that lead to desirable effects are repeated; those that produce undesirable results are not.*
Operant reinforcer *Any event that reliably increases the probability or frequency of responses it follows.*
Conditioning chamber *An apparatus designed for the study of operant conditioning in animals; a Skinner box.*
Response-contingent reinforcement *Reinforcement given only when a particular response is made.*

LIFE IN AN OPERANT COMMUNITY

B. F. Skinner's utopian novel, *Walden Two*, describes a model community based on behavioral engineering. Would such a community work? On a small scale, the answer appears to be yes. At the University of Kansas, college students took part in an experimental living project that was quite successful (Miller, 1976). Thirty men and women shared a large house where work, leadership, and self-government were tied to behavioral principles.

Work sharing illustrates the project's operant approach. Basic jobs such as preparing food and cleaning were divided into approximately 100 tasks. Residents did all of the tasks themselves, and one community member checked daily to see that each job was completed. (This role was rotated.) To maintain job performance, credits were assigned for each task. At the end of the month, residents who had collected 400 credits got a sizable rent reduction.

This system was very effective in maintaining day-to-day work habits. As anyone who has shared living quarters knows, good intentions are no guarantee that the chores will get done. More important, most residents were highly satisfied with the system (Miller, 1976). The experimental living project is a good example of the possibilities of applying conditioning principles to human behavior. While no major "operant communities" exist today, the fact remains that operant principles greatly affect behavior in homes, schools, and businesses. It is always worthwhile to try to arrange reinforcers so that productive and responsible behavior is encouraged.

The Timing of Reinforcement

Operant reinforcement is most effective when it rapidly follows a correct response. For rats in a Skinner box, very little learning occurs when the delay between bar pressing and receiving food reaches 50 seconds. If the food reward is delayed more than about a minute and a half, no learning occurs (Perin, 1943) (❖Fig. 9.12). In general, you will be most successful if you present a reinforcer *immediately* after a response you wish to change. Thus, a child who is helpful or courteous should be praised immediately for her good behavior.

Let's say I work hard all semester in a class to get an A grade. Wouldn't the delay in reinforcement keep me from learning anything? No, for several reasons. First, as a human you can anticipate future reward. Second, you get reinforced by quiz and test grades all through the semester. Third, a single reinforcer can often maintain a long **response chain** (a linked series of actions that lead to reinforcement). A simplified example of response chaining is provided by Barnabus, a rat trained by psychologists at Brown University.

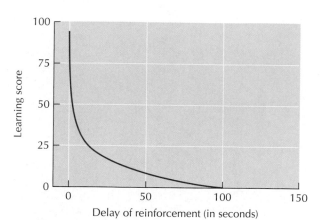

❖ **FIGURE 9.12** *The effect of delay of reinforcement. Notice how rapidly the learning score drops when reward is delayed. Animals learning to press a bar in a Skinner box showed no signs of learning if food reward followed a bar press by more than 100 seconds. (Perin, 1943.)*

The Great Barnabus

By carefully working from the last response to the first, Barnabus was trained to make an ever-longer chain of responses to obtain a single food pellet. When in top form, Barnabus was able to climb a spiral staircase, cross a narrow bridge, climb a ladder, pull a toy car with a chain, get into the car, pedal it to a second staircase, climb the staircase, wriggle through a tube, climb onto an elevator and descend to a platform, press a lever to receive a food pellet, and . . . start over! (Pierrel & Sherman, 1963)

Many of the things we do every day involve similar response chains. The long series of events necessary to prepare a meal is rewarded by the final eating. A violin maker may carry out thousands of steps for the final reward of hearing a first musical note. Tying a shoe is a short but familiar response chain.

SUPERSTITIOUS BEHAVIOR Reinforcers affect not only the response they follow but also other responses that occur shortly before. This helps explain many human superstitions. If a golfer taps her club on the ground three times and then hits an unusually fine shot, what happens? The successful shot reinforces not only the correct swing but also the three taps. During operant training, animals often develop similar unnecessary responses. If a rat scratches its ear just before its first bar press, it may continue to scratch before every bar press. Pressing the bar is all that is required to produce food, but the animal may continue to "superstitiously" scratch its ear, as if doing so was necessary.

Superstitious behaviors are repeated because they appear to produce reinforcement, even though they are actually unnecessary (Pisacreta, 1998). If you get the large half of a wishbone and have good fortune soon after, you may credit your luck to the wishbone. If you walk under a ladder and then break a leg, you may avoid ladders in the future. Each time you avoid a ladder and nothing bad happens, your superstitious action is reinforced. Belief in magic can also be explained along such lines. Rituals to bring rain, ward off illness, or produce abundant crops very likely earn the faith of participants because they occasionally appear to succeed. Besides, better safe than sorry!

Shaping

How is it possible to reinforce responses that rarely occur? Even in a barren Skinner box, it could take a long time for a rat to accidentally press the bar and get a food pellet. We might wait forever for more complicated responses to occur. For example, you would have to wait a long time for a duck to accidentally walk out of its cage, turn on a light, play a toy piano, turn off the light, and walk back to its cage. If this is what you wanted to reward, you would never get the chance.

Then how are the animals on TV and at amusement parks taught to perform complicated tricks? The answer lies in **shaping,** which is the gradual molding of responses to a desired pattern. Let's look again at our subject, Mickey Rat.

Mickey Rat Shapes Up

Assume that the rat has not yet learned to press the bar. He also shows no signs of interest in the bar. Instead of waiting for the first accidental bar press, we can shape his behavior. At first, we settle for just getting him to face the bar. Any time he turns toward the bar, he is reinforced with a bit of food. Soon Mickey spends much of his time facing the bar. Next, we reinforce him every time he takes a step toward the bar. If he turns toward the bar and walks away, nothing happens. But when he faces the bar and takes a step forward, *click!* His responses are being shaped.

By changing the rules about what makes a successful response, we can gradually train the rat to approach the bar and press it. In other words, **successive approximations** (ever-closer matches) to a desired response are reinforced during shaping. B. F. Skinner once taught two pigeons to play Ping-Pong in this way (❖Fig. 9.13). Shaping applies to humans, too. Let's say you want to study more, clean the house more often, or exercise more. In each case, it would be best to set a series of gradual, daily goals. Then you can reward yourself for small steps in the right direction (Watson & Tharp, 1996).

Operant Extinction

Would a rat stop bar pressing if no more food arrived? Yes, but not immediately. Learned responses that are not reinforced gradually fade away. This process is called **operant extinction.** Just as acquiring an operant response takes time, so does extinction. For example, if a TV program repeatedly bores you, watching the program will probably extinguish over time.

Even after extinction seems complete, the previously reinforced response may return. If a rat is removed from a Skinner box after extinction and given a short rest, the rat will press the bar again when returned to the Skinner box. Similarly, a few weeks after they give up on buying state lottery tickets, many people are tempted to try again.

Does extinction take as long the second time? If reinforcement is still withheld, a rat's bar pressing will extinguish again, usually more quickly. The brief return of an operant response after extinction is another example of spontaneous recovery (mentioned earlier regarding classical conditioning). Spontaneous recovery seems to be very adaptive. After a rest period, the rat responds again in a situation that produced food in the past: "Just checking to see if the rules have changed!"

Marked changes in behavior occur when reinforcement and extinction are combined. For example, parents often unknowingly reinforce children for **negative attention seeking** (using misbehavior to gain attention). Children are generally *ignored* when they are playing quietly. They get attention when they become louder and louder, yell, "Hey, Mom!" at the top of their lungs, throw tantrums, show off, or break something. Granted, the attention they get is often a scolding, but attention is a powerful reinforcer, nevertheless. Parents report dramatic improvements when they *ignore* their children's disruptive behavior and praise or attend to a child who is quiet or playing constructively.

Negative Reinforcement

Until now, we have stressed **positive reinforcement,** which occurs when a pleasant or desirable event follows a response. How else could operant learning be reinforced? The time has come to consider **negative reinforcement,** which occurs when making a response removes an unpleasant event. Don't be fooled by the word *negative.* Negative reinforcement also increases responding. However, it does so by ending discomfort.

Let's say that you have a headache and take an aspirin. Your aspirin taking will be negatively reinforced if the headache stops. Likewise, a rat could be taught to press a bar to get food (positive reinforcement), or the rat could be given a continuous mild shock (through the floor of its cage) that is turned off by a bar

❖ **FIGURE 9.13** *Operant conditioning principles were used to train these pigeons to play Ping-Pong.*

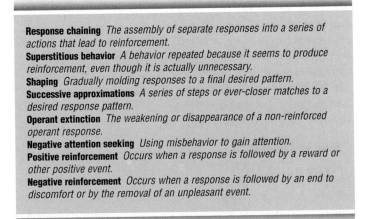

Response chaining *The assembly of separate responses into a series of actions that lead to reinforcement.*
Superstitious behavior *A behavior repeated because it seems to produce reinforcement, even though it is actually unnecessary.*
Shaping *Gradually molding responses to a final desired pattern.*
Successive approximations *A series of steps or ever-closer matches to a desired response pattern.*
Operant extinction *The weakening or disappearance of a non-reinforced operant response.*
Negative attention seeking *Using misbehavior to gain attention.*
Positive reinforcement *Occurs when a response is followed by a reward or other positive event.*
Negative reinforcement *Occurs when a response is followed by an end to discomfort or by the removal of an unpleasant event.*

	CONSEQUENCE OF MAKING A RESPONSE	EXAMPLE	EFFECT ON RESPONSE PROBABILITY
Positive reinforcement	Positive event begins	Food given	Increase
Negative reinforcement	Negative event ends	Pain stops	Increase
Punishment	Negative event begins	Pain begins	Decrease
Punishment (response cost)	Positive event ends	Food removed	Decrease
Non-reinforcement	Nothing	——	Decrease

press (negative reinforcement). Either way, bar pressing would increase. Why? Because it leads to a desired state of affairs (food or an end to pain). Often, positive and negative reinforcement combine. If you are uncomfortably hungry, eating a meal is reinforced by the good-tasting food (positive reinforcement) and by an end to nagging hunger (negative reinforcement).

Punishment

Many people mistake negative reinforcement for punishment. However, **punishment** is any event following a response that decreases its likelihood of occurring again. As noted, negative reinforcement *increases* responding. The difference can be seen in a hypothetical example. Let's say you live in an apartment and your neighbor's stereo is blasting so loudly that your ears hurt. If you pound on the wall and the volume suddenly drops (negative reinforcement), future wall pounding will be more likely. But if you pound on the wall and the volume increases (punishment), or if the neighbor comes over and pounds on you (more punishment), wall pounding becomes less likely.

As another example, consider a drug addict undergoing withdrawal. Taking the drug will temporarily end painful withdrawal symptoms. Drug taking is therefore negatively reinforced. If the drug made the pain worse (punishment), the addict would quickly stop taking it.

Isn't it also punishing to have privileges, money, or other positive things taken away for making a particular response? Yes. Punishment also occurs when a reinforcer or positive state of affairs is removed, such as losing privileges. This second type of punishment is called **response cost.** Parents who "ground" their teenage children for misbehavior are applying response cost. Parking tickets and other fines are also based on response cost. For your convenience, ◆Table 9.3 summarizes four basic consequences of making a response.

OPERANT REINFORCERS—WHAT'S YOUR PLEASURE?

For humans, an effective operant reinforcer may be anything from an M&M candy to a pat on the back. In categorizing such

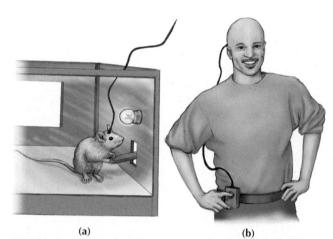

(a)   **(b)**

❖ **FIGURE 9.14** *In the apparatus shown in* (a), *the rat can press a bar to deliver mild electric stimulation to a "pleasure center" in the brain. Humans also have been "wired" for brain stimulation, as shown in* (b). *However, in humans, this has been done only as an experimental way to restrain uncontrollable outbursts of violence. Implants have not been done merely to produce pleasure.*

reinforcers, useful distinctions can be made between *primary reinforcers, secondary reinforcers,* and *feedback.* Operant reinforcers of all types have a large impact on our lives. Let's examine them in more detail.

Primary Reinforcers

Primary reinforcers are natural, non-learned, and rooted in biology: They produce comfort, end discomfort, or fill an immediate physical need. Food, water, and sex are obvious examples. Every time you open the refrigerator, walk to a drinking fountain, turn up the heat, or order a double latte, your actions reflect primary reinforcement.

In addition to obvious examples, there are other less natural primary reinforcers. One of the most powerful is **intracranial stimulation (ICS).** ICS involves direct activation of "pleasure centers" in the brain (Olds & Fobes, 1981) (❖Fig. 9.14).

Wiring a Rat for Pleasure

Use of brain stimulation for reward requires the permanent implantation of tiny electrodes in specific areas of the brain. A rat "wired for pleasure" can be trained to press the bar in a Skinner box to deliver electrical stimulation to its own brain. Some rats will press the bar thousands of times per hour to obtain brain stimulation. After 15 or 20 hours of constant pressing, animals sometimes collapse from exhaustion. When they revive, they begin pressing again. If the reward circuit is not turned off, an animal will ignore food, water, and sex in favor of bar pressing.

Many natural primary reinforcers activate the same pleasure pathways in the brain that make ICS so powerful (McBride, Murphy, & Ikemoto, 1999).

One shudders to think what might happen if brain implants were easy and practical to do. (They are not.) Every company from Playboy to Microsoft would have a device on the market, and we would have to keep a closer watch on politicians than usual!

BRIDGES

Electrical stimulation is a valuable tool for studying the functions of various brain structures.

See Chapter 3, pages 57–58.

Secondary Reinforcers

In some traditional societies, learning is still strongly tied to food, water, and other primary reinforcers. Most of us, however, respond to a much broader range of rewards and reinforcers. Money, praise, attention, approval, success, affection, grades, and the like all serve as learned or **secondary reinforcers.**

How does a secondary reinforcer gain its ability to promote learning? Some secondary reinforcers are simply associated with a primary reinforcer.

The Push-Button Rat

A rat caged in a Skinner box has learned through operant conditioning to press the bar for food pellets. Each rewarded bar press is also followed by a brief auditory tone. After a period of training in which bar pressing, food, and the tone are associated, the rat is moved to a new cage. This cage has no bar, but it does have a button mounted on the wall. If the rat pushes the button, the tone sounds, but no food is delivered. Even though no primary reinforcement (food) is given, the rat learns to press the button to turn on the tone. Because it was associated with food, the tone has become a secondary reinforcer.

TOKENS   Secondary reinforcers that can be *exchanged* for primary reinforcers gain their value more directly. Printed money obviously has little or no value of its own. You can't eat it, drink it, or sleep with it. However, it can be exchanged for food, water, lodging, and other necessities.

A **token reinforcer** is a tangible secondary reinforcer, such as money, gold stars, and poker chips. In a series of classic experiments, chimpanzees were taught to work for tokens. The chimps were first trained to put poker chips into a Chimp-O-Mat vending machine. Each chip dispensed a few grapes or raisins. Once the animals had learned to exchange tokens for food, they would learn new tasks to earn the chips. To maintain the value of the tokens, the chimps were occasionally allowed to use the Chimp-O-Mat (❖Fig. 9.15) (Cowles, 1937; Wolfe, 1936).

A major advantage of tokens is that they don't lose reinforcing value as quickly as primary reinforcers do. For instance, if you use candy to reinforce a retarded child for correctly naming things, the child might lose interest once he is satiated (fully satisfied) or no longer hungry. It would be better to use tokens as immediate rewards for learning. Later, the child could exchange his tokens for food, toys, or a trip to the movies.

Tokens have been used in similar ways with troubled children and adults in special programs and even in ordinary elementary school classrooms (Spiegler & Guevremont, 1998). (See ❖Fig. 9.16.) In each case, the goal is to provide an immediate reward for learning. Typically, tokens may be exchanged for food, desired goods, special privileges, and trips to movies, amusement parks, and so forth.

Many parents find that tokens greatly reduce discipline problems with younger children. For example, children can earn points or gold stars during the week for good behavior. If they earn enough tokens, they are allowed on Sunday to choose one item out of a grab bag of small treats.

❖ **FIGURE 9.15** *Poker chips normally have little or no value for chimpanzees, but this chimp will work hard to earn them once he learns that the Chimp-O-Mat will dispense food in exchange for them.*

Punishment *Any event that follows a response and decreases its likelihood of occurring again.*
Response cost *Removal of a positive reinforcer after a response is made.*
Primary reinforcers *Non-learned reinforcers; usually those that satisfy physiological needs.*
Intracranial stimulation *Direct electrical stimulation and activation of brain tissue.*
Secondary reinforcer *A learned reinforcer; often one that gains reinforcing properties by association with a primary reinforcer.*
Token reinforcer *A tangible secondary reinforcer such as money, gold stars, or poker chips.*

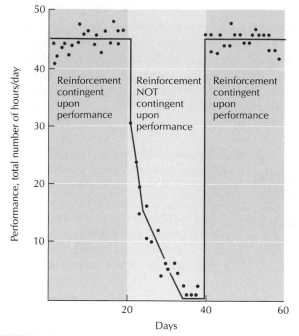

❖ **FIGURE 9.16** *Reinforcement in a token economy. This graph shows the effects of using tokens to reward socially desirable behavior in a mental hospital ward. Desirable behavior was defined as cleaning, bed making, attending therapy sessions, and so forth. Tokens earned could be exchanged for basic amenities such as meals, snacks, coffee, game-room privileges, or weekend passes. The graph shows more than 24 hours per day because it represents the total number of hours of desirable behavior performed by all patients in the ward. (Adapted from Ayllon & Azrin, 1965.)*

SOCIAL REINFORCERS   As we have noted, learned desires for attention and approval, which are called **social reinforcers,** often influence human behavior. This fact can be used in a classic, if somewhat mischievous, demonstration.

Shaping a Teacher

For this activity, about half (or more) of the students in a classroom must participate. First, select a target behavior. This should be something like "lecturing from the right side of the room." (Keep it simple, in case your teacher is a slow learner.) Begin training in this way: Each time the instructor turns toward the right or takes a step in that direction, participating students should look *really* interested. Also, smile, ask questions, lean forward, and make eye contact. If the teacher turns to the left or takes a step in that direction, participating students should lean back, yawn, check out their split ends, close their eyes, or generally look bored. Soon, without being aware of why, the instructor should be spending most of his or her time each class period lecturing from the right side of the classroom.

This trick has been a favorite of psychology graduate students for decades. For a time, one of my professors delivered all of his lectures from the right side of the room while toying with the cords from the venetian blinds. (We added the cords the second week!) The point to remember from this example is that attention and approval can change the behavior of children, family members, friends, roommates, and coworkers. Be aware of what you are reinforcing.

BRIDGES

A token economy is a system for managing and altering behavior through reinforcement of selected responses.

See Chapter 18, pages 612–613.

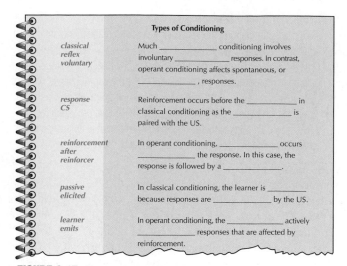

❖ **FIGURE 9.17** *To sample a programmed instruction format, try covering the terms on the left with a piece of paper. As you fill in the blanks, uncover one new term for each response. In this way, your correct (or incorrect) responses will be followed by immediate feedback. (Actually, this is a somewhat simplified example. In true programmed instruction, new ideas are presented along with opportunities to practice them.)*

Feedback

His eyes, driven and blazing, dart from side to side. His left hand twitches, dances, rises, and strikes, hitting its target again and again. At the same time, his right hand furiously spins in circular motions. Does this describe some strange neurological disorder? Actually, it depicts 10-year-old Mark as he plays his favorite video game, an animated skateboarding adventure!

How did Mark learn the complex movements needed to excel at virtual skateboarding? After all, he was not rewarded with food or money. The answer lies in the fact that Mark's favorite video game provides two key elements that underlie learning: *a responsive environment* and *information.*

Every time a player moves, a video game responds instantly with sounds, animated actions, and a higher or lower score. The machine's responsiveness and the information flow it provides can be very motivating if you want to win. The same principle applies to many other learning situations: If you are trying to learn to use a computer, play a musical instrument, cook, or solve math problems, reinforcement comes from knowing that you achieved a desired result.

The adaptive value of information helps explain why much human learning occurs without obvious reinforcement by food, water, and the like. Humans readily learn responses that merely have a desired effect or that bring a goal closer. Let's explore this idea further.

KNOWLEDGE OF RESULTS   Imagine that you are asked to throw darts at a target. Each dart must pass over a screen that prevents you from telling if you hit the target. If you threw 1,000 darts, we would expect little improvement in your performance, because no *feedback* is provided. **Feedback** (information about the effect a response had) is partic-

❖ **FIGURE 9.18** *Computer-assisted instruction. The screen on the left shows a typical drill-and-practice math problem, in which students must find the hypotenuse of a triangle. The center screen presents the same problem as an instructional game to increase interest and motivation. In the game, a child is asked to set the proper distance on a ray gun in the hovering space ship to "vaporize" an attacker. The screen on the right depicts an educational simulation. Here, students place a "probe" at various spots in a human brain. They then "stimulate," "destroy," or "restore" areas. As each area is altered, it is named on the screen, and the effects on behavior are described. This allows students to explore basic brain functions on their own.*

ularly important in human learning. Mark's video game did not explicitly reward him for correct responses. Yet, because it provided feedback, rapid learning took place.

How can feedback be applied? Increased feedback (also called **knowledge of results,** or **KR**) almost always improves learning and performance (Lee & Carnahan, 1990). If you want to learn to play a musical instrument, sing, speak a second language, or deliver a speech, tape-recorded feedback can be very helpful. In sports, videotapes are used to improve everything from tennis serves to pick-off moves in baseball. (Taped replays of this kind are most helpful when a skilled coach directs attention to key details.) Whenever you are trying to learn a complex skill, it pays to get more feedback (Wulf, Shea, & Matschiner, 1998).

Learning Aids

In recent years, operant learning and feedback have been combined in two interesting ways: programmed instruction and computer-assisted instruction.

How do these techniques make use of feedback? Feedback is most effective when it is *frequent, immediate,* and *detailed.* **Programmed instruction** teaches students in a format that presents information in small amounts, gives immediate practice, and provides continuous feedback to learners. Frequent feedback keeps learners from practicing errors. It also lets students work at their own pace. (A small sample of programmed instruction is shown in ❖Figure 9.17 so that you can see what the format looks like.) Programmed learning can be done in book form or presented by a computer (Mabry, 1998).

In **computer-assisted instruction (CAI),** learning is aided by computer-presented information and exercises. In addition to giving immediate feedback, the computer can analyze the answers that learners give. This allows use of a **branching program** that supplies extra information and asks extra questions based on the errors made. CAI programs that use artificial intelligence (see Chapter 11) can even give hints about why an answer was wrong and what is needed to correct it (Light, 1997).

Although the final level of skill or knowledge is not necessarily higher than that gained by conventional methods, CAI can save much time and effort. In addition, people often do better with feedback from a computer because they don't feel they are being watched and evaluated (Schneider & Shugar, 1990). This allows students to freely make mistakes and learn from them. For example, CAI can give medical students unlimited practice at diagnosing diseases from symptoms, such as "acute chest pain" (Papa et al., 1999).

The simplest computerized instruction consists of self-paced **drill and practice.** In this format, students answer questions similar to those in printed workbooks, but they instantly get correct answers. In addition, the computer can give extra KR, such as how fast you worked, your percentage correct, or how your work compared with previous scores.

Higher level CAI programs include instructional games and educational simulations. **Instructional games** use stories, competition with a partner, sound effects, and gamelike graphics to increase interest and motivation (❖Fig. 9.18). The best instructional games show that it is possible to have fun and improve skills at the same time (Stoney & Wild, 1998).

Social reinforcer *Reinforcement based on receiving attention, approval, or affection from another person.*
Feedback *Information returned to a person about the effects a response has had; also known as knowledge of results.*
Knowledge of results *Informational feedback.*
Programmed instruction *Any learning format that presents information in small amounts, gives immediate practice, and provides continuous feedback to learners.*
Computer-assisted instruction (CAI) *Learning aided by computer-presented information, exercises, and feedback.*
Branching program *A computer program that gives learners corrective information and exercises based on the nature of their errors.*
Drill and practice *A basic CAI format, typically consisting of questions and answers.*
Instructional games *Educational computer programs designed to resemble games in order to motivate learning.*

In **educational simulations,** students explore an imaginary situation or "microworld" that simulates real-world problems. By seeing the effects of their choices, students discover basic principles of physics, biology, psychology, or other subjects (Cordova & Lepper, 1996).

Recently, interactive videodisks have added a new dimension to CAI. **Interactive videodisk instruction** (multimedia-based learning) provides a stimulating mixture of text, still photos, motion video, and sound, as well as built-in feedback and coaching (Tannenbaum & Yukl, 1992).

Psychologists are only now beginning to fully explore the value and limits of computer-assisted instruction. Nevertheless, it seems likely that their efforts will improve not only education but also our understanding of human learning.

Let's pause now for some learning exercises so you can get some feedback about your mastery of the preceding ideas.

KNOWLEDGE BUILDER
OPERANT CONDITIONING

RELATE

How have your thoughts about the effects of "rewards" changed, now that you've read about operant conditioning? Can you explain the difference between positive reinforcement, negative reinforcement, and punishment? Can you give an example of each concept from your own experience?

A friend of yours punishes his dog all the time. What advice would you give him about how to use reinforcement, extinction, and shaping instead of punishment?

LEARNING CHECK

1. Responses in operant conditioning are _____, whereas those in classical conditioning are passive, _____ responses.

2. Changing the rules in small steps, so that an animal (or person) is gradually trained to respond as desired, is called _____.

3. Extinction in operant conditioning is also subject to _____ of a response.
   a. successive approximations b. shaping c. automation d. spontaneous recovery

4. Positive reinforcers increase the rate of responding, and negative reinforcers decrease it. T or F?

5. Primary reinforcers are those learned through classical conditioning. T or F?

6. Tokens are basically _____ reinforcers.

7. Superstitious responses are those that are
   a. shaped by secondary reinforcement b. extinguished c. prepotent d. unnecessary to obtain reinforcement

8. Knowledge of results or KR is also known as _____.

9. Branching programs are a basic feature of CAI. T or F?

PARTIAL REINFORCEMENT—LAS VEGAS, A HUMAN SKINNER BOX?

SERENDIPITY *(n):* discovering one thing while looking for another

B. F. Skinner, so the story goes, was studying operant conditioning when he ran short of food pellets. In order to continue, he arranged for a pellet to reward every other response. Thus began the formal study of **schedules of reinforcement** (plans for determining which responses will be reinforced). Until now, we have treated operant reinforcement as if it were continuous. **Continuous reinforcement** means that a reinforcer follows every correct response. This is fine for the lab, but it has little to do with the real world. Most of our responses are more inconsistently rewarded. In daily life, learning is usually based on **partial reinforcement,** in which reinforcers do not follow every response.

Partial reinforcement can be given in several patterns. Each has a distinct effect on behavior. In addition to these (which will be explored in a moment), there is a general effect: Responses acquired by partial reinforcement are highly resistant to extinction. For some obscure reason, lost in the lore of psychology, this is called the **partial reinforcement effect.**

How does getting reinforced part of the time make a habit stronger? If you have ever visited Las Vegas or a similar gambling mecca, you have probably seen row after row of people playing slot machines. To gain insight into partial reinforcement, imagine that you are making your first visit to Las Vegas. You put a dollar in a slot machine and pull the handle. Ten dollars spills into the tray. Using one of your newly won dollars, you pull the handle again. Another payoff! Let's say this continues for 15 minutes. Every pull is followed by a payoff. Suddenly each pull is followed by nothing. Obviously, you would respond several times more before giving up. However, when continuous reinforcement is followed by extinction, the message soon becomes clear: No more payoffs.

Contrast this with partial reinforcement. Again, imagine that this is your first encounter with a slot machine. You put a dollar in the machine five times without a payoff. You are just about to quit but decide to play once more. Bingo! The machine returns $20. After this, payoffs continue on a partial

The one-armed bandit (slot machine) is a dispenser of partial reinforcement.

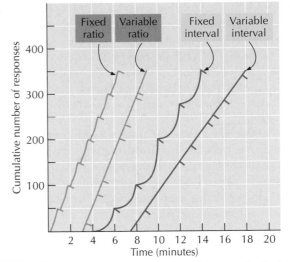

❖ **FIGURE 9.19** *Typical response patterns for reinforcement schedules. Results such as these are obtained when a cumulative recorder is connected to a Skinner box. The device consists of a moving strip of paper and a mechanical pen that jumps upward each time a response is made. Rapid responding causes the pen to draw a steep line; a horizontal line indicates no response. Small tick marks on the lines show when a reinforcer was given.*

schedule; some are large, and some are small. All are unpredictable. Sometimes you hit two in a row, and sometimes 20 or 30 pulls go unrewarded.

Now let's say the payoff mechanism is turned off again. How many times do you think you would respond this time before your handle-pulling behavior extinguished? Because you have developed the expectation that any play may be "the one," it will be hard to resist just one more play . . . and one more . . . and one more. Also, because partial reinforcement includes long periods of non-reward, it will be harder to discriminate between periods of reinforcement and extinction. It is no exaggeration to say that the partial reinforcement effect has left many people penniless. Even psychologists visiting Las Vegas may get "cleaned out"—and they should know better!

Schedules of Partial Reinforcement

Partial reinforcement could be given in many different patterns. Let's consider the four most basic, which have some interesting effects on us.

FIXED RATIO (FR) What would happen if a reinforcer followed only every other response? Or what if we followed every third, fourth, fifth, or other number of responses with reinforcement? Each of these patterns is a **fixed ratio (FR) schedule** (a set number of correct responses must be made to obtain a reinforcer). Notice that in an FR schedule the ratio of reinforcers to responses is fixed: FR-2 means that every other response is rewarded; FR-3 means that every third response is reinforced; in an FR-10 schedule, exactly 10 responses must be made to obtain a reinforcer.

Fixed ratio schedules produce *very high response rates* (❖Fig. 9.19). A hungry rat on an FR-10 schedule will quickly run off 10 responses, pause to eat, and then run off 10 more. A similar situation occurs when factory or farm workers are paid on a piecework basis. When a fixed number of items must be produced for a set amount of pay, work output is high.

VARIABLE RATIO (VR) In a **variable ratio (VR) schedule**, a varied number of correct responses must be made to get a reinforcer. Instead of reinforcing, for example, every fourth response (FR-4), a person or animal on a VR-4 schedule gets rewarded *on the average,* for every fourth response. Sometimes 2 responses must be made to obtain a reinforcer; sometimes it's 5, sometimes 4, and so on. The actual number varies, but it averages out to 4 (in this example). Variable ratio schedules also produce high response rates.

VR schedules seem less predictable than FR. Does that have any effect on extinction? Yes. Because reinforcement is less predictable, VR schedules tend to produce greater resistance to extinction than fixed ratio schedules. Playing a slot machine is

Educational simulations *Computer programs that simulate real-world settings or situations to promote learning.*
Interactive videodisk instruction *Computerized multimedia instruction.*
Schedule of reinforcement *A rule or plan for determining which responses will be reinforced.*
Continuous reinforcement *A schedule in which every correct response is followed by a reinforcer.*
Partial reinforcement *A pattern in which only a portion of all responses are reinforced.*
Partial reinforcement effect *Responses acquired with partial reinforcement are more resistant to extinction.*
Fixed ratio schedule *A set number of correct responses must be made to get a reinforcer. For example, a reinforcer is given for every four correct responses.*
Variable ratio schedule *A varied number of correct responses must be made to get a reinforcer. For example, a reinforcer is given after three to seven correct responses; the actual number changes randomly.*

an example of behavior maintained by a variable ratio schedule. Another would be a child asking for a treat at the supermarket. The number of times the child must ask before getting reinforced varies, so the child becomes quite persistent. Golf, tennis, and many other sports are also reinforced on a variable ratio basis: An average of perhaps one good shot in 5 or 10 may be all that's needed to create a sports fanatic.

FIXED INTERVAL (FI)   In another pattern, reinforcement is given only when a correct response is made after a fixed amount of time has passed. This time interval is measured from the last reinforced response. Responses made during the time interval are not reinforced. In a **fixed interval (FI) schedule** the first correct response made after the time period has passed is reinforced. Thus, a rat on an FI-30-second schedule has to wait 30 seconds after the last reinforced response before a bar press will pay off again. The rat can press the bar as often as it wants during the interval, but it will not be rewarded.

Fixed interval schedules produce *moderate response rates.* These are marked by spurts of activity mixed with periods of inactivity. Animals working on an FI schedule seem to develop a keen sense of the passage of time (Eckerman, 1999). For example:

Mickey Rat Takes a Break

Mickey Rat, trained on an FI-60-second schedule, has just been reinforced for a bar press. What does he do? He saunters around the cage, grooms himself, hums, whistles, reads magazines, and polishes his nails. After 50 seconds, he walks to the bar and gives it a press—just testing. After 55 seconds, he gives it two or three presses, but there's still no payoff. Fifty-eight seconds, and he settles down to rapid pressing, 59 seconds, 60 seconds, and he hits the reinforced press. After one or two more presses (unrewarded), he wanders off again for the next interval.

Is getting paid weekly an FI schedule?   Pure examples of fixed interval schedules are rare, but getting paid each week at work does come close. Notice, however, that most people do not work faster just before payday, as an FI schedule predicts. A closer parallel would be having a report due every 2 weeks for a class. Right after turning in a paper, your work would probably drop to zero for a week or more. Then, as the next due date draws near, a work frenzy occurs. Another fixed interval example is checking a Thanksgiving turkey in the oven. Typically, the frequency of checking increases as the time for the turkey to be done draws near (Schwartz & Robbins, 1995).

VARIABLE INTERVAL (VI)   **Variable interval (VI) schedules** are a variation on fixed intervals. Here, reinforcement is given for the first correct response made after a varied amount of time. On a VI-30-second schedule, reinforcement is available after an interval that *averages* 30 seconds.

The VI schedules produce *slow, steady rates* of response and tremendous resistance to extinction (Lattal et al., 1998). When you dial a phone number and get a busy signal, reward (getting through) is on a VI schedule. You may have to wait 30 seconds or 30 minutes. If you are like most people, you will doggedly dial over and over again until you get a connection. Success in fishing is also on a VI schedule—which may explain the bulldog tenacity of many anglers (Schwartz & Robbins, 1995).

STIMULUS CONTROL—RED LIGHT, GREEN LIGHT

When you are driving, your behavior at intersections is controlled by the red or green light. In similar fashion, many of the stimuli we encounter each day act like stop or go signals that guide our behavior. To state the idea more formally, stimuli that consistently precede a rewarded response tend to influence when and where the response will occur. This effect is called **stimulus control.** Notice how it works with our friend Mickey Rat.

Lights Out for Mickey Rat

While learning the bar-pressing response, Mickey has been in a Skinner box illuminated by a bright light. During several training sessions, the light is alternately turned on and off. When the light is on, a bar press will produce food. When the light is off, bar pressing goes unrewarded. We soon observe that the rat presses vigorously when the light is on and ignores the bar when the light is off.

In this example, the light signals what consequences will follow if a response is made. Evidence for stimulus control could be shown by turning the food delivery *on* when the light is *off.* A well-trained animal might never discover that the rules had changed. A similar example of stimulus control would be a child who learns to ask for candy when her mother is in a good mood but not at other times.

GENERALIZATION   Two important aspects of stimulus control are generalization and discrimination. Let's return to the example

Stimulus control. Operant shaping was used to teach this whale to "bow" to an audience. Fish were used as reinforcers. Notice the trainer's hand signal, which serves as a discriminative stimulus to control the performance.

of the vending machine (from the chapter Preview) to illustrate these concepts. First, generalization.

Is generalization the same in operant conditioning as it is in classical conditioning? Basically, yes. **Operant stimulus generalization** is the tendency to respond to stimuli similar to those that preceded operant reinforcement. That is, a reinforced response tends to be made again when similar antecedents are present. Assume, for instance, that you have been reliably rewarded for kicking one particular vending machine. Your kicking response tends to occur in the presence of that machine. It has come under stimulus control. Now let's say that there are three other machines on campus identical to the one that pays off. Because they are similar, your kicking response will very likely transfer to them. If each of these machines also pays off when kicked, your kicking response may *generalize* to other machines only mildly similar to the original. Similar generalization explains why children may

temporarily call all men *daddy*—much to the embarrassment of their parents.

DISCRIMINATION   Meanwhile, back at the vending machine . . . . As stated earlier, to discriminate means to respond differently to varied stimuli. Because one vending machine reinforced your kicking response, you began kicking other identical machines (generalization). Because these also paid off, you began kicking similar machines (more generalization). If kicking these new machines has no effect, the kicking response that generalized to them will extinguish because of non-reinforcement. Thus, your response to machines of a particular size and color is consistently rewarded, whereas the same response to different machines is extinguished. Through **operant stimulus discrimination,** you have learned to differentiate between antecedent stimuli that signal reward and non-reward. As a result, your response pattern will shift to match these **discriminative stimuli** (stimuli that precede rewarded and non-rewarded responses).

A discriminative stimulus that most drivers are familiar with is a police car on the freeway. This stimulus is a clear signal that a specific set of reinforcement contingencies applies. As you have probably observed, the presence of a police car brings about rapid reductions in driving speed, lane changes, tailgating, and, in Los Angeles, gun battles.

Stimulus discrimination is also aptly illustrated by the sniffer dogs who locate drugs and explosives at airports and border crossings. Operant discrimination is used to teach these dogs to recognize contraband. During training, they are reinforced only for approaching containers baited with drugs or explosives.

Stimulus discrimination clearly has a tremendous impact on human behavior. Learning to recognize different automobile brands, birds, animals, wines, types of music, and even the answers on psychology tests all depends, in part, on operant discrimination learning. (See "Stimulus Control—The Cat's Meow" for a further look at how discriminations are formed.)

A CLOSER LOOK

STIMULUS CONTROL—THE CAT'S MEOW

The role of discriminative stimuli may be clarified by an interesting feat achieved by Jack, a psychologist friend of the author's. Jack decided to teach his cat to say its name. Here is how he proceeded. First, he gave the cat a pat on the back. If the cat meowed in a way that sounded anything like its name, Jack immediately gave the cat a small amount of food. If the cat made this unusual meow at other times, it received nothing. This process was repeated many times each day.

By gradual shaping, the cat's meow was made to sound very much like its name. Also, this peculiar meow came under stimulus control: When it received a pat on the back, the cat said its name; without the pat, it remained silent or meowed normally. Psychologists symbolize a stimulus that precedes reinforced responses as an S+. Discriminative stimuli that precede unrewarded responses are symbolized as S− (Schwartz & Robbins, 1995). Thus, the accompanying diagram summarizes the cat's training.

I should add at this point that I was unaware that Jack had a new cat or that he had trained it. I went to visit him one night and met the cat on the front steps. I gave the cat a pat on the back and said, "Hi kitty, what's your name?" Imagine my surprise when the cat immediately replied, "Ralph"!

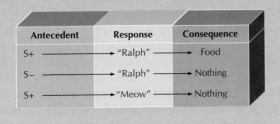

Antecedent	Response	Consequence
S+ ———————→	"Ralph" ———→	Food
S− ———————→	"Ralph" ———→	Nothing
S+ ———————→	"Meow" ———→	Nothing

Fixed interval schedule *A reinforcer is given only when a correct response is made after a set amount of time has passed since the last reinforced response. Responses made during the time interval are not reinforced.*

Variable interval schedule *A reinforcer is given for the first correct response made after a varied amount of time has passed since the last reinforced response. Responses made during the time interval are not reinforced.*

Stimulus control *Stimuli present when an operant response is acquired tend to control when and where the response is made.*

Operant stimulus generalization *The tendency to respond to stimuli similar to those that preceded operant reinforcement.*

Operant stimulus discrimination *The tendency to make an operant response when stimuli previously associated with reward are present and to withhold the response when stimuli associated with non-reward are present.*

Discriminative stimuli *Stimuli that precede rewarded and non-rewarded responses in operant conditioning.*

PARTIAL REINFORCEMENT AND STIMULUS CONTROL

RELATE

Think of something you do that is reinforced only part of the time. Do you pursue this activity persistently? How have you been affected by partial reinforcement?

See if you can think of at least one everyday example of the four basic schedules of reinforcement.

Doors that are meant to be pushed outward have metal plates on them. Those that are meant to be pulled inward have handles. Do these discriminative stimuli affect your behavior? (If they don't, how's your nose doing?)

LEARNING CHECK

1. Two aspects of stimulus control are _____ and _____.

2. Responding tends to occur in the presence of discriminative stimuli associated with reinforcement and tends not to occur in the presence of discriminative stimuli associated with non-reinforcement. T or F?

3. Stimulus generalization refers to making an operant response in the presence of stimuli similar to those that preceded reinforcement. T or F?

4. When a reward follows every response, it is called
   a. continuous reinforcement *b.* fixed reinforcement *c.* ratio reinforcement *d.* controlled reinforcement

5. Partial reinforcement tends to produce slower responding and reduced resistance to extinction. T or F?

6. The schedule of reinforcement associated with playing slot machines and other types of gambling is
   a. fixed ratio *b.* variable ratio *c.* fixed interval *d.* variable interval

CRITICAL THINKING

7. A business owner who pays employees an hourly wage wants to increase productivity. How could the owner make more effective use of reinforcement?

8. How could you use conditioning principles to teach a dog or a cat to come when called?

9. Is the beep on telephone message recorders a discriminative stimulus?

Answers:

1. generalization, discrimination 2. T 3. T 4. a 5. T 6. F 6. b 7. Continuing to use fixed interval rewards (hourly wage or salary) would guarantee a basic level of income for employees. To reward extra effort, the owner could add some fixed ratio reinforcement (such as incentives, bonuses, commissions, or profit sharing) to employees' pay. 8. An excellent way to train a pet to come when you call is to give a distinctive call or whistle each time you feed the animal. This makes the signal a secondary reinforcer and a discriminative stimulus for reward (food). Of course, it also helps to directly reinforce an animal with praise, petting, or food for coming when called. 9. Yes, it is. The beep is a signal that speaking will pay off (your message will be recorded). Most of us are well conditioned to "wait for the beep" before talking.

PUNISHMENT—PUTTING THE BRAKES ON BEHAVIOR

Spankings, reprimands, fines, jail sentences, firings, failing grades, and the like are commonly used to control behavior. Clearly, the story of learning is unfinished without a return to the topic of punishment. Recall that **punishment** lowers the probability that a response will occur again. To be most effective, punishment must be given contingently (only after an undesired response occurs).

Punishers, like reinforcers, are best defined by observing their effects on behavior. A **punisher** is any consequence that reduces the frequency of a target behavior. It is not always possible to know ahead of time what will act as a punisher for a particular person. For example, when Jason's mother reprimanded him for throwing toys, he stopped doing it. In this instance, the reprimand was a punisher. However, Chris is starved for attention of any kind from his parents, who both work full-time. For Chris, a reprimand, or even a spanking, might actually reinforce toy throwing. Remember, too, that a punisher can be either the onset of an unpleasant event or the removal of a positive state of affairs (response cost).

Variables Affecting Punishment

How effective is punishment? Many people assume that punishment stops unacceptable behavior. Is this always true? Actually the effectiveness of punishers depends greatly on their *timing, consistency,* and *intensity.* Punishment works best when it occurs as the response is being made, or *immediately* afterward (timing), and when it is given *each time* a response occurs (consistency). Thus, you could effectively (and humanely) punish a dog that barks incessantly by spraying water on its nose each time it barks. Ten to 15 such treatments are usually enough to greatly reduce barking. This would not be the case if you ap-

Punishers are consequences that lower the probability that a response will be made again. Receiving a traffic citation is directly punishing because the driver is delayed and reprimanded. Paying a fine and higher insurance rates add to the punishment, in the form of response cost.

plied punishment haphazardly or long after the barking stopped. If you discover that your dog dug up a tree and ate it while you were gone, punishing the dog hours later will do little good. Likewise, the commonly heard childhood threat, "Wait till your father comes home, then you'll be sorry," just makes the father a feared brute; it doesn't effectively punish an undesirable response.

Severe punishment (an intensely aversive or unpleasant stimulus) can be extremely effective in stopping behavior. If 3-year-old Beavis sticks his finger in a light socket and gets a shock, that may be the last time he *ever* tries it. More often, however, punishment only temporarily *suppresses* a response. If the response is still reinforced, punishment may be particularly ineffective. Responses suppressed by **mild punishment** usually reappear later. If 7-year-old Alissa sneaks a snack from the refrigerator before dinner and is punished for it, she may pass up snacks for a short time. But because snack sneaking was also rewarded by the sneaked snack, she will probably try sneaky snacking again, sometime later (the sneaky little devil).

This fact was demonstrated by slapping rats on the paw as they were bar pressing in a Skinner box. Two groups of well-trained rats were placed on extinction. One group was punished with a slap for each bar press, while the other group was not. It might seem that the slap would cause bar pressing to extinguish more quickly. Yet, this was not the case, as you can see in ❖Figure 9.20. Punishment temporarily slowed responding, but it did not cause more rapid extinction. Slapping the paws of rats or children has little permanent effect on a reinforced response. It is worth stating again, however, that intense punishment may permanently suppress responding, even for actions as basic as eating. Animals severely punished while eating may never eat again (Bertsch, 1976).

Using Punishment Wisely

In light of its drawbacks, should punishment be used to control behavior? Parents, teachers, animal trainers, and the like have

BRIDGES

Learning principles are only one element of effective child management.

See Chapter 4, pages 116–118, for additional techniques.

three basic tools to control simple learning: (1) Reinforcement strengthens responses, (2) non-reinforcement causes responses to extinguish, and (3) punishment suppresses responses. (Consult ❖Figure 9.21 to refresh your memory about the different types of reinforcement and punishment.) These tools work best in combination.

If punishment is used at all, it should always be mild. But remember that mild punishment will be ineffective if reinforcers are still available in the situation. That's why it is best to also reward an alternate, desired response. For example, a child who has a habit of taking toys from her sister should not just be reprimanded for it. She should also be praised for cooperative play and sharing her toys with others. Punishment tells a person or an animal that a response was "wrong." However, it does not say what the "right" response is, so it *does not teach new behaviors.* If reinforcement is missing from the formula, punishment becomes less effective.

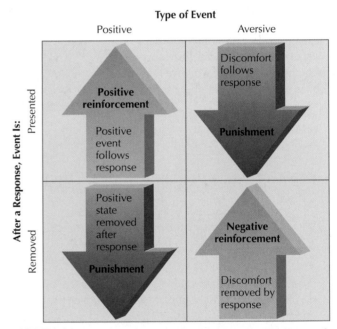

❖ **FIGURE 9.21** *Types of reinforcement and punishment. The impact of an event depends on whether it is presented or removed after a response is made. Each square defines one possibility: Arrows pointing upward indicate that responding is increased; downward-pointing arrows indicate that responding is decreased. (Adapted from Kazdin, 1975.)*

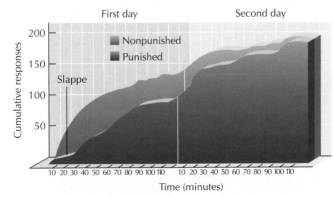

❖ **FIGURE 9.20** *The effect of punishment on extinction. Immediately after punishment, the rate of bar pressing is suppressed, but by the end of the second day, the effects of punishment have disappeared. (After B. F. Skinner,* The Behavior of Organisms. © *1938. D. Appleton-Century Co., Inc. Reprinted by permission of Prentice-Hall, Inc.)*

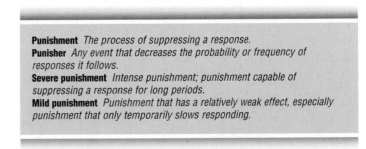

Punishment *The process of suppressing a response.*
Punisher *Any event that decreases the probability or frequency of responses it follows.*
Severe punishment *Intense punishment; punishment capable of suppressing a response for long periods.*
Mild punishment *Punishment that has a relatively weak effect, especially punishment that only temporarily slows responding.*

In a situation that poses immediate danger, such as when a child reaches for something hot or a dog runs into the street, mild punishment may prevent disaster. Punishment in such cases works best when it produces actions *incompatible* with the response you want to suppress. Let's say a child reaches toward a stove burner. Would a swat on the bottom serve as an effective punisher? Probably so. It would be better, however, to slap the child's outstretched hand so it will be *withdrawn* from the source of danger. See "If You Must Punish, Here's How" for some additional tips on using punishment.

Side Effects of Punishment

What are the drawbacks of using punishment? The basic problem with punishment is that it is **aversive** (painful or uncomfortable). As a result, people and situations associated with punishment tend, through classical conditioning, to become feared, resented, or disliked. The aversive nature of punishment makes it especially poor to use when teaching children to eat politely or in toilet training.

ESCAPE AND AVOIDANCE   A second major problem is that aversive stimuli encourage escape and avoidance learning. In **escape learning** we learn to make a response in order to end an aversive stimulus. Escape learning simply reflects the operation of negative reinforcement, as the following example shows.

A dog is placed in a two-compartment cage called a shuttle box. If the dog is shocked while in one of the compartments, it will quickly learn to jump to the other compartment to *escape* the shock. If a buzzer is sounded 10 seconds before each shock begins, the dog will soon learn to associate the buzzer with shock. It will then *avoid* pain by jumping *before* the shock begins. (Solomon & Wynne, 1953)

Avoidance learning appears to involve *both* classical and operant conditioning (Levis, 1989). In a shuttle box, a dog first learns, through classical conditioning, to fear the buzzer. (The buzzer is a CS, which is followed by shock, a US for pain and fear.) Each time the buzzer sounds, the dog becomes fearful. But, by jumping to the "safe" compartment, the dog can end the unpleasant fear it feels. Therefore, learning to jump *before* the onset of the shock is negatively reinforced by fear reduction. This is the operant part of avoidance learning.

Once avoidance is learned, it is very persistent. The electric shock in a shuttle box can be turned off, yet the dog will continue to leap from the compartment each time the buzzer sounds. This fact is rather puzzling: If the buzzer is never followed by shock, why doesn't fear of the buzzer extinguish? The dog, it seems, has learned to *expect* that the buzzer will be followed by shock. If the dog leaves before the shock would normally occur, it gets no new information to change the expectancy (Schwartz & Robbins, 1995).

Escape and avoidance learning are a regular part of daily experience. For example, if you work with a loud and obnoxious person, you may

BRIDGES

The connection between frustration and aggression is strong. But does frustration always produce aggression?

For more information, see Chapter 16, pages 525–527, and Chapter 20, pages 681–682.

For more information, see Chapter 16, pages 525–527, and Chapter 20, pages 681–682.

USING PSYCHOLOGY

IF YOU MUST PUNISH, HERE'S HOW

There are times when punishment may be necessary to manage the behavior of an animal, child, or even another adult. If you feel that you must punish, here are some tips to keep in mind.

1. *Don't use punishment at all if you can discourage misbehavior in other ways.* Make liberal use of positive reinforcement, especially praise, to encourage good behavior. Also, try extinction first: See what happens if you ignore a problem behavior; or shift attention to a desirable activity and then reinforce it with praise.

2. *Apply punishment during, or immediately after, misbehavior.* Of course, immediate punishment is not always possible. With older children and adults, you can bridge the delay by clearly stating what act you are punishing. If you cannot punish an animal *immediately,* wait for the next instance of misbehavior.

3. *Use the minimum punishment necessary to suppress misbehavior.* Often, a verbal rebuke or a scolding is enough. Avoid harsh physical punishment. (Never slap a child's face, for instance.) Taking away privileges or other positive reinforcers (response cost) is usually best

for older children and adults. Frequent punishment may lose its effectiveness, and harsh or excessive punishment has serious negative side effects (discussed in a moment).

4. *Be consistent.* Be very clear about what you regard as misbehavior. Punish every time the misbehavior occurs. Don't punish for something one day and ignore it the next. If you are usually willing to give a child three chances, don't change the rule and explode without warning after a first offense. Both parents should try to punish their children for the same things and in the same way.

5. *Expect anger from a punished person.* Briefly acknowledge this anger, but be careful not to reinforce it. Be willing to admit your mistake if you wrongfully punished someone or if you punished too severely.

6. *Punish with kindness and respect.* Allow the punished person to retain self-respect. For instance, do not punish a person in front of others, if at all possible. A strong, trusting relationship tends to minimize behavior problems. Ideally, others should *want* to behave well to get your praise, not because they fear punishment.

at first escape from conversations with him to obtain relief. Later, you may dodge him altogether. This is an example of **avoidance learning** (making a response in order to postpone or prevent discomfort). Each time you sidestep him, your avoidance is again reinforced by a sense of relief. In many situations involving frequent punishment, similar desires to escape and avoid are activated. For example, children who run away from punishing parents (escape) may soon learn to lie about their behavior (avoidance) or to spend as much time away from home as possible (also an avoidance response).

AGGRESSION A third problem with punishment is that it can greatly increase *aggression*. Animals react to pain by attacking whomever or whatever else is around (Azrin et al., 1965). A common example is the faithful dog that nips its owner during a painful procedure at the veterinarian's office. Likewise, humans who are in pain have a tendency to lash out at others.

We also know that one of the most common responses to frustration is aggression. Generally speaking, punishment is painful, frustrating, or both. Punishment, therefore, sets up a powerful environment for learning aggression. When a child is spanked, the child may feel angry, frustrated, and hostile. What if the child then goes outside and hits a brother, a sister, or a neighbor? The danger is that aggressive acts may feel good because they release anger and frustration. If so, aggression has been rewarded and will tend to occur again in other frustrating situations.

A recent study found that children who are physically punished are more likely to engage in aggressive, impulsive, antisocial behavior (Straus & Mouradian, 1998). Another study of angry adolescent boys found that they were severely punished at home. This suppressed their misbehavior at home but made them more aggressive elsewhere. Parents were often surprised to learn that their "good boys" were in trouble for fighting at school (Bandura & Walters, 1959). Yet another study of classroom discipline problems found that physical punishment, yelling, and humiliation are generally ineffective. Positive reinforcement, in the form of praise, approval, and reward, is much more likely to quell classroom disruptions, defiance, and inattention (Tulley & Chiu, 1995).

SHOULD YOU PUNISH OR NOT? To summarize, the most common error in using punishment is to rely on it alone for training or discipline. The overall emotional adjustment of a child or pet disciplined mainly by reward is usually superior to one disciplined mainly by punishment. Frequent punishment makes a person or an animal unhappy, confused, anxious, aggressive, and fearful.

Parents and teachers should be aware that using punishment can be "habit forming." When children are being noisy, messy, disrespectful, or otherwise misbehaving, the temptation to punish them can be strong. The danger is that punishment often works. When it does, a sudden end to the adult's irritation acts as a negative reinforcer. This encourages the adult to use punishment more often in the future (Alberto & Troutman,

1998). Immediate silence may be golden, but its cost can be very high in terms of a child's emotional health. "Sparing the rod" will not spoil a child. In fact, the reverse is true: Two recent studies found that young children with behavior problems were harshly punished at home (Brenner & Fox, 1998; DeKlyen et al., 1998).

K N O W L E D G E   B U I L D E R

PUNISHMENT

RELATE

Think of how you were punished as a child. Was the punishment immediate? Was it consistent? What effect did these factors have on your behavior? Was the punishment effective? Which side effects of punishment have you witnessed or experienced?

LEARNING CHECK

1. Negative reinforcement increases responding; punishment suppresses responding. T or F?

2. Three factors that greatly influence the effects of punishment are timing, consistency, and _____.

3. Mild punishment tends to only temporarily _____ a response that is also reinforced.
   a. enhance b. aggravate c. replace d. suppress

4. Three undesired side effects of punishment are (1) conditioning of fear and resentment, (2) encouragement of aggression, and (3) the learning of escape or _____ responses.

5. Using punishment can be "habit forming" because putting a stop to someone else's irritating behavior can _____ _____ the person who applies the punishment.

CRITICAL THINKING

6. Using the concept of partial reinforcement, can you explain why inconsistent punishment is especially ineffective?

7. Escape and avoidance learning have been applied to encourage automobile seat belt use. Can you explain how?

Answers:
1. T 2. intensity 3. *d* 4. avoidance 5. negatively reinforce 6. An inconsistently punished response will continue to be reinforced on a partial schedule, which makes it even more resistant to extinction. 7. Many automobiles have an unpleasant buzzer that sounds if the ignition key is turned before the driver's seat belt is fastened. Most drivers quickly learn to fasten the belt to stop the annoying sound. This is an example of escape conditioning. Avoidance conditioning is evident when a driver learns to buckle up before the buzzer sounds.

Aversive stimulus *A stimulus that is painful or uncomfortable.*
Escape learning *Learning to make a response in order to end an aversive stimulus.*
Avoidance learning *Learning to make a response in order to postpone or prevent discomfort.*

COGNITIVE LEARNING—BEYOND CONDITIONING

Is all learning just a connection between stimuli and responses? Some learning can be thought of this way. But, as we have seen, even basic conditioning has "mental" elements. As a human, you can anticipate future reward or punishment and react accordingly. (You may wonder why this doesn't seem to work when a doctor or dentist says, "This won't hurt a bit." Here's why: They lie!) There is no doubt that human learning includes a large *cognitive*, or mental, dimension. As humans, we are greatly affected by information, expectations, perceptions, mental images, and the like.

Loosely speaking, **cognitive learning** refers to understanding, knowing, anticipating, or otherwise making use of information-rich higher mental processes. Cognitive learning extends beyond basic conditioning into the realms of memory, thinking, problem solving, and language. Because these topics are covered in later chapters, our discussion here is limited to a first look at learning beyond conditioning.

COGNITIVE MAPS How do you navigate around the town where you live? Is it fair to assume that you have simply learned to make a series of right and left turns to get from one point to another? It is far more likely that you have an overall mental picture of how the town is laid out. This *cognitive map* acts as a guide, even when you must detour or take a new route. A **cognitive map** is an internal representation of an area, such as a maze, city, or campus. Even the lowly rat—not exactly a mental giant—learns *where* food is found in a maze, not just which turns to make to reach the food (Tolman et al., 1946). In a

It's easy to get lost when visiting a new city if you don't have a cognitive map of the area. Printed maps help, but they may still leave you puzzled until you begin to form a mental representation of major landmarks and directions.

sense, cognitive maps also apply to other kinds of knowledge. For instance, it could be said that you have been developing a "map" of psychology while reading this book. This may be why students sometimes find it helpful to draw pictures or diagrams of how they envision concepts fitting together.

LATENT LEARNING Cognitive learning is also revealed by latent (hidden) learning. **Latent learning** occurs without obvious reinforcement and remains hidden until reinforcement is provided. Here's an example from a classic animal study: Two groups of rats were allowed to explore a maze. The animals in one group found food at the far end of the maze. Soon, they learned to rapidly make their way through the maze when released. Rats in the second group were unrewarded and showed no signs of learning. But later, when the "uneducated" rats were given food, they ran the maze as quickly as the rewarded group (Tolman & Honzik, 1930). Although there was no outward sign of it, the unrewarded animals had learned their way around the maze. Their learning, therefore, remained latent at first (❖Fig. 9.22).

How did they learn if there was no reinforcement? Just satisfying curiosity can be enough to reward learning (Harlow & Harlow, 1962). In humans, latent learning is related to higher level abilities, such as anticipating future reward. For example, if you give an attractive classmate a ride home, you may make mental notes about how to get to his or her house, even if a date is only a remote future possibility.

DISCOVERY LEARNING Much of what is meant by cognitive learning is summarized by the word *understanding*. Each of us has, at times, learned ideas by **rote** (repetition and memorization). Although rote learning is efficient, many psychologists believe that learning is more lasting and flexible when people *discover* facts and principles on their own. In **discovery learning**, skills are gained by insight and understanding instead of by rote. Discovery learning is an important element of computerized educational simulations and instructional games, mentioned earlier (de Jong & van Joolingen, 1998).

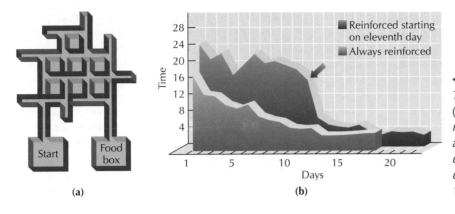

(a)   **(b)**

❖ **FIGURE 9.22** *Latent learning. (a) The maze used by Tolman and Honzik to demonstrate latent learning by rats. (b) Results of the experiment. Notice the rapid improvement in performance that occurred when food was made available to the previously unreinforced animals. This indicates that learning had occurred, but that it remained hidden or unexpressed. (Adapted from Tolman & Honzik, 1930.)*

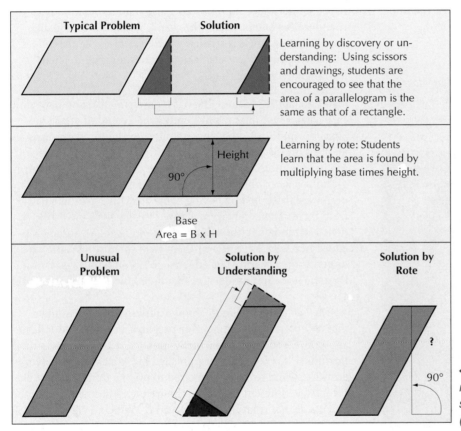

❖ **FIGURE 9.23** *Learning by understanding and by rote. For some types of learning, understanding may be superior, although both types of learning are useful. (After Wertheimer, 1959.)*

As long as learning occurs, what difference does it make if it is by discovery or by rote? ❖Figure 9.23 illustrates the difference. Two groups of students were taught to calculate the area of a parallelogram. Some were encouraged to see that a "piece" of a parallelogram could be "moved" to create a rectangle. Later, they were better able to solve unusual problems. Students who simply memorized a rule were confused by the same problems (Wertheimer, 1959). As this implies, discovery leads to a better understanding of new or unusual problems. Whenever possible, people should try new strategies and discover new solutions during learning (McDaniel & Schlager, 1990).

Cognitive learning *Higher level learning involving thinking, knowing, understanding, and anticipation.*
Cognitive map *Internal images or other mental representations of an area (maze, city, campus, and so forth) that underlie an ability to choose alternate paths to the same goal.*
Latent learning *Learning that occurs without obvious reinforcement and that remains unexpressed until reinforcement is provided.*
Rote learning *Learning that takes place mechanically, through repetition and memorization, or by learning rules.*
Discovery learning *Learning based on insight and understanding.*

MODELING—DO AS I DO, NOT AS I SAY

The class watches intently as a skilled potter pulls a spinning ball of clay into the form of a vase. There is little doubt that many skills are learned by what Albert Bandura (1971) calls *observational learning,* or *modeling.* **Observational learning** is achieved by watching and imitating the actions of another person or by noting the consequences of the person's actions. In other words, modeling is any process in which information is imparted by example, before direct practice is allowed (Rosenthal & Steffek, 1991).

The value of learning by observation is obvious: Imagine trying to *tell* someone how to tie a shoe, do a dance step, crochet, or play a guitar. Bandura believes that anything that can be learned from direct experience can be learned by observation. Often, this allows a person to skip the tedious trial-and-error stage of learning.

Observational Learning

It seems obvious that we learn by observation, but how does it occur? By observing a **model** (someone who serves as an exam-

Observational learning often imparts large amounts of information that would be difficult to obtain by reading instructions or memorizing rules.

ple), a person may (1) learn new responses, (2) learn to carry out or avoid previously learned responses (depending on what happens to the model for doing the same thing), or (3) learn a general rule that can be applied to various situations.

For observational learning to occur, several things must take place. First, the learner must pay *attention* to the model and *remember* what was done. (A beginning auto mechanic might be interested enough to watch an entire tune-up but unable to remember all the steps.) Next, the learner must be able to *reproduce* the modeled behavior. (Sometimes this is a matter of practice, but it may be that the learner will never be able to perform the behavior. I may admire the feats of world-class gymnasts, but with no amount of practice could I ever reproduce them.) If a model is *successful* at a task or *rewarded* for a response, the learner is more likely to imitate the behavior. In general, models who are attractive, trustworthy, capable, admired, powerful, or high in status also tend to be imitated (Bandura & Walters, 1963b; Brewer & Wann, 1998). Finally, once a new response is tried, *normal reinforcement determines if it will be repeated thereafter.* (Notice the similarity to latent learning, described earlier.)

IMITATING MODELS   Modeling has a powerful effect on behavior. In a classic experiment, children watched an adult attack a large blowup Bo-Bo the Clown doll. Some children saw an adult sit on the doll, punch it, hit it with a hammer, and kick it around the room. Others saw a movie of these actions. A third group saw a cartoon version of the aggression. Later, the children were frustrated by having some attractive toys taken away from them. Then, they were allowed to play with the Bo-Bo doll. Most imitated the adult's attack (❖Fig. 9.24). Some even added new aggressive acts of their own! Interestingly, the cartoon was only slightly less effective in encouraging aggression than the live adult model and the filmed model (Bandura et al., 1963).

Then do children blindly imitate adults? No. Remember that observational learning only prepares a person to duplicate a response. Whether it is actually imitated depends on whether the model was rewarded or punished for what was done. Nevertheless, when parents tell a child to do one thing but model a completely different response, children tend to imitate what the parents *do, not* what they *say* (Bryan & Walbek, 1970). Thus, through modeling, children learn not only attitudes, gestures, emotions, and personality traits but also fears, anxieties, and bad habits. A good example is the children of smokers, who are

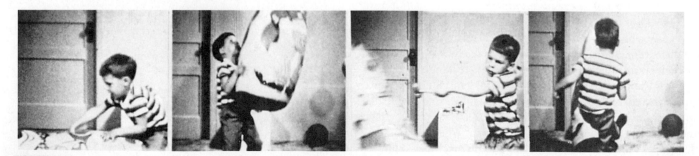

❖ **FIGURE 9.24** *A nursery school child imitates the aggressive behavior of an adult model he has just seen in a movie. (Photos courtesy of Albert Bandura.)*

much more likely to try smoking than children from smoke-free homes (Rowe et al., 1996).

Now, consider a typical situation: Little Shawn-Erin-Ringo-Jeremy Jones has just been interrupted at play by his younger brother, Mildew. Angry and frustrated, he screams at Mildew. This behavior interrupts his father's TV watching. Father promptly spanks little Shawn-Erin-Ringo-Jeremy, saying, "This will teach you to hit your little brother." And it will. Because of modeling effects, it is unrealistic to expect a child to "Do as I say, not as I do." The message the father has given the child is clear: "You have frustrated me; therefore, I will hit you." The next time little Shawn-Erin-Ringo-Jeremy is frustrated, it won't be surprising if he imitates his father and hits his brother.

Modeling and Television

Does television promote observational learning? The impact of TV can be found in these figures: By the time the average person has graduated from high school, she or he will have viewed some 15,000 hours of TV, compared with only 11,000 hours spent in the classroom. In that time, such viewers will have seen some 18,000 murders and countless acts of robbery, arson, bombing, torture, and beatings. It's true that TV programming has improved somewhat during the last decade. Overall, however, violent acts, dynamite blasts, gun battles, high-speed car wrecks, stereotypes, and sexism still prevail. Children watching Saturday morning cartoons see a chilling 26 or more violent acts each hour (Pogatchnik, 1990).

Life after TV

What effect does the North American penchant for TV watching have on behavior? To answer this question, a team of researchers found a town in northwestern Canada that did not receive TV broadcasts. Discovering that the town was about to get TV, the team seized a rare opportunity. Tannis Williams and her colleagues carefully tested residents of the town just before TV arrived and again 2 years later. This natural experiment revealed that after the tube came to town:

- Reading development among children declined (Corteen & Williams, 1986).
- Children's scores on tests of creativity dropped (Harrison & Williams, 1986).

Televised violence may promote observational learning of aggression. In addition to providing poor behavioral models, constant exposure to aggressive imagery can lower viewers' emotional sensitivity to violence.

- Children's perceptions of sex roles became more stereotyped (Kimball, 1986).
- There was a significant increase in both verbal and physical aggression (❖Fig. 9.25). This occurred for both boys and girls, and it applied equally to children who were high or low in aggression before they began watching TV (Joy et al., 1986).

TELEVISED AGGRESSION   The last finding comes as no surprise. Studies show conclusively that if large groups of children watch a great deal of televised violence, they will be more prone to behave aggressively (Hogben, 1998; Hughes & Hasbrouck, 1996). In other words, not all children will become more aggressive, but many will. Incidentally, playing violent video games also tends to encourage greater hostility (Ballard & West, 1996; Dietz, 1998; Kirsch, 1998). The mass murder at Colombine High School in Littleton, Colorado, may be an example. Dylan Klebold and Eric Harris, who killed 12 other students and a teacher before committing suicide were avid fans of violent video games.

Is it fair to say, then, that televised violence causes aggression in viewers, especially children? Fortunately, that would be an exaggeration. Televised violence can make aggression more likely, but it does not invariably "cause" it to occur (Freedman, 1984; Levinger, 1986). Many other factors affect the chances that hostile thoughts will be turned into actions (Berkowitz, 1984). Among children, one such factor is the extent to which a child identifies with aggressive characters (Huesmann et al.,

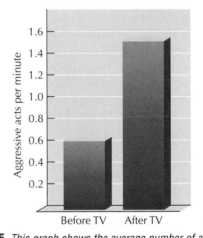

❖ **FIGURE 9.25** *This graph shows the average number of aggressive acts per minute before and after television broadcasts were introduced into a Canadian town. The increase in aggression after television watching began was significant. Two other towns that already had television were used for comparison. Neither showed significant increases in aggression during the same time period. (Data compiled from Joy et al., 1986.)*

Observational learning *Learning achieved by watching and imitating the actions of another or noting the consequences of those actions.*
Model *A person who serves as an example in observational learning.*

TV heroes can act as powerful models for observational learning of aggression.

1983). That's why it is so sad to find TV heroes behaving aggressively, as well as villains.

A case in point is the popular *Power Rangers* TV programs for children. In each episode, the Power Rangers "morph" into superheroes who use karate and other violent actions to conquer monsters. After watching an episode of the Power Rangers, a group of 7-year-old children committed 7 times more aggressive acts than a control group that didn't watch. The aggressive children hit, kicked, and karate-chopped their peers, often directly imitating the Power Rangers (Boyatzis, Matillo, & Nesbitt, 1995). Younger children, in particular, are more likely to be influenced by such programs because they don't fully recognize that the characters and stories are fantasies (McKenna & Ossoff, 1998).

Youngsters who believe that aggression is an acceptable way to solve problems, who believe that TV violence is realistic, and who identify with TV characters are most likely to copy televised aggression (Huesmann, Moise, & Podolski, 1997). In view of such findings, it is understandable that Canada, Norway, and Switzerland have restricted the amount of permissible violence on television. Should all countries do the same?

A LOOK AHEAD   Conditioning principles are often derived from animal experiments. However, it should be apparent that the same principles apply to human behavior. Perhaps the best way to appreciate this fact is to observe how reinforcement affects your own behavior. With this in mind, the upcoming Psychology in Action section proposes a personal experiment in operant conditioning. We'll also consider steps you can take to better manage your learning at school. Don't miss these coming attractions!

RELATE

Try to think of at least one personal example of each of these concepts: cognitive map, latent learning, discovery learning.

Describe a skill you have learned primarily through observational learning. How did modeling help you learn?

What entertainment or sports personalities did you identify with when you were a child? How did it affect your behavior?

LEARNING CHECK

1. An internal representation of relationships is referred to as a
_____ _____.

2. Learning that suddenly appears when a reward or incentive for performance is given is called
   a. discovery learning b. latent learning c. rote learning d. reminiscence

3. Psychologists use the term _____ to describe observational learning.

4. If a model is successful, rewarded, attractive, or high in status, his or her behavior is
   a. difficult to reproduce b. less likely to be attended to c. more likely to be imitated d. subject to positive transfer

5. Children who observed a live adult behave aggressively became more aggressive; those who observed movie and cartoon aggression did not. T or F?

6. Children are most likely to imitate TV characters with whom they identify, but this applies primarily to characters who are nonviolent. T or F?

7. Psychological research indicates that televised violence causes aggressive behavior in children. T or F?

CRITICAL THINKING

8. Draw a map of your school's campus as you picture it now. Draw a map of the campus as you pictured it after your first visit. Why do the maps differ?

9. Children who watch many aggressive programs on television tend to be more aggressive than average. Why doesn't this observation prove that televised aggression causes aggressive behavior?

Answers:

1. cognitive map 2. b 3. modeling 4. c 5. F 6. F 7. F 8. Your cognitive map of the campus has undoubtedly become more accurate and intricate over time as you have added details to it. Your drawings should reflect this change. 9. Because the observation is based on a correlation. Children who are already aggressive may choose to watch more aggressive programs, rather than being made aggressive by them. It took experimental studies to verify that televised aggression promotes aggression by viewers.

BEHAVIORAL SELF-MANAGEMENT

This discussion could be the start of one of the most personal applications of psychology in this book. Many people have learned to use reinforcement to alter or manage their own behavior (Watson & Tharp, 1996). This, then, is an invitation to carry out a self-management project of your own. Would you like to increase the number of hours you spend studying each week? Would you like to exercise more, attend more classes, concentrate longer, or read more books? All these activities and many others can be improved by following the rules described here.

SELF-MANAGED BEHAVIOR—A REWARDING PROJECT

The principles of operant conditioning can be adapted to manage your own behavior. Here's how:

1. **Choose a target behavior.** Identify the activity you want to change.
2. **Record a baseline.** Record how much time you currently spend performing the target activity, or count the number of desired or undesired responses you make each day.
3. **Establish goals.** Remember the principle of shaping, and set realistic goals for gradual improvement on each successive week. Also, set daily goals that add up to the weekly goal.
4. **Choose reinforcers.** If you meet your daily goal, what reward will you allow yourself? Daily rewards might be watching television, eating a candy bar, socializing with friends, playing a musical instrument, or whatever you enjoy. Also establish a weekly reward. If you reach your weekly goal, what reward will you allow yourself? A movie? A dinner out? A weekend hike?
5. **Record your progress.** Keep accurate records of the amount of time spent each day on the desired activity or the number of times you make the desired response.
6. **Reward successes.** If you meet your daily goal, collect your reward. If you fall short, be honest with yourself and skip the reward. Do the same for your weekly goal.
7. **Adjust your plan as you learn more about your behavior.** Overall progress will reinforce your attempts at self-management.

If you have trouble finding rewards, or if you don't want to use the entire system, remember that anything done often can serve as reinforcement. This is known as the **Premack principle.** It is named after

David Premack, a psychologist who popularized its use. For example, if you watch television every night and want to study more, make it a rule not to turn on the set until you have studied for an hour (or whatever length of time you choose). Then lengthen the requirement each week. Here is a sample of one student's plan:

1. *Target behavior:* number of hours spent studying for school.
2. *Recorded baseline:* an average of 25 minutes per day for a weekly total of 3 hours.
3. *Goal for the first week:* an increase in study time to 40 minutes per day; weekly goal of 5 hours total study time. *Goal for second week:* 50 minutes per day and 6 hours per week. *Goal for third week:* 1 hour per day and 7 hours per week. *Ultimate goal:* to reach and maintain 14 hours per week study time.
4. *Daily reward for reaching goal:* 1 hour of guitar playing in the evening; no playing if the goal is not met. Weekly reward for reaching goal: going to a movie or buying a compact disk.

SELF-RECORDING   Even if you find it difficult to give and withhold rewards, you are likely to succeed. Simply knowing that you are reaching a desired goal can be reward enough. The key to any self-management program, therefore, is **self-recording** (keeping records of response frequencies). The concept is demonstrated by students in a psychology course. Some of the students recorded their study time and graphed their daily and weekly study behavior. Even though no extra rewards were offered, these students earned better grades than others who were not required to keep records (Johnson & White, 1971).

As discussed earlier, feedback is also valuable for changing personal behavior. Feedback can help you decrease bad habits as well as increase desirable responses. Keep track of the number of times daily that you arrive late to class, smoke a cigarette, watch an hour of TV, drink a cup of coffee, bite your fingernails, swear, or whatever you are interested in changing. A simple tally on a piece of paper will do, or you can get a small mechanical counter like those used to keep golf scores or count calories. Record keeping helps break patterns, and the feedback can be motivating as you begin to make progress.

Good Ways to Break Bad Habits

How can I use learning principles to break a bad habit?   By using the methods we have discussed, you can reinforce yourself for *decreasing* unwanted behaviors, such as swearing, nail

---

Premack principle *Any high-frequency response can be used to reinforce a low-frequency response.*
Self-recording *Self-management based on keeping records of response frequencies.*

biting, criticizing others, smoking, drinking coffee, excessive TV watching, or any other behavior you choose to target. However, breaking bad habits may require some additional techniques. Here are four strategies to help you change bad habits.

ALTERNATE RESPONSES   A good strategy for change is to try to get the same reinforcement with a new response.

Example: Marta often tells jokes at the expense of others. Her friends sometimes feel hurt by her sharp-edged humor. Marta senses this and wants to change. What can she do? Usually, Marta's joke telling is reinforced by attention and approval. She could just as easily get the same reinforcement by giving other people praise or compliments. Making a change in her behavior should be easy because she will continue to receive the reinforcement she seeks.

EXTINCTION   Try to discover what is reinforcing an unwanted response and remove, avoid, or delay the reinforcement (Ferster et al., 1962).

Example: Tiffany has developed a habit of taking longer and longer "breaks" to watch TV when she should be studying. Obviously, TV watching is reinforcing her break taking. To improve her study habits, Tiffany could delay reinforcement by studying at the library or some other location a good distance from her TV.

RESPONSE CHAINS   Break up response chains that precede an undesired behavior. The key idea is to scramble the chain of events that leads to an undesired response (Watson & Tharp, 1996).

Example: Almost every night Steve comes home from work, turns on the TV, and eats a whole bag of cookies or chips. He then takes a shower and changes clothes. By dinnertime he has lost his appetite. Steve realizes he is substituting junk food for dinner. Steve could solve the problem by breaking the response chain that precedes dinner. For instance, he could shower immediately when he gets home, or he could avoid turning on the television until after dinner.

CUES AND ANTECEDENTS   Try to avoid, narrow down, or remove stimuli that elicit the bad habit.

Example: Raul wants to cut down on smoking. He has taken many smoking cues out of his surroundings by removing ashtrays, matches, and extra cigarettes from his house, car, and office. Raul should try narrowing antecedent stimuli even more. He could begin by smoking only in the lounge at work, never in his office or in his car. He could then limit his smoking to home. Then to only one room at home. Then to one chair at home. If he succeeds in getting this far, he may want to limit his smoking to only one unpleasant place, such as a bathroom, basement, or garage (Goldiamond, 1971).

CONTRACTING   If you try the techniques described here and have difficulty sticking with them, you may want to try behavioral contracting. In a **behavioral contract,** you state a specific problem behavior you want to control or a goal you want to

achieve. Also state the rewards you will receive, privileges you will forfeit, or punishments you must accept. The contract should be typed and signed by you and a person you trust.

A behavioral contract can be quite motivating, especially when mild punishment is part of the agreement. Here's an example reported by Nurnberger and Zimmerman (1970): A student working on his doctorate had completed all requirements but his dissertation, yet for 2 years he had not written a single page. A contract was drawn up for him in which he agreed to meet weekly deadlines on the number of pages he would complete. To make sure he would meet the deadlines, he wrote postdated checks. These were to be forfeited if he failed to reach his goal for the week. The checks were made out to organizations he despised (the Ku Klux Klan and American Nazi Party). From the time he signed the contract until he finished his degree, the student's work output was greatly improved.

Effective learning at school poses a special set of challenges. The next section describes some steps you can take to increase your chances of success.

SELF-REGULATED LEARNING—ACADEMIC ALL-STARS

Think for a moment about a topic that highly interests you, such as music, sports, fashion, automobiles, cooking, politics, or movies. Whatever the topic may be, you have probably learned a large amount of information about it—painlessly. How could you make your college work more like voluntary learning? An approach known as self-regulated learning might be a good start. **Self-regulated learning** is active, self-guided study. You can use the strategies described here to change passive studying into more active, goal-oriented learning (Zimmerman, 1996).

1. *Set specific, objective learning goals.* Try to begin each learning session with specific goals in mind. What knowledge or skills are you trying to master? What do you hope to accomplish? (Schunk, 1990).
2. *Plan a learning strategy.* How will you accomplish your goals? Make daily, weekly, and monthly plans for learning. Then put them into action.
3. *Be your own teacher.* Effective learners silently give themselves guidance and ask themselves questions. For example, when you are reading, you might ask yourself at the end of each paragraph, "What is the main idea here? What do I remember? What don't I understand? What do I need to review? What should I do next?"
4. *Monitor your progress.* Self-regulated learning depends on feedback. Exceptional learners keep records of their progress toward learning goals (pages read, hours of studying, assignments completed, and so forth). They quiz themselves, use study guides, and find other ways to check their understanding while learning.
5. *Use self-reinforcement.* When you meet your daily, weekly, or monthly performance standards, reward your efforts in some way. Be aware that self-praise also rewards learning.

Being able to say, "Hey, I did it!" or "Good work!" and know that you deserve it can be very reinforcing. In the long run, success, feelings of accomplishment, and personal satisfaction provide the real payoffs for self-regulated learning.

6. *Evaluate your progress and goals.* It is a good idea to frequently evaluate your performance records and goals. Are there specific areas of your work that need improvement? If you are not making good progress toward long-range goals, do you need to revise your short-term targets?

7. *Take corrective action.* If you fall short of your goals, you may need to adjust how you budget your time. You may also need to change your learning environment to deal with distractions such as watching TV, daydreaming, talking to friends, or testing the structural integrity of the walls with your stereo system.

8. *Boost your motivation.* One way to keep yourself motivated is to work for self-selected rewards, such as taking a nap, watching TV, eating ice cream, or socializing with friends. Some students also find it helpful to remind themselves that what they are learning is valuable. For example, think of a time in the future when knowing the material will be important (Wolters, 1998).

If you discover that you lack necessary knowledge or skills, ask for help, take advantage of tutoring programs, or look for sources of information beyond your courses and textbooks. Knowing how to regulate and control learning can be a key to lifelong enrichment and personal empowerment.

Getting Help

Attempting to manage or alter your own behavior may be more difficult than it sounds. If you feel you need more information, consult either of the books listed next. You will also find helpful advice in the Psychology in Action section of Chapter 18. If you do try a self-modification project or self-regulated learning but find it impossible to reach your goals, be aware that professional advice is available.

Where to Obtain More Information

- Watson, D. L., & Tharp, R. G. *Self-directed behavior.* Pacific Grove, CA: Wadsworth-Brooks/Cole, 1996.
- Williams, R. L., & Long, J. D. *Toward a self-managed life style.* Boston: Houghton Mifflin, 1991.

KNOWLEDGE BUILDER
BEHAVIORAL SELF-MANAGEMENT

RELATE

Even if you don't expect to carry out a self-management project right now, outline a plan for changing your own behavior. Be sure to describe the behavior you want to change, set goals, and identify reinforcers.

To what extent do you already engage in self-regulated learning? What additional steps could you take to become a more active, goal-oriented learner?

LEARNING CHECK

1. After a target behavior has been selected for reinforcement, it's a good idea to record a baseline so you can set realistic goals for change. T or F?

2. Self-recording, even without the use of extra rewards, can bring about desired changes in target behaviors. T or F?

3. The Premack principle states that behavioral contracting can be used to reinforce changes in behavior. T or F?

4. A self-management plan should make use of the principle of shaping by setting a graduated series of goals. T or F?

5. A key aspect of self-_____ learning is feedback, which means you should find ways to _____ your progress.

6. Self-instruction refers to the process of comparing short-term performance to long-term goals. T or F?

CRITICAL THINKING

7. How does setting daily goals in a behavioral self-management program help maximize the effects of reinforcement?

Answers:

1. T 2. T 3. F 4. T 5. regulated, monitor 6. F 7. Daily performance goals and rewards reduce the delay of reinforcement, which maximizes its impact.

Behavioral contract *A formal agreement stating behaviors to be changed and consequences that apply.*
Self-regulated learning *Active, self-guided learning.*

Focus: How does biology influence learning?

The weaverbird is a curious creature that ties a special grass knot to hold its nest together. How does it learn to make the knot? It doesn't! Weaverbirds raised in total isolation for several generations still tie the knot the first time they build a nest.

Knot tying in the weaverbird is a **fixed action pattern** (FAP). An FAP is an instinctual chain of movements found in almost all members of a species. Like other **innate** (inborn) **behaviors,** fixed action patterns help animals meet major needs in their lives (picture a cat's face-washing routine, for instance). More complicated behaviors, like the maternal instinct in lower animals, combine both fixed action patterns and various reflexes.

Do humans have instincts? Humans do not have instincts as most psychologists define them. To qualify as instinctual, a behavior must be innate, complex, and "species specific." **Species-specific behaviors** occur with little variation in almost all members of a species. Species-specific behaviors appear to be "wired into" the nervous system. Other than reflexes, no human behaviors are so rigidly programmed. However, that doesn't mean that human learning isn't affected by innate behavior.

All species, including humans, engage in a large number of **species-typical behaviors** (actions that are typical of a species, but not automatic). For example, pigeons typically peck at things when they are hungry. If you want to train a pigeon to peck a button to receive food, the pigeon will learn quickly. Likewise, if you want to teach a pigeon to flap its wings to escape an electric shock, learning will be rapid. But just try to teach a pigeon to flap its wings to receive food or to peck a button to turn off a shock to its feet. In both cases, little or no learning will take place.

Such observations suggest that there are **biological constraints,** or limits to learning—especially among animals.

Some associations between stimuli and responses or between responses and consequences are easily learned. Others can be acquired only with great difficulty. For example, many people find it very difficult to do the following: Move the tip of your right foot in a *clockwise* circle on the floor; at the same time, hold your right hand out at waist level and move it in a *counterclockwise* circle, parallel to the floor. Even for a substantial reward, you might find it hard to learn these biologically atypical movements. Perhaps we appreciate gifted musicians and athletes, in part, because they succeed at learning responses that are biologically constrained.

Biological constraints affect both classical conditioning and operant conditioning, as shown by the examples that follow.

Conditioned Fears

Through classical conditioning, it is possible to learn to fear or dislike just about anything. Is it possible, however, that some fears are easier to learn than others? Martin Seligman's (1972b) **prepared fear theory** holds that it is (❖Fig. 9.26). Seligman believes that we are prepared by evolution to readily develop fears to certain stimuli, such as snakes and spiders. Other common objects are more likely to cause pain or harm (a hammer, electric fan, light socket, or skis, for example). Even so, phobias are less likely to develop for such objects than for spiders or snakes. Seligman also believes that our readiness to learn such fears makes them highly resistant to extinction.

Researchers have also found that some fears are learned unconsciously. In one experiment, for example, pictures of snakes and spiders were flashed on a screen for just 30 milliseconds. These were followed by a mild electric shock. Even though subjects were not aware that they had seen the pictures, they began to show fear responses to snake and spider photos. Pictures of flowers and mushrooms didn't have this effect (Oehman &

❖ **FIGURE 9.26** *Which of these stimuli do you think would make a better conditioned stimulus for learned fear? Why did you choose as you did? Fear-relevant stimuli are much more effective conditioned stimuli for learned fears (Oehman & Soares, 1993).*

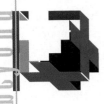

Soares, 1998). Possibly, you have acquired some fears without knowing when or where it happened.

Why should fears of "crawly things" be easier to acquire? According to Seligman's theory, such stimuli posed dangers earlier in human history. Through natural selection, they have become highly effective conditioning stimuli. Experiments in which fear was conditioned to images of spiders, snakes, neutral shapes, and electrical plugs offer some support for Seligman's theory (Hugdahl & Karker, 1981). Maybe, with further evolution, humans will develop proper fears of light sockets and skis, too!

The Reluctant Raccoon

B. F. Skinner's success in shaping pigeons to play Ping-Pong was aided by the fact that pigeons naturally peck objects. At one time, psychologists assumed that almost any voluntary response could be taught by operant conditioning. However, it has become clear that operant responses are also subject to biological constraints. For example, two psychologists, Keller and Marion Breland, went into business training animals for television shows, zoo displays, and amusement parks. Along with their successes came some revealing failures (Bailey & Bailey, 1993).

In one instance, the Brelands tried to condition a raccoon to put coins in a piggy bank for an advertisement. Instead, the raccoon repeatedly rubbed the coins together in a miserly looking fashion (Breland & Breland, 1961). No amount of reinforcement would change this behavior. The Brelands ran into similar snags with other animals. In each case an innate behavior pattern hindered learning. They called this problem **instinctive drift:** Learned responses tend to "drift" toward innate ones. The "miserly" behavior of the raccoon was simply an innate food-washing response. In view of such observations, it is wise to remember that the laws of learning operate within a framework of biological limits and possibilities.

Think about It

An advantage of biologically programmed behavior is that it prepares animals and humans to survive in their natural environments. A disadvantage is that evolution is slow. Natural selection prepares a species only for a future that resembles the biological past (Skinner, 1990).

Under normal circumstances, animals are superbly adapted to their surroundings. But throw them a curve by changing the environment in unexpected ways, and their behavior may suddenly look very "stupid." For example, if a spider begins spinning a cocoon and its silk glands are removed, it will continue to make all 6,400 spinning movements to complete the job. Then it will lay eggs in the nonexistent cocoon. We are indeed fortunate that an overriding feature that emerged in human evolution is our capacity to learn.

CONCLUSION: Not all responses are equal. Responses that are compatible with innate behavior patterns are easy to learn; those that are incompatible with biological programming are difficult to learn.

KNOWLEDGE BUILDER
BIOLOGICAL CONSTRAINTS ON LEARNING

RELATE

What FAPs and species-typical behaviors have you observed? How were they adaptive for the animals that performed them? Under what circumstances would they be inappropriate or maladaptive?

Think of some objects and animals or insects that you fear. Do your own fears seem to support the prepared fear theory?

With the concept of instinctive drift in mind, think of some behaviors that it would be very difficult to condition a dog or cat to do.

LEARNING CHECK

1. An instinctual chain of responses found in nearly all members of a species is called a _____ _____ _____.

2. Biological constraints on learning reflect underlying potentials and limitations imposed by prior conditioning. T or F?

3. A child rapidly learned to fear a neighbor's dog that knocked her down, growled, and showed its teeth. Yet, the same child seems to have no fear of the cars passing by her house. This difference may be explained by _____ _____ theory.

4. Instinctive drift can be said to have occurred any time a non-learned stimulus triggers a reflex. T or F?

CRITICAL THINKING

5. Biologically based patterns of behavior evolve very slowly. Changes based on learning occur very quickly. Can you identify a dimension of human behavior that helps bridge this gap?

Answers:

1. fixed action pattern 2. F 3. prepared fear 4. F 5. B. F. Skinner argued that cultures evolve far more quickly than organisms do. Cultures, therefore, help humans survive and adapt by passing on time-tested behavior patterns.

Fixed action pattern (FAP) *An instinctual chain of movements found in almost all members of a species.*
Innate behavior *Inborn, unlearned behavior.*
Species-specific behavior *Behavior patterns that occur with little variation in almost all members of a species.*
Species-typical behavior *Behavior patterns that are typical of a species but not automatic.*
Biological constraints *Biological limits on what an animal or person can easily learn.*
Prepared fear theory *Holds that people and animals are prepared by evolution to readily learn fears of certain stimuli.*
Instinctive drift *The tendency of learned responses to shift toward innate response patterns.*

CHAPTER IN REVIEW

What is learning?

- Learning is a relatively permanent change in behavior due to experience. Learning resulting from conditioning depends on reinforcement. Reinforcement increases the probability that a particular response will occur.
- Classical (or respondent) conditioning and instrumental (or operant) conditioning are two basic types of learning.
- In classical conditioning, a previously neutral stimulus begins to elicit a response through association with another stimulus.
- In operant conditioning, the frequency and pattern of voluntary responses are altered by their consequences.

How does classical conditioning occur?

- Classical conditioning, studied by Pavlov, occurs when a neutral stimulus (NS) is associated with an unconditioned stimulus (US).
- The US causes a reflex called the unconditioned response (UR). If the NS is consistently paired with the US, it becomes a conditioned stimulus (CS) capable of producing a response by itself. This response is a conditioned (learned) response (CR).
- When the conditioned stimulus is followed by the unconditioned stimulus, conditioning is reinforced (strengthened).
- From an informational view, conditioning creates expectancies, which alter response patterns. In classical conditioning, the CS creates an expectancy that the US will follow.
- Higher order conditioning occurs when a well-learned conditioned stimulus is used as if it were an unconditioned stimulus, bringing about further learning.
- When the CS is repeatedly presented alone, conditioning is extinguished (weakened or inhibited). After extinction seems to be complete, a rest period may lead to the temporary reappearance of a conditioned response. This is called *spontaneous recovery*.
- Through stimulus generalization, stimuli similar to the conditioned stimulus will also produce a response. Generalization gives way to stimulus discrimination when an organism learns to respond to one stimulus but not to similar stimuli.

Does conditioning affect emotions?

- Conditioning applies to visceral or emotional responses as well as simple reflexes. As a result, conditioned emotional responses (CERs) also occur.
- Irrational fears called *phobias* may be CERs. Conditioning of emotional responses can occur vicariously (secondhand) as well as directly.

How does operant conditioning occur?

- Operant conditioning occurs when a voluntary action is followed by a reinforcer. Reinforcement in operant conditioning increases the frequency or probability of a response. This result is based on the law of effect.
- Complex operant responses can be taught by reinforcing successive approximations to a final desired response. This is called *shaping*. It is particularly useful in training animals.

- If an operant response is not reinforced, it may extinguish (disappear). But after extinction seems complete, it may temporarily reappear (spontaneous recovery).

Are there different kinds of operant reinforcement?

- In positive reinforcement, a reward or a pleasant event follows a response. In negative reinforcement, a response that ends discomfort becomes more likely.
- Primary reinforcers are "natural," physiologically based rewards. Intracranial stimulation of "pleasure centers" in the brain can also serve as a primary reinforcer.
- Secondary reinforcers are learned. They typically gain their reinforcing value by direct association with primary reinforcers or because they can be exchanged for primary reinforcers. Tokens and money gain their reinforcing value in this way.
- Feedback, or knowledge of results, aids learning and improves performance. It is most effective when it is immediate, detailed, and frequent.
- Programmed instruction breaks learning into a series of small steps and provides immediate feedback. Computer-assisted instruction (CAI) does the same but has the added advantage of providing alternate exercises and information when needed. Four variations of CAI are drill and practice, instructional games, educational simulations, and interactive videodisk instruction.

How are we influenced by patterns of reward?

- Delay of reinforcement greatly reduces its effectiveness, but long chains of responses may be built up so that a single reinforcer maintains many responses.
- Superstitious behaviors often become part of response chains because they *appear* to be associated with reinforcement.
- Reward or reinforcement may be given continuously (after every response) or on a schedule of partial reinforcement. Partial reinforcement produces greater resistance to extinction.
- The four most basic schedules of reinforcement are fixed ratio, variable ratio, fixed interval, and variable interval. Each produces a distinct pattern of responding.
- Stimuli that precede a reinforced response tend to control the response on future occasions (stimulus control). Two aspects of stimulus control are generalization and discrimination.
- In generalization, an operant response tends to occur when stimuli similar to those preceding reinforcement are present.
- In discrimination, responses are given in the presence of discriminative stimuli associated with reinforcement (S+) and withheld in the presence of stimuli associated with non-reinforcement (S−).

What does punishment do to behavior?

- Punishment decreases responding. Punishment occurs when a response is followed by the onset of an aversive event or by the removal of a positive event (response cost).
- Punishment is most effective when it is immediate, consistent, and intense. Mild punishment tends to only temporarily suppress responses that are also reinforced or were acquired by reinforcement.
- The undesirable side effects of punishment include the conditioning of fear to punishing agents and situations associated

with punishment, the learning of escape and avoidance responses, and the encouragement of aggression.

What is cognitive learning?

- Cognitive learning involves higher mental processes, such as understanding, knowing, or anticipating. Even in relatively simple learning situations, animals and people seem to form cognitive maps (internal representations of relationships).
- In latent learning, learning remains hidden or unseen until a reward or incentive for performance is offered.
- Discovery learning emphasizes insight and understanding, in contrast to rote learning.

Does learning occur by imitation?

- Much human learning is achieved through observation, or modeling. Observational learning is influenced by the personal characteristics of the model and the success or failure of the model's behavior. Studies have shown that aggression is readily learned and released by modeling.
- Television characters can act as powerful models for observational learning. Televised violence increases the likelihood of aggression by viewers.

How does conditioning apply to practical problems?

- Operant principles can be readily applied to manage behavior in everyday settings. When managing one's own behavior, self-reinforcement, self-recording, feedback, and behavioral contracting are all helpful.
- Four strategies that can help change bad habits are reinforcing alternate responses, promoting extinction, breaking response chains, and avoiding antecedent cues.
- In school, self-regulated learners typically do all of the following: They set learning goals, plan learning strategies, use self-instruction, monitor their progress, evaluate themselves, reinforce successes, and take corrective action when required.

How does biology influence learning?

- Many animals are born with innate behavior patterns far more complex than reflexes. These are organized into fixed action patterns (FAPs), which are stereotyped, species-specific behaviors.
- Learning in animals is limited at times by various biological constraints and species-typical behaviors.
- According to prepared fear theory, some stimuli are especially effective conditioned stimuli.

- Many responses are subject to instinctive drift in operant conditioning. Human learning is subtly influenced by many such biological potentials and limits.

PSYCHOLOGY ON THE NET

- **Animal Training at Sea World** Explains how marine mammals are trained at Sea World.
  http://www.seaworld.org/animal_training/atcontents.html
- **Memory** A short tutorial on classical conditioning, operant conditioning, and cognitive learning.
  http://www.science.wayne.edu/~wpoff/memory.html
- **Methods for Changing Behavior** Teaches you how to modify your own behavior. http://www.mentalhelp.net/psyhelp/chap11/
- **Observational Learning** Presents Bandura's original work on modeling, with graphs. http://www.valdosta.peachnet.edu/ ~whuitt/psy702/behsys/social.html
- **Oppatoons** Cartoons of rats undergoing conditioning.
  http://www.thecroft.com/psy/toons/OppaToons.html
- **Studying Television Violence** An article on television violence.
  http://www.ksu.edu/humec/fshs/tv97.htm
  - **InfoTrac® College Edition** For recent articles related to the impact of television, use Key Words search for TELEVISION VIOLENCE.

INTERACTIVE LEARNING

- *PsychNow!* 5a. Classical conditioning. 5b. Operant conditioning. 5c. Observational learning.
- *Psyk.trek* 5a. Overview of classical conditioning. 5b. Basic process in classical conditioning. 5c. Overview of operant conditioning. 5d. Schedule of reinforcement. 5e. Reinforcement and punishment. 5f. Avoidance and escape learning.

10

Memory

Chapter Survey

Theme: *Memory is not like a tape recorder or video camera: Memories change as they are stored and retrieved.*

▼ **KEY QUESTIONS**
● *KEY TOPICS*

▼ Is there more than one type of memory?

- *Sensory memory*
- *Short-term memory*
- *Long-term memory*

▼ What are the features of each type of memory?

- *Characteristics of short-term and long-term memories*

▼ Is there more than one type of long-term memory?

- *Declarative memory*
- *Procedural memory*

▼ How is memory measured?

- *Recall, recognition, and relearning*
- *Implicit memory and priming*

▼ What are "photographic" memories?

- *Eidetic imagery*
- *Exceptional memory*

▼ **KEY QUESTIONS**
● *KEY TOPICS*

▼ What causes forgetting?

- *The curve of forgetting*
- *Theories of forgetting*

▼ How accurate are everyday memories?

- *Repression and suppression*

▼ What happens in the brain when memories are formed?

- *Engrams and memory consolidation*
- *Brain activity and memory*

▼ How can memory be improved?

- *Strategies for enhancing memory*
- *Mnemonic techniques*

▼ What is the "recovered-memory" debate?

- *Repressed memories of childhood sexual abuse*

preview
"WHAT THE HELL'S GOING ON HERE?"

I t's February and Steven is cross-country skiing on the ice of Lake Michigan. He stops for a moment, but quickly realizes that he is very cold. Steven decides to turn back. In a few minutes comes a new realization: He is lost. Wandering on the ice, he grows numb and very, very tired.

Put yourself in Steven's shoes, and you will appreciate the shock of what happened next. Steven clearly recalls wandering lost and alone on the ice. Immediately after that, he remembers waking up in a field. But as he looked around, Steven knew something was wrong. It was spring! The backpack beside him contained running shoes, swimming goggles, and a pair of glasses—all unfamiliar. As he looked at his clothing—also unfamiliar—Steven thought to himself, "What the hell's going on here?" Fourteen months had passed since he left to go skiing (Loftus, 1980). How did he get to the field? Steven couldn't say. He had lost over a year of his life to total amnesia.

As Steven's amnesia vividly shows, life without memory would be meaningless. Imagine the terror and confusion of having all of your memories wiped out. You would have no identity, no knowledge, no life history, no recognition of friends or family. Your past would be a total blank. In a very real sense, we are our memories.

This chapter discusses memory and forgetting. You'll almost certainly discover ways to improve your memory in the information that follows.

Gateways to Memory

REMEMBERING is an active process. Memories are frequently lost, altered, revised, or distorted.

DIFFERENT STRATEGIES are required to make the best use of short-term memory and long-term memory.

REMEMBERING is not an all-or-nothing process. Information that appears to be lost may still reside in memory.

AN INABILITY TO RETRIEVE INFORMATION isn't the only cause of forgetting. Often, memory failures occur because information wasn't stored in the first place.

ALTHOUGH IT'S TRUE THAT SOME PEOPLE HAVE NATURALLY SUPERIOR MEMORIES, everyone can learn to improve his or her memory.

MEMORY SYSTEMS (MNEMONICS) greatly improve immediate memory. However, conventional learning tends to create the most lasting memories.

EXTREME CAUTION is warranted when "recovered" memories are the only basis for believing that a person was sexually abused during childhood.

STAGES OF MEMORY—DO YOU HAVE A MIND LIKE A STEEL TRAP? OR A SIEVE?

Many people think of memory as "a dusty storehouse of facts." In reality, **memory** is an active system that receives, stores, organizes, alters, and recovers information (Baddeley, 1996). In some ways, memory acts like a computer (❖Fig. 10.1). Incoming information is first **encoded**, or changed into a usable form. This step is like typing data into a computer. Next, information is **stored**, or held in the system. (As we will see in a moment, human memory can be pictured as three separate storage systems.) Finally, memories must be **retrieved**, or taken

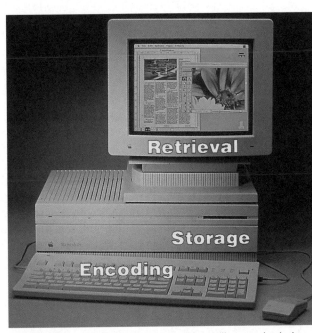

❖ **FIGURE 10.1** In some ways, a computer acts like a mechanical memory system. Both systems process information, and both allow encoding, storage, and retrieval of data.

Memory The mental system for receiving, encoding, storing, organizing, altering, and retrieving information.
Encoding Converting information into a form in which it will be retained in memory.
Storage Holding information in memory for later use.
Retrieval Recovering information from storage in memory.

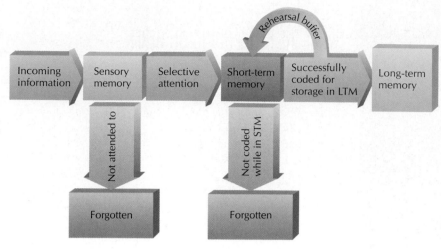

❖ **FIGURE 10.2** *Remembering is thought to involve at least three steps. Incoming information is first held for a second or two by sensory memory. Information selected by attention is then transferred to temporary storage in short-term memory. If new information is not rapidly encoded, or rehearsed, it is forgotten. If it is transferred to long-term memory, it becomes relatively permanent, although retrieving it may be a problem. The preceding is a useful, but highly simplified, model of memory; it may not be literally true of what happens in the brain (Eysenck & Keane, 1995).*

out of storage, to be useful. If you're going to remember all of the 9,856 new terms on your next psychology exam, you must successfully encode, store, and retrieve them.

What are the three separate memory systems just mentioned? Psychologists have identified three stages of memory. To be stored for a long time, information must pass through all three (❖Fig. 10.2).

Sensory Memory

Let's say a friend asks you to pick up several things at a market. How do you remember them? New information first enters **sensory memory,** which can hold an exact copy of what is seen or heard, for a few seconds or less. For instance, look at a flower and then close your eyes. An **icon** (EYE-kon), or fleeting mental image, of the flower will persist for about one-half second. Similarly, when you hear information, it is held in sensory memory as an *echo* for up to 2 seconds (Schweickert, 1993). (An **echo** is a brief continuation of activity in the auditory system.)

Let's say your attention wanders as your friend names the last item on her shopping list. Without thinking, you ask, "What did you say?" But before she can answer, you realize you already know what the last item is. This ability to mentally "play back" what someone else just said is based on echoic memory (Eysenck & Keane, 1995).

In general, sensory memory holds information just long enough to transfer it to the second memory system (Neath, 1998).

Short-Term Memory

Not everything we see or hear is kept in memory. Imagine that a radio is playing in the background as your friend reads her shopping list. Will you remember what the announcer says too? Probably not, because **selective attention** (focusing on a selected portion of sensory input) controls what information moves on to short-term memory. **Short-term memory** (STM) holds small amounts of information for relatively brief periods. By paying attention to your friend, you will place the shopping

list in short-term memory (while you ignore the voice on the radio saying, "Buy Burpo Butter").

How are short-term memories encoded? Short-term memories can be stored as images. But more often they are stored **phonetically** (by sound), especially in recalling words and letters (Neath, 1998). If you are introduced to Tim at a party and you forget his name, you are more likely to call him by a name that sounds like Tim (Jim, Kim, or Slim, for instance) than a name that sounds different, such as Bob or Mike. Your friend with the shopping list may be lucky if you don't bring home jam instead of ham and soap instead of soup!

Short-term memory acts as a *temporary* storehouse for *small amounts* of information. When you dial a phone number or remember a shopping list, you are using STM. Notice that unimportant information is quickly "dumped" from STM and forever lost. Short-term memory prevents our minds from retaining useless names, dates, telephone numbers, and other trivia. At the same time, it provides an area of **working memory,** where we do much of our thinking. Working memory acts as a sort of "mental scratchpad." It holds information for short periods of time while other mental activities are taking place, such as when you do mental arithmetic (Becker & Morris, 1999).

As you may have noticed when dialing a telephone, STM is very sensitive to *interruption* or *interference*. You've probably had this happen with STM: You look up a number and walk to the phone repeating it to yourself. You dial the number and get a busy signal. When you return a few minutes later, you must look up the number again. This time as you are about to dial, someone asks you a question. You answer, turn to the phone, and find that you have forgotten the number. Notice again that working memory can handle only small amounts of information. It is very difficult to do more than one task at a time in STM (Anderson, Reder, & Lebiere, 1996).

Long-Term Memory

If short-term memory is brief, easily interrupted, and limited in "size," how do we remember for greater lengths of time? Information that is important or meaningful is transferred to the third memory system, called long-term memory. In contrast to STM, **long-term memory** (**LTM**) acts as a lasting storehouse for meaningful information. LTM contains everything you know about the world—from aardvark to zucchini, math to Myst, facts to fantasy. And yet, there appears to be no danger of running out of room. LTM has a nearly limitless storage capacity. In fact, the more you know, the easier it is to add new information to memory. This is the reverse of what we would expect if LTM could be "filled up" (Eysenck & Keane, 1995). It is also one of many powerful reasons for getting an education.

Are long-term memories also encoded as sounds?   They can be. But information in LTM is typically stored on the basis of *meaning* and importance, not by sound. If you make an error in LTM, it will probably be related to meaning. For example, if you are trying to recall the word *barn* from a memorized list, you are more likely to mistakenly say *shed* or *farm* than *born*.

When information in STM is associated with knowledge already stored in LTM, it gains meaning. This makes it easier to remember. As an example, try to memorize this story:

> With hocked gems financing him, our hero bravely defied all scornful laughter. "Your eyes deceive," he had said. "An egg, not a table, correctly typifies this unexplored planet." Now three sturdy sisters sought proof. Forging along, days became weeks as many doubters spread fearful rumors about the edge. At last from nowhere welcome winged creatures appeared, signifying momentous success (Adapted from Dooling & Lachman, 1971).

This odd story emphasizes the impact that meaning has on memory. People given the title of the story were able to remember it far better than those not given a title. See if the title helps you as much as it did them. The title is "Columbus Discovers America."

DUAL MEMORY   Most of our memory chores are handled by STM and LTM. To summarize their connection, picture short-term memory as a small desk at the front of a huge warehouse full of filing cabinets (LTM). As information enters the warehouse, it is first placed on the desk. Because the desk is small, it must be quickly cleared off to make room for new information. Unimportant items are simply tossed away. Meaningful or important information is placed in the files (long-term memory).

When we want to use knowledge from LTM to answer a question, the information is returned to STM. Or, in our analogy, a folder is taken out of the files (LTM) and moved to the desk (STM), where it can be used. Computer users may prefer to think of STM as being like RAM and LTM as being like a hard disk. However, it is unlikely that short- and long-term memories are simply stored at different locations in the human brain. STM and LTM appear to be different stages in the storage of information (Best, 1999).

Now that you have a general picture of STM and LTM, it is time to explore both in more detail. But first, here's a chance to rehearse what you've learned.

MEMORY SYSTEMS

RELATE

Wave a pencil back and forth in front of your eyes while focusing on something in the distance. The pencil's image looks transparent. Why? (Because sensory memory briefly holds an image of the pencil. This image persists after the pencil passes by.)

Think of a time today when you used short-term memory (such as briefly remembering a phone number, an Internet address, or someone's name). How long did you retain the information? How did you encode it? How much do you remember now?

How is long-term memory helping you read this sentence? If the words weren't already stored in LTM, could you read at all? How else have you used LTM today?

LEARNING CHECK

Match: **A.** Sensory memory   **B.** STM   **C.** LTM

1. _____ Working memory
2. _____ Holds information for a few seconds or less
3. _____ Stores an icon or echo
4. _____ Permanent, unlimited capacity
5. _____ Temporarily holds small amounts of information
6. _____ Selective attention determines its contents

7. STM is improved by interruption, or interference, because attention is more focused at such times. T or F?

CRITICAL THINKING

8. Why is sensory memory important to filmmakers?

Answers:

1. B 2. A 3. A 4. C 5. B 6. B 7. F 8. Without sensory memory, a movie would look like a flickering series of still pictures. The brief persistence of icons in sensory memory is what blends one movie frame into the next.

SHORT-TERM MEMORY—DO YOU KNOW THE MAGIC NUMBER?

How much information can be held in short-term memory? For an answer, read the following numbers once. Then

---

Sensory memory   *The first stage of memory, which holds an exact record of incoming information for a few seconds or less.*
Icon   *A mental image or visual representation.*
Echo   *A brief continuation of sensory activity in the auditory system after a sound is heard.*
Selective attention   *Voluntarily focusing on a selected portion of sensory input.*
Short-term memory (STM)   *The memory system used to hold small amounts of information for relatively brief time periods.*
Phonetic storage   *Storing a word in memory on the basis of its sound.*
Working memory   *Another name for short-term memory, especially when it is used for thinking and problem solving.*
Long-term memory (LTM)   *The memory system used for relatively permanent storage of meaningful information.*

close the book and write as many as you can in the correct order.

$$8\ 5\ 1\ 7\ 4\ 9\ 3$$

This is called the **digit-span test.** It is a measure of attention and short-term memory. If you were able to correctly repeat seven digits, you have an average short-term memory. Now try to memorize the following list, reading it only once.

$$7\ 1\ 8\ 3\ 5\ 4\ 2\ 9\ 1\ 6\ 3\ 4$$

This series was probably beyond your short-term memory capacity. Psychologist George Miller found that short-term memory is limited to the "magic number" 7 (plus or minus 2) **information bits** (Miller, 1956). A bit is a single meaningful "piece" of information—such as a digit. It is as if short-term memory has seven "slots" or "bins" into which separate items can be placed. Actually, seven bits is the average *upper limit* for short-term memory. For some types of information, five bits is more typical (Neath, 1998).

When all of the slots in STM are filled, there is no room for new information. Picture how this works at a party: Let's say your hostess begins introducing everyone who is there, "Ted, Barbara, Donna, Roseanna, Wayne, Shawn, Linda. . . ." "Stop," you think to yourself. But she continues, "Eddie, Jay, Gordon, Frank, Marietta, Dan, Patty, Glen, Ricky." The hostess leaves, satisfied that you have met everyone. And you spend the evening talking with Ted, Barbara, and Ricky, the only people whose names you remember!

Recoding

Before we continue, try your short-term memory again, this time on letters. Read the following letters once; then look away and try to write them in the proper order.

$$T\ V\ I\quad B\ M\ U\ S\quad N\ Y\quad M\ C\ A$$

Notice that there are 12 letters, or "bits" of information. This should be beyond the seven-item limit of STM. However, because the letters are presented as four groups, or *chunks* of information, many students are able to memorize them. **Information chunks** are made up of bits that have been grouped into larger units.

How does chunking help? Chunking **recodes** (modifies or reorganizes) information into units that are already in LTM. For example, you may have noticed that NY is the abbreviation for New York. If so, the two bits N and Y became one chunk. In an experiment that used lists like the one you read, people remembered best when the letters were grouped into familiar chunks: TV, IBM, USN, and YMCA (Bower & Springston, 1970). If you recoded the letters this way, you undoubtedly remembered the entire list.

Chunking suggests that STM holds about five to seven of whatever units we are using. A single chunk could be made up of numbers, letters, words, phrases, or familiar sentences (Barsalou, 1992). Picture STM as a small desk again. Through chunking, we combine several items into one "stack" of information. This allows us to place seven stacks on the desk, where before there was only room for seven separate items.

Rehearsal

How long do short-term memories last? Short-term memories appear to weaken and disappear very rapidly. However, a short-term memory can be prolonged by silently repeating it until it is needed, a process called **maintenance rehearsal.** You have probably remembered an address or telephone number this way. The more times a short-term memory is rehearsed, the greater its chances of being stored in LTM (Barsalou, 1992).

What if rehearsal is prevented, so a memory cannot be recycled or moved to LTM? Without maintenance rehearsal, STM is incredibly short. In one experiment, subjects heard meaningless syllables, like XAR, followed by a number, like 67. As soon as subjects heard the number, they began counting backward by threes (to prevent them from repeating the syllable). After only 18 seconds of delay, memory scores fell to zero (Peterson & Peterson, 1959).

After *18 seconds* without rehearsal, the short-term memories were gone forever! Keep this in mind when you get only one chance to hear information you want to remember. For example, if you are introduced to someone, and the name slips out of STM, it is gone forever. To escape this awkward situation, you might try saying something like, "I'm curious, how do you spell your name?" Unfortunately, the response is often an icy reply like, "B-O-B S-M-I-T-H, it's really not too difficult." To avoid embarrassment, pay careful attention to the name, repeat it to yourself several times, and try to use it in the next sentence or two—before you lose it (Neath, 1998).

Maintenance rehearsal is not a very good way to transfer information to long-term memory. **Elaborative rehearsal,** which enhances the meaning of information, is far more effective. In other words, it's best to link new information to existing memories and knowledge. That's why passively reading a textbook is a poor way to study. If you don't elaborate, digest, extend, and think about information, you won't remember much later. As you read, try to frequently ask yourself "why" questions, such as "Why would that be true?" (Willoughby et al., 1997). Also, try to relate new ideas to your own experiences (Symons & Johnson, 1997).

LONG-TERM MEMORY—WHERE THE PAST LIVES

An electrode was placed at location number 11 on the patient's brain. She immediately said, "Yes, sir, I think I heard a mother calling her little boy somewhere. It seemed to be something happening years ago. It was somebody in the neighborhood where I live." A short time later, the electrode was applied to the same spot. Again the patient said, "Yes, I hear the same familiar sounds, it seems to be a woman calling, the same lady"

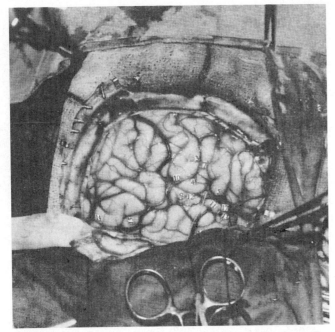

❖ **FIGURE 10.3** *Exposed cerebral cortex of a patient undergoing brain surgery. Numbers represent points that reportedly produced "memories" when electrically stimulated. A critical evaluation of such reports suggests that they are more like dreams than memories. This fact raises questions about claims that long-term memories are permanent. (From Wilder Penfield, The Excitable Cortex in Conscious Man, 1958. Courtesy of the author and Charles C Thomas, Publisher, Springfield, Illinois.)*

(Penfield, 1958). These statements were made by a woman undergoing brain surgery. Only local anesthetics were used (there are no pain receptors in the brain), so the patient was awake as her brain was electrically stimulated (❖Fig. 10.3). When activated, some brain areas seemed to produce vivid memories of long-forgotten events.

PERMANENCE *Is every experience permanently recorded in memory?* Results like those described led neurosurgeon Wilder Penfield to claim that the brain records the past like a "continuous strip of movie film, complete with sound track" (Penfield, 1957). But as you know, this is an exaggeration. Many events never get past short-term memory. Also, brain stimulation produces memory-like experiences in only about 3 percent of cases. Most reports resemble dreams more than memories, and many are clearly imaginary. Memory experts now believe that long-term memories are only *relatively* permanent (Barsalou, 1992; Loftus & Loftus, 1980). Perfect, indelible, eternal memories are a myth.

Constructing Memories

There is another reason to doubt Penfield's claim. As new long-term memories are formed, older memories are often updated, changed, lost, or *revised* (Baddeley, 1990, 1996). To illustrate this point, Elizabeth Loftus and John Palmer (1974) showed people a filmed automobile accident. Afterward, some participants were asked to estimate how fast the cars were going when they "smashed" into each other. For others, the words *bumped*, *contacted*, or *hit* replaced *smashed*. One week later, each person was asked, "Did you see any broken glass?" Those asked earlier about the cars that "smashed" into each other were more likely to say yes. (No broken glass was shown in the film.) The new information ("smashed") was included in memories and altered them.

Revised memories often change in ways that enhance one's self-image. (As long as you're altering memories, you might as well make yourself look good.) For example, college students were asked to remember their high school grades. As a group, they were 90 percent accurate in remembering A grades. However, only 30 percent of D grades were accurately recalled (Bahrick, Hall, & Berger, 1996).

Updating memories is called **constructive processing.** Gaps in memory, which are common, may be filled in by logic, guessing, or new information (Schacter, Norman, & Koutstaal, 1998). Indeed, it is possible to have "memories" for things that never happened (such as remembering broken glass at an accident when there was none). People in Elizabeth Loftus's experiments who had these **pseudo-memories** (false memories) were often quite upset to learn they had given false "testimony" (Loftus & Ketcham, 1991).

Digit-span test *A test of attention and short-term memory in which a string of numbers is recalled.*
Information bits *Meaningful units of information, such as numbers, letters, words, or phrases.*
Information chunks *Information bits grouped into larger units.*
Recoding *Reorganizing or modifying information to assist storage in memory.*
Maintenance rehearsal *Silently repeating or mentally reviewing information to hold it in short-term memory.*
Elaborative rehearsal *Rehearsal that links new information with existing memories and knowledge.*
Constructive processing *Reorganizing or updating memories on the basis of logic, reasoning, or the addition of new information.*
Pseudo-memory *A false memory that a person believes is real or accurate.*

AND NOW, THE RESULTS

Return now and look at the labels you wrote on the "old or new" word list. If you answered as most people do, this exercise may help you appreciate how often we have false memories. All of the listed words are "new." None was on the original list!

If you thought you "remembered" that *sleep* was on the original list, you had a false memory. The word *sleep* is associated with most of the words on the original list, which creates a strong impression that you saw it before (Roediger & McDermott, 1995).

False long-term memories are a common problem in police work. For example, a witness may select a photo of a suspect from police files or see a photo in the news. Later, the witness identifies the suspect in person (in a lineup or in court). Did the witness really remember the suspect from the scene of the crime? Or was it from the more recently seen photograph? Even an innocent person may be "remembered" as the criminal.

Does the new information "overwrite" the original memory? No, the real problem is that we often can't remember the *source* of a memory. This can lead a witness to "remember" a face that she or he saw somewhere other than at the crime scene (Schacter, Norman, & Koutstaal, 1998).

Eyewitness memories are notoriously inaccurate. By the time witnesses are asked to testify in court, information they learned after an incident may blend into their original memories.

HYPNOSIS, IMAGINATION, AND MEMORY

In 1976, near Chowchilla, California, 26 children were abducted from a school bus and held captive for ransom. Under hypnosis, the bus driver recalled the license plate number of the kidnappers' van. This memory helped break the case and led to the children's rescue. Such successes seem to imply that hypnosis can improve memory. But does it? Read on, and judge for yourself.

Research has shown that a hypnotized person is more likely than normal to use imagination to fill in gaps in memory. Also, when hypnotized persons are given false information, they tend to weave it into their memories (Sheehan & Statham, 1989). Even when a memory is completely false, the hypnotized person's confidence in it can be unshakable (Burgess & Kirsch, 1999). Most telling of all is the fact that hypnosis increases false memories more than it does true ones. Eighty percent of the new memories produced by hypnotized subjects in one experiment were *incorrect* (Dywan & Bowers, 1983). Overall, it can be concluded that hypnosis does not greatly improve memory (Burgess & Kirsch, 1999).

Then why did it help in the Chowchilla case? It is true that hypnosis sometimes uncovers more information, as it did in Chowchilla (Schreiber & Schreiber, 1999). However, when it does, there is no sure way to tell which memories are true and which are false (Perry et al., 1996). Clearly, hypnosis is not the "magic bullet" against forgetting that some police investigators hoped it would be (Kebbell & Wagstaff, 1998).

Couldn't hypnosis be used to avoid such problems? News stories often give the impression that it can. Is this true? See "Hypnosis, Imagination, and Memory" for a review of research on this intriguing question.

To summarize, forming and using memories is an active, creative, highly personal process. Our memories are colored by emotions, judgments, and quirks of personality. If you and a friend were lashed together, and you went through life side by side, you would still have different memories. What we remember depends on what we pay attention to, what we regard as meaningful or important, and what we feel strongly about (Schacter, 1996).

Organization

Long-term memory stores a seemingly infinite amount of information in a lifetime. How is it possible to quickly find specific memories? The answer is that each person's "memory index" is highly organized.

Do you mean that information is arranged alphabetically, as in a dictionary? Not a chance! If I ask you to name a black-and-white animal that lives on ice, is related to a chicken, and cannot fly, you don't have to go from aardvark to zebra to find the answer. You will probably only think of black-and-white birds living in the Antarctic. Which of these cannot fly? *Voila*, the answer is penguin.

The arrangement of information in LTM may be based on rules, images, categories, symbols, similarity, formal meaning, or personal meaning (Baddeley, 1990, 1996). In recent years, psychologists have begun to develop a picture of the *structure*, or arrangement, of memories. **Memory structure** is the pattern of associations among items of information stored in memory. One example will serve to illustrate this research.

You are given the following two statements, to which you must answer yes or no: *A canary is an animal. A canary is a bird.* Which do you answer more quickly? Collins and Quillian (1969) found that *A canary is a bird* produced a faster yes than *A canary is an animal.* Why should this be so? Many psychologists believe that a **network model** of memory explains why.

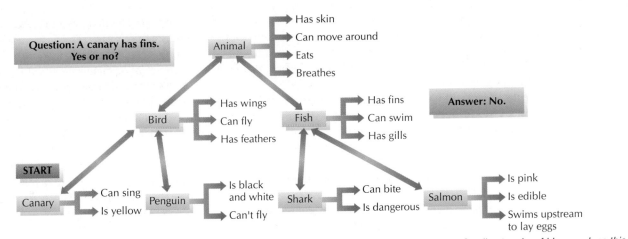

❖ **FIGURE 10.4** *A hypothetical network of facts about animals shows what is meant by the structure of memory. Small networks of ideas such as this are probably organized into larger and larger units and higher levels of meaning. (Adapted from Collins & Quillian, 1969.)*

According to them, LTM is organized as a network of linked ideas (❖Fig. 10.4). When ideas are "farther" apart, it takes a longer chain of associations to connect them. The more two items are separated, the longer it takes to answer. In terms of information links, *canary* is probably "close" to *bird* in your "memory files." *Animal* and *canary* are farther apart. Remember though, this has nothing to do with alphabetical order. We are talking about organization based on linked meanings.

REDINTEGRATIVE MEMORIES   Networks of associated memories may help explain a common experience: Imagine finding a picture taken on your sixth birthday or tenth Christmas. As you look at the photo, one memory leads to another, which leads to another, and another. Soon you have unleashed a flood of seemingly forgotten details. This process is called *redintegration* (ruh-DIN-tuh-GRAY-shun).

Redintegrative memories seem to spread through the "branches" of memory networks. Many people find that such memories are also touched off by distinctive odors out of the past—from a farm visited in childhood, Grandma's kitchen, the seashore, a doctor's office, the perfume or aftershave of a former lover, or a musty museum (Aggleton & Waskett, 1999). The key idea in redintegration is that one memory serves as a cue to trigger another. As a result, an entire past experience may be reconstructed from one small recollection.

Types of Long-Term Memory

How many types of long-term memory are there?   As we have seen, *memory* is an umbrella term that includes both short-term and long-term memory. Beyond this, it is becoming clear that more than one type of long-term memory exists. Let's probe a little further into the mysteries of memory.

SKILL MEMORY AND FACT MEMORY   A curious thing happens to many people who develop amnesia. Amnesic patients may be unable to learn a telephone number, an address, or a person's name. And yet, the same patients can learn to solve complex puzzles in the same amount of time as normal subjects

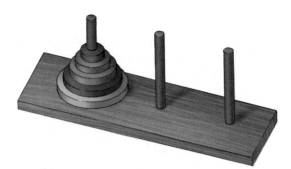

❖ **FIGURE 10.5** *The tower puzzle. In this puzzle, all the colored disks must be moved to another post, without ever placing a larger disk on a smaller one. Only one disk may be moved at a time, and a disk must always be moved from one post to another (it cannot be held aside). An amnesic patient learned to solve the puzzle in 31 moves, the minimum possible. Even so, each time he began, he protested that he did not remember ever solving the puzzle before and that he did not know how to begin. Evidence like this suggests that memories for skills are distinct from memories for facts.*

(Squire & Zola-Morgan, 1988) (❖Fig. 10.5). These and other observations have led many psychologists to conclude that long-term memories fall into at least two categories. One is called *procedural memory* (or skill memory). The other is *declarative memory* (also sometimes called fact memory).

Procedural memory includes basic conditioned responses and learned actions like those involved in typing, solving a

Memory structure *Patterns of associations among bits of information stored in memory.*
Network model *A model of memory that views it as an organized system of linked information.*
Redintegrative memories *Memories that are reconstructed or expanded by starting with one memory and then following chains of association to related memories.*
Procedural memory *Long-term memories of conditioned responses and learned skills.*

puzzle, or swinging a golf club. Memories such as these can be fully expressed only as actions or "know-how." Skill memories appear to register in lower brain areas, especially the cerebellum. They represent the more basic "automatic" elements of conditioning, learning, and memory (Gabrieli, 1998).

Declarative memory stores factual information, such as names, faces, words, dates, and ideas. Declarative memories are expressed as words or symbols. For example, knowing that Steven Spielberg directed both *Close Encounters of the Third Kind* and *Jurassic Park* is a declarative memory. This is the type of memory that a person with amnesia lacks, and that most of us take for granted. Many psychologists believe that declarative memory can be further divided into two other types, called *semantic* and *episodic memory* (Nyberg & Tulving, 1996).

SEMANTIC MEMORY   Most of our basic factual knowledge about the world is almost totally immune to forgetting. The names of objects, the days of the week or months of the year, simple math skills, the seasons, words and language, and other general facts are quite lasting. Such impersonal facts make up a part of LTM called **semantic memory.** Semantic memory serves as a mental dictionary or encyclopedia of basic knowledge. Notice again that long-term memories emphasize *meaning*.

EPISODIC MEMORY   Semantic memory has no connection to times or places. It would be rare, for instance, to remember when and where you first learned the names of the seasons. In contrast, **episodic memory** (ep-ih-SOD-ik) is an "autobiographical" record of personal experiences. It stores life events (or "episodes") day after day, year after year. Can you remember your seventh birthday? Your first date? An accident you

witnessed? The first day of college? What you had for breakfast 3 days ago? All are episodic memories. (See "Memories of a Lifetime" for more information.)

Are episodic memories as lasting as semantic memories?   In general, episodic memories are more easily forgotten than semantic memories. This occurs because new information constantly pours into episodic memory. Stop for a moment and remember what you did last summer. That was an episodic memory. Notice that you now remember that you just remembered something. You have a new episodic memory in which you remember that you remembered while reading this text! It's easy to see how much we ask of our memory system.

HOW MANY TYPES OF MEMORY ARE THERE?   In answer to the question posed at the beginning of this section, it is very likely that three kinds of long-term memories exist: procedural, semantic, and episodic (Mitchell, 1989; Squire et al., 1993) (❖Fig. 10.6). Although other types of memory may be discovered, it appears that some pieces of the puzzle are falling into place.

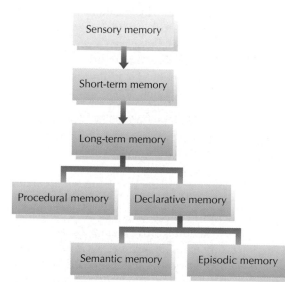

❖ **FIGURE 10.6** *In the model shown here, long-term memory is divided into procedural memory (learned actions and skills) and declarative memory (stored facts). Declarative memories can be either semantic (impersonal knowledge) or episodic (personal experiences associated with specific times and places).*

MEMORIES OF A LIFETIME

A CLOSER LOOK

Ask a 70-year-old person to recall vivid and important autobiographical memories and what do you get? Up to a point, the results are like the memories of people at any age: Most recollections come from the 2 or 3 most recent years. Fewer and fewer autobiographical memories relate to earlier years, and they taper off for childhood. However, something interesting occurs for older adults as they scan over a lifetime. If you tally their memories, you will find a "bulge" or "bump" in the curve between the ages of 10 and 30. In other words, many more memories come from this period than would be expected.

Why do memories from this period of life stand out for older adults? Psychologists David Rubin and Matthew Schulkind believe that memories formed during this time are encoded in ways that make them easier to retrieve later in life. Just why these years are so memorable is not known. However, if you are between the ages of 10 and 30, take note: These are the days, my friend (Rubin & Schulkind, 1997).

K N O W L E D G E   B U I L D E R

STM AND LTM

RELATE

Telephone numbers are divided into an area code (3 digits) and a 7-digit number that is divided into 3 digits, plus 4 more. Can you relate this practice to STM? How about to chunking and recoding?

Think about how you've used your memory in the last hour. See if you can identify an example of each of the following: a procedural memory, a declarative memory, a semantic memory, and an episodic memory.

1. The digit-span test is commonly used to measure LTM. T or F?

2. There is evidence that STM lasts about 18 seconds, without rehearsal. T or F?

3. Information is best transferred from STM to LTM when a person engages in
   a. maintenance chunking   *b.* maintenance recoding
   c. elaborative networking   *d.* elaborative rehearsal

4. Constructive processing is often responsible for creating pseudo-memories. T or F?

5. Electrical stimulation of the brain has shown conclusively that all memories are stored permanently, but not all memories can be retrieved. T or F?

6. Memories elicited under hypnosis are more vivid, complete, and reliable than normal. T or F?

7. _____ of related information are an example of the structure or organization found in LTM.

8. Procedural memories are stored in STM, whereas declarative memories are stored in LTM. T or F?

9. Episodic memories are almost totally immune to forgetting. T or F?

CRITICAL THINKING

10. Parents sometimes warn children not to read comic books, fearing that they will learn less in school if they "fill their heads up with junk." Why is this warning unnecessary?

Answers:

1. F 2. T 3. d 4. T 5. F 6. F 7. Networks 8. F 9. F 10. Because the more information you have in long-term memory, the greater the possibilities for linking new information to it. Generally, the more you know, the more you can learn—even if some of what you know is "junk."

MEASURING MEMORY—THE ANSWER IS ON THE TIP OF MY TONGUE

You either remember something or you don't, right? Wrong. A moment of thought should convince you that partial memories are common. For instance, imagine that a clerk helps you at a clothing store. Will you remember her 6 months later? Probably not—unless you happen to see her again at the mall. If you remember her then, you will have used a form of partial memory called *recognition.*

Partial memory is also demonstrated by the **tip-of-the-tongue (TOT) state.** This is the feeling that a memory is available, but not quite retrievable. It is as if an answer or a memory is just out of reach—on the "tip of your tongue." For instance, in one study, people listened to theme music from popular TV shows. Then they tried to name the program the tune came from. This produced TOT experiences for about 1 out of 5 tunes (Riefer, Keveri, & Kramer, 1995). The items listed next may induce the TOT state. See if you can name the defined words. (*Answers are at the bottom of this page.)

What's on the Tip of Your Tongue?
1. A person who collects and studies postage stamps.
2. A decorative loop of fabric on the shoulder of a coat or dress.
3. A tobacco pipe with a large flared bowl made from a gourd.
4. The dark, dense rock of a lava flow.
5. Thin plant strips pressed together to make a writing material used in ancient Egypt.
6. A small fish that attaches itself to a shark.

In one TOT study, university students read the definitions of words such as *sextant, sampan,* and *ambergris.* Students who "drew a blank" and couldn't name a defined word were asked to give any other information they could. Often, they could guess the first and last letter and the number of syllables of the word they were seeking. They also gave words that sounded like or meant the same thing as the defined word (Brown & McNeill, 1966). Did any of these signs of the TOT state occur as you read the previous definitions?

Closely related to the TOT state is the fact that people can often tell beforehand if they are likely to remember something. This is called the **feeling of knowing** (Nelson, 1987). Feeling-of-knowing reactions are easy to observe on television game shows, where they occur just before contestants are allowed to answer.

Because memory is not an all-or-nothing event, there are several ways of measuring it. Three commonly used **memory tasks** (tests of memory) are recall, recognition, and relearning. Let's see how they differ.

Recall

What is the name of the first song on your favorite compact disk? Who won the World Series last year? Who wrote *Hamlet*? If you can answer these questions, you are demonstrating recall. To **recall** means to supply or reproduce facts or information. Tests of recall often require *verbatim* (word-for-word)

*1. philatelist 2. epaulet 3. calabash 4. basalt 5. papyrus 6. remora

Declarative memory *That part of long-term memory containing specific factual information.*
Semantic memory *A subpart of declarative memory that records impersonal knowledge about the world.*
Episodic memory *A subpart of declarative memory that records personal experiences that are linked with specific times and places.*
Tip-of-the-tongue state *The feeling that a memory is available but not quite retrievable.*
Feeling of knowing *A feeling that allows people to predict beforehand whether they will be able to remember something.*
Memory task *Any task designed to test or assess memory.*
Recall *To supply or reproduce memorized information with a minimum of external cues.*

memory. If you study a poem until you can recite it without looking, you are recalling it. If you complete a fill-in-the-blank question, you are using recall. When you answer an essay question by providing facts and ideas, you are also using recall, even though you didn't learn your essay verbatim.

The order in which information is memorized has an interesting effect on recall. To experience it, try to memorize the following list, reading it only once:

> bread, apples, soda, ham, cookies, rice, lettuce, beets, mustard, cheese, oranges, ice cream, crackers, flour, eggs

If you are like most people, it will be hardest for you to recall items from the middle of the list. ❖Figure 10.7 shows the results of a similar test. Notice that the greatest number of errors is found for middle items of an ordered list. This is the **serial position effect.** The last items on a list are remembered best because they are still in STM. The first items are also remembered well because they entered an "empty" short-term memory. This allows them to be rehearsed, which moves them into long-term memory (Medin & Ross, 1992). The middle items are neither held in short-term memory nor moved to long-term memory, so they are often lost.

Recognition

Try to write down everything you can remember from a class you took last year. (You have 3 minutes, which should be more than enough time!) If you actually did this, you might conclude that you had learned very little. However, we could use a more sensitive test based on recognition. In **recognition memory,** previously learned material is correctly identified. For instance, you could take a multiple-choice test on facts and ideas from the course. Because you would just have to recognize correct answers, we would probably find that you had learned a lot.

Recognition memory can be amazingly accurate for pictures, photographs, or other visual stimuli. One investigator showed people 2,560 photographs at a rate of one every 10 sec-

onds. Each person was then shown 280 pairs of photographs. One in each pair was from the first set of photos and the other was similar but new. Subjects could tell with 85 to 95 percent accuracy which photograph they had seen before (Haber, 1970). This finding may explain why people so often say, "I may forget a name, but I never forget a face." (It's also why we rarely need to see our friends' vacation photos more than once.)

Recognition is usually superior to recall. That's why police departments use photographs or a lineup to identify criminal suspects. Witnesses who disagree in their recall of a suspect's height, weight, age, or eye color often agree completely when recognition is all that is required.

Is recognition always superior? It depends greatly on the kind of **distractors** used. These are false items included with an item to be recognized. If distractors are very similar to the correct item, memory may be poor. A reverse problem sometimes occurs when only one choice looks like it could be correct. This can produce a **false positive,** or false sense of recognition. For example, there have been instances in which witnesses described a criminal as black, tall, or young. Then a lineup was held in which a suspect was the only African American among whites, the only tall suspect, or the only young person. In such cases, a false identification is very likely. A better method is to have all the distractors look like the description witnesses gave. Also, witnesses should be warned that the culprit *may not be present.* This reduces false positives and increases accurate identifications (Wells et al., 1999). The worst situation occurs when only one person is presented as a suspect. In that case, false identifications of look-alike innocent people are a real danger (Yarmey, Yarmey, & Yarmey, 1996).

Police lineups make use of the sensitivity of recognition memory. However, unless great care is taken, false identifications are still possible (Naka, 1998).

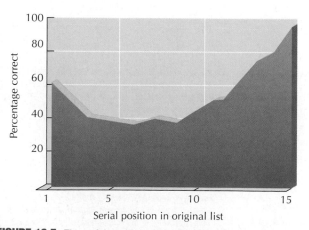

❖ **FIGURE 10.7** *The serial position effect. The graph shows the percentage of subjects correctly recalling each item in a 15-item list. Recall is best for the first and last items. (Data from Craik, 1970.)*

Relearning

In a classic experiment, a psychologist read a short passage in Greek to his son. He did this each day when the boy was between 15 months and 3 years of age. At age 8, the boy was asked if he remembered the Greek passage. He showed no evidence of recall. He was then shown selections from the passage he heard and selections from other Greek passages. Could he recognize the one he heard as an infant? "It's all Greek to me!" he said, indicating no recognition (and drawing a frown from everyone in the room).

Had the psychologist stopped, he might have concluded that no memory of the Greek remained. However, the child was then asked to memorize the original quotation and others of equal difficulty. This time his earlier learning became evident. The boy memorized the passage he heard in childhood 25 percent faster than the others (Burtt, 1941). As this experiment suggests, **relearning** is typically the most sensitive measure of memory.

When a person is tested by relearning, how do we know a memory still exists? As with the boy described, relearning is measured by a **savings score** (the amount of time saved when relearning information). Let's say it takes you 1 hour to memorize all the names in a telephone book. (It's a small town.) Two years later, you relearn them in 45 minutes. Because you "saved" 15 minutes, your savings score would be 25 percent (15 divided by 60 times 100). Savings scores provide a good reason for studying a wide range of subjects. It may seem that learning algebra, history, or a foreign language is wasted if you don't use the knowledge immediately. But when you do need such information, you will be able to relearn it quickly.

Implicit and Explicit Memories

Many memories remain outside of conscious awareness. For example, if you know how to type, it is apparent that you know where the letters are on the keyboard. But how many typists could correctly label blank keys in a drawing of a typewriter? Many people find that they cannot directly remember such information, even though they "know" it.

Who were the last three presidents of the United States? What did you have for breakfast today? What is the title of Michael Jackson's best-selling album? Explicit memory is used in answering each of these questions. **Explicit memories** are past experiences that are consciously brought to mind. Recall, recognition, and the tests you take in school rely on explicit memories. In contrast, **implicit memories** lie outside of awareness (Roediger, 1990). That is, we are not aware that a memory exists. Nevertheless, implicit memories—such as unconsciously

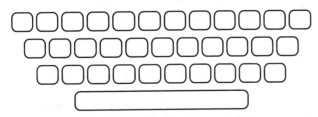

Can you label the letter keys on this blank typewriter? If you can, you probably used implicit memory to do it.

knowing where the letters are on a typewriter—greatly influence our behavior (Neath, 1998).

PRIMING *How is it possible to show that a memory exists if it lies outside of awareness?* Psychologists first noticed implicit memory while studying memory loss caused by brain injuries. Let's say, for example, that a patient is shown a list of common words, such as *chair, tree, lamp, table,* and so on. A few minutes later, the patient is asked to recall words from the list. Sadly, he has no memory of the words.

Now, instead of asking the patient to explicitly recall the list, we could "prime" his memory by giving him the first two letters of each word. "We'd like you to say a word that begins with these letters," we tell him. "Just say whatever comes to mind." Of course, many words could be made from each pair of letters. For example, the first item (from *chair*) would be the letters CH. The patient could say "child," "chalk," "chain," "check," or many other words. Instead, he says, "chair," a word from the original list. The patient is not aware that he is remembering the list, but as he gives a word for each letter pair, almost all are from the list. Apparently, the letters **primed** (activated) hidden memories, which then influenced his answers.

Similar effects have been found for people with normal memories. As the preceding example implies, implicit memories are often revealed by giving a person limited cues, such as the first letter of words or partial drawings of objects. Typically, the person believes that he or she is just saying whatever comes to mind. Nevertheless, information previously seen or heard affects his or her answers (Roediger, 1990). Some nutritionists like to say, "You are what you eat." In the realm of memory, it appears that we are what we experience—to a far greater degree than once realized.

EXCEPTIONAL MEMORY—WIZARDS OF RECALL

Can you remember how many doors there are in your house or apartment? To answer a question like this, many people form **internal images** (mental pictures) of each room and count the

---

Serial position effect *The tendency to make the most errors in remembering the middle items of an ordered list.*
Recognition memory *An ability to correctly identify previously learned information.*
Distractors *False items included with a correct item to form a test of recognition memory (for example, the wrong answers on a multiple-choice test).*
False positive *A false sense of recognition.*
Relearning *Learning again something that was previously learned. Used to measure memory of prior learning.*
Savings score *The amount of time saved (expressed as a percentage) when relearning information.*
Explicit memory *A memory that a person is aware of having; a memory that is consciously retrieved.*
Implicit memory *A memory that a person does not know exists; a memory that is retrieved unconsciously.*
Priming *Facilitating the retrieval of an implicit memory by using cues to activate hidden memories.*
Internal images *Mental images or visual depictions used in memory and thinking.*

❖ **FIGURE 10.8** (a) *"Treasure map" similar to the one used by Kosslyn, Ball, and Reiser (1978) to study images in memory. (b) This graph shows how long it took subjects to move a visualized spot various distances on their mental images of the map. (See text for explanation.)*

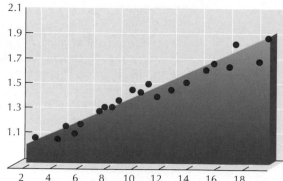

(a)

(b)

doorways they visualize. As this example implies, many memories are stored as mental images (Dewhurst & Conway, 1994).

Stephen Kosslyn, Thomas Ball, and Brian Reiser (1978) found an interesting way to show that memories do exist as images. Participants first memorized a sort of treasure map similar to the one shown in ❖Figure 10.8a. They were then asked to picture a black dot moving from one object, such as one of the trees, to another, such as the hut at the top of the island. Did people really form an image to do this task? It seems they did. As shown in ❖Figure 10.8b, the time it took to "move" the dot was directly related to actual distances on the map.

Is the "treasure map" task an example of photographic memory? In some ways, internal memory images do have "photographic" qualities. However, the term *photographic memory* is more often used to describe a type of memory called *eidetic imagery.*

Eidetic Imagery

Eidetic (eye-DET-ik) **imagery** occurs when a person has visual images clear enough to be "scanned" or retained for at least 30 seconds. Internal memory images can be "viewed" mentally with the eyes closed. In contrast, eidetic images are "projected" out in front of a person. That is, they are best "seen" on a plain surface, such as a blank piece of paper. In this respect, eidetic images are somewhat like the after-images you might have after looking at a flashbulb or a brightly lit neon sign (Kunzendorf, 1989).

Eidetic memory is most common in childhood, with about 8 children out of 100 having eidetic images. In one series of tests, children were shown a picture from *Alice's Adventures in Wonderland* (❖Fig. 10.9). To test your eidetic imagery, look at the picture and read the instructions there.

Now, let's see how much you remember. Can you say (without looking again) which of Alice's apron strings is longer? Are the cat's front paws crossed? How many stripes are on the cat's tail? After the picture was removed from view, one 10-year-old boy was asked what he saw. He replied, "I see the tree, gray tree with three limbs. I see the cat with stripes around its tail." Asked to count the stripes, the boy replied, "There are about 16" (a correct count!). The boy then went on to describe the remainder of the picture in striking detail (Haber, 1969).

❖ **FIGURE 10.9** *A test picture like that used to identify children with eidetic imagery. To test your eidetic imagery, look at the picture for 30 seconds. Then look at a blank surface and try to "project" the picture onto it. If you have good eidetic imagery, you will be able to see the picture in detail. Return now to the text and try to answer the questions there. (Redrawn from an illustration in Lewis Carroll's* Alice's Adventures in Wonderland.*)*

Don't be disappointed if you didn't do too well when you tried your eidetic skills. Most eidetic imagery disappears during adolescence and becomes rare by adulthood (Kunzendorf, 1989). Actually, this may not be too much of a loss. The majority of eidetic memorizers have no better long-term memory than average.

Exceptional Memory

Let's return now to the concept of internal memory images. In rare instances, such images may be so vivid that it is reasonable to say that a person has "photographic memory." A notable example was reported by Aleksandr Luria (1968) in his book, *The Mind of a Mnemonist.* Luria studied a man he called Mr. S who had practically unlimited memory for visual images. Mr. S could remember almost everything that ever happened to him with incredible accuracy. Luria tried to test Mr. S's memory by using longer and longer lists of words or numbers. However, he soon discovered that no matter how long the list, Mr. S was able to recall it without error. Mr. S could memorize, with equal ease, strings of digits, meaningless consonants, mathematical formulas, and poems in foreign languages. His memory was so powerful that he had to devise ways to *forget*—such as writing information on a piece of paper and then burning it.

As fantastic as Mr. S's memory might sound to any student, it caused him great difficulty. He remembered so much that he couldn't separate important facts from trivia or facts from fantasy (Neath, 1998). For instance, if you asked him to read this chapter, he might remember every word. However, he might also recall all the images each word made him think of and all the sights, sounds, and feelings that occurred as he was reading. As a result, finding the answer for a specific question, writing a logical essay, or even understanding a single sentence was very difficult for him.

Few people in history have possessed memory abilities like Mr. S's. Nonetheless, you probably know at least one person who has an especially good memory. Is superior memory a biological gift? Or do excellent memorizers merely make better-than-average use of normal memory capacities? Let's investigate further.

LEARNED STRATEGIES   At first, a student volunteer named Steve could remember 7 digits—a typical score for a college student. Could he improve with practice? For 20 months, Steve practiced memorizing ever-longer lists of digits. Ultimately, he was able to memorize around 80 digits, like this sample:

> 92842048050842268953990190252912807999970
> 66065747173106010805852697260263357332135

How did Steve reach such lofty heights of memory? Basically, he worked by chunking numbers into meaningful groups of three or four digits. Steve's avid interest in long-distance running helped greatly. To him, the first three digits in our example represented 9 minutes and 28 seconds, a good time for a 2-mile run. When running times wouldn't work, Steve used other associations, such as ages or dates, to chunk digits (Ericsson & Chase, 1982).

Psychologist Anders Ericsson believes that exceptional memory is merely a learned extension of normal memory. As evidence, he notes that Steve's short-term memory did not improve during months of practice. For example, Steve could still memorize only seven consonants. Steve's phenomenal memory for numbers grew as he figured out new ways to encode digits and store them in LTM

Researchers studying Rajan Mahadevan have drawn similar conclusions about his spectacular memory for long strings of

digits. In 1981 Rajan earned a place in the *Guinness Book of World Records* by reciting the first 31,811 digits of *pi!* Yet, like Steve, Rajan's memory for most other types of information is average. His exceptional memory seems to be based on highly practiced strategies for encoding and storing digits (Thompson et al., 1993). By using similar memory systems, college students have even managed to duplicate some of Mr. S's feats, such as memorizing a 50-digit matrix in 3 minutes (Higbee, 1997).

Steve and Rajan began with normal memory for digits. Both extended their memory abilities by diligent practice. Clearly, exceptional memory can be learned (Neath, 1998). However, we still have to wonder, do some people have naturally superior memories?

Memory Champions

In 1991, the first World Memory Championship was held in London. There, a variety of mental athletes competed to see who had the best memory. To remain in the running, each contestant had to rapidly memorize daunting amounts of information, such as long lists of unrelated words and numbers. Psychologists John Wilding and Elizabeth Valentine saw an opportunity to study exceptional memory and persuaded the contestants to take some additional memory tests. These ranged from ordinary (recall a story), to challenging (recall the telephone numbers of six different people), to diabolical (recall 48 numerals arranged in rows and columns; recognize 14 previously seen pictures of snowflakes among 70 new photos) (Wilding & Valentine, 1994a).

Wilding and Valentine found that exceptional memorizers:

- Use memory strategies and techniques
- Have specialized interests and knowledge that make certain types of information easier to encode and recall
- Have naturally superior memory abilities, often including vivid mental images

The first two points confirm what we learned from Steve's acquired memory ability. Many of the contestants, for example, actively used memory strategies called *mnemonics* (nee-MON-iks). Specialized interests and knowledge also helped for some tasks. For example, one contestant, who is a mathematician, was exceedingly good at memorizing numbers (Wilding & Valentine, 1994a).

Eidetic imagery *The ability to retain a "projected" mental image long enough to use it as a source of information.*

$$\begin{array}{cccccccc} 8 & 7 & 3 & 7 & 9 & 2 & 6 & 8 \\ 2 & 0 & 1 & 1 & 7 & 4 & 9 & 5 \\ 0 & 1 & 7 & 5 & 8 & 7 & 8 & 3 \\ 1 & 9 & 4 & 7 & 6 & 0 & 6 & 9 \\ 3 & 6 & 1 & 6 & 8 & 1 & 5 & 4 \\ 4 & 5 & 2 & 4 & 0 & 2 & 9 & 7 \end{array}$$

This number matrix is similar to the ones contestants in the World Memory Championship had to memorize. To be scored as correct, digits had to be recalled in their proper positions (Wilding & Valentine, 1994a).

Several of the memory contestants were able to excel on tasks that prevented the use of learned strategies and techniques. This observation implies that superior memory ability can be a "gift" as well as a learned skill. Wilding and Valentine conclude that exceptional memory may be based on either natural ability or learned strategies. Usually it requires both. In fact, most super memorizers use strategies to augment their natural talents, whenever possible. Some mnemonic strategies are described in this chapter's Psychology in Action section. Please do remember to read it.

KNOWLEDGE BUILDER
MEMORY TASKS AND EXCEPTIONAL MEMORY

RELATE

Have you experienced the TOT state recently? Were you able to retrieve the word you were seeking? If not, what could you remember about it?

Do you prefer tests based primarily on recall or recognition? Have you observed a savings effect while relearning information you studied in the past (such as in high school)?

Can you think of things you do that are based on implicit memories? For instance, how do you know which way to turn various handles in your house, apartment, or dorm? Do you have to explicitly think, "Turn it to the right" before you act?

What kinds of information are you good at remembering? Why do you think your memory is better for those topics?

LEARNING CHECK

Unless you have a memory like Mr. S's, it might be a good idea to see if you can answer these questions before reading on.

1. Four techniques for measuring or demonstrating memory are

   _____ _____

   _____ _____

2. Multiple-choice tests primarily require _____ memory.

3. Essay tests require _____ of facts or ideas.

4. As a measure of memory, a savings score is associated with
   a. recognition *b.* eidetic images *c.* relearning *d.* reconstruction

5. Tests of _____ memory are designed to reveal the influences of information that is stored but that remains unconscious.

6. Children with eidetic imagery typically have no better than average long-term memory. T or F?

7. In order to perform well on tests of memory, one must be born with naturally superior memory abilities. T or F?

CRITICAL THINKING

8. Mr. S had great difficulty remembering faces. Can you guess why?

Answers:

1. recall, recognition, relearning, priming 2. recognition 3. recall 4. c 5. implicit 6. T 7. F 8. Mr. S's memory was so specific that faces seemed different and unfamiliar if he saw them from a new angle or if a face had a different expression on it than when Mr. S last saw it.

FORGETTING—WHY WE, UH, LET'S SEE; WHY WE, UH . . . FORGET!

Why are some memories lost so quickly? For example, why is it hard to remember information a week or two after taking a test in class? Most forgetting tends to occur immediately after memorization. In a famous set of experiments, memory researcher Herman Ebbinghaus (1885) tested his own memory at various times after learning. Ebbinghaus wanted to be sure he would not be swayed by prior learning, so he memorized **nonsense syllables.** These are meaningless three-letter words such as GEX, CEF, and WOL. The importance of using meaningless words is shown by the fact that VEL, FAB, and DUZ are no longer used on memory tests. Subjects who recognize these words as detergent names find them very easy to remember.

By waiting various lengths of time before testing himself, Ebbinghaus plotted a **curve of forgetting.** This graph shows the amount of information remembered after varying lengths of time (❖ Fig. 10.10). Because Ebbinghaus took great care in

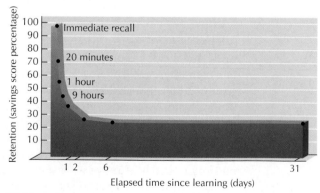

❖ **FIGURE 10.10** *The curve of forgetting. This graph shows the amount remembered (measured by relearning) after varying lengths of time. Notice how rapidly forgetting occurs. The material learned was nonsense syllables. Forgetting curves for meaningful information also show early losses followed by a long gradual decline, but overall, forgetting occurs much more slowly. (After Ebbinghaus, 1885.)*

❖ **FIGURE 10.11** *Some of the distractor items used in a study of recognition memory and encoding failure. Penny A is correct but was seldom recognized. Pennies G and J were popular wrong answers. (Adapted from Nickerson & Adams, 1979.)*

his work, his findings remain valid today. Notice that forgetting is rapid at first and is then followed by a slow decline.

As a student, you should note that a short delay between reviewing and taking a test minimizes forgetting. However, this is no reason for cramming. Most students make the error of *only* cramming. If you cram, you don't have to remember for very long, but you may not learn enough in the first place. If you use short, daily study sessions *and* review intensely before a test, you will get the benefit of good preparation and a minimum time lapse.

The Ebbinghaus curve shows less than 30 percent remembered after only 2 days have passed. Is forgetting really that rapid? No, not always. Meaningful information is not lost nearly as quickly as nonsense syllables. After 3 years, students who took a university psychology course had forgotten about 30 percent of the facts they learned. After that, little more forgetting occurred (Conway et al., 1992). Actually, as learning grows stronger, some knowledge may become nearly permanent (Bahrick, 1984). Semantic memories and implicit memories (both mentioned earlier) appear to be very lasting (Bower, 1990).

"I'll never forget old, old . . . oh, what's his name?" Forgetting is both frustrating and embarrassing. Why *do* we forget? The Ebbinghaus curve gives a general picture of forgetting, but it doesn't explain it. For explanations we must search further.

Encoding Failure

Whose head is on a U.S. penny? Which way is it facing? What is written at the top of a penny? Can you accurately draw and label a penny? In an interesting experiment, Ray Nickerson and Marilyn Adams (1979) asked a large group of students to draw a penny. Few could. Well, then, could the students at least recognize a drawing of a real penny among fakes? (See ❖ Figure 10.11.) Again, few could.

The most obvious reason for forgetting is also the most commonly overlooked. In many cases, we "forget" because of **encoding failure.** That is, a memory was never formed in the first place. Obviously, few of us ever encode the details of a penny. If you are bothered by frequent forgetting, it is wise to ask yourself, "Have I been storing the information in the first place?" If you have a reputation for being absentminded, en-

coding failure is probably to blame (Schachter, 1999). When 140 college professors were asked what strategies they use to improve their memory, the favorite technique was to *write things down* (Park et al., 1990). Making notes ensures that information will not be lost from short-term memory before you can review it and store it more permanently. (Encoding failures also affect our memories of people. See "College Students— They're All Alike!")

Decay

One view of forgetting holds that **memory traces** (changes in nerve cells or brain activity) **decay** (fade or weaken) over time. Decay appears to be a factor in the loss of sensory memories. Such fading also applies to short-term memory. Information stored in STM seems to initiate a brief flurry of activity in the brain that quickly dies out. Short-term memory therefore operates like a "leaky bucket": New information constantly pours in, but it rapidly fades away and is replaced by still newer information. Let's say that you are trying to remember a short list of letters, numbers, or words after seeing or hearing them once. If it takes you more than 4 to 6 seconds to repeat the list, you will forget some of the items (Dosher & Ma, 1998).

DISUSE   Is it possible that the decay of memory traces also explains long-term forgetting? That is, could long-term memory traces fade from **disuse** (infrequent retrieval) and eventually become too weak to retrieve? There is evidence that memories not retrieved and "used" or rehearsed become weaker over time

Nonsense syllables *Invented three-letter words used to test learning and memory.*
Curve of forgetting *A graph that shows the amount of memorized information remembered after varying lengths of time.*
Encoding failure *Failure to store sufficient information to form a useful memory.*
Memory traces *Physical changes in nerve cells or brain activity that take place when memories are stored.*
Memory decay *The fading or weakening of memories assumed to occur when memory traces become weaker.*
Disuse *Theory that memory traces weaken when memories are not periodically used or retrieved.*

HUMAN DIVERSITY

Imagine yourself in this situation: As you are walking on campus, a young man, who looks like a college student, approaches you and asks for directions. While you are talking, two workers carrying a door pass between you and the young man. While your view is blocked by the door, another man takes the place of the first. Now you are facing a different person than the one who was there just seconds earlier. If this happened to you, do you think you would notice the change? Remarkably, only half of the people tested in this way noticed the switch (Simons & Levin, 1998)!

How could anyone fail to notice that one stranger had been replaced by another? The people who didn't remember the first man were all older adults. College students weren't fooled by the switch. The authors of this study, Daniel Simons and Daniel Levin, believe that older adults encoded the first man in very general terms as a "college student." As a result, that's all they remembered about him.

Because his replacement also looked like a college student, they thought he was the same person (Simons & Levin, 1998).

Actually, such memory failures are not as surprising as they might seem. We all tend to categorize strangers according to the groups they belong to: Is the person young or old, male or female, a member of my ethnic group or another? This tendency to encode only general information about strangers is one reason why eyewitnesses are better at identifying members of their own ethnic group than they are at identifying people from other groups (Kassin, Ellsworth, & Smith, 1989). It may seem harsh to say so, but when social contacts are brief or superficial, people really do act like members of other ethnic groups "all look alike." Of course, this bias disappears when we get to know specific members of other groups. Then, we encode more details about each person, which allows us to recognize and appreciate them as individuals.

(Schachter, 1999). However, disuse alone cannot fully explain forgetting.

Disuse doesn't seem to account for our ability to recover seemingly forgotten memories through redintegration, relearning, and priming. It also fails to explain why some unused memories fade, while others are carried for life. A third contradiction will be recognized by anyone who has spent time with the elderly. People growing senile may become so forgetful that they can't remember what happened a week ago. Yet at the same time your Uncle Oscar's recent memories are fading, he may have vivid memories of trivial and long-forgotten events from the past. "Why, I remember it as clearly as if it were yesterday," he will say, forgetting that the story he is about to tell is one he told earlier the same day. In short, disuse offers no more than a partial explanation of long-term forgetting.

If decay and disuse don't fully explain forgetting, what does? Let's briefly consider some additional possibilities.

Cue-Dependent Forgetting

Often, memories appear to be *available*, but not *accessible*. An example is having an answer on the "tip of your tongue." You know the answer is there, but it remains just "out of reach." This suggests that many memories are "forgotten" because **memory cues** (stimuli associated with a memory) are missing when the time comes to retrieve information. For example, if you were asked, "What were you doing on Monday afternoon of the third week in September 2 years ago?" your reply might be "Come on, how should I know?" However, if you were reminded, "That was the day the courthouse burned," or "That was the day Stacy had her automobile accident," you might remember immediately.

The presence of appropriate cues almost always enhances memory. In theory, for instance, memory will be best if you study in the same room where you will be tested. Because this

External cues like those found in a photograph or a scrapbook or during a walk through an old neighborhood often aid recall of seemingly lost memories. For many veterans, finding a familiar name engraved in the Vietnam Veterans Memorial unleashes a flood of memories.

is often impossible, while you are studying try to visualize the room where you will be tested. Doing so can enhance your memory later (Jerabek & Standing, 1992).

STATE-DEPENDENT LEARNING   Have you heard the story about the drunk who misplaced his wallet and had to get drunk again to find it? Although this tale is often told as a joke, it is not too farfetched. The bodily state that exists during learning can be a strong cue for later memory, an effect known as **state-dependent learning** (Neath, 1998). Being very thirsty, for instance, might prompt you to remember events that took place

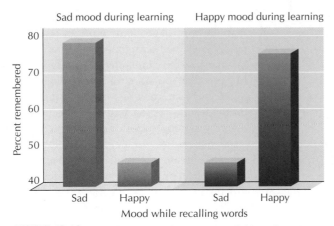

How could anyone lose something as large as a car? If you park your car in a different place every day, you may have experienced forgetting caused by interference. Today's memory about your car's location is easily confused with memories from yesterday, and the day before, and the day before that.

❖ **FIGURE 10.12** *The effect of mood on memory. Subjects best remembered a list of words when their mood during testing was the same as their mood when they learned the list. (Adapted from Bower, 1981.)*

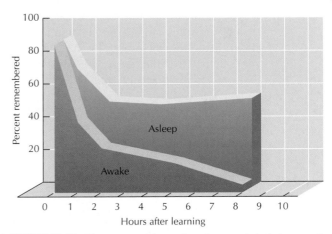

❖ **FIGURE 10.13** *The amount of forgetting after a period of sleep or of being awake. Notice that sleep causes less memory loss than activity that occurs while one is awake. (After Jenkins & Dallenbach, 1924.)*

on another occasion when you were thirsty. Because of such effects, information learned under the influence of a drug is best remembered when the drugged state occurs again (Slot & Colpaert, 1999).

A similar effect applies to emotional states (Eich, 1995). For instance, Gordon Bower (1981) found that people who learned a list of words while in a happy mood recalled them better when they were again happy. People who learned while they felt sad remembered best when they were sad (❖Fig. 10.12). Similarly, if you are in a happy mood, you are more likely to remember recent happy events (Salovey & Singer, 1989). If you are in a bad mood, you will tend to have unpleasant memories (Eich et al., 1990). Such links between emotional cues and memory could explain why couples who quarrel often end up remembering—and rehashing—old arguments.

Interference

Further insight into forgetting comes from a classic experiment in which college students learned lists of nonsense syllables. After studying, students in one group slept for 8 hours and were then tested for memory of the lists. A second group remained awake for 8 hours and went about business as usual. When members of the second group were tested, they remembered *less* than the group that slept (❖Fig. 10.13.) This difference is based on the fact that new learning can interfere with previous learning. **Interference** refers to the tendency for new memories to impair retrieval of older memories (and the reverse). It seems to apply to both short-term and long-term memory.

It is not completely clear if new memories alter existing memory traces or if they make it harder to "locate" (retrieve) earlier memories. In any case, there is no doubt that interference is a major cause of forgetting (Johnson & Hasher, 1987). College students who memorized 20 lists of words (one list each day) were able to recall only 15 percent of the last list.

BRIDGES

Sleep can improve memory in another way: REM sleep and dreaming appear to help us form certain types of memories.

See Chapter 8, page 245.

Students who learned only one list remembered 80 percent (Underwood, 1957) (❖Fig. 10.14).

ORDER EFFECTS   The sleeping college students remembered more because retroactive (RET-ro-AK-tiv) interference was held to a minimum. **Retroactive interference** refers to the tendency for new learning to inhibit retrieval of old learning. Avoiding new learning prevents retroactive interference. This doesn't exactly mean you should hide in a closet after you study for an exam. However,

Memory cue *Any stimulus associated with a particular memory. Memory cues usually enhance retrieval.*
State-dependent learning *Memory influenced by one's bodily state at the time of learning and at the time of retrieval. Improved memory occurs when the bodily states match.*
Interference *The tendency for new memories to impair retrieval of older memories, and the reverse.*
Retroactive interference *The tendency for new memories to interfere with the retrieval of old memories.*

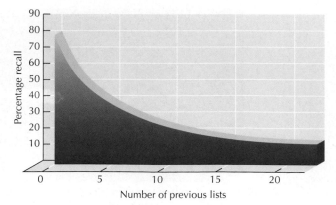

❖ **FIGURE 10.14** *Effects of interference on memory. A graph of the approximate relationship between percentage recalled and number of different word lists memorized. (Adapted from Underwood, 1957.)*

Let's assume that the experimental group remembers less than the control group on a test of task B. In that case, learning task A interfered with memory for task B.

Then proactive interference goes "forward" in time? Yes. Imagine that you cram for a psychology exam. Later the same night, you cram for a history exam. It's likely that your memory for the second subject studied (history) will be less accurate than if you had studied only history. (Because of retroactive interference, your memory for psychology would probably suffer, too.) The greater the similarity in the two subjects studied, the more interference takes place. The moral, of course, is don't procrastinate in preparing for exams.

The interference effects we have described apply primarily to memories of verbal information, such as the contents of this chapter. When you are learning a skill, similarity can sometimes be beneficial rather than disruptive. The next section explains how this occurs.

Transfer of Training

Two people begin mandolin lessons. One already plays the violin. The other is a trumpet player. All other things being equal, which person will initially do better in learning the mandolin? If you chose the violin player, you have an intuitive grasp of what positive transfer is. (The strings on a mandolin are tuned the same as a violin.) **Positive transfer** takes place when mastery of one task aids mastery of a second task. Another example would be learning to balance and turn on a bicycle before learning to ride a motorcycle or motor scooter. Likewise, surfing and skateboarding skills transfer to snowboarding.

Is there such a thing as negative transfer? There is indeed. In **negative transfer,** skills developed in one situation conflict with those required to master a new task. Learning to back a car with a trailer attached to it is a good example. Normally, when you are backing a car, the steering wheel is turned in the direction you want to go, the same as when moving forward. However, when backing a trailer, you must turn the steering wheel *away* from the direction you want the trailer to go. This situation results in negative transfer and often creates comical scenes at campgrounds and boat-launching ramps.

On a more serious note, many tragic crashes caused by negative transfer finally led to greater standardization of airplane cockpits. Fortunately, negative transfer is usually brief, and it occurs less often than positive transfer. Negative transfer is most

you should avoid studying other subjects until the exam. Sleeping after study can help you retain memories, and reading, writing, or even watching TV may cause interference.

Retroactive interference is easily demonstrated in the laboratory by this arrangement:

| Experimental group: | Learn A | Learn B | Test A |
| Control group: | Learn A | Rest | Test A |

Imagine yourself as a member of the experimental group. In task A, you learn a list of telephone numbers. In task B, you learn a list of Social Security numbers. How do you score on a test of task A (the telephone numbers)? If you do not remember as much as the control group that learns *only* task A, then retroactive interference has occurred. The second thing learned interfered with memory of the first thing learned; the interference went "backward," or was "retroactive" (❖Fig. 10.15).

Proactive (pro-AK-tiv) interference is a second basic source of forgetting. **Proactive interference** occurs when prior learning inhibits recall of later learning. A test for proactive interference would take this form:

| Experimental group: | Learn A | Learn B | Test B |
| Control group: | Rest | Learn B | Test B |

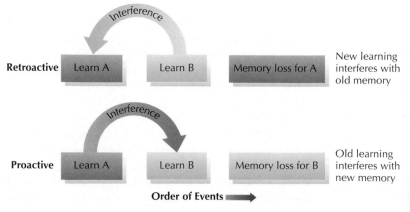

❖ **FIGURE 10.15** *Retroactive and proactive interference. The order of learning and testing shows whether interference is retroactive (backward) or proactive (forward).*

likely to occur when a new response must be made to an old stimulus. If you have ever encountered a pull-type handle on a door that must be pushed open, you will appreciate this point.

Repression and Suppression

Take a moment and scan over the events of the last few years of your life. What kinds of things most easily come to mind? Many people remember happy, positive events better than disappointments and irritations (Linton, 1979). A clinical psychologist would call this tendency **repression,** or *motivated forgetting.* Through repression, painful, threatening, or embarrassing memories are held out of consciousness. An example is provided by soldiers who have repressed some of the horrors they saw during combat (Karon & Widener, 1997, 1998).

The forgetting of past failures, upsetting childhood events, the names of people you dislike, or appointments you don't want to keep may reveal repression. People prone to repression tend to be hypersensitive to emotional events. As a result, they use repression to protect themselves from threatening thoughts (Mendolia, Moore, & Tesser, 1996).

It's possible that some adults who were sexually abused as children have repressed memories of their mistreatment. It's also possible that such memories may surface during psychotherapy or other circumstances. However, as discussed in ❖Figure 10.16, caution is required anytime accusa- tions are made on the basis of seemingly "recovered" memories. (This chapter's A Step Beyond feature discusses some important additional cautions about the recovery of repressed memories.)

If I try to forget a test I failed, am I repressing it? No. Repression can be distinguished from **suppression,** an active, conscious attempt to put something out of mind. By not thinking about the test, you have merely suppressed a memory. If you choose to, you can remember the test. Clinicians consider true repression an *unconscious* event. When a memory is repressed, we may be unaware that forgetting has even occurred.

Psychologists Kenneth Bowers and Peter Farvolden believe that repression is a form of avoidance. If you have experienced a painful emotional event, you will probably avoid all thoughts associated with it. This tends to keep cues out of mind that could trigger a painful memory (Bowers & Farvolden, 1996).

BRIDGES

Clinical psychologists regard repression as one of the major psychological defenses we use against emotional threats.

See Chapter 16, page 530 for details.

Flashbulb Memories

Why are some traumatic events vividly remembered while others are repressed? Psychologists use the term **flashbulb memories** to describe images that seem to be frozen in memory at times of personal tragedy, accident, or other emotionally significant events (Finkenauer, 1998).

Depending on your age, you may have a "flashbulb" memory for the Pearl Harbor attack, the assassinations of John F. Kennedy and Martin Luther King, Jr., the *Challenger* space shuttle disaster, or Princess Diana's death. Flashbulb memories are most often formed when an event is surprising, important, or emotional (Rubin, 1985). They are frequently associated with public tragedies, but memories of positive events may also have "flashbulb" clarity.

Flashbulb memories seem to be very detailed. Often, they focus primarily on how you reacted to the event. ◆Table 10.1 lists some memories that had "flashbulb" clarity for at least 50 percent of a group of college students. How vivid are the memories they trigger for you? (Note again that both positive and negative events are listed.)

The term *flashbulb memories* was first used to describe recall that seemed to be unusually vivid and permanent. It has become clear, however, that flashbulb memories are not always accurate (Harsch & Neisser, 1989). More than anything else, what sets flashbulb memories apart is that we tend to place

❖ **FIGURE 10.16** *In what appeared to be an extreme case of repression, Eileen Franklin testified in court in 1990 that her father, George Franklin, abducted, raped, and killed 8-year-old Susan Nason in 1969. Eileen testified that the memory surfaced one day as she looked into the eyes of her own young daughter. Her father was convicted solely on the basis of her "repressed" memory. However, in 1996, the conviction was overturned when DNA tests cleared her father of a second murder she also accused him of committing. As the Franklin case illustrates, trying to separate true memories from fantasies has become a major headache for psychologists and the courts.*

Proactive interference *The tendency for old memories to interfere with the retrieval of newer memories.*
Positive transfer *Mastery of one task aids learning or performing another.*
Negative transfer *Mastery of one task conflicts with learning or performing another.*
Repression *Unconsciously pushing unwanted memories out of awareness.*
Suppression *A conscious effort to put something out of mind or to keep it from awareness.*
Flashbulb memories *Memories created at times of high emotion that seem especially vivid.*

People who survive earthquakes almost always have flashbulb memories of the event. Typically, people vividly remember where they were when the quake started, what they thought as it was occurring, and how they reacted to it.

◆ **TABLE 10.1** Bright Flashes of Memory

MEMORY CUE	PERCENTAGE OF STUDENTS WITH FLASHBULB MEMORIES
A car accident you were in or witnessed	85
When you first met your college roommate	82
The night of your high school graduation	81
The night of your senior prom (if you went or not)	78
An early romantic experience	77
A time you had to speak in front of an audience	72
When you first got your college admissions letter	65
Your first date—the moment you met him or her	57

(From Rubin, 1985.)

great *confidence* in them—even when they are wrong (Weaver, 1993). Perhaps that's because such memories act as prominent landmarks in our lives. We usually review emotionally charged events over and over and tell others about them. Also, public events such as wars, earthquakes, and assassinations reappear many times in the news, which highlights them in memory (Wright, 1993).

MEMORY FORMATION—SOME "SHOCKING" FINDINGS

One possibility overlooked in our discussion of forgetting is that memories may be lost as they are being formed. For example, a head injury may cause a "gap" in memories preceding the accident. **Retrograde amnesia,** as this is called, involves forgetting events that occurred before an injury or trauma. In contrast, **anterograde amnesia** involves forgetting events that follow an injury or trauma. (An example of this type of amnesia is discussed in a moment.)

Consolidation

Retrograde amnesia can be understood if we assume that it takes a certain amount of time to move information from short-term to long-term memory. The forming of a long-term memory is called **consolidation** (Squire et al., 1993). You can think of consolidation as being somewhat like writing your name in wet concrete. Once the concrete is set, the information (your name) is fairly lasting, but while it is setting, it can be wiped out (amnesia) or scribbled over (interference).

Consider a classic experiment on consolidation, in which a rat is placed on a small platform. The rat steps down to the floor and receives a painful electric shock. After one shock, the rat can be returned to the platform repeatedly, but it will not step down. Obviously, the rat remembers the shock. Would it remember if consolidation were disturbed?

Interestingly, one way to prevent consolidation is to give a different kind of shock called **electroconvulsive shock (ECS).** ECS is a mild electric shock to the brain. It does not harm the animal, but it does destroy any memory that is being formed. If each painful shock (the one the animal remembers) is followed by ECS (which wipes out memories during consolidation), the rat will step down over and over. Each time, ECS will erase the memory of the painful shock.

What would happen if ECS were given several hours after the learning? Recent memories are more easily disrupted than older memories (Gold, 1987). If enough time is allowed to pass between learning and ECS, the memory will be unaffected because consolidation is already complete. That's why people with mild head injuries lose memories only from just before the accident, while older memories remain intact (Baddeley, 1990). Likewise, you would forget more if you studied, stayed awake 8 hours, and then slept 8 hours than you would if you studied, slept 8 hours, and were awake for 8 hours. Either way, 16 hours would pass. However, less forgetting would occur in the second instance, because more consolidation would occur before interference begins (Nesca & Koulack, 1994).

DRUGS AND MEMORY *Can memory be improved with drugs?* The possibility of chemically improving memory has long intrigued psychologists. We have known for some time that various stimulating drugs speed up consolidation if they are given just after learning (McGaugh, 1983). Note, however, that this only reduces the time during which interference can take place; it does not magically improve memory. Also, the drugs in-

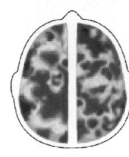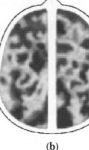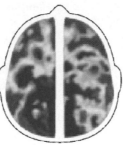

(a)　　　　　　　　(b)　　　　　　　　(c)

❖ **FIGURE 10.17** *Patterns of blood flow in the cerebral cortex (wrinkled outer layer of the brain) change as areas become more or less active. Thus, blood flow can be used to draw "maps" of brain activity. This drawing, which views the brain from the top, shows the results of measuring cerebral blood flow while people were thinking about a semantic memory (a) or an episodic memory (b). In the map, green indicates areas that are more active during semantic thinking. Reds show areas of greater activity during episodic thinking. The brain on the right shows the difference in activity between views a and b. The resulting pattern suggests that the front of the cortex is related to episodic memory. Areas toward the back and sides of the brain, especially the temporal lobes, are more associated with semantic memory (Gabrieli, 1998; Tulving, 1989).*

volved (strychnine, nicotine, caffeine, and amphetamine) must be given in carefully controlled dosages. If the dosage is too high by even a small amount, memory will be *disrupted*. However, other substances are beginning to show promise as memory enhancers (Jaekaelae et al., 1999). Yet, these drugs, too, can disrupt memory if the wrong dosage is given. Also, Mr. S's excessively detailed memory makes it clear that indiscriminately improving memory could be a disaster.

What effect does alcohol have on memory? Memory losses are common when a person overindulges in alcohol. This may be due, in part, to state-dependent learning. At higher levels of intoxication, alcohol seems to directly impair encoding and consolidation of memories. A person suffering an alcohol blackout may lose anywhere from a few minutes to several hours of memory (Goodwin, 1995). Research makes it clear that studying while drunk is an excellent way to *lower* test scores. Even intoxicated eyewitnesses to crimes, which are usually memorable events, suffer impaired memory for what they saw (Yuille & Tollestrup, 1990).

From STM to LTM

Where does consolidation take place in the brain? Actually, many areas of the brain are responsible for memory, but the **hippocampus** is particularly important. This structure, buried deep within the brain, seems to act as a sort of "switching station" between short-term and long-term memory (Gabrieli, 1998).

Humans who have had hippocampal damage show a striking inability to store new memories (Bigler et al., 1996). A patient described by Brenda Milner is typical. Two years after an operation damaged his hippocampus, a 29-year-old patient continued to give his age as 27. He also reported that it seemed as if the operation had just taken place (Milner, 1965). His memory of events before the operation remained clear, but he found forming new long-term memories almost impossible. (He suffered, in other words, from anterograde amnesia.) When his parents moved to a new house a few blocks away on the same street, he could not remember the new address.

BRIDGES

ECS has been employed as a psychiatric treatment for severe depression. Used in this way, electroshock therapy also causes memory loss.

See Chapter 18, page 621.

Month after month, he read the same magazines over and over without finding them familiar. If you were to meet this man, he would seem fairly normal, because he still has short-term memory. But if you were to leave the room and return 15 minutes later, he would act as if he had never seen you before. Years ago, his favorite uncle died, but he suffers the same grief anew each time he is told of the death. Lacking the ability to form new lasting memories, he lives eternally in the present (Hilts, 1995).

The Brain and Memory

Somewhere within the 3-pound mass of the human brain lies all we know: ZIP codes, faces of loved ones, history, favorite melodies, the taste of an apple, and much, much more. Where is this information? Karl Lashley, a pioneering brain researcher, set out in the 1920s to find an **engram,** or memory trace. Lashley taught animals to run mazes and then removed parts of their brains to see how memory of the maze changed. After 30 years he had to concede defeat: Engrams are not located in any one area of the brain. It mattered little which part of the brain's cortex he removed. Only the *amount* removed correlated to memory loss.

Lashley's conclusion remains true for specific memories. However, some areas of the cerebral cortex *are* more important to memory than others (Tulving, 1989). ❖Figure 10.17 explains why.

Retrograde amnesia *Loss of memory for events that preceded a head injury or other amnesia-causing event.*
Anterograde amnesia *Loss of the ability to form or retrieve memories for events that occur after an injury or trauma.*
Consolidation *Process by which relatively permanent memories are formed in the brain.*
Electroconvulsive shock *An electric current passed directly through the brain, producing a convulsion.*
Hippocampus *A brain structure associated with emotion and the transfer of information from short-term memory to long-term memory.*
Engram *A "memory trace" in the brain.*

To summarize (and simplify greatly), the hippocampus handles memory consolidation. Once long-term memories are formed, they appear to be stored in the cortex of the brain (Gabrieli, 1998; Teng & Squire, 1999).

How are memories recorded in the cortex? Scientists are beginning to identify the exact ways in which nerve cells record information. For example, Eric Kandel and his colleagues have studied learning in the marine snail *Aplysia*. Kandel found that learning in *Aplysia* (ah-PLEEZ-yah) occurs when certain nerve cells in a circuit alter the amount of transmitter chemicals they release (Kandel, 1999). Learning also alters the activity, structure, and chemistry of brain cells. Such changes determine which circuits get stronger and which become weaker. This results in a "reprogramming" of the brain that records information (Klintsova & Greenough, 1999; Kolb & Whishaw, 1998).

Is it true that older people have more problems with memory than younger people? Yes, both short-term and long-term memory capacities tend to decline with advancing age. This appears to be caused by a general slowing of information processing in the brain (Frieske & Park, 1999; Luszcz & Bryan, 1999; Swanson, 1999). However, most older people find ways to compensate for occasional gaps in their memories. Memory lapses in the elderly are a problem only when they are frequent or severe.

Scientists continue to study a bewildering array of chemicals and brain processes that affect memory. If their research succeeds, it may be possible to help the millions of persons who suffer from memory impairment. Will researchers ever produce a "memory pill" for those with normal memory? Some neuroscientists are confident that memory can be and will be artificially enhanced. At present, however, the possibility of something like a "physics pill" or a "math pill" seems remote.

BRIDGES

A loss of memory capacity is one of the first signs of Alzheimer's disease and other types of dementia.

For more information, see Chapter 17, page 574.

An *Aplysia*. The relatively simple nervous system of this sea animal allows scientists to study memory as it occurs in single nerve cells.

KNOWLEDGE BUILDER

FORGETTING

RELATE

Which of the following concepts best explain why you have missed some answers on psychology tests: encoding failure, decay, disuse, memory cues, interference?

Do you know someone whose name you have a hard time remembering? Do you like or dislike that person? Do you think your difficulty is an instance of repression? Suppression? Interference? Encoding failure?

Have you had a flashbulb memory? How vivid is the memory today? How accurate do you think it is?

Here's a mnemonic tip: Elephants are supposed to have good memories, but a *hippo campus* is the place to go if you want to learn to consolidate memories.

LEARNING CHECK

1. According to the Ebbinghaus curve of forgetting, we forget slowly at first, and then a rapid decline occurs. T or F?

2. Which explanation seems to account for the loss of short-term memories?
   a. decay *b.* disuse *c.* repression *d.* interference

3. When memories are available but not accessible, forgetting may be cue dependent. T or F?

4. When learning one thing makes it more difficult to recall another, forgetting may be caused by _____.

5. You are asked to memorize long lists of telephone numbers. You learn a new list each day for 10 days. When tested on list 3, you remember less than a person who learned only the first three lists. Your larger memory loss is probably caused by
   a. disuse *b.* retroactive interference
   c. regression *d.* proactive interference

6. _____ _____ is said to occur when skills learned in one situation conflict with those required to master a new task.

7. Repression is thought of as a type of motivated forgetting. T or F?

8. Retrograde amnesia results when consolidation is speeded up. T or F?

9. Researchers have clearly established that engrams are stored in the hippocampus. T or F?

CRITICAL THINKING

10. Based on state-dependent learning, why do you think that music often strongly evokes memories?

11. You must study French, Spanish, psychology, and biology in one evening. What do you think would be the best order in which to study these subjects so as to minimize interference?

12. There may be another way to explain why flashbulb memories are so long lasting. Can you think of one?

Answers:

1. F 2. a and d 3. T 4. interference 5. b 6. Negative transfer 7. T 8. F 9. F 10. Music tends to affect the mood that a person is in, and moods tend to affect memory (Balch & Lewis, 1996). 11. Any order that separates French from Spanish and psychology from biology would work (for instance: French, psychology, Spanish, biology). 12. Memories of emotionally significant events may be unusually strong because such memories are rehearsed more frequently. People usually mentally review emotionally charged events many times.

IMPROVING MEMORY—KEYS TO THE MEMORY BANK

While we're waiting around for the development of a memory pill, let's focus on some ways of improving your memory skills right now.

KNOWLEDGE OF RESULTS   Learning proceeds best when feedback, or **knowledge of results,** allows you to check your progress. Feedback can help you identify ideas that need extra practice. In addition, knowing that you have remembered or answered correctly is rewarding. A prime way to provide feedback for yourself while studying is *recitation.*

RECITATION   If you are going to remember something, eventually you will have to retrieve it. **Recitation** refers to summarizing aloud while you are learning. Recitation forces you to practice retrieving information. When you are reading a text, you should stop frequently and try to remember what you have just read by restating it in your own words. In one experiment, the best memory score was earned by a group of students who spent 80 percent of their time reciting and only 20 percent reading (Gates, 1958). Maybe students who talk to themselves aren't crazy after all.

REHEARSAL   The more you **rehearse** (mentally review) information as you read, the better you will remember it. But remember that maintenance rehearsal alone is not very effective. Elaborative rehearsal, in which you look for connections to existing knowledge, is far better. Thinking about facts helps link them together in memory. To learn college-level information, you must make active use of rehearsal strategies (Nist, Sharman, & Holschuh, 1996).

SELECTION   The Dutch scholar Erasmus said that a good memory should be like a fishnet: It should keep all the big fish in and let the little ones escape. If you boil down the paragraphs in most textbooks to one or two important terms or ideas, your memory chores will be more manageable. Practice very selective marking in your texts and use marginal notes to further summarize ideas. Most students mark their texts too much instead of too little. If everything is underlined, you haven't been selective. And, very likely, you didn't pay much attention in the first place (Peterson, 1992).

ORGANIZATION   Assume that you must memorize the following list of words: *north, man, red, spring, woman, east, autumn, yellow, summer, boy, blue, west, winter, girl, green, south.* This rather difficult list could be reorganized into *chunks* as follows: *north-east-south-west, spring-summer-autumn-winter, red-yellow-green-blue, man-woman-boy-girl.* This simple reordering made the second list much easier to learn when college students were tested on both lists (Deese & Hulse, 1967). Organizing class notes and summarizing chapters can be quite helpful (Dickinson & O'Connell, 1990). You may even want to summarize your summaries, so that the overall network of ideas becomes clearer and simpler. Summaries improve memory by encouraging better encoding of information (Hadwin, Kirby, & Woodhouse, 1999).

WHOLE VERSUS PART LEARNING   If you have to memorize a speech, is it better to try to learn it from beginning to end? Or in smaller parts like paragraphs? Generally, it is better to practice whole packages of information rather than smaller parts (**whole learning**). This is especially true for fairly short, organized information. An exception is that learning parts may be better for extremely long, complicated information. In **part learning,** subparts of a larger body of information are studied (such as sections of a textbook chapter). To decide which approach to use, remember to study the *largest meaningful amount of information* you can at one time.

For very long or complex material, try the **progressive part method,** by breaking a learning task into a series of short sections. At first, you study part A until it is mastered. Next, you study parts A and B; then A, B, and C; and so forth. This is a good way to learn the lines of a play, a long piece of music, or a poem (Ash & Holding, 1990). After the material is learned, you should also practice by starting at points other than A (at C, D, or B, for example). This helps prevent getting "lost" or going blank in the middle of a performance.

SERIAL POSITION   Whenever you must learn something in order, be aware of the **serial position effect.** As you will recall, this is the tendency to make the most errors in remembering the middle of a list. If you are introduced to a long line of people, the names you are likely to forget will be those in the middle, so you should make an extra effort to attend to them. You should also give extra practice to the middle of a list, poem, or speech. Try to break long lists of information into short sublists, and make the middle sublists the shortest of all.

CUES   The best **memory cues** (stimuli that aid retrieval) are those that were present during encoding (Reed, 1996). For example, students in one study had the daunting task of trying to recall a list of 600 words. As they read the list (which they did not know they would be tested on), the students gave three other words closely related in meaning to each listed word. In a test given later, the words each student supplied were used as cues to jog his or her memory. The students recalled an astounding 90 percent of the original word list (Mantyla, 1986).

Knowledge of results *During learning, feedback about the correctness of responses or other aspects of performance.*

Recitation *As a memory aid, repeating aloud information one wishes to retain.*

Rehearsal *Silently repeating or mentally reviewing information to improve memory.*

Whole learning *Studying an entire package of information (such as a complete poem) at once.*

Part learning *Separately studying subparts of a larger body of information (such as sections of a textbook chapter).*

Progressive part method *Breaking information into a series of short units and then learning increasingly longer groups of units.*

Serial position effect *The tendency for the greatest number of memory errors to occur in the middle portion of a list.*

Memory cue *Any stimulus associated with a particular memory. Memory cues usually enhance retrieval.*

❖ **FIGURE 10.18** *Actors can remember large amounts of complex information for many months, even when they learn new roles in between. During testing, they remember their lines best when they are allowed to move and gesture as they would when performing. Apparently, their movements supply cues that aid recall (Noice & Noice, 1999).*

Now read the following sentence: The fish bit the swimmer.

If you were tested a week from now, you would be more likely to recall the sentence if you were given a memory cue. And, surprisingly, the word *shark* would work better as a reminder than *fish* would. The reason for this is that most people think of a shark when they read the sentence. As a result, shark becomes a potent memory cue (Schacter, 1996).

The preceding examples show, once again, that it often helps to *elaborate* information as you learn. When you study, try to use new names, ideas, or terms in several sentences. Also, form images that include the new information, and relate it to knowledge you already have (Pressley et al., 1988). Your goal should be to knit meaningful cues into your memory code to help you retrieve information when you need it (❖Fig. 10.18).

OVERLEARNING Numerous studies have shown that memory is greatly improved when you **overlearn.** That is, study is continued beyond bare mastery. After you have learned material well enough to remember it once without error, you should continue studying. Overlearning is your best insurance against going blank on a test because of nervousness.

SPACED PRACTICE To keep boredom and fatigue to a minimum, try alternating short study sessions with brief rest periods. This pattern, called **spaced practice,** is generally superior to **massed practice,** in which little or no rest is given between learning sessions. By improving attention and consolidation, three 20-minute study sessions can produce more learning than 1 hour of continuous study. There's an old joke that goes "How do you get to Carnegie Hall?" The answer is "Practice, practice, practice." A better answer would be "Practice, wait awhile, practice, wait awhile, practice" (Neath, 1998).

Perhaps the best way to make use of spaced practice is to *schedule* your time. To make an effective schedule, designate times during the week before, after, and between classes when you will study particular subjects. Then treat these times just as if they were classes you had to attend.

SLEEP Remember that sleeping after study reduces interference. However, unless you are a "night person," late evening may not be a very efficient time for you to study. Also, you obviously can't sleep after every study session or study everything just before you sleep. That's why your study schedule (see Spaced Practice) should include ample breaks between subjects. Using your breaks and free time in a schedule is as important as living up to your study periods.

HUNGER People who are hungry almost always score lower on memory tests. So mother was right: It's a good idea to make sure you've had a good breakfast or lunch before you take tests at school (Martin & Benton, 1999; Smith, Clark, & Gallagher, 1999).

EXTEND HOW LONG YOU REMEMBER When you are learning new information, test yourself repeatedly. As you do, gradually lengthen the amount of time that passes before you test yourself again. For example, if you are studying German words on flashcards, look at the first card and then move it a few cards back in the stack. Do the same with the next few cards. When you get to the first "old" card, test yourself on it and check the answer. Then, move it farther back in the stack. Do the same with other "old" cards as they come up. When "old" cards come up for the third time, put them clear to the back of the stack (Cull, Shaughnessy, & Zechmeister, 1996).

REVIEW If you have spaced your practice and overlearned, review will be like icing on your study cake. Reviewing shortly before an exam cuts down the time during which you must remember details that may be important for the test. When reviewing, hold the amount of new information you try to memorize to a minimum. It may be realistic to take what you have actually learned and add a little more to it at the last minute by cramming. But remember that more than a little new learning may interfere with what you already know.

USING A STRATEGY TO AID RECALL Successful recall is usually the result of a planned *search* of memory (Reed, 1996). For example, one study found that students were most likely to recall names that eluded them if they made use of partial information (Reed & Bruce, 1982). The students were trying to answer questions such as "He is best remembered as the scarecrow in the Judy Garland movie *The Wizard of Oz.*" (The answer is Ray Bolger.) Partial information that helped students remember included impressions about the length of the name, letter sounds within the name, similar names, and related information (such as the names of other characters in the movie). A similar helpful strategy is to go through the alphabet, trying each letter as the first sound of a name or word you are seeking.

Using a variety of cues, even partial ones, opens more paths to a memory. The highlight titled "Memory Detectives" gives further hints for recapturing context and jogging memories. After that, the Psychology in Action section covers some of the most powerful memory techniques of all.

A LOOK AHEAD Psychologists still have much to learn about the nature of memory and how to improve it. For now, one thing stands out clearly: People who have good memories excel at or-

MEMORY DETECTIVES

You may not think of yourself as a "memory detective," but active probing often helps improve recall. A case in point is the **cognitive interview,** a technique used to jog the memory of eyewitnesses. The cognitive interview was created by R. Edward Geiselman and Ron Fisher to help police detectives. When used properly, it produces 35 percent more correct information than standard questioning (Geiselman et al., 1986). This improvement comes without adding to the number of false memories elicited, as occurs with hypnosis (Kebbell & Wagstaff, 1998).

By following four simple steps, you can apply cognitive principles to your own memory. The next time you are searching for a "lost" memory—one that you know is in there somewhere—try the following search strategies.

1. Say or write down *everything* you can remember that relates to the information you are seeking. Don't worry about how trivial any of it seems; each bit of information you remember can serve as a cue to bring back others.
2. Try to recall events or information in different orders. Let your memories flow out backward or out of order, or start with whatever impressed you the most.
3. Recall from different viewpoints. Review events by mentally standing in a different place. Or try to view information as another person would remember it. When taking a test, for instance, ask yourself what other students or your professor would remember about the topic.
4. Mentally put yourself back in the situation where you learned the information. Try to mentally re-create the learning environment or relive the event. As you do, in-

clude sounds, smells, details of weather, nearby objects, other people present, what you said or thought, and how you felt as you learned the information (Fisher & Geiselman, 1987).

These strategies help re-create the context in which information was learned, and they provide multiple memory cues. If you think of remembering as a sort of "treasure hunt," you might even learn to enjoy the detective work.

Some police detectives, following the advice of psychologists, re-create crime scenes to help witnesses remember what they saw. Typically, people return to the scene at the time of day the crime occurred. They are also asked to wear the same clothing they wore and go through the same motions as they did before the crime. With so many memory cues available, witnesses sometimes remember key items of information they hadn't recalled before.

ganizing information and making it meaningful. With this in mind, the Psychology in Action discussion for this chapter tells how you can combine organization and meaning into a powerful method for improving memory. In A Step Beyond, we will examine the bitter controversy concerning the recovery of long-repressed memories of childhood sexual abuse.

KNOWLEDGE BUILDER
IMPROVING MEMORY

RELATE

Return to the topic headings in the preceding pages that list techniques for improving memory. Place a check mark next to those that you have used recently. Review any you didn't mark, and think of a specific example of how you could use each technique at school, at home, or at work.

LEARNING CHECK

1. To improve memory, it is reasonable to spend as much or more time reciting as reading. T or F?

2. Organizing information while studying has little effect on memory because long-term memory is already highly organized. T or F?

3. The progressive part method of study is best suited to long and complex learning tasks. T or F?

4. Sleeping immediately after studying is highly disruptive to the consolidation of memories. T or F?

5. As new information is encoded and rehearsed it is helpful to elaborate on its meaning and connect it to other information. T or F?

CRITICAL THINKING

6. What advantages would there be to taking notes as you read a textbook, as opposed to underlining words in the text?

Answers:

1. T 2. F 3. T 4. F 5. T 6. Note-taking is a form of recitation. It encourages elaborative rehearsal and facilitates the organization and selection of important ideas, and your notes can be used for review.

Overlearning *Study or learning that continues after initial mastery of skills or information.*
Spaced practice *A practice schedule that alternates study periods with brief rests.*
Massed practice *A practice schedule in which studying continues for long periods, without interruption.*
Cognitive interview *Use of various cues and strategies to improve the memory of eyewitnesses.*

Some stage performers use memory as part of their acts. Do they have eidetic imagery? Various "memory experts" entertain by memorizing the names of everyone at a banquet, the order of all the cards in a deck, long lists of words, or other seemingly impossible amounts of information. Such feats may seem like magic, but if they are, you can have a magic memory, too. These tricks are performed through the use of mnemonics (nee-MON-iks) (Wilding & Valentine, 1994b). A **mnemonic** is any kind of memory system or aid. In some cases, mnemonic strategies increase recall tenfold (Patten, 1990).

Some mnemonic systems are so common that almost everyone knows them. If you are trying to remember how many days there are in a month, you may find the answer by reciting, "Thirty days hath September. . . ." Physics teachers often help students remember the colors of the spectrum by giving them the mnemonic "Roy G. Biv": **R**ed, **O**range, **Y**ellow, **G**reen, **B**lue, **I**ndigo, **V**iolet. The budding sailor who has trouble telling port from starboard may remember that port and left both have four letters or may remind herself, "I *left* port." And what beginning musician hasn't remembered the notes represented by the lines and spaces of the musical staff by learning "F-A-C-E" and "**E**very **G**ood **B**oy **D**oes **F**ine"?

Mnemonic techniques are ways to avoid *rote* learning (learning by simple repetition). The superiority of mnemonic learning as opposed to rote learning has been demonstrated many times. For example, Gordon Bower (1973) asked college students to study five different lists of 20 unrelated words. At the end of a short study session, subjects tried to recall all 100 items. People using mnemonics remembered an average of 72 items, whereas members of a control group using rote learning remembered an average of 28.

Stage performers rarely have naturally superior memories. Instead, they make extensive use of memory systems to perform their feats (Wilding & Valentine, 1994b). Few of these systems are of practical value to you as a student, but the principles underlying mnemonics are. By practicing mnemonics you should be able to greatly improve your memory with little effort (Dretzke & Levin, 1996).

Here, then, are the basic principles of mnemonics.

1. **Use mental pictures.** Visual pictures, or images, are generally easier to remember than words. Turning information into mental pictures is therefore very helpful. Make these images as vivid as possible (Campos & Perez, 1997).

2. **Make things meaningful.** Transferring information from short-term to long-term memory is aided by making it meaningful. If you encounter technical terms that have little or no immediate meaning for you, *give* them meaning, even if you have to stretch the term to do so. (This point is clarified by the examples following this list.)

3. **Make information familiar.** Connect it to what you already know. Another way to get information into long-term memory is to connect it to information already stored there. If some facts or ideas in a chapter seem to stay in your memory easily, associate more difficult facts with them.

4. **Form bizarre, unusual, or exaggerated mental associations.** Forming images that make sense is better in most situations. However, when associating two ideas, terms, or especially mental images, you may find that the more outrageous and exaggerated the association, the more likely you are to remember. Bizarre images make stored information more *distinctive* and therefore easier to retrieve (Worthen & Marshall, 1996). Imagine, for example, that you have just been introduced to Mr. Rehkop. To remember his name, you could picture him wearing a police uniform. Then replace his nose with a ray gun. This bizarre image will provide two hints when you want to remember Mr. Rehkop's name: *ray* and *cop* (Carney, Levin, & Stackhouse, 1997).

Bizarre images mainly help improve immediate memory, and they work best for fairly simple information (Robinson-Riegler & McDaniel, 1994). Nevertheless, they can be a first step toward learning.

Mnemonics can be an aid in preparing for tests. However, because mnemonics help most in the initial stages of storing information, it is important to follow through with other elaborative learning strategies.

A sampling of typical applications of mnemonics should make these four points clearer to you.

EXAMPLE 1   Let's say you have 30 new vocabulary words to memorize in Spanish. You can proceed by rote memorization (repeat them over and over until you begin to get them), or you can learn them with little effort by using the keyword method (Pressley, 1987). In the **keyword method,** a familiar word or image is used to link two other words or items. To remember that the word *pajaro* (pronounced PAH-hah-ro) means bird, you can link it to a "key" word in English: *Pajaro* (to me) sounds like "parked car-o." Therefore, to remember that *pajaro* means bird, I will visualize a parked car jam-packed full of birds. I will try to make this image as vivid and exaggerated as possible, with birds flapping and chirping and feathers flying everywhere. Similarly, for the word *carta* (which means "letter"), I will imagine a shopping *cart* filled with postal letters.

If you link similar keywords and images for the rest of the list, you may not remember them all, but you will get most without any more practice. As a matter of fact, if you have formed the *pajaro* and *carta* images, it is going to be almost impossible for you to see these words again this week without remembering what they mean. The keyword method is also superior when you want to work "backward" from an English word to a foreign vocabulary word (Hogben & Lawson, 1992).

What about a year from now? How long do keyword memories last?   Mnemonic memories work best in the short run. Later, they may be more fragile than conventional memories. That's why it's usually best to use mnemonics during the initial stages of learning (Carney & Levin, 1998). To create more lasting memories, you'll need to use the techniques discussed earlier in this chapter.

Exaggerated mental images can link two words or ideas in ways that aid memory. Here, the keyword method is used to link the English word *letter* with the Spanish word *carta*.

EXAMPLE 2   Let's say you have to learn the names of all the bones and muscles in the human body for biology. You are trying to remember that the jawbone is the *mandible*. This one is easy because you can associate it to a *man nibbling*, or maybe you can picture a *man dribbling* a basketball with his jaw (make this image as ridiculous as possible). If the muscle name *latissimus dorsi* gives you trouble, familiarize it by turning it into *"the ladder misses the door, sigh."* Then picture a ladder glued to your back where the muscle is found. Picture the ladder leading up to a small door at your shoulder. Picture the ladder missing the door. Picture the ladder sighing like an animated character in a cartoon.

This seems like more to remember, not less, and it seems that it would cause you to misspell things.   Mnemonics are not a complete substitute for normal memory; they are an aid to normal memory. Mnemonics are not likely to be helpful unless you make extensive use of *images* (Willoughby et al., 1997). Your mental pictures will come back to you easily. As for misspellings, mnemonics can be thought of as a built-in hint in your memory. Often, when taking a test, you will find that the slightest hint is all you need to remember correctly. A mnemonic image is like having someone leaning over your shoulder who says, "Psst, the name of that muscle sounds like 'ladder misses the door, sigh.'" If misspelling continues to be a problem, try to create memory aids for spelling, too.

Here are two more examples to help you appreciate the flexibility of a mnemonic approach to studying.

EXAMPLE 3   Your art history teacher expects you to be able to name the artist when you are shown slides as part of exams. You have seen many of the slides only once before in class. How will you remember them? As the slides are shown in class, make each artist's name into an object or image. Then picture the object *in* the paintings done by the artist. For example, you can picture Van Gogh as a *van* (automobile) *going* through the middle of each Van Gogh painting. Picture the van running over things and knocking things over. Or, if you remember that Van Gogh cut off his ear, picture a giant bloody ear in each of his paintings.

EXAMPLE 4   If you have trouble remembering history, try to avoid thinking of it as something from the dim past. Picture each historical personality as a person you know right now (a friend, teacher, parent, and so on). Then picture these people doing whatever the historical figures did. Also, try visualizing battles or other events as if they were happening in your town, or make parks and schools into countries. Use your imagination.

Mnemonic   *Any kind of memory system or aid.*
Keyword method   *As an aid to memory, using a familiar word or image to link two items.*

How can mnemonics be used to remember things in order? Here are three techniques that are helpful.

1. **Form a chain.** To remember lists of ideas, objects, or words in order, try forming an exaggerated association (mental image) connecting the first item to the second, then the second to the third, and so on. To remember the following short list in order—*elephant, doorknob, string, watch, rifle, oranges*—picture a full-sized *elephant* balanced on a *doorknob* playing with a *string* tied to him. Picture a *watch* tied to the string, and a *rifle* shooting *oranges* at the watch. This technique can be used quite successfully for lists of 20 or more items. In a recent test, people who used a linking mnemonic did much better at remembering lists of 15 and 22 errands (Higbee et al., 1990). Try it next time you go shopping and leave your list at home.

2. **Take a mental walk.** Ancient Greek orators had an interesting way to remember ideas in order when giving a speech. Their method was to take a mental walk along a familiar path. As they did, they associated topics with the images of statues found along the walk. You can do the same thing by "placing" objects or ideas along the way as you mentally take a familiar walk (Neath, 1998).

3. **Use a system.** Many times, the first letters or syllables of words or ideas can be formed into another word that will serve as a reminder of order. "Roy G. Biv" is an example. As an alternative, learn the following: 1 is a bun, 2 is a shoe, 3 is a tree, 4 is a door, 5 is a hive, 6 is sticks, 7 is heaven, 8 is a gate, 9 is a line, 10 is a hen. To remember a list in order, form an image associating bun with the first item on your list. For example, if the first item is frog, picture a "frog-burger" on a bun to remember it. Then, associate shoe with the second item, and so on.

If you have never used mnemonics, you may still be skeptical, but give this approach a fair trial. Most people find they can greatly extend their memory through the use of mnemonics. But remember, like most things worthwhile, remembering takes effort.

MNEMONICS

RELATE

As an exercise, see if you can create mnemonics for the words *icon, implicit memory,* and *mnemonic.* The best mnemonics are your own, but here are some examples to help you get started. An icon is a visual image: Picture an *eye* in a *can* to remember that icons store visual information. Implicit memories are "hidden": Picture an *imp* hiding in memory. A mnemonic is a memory aid: Imagine writing a phone number on your knee to remember it. Imagine your *knee moaning,* "*Ick,* you shouldn't write on me."

Now, go through the glossary items in this chapter and make up mnemonics for any terms you have difficulty remembering.

LEARNING CHECK

1. Memory systems and aids are referred to as _____.

2. Which of the following is least likely to improve memory?
   a. using exaggerated mental images
   b. forming a chain of associations
   c. turning visual information into verbal information
   d. associating new information to information that is already known or familiar

3. Picturing your knee moaning as it tries to remember something could serve as a mnemonic for the term *mnemonic.* T or F?

4. Bower's 1973 study showed that, in general, mnemonics improve memory for only related words or ideas. T or F?

CRITICAL THINKING

5. How could you use mnemonics to make the nonsense syllables LAZ, CEF, and WOL easier to remember?

6. How are elaborative rehearsal and mnemonics alike?

Answers:

1. mnemonics 2. c 3. T 4. F 5. How about the "LAZy CHEF is a WOLf"? 6. Both attempt to relate new information to information stored in LTM that is familiar or already easy to retrieve.

THE RECOVERED MEMORY–FALSE MEMORY DEBATE

Focus: Do repressed memories of childhood sexual abuse cause emotional problems in adulthood?

Many sexually abused children develop problems that persist into adulthood. In some instances, a child may repress all memory of the abuse she or he has suffered. According to some psychologists, uncovering these hidden memories can be an important step toward regaining emotional health.

Although the preceding may be true, the search for repressed memories of sexual abuse has itself been a problem. Many cases have surfaced in which families were torn apart by accusations of sexual abuse that later turned out to be completely false.

In recent years, questions about recovered memories have sparked vigorous debate among psychologists. To grasp the nature of this debate, consider the following sketches.

LAURA'S STORY Laura visits a psychotherapist for help with depression and marital difficulties. The therapist tells Laura that her symptoms suggest she was sexually abused as a child. At first, Laura insists that she doesn't remember any abuse. But with the therapist's guidance, Laura begins to bring disturbing memory fragments to the surface. Eventually, in a horrifying rush of flashbacks, Laura remembers that her father raped her.

Through hypnosis, dream analysis, guided visualization, and an incest survivors group, Laura recovers other lost memories of childhood sexual abuse. By doing so, she takes the first painful steps toward healing the long-hidden cause of her problems.

KATHY'S STORY Kathy seeks help from a psychotherapist for depression and marital difficulties. Unbeknownst to her, Kathy has blundered into a "memory mill" run by an incompetent therapist who believes that sexual abuse is the root of nearly all problems. During the very first session, the therapist tells Kathy that she was sexually abused as a child. Kathy resists this idea, saying that she doesn't remember any abuse. But gradually, as she submits to hypnosis, dream analysis, guided visualization, and participation in an incest survivors group, Kathy begins to have detailed memories of childhood abuse.

Kathy's "recovered memories" are actually pure fantasy, spawned by her therapist's suggestions. Nonetheless, she believes them completely. Kathy accuses her father of sexual abuse and breaks all ties with him. Kathy's father loses his job, and her family is shattered. Yet, there is no way of proving Kathy's memories are false.

Recovered Memories?

Laura's and Kathy's stories represent two extremes of the recovered-memory debate. Advocates of recovered-memory therapy view it as an antidote for the long-buried pain of childhood incest and sexual abuse. Critics see it as a nightmare of malpractice that can create false memories and destroy families. Let's examine some points of the debate.

POINT Many adults who suffer from depression, low self-esteem, sexual problems, and other complaints have documented histories of sexual abuse. Many therapists think it is reasonable to suspect hidden abuse when people like Laura or Kathy have similar problems.

COUNTERPOINT The purported symptoms of hidden abuse are dubious, at best. For example, signs of abuse listed in one pop-psychology book include "too much or too little trust of others, high risk-taking or an inability to take risks, too much interest in sex or too little." On the basis of such vague symptoms, almost anyone could be suspected of harboring hidden memories of abuse.

POINT Most victims of childhood sexual abuse vividly remember having been molested. This raises doubt that many victims repress the experience. Childhood memories of other atrocities, such as seeing a family member killed, are usually carried for life. The problem for most victims of abuse is that they can't forget what happened to them, not that they don't remember it.

COUNTERPOINT Sexual abuse may be a special case, because the abuse is repeated and extremely threatening. To cope with ongoing abuse, the child must repress it.

POINT Memory researcher Elizabeth Loftus has shown that false memories are easy to create. Loftus arranged for older relatives to tell college students false stories about how the students got lost in a shopping mall as children. When they were later asked to recall further details, 25 percent described elaborate memories of the fictitious incidents.

Loftus also cites a study of children who were not at their elementary school when a sniper shot at youngsters on the playground. Despite being absent, many of the children later reported intricate memories of the event.

Suggestion and fantasy are major elements of most of the techniques used to recover repressed memories, such as hypnosis and guided visualization. A person seeking an explanation for his or her suffering may be especially susceptible to suggestion. Certainly, some memories that are brought to awareness

Gary Ramona lost his marriage and his $400,000-a-year job as a business executive when his 19-year-old daughter, Holly, alleged that he molested her throughout her childhood. Ramona sued Holly's therapists, claiming that they had been irresponsible. To prove to Holly that her memories were true, the therapists gave her the drug amobarbital and told her that it was a "truth drug." (Amobarbital is a hypnotic drug that induces a twilight state of consciousness. People do not automatically tell the truth while under its influence.) After reviewing the evidence for 2 months, a jury awarded Gary Ramona $500,000 in damages.

by suggestion are genuine. However, there is no way to distinguish real memories from false memories.

COUNTERPOINT   Defenders of recovered memories state that therapists rarely wield enough power to impose false memories on patients. Most survivors unfairly blame themselves, not their abusers.

Summary

As you can see, persuasive arguments exist on both sides of the recovered-memory debate. To summarize, there is evidence that memories of sexual abuse are sometimes repressed. Likewise, there is little doubt that some "recovered" memories are pure fantasy. Researchers have identified many instances in which "recovered" traumatic memories were absolutely false.

Clearly, there is a need to strike a balance between uncovering and treating real repressed trauma and doing damage by fabricating memories.

Protecting Yourself and Others

What can individuals who suspect they were sexually abused do to avoid making false accusations?

1. If you think you may have been sexually abused but aren't sure, consult an experienced psychotherapist. (See the Psychology in Action section of Chapter 18 for information on finding a competent therapist.) Never put yourself in the hands of a self-described "recovered-memory therapist."
2. Be wary of any therapist who tells you within the first few sessions that you were probably sexually abused as a child.
3. If a therapist pressures you to believe that you were sexually abused, discuss your concerns with the therapist. If the pressure continues, report the experience to the therapist's professional association and consider changing therapists.
4. Beware of anyone who treats failure to recall abuse as evidence of abuse. One popular book on abuse states, "If you think you were abused and your life shows the symptoms, then you were," and "If you don't remember your abuse, you are not alone. Many women don't have memories . . . this doesn't mean they weren't abused." Both are dangerously misleading ideas.
5. Maintain a healthy skepticism regarding recovered memories. Remember, unless a memory can be independently confirmed, there is no way to tell if it is real or not.
6. Before making accusations of abuse against anyone, seek confirming evidence. If none is available, consider consulting another therapist before acting on your memories. In the absence of firm evidence, you should be cautious about accusing anyone based on recovered memories alone.

A few years ago, an "epidemic" of recovered memories took place. It subsided as psychologists developed new guidelines for therapists that minimize the risk of influencing clients' memories. Today, both recovered memories and false accusations are

relatively uncommon. Nevertheless, false claims about childhood abuse still occasionally make the news. The saddest thing about such claims is that they deaden public sensitivity to actual abuse. Childhood sexual abuse is widespread. Awareness of its existence must not be repressed.

(Sources: Byrd, 1994; Courtois, 1999; Goldstein, 1997; Lindsay, 1998; Loftus, 1994; Palm & Gibson, 1998; Pendergast, 1995; Reisner, 1996; Schacter, 1999.)

CONCLUSION: Some memories of abuse that return to awareness appear to be genuine. However, in the absence of firm supporting evidence, there is no way to tell if a memory is real or not. No matter how real a recovered memory may seem, it could be false, unless it can be verified by others, or by court or medical records.

K N O W L E D G E   B U I L D E R

THE RECOVERED-MEMORY DEBATE

RELATE

A few years ago, celebrities and talk show hosts by the dozens were revealing that they had recovered long-repressed memories of childhood sexual abuse. Were they victims of a dangerous fad? Were they among the first to reveal one of contemporary society's long-hidden secrets? How do you view the recent epidemic of recovered memories?

LEARNING CHECK

1. Hypnosis, dream analysis, and guided verbalization are methods that are commonly used to "recover" repressed memories. T or F?

2. A reasonable conclusion to be drawn from the recovered-memory debate is that creating false memories is so rare as to be nearly impossible. T or F?

3. Memories of severe, non-sexual traumas in childhood are almost always repressed. T or F?

4. Lab studies have shown that false childhood memories can be created by suggestion. T or F?

5. A competent therapist can usually tell almost immediately that a person was sexually abused as a child, even if the person has repressed all memories of the abuse. T or F?

6. If you think you were abused and your life shows the symptoms, then you were. T or F?

CRITICAL THINKING

7. Why does the use of hypnosis to unlock repressed memories limit the credibility of any "memories" that may be "recovered"?

Answers:

1. T 2. F 3. F 4. T 5. F 6. F 7. As stated earlier in this chapter, hypnosis tends to increase the occurrence of false memories. Also, people have often have unshakable confidence in false memories that are retrieved under hypnosis.

CHAPTER IN REVIEW

Is there more than one type of memory?

- Memory is an active system that encodes, stores, and retrieves information.
- Humans appear to have three interrelated memory systems. These are sensory memory, short-term memory (STM, also called *working memory*), and long-term memory (LTM).

What are the features of each type of memory?

- Sensory memory is exact, but very brief. Through selective attention, some information is transferred to STM.
- STM has a capacity of about seven bits of information, but this can be extended by chunking, or recoding. Short-term memories are brief and very sensitive to interruption, or interference; however, they can be prolonged by maintenance rehearsal.
- LTM functions as a general storehouse of information, especially *meaningful* information. Elaborative rehearsal helps transfer information from STM to LTM. Long-term memories are *relatively permanent*, or lasting. LTM seems to have an almost unlimited storage capacity.
- LTM is subject to constructive processing, or ongoing revision and updating. LTM is highly *organized* to allow retrieval of needed information. The pattern, or structure, of memory networks is the subject of current memory research.
- Redintegrative memories are *reconstructed* as each memory provides a cue for the next memory.

Is there more than one type of long-term memory?

- Within long-term memory, declarative memories for facts seem to differ from procedural memories for skills. Declarative memories may be further categorized as semantic memories or episodic memories. The properties and relationships among types of memory are currently being debated.

How is memory measured?

- The tip-of-the-tongue state shows that memory is not an all-or-nothing event. Memories may therefore be revealed by recall, recognition, or relearning.
- In recall, memory proceeds without specific cues, as in an essay exam. Recall of listed information often reveals a serial position effect (middle items on the list are most subject to errors). A common test of recognition is the multiple-choice question. In relearning, "forgotten" material is learned again, and memory is indicated by a savings score.
- Recall, recognition, and relearning mainly measure explicit memories. Other techniques, such as priming, are necessary to reveal the existence of implicit memories.

What are "photographic" memories?

- Eidetic imagery (photographic memory) occurs when a person is able to project an image onto a blank surface. Such images allow brief, nearly complete recall by some children. Eidetic imagery is rarely found in adults. However, many adults have internal memory images, which can be very vivid.

- Exceptional memory can be learned by finding ways to directly store information in LTM. Learning has no effect on the limits of STM. Some people may have exceptional memories that exceed what can be achieved through learning.

What causes forgetting?

- Forgetting and memory were extensively studied by Herman Ebbinghaus, whose curve of forgetting shows that forgetting is typically most rapid immediately after learning. Although the shape of the curve remains the same, forgetting is much slower for meaningful information.
- Failure to encode information is a common cause of "forgetting." Forgetting in sensory memory and STM probably reflects decay of memory traces in the nervous system. Decay or disuse of memories may also account for some LTM loss, but most forgetting cannot be explained this way.
- Often, forgetting is cue dependent. The power of cues to trigger memories is revealed by state-dependent learning and the link between moods and memory.
- Much forgetting in both STM and LTM can be attributed to interference of memories with one another. When recent learning interferes with retrieval of prior learning, retroactive interference has occurred. If old memories interfere with new memories, proactive interference has occurred.
- Depending on the relationship between prior learning and a new task, skills may show positive transfer or negative transfer (carryover to a new situation).

How accurate are everyday memories?

- Repression is the forgetting of painful, embarrassing, or traumatic memories. Repression is thought to be unconscious, in contrast to suppression, which is a conscious attempt to avoid thinking about something.

What happens in the brain when memories are formed?

- Retrograde amnesia and the effects of electroconvulsive shock (ECS) may be explained by the concept of *consolidation*. Consolidation theory holds that engrams (permanent memory traces) are formed during a critical period after learning. Until they are consolidated, long-term memories are easily destroyed.
- The hippocampus is a brain area that has been linked with consolidation of memories.
- The search within the brain for engrams has now settled on changes in individual nerve cells. The best-documented changes are alterations in the amounts of transmitter chemicals released by the cells and the number of receptor sites on each cell.

How can memory be improved?

- Memory can be improved by using feedback, recitation, and rehearsal, by selecting and organizing information, and by using the progressive part method, spaced practice, overlearning, and active search strategies. Effects of serial position, sleep, hunger, review, cues, and elaboration should also be kept in mind when studying or memorizing.
- Mnemonic systems use mental images and unusual associations to link new information with familiar memories already stored in LTM. Such strategies give information personal meaning and make it easier to recall.

What is the "recovered-memory" debate?

- Experts continue to debate the validity of childhood memories of abuse that reappear after apparently being repressed for decades.
- Independent evidence has verified that some recovered memories are true. However, others have been shown to be false.
- In the absence of confirming or disconfirming evidence, there is currently no way to separate true memories from fantasies. Caution is advised for all concerned with attempts to retrieve supposedly hidden memories.

PSYCHOLOGY ON THE NET

- **Active Brain Areas in Working Memory** A three-dimensional MRI reconstruction of a person's brain while holding letters in working memory. http://www.nimh.nih.gov/events/prfmri2.htm
- **Exploratorium: Memory** Demonstrations and articles related to memory from an exceptional science museum. http://www.exploratorium.edu/memory
- **False-Memory Test** Use the materials in this site to induce false memories in others (for demonstration purposes). http://www.sciam.com/0597issue/0597scicit3.html
- **Memories Are Made of. . . .** Article from *Scientific American* discusses memory-enhancing drugs for Alzheimer's patients. http://www.sciam.com/0397issue/0397techbus1.html

- **Memory Techniques and Mnemonics** Links to information on mnemonics. http://www.demon.co.uk/mindtool/memory.html
- **Questions and Answers about Memories of Childhood Abuse** From APA, a summary of the repressed memory issue. http://www.apa.org/pubinfo/mem.html
- **Repressed and Recovered Memories** Site devoted to the recovered-memory controversy; has links to both sides of the controversy. http://www.ntu.ac.uk/soc/bscpsych/context/recover.htm
- **The Machinery of Thought** *Scientific American* article describes research on the physiology of memory. http://www.sciam.com/0897issue/0897trends.html
- **The Magical Number Seven, Plus or Minus Two** Full text of George Miller's original article. http://www.well.com/user/smalin/miller.html

• **InfoTrac® College Edition** For recent articles on the Psychology in Action feature, use Key Words search for MNEMONICS.

INTERACTIVE LEARNING

- **PsychNow!** 5d. Memory systems. 5e. Forgetting.
- **Psyk.trek** 6a. Memory encoding. 6b. Memory storage. 6c. Physiology of memory. 6d. Problem solving.

Cognition, Language, and Creativity

Chapter Survey

Theme: *The origins of intelligent behavior lie in thinking, language, problem solving, and creativity.*

CARTOONIST RUBE GOLDBERG was famous for drawing wacky machines that did simple tasks in complicated and often hilarious ways. A typical Rube Goldberg device consisted of pulleys, switches, fulcrums, mousetraps, balloons, fans, dancing cows, and other strange items.

Today, thanks to the Theta Tau engineering fraternity, students can honor Goldberg's zany inspiration while testing their own creativity. In a contest held each year at Purdue University, students invent machines to do tasks such as sticking a stamp on a letter, teeing up a golf ball, or screwing a lightbulb into a socket. Of course, any engineering student worth his or her calculator could easily create a machine to do such things. The real challenge in the National Rube Goldberg Machine Contest is to build a gadget that does something simple in the most complicated way imaginable. For instance, Doug Shoenenberger and Paul Calhoun won in 1997 with a contraption that loads a compact disc into a CD player in 35 mind-boggling steps.

Students who enter the contest obviously enjoy complexity, novelty, and problem solving. At higher levels, these are the same qualities that define many of history's geniuses, such as Einstein, Darwin, Mozart, Newton, Michelangelo, Galileo, Madame Curie, Edison, and Martha Graham (Michalko, 1998).

Like all creative activities, the Rube Goldberg contest raises questions about human cognition. How do we think? How are we able to solve problems? How do people create works of art, science, and literature? How many engineering students does it take to screw in a lightbulb? For some preliminary answers, we will investigate thinking, problem solving, and creativity in the pages that follow.

Gateways to Cognition, Language, and Creativity

THINKING is influenced by the form in which information is represented—as images, concepts, or symbols.

LANGUAGE is an especially powerful way to encode information and manipulate ideas.

ANIMALS are capable of rudimentary language use, but only with the aid of human intervention. Language is primarily a human characteristic.

EXPERT PROBLEM SOLVING is based on acquired knowledge and strategies. Experts are not naturally smarter than novices.

CREATIVE THINKING is novel, divergent, and tempered with a dash of practicality.

SOME COMMON THINKING ERRORS an be avoided if you know the pitfalls of intuitive thought.

CREATIVITY can be enhanced by strategies that promote divergent thinking.

MANY ANIMALS appear to engage in elementary forms of thinking.

WHAT IS THINKING?—IT'S ALL IN YOUR HEAD!

Thinking takes many forms, including daydreaming, problem solving, and reasoning (to name but a few). Stated more formally, thinking, or **cognition,** refers to mentally processing information. Studying thinking is similar to figuring out how a computer works by asking, "I wonder what would happen if I did this?" But in **cognitive psychology** (the study of human information processing), the "computer" is the brain, and thinking is the "programming" we seek to understand.

Although thinking is not limited to humans, imagine trying to teach an animal to match the feats of Shakuntala Devi, who holds the world record for mental calculation. Devi once multiplied two 13-digit numbers (7,686,369,774,870 times 2,465,099,745,779) in her head, giving the answer in 28 seconds. (That's 18,947,668,177,995,426,773,730 if you haven't already figured it out yourself.)

Some Basic Units of Thought

At its most basic, thinking is an **internal representation** (mental expression) of a problem or situation. (Picture a chess player who mentally tries out several moves before actually touching a chess piece.) The power of being able to represent problems internally is dramatically illustrated by Chess Grand Master Miguel Najdorf, who once simultaneously played 45 chess games, while blindfolded.

How did Najdorf perform his feat? Like most people, he used the following basic units of thought: (1) images, (2) concepts, and (3) language, or symbols. The three basic units can be defined in this way:

- **Image:** Most often, a mental representation that has picture-like qualities; a visual likeness or icon.
- **Concept:** A generalized idea representing a class of related objects or events.
- **Language:** Words or symbols and rules for combining them, which are used for thinking and communication.

Complex thinking may require all three representations. For example, blindfolded chess players rely on visual images, kinesthetic (muscular) images involving "lines of force," concepts ("Game 2 is an English opening"), and the special notational system, or "language," of chess.

In a moment, we will explore the units of thought identified here. Be aware, however, that thinking involves attention, pattern recognition, memory, decision making, intuition, knowl-

The power of thought is beautifully expressed by Stephen W. Hawking, a theoretical physicist and one of the best-known scientific minds of modern times. Now in his late 50s, Hawking has suffered since age 13 from amyotrophic lateral sclerosis, a disabling condition also known as Lou Gehrig's disease. Today, he can control only his left hand, and he cannot speak. Nevertheless, his brain remains fiercely active. With courage and determination, he has used his intellect to advance our understanding of the universe.

edge, and more. This chapter is only a sample of what cognitive psychologists study.

MENTAL IMAGERY—DOES A FROG HAVE LIPS?

Ninety-seven percent of all people have visual images, and 92 percent have auditory images. More than 50 percent have imagery that includes movement, touch, taste, smell, and pain. When we speak of images, we usually think of mental "pictures" (Kosslyn, 1990). But as you can see, images involve other senses as well. Your image of a bakery, for example, may include its delicious odor, as well as its appearance.

Some people have a rare form of imagery called **synesthesia** (sin-es-THEE-zyah). For these individuals, images cross normal sensory barriers (Cytowic, 1993). For instance, a synesthetic individual listening to music may experience a burst of colors or tastes, as well as sound sensations. Despite such variations, it is generally accepted that most people use images to think, remember, and solve problems. Here are the most common uses for mental images (Kosslyn et al., 1990):

- To make a decision or solve a problem (choosing what clothes to wear, figuring out how to arrange furniture in a room)

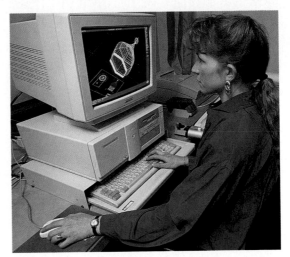

An ability to mentally rotate objects is very valuable for people who work in industrial design and drafting.

- To help understand a verbal description (mentally picturing what a person is talking about, picturing a scene described in a novel)
- To change feelings (thinking of pleasant images to get out of a bad mood, imagining oneself as thin to help stay on a diet)
- To help explain or describe something (visualizing a scene you saw at a party to describe it to a friend)
- To improve a skill or to prepare for some action (using images to improve a swimming stroke, mentally rehearsing how you will ask for a raise)
- To aid memory (picturing Mr. Cook wearing a chef's hat, so you can remember his name)

Properties of Mental Images

Stephen Kosslyn and others have discovered that mental images are not flat, like photographs. To sample Kosslyn's work, think about the following question: Does a frog have lips and a stubby tail? Unless you often kiss frogs, you will probably tackle this question by using mental images. Most people picture a frog, "look" at its mouth, and then mentally rotate the frog to check its tail (Kosslyn, 1983). (**Mental rotation** is the ability to change the position of an image in mental space.) (For a look at some interesting research on mental imagery, see "3-D Images.")

Cognition *The process of thinking or mentally processing information (images, concepts, words, rules, and symbols).*
Cognitive psychology *The study of thinking, knowing, understanding, problem solving, creativity, and information processing.*
Internal representation *Any image, concept, precept, symbol, or process used to mentally represent information during thought.*
Image *Most often, a mental representation that has picture-like qualities; an icon.*
Concept *A generalized idea representing a class of related objects or events.*
Language *Words or symbols, and rules for combining them, that are used for thinking and communication.*
Synesthesia *Experiencing one sense in terms normally associated with another sense; for example, "seeing" colors when a sound is heard.*
Mental rotation *The ability to change the position of an image in mental space.*

3-D IMAGES—NOW SHOWING IN IMAGINATIONS EVERYWHERE

Detective Psyche slowly pushed open the window and stepped into the dingy room. On the opposite wall, above a bed, a mirror reflected her image, startling her. "This is creepy," she thought. Psyche's eyes drifted to the floor at her right. Was that someone's shadow spilling under the closed door?

When you read a description of a scene, how do you remember the locations of objects? Psychologists Nancy Franklin and Barbara Tversky (1990) found that we don't merely remember words, such as "mirror above bed." Typically, we form a spatial image of how objects are arranged.

To explore imagery, Franklin and Tversky had people read descriptions of various environments. Five objects were located in each scene. In a barn scene, for example, the objects

were a saddle, a rake, a pail, a lantern, and shears. People imagined themselves in each setting and were then quizzed about the locations of objects. Periodically, they were asked to change position in the imagined scene ("Turn 90 degrees to the right" or "Face the pail"). Everyone who was tested used imagery to locate the objects. Most, in fact, reported that they mentally "turned" and "looked at" objects to answer questions about them.

Objects above or below a "viewer" were easiest to locate. Finding objects placed to the right or left was the most difficult. This insight may aid the design of such things as airplane cockpits or nuclear power plant controls. To minimize confusion about location, it is better to concentrate on the up-down dimension instead of right-left positioning.

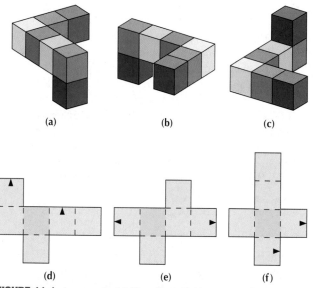

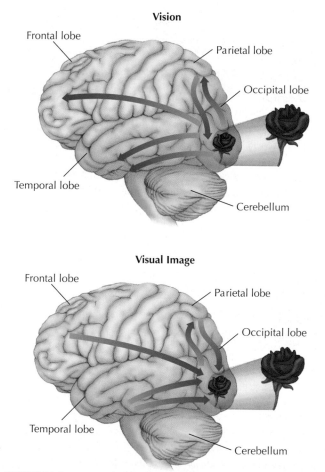

❖ **FIGURE 11.1** *Imagery in thinking. (Top) Subjects were shown a drawing similar to (a) and drawings of how (a) would look in other positions, such as (b) and (c). Subjects could recognize (a) after it had been "rotated" from its original position. However, the more (a) was rotated in space, the longer it took to recognize it. This result suggests that subjects actually formed a three-dimensional image of (a) and rotated the image to see if it matched (Shepard, 1975). (Bottom) Try your ability to manipulate mental images: Each of these shapes can be folded to make a cube; in which do the arrows meet? (After Kosslyn, 1985.)*

In ❖Figure 11.1, notice that mental images of objects can be moved about as needed. This ability is at least partly based on making imagined movements. That is, we mentally pick up an object and turn it around (Wexler, Kosslyn, & Berthoz, 1998).

"REVERSE VISION" *What happens in the brain when a person has visual images?* Seeing something in your "mind's eye" is closely related to seeing real objects. Information from the eyes normally activates the brain's primary visual area, creating an image (❖Fig. 11.2). Other brain areas then help us recognize

❖ **FIGURE 11.2** *When you see a flower, its image is represented by activity in the primary visual area of the cortex, at the back of the brain. Information about the flower is also relayed to other brain areas. If you form a mental image of a flower, information follows a reverse path. The result, once again, is activation of the primary visual area.*

the image by relating it to stored knowledge. When you form a mental image, the system works in reverse. Higher brain areas (where memories are stored) send signals back to the visual cortex, where, once again, an image is created (Farah, 1988; Farah et al., 1989; Kosslyn, Thompson, & Alpert, 1995).

USING MENTAL IMAGES *How are images used to solve problems?* **Stored images** can be retrieved from memory to apply prior experience to problem solving. Let's say you are asked, "How many uses can you think of for an empty egg carton?" You might begin by picturing uses for an egg carton you have already seen, such as sorting buttons. To generate more original solutions, created images may be used. A **created image** is assembled or invented, rather than simply remembered. Thus, an artist may completely picture a sculpture before beginning to work on it. People who have good imaging abilities tend to score higher on tests of creativity (Gonzalez, Campos, & Perez, 1997). In fact, some of history's most original intellects relied heavily on imagery. Examples include Albert Einstein, Thomas Edison, Lewis Carroll, and Winston Churchill (West, 1991).

Does the "size" of a mental image affect thinking? To find out, first picture a cat sitting beside a housefly. Now try to "zoom in" on the cat's ears so you see them clearly. Next, picture a rabbit sitting beside an elephant. How quickly can you "see" the rabbit's front feet? Did it take longer than picturing the cat's ears?

When a rabbit is pictured with an elephant, the rabbit's image must be small because the elephant is large. Using such tasks, Stephen Kosslyn found that the smaller an image is, the harder it is to "see" its details. To put this finding to use, try forming oversized images of things you want to think about. For example, to understand electricity, picture the wires as large pipes with electrons the size of golf balls moving through them; to understand the human ear, explore it (in your mind's eye) like a large cave.

Kinesthetic Imagery

How do muscular responses relate to thinking? In a sense, we think with our bodies as well as our heads. Information can be represented in **kinesthetic images** created from produced, remembered, or imagined muscular sensations (Oyama & Ichikawa, 1990). Such images help us think about movements and actions.

Kinesthetic imagery arises from kinesthetic sensations (feelings from the muscles and joints). As you think and talk, these sensations tend to guide the flow of ideas. For example, if you try to tell a friend how to knead bread dough, you may find it impossible to resist moving your hands in the proper motion. Or, try answering this question: Which direction do you turn the hot-water handle in your kitchen to shut the water off? Most people haven't simply memorized the words "Turn it clockwise," or "Turn it counterclockwise." Instead you will probably "turn" the faucet in your imagination before answering. You may even find yourself making the required hand motions before you answer.

Kinesthetic images are especially important in music, sports, dance, martial arts, and other movement-oriented skills. People with good kinesthetic imagery learn such skills faster than those with poor imagery (Glisky, Williams, & Kihlstrom, 1996).

Thinking is often accompanied by tiny, nearly imperceptible **micromovements** in our muscles. For example, if you imagine lifting a weight, a burst of activity will occur in the muscles of your motionless arm (Bakker, Boschker, & Chung, 1996). Such micromovements are an outward expression of the brain activity that accompanies kinesthetic images (Parsons et al., 1995).

If you would like to demonstrate the link between muscular activity and thinking, ask a friend who was in a sports event to describe what occurred. Along with a description, you will probably get an "instant replay" of the high points!

The Church of the Sacred Family in Barcelona, Spain, was designed by Antonio Gaudi. Could a person lacking mental imagery design such a masterpiece? Three people out of 100 find it impossible to produce mental images, and 3 out of 100 have very strong imagery. Most artists, architects, designers, sculptors, and filmmakers have excellent visual imagery.

Stored image *A mental image retained in memory and retrieved when appropriate.*
Created image *A mental image that has been assembled or invented rather than simply remembered.*
Kinesthetic image *Any mental representation based on produced, remembered, or imagined muscular sensations.*
Micromovements *Tiny, nearly imperceptible motions of the muscles.*

A recent study found that rock climbers use kinesthetic imagery to learn climbing routes and to plan their next few moves (Smyth & Waller, 1998).

CONCEPTS—I'M POSITIVE, IT'S A WHATCHAMACALLIT

A **concept** is an idea that represents a class of objects or events. Concepts are powerful tools because they allow us to think more *abstractly*. Concepts also help us identify important features of objects or events. That's why experts in various areas of knowledge are good at classifying objects. Bird watchers, tropical fish fanciers, 5-year-old dinosaur enthusiasts, and other experts have all learned to look for identifying details that beginners tend to miss. If you are knowledgeable about a particular topic, such as horses, flowers, or football, you literally see things differently than less informed people do (Johnson & Mervis, 1997).

Concept Formation

How are concepts learned? **Concept formation** is the process of classifying information into meaningful categories. At its most basic, concept formation is based on experience with **positive** and **negative instances** (examples that belong, or do not belong, to the concept class).

Concept formation is not as simple as it might seem. Imagine a child learning the concept of *dog*.

Dog Daze

A child and her father go for a walk. At a neighbor's house, they see a medium-sized dog. The father says, "See the dog." As they pass the next yard, the child sees a cat and says, "Dog!" Her father corrects her, "No, that's a *cat*." The child now thinks, "Aha, dogs are large and cats are small." In the next yard, she sees a Pekingese and says, "Cat!" "No, that's a dog," replies her father.

The child's confusion is understandable. At first, she might even mistake a Pekingese for a dust mop. However, with more positive and negative instances, the child will eventually recognize everything from Great Danes to Chihuahuas as examples of the same category—dogs.

As adults, we more often acquire concepts by learning or forming rules. A **conceptual rule** is a guideline for deciding if an object or event belongs to a concept class. For example, a triangle must be a closed shape with three sides made of straight lines. Rules are an efficient way to learn concepts, but examples remain important. It's unlikely that memorizing rules would allow an uninitiated listener to accurately categorize *punk, hip-hop, fusion, salsa, heavy metal, grunge rock,* and *rap* music.

Types of Concepts

Are there different kinds of concepts? Yes, **conjunctive concepts** are defined by the presence of two or more features. In other words, these are "and" concepts: To belong to the concept class, an item must have "this feature *and* this feature *and* this feature." For example, a *motorcycle* must have two wheels *and* an engine *and* handlebars.

Relational concepts are based on how an object relates to something else, or how its features relate to one another. All of the following are relational concepts: *larger, above, left, north,* and *upside down.* Another example is *sister,* which is defined as "a female considered in her relation to another person having the same parents."

Disjunctive concepts refer to objects that have at least one of several possible features. These are "either-or" concepts. To belong, an item must have "this feature *or* that feature *or* another feature." For example, in baseball, a *strike* is *either* a swing and a miss *or* a pitch down the middle *or* a foul ball. The either-or quality of disjunctive concepts makes them hard to learn.

PROTOTYPES When you think of the concept *bird,* do you make a mental list of features that birds have? Probably not. In addition to rules and features, we use **prototypes,** or ideal models, to identify concepts (Rosch, 1977; Smith, 1989). A robin, for instance, is a model bird; an ostrich is not. In other words, some items are better examples of a concept than others are. For instance, which of the drawings in ❖Figure 11.3 best represents a cup? At some point, a cup that is made taller or wider becomes a vase or a bowl. How do we know when the line is crossed? Probably, we mentally compare objects to an "ideal" cup, like number 5. That's why it's hard to identify concepts when we can't

❖ **FIGURE 11.3** *When does a cup become a bowl or a vase? Deciding if an object belongs to a conceptual class is aided by relating it to a prototype, or ideal example. Subjects in one experiment chose number 5 as the "best" cup. (After Labov, 1973.)*

come up with relevant prototypes. What, for example, are the objects shown in ❖Figure 11.4?

CONNOTATIVE MEANING   Generally speaking, concepts have two types of meaning. The **denotative meaning** of a word or concept is its exact definition. The **connotative meaning** is its emotional or personal meaning. The denotative meaning of the word *naked* (having no clothes) is the same for a nudist as it is for a movie censor, but we could expect their connotations to differ. Connotative differences can influence how we think about im-

BRIDGES

Stereotypes have a major impact on social behavior and frequently contribute to prejudice and discrimination.

See Chapter 20, pages 675–676, for more information.

portant issues. For example, the term *enhanced radiation device* has a more positive connotation than *neutron bomb* does (Gruner & Tighe, 1995).

Can you give a clearer statement of what a connotative meaning is?   Researcher Charles Osgood (1916–1991) used a method he called the **semantic differential** to measure connotative meaning (❖Fig. 11.5). When words or concepts are rated on a series of scales, most of their connotative meaning boils down to the dimensions *good-bad, strong-weak,* and *active-passive.* (Sounds like a good movie title, doesn't it: *The Good the Bad the Strong the Weak the Active and the Passive.*) Because concepts vary on these dimensions, words or phrases with roughly the same denotative meaning may have very different connotations. For example, I am *conscientious;* you are *careful;* he is *nitpicky!*

FAULTY CONCEPTS   Using oversimplified concepts often leads to thinking errors. For example, **social stereotypes** are oversimplified concepts of groups of people. Stereotypes are particularly troublesome in human relationships. An inaccurate or rigid picture of men, African Americans, women, conservatives, liberals, police officers, or any other group leads to muddled thinking about individual members of the group. A related problem is **all-or-nothing thinking** (one-dimensional thought). In this case, we classify things as absolutely right or wrong, good or bad, fair or unfair, honest or dishonest. Thinking this way prevents us from appreciating the subtleties of most life problems.

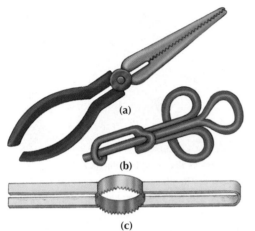

❖ **FIGURE 11.4** *Use of prototypes in concept identification. Even though its shape is unusual, item (a) can be related to a model (an ordinary set of pliers) and thus recognized. But what are items (b) and (c)? If you don't recognize them, look ahead to ❖Figure 11.6. (After Bransford & McCarrell, 1977.)*

Rate this word: **JAZZ**

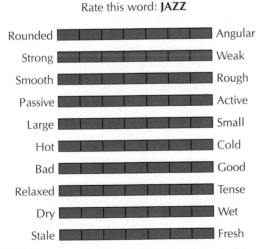

Rounded							Angular
Strong							Weak
Smooth							Rough
Passive							Active
Large							Small
Hot							Cold
Bad							Good
Relaxed							Tense
Dry							Wet
Stale							Fresh

❖ **FIGURE 11.5** *This is an example of Osgood's semantic differential. The connotative meaning of the word* jazz *can be established by rating it on the scales. Mark your own rating by placing dots or Xs in the spaces. Connect the marks with a line; then have a friend rate the word and compare your responses. It might be interesting to do the same for* rock and roll, classical, *and* rap. *You also might want to try the word* psychology. *(From C. E. Osgood. Copyright © 1952, American Psychological Association. Reprinted by permission.)*

Concept *A generalized idea representing a class of related objects or events.*
Concept formation *The process of classifying information into meaningful categories.*
Positive instance *In concept learning, an object or event that belongs to the concept class.*
Negative instance *In concept learning, an object or event that does not belong to the concept class.*
Conceptual rule *A formal rule for deciding if an object or event is an example of a particular concept.*
Conjunctive concept *A class of objects that have two or more features in common. (For example, to qualify as an example of the concept, an object must be both red and triangular.)*
Relational concept *A concept defined by the relationship between features of an object or between an object and its surroundings (for example, "greater than," "lopsided").*
Disjunctive concept *A concept defined by the presence of at least one of several possible features. (For example, to qualify, an object must be either blue or circular.)*
Prototype *An ideal model used as a prime example of a particular concept.*
Denotative meaning *The exact, dictionary definition of a word or concept; its objective meaning.*
Connotative meaning *The subjective, personal, or emotional meaning of a word or concept.*
Semantic differential *A measure of connotative meaning obtained by rating words or concepts on several dimensions.*
Social stereotype *An inaccurate and oversimplified image of members of a social group.*
All-or-nothing thinking *One-dimensional thinking that classifies things in black-and-white terms.*

RELATE

Name some ways in which you have used imagery in the thinking you have done today. Were the images you used created or stored? Were any of them synesthetic or kinesthetic?

Write a conceptual rule for the following idea: *unicycle.* Were you able to define the concept with a rule? Would positive and negative instances help make the concept clearer for others?

A true sports car has two seats, a powerful engine, good brakes, and excellent handling. What kind of a concept is the term *sports car?* What do you think of as a prototypical sports car?

LEARNING CHECK

1. List three basic units of thought:
   _____ _____
   _____

2. Synesthesia is the use of kinesthetic sensations as a vehicle for thought. T or F?

3. Humans appear capable of forming three-dimensional images that can be moved or rotated in mental space. T or F?

4. When a person forms a three-dimensional image of an environment, it is easiest to remember if an object is placed to the right or left of center. T or F?

5. Our reliance on imagery in thinking means that problem solving is impaired by micromovements. T or F?

6. A *mup* is defined as anything that is small, blue, and hairy. *Mup* is a _____ concept.

7. The connotative meaning of the word *naked* is "having no clothes." T or F?

8. Stereotyping is an example of oversimplification in thinking. T or F?

CRITICAL THINKING

9. It takes longer to answer the question "Does a frog have lips and a stubby tail?" than the question "Does a frog have lips?" Can you think of an explanation other than mental rotation to explain this difference?

10. A Democrat and a Republican are asked to rate the word *democratic* on the semantic differential. Under what conditions would their ratings be most alike?

Answers:

1. images, concepts, and language or symbols (others could be listed) 2. F 3. T 4. F 5. F 6. conjunctive 7. F 8. T 9. The first question could simply be more difficult. The difficulty of questions must be carefully matched in studies of mental imagery. 10. If they both assume the word refers to a form of government, not a political party or a candidate.

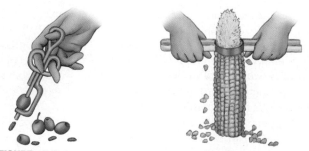

❖ **FIGURE 11.6** *Context can substitute for a lack of appropriate prototypes in concept identification.*

Wine tasting illustrates the encoding function of language. To communicate their experiences to others, wine connoisseurs must put taste sensations into words. The wine you see here is "Marked by deeply concentrated nuances of plum, blackberry, and currant, with a nice balance of tannins and acid, building to a spicy oak finish." (Don't try this with a Pop-tart!)

relies heavily on language, because it allows the world to be **encoded** (translated) into symbols that are easy to manipulate (❖Fig. 11.6).

The study of meaning in words and language is known as **semantics.** It is here that the link between language and thought becomes most evident. Suppose, on an intelligence test, you were asked to circle the word that does not belong in this series:

> SKYSCRAPER CATHEDRAL TEMPLE PRAYER

If you circled *prayer,* you answered as most people do. Now try another problem, again circling the odd item:

> CATHEDRAL PRAYER TEMPLE SKYSCRAPER

Had you seen only this question, you probably would have circled *skyscraper.* There is a subtle change in meaning caused by re-ordering the words (Mayer, 1995). This occurs because words gain much of their meaning from *context.* For example, the word *shot* has different meanings when we are thinking of marksmanship, bartending, medicine, photography, or golf (Miller, 1999).

Semantics may directly influence thinking when the choice of words alters meaning: Has one country's army "invaded" another? Or "effected a protective incursion"? Is the city reservoir

LANGUAGE—DON'T LEAVE HOME WITHOUT IT

As we have seen, thinking sometimes takes place without language. Everyone has searched for a word to express an idea that exists as a vague image or feeling. Nevertheless, most thinking

Bilingualism is the ability to speak two languages. Some people learn both a first and a second language simultaneously. Others learn one language and then another. In either case, age can make a big difference: To gain fluency in a second language and speak it with a native accent, learning must usually begin before age 6 (Genesee, 1994).

Nearly 7 million American children do not speak English at home. At school, many of these children are "immersed" in English, where they are expected to "sink or swim." Others are given a transition period during which they are taught in their home language or in both their home language and English.

For majority speakers, learning a second language is almost always beneficial. It poses no threat to the child's home language, and it improves a variety of general cognitive skills. This has been called "additive bilingualism" because learning a second language adds to a child's overall competence.

For minority children, the picture can be quite different. When minority children are plunged into English-only classrooms, they are likely to experience "subtractive bilingualism." That is, they usually end up losing some proficiency in their native language. Such children are at risk for being less than fully competent in *both* their first and second languages. In addition, they tend to fall behind educationally. As they struggle with English, their grasp of arithmetic, social studies, science, and other subjects may suffer. In short, English-only instruction can leave them poorly prepared to succeed in the majority culture (Genesee, 1994).

An approach called **two-way bilingual education** offers a way to retain the benefits of bilingualism, while avoiding its drawbacks. In such programs, native speakers and children with limited English skills are taught half the day in English and half in a second language. This approach has proved to be very successful. Both native and minority language speakers become fluent in two languages, and they perform as well or better than single-language students in English and general academic abilities.

Then why isn't two-way bilingual education more widely used? For one thing, all types of bilingual education tend to be politically unpopular among majority language speakers. Language is a major sign of group membership. Even where the majority culture is highly dominant, some of its members may feel that their culture is being eroded by recent immigrants and "foreign languages." Yet, an ability to think and communicate in a second language is a wonderful gift. While minority children are certainly at a disadvantage if they do not become proficient in English, native English speakers may be shortchanged by English-only schools as well. Studies of bilingual students in Canada and the United States have found that those who achieve a high level of ability in two languages have better mental flexibility, general language skills, control of attention, and problem-solving abilities (Bialystok, 1999; Cromdal, 1999; Francis, 1999).

PURPLE BLUE GREEN GREEN
RED PURPLE RED GREEN

❖ **FIGURE 11.7** *The Stroop interference task. Test yourself by naming the colors in the top two rows as quickly as you can. Then name the colors of the ink used to print the words in the bottom two rows (do not read the words themselves). The greater difficulty of naming colors in the bottom rows shows how intimately thought is linked to language. The meaning of words has a powerful impact on our response to them. (After Tzeng & Wang, 1983.)*

"half full" or "half empty"? Would you rather eat "prime beef" or "dead cow"? (See ❖ Figure 11.7.)

Cross-culturally, semantic problems may arise when languages are translated. Perhaps the San Jose, California, public library can be excused for displaying a large banner that was supposed to say "You are welcome" in a native Philippine language. The banner actually meant "You are circumcised." Likewise, we may forgive Pepsi for translating "Come alive, you Pepsi generation," into Thai as "Pepsi brings your ancestors back from the dead." However, in more important situations, such as in international diplomacy, avoiding semantic confusion may be vital.

Language plays a major role in defining ethnic communities and other social groups. Thus, language can be a bridge or a barrier between cultures. See "Bilingualism" for a brief discussion of the pros and cons of bilingual education.

The Structure of Language

What does it take to make a language? First of all, a language must provide symbols that can stand for objects and ideas. The symbols we call words are built out of **phonemes** (FOE-neems: basic speech sounds) and **morphemes** (MOR-feems: speech sounds collected into meaningful units, such as syllables or words). For instance, in English the sounds *m*, *b*, *w*, and *a* cannot form a syllable *mbwa*. In Swahili, they can. (Also, see ❖ Figure 11.8.)

Encoding *Changing information into a form that allows it to be manipulated in thought.*
Semantics *The study of meanings in language.*
Bilingualism *An ability to speak two languages.*
Two-way bilingual program *A program in which English-speaking children and children with limited English proficiency are taught half the day in English and half in a second language.*
Phonemes *The basic speech sounds of a language.*
Morphemes *The smallest meaningful units in a language, such as syllables or words.*

As a second point, a language must have a **grammar,** or set of rules for making sounds into words and words into sentences. One part of grammar, known as **syntax,** consists of rules for word order in sentences. Syntax is important because rearranging words almost always changes the meaning of a sentence: "Dog bites man" versus "Man bites dog."

Traditional grammar is concerned with "surface" language—the sentences we actually speak. The revolutionary ideas of linguist Noam Chomsky focus instead on the unspoken rules we use to change core ideas into various sentences. Chomsky (1986) argues that we do not learn all the sentences we might ever say. Rather, we actively *create* them by applying **transformation rules** to universal, core patterns. Such rules allow us to change a simple declarative sentence into other voices or forms. For example, the core sentence "Dog bites man" can be transformed to the following patterns (and others as well):

- **Past:** The dog bit the man.
- **Passive:** The man was bitten by the dog.

Albanian	mak, mak
Chinese	gua, gua
Dutch	rap, rap
English	quack, quack
French	coin, coin
Italian	qua, qua
Spanish	cuá, cuá
Swedish	kvack, kvack
Turkish	vak, vak

❖ **FIGURE 11.8** *Animals around the world make pretty much the same sounds. Notice, however, how various languages use slightly different phonemes to express these sounds.*

- **Negative:** The dog did not bite the man.
- **Question:** Did the dog bite the man?

Children show evidence of using transformation rules when they form sentences such as "I runned home." The child has applied the past tense rule to the irregular verb *to run.*

The third, and perhaps most essential, feature of language is that it is **productive**—it can generate new thoughts or ideas. In fact, words or signs can be rearranged to produce a nearly infinite variety of meaningful sentences. Some are silly: "Please don't feed me to the goldfish." Some are profound: "We hold these truths to be self-evident, that all men are created equal." In either case, the productive quality of language is what makes it such a powerful tool for thought.

GESTURAL LANGUAGES   It is common to think of language only as a system of spoken sounds and written symbols. However, language is not limited to speech. Consider the case of Ildefonso, a young man who was born deaf. At age 24, Ildefonso had never communicated with another human, except by mime. Then at last, Ildefonso had a breakthrough: After much hard work with a sign language teacher, he understood the link between a cat and the gesture for it. At that magic moment, he grasped the idea that "cat" could be communicated to another person, just by signing the word. For Ildefonso, it marked the end of his terrible isolation from others.

Ildefonso's long-awaited breakthrough was made possible by **American Sign Language** (**ASL**), a gestural language. ASL is not pantomime or a code. It is a true language, like German, Spanish, or Japanese. In fact, ASL is not understood by those who use other gestural languages, such as French Sign, Chinese Sign, Yiddish Sign, or Old Kentish Sign.

Similar universal language patterns are evident in both speech and sign. Of course, ASL has a *spatial* grammar, syntax, and semantics all its own (❖Fig. 11.9). Just the same, signing children pass through the same stages of language development at about the same age as speaking children do. Some psychologists believe that speech evolved from gestures, far back in human history. Do you ever make hand gestures when you are speaking on the phone? If so, you may be displaying a remnant of the gestural origins of language (Corballis, 1999).

Sign languages naturally arise out of a need to communicate visually. But they also embody a personal identity and define a

❖ **FIGURE 11.9** *ASL has only 3,000 root signs, compared with roughly 600,000 words in English. However, variations in signs make ASL a highly expressive language. For example, the sign LOOK-AT can be varied in ways to make it mean look at me, look at her, look at each, stare at, gaze, watch, look for a long time, look at again and again, reminisce, sightsee, look forward to, predict, anticipate, browse, and many more variations.*

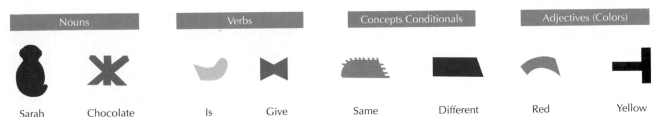

Nouns		Verbs		Concepts Conditionals		Adjectives (Colors)	
Sarah	Chocolate	Is	Give	Same	Different	Red	Yellow

❖ **FIGURE 11.10** *Here is a sample of some of the word-symbols that Sarah, a chimpanzee, used to communicate with humans. (After Premack & Premack, 1972.)*

distinct community. Sign is the true voice of the deaf and hearing impaired. Those who "speak" sign share not just a language, but a rich culture as well (Kemp, 1998; Meier, 1991; Sacks, 1990; Schaller, 1991).

The Animal Language Debate

Do animals use language? Animals do communicate. The cries, gestures, and mating calls of animals have broad meanings immediately understood by other animals of the same species (Premack, 1983). For the most part, however, natural animal communication is quite limited. Even apes and monkeys make only a few dozen distinct cries, which carry messages such as "attack," "flee," or "food here." More important, animal communication lacks the productive quality of human language. For example, when a monkey gives an "eagle distress call," it means something like "I see an eagle." The monkey has no way of saying "I don't see an eagle" or "Thank heavens that wasn't an eagle" or "That sucker I saw yesterday was some huge eagle" (Glass et al., 1979). Let's consider some of psychology's successes and failures in trying to teach animals to use language.

TALKING CHIMPS Early attempts to teach chimps to talk were a dismal failure. The world record was held by Viki, a chimp who could say only four words (*mama, papa, cup,* and *up*) after 6 years of intensive training (Fleming, 1974; Hayes, 1951). (Actually, all four words sounded something like a belch.) Then there was a breakthrough. Beatrix Gardner and Allen Gardner used operant conditioning and imitation to teach a female chimp named Washoe to use American Sign Language.

Washoe's communication skills blossomed rapidly as her "vocabulary" grew. Soon she began to put together primitive sentence strings like "Come-gimme sweet," "Out please," "Gimme tickle," and "Open food drink." Washoe's peak vocabulary was about 240 signs, and she could construct six-word sentences (Gardner & Gardner, 1989).

A chimp named Sarah was another well-known pupil of human language. David Premack taught Sarah to use 130 "words" consisting of plastic chips arranged on a magnetized board (❖Fig. 11.10). From the beginning of her training, Sarah was required to use proper word order. She learned to answer questions, to label things "same" or "different," to classify objects by color, shape, and size, and to form compound sentences (Premack & Premack, 1983). One of Sarah's top achievements was her use of conditional sentences. A **conditional statement** contains a qualification, often in the if-then form: "If Sarah

❖ **FIGURE 11.11** *After reading the message "Sarah insert apple pail banana dish" on the magnetic board, Sarah performed the actions as directed. (From "Teaching Language to an Ape" by Ann J. Premack and David Premack. Copyright © 1972 by Scientific American, Inc. All rights reserved.)*

take apple, then Mary give Sarah chocolate." "If Sarah take banana, then Mary no give Sarah chocolate" (❖Fig. 11.11).

Can it be said with certainty that the chimps understand such interchanges? Most researchers working with chimps believe that they have indeed communicated with them. Especially striking are the chimps' spontaneous responses. Washoe once "wet" on psychologist Roger Fouts's back while riding on his shoulders. When Fouts asked, with some annoyance, why she had done it, Washoe signed, "It's funny!"

Grammar *A set of rules for combining language units into meaningful speech or writing.*
Syntax *Rules for ordering words when forming sentences.*
Transformation rules *Rules by which a simple declarative sentence may be changed to other voices or forms (past tense, passive voice, and so forth).*
Productivity *The capacity of language to generate new ideas and possibilities.*
American Sign Language *A language system of hand gestures used by deaf and hearing-impaired persons.*
Conditional statement *A statement that contains a qualification, often of the if-then form.*

CRITICISMS Such interchanges are impressive. But communication and actual language use are different things. Even untrained chimps use simple gestures to communicate with humans. For example, a chimp will point at a banana that is out of reach, while glancing back and forth between the banana and a nearby human (Leavens & Hopkins, 1998). (The meaning of this gesture is clear. The exasperated look on the chimp's face is more ambiguous, but it probably means "Yes, that one, you idiot.")

Some psychologists doubt that apes can really use language. For one thing, the chimps rarely "speak" without prompting. Many of their seemingly original sentences turn out to be responses to questions or imitations of signs the teacher made. Also, it appears that the apes may be simply performing chains of operant responses to get food, play, or other "goodies" (Hixon, 1998). By using such responses, the apes then manipulate their trainers to get what they want.

You might say critics think the apes have made monkeys out of their trainers. However, psychologists Roger and Debbi Fouts believe they can answer such criticisms. An analysis they performed of some 6,000 conversations between chimps showed that only 5 percent had anything to do with food. The Fouts also videotaped conversations between chimps that took place when no humans were present to cue them (Fouts et al., 1984). Another study of chimps using a special symbol system found that the chimps hold real conversations, in which information is exchanged symbolically (Greenfield & Savage-Rumbaugh, 1993). So, maybe the chimps will make monkeys out of the critics.

PROBLEMS WITH SYNTAX At this point, numerous chimps, a gorilla named Koko, and an assortment of dolphins and sea lions have learned to communicate with word symbols of various kinds. Yet, even if some criticisms can be answered, linguists such as Noam Chomsky remain unconvinced that animals can truly use language. The core issue is that problems with syntax (word order) have plagued almost all animal language experiments. For example, when a chimp named Nim Chimpsky (no relation to Chomsky) wanted an orange, he would typically signal a grammarless string of words: "Give orange me give eat orange me eat orange give me eat orange give me you." This might be communication, but it is not language.

LEXIGRAMS More recently, the flames of controversy were fanned again by Kanzi, a pygmy chimpanzee studied by Duane Rumbaugh and Sue Savage-Rumbaugh. Kanzi communicates using gestures and push buttons on a computer keyboard. Each of the 250 buttons is marked with a **lexigram,** or geometric word-symbol (❖Fig. 11.12). Using the lexigrams, Kanzi can create primitive sentences several words long. He can also understand about 650 spoken sentences. During testing, Kanzi hears spoken words over headphones, so his caretakers cannot prompt him (Savage-Rumbaugh et al., 1990; Savage-Rumbaugh & Lewin, 1996).

Kanzi's sentences consistently follow correct word order. His syntax is good, even for new word combinations he has

❖ **FIGURE 11.12** *Kanzi's language learning has been impressive. He can comprehend spoken English words. He can identify lexigram symbols when he hears corresponding words. He can use lexigrams when the objects they refer to are absent, and he can, if asked, lead someone to the object. All these skills were acquired through observation, not conditioning (Savage-Rumbaugh et al., 1990; Savage-Rumbaugh & Lewin, 1996).*

never made before. Like a child learning language, Kanzi picked up some rules from his caregivers (Savage-Rumbaugh & Lewin, 1996). However, he has developed other patterns on his own. For example, Kanzi almost always places two action symbols in the order he wants to carry them out, such as "chase tickle" or "chase hide." That is, he uses symbols to plan and communicate the order of actions. Psycholinguist Patricia Marks Greenfield says that Kanzi's use of grammar is on a par with that of a 2-year-old child (Savage-Rumbaugh et al., 1993).

Kanzi's ability to invent a simple grammar may help us better understand the roots of human language. It is certainly the strongest answer yet to the critics. On the other hand, Chomsky insists that if chimps were biologically capable of language, they would have made use of it on their own. Although the issue is far from resolved, such research promises to unravel some of the mysteries of language learning. In fact, it has already been helpful for teaching language to children with serious language impairments (Savage-Rumbaugh et al., 1990).

KNOWLEDGE BUILDER
LANGUAGE

RELATE

Here's some mnemonic help: You use a *phone* to send *phonemes*. To *morph* them into words, you have to hit them with a *grammar.* What wrong is with sentence this? (The answer is not a *sin tax,* but it still may tax you.)

Just for fun, see if you can illustrate the productive quality of language by creating a sentence that no one has ever spoken before.

You must learn to communicate with an alien life-form (from the planet Encodon) whose language cannot be reproduced by the human voice. Do you think it would it be better to use a gestural language or lexigrams? Why?

PROBLEM SOLVING—GETTING AN ANSWER IN SIGHT

We have reviewed some of the basic ways that we mentally represent information so that it can be manipulated and used to solve problems. It is now time to take a direct look at problem solving. A good way to start is to solve a problem. Give this one a try.

> A famous ocean liner (the *Queen Ralph*) is steaming toward port at 20 miles per hour. It is 50 miles from shore when a seagull takes off from its deck and flies toward port. At the same instant, a speedboat leaves port at 30 miles per hour. The bird flies back and forth between the speedboat and the *Queen Ralph* at a speed of 40 miles per hour. How far will the bird have flown when the two boats pass?

If you don't immediately see the answer to this problem, read it again. (The answer is revealed shortly in Insightful Solutions.)

We all solve many problems every day. Problem solving can be as commonplace as figuring out how to make a non-poiso-

nous meal out of leftovers or as significant as developing a cure for cancer. How do we find solutions to such problems?

Mechanical Solutions

A **mechanical solution** may be achieved by trial and error or by rote. If I forget the combination to my bike lock, I may be able to discover it by trial and error. In an era of high-speed computers, many trial-and-error solutions are best left to machines. A computer could generate all possible combinations of the five numbers on my lock in a split second. (Of course, it would take me a long time to try them all.)

When a problem is solved by *rote*, thinking is guided by a learned set of rules. If you have a good background in math, you may have solved the problem of the bird and the boats by rote. However, I hope you didn't. There is an easier solution.

Solutions by Understanding

Many problems cannot be solved mechanically or by habitual modes of thought. In that case, **understanding** (deeper comprehension of a problem) is necessary. A classic series of studies on thinking of this type was performed by German psychologist Karl Duncker (1945). Duncker gave college students this problem:

> A person has an inoperable stomach tumor. A device is available that produces rays that, at high intensity, will destroy tissue (both healthy and diseased). How can the tumor be destroyed without damaging surrounding tissue? (Students were also shown the sketch in ❖Figure 11.13.)

What did this problem show about problem solving? Duncker asked his students to think aloud as they worked. He found that there were two phases to successful problem solving. First, students had to discover the *general properties* of a correct solution. A **general solution** states the requirements for success, but not in enough detail for further action. This phase was complete when students realized that the intensity of the rays had to be lowered on their way to the tumor. Then, in the second

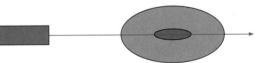

❖ **FIGURE 11.13** *A schematic representation of Duncker's tumor problem. The dark spot represents a tumor surrounded by healthy tissue. How can the tumor be destroyed without injuring surrounding tissue? (After Duncker, 1945.)*

Lexigram *A geometric shape used as a symbol for a word.*
Mechanical solution *A problem solution achieved by trial and error or by a fixed procedure based on learned rules.*
Understanding *In problem solving, a deeper comprehension of the nature of the problem.*
General solution *A solution that correctly states the requirements for success but not in enough detail for further action.*

phase, they proposed a number of **functional** (workable) **solutions** and selected the best one. (One solution is to focus weak rays on the tumor from several angles. Another is to rotate the person's body. That way, the exposure of healthy tissue will be minimized.)

It might help to summarize with another example. Almost everyone who tries the Rubik's cube puzzle begins at the mechanical, *trial-and-error* level. If you want to take the easy route, printed instructions are available that give the steps for a *rote* solution. In time, those who persist begin to *understand* the *general properties* of the puzzle. After that, they can solve it consistently.

Heuristics

"You can't get there from here," or so it often seems when facing a problem. Solving problems often requires a strategy. If the number of alternatives is small, a **random search strategy** may work. This is another example of trial-and-error thinking in which all possibilities are tried, more or less randomly. Imagine that you are traveling and you decide to look up an old friend, J. Smith, in a city you are visiting. You open the phone book and find 47 J. Smiths listed. Of course, you could dial each number until you find the right one. "Forget it," you say to yourself. "Is there any way I can narrow the search?" "Oh, yeah! I remember hearing that Janet lives by the beach." Then you take out a map and call only the numbers with addresses near the waterfront (Ellis & Hunt, 1992).

The approach used in this example is a **heuristic** (hew-RIS-tik: a strategy for identifying and evaluating problem solutions). Typically, a heuristic is a "rule of thumb" that reduces the number of alternatives thinkers must consider. This raises the odds of success, although it does not guarantee a solution. Here are some heuristic strategies that often work:

- Try to identify how the current state of affairs differs from the desired goal. Then find steps that will reduce the difference.
- Try working backward from the desired goal to the starting point or current state.
- If you can't reach the goal directly, try to identify an intermediate goal or subproblem that at least gets you closer.
- Represent the problem in other ways, with graphs, diagrams, or analogies, for instance.
- Find a similar problem. Does the solution to that problem apply to the one you are working on?
- Try to list the assumptions you are making and systematically challenge or reverse each one.
- Generate a possible solution and test it. Doing so may eliminate many alternatives, or it may clarify what is needed for a solution.

IDEAL PROBLEM SOLVING   Perhaps the most valuable heuristic of all is having a *general* thinking strategy. Psychologist John Bransford and his colleagues list five steps that they believe lead to effective problem solving: **i**dentify, **d**efine, **e**xplore, **a**ct, and **l**ook and learn (Bransford et al., 1986; Bransford & Stein, 1984). Notice that the first letters of the steps spell *ideal.*

To apply the ideal thinking strategy, you should *identify* the problem, *define* it clearly, and then *explore* possible solutions and relevant knowledge. Next, you must *act* by trying a possible solution or hypothesis. Finally, you should *look* at the results and *learn* from them. Of course, each attempted solution may identify further subproblems. These can again be tackled with the "ideal" steps until a final satisfactory solution is found.

Insightful Solutions

During problem solving, we say that **insight** has occurred when an answer appears suddenly. Insights are usually so *rapid* and *clear* that we wonder why we didn't see the solution sooner. Insight is usually based on reorganizing the elements of a problem. Seeing the problem in a new way is what makes its solution seem obvious (Durso, Rea, & Dayton, 1994).

Let's return now to the problem of the boats and the bird. The best way to solve it is by insight. Because the boats will cover the 50-mile distance in exactly 1 hour, and the bird flies 40 miles per hour, the bird will have flown 40 miles when the boats meet. No math is necessary if you have insight into this problem. ❖Figure 11.14 lists some additional insight problems you may want to try.

In an interesting experiment, college students rated how "warm" (close to an answer) they felt while solving insight problems. Students who had insights usually jumped directly from "cold" to the correct answer. Students who only got "warmer" usually produced wrong answers (Metcalfe, 1986). Thus, you may be headed for a mistake if an insight is *not* rapid. Real insight tends to be an all-or-nothing event (Smith & Kounios, 1996).

The Nature of Insight

What, really, does it mean to have an insight?   Psychologists Robert Sternberg and Janet Davidson (1982) believe that insight involves three abilities. The first is **selective encoding,** which refers to selecting information that is relevant to a problem, while ignoring distractions. For example, consider the following problem:

> If you have white socks and black socks in your drawer, mixed in the ratio of 4 to 5, how many socks will you have to take out to make sure of having a pair of the same color?

A person who fails to recognize that "mixed in a ratio of 4 to 5" is irrelevant information will be less likely to come up with the correct answer of three socks.

Insight also relies on **selective combination,** or bringing together seemingly unrelated bits of useful information. Try this sample problem:

> With a 7-minute hourglass and an 11-minute hourglass, what is the simplest way to time the boiling of an egg for 15 minutes?

The answer requires using both hourglasses in combination. First, the 7-minute and the 11-minute hourglasses are started running. When the 7-minute hourglass runs out, it's time to begin boiling the egg. At this point, 4 minutes remain on the 11-minute hourglass. Thus, when it runs out, it is simply turned over. When it runs out again, 15 minutes will have passed.

Water lilies

Problem: Water lilies growing in a pond double in area every 24 hours. On the first day of spring, only one lily pad is on the surface of the pond. Sixty days later, the pond is entirely covered. On what day is the pond half-covered?

Twenty dollars

Problem: Jessica and Blair both have the same amount of money. How much must Jessica give Blair so that Blair has $20 more than Jessica?

How many pets?

Problem: How many pets do you have if all of them are birds except two, all of them are cats except two, and all of them are dogs except two?

Between 2 and 3

Problem: What one mathematical symbol can you place between 2 and 3 that results in a number greater than 2 and less than 3?

One word

Problem: Rearrange the letters NEWDOOR to make one word.

Solutions to these problems are listed in ◆Table 11.1.

❖ **FIGURE 11.14.**

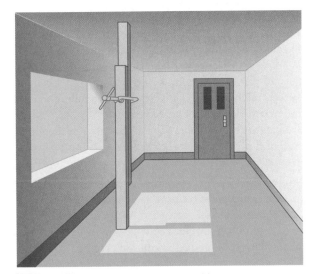

❖ **FIGURE 11.15** *Solution to the hat rack problem.*

A third source of insights is **selective comparison.** This is the ability to compare new problems with old information or with problems already solved. A good example is the hat rack problem, in which subjects must build a structure that can support an overcoat in the middle of a room. Each person is given only two long sticks and a **C**-clamp to work with. The solution, shown in ❖Figure 11.15, is to clamp the two sticks together so that they are wedged between floor and ceiling. If you were given this problem, you would be more likely to solve it if you first thought of the way pole lamps are wedged between floor and ceiling.

Fixations

One of the most important barriers to problem solving is **fixation,** the tendency to get "hung up" on wrong solutions or to become blind to alternatives. Usually this occurs when we place unnecessary restrictions on our thinking (Isaak & Just, 1995). How, for example, could you plant four small trees so that each is an equal distance from all the others? (The answer is shown in ❖Figure 11.16.)

A prime example of restricted thinking is **functional fixedness,** an inability to see new uses (functions) for familiar objects or for objects that were used in a particular way. If you have ever used a dime as a screwdriver, you've overcome functional fixedness.

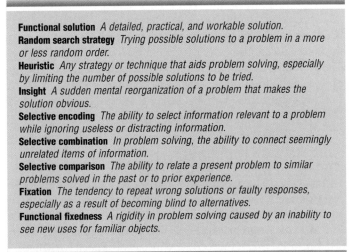

Functional solution *A detailed, practical, and workable solution.*
Random search strategy *Trying possible solutions to a problem in a more or less random order.*
Heuristic *Any strategy or technique that aids problem solving, especially by limiting the number of possible solutions to be tried.*
Insight *A sudden mental reorganization of a problem that makes the solution obvious.*
Selective encoding *The ability to select information relevant to a problem while ignoring useless or distracting information.*
Selective combination *In problem solving, the ability to connect seemingly unrelated items of information.*
Selective comparison *The ability to relate a present problem to similar problems solved in the past or to prior experience.*
Fixation *The tendency to repeat wrong solutions or faulty responses, especially as a result of becoming blind to alternatives.*
Functional fixedness *A rigidity in problem solving caused by an inability to see new uses for familiar objects.*

❖ **FIGURE 11.16** *Four trees can be placed equidistant from one another by piling dirt into a mound. Three of the trees are planted equal distances apart around the base of the mound. The fourth tree is planted on the top of the mound. If you were fixated on arrangements that involve level ground, you may have been blind to this three-dimensional solution.*

How does functional fixedness affect problem solving? Karl Duncker, who coined the term *functional fixedness,* performed a clever study to demonstrate it. Duncker challenged students to mount a candle on a vertical board so that the candle could burn normally. Duncker gave each student three candles, some matches, some cardboard boxes, some thumbtacks, and other items. Half of Duncker's subjects received these items *inside* the cardboard boxes. The others were given all the items, including the boxes, spread out on a tabletop.

Duncker found that when the items were in the boxes, solving the problem was very difficult. This is because the boxes were seen as *containers,* not as items that might be part of the solution. (If you haven't guessed the solution, check ❖Fig. 11.17.) Undoubtedly, we could avoid many fixations if we took a more flexible approach to categorizing the world (Langer & Piper, 1987). For instance, creativity could be facilitated in Duncker's container problem by saying "This *could be* a box," instead of "This *is* a box."

Common Barriers to Problem Solving

Functional fixedness is just one of the mental blocks that prevent insight. Here's an example of another: A $5 bill is placed on a table and a stack of objects is balanced precariously on top of the bill. How can the bill be removed without touching or moving the objects? A good answer is to split the bill on one of its edges. Gently pulling from opposite ends will tear the bill in half and remove it without toppling the objects. Many people fail to see this solution because they have learned not to destroy money (Adams, 1988). Notice again the impact of placing something in a category, in this case, "things of value" (which should not be destroyed). The list that follows identifies other common mental blocks and fixations that can hinder problem solving.

1. **Emotional barriers:** Inhibition and fear of making a fool of oneself, fear of making a mistake, inability to tolerate ambiguity, excessive self-criticism.
   Example: An architect is afraid to try an unconventional design because she fears that other architects will think it is frivolous.

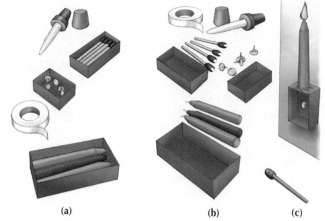

(a)   (b)   (c)

❖ **FIGURE 11.17** *Materials for solving the candle problem were given to subjects in boxes* (a) *or separately* (b). *Functional fixedness caused by condition* (a) *interfered with solving the problem. The solution to the problem is shown in* (c).

2. **Cultural barriers:** Values that hold that fantasy is a waste of time; that playfulness is for children only; that reason, logic, and numbers are good; that feelings, intuitions, pleasure, and humor are bad or have no value in the serious business of problem solving.
   Example: A corporate manager wants to solve a business problem but becomes stern and angry when members of his marketing team joke playfully about possible solutions.
3. **Learned barriers:** Conventions about uses (functional fixedness), meanings, possibilities, taboos.
   Example: A cook doesn't have any clean mixing bowls and fails to see that he could use a frying pan as a bowl.
4. **Perceptual barriers:** Habits leading to a failure to identify important elements of a problem.
   Example: A beginning artist concentrates on drawing a vase of flowers without seeing that the "empty" spaces around the vase are part of the composition, too.

Much of what we know about thinking comes from direct studies of how people solve problems. Yet, surprisingly, much can also be learned from machines. As the next section explains, computerized problem solving provides a fascinating "laboratory" for testing ideas about how you and I think.

◆ **TABLE 11.1** Solutions to Insight Problems

Water lilies: Day 59	
Twenty dollars: $10	
How many pets? Three (one bird, one cat, and one dog)	
Between 2 and 3: A decimal point	
One word: ONE WORD (You may object that the answer is two words, but the problem called for the answer to be "one word," and it is.)	

ARTIFICIAL INTELLIGENCE—I COMPUTE, THEREFORE I AM

It's been a long time since Johann Sebastian Bach, the eighteenth-century German composer, last wrote any music. But listeners can be forgiven if they briefly mistake music created by Kemal Ebcioglu for Bach's work. Ebcioglu devised a computer program that writes harmonies remarkably similar to Bach's. Ebcioglu analyzed Bach's music and came up with 350 rules that govern the harmonizing process. The resulting program displays what is known as artificial intelligence. Its compositions sound like reasonably good classical music. This shows the power of artificial intelligence. Small but glaring defects in the music and a certain lack of inspiration reveal its shortcomings.

Artificial intelligence (**AI**) refers to computer programs capable of doing things that require intelligence when done by people (Best, 1995). Artificial intelligence is based on the fact that many tasks—from harmonizing music to medical diagnosis—can be reduced to a set of rules applied to a body of information. AI is valuable in situations where speed, vast memory, and persistence are required. In fact, AI programs are better at some tasks than humans are. An example can be found in world chess champion Garry Kasparov's loss, in 1997, to a computer called Deep Blue. Kasparov calls Deep Blue—with due respect—"the monster." Deep Blue can calculate 200 million moves a second. That's enough power to check billions of future chess positions before each move.

AI and Cognition

Artificial intelligence provides a way to probe some of the oldest questions about the mind, such as how we comprehend language, make decisions, and solve problems. Increasingly, AI is being used as a research tool in two basic ways: computer simulations and expert systems.

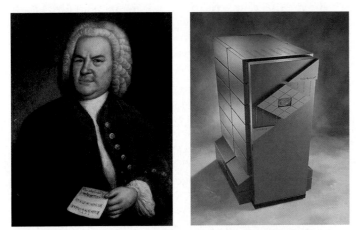

Two composers. The one on the left was a genius who wrote sublime, multivoiced harmonies. The one on the right has created reasonably good, if uninspired, music. Computer models of thought can approximate intelligent human behavior. However, rule-based computer "thinking" still lacks the flexibility, creativity, and common sense of human intelligence.

Computer simulations are programs that attempt to duplicate human behavior, especially thinking, decision making, or problem solving. Here, the computer acts as a "laboratory" for testing models of cognition. If a computer program behaves as humans do (including making the same errors), then the program may be a good model of how we think (Mayer, 1995).

Most computer models of problem solving are based on a **means-ends analysis.** Typically, the program compares the current state of affairs to the desired end-state or goal and attempts to reduce the difference. After each step, the program tests to see if the difference is greater or less than before. This cycle is repeated until the problem is solved. Models such as this may seem removed from real life, but much human thinking and problem solving has a means-ends quality to it (Anderson, 1993). The following quotation provides an everyday example:

> I want to take my son to nursery school. What's the difference between what I have and what I want? Distance. What changes distance? My car. My car won't start. What is needed to make it start? A new battery. What has new batteries? An auto repair shop. I need to have the shop come to my house and put in a new battery. But the shop doesn't know I need a battery. What is the problem? Communication. What allows communication? A telephone. (And so on.) (Adapted from Newell & Simon, 1972.)

Expert systems are a second major form of AI. **Expert systems** are computer programs that respond as a human expert would. They have demystified some human abilities by converting complex skills into clearly stated rules a computer can follow. Expert systems can predict the weather, analyze geological formations, diagnose disease, play chess, read, tell when to buy or sell stocks, and do many other tasks.

EXPERTS AND NOVICES   Working with artificial intelligence has helped especially to clarify differences between novices and experts. Research on chess masters, for example, shows that their skills are based on specific **organized knowledge** (systematic information) and **acquired strategies** (learned tactics). In other words, becoming a star performer does not come from some general strengthening of the mind. Master chess players don't necessarily have better memories than beginners (except

Artificial intelligence *Any artificial system (often a computer program) that is capable of human-like problem solving or intelligent responding.*
Computer simulations *Computer programs that mimic some aspect of human thinking, decision making, or problem solving.*
Means-ends analysis *An analysis of how to reduce the difference between the present state of affairs and a desired goal.*
Expert systems *Computer programs designed to respond as a human expert would; programs based on the knowledge and rules that underlie human expertise in specific topics.*
Organized knowledge *Orderly and highly refined information about a particular topic or skill.*
Acquired strategies *Learned tactics for swiftly solving the problems encountered in one's area of expertise.*

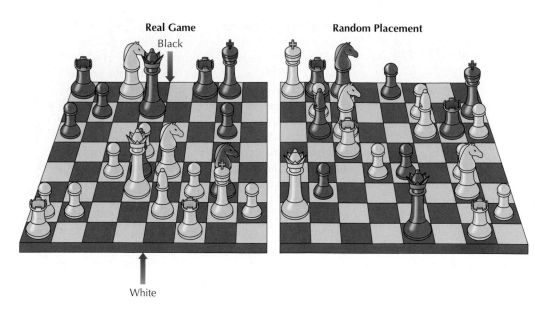

Real Game

Black

White

Random Placement

❖ **FIGURE 11.18** *The left chessboard shows a realistic game. The right chessboard is a random arrangement of pieces. Expert chess players can memorize the left board at a glance, yet they are no better than beginners at memorizing the random board (Saariluoma, 1994). Their superior recall of realistic positions is based on a learned ability to see meaningful patterns among pieces. Such patterns change groups of pieces into large chunks that match knowledge stored in long-term memory (Gorbet & Simon, 1996).*

for realistic chess positions) (Gobet & Simon, 1996). (See ❖Figure 11.18.) And, typically, they don't explore more moves ahead than lesser players.

What does set master players apart is their ability to recognize *patterns* that suggest what lines of play should be explored next (Best, 1995). This helps eliminate a large number of possible moves. The chess master, therefore, does not waste time exploring unproductive pathways. Experts are better able to see the true nature of problems and to define them in terms of general principles (Anderson, 1993). In general, expert performance at most thinking tasks is based on acquired strategies and knowledge. If you would like to excel at a profession or a mental skill, plan on adding to your knowledge every day—for at least 10 years (Ericsson & Charness, 1994).

Expertise also allows more **automatic processing,** or fast, fairly effortless thinking based on experience with similar problems. Automatic processing frees "space" in short-term memory, making it easier to work on the problem. At the highest skill levels, expert performers tend to rise above rules and plans. Their decisions, thinking, and actions become rapid and fluid. Thus, when a chess master recognizes a pattern on the chessboard, the most desirable tactic comes to mind almost immediately (Klein et al., 1995).

LIMITATIONS   What the preceding tells us is that experts in one area do not automatically become better problem solvers elsewhere. Nor do they become generally smarter (Ericsson & Charness, 1994). The same conclusion applies to artificial intelligence. Expert systems have been hailed as a possible remedy for human errors in tasks such as air-traffic control, the operation of nuclear power plants, and the control of weapons systems. However, the truth is that expert systems are "idiot geniuses." They are very adept within a narrow range of problem solving, but they are "stone stupid" at everything else.

Eventually, AI may lead to robots that recognize faces and voices and that speak and act "intelligently" (Best, 1995). But cognitive scientists are becoming aware that machine "intelligence" is ultimately "blind" outside its underlying set of rules.

In contrast, human cognition is much more flexible. For example, u cann understnd wrds thet ar miz↓eld. Computers are very literal and easily stymied by such errors.

Humans are able to take into account exceptions, context, and interpretations as they think. We also make commitments and take responsibility for our actions. A rule-driven expert system processes information without regard for the meaning of actions. Expert systems may never be able to anticipate the infinite number of possible events that could occur. As a result, their actions might be disastrous in unanticipated situations (Denning, 1988).

Clearly, artificial intelligence will play an increasingly visible role in cognitive research and in our lives. However, it is not likely to soon replace the human touch in many areas. Although Bach might have been fascinated by AI, it is doubtful that his musical magic will be eclipsed by a machine.

KNOWLEDGE BUILDER

PROBLEM SOLVING AND ARTIFICIAL INTELLIGENCE

RELATE

Identify at least one problem you have solved mechanically or by rote. Now identify a problem you solved by understanding. Did the second problem involve finding a general solution or a functional solution? Or both? What heuristics did you use to solve the problem?

What is the best insightful solution you've ever come up with? Did it involve selective encoding, combination, or comparison?

Can you think of a time when you overcame functional fixedness to solve a problem?

LEARNING CHECK

1. Insight refers to rote, or trial-and-error, problem solving. T or F?

2. The first phase in problem solving by understanding is to discover the general properties of a correct solution. T or F?

3. Problem-solving strategies that guide the search for solutions are called _____.

4. A common element underlying insight is that information is encoded, combined, and compared
   a. mechanically *b.* by rote *c.* functionally *d.* selectively

5. The term *fixation* refers to the point at which a helpful insight becomes fixed in one's thinking. T or F?

6. Two aspects of artificial intelligence are computer simulations and automatic processing. T or F?

7. Computer simulations are often used to test models of human cognition. T or F?

8. Organized knowledge, acquired strategies, and automatic processing are all characteristics of human expertise. T or F?

9. Expert systems can be described as broadly intelligent because their rules and heuristics apply to almost any problem-solving situation. T or F?

CRITICAL THINKING

10. Do you think that it is true that "a problem clearly defined is a problem half solved"?

11. Is it ever accurate to describe a machine as "intelligent"?

Answers:

1. F 2. T 3. heuristics 4. *d* 5. F 6. T 7. T 8. T 9. F 10. Although that might be an overstatement, it is true that clearly defining a starting point and the desired goal can serve as a heuristic in problem solving. 11. As stated, rule-driven expert systems may appear "intelligent" within a narrow range of problem solving. However, they are idiots at everything else. This is usually not what we have in mind when discussing human intelligence.

Fluency is an important part of creative thinking. Mozart produced more than 600 pieces of music. Picasso (shown here) created more than 20,000 artworks. Shakespeare wrote 154 sonnets. Not all of these works were masterpieces. However, a fluent outpouring of ideas fed the creative efforts of each of these geniuses.

CREATIVE THINKING—DOWN ROADS LESS TRAVELED

As noted earlier, problem solving may be the result of thinking that is mechanical, insightful, or based on understanding. To this, we can add that thought may be **inductive** (going from specific facts or observations to general principles) or **deductive** (going from general principles to specific situations). Thinking may also be **logical** (proceeding from given information to new conclusions on the basis of explicit rules) or **illogical** (intuitive, associative, or personal).

What distinguishes creative thinking from more routine problem solving? Creative thinking involves all these styles of thought (in varying combinations), plus *fluency, flexibility,* and *originality.* The meaning of these terms can be illustrated with an example. Let's say that you would like to find a creative use (or uses) for the millions of automobile tires discarded each year. The creativity of your suggestions could be rated in this way: **Fluency** is defined as the total number of suggestions you are able to make. **Flexibility** is the number of times you shift from one class of possible uses to another. **Originality** refers to how novel or unusual your suggestions are. By totaling the number of times you showed fluency, flexibility, and originality, we could rate the creativity of your thinking on this problem. Speaking more generally, we would be rating your capacity for divergent thinking (Baer, 1993).

Automatic processing *Thinking that can be done with little conscious effort or attention.*

Inductive thought *Thinking in which a general rule or principle is inferred from a series of specific examples; for instance, inferring the laws of gravity by observing many falling objects.*

Deductive thought *Thought that applies a general set of rules to specific situations; for example, using the laws of gravity to predict the behavior of a single falling object.*

Logical thought *Drawing conclusions on the basis of formal principles of reasoning.*

Illogical thought *Thought that is intuitive, haphazard, or irrational.*

Fluency *In tests of creativity, fluency refers to the total number of solutions produced.*

Flexibility *In tests of creativity, flexibility is indicated by the number of different types of solutions produced.*

Originality *In tests of creativity, originality refers to how novel or unusual solutions are.*

Divergent thinking is the most widely used measure of creative problem solving. In routine problem solving or thinking, there is one correct answer, and the problem is to find it. This leads to **convergent thinking** (lines of thought converge on the answer). **Divergent thinking** is the reverse, in which many possibilities are developed from one starting point (Baer, 1993). (See ◆Table 11.2 for some examples.) Rather than repeating learned solutions, creative thinking produces new answers, ideas, or patterns (Michalko, 1998).

Divergent thinking is also a characteristic of daydreaming. Before we discuss divergent thinking further, let's take a brief

BRIDGES

Like fantasy, dreams can also contribute to creative problem solving.

See Chapter 8, pages 267–268.

detour into the realm of fantasy (if you're not there already). See "Daydreams, Fantasy, and Creativity."

Isn't creativity more than divergent thinking? What if a person comes up with a large number of useless answers to a problem? Yes, to be creative, the solution to a problem must be more than novel, unusual, or original. It must also be *practical* if it is an invention and *sensible* if it is an idea (Finke, 1990). This is the dividing line between a "harebrained scheme" and a "stroke of genius" (❖Fig. 11.19). In other words, the creative person brings reasoning and critical thinking to bear on new ideas once they are produced (Feldhusen, 1995).

◆ **TABLE 11.2** Convergent and Divergent Problems

CONVERGENT PROBLEMS
What is the area of a triangle that is 3 feet wide at the base and 2 feet tall?
Erica is shorter than Zoey but taller than Carlo, and Carlo is taller than Jared. Who is the second tallest?
If you simultaneously drop a baseball and a bowling ball from a tall building, which will hit the ground first?

DIVERGENT PROBLEMS
What objects can you think of that begin with the letters BR?
How could discarded aluminum cans be put to use?
Write a poem about fire and ice.

❖ **FIGURE 11.19** *Creative ideas combine originality with feasibility. (Adapted from McMullan & Stocking, 1978.)*

DAYDREAMS, FANTASY, AND CREATIVITY

Has your reading of this chapter been interrupted by a **daydream** (vivid waking fantasy)? Psychologist Eric Klinger (1990) fitted volunteers with pagers and asked them to record what they were doing or thinking whenever he "beeped" them. Surprisingly, Klinger found that about half of our waking thoughts are occupied by daydreams. What do we know about this unique mental state?

CONTENT   In general, daydreams mirror our desires, fears, and anxieties in a fairly direct way. Klinger says, "When you're happy you have happy daydreams, when you're sad you have sad daydreams, and when you're angry you have angry daydreams." Because daydreams are fairly straightforward in meaning, they can be a good source of personal insights. Sleeping dreams, in contrast, tend to be more complex and difficult to analyze (Klinger, 1990).

Two of the most common daydream plots are the *conquering hero* and the *suffering martyr* themes. In a **conquering hero fantasy,** the daydreamer gets the starring role as a famous, rich, or powerful person: a celebrity, athlete, musician, famous surgeon, brilliant lawyer, or magnificent lover. Themes such as these seem to reflect needs for mas-

tery and escape from the frustrations of everyday life. **Suffering martyr daydreams** center on feelings of being neglected, hurt, rejected, or unappreciated by others. In such fantasies, others end up regretting their past actions and realizing what a wonderful person the daydreamer was all along.

BENEFITS   Daydreams often fill a need for stimulation during routine or boring tasks. They also improve our ability to delay immediate pleasures so that future goals can be achieved. And in everyday terms, fantasy can be an outlet for frustrated impulses. If you have a momentary urge to bash the fool in front of you on the highway, substituting fantasy for action may avert disaster.

Perhaps the greatest value of fantasy is its contribution to creativity. In the imaginative realm of fantasy, anything is possible—a quality allowing for tremendous fluency and flexibility of thought. For most people, fantasy and daydreaming are associated with positive emotional adjustment, lower levels of aggression, and greater mental flexibility or creativity (Klinger, 1990; Singer, 1974). Perhaps that's why Albert Einstein was, in his own words, "disorderly and a dreamer."

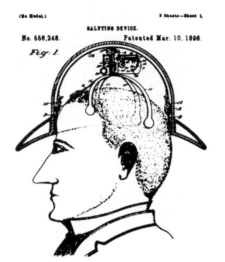

(No Model.)

SALUTING DEVICE.

No. 556,248. Patented Mar. 10, 1896.

Fig. 1.

Hat-tipping device. According to the patent, it is for "automatically effecting polite salutations by the elevation and rotation of the hat on the head of the saluting party when said person bows to the person or persons saluted." In addition to being original or novel, a creative solution must fit the demands of the problem. Is this a creative solution to the "problem" of hat tipping?

Problem finding is another characteristic of creative thinking. Many of the problems we solve are "presented" to us—by employers, teachers, circumstances, or life in general. **Problem finding** involves actively seeking problems to solve. When you are thinking creatively, a spirit of discovery prevails: You are more likely to find unsolved problems and *choose* to tackle them. Thus, problem finding may be a more creative act than the convergent problem solving that typically follows it (Runco & Chand, 1995).

Tests of Creativity

Several tests of divergent thinking have been created. In the **Unusual Uses Test,** a person is asked to think of as many uses as possible for an object (such as the tires mentioned earlier). In the **Consequences Test,** the goal is to list the consequences that would follow a basic change in the world. For example, you might be asked, "What would be the results if everyone suddenly lost the sense of balance and could no longer stay in an upright position?" Subjects try to list as many reactions as possible. In the **Anagrams Test,** people are given a word such as *creativity* and asked to make as many new words as possible by rearranging the letters. Each of these tests can be scored for fluency, flexibility, and originality. (For an example of other tests of divergent thought, see ❖Figure 11.20.)

Creativity tests have been useful, but they are not the whole story. If you want to predict whether a person will be creative in the future, it helps to look at two more kinds of information (Feldhusen & Goh, 1995):

- The *products* of creative thinking (such as essays, poems, drawings, or constructed objects) are often more informative than test results. When creative people are asked to actually produce something, others tend to judge their work as creative.

- A simple listing of a person's *past creative activities and achievements* is an excellent guide to the likelihood that she or he will be creative in the future.

Stages of Creative Thought

Is there any pattern to creative thinking? A good summary of the sequence of events in creative thinking proposes five stages that usually occur:

1. **Orientation.** As a first step, the problem must be defined and important dimensions identified.
2. **Preparation.** In the second stage, creative thinkers saturate themselves with as much information pertaining to the problem as possible.
3. **Incubation.** Most major problems produce a period during which all attempted solutions will have proved futile. At this point, problem solving may proceed on a subconscious level: While the problem seems to have been set aside, it is still "cooking" in the background.
4. **Illumination.** The stage of incubation is often ended by a rapid insight or series of insights. These produce the "Aha!" experience, often depicted in cartoons as a light-bulb appearing over the thinker's head.
5. **Verification.** The final step is to test and critically evaluate the solution obtained during the stage of illumination. If the solution proves faulty, the thinker reverts to the stage of incubation.

Of course, creative thought is seldom so neat. Nevertheless, the stages listed are a good summary of the typical sequence of events.

You may find it helpful to attach the stages to the following more or less true story. Legend has it that the king of Syracuse (a city in ancient Greece) once suspected that his goldsmith had substituted cheaper metals for some of the gold in a crown and had pocketed the difference. Archimedes, a famous mathematician and thinker, was given the problem of discovering whether the king had been cheated.

Archimedes began by defining the problem *(orientation)*: "How can I determine what metals have been used in the crown without damaging it?" He then checked all known

---

Convergent thought *Thinking directed toward discovery of a single established correct answer; conventional thinking.*
Divergent thought *Thinking that produces many ideas or alternatives; a major element in original or creative thought.*
Daydream *A vivid waking fantasy.*
Conquering hero daydream *Fantasy in which the daydreamer is a hero.*
Suffering martyr daydream *Fantasy in which the daydreamer is at first unappreciated, then revealed to be a wonderful person.*
Problem finding *The active discovery of problems to be solved.*
Unusual Uses Test *A test of creativity in which subjects try to think of new uses for a common object.*
Consequences Test *A test of creativity in which subjects try to list as many consequences as possible that would follow if some basic change were made in the world.*
Anagrams Test *A test of creativity in which subjects try to make as many new words as possible from the letters in a given word.*

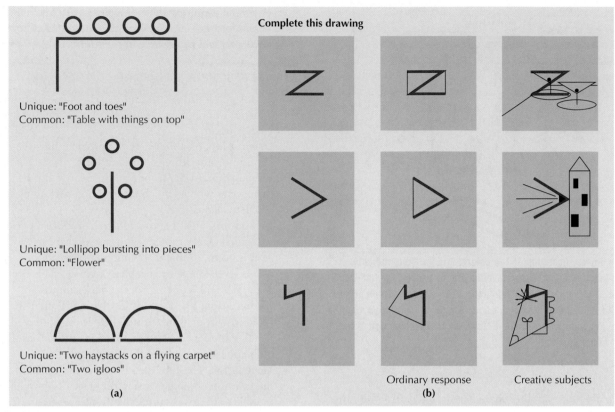

Complete this drawing

Unique: "Foot and toes"
Common: "Table with things on top"

Unique: "Lollipop bursting into pieces"
Common: "Flower"

Unique: "Two haystacks on a flying carpet"
Common: "Two igloos"

(a)

Ordinary response   Creative subjects

(b)

❖ **FIGURE 11.20** *Some tests of divergent thinking. Creative responses are more original and more complex. ([a] after Wallach & Kogan, 1965; [b] after Barron, 1958.)*

methods of analyzing metals *(preparation)*. All involved cutting or melting the crown, so he was forced to temporarily set the problem aside *(incubation)*. Then one day as he stepped into his bath, Archimedes suddenly knew he had the solution *(illumination)*. He was so excited he is said to have run naked through the streets shouting, "Eureka, eureka!" (I have found it, I have found it!).

On observing his own body floating in the bath, Archimedes realized that different metals of equal weight would displace different amounts of water. A pound of brass, for example, occupies more space than a pound of gold, which is denser. All that remained was to test the solution *(verification)*.

Archimedes placed an amount of gold (equal in weight to that given the goldsmith) in a tub of water. He marked the water level and removed the gold. He then placed the crown in the water. Was the crown pure gold? If it was, it would raise the water to exactly the same level. Unfortunately, the purity of the crown and the fate of the goldsmith are to this day unknown!

The preceding account is a good general description of creative thinking. However, creative thinking can be highly complex. Rather than springing from sudden insights, much creative problem solving is **incremental** (Weisenberg, 1986). That is, it is the end result of many small steps. This is certainly true of many inventions, which build on earlier ideas.

Some authors believe that truly exceptional creativity requires a rare combination of thinking skills, personality, and a supportive social environment. This mix, they believe, accounts for creative giants such as Edison, Freud, Mozart, Picasso, and Tolstoy (Tardif & Sternberg, 1988).

The Creative Personality

What makes a person creative? According to the popular stereotype, highly creative people are eccentric, introverted, neurotic, socially inept, unbalanced in their interests, and on the edge of madness. Although some artists and musicians cultivate this public image, there is little truth in it. Direct studies of creative individuals paint a very different picture.

1. For people of normal intelligence, there is a small positive correlation between creativity and IQ. In other words, smarter people have a slight tendency to also be more creative. But, for the most part, at any given level of IQ, some people are creative and others are not. The average college graduate has an IQ of 120. This is more than high enough to allow a person to write novels, do scientific research, or pursue other creative work (Finke, 1990). IQs above 120 do not seem to add anything more to creative ability (Sternberg & Lubart, 1995).
2. Creative people usually have a greater than average range of knowledge and interests, and they are more fluent in combining ideas from various sources.
3. Creative people have an openness to experience. They accept irrational thoughts and are uninhibited about their feelings and fantasies (McCrae, 1987). They also tend to experience

The development of modern aircraft has been highly creative and quite rapid. Even so, it has been marked more by incremental progress than by dramatic breakthroughs.

◆ **TABLE 11.3** Characteristics of Creative Persons

GENERAL TRAITS
Originality
Verbal fluency
Relatively high intelligence
A good imagination

THINKING ABILITIES
Uses metaphors in thinking
Flexible decision maker
Uses broad categories
Makes independent judgments
Uses mental images
Can cope with novelty
Thinks logically
Can break mental sets
Finds order in chaos

THINKING STYLE
Challenges assumptions, asks, "Why?"
Looks for novelty and gaps in knowledge
Draws new ideas out of existing knowledge
Prefers nonverbal communication
Enjoys visualizing
Finds beauty in "good" problems and elegant solutions
Takes advantage of chance

PERSONALITY CHARACTERISTICS
Willing to take intellectual risks
Persistence in problem solving
Curiosity and inquisitiveness
Openness to new experiences
Absorption in tasks of interest
Disciplined and committed to work
High interest in work
Uncomfortable with rules and limits imposed by others
Seeks competence and challenges
Tolerates ambiguity
Broad range of interests
Playful with ideas
Values creativity and originality
Intuitive

Adapted from Tardif and Sternberg (1988).

more unusual states of consciousness, such as vivid dreams and mystical experiences (Ayers, Beaton, & Hunt, 1999).

4. Creative people enjoy symbolic thought, ideas, concepts, and possibilities. They tend to be interested in truth, form, and beauty, rather than in recognition or success. Their creative work is an end in itself (Sternberg & Lubart, 1995).

5. Highly creative people value independence and have a preference for complexity (Dacey, 1989). However, they are unconventional and nonconforming primarily in their work; otherwise, they do not have particularly unusual, outlandish, or bizarre personalities.

It is widely accepted that people are often creative only in particular areas of skill or knowledge. For example, a person who is a creative writer might be an uncreative artist or businessperson. Perhaps this is because creativity favors a prepared mind.

Those who are creative in a particular field often are building on a large store of existing knowledge (Feldhusen, 1995; Sternberg & Lubart, 1995). Yoshiro Nakamats, a Japanese inventor who holds more than 2,000 patents, sees such preparation as a way to gain the freedom to think creatively.

As our discussion has already implied, creative people share a number of general traits, regardless of the field in which they work. ◆Table 11.3 summarizes these characteristics. Of course, a specific creative person may possess many, but not all, of these characteristics.

Incremental problem solving *Thinking marked by a series of small steps that lead to an original solution.*

Can creativity be learned? It is beginning to look as if some creative thinking skills can be taught. In particular, creativity can be increased by practice in divergent thinking (Baer, 1993). Later, in the Psychology in Action section, you will find a discussion of some helpful strategies.

At the same time that irrational, intuitive thought may contribute to creative problem solving, it can also lead to thinking errors. The next section tells how this can happen.

LOGIC AND INTUITION—MENTAL SHORTCUT? OR DANGEROUS DETOUR?

Many thinking errors begin with flawed reasoning. Simple sequences of logic can be arranged as a set of *premises* (assumptions) and a *conclusion.* This format is called a **syllogism.** A syllogism can be evaluated for the *validity* of its reasoning and for the *truth* of its *conclusion.* It is entirely possible to draw true conclusions by using faulty logic or to draw false conclusions by using valid logic. The following examples show how this is possible.

Syllogism 1
All humans are mortal. (Major premise)
All women are humans. (Minor premise)
Therefore, all women are mortal. (Conclusion)

As you can see from ❖Figure 11.21, the logic in this example is valid. Because our premises are true, the conclusion is true. The diagram shows all women included within the boundaries of mortals.

Syllogism 2
All women are humans.
All humans are mortal.
Therefore, all mortals are women.

In this example, the conclusion is false because the reasoning is invalid. The diagram for Syllogism 1 shows that all mortals are not women. Notice how little the information has to be changed to produce a false conclusion. Now consider these statements:

Syllogism 3
All psychologists are weird.
Mary is a psychologist.
Therefore, Mary is weird.

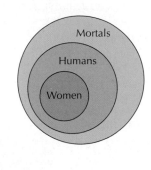

❖ **FIGURE 11.21.**

BRIDGES

Humanistic psychologist Abraham Maslow believed that we must live honestly and creatively to make full use of our potentials.

See Chapter 15, pages 499–500, for a discussion of self-actualization.

In this case, the reasoning is valid, but the conclusion is false because the first premise is false. All psychologists are *not* weird. (Honest!) Now let's analyze one more example.

Syllogism 4
All ducks have wings.
All birds have wings.
Therefore, all ducks are birds.

This sequence shows the importance of paying close attention to logic. The reasoning appears to be valid because the conclusion is true. However, substitute *bats* or *airplanes* for *ducks* and see how the conclusion reads. It is a good idea to get in the habit of questioning the logic used by politicians, advertisers, and, for that matter, psychologists, too.

Intuition

If you are formally trained in logic, you may actually think in logical sequences like the preceding examples. However, in daily life most people take a more intuitive approach to reasoning. For instance, we tend to abandon logical reasoning if a conclusion contradicts our personal beliefs (Markovits & Nantel, 1989). The following problems capture the flavor of much of the reasoning we do.

- *Problem 1.* An epidemic breaks out and 600 people are about to die. Doctors have two choices. If they give drug A, 200 lives will be saved. If they give drug B, there is a one-third chance that 600 people will be saved, and a two-thirds chance that none will be saved. Which drug should they choose?

- *Problem 2.* Again, 600 people are about to die, and doctors must make a choice. If they give drug A, 400 people will die. If they give drug B, there is a one-third chance that no one will die, and a two-thirds chance that 600 will die. Which drug should they choose?

Most people choose drug A for the first problem and drug B for the second. This is fascinating because the two problems are identical. The only difference is that the first is stated in terms of lives saved, the second in terms of lives lost. Yet, even people who realize that their answers are contradictory find it difficult to change them (Kahneman & Tversky, 1972, 1973).

As the example shows, we often make decisions intuitively, rather than logically. **Intuition** is quick, impulsive thought that does not make use of formal reasoning. It may provide fast answers, but it can also be misleading and sometimes disastrous. Two noted psychologists, Daniel Kahneman (KON-eh-man) and Amos Tversky (tuh-VER-ski) (1937–1996), have studied how people make decisions in the face of uncertainty. They have found, to put it bluntly, that human judgment is often seriously flawed (Kahneman et al., 1982). Understanding the thinking errors they have identified may help you to avoid them. Let's explore some common errors.

REPRESENTATIVENESS   One very common pitfall in judgment is illustrated by the following question:
   Which is more probable?
   - A. Steffi Graf will lose the first set of a tennis match but win the match.
   - B. Steffi Graf will lose the first set.

WHICH PARENT?

A couple are divorcing. Both parents seek custody of their only child, but custody can be granted to just one parent. If you had to make a decision based on the following information, to which parent would you award custody of the child?

- **Parent A:** average income, average health, average working hours, reasonable rapport with the child, relatively stable social life.
- **Parent B:** above-average income, minor health problems, lots of work-related travel, very close relationship with the child, extremely active social life.

Most people choose to award custody to Parent B, the parent who has some drawbacks but also several advantages (such as above-average income). That's because people tend to look for *positive qualities* that can be *awarded* to the child. However, how would you choose if you were asked this question: Which parent should be denied custody? In this case, most people choose to deny custody to Parent B. Why is Parent B a good choice one moment and a poor choice the next? It's because the second question asked who should be *denied* custody. To answer this question, people tend to look for *negative qualities* that would *disqualify* a parent.

As you can see, the way a question is framed can channel people down a narrow path where they attend to only part of the information provided, rather than weighing all the pros and cons (Shafir, 1993). If you would like to think more critically and analytically, it is important to pay attention to how you are defining problems before you try to solve them.

Tversky and Kahneman (1982) found that most people regard statements like A as more probable than B. However, this intuitive answer overlooks an important fact: The likelihood of two events occurring together is lower than the probability of either occurring alone. (For example, the probability of getting one head when flipping a coin is one half, or .5. The probability of getting two heads when flipping two coins is one fourth, or .25.) Therefore, A is less likely to be true than B.

Tversky and Kahneman believe that such faulty conclusions are based on an intuitive error called the **representativeness heuristic.** That is, a choice is given greater weight if it seems to be representative of what we already know. Thus, the information about Steffi Graf is compared to a mental model of what a tennis pro's behavior should be like. The first choice seems to better represent this model and therefore seems more likely, even though it isn't.

UNDERLYING ODDS   A second common error in judgment involves ignoring the **base rate,** or underlying probability of an event. People in one experiment were told that they would be given descriptions of 100 people—70 lawyers and 30 engineers. Subjects were then asked to guess, without knowing anything about a person, whether she or he was an engineer or a lawyer. All correctly stated the probabilities as 70 percent for lawyer and 30 percent for engineer. Participants were then given this description:

Dick is a 30-year-old man. He is married with no children. A man of high ability and high motivation, he promises to be quite successful in his field. He is well liked by his colleagues.

Notice that the description gives no new information about Dick's occupation. He could still be either an engineer or a lawyer. Therefore, the odds should again be estimated as 70–30. However, most people changed the odds to 50–50. Intuitively, it seems that Dick has an equal chance of being either an engineer or a lawyer. But this guess completely ignores the underlying odds.

Perhaps it is fortunate that we do at times ignore underlying odds. Were this not the case, how many people would get married in the face of a 50 percent divorce rate? Or how many would start high-risk businesses? On the other hand, people who smoke, drink and then drive, or skip wearing auto seat belts ignore rather high odds of injury or illness. In many high-risk situations, ignoring base rates is the same as thinking you are an exception to the rule.

FRAMING   Perhaps the most general conclusion from Kahneman and Tversky's work is that the way a problem is stated, or **framed,** affects decisions (Tversky & Kahneman, 1981). As the first example in this discussion revealed, people often give different answers to the same problem stated in slightly different ways. Before we continue, read "Which Parent?" to gain some added insight into framing.

Usually, the *broadest* way of framing or stating a problem produces the best decisions. However, people often state problems in increasingly narrow terms until a single, seemingly "obvious" answer emerges. For example, to select a career, it would be wise to consider pay, working conditions, job satisfaction, needed skills, future employment outlook, and many other factors. Instead, such decisions are often narrowed to thoughts such as "I like to write, so I'll be a journalist," "I want to make good money and law pays well," or "I can be creative in photography." Framing decisions so narrowly greatly increases the risk of making a poor choice.

A LOOK AHEAD   We have discussed only some of the intuitive errors made in the face of uncertainty. The study of intuitive reasoning and decision making is being applied to medical diagnosis, business decisions, military strategy, investing and finance, international relations, and more. In each area, people are learning to think twice before they decide. With practice, you, too, can learn to spot errors like those described. Remember that shortcuts to answers often short-circuit clear thinking.

Syllogism *A format for analyzing logical arguments.*
Intuition *Quick, impulsive thought that does not make use of formal logic or clear reasoning.*
Representativeness heuristic *A tendency to select wrong answers because they seem to match preexisting mental categories.*
Base rate *The basic rate at which an event occurs over time; the basic probability of an event.*
Framing *In thought, the terms in which a problem is stated or the way that it is structured.*

In the upcoming "Psychology in Action" section we will return to the topic of creative thinking for a look at ways to promote creativity. After that, we will delve briefly into the fascinating topic of animal intelligence.

psychology in action

ENHANCING CREATIVITY—BRAINSTORMS

Thomas Edison once explained his creativity by saying, "Genius is 1 percent inspiration and 99 percent perspiration." Many studies of creativity show that "genius" and "eminence" owe as much to persistence and dedication as they do to inspiration (Ericsson & Charness, 1994).

Once it is recognized that creativity can be hard work, then something can be done to enhance it. Here are some suggestions on how to begin.

BREAK MENTAL SETS AND CHALLENGE ASSUMPTIONS. A **mental set** is the tendency to perceive a problem in a way that blinds us to possible solutions. Mental sets are a major barrier to creative thinking. Usually, they lead us to see a problem in preconceived terms that impede our problem-solving attempts. (Fixations and functional fixedness, which were described earlier, are specific types of mental sets.)

Try the problems pictured in ❖Figure 11.22. If you have difficulty, try asking yourself what assumptions you are making. The problems are designed to demonstrate the limiting effects of a mental set. (The answers to these problems, along with an explanation of the sets that prevent their solution, are found in ❖Fig. 11.23.)

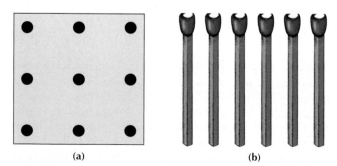

(a)   (b)

❖ **FIGURE 11.22** (a) *Nine dots are arranged in a square. Can you connect them by drawing four continuous straight lines without lifting your pencil from the paper?* (b) *Six matches must be arranged to make four triangles. The triangles must be the same size, with each side equal to the length of one match. (The solutions to these problems appear in* ❖*Figure 11.23.)*

Sometimes, problems themselves produce a disruptive set. For example, see if you can unscramble each group of letters on the following list to make words that use all of the letters:

MEST _____

LFAE _____

DUB _____

STKAL _____

OTOR _____

LTEPA _____

Now try a new list:

FINEK _____

OPONS _____

KROF _____

PUC _____

SDIH _____

LTEPA _____

Did you notice that the last problem was the same in each case? Many people don't and end up solving the problem twice. To complete the first list *(stem, leaf, bud, stalk, root),* the item LTEPA is usually unscrambled as *petal.* In the second list *(knife, spoon, fork, cup, dish),* LTEPA becomes *plate* for many people.

Now that you have been forewarned about the danger of faulty assumptions, see if you can correctly answer the following questions.

1. A farmer had 19 sheep. All but 9 died. How many sheep did the farmer have left?

2. It is not unlawful for a man living in Winston-Salem, North Carolina, to be buried west of the Mississippi River. T or F?

3. Some months have 30 days, some have 31. How many months have 28 days?

4. I have two coins that together total 30 cents. One of the coins is not a nickel. What are the two coins?

5. If there are 12 one-cent candies in a dozen, how many two-cent candies are there in a dozen?

These questions are designed to cause thinking errors. Here are the answers:

1. Nineteen—9 alive and 10 dead. 2. F. It is against the law to bury a living person anywhere. 3. All of them. 4. A quarter and a nickel. One of the coins is not a nickel, but the other one is! 5. 12.

If you got caught on any of the questions, consider it an additional reminder of the value of actively challenging the assumptions you are making in any instance of problem solving.

DEFINE PROBLEMS BROADLY. An effective way to break mental sets is to enlarge the definition of a problem. For instance, assume your problem is: Design a better doorway. This is likely to lead to ordinary solutions. Why not change the problem to: Design a better way to get through a wall? Now your solutions will be more original. Best of all might be to state the problem as: Find a better way to define separate areas for living and working. This could lead to truly creative solutions (Adams, 1988).

Let's say you are leading a group that's designing a new can opener. Wisely, you ask the group to think about *opening* in general, rather than about can openers. This was just the approach that led to the pop-top can. As the design group discussed the concept of opening, one member suggested that nature has its own openers, like the soft seam on a pea pod. Instead of a new can-opening tool, the group invented the self-opening can (Stein, 1974).

RESTATE THE PROBLEM IN DIFFERENT WAYS. Stating problems in novel ways also tends to produce more creative solutions. See if you can cross out six letters to make a single word out of the following:

CSRIEXLEATTTERES

If you're having difficulty, it may be that you need to restate the problem. Were you trying to cross out six letters? The real solution is to cross out the letters in the words *six letters,* which yields the word *create.*

One way to restate a problem is to imagine how another person would view it. What would a child, engineer, professor, mechanic, artist, psychologist, judge, or minister ask about the problem? Also, don't be afraid to ask silly or playful questions. Here are some examples:

- If the problem were alive, what would it look like?
- If the problem were edible, how would it taste?
- How would the problem look from an airplane? How does it look from underneath?
- Is any part of the problem pretty? Ugly? Stupid? Friendly?
- If the problem could speak, what would it say?

At the very least, you should almost always ask the following questions:

- What information do I have?
- What don't I know?
- What can I extract from the known information?
- Have I used all of the information?
- What additional information do I need?

Mental set *A predisposition to perceive or respond in a particular way.*

- What are the parts of the problem?
- How are the parts related?
- How *could* the parts be related?
- Is this in any way like a problem I've solved before?

Remember, to think more creatively, you must find ways to jog yourself out of mental sets and habitual modes of thought (Michalko, 1998).

CREATE THE RIGHT ATMOSPHERE.   Various experiments show that people make more original, spontaneous, and imaginative responses when exposed to others (role models) doing the same. If you want to become more creative, spend more time around creative people. This is the premise underlying much education in art, theater, dance, and music (Sternberg & Lubart, 1995).

ALLOW TIME FOR INCUBATION.   Trying to hurry or to force a solution may simply encourage fixation on a dead end. Creativity takes time. You need to be able to revise or embellish initial solutions, even those based on rapid insight (Tardif & Sternberg, 1988). Incubation is especially fruitful when you are exposed to external cues that relate to the problem (remember Archimedes's bath?). For example, Johannes Gutenberg, creator of the printing press, realized while at a wine harvest that the mechanical pressure used to crush grapes could also be used to imprint letters on paper (Dorfman, Shames, & Kihlstrom, 1996).

SEEK VARIED INPUT.   Remember, creativity requires divergent thinking. Rather than digging deeper with logic, you are attempting to shift your mental "prospecting" to new areas. As an example of this strategy, Edward de Bono (1970, 1992) recommends that you randomly look up words in the dictionary and relate them to the problem. Often the words will trigger a fresh perspective or open a new avenue. For instance, let's say you are asked to come up with new ways to clean oil off a beach. Following de Bono's suggestion, you would read the following randomly selected words, relate each to the problem, and see what thoughts are triggered: *weed, rust, poor, magnify, foam, gold, frame, hole, diagonal, vacuum, tribe, puppet, nose, link, drift, portrait, cheese, coal.* You may get similar benefits from relating various objects to a problem. Or take a walk, skim through a newspaper, or look through a stack of photographs to see what thoughts they trigger (Michalko, 1998).

LOOK FOR ANALOGIES.   Many "new" problems are really old problems in new clothing (Siegler, 1989). Representing a problem in a variety of ways is often the key to the solution. Most problems become easier to solve when they are effectively represented. For example, consider this problem:

Two backpackers start up a steep trail at 6 A.M. They hike all day, resting occasionally, and arrive at the top at 6 P.M. The next day they start back down the trail at 6 A.M. On the way down, they stop several times and vary their pace. They arrive back at 6 P.M. On the way down, one of the hikers, who is a mathematician, tells the other that she has realized that they will pass a point on the trail at exactly the same time as they did the day before. Her non-mathematical friend finds this hard to believe, because on both days they have stopped and started many times and changed their pace. The problem: Is the mathematician right?

Perhaps you will see the answer to this problem immediately. If not, think of it this way: What if there were two pairs of backpackers, one going up the trail, the second coming down, and both hiking on the *same day*? It becomes obvious that the two pairs of hikers will pass each other at some point on the trail. Therefore, they will be at the same place at the same time. The mathematician was right.

TAKE SENSIBLE RISKS.   A willingness to go against the crowd is a key element in doing creative work. Unusual and original ideas may be rejected at first by conventional thinkers. Often, creative individuals must persevere and take some risks before their ideas are widely accepted. For example, Post-it notes were invented by an engineer who accidentally created a weak adhesive. Rather than throw the mixture out, the engineer put it to a highly creative new use. However, it took him some time to convince others that a "bad" adhesive could be a useful product. Today, stick-on note papers are one of the 3M Company's most successful products (Sternberg & Lubart, 1995).

DELAY EVALUATION.   Various studies suggest that people are most likely to be creative when they are given the freedom to play with ideas and solutions without having to worry about whether they will be evaluated. In the first stages of creative thinking, it is important to avoid criticizing your efforts. Worrying about the correctness of solutions tends to inhibit creativity (Amabile, 1983). This idea is expanded in the discussion that follows.

An alternative approach to enhancing creativity is called *brainstorming*. Although brainstorming is a group technique, it can be applied to individual problem solving as well.

Brainstorming

The essence of **brainstorming** is that producing and evaluating ideas are kept separate. In group problem solving, each person is encouraged to produce as many ideas as possible without fear of criticism (Buyer, 1988). This encourages divergent thinking.

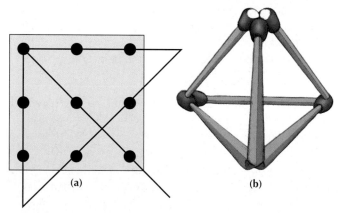

(a)   (b)

❖ **FIGURE 11.23** *Problem solutions. (a) The dot problem can be solved by extending the lines beyond the square formed by the dots. Most people assume incorrectly that they may not do this. (b) The match problem can be solved by building a three-dimensional pyramid. Most people assume that the matches must be arranged on a flat surface. If you remembered the four-tree problem from earlier in the chapter, the match problem may have been easy to solve.*

Some of the most successful brainstorming takes place on computer networks, where each person's fears of being evaluated are minimized (Siau, 1996).

Only at the end of a brainstorming session are ideas reconsidered and evaluated. As ideas are freely generated, an interesting **cross-stimulation effect** takes place, in which one participant's ideas trigger ideas from others (Brown et al., 1998).

The basic rules for successful brainstorming are:

1. Criticism of ideas is absolutely barred. Defer evaluation until later in the session.
2. Modification or combination with other ideas is encouraged. Don't worry about giving credit for ideas or keeping them neat. Mix them up!
3. Quantity of ideas is sought. In the early stages of brainstorming, quantity is more important than quality. Try to generate lots of ideas.
4. Unusual, remote, or wild ideas are sought. Let your imagination run amok!
5. Record ideas as they occur.
6. Elaborate or improve on the most promising ideas (Michalko, 1998).

It is important to be persistent when you are brainstorming. Most groups give up too soon, usually when the flow of new ideas begins to slow (Nijstad, Stroebe, & Lodewijkx, 1999).

How is brainstorming applied to individual problem solving? The essential point to remember is to *suspend judgment.* Ideas should first be produced without regard for logic, organization, accuracy, practicality, or any other evaluation. In writing an essay, for instance, you would begin by writing ideas in any order, the more the better, just as they occur to you. Later, you would go back and reorganize, rewrite, and criticize your efforts.

As an aid to following rules 2, 3, and 4 of the brainstorming method, you might find this checklist helpful for encouraging original thought. It can be used to see if you have overlooked a possible solution.

Creativity Checklist

1. **Redefine.** Consider other uses for all elements of the problem. (This is designed to alert you to fixations that may be blocking creativity.)
2. **Adapt.** How could other objects, ideas, procedures, or solutions be adapted to this particular problem?
3. **Modify.** Imagine changing anything and everything that could be changed.
4. **Magnify.** Exaggerate everything you can think of. Think on a grand scale.
5. **Minify.** What if everything were scaled down? What if all differences were reduced to zero? "Shrink" the problem down to size.
6. **Substitute.** How could one object, idea, or procedure be substituted for another?
7. **Rearrange.** Break the problem into pieces and shuffle them.
8. **Reverse.** Consider reverse orders and opposites, and turn things inside out.
9. **Combine.** This one speaks for itself.

By making a habit of subjecting a problem to each of these procedures, you should be able to greatly reduce the chances that you will overlook a useful, original, or creative solution.

Living More Creatively

Creativity need not be restricted to formal problems. Daily events present many opportunities for living more creatively. Psychologist Mihalyi Csikszentmihalyi (1996) offers the following recommendations for becoming more creative:

- Find something that surprises you every day.
- Try to surprise at least one person every day.
- If something sparks your interest, follow it.
- Make a commitment to doing things well.
- Seek challenges.
- Make time for thinking and relaxing.
- Start doing more of what you really enjoy, less of what you dislike.
- Try to look at problems from as many viewpoints as you can.

Life is not a standardized test with a single set of correct answers. It is much more like a blank canvas on which you can create designs that uniquely express your talents and interests. To live more creatively, you must be willing to keep trying new ways of doing things.

KNOWLEDGE BUILDER
ENHANCING CREATIVITY

RELATE

Review the preceding pages and note which methods you could use more often to improve the quality of your thinking. Now mentally summarize the points you especially want to remember.

LEARNING CHECK

1. Fixations and functional fixedness are specific types of mental sets. T or F?

2. The incubation period in creative problem solving usually lasts just a matter of minutes. T or F?

3. Exposure to creative models has been shown to enhance creativity. T or F?

4. In brainstorming, each idea is critically evaluated as it is generated. T or F?

5. Defining a problem broadly produces a cross-stimulation effect that can inhibit creative thinking. T or F?

CRITICAL THINKING

6. What mode of thinking does the "Creativity Checklist" (redefine, adapt, modify, magnify, and so forth) encourage?

Answers:

1. T 2. F 3. T 4. F 5. F 6. Divergent thinking.

Brainstorming *Method of creative thinking that separates the production and evaluation of ideas.*

Cross-stimulation effect *In group problem solving, the tendency of one person's ideas to trigger ideas from others.*

Focus: Do animals think?

Most pet owners can supply stories of apparent thinking in animals. A friend might say, "Wow, you should have seen Studebaker figure out how to get into the closet where I hid the dog food." Are animals actually thinking in such situations? In a rudimentary sense, they are.

Animals demonstrate an ability to mentally represent situations in **delayed response problems.** These are tasks in which an animal must remember the solution to a problem before responding. For example, a hungry animal could be allowed to watch as food is hidden under one of three goal boxes. After a delay, the animal is released. Can it select the correct box? If the delay is brief, the answer is yes. In fact, some animals can remember the locations of objects for several days or more (Lea & Kiley-Worthington, 1996).

At times, animal behavior implies even higher levels of thought, such as being able to plan ahead (Zentall, 1999). In one recent study, a chimpanzee watched as various objects were hidden outside her cage. Later, when a human approached the chimp, she would gain the person's attention and then touch a lexigram corresponding to the type of object that was hidden. When allowed to leave her enclosure, the chimp pointed toward the object and vocalized until the person found the object (Menzel, 1999).

German psychologist Wolfgang Köhler (VOOLF-gong KEAR-ler) believed that animals such as chimpanzees are actually capable of insight. To test for insight, Köhler challenged Sultan, his brightest chimp, with a **multiple-stick problem.** In this problem, several sticks of increasing length were arranged between the cage and a desired object (a banana in this case) (❖Fig. 11.24). To reach the banana, Sultan had to use the first stick to retrieve the second stick (which was longer than the first). The second stick could then be used to get an even longer stick, which could then be used to reach the banana (Köhler, 1925).

When confronted with this problem, Sultan looked at the banana, then at the sticks . . . then at the banana. Picking up the first stick, Sultan smoothly and without further hesitation solved the problem and raked in the banana.

Psychologists have long debated whether Köhler's chimps actually displayed insight. However, in recent years, evidence for animal intelligence and thinking ability has continued to grow. For example, a recent study suggests that three kinds of apes (chimpanzees, bonobos, and orangutans) can use tools intelligently. Each of the apes was shown a food treat in the middle of a long, narrow, transparent plastic tube. Each was also given a tool that could be used to poke the food out of the tube. The tool was either a straight wooden stick, a bundle of three sticks held tightly together by a rubber band, or a stick

with two shorter sticks stuck through holes drilled in each end (❖Fig. 11.25).

The apes could use the straight stick to directly retrieve the food. The bundle of sticks was too wide to fit in the tube unless the rubber band was removed. The **H**-shaped stick was also too

❖ **FIGURE 11.24** *Psychologist Wolfgang Köhler believed that the solution of a multiple-stick problem revealed a capacity for insight in chimpanzees.*

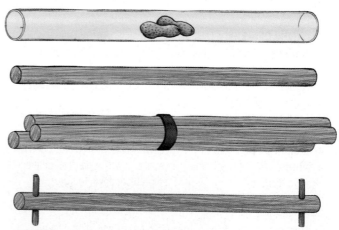

❖ **FIGURE 11.25** *Researchers recently showed that chimpanzees, bonobos, and orangutans can solve problems that appear to require both thinking and comprehension. A transparent plastic tube was baited with a food treat (such as peanuts), and the apes were given one of three tools to use: a straight stick, a bundle of sticks, or a stick with cross-bars. Successful use of the latter two tools required greater comprehension of the problem (Visalberghi, Fragaszy, & Savage-Rumbaugh, 1995).*

wide unless the two short sticks were removed from its ends. The apes were able to successfully use tools in all three of these conditions. They also made fewer errors with practice, suggesting that they had a rudimentary understanding of the problem (Visalberghi, Fragaszy, & Savage-Rumbaugh, 1995).

How Intelligent Are Animals?

Evidence for the idea that animals are capable of intelligent thought is varied and, to many researchers, convincing (Lea & Kiley-Worthington, 1996):

- Monkeys can learn to select, from among three objects, the one that differs from the other two.
- When a container of sugar water is moved a set distance farther from a beehive each day, the bees begin to go to the new location *before* the water is moved.
- Pigeons can learn to select photographs of humans from a group of photos that includes various objects.
- A chimp named Lana has learned to remove one, two, or three objects from a computer screen, after first being shown the numbers 1, 2, or 3.

Do such examples really demonstrate thinking by animals? Some psychologists say yes; some say no. What would it take, then, to verify animal thinking? Psychologist Donald Griffin suggests that we must observe behavior that is *versatile* and *appropriate* to changing circumstances. He also believes that thinking is implied by actions that appear to be planned with an awareness of likely results (Griffin, 1992). As one example, sea otters select suitably sized rocks and use them to hammer shellfish loose for eating. They then use the rock to open the shell.

As convincing as such examples may seem, they have been challenged. For instance, B. F. Skinner conditioned pigeons to duplicate seemingly insightful behavior like that claimed for higher animals. Other psychologists, however, reply that the pigeons achieved only the *appearance* of thinking, because their behavior was strongly guided by reinforcement.

Does the seemingly intelligent behavior of sea otters and other animals reflect thinking ability, instinct, or conditioning? The evidence remains inconclusive, so psychologists disagree.

As stated before, it seems reasonable to assume that animals do think. However, debate is sure to continue about the limits of their intelligence and about whether specific examples demonstrate thinking, instinct, or conditioning.

COUNTING ON SHEBA   Psychologist Sarah Boysen has added to the debate about animal cognition in a fascinating experiment. Boysen and her colleagues taught a chimp named Sheba to count and to recognize numbers from 0 to 8 (Boysen et al., 1995). When Boysen decided to test Sheba's understanding of *more* and *less,* a striking thing happened. Boysen placed two plates of gumdrops in front of Sheba, one holding more gumdrops than the other. Sheba was allowed to select one of the plates. Naturally enough, Sheba selected the plate with more candy. When she did, that plate was given to another chimpanzee. Sheba became visibly agitated at this foul turn of events.

The gumdrop test was repeated many more times. Nonetheless, Sheba could not learn to choose the plate with less candy on it. At that point, Boysen decided to place numbers on the plates, rather than gumdrops. The number Sheba chose determined how many gumdrops the second chimp would receive (❖Fig.11.26). Almost immediately, Sheba learned to point to the smaller number. Clearly, she knew the rule: If she chose the larger number, the larger amount of candy was given away and she kept the smaller amount; if she pointed to the smaller number, she got to keep the larger amount of candy.

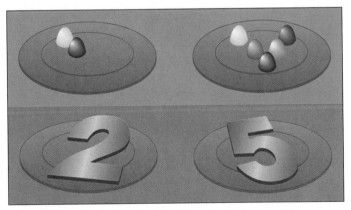

❖ **FIGURE 11.26** *Typical stimuli used in testing chimpanzees for comprehension of the concepts* less *and* more. *The chimps could not resist choosing the larger amount of candy, even when that choice meant they got the smaller amount of candy and another chimp got the larger amount. The use of numeric symbols freed the chimps to choose the smaller amount of food for the other chimp.*

Delayed response problem *A task in which an animal must remember the solution to a problem for a set amount of time before responding.*
Multiple-stick problem *A task in which progressively longer sticks are used to reach a desired object.*

Further testing revealed that knowing the rule and acting on it were two different things. Whenever gumdrops were used, Sheba could not choose the smaller number. When numerals were used, she could. Sheba's behavior suggests that chimpanzees can learn, at a very basic level, to think symbolically. (Symbolic thought uses language or symbols to represent the external world.)

Sheba's inability to choose correctly when faced with plates of candy is intriguing. Very likely, chimps living in the wild are genetically programmed to collect food as efficiently as possible. Only when they have learned to use symbols are chimps freed from the immediate and powerful allure of a plate of gumdrops. In addition to providing insight into the mind of a chimpanzee, Sheba's behavior emphasizes the tremendous advantage that we humans have as symbol-using animals.

Ultimately, we may be asking the wrong questions about animal intelligence. Animals are superbly adapted to the circumstances in which they typically live. If we judge their "intelligence" only in human terms, we may miss the exquisite beauty of their natural behavior.

(Sources: Boysen & Berntson, 1989; S. Budiansky, 1998; Epstein et al., 1981; Griffin, 1992; Herrnstein, 1979; Premack, 1983; Rose, 1984; Rumbaugh et al., 1989.)

CONCLUSION: Animals are capable of delayed responding, planning future actions, tool use, simple problem solving, and other actions that imply at least a basic level of thinking capacity.

KNOWLEDGE BUILDER
ANIMAL INTELLIGENCE

RELATE

What behaviors have you observed in animals that seem to imply that they are capable of thought? Could genetic programming, operant conditioning, or other non-cognitive factors explain what you saw the animal do? Where do you stand on the question of animal intelligence?

LEARNING CHECK

1. There is evidence that chimpanzees are capable of insightful solutions to problems, but some psychologists remain unconvinced that true insight is involved. T or F?

2. Rudimentary thinking abilities are revealed when animals successfully solve _____ _____ problems, which involve mentally representing an external situation.

3. Köhler's ape Sultan was apparently able to solve problems involving numbers and amounts. T or F?

4. Psychologist Donald Griffin suggests that animal cognition is revealed by behavior that is *versatile* and *appropriate* to changing circumstances. T or F?

5. In tests involving the concepts *more* and *less,* Sheba the chimpanzee was able to perform correctly only when the amounts were represented _____.

CRITICAL THINKING

6. Evidence that animals can think becomes more convincing as we ascend the biological scale from lower to higher animals. Why do you think this pattern occurs?

Answers:
1. T 2. delayed response 3. F 4. T 5. symbolically 6. As discussed in Chapter 9, the behavior of lower animals is more rigidly programmed by heredity. Also, as discussed in Chapter 3, the cerebrum is larger in higher animals. In humans, the cerebrum is the brain area most directly responsible for thought.

CHAPTER IN REVIEW

What is the nature of thought?

- Thinking is the manipulation of internal representations of external stimuli or situations.
- Three basic units of thought are images, concepts, and language or symbols.

In what ways are images related to thinking?

- Most people have internal images of one kind or another. Images may be stored or created. Sometimes they cross normal sense boundaries in a type of imagery called synesthesia.
- Images used in problem solving may be three-dimensional, they may be rotated in space, and their size may change.
- Kinesthetic images are created by produced, remembered, or imagined actions. Kinesthetic sensations and micromovements seem to help structure the flow of thought for many people.

How are concepts learned? Are there different kinds of concepts?

- A concept is a generalized idea of a class of objects or events.
- Concept formation may be based on positive and negative instances or, more commonly, on rule learning. In practice, concept identification frequently makes use of prototypes, or general models of the concept class.
- Concepts may be classified as conjunctive ("and" concepts), disjunctive ("either-or" concepts), or relational.
- The denotative meaning of a word or concept is its dictionary definition. Connotative meaning is personal or emotional. Connotative meaning can be measured with the semantic differential.
- Oversimplification and stereotyping contribute to thinking errors.

What is the role of language in thinking?

- Language allows events to be encoded into symbols for easy mental manipulation. Thinking in language is influenced by meaning. The study of meaning is called *semantics*.
- Language carries meaning by combining a set of symbols or signs according to a set of rules (grammar), which includes rules about word order (syntax). A true language is productive, and can be used to generate new ideas or possibilities.
- Complex gestural systems, such as American Sign Language, are true languages.

Can animals be taught to use language?

- Animal communication is relatively limited because it lacks symbols that can be rearranged easily.
- Attempts to teach chimpanzees systems such as American Sign Language suggest to some that primates are capable of language use. Others question this conclusion. Studies that make use of lexigrams provide the best evidence yet of animal language use.

What do we know about problem solving?

- The solution to a problem may be arrived at mechanically (by trial and error or by rote application of rules), but mechanical solutions are frequently inefficient or ineffective, except where aided by computer.

- Solutions by understanding usually begin with discovery of the general properties of an answer. Next comes proposal of a number of functional solutions.
- Problem solving is frequently aided by heuristics. These are strategies that typically narrow the search for solutions. The ideal strategy is a general heuristic.
- When understanding leads to a rapid solution, it is said that insight has occurred. Three elements of insight are selective encoding, selective combination, and selective comparison.
- Insight and other problem solving can be blocked by fixation. Functional fixedness is a common fixation, but emotional blocks, cultural values, learned conventions, and perceptual habits are also problems.

What is artificial intelligence?

- Artificial intelligence refers to any artificial system that can perform tasks that, when done by people, require intelligence.
- Two principal areas of artificial intelligence research are computer simulations and expert systems.
- Computer simulations of human problem solving are usually based on a means-ends analysis.
- Expert human problem solving is based on organized knowledge and acquired strategies, rather than on some general improvement in thinking ability.
- Artificial intelligence is helping scientists explore the nature of human thought, knowledge, and expertise.

What is the nature of creative thinking?

- To be creative, a solution must be practical and sensible as well as original. Creative thinking requires divergent thought, characterized by fluency, flexibility, and originality. Tests of creativity measure these qualities.
- Daydreaming and fantasy are a source of much divergent thinking.
- Five stages often seen in creative problem solving are orientation, preparation, incubation, illumination, and verification. Not all creative thinking fits this pattern. Much creative activity is based on incremental problem solving.
- Studies suggest that creative persons share a number of identifiable characteristics, most of which contradict popular stereotypes. There appears to be only a slight correlation between IQ and creativity.

How accurate is intuition?

- Intuitive thinking often leads to errors. Wrong conclusions may be drawn when an answer seems highly representative of what we already believe is true.
- A second problem is ignoring the base rate (or underlying probability) of an event.
- Clear thinking is usually aided by stating or framing a problem in broad terms.

What can be done to promote creativity?

- Various strategies that promote divergent thinking tend to enhance creative problem solving.
- In group situations, brainstorming may lead to creative solutions. The principles of brainstorming can also be applied to individual problem solving.

Do animals think?

- Animals reveal a rudimentary capacity for thought when they solve delayed-response problems and, in some cases, problems that appear to require understanding or insight.
- There is also evidence that higher animals, such as chimpanzees, can learn to use rudimentary symbolic thought. For the moment, however, some psychologists remain unconvinced about such abilities.

PSYCHOLOGY ON THE NET

- **Creativity Web** Multiple links to resources on creativity. http://www.ozemail.com.au/~caveman/Creative/
- **The Psychology of Invention** An exploration of how invention and discovery happen. http://hawaii.cogsci.uiuc.edu/invent/invention.html

- **The Question of Primate Language** This article from the National Zoo discusses primate communication and intelligence. http://www.fonz.org/Zoogoer/zg1995/primate_language.htm
  - **InfoTrac® College Edition** For recent articles on the controversies surrounding bilingual education, use Key Words search for BILINGUALISM.

INTERACTIVE LEARNING

- **PsychNow!** 5f. Cognition and language. 5g. Problem solving and creativity.
- **Psyk.trek** 6d. Problem solving.

Intelligence

Chapter Survey

Theme: *Measuring intelligence is worthwhile, but tests provide only limited definitions of intelligent behavior.*

▼ **KEY QUESTIONS**

● *KEY TOPICS*

▼ How do psychologists define intelligence?

- ● *A brief history of intelligence testing*
- ● *Intelligence versus aptitudes*

▼ What are the qualities of a good psychological test?

- ● *Reliability, validity, objectivity, and test standardization*

▼ What are typical IQ tests like?

- ● *Individual and group tests of intelligence*

▼ How do IQ scores relate to gender, age, and occupation?

- ● *The concept of IQ*
- ● *Variations in IQ*

▼ What does IQ tell us about genius?

- ● *The mentally gifted*

▼ **KEY QUESTIONS**

● *KEY TOPICS*

▼ What causes mental retardation?

- ● *Degrees of mental retardation*
- ● *Causes of mental retardation*

▼ How do heredity and environment affect intelligence?

- ● *Genetic and environmental influences*

▼ How have views of intelligence changed in recent years?

- ● *Speed of neural processing*
- ● *Cognitive views of intelligence*
- ● *Multiple intelligences*

▼ Are IQ tests fair to all racial and cultural groups?

- ● *IQ in perspective*
- ● *The Larry P. case*

WHAT DAY IS IT?

Ask George, "In which recent years did April 21 fall on a Sunday?" With little hesitation, he will answer, "1996, 1991, 1985, 1974, 1968, 1963, 1957, 1946." Surprisingly, this gives only a hint of his ability. If encouraged, George will go back as far as 1700—with complete accuracy! His calendar calculations cover at least 6,000 years: With equal ease, he can identify February 15, 2002, as a Friday or August 28, 1591, as a Wednesday.

Is he a genius? George's abilities are even more amazing because he is mentally retarded. George cannot add, subtract, multiply, or divide even simple numbers (Horwitz et al., 1965). His strange talent is an example of the savant syndrome, *in which an island of brilliance is found in a sea of retardation. In the savant syndrome, a person of limited intelligence shows exceptional mental ability in a narrow area, such as mental arithmetic, calendar calculations, art, or music ("Savant," 1995).*

How could George be retarded and have such amazing ability at the same time? Perpetual calendars have only 14 different yearly "templates." It appears that many calendar calculators memorize the 14 templates and learn how to tell which one applies to a particular year. This allows persons of below normal intelligence to perform an impressive mental feat (Young, 1994).

The striking contrast between George's general retardation and his unusual ability is a fitting introduction to the challenge of trying to define and measure intelligence. Quite frankly, we are still searching for answers to questions like these: Is intelligence a general trait or a collection of specific skills? Is intelligence affected by the genetic "wheel of fortune"? How much is it nurtured by environment? Is it possible to create an intelligence test that is fair to all people? How important is intelligence for "success"? Because our understanding of intelligence is rapidly changing, we cannot hope to give final answers to all these questions.

For the sake of clarity, let's first assume that intelligence can be measured. That way, we can use IQ scores to answer some important questions about intelligence. Later, we will consider questions that have been raised about intelligence tests and the meaning of their results.

Gateways to Intelligence

INTELLIGENCE TESTS provide a useful but narrow estimate of real-world intelligence.

EVERYONE HAS SPECIAL APTITUDES (talents and potentials). Those who possess a wide range of mental abilities are above average in intelligence.

MOST PEOPLE SCORE IN THE MID-RANGE ON INTELLIGENCE TESTS. Only a small percentage of people have exceptionally high and low IQ scores.

A HIGH IQ DOES NOT AUTOMATICALLY LEAD TO HIGH ACHIEVEMENT. A high IQ reveals potential, but it does not guarantee success.

THE MAJORITY OF PEOPLE WHO ARE MENTALLY RETARDED can master basic adaptive behaviors, and with support they can find a place in the community.

BOTH HEREDITY AND ENVIRONMENT INFLUENCE INTELLIGENCE, but only improved social conditions and education (environment) can raise intelligence.

REAL-WORLD INTELLIGENCE combines a fast nervous system with learned knowledge and skills and an acquired ability to manage one's own thinking and problem solving.

TRADITIONAL IQ TESTS measure linguistic, logical-mathematical, and spatial abilities. It is likely that we all use additional types of intelligence in daily life.

TRADITIONAL IQ TESTS are not universally valid for all cultural groups.

DEFINING INTELLIGENCE—INTELLIGENCE IS . . . YOU KNOW, IT'S . . .

Intelligence cannot be seen: It has no mass, occupies no space, and is invisible. Nevertheless, we feel certain it exists. Consider the following two children:

> When she was 14 months old, Anne H. wrote her own name. She taught herself to read at age 2. At age 5, she astounded her kindergarten teacher by bringing a notebook computer to class, on which she was learning Spanish. At 10, she breezed through an entire high school algebra course in 12 hours.

> At age 10, Billy A. can write his name and can count, but he has trouble with simple addition and subtraction problems and finds multiplication impossible. He has been held back in school twice and is still incapable of doing the work his 8-year-old classmates find easy.

Anne is considered a genius; Billy, a slow learner. There seems little doubt that they differ in intelligence.

Wait! Anne's ability is obvious, but how do we know that Billy isn't just lazy? This is the same question that Alfred Binet faced in 1904. The minister of education in Paris had asked Binet to find a way to distinguish slower students from the more capable (or the capable but lazy). In a flash of brilliance, Binet and an associate created a test made up of "intellectual"

Modern intelligence tests are widely used to measure cognitive abilities. When properly administered, such tests provide an operational definition of intelligence.

questions and problems. Next, they learned which questions an average child could answer at each age. By giving children the test, they could tell if a child was performing up to his or her potential (Kaufman, 2000).

Binet's approach gave rise to modern intelligence tests. At the same time, it launched nearly 100 years of often-heated debate. Part of the debate is related to the basic difficulty of defining intelligence.

Definitions of Intelligence

Is there an accepted definition of intelligence? Most psychologists would probably agree with intelligence test author David Wechsler, who defines **intelligence** as the global capacity to act purposefully, to think rationally, and to deal effectively with the environment. According to a survey of more than 1,000 experts, we should also add the following to any definition of intelligence: abstract thinking or reasoning, problem-solving ability, memory, capacity to acquire knowledge, and adaptation to one's environment (Snyderman & Rothman, 1987).

For the purpose of doing research, many psychologists simply accept an **operational definition** of intelligence. (We define a concept operationally by stating the procedures used to mea-

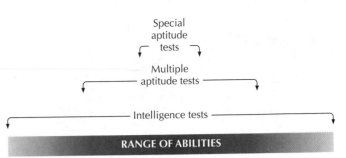

BRIDGES

Psychologists use a variety of aptitude tests to select people for employment and to advise people about choosing careers.

See Appendix A, page A-4.

RANGE OF ABILITIES

❖ **FIGURE 12.1** *Special aptitude tests measure a person's potential for achievement in a limited area of ability, such as manual dexterity. Multiple aptitude tests measure potentials in broader areas, such as college work, law, or medicine. Intelligence tests measure a very wide array of aptitudes and mental abilities.*

sure it.) When psychologists select test items, they are saying in a very direct way, "This is what I mean by intelligence." A test that measures memory, reasoning, and verbal fluency offers a very different definition of intelligence than one that measures strength of grip, shoe size, length of the nose, or a person's best Duke Nukem score.

APTITUDES   As a child, my friend Hedda displayed an aptitude for art. Today, Hedda is a successful graphic artist. How does an aptitude like Hedda's differ from general intelligence? An **aptitude** is a capacity for learning certain abilities. Persons with mechanical, artistic, or musical aptitudes are likely to do well in careers involving mechanics, art, or music, respectively (❖Fig. 12.1).

Are there tests for aptitudes? How are they different from intelligence tests? Aptitude tests measure a narrower range of abilities than intelligence tests do. For example, **special aptitude tests** predict whether you will succeed in a single area, such as clerical work or computer programming (❖Fig. 12.2). **Multiple aptitude tests** measure two or more types of ability. These tests tend to be more like intelligence tests. The well-known *Scholastic Assessment Test* (SAT), which measures aptitudes for language, math, and reasoning, is a multiple aptitude test. So are the tests required to enter graduate schools of law, medicine, business, and dentistry. The broadest aptitude measures are **general intelligence tests,** which assess a wide variety of mental abilities (Anastasi & Urbina, 1996).

Intelligence *An overall capacity to think rationally, act purposefully, and deal effectively with the environment.*
Operational definition *The operations (actions or procedures) used to measure a concept.*
Aptitude *A capacity for learning certain abilities.*
Special aptitude test *Test to predict a person's likelihood of succeeding in a particular area of work or skill.*
Multiple aptitude test *Test that measures two or more aptitudes.*
General intelligence test *Test that measures a wide variety of mental abilities.*

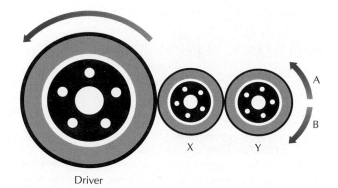

1. If the driver turns in the direction shown, which direction will wheel Y turn?   A   B

2. Which wheel will turn the slowest?   Driver   X   Y

❖ **FIGURE 12.2** *Sample questions like those found on tests of mechanical aptitude. (The answers are A and the Driver.)*

Reliability and Validity

Suppose that a deranged psychologist, Professor Ike Q. Tester, decides to write an intelligence test (the *I. Q. Tester IQ Test*). As a concerned citizen, there are two questions you should ask about Tester's test: "Is it *reliable?*" and "Is it *valid?*"

What does reliability refer to?   If you weigh yourself several times in a row, a reliable bathroom scale gives the same weight each time. Likewise, a **reliable** test must give approximately the same score each time a person takes it. In other words, the scores should be *consistent* and highly correlated. It is easy to see why unreliable tests have little value. Imagine a medical test for pregnancy or breast cancer, for instance, that gives positive and negative responses for the same woman on the same day.

To check the reliability of the *I. Q. Tester IQ Test,* we could give it to a large group of people. Then each person could be tested again a week later to establish *test-retest reliability.* We also might want to know if scores on one half of the test items match scores on the other half *(split-half reliability).* If Professor Tester decides to offer two versions of his test, we could compare scores on one version to scores on the other *(equivalent-forms reliability).*

By comparing such scores, we find that the Tester Test is quite reliable. In fact, the scores are identical each time the test is given: Everyone scores zero (except Professor Tester, who scores 100 percent and thereby proclaims himself the only human with any intelligence).

Let's concede to Tester that his test is reliable (but for the wrong reasons). A more important question then becomes: Is the test valid? Now Tester becomes testy. He knows his test is invalid and that it will have to be withdrawn.

Obviously, we have been playing with a silly example. A test has **validity** when it measures what it claims to measure. By no stretch of imagination could a test of intelligence be valid if the person who wrote it is the only one who can pass it.

How is validity established?   Validity is usually demonstrated by comparing test scores to actual performance. This is called *criterion validity.* Scores on a test of legal aptitude, for example, might be compared to grades in law school. If high scores correlate with high grades or some other standard (criterion) of success, the test might be valid. Unfortunately, many "free" tests you will encounter, such as those found in magazines and on the Internet, have little or no validity.

TESTER'S LAST STAND   Let's return to Professor Tester for a final point. Although he admits that his test has problems, Professor Tester claims that at least it is *objective.* Is he right? Actually, he might be. If the *I. Q. Tester IQ Test* gives the same score when corrected by different people, it is an **objective test.** However, objectivity is not enough to guarantee a fair test. Useful tests must also be *standardized.*

Test standardization refers to two things. First, it means that standard procedures are used in giving the test. The instructions, answer forms, amount of time to work, and so forth are the same for everyone. Second, it means finding the **norm,** or average score, made by a large group of people like those for whom the test was designed. Without standardization, we couldn't fairly compare the scores of people taking the test at different times. And without norms, there would be no way to tell if a score is high, low, or average.

Later in this chapter, we will address the question of whether intelligence tests are valid. For now, let's take a practical approach and learn about some popular standardized tests.

TESTING INTELLIGENCE—THE IQ AND YOU

American psychologists quickly saw the value of Alfred Binet's test. In 1916, **Lewis Terman** and others at Stanford University revised it for use in North America. After more revisions, the **Stanford-Binet Intelligence Scale, Fourth Edition,** continues to be widely used. The original Stanford-Binet assumed that a child's intellectual abilities improve with each passing year. Today, the Stanford-Binet (or Binet-4) is still primarily made up of age-ranked questions. Naturally, these questions get a little harder at each age level. ◆Table 12.1 lists the subtests of the Binet-4.

Intelligence Quotients

Imagine that a child named Yuan can answer questions that an average 7-year-old can answer. How smart is she? Actually, we can't say yet, because we don't know how old Yuan is. If she is 10, she's not very smart. If she's 5, she is very bright. Thus, to estimate a child's intelligence, we need to know both her **chronological age** (age in years) and her **mental age** (average intellectual performance).

A person's mental age is based on the level of age-ranked questions she or he can answer. For example, at ages 8 or 9, very few children can define the word *connection.* At age 10, 10 percent can. At age 13, 60 percent can. In other words, the ability to define *connection* indicates mental ability equal to that of an average 13-year-old. If we had only this one item to test children with, those who answered correctly would be given a mental age of 13. When scores from many items are combined,

VERBAL REASONING

Vocabulary	Name a pictured object or define a word.
Comprehension	Answer questions requiring logic or common sense.
Absurdities	Tell what is wrong with pictures (for example, a bicycle has square wheels).
Verbal relations	Given four words, tell how three are similar.

QUANTITATIVE REASONING

Quantitative	Use numbered blocks to add and count; solve word problems.
Number series	Given a series of numbers, tell what two numbers would come next. For example, 3, 6, 9, would be followed by 12 and 15.
Equation building	Given a set of numbers and mathematical signs, arrange them to make a true equation. For example, 3, 4, 7, +, = would be arranged as 3 + 4 = 7.

ABSTRACT/VISUAL REASONING

Pattern analysis	Put picture puzzles together; reproduce patterns with blocks.
Copying	Copy arrangements of blocks or draw copies of designs.
Matrices	Complete a matrix of shapes that has one part missing.
Paper folding and cutting	Choose pictures that show how a piece of paper would look if folded or cut.

SHORT-TERM MEMORY

Bead memory	Correctly remember the order of beads placed on a stick.
Memory for sentences	Repeat sentences exactly after hearing them once.
Memory for digits	Repeat a series of digits (forward or backward) after hearing them once.
Memory for objects	After seeing several objects, point to the objects in the same order as they were shown.

a child's overall mental age can be found. ◆Table 12.2 is a sample of items that persons of average intelligence can answer at various ages.

Mental age is a good measure of actual ability. But as we have noted, mental age says nothing about whether overall intelligence is high or low, compared with other people of the same age. To find out what a particular mental age means, we must also consider a person's chronological age. Then we can relate mental age to actual age. This yields an **IQ, or intelligence quotient.** When the Stanford-Binet was first used, IQ was defined as mental age (MA) divided by chronological age (CA) and multiplied by 100:

$$\frac{MA}{CA} \times 100 = IQ$$

An advantage of the original IQ was that intelligence could be compared among children with different chronological and mental ages. For instance, 10-year-old Justin has a mental age of 12. Thus, his IQ is 120:

$$\frac{(MA)\ 12}{(CA)\ 10} \times 100 = 120\ (IQ)$$

Justin's friend Suke also has a mental age of 12. However, Suke's chronological age is 12, so his IQ is 100:

$$\frac{(MA)\ 12}{(CA)\ 12} \times 100 = 100\ (IQ)$$

The IQ shows that 10-year-old Justin is brighter than his 12-year-old friend Suke, even though their intellectual skills are about the same. Notice that a person's IQ will be 100 when

mental age equals chronological age. An IQ score of 100 is therefore defined as average intelligence.

Then does a person with an IQ score below 100 have below average intelligence? Not unless the IQ is well below 100. An IQ of 100 is the *mathematical* average (or mean) for such scores. However, average intelligence is usually defined as any score from 90 to 109. The important point is that IQ scores will be over 100 when mental age is higher than age in years (❖Fig. 12.3). IQ scores below 100 occur when a person's age in years exceeds his or her mental age. An example of the second situation would be a 15-year-old with an MA of 12:

$$\frac{12}{15} \times 100 = 80\ (IQ)$$

Reliability *The ability of a test to yield the same score, or nearly the same score, each time it is given to the same person.*
Validity *The ability of a test to measure what it purports to measure.*
Objective test *A test that gives the same score when different people correct it.*
Test standardization *Establishing standards for administering a test and interpreting scores.*
Norm *An average score for a designated group of people.*
Stanford-Binet Intelligence Scale *A widely used individual test of intelligence; a direct descendant of Alfred Binet's first intelligence test.*
Chronological age *A person's age in years.*
Mental age *The average mental ability displayed by people of a given age.*
Intelligence quotient (IQ) *An index of intelligence defined as mental age divided by chronological age and multiplied by 100.*

◆ TABLE 12.2 Sample Items from the Stanford-Binet Intelligence Scale

2 years old	On a large paper doll, points out the hair, mouth, feet, ears, nose, hands, and eyes. When shown a tower built of four blocks, builds one like it.
3 years old	When shown a bridge built of three blocks, builds one like it. When shown a drawing of a circle, copies it with a pencil.
4 years old	Fills in the missing word when asked, "Brother is a boy; sister is a _____." "In daytime it is light; at night it is_____." Answers correctly when asked, "Why do we have houses?" "Why do we have books?"
5 years old	Defines *ball*, *hat*, and *stove*. When shown a drawing of a square, copies it with a pencil.
9 years old	Answers correctly when examiner says, "In an old graveyard in Spain they have discovered a small skull which they believe to be that of Christopher Columbus when he was about 10 years old. What is foolish about that?" Answers correctly when asked, "Tell me the name of a color that rhymes with head." "Tell me a number that rhymes with tree."
Adult	Can describe the difference between laziness and idleness, poverty and misery, character and reputation. Answers correctly when asked, "Which direction would you have to face so your right hand would be toward the north?"

(Terman & Merill, 1960.)

❖ FIGURE 12.3 *With a score of 230, Marilyn Mach vos Savant has the highest IQ ever officially recorded. When she was only 7 years and 9 months old, vos Savant could answer questions that the average 13-year-old can answer. At ages 8, 9, and 10, she got perfect scores on the Stanford-Binet scale. Now in her 40s, she is capitalizing on her celebrity by giving lectures and writing books (Lemley, 1986).*

DEVIATION IQS   The preceding examples may give you insight into the meaning of IQ scores. However, it's no longer necessary to directly calculate IQs. Instead, modern tests use **deviation IQs.** These scores are based on a person's relative standing in his or her age group. That is, they tell how far above or below average the person's score falls. (For more information, see Appendix B.) Tables supplied with the test are then used to convert a person's relative standing in the group to an IQ score (Neisser et al., 1996).

THE STABILITY OF IQ   *How old do children have to be before their IQ scores become stable?*   IQ scores are not very dependable until about age 6 (Schuerger & Witt, 1989). IQ scores measured at age 2 correlate only .31 with those measured at age 18. In other words, knowing a child's IQ at age 2 tells us very little about what his or her IQ will be 16 years later. (Recall that a perfect correlation is 1.00 and a correlation of 0.00 occurs when scores are unrelated.) However, IQs do become more reliable as children grow older. After middle childhood, IQ scores usually change very little (Canivez & Watkins, 1998). The average change during retesting is only about 5 points in either direction (❖Fig. 12.4).

How much are IQs affected by age?   IQs reflect a person's education, maturity, and experience, as well as innate intelligence. As a result, test scores show a small, gradual increase un-

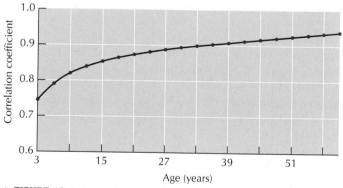

❖ FIGURE 12.4 *The stability or reliability of IQ scores increases rapidly in early childhood. Scores are very consistent from early adulthood to late middle age. (Source: Schuerger & Witt, 1989.)*

til about age 40 (Eichorn et al., 1981). This trend, of course, is an average. Some people make fairly large gains in IQ, whereas others experience sizable losses. How do the two groups differ? In general, those who gain in IQ are exposed to intellectual stimulation during early adulthood. Those who decline typically suffer from chronic illnesses, drinking problems, or unstimulating lifestyles (Honzik, 1984).

Some studies have found slow declines in IQ after middle age, while others indicate little or no change due to aging.

VERBAL SUBTESTS	SAMPLE ITEMS
Information	How many wings does a bird have?
	Who wrote *Paradise Lost?*
Digit span	Repeat from memory a series of digits, such as 3 1 0 6 7 4 2 5, after hearing it once.
General	What is the advantage of keeping money in the bank?
Comprehension	Why is copper often used in electrical wires?
Arithmetic	Three men divided 18 golf balls equally among themselves. How many golf balls did each man receive?
	If 2 apples cost 15¢ what will be the cost of a dozen apples?
Similarities	In what way are a lion and a tiger alike?
	In what way are a saw and a hammer alike?
Vocabulary	The test consists simply of asking, "What is a _____?" or "What does _____ mean?" The words cover a wide range of difficulty or familiarity.

PERFORMANCE SUBTESTS	DESCRIPTION OF ITEM
Picture arrangement	Arrange a series of cartoon panels to make a meaningful story.
Picture completion	What is missing from these pictures?
Block design	Copy designs with blocks (as shown at right).
Object assembly	Put together a jigsaw puzzle.
Digit symbol	Fill in the symbols:

1	2	3	4
X	III	I	0

3	4	1	3	4	2	1	2

(Courtesy of The Psychological Corporation.)

As you may recall from Chapter 5, these contradictory results can be explained in this way: When we emphasize general information or comprehension, there is little decline in IQ until advanced age; however, test items requiring speed, rapid insight, or perceptual flexibility show earlier losses and a rapid decline after middle age (Brody, 1992; Lawrence, Myerson, & Hale, 1998). Overall, age-related losses are small for most healthy, well-educated individuals (Weintraub et al., 1991).

The most striking link between intelligence and aging occurs in the last years of life. Apparently, death is foreshadowed by changes in the brain. An abrupt **terminal decline** in IQ can be measured about 5 years before death, even when a person appears to be in good health (Suedfeld & Piedrahita, 1984).

The Wechsler Tests

Is the Stanford-Binet the only intelligence test?   A widely used alternative to the Stanford-Binet is the **Wechsler Adult Intelligence Scale–Third Edition,** or **WAIS-III.** This test also has a form for use with children, called the **Wechsler Intelligence Scale for Children–Third Edition (WISC-III).**

The Wechsler tests are similar to the Stanford-Binet, but they are also different in important ways. For one thing, the WAIS-III was designed to test adult intelligence. Of course, the Stanford-Binet may be used to test adults, but it tends to be better suited for children and adolescents. The Wechsler tests yield a single overall IQ, just as the Stanford-Binet does. However, the WAIS and WISC also provide separate scores for **performance** (nonverbal) **intelligence** and **verbal** (language- or symbol-oriented) **intelligence**. Verbal and nonverbal abilities can be broken down further to reveal various cognitive strengths and weaknesses. The abilities measured by the Wechsler tests and some sample test items are listed in ◆Table 12.3.

Deviation IQ *An IQ obtained statistically from a person's relative standing in his or her age group; that is, how far above or below average the person's score was, relative to other scores.*

Terminal decline *An abrupt decline in measured intelligence about 5 years before death.*

Wechsler Adult Intelligence Scale–Third Edition (WAIS-III) *An adult intelligence test that rates both verbal and performance intelligence.*

Wechsler Intelligence Scale for Children–Third Edition (WISC-III) *An intelligence test for children that rates both verbal and performance intelligence.*

Performance intelligence *Intelligence measured by solving puzzles, assembling objects, completing pictures, and other nonverbal tasks.*

Verbal intelligence *Intelligence measured by answering questions involving vocabulary, general information, arithmetic, and other language- or symbol-oriented tasks.*

Group Tests

The Binet-4 and the Wechsler tests are **individual intelligence tests,** which must be given to a single person by a trained specialist. In contrast, **group intelligence tests** can be given to a large group of people with minimal supervision. Group tests usually require people to read, to follow instructions, and to solve problems of logic, reasoning, mathematics, or spatial skills. The first group intelligence test was the *Army Alpha,* developed for World War I military inductees. As you can see in ◆Table 12.4, intelligence testing has come a long way since then.

SCHOLASTIC APTITUDE TESTS If you're wondering if you have ever taken an intelligence test, the answer is probably yes. As mentioned earlier, the *Scholastic Assessment Test* is a multiple aptitude test. So are the *American College Test* (ACT) and the *College Qualification Test* (CQT). Each of these group tests is designed to predict your chances for success in college. Because the tests measure a variety of mental aptitudes, each can also be used to estimate general intelligence.

◆ **TABLE 12.4** Items from the Army Alpha Subtest on "Common Sense"

The *Army Alpha* was given to World War I army recruits in the United States as a way to identify potential officers. In these sample questions, note the curious mixture of folk wisdom, scientific information, and moralism (Kessen & Cahan, 1986). Other parts of the test were more like modern intelligence tests.

1. IF PLANTS ARE DYING FOR LACK OF RAIN, YOU SHOULD

[ ] water them
[ ] ask a florist's advice
[ ] put fertilizer around them

2. IF THE GROCER SHOULD GIVE YOU TOO MUCH MONEY IN MAKING CHANGE, WHAT IS THE RIGHT THING TO DO?

[ ] buy some candy for him with it
[ ] give it to the first poor man you meet
[ ] tell him of his mistake

3. IF YOU SAW A TRAIN APPROACHING A BROKEN TRACK YOU SHOULD

[ ] telephone for an ambulance
[ ] signal the engineer to stop the train
[ ] look for a piece of rail to fit in

4. SOME MEN LOSE THEIR BREATH ON HIGH MOUNTAINS BECAUSE

[ ] the wind blows their breath away
[ ] the air is too rare
[ ] it is always cold there

5. WE SEE NO STARS AT NOON BECAUSE

[ ] they have moved to the other side of the earth
[ ] they are much fainter than the sun
[ ] they are hidden behind the sky

INTELLIGENCE TESTS

RELATE

If you were going to write an intelligence test, what kinds of questions would you ask? How much would your questions resemble those on standard intelligence tests? Would you want to measure any mental skills not covered by established tests?

LEARNING CHECK

1. The first successful intelligence test was developed by
   _____ _____.

2. If we define intelligence by writing a test, we are using
   a. a circular definition b. an abstract definition c. an operational definition d. a chronological definition

3. Place an R or a V after each operation to indicate if it would be used to establish the reliability or the validity of a test.
   a. Compare score on one half of test items to score on the other half. ( )
   b. Compare scores on test to grades, performance ratings, or other measures. ( )
   c. Compare scores from the test after administering it on two separate occasions. ( )
   d. Compare scores on alternate forms of the test. ( )

4. IQ was originally defined as _____ times 100.

5. The ability to answer general information and comprehension questions shows the most rapid decline during aging. T or F?

6. The WAIS-III is a group intelligence test. T or F?

7. Establishing norms and uniform procedures for administering a test are elements of standardization. T or F?

8. Scores on modern intelligence tests are based on one's deviation IQ (relative standing among test takers) rather than on the ratio between mental age and chronological age. T or F?

CRITICAL THINKING

9. A person who displays the savant syndrome might score well on a special _____ test, while scoring very low on an _____ test.

Answers:

9. aptitude, intelligence

1. Alfred Binet 2. c 3. a. (R), b. (V), c. (R), d. (R) 4. MA/CA 5. F 6. F 7. T 8. T

VARIATIONS IN INTELLIGENCE—THE NUMBERS GAME

IQ scores are classified as shown in ◆Table 12.5. A look at the percentages reveals a definite pattern. The distribution (or scattering) of IQ scores approximates a **normal** (bell-shaped) **curve.** That is, most scores fall close to the average, and very few are found at the extremes. ❖Figure 12.5 shows this characteristic of measured intelligence.

SEX *On the average, do males and females differ in intelligence?* IQ scores cannot answer this question because test items were

◆ TABLE 12.5 Distribution of Adult IQ Scores on the WAIS-III

IQ	DESCRIPTION	PERCENT
Above 130	Very superior	2.2
120–129	Superior	6.7
110–119	Bright normal	16.1
90–109	Average	50.0
80–89	Dull normal	16.1
70–79	Borderline	6.7
Below 70	Mentally retarded	2.2

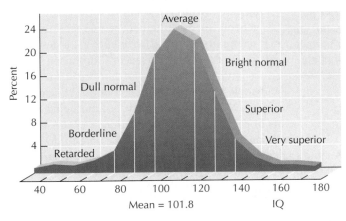

❖ **FIGURE 12.5** *Distribution of Stanford-Binet Intelligence Test scores for 3,184 children. (After Terman & Merrill, 1960.)*

John Kirtley has an IQ score of 174, yet he prefers to do custodial work, feeling that his unusual intellect would be "used" by his employers if he pursued a technical occupation.

selected to be equally difficult for both sexes. However, men and women do not appear to differ in overall intelligence. On the other hand, tests like the WAIS-III allow us to compare the intellectual strengths and weaknesses of men and women. For decades, women, as a group, performed best on items that require verbal ability, vocabulary, and rote learning. Men, in contrast, were best at items that require spatial visualization and arithmetic reasoning. Today, such male-female differences have almost disappeared among children and young adults. The small differences that remain appear to be based on a tendency for parents and educators to encourage males, more than females, to learn math and spatial skills.

IQ AND ACHIEVEMENT *How do IQ scores relate to success in school, jobs, and other endeavors?* IQ differences of a few points tell us little about a person. But if we look at a broader range of scores, the differences do become meaningful. For example, a person with an IQ of 100 would probably struggle with college, whereas one with an IQ of 120 would do just fine.

The correlation between IQ and school grades is .50—a sizable association. If grades depended solely on IQ, the connec-tion would be even stronger. However, motivation, special talents, off-campus educational opportunities, and many other factors influence grades and school success. The same is true of real-world success beyond school. IQ is also not a good predictor of success in art, music, writing, dramatics, science, and leadership. Tests of creativity are much more strongly related to achievement in these areas (Neisser et al., 1996; Wallach, 1985).

As you might expect, IQ and job classification are also related. People holding white-collar, professional positions average higher IQs than those in blue-collar settings. For example, accountants, lawyers, and engineers average about 125 in IQ. In contrast, miners and farm workers average about 90 (Brody, 1992). It is important to note, however, that a range of IQ scores can be found in all occupations. Many people of high intelligence, because of choice or circumstance, have "low-ranking" jobs.

Does the link between IQ and occupation show that professional jobs require more intelligence? Not as clearly as you might think. Higher status jobs often require an academic degree. As a result, hiring for professional jobs is biased in

Individual intelligence test *A test of intelligence designed to be given to a single individual by a trained specialist.*
Group intelligence test *Any intelligence test that can be administered to a group of people with minimal supervision.*

favor of a particular type of intelligence, namely, the kind measured by intelligence tests (McClelland, 1994; Neisser et al., 1996). This bias probably inflates the apparent association between professional jobs and IQ.

When IQs are extreme—below 70 or above 140—their link to an individual's potential for success becomes unmistakable. Only about 3 percent of the population falls in these ranges. Nevertheless, millions of people have exceptionally high or low IQs. Discussions of the mentally gifted and mentally retarded follow.

THE MENTALLY GIFTED—SMART, SMARTER, SMARTEST

How high is the IQ of a genius? Only 2 people out of 100 score above 130 on IQ tests. These bright individuals are usually described as "gifted." Less than half of 1 percent of the population scores above 140. These people are certainly gifted or perhaps even "geniuses." However, some psychologists reserve the term *genius* for people with even higher IQs or those who are exceptionally creative (Kamphaus, 1993).

Gifted Children

Do high IQ scores in childhood predict later ability? To directly answer this question, Lewis Terman selected 1,500 children with IQs of 140 or more. Terman followed this gifted group (the "Termites," as he called them) into adulthood. By doing so, Terman countered a number of popular misconceptions about high intelligence (Shurkin, 1992).

- **Misconception:** The gifted tend to be peculiar, socially backward people.
- **Fact:** On the contrary, Terman's gifted subjects were socially well adjusted and showed above average leadership.
- **Misconception:** Early ripe means later rot; the gifted tend to fizzle out as adults.
- **Fact:** This is false. When they were retested as adults, Terman's subjects again scored in the upper IQ ranges.
- **Misconception:** The very bright are usually physically inferior "eggheads" or weaklings.
- **Fact:** As a group, the gifted were above average in height, weight, and physical appearance.
- **Misconception:** The highly intelligent person is more susceptible to mental illness ("Genius is next to insanity").
- **Fact:** Terman demonstrated conclusively that the gifted have better than average mental health records and a greater *resistance* to mental illness. In general, the highly gifted tend to be very well adjusted psychologically and socially (Garland & Zigler, 1999; Norman et al., 1999). (But see Bridges.)
- **Misconception:** Intelligence has nothing to do with success, especially in practical matters.
- **Fact:** The later success of Terman's subjects was the most striking finding of the study. Far more of them than average had completed college, earned advanced degrees, and held professional positions. As a group, the gifted had produced dozens of

books, thousands of scientific articles, and hundreds of short stories and other publications (Shurkin, 1992; Terman & Oden, 1959).

As noted earlier, IQ scores are not generally good predictors of real-world success. However, when scores are in the gifted range, the likelihood of outstanding achievement does seem to be higher.

GIFTEDNESS AND ACHIEVEMENT *Were all of the gifted children superior as adults?* No. Remember that high IQ reveals *potential*. It does not guarantee success. Marilyn vos Savant, with an IQ of 230, has contributed little to science, literature, or art. Nobel prize–winning physicist Richard Feynman, whom many regarded as a genius, had an IQ of 122 (Michalko, 1998). As adults, some of the Terman's gifted subjects committed crimes, were unemployable, or were poorly adjusted.

How did the more successful gifted people differ from the less successful? Most of the successful Termites had educated parents who valued learning and encouraged them to do the same. In general, successful gifted people tend to have strong *intellectual determination*—a desire to know, excel, and persevere (Tomlinson-Keasey & Little, 1990). Gifted or not, most successful people tend to be *persistent* and *motivated* to learn. No one is paid to sit around being *capable* of achievement. What you do is always more important than what you should be able to do.

A child's talents most often blossom when they are nurtured with support, encouragement, education, and effort (Freeman, 1995).

BRIDGES

One exception exists. Some of history's outstanding writers and composers appear to have suffered from manic-depressive disorder.

See Chapter 17, pages 582–584.

Michael Kearney is the youngest college graduate in the world. He attended high school at 5, earned an A.S. degree in geology at 8, and recieved a B.A. degree in anthropology at age 10. Although it is clear that Michael is gifted, his rapid progress in school required motivation and effort. Also, his experience is atypical. Skipping grades can be risky because even bright children may feel out of place with older students.

It is wise to remember that there are many ways in which a child may be gifted. Many schools now offer Gifted and Talented Education programs for students with a variety of special abilities—not just for those who score well on IQ tests.

IDENTIFYING GIFTED CHILDREN *How might a parent spot an unusually bright child?* Early signs of giftedness are not always purely "intellectual." **Giftedness** can be the possession of either a high IQ or special talents or aptitudes. The following signs may reveal that a child is gifted: a tendency to seek out older children and adults; an early fascination with explanations and problem solving; talking in complete sentences as early as 2 or 3 years of age; an unusually good memory; precocious talent in art, music, or number skills; an early interest in books, along with early reading (often by age 3); showing of kindness, understanding, and cooperation toward others (Alvino, 1996).

Notice that this list goes beyond straight "academic" intelligence. Children may be gifted in ways other than having a high IQ. In fact, if artistic talent, mechanical aptitude, musical aptitude, athletic potential, and so on are considered, 19 out of 20 children have a special "gift" of one kind or another. Limiting giftedness to high IQ can shortchange children with special talents or potentials. This is especially true of ethnic minority children, who may be the victims of subtle biases in standardized intelligence tests. These children, as well as children with physical disabilities, are less likely to be recognized as gifted (Robinson & Clinkenbeard, 1998).

GATE PROGRAMS ▸ Being exceptionally bright is not without its problems. Usually, parents and teachers must make adjustments to help gifted children make the most of their talents (Silverman, 1998). The gifted child may become bored in classes designed for average children. This can lead to misbehavior or clashes with teachers who think the gifted child a

BRIDGES

All children in all IQ ranges benefit from enriched environments.

For a discussion of enrichment and some guidelines for parents, see Chapter 4, pages 113–115.

show-off or smart aleck. The extremely bright child may also find classmates less stimulating than older children or adults. In recognition of these problems, many schools now provide special Gifted and Talented Education (GATE) classes for gifted children. Such programs combine classroom enrichment with fast-paced instruction to satisfy the gifted child's appetite for intellectual stimulation (Gottfried & Gottfried, 1994).

DRAWBACKS OF FORCED TEACHING The value of GATE programs should not be confused with **forced teaching** (accelerated learning at a pace dictated by an adult). Forcing children to learn reading, pre-math skills, gymnastics, swimming, musical skills, and the like can bore or oppress them. These practices, which are sometimes called "hothousing," are like trying to force plants to bloom prematurely (Hyson et al., 1991).

Most educators are aware of the drawbacks of hothousing. However, parents may not be. Understandably, many parents want to help their children excel. However, parents who approach play and learning as if their preschooler is on the fast track for Harvard are filling their own needs at the expense of the child (Alvino et al., 1996).

Normal curve *A bell-shaped curve characterized by a large number of scores in a middle area, tapering to very few extremely high and low scores.*
Giftedness *The possession of either a high IQ or special talents or aptitudes.*
Forced teaching *Accelerated learning in early childhood at a pace dictated by an adult.*

MENTAL RETARDATION—A DIFFERENCE THAT MAKES A DIFFERENCE

A person with mental abilities far below average is termed **mentally retarded** or **developmentally disabled.** Retardation begins at an IQ of approximately 70 or below. However, a person's ability to perform **adaptive behaviors** (basic skills such as dressing, eating, communicating, shopping, and working) also figures into evaluating retardation (DSM-IV, 1994; Kamphaus, 1993).

Levels of Retardation

Below an IQ of 70, retardation is classified as shown in ◆Table 12.6. The listed IQ ranges are approximate because IQ scores normally vary a few points. The terms in the right-hand columns are listed only to give you a general impression of each IQ range. Unless they are used cautiously, such terms can needlessly limit the educational goals of retarded persons (DSM-IV, 1994).

Are the retarded usually placed in institutions? No. Total care is necessary only for the *profoundly* retarded (IQ below 25). Many of these individuals live in group homes or with their families. The *severely* retarded (IQ of 25–40) and *moderately* retarded (IQ of 40–55) are capable of mastering basic language and self-help skills. Many become self-supporting by working in sheltered workshops (special simplified work environments). The *mildly* retarded (IQ of 55–70) make up about 85 percent of all those affected. This group can benefit from carefully structured education. As adults, these persons, as well as the *borderline retarded* (IQ 70–85), are capable of living alone, and they may marry. However, they tend to have difficulties with many of the demands of adult life (Zetlin & Murtaugh, 1990).

Causes of Retardation

What causes mental retardation? In 30 to 40 percent of cases, no known biological problem can be identified. In many such instances, the degree of retardation is mild, in the 50–70 IQ

range. Often, other family members are also mildly retarded. **Familial retardation,** as this is called, occurs mostly in very poor households, where nutrition, intellectual stimulation, medical care, and emotional support may be inadequate. This suggests that familial retardation is based largely on an impov-

These youngsters are participants in the Special Olympics—an athletic event for the mentally retarded. It is often said of the Special Olympics that "everyone is a winner—participants, coaches, and spectators."

◆ **TABLE 12.6** Levels of Mental Retardation

IQ RANGE	DEGREE OF RETARDATION	EDUCATIONAL CLASSIFICATION	REQUIRED LEVEL OF SUPPORT
50–55 to 70	Mild	Educable	Intermittent
35–40 to 50–55	Moderate	Trainable	Limited
20–25 to 35–40	Severe	Dependent	Extensive
Below 20–25	Profound	Life support	Pervasive

(DSM-IV, 1994; Hodapp, 1994.)

erished environment. Thus, better nutrition, education, and early childhood enrichment programs could prevent many cases of retardation (Hunt, 1995; Zigler, 1995).

Organic Sources of Retardation

About half of all cases of mental retardation are *organic,* or related to physical disorders. These include **birth injuries** (such as lack of oxygen during delivery) and **fetal damage** (prenatal damage from disease, infection, or drugs). **Metabolic disorders,** which affect energy production and use in the body, also cause retardation. Some forms of retardation are linked to **genetic abnormalities,** such as missing genes, extra genes, or defective genes. Malnutrition and exposure to lead, PCBs, and other toxins early in childhood can also cause organic retardation (Bryant & Maxwell, 1999). Let's briefly look at several distinctive problems.

PHENYLKETONURIA (PKU)   The problem called **phenylketonuria** (FEN-ul-KEET-uh-NURE-ee-ah) is a genetic disease. Children who have PKU lack an important enzyme. This causes phenylpyruvic (FEN-ul-pye-ROO-vik) acid (a destructive chemical) to collect within their bodies. PKU is also linked to very low levels of dopamine, an important chemical messenger in the brain. If PKU goes untreated, severe retardation typically occurs by age 3.

PKU can be detected in newborn babies by routine medical testing. Affected children are usually placed on a diet low in phenylalanine, the substance the child's body can't handle. Carefully following this diet will usually prevent retardation. (Phenylalanine is present in many foods. You might be interested to know that it is also found in Aspartame, the artificial sweetener in diet colas.)

MICROCEPHALY   The word **microcephaly** (MY-kro-SEF-ah-lee) means small-headedness. The microcephalic person suffers a rare abnormality in which the skull is extremely small or fails to grow. This forces the brain to develop in a limited space, causing severe retardation. Although they are typically institutionalized, microcephalic people are usually affectionate, well behaved, and cooperative.

HYDROCEPHALY   **Hydrocephaly** (HI-dro-SEF-ah-lee: "water on the brain") is caused by a buildup of cerebrospinal fluid within brain cavities. Pressure from this fluid can damage the brain and enlarge the head. Hydrocephaly is not uncommon—about 10,000 hydrocephalic babies are born each year in the United States and Canada. However, thanks to new medical procedures, most of these infants will lead normal lives. A surgically implanted tube drains fluid from the brain into the abdomen. If this is done within the first 3 months of life, retardation can usually be avoided.

CRETINISM   **Cretinism** (KREET-un-iz-um) is another type of retardation that appears in infancy. It results from an insufficient supply of thyroid hormone. In some parts of the world, cretinism is caused by a lack of iodine in the diet (the thyroid glands require iodine to function normally). Iodized salt has

made this source of retardation rare in industrialized nations. Cretinism causes stunted physical and intellectual growth that cannot be reversed. Fortunately, cretinism is easily detected in infancy. Once detected, it can be treated with thyroid hormone replacement before permanent damage occurs.

DOWN SYNDROME   In 1 out of 800 babies, the disorder known as **Down syndrome** causes moderate to severe retardation and a shortened life expectancy (usually around 40 years). Distinctive features of this problem are almond-shaped eyes, a slightly protruding tongue, a stocky build, and stubby hands with deeply creased palms.

It is now known that Down syndrome children have an extra 21st chromosome. This condition, which is called *trisomy-21,* results from flaws in the parents' egg or sperm cells. Thus, although Down syndrome is *genetic,* it is not usually *hereditary* (it doesn't "run in the family").

The age of parents is a major factor in Down syndrome. As people age, their reproductive cells are more prone to errors during cell division. This raises the odds that an extra chromosome will be present. As you can see in the following figures, the older a woman is, the greater the risk:

MOTHER'S AGE	INCIDENCE OF DOWN SYNDROME
Early 20s	1/2,000
Early 40s	1/105
Late 40s	1/12

Older fathers also add to the risk. In about 25 percent of cases, the father is the source of the extra chromosome. Older adults who plan to have children should carefully consider the odds shown here.

There is no "cure" for Down syndrome. However, these children are usually loving and responsive, and they make progress in a caring environment. At a basic level, Down syndrome

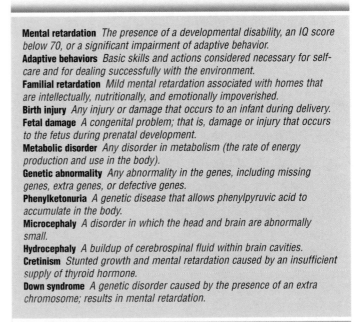

Mental retardation *The presence of a developmental disability, an IQ score below 70, or a significant impairment of adaptive behavior.*
Adaptive behaviors *Basic skills and actions considered necessary for self-care and for dealing successfully with the environment.*
Familial retardation *Mild mental retardation associated with homes that are intellectually, nutritionally, and emotionally impoverished.*
Birth injury *Any injury or damage that occurs to an infant during delivery.*
Fetal damage *A congenital problem; that is, damage or injury that occurs to the fetus during prenatal development.*
Metabolic disorder *Any disorder in metabolism (the rate of energy production and use in the body).*
Genetic abnormality *Any abnormality in the genes, including missing genes, extra genes, or defective genes.*
Phenylketonuria *A genetic disease that allows phenylpyruvic acid to accumulate in the body.*
Microcephaly *A disorder in which the head and brain are abnormally small.*
Hydrocephaly *A buildup of cerebrospinal fluid within brain cavities.*
Cretinism *Stunted growth and mental retardation caused by an insufficient supply of thyroid hormone.*
Down syndrome *A genetic disorder caused by the presence of an extra chromosome; results in mental retardation.*

children can do most of the things that other children can, only more slowly. The best hope for Down syndrome children, therefore, lies in specially tailored educational programs that enable them to lead fuller lives.

FRAGILE-X SYNDROME The second most common form of genetic mental retardation (after Down syndrome) is **fragile-X syndrome** (Hodapp, 1994). Unlike Down syndrome, fragile-X syndrome is hereditary—it *does* run in families. The problem is related to a thin, frail-looking area on the *X* (female) chromosome. Because fragile-X is sex linked (like color-blindness), boys are most often affected, at a rate of about 1 out of every 1,200 (Rose, 1995).

Fragile-X males generally have long, thin faces and big ears. Physically, they are usually larger than average during childhood, but smaller than average after adolescence. Up to three fourths of all fragile-X males suffer from hyperactivity and attention disorders. Many also have a peculiar tendency to avoid eye contact with others.

Fragile-X males are only mildly retarded during early childhood, but they are often severely or profoundly retarded as adults. When learning adaptive behaviors, they tend to do better with daily living skills than with language and social skills (Hodapp, 1994).

Retardation in Perspective

It is important to remember that developmentally disabled persons are not handicapped where their feelings are concerned. They are sensitive to rejection and easily hurt by teasing or ridicule. Likewise, they respond warmly to love and acceptance. Everyone has a right to self-respect and a place in the community. This is especially important during childhood, when the support of others adds greatly to the retarded person's chances of becoming a well-adjusted member of society.

KNOWLEDGE BUILDER
VARIATIONS IN INTELLIGENCE

RELATE

If you measure the heights of all the people in your psychology class, most people will be clustered around an average height. Very few will be extremely tall or extremely short. Does this ring a bell? Do you think it's normal? (It is, of course; most measured human characteristics form a normal curve, just as IQs do.)

Do you think that giftedness should be defined by high IQ or having special talents (or both)? To increase your chances of succeeding in today's society, would you prefer to be smart or talented (or both)? How about smart, talented, motivated, and lucky!

As a psychologist, you are asked to assess a child's degree of retardation. Will you rely more on IQ or the child's level of adaptive behavior? Would you be more confident in your judgment if you took both factors into account?

LEARNING CHECK

1. The distribution of IQs approximates a _____ (bell-shaped) curve.

2. The association between IQ and high-status professional jobs proves that such jobs require more intelligence. T or F?

3. Differences in the intellectual strengths of men and women have grown larger in recent years. T or F?

4. Only about 6 percent of the population scores above 140 on IQ tests. T or F?

5. An IQ score below 90 indicates mental retardation. T or F?

6. Many cases of mental retardation without known organic causes appear to be _____.

Match:

7. _____ PKU   A. Too little thyroid hormone
8. _____ Microcephaly   B. Very small brain
9. _____ Hydrocephaly   C. 47 chromosomes
10. _____ Cretinism   D. Lack of an important enzyme
11. _____ Down syndrome   E. Excess of cerebrospinal fluid
12. _____ Fragile-X   F. Abnormal female chromosome
                     G. Caused by a lack of oxygen at birth

CRITICAL THINKING

13. Lewis Terman took great interest in the lives of many of the "Termites." He even went so far as to advise them about what kinds of careers they should pursue. What error of observation did Terman make?

Answers:

1. normal 2. F 3. F 4. F 5. F 6. familial 7. D 8. B 9. E 10. A 11. C 12. F 13. Terman may have unintentionally altered the behavior of the people he was studying. Although Terman's observations are generally regarded as valid, he did break a basic rule of scientific observation.

HEREDITY AND ENVIRONMENT—SUPER RATS AND FAMILY TREES

Is intelligence inherited? This seemingly simple question is loaded with controversy. Some psychologists believe that intelligence is strongly affected by heredity. Others feel that environment is dominant. Let's examine some evidence for each view.

In a classic study of genetic factors in learning, Tryon (1929) managed to breed separate strains of "maze-bright" and "maze-dull" rats (animals that were extremely "bright" or "stupid" at learning mazes). After several generations of breeding, the slowest "super rat" outperformed the best "dull" rat. This and other studies of **eugenics** (selective breeding for desirable characteristics) suggest that some traits are highly influenced by heredity.

That may be true, but is maze-learning really a measure of intelligence? No, it isn't. Tryon's study seemed to show that intelligence is inherited, but later researchers found that the "bright" rats were simply more motivated by food and less easily distracted during testing. When they weren't chasing after rat chow, the "bright" rats were no more intelligent than the supposedly dull rats. Thus, Tryon's study did demonstrate that behavioral characteristics can be influenced by heredity. However, it was inconclusive concerning intelligence. Because of such problems, animal studies cannot tell us with certainty how heredity and environment affect intelligence. Let's see what human studies reveal.

BRIDGES

Identical twins also tend to have similar personality traits. This suggests that heredity contributes to personality, as well as to intelligence.

See Chapter 15, pages 487–488.

Hereditary Influences

Most people are aware of a moderate similarity in the intelligence between parents and their children or between brothers and sisters. As ❖Figure 12.6 shows, the closer two people are on a family tree, the more alike their IQs are likely to be.

Does that indicate that intelligence is hereditary? Not necessarily. Brothers, sisters, and parents share similar environments as well as similar genes. To separate heredity and environment, we need to make some selected comparisons.

TWIN STUDIES   Notice in ❖Figure 12.6 that the IQ scores of fraternal twins are more alike than those of ordinary brothers and sisters. **Fraternal twins** come from two separate eggs fertilized at the same time. They are no more genetically alike than ordinary siblings. Why, then, should the twins' IQ scores be more similar? The reason is environmental: Parents treat twins more alike than ordinary siblings, resulting in a closer match in IQs.

More striking similarities are observed with **identical twins,** who develop from a single egg and have identical genes. At the top of ❖Figure 12.6, you can see that identical twins who grow up in the same family have highly correlated IQs. This is what we would expect with identical heredity and very similar environments. Now, let's consider what happens when identical twins are reared apart. As you can see, the correlation drops, but only from .86 to .72. Psychologists who

emphasize genetics believe figures like these show that differences in adult intelligence are roughly 50 percent hereditary (Casto, DeFries, & Fulker, 1995; Neisser et al., 1996; Plomin & Rende, 1991).

How do environmentalists interpret the figures? They point out that some separated twins differ by as much as 20 IQ points. In every case where this occurs, there are large educational and environmental differences between the twins. Also, separated twins are almost always placed in homes socially and educationally similar to those of their birth parents. This would tend to inflate apparent genetic effects by making the separated twins' IQs more alike. Another frequently overlooked fact is that twins grow up in the same environment *before birth* (in the womb). If this environmental similarity is taken into account, intelligence would seem to be less than 50 percent hereditary (Devlin, Daniels, & Roeder, 1997).

Environmental Influences

Strong evidence for an environmental view of intelligence comes from families having one adopted child and one biological child. As ❖Figure 12.7 shows, parents contribute genes *and* environment to their biological child. With an adopted child, they contribute only environment. If intelligence is highly genetic, the IQs of biological children should be more like their parents' IQs than the IQs of adopted children are. However, studies show that children reared by the same mother resemble her in IQ to the same degree. It doesn't matter whether they share her genes (Horn et al., 1979; Kamin, 1981; Weinberg, 1989).

Another way to see environmental effects is to compare children adopted by parents of high or low socioeconomic status. As you might predict, children who grow up in high-status

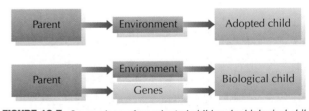

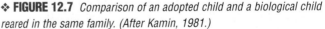

❖ **FIGURE 12.7** *Comparison of an adopted child and a biological child reared in the same family. (After Kamin, 1981.)*

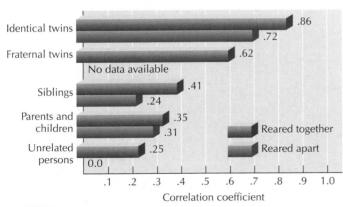

❖ **FIGURE 12.6** *Approximate correlations between IQ scores for persons with varying degrees of genetic and environmental similarity. Notice that the correlations grow smaller as the degree of genetic similarity declines. Also note that a shared environment increases the correlation in all cases. (Estimates from Bouchard, 1983; Henderson, 1982.)*

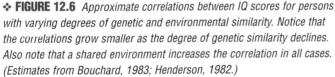

Fragile-X syndrome *A genetic form of mental retardation caused by a defect in the X chromosome.*
Eugenics *Selective breeding for desirable characteristics.*
Fraternal twins *Twins conceived from two separate eggs.*
Identical twins *Twins who develop from a single egg and have identical genes.*

homes develop higher IQs than those reared by lower status parents. Presumably, the higher socioeconomic homes provide an enriched environment, with better nutrition, greater educational opportunities, and other advantages (Capron & Duyme, 1992).

IQ AND ENVIRONMENT   *How much can environment alter intelligence?*   In one study, striking increases in IQ occurred in 25 children who were moved from an orphanage to more stimulating environments. The children, who were all considered mentally retarded and unadoptable, were moved to an institution where they received personal attention from adults. Later, these supposedly retarded children were adopted by parents who gave them love, a family, and a stimulating home environment. These children gained an average of 29 IQ points. For one child, the increase was an amazing 58 points. A second group of initially less "retarded" children, who remained in the orphanage, *lost* an average of 26 IQ points (Skeels, 1966)!

In another encouraging study, children from low-income families were provided with enriched environments from early infancy through preschool. By age 2, their IQ scores were already higher than those in a control group. More important, they were still 5 points higher 7 years after the program ended (Campbell & Ramey, 1994).

A particularly striking environmental effect is the fact that 14 nations have shown average IQ gains of from 5 to 25 points during the last 30 years (Flynn, 1987, 1990; Horgan, 1995). These IQ boosts, averaging 15 points, occurred in far too short a time for genetics to explain them. It is more likely that the gains reflect environmental forces, such as improved education, nutrition, and living in a technologically complex society (Horgan, 1995). Also, if you've ever tried to program a VCR or a watch, you'll understand why people may be getting better at answering IQ test questions that require visual analysis (Neisser, 1997).

BRIDGES

Impoverished and unstimulating environments can severely restrict mental development during early childhood.

See Chapter 4, pages 112–113, for more information.

School can also have a large impact on IQ. Stephen Ceci found that people who leave school lose anywhere from 0.25 point to 6 points in IQ per year. Dropping out of school in the eighth grade can reduce a person's adult IQ by up to 24 points. Conversely, IQ rises as people spend more time in school (Ceci, 1991). This is another clear sign that improved environments can raise intelligence. The highlight titled "Can Intelligence Be Taught?" explores this idea further.

SUMMARY   To sum up, few psychologists seriously believe that heredity is not a major factor in intelligence, and all acknowledge that environment affects it. Estimates of the impact of heredity and environment continue to vary. But ultimately, both camps agree that improving social conditions and education can raise intelligence.

There is probably no limit to how far *down* intelligence can go in an extremely poor environment. On the other hand, heredity does seem to impose upper limits on IQ, even under ideal conditions. It is telling, nevertheless, that gifted children tend to come from homes where parents spend time with their children, answer their questions, and encourage intellectual exploration (Snowden & Christian, 1999).

The fact that intelligence is partly determined by heredity tells us little of any real value. Genes are fixed at birth. Improving the environments in which children learn and grow is the main way in which we can assure that they reach their full potential (Turkheimer, 1998).

As a final summary, it might help to think of inherited intellectual potential as a rubber band that is stretched by outside forces. A long rubber band may be stretched more easily, but a shorter one can be stretched to the same length if enough force is applied. Of course, a superior genetic gift may allow for a higher maximum IQ. In the final analysis, intelligence reflects development as well as potential, nurture as well as nature (Rose, 1995; Weinberg, 1989).

USING PSYCHOLOGY

CAN INTELLIGENCE BE TAUGHT?

The traditional answer to the question "Can intelligence be taught?" is "No." Coaching, for instance, has little positive effect on aptitude and intelligence test scores (Brody, 1992). But is brief coaching a fair test of the elasticity of intelligence? Apparently not. There is growing evidence that extended, in-depth training in thinking skills can increase tested intelligence.

At the forefront of such efforts is Israeli psychologist Reuven Feuerstein (FOY-er-shtine). Feuerstein and his colleagues have developed a program they call Instrumental Enrichment. Through hundreds of hours of guided problem solving, students learn to avoid the thinking flaws that lower IQ scores (Feuerstein et al., 1986b). Feuerstein and others have shown that such training can improve thinking abilities

and even raise IQs (Kozulin, 1999; Skuy et al., 1995; Tzuriel & Alfassi, 1994).

Cognitive skills training is very time consuming. In recognition of this fact, psychologists are writing computer programs to teach problem solving, effective thinking, and other elements of intelligence. With our growing understanding of how people think, and with the tireless aid of computers, it may indeed become common in schools to "teach intelligence." Most important, improved education and training in thinking skills can improve the intellectual abilities of all children, regardless of what their IQ scores are (Hunt, 1995; Perkins, 1995). Even if "teaching intelligence" doesn't raise IQ scores, it can give children the abilities they need to think better and succeed in life (Perkins & Grotzer, 1997).

Stimulus

Processing

Response

❖ **FIGURE 12.8** *Attempts to measure the speed of mental processing have taken several forms. In this example, the person must make a rapid choice based on the position of a colored stimulus flashed on a computer screen. A faster reaction time is assumed to reflect faster processing of information. In some experiments, brain responses are measured directly, through electrodes attached to the scalp.*

NEW APPROACHES TO INTELLIGENCE—INTELLIGENT ALTERNATIVES

Until now, we have treated intelligence as a quality that can be measured, like height or weight. Recently, three new ways of looking at intelligence have emerged:

- Some psychologists are investigating the neural basis for intelligence. How, they ask, does the nervous system contribute to differences in IQ?
- A second new approach views intelligent behavior as an expression of thinking skills. Cognitive psychologists believe that the nervous system is like a fast computer—it's of little value unless you know how to use it.
- A third trend involves newer, broader definitions of intelligence. Many psychologists have begun to question the narrow focus on analytic thinking found in traditional IQ tests (Perkins, 1995).

The Intelligent Nervous System

Do intelligent people have faster nervous systems? In an attempt to answer this question, researchers are measuring how fast people process various kinds of information. For example, psychologists have looked at how long it takes people to react when making a choice (❖Fig. 12.8). The flurry of brain activity that follows exposure to a stimulus has also been recorded. Such studies attempt to measure a person's **speed of processing,** which is assumed to reflect the brain's speed and efficiency (Deary & Stough, 1996).

Does rapid information processing really have anything to do with intelligence? See "Inspecting Intelligence" for an answer.

INTELLIGENT INFORMATION PROCESSING

Much intelligent behavior is an expression of good thinking skills. Cognitive psychologist David Perkins believes that how smart you are depends on three factors:

- Relatively fixed **neural intelligence** (the speed and efficiency of the nervous system)
- **Experiential intelligence** (specialized knowledge and skills acquired over time)
- **Reflective intelligence** (an ability to become aware of one's own thinking habits)

Little can be done to change neural intelligence. However, by adding to personal knowledge and learning to think better, people can become more intelligent (Perkins, 1995). The effects of Feuerstein's Instrumental Enrichment program (described earlier) are a good example of how reflective intelligence can be improved.

Many psychologists now believe that to make full use of innate intelligence a person must have good **metacognitive**

Speed of processing *The speed with which a person can mentally process information.*
Inspection time *The amount of time a person must look at a stimulus to make a correct judgment about it.*
Neural intelligence *The innate speed and efficiency of a person's brain and nervous system.*
Experiential intelligence *Specialized knowledge and skills acquired through learning and experience.*
Reflective intelligence *An ability to become aware of one's own thinking habits.*
Metacognitive skills *An ability to manage one's own thinking and problem-solving efforts.*

INSPECTING INTELLIGENCE

Look quickly at ❖Figure 12.9a. Which "leg" of the drawing is longer, the right or the left? It's a pretty easy question, isn't it? However, if similar drawings are flashed on a screen for only a split second, the task becomes much harder. And, strange as it may seem, it may reveal something about intelligence.

Stimuli like those in ❖Figure 12.9 are used to measure **inspection time**—the amount of time a person must inspect (look at) a stimulus to make a correct judgment about it. In a real inspection time task, a stimulus like the one on the left appears for a few milliseconds. It is then followed immediately by a second stimulus, like 12.9b. (The second stimulus keeps people from using afterimages or sensory memory to make decisions about the first stimulus.)

In inspection time studies, we want to know how quickly a person's nervous system can take in enough information to make a correct decision. As simple as this measure may seem, it correlates about −.45 with IQ scores. (The correla-

tion is negative because shorter inspection times are associated with higher IQs.) So, to a degree, it appears that having a quick nervous system is, indeed, part of what it means to be quick, smart, swift, or brainy. (Sources: Bowling & Mackenzie, 1996; Deary & Stough, 1996.)

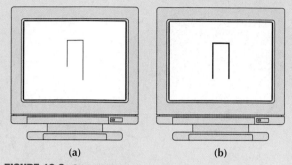

(a)　　　　　(b)

❖ **FIGURE 12.9** *Stimuli like those used in inspection time tasks.*

---

skills. *Meta* means "beyond," so metacognitive skills go above and beyond ordinary thinking. Such skills involve an ability to manage your own thinking and problem solving. Typically, this means breaking problems into parts, establishing goals and subgoals, monitoring your progress, and making corrections. Learning metacognitive skills is the surest avenue to becoming more intelligent (Hunt, 1995).

Multiple Intelligences

At an elementary school, a student who is two grades behind in reading shows his teacher how to solve a difficult computer programming problem. In a nearby room, one of his classmates, who is poor in math, plays an intricate piece of music on a piano. Both of these children show clear signs of intelligence. And yet, each might score below average on a traditional IQ test.

Such observations have convinced many psychologists that it is time to forge new, broader definitions of intelligence. Their basic goal is to better predict real-world success—not just the likelihood of success in school (Sternberg, 1996).

FRAMES OF MIND   One such psychologist is Howard Gardner of Harvard University. Gardner (1993) theorizes that there are actually eight different kinds of intelligence. These are different mental "languages" that people use for thinking. Each is listed next, with examples of pursuits that make use of them.

1. *language*—writer, lawyer, comedian
2. *logic and math*—scientist, accountant, programmer
3. *visual and spatial thinking*—engineer, inventor, artist
4. *music*—composer, musician, music critic
5. *bodily-kinesthetic skills*—dancer, athlete, surgeon
6. *intrapersonal skills* (self-knowledge)—poet, actor, minister
7. *interpersonal skills* (social abilities)—psychologist, teacher, politician

BRIDGES

Having metacognitive skills is a large part of what it means to be an expert in a particular topic or skill.

See Chapter 11, pages 359–360, for a discussion of expertise.

8. *naturalist skills* (an ability to classify plants and animals and understand the natural environment)—biologist, medicine man, organic farmer

Most of us are probably strong in only a few types of intelligence. In contrast, geniuses like Albert Einstein seem to be able to use all of the intelligences, as needed, to solve problems.

If Gardner's theory of **multiple intelligences** is correct, traditional IQ tests measure only a part of real-world intelligence—namely, linguistic, logical-mathematical, and spatial abilities. A further implication is that our schools may be wasting a lot of human potential. For example, some children might find it easier to learn math or reading if these topics were tied into art, music, dance, drama, and so on.

Not all psychologists agree with Gardner's broader definition of intelligence. His view, in fact, is at odds with studies that suggest that scores on IQ tests mainly reflect an underlying "general intelligence" or *general ability factor* (often referred to as *g*) (Neisser et al., 1996). This **g-factor** is said to explain the high correlations found among scores on various tests of intellectual ability and achievement (Robinson, 1999). Gardner's reply would probably be that such correlations show only how narrowly traditional tests define intelligence. In any case, it seems likely that in the future intelligence will not be so strongly equated with IQ. Already, many schools are using Gardner's theory to cultivate a wider range of skills and talents (Woo, 1995).

A LOOK AHEAD   As promised earlier, the Psychology in Action section of this chapter addresses questions concerning the validity of intelligence tests and their fairness to various groups. After that, we will go "a step beyond" to examine the controversies raised by intelligence testing in the school system. In addition to being highly interesting, these topics should round out your understanding of intelligence.

According to Howard Gardner's theory, bodily-kinesthetic skills reflect one of eight distinct types of intelligence.

KNOWLEDGE BUILDER

HEREDITY, ENVIRONMENT, AND NEW VIEWS OF INTELLIGENCE

RELATE

Why do you think studies of hereditary and environmental influences on intelligence have provoked such emotional debate? Which side of the debate would you expect each of the following people to favor: teacher, parent, school administrator, politician, medical doctor, liberal, conservative, bigot?

Would you rather have your own intelligence measured with a speed of processing test or a traditional IQ test? Why?

Here's a mnemonic: *New experiences reflect* three kinds of intelligence. Can you define *neural*, *experiential*, and *reflective* intelligence in your own words?

Make your own list of specialized intelligences. How many items on your list correspond to the eight intelligences identified by Gardner?

LEARNING CHECK

1. Selective breeding for desirable characteristics is called
   _____.

2. The closest similarity in IQs would be observed for
   a. parents and their children
   b. identical twins reared apart
   c. fraternal twins reared together
   d. siblings reared together

3. Most psychologists believe that intelligence is 90 percent hereditary. T or F?

4. Except for slight variations during testing, IQ cannot be changed. T or F?

5. Environmental effects are probably more capable of lowering IQ than of raising it. T or F?

6. Inspection time has been used as a measure of _____ intelligence.
   a. experiential b. neural c. reflective d. analytical

7. According to Howard Gardner's theory, which of the following is not measured by traditional IQ tests?
   a. intrapersonal skills b. spatial skills c. logical skills d. linguistic skills

CRITICAL THINKING

8. Dropping out of school can lower tested IQ and attending school can raise it. What do these observations reveal about intelligence tests?

Answers:

1. eugenics 2. b 3. F 4. F 5. T 6. b 7. a 8. Such observations remind us that intelligence tests are affected by learning and that they measure knowledge, as well as innate cognitive abilities.

Multiple intelligences *Howard Gardner's theory that there are several specialized types of intellectual ability.*
g-factor *A core of general intellectual ability that is assumed to explain the high correlations among various measures of intelligence.*

HOW INTELLIGENT ARE INTELLIGENCE TESTS?

During their lifetimes, most people take an intelligence test or one of the closely related scholastic aptitude tests. If you have ever taken an individually administered IQ test, you may actually know what your IQ is. If not, the following self-administered test will provide a rough estimate of your IQ. Most people are curious about how they would score on an intelligence test. Why not give the Dove Test a try?

Dove Counterbalance Intelligence Test

Time limit: 5 minutes.
Circle the correct answer.

1. T-bone Walker got famous for playing what?
   a. trombone   *b.* piano   *c.* T-flute   *d.* guitar
   e. "hambone"

2. A "gas head" is a person who has a
   a. fast-moving car   *b.* stable of "lace"   *c.* "process"
   d. habit of stealing cars   *e.* long jail record for arson

3. If you throw the dice and 7 is showing on the top, what is facing down?
   a. 7   *b.* snake eyes   *c.* boxcars   *d.* little joes   *e.* 11

4. Cheap chitlings (not the kind you purchase at a frozen-food counter) will taste rubbery unless they are cooked long enough. How soon can you quit cooking them to eat and enjoy them?
   a. 45 minutes   *b.* 2 hours   *c.* 24 hours
   d. 1 week (on a low flame)   *e.* 1 hour

5. Bird or Yardbird was the jacket jazz lovers from coast to coast hung on
   a. Lester Young   *b.* Peggy Lee   *c.* Benny Goodman
   d. Charlie Parker   *e.* Birdman of Alcatraz

6. A "handkerchief head" is
   a. a cool cat   *b.* a porter   *c.* an Uncle Tom   *d.* a hoddi
   e. a preacher

7. Jet is
   a. an East Oakland motorcycle club
   b. one of the gangs in West Side Story
   c. a news and gossip magazine
   d. a way of life for the very rich

8. "Bo Diddly" is a
   a. game for children   *b.* down-home cheap wine
   c. down-home singer   *d.* new dance   *e.* Moejoe call

9. Which word is most out of place here?
   a. splib   *b.* blood   *c.* gray   *d.* black   *e.* spook

10. If a pimp is uptight with a woman who gets state aid, what does he mean when he talks about "Mother's Day"?
    a. second Sunday in May   *b.* third Sunday in June
    c. first of every month   *d.* none of these
    e. first and fifteenth of every month

11. Many people say that "Juneteenth" (June 10) should be made a legal holiday because this was the day when
    a. the slaves were freed in the United States
    b. the slaves were freed in Texas
    c. the slaves were freed in Jamaica
    d. the slaves were freed in California
    e. Martin Luther King was born
    f. Booker T. Washington died

12. If a man is called a "blood," then he is a
    a. fighter   *b.* Mexican-American   *c.* Black
    d. hungry hemophile   *e.* red man or Indian

13. What are the Dixie Hummingbirds?
    a. a part of the KKK
    b. a swamp disease
    c. a modern gospel group
    d. a Mississippi Negro paramilitary strike force
    e. deacons

14. The opposite of square is
    a. round.   *b.* up   *c.* down   *d.* hip   *e.* lame

Answers: 1. *d*   2. *c*   3. *a*   4. *c*   5. *d*   6. *c*   7. *c*   8. *c*   9. *c*   10. *e*   11. *b*   12. *c*   13. *c*   14. *d*

If you scored 14 on this exam, your IQ is approximately 100, indicating average intelligence. If you scored 10 or less, you are mentally retarded. With luck and the help of a special educational program, we may be able to teach you a few simple skills!

Isn't the Dove Test a little unfair?   No, it is *very* unfair. It was written by African American sociologist Adrian Dove as "a half serious attempt to show that we're just not talking the same language." Dove tried to slant his test as much in favor of urban African American culture as he believes the typical intelligence test is biased toward a white middle-class background. (Because of its age, the test is probably now also unfair for anyone under 30.)

Dove's test is a thought-provoking reply to the fact that African American children in the United States score an average of about 15 points lower on standardized IQ tests than Anglo-American children. By reversing the bias, Dove has shown that intelligence tests are not equally valid for all groups. As Jerome Kagan says, "If the Wechsler and Binet scales were translated into Spanish, Swahili, and Chinese and given to every 10-year-old in Latin America, East Africa, or China, the majority would obtain IQ scores in the mentally retarded range." The problem is that people in other cultures do not share the same values, knowledge, and language patterns that underlie IQ tests written for use in North America (Greenfield, 1997).

Culture-Fair Testing

Certainly, we cannot believe that children of different cultures are all retarded. The fault must lie in the test. Cultural values, traditions, and experiences can greatly affect performance on tests designed for Western cultures (Neisser et al., 1996; Nixon, 1990). To avoid this problem, some psychologists have tried to develop culture-fair tests that do not disadvantage certain groups. A **culture-fair test** is designed to minimize the importance of skills and knowledge that may be more common in some cultures than in others. (For a sample of culture-fair test items, see ❖Figure 12.10.) Culture-fair tests attempt to measure intelligence without, as much as possible, being influenced by a person's verbal skills, cultural background, and educational level. Their value lies not just in testing people from other cultures. They are also useful for testing children in the United States who come from poor communities, rural areas, and ethnic minority families (Stephens et al., 1999).

THE BELL CURVE—RACE, CULTURE, AND IQ

Biased tests are not the only IQ issue blacks have confronted. In 1994, Richard Herrnstein and Charles Murray proclaimed, in a book titled *The Bell Curve*, that African Americans score below average in IQ because of their "genetic heritage." Herrnstein and Murray's most inflammatory claim is that the poor, whatever ethnic group they may belong to, are genetically incapable of climbing out of poverty (Herrnstein & Murray, 1994).

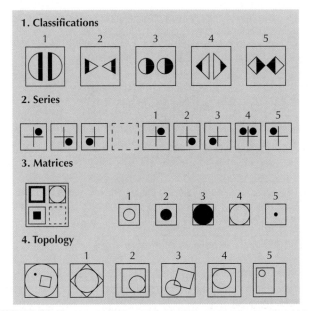

1. Classifications

2. Series

3. Matrices

4. Topology

❖ **FIGURE 12.10** *No intelligence test can be entirely free of cultural bias. However, culture-fair intelligence tests try to minimize the effects of growing up in various cultures. The sample items above are from a culture-fair test. 1. Which pattern is different from the remaining four? (Number 3.) 2. Which of the five figures on the right would properly continue the three on the left—that is, fill the blank? (Number 5.) 3. Which of the figures on the right should go in the square on the left to make it look right? (Number 2.) 4. At left, the dot is outside the square and inside the circle. In which of the figures on the right could you put a dot outside the square and inside the circle? (Number 3.) (Courtesy of R. B. Cattell.)*

Psychologists have responded to such claims with a number of counterarguments. First, it is no secret that as a group blacks in the United States are more likely than whites to live in environments that are physically, educationally, and intellectually impoverished. When unequal education is part of the equation, IQs tell us little about how heredity affects intelligence (Neisser et al., 1996).

A second argument against Herrnstein and Murray is that they overlook the point made by the Dove Test. The assumptions, biases, and content of standard IQ tests do not always allow meaningful comparisons between ethnic, cultural, and racial groups (Helms, 1992; Miller-Jones, 1989). As Leon Kamin (1981) says, "The important fact is that we cannot say which sex (or race) might be more intelligent, because we have no way of measuring 'intelligence.' We have only IQ tests."

Kamin's point is that the makers of IQ tests decided in advance to use test items that would give men and women equal IQ scores. It would be just as easy to put together an IQ test that would give blacks and whites equal scores. Differences in IQ scores are not a fact of nature but a decision by the test makers. This is why whites do better on IQ tests written by whites, and blacks do better on IQ tests devised by blacks. Another example of this fact is an intelligence test made up of 100 words selected from the *Dictionary of Afro-American Slang*. Williams (1975) gave the test to 100 black and 100 white high school students in St. Louis and found that the black group averaged 36 points higher than the white group.

Recently, a distinguished group of psychologists evaluated the claims made in *The Bell Curve*. They concluded there is no scientific evidence that group differences in average IQ are based on genetics. In fact, studies that used actual blood-group testing found no significant correlations between ethnic ancestry and IQ scores. The conclusions that Herrnstein and Murray drew in *The Bell Curve* reflect their political beliefs and biases, not scientific facts. Group differences in IQ scores are based on cultural and environmental differences, not on heredity (Neisser et al., 1996; Williams & Ceci, 1997).

QUESTIONING IQ—BEYOND THE NUMBERS GAME

African Americans are not the only segment of the population with reason to question the validity of intelligence testing and the role of heredity in determining intelligence. The clarifications they have won extend to others as well.

Consider the 9-year-old child confronted with this question on an intelligence test: "Which of the following does not belong with the others? Roller skates, airplane, train, bicycle." If the child fails to answer "airplane," does it reveal a lack of intelligence? It can be argued that an intelligent choice could be based on any of these alternatives: Roller skates are not typically used

Culture-fair test *A test designed to minimize the importance of skills and knowledge that may be more common in some cultures than in others.*

for transportation; an airplane is the only non-land item; a train can't be steered; a bicycle is the only item with just two wheels. The parents of a child who misses this question may have reason to be angry because educational systems tend to classify children and then make the label stick.

Recent court decisions have led some states to outlaw the use of intelligence tests in public schools (see the A Step Beyond section). Criticism of intelligence testing has also come from the academic community. Harvard University psychologist David McClelland believes that IQ is of little value in predicting real competence to deal effectively with the world. McClelland concedes that IQ predicts school performance, but when he compared a group of college students with straight A's to another group with poor grades, he found no differences in later career success (McClelland, 1973, 1994).

STANDARDIZED TESTING

In addition to IQ tests, 400 to 500 million standardized multiple-choice tests are given in schools and workplaces around the nation each year. Many, like the *Scholastic Assessment Test,* may determine whether a person is admitted to college. Other tests—for employment, licensing, and certification—directly affect the lives of thousands by qualifying or disqualifying them for jobs.

Widespread reliance on standardized intelligence tests and aptitude tests raises questions about the relative good and harm they do. On the positive side, tests can open opportunities as well as close them. A high test score may allow a disadvantaged youth to enter college, or it may identify a child who is bright but emotionally disturbed. Test scores may also be fairer and more objective than arbitrary judgments made by admissions officers or employment interviewers. Also, tests *do* accurately predict academic performance. The fact that academic performance *does not* predict later success may call for an overhaul of college course work, not an end to testing.

On the negative side, mass testing can occasionally exclude people of obvious ability. In one case, a student who was seventh in his class at Columbia University, and a member of Phi Beta Kappa, was denied entrance to law school because he had low scores on the *Law School Admissions Test.* Other complaints relate to the frequent appearance of bad or ambiguous questions on standardized tests, overuse of class time to prepare students for the tests (instead of teaching general skills), and in the case of intelligence tests, the charge that tests are often biased. Also, most standardized tests demand passive recognition of facts, assessed with a multiple-choice format. They do not, for the most part, test a person's ability to think critically or creatively or to apply knowledge to solve problems (Jones & Appelbaum, 1989).

What should we make of the positive and negative aspects of standardized testing? Robert Glaser says we should remember that tests are "limited tools for limited purposes." Glaser also says that tests are now used primarily to *select* people. In schools, they could instead be used to *adapt* instruction to the

strengths, weaknesses, and needs of each student—thereby increasing the chances of success.

CONCLUSION

An application of the preceding discussion to your personal understanding of intelligence can be summarized in this way: Intelligence tests are a two-edged sword; we have learned much from their use, yet they have the potential to do great harm. In the final analysis, it is important to remember—as Howard Gardner has pointed out—that creativity, motivation, physical health, mechanical aptitude, artistic ability, and numerous other qualities not measured by intelligence tests contribute to the achievement of life goals. Also remember that IQ is not intelligence. IQ is an *index* of intelligence (as narrowly defined by a particular test). Change the test and you change the score. An IQ is not some permanent number stamped on the forehead of a child that forever determines his or her potential. The real issue is what skills people have, not what their test scores are (Hunt, 1995).

KNOWLEDGE BUILDER

INTELLIGENCE TESTING IN PERSPECTIVE

RELATE

Do you think it would be possible to create an intelligence test that is universally culture-fair? What would its questions look like? Can you think of any type of question that wouldn't favor the mental skills emphasized by some culture, somewhere in the world?

Funding for schools in some states varies greatly in rich and poor neighborhoods. Imagine that a politician opposes spending more money on disadvantaged students because she believes it would "just be a waste." Using the controversy surrounding *The Bell Curve* as a guide, what arguments can you offer against her assertion?

In your own opinion, what are the advantages of using standardized tests to select applicants for college, graduate school, and professional schools? What are the disadvantages?

LEARNING CHECK

1. The WAIS-III, Binet-4, and Dove Test are all culture-fair intelligence scales. T or F?

2. Herrnstein and Murray's claim that heredity accounts for racial differences in average IQ ignores environmental differences and the cultural bias inherent in standard IQ tests. T or F?

3. IQ scores predict school performance. T or F?

4. IQ is not intelligence; it is one index of intelligence. T or F?

CRITICAL THINKING

5. Assume that a test of memory for words is translated from English to Spanish. Would the Spanish version of the test be equal in difficulty to the English version?

Answers:

1. F 2. T 3. T 4. T 5. Probably not, because the Spanish words might be longer or shorter than the same words in English. The Spanish words might also sound more or less alike than words on the original test. Translating an intelligence test into another language can subtly change the meaning and difficulty of test items.

Focus: Should IQ tests be used to classify children for placement in school?

- **The Case:** *Larry P. v. the California State Superintendent of Education.*
- **The Issue:** Larry P. is one of six African American children who claim that biased IQ test scores were wrongly used to place them in classes for the educable mentally retarded (EMR).
- **The Outcome:** In a landmark decision, a federal judge ruled that IQ test scores alone can no longer be used for EMR placement.

The ruling has virtually eliminated IQ testing in California schools. Similar rulings in other states have had the same effect (Kamphaus, 1993). The bare facts of the Larry P. case only hint at the interesting issues it raised. Testimony during the trial brought out the following:

- **For Larry P.:** All six youngsters suing the state had scored below 75 on standardized IQ tests. But they scored from 17 to 35 points higher when retested by psychologists who used language and examples the children were familiar with.
- **For the State:** Experts admitted that IQ test questions can be easier for some groups than for others. However, they held that IQ tests accurately predict school performance and are therefore valid.
- **For Larry P.:** Witnesses pointed out that EMR assignments are almost always permanent. They also described the devastating effects of placing a child of normal intelligence in an EMR class. One researcher found that other students commonly refer to EMR students with cruel nicknames. EMR students are not expected to progress beyond the third- to fifth-grade level. Thus, by the time of graduation, a child of normal intelligence would be hopelessly behind other students. After graduation, EMR students find it difficult to get jobs, because they have been labeled "retarded."
- **For the State:** Defense experts claimed that IQ tests help prevent mistakes in EMR assignments—for example, by revealing the true potential of a child who might be considered "slow" by a biased teacher. They also defended the EMR program as an effort to help less able students.
- **For Larry P.:** Roughly twice as many African American and Latino children are found in EMR classes than would be expected based on the percentage of African Americans and Latinos in the general population. This fact suggests a defect in the tests, not in the children.

IGNORANCE VS. STUPIDITY In the end, the judge ruled that IQ tests violate federal antidiscrimination laws. He was convinced, he said, that they are based mainly on verbal tasks that are unfair to children whose home environment does not provide practice in formal English or verbal skills. He further held that "if tests suggest that a young child is probably going to be a poor student, the school cannot, on that basis alone, deny that child the opportunity to develop and improve the academic skills necessary for success in our society."

Supporters of the Larry P. decision believe that it affirms the rights of disadvantaged children, whose ignorance—a lack of knowledge—has been mistaken for stupidity—a lack of intelligence. One such supporter is Jane Mercer, a sociologist who gave key testimony in the case.

SIX-HOUR RETARDATES Mercer testified that the more a child's family is like the average white Anglo middle-class norm, the better the child scores on IQ tests. Mercer believes that schools often label children retarded, when actually the children lack only culturally tied knowledge. Mercer has found that many African American or Latino EMR students show abundant signs of normal intelligence. A child who does poorly in the classroom or on an IQ test may function perfectly well at home and in the community. Mercer refers to such children as "six-hour retardates"—youngsters who are "retarded" only during the school day.

SOMPA *If standardized IQ tests cannot be used to assess student abilities, what can?* Mercer and her associate June Lewis think they have an answer. They call it SOMPA, which stands for *System of Multicultural Pluralistic Assessment*. SOMPA is not a new test. Rather, it's a different way of looking at children.

How does SOMPA differ from standard IQ tests? SOMPA combines three ways of assessing a child. First, it looks for any medical problems that may be causing low school performance. Next, the child's behavior outside the classroom is evaluated to avoid the mistake of creating a "six-hour retardate" on the basis of a test score. Third, SOMPA assumes that when everything else is held constant (educational advantages at home, especially), the child who has learned the most probably has the most "learning potential." Off-campus environments, however, are not equal. SOMPA therefore assumes that true potential can be masked by a child's cultural background. To avoid this problem, SOMPA compares each child's WISC score with that of children from similar backgrounds.

To show how SOMPA works, Mercer offers an example. Maria Gonzales is 7. She lives with her mother, father, and five brothers and sisters in an inner-city barrio. Maria's mother and father both grew up in rural Mexico, where the mother finished fourth grade and the father second grade. Maria's family speaks only Spanish.

The average score for a child like Maria—with a background so different from core Anglo culture—is about 85. Maria's score on the WISC was 114, almost 30 points above this

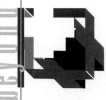
average. Mercer estimates Maria's real learning potential at 133. If her family had been more like the middle-class norm, Maria's score of 114 would have been accepted as accurate. Considering her age and background, Maria's performance on the WISC is truly outstanding. Maria is probably a gifted child whose potential should not be wasted.

MORE IQ CONTROVERSY   In 1986, Judge Robert Peckham, who issued the original opinion, reiterated the California IQ test ban. In fact, he added to it, saying, "The prohibition on IQ tests goes further and prohibits any use of an IQ test as part of an assessment which could lead to special education placement or services, even if the test is only part of a comprehensive assessment plan" (Landers, 1986). This directive pretty much eliminated any form of IQ tests, even SOMPA, for evaluating African American children.

Soon after Judge Peckham's ruling, a group of African American parents filed a suit claiming that the ban on IQ testing discriminated against their children. It was nearly impossible, they pointed out, to use tests to identify learning disabilities or other problems if a child was making poor progress in school. In 1992, Judge Peckham revised his decision again. Children could be tested for learning disabilities, he decided, if their parents requested it. The ban on routine use of IQ tests for placement in EMR classes remains in effect, however (Turkington, 1992).

THE STATE OF THE DEBATE   Understandably, the Larry P. decision and those that followed remain controversial. Some psychologists object to the courts making educational decisions. Others point out that they must now resort to nonstandard alternative measures. Many of these alternatives are subjective and open to potential abuse. It may become easier, for instance, to rid classrooms of "problem children"—late bloomers, troublemakers, quirky learners—who may not be intellectually deficient but just need more attention and understanding. Without IQ tests, how can such children be identified?

A typical reply from critics of IQ testing is that an IQ gives little information about the cause of a low score. It therefore tells little about what corrective action should be taken. To improve mental ability, IQ scores are not needed. The purpose of school is to help children learn and develop skills needed in adjusting to life and work (Baumeister, 1987).

In the years since the Larry P. case, studies of traditional intelligence tests continue to show that IQ tests predict school performance quite well (Neisser et al., 1996). Thus, it is fair to ask: Should a child who is intelligent, but educationally disadvantaged, be placed in a class that is too advanced for his or her ability level? Certainly, it is damaging to be falsely labeled "retarded." However, it can also be damaging to place children in

classes for which they are unprepared. In view of such dilemmas, some psychologists believe it is a serious mistake to ban IQ testing in the schools (Lopez, 1997).

WHAT DO YOU THINK?   If you were the judge in the Larry P. case, how would you have ruled? If you were a school psychologist, how would you feel about using IQ tests or alternatives such as SOMPA? In your opinion, what role should IQ tests have in a democratic society?

Conclusion: There are no simple answers to questions concerning IQ testing in public schools. Testing benefits some students, but it can be unfair to others. The goal of placing students in appropriate educational settings may be better served by measures other than traditional IQ tests.

K N O W L E D G E   B U I L D E R

IQ TESTING AND SCHOOL PLACEMENT

RELATE

How much impact do you think classification and labeling have on children in the school system? Do you think that a child could be harmed by being inaccurately labeled as a slow learner? What if an average child is labeled as gifted or placed in accelerated classes? Should children be assessed and classified for placement in schools? If so, how?

LEARNING CHECK

1. The basic issue of the Larry P. case was whether children's IQs are lowered by placement in EMR classes. T or F?

2. Before the Larry P. case, placement in EMR classes was almost always done on the basis of group IQ test scores. T or F?

3. SOMPA is designed to obtain IQ scores from an assessment of a child's physical health and social functioning. T or F?

4. In the SOMPA system, IQ scores are compared to norms for children of similar cultural and social backgrounds. T or F?

5. According to the latest ruling, IQ tests can be used for educational placement in California EMR programs only when they are part of a comprehensive assessment plan. T or F?

CRITICAL THINKING

6. Much of the Larry P. case centered on whether IQ tests are accurate measures of intelligence for all children. In other words, the debate revolved around the _____ of IQ tests.

Answers:

1. F 2. T 3. F 4. T 5. F 6. validity

CHAPTER IN REVIEW

How do psychologists define intelligence?

- Intelligence refers to one's general capacity to act purposefully, think rationally, and deal effectively with the environment.
- In practice, intelligence is operationally defined by the creation of intelligence tests.
- General intelligence is distinguished from specific aptitudes. Special aptitude tests and multiple aptitude tests are used to assess a person's capacities for learning various abilities. Aptitude tests measure a narrower range of abilities than general intelligence tests do.

What are the qualities of a good psychological test?

- To be of any value, a psychological test must be reliable (give consistent results). A worthwhile test must also have validity, meaning that it measures what it claims to measure.
- Widely used intelligence tests are objective (they give the same result when scored by different people) and standardized (the same procedures are always used in giving the test, and norms have been established so that scores can be interpreted).

What are typical IQ tests like?

- The first practical intelligence test was assembled by Alfred Binet. A modern version of Binet's test is the *Stanford-Binet Intelligence Scale, Fourth Edition*. A second major intelligence test is the *Wechsler Adult Intelligence Scale–Third Edition (WAIS-III)*. The WAIS-III measures both verbal and performance intelligence.
- In addition to individual tests, intelligence tests have also been produced for use with groups. A group test of historical interest is the *Army Alpha*. The SAT, the ACT, and the CQT are group scholastic aptitude tests. Although narrower in scope than IQ tests, they bear some similarities to them.

How do IQ scores relate to gender, age, and occupation?

- Intelligence is expressed in terms of an intelligence quotient (IQ). IQ is defined as mental age (MA) divided by chronological age (CA) and then multiplied by 100. An "average" IQ of 100 occurs when mental age equals chronological age.
- Modern IQ tests no longer calculate IQs directly. Instead, the final score reported by the test is a deviation IQ.
- IQ scores become fairly stable at about age 6, and they become increasingly reliable thereafter. On the average, IQ scores continue to gradually increase until middle age. Later intellectual declines are moderate for most people until their 70s. A few years before death, a more significant terminal decline in intelligence is often observed.
- The distribution of IQ scores approximates a normal curve. There are no overall differences between males and females in tested intelligence. However, very small gender differences may result from the intellectual skills our culture encourages males and females to develop.
- IQ is related to school grades and job status. The second association may be somewhat artificial because educational credentials are required for entry into many occupations.

What does IQ tell us about genius?

- People with IQs in the gifted or "genius" range of above 140 tend to be superior in many respects.
- By criteria other than IQ, a large proportion of children might be considered gifted or talented in one way or another. Intellectually gifted children often have difficulties in average classrooms and benefit from special accelerated programs.

What causes mental retardation?

- The terms *mentally retarded* and *developmentally disabled* are applied to those whose IQ falls below 70 or who lack various adaptive behaviors.
- Further classifications of retardation are mild (50–55 to 70), moderate (35–40 to 50–55), severe (20–25 to 35–40), and profound (below 20–25). Chances for educational success are related to the degree of retardation.
- About 50 percent of the cases of mental retardation are organic, being caused by birth injuries, fetal damage, metabolic disorders, or genetic abnormalities. The remaining cases are of undetermined cause.
- Many cases of subnormal intelligence are thought to be the result of familial retardation, a generally low level of educational and intellectual stimulation in the home, coupled with poverty and poor nutrition.
- Six distinct forms of organic retardation are phenylketonuria (PKU), microcephaly, hydrocephaly, cretinism, Down syndrome, and fragile-X syndrome.

How do heredity and environment affect intelligence?

- Studies of eugenics in animals and familial relationships in humans demonstrate that intelligence is partially determined by heredity. However, environment is also important, as revealed by changes in tested intelligence induced by schooling and stimulating environments.
- There is evidence that some elements of intelligence can be taught. Intelligence therefore reflects the combined effects of both heredity and environment in the development of intellectual abilities.

How have views of intelligence changed in recent years?

- Some psychologists are investigating the *neural basis* for intelligence, especially the speed of processing various kinds of information.
- Cognitive psychologists believe that successful intelligence depends on thinking and problem-solving skills. Metacognitive skills, in particular, contribute greatly to intelligent behavior.
- Many psychologists have begun to forge new, broader definitions of intelligence. Howard Gardner's theory of multiple intelligences is a good example of this trend.

Are IQ tests fair to all racial and cultural groups?

- Traditional IQ tests often suffer from a degree of cultural bias. For this and other reasons, it is wise to remember that IQ is merely an index of intelligence and that intelligence is narrowly defined by most tests.
- The use of standard IQ tests for educational placement of students (especially into special education classes) has been prohibited by law in some states. Whether this is desirable and beneficial to students is currently being debated.

PSYCHOLOGY ON THE NET

- **Be Careful of How You Define Intelligence** An article about cross-cultural differences in intelligence. http://www.apa.org/monitor/oct97/define.html
- **Helping Your Highly Gifted Child** Advice for parents of gifted children. http://www.kidsource.com/kidsource/content/help.gift.html
- **Introduction to Mental Retardation** Answers to basic question about mental retardation. http://TheArc.org/faqs/mrqa.html
- **IQ Tests** Provides links to a number of IQ tests. http://www.stud.ntnu.no/studorg/mensa/iq.html
- **The Bell Curve Flattened** An article that summarizes objections to *The Bell Curve*. http://www.slate.com/Features/BellCurve/BellCurve.asp

- **The Knowns and Unknowns of Intelligence** From the APA, what is known about intelligence and intelligence tests. http://www.apa.org/releases/intell.html
  - **InfoTrac® College Edition** For more information on the controversy concerning the book *The Bell Curve*, use Key Words search for BELL CURVE.

INTERACTIVE LEARNING

- *Psyk.trek* 7a. Types of psychological tests. 7b. Key concepts in testing. 7c. Understanding IQ. 7d. Heredity, environment, and intelligence.

13

Motivation and Emotion

FLIGHT OF THE *GOSSAMER ALBATROSS*

What would it feel like to pedal an airplane over the English Channel? Bryan Allen found out the hard way as he fought head winds, searing thirst, leg cramps, and exhaustion. Allen was the pilot and "engine" for the first human-powered flight from England to France. Bryan's 3-hour ordeal in the Gossamer Albatross, a delicate aircraft, took him to the limits of human endurance. The following excerpts are from his (1979) personal account:

> 6:59 A.M. At last, word comes over the radio. . . . "We have France in sight—four miles to go. . . ."
>
> Four miles or four hundred. I'm fading now and know it. Gradually the head winds have been building up. . . . I talk to myself. . . . Don't give up now, you *can* do it! As I waver between hope and despair, the radio crackles again:
>
> "Altitude six inches, six inches; get it up, you've got to get it up!"
>
> 7:29 A.M. One mile. Less distance than I had flown *Gossamer Condor* two years before for the original Kremer prize. Then, however, there were no head winds or turbulence, no thirst, no cramps. . . . Despite the cramps, I struggle back up to five feet. "Against all hope," I repeat to myself, "against all hope."
>
> 7:36 A.M. Four hundred yards to shore. . . . One hundred yards now. I am running on reserves I never knew I had. . . .

This chapter is about the motives and emotions underlying Bryan Allen's behavior—and your own. Bryan's final burst of effort ("I am running on reserves I never knew I had") is but one example of the many links between emotion and motivation. Our discussion will begin with basic motives, such as hunger and thirst, and

end with a look at how emotions affect us. Although emotion can be the spice of life, it is sometimes the spice of death as well. Read on to find out why.

Gateways to Motivation and Emotion

MOTIVES AND GOALS *greatly influence what we do and how we expend our energies.*

BASIC MOTIVES, *such as hunger and thirst, are controlled by internal signals monitored within the brain.*

MOTIVATED BEHAVIOR *is also influenced by learned habits, external cues, and cultural values.*

NUMEROUS ACTIVITIES *are related to our needs for stimulation and our efforts to maintain desired levels of arousal.*

MANY NEEDS AND MOTIVES *are learned.*

EMOTIONS *can be disruptive, but overall they help us adapt to environmental challenges.*

THE MOST EFFECTIVE "DIET" *is one that changes eating habits and exercise levels.*

IN ITS IDEAL FORM, ROMANTIC LOVE *is a combination of passion, intimacy, and commitment. However, many long-term relationships are built on companionship, intimacy, mutual respect, shared interests, and firm friendship.*

MOTIVATION—FORCES THAT PUSH AND PULL

We move. We seek some goals more vigorously than others. People may pursue the same goal for different reasons. Or, we may strive to reach different goals for the same reason. The concept **motivation** refers to these dynamics of behavior—the ways in which our actions are *initiated, sustained,* and *directed* (Petri, 1996).

Can you clarify that? Yes. Let's relate the concept of motivation to a simple sequence of activity:

> Marcelina is studying (psychology, of course) in the library. She begins to feel hungry and can't concentrate. Her stomach growls. She grows restless and decides to buy an apple from a vending machine. The machine is empty, so she goes to the cafeteria. Closed. Marcelina drives home, where she prepares a meal and eats. At last her hunger is satisfied, and she again resumes studying.

Marcelina's food seeking was *initiated* by her bodily need for food, it was *sustained* because her need was not immediately met, and her activities were *directed* by possible sources of food. Notice, too, that her food seeking was *terminated* by achieving her goal.

A Model of Motivation

Many motivated activities begin with a **need** (an internal deficiency). The need that initiated Marcelina's search was a depletion of substances within the cells of her body. Needs cause a **drive** (an energized motivational state) to develop. The drive was hunger, in Marcelina's case. Drives activate a **response** (an action or series of actions) designed to attain a **goal** (the target of motivated behavior). A goal that satisfies the original need ends the motivational sequence. Thus, a simple model of motivation can be shown in this way:

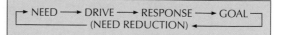

$$\rightarrow \text{NEED} \longrightarrow \text{DRIVE} \longrightarrow \text{RESPONSE} \longrightarrow \text{GOAL} \neg$$
$$\text{(NEED REDUCTION)} \longleftarrow$$

Why use the terms need *and* drive? *Aren't they the same thing?* No, we need both terms because the strength of needs and drives can differ. If you begin fasting today, your bodily need for food will increase every day. However, you would probably be less "hungry" on the seventh day of fasting than you were on the first. While your need for food steadily increases, the hunger drive comes and goes.

Before we assume that we have a complete model of motivation, let us observe Marcelina's eating behavior on another occasion:

> For dinner, Marcelina has just eaten soup, salad, a large steak, a large baked potato, one half of a loaf of bread, two pieces of cheesecake, and four cups of coffee. After the meal, she complains that she is "too full" from eating so much food. Soon after, Marcelina's roommate arrives with a strawberry pie. Marcelina exclaims that strawberry pie is her favorite dessert and eats three good-sized pieces!

Is this hunger? Certainly, Marcelina's extra-large meal was enough to satisfy her biological needs for food.

How does that change the model of motivation? Marcelina's story illustrates that motivated behavior can be energized by the "pull" of external stimuli, as well as by the "push" of internal needs.

<u>INCENTIVES</u> The pull exerted by a goal is called its **incentive value** (a goal's appeal beyond its ability to fill a need). Some goals are so desirable (strawberry pie, for example) that they motivate behavior in the absence of an internal need. Other goals are so low in incentive value that they will be rejected even though they might meet the internal need. Fresh, live grubworms, for instance, are considered a delicacy in some parts of the world, but it is doubtful that you would eat one no matter how hungry you might be.

In most cases, actions are energized by both internal needs *and* external incentives. In addition, a strong need may make a less attractive incentive into a desirable goal. You may never have eaten a grubworm, but chances are you've eaten some pretty horrible leftovers when the refrigerator was bare. Incentives also help account for motives that do not seem to have any identifiable internal need, such as drives for success, status, or approval (❖Fig. 13.1).

<u>TYPES OF MOTIVES</u> For the purpose of study, motives can be divided into three major categories:

1. **Primary motives** are based on biological needs that must be met for survival. The most important primary motives are hunger, thirst, pain avoidance, and needs for air, sleep, elimination of wastes, and regulation of body temperature. Primary motives are innate.
2. **Stimulus motives** are needs for stimulation and information. Examples include activity, curiosity, exploration, manipulation, and physical contact. Although such motives also appear to be innate, they are not strictly necessary for survival.
3. **Secondary motives** are based on learned needs, drives, and goals. Learned motives account for the great diversity of activities suggested by Bryan Allen's historic flight. Many secondary motives are related to learned needs for power, affiliation (the need to be with others), approval, status, security, and achievement. Fear and aggression also appear to be affected by learning.

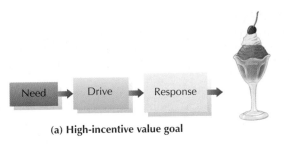

(a) High-incentive value goal

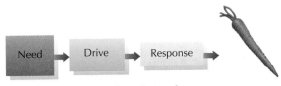

(b) Low-incentive value goal

❖ **FIGURE 13.1** *Needs and incentives interact to determine drive strength (above). (a) Moderate need combined with a high-incentive goal produces a strong drive. (b) Even when a strong need exists, drive strength may be moderate if a goal's incentive value is low. It is important to remember, however, that incentive value lies "in the eye of the beholder" (photo). No matter how hungry, few people would be able to eat the pictured grubworms.*

Motivation *Internal processes that initiate, sustain, and direct activities.*
Need *An internal deficiency that may energize behavior.*
Drive *The psychological expression of internal needs or valued goals, for example, hunger, thirst, or a drive for success.*
Response *Any action, glandular activity, or other identifiable behavior.*
Goal *The target or objective of motivated behavior.*
Incentive value *The value of a goal above and beyond its ability to fill a need.*
Primary motives *Innate motives based on biological needs.*
Stimulus motives *Innate needs for stimulation and information.*
Secondary motives *Motives based on learned needs, drives, and goals.*

PRIMARY MOTIVES AND HOMEOSTASIS—KEEPING THE HOME FIRES BURNING

How important is food in your life? Water? Sleep? Air? Temperature regulation? Finding a public rest room? For most of us, satisfying biological needs is so routine that we tend to overlook how much of our behavior they direct. But exaggerate any of these needs through famine, shipwreck, poverty, near-drowning, bitter cold, or drinking 10 cups of coffee, and their powerful grip on behavior becomes evident. We are, after all, still animals in many ways.

Biological drives are essential because they maintain **homeostasis** (HOE-me-oh-STAY-sis), or bodily equilibrium (Cannon, 1932).

What is homeostasis? The term *homeostasis* means "standing steady," or "steady state." Within the body there are "ideal" levels for body temperature, for the concentration of chemicals in the blood, for blood pressure, and so forth. When the body deviates from these ideal levels, automatic reactions restore equilibrium. You might find it helpful to think of homeostatic mechanisms as being similar to a thermostat set at a particular temperature.

A (Very) Short Course on Thermostats

When room temperature falls below the level set on a thermostat, the heat is automatically turned on to warm the room. When the heat equals or slightly exceeds the ideal temperature, it is automatically turned off. In this way, room temperature is kept in a state of equilibrium hovering around the ideal level.

In the human body, the first reactions to disequilibrium are also automatic. For example, if you become too hot, blood flow to the surface of your body will increase, and you will begin to perspire, thus lowering body temperature. We become aware of homeostasis only when disequilibrium drives us to seek shade, warmth, food, or water.

Because hunger is one of the most interesting and better understood of the primary drives, we will examine it in detail before we discuss biological drives in general. Before reading more, you may find it helpful to complete the learning exercises that follow.

KNOWLEDGE BUILDER

OVERVIEW OF MOTIVATION

RELATE

Motives help explain why we do what we do. See if you can think of something you do that illustrates the concepts of need, drive, response, and goal. Does the goal in your example vary in incentive value? What effects do high- and low-incentive value goals have on your behavior?

Mentally list some primary motives you have satisfied today. Some stimulus motives. Some secondary motives. How did each influence your behavior?

LEARNING CHECK

1. Motives _____, sustain, and _____ activities.

2. Needs provide the _____ of motivation, whereas incentives provide the _____.

Classify the following needs or motives by placing the correct letter in the blank.

A. Primary motive   **B.** Stimulus motive   **C.** Secondary motive

3. _____ curiosity   6. _____ thirst

4. _____ status   7. _____ achievement

5. _____ sleep   8. _____ physical contact

9. The maintenance of bodily equilibrium is called thermostasis. T or F?

10. A goal high in incentive value may create a drive in the absence of any internal need. T or F?

CRITICAL THINKING

11. There's an old saying that "You can lead a horse to water, but you can't make him drink." Can you restate this in motivational terms?

12. Many people mistakenly believe that they suffer from "hypoglycemia," which is often blamed for fatigue, difficulty in concentrating, irritability, and other symptoms. Why is it unlikely that many people actually have hypoglycemia?

Answers:

1. initiate, direct 2. push, pull 3. B 4. C 5. A 6. A 7. C 8. B 9. F 10. T 11. Providing an incentive (water) will not automatically lead to drinking in the absence of an internal need for water. 12. Because of homeostasis: Blood sugar is normally maintained within narrow bounds. Although blood sugar levels fluctuate enough to affect hunger, true hypoglycemia is an infrequent medical problem.

HUNGER—PARDON ME, THAT'S JUST MY HYPOTHALAMUS GROWLING

What causes hunger? When you feel hungry, you probably associate a desire for food with sensations from your stomach. This, sensibly enough, is where the search for hunger began. In an early study, Cannon and Washburn decided to see if the contractions of an empty stomach cause hunger. To do this, Washburn trained himself to swallow a balloon. The balloon was then inflated inside his stomach, through an attached tube. This allowed Washburn's stomach contractions to be recorded (❖Fig. 13.2). Cannon and Washburn observed that when Washburn's stomach contracted, he felt "hunger pangs." They concluded that hunger is nothing more than stomach contractions (Cannon & Washburn, 1912). (Unfortunately, this proved to be an inflated conclusion.)

Perhaps you already guessed that something more than the stomach is involved in hunger. For many people, hunger produces an overall feeling of weakness or shakiness that seems unrelated to the stomach. Of course, eating *is* limited when the stomach is distended (full). (Remember last Thanksgiving?)

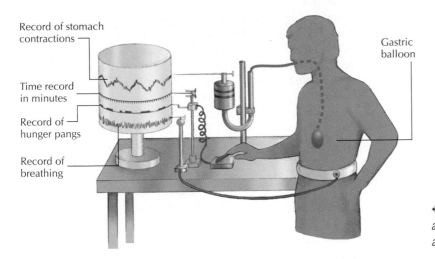

Record of stomach contractions

Time record in minutes

Record of hunger pangs

Record of breathing

Gastric balloon

❖ **FIGURE 13.2** *In Cannon's early study of hunger, a simple apparatus was used to simultaneously record hunger pangs and stomach contractions. (After Cannon, 1934.)*

However, we now know that the stomach is not essential for feeling hunger (Woods et al., 2000).

How has that been demonstrated? For medical reasons, many people have had their stomachs removed surgically. Despite this, they continue to feel hungry and to eat regularly. It would seem that some *central* factor must cause hunger. One important element appears to be the level of glucose (sugar) in the blood (Campfield et al., 1996). If insulin is injected in humans, it causes **hypoglycemia** (HI-po-gly-SEE-me-ah: low blood sugar) and stimulates feelings of hunger and stomach contractions. Strange as it may seem, the liver also affects hunger.

The liver? Yes, the liver responds to a lack of bodily "fuel" by sending nerve impulses to the brain, which contribute to a desire to eat (Woods et al., 2000).

Brain Mechanisms

What part of the brain controls hunger? When you are hungry, many parts of the brain are affected, so no single "hunger center" exists. However, a small area called the **hypothalamus** (HI-po-THAL-ah-mus) does regulate many aspects of motivation and emotion, including hunger, thirst, and sexual behavior (❖Fig. 13.3).

The hypothalamus is sensitive to levels of sugar in the blood (and other substances described in a moment). It also receives neural messages from the liver and the stomach. When combined, these messages regulate hunger (Woods et al., 2000).

One part of the hypothalamus acts as a **feeding system** that initiates eating. If the *lateral hypothalamus* is "turned on" with an electrified probe, even a well-fed animal will immediately begin eating. (The term *lateral* simply means the sides of the hypothalamus. See ❖Figure 13.4.) If the same area is destroyed, the animal will never eat again.

A second area within the hypothalamus seems to be part of a **satiety system,** or "stop mechanism" for eating. If the *ventro-*

Hypothalamus

❖ **FIGURE 13.3** *Location of the hypothalamus in the human brain.*

BRIDGES

The hypothalamus directly affects many basic motives.

For more information about its role in controlling behavior, see Chapter 3, pages 69–70.

medial hypothalamus (VENT-ro-MEE-dee-al) is destroyed, dramatic overeating results. (*Ventromedial* refers to the bottom middle of the hypothalamus.) Rats with such damage will overeat until they balloon up to weights of 1,000 grams or more (❖Fig. 13.5). A normal rat weighs about 180 grams. To put this weight gain in human terms, picture someone you know who weighs 180 pounds growing to a weight of 1,000 pounds.

Homeostasis *A steady state of bodily equilibrium.*
Hypoglycemia *Below-normal blood sugar level.*
Hypothalamus *A small area at the base of the brain that regulates many aspects of motivation and emotion, especially hunger, thirst, and sexual behavior.*
Feeding system *Areas in the hypothalamus that initiate eating when stimulated.*
Satiety system *Areas in the hypothalamus that terminate eating.*

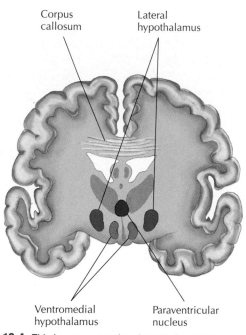

Corpus callosum   Lateral hypothalamus

Ventromedial hypothalamus   Paraventricular nucleus

❖ **FIGURE 13.4** *This is a cross section through the middle of the brain (viewed from the front of the brain). Indicated areas of the hypothalamus are associated with hunger and the regulation of body weight.*

The *paraventricular nucleus* (PAIR-uh-ven-TRICK-you-ler) is a third hunger-related part of the hypothalamus (❖Fig. 13.4). This area helps keep blood sugar levels steady in the body. As a result, it is involved in both starting and stopping eating. The paraventricular nucleus is very sensitive to a substance called **neuropeptide Y** (**NPY**). If NPY is present in large amounts, an animal will eat until it cannot hold another bite (Woods et al., 2000).

How do you know when to stop eating? A chemical called **glucagon-like peptide 1** (**GLP-1**) causes eating to cease. GLP-1 is released by the intestines after you eat a meal. From there, it travels in the bloodstream to the brain. When enough GLP-1 arrives, your desire to eat ends (Nori, 1998; Turton et al., 1996).

The substances we have reviewed are only some of the chemical signals that start and stop eating. Others continue to be discovered. In time, they may make artificial control of hunger possible. If so, better treatments for eating disorders, such as extreme obesity and self-starvation, could follow (Scott, 1996; Woods et al., 2000).

SET POINT   In addition to knowing when to start eating and when a meal is over, your body needs to regulate weight over longer periods of time. This task appears to be handled by a system that is sensitive to the amount of fat stored in the body (Woods, Seeley, & Porte, 1998).

Basically, your body has a **set point** for the proportion of fat it maintains. The set point acts like a thermostat for fat levels. Your own set point is the weight you maintain when you are making no effort to gain or lose weight. When your body goes below its set point, you will feel hungry most of the time. On the other hand, fat cells release a substance called *leptin* when your "spare tire" is well inflated. **Leptin** is carried in the bloodstream to the brain, where it acts as a signal to eat less (Considine et al., 1996; Mercer et al., 1998).

Do people have different set points? Yes. The set point is partly inherited and partly determined by early feeding patterns. Adopted children whose birth parents were overweight are likely to become heavy adults (Stunkard et al., 1986). This

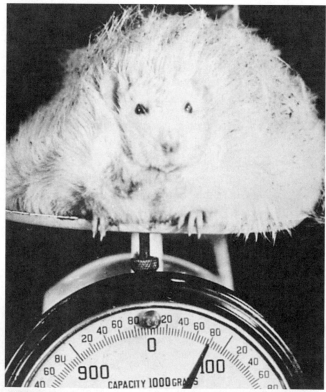

❖ **FIGURE 13.5** *Damage to the hunger satiety system in the hypothalamus can produce a very fat rat, a condition called hypothalamic hyperphagia (HI-per-FAGE-yah: overeating). This rat weighs 1,080 grams. (The pointer has gone completely around the dial and beyond.) (Photo courtesy of Neal Miller.)*

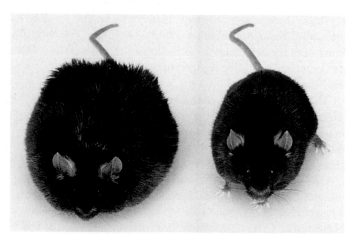

The mouse on the left has a genetic defect that prevents its fat cells from producing normal amounts of leptin. Without this chemical signal, the mouse's body acts as if its set point for fat storage is, shall we say, rather high.

shows that genes greatly influence adult weight. Overfeeding a child can also raise the set point. Adults who were overweight as children have *more* fat cells and *larger* fat cells. A person who does not become heavy until adulthood will have larger fat cells, but the overall number stays approximately the same. Thus, weight problems that begin in childhood are much harder to control.

Set points are only one piece in a complex puzzle that's worth solving. Obesity is a major health risk and, for many, a source of social stigma and low self-esteem.

Obesity

Why do people overeat?   If internal needs alone controlled eating, fewer people would overeat. However, most of us are sensitive to **external eating cues** (signs and signals linked with food). If you are sensitive to external cues, you are most likely to eat when food is attractive, highly visible, and easy to get. Thus, your lifestyle and opportunities to eat may have more to do with your food intake than bodily needs do (Woods et al., 2000). In a culture where food is plentiful, people of all weights can be susceptible to external eating cues, so this is not strictly a problem of the obese (Rodin, 1981). Just the same, eating cues contribute to many cases of overeating.

DIET   A diet is not just something you go on to lose weight. Your current **diet** is defined by the types and amounts of food

you regularly consume. Some diets actually encourage overeating. For instance, placing animals on a "supermarket" diet can lead to gross obesity. In one experiment, rats were given meals of chocolate chip cookies, salami, cheese, bananas, marshmallows, milk chocolate, peanut butter, and fat. Rats on this diet gained almost three times as much weight as animals that ate only laboratory rat chow (Sclafani & Springer, 1976). (Rat chow is a dry mixture of several bland grains. If you were a rat, you'd probably eat more cookies than rat chow, too.)

Humans are also sensitive to dietary content. In general, *sweetness,* high *fat content,* and *variety* tend to encourage overeating (Ball & Grinker, 1981; Lucas & Sclafani, 1990). Sadly, our culture may provide the worst possible kinds of foods for those with a tendency toward obesity.

It is tempting to assume that fatness comes from constant overeating, but this is a myth. Overeating occurs mainly when a person is gaining weight. Once excess weight is gained, it can be maintained with a normal diet. An added problem is that as people gain weight, they reduce their activity levels and burn fewer calories. As a result, some overweight people continue to gain weight while consuming fewer calories than their slimmer neighbors.

Is it true that people also overeat when they are emotionally upset?   Yes. People with weight problems are just as likely to eat when they are anxious, angry, or sad as when they are hungry (Schotte, Cools, & McNally, 1990). Furthermore, the obese are often unhappy in our fat-conscious culture. The result is overeating that leads to emotional distress and still

Plentiful, eye-catching foods provide powerful incentives for overeating. In North America, numerous external eating cues and diets high in sweetness, fat, and variety have contributed to excessive weight gains in one adult out of every three.

Neuropeptide Y *A substance in the brain that initiates eating.*
Glucagon-like peptide 1 *A substance in the brain that terminates eating.*
Set point *The proportion of body fat that tends to be maintained by changes in hunger and eating.*
Leptin *A substance released by fat cells that inhibits eating.*
External eating cue *Any external stimulus that tends to encourage hunger or to elicit eating.*
Diet *The types and amounts of food and drink regularly consumed over a period of time.*

more overeating. This makes weight control extremely difficult (Rutledge & Linden, 1998).

To summarize, overeating results from a complex interplay of internal and external influences, diet, emotions, genetics, exercise, and many other factors. To answer the question we began with, people become obese in different ways and for different reasons. Clearly, scientists are still a long way from winning the "battle of the bulge." For another perspective on overeating, see "The Paradox of Yo-Yo Dieting."

Other Factors in Hunger

As research on overeating suggests, "hunger" is affected by more than bodily needs for food. Let's consider some additional factors of interest.

CULTURAL FACTORS   Learning to think of some foods as desirable and others as revolting has much to do with eating habits. In North America, we would never consider eating the eyes out of the steamed head of a monkey, but in some parts of the world this dish is considered a real delicacy. By the same token, vegans and vegetarians consider the eating of meat to be cruel and barbaric. In short, cultural values greatly affect the incentive value of foods. (**Cultural values** are widely held beliefs about the desirability of various objects and activities.)

TASTE   Even tastes for "normal" foods may vary considerably. For example, the hungrier you are, the more pleasant a sweet food tastes (Cabanac & Duclaux, 1970). When you are anxious, you are more likely to choose familiar foods to eat, rather than unusual foods (Pliner, Eng, & Krishnan, 1995). If you have some favorite "comfort foods" that you eat when you are upset, this effect will be familiar to you.

As you may have noticed, it is easy to acquire a **taste aversion,** or active dislike, for a particular food. This happens whenever a food causes sickness or is merely associated with nausea (Jacobsen et al., 1993). Not only do we learn to avoid such foods, but they, too, can become nauseating. A friend of the author's, who once became ill after eating a cheese Danish (well, actually, *several*), has never again been able to come face to face with this delightful pastry.

If getting sick occurs long after eating, how does it become associated with a particular food?   A good question. Taste aversions are a type of classical conditioning. As stated in Chapter 9, a long delay between the CS and US usually prevents conditioning. However, psychologists theorize that we have a biological tendency to associate an upset stomach with foods eaten earlier. Such learning is usually protective (Garcia et al., 1974). Yet, sadly, many human cancer patients suffer taste aversions long after the nausea of their drug treatments has passed (Stockhorst et al., 1998).

A CLOSER LOOK

THE PARADOX OF YO-YO DIETING

If dieting works, why are hundreds of "new" diets published each year? The answer is that while dieters do lose weight, most regain it soon after they quit dieting. Indeed, many people suffer a rebound that pushes weight higher than it was before they began dieting. Why should this be so? The answer is that dieting (starving) slows the body's rate of metabolism (Leibel, Rosenbaum, & Hirsch, 1995).

In effect, a dieter's body becomes highly efficient at *conserving* calories and storing them as fat. Any low-calorie diet may have this effect, but "yo-yo dieting," or repeated weight loss and gain, is especially troublesome. Frequent **weight cycling** (losing and gaining weight) tends to slow the body's **metabolic rate** (the rate at which energy is used up). This makes it harder to lose weight each time a person diets and easier to regain weight when the diet ends. Frequent changes in weight also increase the risk of heart disease and premature death (Brownell & Rodin, 1994; Lissner et al., 1991).

Apparently, evolution prepared us to save energy when food is scarce and to stock up on fat when food is plentiful. Briefly starving yourself, therefore, may have little lasting effect on weight. To avoid bouncing between feast and famine requires a permanent change in eating habits and exercise—a topic we will return to in this chapter's Psychology in Action section.

Fans cheered as daytime TV host Oprah Winfrey lost 67 pounds on a commercial diet. Over the next year, viewers watched in morbid fascination as Oprah regained all of the weight she had lost. Oprah's rebound came as no surprise to psychologists. Numerous studies show that you can lose weight on almost any diet. However, you will almost certainly gain it back in a few years. Only recently has Oprah been able to stabilize her weight through exercise and revised eating habits (Seligman, 1994).

If you like animals, you will be interested in an imaginative approach to an age-old problem. In many rural areas, predators are poisoned, trapped, or shot by ranchers. These practices have nearly wiped out the timber wolf, and in some areas the coyote faces a similar end. How might the coyote be saved without a costly loss of livestock?

In a classic experiment, coyotes were given lamb tainted with lithium chloride. Coyotes who took the bait became nauseated and vomited. After one or two such treatments, they developed **bait shyness**—a lasting distaste for the tainted food (Gustavson & Garcia, 1974). If applied consistently, taste aversion conditioning might solve many predator-livestock problems. (Perhaps this technique could even be used to protect roadrunners from the Wile E. Coyote!)

Taste aversions may also help people avoid severe nutritional imbalances. For example, if you go on a fad diet and eat only grapefruit, you will eventually begin to feel ill. In time, associating your discomfort with grapefruit may create an aversion to it and restore some balance to your diet.

Eating Disorders

Under the sheets of her hospital bed, Krystal looks like a starved skeleton. If her self-starvation cannot be stopped, Krystal may die of malnutrition.

Serious cases of undereating like Krystal's are called **anorexia nervosa** (AN-uh-REK-see-yah ner-VOH-sah). Victims of anorexia, who are mostly adolescent females (5 to 10 percent are male), suffer devastating weight losses from active, self-inflicted starvation (Wakeling, 1996).

Do anorexics lose their appetite? No, many continue to feel hungry yet struggle to starve themselves. What they suffer from

BRIDGES

Bait shyness is similar to human aversion conditioning, which is used to help people control bad habits, such as smoking, drinking, or nail-biting.

See Chapter 18, pages 606–607.

is a relentless pursuit of excessive thinness. Often, anorexia starts with "normal" dieting that gradually begins to dominate the person's life. In time, anorexics suffer weakness, an absence of menstrual cycles, and frequent infections. Five to 8 percent (more than 1 in 20) die of malnutrition or related problems. ◆Table 13.1 lists the symptoms of anorexia nervosa.

Bulimia nervosa (bue-LIHM-ee-yah), also known as the *binge-purge syndrome*, is a second major eating disorder. Bulimic people gorge on food, then induce vomiting or take laxatives to avoid gaining weight (see ◆Table 13.1). As with anorexia, most victims of bulimia are girls or women. Approximately 5 percent of college women are bulimic, and as many as 61 percent have milder eating problems. Like self-starvation, bingeing and purging can seriously damage health. Typical risks include sore throat, hair loss, muscle spasms, kidney damage, dehydration, tooth erosion, swollen salivary glands, menstrual irregularities, loss of sex drive, and even heart attack.

◆ TABLE 13.1 Recognizing Eating Disorders

ANOREXIA NERVOSA

Body weight below 85 percent of normal for one's height and age.
Refusal to maintain body weight in normal range.
Intense fear of becoming fat or gaining weight, even though underweight.
Disturbance in one's body image or perceived weight.
Self-evaluation is unduly influenced by body weight.
Denial of seriousness of abnormally low body weight.
Absence of menstrual periods.
Purging behavior (vomiting or misuse of laxatives or diuretics).

BULIMIA NERVOSA

Normal or above-normal weight.
Recurring binge eating.
Eating within an hour or two an amount of food that is much larger than most people would consume.
Feeling a lack of control over eating.
Purging behavior (vomiting or misuse of laxatives or diuretics).
Excessive exercise to prevent weight gain.
Fasting to prevent weight gain.
Self-evaluation is unduly influenced by body weight.

(DSM-IV, 1994.)

Weight cycling *Repeated swings between losing and gaining weight.*
Metabolic rate *The rate at which energy is consumed by bodily activity.*
Cultural values *The values attached to various objects and activities by people in a given culture.*
Taste aversion *An active dislike for a particular food.*
Bait shyness *An unwillingness or hesitation on the part of animals to eat a particular food.*
Anorexia nervosa *Active self-starvation or a sustained loss of appetite that has psychological origins.*
Bulimia nervosa *Excessive eating (gorging) usually followed by self-induced vomiting and/or taking laxatives.*

Like humans and other animals, coyotes develop taste aversions when food is associated with nausea.

CAUSES *What causes anorexia and bulimia?* Anorexic and bulimic people have distorted views of themselves and exaggerated fears of becoming fat (Gardner & Bokenkamp, 1996). Many overestimate their body size by 25 percent or more. As a result, they see themselves as "fat" when they are actually wasting away (❖Fig. 13.6) (Wichstrom, 1995). In some cases, their body image can actually change after a meal. For example, after eating nothing more than a candy bar and a soft drink, bulimic women thought they had grown larger. It's no wonder that they often panic and attempt to purge themselves of food (McKinzie et al., 1993).

Anorexic teens are usually described as "perfect" daughters—helpful, considerate, conforming, and obedient. Many seem to be trying to have perfect control in one area of their lives, by being perfectly slim (Pliner & Haddock, 1996). People suffering from bulimia are also concerned with control. Typically they are obsessed with thoughts of weight, food, eating, and ridding themselves of food. As a result, most feel guilt, shame, self-contempt, and anxiety after a binge. Vomiting reduces this anxiety, which makes purging highly reinforcing (Powell & Thelen, 1996). Depression is also a factor in some eating disorders (Nagel & Jones, 1992).

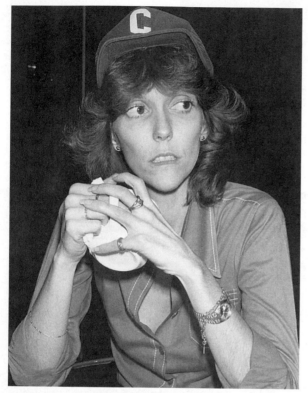

Anorexia nervosa can be far more dangerous than many people realize. This haunting photo shows popular singer Karen Carpenter shortly before her death. Carpenter died of starvation-induced heart failure. More recently, Christy Henrich, a former member of the U.S. National Gymnastics Team, died at age 22. Henrich, too, suffered from anorexia. Many more victims of eating disorders die each year (Witherspoon, 1994).

The relentless parade of atypically thin models in the media contributes to eating disorders. People with eating disorders are much more likely to report being influenced by unrealistic body ideals in the media (Murray, Touyz, & Beumont, 1996).

❖ **FIGURE 13.6** *Women with abnormal eating habits were asked to rate their body shape on a scale similar to the one you see here. As a group, they chose ideal figures much thinner than what they thought their current weights were. (Most women say they want to be thinner than they currently are, but to a lesser degree than women with eating problems.) Notice that the women with eating problems chose an ideal weight that was even thinner than what they thought men prefer. This is not typical of most women. In this study, only women with eating problems wanted to be thinner than what they thought men find attractive (Zellner, Harner, & Adler, 1989).*

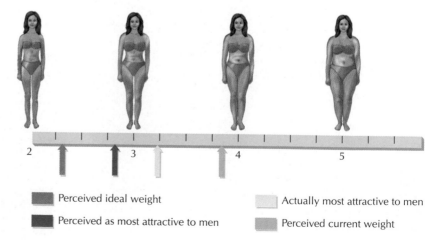

Perceived ideal weight

Perceived as most attractive to men

Actually most attractive to men

Perceived current weight

TREATMENT In almost all cases, people suffering from eating disorders need professional help. Treatment for anorexia usually begins with a medical diet to restore weight and health. Next, the client enters counseling to work on the emotional conflicts that led to weight loss. For bulimia, behavioral counseling may include self-monitoring of food intake. The urge to vomit can be treated with extinction training. A related cognitive-behavioral approach focuses on changing the thinking patterns and beliefs about weight and body shape that perpetuate eating disorders (Whittal, Agras, & Gould, 1999).

Most anorexics do not seek help, and many actively resist it. Bulimics will sometimes seek treatment, but usually not until their eating habits become intolerable. In either case, it may take strong urging by family or friends to get victims into treatment.

Culture, Ethnicity, and Dieting

Women with eating disorders are not alone in having body image problems. In Western cultures, many women learn to see themselves as "objects" that are evaluated by others. As a result, they try to shape their bodies to the cultural ideal of slimness through dieting (Fredrickson et al., 1998).

Just looking at a fashion magazine tends to leave women less satisfied with their weight and anxious to be thinner (Turner et al., 1997). However, women from some cultural backgrounds appear to be less susceptible to the glorification of slimness. For example, Asian-American college students are only half as likely to diet as other college women are (Tsai, Hoerr, & Song, 1998). Within the African American and Pacific Islander communities, there is a general preference for a fuller and shapelier figure. In these groups, a larger body size is associated with high social status, health, and beauty (Flynn & Fitzgibbon, 1998; Hebl & Heatherton, 1998; Ofosu, Lafreniere, & Senn, 1998). Clearly, what constitutes an attractive body style is a matter of opinion.

PRIMARY MOTIVES REVISITED—THIRST, SEX, AND PAIN

The control of most other primary motives is similar to that observed in hunger. For example, thirst is only partially related to dryness of the mouth and throat. When drugs are used to keep the mouth constantly wet or dry, thirst and water intake remain normal. Like hunger, thirst appears to be regulated by the hypothalamus, where separate *thirst* and *thirst satiety* systems are found. Also like hunger, thirst is strongly affected by individual learning and by cultural values.

Thirst

You may not have noticed, but there are actually two kinds of thirst. **Extracellular thirst** occurs when water is lost from the fluids surrounding the cells of your body. Bleeding, vomiting, diarrhea, sweating, and drinking alcohol cause this type of thirst (Petri, 1996). When a person loses both water and minerals in any of these ways—especially by perspiration—a slightly salty liquid may be more satisfying than plain water.

Why would a thirsty person want to drink salty water? The reason is that before the body can retain water, minerals lost through perspiration (mainly salt) must be replaced. In lab tests, animals greatly prefer saltwater after salt levels in their bodies are lowered (Strickler & Verbalis, 1988). Similarly, some nomadic peoples of the Sahara Desert prize blood as a beverage, probably because of its saltiness. (Maybe they should try Gatorade?)

A second type of thirst occurs when you eat a salty meal. In this instance, your body does not lose fluid. Instead, excess salt causes fluid to be drawn out of cells. As the cells "shrink," **intracellular thirst** is triggered. Thirst of this type is best quenched by plain water.

The drives for food, water, air, sleep, and elimination are all fairly similar in that they are generated by a combination of activities in the body and the brain, are modified by learning and culture, and are influenced by external factors. Two unusual primary drives are the sex drive and the drive to avoid pain.

Pain

How is the drive to avoid pain different? Drives such as hunger, thirst, and sleepiness come and go in a fairly regular cycle each day. Pain avoidance, by contrast, is an **episodic drive** (ep-ih-SOD-ik). That is, it occurs in distinct episodes when damage to the body takes place or is imminent. Most of the

It may seem contradictory, but thirst caused by perspiring is best quenched by slightly salty liquids. The salty snacks offered at taverns are intended to increase beer sales, but they also appeal to people who have perspired heavily at work or play.

Extracellular thirst *Thirst caused by a reduction in the volume of fluids found between body cells.*
Intracellular thirst *Thirst triggered when fluid is drawn out of cells because of an increased concentration of salts and minerals outside the cell.*
Episodic drive *A drive that occurs in distinct episodes.*

Tolerance for pain and the strength of a person's motivation to avoid discomfort are greatly affected by cultural practices and beliefs.

primary drives cause us to actively seek a desired goal (food, drink, warmth, and so forth). The goal in pain avoidance is to eliminate pain.

Some people feel they must be "tough" and not show any discomfort. Others complain loudly at the smallest ache or pain. The first attitude raises pain tolerance, and the second lowers it. As this suggests, the drive to avoid pain is partly learned. That's why members of some societies endure cutting, burning, whipping, tattooing, and piercing of the skin that would agonize you or me (but apparently not members of college basketball teams). In general, we learn how to react to pain by observing family members, peers, and other social role models (Rollman, 1998).

The Sex Drive

The sex drive is an unusual motive. In fact, many psychologists do not think of sex as a primary motive because sex (contrary to anything your personal experience might suggest) is not necessary for *individual* survival. It is necessary, of course, for *group* survival among humans and other creatures.

In lower animals, the sex drive is directly related to the effects of hormones. Female mammals (other than humans) are interested in mating only when their fertility cycles are in the stage of **estrus,** or "heat." Estrus is caused by a release of **estrogen** (a female sex hormone) into the bloodstream. Hormones are important in the male animal as well. In most lower animals, castration will abolish the sex drive. But in contrast to the female, the normal male animal is almost always ready to mate. His sex drive is primarily aroused by the behavior of a recep-

tive female. In many species, mating is therefore closely tied to female fertility cycles.

How much do hormones affect the sex drive in humans? The link between hormones and the sex drive grows weaker as we ascend the biological scale. Hormones do affect the human sex drive, but only to a limited degree. For example, there is no connection between female sexual activity and women's monthly menstrual cycles (Udry & Morris, 1977). In humans, mental, cultural, and emotional factors determine sexual expression. However, our liberation from hormones is not total. Human males show a loss of sex drive after castration, and some women lose sexual desire when taking birth control pills.

Human sexual behavior and attitudes are discussed in detail in Chapter 14. For now, it is enough to note that the sex drive is largely **non-homeostatic** (relatively independent of bodily need states). In humans, the sex drive can be aroused at virtually any time by almost anything. It therefore shows no clear relationship to deprivation (the amount of time since the drive was last satisfied). Certainly, an increase in desire may occur as time passes. But recent sexual activity does not prevent sexual desire from occurring again. Notice, too, that people may seek to arouse the sex drive as well as to reduce it. This unusual quality makes the sex drive capable of motivating a wide range of behaviors. It also explains why sex is used to sell almost everything imaginable.

The non-homeostatic quality of the sex drive can be shown in this way: A male animal is allowed to copulate until it seems to have no further interest in sexual behavior. Then a new sexual partner is provided. Immediately, the animal resumes sexual activity. This pattern is called the *Coolidge effect* after former U.S. president Calvin Coolidge. What, you might ask, does Calvin Coolidge have to do with the sex drive? The answer is found in the following story.

While touring an experimental farm, Coolidge's wife reportedly asked if a rooster mated just once a day. "No ma'am," she was told, "he mates dozens of times each day." "Tell that to the president," she said, with a faraway look in her eyes. When President Coolidge reached the same part of the tour, his wife's message was given to him. His reaction was to ask if the dozens of matings were with the same hen. No, he was told, different hens were involved. "Tell *that* to Mrs. Coolidge," the president is said to have replied.

KNOWLEDGE BUILDER

HUNGER, THIRST, PAIN, AND SEX

RELATE

Think of the last meal you ate. What caused you to feel hungry? What internal signals told your body to stop eating? How sensitive are you to external eating cues? Have you developed any taste aversions?

A friend of yours seems to be engaging in yo-yo dieting. Can you explain to her or him why such dieting is ineffective?

If you wanted to provoke extracellular thirst in yourself, what would you do? How could you make intracellular thirst occur?

STIMULUS DRIVES—SKYDIVING, HORROR MOVIES, AND THE FUN ZONE

Many people find browsing the Internet to be nearly irresistible. But satisfying curiosity is more than just entertaining. **Stimulus drives,** which reflect needs for exploration, manipulation, curiosity, and stimulation, clearly aid survival. As mentioned earlier, such drives reflect the life-and-death necessity of keeping track of sources of food, danger, and other important details of the environment. However, stimulus drives seem to go beyond such elemental needs.

Monkey Business

In an experiment, monkeys confined to a dimly lit box learned to perform a simple task in order to open a window that allowed them to view the outside world (Butler & Harlow, 1954). In a similar experiment, monkeys quickly learned to solve a mechanical puzzle made up of interlocking metal pins, hooks, and hasps (Butler, 1954) (❖Fig. 13.7). In both situations, no external reward was offered for exploration or manipulation.

❖ **FIGURE 13.7** *Monkeys happily open locks that are placed in their cage. Because no reward is given for this activity, it provides evidence for the existence of stimulus needs. (Photo courtesy of Harry F. Harlow.)*

The puzzle-solving monkeys seemed to work for the sheer fun of it. An interest in video games, chess, puzzles, Rubik's cube, and the like offers a human parallel. Curiosity—the drive to *know*—is powerful in humans. Scientific investigation, intellectual curiosity, surfing the Net, and other advanced activities express this basic drive. The drive for stimulation can even be observed in infants. By the time a child can walk, there are few things in the home that have not been tasted, touched, viewed, handled, or, in the case of toys, destroyed!

Arousal Theory

Are stimulus drives homeostatic? By combining homeostasis with drives for stimulation, we get a useful model of human behavior. **Arousal theory** states that there are ideal levels of arousal for various activities. It further assumes that people try to keep arousal near these ideal levels (Hebb, 1966).

What do you mean by arousal? **Arousal** refers to activation of the body and the nervous system. Arousal is zero at death, it is low during sleep, it is moderate during normal daily activities, and it is high at times of excitement, emotion, or panic. Arousal theory assumes that we become uncomfortable when arousal is too low ("I'm bored") or when it is too high, as in fear, anxiety, or panic ("The dentist will see you now").

Estrus *Changes in the sexual drives of animals that create a desire for mating; particularly used to refer to females in heat.*
Estrogen *Any of a number of female sex hormones.*
Non-homeostatic drive *A drive that is relatively independent of physical deprivation cycles or bodily need states.*
Stimulus drives *Drives based on needs for exploration, manipulation, curiosity, and stimulation.*
Arousal theory *Assumes that people prefer to maintain ideal, or comfortable, levels of arousal.*
Arousal *The overall level of activation in the body and nervous system of a person or animal.*

Curiosity and stimulation seeking can be interpreted as attempts to raise the level of arousal when it is too low. Most adults vary their activities to maintain a comfortable level of activation. Music, parties, sports, conversation, sleep, and the like are mixed to keep arousal at moderate levels, thus preventing both boredom and overstimulation.

SENSATION SEEKERS *Do people vary in their needs for stimulation?* The city dweller who visits the country complains that it is "too quiet" and seeks some "action." The country dweller finds the city "hectic," "overwhelming," or "too much" and seeks peace and quiet. Arousal theory also assumes that each of us learns to seek a personal "ideal" or preferred level of arousal.

Marvin Zuckerman (1990) has devised a test to measure such differences. The *Sensation-Seeking Scale* (SSS), as he calls it, includes statements like the samples shown here (from Zuckerman, 1996; Zuckerman et al., 1978):

Thrill and adventure seeking
- I would like to try parachute jumping.
- I think I would enjoy the sensations of skiing very fast down a high mountain slope.

Experience seeking
- I like to explore a strange city or section of town myself, even if it means getting lost.
- I like to try new foods that I have never tasted before.

Disinhibition
- I like wild, "uninhibited" parties.
- I often like to get high (drinking liquor or smoking marijuana).

Boredom susceptibility
- I can't stand watching a movie that I've seen before.
- I like people who are sharp and witty, even if they do sometimes insult others.

Sensation seeking is a trait of individuals who prefer high levels of stimulation. Whether you are high or low in sensation seeking is probably based on how your body responds to new, unusual, or intense stimulation (Zuckerman, 1990). People who score high on the entire SSS tend to be bold, independent individuals who value change. They also report more sexual partners than low scorers; they are more likely to smoke, and they prefer spicy, sour, and crunchy foods over bland foods. Tourists who take "adventure" holidays tend score high on the SSS (Gilchrist et al., 1995)! Low sensation seekers are orderly, nurturant, and giving, and they enjoy the company of others. Which are you? (Most people fall somewhere between the extremes.)

Levels of Arousal

Is there an ideal level of arousal for peak performance? If we set aside individual differences, performance is usually best when arousal is *moderate*. Let's say that you have to take an essay exam. If you are sleepy or feeling lazy (arousal level too low), your performance will suffer. If you are in a

Thrill seeking is an element of the sensation-seeking personality.

state of anxiety or panic about the test (arousal level too high), you will also perform below par. This relationship between arousal and efficiency of behavior can be expressed as an **inverted U function** (a curve, roughly in the shape of an upside-down **U**) (❖Fig. 13.8) (Anderson, 1990).

At very low levels of arousal, the body is not sufficiently energized to perform well. With increased arousal, performance continues to improve up to the middle regions of the curve. Then it begins to drop off, as an individual becomes emotional, frenzied, or disorganized. (Imagine trying to start a car stalled on a railroad track, with a speeding train bearing down on you.) Even when life and death are not at stake, excess arousal is disruptive. For example, the batting averages of professional baseball players drop dramatically during the late innings of close games (Davis & Harvey, 1992).

Is performance always best at moderate levels of arousal? No, the optimal level of arousal depends on the complexity of the task you are performing. For simple tasks, activation is less harmful. If a task is relatively simple, the optimal level of arousal will be high. When a task is more complex, the best performance occurs at lower levels of arousal. This relationship is called the **Yerkes-Dodson law** (see ❖Fig. 13.8). It applies to a wide variety of tasks and to measures of motivation other than arousal.

Some examples of the Yerkes-Dodson law might be helpful. In track, it is almost impossible for a sprinter to get too aroused for a race. The task is direct and uncomplicated: Run as fast as you can for a short distance. On the other hand, a basketball player making a game-deciding free throw faces a more sensitive and complex task. Excessive arousal is almost certain to

BRIDGES

One of the best ways to avoid test anxiety is to improve your study skills. See the Introduction in this text and review the learning and test-taking skills described there.

See pages xli–xlix.

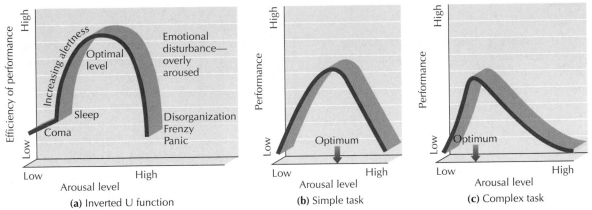

(a) Inverted U function   **(b)** Simple task   **(c)** Complex task

❖ **FIGURE 13.8** (a) *The general relationship between arousal and efficiency can be described by an inverted U curve. The optimal level of arousal or motivation is higher for a simple task* (b) *than for a complex task* (c).

COPING WITH TEST ANXIETY

Test anxiety is a combination of *heightened physiological arousal* (nervousness, sweating, pounding heart) and *excessive worry*. This combination—worry plus arousal—tends to distract test takers with a rush of upsetting thoughts and feelings (Gierl & Rogers, 1996).

Let's see what we can learn about alleviating test anxiety.

PREPARATION   The most direct antidote for test anxiety is *hard work*. Many test-anxious students simply study too little and too late for exams. That's why improving your study skills is a good way to reduce test anxiety (Jones & Petruzzi, 1995).

Apparently, students know when they are not ready for an exam. Test anxiety is highest before exams on which students expect to do poorly. The best solution is to *overprepare* by studying well in advance of the "big day." Students who are well prepared score higher, worry less, and are less likely to panic (Zohar, 1998).

RELAXATION   Learning to relax is another way to lower test anxiety (Ricketts & Galloway, 1984). You can learn self-relaxation skills by looking at Chapter 18, where a relaxation technique is described. Test taking is also less threatening if you feel that you have emotional support from others (Sarason, 1981). If you are test anxious, it might help to discuss the problem with your professors. Preparing for tests with a supportive friend or classmate can also help.

REHEARSAL   Nervousness during tests can be lessened by rehearsing how you will cope with upsetting events. Before taking a test, imagine yourself going blank, running out of time, or feeling panicked. Then calmly plan how you will handle each situation—by keeping your attention on the task, by focusing on one question at a time, and so forth (Watson & Tharp, 1996).

RESTRUCTURING THOUGHTS   What can be done about worries and self-defeating thinking patterns? Many test-anxious students benefit from listing the distracting and upsetting thoughts they have during exams. They then learn to combat their worries with calming, rational replies (Jones & Petruzzi, 1995). (These are called *coping statements;* see the "Psychology in Action" section in Chapter 16 for more information.)

Let's say that a student thinks, "I'm going to fail this test, and everybody will think I'm stupid." To counter this upsetting thought, she or he might say, "If I prepare well and control my worries, I will probably pass the test. Even if I don't, it won't be the end of the world. My friends will still like me, and I can try to improve on the next test."

Students who cope well with testing take a practical attitude and try to do the best they can, even under trying circumstances. With practice, most students can learn to be less testy at test-taking time (Zeidner, 1995).

hurt his or her performance. In school, most students have had experience with "test anxiety," a familiar example of how excessive arousal can lower performance.

Then is it true that by learning to calm down, a person would do better on tests?   Usually, but not always. Studies show that students are typically most anxious when they don't know the material. If this is the case, calming down simply means you will remain calm while failing. See "Coping with Test Anxiety" to learn how to lower test anxiety.

Sensation seeking *A personality characteristic of people who prefer high levels of stimulation.*
Inverted U function *A curve, roughly in the shape of an upside-down U, that relates performance to levels of arousal.*
Yerkes-Dodson law *A summary of the relationships among arousal, task complexity, and performance.*
Test anxiety *High levels of arousal and worry that seriously impair test performance.*

Circadian Rhythms

We have seen that moment-to-moment changes in activation can have a major impact on performance. What about larger cycles of arousal? Do they also affect energy levels, motivation, and performance? Scientists have long known that bodily activity is guided by internal "biological clocks." Every 24 hours, your body undergoes a cycle of changes called **circadian** (sur-KAY-dee-an) **rhythms** (*circa*: about; *diem*: a day) (Orlock, 1993).

Throughout the day, large changes take place in body temperature, blood pressure, urine volume, and amino acid levels (❖Fig. 13.9). Also affected are the activities of the liver, kidneys, and endocrine glands. These activities, and many others, peak sometime each day. Output of the hormone adrenaline, which arouses the body, is often three to five times greater during the day. Most people are more energetic and alert at the high point of their circadian rhythms (Natale & Cicogna, 1996).

Differences in such peaks are so basic that when a "day person" rooms with a "night person," both are more likely to give their relationship a negative rating (Carey et al., 1988). This is easy to understand: What could be worse than having someone bounding around cheerily when you're half asleep, or the reverse?

SHIFT WORK AND JET LAG   Circadian rhythms are most noticeable whenever there is a major shift in time schedules. Businesspeople, diplomats, athletes, and other time zone travelers tend to make errors or perform poorly when their body rhythms are disturbed (Rader & Hicks, 1987). If you travel great distances east or west, the peaks and valleys of your circadian rhythms will be out of phase with the sun and clocks. For example, you might find that you are wide-awake and alert at midnight. Your low point, in contrast, occurs during the middle of the day (return to ❖Fig. 13.9). Shift work has the same effect, causing fatigue, inefficiency, irritability, upset stomach, and depression (Akerstedt, 1990).

How fast do people adapt to time shifts?   For major time zone shifts (5 hours or more), it can take from several days to 2 weeks to resynchronize. Adaptation to jet lag is slowest when you stay indoors, where you can sleep and eat on "home time." Getting outdoors, where you must sleep, eat, and socialize on the new schedule, speeds adaptation. A 5-hour dose of bright sunlight early each day is particularly helpful for resetting your circadian rhythm in a new time zone (Czeisler et al., 1989). The same principle can be applied to shift work by bathing workers in bright light during their first few night shifts (Eastman et al., 1994).

The *direction* of travel also affects adaptation (Harma et al., 1994). If you fly west, adapting is relatively easy, taking an average of 4 to 5 days. If you fly east, adapting takes 50 percent longer, or more (❖Fig. 13.10). Why is there a difference? The answer is that when you fly east, the sun comes up *earlier* (relative to your "home" time). Let's say that you live in Los Angeles

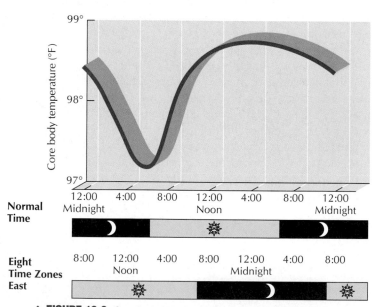

❖ **FIGURE 13.9** *Core body temperature is a good indicator of a person's circadian rhythm. Most people reach a low point 2 to 3 hours before their normal waking time. It's no wonder that both the Chernobyl and Three Mile Island nuclear power plant accidents occurred around 4 A.M. Rapid travel to a different time zone, shift work, depression, and illness can throw sleep and waking patterns out of synchronization with the body's core rhythm. Mismatches of this kind are very disruptive (Hauri & Linde, 1990).*

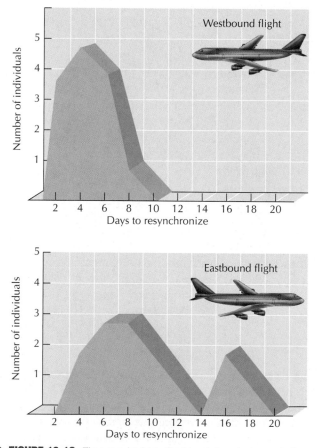

❖ **FIGURE 13.10** *Time required to adjust to air travel across six time zones. The average time to resynchronize was shorter for westbound travel than for eastbound flights. (Data from Beljan et al., 1972; cited by Moore-Ede et al., 1982.)*

and fly to New York. Getting up at 7 A.M. in New York will be like getting up at 4 A.M. in Los Angeles. If you fly west, the sun comes up later, and it is easier for most people to "advance" (stay up later and sleep in) than it is to shift backward. Likewise, work shifts that "rotate" backward (night, evening, day) are more disruptive than those that advance (day, evening, night). Best of all are work shifts that do not change: Even continuous night work is less upsetting than rotating shifts (Williamson & Sanderson, 1986).

What does all of this have to do with those of us who are not shift workers or world travelers? There are few college students who have not at one time or another "burned the midnight oil," especially for final exams. During any strenuous period, it is wise to remember that departing from your regular schedule is likely to cost more than it's worth. Often, you can do as much during 1 hour in the morning as you could have in 3 hours of work after midnight. The 2-hour difference in efficiency might as well be spent sleeping. If you feel you must deviate from your normal schedule, do it gradually over a period of days.

In general, if you can anticipate an upcoming body rhythm change (when traveling, before finals week, or when doing shift work), it is best to *preadapt* to your new schedule. **Preadaptation** is the gradual matching of sleep-wake cycles to a new time schedule. Before traveling, for instance, you should go to sleep 1 hour later (or earlier) each day until your sleep cycle matches the time at your destination. If you are unable to do that, it at least helps to fly early in the day when you fly east. When you fly west, it is better to fly late. (Remember, the *E* in *east* matches the *E* in *early.*)

Studies of flight crews show that jet lag can also be minimized by a hormone called **melatonin** (mel-ah-TONE-in).

BRIDGES

Changes in melatonin levels are thought to partly explain winter depressions that occur when people endure several months of long, dark days.

See Chapter 17, page 585.

Melatonin is normally produced at night by the pineal gland and suppressed during daylight (Brown, 1994). Melatonin has a strong impact on the timing of body rhythms and sleep cycles. As far as the brain is concerned, it's bedtime when melatonin levels rise (Attenburrow, Cowen, & Sharpley, 1996).

To reset the body's clock in a new time zone, a small amount of melatonin can be taken about an hour before bedtime. This dose is continued for as many days as necessary to ease jet lag. The same treatment can be used for rotating work shifts (Arendt, 1994; Brown, 1994; Comperatore et al, 1996).

LEARNED MOTIVES—THE PURSUIT OF EXCELLENCE

Many motives are acquired directly. It is easy enough to see that praise, money, success, pleasure, and similar reinforcers affect our goals and desires. But how do people learn to enjoy activities that are at first painful or frightening? Why do people climb rocks, jump out of airplanes, run marathons, take sauna baths, or swim in frozen lakes? For an answer, let's examine a related situation.

When a person first tries a drug such as heroin, he or she feels a "rush" of pleasure. However, as the drug wears off, discomfort and craving occurs. The easiest way to end the discomfort is to take another dose—as most drug users quickly learn. But in time, habituation takes place; the drug stops producing pleasure, although it will end discomfort. At the same time, the aftereffects of the drug grow more painful. At this point, the drug user has acquired a powerful new motive. In a vicious cycle, heroin relieves discomfort, but it guarantees that withdrawal will occur again in a few hours.

Opponent-Process Theory

Psychologist Richard Solomon (1980) offers an intriguing explanation for drug addiction and other learned motives. According to his **opponent-process theory**, if a stimulus causes a strong emotion, such as fear or pleasure, an opposite emotion tends to occur when the stimulus ends. For example, if you are in pain and the pain ends, you will feel a pleasant sense of relief. If a person feels pleasure, as in the case of drug use, and the pleasure ends, it will be followed by craving or discomfort. If you are in love and feel good when you are with your lover, you will be uncomfortable when she or he is absent.

Flight crews often suffer severe disruptions in their sleep cycles. For example, a crew that leaves Los Angeles at 4 P.M., bound for London, will arrive in 8 hours. Crew members' bodies, which are on California time, will act as if it is 12 A.M. Yet in London, it will be 8 A.M. Recent studies confirm that melatonin can help people adjust more rapidly to such time-zone changes.

Circadian rhythms *Cyclical changes in bodily functions and arousal levels that vary on a schedule approximating a 24-hour day.*
Preadaptation *Gradual matching of sleep-waking cycles to a new time schedule before an anticipated change in circadian rhythms.*
Melatonin *A hormone produced by the pineal gland in response to cycles of light and dark.*
Opponent-process theory *States that strong emotions tend to be followed by an opposite emotional state; also the strength of both emotional states changes over time.*

❖ **FIGURE 13.11** *A sport parachutist takes the plunge. The typical emotional sequence for a first jump is anxiety before, terror during, and relief after the jump. After many jumps, the emotional sequence becomes eagerness before, a thrill during, and exhilaration after a jump. The new sequence strongly reinforces skydiving.*

What happens if the stimulus is repeated? Solomon assumes that when a stimulus is repeated, our response to it habituates, or gets weaker. First-time skydivers, for instance, are almost always terrified. But with repeated jumps, fear decreases, until finally the skydiver feels a "thrill" instead of terror (Roth et al., 1996). In contrast, emotional aftereffects get stronger with repetition. After a first jump, beginning parachutists feel a brief but exhilarating sense of relief. After many such experiences, seasoned skydivers can get a "rush" of euphoria that lasts for hours after a jump (❖Fig. 13.11). With repetition, the pleasurable aftereffect gets stronger and the initial "cost" (pain or fear) gets weaker. The opponent-process theory thus explains how skydiving, rock climbing, ski jumping, and other hazardous pursuits become reinforcing. If you are a fan of horror movies, carnival rides, or bungee jumping, your motives may be based on the same effect. (Notice, too, the strong link between motivation and emotion in such examples. We will return to this idea later.)

Social Motives

Competition and achievement are highly valued in Western culture. In less industrialized nations, the desire to achieve may be low. Some of your friends are more interested than others in success, money, possessions, status, love, approval, grades, dominance, power, or belonging to groups. In each case, we are referring to differences in *social motives* or goals. **Social motives** are acquired in complex ways through socialization and cultural conditioning. The behavior of outstanding artists, scientists, athletes, educators, and leaders is best understood in terms of such learned needs, particularly the need for achievement.

The Need for Achievement

To many people, being "motivated" means being interested in achievement. In later chapters, we will investigate aggression, helping, affiliation, seeking approval, and other social motives. For now, let us focus on the need for achievement.

The **need for achievement (nAch)** can be defined as a desire to meet some internal standard of excellence (McClelland, 1961). The person with high needs for achievement strives to do well in any situation in which evaluation takes place.

Is that like the aggressive businessperson who strives for success? Not necessarily. Needs for achievement may lead to wealth and prestige, but a person who is a high achiever in art, music, science, or amateur sports may attain excellence without seeking riches. People high in the need for achievement enjoy challenges and a chance to test their abilities (Puca & Schmalt, 1999).

POWER The need for achievement differs from a **need for power,** which is a desire to have impact or control over others (McClelland, 1975). People with strong needs for power want their importance to be visible: They buy expensive possessions, wear prestigious clothes, and exploit relationships. In some ways, the pursuit of power and financial success is the dark side of the American dream. People whose main goal in life is to make lots of money tend to be poorly adjusted and unhappy (Kasser & Ryan, 1993).

The person with high needs for achievement strives to do well in any situation in which evaluation takes place.

ACHIEVEMENT David McClelland and others have probed the effects of needs for achievement. Using a simple measure of nAch, McClelland found that he could predict the behavior of high and low achievers in many situations. In one study, the occupations of college graduates were compared with scores on a need-for-achievement test they took as sophomores. Fourteen years after graduation, those who scored high in nAch were found more often in careers involving risk and responsibility (McClelland, 1965).

CHARACTERISTICS OF ACHIEVERS In front of you are five targets. Each is placed at an increasing distance from where you are standing. You are given a beanbag to toss at the target of your choice. Target A, anyone can hit; target B, most people can hit; target C, some people can hit; target D, very few people can hit; target E is rarely if ever hit. If you hit A, you will receive $2; B, $4; C, $8; D, $16; and E, $32. You get only one toss. Which one would you choose? McClelland's research suggests that if you have a high need for achievement, you will select C or perhaps D. Those high in nAch are *moderate* risk takers. When faced with a problem or a challenge, persons high in nAch avoid goals that are too easy.

MAIL-ORDER MOTIVATION?

CRITICAL THINKING

Each year, consumers spend millions of dollars on so-called subliminal self-help audiotapes. These tapes supposedly contain messages presented below the level of conscious awareness. Usually, "subliminal messages" are embedded in relaxing music or the soothing sounds of ocean waves. The tapes are purported to "subconsciously" influence motivation to help listeners lose weight, relieve pain, gain intimacy, succeed financially, improve grades, and so forth. Do the tapes work? Tanya Russell, Wayne Rowe, and Albert Smouse (1991) decided to test them under controlled conditions.

Russell, Rowe, and Smouse obtained the tapes "Improve Study Habits" and "Passing Exams" from the largest U.S. manufacturer of subliminal audiotapes. Three groups of university students took part in a 10-week evaluation. An "active treatment group" listened to tapes containing subliminal suggestions. An "inactive treatment group" listened to placebo tapes with ocean wave sounds but no subliminal messages. Students in a control group did not listen to any tapes.

The results of the experiment were certainly not subliminal. The message came through loud and clear: Average final exam grades and semester grade point averages for all three groups revealed no effects or benefits from listening to the tapes (Russell, Rowe, & Smouse, 1991). People who think they have been helped by subliminal tapes apparently have experienced nothing more than a placebo effect (Benoit & Thomas, 1992; Greenwald et al., 1991; Merikle & Skanes, 1992; Moore, 1995; Staum & Brotons, 1992).

Why do they pass up sure success? It's because easy goals offer no sense of satisfaction. They also avoid long shots because there is either no hope of success, or it will be due to luck rather than skill. Persons low in nAch select either sure things or impossible goals. Either way, there is no risk of personal responsibility for failure.

Desires for achievement and calculated risk taking lead to success in many situations. People high in nAch complete difficult tasks, they earn better grades, and they tend to excel in their occupations. College students high in nAch attribute success to their own ability, and failure to insufficient effort. Thus, high-nAch students are more likely to renew their efforts when they perform poorly. When the going gets tough, high achievers get going.

In college, a great deal of importance is placed on academic achievement. In light of this, it is understandable that students are sometimes tempted to buy self-help tapes that promise to improve their motivation to study. Such tapes are aggressively advertised and available in many campus bookstores. However, if you're ever tempted to buy one of these tapes, you should ask a crucial question: Do they work? Read "Mail-Order Motivation?" for an answer.

The Key to Success?

What does it take to achieve extraordinary success? Psychologist Benjamin Bloom did an interesting study of America's top concert pianists, Olympic swimmers, sculptors, tennis players, mathematicians, and research neurologists. Bloom (1985) found that drive and determination, not great natural talent, led to exceptional success.

The first steps toward high achievement began when parents exposed the child to music, swimming, scientific ideas, and so forth, "just for fun." At first many of the children were quite ordinary in their skills. One Olympic swimmer, for instance, remembers repeatedly losing races as a 10-year-old. At some point, however, the children began to more actively cultivate their abilities. Before long, parents noticed the child's rapid progress and sought out an expert instructor or coach. After more successes, the youngsters began "living" for their talent, practicing many hours daily. This continued for many years before they reached truly extraordinary heights of achievement.

The upshot of Bloom's work is that talent is nurtured by dedication and hard work. It is most likely to blossom when parents actively support a child's special interest and emphasize doing one's best at all times. Studies of child prodigies and eminent adults also show that intensive practice and expert coaching are common ingredients of high achievement. Elite performance in music, sports, chess, the arts, and many other

Social motives *Learned motives acquired as part of growing up in a particular society or culture.*
Need for achievement *The desire to excel or meet some internalized standard of excellence.*
Need for power *The desire to have social impact and control over others.*

MOTIVATION AND EMOTION **421**

pursuits requires at least 10 years of dedicated practice (Ericsson & Charness, 1994). The old belief that "talent will out" of its own accord is largely a myth. This is especially true for talented women, who face a wide variety of social obstacles to exceptional achievement (Noble, Subotnik, & Arnold, 1996).

SELF-CONFIDENCE   Achieving elite performance may be reserved for the dedicated few. Nevertheless, anyone can improve everyday motivation by increasing his or her self-confidence. A person with **self-confidence** believes she or he can successfully carry out an activity or reach a goal. To enhance self-confidence, it is wise to do the following (Druckman & Bjork, 1994):

- Set goals that are specific and challenging, but attainable.
- Advance in small steps.
- When you first acquire a skill, your goal should be to make progress in learning. Later, you can concentrate on improving your performance, compared with other people.
- Get expert instruction that helps you master the skill.
- Find a skilled model (someone good at the skill) to emulate.
- Get support and encouragement from an observer.

If you fail, regard it as a sign that you need to try harder, not that you lack ability.

Self-confidence affects motivation because it influences the challenges you will undertake, the effort you will make, and how long you will persist when things don't go well. Psychologists are confident that self-confidence is well worth cultivating.

MOTIVES IN PERSPECTIVE—A VIEW FROM THE PYRAMID

As you may recall from Chapter 1, humanistic psychologist Abraham Maslow defined self-actualization as the full development of personal potential. As a sidelight to his work on self-actualization, Maslow proposed that there is a **hierarchy of human needs.** By this, he meant that some needs are more basic or powerful than others. Think for a moment about the needs that influence your behavior. Which seem strongest? Which do you spend the most time and energy satisfying? Now look at Maslow's hierarchy (❖Fig. 13.12). Note that physiological needs are at the bottom. Because these are necessary for survival, they tend to be prepotent, or dominant over the higher needs. It could be said, for example, that "to a starving person, food is god."

Maslow believed that higher needs are expressed only after the prepotent physiological needs are satisfied. This is also true of needs for safety and security. Until there is a basic amount of order and stability in meeting such needs, a person may have little interest in higher pursuits. A person who is extremely thirsty, for instance, might have little interest in writing poetry or even just talking with friends. For this reason, Maslow described the first four levels of the hierarchy as **basic needs.** Other basic needs include love and belonging (family, friendship, caring) and esteem and self-esteem (recognition and self-respect).

All of the basic needs are *deficiency* motives. That is, they are activated by a *lack* of food, water, security, love, esteem, or other basic needs. At the top of the hierarchy we find **growth needs,** represented by the need for self-actualization. The need for self-actualization is not based on deficiencies. Rather, it is a positive, life-enhancing force for personal growth. Like other humanists, Maslow believed that people are basically good. If their basic needs are met, they will actualize their potentials.

How are needs for self-actualization expressed?   Maslow called the less powerful but humanly important actualization motives **meta-needs** (Maslow, 1970). They are listed in ◆Table 13.2. According to Maslow, we have a tendency to move up the hierarchy to the meta-needs. A person whose survival needs are met, but whose meta-needs are unfulfilled, falls into a "syndrome of decay." Such people experience despair, apathy, and alienation.

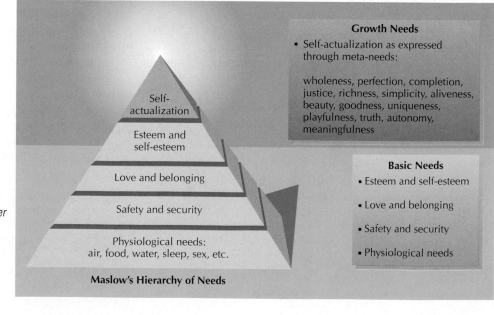

❖ **FIGURE 13.12** *Maslow believed that lower needs in the hierarchy are dominant. Basic needs must be satisfied before growth motives are fully expressed. Desires for self-actualization are reflected in various meta-needs (see text).*

Growth Needs
- Self-actualization as expressed through meta-needs:

  wholeness, perfection, completion, justice, richness, simplicity, aliveness, beauty, goodness, uniqueness, playfulness, truth, autonomy, meaningfulness

Basic Needs
- Esteem and self-esteem
- Love and belonging
- Safety and security
- Physiological needs

Self-actualization
Esteem and self-esteem
Love and belonging
Safety and security
Physiological needs: air, food, water, sleep, sex, etc.

Maslow's Hierarchy of Needs

Wheelchair athletes engage in vigorous competition. Maslow considered such behavior an expression of the need for self-actualization.

◆ **TABLE 13.2** Maslow's List of Meta-Needs

Meta-needs are seen as an expression of tendencies for self-actualization, the full development of personal potential.

1. Wholeness (unity)

2. Perfection (balance and harmony)

3. Completion (ending)

4. Justice (fairness)

5. Richness (complexity)

6. Simplicity (essence)

7. Aliveness (spontaneity)

8. Beauty (rightness of form)

9. Goodness (benevolence)

10. Uniqueness (individuality)

11. Playfulness (ease)

12. Truth (reality)

13. Autonomy (self-sufficiency)

14. Meaningfulness (values)

Maslow's point is that mere survival or comfort is usually not enough to make a full and satisfying life. It's interesting to note, in this regard, that college students who are primarily concerned with financial success, personal appearance, and social recognition score lower than average in vitality, self-actualization, and general well-being (Kasser & Ryan, 1996).

Maslow's hierarchy is not well documented by research, and many questions can be raised about it. How, for instance, do we explain the use of fasting as a means of social protest? How has the meta-need for justice overcome the more basic need for food? (Perhaps the answer is that fasting is temporary and self-imposed.) Despite such objections, Maslow's views have been influential as a way of understanding and appreciating the rich interplay of human motives. Rather than being a scientific theory, Maslow's hierarchy represents a philosophical viewpoint.

Did Maslow believe that many people are motivated by meta-needs? Maslow estimated that few people are primarily motivated by self-actualization needs. Most are more concerned with esteem, love, or security. Perhaps this is because incentives and rewards in our society are slanted to encourage conformity, uniformity, and security in schools, jobs, and relationships. When was the last time you met a meta-need?

Intrinsic and Extrinsic Motivation

Some people cook for a living and consider it hard work. Others cook for pleasure and dream of opening a restaurant. For some people, carpentry, gardening, writing, photography, or jewelry making is fun. For others, the same activities are

BRIDGES

Maslow provided few guidelines for promoting self-actualization. However, some suggestions can be gleaned from his writings.

See Chapter 15, pages 499–500.

drudgery they must be paid to do. How can the same activity be "work" for one person and "play" for another?

When you perform an activity for enjoyment, to show your ability, or to gain skill, your motivation is usually *intrinsic*. **Intrinsic motivation** occurs when there is no obvious external reward or ulterior purpose behind your actions. You simply enjoy the activity as an end in itself, as a new challenge, as a way to enhance your

Self-confidence *Belief that one can successfully carry out an activity or reach a goal.*
Hierarchy of human needs *Abraham Maslow's ordering of needs, based on their presumed strength or potency.*
Basic needs *The first four levels of needs in Maslow's hierarchy; lower needs tend to be more potent than higher needs.*
Growth needs *In Maslow's hierarchy, the higher level needs associated with self-actualization.*
Meta-needs *In Maslow's hierarchy, needs associated with impulses for self-actualization.*
Intrinsic motivation *Motivation that comes from within, rather than from external rewards; motivation based on personal enjoyment of a task or activity.*

abilities, or as a chance to explore and learn. In contrast, **extrinsic motivation** stems from obvious external factors, such as pay, grades, rewards, obligations, and approval. Most of the activities we think of as "work" are extrinsically rewarded (Ryan & Deci, 2000).

Turning Play into Work

It might seem that increasing extrinsic incentives would strengthen motivation, but this is not always the case (Lepper, Keavney, & Drake, 1996). Research with children shows that excessive rewards can undermine spontaneous interest (Ross et al., 1976). For instance, children lavishly rewarded for drawing with felt-tip pens later showed little interest in playing with them again (Greene & Lepper, 1974). Apparently, "play" can be turned into "work" by *requiring* a person to do something he or she would otherwise enjoy. In general, strong extrinsic rewards tend to decrease intrinsic motivation (Tang & Hall, 1995). People who are coerced or "bribed" to act tend to become alienated and feel as if they are "faking it." Examples of such reactions are employees who show no initiative and teenagers who reject school and learning (Ryan & Deci, 2000).

CREATIVITY   People are more likely to be creative when they are intrinsically motivated. On the job, for instance, salaries and bonuses may increase the amount of work done. However, work *quality* is tied more to intrinsic factors, such as interest, freedom to choose, and useful feedback (Kohn, 1987). Intrinsic motivation also promotes personal involvement in a task. This, in turn, tends to lead to greater creativity (Ruscio, Whitney, & Amabile, 1998).

People who are intrinsically motivated feel free to explore creative solutions to problems.

Psychologist Teresa Amabile lists the following as "creativity killers" on the job:

- Working under surveillance
- Having your choices restricted by rules
- Working primarily to get a good evaluation (or avoid a bad one)
- Working mainly to get more money

When a person is intrinsically motivated, a certain amount of challenge, surprise, and complexity makes a task rewarding. When extrinsic motivation is stressed, complexity, surprise, and challenge just become barriers to reaching a goal (Pittman & Heller, 1987). A person who is extrinsically motivated wants to take the fastest, most direct route to a goal. Typically, this undermines creativity (Sternberg & Lubart, 1995).

How can the concept of intrinsic motivation be applied?   Motivation can't always be intrinsic. Nor should it be. Not every worthwhile activity is intrinsically satisfying. In addition, extrinsic motivation is often needed if we are to develop enough skill or knowledge for an activity to become intrinsically rewarding. This effect can be observed in learning to read, play a musical instrument, or enjoy a sport.

In summary, both types of motivation are necessary. But extrinsic motivation should not be overused, especially with children. Greene and Lepper (1974) summarize: (1) If there's no intrinsic interest in an activity to begin with, you have nothing to lose by using extrinsic rewards; (2) if basic skills are lacking, extrinsic rewards may be necessary at first; (3) extrinsic rewards can focus attention on an activity so real interest will develop; (4) if extrinsic rewards are used, they should be small and faded out as soon as possible. It also helps to tell children they seem to be *really interested* in drawing, playing the piano, learning a language, or whatever activity you are rewarding (Cialdini et al., 1998).

At work, managers should try to find out what each employee's interests and career goals are. It can be a mistake to assume that people are motivated only by money. A chance to do challenging, interesting, and intrinsically rewarding work is often just as important. If you are aware of intrinsic motivation, you can do much to avoid taking spontaneous interest and satisfaction out of activities, especially for children learning new skills.

KNOWLEDGE BUILDER

STIMULUS MOTIVES, LEARNED MOTIVES, MASLOW, AND INTRINSIC MOTIVATION

RELATE

Does arousal theory seem to explain any of your own behavior? Think of at least one time when your performance was impaired by arousal that was too low or too high. Now think of some personal examples that illustrate the Yerkes-Dodson law.

In situations involving risk and skill, do you like to "go for broke"? Or do you prefer sure things? Do you think you are high, medium, or low in nAch?

Which levels of Maslow's hierarchy of needs occupy most of your time and energy?

Name an activity you do that is intrinsically motivated and one that is extrinsically motivated. How do they differ?

DISSECTING AN EMOTION—HOW DO YOU FEEL?

If a mad scientist were to replace your best friend's brain with a computer, how would you know that something was different? One of the first telltale signs might be an absence of emotion. **Emotion** is a state characterized by physiological arousal and changes in facial expressions, gestures, posture, and subjective feelings.

The root of the word *emotion* means "to move," and emotions do indeed move us. First, the body is physically aroused during emotion. Such bodily stirrings are what cause us to say we were "moved" by a play, a funeral, or an act of kindness. Second, we are often motivated, or moved to take action, by emotions such as fear, anger, or joy. Many of the goals we seek make us feel good. Many of the activities we avoid make us feel bad. Success is usually accompanied by pleasant emotions, and failure by unpleasant emotions. For such reasons, the story of human motivation is also an emotional tale (Oatley & Jenkins, 1992).

Underlying all this, perhaps, is the fact that emotions are linked to basic *adaptive behaviors,* such as attacking, retreating, seeking comfort, helping others, and reproducing. **Adaptive behaviors** aid our attempts to survive and adjust to changing conditions (Plutchik, 1990, 1994). It is equally apparent, however, that emotions can have a negative effect. Stage fright or choking up in sports can spoil performances. Hate, anger, contempt, disgust, and fear all disrupt behavior and relationships. But more often, emotions aid survival.

A pounding heart, sweating palms, "butterflies" in the stomach, and other bodily reactions are a major element of fear, anger, joy, and other emotions. These **physiological changes** include alterations in heart rate, blood pressure, perspiration, and other bodily stirrings. (More on this in a moment.) Most of these changes in activity are caused by **adrenaline,** a hormone produced by the adrenal glands. Adrenaline enters the bloodstream when the sympathetic nervous system is activated. People who have had their adrenal glands removed for medical reasons display much less emotional arousal (Hepburn, Deary, & MacLeod, 1996).

Emotional expressions, or outward signs of what a person is feeling, are another major element of emotion. For example, when you are intensely afraid, your hands tremble, your face contorts, and your posture becomes tense and defensive. Emotion is also revealed by marked shifts in voice tone or modulation. Such expressions are important because they communicate emotion from one person to another (❖Fig. 13.13). **Emotional feelings** (a person's private emotional experience) are a final major element of emotion. This is the part of emotion with which we are usually most familiar.

Primary Emotions

Are some emotions more basic than others? Based on his research, Robert Plutchik (1990, 1994) believes there are eight **primary emotions:** fear, surprise, sadness, disgust, anger, antic-

Extrinsic motivation *Motivation based on obvious external rewards, obligations, or similar factors.*
Emotion *A state characterized by physiological arousal, changes in facial expression, gestures, posture, and subjective feelings.*
Adaptive behaviors *Actions that aid attempts to survive and adapt to changing conditions.*
Physiological changes (in emotion) *Alterations in heart rate, blood pressure, perspiration, and other involuntary responses.*
Adrenaline *A hormone produced by the adrenal glands that tends to arouse the body.*
Emotional expression *Outward signs that an emotion is occurring.*
Emotional feelings *The private, subjective experience of having an emotion.*
Primary emotions *According to Robert Plutchik, the most basic emotions are fear, surprise, sadness, disgust, anger, anticipation, joy, and acceptance.*

❖ **FIGURE 13.13** *How accurately do facial expressions reveal emotion? After you have guessed what emotion these people are feeling, turn to* ❖*Figure 13.20.*

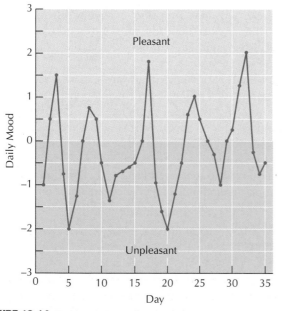

❖ **FIGURE 13.14** *Folklore holds that people who work or attend school on a weekly schedule experience their lowest moods on "Blue Monday." Actually, moods tend to be generally lower for most weekdays than they are on weekends. The graph shown here plots the average daily mood ratings made by a group of college students over a 5-week period. As you can see, many people find that their moods rise and fall on a 7-day cycle. For most students, a low point tends to occur around Monday or Tuesday and a peak on Friday or Saturday. (Adapted from Larsen & Kasimatis, 1990.) In other words, moods are often entrained (pulled along) by weekly schedules.*

ipation, joy, and acceptance (receptivity). If the list seems too short, it's because each emotion can vary in *intensity*. Anger, for instance, may vary from rage to simple annoyance.

The mildest forms of various emotions are called *moods* (❖Fig. 13.14). A **mood** is a low-intensity, long-lasting emotional state. Moods act as a subtle emotional undercurrent that

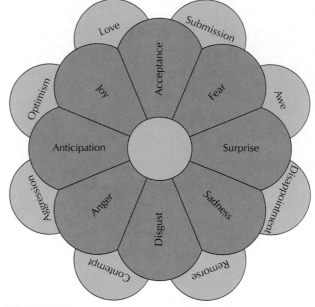

❖ **FIGURE 13.15** *Primary and mixed emotions. In Robert Plutchik's model, there are eight primary emotions, as listed in the inner areas. Adjacent emotions may combine to give the emotions listed around the perimeter. Mixtures involving more widely separated emotions are also possible. For example, fear plus anticipation produces anxiety. (Adapted from Plutchik, 1980.)*

affects day-to-day behavior (Clark & Williamson, 1989). Emotions typically last from a few seconds to a few hours. Moods can last for many hours, or even days. Moods often prepare us to act in certain ways. For example, when your neighbor Roseanne is in an irritable mood, she may react angrily to almost anything you say. When she is in a happy mood, she can easily laugh off an insult (Oatley & Jenkins, 1992). Our moods are closely tied to circadian rhythms. When body temperature is at its daily low point, people tend to feel "down," emotionally. When body temperature is at its peak, your mood is likely to be positive—even if you missed a night of sleep (Boivin, Czeisler, & Waterhouse, 1997).

One of Plutchik's most interesting ideas concerns the mixing of primary emotions. As shown in ❖Figure 13.15, each pair of adjacent emotions can be mixed to yield a third, more complex emotion. Other mixtures are also possible. For example, 5-year-old Shannon feels both joy and fear as she eats a stolen cookie. The result? Guilt—as you may recall from your own childhood. Likewise, jealousy could be a mixture of love, anger, and fear.

The Brain and Emotion

The primary emotions we have discussed can be further reduced to just two categories: positive and negative emotions. Ordinarily, we might think that positive and negative emotions are opposites. But this is not the case. As Shannon's "cookie guilt" implies, people can experience positive and negative emotions at the same time. How is that possible? Recordings of brain activity show that positive emotions are processed mainly

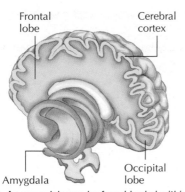

Frontal lobe

Cerebral cortex

Amygdala

Occipital lobe

❖ **FIGURE 13.16** *An amygdala can be found buried within the temporal lobes on each side of the brain (see Chapter 3). The amygdala appears to provide "quick and dirty" processing of emotional stimuli that allows us to react involuntarily to danger.*

in the left hemisphere of the brain. In contrast, negative emotions are processed in the right hemisphere. The fact that positive and negative emotions are based on different brain areas helps explain why we can feel happy and sad at the same time (Canli, 1998).

Scientists used to think that all emotions are processed by the cerebral cortex. However, this is not always the case. Imagine this test of willpower: Go to a zoo and place your face close to the glass in front of a rattlesnake display. Suddenly, the rattlesnake strikes at your face. Do you flinch? Even though you know you are safe, researcher Joseph LeDoux predicts that you will recoil from the snake's attack (LeDoux, 1999).

LeDoux and other researchers have found that an area of the brain called the **amygdala** (ah-MIG-duh-la) specializes in producing fear (❖Fig. 13.16). (See Chapter 3 for more information.) The amygdala receives sensory information very directly and quickly, bypassing the cortex. As a result, it allows us to respond to potentially dangerous stimuli before we really know what's happening. This primitive fear response is not under the control of higher brain centers. The role of the amygdala in emotion may explain why people who suffer from phobias and disabling anxiety often feel afraid without knowing why (LeDoux, 1999).

People who suffer damage to the amygdala become "blind" to emotion. An armed robber could hold a gun to the person's head and the person wouldn't feel fear. Such people are also unable to "read" or understand other people's emotions. Many lose their ability to relate normally to friends, family, and coworkers (Goleman, 1995).

Later we will attempt to put all the elements of emotion together into a single picture. But first, we need to look more closely at physiological arousal and emotional expressions.

PHYSIOLOGY AND EMOTION—AROUSAL, SUDDEN DEATH, AND LYING

To a large degree, the physical aspects of emotion are innate, or built into the body. The physical reactions of an African Bush-man frightened by a wild animal and an urbane city dweller frightened by a prowler are quite similar (Mesquita & Frijda, 1992). Reactions to unpleasant emotions are especially consistent. Typically, they include muscle tension, a pounding heart, irritability, dryness of the throat and mouth, sweating, butterflies in the stomach, frequent urination, trembling, restlessness, sensitivity to loud noises, and a large number of internal changes. These reactions are nearly universal because they are caused by the **autonomic nervous system** (**ANS**) (the neural system that connects the brain with the internal organs and glands).

As you may recall from Chapter 3, activity of the ANS is *automatic* and not normally under voluntary control. There are two divisions of the ANS, one called the sympathetic branch and the other the parasympathetic branch. The two branches are active at all times. Whether you are relaxed or aroused depends on the combined activity of both.

Fight or Flight

What does the ANS do during emotion? In general, the **sympathetic branch** activates the body for emergency action—for "fighting or fleeing." It does this by arousing a number of bodily systems and inhibiting others. (Sympathetic nervous system effects are listed in ◆Table 13.3.) These changes have a purpose. Sugar is released into the bloodstream for quick energy, the heart beats faster to supply blood to the muscles, digestion is temporarily slowed, blood flow in the skin is restricted to reduce bleeding, and so forth. Most sympathetic reactions improve the chances of surviving an emergency. To learn about an interesting sidelight of sympathetic arousal, see "Emotion—Do the Eyes Have It?"

The **parasympathetic branch** generally reverses emotional arousal and calms and relaxes the body. After a period of high emotion, the heart is slowed, the pupils return to normal size, blood pressure drops, and so forth. In addition to restoring balance, the parasympathetic system helps build up and conserve bodily energy.

The parasympathetic system responds much more slowly than the sympathetic system. That's why increased heart rate, muscle tension, and other signs of arousal do not fade for 20 or 30 minutes after you feel an intense emotion, such as fear. Moreover, after a strong emotional shock, the parasympathetic system may overreact and lower blood pressure too much. This is why people sometimes become dizzy or faint at the sight of blood and other such shocks (Kleinknecht, 1986).

Mood *A low-intensity, long-lasting emotional state.*
Amygdala *A part of the limbic system (within the brain) that produces fear responses.*
Autonomic nervous system (ANS) *The system of nerves that connects the brain with the internal organs and glands.*
Sympathetic branch *A part of the ANS that activates the body at times of stress.*
Parasympathetic branch *A part of the autonomic system that quiets the body and conserves energy.*

◆ **TABLE 13.3** Autonomic Nervous System Effects

ORGAN	PARASYMPATHETIC SYSTEM	SYMPATHETIC SYSTEM
Pupils of eyes Tear glands Mucous membranes of nose and throat Salivary glands	Constricts to diminish light Stimulates secretion	Dilates to increase light Inhibits secretion, causes dryness
Heart Blood vessels	Slowing of heart, constriction of blood vessels	Acceleration of heart; dilation of blood vessels to increase blood flow
Lungs, windpipe	Constricts bronchi of lungs to relax breathing	Dilates bronchi to increase breathing
Esophagus Stomach Abdominal blood vessels	Stimulates secretion and movement	Inhibits secretion and movement, diverts blood flow
Liver	Liberates bile	Retains bile, releases blood sugar
Pancreas	Stimulates secretion	Inhibits secretion
Intestines Rectum Kidney Bladder	Excitation, expulsion of feces and urine	Inhibition, retention of feces and urine
Skin blood vessels	Dilate, increase blood flow	Constrict; skin becomes cold and clammy
Sweat glands	Inhibited	Stimulated to increase perspiration
Hair follicles	Relaxed	Tensed to make hair stand on end

EMOTION—DO THE EYES HAVE IT?

Is there any truth to the idea that the eyes can reveal emotion? The eyes have long been called "windows on the soul" and regarded as clues to emotion. If you doubt someone's word, you may ask them to "look you in the eye." Many seasoned poker players claim to have detected a bluff by watching the eyes of their opponents. Psychologist Eckhard Hess believes that in such instances we are mainly interested in the size of a person's *pupils.* As shown in ◆ Table 13.3, emotion affects the pupils. Specifically, *arousal, interest,* or *attention* can activate the sympathetic nervous system and cause the pupils to dilate (enlarge).

Dilation of the pupils can occur during both pleasant and unpleasant emotions. Despite this fact, most people tend to interpret *large* pupils as a sign of pleasant feelings and *small* pupils as a sign of negative feelings. To illustrate, Hess (1975a) showed two photos of an attractive young woman to a group of men. In one photograph, the woman's pupils were large. In the other, they were small. The men consistently described the woman with large pupils as "soft," "feminine," or "pretty." The same woman, with small pupils, was described as "hard," "selfish," and "cold" (❖ Fig. 13.17).

This effect, of course, does not apply only to women. In another experiment, subjects were introduced to two individuals of the opposite sex and asked to choose one as a partner for the experiment. One person in each pair had been given eye drops to dilate his or her pupils, and the other had not. Subjects of both sexes tended to select the person with the larger pupils as a partner. (Perhaps at long last we know why the bad guys in movies always have beady eyes!)

❖ **FIGURE 13.17** *Select the face you think looks more attractive, warm, or friendly. Research by Eckhard Hess (1975b) suggests you will choose the face on the left because the pupils of the eyes are larger.*

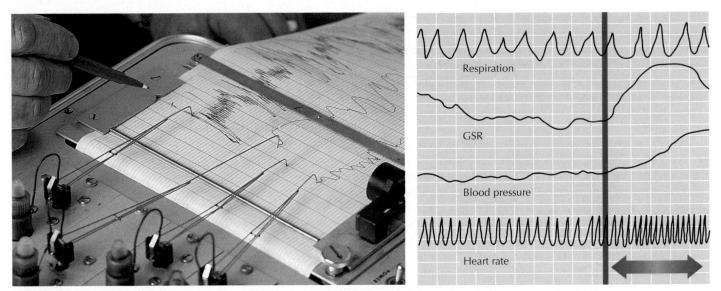

❖ FIGURE 13.18 (left) *A typical polygraph includes devices for measuring heart rate, blood pressure, respiration, and galvanic skin response. Pens mounted on the top of the machine make a record of bodily responses on a moving strip of paper.* (right) *Changes in the area marked by the arrow indicate emotional arousal. If such responses appear when a person answers a question, he or she may be lying, but other causes of arousal are also possible.*

SUDDEN DEATH   As noted, the parasympathetic system may overreact during intense fear or after any period of intense emotion. This response is called a **parasympathetic rebound.** When it is severe, it can sometimes cause death. In times of war, combat can be so savage that some soldiers literally die of fear (Moritz & Zamchech, 1946). Apparently, such deaths are caused when the parasympathetic nervous system overreacts and slows the heart to a stop. Even in civilian life, this is possible. In one case, a terrified young woman was admitted to a hospital because she felt she was going to die. A backwoods midwife had predicted that the woman's two sisters would die before their sixteenth and twenty-first birthdays. Both died as predicted. The midwife also predicted that this woman would die before her twenty-third birthday. She was found dead in her hospital bed the day after she was admitted. It was 2 days before her twenty-third birthday (Seligman, 1989). The woman was an apparent victim of her own terror.

Is the parasympathetic nervous system always responsible for such deaths?   Probably not. In the case of older people or those with heart problems, the direct effects of sympathetic activation may be enough to bring about heart attack and collapse. For example, five times more people than usual died of heart attacks on the day of a major 1994 earthquake in Los Angeles (Leor, Poole, & Kloner, 1996). Psychiatrist George Engel (1977) studied hundreds of similar occurrences and concluded that almost half of all sudden deaths are associated with the traumatic disruption of a close relationship, such as the anniversary of the death of a loved one. Recently widowed men, for instance, have a sudden death rate 40 percent higher than married men of the same age. Clearly, relationships are one of the most potent sources of human emotional response.

Lie Detectors

Did O.J. do it? Did Monica tell the whole truth? Has a trusted employee been stealing from the business? There are many situations in which we would like to be able to detect lying. The most popular method for detecting lies measures some of the bodily changes that accompany emotion. However, "lie detection" must be questioned for two reasons: First, the lie detector's accuracy is doubtful; second, such testing is often a serious invasion of privacy (Iacono & Lykken, 1997; Lykken, 1998; Saxe, 1994).

What is a lie detector? Do lie detectors really detect lies?   The lie detector is more accurately called a *polygraph*, a word that means "many writings" (❖Fig. 13.18). A **polygraph** is a device that records changes in heart rate, blood pressure, breathing rate, and the galvanic skin response. The **galvanic skin response** (GSR) is recorded from the surface of the hand by electrodes that measure skin conductance or, more simply, sweating. The polygraph is popularly known as a lie detector because police use it. In reality, the polygraph is not a lie detector at all. As critic David Lykken points out, there is no unique "lie response" that everyone gives when not telling the truth. The machine records only *general emotional arousal*—it can't tell the difference between lying and fear, anxiety, or excitement (Lykken, 1998).

Parasympathetic rebound *Excess activity in the parasympathetic nervous system following a period of intense emotion.*
Polygraph *A device for recording heart rate, blood pressure, respiration, and galvanic skin response; commonly called a "lie detector."*
Galvanic skin response (GSR) *A change in the electrical resistance (or inversely, the conductance) of the skin, due to sweating.*

When trying to detect a lie, the polygraph operator begins by asking **irrelevant** (neutral, nonemotional) **questions,** such as "Is your name (person's name)?" and "Did you eat lunch today?" This establishes a "baseline" for normal emotional responsiveness. Then relevant questions can be asked: "Did you murder Hensley?" **Relevant questions** are those to which only a guilty person should react. A person who lies will presumably become anxious or emotional when answering relevant questions.

Wouldn't a person be nervous just from being questioned? Yes, but to minimize this problem, skilled polygraph examiners ask a *series* of questions, with critical items mixed among them. An innocent person may respond emotionally to the whole procedure, but only a guilty person is supposed to respond more to key questions. For example, a suspected bank robber might be shown several pictures and asked, "Was the teller who was robbed this person? Was it this person?"

As an alternative, subjects may be asked control questions that can be compared with critical questions. **Control questions** are designed to make almost anyone anxious: "Have you ever stolen anything from your place of work?" Typically, control questions are very difficult to answer truthfully with an unqualified no. In theory, they allow the examiner to see how a person reacts to doubt or misgivings. The person's reaction to critical questions can then be compared with responses to control questions.

Even when questioning is done properly, lie detection may be inaccurate (Dawson, 1990). For example, a man named Floyd Fay was convicted of murdering his friend Fred Ery. To prove his innocence, Fay volunteered to take a lie detector test, which he failed. Fay spent 2 years in prison before the real killer confessed to the crime. Psychologist David Lykken (1998) has documented many cases in which innocent people were jailed after being convicted on the basis of polygraph evidence.

If Floyd Fay was innocent, why did he fail the test? Put yourself in his place, and it's easy to see why. Imagine the examiner asking, "Did you kill Fred?" Because you knew Fred, and you are a suspect, it's no secret that this is a critical question. What would happen to *your* heart rate, blood pressure, breathing, and perspiration under such circumstances?

Proponents of lie detection claim from 90 to 95 percent accuracy. But in one laboratory experiment, accuracy was dramatically lowered when people thought about past emotional situations as they answered irrelevant questions (Ben-Shakhar & Dolev, 1996). Similarly, the polygraph may be thrown off by self-inflicted pain, by tranquilizing drugs, or by people who can lie without anxiety (Waid & Orne, 1982). Worst of all, the test's most common error is to label an innocent person guilty, rather than a guilty person innocent (Lykken, 1981; Patrick & Iacono, 1989).

In field studies involving real crimes and criminal suspects, an average of approximately 1 innocent person in 5 was rated as guilty by the lie detector (Saxe et al., 1985). In some instances, these false positives caused 3 out of 4 innocent persons to be labeled guilty. Individuals who believe the polygraph is highly accurate may actually change their statements to be consistent with the test. This, too, can leave an innocent person open to false accusations (Meyer & Youngjohn, 1991).

Despite the lie detector's unreliability, you may be tested for employment or other reasons. Should this occur, the best advice is to remain calm; then, actively challenge the outcome if the machine wrongly questions your honesty.

KNOWLEDGE BUILDER

EMOTION AND PHYSIOLOGICAL AROUSAL

RELATE

How did your most emotional moment of the past week affect your behavior, expressions, feelings, and bodily state? Could you detect both sympathetic and parasympathetic effects?

Make a list of the emotions you consider to be most basic. To what extent do they agree with Plutchik's list?

What did you think about the lie detector test before reading this chapter? What do you think now?

LEARNING CHECK

1. Many of the physiological changes associated with emotion are caused by secretion of the hormone
   a. atropine *b.* adrenaline *c.* attributine *d.* amoduline

2. Emotional _____ often serve to communicate a person's emotional state to others.

3. Awe, remorse, and disappointment are among the primary emotions listed by Robert Plutchik. T or F?

4. Emotional arousal is closely related to activity of the _____ nervous system.

5. The sympathetic system prepares the body for "fight or flight" by activating the parasympathetic system. T or F?

6. The parasympathetic system inhibits digestion and raises blood pressure and heart rate. T or F?

7. What bodily changes are measured by a polygraph?

   _____

   _____

CRITICAL THINKING

8. Can you explain why people "cursed" by shamans or "witch doctors" sometimes actually die?

Answers:

1. *b* 2. expressions 3. F 4. autonomic 5. F 6. F 7. heart rate, blood pressure, breathing rate, galvanic skin response 8. In cultures where there is deep belief in magic or voodoo, a person who thinks that she or he has been cursed may become uncontrollably emotional. After several days of intense terror, a parasympathetic rebound is likely. If the rebound is severe enough, it can lead to physical collapse and death.

EXPRESSING EMOTIONS—MAKING FACES AND TALKING BODIES

Are human emotional expressions a carryover from more primitive stages of human evolution? Charles Darwin thought so. Darwin (1872) observed that tigers, monkeys, dogs, and humans all bare their teeth in the same way during rage. Darwin believed that emotional expressions were retained during the course of human evolution because communicating feelings to others is an aid to survival. Today, emotional expressions give us valuable hints about what others are feeling (Oatley & Jenkins, 1992). It would be difficult to live, work, or play with others without such messages. Among other things, emotional expressions provide a major clue as to what another person is about to do next (Ekman & Rosenberg, 1997).

Facial Expressions

Are emotional expressions the same for all people? The most basic expressions appear to be fairly universal (❖Fig. 13.19). Children who are born blind have little opportunity to learn emotional expressions from others. Even so, they use the same facial gestures as others to display joy, sadness, disgust, and so on. In fact, the gestures of such children may be one of the few examples of "pure" emotional expression (Galati, Scherer, & Ricci-Bitti, 1997).

Many adult facial expressions are influenced by learning. As a result, some are unique to certain cultures. Among the Chinese, for example, sticking out the tongue is a gesture of surprise, not disrespect or teasing. If a person comes from a

❖ **FIGURE 13.19** *Facial expressions of anger often act as a warning of threat or impending attack. Is anger expressed the same way in different cultures? A study of masks from 18 cultures found that those meant to be frightening or threatening were strikingly similar. Shared features included angular, diagonal, or triangular eyes, eyebrows, nose, cheeks, and chin, together with an open, downward-curved mouth. (Keep this list in mind next Halloween.) Obviously, the pictured mask is not meant to be warm and cuddly. Your ability to "read" its emotional message suggests that basic emotional expressions have universal biological roots (Aronoff, Barclay, & Stevenson, 1988).*

The expression of emotion is strongly influenced by learning. As you have no doubt observed, women cry more often, longer, and more intensely than men do. Men begin learning early in childhood to suppress crying—possibly to the detriment of their emotional health (Williams & Morris, 1996).

culture other than your own, it is wise to remember that you can easily misunderstand his or her expressions. At such times, the social *context* in which the expression occurred helps us interpret what others are feeling (Carroll & Russell, 1996; Ekman, 1993).

Despite cultural differences, facial expressions of *fear, anger, disgust, sadness,* and *happiness* (enjoyment) are recognized around the world. *Contempt, surprise,* and *interest* may also be universal, although researchers are less certain of these expressions (Ekman, 1993). Notice that this list covers most of the primary emotions described earlier. It's also nice to note that a smile is the most universal and easily recognized facial expression of emotion.

CULTURAL DIFFERENCES IN EMOTION How many times have you been angry this week? Once? Twice? Several times? If it was more than once, you're not unusual. Anger is a very common emotion in Western cultures. Very likely this is because our culture emphasizes personal independence and a free expression of individual rights and needs. In North America, anger is widely viewed as a "natural" reaction to feeling that you have been treated unfairly. On a broad scale, our willingness to freely express anger upholds and reinforces a valued cultural belief—namely, that personal rights should be protected.

Irrelevant questions *In a polygraph exam, neutral, nonthreatening, or nonemotional questions.*
Relevant questions *In a polygraph exam, questions to which only a guilty person should react.*
Control questions *In a polygraph exam, questions that almost always provoke anxiety.*

On the opposite side of the globe, many Asian cultures place a high value on group harmony. In Asian cultures, expressing anger in public is less common, and anger is regarded as less "natural." The reason for this is that anger tends to separate people. Thus, being angry is at odds with a culture that values interdependence among individuals.

It is common to think of emotion as an individual event. However, as you can see, emotion is shaped by cultural ideas, values, and practices (Markus, Kitayama, & VandenBos, 1996).

GENDER DIFFERENCES IN EMOTION *Women have a reputation for being "more emotional" than men. Are they?* There is little reason to think that men and women differ in their private experiences of emotion. However, in Western cultures, women do tend to be more emotionally expressive (Kring & Gordon, 1998). Why should this be so? The answer again lies in the impact of learning: As they are growing up, boys learn to suppress their emotional expressions; girls tend to increase theirs (Polce-Lynch, 1998). For many men, an inability to express feelings is a major barrier to having close, satisfying relationships with others (Bruch, Berko, & Haase, 1998). It may even contribute to tragedies like the mass murders at Columbine High School in Littleton, Colorado. For many young males, anger becomes the only emotion they can freely express.

Body Language

If a friend approached you and said, "Hey, ugly, what are you doing?" would you be offended? Probably not, because such expressions are usually accompanied by a big grin. The facial and bodily gestures of emotion speak a language all their own and add an extra message to what a person says. The study of communication through body movement, posture, gestures, and facial expressions is called **kinesics** (kih-NEEZ-iks). Informally,

we call it body language. To see a masterful use of body language, turn off the TV sound sometime and watch a popular entertainer or politician at work.

What kinds of messages are sent with body language? Popular books on body language tend to list particular meanings for gestures. For instance, a woman who stands rigidly, crosses her arms over her chest, or sits with her legs tightly crossed is supposedly sending a "hands off" message. But experts in kinesics emphasize that gestures are rarely this fixed in meaning. The message might simply be "This room is cold."

It is also important to realize cultural learning also affects the meaning of gestures. What, for instance, does it mean if you touch your thumb and first finger together to form a circle? In North America it means "Everything is fine" or "A-okay." In France and Belgium, it means "You're worth zero." In southern Italy it means "You're an ass!" (Ekman et al., 1984). Thus, when the layer of culturally defined meanings is removed, it is more realistic to say that body language reveals an overall **emotional tone** (underlying emotional state).

The human face is capable of producing some 20,000 different expressions, which makes it the most expressive part of the body. Most of these are **facial blends** that mix two or more basic expressions. Imagine, for example, that you just received an F on an unfair test. Quite likely, your eyes, eyebrows, and forehead would show anger, while your mouth would express sadness.

Most of us believe we can fairly accurately tell what others are feeling by observing facial expressions. If thousands of facial blends occur, how do we make such judgments? The answer lies in the fact that facial expressions can be boiled down to basic dimensions of **pleasantness-unpleasantness, attention-rejection,** and **activation** (or arousal) (Schlosberg, 1954). By smiling when giving a friend a hard time, you add an emotional message of pleasantness and acceptance to the verbal insult and change its meaning. As they say in movie

Emotions are often unconsciously revealed by gestures and body positioning.

❖ **FIGURE 13.20** *Facial displays and gestures that express complex emotions can be difficult to judge accurately. The agonized expression on the face of Frank De Vito is deceptive. When this photograph was taken, Mr. De Vito and his wife had just learned that he won $1 million in a state lottery.*

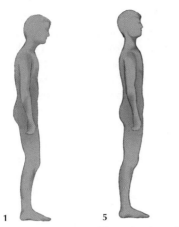

❖ **FIGURE 13.21** *Posture and success. These drawings show the end points of a five-point scale used to measure erectness of posture. Success by people in various situations was found to be reflected by a more upright posture. (Adapted from Weisfeld & Beresford, 1982.)*

BEHAVIORAL LIE CATCHING

The salesman swears that he is giving you "the buy of a lifetime." If you can't touch his tongue to a hot knife, how else can you tell if he's lying?

Most people assume that shifty eyes and squirming are clear signs of lying. But Paul Ekman (1986) found that neither of these clues increases when a person is fibbing. Also contrary to what you might expect, nervous movements that involve touching one's own body (rubbing, grooming, scratching, twisting hair, rubbing hands, biting lips, stroking the chin, and so on) are not consistently related to lying.

On the other hand, the gestures people use to illustrate what they are saying may reveal lying. These gestures, called **illustrators,** tend to *decrease* when a person is telling a lie. In other words, people who usually "talk with their hands" may be much less animated when they are lying.

Other movements, called *emblems,* can also reveal lying. **Emblems** are gestures that have widely understood meanings within a particular culture. Some examples are the thumbs-up sign, the A-OK sign, the middle-finger insult, a head nod for yes, and a head shake for no. Emblems tend to *increase* when a person is lying. More important, they often reveal true feelings contrary to what the liar is saying. For example, a person might smile and say, "Yes, I'd love to try some of your homemade candied pig's feet," while slowly shaking her head from side to side.

Among the best clues to lying are the signs of strong emotion produced by the ANS. These include blinking, blushing, blanching, pupil dilation, rapid or irregular breathing, perspiration, frequent swallowing, speech errors, and a louder, higher pitched voice. All of these clues are hard for the liar to censor. But such clues are like the polygraph: They reveal emotions; they do not always mean a person is lying. Remember, good liars can fool most people most of the time—and that's no lie (Ekman & O'Sullivan, 1991).

Westerns, it makes a big difference to "Smile when you say that, partner."

Other feelings are telegraphed by the body. The most general seem to be *relaxation* or *tension* and *liking* or *disliking.* Relaxation is expressed by casually positioning the arms and legs, leaning back (if sitting), and spreading the arms and legs. Liking is expressed mainly by leaning toward a person or object. Thus, body positioning can reveal feelings that would normally be concealed. Who do you "lean toward"?

Psychologists John Bargh and Tanya Chartrand recently identified an aspect of body language they call the "chameleon effect." This refers to the fact that we often unconsciously mimic the postures, mannerisms, and facial expressions of other people as we interact with them. (We change our gestures to match our surroundings, like a chameleon changes color.) Bargh and Chartrand also found that if another person copies your gestures and physical postures, you are more inclined to like them (Chartrand & Bargh, 1999). This implies that to make a stronger connection with others, it helps to subtly mimic their gestures.

Imagine that you are standing 30 yards from a classroom in which test grades are being announced. As students file out, do you think you could tell—without the aid of facial expressions—who got an A and who got an F? Actually, your task might not be too difficult. Overall *posture* can also indicate one's emotional state. Specifically, when a person is successful, his or her posture is likely to be more erect (Weisfeld & Beresford, 1982) (❖Fig. 13.21). Psychologists debate whether this tendency is a product of evolution or is simply learned. In any case, standing tall with pride and slumping with dejection do seem to be consistent patterns.

Does body positioning or movement ever reveal lying or deception? If you know a person well, you may be able to detect deception from expressive changes. But don't count on it. Most people learn to maintain careful control over their facial expressions. A good example is smiling so you won't hurt someone's feelings when you have received a disappointing gift. Because of such control, deception is often best revealed by body language (Ekman & O'Sullivan, 1991). Even a good con artist may be too busy attending to his or her words and face to control certain bodily clues. See "Behavioral Lie Catching" for details.

Kinesics *Study of the meaning of body movements, posture, hand gestures, and facial expressions; commonly called body language.*
Emotional tone *The underlying emotional state an individual is experiencing at any given moment.*
Facial blend *A mix of two or more basic facial expressions.*
Pleasantness-unpleasantness *As reflected by facial expressions, the degree to which a person is experiencing pleasure or displeasure.*
Attention-rejection *As reflected by facial expressions, the degree of attention given to a person or object.*
Activation *As reflected by facial expressions, the degree of arousal a person is experiencing.*
Illustrators *Gestures people use to illustrate what they are saying.*
Emblems *Gestures that have widely understood meanings within a particular culture.*

USING PSYCHOLOGY

THEORIES OF EMOTION—SEVERAL WAYS TO FEAR A BEAR

Is it possible to explain what takes place during emotion? How are arousal, behavior, cognition, expression, and feelings interrelated? Theories of emotion offer different answers to these questions. Let's investigate some prominent views. Each appears to have a part of the truth, so we will try to put them all together in the end.

The James-Lange Theory (1884–1885)

Common sense tells us that we see a bear, feel fear, become aroused, and run (and sweat and yell). But is this the true order of events? In the 1880s, American psychologist William James (the functionalist) and Danish psychologist Carl Lange proposed that common sense had it backward. According to James and Lange, bodily arousal (such as increased heart rate) does not follow a feeling such as fear. Instead, they argued, *emotional feelings follow bodily arousal.* Thus, we see a bear, run, are aroused, and *then* feel fear as we become aware of our bodily reactions (❖Fig. 13.22).

To support this line of thought, James pointed out that we often do not experience an emotion until after reacting. For example, imagine that you are driving and that a car suddenly pulls out in front of you. You swerve and skid to an abrupt halt at the side of the road. Only after you have come to a stop do you notice your pounding heart, rapid breathing, and tense muscles—and recognize your fear.

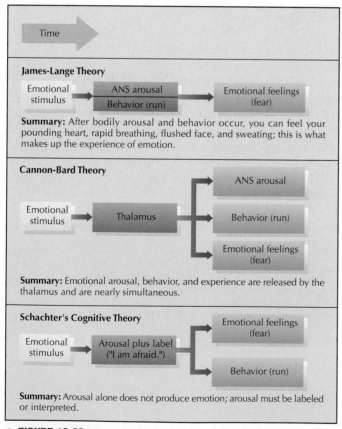

❖ **FIGURE 13.22** *Theories of emotion.*

The Cannon-Bard Theory (1927)

American physiologists Walter Cannon and Phillip Bard disagreed with the James-Lange theory. Cannon (1932) and Bard proposed that emotional feelings and bodily arousal *occur at the same time.* Both are organized in the brain, where seeing a bear activates the thalamus. The thalamus, in turn, alerts both the cortex and the hypothalamus for action. The cortex produces our emotional feelings and emotional behavior. The hypothalamus is responsible for arousing the body. Thus, if you see a dangerous-looking bear, bodily arousal, running, and feelings of fear will all be generated simultaneously by brain activity (see ❖Fig. 13.22).

Schachter's Cognitive Theory of Emotion (1971)

The previous theories are mostly concerned with physical responses. Stanley Schachter realized that cognitive (mental) factors also enter into emotion. According to Schachter, emotion occurs when a particular *label* is applied to general physical *arousal.* Schachter believes that when we are aroused, we have a need to interpret our feelings. Assume, for instance, that someone sneaks up behind you on a dark street and says, "Boo!" No matter who the person is, your body will be aroused (pounding heart, sweating palms, and so on). If the person is a total stranger, you may interpret this arousal as fear; if the person is a close friend, the arousal may be labeled as surprise or delight. The label (such as anger, fear, or happiness) applied to bodily arousal is influenced by past experience, the situation, and the reactions of others (see ❖Fig. 13.22).

The cognitive theory of emotion is supported by an experiment in which subjects watched a slapstick movie (Schachter & Wheeler, 1962). Before viewing the movie, one third of the subjects received an injection of adrenaline, one third got a placebo injection, and the remaining subjects were given a tranquilizer. Subjects who received the adrenaline rated the movie funniest and showed the most amusement while watching it. In contrast, those given the tranquilizer were least amused. The placebo group fell in between.

According to the cognitive theory of emotion, individuals who received adrenaline had a stirred-up body but no explanation for the way they were feeling. Consequently, they became happy when the movie implied that their arousal was due to amusement. This and similar experiments make it clear that emotion is much more than just an agitated body. Perception, experience, attitudes, judgment, and many other mental factors also affect emotion. Schachter's theory would predict, then, that if you met a bear, you would be aroused. If the bear seemed unfriendly, you would interpret your arousal as fear, and if the bear offered to shake your "paw," you would be happy, amazed, and relieved!

ATTRIBUTION We now move from slapstick movies and fear of bear bodies to appreciation of bare bodies. Researcher Stuart Valins (1967) added an interesting wrinkle to Schachter's theory of emotion. According to Valins, arousal can be attributed to various sources—a process that alters perceptions of emo-

Which theory of emotion best describes the reactions of these people? Given the complexity of emotion, each theory appears to possess an element of truth.

tion. To demonstrate **attribution,** Valins (1966) showed male college students a series of slides of nude females. While watching the slides, each subject heard an amplified heartbeat that he believed was his own. In reality, subjects were listening to a recorded heartbeat carefully designed to beat *louder* and *stronger* when some (but not all) of the slides were shown.

After viewing the slides, each subject was asked to say which slide he found most attractive. Students exposed to the false heartbeat consistently rated slides paired with a "pounding heart" as the most attractive. In other words, when a student saw a slide and heard his heartbeat become more pronounced, he attributed his "emotion" to the slide. His interpretation seems to have been, "Now that one I like!" His next reaction, perhaps, was "But why?" Later research suggests that subjects persuade themselves that the slide really is more attractive, in order to explain their apparent arousal (Truax, 1983).

That seems somewhat artificial. Does it really make any difference what arousal is attributed to? Yes. To illustrate attribution in the "real world," consider what happens when parents interfere with the budding romance of a son or daughter. Often, trying to break up a young couple *intensifies* their feelings for one another. Parental interference adds frustration, anger, and fear or excitement (as in seeing each other "on the sly") to the couple's feelings. Because they already care for one another, they are likely to attribute all this added emotion to "true love" (Walster, 1971).

Attribution theory predicts that you are most likely to "love" someone who gets you stirred up emotionally (Foster et al., 1998). This is true even when fear, anger, frustration, or rejection is part of the formula. Thus, if you want to successfully propose marriage, take your intended to the middle of a nar-

row, windswept suspension bridge over a deep chasm and look deeply into his or her eyes. As your beloved's heart pounds wildly (from being on the bridge, not from your irresistible charms), say, "I love you." Attribution theory predicts that your companion will conclude, "Oh wow, I must love you, too."

The preceding is not as farfetched as it may seem. In an ingenious study, a female experimenter interviewed men in a park. Some were on a swaying suspension bridge 230 feet above a river, and others on a solid wooden bridge just 10 feet above the ground. After the interview, each subject was given the experimenter's telephone number, so he could "find out about the results" of the study. Men interviewed on the suspension bridge were much more likely to give the "lady from the park" a call (Dutton & Aron, 1974). Apparently, these men experienced heightened arousal, which they interpreted as attraction to the experimenter—a clear case of love at first fright! (Love is discussed further in this chapter's A Step Beyond.)

The Facial Feedback Hypothesis

Schachter added thinking and interpretation (cognition) to our view of emotion, but the picture still seems incomplete. What about expressions? How do they influence emotion? As Charles Darwin observed, the face seems very central to emotion. Is it really just an "emotional billboard"?

Psychologist Carrol Izard (1977, 1990) was among the first to suggest that the face does, indeed, affect emotion. According to Izard and others, emotional activity causes innately programmed changes in facial expression. Sensations from the face then provide cues to the brain that help us determine what emotion we are feeling. This idea is known as the **facial feedback hypothesis** (Adelmann & Zajonc, 1989). Stated another way, it says that having facial expressions and becoming aware of them is what leads to emotional experience. Exercise, for instance, arouses the body, but this arousal is not experienced as emotion because it does not trigger emotional expressions.

Psychologist Paul Ekman takes the idea one step further. Ekman believes that "making faces" can actually cause emotion (Ekman, 1993). In one study, participants were guided as they arranged their faces, muscle by muscle, into expressions

> **BRIDGES**
>
> Love is one basis for interpersonal attraction, but there are others, such as similarity and proximity.
>
> To learn more about what brings people together, see Chapter 19, pages 641–646.

James-Lange theory *States that emotional feelings follow bodily arousal and come from awareness of such arousal.*
Cannon-Bard theory *States that activity in the thalamus causes emotional feelings and bodily arousal to occur simultaneously.*
Schachter's cognitive theory *States that emotions occur when physical arousal is labeled or interpreted on the basis of experience and situational cues.*
Attribution *The mental process of assigning causes to events. In emotion, the process of attributing arousal to a particular source.*
Facial feedback hypothesis *States that sensations from facial expressions help define what emotion a person feels.*

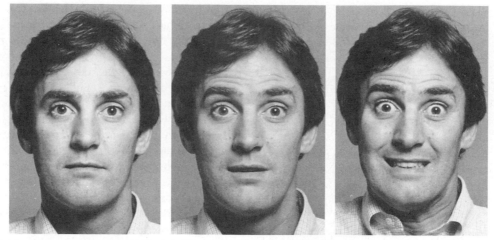

❖ **FIGURE 13.23** *Facial feedback and emotion. Participants in Ekman's study formed facial expressions like those normally observed during emotion. When they did this, emotion-like changes took place in their bodily activity. (After Ekman et al., 1983.)*

◆ **TABLE 13.4** Facial Muscles and Felt Emotion

CONTRACTED FACIAL MUSCLES	FELT EMOTION
Forehead	Surprise
Brow	Anger
Mouth (down)	Sadness
Mouth (smile)	Joy

Adelmann & Zajonc, 1989.

of surprise, disgust, sadness, anger, fear, and happiness (❖Fig. 13.23). At the same time, each person's bodily reactions were monitored.

Contrary to what might be expected, "making faces" brought about changes in the autonomic nervous system, as reflected by heart rate and skin temperature. In addition, each facial expression produced a different pattern of activity. An angry face, for instance, raised heart rate and skin temperature, whereas disgust lowered heart rate and skin temperature (Ekman et al., 1983). In a related experiment, people rated how funny they thought cartoons were while holding a pen crosswise in their mouths. Those who held the pen in their teeth thought the cartoons were funnier than did people who held the pen in their lips. Can you guess why? The answer is that if you hold a pen with your teeth, you are forced to form a smile; holding it with the lips makes a frown. As predicted by the facial feedback hypothesis, subjects' emotional experiences were influenced by their facial expressions (Strack, Martin, & Stepper, 1988). Next time you're feeling sad, bite a pen!

BRIDGES

Emotional appraisals have a major impact on the ability to cope with threats and stress, which may ultimately affect your health.

See Chapter 16, pages 523–525.

It appears, then, that not only do emotions influence expressions but also expressions may influence emotions (McIntosh, 1996) (◆Table 13.4). This could explain an interesting effect you have probably observed. When you are feeling "down," forcing yourself to smile will sometimes be followed by an actual improvement in your mood (Kleinke, Peterson, & Rutledge, 1998).

A Contemporary Model of Emotion

Each of the theories we have described is partly true. James and Lange were right that feedback from arousal and behavior adds to emotional experience. Cannon and Bard were right about the timing of events (although we now know that the amygdala provides an alternate, faster pathway to fear arousal). Schachter showed that cognition is important. Today, psychologists are increasingly aware that the way a situation is *appraised* greatly affects the course of emotion (Strongman, 1996).

Emotional appraisal refers to evaluating the personal meaning of a stimulus: Is it good or bad, threatening or supportive, relevant or irrelevant, and so on. However, Schachter's theory tends to overlook the role of other parts of emotion, such as facial expressions. Also, the theory doesn't seem to fit all circumstances. For example, how can a child who hasn't learned to label emotion have an emotion?

In recent years, many new theories of emotion have appeared. Rather than pick one "best" theory, let's put the main points of several theories together in a single contemporary model of emotion (❖Fig. 13.24).

Imagine that a large, snarling dog has just lunged at you with its teeth bared. A modern view of emotion goes something like this: An *emotional stimulus* (the dog) is *appraised* (judged) as a threat or other cause for emotional response (◆Table 13.5). (You think to yourself, "Uh-oh, big trouble!") Your emotional appraisal gives rise to *ANS arousal* (your heart

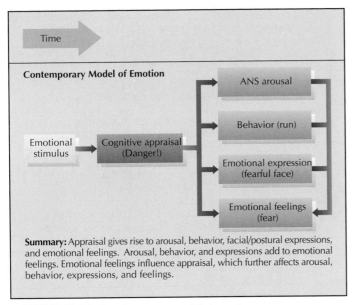

Time

Contemporary Model of Emotion

Emotional stimulus → Cognitive appraisal (Danger!) → ANS arousal / Behavior (run) / Emotional expression (fearful face) / Emotional feelings (fear)

Summary: Appraisal gives rise to arousal, behavior, facial/postural expressions, and emotional feelings. Arousal, behavior, and expressions add to emotional feelings. Emotional feelings influence appraisal, which further affects arousal, behavior, expressions, and feelings.

❖ **FIGURE 13.24** *A contemporary model of emotion.*

◆ **TABLE 13.5** Appraisals and Corresponding Emotions

APPRAISAL	EMOTION
You have been slighted or demeaned	Anger
You feel threatened	Anxiety
You have experienced a loss	Sadness
You have broken a moral rule	Guilt
You have not lived up to your ideals	Shame
You desire something another has	Envy
You are near something repulsive	Disgust
You fear the worst but yearn for better	Hope
You are moving toward a desired goal	Happiness
You are linked with a valued object or accomplishment	Pride
You have been treated well by another	Gratitude
You desire affection from another person	Love
You are moved by someone's suffering	Compassion

(Paraphrased from Lazarus, 1991a.)

pounds and your body becomes stirred up). The appraisal also releases *innate emotional expressions* (your face twists into a mask of fear and your posture becomes tense). At the same time, the appraisal leads to *adaptive behavior* (running from

the dog). It also causes a change in consciousness that you recognize as the subjective experience of fear. (The intensity of this *emotional feeling* is directly related to the amount of ANS arousal.)

Each element of emotion—ANS arousal, adaptive behavior, subjective experience, and emotional expressions—may feed back into your appraisal and alter it. In other words, this feedback changes your thoughts, judgments, or perceptions of emotion. Such changes further alter all of the other reactions, which again alter the appraisal or interpretation of events. Thus, emotion may blossom, change course, or diminish as it proceeds. Note, too, that the original emotional stimulus can be external, like the attacking dog, or internal, such as a memory of being chased by a dog, rejected by a lover, or praised by a friend. That's why mere thoughts and memories can make us fearful, sad, or happy (Strongman, 1996).

Our discussion suggests that emotion is greatly influenced by how you think about an event. For example, if another driver "cuts you off" on the highway, you could become very angry. But if you do, you will add 5 or 10 minutes of emotional upset to your day. By changing your appraisal, you could just as easily choose to laugh at the other driver's childish behavior—and minimize the emotional wear-and-tear.

Emotional Intelligence

The Greek philosopher Aristotle had a recipe for handling relationships smoothly. You must be able, he said, "to be angry with the right person, to the right degree, at the right time, for the right purpose, and in the right way." Psychologists Peter Salovey and John Mayer call such self-control "emotional intelligence." **Emotional intelligence** refers to a combination of skills. These include empathy, self-control, self-awareness, sensitivity to the feelings of others, persistence, and self-motivation, among others (Salovey & Mayer, 1997).

Psychologist and writer Daniel Goleman believes that people who excel in life tend to be emotionally intelligent. Indeed, the costs of poor emotional skills can be high. They range from problems in marriage and parenting to poor physical health. A lack of emotional intelligence can ruin careers and sabotage achievement. Perhaps the greatest toll falls on children and teenagers. For them, poor emotional skills can contribute to depression, eating disorders, unwanted pregnancy, aggression, and violent crime.

Understandably, many psychologists believe that schools should promote emotional competence as well as intellectual skills. The result, they feel, would be greater self-control, altruism, and compassion—all basic capacities needed if our society is to thrive (Goleman, 1995).

Emotional appraisal *Evaluating the personal meaning of a stimulus or situation.*
Emotional intelligence *Emotional competence, including empathy, self-control, self-awareness, and other skills.*

A LOOK AHEAD   At one point or another, weight control becomes a challenge for many people. In this chapter's Psychology in Action section, we will return to the topic of hunger to summarize some strategies for winning the battle of the bulge. After that, we will end on a positive note by exploring the powerful emotion of love.

KNOWLEDGE BUILDER

EMOTIONAL EXPRESSION AND THEORIES OF EMOTION

RELATE

Write a list of emotions that you think you can accurately detect from facial expressions. Does your list match Paul Ekman's? Would you be more confident in rating pleasantness-unpleasantness, attention-rejection, and activation? Why?

Which theory seems to best explain your own emotional experiences? Try frowning or smiling for 5 minutes. Did facial feedback have any effect on your mood? Cover the left column of ◆Table 13.5. Read each emotional label in the right column. What appraisal do you think would lead to the listed emotion? Do the appraisals in the table match your predictions?

LEARNING CHECK

1. Charles Darwin held that emotional expressions aid survival for animals. T or F?

2. A formal term for "body language" is _____.

3. Which three dimensions of emotion are communicated by facial expressions?
   a. pleasantness-unpleasantness b. complexity c. attention-rejection d. anger e. curiosity-disinterest f. activation

4. According to the James-Lange theory, emotional experience precedes physical arousal and emotional behavior. (We see a bear, are frightened, and run.) T or F?

5. The Cannon-Bard theory of emotion says that bodily arousal and emotional experience occur _____.

6. According to Schachter's cognitive theory, bodily arousal must be labeled or interpreted for an emotional experience to occur. T or F?

7. Subjects in Valins's false heart rate study attributed increases in their heart rate to the action of a placebo. T or F?

8. As you try to wiggle your ears, you keep pulling the corners of your mouth back into a smile. Each time you do, you find yourself giggling. Which of the following provides the best explanation for this reaction?
   a. attribution b. the Cannon-Bard theory c. appraisal d. facial feedback

CRITICAL THINKING

9. People with high spinal injuries may feel almost no signs of physiological arousal from their bodies. Nevertheless, they still feel emotion, which can be intense at times. What theory of emotion does this observation contradict?

Answers:

1. T 2. kinesics 3. a, c, f 4. F 5. simultaneously 6. T 7. F 8. d 9. The James-Lange theory and Schachter's cognitive theory. The facial feedback hypothesis also helps explain the observation.

psychology in action

BEHAVIORAL DIETING—FAT CHANCE FOR A SLIM FUTURE

The goal of the previous discussion was to help you better understand a number of basic motives and emotions. In this section, we will apply motivational research by looking at psychological techniques for weight control. The average American gains 5 to 10 pounds each decade after age 20. Thus, by age 50, the average person is 15 to 30 pounds overweight. The percentage of overweight people in North America is increasing, so it's apparent that many don't know how to control their weight (Serdula et al., 1999).

What can be done to control weight?   The basic approach for years has been to "diet"—that is, to restrict food intake drastically for a brief period. This, of course, is perfectly sensible in theory: You must eat less to lose weight. As noted earlier, however, most people who lose weight by dieting regain it rapidly. A study of an expensive commercial diet program found that most of the weight lost was regained within about 4 years (Walsh & Flynn, 1995).

If you really want to permanently lose weight, you must overhaul eating habits and control cues for eating. This approach, called **behavioral dieting,** is greatly superior to simple dieting for weight control. The following list summarizes several helpful behavioral techniques.

1. **Begin any weight-control program with a physical checkup.** About 5 percent of all weight problems are physical.

2. **Get yourself committed to weight loss.** Involve other people in your efforts. Formal programs such as Overeaters Anonymous or Take Off Pounds Sensibly can be a good source of social support (Foreyt, 1987b).

3. **Exercise.** If you would like to lose weight, your first goal should be to get more exercise. Physical activity burns calories. Stop saving steps and riding elevators. Add activity to your routine in every way you can think of. Contrary to popular opinion, regular exercise does not

increase appetite. For reasons that are not well understood, exercise lowers the body's set point for fat storage. Many psychologists are now convinced that no diet can succeed for long without an increase in exercise. Also, being fit may be more important than being fat. You can be moderately overweight and still be healthy if you get lots of exercise (Miller, 1999).

Burning as little as 200 extra calories a day can play a major role in preventing regain of weight. A recent study found that you're more likely to maintain a weight loss if you exercise regularly (Wadden et al., 1998).

4. **Learn your eating habits by observing yourself and keeping a "diet diary."** Begin by making a complete record of your eating habits for 2 weeks. Record when and where you eat, what you eat, and the feelings and events that occur just before and after eating. How do others around you respond to your eating? Is a roommate, relative, or spouse encouraging you to overeat?

5. **Count calories, but don't starve yourself.** To lose, you must eat less, and calories allow you to keep a record of your food intake. If you have trouble eating less every day, try dieting 4 days a week. People who diet intensely every other day lose as much as those who diet moderately every day (Viegener et al., 1990).

Only about 20 percent of the men and women in the United States who are trying to lose weight are eating fewer calories and getting more exercise. Thus, most will fail. Cutting down on fat in your diet is not enough, and reducing calories is effective only if you also exercise (Serdula et al., 1999).

6. **Develop techniques to control the act of eating.** Begin by taking smaller portions. Carry to the table only what you plan to eat. Put all other food away before leaving the kitchen. Eat slowly, finish one mouthful before taking another, sip water between bites of food, count your mouthfuls, and leave food on your plate.

Generally, avoid eating alone, because you're less likely to overeat in front of others. (One exception is eating at social events where food is plentiful and you are urged to eat. Another is eating with someone else who is overeating. In either case, eating may be facilitated.)

7. **Try to base eating on hunger, not on taste or learned habits that dictate leaving a clean plate.** When you see something really appealing, ask yourself, "Am I hungry? Do I need to eat? Or do I just want a good taste?" If your desire to eat is based on taste, turn the food down. Also, during meals, pause for a minute or two and then ask yourself, "Am I full?" If the answer is yes, or if the taste of the food has become less pleasant, stop eating (Poothullil, 1999; Seligman, 1994). Also, be especially careful during the holiday season. People gain more weight per week between Thanksgiving and New Year's Day than at any other time during the year (Baker & Kirschenbaum, 1998).

8. **Learn to weaken your personal eating cues.** When you have learned when and where you do most of your eating, avoid these situations. Try to restrict your eating to one room, and do not read, watch TV, study, or talk on the phone while eating. Require yourself to interrupt what you are doing in order to eat. Be especially aware of the "night eating syndrome." Most calories are consumed late in the day or at night. Keep food out of sight and find things to do to keep yourself busy during this dangerous period.

9. **Avoid snacks.** It is generally better to eat several small meals a day than three large ones (Assanand, Pinel, & Lehman, 1998). However, high-calorie snacks tend to be eaten *in addition to* meals. Buy low-calorie foods that require preparation, and fix only a single portion at a time. If you have an impulse to snack, set a timer for 20 minutes and see if you are still hungry then. Delay the impulse to snack several times if possible. Dull your appetite by filling up on raw carrots, bouillon, water, coffee, or tea.

10. **Make a list of rewards you will receive if you change your eating habits and punishments that will occur if you don't.** You may find it helpful to set up specific rewards (see Chapter 18 for more details). Don't reward yourself with food!

11. **Chart your progress daily.** Record your weight, the number of calories eaten, and whether you met your daily

Behavioral dieting *Weight reduction based on changing exercise and eating habits, rather than temporary self-starvation.*

goal. Set realistic goals by cutting down calories gradually. Losing about a pound per week is realistic, but remember, you are changing habits, not just dieting. Diets don't work! Take pride in your successes. Post your chart in a prominent place. This record of your progress is possibly the most important of all the techniques.

12. **Beware of relapses.** Try to identify specific high-risk situations in which you are likely to overeat. Then form a plan using the principles already described to help you cope with the risk of relapse (Foreyt, 1987b). It also helps to tell yourself that a single overeating incident does not mean that you have "blown it." Faltering should be interpreted as an isolated slip, not as a sign that you might as well give up (Marlatt & Gordon, 1985).

13. **Set a "threshold" for weight control.** A study of Weight Watchers members found that those who successfully maintained their weight loss had a regain limit of 3 pounds or less. In other words, if they gained more than 2 or 3 pounds, they immediately began to make corrections in their eating habits and exercise (Brownell et al., 1986).

Be patient with this program. It takes years to develop eating habits. You can expect it to take at least several months to change them. If you are unsuccessful at losing weight with these techniques, you might find it helpful to seek the aid of a psychologist familiar with behavioral weight-loss techniques.

BEHAVIORAL DIETING

RELATE

Even if you're not overweight, reread each of the weight-control techniques and visualize how you would carry out the suggested behaviors.

LEARNING CHECK

1. According to behavioral dieting specialists, about 45 percent of all weight problems are physical. T or F?

2. In addition to burning calories, physical exercise can lower the body's set point. T or F?

3. For behavioral dieting, you should maintain a diet diary and chart your progress, but you should avoid the trap of counting calories. T or F?

4. Those who successfully control their weight are willing to admit to themselves that they have "blown it" if they deviate from their diet. T or F?

CRITICAL THINKING

5. Charting weight loss makes use of a behavioral principle discussed in Chapter 9, "Conditioning and Learning." Can you name it?

Answers:

1. F 2. T 3. F 4. F 5. Feedback.

---

a step beyond

LOVE—STALKING AN ELUSIVE EMOTION

Focus: What is the nature of love?

Love is one of the most intense of all human experiences. Moreover, at one time or another, most people must ask themselves, "Is this love or lust?" "Is it real or infatuation?" "What am I really feeling?" All of which raises the question: What is love? Think, for instance, about the different ways we love our parents, friends, and spouses or lovers.

How do various kinds of love differ from one another? This is the question that led psychologist Robert Sternberg to propose his *triangular theory of love.* Although the theory is preliminary, others have confirmed the value of its core ideas (Aron & Westbay, 1996). Perhaps they will help you think more clearly about your own loving relationships.

Love Triangles

According to Sternberg's **triangular theory of love** (1988), love is made up of three elements: intimacy, passion, and commitment. As you can see in ❖Figure 13.25, each factor can be visu-

alized as one side of a triangle. Notice also that the three elements can combine to produce seven different types of love. We will return to these types in a moment, but first let's briefly explore love's three "ingredients."

INTIMACY   A relationship has **intimacy,** or closeness, if affection, sharing, communication, and support are present. Intimacy grows steadily at first, but in time it levels off. After it does, people in long-term relationships may gradually lose sight of the fact that they are still very close and mutually dependent.

PASSION   **Passion** refers mainly to physiological arousal. This arousal may be sexual, but it includes other sources, too. As discussed earlier in this chapter, arousal, no matter what its cause, may be interpreted as passion in a romantic relationship (Bersheid & Walster, 1974). This is probably why passionate love often occurs against a backdrop of danger, adversity, or frustration—especially in soap operas and romance novels! Passion is the primary source of love's *intensity.* It's not surpris-

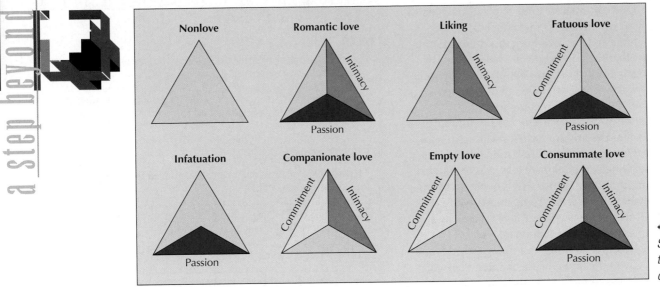

❖ **FIGURE 13.25**
Sternberg's triangular theory of love.

ing, then, that romance inspires the strongest feelings of love. In contrast, love for siblings is least intense (Sternberg & Grajeck, 1984).

COMMITMENT   The third side of the love triangle consists of commitment—your decision to love another person and your degree of commitment to stay with that person. Commitment starts at zero before you meet a person, and it grows steadily as you get acquainted. Like intimacy, commitment tends to level off. However, it may waver up and down with a relationship's good times and bad times. Commitment drops rapidly when a relationship is in serious trouble.

Seven Flavors of Love

The presence or absence of intimacy, passion, and/or commitment produces eight triangles. The first defines **nonlove,** a total absence of all three elements.

In **liking,** you feel close to a person and communicate well with her or him. However, you do not feel any passion or deep commitment to the person. A likable classmate might fall into this category.

Romantic love mixes intimacy (closeness and sharing) with passion (often in the form of physical attraction). Despite its intensity, romantic love does not involve much commitment at first. Think, for example, of a summer romance that ends in a relatively easy parting of ways.

Fatuous love describes commitments made rapidly on the basis of physical attraction (passion) but without much emotional intimacy. Fatuous love is of the boy-meets-girl-and-they-get-married-a-month-later type. Relationships started this way risk failure because lovers make a commitment before they really get to know each other well.

Infatuation is an even more superficial form of love. In this case, a person is inflamed with passion but shares no intimacy or commitment with the beloved. In time, of course, infatuation may lead to more lasting kinds of love.

Companionate love refers to affection and deep attachment that is built on respect, shared interests, and firm friendship. Companionate love is lower key emotionally. However, it is steady and long term and tends to grow in time. Companionate love is the "kind of affection we feel for those with whom our lives are deeply intertwined" (Walster & Walster, 1978).

Couples sometimes reach a point where there is little passion or intimacy left in their relationship. If they stay together merely out of commitment or habit, they experience **empty love.**

Consummate love occurs when two people are passionate, committed to one another, and emotionally close. Complete, balanced love of this kind occurs only in very special relationships. When all three factors are present, a relationship is more likely to be lasting (Whitley, 1993).

HOW DO I LOVE THEE?   The categories described here are certainly not the last word on love. Undoubtedly, other kinds of love also exist. In addition, Sternberg's theory may place too much emphasis on passion. In most relationships, intimacy and commitment are a bigger part of love than passion is (Clark & Reis, 1988; Tucker & Aron, 1993).

Triangular theory of love *Robert Sternberg's theory that love is made up of intimacy, passion, and commitment.*
Intimacy *Affection, sharing, communication, and support in a relationship.*
Passion *High levels of physical arousal in a relationship, especially sexual arousal.*
Commitment *Decision to love and stay with another person.*
Nonlove *An absence of passion, intimacy, and commitment.*
Liking *Intimacy without passion or commitment.*
Romantic love *Intimacy plus passion.*
Fatuous love *Passion with commitment, but lacking intimacy.*
Infatuation *Passion without commitment or intimacy.*
Companionate love *Intimacy and commitment without passion.*
Empty love *Commitment without intimacy or passion.*
Consummate love *Passion, intimacy, and commitment.*

Our culture also tends to place much emphasis on passion as the main basis for "falling" in love. However, this overlooks the fact that the passionate, breathless stage of love typically lasts only about 6 to 30 months (Walster & Walster, 1978). What happens when this period ends? Quite often, people separate.

There is a degree of danger in expecting to live forever on a romantic cloud. People who are primarily caught up in passionate love may neglect to build a more lasting relationship. Rather than downplaying companionate love, it is helpful to realize that lovers must also be friends. High-quality relationships are frequently based on secure, companionate love (Hecht et al., 1994). In fact, consummate love is basically a blending of romantic love and companionate love.

You may be tempted to match the love triangles with your own relationships. If you do apply the theory, remember that each love relationship is a unique story, and few are perfect (Sternberg, 1995). In another study, Sternberg and Michael Barnes (1986) found that relationships are generally satisfying if you think the other person feels about you the way you would *like* her or him to feel about you.

Some politicians have belittled the study of love as "unscientific." But in a world often wracked by violence, hatred, and despair, what could be more important than understanding the elusive state we call love?

CONCLUSION: Romantic love takes many forms, depending on the amount of passion, intimacy, and commitment in a relationship. In many long-term relationships, intimacy and commitment are the main ingredients of love.

KNOWLEDGE BUILDER

THE NATURE OF LOVE

RELATE

See if you can think of specific people you know whose relationships fit into each of these categories: liking, romantic love, fatuous love, infatuation, companionate love, empty love, consummate love. Think of the three best long-term relationships you know; would it be more accurate to describe them as consummate love or companionate love?

LEARNING CHECK

1. Essentially, all types of love can be described as a passion for another person. T or F?

2. According to Sternberg's theory, all forms of love involve commitment to another person or to a relationship. T or F?

3. Passion is the primary element of infatuation. T or F?

4. Fatuous love can be defined as commitment based on passion but lacking in intimacy. T or F?

5. The passionate stage of love usually lasts only 6 to 30 weeks. T or F?

CRITICAL THINKING

6. Passionate love tends to decline at each of three major transitions in marriage. Based on your own observations of relationships, what do you think they are?

Answers:

1. F 2. F 3. T 4. T 5. F 6. The transitions are: from engagement to marriage, from childlessness to parenthood, and from children living at home to an empty nest (Tucker & Aron, 1993).

CHAPTER IN REVIEW

What is motivation? Are there different types of motives?

- Motives initiate, sustain, and direct activities. Motivation typically involves the sequence need, drive, goal, and goal attainment (need reduction).
- Behavior can be activated either by needs (push) or by goals (pull). The attractiveness of a goal and its ability to initiate action are related to its incentive value.
- Three principal types of motives are primary motives, stimulus motives, and secondary motives. Most primary motives operate to maintain homeostasis.

What causes hunger? Overeating? Eating disorders?

- Hunger is influenced by a complex interplay of fullness of the stomach, blood sugar levels, metabolism in the liver, and fat stores in the body.
- Eating is most directly controlled by the hypothalamus, which has areas that act like feeding and satiety systems. The hypothalamus is sensitive to both neural and chemical messages, which affect eating.
- Other factors influencing hunger are the body's set point, external eating cues, the attractiveness and variety of diet, emotions, learned taste preferences and taste aversions, and cultural values.
- Obesity is the result of a complex interplay of internal and external influences, diet, emotions, genetics, and exercise.
- Anorexia nervosa (self-starvation) and bulimia nervosa (gorging and purging) are two prominent eating disorders. Both problems tend to involve conflicts about self-image, self-control, and anxiety.

Is there more than one type of thirst?

- Like hunger, thirst and other basic motives are affected by a number of bodily factors but are primarily under the central control of the hypothalamus. Thirst may be either intracellular or extracellular.

In what ways are pain avoidance and the sex drive unusual?

- Pain avoidance is unusual because it is episodic as opposed to cyclic. Pain avoidance and pain tolerance are partially learned.
- The sex drive is also unusual in that it is non-homeostatic.

How does arousal relate to motivation?

- The stimulus motives include drives for exploration, manipulation, change, and sensory stimulation.
- Drives for stimulation are partially explained by arousal theory, which states that an ideal level of bodily arousal will be maintained if possible. The desired level of arousal or stimulation varies from person to person, as measured by the *Sensation-Seeking Scale*.
- Optimal performance on a task usually occurs at *moderate* levels of arousal. This relationship is described by an inverted **U** function. The Yerkes-Dodson law further states that for simple tasks the ideal arousal level is higher, and for complex tasks it is lower.
- Circadian rhythms of bodily activity are closely tied to sleep, activity, and energy cycles. Time zone travel and shift work can seriously disrupt sleep and bodily rhythms.

What are social motives? Why are they important?

- Social motives are learned through socialization and cultural conditioning. Such motives account for much of the diversity of human motivation. Opponent-process theory explains the operation of some acquired motives.
- One of the most prominent social motives is the need for achievement (nAch). High nAch is correlated with success in many situations, with occupational choice, and with *moderate* risk taking.
- There is evidence that at times both men and women experience a fear of success. This is especially true if achievement is seen as conflicting with social acceptance.
- Self-confidence greatly affects motivation in everyday life.

Are some motives more basic than others?

- Maslow's hierarchy of motives categorizes needs as basic and growth oriented. Lower needs in the hierarchy are assumed to be prepotent (dominant) over higher needs. Self-actualization, the highest and most fragile need, is reflected in meta-needs.
- Higher needs in Maslow's hierarchy are closely related to the concept of intrinsic motivation. In many situations, extrinsic motivation can reduce intrinsic motivation, enjoyment, and creativity.

What happens during emotion?

- Emotions are linked to many basic adaptive behaviors. Other major elements of emotion are physiological changes in the body, emotional expressions, and emotional feelings.
- The following are considered to be primary emotions: *fear, surprise, sadness, disgust, anger, anticipation, joy,* and *acceptance.* Other emotions seem to represent mixtures of the primaries.
- The left hemisphere of the brain primarily processes positive emotions. Negative emotions are processed in the right hemisphere.
- The amygdala provides a "quick and dirty" pathway for the arousal of fear that bypasses the cerebral cortex.
- Physical changes associated with emotion are caused by the action of adrenaline, a hormone released into the bloodstream, and by activity in the autonomic nervous system (ANS).
- The sympathetic branch of the ANS is primarily responsible for arousing the body, the parasympathetic branch for quieting it.

Can "lie detectors" really detect lies?

- The polygraph, or "lie detector," measures emotional arousal by monitoring heart rate, blood pressure, breathing rate, and the galvanic skin response (GSR).
- The accuracy of the lie detector can be disturbingly low.

How accurately are emotions expressed by "body language" and the face?

- Basic emotional expressions, such as smiling or baring one's teeth when angry, appear to be unlearned. Facial expressions appear to be central to emotion.
- Body gestures and movements (body language) also express feelings, mainly by communicating emotional tone. Three dimensions of facial expressions are pleasantness-unpleasantness, attention-rejection, and activation. The study of body language is known as *kinesics.*
- Lying can sometimes be detected from changes in illustrators or emblems and from signs of general arousal.

How do psychologists explain emotions?

- The James-Lange theory says that emotional experience follows the bodily reactions. In contrast, the Cannon-Bard theory says that bodily reactions and emotional experiences are organized in the brain and occur simultaneously.
- Schachter's cognitive theory of emotion emphasizes the importance of the labels we apply to feelings of bodily arousal. In addition, emotions are affected by attribution (ascribing bodily arousal to a particular source).
- The facial feedback hypothesis holds that emotional expressions help define what emotion a person is feeling.
- Contemporary views of emotion place greater emphasis on the effects of cognitive appraisals. Also, all of the elements of emotion are seen as interrelated and interacting.

Can psychology be applied to weight control?

- Changing eating patterns and exercise habits is usually more effective than traditional dieting. Behavioral dieting is based on various self-control and self-management techniques.

What is the nature of love?

- Robert Sternberg's triangular theory describes love as a combination of passion, intimacy, and commitment. Combinations of these three factors produce nonlove, liking, infatuation, romantic love, fatuous love, companionate love, empty love, and consummate love.

PSYCHOLOGY ON THE NET

- **Controlling Anger** Discusses anger and some strategies for its control. http://www.apa.org/pubinfo/anger.html

- **Eating Disorders Website** Home page of a self-help group for those afflicted with eating disorders. http://www.something-fishy.org
- **Emotions and Emotional Intelligence** Discusses emotional intelligence. http://trochim.human.cornell.edu/gallery/young/emotion.htm
- **Gestures around the World** A description of body language practices in a variety of cultures. http://www.webofculture.com/refs/gestures.html
- **Research on Human Emotions** Links to a variety of sources on emotion. http://www.white.media.mit.edu/vismod/demos/affect/AC_research/emotions.html
- **The Validity of Polygraph Examinations** Information about the doubtful validity of polygraph examinations. http://www.apa.org/releases/liedetector.html
- **What's Your Emotional Intelligence Quotient?** Visitors may take an on-line quiz about their E-IQ. http://www.utne.com/lens/bms/9bmseq.html

- •**InfoTrac® College Edition** For recent articles on lie detection, use Key Words search for POLYGRAPH.

INTERACTIVE LEARNING

- *Psych Now!* 4a. Motivation. 4b. Emotion.
- *Psyk.trek* 8a. Hunger. 8b. Achievement motivation. 8c. Elements of emotion. 8d. Theories of emotion.

14

Gender and Sexuality

Chapter Survey

Theme: *The sexes are more alike than different. Sexuality is a normal and healthy part of human behavior.*

THAT MAGIC WORD

Sex\seks n 1. One of the two divisions of organisms formed on the distinction of male and female.

"S EX" HAS MANY MEANINGS: *reproduction, lovemaking, sexual identity, and much more. Of the various meanings, the simplest would seem to be biological sex. What, really, could be simpler? Females are females, and males are males, right? Wrong. Even something as basic as biological sex is many sided.*

The complexity of sexual identity is illustrated by Dr. Renée Richards's attempt to enter a women's tennis tournament. Richards is a transsexual. Formerly, she was Richard Raskin, an ophthalmologist. As a man, Richard Raskin was a modestly successful tennis player. After a sex-change operation, Richards tried to launch a new tennis career as a woman. Understandably, other women players protested. Officials finally decided to use a genetic sex test to decide if Richards could compete. She, in turn, protested the test. Genetically, she is still male, but psychologically she is female—she has female genitals, and she functions socially as a female (Hyde, 1996). Is Dr. Richards, then, female or male?

You might view Renée Richards as an unfair example because transsexuals seek to alter their natural sex. For most people, the indicators of maleness or femaleness are in agreement. Nevertheless, it is not unusual to find ambiguities among various aspects of a person's sex.

Contrary to common belief, classifying a person as male or female is not a simple either/or proposition. In the first part of this chapter, we will consider the basic dimensions that define each person as male or female.

Each of us is, by nature, a sexual creature. With this in mind, later sections of this chapter discuss sexual behavior, sexual arousal and response, sexual problems, and attitudes toward sexuality.

Sex is probably a topic you already know a lot about. It should be interesting, then, for you to compare your knowledge with the

information that follows. Sexuality has a tremendous impact on relationships, personal identity, and health. It is important to be well informed about it.

Gateways to Gender and Sexuality

MALE AND FEMALE are not simple either/or categories. Sexual identity is complex, multifaceted, and influenced by biology, socialization, and learning.

WOMEN AND MEN are more alike than different. The core of humanity in each person is more important than superficial gender differences.

IT IS POSSIBLE, AND GENERALLY DESIRABLE, to have both masculine and feminine gender traits.

SIMILAR FACTORS (heredity, biology, and socialization) underlie all sexual orientations.

AN UNDERSTANDING OF HUMAN SEXUAL RESPONSE contributes to responsible and satisfying sexual behavior.

ADULTS normally engage in a wide variety of sexual behaviors. However, coercive and/or compulsive sexual behaviors are emotionally unhealthy.

EACH PERSON must take responsibility for practicing safer sex and for choosing when, where, and with whom to express his or her sexuality.

SOLUTIONS EXIST for many sexual adjustment problems, but good communication and a healthy relationship are the real keys to sexual satisfaction.

MOST TOUCHING IS NONSEXUAL. However, touching tends to be highly restricted in North America because of social norms and fears that touching will be perceived as erotic or inappropriate.

SEXUAL DEVELOPMENT—CIRCLE ONE: *XX* OR *XY*?

One thing we never forget about a person is his or her sex. Considering the number of activities, relationships, conflicts, and choices influenced by sex, it is no wonder that we pay such close attention to it.

Being male or female is partly a matter of biology and partly psychological. The term **sex** refers to whether you are biologically female or male. In contrast, **gender** refers to all the psychological and social characteristics associated with being male or female (Crooks & Baur, 1999). In other words, after we establish that you are male or female, gender tells us if you are masculine

or feminine (as defined by the culture in which you live). Two important aspects of gender are *gender roles* and *gender identity,* which we will discuss later. For the moment, let's begin with two basic questions: Biologically, what does it mean to be female or male? How do male and female differences develop?

Female or Male?

Basic physical differences between males and females can be divided into *primary* and *secondary* sexual characteristics. **Primary sexual characteristics** refer to the sexual and reproductive organs themselves: the vagina, ovaries, and uterus in females and the penis, testes, and scrotum in males. (See

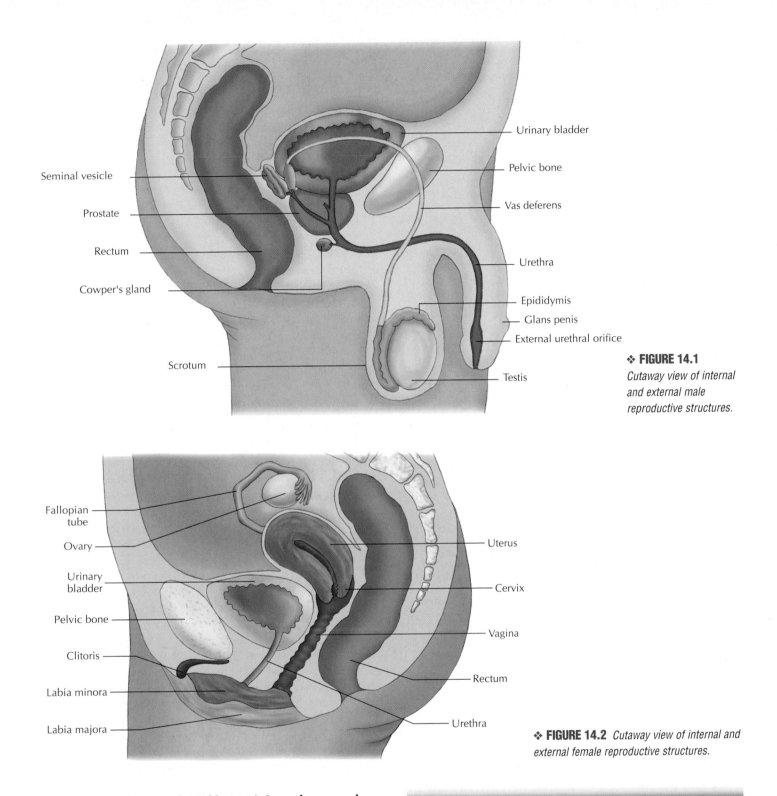

Seminal vesicle

Prostate

Rectum

Cowper's gland

Scrotum

Urinary bladder

Pelvic bone

Vas deferens

Urethra

Epididymis

Glans penis

External urethral orifice

Testis

❖ **FIGURE 14.1**
Cutaway view of internal and external male reproductive structures.

Fallopian tube

Ovary

Urinary bladder

Pelvic bone

Clitoris

Labia minora

Labia majora

Uterus

Cervix

Vagina

Rectum

Urethra

❖ **FIGURE 14.2** *Cutaway view of internal and external female reproductive structures.*

❖Figs. 14.1 and 14.2 and ◆Table 14.1.) **Secondary sexual characteristics** are more superficial physical features that appear at puberty. These features develop in response to hormonal signals from the pituitary gland. In females, secondary sexual characteristics include development of the breasts, broadening of the hips, and other changes in body shape. Males grow facial and body hair, and the voice deepens. These changes signal biological readiness for reproduction. Reproductive maturity is especially evident in the female **menarche** (MEN-ar-kee: the onset of menstruation). Soon

Sex *One's biological classification as female or male.*
Gender *Psychological and social characteristics associated with being male or female; defined especially by one's gender identity and learned gender roles.*
Primary sexual characteristics *Sex as defined by the genitals and internal reproductive organs.*
Secondary sexual characteristics *Sexual features other than the genitals and reproductive organs—breasts, body shape, facial hair, and so forth.*
Menarche *The onset of menstruation; a woman's first menstrual period.*

◆ TABLE 14.1 Female and Male Sexual Anatomy

FEMALE REPRODUCTIVE STRUCTURES

Cervix (SER-vix) The lower end of the uterus that projects into the vagina.
Clitoris (KLIT-er-iss) Small, sensitive organ made up of erectile tissue; located above the vaginal opening.
Fallopian tube (feh-LOPE-ee-en) One of two tubes that carry eggs from the ovaries to the uterus.
Labia majora (LAY-bee-ah mah-JOR-ah) The larger outer lips of the vulva.
Labia minora (LAY-bee-ah mih-NOR-ah) Inner lips of the vulva, surrounding the vaginal opening.
Ovary (OH-vah-ree) One of the two female reproductive glands; ovaries are the source of hormones and eggs.
Uterus (YOO-ter-us) The pear-shaped muscular organ in which the fetus develops during pregnancy; also known as the *womb*.
Vagina (vah-JINE-ah) Tubelike structure connecting the external female genitalia with the uterus.

MALE REPRODUCTIVE STRUCTURES

Cowper's glands Two small glands that secrete a clear fluid into the urethra during sexual excitement.
Epididymis (ep-ih-DID-ih-mus) A coiled structure at the top of the testes in which sperm are stored.
External urethral orifice (yoo-REE-thral OR-ih-fis) The opening at the tip of the penis through which urine and semen pass.
Glans penis (glanz PEA-nis) The tip of the penis.
Prostate (PROSS-tate) A gland located at the base of the urinary bladder that supplies most of the fluid that makes up semen.
Scrotum (SKROE-tehm) The saclike pouch that holds the testes.
Seminal vesicles (SEM-in-uhl VES-ih-kuhlz) These two small organs (one on each side of the prostate) supply fluid that becomes part of semen.
Testis (TES-tis, singular; *testes*, plural) One of the two male reproductive glands; the testes are a source of hormones and sperm.
Vas deferens (vaz DEH-fur-enz) The duct that carries sperm from the testes to the urethra.

RELATED STRUCTURES

Pelvic bone One of the bones at the front of the pelvis (the pelvis connects the spine with the legs).
Rectum The lowest section of the large intestine.
Urethra (yoo-REE-thra) The tube through which urine drains as it leaves the body. In males, semen also passes through the urethra.
Urinary bladder The sac that collects urine before it is eliminated from the body.

---

after menarche, monthly ovulation begins. **Ovulation** refers to the release of ova (eggs) from the ovaries. From the first ovulation until **menopause** (the end of regular monthly fertility cycles in the late 40s or early 50s), women can bear children.

SEX HORMONES *What causes the development of sex differences?* In general, sexual characteristics are related to the effects of sex hormones. (Hormones are chemical substances secreted by endocrine glands.) The **gonads** (or sex glands) affect sexual development and behavior by secreting **estrogens** (female hormones) and **androgens** (male hormones). The gonads in the male are the testes; female gonads are the ovaries. The adrenal glands (located above the kidneys) also

BRIDGES

The first signs of sexual maturity during puberty start the transition to adult status. Menopause is a clear sign of aging.

See Chapter 5, pages 138 and 147.

supply sex hormones in both females and males. At puberty, adrenal hormones add to the development of secondary sexual characteristics.

Interestingly, everyone normally produces both estrogens and androgens. Sex differences are related to the *proportion* of these hormones found in the body. In fact, prenatal development of male or female anatomy is largely due to the presence or absence of **testosterone** (tes-TOSS-teh-rone: one of the androgens, secreted mainly by the testes) (Breedlove, 1994).

Then is biological sex determined by the sex hormones? Not entirely. As suggested by the chapter Preview, sex cannot be reduced to a single dimension.

DIMENSIONS OF SEX At the very least, classifying a person as female or male must take into account the following biological factors: (1) **genetic sex** (*XX* or *XY* chromosomes), (2) **gonadal sex** (ovaries or testes), (3) **hormonal sex** (predominance of androgens or estrogens), and (4) **genital sex** (clitoris and vagina in females, penis and scrotum in males). An important nonbiological part of a person's sexual makeup is (5) **gender identity** (one's subjective sense of being male or female). To see why sex must be defined along these five dimensions, let's follow the sequence of events involved in becoming female or male.

Prenatal Sexual Development

Becoming male or female starts simply enough. Genetic sex is determined at the instant of conception: Two *X* **chromosomes** initiate the development of a female; an *X* chromosome plus a *Y* **chromosome** produces a male. A woman's ovum always provides an *X* chromosome, because she has two *X*'s in her own genetic makeup. In contrast, half of the male's sperm carry *X* chromosomes and the other half *Y*'s.

Genetic sex stays the same throughout life. But it alone does not determine biological sex. We must also consider hormonal effects before birth. For the first 6 weeks of prenatal growth, genetically female and male embryos look identical. However, if a *Y* chromosome is present, testes develop in the embryo and supply testosterone. This stimulates growth of the penis and other male structures (❖Fig. 14.3). In the absence of testosterone, the embryo will develop female reproductive organs and genitals, regardless of genetic sex (Breedlove, 1994). It might be said, then, that nature's primary impulse is to make a female.

Prenatal growth usually matches genetic sex, but not always. A genetic male won't develop male genitals if too little testosterone is available. Even if testosterone is present, an inherited **androgen insensitivity** (unresponsiveness to testosterone) may exist. Again, the result is female development (Breedlove, 1994).

Similarly, androgens must be at low levels or absent for an *XX* embryo to develop as a female. Thus, for both genetic females and males, hormonal problems before birth may result in **hermaphroditism** (her-MAF-ro-dite-ism: dual or ambiguous sexual anatomy). For instance, a developing female may be masculinized by the antimiscarriage drug progestin, or by a problem known as the

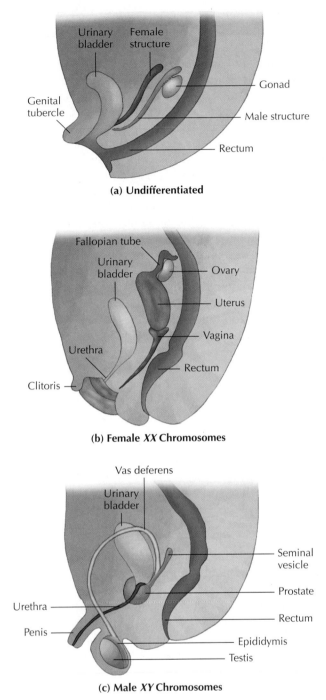

(a) Undifferentiated

(b) Female *XX* Chromosomes

(c) Male *XY* Chromosomes

❖ **FIGURE 14.3** *Prenatal development of the reproductive organs. Early development of ovaries or testes affects hormonal balance and alters sexual anatomy. (a) At first, the sex organs are the same in the human female and male. (b) When androgens are absent, female structures develop. (c) Male sex organs are produced when androgens are present.*

androgenital syndrome (an-dro-JEN-ih-tal). In the androgenital syndrome, the child's body produces estrogen, but a genetic abnormality causes the adrenal glands to release too much androgen. In such cases, a female child may be born with male genitals.

Would such a child be reared as a male? Some are. Usually, however, the condition is detected and corrected by surgery. If necessary, extra estrogen may be given after birth.

ORIGINS OF MALE-FEMALE DIFFERENCES Some experts believe that the interplay of sex hormones before birth may "sex-type" the brain (Breedlove, 1994; Money, 1987). Changes in the brain are then thought to alter the chances of developing feminine or masculine traits (Witelson, 1991).

Does that mean there is a physical basis for female and male traits? In animals, clear links exist between prenatal hormones and male or female behaviors. For humans, however, the evidence suggests that most sex-linked behavior is learned (Caplan et al., 1985, 1987; Hare-Mustin & Marecek, 1988). Be that as it may, some researchers think that a **biological biasing effect** occurs. According to them, prenatal androgens and estrogens subtly influence development of the body, nervous system, and later behavior patterns.

Is there any evidence for that? Consider females exposed to androgens before birth. After birth, their hormone balance shifts to female, and they are raised as girls. Does their prenatal exposure to male hormones have a masculinizing effect? Up to a point, the answer is yes. During childhood, such girls are typically "tomboys" who prefer the company of boys to girls. However, their masculinization does not persist. After adolescence, the girls' tomboyism usually gives way to female interests and gender characteristics (Money, 1987; Money & Mathews, 1982). Cases like these seem to show that both prenatal hormones and later social factors contribute to adult sexual identity (Breedlove, Cooke, & Jordan, 1999).

Ovulation *The release of an ovum (egg cell) by the ovaries; ova combine with sperm cells to begin the growth of an embryo.*

Menopause *An end to regular monthly menstrual periods.*

Gonads *The primary sex glands—the testes in males and ovaries in females.*

Estrogen *Any of a number of female sex hormones.*

Androgen *Any of a number of male sex hormones, especially testosterone.*

Testosterone *A male sex hormone, secreted mainly by the testes and responsible for the development of many male sexual characteristics.*

Genetic sex *Sex as indicated by the presence of XX (female) or XY (male) chromosomes.*

Gonadal sex *Sex as indicated by the presence of ovaries (female) or testes (male).*

Hormonal sex *Sex as indicated by a preponderance of estrogens (female) or androgens (male) in the body.*

Genital sex *Sex as indicated by the presence of male or female genitals.*

Gender identity *One's personal, private sense of maleness or femaleness.*

***X* chromosome** *The female chromosome contributed by the mother; produces a female when paired with another X chromosome and a male when paired with a Y chromosome.*

***Y* chromosome** *The male chromosome contributed by the father; produces a male when paired with an X chromosome. Fathers may give either an X or a Y chromosome to their offspring.*

Androgen insensitivity *An inherited disorder in which male embryos fail to develop male genitals because of an unresponsiveness to testosterone.*

Hermaphroditism *Having genitals suggestive of both sexes; ambiguous genital sexuality.*

Androgenital syndrome *An inherited disorder that causes the adrenal glands to produce excess androgens, sometimes masculinizing developing females before birth.*

Biological biasing effect *Hypothesized effect that prenatal exposure to sex hormones has on development of the body, nervous system, and later behavior patterns.*

At the risk of getting mired in the "battle of the sexes," let's consider one more idea. Some researchers believe that women and men have different thinking abilities. This occurs, they contend, because women are more often "left brained," and men, "right brained." The left brain, you may recall, is largely responsible for language and rote learning. The right brain is superior at spatial reasoning. Thus, some psychologists think that biological differences explain why men (as a group) do slightly better on spatial tasks and math and why women are slightly better at language skills (Wisniewski, 1998). Others, however, strongly reject this theory. To them, such claims are based on shaky evidence and sexist thinking (Caplan et al., 1985; Hellige, 1990). The most telling evidence on this point may be the fact that differences between female and male scores on the Scholastic Assessment Test are rapidly declining. The same applies to tests of math ability (Buss, 1995). The narrowing gap is probably explained by a growing similarity in male and female interests, experiences, and educational goals.

Note that the differences that do exist between women and men are based on *averages* (❖Fig. 14.4). Many women are better at math than most men are. Likewise, many men are better at verbal skills than most women are. Scores for women and men overlap so much that it is impossible to predict if any one person will be good or bad at math or language simply from knowing his or her sex. There is no biological basis for the unequal treatment women have faced at work, school, and elsewhere. The important differences between women and men are not in our genes or hormones. Instead, most male-female performance gaps can be traced to *social* differences in the power and opportunities given to men and women (Tavris, 1992).

GENDER IDENTITY   As stated earlier, your personal, private sense of being female or male is known as gender identity. Gender identity is a learned self-perception. This point is emphasized by cases of hermaphroditism. Consider, for instance, two persons with ambiguous sex, one raised as a girl and the other as a boy. Usually, the person raised as a girl will regard herself as a girl and act like a girl. Likewise, the individual raised as a boy will act like a boy and identify himself as a boy (Money, 1987).

BRIDGES

Differences in male and female brains may affect the odds of retaining language after a stroke.

See "His and Her Brains?" in Chapter 3, page 67.

At what age is gender identity acquired?   Gender identity is essentially formed by 3 or 4 years of age. Children born with ambiguous sex have few problems as long as a final decision about whether they are male or female is made by the age of 18 months. If parents consistently treat the child only as a girl, or only as a boy, the child will develop a stable gender identity. If the decision is delayed, the child may have a confused gender identity or one at odds with his or her genetic sex.

How is gender identity acquired?   Obviously, it begins with *labeling* ("It's a girl," "It's a boy") (Burnham & Harris, 1992). Thereafter, it is shaped by **gender role socialization** (the process of learning gender behaviors regarded as appropriate for one's sex in a given culture). Gender role socialization reflects all the subtle pressures from parents, peers, and cultural forces that urge boys to "act like boys" and girls to "act like girls." By the time they are just 2 years of age, children are aware of gender role differences (Witt, 1997). Let's investigate gender roles and gender role socialization in more detail.

Gender Roles

Gender roles are probably as important as chromosomal, genital, or hormonal sex in their influence on adult sexual behavior. A **gender role** is the favored pattern of behavior expected of each sex. In our culture, boys are usually encouraged to be strong, fast, aggressive, dominant, and achieving. Traditional females are expected to be sensitive, intuitive, passive, emotional, and "naturally" interested in child-rearing. All cultures define gender roles. As "Gender Role Stereotypes" points out, this often leads to stereotyped thinking about females and males.

CULTURE   A look at other cultures shows that our gender roles are by no means "natural" or universal. For example, in many cultures women do the heavy work because men are considered too weak for it (Albert, 1963). In Russia, roughly 75 percent of all medical doctors are women, and women make up a large portion of the workforce. Many more examples could be cited, but one of the most interesting is anthropologist Margaret Mead's (1935) classic observations of the Tchambuli people of New Guinea.

❖ **FIGURE 14.4** *Recorded differences in various abilities that exist between women and men are based on averages. For example, if we were to record the number of men and women who have low, medium, or high scores on tests of language ability, we might obtain graphs like those shown. For other abilities, men would have a higher average. However, such average differences are typically small. As a result, the overlap in female abilities and male abilities is very large (Breedlove, 1994).*

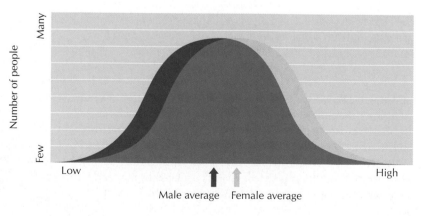

GENDER ROLE STEREOTYPES

Question: How many men does it take to change a light bulb?
Answer: None. Real men aren't afraid of the dark.

This joke pokes fun at the North American stereotype of manhood. Despite much progress in the last 20 years, gender role stereotypes continue to have a major impact on women and men. **Gender role stereotypes** are oversimplified beliefs about what men and women are actually like. Gender roles influence how we act. Gender role stereotypes, in contrast, treat gender roles as if they were real biological differences. That is, culturally defined ways of acting are turned into false beliefs about what men and women can and can't do.

Are women suited to be fighter pilots, corporate presidents, military commanders, or race car drivers? A person with strong gender role stereotypes might say, "No, because women are not sufficiently aggressive, dominant, or mechanically inclined for such roles." Yet, today we know that women have performed successfully in virtually all realms. Nevertheless, gender role stereotypes persist. The United States has never had a woman president and it wasn't until 1999 that Elizabeth Dole had a serious chance of winning a presidential nomination.

In many occupations, women continue to score "firsts" of the kind just mentioned. Nonetheless, gender role stereotypes are a major career obstacle. Unequal pay for comparable work and experience is a major problem for women (Frieze, Olson, & Good, 1990). For many jobs, your chances of being hired could be reduced by your sex, be it male or female. Like all stereotypes, those based on gender roles ignore the wonderful diversity of humanity. Fortunately, extreme gender stereotyping has declined somewhat in the last 20 years (Helwig, 1998; Loo & Thorpe, 1998).

"The committee on women's rights will now come to order."

Gender roles for the Tchambuli are a nearly perfect reversal of North American stereotypes. Tchambuli women do the fishing and manufacturing, and they control the power and economic life of the community. Women also take the initiative in courting and sexual relations. Tchambuli men, on the other hand, are expected to be dependent, flirtatious, and concerned

Behaviors that are considered typical and appropriate for each sex (gender roles) vary a great deal from culture to culture. Undoubtedly some cultures magnify sex differences more than others (Breedlove, 1994).

with their appearance. Art, games, and theatrics occupy most of the Tchambuli males' time, and men are particularly fond of adorning themselves with flowers and jewelry.

As the Tchambuli show, men and women are expected to act in quite different ways in various cultures. The arbitrary nature of gender roles is also apparent. A man is no less a man if he cooks, sews, or cares for children. A woman is no less a woman if she excels in sports, succeeds in business, or works as an auto mechanic. Still, adult personality and gender identity are closely tied to cultural definitions of "masculinity" and "femininity."

An interesting side effect of gender role socialization is the imprint it leaves on activities that have nothing to do with sex. For example, boys are more aggressive than girls, and girls have more emotional empathy than boys (Block, 1979; Maccoby & Jacklin, 1974).

Gender Role Socialization

How are gender differences created? Learning gender roles begins immediately. Infant girls are held more gently and treated more tenderly than boys. Both parents play more roughly with sons than with daughters (who are presumed to be more "delicate"). Later, boys are allowed to roam over a wider area without special permission. They are also expected to run errands earlier than girls. Daughters are told that they are pretty and

Gender role socialization *The process of learning gender behaviors considered appropriate for one's sex in a given culture.*
Gender role *The pattern of behaviors that is regarded as "male" or "female" by one's culture; sometimes also referred to as a sex role.*
Gender role stereotypes *Oversimplified and widely held beliefs about the basic characteristics of men and women.*

❖ **FIGURE 14.5** *One study found that even 2-year-olds are strongly encouraged by their parents to play with "sex-appropriate" toys. Parents' nonverbal responses to toys were consistently more positive when a toy matched stereotypes for the child's gender (Caldera, Huston, & O'Brien, 1989).*

that "nice girls don't fight." Boys are told to be strong and that "tough guys don't cry." Sons are more often urged to control their emotions, except for anger and aggression, which parents tolerate more in boys than in girls.

Toys are strongly sex typed: Parents buy dolls for girls and trucks, tools, and sports equipment for boys. Fathers, especially, tend to encourage their children to play with "appropriate" sex-typed toys (Raag & Rackliff, 1998) (❖Fig. 14.5). By the time children reach kindergarten, they have learned to think that doctors, firefighters, and pilots are men and that nurses, secretaries, and hairdressers are women (Blaske, 1984; Stroeher, 1994). And why not? The workforce is still highly segregated by sex, and children learn from what they observe. Stereotyped gender roles are even the norm in TV commercials, children's picture books, and video games (Browne, 1998; Dietz, 1998; McDonald, 1989)!

"FEMALE" AND "MALE" BEHAVIOR Overall, parents tend to encourage their sons to engage in **instrumental** (goal-directed) **behaviors,** to control their emotions, and to prepare for the world of work. Daughters, on the other hand, are encouraged in **expressive** (emotion-oriented) **behaviors** and, to a lesser degree, are socialized for motherhood.

When parents are told they treat girls and boys differently, many explain that the sexes are just "naturally" different. But what comes first, "natural differences" or the gender-based ex-

BRIDGES

In males, a restricted ability to express emotion is one of the costs of adopting a masculine gender role, as it is defined in North America.

See Chapter 13, page 432.

pectations that create them? In our culture, "male" seems—for many—to be defined as "not female." That is, parents often have a vague fear of expressive and emotional behavior in male children. To them, such behavior implies that a boy is effeminate or a sissy. Many parents who would not be troubled if their daughters engaged in "masculine" play might be upset if their sons played with dolls or imitated "female" mannerisms.

To summarize, gender role socialization in our society prepares children for a world in which men are expected to be instrumental, conquering, controlling, and unemotional. Women, in contrast, are expected to be expressive, emotional, passive, and dependent. Thus, gender role socialization teaches us to be highly competent in some respects and handicapped in others (Levant, 1996).

Of course, many people find traditional gender roles acceptable and comfortable. It seems evident, however, that just about everyone will benefit when the more stereotyped and burdensome aspects of gender roles are set aside. The next section explains why.

ANDROGYNY—ARE YOU MASCULINE, FEMININE, OR ANDROGYNOUS?

Are you aggressive, ambitious, analytical, assertive, athletic, competitive, decisive, dominant, forceful, independent, individualistic, self-reliant, and willing to take risks? If so, you are quite "masculine." Are you affectionate, cheerful, childlike, compassionate, flatterable, gentle, gullible, loyal, sensitive, shy, soft-spoken, sympathetic, tender, understanding, warm, and yielding? If so, then you are quite "feminine." What if you have traits from both lists? In that case, you may be *androgynous* (an-DROJ-ih-nus).

The two lists you just read are from the work of psychologist Sandra Bem. By combining 20 "masculine" traits (self-reliant, assertive, and so forth), 20 "feminine" traits (affectionate, gentle), and 20 neutral traits (truthful, friendly), Bem created the **Bem Sex Role Inventory (BSRI).** (Some psychologists prefer to use the term *sex role* instead of gender role.) Next, she and her associates gave the BSRI to thousands of people, asking them to say whether each trait applied to them. Of those surveyed, 50 percent fell into traditional feminine or masculine categories; 15 percent scored higher on traits of the opposite sex; and 35 percent were androgynous, getting high scores on both feminine and masculine items.

Psychological Androgyny

The word **androgyny** (an-DROJ-ih-nee) literally means "man-woman." Androgyny sounds as if it might have something to do with androids, asexuality, or sex-change operations, but it actually refers to having both feminine and masculine traits.

Bem is convinced that our complex society requires flexibility with respect to gender roles. She believes that it is necessary

Androgynous individuals adapt easily to both traditionally "feminine" and "masculine" situations.

for men to be gentle, compassionate, sensitive, and yielding and for women to be forceful, self-reliant, independent, and ambitious—*as the situation requires*. In short, Bem feels that more people should be androgynous.

ADAPTABILITY   Bem has shown that androgynous individuals are more adaptable. They seem especially to be less hindered by images of "feminine" or "masculine" behavior. For example, in one study people were given the choice of doing either a "masculine" activity (oil a hinge, nail boards together, and so forth) or a "feminine" activity (prepare a baby bottle, wind yarn into a ball, and so on). Masculine men and feminine women consistently chose to do gender-appropriate activities, even when the opposite choice paid more!

Bem has concluded that rigid gender stereotypes and gender roles can seriously restrict behavior, especially for men (Bem, 1975, 1981). She believes that masculine males have great difficulty expressing warmth, playfulness, and concern—even when they are appropriate. Masculine men, it seems, tend to view such feelings as unacceptably "feminine." Masculine men also find it hard to accept emotional support from others, particularly from women (Ashton & Fuehrer, 1993). Problems faced by highly feminine women are the reverse of those faced by masculine men. Such women have trouble being independent and assertive, even when these qualities are desirable.

Over the years, androgyny has been variously supported, attacked, and debated. Now, as the dust begins to settle, the picture looks like this:

- Having "masculine" traits primarily means that a person is independent and assertive. Scoring high in "masculinity," therefore, is related to high self-esteem and to success in many situations (Long, 1989).
- Having "feminine" traits primarily means that a person is nurturant and interpersonally oriented. People who

score high in "femininity," therefore, tend to experience greater social closeness with others and more happiness in marriage.

In sum, there are advantages to possessing both "feminine" and "masculine" traits (Ickes, 1993; Spence, 1984). In general, androgynous persons are more flexible when it comes to coping with difficult situations (Jurma & Powell, 1994; Spangenberg & Lategan, 1993). (See ❖Figure 14.6.) Androgynous people also tend to be more satisfied with their lives. Apparently, they can use both instrumental and emotionally expressive capacities to enhance their lives and relationships (Dean-Church & Gilroy, 1993; Ramanaiah, Detwiler, & Byravan, 1995).

Interestingly, some men appear to be moving toward more balanced definitions of manhood. For instance, more Mexican American men than European American men are androgynous (Sugihara & Warner, 1999). Along the same lines, some Asian American men, especially those who were born in the United States, appear to be creating a more flexible masculinity free from male dominance. These men link their masculinity with a capacity for caring, and they are not afraid of doing "feminine tasks," such as cooking or housework (Chua & Fujino, 1999).

Instrumental behaviors *Behaviors directed toward the achievement of some goal; behaviors that are instrumental in producing some effect.*
Expressive behaviors *Behaviors that express or communicate emotion or personal feelings.*
Bem Sex Role Inventory (BSRI) *A list of 60 personal traits including "masculine," "feminine," and "neutral" traits; used to rate one's degree of androgyny.*
Androgyny *The presence of both "masculine" and "feminine" traits in a single person (as masculinity and femininity are defined within one's culture).*

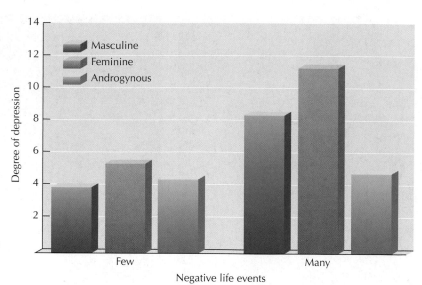

❖ **FIGURE. 14.6** *Another indication of the possible benefits of androgyny is found in a study of reactions to stress. When confronted with an onslaught of negative events, strongly masculine or feminine persons become more depressed than androgynous individuals do (adapted from Roos & Cohen, 1987).*

It is worth saying again that many people remain comfortable with traditional views of gender. Nevertheless, "feminine" traits and "masculine" traits can exist in the same person, and androgyny can be a highly adaptive balance.

SEXUAL DEVELOPMENT, GENDER, AND ANDROGYNY

RELATE

You are a pediatrician who has been asked to evaluate a child whose sex seems to be ambiguous. What indicators of sex would you want to check?

Can you remember an example of gender role socialization you experienced as a child? Do you think you were encouraged to engage in more instrumental behaviors or expressive behaviors?

Mentally change your male friends to females and your female friends to males. Can you separate the "human being" or "core person" from your friends' normal gender identities and gender roles?

Think of three people you know, one who is androgynous, one who is traditionally feminine, and one who is traditionally masculine. What advantages and disadvantages do you see in each collection of traits? How do you think you would be classified if you took the BSRI?

LEARNING CHECK

1. _____ sexual characteristics refer to the sexual and reproductive organs; _____ sexual characteristics refer to other bodily changes that take place at puberty.

2. All individuals normally produce both androgens and estrogens, although the proportions differ in females and males. T or F?

3. The four basic dimensions of biological sex are:

    _____   _____

    _____   _____

4. In females, hermaphroditism may result from
   a. an androgen insensitivity *b.* the androgenital syndrome *c.* excessive estrogen. *d.* all of these

5. For humans, the biological biasing effect of prenatal hormones tends to override all other influences. T or F?

6. One's private sense of maleness or femaleness is referred to as

    _____   _____.

7. Traditional gender role socialization encourages _____ behavior in males.
   a. instrumental *b.* emotional *c.* expressive *d.* dependent

8. A person who is androgynous is one who scores high on ratings of traits usually possessed by the opposite sex. T or F?

9. For both women and men, having masculine traits is associated with greater happiness in marriage. T or F?

CRITICAL THINKING

10. A problem known as transsexualism exists when a person feels that she or he is trapped in a body of the wrong sex. This problem is therefore defined almost entirely on the basis of which dimension of gender?

11. As children are growing up, the male emphasis on instrumental behavior comes into conflict with the female emphasis on expressive behavior. At what age do you think such conflicts become prominent?

12. Could a person be androgynous in a culture where "masculine" and "feminine" traits differ greatly from those on Bem's list?

Answers:

1. Primary, secondary 2. T 3. genetic sex, gonadal sex, hormonal sex, genital sex 4. b 5. F 6. gender identity 7. a 8. F 9. F 10. Gender identity. 11. Children segregate themselves into same-sex groups during much of childhood, which limits conflicts between male and female patterns of behavior. However, as children move into adolescence, they begin to spend more time with members of the opposite sex. This brings the dominant, competitive style of boys into conflict with the nurturant, expressive style of girls, often placing girls at a disadvantage (Maccoby, 1990). 12. Yes. Being androgynous means having both masculine and feminine traits *as they are defined within one's culture.*

SEXUAL BEHAVIOR—MAPPING THE EROGENOUS ZONE

When does sexual behavior first appear in humans? A capacity for sexual arousal is apparent at birth or soon after. Researcher Alfred Kinsey verified instances of orgasm (sexual climax) in boys as young as 5 months old and girls as young as 4 months (Kinsey et al., 1948, 1953). Kinsey also found that 2- to 5-year-old children spontaneously touch and exhibit their genitals.

Various types of sexual behavior continue throughout childhood. But as a child matures, cultural norms place greater restrictions on sexual activities. Still, 25 percent of females and 50 percent of males engage in preadolescent sex play. In adulthood, norms continue to shape sexual activity along socially approved lines. In our culture, sex between children, incest (sex between close relatives), prostitution, and extramarital sex all tend to be discouraged.

As was true of gender roles, it's apparent that such restrictions are somewhat arbitrary. Sexual activities of all kinds are more common in cultures that place fewer restrictions on sexual behavior. Apart from cultural norms, it can be said that any sexual act engaged in by consenting adults is "normal" if it does not hurt anyone. (Atypical sexual behavior is discussed later in this chapter.)

Sexual Arousal

Human sexual arousal is complex. It may, of course, be produced by direct stimulation of the body's **erogenous zones** (eh-ROJ-eh-nus: productive of pleasure or erotic desire). Human erogenous zones include the genitals, mouth, breasts, ears, anus, and, to a lesser degree, the surface of the entire body. It is clear, however, that more than physical contact is involved: A urological or gynecological exam rarely results in any sexual arousal. Likewise, an unwanted sexual advance may produce only revulsion. Human sexual arousal obviously includes a large cognitive element. Indeed, arousal may be triggered by mere thoughts or mental images.

SEXUAL SCRIPTS   In a restaurant, we commonly expect certain things to occur. It could even be said that each of us has a restaurant "script" that defines a plot, dialogue, and actions that should take place. Researcher John Gagnon (1977) has pointed out that, similarly, we learn a variety of **sexual scripts,** or unspoken mental plans that guide our sexual behavior. Such scripts determine when and where we are likely to express sexual feelings, and with whom. They provide a "plot" for the order of events in lovemaking, and they outline "approved" actions, motives, and outcomes.

When two people follow markedly different scripts, misunderstandings are almost sure to occur. Consider, for instance, what happens when a woman acting out a "friendly-first-date" script is paired with a man following a "seduction" script: The result is often anger, hurt feelings, or worse. Even newlyweds may find that their sexual "agendas" differ. In such cases, considerable "rewriting" of scripts is often needed for sexual compatibility. For humans, the mind (or brain) is the ultimate erogenous zone.

Ziggy

Are men more easily sexually aroused than women? Women are no less *physically* responsive than men (Laan et al., 1995). However, compared with men, women more often have a negative *emotional* response to erotic stimuli, such as explicit pictures of sex. That is, women more often say they are upset or disgusted by these stimuli (Mosher & MacIan, 1994).

One reason for women's emotional responses may lie in the erotic stimuli themselves. Most erotic materials (such as films and videos) are made by men, for men. See "What Do Women Want?" for more information about this interesting aspect of female sexuality.

Based on the frequency of orgasm (from masturbation or intercourse), the peak of male sexual activity is at age 18. The peak rate of female sexual activity appears to occur a little later (Janus & Janus, 1993). However, male and female sexual patterns are rapidly becoming more alike (Oliver & Hyde, 1993). ❖Figure 14.7 shows the results of a major survey of sexual behavior among American adults. As you can see, the frequency of sexual intercourse is very similar for men and women (Laumann et al., 1994).

SEX DRIVE   *What causes differences in sex drive?* The term **sex drive** refers to the strength of one's motivation to engage in sexual behavior. Attitudes toward sex, sexual experience, and recency of sexual activity are all important, but physical factors also play a role. In males, the strength of the sex drive is related to the amount of androgens secreted by the testes. When the supply of androgens dramatically increases at puberty, sex drive increases, too. Likewise, the sex drive in women is related to their estrogen levels (Graziottin, 1998).

Erogenous zones *Areas of the body that produce pleasure and/or provoke erotic desire.*
Sexual script *An unspoken mental plan that defines a "plot," dialogue, and actions expected to take place in a sexual encounter.*
Sex drive *The strength of one's motivation to engage in sexual behavior.*

"WHAT DO WOMEN WANT?"

Sigmund Freud was perplexed by what he regarded as a great mystery. "What," he wondered, "do women want?" Psychologist Ellen Laan thinks she may have an answer. Laan is studying differences between subjective sexual arousal (whether a woman says she feels sexually aroused) and physical arousal (how her body is actually responding) (Laan et al., 1995).

In one of Laan's studies, women watched excerpts from two erotic films. One was made by a man for male viewers. The other was directed by a woman and presented from a female point of view. Using a medical recording device, Laan found that women's physical arousal was nearly identical for both films. However, their subjective experiences differed greatly. Many women reported being repulsed, disgusted, and decidedly not aroused by the male-oriented film. When they watched the film made for women, Laan's

subjects reported more subjective feelings of sexual arousal, more positive emotions, and more interest in the film (Laan et al., 1994).

Why did the women respond so differently? Basically, the male-centered film was a macho fantasy in which the woman was little more than a sexual prop—her pleasure and fulfillment were portrayed as largely unimportant. In the woman-made film, the female character took the initiative in lovemaking and obviously enjoyed it.

Clearly, women and men have equal potential for sexual arousal. However, a woman's subjective feelings of arousal tend to be more closely tied to her emotional response to erotic cues. It would appear that many women want to be active partners in lovemaking, and they want their needs and preferences to be acknowledged. There's no mystery in that, Dr. Freud.

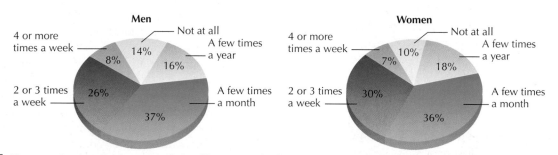

❖ **FIGURE 14.7** *These graphs show the frequency of sexual intercourse for American adults. To generalize, about one third of the people surveyed have sex twice a week or more, one third a few times a month, and one third a few times a year or not at all. The overall average is about once a week (Laumann et al., 1994).*

Surprisingly, "male" hormones also affect the female sex drive. In addition to estrogen, a woman's body produces small amounts of androgens, which can increase the sex drive in women, just as they do in men. When women are given androgens for medical reasons, they report increased sexual desire (Van Goozen et al., 1995). Some women also report changes in sex drive at various times during their monthly cycles. However, such effects are probably small, because women may have sex at any time, including during menstruation.

Do nocturnal emissions ("wet dreams") reveal an unusually strong sex drive? Do they ever indicate sexual disorders? Do both sexes have nocturnal orgasms? About 85 percent of males and 35 percent of females have had erotic dreams that resulted in sexual climax (**nocturnal orgasms**). These incidents typically begin during adolescence and may continue throughout adulthood. Nocturnal orgasm, therefore, may be considered a completely normal (if relatively infrequent) form of sexual release.

Does alcohol stimulate the sex drive? In general, no. Alcohol is a *depressant*. As such, it may, in small doses, stimulate erotic desire by lowering inhibitions. This effect no doubt accounts for alcohol's rep-

utation as an aid to seduction. (Humorist Ogden Nash once summarized this bit of folklore by saying "Candy is dandy, but liquor is quicker.") However, in larger doses, alcohol suppresses orgasm in women and erection in men. Getting drunk *decreases* sexual desire, arousal, pleasure, and performance (Crowe & George, 1989).

Does removal of the testes or ovaries abolish the sex drive? In lower animals, **castration** (surgical removal of the testicles or ovaries) tends to abolish sexual activity in *inexperienced* animals. In humans, the effects of male and female castration vary. At first, some people experience a loss of sex drive; in others, there is no change. (That's why castration of sex offenders is not likely to curb their behavior.) However, after several years, almost all subjects report a decrease in sex drive unless they take hormone supplements.

The preceding observations have nothing to do with **sterilization** (surgery to make a man or woman infertile). The vast majority of women and men who choose surgically based birth control (such as a tubal ligation or a vasectomy) experience no loss of sex drive. If anything, they may become more sexually active when pregnancy is no longer a concern.

BRIDGES

Sexual arousal normally occurs during rapid-eye-movement sleep (REM), when most dreaming takes place.

See Chapter 8, page 240.

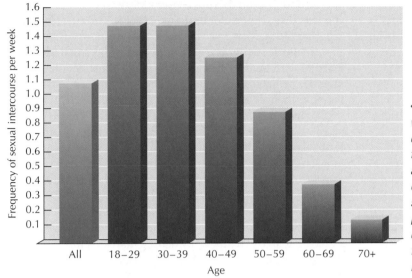

❖ **FIGURE 14.8** *Average frequency of sexual intercourse per week for adults in the United States. Average intervals for intercourse decline from once every 4 or 5 days in young adulthood, to once every 16 days in the 60s. Remember that averages such as these are lowered by the inclusion of people who are abstinent or who do not have sexual partners (such as many widowed persons). However, the age declines noted here also show up for people who are married, ranging from an average rate of intercourse of twice a week for couples under 30 to once every 3 weeks for those over 70. This suggests that the average frequency of intercourse does decline with advancing age (Smith, 1990).*

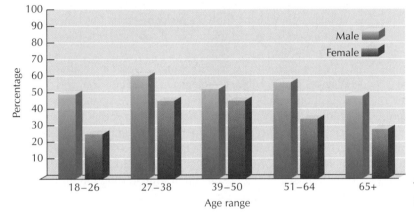

❖ **FIGURE 14.9** *Percentage of women and men who masturbate. (Data from Janus & Janus, 1993.)*

What happens to the sex drive in old age? A natural decline in sex drive typically accompanies aging and reduced sex hormone output (Segraves & Segraves, 1995) (❖Fig. 14.8). However, sexual activity need not come to an unavoidable end. Some people in their 80s and 90s continue to have active sex lives (Skoog, 1996). The crucial factor for an extended sex life appears to be regularity and opportunity. ("Use it or lose it.") People who fairly regularly engage in intercourse have little difficulty in later years. Many in their 70s, 80s, and 90s report that sex is at least as gratifying as ever (Janus & Janus, 1993).

MASTURBATION   One of the most basic sexual behaviors is **masturbation,** or deliberate self-stimulation that causes sexual pleasure or orgasm. Self-stimulation has been observed in infants under 1 year of age. In adulthood, female masturbation most often involves stimulating the clitoris or areas near it. Masturbation in the male usually takes the form of stroking or other manipulation of the penis.

Do more men masturbate than women? Yes. Of the women who took part in a recent national survey, 89 percent reported that they had masturbated at some time. Of the males, 95 percent reported that they had masturbated. (Some cynics add, "And the other 5 percent lied!") As ❖Figure 14.9 shows, mas-

turbation is a regular feature of the sex lives of many people (Janus & Janus, 1993).

What purpose does masturbation serve? Through masturbation, people discover what pleases them sexually and what their natural rhythms and preferences are. Masturbation is an important part of the psychosexual development of most adolescents. Among other things, it provides a healthy substitute for sexual involvement at a time when young people are maturing emotionally (Strong & DeVault, 1994).

Is it immature for masturbation to continue after marriage? If it is, there are many "immature" people around! Approximately 70 percent of married women and men masturbate at least occasionally. Generally speaking, masturbation is valid at

Nocturnal orgasm *An orgasm that occurs spontaneously during sleep or dreaming.*
Castration *Surgical removal of the testicles or ovaries.*
Sterilization *Medical procedures such as vasectomy or tubal ligation that make a man or a woman infertile.*
Masturbation *Producing sexual pleasure or orgasm by directly stimulating the genitals.*

any age and usually has no effect on marital relationships. Contrary to popular myths, people are not compelled to masturbate because they lack a sexual partner. Actually, people who are most sexually active are also the ones who masturbate the most. Masturbation is just "one more item on the menu" for people with active sex lives (Laumann et al., 1994).

Is there any way in which masturbation can cause harm? Fifty years ago, a child might have been told that masturbation would cause insanity, acne, sterility, or other such nonsense. "Self-abuse," as it was often called, has enjoyed a long and unfortunate history of religious and medical disapproval. The modern view is that masturbation is a normal sexual behavior. Enlightened parents are well aware of this fact. Still, many children are punished or made to feel guilty for touching their genitals. This is unfortunate in that masturbation itself is harmless. Typically, its only negative effects are fear, guilt, or anxiety, which arises when people learn to think of masturbation as "bad" or "wrong." In an age when people are being urged to practice "safer sex," masturbation remains the safest sex of all.

SEXUAL ORIENTATION—WHO DO YOU LOVE?

Sexual behavior and romantic relationships are strongly influenced by a person's sexual orientation. **Sexual orientation** refers to your degree of emotional and erotic attraction to members of the same sex, opposite sex, or both sexes. **Heterosexual** people are romantically and erotically attracted to members of the opposite sex. Those who are **homosexual** are attracted to people whose sex matches their own. A person who is **bisexual** is attracted to both men and women. In short, sexual orientation answers these questions: Whom are you

attracted to? Whom do you have erotic fantasies about? Do you love men, women, or both? (Garnets & Kimmel, 1991; Seligman, 1994).

Sexual orientation is a very deep part of personal identity. Starting with their earliest erotic feelings, most people remember being attracted to either the opposite sex or the same sex. The chances are practically nil of an exclusively heterosexual or homosexual person being "converted" from one orientation to the other. If you are heterosexual, you are probably certain that nothing could ever make you have homoerotic feelings. If so, then you know how homosexual persons feel about the prospects for changing *their* sexual orientation (Seligman, 1994).

But what about people who have had both heterosexual and homosexual relationships? Many such instances involve homosexual people who temporarily date or marry members of the opposite sex because of pressures to fit into a predominantly heterosexual society. When these people realize they are being untrue to themselves, their identity and relationships may shift accordingly. Other apparent shifts in orientation probably involve people who are fundamentally bisexual. Overall, sexual orientation is a very stable personal characteristic (Garnets & Kimmel, 1991).

What determines a person's sexual orientation? Research suggests that hereditary, biological, social, cultural, and psychological influences combine to produce one's sexual orientation (Money, 1987; Van Wyk & Geist, 1995). As one author summarizes, "Like much of human behavior, a combination of biological and social factors are most likely involved in the development of sexuality" (Gladue, 1987). "Genes, the Brain, and Sexual Orientation" summarizes some interesting findings about the origins of sexual orientation.

GENES, THE BRAIN, AND SEXUAL ORIENTATION

FOCUS ON RESEARCH

Why are some people attracted to the opposite sex while others prefer members of the same sex? New evidence suggests that sexual orientation is at least partly hereditary. One study found that if one identical twin is homosexual or bisexual, there is a 50 percent chance that the other twin is, too. Similar findings lead some researchers to estimate that sexual orientation is from 30 to 70 percent genetic (Bailey et al., 1993; Bailey & Pillard, 1991).

How could genes affect sexual orientation? Possibly, heredity shapes areas of the brain that orchestrate sexual behavior. Support for this idea comes from the work of neurobiologist Simon LeVay. He and other scientists have shown that various brain structures do indeed differ in heterosexuals and homosexuals (LeVay, 1993). Other research suggests that sexual orientation is influenced by a gene or genes found on the X chromosome. Thus, genetic tendencies for homosexuality may be passed from mothers to their children (Hamer et al., 1993; Hu et al., 1995).

Many people mistakenly believe that homosexuality is caused by a hormone imbalance. However, it is *highly un-*

likely that hormone levels during adulthood affect sexual orientation. Hormone levels of most gay men and lesbians are within the normal range (Banks & Gartrell, 1995). If hormones do have a role in determining sexual orientation, their impact occurs before birth (Berenbaum & Snyder, 1995; Meyer-Bahlburg et al., 1995).

It is also a mistake to think that parenting makes children homosexual. There is little difference between the development of children with gay or lesbian parents and those who have heterosexual parents (Chan, Raboy, & Patterson, 1998; Parks, 1998).

All of these findings tend to discredit myths about parental behavior making children homosexual or claims that homosexuality is merely a preference. Although learning contributes to one's sexual orientation, it appears that nature strongly prepares people to be either homosexual or heterosexual (LeVay, 1993). In view of this, discriminating against homosexuals is much like rejecting a person for being blue-eyed or left-handed (Hamill, 1995).

Homosexuality

As the preceding discussion implies, homosexuality is part of the normal range of variations in sexual orientation (Garnets & Kimmel, 1991). Gay men, lesbians, and bisexuals encounter hostility because they are members of minority groups, not because there is anything inherently wrong with them (Meyer, 1995).

Based on a national survey, it is estimated that about 7 percent of all adults regard themselves as homosexual or bisexual (Janus & Janus, 1993). Here are the figures:

	MEN	WOMEN
Heterosexual	91%	95%
Homosexual	4%	2%
Bisexual	5%	3%

A more recent survey of young men found that 6 percent identified themselves as homosexual, so the preceding figures may be low estimates (Bagley & Tremblay, 1998). Nevertheless, among men, *at least* 1 in 25 is homosexual. Among women, *at least* 1 in 50 is a lesbian. About 1 person in 25 is bisexual. Together, these percentages indicate that at least 7 people out of every 100 are bisexual or homosexual (Janus & Janus, 1993). That means about 50 million people in the United States alone are gay, lesbian, or have a family member who is homosexual (Patterson, 1995).

When evaluating homosexuality, it is important to remember that cultural standards vary greatly. A survey of 76 cultures found that almost two thirds accept some form of homosexuality. About 20 percent of all females and 25 percent of all males have had at least one homosexual experience. Historically, homosexuality has been a part of human sexuality since the dawn of time.

In contrast to heterosexuals, homosexual persons tend to discover their sexual orientation at a fairly late date—often not until early adolescence. Very likely, this is because they are surrounded by powerful cultural images that contradict their natural feelings. However, most homosexual persons begin to sense that they are different in childhood. By early adolescence, gay men and lesbians begin to feel an attraction to members of the same sex. Gradually, this leads them to question their sexual identity and accept their same-sex orientation (Diamond, 1998).

It is probably difficult for most heterosexual persons to imagine how stressful it is to deny something as basic as one's sexual orientation. Yet, understandably, homosexual persons may be reluctant to accept or acknowledge their sexual orientation. Doing so risks rejection by family, friends, and others (Krivascka, Savin-Williams, & Slater, 1992).

Testing consistently shows no differences in personality or adjustment between heterosexuals and homosexuals (Bell et al., 1981; Marmor, 1980). Emotional health, then, appears to be independent of sexual preference (Siegelman, 1987). Sexual orientation is not related to a person's ability to function in society, work constructively, maintain mental health, care for children, or form caring relationships (Seligman, 1994).

The problems faced by lesbians and gay men tend to be related to rejection by family, discrimination in employment and housing, and the undercurrents of *homophobia* and *heterosex-*ism in our society (Meyer, 1995). (**Homophobia** refers to prejudice, fear, and dislike directed at homosexuals. **Heterosexism** is the belief that heterosexuality is better or more natural than homosexuality.)

Most homosexual people have at one time or another suffered verbal abuse—or worse—because of their sexual orientation (Pilkington & D'Augelli, 1995). Much of this rejection is based on false stereotypes about gay and lesbian people. The following points are a partial reply to such stereotypes (Melton, 1989). Gay and lesbian people:

- Do not try to convert others to homosexuality.
- Do not molest children.
- Are not mentally ill.
- Do not hate persons of the opposite sex.
- Do not, as parents, make their own children gay.
- Do have long-term, caring, monogamous relationships.
- Are no less able to contribute to society than heterosexuals.

Homosexual people are found in all walks of life, at all social and economic levels, and in all cultural groups. They are as diverse in terms of race, ethnicity, age, parenthood, relationships, careers, health, education, politics, and sexual behavior as the heterosexual community (Garnets & Kimmel, 1991). Perhaps as more people come to see gay and lesbian people in terms of their humanity, rather than their sexuality, the prejudices they have faced will wane.

KNOWLEDGE BUILDER

SEXUAL BEHAVIOR AND SEXUAL ORIENTATION

RELATE

How would you explain the following statement to students in a high school biology class: "Human sexual arousal obviously includes a large cognitive element"?

To what extent does the discussion of sexual arousal and sex drive agree with your own experiences and beliefs? What do you want to remember that you didn't know before?

Which of your prior beliefs about sexual orientation are true? Which are false?

LEARNING CHECK

1. A capacity for sexual arousal is apparent at birth or soon after. T or F?

2. Areas of the body that produce erotic pleasure are called _____ zones.

Sexual orientation *One's degree of emotional and erotic attraction to members of the same sex, opposite sex, or both sexes.*
Heterosexual *A person romantically and erotically attracted to members of the opposite sex.*
Homosexual *A person romantically and erotically attracted to same-sex persons.*
Bisexual *A person romantically and erotically attracted to both men and women.*
Homophobia *A powerful fear of homosexuality.*
Heterosexism *The belief that heterosexuality is better or more natural than homosexuality.*

HUMAN SEXUAL RESPONSE–SEXUAL INTERACTIONS

The pioneering work of gynecologist William Masters and psychologist Virginia Johnson greatly expanded our understanding of sexual response (Masters & Johnson, 1966; 1970). In a series of experiments, interviews, and controlled observations, Masters and Johnson directly studied sexual intercourse and masturba-

tion in nearly 700 males and females. This objective information has given us a much clearer picture of human sexuality.

According to Masters and Johnson, sexual response can be divided into four phases: (1) *excitement,* (2) *plateau,* (3) *orgasm,* and (4) *resolution* (❖Figs. 14.10 and 14.11). These four phases can be described as follows:

- **Excitement phase:** The first level of sexual response, indicated by initial signs of sexual arousal.
- **Plateau phase:** The second level of sexual response, during which physical arousal intensifies.
- **Orgasm:** A climax and release of sexual excitement.
- **Resolution:** The final phase of sexual response, involving a return to lower levels of sexual tension and arousal.

The four phases are the same for people of all sexual orientations (Garnets & Kimmel, 1991).

FEMALE RESPONSE   In women, the excitement phase is marked by a complex pattern of changes that prepare the vagina for intercourse. At the same time, the nipples become erect, pulse rate rises, and the skin may become flushed. If sexual stimulation ends, the excitement phase will gradually subside. If the person moves into the plateau phase, physical changes and subjective feelings of arousal become more intense. Sexual arousal that ends during this phase tends to ebb more slowly, which may produce considerable frustration. Occasionally, women skip the plateau phase (see ❖Fig. 14.10). For some women, this is almost always the case.

During orgasm, from 3 to 10 muscular contractions of the vagina, uterus, and related structures discharge sexual tension. A small amount of fluid is sometimes released from the urethra during orgasm. However, vaginal lubrication produced during the excitement phase probably accounts for the perceptions of women who believe they have ejaculated. Orgasm is usually followed by resolution, a return to lower levels of sexual tension and arousal. After orgasm, about 15 percent of all women return to the plateau phase and may have one or more additional orgasms.

Before the work of Masters and Johnson, theorists debated whether "vaginal orgasms" are different from those derived

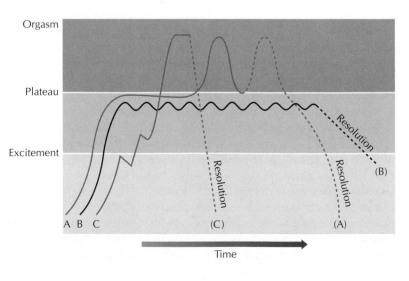

❖ **FIGURE 14.10** *Female sexual response cycle. The green line shows that sexual arousal rises through the excitement phase and levels off for a time during the plateau phase. Arousal peaks during orgasm and then returns to pre-excitement levels. In pattern A, arousal rises from excitement, through the plateau phase, and peaks in orgasm. Resolution may be immediate, or it may first include a return to the plateau phase and a second orgasm (dotted line). In pattern B, arousal is sustained at the plateau phase and slowly resolved without sexual climax. Pattern C shows a fairly rapid rise in arousal to orgasm. Little time is spent in the plateau phase, and resolution is fairly rapid. (Reproduced by permission from Frank A. Beach, ed., Sex and Behavior, New York: John Wiley & Sons, Inc., 1965.)*

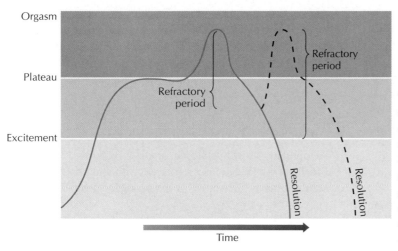

❖ **FIGURE 14.11** *Male sexual response cycle. The green line shows that sexual arousal rises through the excitement phase and levels off for a time during the plateau phase. Arousal peaks during orgasm and then returns to pre-excitement levels. During the refractory period, immediately after orgasm, a second sexual climax is typically impossible. However, after the refractory period has passed, there may be a return to the plateau phase, followed by a second orgasm (dotted line). (Reproduced by permission from Frank A. Beach, ed., Sex and Behavior, New York: John Wiley & Sons, Inc., 1965.)*

from stimulation of the clitoris. Sigmund Freud claimed that a "clitoral orgasm" is an "immature" form of female response. Because the clitoris is the female structure comparable to the penis, Freud believed that women whose orgasms centered on the clitoris had not fully accepted their femininity.

Masters and Johnson exploded the Freudian myth by showing that physical responses are the same no matter how an orgasm is produced. As a matter of fact, the inner two thirds of the vagina is relatively insensitive to touch. Most sensations during intercourse come from stimulation of the clitoris and other external areas.

Apparently, sensations from many sources are fused together into the total experience of orgasm. For most women, the clitoris is an important source of pleasurable sensations. When women in one study were asked to express a preference for vaginal or clitoral stimulation, most said they would rather not choose. But if they were forced to choose, two thirds said they would prefer clitoral sensations (Fisher, 1973). Similarly, researcher Shere Hite reported the results of an unscientific yet thought-provoking survey of 3,000 women. Among these women, only 26 percent reported regularly reaching orgasm during intercourse without separate massaging of the clitoris (Hite, 1976). Thus, to downgrade the "clitoral orgasm" ignores the basic physiology of female sexual response.

MALE RESPONSE   Sexual arousal in the male is signaled by erection of the penis during the excitement phase. There is also a rise in heart rate, increased blood flow to the genitals, enlargement of the testicles, erection of the nipples, and numerous other bodily changes. As is true of female sexual response, continued stimulation moves the male into the plateau phase. Again, physical changes and subjective feelings of arousal become more intense. Further stimulation during the plateau phase brings about a reflex release of sexual tension, resulting in orgasm.

In the mature male, orgasm is usually accompanied by **ejaculation** (release of sperm and seminal fluid). Afterward, it is followed by a short **refractory period,** during which a second orgasm is impossible. (Many men cannot even have an erection until the refractory phase has passed.) Only rarely is the male

refractory period immediately followed by a second orgasm. Both orgasm and resolution in the male usually do not last as long as they do for females.

Comparing Male and Female Responses

Male and female sexual responses are generally quite similar. However, the differences that do exist can affect sexual adjustment. For example, women typically go through the sexual phases more slowly than men do. During lovemaking, from 10 to 20 minutes is often required for a woman to go from excitement to orgasm. Males may experience all four stages in as little as 4 minutes. However, there is much variation, especially in women. A study of married women found that 50 percent of them reached orgasm if intercourse lasted 1 to 11 minutes; when intercourse lasted 15 minutes or more, the rate increased to 66 percent. Twenty-five percent of the wives said that orgasm occurred within 1 minute of the start of intercourse (Brewer, 1981). (Note that these times refer only to intercourse, not to an entire arousal sequence.) Such differences should be kept in mind by couples seeking sexual compatibility.

Does that mean that a couple should try to time lovemaking to promote simultaneous orgasm?   At one time, simultaneous orgasm (both partners reaching sexual climax at the same time) was considered the "goal" of lovemaking. Now, it is regarded as an artificial concern that may reduce sexual enjoyment. It is more advisable for couples to seek mutual satisfaction through a combination of intercourse and erotic touching than it is to

Excitement phase *The first phase of sexual response, indicated by initial signs of sexual arousal.*
Plateau phase *The second phase of sexual response, during which physical arousal is further heightened.*
Orgasm *A climax and release of sexual excitement.*
Resolution *The fourth phase of sexual response, involving a return to lower levels of sexual tension and arousal.*
Ejaculation *The release of sperm and seminal fluid by the male at the time of orgasm.*
Refractory period *A short time period after orgasm during which males are unable to again reach orgasm.*

inhibit spontaneity, communication, and pleasure. A national survey found that the vast majority of American adults no longer feel that simultaneous orgasm is necessary for satisfying lovemaking (Janus & Janus, 1993).

Does the slower response just described mean that women are less sexual than men? Definitely not. During masturbation, 70 percent of females reach orgasm in 4 minutes or less. This casts serious doubts on the idea that women respond more slowly. Slower female response during intercourse probably occurs because stimulation to the clitoris is less direct. It might be said that men simply provide too little stimulation for more rapid female response, not that women are in any way inferior.

Does penis size affect female response? Masters and Johnson found that the vagina adjusts to the size of the penis and that subjective feelings of pleasure and intensity of orgasm are not related to penis size. They also found that while individual differences exist in flaccid penis size, there tends to be much less variation in size during erection. That's why erection has been called the "great equalizer." Contrary to popular belief, there is no relationship between penis size and male sexual potency. Lovemaking involves the entire body. Preoccupation with the size of a woman's breasts, a man's penis, and the like are based on myths that undermine genuine caring, sharing, and sexual satisfaction.

Men almost always reach orgasm during intercourse, but many women do not. Does this indicate that women are less sexually responsive? Again, the evidence argues against any lack of female sexual responsiveness. It is true that about 1 woman in 3 does not experience orgasm during the first year of marriage, and only about 30 percent regularly reach orgasm through intercourse alone. However, this does not imply lack of physical responsiveness because 90 percent of all women reach orgasm when masturbating.

In another regard, the female is clearly more responsive. Only about 5 percent of males are capable of multiple orgasm (and then only after an unavoidable refractory period). Most men are limited to a second orgasm at best. In contrast, Masters and Johnson's findings suggest that most women who regularly experience orgasm are capable of multiple orgasm. According to one survey, 48 percent of all women have had multiple orgasms (Darling et al., 1992). Remember though, that only about 15 percent regularly have multiple orgasms. A woman should not automatically assume that something is wrong if she isn't orgasmic or multi-orgasmic. Many women have satisfying sexual experiences even when orgasm is not involved.

ATYPICAL SEXUAL BEHAVIOR—TRENCH COATS, WHIPS, LEATHERS, AND LACE

By strict standards (including the law in some states), any sexual activity other than face-to-face heterosexual intercourse between married adults is atypical or "deviant." But public standards are often at odds with private behavior. Just as the hunger drive is expressed and satisfied in many ways, the sex drive also leads to an immense range of behaviors.

When do variations in sexual behavior become sufficiently atypical to be a problem? Psychologically, the mark of true sexual deviations is that they are compulsive and destructive.

Paraphilias

Sexual deviations, or **paraphilias** (PAIR-eh-FIL-ih-ahs) typically cause guilt, anxiety, or discomfort for one or both participants. The paraphilias cover a wide variety of behaviors, including:

- **Pedophilia**—sex with children, or child molesting
- **Fetishism**—sexual arousal associated with inanimate objects
- **Exhibitionism**—"flashing," or displaying the genitals to unwilling viewers
- **Voyeurism**—"peeping," or viewing the genitals of others without their permission
- **Transvestic fetishism**—achieving sexual arousal by wearing clothing of the opposite sex
- **Sexual sadism**—deriving sexual pleasure from inflicting pain
- **Sexual masochism**—desiring pain as part of the sex act
- **Frotteurism**—sexually touching or rubbing against a nonconsenting person, usually in a public place such as a subway

Sexual deviance is a highly emotional subject, and many people have misconceptions about it. Two of the most misunderstood problems are exhibitionism and pedophilia. Check your understanding against the information that follows.

EXHIBITIONISM Exhibitionism is a common problem. Roughly 35 percent of all sexual arrests are for "flashing." Exhibitionists are typically male and married, and most come from strict and repressive backgrounds. Exhibitionists have the highest repeat rate among sexual offenders. Most of them feel a deep sense of inadequacy, which produces a compulsive need to prove their "manhood" by frightening women. Although exhibitionists are usually harmless, those who approach closer than arm's reach may be dangerous (Sue et al., 1996). In general, a woman confronted by an exhibitionist can assume that his goal is to shock and alarm her. By becoming visibly upset, she actually encourages him (Hyde, 1996).

CHILD MOLESTATION Child molesters, who also are usually male, are often pictured as despicable perverts lurking in dark alleys. In fact, most are married, and two thirds are fathers. Many are rigid, passive, puritanical, or religious. In half to two thirds of all cases of pedophilia, the offender is a friend, acquaintance, or relative of the child. Molesters are also often thought of as child rapists, but most molestations rarely exceed fondling (Sue et al., 1996).

How serious are the effects of a molestation? The impact varies widely. It is affected by how long the abuse lasts and by whether genital sexual acts are involved (Freize, 1987). Many authorities believe that a single incident of fondling is unlikely to cause severe emotional harm to a child. For most children, the event is frightening but not a lasting trauma. This is why parents are urged not to overreact to such incidents or to become hysterical. Doing so only further frightens the child. This does not mean, however, that parents should ignore hints from a child that a molestation may have occurred. Here are some hints of trouble that parents should watch for.

Recognizing Signs of Child Molestation

1. The child fears being seen nude (for instance, during bathing), when such fears were absent before.
2. The child develops physical complaints, such as headaches, stomachaches, and other stress symptoms.
3. The child displays anxiety, fidgeting, shame, or discomfort when any reference to sexual behavior occurs.
4. The child becomes markedly emotional and irritable.
5. The child engages in hazardous risk taking, such as jumping from high places or riding a bicycle dangerously in traffic.
6. The child reveals self-destructive or suicidal thoughts and self-blame.
7. The child shows a loss of self-esteem or self-worth.

(Adapted from Frederick, 1987.)

How can children protect themselves? Children should be taught to shout "No" if an adult tries to engage them in sexual activity. If children are asked to keep a secret, they should reply that they don't keep secrets. Parents and children also need to be aware that some pedophiles now try to make contact with children on the Internet. If an adult suggests to a child on-line that they could meet in person, the child should immediately tell his or her parents.

It also helps if children know the tactics typically used by molesters. Interviews with convicted sex offenders revealed the following (Elliott, Browne, & Kilcoyne, 1995):

Tactics of Child Molesters

1. Most molesters act alone.
2. Most assaults take place in the abuser's home.
3. Many abusers gain access to the child through caretaking.
4. Children are targeted at first through bribes, gifts, and games.
5. The abuser tries to lull the child into participation through touch, talking about sex, and persuasion. (This can take place through e-mail or chat rooms on the Internet.)
6. The abuser then uses force, anger, threats, and bribes to gain continued compliance.

Repeated molestations, those that involve force or threats, and incidents that exceed fondling can leave lasting emotional scars. As adults, many victims of incest or molestation develop sexual phobias. For them, lovemaking may evoke vivid and terrifying memories of the childhood victimization. Serious harm is especially likely if the molester is someone the child deeply trusts. Molestations by parents, close relatives, teachers, clergy, youth leaders, and similar persons can be quite damaging. In such cases, professional counseling is often needed.

As the preceding discussion suggests, the picture of sexual deviance that most often emerges is one of sexual inhibition and immaturity. Typically, some relatively infantile sexual expression (like exhibitionism or pedophilia) is selected because it is less threatening than more mature sexuality.

Many sadists, masochists, fetishists, and transvestites voluntarily associate with people who share their sexual interests. Thus, their behavior may not harm anyone, except when it is extreme. In contrast, pedophilia, exhibitionism, voyeurism, and frotteurism do victimize unwilling participants (Crooks & Bauer, 1999).

All of the paraphilias, unless they are very mild, involve compulsive behavior. As a result, they tend to emotionally handicap people. There is room in contemporary society for a large array of sexual behaviors. Nevertheless, any behavior that becomes compulsive (be it eating, gambling, drug abuse, or sex) is psychologically unhealthy.

ATTITUDES AND SEXUAL BEHAVIOR—THE CHANGING SEXUAL LANDSCAPE

Has there been a "sexual revolution"? If a woman and a man living 100 years ago could be transported to the present, what would they think about today's sexual values and practices? Undoubtedly, they would be stunned by the changes that have taken place. Unmarried couples falling into bed on television; advertisements for bras, skimpy men's underwear, tampons, and cures for "jock itch"; near nudity at the beaches; sexually explicit movies—these and many other elements of contemporary culture would shock a person from the Victorian era (Strong & DeVault, 1994).

The word *revolution*, however, suggests rapid change. Has there been a sexual revolution? A look at social changes in the 1960s and 1970s makes it clear that some fundamental alterations have occurred. Liberalized sexual attitudes and access to effective birth control significantly changed sexual behavior. Compared with earlier times, the gap between sexual values and actual behavior has narrowed. For example, traditional morality called for female virginity before marriage. Yet, by the 1940s and 1950s, as many as 75 percent of married women had engaged in premarital sex (Strong & DeVault, 1994).

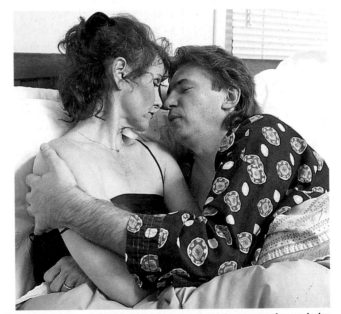

Twenty years ago, television soap operas were tame, gossipy melodramas. Today they are sexy, gossipy melodramas that frequently feature steamy on-screen lovemaking.

Paraphilias *Compulsive or destructive deviations in sexual preferences or behavior.*

ATTITUDES   Changing attitudes can be seen in national polls about premarital intercourse. In a 1959 Roper Poll, 88 percent of those interviewed agreed that premarital sex is wrong. By 1973, only 48 percent felt likewise. In a more recent Gallup Poll, only 40 percent of adults believed that premarital sex is unacceptable (Gallup Poll, 1991). Similar changes have occurred in attitudes toward extramarital sex, homosexuality, sex education, and related issues.

BEHAVIOR   *Have changing attitudes been translated into behavior?*   Changes in attitudes are still larger than changes in actual sexual behavior. Mostly, there is greater *tolerance* for sexual activity, especially that *engaged in by others.* For example, a magazine poll found that 80 percent of all readers considered extramarital sex acceptable under some circumstances (Athenasiou et al., 1970). But two other polls found that, in practice, only about 30 percent of married persons actually had extramarital sexual experience (Rubenstein, 1983; Rubenstein & Tavris, 1987). These are older studies, but the percentage has not changed greatly in the last 50 years. More important, faithfulness in marriage is a widely shared norm. Over a year, only 1.5 percent of married people have sex partners other than their spouse. Americans actually seem to live up to the norm of marital fidelity fairly well (Laumann et al., 1994; Smith, 1990).

Premarital intercourse rates are a good indication of overall sexual activity. The social upheaval that began in the 1960s led to an especially sharp rise in sexual activity among teenagers. This increase continued into the 1980s, although it has slowed recently. In the 1950s, Kinsey found that 70 percent of males and 33 percent of females had premarital intercourse by age 25. In the 1970s, Morton Hunt obtained premarital intercourse rates of 97 percent for males and about 70 percent for females. Now, 83 percent of all women and 91 percent of all men have premarital sexual experience (Janus & Janus, 1993). To some extent, these changes are related to a tendency to postpone marriage. In the United States alone, more than 2 million unmarried couples are living together.

Another major change is that both sexes engage in sexual behavior at earlier ages. A poll conducted in 1986 found that 57 percent of the nation's 17-year-olds were sexually experienced. For 16-year-olds, the figure was 46 percent; for 15-year-olds it was 29 percent; and for 14-year-olds, 19 percent. Pressures to engage in adult behaviors, early physical maturity, and the use of drugs all contribute to early sexual activity (Rosenthal, Smith, & de Visser, 1999).

The increase in sexual behavior during early adolescence is troubling. The United States has one of the highest teenage pregnancy rates among all industrialized nations. A partial solution to this problem may be to give youths a better understanding of their sexuality. A recent study confirmed that sex education *delays* the age at which young people first engage in sexual intercourse (Sawyer & Smith, 1996).

Is the Revolution Over?

Talk of a sexual revolution has quieted somewhat in recent years, and a conservative countermovement has been visible. Some of the reaction may reflect concern about sexually transmitted diseases. However, a gradual liberalization continues, albeit at a much slower pace (Janus & Janus, 1993).

In all, there is ample evidence that sexual behavior has increased in the last 40 years. Although this trend has brought problems, it does not seem to represent a wholesale move toward sexual promiscuity. It's true that sexual intercourse by unmarried couples is more common today. However, most couples continue to emphasize mutual commitment and love as requirements for sexual involvement (Strong & DeVault, 1994). In this regard, premarital sex can be said to parallel the behavior of engaged couples in past years. Or, as one author noted (Hyde, 1996), many young people today have just changed the sequence of events. For their parents, the sequence was fall in love, marry, and begin a sexual relationship. For many, the sequence now is fall in love, begin a sexual relationship, and marry. Most women have only one premarital sexual partner, whom they eventually marry. And men typically have about six premarital partners (Hyde, 1996). Overall, the evidence doesn't paint a picture of rampant sexual behavior.

Even premarital intercourse does not appear to represent a major rejection of traditional values and responsible behavior. The connection between sexuality and love or affection remains strong for most people. Both premarital sex and cohabitation are still widely viewed as preludes to marriage or as temporary substitutes for it (Strong & DeVault, 1994). Likewise, other changes in attitudes and behavior appear to reflect a greater acceptance of sexuality rather than a total rejection of earlier values.

SLOW DEATH OF THE DOUBLE STANDARD   A good summary of one major change that has occurred in sexual behavior is found in the phrase "the slow death of the double standard."

The **double standard** refers to using different rules to judge the appropriateness of male and female sexual behavior. In past decades, for example, males were largely forgiven for engaging in premarital sex. Young males who "sowed some wild oats" were widely tolerated. In fact, many were tacitly encouraged to seek casual sex as a step toward manhood. On the other hand, women who were sexually active before marriage ran the risk of being labeled "easy," "bad," or "promiscuous." Clearly, women are more aware of the double standard than men are: 79 percent of men believe it exists, whereas 91 percent of women do (Janus & Janus, 1993).

Similar differences pervade sexual mores and frequently place women in a "separate but not equal" position with regard to sexual behavior (Sprecher & Hatfield, 1996). However, as the gap between female and male sexual patterns continues to close, it is increasingly likely that an end to the double standard is in sight.

CHOICES   A more comfortable acceptance of human sexuality is the positive side of changing sexual attitudes and values. The negative side is revealed by the plight of people who are not ready for, or interested in, greater sexual freedom. Apparently, some individuals feel pressured into sexual behavior because it is "expected." Six percent of first sexual intercourse experiences are against the person's will (Bajracharya, Sarvela, & Isberner, 1995).

Pressures to engage in sex probably come as much from the individual as from others. For a greater acceptance of sexuality

GENDER ROLE STEREOTYPING AND RAPE

Rape is related to traditional gender role socialization. Many people learn to believe that women should not show direct interest in sex. Men, on the other hand, are taught to take the initiative and to persist in attempts at sexual intimacy—even when a woman says no.

Psychologists James Check and Neil Malamuth believe that such attitudes create a "rape-supportive culture." In their view, rape is only an extreme expression of a system that condones coercive (forced) sexual intimacy. They point out, for instance, that the single most used cry of rapists to their victims is "You know you want it." And afterward, "There now, you really enjoyed it, didn't you."

To test the hypothesis that stereotyped images contribute to rape, male college students were classified as either high or low in gender role stereotyping. Each student then read one of three stories: The first described voluntary intercourse, the second depicted stranger rape, and the third described date rape.

As predicted, college males high in gender role stereotyping were more aroused by the rape stories. Their arousal patterns, in fact, were similar to those found among actual rapists. Moreover, a chilling 44 percent of those tested indicated they would consider rape—especially if they could be sure of not being caught (Check & Malamuth, 1983).

In view of such findings—and the continuing widespread belief that when a woman says no she means yes—it is little wonder that rape occurs every 6 minutes in the United States. Perhaps the time has come for our culture to make it clear that no means no. Educating men about rape myths has been one of the most successful ways of preventing sexual assault (Reppucci, Woolard, & Fried, 1999).

---

to be constructive, people must feel that they have the right to say no, as well as the right to choose when, where, how, and with whom they will express their sexuality. As is true elsewhere, freedom must be combined with responsibility, commitment, and caring if it is to have meaning.

The Crime of Rape

The importance of respecting the right to say no is underscored by a recent dramatic increase in **acquaintance** (or **date**) **rape** (forced intercourse that occurs in the context of a date or other voluntary encounter). From *5 to 15 percent* of all female college students report having been raped. Roughly half of these rapes were by first dates, casual dates, or romantic acquaintances (Finkelson & Oswalt, 1995; Koss et al., 1987).

Men who commit date rape often believe they have done nothing wrong. A typical explanation is "Her words were saying no, but her body was saying yes" (see "Gender Role Stereotyping and Rape"). But forced sex is rape, even if the rapist doesn't use a knife or become violent. The effects of acquaintance rape are no less devastating than rape committed by a stranger.

RAPE MYTHS   A study of college men found that many tend to blame *women* for date rape. According to them, women who are raped by an acquaintance actually wanted to have sex (Proite et al., 1993). This is just one of several widely held beliefs that qualify as **rape myths** (Jones, Russell, & Bryant, 1998). All of these statements are myths:

- A woman who appears alone in public and dresses attractively is "asking for it."
- When a woman says no, she really means yes.
- Many women who are raped actually enjoy it.
- If a woman goes home with a man on a first date, she is interested in sex.
- If a woman is sexually active, she is probably lying if she says she was raped.

Men who believe rape myths are more likely to misread a woman's resistance to unwanted sexual advances, assuming that she really means yes when she says no (Garcia, 1998). Add some alcohol to the situation, and the risk of sexual assault is even greater: Men who believe rape myths and who have been drinking are especially likely to ignore signals that a woman wants sexual advances to stop (Abbey, McAuslan, & Ross, 1998; Bernat, Calhoun, & Stolp, 1998; Marx, Gross, & Adams, 1999).

FORCIBLE RAPE   Date rape is coercive, but not necessarily violent. **Forcible rape,** which is distressingly common, is carried out under the threat of bodily injury. Rapists often inflict more violence on their victims than is necessary to achieve their goal. Many women feel confident that their chances of being raped are low. But the facts tell a different story (Koss, 1993):

- At least 1 woman in 7 will be raped in her lifetime. Because many rapes go unreported, the true figure is probably 1 in 4.
- In 65 to 80 percent of all cases, the rapist is a friend or acquaintance of the victim.
- Five percent of rapes result in pregnancy.
- Four to 30 percent of rape victims contract sexually transmitted diseases.

Most authorities no longer think of forcible rape as a primarily sexual act. Rather, it is an act of brutality or aggression based on the need to debase others. Many rapists impulsively take

---

Double standard *Applying different standards for judging the appropriateness of male and female sexual behavior.*
Acquaintance (date) rape *Forced intercourse that occurs in the context of a date or other voluntary encounter.*
Rape myths *False beliefs about rape that tend to blame the victim and increase the likelihood that some men will think that rape is justified.*
Forcible rape *Sexual intercourse carried out against the victim's will, under the threat of violence or bodily injury.*

what they want without concern for the feelings of the victim or guilt about their deed. Others harbor deep-seated resentment or outright hatred of women.

Quite often, the rapist's goal is not strictly sexual intercourse; it is to attack, subordinate, humiliate, and degrade the victim. Typical aftereffects for the victim include rage, guilt, depression, loss of self-esteem, shame, sexual adjustment problems, and, in many cases, a lasting mistrust of male-female relationships. The impact is so great that most women continue to report fear, anxiety, and sexual dysfunction a year or two after being raped. Even years later, rape survivors are more likely to suffer from depression, alcohol or drug abuse, and other emotional problems (Koss, 1993).

Any man who doubts the seriousness of rape should imagine himself mistakenly placed in jail, where he is violently raped (sodomized) by other inmates. There is no pleasure in rape for victims of either sex. It is truly a despicable crime.

STDs AND SAFER SEX—CHOICE, RISK, AND RESPONSIBILITY

In general, most adults favor greater freedom of choice for themselves, including choice about sexual behavior. Yet, as noted, there is some ambivalence toward greater sexual free-dom. As the upcoming discussion of AIDS suggests, there are new and compelling reasons for caution in sexual behavior.

A **sexually transmitted disease (STD)** is passed from one person to another by intimate physical contact. The incidence of STDs has been rising for the last 20 years. Today, sexually active people run an elevated risk of getting chlamydia (klah-MID-ee-ah), gonorrhea, hepatitis B, herpes, syphilis, and other STDs (see ◆Table 14.2). As you read through ◆Table 14.2, remember that many people who carry STDs remain **asymptomatic** (a-SIMP-teh-mat-ik: lacking obvious symptoms). It is quite possible to be infected without knowing it. Likewise, it is often impossible to tell if a sexual partner is infectious. Thus, sexual risk taking poses a serious health hazard (Ramirez-Valles, Zimmerman, & Newcomb, 1998).

For many sexually active people, the **human immunodeficiency virus (HIV)** has added a new threat. HIV is a sexually transmitted virus that disables the immune system. Whereas most other STDs are treatable, HIV infections can be lethal. Check your knowledge about HIV against the following summary.

AIDS

Acquired immune deficiency syndrome (AIDS) is caused by an HIV infection. As the immune system weakens, other "opportunistic" diseases invade the body without resistance. Most AIDS victims eventually die of multiple infections (although a

◆TABLE 14.2 Common Sexually Transmitted Diseases

STD	MALE SYMPTOMS	FEMALE SYMPTOMS	PREVENTION	TREATMENT
Gonorrhea	Milky discharge from urethra; painful, frequent urination	Vaginal discharge and inflammation, painful urination	Condom/safer sex practices	Antibiotics
Chlamydia	Painful urination, discharge from urethra	Painful urination, discharge from vagina, abdominal pain	Condom/safer sex practices	Antibiotics
Syphilis	Painless sores on genitals, rectum, tongue, or lips; skin rash, fever, headache, aching bones and joints	Same	Condom/safer sex practices	Antibiotics
Genital herpes	Pain or itching on the penis; water blisters or open sores	Pain or itching in the genital area; water blisters or open sores	Condom/safer sex practices	Symptoms can be treated but not cured
Genital warts	Warty growths on genitals	Same	Condom/safer sex practices	Removal by surgery or laser
HIV/AIDS	Prolonged fatigue, swollen lymph nodes, fever lasting more than 10 days, night sweats, unexplained weight loss, purplish lesions on skin, persistent cough or sore throat, persistent colds, persistent diarrhea, easy bruising or unexplained bleeding	Same	Condom/safer sex practices	Can be treated with various drugs, but not cured
Hepatitis B	Mild cases may have no symptoms, but infection can cause chronic liver disease, cirrhosis of the liver, or liver cancer	Same	Vaccination	None available
Pelvic inflammatory disease	Does not apply	Intense pain in lower back and/or abdomen, fever	Condom/safer sex practices	Antibiotics

new three-drug therapy has greatly improved the odds of survival). The first symptoms of AIDS may show up as little as 2 months after infection, or they may not appear for up to 7 years. Because of this long incubation period, infected persons often pass the AIDS virus to others without knowing it. Medical testing can detect an HIV infection. However, for at least the first 6 months after becoming infected, a person can test negative while carrying the virus. A negative test result, therefore, is no guarantee that a person is a "safe" sex partner.

HIV infections are spread by direct contact with body fluids—especially blood, semen, and vaginal secretions. The AIDS virus cannot be transmitted by casual contact. People do not get AIDS from shaking hands, touching or using objects used by an AIDS patient, eating food prepared by an infected person, social kissing, sweat or tears, sharing drinking glasses, or sharing towels.

POPULATIONS AT RISK   AIDS has been called the gay plague because male homosexuals were its first highly visible victims. However, this label is in error. AIDS can be spread by all forms of sexual intercourse, and it has affected persons of all sexual orientations. Recently, the AIDS epidemic has spread more quickly among heterosexuals, women, African Americans, Hispanics, and children. HIV infection is the leading cause of death among women and men between the ages of 25 and 44 (Knowles, 1995).

In North America, those who are at greatest risk for HIV infection remain men who have had sex with other men (homosexual and bisexual men), people who have shared needles (for tattoos or for intravenous drug use), blood transfusion recipients (between 1977 and spring 1985), hemophiliacs (who require frequent blood transfusions), sexual partners of people in the preceding groups, and heterosexuals with a history of multiple partners. Thus, the vast majority of people are not at high risk of HIV infection. Still, 1 in 75 men and 1 in 700 women in North America are now infected with HIV. As a result, people who engage in unsafe sex are gambling with their lives—at very poor odds (❖Fig. 14.12). Six percent of all new AIDS cases are

The AIDS Memorial Quilt was begun in 1985 to commemorate those who have died from AIDS. Today, the quilt has grown to immense size, symbolizing the extent of the AIDS epidemic. Originally, the quilt memorialized only homosexual victims. It now includes heterosexual men, women, and children, signifying that AIDS respects no boundaries (Zucker, 1995).

❖ **FIGURE 14.12** *Popular professional basketball star Earvin "Magic" Johnson stunned fans in 1991 when he announced that he had tested positive for the HIV virus. Johnson, who is heterosexual, emphasized that his infection is a warning that anyone who is sexually active can contract the AIDS virus if they don't follow safe sex practices. Johnson further stressed that abstinence is the surest way to prevent AIDS. Johnson's infection increased public awareness about AIDS. Unfortunately, though, it has resulted in little real change in risky behavior (Brown et al., 1996).*

Sexually transmitted disease (STD) *A disease that is typically passed from one person to the next by intimate physical contact; a venereal disease.*
Asymptomatic *Refers to having a disease while lacking obvious symptoms of illness.*
Human immunodeficiency virus (HIV) *A sexually transmitted virus that disables the immune system.*
Acquired immune deficiency syndrome (AIDS) *A frequently fatal disease caused by HIV infection. In AIDS, the immune system is weakened, allowing other diseases to invade the body.*

now heterosexual—and the incidence is rising. In addition, new strains of the HIV virus are appearing. One in particular, which has spread explosively among heterosexuals in Africa, has been detected in North America (Knowles, 1995).

Behavioral Risk Factors

Sexually active people can do much to protect their own health. The behaviors listed here are risky when performed with an infected person.

Risky Behaviors
- Sharing drug needles and syringes
- Anal sex, with or without a condom
- Vaginal or oral sex with someone who injects drugs or engages in anal sex
- Sex with someone you don't know well, or with someone you know has several partners
- Unprotected sex (without a condom) with an infected partner
- Having two or more sex partners (additional partners further increase the risk)

It's important to remember that you can't tell from appearance if a person is infected. Many people would be surprised to learn that their partners have engaged in behavior that places them both at risk (Seal & Palmer-Seal, 1996).

The preceding high-risk behaviors can be contrasted with the following list of safer sexual practices. Note, however, that unless a person completely abstains, sex can be made safer, but not risk-free (Hawkins, Gray, & Hawkins, 1995).

Safer Sex Practices
- Not having sex
- Sex with one mutually faithful, uninfected partner
- Not injecting drugs
- Discussing contraception with partner
- Being selective regarding sexual partners
- Reducing the number of sexual partners
- Discussing partner's sexual health prior to engaging in sex
- Not engaging in sex while intoxicated
- Using a condom

Sexually active persons should practice safer sex until their partner's sexual history and/or health has been clearly established. And remember, a condom offers little or no protection if it is misused. Positive attitudes towards condoms, planning to use them, and knowing how to use them contribute greatly to safer sex practices (Elkins et al., 1998; Sheeran, Abraham, & Orbell, 1999).

Perhaps because it is fatal, AIDS is having a strong impact on sexual behavior in some groups. Among gay men, there has been a sharp increase in monogamous relationships and in abstention from sex. Gay men have also significantly reduced their high-risk sexual behaviors.

Other groups are not getting the message. The AIDS epidemic has thus far had little impact on the willingness of high school and college-age students to engage in risky behavior (casual sex) or to use condoms (Clark, 1990; Ramirez-Valles, Zimmerman, & Newcomb, 1998). A recent study of heterosex-

◆ **TABLE 14.3** Common Excuses for Not Practicing Safer Sex

REASONS FOR NOT HAVING SAFER SEX	PERCENTAGE GIVING EXCUSE
Condom not available	20
Didn't want to use a condom	19
"Couldn't stop ourselves"	15
Partner didn't want to use a condom	14
Alcohol or drug use	11

(Kusseling et al., 1996.)

ually active adults found that 62 percent did not practice safer sex with their last partner. Most of these "gamblers" knew too little about their partners to be assured that they were not taking a big risk. ◆Table 14.3 lists the excuses they gave for engaging in risky sex (Kusseling et al., 1996).

Apparently, heterosexual people still don't feel that they are truly at risk. However, of adolescent females in North America who get AIDS, 52 percent contracted it through heterosexual intercourse. For adolescent males, the figure is 32 percent. Worldwide, *75 percent* of people with the AIDS virus were infected through heterosexual sex. Over the next 20 to 30 years, heterosexual transmission is expected to become the primary means of spreading HIV infection in most industrialized countries. A special concern is the fact that approximately 20 percent of all AIDS victims are teenagers. Adolescents tend to see themselves as invulnerable and take risks that range from speeding to unprotected sex. Many sexually active teens are under the mistaken impression that precautions are unnecessary. However, among North American adolescents, straight sex has surpassed gay sex as the primary source of HIV infections (Radetsky, 1992; Reppucci, Woolard, & Fried, 1999).

Risk and Responsibility

The threat of AIDS has forced many people to face new issues of risk and responsibility. People who do not ensure their own safety are playing Russian roulette with their health. One chilling study of HIV patients—who knew they were infectious—found that 41 percent of those who were sexually active did not always use condoms (Sobel et al., 1996)! Thus, responsibility for "safer sex" rests with each sexually active individual. It is unwise to count on a sexual partner for protection against HIV infection.

Unprotected sex might seem safe if both partners know that they are HIV-negative. However, HIV can be extremely contagious during the first 2 months of infection. During that time, routine HIV testing cannot detect the infection. A special risk that befalls people in committed relationships is that they often interpret practicing safer sex as a sign of mistrust. Taking precautions could, instead, be defined as a way of showing that you really care about the welfare of your partner (Hammer et al., 1996). Likewise, dating couples who have high levels of emotional, social, and intellectual intimacy are more likely to use contraceptives (Davis & Bibace, 1999).

The sexual revolution was fueled, in part, by "the pill" and other birth control methods. Will the threat of AIDS reverse the tide of changes that occurred in previous decades? Will STD come to mean Sudden Total Disinterest in sex? Will the "germs of endearment" change the terms of endearment? The answers may depend on how quickly people learn to respect the AIDS virus and whether its prevention or cure can be achieved.

A LOOK AHEAD   Even without STDs to worry about, sexual problems are quite common. In the Psychology in Action section, we will consider the most frequent complaints and how they are remedied. After that, we will explore our culture's socially approved patterns of touching. Stay in touch with these final topics!

KNOWLEDGE BUILDER
SEXUAL RESPONSE, ATTITUDES, AND BEHAVIOR

RELATE

In what ways are sexual responses of members of the opposite sex similar to your own? In what ways are they different?

Based on your own observations of attitudes toward sex and patterns of sexual behavior, do you think there has been a sexual revolution?

You work in a program that provides counseling to AIDS patients. Should you be worried about contracting the disease? Why or why not?

To what extent do movies, music videos, and video games contribute directly to the perpetuation of rape myths? What about indirectly, by portraying gender role stereotypes?

As a counselor, you are working with a young person who seems to be sexually active. What can you tell this person about STDs and safer sex practices?

LEARNING CHECK

1. List the four phases of sexual response identified by Masters and Johnson: _____ _____
   _____ _____

2. Males typically experience _____ after ejaculation.
   a. an increased potential for orgasm *b.* a short refractory period
   c. the excitement phase *d.* muscular contractions of the uterus

3. The research of Masters and Johnson suggests that the similarities between female and male sexual responses outweigh the differences. T or F?

4. During lovemaking, from 10 to 20 minutes is often required for a woman to go from excitement to orgasm, while a male may experience all four stages of sexual response in as little as 4 minutes. T or F?

5. Simultaneous orgasm of the female and male should be the ultimate goal in lovemaking. T or F?

6. Recent research shows that more liberal views regarding sexual behavior have erased the traditional values that link sexual involvement with committed relationships. T or F?

7. Contrary to long-standing belief, it now appears that much female sexual pleasure is focused on
   a. the uterus *b.* the clitoris *c.* the urethra *d.* the cervix

8. One woman in 70 will be raped in her lifetime, and chances are greater than 50 percent that the rapist will be a friend or acquaintance. T or F?

9. The term _____ _____ describes the tendency for the sexual behavior of women and men to be judged differently.

10. Because AIDS is spread by direct contact with body fluids, it can be transmitted by social kissing or contact with food or dishes handled by an AIDS patient. T or F?

CRITICAL THINKING

11. Of the following reasons that teenage boys and girls give for engaging in sex—love, curiosity, sexual gratification, peer pressure, and "everyone's doing it"—which do you think they rank first, and which last?

Answers

1. excitement, plateau, orgasm, resolution 2. b 3. T 4. T 5. F 6. F 7. b 8. F 9. double standard 10. F 11. Peer pressure ranks first (cited by 30 percent of those surveyed) and love ranks last (cited by 8 percent) ("Teen sex," 1989).

psychology in action

SEXUAL PROBLEMS—WHEN PLEASURE FADES

Sexual dysfunctions are far more common than many people realize. Most people who seek sexual counseling have one or more of the following types of problems (DSM-IV, 1994):

1. **Desire Disorders:** The person has little or no sexual motivation or desire.
2. **Arousal Disorders:** The person desires sexual activity but does not become sexually aroused.
3. **Orgasm Disorders:** The person does not have orgasms or experiences orgasm too soon or too late.
4. **Sexual Pain Disorders:** The person experiences pain that makes lovemaking uncomfortable or impossible.

There was a time when people suffered such problems in silence. However, in recent years, effective treatments have been found for many of the major complaints. Let's briefly investigate the nature, causes, and treatments of sexual dysfunctions.

Desire Disorders

Desire disorders, like most sexual problems, must be defined in relation to a person's age, sex, partner, expectations, and sexual history. It is not at all unusual for a person to briefly lose sexual desire. Typically, erotic feelings return when anger toward a partner fades, or fatigue, illness, and similar temporary problems end. Under what circumstances, then, is loss of desire a dysfunction? First, the loss of desire must be *persistent*. Second, the person must be *troubled by it*. When these two conditions are met, **hypoactive sexual desire** is said to exist. Diminished desire can apply to both sexes. However, it is somewhat more common in women (Beck, 1995; Read, 1995).

Some people don't merely lack sexual desire; they are *repelled* by sex and seek to avoid it. A person who suffers from **sexual aversion** feels fear, anxiety, or disgust about engaging in sex. Often, the afflicted person still has some erotic feelings. For example, he or she may still masturbate or have sexual fantasies. Nevertheless, the prospect of having sex with another person causes panic or revulsion (DSM-IV, 1994).

Sexual desire disorders are common. Possible physical causes include illness, fatigue, hormonal difficulties, and the side effects of medicines. Desire disorders are also associated with psychological factors such as depression, fearing loss of control over sexual urges, strict religious beliefs, fear of pregnancy, marital conflict, fear of closeness, and simple loss of attraction to one's partner (Allgeier & Allgeier, 1995; Read, 1995). It is also not uncommon to find that people with desire disorders were sexually mistreated as children (Bakich, 1995).

TREATMENT   Desire disorders are complex problems. Unless they have a straightforward physical cause, they are difficult to treat. Desire disorders are often deeply rooted in a person's childhood, sexual history, personality, and relationships. In such instances, counseling or psychotherapy is recommended (Allgeier & Allgeier, 1995).

Arousal Disorders

A person suffering from an arousal disorder wants to make love but experiences little or no physical arousal. For women, this means vaginal dryness. For men, it means an inability to maintain an erection. Basically, in arousal disorders, the body does not cooperate with the person's desire to make love.

MALE ERECTILE DISORDER   An inability to maintain an erection for lovemaking is called male **erectile disorder.** This problem, which is also known as erectile dysfunction, was once referred to as *impotence.* However, psychologists now discourage use of the term *impotence* because of its many negative connotations.

Erectile disorders can be primary or secondary. Men suffering from primary erectile dysfunction have never had an erection. Those who previously performed successfully, but then developed a problem, suffer from secondary erectile dysfunction. Either way, persistent erectile difficulties tend to be very disturbing to the man and his sexual partner.

How often must a man experience failure for a problem to exist? Ultimately, only the man and his partner can make this judgment. Nevertheless, sex therapists Masters and Johnson (1970) believe that a problem exists when failure occurs on 25 percent or more of a man's lovemaking attempts. Repeated erectile dysfunction should therefore be distinguished from *occasional* erectile problems. Fatigue, anger, anxiety, and drinking too much alcohol can cause temporary erectile difficulties in healthy males. True erectile disorders typically persist for months or years.

It is important to recognize that occasional erectile problems are normal. In fact, "performance demands" or overreaction to the temporary loss of an erection may generate fears and doubts that contribute to a further inhibition of arousal (Abrahamson et al., 1989). At such times, it is particularly important for the man's partner to avoid expressing anger, disappointment, or embarrassment. Patient reassurance helps prevent the establishment of a vicious cycle.

What causes erectile disorders?   For years, experts held that erectile disorders are rarely caused by physical illness, disease, or damage. Now it is recognized that roughly 40 percent of all cases are organic, or physically caused. The origin of the remaining cases is **psychogenic** (a result of emotional factors). Even when erectile dysfunction is organic, however, it is almost always made worse by anxiety, anger, and dejection. If a man can have an erection at times other than lovemaking (during sleep, for instance), the problem probably is not physical (Ackerman & Carey, 1995).

Organic erectile problems have many causes. Typical sources of trouble include alcohol or drug abuse, diabetes, vascular disease, prostate and urological disorders, neurological problems, and reactions to medication for high blood pressure, heart disease, or stomach ulcers. Erectile problems are also a normal part of aging. As men grow older, they typically experience a decline in sexual desire and arousal and an increase in sexual dysfunction (Segraves & Segraves, 1995).

According to Masters and Johnson (1970), primary erectile disorders are often related to harsh religious training, early sexual experiences with a seductive mother, sexual molestation in childhood, or other experiences leading to guilt, fear, and sexual inhibition.

Secondary erectile disorders may be related to anxiety about sex in general, guilt because of an extramarital affair, resentment or hostility toward a sexual partner, fear of inability to perform, concerns about STDs, and similar emotions and conflicts (Shires & Miller, 1998). Often the problem starts with repeated sexual failures caused by drinking too much alcohol or by premature ejaculation. In any event, initial doubts soon become severe fears of failure—which further inhibit sexual response.

TREATMENT Drugs or surgery may be used in medical treatment of organic erectile disorders. The drug Viagra is successful for about 70 to 80 percent of men with erectile disorders. However, effective treatment should also include counseling to remove fears and psychological blocks (Althof & Seftel, 1995). Fixing the "hydraulics" of erectile problems may not be enough to end the problem. It is important for the man to also regain confidence, improve his relationship with his partner, and learn better lovemaking skills. To free him of conflicts, the man and his partner may be assigned a series of exercises to perform. This technique, called **sensate focus,** directs attention to natural sensations of pleasure and builds communication skills (McCabe, 1992).

In sensate focus, the couple is told to take turns caressing various parts of each other's bodies. They are further instructed to carefully avoid any genital contact. Instead, they are to concentrate on giving pleasure and on signaling what feels good to them. This takes the pressure to perform off the man and allows him to learn to give pleasure as a means of receiving it. For many men, sensate focus is a better solution than depending on an expensive drug to perform sexually.

Over a period of days or weeks, the couple proceeds to more intense physical contact involving the breasts and genitals. As inhibitions are reduced and natural arousal begins to replace fear, the successful couple moves on to mutually satisfying lovemaking.

FEMALE SEXUAL AROUSAL DISORDER Women who suffer from **female sexual arousal disorder** respond with little or no physical arousal to sexual stimulation. The problem thus appears to correspond directly to male erectile difficulties. As in the male, female sexual arousal disorder may be primary or secondary. Also, it is again important to remember that all women occasionally experience inhibited arousal. In some instances, the problem may reflect nothing more than a lack of sufficient sexual stimulation before attempting lovemaking (Allgeier & Allgeier, 1995; Read, 1995).

The causes of inhibited arousal in women are similar to those seen in men. Sometimes the problem is medical, related to illness or the side effects of medicines or contraceptives. Psychological factors include anxiety, anger or hostility toward one's partner, depression, stress, or distracting worries. Some women can trace their arousal difficulties to frightening childhood experiences, such as molestations (often by older relatives), incestuous relations that produced lasting guilt, a harsh religious background in which sex was considered evil, or cold, unloving childhood relationships. Also common is a need to maintain control over emotions, deep-seated conflicts over being female, and extreme distrust of others, especially males (Read, 1995).

TREATMENT *How does treatment proceed?* Treatment typically includes sensate focus, genital stimulation by the woman's partner, and "nondemanding" intercourse controlled by the woman. With success in these initial stages, full intercourse is gradually introduced. As sexual training proceeds, psychological conflicts and dynamics typically appear, and as they do, they are treated in separate counseling sessions.

Orgasm Disorders

A person suffering from an orgasm disorder either fails to reach orgasm during sexual activity or reaches orgasm too soon or too late. Notice that such disorders are very much based on expectations. For instance, if a man experiences delayed orgasm, one couple might define it as a problem, whereas another might welcome it. It is also worth noting again that some women rarely or never have orgasms and still find sex pleasurable (Allgeier & Allgeier, 1995; Read, 1995).

FEMALE ORGASMIC DISORDER The most prevalent sexual complaint among women is a persistent inability to reach orgasm during lovemaking. It is often clear in **female orgasmic disorder** that the woman is not completely unresponsive. Rather, she is unresponsive in the context of a relationship—she may easily reach orgasm by masturbation, but not in lovemaking with her partner.

Then couldn't the woman's partner be at fault? Sex therapists try to avoid finding fault or placing blame. However, it is true that the woman's partner must be committed to ensuring

---

Hypoactive sexual desire *A persistent, upsetting loss of sexual desire.*
Sexual aversion *Persistent feelings of fear, anxiety, or disgust about engaging in sex.*
Erectile disorder *An inability to maintain an erection for lovemaking.*
Psychogenic *Having psychological origins, rather than physical causes.*
Sensate focus *Form of therapy that directs a couple's attention to natural sensations of sexual pleasure.*
Female sexual arousal disorder *A lack of physical arousal to sexual stimulation.*
Female orgasmic disorder *A persistent inability to reach orgasm during lovemaking.*

her gratification. Roughly two thirds of all women need direct stimulation of the clitoris to reach orgasm. Therefore, some apparent instances of female orgasmic disorder can be traced to inadequate stimulation or faulty technique on the part of the woman's partner. Even when this is true, sexual adjustment difficulties are best viewed as a problem the couple shares, not just as the "woman's problem," the "man's problem," or her "partner's problem."

TREATMENT   If we focus only on the woman, the most common source of orgasmic difficulties is overcontrol of sexual response. Orgasm requires a degree of abandonment to erotic feelings. It is inhibited by ambivalence or hostility toward the relationship, by guilt, by fears of expressing sexual needs, and by tendencies to control and intellectualize erotic feelings. The woman is unable to let go and enjoy the flow of pleasurable sensations.

In Helen Kaplan's treatment program at Cornell University, anorgasmic women (those who do not have orgasms) are first trained to focus on their sexual responsiveness through masturbation or vigorous stimulation by a partner. As the woman becomes consistently orgasmic in these circumstances, her responsiveness is gradually transferred to lovemaking with her partner. Couples also typically learn alternative positions and techniques of lovemaking designed to increase clitoral stimulation (Hurlbert & Apt, 1995). At the same time, communication between partners is stressed, especially with reference to the woman's sexual value system (expectations, motivations, and preferences).

MALE ORGASMIC DISORDER   Among males, an inability to reach orgasm was once considered a rare problem. But milder forms of **male orgasmic disorder** account for increasing numbers of clients seeking therapy. Typical background factors are strict religious training, fear of impregnating, lack of interest in the sexual partner, symbolic inability to give of oneself, unacknowledged homosexuality, or the recent occurrence of traumatic life events. Power and commitment struggles within relationships may be important added factors.

TREATMENT   Treatment for male orgasmic disorder (also known as *retarded ejaculation*) consists of sensate focus, manual stimulation by the man's partner (which is designed to orient the male to his partner as a source of pleasure), and stimulation to the point of orgasm followed by immediate intercourse and ejaculation. Work also focuses on resolving personal conflicts and marital difficulties underlying the problem.

PREMATURE EJACULATION   Defining premature ejaculation is tricky because of large variations in the time different women take to reach orgasm. Helen Kaplan says that **premature ejaculation** exists when it occurs reflexively or the man cannot tolerate high levels of excitement at the plateau stage of arousal. Basically, ejaculation is premature if it consistently occurs before the man and his partner want it to occur.

Do many men have difficulties with premature ejaculation? Approximately 50 percent of young adult men have problems

with premature ejaculation. Theories advanced to explain it have ranged from the idea that it may represent hostility toward the man's sexual partner (because it deprives the partner of satisfaction) to the suggestion that most early male sexual experiences tend to encourage rapid climax (such as those taking place in the back seat of a car and masturbation). Kaplan (1974) adds that excessive arousal and anxiety over performance are usually present. Also, some men simply engage in techniques that maximize sensation and make rapid orgasm inevitable.

Ejaculation is a reflex. To control it, a man must learn to recognize the physical signals that it is about to occur. Some men have simply never learned to be aware of these signals. Whatever the causes, premature ejaculation can be a serious difficulty, especially in the context of long-term relationships.

TREATMENT   Treatment for premature ejaculation is highly successful and relatively simple. The most common treatment is a "stop-start" procedure called the **squeeze technique** (Grenier & Byers, 1995). The man's sexual partner stimulates him manually until he signals that ejaculation is about to occur. The man's partner then firmly squeezes the tip of his penis to inhibit orgasm. When the man feels he has control, stimulation is repeated. Later, the squeeze technique is used during lovemaking. Gradually, the man acquires the ability to delay orgasm sufficiently for mutually satisfactory lovemaking. During treatment, skills that improve communication between partners are developed, along with a better understanding of the male's sexual response cues (Larson, 1990).

Sexual Pain Disorders

Pain in the genitals before, during, or after sexual intercourse is called **dyspareunia** (DIS-pah-ROO-nee-ah). Both females and males can experience dyspareunia. However, this problem is actually rare in males. In women, dyspareunia is often related to **vaginismus** (VAJ-ih-NIS-mus), a condition in which muscle spasms of the vagina prevent intercourse (DSM-IV, 1994). Vaginismus is often accompanied by obvious fears of intercourse, and where fear is absent, high levels of anxiety are present. Vaginismus therefore appears to be a phobic response to intercourse. Predictably, its causes include experiences of painful intercourse, rape or other brutal and frightening sexual encounters, fear of men and of penetration, misinformation about sex (belief that it is injurious), fear of pregnancy, and fear of the specific male partner (Read, 1995; Ward & Ogden, 1994).

TREATMENT   Treatment of vaginismus is similar to what might be done for a nonsexual phobia. It includes extinction of conditioned muscle spasms by progressive relaxation of the vagina, desensitization of fears of intercourse, and masturbation or manual stimulation to associate pleasure with sexual approach by the woman's partner. Hypnosis has also been used successfully in some cases.

SUMMARY   Solving sexual problems can be difficult. The problems described here are rarely solved without professional help (with the possible exception of premature ejaculation). If a serious sexual difficulty is not resolved in a reasonable amount of time, the aid of an appropriately trained psychologist, physician, or counselor should be sought. The longer the problem is ignored, the more difficult it is to solve. But professional help is available.

RELATIONSHIPS AND SEXUAL ADJUSTMENT

What can be done to improve sexual adjustment? Often, it is best to view sexual adjustment within the broader context of a relationship. Conflict and unresolved anger in other areas frequently take their toll in sexual adjustment, and mutually satisfying relationships tend to carry over into sexual relations. Sex is not a performance or a skill to be mastered like playing tennis. It is a form of communication within a relationship. Couples with strong and caring relationships can probably survive most sexual problems. A couple with a satisfactory sex life but a poor relationship rarely lasts. Marriage expert John Gottman believes that a couple must have at least five times as many positive as negative moments in their marriage if it is to survive (Gottman, 1994).

DISAGREEMENTS ABOUT SEX When disagreements arise over issues such as frequency of lovemaking, who initiates lovemaking, or what behavior is appropriate, Masters and Johnson believe that the rule should be: "Each partner must accept the other as the final authority on his or her own feelings." Partners are urged to give feedback about their feelings by following what therapists call the "touch and ask" rule: Touching and caressing should often be followed by questions such as, "Does that feel good?" "Do you like that?" and so forth (Knox, 1984). Satisfying erotic relationships focus on enhancing sexual pleasure for both partners, not on selfish interest in one's own gratification (Kleinplatz, 1996).

When problems do arise, partners are urged to be *responsive* to each other's needs at an *emotional* level and to recognize that all sexual problems are *mutual.* "Failures" should always be shared without placing blame. Masters and Johnson believe that it is particularly important to avoid the "numbers game." That is, couples should avoid being influenced by statistics on the average frequency of lovemaking, by stereotypes about sexual potency, and by the superhuman sexual exploits portrayed in movies and magazines.

BRIDGES TO SEXUAL SATISFACTION According to sex therapist Barry McCarthy, four elements are necessary for a continuing healthy sexual relationship:

1. *Sexual anticipation.* Looking forward to lovemaking is inhibited by routine and poor communication between partners. It is wise for busy couples to set aside time to spend together. Unexpected, spontaneous lovemaking should also be encouraged.
2. *Valuing one's sexuality.* This is most likely to occur when you develop a respectful, trusting, and intimate relationship with your partner. Such relationships allow both part-

ners to deal with negative sexual experiences when they occur.
3. *Feeling that you deserve sexual pleasure.* As previously noted, the essence of satisfying lovemaking is the giving and receiving of pleasure.
4. *Valuing intimacy.* A sense of closeness and intimacy with one's partner helps maintain sexual desire, especially in long-term relationships (McCarthy, 1995).

Intimacy and Communication

Are there any other guidelines for maintaining a healthy relationship? A study that compared happily married couples with unhappily married couples found that, in almost every regard, the happily married couples showed superior *communication* skills. Three patterns that are almost always related to serious long-term problems in relationships are defensiveness (including whining), stubbornness, and refusal to talk with your partner (the "big freeze") (Gottman & Krokoff, 1989). Many couples find that communication is facilitated by observing the following guidelines:

AVOID "GUNNYSACKING" Persistent feelings, whether positive or negative, need to be expressed. *Gunnysacking* refers to saving up feelings and complaints. These are then "dumped" during an argument or are used as ammunition in a fight. Gunnysacking is very destructive to a relationship.

BE OPEN ABOUT FEELINGS Happy couples not only talk more but also convey more personal feelings and show greater sensitivity to their partners' feelings. As one expert put it, "In a healthy relationship, each partner feels free to express his likes, dislikes, wants, wishes, feelings, impulses, and the other person feels free to react with like honesty to these. In such a relationship, there will be tears, laughter, sensuality, irritation, anger, fear, babylike behavior, and so on" (Jourard, 1963).

DON'T ATTACK THE OTHER PERSON'S CHARACTER Whenever possible, expressions of negative feelings should be given as statements of one's own feelings, not as statements of blame. It is far more constructive to say, "It makes me angry when you leave things around the house" than it is to say, "You're a slob!" Remember, too, that if you use the words *always* or *never,* you are probably mounting a character attack.

DON'T TRY TO "WIN" A FIGHT Constructive fights are aimed at resolving shared differences, not at establishing who is right or wrong, superior or inferior.

Male orgasmic disorder *A persistent inability to reach orgasm during lovemaking.*
Premature ejaculation *Ejaculation that consistently occurs before the man and his partner want it to occur.*
Squeeze technique *Method for inhibiting ejaculation by compressing the tip of the penis.*
Dyspareunia *Genital pain before, during, or after sexual intercourse.*
Vaginismus *Muscle spasms of the vagina.*

RECOGNIZE THAT ANGER IS APPROPRIATE Constructive and destructive fights are not distinguished by whether anger is expressed. A fight is a fight, and anger is appropriate. As is the case with any other emotion in a relationship, anger should be expressed. However, constructive expression of anger requires that couples fight fair by sticking to the real issues and not "hitting below the belt." Resorting to threats, such as announcing "This relationship is over," is especially damaging.

TRY TO SEE THINGS THROUGH YOUR PARTNER'S EYES Marital harmony is closely related to the ability to put yourself in another person's place (Long & Andrews, 1990). When a conflict arises, always pause and try to take your partner's perspective. Seeing things through your partner's eyes can be a good reminder that no one is ever totally right or wrong in a personal dispute.

DON'T BE A "MIND READER" The preceding suggestion should not be taken as an invitation to engage in "mind reading." Assuming that you know what your partner is thinking or feeling can muddle or block communication. Hostile or accusatory mind reading, like the following examples, can be very disruptive: "You're just looking for an excuse to criticize me, aren't you?" "You don't really want my mother to visit, or you wouldn't say that." Rather than *telling* your partner what she or he thinks, *ask*.

To add to these guidelines, Bryan Strong and Christine DeVault (1994) suggest that if you really want to mess up a relationship, you can almost totally avoid intimacy and communication by doing the following.

Ten Ways to Avoid Intimacy
1. Don't talk about anything meaningful, especially about feelings.
2. Never show your feelings; remain as expressionless as possible.
3. Always be pleasant and pretend everything is okay, even if you are upset or dissatisfied.
4. Always win; never compromise.
5. Always keep busy; that way you can avoid intimacy and make your partner feel unimportant in your life.
6. Always be right; don't let on that you are human.
7. Never argue or you may have to reveal differences and make changes.
8. Make your partner guess what you want. That way, you can tell your partner that she or he doesn't really understand or love you.
9. Always take care of your own needs first.
10. Keep the television set on. Wouldn't you rather be watching TV than talking with your partner?

Remember, to encourage intimacy, wise couples *avoid* the practices in the preceding list.

As a last point, it is worth restating that sexual adjustment and loving relationships are interdependent. As one observer put it, when sex goes well, it's 15 percent of a relationship, and when it goes badly it's 85 percent (Knox, 1984). As a shared pleasure, a form of intimacy, a means of communication, and a haven from everyday tensions, a positive sexual relationship can do much to enhance a couple's mutual understanding and caring. Likewise, an honest, equitable, and affectionate out-of-bed relationship contributes greatly to sexual satisfaction (Hatfield et al., 1982).

KNOWLEDGE BUILDER

SEXUAL PROBLEMS

RELATE

In plain language, sexual disorders can be summarized this way: The person doesn't want to do it. The person wants to do it but can't get aroused. The person wants to do it, gets aroused, but has problems with orgasm. The person wants to do it and gets aroused, but lovemaking is uncomfortable. What are the formal terms for each of these possibilities?

We all make mistakes in relationships. Using the discussion in the "Psychology in Action" section as a guide, which mistakes have you avoided? Which would you like to avoid or correct?

LEARNING CHECK

1. Males suffering from primary erectile dysfunction have never been able to have or maintain an erection. T or F?

2. According to the latest figures, most erectile disorders are caused by castration fears. T or F?

3. Sensate focus is the most common treatment for premature ejaculation. T or F?

4. Premature ejaculation is considered the rarest of the male sexual adjustment problems. T or F?

5. As it is for female sexual arousal disorder, the sensate focus technique is a primary treatment mode for male sexual arousal disorder. T or F?

6. Vaginismus, which appears to be a phobic response to sexual intercourse, can also cause dyspareunia. T or F?

7. Masters and Johnson urge sexual partners to recognize that all sexual problems are mutual and not just one partner's problem. T or F?

8. The term *gunnysacking* refers to the constructive practice of hiding anger until it is appropriate to express it. T or F?

CRITICAL THINKING

9. Who would you expect to have the most frequent sex and the most satisfying sex, married couples or single people?

Answers:

1. T 2. F 3. F 4. F 5. T 6. T 7. T 8. F 9. Contrary to mass media portrayals of sexy singles, married couples have the most sex and are most likely to have orgasms when they do. Greater opportunity, plus familiarity with a partner's needs and preferences, probably account for these findings (Laumann et al., 1994).

Focus: What is the role of touching in personal relationships?

The whole thing began because Sidney Jourard is a people watcher. One day, sitting in a coffeehouse in San Juan, Puerto Rico, where he was a Peace Corps consultant, he wondered how many times the couple at the next table would touch each other in 1 hour. During the next 2 years, he did the same thing in London and Paris while studying at London's Tavistock Clinic. When he went to Gainesville, Florida, to teach psychology at the University of Florida, he checked out an American couple for the 1 hour. The two people at the Gainesville table touched each other twice in 1 hour. In Paris, the touch total for 1 hour was 110; in San Juan, 180. And in London? In London, the two people touched each other not at all.

From this information, you must draw your own conclusions. Jourard—back at Gainesville, Florida, teaching, being a therapist, and practicing hatha yoga—refused to. But his interest led him to make further surveys.

He gave booklets to his Gainesville students, 54 males and 84 females. Each booklet contained four diagrams of the body divided into 24 zones, the idea lifted (he says with a straight face) from a butcher's meat chart. He then asked his students to report—anonymously, of course—which area of their bodies had been touched by mother, father, best-friend-same-sex, and best-friend-opposite-sex. Furthermore, each student was asked to show which zones he or she had touched on these four persons. Time range: within the last year. The charts in ❖Figure 14.13 show the result. Here Jourard will draw conclusions about "body accessibility."

"If you're out of love," says the professor, "you're out of touch."

"There isn't a great deal of body contact going on outside the strictly sexual context. It's almost as if all possible meanings of a touch are eliminated except the caress with the sexually arousing intent. . . . Most regions of a young adult's body remain untouched unless one has a close friend of the opposite sex, and that depends on the relationship going on between them."

Where American Males Are Touched

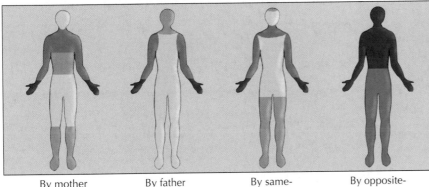

By mother   By father   By same-sex friend   By opposite-sex friend

Where American Females Are Touched

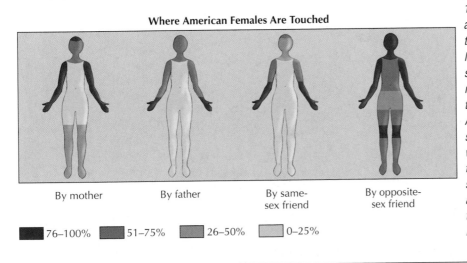

By mother   By father   By same-sex friend   By opposite-sex friend

■ 76–100%   ■ 51–75%   ■ 26–50%   ■ 0–25%

❖ **FIGURE 14.13** *Results of Jourard's study of interpersonal touch. Figures shown are the percentages of young adults touched in each body area, during a 1-year period, by the persons listed. Touching patterns are highly influenced by culture. People in other countries touch much more, or less, than is customary in North America. (After Jourard, 1966.) A more recent study found that women and androgynous persons are more likely to touch same-sex friends and acquaintances than shown here (Crawford, 1994a, 1994b). Also, touching patterns change over time. More recent studies of touching show significant increases in women's reports of being touched in the area from the thighs to the shoulders by an opposite-sex friend. Men show similar increases in being touched in the pelvic area and upper torso by an opposite-sex friend. These trends seem to reflect a liberalization of intimate touching in love and dating relationships (Thayer, 1988).*

One of our touch taboos, then, is that we equate touch with sexuality. Therefore, unless the relationship is sexual, *mustn't touch.*

Jourard goes on to say that in family physical contact, the daughters are "the favored ones." A girl's parents touch her more than they would if she were a boy, right up into her 20s. Parents stop touching boys about the time they reach what used to be called the age of reason—when one can commit sin. Furthermore, a girl's mother is allowed, or allows herself (having herself once been a favored one), to give frequent touches to a girl's hair. Half of the parents get to touch her on the lips, and half manage a literal pat on the back. But—taboo, taboo—only 13 percent of the girls received a paternal pat on the bottom, and none of the girls touched or were touched by their fathers in the genital area.

Outside the best-friend-opposite-sex category, very little touching goes on, but when it does happen between lovers, the professor says, "There is a virtual deluge of physical contact all over the body. . . . I suspect that the transformation from virginity or even pre-orgasmic existence to the experience of having a sexual climax is so radical as to be equivalent to a kind of rebirth."

For Jourard, in our maddeningly crowded world, touch may be our salvation. "I think that body contact has the function of confirming one's bodily being," he says. Yet, how can one learn to touch lovingly if one is not permitted to touch and be touched when young? To touch and be touched at times other than when making love?

"It's a blunted way of life," Jourard says. "People need physical contact to increase awareness and sensitivity to the body. But, instead, we use our relationship with others as a means to increase our status and social position. We are afraid to let others get close because then we are trapped. . . . The price we pay for this estrangement is loneliness." (The preceding article was written by H. E. F. Donohue, 1968.)

CONCLUSION: The amount of physical contact and touching that occurs between people is very limited, except for lovers. Social norms that restrict touching appear to be based on fears that touching will be perceived as erotic.

PATTERNS OF TOUCHING

RELATE

Do your patterns of touching and being touched correspond to those found by Jourard?

In what ways does sexual contact differ from nonsexual touching? Do you feel, as Jourard did, that people should touch more?

Would you be jealous if your spouse or lover were touched (in a nonsexual way) by a person of the same sex? Opposite sex?

In recent years, there has been a dramatic increase in child molestation trials involving day-care workers. Some teachers and child-care workers complain that they are now afraid to touch or hug children. Is this new reticence to touch an overdue correction or a saddening loss?

LEARNING CHECK

1. In his first casual observations, Jourard noted the highest rates of touching in
   a. Florida b. France c. Puerto Rico d. England

2. Within the family, boys are typically touched more by parents than girls are. T or F?

3. Jourard recorded the highest rates of touching by
   a. mothers b. fathers c. same-sex friends d. opposite-sex friends

4. In North American culture, the hands are the most accepted areas of the body for touching by others. T or F?

CRITICAL THINKING

5. If a man touches a woman on the arm or shoulder while talking to her at work, has he sexually harassed her?

Answers:

1. c 2. F 3. d 4. T 5. It depends on her wishes: Even touching that involves "public" areas of the body can be harassing if it is an unwanted intrusion on personal privacy.

CHAPTER IN REVIEW

What are the basic dimensions of sex?

- Physically, males and females differ in primary and secondary sexual characteristics.
- Estrogens (female sex hormones) and androgens (male sex hormones) influence the development of primary and secondary sexual characteristics.
- Biological sex consists of genetic sex, gonadal sex, hormonal sex, and genital sex. Sexual character is also affected by gender identity.
- Sexual development begins with genetic sex (*XX* or *XY* chromosomes) and is then influenced by prenatal hormone levels.
- Androgen insensitivity, exposure to progestin, the androgenital syndrome, and similar problems can cause hermaphroditism.
- Many researchers believe that prenatal hormones exert a biological biasing effect that combines with social factors to influence psychosexual development.
- On most psychological dimensions, women and men are more alike than they are different.

How does one's sense of maleness or femaleness develop?

- Male and female behavior patterns are related to learned gender identity and gender role socialization.
- Gender role stereotypes often distort perceptions about the kinds of activities for which men and women are suited.
- Gender identity usually becomes stable by age 3 or 4 years.
- Gender role socialization seems to account for most observed female-male gender differences. Parents tend to encourage boys in instrumental behaviors and girls in expressive behaviors.

What is psychological androgyny (and is it contagious)?

- Roughly one third of all persons are androgynous. Approximately 50 percent are traditionally feminine or masculine.
- Psychological androgyny is related to greater behavioral adaptability and flexibility.

What are the most typical patterns of human sexual behavior?

- "Normal" sexual behavior is defined differently by various cultures. There appears to be little difference in sexual responsiveness between females and males.
- Sexual arousal is related to the body's erogenous zones, but mental and emotional reactions are the ultimate source of sexual responsiveness.
- There is evidence that the sex drive peaks at a later age for females than it does for males, although this difference is diminishing.
- Castration may or may not influence sex drive in humans. Sterilization does not alter the sex drive.
- There is a gradual decline in the frequency of sexual intercourse with increasing age. However, many elderly persons remain sexually active, and large variations exist at all ages.
- Masturbation is a normal and completely acceptable behavior.
- Sexual orientation refers to one's degree of emotional and erotic attraction to members of the same sex, opposite sex, or both sexes. A person may be heterosexual, homosexual, or bisexual.

- A combination of hereditary, biological, social, and psychological influences combine to produce one's sexual orientation.
- As a group, homosexual men and women do not differ psychologically from heterosexuals.

To what extent do females and males differ in sexual response?

- Human sexual response can be divided into four phases: (1) excitement, (2) plateau, (3) orgasm, and (4) resolution.
- There do not appear to be any differences between "vaginal orgasms" and "clitoral orgasms." Fifteen percent of women are consistently multi-orgasmic, and at least 50 percent are capable of multiple orgasm.
- Males experience a refractory period after orgasm, and only 5 percent of men are multi-orgasmic.
- Mutual orgasm has been abandoned by most sex counselors as the ideal in lovemaking.

What are the most common sexual disorders?

- Atypical sexual behaviors that often cause difficulty are called *paraphilias*. The paraphilias include pedophilia, fetishism, voyeurism, exhibitionism, transvestic fetishism, sexual sadism, sexual masochism, and frotteurism.
- Exhibitionists are rarely dangerous and can best be characterized as sexually inhibited and immature.
- The effects of child molestation vary greatly, depending on the severity of the molestation and the child's relationship to the molester.

Have recent changes in attitudes affected sexual behavior?

- Attitudes toward sexual behavior have become more liberal, but actual changes in sexual behavior have been more gradual.
- Adolescents and young adults engage in more frequent sexual activity than they did 40 years ago.
- In recent years, there has been a greater acceptance of female sexuality and a narrowing of differences in female and male patterns of sexual behavior.
- Forcible rape, acquaintance rape, and rape-supportive attitudes and beliefs are major problems in North America.

What impacts have sexually transmitted diseases had on sexual behavior?

- During the last 20 years, the incidence of sexually transmitted diseases has steadily increased.
- STDs and the spread of AIDs have had a sizable impact on patterns of sexual behavior, including some curtailment of risk taking.
- Many sexually active people continue to take unnecessary risks with their health by failing to follow safer sex practices.

What are the most common sexual adjustment problems? How are they treated?

- The principal sexual problems are desire disorders, arousal disorders, orgasm disorders, and sexual pain disorders.
- Behavioral methods and counseling techniques have been developed to alleviate many sexual problems.
- Most sexual adjustment problems are closely linked to the general health of a couple's relationship.
- Communication skills that foster and maintain intimacy are the key to successful relationships.

What is the role of touching in personal relationships?

- Patterns of touching vary from culture to culture, and they depend on the nature of the relationship between two people. Touch can therefore have a variety of meanings, most of which are nonsexual.

PSYCHOLOGY ON THE NET

- **"Friends" Raping Friends** Information about date rape. http://www.cs.utk.edu/~bartley/acquaint/acquaintRape.html
- **Go Ask Alice** The Sexual Health section of this question-and-answer site offers valuable information and links about sexuality. http://www.goaskalice.columbia.edu/index.html
- **Online Sexual Disorders Screening Test for Men** A self-scoring test for sexual problems. http://www.med.nyu.edu/Psych/screens/sdsm.html

- **Online Sexual Disorders Screening Test for Women** A self-scoring test for sexual problems. http://www.med.nyu.edu/Psych/screens/sdsf.html
- **Preventing HIV Infection** Advice on how to prevent HIV. http://www.tht.org.uk/pubs/prvinfec.htm
- **Sexual Orientation and Homosexuality—FAQ** Answers basic questions about sexual orientation and homosexuality. http://www.apa.org/pubinfo/orient.html

- **•Info Trac® College Edition** For recent articles related to what traits attract humans to one another, use Key Words search for INTERPERSONAL ATTRACTION.

INTERACTIVE LEARNING

- **PsychNow!** 4e. Human sexuality. 8g. Gender and stereotyping.

CHAPTER 15

Personality

Chapter Survey

Theme: Personality refers to the consistency we see in personal behavior patterns. Measures of personality reveal individual differences and help predict future behavior.

THE HIDDEN ESSENCE

RURAL COLORADO. *Our car lurched toward the dilapidated farmhouse, banging over one last brain-jarring rut. Annette was out of the door—hooting and whooping—before we had stopped.*

If anyone was suited for the "wilds" of Colorado, it was Annette, a strong and resourceful woman. Still, it was hard to imagine a more radical change. After separating from her husband, she had traded a comfortable life in the city for survival in the high country. Survival, by the way, is no exaggeration. Annette was working as a ranch hand and a lumberjack (lumberjill?), trying to make it through some hard winters.

So radical were the changes in Annette's life, I was afraid that she, too, would be entirely different. She was, on the contrary, more her "old self" than ever.

Perhaps you have had a similar experience. After several years of separation, it is always intriguing to see an old friend. At first, you may be struck by how the person has changed. Soon, however, you will probably be delighted to discover that the semi-stranger before you is still the person you once knew. It is exactly this core of consistency that psychologists have in mind when they use the term personality.

Without doubt, personality touches our daily lives. Falling in love, choosing friends, getting along with coworkers, voting for a president, and coping with your zaniest relatives all raise questions about personality.

What is personality? How does it differ from temperament, character, or attitudes? Is it possible to measure personality? These and related questions are the concerns of this chapter.

Gateways to Personality

EACH OF US displays consistent behavior patterns that define our own personalities and allow us to predict how other people will act.

PERSONALITY can be understood by identifying traits, by probing mental conflicts and dynamics, by noting the effects of prior learning and situations, and by knowing how people perceive themselves.

PSYCHOLOGISTS use interviews, direct observation, questionnaires, and projective tests to measure and assess personality.

SHYNESS is related to public self-consciousness and other psychological factors that can be altered, which makes it possible for some people to overcome shyness.

OUR BEHAVIOR is influenced by self-monitoring, the process of observing, regulating, and controlling the personal image we display to others.

DO YOU HAVE PERSONALITY?

"Jim's not handsome, but he has a great personality." "My father's business friends think he's a nice guy. They should see him at home where his real personality comes out." "It's hard to believe Tanya and Nikki are sisters. They have such opposite personalities."

It's obvious that we all frequently use the term *personality*, but many people seem hard-pressed to define it. Most simply end up saying something about "charm," "charisma," or "style." If you use *personality* in such ways, you are giving it a different meaning than psychologists do.

Then how do psychologists use the term? Most regard **personality** as a person's unique and relatively stable behavior patterns. In other words, personality refers to the consistency in who you are, have been, and will become. It also refers to the special blend of talents, attitudes, values, hopes, loves, hates, and habits that makes each of us a unique person.

How is that different from the way most people use the term? Many people confuse personality with *character*. The term **character** implies that a person has been judged or evaluated, not just described (Skipton, 1997). If, by saying someone has "personality," you mean the person is friendly, outgoing, and attractive, you are really referring to what we regard as good character in our culture. But in some cultures, it is deemed

Do these men have personality? Do you?

good for a person to be fierce, warlike, and cruel. So, although everyone in a particular culture has personality, not everyone has character—or at least not good character. (Do you know any good characters?)

Personality is also distinct from *temperament.* Temperament is the "raw material" from which personality is formed. **Temperament** refers to the hereditary aspects of personality, including sensitivity, activity levels, prevailing mood, irritability, and adaptability (Kagan, 1989).

Psychology Looks at Personality

Psychologists use a large number of terms to explain personality. It might be wise, therefore, to start with a few key concepts. These ideas should help you keep your bearings as you read this chapter.

Traits

We use the idea of traits every day in talking about the personalities of others. For instance, my friend Dan is *sociable, orderly,* and *intelligent.* His sister Kayla is *shy, sensitive,* and *creative.* In general, **personality traits** are stable qualities that a person shows in most situations. Typically, traits are inferred from behavior. If you see Dan talking to strangers—first at a supermarket and later at a party—you might deduce that he is "sociable." You might then predict from this trait that he will also be sociable at school or at work.

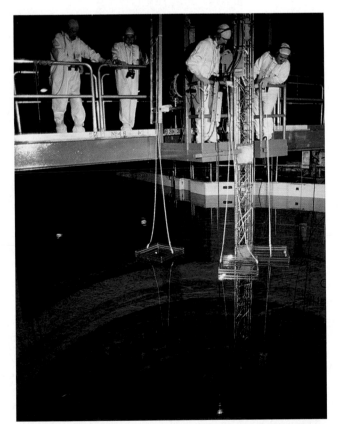

Psychologists and employers are especially interested in the personality traits of individuals who hold high-risk, high-stress positions involving public safety, such as police, air-traffic controllers, and nuclear power plant employees.

BRIDGES

Even newborn babies differ in temperament, which implies that it is hereditary. Temperament has a large impact on how infants interact with their parents.

See Chapter 4, page 87.

As you can see, traits can predict future behavior. For example, students who are extroverted, agreeable, and conscientious tend to make more friends and have less conflict with other students. They are also more likely to fall in love (Asendorpf & Wilpers, 1998).

WHEN IS THE PLASTER SET?   Personality traits are usually quite stable (Gustavsson et al., 1997). As an example, think about how little the traits of your best friends have changed in the last 5 years. It would be strange indeed to feel like you were talking with a different person every time you met a friend or acquaintance.

At what age are the major outlines of personality firmly established?   It is rare for personality to change dramatically. However, between college age and middle age, most people do gradually become less emotional, extroverted, and intellectually inquisitive. Most also become more agreeable and conscientious (McCrae et al., 1999). (This, no doubt, is a dream come true for many parents.)

During the 20s, personality slowly begins to harden. By age 30, your personality is usually quite stable. After that, major shifts in who you are tend to be unusual. When major changes do occur, they are associated with dramatic life events, such as personal catastrophes or tragedies. After age 30, simply moving to a new city, changing your looks, or finding new friends won't reshape your basic personality. The person you are at age 30 is, for the most part, the person you will be at age 60. (Additional sources: Costa & McCrae, 1992; Roan, 1992.)

Types

Have you ever asked the question, "What type of person is she (or he)?" A **personality type** refers to people who have *several traits in common* (Potkay & Allen, 1986). Informally, your own thinking might include categories such as the executive type, the athletic type, the motherly type, the hip-hop type, and the strong silent type. If I asked you to define these informal types, you would probably list a different collection of traits for each one.

How valid is it to speak of personality "types"?   Over the years, psychologists have proposed many ways to categorize personalities into types. Consider the idea, first advanced by Swiss psychiatrist Carl Jung (yoong), that a person is either an

Personality *A person's unique and relatively stable behavior patterns.*
Character *Personal characteristics that have been judged or evaluated; a person's desirable or undesirable qualities.*
Temperament *The hereditary aspects of personality, including sensitivity, activity levels, prevailing mood, irritability, and adaptability.*
Personality trait *A stable, enduring quality that a person shows in most situations.*
Personality type *A style of personality defined by a group of related traits.*

The four basic personality types

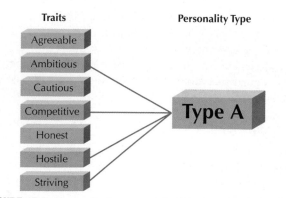

❖ **FIGURE 15.1** *Personality types are defined by the presence of several specific traits. For example, several possible personality traits are shown in the left column. A person who has a Type A personality typically possesses all or most of the highlighted traits. Type A people are especially prone to heart disease (see Chapter 16).*

introvert or *extrovert*. An **introvert** is a shy, self-centered person whose attention is focused inward. An **extrovert** is a bold, outgoing person whose attention is directed outward. These terms are so widely used that you may think of yourself and your friends as being one type or the other. However, the wildest, wittiest, most party-loving "extrovert" you know is introverted at times, and extremely introverted persons are assertive and sociable in some situations. In short, two categories (or even several) are often inadequate to fully describe differences in personality. That's why rating people on a list of traits is often more informative than classifying them into two or three types.

Even though types tend to oversimplify personality, they do have value. Most often, types are a shorthand way of labeling people who have several key traits in common. For example, in Chapter 16 we will discuss Type A personalities. These are people whose traits increase their chance of suffering a heart attack (see ❖Fig. 15.1). Similarly, you will read in Chapter 17 about unhealthy personality types such as the paranoid personality, the dependent personality, and the antisocial personality. Each is defined by a specific collection of maladaptive traits.

Self-Concept

Another way of understanding personality is to focus on a person's self-concept. The rough outlines of your self-concept would be revealed by this request: "Please tell us about yourself." In other words, your **self-concept** consists of all your ideas, perceptions, and feelings about who you are (Potkay & Allen, 1986).

Self-concepts can be remarkably consistent. In a recent study, very old people were asked how they had changed over the years. Almost all thought they were essentially the same person they were when they were young (Troll & Skaff, 1997).

Self-concepts have a major impact on behavior. We creatively build our self-concepts out of daily experiences. Then we slowly revise them as we have new experiences. Once a stable self-concept exists, it tends to shape our subjective world by guiding what we pay attention to, remember, and think about (Markus & Nurius, 1986).

Self-concepts can greatly affect personal adjustment—especially when they are *inaccurate* or *inadequate* (Potkay & Allen, 1986). As an example, consider Maryanne, a student who thinks she is stupid, worthless, and a failure, despite getting good grades in college. With such a negative self-concept, Maryanne will probably be depressed or anxious no matter how well she does.

SELF-ESTEEM AND CULTURE— HOTSHOT OR TEAM PLAYER?

You and some friends are playing an informal game of volleyball. Your team wins, in part because you make some good plays. After the game, you bask in the glow of having performed well. You don't want to brag about being a hotshot, but your self-esteem does get a boost from your personal success.

In Japan, Shinobu is playing volleyball with some friends. His team wins, in part because he makes some good plays. After the game, Shinobu is happy because his team did well. However, Shinobu also dwells on the ways in which he let his team down. He thinks about how he could improve in the future, and he resolves to be a better team player.

These sketches illustrate a basic difference in Eastern and Western psychology. In individualistic cultures such as the United States and Canada, self-esteem is based on success, competence, and outstanding performance. For us, the path to higher self-esteem lies in self-enhancement. We are pumped up by our successes and tend to ignore our faults and failures.

Japanese and other Asian cultures place a greater emphasis on collectivism or mutual interdependence among people. In such cultures, self-esteem is related to group success. It is also based on identifying personal failures and correcting them, because self-improvement contributes to the welfare of the group. As a result, Japanese people tend to be more self-critical than we are in North America. For them, self-esteem is based on a secure sense of belonging to social groups. This makes self-criticism a way of contributing to the success and well-being of the entire group.

Perhaps it is still fair to say that self-esteem is based on success in both Eastern and Western cultures. However, it is interesting to note that cultures define success in different ways. The North American emphasis on winning is not the only way to feel good about yourself.

(Sources: Heine & Lehman, 1999; Kitayama et al., 1997; Lay & Verkuyten, 1999; Markus & Kitayama, 1998.)

SELF-ESTEEM Note that Maryanne also suffers from low **self-esteem** (how she evaluates herself). A person who has high self-esteem is confident, proud, and self-respecting. A person who is self-critical, insecure, and lacking in confidence has low self-esteem. Like Maryanne, people with low self-esteem are usually anxious and unhappy.

Self-esteem tends to rise when we experience success. It is also enhanced by praise from others. Thus, a person who is competent and effective and who is loved, admired, and respected by others will almost always have high self-esteem (Baumeister, 1994). (The reasons for having high self-esteem

can vary in different cultures. See "Self-Esteem and Culture" for more information.)

People who have low self-esteem typically also suffer from poor self-knowledge. Like Maryanne, their self-concepts are inconsistent, inaccurate, and confused. Problems of this type are explored later in this chapter.

Can self-esteem ever be too high? Yes, at least in group situations. People who think very highly of themselves (and let others know it) may at first appear confident and interesting. However, their arrogance quickly becomes obvious, which tends to turn off other people (Paulhus, 1998). A related problem plagues people who are incompetent. Such people grossly overestimate their own abilities. For instance, a recent study found that people who score very low on tests of logic, grammar, and humor think that their abilities are well above average in these areas. Basically, they seem to be too incompetent to recognize their own incompetence. This finding may explain why humor-impaired people (we all know at least one) insist on telling jokes that are not funny (Kruger & Dunning, 1999).

Personality Theories

It would be easy to get lost without a framework for understanding personality. How do our actions and feelings relate to personality? How does personality develop? Why do some people suffer from psychological problems? How can they be helped? To answer such questions, psychologists have created a dazzling array of theories. A **personality theory** is a system of concepts, assumptions, ideas, and principles proposed to explain personality (❖Fig. 15.2).

Many personality theories have been created, so it is possible to introduce only a few here.

1. **Trait theories** attempt to learn what traits make up personality and how they relate to actual behavior.
2. **Psychodynamic theories** focus on the inner workings of personality, especially internal conflicts and struggles.
3. **Behavioristic theories** place importance on the external environment and on the effects of conditioning and learning.
4. **Humanistic theories** stress private, subjective experience and personal growth.

Now that you are oriented, let's take a deeper look at personality.

Introvert *A person whose attention is focused inward; a shy, reserved, self-centered person.*
Extrovert *A person whose attention is directed outward; a bold, outgoing person.*
Self-concept *A person's perception of his or her own personality traits.*
Self-esteem *Regarding oneself as a worthwhile person; a positive evaluation of oneself.*
Personality theory *A system of concepts, assumptions, ideas, and principles used to understand and explain personality.*

❖ **FIGURE 15.2** *English psychologist Hans Eysenck believes that many personality traits are related to whether you are mainly introverted or extroverted and whether you tend to be emotionally stable or unstable (highly emotional). These characteristics, in turn, are related to four basic types of temperament first recognized by the early Greeks. The types are melancholic (sad, gloomy), choleric (hot-tempered, irritable), phlegmatic (sluggish, calm), and sanguine (cheerful, hopeful). (Adapted from Eysenck, 1981.)*

THE TRAIT APPROACH—DESCRIBE YOURSELF IN 18,000 WORDS OR LESS

How many words can you think of to describe the personality of a close friend? Your list might be long: More than 18,000 English words refer to personal characteristics. As you now know, traits are stable and enduring qualities that a person shows in most situations. For example, if you are usually optimistic, reserved, and friendly, these qualities could be stable traits of your personality.

What if I am sometimes pessimistic, uninhibited, or shy? The original three qualities are still traits as long as they are most *typical* of your behavior. Let's say Ima Student approaches most situations with optimism but tends to expect the worst each time she takes a test. If her pessimism is limited to this situation or a few others, it is still accurate and useful to describe her as an optimistic person.

Predicting Behavior

As we have noted, separating people into broad types, such as "introvert" or "extrovert," may oversimplify personality. However, introversion-extroversion can also be thought of as a trait. Knowing how you rate on this single dimension would allow us to predict how you will behave in a variety of settings. Where, for example, do you prefer to study in the library?

Researchers have found that students high in the trait of extroversion study in locations with high noise levels and more chances for socializing (Campbell & Hawley, 1982). In the library at Colgate University (where the study was done), you can find extroverted students in the second floor lounge. Or, if you prefer, more introverted students can be found in the carrels on the first and third floors!

An analysis of U.S. President Bill Clinton's personality traits showed that he is self-assertive, self-promoting, extroverted, and sociable. These traits probably helped Clinton maintain a surprisingly high degree of public approval during the "Monicagate" scandal (Immelman, 1998).

Describing People

In general, psychologists try to identify traits that best describe a person. Take a moment to check the traits in ◆Table 15.1 that describe your personality. Are the traits you checked of equal importance? Are some stronger or more basic than others? Do any overlap? For example, if you checked "dominant," did you also check "confident" and "bold"? Answers to these questions would interest a trait theorist. To better un-

TABLE 15.1 Adjective Checklist

CHECK THE TRAITS YOU FEEL ARE CHARACTERISTIC OF YOUR PERSONALITY. ARE SOME MORE BASIC THAN OTHERS?

aggressive	organized	ambitious	clever
confident	loyal	generous	calm
warm	bold	cautious	reliable
sensitive	mature	talented	jealous
sociable	honest	funny	religious
dominant	dull	accurate	nervous
humble	uninhibited	visionary	cheerful
thoughtful	serious	helpful	emotional
orderly	anxious	conforming	good-natured
liberal	curious	optimistic	kind
meek	neighborly	passionate	compulsive

derstand personality, **trait theorists** attempt to analyze, classify, and interrelate traits.

Classifying Traits

Are there different types of traits? Yes, psychologist Gordon Allport (1961) identified several kinds. **Common traits** are characteristics shared by most members of a culture. Common traits tell us how people from a particular nation or culture are similar, or which traits a culture emphasizes. In America, for example, competitiveness is a fairly common trait. Among the Hopi of Northern Arizona, it is a relatively rare trait.

Of course, common traits tell us little about individuals. Although many people are competitive in American culture, each person may rate high, medium, or low in this trait. Usually we are also interested in these **individual traits,** which define a person's unique personal qualities.

Here's an analogy to help you separate common traits from individual traits: If you were going to buy a pet dog, you would want to know the general characteristics of the dog's breed (its common traits). In addition, you would want to know about the "personality" of a specific dog (its individual traits) before you decided to take it home.

Allport also made distinctions between *cardinal traits, central traits,* and *secondary traits.* A **cardinal trait** is so basic that all of a person's activities can be traced to the trait. For instance, an overriding factor in the life of Albert Schweitzer was "reverence for every living thing." Likewise, Abraham Lincoln's personality was dominated by the cardinal trait of honesty. According to Allport, few people have cardinal traits.

CENTRAL TRAITS *How do central and secondary traits differ from cardinal traits?* **Central traits** are the core qualities or basic building blocks of personality. A surprisingly small number of central traits can capture the essence of a person. When college students were asked to describe someone they knew well, they mentioned an average of only seven central traits (Allport, 1961).

In contrast, **secondary traits** are less consistent, relatively superficial aspects of a person. Any number of secondary traits could be listed in a personality description. Your own secondary traits include such things as food preferences, attitudes, political opinions, musical tastes, and so forth. In Allport's terms, a personality description might therefore include the following items.

- **Name:** Jane Doe
- **Age:** 22
- **Cardinal traits:** None
- **Central traits:** Possessive, autonomous, artistic, dramatic, self-centered, trusting
- **Secondary traits:** Prefers colorful clothes, likes to work alone, politically liberal, always late

SOURCE TRAITS A second major approach to traits is illustrated by the work of Raymond B. Cattell (1906–1998). Cattell wanted to reach deeper into personality to learn how traits are interlinked. He began by studying features that make up the visible areas of personality. He called these **surface traits.** Through the use of questionnaires, direct observations, and life records, Cattell assembled data on the surface traits of a large number of people. He then noted that surface traits often appear in *clusters,* or groups. In fact, some traits appeared together so often that they seemed to represent a single more basic trait. Cattell called such underlying personality characteristics **source traits** (Cattell, 1965).

How do source traits differ from Allport's central traits? The main difference is that Allport classified traits subjectively, whereas Cattell used a statistical technique called *factor analysis* to reduce surface traits to source traits.

In a **factor analysis,** psychologists look at the correlations among several measurements. If patterns emerge in these correlations, they are assumed to reflect general, underlying

Trait theorist *A psychologist interested in classifying, analyzing, and interrelating traits to understand personality.*
Common traits *Personality traits that are shared by most members of a particular culture.*
Individual traits *Personality traits that define a person's unique individual qualities.*
Cardinal trait *A personality trait so basic that all of a person's activities relate to it.*
Central traits *The core traits that characterize an individual personality.*
Secondary traits *Traits that are inconsistent or relatively superficial.*
Surface traits *The visible or observable traits of one's personality.*
Source traits *Basic underlying traits of personality; each source trait is reflected in a number of surface traits.*
Factor analysis *A statistical technique used to correlate multiple measurements and identify general underlying factors.*

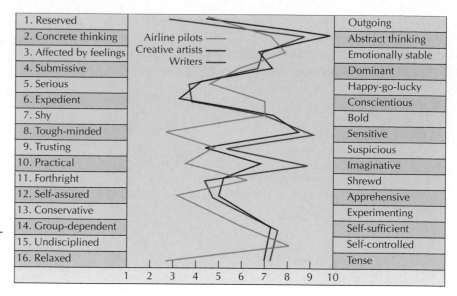

1. Reserved		Outgoing
2. Concrete thinking		Abstract thinking
3. Affected by feelings		Emotionally stable
4. Submissive		Dominant
5. Serious		Happy-go-lucky
6. Expedient		Conscientious
7. Shy		Bold
8. Tough-minded		Sensitive
9. Trusting		Suspicious
10. Practical		Imaginative
11. Forthright		Shrewd
12. Self-assured		Apprehensive
13. Conservative		Experimenting
14. Group-dependent		Self-sufficient
15. Undisciplined		Self-controlled
16. Relaxed		Tense

Airline pilots ——
Creative artists ——
Writers ——

1 2 3 4 5 6 7 8 9 10

❖ **FIGURE 15.3** *The 16 source traits measured by Cattell's 16 PF are listed beside the graph. Scores can be plotted as a profile for an individual or a group. The profiles shown here are group averages for airline pilots, creative artists, and writers. Notice the similarity between artists and writers and the difference between these two groups and pilots. (After Cattell, 1973.)*

factors. Using this approach, Cattell developed a list of 16 source traits. He considered this the basic number necessary to describe a personality.

Cattell's source traits are measured by a test called the *Sixteen Personality Factor Questionnaire* (often referred to as the 16 PF). Like many tests of its type, the 16 PF can be used to produce a **trait profile,** or graph of a person's score on each trait. Trait profiles draw a "picture" of individual personalities, which makes it easier to compare them (❖Fig. 15.3).

The Big Five

Noel is outgoing and friendly, conscientious, emotionally stable, and smart. His brother Joel is introverted, hostile, irresponsible, emotionally unpredictable, and uninterested in ideas (stupid). You will be spending a week in a space capsule with either Noel or Joel. Which would you choose? If the answer seems obvious, it's because Noel and Joel were described with the **five-factor model,** a system that identifies the five most basic dimensions of personality.

The "Big Five" factors listed in ❖Figure 15.4 attempt to further reduce Cattell's 16 factors to just five universal dimensions (Digman, 1990; Goldberg, 1993). The Big Five may be the best answer of all to the question, What is the essence of human personality? (De Raad, 1998; McCrae & Costa, 1997).

FIVE KEY DIMENSIONS   If you would like to compare the personalities of two people, try rating them informally on the five dimensions shown in ❖Figure 15.4. For factor 1, *extroversion,* rate how introverted or extroverted each person is. Factor 2, *agreeableness,* refers to how friendly, nurturant, and caring a person is, as opposed to cold, indifferent, self-centered, or spiteful. A person who is *conscientious* (factor 3) is self-disciplined, responsible, and achieving. People low on this factor are irresponsible, careless, and undependable. Factor 4, *neuroticism,* refers to negative, upsetting emotions. People who are high in neuroticism tend to be anxious, emotionally "sour," irritable, and unhappy (DeNeve & Cooper, 1998). Finally, people who

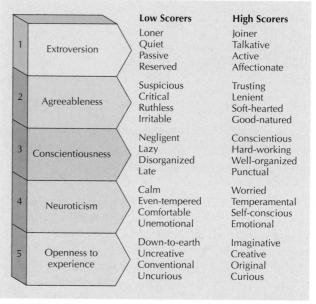

		Low Scorers	High Scorers
1	Extroversion	Loner Quiet Passive Reserved	Joiner Talkative Active Affectionate
2	Agreeableness	Suspicious Critical Ruthless Irritable	Trusting Lenient Soft-hearted Good-natured
3	Conscientiousness	Negligent Lazy Disorganized Late	Conscientious Hard-working Well-organized Punctual
4	Neuroticism	Calm Even-tempered Comfortable Unemotional	Worried Temperamental Self-conscious Emotional
5	Openness to experience	Down-to-earth Uncreative Conventional Uncurious	Imaginative Creative Original Curious

❖ **FIGURE 15.4** *The Big Five. According to the five-factor model, basic differences in personality can be "boiled down" to the dimensions shown here. The five-factor model answers these essential questions about a person: Is she or he extroverted or introverted? Agreeable or difficult? Conscientious or irresponsible? Emotionally stable or unstable? Smart or unintelligent? These questions cover a large measure of what we might want to know about someone's personality. (Trait descriptions adapted from McCrae & Costa, 1990.)*

rate high on factor 5, *openness to experience,* are intelligent and open to new ideas (Digman, 1990). The beauty of this model is that almost any trait you can name will be related to one of the five factors. If you were selecting a college roommate, hiring an employee, or answering a singles ad, you would probably like to know all of the personal dimensions covered by the Big Five.

Knowing where a person stands on the "Big Five" personality factors helps predict his or her behavior. For example, people who score high on conscientiousness tend to be safe drivers who are unlikely to have automobile accidents (Arthur & Graziano, 1996).

Before you read the next section, take a moment to answer the questions that follow. Doing so will add to your understanding of a long-running controversy in the psychology of personality.

RATE YOURSELF
HOW DO YOU VIEW PERSONALITY?

1. My friends' actions are fairly consistent from day to day and in different situations. T or F?
2. Whether a person is honest or dishonest, kind or cruel, a hero or a coward, depends mainly on circumstances. T or F?
3. Most people that I have known for several years have pretty much the same personalities now as they did when I first met them. T or F?
4. The reason that people in some professions (such as teachers, lawyers, or doctors) seem so much alike is because their work requires that they act in particular ways. T or F?
5. One of the first things I would want to know about a potential roommate is what the person's personality is like. T or F?
6. I believe that immediate circumstances usually determine how people act at any given time. T or F?
7. To be comfortable in a particular job, a person's personality must match the nature of the work. T or F?
8. Almost anyone would be polite at a wedding reception; it doesn't matter what kind of personality the person has. T or F?

Now count the number of times you marked true for the odd-numbered items. Do the same for the even-numbered items.

If you agreed with most of the odd-numbered items, you tend to view behavior as strongly influenced by personality traits or lasting personal dispositions.

If you agreed with most of the even-numbered items, you view behavior as strongly influenced by external situations and circumstances.

If the number of times you answered true is nearly equal for odd and even items, you place equal weight on traits and situations as sources of behavior. This is the view now held by many personality psychologists (Mischel & Shoda, 1998).

Traits, Consistency, and Situations

To predict how a person will act, is it better to focus on personality traits or external circumstances? Actually, it's best to take both into account. Personality traits are quite consistent (Costa & McCrae, 1992; Roan, 1992). Yet, *situations* also greatly influence our behavior. For instance, it would be unusual for you to dance at a movie or read a book at a football game. Likewise, few people sleep on roller coasters or tell off-color jokes at funerals. However, your personality traits may predict whether you choose to read a book, go to a movie, or attend a football game in the first place. Typically, traits *interact* with situations to determine how we will act (Sheldon et al., 1997).

Trait-situation interactions occur when external circumstances influence the expression of personality traits. For instance, imagine what would happen if you moved from a church to a classroom to a party to a football game. As the setting changed, you would probably become louder and more boisterous. This change would demonstrate situational effects on behavior. At the same time, your personality traits would also be apparent: If you were quieter than average in class, you would probably be quieter than average in the other settings, too (Rorer & Widiger, 1983). Where do such differences come from? The next section explores one source of personality traits.

Do We Inherit Personality?

How much does heredity affect personality traits? Some breeds of dogs have reputations for being friendly, aggressive, intelligent, calm, or emotional. Such differences fall in the realm of **behavioral genetics**—the study of inherited behavioral traits. We know that facial features, eye color, body type, and other physical characteristics are inherited. So, too, are many behavioral tendencies. For example, selective breeding of animals can lead to striking differences in social behavior, emotionality, learning ability, aggression, activity, and other behaviors (Steen, 1996; Trut, 1999).

To what extent do such findings apply to humans? Genetic studies of humans must rely on comparisons of identical twins and other close relatives. As a result, they are not as conclusive as animal studies (Rose, 1995). Nonetheless, they show that intelligence, some mental disorders, temperament, and other complex qualities are influenced by heredity. In view of findings like these, we also might wonder, Do genes affect personality?

Trait profile *A graph of the scores obtained on several personality traits.*
Five-factor model *Proposes that there are five universal dimensions of personality.*
Trait-situation interaction *The influence that external settings or circumstances have on the expression of personality traits.*
Behavioral genetics *The study of inherited behavioral traits and tendencies.*

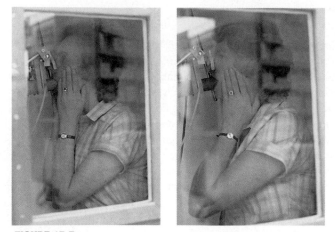

❖ **FIGURE 15.5** *Reunited identical twins Terry and Margaret undergo lung function tests at the University of Minnesota. Researchers collected a wide range of medical and psychological data for each set of twins.*

Wouldn't comparing the personalities of identical twins help answer the question? It would indeed—especially if the twins were separated at birth or soon after.

TWINS AND TRAITS For two decades, psychologists at the University of Minnesota have been studying identical twins who grew up in different homes. At the university, reunited twins take a wide range of medical and psychological tests (❖Fig. 15.5). Test results show that identical twins are very much alike, even when they are reared apart (Bouchard et al., 1990; Lykken et al., 1992).

BRIDGES

Behavioral genetic research has helped us understand the hereditary origins of intelligence and psychological disorders.

See pages 290–291, 579, and 584.

Like all identical twins, reunited twins are astonishingly similar in appearance and voice quality. Observers are struck by how often twins display identical facial gestures, hand movements, and nervous tics, such as nail biting or finger tapping. Separated twins also tend to have similar talents. If one twin excels at art, music, dance, drama, or athletics, the other is likely to as well—despite wide differences in childhood environment. However, as the highlight titled "The Minnesota Twins" explains, it's wise to be cautious about some reports of extraordinary similarities in reunited twins.

Studies of twins make it clear that heredity has a sizable effect on each of us. All told, it seems reasonable to conclude that there is a genetic factor in personality. Heredity appears to be responsible for about 25 to 50 percent of the variation in many personality traits (Jang & Livesley, 1998; Loehlin et al., 1998). Notice, however, that the same figures imply personality is shaped as much, or more, by environment as it is by heredity (Gatz, 1990). That's why separated twins become more different the longer they live apart (Baker & Daniels, 1990; McCartney, Bernieri, & Harris, 1990).

In summary, each personality is a unique blend of heredity and environment, biology and culture. We are not—thank goodness!—genetically programmed robots whose behavior and personality traits are "wired in" for life. Where you go in life is the result of the choices you make. To a degree, these choices may be influenced by inherited tendencies (Saudino et al., 1997). However, they are not merely a result of our genetic fortunes (Rose, 1995).

THE MINNESOTA TWINS

CRITICAL THINKING

Many reunited twins in the Minnesota study have displayed similarities far beyond what would be expected on the basis of heredity. A good example is provided by the "Jim twins," James Lewis and James Springer. Both Jims had married and divorced women named Linda. Both had undergone police training. Both had named their firstborn sons James Allan. Both drove Chevrolets and vacationed at the same beach each summer. Both listed carpentry and mechanical drawing among their hobbies. Both had built benches around trees in their yards. And so forth (Holden, 1980).

Does heredity actually control such details of our lives? Are there child-naming genes and bench-building genes? Of course, the idea is preposterous. How, then, do we explain the eerie similarities in separated twins' lives?

The astute reader will realize that completely unrelated persons can also share "amazing" similarities. One study, for instance, compared twins to unrelated pairs of students. The unrelated pairs, who were the same age and sex, were almost as alike as the twins. They had highly similar political beliefs,

musical interests, religious preferences, job histories, hobbies, favorite foods, and so on (Wyatt et al., 1984). Why were the unrelated students so similar? Basically, it's because people of the same age and sex live in the same historical times and select from similar societal options.

Imagine that you were separated at birth from a twin brother or sister. If you were reunited with your twin today, what would you do? Quite likely, you would spend the next several days comparing every imaginable detail of your lives. Under such circumstances, it is virtually certain that you and your twin would compile a long list of similarities. ("Wow! I use the same brand of toothpaste you do!") Yet, two unrelated persons of the same age, sex, and race could probably rival your list—*if* they were as motivated to find similarities.

To summarize, many of the seemingly "astounding" coincidences shared by reunited twins may be a special case of the fallacy of positive instances, described in Chapter 1. Similarities blaze brightly in the memories of reunited twins, while differences are ignored.

PERSONALITY AND TRAIT THEORIES

RELATE

See if you can define or describe the following terms in your own words: personality, character, temperament, trait, type, self-concept, self-esteem.

List six or seven traits that best describe your personality. Which system of traits seems to best match your list, Allport's, Cattell's, or the Big Five?

Choose a prominent trait from your list. Does its expression seem to be influenced by specific situations? Do you think that heredity contributed to the trait?

LEARNING CHECK

1. _____ refers to the hereditary aspects of a person's emotional nature.

2. The term _____ refers to the presence or absence of desirable personal qualities.
   a. personality *b.* source trait *c.* character *d.* temperament

3. A system that classifies all people as either introverts or extroverts is an example of a _____ approach to personality.

4. An individual's perception of his or her own personality constitutes that person's _____.

5. According to Allport, few people have _____ traits.

6. Central traits are those shared by most members of a culture. T or F?

7. Cattell believes that clusters of _____ traits reveal the presence of underlying _____ traits.

8. Cattell's personality questionnaire provides ratings on 16 surface traits. T or F?

9. Which of the following is *not* one of the Big Five personality factors?
   a. submissiveness *b.* agreeableness *c.* extroversion *d.* neuroticism

10. To understand personality, it is wise to remember that traits and situations _____ to determine our behavior.

CRITICAL THINKING

11. In what way would memory contribute to the formation of an accurate or inaccurate self-image?

12. Are situations equally powerful in their impact on behavior?

Answers:

1. Temperament 2. *c* 3. type 4. self-concept 5. cardinal 6. F 7. surface, source 8. F 9. *a* 10. interact 11. As discussed in Chapter 9, memory is highly selective, and long-term memories are often distorted by recent information. Such properties add to the moldability of self-concept. 12. No. Circumstances can have a strong or weak influence. In some situations, almost everyone will act the same, no matter what their personality traits may be. In other situations, traits may be of greater importance.

PSYCHOANALYTIC THEORY—ID CAME TO ME IN A DREAM

Psychodynamic theorists are not content with studying traits. Instead, they try to probe under the surface of personality—to learn what drives, conflicts, and energies animate us. **Psychoanalytic theory,** the best-known psychodynamic approach, grew out of the work of Sigmund Freud, a Viennese physician. As a doctor, Freud was fascinated by patients whose problems seemed to be more emotional than physical. From about 1890 until he died in 1939, Freud evolved a theory of personality that deeply influenced modern thought. Let's consider some of its main features.

The Structure of Personality

How did Freud view personality? Freud's model portrays personality as a dynamic system directed by three mental structures, the **id,** the **ego,** and the **superego.** According to Freud, most behavior involves activity of all three systems. (Freud's theory includes a large number of concepts. For your convenience, they are defined in ◆Table 15.2 rather than in the running glossary.)

THE ID   The id is made up of innate biological instincts and urges. It is self-serving, irrational, impulsive, and totally unconscious. The id operates on the **pleasure principle.** That is, it seeks to freely express pleasure-seeking urges of all kinds. If we were solely under control of the id, the world would be chaotic beyond belief.

The id acts as a well of energy for the entire **psyche** (sie-KEY), or personality. This energy, called **libido** (lih-BEE-doe), flows from the **life instincts** (or **Eros**). According to Freud, libido underlies our efforts to survive, as well as our sexual desires and pleasure seeking. Freud also described a **death instinct. Thanatos,** as he called it, produces aggressive and destructive urges. Freud offered humanity's long history of wars and violence as evidence of such urges. Most id energies, then, are aimed at discharging tensions related to sex and aggression.

THE EGO   The ego is sometimes described as the "executive," because it directs energies supplied by the id. The id is like a blind king or queen whose power is awesome but who must rely on others to carry out orders. The id can only form mental images of things it desires. The ego wins power to direct behavior by relating the desires of the id to external reality.

Are there other differences between the ego and the id? Yes. Recall that the id operates on the pleasure principle. The ego, in contrast, is guided by the **reality principle.** That is, the ego delays action until it is practical or appropriate. The ego is the system of thinking, planning, problem solving, and deciding. It is in conscious control of the personality.

Psychoanalytic theory *Freudian theory of personality that emphasizes unconscious forces and conflicts.*

Anal stage *The psychosexual stage corresponding roughly to the period of toilet training (ages 1 to 3).*

Anal-expulsive personality *A disorderly, destructive, cruel, or messy person.*

Anal-retentive personality *A person who is obstinate, stingy, or compulsive, and who generally has difficulty "letting go."*

Conscience *The part of the superego that causes guilt when its standards are not met.*

Conscious *Region of the mind that includes all mental contents a person is aware of at any given moment.*

Ego *The executive part of personality that directs rational behavior.*

Ego ideal *The part of the superego representing ideal behavior; a source of pride when its standards are met.*

Electra conflict *A girl's sexual attraction to her father and feelings of rivalry with her mother.*

Erogenous zone *Any body area that produces pleasurable sensations.*

Eros *Freud's name for the "life instincts."*

Fixation *A lasting conflict developed as a result of frustration or overindulgence.*

Genital stage *Period of full psychosexual development, marked by the attainment of mature adult sexuality.*

Id *The primitive part of personality that remains unconscious, supplies energy, and demands pleasure.*

Latency *According to Freud, a period in childhood when psychosexual development is more or less interrupted.*

Libido *In Freudian theory, the force, primarily pleasure oriented, that energizes the personality.*

Moral anxiety *Apprehension felt when thoughts, impulses, or actions conflict with the superego's standards.*

Neurotic anxiety *Apprehension felt when the ego struggles to control id impulses.*

Oedipus conflict *A boy's sexual attraction to his mother and feelings of rivalry with his father.*

Oral stage *The period when infants are preoccupied with the mouth as a source of pleasure and means of expression.*

Oral-aggressive personality *A person who uses the mouth to express hostility by shouting, cursing, biting, and so forth. Also, one who actively exploits others.*

Oral-dependent personality *A person who wants to passively receive attention, gifts, love, and so forth.*

Phallic personality *A person who is vain, exhibitionistic, sensitive, and narcissistic.*

Phallic stage *The psychosexual stage (roughly ages 3 to 6) when a child is preoccupied with the genitals.*

Pleasure principle *A desire for immediate satisfaction of wishes, desires, or needs.*

Preconscious *An area of the mind containing information that can be voluntarily brought to awareness.*

Psyche *The mind, mental life, and personality as a whole.*

Psychosexual stages *The oral, anal, phallic, and genital stages, during which various personality traits are formed.*

Reality principle *Delaying action (or pleasure) until it is appropriate.*

Superego *A judge or censor for thoughts and actions.*

Thanatos *The death instinct postulated by Freud.*

Unconscious *The region of the mind that is beyond awareness, especially impulses and desires not directly known to a person.*

Freud considered personality an expression of two conflicting forces, life instincts and the death instinct. Both are symbolized in this drawing by Allan Gilbert. (If you don't immediately see the death symbolism, stand farther from the drawing.)

THE SUPEREGO   *What is the role of the superego?*   The superego acts as a judge or censor for the thoughts and actions of the ego. One part of the superego, called the **conscience,** reflects actions for which a person has been punished. When standards of the conscience are not met, you are punished internally by *guilt* feelings.

A second part of the superego is the **ego ideal.** The ego ideal reflects all behavior one's parents approved of or rewarded. The ego ideal is a source of goals and aspirations. When its standards are met, we feel *pride.*

The superego acts as an "internalized parent" to bring behavior under control. In Freudian terms, a person with a weak superego will be a delinquent, criminal, or antisocial personality. In contrast, an overly strict or harsh superego may cause inhibition, rigidity, or unbearable guilt.

The Dynamics of Personality

How do the id, ego, and superego interact?   Freud didn't picture the id, ego, and superego as parts of the brain or as "little people" running the human psyche. Instead, they are conflicting mental processes. Freud theorized a delicate balance of power among the three. For example, the id's demands for immediate pleasure often clash with the superego's moral restrictions. Perhaps an example will help clarify the role of each part of the personality.

Freud in a Nutshell

Let's say you are sexually attracted to an acquaintance. The id clamors for immediate satisfaction of its sexual desires, but is opposed by the superego (which finds the very thought of sex shocking). The id says, "Go for it!" The superego icily replies, "Never even think that again!" And what does the ego say? The ego says, "I have a plan!"

Of course, this is a drastic simplification, but it does capture the core of Freudian thinking. To reduce tension, the ego could begin actions leading to friendship, romance, courtship, and marriage. If the id is unusually powerful, the ego may give in and attempt a seduction. If the superego prevails, the ego may be forced to *displace* or *sublimate* sexual energies to other activities (sports, music, dancing, push-ups, cold showers). According to Freud, internal struggles and rechanneled energies typify most personality functioning.

Is the ego always caught in the middle? Basically yes, and the pressures on it can be intense. In addition to meeting the conflicting demands of the id and superego, the overworked ego must deal with external reality.

According to Freud, you feel anxiety when your ego is threatened or overwhelmed. Impulses from the id cause **neurotic anxiety** when the ego can barely keep them under control. Threats of punishment from the superego cause **moral anxiety.** Each person develops habitual ways of calming these anxieties, and many resort to using *ego-defense mechanisms* to lessen internal conflicts. Defense mechanisms are mental processes that deny, distort, or otherwise block out sources of threat and anxiety.

LEVELS OF AWARENESS   Like other psychodynamic theorists, Freud believed that our behavior often expresses unconscious (or hidden) internal forces. The **unconscious** holds repressed memories and emotions, plus the instinctual drives of the id. Interestingly, modern scientists have found that the brain's limbic system does, in fact, seem to trigger unconscious emotions and memories (LeDoux, 1996).

Even though they are beyond awareness, unconscious thoughts, feelings, or urges may slip into behavior in disguised or symbolic form. For example, if you meet someone you would like to know better, you may unconsciously leave a book or a jacket at that person's house to ensure another meeting.

Earlier you said that the id is completely unconscious. Are the actions of the ego and superego unconscious? At times, yes, but they also operate on two other levels of awareness (❖Fig. 15.6). The **conscious** level includes everything you are aware of at a

BRIDGES

The ego defense mechanisms that Freud identified are used as a form of protection against stress, anxiety, and threatening events.

See Chapter 16, pages 530–532.

given moment, including thoughts, perceptions, feelings, and memories. The **preconscious** contains material that can be easily brought to awareness. If you stop to think about a time when you felt angry or rejected, you will be moving this memory from the preconscious to the conscious level of awareness.

The superego's activities also reveal differing levels of awareness. At times, we consciously try to live up to moral codes or standards. Yet, at other times a person may feel guilty without knowing why. Psychoanalytic theory credits such guilt to unconscious workings of the superego. Indeed, Freud believed that the unconscious origins of many feelings cannot be easily brought to awareness.

Personality Development

How does psychoanalytic theory explain personality development? Freud theorized that the core of personality is formed before age 6 in a series of **psychosexual stages.** Freud believed that erotic childhood urges have lasting effects on development. As you might expect, this is a controversial idea. However, Freud used the terms *sex* and *erotic* very broadly to refer to many physical sources of pleasure.

A FREUDIAN FABLE?   Freud identified four psychosexual stages, the **oral, anal, phallic,** and **genital.** (He also described a period of "latency" between the phallic and genital stages. Latency is explained in a moment.) At each stage, a different part of the body becomes a child's primary **erogenous zone** (an area capable of producing pleasure). Each area then serves as the main source of pleasure, frustration, and self-expression. Freud believed that many adult personality traits can be traced to **fixations** in one or more of the stages.

What is a fixation? A fixation is an unresolved conflict or emotional hang-up caused by overindulgence or by frustration. As we describe the psychosexual stages, you'll see why Freud considered fixations important.

THE ORAL STAGE   During the first year of life, most of an infant's pleasure comes from stimulation of the mouth. If a child is overfed or frustrated, oral traits may be created. Adult expressions of oral needs include gum chewing, nail biting, smoking, kissing, overeating, and alcoholism.

What if there is an oral fixation? Fixation early in the oral stage produces an **oral-dependent** personality. Oral-dependent persons are gullible (they swallow things easily!) and passive and need lots of attention (they want to be mothered and showered with gifts). Frustrations later in the oral stage may cause aggression, often in the form of biting. Fixations here create cynical, **oral-aggressive** adults who exploit others. They also like to argue ("biting sarcasm" is their forte!).

THE ANAL STAGE   Between the ages of 1 and 3, the child's attention shifts to the process of elimination. When parents attempt toilet training, the child can gain approval or express rebellion or aggression by "holding on" or by "letting go." Therefore,

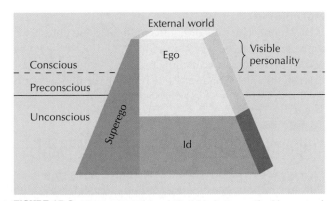

❖ **FIGURE 15.6** *The approximate relationship between the id, ego, and superego and the levels of awareness.*

Was Freud's ever-present cigar a sign of an oral fixation? Was it a phallic symbol? Was it both? Or was it neither? An inability to say for sure is one of the shortcomings of psychoanalytic theory.

LATENCY   According to Freud there is a period of **latency** from age 6 to puberty. Latency is not actually a stage. Rather, it is a quiet time during which psychosexual development is dormant. Freud's belief that psychosexual development is "on hold" at this time is hard to accept. Nevertheless, Freud saw latency as a relatively quiet time, compared with the stormy first 6 years of life.

THE GENITAL STAGE   At puberty, an upswing in sexual energies activates all the unresolved conflicts of earlier years. This upsurge, according to Freud, is the reason why adolescence can be filled with emotion and turmoil. The genital stage begins at puberty. It is marked, during adolescence, by a growing capacity for responsible social-sexual relationships. The genital stage ends with a mature capacity for love and the realization of full adult sexuality.

CRITICAL COMMENTS   As bizarre as Freud's theory might seem, it has been influential for several reasons. First, it pioneered the idea that the first years of life help shape adult personality. Second, it identified feeding, toilet training, and early sexual experiences as critical events in personality formation. Third, Freud was among the first to propose that development proceeds through a series of stages.

Is the Freudian view of development widely accepted?   Few psychologists wholeheartedly embrace Freud's theory today. In some cases, Freud was clearly wrong. His portrayal of the elementary school years (latency) as free from sexuality and unimportant for personality development is hard to believe. His idea of the role of a stern or threatening father in the development of a strong conscience in males has also been challenged. Studies show that a son is more likely to develop a strong conscience if his father is affectionate and accepting, rather than stern and punishing. Freud also overemphasized sexuality in personality development. Other motives and cognitive factors are of equal importance.

Recently, Freud has been criticized for his views of patients who believed they were sexually molested as children. Freud assumed that such events were merely childhood fantasies. This view led to a long-standing tendency to disbelieve children who have been molested and women who have been raped (Brannon, 1996).

Many more criticisms of Freud could be listed, but the fact remains that there is an element of truth to much of what he said. However, a major remaining problem with Freud's theory is insurmountable: Whatever value it may have clinically, it has been almost impossible to verify scientifically.

harsh or lenient toilet training can cause an anal fixation that may lock such responses into personality. Freud described the **anal-retentive** (holding-on) personality as obstinate, stingy, orderly, and compulsively clean. The **anal-expulsive** (letting-go) personality is disorderly, destructive, cruel, or messy.

THE PHALLIC STAGE   Adult traits of the **phallic personality** are vanity, exhibitionism, sensitive pride, and narcissism (self-love). Freud theorized that phallic fixations develop between the ages of 3 and 6. At this time, increased sexual interest causes the child to be physically attracted to the parent of the opposite sex. In males, this attraction leads to an **Oedipus conflict.** In it, the boy feels a rivalry with his father for the affection of his mother. Freud believed that the male child feels threatened by the father (specifically, the boy fears castration). To ease his anxieties, the boy must **identify** with the father. Their rivalry ends when the boy seeks to become more like his father. As he does, he begins to accept the father's values and forms a conscience.

What about the female child?   Girls experience an **Electra conflict.** In this case, the girl loves her father and competes with her mother. However, according to Freud, the girl identifies with the mother more gradually.

Freud believed that females already feel castrated. Because of this, they are less driven to identify with their mothers than boys are with their fathers. This, he said, is less effective in creating a conscience. This particular part of Freudian thought has been thoroughly (and rightfully) rejected by modern feminists. It is probably best understood as a reflection of the male-dominated times in which Freud lived.

BRIDGES

Erik Erikson's psychosocial stages, which cover development from birth to old age, are a modern offshoot of Freudian thinking.

See Chapter 5, pages 126–129.

PSYCHODYNAMIC THEORIES—FREUD'S DESCENDANTS

Freud's ideas quickly attracted a brilliant following. Just as rapidly, the importance Freud placed on instinctual drives and sexuality caused many to disagree with him. Those who stayed close to the core of Freud's thinking are called *neo-Freudians* (*neo* means "new"). **Neo-Freudians** accepted the broad features of Freud's theory but revised parts of it. Some of the better-known neo-Freudians are Karen Horney, Anna Freud (Freud's daughter), Otto Rank, and Erich Fromm. Other early followers broke away more completely from Freud and created their own opposing theories. This group includes people such as Alfred Adler, Harry Sullivan, and Carl Jung.

The full story of other psychodynamic theories must await your first course in personality. For now, let's sample three views. The first represents an early rejection of Freud's thinking (Adler). The second embraces most but not all of Freud's theory (Horney). The third involves a carryover of Freudian ideas into a related but unique theory (Jung).

Alfred Adler (1870–1937)

Adler broke away from Freud because he disagreed with Freud's emphasis on the unconscious, on instinctual drives, and on the importance of sexuality. Adler believed that we are social creatures governed by social urges, not by biological instincts. In Adler's view, the main driving force in personality is a **striving for superiority.** This striving, he said, is a struggle to overcome imperfections, an upward drive for competence, completion, and mastery of shortcomings.

What motivates "striving for superiority"? Adler believed that everyone experiences feelings of inferiority. This occurs mainly because we begin life as small, weak, and relatively powerless children surrounded by larger and more powerful adults. Feelings of inferiority may also come from our personal limitations. The struggle for superiority arises from such feelings.

Although everyone strives for superiority, each person tries to **compensate** for different limitations, and each chooses a different pathway to superiority. Adler believed that this situation creates a unique **style of life** (or personality pattern) for each individual. According to Adler, the core of each person's style of life is formed by age 5. (Adler also believed that valuable clues to a person's style of life are revealed by the earliest memory that can be recalled. You might find it interesting to search back to your earliest memory and contemplate what it tells you.) However, later in his life Adler began to emphasize the existence of a **creative self.** By this, he meant that humans create their personalities through choices and experiences.

Karen Horney (1885–1952)

Karen Horney (HORN-eye) remained faithful to most of Freud's theory, but she resisted his more mechanistic, biological, and instinctive ideas. For example, as a woman, Horney rejected Freud's claim that "anatomy is destiny." This view, woven into Freudian psychology, held that males are dominant or superior to females. Horney was among the first to challenge the obvious male bias in Freud's thinking.

Horney also disagreed with Freud about the causes of neurosis. Freud held that neurotic (anxiety-ridden) individuals are struggling with forbidden id drives that they fear they cannot control. Horney's view was that a core of **basic anxiety** occurs when people feel isolated and helpless in a hostile world. These feelings, she believed, are rooted in childhood. Trouble occurs when an individual tries to control basic anxiety by exaggerating a single mode of interacting with others.

What do you mean by "mode of interacting"? According to Horney, each of us can move toward others (by depending on them for love, support, or friendship), we can move away from others (by withdrawing, acting like a "loner," or being "strong" and independent), or we can move against others (by attacking, competing with, or seeking power over them). Horney believed that emotional health reflects a balance in moving toward, away from, and against others. In her view, emotional problems tend to lock people into overuse of one of the three modes—an insight that remains valuable today.

Carl Jung (1875–1961)

Carl Jung was a student of Freud's, but the two parted ways as Jung began to develop his own ideas. Like Freud, Jung called the conscious part of the personality the ego. However, he further noted that a *persona*, or "mask," exists between the ego and the outside world. The **persona** is the "public self" presented to others. It is most apparent when we adopt particular roles or hide our deeper feelings. As mentioned earlier, Jung believed that actions of the ego may reflect attitudes of introversion (in which energy is mainly directed inward) or of extroversion (in which energy is mainly directed outward).

Was Jung's view of the unconscious the same as Freud's? Jung used the term *personal unconscious* to refer to what Freud simply called the unconscious. The **personal unconscious** is a mental storehouse for a single individual's experiences, feelings, and memories. But Jung also described a deeper **collective unconscious,** or mental storehouse for unconscious ideas and images shared by all humans. Jung believed that, from the beginning of time, all humans have had experiences with birth, death, power, god figures, mother and father figures, animals, the earth, energy, evil, rebirth, and so on. According to Jung, such universals create **archetypes** (AR-KEH-types: original ideas, images, or patterns).

Neo-Freudian *A psychologist who has revised Freud's theory, while still accepting some of its basic features.*

Striving for superiority *According to Adler, this basic drive propels us toward perfection.*

Compensation *Any attempt to overcome feelings of inadequacy or inferiority.*

Style of life *The pattern of personality and behavior that defines the pathway each person takes through life.*

Creative self *The "artist" in each of us that creates a unique identity and style of life.*

Basic anxiety *A primary form of anxiety that arises from living in a hostile world.*

Persona *The "mask" or public self presented to others.*

Personal unconscious *A mental storehouse for a single individual's unconscious thoughts.*

Collective unconscious *A mental storehouse for unconscious ideas and images shared by all humans.*

Archetype *A universal idea, image, or pattern, found in the collective unconscious.*

Archetypes, found in the collective unconscious, are unconscious images that cause us to respond emotionally to symbols of birth, death, energy, animals, evil, and the like (Maloney, 1999). Jung believed that he detected symbols of such archetypes in the art, religion, myths, and dreams of every culture and age. Let us say, for instance, that a man dreams of dancing with his sister. To Freud, this would probably be a sign of hidden incestuous feelings. To Jung, the image of the sister might represent an unexpressed feminine side of the man's personality, and the dream might represent the cosmic dance that intertwines "maleness" and "femaleness" in all lives.

Are some archetypes more important than others? Two particularly important archetypes are the **anima** (female principle) and the **animus** (male principle). In men, the anima is an unconscious, idealized image of women. This image is based, in part, on real experiences with women (the man's mother, sister, friends). However, the experiences men have had with women throughout history form the true core of the anima. The reverse is true of women, who possess an animus, or idealized image of men. The anima in males and the animus in females enable us to relate to members of the opposite sex. The anima and animus also make it possible for people to learn to express both "masculine" and "feminine" sides of their personalities.

Jung regarded the *self archetype* as the most important of all. The **self archetype** represents unity. Its existence causes a gradual movement toward balance, wholeness, and harmony within the personality. Jung felt that we become richer and more completely human when a balance is achieved between the conscious and unconscious, the anima and animus, thinking and feeling, sensing and intuiting, the persona and the ego, introversion and extroversion.

Was Jung talking about self-actualization? Essentially, he was. Jung was the first to use the term *self-actualization* to describe a striving for completion and unity. He believed that the self archetype is symbolized in every culture by **mandalas** (magic circles) of one kind or another.

Jung regarded circular designs as symbols of the self archetype and representations of unity, balance, and completion within the personality.

Jung's theory may not be scientific, but clearly he was a man of genius and vision. If you would like to know more about Jung and his ideas, a good starting place is his autobiography, *Memories, Dreams, Reflections.*

LEARNING THEORIES OF PERSONALITY—HABIT I SEEN YOU BEFORE?

How do behaviorists approach personality? According to some critics, as if people were robots like R2D2 of *Star Wars* fame. Actually, the behaviorist position is not nearly that mechanistic, and its value is well established. Behaviorists have shown repeatedly that children can *learn* things like kindness, hostility, generosity, or destructiveness. What does this have to do with personality? Everything, according to the behavioral viewpoint.

Behavioral personality theories emphasize that personality is no more (or less) than a collection of learned behavior patterns. Personality, like other learned behavior, is acquired through classical and operant conditioning, observational learning, reinforcement, extinction, generalization, and discrimination. When Mother says, "It's not nice to make mud pies with Mommy's blender. If we want to grow up to be a big girl, we won't do it again, will we?" she serves as a model and in other ways shapes her daughter's personality.

Strict **learning theorists** reject the idea that personality is made up of traits. They would assert, for instance, that there is no such thing as a trait of "honesty" (Bandura, 1973; Mischel, 1968).

Certainly, some people are honest, and others are not. How can honesty not be a trait? A learning theorist would agree that some people are honest *more often* than others. But knowing this does not allow us to predict for certain whether a person will be honest in a specific situation. It would not be unusual, for example, to find that a person honored for returning a lost wallet had cheated on a test, bought a term paper, or broken the speed limit. If you were to ask a learning theorist, "Are you an honest person?" the reply might be "In what situation?"

A good example of how situations influence behavior is shown in ❖Figure 15.7. The graphs give the results of a role-playing experiment in which college students had to ask a professor for an extension on an assigned paper. For some students, the paper was worth 15 percent of their final grade; for others, it was worth 75 percent. Each student was assigned one of three reasons why the paper was late: They had a hangover, had too much work to do, or had the flu. The students were then sent in to plead their cases. As ❖Figure 15.7 shows, most students lied about why their paper was late when they had an illegitimate excuse (a hangover) and the paper was critical to their grade. When their excuse was legitimate (the flu), none lied (Greene & Saxe, 1990). In another study, people were intentionally overpaid for doing an assigned task. Under normal circumstances, 80 percent kept the extra money without saying anything about it. But as few as 17 percent were

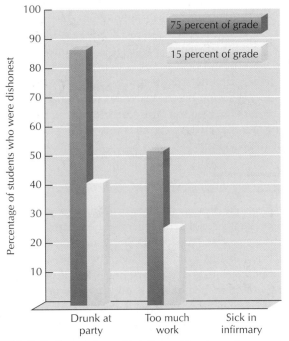

❖ **FIGURE 15.7** *Honesty is greatly influenced by circumstances. Many students were dishonest when the true reason for wanting an extension on an overdue paper was a poor excuse ("drunk at party"). Fewer were dishonest when the excuse was semi-legitimate ("too much work"), and none lied when their excuse was legitimate ("sick in infirmary"). The importance of the paper for a course grade also influenced honesty. (Data from Greene & Saxe, 1990.)*

Freud believed that aggressive urges are "instinctual." In contrast, behavioral theories assume that personal characteristics such as aggressiveness are learned. Is this boy's aggression the result of observational learning, harsh punishment, or prior reinforcement?

Anima *An archetype representing the female principle.*
Animus *An archetype representing the male principle.*
Self archetype *An unconscious image representing unity, wholeness, completion, and balance.*
Mandala *A circular design representing balance, unity, and completion.*
Behavioral personality theory *Any model of personality that emphasizes learning and observable behavior.*
Learning theorist *A psychologist interested in the ways that learning shapes behavior and explains personality.*

dishonest if the situation was restructured. For instance, if people thought the money was coming out of the pocket of the person doing the study, far fewer were dishonest (Bersoff, 1999).

As you can see, learning theorists are interested in the **situational determinants** (external causes) of our actions. However, this does not entirely remove the person from the picture. Situations always interact with a person's prior learning history to activate behavior.

Situations vary greatly in their impact. Some are powerful. Others are trivial and have little effect on behavior. The more powerful the situation, the easier it is to see what is meant by situational determinants. For example, each of the following situations would undoubtedly have a strong influence on behavior: An escaped lion walks into a supermarket; you accidentally sit on a lighted cigarette; you find your lover in bed with your best friend. Yet even these situations could provoke very different reactions from different personalities. That's why behavior is always a product of both prior learning and the situations in which people find themselves (Mischel & Shoda, 1998).

As discussed earlier, trait theorists also believe that situations affect behavior. But in their view, situations interact with *traits*, rather than a person's learning history. So, in essence, learning theorists favor replacing "traits" with "prior learning" to explain behavior.

Personality = Behavior

How do learning theorists view the structure of personality? The behavioral view of personality can be illustrated with an early theory proposed by John Dollard and Neal Miller (1950). In their view, **habits** (learned behavior patterns) make up the structure of personality. As for the dynamics of personality, Dollard and Miller believe that habits are governed by four elements of learning: *drive, cue, response,* and *reward.* A **drive** is any stimulus strong enough to goad a person to action (such as hunger, pain, lust, frustration, or fear). **Cues** are signals from the environment. These signals guide **responses** (actions) so that they are most likely to bring about **reward** (positive reinforcement).

How does that relate to personality? Let's say a child named Kindra is frustrated by her older brother Kelvin, who takes a toy from her. Kindra could respond in several ways: She could throw a temper tantrum, hit Kelvin, tell Mother, and so forth. The response she chooses is guided by available cues and the previous effects of each response. If telling Mother has paid off in the past, and the mother is present, telling again may be her immediate response. If a different set of cues exists (if Mother is absent or if Kelvin looks particularly menacing), Kindra may select some other response. To an outside observer, Kindra's actions seem to reflect her personality. To the learning theorist, they are a direct reaction to the combined effects of drive, cue, response, and reward.

Doesn't this analysis leave out a lot? Yes. Learning theorists first set out to provide a simple, clear model of personality. But

BRIDGES

Behavioral theories have contributed greatly to the creation of therapies for various psychological problems and disorders.

See Chapter 18, pages 605–612.

in recent years, they have had to face a fact that they originally tended to overlook: People think. The new breed of behavioral psychologists—who include perception, thinking, expectations, and other mental events in their views—are called social learning theorists. Learning principles, modeling, thought patterns, perceptions, expectations, beliefs, goals, emotions, and social relationships are combined in **social learning theory** to explain personality (Mischel & Shoda, 1998).

Social Learning Theory

The "cognitive behaviorism" of social learning theory can be illustrated by three concepts proposed by Julian Rotter: the *psychological situation, expectancy,* and *reinforcement value* (Rotter & Hochreich, 1975). Let's examine each.

Someone trips you. How do you respond? Your response probably depends on whether you think it was planned or an accident. It is not enough to know the setting in which a person responds. We also need to know the person's **psychological situation** (how the person interprets or defines the situation). As another example, let's say you score low on an exam. Do you consider it a challenge to work harder, a sign that you should drop the class, or an excuse to get drunk? Again, your interpretation is important.

An **expectancy** refers to your anticipation that making a response will lead to reinforcement. To continue the example, if working harder has paid off in the past, it is a likely reaction to a low test score. But to predict your response, we would also have to know if you *expect* your efforts to pay off in the present situation. In fact, expected reinforcement may be more important than actual past reinforcement. And what about the *value* you attach to grades, school success, or personal ability? Rotter's third concept, **reinforcement value,** states that humans attach different subjective values to various activities or rewards. This, too, must be taken into account to understand personality.

Through self-reinforcement, we reward ourselves for personal achievements and other "good" behavior.

One more idea deserves mention. At times, we all evaluate our actions and may reward ourselves with special privileges or treats for "good behavior." With this in mind, social learning theory adds the concept of *self-reinforcement* to the behavioristic view. **Self-reinforcement** refers to praising or rewarding oneself for having made a particular response (such as completing a school assignment). Thus, habits of self-praise and self-blame become an important part of personality. In fact, self-reinforcement can be thought of as the behaviorist's counterpart to the superego. To find out how self-reinforcement affects your behavior, check the items in the following scale that apply to you:

RATE YOURSELF

BEING GOOD TO YOURSELF
- I often think positive thoughts about myself.
- I frequently meet standards that I set for myself.
- I try not to blame myself when things go wrong.
- I usually don't get upset when I make mistakes because I learn from them.
- I can get satisfaction out of what I do even if it's not perfect.
- When I make mistakes, I take time to reassure myself.
- I don't think talking about what you've done right is too boastful.
- Praising yourself is healthy and normal.
- I don't think I have to be upset every time I make a mistake.
- My feelings of self-confidence and self-esteem stay pretty steady.

People who agree with most of these statements tend to have high rates of self-reinforcement (Heiby, 1983).

As the last item suggests, self-reinforcement is related to high self-esteem. The reverse is also true: Mildly depressed college students tend to have low rates of self-reinforcement. It is not known if low self-reinforcement leads to depression, or the reverse. In either case, self-reinforcement is associated with less depression and greater life satisfaction (Seybolt & Wagner, 1997; Wilkinson, 1997). From a behavioral viewpoint, there is value in learning to be "good to yourself."

Behavioristic View of Development

How do learning theorists account for personality development? Many of Freud's ideas can be restated in terms of learning theory. Miller and Dollard (1950) agree with Freud that the first 6 years are crucial for personality development, but for different reasons. Rather than thinking in terms of psychosexual urges and fixations, they ask, "What makes early learning experiences so lasting in their effects?" Their answer is that childhood is a time of urgent and tearing drives, powerful rewards and punishments, and crushing frustrations. Also important is **social reinforcement,** which is based on praise, attention, or approval from others. These forces combine to shape the core of personality.

CRITICAL SITUATIONS   Miller and Dollard believe that during childhood four **critical situations** are capable of leaving a lasting imprint on personality. These are (1) feeding, (2) toilet or

cleanliness training, (3) sex training, and (4) learning to express anger or aggression.

Why are these of special importance?   Feeding serves as an illustration. If children are fed when they cry, it encourages them to actively manipulate their parents. The child allowed to cry without being fed learns to be passive. Thus, a basic active or passive orientation toward the world may be created by early feeding experiences. Feeding can also affect later social relationships because the child learns to associate people with satisfaction and pleasure or with frustration and discomfort.

Toilet and cleanliness training can be a particularly strong source of emotion for both parents and children. Rashad's parents were aghast the day they found him smearing feces about with gay abandon. They reacted to this with sharp punishment, which frustrated and confused Rashad. Many attitudes toward cleanliness, conformity, and bodily functions are formed at such times. Studies also show that severe, punishing, or frustrating toilet training can have undesirable effects on personality development (Sears et al., 1957). Toilet and cleanliness training therefore demand patience and a sense of humor.

What about sex and anger?   When, where, and how a child learns to express anger and aggression is of obvious importance. So, too, is expression of sexual behavior. Both types of experiences can leave an imprint on personality. Specifically, permissiveness for sexual and aggressive behavior in childhood is linked to adult needs for power (McClelland & Pilon, 1983). This link probably occurs because permitting such behaviors allows children to get pleasure from asserting themselves.

Sex training also involves learning "male" and "female" behaviors—which creates an even broader basis for shaping personality.

BECOMING MALE OR FEMALE   From birth onward, children are labeled as boys or girls and encouraged to learn sex-appropriate behavior. According to social learning theory, identification and imitation contribute greatly to personality development

Situational determinants *External conditions that strongly influence behavior.*
Habit *A deeply ingrained, learned pattern of behavior.*
Drive *Any stimulus (especially an internal stimulus such as hunger) strong enough to goad a person to action.*
Cue *External stimuli that guide responses, especially by signaling the presence or absence of reinforcement.*
Response *Any behavior, either observable or internal.*
Reward *Anything that produces pleasure or satisfaction; a positive reinforcer.*
Social learning theory *An explanation of personality that combines learning principles, cognition, and the effects of social relationships.*
Psychological situation *A situation as it is perceived and interpreted by an individual, not as it exists objectively.*
Expectancy *Anticipation about the effect a response will have, especially regarding reinforcement.*
Reinforcement value *The subjective value a person attaches to a particular activity or reinforcer.*
Self-reinforcement *Praising or rewarding yourself for having made a particular response (such as completing a school assignment).*
Social reinforcement *Praise, attention, approval, and/or affection from others.*
Critical situations *Situations during childhood that are capable of leaving a lasting imprint on personality.*

and to sex training. **Identification** refers to the child's emotional attachment to admired adults, especially those who provide love and care. Identification typically encourages **imitation,** a desire to act like the admired person. Many "male" or "female" traits come from children's attempts to imitate a same-sex parent with whom they identify.

If children are around parents of both sexes, why don't they imitate behavior typical of the opposite sex as well as of the same sex? You may recall from Chapter 9 that Albert Bandura and others have shown that learning takes place vicariously as well as directly. This means that we can learn without direct reward by observing and remembering the actions of others. But the actions we choose to imitate depend on their outcomes. For example, boys and girls have equal chances to observe adults and other children acting aggressively. However, girls are less likely than boys to imitate aggressive behavior because they rarely see female aggression rewarded or approved. Thus, many arbitrary "male" and "female" qualities are passed on at the same time sexual identity is learned.

A study of preschool children found that teachers are three times more likely to pay attention to aggressive or disruptive boys than to girls acting the same way. Boys who hit other students or who broke things typically got loud scoldings. This made them the center of attention for the whole class. When teachers responded to disruptive girls, they gave brief, soft rebukes that others couldn't hear (Serbin & O'Leary, 1975). We know that attention of almost any kind reinforces children's behavior. Therefore, it is clear that the boys were being encouraged to be active and aggressive. Girls got the most attention when they were within arm's reach, more or less clinging to the teacher.

The pattern just described grows stronger throughout elementary school. In all grades, boys are louder, faster, and more boisterous than girls. Day after day, boys receive a disproportionate amount of the teacher's attention (Sadker & Sadker, 1994).

It's easy to see that teachers unwittingly encourage girls to be submissive, dependent, and passive. Similar differences in reinforcement probably explain why males are responsible for much more aggression in society than females are. By age 10, boys expect to get less disapproval from parents for aggression than girls do. This is especially true if the aggression is provoked by another boy (Perry, Perry, & Weiss, 1989). Among adults, rates of murder and assault are consistently higher for men. The roots of this difference appear to lie in childhood.

Adult personality is influenced by identification with parents.

KNOWLEDGE BUILDER
BEHAVIORAL AND SOCIAL LEARNING THEORIES

RELATE

What is your favorite type of food? Can you relate Miller and Dollard's concepts of habit, drive, cue, response, and reward to explain your preference?

Some people love to shop. Others hate it. How have the psychological situation, expectancy, and reinforcement value affected your willingness to "shop till you drop"?

Whom did you identify with as a child? What aspects of that person's behavior did you imitate?

LEARNING CHECK

1. Learning theorists believe that personality "traits" really are
   _____ acquired through prior learning.
   They also emphasize _____ determinants
   of behavior.

2. Dollard and Miller consider cues the basic structure of personality. T or F?

3. To explain behavior, social learning theorists include mental elements, such as _____ (the anticipation that a response will lead to reinforcement).

4. Self-reinforcement is to behavioristic theory as superego is to psychoanalytic theory. T or F?

5. Which of the following is *not* a "critical situation" in the behaviorist theory of personality development?
   a. feeding *b.* sex training *c.* language training *d.* anger training

6. In addition to basic rewards and punishments, a child's personality is also shaped by _____ reinforcement.

7. Social learning theories of development emphasize the impact of identification and _____.

CRITICAL THINKING

8. Julian Rotter's concept of *reinforcement value* is closely related to a motivational principle discussed in Chapter 13. Can you name it?

Answers:

1. habits, situational 2. F 3. expectancies 4. T 5. c 6. social 7. imitation
8. incentive value

HUMANISTIC THEORY—PEAK EXPERIENCES AND PERSONAL GROWTH

Humanism focuses on human experience, problems, potentials, and ideals. It is a reaction to the static quality of trait theories, the pessimism of psychoanalytic theory, and the mechanical nature of learning theory. At its core is a positive image of what it means to be human. Humanists reject the Freudian view of personality as a battleground for instincts and unconscious forces. Instead, they view human nature as inherently good. (**Human nature** consists of the traits, qualities, potentials, and behavior patterns most characteristic of the human species.) Humanists also oppose the mechanical, "thing-like" overtones of the behaviorist viewpoint. We are not, they say, merely a bundle of moldable responses. Rather, we are creative beings capable of **free choice** (an ability to choose that is not controlled by genetics, learning, or unconscious forces). In short, humanists seek ways to encourage our potentials to blossom.

To a humanist, the person you are today is largely the product of all the choices you have made. The humanistic viewpoint also emphasizes immediate **subjective experience** (private perceptions of reality), rather than prior learning. Humanists believe that there are as many "real worlds" as there are people. To understand behavior, we must learn how a person subjectively views the world—what is "real" for her or him.

Who are the major humanistic theorists? Many psychologists have added to the humanistic tradition. Of these, the best known are Carl Rogers (1902–1987) and Abraham Maslow (1908–1970). Because Maslow's idea of self-actualization was introduced in Chapter 1, let's begin with a more detailed look at this facet of his thinking.

Maslow and Self-Actualization

Abraham Maslow became interested in people who were living unusually effective lives. How were they different? To find an answer, Maslow began by studying the lives of great men and women, such as Albert Einstein, William James, Jane Addams, Eleanor Roosevelt, Abraham Lincoln, John Muir, and Walt Whitman. From there, he moved on to directly study living artists, writers, poets, and other creative individuals.

Along the way, Maslow's thinking changed radically. At first, he studied only people of obvious creativity or high achievement. However, it eventually became clear that a housewife, carpenter, clerk, or student could be living a rich, creative, and satisfying life. Maslow referred to the process of fully developing personal potentials as **self-actualization** (Maslow, 1954). The heart of self-actualization is a continuous search for personal fulfillment (Sumerlin, 1997).

CHARACTERISTICS OF SELF-ACTUALIZERS A **self-actualizer** is a person who is living creatively and fully using his or her potentials. In his studies, Maslow found that self-actualizers share many similarities. Whether famous or unknown, well schooled or uneducated, rich or poor, self-actualizers tend to fit the following profile.

1. **Efficient perceptions of reality.** Self-actualizers are able to judge situations correctly and honestly. They are very sensitive to the fake and dishonest.
2. **Comfortable acceptance of self, others, nature.** Self-actualizers accept their own human nature with all its flaws. The shortcomings of others and the contradictions of the human condition are accepted with humor and tolerance.
3. **Spontaneity.** Maslow's subjects extended their creativity into everyday activities. Actualizers tend to be unusually alive, engaged, and spontaneous.
4. **Task centering.** Most of Maslow's subjects had a mission to fulfill in life or some task or problem outside of themselves to pursue. Humanitarians such as Albert Schweitzer and Mother Teresa represent this quality.
5. **Autonomy.** Self-actualizers are free from reliance on external authorities or other people. They tend to be resourceful and independent.
6. **Continued freshness of appreciation.** The self-actualizer seems to constantly renew appreciation of life's basic goods. A sunset or a flower will be experienced as intensely time after time as it was at first. There is an "innocence of vision," like that of an artist or child.
7. **Fellowship with humanity.** Maslow's subjects felt a deep identification with others and the human situation in general.
8. **Profound interpersonal relationships.** The interpersonal relationships of self-actualizers are marked by deep, loving bonds.
9. **Comfort with solitude.** Despite their satisfying relationships with others, self-actualizing people value solitude and are comfortable being alone (Sumerlin & Bundrick, 1996).
10. **Nonhostile sense of humor.** This refers to the wonderful capacity to laugh at oneself. It also describes the kind of humor a man like Abraham Lincoln had. Lincoln probably never made a joke that hurt anybody. His wry comments were a gentle prodding of human shortcomings.
11. **Peak experiences.** All of Maslow's subjects reported the frequent occurrence of **peak experiences** (temporary

Identification *Feeling emotionally connected to a person and seeing oneself as like him or her.*
Imitation *An attempt to match one's own behavior to another person's behavior.*
Humanism *An approach that focuses on human experience, problems, potentials, and ideals.*
Human nature *Those traits, qualities, potentials, and behavior patterns most characteristic of the human species.*
Free choice *The ability to freely make choices that are not controlled by genetics, learning, or unconscious forces.*
Subjective experience *Reality as it is perceived and interpreted, not as it exists objectively.*
Self-actualization *The process of fully developing personal potentials.*
Self-actualizer *One who is living creatively and making full use of his or her potentials.*
Peak experiences *Temporary moments of self-actualization.*

moments of self-actualization). These occasions were marked by feelings of ecstasy, harmony, and deep meaning. Self-actualizers reported feeling at one with the universe, stronger and calmer than ever before, and filled with light, beautiful, and good.

In summary, self-actualizers feel safe, nonanxious, accepted, loved, loving, and alive.

Maslow's choice of self-actualizing people for study seems pretty subjective. Is it really a fair representation of self-actualization? Although Maslow tried to investigate self-actualization empirically, his choice of people for study was subjective. Undoubtedly, there are many ways to make full use of personal potential. Maslow's primary contribution was to draw attention to the possibility of lifelong personal growth.

What steps can be taken to promote self-actualization? Maslow made few specific recommendations about how to proceed. Nevertheless, some helpful suggestions can be gleaned from his writings (Maslow, 1954, 1967, 1971). See "Steps toward Self-Actualization."

Carl Rogers's Self Theory

Like Freud, Carl Rogers based his theory on clinical experience. Unlike Freud, who portrayed the normal personality as "adjusted" to internal conflict, Rogers saw a greater possibility for inner harmony. The **fully functioning person,** he said, lives in harmony with her or his deepest feelings and impulses. Such people are open to their experiences, and they trust their inner urges and intuitions (Rogers, 1961). Rogers believed that this attitude is most likely to occur when a person receives ample amounts of love and acceptance from others.

PERSONALITY STRUCTURE AND DYNAMICS   Rogers's theory emphasizes the **self,** a flexible and changing perception of personal identity. The self is made up of experiences that fit our self-perceptions. It tends to exclude experiences that are labeled "not-me." Much human behavior can be understood as an attempt to maintain consistency between our *self-image* and our actions. (**Self-image** is your total subjective perception of your body and personality.) For example, individuals who think of themselves as kind will act with consideration in most situations.

Let's say I know a person who thinks she is kind, but she really isn't. How does that fit Rogers's theory? According to Rogers, experiences that match the self-image are **symbolized** (admitted to awareness) and contribute to gradual changes in the self. Information or feelings inconsistent with the self-image are said to be incon-

BRIDGES

Rogers and other humanistic theorists believe that some psychological disorders are caused by a faulty or incongruent self-image.

See Chapter 17, page 570.

USING PSYCHOLOGY

STEPS TOWARD SELF-ACTUALIZATION

There is no magic formula for leading a more creative life. Self-actualization is primarily a *process,* not a goal or an end-point. As such, it requires hard work, patience, and commitment. Here are some ways to begin.

1. **Be willing to change.** Begin by asking yourself, "Am I living in a way that is deeply satisfying to me and that truly expresses me?" If not, be prepared to make changes in your life. Indeed, ask yourself this question often, and accept the need for continual change.

2. **Take responsibility.** You can become an architect of self by acting as if you are personally responsible for every aspect of your life. Shouldering responsibility in this way helps end the habit of blaming others for your own shortcomings.

3. **Examine your motives.** Self-discovery involves an element of risk. If your behavior is restricted by a desire for safety or security, it may be time to test some limits. Try to make each life decision a choice for growth, not a response to fear or anxiety.

4. **Experience honestly and directly.** Wishful thinking is another barrier to personal growth. Self-actualizers trust themselves enough to accept all kinds of information without distorting it to fit their fears and desires. Try to see yourself as others do. Be willing to admit "I was wrong" or, "I failed because I was irresponsible."

5. **Make use of positive experiences.** Maslow considered peak experiences temporary moments of self-actualization. Therefore, you might actively repeat activities that have caused feelings of awe, amazement, exaltation, renewal, reverence, humility, fulfillment, or joy.

6. **Be prepared to be different.** Maslow felt that everyone has a potential for "greatness," but most fear becoming what they might. As part of personal growth, be prepared to trust your own impulses and feelings; don't automatically judge yourself by the standards of others. Accept your uniqueness.

7. **Get involved.** With few exceptions, self-actualizers tend to have a mission or "calling" in life. For these people, "work" is not done just to fill deficiency needs but to satisfy higher yearnings for truth, beauty, community, and meaning. Get personally involved and committed. Turn your attention to problems outside yourself.

8. **Assess your progress.** There is no final point at which one becomes self-actualized. It's important to gauge your progress frequently and to renew your efforts. If you feel bored at school, at a job, or in a relationship, consider it a challenge. Have you been taking responsibility for your own personal growth? Almost any activity can be used as a chance for self-enhancement if it is approached creatively.

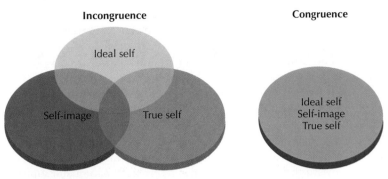

Incongruence | Congruence

Ideal self

Self-image | True self

Ideal self
Self-image
True self

❖ **FIGURE 15.8** *Incongruence occurs when there is a mismatch between any of these three entities: the ideal self (the person you would like to be), your self-image (the person you think you are), and the true self (the person you actually are). Self-esteem suffers when there is a large difference between one's ideal self and self-image. Anxiety and defensiveness are common when the self-image does not match the true self.*

Humanists consider self-image a central determinant of behavior and personal adjustment.

gruent. Thus, a state of **incongruence** exists when there is a discrepancy between people's experiences and their self-images. It is incongruent, for example, to think of yourself as a considerate person if others frequently mention your rudeness. It is also incongruent to pretend you are kind when you are feeling callous or to say you are not angry when you are seething inside.

Experiences seriously incongruent with the self-image can be threatening, and they are often distorted or denied conscious recognition. Blocking, denying, or distorting experiences prevents the self from changing. This creates a gulf between the self-image and reality. As the self-image grows more unrealistic, the **incongruent person** becomes confused, vulnerable, dissatisfied, or seriously maladjusted (❖Fig. 15.8). In line with Rogers's observations, a study of college students confirmed that being *authentic* is vital for healthy functioning. That is, we need to feel that

our behavior accurately expresses who we are (Sheldon et al., 1997). Please note, however, that being authentic doesn't mean you can do whatever you want. Being true to yourself is no excuse for acting irresponsibly or ignoring the feelings of others.

When your self-image is consistent with what you really think, feel, do, and experience, you are best able to actualize your potentials. Rogers also considered it essential to have congruence between the self-image and the **ideal self.** The ideal self is similar to Freud's ego ideal. It is an image of the person you would most like to be.

Is it really incongruent not to live up to one's ideal self? Rogers was aware that we never fully attain our ideals. Nevertheless, the greater the gap between the way you see yourself and the way you would like to be, the more tension and anxiety you will experience.

Rogers emphasized that, to maximize our potentials, we must accept information about ourselves as honestly as possible. In accord with his thinking, researchers have found that people with a close match between their self-image and ideal self tend to be socially poised, confident, and resourceful. Those with a poor match tend to be depressed, anxious, and insecure (Alfeld-Liro & Sigelman, 1998; Scott & O'Hara, 1993). (See "Possible Selves" for another perspective on the ways in which self-image can influence our behavior.)

Humanistic View of Development

Why do mirrors, photographs, video cameras, and the reactions of others hold such fascination and threat for many people? Carl Rogers's theory suggests it is because they provide information about one's self. The development of a self-image depends greatly on information from the environment. It

---

Fully functioning person *A person living in harmony with her or his deepest feelings, impulses, and intuitions.*
Self *A continuously evolving conception of one's personal identity.*
Self-image *Total subjective perception of one's body and personality (another term for self-concept).*
Symbolization *The process of admitting an experience to awareness.*
Incongruence *State that exists when there is a discrepancy between one's experiences and self-image or between one's self-image and ideal self.*
Incongruent person *A person who has an inaccurate self-image or whose self-image differs greatly from the ideal self.*
Ideal self *An idealized image of oneself (the person one would like to be).*

POSSIBLE SELVES—TRYING ON A SELF FOR SIZE

Your ideal self is only one of many personal identities you may have pondered. Psychologists Hazel Markus and Paula Nurius (1986) believe that each of us harbors images of many **possible selves** (persons one could become). These selves include the person we would most like to be (the ideal self), as well as other selves we could become or are afraid of becoming.

Possible selves translate our hopes, fears, fantasies, and goals into specific images of who we *could* be. Thus, a beginning law student might picture herself as a successful attorney, the husband in a troubled marriage might picture himself as a divorcé, and a person on a diet might imagine both slim and grossly obese possible selves. Such self-images tend to direct future behavior. They also give meaning to current behavior and help us evaluate it. For example, the unhappy spouse might be moved by upsetting images of his "divorcé self" to try saving the marriage.

Even day-to-day decisions may be guided by possible selves. Purchasing clothes, a car, cologne, membership in a health club, and the like may be influenced by images of a valued future self. Of course, identities are not all equally possible. As Markus and Nurius point out, almost everyone over age 30 has probably felt the anguish of realizing that some cherished possible selves will never be realized.

begins with a sorting of perceptions and feelings: my body, my toes, my nose, I want, I like, I am, and so on. Soon, it expands to include self-evaluation: I am a good person, I did something bad just now, and so forth.

How does development of the self contribute to later personality functioning? Rogers believed that others' positive and negative evaluations cause children to develop internal standards of evaluation he called **conditions of worth.** In other words, we learn that some actions win our parents' love and approval whereas others are rejected. More important, parents often label many of a child's *feelings* as bad or wrong. For example, a child might be told that it is wrong to feel angry toward a brother or sister—even when anger is justified. Likewise, a little boy might be told that he must not cry or be afraid, two very normal emotions.

Learning to evaluate some experiences or feelings as "good" and others as "bad" is directly related to a later capacity for self-esteem, positive self-evaluation, or **positive self-regard,** to use Rogers's term. To think of yourself as a good, lovable, worthwhile person, your behavior and experiences must match your internal conditions of worth. The problem is that this can cause incongruence by leading to the denial of many true feelings and experiences.

To put it simply, Rogers blamed many adult emotional problems on attempts to live by the standards of others. He believed that congruence and self-actualization are encouraged by replacing conditions of worth with **organismic valuing** (a natural, undistorted, full-body reaction to an experience). Organ-

ismic valuing is a direct, gut-level response to life that avoids the filtering and distortion of incongruence. It involves trusting one's own feelings and perceptions and being one's own "locus of evaluation." Organismic valuing is most likely to develop, Rogers felt, when children (or adults) receive **unconditional positive regard** (unshakable love and approval) from others. That is, when they are "prized" as worthwhile human beings, just for being themselves, without any conditions or strings attached. Although this may be a luxury few people enjoy, a recent study confirmed that people are more likely to move toward their ideal selves if they receive affirmation and support from a close partner (Drigotas et al., 1999).

KNOWLEDGE BUILDER

HUMANISTIC THEORY

RELATE

How do your views of human nature and free choice compare with those of the humanists?

Do you know anyone who seems to be making especially good use of her or his personal potentials? Does that person fit Maslow's profile of a self-actualizer?

How much difference do you think there is between your self-image, your ideal self, and your true self? Do you think Rogers is right about the effects of applying conditions of worth to your perceptions and feelings?

LEARNING CHECK

1. Humanists view human nature as basically good, and they emphasize the effects of subjective learning and unconscious choice. T or F?

2. Maslow used the term _____ to describe the tendency of certain individuals to fully use their talents and potentials.

3. According to Rogers, a close match between the self-image and the ideal self creates a condition called incongruence. T or F?

4. Markus and Nurius describe alternative self-concepts that a person may have as "possible selves." T or F?

5. Rogers's theory considers acceptance of conditions of _____ a troublesome aspect of development of the self.

6. According to Maslow, a preoccupation with one's own thoughts, feelings, and needs is characteristic of self-actualizing individuals. T or F?

7. Maslow regarded _____ experiences as times of temporary self-actualization.

CRITICAL THINKING

8. What role would "possible selves" have in the choice of a college major?

Answers:

1. F 2. self-actualization 3. F 4. T 5. worth 6. F 7. peak 8. Career decisions almost always involve, in part, picturing oneself occupying various occupational roles.

◆ TABLE 15.3 Comparison of Four Views of Personality

	TRAIT THEORIES	PSYCHOANALYTIC THEORY	BEHAVIORISTIC THEORY	HUMANISTIC THEORY
View of human nature	neutral	negative	neutral	positive
Is behavior free or determined?	determined	determined	determined	free choice
Principal motives	depends on one's traits	sex and aggression	drives of all kinds	self-actualization
Personality structure	traits	id, ego, superego	habits	self
Role of unconscious	minimized	maximized	practically nonexistent	minimized
Conception of conscience	traits of honesty, etc.	superego	self-reinforcement punishment history	ideal self, valuing process
Developmental emphasis	combined effects of heredity and environment	psychosexual stages	critical learning situations identification and imitation	development of self-image
Barriers to personal growth	unhealthy traits	unconscious conflicts, fixations	maladaptive habits; unhealthy environment	conditions of worth; incongruence

PERSONALITY THEORIES—OVERVIEW AND COMPARISON

Which personality theory is right?   Although each theory has added to our understanding, no theory can be fully proved or disproved. We can only ask, Does the evidence support this theory or disconfirm it? Thus, it is best to judge a theory in terms of its *usefulness.* Does the theory adequately predict and explain behavior? Does it stimulate new research? Does it suggest how to treat psychological disorders? Each theory has fared differently in these areas.

TRAIT THEORIES   Traits are very useful for describing and comparing personalities. Many of the personality tests used by clinical psychologists are based on trait theories. However, trait theories tend to have a circular quality. For example, how do we know that a young woman named Carrie has the trait of shyness? Because we frequently observe Carrie avoiding conversations with others. And why doesn't Carrie socialize with others? Because shyness is a trait of her personality. And how do we know she has the trait of shyness? Because we observe that she avoids socializing with others. And so on.

PSYCHOANALYTIC THEORY   By present standards, psychoanalytic theory seems to overemphasize sexuality and biological instincts. These distortions were corrected somewhat by the neo-Freudians, but problems remain. One of the most telling criticisms of Freudian theory is that it can explain any psychological event *after* it has occurred. But beforehand, it offers little help in predicting future behavior. For this reason, many psychoanalytic concepts are difficult or impossible to test scientifically (Schick & Vaughn, 1995).

BEHAVIORISTIC THEORY   Learning theories have provided a good framework for personality research. Of the three major per-

spectives, the behaviorists have made the best effort to rigorously test and verify their ideas. They have, however, been criticized for understating the impact that temperament, emotion, thinking, and subjective experience have on personality. Social learning theory answers some of these criticisms, but it may still understate the importance of private experience.

HUMANISTIC THEORY   A great strength of the humanists is the attention they have given to positive dimensions of personality. As Maslow (1968) put it, "Human nature is not nearly as bad as it has been thought to be. It is as if Freud supplied us with the sick half of psychology and we must now fill it out with the healthy half." Despite their contributions, humanists can be criticized for using "fuzzy" concepts that are difficult to measure and study objectively. Even so, humanistic thought has encouraged many people to seek greater self-awareness and personal growth. Also, humanistic concepts have been very useful in counseling and psychotherapy.

   In the final analysis, we need all four major perspectives to explain personality. Each provides a sort of lens through which human behavior can be viewed. In many instances, a balanced picture emerges only when each theory is considered. ◆Table 15.3 provides a final overview of the four principal approaches to personality.

Possible self *A collection of thoughts, beliefs, feelings, and images concerning the person one could become.*
Conditions of worth *Internal standards used to judge the value of one's thoughts, actions, feelings, or experiences.*
Positive self-regard *Thinking of oneself as a good, lovable, worthwhile person.*
Organismic valuing *A natural, undistorted, full-body reaction to an experience.*
Unconditional positive regard *Unshakable love and approval given without qualification.*

PERSONALITY ASSESSMENT—PSYCHOLOGICAL YARDSTICKS

Studies of personality have greatly improved personality measurement in industry, education, and clinical work.

How is personality "measured"?   Psychologists use interviews, observation, questionnaires, and projective tests to assess personality. Each method has strengths and limitations. For this reason, they are often used in combination.

Formal personality measures are refinements of more casual ways of judging a person. At one time or another, you have probably "sized up" a potential date, friend, or employer by engaging in conversation (interview). Perhaps you have asked a friend, "When I am delayed, I get angry. Do you?" (questionnaire). Maybe you watch your professors when they are angry or embarrassed to learn what they are "really" like (observation). Or possibly you have noticed that when you say, "I think people feel . . . ," you may be expressing your own feelings (projection). Let's see how psychologists apply each of these approaches to probe personality.

What is your initial impression of the person wearing the gray jacket? If you think that she looks friendly, attractive, or neat, your subsequent perceptions might be altered by a positive first impression. Interviewers are often influenced by the halo effect (see text).

The Interview

In an **interview,** questioning is used to gain information about an individual's personal history, personality traits, or current psychological state. In an **unstructured interview,** conversation is informal, and topics are taken up freely as they arise. In a **structured interview,** the interviewer obtains information by asking a planned series of questions.

How are interviews used?   Interviews are used to identify personality disturbances; to select people for employment, college, or special programs; and to study the dynamics of personality. Interviews also provide information for counseling or therapy. For instance, a counselor might ask a depressed person, "Have you ever contemplated suicide? What were the circumstances?" The counselor might then follow by asking, "How did you feel about it?" or "How is what you are now feeling different from what you felt then?"

In addition to providing information, interviews make it possible to observe a person's tone of voice, hand gestures, posture, and facial expressions. Such "body language" cues are important because they may radically alter the message sent, as when a person claims to be "completely calm" but trembles uncontrollably.

COMPUTERIZED INTERVIEWS   If you were distressed and went to a psychologist or psychiatrist, what is the first thing she or he might do? Typically, a **diagnostic interview** is used to find out how a person is feeling and what complaints or symptoms he or she has. In many cases, such interviews are based on a specific series of questions. Because the questions are always the same, some researchers have begun to wonder, Why not let a computer ask them?

So far, the results of computer-administered interviews have been promising. In one study, people were interviewed by both a computer and a psychiatrist. Eighty-five percent of these people thought the computer did an acceptable interview (Dignon, 1996). Another study examined the ability of a computerized

interview to identify psychiatric disorders and symptoms. The computer-based interview proved to be highly accurate and in close agreement with psychiatrists (Marion, Shayka, & Marcus, 1996). Thus, it may soon become common for people to "Tell it to the computer," at least in the first stages of seeking help (Peters, Clark, & Carroll, 1998).

LIMITATIONS   Interviews give rapid insight into personality, but they have certain limitations. For one thing, interviewers can be swayed by preconceptions. A person identified as a "housewife," "college student," "high school athlete," "punk," or "ski bum" may be misjudged because of an interviewer's bias toward a particular lifestyle. Second, an interviewer's own personality, or even gender, may influence a client's behavior. When this occurs, it can accentuate or distort the person's apparent traits (Pollner, 1998). A third problem is that people sometimes try to deceive interviewers. For example, a person accused of a crime might pretend to be mentally disabled to avoid punishment.

A fourth problem is the **halo effect,** which is the tendency to generalize a favorable or unfavorable impression to unrelated details of personality. A person who is likable or physically attractive may be rated more mature, intelligent, or adjusted than she or he actually is. The halo effect is something to keep in mind when interviewing for employment. First impressions do make a difference (Lance, LaPointe, & Stewart, 1994).

Even with their limitations, interviews are a respected method of personality assessment. In many cases, interviews are an essential step to additional personality testing and to counseling or therapy.

Direct Observation and Rating Scales

Are you fascinated by beaches, bus depots, airports, subway stations, or other public places? Many people relish a chance to observe the actions of others. When used as an assessment procedure, **direct observation** (looking at behavior) is a sim-

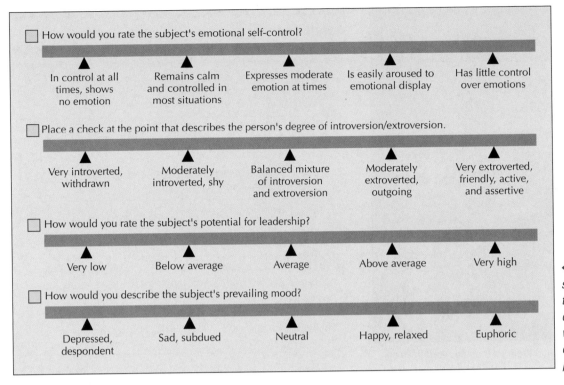

How would you rate the subject's emotional self-control?

| In control at all times, shows no emotion | Remains calm and controlled in most situations | Expresses moderate emotion at times | Is easily aroused to emotional display | Has little control over emotions |

Place a check at the point that describes the person's degree of introversion/extroversion.

| Very introverted, withdrawn | Moderately introverted, shy | Balanced mixture of introversion and extroversion | Moderately extroverted, outgoing | Very extroverted, friendly, active, and assertive |

How would you rate the subject's potential for leadership?

| Very low | Below average | Average | Above average | Very high |

How would you describe the subject's prevailing mood?

| Depressed, despondent | Sad, subdued | Neutral | Happy, relaxed | Euphoric |

❖ **FIGURE 15.9** *Sample rating scale items. To understand how the scale works, imagine someone you know well. Where would you place check marks on each of the scales to rate that person's characteristics?*

ple extension of this natural interest in "people watching." For instance, a psychologist might arrange to observe a disturbed child as she plays with other children. Is the child withdrawn from others? Does she become hostile or aggressive without warning? By careful observation, the psychologist will identify personality characteristics and clarify the nature of the child's problems.

Wouldn't observation be subject to the same problems of misperception as an interview? Yes. Misperceptions can be a difficulty, which is why rating scales are sometimes used (❖Fig. 15.9). A **rating scale** is a list of personality traits or aspects of behavior that can be used to evaluate a person. Rating scales limit the chance that some traits will be overlooked while others are exaggerated (Merenda, 1996). Perhaps they should be standard procedures for choosing a roommate, spouse, or lover!

An alternative is to do a **behavioral assessment** by recording the frequency of specific behaviors. In this case, observers record *actions*, not what traits they think a person has. For example, a psychologist working with hospitalized mental patients might find it helpful to record the frequency of patients' aggression, self-care, speech, and unusual behaviors. Behavioral assessments are not strictly limited to visible actions. They can also be helpful in probing thought processes. In one study, for example, students high in math anxiety were asked to think aloud while doing math problems. Afterward, their thoughts were analyzed to pinpoint the causes of their math fears (Blackwell et al., 1985).

SITUATIONAL TESTING   In **situational testing,** real-life conditions are simulated so that a person's spontaneous reactions can be

recorded. Such tests assume that the best way to learn how people react to certain situations is to put them in those situations and watch what happens. Situational tests expose people to frustration, temptation, pressure, boredom, or other conditions capable of revealing personality characteristics (Weekley & Jones, 1997).

How are situational tests done? An interesting example of situational testing is the judgmental firearms training provided by many police departments. At times, police officers must make split-second decisions about using their weapons. A mistake may be fatal. In a typical shoot or don't shoot test, actors play the part of armed criminals. As various high-risk scenes are acted out live or on videotape, officers must decide to shoot

Interview (personality) *A face-to-face meeting held for the purpose of gaining information about an individual's personal history, personality traits, current psychological state, and so forth.*
Unstructured interview *An interview in which conversation is informal and topics are taken up freely as they arise.*
Structured interview *An interview that follows a prearranged plan, usually a series of planned questions.*
Diagnostic interview *An interview used to find out how a person is feeling and what complaints or symptoms he or she has.*
Halo effect *The tendency to generalize a favorable or unfavorable first impression to unrelated details of personality.*
Direct observation *Assessing behavior through direct surveillance.*
Rating scale *A list of personality traits or aspects of behavior on which a person is rated.*
Behavioral assessment *Recording the frequency of various behaviors.*
Situational test *Simulating real-life conditions so that a person's reactions may be directly observed.*

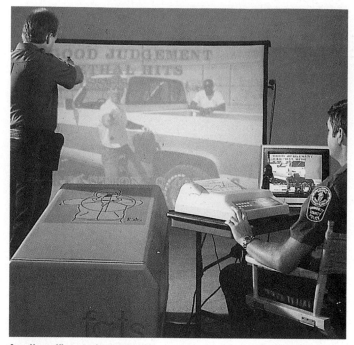

A police officer undergoes judgmental firearms training. Variations on this situational test are used by a growing number of police departments. All officers must score a passing grade.

1. **Hypochondriasis** (HI-po-kon-DRY-uh-sis). Exaggerated concern about one's physical health.

2. **Depression.** Feelings of worthlessness, hopelessness, and pessimism.

3. **Hysteria.** The presence of physical complaints for which no physical basis can be established.

4. **Psychopathic deviate.** Emotional shallowness in relationships and a disregard for social and moral standards.

5. **Masculinity/femininity.** One's degree of traditional "masculine" aggressiveness or "feminine" sensitivity.

6. **Paranoia.** Extreme suspiciousness and feelings of persecution.

7. **Psychasthenia** (sike-as-THEE-nee-ah). The presence of obsessive worries, irrational fears (phobias), and compulsive (ritualistic) actions.

8. **Schizophrenia.** Emotional withdrawal and unusual or bizarre thinking and actions.

9. **Mania.** Emotional excitability, manic moods or behavior, and excessive activity.

10. **Social introversion.** One's tendency to be socially withdrawn.

or hold fire. A newspaper reporter who once took the test (and failed it) gives this account (Gersh, 1982):

> I judged wrong. I was killed by a man in a closet, a man with a hostage, a woman interrupted when kissing her lover, and a man I thought was cleaning a shotgun. . . . I shot a drunk who reached for a comb, and a teenager who pulled out a black water pistol. Looked real to me.

In addition to the training it provides, situational testing uncovers police cadets who lack the good judgment needed to carry a gun out on the street.

Personality Questionnaires

Most **personality questionnaires** are paper-and-pencil tests that reveal personality characteristics. Questionnaires are more objective than interviews or observation. (An **objective test** gives the same score when different people correct it.) Questions, administration, and scoring are all standardized so that scores are unaffected by the opinions or prejudices of the examiner. However, this is not enough to ensure a test's accuracy. A good test must also be reliable and valid. A test is **reliable** if it yields close to the same score each time it is given to the same person. A test has **validity** when it measures what it claims to measure. Unfortunately, many personality tests you will encounter, such as those in magazines or on the Internet, have little or no validity.

Many personality tests have been devised, including the *Guilford-Zimmerman Temperament Survey,* the *California Psychological Inventory,* the *Allport-Vernon Study of Values,* and the 16 PF. One of

BRIDGES

Reliability and validity are important features of all psychological tests, especially intelligence and aptitude tests.

See Chapter 12, page 380.

the best-known and most widely used objective tests is the **Minnesota Multiphasic Personality Inventory-2** (**MMPI-2**). The MMPI-2 is composed of 567 items to which a test taker must respond "true" or "false." Items include statements such as the following.

- Everything tastes the same.
- There is something wrong with my mind.
- I enjoy animals.
- Whenever possible I avoid being in a crowd.
- I have never indulged in any unusual sex practices.
- Someone has been trying to poison me.
- I daydream often.*

How can these items show anything about personality? For instance, what if a person has a cold so that "everything tastes the same"? For an answer (and a little bit of fun), read "Personality Tests—A Roast and a Rationale."

The MMPI-2 measures 10 major aspects of personality (listed in ❖Table 15.4). After the MMPI-2 is scored, results are charted graphically as an **MMPI-2 profile** (❖Fig. 15.10). By comparing a person's profile to scores produced by normal adults, a psychologist can identify various personality disorders. Additional scales are capable of identifying substance abuse, eating disorders,

*Reproduced by permission. Copyright 1989, by the University of Minnesota Press.

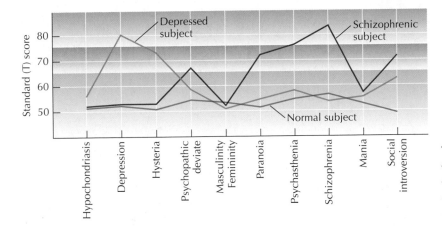

❖ **FIGURE 15.10** *An MMPI-2 profile showing hypothetical scores indicating normality, depression, and psychosis. High scores begin at 66 and very high scores at 76. An unusually low score (40 and below) may also reveal personality characteristics or problems.*

Type A behavior, repression, anger, cynicism, low self-esteem, family problems, inability to function in a job, and other problems (Hathaway & McKinley, 1989).

How accurate is the MMPI-2? Personality questionnaires are accurate only if people tell the truth about themselves. Because of this, the MMPI-2 has additional **validity scales** that tell whether a person's scores should be discarded. The validity scales detect attempts by test takers to "fake good" (make themselves look good) or "fake bad" (make it look like they have problems). Other scales reveal defensiveness or tendencies to exaggerate shortcomings and troubles. When taking the MMPI-2, it is best to answer honestly, without trying to second-guess the test.

A clinical psychologist trying to decide if a person has emotional problems would be wise to take more than the MMPI-2 into account. Test scores are informative, but they can incorrectly label some people (Cronbach, 1990). ("Honesty Tests"

discusses a related problem.) Fortunately, clinical judgments usually rely on information from interviews, tests, and other sources.

Personality questionnaire *A paper-and-pencil test consisting of questions that reveal aspects of personality.*
Objective test *A test that gives the same score when different people correct it.*
Reliability *The ability of a test to yield nearly the same score each time it is given to the same person.*
Validity *The ability of a test to measure what it purports to measure.*
Minnesota Multiphasic Personality Inventory-2 (MMPI-2) *One of the best-known and most widely used objective personality questionnaires.*
MMPI-2 profile *A graphic representation of an individual's scores on each of the primary scales of the MMPI-2.*
Validity scales *Scales that tell whether test scores should be invalidated for lying, inconsistency, or "faking good."*

HONESTY TESTS—DO THEY TELL THE TRUTH?

Each year, millions of anxious job seekers take paper-and-pencil honesty tests given by companies that hope to avoid hiring dishonest workers. **Honesty tests** (also known as integrity tests) assume that poor attitudes toward dishonest acts predispose a person to dishonest behavior. Examples include attitudes toward taking office supplies home or leaving work early. Most of the tests also ask people how honest they think the average person is and how honest they are in comparison. Surprisingly, many job applicants willingly rate their own honesty as below average (Neuman & Baydoun, 1998). (You have to admire them for being honest about it!) Honesty tests also ask about prior brushes with the law, past acts of theft or deceit, and attitudes toward alcohol and drug use.

Is honesty testing valid? This question is still very much in dispute. Some psychologists believe that the best honesty tests are sufficiently valid to be used for making hiring decisions

(Ones et al., 1993). Others, however, remain unconvinced. Most studies have failed to demonstrate that honesty tests can accurately *predict* if a person will be a poor risk on the job (Saxe, 1991). Psychologists are also concerned because honesty tests are often administered by untrained people. Yet another cause for concern is the fact that 96 percent of test takers who fail are falsely labeled as dishonest (Camara & Schneider, 1994). In North America alone, that means well over a million workers a year are wrongly accused of being dishonest (Rieke & Guastello, 1995).

Some states have banned the use of honesty tests as the sole basis for deciding whether to hire a person. Yet, it's easy to understand why employers want to do whatever they can to reduce theft and dishonesty in the workplace. The pressures to use honesty tests are intense. No doubt, the debate about honesty testing will continue. Honest.

PROJECTIVE TESTS OF PERSONALITY—INKBLOTS AND HIDDEN PLOTS

Projective tests take a decidedly different approach to personality. Interviews, observation, rating scales, and inventories try to directly identify overt, observable traits (Vane & Guarnaccia, 1989). By contrast, projective tests seek to uncover deeply hidden or *unconscious* wishes, thoughts, and needs.

As a child, you may have delighted in finding faces and objects in cloud formations. Or perhaps you have learned something about your friends' personalities from their reactions to movies or paintings. If so, you will have some insight into the rationale for projective tests. In a **projective test,** a person is asked to describe ambiguous stimuli or make up stories about them. Describing an unambiguous stimulus (a picture of an automobile, for example) tells little about your personality. But when you are faced with an unstructured stimulus, you must organize what you see in terms of your own life experiences. Everyone sees something different in a projective test, and what is perceived can reveal the inner workings of personality.

Projective tests have no right or wrong answers. This makes it difficult for people to fake or "see through" such tests (Vane & Guarnaccia, 1989). Moreover, projective tests can be a rich source of information, because responses are not restricted to simple true-false or yes-no answers.

The Rorschach Inkblot Test

Is the inkblot test a projective technique? The inkblot test, or **Rorschach Technique** (ROR-shock), is one of the oldest and most widely used projective tests. Developed by Swiss psychologist Hermann Rorschach in the 1920s, it consists of 10

standardized inkblots. These vary in color, shading, form, and complexity.

How does the test work? First, a person is shown each blot and asked to describe what she or he sees in it (❖Fig. 15.11). Later, the psychologist may return to a blot, asking the person to identify specific sections of it, to expand previous descriptions, or to give new impressions about what it contains. Obvious differences in content—such as "blood dripping from a dagger" versus "flowers blooming in a field"—are important for identifying personal conflicts and fantasies. But surprisingly, content is less important than what parts of the inkblot are used to organize images. These factors allow psychologists to detect emotional disturbances by observing how a person perceives the world. The Rorschach is especially good at detecting psychosis, one of the most serious of all mental disorders (Ganellen, 1996).

The Thematic Apperception Test

Another popular projective test is the **Thematic Apperception Test** (**TAT**) developed by personality theorist Henry Murray (1893–1988).

How does the TAT differ from the Rorschach? The TAT consists of 20 sketches depicting various scenes and life situations (❖Fig. 15.12). During testing, a person is shown each sketch and asked to make up a story about the people in it. Later the person is shown each sketch a second or a third time and asked to elaborate on previous stories or to construct new stories.

To score the TAT, a psychologist analyzes the content of the stories. Interpretations focus on how people feel, how they interact, what events led up to the incidents depicted in the sketch, and how the story will end. For example, TAT stories told by bereaved college students typically include themes of death, grief, and coping with loss (Balk et al., 1998).

BRIDGES

Psychotic disorders involve severe disturbances in thinking and perception, which are apparent during projective testing.

See pages 372–377.

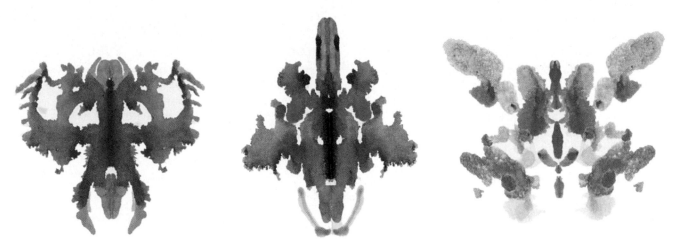

❖ **FIGURE 15.11** *Inkblots similar to those used on the Rorschach. What do you see?*

❖ **FIGURE 15.12** *This is a picture like those used for the Thematic Apperception Test. If you wish to simulate the test, tell a story that explains what led up to the pictured situation, what is happening now, and how the action will end.*

A psychologist might also count the number of times the central figure in a TAT story is angry, overlooked, apathetic, jealous, or threatened. Here is a story written by a student to describe ❖Figure 15.12:

> The girl has been seeing this guy her mother doesn't like. The mother is telling her that she better not see him again. The mother says, "He's just like your father." The mother and father are divorced. The mother is smiling because she thinks she is right. But she doesn't really know what the girl wants. The girl is going to see the guy again, anyway.

As this example implies, the TAT is especially good at revealing feelings about a person's social relationships (Alvarado, 1994).

LIMITATIONS OF PROJECTIVE TESTING Although projective tests have been popular, their validity is considered lowest among tests of personality (Lilienfeld, 1999). Objectivity and reliability (consistency) of judgments are also low among different users of the TAT and Rorschach. Note that after a person interprets an ambiguous stimulus, the scorer must interpret the person's (sometimes) ambiguous responses. In a sense, the interpretation of a projective test may be a projective test for the scorer!

Despite their drawbacks, projective tests still have value (Weiner, 1997). This is especially true when they are used as part of a **test battery** (collection of assessment devices and interviews). In the hands of a skilled clinician, projective tests can detect major conflicts and aid in setting goals for therapy (Weiner, 1996). Moreover, because projective tests are unstructured, they can be a good way to get clients to talk about anxiety-provoking topics.

SUDDEN MURDERERS—A RESEARCH EXAMPLE

Personality assessments provide us with clues to some of the most perplexing human events. Consider Fred Cowan, a model student in school and described by those who knew him as quiet, gentle, and a man who loved children. Despite his size (6 feet tall, 250 pounds), Fred was described by a coworker as "someone you could easily push around."

Honesty test *A paper-and-pencil test designed to detect attitudes, beliefs, and behavior patterns that predispose a person to dishonest behavior.*
Projective tests *Psychological tests making use of ambiguous or unstructured stimuli.*
Rorschach Technique *A projective test comprised of 10 standardized inkblots.*
Thematic Apperception Test (TAT) *A projective test consisting of 20 different scenes and life situations about which respondents make up stories.*
Test battery *A group of tests and interviews given to the same individual.*

Fred Cowan represents a puzzling phenomenon: We occasionally read in the news about sudden murderers—gentle, quiet, shy, good-natured people who explode without warning into violence (Lee et al., 1977). Two weeks after he was suspended from his job, Fred returned to work determined to get even with his supervisor. Unable to find the man, he killed four coworkers and a policeman before taking his own life.

Isn't such behavior contrary to the idea of personality traits? It might seem that sudden murderers are newsworthy simply because they are unlikely candidates for violence. On the contrary, research conducted by Melvin Lee, Philip Zimbardo, and Minerva Bertholf suggests that sudden murderers explode into violence *because* they are shy, restrained, and inexpressive, not in spite of it. These researchers studied prisoners at a California prison. Ten were inmates whose homicide was an unexpected first offense. Nine were criminals with a record of habitual violence prior to murder. Sixteen were inmates convicted of non-violent crimes.

Did the inmates differ in personality makeup? Each of the inmates took a battery of tests, including the MMPI, a measure of shyness, and an adjective checklist. Personal interviews were also done with each inmate. As expected, the sudden murderers were passive, shy, and overcontrolled (restrained) individuals. The habitually violent inmates were "masculine" (aggressive), undercontrolled (impulsive), and less likely to view themselves as shy than the average person (Lee et al., 1977).

Psychologists have learned that quiet, overcontrolled individuals are likely to be especially violent if they ever lose control. Their attacks are usually triggered by a minor irritation or frustration, but the attack reflects years of unexpressed feelings of anger and belittlement. When sudden murderers finally release the strict controls they have maintained on their behavior, a furious and frenzied attack ensues. Usually it is totally out of proportion to the offense against them, and many have amnesia for their violent actions.

In comparison, the previously violent murderers showed very different reactions. Although they killed, their violence was moderate—usually only enough to do the necessary damage. Typically, they felt they had been cheated or betrayed and that they were doing what was necessary to remedy the situation or maintain their manhood (Lee et al., 1977).

A LOOK AHEAD   The preceding example illustrates how some of the concepts and techniques discussed in this chapter can be applied to further our understanding. The Psychology in Action section that follows should add balance to your view of personality. After that, A Step Beyond discusses some interesting ideas about how we present ourselves to others. Don't be shy. Read on!

KNOWLEDGE BUILDER
PERSONALITY ASSESSMENT

RELATE

How do *you* assess personality? Do you informally make use of any of the methods described in this chapter?

You are a candidate for a desirable job. Your personality is going to be assessed by a psychologist. What method (or methods) would you prefer that she or he use? Why?

LEARNING CHECK

1. Planned questions are used in a _____ interview.

2. The halo effect is the tendency of an interviewer to influence what is said by the interviewee. T or F?

3. Which of the following is considered the most objective measure of personality?
   a. rating scales *b.* personality questionnaires *c.* projective tests *d.* TAT

4. Situational testing allows direct _____ of personality characteristics.

5. A psychotic person would probably score highest on which MMPI-2 scale?
   a. depression *b.* hysteria *c.* schizophrenia *d.* mania

6. The use of ambiguous stimuli is most characteristic of
   a. interviews *b.* projective tests *c.* personality inventories *d.* direct observation

7. The content of one's responses to the MMPI-2 is considered an indication of unconscious wishes, thoughts, and needs. T or F?

8. Doing a behavioral assessment requires direct observation of the person's actions or a direct report of the person's thoughts. T or F?

9. A surprising finding is that sudden murderers are usually undercontrolled, very masculine, and more impulsive than average. T or F?

10. A test is considered valid if it consistently yields the same score when the same person takes it on different occasions. T or F?

CRITICAL THINKING

11. Can you think of one more reasons why personality traits may not be accurately revealed by interviews?

12. Projective testing would be of greatest interest to which type of personality theorist?

Answers:

1. structured 2. F 3. *b* 4. observation 5. *c* 6. *b* 7. F 8. F 9. F 10. F 11. Because of trait-situation interactions, a person may not behave in a normal fashion while being evaluated in an interview. 12. Psychodynamic: Because projective testing is designed to uncover unconscious thoughts, feelings, and conflicts.

BARRIERS AND BRIDGES—UNDERSTANDING SHYNESS

As a personality trait, **shyness** refers to a tendency to avoid others, as well as feelings of social inhibition (uneasiness and strain when socializing) (Buss, 1980). Shy persons fail to make eye contact, retreat when spoken to, speak too quietly, and display little interest or animation in conversations. Do you:

- Find it hard to talk to strangers?
- Lack confidence with people?
- Feel uncomfortable in social situations?
- Feel nervous with people who are not close friends?

If so, you may be part of the *50 percent* of college students who consider themselves shy (Carducci & Stein, 1988). Mild shyness may be no more than a nuisance. However, extreme shyness is often associated with depression, loneliness, fearfulness, social anxiety, inhibition, and low self-esteem (Henderson, 1997; Schmidt & Fox, 1995).

Elements of Shyness

What causes shyness? To begin with, shy persons often lack **social skills** (proficiency at interacting with others). Many simply have not learned how to meet people or how to start a conversation and keep it going. **Social anxiety** (a feeling of apprehension in the presence of others) is also a factor in shyness. Almost everyone feels nervous in some social situations (such as meeting an attractive stranger). Typically, this is a reaction to **evaluation fears** (fears of being inadequate, embarrassed, ridiculed, or rejected). Although fears of rejection are common, they are much more frequent or intense for shy people (Jackson, Towson, & Narduzzi, 1997). A third problem for shy people is a **self-defeating bias** (distortion) in their thinking. Specifically, shy people almost always blame themselves when a social encounter doesn't go well.

SITUATIONAL CAUSES OF SHYNESS   Shyness is most often triggered by *novel* or *unfamiliar* social situations. A person who does fine with family or close friends may become shy and awkward when meeting a stranger. Shyness is also magnified by formality, by meeting someone of higher status, by being noticeably different from others, or by being the focus of attention (as in giving a speech) (Buss, 1980).

Don't most people become cautious and inhibited in such circumstances? Yes. That's why we need to see how the personalities of shy and nonshy people differ.

Dynamics of the Shy Personality

There is a tendency to think that shy people are wrapped up in their own feelings and thoughts. But surprisingly, researchers

Jonathan Cheek and Arnold Buss (1979) found no connection between shyness and **private self-consciousness** (attention to inner feelings, thoughts, and fantasies). Instead, they discovered that shyness is linked to **public self-consciousness** (acute awareness of oneself as a social object).

People who rate high in public self-consciousness are intensely concerned about what others think of them (Buss, 1980). They worry about saying the wrong thing or appearing foolish. In public, they may feel "naked" or as if others can "see through them." Such feelings trigger anxiety or outright fear during social encounters, leading to awkwardness and inhibition (Buss, 1986). The shy person's anxiety, in turn, often causes her or him to misperceive others in social situations (Schroeder, 1995).

As mentioned, almost everyone feels anxious in at least some social situations. But there is a key difference in the way shy and nonshy persons *label* this anxiety. Shy people tend to consider their social anxiety a *lasting personality trait*. Shyness, in other words, becomes part of their self-concept. In contrast, nonshy people believe that *external situations* cause their occasional feelings of shyness. When nonshy people feel anxiety or "stage fright," they assume that almost anyone would feel as they do under the same circumstances (Zimbardo et al., 1978).

Labeling is important because it affects *self-esteem*. In general, nonshy people tend to have higher self-esteem than shy people. This is because nonshy people give themselves credit for their social successes and they recognize that failures are often due to circumstances. In contrast, shy people blame themselves for social failures and never give themselves credit for successes (Buss, 1980; Girodo, 1978).

Shy Beliefs

What can be done to reduce shyness? While directing a shyness clinic, psychologist Michel Girodo (1978) observed that shyness is often maintained by unrealistic or self-defeating beliefs. Here's a sample of such beliefs.

BRIDGES

Three to 5 percent of North Americans are so shy that they suffer from "social phobia" and need treatment.

See Chapter 17, page 567, for more information.

Shyness *A tendency to avoid others plus uneasiness and strain when socializing.*
Social skills *Proficiency at interacting with others.*
Social anxiety *A feeling of apprehension in the presence of others.*
Evaluation fears *Fears of being inadequate, embarrassed, ridiculed, or rejected.*
Self-defeating bias *A distortion of thinking that impairs behavior.*
Private self-consciousness *Preoccupation with inner feelings, thoughts, and fantasies.*
Public self-consciousness *Intense awareness of oneself as a social object.*

1. *If you wait around long enough at a social gathering, something will happen.*
   Comment: This is really a cover-up for fear of starting a conversation. For two people to meet, at least one has to make an effort, and it might as well be you.

2. *Other people who are popular are just lucky when it comes to being invited to social events or asked out.*
   Comment: Except for times when a person is formally introduced to someone new, this is false. People who are more active socially typically make an effort to meet and spend time with others. They join clubs, invite others to do things, strike up conversations, and generally leave little to luck.

3. *The odds of meeting someone interested in socializing are always the same, no matter where I am.*
   Comment: This is another excuse for inaction. It pays to seek out situations that have a higher probability of leading to social contact, such as clubs, teams, and school events.

4. *If someone doesn't seem to like you right away, they really don't like you and never will.*
   Comment: This belief leads to much needless shyness. Even when a person doesn't show immediate interest, it doesn't mean the person dislikes you. Liking takes time and opportunity to develop.

Unproductive beliefs like the preceding can be replaced with statements such as the following.

1. I've got to be active in social situations.
2. I can't wait until I'm completely relaxed or comfortable before taking a social risk.
3. I don't need to pretend to be someone I'm not; it just makes me more anxious.
4. I may think other people are harshly evaluating me, but actually I'm being too hard on myself.
5. I can set reasonable goals for expanding my social experience and skills.
6. Even people who are very socially skillful are never successful 100 percent of the time. I shouldn't get so upset when an encounter goes badly. (Adapted from Girodo, 1978.)

Social Skills

Learning social skills takes practice. There is nothing "innate" about knowing how to meet people or start a conversation. Social skills can be directly practiced in a variety of ways. It can be helpful, for instance, to get a tape recorder and listen to several of your conversations. You may be surprised by the way you pause, interrupt, miss cues, or seem uninterested. Similarly, it can be useful to look at yourself in a mirror and exaggerate facial expressions of surprise, interest, dislike, pleasure, and so forth. By such methods, most people can learn to put more animation and skill into their self-presentation. (For a discussion of related skills, see the section on self-assertion in Chapter 19.)

CONVERSATION One of the simplest ways to make better conversation is by learning to ask questions. A good series of questions shifts attention to the other person and shows you are interested. Nothing fancy is needed. You can do fine with questions such as, "Where do you (work, study, live)? Do you like (dancing, travel, music)? How long have you (been at this school, worked here, lived here)?" After you've broken the ice, the best questions are often those that are *open ended*:

- "What parts of the country have you seen?" (as opposed to: "Have you ever been to Florida?")
- "What's it like living on the west side?" (as opposed to: "Do you like living on the west side?")
- "What kinds of food do you like?" (as opposed to: "Do you like Chinese cooking?")

It's easy to see why open-ended questions are helpful. In replying to open-ended questions, people often give "free information" about themselves. This extra information can be used to ask other questions or to lead into other topics of conversation.

This brief sampling of ideas is no substitute for actual practice. Overcoming shyness requires a real effort to learn new skills and test old beliefs and attitudes. It may even require the help of a counselor or therapist. At the very least, a shy person must be willing to take social risks. Breaking down the barriers of shyness will always include some awkward or unsuccessful encounters. Nevertheless, the rewards are powerful: human companionship and personal freedom.

KNOWLEDGE BUILDER

SHYNESS AND SOCIAL SKILLS

RELATE

If you are shy, see if you can summarize how social skills, social anxiety, evaluation fears, self-defeating thoughts, and public self-consciousness contribute to your social inhibition. If you're not shy, imagine how you would explain these concepts to a shy friend.

LEARNING CHECK

1. Surveys show that 14 percent of American college students consider themselves shy. T or F?

2. Social anxiety and evaluation fears are seen almost exclusively in shy individuals; the nonshy rarely have such experiences. T or F?

3. Unfamiliar people and situations most often trigger shyness. T or F?

4. Public self-consciousness plus a tendency to label oneself as shy are major characteristics of the shy personality. T or F?

5. Changing personal beliefs and practicing social skills can be helpful in overcoming shyness. T or F?

CRITICAL THINKING

6. Shyness is a trait of Vonda's personality. Like most shy people, Vonda is most likely to feel shy in unfamiliar social settings. Vonda's shy behavior demonstrates that the expression of traits is governed by what concept?

Answers:

1. F 2. F 3. T 4. T 5. T 6. trait-situation interactions (again)

Focus: How does self-monitoring affect behavior?

You walk into a room and face a dilemma that challenges partygoers everywhere: On the left, a conversation is taking place between three similar people—a film lover, an art lover, and a music lover. On the right side of the room, a mixed group has formed, including a member of the peace movement, a military "hawk," and a feminist. Which group do you join? Your answer may depend on whether you are high or low in *self-monitoring* (Snyder & Harkness, 1984).

Self-monitoring refers to how much we monitor (observe, regulate, and control) the image of ourselves we display to others. Some of us are **high self-monitors,** who actively change the impression we make to fit situations and expectations. It is as if high self-monitors ask, "Who does this situation want me to be, and how can I be that person?" In contrast, **low self-monitors** are less interested in controlling the impression they make. Such people seek to faithfully express what they really think and feel. It is as if they want to know, "Who am I, and how can I be me in this situation?" (Snyder, 1987).

The Public Self

Psychologist Mark Snyder has found that people who are high in self-monitoring have a flexible definition of themselves. They are also very interested in their public "image." Low self-monitors, on the other hand, try to accurately present their beliefs and principles no matter what the situation is. Snyder believes that such differences have an impact on our lives and behavior.

To return to the party, Snyder and Harkness (1984) found that in similar situations high self-monitors preferred to join clearly defined groups. At the party, for example, they could strike a "cultured" pose if they joined the first group. However, the second group would put them in a difficult position: Any image they projected could offend at least one member of the group. Such group differences had far less impact on low self-monitors. Basically, they chose whichever group had someone they could identify with.

HIGH OR LOW? *How can you tell if you are high or low in self-monitoring?* To measure this characteristic, Snyder developed the *Self-Monitoring Scale.* Although the entire scale cannot be reprinted here, the items that follow are examples of statements that separate highs from lows.

High Self-Monitors
- I would probably make a good actor.
- I'm not always the person I appear to be.
- I guess I put on a show to impress and entertain others.

Low Self-Monitors
- I have never been good at games like charades or improvisational acting.
- In a group, I am rarely the center of attention.
- At a party, I let others keep the jokes and stories going.

If you are still not sure what your self-monitoring style is, the following comparisons may be helpful. Each difference has been verified by studies of self-monitoring (Snyder, 1987).

- **Highs** are keenly interested in the actions of others and in trying to "read" their motives, attitudes, and traits. Presumably, high self-monitors do this so that they will know how to present themselves to a particular person, such as a date.
- **Lows** seek to match their public behavior to their private attitudes, feelings, and beliefs. Lows tend to speak their minds no matter who is listening.
- **Highs** are flexible and adaptable, and they display different behavior from situation to situation.
- **Lows** change little from situation to situation. They want what they do to match who they are. Lows do not change their opinions to please others or win favor.
- **Highs** tend to declare who they are by listing their roles and memberships (student, post office employee, member of the school orchestra, third-ranking player of the tennis team, and so on).
- **Lows** identify themselves in terms of their beliefs, emotions, values, and personality.
- **Highs** choose friends who are skilled or knowledgeable in various areas. They also tend to have specific friends for specific activities.
- **Lows** have friends who tend to all be alike in basic ways. No matter what the activity, they prefer to get together with the same friends.
- **Highs** are concerned with outer appearances. They choose their clothes, hairstyle, and jewelry to project an image (Graeff, 1996).
- **Lows** have a wardrobe that is less varied; they do not have to change their appearance as often as high self-monitors do.
- **Highs** are mainly interested in dating attractive people. (In the personals columns, their ads are the ones that emphasize appearance.)
- **Lows** are more interested in a potential date's personality.
- **Highs** believe it is possible to love two people at the same time.
- **Lows** believe that there is only one real love for a person.
- **Highs** prefer jobs where their role is very clearly defined.
- **Lows** prefer jobs where they can "just be themselves."

Self-monitoring *Regulation and control of the image one displays to others in public.*
High self-monitor *A person who actively changes the impression she or he makes to fit situations and expectations.*
Low self-monitor *A person who seeks to faithfully express who he or she is, regardless of the situation.*

IMPLICATIONS   As you can see, there are advantages and disadvantages to being either high or low in self-monitoring. In general, high self-monitors are adaptable and present themselves well in social situations. However, they tend to reveal little about their private feelings, beliefs, and intentions. This, along with gaps between their attitudes and actions, may have a negative effect on relationships. The primary drawback to being low in self-monitoring is a tendency to ignore the demands of different situations. Low self-monitors want to "just be themselves," even when adjustments in self-presentation would make them more effective.

ONE TRUE SELF?   Is there a single "true self" that underlies the many roles we play in daily life? Studies of self-monitoring raise questions about the idea that each person has a true self. High self-monitors, in particular, act as if they have many selves. For these people, controlling the image they impart is a way of life at parties, in meetings, in classes, and elsewhere. The "public self" of high self-monitors may or may not be backed by a perceived "real me" on the inside. In many cases, it may be better to try to understand the self *in action* by looking at the ways people define themselves. Just as the answer to the question "Who am I?" varies for each person, the answer to the question "Do I have a single true self?" may vary, too.

Do you have a single true self? Give the question some thought the next time you go to a party!

CONCLUSION: People who are high or low in self-monitoring take very different approaches to interacting with other people. People at each extreme could probably learn something from their counterparts at the other end of the scale. There are benefits in both flexible self-presentation and in being true to oneself.

SELF-MONITORING

RELATE

Identify a person you know who appears to be a high self-monitor. Identify a person who seems to be low in self-monitoring. What are the consequences of each orientation? What are the advantages and disadvantages? Do you think you rate high or low in self-monitoring?

LEARNING CHECK

1. Self-monitoring refers to how much people compare their self-image to the images others hold of them. T or F?

2. Low self-monitors tend to ask, "Who does this situation want me to be?" T or F?

3. In social situations, high self-monitors prefer clearly defined groups that do not create self-presentation conflicts. T or F?

4. A low self-monitor would probably agree with the statement "I usually prefer to wear my most comfortable clothes, no matter what the occasion is." T or F?

5. "Handsome Tom Cruise look-alike seeking slim fashion-model-type fox for flights of fancy." This ad would most likely be placed by a person high in self-monitoring. T or F?

CRITICAL THINKING

6. Which of Carl Jung's concepts is most relevant to the behavior of high self-monitors?

Answers:

1. F 2. F 3. T 4. T 5. T 6. persona

CHAPTER IN REVIEW

How do psychologists use the term *personality*?

- Personality is made up of one's unique and enduring behavior patterns.
- Character is personality evaluated, or the possession of desirable qualities.
- Temperament refers to the hereditary and physiological aspects of one's emotional nature.

What core concepts make up the psychology of personality?

- Personality traits are lasting personal qualities that are inferred from behavior.
- Personality types group people into categories on the basis of shared traits or similar characteristics.
- Behavior is influenced by self-concept, which is a perception of one's own personality traits.
- A positive self-evaluation leads to high self-esteem. Low self-esteem is associated with stress, unhappiness, and depression.
- Personality theories combine interrelated assumptions, ideas, and principles to explain personality.

Are some personality traits more basic or important than others?

- Trait theories identify qualities that are most lasting or characteristic of a person.
- Allport made useful distinctions between common traits and individual traits and between cardinal, central, and secondary traits.
- Cattell's trait theory attributes visible surface traits to the existence of underlying source traits. Cattell used factor analysis to identify 16 source traits.
- Source traits are measured by the *Sixteen Personality Factor Questionnaire* (16 PF). Like other trait measures, the outcome of the 16 PF may be graphed as a trait profile.
- The five-factor model identifies five universal dimensions of personality: extroversion, agreeableness, conscientiousness, neuroticism, and openness to experience.
- Traits interact with situations to determine behavior. Neither factor alone fully explains our actions.
- Behavioral genetics and studies of separated identical twins suggest that heredity contributes significantly to adult personality traits.

How do psychodynamic theories explain personality?

- Like other psychodynamic approaches, Sigmund Freud's psychoanalytic theory emphasizes unconscious forces and conflicts within the personality.
- In Freud's theory, personality is made up of the id, ego, and superego.
- Libido, derived from the life instincts, is the primary energy running the personality. Conflicts within the personality may cause neurotic anxiety or moral anxiety and motivate use of ego-defense mechanisms.
- The personality operates on three levels, the conscious, preconscious, and unconscious.
- The Freudian view of personality development is based on a series of psychosexual stages: the oral, anal, phallic, and genital stages. Fixation at any stage can leave a lasting imprint on personality.

What do behaviorists emphasize in their approach to personality?

- Behavioral theories of personality emphasize learning, conditioning, and immediate effects of the environment.
- Learning theorists generally stress the effects of prior learning and situational determinants of behavior.
- Learning theorists John Dollard and Neal Miller consider habits the basic core of personality. Habits express the combined effects of drive, cue, response, and reward.
- Social learning theory adds cognitive elements, such as perception, thinking, and understanding, to the behavioral view of personality. Examples of such concepts include the psychological situation, expectancies, and reinforcement value. Some social learning theorists treat "conscience" as a case of self-reinforcement.
- The behavioristic view of personality development holds that social reinforcement in four situations is critical. The critical situations are feeding, toilet or cleanliness training, sex training, and anger or aggression training. Identification and imitation are of particular importance in sex training.

How do humanistic theories differ from other perspectives?

- Humanistic theory emphasizes subjective experience and needs for self-actualization.
- Abraham Maslow's study of self-actualizers identified characteristics they share, ranging from efficient perceptions of reality to frequent peak experiences.
- Carl Rogers's theory views the self as an entity that emerges from personal experience. Experiences that match the self-image are symbolized (admitted to consciousness), while those that are incongruent are excluded.
- The incongruent person has a highly unrealistic self-image and/or a mismatch between the self-image and the ideal self. The congruent or fully functioning person is flexible and open to experiences and feelings.
- In the development of personality, humanists are primarily interested in the emergence of a self-image and in self-evaluations.
- As parents apply conditions of worth to children's behavior, thoughts, and feelings, children begin to do the same. Internalized conditions of worth then contribute to incongruence and disrupt the organismic valuing process.

How do psychologists measure personality?

- Techniques typically used for personality assessment are interviews, observation, questionnaires, and projective tests.
- Structured and unstructured interviews provide much information, but they are subject to interviewer bias and misperceptions. The halo effect may also lower the accuracy of an interview.
- Direct observation, sometimes involving situational tests, behavioral assessment, or the use of rating scales, allows evaluation of a person's actual behavior.
- Personality questionnaires, such as the *Minnesota Multiphasic Personality Inventory-2* (MMPI-2), are objective and reliable, but their validity is open to question.
- Honesty tests, which are essentially personality questionnaires, are widely used by businesses to make hiring decisions. Their validity is hotly debated.

- Projective tests ask a subject to project thoughts or feelings to an ambiguous stimulus or unstructured situation.
- The *Rorschach Technique,* or inkblot test, is a well-known projective technique. A second is the *Thematic Apperception Test* (TAT).
- The validity and objectivity of projective tests are quite low. Nevertheless, projective techniques are considered useful by many clinicians, particularly as part of a test battery.

What causes shyness? What can be done about it?

- Shyness is a mixture of social inhibition and social anxiety. It is marked by heightened public self-consciousness and a tendency to regard one's shyness as a lasting trait.
- Shyness can be lessened by changing self-defeating beliefs and by improving social skills.

How does self-monitoring affect behavior?

- People vary in their degree of self-monitoring or desire to control the impression they make on others.
- High self-monitoring persons try to fit their public image to various situations. Low self-monitors are interested in accurately expressing their feelings, beliefs, and values, regardless of the situation.

PSYCHOLOGY ON THE NET

- **About Humanistic Psychology** Discusses the history and future of humanistic psychology. http://ahpweb.org/aboutahp/whatis.html

- **Freud Net** Offers links to information on Freud and psychoanalysis. http://plaza.interport.net/nypsan/
- **Great Ideas in Personality** Summarizes major models of personality and relevant research. http://galton.psych.nwu.edu/GreatIdeas.html
- **Personality and IQ Tests** Multiple links to personality tests and IQ tests that are scored on-line. http://www.davideck.com/online-tests.html
- **The Big Five Dimensions** Provides additional information about the Big Five, with links to related sites. http://galton.psych.nwu.edu/GreatIdeas/bigfive.html
  - **InfoTrac® College Edition** For recent articles related to heritability of personality traits, use Key Words search for TWIN STUDIES.

INTERACTIVE LEARNING

- *PsychNow!* 7a. Theories of personality. 7e. Assessment.
- *Psyk.trek* 10a. Freudian theory. 10b. Behavioral theory. 10c. Humanistic theory. 10d. Biological theory.

16

Health, Stress, and Coping

Chapter Survey

Theme: *Health is affected greatly by lifestyle and behavior patterns, especially those related to stress.*

▼ **KEY QUESTIONS**

● *KEY TOPICS*

▼ What is health psychology? How does behavior affect health?

- ● *Health psychology*
- ● *Behavioral risk factors*
- ● *Health-promoting behaviors*

▼ What is stress? What factors determine its severity?

- ● *Dimensions of stress*
- ● *Emotional appraisals*

▼ What causes frustration and what are typical reactions to it?

- ● *Variables affecting frustration*
- ● *Typical reactions to frustration*

▼ Are there different types of conflict? How do people react to conflict?

- ● *Types of conflict*
- ● *Typical reactions to conflict*

▼ What are defense mechanisms?

- ● *Anxiety and psychological defense*
- ● *Types of defense mechanisms*

▼ **KEY QUESTIONS**

● *KEY TOPICS*

▼ What do we know about coping with feelings of helplessness and depression?

- ● *Learned helplessness*
- ● *Mastery training*
- ● *Depression and the college blues*

▼ How is stress related to health and disease?

- ● *Life events, hassles, and stress*
- ● *Psychosomatic disorders*
- ● *Biofeedback*
- ● *The general adaptation syndrome*

▼ What are the best strategies for managing stress?

- ● *Stress management and coping skills*

▼ Is meditation useful for coping with stress?

- ● *Meditation and the relaxation response*

TAYLOR'S (NOT SO VERY) FINE ADVENTURE

SOMEHOW, TAYLOR HAD MANAGED TO SURVIVE the rush of make-or-break term papers, projects, and classroom speeches. Then it was on to finals, where his tests seemed perfectly timed to inflict as much suffering as possible. His two hardest exams fell on the same day! Great. What luck!

On the last day of finals, Taylor got caught in a traffic jam on his way to school. Two drivers cut him off, and another gave him a one-finger salute. When Taylor finally got to campus, the parking lot was swarming with frantic students. Most of them, like him, were within minutes of missing a final exam. At last, Taylor spied an empty space. As he started toward it, a Volkswagen darted around the corner and into "his" place. The driver of the car behind him began to honk impatiently. For a moment, Taylor was seized by a colossal desire to run over anything in sight.

Finally, after a week and a half of stress, pressure, and frustration, Taylor's finals were over. Sleep deprivation, gallons of coffee, junk food, and equal portions of cramming and complaining had carried him through. He was off for the summer. At last, he could kick back, relax, and have some fun. Or could he? Just four days after the end of school, Taylor got a bad cold, followed by bronchitis that lasted for nearly a month.

Taylor's experience illustrates what happens when stress, emotion, personal habits, and health collide. Although the timing of his cold might have been a coincidence, odds are it wasn't. Periods of stress are frequently followed by illness (Biondi & Zannino, 1997).

Stress occurs whenever a challenge or a threat forces a person to adjust or adapt. Stress is a normal part of life. But when stress is chronic or severe, it can damage health. Stress, in other words, is a behavioral factor that directly affects personal well-being.

In the first part of this chapter, we will explore a variety of behavioral health risks. Then we will look more closely at what stress is and how it affects us. After that, we will stress ways of coping with stress, so you can do a better job of staying healthy than Taylor did.

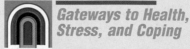

Gateways to Health, Stress, and Coping

A VARIETY OF PERSONAL HABITS AND BEHAVIOR PATTERNS affect health.

MAINTAINING GOOD HEALTH is a personal responsibility, not a matter of luck. Wellness is based on minimizing risk factors and engaging in health-promoting behaviors.

STRESS is a normal part of life; however, it is also a major risk factor for illness and disease.

ALTHOUGH SOME EVENTS ARE MORE STRESSFUL than others, stress always represents an interaction between people and the environments in which they live.

PERSONALITY CHARACTERISTICS affect the amount of stress a person experiences and the subsequent risk of illness.

THE BODY'S REACTIONS TO STRESS can directly damage internal organs, and stress impairs the body's immune system, increasing susceptibility to disease.

THE DAMAGING EFFECTS OF STRESS can be reduced with stress management techniques.

HEALTH PSYCHOLOGY—HERE'S TO YOUR GOOD HEALTH

Most people agree that health is important—especially their own. Yet, almost half of all deaths in North America are primarily due to unhealthy behavior. **Health psychology** aims to do something about such deaths. Health psychologists use behavioral principles to promote health and prevent illness (Terborg, 1998). Psychologists working in the allied field of **behavioral medicine** apply psychology to manage medical problems, such as diabetes or asthma. Their interests include pain control, helping people cope with chronic illness, stress-related diseases, self-screening for diseases (such as breast cancer), and similar topics (Luiselli, 1994).

Behavioral Risk Factors

Around the turn of the twentieth century, people primarily died from infectious diseases and accidents. Today, people generally die from **lifestyle diseases,** which are related to health-damaging personal habits. Examples include heart disease, stroke, and lung cancer (McGinnis & Foege, 1993) (❖Fig. 16.1). Clearly, some lifestyles promote health, whereas others lead to illness and death. As the cartoon character Pogo put it, "We have met the enemy and he is us."

What kinds of behavior are you referring to as unhealthy? Some causes of poor health are beyond our control. Nevertheless, a number of behavioral risk factors can be controlled. **Behavioral risk factors** are behaviors that increase the chances of disease, injury, or early death. For example, just being overweight is enough to double a person's chances of dying from cancer or heart disease. Thus, being fat is not just a matter of fashion—in the long run, it could kill you (Calle et al., 1999).

Each of the following is a major behavioral risk factor (Baum & Posluszny, 1999; Groth-Marnat & Schumaker, 1995):

- high levels of stress
- untreated high blood pressure
- cigarette smoking
- abuse of alcohol or other drugs

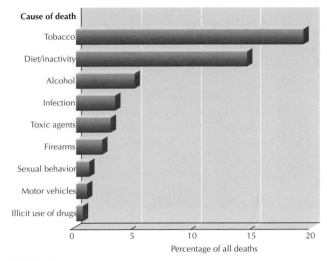

Cause of death

Percentage of all deaths

❖ **FIGURE 16.1** *The nine leading causes of death in the United States are shown in this graph. As you can see, eight of the top nine causes are directly related to behavioral risk factors (infection is the exception). At least 45 percent of all deaths can be traced to unhealthful behavior. The percentage of day-to-day health problems related to unhealthful behavior is even higher. (Data from McGinnis & Foege, 1993.)*

- overeating
- inadequate exercise
- unsafe sexual behavior
- exposure to toxic substances
- violence
- excess sun exposure
- driving at excessive speeds
- disregarding personal safety

Lifestyle diseases related to just six behaviors—smoking, alcohol and drug abuse, poor diet, insufficient exercise, and risky sexual practices—account for 70 percent of all medical costs (Orleans, Gruman, & Hollendonner, 1999).

◆Table 16.1 shows how many U.S. high school students engage in risky behaviors of the kind listed here. As you can see, health-damaging behavior is usually well established before adulthood (Kolbe, Collins, & Cortese, 1997).

In addition to specific risk factors, a general **disease-prone personality** type also exists. Such people tend to be chronically depressed, anxious, hostile, and . . . frequently ill (Taylor, 1990). In contrast, people who are intellectually resourceful, compassionate, optimistic, and non-hostile tend to enjoy good health (Lawler et al., 1999; Taylor et al., 1999).

LIFESTYLE   In your mind's eye, fast-forward an imaginary film of your life all the way to old age. Do it twice—once with a lifestyle including a large number of behavioral risk factors, and again without them. It should be obvious that countless small risks can add up to dramatically raise the chance of illness. If stress is a frequent part of your life, visualize your body seething with emotion, day after day. If you smoke, picture a lifetime's worth of cigarette smoke blown through your lungs in a week. If you drink, take a lifetime of alcohol's assaults on the brain, stomach, and liver, and squeeze them into a month:

◆ **TABLE 16.1** Percentage of U.S. High School Students Who Engaged in Health-Endangering Behaviors

RISKY BEHAVIOR	PERCENTAGE
Rode with drinking driver (previous month)	35
Were in a physical fight (previous year)	42
Carried a weapon (previous month)	22
Had 5 or more drinks on one occasion (previous month)	30
Have used marijuana	33
Have engaged in sexual intercourse	53
Did not use condom during last sexual intercourse	47
Smoked cigarettes (previous month)	31
Ate high-fat food (previous day)	34
No vigorous exercise (previous week)	34

(Source: Kolbe, Collins, & Cortese, 1997.)

Your body would be poisoned, ravaged, and soon dead. If you eat a high-fat, high-cholesterol diet, fast-forward to a lifetime of heart-killing plaque clogging your arteries.

Although it may sound like it, this discussion is not meant to be a sermon. It is merely a reminder that risk factors do make a difference. To make matters worse, unhealthy lifestyles almost always create multiple risks. That is, people who smoke are also likely to drink excessively. Those who overeat usually do not get enough exercise (Emmons et al., 1998). And so on.

Health-Promoting Behaviors

To prevent disease and promote well-being, health psychologists first try to remove behavioral risk factors. All the medicine in the world may not be enough to restore health without changes in behavior. We all know someone who has had a heart attack or lung disease who cannot or will not change the habits that led to the illness.

Health psychology *Study of the ways in which behavioral principles can be used to prevent illness and promote health.*
Behavioral medicine *The study of behavioral factors in medicine, physical illness, and medical treatment.*
Lifestyle disease *A disease related to health-damaging personal habits.*
Behavioral risk factors *Behaviors that increase the chances of disease, injury, or premature death.*
Disease-prone personality *A personality type associated with poor health; marked by persistent negative emotions, including anxiety, depression, and hostility.*

In the long run, behavioral risk factors and lifestyles do make a difference in health and life expectancy.

Beyond this, psychologists are also interested in getting people to increase behaviors that promote health. **Health-promoting behaviors** include such obvious practices as getting regular exercise, controlling smoking and alcohol use, maintaining a balanced diet, getting good medical care, and managing stress (Glik, Kronenfeld, & Jackson, 1996). Even something as simple as using seat belts in a car greatly ups life expectancy.

Basic health practices *should* extend a person's life. But do they? A major study done in California provides an answer (Belloc, 1973; Belloc & Breslow, 1972; Breslow & Enstrom, 1980). Nearly 7,000 people filled out a detailed questionnaire about their health practices. In ensuing years, researchers kept a close watch on the medical and death records of these people. Before we discuss the results, you might find it interesting to check the items listed here that apply to you.

1. I get 7 to 8 hours of sleep a night.
2. I am currently at or near the ideal weight for my height.
3. I have never smoked cigarettes.
4. I use alcohol moderately or not at all.
5. I get regular physical exercise.

Men who engaged in all five practices had a death rate almost four times lower than men who engaged in zero to three practices. The death rate was two times lower for women who engaged in all five practices. (Note, however, that these are not the only elements of a healthy lifestyle. They are just the ones investigated in this study.)

In some cases, diseases can be treated or prevented by making specific changes in behavior. For example, hypertension (high blood pressure) is often deadly. Yet, for some people, simple lifestyle changes will fend off this "silent killer." Here's the recipe for lower blood pressure: lose weight, consume less sodium (salt), use alcohol sparingly, and get more exercise (Dubbert, 1995).

To summarize, a small number of behavioral patterns account for many common health problems (Kolbe, Collins, & Cortese, 1997). ◆Table 16.2 lists several major ways to promote good health.

EARLY PREVENTION   Smoking is the largest preventable cause of death and the single most lethal behavioral risk factor (McGinnis & Foege, 1993). As such, it illustrates the prospect for preventing illness.

◆ **TABLE 16.2** Major Health-Promoting Behaviors

	SOURCE	DESIRABLE BEHAVIORS
	Nutrition	Eating a balanced, low-fat diet; appropriate caloric intake; maintenance of healthy body weight
	Exercise	At least 30 minutes of aerobic exercise, 5 days per week
	Blood pressure	Lower blood pressure with diet and exercise, or drugs if necessary
	Alcohol and drugs	No more than 2 drinks per day; abstain from using drugs
	Tobacco	Do not smoke; do not use smokeless tobacco
	Sleep and relaxation	Avoid sleep deprivation; provide for periods of relaxation every day
	Sex	Practice safer sex; avoid unplanned pregnancy
	Injury	Curb dangerous driving habits, use seat belts; minimize sun exposure; forgo dangerous activities
	Stress	Learn stress management; lower hostility

What have health psychologists done to lessen the risks? Attempts to "immunize" youths against pressures to start smoking provide a good example. The smoker who says, "Quitting is easy, I've done it dozens of times" states a basic truth—only 1 smoker in 10 has long-term success at quitting. Thus, the best way to deal with smoking is to prevent it before it becomes a lifelong habit.

Smoking develops slowly, which gives time to expose young people to prevention efforts. Examples include peer quizzes about the effects of smoking, anti-smoking art contests, poster and T-shirt giveaways, anti-smoking pamphlets for parents, and student quizzes of parents (Biglan et al., 1996). Such efforts persuade kids that smoking is dangerous and "uncool."

Some of the best anti-smoking programs include **refusal skills training.** In this case, youths learn to resist pressures to begin smoking (or using other drugs) (Botvin et al., 1997). For example, junior high students can role-play ways to resist smoking pressures from peers, adults, and cigarette ads. Similar methods can be applied to other health risks, such as sexually transmitted diseases and unwanted pregnancy (Botvin et al., 1995).

The latest health programs also teach students general life skills. The idea is to give kids skills that will help them cope with day-to-day stresses. That way, they will be less tempted to escape problems through drug use or other destructive behaviors. **Life skills training** includes practice in stress reduction, self-protection, decision making, self-control, and social skills (Jones et al., 1995).

Health Campaigns

In addition to projects like the ones described, health psychologists have had success with **community health campaigns.** These are community-wide education projects designed to lessen a combination of major risk factors. Health campaigns inform people of risks such as stress, alcohol abuse, high blood pressure, high cholesterol, smoking, sexually transmitted diseases, or excessive sun exposure. This is followed by efforts to motivate people to change their behavior. Campaigns sometimes provide **role models** (positive examples), who show people how to improve their own health. They also direct people to community services for health screening, advice, and treatment (Cheadle et al., 1992–93). People may be reached through the mass media, public schools, health fairs, their work, or self-help programs (Calvert & Cocking, 1992; Schooler et al., 1993). Recently, psychologists have concentrated more on reaching previously neglected people, such as elderly members of ethnic minority groups, African-Americans, Latinos, Native Americans, and people living in rural areas (Reppucci, Woolard, & Fried, 1999).

A MODEL PROGRAM   A good example of a community health campaign in action is the Stanford Heart Disease Prevention Program (Meyer et al., 1980). In the Stanford project, a media campaign about risk factors in heart disease—smoking, diet, and exercise—was combined with special group "workshops" for high-risk individuals. After the program had run for 2 years, smokers decreased by 17 percent in two test communities. Compare this figure with the 12 percent *increase* observed in similar, untreated communities.

Such progress may seem modest, but it is, in fact, worthwhile, cost effective, and highly promising. Similar projects have lowered the risk of heart disease in target communities by at least 15 percent (Farquhar et al., 1984, 1997). All you have to

The page shown here is reproduced from a booklet prepared as part of a public health campaign conducted in southern Arizona. Such campaigns promote health by calling attention to psychological risk factors and by telling what to do about them. (From Marques et al., 1982.)

do is picture someone you love staying healthy or living longer to appreciate the value of such efforts.

Wellness

Health is not just an absence of disease. People who are truly healthy enjoy a positive state of **wellness** or well-being. Maintaining wellness is a life-long pursuit and, hopefully, a labor of love. People who attain optimal wellness are both physically and psychologically healthy. They engage in positive thinking, show emotional resilience, and are optimistic and self-confident (Lightsey, 1996).

People who enjoy a sense of well-being also have supportive relationships with others, they do meaningful work, and they live in a clean environment. Many of these aspects of wellness are addressed in other chapters of this book. In this chapter, we

Health-promoting behavior *Any practice that tends to maintain or enhance good health.*
Refusal skills training *Program that teaches youths how to resist pressures to begin smoking. (Can also be applied to other drugs, and health risks.)*
Life skills training *A program that teaches stress reduction, self-protection, decision making, self-control, and social skills.*
Community health campaign *A community-wide education program that provides information about how to lessen risk factors and promote health.*
Role model *A person who serves as a positive example of desirable behavior.*
Wellness *A positive state of good health; more than the absence of disease.*

will give special attention to the role that stress plays in health and sickness. As stated earlier, stress management is a major activity of health psychologists. Understanding stress, and learning to control it, can improve not only your health but the quality of your life as well. For these reasons, a discussion of stress and stress management follows.

KNOWLEDGE BUILDER

HEALTH PSYCHOLOGY

RELATE

If you were to work as a health psychologist, would you be more interested in preventing disease or managing it?

Make a list of the major behavioral risk factors that apply to you. Are you laying the foundation for a lifestyle disease?

Which of the health-promoting behaviors listed in ◆Table 16.2 would you like to increase?

If you were designing a community health campaign, whom would you use as role models of healthful behavior?

LEARNING CHECK

1. Adjustment to chronic illness and the control of pain are topics that would more likely be of interest to a specialist in

   _____ _____

   rather than a health psychologist.

2. With respect to health, which of the following is *not* a major behavioral risk factor?
   a. overexercise *b.* cigarette smoking *c.* stress *d.* high blood pressure

3. Eating breakfast almost every day and rarely eating between meals proved to be the two most important health-promoting behaviors in the Alameda County study. T or F?

4. Health psychologists tend to prefer _____ rather than modifying habits (like smoking) that become difficult to break once they are established.

5. The disease-prone personality is marked by _____, anxiety, and hostility.

CRITICAL THINKING

6. The general public is increasingly well informed about health risks and healthful behavior. Can you apply the concept of reinforcement to explain why so many people fail to act on this information?

Answers:

1. behavioral medicine 2. *a* 3. F 4. prevention 5. depression 6. Many health payoffs are delayed by months or years, greatly lessening the immediate rewards for healthful behavior.

STRESS—THRILL OR THREAT?

Stress isn't always bad. As stress researcher Hans Selye (SEL-yay) (1976) observed, "To be totally without stress is to be dead." As noted earlier, **stress** is the mental and physical con-

dition that occurs when a person must adjust or adapt to the environment. Unpleasant events such as work pressures, marital problems, or financial woes naturally produce stress. But so do travel, sports, a new job, mountain climbing, dating, and other positive activities. Even if you aren't a thrill seeker, a healthy lifestyle may include a fair amount of *eustress* (good stress). Eustress can be energizing. Activities that provoke "good stress" are usually experienced as challenging and rewarding.

A **stress reaction** begins with the same autonomic nervous system arousal that occurs during emotion. Imagine standing at the top of a wind-whipped ski jump for the first time. Internally, there would be a rapid surge in your heart rate, blood pressure, respiration, muscle tension, and other ANS responses. *Short-term* stresses of this kind can be uncomfortable, but they rarely do any damage. (Your landing might be another matter, however.) Later, we will describe the *long-term* physical impact of prolonged stress—which *can* do harm. For now, ◆Table 16.3 gives an overview of typical signs or symptoms of prolonged stress.

Other than when it is long lasting, why is stress sometimes damaging and sometimes not? Stress reactions are complex. Let's examine some of the chief factors that determine whether stress is harmful.

When Is Stress a Strain?

It goes almost without saying that some events are more likely to cause stress than others. A **stressor** is a condition or event in the environment that challenges or threatens a person. Police officers, for instance, suffer from a high rate of stress-related diseases. The threat of injury or death, plus occasional confrontations with drunk or belligerent citizens, takes a toll. A major factor here is the *unpredictable* nature of police work. An officer who stops to issue a traffic ticket

---

◆ TABLE 16.3 Warning Signs of Stress

EMOTIONAL SIGNS
Anxiety
Apathy
Irritability
Mental fatigue

BEHAVIORAL SIGNS
Avoidance of responsibilities and relationships
Extreme or self-destructive behavior
Self-neglect
Poor judgment

PHYSICAL SIGNS
Excessive worry about illness
Frequent illness
Exhaustion
Overuse of medicines
Physical aliments and complaints

(Doctor & Doctor, 1994)

Although it may not seem so, assembly line work can be quite stressful, because of the lack of control employees have over the pace of work.

◆ **TABLE 16.4** The 10 Most Stressful Jobs

JOB	RANK
U.S. president	1
firefighter	2
senior corporate executive	3
Indy-class race car driver	4
taxi driver	5
surgeon	6
astronaut	7
police officer	8
NFL football player	9
air-traffic controller	10

(Krantz, 1995.)

never knows if a cooperative citizen or an armed gangster is waiting in the car.

A study done with rats shows how unpredictable events add to stress. Rats in one group were given shocks preceded by a warning tone. A second group got shocks without warning. The third group received no shocks but heard the tone. After a few weeks, the animals that received unpredictable shocks had severe stomach ulcers. Those given predictable shocks showed little or no ulceration. The lucky group that received no shocks also had no ulcers (Weiss, 1972).

Pressure is another element in stress, especially job stress. **Pressure** occurs when a person must meet urgent external demands or expectations (Weiten, 1998). For example, we feel pressured when activities must be speeded up, when deadlines must be met, when extra work is added unexpectedly, or when we must work near maximum capacity for long periods. Most students who have survived final exams are familiar with the effects of pressure.

What if I set deadlines for myself? Does it make a difference where the pressure comes from? Yes. People generally feel more stress in situations over which they have little or no control (Taylor et al., 1999). For example, Douglas DeGood (1975) subjected college students to an unpleasant shock-avoidance task. Some students were allowed to select their own rest periods; others rested at times selected for them. Participants allowed to control their own rest periods showed lower stress levels (as measured by blood pressure) than those given no choice.

To summarize, when emotional "shocks" are *intense* or *repeated, unpredictable, uncontrollable,* and linked to *pressure,* stress will be magnified and damage is likely to result. (See ◆Table 16.4 for a rating of jobs that contain these elements.) At work, chronic stress sometimes results in *burnout,* a pattern of emotional exhaustion described in the highlight "Burnout—The High Cost of Caring."

Appraising Stressors

External events are not the whole story of stress. As noted in Chapter 13, the emotions we feel are greatly affected by the ways in which we appraise situations. That's why some people are distressed by events that others view as a thrill or a challenge (eustress). Ultimately, stress depends on how a situation is perceived. I have a friend who would find it stressful to listen to five of his son's rap CDs in a row. He has a son who would find it stressful to listen to one of his father's opera CDs. To know if you are stressed, we must know what meaning you place on events. As we will see in a moment, whenever a stressor is appraised as a **threat** (potentially harmful), a powerful stress reaction follows (Lazarus, 1991a).

"AM I OKAY OR IN TROUBLE?" Situation: You have been selected to give a speech to 300 people. Or a doctor tells you that you must undergo a dangerous and painful operation. Or the one true love of your life walks out the door. What would your emotional response to these events be? How do you cope with an emotional threat?

Stress *The mental and physical condition that occurs when a person must adjust or adapt to the environment.*
Stress reaction *The physical response to stress, consisting mainly of bodily changes related to autonomic nervous system arousal.*
Stressor *A specific condition or event in the environment that challenges or threatens a person.*
Pressure *A stressful condition that occurs when a person must meet urgent external demands or expectations.*
Threat *An event or situation perceived as potentially harmful.*

A CLOSER LOOK

BURNOUT—THE HIGH COST OF CARING

Margo, a young nurse, realizes with dismay that she has "lost all patience with her patients" and wishes they would "go somewhere else to be sick."

Reactions like Margo's are clear signs of job **burnout,** a condition in which workers are physically, mentally, and emotionally drained. What does it mean to be "burned out"? The problem has three aspects (Maslach, 1982; Yadama & Drake, 1995).

First of all, burnout involves *emotional exhaustion.* Affected people are fatigued, tense, apathetic, and suffering from physical ailments. They feel "used up" and have an "I don't give a damn anymore" attitude toward work.

A second problem is *depersonalization,* or detachment from others. Burned-out workers no longer care about their clients and coldly treat them like objects.

The third aspect of burnout is a feeling of *reduced personal accomplishment.* Burned-out workers do poor work and feel helpless, hopeless, or angry. Their self-esteem slumps, and they yearn to change jobs or careers.

Burnout may occur in any job, but it is a marked problem in emotionally demanding helping professions, such as nursing, teaching, social work, child care, counseling, caring for AIDS patients, or police work (Bellani et al., 1996; Matthews, 1990; Poulin & Walter, 1993; Yadama & Drake, 1995).

It's ironic that the same work that produces burnout can also be highly rewarding. If our society wishes to keep caring people in the helping professions, some changes may be needed. A good start would be to redesign jobs to create a better balance between demands and satisfactions. As in other stressful situations, people are more likely to burn out if they feel they have little control over their work (McKnight & Glass, 1995).

Building stronger social support systems could also help prevent burnout. A good example is the growing use of support groups for nurses and other caregivers. In a **support group,** workers give and receive emotional encouragement as they talk about feelings, problems, and stresses (Greenglass, Burke, & Konarski, 1998).

Ultimately, the best solution for burnout may be for each of us to better appreciate the stresses felt by people whose work requires caring about the needs of others (Capner & Caltabiano, 1993).

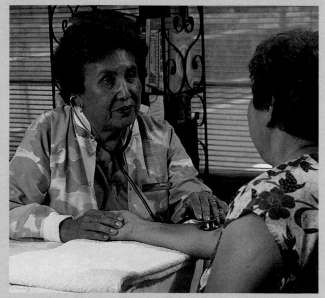

The helping professions require empathy, caring, and emotional involvement. As a result, caregivers risk depleting their emotional resources and ability to cope. Over time, this can lead to burnout.

According to Richard Lazarus (1991a), there are two important steps in managing a threat. The first is a **primary appraisal,** in which you decide if a situation is relevant or irrelevant, positive or threatening. In essence, this step answers the question, "Am I okay or in trouble?" Then you make a **secondary appraisal,** in which you assess your resources and choose a way to meet the threat or challenge. ("What can I do about this situation?") Thus, the way a situation is "sized up" greatly affects one's ability to cope with it (❖Fig. 16.2). Public speaking, for instance, can be appraised as an intense threat, a challenge, or a chance to perform. Emphasizing the threat—by imagining failure, rejection, or embarrassment—obviously invites disaster (Lazarus, 1993).

THE NATURE OF THREAT   What does it mean to feel threatened by a stressor? Certainly, in most day-to-day situations, it doesn't mean you think your life is in danger. (Unless, of course, you owe money to Enrico the Enforcer.) Threat has more to do with the idea of control. We are particularly prone to feel stressed when we can't—or think we can't—control our imme-

Primary Appraisal ⟶ **Secondary Appraisal**
relevant?   coping resources available?
threatening?   course of action?

Stressor
intense?
repeated?
unpredictable?
uncontrollable?
pressure?

Notice of Workforce Reduction

❖ **FIGURE 16.2** *Stress is the product of an interchange between a person and the environment.*

© 1985 FarWorks, Inc./Dist. by Universal Press Syndicate

Larson 3-19

"The fuel light's on, Frank! We're all going to die! ... Wait, wait. ... Oh, my mistake—that's the intercom light."

diate environment. In short, a *perceived lack of control* is just as threatening as an actual lack of control (DasGupta, 1992). If your answer to the question "What can I do about this situation?" is "nothing," you will feel emotionally stressed.

A sense of control also comes from believing you can reach desired goals. It is threatening to feel that we lack *competence* to cope with life's demands (Bandura, 1986). Thus, the intensity of the body's stress reaction often depends on what we think and tell ourselves about stressors. That's why it's valuable to learn to think in ways that ward off the body's stress response. (Some strategies for controlling upsetting thoughts are described in this chapter's Psychology in Action section.)

Coping with Threat

You have appraised a situation as threatening. What will you do next? There are two major choices. **Problem-focused coping** is aimed at managing or altering the distressing situation itself. In **emotion-focused coping,** people try instead to control their emotional reactions to the situation (Lazarus, 1993).

Couldn't both types of coping occur together? Yes. Sometimes the two types of coping aid one another. Say, for example, that a woman feels anxious as she steps to the podium to give a speech. If she does some deep breathing to reduce her anxiety (emotion-focused coping), she will be better able to glance over her notes to improve her delivery (problem-focused coping).

It is also possible for coping efforts to clash. For instance, if you have to make a difficult decision, you may suffer intense

emotional distress. In such circumstances, there is a temptation to make a quick and ill-advised choice, just to end the suffering. Doing so may allow you to cope with your emotions, but it shortchanges problem-focused coping.

In general, problem-focused coping tends to be especially useful when you are facing a controllable stressor—that is, a situation you can actually do something about. Emotion-focused efforts are best suited to managing stressors that you cannot control (Lazarus, 1993; Taylor, 1990). To improve your chances of coping effectively, the stress-fighting strategies described in this chapter include a mixture of both techniques.

We will soon return to another look at stress and its effects. But first, let's examine two major (and all too familiar) causes of stress: frustration and conflict.

FRUSTRATION—BLIND ALLEYS AND LEAD BALLOONS

Do you remember how frustrated Taylor was when he couldn't find a parking place? **Frustration** is a negative emotional state that occurs when people are prevented from reaching desired goals. In Taylor's case, the goal of finding a parking space was blocked by another car.

Obstacles of many kinds cause frustration. A useful distinction can be made between external and personal sources of frustration. **External frustration** is based on conditions outside the individual that impede progress toward a goal. All of the following are external frustrations: getting stuck with a flat tire, having a marriage proposal rejected, finding the cupboard bare when you go to get your poor dog a bone, finding the refrigerator bare when you go to get your poor tummy a T-bone, finding the refrigerator gone when you return home, and being chased out of the house by your starving dog. In other words, external frustrations are based on *delays, failure, rejection, loss,* and other direct blocking of motivated behavior.

Notice that external obstacles can be either *social* (slow drivers, tall people in theaters, people who cut into lines) or *nonsocial* (stuck doors, a dead battery, rain on the day of the game). If you ask 10 of your friends what has frustrated them recently, most will probably mention someone's behavior ("My sister wore one of my dresses when I wanted to wear it," "My

Burnout *A job-related condition of mental, physical, and emotional exhaustion.*
Support group *A group formed to provide emotional support for its members through discussion of stresses and shared concerns.*
Primary appraisal *Deciding if a situation is relevant to oneself and if it is a threat.*
Secondary appraisal *Deciding how to cope with a threat or challenge.*
Problem-focused coping *Directly managing or remedying a stressful or threatening situation.*
Emotion-focused coping *Managing or controlling one's emotional reaction to a stressful or threatening situation.*
Frustration *A negative emotional state that occurs when one is prevented from reaching a goal.*
External frustration *Distress caused by external conditions that impede progress toward a goal.*

supervisor is unfair," or "My history teacher grades too hard"). As social animals, we humans are highly sensitive to social sources of frustration (Peeters, Buunk, & Schaufeli, 1995).

Frustration usually increases as the *strength, urgency,* or *importance* of a blocked motive increases. Taylor was especially frustrated in the parking lot because he was late for an exam. Likewise, an escape artist submerged in a tank of water and bound with 200 pounds of chain would become *quite* frustrated if a trick lock jammed. Remember, too, that motivation becomes stronger as we near a goal. As a result, frustration is more intense when a person runs into an obstacle very close to a goal. If you've ever missed an A grade by 5 points, you were probably very frustrated. If you've missed an A by 1 point—well, frustration builds character, right?

A final factor affecting frustration is summarized by the old phrase "the straw that broke the camel's back." The effects of *repeated* frustrations can accumulate until a small irritation sets off an unexpectedly violent response. A case in point is the fact that people with long commutes are more likely to display "road rage" (angry, aggressive driving) (Harding et al., 1998).

Personal frustrations are based on personal characteristics. If you are 4 feet tall and aspire to be a professional basketball player, you very likely will be frustrated. If you want to go to medical school, but can earn only D grades, you will likewise be frustrated. In both examples, frustration is actually based on personal limitations. Yet, failure may be *perceived* as externally caused. We will return to this point in the Psychology in Action section. In the meantime, let's look at some typical reactions to frustration.

Reactions to Frustration

Aggression is any response made with the intent of harming a person or an object. It is one of the most persistent and frequent responses to frustration (Berkowitz, 1988). The frustration-aggression link is so common, in fact, that experiments are hardly necessary to show it. A glance at almost any newspaper will provide examples like the one that follows.

Justifiable Autocide

Burien, Washington (AP)—Barbara Smith committed the assault, but police aren't likely to press charges. Her victim was a 1964 Oldsmobile which failed once too often to start.

When Officer Jim Fuda arrived at the scene, he found one beat-up car, a broken baseball bat and a satisfied 23-year-old Seattle woman.

"I feel good," Ms. Smith reportedly told the officer. "That car's been giving me misery for years and I killed it."

Does frustration always cause aggression? Aren't there other reactions? Although the connection is strong, frustration does not always provoke aggression. Later, in Chapter 20, we will explore factors that influence when and where aggression is likely to occur. For now, it is enough to note that aggression is not usually the first, or only, reaction to frustration. More often, frustration is met first with *persistence*. This is characterized by more *vigorous efforts* and *varied responses* (❖Fig. 16.3). For example, if you put your last quarter in a vending machine, and pressing the button has no effect, you will probably press

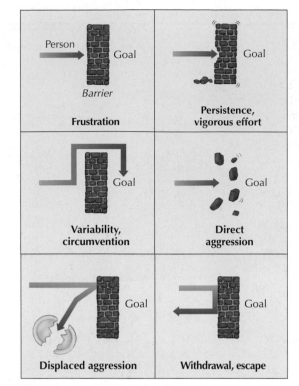

❖ **FIGURE 16.3** *Frustration and common reactions to it.*

harder and faster (vigorous effort). Then you will press all the other buttons (varied response). Persistence may help you get *around* a barrier in order to reach your goal. However, if the machine *still* refuses to deliver, or return your quarter, you may become aggressive and kick the machine (or at least tell it what you think of it).

Persistence can be very adaptive. Overcoming a barrier ends the frustration and allows the need or motive to be satisfied. The same is true of aggression that removes or destroys a barrier. Picture a small band of nomadic humans, parched by thirst but separated from a water hole by a menacing animal. It is easy to see that attacking the animal may ensure their survival. In modern society, such direct aggression is seldom acceptable. If you find a long line at the drinking fountain, aggression is hardly appropriate. Because direct aggression is discouraged, it is frequently *displaced*.

How is aggression displaced? Does displaced aggression occur often? Directing aggression toward a source of frustration may be impossible, or it may be too dangerous. If you are frustrated by your boss at work or by a teacher at school, the cost of direct aggression may be too high (losing your job or failing a needed class). Instead, the aggression may be displaced, or redirected, toward whomever or whatever is available. Targets of **displaced aggression** tend to be safer, or less likely to retaliate, than the original source of frustration.

Sometimes long *chains* of displacement occur, in which one person displaces aggression to the next. For instance, a businesswoman who is frustrated by high taxes reprimands an employee, who swallows his anger until he reaches home and then yells at his wife, who in turn yells at the children, who then

Some organizations raise money by charging people for the "privilege" of smashing a junk car with a sledge hammer. Are some participants displacing aggressive urges related to frustration in other areas of their lives?

tease the dog. The dog chases the cat, who later knocks over the canary cage.

Psychologists attribute much hostility and violence to displaced aggression. A disturbing example is the finding that when unemployment increases, so does child abuse (Steinberg et al., 1981). A pattern known as **scapegoating,** in which a person or group of people are blamed for conditions not of their making, is particularly troubling. A **scapegoat** is a person who has become a habitual target of displaced aggression. A tragic example of scapegoating on a large scale is the fact that in the United States between 1880 and 1930 there was a strong correlation between the price of cotton and the number of lynchings of African Americans in the South. As the price of cotton went down (and frustration increased), the number of lynchings increased (Dollard et al., 1939). Despite recent progress, many minority groups continue to suffer from hostility based on scapegoating. Think, for example, about the hostility expressed toward recent immigrants during times of economic hardship. In many communities, layoffs and job losses continue to be associated with increases in violence (Catalano, Novaco, & McConnell, 1997).

I have a friend who dropped out of school to hitchhike around the country. He seemed very frustrated before he quit. What type of response to frustration is that? Another major reaction to frustration is escape, or withdrawal. It is stressful and unpleasant to be frustrated. If other reactions do not reduce feelings of frustration, a person may try to escape. **Escape** may mean actually leaving a source of frustration (dropping out of school,

quitting a job, leaving an unhappy marriage), or it may mean psychologically escaping. Two common forms of psychological escape are *apathy* (pretending not to care) and the *use of drugs* such as cocaine, alcohol, marijuana, or narcotics. (See ❖Fig. 16.3 for a summary of common reactions to frustration.)

CONFLICT—YES, NO, YES, NO, YES, NO, WELL, MAYBE

Conflict occurs whenever a person must choose between contradictory needs, desires, motives, or demands. Choosing between college and work, marriage and single life, or study and failure are common conflicts. There are four basic forms of conflict. As we will see, each has its own properties (❖ Figs. 16.4 and 16.5).

APPROACH-APPROACH CONFLICTS   A simple **approach-approach conflict** comes from having to choose between two positive, or desirable, alternatives. Choosing between tutti-frutti-coconut-mocha-champagne ice and orange-marmalade-peanut

❖ **FIGURE 16.4** *Three basic forms of conflict. For this woman, choosing between pie and ice cream is a minor approach-approach conflict, deciding whether to take a job that will require weekend work is an approach-avoidance conflict, and choosing between paying higher rent and moving is an avoidance-avoidance conflict.*

Personal frustration *Distress caused by personal characteristics that impede progress toward a goal.*
Aggression *Any response made with the intent of harming some person or object.*
Displaced aggression *Redirecting aggression to a target other than the actual source of one's frustration.*
Scapegoating *Blaming a person or a group of people for conditions not of their making.*
Scapegoat *A person who has become a habitual target of displaced aggression.*
Escape *Reducing discomfort by leaving frustrating situations or by psychologically withdrawing from them.*
Conflict *A stressful condition that occurs when a person must choose between incompatible or contradictory alternatives.*
Approach-approach conflict *Choosing between two positive, or desirable, alternatives.*

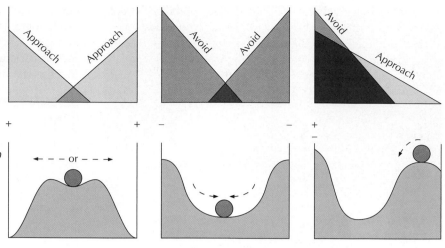

❖ **FIGURE 16.5** *Conflict diagrams. As shown by the colored areas in the graphs, desires to approach and to avoid increase near a goal. The effects of these tendencies are depicted below each graph. The "behavior" of the ball in each example illustrates the nature of the conflict above it. An approach conflict (left) is easily decided. Moving toward one goal will increase its attraction (graph) and will lead to a rapid resolution. (If the ball moves in either direction, it will go all the way to one of the goals.) In an avoidance conflict (center), tendencies to avoid are deadlocked, resulting in inaction. In an approach-avoidance conflict (right), approach proceeds to the point where desires to approach and avoid cancel each other. Again, these tendencies are depicted (below) by the action of the ball. (Graphs after Miller, 1944.)*

butter-coffee swirl at the ice cream parlor may throw you into a temporary conflict. However, if you really like both choices, your decision will be quickly made. Even when more important decisions are at stake, approach-approach conflicts tend to be the easiest to resolve. The old fable about the mule that died of thirst and starvation while standing between a bucket of water and a bucket of oats is obviously unrealistic. When both options are positive, the scales of decision are easily tipped in one direction or the other.

AVOIDANCE-AVOIDANCE CONFLICTS   Being forced to choose between two negative, or undesirable, alternatives creates an **avoidance-avoidance conflict.** A person in an avoidance conflict is caught between "the devil and the deep blue sea" or between "the frying pan and the fire." In real life, double-avoidance conflicts involve dilemmas such as choosing between unwanted pregnancy and abortion, the dentist and tooth decay, a monotonous job and poverty, or dorm food and starvation.

Suppose I don't object to abortion. Or suppose that I consider any pregnancy sacred and not to be tampered with?   Like many other stressful situations, these examples can be defined as conflicts only on the basis of personal needs and values. If a woman wants to end a pregnancy and does not object to abortion, she experiences no conflict. If she would not consider abortion under any circumstances, there is no conflict.

Avoidance conflicts often have a "damned if you do, damned if you don't" quality. In other words, both choices are negative, but *not choosing* may be impossible or equally undesirable. To illustrate, imagine the plight of a person trapped in a hotel fire 20 stories from the ground. Should she jump from the window and almost surely die on the pavement? Or should she try to dash through the flames and almost surely die of smoke inhalation and burns? When faced with a choice such as this, it is easy to see why people often *freeze*, finding it impossible to decide or take action. A trapped individual may first think about the window, approach it, and then back away after looking down 20 stories. Next, she may try the door and again back away as heat and smoke billow in. In actual disasters of this

sort, people are often found dead in their rooms, victims of an inability to take action.

Indecision, inaction, and freezing are not the only reactions to double-avoidance conflicts. Because avoidance conflicts are stressful and rarely solved, people sometimes pull out of them entirely. This reaction, called *leaving the field*, is another form of escape. It may explain the behavior of a student the author knew who could not attend school unless he worked. However, if he worked, he could not earn passing grades. His solution, after much conflict and indecision? He joined the navy.

APPROACH-AVOIDANCE CONFLICTS   Approach-avoidance conflicts are also difficult to resolve. In some ways, they are more troublesome than avoidance conflicts because people seldom escape them. A person in an **approach-avoidance conflict** is "caught" by being attracted to, and repelled by, the same goal or activity. Attraction keeps the person in the situation, but its negative aspects cause turmoil and distress. For example, a high school student arrives to pick up his date for the first time. He is met at the door by her father, who is a professional wrestler—7 feet tall, 300 pounds, and entirely covered with hair. The father gives the boy a crushing handshake and growls that he will break him in half if the girl is not home on time. The student considers the girl attractive and has a good time. But does he ask her out again? It depends on the relative strength of his attraction and his fear. Almost certainly he will feel *ambivalent* about asking her out again, knowing that another encounter with her father awaits him.

Ambivalence (mixed positive and negative feelings) is a central characteristic of approach-avoidance conflicts. Ambivalence is usually translated into *partial approach* (Miller, 1944). Because our student is still attracted to the girl, he may spend time with her at school and elsewhere, but he may not actually date her again. Some more realistic examples of approach-avoidance conflicts are planning to marry someone your parents strongly disapprove of, wanting to be in a play but suffering stage fright, wanting to buy a car but not wanting to make monthly payments, and wanting to eat when overweight. Many of life's important decisions have approach-avoidance dimensions.

Aren't real-life conflicts more complex than the ones described here? Yes. Conflicts are rarely as clear-cut as those described. People in conflict are usually faced with several dilemmas at once, so several types of conflict may be intermingled. The fourth type of conflict moves us closer to reality.

MULTIPLE CONFLICTS   You are offered two jobs: One has good pay but poor hours and dull work; the second has interesting work and excellent hours but low pay. Which do you select? This situation is more typical of the choices we must usually make. It offers neither completely positive nor completely negative options. It is, in other words, a **double approach-avoidance conflict,** in which each alternative has both positive and negative qualities.

As with single approach-avoidance conflicts, people faced with double approach-avoidance conflicts feel ambivalent about each choice. This causes them to *vacillate,* or waver between the alternatives. Just as you are about to choose one such alternative, its undesirable aspects tend to loom large. So, what do you do? You swing back toward the other choice. If you have ever been romantically attracted to two people at once— each having qualities you like and dislike—then you have probably experienced **vacillation.** Another example that may be familiar is trying to decide between two college majors, each with advantages and disadvantages.

In real life, it is common to face **multiple approach-avoidance conflicts,** in which several alternatives each have positive and negative features. An example would be trying to choose which automobile to buy among several brands. On a day-to-day basis, most multiple approach-avoidance conflicts are little more than an annoyance. When they involve major life decisions, such as choosing a career, a school, a mate, or a job, they can add greatly to the amount of stress we experience.

KNOWLEDGE BUILDER
STRESS, FRUSTRATION, AND CONFLICT

RELATE

What impact did pressure, control, predictability, repetition, and intensity have on your last stress reaction?

What type of coping do you tend to use when you face a stressor such as public speaking or taking an important exam?

Think of a time when you were frustrated. What was your goal? What prevented you from reacting to it? Was your frustration external or personal?

Have you ever displaced aggression? Why did you choose another target for your hostility?

Review the major types of conflict and think of a conflict you have faced that illustrates each type. Did your reactions match those described in the text?

LEARNING CHECK

1. Greater perceived control over a stressor is usually associated with a reduction in the amount of stress experienced. T or F?

2. Emotional exhaustion, depersonalization, and reduced accomplishment are characteristics of job _____.

3. Stress tends to be greatest when a situation is appraised as a _____ and a person does not feel _____ to cope with the situation.

4. According to Lazarus, coping with threatening situations can be both problem focused and _____ focused.

5. Which of the following is *not* a common reaction to frustration? *a.* ambivalence *b.* aggression *c.* displaced aggression *d.* persistence

6. Sampson Goliath is 7 feet tall and weighs 300 pounds. He has failed miserably in his aspirations to become a jockey. The source of his frustration is mainly _____.

7. As a reaction to frustration, apathy may be viewed as a form of _____.

8. Inaction and freezing are most characteristic of avoidance-avoidance conflicts. T or F?

9. Approach-avoidance conflicts produce mixed feelings called _____.

CRITICAL THINKING

10. Which do you think would produce more stress: (a) appraising a situation as mildly threatening but feeling like you are totally incompetent to cope with it? Or (b) appraising a situation as very threatening but feeling that you have the resources and skills to cope with it?

11. Being frustrated is unpleasant. If some action, including aggression, ends frustration, why might we expect the action to be repeated on other occasions?

12. What kind of conflict would you expect a first-time skydiver to experience?

Answers:
1. T 2. burnout 3. threat, competent 4. emotion 5. *a* 6. personal 7. escape 8. T 9. ambivalence 10. There is no correct answer here because individual stress reactions vary greatly. However, the secondary appraisal of a situation often determines just how stressful it is. Feeling incapable of coping is very threatening. 11. If a response ends discomfort, the response has been negatively reinforced. This makes it more likely to occur in the future (see Chapter 8). 12. Again, the answer depends on the person. The dilemma could be a simple approach-avoidance conflict (a desire to jump, coupled with fear). Or it could be a double approach-avoidance conflict (a desire to jump coupled with fear on one side, and on the other side, a desire for safety coupled with fear of being ridiculed as a "chicken").

Avoidance-avoidance conflict *Choosing between two negative, or mutually undesirable, alternatives.*
Approach-avoidance conflict *Being attracted to and repelled by the same goal or activity.*
Ambivalence *Mixed positive and negative feelings or simultaneous attraction and repulsion.*
Double approach-avoidance conflict *Being simultaneously attracted to and repelled by each of two alternatives.*
Vacillation *Wavering in intention or feelings.*
Multiple approach-avoidance conflict *Being simultaneously attracted to and repelled by each of several alternatives.*

PSYCHOLOGICAL DEFENSE—MENTAL KARATE?

Threatening situations are often accompanied by an unpleasant emotion called **anxiety.** A person who is anxious feels tense, uneasy, apprehensive, worried, and vulnerable. This can lead to emotion-focused coping that is *defensive* in nature (Lazarus, 1991b). Because anxiety is unpleasant and uncomfortable, we are usually motivated to avoid it. Psychological defense mechanisms allow us to reduce anxiety caused by stressful situations or our shortcomings.

What are psychological defense mechanisms, and how do they reduce anxiety? A **defense mechanism** is any process used to avoid, deny, or distort sources of threat or anxiety. Defense mechanisms also help protect an idealized self-image so that we can comfortably live with ourselves. Many of the defenses were first identified by Sigmund Freud, who assumed they operate *unconsciously.* Often, defense mechanisms create large blind spots in awareness. For instance, I know an extremely stingy person who is completely unaware that he is a tightwad.

Everyone has at one time or another used defense mechanisms. Let's consider some of the most common. (A more complete listing is given in ◆Table 16.5.)

DENIAL   One of the most basic defenses is **denial** (protecting oneself from an unpleasant reality by refusing to accept it or believe it). Denial is closely linked with death, illness, and similar painful and threatening events. For instance, if you were told that you had only 3 months to live, how would you react? Your first thoughts might be "Aw, come on, someone must have mixed up the X-rays" or "The doctor must be mistaken" or simply "It can't be true!" Similar denial and disbelief are common reactions to the unexpected death of a friend or relative: "It's just not real. I don't believe it. I just don't believe it!"

REPRESSION   Freud noticed that his patients had tremendous difficulty recalling shocking or traumatic events from childhood. It seemed that powerful forces were holding these painful memories from awareness. Freud called this **repression.** He believed that we protect ourselves by repressing threatening thoughts and impulses. Feelings of hostility toward a family member, the names of people we dislike, and past failures are common targets of repression.

REACTION FORMATION   In a **reaction formation,** impulses are not just repressed; they are also held in check by exaggerating

BRIDGES

Severe anxiety can be extremely disruptive. It is the basis for some of the most common psychological disorders.

See Chapter 17, pages 565–569.

opposite behavior. For example, a mother who unconsciously resents her children may, through reaction formation, become absurdly overprotective and overindulgent. Her real thoughts of "I hate them" and "I wish they were gone" are replaced by "I love them" and "I don't know what I would do without them." The mother's hostile impulses are traded for "smother" love, so that she won't have to admit she hates her children. Thus, the basic idea in a reaction formation is that the individual acts out an opposite behavior to block threatening impulses or feelings.

◆ **TABLE 16.5** Psychological Defense Mechanisms

Compensation Counteracting a real or imagined weakness by emphasizing desirable traits or seeking to excel in the area of weakness or in other areas.

Denial Protecting oneself from an unpleasant reality by refusing to perceive it.

Fantasy Fulfilling unmet desires in imagined achievements or activities.

Identification Taking on some of the characteristics of an admired person, usually as a way of compensating for perceived personal weaknesses or faults.

Intellectualization Separating emotion from a threatening or anxiety-provoking situation by talking or thinking about it in impersonal "intellectual" terms.

Isolation Separating contradictory thoughts or feelings into "logic-tight" mental compartments so that they do not come into conflict.

Projection Attributing one's own feelings, shortcomings, or unacceptable impulses to others.

Rationalization Justifying your behavior by giving reasonable and "rational," but false, reasons for it.

Reaction formation Preventing dangerous impulses from being expressed in behavior by exaggerating opposite behavior.

Regression Retreating to an earlier level of development or to earlier, less demanding habits or situations.

Repression Unconsciously preventing painful or dangerous thoughts from entering awareness.

Sublimation Working off unmet desires, or unacceptable impulses, in activities that are constructive.

JUMP START REPRINTED BY PERMISSION OF UFS, INC.

REGRESSION In its broadest meaning, **regression** refers to any return to earlier, less demanding situations or habits. Most parents who have a second child have to put up with at least some regression by the older child. Threatened by a new rival for affection, an older child may regress to childish speech, bedwetting, or infantile play after the new baby arrives. If you've ever seen a child get homesick at summer camp or on a vacation, you've observed regression. An adult who throws a temper tantrum or a married adult who "goes home to mother" is also regressing.

PROJECTION Projection is an unconscious process that protects us from the anxiety we would feel if we were to discern our faults. A person who is projecting tends to see his or her own feelings, shortcomings, or unacceptable impulses in others. **Projection** lowers anxiety by exaggerating negative traits in others. This justifies one's own actions and directs attention away from personal failings.

Your author once worked for a greedy shop owner who cheated many of his customers. This same man considered himself a pillar of the community and a good Christian. How did he justify to himself his greed and dishonesty? He believed that everyone who entered his store was bent on cheating *him* any way they could. In reality, few, if any, of his customers shared his motives, but he projected his own greed and dishonesty onto them.

RATIONALIZATION Every teacher is familiar with this strange phenomenon: On the day of an exam, an incredible wave of disasters sweeps through the city. Mothers, fathers, sisters, brothers, aunts, uncles, grandparents, friends, and pets become ill or die. Motors suddenly fall out of automobiles. Books are lost or stolen. Alarm clocks go belly-up and ring no more.

The making of excuses comes from a natural tendency to explain our behavior. **Rationalization** refers to justifying personal actions by giving "rational" but false reasons for them. When the explanation you give for your behavior is reasonable and convincing—but not the real reason—you are *rationalizing*. For example, Taylor failed to turn in an assignment made at the beginning of the semester in one of his classes. Here's the explanation he gave his professor:

> My car broke down 2 days ago, and I couldn't get to the library until yesterday. Then I couldn't get all the books I needed because some were checked out, but I wrote what I could. Then last night, as the last straw, the cartridge in my printer ran out, and since all the stores were closed, I couldn't finish the paper on time.

When asked why he left the assignment until the last minute (the real reason it was late), Taylor offered another set of rationalizations. Like many people, Taylor had difficulty seeing himself without the protection of his rationalizations.

All of the defense mechanisms described seem pretty undesirable. Do they have a positive side? People who overuse defense mechanisms become less adaptable, because they consume great amounts of emotional energy to control anxiety and maintain an unrealistic self-image. Defense mechanisms do have value, though. Often, they help keep us from being over-whelmed by immediate threats. This can provide time for a person to learn to cope in a more effective, problem-focused manner. If you recognize some of your own behavior in the descriptions here, it is hardly a sign that you are hopelessly defensive. As noted earlier, most people occasionally use defense mechanisms.

Two defense mechanisms that have a decidedly more positive quality are compensation and sublimation.

COMPENSATION Compensatory reactions are defenses against feelings of inferiority. A person who has a defect or weakness (real or imagined) may go to unusual lengths to overcome the weakness or to *compensate* for it by excelling in other areas. One of the pioneers of "pumping iron" in America is Jack LaLanne. LaLanne made a successful career out of bodybuilding in spite of the fact that he was thin and sickly as a young man. Or perhaps it would be more accurate to say *because* he was thin and sickly. There are dozens of examples of **compensation** at work. A childhood stutterer may excel in debate at college. Franklin D. Roosevelt's outstanding achievements in politics came after he was stricken with polio. As a child, Helen Keller was unable to see or hear, but she became an outstanding thinker and writer. Doc Watson, Ray Charles, Stevie Wonder, and a number of other well-known musicians are blind.

SUBLIMATION The defense called **sublimation** (sub-lih-MAY-shun) is defined as working off frustrated desires (especially sexual desires) through socially acceptable activities. Freud believed that art, music, dance, poetry, scientific investigation, and other creative activities can serve to rechannel sexual energies into productive behavior. Freud also felt that almost any strong desire can be sublimated. For example, a very aggressive person may find social acceptance as a professional soldier, boxer, or football player. Greed may be refined into a successful business career. Lying may be sublimated into storytelling, creative writing, or politics.

Anxiety *Apprehension, dread, or uneasiness similar to fear but based on an unclear threat.*

Defense mechanism *A habitual and often unconscious psychological process used to reduce anxiety.*

Denial *Protecting oneself from an unpleasant reality by refusing to perceive it or believe it.*

Repression *Unconsciously preventing painful or dangerous thoughts from entering awareness.*

Reaction formation *Preventing dangerous impulses from being expressed in behavior by exaggerating opposite behavior.*

Regression *Retreating to an earlier stage of development or to earlier, less demanding habits or situations.*

Projection *Attributing one's own feelings, shortcomings, or unacceptable impulses to others.*

Rationalization *Justifying personal behavior by giving reasonable and "rational" but false reasons for it.*

Compensation *Counteracting a real or imagined weakness by emphasizing desirable traits or seeking to excel in the area of weakness or in other areas.*

Sublimation *Working off frustrated desires or unacceptable impulses in substitute activities that are constructive or accepted by society.*

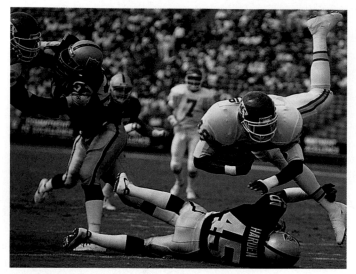

For some players—and fans—football probably allows sublimation of aggressive urges. *Mortal Kombat* and similar computer games may serve the same purpose.

Sexual motives appear to be the most easily and widely sublimated. Freud would have had a field day with such modern pastimes as surfing, motorcycle riding, drag racing, and dancing to or playing rock music, to name but a few. People enjoy each of these activities for a multitude of reasons, but it is hard to overlook the rich sexual symbolism apparent in each.

LEARNED HELPLESSNESS—IS THERE HOPE?

What would happen if a person's defenses failed or if the person appraised a threatening situation as hopeless?   Bruno Bettelheim (1960), who survived the Nazi concentration camps, described a reaction he called "give-up-itis." Many prisoners felt so helpless that they displayed a "zombie-like" detachment and became "walking corpses." Martin Seligman has described a similar reaction in Vietnam prisoner of war camps. Seligman reports the case of a young marine who had adapted unusually well to the stresses of being a POW. His health was related to a promise made by his captors: If he cooperated, they said, he would be released on a certain date. As the date approached, his spirits soared. Then came a devastating blow. He had been deceived. His captors had no intention of ever releasing him. He immediately lapsed into a deep depression, refused to eat or drink, and died shortly thereafter.

Those seem like extreme examples. Does anything similar occur outside of concentration camps?   Apparently so. For example, researchers in Finland recently discovered that even in everyday life, people who feel a sense of hopelessness die at elevated rates (Everson, Goldberg, & Salonen, 1996).

How can we explain such patterns? Psychologists have focused on the concept of learned helplessness (Seligman, 1989). **Learned helplessness** is an acquired inability to overcome obstacles and avoid aversive stimuli. To observe learned helplessness, let's see what happens when animals are tested in a shuttle box (❖ Fig. 16.6). If placed in one side of a divided box, dogs will quickly learn to leap to the other side to escape an electric shock. If they are given a warning before the shock occurs (for example, a light that dims), most dogs learn to avoid the shock by leaping the barrier before the shock arrives. This is true of most dogs, but not those who have learned to feel helpless (Overmier & LoLordo, 1998).

How is a dog made to feel helpless?   Before being tested in the shuttle box, a dog can be placed in a harness (from which the dog cannot escape). The dog is then given several painful shocks. The animal is helpless to prevent these shocks. When placed in the shuttle box, dogs pretreated this way react to the first shock by crouching, howling, and whining. None of them try to escape. They helplessly resign themselves to their fate. After all, they have already learned that there is nothing they can do about shock.

As the shuttle box experiments suggest, helplessness is a psychological state that occurs when events *appear to be uncontrollable* (Seligman, 1989). Helplessness also afflicts humans. It is a common reaction to repeated failure and to unpredictable or unavoidable punishment. A prime example is college students who feel helpless about their schoolwork. Such students tend to procrastinate and give up easily (McKean, 1994).

Where humans are concerned, attributions (discussed in Chapter 13) have a large effect on helplessness. People who are made to feel helpless in one situation are more likely to act helpless in other situations if they attribute their failure to *lasting, general* factors. An example would be concluding "I must be stupid" after failing to solve a series of puzzles. In contrast, attributing failure to specific factors in the original situation ("I'm not too good at puzzles" or "I wasn't really interested") tends to prevent learned helplessness from spreading (Alloy et al., 1984; Anderson et al., 1984).

Depression

Seligman and others have pointed out the similarities between learned helplessness and **depression.** Both are marked by feelings of despondency, powerlessness, and hopelessness. "Helpless" animals display decreased activity, lowered aggression, blunted appetite, and a loss of sex drive. Humans suffer from similar effects and also tend to see themselves as failing, even when they're not (Seligman, 1989).

BRIDGES

Depression is a complex problem that takes many forms and has many causes.

See Chapter 17, pages 582–584.

Depression is one of the most widespread emotional problems, and it undoubtedly has many causes. However, learned helplessness seems to explain many cases of depression and hopelessness. For example, Seligman (1972a) describes the fate of Archie, a 15-year-old boy. For Archie, school is an unending series of shocks and failures. Other students treat him as if he's stupid; in class, he rarely answers questions because he doesn't know some of the words. He feels knocked down

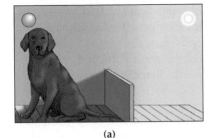 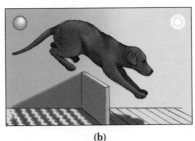
(a)   (b)

(c)   (d)

❖ **FIGURE 16.6** *In the normal course of escape and avoidance learning, a light dims shortly before the floor is electrified (a). Because the light does not yet have meaning for the dog, the dog receives a shock (non-injurious, by the way) and leaps the barrier (b). Dogs soon learn to watch for the dimming of the light (c) and to jump before receiving a shock (d). Dogs made to feel "helpless" rarely even learn to escape shock, much less avoid it.*

everywhere he turns. These may not be electric shocks, but they are certainly emotional "shocks," and Archie has learned to feel helpless to prevent them. When he leaves school, his chances of success will be poor. He has learned to passively endure whatever shocks life has in store for him. Archie is not alone in this regard. Hopelessness is almost always a major element of depression (Alloy & Clements, 1998).

HOPE *Does Seligman's research give any clues about how to "unlearn" helplessness?* With dogs, an effective technique is to forcibly drag them away from shock into the "safe" compartment. After this is done several times, the animals regain "hope" and feelings of control over their environment. Just how this can be done with humans is a question psychologists are exploring. It seems obvious, for instance, that someone like Archie would benefit from an educational program that would allow him to "succeed" repeatedly.

In **mastery training,** responses are reinforced that lead to mastery of a threat or control over one's environment. Animals who undergo such training become more resistant to learned helplessness (Volpicelli et al., 1983). For example, animals that first learn to escape shock become more persistent in trying to flee inescapable shock. In effect, they won't give up, even when the situation really is "hopeless."

Such findings suggest that we might be able to "immunize" people against helplessness and depression by allowing them to master difficult challenges. The Outward Bound schools, in which people pit themselves against the rigors of mountaineering, white-water canoeing, and wilderness survival, might serve as a model for such a program. Similarly, psychologists have found that the mental and physical health of elderly persons who live in nursing homes can be improved by giving them more control over their lives (Seligman, 1989). Things as small as choosing what to eat for lunch or being allowed to decorate one's room can be enough to counteract feelings of helplessness.

Mastery training can occur informally when people learn to cope with challenges. For example, 18- to 21-year-old trainees on a transatlantic sailing voyage showed marked improvements in their ability to cope with stress (Norris & Weinman, 1996).

Learned helplessness *A learned inability to overcome obstacles or to avoid punishment; learned passivity and inaction to aversive stimuli.*
Depression *A state of despondency marked by feelings of powerlessness and hopelessness.*
Mastery training *Reinforcement of responses that lead to mastery of a threat or control over one's environment.*

The value of hope should not be overlooked. As fragile as this emotion seems to be, it is a powerful antidote to depression and helplessness. As an individual, you may find hope in religion, nature, human companionship, or even technology. Wherever you find it, remember its value: Hope is among the most important of all human emotions. Having positive beliefs, such as optimism, hope, and a sense of meaning and control, is closely related to personal well-being (Lachman & Weaver, 1998; Taylor et al., 1999).

Depression, a Problem for Everyone

During the school year, up to 78 percent of all college students suffer some symptoms of depression. At any given time, from 16 to 30 percent of the student population is depressed (McLennan, 1992; Wong & Whitaker, 1993).

WHY STUDENTS GET THE BLUES

Why should so many students be "blue"? Various problems contribute to depressive feelings. Here are some of the most common:

1. Stresses from college work and pressures to choose a career can leave students feeling that they are missing out on fun or that all their hard work is meaningless.
2. Isolation and loneliness are common when students leave their support groups behind. In the past, family, a circle of high school friends, and often a boyfriend or girlfriend could be counted on for support and encouragement.
3. Problems with studying and grades frequently trigger depression. Many students start college with high aspirations and little prior experience with failure. At the same time, many lack basic skills necessary for academic success.

4. Another common problem is the breakup of an intimate relationship, either with a former boyfriend or girlfriend or with a newly formed college romance.
5. Students who find it difficult to live up to their idealized images of themselves are especially prone to depression (Scott & O'Hara, 1993).
6. An added danger is that depressed students are more likely to abuse alcohol, which is a depressant (Camatta & Nagoshi, 1995).

RECOGNIZING DEPRESSION

Most people know, obviously enough, when they are "down." Aaron Beck, an authority on depression, suggests you should assume that more than a minor fluctuation in mood is involved when five conditions exist:

1. You have a consistently negative opinion of yourself.
2. You engage in frequent self-criticism and self-blame.
3. You place negative interpretations on events that usually wouldn't bother you.
4. The future looks bleak and negative.
5. You feel that your responsibilities are overwhelming.

What can be done to combat depression? Bouts of the college blues are closely related to stressful events. Learning to manage college work and to challenge self-critical thinking can help alleviate mild school-related depression. See "Coping with Depression" for some helpful suggestions.

Attacks of the college blues are common and should be distinguished from more serious cases of depression. Severe depression is a serious problem that can lead to suicide or a major impairment of emotional functioning. In such cases, it would be wise to seek professional help.

COPING WITH DEPRESSION

If you don't do well on a test or a class assignment, how do you react? If you see it as a small, isolated setback, you probably won't feel too bad. However, if you feel that you have "blown it" in a big way, depression may follow. Students who strongly link everyday events to long-term goals (such as a successful career or high income) tend to overreact to day-to-day disappointments (McIntosh, Harlow, & Martin, 1995).

What does the preceding tell us about the college blues? The implication is that it's important to take daily tasks one step at a time and chip away at them. That way, you are less likely to feel overwhelmed, helpless, or hopeless. Beck and Greenberg (1974) suggest that when you feel "blue," you should make a *daily schedule* for yourself. Try to schedule activities to fill up every hour during the day. It is best to start with easy activities and progress to more difficult tasks. Check off each item as it is completed. That way, you will begin to break the self-defeating cycle of feeling helpless and

falling further behind. (Depressed students spend much of their time sleeping.) A series of small accomplishments, successes, or pleasures may be all that you need to get going again. However, if you are lacking skills needed for success in college, ask for help in getting them. Don't remain "helpless."

Feelings of worthlessness and hopelessness are usually supported by self-critical or negative thoughts. Beck and Greenberg recommend writing down such thoughts as they occur, especially those that immediately precede feelings of sadness. After you have collected these thoughts, write a rational answer to each. For example, the thought "No one loves me" should be answered with a list of those who do care. (See Chapter 18 for more information.) One more point to keep in mind is this: When events begin to improve, try to accept it as a sign that better times lie ahead. Positive events are most likely to end depression if you view them as stable and continuing, rather than temporary and fragile (Needles & Abramson, 1990).

USING PSYCHOLOGY

In a survey, college students reported that they were depressed once or twice a month. These episodes lasted from a few hours to several days (Snyder & Smith, 1985).

KNOWLEDGE BUILDER
DEFENSE MECHANISMS, HELPLESSNESS, AND DEPRESSION

RELATE

We tend to be blind to our own reliance on defense mechanisms. Return to the definitions in Table 16.5 and see if you can think of one example of each defense that you have observed someone else using.

Have you ever felt helpless in a particular situation? What caused you to feel that way? Does any part of Seligman's description of learned helplessness match your own experience?

Imagine that a friend of yours is suffering from the college blues. What advice would you give your friend?

LEARNING CHECK

1. The psychological defense known as denial refers to the natural tendency to explain or justify one's actions. T or F?

2. Fulfilling frustrated desires in imaginary achievements or activities defines the defense mechanism of
   a. compensation b. isolation c. fantasy d. sublimation

3. In compensation, one's own undesirable characteristics or motives are attributed to others. T or F?

4. Of the defense mechanisms, two that are considered relatively constructive are
   a. compensation b. denial c. isolation d. projection e. regression f. rationalization g. sublimation

5. Depression in humans is similar to _____ _____ observed in animal experiments.

6. At any given time, more than half of the college student population suffers symptoms of depression. T or F?

7. Frequent self-criticism and self-blame are a natural consequence of doing college work. T or F?

8. Countering negative, self-critical thoughts only calls attention to them and makes depression worse. T or F?

CRITICAL THINKING

9. Learned helplessness is closely related to which of the factors that determine the severity of stress?

Answers:

1. F 2. c 3. F 4. a, g 5. learned helplessness 6. F 7. F 8. F 9. Feelings of in- competence and lack of control.

STRESS AND HEALTH—UNMASKING A HIDDEN KILLER

Disaster, depression, and sorrow often precede illness. As Taylor (our intrepid student) found after finals week, stressful events reduce the body's natural defenses against disease. More surprising is the finding that major *life changes*—both good and bad—can increase susceptibility to accidents or illness.

Life Events and Stress

How can I tell if I am subjecting myself to too much stress? Some 30 years ago, Thomas Holmes and his associates developed a rating scale to estimate the health hazards faced when stresses add up (Holmes & Masuda, 1972). More recently, Mark Miller and Richard Rahe updated the scale for use today. The *Social Readjustment Rating Scale* (**SRRS**) is reprinted in ◆Table 16.6. Notice that the effect of life events is expressed in **life change units** (**LCUs**) (numerical values assigned to each life event).

As you read the scale, note again that positive life events may be as costly as disasters. Marriage rates 50 life change units, even though it is usually a happy event. You'll also see

Social Readjustment Rating Scale (SRRS) *A scale that rates the impact of various life events on the likelihood of illness.*
Life change units (LCUs) *Numerical values assigned to each life event on the SRRS.*

◆ TABLE 16.6 Social Readjustment Rating Scale

RANK	LIFE EVENT	LIFE CHANGE UNITS
1	Death of spouse or child	119
2	Divorce	98
3	Death of a close family member	92
4	Marital separation	79
5	Fired from work	79
6	Major personal injury or illness	77
7	Jail term	75
8	Death of close friend	70
9	Pregnancy	66
10	Major business readjustment	62
11	Foreclosure on a mortgage or loan	61
12	Gain of new family member	57
13	Marital reconciliation	57
14	Change in health or behavior of family member	56
15	Change in financial state	56
16	Retirement	54
17	Change to different line of work	51
18	Change in number of arguments with spouse	51
19	Marriage	50
20	Spouse begins or ends work	46
21	Sexual difficulties	45
22	Child leaving home	44
23	Mortgage or loan greater than $10,000	44
24	Change in responsibilities at work	43
25	Change in living conditions	42
26	Change in residence	41
27	Begin or end school	38
28	Trouble with in-laws	38
29	Outstanding personal achievement	37
30	Change in work hours or conditions	36
31	Change in schools	35
32	Christmas	30
33	Trouble with boss	29
34	Change in recreation	29
35	Mortgage or loan less than $10,000	28
36	Change in personal habits	27
37	Change in eating habits	27
38	Change in social activities	27
39	Change in number of family get-togethers	26
40	Change in sleeping habits	26
41	Vacation	25
42	Change in church activities	22
43	Minor violations of the law	22

(Source: Miller & Rahe, 1997; reproduced by permission.)

Marriage is usually a positive life event. Nevertheless, the many changes it brings can be stressful.

According to Holmes, there is a high chance of illness or accident when your LCU total exceeds 300 points. A more conservative rating of stress can be obtained by totaling LCU points for only the previous 6 months. Studies of U.S. Navy personnel produced the figures shown here for 6-month totals (Rahe, 1972).

LCUs	AVERAGE NUMBER OF ILLNESSES REPORTED FOR 6-MONTH PERIOD
0–100	1.4
300–400	1.9
500–600	2.1

Many of the listed life changes don't seem relevant to young adults or college students. Does the SRRS apply to these people? The SRRS tends to be more appropriate for older, more established adults. However, research has shown that the health of college students is also affected by stressful events, such as entering college, changing majors, or the breakup of a steady relationship (Crandall, Preisler, & Aussprung, 1992).

EVALUATION The SRRS is not a foolproof way to rate stress, and some studies have failed to confirm the LCU-illness link (Weinberger, 1987). Furthermore, it is debatable whether positive life events are always stressful (Feuerstein et al., 1986a). Perhaps the most important criticism of the scale is based on a point made earlier: People differ greatly in their reactions to the same event. For such reasons, the SRRS is, at best, only a rough index of stress. Nevertheless, it's hard to ignore a study in which people were deliberately exposed to the virus that causes common colds. The results were nothing to sneeze at: If

many items that read "Change in. . . ." This means that an improvement in life conditions can be as costly as a decline. A stressful adjustment may be required in either case.

To use the scale, add up the LCUs for all life events you have experienced during the last year and compare the total to the following standards.

0–150: No significant problems
150–199: Mild life crisis (33 percent chance of illness)
200–299: Moderate life crisis (50 percent chance of illness)
300 or more: Major life crisis (80 percent chance of illness)

a person had a high stress score, she or he was much more likely to actually get a cold (Cohen et al., 1993).

To summarize, a high LCU score should be taken seriously. If your score goes much over 300, an adjustment in your activities or lifestyle may be needed. Remember: "To be forewarned is to be forearmed."

THE HAZARDS OF HASSLES *There must be more to stress than major life changes. Isn't there a link between ongoing stresses and health?* In addition to having a direct impact, major life events spawn countless daily frustrations and irritations (Pillow, Zautra, & Sandler, 1996). Also, many of us face ongoing stresses at work or at home that do not involve major life changes. In view of these facts, psychologist Richard Lazarus and his associates studied the impact of minor but frequent stresses. Lazarus (1981) aptly refers to such distressing daily annoyances as **hassles,** or microstressors. Hassles range from traffic jams to losing classroom notes, from an argument with a roommate to an employer's unrealistic demands (see ◆Table 16.7).

In a year-long study, Lazarus had 100 men and women keep track of the frequency and severity of the hassles they endured. Participants also reported on their physical and mental health. As Lazarus suspected, frequent and severe hassles turned out to be better predictors of day-to-day health than major life events were. However, major life events did predict changes in health 1 or 2 years after the events took place. It appears that daily hassles are closely linked to immediate health and psychological well-being (Johnson & Sherman, 1997; Roberts, 1995). Major life changes have more of a long-term impact.

In follow-up work, Lazarus and others found that the personal importance of hassles affects the amount of stress they produce (Lazarus et al., 1985). Microstressors that are viewed as central to one's self-worth are many times more likely to cause trouble. For many people, central hassles are linked to work, family, and relationships. But as psychologist Rand Gruen notes, "Taking care of paperwork or being organized

◆ **TABLE 16.7** Examples of Daily Hassles

Too many responsibilities or commitments
Problems with work, boss, or coworkers
Unexpected house guests
Inconsiderate neighbors
Noisy, messy, or quarreling children
Regrets over past decisions
Having trouble making decisions
Money worries or concerns
Not enough time for family, relaxation, entertainment
Loneliness, social isolation, separated from family
Physical illness, symptoms, complaints
Concerns about weight, appearance
Frustrations with daily chores
Delays, transportation problems
Paperwork, filling out forms
Misplacing or losing things
Noise, pollution, deteriorating neighborhoods
Bad weather
Crime, disturbing news events

can be central for some people" (Fisher, 1984). This observation again emphasizes that stress occurs in people, not in the environment. Stress is always related to personality, values, perceptions, and personal resources (Moos & Swindle, 1990).

What can be done about a high LCU score or feeling excessively hassled? A good response is to use stress management skills. For serious problems, stress management should be learned directly from a therapist or a stress clinic. When ordinary stresses are involved, there is much you can do on your own. This chapter's Psychology in Action section will give you a start. In the meantime, take it easy!

One way to guarantee that you will experience a large number of life changes and hassles is to live in a foreign culture. The discussion "Acculturative Stress" offers a brief glimpse into some of the consequences of culture shock.

Psychosomatic Disorders

As we have seen, chronic or repeated stress can damage physical health, as well as upset emotional well-being. Prolonged stress reactions are closely related to a large number of psychosomatic (SIKE-oh-so-MAT-ik) illnesses. In **psychosomatic disorders** (*psyche:* mind; *soma:* body), psychological factors contribute to actual bodily damage or to damaging changes in bodily functioning. Psychosomatic problems, therefore, are *not* the same as hypochondria. **Hypochondriacs** (HI-po-KON-dree-aks) imagine that they suffer from diseases. There is nothing imaginary about asthma, a migraine headache, or high blood pressure. Severe psychosomatic disorders can be fatal. The person who says, "Oh it's *just* psychosomatic" misunderstands the seriousness of stress-related diseases.

Are stomach ulcers psychosomatic? For many years, stomach ulcers were thought to be primarily caused by stress. However, recent medical research has traced some ulcers to bacterial infections of the stomach. This does not rule out the possibility that ulcers may occasionally be psychosomatic. Stress and lifestyle factors may contribute to the development of stomach infections (Doctor & Doctor, 1994). However, it is more likely that a person suffering from stomach pain has *functional dyspepsia.* This psychosomatic disorder causes ulcer-like pain, but does not make holes in the stomach lining (Whitehead, 1992).

The most common psychosomatic problems are gastrointestinal and respiratory (dyspepsia and asthma, for example), but many others exist. Typical problems include eczema (skin rash), hives, migraine headaches, rheumatoid arthritis, hypertension (high blood pressure), colitis (ulceration of the colon), and heart disease. Actually, these are only the major problems. Lesser health complaints are also frequently stress related. Typical examples include sore muscles, headaches, neckaches, back-

Hassle *Any distressing, day-to-day annoyance; also called a* microstressor.
Psychosomatic disorders *Illnesses in which psychological factors contribute to bodily damage or to damaging changes in bodily functioning.*
Hypochondriac *A person who complains about illnesses that appear to be imaginary.*

How stressful is it to be a "stranger in a strange land"? Around the world, an increasing number of emigrants and refugees must adapt to dramatic changes in language, dress, values, and social customs. For many, the result is a period of culture shock or **acculturative stress** (stress caused by adapting to a foreign culture). Typical reactions to acculturative stress are anxiety, hostility, depression, alienation, physical illness, or identity confusion (Thomas, 1995).

The severity of acculturative stress is related, in part, to how a person adapts to a new culture. Four main patterns are:

- **Integration:** maintain your old cultural identity but participate in the new culture
- **Separation:** maintain your old cultural identity and avoid contact with the new culture
- **Assimilation:** adopt the new culture as your own and have contact with its members
- **Marginalization:** reject your old culture but suffer rejection by members of the new culture

To illustrate each pattern, let's consider a family that has immigrated to the United States from the imaginary country of Farlandia.

The father favors integration. He is learning English and wants to get involved in American life. At the same time, he is a leader in the Farlandian-American community and spends much of his leisure time with other Farlandian-Americans. His level of acculturative stress is low.

The mother speaks only Farlandish and interacts only with other Farlandian-Americans. She remains almost completely separate from American society. Her stress level is high.

The teenage daughter is annoyed by hearing Farlandish spoken at home, by her mother's serving only Farlandian food, and by having to spend her leisure time with her extended Farlandian family. She would prefer to speak English and to be with her American friends. Her desire to assimilate creates moderate stress.

The son doesn't particularly value his Farlandian heritage, yet he is rejected by his schoolmates because he speaks with a Farlandian ac-

cent. He feels trapped between two cultures. His position is marginal, and his stress level is high.

To summarize, those who feel marginalized tend to be highly stressed, those who seek to remain separate are also highly stressed, those who pursue integration into their new culture are minimally stressed, and those who assimilate are moderately stressed.

As you can see, integration and assimilation are the best options. However, a big benefit of assimilating is that people who embrace their new culture experience fewer social difficulties. For many, this justifies the stress of adopting new customs and cultural values. (Sources: Berry, 1990; Rogler, Cortes, & Malgady, 1991; Ward & Rana-Deuba, 1999; Williams & Berry, 1991.)

One of the best antidotes for acculturative stress is a society that tolerates or even celebrates ethnic diversity. Although some people find it hard to accept new immigrants, the fact is, nearly everyone's family tree includes people who were once strangers in a strange land.

aches, indigestion, constipation, chronic diarrhea, fatigue, insomnia, premenstrual problems, and sexual dysfunctions (Brown, 1980; De Benedittis et al., 1990). For some of these problems, biofeedback may be helpful. The next section explains how.

Biofeedback

Psychologists have discovered that people can learn to control bodily activities once thought to be involuntary. This is done by applying informational feedback to bodily control, a process called **biofeedback.** If I were to say to you, "Raise the temperature of your right hand," you probably couldn't, because you wouldn't know if you were succeeding. To make your task eas-

ier, we could attach a sensitive thermometer to your hand. The thermometer could be wired so that an increase in temperature would activate a signal light. Then, all you would have to do is try to keep the light on as much as possible. With practice and the help of biofeedback, you could learn to raise your hand temperature at will.

Biofeedback holds promise as a way to treat some psychosomatic problems (❖Fig. 16.7). For instance, people have been trained to prevent migraine headaches with biofeedback. Sensors are taped to patients' hands and foreheads. Patients then learn to redirect blood flow away from the head to their extremities. Because migraine headaches involve excessive blood flow to the head, biofeedback helps patients reduce the frequency of their headaches (Gauthier et al., 1994; Kropp et al., 1997).

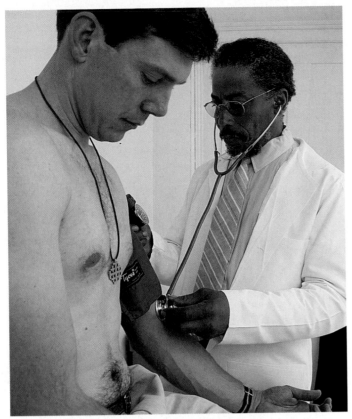

It is estimated that at least half of all patients who see a doctor have a psychosomatic disorder or an illness that is complicated by psychosomatic symptoms.

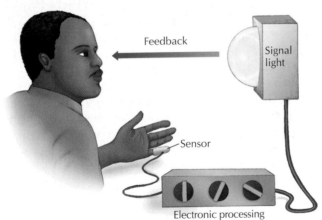

❖ **FIGURE 16.7** *In biofeedback training, bodily processes are monitored and processed electronically. A signal is then routed back to the patient through headphones, signal lights, or other means. This information helps the patient alter bodily activities not normally under voluntary control.*

Early successes led many to predict that biofeedback would offer a cure for psychosomatic illnesses, anxiety, phobias, drug abuse, and a long list of other problems. In reality, biofeedback has proved helpful, but not an instant cure (Amar, 1993). Biofeedback can help relieve muscle-tension headaches, migraine headaches, and chronic pain (Arena et al., 1995; Buckelew et al., 1998; Gauthier et al., 1994). It shows promise for lowering blood pressure and controlling heart rhythms

(Blanchard et al., 1996; Lal et al., 1998). The technique has been used with some success to control epileptic seizures and hyperactivity in children (Potashkin & Beckles, 1990; Sterman, 1996). Insomnia also responds to biofeedback therapy (Barowsky et al., 1990).

How does biofeedback help? Some researchers believe that many of its benefits arise from *general relaxation.* Others stress that there is no magic in biofeedback itself. The method simply acts as a "mirror" to help a person perform tasks involving *self-regulation.* Just as a mirror does not comb your hair, biofeedback does not do anything by itself. It can, however, help people make desired changes in their behavior (Amar, 1993; Weems, 1998).

ELECTRONIC YOGA? *Does biofeedback apply to brain activity?* Alpha waves are one of several brain-wave patterns that can be recorded with the EEG (electroencephalograph; see Chapter 8). Using an EEG, psychologist Joseph Kamiya developed a system that signals subjects with a tone or light whenever they produce alpha waves (Kamiya, 1968). Subjects typically report that high levels of alpha are linked with sensations of pleasure, relaxation, passive alertness, or peaceful images.

Some researchers have successfully used alpha-wave biofeedback to reduce anxiety in emotionally troubled patients (Rice et al., 1993). However, questions remain about the ability of alpha training to promote deep relaxation. Research has shown that for some people increased alpha waves are related to relaxation; for others, alpha waves occur at times of *heightened* arousal.

For the moment, it seems that we have not yet reached the age of "electronic yoga" or "instant bliss." This is especially true of low-cost home "alpha-feedback" machines. These devices are so inaccurate that many "blissed out" users are actually listening to electrical noise from their house wiring, rather than their own brain waves (Beyerstein, 1985). Likewise, commercial programs that claim to teach people to produce alpha waves are essentially worthless (Beyerstein, 1990). Although biofeedback is a useful therapy, it must be applied skillfully to be of value (Amar, 1993).

The Cardiac Personality

It would be a mistake to assume that stress is the sole cause of psychosomatic diseases. Hereditary differences, organ weaknesses, and learned reactions to stress combine to do damage. Personality also enters the picture. As mentioned earlier, a general disease-prone personality type exists. To a degree, there are also "headache personalities," "asthma personalities," and so on. The best documented of such patterns is the "cardiac personality"—a person at high risk for heart disease.

BAcculturative stress *Stress caused by the many changes and adaptations required when a person moves to a foreign culture.*
Biofeedback *Information given to a person about his or her ongoing bodily activities; aids voluntary regulation of bodily states.*

Individuals with Type A personalities feel a continuous sense of anger, irritation, and hostility.

◆ TABLE 16.8 Characteristics of the Type A Person

CHECK THE ITEMS THAT APPLY TO YOU. DO YOU:

_____ Have a habit of explosively accentuating various key words in ordinary speech even when there is no need for such accentuation?
_____ Finish other persons' sentences for them?
_____ *Always* move, walk, and eat rapidly?
_____ Quickly skim reading material and prefer summaries or condensations of books?
_____ Become easily angered by slow-moving lines or traffic?
_____ Feel an impatience with the rate at which most events take place?
_____ Tend to be unaware of the details or beauty of your surroundings?
_____ Frequently strive to think of or do two or more things simultaneously?
_____ Almost always feel vaguely guilty when you relax, vacation, or do absolutely nothing for several days?
_____ Tend to evaluate your worth in quantitative terms (number of A's earned, amount of income, number of games won, and so forth)?
_____ Have nervous gestures or muscle twitches, such as grinding your teeth, clenching your fists, or drumming your fingers?
_____ Attempt to schedule more and more activities into less time and in so doing make fewer allowances for unforeseen problems?
_____ Frequently think about other things while talking to someone?
_____ Repeatedly take on more responsibilities than you can comfortably handle?

Shortened and adapted from Meyer Friedman and Ray H. Rosenman, *Type A Behavior and Your Heart* (New York: Knopf, 1983).

Two noted cardiologists, Meyer Friedman and Ray Rosenman, offer a glimpse at how some people create stress for themselves. In a landmark study of heart problems, Friedman and Rosenman (1974) classified people as either **Type A personalities** (those who run a high risk of heart attack) or **Type B personalities** (those who are unlikely to have a heart attack). Then they did an 8-year follow-up, finding more than twice the rate of heart disease in Type As than in Type Bs (Rosenman et al., 1975).

TYPE A   *What is the Type A personality like?*   Type A people are hard driving, ambitious, highly competitive, achievement oriented, and striving. Type A people believe that, with enough effort, they can overcome any obstacle, and they "push" themselves accordingly.

Perhaps the most telltale signs of a Type A personality are *time urgency* and chronic *anger* or *hostility*. Type A people seem to chafe at the normal pace of events. They hurry from one activity to another, racing the clock in self-imposed urgency. As they do, they feel a constant sense of frustration and anger. Feelings of anger and hostility, in particular, are strongly related to increased risk of heart attack (Miller et al., 1996). One study found that 15 percent of a group of 25-year-old doctors and lawyers who scored high on a hostility test were dead by age 50. The most damaging pattern may occur in hostile people who "bottle up" their anger. Such people seethe with anger but don't express it outwardly. This increases cardiac rate and blood pressure and puts a tremendous strain on the heart (Bongard, al'Absi, & Lovallo, 1998).

To summarize, there is growing evidence that anger or hostility may be the core lethal factor of Type A behavior (King, 1997). To date, hundreds of studies have supported the validity of the Type A concept. In view of this, Type A people would be wise to take their increased health risks seriously (Miller et al., 1991; Sprafka et al., 1990).

How are Type A people identified?   Characteristics of Type A people are summarized in the short self-identification test presented in ◆Table 16.8. If most of the list applies to you, you may be a Type A. However, confirmation of your type would require more powerful testing methods. Also, remember that the original definition of Type A behavior was probably too broad. The key psychological factors that increase heart disease risk appear to be anger, hostility, and mistrust (Suls & Swain, 1994).

Because our society places a premium on achievement, competition, and mastery, it is not surprising that many people develop Type A personalities. The best way to avoid the self-made stress this causes is to adopt behavior that is the opposite of that listed in ◆Table 16.8 (Karlberg, Krakau, & Unden, 1998).

It is entirely possible to succeed in life without sacrificing your health or happiness in the process. People who frequently feel angry and hostile toward others may benefit from the advice of Redford Williams, a physician interested in Type A behavior. "Strategies for Reducing Hostility" summarizes his advice.

Hardy Personality

How do Type A people who do not develop heart disease differ from those who do?   Psychologists Salvatore Maddi and others

STRATEGIES FOR REDUCING HOSTILITY

According to Redford Williams, reducing hostility involves three goals. First, you must stop mistrusting the motives of others. Second, you must find ways to reduce how often you feel anger, indignation, irritation, and rage. Third, you must learn to be kinder and more considerate. Based on his clinical experience, Williams (1989) recommends 12 strategies for reducing hostility and increasing trust.

1. Become aware of your angry, hostile, and cynical thoughts by logging them in a notebook. Record what happened, what you thought and felt, and what actions you took. Review your hostility log at the end of each week.
2. Admit to yourself and to someone you trust that you have a problem with excessive anger and hostility.
3. Interrupt hostile, cynical thoughts whenever they occur. (The Psychology in Action section of Chapter 18 explains a thought-stopping method you can use for this step.)
4. When you have an angry, hostile, or cynical thought about someone, silently look for the ways in which it is irrational or unreasonable.
5. When you are angry, try to mentally put yourself in the other person's shoes.
6. Learn to laugh at yourself and use humor to defuse your anger.
7. Learn reliable ways to relax. Two methods are described in this chapter's Psychology in Action section. Another can be found in the Psychology in Action discussion of Chapter 18.
8. Practice trusting others more. Begin with situations where no great harm will be done if the person lets you down.
9. Make an effort to listen more to others and to really understand what they are saying.
10. Learn to be assertive, rather than aggressive in upsetting situations. (See Chapter 19 for information about self-assertion skills.)
11. Rise above small irritations by pretending that today is the last day of your life.
12. Rather than blaming people for mistreating you and becoming angry over it, try to forgive them. We all have shortcomings.

typical of the Type A personality, so that wasn't the explanation. They were also quite similar in most other respects. The main difference was that the hardy group seemed to hold a worldview that consisted of three traits (Maddi, Kahn, & Maddi, 1998):

1. They had a sense of personal *commitment* to self, work, family, and other stabilizing values.
2. They felt that they had *control* over their lives and their work.
3. They had a tendency to see life as a series of *challenges*, rather than as a series of threats or problems.

How do such traits protect people from the effects of stress? Persons strong in *commitment* find ways of turning whatever they are doing into something that seems interesting and important. They tend to get involved rather than feeling alienated.

Persons strong in *control* believe that they can more often than not influence the course of events around them. This prevents them from passively seeing themselves as victims of circumstance.

Finally, people strong in *challenge* believe that fulfillment is found in continual growth. They seek to learn from their experiences, rather than accepting easy comfort, security, and routine (Maddi, Kahn, & Maddi, 1998).

HARDINESS AND HAPPINESS   Good and bad events occur in all lives. What separates happy people from those who are unhappy is largely a matter of attitude. Happy people tend to see their lives in more positive terms, even when trouble comes their way. For example, happier people tend to find humor in disappointments. They look at setbacks as challenges. They are strengthened by losses (Lyubomirsky & Tucker, 1998). In short, happiness tends to be related to hardiness. It is a general personal characteristic, not simply a reaction to circumstances (Brebner, 1998).

At this point, we have left a very basic issue unexplained: How does stress, and our response to it, translate into disease? The answer seems to lie in the body's defenses against stress, a pattern known as the general adaptation syndrome.

The General Adaptation Syndrome

The **general adaptation syndrome** (**G.A.S.**) is a series of bodily reactions to prolonged stress. Canadian physiologist Hans Selye (1976) noticed that the first symptoms of almost any disease or trauma (poisoning, infection, injury, or stress) are almost

have studied people who have a **hardy personality.** Such people seem to be unusually resistant to stress. The study of hardiness began with two groups of managers at a large utility company. All of the managers held high-stress positions. Yet, some tended to get sick after stressful events, while others were rarely ill. How did the people who were thriving differ from their "stressed-out" colleagues? Both groups seemed to have traits

Type A personality *A personality type with an elevated risk of heart disease; characterized by time urgency, anger, and hostility.*
Type B personality *All personality types other than Type A; a low cardiac-risk personality.*
Hardy personality *A personality style associated with superior stress resistance.*
General adaptation syndrome (G.A.S.) *A series of bodily reactions to prolonged stress; occurs in three stages: alarm, resistance, and exhaustion.*

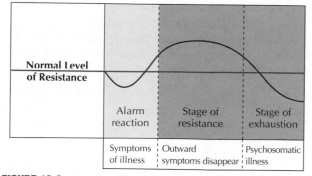

FIGURE 16.8 *The general adaptation syndrome. During the initial alarm reaction to stress, resistance falls below normal. It rises again as bodily resources are mobilized, and it remains high during the stage of resistance. Eventually, resistance falls again as the stage of exhaustion is reached. (Adapted from* The Stress of Life *by Hans Selye. Copyright © 1976 by Hans Selye. Used by permission of McGraw-Hill Book Company.)*

STRESS AND THE IMMUNE SYSTEM

How else might stress affect health? An answer can be found in the **immune system,** which mobilizes defenses (such as white blood cells) against invading microbes and other disease agents (Ader & Cohen, 1993). The immune system is regulated, in part, by the brain. Because of this link, stress and upsetting emotions can affect the immune system in ways that increase susceptibility to disease (Miller, 1998; Pike et al., 1997). (By the way, the study of links among behavior, stress, disease, and the immune system is called **psychoneuroimmunology.** Try dropping that into a conversation sometime if you want to see a stress reaction!)

Studies show that the immune system is weakened in students during major exam times. Immunity is also lowered by divorce, bereavement, a troubled marriage, job loss, depression, and similar stresses (Gilbert et al., 1996; Herbert & Cohen, 1993; Stein et al., 1990). Lowered immunity explains why the "double whammy" of getting sick when you are trying to cope with prolonged or severe stress is so common (Biondi & Zannino, 1997).

Could reducing stress help prevent illness? Yes. Various psychological approaches, such as support groups, relaxation exercises, guided imagery, and stress management training can actually boost immune system functioning (Kiecolt-Glaser & Glaser, 1992). By doing so, they help promote and restore health. There is even evidence that such measures improve the chances of survival following life-threatening diseases, such as cancer (Anderson et al., 1994).

No one is immune to stress. Nevertheless, it's reassuring to know that managing stress can help protect your immune system and your health.

identical. Selye's studies showed that the body responds in the same way to any stress, be it infection, failure, embarrassment, a new job, trouble at school, or a stormy romance.

What pattern does the body's response to stress take? The G.A.S. consists of three stages: an alarm reaction, a stage of resistance, and a stage of exhaustion (Selye, 1976).

In the **alarm reaction,** the body mobilizes its resources to cope with added stress. The pituitary gland signals the adrenal glands to produce more adrenaline and noradrenaline. As these hormones are dumped into the bloodstream, some bodily processes are speeded up and others are slowed. This allows bodily resources to be applied where they are needed.

We should all be thankful that our bodies automatically respond to emergencies. But brilliant as this emergency system is, it can also cause problems. In the first phase of the alarm reaction, people have such symptoms as headache, fever, fatigue, sore muscles, shortness of breath, diarrhea, upset stomach, loss of appetite, and a lack of energy. Notice that these are also the symptoms of being sick, of stressful travel, of high-altitude sickness, of final exams week, and (possibly) of falling in love!

During the **stage of resistance,** bodily adjustments to stress stabilize. As the body's defenses come into balance, symptoms of the alarm reaction disappear. Outwardly, everything seems normal. However, this appearance of normality comes at a high cost. The body is better able to cope with the original stressor, but its resistance to other stresses is lowered (❖ Fig. 16.8). For example, animals placed in extreme cold become more resistant to the cold but more susceptible to infection. It is during the stage of resistance that the first signs of psychosomatic disorders begin to appear.

Continued stress leads to the **stage of exhaustion,** in which the body's resources are drained and stress hormones are depleted. Unless a way of relieving stress is found, the result will be a psychosomatic disease, a serious loss of health, or complete collapse.

The G.A.S. may sound melodramatic if you are young and healthy or if you've never endured prolonged stress. However, stress should not be taken lightly. When Selye examined animals in the later stages of the G.A.S., he found that their adrenal glands were enlarged and discolored. There was intense shrinkage of the thymus, spleen, and lymph nodes. Many animals also suffered from deep bleeding stomach ulcers. In addition to such direct effects, stress can disrupt the body's immune system, as described in "Stress, Illness, and the Immune System."

A LOOK AHEAD   The work we have reviewed here has drawn new attention to the fact that each of us has a personal responsibility for maintaining and promoting health. In the Psychology in Action section that follows, we will look at what you can do to better cope with stress and the health risks that it entails. The concluding A Step Beyond looks at meditation as a potential stress-reducing technique. But first, the following questions may help you maintain a healthy grade on your next psychology test.

STRESS AND HEALTH

RELATE

Pick a year from your life that was unusually stressful. Use the SRRS to find your LCU score for that year. Do you think there was a connection between your LCU score and your health? Or have you observed more of a connection between microstressors and your health?

Mindy complains about her health all the time, but she actually seems to be just fine. An acquaintance of Mindy's dismisses her problems by saying, "Oh, she's not really sick. It's just psychosomatic." What's wrong with this use of the term *psychosomatic*?

Do you think you are basically a Type A or a Type B personality? To what extent do you possess traits of the hardy personality?

Can you say psychoneuroimmunology? Have you impressed anyone with the word yet?

LEARNING CHECK

1. Holmes's SRRS appears to predict long-range changes in health, whereas the frequency and severity of daily microstressors is closely related to immediate ratings of health. T or F?

2. Ulcers, migraine headaches, and hypochondria are all frequently psychosomatic disorders. T or F?

3. Which of the following is *not* classified as a psychosomatic disorder?
   a. hypertension *b.* colitis *c.* eczema *d.* thymus

4. Biofeedback is a type of meditation in which the body is made very quiet so that bodily functioning can be detected. T or F?

5. Two major elements of biofeedback training appear to be relaxation and self-regulation. T or F?

6. Evidence is beginning to suggest that the most important feature of the Type A personality is a sense of time urgency, rather than feelings of anger and hostility. T or F?

7. A sense of commitment, challenge, and control characterizes the hardy personality. T or F?

8. The first stage of the G.A.S. is called the _____ reaction.

9. Whereas stressful incidents suppress the immune system, stress management techniques have almost no effect on immune system functioning. T or F?

10. Acculturative stress tends to be minimal when a person who has moved to a different country maintains a high degree of separation from the new "host" culture. T or F?

CRITICAL THINKING

11. People with a hardy personality type appear to be especially resistant to which of the problems discussed earlier in this chapter?

Answers:

1. T 2. F 3. *d* 4. F 5. T 6. T 7. T 8. alarm 9. F 10. F 11. Learned helplessness.

Alarm reaction *First stage of the G.A.S., during which bodily resources are mobilized to cope with a stressor.*

Stage of resistance *Second stage of the G.A.S., during which bodily adjustments to stress stabilize, but at a high physical cost.*

Stage of exhaustion *Third stage of the G.A.S., at which time the body's resources are exhausted and serious health consequences occur.*

Immune system *System that mobilizes bodily defenses (such as white blood cells) against invading microbes and other disease agents.*

Psychoneuroimmunology *Study of the links among behavior, stress, disease, and the immune system.*

psychology in action

Stress management is the use of behavioral strategies to reduce stress and improve coping skills. As promised, this section describes strategies for managing stress. Before you continue, you may want to assess your level of stress again, this time using a scale developed for undergraduate students. (See ◆Table 16.9.) Like the SRRS, high scores on the *College Life Stress Inventory* suggest that you have been exposed to health-threatening levels of stress. (Source: Renner & Mackin, 1998.)

The *College Life Stress Inventory* is scored by adding the ratings for all of the items that have happened to you in the last year. The scale below is an approximate guide to the meaning of your score. But remember, stress is an internal state. If you are good at coping with stressors, a high score may not be a problem for you.

2351+	extremely high
1911–2350	very high
1471–1910	high
1031–1470	average
591–1030	below average
151–590	low
0–150	very low

Now that you have a picture of your current level of stress, what can you do about it? The simplest way of coping with stress is to modify or remove its source—by leaving a stressful job, for example. Obviously this is often impossible, which is why learning to manage stress is so important.

As shown in ❖ Figure 16.9, stress triggers *bodily effects, upsetting thoughts,* and *ineffective behavior.* Also shown is the fact that each element worsens the others in a vicious cycle. Indeed, the basic idea of the "Stress Game" is that once it begins, *you lose*—unless you take action to break the cycle. The information that follows tells how.

Managing Bodily Reactions

Much of the immediate discomfort of stress is caused by fight-or-flight emotional responses. The body is ready to act, with tight muscles and a pounding heart. If action is prevented, we merely remain "uptight." A sensible remedy is to learn a reliable, drug-free way of relaxing.

EXERCISE   Stress-based arousal can be dissipated by using the body. Any full-body exercise can be effective. Swimming, danc-

◆ **TABLE 16.9** College Life Stress Inventory

Circle the "stress rating" number for any item that has happened to you in the last year, then add them.

EVENT	STRESS RATING
Being raped	100
Finding out that you are HIV-positive	100
Being accused of rape	98
Death of a close friend	97
Death of a close family member	96
Contracting a sexually transmitted disease (other than AIDS)	94
Concerns about being pregnant	91
Finals week	90
Concerns about your partner being pregnant	90
Oversleeping for an exam	89
Flunking a class	89
Having a boyfriend or girlfriend cheat on you	85
Ending a steady dating relationship	85
Serious illness in a close friend or family member	85
Financial difficulties	84
Writing a major term paper	83
Being caught cheating on a test	83
Drunk driving	82
Sense of overload in school or work	82
Two exams in one day	80
Cheating on your boyfriend or girlfriend	77
Getting married	76
Negative consequences of drinking or drug use	75
Depression or crisis in your best friend	73
Difficulties with parents	73
Talking in front of a class	72
Lack of sleep	69
Change in housing situation (hassles, moves)	69
Competing or performing in public	69
Getting in a physical fight	66
Difficulties with a roommate	66
Job changes (applying, new job, work hassles)	65
Declaring a major or concerns about future plans	65
A class you hate	62
Drinking or use of drugs	61
Confrontations with professors	60
Starting a new semester	58
Going on a first date	57
Registration	55
Maintaining a steady dating relationship	55
Commuting to campus or work, or both	54
Peer pressures	53
Being away from home for the first time	53
Getting sick	52
Concerns about your appearance	52
Getting straight A's	51
A difficult class that you love	48
Making new friends; getting along with friends	47
Fraternity or sorority rush	47
Falling asleep in class	40
Attending an athletic event (e.g., football game)	20

(Source: Renner & Mackin, 1998.)

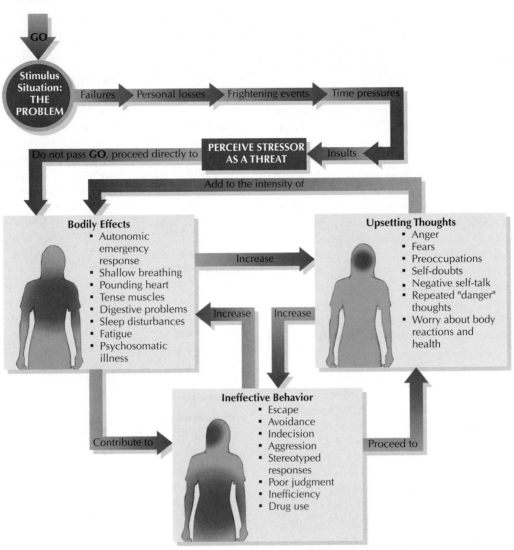

❖ **FIGURE 16.9** *The stress game. (Adapted from Rosenthal & Rosenthal, 1980.)*

ing, jumping rope, yoga, most sports, and especially walking are valuable outlets (Anshel, 1995b). Regular exercise alters hormones, circulation, muscle tone, and a number of other aspects of physical functioning. Together, such changes can lower the risks for disease (Baum & Posluszny, 1999).

Be sure to choose activities that are vigorous enough to relieve tension yet enjoyable enough to be done repeatedly. Exercising for stress management is most effective when it is done daily (Wheeler & Frank, 1988). Remember, though, that this refers to light exercise, such as walking. If you do more vigorous exercise to maintain aerobic fitness, three or four times a week is about right.

MEDITATION   Many stress counselors recommend *meditation* for quieting the body and promoting relaxation. We will consider meditation techniques and their effects in the upcoming A Step Beyond section. For now, it is enough to note that meditation is easy to learn—taking an expensive commercial course is unnecessary.

Meditation is one of the most effective ways to relax (Eppley, Abrams, & Shear, 1989). But be aware that listening to or playing music, taking nature walks, enjoying hobbies, and the like can be meditations of sorts. Anything that reliably interrupts upsetting thoughts and promotes relaxation can be helpful.

PROGRESSIVE RELAXATION   It is possible to relax systematically, completely, and by choice. To learn the details of how this is done, consult Chapter 18 of this book. The basic idea of **progressive relaxation** is to tighten all the muscles in a given area of your body (the arms, for instance) and then voluntarily

Stress management *The application of behavioral strategies to reduce stress and improve coping skills.*
Progressive relaxation *A method for producing deep relaxation of all parts of the body.*

relax them. By first tensing and relaxing each area of the body, you can learn what muscle tension feels like. Then when each area is relaxed, the change is more noticeable and more controllable. In this way, it is possible, with practice, to greatly reduce tension.

GUIDED IMAGERY   In a technique called **guided imagery,** people visualize images that are calming, relaxing, or beneficial in other ways. Relaxation, for instance, can be promoted by visualizing peaceful scenes. Pick several places where you feel safe, calm, and at ease. Typical locations might be a beach or lake, the woods, floating on an air mattress in a warm pool, or lying in the sun at a quiet park. To relax, vividly imagine yourself in one of these locations. In the visualized scene, you should be alone and in a comfortable position. It is important to visualize the scene as realistically as possible. Try to feel, taste, smell, hear, and see what you would actually experience in the calming scene. Practice forming such images several times a day for about 5 minutes each time. When your scenes become familiar and detailed, they can be used to reduce anxiety and encourage relaxation (Rosenthal, 1993).

Modifying Ineffective Behavior

Stress is often made worse by our misguided responses to it. The following suggestions may help you deal with stress more effectively.

SLOW DOWN   Remember that stress can be self-generated. Try to deliberately do things at a slower pace—especially if your pace has speeded up over the years. Tell yourself, "What counts most is not if I get there first, but if I get there at all" or "My goal is distance, not speed."

ORGANIZE   Disorganization creates stress. Try to take a fresh look at your situation and get organized. Setting priorities can be a real stress fighter. Ask yourself what's really important and concentrate on the things that count. Learn to let go of trivial but upsetting irritations. And above all, when you are feeling stressed, remember to K.I.S.: **K**eep **I**t **S**imple. (Some people prefer K.I.S.S.: Keep It Simple, Stupid.)

STRIKE A BALANCE   Work, school, family, friends, interests, hobbies, recreation, community, religion—there are many important elements in a satisfying life. Damaging stress often comes from letting one element—especially work or school—get blown out of proportion. Your goal should be quality in life, not quantity. Try to strike a balance between challenging "good stress" and relaxation (Wheeler & Frank, 1988). Remember, when you are "doing nothing," you are actually doing something very important: Set aside time for "me acts" such as loafing, browsing, puttering, playing, and napping.

RECOGNIZE AND ACCEPT YOUR LIMITS   Many of us set unrealistic and perfectionistic goals. Given that no one can ever be perfect, this attitude leaves many people feeling inadequate, no matter how well they have performed. Set gradual, achievable

goals for yourself. Also, set realistic limits on what you try to do on any given day. Learn to say no to added demands or responsibilities.

SEEK SOCIAL SUPPORT   **Social support** (close, positive relationships with others) facilitates good health and morale (Greenglass, Burke, & Konarski, 1998). One reason for this is that support from family and friends serves as a buffer to cushion the impact of stressful events (Taylor, 1990). Talking out problems and expressing tensions can be incredibly helpful. If things really get bad, seek help from a therapist, counselor, or clergy (please note that bartender is not on the list).

WRITE ABOUT YOUR FEELINGS   If you don't have someone you can talk to about stressful events, you might try expressing your thoughts and feelings in writing. Several studies have found that students who write about their upsetting experiences, thoughts, and feelings are better able to cope with stress. They also experience fewer illnesses, and they get better grades (Esterling et al., 1999; Pennebaker & Francis, 1996). For some people, just expressing their feelings is beneficial. For many, though, it also helps to make specific plans for coping with upsetting experiences after writing about them (Cameron & Nicholls, 1998).

Avoiding Upsetting Thoughts

Assume you are taking a test. Suddenly you realize that you are running short of time. If you say to yourself, "Oh no, this is terrible, I've blown it now," your body's response will probably be sweating, tenseness, and a knot in your stomach. On the other hand, if you say, "I should have watched the time, but getting upset won't help, I'll just take one question at a time," your stress level will be much lower.

As stated earlier, stress is greatly affected by the views we take of events. Physical symptoms and a tendency to make poor decisions are increased by negative thoughts or "self-talk." In many cases, what you say to yourself can be the difference between coping and collapsing (Matheny et al., 1996).

COPING STATEMENTS   Psychologist Donald Meichenbaum has popularized a technique called **stress inoculation.** In it, clients learn to fight fear and anxiety with an internal monologue of positive coping statements. First, clients learn to identify and monitor **negative self-statements** (self-critical thoughts that increase anxiety). Negative thoughts are a problem because they tend to directly elevate physical arousal. To counter this effect, clients learn to replace negative statements with coping statements from a supplied list. Eventually, they are encouraged to make their own lists (Saunders et al., 1996).

How are coping statements applied?   **Coping statements** are reassuring and self-enhancing. They are used to block out, or counteract, negative self-talk in stressful situations. Before giving a short speech, for instance, you would replace "I'm scared," "I can't do this," "My mind will go blank and

I'll panic," or "I'll sound stupid and boring" with "I'll give my speech on something I like," "I'll breathe deeply before I start my speech," or "My pounding heart just means I'm psyched up to do my best." Additional examples of coping statements follow.

Preparing for Stressful Situation
- I'll just take things one step at a time.
- If I get nervous, I'll just pause a moment.
- Tomorrow I'll be through it.
- I've managed to do this before.
- What exactly do I have to do?

Confronting the Stressful Situation
- Relax now, this can't really hurt me.
- Stay organized, focus on the task.
- There's no hurry, take it step by step.
- Nobody's perfect, I'll just do my best.
- It will be over soon, just be calm.

Meichenbaum cautions that saying the "right" things to yourself may not be enough to improve stress tolerance. You must practice this approach in actual stress situations. Also, it is important to develop your own personal list of coping statements by finding what works for you. Ultimately, the value of learning this, and other stress management skills, ties back into the idea that much stress is self-generated. Knowing that you can manage a demanding situation is in itself a major antidote for stress.

LIGHTEN UP   Humor is worth cultivating as a way to reduce stress. A good sense of humor can lower your distress or stress reaction to difficult events (Lefcourt & Thomas, 1998). In addition, an ability to laugh at life's ups and downs is associated with better immunity to disease (McCelland & Cheriff, 1997). Don't be afraid to laugh at yourself and at the many ways in which we humans make things difficult for ourselves. Humor is one of the best antidotes for anxiety and emotional distress (Cann, Holt, & Calhoun, 1999).

Coping with Frustration and Conflict

In a classic experiment, a psychologist studying frustration placed rats on a small platform at the top of a tall pole. Then he forced them to jump off the platform toward two elevated doors, one locked and the other unlocked. If the rat chose the correct door, it swung open and the rat landed safely on another platform. Rats who chose the locked door bounced off it and fell into a net far below.

The problem of choosing the open door was made unsolvable and very frustrating by randomly alternating which door was locked. After a time, most rats adopted a stereotyped response. That is, they chose the same door every time. This door was then permanently locked. All the rat had to do was to jump to the other door to avoid a fall, but time after time the rat bounced off the locked door (Maier, 1949).

Isn't that an example of persistence?   No. Persistence that is *inflexible* can turn into "stupid," stereotyped behavior like that of a rat on a jumping stand. When dealing with frustration, you must know when to quit and establish a new direction. Here are some suggestions to help you avoid needless frustration.

1. Try to identify the source of your frustration. Is it external or personal?
2. Is the source of frustration something that can be changed? How hard would you have to work to change it? Is it under your control at all?
3. If the source of your frustration can be changed or removed, are the necessary efforts worth it?

The answers to these questions help determine if persistence will be futile. There is value in learning to accept gracefully those things that cannot be changed.

It is also important to distinguish between *real* barriers and *imagined* barriers. All too often, we create our own imaginary barriers. For example, Anita wants a part-time job to earn extra money. At the first place she applied, she was told that she didn't have enough "experience." Now she complains of being frustrated because she wants to work but cannot. She needs "experience" to work, but can't get experience without working. She has quit looking for a job.

Is Anita's need for experience a real barrier? Unless she applies for *many* jobs, it is impossible to tell if she has overestimated its importance. For her, the barrier is real enough to prevent further efforts, but with persistence she might locate an "unlocked door." If a reasonable amount of effort does show that experience is essential, it might be obtained in other ways—through temporary volunteer work, for instance.

How can I handle conflicts more effectively?   Most of the suggestions just made also apply to conflicts. However, here are some additional things to remember when you are in conflict or must make a difficult decision.

1. Don't be hasty when making important decisions. Take time to collect information and to weigh pros and cons. Hasty decisions are often regretted. Even if you do make a faulty decision, it will trouble you less if you know that you did everything possible to avoid a mistake.
2. Try out important decisions *partially* when possible. If you are thinking about moving to a new town, try to spend a few days there first. If you are choosing between colleges, do

---

Guided imagery *Intentional visualization of images that are calming, relaxing, or beneficial in other ways.*
Social support *Close, positive relationships with other people.*
Stress inoculation *Use of positive coping statements to control fear and anxiety.*
Negative self-statements *Self-critical thoughts that increase anxiety and lower performance.*
Coping statements *Reassuring, self-enhancing statements that are used to stop self-critical thinking.*

the same. If classes are in progress, sit in on some. If you want to learn to scuba dive, rent equipment for a reasonable length of time before buying.

3. Look for workable compromises. Again it is important to get all available information. If you think that you have only one or two alternatives and they are undesirable or unbearable, seek the aid of a teacher, counselor, minister, or social service agency. You may be overlooking possible alternatives these people will know about.

4. When all else fails, make a decision and live with it. Indecision and conflict exact a high cost. Sometimes it is best to select a course of action and stick with it unless it is very obviously wrong after you have taken it.

In class, you may want to describe some of the frustrations and conflicts you have experienced and how you handled them. Prepare to discuss frustrations and conflicts you have resolved unusually effectively or that you might have handled better. Do you have some additional hints to share with other students?

a step beyond

MEDITATION—THE 20-MINUTE VACATION

Focus: Is meditation useful for coping with stress?

Meditation refers to mental exercises that focus attention and interrupt the typical flow of thoughts, worries, and analysis (Wilson, 1986). Meditation takes many forms and has many meanings in various cultures. Here we are interested in meditation as a self-control strategy for lowering physical and mental arousal. People who regularly use meditation as a stress reduction technique often report less daily physical arousal and anxiety. Even if meditation is not practiced daily, it may be a useful technique for interrupting worries and fearful thinking (Wilson, 1986).

TYPES OF MEDITATION   Meditation takes two major forms. In **concentrative meditation,** attention is given to a single focal point, such as an object, a thought, or one's own breathing. In contrast, **receptive meditation** is "open," or expansive. That is, the person widens attention to embrace a total, nonjudgmental awareness of his or her experience of the world (Walsh, 1984). An example of this type of meditation is losing all self-consciousness while walking in the wilderness with a quiet and receptive mind. To gain insight into receptive meditation, try the following exercise sometime.

While walking outdoors, silently complete this statement four or five times: Right now I see. . . . Then complete each of the following statements four or five times and proceed to the next one: Right now I hear. . . . Right now I smell. . . . Right now I feel. . . . Each time, become aware of what you see, hear, smell, and feel. Then repeat the process as many times as you like.

At first, you will tend to name what you are experiencing. If you can stop doing that and just be intensely aware of your surroundings—without thinking—you will have some idea of

what receptive meditation is like. If you can learn to be openly aware without using any words, you will be even closer.

Although it may not seem so, receptive meditation is regarded as more difficult to attain than concentrative meditation (Smith, 1986). For this reason, we will discuss concentrative meditation as a practical self-control method.

Performing Concentrative Meditation

How is concentrative meditation done? The basic idea in concentrative meditation is to sit still and quietly focus on some external object or on a repetitive internal stimulus such as a word or your own breathing (Wilson, 1986). In one experiment, college students were instructed to concentrate on breathing:

> While you are sitting, let your breath become relaxed and natural. Let it set its own pace and depth if you can. Then focus your attention on your own breathing: the movements of your belly, not your nose and throat. Do not allow extraneous thoughts or stimuli to pull your attention away from your breathing. This may be hard to do at first, but keep directing your attention back to it. Turn everything else aside if it comes up (Maupin, 1965).

Not all subjects responded to this exercise, but at the end of a 2-week period, those who did reported experiences of deep concentration, pleasant bodily sensations, and extreme detachment from outside worries and distractions.

Using a *mantra* is an alternative approach you may want to try. A **mantra** consists of words used as the focus of attention in concentrative meditation. Typical mantras are smooth, flowing sounds that are easily repeated. A widely used mantra is the word *om*. A mantra could also be a phrase from a familiar prayer, a positive affirmation, a short line from a poem, or just a beautiful thought. If other thoughts arise as you repeat a mantra, just return attention to it as often as necessary to maintain meditation.

THE RELAXATION RESPONSE Many commercial meditation courses claim to offer mantras tailored to each individual. But medical researcher Herbert Benson found that the physical benefits of meditation are the same no matter what word is used. They include lowered heart rate, blood pressure, muscle tension, and other signs of stress.

Benson believes that the core of meditation is the **relaxation response**—an innate physiological pattern that opposes activation of the body's fight-or-flight mechanisms. Benson feels, quite simply, that most of us have forgotten how to relax deeply. Subjects in his experiments have had considerable success in producing the relaxation response by following these instructions:

> Sit quietly in a comfortable position. Close your eyes. Deeply relax all your muscles, beginning at your feet and progressing up to your face. Keep them deeply relaxed.
> Breathe through your nose. Become aware of your breathing. As you breathe out, say the word *one* silently to yourself.

Do not worry about whether you are successful in achieving a deep level of relaxation. Maintain a passive attitude and permit relaxation to occur at its own pace. Expect distracting thoughts. When these distracting thoughts occur, ignore them and continue repeating "one" (Adapted from Benson, 1977).

EFFECTS OF MEDITATION *What effects does meditation have, other than producing relaxation?* Many extravagant claims have been made about meditation. For example, members of the Transcendental Meditation (TM) movement have stated that 20 minutes of meditation is as restful as a full night's sleep. This, however, is simply not true. One study, for instance, found that merely "resting" for 20 minutes produces the same bodily effects as meditation (Holmes, 1984; Holmes et al., 1983). Long-term meditators have also claimed improvement in memory, alertness, creativity, and intuition. Again, such claims must be regarded as unproven. Most are based on personal testimonials or poorly controlled studies. A major problem with most studies of TM is that they use devoted meditators. It is quite likely that the beliefs and lifestyles of these people influence the results of the studies as much as meditation does (Druckman & Bjork, 1994).

In defense of meditation, it is important to remember that relaxation can be mental as well as physical. As a stress-control technique, meditation may be a good choice for people who find it difficult to "turn off" upsetting thoughts when they need to relax. For example, college students who tried meditation felt happier, less anxious, and less depressed after just 2 weeks of twice-a-day meditation (Smith, Compton, & West, 1995). On the other side of the educational fence, teachers who learned meditation also experienced lowered stress levels (Winzelberg & Luskin, 1999).

Although many of the claimed benefits of meditation appear to be overstated, meditation does reliably elicit the relaxation response (Janowiak & Hackman, 1994; Kelly, 1996). Benson (1975) believes that the following elements are the keys for inducing relaxation.

1. A quiet environment
2. Decreased muscle tension
3. A mental device (such as a repeated word) that helps shift thoughts away from ordinary, rational concerns
4. A passive attitude toward whether you are "succeeding" at becoming relaxed

---

Meditation *A mental exercise for producing relaxation or heightened awareness.*
Concentrative meditation *Mental exercise based on attending to a single object or thought.*
Receptive meditation *Mental exercise based on widening attention to become aware of everything experienced at any given moment.*
Mantra *A flowing word or sound repeated silently during concentrative meditation.*
Relaxation response *The pattern of internal bodily changes that occurs at times of relaxation.*

SUMMARY To summarize, research suggests that concentrative meditation is only one of several ways to elicit the relaxation response. For many people, sitting quietly and "resting" can be as effective. Similar stress reduction occurs when people set aside time daily to engage in other restful activities, such as muscle relaxation, positive daydreaming, and even leisure reading. However, if you are the type of person who finds it difficult to ignore upsetting thoughts, then concentrative meditation might be a good way to promote relaxation. Meditation and similar techniques provide a valuable, stress-lowering "time-out" from the normal clamor of thoughts and worries—something almost everyone could use in our fast-paced society.

CONCLUSION: Concentrative meditation reliably produces the relaxation response, which makes it valuable for stress reduction.

KNOWLEDGE BUILDER
MEDITATION AND STRESS REDUCTION

RELATE

Various activities can produce the relaxation response. When do you experience states of deep relaxation, coupled with a sense of serene awareness? What similarities do these occurrences have to meditation?

LEARNING CHECK

1. The focus of attention in concentrative meditation is "open," or expansive. T or F?

2. Mantras are words said silently to oneself to end a session of meditation. T or F?

3. Research conducted by Herbert Benson indicates that careful selection of a mantra is necessary to obtain the physical benefits of meditation. T or F?

4. The most immediate benefit of meditation appears to be its capacity for producing the relaxation response. T or F?

CRITICAL THINKING

5. Meditation tends to interrupt negative self-statements and other upsetting internal "talk." In this sense, the effects of meditation are similar to what technique?

Answers:

1. F 2. F 3. F 4. T 5. Stress inoculation (the use of coping statements).

What is health psychology? How does behavior affect health?

- Health psychologists are interested in behavior that helps maintain and promote health.
- Studies of health and illness have identified a number of behavioral risk factors and health-promoting behaviors.
- Health psychologists have pioneered efforts to prevent the development of unhealthy habits and to improve well-being through community health campaigns.

What is stress? What factors determine its severity?

- Stress occurs when demands are placed on an organism to adjust or adapt.
- Stress is more damaging in situations involving pressure, a lack of control, unpredictability of the stressor, and intense or repeated emotional shocks.
- Stress is intensified when a situation is perceived as a threat and when a person does not feel competent to cope with it.
- In work settings, prolonged stress can lead to burnout.
- The primary appraisal of a situation greatly affects our emotional response to it. Stress reactions, in particular, are related to an appraisal of threat.
- During a secondary appraisal, some means of coping with a situation is selected. Coping may be problem focused, emotion focused, or both.

What causes frustration and what are typical reactions to it?

- Frustration is the negative emotional state that occurs when progress toward a goal is blocked. Sources of frustration may be usefully classified as external or personal.
- External frustrations are based on delay, failure, rejection, loss, and other direct blocking of motives. Personal frustration is related to personal characteristics over which one has little control.
- Frustrations of all types become more intense as the strength, urgency, or importance of the blocked motive increases.
- Major behavioral reactions to frustration include persistence, more vigorous responding, circumvention, direct aggression, displaced aggression (including scapegoating), and escape or withdrawal.

Are there different types of conflict? How do people react to conflict?

- Conflict occurs when one must choose between contradictory alternatives.
- Five major types of conflict are approach-approach, avoidance-avoidance, approach-avoidance, double approach-avoidance, and multiple approach-avoidance.
- Approach-approach conflicts are usually the easiest to resolve.
- Avoidance conflicts are difficult to resolve and are characterized by inaction, indecision, freezing, and a desire to escape (called "leaving the field").
- People usually remain in approach-avoidance conflicts but fail to fully resolve them. Approach-avoidance conflicts are associated with ambivalence and partial approach.
- Vacillation is a common reaction to double approach-avoidance conflicts.

What are defense mechanisms?

- Anxiety, threat, or feelings of inadequacy frequently lead to the use of defense mechanisms. These are habitual psychological strategies used to avoid or reduce anxiety.
- A large number of defense mechanisms have been identified, including compensation, denial, fantasy, intellectualization, isolation, projection, rationalization, reaction formation, regression, repression, and sublimation.

What do we know about coping with feelings of helplessness and depression?

- Learned helplessness has been used as a model for understanding depression. Mastery training acts as one major antidote to helplessness.
- Depression is a major and surprisingly common emotional problem. Actions and thoughts that counter feelings of helplessness tend to reduce depression.
- The college blues are a relatively mild form of depression. Learning to manage college work and to challenge self-critical thinking can help alleviate the college blues.

How is stress related to health and disease?

- Work with the *Social Readjustment Rating Scale* indicates that multiple life changes can increase long-range susceptibility to accident or illness.
- Immediate psychological and mental health is more closely related to the intensity and severity of daily hassles or microstressors.
- Intense or prolonged stress may cause damage in the form of psychosomatic problems.
- Psychosomatic (mind-body) disorders have no connection to hypochondria, the tendency to imagine that one has some terrible disease.
- During biofeedback training, bodily processes are monitored and converted to a signal that tells what the body is doing. With practice, biofeedback allows alteration of many bodily activities. It shows promise for the alleviation of some psychosomatic illnesses.
- People with Type A personalities are competitive, striving, hostile, and impatient. These characteristics—especially hostility—double the risk of heart attack.
- People who have traits of the hardy personality seem to be resistant to stress, even if they also have Type A traits.
- The body reacts to stress in a series of stages called the general adaptation syndrome (G.A.S.).
- The stages of the G.A.S. are alarm, resistance, and exhaustion. The pattern of bodily reactions and changes in resistance observed in the G.A.S. follows closely the pattern observed in the development of psychosomatic disorders.
- Studies of psychoneuroimmunology show that stress also lowers the body's immunity to disease.

What are the best strategies for managing stress?

- A sizable number of coping skills can be applied to manage stress. Most of these focus on one of three areas: bodily effects, ineffective behavior, and upsetting thoughts.

Is meditation useful for coping with stress?

- Receptive meditation and concentrative meditation are self-control techniques that can be used to reduce stress. Two major benefits of meditation are its ability to interrupt anxious thoughts and its ability to elicit the relaxation response.

PSYCHOLOGY ON THE NET

- **Burnout Test** A short questionnaire on job burnout. http://www.prohealth.com/articles/burnout.htm
- **Focus on Stress** A series of articles about stress. http://helping.apa.org/work/index.html
- **HealthyWay** A set of pages on health, nutrition, addictions, disabilities, sexuality, fitness, and much more. http://sympatico.healthcentral.ca/home/home.cfm
- **Preventive Health Center** A general source of information on how to maintain health and prevent disease. http://www.md-phc.com/index.html

- **Stress Management: Review of Principles** Links to articles on stress management. http://www.unl.edu/stress/mgmt/
- **Type A Behavior** Describes Type A behavior, with links to an on-line test and related sites. http://www.msnbc.com/onair/nbc/nightlynews/stress/default.asp

- •**InfoTrac® College Edition** For recent articles related to the college blues and more serious forms of depression, use Key Words search for MENTAL DEPRESSION.

INTERACTIVE LEARNING

PsychNow! 4c. Coping with Emotion 4d. Stress and Health

CHAPTER 17

Psychological Disorders

Chapter Survey

Theme: *Judgments of normality are relative, but psychological disorders clearly exist and need to be classified, explained, and treated.*

BEWARE THE HELICOPTERS

"THE HELICOPTERS. OH NO, NOT THE HELI-COPTERS. Have come to tear the feathers out of my frontal lobes. Help me, nurse, help me, can't you hear them? Gotta get back into my body to save it. . . . The doctor is thinking I would make good glue."

These are the words of Carol North, a psychiatrist who survived schizophrenia. In addition to her hallucinated helicopters, she was plagued by voices that said: "Be good," "Do bad," "Stand up," "Sit down," "Collide with the other world," "Do you want a cigar?" (North, 1987).

Carol North's painful journey into the shadows of madness left her incapacitated for nearly two decades. Her case is but one hint of the magnitude of mental health problems. Here are the facts on psychopathology:

- One out of every 100 persons will become so severely disturbed as to require hospitalization at some point in his or her lifetime.
- Some 3 to 6 percent of the aged suffer from organic psychoses.
- In any given week, 7 percent of the population is experiencing an anxiety-related disorder.
- One out of every 8 school-age children is seriously maladjusted.
- Ten to 20 percent or more of all adults suffer a major depression in their lifetime.
- Each year more than 2 million people are admitted or readmitted to outpatient services or psychiatric treatment in general hospitals.

The scientific study of mental, emotional, and behavioral disorders is known as **psychopathology**. The term psychopathology also refers to mental disorders themselves or to psychologically unhealthy behavior. Thus, it covers not only obviously maladaptive behavior, such as drug addiction, compulsive gambling, or a loss of contact with reality, but also any behavior that interferes with personal growth and self-fulfillment (Carson, Butcher, & Mineka, 1997).

What does it mean to be "crazy"? In the 1800s, doctors and nonprofessionals alike used terms such as "crazy," "insane," "cracked," and "lunatic" quite freely. The "insane" were thought of as bizarre and definitely different from you or me. Today, our understanding of psychological disorders is growing ever more sophisticated. To draw the line between normal and abnormal, we must weigh some complex issues. In this chapter, we will address some of those issues, while describing an array of psychological problems.

Gateways to Understanding Psychological Disorders

PSYCHOLOGICAL DISORDERS damage the quality of life, in varying degrees, for many people.

PSYCHOPATHOLOGY, which involves identifying, classifying, and explaining psychological disorders, is worthwhile and necessary.

PSYCHOLOGICALLY UNHEALTHY BEHAVIOR is maladaptive, and it involves a loss of adequate control over thoughts, feelings, and actions.

MALADAPTIVE BEHAVIOR PATTERNS, UNHEALTHY PERSONALITY TYPES, AND EXCESSIVE LEVELS OF ANXIETY underlie many mental disorders.

THE MOST SEVERE FORMS OF PSYCHOPATHOLOGY involve emotional extremes and/or a break with reality.

PSYCHOLOGICAL DISORDERS are complex and have multiple causes.

SUICIDE is a relatively frequent cause of death that can, in many cases, be prevented.

DESPITE ITS VALUE, THE MEDICAL MODEL OF PSYCHOLOGICAL DISORDERS sometimes leads to a limited view of human behavior and problems.

NORMALITY—WHAT IS NORMAL?

"That guy is really wacko. His porch lights are dimming." "Yeah, the butter's sliding off his waffle. I think he's ready to go postal." Informally, it's tempting to make snap judgments about mental health. However, to seriously classify people as psychologically unhealthy raises complex and age-old issues.

Defining abnormality can be tricky. We might begin by saying that psychopathology is characterized by **subjective discomfort.** That is, the unhealthy personality is marked by unhappiness, anxiety, depression, or other signs of emotional distress.

But couldn't a person be seriously disturbed without feeling subjective discomfort? Yes. Psychopathology doesn't always

cause personal anguish. A person displaying obviously bizarre behavior might feel "on top of the world." Also, a *lack* of discomfort may reveal a problem. If you were to show no signs of grief or depression after the death of a close friend or loved one, we might suspect psychopathology. In practice, subjective discomfort accounts for most instances in which people voluntarily seek professional help.

Some psychologists try to pin down normality more objectively by using statistical definitions. **Statistical abnormality** refers to extreme scores on some dimension, such as intelligence or anxiety. For example, because anxiety is a feature of several psychological disorders, we could devise a test to learn how many people show low, medium, or high levels of anxiety. Usually, the results of such a test will form a **normal** (bell-shaped) **curve** (❖Fig. 17.1). (*Normal* in this case is a statistical

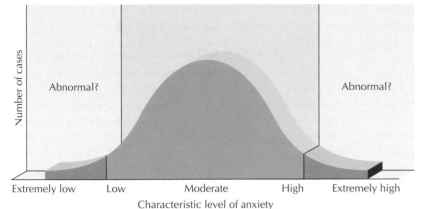

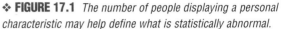
❖ **FIGURE 17.1** *The number of people displaying a personal characteristic may help define what is statistically abnormal.*

concept. It refers only to the shape of the curve.) Notice that most people score in the central region of such curves. A person who deviates from the average by being anxious all the time (high anxiety) might be considered abnormal. So, too, might a person who never feels anxiety.

Then a statistical definition of abnormality tells us nothing about the meaning of deviations from the norm? Right. It is as statistically "abnormal" (unusual) for a person to score above 145 on an IQ test as it is to score below 55. However, only the lower score is regarded as "abnormal" or undesirable (Wakefield, 1992).

Another problem with statistical definitions is the issue of *where to draw the line* between normality and abnormality. To take a new example, we could obtain the average frequency of sexual intercourse for persons of a particular age, sex, sexual orientation, and marital status. It is probably fair to say that a person who feels driven to have sex dozens of times a day has a problem. But as we move back toward the norm we face the statistical problem of drawing lines. How often does an otherwise normal behavior have to occur before it becomes abnormal? As you can see, statistical boundary lines tend to be somewhat arbitrary (Widiger & Trull, 1991).

Nonconformity may also reveal the existence of a psychological disorder. **Social nonconformity** refers to disobeying societal standards for acceptable conduct. In such cases, faulty socialization leads to destructive or self-destructive behavior. (Think, for instance, of a drug abuser or a prostitute.) However, we must be careful to separate unhealthy nonconformity from creativity and unique lifestyles. Many eccentric "characters" are charming and emotionally stable. Note, too, that strictly following social norms is no guarantee of mental health. In some cases, psychopathology takes the form of rigid conformity.

Before any behavior can be defined as abnormal, we must consider the **situational context** (social situation, behavioral setting, or general circumstances) in which it occurs. Is it normal to stand outside and water a lawn with a hose? It depends on whether it is raining. Is it abnormal for a grown man to remove his pants and expose himself to another man or woman in a place of business? It depends on whether the other person is a bank clerk or a doctor! Almost any imaginable behavior can be considered normal in some contexts, as the following example indicates.

In mid-October, 1972, an airplane carrying a rugby team called the Old Christians crashed in the snow-capped Andes of South America. Incredibly, 16 of the 45 people who had been aboard at the time of the crash survived 73 days in deep snow and subfreezing temperatures. They were forced to use extremely grim measures to do so—they ate the bodies of those who had died in the crash.

Social nonconformity does not automatically indicate psychopathology.

Psychopathology *The scientific study of mental, emotional, and behavioral disorders; also, abnormal or maladaptive behavior.*
Subjective discomfort *Personal, private feelings of discomfort, unhappiness, or emotional distress.*
Statistical abnormality *Abnormality defined on the basis of an extreme score on some dimension, such as IQ or anxiety.*
Normal curve *A bell-shaped curve with a large number of scores in the middle, tapering to very few extremely high and low scores.*
Social nonconformity *Failure to conform to societal norms or the usual minimum standards for social conduct.*
Situational context *The social situation, behavioral setting, or general circumstances in which an action takes place.*

Culture is one of the most influential contexts in which any behavior is judged. In some cultures it is considered normal to defecate or urinate in public or to appear naked in public. In our culture, such behaviors would be considered unusual or abnormal. In some Muslim cultures, women who remain completely housebound are considered normal or even virtuous. In Western cultures, they might be diagnosed as suffering from agoraphobia (Widiger & Sankis, 2000).

Thus, **cultural relativity** (the idea that judgments are made relative to the values of one's culture) can affect the diagnosis of psychological disorders (Alarcon, 1995). (See "The Politics of 'Madness.'") Still, all cultures classify people as abnormal if they fail to communicate with others or are consistently unpredictable in their actions.

Core Features of Disordered Behavior

If abnormality is so hard to define, how are judgments of psychopathology made? It's clear that all of the standards we have discussed are *relative.* However, abnormal behavior does have two core features. First, it is **maladaptive.** Rather than helping people to cope successfully, abnormal behavior makes it more difficult for them to meet the demands of day-to-day life. Second, psychological disorders involve a *loss of the ability to control* one's thoughts, behaviors, or feelings adequately. For example, gambling is not a problem if people gamble voluntarily and with adequate self-control. However, compulsive gambling is a sign of psychopathology (Widiger & Sankis, 2000).

Various levels of functioning—from superior to severely disturbed—are described in ◆Table 17.1. Note that the bottom of the scale reads, "persistent danger of hurting self or others." Obviously, behavior at that level is maladaptive and involves a serious loss of control.

In practice, the judgment that a person needs help usually occurs when the person *does something* (hits a person, hallucinates, stares into space, collects rolls of toilet paper, and so forth) that *annoys* or *gains the attention* of a person in a *position of power* in the person's life (an employer, teacher, parent, spouse, or the person himself or herself). That person then *does something* about it. (A police officer may be called, the person may be urged to see a psychologist, a relative may start commitment proceedings, or the person may voluntarily seek help.)

Psychiatric Labeling

Before we proceed, a caution is in order. The terms reviewed in this chapter aid communication about human problems. But if used carelessly, they can hurt people. Everyone has felt or acted "crazy" during brief periods of stress or high emotion. People with psychological disorders have problems that are more severe or long lasting than most of us experience. Otherwise, they may not be that different from you or me.

A fascinating study done by David Rosenhan of Stanford University illustrates the impact of psychiatric labeling. Rosenhan and several colleagues had themselves committed to mental hospitals with a diagnosis of "schizophrenia" (Rosenhan, 1973). After being admitted, each of these pseudo-patients dropped all pretense of mental illness. Yet, even though they acted completely normal, none of the researchers was ever recognized by hospital *staff* as a phony patient. Real patients were not so easily fooled. It was not unusual for a patient to say to one of the researchers, "You're not crazy, you're checking up on the hospital!" or "You're a journalist."

To record his observations, Rosenhan took notes by carefully jotting things on a small piece of paper hidden in his hand. However, he soon learned that stealth was totally unnecessary. Rosenhan simply walked around with a clipboard, recording observations and collecting data. No one questioned this behavior. Rosenhan's note taking was just regarded as a symptom of his "illness." This observation clarifies why staff members failed to detect the fake patients. Because they were in a mental ward, and because they had been *labeled* schizophrenic, anything the pseudo-patients did was seen as a symptom of psychopathology.

CRITICAL THINKING

THE POLITICS OF "MADNESS"

The year is 1840. You are a slave who has tried repeatedly to escape from a cruel and abusive master. An expert is consulted about your "abnormal" behavior. His conclusion? You are suffering from "drapetomania," a mental "disorder" that causes slaves to run away (Wakefield, 1992).

As this example suggests, psychiatric terms are easily abused. Historically, some have been applied to culturally disapproved behaviors that are not really disorders. For example, all of the following were once considered disorders: drapetomania, childhood masturbation, lack of vaginal orgasm, self-defeating personality (applied mainly to women), and nymphomania (a woman with a healthy sexual appetite) (Wakefield, 1992). Even today, race, gender, and social class continue to affect the diagnosis of various disorders (Nathan & Langenbucher, 1999).

Gender is probably the most common source of bias in judging normality because standards tend to be based on males (Hartung & Widiger, 1998). According to psychologist Paula Caplan (1995) and others, women are penalized both for conforming to female stereotypes and for ignoring them. If a woman is independent, aggressive, and unemotional, she may be considered "unhealthy." Yet at the same time, a woman who is vain, emotional, irrational, and dependent on others (all "feminine" traits in our culture) may be classified as a histrionic or dependent personality (Bornstein, 1996). Indeed, a majority of persons classified as having dependent personality disorder are women. In view of this, Paula Caplan asks, Why isn't there a category called "delusional dominating personality disorder" for obnoxious men (Caplan, 1995)?

The differences we have reviewed illustrate the subtle influence that culture can have on perceptions of disorder and normality. Be cautious before you leap to conclusions about the mental health of others.

SCALE	LEVEL OF FUNCTIONING	EXAMPLES
100	Superior functioning in a wide range of activities. No symptoms.	Life's problems never seem to get out of hand. Person is sought out by others because of his or her many positive qualities.
90	Absent or minimal symptoms, functioning well in all areas, no more than everyday problems.	Has mild anxiety before exams, occasional arguments with family members.
80	If symptoms are present, they are brief and common reactions to stressors. No more than slight impairment in relationships, work, or school.	Has difficulty concentrating after family arguments, is falling behind in schoolwork.
70	Some mild symptoms, or some difficulty with relationships, work, or school.	Mood is depressed and has mild insomnia. Has been truant at school and has stolen things at home.
60	Moderate symptoms or moderate problems with relationships, work, or school.	Emotions are blunted, speech evasive, occasional panic attacks, no friends, unable to keep a job.
50	Serious symptoms or any serious impairments in relationships, work, or school.	Person has suicidal thoughts, engages in obessional rituals, shoplifts, has no friends, unable to keep a job.
40	Some impairment in grasp of reality or in communication, plus major impairments in work or school, relationships, judgment, thinking, or mood.	Speech is illogical, obscure, or irrelevant. Person is depressed and avoids friends, neglects family, and is unable to work.
30	Behavior is considerably affected by delusions or hallucinations; or, person is seriously impaired in communication or judgment; or, is unable to function in almost all areas.	Person is sometimes incoherent, acts grossly inappropriately, is preoccupied with suicide, stays in bed all day, has no job, home, or friends.
20	Some danger of hurting self or others; or, occasionally fails to maintain minimal personal hygiene; or, communication is grossly impaired.	Person makes tentative suicide attempts, is frequently violent and manically excited, smears own feces, is either incoherent or mute.
10	Persistent danger of severely hurting self or others; or, persistent inability to maintain minimal personal hygiene; or, serious suicidal acts.	Repeatedly violent, maintains almost no personal hygiene, has made potentially lethal suicide attempts.

(Adapted from *Global Assessment of Functioning Scale*, DSM-IV, 1994.)

As Rosenhan's study shows, it is far better to label *problems* than to label people. Think of the difference in impact between saying "You are experiencing a serious psychological disorder" and saying "You are a schizophrenic." Which statement would you prefer to have said about yourself?

SOCIAL STIGMA An added problem with psychiatric labeling is that it frequently leads to prejudice and discrimination. That is, it is common for the mentally ill in our culture to be *stigmatized* (rejected and disgraced). People who have been labeled mentally ill (at any time in their lives) are less likely to be hired. They also tend to be denied housing, and they are more likely to be falsely accused of crimes. Thus, people who are grappling with mental illness may be harmed as much by social stigma as they are by their immediate psychological problems (Corrigan & Penn, 1999).

BRIDGES

Labels and categories greatly influence our perceptions in many circumstances.

See Chapter 7, pages 223–224.

CLASSIFYING MENTAL DISORDERS—PROBLEMS BY THE BOOK

Psychological problems can be grouped into broad categories. The most widely used classification system is found in the *Diagnostic and Statistical Manual of Mental Disorders* (DSM-IV, 1994). The manual provides a common language for therapists, researchers, social agencies, and health

Cultural relativity *Perceptions and judgments made relative to the values of one's culture.*
Maladaptive behavior *Behavior that makes it difficult to adapt to the environment and meet the demands of day-to-day life.*

workers. It also helps professionals diagnose specific mental disorders and select appropriate therapies. The current DSM has its problems, but it is a big improvement over previous versions (Nathan & Langenbucher, 1999).

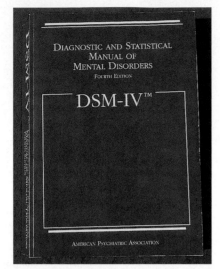

DSM-IV is not the only system for classifying mental disorders. Nevertheless, most activities in mental health settings—from diagnosis to therapy to billing of insurance companies—are influenced by the DSM. DSM-IV is both a scientific document and a social one. Major disorders are well-documented problems. Some problems, however, have little to do with "mental illness." Instead, they are primarily socially disapproved behaviors.

A **mental disorder** is a significant impairment in psychological functioning (Widiger & Trull, 1991). If you were to glance through DSM-IV, you would find a wide range of disorders described, including those in ◆Table 17.3 (on page 559). It's impossible here to discuss all of the problems in the table. An entire list of major disorders is provided so you can see the range of problems covered by the DSM. (You don't need to memorize all of them.) The descriptions that follow will give you an overview of some selected problems.

An Overview of Psychological Disorders

Psychotic disorders are characterized by hallucinations and delusions, social withdrawal, and a retreat from reality. Psychotic disorders, which tend to be severely disabling, may lead to hospitalization. At times, psychotic patients cannot separate their hallucinations from reality. In addition, their ability to control their thoughts and actions is severely impaired. Here's what a young college student who became psychotic told his father:

> It's the strangest thing. I hear voices, hundreds of them, telling me that everyone wants me dead. It's like all the radios of the world blaring all the stations at once, and it doesn't stop. It jams my brain (Weisburd, 1990).

Schizophrenia, delusional disorders, and some mood disorders include psychotic symptoms. Such symptoms may also accompany medical problems (such as brain diseases), drug abuse, and other conditions (DSM-IV, 1994). (◆Table 17.2 provides a simplified list of major disorders.)

◆**TABLE 17.2** Some Selected Categories of Psychopathology

PROBLEM	PRIMARY SYMPTOM	TYPICAL SIGNS OF TROUBLE
Psychotic disorders	Loss of contact with reality	You hear or see things that others don't; your mind has been playing tricks on you
Mood disorders	Mania or depression	You feel sad and hopeless; or you talk too loud and too fast and have a rush of ideas and feelings that others think are unreasonable
Anxiety disorders	High anxiety, or anxiety-based distortions of behavior	You have anxiety attacks and feel like you are going to die; or you are afraid to do things that most people can do; or you spend unusual amounts of time doing things like washing your hands or counting your heartbeats
Somatoform disorders	Bodily complaints without an organic (physical) basis	You feel physically sick, but your doctor says nothing is wrong with you; or you suffer from pain that has no physical basis; or you are preoccupied with thoughts about being sick
Dissociative disorders	Amnesia, feelings of unreality, multiple identities	There are major gaps in your memory of events; you feel like you are a robot or a stranger to yourself; others tell you that you have done things that you don't remember doing
Personality disorders	Unhealthy personality patterns	Your behavior patterns repeatedly cause problems at work, school, and in your relationships with others
Sexual and gender identity disorders	Disturbed gender identity, deviant sexual behavior, problems in sexual adjustment	You feel that you are a man trapped in a woman's body (or the reverse); or you can gain sexual satisfaction only by engaging in highly atypical sexual behavior; or you have problems with sexual desire, arousal, or performance
Substance related disorders	Disturbances related to drug abuse or dependence	You have been drinking too much, using illegal drugs, or taking prescription drugs more often than you should

DISORDERS USUALLY FIRST DIAGNOSED IN INFANCY, CHILDHOOD, OR ADOLESCENCE
Mental retardation
Example: Mild mental retardation
Learning disorders
Example: Reading disorder
Motor skills disorder
Example: Developmental coordination disorder
Pervasive developmental disorders
Example: Autistic disorder
Disruptive behavior and attention-deficit disorders
Example: Attention-deficit/hyperactivity disorder
Feeding and eating disorders of infancy or early childhood
Example: Pica
Tic disorders
Example: Transient tic disorder
Communication disorders
Example: Stuttering
Elimination disorders
Example: Enuresis
Other disorders of infancy, childhood, or adolescence
Example: Separation anxiety disorder

DELIRIUM, DEMENTIA, AMNESTIC AND OTHER COGNITIVE DISORDERS
Delirium
Example: Delirium due to a general medical condition
Dementia
Example: Dementia of the Alzheimer's type
Amnestic disorders (memory loss)
Example: Amnestic disorder due to a general medical condition
Cognitive disorder not otherwise specified

MENTAL DISORDERS DUE TO A GENERAL MEDICAL CONDITION NOT ELSEWHERE CLASSIFIED
Catatonic disorder due to a general medical condition
Personality change due to a general medical condition
Mental disorder not otherwise specified due to a general medical condition

SUBSTANCE RELATED DISORDERS
Example: Cocaine use disorders

SCHIZOPHRENIA AND OTHER PSYCHOTIC DISORDERS
Schizophrenia
Example: Schizophrenia, paranoid type
Schizophreniform disorder
Schizoaffective disorder
Delusional disorder
Example: Delusional disorder, grandiose type
Brief psychotic disorder
Shared psychotic disorder (folie à deux)
Psychotic disorder due to a general medical condition
Substance-induced psychotic disorder
Psychotic disorder not otherwise specified

MOOD DISORDERS
Depressive disorders
Example: Major depressive disorder
Bipolar disorders
Example: Bipolar I disorder
Mood disorder due to a general medical condition
Substance-induced mood disorder
Mood disorder not otherwise specified

ANXIETY DISORDERS
Example: Panic disorder

SOMATOFORM DISORDERS
Example: Conversion disorder

FACTITIOUS DISORDERS (FAKED DISABILITY OR ILLNESS)
Example: Factitious disorder

DISSOCIATIVE DISORDERS
Example: Dissociative identity disorder

SEXUAL AND GENDER IDENTITY DISORDERS
Sexual dysfunctions
Example: Sexual arousal disorders
Paraphilias
Example: Voyeurism
Sexual disorder not otherwise specified
Gender identity disorders
Example: Gender identity disorder

EATING DISORDERS
Example: Anorexia nervosa

SLEEP DISORDERS
Primary sleep disorders
  Dyssomnias
  Example: Primary insomnia
  Parasomnias
  Example: Sleep terror disorder
Sleep disorders related to another mental disorder
Example: Insomnia related to post-traumatic stress disorder
Other sleep disorders
Example: Substance-induced sleep disorder

IMPULSE CONTROL DISORDERS NOT ELSEWHERE CLASSIFIED
Example: Kleptomania

ADJUSTMENT DISORDERS
Example: Adjustment disorder

PERSONALITY DISORDERS
Example: Antisocial personality disorder

Organic mental disorders are problems caused by brain pathology—that is, by drug damage, diseases of the brain, injuries, poisons, and so on (❖Fig. 17.2). Organic disorders may be accompanied by severe emotional disturbances, impaired thinking, memory loss, personality changes, delirium, or psychotic symptoms (Costello & Costello, 1992).

It could be argued that almost all mental disorders are partly biological (Widiger & Sankis, 2000). For this reason, DSM-IV does not list "organic mental disorders" as a separate category. Nevertheless, all of the following problems are closely associated with organic damage: delirium, dementia, amnestic, and other cognitive disorders; mental disorders due to a general medical condition; and substance related disorders.

Mental disorder *A significant impairment in psychological functioning.*
Psychotic disorder *A severe mental disorder characterized by a retreat from reality, by hallucinations and delusions, and by social withdrawal.*
Organic mental disorder *A mental or emotional problem caused by brain diseases or injuries.*

Substance related disorders involve abuse of, or dependence on, mood- or behavior-altering drugs. Typical culprits include alcohol, barbiturates, opiates, cocaine, amphetamines, hallucinogens, marijuana, and nicotine. Problems of this type center on damaged functioning at home or on the job and an inability to stop using the drug. Active drug intoxication or drug withdrawal, delirium, dementia, amnesia, psychosis, emotional problems, sexual problems, and sleep disturbances may also be substance related (Boutros & Bowers, 1996).

BRIDGES

Problems with drug abuse and dependence are discussed in Chapter 8.

See pages 251–265 and 269–271.

Mood disorders primarily involve disturbances in affect (emotion). Afflicted persons may be *manic,* meaning agitated, euphoric, and hyperactive, or they may be *depressed.* Some people actually cycle between mania and depression. In each case, extremes of mood are intense or long lasting. Mood disorders may include psychotic symptoms, and they are sometimes caused by medical conditions or by drug abuse (DSM-IV, 1994).

Anxiety disorders are marked by feelings of fear, apprehension, or anxiety, as well as anxiety-based distortions of behavior. Anxiety disorders may take the form of *panic* (in which the person suffers sudden unexplainable feelings of panic), *phobias* (excessive, irrational fears), or *generalized anxiety* (chronic and persistent anxiety). Other anxiety disorders are *post-traumatic stress disorder* (high anxiety that persists long after an extremely distressing event, such as military combat) and *acute stress disorder* (high anxiety that occurs immediately after a highly distressing event, such as an airliner crash). A pattern known as *obsessive-compulsive* behavior is also associated with anxiety (more on this later).

Somatoform disorders (so-MAT-oh-form) occur when a person has physical symptoms that mimic disease or injury (paralysis, blindness, illness, or chronic pain, for example), for which there is no identifiable physical cause. In such cases, it is assumed that psychological factors underlie the symptoms.

Dissociative disorders include cases of sudden temporary amnesia and instances of multiple identity (multiple personality). Also included in this category are frightening episodes of depersonalization. Depersonalization refers to feelings of being outside one's body, of behaving like a robot, or of being in a dream world.

Personality disorders are deeply ingrained, unhealthy personality patterns. Such patterns usually appear by adolescence, and they continue through much of adult life. They include paranoid (overly suspicious), narcissistic (self-loving), dependent, borderline, and antisocial personality types, as well as others.

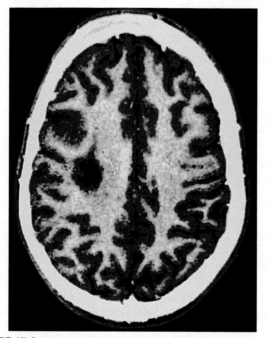

❖ **FIGURE 17.2** *This MRI scan of a human brain (viewed from the top) reveals a tumor (dark spot). Mental disorders sometimes have organic causes of this sort. However, in many instances, no organic damage can be found.*

The self-portraits shown here were painted by Andy Wilf between 1978 and 1981. During that time, Wilf is said to have increasingly abused drugs and alcohol. This dramatic series of images is a record of his self-destructive descent into a private hell. The third painting shows a shrouded skull—and foretells the artist's fate. Wilf died of a drug overdose. Drug abuse is but one of the many psychopathologies, or "problems in living," psychologists seek to alleviate. (Courtesy of Ulrike Kantor, Ulrike Kantor Gallery.)

Every culture recognizes the existence of psychopathology, and most have at least a few folk terms to name afflictions you won't find in DSM-IV. Here are some examples from around the world:

- **Amok:** Men in Malaysia, Laos, the Philippines, and Polynesia who believe they have been insulted are sometimes known to go amok. After a period of brooding, they erupt into an outburst of violent, aggressive, or homicidal behavior randomly directed at people and objects.
- **Ataque de nervios:** Among Latinos from the Caribbean, the symptoms of an *ataque de nervios* (attack of nerves) include shouting, crying, trembling, aggression, threats of suicide, and seizures or fainting. *Ataques de nervios* frequently occur after a stressful event, such as the death of a close relative, divorce, or an accident involving a family member.
- **Ghost sickness:** Among many American Indian tribes, people who become preoccupied with death and the deceased are said to suffer from ghost sickness. The symptoms of ghost sickness include bad dreams, weakness, loss of appetite, fainting, dizziness, fear, anxiety, hallucinations, loss of consciousness, confusion, feelings of futility, and a sense of suffocation.
- **Koro:** In southern and eastern Asia, a man may experience sudden and intense anxiety that his penis (or, in females, the vulva and nipples) will recede into the body. In addition to the terror this incites, victims also believe that advanced cases of *koro* can cause death.
- **Locura:** Latinos in the United States and Latin America use the term *locura* to refer to people who suffer from chronic psychotic symptoms such as incoherence, agitation, auditory and visual hallucinations, inability to follow social rules, unpredictability, and violence.
- **Zar:** In North African and Middle Eastern societies, *zar* is said to occur when spirits possess an individual. *Zar* is marked by shouting, laughing, hitting the head against a wall, singing, or weeping. Victims may become apathetic or withdrawn, and they may refuse to eat or carry out daily tasks.

The existence of such terms emphasizes that people have a need to label and categorize disturbed behavior. As you can see, however, folk terminology tends to be vague. Most of the problems listed here include symptoms from more than one of the psychological disorders described in DSM-IV. As a result, they provide little guidance about the true nature of a person's problems or the best ways to treat them. That's why DSM-IV is based on empirical data and clinical observations. Otherwise, psychologists and psychiatrists would be no better than folk healers or shamans when making diagnoses ("Outline for Cultural," 1994; Regeser López & Guarnaccia, 2000).

Sexual and gender identity disorders include any of a wide range of difficulties with sexual identity, deviant sexual behavior, or sexual adjustment. In gender identity disorders, sexual identity does not match a person's physical sex. Deviations in sexual behavior known as *paraphilias* include exhibitionism, fetishism, and voyeurism. Also found in this category are a variety of *sexual dysfunctions* (problems in sexual desire, arousal, or response). (Paraphilias and sexual dysfunctions are discussed in Chapter 14.)

Shouldn't neurosis be listed? Neurosis was once a recognized mental disorder. However, it is no longer included in the DSM because the term *neurosis* is too imprecise. Behavior once considered "neurotic" is now included in categories such as anxiety, somatoform, or dissociative disorders. Even though **neurosis** is an outdated term, you may hear it used to loosely refer to problems involving excessive anxiety.

In addition to the formal mental disorders we have reviewed, many cultures have names for "unofficial" psychological "disorders." See "Running Amok with Cultural Maladies" for some samples.

General Risk Factors

What causes mental and psychological disorders like those listed in ◆ Table 17.2? In upcoming discussions, we will explore the causes of some specific problems. For now, it is worth noting that a variety of risk factors contribute to various instances of psychopathology.

- **Social conditions:** poverty, stressful living conditions, homelessness, social disorganization, overcrowding
- **Family factors:** parents who are immature, mentally disturbed, criminal, or abusive; severe marital strife; extremely poor child discipline; disordered family communication patterns
- **Psychological factors:** stress, low intelligence, learning disorders, lack of control or mastery
- **Biological factors:** genetic defects or inherited vulnerabilities, poor prenatal care, very low birth weight, chronic physical illness or disability, exposure to toxic chemicals or drugs, head injuries

ETHNIC GROUP MEMBERSHIP Culture also influences our susceptibility to various psychological disorders. For example, a recent study found that some disorders are less common in three

Substance related disorder *Abuse of or dependence on a mood- or behavior-altering drug.*
Mood disorder *A major disturbance in mood or emotion, such as depression or mania.*
Anxiety disorder *Disruptive feelings of fear, apprehension, or anxiety, or distortions in behavior that are anxiety related.*
Somatoform disorder *Physical symptoms that mimic disease or injury for which there is no identifiable physical cause.*
Dissociative disorder *Temporary amnesia, multiple personality, or depersonalization.*
Personality disorder *A maladaptive personality pattern.*
Sexual and gender identity disorders *Any of a wide range of difficulties with sexual identity, deviant sexual behavior, or sexual adjustment.*
Neurosis *An outdated term once used to refer, as a group, to anxiety disorders, somatoform disorders, dissociative disorders, and some forms of depression.*

ethnic groups than they are among European Americans (Zhang & Snowden, 1999).

- Compared with European Americans, African Americans are less likely to suffer from depression, obsessive-compulsive disorder, substance abuse, antisocial personality disorder, and anorexia nervosa.
- Compared with European Americans, Asian Americans are less likely to suffer from schizophrenia, mania or bipolar disorders, panic, somatization, substance abuse, and antisocial personality.
- Hispanic Americans have lower rates of schizophrenia, obsessive-compulsive disorder, panic, and substance abuse than European Americans do.

It is probably fair to say that the social world and the psychological world interact on an equal footing to produce human behavior. For this reason, cultural factors can influence the expression of psychological disorders. Different values, support networks, stress levels, behavior patterns, family ties, and cultural beliefs can have a big impact on overall mental health (López & Guarnaccia, 2000).

Insanity

Which of the mental disorders causes insanity? None. **Insanity** is a legal term that refers to an inability to manage one's affairs or foresee the consequences of one's actions. People who are declared insane are not legally responsible for their actions. If necessary, they can be involuntarily committed to a mental hospital. (See this chapter's A Step Beyond for more information.)

Legally, insanity is established by testimony from expert witnesses (psychologists and psychiatrists). An **expert witness** is a person recognized by a court of law as qualified to give opinions on a specific topic. In practice, those who are involuntarily committed are usually judged to be a danger to themselves or to others, or they are severely mentally disabled (Turkheimer & Parry, 1992). Involuntary commitments happen most often when people are brought to hospital emergency rooms by the police or paramedics. Then, two doctors must agree that the person will either commit suicide or hurt someone else if she or he is not put into the hospital right away (Gorman, 1996).

PERSONALITY DISORDERS—BLUEPRINTS FOR MALADJUSTMENT

"Get out of here and leave me alone so I can die in peace," Judy screamed at her nurses. Although normally very attractive, Judy looked old, disheveled, and haggard in the seclusion room of the psychiatric hospital. On one of her arms, long dark red marks mingled with the scars of previous suicide attempts. Judy once bragged that her record was 67 stitches. Today, the nurses had to strap her into restraints to keep her from gouging her own eyes. She was given a sedative and slept for 12 hours. She woke calmly and asked for her therapist—even

though this latest incident was ostensibly triggered by his canceling her morning appointment and rescheduling it for that afternoon.

Judy has a borderline personality disorder. Although she is capable of working, Judy has repeatedly lost jobs because of her turbulent relationships with others. At times, she can be friendly and a real charmer. At other times, she is extremely unpredictable, moody, and even suicidal. Being a friend to Judy means accepting a burden that is nearly unbearable at times. The cancellation of an appointment, special dates that are forgotten, a wrong turn of phrase—these and similar small incidents may trigger Judy's anger or, worse yet, a suicide attempt.

Maladaptive Personality Patterns

As stated earlier, personality disorders are deeply ingrained maladaptive personality patterns. For example, people who have paranoid personality disorder are overly suspicious, hypersensitive, guarded, and distrusting of others. Narcissistic people are preoccupied with their own self-importance: They need constant admiration, and they are absorbed in fantasies of power, wealth, brilliance, beauty, and love. The dependent personality is marked by an extreme lack of self-confidence. Dependent persons allow others to run their lives, and they place their own needs second to others. In a histrionic personality disorder, the person seeks attention by exaggerating emotion and acting very dramatically. Typically, patterns such as these can be traced back to adolescence or even to childhood.

The list of personality disorders is long (◆Table 17.4), so let us focus on a single frequently misunderstood problem, the antisocial personality.

◆ TABLE 17.4 Personality Disorders and Typical Degree of Impairment

MODERATE IMPAIRMENT
Dependent: Unhealthy submissiveness and dependence on others (clinging)
Histrionic: Excessive emotion and attention-seeking behavior
Narcissistic: Exaggerated self-importance and desire for constant admiration
Antisocial: Irresponsible and antisocial behavior, such as aggression, deceit, recklessness, and lack of remorse

HIGH IMPAIRMENT
Obsessive-compulsive: Orderliness, perfectionism, and rigid routine
Schizoid: Limited emotion and a lack of interest in close personal relationships with others
Avoidant: Discomfort in social situations, fear of evaluation, timidity

SEVERE IMPAIRMENT
Borderline: Extremely unstable self-image, relationships, moods, and impulses
Paranoid: A deep distrust and suspiciousness of the motives of others, which are seen as demeaning or threatening
Schizotypal: Social isolation, extremely odd behavior, and disturbed thought patterns, but not actively psychotic

(From DSM-IV, 1994; Millon, 1981.)

Antisocial Personality

What are the characteristics of an antisocial personality? A person with an **antisocial personality** lacks a conscience. Typically, they are impulsive, selfish, emotionally shallow, and manipulative toward others (Lykken, 1995). Such people often have a long history of conflict with society. Antisocial people, who are sometimes called *sociopaths* or *psychopaths*, are irresponsible and dishonest, and they lack judgment and morals. Most seem to be incapable of having deep feelings, such as guilt, shame, fear, loyalty, or love. In short, sociopaths are poorly socialized, and they have a general disregard for the truth (DSM-IV, 1994).

Are sociopaths dangerous? Many sociopaths are delinquents or criminals who may be a threat to the general public (Rice, 1997). However, sociopaths are rarely the crazed murderers you have seen portrayed on TV and in movies. In fact, many sociopaths are "charming" and create a good first impression. Their lying, self-serving manipulation, and lack of dependability only gradually become evident. Many successful businesspeople, entertainers, politicians, and other seemingly normal people have psychopathic leanings. Basically, psychopaths coldly use others to cheat their way through life (Rice, 1997).

What causes sociopathy? People with antisocial personalities usually have a childhood history of emotional deprivation, neglect, and physical abuse (Pollock et al., 1990). As mentioned

BRIDGES

Personality patterns usually become stable by age 30. This makes personality disorders difficult to treat.

See Chapter 15, page 481.

in Chapter 4, infants who fail to form a healthy emotional attachment to a caregiver may later be prone to antisocial behavior (Magid, 1988). Adult sociopaths also display some subtle neurological problems (❖Fig. 17.3). For example, they have unusual brain-wave patterns that suggest underarousal of the brain. This may explain why many sociopaths are thrill seekers. Quite likely, they are searching for stimulation strong enough to overcome their chronic underarousal and "boredom" (Carson, Butcher, & Mineka, 1997; Hare, 1996).

In a revealing study, psychopaths were shown extremely grisly and unpleasant photographs. The photos were so upsetting that normal people are visibly startled by them. The psychopaths, however, showed no startle response to the photos (Patrick et al., 1993). (They didn't "bat an eyelash.") Those with antisocial personalities might therefore be described as *emotionally cold.* They simply do not feel normal pangs of conscience, guilt, or anxiety (Hare, 1996). This coldness seems to account for an unusual ability to calmly lie, cheat, steal, or take advantage of others (Lykken, 1995).

Can sociopathy be treated? Antisocial personality disorders are rarely treated with success. All too often, sociopaths manipulate therapy, just like any other situation. If it is to their advantage to act "cured," they will do so. However, they return to their former behavior patterns as soon as possible. On a more positive note, antisocial behavior does tend to decline somewhat after age 40, even without treatment.

Studies show that more than 65 percent of all people with antisocial personalities have been arrested, usually for crimes such as robbery, vandalism, or rape.

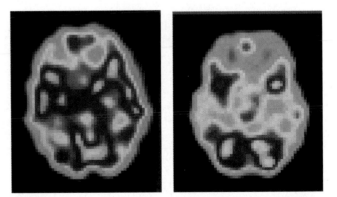

❖ **FIGURE 17.3** *Using PET scans, Canadian psychologist Robert Hare found that the normally functioning brain (left) lights up with activity when a person sees emotion-laden words such as maggot or cancer. But the brain of a psychopath (right) remains inactive, especially in areas associated with feelings and self-control. When Hare showed the right image to several neurologists, one asked, "Is this person from Mars?" (Images courtesy of Robert Hare.)*

Insanity *A legal term that refers to a mental inability to manage one's affairs or to be aware of the consequences of one's actions.*
Expert witness *A person recognized by a court of law as being qualified to give expert testimony on a specific topic.*
Antisocial personality *A person who lacks a conscience; is emotionally shallow, impulsive, and selfish; and tends to manipulate others.*

NORMALITY, PSYCHOPATHOLOGY, AND PERSONALITY DISORDERS

RELATE

Think of an instance of abnormal behavior you have witnessed. By what formal standards would the behavior be regarded as abnormal? In what way was the behavior maladaptive?

What disorders would the following sentences help you remember? An anxious psychotic in a bad mood asked for an organic substance. "First you have to fill out a somato form and tell us what sex or gender you are," he was told. "Don't diss my personality," he replied.

Many of the qualities that define personality disorders exist to a minor degree in normal personalities. Try to think of a person you know who has some of the characteristics described for each type of personality disorder.

LEARNING CHECK

1. Statistical definitions of abnormality successfully avoid the limitations of other approaches. T or F?

2. One of the most powerful contexts in which judgments of normality and abnormality are made is
   a. the family b. occupational settings c. religious systems d. culture

3. In a court of law, sanity is determined by a test administered by court-appointed lawyers. T or F?

4. Amnesia, multiple identities, and depersonalization are possible problems in
   a. mood disorders b. somatoform disorders c. psychosis d. dissociative disorders

5. Which among the following is *not* a major psychological problem listed in DSM-IV?
   a. mood disorders b. personality disorders c. insanity d. anxiety disorders

6. A major difference between psychotic disorders and anxiety disorders (or other milder problems) is that in psychosis the individual has lost contact with reality as shown by the presence of
   _____ or _____ .

7. Which of the following personality disorders is associated with an inflated sense of self-importance and a constant need for attention and admiration?
   a. narcissistic b. antisocial c. paranoid d. manipulative

8. More than half of all people with antisocial personalities have been arrested. T or F?

9. Antisocial personality disorders are difficult to treat, but there is typically a decline in antisocial behavior a year or two after adolescence. T or F?

10. Alzheimer's disease is thought to be caused by lead poisoning of the hippocampus. T or F?

CRITICAL THINKING

11. Brian, a fan of grunge rock, occasionally wears a skirt in public. Does Brian's cross-dressing indicate that he has a mental disorder?

12. Many states began to restrict use of the insanity defense after John Hinckley Jr., who tried to murder former U.S. President Ronald Reagan, was acquitted by reason of insanity. What does this trend reveal about insanity?

Answers:

1. F 2. d 3. F 4. d 5. c 6. delusions, hallucinations 7. a 8. T 9. F 10. F 11. Probably not. Undoubtedly, Brian's cross-dressing is socially disapproved by many people. Nevertheless, to be classified as a mental disorder, it must cause him to feel disabling shame, guilt, depression, or anxiety. The cultural relativity of behavior like Brian's is revealed by the fact that it is fashionable and acceptable for women to wear men's clothing. 12. It emphasizes that insanity is a legal concept, not a psychiatric diagnosis. Laws reflect community standards. When those standards change, lawmakers may seek to alter definitions of legal responsibility. (See A Step Beyond in this chapter for more information.)

ANXIETY-BASED DISORDERS—WHEN ANXIETY RULES

Imagine the feeling of waiting to take an important test for which you are unprepared, waiting to give a speech to a large audience of strangers, or being followed by a police car while you are driving. You've almost certainly felt *anxiety* in one of these situations.

Anxiety refers to feelings of apprehension, dread, or uneasiness. As you may have noticed, the physical reactions that accompany anxiety are similar to fear. However, anxiety is a response to an *unclear* or *ambiguous* threat. For instance, what we commonly call "stage fright" is actually anxiety, because an audience poses no real threat to safety. (Except, perhaps, at extremely bad talent shows!) Compared to anxiety, fear is more focused and intense. Typically, it is the result of a specific, identifiable threat. When we are afraid, we say to ourselves, "A terrible event is happening and I must take action right now to stop it." When we are anxious, we say, "A terrible event may happen. I may not be able to deal with it, but I've got to be ready to try" (Zinbarg et al., 1992).

Disruptive Anxiety

We all feel anxiety, but anxiety that is out of proportion to a situation may reveal a problem. An example is a college student named Jian, who became unbearably anxious when he had to take tests. By the time Jian went to see a counselor, he had already skipped several exams and was in danger of dropping out of school. In general, anxiety-related problems like Jian's involve:

- High levels of anxiety and/or restrictive, self-defeating behavior patterns
- A tendency to use elaborate defense mechanisms or avoidance responses to get through the day
- Pervasive feelings of stress, insecurity, inferiority, unhappiness, and dissatisfaction with life

Typically, people with anxiety-related problems feel threatened, but they don't do anything constructive about it. In short, they struggle to preserve control, but they remain ineffective and unhappy (Zinbarg et al., 1992).

If fear and anxiety are normal emotions, when do they signify a problem? A problem exists when intense or persistent anxiety prevents people from doing what they want or need to do. Also, their anxieties are typically out of control—they simply cannot stop worrying. Anxiety, fears, and phobias are probably the most common psychological disturbances today. On any given day, roughly 7 percent of the adult population could be diagnosed as having an anxiety disorder (Landers, 1989).

Adjustment Disorders

Do such problems cause a "nervous breakdown"? Anxiety-based problems cause misery and seriously disrupt people's lives. However, they rarely bring about a total "breakdown." Actually, the term *nervous breakdown* has no formal meaning. What many people have in mind when they speak of a "breakdown" is usually an *adjustment disorder.*

Adjustment disorders occur when ordinary life stresses push people beyond their ability to cope effectively. Examples of such stresses are prolonged unemployment, intense marital strife, and chronic physical illness. People suffering from an adjustment disorder are extremely irritable, anxious, apathetic, or depressed. They also experience sleep disturbances, a loss of appetite, and physical complaints (DSM-IV, 1994). Often, these problems can be relieved by rest, sedation, supportive counseling, and a chance to "talk through" fears and anxieties.

How is an adjustment disorder different from an anxiety disorder? The outward symptoms are similar. However, adjustment disorders typically disappear when a person's life circumstances improve. This shows that they are linked to stressful events. Anxiety disorders, in contrast, appear to be self-generated.

Anxiety Disorders

In most anxiety disorders, people's distress seems greatly out of proportion to the situations in which they find themselves. Consider, for example, the following description of Ethel B:

> She was never completely relaxed, and complained of vague feelings of restlessness, and a fear that something was "just around the corner." Although she felt that she had to go to work to help pay the family bills, she could not bring herself to start anything new for fear that something terrible would happen on the job. She had experienced a few extreme anxiety attacks during which she felt "like I couldn't breathe, like I was sealed up in a transparent envelope. I thought I was going to have a heart attack. I couldn't stop shaking." (Suinn, 1975*)

Distress like Ethel B's is a key element in anxiety disorders. Many psychologists believe that it also underlies dissociative and somatoform disorders, where maladaptive behavior serves to reduce anxiety and discomfort. To deepen your understanding, let's

*From *Fundamentals of Behavior Pathology* by R. M. Suinn. Copyright © 1975. Reprinted by permission of John Wiley & Sons, Inc. Additional Suinn quotes in this chapter are from the same source.

BRIDGES

Excessive use of psychological defense mechanisms is a feature of many anxiety disorders.

See Chapter 16, pages 530–532.

first examine the anxiety disorders themselves (◆Table 17.5). Then we will see how anxiety contributes to other problems.

GENERALIZED ANXIETY DISORDER The essential feature of a **generalized anxiety disorder** is at least 6 months of unrealistic or excessive anxiety and worry (DSM-IV, 1994). The person's discomfort is sometimes described as **free-floating anxiety** because it is triggered by so many different situations. Sufferers worry especially about future events (Dugas et al. 1998). They also typically complain of sweating, a racing heart, clammy hands, dizziness, upset stomach, rapid breathing, irritability, and poor concentration. Overall, more women than men suffer from these symptoms (Brawman-Mintzer & Lydiard, 1996).

Was Ethel B's problem a generalized anxiety disorder? No. The added presence of *anxiety attacks* indicates she suffered from panic disorder.

PANIC DISORDER (WITHOUT AGORAPHOBIA) In a **panic disorder (without agoraphobia),** the person is in a chronic state of anxiety and also has moments of sudden, intense, unexpected panic. During a panic attack, victims experience heart palpitations or chest pain, choking or smothering sensations, vertigo, feelings of unreality, trembling, and fears of losing control. Many believe that they are having a heart attack, are going insane, or are about to die. Needless to say, this pattern leaves victims unhappy and uncomfortable much of the time. Again, the majority of people who suffer from panic disorder are women (Sansone, Sansone, & Righter, 1998).

◆ **TABLE 17.5** Anxiety Disorders

Generalized anxiety disorder
Panic disorder
  Without Agoraphobia
  With Agoraphobia
Agoraphobia (without a history of panic disorder)
Specific phobia
Social phobia
Obsessive-compulsive disorder
Post-traumatic stress disorder
Acute stress disorder

(DSM-IV, 1994.)

Anxiety *Apprehension, dread, or uneasiness similar to fear but based on an unclear threat.*
Adjustment disorder *An emotional disturbance caused by ongoing stressors within the range of common experience.*
Generalized anxiety disorder *The person is in a chronic state of tension and worries about work, relationships, ability, or impending disaster.*
Free-floating anxiety *Anxiety that is very general and pervasive.*
Panic disorder (without agoraphobia) *The person is in a chronic state of anxiety and also has brief moments of sudden, intense, unexpected panic.*

To get an idea of what a panic attack feels like, imagine that you are trapped in your stateroom on a sinking ocean liner (the *Titanic*?). The room fills with water. When only a small air space remains near the ceiling and you are gasping for air, you'll know what a panic attack feels like.

Panic attacks may also occur in other anxiety disorders. What sets a panic disorder apart is that the panic attacks seem to appear without warning ("out of the blue"), rather than just in certain situations (DSM-IV, 1994).

PANIC DISORDER (WITH AGORAPHOBIA) In a **panic disorder (with agoraphobia)** the person suffers from chronic anxiety and brief moments of sudden panic. In addition, the person suffers from **agoraphobia** (ah-go-rah-FOBE-ee-ah), which is an intense, irrational fear that a panic attack will occur in a public place or unfamiliar situation. More simply, agoraphobics have an intense fear of leaving the house and familiar surroundings. Typically, they find ways of avoiding areas of insecurity—such as crowds, open roads, supermarkets, and automobiles. As a result, some agoraphobics are literally house-bound (DSM-IV, 1994).

AGORAPHOBIA The problem known as agoraphobia can also occur without panic. In this case, people fear that something extremely embarrassing will happen if they leave home or enter an unfamiliar situation. For example, agoraphobic people may refuse to go outside because they fear having a sudden attack of dizziness, diarrhea, or shortness of breath. Going outside the home alone, being in a crowd, standing in line, crossing a bridge, or riding in a car, bus, or train can be impossible for an agoraphobic person (DSM-IV, 1994). About 7 percent of all adults suffer from agoraphobia (with or without panic) during their lifetime (Magee et al., 1996).

SPECIFIC PHOBIA As we noted earlier, phobias are intense, irrational fears that persist even when there is no real danger. In a **specific phobia,** persistent fears, anxiety, and avoidance are focused on particular objects, activities, or situations. People affected by phobias recognize that their fears are unreasonable and excessive, but they cannot control them.

Phobias can be classified according to the type of object or situation that is feared. The most common types are:

- **Animal type**—fear of a specific type of animal, such as a dog, spider, or snake
- **Natural environment type**—fear of heights, storms, the ocean, caves, and the like
- **Blood, injection, injury type**—fear of blood, injections, injuries, medical procedures
- **Situational type**—fear of specific situations, such as airplanes, elevators, enclosed spaces
- **Other type**—fear of a wide range of other situations, such as those that may lead to choking, vomiting, or catching an illness

These types, of course, only outline the possibilities. Specific phobias can be associated with nearly any object or situation. Many of the more common specific phobias have been given names, such as those listed in ◆Table 17.6.

By combining the appropriate root word with the word *phobia,* any number of unlikely fears can be named. Some are

◆ **TABLE 17.6** Common Phobias
Acrophobia—fear of heights
Astraphobia—fear of storms, thunder, lightning
Arachnophobia—fear of spiders
Aviophobia—fear of airplanes
Claustrophobia—fear of closed spaces
Hematophobia—fear of blood
Microphobia—fear of germs
Nyctophobia—fear of darkness
Pathophobia—fear of disease
Pyrophobia—fear of fire
Xenophobia—fear of stranger
Zoophobia—fear of animals

For a person with a strong fear of snakes (ophidiophobia), merely looking at this picture may be unsettling.

acarophobia, a fear of itching; *zemmiphobia,* fear of the great mole rat; *phobosophobia,* fear of fear; *arachibutyrophobia,* fear of peanut butter sticking to the roof of the mouth, and *hippopotomonstrosesquipedaliophobia,* fear of long words!

Almost everyone has a few mild phobias: Fears of heights, closed spaces, or bugs and crawly things are common. A phobic disorder differs from such garden-variety fears in that it produces overwhelming anxiety. This may lead to vomiting, wild climbing and running, or fainting. For a phobic disorder to exist, the person's fear must disrupt his or her daily life. Phobic persons are so threatened that they will go to almost any length to avoid the feared object or situation. About 11 percent of all adults have phobic disorders during their lifetime (Magee et al., 1996).

SOCIAL PHOBIA   In a **social phobia,** people fear social situations in which they can be observed, evaluated, embarrassed, or humiliated by others. This leads them to avoid certain social situations, such as eating, writing, using the rest room, or speaking in public. When such situations cannot be avoided, they are endured with intense anxiety or distress. Social phobias greatly impair functioning at work, at school, in social activities, and in personal relationships (DSM-IV, 1994). About 13 percent of all adults are affected by social phobias at one time or another (Fones et al., 1998).

Obsessive-Compulsive Disorder

People who suffer from **obsessive-compulsive disorder** are preoccupied with certain distressing thoughts, and they feel compelled to perform certain behaviors. You have probably experienced a mild obsessional thought, such as a song or stupid commercial jingle, that repeats over and over in your mind. This may be irritating, but it's usually not terribly disturbing. True **obsessions** are images or thoughts that intrude into consciousness against a person's will. They are so disturbing that they cause anxiety or extreme discomfort. The most common obsessions are about violence or harm (such as poisoning one's spouse or being hit by a car), about being "dirty" or "unclean," about whether one has performed some action (such as turning off the stove), and about committing immoral acts (Wilson, 1986).

Obsessions usually give rise to **compulsions.** These are irrational acts that people feel driven to repeat. Often, compulsive

acts help control or block out anxiety caused by an obsession. For example, a minister who finds profanities popping into her mind might start compulsively counting her heartbeat. Doing this would prevent her from thinking "dirty" words.

Many people with compulsions can be classified as *checkers* or *cleaners.* For instance, people who feel guilty and unclean because they masturbate or "think dirty thoughts" may be driven to wash their hands hundreds of times a day. Typically, such compulsive behavior will continue even after the person's hands become raw and painful (Tallis, 1996). Likewise, a young mother who repeatedly has images of a knife plunging into her infant might check once an hour to make sure all the knives in her house are locked away. Doing so may reduce her anxieties, but it will probably also take over her life.

Of course, not all obsessive-compulsive disorders are so dramatic. Many simply involve extreme orderliness and rigid routine. Compulsive attention to detail and rigidly following procedures and rules makes the highly anxious person feel more secure. Doing so helps keep activities totally under control. (Notice that when such patterns are long-standing, but less intense, they are classified as a personality disorder.)

Stress Disorders

Most anxiety disorders have little connection to the actual degree of threat. A notable exception is found in **stress disorders.** These problems occur when stresses outside the range of normal human experience cause a major emotional disturbance (DSM-IV, 1994). Such reactions frequently follow sudden disasters, such as floods, tornadoes, earthquakes, or serious accidents. Stress disorders also affect many political hostages, combat veterans, prisoners of war, and victims of terrorism, violent crime, child molestation, rape, or witnessing the death or injury of another person (Berman et al., 1996; Coyne & Downey, 1991). Even medical workers who merely help the victims of disasters risk suffering from stress disorders (Epstein, Fullerton, & Ursano, 1998).

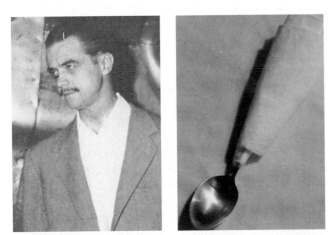

The severe obsessions and compulsions of billionaire Howard Hughes led him to live as a recluse for more than 20 years. Hughes had an intense fear of contamination. To avoid infection, he constructed sterile, isolated environments in which his contact with people and objects was strictly limited by complicated rituals. Before handling a spoon, for instance, Hughes had his attendants wrap the handle in tissue paper and seal it with tape. A second piece of tissue was then wrapped around the first before he would touch it (Hodgson & Miller, 1982). A spoon prepared as Hughes required is shown at right.

Panic disorder (with agoraphobia) *A chronic state of anxiety and brief moments of sudden panic. The person fears that these panic attacks will occur in public places or unfamiliar situations.*
Agoraphobia (without panic) *The person fears that something extremely embarrassing will happen if he or she leaves the house or enters unfamiliar situations.*
Specific phobia *An intense, irrational fear of specific objects, activities, or situations.*
Social phobia *An intense, irrational fear of being observed, evaluated, embarrassed, or humiliated by others in social situations.*
Obsessive-compulsive disorder *An extreme preoccupation with certain thoughts and compulsive performance of certain behaviors.*
Obsession *Recurring irrational or disturbing thoughts or mental images that a person cannot prevent.*
Compulsion *An act an individual feels driven to repeat, often against his or her will.*
Stress disorder *A significant emotional disturbance caused by stresses outside the range of normal human experience.*

A terrorist bomb destroyed the Alfred P. Murrah Building in Oklahoma City on April 19, 1995. The bomb killed 169 people and left more than 600 injured. In the aftermath of such disasters, many survivors suffer from acute stress reactions. For some, the flare-up of anxiety and distress may occur months or years after the stressful event is over, an example of a post-traumatic stress reaction. Many witnesses, survivors, and rescue workers have suffered PTSD in the years following the Oklahoma City bombing.

Symptoms of stress disorders include repeatedly reliving the traumatic event, avoiding stimuli associated with the event, and a numbing of emotions. Also common are insomnia, nightmares, wariness, poor concentration, irritability, and explosions of anger or aggression. If such reactions last *less* than a month after a traumatic event, the problem is called an **acute stress disorder.** If they last *more* than a month, the person is suffering from **post-traumatic stress disorder** (**PTSD**) (DSM-IV, 1994).

PTSD may persist for years after the stress has passed—as has happened to many veterans of the Vietnam War (Fontana et al., 1992). PTSD is far more common than once believed. Nearly 1 adult out of 12 in the United States has suffered from post-traumatic stress disorder at some time during his or her life (Kessler, Sonnega, & Nelson, 1995).

Dissociative Disorders

In dissociative reactions, we see striking episodes of *amnesia, fugue,* or *multiple identity.* **Dissociative amnesia** is an inability to recall one's name, address, or past. **Dissociative fugue** (sounds like "fewg") involves sudden travel away from home and confusion about personal identity. Dissociations are often triggered by highly traumatic events, as the following case illustrates (Lipschitz et al., 1996).

> An American soldier in the Vietnam war wandered into the countryside and ambushed Vietcong soldiers without any memory of his actions. His fugue and amnesia were triggered when he discovered the dead body of a Vietnamese child he had adopted. Later, in therapy, he was able to remember the incident: "After 15 years in the Army, he was all I had. It's all my fault! It's all my fault! If I had just taken you over to the hooch, you wouldn't be there, man! It's not fair. They ain't gotta kill kids" (Spiegel, 1986).

As you can see, forgetting personal identity and fleeing unpleasant situations can serve as defenses against intolerable anxiety.

A person suffering from a **dissociative identity disorder** has two or more separate identities or personality states (DSM-IV, 1994). (Note that identity disorders are not the same as schizophrenia. Schizophrenia, which is a psychotic disorder, is discussed later in this chapter.) A dramatic example of multiple identity is described in the book *Sybil* (Schreiber, 1973). Sybil reportedly had 16 different personality states. Each identity had a distinct voice, vocabulary, and posture. One personality could play the piano (not Sybil), but the others could not.

When an identity other than Sybil was in control, Sybil experienced a "time lapse," or memory blackout. Sybil's amnesia and alternate identities first appeared during childhood. As a girl she was beaten, locked in closets, perversely tortured, sexually abused, and almost killed. Sybil's first dissociations allowed her to escape by creating another person who would suffer torture in her place. Dissociative identity disorders often begin with unbearable childhood experiences, like those Sybil endured. A history of childhood trauma, especially sexual abuse, is found in more than 95 percent of people whose personalities split into multiple identities (Scroppo et al., 1998; Tutkun, Yargic, & Sar, 1995).

Flamboyant cases like Sybil's have led some experts to question the existence of multiple personalities (Rieber, 1999). However, a majority of psychologists continue to believe that multiple identity is a real, if rare, problem (Cormier & Thelen, 1998).

Therapy for dissociative identity disorders may make use of hypnosis, which allows contact with the various personality states. The goal of therapy is *integration* and *fusion* of the various identities into a single, balanced personality. Fortunately, multiple identity disorders are far rarer in real life than they are in TV dramas!

Somatoform Disorders

Perhaps you have known someone, particularly someone prone to anxiety, who seems to be obsessed with fears of having a serious disease. These people are preoccupied with bodily functions, such as their heartbeat or breathing or digestion. Minor physical problems, such as a small sore or an occasional cough, may convince them that they have cancer or some other dreaded disease. Typically, their unwarranted fear of illness persists, despite the fact that there is no medical basis for their complaints (DSM-IV, 1994).

Are you describing hypochondria? Yes. In **hypochondriasis** (HI-po-kon-DRY-uh-sis), people interpret normal sensations and small bodily signs as proof that they have a terrible disease. People who have a related problem called **somatization disorder** (som-ah-tuh-ZAY-shun) express their anxieties in the form of various bodily complaints. Examples include vomiting or nausea, shortness of breath, difficulty swallowing, and painful menstrual periods. Typically, the person feels ill much of the time and visits doctors repeatedly. Most sufferers take medicines or other treatments, but no organic cause can be found for their distress (Ford, 1995). Similarly, a person with **pain disorder** is disabled by pain that has no identifiable physical basis (DSM-IV, 1994).

A rarer somatoform disorder ("body-form" disorder) is called a *conversion reaction.* In a **conversion disorder,** severe emotional conflicts are "converted" into symptoms that actually disturb physical functioning or closely resemble a physical disability. For instance, a soldier might become deaf or lame or develop "glove anesthesia" just before a battle.

What is "glove anesthesia"? "Glove anesthesia" is a loss of sensitivity in the areas of the skin that would normally be covered by a glove. Glove anesthesia shows that conversion symptoms often contradict known medical facts. The system of nerves in the

BRIDGES

Don't confuse so-matoform disorders with psychosomatic illnesses, which occur when stress causes real physical damage to the body.

See Chapter 16, pages 537–538.

hands does not form a glove-like pattern and could not cause the observed symptoms (❖Fig. 17.4).

If symptoms disappear when a victim is asleep, hypnotized, or anesthetized, a conversion reaction must be suspected (Russo et al., 1998). Another sign to watch for is a victim's seeming lack of concern about suddenly becoming disabled.

ANXIETY AND DISORDER—FOUR PATHWAYS TO TROUBLE

What causes the problems described in the preceding discussion? Because we are both biological and social creatures, it is not surprising that susceptibility to anxiety-based disorders appears to be partly inherited. Studies of parents suffering from panic disorder, for instance, show that an unusually large number (60 percent) of their children are born with a fearful, inhibited temperament (Rosenbaum et al., 1989). Such children are irritable and wary as infants, shy and fearful as toddlers, and quiet and cautious introverts in elementary school. Authorities believe that such children are at high risk for anxiety problems, such as panic attacks, in adulthood (Rosenbaum et al., 1991).

At least four major perspectives on the causes of dissociative, anxiety, and somatoform disorders exist. These are (1) the *psychodynamic* approach, (2) the *humanistic-existential* approach, (3) the *behavioral* approach, and (4) the *cognitive* approach.

Psychodynamic Approach

Recall that the term **psychodynamic** refers to internal motives, conflicts, unconscious forces, and other dynamics of mental life. Freud was the first to propose a psychodynamic explanation for what was then known as neurosis. According to Freud,

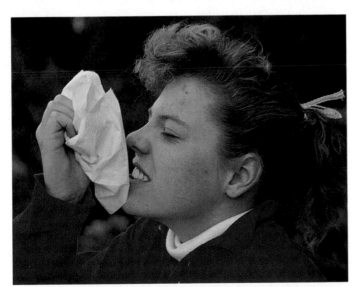

Uncontrollable sneezing, which may continue for days or weeks, is often a conversion disorder. In such cases, sneezing is atypical in rate and rhythm. In addition, the person's eyes do not close during a sneeze and sneezing does not occur during sleep. (A normal sneeze is shown here.) All of these signs suggest that the cause of the sneezing is psychological, not physical (Fochtmann, 1995).

Acute stress disorder *A psychological disturbance lasting up to 1 month following stresses that would produce anxiety in anyone who experienced them.*

Post-traumatic stress disorder *A psychological disturbance lasting more than 1 month following stresses that would produce anxiety in anyone who experienced them.*

Dissociative amnesia *Loss of memory (partial or complete) for important information related to personal identity.*

Dissociative fugue *Sudden travel away from home, plus confusion about one's personal identity.*

Dissociative identity disorder *The presence of two or more distinct personalities (multiple personality).*

Hypochondriasis *A preoccupation with fears of having a serious disease. Ordinary physical signs are interpreted as proof that the person has a disease, but no physical disorder can be found.*

Somatization disorder *Afflicted persons have numerous physical complaints. Typically, they have consulted many doctors, but no organic cause for their distress can be identified.*

Pain disorder *Pain that has no identifiable physical cause and appears to be of psychological origin.*

Conversion disorder *A bodily symptom that mimics a physical disability but is actually caused by anxiety or emotional distress.*

Psychodynamic *Pertaining to internal motives, conflicts, unconscious forces, and other dynamics of mental life.*

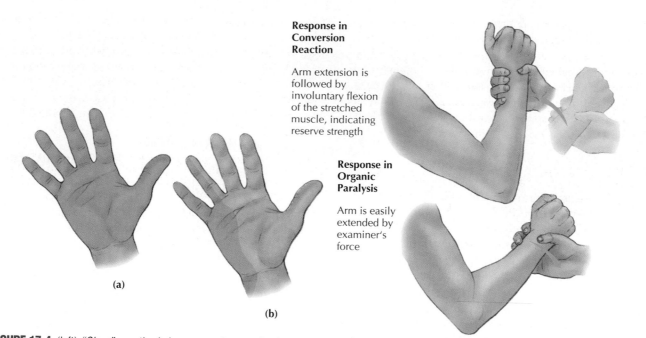

Response in Conversion Reaction

Arm extension is followed by involuntary flexion of the stretched muscle, indicating reserve strength

Response in Organic Paralysis

Arm is easily extended by examiner's force

(a)

(b)

❖ **FIGURE 17.4** (left) *"Glove" anesthesia is a conversion reaction involving loss of feeling in areas of the hand that would be covered by a glove* (a). *If the anesthesia were physically caused, it would follow the pattern shown in* (b). (right) *To test for organic paralysis of the arm, an examiner can suddenly extend the arm, stretching the muscles. A conversion reaction is indicated if the arm pulls back involuntarily. (Adapted from Weintraub, 1983.)*

disturbances like those we have described represent a raging conflict among subparts of the personality—the id, ego, and superego.

Freud emphasized that intense anxiety can be caused by forbidden id impulses for sex or aggression that threaten to break through into behavior. The person constantly fears doing something "crazy" or forbidden. She or he may also be tortured by guilt, which the superego generates in response to forbidden impulses. Caught in the middle, the ego is eventually overwhelmed. This forces the person to adopt rigid defense mechanisms and misguided, inflexible behavior to prevent a disastrous loss of control.

Humanistic-Existential Approaches

Humanistic thought emphasizes subjective experience, human problems, and personal potentials. Humanistic psychologist Carl Rogers regarded emotional disorders as the end product of a faulty **self-image** (your total perception of yourself; in other words, your self-concept) (Rogers, 1959). Rogers believed that anxious individuals have built up unrealistic mental images of themselves. This leaves them vulnerable to contradictory information. Let's say, for example, that an essential part of Carli's self-image is the idea that she is highly intelligent. If Carli does poorly in school, she may deny or distort her perceptions of herself and her perceptions of the situation. Should Carli's anxiety become severe, she may resort to the rigid use of defense mechanisms. A conversion reaction, anxiety attacks, or similar symptoms could also result from threats to her self-image. These symptoms, in turn, would become new threats that provoke further distortions. We would have, in other words, a classic example of a vicious cycle of maladjustment and anxiety that feeds on itself once started.

Existentialism focuses on the elemental problems of existence, such as death, meaning, choice, and responsibility. Some psychologists take a more existential view and stress that unhealthy anxiety reflects a loss of *meaning* in one's life. According to them, we must show *courage* and *responsibility* in our choices if life is to have meaning. Too often, they say, we give in to "existential anxiety" and back away from life-enhancing choices. Existential anxiety is the unavoidable anguish that comes from knowing that we are personally responsible for our lives. Hence, we have a crushing need to choose wisely and courageously as we face life's empty and impersonal void.

From the existential view, people who are unhappy and anxious are living in "bad faith." That is, they have collapsed in the face of the awesome responsibility to choose a meaningful existence. In short, they have lost their way in life. From this point of view, making choices that don't reflect what you really value, feel, and believe can make you sick.

Behavioral Approach

Behavioristic approaches emphasize overt, observable behavior and the effects of learning and conditioning. Behaviorists assume that the "symptoms" we have discussed are learned, just as other behaviors are. You might recall from Chapter 9, for instance, that phobias can be acquired through classical conditioning. Similarly, anxiety attacks may reflect conditioned emotional responses that generalize to new situations. As another example, the hypochondriac's "sickness behavior" may be reinforced by the sympathy and attention he or she gets.

One point that all theorists agree on is that disordered behavior is ultimately self-defeating and *paradoxical*. A paradox is a contradiction. The contradiction in self-defeating behavior is that it makes the person more miserable in the long run, even though it temporarily lowers anxiety.

But if the person becomes more miserable in the long run, how does the pattern get started? The behavioral explanation is that self-defeating behavior begins with avoidance learning (described in Chapter 9). **Avoidance learning** occurs when making a particular response delays or prevents the onset of a painful or unpleasant stimulus. Here's a quick review to refresh your memory:

> An animal is placed in a special cage. After a few minutes, a light comes on, followed a moment later by a painful shock. Quickly, the animal escapes into a second chamber. After a few minutes, a light comes on in this chamber, and the shock is repeated. Soon the animal learns to avoid pain by moving before the shock occurs. Once an animal learns to avoid the shock, it can be turned off altogether. A well-trained animal may avoid the nonexistent shock indefinitely.

The same analysis can be applied to disordered human behavior. A behaviorist would say that the powerful reward of immediate relief from anxiety keeps self-defeating avoidance behavior alive. This view, known as the **anxiety reduction hypothesis,** seems to explain why the behavior patterns we have discussed often look very "stupid" to outside observers.

Cognitive Approach

The **cognitive view** is that distorted thinking causes people to magnify ordinary threats and failures, which leads to distress (Foa et al., 1996). For example, Terrie, who is socially phobic, constantly has upsetting thoughts about being evaluated. One reason for this is that social phobics tend to be perfectionists. Like other social phobics, Terrie is excessively concerned about mistakes. She also perceives criticism where none exists (Juster et al., 1996). Terrie tends to focus too much attention on herself, which intensifies her anxiety in social situations (Woody, 1996). Even when socially phobic people are successful, distorted thinking leads them to think they have failed (Alden & Wallace, 1995). In short, changing the thinking patterns of anxious individuals can greatly lessen their fears (Poulton & Andrews, 1996).

SUMMARY   There is probably a core of truth to all four psychological explanations. For this reason, understanding anxiety-based disorders may be aided by combining parts of each perspective. Each viewpoint also suggests a different approach to treatment. Because there are many possibilities, a full discussion of therapy is found later, in Chapter 18.

KNOWLEDGE BUILDER
ANXIETY-BASED DISORDERS

RELATE

Which of the anxiety disorders would you *least* want to suffer from? Why?

What minor obsessions or compulsions have you experienced?

What is the key difference between a stress disorder and an adjustment disorder? (Review both discussions if you don't immediately know the answer.)

Which of the four main explanations of anxiety-based disorders do you find most convincing?

LEARNING CHECK

1. Excessive anxiety over ordinary life stresses is characteristic of which of the following disorders?
   a. free-floating anxiety disorder b. agoraphobia c. hypochondriasis d. adjustment disorder

2. Panic disorder can occur with or without agoraphobia, but agoraphobia cannot occur alone, without the presence of a panic disorder. T or F?

3. Alice has a phobic fear of blood. The formal term for her fear is
   a. nyctophobia b. hematophobia c. pathophobia d. pyrophobia

4. A person who intensely fears eating, writing, or speaking in public suffers from _____

   _____ .

5. "Checkers" and "cleaners" suffer from which disorder?
   a. acarophobia b. panic disorder with agoraphobia c. generalized anxiety disorder d. obsessive-compulsive disorder

6. The symptoms of acute stress disorders last less than 1 month; post-traumatic stress disorders last more than 1 month. T or F?

7. Which of the following is *not* a dissociative disorder?
   a. fugue b. amnesia c. conversion reaction d. multiple identity

8. Freud's original psychodynamic explanation of "neurosis" was based on the avoidance learning hypothesis. T or F?

CRITICAL THINKING

9. Many of the physical complaints associated with anxiety disorders are closely related to activity of what part of the nervous system?

10. American veterans of the Vietnam War have experienced an elevated rate of PTSD. Can you explain why?

Answers:

1. d 2. F 3. b 4. social phobia 5. d 6. T 7. c 8. F 9. The autonomic nervous system (ANS), especially the sympathetic branch of the ANS. 10. Veterans of WWII were welcomed home as heroes. In addition to the unusual combat stresses they experienced, veterans of the Vietnam War were ignored or even reviled and spat upon when they first returned.

Humanistic *Any system of thought focused on subjective experience and human problems and potentials.*

Self-image *Total subjective perception of oneself; another term for self-concept.*

Existentialism *A system of thought that focuses on the elemental problems of existence, such as death, meaning, choice, and responsibility.*

Behavioristic *Any approach that emphasizes overt, observable behavior and the effects of learning and conditioning.*

Avoidance learning *Learning that occurs when making a particular response delays or prevents the onset of a painful or unpleasant stimulus.*

Anxiety reduction hypothesis *Explains the self-defeating nature of avoidance responses as a result of the reinforcing effects of relief from anxiety.*

Cognitive view *Holds that distorted thinking causes people to magnify ordinary threats and failures, leading to anxiety and distress.*

PSYCHOTIC DISORDERS—LIFE IN THE SHADOW OF MADNESS

Psychotic disorders are among the most serious of all mental problems. A person who is psychotic undergoes a number of striking changes in thinking, behavior, and emotion. Basic to all of these changes is the fact that **psychosis** reflects a loss of contact with shared views of reality (psycho*sis*, singular; psycho*ses*, plural). The following comments, made by several psychotic patients, illustrate what is meant by a "split" from reality (Torrey, 1988).

> Everything is in bits. You put the picture up bit by bit into your head. It's like a photograph that's torn in bits and put together again. If you move it's frightening.
>
> I felt I had the power to determine the weather, which responded to my inner moods, and even to control the movement of the sun.
>
> Last week I was with a girl and suddenly she seemed to get bigger and bigger, like a monster coming nearer and nearer.

What are the major features of psychotic disorders? Delusions and hallucinations are core features, but there are others as well.

DELUSIONAL THINKING   People who suffer from **delusions** hold false beliefs that they insist are true, regardless of how much the facts contradict them. An example is a 43-year-old schizophrenic man who was convinced he was pregnant (Mansouri & Adityanjee, 1995).

Are there different types of delusions? Yes, some common types of delusions are (1) *depressive* delusions, in which people feel that they have committed horrible crimes or sinful deeds; (2) *somatic* delusions, such as believing your body is "rotting away" or that it is emitting foul odors; (3) delusions of *grandeur,* in which people think they are extremely important; (4) delusions of *influence,* in which people feel they are being controlled or influenced by others or by unseen forces; (5) delusions of *persecution,* in which people believe that others are "out to get them"; and (6) delusions of *reference,* in which people assign great personal meaning to unrelated events. For instance, people sometimes think that television programs are giving them a special personal message (DSM-IV, 1994).

HALLUCINATIONS AND SENSATIONS   **Hallucinations** are imaginary sensations, such as seeing, hearing, or smelling things that don't exist in the real world. The most common psychotic hallucination is hearing voices. Sometimes these voices command patients to hurt themselves. Unfortunately, many people obey (Kasper, Rogers, & Adams, 1996).

More rarely, psychotic people may feel "insects crawling under their skin," taste "poisons" in their food, or smell "gas" their "enemies" are using to "get" them. Sensory changes, such as anesthesia (numbness, or a loss of sensation) or extreme sensitivity to heat, cold, pain, or touch, can also occur.

DISTURBED EMOTIONS   Emotions may swing violently between the extremes of elation and depression, or the psychotic person may be hyperemotional, depressed, emotionally "flat," or apa-

thetic. In instances of **flat affect,** almost no signs of emotion are visible. Typically, the person's face is frozen in a blank expression. However, behind their "frozen masks," people suffering from psychotic disorders continue to feel emotions just as strongly as ever (Sison et al., 1996).

DISTURBED COMMUNICATION   Some psychotic symptoms can be thought of as a primitive type of communication. That is, many patients can use only their actions to say, "I need help" or "I can't handle it any more." Disturbed verbal communication is a nearly universal symptom of psychotic disorders, which is why nonverbal pleas for help may become a necessity. Psychotic speech tends to be garbled and chaotic. Sometimes it sounds like a "word salad."

PERSONALITY DISINTEGRATION   Major disturbances such as those just described—as well as added problems in thought, memory, and attention—bring about personality disintegration and a break with reality. **Personality disintegration** occurs when a person's thoughts, actions, and emotions are no longer coordinated. Personality disintegration seriously impairs a person's work, social relations, and self-care.

When psychotic disturbances and a fragmented personality are evident for weeks or months (often including a period of deterioration, an active phase, and a residual phase), the person has suffered a psychosis (DSM-IV, 1994).

How could a person function with such problems? Actually, the preceding description is somewhat exaggerated. It is rare to find all these changes occurring at once. As a matter of fact, you would probably find a trip to a psychiatric ward dull if you

A scene in a state mental hospital.

TABLE 17.7 Warning Signs of Psychotic Disorders and Major Mood Disorders

You express bizarre thoughts or beliefs that defy reality.
You have withdrawn from family members and other relationships.
You hear unreal voices or sees things others don't.
You are extremely sad, persistently despondent, or suicidal.
You are excessively energetic and have little need for sleep.
You lose your appetite, sleep excessively, and have no energy.
You exhibit extreme mood swings.
You believe someone is trying to get you.
You have engaged in antisocial, destructive, or self-destructive behavior.

(Sources: Harvey et al., 1996; Sheehy & Cournos, 1992.)

❖ **FIGURE 17.5** *The Mad Hatter, from Lewis Carroll's* Alice's Adventures in Wonderland. *History provides numerous examples of psychosis caused by toxic chemicals. Carroll's Mad Hatter character is modeled after an occupational disease of the eighteenth and nineteenth centuries. In that era, hatmakers were heavily exposed to mercury used in the preparation of felt. Consequently, many suffered brain damage and became psychotic, or "mad" (Kety, 1979).*

expected to see flamboyant, dramatic, or bizarre behavior. Extreme, psychotic behavior typically occurs in brief *episodes* (see ❖Table 17.7). The symptoms of psychotic disorders come and go; much of the time, they are quite subtle.

Are there different types of psychotic disorders? Two major types of psychosis are *delusional disorders* and *schizophrenia.* Mood disorders, which primarily involve extremes of emotion, can also have psychotic features. Information on each is provided in upcoming discussions. (Remember, too, that a general category called *psychotic disorders not otherwise specified* also exists.)

Some psychotic disorders are clearly *organic* or based on known physical causes, such as brain diseases, gunshot wounds, and accidental brain injuries. In contrast, most psychotic disorders are **functional:** there is clear evidence that the patient is severely disturbed, but the causes of his or her illness are unknown.

As we will see later, all of the psychotic disorders appear to involve physical changes in the brain. In a sense, then, all psychoses are partly organic. However, the general term **organic psychosis** is usually reserved for problems involving clear-cut brain injuries or diseases. For example, a condition called *general paresis* (pah-REE-sis) occurs when syphilis attacks brain cells. In advanced cases of untreated syphilis, a patient's behavior may become disorganized and uninhibited. This can lead to shocking profanity and obscene behavior—the "dirty old man" syndrome.

A source of organic psychosis that gives special cause for alarm is poisoning by lead and mercury (❖Fig. 17.5). Although relatively rare, such poisoning can damage the brain and cause hallucinations, delusions, and a loss of emotional control. A particularly dangerous situation is found in old buildings that contain leaded paints. Lead tastes sweet. Thus, young children may be tempted to eat leaded paint flakes as if they were candy. Children who eat leaded paint can become psychotic or retarded (Dyer, 1993; Mielke, 1999).

Leaded paints also release powdered lead into the air. Children may breathe the powder or eat it after handling contaminated toys. Other sources of lead are soldered water pipes, old lead-lined drinking fountains, lead-glazed pottery, and lead from automobile exhaust. On a much larger scale, "poisoning" of another type, in the form of drug abuse, can also produce psychosis (DSM-IV, 1994).

The soil and dust in cities and near busy streets is often heavily contaminated with lead. This lead came from automobile exhaust before leaded gasoline was banned. Young children frequently put objects and their hands in their mouths. This, then, is a major source of lead poisoning for many children. Paving play areas or covering them with clean soil can greatly reduce lead exposure (Mielke, 1999).

Psychosis *A withdrawal from reality marked by hallucinations and delusions, disturbed thought and emotions, and personality disorganization.*
Delusion *A false belief held against all contrary evidence.*
Hallucination *An imaginary sensation, such as seeing, hearing, or smelling things that don't exist in the real world.*
Flat affect *An extreme lack of emotional responsiveness.*
Personality disintegration *A shattering of the coordination among thoughts, actions, and emotions normally found in personality.*
Functional psychosis *A psychosis of unknown origin or one presumed to be caused by psychological factors.*
Organic psychosis *A psychosis caused by brain injury or disease.*

The most common organic problem is **dementia** (duh-MEN-sha), a serious mental impairment in old age caused by deterioration of the brain. In dementia, we see major disturbances in memory, reasoning, judgment, impulse control, and personality. This combination usually leaves people confused, suspicious, apathetic, or withdrawn (Larson, 1990). The most common cause of dementia is *Alzheimer's disease*. Other common causes are circulatory problems, repeated strokes, or general shrinkage and atrophy of the brain (see "Alzheimer's Disease"). The majority of people who suffer from dementia slowly lose their mental abilities without becoming psychotic. However, some do develop delusions and lose contact with reality.

DELUSIONAL DISORDERS—AN ENEMY BEHIND EVERY TREE

People with delusional disorders usually do not suffer from hallucinations, emotional excesses, or personality disintegration. Even so, their break with reality is unmistakable. The main feature of **delusional disorders** is the presence of deeply held false beliefs. Such delusions may involve grandiosity, jealousy, persecution, bodily complaints, or romantic attraction (DSM-IV, 1994). Five types of delusional disorders have been identified:

- **Erotomanic type:** In this disorder, people have erotic delusions that they are loved by another person, especially by someone famous or of higher status.
- **Grandiose type:** In this case, people suffer from the delusion that they have some great, unrecognized talent, knowledge, or

insight. They may also believe that they have a special relationship with an important person or with God or that they are a famous person. (If the famous person is alive, the deluded person regards her or him as an imposter.)

- **Jealous type:** Typical of this type of delusion is an all-consuming, unfounded belief that one's spouse or lover is unfaithful.
- **Persecutory type:** Delusions of persecution involve belief that one is being conspired against, cheated, spied on, followed, poisoned, maligned, or harassed.
- **Somatic type:** People suffering from somatic delusions typically believe that their bodies are diseased or rotting or infested with insects or parasites, or that parts of their bodies are misshapen or defective.

Although they are false, and sometimes far-fetched, all of these delusions are about experiences that could conceivably occur in real life (Manschreck, 1996).

PARANOID PSYCHOSIS   The most common delusional disorder, often called **paranoid psychosis,** centers on delusions of persecution. Many self-styled reformers, crank letter writers, "communist hunters," "UFO abductees," and the like suffer paranoid delusions. Paranoid individuals often believe that they are being cheated, spied on, followed, poisoned, harassed, or plotted against. Usually they are intensely suspicious, believing they must be on guard at all times.

The evidence such people find to support their beliefs is usually unconvincing to others. Every detail of the paranoid person's existence is woven into a private version of "what's really going on." Buzzing during a telephone conversation may be

ALZHEIMER'S DISEASE

Alzheimer's disease (ALLS-hi-merz) is one of the most fearsome problems of aging. **Alzheimer's disease** is an age-related disorder characterized by impaired memory, confusion, and a progressive loss of mental abilities.

Alzheimer's victims at first have difficulty remembering recent events. Then they slowly become more disoriented, suspicious, and confused. In time, they lose the ability to work, cook, drive, or use tools. As their condition worsens, victims can no longer read, write, or calculate. Eventually they are mute, bedridden, and unable to walk, sit up, or smile (Larson, 1990).

Researchers suspect that Alzheimer's disease is caused by unusual webs and tangles in brain cells leading to and from the hippocampus (Nagy et al., 1996). (This area, you may recall, is important for learning and memory.) Changes also take place in an area called the nucleus basalis and in chemicals that carry messages within the brain. In roughly 20 percent of all cases of Alzheimer's disease, the cause is genetic. Hereditary Alzheimer's disease runs in families and strikes its victims early, between the ages of 45 and 55 (Murrell et al., 1991).

One out of every 10 adults over age 65 is a victim of Alzheimer's disease. Although the disease tends to progress slowly, it is ultimately fatal. Yet, there is no known remedy.

Understandably, efforts to find a cure for Alzheimer's disease are expanding. For some of us, such efforts may be a race against time.

Former U.S. President Ronald Reagan was diagnosed with Alzheimer's disease in 1994. Like many Alzheimer's victims, Reagan slipped into a slow mental decline that severely restricted his activities.

interpreted as "someone listening"; a stranger who comes to the door asking for directions may be seen as "really trying to get information."

Persons suffering paranoid delusions are rarely treated. It is almost impossible for them to accept that they need help. Anyone who suggests that they have a problem simply becomes part of the "conspiracy" to persecute them.

Paranoid people frequently lead lonely, isolated, and humorless lives dominated by constant suspicion and hostility. Although they are not necessarily dangerous to others, they can be. People who believe that the Mafia, government agents, space aliens, or a street gang is slowly closing in on them may be moved to violence by their irrational fears. Imagine that a stranger comes to the door to ask a paranoid person for directions. If the stranger has his hand in his coat pocket, he could become the target of a paranoid attempt at self-defense.

Because the topics we will consider next involve several new terms and ideas, let's stop for a quick review.

KNOWLEDGE BUILDER
PSYCHOSIS AND DELUSIONAL DISORDERS

RELATE

What did you think psychosis was like before you read about it? How has your understanding changed?

If you were writing a "recipe" for psychosis, what would the main "ingredients" be?

If you were asked to play the role of a paranoid for a theater production, what symptoms would you emphasize?

LEARNING CHECK

1. A person who wrongly believes that his or her body is "rotting away" is suffering from
   a. depressive delusions *b.* somatic delusions *c.* delusions of grandeur *d.* delusions of persecution

2. Colin, who has suffered a psychotic break, is hearing voices. This symptom is referred to as
   a. flat affect *b.* hallucination *c.* a word salad *d.* delusions of influence

3. A psychosis caused by lead poisoning would be termed a *functional* disorder. T or F?

4. Hallucinations and personality disintegration are the principal features of paranoid psychosis. T or F?

5. Some cases of organic psychosis are caused by drug abuse. T or F?

CRITICAL THINKING

6. The following quotation is an example of which symptom of psychosis? "I felt I had the power to determine the weather, which responded to my inner moods, and even to control the movement of the sun."

Answers:

1. b 2. b 3. F 4. F 5. T 6. Delusions of grandeur.

SCHIZOPHRENIA—SHATTERED REALITY

Schizophrenia (SKIT-soh-FREE-nee-uh) is a psychotic disorder marked by delusions, hallucinations, apathy, thinking abnormalities, and a "split" between thought and emotion. One person in 100 will become schizophrenic, and roughly half of all the people admitted to mental hospitals are schizophrenic. Most are young adults, but schizophrenia can occur at any age.

In schizophrenia, emotions may become blunted or very inappropriate. For example, if a schizophrenic person is told his mother just died, he might smile, giggle, or show no emotion at all. In addition, schizophrenia involves withdrawal from contact with others, a loss of interest in external activities, a breakdown of personal habits, and an inability to deal with daily events.

Remember the schizophrenic person who said, "Everything is in bits. . . . It's like a photograph that's torn in bits and put together again"? Many schizophrenic symptoms appear to arise from impaired *selective attention* (Hirt & Pithers, 1991; Lenzenweger et al., 1991; Ward et al., 1991). In other words, it is hard for schizophrenic people to focus on one item of information at a time. This may be why they are overwhelmed by a jumble of thoughts, sensations, images, and feelings.

Schizophrenic delusions can be bizarre. They often include the idea that the person's thoughts and actions are being controlled, that thoughts are being broadcast (so others can hear them), that thoughts have been "inserted" into the person's mind, or that thoughts have been removed.

Do schizophrenic people have two personalities? No, schizophrenia does not refer to having more than one personality. Recall from our earlier discussion that multiple identity is a non-psychotic disorder. "Schizophrenic Confusion" clarifies the differences between schizophrenia and other problems that are easily confused with it.

Is there more than one type of schizophrenia? Schizophrenia appears to be a group of related disturbances. It has four major subtypes (DSM-IV, 1994):

- **Disorganized type:** Schizophrenia marked by incoherence, grossly disorganized behavior, bizarre thinking, and flat or grossly inappropriate emotions.
- **Catatonic type:** Schizophrenia marked by stupor, rigidity, unresponsiveness, posturing, mutism, and, sometimes, agitated, purposeless behavior.

Dementia *Serious mental impairment in old age caused by physical deterioration of the brain.*
Alzheimer's disease *An age-related disease characterized by memory loss, mental confusion, and, in its later stages, by a nearly total loss of mental abilities.*
Delusional disorder *A psychosis marked by severe delusions of grandeur, jealousy, persecution, or similar preoccupations.*
Paranoid psychosis *A delusional disorder centered especially on delusions of persecution.*
Schizophrenia *A psychosis characterized by delusions, hallucinations, apathy, and a "split" between thought and emotion.*

CRITICAL THINKING

SCHIZOPHRENIC CONFUSION

"David was so warm and friendly yesterday, but today he's as cold as ice. He's so schizophrenic sometimes that I don't know how to react." Such statements illustrate how often the term *schizophrenic* is misused. As you know, even a person who displays two or more personalities (a dissociative disorder) is not "schizophrenic." Neither, of course, is a person like David, whose behavior is merely inconsistent.

On a more technical level, schizophrenia is often confused with a personality disorder that resembles it somewhat. Recall that personality disorders are maladaptive personality patterns. One such pattern is the **schizotypal personality,** a nonpsychotic disorder involving withdrawal, social isolation, and odd behavior—but no break with reality. Starting in adolescence, affected persons slowly become isolated, emotionally withdrawn, listless, and apathetic. Many are considered odd, shiftless, or eccentric. Their behavior at times may be markedly peculiar (collecting garbage, eating cigarette butts, talking to themselves, and so forth).

Problems of this type do resemble some aspects of schizophrenia. But the schizotypal personality, like other personality disorders, does not involve a psychotic "break with reality." Many individuals with a schizotypal personality simply live colorless and isolated lives on the fringes of society as vagrants, eccentrics, derelicts, or prostitutes.

In disorganized schizophrenia, behavior is marked by silliness, laughter, and bizarre or obscene behavior.

- **Paranoid type:** Schizophrenia marked by a preoccupation with delusions or by frequent auditory hallucinations related to a single theme, especially grandeur or persecution.
- **Undifferentiated type:** Schizophrenia in which there are prominent psychotic symptoms but none of the specific features of catatonic, disorganized, or paranoid types.

Disorganized Schizophrenia

The disorder known as disorganized schizophrenia (sometimes called hebephrenic schizophrenia) comes close to matching the stereotyped images of "madness" seen in movies. In **disorganized schizophrenia,** personality disintegration is almost complete: Emotions, speech, and behavior are all highly disorganized. The result is silliness, laughter, and bizarre or obscene behavior, as shown by this intake interview of a patient:

Dr. I am Dr. _____. I would like to know something more about you.
Patient You have a nasty mind. Lord! Lord! Cat's in a cradle.
Dr. Tell me, how do you feel?
Patient London's bell is a long, long dock. Hee! Hee! (Giggles uncontrollably.)
Dr. Do you know where you are now?
Patient D_____n! S_____t on you all who rip into my internals! The grudgerometer will take care of you all! (Shouting) I am the Queen, see my magic, I shall turn you all into smidgelings forever!
Dr. Your husband is concerned about you. Do you know his name?
Patient (Stands, walks to and faces the wall) Who am I, who are we, who are you, who are they (turns). I . . . I . . . I . . . I! (Makes grotesque faces.)

Edna was placed in the women's ward where she proceeded to masturbate. Occasionally, she would scream or shout obscenities. At other times she giggled to herself. She was known to attack other patients. She began to complain that her uterus was attached to a "pipeline to the Kremlin" and that she was being "infernally invaded" by Communism (Suinn, 1975).

Disorganized schizophrenia typically develops in early adolescence or young adulthood. It is often preceded by serious personality disorganization in earlier years. Chances of improvement are limited, and social impairment is usually extreme (DSM-IV, 1994).

Catatonic Schizophrenia

The catatonic person seems to be in a state of total panic. **Catatonic schizophrenia** brings about a stuporous condition in which odd positions may be held for hours or even days. Sometimes, a condition called *waxy flexibility* occurs. While in this state, the catatonic person can be arranged into any position, like a mannequin. These periods of immobility may be similar to the tendency to "freeze" at times of great emergency or panic. Catatonic individuals appear to be struggling desperately to control their inner turmoil. One sign of this is the fact that stupor may occasionally give way to agitated outbursts or violent behavior. The following excerpt describes a **catatonic episode** (a period of extreme stupor, immobility, and unresponsiveness).

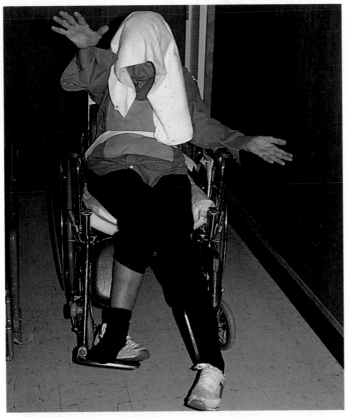

Can the catatonic's rigid postures and stupor be understood in terms of abnormal body chemistry? Environment? Heredity?

Manuel appeared to be physically healthy upon examination. Yet he did not regain his awareness of his surroundings. He remained motionless, speechless, and seemingly unconscious. One evening an aide turned him on his side to straighten out the sheet, was called away to tend another patient, and forgot to return. Manuel was found the next morning, still on his side, his arm tucked under his body, as he had been left the night before. His arm was turning blue from lack of circulation, but he seemed to be experiencing no discomfort. Further examination confirmed that he was in a state of waxy flexibility (Suinn, 1975).

Notice that Manuel did not speak. *Mutism,* along with a marked decrease in responsiveness to the environment, makes the catatonic patient difficult to "reach." Fortunately, this bizarre form of schizophrenia has become rare in Europe and North America (DSM-IV, 1994).

Paranoid Schizophrenia

Paranoid schizophrenia is the most common schizophrenic disorder. **Paranoid schizophrenia,** like a paranoid delusional disorder, centers around delusions of grandeur and persecution. However, paranoid schizophrenics also hallucinate, and their delusions are more bizarre and unconvincing than those seen in a delusional disorder.

Thinking that their minds are being controlled by God, the government, or "cosmic rays from space," or that someone is trying to poison them, people suffering from paranoid schizo-

phrenia may feel forced into violence to "protect" themselves. An example is James Huberty, who brutally murdered 21 people at a McDonald's restaurant in San Ysidro, California. Huberty was a paranoid schizophrenic who felt persecuted and cheated by life. Shortly before he announced to his wife that he was "going hunting humans," Huberty had been hearing hallucinated voices (❖Fig. 17.6).

How dangerous are the mentally ill? Depictions in the news certainly give the impression that practically everyone who is mentally ill is dangerous. Consider, for example, the ghastly case of Jeffrey Dahmer. Dahmer was everyone's worst nightmare brought to life. Dahmer drugged his victims, drilled holes in their skulls, sexually molested their lifeless bodies, dismembered them, and ate their body parts, which he stored in a refrigerator.

How accurately does a case like Dahmer's reflect the risk of violence by the mentally ill? You might be surprised by the answer, found in "Are the Mentally Ill Prone to Violence?"

The sections that follow continue our discussion by describing in greater detail some of the problems already mentioned.

❖ **FIGURE 17.6** *Over a period of years, Theodore Kaczynski mailed bombs to unsuspecting victims, many of whom were maimed or killed. As a young adult, Kaczynski was a brilliant mathematician. At the time of his arrest, he had become the Unabomber—a reclusive "loner" who deeply mistrusted other people and modern technology. After his arrest, Kaczynski was judged to be suffering from paranoid schizophrenia.*

Schizotypal personality *A non-psychotic personality disorder involving withdrawal, social isolation, and odd behavior, but no break with reality.*
Disorganized schizophrenia *Schizophrenia marked by incoherence, grossly disorganized behavior, bizarre thinking, and flat or grossly inappropriate emotions.*
Catatonic schizophrenia *Schizophrenia marked by stupor, rigidity, unresponsiveness, posturing, mutism, and, sometimes, agitated, purposeless behavior.*
Catatonic episode *Period of extreme stupor, immobility, and unresponsiveness.*
Paranoid schizophrenia *Schizophrenia marked by a preoccupation with delusions or by frequent auditory hallucinations related to a single theme, especially grandeur or persecution.*

ARE THE MENTALLY ILL PRONE TO VIOLENCE?

News reports and television programs tend to greatly exaggerate the connection between mental illness and violence (Diefenbach, 1997). In reality, research on this question leads to these conclusions:

- Only people who are *actively psychotic* are more violence prone than non-patients. That is, if a person is experiencing delusions and hallucinations, the risk of violence is elevated. Other mental problems are unrelated to violence.
- Only people *currently* experiencing psychotic symptoms are at increased risk for violence. Violent behavior is not related to having been a mental patient or having had psychotic symptoms *in the past.*

Thus, most news stories give a false impression. Even when we consider people who are actively psychotic, we find that the vast majority are not violent. The risk of violence from mental patients is actually many times lower than that posed by people who have the following attributes: young, male, poor, and intoxicated.

Beliefs about mental disorders are important because they affect laws and personal attitudes toward the mentally ill. People who strongly believe that the mentally ill are prone to violence are typically afraid to have former mental patients as neighbors, coworkers, or friends. But as you can see, only a small minority of the actively mentally ill pose an increased risk. Former mental patients, in particular, are no more likely to be violent than people in general. No matter how disturbed a person may have been, she or he merits respect and compassion. Consider the ill-informed reception one former patient received:

> After I got back from the hospital, my friends tried to *act* like nothing had changed. But I could tell they weren't being honest. For instance, a friend invited me to dinner and everything went fine until I dropped my fork. Both my friend and his wife jumped up and stared at me like they thought I might explode. I was quite embarrassed.

Remember, the overwhelming majority of violent crimes are committed by people who are not mentally ill. (Sources: Monahan, 1992; Noble, 1997; Rice, 1997; Teplin, Abram, & McClelland, 1994.)

Although Jeffrey Dahmer's case is extreme, he is typical of the mentally disordered persons who make the evening news. Most have committed murder or some other heinous crime. This gives the impression that the mentally ill are violent and dangerous. In reality, only a tiny percentage of all mentally disordered persons are more violent than average. (Dahmer was killed in prison by another inmate in 1994.)

Undifferentiated Schizophrenia

The three types of schizophrenia just described occur most often in textbooks. In reality, patients may shift from one pattern to another at different times (Heinrichs, 1993). Many patients, therefore, are simply classified as suffering from **undifferentiated schizophrenia,** in which the specific features of catatonic, disorganized, or paranoid types are missing.

The diagnosis of schizophrenia is fairly subjective and open to error. For example, when 72 "schizophrenic" patients in a state hospital were re-evaluated, only 45 were confirmed to be schizophrenic (Wilson, 1989). All things considered, however, there is no doubt that schizophrenia is real or that its treatment is a major challenge.

The Causes of Schizophrenia

Former British Prime Minister Winston Churchill once described a question that perplexed him as "a riddle wrapped in a mystery inside an enigma." The same words might describe the causes of schizophrenia.

ENVIRONMENT *What causes schizophrenia?* An increased risk of developing schizophrenia may begin at birth or even before. Women who are exposed to the influenza (flu) virus during the middle of pregnancy have children who are more likely to become schizophrenic. Malnutrition during pregnancy and complications at the time of birth can have a similar impact. Possibly, such events disturb brain development, leaving people more vulnerable to a psychotic break with reality (Cannon 1998; Takei et al., 1994; Woods, 1998).

Early **psychological trauma** (a psychological injury or shock) may also add to the risk. Often, the victims of schizophrenia were exposed to violence, sexual abuse, death, divorce, separation, or other stresses in childhood (Mirsky & Duncan, 1986). Living in a troubled family is a related risk factor. In a **disturbed family environment,** stressful relationships, communication patterns, and negative emotions prevail. For example,

THE GENAIN SISTERS—TROUBLE TIMES FOUR

By the time the Genain quadruplets reached high school, they began to act strangely. Hester broke light bulbs and tore buttons off her clothes. By age 20, Nora moaned at meals and complained that the bones in her neck were slipping. At night she stood on her knees and elbows in bed until they bled. At age 22, Iris quit her job, complaining that "I am pinned down. Someone wants to fight and I don't want to." Soon after, she "went to pieces." She screamed, drooled at meals, and talked of hearing voices. Myra, who was the fourth identical quad, panicked easily and couldn't be reassured, but did not actually break down until age 24 (Rosenthal & Quinn, 1977).

In addition to sharing identical heredity, the Genain sisters—Nora, Iris, Myra, and Hester—have something else in common: All four became schizophrenic before age 25. The women, who are now in their early 60s, have been in and out of mental hospitals all their lives.

You may be immediately tempted to assume that the Genain quads' psychoses were caused by heredity. However, it would be a mistake to overlook the nightmarish family life in which the girls grew up. Mr. Genain was an alcoholic who hounded, spied on, terrorized, and sexually molested the girls.

For the most part, Mrs. Genain was curiously blind to her husband's actions and offered the girls little support. Instead, she added her own bizarre thinking and sexual preoccupations to the family's already warped relationships. To put it mildly, the girls' mother and father failed spectacularly as parents.

In the final analysis, it seems that both heredity and an unhealthy environment led to the Genain sisters' problems (Carson, Butcher, & Mineka, 1997). Further support for this conclusion comes from the fact that Myra, the least ill of the four, was her mother's favorite. Myra also was the only sister able to keep some distance from her father.

In sum, it appears that heredity may set higher or lower thresholds for psychosis. Whether a person becomes actively disturbed, however, may depend on the kind of stresses to which she or he is exposed (Ventura et al., 1989).

---

a 15-year study found that the chance of developing schizophrenia is related to deviant communication within families (Goldstein, 1985). **Deviant communication patterns** cause anxiety, confusion, anger, conflict, and turmoil. Typically, disturbed families interact in ways that are laden with guilt, prying, criticism, negativity, and emotional attacks (Bressi, Albonetti, & Razzoli, 1998; Docherty et al., 1998).

Although they are attractive, environmental explanations alone are not enough to account for schizophrenia (Fowles, 1992). For example, when the children of schizophrenic parents are raised away from their chaotic home environment, they are still more likely to become psychotic.

Does that mean that heredity affects the risk of developing schizophrenia?

HEREDITY Evidence has grown stronger in recent years that heredity is a factor in schizophrenia. It now appears that some individuals inherit a *potential* for developing schizophrenia. They are, in other words, more *vulnerable* to the disorder than others are (Cannon et al., 1998; Fowles, 1992).

How has that been shown? If one identical twin becomes schizophrenic (remember, identical twins have identical genes), then the other twin has a *48 percent* chance of also becoming schizophrenic (Lenzenweger & Gottesman, 1994). There's even a case on record of *four* identical quadruplets *all* developing schizophrenia (see "The Genain Sisters").

The figure for twins can be compared with the risk of schizophrenia for the population in general, which is 1 percent. (See ❖Fig. 17.7 for other relationships.) In general, it is clear that schizophrenia is more common among close relatives and it tends to run in families (Plomin & Rende, 1991). Researchers are even beginning to identify specific genes related to schizophrenia (Gershon et al., 1998).

BRAIN CHEMISTRY *How could someone inherit a susceptibility to schizophrenia?* Amphetamine, LSD, PCP ("angel dust"), and similar drugs produce effects that partially mimic the symptoms of schizophrenia. Also, the same drugs (phenothiazines) used to treat LSD overdoses tend to alleviate psychotic symptoms. Facts such as these suggest that **biochemical abnormalities** (disturbances in brain chemicals or neurotransmitters) may occur in schizophrenic people. It is possible that the schizophrenic brain produces some substance similar to a *psychedelic* (mind-altering) drug. At present, one likely candidate is **dopamine** (DOPE-ah-meen), an important chemical messenger found in the brain (Abi-Dargham et al., 1998).

Many researchers now believe that schizophrenia is related to overactivity in brain dopamine systems (Heinrichs, 1993). Another possibility is that dopamine receptors become superresponsive to normal amounts of dopamine (Port & Seybold, 1995). Dopamine appears to trigger a flood of unrelated thoughts, feelings, and perceptions, which may account for the

---

Undifferentiated schizophrenia *Schizophrenia lacking the specific features of catatonic, disorganized, or paranoid types.*

Psychological trauma *A psychological injury or shock, such as that caused by violence, abuse, neglect, or separation.*

Disturbed family environment *Stressful or unhealthy family relationships, communication patterns, and emotional atmosphere.*

Deviant communication patterns *Patterns of communication that cause guilt, anxiety, confusion, anger, conflict, and emotional turmoil.*

Biochemical abnormality *A disturbance of the body's chemical systems, especially in brain chemicals or neurotransmitters.*

Dopamine *An important transmitter substance found in the brain, especially in the limbic system, an area associated with emotional response.*

Genetic relatedness	Relationship	Risk
100%	Identical twin	48%
—	Offspring of two patients	46%
50%	Fraternal twin	17%
50%	Offspring of one patient	17%
50%	Sibling	9%
25%	Nephew or niece	4%
0%	Spouse	2%
0%	Unrelated person in the general population	1%

❖ **FIGURE 17.7** *Lifetime risk of developing schizophrenia is associated with how closely a person is genetically related to a schizophrenic person. A shared environment also increases the risk. (Estimates from Lenzenweger & Gottesman, 1994.)*

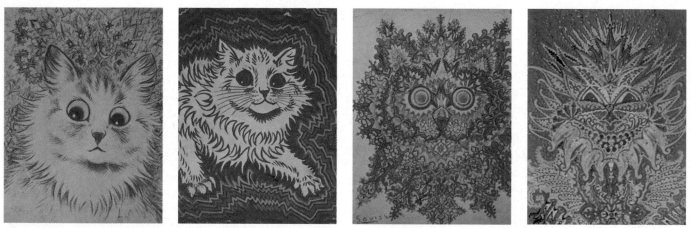

This series of paintings by Louis Wain reflects a troubled personality. Wain was a British illustrator who became schizophrenic in middle age. As Wain's psychosis progressed, his cat paintings became highly abstract and fragmented. In many ways, Wain's paintings resemble the perceptual changes caused by psychedelic drugs such as mescaline and LSD. Recent research suggests that psychosis may, in fact, be the result of mind-altering changes in brain chemistry. (Derik Bayes/Courtesy Guttman-Maclay *Life* Picture Service.)

voices, hallucinations, and delusions of schizophrenia (Gottesman, 1991). The implication is that schizophrenic people may be on a sort of drug trip caused by their own bodies (❖Fig. 17.8). In short, most evidence suggests that schizophrenia is a brain disease (Heinrichs, 1993).

The Schizophrenic Brain

Medical researchers have long hoped for a way to directly observe the schizophrenic brain. Three medical techniques are now making it possible. One, called a **CT scan,** provides an X-ray picture of the brain. (CT stands for computed tomography, or computer-enhanced X-ray images.) ❖Figure 17.9 shows a CT scan of the brain of John Hinkley Jr, who shot former U.S. President Ronald Reagan and three other men in 1981. In the ensuing trial, Hinkley was declared insane.

BRIDGES

Brain scans have provided valuable new insights into brain structures and activities.

See Chapter 3, pages 58–60.

As you can see, his brain differed from the norm. Specifically, it had wider surface fissuring.

MRI scans (magnetic resonance imaging) are allowing researchers to peer inside the schizophrenic brain. What they find is that schizophrenic people tend to have enlarged ventricles (fluid-filled spaces within the brain) (Sharma et al., 1998). Other brain regions also appear to be abnormal. It is telling that the affected areas are crucial for regulating motivation, emotion, perception, actions, and attention (Degreef et al., 1992; Frazier et al., 1996; Gur et al., 1998).

A third technique, called a **PET scan** (positron emission tomography), provides an image of brain activity. To make a PET scan, a radioactive sugar solution is injected into a vein. When the sugar reaches the brain, an electronic device measures how much is used in each area. These data are then translated into a

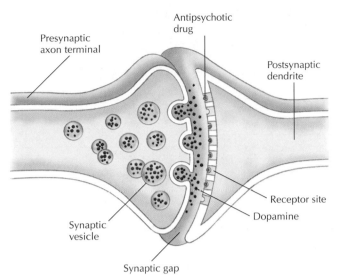

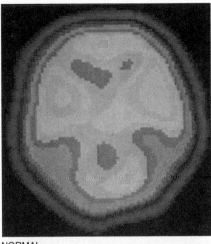

NORMAL

❖ **FIGURE 17.8** *Dopamine normally crosses the synapse between two neurons, activating the second cell. Antipsychotic drugs bind to the same receptor sites as dopamine does, blocking its action. In people suffering from schizophrenia, a reduction in dopamine activity can quiet a person's agitation and psychotic symptoms.*

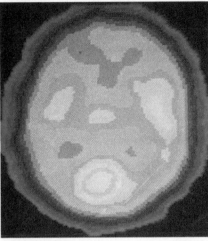

SCHIZOPHRENIC

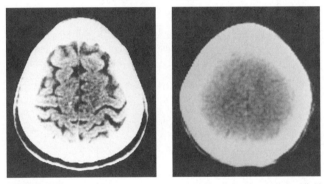

❖ **FIGURE 17.9** (left) *CT scan of would-be presidential assassin John Hinkley Jr., taken when he was 25. The X-ray image shows widened fissures in the wrinkled surface of Hinkley's brain. (right) CT scan of a normal 25-year-old's brain. In most young adults, the surface folds of the brain are pressed together too tightly to be seen. As a person ages, surface folds of the brain normally become more visible. Pronounced brain fissuring in young adults may be a sign of schizophrenia, chronic alcoholism, or other problems.*

❖ **FIGURE 17.10** *Positron emission tomography produces PET scans of the human brain. In the scans shown here, red, pink, and orange indicate lower levels of brain activity; white and blue indicate higher activity levels. Notice that activity in the schizophrenic brain is quite low in the frontal lobes (top area of each scan) (Velakoulis & Pantelis, 1996). Activity in the manic-depressive brain is low in the left brain hemisphere and high in the right brain hemisphere. The reverse is more often true of the schizophrenic brain. Researchers are trying to identify consistent patterns like these to aid diagnosis of mental disorders.*

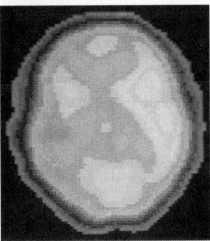

MANIC-DEPRESSIVE

color map, or scan, of brain activity (❖Fig. 17.10). Researchers are finding patterns in such scans that are consistently linked with schizophrenia, affective disorders, and other problems. For instance, activity tends to be abnormally low in the frontal lobes of the schizophrenic brain (Velakoulis & Pantelis, 1996). In the future, PET scans may be used to accurately diagnose schizophrenia. For now, PET scans show that there is a clear difference in schizophrenic brain activity.

SUMMARY   In summary, the emerging picture of psychotic disorders such as schizophrenia takes this form: Anyone subjected to enough stress may be pushed to a psychotic break. (Battlefield psychosis is an example.) However, some people inherit a

CT scan *Computed tomography scan; a computer-enhanced X-ray image of the brain or body.*
MRI scan *Magnetic resonance imaging; a computer-enhanced three-dimensional representation of the brain or body, based on the body's response to a magnetic field.*
PET scan *Positron emission tomography; a computer-generated color image of brain activity, as revealed by the consumption of radioactive sugar.*

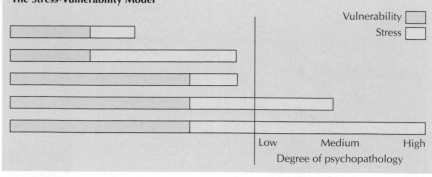

❖ **FIGURE 17.11** *Various combinations of vulnerability and stress may produce psychological problems. The top bar shows low vulnerability and low stress. The result? No problem. The same is true of the next bar down, where low vulnerability is combined with moderate stress. Even high vulnerability (third bar) may not lead to problems if stress levels remain low. However, when high vulnerability combines with moderate or high stress (bottom two bars), the person "crosses the line" and suffers from psychopathology.*

◆ **TABLE 17.8** DSM-IV Classification of Mood Disorders

PROBLEM	PRIMARY SYMPTOM	TYPICAL SIGNS OF TROUBLE
DEPRESSIVE DISORDERS		
Major depressive disorder	Extreme emotional depression for at least two weeks	You feel extremely sad, worthless, fatigued, and empty; you are unable to feel pleasure; you are having thoughts of suicide
Dysthymic disorder	Moderately depressed mood on most days during the last two years	You feel down and depressed more days than not; your self-esteem and energy levels have been low for many months
BIPOLAR DISORDERS		
Bipolar I disorder	Extreme mania and depression	At times you have little need for sleep, can't stop talking, your mind races, and everything you do is of immense importance; at other times you feel extremely sad, worthless, and empty
Bipolar II disorder	Emotional depression and at least one episode of mild mania	Most of the time you feel extremely sad, worthless, fatigued, and empty; however, at times you feel unusually good, cheerful, energetic, or "high."
Cyclothymic disorder	Periods of moderate depression and moderate mania for at least two years	You have been experiencing upsetting emotional ups and downs for many months

difference in brain chemistry or brain structure that makes them more susceptible—even to normal life stresses.

Thus, the right combination of inherited potential and environmental stress brings about mind-altering changes in brain chemicals and brain structure. This explanation is called a **stress-vulnerability model.** It attributes psychotic disorders to a combination of environmental stress and inherited susceptibility. The model seems to apply to other forms of psychopathology as well, such as depression (Fowles, 1992; Gottesman, 1991; Yank et al., 1993) (❖Fig. 17.11).

Ultimately, distinctions between organic and functional psychoses may be dropped, and treatment of major disturbances may become more chemical than psychological. But for now, psychosis remains "a riddle wrapped in a mystery inside an enigma." Let us hope the recent advances that we have so briefly explored are as promising as they appear to be.

MOOD DISORDERS—PEAKS AND VALLEYS

Nobody loves you when you're down and out—or so it seems. Psychologists have come to realize that **mood disor-**ders (major disturbances in emotion) are among the most serious of all. Two general types of mood disorder are depressive disorders and bipolar disorders. (See ◆Table 17.8.) In **depressive disorders,** sadness and despondency are exaggerated, prolonged, or unreasonable. Signs of a depressive disorder are dejection, hopelessness, and an inability to feel pleasure or to take interest in anything. Also common are fatigue, disturbed sleep and eating patterns, feelings of worthlessness, a very negative self-image, and thoughts of suicide. In **bipolar disorders,** people go both "up" and "down" emotionally (DSM-IV, 1994).

In Europe and North America, between 10 and 20 percent of the adult population has had a major depressive episode at some time (DSM-IV, 1994). At any given time, roughly 5 percent of the population is suffering from a mood disorder (Landers, 1989).

Moderate Mood Disorders

If a person is moderately depressed for at least 2 years, the problem is called a **dysthymic disorder** (dis-THY-mik). If depression alternates with periods when the person's mood is elevated, cheerful, expansive, or irritable, the problem is a **cyclothymic disorder** (SIKE-lo-THY-mik) (DSM-IV, 1994).

In serious cases of depression, it is impossible for a person to function at work or at school. Sometimes, depressed individuals cannot even feed or dress themselves. When depression and/or mania is even more severe, the person may also lose touch with reality.

How are mood disorders different from milder feelings of depression? It is normal for depression to follow events such as failures, losses, setbacks, or the death of a loved one. However, mood disorders seem to have a life of their own. Often, there doesn't seem to be any obvious reason why people suffering from mood disorders become depressed. Sometimes, of course, clinical depression does follow a specific event, such as a loss or a failure. However, such **reactive depressions** last longer and are more severe than the event would seem to warrant (Gorman, 1996).

When someone is continuously or intensely depressed, we must look for causes that go beyond the apparent triggering incident. In many reactive depressions, we find that the person was unprepared to cope with a major loss, perhaps because of a previous series of disappointments. For example, after his car is stolen and he fails a class, a college student learns that his girlfriend back home is engaged to someone else. The student stops eating regularly, withdraws from friends, and neglects studying. In many reactive depressions, the triggering incident is merely the "last straw" that reveals an underlying emotional disturbance.

Major Mood Disorders

Major mood disorders are marked by lasting extremes of emotion. About 14 percent of patients admitted to mental hospitals suffer from major mood disorders. The person who goes only "down" emotionally suffers from a **major depressive disorder.** During major depressive episodes, people reach an extreme low point emotionally. Everything looks bleak and hopeless, and the person's suffering is intense.

In a **bipolar I disorder,** people experience both extreme mania and deep depression. During manic episodes, the person is loud, elated, hyperactive, grandiose, and energetic. Manic patients may go bankrupt in a matter of days, get arrested, or go on a binge of promiscuous sex. During periods of depression, the person is deeply despondent and possibly suicidal.

In a **bipolar II disorder,** the person is mostly sad and guilt ridden but has had one or more mildly manic episodes (called *hypomania*). That is, in a bipolar II disorder, both elation and depression occur, but the person's mania is not as extreme as it is in a bipolar I disorder. Bipolar II patients who are hypomanic usually just manage to irritate everyone around them. They are excessively cheerful, aggressive, or irritable, and they may brag, talk too fast, interrupt conversations, or spend too much money (Gorman, 1996).

Major mood disorders primarily involve emotional extremes. Quite often, however, people with major mood disorders also have psychotic symptoms. This combination of mood disorder and a break with reality is called an **affective psychosis.**

How do such problems differ from other types of psychosis?

AFFECTIVE PSYCHOSES   Manic individuals throw themselves into fits of activity characterized by extreme distractibility, rapid shifts in thoughts ("flights of ideas"), constant talking, and restless movement. In advanced stages, manic behavior becomes more and more incoherent, agitated, and out of control. Eating or sleeping may be ignored until manic individuals push themselves into states of total delirium. (This behavior accounts for public images of the "raving maniac.") The following excerpt illustrates manic behavior that includes psychotic features.

> Her husband had returned home to find her twirling around the living room bizarrely draped in her wedding gown tied with a bath towel and wearing a lamp shade. She gaily greeted him, laughed with an ear-piercing shrillness, and invited him to stay for the exciting "coming-out" party she was giving. Strewn on the table were a thousand handwritten invitations signed with a flourish and addressed to such dignitaries as the president of the United States, the justices of the Supreme Court, the emperor of Japan. She made incessant noises: singing her own ballads, shouting mottoes, which she devised, reciting limericks, making rhyming sounds, and yelling obscenities (Suinn, 1970).

Depressive reactions show a reverse pattern in which feelings of failure, sinfulness, worthlessness, and total despair are dominant. The person becomes extremely subdued or withdrawn and may be intensely suicidal. Depressive reactions pose a serious threat to survival. Suicide attempted during a major depression is rarely a simple "plea for help." Usually, the person intends to succeed and may give no prior warning.

Stress-vulnerability model *Attributes psychosis to a combination of environmental stress and inherited susceptibility.*
Mood disorder *Major disturbances in mood or emotion, such as depression or mania.*
Depressive disorders *Emotional disorders primarily involving sadness, despondency, and depression.*
Bipolar disorders *Emotional disorders involving both depression and mania or hypomania.*
Dysthymic disorder *Moderate depression that persists for 2 years or more.*
Cyclothymic disorder *Moderate manic and depressive behavior that persists for 2 years or more.*
Reactive depression *A serious depression that appears to be a reaction to some identifiable event but that is more severe than the event seems to warrant.*
Major mood disorders *Disorders marked by lasting extremes of mood or emotion and sometimes accompanied by psychotic symptoms.*
Major depressive disorder *A mood disorder in which the person has suffered one or more intense episodes of depression.*
Bipolar I disorder *A mood disorder in which a person has episodes of mania (excited, hyperactive, energetic, grandiose behavior) and also periods of deep depression.*
Bipolar II disorder *A mood disorder in which a person is mostly depressed (sad, despondent, guilt ridden) but has also had one or more episodes of mild mania (hypomania).*
Affective psychosis *A general term for any major mood disorder that includes psychotic symptoms.*

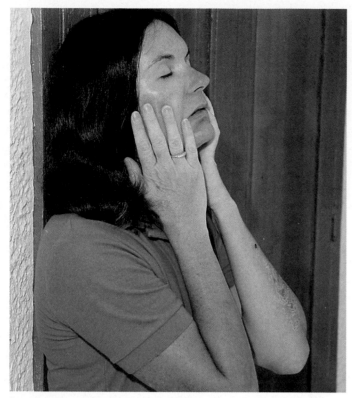

In major depressive disorders, suicidal impulses can be intense and despair total.

or self-defeating thoughts underlie many cases of depression. (This view is discussed in Chapter 18.) Clearly, life stresses trigger many mood disorders (Kessler, 1997). This is especially true for people who have personality traits and thinking patterns that make them vulnerable to depression (Franche & Dobson, 1992; Gatz, 1990; Miranda, 1992).

Overall, women are twice as likely as men to experience depression (Culertson, 1997). Authorities believe that social and environmental conditions are the main reason for this difference. Factors that contribute to women's greater risk of depression include reproductive stresses, conflicts between work and parenting, and the strain of providing emotional support for others. Marital strife, sexual and physical abuse, and poverty are also factors. Nationwide, poverty is concentrated among women and children. As a result, poor women frequently suffer the stresses associated with single parenthood, loss of control over their lives, poor housing, and dangerous neighborhoods (Russo, 1990).

As you might guess, the fact that major mood disorders appear to be endogenous implies that genetics may be involved, especially in bipolar disorders (Gershon et al., 1998). As a case in point, if one identical twin is depressed, the other has an 80 percent chance of suffering depression, too. For non-twin siblings the probability is 35 percent. As we have noted, psychological causes are important in many cases of depression. But for major mood disorders, biological factors seem to play a larger role. (For an interesting look at another cause of depression, see "Feeling Sad?")

How do major mood disorders differ from dysthymic and cyclothymic disorders? The major mood disorders involve more severe emotional changes. Also, as just noted, the person's emotional excesses may be accompanied by delusions or hallucinations. As a further distinction, major mood disorders and affective psychoses more often appear to be **endogenous** (en-DODGE-eh-nus: produced from within) rather than a reaction to external events.

The Causes of Mood Disorders

How is depression explained? Depression and other mood disorders have resisted adequate explanation and treatment. Some scientists are focusing on the biology of mood changes. They are interested in brain chemicals and transmitter substances, especially serotonin, noradrenaline, and dopamine levels (Ricci & Wellman, 1990). Their findings are complex and incomplete, but progress has been made. For example, the chemical *lithium carbonate* can be effective for treating some cases of bipolar depression.

Other researchers seek psychological explanations. Psychoanalytic theory, for instance, holds that depression is caused by repressed anger. This rage is displaced and turned inward as self-blame and self-hate (Isenberg & Schatzberg, 1976). As discussed in Chapter 16, behavioral theories of depression emphasize learned helplessness (Seligman, 1989). Cognitive psychologists believe that self-criticism and negative, distorted,

BRIDGES

In addition to its role in producing SAD, melatonin regulates normal circadian rhythms.

See Chapter 13, pages 418–419.

MENTAL HOSPITALIZATION—TREATING MAJOR MENTAL DISORDERS

What can be done about major mental disorders? Two basic forms of treatment exist for psychological disorders of all types. The first, called **psychotherapy,** is any psychological treatment for behavioral or emotional problems. Psychotherapy is based on a special relationship between a psychologist and a person in trouble. It typically involves two people talking about one person's problems. **Medical therapies** range from prescribing drugs to performing brain surgery. Because treatment approaches vary greatly, a complete discussion of therapies is found in the next chapter.

Hospitalization

For major mental disorders, therapy is often best done in a controlled setting, such as a psychiatric hospital. **Mental hospitalization** involves placing a person in a protected, therapeutic environment staffed by mental health professionals. This, by itself, can be a form of treatment. Staying in a hospital removes patients from situations that may be provoking or maintaining their problems. For example, people with drug addictions may find it nearly impossible to resist the temptations for drug abuse in their daily lives. Hospitalization can help them make a clean break from their former self-destructive behavior patterns (Gorman, 1996).

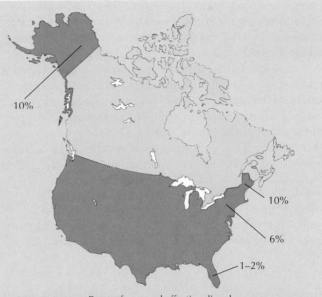

FEELING SAD? IT COULD BE SAD

Unless you have experienced a winter of "cabin fever" in the far north, you may be surprised to learn that the rhythms of the seasons underlie some depressions. Researcher Norman Rosenthal has found that some people suffer from **seasonal affective disorder (SAD)**, or depression that occurs only during the fall and winter months. Almost anyone can get a little depressed when days are short, dark, and cold. But when a person's symptoms are lasting and disabling, the problem may be SAD. Here are some of the major symptoms of SAD (Rosenthal, 1993):

- **Oversleeping and difficulty staying awake:** Your sleep patterns may be disturbed, and waking very early in the morning is common.
- **Fatigue:** You feel too tired to maintain a normal routine.
- **Craving:** You hunger for carbohydrates and sweets, leading to overeating and weight gain.
- **Inability to cope:** You feel irritable and stressed.
- **Social withdrawal:** You become unsocial in the winter but are socially active during other seasons.

Starting in the fall, people with SAD sleep longer but more poorly. During the day, they feel tired and drowsy, and they tend to overeat. With each passing day, they become sadder and more anxious, irritable, and socially withdrawn.

Although their depressions are usually only moderately severe, many victims of SAD face each winter with a sense of foreboding. SAD is especially prevalent in northern latitudes, where days are very short during the winter (Booker & Hellekson, 1992) (❖Fig. 17.12). One recent study found that among college students living in northern New England, 13 percent showed signs of suffering from SAD (Low & Feissner, 1998). The students most likely to be affected were those who had moved from the south to attend college!

Seasonal depressions are related to the release of more melatonin during the winter. This hormone, which is secreted by the pineal gland, regulates the body's response to changing light conditions. That's why 80 percent of SAD patients can be helped by extra doses of bright light, an approach called phototherapy (❖Fig. 17.13). **Phototherapy** involves exposing SAD patients to one or more hours of very bright fluorescent light each day. Light therapy works best when it is used early in the

Rates of seasonal affective disorder, by latitude

❖ **FIGURE 17.12** *Seasonal affective disorder appears to be related to reduced exposure to daylight during the winter. SAD affects 1 to 2 percent of Florida's population, about 6 percent of the people living in Maryland and New York City, and nearly 10 percent of the residents of New Hampshire and Alaska (Booker & Hellekson, 1992).*

❖ **FIGURE 17.13** *An hour or more of bright light a day can dramatically reduce the symptoms of seasonal affective disorder. Treatment is usually necessary from fall through spring. Light therapy typically works best when it is used early in the morning (Lewy et al., 1998).*

morning (Lewy et al., 1998). For many SAD sufferers a hearty dose of light appears to be the next best thing to vacationing in the tropics.

At its best, the hospital is a sanctuary that provides diagnosis, support, refuge, and therapy. This is generally true of psychiatric units in general hospitals and private psychiatric hospitals. At worst, confinement to an institution can be a brutalizing experience that leaves people less prepared to face the world than they were before they arrived. This is more often the case in large state mental hospitals (Gorman, 1996).

In most instances, hospitals are best used as a last resort, after other forms of treatment within the community have been exhausted. Actually, most psychiatric patients do as well with short-term hospitalization as they do with longer periods. For this reason, the average stay in psychiatric hospitals is now just 20 days, rather than 3 to 4 months, as it was 20 years ago.

Endogenous depression *Depression that appears to be produced from within (perhaps by chemical imbalances in the brain), rather than as a reaction to life events.*
Seasonal affective disorder *Depression that occurs only during fall and winter; presumably related to decreased exposure to sunlight.*
Phototherapy *A treatment for seasonal affective disorder that involves exposure to bright, full-spectrum light.*
Psychotherapy *Any psychological treatment for behavioral or emotional problems.*
Medical therapies *Any bodily therapy, such as drug therapy, electroshock, or psychosurgery.*
Mental hospitalization *Placing a person in a protected, therapeutic environment staffed by mental health professionals.*

A new trend in psychiatric treatment is **partial hospitalization.** In this approach, patients spend only part of their time at the hospital. Even for the acutely disturbed, overnight hospital stays are becoming less common. For example, some patients spend their days in the hospital, but go home at night. Others attend therapy sessions during the evening. A major advantage of partial hospitalization is that patients can go home and practice what they've been learning. Gradually, the amount of time patients spend at the hospital is reduced. Eventually, most people return to normal life. Overall, partial hospitalization is comparable to full hospitalization in its effectiveness (Sledge et al., 1996).

DEINSTITUTIONALIZATION   The population in large mental hospitals has dropped by two thirds in the last 30 years. This is mostly the result of a trend toward **deinstitutionalization,** or reduced use of full-time commitment to mental institutions.

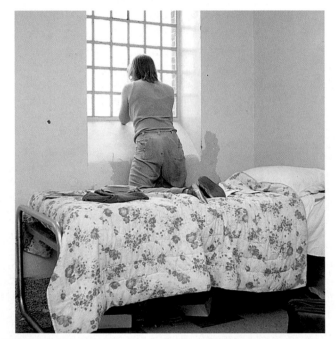

Depending on the quality of the institution, hospitalization may be a refuge or a brutalizing experience. Many state "asylums" or mental hospitals are antiquated and in need of drastic improvement.

Limiting hospitalization makes it easier for patients to successfully return to their communities. Long-term "institutionalization," in contrast, tends to keep patients dependent and isolated. Too often, this perpetuates their emotional disturbances (Chamberlin & Rogers, 1990).

How successful has deinstitutionalization been?   In truth, its success has been limited. Some states reduced mental hospital populations as a way to save money. The upsetting result is that many chronic patients were discharged to a lonely existence in hostile communities without adequate care. Many former patients have joined the ranks of the homeless. Others are repeatedly jailed for minor crimes. All too often, patients who move from hospitalization to unemployment, homelessness, and social isolation just end up rehospitalized or in jail (Goldman, 1998).

Large mental hospitals may no longer be warehouses for society's unwanted, but many former patients are no better off in bleak nursing homes, single-room hotels, board-and-care homes, jails, or shelters (Isaac & Armat, 1990). Ironically, high-quality care is available in most communities. A simple lack of funding prevents people from getting the help they need (Torrey, 1996).

It would help greatly if better rehabilitation programs were offered after hospital treatment (Anthony, Cohen, & Kennard, 1990). One such approach is the use of *half-way houses,* which can ease a patient's return to the community. **Half-way houses** are short-term group living facilities for individuals making the transition from an institution (mental hospital, prison, and so forth) to independent living. Typically, they offer supervision and support, without being as restrictive and medically slanted as hospitals. They also keep people near their families. Most important, half-way houses can reduce a person's chances of being readmitted to a hospital (Coursey, Ward-Alexander, & Katz, 1990).

PROSPECT   Major mental disorders that have organic causes usually cannot be "cured," but their symptoms may be controlled with drugs and other techniques. With psychoses, the outlook is still rather negative, but many people do recover (❖Fig. 17.14). It is wrong to fear "former mental patients" or to exclude them from work, friendships, and other social situations. A psychotic episode does not inevitably lead to lifelong dysfunction. Too often, however, it leads to unnecessary rejection based on groundless fears (Monahan, 1992).

A well-run half-way house can be a humane and cost-effective way to ease former mental patients back into the community (Coursey, Ward-Alexander, & Katz, 1990).

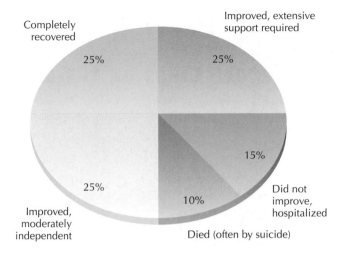

Schizophrenic patients 10 years after diagnosis

❖ **FIGURE 17.14** *At least one schizophrenic patient in four had completely recovered 10 years after being diagnosed. Three out of four had improved. New treatments for schizophrenia and other major mental disorders may improve these odds. (Source:* FDA Consumer, *1993.)*

A Final Note—You're Okay, Really!

It is your author's hope that you will not fall prey to the psychological equivalent of "medical student's disease" after reading this chapter. Medical students, it seems, have a predictable tendency to notice in themselves the symptoms of each dreaded disease they study. As a psychology student, you may have noticed what seem to be abnormal tendencies in your own behavior. If so, don't panic. In the majority of instances, this shows only that pathological behavior is an *exaggeration* of normal defenses and reactions, not that your behavior is abnormal.

A LOOK AHEAD   By the time you finish reading this page, someone in the United States or Canada will have attempted suicide. Suicide is a disturbing and widely misunderstood problem. What can be done about it? This chapter's Psychology in Action section will provide some answers. After that, in A Step Beyond, we will address the question, Who is "crazy" and what should be done about it?

K N O W L E D G E   B U I L D E R
SCHIZOPHRENIA, MOOD DISORDERS, AND HOSPITALIZATION

RELATE

As a psychologist, you are seeing a patient who has the following symptoms: hallucinations, waxy flexibility, incoherence, and delusions of persecution. What type of schizophrenia does the patient have?

You have been asked to explain the causes of schizophrenia to the parents of a schizophrenic teenager. What would you tell them?

On a piece of paper, write "Bipolar Disorders" and "Depressive Disorders." How much of ◆Table 17.8 can you fill in under these headings? Keep reviewing until you can recreate the table (in your own words).

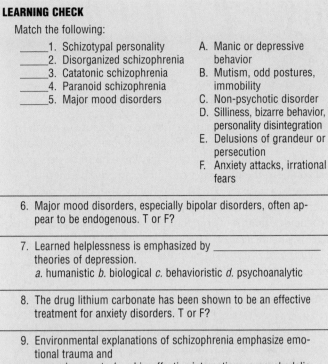

Partial hospitalization *An approach in which patients receive treatment at a hospital during the day but return home at night.*
Deinstitutionalization *Reduced use of full-time commitment to mental institutions to treat mental disorders.*
Half-way house *A community-based facility for individuals making the transition from an institution (mental hospital, prison, and so forth) to independent living.*

SUICIDE—LIVES ON THE BRINK

"Suicide: A permanent solution to a temporary problem."

Suicide ranks as the seventh cause of death in North America. Roughly 1 person out of 100 attempts suicide during his or her life. We tend to be very concerned about the high rates of murder in North America. However, for every 2 people who die by homicide, 3 die as a result of suicide. Sooner or later, you are likely to be affected by the suicide attempt of someone you know. Check your knowledge of suicide against the following information.

What factors affect suicide rates? Suicide rates vary greatly, but some general patterns do emerge.

SEASON Contrary to popular belief, suicide rates are lower than average between Thanksgiving and Christmas (Phillips & Wills, 1987). On the other hand, more suicides take place at New Year's than on any other day. A "Monday effect" also exists, with higher suicide rates occurring on the first day of the week (McCleary et al., 1991).

SEX Men have the questionable honor of being better at suicide than women. Three times as many men as women *complete* suicide, but women make more attempts. Male suicide attempts are more lethal because men typically use a gun or an equally fatal method (Garland & Zigler, 1993). Women most often attempt a drug overdose, so there's more chance of help arriving before death occurs. Sadly, women are beginning to use more deadly methods than in the past (Rogers, 1990). This, combined with a higher rate of attempts, may soon place women and men at equal risk of death by suicide.

AGE Age is also a factor in suicide. Suicide rates gradually rise during adolescence. They then sharply increase during young adulthood (ages 20 to 24). From then until age 84, the rate continues to gradually rise with advancing age. As a result, more than half of all suicide victims are over 45 years old. White men 65 years and older are particularly at risk. However, there has been a steady increase in the suicide rates for adolescents and young adults (Diekstra & Garnefski, 1995). In the United States, about 19 teenagers a day (more than 7,000 a year) commit suicide. This is triple the rate reported 20 years ago (Garland & Zigler, 1993). (See ❖Figure 17.15.)

Part of the increase in youth suicide comes from the ranks of college students, where suicide is the leading cause of death. Contrary to popular belief, the most dangerous time for student suicide is the first 6 weeks of a semester, not during final exams.

School is a factor in some suicides, but only in the sense that suicidal students were not living up to their own extremely high standards. Many were good students. Other important factors in student suicide are chronic health problems (real or imagined)

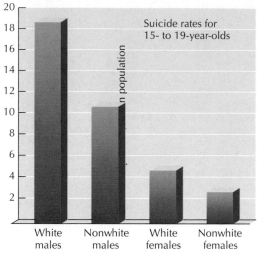

❖ **FIGURE 17.15** *Adolescent suicide rates vary for different racial and ethnic groups. Higher rates occur among whites than among non-whites. White male adolescents run the highest risk of suicide. Considering gender alone, it is apparent that more male than female adolescents commit suicide. This is the same as the pattern observed for adults.*

and interpersonal difficulties (some suicides are rejected lovers, but others are simply withdrawn and friendless people).

INCOME Some professions, such as medicine and psychiatry, have higher than average suicide rates. Overall, however, suicide is quite democratic. It is equally a problem of the rich and the poor.

MARITAL STATUS Marriage (when successful) may be the best natural guard against suicidal impulses. The highest suicide rates are found among the divorced, the next-highest rates occur among the widowed, lower rates are recorded for single persons, and married individuals have the lowest rates of all.

Immediate Causes of Suicide

Why do people try to kill themselves? The best explanation for suicide may simply come from a look at the conditions that precede it. The following are all major *risk factors* for suicide (Gould et al., 1998; Hall, Platt, & Hall, 1999):

- Drug or alcohol abuse
- A prior suicide attempt
- Depression or other mood disorder
- Feelings of hopelessness, worthlessness
- Antisocial, impulsive, or aggressive behavior
- Severe anxiety, panic attacks
- Family history of suicidal behavior
- Shame, humiliation, failure, or rejection
- Availability of a firearm

As you can see, usually there is a history of interpersonal troubles with family, in-laws, or a lover or spouse. Often there may be drinking or drug abuse problems, sexual adjustment problems, or job difficulties. Depression is a factor in 70 percent of all suicides (Lecomte & Fornes, 1998).

Factors such as these lead to a preoccupation with death as the "answer" to the person's suffering. There is usually a break in communication with others, which causes the person to feel isolated and misunderstood. Self-image becomes very negative. The person feels worthless and helpless and wants to die. Severe feelings of *hopelessness* are a warning that the risk of suicide is very high (Beck et al., 1990; Boergers, Spirito, & Donaldson, 1998).

A long history of such conditions is not always necessary to produce a desire for suicide. Anyone may temporarily reach a state of depression severe enough to attempt suicide. Most dangerous for the average person are times of divorce, separation, rejection, failure, and bereavement. Each situation can seem intolerable and motivate an intense desire to die, to escape, or to obtain relief (Boergers, Spirito, & Donaldson, 1998).

The causes of increased adolescent suicide remain unclear. As with adults, there is often a backdrop of problems with drugs, depression, school, peers, family, divorced parents, or the breakup of a romance. To make matters worse, most adolescents who attempt suicide are socially isolated and poor at solving problems in their personal relationships (Cole et al., 1992; Sadowski & Kelley, 1993).

Many cases of adolescent suicide result from *perfectionism* and unrealistic expectations. For example, parents may create feelings of despair by pressuring their children to meet impossibly high standards. Even without parental pressure, teenagers may expect the impossible of themselves in school, sports, or romance. Extremely high expectations and an unusual degree of sensitivity to hurt and disappointment can bring self-esteem to rock bottom over even the smallest "failure" (Cole et al., 1992; Mack, 1986). Again, the outcome is feelings of helplessness, hopelessness, and a desire to escape (Boergers, Spirito, & Donaldson, 1998).

Preventing Suicide

Is it true that people who talk about or threaten suicide are rarely the ones who try it? No, this is a major fallacy. Of every 10 potential suicides, 8 give warning beforehand. A person who threatens suicide should be taken seriously. (See ❖ Figure 17.16.) A suicidal person may say nothing more than "I feel sometimes like I'd be better off dead." Warnings may also come indirectly. If a friend gives you a favorite ring and says, "Here, I won't be needing this anymore," or comments, "I guess I won't get my watch fixed—it doesn't matter anyway," it may be a plea for help. The warning signs listed in ◆ Table 17.9—especially if observed in combination—can signal an impending suicide attempt (Leenaars, 1995; Slaby, Garfinkel, & Garfinkel, 1994).

Is it true that suicide can't be prevented, that the person will find a way to do it anyway? No. Suicide attempts usually come when a person is alone, depressed, and unable to view matters

❖ **FIGURE 17.16** *Suicidal behavior usually progresses from suicidal thoughts, to threats, to attempts. A person is unlikely to make an attempt without first making threats. Thus, suicide threats should be taken seriously (Garland & Zigler, 1993).*

◆ **TABLE 17.9** Warning Signs of Potential Suicide

Withdrawal from contact with others
Sudden swings in mood
Recent occurrence of life crisis or emotional shock
Personality change
Gift giving of prized possessions
Depression and/or hopelessness
Aggression and/or risk taking
Single-car accident
Preoccupation with death
Drug use
Death imagery in art
Direct threats to commit suicide

objectively. You *should* intervene if someone seems to be threatening suicide.

It is estimated that about two thirds of all suicide attempts fall in the "to be" category. That is, they are made by people who do not really want to die. Almost a third more are characterized by a "to be or not to be" attitude. These people are *ambivalent* or undecided about dying.

Only 3 to 5 percent of suicide cases involve people who really want to die. Most people, therefore, are relieved when someone comes to their aid. Remember that suicide is almost always a cry for help and that you *can* help. As suicide expert Edwin Shneidman (1987a) puts it, "Suicidal behavior is often a form of communication, a cry for help born out of pain, with clues and messages of suffering and anguish and pleas for response."

How to Help

What is the best thing to do if someone hints they are thinking about suicide? It helps to know some of the common characteristics of suicidal thoughts and feelings. Edwin Shneidman (1987b) has identified several.

1. **Escape.** Everyone at times feels like running away from an upsetting situation. Running away from home, quitting school, abandoning a marriage—these are all departures. Suicide, of course, is the ultimate escape. It helps when suicidal people see that the natural wish for escape doesn't have to be expressed by ending it all.
2. **Unbearable psychological pain.** Emotional pain is what the suicidal person is seeking to escape. A goal of anyone hoping to prevent suicide should be to reduce the pain in any way possible. Ask the person, "Where does it hurt?"
3. **Frustrated psychological needs.** Often, suicide can be prevented if a distraught person's frustrated needs can be

identified and eased. Is the person deeply frustrated in his or her search for love, achievement, trust, security, or friendship?

4. **Constriction of options.** The suicidal person feels helpless and decides that death is the *only* solution. The person has narrowed all his or her options solely to death. The rescuer's goal, then, is to help broaden the person's perspective. Even when all the choices are unpleasant, suicidal people can usually be made to see that their *least unpleasant option* is better than death.

Knowing these patterns will give you some guidance in talking to a suicidal person. In addition, your most important task may be to establish *rapport* with the person. You should offer support, acceptance, and legitimate caring.

Remember that a suicidal person feels misunderstood. Try to accept and understand the feelings the person is expressing. Acceptance should also extend to the idea of suicide itself. It is completely acceptable to ask, "Are you thinking of suicide?"

Establishing communication with suicidal people may be enough to carry them through a difficult time. You may also find it helpful to get day-by-day commitments from them to meet for lunch, share a ride, and the like. Let the person know you *expect* her or him to be there. Such commitments, even though small, can be enough to tip the scales when a person is alone and thinking about suicide.

Don't end your efforts too soon. A dangerous time for suicide is when a person suddenly seems to get better after a severe depression. This often means the person has finally decided to end it all. The improvement in mood is deceptive because it comes from an anticipation that suffering is about to end.

CRISIS INTERVENTION   Most cities have mental health crisis intervention teams or centers for suicide prevention. Both have staff members trained to talk with suicidal people over the phone. Give a person who seems to be suicidal the number of one of these services. Urge the person to call you or the other number if she or he becomes frightened or impulsive. Or better yet, help the person make an appointment to get psychological treatment (Garland & Zigler, 1993).

The preceding applies mainly to people who are having mild suicidal thoughts. If a person actually threatens suicide, you must act more quickly. Ask how the person plans to carry out the suicide. A person who has a *concrete, workable plan,* and the means to carry it out, should be asked to accompany you to the emergency ward of a hospital.

If a person seems on the verge of attempting suicide, don't worry about overreacting. Call the police, crisis intervention, or a rescue unit. Needless to say, you should call immediately if a person is in the act of attempting suicide or if a drug has already been taken. The majority of suicide attempts come at temporary low points in a person's life and may never be repeated. Get involved—you may save a life!

KNOWLEDGE BUILDER

SUICIDE AND SUICIDE PREVENTION

RELATE

You're working a suicide hotline, and you take a call from a very distressed young man. What risk factors will you look for as he tells you about his anguish?

What are the common characteristics of suicidal thoughts and feelings identified by Edwin Shneidman? If a friend of yours were to express any of these thoughts or feelings, how would you respond?

LEARNING CHECK

1. More women than men use guns in their suicide attempts. T or F?

2. Although the overall suicide rate has remained about the same, there has been a decrease in adolescent suicides. T or F?

3. Suicide is equally a problem of the rich and the poor. T or F?

4. The highest suicide rates are found among the divorced. T or F?

5. The majority (two thirds) of suicide attempts fall in the "to be" category. T or F?

CRITICAL THINKING

6. If you follow popular music, see if you can answer this question: What two major risk factors contributed to the 1994 suicide of Kurt Cobain, lead singer for the rock group Nirvana?

Answers:

1. F 2. F 3. T 4. T 5. T 6. Drug or alcohol abuse and availability of a firearm.

Focus: What should we, as a society, do about people whose behavior is seriously disturbed or disturbing?

Mark David Chapman claimed that devils forced him to kill former Beatle John Lennon. In court, his lawyer asserted that Chapman was "not guilty by reason of insanity." However, at mid-trial Chapman decided to plead guilty to second-degree murder. His reason? He said that God had visited him in his cell and told him to confess.

Chapman's case was one of thousands each year that mingle law, psychiatry, psychology, and public opinion. For more than 150 years, the insanity defense has bedeviled the courts and raised difficult legal, moral, and psychological questions.

What exactly is the insanity defense? The **insanity defense** is based on claims that a person was incapable of knowing right from wrong while committing a crime.

Insanity

The insanity defense began with the **M'Naghten rule,** a standard for judging legal responsibility in English common law. In 1843, the British House of Lords ruled on the case of Daniel M'Naghten, a "madman" who attempted to kill a member of Parliament, but murdered another man instead. The court held that defendants like M'Naughten must understand the wrongfulness of their actions to be held responsible for them. People suffering from "mental disease or other defects" that prevent them from knowing right from wrong are "insane." In the United States, the taking of life by an insane person is not murder.

Defendants may also claim they knew their deed was wrong, but they had an **irresistible impulse** (uncontrollable urge) to act. An example is the person who finds his or her lover in a stranger's arms and kills in a jealous rage. **Diminished capacity** is a related defense. In this case, people claim a temporary loss of ability to control their actions or to know right from wrong. A person who commits a crime under the influence of drugs might make this plea.

THE TWINKIE DEFENSE   The problems posed by the insanity defense are vividly shown by three legal cases. In Oakland, California, a jury declared Darlin June Cromer sane in the racial killing of a 5-year-old boy. This was the verdict, despite the fact that one psychiatrist testified that Cromer was "the most psychotic person" he'd ever seen. Cromer was sentenced to life in prison.

On the opposite side of the bay, Dan White admitted he killed San Francisco Mayor George Moscone and Supervisor Harvey Milk. However, White's lawyer convinced the jury that White acted with diminished capacity. The lawyer claimed, among other things, that White was deranged from eating too much junk food—an argument that became known as the "Twinkie Defense." (For those unschooled in junk food, a Twinkie is a small sponge cake with a sugary cream filling.)

White planned the murders beforehand and carefully avoided security guards to reach his victims. This certainly sounds like premeditated murder, but White received only a 7-year jail sentence. He was paroled after just 3 years in prison. The verdict so outraged many citizens that a law in California now bans claims of "diminished capacity." In yet another case, "Vampire Killer" Richard Chase was convicted of killing six people and drinking the blood of some of his victims. Chase was declared sane.

These cases point to the inconsistencies of a system that allows people who appear sane to be judged insane, and apparently insane people to be judged sane.

Expert Testimony

How is sanity determined? The most sensational trials have a typical pattern: Defense psychiatrists or psychologists testify that the defendant was insane at the time of the crime. Prosecution psychiatrists or psychologists testify that the defendant was sane. After these expert witnesses contradict one another, it's up to the jury to decide who is right.

More often, this "battle of the experts" never takes place. In almost all cases, prosecutors, defense attorneys, medical experts, psychologists, and judges agree *before* trial that the defendant is mentally ill. Thus, if a person really is psychotic, experts usually agree fairly readily (Janofsky et al., 1996).

OPINION, PLEASE   The preceding discussion raises several interesting questions.

1. The states of Montana, Idaho, and Utah have banned the insanity plea, but in most states it remains intact. Several other states now allow only a "guilty, but insane" plea. In your opinion, should questions of sanity be considered in criminal trials? Should the insanity defense be allowed?

    Before you answer, you should know that pleas of insanity are actually relatively rare, used in only about 1 out of every 100 court cases. In only about 1 out of 500 of these cases does the insanity defense succeed. Nationally, this

---

Insanity defense *Legal plea that says a person who was incapable of knowing right from wrong at the time of a crime is not guilty.*
M'Naghten rule *A rule in English common law for judging sanity and legal responsibility.*
Irresistible impulse *An uncontrollable impulse to act.*
Diminished capacity *Impaired mental competence to control actions or know right from wrong.*

amounts to about 150 cases a year in the United States (Silver et al., 1994).

More important, a verdict of innocence by reason of insanity does not set a person free. In most states, it requires automatic commitment to a mental hospital. Thereafter, the law places the burden of proof on patients. To be released, they must show they are no longer a danger to themselves or others. In most cases, people declared "insane" are hospitalized longer than they would have been imprisoned for a criminal conviction. The average hospital stay is about 3 years (Silver et al., 1994). Nevertheless, in some instances, the public may still rightly ask if justice has been served.

2. Should the courts accept pleas of diminished capacity? Before you answer this question, think about the "guilt" of a severely retarded person or someone with a brain tumor who commits a crime.

3. In your opinion, who should decide if a person should be committed? Should it be a judge? A jury? A psychiatrist? A psychologist? Who should decide when an "insane" person can be released? Should a person have the right to refuse treatment? What if the person committed a crime?

Before you answer, it may be useful to know that psychiatric predictions of violent behavior are largely inaccurate. From 60 to 90 percent of the time, experts are *wrong* in forecasting violence. At present, there is no way to accurately predict which individuals are likely to be dangerous to themselves or to others (Teplin, Abram, & McClelland, 1994).

As you can see, there are no easy answers to the preceding questions. Nevertheless, when the issues are "madness," personal freedom, criminal responsibility, and justice, everyone has an opinion. What's yours?

The Medical Model and Psychological Disorders

Medicine has had an even greater impact on how we think about human problems than the law has. The **medical model** treats such problems as "diseases" with "symptoms" that can be "cured." Generally, this approach has served well to advance our knowledge of mental disorders. However, it also has limitations. The best-known critic of the psychiatric concept of "mental illness" is psychiatrist Thomas Szasz (pronounced *saz*). Szasz asserts that mental illness is a myth. Traditional medical concepts of disease, he believes, have been wrongly applied to emotional and psychological problems (Szasz, 1966, 1983, 1987).

In Szasz's opinion, thinking in terms of "mental illness" is a poor way to deal with unusual or disturbing behavior. If "mental patients" starve themselves, attack members of their families, commit arson or theft, or even kill prominent persons, what does psychiatry do? It pardons them (says they are not responsible for their actions) and imprisons them (commits them to a mental hospital for "treatment"). Or it says they are sane, responsible, and guilty of a crime. In this case, they are put in jail. Thus, Szasz believes that labels such as *psychotic* are used mainly to transform people from being responsible for their actions to being non-responsible "patients" who need pity and therapy.

According to Szasz, the concept of mental illness is often used to deal with people whose behavior creates a *social disturbance* or violates social rules. If a person acts in a way that "offends" society and a law exists against such acts, the person may be jailed. If no law exists, the person may be "treated." In this sense, the distinction between madness and badness, or mental illness and criminality, is a *moral judgment,* not a medical reality. Involuntary commitment to mental hospitals, Szasz says, is "punishment without trial, imprisonment without limit, and stigmatization without hope of redress."

In light of such thinking, Szasz and a number of other experts prefer to view emotional disturbances as "problems in living." This view makes the goal of therapy "change" rather than "cure," and it transforms "patients" into "clients."

Szasz does not assert that bizarre behavior is normal. His position is merely that it cannot be explained or sensibly treated by using a strict medical model. Szasz's critics reply that advances in neuroscience increasingly call his ideas into question. Certainly, a brain damaged by disease, accident, or drugs can lead to illness, including mental or emotional illness. Szasz's reply is that only a small percentage of all mental problems involve clearly identified brain abnormalities.

Even if Szasz's views are overstated, it is readily apparent that biological factors are only part of the explanation for disordered behavior. Most mental problems also have psychological, emotional, and social origins (Widiger & Sankis, 2000).

Point and Counterpoint

All societies have classified some of their members into categories analogous to our term "mentally ill." The social problems created by "crazy" behavior will not vanish by changing the words used to describe it. However, the points that Szasz and others have made do raise serious questions about civil rights and involuntary commitment. At its best, the medical model of mental illness offers hope of recovery to patients and their families. At its worst, it can strip people of their humanity, autonomy, and self-respect (Hall, 1996). Fortunately, a growing number of psychiatrists recognize that people with mental disorders should be treated with respect and compassion (Gorman, 1996).

The risk of running roughshod over the civil rights of the mentally ill "for the good of the community" is still a problem. Recently, several states have made it easier to force the mentally ill into hospitals (Shogren, 1994). This is primarily a reaction to the increased number of mentally ill people living on the streets. Forced treatment might appear to be humane in some instances. But as a final bit of food for thought, consider the following incident, recorded by a reporter visiting a large state mental hospital.

> A thin man, old and dry, stopped the guide and said, "When the hell you gonna get me a suit and let me outa here? How about it? . . ." The guide said something indefinite and the man walked away, nodding. This was the section for killers, I had been told, so I asked what the thin man had done. "He painted a horse." "He what?" "He painted a horse." "What's wrong with that?" "It was in a field. A live horse. He was drunk and somebody bet him he couldn't make a horse look like

a zebra, I think, so he painted it and they put him here. For being drunk probably." "How long has he been in?" "Thirty-seven years. By the time they got around to letting him out he really was crazy. . . . For his own good we just can't let him go out of here."*

On what basis should we as a society involuntarily commit people? How often would an end to involuntary commitment mean freedom to wander alone—lost, neglected, and without hope? Is it better to force mentally ill people off the streets and into hospitals? What do you think is the right way to deal with "crazy" behavior?

CONCLUSION: The law, medicine, and psychology must simultaneously protect people from being wrongly deprived of personal freedom while also providing ways to treat people who desperately need help. This creates conflicts that are difficult to solve. Continuing debate about the role of involuntary commitment in a free society is warranted.

*Bruce Jackson, "Our prisons are criminal," *New York Times Magazine*, September 22, 1973, pp. 54–57.

INSANITY, THE MEDICAL MODEL, AND INVOLUNTARY COMMITMENT

RELATE

Under what conditions would you regard a close friend as being not legally responsible for committing a crime? Do you think that insanity should be allowed as a defense in court cases?

Under what conditions do you think a person should be involuntarily committed? Would it be possible for a person to be involuntarily committed by accident or by a conspiracy among family members?

LEARNING CHECK

1. Daniel M'Naghten was a lawyer who defended a member of the British House of Lords who was accused of murder, but who pleaded insanity. T or F?

2. In a court of law, the insanity defense is based on the premise that people who are mentally defective cannot be held fully responsible for their actions. T or F?

3. A person who commits a crime while suffering from a mind-altering reaction to a prescription medicine might have some success in claiming innocence due to diminished capacity. T or F?

4. In every state of the United States, insanity can be used as a legal defense as long as expert witnesses are willing to testify that the defendant was insane at the time of the crime. T or F?

5. Psychiatric predictions of future violence are correct only in about one tenth to one third of all forecasts. T or F?

6. Szasz has argued that it is inappropriate to apply a medical or disease model to what he terms "problems in living." T or F?

7. Psychosis is the only disorder that Szasz recognizes as a legitimate mental disease. T or F?

CRITICAL THINKING

8. The new trend that favors forcing the chronically mentally ill off the streets and into hospitals is a reversal of an earlier trend. Can you name the former pattern?

Answers:

1. F 2. T 3. T 4. F 5. T 6. T 7. F 8. Deinstitutionalization.

Medical model *An approach that treats psychological disorders as "diseases" with "symptoms" that can be "cured."*

CHAPTER IN REVIEW

How is normality defined, and what are the major psychological disorders?

- Psychopathology refers to maladaptive behavior and to the scientific study of mental, emotional, and behavioral disorders.
- Definitions of normality usually take into account the following: subjective discomfort, statistical abnormality, social nonconformity, and the cultural or situational context of behavior.
- Two key elements in judgments of disorder are that a person's behavior must be maladaptive and it must involve a loss of control.
- Major mental disorders include psychotic disorders, dementia, substance related disorders, mood disorders, anxiety disorders, somatoform disorders, dissociative disorders, personality disorders, and sexual or gender identity disorders.
- Traditionally, the term *neurosis* has been used to describe milder, anxiety-related disorders. However, the term is fading from use.
- Insanity is a legal term defining whether a person may be held responsible for his or her actions. Sanity is determined in court on the basis of testimony by expert witnesses.

What is a personality disorder?

- Personality disorders are deeply ingrained maladaptive personality patterns.
- Sociopathy is a common personality disorder. Antisocial people seem to lack a conscience. They are emotionally unresponsive, manipulative, shallow, and dishonest.

What problems result when a person suffers high levels of anxiety?

- Anxiety disorders, dissociative disorders, and somatoform disorders are characterized by high levels of anxiety, rigid defense mechanisms, and self-defeating behavior patterns.
- The term *nervous breakdown* has no formal meaning. However, "emotional breakdowns" do correspond somewhat to adjustment disorders.
- Anxiety disorders include generalized anxiety disorder, panic disorder with or without agoraphobia, agoraphobia (without panic), specific phobias, social phobia, obsessive-compulsive disorders, post-traumatic stress disorder, and acute stress disorder.
- Dissociative disorders may take the form of dissociative amnesia, dissociative fugue, or dissociative identity disorder.
- Somatoform disorders center on physical complaints that mimic disease or disability. Four examples of somatoform disorders are hypochondriasis, somatization disorder, somatoform pain disorder, and conversion disorders.

How do psychologists explain anxiety-based disorders?

- The psychodynamic approach emphasizes unconscious conflicts as the cause of disabling anxiety.
- The humanistic approach emphasizes the effects of a faulty self-image.
- The behaviorists emphasize the effects of previous learning, particularly avoidance learning.

- Cognitive theories of anxiety focus on distorted thinking, judgment, and attention.

What are the general characteristics of psychosis?

- Psychosis is a break in contact with reality that is marked by delusions, hallucinations, sensory changes, disturbed emotions, disturbed communication, and, in some cases, personality disintegration.
- An organic psychosis is based on known injuries or diseases of the brain. Other problems of unknown origin are termed functional psychoses.
- Some common causes of organic psychosis are untreated syphilis, poisoning, drug abuse, and dementia (especially Alzheimer's disease).

How do delusional disorders differ from other forms of psychosis?

- A diagnosis of delusional disorder is almost totally based on the presence of delusions of grandeur, persecution, infidelity, romantic attraction, or physical disease.
- The most common delusional disorder is paranoid psychosis. Paranoids may be violent if they believe they are threatened.

What forms does schizophrenia take? What causes it?

- Schizophrenia involves a split between thought and emotion, delusions, hallucinations, and communication difficulties.
- Disorganized schizophrenia is marked by extreme personality disintegration and silly, bizarre, or obscene behavior. Social impairment is usually extreme.
- Catatonic schizophrenia is associated with stupor, mutism, and odd postures. Sometimes violent and agitated behavior also occurs.
- In paranoid schizophrenia (the most common type), outlandish delusions of grandeur and persecution are coupled with psychotic symptoms and personality breakdown.
- Undifferentiated schizophrenia is the term used to indicate a lack of clear-cut patterns of disturbance.
- Current explanations of schizophrenia emphasize a combination of early trauma, environmental stress, inherited susceptibility, and abnormalities in the brain.
- Environmental factors that increase the risk of schizophrenia include viral infection or malnutrition during the mother's pregnancy, birth complications, early psychological trauma, and a disturbed family environment.
- Heredity is a major factor in schizophrenia.
- Recent biochemical studies have focused on the brain transmitter dopamine and its receptor sites.
- The dominant explanation of schizophrenia, and other problems as well, is the stress-vulnerability model.

What are mood disorders? What causes depression?

- Mood disorders primarily involve disturbances of mood or emotion, producing manic or depressive states.
- Long-lasting, though relatively moderate, depression is called a dysthymic disorder. Chronic, though moderate, swings in mood between depression and elation are called a cyclothymic disorder. Reactive depressions are triggered by external events.

- Bipolar disorders combine mania and depression. In a bipolar I disorder, the person alternates between mania and depression. In a bipolar II disorder, the person is mostly depressed, but also has periods of mild mania.
- The problem known as major depressive disorder involves extreme sadness and despondency but no evidence of mania.
- A major mood disorder accompanied by psychotic symptoms is called an affective psychosis.
- Seasonal affective disorder (SAD), which occurs during the winter months, is another common form of depression. SAD is typically treated with phototherapy.
- Biological, psychoanalytic, cognitive, and behavioral theories of depression have been proposed. Heredity is clearly a factor in susceptibility to mood disorders. Research on the causes and treatment of depression continues.

Why do people commit suicide? Can suicide be prevented?

- Suicide is statistically related to such factors as age, sex, and marital status.
- In individual cases, the potential for suicide is best identified by a desire to escape, unbearable psychological pain, frustrated psychological needs, and a constriction of options.
- Suicide can often be prevented by the efforts of family, friends, and mental health professionals.

What does it mean to be "crazy"? What should be done about it?

- In Western law, the insanity defense evolved from the M'Naghten rule.
- Insanity is closely related to claims of diminished capacity or claims that a person had an irresistible impulse.
- Inconsistencies in the application of the insanity defense have fueled debate about its validity.
- Thomas Szasz has raised questions about the nature of abnormal behavior and its relationship to personal responsibility and civil rights.
- Public policies concerning treatment of the chronically mentally ill continue to evolve as authorities try to strike a balance between providing help and taking away personal freedoms.

PSYCHOLOGY ON THE NET

- **A Guide to Depressive and Manic Depressive Illness** A complete overview of mood disorders. http://www.ndmda.org/id.htm
- **Anxiety Disorders** Information and links to sites about anxiety disorders. http://www.adaa.org/consumerresources/links/
- **DSM-IV Questions and Answers** Answers to common questions about the DSM-IV. http://www.psych.org/clin_res/q_a.html
- **Internet Mental Health** Comprehensive page on mental health, with links to many other sites. http://www.mentalhealth.com/
- **National Alliance for the Mentally Ill** Home page of the group, with links. http://www.nami.org/
- **National Institute of Mental Health** Links to public information, news and events, and research activities. http://www.nimh.nih.gov/
- **Personality Disorders** Multiple links to information on personality disorders and their treatment. http://www.health-center.com/brain/personality/default.htm
- **Understanding Schizophrenia** An extensive look at schizophrenia. http://www.mhsource.com/schizophrenia/index.html
  - **InfoTrac® College Edition** For recent articles related to the Psychology in Action feature, use Key Words search for SUICIDE PREVENTION.

INTERACTIVE LEARNING

- *PsychNow!* 7c. Abnormality and Psychopathology, 7d. Nonpsychotic, Psychotic, and Affective Disorders.
- *Psyk.trek* 11a. Anxiety disorder. 11b. Mood disorder. 11c. Schizophrenic disorders.

COLD TERROR ON A WARM AFTERNOON

THE WARM ARIZONA SUN *was shining brightly. Outside my office window an assortment of small birds sang sweetly. I could hear them between Susan's frightened sobs.*

As a psychologist, I see many students with personal problems. Still, I was surprised to see Susan at my office door. Her excellent work in class and her healthy, casual appearance left me unprepared for her first words. "I feel like I'm losing my mind," she said. "Can I talk to you?"

In the next hour, Susan described her own personal hell. Her calm appearance hid a world of overwhelming fear, anxiety, and depression. At work, she was deathly afraid of talking to coworkers and customers. Her social phobia led to frequent absenteeism and embarrassing behavior. At each job she held, it was only a matter of time until she got fired.

At school, Susan felt "different" and was sure that other students could tell she was "weird." Several disastrous romances had left her terrified of men. Lately, she had been so depressed that she had thoughts of suicide. Often, she became terrified for no apparent reason. Each time, her heart pounded wildly, and she felt she was about to completely lose control.

Susan's visit to my office was an important turning point. Emotional conflicts had made her existence a nightmare. At a time when she was becoming her own worst enemy, Susan realized she needed help from another person. In Susan's case, that person was a talented psychologist to whom I referred her. By combining various forms of psychotherapy, the psychologist was able to help Susan come to grips with her emotions and restore her balance.

This chapter discusses methods used to alleviate problems like Susan's. First, we will describe therapies that emphasize the value of gaining insight into personal problems. Then, we will focus on behavior therapies and cognitive therapies, which are used to directly change troublesome actions and thoughts. Later, we will conclude with medical therapies, which employ psychiatric drugs and other physical treatments. The following "Gateways" will open the path to these interesting topics.

Gateways to Therapy

PSYCHOTHERAPY facilitates positive changes in personality, behavior, or adjustment.

BEFORE THE DEVELOPMENT OF MODERN THERAPIES, superstition dominated attempts to treat psychological problems.

FIVE MAJOR CATEGORIES OF PSYCHOTHERAPY are psychodynamic, insight, behavioral, cognitive, and group therapies.

PSYCHOTHERAPY is generally effective, although no single form of therapy is superior to others.

ALL MEDICAL TREATMENTS FOR PSYCHOLOGICAL DISORDERS have pros and cons. Overall, however, their effectiveness is improving.

SOME PERSONAL PROBLEMS can be successfully treated by using self-management techniques.

EVERYONE SHOULD KNOW how to obtain high-quality mental health care in his or her community.

TO BE EFFECTIVE, THERAPISTS must be aware of the special needs of clients from diverse cultural backgrounds.

PSYCHOTHERAPY—GETTING BETTER BY THE HOUR

> Humpty-Dumpty sat on a wall.
> Humpty-Dumpty had a great fall.
> All the King's horses and all the King's men,
> Couldn't put Humpty together again.

In our age of stress, conflict, and anxiety, who will put you together again, and how will they do it? Actually, the odds are that you will *not* experience an emotional problem like Susan's. But if you did, what help is available? In most cases, the answer is some form of *psychotherapy.*

Psychotherapy is any psychological technique used to facilitate positive changes in personality, behavior, or adjustment. Psychotherapy most often refers to verbal interaction between trained mental health professionals and their clients. Many therapists also use learning principles to directly alter troublesome behaviors.

Dimensions of Therapy

Psychotherapists have many approaches to choose from: psychoanalysis, desensitization, Gestalt therapy, logotherapy, client-centered therapy, reality therapy, and behavior therapy—to name but a few. With so many therapies in use, some confusion may exist about how they differ. To begin, it is helpful to recognize that psychotherapies vary widely in emphasis. For this reason, the best approach for a particular person or problem may also vary.

The terms listed here describe basic aspects of various therapies. Notice that more than one term may apply to a particular therapy. For example, it is possible to have a directive,

Psychotherapy *Any psychological technique used to facilitate positive changes in a person's personality, behavior, or adjustment.*

action-oriented group therapy or a nondirective, individual, insight-oriented therapy.

- **Individual therapy**: A therapy involving only one client and one therapist.
- **Group therapy**: A therapy session in which several clients participate at the same time.
- **Insight therapy**: Any psychotherapy whose goal is to lead clients to a deeper understanding of their thoughts, emotions, and behavior.
- **Action therapy**: Any therapy designed to bring about direct changes in troublesome thoughts, habits, feelings, or behavior, without seeking insight into their origins or meanings.
- **Directive therapy**: Any approach in which the therapist provides strong guidance.
- **Nondirective therapy**: A style of therapy in which clients assume responsibility for solving their own problems; the therapist assists but does not guide or give advice.
- **Time-limited therapy**: Any therapy begun with the expectation that it will last only a limited number of sessions.
- **Supportive therapy**: An approach in which the therapist's goal is to offer support, rather than to promote personal change. A person trying to get through an emotional crisis or one who wants to solve day-to-day problems may benefit from supportive therapy.

MYTHS Psychotherapy has been depicted as a complete personal transformation—a sort of "major overhaul" of the psyche. But this ignores the realities of solving human problems. Therapy is *not* equally effective for all problems. Chances of improvement are fairly good for phobias, low self-esteem, some sexual problems, and marital conflicts. More complex problems, however, can be difficult to solve. Also, contrary to what many people think, therapy usually does not bring about dramatic changes in behavior or an end to personal difficulties. For many people, the major benefit of therapy is that it provides comfort, support, and a way to make constructive changes (Hellerstein et al., 1998).

In short, it is often unrealistic to expect psychotherapy to undo a person's entire past history. Yet even when problems are severe, therapy may help a person gain a new perspective or learn behaviors to better cope with life. Psychotherapy can be hard work for both clients and therapists. But when it succeeds, there are few activities more worthwhile.

It is also worth noting that psychotherapy is not always undertaken to solve problems or end a crisis. Therapy can promote personal growth and enrichment for people who are already doing well (Buck, 1990). ◆Table 18.1 lists some of the elements of positive mental health that therapists seek to restore or promote (Bergin, 1991).

ORIGINS OF THERAPY—BORED SKULLS AND HYSTERIA ON THE COUCH

Early treatments for mental problems give ample reason for appreciating modern therapies. Archaeological findings dating

◆ **TABLE 18.1** Elements of Positive Mental Health

- Personal autonomy and independence
- A sense of identity
- Feelings of personal worth
- Skilled in interpersonal communication
- Sensitivity, nurturance, and trust
- Genuine and honest with self and others
- Self-control and personal responsibility
- Committed and loving in personal relationships
- Capacity to forgive others and oneself
- Personal values and a purpose in life
- Self-awareness and motivation for personal growth
- Adaptive coping strategies for managing stresses and crises
- Fulfillment and satisfaction in work
- Good habits of physical health

(Adapted from Bergin, 1991.)

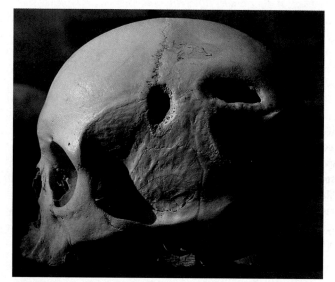

❖ **FIGURE 18.1** Primitive "treatment" for mental disorders sometimes took the form of boring a hole in the skull. This example shows signs of healing, which means the patient survived the treatment. Many didn't.

to the Stone Age suggest that most primitive approaches were marked by fear and superstitious belief in demons, witchcraft, and magic. One of the more dramatic "cures" practiced by primitive "therapists" was a process called *trepanning* (treh-PAN-ing; also sometimes spelled *trephining*). In modern usage, **trepanning** is any surgical procedure in which a hole is bored in the skull. In the hands of primitive therapists, it meant boring, chipping, or bashing holes into a patient's head. Presumably this was done to relieve pressure or release evil spirits (❖Fig. 18.1). Actually, trepanning may have simply been an excuse to kill people who were unusual, because many "patients" didn't survive the "treatment."

During the Middle Ages, treatments for mental illness in Europe focused on **demonology**, the study of demons and persons plagued by spirits. Medieval "therapists" commonly

(Top) Supernatural explanations attributed abnormal behavior to the work of the devil or "possession" by demons. A modern analysis of "demonic possession" suggests that some victims were suffering from dissociative disorders (van der Hart, Lierens, & Goodwin, 1996). *(Bottom)* Many other cases of "possession" in medieval Europe and "bewitchment" in colonial New England may be explained by the psychedelic effects of ergot fungus. Two ears of rye infested with the fungus (dark areas) are shown here.

(Top) Many early asylums were no more than prisons with inmates held in chains. *(Bottom)* One late-nineteenth-century "treatment" was based on swinging the patient in a harness—presumably to calm the patient's nerves.

blamed abnormal behavior on supernatural forces, such as possession by the devil, or on curses from witches and wizards. As a cure, they used **exorcism** to "cast out evil spirits." For the fortunate, exorcism was a religious ritual. More often, physical torture was used to make the body an inhospitable place for the devil to reside.

One reason for the rise of demonology may lie in **ergotism** (AIR-got-ism), a psychotic-like condition caused by ergot poisoning. In the Middle Ages, rye fields were often infested with ergot fungus. Ergot, we now know, is a natural source of LSD and other mind-altering chemicals. Eating tainted bread could have caused symptoms that were easily mistaken for possession, bewitchment, or madness. Pinching sensations, muscle twitches, facial spasms, delirium, and hallucinations are all signs of ergot poisoning (Kety, 1979; Matossian, 1982). Thus, many people "treated" with demonology may have been doubly victimized.

It wasn't until 1793 that the emotionally disturbed were regarded as "mentally ill" and given compassionate treatment. That

Trepanning *In modern usage, any surgical procedure in which a hole is bored in the skull; historically, the chipping or boring of holes in the skull to "treat" mental disturbance.*
Demonology *In medieval Europe, the study of demons and the treatment of persons "possessed" by demons.*
Exorcism *In medieval Europe, the practice of driving off an "evil spirit," especially from the body of a person who is "possessed."*
Ergotism *A pattern of psychotic-like symptoms that accompanies poisoning by ergot fungus.*

was the year French physician **Philippe Pinel** changed the Bicêtre Asylum in Paris from a squalid "madhouse" into a mental hospital by personally unchaining inmates. Although more than 200 years have passed since Pinel began humane treatment, the process of improving psychiatric care continues today.

When was psychotherapy developed? The first true psychotherapy was developed around the turn of the century by Sigmund Freud. As a physician in Vienna, Freud was intrigued by cases of **hysteria,** in which physical symptoms (such as paralysis or numbness) occur without known physical causes. As you may recall, such problems are now called somatoform disorders (see Chapter 17). Slowly, Freud became convinced that hysteria was caused by deeply hidden unconscious conflicts. Based on this insight, Freud developed a therapy called psychoanalysis. Because it is the "granddaddy" of more modern therapies, let us examine psychoanalysis in some detail.

PSYCHOANALYSIS—EXPEDITION INTO THE UNCONSCIOUS

Isn't psychoanalysis the therapy where the patient lies on a couch? Freud's patients usually reclined on a couch during therapy, while Freud sat out of sight taking notes and offering interpretations. This arrangement was supposed to encourage relaxation and a free flow of thoughts and images from the unconscious. However, it is the least important characteristic of psychoanalysis, and many modern analysts have abandoned it.

How did Freud treat emotional problems? Freud's theory stressed that "neurosis" and "hysteria" are caused by repressed memories, motives, and conflicts—particularly those stemming from instinctual drives for sex and aggression. Although they are hidden, these factors remain active in the personality. This forces the person to develop rigid ego-defense mechanisms. Such people then devote excessive amounts of time and energy to compulsive and self-defeating behavior. Thus, the main goal of

psychoanalysis is to resolve internal conflicts that lead to emotional suffering (Wolitzky, 1995).

Freud relied on four basic techniques to uncover the unconscious roots of neurosis (Freud, 1949). These are *free association, dream analysis, analysis of resistance,* and *analysis of transference.*

FREE ASSOCIATION   The process of **free association** involves saying whatever comes to mind. Patients must speak without concern for whether ideas are painful, embarrassing, or illogical. Thoughts are simply allowed to move freely from one association to the next. The purpose of free association is to lower defenses so that unconscious material can emerge (Wolitzky, 1995).

DREAM ANALYSIS   Freud believed that dreams provide a "royal road to the unconscious" because they freely express forbidden desires and unconscious feelings. Such feelings are found in the **latent content** (hidden, symbolic meaning) of dreams. A dream's **manifest content** (obvious, visible meaning) tends to disguise information from the unconscious.

Freud was very interested in unconscious messages revealed by **dream symbols** (images that have personal or emotional meanings). Let's say a young man reports a dream in which he pulls a pistol from his waistband and aims at a target while his wife watches. The pistol repeatedly fails to discharge, and the man's wife laughs at him. Freud might have seen this as an indication of repressed feelings of sexual impotence, with the gun serving as a disguised image of the penis.

BRIDGES

Some theorists dispute the psychodynamic claim that dreams have symbolic meaning.

See Chapter 8, page 246

ANALYSIS OF RESISTANCE   When free associating or describing dreams, patients may *resist* talking about or thinking about certain topics. Such **resistances** (blockages in the flow of ideas) are said to reveal particularly important unconscious conflicts. As analysts become aware of resistances, they bring them to the patient's awareness so the patient can deal with them realistically (Wolitzky, 1995).

Rather than being roadblocks in therapy, resistances can be challenges and guides (May, 1996).

Pioneering psychotherapist Sigmund Freud in his office.

ANALYSIS OF TRANSFERENCE **Transference** is the tendency to "transfer" feelings to a therapist that match those the patient had for important persons in his or her past. At times, the patient may act as if the analyst is a rejecting father, an unloving or overprotective mother, or a former lover. As the patient re-experiences repressed emotions, the therapist can help the patient recognize and understand them. Troubled persons often provoke anger, rejection, boredom, criticism, and other negative reactions from others. Effective therapists learn to avoid reacting as others do and playing the patient's habitual "games." This, too, contributes to therapeutic change (Strupp, 1989).

PSYCHOANALYSIS TODAY *What is the status of psychoanalysis today?* Traditional psychoanalysis called for three to five therapy sessions a week, often for many years. Today, most patients are seen only once or twice per week, but treatment may still go on for years (Friedman et al., 1998). Because of the huge amounts of time and money this requires, psychoanalysts have become relatively rare.

Many therapists have switched to doing **brief psychodynamic therapy,** which uses direct questioning to reveal unconscious conflicts (Book & Luborsky, 1998). Modern therapists also actively provoke emotional reactions that will lower defenses and provide insights (Davanloo, 1995). Interestingly, brief therapy seems to accelerate recovery. It is as if patients realize that they need to get to the heart of their problems quickly (Reynolds et al., 1996).

The development of newer, more streamlined dynamic therapies is in part due to questions about the effectiveness of traditional psychoanalysis. One critic, Hans J. Eysenck (1967, 1994), suggested that psychoanalysis simply takes so long that patients experience a **spontaneous remission** of symptoms (improvement due to the mere passage of time). How could we tell if a particular therapy or the passage of time is responsible for a person's improvement? Typically, some patients are randomly assigned for treatment, while others are placed on a waiting list. If members of this **waiting-list control group,** who receive no treatment, improve at the same rate as those in therapy, the therapy may be of little value.

How seriously should the possibility of spontaneous remission be taken? It is true that problems ranging from hyperactivity to anxiety improve with the passage of time. However, researchers have confirmed psychoanalysis does, in fact, produce improvement in a majority of patients (Doidge, 1997).

The real value of Eysenck's critique is that it encouraged psychologists to try new ideas and techniques. Researchers began to ask: "When psychoanalysis works, why does it work? What procedures are essential, and which are unnecessary?" Modern therapists have given surprisingly varied answers to these questions. Upcoming sections will acquaint you with some of the therapies currently in use.

KNOWLEDGE BUILDER
PSYCHOTHERAPY AND PSYCHOANALYSIS

RELATE

How has your understanding of psychotherapy changed? How many types of therapy can you name?

Make a list describing what you think it means to be mentally healthy. How well does your list match the items in ◆Table 18.1?

The use of trepanning, demonology, and exorcism all implied that the mentally ill are "cursed." To what extent are the mentally ill rejected and stigmatized today?

Try to free associate (aloud) for 10 minutes. How difficult was it? Did anything interesting surface?

Can you explain, in your own words, the role of dream analysis, resistances, and transference in psychoanalysis?

LEARNING CHECK

Match:

_____ 1. Directive therapies	A. Change behavior
_____ 2. Action therapies	B. Place responsibility on the client
_____ 3. Insight therapies	C. The client is guided strongly
_____ 4. Nondirective therapies	D. Seek understanding

5. Pinel is famous for his use of exorcism. T or F?

6. Freud developed trepanning. T or F?

7. In psychoanalysis, an emotional attachment to the therapist by the patient is called
a. free association b. manifest association c. resistance d. transference

CRITICAL THINKING

8. Waiting-list control groups help separate the effects of therapy from improvement related to the mere passage of time. What other type of control group might be needed to learn if therapy is truly beneficial?

Answers:

1. C 2. A 3. D 4. B 5. F 6. F 7. d 8. Placebo therapy is sometimes used to assess the benefits of real therapy. Placebo therapy superficially resembles the real thing but lacks key elements that are thought to be therapeutic.

Philippe Pinel *The French physician who initiated humane treatment of mental patients in 1793.*

Hysteria *Wild emotional excitability sometimes associated with the development of apparent physical disabilities (numbness, blindness, and the like) without known physical cause.*

Psychoanalysis *A Freudian therapy that emphasizes the use of free association, dream interpretation, resistances, and transference to uncover unconscious conflicts.*

Free association *In psychoanalysis, the technique of having a client say anything that comes to mind, regardless of how embarrassing or unimportant it may seem.*

Latent dream content *The hidden or symbolic meaning of a dream, as revealed by dream interpretation and analysis.*

Manifest dream content *The surface, "visible" content of a dream; dream images as they are remembered by the dreamer.*

Dream symbols *Images in dreams whose personal or emotional meanings differ from their literal meanings.*

Resistance *A blockage in the flow of free association; topics the client resists thinking or talking about.*

Transference *The tendency of patients to transfer feelings to a therapist that correspond to those the patient had for important persons in his or her past.*

Brief psychodynamic therapy *A modern therapy based on psychoanalytic theory but designed to produce insights more quickly.*

Spontaneous remission *The disappearance of a psychological disturbance without the aid of therapy.*

Waiting-list control group *People who receive no treatment as a test of the effectiveness of psychotherapy.*

HUMANISTIC THERAPIES—RESTORING HUMAN POTENTIAL

The goal of traditional psychoanalysis is adjustment. Freud claimed that his patients could expect only to change their "hysterical misery into common unhappiness"! Humanistic therapies are generally more optimistic. Most assume that it is possible for people to use their potentials fully and live rich, rewarding lives. Psychotherapy is seen as a way to give natural tendencies toward mental health a chance to emerge.

Client-Centered Therapy

What is client-centered therapy? How is it different from psychoanalysis? Psychoanalysts delve into the unconscious. Psychologist Carl Rogers (1902–1987) found it more beneficial to explore *conscious* thoughts and feelings. The psychoanalyst tends to take a position of authority, stating what dreams, thoughts, or memories "mean." In contrast, Rogers believed that what is right or valuable for the therapist may not be right or valuable for the client. Consequently, the client determines what will be discussed during each session. (Rogers preferred the term *client* to *patient* because "patient" implies a person is "sick" and needs to be "cured.") In summary, **client-centered therapy** (also called *person-centered therapy*) is nondirective and based on insights from conscious thoughts and feelings (Bohart, 1995).

If the client runs things, what does the therapist do? The therapist's job is to create an "atmosphere of growth." The therapist provides opportunities for change, but the client must actively seek to solve his or her problems. The therapist cannot "fix" the client (Bohart & Tallman, 1996).

HEALTH-PROMOTING CONDITIONS Rogers believed that effective therapists maintain four basic conditions. First, the therapist offers the client **unconditional positive regard** (unshakable personal acceptance). The therapist refuses to react with shock, dismay, or disapproval to anything the client says or feels. Total acceptance by the therapist is the first step to self-acceptance by the client.

Second, the therapist attempts to achieve genuine **empathy** by trying to see the world through the client's eyes and feeling some part of what the client is feeling.

As a third essential condition, the therapist strives to be **authentic** (genuine and honest). The therapist must not hide behind a professional role. Rogers believed that phony fronts destroy the growth atmosphere sought in client-centered therapy.

Fourth, the therapist does not make interpretations, propose solutions, or offer advice. Instead, the therapist **reflects** (rephrases, summarizes, or repeats) the client's thoughts and feelings. This allows the therapist to act as a psychological "mirror" so clients can see themselves more clearly. Rogers believed that a person armed with a realistic self-image and greater self-acceptance will gradually discover solutions to life's problems.

PERSONAL GROWTH Like other humanistic psychologists, Carl Rogers (1980) believed deeply that humans have a natural urge

Psychotherapist Carl Rogers, who originated client-centered therapy.

to seek health and self-growth. Rogers's belief is movingly expressed by the following words:

> I remember that in my boyhood the bin in which we stored our winter's supply of potatoes was in the basement, several feet below a small window. The conditions were unfavorable, but pale white sprouts . . . would grow two or three feet in length as they reached toward the light of the distant window. The sprouts were, in their bizarre, futile growth, a sort of desperate expression of the directional tendency I have been describing. . . . In dealing with clients whose lives have been terribly warped, in working with men and women on the back wards of state hospitals, I often think of those potato sprouts. . . . The clue to understanding their behavior is that they are striving, in the only ways that they perceive as available to them, to move toward growth, toward becoming. To healthy persons, the results may seem bizarre and futile but they are life's desperate attempt to become itself. This potent constructive tendency is an underlying basis of the person-centered approach.

Existential Therapy

According to the existentialists, "being in the world" (existence) creates deep conflicts. Each of us, they say, must deal with the realities of death. We must face the fact that we create our private world by making choices. We must overcome isolation on a vast and indifferent planet. Most of all, we must confront feelings of meaninglessness.

What do these concerns have to do with psychotherapy? **Existential therapy** focuses on the problems of existence, such as meaning, choice, and responsibility. Like client-centered therapy, it promotes self-knowledge and self-actualization. However, there are important differences. Client-centered therapy seeks to uncover a "true self" hidden behind a screen of defenses. In contrast, existential therapy emphasizes **free will,** the human ability to make choices. Accordingly, existential therapists believe you can *choose to become* the person you want to be.

Existential therapists try to give clients the *courage* to make rewarding and socially constructive choices. Typically, therapy focuses on **death, freedom, isolation,** and **meaninglessness,** the "ultimate concerns" of existence (Yalom, 1980). These universal human challenges include an awareness of one's mortality, the responsibility that comes with freedom to choose, being alone in one's private world, and the reality that meaning must be created in life.

What does the existential therapist do? The therapist helps clients discover self-imposed limitations in personal identity. To be successful, the client must fully accept the challenge of changing his or her life (Bugental & Sterling, 1995).

One example of existential therapy is Victor Frankl's **logotherapy,** which emphasizes the need to find and maintain meaning in life. Frankl (1904–1997) based his approach on experiences he had as a prisoner in a Nazi concentration camp. In the camp, Frankl saw countless prisoners break down as they were stripped of all hope and human dignity (Frankl, 1955). Those who survived with their sanity did so because they managed to hang on to a sense of meaning *(logos).* Even in less dire circumstances, a sense of purpose in life adds greatly to psychological well-being (Lantz, 1998).

A key aspect of existential therapy is **confrontation,** in which clients are challenged to examine their values and choices. Frankl emphasized that we have choices under all circumstances (Gerwood, 1998). Ideally, accepting this reality prompts people to take responsibility for the quality of their existence.

An important part of confrontation is the unique, intense, here-and-now *encounter* between two human beings. When existential therapy is successful, it brings about a renewed sense of purpose and a reappraisal of what's important in life. Some clients even experience an emotional rebirth like that seen after people survive a close brush with death. As Marcel Proust wrote, "The real voyage of discovery consists not in seeing new landscapes but in having new eyes."

Gestalt Therapy

Gestalt therapy, which is most often associated with Frederick (Fritz) Perls (1969), is built around the idea that perception, or *awareness,* is disjointed and incomplete in the maladjusted individual.

What does Gestalt *mean?* The German word *Gestalt* means "whole," or "complete." **Gestalt therapy** helps individuals rebuild thinking, feeling, and acting into connected wholes. This is achieved by expanding personal awareness, by accepting responsibility for one's thoughts, feelings, and actions, and by filling in gaps in experience (Yontef, 1995).

What do you mean by gaps in experience? Gestalt therapists believe that we often shy away from expressing or "owning" up-

setting feelings. This creates a gap in self-awareness that may become a barrier to personal growth. For example, a person who feels anger after the death of a parent might go for years without expressing it. This and similar threatening gaps may impair emotional health.

The Gestalt approach is more directive than client-centered or existential therapy, and it emphasizes immediate experience. Working either one-to-one or in a group setting, the Gestalt therapist encourages clients to become more aware of their moment-to-moment thoughts, perceptions, and emotions (Cole, 1998). Rather than discussing *why* clients feel guilt, anger, fear, or boredom, they are encouraged to have these feelings in the "here and now" and become fully aware of them. The therapist promotes awareness by drawing attention to a client's posture, voice, eye movement, and hand gestures. Clients may also be asked to exaggerate vague feelings until they become clear. Gestalt therapists believe that expressing such feelings allows people to "take care of unfinished business" and break through emotional impasses.

In all his writings, Perls's basic message comes through clearly: Emotional health comes from knowing what you *want* to do, not dwelling on what you *should* do, *ought* to do, or *should want* to do. Another way of stating this idea is that emotional health comes from taking full responsibility for one's feelings and actions. For example, it means changing "I can't" to "I won't," or "I must" to "I choose to."

How does Gestalt therapy help people discover their real wants? Above all else, Gestalt therapy emphasizes *present* experience. Clients are urged to stop intellectualizing and talking

Client-centered therapy *A nondirective therapy based on insights gained from conscious thoughts and feelings; emphasizes accepting one's true self.*

Unconditional positive regard *An unqualified, unshakable acceptance of another person.*

Empathy *A capacity for taking another's point of view; the ability to feel what another is feeling.*

Authenticity *In Carl Rogers's terms, the ability of a therapist to be genuine and honest about his or her own feelings.*

Reflection *In client-centered therapy, the process of rephrasing or repeating thoughts and feelings expressed by clients so they can become aware of what they are saying.*

Existential therapy *An insight therapy that focuses on the elemental problems of existence, such as death, meaning, choice, and responsibility; emphasizes making courageous life choices.*

Free will *The presumed ability of humans to freely make choices not determined by heredity, past conditioning, or other dictates.*

Death, freedom, isolation, meaninglessness *The universal challenges of existence, including an awareness that everyone will die, the responsibility that comes with freedom to choose, the fact that each person is ultimately isolated and alone in his or her private world, and the reality that meaning must be created in life.*

Logotherapy *A form of existential therapy that emphasizes the need to find and maintain meaning in one's life.*

Confrontation *In existential therapy, the process of confronting clients with their own values and with the need to take responsibility for the quality of their existence.*

Gestalt therapy *An approach that focuses on immediate experience and awareness to help clients rebuild thinking, feeling, and acting into connected wholes; emphasizes the integration of fragmented experiences.*

about feelings. Instead, they learn to live now; live here; stop imagining; experience the real; stop unnecessary thinking; taste and see; express rather than explain, justify, or judge; give in to unpleasantness and pain just as to pleasure; and surrender to being as you are (Naranjo, 1970). Gestalt therapists believe that, paradoxically, the best way to change is to become who you really are (Yontef, 1995).

Because of their emphasis on verbal interaction, humanistic therapies may be conducted at a distance, by telephone or e-mail. Let's investigate this possibility.

PSYCHOTHERAPY AT A DISTANCE—PSYCH JOCKEYS AND CYBERTHERAPY

How valid are psychological services offered over the phone and on the Internet? For better or worse, psychotherapy and counseling are rapidly entering the electronic age. Today, psychological services are available through radio, telephone, videoconferencing, and e-mail. What are the advantages and disadvantages of getting help "on-line"? What are the risks and possible benefits?

Media Psychologists

By now, you have probably heard a phone-in radio psychologist. On a typical program, callers describe problems arising from child abuse, loneliness, love affairs, phobias, sexual adjustment, or depression. The radio psychologist then offers reassurance, advice, or suggestions for getting help.

Talk-radio psychology may seem harmless, but it raises some important questions. For instance, is it reasonable to give advice without knowing anything about a person's background? Might the advice do harm? What good can a psychologist do in 3 minutes?

Media psychologists have been urged to educate without actually doing therapy on the air. Some overstep this boundary, however.

In defense of themselves, radio psychologists point out that listeners may learn solutions to their problems by hearing others talk. Many also stress that their work is educational, not therapeutic. Nevertheless, the question arises, When does advice become therapy? The American Psychological Association urges media psychologists to discuss problems only of a general nature, instead of actually counseling anyone. For example, if a caller complains about insomnia, the radio psychologist should talk about insomnia in general, not probe the caller's personal life.

By giving information, advice, and social support, radio psychologists probably do help some listeners (Levy, 1989). Even so, a good guide for anyone tempted to call a radio psychologist might be "let the consumer beware."

Telephone Therapists

The same caution applies to telephone therapists. These "counselors" can be reached through 900-number services for $3 to $4 per minute. To date, there is no evidence that telephone counseling is effective. Successful face-to-face therapy is based on a continuing *relationship* between two people. Telephone therapy is seriously undermined by a lack of visual cues (such as facial expressions and body language) and by limited personal contact (Haas, Benedict, & Kobos, 1996).

It's important to note that legitimate therapists occasionally use the phone to calm, console, or advise clients between therapy sessions. Others are experimenting with actually doing therapy by telephone (Sanders & Rosenfield, 1998). Also, use of the telephone for suicide hotlines and crisis counseling is well established. However, where commercial telephone therapists are concerned, consumers might well ask themselves, How much confidence would I place in a physician who would make a diagnosis over the phone? Many telephone "therapists" may be nothing more than untrained operators (Newman, 1994).

Cybertherapy

You can find almost anything on the Internet. Recently, "cybertherapy," psychological advice, support groups, and self-help magazines have been added to the list. Some services, such as support groups, are free. On-line counseling or advice, in contrast, is typically offered for a fee. Some on-line therapists will "discuss" problems with you through e-mail messages. Others merely answer questions or give advice concerning specific problems.

Psychologists who have gone on-line emphasize that they're not engaged in therapy. Rather, they offer guidance and advice to help people solve everyday problems in living. However, many on-line services imply in advertising that they are a substitute for therapy. Consequently, some people may be contacting on-line counselors when they actually need face-to-face therapy.

On-line counseling and advice services do have some advantages. For one thing, clients can remain anonymous. Thus, a person who might hesitate to see a psychologist can seek help privately, on-line. Likewise, the Internet can link people who live in rural areas with professional psychologists living in large cities. And, compared with traditional office visits, cybertherapy is relatively inexpensive.

As with radio talk shows and telephone counselors, many objections can be raised about on-line psychological services. Clearly, brief e-mail messages are no way to make a diagnosis. And forget about facial expressions or body language—not even tone of voice reaches the cybertherapist. Typing little smiley faces or frowns is a poor substitute for real human interaction. Another problem is that e-mail counseling may not be completely confidential. In some cases, highly personal messages could be intercepted and misused. Of special concern is the fact that "cybershrinks" may or may not be trained professionals (Bloom, 1998). And even if they are, questions have been raised about whether a psychologist licensed in one state can legally conduct therapy in another state, via the Internet.

Telehealth

Many of the limitations and drawbacks we have discussed can be avoided with videoconferencing. In this emerging approach, therapists provide services to people who live too far away to be seen in person on a regular basis. A two-way audio-video link allows the client and therapist to see one another on TV screens and talk via speakerphones. Doing therapy this way still lacks the immediacy of face-to-face interaction. However, it does remove many of the objections to doing therapy at a distance. Some experts predict that "telehealth" services will become a major source of mental health care in coming years (Nickelson, 1998; Stamm, 1998).

SUMMARY   As you can see, psychological services that rely on electronic communication may serve some useful purposes. However, the effectiveness of therapy conducted by telephone or over the Internet has not been established. As a result, the very best advice given by media psychologists, telephone counselors, or cybertherapists may be "You should consider discussing this problem with a psychologist or counselor in your own community" (additional sources: Hannon, 1996; Sleek, 1995; Zgodzinski, 1996).

KNOWLEDGE BUILDER

INSIGHT THERAPIES

RELATE

Here's a mnemonic for the elements of client-centered therapy: Picture a therapist saying "I ear u" to a client. The *E* stands for empathy, *A* for authenticity, *R* for reflection, and *U* for unconditional positive regard.

What would an existential therapist say about the choices you have made so far in your life? Should you be choosing more "courageously"?

You are going to play the role of a therapist for a classroom demonstration. How would you act if you were a client-centered therapist? An existential therapist? A Gestalt therapist?

A neighbor of yours is thinking about getting counseling on the Internet. What would you tell her about the pros and cons of distance therapy?

BEHAVIOR THERAPY—HEALING BY LEARNING

Five times a day, for several days, Brooks Workman stopped what she was doing and vividly imagined opening a soft-drink can. She then pictured herself bringing the can to her mouth and placing her lips on it. Just as she was about to drink, hordes of roaches poured out of the can and scurried into her mouth—writhing, twitching, and wiggling their feelers (Williams & Long, 1991).

Why would anyone imagine such a thing?   Brooks Workman's behavior is not as strange as it may seem. Her goal was self-control: Brooks was drinking too many colas, and she wanted to cut down. The method she chose (called *covert sensitization*) is a form of behavior therapy (Cautela & Kearney, 1986). **Behavior therapy** is the use of learning principles to make constructive changes in behavior. Behavioral approaches

Behavior therapy *Any therapy designed to actively change behavior.*

include behavior modification, aversion therapy, desensitization, token economies, and other techniques.

Behavior therapists believe that deep insight into one's problems is often unnecessary for improvement. Instead, they try to directly alter troublesome thoughts and actions. Brooks Workman didn't need to probe into her past or her emotions and conflicts; she simply wanted to break her habit of drinking too many colas. Even when more serious problems are at stake, techniques like the one she used have proved valuable.

In general, how does behavior therapy work? Behavior therapists assume that people have *learned* to be the way they are. If they have learned responses that cause problems, then they can change them by *relearning* more appropriate responses. Broadly speaking, **behavior modification** is any use of classical or operant conditioning to directly alter human behavior (Spiegler & Guevremont, 1998).

How does classical conditioning work? I'm not sure I remember. **Classical conditioning** is a form of learning in which simple responses (especially reflexes) are associated with new stimuli. Here is a brief review of conditioning principles:

A neutral stimulus is followed by an *unconditioned stimulus (US)* that consistently produces an unlearned reaction, called the *unconditioned response (UR)*. Eventually, the previously neutral stimulus begins to produce this response directly. The response is then called a *conditioned response (CR)*, and the stimulus becomes a *conditioned stimulus (CS)*. Thus, for a child the sight of a hypodermic needle (CS) is followed by an injection (US), which causes anxiety or fear (UR). Eventually the sight of a hypodermic (the conditioned stimulus) may produce anxiety or fear (a conditioned response) *before* the child gets an injection.

What does classical conditioning have to do with behavior modification? Classical conditioning can be used to associate discomfort with a bad habit, as in the case of the woman who wanted to drink fewer colas. More powerful versions of this approach are called aversion therapy.

Aversion Therapy

Imagine that you are eating an apple. Suddenly you discover that you just bit a large green worm in half. You vomit. Months pass before you can eat an apple again without feeling ill. You now have a *conditioned aversion* to apples. (A **conditioned aversion** is a learned dislike or negative emotional response to some stimulus.)

How are conditioned aversions used in therapy? In **aversion therapy,** an individual learns to associate a strong aversion to an undesirable habit such as smoking, drinking, or gambling. Aversion therapy has been used to cure hiccups, sneezing, stuttering, vomiting, nail-biting, bed-wetting, compulsive hair-pulling, alcoholism, and the smoking of tobacco, marijuana, and crack cocaine. It is also used to treat fetishism, transvestism, pedophilia, and other "maladaptive" sexual behaviors. (To learn how aversion therapy can help people quit smoking, see "Puffing Up an Aversion.") There is little doubt that aversive conditioning is an everyday occurrence. For example, not many physicians who treat lung cancer are smokers, nor do many emergency room doctors drive without using their seat belts (Rosenthal & Steffek, 1991).

An excellent example of aversion therapy is provided by the work of Roger Vogler and his associates (1977). Vogler works with alcoholics who were unable to stop drinking. For many clients, aversion therapy is a last chance. Here is a typical aversion procedure:

While drinking an alcoholic beverage, painful (although noninjurious) electric shocks are delivered to the client's hand. From the client's point of view, the shocks are unpredictable; he or she never knows for sure when one is due. Most of the time, however, the shocks come as the client is beginning to take a drink of alcohol.

This **response-contingent** (response-connected) shock obviously takes the pleasure out of drinking. Shocks also cause the alcohol abuser to develop a conditioned aversion to drinking.

PUFFING UP AN AVERSION

The fact that nicotine is toxic makes it easy to create an aversion to smoking. Behavior therapists have found that electric shock, nauseating drugs, and similar aversive stimuli are not required to make smokers uncomfortable. All that is needed is for the smoker to smoke—rapidly and for a long time.

Rapid smoking (prolonged smoking at a forced pace) is the most widely used aversion therapy for smoking (Lichtenstein, 1982). In this method, clients are told to smoke continuously, taking a puff every 6 to 8 seconds. Rapid smoking continues until the smoker is miserable and can stand it no more. By then, most people are thinking, "I never want to see another cigarette for the rest of my life."

Studies suggest that rapid smoking is one of the most effective behavior therapies for smoking (Tiffany et al., 1986). Nevertheless, anyone tempted to try rapid smoking should realize that it is very unpleasant. Without the help of a therapist, most people quit too soon for the procedure to succeed. (An alternative method that is more practical is described in the "Psychology in Action" section of this chapter.)

The most basic problem with rapid smoking—as with other stop-smoking methods—is that about half of those who quit smoking begin again. During at least the first year after quitting, there is no "safe point" after which relapse becomes less likely (Swan & Denk, 1987).

Because the "evil weed" calls so strongly to former smokers, support from a stop-smoking group or a close, caring person can make a big difference. Former smokers who get encouragement from others are much more likely to stay smoke free (Gruder et al., 1993). Those whose social groups include many smokers are more likely to begin smoking again (Mermelstein, 1986).

USING PSYCHOLOGY

Aversion therapy for drinking. The sights, smells, and tastes of drinking are associated with unpleasant electric shocks applied to the hand.

Normally, the misery caused by alcohol abuse comes long after the act of drinking—too late to have much effect. But if alcohol can be linked with *immediate* discomfort, then drinking will begin to make the individual very uncomfortable.

But can't the person tell when it is "safe" to drink and when it is not? Yes, *generalization* of aversion conditioning to the "real world" is a problem. With this in mind, Vogler constructed in his office a vivid re-creation of a "friendly neighborhood tavern," complete with a bar, tables, soft lights, music, and a bartender. Also provided are a "living room," a "bedroom," and a "kitchen." Clients undergo aversion therapy in a setting as much like the normal site of their drinking as possible, and carryover of the aversion training is improved.

Vogler also added an interesting twist to his program: Alcohol abusers are videotaped as they go from sober to drunk. Later, they watch the videotaped drinking bout and see themselves with slurred speech, dropping cigarette ashes in their drinks and saying stupid and belligerent things. Most are ashamed and embarrassed when they see the tapes. Apparently, few people have any idea how unattractive they are when drunk.

To add to the effect, the bartender is trained to provoke clients into becoming argumentative and obnoxious. Presumably, this is not too hard to do by the time the client is saying, "I am 'masshhhed.'" In the videotape self-confrontation held later, grossly drunken behaviors are replayed until the client says, "Okay, okay, I've seen enough." Seeing themselves as obnoxious drunks adds to the aversion people feel for drinking, and it increases their determination to quit.

Is it really acceptable to treat clients this way? People are often disturbed (shocked?) by such methods. However, clients

usually *volunteer* for aversion therapy because it helps them overcome a destructive habit. Indeed, commercial aversion programs for overeating, smoking, and alcohol abuse have attracted many willing customers. And more important, aversion therapy can be justified by its long-term benefits. As behaviorist Donald Baer put it, "A small number of brief, painful experiences is a reasonable exchange for the interminable pain of a lifelong maladjustment."

Desensitization

Assume that you are a swimming instructor who wants to help a child named Jamie overcome fear of the high diving board. How might you proceed? Directly forcing Jamie off the high board could be a psychological disaster. Obviously, a better approach would be to begin by teaching her to dive off the edge of the pool. Then she could be taught to dive off the low board, followed by a platform 6 feet above the water, and then an 8-foot platform. As a last step, Jamie could try the high board.

WHO'S AFRAID OF A HIERARCHY? This rank-ordered series of steps is called a **hierarchy.** The hierarchy allows Jamie to undergo *adaptation*. Gradually, she adapts to the high dive and overcomes fear, much as one adapts to a cool swimming pool on a hot day. When Jamie has overcome her fear, we can say that *desensitization* (dee-SEN-sih-tih-ZAY-shun) has occurred (Spiegler & Guevremont, 1998).

Desensitization is also based on reciprocal inhibition, a term coined by Joseph Wolpe (Wolpe & Plaud, 1997). In **reciprocal inhibition,** one emotional state is used to block another. For instance, it is impossible to be anxious and relaxed at the same time. If we can get Jamie onto the high board in a relaxed state, her anxiety and fear will be inhibited. Repeated visits to the high board should cause fear in this situation to disappear. Again, we would say that Jamie has been desensitized. Typically, **systematic desensitization** (a guided reduction in fear, anxiety, or aversion) is attained by gradually approaching a feared stimulus while maintaining relaxation.

Behavior modification *The application of learning principles to change human behavior, especially maladaptive behavior.*
Classical conditioning *A form of learning in which reflex responses are associated with new stimuli.*
Conditioned aversion *A learned dislike or conditioned negative emotional response to a particular stimulus.*
Aversion therapy *Suppressing an undesirable response by associating it with aversive (painful or uncomfortable) stimuli.*
Rapid smoking *Prolonged smoking at a forced pace; used to produce discomfort in aversion therapy for smoking.*
Response-contingent consequences *Reinforcement, punishment, or other consequences that are applied only when a certain response is made.*
Hierarchy *A rank-ordered series of higher and lower amounts, levels, degrees, or steps.*
Reciprocal inhibition *The presence of one emotional state can inhibit the occurrence of another, such as joy preventing fear or anxiety inhibiting pleasure.*
Systematic desensitization *A reduction in fear, anxiety, or aversion brought about by planned exposure to aversive stimuli.*

Programs for treating fears of flying combine relaxation, systematic desensitization, group support, and lots of direct exposure to airliners. Many such programs conclude with a brief flight, so that participants can "test their wings" (Roberts, 1989).

What is desensitization used for? Desensitization is primarily used to help people unlearn or countercondition **phobias** (intense, unrealistic fears) or strong anxieties. Almost everyone has a phobia or two. Many people fear heights, snakes, public speaking, spiders, and so forth. Usually, these cause little difficulty because the person carefully avoids feared situations. However, consider the following: a teacher with stage fright, a student with test anxiety, a salesperson who fears people, an aspiring pole-vaulter who fears heights, or a newlywed with a fear of sexual intimacy. Each may be hampered enough by fears or anxieties to seek aid.

PERFORMING DESENSITIZATION   *How is desensitization done?* Systematic desensitization usually involves three steps. First, the client and the therapist *construct a hierarchy.* This is a list of fear-provoking situations, arranged from least disturbing to most frightening. Second, the client is taught *exercises that produce deep relaxation.* (These are described later in this chapter.) Once the client is relaxed, she or he proceeds to the third step by trying to *perform the least disturbing item* on the list. For a fear of heights (acrophobia), this might be: "(1) Stand on a chair." The first item is repeated until no anxiety is felt. Any change from complete relaxation is a signal that clients must repeat the relaxation process before continuing. Slowly, clients move up the hierarchy: "(2) Climb to the top of a small stepladder"; "(3) Look down a flight of stairs"; and so on, until the last item is performed without fear: "(20) Fly in an airplane."

For many fears, desensitization works best when people are directly exposed to the stimuli and situations they fear (Menzies & Clarke, 1993). For something like a simple spider phobia, this exposure can even be done in groups (Ost, 1996). Also, for some fears (such as fear of riding an elevator) desensitization may be completed in a single session (Sturges & Sturges, 1998).

VICARIOUS DESENSITIZATION   *I understand how some fears could be desensitized by gradual approach—as in the case of the child on the high dive. But how would a therapist use desensitization to combat fear of sexual intimacy?* For a person with a fear of heights, the steps of the hierarchy might be acted out. Often, however, this is impractical. In some cases, the problem can be handled by having clients observe models who are performing the feared behavior (❖Fig. 18.2) (Rosenthal & Steffek, 1991). A **model** is a person who serves as an example for observational learning. If such **vicarious desensitization** (secondhand learning) is not practical, there is yet another option. Fortunately, desensitization works almost as well when a person *vividly imagines* each step in the hierarchy (Deffenbacher & Suinn, 1988). If the steps can be visualized without anxiety, fear in the actual situation is reduced.

Here is a sample of the hierarchy imagined by a 24-year-old married woman to overcome the fear and disgust she felt for sexual intercourse. (Some steps are left out to shorten the list.)

1. Dancing with and embracing husband while fully clothed.
2. Being kissed on cheeks and forehead.
3. Being kissed on lips.
4. Sitting on husband's lap, both fully dressed.
5. Husband kisses neck and ears.
6. Husband caresses hair and face.
   •
   •
   •
17. Having intercourse in bed in the dark.
18. Having intercourse in the nude in a dining room or living room.
19. Changing positions during intercourse.
20. Having intercourse in the nude while sitting on husband's lap. (Adapted from Lazarus, 1964.)

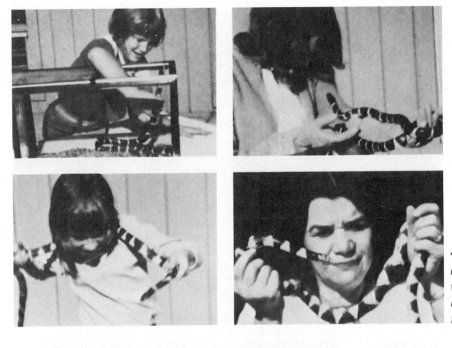

❖ **FIGURE 18.2** *Treatment of a snake phobia by vicarious desensitization. The photographs show models interacting with snakes. To overcome their own fears, phobic subjects observed the models. (Bandura et al., 1969. Photos courtesy of Albert Bandura.)*

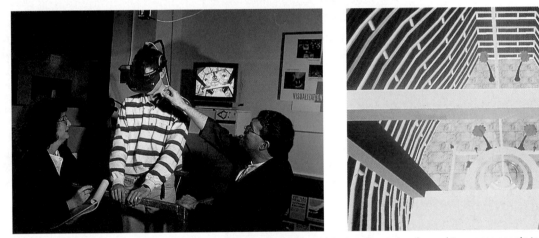

❖ **FIGURE 18.3** (Left) *Barbara Rothbaum and Larry Hodges show how a virtual reality system is used to expose people to feared stimuli. Many patients say that they would rather face exposure to feared stimuli in a virtual environment than in a real physical environment. (Right) A computer image from a virtual elevator. Over an 8-week period, patients who suffered from acrophobia "rode" in the elevator. Each session took them to greater heights. (Image courtesy of Larry Hodges, Thomas Meyer, and Rob Kooper.)*

Mrs. A was able to imagine the last steps in this hierarchy without anxiety after a 3-month period of desensitization. Accordingly, she and her husband reported that their sexual relationship was greatly improved.

VIRTUAL REALITY EXPOSURE   In an important new development, psychologists are beginning to use virtual reality to treat phobias. Virtual reality is a computer-generated, three-dimensional "world" that viewers enter by wearing a head-mounted video display. **Virtual reality exposure** presents computerized fear stimuli to patients in a controlled fashion. It has already been used to treat acrophobia (fear of heights), fear of flying, spider phobias, and claustrophobia (Botella et al., 1998; Rothbaum et al., 1995, 1996; Rothbaum, Hodges, & Kooper, 1997) (❖Fig. 18.3).

Desensitization has been one of the most successful behavior therapies. A second new technique may provide yet another way to lower fears, anxieties, and psychological pain. The highlight titled "Eye Movement Desensitization" has the details.

Phobia *An intense and unrealistic fear of some object or situation.*
Model *A person (either live or filmed) who serves as an example for observational learning or vicarious conditioning.*
Vicarious desensitization *A reduction in fear or anxiety that takes place vicariously ("secondhand") when a client watches models perform the feared behavior.*
Virtual reality exposure *Use of computer-generated images to present fear stimuli. The virtual environment responds to a viewer's head movements and other inputs.*

EYE MOVEMENT DESENSITIZATION— WATCHING TRAUMA FADE?

Traumatic events produce painful memories. Victims of accidents, disasters, molestations, muggings, rapes, or emotional abuse are often haunted by disturbing flashbacks. Recently, Francine Shapiro developed **eye movement desensitization and re-processing** (**EMDR**) to help ease traumatic memories and post-traumatic stress.

In a typical EMDR session, the client is asked to visualize the images that most upset her or him. At the same time, a pencil (or other object) is moved rapidly from side to side in front of the person's eyes. Watching the moving object causes the person's eyes to dart swiftly back and forth. After about 30 seconds, patients describe any memories, feelings, and thoughts that emerged and discuss them with the therapist. These steps are repeated until troubling thoughts and emotions no longer surface (Shapiro, 1995).

A number of studies indicate that EMDR lowers anxieties and takes the pain out of traumatic memories (Carlson et al., 1998; Lazgrove et al., 1998; Scheck, Schaeffer, & Gillette, 1998). However, EMDR is highly controversial. Some studies, for example, have found that eye movements add nothing to the treatment. The apparent success of EMDR may simply be based on gradual exposure to upsetting stimuli, as in other forms of desensitization (Cahill, Carrigan, & Frueh, 1999; Lohr, Tolin, & Lilienfeld, 1998; Muris & Merckelbach, 1999).

Is EMDR a breakthrough? Or will it prove to be a case of wishful thinking? Given the frequency of traumas in modern society, it shouldn't be long before we find out.

3. If shock is used to control drinking, it must be _____ contingent.

4. A potential problem with aversion therapy is transfer of the aversion to settings outside the clinic or laboratory. T or F?

5. What two principles underlie systematic desensitization? _____ and _____

6. When desensitization is carried out through the use of live or filmed models, it is called
a. cognitive therapy b. flooding c. covert desensitization d. vicarious desensitization

7. The three basic steps in systematic desensitization are: Construct a hierarchy, flood the person with anxiety, and imagine relaxation. T or F?

8. In EMDR therapy, computer-generated virtual reality images are used to expose patients to fear-provoking stimuli. T or F?

CRITICAL THINKING

9. Alcoholics who take a drug called Antabuse become ill after drinking alcohol. Why, then, don't they develop an aversion to drinking?

10. A natural form of desensitization often takes place in hospitals. Can you guess what it is?

Answers:

1. classical (or respondent), operant 2. c 3. response 4. T 5. adaptation, reciprocal inhibition 6. d 7. F 8. F 9. Their discomfort is delayed enough to prevent it from being closely associated with drinking. Fortunately, there are safer, better ways to do aversion therapy (Wilson, 1987). 10. Doctors and nurses learn to relax and remain calm at the sight of blood because of their frequent exposure to it.

KNOWLEDGE BUILDER

BEHAVIOR THERAPY

RELATE

Can you describe three problems for which you think behavior therapy would be an appropriate treatment?

When pain is used to create an aversion to drinking alcohol, what is the CS and what is the US?

A friend of yours has a dog that goes berserk during thunderstorms. You own an audiotape of a thunderstorm. How could you use the tape to desensitize the dog? (Hint: The tape player has a volume control.)

Have you ever become naturally desensitized to a stimulus or situation that at first made you anxious (for instance, heights, public speaking, or driving on freeways)? How would you explain your reduced fear?

LEARNING CHECK

1. What two types of conditioning are used in behavior modification? _____ and _____

2. Shock, pain, and discomfort play what role in conditioning an aversion?
a. conditioned stimulus b. unconditioned response c. unconditioned stimulus d. conditioned response

OPERANT THERAPIES—ALL THE WORLD IS A SKINNER BOX?

Aversion therapy and desensitization are based on classical conditioning. Where does operant conditioning fit in? The principles of operant conditioning were developed by B. F. Skinner and other psychologists. As you may recall, **operant conditioning** refers to learning based on the consequences of making a response. The operant principles most often used by behavior therapists to deal with human behavior are:

1. **Positive reinforcement.** Responses that are followed by reward tend to occur more frequently. If children whine and get attention, they will whine more frequently. If you get A's in your psychology class, you may become a psychology major.

2. **Nonreinforcement.** A response that is not followed by reward will occur less frequently.

3. **Extinction.** If a response is not followed by reward after it has been repeated many times, it will go away. After win-

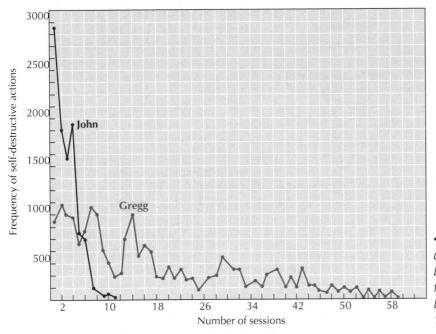

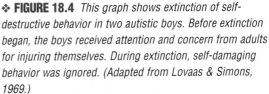

❖ **FIGURE 18.4** *This graph shows extinction of self-destructive behavior in two autistic boys. Before extinction began, the boys received attention and concern from adults for injuring themselves. During extinction, self-damaging behavior was ignored. (Adapted from Lovaas & Simons, 1969.)*

ning three times, you pull the handle on a slot machine 30 times more without a payoff. What do you do? You go away. So does the response of handle pulling (for that particular machine, at any rate).

4. **Punishment.** If a response is followed by discomfort or an undesirable effect, the response will be suppressed (but not necessarily extinguished).

5. **Shaping.** Shaping means rewarding actions that are closer and closer approximations to a desired response. For example, if I want to reward a retarded child for saying, "ball," I may begin by rewarding the child for saying anything that starts with a *b* sound.

6. **Stimulus control.** Responses tend to come under the control of the situation in which they occur. If I set my clock 10 minutes fast, I can get to work on time in the morning. My departure is under the stimulus control of the clock, even though I know it is fast.

7. **Time out.** A time-out procedure usually involves removing the individual from a situation in which reinforcement occurs. Time out is a variation of nonreinforcement: It prevents reward from following an undesirable response. For example, children who fight with each other can be sent to separate rooms and allowed out only when they are able to behave more calmly (Olson & Roberts, 1987). (For a more thorough review of operant learning, return to Chapter 9.)

As simple as these principles may seem, they have been used very effectively to overcome difficulties in work, home, school, and industrial settings. Let's see how.

Nonreinforcement and Extinction

An extremely overweight mental patient had a persistent and disturbing habit: She stole food from other patients. No one could persuade her to stop stealing or to diet. For the sake of her health, a behavior therapist assigned her a special table in the ward dining room. If she approached any other table, she was immediately removed from the dining room. Because her attempts to steal food went unrewarded, they rapidly disappeared. Additionally, any attempt to steal from others caused the patient to miss her own meal (Ayllon, 1963).

What operant principles did the therapist in this example use? The therapist used *nonreward* to produce *extinction.* The most frequently occurring human behaviors lead to some form of reward. An undesirable response can be eliminated by *identifying* and *removing* the rewards that maintain it. But people don't always do things for food, money, or other obvious rewards. Most of the rewards maintaining human behavior are subtler. *Attention, approval,* and *concern* are common yet powerful reinforcers for humans (❖Fig. 18.4).

In school, we often find that misbehaving children are surrounded by others who giggle and pay attention to them. If seating is rearranged so that the disruptive children are surrounded by less responsive students, misbehavior decreases. Attention from a teacher (even a scolding) can also be a reinforcer. An experiment showed that when teachers paid extra attention to classroom misbehavior, it increased. It increased even when the attention took the form of saying things such as "Sit down!" When misbehaving children were *ignored* and attention was given to children who were *not* misbehaving, misbehavior decreased (Madsen et al., 1968).

How are nonreward and extinction applied in therapy? Nonreward and extinction can eliminate many problem behav-

Eye movement desensitization and reprocessing (EMDR) *A technique for reducing fear or anxiety; based on holding upsetting thoughts in mind while rapidly moving the eyes from side to side.*
Operant conditioning *A type of learning that occurs when the behavior of a person or an animal changes in response to the consequences of actions.*

iors, especially in schools, hospitals, and institutions. Often, difficulties center around a limited number of particularly disturbing responses. Time out is a good way to remove such responses, usually by refusing to play the *attention* game. Another form of time out is to remove an individual immediately from the setting in which an undesirable response occurs, so that the response will not be rewarded. For example:

> Fourteen-year-old Zeke periodically appeared in the nude in the activity room of a training center for disturbed juveniles. This behavior always generated a great deal of attention from staff and other patients. Usually Zeke was returned to his room and confined there. During this "confinement," he often missed doing his usual chores. As an experiment he was placed on time out. The next time he appeared nude, counselors and other staff members greeted him normally and then ignored him. Attention from other patients rapidly subsided. Sheepishly he returned to his room and dressed.

Reinforcement and Token Economies

This section might be called "Throwing a Lifeline to the Unreachable." A distressing problem faced in dealing with the severely disturbed is how to "break through" to a patient who cannot, or will not, communicate. Mental patients sometimes spend years in hospitals without noticeable improvement.

What can be done in such circumstances? One widely used approach is based on **tokens** (symbolic rewards, such as plastic chips, that can be exchanged for real rewards). Tokens may be printed slips of paper, check marks, points, or gold stars. What-

BRIDGES

Tokens provide an effective way to change behavior because they are secondary reinforcers.

See Chapter 9, page 287

ever form they take, tokens serve as rewards because they may be exchanged for candy, food, cigarettes, recreation, or other privileges, such as private time with a therapist, outings, or watching TV. Tokens are used in mental hospitals, halfway houses, schools for the retarded, programs for delinquents, and ordinary classrooms. They usually produce dramatic improvements in behavior (Foxx, 1998; Mohanty, Pati, & Kumar, 1998; Truchlicka, McLaughlin, & Swain, 1998).

By using tokens, a therapist can *immediately reward* a positive response. This allows a therapist to influence behavior directly, through operant shaping, instead of vaguely urging patients to "get themselves together." For maximum impact, the therapist selects specific **target behaviors** (actions or other behaviors the therapist seeks to modify). Target behaviors are then reinforced with tokens. For example, a mute mental patient might first be given a token each time he or she says a word. Next, tokens may be given for speaking a complete sentence. Later, the patient could gradually be required to speak more often, then to answer questions, and eventually to carry on a short conversation in order to receive tokens. In this way, patients who rarely spoke more than a few words have been returned to the world of normal communication.

Full-scale use of tokens in an institutional setting produces a *token economy*. In a **token economy,** patients are rewarded with tokens for a wide range of socially desirable or productive activities (Spiegler & Guevremont, 1998). They must *pay* tokens for privileges and for engaging in problem behaviors (❖Fig. 18.5). For example, tokens are given to patients who get out of bed,

Credit Card

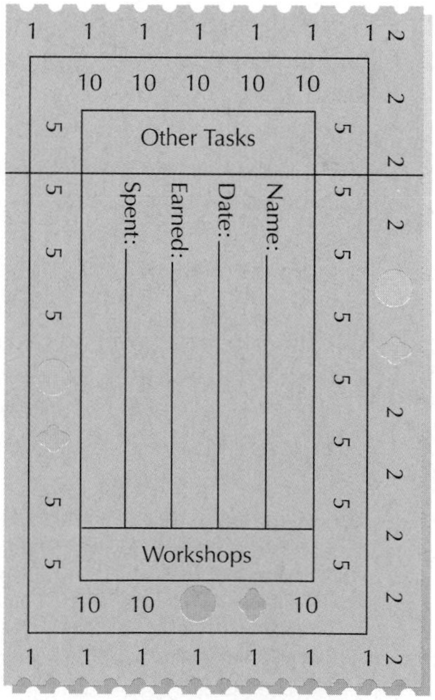

❖ **FIGURE 18.5** *Shown here is a token used in one token economy system; also pictured is a list of credit values for various activities. Tokens may be exchanged for items or for privileges listed on the board. (After photographs by Robert P. Liberman.)*

OXNARD DAY TREATMENT CENTER
CREDIT INCENTIVE SYSTEM

EARN CREDITS BY		SPEND CREDITS FOR	
MONITOR DAILY	15	COFFEE	5
MENU PLANNING CHAIRMAN	50	LUNCH	10
PARTICIPATE	5	EXCEPT THURSDAY	15
BUY FOOD AT STORE	10	BUS TRIP	5
COOK FOR/PREPARE LUNCH	5	BOWLING	8
WIPE OFF KITCHEN TABLE	3	GROUP THERAPY	5
WASH DISHES	5-10	PRIVATE STAFF TIME	5
DRY AND PUT AWAY DISHES	5	DAY OFF	5-20
MAKE COFFEE AND CLEAN URN	15	WINDOW SHOPPING	5
CLEAN REFRIGERATOR	20	REVIEW WITH DR.	10
ATTEND PLANNING CONFERENCE	1	DOING OWN THING	1
OT PREPARATION	1-5	LATE 1 PER EVERY 10 MIN	
COMPLETE OT PROJECT	5	PRESCRIPTION FROM DR.	10
RETURN OT PROJECT	2		
DUST AND POLISH TABLES	5		
PUT AWAY GROCERIES	3		
CLEAN TABLE	5		
CLEAN 6 ASH TRAYS	2		
CLEAN SINK	5		
CARRY OUT CUPS & BOTTLES	5		
CLEAN CHAIRS	5		
CLEAN KITCHEN CUPBOARDS	5		
ASSIST STAFF	5		
ARRANGE MAGAZINES NEATLY	3		
BEING ON TIME	5		
MONITOR-ANN			

dress themselves, take required medication, arrive for meals on time, and so on. Constructive activities, such as gardening, cooking, or cleaning, may also earn tokens. Patients must *exchange* tokens for meals and private rooms, movies, passes, off-ward activities, and other privileges. They are *charged* tokens for staying in bed, disrobing in public, talking to themselves, fighting, crying, and similar target behaviors (Morisse et al., 1996).

Token economies can radically change a patient's overall adjustment and morale. Patients are given an incentive to change, and they are held responsible for their actions. The use of tokens may seem manipulative, but it actually empowers patients. Many "hopelessly" retarded, mentally ill, and delinquent people have been returned to productive lives by means of token economies (Corrigan, 1997).

Wouldn't there be a problem with generalization of improvements brought about by a token economy? Yes. Lack of generalization can again be a problem. To minimize this, patients are praised and given *social* recognition when they receive tokens. Each time a token is given, the therapist says something like "That was very good," or "You're doing so well."

By the time they are ready to leave the program, patients may be earning tokens on a weekly basis for maintaining sane, responsible, and productive behavior (Binder, 1976). Typically, the most effective token economies are those that gradually switch from tokens to *social rewards* such as recognition and approval. Such rewards are what patients will receive when they return to family, friends, and community.

COGNITIVE THERAPY—THINK POSITIVE!

How would a behavior therapist treat a problem like depression? None of the techniques described seem to apply. As we have discussed, behavior therapists usually try to change troublesome actions. However, in recent years a new breed of therapist has appeared. *Cognitive therapists,* as they are called, are interested in what people think, believe, and feel, as well as how they act. In general, **cognitive therapy** helps clients change thinking patterns that lead to troublesome emotions or behaviors (Freeman & Reinecke, 1995). For example, compulsive handwashing can be greatly reduced just by changing a client's thoughts and beliefs about dirt and contamination (Jones & Menzies, 1998).

Cognitive Therapy for Depression

Cognitive therapy has been especially effective for treating depression. As you may recall from Chapter 17, Aaron Beck (1991) believes that negative, self-defeating thoughts underlie depression. According to Beck, depressed people see themselves, the world, and the future in negative terms. Beck believes this occurs because of major distortions in thinking. The first is **selective perception,** which refers to perceiving only certain stimuli in a larger array. If five good things happen during the day and three bad things, depressed people focus only on the bad. A second thinking error underlying depression is **overgeneralization,** the tendency to let upsetting events affect unrelated situations. An example would be considering yourself a total failure, or completely worthless, if you were to lose a job or fail a test. To complete the picture, Beck says that depressed people tend to magnify the importance of undesirable events, and they engage in **all-or-nothing thinking,** by seeing each event as completely good or bad, right or wrong, successful or a failure (Beck, 1985).

How do cognitive therapists alter such patterns? Cognitive therapists make a step-by-step effort to correct negative thoughts that lead to depression or similar problems. At first, clients are taught to recognize and keep track of their own thoughts. The client and therapist then look for ideas and beliefs that cause depression, anger, and avoidance. For example, here's how a therapist might challenge all-or-nothing thinking (Burns & Persons, 1982):

Patient: I'm feeling even more depressed. No one wants to hire me, and I can't even clean up my apartment. I feel completely incompetent!
Therapist: I see. The fact that you are unemployed and have a messy apartment proves that you are completely incompetent?
Patient: Well . . . I can see that doesn't add up.

Next, clients are asked to gather information to test their beliefs. For instance, a depressed person might list his or her activities for a week. The list is then used to challenge all-or-nothing thoughts, such as "I had a terrible week" or "I'm a complete failure." With more coaching, clients learn to alter their thoughts in ways that improve their moods, actions, and relationships.

Cognitive therapy is as effective as drugs for treating many cases of depression. More important, people who have adopted new thinking patterns are less likely to become depressed again—a benefit that drugs can't impart (Fava et al., 1998; Gloaguen et al., 1998).

In an alternate approach, cognitive therapists look for an *absence* of effective coping skills and thinking patterns, not for the *presence* of self-defeating thoughts (Freeman & Reinecke, 1995). The aim is to teach clients how to cope with anger, depression, shyness, stress, and similar problems. Stress inoculation, which was described in Chapter 16, is a good example of this approach.

Tokens *Symbolic rewards, or secondary reinforcers (such as plastic chips, gold stars, or points), that can be exchanged for real reinforcers.*
Target behaviors *Actions or other behaviors (such as speech) that a therapist selects as the focus for behavior modification efforts.*
Token economy *A therapeutic program in which desirable behaviors are reinforced with tokens that can be exchanged for goods, services, activities, and privileges.*
Cognitive therapy *A therapy directed at changing the maladaptive thoughts, beliefs, and feelings that underlie emotional and behavioral problems.*
Selective perception *Perceiving only certain stimuli among a larger array of possibilities.*
Overgeneralization *Blowing a single event out of proportion by extending it to a large number of unrelated situations.*
All-or-nothing thinking *Classifying objects or events as absolutely right or wrong, good or bad, acceptable or unacceptable, and so forth.*

Cognitive therapy is a rapidly expanding specialty. Before we leave the topic, let's explore another widely used cognitive therapy.

Rational-Emotive Behavior Therapy

Rational-emotive behavior therapy (**REBT**) attempts to change irrational beliefs that cause emotional problems. According to Albert Ellis (1973, 1995), the basic idea of rational-emotive behavior therapy is as easy as ABC. Ellis assumes that people become unhappy and develop self-defeating habits because they have unrealistic or faulty *beliefs.*

How are beliefs important? Ellis analyzes problems in this way: The letter A stands for an *activating experience,* which the person assumes to be the cause of C, an *emotional consequence.* For instance, a person who is rejected (the activating experience) feels depressed, threatened, or hurt (the consequence). Rational-emotive behavior therapy shows the client that the real problem is what comes between A and C: In between is B, the client's irrational and unrealistic *beliefs.* In this example, the unrealistic belief leading to unnecessary suffering is: "I must be loved and approved by almost everyone at all times." REBT holds that events do not *cause* us to have feelings. We feel as we do because of our beliefs (Kottler & Brown, 1999). (For some examples, see "Ten Irrational Beliefs.")

BRIDGES

The REBT explanation of emotional distress is related to the effects of emotional appraisals.

See Chapter 13, pages 436–437.

Ellis (1979, 1987) says that most irrational beliefs come from three core ideas, each of which is unrealistic:

1. I *must* perform well and be approved of by significant others. If I don't, then it is awful, I cannot stand it, and I am a rotten person.
2. You *must* treat me fairly. When you don't, it is horrible, and I cannot bear it.
3. Conditions *must* be the way I want them to be. It is terrible when they are not, and I cannot stand living in such an awful world.

It's easy to see that such beliefs can lead to much grief and needless suffering in a less than perfect world. Rational-emotive behavior therapists are very directive in their attempts to change a client's irrational beliefs and "self-talk." The therapist may directly attack clients' logic, challenge their thinking, confront them with evidence contrary to their beliefs, and even assign "homework." Here, for instance, are some examples of statements that dispute irrational beliefs (after Kottler & Brown, 1999):

- "Where is the evidence that you are a loser just because you didn't do well this one time?"
- "Who said the world should be fair? That's your rule."
- "What are you telling yourself to make yourself feel so upset?"
- "Is it really terrible that things aren't working out as you would like? Or is it just inconvenient?"

TEN IRRATIONAL BELIEFS—WHICH DO YOU HOLD?

Rational-emotive behavior therapists have identified numerous beliefs that commonly lead to emotional upsets and conflicts. See if you recognize any of the following irrational beliefs:

1. I must be loved and approved of by almost every significant person in my life or it's awful and I'm worthless.
   Example: "One of my roommates doesn't seem to like me. I must be a total zero."
2. I should be completely competent and achieving in all ways to be a worthwhile person.
   Example: "I don't understand my chemistry class. I guess I really am a stupid person."
3. Certain people I must deal with are thoroughly bad and should be severely blamed and punished for it.
   Example: "The old man next door is such a pain. I'm going to play my stereo even louder the next time he complains."
4. It is awful and upsetting when things are not the way I would very much like them to be.
   Example: "I should have gotten a B in that class. The teacher is unfair."
5. My unhappiness is always caused by external events; I cannot control my emotional reactions.
   Example: "You make me feel awful. I would be happy if it weren't for you."
6. If something unpleasant might happen, I should keep dwelling on it.
   Example: "I'll never forget the time my boss insulted me. I think about it every day at work."
7. It is easier to avoid difficulties and responsibilities than to face them.
   Example: "I don't know why my wife seems angry. Maybe it will just pass by if I ignore it."
8. I should depend on others who are stronger than I am.
   Example: "I couldn't survive if he left me."
9. Because something once strongly affected my life, it will do so indefinitely.
   Example: "My girlfriend dumped me during my junior year in college. I don't know if I can ever trust a woman again."
10. There is always a perfect solution to human problems and it is awful if this solution is not found.
    Example: "I'm so depressed about politics in this country. It all seems hopeless."
    (Adapted from Rohsenow & Smith, 1982.)

If any of the listed beliefs sound familiar, you may be creating unnecessary emotional distress for yourself by holding on to unrealistic expectations.

Many of us would probably do well to give up our irrational beliefs. Improved self-acceptance and a better tolerance of daily annoyances are the benefits of doing so.

The value of cognitive approaches is further illustrated by three techniques (*covert sensitization, thought stopping,* and *covert reinforcement*) described in this chapter's "Psychology in Action" section. A little later you can see what you think of them.

GROUP THERAPY—PEOPLE WHO NEED PEOPLE

Group therapy is psychotherapy done with more than one person. Most of the therapies we have discussed can be adapted for use in groups. Psychologists first tried working with groups as a practical response to the need for more therapists. Surprisingly, group therapy has turned out to be just as effective as individual therapy. In addition, it offers some special advantages (McRoberts, Burlingame, & Hoag, 1998).

What are the advantages of group therapy? In group therapy, a person can *act out* or directly experience problems. Doing so often produces insights that might not occur from merely talking about one person's difficulties. In addition, other group members with similar problems can offer support and useful input. Groups can help form a bridge between therapy and real-life problems (Corey & Corey, 1996). For reasons such as these, a number of specialized group techniques have emerged. Because they range from Alcoholics Anonymous to Marriage Encounter, we will sample only a few representative approaches.

Psychodrama

One of the first groups was developed by Jacob L. Moreno (1953), who called his technique psychodrama. In **psychodrama,** clients act out personal conflicts and feelings with others who play supporting roles. Through **role-playing,** the client re-enacts incidents that cause problems in real life. For example, Don, a disturbed teenager, might act out a typical family fight, with the therapist playing his father and with other clients playing his mother, brothers, and sisters. Moreno believed that insights gained in this way transfer to real-life situations.

Therapists using psychodrama often find role reversals especially helpful. A **role reversal** involves taking the part of another person to learn how he or she feels. For instance, Don could be asked to role-play his father or mother, to better understand their feelings. A related method is the **mirror technique,** in which a client observes another person re-enact the client's behavior. Thus, Don might briefly join the audience and watch as another group member plays his role. This would allow him to see himself as others do. Later, the group may summarize what happened and reflect on its meaning (Turner, 1997).

Family Therapy

Family relationships are the source of great pleasure and, all too often, of great pain for many people. In **family therapy,** husband, wife, and children work as a group to resolve the

Rational-emotive behavior therapy (REBT) *An approach that states that irrational beliefs cause many emotional problems and that such beliefs must be changed or abandoned.*

Group therapy *Psychotherapy conducted in a group setting to make therapeutic use of group dynamics.*

Psychodrama *A therapy in which clients act out personal conflicts and feelings in the presence of others, who play supporting roles.*

Role-playing *The dramatic enactment or re-enactment of significant life events.*

Role reversal *Taking the role of another person to learn how one's own behavior appears from the other person's perspective.*

Mirror technique *Observing another person re-enact one's own behavior, like a character in a play; designed to help people see themselves more clearly.*

Family therapy *Technique in which all family members participate, both individually and as a group, to change destructive relationships and communication patterns.*

A group therapy session. Group members offer mutual support while sharing problems and insights.

problems of each family member. Family therapy tends to be brief and focused on specific problems, such as frequent fights or a depressed teenager. For some types of problems, family therapy may be superior to other approaches (Pinsof, Wynne, & Hambright, 1996).

Family therapists believe that problems are rarely limited to a single family member: A problem for one is considered a problem for all. That is, families often contribute to and maintain maladaptive behavior. If changes are not made in the *family system,* changes in any single family member may not last. A **family system** is an entire family unit, including all its members, their relationships, and their typical patterns of behavior. Thus, family members work together to improve communication, to change destructive patterns, and to see themselves and each other in new ways. This helps them reshape distorted perceptions and interactions directly, with the very persons with whom they have troubled relationships (Goldfried, Greenberg, & Marmar, 1990).

Does the therapist work with the whole family at once? Family therapists treat the family as a unit, but they may not meet with the entire family at each session. If a family crisis is at hand, the therapist may first try to identify the most resourceful family members, who can help solve the immediate problem. The therapist and family members may then work on resolving more basic conflicts and on improving family relationships (Dies, 1995).

Group Awareness Training

During the 1960s and 1970s, the human potential movement led many people to seek personal growth experiences. Often, their interest was expressed by participation in sensitivity training or encounter groups.

What is the difference between sensitivity and encounter groups? Sensitivity groups tend to be less confrontive than en-

counter groups. Participants in **sensitivity groups** take part in exercises that gently enlarge self-awareness and sensitivity to others. For example, in a "trust walk," participants expand their confidence in others by allowing themselves to be led about while blindfolded.

Encounter groups are based on an honest expression of feelings and reactions to other participants. Intense emotion and communication may take place in an encounter group. Typically, the emphasis is on tearing down defenses and false fronts. Because there is a danger of hostile confrontation and psychological damage, encounter group participation is safest when members are carefully screened and when a trained leader guides the group. Encounter group "casualties" are rare, but they do occur (Shaffer & Galinsky, 1989).

In business settings, psychologists still use the basic principles of sensitivity and encounter groups—truth, self-awareness, and self-determination—to improve employee relationships. Specially designed encounter groups for married couples are also widely held.

There has also been much public interest in various forms of large-group awareness training (Finkelstein et al., 1982). **Large-group awareness training** refers to programs that claim to increase self-awareness and facilitate constructive personal change. Lifespring, Actualizations, est, the Forum, and similar commercial programs are well-known examples. Like the smaller groups that preceded them, large-group trainings combine psychological exercises, confrontation, new viewpoints, and group dynamics to promote personal change.

Are sensitivity, encounter, and awareness groups really psychotherapies? These experiences tend to be positive, but they produce only moderate benefits (Faith, Wong, & Carpenter, 1995). Moreover, many of the claimed benefits may simply result from a kind of **therapy placebo effect,** in which improvement is based on a client's belief that therapy will help. Positive expectations, a break in daily routine, and an excuse to act differently can have quite an impact. The importance of such factors is easily illustrated: Participants in a weekend "retreat" that featured nothing more than volleyball, charades, and ballroom dancing reported enhanced mental health (McCardel & Murray, 1974)!

Perhaps it is naive to think that anyone's life might be transformed by a large-group experience. However, less ambitious goals often can be attained. For example, one recent program succeeded in teaching stress-management techniques in a large group setting (Timmerman, Emmelkamp, & Sanderman, 1998). Because of their versatility, groups undoubtedly will continue to be a major tool for solving problems and improving lives.

PSYCHOTHERAPY—AN OVERVIEW

How effective is psychotherapy?   Judging the outcome of therapy is tricky. Nevertheless, there is ample evidence that therapy is beneficial. Hundreds of studies show a strong pattern of positive effects for psychotherapy and counseling (Lambert & Cattani-Thompson, 1996; Lipsey & Wilson, 1993). Even more convincing, perhaps, are the findings of a national survey. Nearly 9 out of 10 people who have sought mental health care say their lives improved as a result of the treatment (Consumer, 1995; Kotkin, Daviet, & Gurin, 1996).

In general, then, psychotherapy works (Kopta et al., 1999). Of course, results vary in individual cases. For some people, therapy is immensely helpful; for others it is unsuccessful; overall, it is effective for more people than not. Speaking more subjectively, a real success, in which a person's life is changed for the better, can be worth the frustration of several cases in which little progress is made.

It is common to think of therapy as a long, slow process. But this is not always the case. Research shows that about 50 percent of all patients feel better after only 8 therapy sessions. After 26 sessions, roughly 75 percent have improved (Howard et al., 1986b) (❖Fig. 18.6). The typical "dose" of therapy is one hourly session per week. This means that the majority of patients improve after 6 months of therapy, and half feel better in just 2 months. Keep in mind that people often suffer for several years before seeking help. In view of this, such rapid improvement is impressive.

Core Features of Psychotherapy

What do psychotherapies have in common?   We have sampled only a few of the many therapies in use today. For a summary of major differences among psychotherapies, see ◆Table 18.2. To add to your understanding, let us briefly summarize what all techniques have in common.

All the psychotherapies we have discussed include some combination of the following goals: restoring hope, courage, and optimism; gaining insight; resolving conflicts; improving one's sense of self; changing unacceptable patterns of behavior; finding purpose; mending interpersonal relations; and learning to approach problems rationally (Seligman, 1998). To accomplish these goals, psychotherapies offer the following.

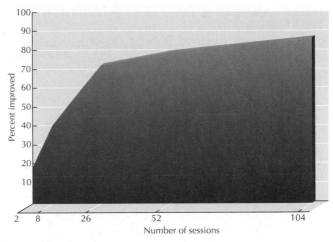

❖ **FIGURE 18.6** *The dose-improvement relationship in psychotherapy. This graph shows the percentage of patients who improved after varying numbers of therapy sessions. Notice that the most rapid improvement took place during the first 6 months of once-a-week sessions. (From Howard et al., 1986b.)*

1. Therapy provides a *caring relationship* between the client and therapist, called a **therapeutic alliance.** Emotional rapport, warmth, friendship, understanding, acceptance, and empathy are the basis for this relationship. The therapeutic alliance unites the client and therapist as they work together to solve the client's problems. The strength of this alliance has a major impact on whether therapy succeeds (Gaston et al., 1998; Stiles et al., 1998).

2. Therapy offers a *protected setting* in which emotional *catharsis* (release) can take place. Therapy is a sanctuary in which the client is free to express fears, anxieties, and personal secrets without fearing rejection or loss of confidentiality (Weiss, 1990).

3. All therapies to some extent offer an *explanation* or *rationale* for the client's suffering. Additionally, they propose a line of action that will end this suffering.

4. Therapy provides clients with a *new perspective* about themselves and their situations and a chance to practice *new behaviors* (Crencavage & Norcross, 1990; Stiles et al., 1986).

Family system *The family as an entire unit, including all its members, their relationships, and their typical patterns of behavior.*
Sensitivity group *A group experience consisting of exercises designed to increase self-awareness and sensitivity to others.*
Encounter group *A group experience that emphasizes intensely honest interchanges among participants regarding feelings and reactions to one another.*
Large-group awareness training *Any of a number of programs (many of them commercialized) that claim to increase self-awareness and facilitate constructive personal change.*
Therapy placebo effect *Improvement caused not by the actual process of therapy but by a client's expectation that therapy will help.*
Therapeutic alliance *A caring relationship that unites a therapist and a client in working to solve the client's problems.*

	INSIGHT OR ACTION?	DIRECTIVE OR NONDIRECTIVE?	INDIVIDUAL OR GROUP?	THERAPY'S STRENGTH*
Psychoanalysis	Insight	Directive	Individual	Searching honesty
Brief psychodynamic therapy	Insight	Directive	Individual	Productive use of conflict
Client-centered therapy	Insight	Nondirective	Both	Acceptance, empathy
Existential therapy	Insight	Both	Individual	Personal empowerment
Gestalt therapy	Insight	Directive	Both	Focus on immediate awareness
Behavior therapy	Action	Directive	Both	Observable changes in behavior
Cognitive therapy	Action	Directive	Individual	Constructive guidance
Rational-emotive behavior therapy	Action	Directive	Individual	Clarity of thinking and goals
Psychodrama	Insight	Directive	Group	Constructive re-enactments
Family therapy	Both	Directive	Group	Shared responsibility for problems

*This column based in part on Andrews (1989).

If you recall that our discussion began with trepanning and demonology, it is clear that psychotherapy has come a long way. Still, the search for ways to improve psychotherapy remains an urgent challenge for those who devote their lives to helping others.

MASTER THERAPISTS   Because therapies have much in common, a majority of psychologists have become *eclectic* in their work (Kopta et al., 1999). Eclectic therapists use whatever methods best fit a particular problem. In addition, some seek to combine the best elements of various therapies into more general systems.

What do the most capable therapists have in common?   A recent study of master therapists found that they share several characteristics (Jennings & Skovholt, 1999). The most effective therapists:

- Are enthusiastic learners
- Draw on their experience with similar problems
- Value complexity and ambiguity
- Are emotionally open
- Are mentally healthy and mature
- Nurture their own emotional well-being
- Realize that their emotional health affects their work
- Have strong social skills
- Cultivate a working alliance
- Expertly use their social skills in therapy

Notice that this list could also describe the kind of person most of us would want to talk to when facing a life crisis.

Basic Counseling Skills

A number of general helping skills can be distilled from the various approaches to therapy. These are points to keep in mind if you would like to comfort a person in distress, such as a troubled friend or relative (◆Table 18.3.)

ACTIVE LISTENING   People frequently talk "at" each other without really listening. A person with problems needs to be heard. Make a sincere effort to listen to and understand the person. Try to accept the person's message without judging it or leaping to conclusions. Let the person know you are listening, through eye contact, posture, your tone of voice, and your replies (Kottler & Brown, 1999).

CLARIFY THE PROBLEM   People who have a clear idea of what is wrong in their lives are more likely to discover solutions. Try to understand the problem from the person's point of view. As you do, check your understanding often. For example, you might ask, "Are you saying that you feel depressed just at school? Or in general?" Remember, a problem well defined is often half solved.

◆ TABLE 18.3 Helping Behaviors

To help another person gain insight into a personal problem, it is valuable to keep the following comparison in mind.

BEHAVIORS THAT HELP	BEHAVIORS THAT HINDER
Active listening	Probing painful topics
Acceptance	Judging or moralizing
Reflecting feelings	Criticism
Open-ended questioning	Threats
Supportive statements	Rejection
Respect	Ridicule or sarcasm
Patience	Impatience
Genuineness	Placing blame
Paraphrasing	Opinionated statements

(Adapted from Kottler & Brown, 1999.)

Teams of psychologists and counselors are often assembled to provide support to victims of major accidents and natural disasters. Because their work is stressful and often heart breaking, relief workers also benefit from on-site counseling. Expressing emotions and talking about feelings are major elements of disaster counseling.

FOCUS ON FEELINGS Feelings are neither right nor wrong. By focusing on feelings, you can encourage the outpouring of emotion that is the basis for catharsis. Passing judgment on what is said just makes people defensive. For example, a friend confides that he has failed a test. Perhaps you know that he studies very little. If you say, "Just study more and you would do better," he will probably become defensive or hostile. Much more can be accomplished by saying, "You must feel very frustrated" or simply "How do you feel about it?" (Ivey & Galvin, 1984).

AVOID GIVING ADVICE Many people mistakenly think that they must solve problems for others. Remember that your goal is to provide understanding and support, not solutions. Of course, it is reasonable to give advice when you are asked for it, but beware of the trap of the "Why don't you . . ? Yes, but . . ." game. According to psychotherapist Eric Berne (1964), this "game" follows a pattern: Someone says, "I have this problem." You say, "Why don't you do thus and so?" The person replies, "Yes, but . . ." and then tells you why your suggestion won't work. If you make a new suggestion, the reply will once again be "Yes, but. . . ." Obviously, the person either knows more about his or her personal situation than you do, or he or she has reasons for avoiding your advice. The student described earlier knows he needs to study. His problem is to understand why he doesn't *want* to study.

ACCEPT THE PERSON'S FRAME OF REFERENCE W. I. Thomas said, "Things perceived as real are real in their effects." Try to resist imposing your views on the problems of others. Because we all live in different psychological worlds, there is no "correct" view of a life situation. A person who feels that his or her viewpoint has been understood feels freer to examine it objectively and to question it. (Accepting and understanding the perspective of another person can be especially difficult when cultural differences exist. See this chapter's "A Step Beyond" for more information.)

REFLECT THOUGHTS AND FEELINGS One of the best things you can do when offering support to another person is to give feedback by simply restating what is said. This is also a good way to encourage a person to talk. If your friend seems to be at a loss for words, *restate* or *paraphrase* his or her last sentence. Here's an example.

Friend: *I'm really down about school. I can't get interested in any of my classes. I flunked my Spanish test, and somebody stole my notebook for psychology.*
You: *You're really upset about school, aren't you?*
Friend: *Yeah, and my parents are hassling me about my grades again.*
You: *You're feeling pressured by your parents?*
Friend: *Yeah, damn.*
You: *It must make you angry to be pressured by them.*

As simple as this sounds, it is very helpful to someone trying to sort out feelings. Try it. If nothing else, you'll develop a reputation as a fantastic conversationalist!

SILENCE Studies show that counselors tend to wait longer before responding than do people in everyday conversations. Pauses of 5 seconds or more are not unusual, and interrupting is rare. Listening patiently lets the person feel unhurried and encourages her or him to speak freely (Goodman, 1984).

QUESTIONS Because your goal is to encourage free expression, *open questions* tend to be the most helpful (Goodman, 1984). A *closed question* is one that can be answered yes or no. Open questions call for an open-ended reply. Say, for example, that a friend tells you, "I feel like my boss has it in for me at work." A closed question would be, "Oh yeah? So, are you going to quit?" Open questions such as "Do you want to tell me about it?" or "How do you feel about it?" are more likely to be helpful.

MAINTAIN CONFIDENTIALITY Your efforts to help will be wasted if you fail to respect the privacy of someone who has confided in you. Put yourself in the person's place. Don't gossip.

These guidelines are not an invitation to play "junior therapist." Professional therapists are trained to approach serious problems with skills far exceeding those described here. However, the points made help define the qualities of a therapeutic relationship. They also emphasize that each of us can supply two of the greatest mental health resources available at any cost: friendship and honest communication.

MEDICAL THERAPIES—PSYCHIATRIC CARE

Psychotherapy may be applied to anything from a brief crisis to a full-scale psychosis. However, most psychotherapists *do not* treat patients with major depressive disorders, schizophrenia, or other severe conditions. Major mental disorders are more often treated medically (Knesper et al., 1989; Kopta et al., 1999).

Three main types of **somatic** (bodily) **therapy** are *pharmacotherapy, electroconvulsive therapy,* and *psychosurgery.* Somatic therapy is often done in the context of psychiatric *hospitalization.* All the somatic approaches have a strong medical slant, and they are typically administered by psychiatrists.

Drugs

The atmosphere in psychiatric wards and mental hospitals changed radically in the mid-1950s with the widespread adoption of *pharmacotherapy* (FAR-meh-koe-THER-eh-pea). **Pharmacotherapy** is the use of drugs to alleviate the symptoms of emotional disturbance. Drugs may relieve the anxiety attacks

BRIDGES

Open questions are an effective way to begin and sustain a conversation.

See Chapter 15, page 512.

and other discomforts of milder psychological disorders. More often, however, they are used to combat schizophrenia and major mood disorders.

What types of drugs are used in pharmacotherapy? Three major classes of drugs are used. **Minor tranquilizers** (such as Valium) produce relaxation or reduce anxiety. **Antidepressants** are mood-elevating drugs that combat depression. **Antipsychotics** (also called **major tranquilizers**) have tranquilizing effects and, in addition, reduce hallucinations and delusional thinking. (See ◆Table 18.4 for examples of each class of drugs.)

Are drugs a valid approach to treatment? Drugs have shortened hospital stays, and they have greatly improved the chances that people will recover from major psychological disorders. Drug therapy has also made it possible for many people to return to the community, where they can be treated on an outpatient basis.

LIMITATIONS OF DRUG THERAPY Few experts would argue for a return to the conditions that existed before pharmacotherapy became available. However, drugs do have drawbacks. For example, 15 percent of patients taking major tranquilizers for long periods develop **tardive dyskinesia** (TAR-div dis-cah-NEE-zyah). This neurological disorder is marked by rhythmic facial and mouth movements, such as chewing, sucking, or smacking the lips. Unusual arm movements (such as "fly-catching" motions) and other restless actions are also common (Chakos et al., 1996).

New psychiatric drugs are often hailed as medical "miracles." However, all drugs involve a trade-off between benefits and risks. For example, the drug Clozaril (clozapine) can relieve the symptoms of schizophrenia in some previously "hopeless" cases (Buchanan et al., 1998). But Clozaril is nearly as dangerous as it is helpful: Two out of 100 patients taking the drug suffer from a potentially fatal blood disease.

Is the risk worth it? Many experts think it is, because chronic schizophrenia robs people of almost everything that makes life worth living.

It's possible, of course, that newer drugs will improve the risk-benefit ratio in the treatment of severe problems like schizophrenia. For example, the recently approved drug Risperdal (risperidone) appears to be as effective as Clozaril, without the lethal risk. It also shows no signs of causing tardive dyskinesia.

◆ **TABLE 18.4** Commonly Prescribed Psychiatric Drugs

CLASS	EXAMPLES (TRADE NAMES)	EFFECTS
Minor tranquilizers (anti-anxiety drugs)	Ativan, Halcion, Librium, Restoril, Valium, Zanax	Reduce anxiety, tension, fear
Antidepressants	Anafranil, Elavil, Nardil, Norpramin, Parnate, Paxil, Prozac, Tofranil, Zoloft	Counteract depression
Antipsychotics (major tranquilizers)	Clozaril, Haldol, Mellaril, Navane, Risperdal, Thorazine	Reduce agitation, delusions, hallucinations, thought disorders

THE RISKS OF SELF-MEDICATION

Some people are tempted to try folk remedies for emotional problems. For example, the herbal extract *Hypericum perforatum*, commonly known as St. John's wort, is being promoted as an alternative treatment for depression.

St. John's wort does appear to have some value for treating mild to moderate depression. However, until it has been thoroughly tested, we won't know how effective it is, what the correct dosage is, its possible side effects, or its long-term risks. In addition, many of the popular herbal remedies can interact with other drugs in ways that can pose serious dangers to the unwary.

Emotional problems and physical illnesses sometimes cause similar symptoms. As a result, self-medicating could delay treatment for a serious medical condition. In most cases, the risks of self-medication far outweigh the potential benefits. In the long run, professional mental health care is a bargain. (Sources: Bloomfield, Nordfors, & McWilliams, 1997; Gotlib, 1997; Linde et al., 1996.)

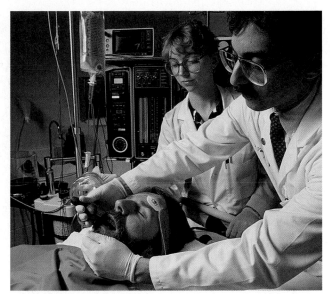

In electroconvulsive therapy, electrodes are attached to the head, and a brief electrical current is passed through the brain. ECT is used in the treatment of severe depression.

Even the best new drugs are not cure-alls. They help some people and relieve some problems, but not all. It is noteworthy that for serious mental disorders a combination of medication and psychotherapy almost always works better than drugs alone. Nevertheless, where schizophrenia and major mood disorders are concerned, drugs will undoubtedly remain the primary mode of treatment (Thase & Kupfer, 1996). (See "The Risks of Self-Medication.")

Shock

In **electroconvulsive therapy** (**ECT**), a 150-volt electrical current is passed through the brain for slightly less than a second. This rather drastic medical treatment for depression triggers a convulsion and causes the patient to lose consciousness for a short time. Muscle relaxants and sedative drugs are given before ECT to soften its impact. Treatments are given in a series of six to eight sessions spread over 3 to 4 weeks.

How does shock help? Actually, it is the seizure activity that is believed to be helpful. Proponents of ECT claim that shock-induced seizures alter the biochemical balance in the brain, bringing an end to severe depression and suicidal behavior (Swartz, 1993). Others have charged that ECT works only by confusing patients so they can't remember why they were depressed (Kohn, 1988).

THE ECT DEBATE   Many people consider ECT a distasteful procedure, and not all professionals support its use. However, most experts seem to agree on the following: (1) At best, ECT produces only temporary improvement that gets the patient out of a bad spot, and it must be combined with other treatments; (2) ECT does cause permanent memory losses in many patients; and (3) ECT should be used only as a last resort after drug therapy has failed (Kohn, 1988). All told, ECT is consid-

ered by many to be a valid treatment for selected cases of depression—especially when it rapidly ends wildly self-destructive or suicidal behavior (Abrams, 1997; Kellner, 1998). It's interesting to note that most ECT patients feel that the treatment helped them. Most, in fact, would have it done again (Bernstein et al., 1998).

Psychosurgery

The most extreme medical treatment is **psychosurgery** (any surgical alteration of the brain). The best-known psychosurgery is the lobotomy. In the **prefrontal lobotomy,** the frontal lobes were surgically disconnected from other brain areas. This procedure was supposed to calm people who didn't respond to any other type of treatment.

Somatic therapy *Any bodily therapy, such as drug therapy, electroconvulsive therapy, or psychosurgery.*
Pharmacotherapy *The use of drugs to alleviate the symptoms of emotional disturbance.*
Minor tranquilizers *Drugs (such as Valium) that produce relaxation or reduce anxiety.*
Antidepressants *Mood-elevating drugs.*
Antipsychotics *Drugs that, in addition to having tranquilizing effects, also tend to reduce hallucinations and delusional thinking. (Also called major tranquilizers.)*
Tardive dyskinesia *A neurological disorder associated with excessive use of antipsychotic drugs.*
Electroconvulsive therapy (ECT) *A treatment for severe depression, consisting of an electric shock passed directly through the brain, which induces a convulsion.*
Psychosurgery *Any surgical alteration of the brain designed to bring about desirable behavioral or emotional changes.*
Prefrontal lobotomy *An antiquated surgery in which portions of the frontal lobes were destroyed or disconnected from other brain areas.*

When the lobotomy was first introduced in the 1940s, there were enthusiastic claims for its success. But later studies suggested that some patients were calmed, some showed no change, and some became "vegetables." Lobotomies also produced a high rate of undesirable side effects, such as seizures, extreme lack of emotional response, major personality changes, and stupor. At about the same time that such problems became apparent, the first antipsychotic drugs became available. Soon after, the lobotomy was abandoned (Pressman, 1998; Swayze, 1995).

To what extent is psychosurgery used now?　Psychosurgery is still considered valid by many neurosurgeons. However, most now use **deep lesioning,** in which small target areas are destroyed in the brain's interior. The appeal of deep lesioning is that it can have fairly specific effects. For instance, patients suffering from a severe type of obsessive-compulsive disorder may be helped by psychosurgery (Cumming et al., 1995).

It is worth remembering that all forms of psychosurgery are *irreversible.* A drug can be given or taken away. You can't take back psychosurgery. Many critics argue that psychosurgery should be banned altogether. Others continue to report success with brain surgery. All things considered, it is perhaps most accurate, even after decades of use, to describe psychosurgery as an experimental technique. Nevertheless, it may have value as a remedy for some very specific disorders (Fenton, 1998).

Community Mental Health Programs

Community mental health centers are a bright spot in the area of mental health care. **Community mental health centers** offer a wide range of mental health services, such as prevention, counseling, consultation, and crisis intervention. Such centers try to minimize hospitalization and seek new answers to mental health problems. Typically, they provide short-term treatment, outpatient care, and special crisis or emergency services.

If it is like most, the primary aim of the mental health center in your community is to directly aid troubled citizens. The second goal of mental health centers is *prevention.* Consultation, education, and **crisis intervention** (skilled management of a psychological emergency) are used to end or prevent problems before they become serious. Also, some centers attempt to raise the general level of mental health in target areas by combating problems such as unemployment, delinquency, and drug abuse (Levine et al., 1993).

How have community mental health centers fared in meeting their goals?　In practice, they have concentrated much more on providing clinical services than they have on prevention. This appears to be primarily the result of wavering government support (translation: money). Overall, community mental health centers have succeeded in making mental health services more accessible than ever before. Many of their programs are made possible by **paraprofessionals** (individuals who work in a near-professional capacity under the supervision of more highly trained staff). Some paraprofessionals are ex-addicts, ex-alcoholics, or ex-patients who have "been there." Many more

BRIDGES

Deep lesioning is one of several methods used to investigate the brain's inner workings.

For more information, see Chapter 3, page 58.

are people (paid or volunteer) who have skills in tutoring, crafts, or counseling or who are simply warm, understanding, and skilled at communication. A career as a paraprofessional should not be overlooked by students planning to work in the field of mental health.

A LOOK AHEAD　In the "Psychology in Action" section that follows, we will return briefly to behavioral approaches. There you will find a number of useful techniques that you may be able to apply to your own behavior. You'll also find a discussion of when to seek professional help and how to find it. Here's your author's professional advice: This is information you won't want to skip.

KNOWLEDGE BUILDER
GROUP THERAPIES, PSYCHOTHERAPY SKILLS, AND MEDICAL THERAPIES

RELATE

Would you rather participate in individual therapy or group therapy? What advantages and disadvantages do you think each has?

Based on your own experience, how valid do you think it is to say that within families "a problem for one is a problem for all"?

What lies at the "heart" of psychotherapy? How would you describe it to a friend?

Which of the basic counseling skills do you already use? Which would improve your ability to help a person in distress?

If a family member of yours became severely depressed, what therapies would be available to him or her? What are the pros and cons of each choice?

LEARNING CHECK

1. In psychodrama, people attempt to form meaningful wholes out of disjointed thoughts, feelings, and actions. T or F?

2. Most large-group awareness trainings make use of Gestalt therapy. T or F?

3. Which therapy places great emphasis on role-playing?
   a. psychodrama *b.* awareness training *c.* family therapy *d.* encounter

4. Emotional _____ (release) in a protected setting is an element of most psychotherapies.

5. To aid a troubled friend, you should focus on facts rather than feelings, and you should critically evaluate what the person is saying to help him or her grasp reality. T or F?

6. One danger of giving advice is the tendency for the interchange to slip into the "Yes, but" game. T or F?

7. ECT is a modern form of pharmacotherapy. T or F?

8. Tardive dyskinesia is a possible complication in long-term use of
   a. major tranquilizers *b.* antidepressants *c.* minor tranquilizers *d.* ECT

9. Currently, the frontal lobotomy is the most widely used form of psychosurgery. T or F?

10. In your opinion, do psychologists have a duty to protect others who may be harmed by their clients? For example, if a patient has homicidal fantasies about his ex-wife, should she be informed?

11. In 1982, residents of Berkeley, California, voted on a referendum to ban the use of ECT within city limits. Do you think that the use of certain psychiatric treatments should be controlled by law?

Answers:

1. F 2. F 3. a 4. catharsis 5. F 6. T 7. F 8. a 9. F 10. According to the law, there is a duty to protect others where a therapist could, with little effort, prevent serious harm. However, this duty can conflict with a client's rights to confidentiality and with client–therapist trust. Therapists often make difficult choices in such situations. 11. The question of who can prescribe drugs, do surgery, and administer ECT *is* controlled by law. However, psychiatrists strongly object to residents, city councils, or government agencies making *medical* decisions.

psychology in action

SELF-MANAGEMENT AND SEEKING PROFESSIONAL HELP

"Throw out the snake oil, ladies and gentlemen, and throw away your troubles. Doctor B. Havior Modification is here to put an end to all human suffering."

True? Well, not quite. Behavior therapy is not a cure-all. Its use is often quite complicated and requires a great deal of expertise. Still, behavior therapy offers a straightforward solution to many problems.

As mentioned elsewhere in this book, you should seek professional help when a significant problem exists. For lesser difficulties, you may want to try applying behavioral principles yourself. Let us see how this might be done.

COVERT REWARD AND PUNISHMENT—BOOSTING YOUR "WILLPOWER"

"Have you ever decided to quit smoking cigarettes, watching television too much, eating too much, drinking too much, or driving too fast?"

"Well, one of those applies. I have decided several times to quit smoking."

"When have you decided?"

"Usually after I am reminded of how dangerous smoking is—like when I heard that my uncle had died of lung cancer. He smoked constantly."

"If you have decided to quit 'several times,' I assume you haven't succeeded."

"No, the usual pattern is for me to become upset about smoking and then to cut down for a day or two."

"You forget the disturbing image of your uncle's death, or whatever, and start smoking again."

"Yes, I suppose if I had an uncle die every day or so, I might actually quit!"

The use of electric shock to condition an aversion seems remote from everyday problems. Even naturally aversive actions

are difficult to apply to personal behavior. As mentioned earlier, for instance, rapid smoking is difficult for most smokers to carry out on their own. And what about a problem like overeating? It would be difficult indeed to eat enough to create a lasting aversion to overeating. (Although it's sometimes tempting to try.)

In view of such limitations, psychologists have developed an alternative procedure that can be used to curb smoking, overeating, and other habits (Cautela & Bennett, 1981; Cautela & Kearney, 1986).

COVERT SENSITIZATION   In **covert sensitization,** aversive imagery is used to reduce the occurrence of an undesired response. Here's how it's done: Obtain six 3-by-5 cards, and on each write a brief description of a scene related to the habit you wish to control. The scene should be so *disturbing* or *disgusting* that thinking about it would temporarily make you very uncomfortable about indulging in the habit. For smoking, the cards might read:

- I am in a doctor's office. The doctor looks at some reports and tells me I have lung cancer. He says a lung will have to be removed and sets a date for the operation.
- I am in bed under an oxygen tent. My chest feels caved in. There is a tube in my throat. I can barely breathe.
- I wake up in the morning and smoke a cigarette. I begin coughing up blood.

Deep lesioning *Use of an electrode (electrified wire) to destroy small areas deep within the brain.*
Community mental health center *A facility offering a wide range of mental health services, such as prevention, counseling, consultation, and crisis intervention.*
Crisis intervention *Skilled management of a psychological emergency.*
Paraprofessional *An individual who works in a near-professional capacity under the supervision of a more highly trained person.*
Covert sensitization *Use of aversive imagery to reduce the occurrence of an undesired response.*

Other cards would continue along the same line. For overeating, the cards might read:

- I am at the beach. I get up to go for a swim and I overhear people whispering to each other, "Isn't that fat disgusting?"
- I am at a store buying clothes. I try on several things that are too small. The only things that fit look like rumpled sacks. Salespeople are staring at me.

Other cards would continue along the same line.

The trick, of course, is to get yourself to imagine or picture vividly each of these disturbing scenes *several times* a day. Imagining the scenes can be accomplished by placing them under *stimulus control.* Simply choose something you do *frequently* each day (such as getting a cup of coffee or getting up from your chair). Next make a rule: Before you can get a cup of coffee or get up from your chair, or whatever you have selected as a cue, you must take out your cards and *vividly picture* yourself engaging in the action you wish to curb (eating or smoking, for example). Then *vividly picture* the scene described on the top card. Imagine the scene for 30 seconds.

After visualizing the top card, move it to the bottom so the cards are rotated. Make up new cards each week. The scenes can be made much more upsetting than the samples given here. The samples are toned down to keep you from being "grossed out."

Covert sensitization can also be used directly in situations that test your self-control. If you are trying to lose weight, for instance, you might be able to turn down a tempting dessert in this way: As you look at the dessert, visualize maggots crawling all over it. If you make this image as vivid and nauseating as possible, losing your appetite is almost a certainty. If you want to apply this technique to other situations, be aware that vomiting scenes are especially effective. Covert sensitization may sound as if you are "playing games with yourself," but it can be a great help if you want to cut down on a bad habit (Cautela & Kearney, 1986). Try it!

THOUGHT STOPPING   As discussed earlier, behavior therapists accept that thoughts, like visible responses, can also cause trouble. Think of times when you have repeatedly "put yourself down" mentally or when you have been preoccupied by needless worries, fears, or other negative and upsetting thoughts. If you would like to gain control over such thoughts, thought stopping may help you do it.

In **thought stopping,** aversive stimuli are used to interrupt or prevent upsetting thoughts. The simplest thought-stopping technique makes use of mild punishment to suppress upsetting mental images and internal "talk." Simply place a large, flat rubber band around your wrist. As you go through the day, apply this rule: Each time you catch yourself thinking the upsetting image or thought, pull the rubber band away from your wrist and snap it. You need not make this terribly painful. Its value lies in drawing your attention to how often you form negative thoughts and in interrupting the flow of thoughts. Strong punishment is not required.

It seems like this procedure might be abandoned rapidly. Is there an alternative?   A second thought-stopping procedure requires only that you interrupt upsetting thoughts each time they occur. Begin by setting aside time each day during which you will deliberately think the unwanted thought. As you begin to form the thought, shout "Stop!" aloud, with conviction. (Obviously, you should choose a private spot for this part of the procedure!)

Repeat the thought-stopping procedure 10 to 20 times for the first 2 or 3 days. Then switch to shouting "Stop!" covertly (to yourself) rather than aloud. Thereafter, thought stopping can be carried out throughout the day, whenever upsetting thoughts occur (Williams & Long, 1991). After several days of practice, you should be able to stop unwanted thoughts whenever they occur.

COVERT REINFORCEMENT   Earlier, we discussed how punishing images can be used to decrease undesirable responses, such as smoking or overeating. Many people also find it helpful to covertly *reinforce* desired actions. **Covert reinforcement** is the use of positive imagery to reinforce desired behavior. For example, suppose your target behavior is, once again, not eating dessert. If this were the case, you could do the following (Cautela & Bennett, 1981; Cautela & Kearney, 1986):

Imagine that you are standing at the dessert table with your friends. As dessert is passed, you politely refuse and feel good about staying on your diet.

These images would then be followed by imagining a pleasant, reinforcing scene:

Imagine that you are your ideal weight. You look really slim in your favorite color and style. Someone you like says to you, "Gee, you've lost weight. I've never seen you look so good."

For many people, of course, actual direct reinforcement (as described in the "Psychology in Action" section of Chapter 9) is the best way to alter behavior. Nevertheless, covert or "visualized" reinforcement can have similar effects. To make use of covert reinforcement, choose one or more target behaviors and rehearse them mentally. Then follow each rehearsal with a vivid, rewarding image.

SELF-DIRECTED DESENSITIZATION—OVERCOMING COMMON FEARS

You have prepared for 2 weeks to give a speech in a large class. As your turn approaches, your hands begin to tremble. Your heart pounds, and you find it difficult to breathe. You say to your body, "Relax!" What happens? Nothing!

RELAXATION   The key to desensitization is relaxation. To inhibit fear, one must *learn* to relax. Here is a description of how the **tension-release method** can be used to achieve deep-muscle relaxation.

Tense the muscles in your right arm until they tremble. Hold them tight for about 5 seconds and then let go. Allow your hand and arm to go limp and to relax completely. Repeat the procedure. Releasing tension two or three times will allow you to feel whether or not your arm muscles have relaxed. Repeat the tension-release procedure with your left arm. Compare it with your right arm. Repeat until the left arm is equally relaxed. Apply the tension-release technique to your right leg; to your left leg; to your abdomen; to your chest and shoulders. Clench and release your chin, neck, and throat. Wrinkle and release your forehead and scalp. Tighten and release your mouth and face muscles. As a last step, curl your toes and tense your feet. Then release.

Practice the tension-release method until you can achieve complete relaxation quickly (5 to 10 minutes).

After you have practiced relaxation once a day for a week or two, you will begin to be able to tell when your body (or a group of muscles) is tense. Also, you will begin to be able to relax on command. As an alternative, you might want to try imagining a very safe, pleasant, and relaxing scene. Some people find such images as relaxing as the tension-release method (Rosenthal, 1993b). Once you have learned to relax, the next step is to identify the fear you would like to control and construct a hierarchy.

PROCEDURE FOR CONSTRUCTING A HIERARCHY   Make a list of situations (related to the fear) that make you anxious. Try to list at least 10 situations. Some should be very frightening and others only mildly frightening. Write a short description of each situation on a separate 3-by-5 card. Place the cards in order from the least disturbing situation to the most disturbing. Here is a sample hierarchy for a student afraid of public speaking:

1. Being given an assignment to speak in class
2. Thinking about the topic and the date the speech must be given
3. Writing the speech; thinking about delivering the speech
4. Watching other students speak in class the week before the speech date
5. Rehearsing the speech alone; pretending to give it to the class
6. Delivering the speech to my roommate; pretending my roommate is the teacher
7. Reviewing the speech on the day it is to be presented
8. Entering the classroom; waiting and thinking about the speech
9. Being called; standing up; facing the audience
10. Delivering the speech

USING THE HIERARCHY   When you have mastered the relaxation exercises and have the hierarchy constructed, set aside time each day to work on reducing your fear. Begin by performing the relaxation exercises. When you are completely relaxed, visualize the scene on the first card (the least frightening scene). If you can *vividly* picture and imagine yourself in the first situation twice *without a noticeable increase in muscle tension*, proceed to the next card. Also, as you progress, relax yourself between cards.

Each day, stop when you reach a card that you cannot visualize without becoming tense in three attempts. Each day, begin one or two cards before the one on which you stopped the pre-

vious day. Continue to work with the cards until you can visualize the last situation without experiencing tension (techniques are based on Wolpe, 1974).

By using this approach, you should be able to reduce the fear or anxiety associated with things such as public speaking, entering darkened rooms, asking questions in large classes, heights, talking to members of the opposite sex, and taking tests. Even if you are not always able to reduce a fear, you will have learned to place relaxation under voluntary control. This alone is valuable because controlling unnecessary tension can increase energy and efficiency.

SEEKING PROFESSIONAL HELP—WHEN, WHERE, AND HOW?

How would I know if I should seek professional help at some point in my life?   Although there is no simple answer to this question, the following guidelines may be helpful.

1. If your level of psychological discomfort (unhappiness, anxiety, or depression, for example) is comparable to a level of physical discomfort that would cause you to see a doctor or dentist, you should consider seeing a psychologist or a psychiatrist.
2. Another signal to watch for is significant changes in behavior, such as the quality of your work (or schoolwork), your rate of absenteeism, your use of drugs (including alcohol), or your relationships with others.
3. Perhaps you have urged a friend or relative to seek professional help and were dismayed because he or she refused to do so. If *you* find friends or relatives making a similar suggestion, recognize that they may be seeing things more clearly than you are.
4. If you have persistent or disturbing suicidal thoughts or impulses, you should seek help immediately.

◆Table 18.5 lists the reasons most often given by people who voluntarily sought help from a mental health professional.

Locating a Therapist

If I wanted to talk to a therapist, how would I find one?   Here are some suggestions that could help you get started.

1. *The yellow pages.* Psychologists are listed in the telephone book under "Psychologist" or in some cases under "Counseling Services." Psychiatrists are generally listed as a subheading under "Physicians." Counselors are usually found under the heading "Marriage and Family Counselors." These listings will usually put you in touch with individuals in private practice.

Thought stopping   *Use of aversive stimuli to interrupt or prevent upsetting thoughts.*
Covert reinforcement   *Using positive imagery to reinforce desired behavior.*
Tension-release method   *A procedure for systematically achieving deep relaxation of the body.*

2. *Community or county mental health centers.* Most counties and many cities offer public mental health services. (These are listed in the phone book.) Public mental health centers usually provide counseling and therapy services directly, and they can refer you to private therapists.

3. *Mental health associations.* Many cities have mental health associations organized by concerned citizens. Groups such as these usually keep listings of qualified therapists and other services and programs in the community.

4. *Colleges and universities.* If you are a student, don't overlook counseling services offered by a student health center or special student counseling facilities.

5. *Newspaper advertisements.* Some psychologists advertise their services in newspapers. Also, low-cost "outreach" clinics occasionally try to make their presence known to the public by advertising. In either case, you should carefully inquire into a therapist's training and qualifications. Without the benefit of a referral from a trusted person, it is wise to be cautious.

6. *Crisis hotlines.* The typical crisis hotline is a telephone service staffed by community volunteers. These people are trained to provide information concerning a wide range of mental health problems. They also have lists of organizations, services, and other resources in the community to which you can go for help.

◆Table 18.6 summarizes all of the sources for psychotherapy, counseling, and referrals we have discussed, as well as some additional possibilities.

OPTIONS   *How would I know what kind of a therapist to see? How would I pick one?*   The choice between a psychiatrist and a psychologist is somewhat arbitrary. Both are trained to do psychotherapy. Although a psychiatrist can administer somatic therapy and prescribe drugs, a psychologist can work in conjunction with a physician if such services are needed. Psychologists and psychiatrists are equally effective as therapists (Consumer, 1995; Seligman, 1995).

Fees for psychiatrists are usually higher, averaging about $100 an hour. Psychologists average about $85 an hour. Counselors and social workers typically charge about $70 per hour. Group therapy averages only $40 because the therapist's fee is divided among several people (Engler & Goleman, 1992).

With fees in mind, your decision may be influenced by whether you have health insurance that will cover the expense. If fees are a problem, keep in mind that many therapists charge on a sliding scale, or ability-to-pay basis, and that community mental health centers almost always charge on a sliding scale.

Some communities and college campuses have counseling services staffed by sympathetic paraprofessionals or peer counselors. These services are free or very low cost. As mentioned earlier, paraprofessionals are people who work in a near-professional capacity under professional supervision. **Peer counselors** are nonprofessional persons who have learned basic counseling skills. There is a natural tendency, perhaps, to doubt the abilities of paraprofessionals. However, many studies have shown that paraprofessional counselors are often as effective as professionals (Christensen & Jacobson, 1994).

Also, don't overlook self-help groups, which can add valuable support to professional treatment. Members of a self-help group typically share a particular type of problem, such as eat-

◆ **TABLE 18.5** Reasons for Consulting a Mental Health Professional

REASON	PERCENT
Depression	21.2
Marital problems	16.8
Child-rearing problems	9.7
Difficulty in social relationships	5.3
Difficulty in work relationships	5.3
Suicidal thoughts	5.3
Alcohol or drug dependence	3.5
Desire to quit smoking	2.6
Obsession about something	2.6
Sexual dysfunction	2.6
Weight loss or eating disorders	1.8
Spousal or partner abuse	1.8
Hallucinations or hearing voices	1.8
Other	19.5

Note: Respondents could list more than one reason.
(Adapted from Murstein & Fontaine, 1993.)

◆ **TABLE 18.6** Mental Health Resources

- Family doctors
- Mental health specialists, such as psychiatrists, psychologists, social workers, or mental health counselors
- Health maintenance organizations
- Community mental health centers
- Hospital psychiatry departments and outpatient clinics
- University- or medical school-affiliated programs
- State hospital outpatient clinics
- Family service and social agencies
- Private clinics and facilities
- Employee assistance programs
- Local medical, psychiatric, or psychological societies

(Source: National Institute of Mental Health.)

ing disorders or coping with an alcoholic parent. **Self-help groups** offer members mutual support and a chance to discuss problems. In many instances, helping others also serves as therapy for those who give help (Levine, Toro, & Perkins, 1993). For some problems, self-help groups may be the best choice of all (Christensen & Jacobson, 1994; Fobair, 1997).

What about self-help books?   Many people turn to self-help books each year. At their best, self-help books can provide valuable information and advice. At their worst, self-help books are like a fast-food version of psychotherapy: They are quick and inexpensive, but low in nutritional value (Marx et al., 1992).

Some self-help books simply promise too much or make personal change sound too easy. Such books can lead readers to unfairly blame themselves for conditions over which they have little control. People who are already feeling overwhelmed might end up feeling utterly hopeless if they can't follow the advice given in a self-help book (Gambrill, 1992).

About one third of all therapists at least occasionally recommend self-help books to their clients. This practice, which is called **bibliotherapy** (book therapy), suggests that certain books do have value. Bibliotherapy is typically used to support traditional therapy. People who read self-help books on their own run a risk of getting bad advice or actually being harmed by what they read (Gambrill, 1992; Marx et al., 1992). Nevertheless, for some problems, such as passivity, anxiety, and milder forms of depression and sexual dysfunction, bibliotherapy can be effective (Ackerson et al., 1998; Cuijpers, 1997; Marrs, 1995).

In summary, if the problem is not too serious, and you read with a healthy dose of skepticism, some self-help books can actually be helpful. ◆Table 18.7 lists several books given favorable ratings by therapists and other experts (Marx et al., 1992; Santrock, Minnett, & Campbell, 1994.).

◆ TABLE 18.7 Favorably Rated Self-Help Books

Adult Children of Alcoholics (Woititz, 1983)
Anger: The Misunderstood Emotion (Tavris, 1989)
Anxiety Disorders and Phobias (Beck & Emery, 1985)
Cognitive Therapy and Emotional Disorders (Beck, 1976)
Feeling Good (Burns, 1980)
Learned Optimism (Seligman, 1991)
On Death and Dying (Kübler-Ross, 1969)
Parent Effectiveness Training (Gordon, 1970)
Passages (Sheehy, 1977)
Shyness (Zimbardo, 1977)
The Hurried Child (Elkind, 1981)
The Relaxation Response (Benson, 1975)
The Road Less Traveled (Peck, 1980)
What Color Is Your Parachute (Bolles, 1987)
When Bad Things Happen To Good People (Kushner, 1981)
When I Say No I Feel Guilty (Smith, 1975)
Women Who Love Too Much (Norwood, 1985)
You Just Don't Understand (Tannen, 1990)

(Marx et al., 1992; Santrock, Minnett, & Campbell, 1994.)

QUALIFICATIONS   You can usually find out about a therapist's qualifications simply by asking. A reputable therapist will be glad to reveal his or her background. If you have any doubts, credentials may be checked and other helpful information can be obtained from local branches of any of the following organizations. You can also write to the addresses listed here.

- American Family Therapy Association
  2020 Pennsylvania Ave. N.W., Suite 273
  Washington, DC 20006
- American Psychiatric Association
  1400 K Street N.W.
  Washington, DC 20005
- American Psychological Association
  750 1st Street N.E.
  Washington, DC 20002
- American Association of Humanistic Psychology
  7 Hartwood Dr.
  Amherst, NY 14226
- Canadian Psychiatric Association
  200–237 Argyle
  Ottawa, ONT K2P1B8
- National Mental Health Association
  1021 Prince St.
  Alexandria, VA 22314

The question of how to pick a particular therapist remains. The best way is to start with a short consultation with a respected psychiatrist, psychologist, or counselor. This will allow the person you consult to evaluate your difficulty and recommend a type of therapy or a therapist who is likely to be helpful. As an alternative, you might ask the person teaching this course for a referral.

EVALUATING A THERAPIST   *How would I know whether to quit or ignore a therapist?*   A balanced look at psychotherapies suggests that all *techniques* are about equally successful (Wampold et al., 1997). However, all *therapists* are not equally successful. Far more important than the approach used are the therapist's personal qualities (Luborsky et al., 1997). The most consistently successful therapists are those who are willing to use whatever method seems most helpful for a client. They are also marked by personal characteristics of warmth, integrity, sincerity, and empathy (Patterson, 1989; Strupp, 1989).

It is perhaps most accurate to say that, at this stage of development, psychotherapy is an art, not a science. The *relationship* between a client and therapist is the therapist's most basic tool (Hubble, Duncan, & Miller, 1999). This is why you must trust and easily relate to a therapist for therapy to be effective. Here are some danger signals to watch for in psychotherapy:

Peer counselor *A nonprofessional person who has learned basic counseling skills.*
Self-help group *A group of people who share a particular type of problem and provide mutual support to one another.*
Bibliotherapy *Therapy based on information presented in a book.*

- Sexual advances by therapist
- Therapist makes repeated verbal threats or is physically aggressive
- Therapist is excessively blaming, belittling, hostile, or controlling
- Therapist makes excessive small talk; talks repeatedly about his or her own problems
- Therapist encourages prolonged dependence on him or her
- Therapist demands absolute trust or tells client not to discuss therapy with anyone else

Clients who like their therapist are generally more successful in therapy (Talley et al., 1990). An especially important part of the therapeutic alliance is agreement about the goals of therapy. It is therefore a good idea to think about what you would like to accomplish by entering therapy. Write down your goals and discuss them with your therapist during the first session (Goldfried et al., 1990). Your first meeting with a therapist should also answer all of the following questions (Somberg et al., 1993):

- Will the information I reveal in therapy remain completely confidential?
- What risks do I face if I begin therapy?
- How long do you expect treatment to last?
- What form of treatment do you expect to use?
- Are there alternatives to therapy that might help me as much or more?

It's always tempting to avoid facing up to personal problems. With this in mind, you should give a therapist a fair chance and not give up too easily. But don't hesitate to change therapists or to terminate therapy if you lose confidence in the therapist or if you don't relate well to the therapist as a person.

SELF-MANAGEMENT AND FINDING PROFESSIONAL HELP

RELATE

How could you use covert sensitization, thought stopping, and covert reinforcement to change your behavior? Try to apply each technique to a specific example.

Just for practice, make a fear hierarchy for a situation you find frightening. Does vividly picturing items in the hierarchy make you tense or anxious? If so, can you intentionally relax by using the tension-release method?

Assume that you want to seek help from a psychologist or other mental health professional. How would you proceed? Take some time to actually find out what mental health services are available to you.

LEARNING CHECK

1. Covert sensitization and thought stopping combine aversion therapy and cognitive therapy. T or F?
2. Like covert aversion conditioning, covert reinforcement of desired responses is also possible. T or F?
3. Exercises that bring about deep-muscle relaxation are an essential element in covert sensitization. T or F?
4. Items in a desensitization hierarchy should be placed in order from the least disturbing to the most disturbing. T or F?
5. The first step in desensitization is to place the visualization of disturbing images under stimulus control. T or F?
6. Persistent emotional discomfort is a clear sign that professional psychological counseling should be sought. T or F?
7. Community mental health centers rarely offer counseling or therapy themselves; they only do referrals. T or F?
8. In many instances, a therapist's personal qualities have more of an effect on the outcome of therapy than does the type of therapy used. T or F?

CRITICAL THINKING

9. Would it be acceptable for a therapist to urge a client to break all ties with a troublesome family member?

Answers:

1. T 2. T 3. F 4. T 5. F 6. T 7. F 8. T 9. Such decisions must be made by clients themselves. Therapists can help clients evaluate important decisions and feelings about significant persons in their lives. However, actively urging a client to sever a relationship borders on unethical behavior.

Focus: Do cultural differences affect counseling and psychotherapy?

Our multi-ethnic society increasingly calls for therapists who can work with clients from varied cultural backgrounds (Montague, 1996; Storck, 1997). Consider the following case history:

David Chan

David Chan, a 21-year-old engineering student, was failing his classes and suffering from headaches, indigestion, and insomnia. During his first counseling session, David seemed depressed and anxious. He responded to questions with polite statements that revealed little about his feelings. After several more sessions, the counselor realized that David disliked engineering, but felt pressured by his parents to enter this career. The counselor thought that David was too dependent on his parents and unable to express his anger towards them. To help him vent his feelings, the counselor used a Gestalt technique called the "empty chair." The counselor asked David to imagine that his parents were seated in two chairs. After much prompting, David was able to express his true feelings toward his parents. However, in the following sessions, David seemed even more withdrawn and guilt-ridden than before (Sue & Sue, 1991).

David's counselor had a history of success with other clients. What went wrong with David? The fault lies in subtle cultural differences between the counselor, a European American, and David, a Chinese American.

David's cultural heritage emphasizes moderation, self-discipline, patience, humility, and respect for one's parents. David's counselor was trained to value independence, openness, and the free expression of thoughts and feelings. Using his own values as a guide, the counselor misunderstood David's restrained answers to questions, which merely showed proper deference to authority. The counselor's use of the empty chair technique was also a mistake. "Honor thy parents" is a very basic Chinese American value. Asking David to "talk back" to his parents actually made his conflicts worse. For David, a less direct, more culturally aware approach might have been more helpful (Sue & Sue, 1991).

Traditional therapies tend to emphasize values like those listed in ◆Table 18.1. However, these values are not shared by all cultures or ethnic groups. For example, North American culture strongly emphasizes competition and individualism, whereas others stress cooperation and group effort. The behavior that David's counselor saw as overly passive is actually preferred in Chinese American culture. In short, therapists need to use techniques that are consistent with the life experiences and cultural values of their clients (Lee, 1991b).

Cultural Barriers

When a client and therapist come from different cultural backgrounds, misunderstandings are common (Clauss, 1998; Storck, 1997). Cultural groups vary greatly in their beliefs, values, religious convictions, lifestyles, sexual attitudes, and family structures. The culturally aware therapist must be careful to not make false assumptions about a client's personal history, values, goals for therapy, or expectations (Montague, 1996).

Psychologists Derald Sue and David Sue (1990) believe there are four main **cultural barriers** to counseling. These include differences in language, social class, cultural values, and nonverbal communication. Nonverbal communication provides an example of how even small cultural differences cause misunderstandings. Most Native American people show respect by not making eye contact. In fact, Native Americans who enter therapy often spend much of their time looking at their feet or at the ground. But if a therapist doesn't understand this behavior, it looks like a sign of poor self-esteem. In light of such misunderstandings, it's not surprising that more than half of all Native Americans do not return after a first therapy session with non-native therapists (Heinrich, Corbine, & Thomas, 1990). Misunderstanding such nonverbal communication can lead to serious mistakes by therapists (Singh, McKay, & Singh, 1998).

Culturally Skilled Counselors

A **culturally skilled counselor** is a therapist who has the awareness, knowledge, and skills to intervene successfully in the lives of clients from diverse cultural backgrounds. Counselors, of course, need to be aware of issues faced by almost everyone. In addition, the culturally skilled counselor must know about the special conflicts and problems typical of members of various racial or ethnic groups (Montague, 1996; Zayas et al., 1996).

A major step toward becoming a culturally skilled counselor is to be more aware of one's own cultural values and biases. Therapists must also sincerely accept that different cultural beliefs are not inferior to their own (Heinrich, Corbine, & Thomas, 1990). They need to learn about the history and culture of diverse groups of people, ideally through direct experience (Lee, 1991b). In particular, culturally skilled counselors must be able to mentally take the role of a client (Scott & Borodovsky, 1990).

Cultural barriers *Differences in language, social class, cultural values, and nonverbal communication that lead to misunderstandings between people with different cultural backgrounds.*
Culturally skilled counselor *A therapist who has the awareness, knowledge, and skills necessary to treat clients from diverse cultural backgrounds.*

What do you mean by "mentally take the role of a client"? Multicultural counselors attempt to put themselves in their clients' shoes by making sure they understand the client's sense of ethnic identity, degree of acculturation, family influences, sex role socialization, religious beliefs, and immigration experiences (Lee, 1991a). The more the counselor's and client's backgrounds differ, the more important it is for such factors to guide therapy. In summary, the culturally skilled counselor must be able to do all of the following (Lee, 1991b):

- Be aware of his or her own cultural values and biases
- Establish rapport with a person from a different cultural background
- Adapt traditional theories and techniques to meet the needs of clients from non-European ethnic or racial groups
- Be sensitive to cultural differences without resorting to stereotypes
- Treat members of racial or ethnic communities as individuals
- Be aware of a client's ethnic identity and degree of acculturation to the majority society
- Use existing helping resources within a cultural group to support efforts to resolve problems

SUMMARY Multicultural awareness has helped broaden our ideas about mental health. Furthermore, the lessons learned in cross-cultural counseling draw attention to other differences that may affect therapy. Skilled therapists must be sensitive not only to racial and ethnic differences but also to differences based on a client's sex, age, education, sexual orientation, religious beliefs, and handicaps.

Ultimately, it is worth remembering that cultural barriers apply to communication in all areas of life, not just therapy. Although such differences can be challenging, they are also frequently enriching (Sue, 1998).

CONCLUSION: To be fully effective in today's multicultural society, therapists and counselors must be sensitive to cultural differences and capable of adjusting their methods to fit the needs of a culturally diverse clientele.

KNOWLEDGE BUILDER
CULTURALLY SKILLED THERAPISTS

RELATE

To be effective, what should a therapist know about your ethnic identity, degree of acculturation, family influences, gender role socialization, religious beliefs, sex, sexual orientation, age, and abilities? Would you expect for it to be easy or difficult to find a counselor well suited to your unique personal profile?

LEARNING CHECK

1. As the case history of David Chan shows, it is almost impossible for counseling or psychotherapy to succeed when the cultural backgrounds of a client and therapist are very different. T or F?

2. A major difference in social class between a client and a therapist, such as urban poor versus upper middle class, is considered less of a barrier than differences in nonverbal communication. T or F?

3. The culturally skilled counselor must be highly aware of his or her own cultural background, as well as that of clients. T or F?

4. Although Marsha cannot really know what it is like to leave a war-torn nation and emigrate to a strange country, she has talked extensively with members of the Vietnamese American community and feels great empathy for them. Marsha has met a key requirement for effective cross-cultural counseling of Vietnamese immigrants. T or F?

CRITICAL THINKING

5. The essence of culturally skilled counseling could be summarized as an awareness of the social and cultural _____ in which people live.

Answers:

1. F 2. F 3. T 4. T 5. contexts

CHAPTER IN REVIEW

How do psychotherapies differ? How did psychotherapy originate?

- Psychotherapies may be classified as insight, action, directive, nondirective, or supportive therapies, and combinations of these.
- Therapies may be conducted either individually or in groups, and they may be time limited.
- Primitive approaches to mental illness were often based on belief in supernatural forces.
- Trepanning involved boring a hole in the skull.
- Demonology attributed mental disturbance to demonic possession and prescribed exorcism as the cure.
- In some instances, the actual cause of bizarre behavior may have been ergot poisoning.
- More humane treatment began in 1793 with the work of Philippe Pinel in Paris.

Is Freudian psychoanalysis still used?

- Freud's psychoanalysis was the first formal psychotherapy. Psychoanalysis seeks to release repressed thoughts and emotions from the unconscious.
- The psychoanalyst uses free association, dream analysis, and analysis of resistance and transference to reveal health-producing insights.
- Some critics argue that traditional psychoanalysis receives credit for spontaneous remissions of symptoms. However, psychoanalysis has been shown to be successful for many patients.
- Brief psychodynamic therapy (which relies on psychoanalytic theory but is brief and focused) is as effective as other major therapies.

What are the major humanistic therapies?

- Client-centered (or person-centered) therapy is nondirective and is dedicated to creating an atmosphere of growth.
- Unconditional positive regard, empathy, authenticity, and reflection are combined to give the client a chance to solve his or her own problems.
- Existential therapies, such as Frankl's logotherapy, focus on the end result of the choices one makes in life. Clients are encouraged through confrontation and encounter to exercise free will and to take responsibility for their choices.
- Gestalt therapy emphasizes immediate awareness of thoughts and feelings. Its goal is to rebuild thinking, feeling, and acting into connected wholes and to help clients break through emotional blockages.
- Media psychologists, telephone counselors, and cybertherapists may, on occasion, do some good. However, each has serious drawbacks, and the effectiveness of telephone counseling and cybertherapy has not been established.
- Therapy by videoconferencing shows more promise as a way to provide mental health services at a distance.

What is behavior therapy?

- Behavior therapists use various behavior modification techniques that apply learning principles to change human behavior.

- In aversion therapy, classical conditioning is used to associate maladaptive behavior (such as smoking or drinking) with pain or other aversive events in order to inhibit undesirable responses.

How is behavior therapy used to treat phobias, fears, and anxieties?

- Classical conditioning also underlies systematic desensitization, a technique used to overcome fears and anxieties. In desensitization, gradual adaptation and reciprocal inhibition break the link between fear and particular situations.
- Typical steps in desensitization are: Construct a fear hierarchy, learn to produce total relaxation, and perform items on the hierarchy (from least to most disturbing).
- Desensitization may be carried out with real settings, or it may be done by vividly imagining the fear hierarchy.
- Desensitization is also effective when it is administered vicariously—that is, when clients watch models perform the feared responses.
- In some cases, virtual reality exposure can be used to present fear stimuli in a controlled manner.
- A new technique called eye movement desensitization and reprocessing (EMDR) shows promise as a treatment for traumatic memories and stress disorders. At present, however, EMDR is highly controversial.

What role does reinforcement play in behavior therapy?

- Behavior modification also makes use of operant principles, such as positive reinforcement, nonreinforcement, extinction, punishment, shaping, stimulus control, and time out. These principles are used to extinguish undesirable responses and to promote constructive behavior.
- Nonreward can extinguish troublesome behaviors. Often this is done by simply identifying and eliminating reinforcers, particularly attention and approval.
- To apply positive reinforcement and operant shaping, symbolic rewards known as tokens are often used. Tokens allow immediate reinforcement of selected target behaviors.
- Full-scale use of tokens in an institutional setting produces a token economy. Toward the end of a token economy program, patients are shifted to social rewards such as recognition and approval.

Can therapy change thoughts and emotions?

- Cognitive therapy emphasizes changing thought patterns that underlie emotional or behavioral problems. Its goals are to correct distorted thinking and/or teach improved coping skills.
- In a variation of cognitive therapy called rational-emotive behavior therapy (REBT), clients learn to recognize and challenge their own irrational beliefs.

Can psychotherapy be done with groups of people?

- Group therapy may be a simple extension of individual methods, or it may be based on techniques developed specifically for groups.
- In psychodrama, individuals enact roles and incidents resembling their real-life problems. In family therapy, the family group is treated as a unit.

- Although they are not literally psychotherapies, sensitivity and encounter groups attempt to encourage positive personality change. In recent years, commercially offered large-group awareness trainings have become popular. However, the therapeutic benefits of such programs are questionable.

What do various therapies have in common?

- To alleviate personal problems, all psychotherapies offer a caring relationship, emotional rapport, a protected setting, catharsis, explanations for the client's problems, a new perspective, and a chance to practice new behaviors.
- Many basic counseling skills underlie a variety of therapies. These include listening actively, helping to clarify the problem, focusing on feelings, avoiding the giving of unwanted advice, accepting the person's perspective, reflecting thoughts and feelings, being patient during silences, using open questions when possible, and maintaining confidentiality.

How do psychiatrists treat psychological disorders?

- Three medical, or somatic, approaches to treatment are pharmacotherapy, electroconvulsive therapy (ECT), and psychosurgery. All three techniques are controversial to a degree because of questions about effectiveness and side effects.
- Community mental health centers seek to avoid or minimize mental hospitalization. They also seek to prevent mental health problems through education, consultation, and crisis intervention.

How are behavioral principles applied to everyday problems?

- Cognitive techniques can be an aid to managing personal behavior.
- In covert sensitization, aversive images are used to discourage unwanted behavior.
- Thought stopping uses mild punishment to prevent upsetting thoughts.
- Covert reinforcement is a way to encourage desired responses by mental rehearsal.
- Desensitization pairs relaxation with a hierarchy of upsetting images in order to lessen fears.

How could a person find professional help?

- In most communities, a competent and reputable therapist can be located with public sources of information or through a referral.
- Practical considerations such as cost and qualifications enter into choosing a therapist. However, the therapist's personal characteristics are of equal importance.

Do cultural differences affect counseling and psychotherapy?

- Many cultural barriers to effective counseling and therapy have been identified.

- Aware therapists are beginning to seek out the knowledge and skills needed to intervene successfully in the lives of clients from diverse cultural backgrounds.
- The culturally skilled counselor must be able to establish rapport with a person from a different cultural background and adapt traditional theories and techniques to meet the needs of clients from non-European ethnic or racial groups.

PSYCHOLOGY ON THE NET

- **Basics of Cognitive Therapy** An overview of cognitive therapy, with suggested readings. http://mindstreet.com/cbt.html
- **How to Find Help for Life's Problems** Provides information on psychotherapy and advice on how to choose a psychotherapist. http://helping.apa.org/brochure/index.html
- **NetPsychology** Explores the delivery of psychological services on the Internet. http://netpsych.com/
- **Psychological Self-Help** An on-line book about self-improvement. http://www.cmhc.com/psyhelp/
- **The Effectiveness of Psychotherapy** A summary of the *Consumer Reports* survey on the effectiveness of psychotherapy. http://www.cmhc.com/articles/seligm.htm
- **Types of Therapies** Describes four different approaches to therapy. Also has information about choosing a therapist. http://www.grohol.com/therapy.htm
- **Web Counselor** Typical personal problems are presented along with examples of advice. http://www.queendom.com/shrink.html
- **•InfoTrac® College Edition** For more information about topics in the "Psychology in Action" feature, use Key Words search for PSYCHOTHERAPY.

INTERACTIVE LEARNING

- *PsychNow!* 7b. Major psychological therapies.
- *Psyk.trek* 11d. Insight therapies. 11e. Behavioral and biomedical therapies.

Social Behavior

Chapter Survey

Theme: *Humans are social animals. We live in a social world in which our behavior is frequently influenced by the presence of others.*

▼ **KEY QUESTIONS**

● ***KEY TOPICS***

▼ How does group membership affect individual behavior?

- ● *Culture, roles, status, group structure, and norms*

▼ What unspoken rules govern the use of personal space?

- ● *Proxemics and personal space*
- ● *Spatial norms*

▼ How do we perceive the motives of others and the causes of our own behavior?

- ● *Attribution theory and errors in attribution*
- ● *Self-handicapping*

▼ Why do people affiliate?

- ● *The need to affiliate*
- ● *Social comparison theory*

▼ **KEY QUESTIONS**

● ***KEY TOPICS***

▼ What factors influence interpersonal attraction?

- ● *Patterns of interpersonal attraction*
- ● *Self-disclosure*
- ● *Social exchange theory*
- ● *Romantic love and attachment*

▼ What have social psychologists learned about conformity, social power, obedience, and compliance?

- ● *Conformity, groupthink, social power, obedience, and compliance*

▼ How does self-assertion differ from aggression?

- ● *Assertiveness training*

▼ What is a social trap?

- ● *Social traps and the tragedy of the commons*

THE SOCIAL ANIMAL

To live alone, one must be either an animal or a god.
Aristotle

No man is an Iland, intire of itselfe.
John Donne

HERE'S YOUR ASSIGNMENT: *You have been given a written message and the name, address, and occupation of the person who should receive it. The "target person" lives more than 1,500 miles away, in a city you have never visited. You can move the message by mail, but you may send it only to a first-name acquaintance. That person, in turn, must mail the message to a first-name acquaintance. The message is to be moved in this fashion until it reaches the target person, whom the previous person must know by name.*

Sound impossible? Social psychologist Stanley Milgram asked people to try moving messages in this way. Amazingly, about one in five made it. Many were handed to the target person by a friend or an acquaintance. Even more amazing is the fact that, on average, only seven people were needed to link two strangers separated by half a continent (Korte & Milgram, 1970; Milgram, 1967)!

How is that possible? *Each of us is part of a rich tapestry of social relationships. You probably know at least dozens of people by name. Each of them knows dozens more people, who each know still more people, and so on. Thus, each social relationship connects with many others. By following all the social links, you could reach millions of people, just seven "layers" out. Undeniably, humans are social animals.*

Social psychology *is the scientific study of how individuals behave, think, and feel in social situations (that is, in the presence, actual or implied, of others) (Baron & Byrne, 1997). Every day, there is a fascinating interplay between our own behavior and that of people around us. Social behavior has been the target of*

an immense amount of study—too much, in fact, for us to cover in detail. Therefore, this chapter and the next are social psychology "samplers." It is hoped that you will find the topics interesting and thought provoking.

Gateways to Social Behavior

SOCIAL PSYCHOLOGY studies how we behave, think, and feel in social situations.

THE NATURE OF MANY RELATIONSHIPS is revealed by the distance you are comfortable maintaining between yourself and another person.

SOCIAL BEHAVIOR cannot be fully understood unless we know to what causes people attribute their behavior and how they explain the behavior of others.

WE ARE ATTRACTED TO OTHER PEOPLE—even potential mates—for reasons that are predictable and fairly universal.

MANY SOCIAL INTERACTIONS can be understood as an exchange of attention, information, affection, or favors between two people.

A MAJOR FACT OF SOCIAL LIFE is that our behavior is influenced in numerous ways by the actions of other people.

EVERYONE is affected by pressures to conform, obey, and comply. There are times when it is valuable to know how to recognize and resist such pressures.

ASSERTIVENESS is a valuable alternative to becoming aggressive or being victimized in social situations.

A NUMBER OF SOCIAL PROBLEMS are based on social traps—situations that provide immediate rewards for actions that have damaging effects in the long run.

HUMANS IN A SOCIAL CONTEXT—PEOPLE, PEOPLE, EVERYWHERE

We are born into an organized society. Established values, expectations, and behavior patterns are present when we arrive. So, too, is **culture,** an ongoing pattern of life that is passed from one generation to the next. To appreciate the impact of culture, think about how you have been affected by language, marriage customs, concepts of ownership, and gender roles.

Roles

Each person in society is a member of many overlapping social groups: families, teams, church groups, work groups, and so on. In each group, we occupy a *position* in the *structure* of the group. **Social roles** are patterns of behavior expected of persons in various social positions. For instance, playing the roles mother, boss, and student involves different sets of behaviors and expectations. Some roles are **ascribed** (they are assigned to a person or are not under personal control): male or female, son, adolescent, inmate. **Achieved roles** are attained voluntarily or by special effort: spouse, teacher, scientist, band leader.

What effect does role-playing have on behavior? Roles streamline daily interactions by allowing us to anticipate the behavior of others. When a person is acting as a doctor, mother, clerk, or police officer, we expect certain behaviors. However, roles have a negative side, too. Many people experience **role conflicts,** in which two or more roles make conflicting demands on behavior. Consider, for example, a judge whose neighbor's son is brought in with a traffic violation or the teacher who must flunk a close friend's daughter. Likewise, the clashing demands of work, family, and school create role conflicts for many students (Hammer, Grigsby, & Woods, 1998).

Roles have a powerful impact on social behavior. What kinds of behavior do you expect from your teachers? What behaviors do they expect from you? What happens if either of you fails to match the other's expectations?

A study done by Philip Zimbardo and his students at Stanford University dramatically shows the impact of social roles. In this experiment, normal, healthy, male college students were paid to serve as "inmates" and "guards" in a simulated prison (Zimbardo et al., 1973).

After just 2 days in "jail," the prisoners grew restless and defiant. When they staged a disturbance, the guards unmercifully suppressed the rebellion. Over the next few days, the guards clamped down with increasing brutality. In a surprisingly short time, the sham convicts looked like real prisoners: They were dejected, traumatized, passive, and dehumanized. Four of them had to be released because of hysterical crying, confusion, or severe depression. Each day, the guards tormented the prisoners with more frequent commands, insults, and demeaning tasks. After 6 days, the experiment was halted.

What had happened? Apparently, the assigned roles—prisoner and guard—were so powerful that in just a few days the experiment became "reality" for those involved. Afterward, it was difficult for many of the guards to believe their own behavior. As one recalls, "I was surprised at myself. I made them call each other names and clean toilets out with their bare hands. I practically considered the prisoners cattle" (Zimbardo, 1973). Clearly, the origins of many destructive human relationships can be found in destructive roles.

Group Structure and Cohesion

Are there other dimensions of group membership? Two important dimensions of any group are its structure and its cohesiveness. **Group structure** consists of the network of roles, communication pathways, and power in a group. Organized groups such as an army or an athletic team have a high degree of structure. Informal friendship groups may or may not be very structured.

Group cohesiveness is basically the degree of attraction among group members or their commitment to remaining in the group. Members of cohesive groups literally stick together: They tend to stand or sit close together, they pay more attention to one another, and they show more signs of mutual affection. Also, their behavior tends to be closely coordinated (Levine & Moreland, 1990). Cohesiveness is the basis for much of the power that groups exert over their members. Therapy groups, businesses, sports teams, and the like often actively seek to strengthen group cohesion. One reason for this is because cohesive groups tend to work together better and they are better at solving problems (Craig & Kelly, 1999).

STATUS   In addition to defining roles, a person's social position within groups determines his or her **status,** or level of social power and importance. In most groups, higher status bestows special privileges and respect. For example, in a classic experiment, researchers left dimes in phone booths. When people entered the booths, a researcher approached and said, "Excuse me, I think I left a dime in this phone booth a few minutes ago. Did you find it?" Seventy-seven percent of the people who were approached returned the money when the researcher was well dressed. Only 38 percent returned it to poorly dressed researchers (Bickman, 1974). Perhaps the better treatment given "higher-status" persons in this example explains some of our society's preoccupation with expensive clothes, cars, and other status symbols. (For another perspective on the effects of status differences, see "Touch and Status.")

NORMS   We are also greatly affected by group norms. A **norm** is an accepted (but often unspoken) standard for appropriate behavior. If you have the slightest doubt about the power of group norms, try this test: Board a crowded bus, find a seat, and begin singing loudly in your fullest voice. Probably only 1 person in 100 could actually carry out these instructions.

Social psychology *The scientific study of how individuals behave, think, and feel in social situations.*
Culture *An ongoing pattern of life, characterizing a society at a given point in history.*
Social role *Expected behavior patterns associated with particular social positions (such as daughter, worker, student).*
Ascribed role *A role that is assigned to a person; a role one has no choice about playing.*
Achieved role *A role that is assumed voluntarily.*
Role conflict *Trying to occupy two or more roles that make conflicting demands on behavior.*
Group structure *The network of roles, communication pathways, and power in a group.*
Group cohesiveness *The degree of attraction among group members or their commitment to remaining in the group.*
Status *An individual's position in a social structure, especially with respect to power, privilege, or importance.*
Norm *An accepted (but often unspoken) standard of conduct for appropriate behavior.*

TOUCH AND STATUS

Pause for a moment and think about who you touch during a typical day. Do you think that social status affects your patterns of touching and being touched by others?

It would be surprising if touching weren't affected by status. Touch is one of the most basic forms of communication. Its message can be one of warmth, friendship, caring, nurturance, or sexual interest (see Chapter 14). In addition, touching is a "privilege" of power and high status. Older people, for instance, are more likely to touch younger people than the reverse. Likewise, people of high socioeconomic status are more likely to touch those of lower status.

Even in situations where people touch each other equal amounts, there is an important difference. When a person of higher status touches one of lower status, the contact is more likely to be "personal" or familiar. When lower status people touch those of higher status, it is more likely to be formal or impersonal, such as a handshake (Hall, 1996b).

There is one more difference worth noting. Men, by virtue of their higher status and greater power in society, are more likely to touch women than women are to touch men (Major, Schmidlin, & Williams, 1990). This difference is highly visible in most work settings: Picture a male boss touching his female secretary on the shoulder or arm to get her attention; she, in turn, never touches him. Although women have moved toward equal status with men, patterns of social touching suggest that subtle inequalities in power and dominance persist.

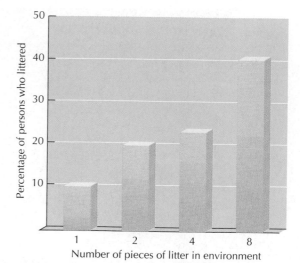

❖ **FIGURE 19.1** *Results of an experiment on norms concerning littering. The prior existence of litter in a public setting implies that littering is acceptable. This encourages others to "trash" the area. (From Cialdini, Reno, & Kallgren, 1990.)*

The impact of norms is shown by an interesting experiment on littering. The question was, Does the amount of trash discarded in an area affect whether people will add to the litter? To find out, people were given handbills as they walked into a public parking garage. As you can see in ❖Figure 19.1, the more litter there was in the garage, the more likely people were to add to it—by dropping their handbills on the floor. Apparently, seeing that others had already littered implied a lax norm about whether littering is acceptable. The moral? The cleaner a public area is kept, the less likely people are to "trash" it (Cialdini, Reno, & Kallgren, 1990).

How are norms formed? One early study of group norms made use of a striking illusion called the **autokinetic effect.** In a completely darkened room, a stationary pinpoint of light will appear to drift or move about. (The light is therefore *autokinetic,* or "self-moving.") Muzafer Sherif (1906–1988) found that people give very different estimates of how far the light moves. However, when two or more people announce their estimates at the same time, their judgments rapidly converge. This is an example of *social influence,* in which one person's behavior is changed by the actions of others. We will return to social influence later. For now, it is enough to note that a convergence of attitudes, beliefs, and behaviors tends to take place in many groups.

Norms are often based on our *perceptions* of what others think and do. For example, a majority of college students believe that they are more troubled about excessive drinking on campus than other students are. Apparently, many students are fooled by a false norm. Ironically, they help create this false impression by not speaking up. If disapproving students actually outnumber "party animals," then campus norms for acceptable drinking should be fairly conservative, which is usually not the case (Prentice & Miller, 1993).

A vivid example of how norms influence behavior is found in unspoken rules that govern the use of *personal space.* Because personal space is an intriguing topic in its own right, let's take a moment to examine it.

PERSONAL SPACE—INVISIBLE BOUNDARIES

An interesting aspect of social behavior is the effort people make to regulate the space around their bodies. Each person has an invisible "spatial envelope" that defines his or her **personal space.** This is an area surrounding the body that is regarded as private and subject to personal control. Basically, personal space extends "I" or "me" boundaries past the skin.

What effect does personal space have on behavior? Maintaining and regulating personal space affects many social interactions. Powerful norms define the interpersonal distance we regard as appropriate for formal business, casual conversation, waiting in line with strangers, and other situations.

The systematic study of rules for the use of personal space is called **proxemics** (Hall, 1974b). You can demonstrate personal space and the nature of proxemics by "invading" the space of another person. The next time you are talking with an acquaintance, move closer and watch the reaction. Most people show

The use of space in public places is governed by unspoken norms, or "rules," about what is appropriate.

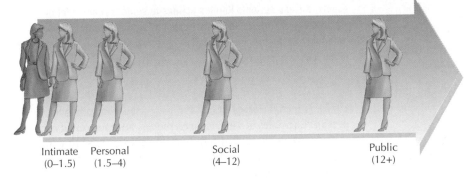

Intimate
(0–1.5)

Personal
(1.5–4)

Social
(4–12)

Public
(12+)

❖ **FIGURE 19.2** *Typical spatial zones (in feet) for face-to-face interactions in North America. Often, we must stand within intimate distance of others in crowds, buses, subways, elevators, and other public places. At such times, privacy is maintained by avoiding eye contact, by standing shoulder to shoulder or back to back, and by positioning a purse, bag, package, or coat as a barrier to spatial intrusions.*

signs of discomfort and step back to re-establish their original distance. Those who hold their ground will turn to the side, look away, or position an arm in front of themselves as a barrier. If you persistently edge toward your subjects, it should be easy to move them back several feet. Such norms may explain why people who feel offended by another person sometimes say, "Get out of my face."

Would this technique work with a good friend? Possibly not. Norms governing comfortable or acceptable distances vary according to relationships as well as activities. Hall (1966b) identified four basic zones: *intimate, personal, social,* and *public* distance (❖Fig. 19.2).

Spatial Norms

In addition to situations and relationships, cultural differences also affect spatial norms. The distances listed here apply to face-to-face interactions in North America. In many Middle Eastern countries, people hold their faces only inches apart while talking. In Western Europe, the English sit closer together when conversing than the French do. The Dutch, on the other hand, sit farther apart than the French (Remland, Jones, & Brinkman, 1991). In many parts of the world, merely crossing a border can dramatically change spatial behavior.

1. **Intimate distance.** For the majority of North American adults, the most private and exclusive space extends about 18 inches out from the skin. Entry within this space (face to face) is reserved for special people or special circumstances. Lovemaking, comforting others, and cuddling children all take place within this space.
2. **Personal distance.** This is the distance maintained in comfortable interaction with friends. It extends from about 18 inches to 4 feet from the body. Personal distance basically keeps people within "arm's reach" of each other.
3. **Social distance.** Impersonal business and casual social gatherings take place in a range of about 4 to 12 feet. This

Autokinetic effect *The apparent movement of a stationary pinpoint of light displayed in a darkened room.*
Personal space *An area surrounding the body that is regarded as private and subject to personal control.*
Proxemics *Systematic study of the human use of space, particularly in social settings.*
Intimate distance *The most private space immediately surrounding the body (up to about 18 inches from the skin).*
Personal distance *The distance maintained when interacting with close friends (about 18 inches to 4 feet from the body).*

distance eliminates most touching, and it formalizes conversation by requiring greater voice projection. "Important people" in many business offices use the imposing width of their desks to maintain social distance. A big smelly cigar helps, too.

4. **Public distance.** This is the distance at which formal interactions occur (about 12 feet or more from the body). When people are separated by more than 12 feet, people look "flat," and they must raise their voices to speak to one another. Formal speeches, lectures, business meetings, and the like are conducted at public distance.

Because spatial behavior is very consistent, you can learn much about your relationship to others by observing the distance you comfortably hold between yourselves. Watch for this dimension in your daily social activities. But be aware of cultural differences, too. Otherwise, you might misread another person's spatial behavior. People of different nationalities often have different norms for personal space. When they do, both are likely to be uncomfortable when talking, as one tries to move closer and the other keeps moving back. This can lead to misunderstandings in which one person feels that the other is being too familiar, while that person feels rejected.

We have now explored some basic facts of social life and a striking example of group norms. In the next section, we will consider a kind of impromptu detective work that we engage in as we try to guess the motives of others and the causes of their actions. Let's see how this is done.

During the 1996 Olympics, U.S. gymnast Kerri Strug performed an important vault after severely spraining her ankle. Later, she was carried to the award stand by her coach, Bela Karoli. As you watched these events, did you attribute Karoli's actions to selfless concern for his young protégé? Or was Karoli motivated by a selfish desire to hog the limelight? Such attributions greatly affect how we perceive and respond to the social behavior of others.

SOCIAL PERCEPTION—BEHIND THE MASK

It is probably impossible to completely know another person. In fact, every day we must form impressions of people from only the smallest shreds of evidence. How do we form such impressions? How do they affect our behavior? Many of the answers lie in **attribution.** As we observe others, we tend to make inferences about their actions. Why did Vonda insult Sutchai? Why did Nick change his college major? Why does Kirti talk so fast when she's around men? In answering such questions, we *attribute* people's behavior to various causes. Sometimes we are right about the causes of behavior, and sometimes we are wrong. Either way, it affects how we act in social situations. To learn how we fill in the "person behind the mask," let's explore the making of attributions.

Attribution Theory

Two people enter a restaurant and order different meals. Nell tastes her food, then salts it. Bert salts his food before he tastes it. How would you explain their behavior? In Nell's case, you might assume that the *food* needed salt. If so, you have attributed her actions to an **external cause** (one assumed to lie outside a person). With Bert, you might be more inclined to conclude that he must really *like* salt. If so, you would be saying that the cause of his behavior is internal (McGee & Snyder,

1975). **Internal causes** of behavior are assumed to lie within a person. Examples are needs, preferences, and personality traits.

What effects do such interpretations have? It is difficult to fully understand social behavior without considering the attributions that we make. For instance, let's say that Tam, who is in one of your classes, seems to avoid you. You see Tam at a market. Do you say hello to him? It could depend on how you have explained Tam's actions to yourself. Have you assumed his avoidance is caused by shyness? Coincidence? Dislike? Many factors affect such judgments. Let's examine a few.

MAKING ATTRIBUTIONS   When we make attributions, we are sensitive to how *consistent* and *distinctive* a person's behavior is (Kelly, 1967). A person's behavior is **consistent** if it changes very little when we observe it on many different occasions. The first time that Tam avoided you, he might have just been in a bad mood. However, if Tam has consistently avoided you, it's not likely that he was in a bad mood every time. That rules out coincidence. Still, Tam's avoidance could mean he is shy, not that he dislikes you. That's why distinctiveness is also important. When we watch other people, **distinctiveness** refers to noting that their behavior occurs only under specific circumstances. If you notice that Tam seems to avoid other people too, you may conclude that he is shy or unfriendly. If his avoidance is consistently and distinctively linked only with you, you will probably assume he dislikes you. You could be wrong, of course, but your behavior toward him will change just the same.

BRIDGES

Attributing bodily arousal to various sources can also have a large impact on emotions.

See Chapter 13, pages 434–435.

SELF-HANDICAPPING—SMOKE SCREEN FOR FAILURE

Have you ever known someone who got drunk before taking an exam or making a speech? Why would a person risk failure in this way? Often, the reason lies in **self-handicapping** (arranging to perform under conditions that impair performance). By providing an excuse for poor performance, self-handicapping makes people feel better in situations where they might fail (Drexler, Ahrens, & Haaga, 1995).

What if a person succeeds while "handicapped"? Well, then, so much the better. The person's self-image then gets a boost because she or he succeeded under conditions that normally lower performance (Murray & Warden, 1992).

Do you believe that "you either have it or you don't" where ability is concerned? If so, you may be particularly prone to self-handicapping. By working with a handicap, people can avoid any chance of discovering that they "don't have it" (Rhodewalt, 1994)!

Drinking alcohol is one of the most popular—and dangerous—self-handicapping strategies. A person who is drunk can attribute failure to being "loaded," while accepting success if it occurs. Examples of using alcohol for self-handicapping include being drunk for school exams, job interviews, or an important first date. A person who gets drunk at such times should be aware that coping with anxiety in this way can lead to serious alcohol abuse.

Any time you set up excuses for a poor performance, you are self-handicapping. Other examples of self-handicapping include making a half-hearted effort, claiming to be ill, and procrastinating. Most of us have used self-handicapping at times. Indeed, life would be harsh if we didn't sometimes give ourselves a break from accepting full responsibility for success or failure. Self-handicapping is mainly a problem when it becomes habitual. When it does, it typically leads to poor adjustment and lower self-esteem (Zuckerman, Kieffer, & Knee, 1998). So, watch out for self-handicapping, but try not to be too hard on yourself.

To deduce causes, we typically take into account the behavior of the **actor** (the person of interest), the **object** the person's action is directed toward, and the **setting** (social or physical environment) in which the action occurs (Kelly, 1967). Imagine, for example, that someone compliments you on your taste in clothes. If you are at a picnic, you may attribute this compliment to what you are wearing (the "object") unless, of course, you're wearing your worst "grubbies." If you are, you may simply assume that the person (or "actor") is friendly or tactful. However, if you are in a clothing store and a salesperson compliments you, you will probably attribute the compliment to the setting. It's still possible that the salesperson actually likes what you are wearing. Nevertheless, when we make attributions, we are very sensitive to the *situational demands* affecting other people's behavior. **Situational demands** are pressures to behave in certain ways in particular settings and social situations. If you see Tam at a funeral, and he is quiet and polite, it will tell you little about his motives and personality traits. The situation demands such behavior.

When situational demands are strong, we tend to **discount** (downgrade) internal causes as a way of explaining a person's behavior. Actually, this is true whenever strong external causes for behavior are present. For example, you have probably discounted the motives of professional athletes who praise shaving creams, hair tonics, deodorants, and the like. Obviously, the large sums of money they receive fully explain their endorsements. It's not necessary to assume they actually *like* the potions they sell. ("Self-Handicapping" discusses a related phenomenon.)

Yet another factor affecting attribution is **consensus** (or agreement). When many people act alike (there is a consensus in their behavior), it implies that their behavior is externally caused. For example, if millions of people go to see the latest episode of the Star Wars series, we tend to say *the movie* is good. If someone you know goes to see a movie six times, while others are staying away in droves, the tendency is to assume that *the person* likes "that type of movie."

Actor and Observer

Let's say that at the last five parties you have attended, you've seen a woman named Macy. Based on this, you assume that Macy is very outgoing and likes to socialize. You see Macy at yet another gathering and mention that she seems to like

---

Social distance *Distance at which impersonal interaction takes place (about 4 to 12 feet from the body).*

Public distance *Distance at which formal interactions, such as giving a speech, occur (about 12 feet or more from the body).*

Attribution *The process of making inferences about the causes of one's own behavior and that of others.*

External cause *A cause of behavior that is assumed to lie outside a person.*

Internal cause *A cause of behavior assumed to lie within a person—for instance, a need, preference, or personality trait.*

Consistency *In making attributions, noticing that a behavior changes very little on many different occasions.*

Distinctiveness *In making attributions, noticing that a behavior occurs only under specific circumstances.*

Actor *In making attributions, the person whose behavior is being interpreted.*

Object *In making attributions, the aim, motive, or target of an action.*

Setting *In making attributions, the social and/or physical environment in which an action occurs.*

Situational demands *Unstated expectations that define desirable or appropriate behavior in various settings and social situations.*

Discounting *Downgrading internal explanations of behavior when a person's actions appear to have strong external causes.*

Consensus *The degree to which people respond alike. In making attributions, consensus implies that responses are externally caused.*

Self-handicapping *Arranging to perform under conditions that usually impair performance, so as to have an excuse for a poor showing.*

Distressed couples tend to attribute their partners' actions to the worst possible motives, such as bad intentions or selfishness. Thus, attributional styles may lead to serious conflicts in marriage and other relationships (Holtzworth-Munroe & Hutchinson, 1993; Noller & Ruzzene, 1991).

parties. She says, "Actually, I hate these parties, but I get invited to play my tuba at them. My music teacher says I need to practice in front of an audience, so I keep attending these dumb events. Want to hear a Sousa march?"

We seldom know the real reasons for others' actions. That is why we tend to infer causes from *circumstances.* However, in doing so, we often make mistakes like the one with Macy. The most common error is to attribute the actions of others to internal causes (Jones & Nisbett, 1971). This mistake is called the **fundamental attributional error.** We tend to think the actions of others have internal causes, even if they are actually caused by external forces or circumstances.

Where our own behavior is concerned, we are more likely to think that external causes explain most of our actions. In other words, there is an **actor-observer bias** in how we explain behavior. As *observers,* we consistently attribute the behavior of others to their wants, motives, and personality traits (this is the fundamental attributional error). As *actors,* we tend to find external explanations for our own behavior (Krueger, Ham, & Linford, 1996). No doubt you chose your major in school because of what it has to offer. Other students choose *their* majors because of the kind of people they are. Other people who don't leave tips in restaurants are cheapskates. If you don't leave a tip, it's because the service was bad. And, of course, other people are always late because they are irresponsible. I am late because I was held up by events beyond my control.

As you can see, attribution theory summarizes how we think about ourselves and others, including the errors we tend to make. In addition, attribution theory has highlighted some practical problems. Let's conclude with a brief example.

YE OLDE DOUBLE STANDARD   Research on attribution has revealed an interesting double standard regarding the abilities of men and women. In a study by Kay Deaux and Tim Emswiller (1974), men and women overheard a male or female perform extremely well on a perception task. Each person was then asked to rate whether the test taker's success was due to ability, luck, or some combination of the two. Both men and women attributed male success mainly to skill and women's perfor-

mances mainly to luck! This was true even though male and female performances were identical.

As early as *kindergarten,* boys tend to take credit for successes. Girls, in contrast, tend to discount their own performances ("put themselves down") (Burgner & Hewstone, 1993). In general, there is a strong tendency to assume "He's skilled, she's lucky" when assessing the performances of men and women (Swim & Sanna, 1996). Throughout life, such attributions no doubt dog the heels of many talented and successful women.

4. The Stanford prison experiment demonstrated the powerful influence of the autokinetic effect on behavior. T or F?

5. Social psychology is the study of how people behave in
_____.

6. If two people position themselves 5 feet apart while conversing, they are separated by a gap referred to as
_____ distance.

7. When situational demands are strong, we tend to attribute a person's actions to internal causes. T or F?

8. The fundamental attributional error is to attribute the actions of others to internal causes. T or F?

CRITICAL THINKING

9. The Stanford prison experiment also illustrates a major concept of personality theory (Chapter 15), especially social learning theory. Can you name it?

10. How could the autokinetic effect contribute to UFO sightings?

Answers:
1. ascribed 2. F 3. T 4. F 5. social situations or the presence of others 6. social 7. F 8. T 9. It is the idea that behavior is often strongly influenced by situations rather than by personal traits. 10. Any point of light in the night sky may appear to move because of the autokinetic effect. This could cause a stationary light to look like it is flying or changing direction rapidly.

THE NEED FOR AFFILIATION—COME TOGETHER

Why do people choose to congregate with others? We have already observed that the **need to affiliate** (a desire to associate with other people) appears to be a basic human trait. But why? Probably because affiliation helps meet needs for approval, support, friendship, and information. We also seek the company of others to alleviate fear or anxiety. An experiment in which college women were threatened with electric shock serves as an illustration.

Zilstein's Shock Shop

A man introduced as Dr. Gregor Zilstein ominously explained to arriving subjects, "We would like to give each of you a series of electric shocks . . . these shocks will hurt, they will be painful." In the room was a frightening electrical device that seemed to verify Zilstein's plans. While waiting to be shocked, each subject was given a choice of waiting alone or with other subjects. Women frightened in this way more often chose to wait with others; those who expected the shock to be "a mild tickle or tingle" were more willing to wait alone (Schachter, 1959).

Apparently, the frightened women found it comforting to be with others. The tempting conclusion is that "misery loves company," but this is not completely accurate. In a later experiment, women expecting to be shocked were given the option of waiting with other shock subjects, with women waiting to see their college advisors, or alone. Most women chose to wait with

other future "victims." In short, misery seems to love miserable company! In general, we tend to prefer the company of people in circumstances similar to our own (Gump & Kulik, 1997).

Is there a reason for that? Yes. Other people provide information for evaluating our own reactions. When a situation is threatening or unfamiliar, or when a person is in doubt, *social comparisons* act as a guide for behavior (Banaji & Prentice, 1994).

Social Comparison Theory

In many cases, objective standards for self-evaluation exist. If I want to know how tall I am, I simply get out a tape measure. But how do I know if I am a good athlete, guitarist, worker, parent, or friend? How do I know if my views on politics, religion, or grunge rock are unusual or widely shared? When there are no objective standards, the only available yardstick is provided by comparing yourself to others.

High school class reunions are notorious for the rampant social comparison they often encourage. Apparently, it's hard to resist comparing yourself to former classmates to see how you are doing in life.

Fundamental attributional error *The tendency to attribute the behavior of others to internal causes (personality, likes, and so forth).*
Actor-observer bias *In making attributions, the tendency to attribute the behavior of others to internal causes while attributing one's own behavior to external causes (situations and circumstances).*
Need to affiliate *The desire to associate with other people.*

Social psychologist Leon Festinger (1919–1989) theorized that group membership fills needs for **social comparison** (comparing your own actions, feelings, opinions, or abilities to those of other people). When there are no objective standards, we must use other people to evaluate our actions, feelings, opinions, or abilities (Festinger, 1954). Have you noticed how students gather and "compare notes" after taking an exam? Many are satisfying needs for social comparison.

Social comparisons are not made randomly or on some ultimate scale. To illustrate, let's ask a student named Wendy if she is a good tennis player. If Wendy compares herself to a professional, the answer will be no. But this tells us little about her *relative* ability. Within her tennis group, Wendy is regarded as an excellent player. Meaningful evaluations are based on comparing yourself with people of similar backgrounds, abilities, and circumstances (Miller, Turnbull, & McFarland, 1988). On a fair scale of comparison, Wendy knows she is good, and she takes pride in her tennis skills. In the same way, thinking of yourself as successful, talented, responsible, or fairly paid depends entirely on whom you compare yourself with.

In addition to providing information, social comparisons may, at times, be made in ways that reflect desires for self-protection or self-enhancement. If you feel threatened, you may make a **downward comparison** by contrasting yourself with a person who ranks lower on some dimension (Banaji & Prentice, 1994). For example, if you have a part-time job and your employer cuts your hours, you may comfort yourself by thinking about a friend who just lost a job.

What about upward comparisons? Do they occur, too? As Wendy's tennis playing suggests, comparing yourself with people of much higher ability will probably just make you feel bad (Wheeler and Miyake, 1992). However, **upward comparisons,** in which we compare ourselves to a person who ranks higher on some dimension, are sometimes used for self-improvement. One way that Wendy can learn to improve her tennis skills is to compare herself with players who are only a little better than she is (Collins, 1996).

In general, social comparison theory holds that desires for self-evaluation, self-protection, and self-enhancement provide motives for associating with others. In doing so, they influence which groups we join.

Don't people also affiliate out of attraction for one another? They do, of course. The next section tells why.

INTERPERSONAL ATTRACTION—SOCIAL MAGNETISM?

"Birds of a feather flock together." "Familiarity breeds contempt." "Opposites attract." "Absence makes the heart grow fonder." Are these statements true? Actually, the folklore about friendship is, at best, a mixture of fact and fiction.

What does attract people to each other? **Interpersonal attraction** (affinity to another person) is the basis for most voluntary social relationships. As you might expect, we look for friends and lovers who are kind and understanding, who have attractive personalities, and who like us in return (Sprecher, 1998). In addition, several less obvious factors influence attraction.

What attracts people to each other? Proximity and frequency of contact have a surprisingly large impact.

Physical Proximity

Our choice of friends (and even lovers) is based more on **physical proximity** (nearness) than we might care to believe. For example, the closer people live to each other in a housing complex, the more likely they are to become friends (Festinger et al., 1950). Likewise, lovers like to think they have found the "one and only" person in the universe for them. In reality, they have probably found the best match in a 5-mile radius—or at least within driving distance (Buss, 1985)! The implication is that marriages are not made in heaven—they are made in schools, businesses, and neighborhoods.

A main reason for proximity's effect is that it increases the *frequency of contact* between people. A variety of experiments show that we are generally attracted to people with whom we have frequent contact (Saegert et al., 1973). (If you have a reluctant sweetheart, be careful not to send too many love letters—she or he might run off with the letter carrier!) In short, there does seem to be a "boy-next-door" or "girl-next-door" effect in romantic attraction, and a "folks-next-door" effect in friendship.

Physical Attractiveness

Physical attractiveness refers to a person's degree of physical beauty, as defined by his or her culture. Beautiful people tend to be rated as more appealing than those of average appearance. This is due, in part, to the **halo effect,** a tendency to generalize a favorable impression to unrelated personal characteristics. Because of it, we assume that attractive people are also likable, intelligent, warm, witty, mentally healthy, and socially skilled (Feingold, 1992a). Basically, we act as if "what is beautiful is good." Even characters in Hollywood movies tend to be portrayed more favorably if they are beautiful (Smith, McIntosh, & Bazzini, 1999).

Physical beauty can be socially advantageous because of the widespread belief that "what is beautiful is good." However, physical beauty is generally unrelated to actual personal traits and talents.

There are limits to the traits we associate with beauty. For instance, we do not expect beautiful people to be more honest or concerned about others (Johnson, 1991)! And in reality, physical attractiveness has almost *no* connection to intelligence, talents, or abilities (Feingold, 1992a).

Being physically attractive can be an advantage for both males and females. Good-looking people are less lonely, less socially anxious, more popular, more socially skilled, and more sexually experienced than unattractive people (Feingold, 1992a). Where romance is concerned, physical attractiveness has more influence on a woman's fate than on a man's (Feingold, 1990). For instance, there is a strong relationship between a woman's physical beauty and her frequency of dating. For men, looks are unrelated to dating frequency.

Do these findings seem shallow and sexist? If so, it may be reassuring to know that beauty is a factor mainly in initial acquaintance (Keller & Young, 1996). Later, more substantial personal qualities become important (Berscheid, 1994). It takes more than appearance to make a lasting relationship. Even first impressions are less affected by beauty if we are given information that helps us see a person as an individual (Johnson, 1991).

Competence

Competence is the degree of ability or proficiency a person displays. All other things being equal, we are more attracted to people who are talented or competent. However, there is an interesting twist to this, as revealed in the following example.

Clever but Clumsy

In an experiment on attraction, college students listened to tapes of supposed candidates for a "College Quiz Bowl." Two of the candidates were presented as highly intelligent. The other two were depicted as average in ability. One of the "intelligent" and one of the "average" tapes included an incident in which the candidate clumsily spilled coffee on himself. Those listening to the tapes rated the superior candidate who blundered as *most* attractive. The *least* attractive person was the student who was average and clumsy (Aronson, 1969).

Note that the superior but clumsy student was more attractive than the student who was only superior. The upshot of this experiment seems to be that we like people who are competent but imperfect—which makes them more "human."

Similarity

Take a moment to make a list of your closest friends. What do they have in common (other than the joy of knowing you)? It is likely that most are similar to you in age and the same sex and race as you. There will be exceptions, of course. But similarity on these three dimensions is the general rule for friendships.

Social comparison *Making judgments about ourselves through comparison with others.*
Downward comparison *Comparing yourself with a person who ranks lower than you on some dimension.*
Upward comparison *Comparing yourself with a person who ranks higher than you on some dimension.*
Interpersonal attraction *Social attraction to another person.*
Physical proximity *One's actual physical nearness to others in terms of housing, work, school, and so forth.*
Physical attractiveness *A person's degree of physical beauty, as defined by his or her culture.*
Halo effect *The tendency to generalize a favorable first impression to unrelated personal characteristics.*
Competence *The degree of general ability or proficiency a person displays.*

Similarity refers to the extent to which two people are alike in background, age, interests, attitudes, beliefs, and so forth. Social psychologists have repeatedly found that similar people are attracted to each other (Carli, Ganley, & Pierce-Otay, 1991). And why not? It's reinforcing to see our beliefs and attitudes shared by others. It shows we are "right" and reveals that they are clever people as well (Alicke, Yurak, & Vredenburg, 1996)!

Does similarity also influence mate selection? For an answer to this question, read "Selecting a Mate."

In college dormitories, roommates who are similar in personality and physical attractiveness tend to be more satisfied with their relationship (Carli, Ganley, & Pierce-Otay, 1991).

Self-Disclosure

How do people who are not yet friends learn if they are similar? Getting to know others requires a willingness to talk about more than just the weather, sports, or nuclear physics. At some point, you must begin to share private thoughts and feelings and reveal yourself to others. This process, which is called **self-disclosure,** is essential for developing close relationships. Lack of self-disclosure is associated with anxiety, unhappiness, and loneliness (Meleshko & Alden, 1993; Mikulincer & Nachshon, 1991).

We more often reveal ourselves to persons we like than to those we find unattractive. Disclosure also requires a degree of trust. Many people play it safe, or "close to the vest," with people they do not know well. Indeed, self-disclosure is governed by definite norms about what's acceptable. Moderate self-disclosure leads to **reciprocity** (a return in kind). Overdisclosure, however, gives rise to suspicion and reduced attraction. **Overdisclosure** is self-disclosure that exceeds what is appropriate for a relationship or social situation. For example, imagine standing in line at a market and having the stranger in front of you say, "Lately I've been thinking about how I really feel about myself. I think I'm pretty well adjusted, but I occasionally have some questions about my sexual adequacy."

When self-disclosure proceeds at a moderate pace, it is accompanied by growing trust and intimacy. When it is too rapid or inappropriate, we are likely to back off and wonder about the person's motives. Thus, as friends talk, they influence each other in ways that gradually deepen the level of liking, trust, and self-disclosure (Miller, 1990). However, women and men display an interesting difference in patterns of self-disclosure, as described next.

GENDERED FRIENDSHIPS   Two male friends share lunch at a restaurant. In the next hour, they talk about sports, cars, sports cars, the *Sports Illustrated* swimsuit edition, sports, cars, and

SELECTING A MATE—REFLECTIONS IN A SOCIAL MIRROR

Ninety percent of all people in Western societies marry at some point. What, beyond attraction, determines how people pair up? The answer is that we tend to marry someone who is like us in almost every way, a pattern called **homogamy** (huh-MOG-ah-me) (Caspi & Herbener, 1990).

Studies show that married couples are highly similar in age, education, race, religion, and ethnic background. In addition, the correlation between their attitudes and opinions is .5. For mental abilities it is .4, and for socioeconomic status, height, weight, and eye color it is .3. In general, you are far more likely to choose someone similar to yourself as a mate than someone very different. This is probably a good thing. Personality traits tend to be closely matched in the most stable marriages (Kim, Martin, & Martin, 1989). Conversely, the risk of divorce is highest among couples with sizable differences in age and education (Tzeng, 1992). Most

dangerous of all are "fatal attractions," in which qualities that originally made a partner appealing are later disliked. Fatal attractions are likely when an individual is drawn to someone who seems "different," "unique," or "extreme." When two people are similar, disenchantment is less likely to occur (Felmlee, 1998).

Do people look for specific traits in a potential mate? Yes, in the United States, both men and women agree that the most important qualities are kindness and understanding, intelligence, exciting personality, good health, adaptability, and physical attractiveness (Buss, 1985). However, women apparently season romance with a dash of practicality. Women regard intelligence, ambition, success, and status as more important in a potential mate than men do (Townsend & Wasserman, 1998). Notice, though, that kindness and understanding are still ranked first by both men and women (Hatfield & Sprecher, 1995).

FOCUS ON RESEARCH

Excessive self-disclosure is a staple of many television talk shows. Guests frequently reveal intimate details about their personal lives, including private family matters, sex and dating, physical or sexual abuse, major embarrassments, and criminal activities. Viewers probably find such intimate disclosures entertaining, rather than threatening, because they don't have to reciprocate.

golf. (Did I mention sports and cars?) Janis, who was at a nearby table, overheard the entire conversation. Here's her summary of what the men said to each other: "Absolutely nothing!"

In North American culture, most male friendships are *activity based*. That is, men tend to do things together—a pattern that provides companionship without closeness.

The friendships of women are more often based on *shared feelings and confidences*. If two female friends spent an afternoon together and did not reveal problems, private thoughts, and feelings to one another, they would assume that something was wrong. For women, friendship is a matter of talking about shared concerns and intimate matters.

Actually, the differences between male and female friendships are smaller than implied here. Men do know *something* about the private thoughts and feelings of their friends. Nevertheless, most contemporary men do not form close friendships with other men. Many could probably learn something from female friendships: Men live their friendships side by side; women live them face to face (Archer, 1996; Nardi, 1992; Reid & Fine, 1992).

Social Exchange Theory

Self-disclosure involves an exchange of personal information, but other exchanges also occur. In fact, many relationships can be understood as an ongoing series of **social exchanges** (transfers of attention, information, affection, favors, and the like, between two people). In many social exchanges, people try to maximize their rewards while minimizing their "costs." When a friendship or love relationship ceases to be attractive, people often say, "I'm not getting anything out of it any more." Actually, they probably are, but their costs—in terms of effort, irritation, or lowered self-esteem—have exceeded their rewards.

According to **social exchange theory,** we unconsciously weigh social rewards and costs. For a relationship to last, it must be *profitable* (its rewards must exceed its costs) for both parties. For instance, John and Helen have been dating for 2 years. Although they still have fun at times, they also frequently argue and bicker. If the friction in their relationship gets much stronger, it will exceed the rewards of staying together. When that happens, they will probably split up (Gottman, 1994).

Actually, just being profitable is not the whole story. It is more accurate to say that a relationship needs to be *profitable enough*. Generally, the balance between rewards and costs is judged in comparison with what we have come to expect from past experience. The personal standard a person uses to evaluate rewards and costs is called the **comparison level.** The comparison level is high for people with histories of satisfying and rewarding relationships. It is lower for someone whose relationships have been unsatisfying. Thus, the decision to continue a relationship is affected by your personal comparison level. A lonely person or one whose friendships have been marginal might stay in a relationship that you would consider unacceptable.

LOVING AND LIKING—DATING, RATING, MATING

Does romantic attraction differ from interpersonal attraction? In Chapter 13, we noted that **romantic love** is marked by high levels of interpersonal attraction and emotional arousal. We also discussed various types of love that result from combinations of intimacy, passion, and commitment. In Western cultures, sexual desire is also regarded as an important part of romantic attraction (Regan, 1998).

Similarity *The extent to which two people are alike in background, age, interests, attitudes, beliefs, and so forth.*
Homogamy *Marriage of two people who are similar to one another.*
Self-disclosure *The process of revealing private thoughts, feelings, and one's personal history to others.*
Reciprocity *A reciprocal interchange or return in kind.*
Overdisclosure *Self-disclosure that exceeds what is appropriate for a particular relationship or social situation.*
Social exchange *Any exchange between two people of attention, information, affection, favors, or the like.*
Social exchange theory *Theory stating that rewards must exceed costs for relationships to endure.*
Comparison level *A personal standard used to evaluate rewards and costs in a social exchange.*
Romantic love *Love that is associated with high levels of interpersonal attraction, heightened arousal, mutual absorption, and sexual desire.*

To get another angle on love, psychologist Zick Rubin (1973) chose to think of it as an attitude held by one person toward another. This allowed him to develop "liking" and "love" scales to measure each "attitude" (❖Fig. 19.3). Next, he asked dating couples to complete each scale twice—once with their date in mind and once for a close friend of the same sex.

What were the results? Love for partners and friends differed more than liking did (◆Table 19.1). (**Liking** is affection without passion or deep commitment.) Basically, dating couples like *and* love their partners, but mostly just like their friends. Women, however, were a little more "loving" of their friends than were men. Does this reflect real differences in the strength of male friendships and female friendships? Maybe not, because it is more acceptable in our culture for women to express love for one another than it is for men. Nevertheless, another study confirmed that dating couples feel a mixture of love and friendship for their partners. In fact, 44 percent of a group of dating people named their romantic partner as their closest friend (Hendrick & Hendrick, 1993).

Love and friendship differ in another interesting way. Romantic love, in contrast to simple liking, usually involves deep **mutual absorption** of the lovers. In other words, lovers (unlike friends) attend almost exclusively to one another. It's not surprising, then, that couples scoring high on Rubin's love scale spend more time gazing into each other's eyes than do couples who score low on the scale.

What do romantic partners see when they gaze into each other's eyes? A final interesting characteristic of romantic love is lovers' ability to see their partners in idealized ways. Nobody's perfect, of course. That's why it's no surprise that relationships are most likely to persist when lovers idealize one another. Doing so doesn't just blind them to their partner's faults, it actually helps them create the relationship they wish for (Murray, Holmes, & Griffin, 1996).

Love and Attachment

Sheela has been dating Paul for over a year. Although they have had some rough spots, Sheela is comfortable, secure, and trusting in her love for Paul. Charlene, in contrast, has had a long series of unhappy romances with men. She is basically a loner who has difficulty trusting others. Like Sheela, Eduardo has been dating the same person for a year. However, his relationship with Tanya has been stormy and troubled. Eduardo is strongly attracted to Tanya. Yet, he is also in a constant state of anxiety over whether she really loves him.

Sheela, Charlene, and Eduardo might be surprised to learn that the roots of their romantic relationships may lie in childhood. There is growing evidence that early attachments to caregivers (see Chapter 4) can have a lasting impact on how we relate to others (Shaver & Hazan, 1993). For example, studies of dating couples have identified secure, avoidant, and ambivalent attachment patterns similar to those seen in early child development (Mikulincer & Nachshon, 1991). Nationally, about 59 percent of all adults have a secure attachment style, 25 percent are avoidant, and 11 percent have anxious attachment styles (Mickelson, Kessler, & Shaver, 1997).

Secure attachment is a stable and positive emotional bond. A secure attachment style like Sheela's is marked by caring, intimacy, supportiveness, and understanding in love relationships. Secure people regard themselves as friendly, good-natured, and likable. They think of others as generally well intentioned, reliable, and trustworthy. People with a secure attachment style find it relatively easy to get close to others. They are comfortable depending on others and having others depend on them. In general, they don't worry too much about being abandoned or about having someone become too emotionally close to them. Most people prefer to have a secure partner, whatever their own style might be (Latty-Mann & Davis, 1996).

Charlene's **avoidant attachment** style reflects a fear of intimacy and a tendency to resist commitment to others. Avoidant people tend to pull back when things don't go well in a rela-

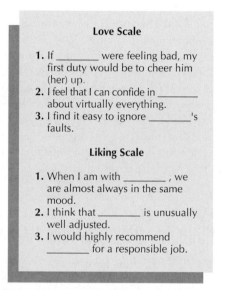

❖ **FIGURE 19.3** *Sample love scale and liking scale items. Each scale consists of 13 items similar to those shown. Scores on these scales correspond to other indications of love and liking. (Reprinted by permission of Zick Rubin.)*

◆ **TABLE 19.1** Average Love and Liking Scores for Date and Same-Sex Close Friend

Attitude toward dating partner

	LOVE SCORE	LIKING SCORE
Women	89.5	88.5
Men	89.4	84.7

Attitude toward close friend

	LOVE SCORE	LIKING SCORE
Women	65.3	80.5
Men	55.0	79.1

Source: Rubin, 1970.

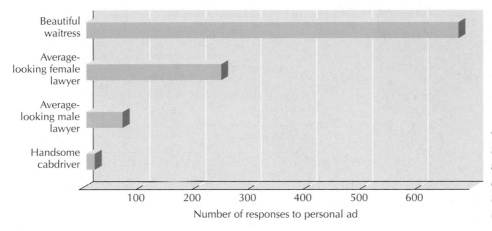

❖ **FIGURE 19.4** *What do people look for in potential dating partners? Here are the results of a study in which personal ads were placed in newspapers. As you can see, men were more influenced by looks, and women by success (Goode, 1996).*

tionship. The avoidant person is suspicious, aloof, and skeptical about love. She or he tends to see others as either unreliable or overly eager to commit to a relationship. As a result, avoidant people find it hard to completely trust and depend on others. Avoidant people get nervous when anyone gets too close emotionally. Basically, they avoid intimacy (Tidwell, Reis, & Shaver, 1996).

People like Eduardo have an **ambivalent attachment** style, marked by mixed emotions about relationships. Conflicting feelings of affection, anger, emotional turmoil, physical attraction, and doubt leave them in an unsettled, ambivalent state. Often, ambivalent people regard themselves as misunderstood and unappreciated. They tend to see their friends and lovers as unreliable and unable or unwilling to commit themselves to lasting relationships. Ambivalent people worry that their romantic partners don't really love them or may leave them. While they want to be extremely close to their partners, they are also preoccupied with doubts about the partner's dependability and trustworthiness.

How could emotional attachments early in life affect adult relationships? It appears that we use early attachment experiences to build mental models about affectionate relationships. Later, we use these models as a sort of blueprint for forming, maintaining, and breaking bonds of love and affection (Simpson, 1990). Thus, the quality of childhood bonds to parents or other caregivers may hold a key to understanding how we approach romantic relationships (Shaver & Hazen, 1993). Maybe it's no accident that people who are romantically available are often described as "unattached."

It is fascinating to think that our relationships may be influenced by events early in childhood. Could the source of adult mating patterns reach even further back? The next section explores that possibility.

Evolution and Mate Selection

Evolutionary psychology is the study of the evolutionary origins of human behavior patterns. Many psychologists have come to believe that evolution left an imprint on men and women that influences everything from sexual attraction and

BRIDGES

Forming a secure attachment to a caregiver is a major event in early child development.

See Chapter 4, pages 96–97.

infidelity to jealousy and divorce. According to David Buss, the key to understanding human mating patterns is not found just in learning, socialization, attachment, or culture. Rather, we must also understand how evolved behavior patterns guide our choices (Buss, 1994).

In a study of 37 cultures on six continents, Buss found the following patterns: Compared with women, men are more interested in casual sex; they prefer younger, more physically attractive partners; and they get more jealous over real or imagined sexual infidelities than they do over a loss of emotional commitment. Compared with men, women prefer slightly older partners who appear to be industrious, higher in status, or economically successful; women are more upset by a partner who becomes emotionally involved with someone else, rather than one who is sexually unfaithful (Buss, 1994; Buss et al., 1992) (❖Fig. 19.4).

Why do such differences exist? Buss and other researchers believe that evolutionary psychology explains many human mating patterns. Mating preferences, they say, evolved in response to the differing reproductive challenges faced by men and women.

As a rule, women must invest more time and energy in reproduction and in nurturing their young than men do. Consequently, women evolved an interest in whether their partners will stay with them and whether their mates have the resources to provide for their children (Archer, 1996).

Liking *A relationship based on intimacy but lacking passion and commitment.*
Mutual absorption *With regard to romantic love, the nearly exclusive attention lovers give to one another.*
Secure attachment *A stable and positive emotional bond.*
Avoidant attachment *An emotional bond marked by a tendency to resist commitment to others.*
Ambivalent attachment *An emotional bond marked by conflicting feelings of affection, anger, and emotional turmoil.*
Evolutionary psychology *Study of the evolutionary origins of human behavior patterns.*

According to evolutionary psychologists, women tend to be concerned with whether mates will devote time and resources to a relationship. Men place more emphasis on physical attractiveness and sexual fidelity.

In contrast, the reproductive success of men depends on their mates' fertility. Men, therefore, tend to look for health, youth, and beauty in a prospective mate as signs of suitability for reproduction (Pines, 1998). This preference, perhaps, is why some older men abandon their first wives in favor of young, beautiful "trophy wives." Evolutionary theory further explains that the male emphasis on mates' sexual fidelity is based on concerns about the paternity of offspring. From a biological perspective, men do not benefit from investing resources in children they did not sire (Schmitt & Buss, 1996).

A sizable body of evidence supports the evolutionary view of mating preferences. However, it is important to remember that evolved mating tendencies are subtle at best and easily overruled by other factors. Indeed, some mating patterns may simply reflect the fact that men still tend to control the power and resources in most societies (Feingold, 1992a). Most important of all, remember that when either men or women choose mates, kindness and intelligence still rate highest. They are love's greatest allies.

KNOWLEDGE BUILDER
AFFILIATION, LOVE, FRIENDSHIP, AND ATTACHMENT

RELATE

How has social comparison affected your behavior? Has it influenced whom you associate with?

Think of three close friends. Which of the attraction factors described earlier apply to your friendships?

To what extent do Rubin's findings about love and liking match your own experiences?

Can you think of people you know whose adult relationships seem to illustrate each of the three attachment styles described in the preceding section?

LEARNING CHECK

1. Women threatened with electric shock in an experiment generally chose to wait alone or with other women not taking part in the experiment. T or F?

2. The need to affiliate is related to interest in social comparison. T or F?

3. Social comparisons are made pretty much at random. T or F?

4. Interpersonal attraction is increased by all but one of the following. (Which does not fit?)
   a. physical proximity b. competence c. similarity d. social costs

5. High levels of self-disclosure are reciprocated in most social encounters. T or F?

6. Women rate their friends higher on the love scale than do men. T or F?

7. The most striking finding about marriage patterns is that most people choose mates whose personalities are quite unlike their own. T or F?

8. Both ambivalent and avoidant attachment patterns are associated with difficulties in trusting a romantic partner. T or F?

9. Compared with men, women tend to be more upset by sexual infidelity than by a loss of emotional commitment on the part of their mates. T or F?

CRITICAL THINKING

10. How have contemporary communications networks altered the effects of proximity on interpersonal attraction?

Answers:
1. F 2. T 3. F 4. d 5. F 6. T 7. F 8. T 9. F 10. It is now possible to interact with another person by telephone, fax, short-wave radio, modem, or similar means. This makes actual physical proximity less crucial in interpersonal attraction, because frequent contact is possible even at great distances.

SOCIAL INFLUENCE—FOLLOW THE LEADER

No topic lies nearer the heart of social psychology than **social influence,** or changes in a person's behavior induced by the actions of others. When people interact, they almost always affect one another's behavior. Let's probe the ways in which this takes place.

Imagine a traffic signal brightly flashing the word WAIT. As you and other pedestrians wait for it to change, a well-dressed man in a suit crosses against the light. How many people will follow him? Do you think the answer would be different if the man were dressed in a denim shirt, patched pants, and scuffed shoes? This street-corner scenario was used in an early experiment on social influence. As you might have guessed, more people followed the well-dressed man than the one dressed in shabby clothes (Lefkowitz et al., 1955).

In another sidewalk experiment, various numbers of people were assembled on a busy New York City street. On cue, they all looked at a sixth-floor window across the street. A camera recorded the number of passersby who also stopped to stare. The larger the influencing group, the more people were swayed to join in staring at the window (Milgram et al., 1969).

Are there different kinds of social influence? Social influence ranges from simple suggestion to intensive indoctrination (brainwashing). Our daily behavior is probably most influenced by group pressures for conformity. Conformity typically occurs when people become aware of differences between themselves and the actions, norms, or values of other group members (Baron & Byrne, 1997).

Conformity

When John first started working at the Fleegle Flange Factory, he found it easy to process 300 flanges an hour. Others around him averaged only 200. John's coworkers told him to slow down and take it easy. "I get bored," he said, and he continued to do 300 flanges an hour. At first, John was welcomed, but now conversations broke up when he approached. Other workers laughed at him or ignored him when he spoke. Although he never made a conscious decision to conform, in another week John's output had slowed to 200 flanges an hour.

As mentioned earlier, all groups have unspoken rules of conduct called *norms*. The broadest norms, defined by society as a whole, establish "normal" or acceptable behavior in most situations. Comparing hairstyles, habits of speech, dress, eating habits, and social customs in two or more cultures makes it clear that we all conform to social norms. In

Conformity is a subtle dimension of daily life. Notice the similarities in clothing and hairstyles among these couples.

fact, a degree of uniformity is necessary if we are to interact comfortably. Imagine being totally unable to anticipate the actions of others. In stores, schools, and homes, this would be frustrating and disturbing. On the highways, it would be lethal.

Perhaps the most basic of all group norms is, as John discovered, "Thou shalt conform." This is equally true for the Hell's Angels, the Daughters of the American Revolution, a street-corner gang, or the board of directors of a large corporation. Groups of all kinds exert considerable pressures toward uniformity on their members. Like it or not, life is filled with instances of **conformity** (bringing one's own behavior into agreement with norms or the behavior of others).

THE ASCH EXPERIMENT *How strong are group pressures for conformity?* One of the better-known experiments on conformity was staged by Solomon Asch (1907–1996) in the early 1950s. Asch's study is best appreciated by imagining yourself as a subject. Assume that you are seated at a table with six other students. Your task is actually quite simple. On each trial, you are shown three lines. Your job is to select the line that matches a "standard" line (❖Fig. 19.5).

As the testing begins, each subject announces an answer for the first card. When your turn comes, you find yourself in complete agreement with the others. "This isn't hard at all," you say to yourself. For several more trials, your answers agree with those of the group. Then comes a shock. All six people announce that line 1 matches the standard, and you were about to say that line 2 matches. Suddenly you feel alone and upset. You nervously look at the lines again. The room falls silent. Everyone seems to be staring at you. The experimenter awaits your answer. Do you yield to the group?

In this experiment, the other "students" were all accomplices who gave the wrong answer on about a third of the trials. Few real subjects suspected trickery; hence, the group pressure created was very realistic (Asch, 1956).

How many people yielded to group pressure? People conformed to the group on about one third of the critical trials. Of those tested, 75 percent yielded at least once. In contrast,

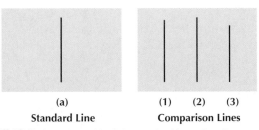

(a)
Standard Line

(1) (2) (3)
Comparison Lines

❖ **FIGURE 19.5** *Stimuli used in Solomon Asch's conformity experiments.*

Social influence *Changes in a person's behavior induced by the presence or actions of others.*
Conformity *Bringing one's behavior into agreement or harmony with norms or with the behavior of others in a group.*

people tested alone erred in less than 1 percent of their judgments. Those who yielded to group pressures were clearly denying what their eyes told them.

Are some people more susceptible to group pressures than others? People with high needs for structure or certainty are more likely to conform. So are people who are anxious, low in self-confidence, or concerned with the approval of others. People who live in cultures that emphasize group cooperation (such as many Asian cultures) are also more likely to conform (Bond & Smith, 1996).

CRITICAL THINKING

GROUPTHINK—AGREEMENT AT ANY COST

What happens when people in positions of power fall prey to pressures for conformity? To find out, Yale psychologist Irving Janis (1918–1990) analyzed a series of disastrous decisions made by government officials. His conclusion? Many such fiascoes are the result of **groupthink**—a compulsion by decision makers to maintain each other's approval, even at the cost of critical thinking (Janis, 1989).

Groupthink has been blamed for many embarrassments, such as John F. Kennedy's backing of the Bay of Pigs invasion in Cuba or Ronald Reagan's Iran-Contra scandal. It also seems to have contributed to the *Challenger* space shuttle disaster and the loss, in 1999, of the $165 million *Mars Climate Orbiter*. An analysis of 19 international crises found that groupthink contributed to most (Schafer & Crichlow, 1996).

The core of groupthink is misguided loyalty. Group members are hesitant to "rock the boat" or question sloppy thinking. This self-censorship leads people to believe they agree more than they actually do (Bernthal & Insko, 1993; Esser, 1998).

To prevent groupthink, group leaders should take the following steps:

- Define each group member's role as a "critical evaluator."
- Avoid revealing any personal preferences in the beginning.
- State the problem factually, without bias.
- Invite a group member or outside person to play devil's advocate.
- Make it clear that group members will be held accountable for decisions.
- Encourage open inquiry and a search for alternate solutions (Chen et al., 1996; Kroon et al., 1992).

In addition, Janis suggested that there should be a "second-chance" meeting to re-evaluate important decisions. That is, each decision should be reached twice.

In an age clouded by the threat of war, meltdowns, and similar disasters, even stronger solutions to the problem of groupthink would be welcome. Perhaps we should form a group to think about it!

In addition to personal characteristics, certain situations tend to encourage conformity—sometimes with disastrous results. "Groupthink—Agreement at Any Cost" offers a prime example.

GROUP FACTORS IN CONFORMITY *How do groups enforce norms?* In most groups, we have been rewarded with acceptance and approval for conformity and threatened with rejection or ridicule for nonconformity. These reactions are called **group sanctions** (rewards and punishments administered by groups to enforce conformity). Negative sanctions range from laughter, staring, or social disapproval to complete rejection or formal ostracism. If you've ever felt the sudden chill of disapproval by others, you will understand the power of group sanctions.

The power of group sanctions is illustrated by experiments in which Asch made up groups of six real subjects and one trained dissenter. When "Mr. Odd" announced his wrong answers, he was greeted with derisive laughter and sidelong glances. Treatment such as this helps explain why we are especially likely to conform when we are concerned about whether our views are right or wrong (Alicke & Doherty, 1992).

Wouldn't the effectiveness of group sanctions depend on the importance of the group? Yes. The more important group membership is to a person, the more he or she will be influenced by other group members. That's why the Asch experiments are impressive. Because these were only temporary groups, sanctions were informal, and rejection had no lasting importance. Just the same, the power of the group was evident.

What other factors, besides the importance of the group, affect the degree of conformity? Earlier, we described an experiment in which passersby were influenced by people staring at a building. We noted that the larger the group, the greater the number of people influenced. In Asch's face-to-face groups, the size of the majority also made a difference, but a surprisingly small one. In other experiments, the number of conforming subjects increased dramatically as the majority grew from two to three people. However, a majority of three produced about as much yielding as a majority of eight. The next time you want to talk someone into (or out of) something, take two friends along and see what a difference it makes! (Sometimes it helps if the two are large and mean looking.)

Even more important than the size of the majority is its **unanimity** (unanimous agreement). Having at least one person in your corner can greatly reduce pressures to conform. When Asch gave subjects an ally (who also opposed the majority by giving the correct answer), conformity was lessened. In terms of numbers, a unanimous majority of three is more powerful than a majority of eight with one dissenting. Perhaps this accounts for the rich diversity of human attitudes, beliefs, opinions, and lifestyles. If you can find at least one other person who sees things as you do (no matter how weird), you can be relatively secure in your opposition to other viewpoints. Incidentally, the Internet is a perfect way to find that other person (McKenna & Bargh, 1998)!

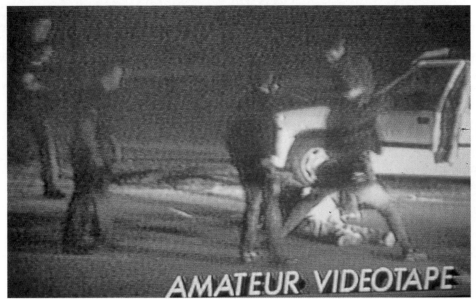

AMATEUR VIDEOTAPE

In 1991, television viewers all over the world saw a graphic videotape of Los Angeles police officers beating Rodney King as they arrested him. Jurors at the officers' assault trial saw the same incriminating videotape. Nevertheless, the officers were acquitted. In response to social pressure from other jurors, one key juror had changed her vote from "guilty" to "not guilty." You may be confident that you would not change your vote under similar circumstances. However, social pressures can be intense in the jury room.

KNOWLEDGE BUILDER
SOCIAL INFLUENCE AND CONFORMITY

RELATE

Identify a recent time when you conformed in some way. How did norms, group pressure, sanctions, and unanimity contribute to your tendency to conform?

What group sanctions have you experienced? What sanctions have you applied to others?

Have you ever been part of a group that seemed to make a bad decision because of groupthink? How could the group have avoided its mistake?

LEARNING CHECK

1. The effect one person's behavior has on another is called
_____ _____.

2. Conformity is a normal aspect of social life. T or F?

3. Subjects in Solomon Asch's conformity study yielded on about 75 percent of the critical trials. T or F?

4. Nonconformity is punished by negative group _____.

5. Janis used the term _____ to describe a compulsion among decision-making groups to maintain an illusion of unanimity.

CRITICAL THINKING

6. Would it be possible to be completely nonconforming (that is, to not conform to some group norm)?

Answers:
1. social influence 2. T 3. F 4. sanctions 5. groupthink 6. A person who did not follow at least some norms concerning normal social behavior would very likely be perceived as extremely bizarre, disturbed, or psychotic.

SOCIAL POWER—WHO CAN DO WHAT TO WHOM?

Here's something to think about: Strength is a quality possessed by individuals; power is always social—it arises when people come together and disappears when they disperse. In trying to understand the ways in which people are able to influence each other, it is helpful to distinguish among five types of **social power** (the capacity to control, alter, or influence the behavior of another person) (Raven, 1974).

Reward power lies in the ability to reward a person for complying with desired behavior. Teachers try to exert reward power over students with grades. Employers command reward power by their control of wages and bonuses.

Coercive power is based on an ability to punish a person for failure to comply. Coercive power is the basis for most laws, in that fines or imprisonment are used to control behavior.

Legitimate power comes from accepting a person as an agent of an established social order. For example, elected leaders

Groupthink *A compulsion by members of decision-making groups to maintain agreement, even at the cost of critical thinking.*
Group sanctions *Rewards and punishments (such as approval or disapproval) administered by groups to enforce conformity among members.*
Unanimity *Being unanimous or of one mind; agreement.*
Social power *The capacity to control, alter, or influence the behavior of another person.*
Reward power *Social power based on the capacity to reward a person for acting as desired.*
Coercive power *Social power based on the ability to punish others.*
Legitimate power *Social power based on a person's position as an agent of an accepted social order.*

and supervisors have legitimate power. So does a teacher in the classroom. Outside the classroom that power would have to come from another source.

Referent power is based on respect for or identification with a person or a group. The person "refers to" the source of referent power for direction. Referent power is responsible for much of the conformity we see in groups.

Expert power is based on recognition that another person has knowledge necessary for achieving a goal. We allow teachers, lawyers, and other experts to guide behavior because of their ability to produce desired results. Physicians, psychologists, programmers, and plumbers have expert power.

A person who has power in one situation may have very little in another. In those situations where a person has power, she or he is described as an *authority.* In the next section we will investigate **obedience,** a special type of conformity to the demands of an authority.

OBEDIENCE—WOULD YOU ELECTROCUTE A STRANGER?

The question is this: If ordered to do so, would you shock a man with a known heart condition who is screaming and asking to be released? Certainly, we can assume that few people would do so. Or can we? In Nazi Germany, obedient soldiers (once average citizens) helped slaughter more than 6 million people in concentration camps. Another example of the same phenomenon was an infamous incident during the Vietnam War. To the horror of many under his command, Lt. William Calley led a bloody massacre of helpless civilians at a village called My Lai. Do such inhumane acts reflect deep character flaws? Are they the acts of heartless psychopaths or crazed killers? Or are they simply the result of obedience to authority? What are the limits of obedience? These are the questions that puzzled social psychologist Stanley Milgram (1965) when he began a provocative series of studies on obedience.

How did Milgram study obedience? As was true of the Asch experiments, Milgram's research is best appreciated by imagining yourself as a subject. Place yourself in the following situation.

Milgram's Obedience Studies

Imagine answering a newspaper ad to take part in a "learning" experiment at Yale University. When you arrive, a coin is flipped and a second subject, a pleasant-looking man in his 50s, is designated the "learner." By chance, you have become the "teacher."

Your task is to read a list of word pairs. The learner's task is to memorize them. You are to punish him with an electric shock each time he makes a mistake. The learner is taken to an adjacent room, and you watch as he is seated in an "electric chair" apparatus. Electrodes are attached to his wrists. You are then escorted to your position in front of a "shock generator." On this device is a row of 30 switches labeled from 15 to 450 volts. Accompanying descriptions range from "Slight Shock" to "Extreme Intensity Shock" and finally "Danger Severe Shock." Your instructions are to administer a shock each time the learner makes a mistake. You are to begin with 15 volts and then move one switch (15 volts) higher for each additional mistake (❖Fig. 19.6).

The experiment begins, and the learner soon makes his first error. You flip a switch. More mistakes. Rapidly you reach the 75-volt level. The learner moans after each shock. At 100 volts, he complains that he has a heart condition. At 150 volts, he says he no longer wants to continue and demands release. At 300 volts, he screams and says he can no longer give answers.

At some point during the experiment, you begin to protest to the experimenter. "That man has a heart condition," you say. "I'm not going to kill that man." The experimenter says, "Please continue." Another shock and another scream from the learner and you say, "You mean I've got to keep going up the scale? No, sir. I'm not going to give him 450 volts!" The experimenter says, "The experiment requires that you continue." For a time, the learner refuses to answer any more questions and screams with each shock (Milgram, 1965). Then he falls chillingly silent for the remainder of the experiment.

It's hard to believe many people would do this. What happened? Milgram also doubted that many people would obey his orders. When he polled a group of psychiatrists before the experiment, they predicted that fewer than 1 percent of those tested would obey. The astounding fact is that 65 percent

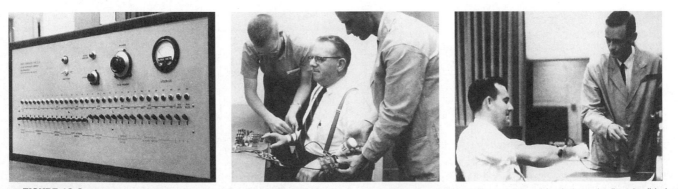

❖ **FIGURE 19.6** *Scenes from Stanley Milgram's study of obedience: the "shock generator," strapping a "learner" into his chair, and a "teacher" being told to administer a severe shock to the learner.*

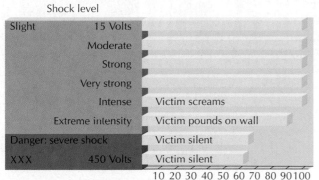

❖ **FIGURE 19.7** *Results of Milgram's obedience experiment. Only a minority of subjects refused to provide shocks, even at the most extreme intensities. The first substantial drop in obedience occurred at the 300-volt level (Milgram, 1963).*

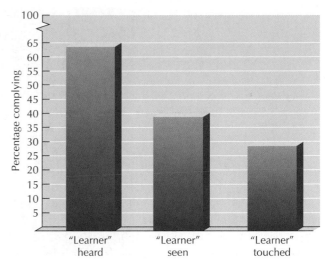

❖ **FIGURE 19.8** *Physical distance from the "learner" had a significant effect on the percentage of subjects obeying orders.*

obeyed completely by going all the way to the 450-volt level. Virtually no one stopped short of 300 volts ("Severe Shock") (❖Fig. 19.7).

Was the learner injured? The time has come to reveal that the "learner" was actually an actor who turned a tape recorder on and off in the shock room. No shocks were ever administered, but the dilemma for the "teacher" was quite real. Subjects protested, sweated, trembled, stuttered, bit their lips, and laughed nervously. Clearly, they were disturbed by what they were doing. Nevertheless, most obeyed the experimenter's orders.

MILGRAM'S FOLLOW-UP *Why did so many people obey?* Some have suggested that the prestige of Yale University contributed to subjects' willingness to obey. Might it be that they assumed the professor running the experiment would not really allow anyone to be hurt? To investigate this possibility, the experiment was rerun in a shabby office building in nearby Bridgeport, Connecticut. There was nothing in either the location or the experimenter's appearance to inspire confidence. Under these conditions, fewer people obeyed (48 percent), but the reduction was minor.

Milgram was disturbed by the willingness of people to knuckle under to authority and senselessly shock someone. In later experiments, he tried to reduce obedience. He found that the distance between the teacher and the learner was important. When subjects were in the *same room* as the learner, only 40 percent obeyed fully. When they were *face to face* with the learner and required to force his hand down on a simulated "shock plate," only 30 percent obeyed (❖Fig. 19.8). Distance from the authority also had an effect. When the experimenter gave his orders over the phone, only 22 percent obeyed. You may doubt that Milgram's study of obedience applies to you. If so, take a moment to read the following description:

BRIDGES

Milgram's studies of obedience raised questions about the ethics of psychological research.

See Chapter 2, pages 46–47.

Quack Like a Duck

The demonstration described here has become a favorite of many psychology teachers (Halonen, 1986). Imagine your response to the following events. On the first day of class, your professor begins to establish the basic rules of behavior for the course. Seats are assigned and you must move to a new location. You are told not to talk during class. Your professor tells you that you must have permission to leave early. You are told to bring your textbook to class at all times. Up to this point you might not have any difficulty obeying your professor's orders. Then the demands become less reasonable. The professor says, "Use only a pencil for taking notes. Borrow one if you must." "Take off your watch." "Keep both hands on your desktop at all times." "All students who are freshmen stand at the back of the class." The demonstration is capped by orders that you cannot follow without looking silly: "Stick two fingers up your nose and quack like a duck."

Where do you think you would draw the line in obeying such orders? In reality, you might find yourself obeying a legitimate authority long after that person's demands had become unreasonable. What would happen, though, if a few students resisted orders early in the sequence? Would that help free others to disobey? For an answer, let's return to some final remarks on Milgram's experiment.

IMPLICATIONS Milgram's research raises nagging questions about our willingness to commit antisocial or inhumane acts

Referent power *Social power gained when one is used as a point of reference by others.*
Expert power *Social power derived from possession of knowledge or expertise.*
Obedience *Conformity to the demands of an authority.*

Obedience to authority is often necessary and reasonable; however, it can also be destructive.

commanded by a "legitimate authority." The excuse so often given by war criminals—"I was only following orders"—takes on new meaning in this light. Milgram suggested that when directions come from an authority, people rationalize that they are not personally responsible for their actions. Others have pointed out that "crimes of obedience" may be committed by ordinary people responding to normal social psychological processes. In locales as diverse as Vietnam, Rwanda, Bosnia, South Africa, Nicaragua, Sri Lanka, and Laos, the tragic result has been "sanctioned massacres" of chilling proportions (Kelman & Hamilton, 1989). Even in everyday life, crimes of obedience are common. In order to keep their jobs, many people obey orders to do things that they personally regard as dishonest, unethical, or harmful (Hamilton & Sanders, 1995).

Aren't you taking an overly dim view of obedience? Obedience to authority is obviously necessary and desirable in many circumstances. Just the same, it is probably true, as C. P. Snow (1961) observed, "When you think of the long and gloomy history of man, you will find more hideous crimes have been committed in the name of obedience than in the name of rebellion." With this in mind, let us end on a more positive note. In one of his experiments, Milgram found that group support can greatly reduce destructive obedience. When real subjects saw two other "teachers" (both actors) resist orders and walk out of the experiment, only 10 percent continued to obey. Thus, a personal act of courage or moral fortitude by one or two members of a group may free others to disobey misguided or unjust authority.

COMPLIANCE—A FOOT IN THE DOOR

In *conformity* situations, the pressure to "get in line" is usually indirect. When an authority commands obedience, the pressure is direct and difficult to resist. There is a third possibility. The term **compliance** refers to situations in which one person bends to the requests of another person who has little or no authority or social power (Deaux, Dane, & Wrightsman, 1993).

Pressures to comply are quite common. For example, a stranger might ask you to yield a phone booth so he can make a call, a saleswoman might suggest that you buy a more expensive watch than you had planned on, or a coworker might ask you for 50 cents to buy a cup of coffee.

What determines whether a person will comply with a request? Many factors could be listed, but three stand out as especially interesting. Let's briefly consider each.

THE FOOT-IN-THE-DOOR EFFECT   People who sell door-to-door have long recognized that once they get a foot in the door, a sale is almost a sure thing. To state the **foot-in-the-door principle** more formally, a person who first agrees to a small request is later more likely to comply with a larger demand (Dillard, 1991). For instance, if someone asked you to put a large, ugly sign in your front yard to promote safe driving, you would probably refuse. If, however, you had first agreed to put a small sign in your window, you would later be much more likely to allow the big sign in your yard (Freedman & Fraser, 1966).

Apparently, the foot-in-the-door effect is based on observing one's own behavior. Seeing yourself agree to a small request helps convince you that you didn't mind doing what was asked. After that, you are more likely to comply with a larger request (Dillard, 1991).

THE DOOR-IN-THE-FACE EFFECT   Let's say that a neighbor comes to your door and asks you to feed his dogs, water his plants, and mow his yard while he is out of town for a month. This is quite a major request—one that most people would probably turn down. Feeling only slightly guilty, you tell your neighbor that you're sorry but you can't help him. Now, what if the same neighbor returns the next day and asks if you would at least pick up his mail while he is gone. Chances are very good that you would honor this request, even if you might have resisted it otherwise.

Psychologist Robert Cialdini coined the term **door-in-the-face effect** to describe the tendency for a person who has refused a major request to comply with a smaller request (Cialdini et al., 1975). In other words, after a person has turned down a major request ("slammed the door in your face"), he or she may be more willing to agree to a lesser demand. This

USING PSYCHOLOGY

HOW TO DRIVE A HARD BARGAIN

Your local car lot is a good place to see compliance take place. Automobile salespeople play the compliance game daily and get very good at it. If you understand what they are up to, you will have a far better chance of resisting their tactics.

A FOOT IN THE DOOR   The salesperson offers you a test drive. If you accept, you will have made a small commitment of time to a particular car and to the salesperson. The salesperson will then ask you to go to an office and fill out some papers, "just to see what kind of a price" she or he can offer. If you go along, you will be further committed.

THE LOW-BALL TECHNIQUE   To get things underway, the salesperson will offer you a very good price for your trade-in or will ask you to make an offer on the new car, "any offer, no matter how low." The salesperson will then ask if you will buy the car if she or he can sell it for the price you state. If you say yes, you have virtually bought the car. Most people find it very difficult to walk away once bargaining has reached this stage.

THE HOOK IS SET   Once buyers are "hooked" by a low-ball offer, the salesperson goes to the manager to have the sale "approved." On returning, the salesperson will tell you with great disappointment that the dealership would lose money on the deal. "Couldn't you just take a little less for the trade-in or pay a little more for the car?" the salesperson will ask. At this point, many people hesitate and grumble, but most

give in and accept some "compromise" price or trade-in amount.

MILKING THE SALE   By the time you strike a deal, you can be sure that the price you accept will give the dealership the minimum profit it requires on all sales—and probably much more. To add insult to injury, the salesperson will then try to increase the profit by convincing you to add various options to your car—extra mirrors, a stereo system, cruise control, and so forth. All of these items cost less from independent suppliers, so many people pay hundreds of dollars too much for them alone.

EVENING THE ODDS   To combat all of the preceding, you must arm yourself with accurate information. In the past, salespeople had a great advantage in negotiating because they knew exactly how much the dealership paid for each car. Now, you can obtain detailed automobile pricing information on the Internet. With such information in hand, you will find it easier to challenge a salesperson's manipulative tactics.

After you've negotiated a final "best offer," get it in writing. Then walk out. Go to another dealer and see if the salesperson will better the price, in writing. When he or she does, return to the first dealership and negotiate for an even better price. Then decide where to buy. Now that you know some of the rules of the "New Car Game," you might even enjoy playing it.

strategy works because a person who abandons a large request appears to have given up something. In response, many people feel that they must repay her or him by giving in to the smaller request (Dillard, 1991). In fact, a good way to get another person to comply with a request is to first do a small favor for the person (Whatley et al., 1999).

THE LOW-BALL TECHNIQUE   Anyone who has purchased an automobile will recognize a third way of inducing compliance. Automobile dealers are notorious for convincing customers to buy cars by offering "low-ball" prices that undercut the competition. The dealer first gets the customer to agree to buy at an attractively low price. Then, once the customer is committed,

various techniques are used to bump the price up before the sale is concluded. (This ploy is described further in "How to Drive a Hard Bargain.")

Compliance   *Bending to the requests of a person who has little or no authority or other form of social power.*
Foot-in-the-door effect   *The tendency for a person who has first complied with a small request to be more likely later to fulfill a larger request.*
Door-in-the-face effect   *The tendency for a person who has refused a major request to subsequently be more likely to comply with a minor request.*

The **low-ball technique** consists of getting a person committed to act and then making the terms of acting less desirable. Here's another example: A fellow student asks to borrow $25 for a day. This seems reasonable and you agree. However, once you have given your classmate the money, he explains that it would be easier to repay you after payday, in 2 weeks. If you agree, you've succumbed to the low-ball technique. Here's one more example: Let's say you ask someone to give you a ride to school in the morning. Only after the person has agreed do you tell her that you have to be there at 6 A.M.

BRIDGES

For some people, passive compliance may be an expression of learned helplessness.

See Chapter 16, pages 532–533.

Passive Compliance

Complying with requests is a normal part of daily social life. At times, however, a willingness to comply can exceed what is reasonable. Researcher Thomas Moriarty (1975) has demonstrated excessive, passive compliance under realistic conditions. **Passive compliance** refers to quietly bending to unreasonable demands or unacceptable conditions. Moriarty became interested in the "little murders" of daily life—the personal insults, rebuffs, and sacrifices of dignity that have become so common. Moriarty observed that many people will put up with almost anything to avoid a confrontation. He decided to put this passive, "no-hassle" attitude to experimental test.

In one experiment, two people (one actually an accomplice) were given a difficult test in a very small room. The subjects were seated back to back and left alone to work. As soon as the experimenter left, the phony subject turned on a portable cassette player at full volume. Real subjects who failed to complain were treated to a 17-minute blast of nerve-wracking rock music. The accomplice was instructed to turn the music off only after a third request. In this particular experiment, 80 percent of the subjects said nothing, although they glared, covered their ears, stopped work, and so forth. An interview later showed that most were angry or annoyed but were afraid to tell the other person to be quiet.

Could it be that people failed to complain because they didn't want to disrupt the testing? Yes, it is possible that the passivity observed in this study is unique to the experimental setting. However, when Moriarty and his students staged loud conversations behind theater patrons or people studying in a library, very few protested. In other naturalistic experiments, people were accosted in phone booths. The experimenter explained that he had left a ring in the booth and asked if the person had found it. When subjects said no, the experimenter demanded that they empty their pockets. Most did.

In these and similar situations, people passively accepted having their personal rights trampled, even when objecting presented no threat to their safety (❖Fig. 19.9). Overly passive women, in particular, tend to be ripe targets for exploitation, especially by men (Richards, Rollerson, & Phillips, 1991). Have we become "a nation of willing victims"? Certainly, we hope not. Nevertheless, researchers such as Milgram and Moriarty have identified a significant social problem. We will address the

problem again in the "Psychology in Action" section of this chapter.

A LOOK AHEAD   In the upcoming discussion of "Psychology in Action," we will return to the problem of passive behavior to learn how you can better handle difficult social situations. Then, in "A Step Beyond," we will examine the nature of social traps. A social trap is a situation in which individuals blindly act in ways that do collective harm.

❖ **FIGURE 19.9** *In an experiment done at an airport, a smoker intentionally sat or stood near nonsmokers. Only 9 percent of the nonsmokers asked the smoker to stop smoking, even when no-smoking signs were clearly visible nearby (Gibson & Werner, 1994).*

KNOWLEDGE BUILDER
SOCIAL POWER, OBEDIENCE, AND COMPLIANCE

RELATE

Return to the description of various types of social power. Can you think of a setting in which you have (to a greater or lesser degree) each type of power?

Are you surprised that so many people obeyed orders in Milgram's experiments? Do you think you would have obeyed? How actively do you question authority?

You would like to persuade people to donate to a deserving charity. How, specifically, could you use compliance techniques to get people to donate?

LEARNING CHECK

1. An ability to punish others for failure to obey is the basis for
   a. referent power b. legitimate power c. expert power d. coercive power

2. The term *compliance* refers to situations in which a person complies with commands made by a person who has authority. T or F?

3. Obedience in Milgram's experiments was related to
   a. distance between learner and teacher
   b. distance between experimenter and teacher
   c. obedience of other teachers
   d. all of these

4. Obedience is conformity to the commands of an
   _____.

5. By repeating his obedience experiment in a downtown office building, Milgram demonstrated that the prestige of Yale University was the main reason for subjects' willingness to obey in the original experiment. T or F?

6. The research of Thomas Moriarty and others has highlighted the problem of _____ _____, rather than obedience to authority.

CRITICAL THINKING

7. Modern warfare allows killing to take place impersonally and at a distance. How does this relate to Milgram's experiments?

Answers:

1. d 2. F 3. d 4. authority 5. F 6. passive compliance 7. There is a big difference between killing someone in hand-to-hand combat and killing someone by lining up images on a video screen. Milgram's research suggests that it is easier for a person to follow orders to kill another human when the victim is at a distance and removed from personal contact.

psychology in action

ASSERTIVENESS TRAINING—STANDING UP FOR YOUR RIGHTS

Most of us have been rewarded, first as children and later as adults, for compliant, obedient, or "good" behavior. Perhaps this is why so many people find it difficult to assert themselves. Or perhaps nonassertion is related to anxiety about "making a scene" or feeling disliked by others. Whatever the causes, some people suffer tremendous anguish in any situation requiring poise, self-confidence, or self-assertion. Have you ever done any of the following?

- Hesitated to question an error on a restaurant bill because you were afraid of making a scene?
- Backed out of asking for a raise or a change in working conditions?
- Said yes when you wanted to say no?
- Been afraid to question a grade that seemed unfair?

If you have ever had difficulty in asserting yourself in similar situations, behavior therapist Joseph Wolpe has a solution for you: a technique called **assertiveness training** (instruction in how to be self-assertive).

What is done in assertiveness training?   Assertiveness training is a very direct procedure. By using group exercises, videotapes, mirrors, and staged conflicts, the instructor teaches assertive behavior. People learn to practice honesty, disagreeing, questioning authority, and assertive postures and gestures. As their self-confidence improves, nonassertive clients are taken on "field trips" to shops and restaurants where they practice what they have learned.

Nonassertion requiring therapy is unusual. Nevertheless, many people become tense or upset in at least some situations in which they must stand up for their rights. For this reason,

many people have found the techniques and exercises of assertiveness training helpful. If you have ever eaten a carbonized steak when you ordered it rare or stood in silent rage as a clerk ignored you, the following discussion will be of interest.

Self-Assertion

The first step in assertiveness training is to convince yourself of three basic rights: You have the right to refuse, to request, and to right a wrong. **Self-assertion** involves standing up for these rights by speaking out in your own behalf.

Is self-assertion just getting things your own way?   Not at all. A basic distinction can be made between *self-assertion* and *aggressive* behavior. Self-assertion is a direct, honest expression of feelings and desires. It is not exclusively self-serving. People who are nonassertive are usually patient to a fault. Sometimes their pent-up anger explodes with unexpected fury, which can be very destructive to relationships. In contrast to assertive behavior, **aggression** involves hurting another person or

Low-ball technique *A strategy in which commitment is gained first to reasonable or desirable terms, which are then made less reasonable or desirable.*
Passive compliance *Passively bending to unreasonable demands or circumstances.*
Assertiveness training *Instruction in how to be self-assertive.*
Self-assertion *A direct, honest expression of feelings and desires.*
Aggression *Hurting another person or achieving one's goals at the expense of another person.*

achieving one's goals at the expense of another. Aggression does not take into account the feelings or rights of others. It is an attempt to get one's own way no matter what. Assertion techniques emphasize firmness, not attack (◆Table 19.2).

Assertiveness Training

The basic idea in assertiveness training is that each assertive action is practiced until it can be repeated even under stress. For example, let's say it really angers you when a store clerk waits on several people who arrived after you did. To improve your assertiveness in this situation, you would begin by *rehearsing* the dialogue, posture, and gestures you would use to confront the clerk or the other customer. Working in front of a mirror can be very helpful. If possible, you should *role-play* the scene with a friend. Be sure to have your friend take the part of a really aggressive or irresponsible clerk, as well as a cooperative one. Rehearsal and role-playing should also be used when you expect a possible confrontation with someone—for example, if you are going to ask for a raise, challenge a grade, or confront a landlord.

Is that all there is to it? No. Another important principle is **overlearning** (practice that continues after initial mastery of a skill). When you rehearse or role-play assertive behavior, it is essential to continue to practice until your responses become almost automatic. This helps prevent you from getting flustered in the actual situation.

One more technique you may find useful is the **broken record.** This is a self-assertion technique involving repeating a request until it is acknowledged. (In ancient times, when people played phonograph records, the needle sometimes got "stuck in a groove." When this happened, part of a song might repeat over and over. Hence, the term *broken record* refers to repeating yourself.)

A good way to prevent assertion from becoming aggression is to simply restate your request as many times and in as many ways as necessary. As an illustration, let's say you are returning a pair of shoes to a store. After two wearings, the shoes fell apart, but you bought them 2 months ago and no longer have a receipt. The broken record could sound something like this:

Customer: *I would like to have these shoes replaced.*
Clerk: *Do you have a receipt?*
Customer: *No, but I bought them here, and since they are defective, I would like to have you replace them.*
Clerk: *I can't do that without a receipt.*
Customer: *I understand that, but I want them replaced.*
Clerk: *Well, if you'll come back this afternoon and talk to the manager.*
Customer: *I've brought these shoes in because they are defective.*
Clerk: *Well, I'm not authorized to replace them.*
Customer: *Yes, well, if you'll replace these, I'll be on my way.*

Notice that the customer did not attack the clerk or create an angry confrontation. Simple persistence is often all that is necessary for successful self-assertion.

How would I respond assertively to a put-down? Responding assertively to verbal aggression (a "put-down") is a real challenge. The tendency is to respond aggressively, which usually makes things worse. A good way to respond to a put-down uses the following steps: (1) If you are wrong, admit it; (2) acknowledge the person's feelings; (3) assert yourself about the other person's aggression; (4) briskly end the interchange.

Psychologists Robert Alberti and Michael Emmons (1995) offer an example of how to use the four steps. Let's say you accidentally bump into someone. The person responds angrily, "Damn it! Why don't you watch where you're going! You fool, you could have hurt me!" A good response would be to say, "I'm sorry I bumped you. I didn't do it intentionally. It's obvious you're upset, but I don't like your calling me names, or yelling. I can get your point without that."

Now, what if someone insults you indirectly ("I love your taste in clothes, it's so folksy")? Alberti and Emmons suggest you ask for a clarification ("What are you trying to say?"). This will force the person to take responsibility for the aggression. It can also provide an opportunity to change the way the person interacts with you: "If you really don't like what I'm wearing, I'd like to know it. I'm not always sure I like the things I buy, and I value your opinion."

◆ **TABLE 19.2** Comparison of Assertive, Aggressive, and Nonassertive Behavior

	ACTOR	RECEIVER OF BEHAVIOR
Nonassertive behavior	Self-denying, inhibited, hurt, and anxious; lets others make choices; goals not achieved	Feels sympathy, guilt, or contempt for actor; achieves goals at actor's expense
Aggressive behavior	Achieves goals at others' expense; expresses feelings, but hurts others; chooses for others or puts them down	Feels hurt, defensive, humiliated, or taken advantage of; does not meet own needs
Assertive behavior	Self-enhancing; acts in own best interests; expresses feelings; respects rights of others; goals usually achieved, self-respect maintained	Needs respected and feelings expressed; may achieve goal; self-worth maintained

psychology in action

To summarize, self-assertion does not supply instant poise, confidence, or self-assurance. However, it is a way of combating anxieties associated with life in an impersonal and sometimes intimidating society. If you are interested in more information, you can consult the book *Your Perfect Right* by Alberti and Emmons (1995).

ASSERTIVENESS TRAINING

RELATE

Pick a specific instance when you could have been more assertive. How would you handle the situation if it occurs again?

Think of a specific instance when you were angry and acted aggressively. How could you have handled the situation through self-assertion, instead of aggression?

LEARNING CHECK

1. In assertiveness training, people learn techniques for getting their way in social situations and angry interchanges. T or F?

2. Nonassertive behavior causes hurt, anxiety, and self-denial in the actor, and sympathy, guilt, or contempt in the receiver. T or F?

3. Overlearning should be avoided when rehearsing assertive behaviors. T or F?

4. The "broken record" must be avoided, because it is a basic nonassertive behavior. T or F?

CRITICAL THINKING

5. When practicing self-assertion, do you think it would be better to improvise your own responses or imitate those of a person skilled in self-assertion?

Answers:

1. F 2. T 3. F 4. F 5. A recent study found that imitating an assertive model is more effective than improvising your own responses (Kipper, 1992). If you know an assertive and self-assured person, you can learn a lot by watching how that person handles difficult situations.

a step beyond

SOCIAL TRAPS—THE TRAGEDY OF THE COMMONS

Focus: Why is group behavior sometimes misguided and destructive?

You are in a packed theater in an older building. Halfway through the feature movie (*Bambi Meets Godzilla*), you begin to smell smoke. The screen goes dark. You try to stay calm as you shuffle toward a distant exit sign. Suddenly someone screams. You lunge for the door. Instantly, you are caught in a crush of people. The crowd jams together so tightly that only a few people can squeeze through the door. If the fire moves swiftly, many lives will be lost.

This situation—panic during a fire—is a classic example of a *social trap*. Each person in a theater who runs toward the exits has acted in his or her immediate self-interest. Yet if everyone bolts at once, the chances that anyone will survive may be very low.

Social Traps

What exactly is a social trap? A **social trap** is any social situation that rewards individual actions that have undesired collective effects in the long run (Cross & Guyer, 1980). On an individual level, it is quite common for people to be "trapped"

Overlearning *Learning or practice that continues after initial mastery of a skill.*

Broken record *A self-assertion technique involving repeating a request until it is acknowledged.*

Social trap *A social situation that tends to provide immediate rewards for actions that will have undesired effects in the long run.*

by immediate rewards that are followed by delayed costs or suffering. For instance, many people are enticed into drinking too much at parties because their pleasure is immediate and their discomfort (a hangover) comes later.

Many people go into debt because they get the immediate reward of owning desirable goods; only later do they suffer when a staggering credit card bill arrives. For the immediate pleasures of intimacy, many teenagers later pay the price of pregnancy, forced marriage, early divorce, curtailed education, and so on.

Behavioral traps that involve groups of people, or social traps, as we have called them, are especially interesting. In a social trap, no one individual intentionally acts against the group interest, but if many people act alike, collective harm is done. For example, each person who leaves work at 5 P.M. in a congested city expects to gain by getting home earlier. Yet if everyone leaves at 5:00, the resulting traffic jam ensures that everyone will, in fact, arrive home late and emotionally frazzled. The problem could be solved if some people would wait a half hour or more before leaving. However, no one does this because immediate self-interest encourages a "fast getaway."

A related example is the fact that many large cities now have rapid transit systems that are underused by their citizens. Each person decides that it is more convenient to own and drive a separate car (in order to run errands and so on). However, we see again that individual behavior affects the welfare of others. Because everyone wants to drive for "convenience," driving becomes inconvenient: The mass of cars in most cities causes irritating traffic snarls and a lack of parking spaces. Each car owner has been drawn into a trap.

The Tragedy of the Commons

Social traps are especially damaging when we are enticed into overuse of scarce resources. Again, each person acts in his or her self-interest. But collectively, everyone ends up suffering. This is exactly what happened a few years ago to crab fishermen in Alaska.

Initially, crabs were plentiful and fishermen were few. Each fisherman was therefore able to make large, lucrative catches. To raise their profits, fishermen began to add second, third, and fourth boats to their operations. For a while this did, in fact, increase individual profits. But as the size of the fishing fleet continued to grow, the number of crabs available to be caught by any boat decreased.

Eventually, so many crabs were caught that their rate of reproduction slowed. As a result, crab fishermen began to go bankrupt in large numbers. Individually, their actions made sense. But collectively, the group suffered greatly.

Ecologist Garrett Hardin (1968, 1985) calls situations like the one just described the **tragedy of the commons.** Tragedies of this sort occur when people share a scarce resource. Each person acts in his or her self-interest, which causes the resource to be used up so that everyone suffers. More familiar examples of this dilemma are the lack of indi-

vidual incentives to conserve gasoline, water, or electricity. Whenever one's personal comfort or convenience is involved, it is highly tempting to "let others worry about it." Yet in the long run, everyone stands to lose. The tragedy of the commons is especially likely to occur when people are uncertain about how much of a resource exists or how fast it is being replaced (Hine & Gifford, 1996).

Social Problems

Many major social problems can be thought of as social traps. In most cases of environmental pollution, for instance, there are immediate benefits for polluting and major long-term costs. If one person pollutes a river or trashes the roadside, it has little noticeable effect. But as many people do the same, problems that affect everyone quickly mount. As another example, consider the farmer who applies pesticides to a crop to save it from insect damage. The farmer benefits immediately. However, if other farmers follow suit, the local water system may be permanently damaged.

Traps also exist at the international level. Countries that add to their nuclear stockpiles hope to be more "secure." Yet, doing so may eventually increase the chances of a final nuclear holocaust (Nevin & Fuld, 1993). It's no wonder that people who study international conflicts often come away shaking their heads and wondering, "How did we get into this mess?"

ESCAPING TRAPS   *What can be done to avoid social traps?* In some situations, it might be possible to dismantle social traps by rearranging rewards and costs. For example, many companies are tempted to pollute because it saves them money and increases profits. To reverse the situation, a pollution tax could be levied so that it would cost more, not less, for a business to pollute. As another example, we could reward lower individual consumption of resources. Some power companies have already experimented with a meter that charges lower rates for using power at off-peak periods (also see Appendix A).

There is evidence that in real social traps, people are more likely to restrain themselves when they believe others will, too (Messick et al., 1983). Otherwise, they are likely to think, "Why should I be a sucker? I don't think anyone else is going to conserve" (fuel, electricity, water, paper, crabs, or whatever). In some cases, people can be forced to limit their use of a scarce resource. However, some will see this as an infringement of their rights. Others, who are already nonabusers, may feel that they are being punished for a problem they did not cause (Baron & Jurney, 1993). Fortunately, just being aware that a social trap exists is sometimes enough to help people avoid it (Neidert & Linder, 1990).

Some problems may be harder to solve. What, for instance, can be done about truck drivers who cause dangerous traffic jams because they will not pull over on narrow roads? How can littering be discouraged or prevented? How would you make car-pooling or using public transportation the first choice for most people? Or how could people simply be encouraged to

stagger their departure times to and from work? All of these and more are social traps that need springing. It is important that we not fall into the trap of ignoring them.

CONCLUSION: Some social behaviors produce immediate rewards but have destructive effects in the long run. Rearranging the rewards and costs associated with such behaviors can help prevent people from falling into social traps.

KNOWLEDGE BUILDER

SOCIAL TRAPS

RELATE

Think of at least one specific situation in which your behavior was influenced by immediate rewards that were later followed by delayed costs or suffering. Was the situation an individual behavioral trap or a social trap? Describe at least three situations you have observed that appear to be social traps. Choose one of the situations and devise a plan for preventing people from doing group harm.

LEARNING CHECK

1. A social trap is any situation in which undesired actions are rewarded in the long run. T or F?

2. Individuals in a social trap act in ways that appear to be rational but that create problems for the group as a whole. T or F?

3. The tragedy of the commons occurs when individuals use a shared resource too quickly because they get immediate rewards for doing so. T or F?

4. Rearranging individual rewards and costs is one way to dismantle social traps. T or F?

CRITICAL THINKING

5. What social trap accompanies most major holidays?

Answers:

1. F 2. T 3. T 4. T 5. Travel nightmares are the rule as people jam trains, planes, and highways on major holidays.

Tragedy of the commons *A social trap in which individuals, each acting in his or her immediate self-interest, overuse a scarce group resource.*

CHAPTER IN REVIEW

How does group membership affect individual behavior?

- Humans are social animals enmeshed in a complex network of social relationships. Social psychology studies how individuals behave, think, and feel in social situations.
- Culture provides a broad social context for our behavior. One's position in groups defines a variety of roles to be played.
- Social roles, which may be achieved or ascribed, are particular behavior patterns associated with social positions. When two or more contradictory roles are held, role conflict may occur. The Stanford prison experiment showed that destructive roles may override individual motives for behavior.
- Positions within groups typically carry higher or lower levels of status. High status is associated with special privileges and respect.
- Group structure refers to the organization of roles, communication pathways, and power within a group. Group cohesiveness is basically the degree of attraction among group members.
- Norms are standards of conduct enforced (formally or informally) by groups. The autokinetic effect has been used to demonstrate that norms rapidly form even in temporary groups.

What unspoken rules govern the use of personal space?

- The study of personal space is called proxemics. Four basic spatial zones around each person's body are intimate distance (0 to 18 inches), personal distance (1 ½ to 4 feet), social distance (4 to 12 feet), and public distance (12 feet or more).

How do we perceive the motives of others and the causes of our own behavior?

- Attribution theory is concerned with how we make inferences about behavior. A variety of factors affect attribution, including consistency, distinctiveness, situational demands, and consensus.
- The fundamental attributional error is to ascribe the actions of others to internal causes. Because of actor-observer differences, we tend to attribute our own behavior to external causes.
- Self-handicapping involves arranging excuses for poor performance as a way to protect one's self-image or self-esteem.

Why do people affiliate?

- The need to affiliate is tied to additional needs for approval, support, friendship, and information. Additionally, research indicates that affiliation is related to reducing anxiety and uncertainty.
- Social comparison theory holds that we affiliate to evaluate our actions, feelings, and abilities. Social comparisons are also made for purposes of self-protection and self-enhancement.

What factors influence interpersonal attraction?

- Interpersonal attraction is increased by physical proximity (nearness), frequent contact, physical attractiveness, competence, and similarity. A large degree of similarity on many dimensions is characteristic of mate selection.

- Self-disclosure occurs more when two people like one another. Self-disclosure follows a reciprocity norm: Low levels of self-disclosure are met with low levels in return, whereas moderate self-disclosure elicits more personal replies. However, overdisclosure tends to inhibit self-disclosure by others.
- According to social exchange theory, we tend to maintain relationships that are profitable—that is, those for which perceived rewards exceed perceived costs.
- Romantic love has been studied as a special kind of attitude. Love can be distinguished from liking by the use of attitude scales. Dating couples like and love their partners but only like their friends. Love is also associated with greater mutual absorption between people.
- Adult love relationships tend to mirror patterns of emotional attachment observed in infancy and early childhood. Secure, avoidant, and ambivalent patterns can be defined on the basis of how a person approaches romantic and affectionate relationships with others.
- Evolutionary psychology attributes human mating patterns to the differing reproductive challenges faced by men and women since the dawn of time.

What have social psychologists learned about conformity, social power, obedience, and compliance?

- In general, social influence refers to alterations in behavior brought about by the behavior of others. Conformity to group pressure is a familiar example of social influence.
- Virtually everyone conforms to a variety of broad social and cultural norms. Conformity pressures also exist within smaller groups. The famous Asch experiments demonstrated that various group sanctions encourage conformity.
- Groupthink refers to compulsive conformity in group decision making. Victims of groupthink seek to maintain each other's approval, even at the cost of critical thinking.
- Social influence is also related to five types of social power: reward power, coercive power, legitimate power, referent power, and expert power.
- Obedience to authority has been investigated in a variety of experiments, particularly those by Milgram. Obedience in Milgram's studies decreased when the victim was in the same room, when the victim and subject were face to face, when the authority figure was absent, and when others refused to obey.
- Compliance with direct requests is another means by which behavior is influenced. Three strategies for inducing compliance are the foot-in-the-door technique, the door-in-the-face approach, and the low-ball technique.
- Recent research suggests that, in addition to excessive obedience to authority, many people show a surprising passive compliance to unreasonable requests.

How does self-assertion differ from aggression?

- Self-assertion, as opposed to aggression, involves clearly stating one's wants and needs to others. Learning to be assertive is accomplished by role-playing, rehearsing assertive actions, overlearning, and using specific techniques, such as the "broken record."

What is a social trap?

- A social trap is a social situation in which immediately rewarded actions have undesired effects in the long run.
- One prominent social trap occurs when limited public resources are overused, a problem called the tragedy of the commons.

PSYCHOLOGY ON THE NET

- **Social Psychology Network** A comprehensive site with many links to information about social psychology. http://www.wesleyan.edu/spn/
- **In Your Face** Discusses research on facial attractiveness. http://www.sp.uconn.edu/marshall/html/afigure5.html
- **Center for Evolutionary Psychology** A primer on evolutionary psychology, a reading list, and links. http://www.psych.ucsb.edu/research/cep/
- **Evolutionary Psychology for the Common Person** Introduces evolutionary psychology; with links to other information on EP. http://www.evoyage.com/

- **Preventing Groupthink** Offers five ways to prevent groupthink. http://www.fis.utoronto.ca/people/faculty/choo/FIS/Courses/LIS 2149/PreventGTl.html
- **Social Psychology Humor** Links to cartoons that relate to principles of social psychology. http://miavx1.muohio.edu/~shermarc/p324cart.html
- **InfoTrac® College Edition** For recent articles on the "Psychology in Action" feature, use Key Words search for ASSERTIVENESS.

INTERACTIVE LEARNING

- *PsychNow!* 8a. Helping others. 8b. Attribution. 8c. Social influence.
- *Psyk.trek* 12a. Attribution processes. 12b. Theories of love.

CHAPTER 20

Attitudes, Culture, and Human Relations

Chapter Survey

Theme: *Social life is complex, but consistent patterns can be found in our attitudes, as well as in our positive and negative interactions with others.*

▼ **KEY QUESTIONS**

● **KEY TOPICS**

▼ What are attitudes? How are they acquired?

- *Attitudes and attitude formation*

▼ How are attitudes measured and changed?

- *Measuring attitudes*
- *Sources of attitude change*

▼ Under what conditions is persuasion most effective?

- *Persuasion*
- *Characteristics of the communicator, message, and audience*

▼ What is cognitive dissonance? What does it have to do with attitudes and behavior?

- *Cognitive dissonance theory*

▼ Is brainwashing actually possible?

- *Brainwashing and forced attitude change*

▼ How are people converted to cult membership?

- *Cult recruitment and membership*

▼ **KEY QUESTIONS**

● **KEY TOPICS**

▼ What causes prejudice and intergroup conflict?

- *Types and sources of prejudice*
- *Stereotypes and group conflict*

▼ What can be done about these problems?

- *Reducing prejudice*

▼ How do psychologists explain human aggression?

- *Theories of aggression*

▼ Why are bystanders so often unwilling to help in an emergency?

- *Bystander apathy and helping others*

▼ What can be done to lower prejudice and promote social harmony?

- *Living with diversity*

▼ How does the theory of sociobiology try to explain social behavior?

- *Sociobiology and biological determinism*

DOOMSDAY FOR THE SEEKERS

HARDLY A YEAR PASSES without a doomsday group of one kind or another making the news. In one classic example of such groups, a woman named Mrs. Keech claimed she was receiving messages from beings on a planet called Clarion. The aliens told Mrs. Keech they had detected a fault in the earth's crust that would plunge North America into the sea on December 21. However, Mrs. Keech and her followers, who called themselves the Seekers, had no fear: On December 20, they expected to be met at midnight by a flying saucer and taken to safety in outer space.

December 20 arrived, and the Seekers gathered at Mrs. Keech's house. Many had given up jobs and possessions to prepare for departure. Expectations were high, and commitment was total. But as the night wore on, midnight passed, and the world continued to exist. It was a bitter and embarrassing disappointment for the Seekers.

Did the group break up then?   Our story now takes an amazing twist—one that intrigued social psychologists. Instead of breaking up, the Seekers became more convinced than ever before that they were right. At about 5 A.M., Mrs. Keech said she had received a new message, explaining that the Seekers had saved the world.

Before December 20, the Seekers were uninterested in persuading other people that the world was coming to an end. Now, they called newspapers and radio stations to convince others of their accomplishment.

How do we explain this strange turn in the behavior of Mrs. Keech's doomsday group? An answer may lie in the concept of cognitive dissonance. Cognitive dissonance also helps explain many aspects of attitude change. Watch for Mrs. Keech and a discussion of cognitive dissonance later in this chapter.

 Gateways to Attitudes, Culture, and Human Relations

ATTITUDES subtly affect nearly all aspects of social behavior.

TO PERSUADE OTHERS, you must be aware of your role as a communicator, the characteristics of the audience, and the type of message that will appeal to them.

FORCED ATTITUDE CHANGE (BRAINWASHING) is possible and sometimes used by cults and other coercive groups.

PREJUDICE, DISCRIMINATION, INTOLERANCE, AND STEREOTYPING damage the lives of many people.

PREJUDICE is reduced by equal-status contact with members of other groups and by mutual interdependence, which promotes cooperation.

AGGRESSION is a fact of life, but humans are not inevitably aggressive.

BY UNDERSTANDING BARRIERS TO PROSOCIAL BEHAVIOR, we can encourage acts of helping and altruism.

MULTICULTURAL HARMONY is attainable through conscious efforts to be more tolerant of others.

SOCIOBIOLOGY is an extreme form of evolutionary psychology that has drawn attention to the biological origins of human behavior.

ATTITUDES—BELIEF + EMOTION + ACTION

What is your attitude toward affirmative action, environmental groups, the death penalty, imported automobiles, k. d. lang, psychology? The answers can have far-reaching effects on your behavior. Attitudes are intimately woven into our actions and views of the world. Our tastes, friendships, votes, preferences, and goals are all touched by attitudes.

What specifically is an attitude?   An **attitude** is a mixture of belief and emotion that predisposes a person to respond to other people, objects, or institutions in a positive or negative way. Attitudes summarize your *evaluation* of objects (Petty, Wegener, & Fabrigar, 1997). As a result, they predict or direct future actions. For example, an approach known as the *misdirected letter technique* demonstrates that actions are closely connected to attitudes.

The Luck of the Irish

During a period of violence in Northern Ireland, attitudes toward the Irish were measured in a sample of English households. Later, wrongly addressed letters were sent to the same households. Each letter had either an English name or an Irish name on it. The question was: Would the "Irish" letters be returned to the Post Office or thrown away? As predicted, letters were more often thrown away by people living in households where anti-Irish attitudes had been measured earlier. (Howitt et al., 1977)

"Your attitude is showing" is sometimes said. Actually, attitudes are expressed in three ways: through beliefs, emotions, and actions. The **belief component** of an attitude is what a person believes about the attitudinal object. The **emotional component** consists of feelings toward the attitudinal object. The **action component** refers to one's actions toward various people, objects, or institutions. Consider, for example, your attitude

---

Attitude *A learned tendency to respond to people, objects, or institutions in a positive or negative way.*
Belief component *What a person thinks or believes about the object of an attitude.*
Emotional component *One's feelings toward the object of an attitude.*
Action component *How one tends to act toward the object of an attitude.*

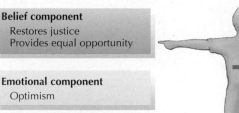
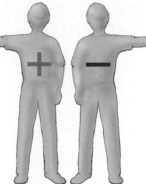

Belief component
Restores justice
Provides equal opportunity

Emotional component
Optimism

Action component
Vote for affirmative action
Donate to groups that support
affirmative action

Belief component
Unfair to majority
Reverse discrimination

Emotional component
Anger

Action component
Vote against affirmative action
Donate to groups that oppose
affirmative action

❖ **FIGURE 20.1** *Elements of positive and negative attitudes toward affirmative action.*

toward gun control. You will have beliefs about whether gun control would affect rates of crime or violence. You will have emotional responses to guns, finding them either attractive and desirable or threatening and destructive. And you will have a tendency to seek out or avoid gun ownership. The action component of your attitude will probably also include support of organizations that urge or oppose gun control.

As you can see, attitudes orient us to the social world. In doing so, they prepare us to act in certain ways (Olson & Zanna, 1993). (For another example, see ❖Fig. 20.1.)

Attitude Formation

How do people acquire attitudes? Attitudes are acquired in several basic ways. Sometimes, attitudes come from **direct contact** (personal experience) with the object of the attitude—such as opposing pollution when a nearby factory ruins your favorite river. Attitudes are also learned through **interaction with others**—that is, through discussion with people holding a particular attitude. For instance, if three of your friends are volunteers at a local recycling center, and you talk with them about their beliefs, you will probably come to favor recycling, too. **Child rearing** (the effects of parental values, beliefs, and practices) also affects attitudes. For example, if both parents belong to the same political party, chances are 2 out of 3 that their children will belong to that party as adults.

In the previous chapter, we discussed group forces that operate to bring about conformity. There is little doubt that many of our attitudes are influenced by **group membership** (affiliation with others). In one classic study, for example, groups were formed to discuss the case of a juvenile delinquent. Most participants believed the boy needed love, kindness, and friendship. To test group pressures on attitudes, a person who advocated severe punishment was added to each group.

How did group members react to the "deviate"? At first, they directed almost all of their comments to him. But when he stuck to his position, an interesting thing happened. Soon, he was almost completely excluded from conversation. And later, the deviate was strongly rejected in ratings made by other group members (Schachter, 1951). Group pressures for conformity and the difficulty of holding deviant attitudes can be clearly seen in this outcome.

Attitudes are an important dimension of social behavior. They are often greatly influenced by the groups to which we belong.

Attitudes are also influenced by the **mass media** (all media, such as magazines and television, that reach large audiences). As Marshall McLuhan put it, we are "massaged" by the media, meaning we are coaxed, persuaded, and skillfully manipulated. Ninety-nine percent of North American homes have a television set, which is turned on an average of over 7 hours a day. The information thus channeled into homes has a powerful impact. For instance, frequent viewers mistrust others and overestimate their chances of being harmed. This suggests that a steady diet of TV violence leads some people to develop a **mean worldview,** in which they regard the world as a dangerous and threatening place (Heath & Gilbert, 1996).

Some attitudes are simply formed through **chance conditioning** (learning that takes place by chance or coincidence) (Olson & Zanna, 1993). Let's say, for instance, that you have had three encounters in your lifetime with psychologists. If all three were negative, you might take an unduly dim view of

FOR BETTER OR WORSE, COPYRIGHT © 1991 UFS, INC. ALL RIGHTS RESERVED.

ROCK MUSIC VIDEOS AND ANTISOCIAL ATTITUDES

Many rock music videos are filled with rebellion, violence, intoxication, sexual promiscuity, and degrading images of women. Rock videos almost always show such behavior in a positive light, making it seem commonplace. Does this affect viewers' attitudes toward antisocial behavior? To find out, Christine and Ranald Hansen (1990) staged an experiment in which college students watched three antisocial rock videos or three neutral music videos. Afterward, subjects "accidentally" saw one of two "job applicants" (who were actually accomplices in the experiment) make an obscene gesture with his hand. Later, each student was asked how likable the job applicants were and if they should be hired.

As you might expect, students who watched only neutral videos liked the antisocial job applicant less and gave him low ratings.

What about the students who had watched antisocial videos? Were their attitudes influenced? Clearly they were. Subjects who had just seen a barrage of antisocial images rated the "job applicant" who made the obscene gesture just as highly as the one who didn't.

As the Hansens point out, music elicits positive emotions. What if these good feelings are associated with antisocial themes? Quite likely, classical conditioning will contribute to the creation of positive attitudes toward antisocial behavior (Hansen & Hansen, 1990).

psychology and psychologists. In the same way, people often develop strong attitudes toward cities, restaurants, or parts of the country on the basis of one or two unusually good or bad experiences. The highlight "Rock Music Videos and Antisocial Attitudes" provides an interesting example of how conditioning contributes to attitude formation.

Why are some attitudes acted on and others are not? To answer this question, let's consider an example. Assume that a woman named Lorraine knows that automobiles add to air pollution and strongly objects to smog. Why would Lorraine continue to drive to work every day? Probably it is because the *immediate consequences* of our actions weigh heavily on the choices we make. No matter what Lorraine's attitude may be, it is difficult for her to resist the immediate convenience of driving. Our expectations of how *others will evaluate* our actions are also important. By taking this factor into account, researchers have been able to predict family planning choices, alcohol use by adolescents, re-enlistment in the National Guard, voting on a nuclear power plant initiative, and so forth (Cialdini et al., 1981). Finally, we must not overlook the effects of long-standing *habits* (Petty, Wegener, & Fabrigar, 1997). Let's say that a "male chauvinist" boss vows to change his sexist attitudes toward female employees. Two months later it would not be unusual for his behavior to show the effects of habit rather than his intention to change.

In short, there are often large differences between attitudes and behavior—particularly between privately held attitudes and public behavior. However, barriers to action typically fall when a person holds an attitude with *conviction*. If you have **conviction** about an issue, it evokes strong feelings, you think about it and discuss it often, and you are knowledgeable about it (Abelson, 1988). Attitudes held with passionate conviction often lead to major changes in personal behavior (Petty, Wegener, & Fabrigar, 1997).

Attitude Measurement

Can attitudes be measured? Attitudes can be measured several ways. In an **open-ended interview,** individuals are simply

---

Direct contact *In forming attitudes, the effects of direct experience with the object of the attitude.*
Interaction with others *In forming attitudes, the influence of discussions with others who hold particular attitudes.*
Child rearing *In forming attitudes, the effects of parental values, beliefs, and practices.*
Group membership *As a factor in forming attitudes, social influences associated with belonging to various groups.*
Mass media *Collectively, all media that reach very large audiences (magazines, for instance, are a medium of mass communication).*
Mean worldview *Viewing the world and other people as dangerous and threatening.*
Chance conditioning *Conditioning that takes place by chance or coincidence.*
Conviction *Beliefs that are important to a person and that evoke strong emotion.*
Open-ended interview *An interview in which people are allowed to freely state their views.*

asked to freely express attitudes toward a particular issue. For example, a person might be asked, "What are your thoughts about freedom of speech on college campuses?" Attitudes toward social groups can be measured with a **social distance scale.** On such scales, people state their willingness to admit members of a particular group to various levels of social closeness. These levels range from "would exclude from my country" to "would admit to marriage in my family." If a person is prejudiced toward a group, she or he will prefer to remain socially distant from members of the group (Cover, 1995).

The use of *attitude scales* is one of the most common methods of measurement. **Attitude scales** consist of statements expressing various possible views on an issue (for example, "Socialized medicine would destroy the quality of health care in this country" or "This country needs a national health care program"). People typically respond to each item on a 5-point scale by ranking it from "strongly agree" to "strongly disagree." By combining scores on all items, a person can be rated for overall acceptance or rejection of a particular issue. When used in public polls, attitude scales provide useful information about the feelings of large segments of the population.

ATTITUDE CHANGE—WHY THE "SEEKERS" WENT PUBLIC

Although attitudes are relatively stable, they do change. Some attitude change can be understood in terms of **reference groups** (any group a person identifies with and uses as a standard for social comparison). It is not necessary to have face-to-face contact with other people for them to serve as a reference group. It depends instead on whom you identify with or whose attitudes and values you care about.

In the 1930s, Theodore Newcomb studied real-life attitude change among students at Bennington College. Most students came from conservative homes, but Bennington was a very

liberal school. Newcomb found that most students shifted significantly toward more liberal attitudes during their 4 years at Bennington. Those who didn't change kept their parents and hometown friends as primary reference groups. This is typified by one student's statement, "I decided I'd rather stick to my father's ideas." Those who did change identified primarily with the campus community. Notice that all students could count the college and their families as *membership* groups. However, one group or the other tended to become their point of reference.

Persuasion

What about advertising and other direct attempts to change attitudes? Are they effective? **Persuasion** is any deliberate attempt to change attitudes or beliefs through information and arguments. Businesses, politicians, and others who seek to persuade us obviously believe that attitudes can be changed. More than $12 billion is spent yearly on television advertising in the United States and Canada alone. Persuasion can range from the daily blitz of media commercials to personal discussion among friends. In most cases, the success or failure of persuasion can be understood if we consider the **communicator,** the **message,** and the **audience.**

Persuasion. Would you be likely to be swayed by this group's message? Successful persuasion is related to characteristics of the communicator, the message, and the audience.

Do you exercise regularly? Like students in the Bennington study, your intentions to exercise are probably influenced by the exercise habits of your reference groups (Terry & Hogg, 1996).

CONSUMER PSYCHOLOGY

Whether it's buying a car, toothpaste, a record, or lunch, we are all consumers. **Consumer psychology** is an applied field that focuses on how consumers behave (Robertson & Kassarjian, 1991).

Many people give little thought to why they buy what they do. But, in fact, **consumer behavior** consists of deciding to spend, selecting a brand, shopping, making a purchase, and evaluating the product in use (Robertson & Kassarjian, 1991). At each step, advertising, packaging, and a host of other factors affect our behavior. To pinpoint such factors, **marketing research** is often done. This is a type of public opinion polling in which people are asked to give their personal impressions of products, services, or advertising. In this way, researchers have learned that powerful, widely held *brand images* often develop. A **brand image** is the mental "picture" that consumers have of a product, especially with regard to its emotional meaning. A case in point is the images many people have of automobiles, such as Mercedes-Benz (high status), Corvette (power and sportiness), Buick

(conservatism), and so forth (Robertson & Kassarjian, 1991). Brand images tend to direct buying behavior, and they help explain why many people purchase products for their labels as much as for their performance. (The importance of product names is illustrated by the difficulty Chevrolet had in initial attempts to market its *Nova* model in South America. Until the name was changed, consumers shunned the car. The problem? In Spanish, *no va* means "doesn't go"!)

It sounds like consumer psychology is concerned with persuading people to buy things they don't need. Is that the case? Not all consumer psychology is profit oriented. For instance, principles of consumer behavior may be used to encourage people to conserve gasoline, water, and electricity or to use "green" (environmentally friendly) products (Shrum et al., 1995). The same principles that are used to get us to buy products can persuade us to act in our own best interest. Advertising campaigns concerning auto seat belt use, drug abuse prevention, healthful behavior, and the like all draw on an understanding of consumer behavior (Olander, 1990).

Let's say you have a chance to promote an issue important to you (for or against nuclear power, for instance) at a community gathering. Whom should you choose to make the presentation, and how should that person present it? Research suggests that attitude change is encouraged when the following conditions are met.

1. The communicator is likable, expressive, trustworthy, an expert on the topic, and similar to the audience in some respect.
2. The message appeals to emotions, particularly to fear or anxiety.
3. The message also provides a clear course of action that will, if followed, reduce fear or produce personally desirable results.
4. The message states clear-cut conclusions.
5. The message is backed up by facts and statistics.
6. Both sides of the argument are presented in the case of a well-informed audience.
7. Only one side of the argument is presented in the case of a poorly informed audience.
8. The persuader appears to have nothing to gain if the audience accepts the message.
9. The message is repeated as frequently as possible (Aronson, 1992; Eagly & Chaiken, 1992; Petty, Wegener, & Fabrigar, 1997).

You should have little trouble seeing how these principles are applied to sell everything from underarm deodorants to presidents. With selling in mind, take a moment to read "Consumer Psychology" for a brief side visit to an interesting topic.

ROLE-PLAYING We all know from personal observation that emotional experiences can dramatically alter attitudes. A good example is the person who gives up drinking after nearly dying

in an automobile accident caused by drunkenness. To actively bring about such attitude change, psychologists sometimes create similar experiences through role-playing. For instance, Janis and Mann (1965) asked women who were known smokers to play the role of cancer patients. A doctor told each of the women that he had some bad news: She had lung cancer and would have to undergo immediate surgery. The women played out the part by asking questions about the surgery, if it might fail, and so on. Women in the role-playing group drastically reduced their smoking. Those who listened to a tape recording of similar information showed little change.

Social distance scale *A rating of the degree to which a person would be willing to have contact with a member of another group.*
Attitude scale *A collection of attitudinal statements with which respondents indicate agreement or disagreement.*
Reference group *Any group that an individual identifies with and uses as a standard for social comparison.*
Persuasion *A deliberate attempt to change attitudes or beliefs with information and arguments.*
Communicator *In persuasion, the person presenting arguments or information.*
Message *In persuasion, the content of a communicator's arguments or presentation.*
Audience *The person or group toward whom a persuasive message is directed.*
Consumer psychology *Specialty area that seeks to understand consumer behavior and apply psychology to advertising, marketing, and product testing.*
Consumer behavior *All of the actions involved in deciding to spend, selecting a brand, shopping, making the purchase, and evaluating a product in use.*
Marketing research *A type of public opinion polling used to assess consumer views of products, services, and advertising.*
Brand image *The image that consumers have of various products, especially with regard to their personal or emotional meanings.*

Cognitive Dissonance Theory

Why does role-playing have more effect than hearing the same information? Certainly, emotional impact and realism have some effect, but part of the explanation also lies in *cognitive dissonance.* Cognitions are thoughts. Dissonance means clashing. The influential theory of **cognitive dissonance** states that contradicting or clashing thoughts cause discomfort. That is, we have a need for *consistency* in our thoughts, perceptions, and images of ourselves (Festinger, 1957; Thibodeau & Aronson, 1992).

What happens if people act in ways that are inconsistent with their attitudes or self-images? Typically, the contradiction makes them uncomfortable. Such discomfort can motivate people to make their thoughts or attitudes agree with their actions (Petty, Wegener, & Fabrigar, 1997). For example, smokers are told on every pack that cigarettes endanger their lives. They light up and smoke anyway. How do they resolve the tension between this information and their actions? They could quit smoking, but it may be easier to convince themselves that smoking is not really so dangerous. To do this, many smokers seek examples of heavy smokers who have lived long lives, they spend their time with other smokers, and they avoid information about the link between smoking and cancer. According to cognitive dissonance theory, we also tend to reject new information that contradicts ideas we already hold. At times, we're all guilty of this "don't bother me with the facts, my mind is made up" strategy.

Now recall Mrs. Keech and her doomsday group. Why did their belief in Mrs. Keech's messages *increase* after the world failed to end? Why did the group suddenly become interested in convincing others that their beliefs were correct? Cognitive dissonance theory explains that, after publicly committing themselves to their beliefs, they had a strong need to maintain their consistency. In effect, convincing others was a way of adding proof that they were right (see ◆Table 20.1).

Cognitive dissonance also underlies attempts to convince *ourselves* that we've done the right thing. Here's an example you may recognize: As romantic partners become better acquainted, they sooner or later begin to notice things they don't like about each other. How do they reduce the cognitive dissonance and doubts caused by their partners' shortcomings? A recent study found that we tend to create stories that change our partners' faults into virtues: He seems cheap, but he's really frugal; she seems egotistical, but she's really self-confident; he's not stubborn, he just has integrity; she's not undependable, she's a free spirit; and so on (Murray & Holmes, 1993).

Acting contrary to one's attitudes doesn't always bring about change. How does cognitive dissonance account for that? The amount of justification for acting contrary to your attitudes and beliefs affects how much dissonance you feel. (**Justification** is the degree to which a person's actions are explained by rewards or other circumstances.) In a classic study, college students did an extremely boring task (turning wooden pegs on a board) for a *long* time. Afterward, they were asked to help lure others into the experiment by pretending that the task was interesting and enjoyable. Students paid $20 for lying to others

◆ **TABLE 20.1** Strategies for Reducing Cognitive Dissonance

Celia, who is a college student, has always thought of herself as an environmental activist. Recently, Celia "inherited" a car from her parents, who were replacing the family "barge." In the past, Celia biked or used public transportation to get around. Her parents' old car is an antiquated gas-guzzler, but she has begun to drive it on a daily basis. How might Celia reduce the cognitive dissonance created by the clash between her environmentalism and her use of an inefficient automobile?

STRATEGY	EXAMPLE
Change your attitude	"Cars are not really a major environmental problem."
Add consonant thoughts	"This is an old car, so keeping it on the road makes good use of the resources consumed when it was manufactured."
Change the importance of the dissonant thoughts	"It's more important for me to support the environmental movement politically than it is to worry about how I get to school and work."
Reduce the amount of perceived choice	"My schedule has become too hectic. I really can't afford to bike or take the bus anymore."
Change your behavior	"I'm only going to use the car when it's impossible to bike or take the bus."

(After Franzoi, 1996.)

True State of Affairs →	Task was dull.
Conflicting Behavior →	"I told others that the task was interesting."
Dissonance Aroused →	"I wouldn't lie for $1." (Action not justified by payment.)
Result →	Change attitude: "I didn't lie; the task really was interesting."
	Dissonance reduced.

❖ **FIGURE 20.2** *Summary of the Festinger and Carlsmith (1959) study from the viewpoint of a person experiencing cognitive dissonance.*

did not change their own negative opinion of the task. Those who were paid only $1 later rated the experience as actually being pleasant and interesting. How can we explain these results? Apparently, students paid $20 experienced no dissonance. These students could reassure themselves that anybody would tell a little white lie for $20. Those paid $1 were faced with the conflicting thoughts, "I lied. But I had no good reason to do it." Rather than admit to themselves that they had lied, these students changed their attitudes toward what they had done (Festinger & Carlsmith, 1959) (❖Fig. 20.2).

Making choices often causes dissonance. This is especially true if the rejected alternative is perceived as better than the one selected. To minimize such dissonance, we tend to emphasize positive aspects of what we choose, while downgrading other alternatives. Thus, college students are more likely to think their courses will be good after they have registered than they did before making a commitment (Rosenfeld et al., 1983).

We are especially likely to experience dissonance after we cause an event to occur that we wish hadn't taken place (Cooper & Fazio, 1984). Let's say that you agree to help a friend move to a new apartment. The big day arrives, and you feel like staying in bed. Actually, you wish you hadn't promised to help. To reduce dissonance, you may convince yourself that the work will actually be "good exercise," "sort of fun," or that your friend really deserves the help. We often make such adjustments in attitudes to minimize cognitive dissonance.

FORCED ATTITUDE CHANGE—BRAINWASHING AND CULTS

It you're a history enthusiast, you may associate *brainwashing* with techniques used by the Communist Chinese on prisoners during the Korean War. Through various types of "thought reform," the Chinese were able to coerce approximately 16 percent of these prisoners to sign false confessions (Schein et al., 1957). More recently, the mass murder-suicide at Jonestown, the Branch Davidian tragedy at Waco, and the Heaven's Gate group suicide in San Diego have rekindled public interest in forced attitude change.

What is brainwashing? How does it differ from other persuasive techniques? As we have noted, advertisers, politicians, educators, religious organizations, and others actively seek to alter attitudes and opinions. To an extent, their persuasive efforts resemble brainwashing, but there is an important difference: **Brainwashing,** or forced attitude change, requires a captive audience. If you are offended by a television commercial, you can tune it out. Prisoners in the POW camps in Korea (and later in Vietnam) were completely at the mercy of their captors. Complete control over the environment allows a degree of psychological manipulation that would be impossible in a normal setting.

Brainwashing

How does captivity facilitate persuasion? Psychologist James McConnell identified three techniques used in brainwashing: (1) The target person is isolated from other people who would support his or her original attitudes, (2) the target is made completely dependent on his or her captors for satisfaction of needs, and (3) the indoctrinating agent is in a position to reward the target for changes in attitudes or behavior.

Brainwashing typically begins with an attempt to make the target person feel completely helpless. Physical and psychological abuse, lack of sleep, humiliation, and isolation serve to **unfreeze,** or loosen, former values and beliefs. When exhaustion, pressure, and fear become unbearable, **change** occurs, as the person abandons former beliefs. Typically, prisoners who reach the breaking point sign a false confession or cooperate to gain relief. When they do, they are suddenly rewarded with praise, privileges, food, or rest. Continued coupling of hope and fear with additional pressures to conform then serves to **refreeze** (solidify) new attitudes (Schein et al., 1961).

How permanent are changes caused by brainwashing? In most cases, the dramatic shift in attitudes brought about by brainwashing is temporary. Most "converted" prisoners who returned to the United States after the Korean War eventually reverted to their original beliefs and repudiated their indoctrinators. Nevertheless, brainwashing can be powerful, as shown by the success of cults in recruiting new members.

Cults

Exhorted by their leader, some 900 members of the Reverend Jim Jones's People's Temple picked up paper cups and drank purple Kool-Aid laced with the deadly poison cyanide. Psychologically, the mass suicide at Jonestown in 1978 is not so

Cognitive dissonance *An uncomfortable clash between self-image, thoughts, beliefs, attitudes, or perceptions and one's behavior.*
Justification *In cognitive dissonance theory, the degree to which one's actions are justified by rewards or other circumstances.*
Brainwashing *Engineered or forced attitude change involving a captive audience.*
Unfreezing *In brainwashing, a loosening of convictions about former values, attitudes, and beliefs.*
Change *In brainwashing, the point at which a person begins to repudiate former attitudes and beliefs.*
Refreezing *In brainwashing, the process of rewarding and strengthening new attitudes and beliefs.*

In April 1993, David Koresh and members of his Branch Davidian group perished in an inferno at their Waco, Texas, compound. Authorities believe the fire was set by a cult member, under the direction of Koresh. Like Jim Jones had done years before in Jonestown, Koresh took nearly total control of his followers' lives. He told them what to eat, dictated sexual mores, and directed the paddling of errant followers. Followers were persuaded to surrender money, property, and even their children and wives. Like Jones, Koresh also took mistresses and had children out of wedlock. Like other cult leaders, Jones and Koresh demanded absolute loyalty and obedience, with tragic results (Reiterman, 1993).

incredible as it might seem. The inhabitants of Jonestown were isolated in the jungles of Guyana, intimidated by guards and lulled with sedatives. They were also cut off from friends and relatives and totally accustomed to obeying rigid rules of conduct, which primed them for Jones's final "loyalty test." Of greater psychological interest is the question of how people reach such a state of commitment and dependency.

Why do people join groups such as the People's Temple? The People's Temple was a classic example of a *cult*. A **cult** is a group in which the leader's personality is more important than the beliefs she or he preaches. Cult members give their allegiance to this person, who is regarded as infallible, and they follow his or her dictates without question. Almost always, cult members are victimized by their leaders in one way or another.

Psychologist Margaret Singer has studied and aided hundreds of former cult members. Her interviews reveal that, in recruiting new members, cults use a powerful blend of guilt, manipulation, isolation, deception, fear, and escalating commitment. In this respect, cults employ high-pressure indoctrination techniques not unlike those used in brainwashing (Isser, 1991; Singer & Addis, 1992). In the United States alone, an estimated 2 to 5 million people have succumbed to the lure of cults (Robinson, Frye, & Bradley, 1997).

RECRUITMENT   Some of those interviewed by Singer were suffering from marked psychological distress when they joined a cult. Most, however, were simply undergoing a period of mild depression, indecision, or alienation from family and friends (Hunter, 1998). Cult members try to catch potential converts at a time of need—especially when a sense of belonging will be attractive to the convert. For instance, many converts were approached just after a romance had broken up, or when they were struggling with exams, were trying to choose a major, or were simply at loose ends and "on the street." Another danger-

BRIDGES

People suffering from identity confusion, which is common during adolescence, are more susceptible to recruitment by coercive groups.

See Chapter 5, pages 139–141.

ous time is when young adults are having difficulty becoming independent from their families (Sirkin, 1990). At such times, people are easily persuaded that joining the group is all they must do to be happy again (Hunter, 1998; Schwartz, 1991).

CONVERSION   *How is conversion achieved?*   Often it begins with intense displays of affection and understanding ("love bombing"). Next comes isolation from noncult members and drills, discipline, and rituals (all-night meditation or continuous chanting, for instance). These rituals wear down physical and emotional resistance and generate feelings of commitment. In short, cults tend to appeal to recruits' emotions, while discouraging critical thinking (Galanti, 1993).

Many cults make clever use of the foot-in-the-door technique (described in Chapter 19). At first, recruits make small commitments (to stay after a meeting, for example). Then, larger commitments are encouraged (to stay an extra day, to call in sick at work, and so forth). Making a major commitment is usually the final step. The new devotee signs over a bank account or property to the group, moves in with the group, and so forth. Making such major public commitments creates a powerful cognitive dissonance effect. Before long, it becomes virtually impossible for converts to admit they have made a mistake.

Once in the group, members are cut off from family and friends (former reference groups), and the cult can control the flow and interpretation of information to them. Members are isolated from their former value systems and social structures. Conversion is complete when they come to think of themselves more as group members than as individuals. At this point, obedience is nearly total (Schwartz, 1991; Wexler, 1995).

Why do people stay in cults?   Most former members mention guilt and fear as the main reasons for not leaving when they wished they could. Most had been reduced to child-like dependency on the group for meeting all their daily needs (Singer, 1979). After they leave, many former cult members

Aftermath of the mass suicide at Jonestown. How do cult-like groups recruit new devotees? (See text.)

suffer from anxiety, panic attacks, and emotional disturbances much like post-traumatic stress syndrome (West, 1993).

Behind the "throne" from which Jim Jones ruled Jonestown was a sign bearing these words: "Those who do not remember the past are condemned to repeat it." If we are to take the Reverend Jones at his word, then we should remember that cults are but one example of the danger of trading independence for security. Cults are merely the most visible sign of how we all can be influenced by sophisticated psychological coercion and by our need for approval from others.

KNOWLEDGE BUILDER

ATTITUDES AND PERSUASION

RELATE

Describe an attitude that is important to you. What are its three components?

Which of the various sources of attitudes best explain your own attitudes?

Who belongs to your most important reference group?

Imagine that you would like to persuade voters to support an initiative to preserve a small wilderness area by converting it to a park. Using research on persuasion as a guide, what could you do to be more effective?

How would you explain cognitive dissonance theory to a person who knows nothing about it?

LEARNING CHECK

1. Attitudes have three parts, a _____ component, an _____ component, and an _____ component.

2. Which of the following is associated with attitude formation?
   a. group membership b. mass media c. chance conditioning
   d. child rearing e. all of the preceding f. a and d only

3. Because of the immediate consequences of actions, behavior contrary to one's stated attitudes is often enacted. T or F?

4. Items such as "would exclude from my country" or "would admit to marriage in my family" are found in which attitude measure?
   a. a reference group scale b. a social distance scale
   c. an attitude scale d. an open-ended interview

5. In presenting a persuasive message, it is best to give both sides of the argument if the audience is already well informed on the topic. T or F?

6. Consumer psychology is exclusively concerned with profits and increasing the sales of commercial products. T or F?

7. Much attitude change is related to a desire to avoid clashing or contradictory thoughts, an idea summarized by _____ _____ theory.

8. Brainwashing differs from other persuasive attempts in that brainwashing requires a _____ _____.

9. Which statement about brainwashing is *false*?
   a. The target person is isolated from others.
   b. Attitude changes brought about by brainwashing are usually permanent.
   c. The first step is unfreezing former values and beliefs.
   d. Cooperation with the indoctrinating agent is rewarded.

10. Margaret Singer found that most former cult members had experienced a major psychological disturbance just prior to joining the cult. T or F?

CRITICAL THINKING

11. Students entering a college gym are asked to sign a banner promoting water conservation. Later, the students shower at the gym. What effect would you expect signing the banner to have on how long students stay in the showers?

12. Cognitive dissonance theory predicts that false confessions obtained during brainwashing are not likely to bring about lasting changes in attitudes. Why?

Answers:

1. belief, emotional, action 2. e 3. T 4. b 5. d 6. F 7. cognitive dissonance 8. captive audience 9. b 10. F 11. Cognitive dissonance theory predicts that students who sign the banner will take shorter showers, to be consistent with their publicly expressed support of water conservation. This is exactly the result observed in a study done by social psychologist Elliot Aronson. 12. Because there is strong justification for such actions. As a result, little cognitive dissonance is created when a prisoner makes statements that contradict his or her beliefs.

Cult *A group that professes great devotion to some person and follows that person almost without question; cult members are typically victimized by their leaders in various ways.*

PREJUDICE—ATTITUDES THAT INJURE

Love and friendship bind people together. Prejudice, which is marked by suspicion, fear, or hatred, has the opposite effect. **Prejudice** is a negative emotional attitude held toward members of a specific social group. Prejudices may be reflected in the policies of police departments, schools, or government institutions. In such cases, prejudice is referred to as **racism**, **sexism**, **ageism**, or **heterosexism,** depending on the group affected. Because sexism, ageism, and heterosexism were discussed in earlier chapters, let's focus on racism.

Both racial prejudice and racism lead to **discrimination,** or unequal treatment of people who should have the same rights as others. Discrimination frequently prevents people from doing things they should be able to do, such as buying a house, riding a bus, or attending a high-quality school.

Discrimination is deeply woven into society. One remarkable study, for instance, involved 15 college students who had received no traffic citations in the previous year. Each student attached a bumper sticker for a well-known, militant black organization to his or her car (Heussenstamm, 1971). During the next 17 days, the group received a total of 33 traffic citations! The power relationship between the white establishment and black militants in this instance (at least as interpreted by individual police officers) is clear.

Actually, it's not necessary to flaunt one's political views in order to provoke racial discrimination. In many cities, African Americans have been stopped by police for DWB—Driving While Black. Usually, drivers who are the target of "racial profiling" are merely detained and questioned. Sometimes, they are cited for minor infractions, such as a cracked taillight or an illegal lane change. In any event, in some cities black drivers and other people of color are frequently stopped without reason. For many law-abiding citizens, being detained in this manner is a rude awakening (Davis, 1999).

Becoming Prejudiced

How do prejudices develop? One major theory suggests that prejudice is a form of **scapegoating** (blaming a person or a group for the actions of others or for conditions not of their making). Scapegoating, you may recall, is a type of *displaced aggression* in which hostilities triggered by frustration are redirected at "safe" targets. One interesting test of this hypothesis was conducted at a summer camp for young men. The men were given a difficult test they were sure to fail. Additionally, completing the test caused them to miss a trip to the theater, which was normally the high point of their weekly entertainment. Attitudes toward Mexicans and Japanese were measured before the test and after the men had failed the test and missed the entertainment. Subjects in this study, all European Americans, consistently rated members of these two groups lower after being frustrated (Miller & Bugelski, 1970).

At times, the development of prejudice (like other attitudes) can be traced to direct experiences with members of the rejected group. A child who is repeatedly bullied by members of

a particular racial or ethnic group might develop a lifelong dislike for all members of the group. The tragedy is that, once prejudices are established, they prevent us from accepting more positive experiences that could reverse the damage (Wilder, Simon, & Faith, 1996).

Distinguished psychologist Gordon Allport (1958) concluded that there are two important sources of prejudice. **Personal prejudice** occurs when members of another racial or ethnic group are perceived as a threat to one's own interests. For example, members of another group may be viewed as competitors for jobs. **Group prejudice** occurs when a person conforms to group norms. Let's say, for instance, that you have no personal reason for disliking out-group members. Nevertheless, your friends, acquaintances, or coworkers expect it of you.

The Prejudiced Personality

Other research suggests that prejudice can also be a general personality characteristic.

Do you mean some people are more prone to prejudice than others? Apparently, some are. Theodore Adorno and his associates (1950) carefully probed what they called the *authoritarian personality* (ah-thor-ih-TARE-ee-un). These researchers started out by studying anti-Semitism as a means of understanding the social climate that existed in Germany during World War II. In the process, they found that people who are prejudiced against one group tend to be prejudiced against *all* out-groups.

What are the characteristics of the prejudice-prone personality? The **authoritarian personality** is marked by rigidity, inhibition, prejudice, and oversimplification. Authoritarians also tend to be very *ethnocentric*. **Ethnocentrism** refers to placing one's own group "at the center," usually by rejecting all other groups. Put more simply, authoritarians consider their own ethnic or racial group superior to others. In fact, authoritarians are prejudiced against almost everyone who is different, including homosexuals (Whitley, 1999).

In addition to rejecting out-groups, authoritarians are overwhelmingly concerned with power, authority, and obedience. To measure these qualities, the *F scale* was created (the *F* stands for "fascism"). This attitude scale is made up of statements such as the ones that follow—to which authoritarians readily agree (Adorno et al., 1950).

Authoritarian Beliefs

- Obedience and respect for authority are the most important virtues children should learn.
- People can be divided into two distinct classes: the weak and the strong.
- If people would talk less and work more, everybody would be better off.
- What this country needs most, more than laws and political programs, is a few courageous, tireless, devoted leaders, in whom the people can put their faith.
- Nobody ever learns anything really important except through suffering.
- Every person should have complete faith in some supernatural power whose decisions are obeyed without question.
- Certain religious sects that refuse to salute the flag should be forced to conform to such patriotic action or else be abolished.

As children, authoritarians were usually severely punished. Most learned to fear authority (and to covet it) at an early age. In general, people are more likely to express authoritarian beliefs when they feel threatened (Doty, Peterson, & Winter, 1991). An example would be calling for more severe punishment in schools when the economy is bad and job insecurities are high. Authoritarians are not happy people.

It should be readily apparent from the list of authoritarian beliefs that the F scale is slanted toward politically conservative authoritarians. To be fair, psychologist Milton Rokeach (1918–1988) noted that rigid and authoritarian personalities can be found at both ends of the political spectrum. Rokeach, therefore, preferred to describe rigid and intolerant thinking as *dogmatism*. (**Dogmatism** is an unwarranted positiveness or certainty in matters of belief or opinion.) Dogmatic people find it difficult to change their beliefs, even when the evidence contradicts them (Davies, 1993).

Even if we discount the obvious bigotry of the dogmatic or authoritarian personality, racial prejudice runs deep in many nations. To illustrate, one experiment showed that liberal, white, male college students were more willing to give shocks (under laboratory conditions) to a black victim than to a white victim (Shulman, 1974). We will probe deeper into the roots of such prejudiced behavior in the next discussion.

INTERGROUP CONFLICT—THE ROOTS OF PREJUDICE

An unfortunate by-product of group membership is that it often limits contact with people in other groups. Additionally, groups themselves may come into conflict. Both events tend to foster unpleasant feelings and prejudices toward the out-group. The bloody clash of opposing forces in Bosnia, Israel, Ireland, South Africa, and Hometown, U.S.A., are reminders that intergroup conflict is widespread. Daily, we read of jarring strife between nations, communities, and political, religious, and ethnic groups. In many cases, intergroup conflict is accompanied by *stereotyped* images of out-group members and by bitter prejudice.

What exactly do you mean by a stereotype?   **Social stereotypes** are oversimplified images of people who belong to a particular social group. There is a good chance that you have stereotyped images of some of the following categories: redneck, politician, show-off, do-gooder, juvenile delinquent, business executive, housewife, snob, playboy, teenager, slob, spoiled brat, billionaire. Stereotypes have a powerful effect on how we treat others (Andersen, Klatzky, & Murray, 1990). In general, the top three categories on which most stereotypes are based are gender, age, and race (Fiske, 1993a).

Stereotypes tend to simplify people into "us" and "them" categories. Actually, aside from the fact that they always oversimplify, stereotypes may be either *positive* or *negative* (❖Fig. 20.3). ◆Table 20.2 shows stereotyped images of various national and ethnic groups and their changes over a 34-year period. Notice that many of the qualities listed are desirable. Note, too, that although the overall trend was a decrease in negative stereotypes, belief in the existence of some negative traits increased.

❖ **FIGURE 20.3** *Racial stereotypes are common in sports. For example, a recent study confirmed that many people actually do believe that "white men can't jump." This stereotype implies that black basketball players are naturally superior in athletic ability. White players, in contrast, are falsely perceived as smarter and harder working than blacks. Such stereotypes set up expectations that distort the perceptions of fans, coaches, and sportswriters. The resulting misperceptions, in turn, help perpetuate the stereotypes (Stone, Perry, & Darley, 1997).*

Prejudice *A negative emotional attitude held against members of a particular group of people.*
Racism *Racial prejudice that has become institutionalized (that is, it is reflected in government policy, schools, and so forth) and that is enforced by the existing social power structure.*
Sexism *Institutionalized prejudice against members of either sex, based solely on their gender.*
Ageism *An institutionalized tendency to discriminate on the basis of age; prejudice based on age.*
Heterosexism *The belief that heterosexuality is better or more natural than homosexuality.*
Discrimination *Treating members of various social groups differently in circumstances where their rights or treatment should be identical.*
Scapegoating *Blaming a person or a group for the actions of others or for conditions not of their making.*
Displaced aggression *Redirecting aggression to a target other than the actual source of one's frustration.*
Personal prejudice *Prejudicial attitudes held toward people who are perceived as a direct threat to one's own interests.*
Group prejudice *Prejudice held out of conformity to group views.*
Authoritarian personality *A personality pattern characterized by rigidity, inhibition, prejudice, and an excessive concern with power, authority, and obedience.*
Ethnocentrism *Placing one's own group or race at the center—that is, tending to reject all other groups but one's own.*
Dogmatism *An unwarranted positiveness or certainty in matters of belief or opinion.*
Social stereotypes *Oversimplified images of the traits of individuals who belong to a particular social group.*

TRAIT	PERCENT CHECKING TRAIT		TRAIT	PERCENT CHECKING TRAIT		TRAIT	PERCENT CHECKING TRAIT	
	1933	1967		1933	1967		1933	1967
Americans			**Italians**			**Jews**		
Industrious	48	23	Artistic	53	30	Shrewd	79	30
Intelligent	47	20	Impulsive	44	28	Mercenary	49	15
Materialistic	33	67	Musical	32	9	Grasping	34	17
Progressive	27	17	Imaginative	30	7	Intelligent	29	37
Germans			**Irish**			**Blacks**		
Scientific	78	47	Pugnacious	45	13	Superstitious	84	13
Stolid	44	9	Witty	38	7	Lazy	75	26
Methodical	31	21	Honest	32	17	Ignorant	38	11
Efficient	16	46	Nationalistic	21	41	Religious	24	8

Source: M. Karlins, T. L. Coffman, and G. Walters, "On the fading of social stereotypes: Studies in three generations of college students," *Journal of Personality and Social Psychology* 13 (1969): 116.

HUMAN DIVERSITY

CHOKING ON STEREOTYPES

Bill, a retired aircraft mechanic, has agreed to talk to a group of high school students about the early days of commercial aviation. During his talk, Bill is concerned that any slip in his memory will confirm stereotypes about older people being forgetful. Because he is anxious and preoccupied about possible memory lapses, Bill actually does have problems with his memory.

As Bill's example suggests, negative stereotypes can have a self-fulfilling quality. This is especially true in situations in which a person's abilities are evaluated. For example, African Americans must often cope with negative stereotypes about their academic abilities. Could such stereotypes actually impair school performance?

Psychologist Claude Steele has amassed evidence that people tend to feel threatened when they think they are being judged in terms of a stereotype. The anxiety that this causes can then lower performance, seemingly confirming the stereotype. An experiment, Steele did demonstrate this effect. In the study, black and white college students took a very difficult verbal test. Some students were told the test measured *academic ability*. Others were told that the test was a laboratory *problem-solving task* unrelated to ability. In the ability condition, black students performed worse than whites. In the problem-solving condition, they performed the same as whites.

In light of such findings, Steele and his colleagues are currently working on ways to remove stereotype threat, so that all students can use their potentials more fully (Steele, 1997).

Ethnic pride is gradually replacing stereotypes and discrimination. For example, the African American festival of Kwanzaa, a holiday celebrated late in December, emphasizes commitment to family, community, and African culture. However, despite affirmations of ethnic heritage, the problem of prejudice is far from solved.

Even though stereotypes sometimes include positive traits, they are mainly used to maintain control over other people. When a person is stereotyped, the easiest thing for her or him to do is to abide by others' expectations—even if the expectations

are demeaning. That's why no one likes to be stereotyped. Being forced into a small, distorted social "box" by stereotyping is limiting and insulting. Stereotypes rob people of their individuality. (See "Choking on Stereotypes.") Without stereotypes, there would be far less hate, prejudice, exclusion, and conflict (Fiske, 1993b).

In the years since 1967, there have been further declines in negative stereotypes, but also some recent reversals. Some observers believe that racial and ethnic prejudice is on the upswing. But often, today's racism takes the form of **symbolic prejudice,** which is expressed in a disguised fashion (Brewer & Kramer, 1985). That is, many people realize that crude and obvious racism is socially unacceptable. However, this may not stop them from expressing prejudice in thinly veiled forms when they state their opinions on issues such as affirmative action programs, busing, immigration, and crime. In effect, modern racists find ways to rationalize their prejudice so that it seems to be based on issues other than raw racism.

CRITICAL THINKING

ENEMY IMAGES

"Huns, Krauts, Japs." If you've watched many vintage war movies, you've probably heard these ugly and hateful terms. During World War II, as in all wars, public images of "the enemy" were monstrous and dehumanizing. Even today, in the absence of active hostilities, enemy images tend to depict our national rivals as evil or less than human. For example, media images of Russians have long depicted them as inhumane, vicious torturers who enjoy murder and inflicting pain. In the movie *Rambo*, for instance, two Russian soldiers are shown enjoying themselves as they torture Sylvester Stallone with electric shock and hot knives (Silverstein, 1989). (Given a chance, some movie critics might join in.)

In times of war, dehumanizing images are used to make it seem that a nation's enemies *deserve* hatred and even death. Undoubtedly, such images provide a degree of emotional insulation that makes it easier for soldiers to harm other humans. Yet during times of peace, enemy images can lead to dangerous misperceptions of the motives and actions of other nations (Silverstein, 1989).

In many ways, ethnic jokes, racial stereotypes, degrading names, out-group slurs, and the like are small-scale examples of the damage that "enemy" images can do. Clashes ranging from those between street gangs to those between nations are fueled, in part, by dehumanizing images of "the enemy."

During the recent civil war in parts of the former Yugoslavia, Bosnian Serbs described mass killing of Muslim civilians as "ethnic cleansing." In reality, the Serb attacks were genocide, in which mothers, fathers, daughters, and sons were slaughtered.

Stereotypes held by the prejudiced tend to be unusually irrational. When given a list of negative statements about other groups, prejudiced individuals agree with most of them. It's particularly revealing that they often agree with conflicting statements. Thus, a prejudiced person may say that Jews are both "pushy" and "standoffish" or that African Americans are both "ignorant" and "sly." In one study, prejudiced persons even expressed negative attitudes toward two nonexistent groups, the "Piraneans" and the "Danirians." (See "Enemy Images" for further information.) Note, too, that when a prejudiced person meets a pleasant or likable member of a rejected group, the out-group member tends to be perceived as "an exception to the rule," not as evidence against the stereotype. Even when such "exceptional" experiences begin to accumulate, a prejudiced person may not change his or her stereotyped belief (Fiske, 1993a; Wilder, Simon, & Faith, 1996).

How do stereotypes and intergroup tensions develop? Two experiments, both in unlikely settings and both using children as subjects, offer some insight into these problems.

Experiments in Prejudice

What is it like to be discriminated against? Those who have never experienced discrimination probably can't imagine it. In a unique experiment, elementary school teacher Jane Elliot sought to give her pupils direct experience with prejudice.

On the first day of the experiment, Elliot announced that brown-eyed children were to sit in the back of the room and that they could not use the drinking fountain. Blue-eyed children were given extra recess time and got to leave first for lunch. At lunch, brown-eyed children were prevented from taking second helpings because they would "just waste it." Brown-eyed and blue-eyed children were kept from mingling, and the blue-eyed children were told they were "cleaner" and "smarter" (Peters, 1971). Eye color might seem like an unrealistic basis for creating prejudices. However, people primarily use skin color to make decisions about the race of another person (Brown, Danc, & Durham, 1998). Surely, this is just as superficial a way of evaluating people as eye color is. (See this chapter's "Psychology in Action" for further information about the concept of race.)

At first, Elliot had to maintain these imposed conditions of prejudice. She also made an effort to constantly criticize and belittle the brown-eyed children. To her surprise, the blue-eyed children rapidly joined in and were soon outdoing her in the viciousness of their attacks. The blue-eyed children began to feel superior, and the brown-eyed children felt just plain awful. Fights broke out. Test scores of the brown-eyed children fell.

How lasting were the effects of this experiment? The effects were short-lived, because two days later the roles of the children were reversed. Before long, the same destructive effects occurred again, but this time in reverse. The implications of

Symbolic prejudice *Prejudice that is expressed in disguised fashion.*

this experiment are unmistakable. In less than 1 day, it was possible to get children to hate each other because of eye color and **status inequalities** (differences in power, prestige, or privileges). Certainly, the effects of a lifetime of real racial or ethnic prejudice are infinitely more powerful and destructive. Racism is a major source of stress in the lives of many people of color. Over time, prejudice can have a negative impact on a person's physical and emotional health (Clark et al., 1999).

EQUAL-STATUS CONTACT *What can be done to combat prejudice?* Progress has been made through attempts to educate the general public about the lack of justification for prejudice. Changing the belief component of an attitude is one of the most direct means of changing the entire attitude. Thus, when people are made aware that members of various racial and ethnic groups share the same goals, ambitions, feelings, and frustrations as they do, intergroup relations may be improved.

However, this is not the whole answer. As we noted earlier, there is often a wide difference between attitudes and actual behavior. Until unprejudiced behavior is engineered, changes can be quite superficial. Several lines of thought (including cognitive dissonance theory) suggest that more frequent *equal-status contact* between groups in conflict should reduce prejudice and stereotyping (Olson & Zanna, 1993).

Equal-status contact refers to social interaction that occurs on an equal footing, without obvious differences in power or status. Much evidence suggests that equal-status contact does, in fact, lessen prejudice. For example, in one early study, white women who lived in integrated and segregated housing projects were compared for changes in attitude toward their African American neighbors. Women in the integrated project showed a favorable shift in attitudes toward members of the other racial group. Those in the segregated project showed no change or actually became more prejudiced than before (Deutsch & Collins, 1951). In other studies, mixed-race groups have been formed at work, in the laboratory, and at schools. The conclusion from such research is that personal contact with a disliked group will induce friendly behavior, respect, and liking. However, these benefits occur only when personal contact is cooperative and on an equal footing (Grack & Richman, 1996).

To test the importance of equal-status contact directly, Gerald Clore and his associates set up a unique summer camp for children. The camp was directed by one white male, one white female, one black male, and one black female. Each campsite had three black and three white campers and one black and one white counselor. Thus, blacks and whites were equally divided in number, power, privileges, and duties. Did the experience make a difference? Apparently it did: Testing showed that the children had significantly more positive attitudes toward opposite-race children after the camp than they did before (Clore, 1976).

SUPERORDINATE GOALS Let us now consider a revealing study of intergroup conflict. Muzafer Sherif and his associates did an ingenious experiment at a summer camp, with 11-year-old boys. When the boys arrived at camp, they were split into two

Many school districts in the United States have begun requiring students to wear uniforms. Appearance (including gang colors) is one of the major reasons why kids treat each other differently. Uniforms help minimize status inequalities and in-group, out-group distinctions. In Long Beach, California, a switch to uniforms was followed by a 91 percent drop in student assaults, thefts, vandalism, and weapons and drug violations (Ritter, 1998).

groups and housed in separate cabins. At first, the groups were kept apart to build up in-group friendships. During this time, cooperative games and activities were used to develop group pride and identification. Soon, each group had a flag and a name (the "Rattlers" and the "Eagles"), and each had staked out its territory. At this point, the two groups were placed in competition with each other. After a number of clashes, dislike between the groups bordered on hatred: The boys baited each other, started fights, and raided each other's cabins (Sherif et al., 1961).

Were they allowed to go home hating each other? As an experiment in reducing intergroup conflict, and to prevent the boys from remaining enemies, various strategies to reduce tensions were tried. Holding meetings between leaders from each group did nothing. Just getting the groups together also did little. When the groups were invited to eat together, the event became a free-for-all.

Finally, emergencies that required cooperation among members of both groups were staged at the camp. For example, the water supply was damaged in a way so that all the boys had to work together to repair it. Creation of this and other *superordinate goals* helped restore peace between the two groups. (A **superordinate goal** exceeds or overrides other lesser goals.)

As members of the groups were forced to cooperate, hostilities subsided. Cooperation and shared goals seem to help reduce conflict by encouraging people in opposing groups to see themselves as members of a single, larger group (Gaertner et al., 1990). Superordinate goals, in other words, have a "we're all in the same boat" effect on perceptions of group membership (Olson & Zanna, 1993). (For a broader perspective, read "Superordinate Goals.")

"JIGSAW" CLASSROOMS   Contrary to the hopes of many, integrating public schools often has little positive effect on racial prejudice. In fact, prejudice may be made worse, and the self-esteem of minority students frequently decreases (Aronson, 1992).

If integrated schools provide equal-status contact, shouldn't prejudice be reduced?   Theoretically, yes. But in practice, minority group children often enter newly integrated schools unprepared to compete on an equal footing. Elliot Aronson and his colleagues argue that the competitive nature of schools almost guarantees that children will *not* learn to like and understand each other. In the typical classroom, children compete

SUPERORDINATE GOALS—FINDING COMMON GROUND

Superordinate goals unite groups in the pursuit of a common goal. Can such goals exist on a global scale? One example might be a desire to avoid nuclear holocaust. Politically, this goal may be far from universal. But its superordinate quality is clearly evident. Scientists now project that if *any* country suffers a nuclear attack, all other countries would suffer a terrifying "nuclear winter." In effect, almost everyone, friend and foe alike, would share the same fate (Sagan & Turco, 1990).

Nuclear winter refers to a devastating drop in global temperature that would follow the firestorms, dust, and smoke of a nuclear strike. The probable result would be global crop failure, famine, and death on a large scale. Even if there were no counterattack, a hostile country could pay dearly for its aggression (Turco et al., 1983).

It is probably fair to say that nations need to find more commonalities and shared goals. It's true that the former Soviet Union has become less of a threat to world peace. But at the same time, other "unstable" nations are gaining nuclear weapons capability. In view of the implications of nuclear winter, perhaps finding a way to reduce the threat of nuclear warfare will prove to be a superordinate goal. Another that comes quickly to mind is the need to preserve the natural environment on a global scale.

fiercely for the teacher's approval. Successful students learn to feel superior and often show contempt for unsuccessful students. This is a high-stakes game in which only a few can win. It is clearly not a good way to reduce prejudice.

With the preceding in mind, Aronson pioneered a way to apply the concept of superordinate goals to ordinary classrooms. According to Aronson, such goals are effective because they create **mutual interdependence.** That is, people must depend on one another to meet each person's goals. When each person's needs are linked to those of others in the group, cooperation is encouraged (Deutsch, 1993).

How has this idea been applied?   Aronson has successfully created "jigsaw" classrooms that emphasize cooperation rather than competition. The term *jigsaw* refers to the pieces of a jigsaw puzzle. In a **jigsaw classroom,** each child is given a "piece" of the information needed to complete a project or prepare for a test.

In a typical session, children are divided into groups of five or six and given a topic to study for a later exam. Each child is given his or her "piece" of information and asked to learn it. For example, one child might have information on Thomas

In a "jigsaw" classroom, children help each other prepare for tests. As they teach each other what they know, the children learn to cooperate and to respect the unique strengths of each individual.

Status inequalities *Differences in the power, prestige, or privileges of two or more persons or groups.*
Equal-status contact *Social interaction that occurs on an equal footing, without obvious differences in power or status.*
Superordinate goal *A goal that exceeds or overrides all others; a goal that renders other goals relatively less important.*
Mutual interdependence *A condition in which two or more people must depend on one another to meet each person's needs or goals.*
Jigsaw classroom *A method of reducing prejudice; each student receives only part of the information needed to complete a project or prepare for a test.*

Edison's invention of the lightbulb; another, facts about his invention of the long-playing phonograph record; and a third, information about Edison's childhood. After the children have learned their parts, they teach them to others in the group. Even the most competitive children quickly realize that they cannot do well without the aid of everyone in the group. Each child makes a unique and essential contribution, so the children learn to listen to and respect each other.

Does the jigsaw method work? Compared to children in traditional classrooms, children in jigsaw groups are less prejudiced, they like their classmates more, they have more positive attitudes toward school, their grades improve, and their self-esteem increases (Walker & Crogan, 1998; Webb & Farivar, 1994). Such results are quite encouraging. As Kenneth Clark (1965) has said, "Racial prejudice . . . debases all human beings—those who are its victims, those who victimize, and in quite subtle ways, those who are merely accessories."

To summarize, prejudice will be reduced when:

- Members of different groups have equal status *within the situation* that brings them together.
- Members of all groups seek a common goal.
- Group members must cooperate to reach the goal.
- Group members spend enough time together for cross-group friendships to develop (Pettigrew, 1998).

Sports teams are an excellent example of a situation in which all of these conditions apply. The close contact and interdependent effort required in team sports often creates lifelong friendships and breaks down the walls of prejudice.

K N O W L E D G E   B U I L D E R

PREJUDICE AND INTERGROUP CONFLICT

RELATE

Mentally scan over the events of the last week. How would they have changed if prejudices of all types ceased to exist?

Think of the most rigid or dogmatic person you know. Does he or she match the profile of the authoritarian personality?

Stereotypes exist for many social categories, even ordinary ones such as "college student" or "unmarried young adult." What stereotypes do you think you face in daily life?

The director of a youth recreation center is concerned about the amount of conflict she is seeing between boys and girls from different racial and ethnic groups. What advice can you give the director?

LEARNING CHECK

1. As a basis for prejudice, _____ is frequently related to frustration and displaced _____.

2. The authoritarian personality tends to be prejudiced against all out-groups, a quality referred to as _____.

3. Social stereotypes may be both positive and negative. T or F?

4. The stereotypes underlying racial and ethnic prejudice tend to evolve from the superordinate goals that often separate groups. T or F?

5. The term *symbolic prejudice* refers to racism or prejudice that is expressed in disguised or hidden form. T or F?

6. Jane Elliot's classroom experiment in prejudice showed that children could be made to dislike one another
   a. by setting up group competition
   b. by imposing status inequalities
   c. by role-playing
   d. by frustrating all the students

7. Research suggests that prejudice and intergroup conflict may be reduced by _____ interaction and _____ goals.

CRITICAL THINKING

8. In court trials, defense lawyers sometimes try to identify and eliminate prospective jurors who have authoritarian personality traits. Can you guess why?

Answers:

1. scapegoating, aggression 2. ethnocentrism 3. T 4. F 5. T 6. T 7. equal-status, superordinate 8. Because authoritarians tend to believe that punishment is effective, they are more likely to vote for conviction.

AGGRESSION—THE WORLD'S MOST DANGEROUS ANIMAL

For a time, the City Zoo of Los Angeles, California, had on display two examples of the world's most dangerous animal—the only animal capable of destroying the earth and all other animal species. Perhaps you have already guessed which animal it was. In the cage were two college students, representing the species *Homo sapiens!*

The human capacity for aggression seems staggering. It has been estimated that during the 125-year period ending with World War II, 58 million humans were killed by other humans (an average of nearly one person per minute). Murder ranks as a major cause of death in the United States. One American kills another every 23 minutes—making the United States one of the world's most violent nations. It is estimated that more than 1.4 million American children are subjected to physical abuse by parents each year. More than 25 percent of all married American men and women have physically attacked their spouses (O'Leary et al., 1989). War, homicide, riots, family violence, assassination, rape, assault, forcible robbery, and other violent acts offer sad testimony to the realities of human aggression.

What causes aggression? **Aggression** refers to any action carried out with the intention of harming another person. The complexity of aggression has given rise to a number of potential explanations for its occurrence. Brief descriptions of some of the major possibilities follow.

Instincts

Some theorists argue that, as humans, we are naturally aggressive, having inherited a "killer instinct" from our animal ances-

Ritualized human aggression. Violent and aggressive behavior is so commonplace it may be viewed as entertainment. How "natural" is aggressive behavior?

tors. *Ethologists* theorize that aggression is a biologically rooted behavior observed in all animals, including humans. (An **ethologist** is a person who studies the natural behavior patterns of animals.) Noted ethologist Konrad Lorenz (1966, 1974) also believed that humans lack certain innate patterns that inhibit aggression in animals. For example, in a dispute over territory or dominance, two wolves may growl, lunge, bare their teeth, and fiercely threaten each other. In most instances, though, neither is killed or even wounded. One wolf, recognizing the dominance of the other, will typically bare its throat in a gesture of submission. The dominant wolf could kill in an instant, but it is inhibited by the submissive gesture. In contrast, human confrontations of equal intensity almost always end in injury or death.

The idea that humans are "naturally" aggressive has an intuitive appeal, but many psychologists question it. Many of Lorenz's "explanations" of aggression are little more than loose comparisons between human and animal behavior. Just labeling a behavior as "instinctive" does little to explain it. More important, we are left with the question of why some individuals or human groups (the Arapesh, the Senoi, the Navajo, the Eskimo, and others) show little hostility or aggression. And, thankfully, the vast majority of humans *do not* kill or harm others.

Biology

Despite problems with the instinctive view, there is evidence that aggression may have a biological basis. Physiological studies have shown that there are brain areas capable of triggering or ending aggressive behavior. Also, researchers have found a relationship between aggression and such physical factors as hypoglycemia (low blood sugar), allergy, and specific brain injuries and disorders. For both men and women, higher levels of the hormone testosterone are associated with more aggressive behavior (Banks & Dabbs, 1996; Dabbs, Hargrove, & Heusel, 1996; Harris et al., 1996). None of these conditions, however, can be considered a direct *cause* of aggression. Instead, they probably lower the threshold for aggression, making hostile behavior more likely to occur (Baron & Richardson, 1994).

The effects of alcohol and other drugs provide another indication of the role of the brain and biology in violence and aggression. A variety of studies show that alcohol is involved in large percentages of murders and violent crimes. Like the conditions already noted, intoxicating drugs seem to lower inhibitions to act aggressively—often with tragic results (Bushman & Cooper, 1990; Ito, Miller, & Pollock, 1996).

To summarize, the fact that we are biologically *capable* of aggression does not mean that aggression is inevitable or "part of human nature." Twenty eminent scientists who studied the question concluded, "Biology does not condemn humanity to war. . . . Violence is neither in our evolutionary legacy nor in our genes. The same species that invented war is capable of inventing peace" (Scott & Ginsburg, 1994; UNESCO, 1990). Humans are fully capable of learning to inhibit their use of violence (Lore & Schultz, 1993).

BRIDGES

Various parts of the limbic system in the brain are closely linked with anger and aggression.

See Chapter 3, page 70.

Frustration

Step on a dog's tail, and you may get nipped. Frustrate a human, and you may get insulted. The **frustration-aggression hypothesis** states that frustration tends to lead to aggression (Dollard et al., 1939). At several points in earlier chapters, we have considered examples of the link between frustration and aggression.

Does frustration always produce aggression? Although the connection is strong, a moment's thought will show that frustration does not *always* lead to aggression. Frustration, for instance, may lead to stereotyped responding or perhaps to a state of "learned helplessness" (see Chapter 16). Also, aggression can occur in the absence of frustration. This possibility is illustrated by sports spectators who start fights, throw bottles, tear down goalposts, and so forth, after their team has *won*.

AVERSIVE STIMULI Frustration probably encourages aggression because it is uncomfortable. Various **aversive stimuli,** which produce discomfort or displeasure, can heighten hostility and aggression (Anderson, Anderson, & Deuser, 1996; Berkowitz, 1990) (❖Fig. 20.4). Examples include insults, high temperatures, pain, and even disgusting scenes or odors. Such stimuli probably raise overall arousal levels so that we become more

Aggression *Any action carried out with the intention of harming another person.*
Ethologist *A person who studies the natural behavior patterns of animals.*
Frustration-aggression hypothesis *States that frustration tends to lead to aggression.*
Aversive stimulus *Any stimulus that produces discomfort or displeasure.*

Road rage and some freeway shootings may be a reaction to the frustration of traffic congestion. The fact that automobiles provide anonymity, or a loss of personal identity, may also encourage aggressive actions that would not otherwise occur.

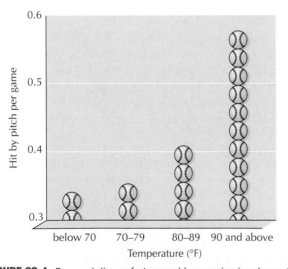

❖ **FIGURE 20.4** *Personal discomfort caused by aversive (unpleasant) stimuli can make aggressive behavior more likely. For example, studies of crime rates show that the incidence of highly aggressive behavior, such as murder, rape, and assault, rises as the air temperature goes from warm to hot to sweltering (Anderson, 1989). The results you see here further confirm the heat-aggression link. The graph shows that there is a strong association between the temperatures at major league baseball games and the number of batters hit by a pitch during those games. When the temperature goes over 90°, watch out for that fastball! (Reifman, Larrick, & Fein, 1991.)*

sensitive to **aggression cues** (signals that are associated with aggression) (Carlson, Marcus-Newhall, & Miller, 1990). Aversive stimuli also tend to activate ideas, memories, and expressions associated with anger and aggression (Berkowitz, 1990).

Some cues for aggression are internal (angry thoughts, for instance). Many are external: Certain words, actions, and gestures made by others are strongly associated with aggressive responses. A raised middle finger, for instance, is an almost universal invitation to aggression in North America.

Even inanimate objects may serve as aggression cues. In one classic experiment, subjects gave shocks to another person in a laboratory. Before doing so, they were ridiculed and shocked by the other person. Just before subjects got a chance to "return the favor," they saw either two badminton rackets or a shotgun and a revolver on a table in the testing room. In either case, the experimenter explained that someone had left the objects there, and he casually moved them aside. Subjects who glimpsed the guns gave stronger shocks to the person who had angered them than did subjects who saw the sports equipment (Berkowitz, 1968). Thus, we see that weapons serve as strong cues for aggressive behavior. The implication of this **weapons effect** seems to be that the symbols and trappings of aggression encourage aggression. A prime example is the fact that murders are almost three times more likely to occur in homes where guns are kept. Nearly 80 percent of the victims in such homes are killed by a family member or acquaintance. Only 4 percent are murdered by strangers (Kellermann et al., 1993).

Social Learning

One of the most widely accepted explanations of aggression is also the simplest. Social learning theory holds that we learn to be aggressive by observing aggression in others (Bandura, 1973). To explain behavior, **social learning theory** combines learning principles with cognitive processes, socialization, and modeling. According to this view, there is no instinctive human programming for fistfighting, pipe-bombing, knife wielding, gun loading, 95-mile-an-hour "beanballs," or other violent or aggressive behaviors. Hence, aggression must be learned (❖Fig. 20.5).

Social learning theorists predict that individuals growing up in nonaggressive cultures will themselves be nonaggressive. Those raised in a culture with aggressive models and heroes will learn aggressive responses. Considered in such terms, it is no wonder that America has become one of the most violent of all countries. It is estimated that a violent crime occurs every 54 seconds in the United States. Approximately 40 percent of the population owns firearms. Nationally, 70 percent agree that "When a boy is growing up, it is very important for him to have a few fistfights." Eighteen percent of the population admit to having slapped or kicked another person. Children and adults are treated to an almost nonstop parade of aggressive models, in the media as well as in actual behavior. We are, without a doubt, an aggressive culture.

THE WORLD ACCORDING TO TV Did you know that the world is populated primarily by males, professionals, whites, and members of the middle class? Did you know that women make up

Minor Aggression Bullying, annoying others	→	Physical Fighting Fighting, gang fighting	→	Violence Rape, attack, mugging

❖ **FIGURE 20.5** *Violent behavior among delinquent boys doesn't appear overnight. Usually, their capacity for violence develops slowly, as they move from minor aggression to increasingly brutal acts. Overall aggression increases dramatically in early adolescence as boys gain physical strength and more access to weapons (Loeber & Hay, 1997).*

FOCUS ON RESEARCH

AGGRESSION AND PORNOGRAPHY—IS THERE A LINK?

The debate on the effects of pornography is heating up again. Until recently, most evidence suggested that viewing pornography has no major adverse effects. This conclusion appears to remain valid for stimuli that can be described as merely erotic or sexual in content (Pollard, 1995). However, in the last 10 years, there has been a dramatic increase in aggressive-pornographic stimuli in the mass media. **Aggressive pornography** refers to depictions in which violence, threats, or obvious power differences are used to force someone (usually a woman) to engage in sex.

The principal finding of studies on aggressive-pornographic stimuli is that they do increase male aggression against females (Pollard, 1995). In a summary of various experiments, researchers Neil Malamuth and Ed Donnerstein

(1982) concluded that "exposure to mass media stimuli that have violent *and* sexual content increases the audience's aggressive-sexual fantasies, beliefs in rape myths, and aggressive behavior." Donnerstein and Daniel Linz (1986) further conclude that it is media *violence* that is most damaging. As they put it, "Violent images, rather than sexual ones, are most responsible for people's attitudes about women and rape." The problem, then, extends far beyond X-rated films and books. Mainstream movies, magazines, music videos (like those mentioned earlier), and television programs are equally to blame for reinforcing the myth that women find force or aggression pleasurable. It is very telling that rapists respond with sexual arousal to both sexual and nonsexual violence. Clearly, violence is a major dimension of rape (Seto & Kuban, 1996).

---

only 28 percent of the population, that half of all women are teenagers or in their early 20s, and that more than one third are unemployed or have no purpose beyond offering emotional support to men or serving as objects of sexual desire? That minorities are generally service workers, criminals, victims, or students? That more than half of all villains have accents? That most victims are single women, young boys, or nonwhites? If you watch much TV, these are the impressions you get daily on the tube (Carlson, 1986; Charren & Sandler, 1983).

TELEVISED VIOLENCE   It is clear that TV reality does not match the real world. Every day, TV provides an endless stream of bad models, especially concerning violence. In the United States, there are about 188 hours of violent programs per week on network TV. Eighty-one percent of all programs contain violence. Murder, robbery, kidnapping, and assault make up 85 percent of TV crimes. In real life, they total about 5 percent. Television is particularly unrealistic about the effects of violence. An astounding 73 percent of violent characters go unpunished, and 58 percent of violent acts don't lead to painful results. Only 16 percent of all programs show any realistic long-term consequences for violence. For children's programs, the rate falls to just 5 percent (*National Television Violence Study,* 1995–96).

How much does TV violence affect children?   As Albert Bandura showed in his studies of imitation (Chapter 9), children may

BRIDGES

Modeling and observational learning explain much of television's impact on our behavior.

See Chapter 9, pages 300–302.

learn new aggressive actions by watching violent or aggressive behavior, or they may learn that violence is "okay." Either way, they are more likely to act aggressively. It is important to remember that younger children do not grasp the nuances of TV plots. A child may simply remember that when good guys were bothered in some way by others, they aggressed. Heroes on TV are as violent as the villains, and they usually receive praise for their violence.

In addition to teaching new antisocial actions, television may *disinhibit* dangerous impulses that viewers already have. **Disinhibition** (the removal of inhibition) results in acting out behavior that normally would be restrained. For example, many TV programs give the message that violence is

---

Aggression cues *Stimuli or signals that are associated with aggression and that tend to elicit it.*
Weapons effect *The observation that weapons serve as strong cues for aggressive behavior.*
Social learning theory *To explain behavior, combines learning principles with cognitive processes, socialization, and modeling.*
Aggressive pornography *Media depictions of sexual violence or of forced participation in sexual activity.*
Disinhibition *The removal of inhibition; results in acting out behavior that normally would be restrained.*

acceptable behavior that leads to success and popularity. For some people, this message can lower inhibitions against acting out hostile feelings (Berkowitz, 1984).

Another effect of TV violence is that it tends to lower sensitivity to violent acts. As anyone who has seen a street fight or a mugging can tell you, TV violence is sanitized and unrealistic. The real thing is gross, ugly, and gut wrenching. Even when it is graphic, TV violence is viewed in the relaxed and familiar setting of the home. For at least some viewers, this combination diminishes emotional reactions to violent scenes. When Victor Cline and his associates showed a bloody fight film to a group of boys, they found that heavy TV viewers (averaging 42 hours a week) showed much less emotion than those who watched little or no TV (Cline et al., 1972). Television, it seems, can cause a **desensitization** (reduced emotional sensitivity) to violence.

Preventing Aggression

What can be done about aggression? Social learning theory implies that "aggression begets aggression." For example, children who are physically abused at home, those who suffer severe physical punishment, and those who merely witness violence in the community are more likely to be involved in fighting, aggressive play, and antisocial behavior at school (Margolin & Gordis, 2000).

According to social learning theorists, watching a prizefight, sporting event, or violent television program may increase aggression, rather than drain off aggressive urges. A case in point is provided by psychologist Leonard Eron, who spent 22 years following more than 600 children into adulthood. Eron (1987) observes, "Among the most influential models for children were those observed on television. One of the best predictors of how aggressive a young man would be at age 19 was the violence of the television programs he pre-

BRIDGES

Abused children frequently become abusive adults, which is another indication that "aggression begets aggression."

See Chapter 5, pages 136-137.

ferred when he was 8 years old" (❖Fig. 20.6). According to Eron, children learn aggressive strategies and actions from TV violence (also see Chapter 9). Because of this, they are more prone to aggress when they face frustrating situations or cues. Others have found that viewers who watch violent videotapes have more aggressive thoughts. As we have noted, violent thoughts often precede violent actions (Bushman & Geen, 1990). Thus, the spiral of aggression might be broken if we did not so often portray it, reward it, and glorify it (Hughes & Hasbrouck, 1996).

TV AS A POSITIVE MODEL   *Couldn't TV's impact also be used constructively?*   There is no denying TV's tremendous power to inform and to entertain. When these features are combined, as they were in specials such as *Roots* or *Holocaust,* the effect can be quite constructive. Perhaps the best examples of TV as a positive social force are educational programs such as *Barney and Friends, Sesame Street,* and *Mr. Rogers' Neighborhood.* Numerous research reports have found that the impact of these programs is positive. Clearly, television can teach children while holding their interest and attention.

Prosocial behavior consists of actions toward others that are helpful, constructive, or altruistic. As a model for positive attitudes and responses, TV could be used to promote helping, cooperation, charity, and brotherhood in the same way that it has tended to stereotype and encourage aggression. More than 200 studies have now shown that prosocial behavior on TV increases prosocial behavior by viewers (Hearold, 1987). To illustrate, a program called "Youth against Violence: Choose to De-Fuse" was developed in New York City to help inner-city youths resist violence. The program focused on creating positive peer pressure for choosing nonviolent solutions to conflict. The use of real-life situations, speech, and body language added to the effectiveness of the program (Zimmerman, 1996b).

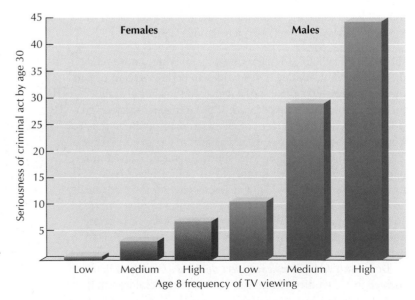

❖ **FIGURE 20.6** *Although TV violence does not cause aggression, it can encourage it. The likelihood of committing criminal acts by age 30 is related to the amount of TV watching a person did as a child (Eron, 1987). (Graph copyright 1987 by the American Psychological Association, Inc. Reprinted by permission of the author.)*

BUFFERING TELEVISION'S IMPACT

Other than pulling the plug, what can parents do about television's negative effects on children? Actually, quite a lot. Children typically model parents' TV viewing habits, and they are guided by parents' reactions to programs. Parents can make a big difference if they do the following (Eron, 1986; Huesmann, 1986; Schneider, 1987).

Parents as TV Guides

1. Limit total viewing time so that television does not dominate your child's view of the world. If necessary, set schedules for when watching TV is allowed. Don't use television as a babysitter.
2. Closely monitor what your child does watch. Change channels or turn off the TV if you object to a program. Be prepared to offer games and activities that stimulate your child's imagination and creativity.
3. Actively seek programs your child will enjoy, especially those that model positive behavior and social attitudes.
4. Watch television with your child so that you can counter what is shown. Help your child distinguish between reality and TV fantasies. Reply to distortions and stereotypes as they appear on screen.
5. Discuss the social conflicts and violent solutions shown on television. Ask your child in what ways the situations are unrealistic and why the violence shown would not work in the real world. Encourage the child to propose more mature, realistic, and positive responses to situations.
6. Show by your own disapproval that violent TV heroes are not the ones to emulate. Remember, children who identify with TV characters are more likely to be influenced by televised aggression.

By following these guidelines you can help children learn to enjoy television without being overly influenced by programs and advertisers.

ANGER CONTROL   On a personal level, psychologists have succeeded in teaching some people to control their anger and aggressive impulses. **Anger control** refers to personal strategies for reducing or curbing anger. The key to remaining calm is to define upsetting situations as *problems to be solved*. Therefore, to limit anger, people are taught to:

1. Define the problem as precisely as possible.
2. Make a list of possible solutions.
3. Rank the likely success of each solution.
4. Choose a solution and try it.
5. Assess how successful the solution was, and make adjustments if necessary.

Taking these steps has helped many people to lessen tendencies toward child abuse, family violence, and other destructive outbursts (Meichenbaum et al., 1982).

Beyond this, the question remains, How shall we tame the world's most dangerous animal? There is no easy answer—only

A study by Jerome and Dorothy Singer found that preschoolers who watch *Barney and Friends* show improved cognitive skills and knowledge—such as knowing colors and shapes, numbers, vocabulary, good manners, and facts about nature and health (deGroot, 1994).

a challenge of pressing importance. The solution will undoubtedly involve the best efforts of thinkers and researchers from many disciplines.

For the more immediate future, it is clear that we need more people who are willing to engage in helpful, altruistic, prosocial behavior. In the next section, we will examine some of the forces that operate to prevent people from helping others. Also discussed are a few glimmerings about how to encourage prosocial behavior.

PROSOCIAL BEHAVIOR—HELPING OTHERS

Late one night, tenants of a Queens, New York, apartment building watched and listened in horror as a young woman named Kitty Genovese was murdered on the sidewalk outside. From the safety of their rooms, no fewer than 38 people heard her agonized screams as her assailant stabbed her, was frightened off, and returned to stab her again.

Desensitization *A reduction in emotional sensitivity to a stimulus.*
Prosocial behavior *Behavior toward others that is helpful, constructive, or altruistic.*
Anger control *Personal strategies for reducing or curbing anger.*

Kitty Genovese's murder took more than 30 minutes, but none of her neighbors tried to help. None even called the police until after the attack had ended. Perhaps it is understandable that no one wanted to get involved. After all, it could have been a violent lovers' quarrel. Or helping might have meant risking personal injury. But what prevented these people from at least calling the police?

Isn't this an example of the alienation of city life? News reports treated this incident as evidence of a breakdown in social ties caused by the impersonality of the city. Although it is true that urban living can be dehumanizing, this does not fully explain such **bystander apathy** (unwillingness of bystanders to offer help during emergencies). According to psychologists Bibb Latané and John Darley (1968), failure to help is related to the number of people present. Over the years, many studies have shown that the *more* potential helpers present, the *lower* the chances that help will be given (Latané et al., 1981).

Why would people be less willing to help when others are present? In Kitty Genovese's case, the answer is that everyone

Does the person lying on the ground need help? What factors determine whether a person in trouble will receive help in an emergency? Surprisingly, more potential helpers tend to lower the chances that help will be given.

thought *someone else* would help. The dynamics of this effect are easily illustrated: Suppose that two motorists have stalled at roadside, one on a sparsely traveled country road and the other on a busy freeway. Who gets help first?

On the freeway, where hundreds of cars pass every minute, each driver can assume that someone else will help. Personal responsibility for helping is spread so thin that no one takes action. On the country road, one of the first few people to arrive will probably stop, because the responsibility is clearly theirs. In general, Latané and Darley assume that bystanders are not apathetic or uncaring; they are inhibited by the presence of others.

Bystander Intervention

People must pass through four decision points before giving help. First, they must notice that something is happening. Next, they must define the event as an emergency. Then, they must take responsibility. Finally, they must select a course of action (❖Fig. 20.7). Laboratory experiments have shown that each step can be influenced by the presence of other people.

NOTICING What would happen if you fainted and collapsed on the sidewalk? Would someone stop to help? Would people think you were drunk? Would they even notice you? Latané and Darley suggest that if the sidewalk is crowded, few people will even see you. This has nothing to do with people blocking each other's vision. Instead, it is related to widely accepted norms against staring at others in public. People in crowds typically "keep their eyes to themselves."

Is there any way to show that this is a factor in bystander apathy? To test this idea, students were asked to fill out a questionnaire either alone or in a room full of people. While the students worked, a thick cloud of smoke was blown into the room through a vent.

Most students left alone in the room noticed the smoke immediately. Few of the people in groups noticed the smoke until it actually became difficult to see through it. Subjects working in groups politely kept their eyes on their papers and avoided looking at others (or the smoke). In contrast, those who were alone scanned the room from time to time.

DEFINING AN EMERGENCY The smoke-filled room also shows the influence others have on defining a situation as an emergency.

❖ **FIGURE 20.7** *This decision tree summarizes the steps a person must take before making a commitment to offer help, according to Latané and Darley's model.*

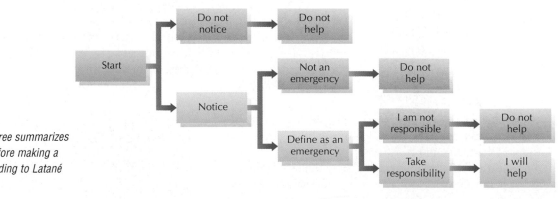

When subjects in groups finally noticed the smoke, they cast sidelong glances at others in the room. Apparently, they were searching for clues to help interpret what was happening. No one wanted to overreact or act like a fool if there was no emergency. However, as subjects coolly surveyed the reactions of others, they were themselves being watched. In real emergencies, people sometimes "fake each other out" and underestimate the need for action because each person attempts to appear calm. In short, until someone acts, no one acts.

TAKING RESPONSIBILITY Perhaps the most crucial step in helping is assuming responsibility. In this case, groups limit helping by causing a **diffusion of responsibility** (spreading responsibility among several people).

Is that like the unwillingness of drivers to offer help on a crowded freeway? Exactly. It is the feeling that no one is personally responsible for helping. This problem was demonstrated in an experiment in which students took part in a group discussion over an intercom system. Actually, there was only one real subject in each group; the others were tape-recorded actors. Each subject was placed in a separate room (supposedly to maintain confidentiality), and discussions of college life were begun. During the discussion, one of the "students" simulated an epileptic-like seizure and called out for help. In some cases, subjects thought they were alone with the seizure victim. Others believed they were members of three- or six-person groups.

Subjects who thought they were alone with the "victim" of this staged emergency reported it immediately or tried to help. Some subjects in the three-person groups failed to respond, and those who did were slower. In the six-person groups, more than a third of the subjects took no action at all. People in this experiment were obviously faced with a conflict like that in many real emergencies: Should they be helpful and responsible, or should they mind their own business? Many were influenced toward inaction by the presence of others.

People do help in some emergencies. How are these different? It is not always clear what makes the difference. Helping behavior is complex and influenced by many variables. One naturalistic experiment staged in a New York City subway gives a hint of the kinds of things that may be important. When a "victim" (actor) "passed out" in a subway car, he received more help when he carried a cane than when he carried a liquor bottle. More important, however, was the fact that most people were willing to help in either case (Piliavin et al., 1969).

To better answer the question, we need to consider some factors not included in Latané and Darley's account of helping.

Who Will Help Whom?

Many studies suggest that when we see a person in trouble, it tends to cause *heightened arousal* (Dovido, 1984). This aroused, keyed-up feeling can motivate us to give aid, but only if the rewards of helping outweigh the costs. Higher costs (such as great effort, personal risk, or possible embarrassment) almost always decrease helping (Foss, 1986). In addition to general arousal, potential helpers may also feel **empathic arousal.** This means they empathize with the person in need or feel some of

the person's pain, fear, or anguish. Helping is much more likely when we are able to take the perspective of others and feel sympathy for their plight (Eisenberg, 1991).

If people feel sad or distressed when another person is in trouble, couldn't it be that they help just to make themselves feel better? It is certainly possible that some helping is actually "selfish." But research has shown that empathy (empathic arousal) really does unleash altruistic motivation based on sympathy and compassion. Most helping, including such altruistic acts as making donations or being kind, is motivated by a true desire to relieve the distress of others (Dovido, Allen, & Schroeder, 1990).

Empathic arousal is especially likely to motivate helping when the person in need seems to be similar to ourselves (Eisenberg & Miller, 1987). In fact, a feeling of connection to the victim may be one of the most important factors in helping. This, perhaps, is why being in a good mood also increases helping. When we are feeling successful, happy, or fortunate, we may also feel more connected to others (Dovido, 1984). In summary, there is a strong **empathy-helping relationship:** We are most likely to help someone in need when we "feel for" that person and experience emotions such as empathy, sympathy, and compassion (Batson, 1990).

Is there anything that can be done to encourage prosocial behavior? People who see others helping are more likely to offer help themselves. As you may recall from Chapter 2, for example, motorists were much more likely to stop to help a woman fix a tire when they had just passed another woman being helped by someone (Bryan & Test, 1967). Also, people who give help in one situation tend to perceive themselves as helpful people. This change in self-image encourages them to help in other situations. One more point is that norms of fairness encourage us to help others who have helped us (Dovido, 1984). For all these reasons, helping others not only assists them directly but also encourages others to help.

"DE-VICTIMIZE" YOURSELF If you should find yourself in need of help during an emergency, what can you do to avoid being a victim of bystander apathy? The work we have reviewed here suggests that you should make sure that you are noticed, that people realize there's an emergency, and that they need to take action. Being noticed can be promoted in some situations by shouting "Fire!" Bystanders who might run away from a robbery or an assault may rush to see where the fire is. At the very least, remember not to just scream. Instead, you should call out, "Help" or "I need help right now." Whenever possible,

---

Bystander apathy *Unwillingness of bystanders to offer help during emergencies or to become involved in others' problems.*
Diffusion of responsibility *Spreading the responsibility to act among several people; reduces the likelihood that help will be given to a person in need.*
Empathic arousal *Emotional arousal that occurs when you feel some of another person's pain, fear, or anguish.*
Empathy-helping relationship *Observation that we are most likely to help someone else when we feel emotions such as empathy and compassion.*

define your situation for bystanders. Say, for instance, "I'm being attacked, call the police" or "Stop that man, he has my purse." You can also directly assign responsibility to a bystander by pointing to someone and saying, "You, call the police" or "I'm injured, I need you to call an ambulance" (Cummins, 1995).

A LOOK AHEAD The Psychology in Action section of this chapter returns to the topic of prejudice for some further thoughts about how to promote tolerance. Sociobiology, which is discussed in the A Step Beyond section, is a controversial theory that relates social behavior to heredity and evolution. Don't miss this interesting conclusion to our discussion of social psychology.

KNOWLEDGE BUILDER
AGGRESSION AND PROSOCIAL BEHAVIOR

RELATE

Most people have been angry enough at some time to behave aggressively. Which concepts or theories do you think best explain your own aggressive actions?

An elderly woman is at the side of the road, trying to change a flat tire. She obviously needs help. You are approaching her in your car. What must happen before you are likely to stop and help her?

LEARNING CHECK

1. The position of ethologists is that there is no biological basis for aggression. T or F?

2. Higher levels of testosterone are associated with more aggressive behavior. T or F?

3. Frustration and aversive stimuli are more likely to produce aggression when cues for aggressive behavior are present. T or F?

4. Social learning theorists view aggression as primarily related to biological instincts. T or F?

5. Social learning theory holds that exposure to aggressive models helps drain off aggressive energies. T or F?

6. Heavy exposure to television results in lowered emotional sensitivity to violence. T or F?

7. _____ behavior refers to actions that are constructive, altruistic, or helpful to others.

8. Defining an event as an emergency is the first step toward bystander intervention. T or F?

9. Seeing that a person in need is similar to ourselves tends to increase empathic arousal and the likelihood that help will be given. T or F?

CRITICAL THINKING

10. If televised violence contributes to aggressive behavior in our society, do you think it is possible that television could also promote prosocial behavior?

Answers:

1. F 2. T 3. T 4. F 5. F 6. T 7. Prosocial 8. F 9. T 10. Yes, TV could be used to promote helping, cooperation, charity, and brotherhood in the same way that it has encouraged aggression. Numerous studies show that prosocial behavior on TV increases prosocial behavior by viewers.

psychology in action

MULTICULTURALISM—LIVING WITH DIVERSITY

Today's society is more like a tossed salad than like a cultural melting pot. Rather than expecting everyone to be alike, psychologists believe that we must learn to respect and appreciate our differences. **Multiculturalism,** as this is called, gives equal status to different ethnic, racial, and cultural groups. It is a recognition and acceptance of human diversity (Fowers & Richardson, 1996).

Breaking the Prejudice Habit

Most people publicly support policies of equality and fairness. Yet, many still have lingering biases and negative images of blacks, Latinos, Asians, and other racial and ethnic minorities. How can we make sense of such conflicting attitudes? Patricia Devine, a social psychologist, has shown that a decision to forsake prejudice does not immediately eliminate prejudiced thoughts and feelings. Unprejudiced people may continue to respond emotionally to members of other racial or ethnic groups. Quite likely this reflects lingering stereotypes and prejudices learned in childhood (Devine et al., 1991).

Devine's work gives insight into how prejudice reduction takes place. For many people, the process begins with sincerely accepting values of tolerance and equality. People who count tolerance as an important personal value feel pangs of guilt, conscience, or self-criticism when they have intolerant thoughts or feelings (Zuwerink et al., 1996). This motivates them to try to alter their own biased reactions (Dovidio & Gaertner, 1999). But doing so is not easy. Typically, it requires repeated efforts to learn to think, feel, and act differently. Fully overcoming the "prejudice habit" can be challenging. Nevertheless, many people are succeeding (Devine et al., 1991). If you would like to be more tolerant, the following points may be helpful to you.

BEWARE OF STEREOTYPING Stereotypes make the social world more manageable. But placing people in categories almost always causes them to appear more similar than they really are. As a result, we tend to see out-group members as very much alike, even when they are as varied as our friends and family.

Patricia Devine found that both prejudiced and unprejudiced people are equally aware of stereotypes. Unprejudiced people, however, work hard to actively inhibit stereotyped thoughts and to emphasize fairness and equality (Devine, 1990). A good way to tear down stereotypes is to get to know individuals from various racial, ethnic, and cultural groups.

SEEK INDIVIDUATING INFORMATION When are we most tempted to apply stereotypes? Typically, it is when we have only minimal information about a person. Stereotypes help us guess what a person is like and how she or he will act. Unfortunately, these inferences are usually wrong.

One of the best antidotes for stereotypes is **individuating information** (information that helps us see a person as an individual, rather than as a member of a group) (Click, Zion, & Nelson, 1988). Anything that keeps us from placing a person in a particular social category tends to negate stereotyped thinking. When you meet individuals from various backgrounds, focus on the *person*, not the *label* attached to her or him.

A good example of the effects of individuating information comes from a study in Canada of English-speaking students in a French language program. Students who were "immersed" (spent most of their waking hours with French Canadians) became more positive toward them. Immersed students were more likely to say they had come to appreciate and like French Canadians, they were more willing to meet and interact with them, and they saw themselves as less different from French Canadians (Lambert, 1987). In fact, with more subtle kinds of symbolic prejudice, such contact may be the best way to reduce intergroup conflict (Dovidio & Gaertner, 1999).

DON'T FALL PREY TO JUST-WORLD BELIEFS Do you believe that the world is basically fair? Even if you don't, you may believe that the world is sufficiently just that people generally get what they deserve. It may not be obvious, but beliefs of this sort can directly increase prejudiced thinking.

As a result of discrimination, social conditions, and circumstances (such as recent immigration), minorities may occupy lower socioeconomic positions. **Just-world beliefs** (belief that people generally get what they deserve) can lead us to assume that minority group members wouldn't be in such positions if they weren't inferior in some way. This bit of faulty thinking amounts to blaming people who are *victims* of prejudice and discrimination for their plight.

BE AWARE OF SELF-FULFILLING PROPHECIES You may recall from Chapter 2 that people tend to act in accordance with the behavior expected by others. If you hold strong stereotypes about members of various groups, a vicious cycle can be set up. When you meet someone who is different from yourself, you may treat her or him in a way that is consistent with your stereotypes. If the other person is influenced by your behavior, she or he may act in ways that seem to match your stereotype. This creates a self-fulfilling prophecy and reinforces your belief in the stereotype. (A **self-fulfilling prophecy** is an expectation that prompts people to act in ways that make the expectation come true.)

REMEMBER, DIFFERENT DOES NOT MEAN INFERIOR Some conflicts between groups cannot be avoided. What *can* be avoided is unnecessary **social competition** (rivalry among groups, each of which regards itself as superior to others). The concept of social competition refers to the fact that some individuals seek to enhance their self-esteem by identifying with a group. However, this works only if the group can be seen as superior to others. Because of social competition, groups tend to view themselves as better than their rivals (Baron & Byrne, 1997). In a survey, every major ethnic group in the United States rated itself as better than any other group (Njeri, 1991). This is a little like the fabled town of Lake Woebegone, where all the children are above average.

A person who has high self-esteem does not need to treat others as inferior in order to feel good about himself or herself. Similarly, it is not necessary to degrade other groups in order to feel positive about one's own group identity (Messick & Mackie, 1989). In fact, each ethnic group has strengths that members of other groups could benefit from emulating. For instance, African Americans, Asians, and Latinos emphasize family networks that help buffer them from some of the stresses of daily life (Suinn, 1999).

UNDERSTAND THAT RACE IS A SOCIAL CONSTRUCTION From the viewpoint of modern genetics, the concept of race has absolutely no meaning. Members of various groups are so varied genetically and human groups have intermixed for so many centuries that it is impossible to tell, biologically, to what "race" any given individual belongs. Thus, race is an illusion based on superficial physical differences and learned ethnic identities. Certainly, people *act as if* different races exist. But this is a matter of social labeling, not biological reality. To assume that any human group is biologically superior or inferior to another is simply wrong. In fact, the best available evidence suggests that all people are descended from the same ancient ancestors. The origins of our species lie in Africa, about 100,000 years ago. Biologically, we are all brothers and sisters under the skin (Cavalli-Sforza, 1991; Segall, Lonner, & Berry, 1998).

Multiculturalism *Giving equal status, recognition, and acceptance to different ethnic and cultural groups.*
Individuating information *Information that helps define a person as an individual, rather than as a member of a group or social category.*
Just-world beliefs *Belief that people generally get what they deserve.*
Self-fulfilling prophecy *An expectation that prompts people to act in ways that make the expectation come true.*
Social competition *Rivalry among groups, each of which regards itself as superior to others.*

LOOK FOR COMMONALITIES We live in a society that puts a premium on competition and individual effort. One problem with this is that competing with others fosters desires to demean, defeat, and vanquish them. When we cooperate with others, we tend to share their joys and suffer when they are in distress (Lanzetta & Englis, 1989). If you feel that you have nothing in common with people whose backgrounds are very different from your own, remember this: If we don't find ways to cooperate and live in greater harmony, everyone will suffer. That, if nothing else, is one thing that we all have in common.

Everyone knows what it feels like to be different. Greater tolerance comes from remembering those times.

Cultural Awareness

Living comfortably in a multicultural society means getting to know a little about other groups. Getting acquainted with a person whose cultural background is different from your own can be a wonderful learning experience. No one culture has all the answers or the best ways of doing things. Multicultural populations enrich a community's food, music, arts, and philosophy. Likewise, learning about different racial, cultural, and ethnic groups can be personally rewarding.

The importance of cultural awareness often lies in subtleties and details. For example, in large American cities, many small stores are owned by Korean immigrants. Some of these Korean American merchants have been criticized for being cold and hostile to their customers. Refusing to place change directly in customers' hands, for instance, helped trigger an African American boycott of Korean grocers in New York City. The core of the problem was a lack of cultural awareness on both sides.

In America, if you walk into a store, you expect the clerk to be courteous to you. One way of showing politeness is by smiling. But in the Confucian-steeped Korean culture, a smile is reserved for family members and close friends. If a Korean or Korean American has no reason to smile, he or she just doesn't smile. There's a Korean saying: "If you smile a lot, you're silly." Expressions such as "thank you" and "excuse me" are also used sparingly, and strangers rarely touch each other—not even to return change.

Here's another example of how ignorance of cultural practices can lead to needless friction and misunderstanding: An African American woman who wanted to ease racial tensions took a freshly baked pie to her neighbors across the way, who were Orthodox Jews. At the front door the woman extended her hand, not knowing that Orthodox Jews don't shake women's hands, unless the woman is a close family member. Once she was inside, she picked up a kitchen knife to cut the pie, not knowing the couple kept a kosher household and used different knives for different foods. The woman's well-intentioned attempt at neighborliness ended in an argument! Knowing a little more about each other's cultures could have prevented both of the conflicts just described.

KNOWLEDGE BUILDER
MULTICULTURALISM

RELATE

Which strategies for breaking the prejudice habit do you already use? How could you apply the remaining strategies to become more tolerant?

LEARNING CHECK

1. Multiculturalism refers to the belief that various subcultures and ethnic groups should be blended into a single emergent culture. T or F?

2. Patricia Devine found that many people who hold unprejudiced beliefs still have prejudiced thoughts and feelings in the presence of minority group individuals. T or F?

3. Individuating information tends to be a good antidote for stereotypes. T or F?

4. Just-world beliefs are the primary cause of social competition. T or F?

CRITICAL THINKING

5. Why is it valuable to learn the terms by which members of various groups prefer to be addressed (for example, Mexican American, Latino [or Latina], Hispanic, or Chicano [Chicana])?

Answers:

1. F 2. T 3. T 4. F 5. Because labels might have negative meanings that are not apparent to people outside the group. People who are culturally aware allow others to define their own identities, rather than imposing labels on them.

Focus: To what extent does heredity explain social behavior?

A small band of men moves cautiously through a rubble-strewn battlefield. Without warning, a grenade sails overhead and lands at their feet. There is no time for escape. Instinctively, one of the men dives at the grenade, covers it with his own body, and shields his comrades from certain death. Scenes such as this have occurred in almost every modern war. How are such altruistic actions explained?

Sociobiology

According to a viewpoint called **sociobiology,** many human social behaviors have roots in heredity. Sociobiology is a more extreme form of evolutionary psychology, discussed briefly in Chapter 19 Sociobiologists, such as Harvard zoologist Edward Wilson, believe that competition, war, territoriality, aggression, sibling rivalry, conformity, male-female differences, fear of strangers, altruism, and many other behaviors are "in our genes."

The core idea in sociobiology is that social behavior evolves in ways that maximize fitness for survival. For instance, animals who compete successfully for food, territory, mates, and so forth are more likely to survive and reproduce. Thus, competitiveness gradually becomes an inborn trait. Sociobiologists believe that many human traits evolved through similar patterns of natural selection.

Applying the concept of natural selection to explain human nature may make sense for some behaviors. But how do sociobiologists explain altruistic actions like the selfless heroism of the soldier described earlier? The answer is intriguing. Sociobiologists point out that altruistic suicides can be observed in many animal species. For example, if a honeybee stings an intruder to protect its hive, the bee will die. How could such behavior evolve if altruistic bees never get a chance to reproduce and pass on their genes? Sociobiologists reply that altruistic actions help improve chances that an animal's *kin* will survive.

Each individual shares some genes in common with close family members. So, although the altruistic individual's genes may not be passed on directly, they are perpetuated by close kin. In human terms, sociobiologists argue that a person might sacrifice his or her own chance of survival to ensure the survival of several close relatives. Of course, heroic soldiers are typically unrelated to their comrades. Nevertheless, a soldier may act for the good of the group because altruism was "bred into" humans during eons of evolution.

BIOLOGICAL DETERMINISM   Sociobiology deserves credit for offering a fresh perspective on human behavior. In fact, sociobi-

ology produces some fascinating images when it is taken to its logical extremes: It is almost as if genes are at the helms of great hulking machines (our bodies) that they use for protection and self-preservation. Sociobiology seems to say that genes manipulate our behavior to ensure *their* survival (or at least the survival of duplicate genes in the bodies of our relatives).

Sociobiology's major strength is that it helps relate human behavior to biology. Its major weakness is that it probably overstates its case. The degree of **biological determinism** assumed by sociobiologists is so extreme that even most biologists question it.

CRITIQUE   Thinking about the biological foundations of human behavior is always interesting. However, the conclusions drawn by sociobiologists are highly questionable (Lerner & von Eye, 1992). Evolution and natural selection, for instance, may have favored development of the human brain, rather than of specific behavioral traits. Humans equipped with large brains are resourceful, adaptable, and flexible. Intelligence, in fact, would seem to have much more to do with our survival than strict genetic programming does. Likewise, development during each person's own lifetime provides a powerful explanation for most behavior patterns (Lerner & von Eye, 1992).

Critics of sociobiology point out that evolution progresses too slowly to account for many behavioral adaptations. The spread of ideas, traditions, and cultural patterns is much more rapid. To return to our earlier example, altruism may indeed be a necessity for a society to endure. However, selfless acts need not be coded into our nature by genes; they may be explained equally well by learning.

The danger inherent in sociobiology is that it can be used to support the social status quo. By defining human nature as relatively fixed and (in the short run) unchanging, sociobiology discourages attempts to change current cultural practices. Edward Wilson has said, for instance, that because males are typically more aggressive than females, "Even with identical education and equal access to all professions, men are more likely to continue to play a disproportionate role in political life, business, and science." If you are female, that should make you angry. If you are male, it should make you angry on behalf of your mother, sisters, daughters, wife, lover, or female friends.

Sociobiology *Theory that social behavior evolved in ways that maximize fitness for survival of the species.*
Biological determinism *Belief that behavior is controlled by biological processes, such as heredity or evolution.*

CONCLUSION   In the realm of ideas, it's also a matter of survival of the fittest. To many observers, it appears that sociobiology will have to evolve greatly if it is going to survive. In the meantime, the sociobiology debate should prove interesting. (Sources: Blaustein, 1983; Gould, 1976; Kamin, 1985; Kitcher, 1985; Lerner & von Eye, 1992; Lumsden & Wilson, 1983; Snowdon, 1983; Wilson, 1975.)

CONCLUSION: It is likely that some social behavior is based on genetics and evolution. However, extreme biological determinism tends to ignore the social, cultural, emotional, and intellectual origins of human behavior.

KNOWLEDGE BUILDER

SOCIOBIOLOGY

RELATE

What arguments can you make in support of sociobiology? Which criticisms of sociobiology do you find most convincing?

LEARNING CHECK

1. The core idea of sociobiology is that social behavior evolved in ways that maximize individual fitness for survival. T or F?

2. Sociobiologists believe that altruistic behavior evolved because individual sacrifice can improve chances that immediate family members and close kin will survive. T or F?

3. The majority of biologists endorse sociobiological explanations of behavior. T or F?

4. Critics of sociobiology point out that natural selection among humans might have favored enlargement of the brain and behavioral flexibility—not selection of specific behavioral traits. T or F?

CRITICAL THINKING

5. Sociobiology is highly controversial because it takes an extreme position in an age-old debate that also applies to human development, intelligence, and personality. What is the debate and what is sociobiology's position?

Answers:

1. F 2. T 3. F 4. T 5. The nature-nurture debate. Sociobiology places an extreme emphasis on nature (inborn behavioral tendencies).

CHAPTER IN REVIEW

What are attitudes? How are they acquired?

- Attitudes are learned dispositions made up of a belief component, an emotional component, and an action component.
- Attitudes may be formed by direct contact, interaction with others, child-rearing practices, and group pressures. Peer group influences, the mass media, and chance conditioning also appear to be important in attitude formation.

How are attitudes measured and changed?

- Attitudes are typically measured by use of techniques such as open-ended interviews, social distance scales, and attitude scales. Attitudes expressed in these ways do not always correspond to actual behavior.
- Attitude change is related to reference group membership, to deliberate persuasion, and to significant personal experiences (which may be engineered through role-playing).

Under what conditions is persuasion most effective?

- Effective persuasion occurs when characteristics of the communicator, the message, and the audience are well matched. In general, a likable and believable communicator who repeats a credible message that arouses emotion in the audience and states clear-cut conclusions will be persuasive.

What is cognitive dissonance? What does it have to do with attitudes and behavior?

- The maintenance and change of attitudes is closely related to needs for consistency in thoughts and actions. Cognitive dissonance theory explains the dynamics of such needs.
- Cognitive dissonance occurs when there is a clash between thoughts or between thoughts and actions. The amount of reward or justification for one's actions influences whether dissonance occurs. We are motivated to reduce dissonance when it occurs, often by changing beliefs or attitudes.

Is brainwashing actually possible? How are people converted to cult membership?

- Brainwashing is a form of forced attitude change. It depends on control of the target person's total environment. Three steps in brainwashing are unfreezing, changing, and refreezing attitudes and beliefs.
- Many cults recruit new members with high-pressure indoctrination techniques resembling brainwashing. Such groups attempt to catch people when they are vulnerable. Then they combine isolation, displays of affection, discipline and rituals, intimidation, and escalating commitment to bring about conversion.

What causes prejudice and intergroup conflict? What can be done about these problems?

- Prejudice is a negative attitude held toward members of various out-groups. One theory attributes prejudice to scapegoating. A second account says that prejudices may be held for personal reasons (personal prejudice) or simply through adherence to group norms (group prejudice).
- Prejudiced individuals tend to have an authoritarian or dogmatic personality, characterized by rigidity, inhibition, intolerance, oversimplification, and ethnocentrism.
- Intergroup conflict gives rise to hostility and the formation of social stereotypes. Status inequalities tend to build prejudice. Equal-status contact tends to reduce it.
- Psychologists have emphasized the concept of superordinate goals as a key to reducing intergroup conflict, be it racial, religious, ethnic, or national. On a smaller scale, jigsaw classrooms (which encourage cooperation through mutual interdependence) have been shown to be an effective way of combating prejudice.

How do psychologists explain human aggression?

- Aggression and violence are serious social problems and the subject of much current research. Ethological explanations of aggression attribute it to inherited instincts. Biological explanations emphasize brain mechanisms and physical factors related to thresholds for aggression.
- According to the frustration-aggression hypothesis, frustration and aggression are closely linked. Frustration is only one of many aversive stimuli that can arouse a person and make aggression more likely. Aggression is especially likely to occur when aggression cues are present.
- Social learning theory has focused attention on the role of aggressive models in the development of aggressive behavior.

Why are bystanders so often unwilling to help in an emergency?

- Four decision points that must be passed before a person gives help are noticing, defining an emergency, taking responsibility, and selecting a course of action. Helping is less likely at each point when other potential helpers are present.
- Helping is encouraged by general arousal, empathic arousal, being in a good mood, low effort or risk, and perceived similarity between the victim and the helper. For several reasons, giving help tends to encourage others to help, too.

What can be done to lower prejudice and promote social harmony?

- Multiculturalism is an attempt to give equal status to different ethnic, racial, and cultural groups.
- Greater tolerance can be encouraged by neutralizing stereotypes with individuating information, by looking for commonalities with others, and by avoiding the effects of just-world beliefs, self-fulfilling prophecies, and social competition.
- Cultural awareness is a key element in promoting greater social harmony.

How does the theory of sociobiology try to explain social behavior?

- Sociobiology attempts to explain human social behavior by relating it to natural selection and human evolution. Although some elements of the theory are difficult to defend, sociobiology has prompted a healthy debate about the biological origins of human behavior.

PSYCHOLOGY ON THE NET

INTERACTIVE LEARNING

- **Information about Cults and Psychological Manipulation**
  http://www.csj.org/
- **Ethnic Images in the Comics** Articles on the history of ethnic stereotyping in the comics. http://www.libertynet.org/~balch/comics/comics.html
- **Implicit Association Test** On-line tests that purportedly reveal the unconscious roots of prejudice. http://depts.washington.edu/iat/
- **Social Psychology Network** A comprehensive site with many links to information about social psychology. http://www.wesleyan.edu/spn/
- **Violence on Television** Discusses research and implications of watching violence on television. http://www.apa.org/pubinfo/violence.html

  •**InfoTrac® College Edition** For recent articles on coercive attitude change, use Key Words search for CULTS and BRAINWASHING.

- **PsychNow!** 8a. Helping others. 8b. Attribution. 8c. Social influence. 8d. Attitudes and prejudice. 8e. Aggression. 8g. Gender and stereotyping.
- **Psyk.trek** 12c. Attitude change. 12d. Prejudice.

Applied Psychology

Chapter Survey

Theme: Psychological principles are highly useful; psychology can be used to solve practical problems in a variety of settings.

▼ **KEY QUESTIONS**
● *KEY TOPICS*

▼ How is psychology applied in business and industry?

- *Industrial-organizational psychology*
- *Personnel psychology*
- *Theories of management*

▼ What have psychologists learned about the effects of our physical and social environments?

- *Environmental psychology*
- *Stressful environments*
- *Environmental problem solving*

▼ How has psychology improved education?

- *Educational psychology*

▼ **KEY QUESTIONS**
● *KEY TOPICS*

▼ What does psychology reveal about juries and court verdicts?

- *Law and psychology*
- *Jury selection and juror behavior*

▼ Can psychology enhance athletic performance?

- *Sports psychology*
- *Motor skills and peak performance*

▼ What can be done to improve communication at work?

- *Effective communication*
- *Being a good listener*

▼ How is psychology being applied in space missions?

- *Space psychology*
- *Designing space habitats*

preview

THE TOWERING INFERNO

ALARMED, YOU SNIFF THE AIR. "Is that smoke?" you ask yourself. "Yes, something's definitely burning!" You throw open your hotel room door. Outside, a thick black cloud fills the hallway. Somewhere in the choking haze, you hear someone shout, "Fire!" "Oh my," you think, "I'm on the twenty-second floor. I'd better find the elevator—fast." At that instant, you hear the following:

Female voice: "May I have your attention, please. May I have your attention, please."

Male voice: "There has been a fire reported on the 20th floor. While this report is being verified, the building manager would like you to proceed to the stairways and walk down to the 18th floor. Please do not use the elevators, as they may be needed. Please do not use the elevators, but proceed to the stairways." (Loftus, 1979)

All too often, fires in high-rise buildings lead to needless deaths. Using the elevators, for instance, can be fatal. During a fire, they act as chimneys for smoke and poisonous fumes.

In the confusion following a fire alarm, many people ignore posted instructions for safe escape. To remedy the situation, psychologists Jack Keating and Elizabeth Loftus created an unusual, life-saving "fire alarm." The best alarm, they found, is a voice that tells people exactly what to do, like the message reproduced here.

As simple as the message seems, it contains certain key elements: (1) Research has shown that switching from a female to a male voice (or the reverse) is very attention getting; (2) during emergencies, people like to feel that some authority is in control (the "building manager" in this case); (3) the crucial reminder to avoid the elevators is repeated, so it will be remembered.

Applied psychology refers to the use of psychological principles and research methods to solve practical problems. Escaping from fires may be a dramatic example of applying psychology, but it is far from unusual. The largest applied areas are clinical and counseling psychology, but there are many others. In fields as diverse as business, education, sports, law, and the environment, psychology is being applied to our lives. Let's see how.

Gateways to Applied Psychology

INDUSTRIAL-ORGANIZATIONAL PSYCHOLOGISTS enhance the quality of work by matching people with jobs and by improving human relations at work.

SELECTING THE RIGHT PERSON for a job or the right job for a person can be improved by using biographical information, interviews, and psychological tests.

EFFECTIVE MANAGEMENT AT WORK must take human behavior into account.

ENVIRONMENTAL PSYCHOLOGISTS study the relationship between environments and human behavior.

ENVIRONMENTAL PROBLEMS such as crowding, pollution, and wasted resources are based on human behavior; they can be solved only by changing behavior patterns.

EDUCATIONAL PSYCHOLOGISTS improve the quality of learning and teaching.

PSYCHOLOGICAL FACTORS greatly affect the law and jury decisions.

SPORTS PSYCHOLOGISTS enhance sports performance and the value of participating in sports.

EFFECTIVE COMMUNICATION is essential for success in most settings. Good communicators speak effectively and listen attentively.

SPACE HABITATS magnify many of the psychological challenges we face in daily life. Living in space has provided valuable lessons about how we can live in greater harmony here on Earth.

INDUSTRIAL-ORGANIZATIONAL PSYCHOLOGY— PSYCHOLOGY AT WORK

Do you consider work a blessing? Or a curse? Or do you simply agree that it is "better to wear out than to rust out"? Whatever your attitude, the simple fact is that most adults work for a living.

Industrial-organizational psychologists study the behavior of people at work and in organizations. Very likely, their efforts will affect how you are selected for a job and tested, trained, or evaluated for promotion. Most I-O psychologists are employed by the government, industry, and businesses. Typically, they work in two major areas: (1) testing and placement (personnel psychology) and (2) human relations at work. To get a fuller flavor of what I-O psychologists do, look at ◆Table A.1. As you can see, their interests are quite varied.

◆**TABLE A.1** Topics of Special Interest to Industrial-Organizational Psychologists

Absenteeism	Pay schedules
Decision making	Personnel selection
Design of organizations	Personnel training
Employee stress	Productivity
Employee turnover	Promotion
Interviewing	Task analysis
Job enrichment	Task design
Job satisfaction	Work behavior
Labor relations	Work environment
Machine design	Worker evaluations
Management styles	Work motivation
Minority workers	

❖ **FIGURE A.1** *Analyzing complex skills has also been valuable to the U.S. Air Force. When million-dollar aircraft and the lives of pilots are at stake, it makes good sense to do as much training and research as possible on the ground. Air Force psychologists use flight simulators like the one pictured here to analyze the complex skills needed to fly jet fighters. Skills can then be taught without risk on the ground. The General Electric simulator shown here uses a computer to generate full-color images that respond realistically to a pilot's use of the controls. (Photograph supplied courtesy of General Electric Company.)*

The mark of maturity, Sigmund Freud said, is a capacity for love and work. Although most people gladly embrace love, many would just as soon forget work. Yet the fact is that employed adults spend an average of more than 2,000 hours a year at their jobs. With so much time at stake, understanding the world of work is clearly a "survival skill." Let's begin with personnel psychology.

Personnel Psychology

At present, the odds are 9 out of 10 that you are, or will be, employed in business or industry. Thus, nearly everyone who holds a job is sooner or later placed under the "psychological microscope" of personnel selection. **Personnel psychology** is concerned with testing, selection, placement, and promotion of employees. Clearly, there is value in knowing how selection for hiring and promotion is done.

Job Analysis

How do personnel psychologists make employee selections?   Personnel selection begins with **job analysis,** a detailed description of the skills, knowledge, and activities required by a particular job (Borman et al., 1997). A job analysis may be done by interviewing expert workers or supervisors, by giving them questionnaires, by directly observing work, or by identifying *critical incidents.* **Critical incidents** are situations with which competent employees must be able to cope. The ability to deal calmly with a mechanical emergency, for example, is a critical incident for airline pilots. Once job requirements are known, psychologists can state what skills, aptitudes, and interests are needed (❖Fig. A.1). In addition, some psychologists are now doing a broader "work analysis." In this case, they try to identify general characteristics that a person must have to succeed in a variety of work roles, rather than in just a specific job (Hough & Oswald, 2000).

Selection Procedures

After desirable skills and traits are identified, the next step is to learn who has them. Today, the methods most often used for evaluating job candidates include collecting *biodata,* conducting *interviews,* giving *standardized psychological tests,* and the *assessment center* approach. Let's see what each entails.

BIODATA   As simple as it may seem, one good way to predict job success is to collect **biodata** (detailed biographical information) from applicants (Borman et al., 1997). The idea behind biodata is that looking at past behavior is a good way to predict future behavior. By learning in detail about a person's life, it is often possible to say whether the person is suited for a particular type of work (Hough & Oswald, 2000).

Some of the most useful items of biodata include past athletic interests, academic achievements, scientific interests, extracurricular activities, religious activities, social popularity, conflict with brothers and sisters, attitudes toward school, and parents' socio-economic status (Eberhardt & Muchinsky, 1982). Such facts tell quite a lot about personality, interests, and abilities. In addition to past experiences, a person's recent life activities also help predict job success (Schmidt, Ones, & Hunter, 1992). For instance, you might think that college grades are unimportant, but college GPA predicts success in many types of work (Hough & Oswald, 2000).

INTERVIEWS   The traditional personal interview is still one of the most popular ways to select people for jobs or promotions.

Applied psychology *The use of psychological principles and research methods to solve practical problems.*
Industrial-organizational psychology *A field that focuses on the psychology of work and on behavior within organizations.*
Personnel psychology *Branch of industrial-organizational psychology concerned with testing, selection, placement, and promotion of employees.*
Job analysis *A detailed description of the skills, knowledge, and activities required by a particular job.*
Critical incidents *Situations that arise in a job, with which a competent worker must be able to cope.*
Biodata *Detailed biographical information about a job applicant.*

In a **personal interview,** job applicants are questioned about their qualifications. At the same time, interviewers gain an impression of the applicant's personality (Borman et al., 1997). (Or personalities—but that's another story!)

As we discussed in Chapter 15, interviews are subject to the halo effect and similar problems. (Recall that the **halo effect** is the tendency of interviewers to extend favorable or unfavorable impressions to unrelated aspects of an individual's personality.) That's why psychologists continue to look for ways to improve the accuracy of interviews (see "The Sweet Smell of Success"). For instance, recent studies suggest that interviews can be improved by giving them more structure (Hough & Oswald, 2000). For example, each job candidate should be asked the same questions (Campion, Palmer, & Campion, 1998). However, even with their limitations, interviews are a valid and effective way of predicting how people will perform on the job (Landy et al., 1994).

PSYCHOLOGICAL TESTING   *What kinds of tests do personnel psychologists use?*   General mental ability tests (intelligence tests) tell a great deal about a person's chances of succeeding in various jobs (Schmidt, & Hunter, 1998). So do general personality tests and honesty tests (described in Chapter 15) (Hough &

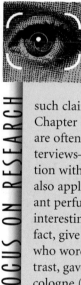

FOCUS ON RESEARCH

THE SWEET SMELL OF SUCCESS? NOT ALWAYS

Each year, clothing and cosmetics manufacturers spend huge sums to convince us that their products make us more attractive. Actually, such claims are somewhat justified. You might recall from Chapter 15, for instance, that physically attractive people are often given more positive evaluations in interviews—even on traits that have no connection with appearance. Presumably, this might also apply to the effects of wearing a pleasant perfume or cologne. But does it? In an interesting study, *female* interviewers did, in fact, give higher ratings to job applicants who wore pleasant scents. But *males,* in contrast, gave *lower* ratings to people who wore perfume or cologne (Baron, 1983).

Psychologist Robert Baron, who did this experiment, speculates that the male interviewers were more aware of the scents and resented the implied attempt to influence their ratings. Whatever the case, one thing is clear: If possible, you should learn an interviewer's sex beforehand—if you want to avoid making a flagrant, fragrant error, that is.

In general, a direct effort to make a good impression—such as emphasizing your positive traits and past successes—is most effective in interviews (Gilmore & Ferris, 1989). However, beware of blatant self-promotion. Excessively "blowing your own horn" tends to lower interviewers' perceptions of competence and suitability for a job (Howard & Ferris, 1996).

Oswald, 2000). In addition, personnel psychologists often use **vocational interest tests.** These paper-and-pencil tests assess people's interests and match them to interests found among successful workers in various occupations. Tests such as the *Kuder Occupational Interest Survey* and the *Strong-Campbell Interest Inventory* probe interests with items like the following:

- I would prefer to
  - *a.* visit a museum
  - *b.* read a good book
  - *c.* take a walk outdoors

Interest inventories typically measure six major themes identified by John Holland (see ◆Table A-2). If you take an interest test and your choices match those of people in a given occupation, it is assumed that you, too, would be comfortable doing the work they do (Holland, 1997).

Aptitude tests are another mainstay of personnel psychology. Such tests rate a person's potential to learn tasks or skills used in various occupations. Tests exist for clerical, verbal, mechanical, artistic, legal, and medical aptitudes, plus many others. For example, tests of clerical aptitude emphasize the capacity to do rapid, precise, and accurate office work. One section of a clerical aptitude test might therefore ask a person to mark all identical numbers and names in a long list of pairs like those shown here.

49837266	49832766
Global Widgets, Inc.	Global Wigets, Inc.
874583725	874583725
Sevanden Corp.	Sevanden Corp.
Wadsworth Publishing	Wadsworth Puhlishing

Paper-and-pencil tests sometimes seem far removed from the day-to-day challenges of work. In recent years, psychologists have tried to make employment testing more interesting and relevant. For example, personnel psychologists are developing **multimedia computerized tests.** These tests use computers to present realistic work situations—in living color and stereo sound. As potential employees watch typical work scenes unfold, the action freezes on

◆ **TABLE A.2** Vocational Interest Themes

THEMES	SAMPLE COLLEGE MAJORS	SAMPLE OCCUPATIONS
Realistic	Agriculture	Mechanic
Investigative	Physics	Chemist
Artistic	Music	Writer
Social	Education	Counselor
Enterprising	Business	Sales
Conventional	Economics	Clerk

(Holland, 1997.)

various problems. The applicant is then asked what she or he would do in that situation. In addition to screening job applicants, multimedia presentations can be used to improve the job skills of current employees. It won't be long before multimedia tests are widely used (Landy et al., 1994).

After college, chances are good that you will encounter an *assessment center*. Many large organizations use **assessment centers** to do in-depth evaluations of job candidates. This approach has become so popular that the list of businesses using it—Ford, IBM, Kodak, Exxon, Sears, AT&T, and thousands of others—reads like a corporate *Who's Who*.

How do assessment centers differ from the selection methods already described? Assessment centers are primarily used to fill management and executive positions. First, applicants are tested and interviewed. Then they are observed and evaluated in simulated work situations. Specifically, **situational judgment tests** are used to present difficult but realistic work situations to applicants (Borman et al., 1997). For example, in one exercise applicants are given an **in-basket test** that simulates the decision-making challenges executives face. The test consists of a basket full of memos, requests, and typical business problems. Each applicant is asked to quickly read all of the materials and take appropriate action. In a more stressful test, applicants take part in a **leaderless group discussion.** This is a test of leadership that simulates group decision making and problem solving. While the group grapples with a realistic business problem, "clerks" bring in price changes, notices about delayed supplies, and so forth. By observing applicants, it is possible to evaluate leadership skills and see how job candidates cope with stress.

How well does this approach work? Assessment centers have had considerable success in predicting performance in a variety of jobs, careers, and advanced positions (Landy et al., 1994). One study of

BRIDGES

Aptitude tests are related to intelligence tests.

See Chapter 12, pages 379–380, to learn how they differ

BRIDGES

Situational tests are also used to investigate personality differences.

See Chapter 15, pages 505–506.

women, for instance, found that assessment center predictions of management potential were closely related to career progress 7 years later (Ritchie & Moses, 1983). On the basis of long-range studies, it appears that future success is most clearly predicted by oral communication skills, leadership, energy, resistance to stress, tolerance for uncertainty, need for advancement, and planning skills (Ritchie & Moses, 1983).

As you will soon learn, psychologists working in business do far more than match people with jobs. Let's see how they contribute to management and the quality of work.

THEORIES OF MANAGEMENT—WHAT WORKS AT WORK?

At 7 A.M. each morning at a major manufacturing plant, more than 400 assembly line workers, supervisors, and top executives begin their day talking, joking, and exercising together, all to the beat of amplified music. To say the least, these are unusual working conditions. To understand the rationale behind them, let's consider two basic theories of employee management.

Theory X and Theory Y

One of the earliest attempts to improve worker efficiency was made in 1923 by Frederick Taylor, an engineer. To speed up production, Taylor standardized work routines and stressed careful planning, control, and orderliness. Today, modern versions of Taylor's approach are called *scientific management* (also known as **Theory X,** for reasons explained shortly). **Scientific management** uses time-and-motion studies, task analysis, job specialization, assembly lines, pay schedules, and the like to increase productivity.

It sounds like scientific management treats people as if they were machines. Is that true? To some extent,

Aptitude tests are used to select job candidates and to advise people about what types of work they are likely to be good at.

Personal interview *Formal or informal questioning of job applicants to learn their qualifications and to gain an impression of their personalities.*
Halo effect *The tendency of an interviewer to extend a favorable or unfavorable impression to unrelated aspects of an individual's personality.*
Vocational interest test *A paper-and-pencil test that assesses a person's interests and matches them to interests found among successful workers in various occupations.*
Aptitude test *A test that rates a person's potential to learn skills required by various occupations.*
Multimedia computerized test *A test that uses a computer to present lifelike situations; test takers react to problems posed by the situations.*
Assessment center *A program set up within an organization to conduct in-depth evaluations of job candidates.*
Situational judgment test *Presenting realistic work situations to applicants in order to observe their skills and reactions.*
In-basket test *A testing procedure that simulates the individual decision-making challenges that executives face.*
Leaderless group discussion *A test of leadership that simulates group decision making and problem solving.*
Scientific management (Theory X) *An approach to managing employees that emphasizes work efficiency.*

it is. Managers who follow Theory X tend to assume that workers must be goaded or guided into being productive. Many psychologists working in business, of course, are concerned with improving **work efficiency** (defined as maximum output at lowest cost). As a result, they alter conditions they believe will affect workers (such as time schedules, work quotas, and bonuses). Some might even occasionally wish that people would act like well-oiled machines. However, most recognize that psychological efficiency is just as important as work efficiency. **Psychological efficiency** refers to maintaining good morale, labor relations, employee satisfaction, and similar aspects of work behavior. Management styles that ignore or mishandle the human element can be devastatingly costly. Studies have consistently found that happy workers are productive workers (Cote, 1999; Wright, & Cropanzano, 2000).

The term *Theory X* was coined by psychologist Douglas McGregor (1960) as a way to distinguish scientific management from a newer management style. McGregor dubbed this newer approach, which emphasizes human relations at work, *Theory Y.*

How is this approach different? **Theory Y** managers assume that workers enjoy autonomy and are willing to accept responsibility. They also assume that worker needs and goals can be meshed with the company's goals, and that people are not naturally passive or lazy. In short, Theory Y assumes that people are industrious, creative, and rewarded by challenging work. It appears that, given the proper conditions of freedom and responsibility, many people will work hard to gain competence and use their talents.

Many features of Theory Y are illustrated by the Honda plant at Marysville, Ohio. As you may already know, the automobile industry has a long history of labor-management clashes and worker discontent. In fact, outright sabotage by assembly line workers is not uncommon. To avoid such problems, Honda initiated a series of simple, seemingly successful measures. They include the following practices.

- Regardless of their position, all employees wear identical white uniforms. This allows workers and supervisors to interact on a more equal footing and builds feelings of teamwork.

- To further minimize status differences, all employees hold the title *associate.*
- Private offices, separate dining halls, and reserved parking spaces for executives were abolished.
- Employees work alongside company executives, to whom they have easy access.
- Every employee has a say in, and responsibility for, quality control and safety.
- Departmental meetings are held daily. At this time, announcements are discussed, decisions are made, and thoughts are freely shared (Abrams, 1983).

MANAGEMENT STRATEGIES Two elements that make Theory Y methods effective are *participative management* and *management by objectives.* In **participative management,** employees at all levels are directly involved in decision making. By taking part in decisions that affect them, employees like those at the Honda factory come to see work as a cooperative effort—not as something imposed on them by an egotistical boss. The benefits include greater productivity, more involvement in work, greater job satisfaction, and less job-related stress (Coye & Belohlav, 1995; Jackson, 1983).

What does "management by objectives" refer to? In **management by objectives,** workers are given specific goals to meet, so they can tell if they are doing a good job. Typical objectives include reaching a certain sales total, making a certain number of items, or reducing waste by a specific percentage. In any case, workers are free to choose (within limits) how they will achieve their goals. As a result, they feel more independent and take personal responsibility for their work. Workers are especially productive when they receive feedback about their progress toward goals. Clearly, people like to know what the target is and whether they are succeeding (Neubert, 1998).

Recently, many companies have begun to give *groups* of workers greater freedom and responsibility as well. This is typically done by creating self-managed teams. A **self-managed team** is a group of employees who work together toward shared goals. Self-managed teams can typically choose their

Participative management techniques encourage employees at all levels to become involved in decision making. Quite often, this arrangement leads to greater job satisfaction.

own methods of achieving results, as long as they are effective. Self-managed teams tend to make good use of the strengths and talents of individual employees. They also promote new ideas and improve motivation. Most of all, they encourage cooperation and teamwork within organizations (Lewis, Goodman, & Fandt, 1995).

How can workers below the management level be involved more in their work? One popular answer is the use of **quality circles.** These are voluntary discussion groups that seek ways to solve business problems and improve efficiency (Jewell, 1990). In contrast to self-managed teams, quality circles usually do not have the power to put their suggestions into practice directly. But good ideas speak for themselves, and many are adopted by management. Quality circles have many limitations. Nevertheless, studies verify that greater personal involvement can lead to better performance and job satisfaction (Buch & Spangler, 1990; Geehr et al., 1995).

Job Satisfaction

It often makes perfect sense to apply Theory X methods to work. However, doing so without taking worker needs into account can be a case of winning the battle while losing the war. That is, immediate productivity may be enhanced while job satisfaction is lowered. And when job satisfaction is low, absenteeism skyrockets, morale falls, and there is a high rate of employee turnover (leading to higher training costs and inefficiency). Understandably, many of the methods used by enlightened Theory Y managers ultimately improve **job satisfaction,** or the degree to which a person is pleased with his or her work.

Under what conditions is job satisfaction highest? Basically, job satisfaction comes from a good fit between work and a person's interests, abilities, needs, and expectations (Lubinski, 2000). What, then, do workers consider important? In the early 1970s, American workers were asked to rate the importance of 25 aspects of work. Their first eight choices were as follows (*Work in America,* 1973):

1. Interesting work
2. Enough help and equipment to get the job done
3. Enough information to get the job done
4. Enough authority to get the job done
5. Good pay
6. Opportunity to develop special abilities
7. Job security
8. Seeing the results of one's work

A second survey in the early 1980s again found that satisfying, rewarding work ranked first in worker preference. However, high income rose to second place (Weaver & Mathews, 1987). Some observers worry that a swing toward greater materialism has occurred in the last 10 to 15 years. Even if this is true, intrinsically interesting work still tops the list. To summarize much research, we can say that job satisfaction is highest when workers are (1) allowed ordinary social contacts with others, (2) given opportunities to use their own judgment and intelligence, (3) recognized for doing well, (4) given a chance to apply their skills, (5) given relative freedom from close supervision, and (6) given opportunities for promotion and advancement. Understandably, the most productive employees are those who are happy at work (Elovainio et al., 2000; Staw et al., 1994). This connection can be seen clearly in the research reported in "Flextime."

FOCUS ON RESEARCH

FLEXTIME

If you've ever worked "9 to 5," you know that traditional time schedules can be confining. They also doom many workers to a daily battle with rush-hour traffic. To improve worker morale, I-O psychologists recommend the use of **flextime,** or flexible working hours. The basic idea of flextime is that starting and quitting times are flexible, as long as employees are present during a core work period (Owen, 1976). For example, employees might be allowed to arrive between 7:30 A.M. and 10:30 A.M. and depart between 3:30 P.M. and 6:30 P.M.

Is flextime really an improvement? A recent analysis of more than 30 studies found that flextime has a positive effect on workers' productivity, job satisfaction, absenteeism, and comfort with their work schedules (Baltes et al., 1999).

How does flextime help? Psychologists theorize that it lowers stress and increases feelings of independence, both of which increase productivity and job satisfaction. Another benefit is that flextime is "family friendly." Parents working on a flexible schedule find it much easier to coordinate their work and child-care responsibilities (Frone & Yardley, 1996). When conflicts between work and private life decline, absenteeism usually does, too (Baltes, 1999).

In view of such benefits, two of three large organizations now use flextime. Perhaps we can conclude that it is better, when possible, to bend hours instead of people.

Work efficiency *Maximum output (productivity) at lowest cost.*
Psychological efficiency *Maintenance of good morale, labor relations, employee satisfaction, and similar aspects of work behavior.*
Theory Y *A management style that emphasizes human relations at work and that views people as industrious, responsible, and interested in challenging work.*
Participative management *An approach to management that allows employees at all levels to participate in decision making.*
Management by objectives *A management technique in which employees are given specific goals to meet in their work.*
Self-managed team *A work group that has a high degree of freedom with respect to how it achieves its goals.*
Quality circle *An employee discussion group that makes suggestions for improving quality and solving business problems.*
Job satisfaction *The degree to which a person is comfortable with or satisfied with his or her work.*
Flextime *A work schedule that allows flexible starting and quitting times.*

JOB ENRICHMENT For years, the trend in business and industry was to make work more streamlined and efficient and to tie better pay to better work. There is now ample evidence that incentives such as bonuses, earned time off, and profit sharing can increase productivity (Horn, 1987). However, in recent years far too many jobs have become routine, repetitive, boring, and unfulfilling. To combat the discontent this can breed, many psychologists recommend a strategy called *job enrichment.*

Job enrichment involves making a job more personally rewarding, interesting, or intrinsically motivating. Job enrichment has been used with great success by large corporations such as IBM, Maytag, Western Electric, Chrysler, and Polaroid. It usually leads to lower production costs, increased job satisfaction, reduced boredom, and less absenteeism (Lewis, Goodman, & Fandt, 1995).

How is job enrichment done? Job enrichment applies many of the principles we have discussed. Usually it involves removing some of the controls and restrictions on employees, giving them greater freedom, choice, and authority. In some cases, employees also switch to doing a complete cycle of work. That is, they complete an entire item or project, instead of doing an isolated part of a larger process. Whenever possible, workers are given direct feedback about their work or progress.

Merely assigning a person more tasks is usually not enriching. Overloaded workers just feel stressed, and they tend to make more errors. True job enrichment increases workers' *knowledge.* That is, workers are encouraged to learn a broad range of skills and information related to their occupations (Campion & McClelland, 1993). In short, most people seem to enjoy being good at what they do.

Making Career Decisions

When people become seriously dissatisfied with their work, it may be time to seek a new job. This can be a difficult step to take. One way to improve career decisions is to examine how you approach them. Psychologist Irving Janis and Dan Wheeler (1978) have described how people typically deal with work dilemmas, especially those that lead to a major change in jobs or careers. Their analysis suggests that there are four basic coping styles. See if you recognize yourself in any of the following descriptions.

- **The Vigilant Style:** This style is the most effective of the four. It describes individuals who evaluate information objectively and make decisions with a clear understanding of the alternatives. Persons using this style make mental "balance sheets" to weigh possible gains and losses before taking action.
- **The Complacent Style:** People of this type drift along with a nonchalant attitude toward job decisions. They tend to let chance direct their careers and to take whatever comes along without really making plans.
- **The Defensive-Avoidant Style:** These people are fully aware of the risks and opportunities presented by career choices and

BRIDGES

Job enrichment can be thought of as a way of increasing intrinsic motivation.

See Chapter 13, pages 423–424.

dilemmas. However, they are uncomfortable making decisions. This leads them to procrastinate, rationalize, and make excuses for their inaction and indecision.
- **The Hypervigilant Style:** People with this style more or less panic when forced to make career decisions. They may collect hundreds of job announcements and brochures, but they become so frantic that making logical decisions is nearly impossible.

These coping styles may seem exaggerated, but they are easy to observe when people are forced to change jobs or make major alterations in career plans. To relate them to yourself, think about how you have handled vocational decisions to date, or decisions about your college career. Of the four, Janis and Wheeler consider only the vigilant style to be constructive. With this insight, you may be able to improve the quality of your career decisions.

Although we have only scratched the surface of industrial-organizational psychology, it is time to move on for a look at another applied area of great personal relevance. Before we begin, here's a chance to enhance your learning.

KNOWLEDGE BUILDER
INDUSTRIAL-ORGANIZATIONAL PSYCHOLOGY

RELATE

Which of the various ways of evaluating job applicants do you regard as most valid? Which would you prefer to have applied to yourself?

If you were managing people in a business setting, which of the management concepts discussed in the text do you think you would be most likely to use?

Think of a job you know well (something you have done yourself, or something a person you know does). Could job enrichment be applied to the work? What would you do to increase job satisfaction for people doing similar work?

LEARNING CHECK

1. To gain attention for an emergency announcement, it is better to switch from a male voice to a female voice than it is to do the reverse. T or F?

2. Identifying critical work incidents is sometimes included in a thorough _____ _____.

3. Detailed biographical information about a job applicant is referred to as _____.

4. The *Strong-Campbell Inventory* is a typical aptitude test. T or F?

5. A leaderless group discussion is most closely associated with which approach to employee selection?
   a. aptitude testing *b.* personal interviews *c.* job analysis *d.* assessment center

6. Theory X, or scientific management, is concerned primarily with improving _____ _____.

7. Participative management is often a feature of businesses that adhere to Theory Y. T or F?

8. For the majority of workers, job satisfaction is almost exclusively related to the amount of pay received. T or F?

9. Job enrichment is a direct expression of scientific management principles. T or F?

CRITICAL THINKING

10. In what area of human behavior other than work would a careful task analysis be helpful?

Answers:

1. F 2. job analysis 3. biodata 4. F 5. d 6. work efficiency 7. T 8. F 9. F 10. One such area is sports psychology. As described later in this appendix, sports skills can be broken into subparts, so key elements can be identified and taught. Such methods are an extension of techniques first used for job analyses. To a large extent, attempts to identify the characteristics of effective teaching also rely on task analysis.

Various behavioral settings place strong demands on people to act in expected ways.

ENVIRONMENTAL PSYCHOLOGY—LIFE IN THE BIG CITY

If cities were drivers, some would get lots of speeding tickets. Others would spend most of their time in the slow lane, watching the scenery go by. Informally, you may have noticed that the pace of life varies from city to city. Psychologist Robert Levine and his students decided to measure the overall tempo of 36 American cities to see how they compare (Levine, 1998).

To rate a city's pace, Levine looked at four indicators: walking speed, working speed, talking speed, and the percentage of men and women wearing watches. The results? The three fastest American cities were Boston, Buffalo, and New York—all in the Northeast. The three slowest cities were in the South and West: Shreveport, Sacramento, and Los Angeles. No surprises here. But Levine's other findings are surprising. Levine and his team also found that there is a correlation between the pace of life and heart disease. Just as there are Type A personalities (heart attack–prone personalities, see Chapter 16), there also seem to be Type A cities. Very likely, Type A people are attracted to fast-paced Type A cities—where they then do their best to keep the pace (Levine, 1998).

The work of Robert Levine, and psychologists like him, falls into an area known as **environmental psychology,** a specialty concerned with the relationship between environments and human behavior (Stokols, 1995). Environmental psychologists are interested in both **physical environments** (natural or constructed) and **social environments** (defined by groups of people, such as a dance, business meeting, or party) (Gifford, 1987). They also give special attention to **behavioral settings** (smaller areas within an environment whose use is well defined, such as an office, locker room, church, casino, or classroom) (Schoggen, 1989). As you have no doubt noticed, various environments and behavioral settings tend to "demand" certain actions. Consider, for example, the difference between a library and a campus center lounge. In which would a conversation be more likely to occur?

◆ **TABLE A.3** Topics of Special Interest to Environmental Psychologists

Architectural design	Noise
Behavioral settings	Personal space
Cognitive maps	Personality and environment
Constructed environments	Pollution
Crowding	Privacy
Energy conservation	Proxemics
Environmental stressors	Resource management
Heat	Territoriality
Human ecology	Urban planning
Littering	Vandalism
Natural environment	

Other major interests of environmental psychologists are personal space, **territorial behavior** (discussed in the highlight "Territoriality"), stressful environments, architectural design, environmental protection, and many related topics (◆Table A.3).

Job enrichment *Making a job more personally rewarding, interesting, or intrinsically motivating; typically involves increasing worker knowledge.*
Environmental psychology *The formal study of how environments affect behavior.*
Physical environments *Natural settings, such as forests and beaches, as well as environments built by humans, such as buildings, ships, and cities.*
Social environment *An environment defined by a group of people and their activities or interrelationships (such as a parade, revival meeting, or sports event).*
Behavioral setting *A smaller area within an environment whose use is well defined, such as a bus depot, waiting room, or lounge.*
Territorial behavior *Any behavior that tends to define a space as one's own or that protects it from intruders.*

TERRITORIALITY

In Chapter 19, we noted that powerful norms govern the use of the space immediately surrounding each person's body. As we move farther from the body, it becomes apparent that personal space also extends to adjacent areas that we claim as our "territory." Territorial behavior refers to actions that define a space as one's own or that protect it from intruders. For example, in the library, you might protect your space with a coat, handbag, book, or other personal belongings. "Saving a place" at a theater or a beach also demonstrates the tendency to identify a space as "ours."

Respect for the temporary ownership of space is widespread. It is not unusual for a person to "take over" an entire table or study room by looking annoyed when others intrude. Your own personal territory may include your room, specific seats in many of your classes, or a particular table in the cafeteria or library that "belongs" to you and your friends.

Researchers have found that the more attached you are to an area, the more likely you are to adorn it with obvious **territorial markers** that signal your "ownership." Typical markers include decorations, plants, photographs, or posters. College dorms and business offices are prime places to observe this type of territorial marking. Interestingly, burglars are less likely to break into houses that have lots of obvious territorial cues, such as fences (even if small), parked cars, lawn furniture, exterior lights, and security signs (Brown & Bentley, 1993). "Gated communities" have sprung up in many cities because they mark out a "defensible space" that discourages intrusions (Tijerino, 1998). (A highly territorial bulldog may help, too.)

Graffiti, one of the blights of urban life, is an obvious form of territorial marking.

Environmental Influences

A major finding of environmental research is that much of our behavior is controlled, in part, by specific types of environments (Gifford, 1987). For example, many shopping malls and department stores are designed like mazes. Their twisting pathways encourage shoppers to linger and wander while looking at merchandise. Likewise, many college classrooms clearly define a speaker-audience relationship. Discussion among students tends to be discouraged by seats that are bolted to the floor, facing an authority at the front of the room (Wong, Somer, & Cook, 1992). Even public bathrooms influence behavior. Because the seating is limited, few people hold meetings there!

Psychologists have also found that a variety of environmental factors influence the amount of vandalism that occurs in public places. On the basis of psychological research, many architects now "harden" and "de-opportunize" public settings to discourage vandalism and graffiti (Wise, 1982). Some such efforts limit opportunities for vandalism (doorless toilet stalls, tiled walls). Others weaken the lure of likely targets. (Strangely enough, a raised flowerbed around signs helps protect them because people resist trampling the flowers to get to the sign.)

Given the personal impact that environments have, it is important to know how we are affected by stressful or unhealthy environments—a topic we will consider next.

Stressful Environments

Everyone has his or her own list of complaints about large cities. Traffic congestion, pollution, crime, and impersonality are urban problems that immediately come to mind. To this list, psychologists have added crowding, noise, and overstimulation as major sources of urban stress. Psychological research has begun to clarify the impact of each of these conditions on human functioning (Marsella, 1998).

CROWDING   Overpopulation ranks as one of the most serious problems facing the world today. The world's population is now more than 6 billion people. World population doubled in the period from 1950 to 1987. It will double again by about 2040 (❖Fig. A.2). Each day, the world population grows by 250,000 (a quarter of a million) people (United Nations Population Fund, 1993).

Experts estimate that the maximum sustainable population of Earth is between 5 billion and 20 billion persons. This means the Earth has already entered the lower range of its carrying capacity (Cohen, 1995). Further population increases at the present rate could be disastrous. How many more people can the forests, oceans, croplands, and atmosphere support? The most pessimistic experts believe we have *already* exceeded the number of people Earth can sustain indefinitely (Oskamp, 1995a).

Nowhere are the effects of overpopulation more evident than in the teeming cities of many underdeveloped nations. Closer to home, the jammed buses, subways, and living quarters of our own large cities are ample testimony to the stresses of crowding.

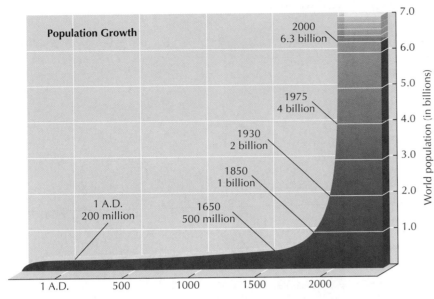

Population Growth

2000
6.3 billion

1975
4 billion

1930
2 billion

1850
1 billion

1 A.D.
200 million

1650
500 million

World population (in billions)

1 A.D.   500   1000   1500   2000

❖ **FIGURE A.2** *Population growth has slowed slightly in recent years, but world population still threatens to double again in less than 40 years (graph source: Population Institute). Overpopulation and rapid population growth are closely connected with environmental damage, international tensions, and rapid depletion of nonrenewable resources. Some demographers predict that if population growth is not limited voluntarily before it reaches 10 billion, it will be limited by widespread food shortages, disease, infant mortality, and early death (Erlich & Erlich, 1990).*

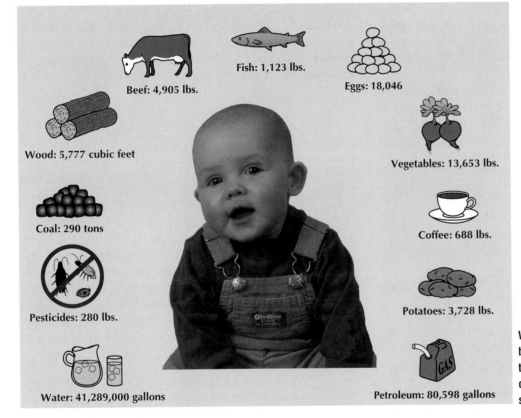

Beef: 4,905 lbs.

Fish: 1,123 lbs.

Eggs: 18,046

Wood: 5,777 cubic feet

Vegetables: 13,653 lbs.

Coal: 290 tons

Coffee: 688 lbs.

Pesticides: 280 lbs.

Potatoes: 3,728 lbs.

Water: 41,289,000 gallons

Petroleum: 80,598 gallons

What will it cost the world to provide for a baby born in the year 2000? Over a lifetime, a person born in North America will consume, on average, the resources shown here ("Bringing Up Baby," 1999).

Is there any way to assess the effect crowding has on people? One approach is to study the effects of overcrowding among animals. Although the results of animal experiments cannot be considered conclusive for humans, they point to some disturbing effects.

For example? In an interesting experiment, John Calhoun (1962) let a group of laboratory rats breed without limit in a confined space. Calhoun provided plenty of food, water, and nesting material for the rats. All that the rats lacked was space. At its peak, the colony numbered 80 rats. Yet, it was housed in

a cage designed to comfortably hold about 50. Overcrowding in the cage was heightened by the actions of the two most dominant males. These rascals staked out private territory at opposite ends of the cage, gathered harems of 8 to 10 females, and

Territorial markers *Objects and other signals whose placement indicates to others the "ownership" or control of a particular area.*

prospered. Their actions forced the remaining rats into a small, severely crowded middle area.

What effect did crowding have on the animals? A high rate of pathological behavior developed in both males and females. Females gave up nest building and caring for their young. Pregnancies decreased, and infant mortality ran extremely high. Many of the animals became indiscriminately aggressive and went on rampaging attacks against others. Abnormal sexual behavior was rampant, with some animals displaying hypersexuality and others total sexual passivity. Many of the animals died, apparently from stress-caused diseases. The link between these problems and overcrowding is unmistakable.

But does that apply to humans? Many of the same pathological behaviors can be observed in crowded inner-city areas. It is therefore tempting to assume that violence, social disorganization, and declining birthrates as seen in these areas are directly related to crowding. However, the connection has not been so clearly demonstrated with humans. People living in the inner city suffer disadvantages in nutrition, education, income, and health care. These, more than crowding, may deserve the blame. In fact, most laboratory studies using human subjects have failed to produce any serious ill effects by crowding people into small places. Most likely, this is because *crowding* is a psychological condition that is separate from **density** (the number of people in a given space).

How does crowding differ from density? **Crowding** refers to subjective feelings of being overstimulated by social inputs or a loss of privacy. Whether high density is experienced as crowding may depend on relationships among those involved. In an elevator, subway, or prison, high densities may be uncomfortable. In contrast, a musical concert, party, or reunion may be most pleasant at high density levels. Thus, physical crowding may interact with situations to intensify existing stresses or pleasures. However, when crowding causes a *loss of control* over one's immediate social environment, stress is likely to result (Fuller et al., 1996; Lepore, Evans, & Schneider, 1992; Pandey, 1999).

Stress probably explains why death rates increase among prison inmates and mental hospital patients who live in crowded conditions. Even milder instances of crowding can have a negative impact. People who live in crowded conditions often become guarded and withdrawn from others (Evans & Lepore, 1993).

OVERLOAD One unmistakable result of high densities and crowding is a state that psychologist Stanley Milgram called **attentional overload.** This is a stressful condition that occurs when sensory stimulation, information, and social contacts make excessive demands on attention. Large cities, in particular, tend to bombard residents with continuous input. The resulting sensory and cognitive overload can be quite stressful.

Milgram (1970) believed that city dwellers learn to prevent attentional overload by engaging in only brief, superficial social contacts, by ignoring nonessential events, and by fending off others with cold and unfriendly expressions. In short, many city dwellers find that a degree of callousness is essential for survival.

Woodstock '94. High densities do not automatically produce feelings of crowding. The nature of the situation and the relationship between crowd members are also important.

Is there any evidence that such strategies are actually adopted? A fascinating study suggests they are. In several large American cities and smaller nearby towns, a young child stood on a busy street corner and asked passing strangers for help, saying, "I'm lost. Can you call my house?" About 72 percent of those approached in small towns offered to help. Only about 46 percent of those who were asked for help in the cities gave aid. In some cities (Boston and Philadelphia) only about one third were willing to help (Takooshian et al., 1977). An analysis of 65 studies confirmed that country people are more likely to help than city people (Steblay, 1987). Thus, a blunting of sensitivity to the needs of others may be one of the more serious costs of urban stresses and crowding. As described next, noise also contributes to the sensory assault many people endure in urban environments.

THE HIGH COST OF NOISE How serious are the effects of daily exposure to noise? A study of children attending schools near Los Angeles International Airport suggests that constant noise can be quite damaging. Children from the noisy schools were compared with similar students attending schools farther from the airport (Cohen et al., 1981). These comparison students were from families of comparable social and economic makeup. Testing showed that children attending the noisy schools had higher blood pressure than those from the quieter schools. They were more likely to give up attempts to solve a difficult puzzle. And they were poorer at proofreading a printed paragraph—a task that requires close attention and concentration. A recent study of children living near a new airport in Munich, Germany, found similar damaging effects (Evans, Bullinger, & Hygge, 1998).

Noise pollution is a source of stress in many urban environments.

People tend to have prolonged emotional responses to technological disasters. Long after an accidental release of radioactivity by the Three Mile Island Nuclear Power Plant, nearby residents continued to feel stressed and apprehensive (Baum & Fleming, 1993).

As the late Carl Sagan once said, "When you look closely, you find so many things going wrong with the environment, you are forced to reassess the hypothesis of intelligent life on Earth."

The greater tendency of the noisy-school children to give up or become distracted is a serious handicap. It may even reveal a state of "learned helplessness" (described in Chapter 16) caused by daily, uncontrollable blasts of sound. Even if such damage proves to be temporary, it is clear that **noise pollution** (annoying and intrusive noise) is a major source of environmental stress. Other researchers have linked noise with impaired learning ability, less tolerance for frustration, and a reduced willingness to help others (Staples, 1996).

TOXIC ENVIRONMENTS   Human activities drastically change the natural environment. We burn fossil fuels, destroy forests, use chemical products, and strip, clear, and farm the land. In doing so, we alter natural cycles, animal populations, and the very face of the Earth. The long-range impact of such activities is already becoming evident through global warming, the extinction of plants and animals, a hole in the ozone layer, and polluted land, air, water, and oceans (McKenzie-Mohr & Oskamp, 1995).

On a smaller scale, there is plenty of evidence that unchecked environmental damage will be costly to our children and descendants. For example, studies show that exposure to toxic hazards, such as radiation, pesticides, and industrial chemicals, leads to an elevated risk of physical and mental disease (Baum & Fleming, 1993).

How can people be encouraged to help preserve the environment?   Research has shown that it is best to combine several strategies. Persuasion and education can be used to get individuals and businesses to voluntarily reduce activities that damage the environment. Effective appeals may be based on self-interest

Density *The number of people in a given space or, inversely, the amount of space available to each person.*
Crowding *A subjective feeling of being overstimulated by a loss of privacy or by the nearness of others (especially when social contact with them is unavoidable).*
Attentional overload *A stressful condition caused when sensory stimulation, information, and social contacts make excessive demands on attention.*
Noise pollution *Stressful and intrusive noise; usually artificially generated by machinery, but also including noises made by animals and humans.*

(cost savings), the collective good (protecting one's own children and future generations), or simply a personal desire to take better care of the planet. Changing the consequences of wasteful energy use, polluting, and the like can also alter behavior. For example, energy taxes can be used to increase the cost of using fossil fuels, rebates can be offered for installing insulation or buying energy-efficient appliances, and tax breaks can be given to companies that take steps to preserve the environment (Dwyer et al., 1993; Kempton, Darley, & Stern, 1992).

Environmental Problem Solving

Although overcrowding and pollution rank high on the list of environmental stresses, they are only two of the many challenges that press for attention. To conclude, let's sample some of the solutions that psychologists have provided for environmental problems.

PROBLEM: URBAN FEARS   The way people think about the environment greatly affects their behavior. Mental "maps" of various areas, for instance, often guide actions and alter decisions. A case in point is a study done in Philadelphia. There, researchers found that an existing school bus route contributed to truancy. The problem was that many of its stops were at corners where children were afraid of being attacked and beaten (Conyne & Clack, 1981).

SOLUTION   By doing an **environmental assessment,** psychologists develop a picture of environments as they are perceived by the people using them. An assessment often includes such things as charting areas of highest use in buildings, using attitude scales to measure reactions to various settings (such as schools, businesses, and parks), and even having people draw a version of their cognitive map of a building, campus, or city (Coulton et al., 1996).

In the case of the schoolchildren, residents of the neighborhood were asked to rate how much stress they felt when walking in various areas. The result was a contour map (somewhat like a high- and low-pressure weather map) that showed the areas

BRIDGES

Learned cognitive maps guide our behavior in a variety of situations.

See Chapter 9, page 298.

of highest perceived stress. This "stress map" was then used to reroute school buses to "low-pressure" areas.

PROBLEM: RESIDENTIAL CROWDING   Anyone who has ever lived in a college dorm knows that at times a dorm hall can be quite a "zoo." Most architects aim to create buildings in which people will be comfortable, happy, and healthy. But sometimes they miss the mark with human behavior. In one well-known experiment, Baum and Valins (1977) found that students housed in long, narrow, corridor-design dormitories often feel crowded and stressed. The crowded students tended to withdraw from others and even made more trips to the campus health center than students living in less crowded buildings.

SOLUTION   **Architectural psychology** is the study of the effects buildings have on behavior. By analyzing buildings, psychologists are often able to suggest design changes that solve or avoid problems. For example, Baum and Valins (1979) studied two basic dorm arrangements. One dorm had a long corridor with one central bathroom. As a result, residents were constantly forced into contact with one another. The other dorm had rooms clustered in threes. Each of these suites shared a small bathroom. Even though the amount of space available to each student was the same in both dorms, students in the long-corridor dorm reported feeling more crowded. They also made fewer friends in their dorm and showed greater signs of withdrawing from social contact.

What sort of solution does this suggest?   A later study showed that small architectural changes can greatly reduce stress in high-density living conditions. Baum and Davis (1980) compared students living in a long-corridor dorm housing 40 students to those living in an altered long-corridor dorm. In the altered dorm, Baum and Davis divided the hallway in half with unlocked doors and made three center bedrooms into a lounge area (❖Fig. A.3). At the end of the term, students living in the divided dorm reported less stress from crowding. They also formed more friendships and were more open to social contacts. In comparison, students in the long-corridor dorm felt more crowded, stressed, and unfriendly, and they

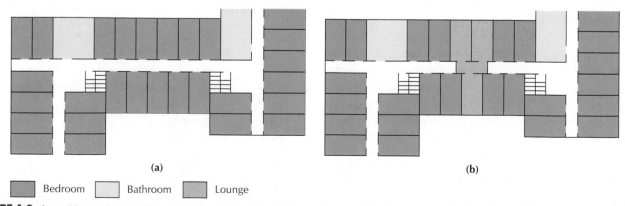

(a)   (b)

◼ Bedroom   ◻ Bathroom   ◼ Lounge

❖ **FIGURE A.3** *An architectural solution for crowding. Psychologists divided a dorm hall like that shown in the left diagram* (a) *into two shorter halls separated by unlocked doors and a lounge area* (b). *This simple change minimized unwanted social contacts and greatly reduced feelings of crowding among dorm residents. (Adapted from Baum & Davis, 1980.)*

Shown here are the Skeen family of Pearland, Texas, and the Yadev family of Ahraura, India. Each was photographed by the Material World Project, which documented typical families and their possessions around the world. Developed countries presently consume the largest share of world resources. However, population growth is fastest in developing countries, and their hunger for material possessions is rapidly expanding. Achieving sustainable levels of population and consumption are two of the greatest challenges of the coming century. (From *Material World,* Menzel et al, 1994.)

kept their doors shut much more frequently—presumably because they "vahnted to be alone." Similar improvements have been made by altering the interior design of businesses, schools, apartment buildings, mental hospitals, and prisons. In general, the more spaces one must pass through to get from one part of a building to another, the less stressed and crowded people feel (Evans et al., 1996).

PROBLEM: WASTED RESOURCES   The rapid worldwide consumption of natural resources is one of the most devastating of all social problems. Industrialized nations, in particular, are consuming world resources at an alarming rate. The United States and Canada, for instance, have a little over 5 percent of the world's population. Yet we consume 25 to 30 percent of all the fossil fuels and raw materials used annually. The typical resident of Vancouver, Chicago, or Miami consumes 10 to 1,000 times more resources each day than the average resident of Chile, Ghana, or Zaire (Cohen, 1995). In the face of projected shortages and squandered resources, what can be done to encourage conservation on a personal level?

SOLUTION   Try as you might to reduce your use of energy (electricity, for instance), you would probably find it difficult to do. A major problem is that *feedback* about energy use (the monthly bill) arrives long after the temptation to turn up the heat or to leave lights on (see Chapter 9). Psychologists aware of this problem have shown that lower energy bills result from simply giving families daily feedback about their use of gas or electricity.

Programs that give monetary rewards for energy conservation are even more effective. This is especially true for "master-metered" apartment complexes. In such apartments, families do not receive individual bills for their utilities. Consequently,

Environmental assessment   *Measurement and analysis of the effects an environment has on the behavior of people within that environment.*
Architectural psychology   *Study of the effects buildings have on behavior and the design of buildings using behavioral principles.*

REDUCE, REUSE, RECYCLE

What can be done to lighten the environmental impact of our "throwaway" society? As we have discussed, reducing consumption is a start. Personally reusing products and materials that would normally be thrown away is also important. In addition, we can recycle materials such as paper, steel, glass, aluminum, and plastic that can be used to make new products.

What can be done to encourage people to recycle? Psychological research has shown that all of the following strategies promote recycling (Oskamp, 1995b).

- **Educate.** Learning about environmental problems and pro-environment values at school has been one of the most effective ways to encourage pro-environmental behavior (Zelezny, 1999).
- **Provide monetary rewards.** As mentioned before, monetary rewards encourage conservation. Requiring refundable deposits on glass bottles is a good example of using incentives to increase recycling.
- **Remove barriers.** Anything that makes recycling more convenient helps. A good example is cities that offer curbside pickup of household recyclables. Some cities even accept unsorted recycling materials, which greatly increases participation in recycling programs. On campus, simply putting marked containers in classrooms is a good way to encourage recycling (Ludwig, Gray, & Rowell, 1998).
- **Use persuasion.** Many recycling programs benefit from media campaigns to persuade people to participate.
- **Obtain public commitment.** People who feel they have committed themselves to recycling are more likely to follow through and actually recycle. Sometimes, people are asked to sign "pledge cards" on which they promise to recycle. Another technique involves having people sign a list committing themselves to recycling. Such lists may or may not be published in a local newspaper. They are just as effective either way.
- **Encourage goal setting.** People who set their own goals for recycling tend to meet them. Goal setting has been used successfully with families, dorms, neighborhoods, offices, factories, and so forth.

- **Give feedback.** Again, feedback proves to be very valuable. Recycling typically increases when families, work groups, dorms, and the like are simply told, on a weekly basis, how much they recycled. Even impersonal feedback can be effective. In one study, signs were placed on recycling containers on a college campus. The signs showed how many aluminum cans had been deposited in the previous week. This simple procedure increased recycling by 65 percent (Larson et al., 1995).
- **Revise attitudes.** Even people who believe that recycling is worthwhile are likely to regard it as a boring task. Thus, people are most likely to continue recycling if they emphasize the sense of satisfaction they get from contributing to the environment (Werner & Makela, 1998).

People are much more likely to recycle if proper attention is given to psychological factors that promote recycling behavior.

they have no reason to save gas and electricity. Often, they consume about 25 percent more energy than they would in an individually metered apartment (McClelland & Cook, 1980). At this rate of waste, apartment owners can split any savings (from reduced consumption) with their tenants—and still be ahead. Similar factors can greatly increase recycling, as described in "Reduce, Reuse, Recycle."

Conclusion

We have had room here only to hint at the creative and highly useful work being done in environmental psychology. Although many environmental problems remain, it is encouraging to see that behavioral solutions exist for at least some of them. Surely, creating and maintaining healthy environments is one of the major challenges facing coming generations (Oskamp, 1995a).

We have discussed work and the environment at some length because both have major effects on our lives. To provide a fuller account of the diversity of applied psychology, let's conclude by briefly sampling three additional topics of interest: educational psychology, psychology and law, and sports psychology.

KNOWLEDGE BUILDER
ENVIRONMENTAL PSYCHOLOGY

RELATE

What is the nature of the natural environment, constructed environment, social environment, and behavioral setting you are in right now?

What forms of territorial behavior are you aware of in your own actions?

Have you ever experienced a stressful level of crowding? Was density or control the key factor?

If you were setting up a program to promote recycling on campus, what techniques would you apply?

LEARNING CHECK

1. Although male rats in Calhoun's crowded animal colony became quite pathological, female rats continued to behave in a relatively normal fashion. T or F?

2. To clearly understand behavior, it is necessary to make a distinction between crowding and _____ (the number of people in a given space).

3. Milgram believed that many city dwellers prevent attentional overload by limiting themselves to superficial social contacts. T or F?

4. Performing an environmental _____ might be a good prelude to redesigning college classrooms to make them more comfortable and conducive to learning.

5. So far, the most successful approach for bringing about energy conservation is to add monetary penalties to monthly bills for excessive consumption. T or F?

CRITICAL THINKING

6. Many of the most damaging changes to the environment being caused by humans will not be felt until sometime in the future. How does this complicate the problem of preserving environmental quality?

Answers:

1. F 2. density 3. T 4. assessment 5. F 6. A delay of consequences (rewards, benefits, costs, and punishers) tends to reduce their impact on immediate behavior.

Educational psychologists are interested in enhancing learning and improving teaching.

◆ **TABLE A.4** Topics of Special Interest to Educational Psychologists

Aptitude testing	Language learning
Classroom management	Learning theory
Classroom motivation	Moral development
Classroom organization	Student adjustment
Concept learning	Student attitudes
Curriculum development	Student needs
Disabled students	Teacher attitudes
Exceptional students	Teaching strategies
Gifted students	Teaching styles
Individualized instruction	Test writing
Intellectual development	Transfer of learning
Intelligence testing	

EDUCATIONAL PSYCHOLOGY—AN INSTRUCTIVE TOPIC

You have just been asked to teach a class of fourth-graders for a day. What will you do? (Assume that bribery, showing them films, and a field trip to a video arcade are out.) If you ever do try teaching, you might be surprised at how challenging it is. Effective teachers must understand learning, instruction, classroom dynamics, and testing.

What are the best ways to teach? Is there an optimal teaching style for different age groups, topics, or individuals? These and related questions lie at the heart of educational psychology (◆Table A.4). Specifically, **educational psychology** seeks to understand how people learn and how teachers instruct.

Elements of a Teaching Strategy

Whether it's "breaking in" a new coworker, instructing a friend in a hobby, or helping a child learn to read, the fact is, we all teach at times. The next time you are asked to share your knowledge, how will you do it? One good way to become more effective is to use a specific **teaching strategy,** or planned

method of instruction. The example that follows was designed for classroom use, but it applies to many other situations as well (Thornburg, 1984).

- **Step 1: Learner preparation.** Begin by gaining the learner's attention, and focus interest on the topic at hand.
- **Step 2: Stimulus presentation.** Present instructional stimuli (information, examples, and illustrations) deliberately and clearly.
- **Step 3: Learner response.** Allow time for the learner to respond to the information presented (by repeating correct responses or asking questions, for example).

Educational psychology *The field that seeks to understand how people learn and how teachers instruct.*
Teaching strategy *A plan for effective teaching.*

- **Step 4: Reinforcement.** Give positive reinforcement (praise, encouragement) and feedback ("Yes, that's right," "No, this way," and so on) to strengthen correct responses.
- **Step 5: Evaluation.** Test or assess the learner's progress so that both you and the learner can make adjustments when needed.
- **Step 6: Spaced review.** Periodic review is an important step in teaching because it helps strengthen responses to key stimuli.

BRIDGES

Many effective teaching strategies apply the basic principles of operant conditioning.

See Chapter 9, pages 282–286.

EFFECTS OF TEACHING STYLES *As a student, I've encountered many different teaching styles. Do different styles affect classroom learning?* There is little doubt that teachers can greatly affect student interest, motivation, and creativity. But what styles have what effects? To answer this question, psychologists have compared a number of teaching styles. Two of the most basic are *direct instruction* and *open teaching*.

In **direct instruction,** factual information is presented by lecture, demonstration, and rote practice. In **open teaching,** active teacher-student discussion is emphasized (Peterson, 1979). And now, the winner: As it turns out, both approaches have certain advantages. Students of direct instruction do slightly better on achievement tests than students in open classrooms (Thornburg, 1984). However, students of open teaching do somewhat better on tests of abstract thinking, creativity, and problem solving. They also tend to be more independent, curious, and positive in their attitudes toward school (Peterson, 1979). At present, it looks as if a balance of teaching styles goes hand in hand with a balanced education.

Although we have viewed only a small sample of educational research, its value for improving teaching and learning should be apparent. Before we leave the topic of education, "The School of the Future" offers a peek at where education is going in the new millennium.

PSYCHOLOGY AND LAW—JUDGING JURIES

One of the best places to see psychology in action is the local courthouse. Jury trials are often fascinating studies in human behavior. Does the defendant's appearance affect the jury's decision? Do the personality characteristics or attitudes of jurors influence how they vote? These and many more questions have been investigated by psychologists interested in law (Davis, 1989). Specifically, the **psychology of law** is the study of the behavioral dimensions of the legal system (see ◆Table A.5).

◆ **TABLE A.5** Topics of Special Interest in the Psychology of Law

Arbitration	Juror attitudes
Attitudes toward law	Jury decisions
Bail setting	Jury selection
Capital punishment	Mediation
Conflict resolution	Memory
Criminal personality	Parole board decisions
Diversion programs	Police selection
Effects of parole	Police stress
Expert testimony	Police training
Eyewitness testimony	Polygraph accuracy
Forensic hypnosis	Sentencing decisions
Insanity plea	White-collar crime

THE SCHOOL OF THE FUTURE

A CLOSER LOOK

What will schools of the future look like? Psychologist Wayne Holtzman offers an intriguing answer. Holtzman believes schools should enhance children's mental and physical health just as actively as they encourage learning the "three R's." To explore the possibilities, Holtzman and his colleagues have created several "full-service" Schools of the Future.

How are these schools different? First, they integrate a large array of health services and human services into the schools themselves. In conventional schools, children and families needing special help must travel all over town to get it. Many parents simply never make the effort or find the appropriate agencies. In the School of the Future, everything is available on campus. In this way, efforts to prevent mental health problems, drug abuse, school dropouts, teen pregnancy, and gang activity are made an integral part of each school.

A second major feature of the School of the Future is a very high level of teacher, parent, and community involvement. Parents, in particular, are encouraged to help set goals for the schools and to identify their children's needs. Many parents participate on campus as volunteers, and they meet frequently with teachers to monitor their children's progress. In addition, the schools form links with neighborhood groups, churches, recreation programs, and volunteer organizations. As a result, the School of the Future is an active part of the surrounding community (Holtzman, 1997). Such schools serve as a hub of child and family life. By bringing together childcare, education, and mental health services, schools can enhance the lives of children in ways that traditional schools haven't (Zigler & Gilman, 1998).

The first School of the Future program has been highly successful. Perhaps it could be in other communities, too.

Jury Behavior

When a case goes to trial, jurors must listen to days or weeks of testimony and then decide guilt or innocence. How do they reach their decision? Psychologists use **mock juries** (simulated juries) to probe such questions. In some mock juries, volunteers are simply given written evidence and arguments to read before making a decision. Others watch videotaped trials staged by actors. Either way, studying the behavior of mock juries helps us understand what determines how real jurors vote.

Some of the findings of jury research are unsettling. Studies show that jurors are rarely able to put aside their biases, attitudes, and values while making a decision (Watson et al., 1984). For example, jurors are less likely to find attractive defendants guilty (on the basis of the same evidence) than unattractive defendants (Perlman & Cozby, 1983). There is an interesting twist, however. If good looks helped a person commit a crime, it can work against her or him in court (Tedeschi et al., 1985). An example would be a handsome man accused of swindling money from an unmarried middle-aged woman.

A second major problem is that jurors are not very good at separating evidence from other information, such as their perceptions of the defendant, attorneys, witnesses, and what they think the judge wants. For example, if complex scientific evidence is presented, jurors tend to be swayed more by the expertise of the witness than by the evidence itself (Cooper et al., 1996).

Often, jurors' final verdict is influenced by inadmissible evidence, such as mention of a defendant's prior conviction. When jurors are told to ignore information that slips out in court, they find it very hard to do so. A related problem occurs when jurors take into account the severity of the punishment a defendant faces (Sales & Hafemeister, 1985). Jurors are not supposed to let this affect their verdict, but many do.

A fourth area of difficulty arises because jurors usually cannot suspend judgment until all the evidence is in. Typically, they form an opinion early in the trial. It then becomes hard for them to fairly judge evidence that contradicts their opinion.

Problems like these are troubling in a legal system that prides itself on fairness. However, all is not lost. The more severe the crime and the more clear-cut the evidence, the less a jury's quirks affect the verdict (Tedeschi et al., 1985). Although it is far from perfect, the jury system works reasonably well in most cases.

Jury Selection

Before a trial begins, opposing attorneys are allowed to disqualify potential jurors who may be biased. For example, a person who knows anyone connected with the trial can be excluded. Beyond this, attorneys try to use jury selection to remove people who may cause trouble for them. For instance, jurors who believe rape myths (that some women "ask for it" by their actions or style of dress, for example) are less likely to convict an accused rapist (Watson et al., 1984).

Only a limited number of potential jurors can be excused. As a result, many attorneys ask psychologists for help in identi-

The behavior of juries and jurors has been extensively studied. The findings of such studies are applied by psychologists who act as advisors to attorneys during the jury selection process. Jury selection in the O. J. Simpson murder trial took 2 months, as defense and prosecution lawyers struggled for the advantage in jury makeup.

fying people who will favor or harm their efforts. In **scientific jury selection,** social science principles are applied to the process of choosing a jury. Several techniques are typically used. As a first step, *demographic information* may be collected for each juror. Much can be guessed by knowing a juror's age, sex, race, occupation, education, political affiliation, religion, and socioeconomic status. Most of this information is available from public records.

To supplement demographic information, a *community survey* may be done to find out how local citizens feel about the case. The assumption is that jurors probably have attitudes similar to people with backgrounds like their own. Although talking with potential jurors outside the courtroom is not permitted, other information networks are available. For instance, a psychologist may interview relatives, acquaintances, neighbors, and coworkers of potential jurors.

Back in court, psychologists also often watch for *authoritarian personality* traits in potential jurors. Authoritarians tend to believe that punishment is effective, and they are more likely to vote for conviction (Narby et al., 1993). At the same time, the

Direct instruction *Presentation of factual information by lecture, demonstration, and rote practice.*
Open teaching *Instruction based on active teacher-student discussion.*
Psychology of law *Study of the psychological and behavioral dimensions of the legal system.*
Mock jury *A group that realistically simulates a courtroom jury.*
Scientific jury selection *Using social science principles to choose members of a jury.*

psychologist typically observes potential jurors' *non-verbal behavior*. The idea is to try to learn from body language which side the person favors (Sales & Hafemeister, 1985).

In the United States, murder trials require a special jury—one made up of people who are not opposed to the death penalty. "Death-Qualified Juries" examines the implications of this practice.

In the well-publicized case of O. J. Simpson, a majority of African Americans thought Simpson was innocent during the early stages of the trial. In contrast, the majority of European Americans thought he was guilty. The opinions of both groups changed little over the course of the yearlong trial. (Simpson was eventually acquitted.) The fact that emerging evidence and arguments had little effect on what people believed shows why jury makeup can sometimes decide the outcome of a trial (Brigham & Wasserman, 1999).

Cases like O. J. Simpson's, the Menendez brothers', and William Kennedy Smith's raise troubling ethical questions. In each case, wealthy clients had the advantage of psychological jury selection—something most people cannot afford. Attorneys, of course, can't be blamed for trying to improve their

BRIDGES

Authoritarian personality traits are also related to ethnocentrism and racial prejudice.

See Chapter 20, pages 674–675.

odds of winning a case. And because both sides help select jurors, the net effect in most instances is probably a more balanced jury (Sales & Hafemeister, 1985). At its worst, jury analysis leads to unjust verdicts. At its best, it helps to identify and remove only people who would be highly biased (Strier, 1999).

Jury research is perhaps the most direct link between psychology and law, but there are others. Psychologists evaluate people for sanity hearings, do counseling in prisons, advise lawmakers on public policy, help select and train police cadets, and more (Sales & Hafemeister, 1985). In the future, it is quite likely that psychology will have a growing impact on law and the courts.

SPORTS PSYCHOLOGY—THE ATHLETIC MIND

What does psychology have to do with sports? **Sports psychology** is the study of the behavioral dimensions of sports performance. As almost all serious athletes soon learn, peak performance requires more than physical training. Mental and emotional "conditioning" are also important. Recognizing this fact, many teams, both professional and amateur, now include psychologists on their staffs. On any given day, a sports psychologist might teach an athlete how to relax, how to ignore distractions, or how to cope with emotions. The sports psy-

DEATH-QUALIFIED JURIES

CRITICAL THINKING

People in a **death-qualified jury** must favor the death penalty or at least be indifferent to it. That way, jurors are capable of voting for the death penalty if they think it is justified.

In order for the death penalty to have meaning, death-qualified juries may be a necessity. However, psychologists have discovered that the makeup of such juries tends to be biased. Specifically, death-qualified juries are likely to contain a disproportionate number of people who are male, white, high income, conservative, and authoritarian. Such juries are much more likely than average to convict a defendant (Haney et al., 1994; Narby et al., 1993). Given the same facts, jurors who favor the death penalty are more likely to read criminal intent into a defendant's actions (Goodman-Delahunty, Greene, & Hsiao, 1998). Overall, pro-death jurors are a whopping 44 percent more likely to favor conviction (Allen, Mabry, & McKelton, 1998).

Could death-qualified juries be too willing to convict? It is nearly impossible to say how often the bias inherent in death-qualified juries results in bad verdicts. However, the possibility that some innocent persons have been executed may be one of the inevitable costs of using death as the ultimate punishment.

Sports psychologists have played a significant role in helping prepare athletes for peak performance in the Olympic Games. Stress management, attention regulation, mental imagery, motivation, self-confidence, and many other psychological factors greatly affect athletic performance.

◆ **TABLE A.6** Topics of Special Interest to Sports Psychologists

Achievement motivation	Hypnosis
Athletic personality	Mental practice
Athletic task analysis	Motor learning
Coaching styles	Peak performance
Competition	Positive visualization
Control of attention	Self-regulation
Coping strategies	Skill acquisition
Emotions and performance	Social facilitation
Exercise and mental health	Stress reduction
Goal setting	Team cooperation
Group (team) dynamics	Training procedures

Testing by psychologists has shown that umpires can call balls and strikes more accurately if they stand behind the outside corner of home plate. This position supplies better height and distance information because umpires are able to see pitches pass in front of the batter (Ford et al., 1999).

chologist might also provide personal counseling for performance-lowering stresses and conflicts (Neff, 1990). Other psychologists are interested in studying factors that affect athletic achievement, such as skill learning, the personality profiles of champion athletes, the effects of spectators, and related topics (◆Table A.6). In short, sports psychologists seek to understand and improve sports performance and to enhance the benefits of participating in sports (Williams, 1995).

Sports often provide valuable information on human behavior in general. For example, a study of Little League baseball found that children's self-esteem improved significantly after a season of play (Hawkins & Gruber, 1982). In other work, psychologists have learned that such benefits are most likely to occur when competition, rejection, criticism, and the "one-winner mentality" are minimized. In working with children in sports, it is also important to emphasize fair play, intrinsic rewards, self-control of emotions, independence, and self-reliance (Orlick, 1975). A recent study provides another example of using sports to test ideas about human behavior. Researchers found that when sports teams travel eastward over one or more time zones, they perform more poorly than they do when they travel westward. This is exactly what we would expect from people whose circadian rhythms are disrupted. It provides "real-world" support for other observations about bodily rhythms (Worthen & Wade, 1999).

Adults, of course, may also benefit from sports. For many, the payoffs are stress reduction, a better self-image, and improved general health. Researchers have reported, for instance, that running is associated with lower levels of tension, anxiety, fatigue, and depression than are found in the nonrunning population (Gondola & Tuckman, 1982).

Before the advent of sports psychology, it was debatable whether athletes improved because of "homespun" coaching methods, or in spite of them. For example, in early studies of volleyball and gymnastics, it became clear that people teaching these sports had very little knowledge of crucial, underlying skills (Salmela, 1974, 1975).

How has psychology helped? An ability to do detailed studies of complex skills has been one of the major contributions. In a **task analysis,** sports skills are broken into subparts, so that

key elements can be identified and taught. Such methods are an extension of techniques first used for job analyses, as described earlier. For example, it doesn't take much to be off target in the Olympic sport of marksmanship. The object is to hit a bull's-eye the size of a dime at the end of a 165-foot-long shooting range. Nevertheless, an average of 50 bull's-eyes out of 60 shots is not unusual in international competition (prone position).

What does it take—beyond keen eyes and steady hands—to achieve such accuracy? The answer is surprising. Sports psychologists have found that top marksmen consistently squeeze the trigger *between* heartbeats (❖Fig. A.4). Apparently, the tiny tremor induced by a heartbeat is enough to send the shot astray (Pelton, 1983). Without careful psychological study, it is doubtful that this element of marksmanship would have been identified. Now that its importance is known, competitors have begun to use various techniques—from relaxation training to biofeedback—to steady and control their heartbeat. In the future, the best marksmen may be those who set their sights on mastering their hearts.

Death-qualified jury *A jury composed of people who favor the death penalty or at least are indifferent to it.*
Sports psychology *Study of the psychological and behavioral dimensions of sports performance.*
Task analysis *Breaking complex skills into their subparts.*

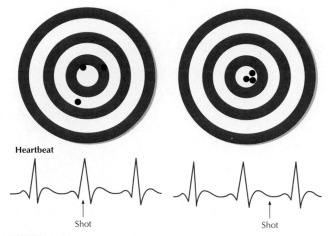

FIGURE A.4 *The target on the left shows what happens when a marksman fires during the heart's contraction. Higher scores, as shown by the three shots on the right, are more likely when shots are made between heartbeats. (Adapted from Pelton, 1983.)*

MOTOR SKILLS   Sports psychologists are very interested in how we learn motor skills. A **motor skill** is a series of actions molded into a smooth and efficient performance. Typing, walking, pole-vaulting, shooting baskets, playing golf, driving a car, writing, and skiing are all motor skills.

A basketball player may never make exactly the same shot twice in a game. This makes it almost impossible to practice every shot that might occur. How, then, do athletes become skillful? Typically, athletic performances involve learning *motor programs.* A **motor program** is a mental plan or model of what a skilled movement should be like. Motor programs allow an athlete—or a person simply walking across a room—to perform complex movements that fit changing conditions. If, for example, you have learned a "bike-riding" motor program, you can easily ride bicycles of different sizes and types on a large variety of surfaces.

Throughout life, you will face the challenge of learning new motor skills. How can psychology make your learning more effective? Studies of sports skills suggest that you should keep the following points in mind for optimal skill learning:

1. Begin by observing and imitating a *skilled model.* Modeling provides a good mental picture of the skill. At this point, try simply to grasp a visual image of the skilled movement.
2. Learn *verbal rules* to back up motor learning. Such rules are usually most helpful in the early phases of skill learning. When first learning cross-country skiing, for example, it is helpful to say, "left arm, right foot, right arm, left foot." Later, as a skill becomes more automated, internal speech may actually get in the way.
3. Practice should be as *lifelike* as possible so that artificial cues and responses do not become a part of the skill. A competitive diver should practice on the board, not on a trampoline. If you want to learn to ski, try to practice on snow, not straw.

4. Get *feedback* from a mirror, videotape, coach, or observer. Whenever possible, get someone experienced in the skill to direct attention to *correct responses* when they occur.
5. When possible, it is better to practice *natural units* rather than breaking the task into artificial parts. In learning to type, it is better to start with real words rather than nonsense syllables.
6. Learn to *evaluate* and *analyze* your own performance. Remember, you are trying to learn a motor program, not just train your muscles. Motor skills are actually very mental.

The last point leads to one more suggestion. Research has shown that **mental practice,** or merely imagining a skilled performance, can aid learning (Martin, Moritz, & Hall, 1999). This technique seems to help by refining motor programs. Of course, mental practice is not superior to actual practice. Mental practice tends to be most valuable after you have mastered a task at a basic level (Tenenbaum et al., 1996). When you begin to get really good at a skill, give mental practice a try. You may be surprised at how effective it can be.

PEAK PERFORMANCE   One of the most interesting topics in sports psychology is the phenomenon of *peak performance.* During **peak performance,** physical, mental, and emotional states are harmonious and optimal. Many athletes report episodes during which they felt almost as if they were in a trance. The experience has also been called "flow" because the athlete becomes one with his or her performance and flows with it. At such times, athletes experience intense concentration, detachment, a lack of fatigue and pain, a subjective slowing of time, and feelings of unusual power and control (Csikszmentmihalyi, 1999). It is at just such times that "personal bests" tend to occur.

A curious aspect of flow is that it cannot be forced to happen. In fact, if a person stops to think about it, the flow state goes away. Psychologists are now seeking to identify conditions that facilitate peak performance and the unusual mental state that usually accompanies it (Csikszmentmihalyi, 1999).

Even though flow may be an elusive state, there is much that athletes can do mentally to improve performance. A starting point is to make sure that their *arousal level is appropriate for the task* at hand. For a sprinter at a track meet, that may mean elevating arousal to a very high level. The sprinter could, for example, try to become angry by picturing a rival cheating. For a golfer or a gymnast, lowering arousal may be crucial, in order to avoid "choking" during a big event. One way of controlling arousal is to go through a *fixed routine* before each game or event. Athletes also learn to use *imagery and relaxation techniques* to adjust their degree of arousal (Gould & Udry, 1994).

Imaging techniques can be used to *focus attention* on the athlete's task and to *mentally rehearse* it beforehand. For example, golf great Jack Nicklaus "watches a movie" in his head before each shot. During events, athletes learn to *use cognitive-behavioral strategies to guide their efforts* in a supportive, positive way (Beauchamp et al., 1996). For

BRIDGES

Many of the mental strategies developed by sports psychologists are an extension of stress inoculation techniques.

See Chapter 16, pages 546–547.

instance, instead of berating herself for being behind in a match, a tennis player could use the time between points to savor a good shot or put an error out of mind. In general, athletes benefit from avoiding negative, self-critical thoughts that distract them and undermine their confidence. Finally, top athletes tend to use more *self-regulation strategies,* in which they evaluate their performance and make adjustments to keep it at optimum levels (Anshel, 1995a; Kim et al., 1996).

At present, sports psychology is a very young field, and still much more an art than a science. Nevertheless, interest in the field is rapidly expanding (Petrie & Diehl, 1995).

A LOOK AHEAD   Although we have sampled several major areas of applied psychology, they are by no means the only applied specialties. Others that immediately come to mind are community psychology, school psychology, military psychology, health psychology (discussed in Chapter 16), and space psychology (a skyrocketing field that is really looking up—see this chapter's A Step Beyond). Before we explore the "final frontier," the upcoming Psychology in Action section returns to the work environment with some advice on how to be an effective communicator.

K N O W L E D G E   B U I L D E R
PSYCHOLOGY APPLIED TO EDUCATION, THE LAW, AND SPORTS

RELATE

You are going to tutor a young child in arithmetic. How could you use a teaching strategy to improve your effectiveness?

As a student, do you prefer direct instruction or open teaching?

What advice would you give a person who is about to serve on a jury, if she or he wants to make an impartial judgment?

How could you apply the concepts of task analysis, mental practice, and peak performance to a sport you are interested in?

LEARNING CHECK

1. Evaluation of learning is typically the first step in a systematic teaching strategy. T or F?

2. Compared to direct instruction, open teaching produces better scores on achievement tests. T or F?

3. The School of the Future program created _____ schools with close links to the surrounding community. T or F

4. Despite their many limitations, one thing that jurors are good at is setting aside inadmissible evidence. T or F?

5. Which of the following is *not* commonly used by psychologists to aid jury selection?
   a. mock testimony *b.* information networks *c.* community surveys *d.* demographic data

6. Mental models, called _____
   _____, appear to underlie well-learned motor skills.

7. Learning verbal rules to back up motor learning is usually most helpful in the early stages of acquiring a skill. T or F?

8. The flow experience is closely linked with instances of _____ performance.

CRITICAL THINKING

9. When an athlete follows a set routine before an event, what source of stress has she or he eliminated?

Answers:

1. F 2. F 3. full-service 4. F 5. a 6. motor programs 7. T 8. peak 9. As discussed in Chapter 16, stress is reduced when a person feels in control of a situation. Following a routine helps athletes maintain a sense of order and control so that they are not over-aroused when the time comes to perform.

Motor skill *A series of actions molded into a smooth and efficient performance.*
Motor program *A mental plan or model that guides skilled movement.*
Mental practice *Imagining a skilled performance to aid learning.*
Peak performance *A performance during which physical, mental, and emotional states are harmonious and optimal.*

psychology in action
IMPROVING COMMUNICATION AT WORK

• Just a minute, I want to expand on the confusion. This is where I'm assuming we're just going to throw it up for air. I mean, let's tie all this up in loose ends.
• The bottom line is we've got to round-file this puppy ASAP before it goes belly-up. Stan says we're talking mouth-

breather here. Copy Monica, Steve, and the bean-counters with your input and let's circle the wagons in the A.M.
• I was just, like, totally embarrassed, I mean, like abso-double-lutely, totally incinerated, you know? I mean, to the max. I'm all, "I'm just totally sorry, Mr. Thompson." And he's all, "If this is the way you do business, I'm not interested."

Each of the people just quoted probably intended to express his or her ideas clearly. As you can see, however, their efforts are less than a model of clarity.

GETTING THE MESSAGE ACROSS Effective communication is crucial in many work settings. When communication is muddled, important messages may get lost. Feelings can be crushed. Trust may be damaged. Poor decisions are made. Almost always, group effectiveness is impaired.

Clearly, people who work together depend on good communication. Service-oriented work with customers and ethnocultural diversity in the work force also put a premium on communication skills. For such reasons, getting a job, keeping it, and excelling in your work all depend on knowing how to communicate clearly with others (Goldstein & Gilliam, 1990).

Effective Communication

To improve your communication skills, or to keep them sharp, remember the following points.

1. **State your ideas clearly and decisively.** News reporters learn to be precise about the "who, what, when, where, how, and why" of events. At work, the same list is a good guide when you are making a request, giving instructions, or answering a question. Rather than saying "I need someone to give me a hand sometime with some stuff," it would be better to say, "Blake, would you please meet me in the storeroom in 5 minutes? I need help lifting a box." Notice that the second request answers all of these questions: Who? Blake. What? Could you help me? How? By lifting a box. When? In 5 minutes. Where? In the storeroom. Why? It takes two people.

   As you speak, avoid overuse of ambiguous words and phrases ("wiggle words") such as *I guess, I think, kinda, sort of, around, some, about, you know,* and *like.* Here's an example: "Basically, I sort of feel like we should kinda pause. I mean, and, let's see, maybe reconsider, you know, rethink some of this stuff." It would be better to say: "I believe we should revise our plans immediately." Ambiguous messages leave others in doubt as to your true thoughts and wishes.

   Also try not to overuse intensifiers (*very, really, absolutely, extra, super, awesome, ultimate, completely,* and so on). Super extra frequent use of such awesome words really causes them to completely lose their ultimate effectiveness.

2. **Eschew the meretricious utilization of polysyllabic locutions. (Don't overuse big words.)** Overuse of obscure vocabulary is often a sign of insecurity. Big words may make you sound important, but they can also blur your message. Which of the following two statements is clearer? "Pulchritude possesses solely cutaneous profundity," or "Beauty is only skin deep."

   Trendy, overused "buzz words" or phrases should also be avoided. Often, they are just a way of *sounding like* you are saying something: "Personally, I feel we've got to be more synergistically proactive and start networking in a programmatic fashion if we want to avoid being negatively impacted by future megatrends in the client-purveyor interface." Translation: "I don't have any worthwhile thoughts on the topic."

3. **Avoid excessive use of jargon or slang.** Most professions have their own specialized terminology. Here's an example of some printers' jargon: "TR the last two lines but STET the leading." (Reverse the order of the last two lines but don't change the spacing between them.) Jargon can provide a quick, shorthand way of expressing ideas. However, jargon and technical lingo should be avoided unless you are sure that others are familiar with it. Otherwise, people may misunderstand you or feel left out. Using slang can have the same effect as jargon. Slang that excludes people from a conversation makes them feel belittled. (The second quotation at the beginning of this Application is full of slang.)

4. **Avoid loaded words.** Words that have strong emotional meanings (loaded words) can have unintended effects on listeners. For example, the observation "What a stupid-looking tie" implies that anyone who likes the tie is stupid. In the same way, saying "I think the supervisor's new schedule is a *dumb* idea" brands anyone who agrees with the schedule as foolish. Good decision making and problem solving require an atmosphere in which people feel that their ideas are respected, even when they disagree.

5. **Use people's names.** Work relationships go more smoothly when you learn names and use them. An impersonal request such as "Hey you, could you make five copies of this for me?" is not likely to promote future cooperation. Of course, whether you use a first or last name will depend on how formal your relationship to a person is. In any case, learning names is well worth the effort. (The "Psychology in Action" section of Chapter 10 tells how to improve your memory for names.)

6. **Be polite and respectful.** Being polite is important, but don't be artificially servile or stilted. Overuse of expressions such as *sir, madam, with your permission,* and *if you would be ever so kind* can actually be insulting. True politeness puts others at ease. Phony politeness makes people feel that they are being made fun of or manipulated, or that you are faking it to win approval. Being polite can be difficult when tempers flare. If you have a dispute with someone at work, remember to use the techniques of self-assertion described in Chapter 20.

   In addition to *what* you say, *how* you say it can be important. Psychologist Chris Kleinke (1986) has noted several speech cues that communicate self-confidence and add credibility to your message.

7. **Use an expressive tone of voice.** People who know a subject well or who believe in their point of view usually speak with an expressive, animated tone of voice. Speaking energetically, with good voice inflection, typically adds to one's credibility. Don't, however, use a higher pitched voice, as this suggests nervousness.

8. **Speak fluently.** Before you speak, try to collect your thoughts so that you can get right to the point. Stammer-

psychology in action

ing, repeating yourself, frequent pauses, and overuse of "ahs," "uhms," and "you knows" imply incompetence or nervousness.

9. **Speak quickly.** A brisk rate of speech tends to be persuasive because it implies knowledge, competence, enthusiasm, and confidence. It also helps hold your listener's attention.

10. **Make use of nonverbal cues.** Remember that nonverbal cues, such as facial expressions and hand gestures, can help accentuate your message and structure it for listeners. In Western cultures, making eye contact while speaking is a particularly important nonverbal cue. In a group, don't talk to the ceiling or to just one person. Try to make eye contact with each person in the group. That way, each feels included and knows that your message is meant for her or him. Another advantage of eye contact is that it lets you watch for feedback from listeners, whose reactions can guide your communication efforts.

Be aware that your behavior sends messages, too. Actions can parallel, amplify, contradict, or undermine what you are saying. For example, being late for a meeting tells others that they are not very important to you. Likewise, your manner of dress and personal grooming—even the way you decorate your personal work space—all send messages. Think about the message you want to send, and be sensitive to nonverbal channels of information.

Being a Good Listener

Effective communication is a two-way street. In addition to expressing yourself clearly, you must also be a good listener. We have already discussed good classroom listening habits (Introduction) and listening in counseling situations (Chapter 18). Here are some additional pointers that apply to work settings.

1. **Make an honest effort to pay attention.** Stop what you are doing, actively give the speaker your attention, and resist distractions. Communicate your interest by posture and body position. Make eye contact with the speaker to show your interest.

2. **Try to identify the speaker's purpose.** Is he or she informing, requesting, discussing, persuading, correcting, digressing, or entertaining? Listen for main themes rather than isolated facts. A good listener will be able to answer the question: What is this person's central message? Thus, as you listen, pretend that you will have to summarize the speaker's message for someone else.

3. **Suspend evaluation.** As you listen, try to keep an open mind. Avoid hasty judging, disagreeing, rejecting, or criticizing. There will be time later to think about what was said. After you have heard an entire message, evaluate the information it contains and decide how to use it. Then reply or take action.

4. **Check your understanding.** Let the other person talk, but occasionally acknowledge and confirm what she or he is

saying. Restate important parts of the message in your own words to make sure you understand it. Ask questions and clarify points you don't understand. Don't let doubts or ambiguities go unresolved.

5. **Pay attention to nonverbal messages.** Listeners must also be aware of the information provided by gestures, facial expressions, eye contact, touching, body positioning, and voice qualities such as volume, rate, pitch, emphasis, hesitations, and silences. Good listeners are also good observers.

6. **Accept responsibility for effective communication.** As a listener, it is up to you to actively search for meaning and value in what is said. You can facilitate communication as much by being a good listener as you can by being an effective speaker.

The art of effective communication is well worth cultivating. The points made here are basic, but they can go a long way toward ensuring your success at work—like, totally, abso-double-lutely, you know what I mean?

(Sources: Hartgrove-Freile, 1990; Hellriegel, Slocum, & Woodman, 1995; Jewell, 1989; Kleinke, 1986; Timm & Peterson, 1993.)

Focus: What have the problems of space travel taught us about living harmoniously on Earth?

The first long-term outpost in space is drawing nearer. By the year 2002, the United States, Canada, France, Japan, Russia, and other countries hope to orbit a continuously inhabited space station. Many engineering problems must be solved before the International Space Station becomes a reality (Guterl, 1997). Yet, the real challenge may lie in the psychological adjustments needed for life in space (Preiser, 1997; Suedfeld & Steel, 2000).

The Challenge of Living Aloft

Life in the "mini-world" of a space station won't be easy, physically or mentally. For months at a time, space station residents will be restricted to tiny living quarters with little privacy. Living aloft would be similar to spending several months among strangers in a small room from which you cannot escape. In addition to confinement, long-term space inhabitants will face other trying conditions. These include restricted movement, separation from loved ones, sensory monotony, noise, limited recreation, and other stresses (Suedfeld & Steel, 2000).

Space Habitats

Space psychologists study the many behavioral challenges that accompany space flight and life in restricted environments. Clearly, space habitats must be designed with human behavior in mind. What will it take to sustain emotional well-being and effi-

cient performance? To begin, the *social* environment on a space station must operate as smoothly as possible. For this reason, many problems can be avoided by carefully selecting and training future space residents *before* they go aloft. The qualities space psychologists look for include special abilities, self-reliance, sociability, emotional stability, and a sense of humor. To identify the best candidates, they use the same methods as I-O psychologists do: collecting biodata, interviewing, situational testing, and giving standardized psychological tests. Because group cooperation is so important in a confined living space, some national space programs emphasize selecting compatible groups of people rather than just individuals (Suedfeld & Steel, 2000).

It also would be wise to identify—and ease—stressors in space station living quarters. To this end, psychologists have studied people confined to submarines, missile silos, Antarctic stations, simulated space stations on Earth, and the like. Let's sample some expected problems and possible solutions.

GENERAL ENVIRONMENT   Space station design must take many human factors into account. For instance, researchers have learned that astronauts prefer rooms with clearly defined "up" and "down"—even in the weightlessness of space. This can be done by color-coding walls, floors, and ceilings and by orienting furniture and controls so they all face the "ceiling." Provision must be made for regular exercise and full-body showers. As trivial as it might seem, a lack of showers has been a major complaint among people in confinement experiments (Suedfeld & Steel, 2000).

Ideally there should be some flexibility in the use of living and work areas inside a space station. Behavior patterns change

Assembly of the International Space Station by space shuttle crews began in 1998. By 2002, the station should be permanently inhabited. It will provide the United States and its partners—Canada, Japan, and nine European nations—with a habitat in which men and women will live and work in space for extended periods of time. Solving the behavioral problems of living in space will be an important step toward human exploration of the solar system. (Art courtesy of NASA.)

over time, and being able to control one's environment helps lower stress. At the same time, people need stability. Psychologists have found, for instance, that eating becomes an important high point in monotonous environments. Eating at least one meal together each day can help keep crew members working as a social unit.

Sleep cycles must be carefully controlled in space to avoid disrupting bodily rhythms (Suedfeld & Steel, 2000). In past space missions, some astronauts found they couldn't sleep while other crew members continued to work and talk. Problems with sleep will be worsened by the constant noise on a space station. At first, such noise is annoying. After weeks or months, it can become a serious stressor. Researchers are experimenting with various earmuffs, eyeshades, and sleeping arrangements to alleviate such difficulties.

PRIVACY   Psychologists are helping engineers design space habitats so they meet human needs for privacy. However, privacy must be based mainly on temporarily blocking out visual and auditory contact with others. In the first permanent space station, there will be too little room for separate quarters.

Forced togetherness is stressful mainly because temporary retreat from others is difficult or impossible. Thus, control over the amount of group contact is more important than actually having a private room. Designers do recognize, however, the need to define private territories. It will be important to identify small areas that can be personalized and "owned" by each individual. Desks, lockers, and sleep stations could fill this need if they are not shared with others.

SENSORY RESTRICTION   Sensory monotony will be a problem in space, even with the magnificent vistas of Earth below. (How many times would you have to see the North American continent before you lost interest?)

Researchers are developing stimulus environments that will use music, videotapes, and other diversions to combat monotony and boredom. Again, they are trying to provide choice and control for space crews. Studies of confined living make it clear that one person's symphony is another's grating noise. Where music is concerned, individual earphones may be all that is required to avoid problems.

Most people in restricted environments find that they prefer noninteractive pastimes such as reading, listening to music, looking out windows, writing, and watching films or television. As much as anything, this preference may show again the need for privacy. Reading or listening to music is a good way to psychologically withdraw from the group. A variety of passive entertainment looks like a must for any space station. Russian astronauts, who make much use of music, have also reacted with delight to grab bags containing unexpected toys or novelties. Experiences with confining environments on Earth (such as Biosphere 2) suggest that including live animals and plants in space habitats could reduce stress and boredom (Suedfeld & Steel, 2000).

CULTURAL DIFFERENCES   The International Space Station will pose a special psychological challenge only hinted at in previ-

ous space missions. Astronauts from different cultures will live and work together for many months at a time. In previous space flights, crew members from different countries have reported occasional incidents of misunderstanding and interpersonal friction (Santy et al., 1993).

How important will such differences become when time aloft stretches beyond 6 months? Most likely, they will be magnified. For instance, Japanese astronauts felt that Americans paid too much attention to hair care and personal grooming. Americans, in turn, were surprised by the Japanese indifference to tooth brushing. Likewise, European astronauts felt that Americans did not appreciate the ritual of eating. For their part, Americans were troubled by the fuss European astronauts made over food (Preiser, 1997).

Food itself may be a problem. Norm Thagard, who spent time aboard the Russian space station *Mir,* gagged on canned, jellied fish, a major part of the Russian diet in space. Russians, in contrast, are repulsed by steamed green beans, buttered carrots, and other plain vegetables, all typical foods on American space missions (Preiser, 1997).

Clearly, long-term space inhabitants could benefit from training in cultural awareness. Beyond that, one saving grace is that crew members will have common backgrounds in aviation and space flight. Such similarities may, in fact, create a shared "space culture" capable of bridging national differences.

SOCIAL ISOLATION   Separation from family, friends, and one's home community will be a major source of stress. However, the ability to talk regularly with family via two-way televised meetings, satellite phones, and the Internet should help ease feelings of social isolation (Suedfeld & Steel, 2000). Emotional problems could also be prevented by allowing crew members to talk with a psychological support group on Earth. In short, the best antidote for social isolation will probably be abundant opportunities to communicate with associates and loved ones back home (Kelly & Kanas, 1993).

CONFLICT RESOLUTION AND MENTAL HEALTH   Many studies of long-term isolation show steady declines in motivation. Most inhabitants intend to use their free time for creative pursuits. In reality, they end up marking time and may become apathetic. Judging from submarine missions and Antarctic bases, as many as 5 percent of space inhabitants might experience some psychological disturbance. Most often, the problem will be depression. However, in rare instances people have become paranoid, psychotic, suicidal, or uncontrollably aggressive. After many months in close quarters, the way another person chews his or her food can become a major source of irritation. As stated earlier, the risk of such problems can be minimized by carefully selecting personnel. Even so, it will be important to teach crew members basic counseling skills for solving conflicts. Effective leaders, in particular, will need to be sensitive to

Space psychology *Study of the behavioral dimensions of space flight and life in restricted environments.*

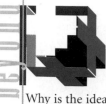

crew members' feelings and able to maintain group harmony and cohesion (Nicholas & Penwell, 1995).

Life on Spaceship Earth

Why is the idea of living in space so fascinating? Perhaps it is because human strengths and weaknesses are magnified in the miniature world of a space station. As psychologist Yvonne Clearwater (1985) says:

> The space station represents the first glimmerings of recognition that some of the toughest challenges in space—as on Earth—concern human behavior, not technology. . . . Ironically, the farther we go from Earth and the longer we stay away, the more we will need to know about ourselves. Scientists working on the space effort believe that psychological factors will become increasingly important for the success or failure of future space missions.

In fact, plans are now being made to expand psychological testing and preparation for NASA's new "expedition" astronauts—those who will live on the space station or go to bases on the moon and Mars (Suedfeld & Steel, 2000).

It is curiously fitting that the dazzling technology of space travel has highlighted the inevitable importance of human be-

havior. Here on Earth, as in space, we cannot count on technology alone to solve problems. The threat of nuclear war, social conflict, crime, prejudice, infectious disease, overpopulation, environmental damage, famine, homicide, economic disaster—these and most other major problems facing us are behavioral (Kirk & Picard, in press).

Will spaceship Earth endure? It's a psychological question.

CONCLUSION: Work, leisure, family, community, and environment all contribute to the quality of our lives. And as we have seen throughout this text, psychology has much to offer in each of these areas. It is my sincere hope that you have found enough relevance and value in this book to kindle a lifelong interest in psychology. Psychology's future looks exciting. What role will it play in your life?

KNOWLEDGE BUILDER

SPACE PSYCHOLOGY

RELATE

Imagine that you have agreed to sail across the Atlantic in a small boat with five other people. What potential problems does space psychology suggest you should be aware of?

LEARNING CHECK

1. Depression is the most common major psychological disturbance that occurs during prolonged isolation in confined living conditions. T or F?

2. Researchers have learned that astronauts don't really care if living quarters have clearly defined "up" and "down" orientations. T or F?

3. Research shows that needs for privacy can be met by providing ways to temporarily withdraw from social contact with a group, even when physical withdrawal is impossible. T or F?

4. Most people in restricted environments prefer group pastimes, such as playing card games, skits, or group singing. T or F?

CRITICAL THINKING

5. On a spacecraft, how would blocking visual and auditory contact with others affect crowding?

Answers:

1. T 2. F 3. T 4. F 5. While density would remain high, the sense of crowding would be reduced because crew members would feel that they have some control over their immediate social environment.

APPENDIX IN REVIEW

How is psychology applied in business and industry?

- Applied psychology refers to the use of psychological principles and research methods to solve practical problems.
- Industrial-organizational psychologists are interested in the problems people face at work and in organizations. Typically, they specialize in personnel psychology and human relations at work.
- Personnel psychologists try to match people with jobs by combining job analysis with a variety of selection procedures. These include gathering biodata, interviewing, giving standardized psychological tests (interest inventories, aptitude tests, and computerized tests), and using assessment centers.
- Two basic approaches to business and industrial management are scientific management (Theory X) and human relations approaches (Theory Y). Theory X is most concerned with work efficiency, whereas Theory Y emphasizes psychological efficiency.
- Theory Y methods include participative management, management by objectives, self-managed teams, and quality circles.
- Job satisfaction is related to productivity, absenteeism, morale, employee turnover, and other factors that affect overall business efficiency.
- Job satisfaction comes from a good fit between work and a person's interests, abilities, needs, and expectations. Job enrichment tends to increase job satisfaction.
- An active, vigilant coping style is most likely to produce good career decisions.

What have psychologists learned about the effects of our physical and social environments?

- Environmental psychologists are interested in the effects of behavioral settings, physical or social environments, and human territoriality, among many other topics.
- Overpopulation is a major world problem, often reflected at an individual level in crowding.
- Animal experiments indicate that excessive crowding can be unhealthy. However, human research shows that psychological feelings of crowding do not always correspond to density (the number of people in a given space).
- One major consequence of crowding is attentional overload.
- A large number of practical problems—from noise pollution to architectural design—have come under the scrutiny of environmental psychologists. In many cases, effective behavioral solutions to such problems have been found, often as a result of first doing a careful environmental assessment.
- Research has shown that various psychological strategies can promote recycling.

How has psychology improved education?

- Educational psychologists seek to understand how people learn and teachers instruct. They are particularly interested in teaching strategies and in teaching styles, such as direct instruction and open teaching.

What does psychology reveal about juries and court verdicts?

- The psychology of law includes studies of courtroom behavior and other topics that pertain to the legal system. Psychologists also serve various consulting and counseling roles in legal, law enforcement, and criminal justice settings.
- Studies of mock juries show that jury decisions are often far from objective.
- Scientific jury selection is used in attempts to choose jurors who have particular characteristics. In some instances, this may result in juries that have a particular bias or that do not represent the community as a whole.
- A bias toward convicting defendants is characteristic of many death-qualified juries.

Can psychology enhance athletic performance?

- Sports psychologists seek to enhance sports performance and the benefits of sports participation. A careful task analysis of sports skills is one of the major tools for improving coaching and performance.
- A motor skill is a nonverbal response chain assembled into a smooth performance. Motor skills are guided by internal mental models called motor programs.
- Motor skills are refined through direct practice, but mental practice can also contribute to improvement.
- During moments of peak performance, physical, mental, and emotional states are optimal.

What can be done to improve communication at work?

- State your message clearly and precisely. Try to avoid overuse of obscure vocabulary, jargon, slang, and loaded words. Learn and use people's names. Be polite, but not servile. Be expressive when you speak. Pay attention to nonverbal cues and the messages they send.
- To be a good listener, actively pay attention, identify the speaker's purpose and core message, suspend evaluation while listening, check your understanding, and make note of nonverbal information.

How is psychology being applied in space missions?

- Space psychologists study the many behavioral challenges that accompany space flight and life in restricted environments.
- Space habitats must be designed with special attention to environmental stressors, privacy, social isolation, conflict resolution, and the maintenance of mental health.

PSYCHOLOGY ON THE NET

- **Living in Space** Articles about the challenges of living in space. http://www.tv.cbc.ca/national/pgminfo/space/livingspace.html
- **Mars Academy** A discussion of crew selection issues for possible trips to Mars. http://www.marsacademy.com/text/crew.htm

- **Newsletter for Educational Psychologists** Information and articles about the activities of educational psychologists. http://www.apa.org/divisions/div15/
- **Environmental Psychology** From the Canadian Psychological Association; features articles on environmental psychology, with links to other sites. http://home.uleth.ca/%7Esandilands/sec7default1.html
- **Sport Psychology** Articles, information, and links related to sports psychology. http://www.cop.es/docs_web/otros/sport.htm

- **The Industrial-Organizational Psychologist** Online journal concerning I-O psychology. http://www.siop.org/tip/TIP.html
  - **InfoTrac® College Edition** For recent articles related to the application of psychology to athletics, use Key Words search for: SPORTS PSYCHOLOGY.

INTERACTIVE LEARNING

- **PsychNow!** 8f. Environmental psychology.

Behavioral Statistics

Survey

Theme: *Statistics allow us to summarize the results of psychological studies and draw valid conclusions about behavior.*

▼**KEY QUESTIONS**

●*KEY TOPICS*

▼What are descriptive statistics?

● *Summarizing the results of psychological studies*
● *Graphs and distributions*

▼ How are statistics used to identify an average score?

● *Measures of central tendency*
● *The mean, median, and mode*

▼ What statistics do psychologists use to measure how much scores differ from one another?

● *Measures of variability*
● *The range, standard deviation, and z-scores*
● *The normal curve*

▼**KEY QUESTIONS**

●*KEY TOPICS*

▼ What are inferential statistics?

● *Making generalizations and drawing conclusions*
● *Samples and populations*
● *Statistical significance*

▼ How are correlations used in psychology?

● *Scatter diagrams and correlations*
● *Positive and negative relationships*
● *Correlation and causation*

STATISTICS FROM "HEADS" TO "TAILS"

L ET'S SAY A FRIEND OF YOURS *invites you to try your hand at a "game of chance." He offers to flip a coin and pay you a dollar if the coin comes up heads. If the coin shows tails, you must pay him a dollar. He flips the coin: tails—you pay him a dollar. He flips it again: tails. Again: tails. And again: tails. And again: tails.*

At this point you are faced with a choice. Should you continue the game in an attempt to recoup your losses? Or should you assume that the coin is biased and quit before you really get "skinned"? Taking out a pocket calculator (and the statistics book you carry with you at all times), you compute the odds of obtaining 5 tails in a row from an unbiased coin. The probability is 0.031 (roughly 3 times out of 100).

If the coin really is honest, 5 consecutive tails is a rare event. Wisely, you decide that the coin is probably biased and refuse to play again. (Unless, of course, your "friend" is willing to take "tails" for the next 5 tosses!)

Perhaps a decision could have been made in this hypothetical example without using statistics. But notice how much clearer the situation becomes when it is expressed statistically.

Psychologists try to extract and summarize useful information from the observations they make. To do so, they use two major types of statistics. **Descriptive statistics,** *summarize or "boil down" numbers so that they become more meaningful and easier to communicate to others. In comparison,* **inferential statistics,** *are used for decision making, for generalizing from small samples and for drawing conclusions. As was the case in the coin-flipping example, psy-chologists must often base decisions on limited data. Such decisions are much easier to make with the help of inferential statistics. Let's see how statistics are used in psychology.*

Gateways to Behavioral Statistics

THE RESULTS OF PSYCHOLOGICAL STUDIES are often expressed as numbers, which must be summarized and interpreted before they have any meaning.

SUMMARIZING NUMBERS VISUALLY, by using various types of graphs, makes it easier to see trends and patterns in the results of psychological investigations.

WE USUALLY WANT TO KNOW THE "AVERAGE" of a group of scores as well as how much they vary.

MANY PSYCHOLOGICAL MEASURES PRODUCE SCORES that form a normal curve. This is useful because the characteristics of normal curves are well known.

SOME STATISTICAL TECHNIQUES can be used to generalize results from samples to populations, to draw conclusions, and to tell if the results of a study could have occurred by chance.

WHEN THERE IS A CORRELATION, or consistent relationship, between scores on two measures, knowing a person's score on one measure allows us to predict his or her score on the second measure.

DESCRIPTIVE STATISTICS

Statistics bring greater clarity and precision to psychological thought and research. To see how, let's begin by considering three basic types of descriptive statistics: *graphical statistics,* measures of *central tendency,* and measures of *variability.* Let's start with **graphical statistics,** *which present numbers pictorially, so they are easier to visualize.*

GRAPHICAL STATISTICS ◆Table B.1 shows simulated scores on a test of hypnotic susceptibility given to 100 college students. With such disorganized data, it is hard to form an overall picture of the differences in hypnotic susceptibility. But by using a *frequency distribution,* large amounts of information can be neatly organized and summarized. A **frequency distribution** is made by breaking down the entire range of possible scores into classes of equal size. Next, the number of scores falling into each

◆ **TABLE B.1** Raw Scores of Hypnotic Susceptibility

55	86	52	17	61	57	84	51	16	64
22	56	25	38	35	24	54	26	37	38
52	42	59	26	21	55	40	59	25	57
91	27	38	53	19	93	25	39	52	56
66	14	18	63	59	68	12	19	62	45
47	98	88	72	50	49	96	89	71	66
50	44	71	57	90	53	41	72	56	93
57	38	55	49	87	59	36	56	48	70
33	69	50	50	60	35	67	51	50	52
11	73	46	16	67	13	71	47	25	77

◆ TABLE B.2 Frequency Distribution of Hypnotic Susceptibility Scores	
CLASS INTERVAL	NUMBER OF PERSONS IN CLASS
0–19	10
20–39	20
40–59	40
60–79	20
80–99	10

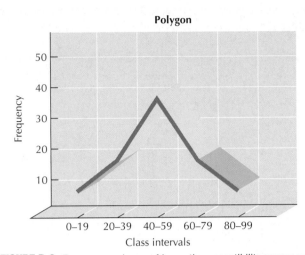

Polygon

❖ **FIGURE B.2** *Frequency polygon of hypnotic susceptibility scores contained in Table B.2.*

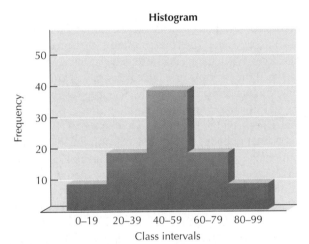

Histogram

❖ **FIGURE B.1** *Frequency histogram of hypnotic susceptibility scores contained in Table B.2.*

class is recorded. In ◆Table B.2, the raw data from ◆Table B.1 have been condensed into a frequency distribution. Notice how much clearer the pattern of scores for the entire group becomes.

Frequency distributions are often shown *graphically* to make them more "visual." A **histogram,** or graph of a frequency distribution, is made by labeling class intervals on the *abscissa* (horizontal line) and frequencies (the number of scores in each class) on the *ordinate* (vertical line). Next, bars are drawn for each class interval; the height of each bar is determined by the number of scores in each class (❖Fig. B.1). An alternate way of graphing scores is the more familiar **frequency polygon** (❖Fig. B.2). Here, points are placed at the center of each class interval to indicate the number of scores. Then the dots are connected by straight lines.

MEASURES OF CENTRAL TENDENCY   Notice in ◆Table B.2 that more scores fall in the range 40–59 than elsewhere. How can we show this fact? A measure of **central tendency** is simply a number describing a "typical score" around which other scores fall. A familiar measure of central tendency is the mean, or "average." But as we shall see in a moment, there are other types of "averages" that can be used. To illustrate each, we need an example: ◆Table B.3 shows the raw data for an imaginary experiment in which two groups of subjects were given a test of

memory. Assume that one group was given a drug that might improve memory (let's call the drug Rememberine). The second group received a placebo. Is there a difference in memory scores between the two groups? It's difficult to tell without computing an average.

As one type of "average," the **mean** is calculated by adding all the scores for each group and then dividing by the total number of scores. Notice in ◆Table B.3 that the means reveal a difference between the two groups.

The mean is sensitive to extremely high or low scores in a distribution. For this reason, it is not always the best measure of central tendency. (Imagine how distorted it would be to calculate average yearly incomes from a small sample of people that happened to include a multimillionaire.) In such cases, the middle score in a group of scores—called the *median*—is used instead.

The **median** is found by arranging scores from the highest to the lowest and selecting the score that falls in the middle. In

Descriptive statistics *Mathematical tools used to describe and summarize numeric data.*
Inferential statistics *Mathematical tools used for decision making, for generalizing from small samples, and for drawing conclusions.*
Graphical statistics *Techniques for presenting numbers pictorially, often by plotting them on a graph.*
Frequency distribution *A table that divides an entire range of scores into a series of classes and then records the number of scores that fall into each class.*
Histogram *A graph of a frequency distribution in which the number of scores falling in each class is represented by vertical bars.*
Frequency polygon *A graph of a frequency distribution in which the number of scores falling in each class is represented by points on a line.*
Central tendency *The tendency for a majority of scores to fall in the midrange of possible values.*
Mean *A measure of central tendency calculated by adding a group of scores and then dividing by the total number of scores.*
Median *A measure of central tendency found by arranging scores from the highest to the lowest and selecting the score that falls in the middle. That is, half the values in a group of scores fall above the median and half fall below.*

◆ TABLE B.3 Raw Scores on a Memory Test for Subjects Taking Rememberine or a Placebo

SUBJECT	GROUP 1 REMEMBERINE	GROUP 2 PLACEBO
1	65	54
2	67	60
3	73	63
4	65	33
5	58	56
6	55	60
7	70	60
8	69	31
9	60	62
10	68	61
Sum	650	540
Mean	65	54
Median	66	60

$$\text{Mean} = \frac{\Sigma X}{N} \text{ or } \frac{\text{Sum of all scores, } X}{\text{number of scores}}$$

$$\text{Mean Group 1} = \frac{65 + 67 + 73 + 65 + 58 + 55 + 70 + 69 + 60 + 68}{10}$$

$$= \frac{650}{10} = 65$$

$$\text{Mean Group 2} = \frac{54 + 60 + 63 + 33 + 56 + 60 + 60 + 31 + 62 + 61}{10}$$

$$= \frac{540}{10} = 54$$

Median = the middle score or the mean of the two middle scores*

Median Group 1 = 55 58 60 65 [65 67] 68 69 70 73

$$= \frac{65 + 67}{2} = 66$$

Median Group 2 = 31 33 54 56 [60 60] 60 61 62 63

$$= \frac{60 + 60}{2} = 60$$

* ☐ indicates middle score(s).

other words, half the values in a group of scores fall below the median and half fall above. Consider, for example, the following weights obtained from a small class of college students: 105, 111, 123, 126, 148, 151, 154, 162, 182. The median for the group is 148, the middle score. Of course, if there is an even number of scores, there will be no "middle score." This problem is handled by averaging the two scores that share the middle spot. This procedure yields a single number to serve as the median (see bottom panel of ◆Table B.3).

A final measure of central tendency is the *mode.* The **mode** is simply the most frequently occurring score in a group of scores. If you were to take the time to count the scores in ◆Table B.3, you would find that the mode of Group l is 65, and

the mode of Group 2 is 60. The mode is usually easy to obtain. However, the mode can be an unreliable measure, especially in a small group of scores. The mode's advantage is that it gives the score actually obtained by the greatest number of people.

MEASURES OF VARIABILITY Let's say a researcher discovers two drugs that lower anxiety in agitated patients. However, let's also assume that one drug consistently lowers anxiety by moderate amounts, whereas the second sometimes lowers it by large amounts, sometimes has no effect, or sometimes may even increase anxiety in some patients. Overall, there is no difference in the *average* (mean) amount of anxiety reduction. Even so, an important difference exists between the two drugs. As this example shows, it is not enough to simply know the average score in a distribution. Usually, we would also like to know if scores are grouped closely together or scattered widely.

Measures of **variability** provide a single number that tells how "spread out" scores are. When the scores are widely spread, this number gets larger. When they are close together, it gets smaller. If you look again at the example in ◆Table B.3, you will notice that the scores within each group vary widely. How can we show this fact?

The simplest way would be to use the **range,** which is the difference between the highest and lowest scores. In Group 1 of our experiment, the highest score is 73, and the lowest is 55; thus, the range is 18 (73 − 55 = 18). In Group 2, the highest score is 63, and the lowest is 31; this makes the range 32. Scores in Group 2 are more spread out than those in Group 1.

A better measure of variability is the **standard deviation** (an index of how much a typical score differs from the mean of a group of scores). To obtain the standard deviation, we find the deviation (or difference) of each score from the mean and then square it (multiply it by itself). These squared deviations are then added and averaged (the total is divided by the number of deviations). Taking the square root of this average yields the standard deviation (◆Table B.4). Notice again that the variability for Group 1 (5.4) is smaller than that for Group 2 (where the standard deviation is 11.3).

STANDARD SCORES A particular advantage of the standard deviation is that it can be used to "standardize" scores in a way that gives them greater meaning. For example, John and Susan both took psychology midterms, but in different classes. John earned a score of 118, and Susan scored 110. Who did better? It is impossible to tell without knowing what the average score was on each test, and whether John and Susan scored at the top, middle, or bottom of their classes. We would like to have one number that gives all this information. A number that does this is the *z-score.*

To convert an original score to a **z-score,** we subtract the mean from the score. The resulting number is then divided by the standard deviation for that group of scores. To illustrate, Susan had a score of 110 in a class with a mean of 100 and a standard deviation of 10. Therefore, her z-score is +1.0 (◆Table B.5). John's score of 118 came from a class having a mean of 100 and a standard deviation of 18; thus his z-score is also +1.0 (see ◆Table B.5). Originally, it looked as if John did better on his

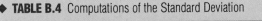

◆ TABLE B.4 Computations of the Standard Deviation

		GROUP 1 MEAN = 65	
SCORE MEAN		DEVIATION (d)	DEVIATION SQUARED (d²)
65 − 65 =		0	0
67 − 65 =		2	4
73 − 65 =		8	64
65 − 65 =		0	0
58 − 65 =		−7	49
55 − 65 =		−10	100
70 − 65 =		5	25
69 − 65 =		4	16
60 − 65 =		−5	25
68 − 65 =		3	9
			292

$$SD = \sqrt{\frac{\text{sum of } d^2}{n}} = \sqrt{\frac{292}{10}} = \sqrt{29.2} = 5.4$$

		GROUP 1 MEAN = 54	
SCORE MEAN		DEVIATION (d)	DEVIATION SQUARED (d²)
54 − 54 =		0	0
60 − 54 =		6	36
63 − 54 =		9	81
33 − 54 =		−21	441
56 − 54 =		2	4
60 − 54 =		6	36
60 − 54 =		6	36
31 − 54 =		−23	529
62 − 54 =		8	64
61 − 54 =		7	49
			1276

$$SD = \sqrt{\frac{\text{sum of } d^2}{n}} = \sqrt{\frac{1276}{10}} = \sqrt{127.6} = 11.3$$

◆ TABLE B.5 Computation of a z-Score

$$z = \frac{X - \bar{X}}{SD} = \text{ or } \frac{\text{score} - \text{mean}}{\text{standard deviation}}$$

$$\text{Susan: } z = \frac{110 - 100}{10} = \frac{+10}{10} = +1.0$$

$$\text{John: } z = \frac{118 - 100}{18} = \frac{+18}{18} = +1.0$$

midterm than Susan did. But we now see that, relatively speaking, their scores were equivalent. Compared to other students, each was an equal distance above average.

THE NORMAL CURVE

When chance events are recorded, we find that some outcomes have a high probability and occur very often; others

have a low probability and occur infrequently; still others have little probability and occur rarely. As a result, the distribution (or tally) of chance events typically resembles a *normal curve* (❖Fig. B.3). A **normal curve** is bell-shaped, with a large number of scores in the middle, tapering to very few extremely high and low scores. Most psychological traits or events are determined by the action of a large number of factors. Therefore, like chance events, measures of psychological variables tend to roughly match a normal curve. For example, direct measurement has shown such characteristics as height, memory span, and intelligence to be distributed approximately along a normal curve. In other words, many people have average height, memory ability, and intelligence. However, as we move above or below average, fewer and fewer people are found.

It is very fortunate that so many psychological variables tend to form a normal curve, because much is known about the curve. One valuable property concerns the relationship between the standard deviation and the normal curve. Specifically, the standard deviation measures offset proportions of the curve above and below the mean. For example, in ❖Figure B.4, notice that roughly 68 percent of all cases (IQ scores, memory scores, heights, or whatever) fall between one standard deviation above and below the mean (± 1 SD), 95 percent of all cases fall between ± 2 SD, and 99 percent of the cases can be found between ± 3 SD from the mean.

◆Table B.6 gives a more complete account of the relationship between z-scores and the percentage of cases found in a particular area of the normal curve. Notice, for example, that 93.3 percent of all cases fall below a z-score of +1.5. A z-score of 1.5 on a test (no matter what the original, or "raw," score was) would be a good performance, because roughly 93 percent of all scores fall below this mark. Relationships between the standard deviation (or z-scores) and the normal curve do not change. This makes it possible to compare various tests or groups of scores if they come from distributions that are approximately normal.

Mode *A measure of central tendency found by identifying the most frequently occurring score in a group of scores.*
Variability *The tendency for a group of scores to differ in value. Measures of variability indicate the degree to which a group of scores differ from one another.*
Range *The difference between the highest and lowest scores in a group of scores.*
Descriptive statistics *Mathematical tools used to describe and summarize numeric data.*
Inferential statistics *Mathematical tools used for decision making, for generalizing from small samples, and for drawing conclusions.*
Graphical statistics *Techniques for presenting numbers pictorially, often by plotting them on a graph.*
Standard deviation *An index of how much a typical score differs from the mean of a group of scores.*
z-score *A number that tells how many standard deviations above or below the mean a score is.*
Normal curve *A bell-shaped distribution, with a large number of scores in the middle, tapering to very few extremely high and low scores.*

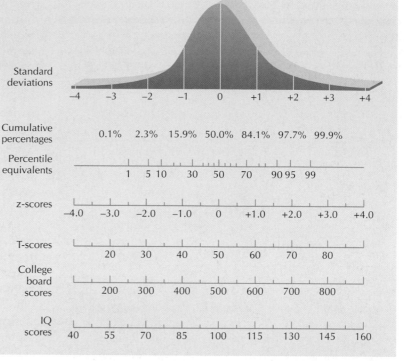

❖ **FIGURE B.3** *The normal curve. The normal curve is an idealized mathematical model. However, many measurements in psychology closely approximate a normal curve. The scales you see here show the relationship of standard deviations, z-scores, and other measures to the curve.*

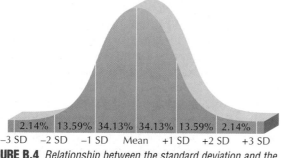

❖ **FIGURE B.4** *Relationship between the standard deviation and the normal curve.*

◆ **TABLE B.6** Area Under the Normal Curve as a Percentage of Total Area for a Variety of z-Scores

Z-SCORE	PERCENTAGE OF AREA TO THE LEFT OF THIS VALUE	PERCENTAGE OF AREA TO THE RIGHT OF THIS VALUE
−3.0 SD	00.1	99.9
−2.5 SD	00.6	99.4
−2.0 SD	02.3	97.7
−1.5 SD	06.7	93.3
−1.0 SD	15.9	84.1
−0.5 SD	30.9	69.1
0.0 SD	50.0	50.0
+0.5 SD	69.1	30.9
+1.0 SD	84.1	15.9
+1.5 SD	93.3	06.7
+2.0 SD	97.7	02.3
+2.5 SD	99.4	00.6
+3.0 SD	99.9	00.1

KNOWLEDGE BUILDER

LEARNING CHECK

1. _____ statistics summarize numbers so they become more meaningful or easier to communicate; _____ statistics are used for decision making, generalizing, or drawing conclusions.

2. Histograms and frequency polygons are graphs of frequency distributions. T or F?

3. Three measures of central tendency are the mean, the median, and the _____.

4. If scores are placed in order, from the smallest to the largest, the median is defined as the middle score. T or F?

5. As a measure of variability, the standard deviation is defined as the difference between the highest and lowest scores. T or F?

6. A z-score of −1 tells us that a score fell one standard deviation below the mean in a group of scores. T or F?

7. In a normal curve, 99 percent of all scores can be found between +1 and −1 standard deviations from the mean. T or F?

Answers:

1. Descriptive, inferential 2. T 3. mode 4. T 5. F 6. T 7. F

INFERENTIAL STATISTICS

Let's say that a researcher studies the effects of a new therapy on a small group of depressed individuals. Is she or he interested only in these particular individuals? Usually not. Except in rare instances, psychologists seek to discover general laws of behavior that apply widely to humans and animals. Undoubtedly, the researcher would like to know if the therapy holds any promise for all depressed people. As stated earlier, inferential statistics *are techniques that allow us to make inferences.* That is, they allow us to generalize from the behavior of small groups of subjects to that of the larger groups they represent.

SAMPLES AND POPULATIONS   In any scientific study, we would like to observe the entire set, or **population,** of subjects, objects, or events of interest. However, this is usually impossible or impractical. Observing all Catholics, all cancer patients, or all mothers-in-law could be both impractical (in that all are large populations) and impossible (in that people change denominations, may be unaware that they have cancer, and change their status as relatives). In such cases, **samples** *(smaller cross-sections of a population)* are selected, and observations of the sample are used to draw conclusions about the entire population.

For any sample to be meaningful, it must be **representative.** That is, the sample group must truly reflect the membership and characteristics of the larger population. In our earlier hypothetical study of a memory drug, it would be essential for the sample of 20 people to be representative of the general population. A very important aspect of representative samples is that their members are chosen at **random.** In other words, each member of the population must have an equal chance of being included in the sample.

SIGNIFICANT DIFFERENCES   In our imaginary drug experiment, we found that the average memory score was higher for the group given the drug than it was for people who didn't take the drug (the placebo group). Certainly, this result is interesting, but could it have occurred by chance? If two groups were repeatedly tested (with neither receiving any drug), their average memory scores would sometimes differ. How much must two means differ before we can consider the difference "real" (not due to chance)?

Notice that the question is similar to one discussed earlier: How many tails in a row must we obtain when flipping a coin before we can conclude that the coin is biased? In the case of the coin, we noted that obtaining five tails in a row is a rare event. Thus, it became reasonable to assume that the coin was biased. Of course, it is possible to get five tails in a row when flipping an honest coin. But because this outcome is unlikely, we have good reason to suspect that something other than chance (a loaded coin, for instance) caused the results. Similar reasoning is used in tests of statistical significance.

Tests of **statistical significance** provide an estimate of how often experimental results could have occurred by chance alone. The results of a significance test are stated as a probability. This probability gives the odds that the observed difference was due to chance. In psychology, any experimental result that could have occurred by chance 5 times (or less) out of 100 (in other words, a probability of .05 or less) is considered *significant.* In our memory experiment, the probability is .025 ($p = .025$) that the group means would differ as they do by chance

alone. This allows us to conclude with reasonable certainty that the drug actually did improve memory scores.

CORRELATION

Many of the statements that psychologists make about behavior do not result from the use of experimental methods. Rather, they come from keen observations and measures of existing phenomena. A psychologist might note, for example, that the higher a couple's socioeconomic and educational status, the smaller the number of children they are likely to have. Or that grades in high school are related to how well a person is likely to do in college. Or even that as rainfall levels increase within a given metropolitan area, crime rates decline. In these instances, we are dealing with the fact that two variables are **correlating** (varying together in some orderly fashion).

The simplest way of visualizing a correlation is to construct a **scatter diagram.** In a scatter diagram, two measures (grades in high school and grades in college, for instance) are obtained. One measure is indicated by the X axis and the second by the Y axis. The scatter diagram plots the intersection (crossing) of each pair of measurements as a single point. Many such measurement pairs give pictures like those shown in ❖Figure B.5.

❖Figure B.5 also shows scatter diagrams of three basic kinds of relationships between variables (or measures). Graphs A, B, and C show *positive relationships* of varying strength. As you can see, in a **positive relationship,** increases in the X measure (or score) are matched by increases on the Y measure (or score). An example would be finding that higher IQ scores (X) are associated with higher college grades (Y). A **zero correlation** suggests that no relationship exists between two measures (see graph D). This might be the result of comparing subjects' hat sizes (X) to their college grades (Y). Graphs E and F both show a **negative relationship** (or correlation). Notice that as

Population *An entire group of animals, people, or objects belonging to a particular category (for example, all college students or all married women).*

Sample *A smaller subpart of a population.*

Representative sample *A small, randomly selected part of a larger population that accurately reflects characteristics of the whole population.*

Random selection *Choosing a sample so that each member of the population has an equal chance of being included in the sample.*

Statistical significance *The degree to which an event (such as the results of an experiment) is unlikely to have occurred by chance alone.*

Correlation *The existence of a consistent, systematic relationship between two events, measures, or variables.*

Scatter diagram *A graph that plots the intersection of paired measures; that is, the points at which paired X and Y measures cross.*

Positive relationship *A mathematical relationship in which increases in one measure are matched by increases in the other (or decreases correspond with decreases).*

Zero correlation *The absence of a (linear) mathematical relationship between two measures.*

Negative relationship *A mathematical relationship in which increases in one measure are matched by decreases in the other.*

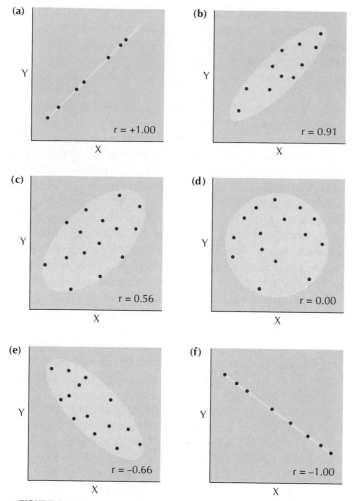

❖ **FIGURE B.5** *Scatter diagrams showing various degrees of relationship for a positive, zero, and negative correlation. (Adapted from Pagano, 1981.)*

values of one measure increase, those of the second become smaller. An example might be the relationship between amount of alcohol consumed and scores on a test of coordination: Higher alcohol levels are correlated with lower coordination scores.

The strength of a correlation can also be expressed as a **coefficient of correlation.** This coefficient is simply a number falling somewhere between +1.00 and −1.00. If the number is zero or close to zero, it indicates a weak or nonexistent relationship. If the *correlation is* + 1.00, a **perfect positive relationship** exists; if the correlation is −1.00, a **perfect negative relationship** has been discovered. The most commonly used correlation coefficient is called the Pearson *r.* Calculation of the Pearson *r* is relatively simple, as shown in ◆Table B.7. (The numbers shown are hypothetical.)

As stated in Chapter 2, correlations in psychology are rarely perfect. Most fall somewhere between zero and plus or minus 1. The closer the correlation coefficient is to +1.00 or −1.00, the stronger the relationship. An interesting example of some typical correlations is provided by a study that compared the IQs of adopted children with the IQs of their biological moth-

ers. At age 4, the children's IQs correlated .28 with their mothers' IQs. By age 7, the correlation was .35. And by age 13, it had grown to .38.

Correlations often provide highly useful information. For instance, it is valuable to know that there is a correlation between cigarette smoking and lung cancer rates. Another example is the fact that higher consumption of alcohol during pregnancy is correlated with lower birth weight and a higher rate of birth defects. There is a correlation between the number of recent life stresses experienced and the likelihood of emotional disturbance. Many more examples could be cited, but the point is that correlations help us to identify relationships that are worth knowing.

Correlations are particularly valuable for making *predictions.* If we know that two measures are correlated, and we know a person's score on one measure, we can predict his or her score on the other. For example, most colleges have formulas that use multiple correlations to decide which applicants have the best chances for success. Usually the formula includes such predictors as high school GPA, teacher ratings, extracurricular activities, and scores on the *Scholastic Assessment Test* (SAT) or some similar test. Although no single predictor is perfectly correlated with success in college, together the various predictors correlate highly and provide a useful technique for screening applicants.

There is an interesting "trick" you can do with correlations that you may find useful. It works like this: If you *square* the correlation coefficient (multiply *r* by itself), you will get a number telling the **percent of variance** (amount of variation in scores) accounted for by the correlation. For example, the correlation between IQ scores and college grade point average is .5. Multiplying .5 times .5 gives .25, or 25 percent. This means that 25 percent of the variation in college grades is accounted for by knowing IQ scores. In other words, with a correlation of .5, college grades are "squeezed" into an oval like the one shown in graph C, ❖Figure B.5. IQ scores take away some of the possible variation in corresponding grade point averages. If there were no correlation between IQ and grades, grades would be completely free to vary, as shown in ❖Figure B.5, graph D.

Along the same line, a correlation of +1.00 or −1.00 means that 100 percent of the variation in the Y measure is accounted for by knowing the X measure: If you know a person's X score, you can tell exactly what the Y score is. An example that comes close to this state of affairs is the high correlation (.86) between the IQs of identical twins. In any group of identical twins, 74 percent of the variation in the "Y" twins' IQs is accounted for by knowing the IQs of their siblings (the "X's").

CORRELATION AND CAUSATION   It is very important to recognize that finding a correlation between two measures does not automatically mean that one causes the other: *Correlation does not demonstrate* **causation.** When a correlation exists, the best we can say is that two variables are related. Of course, this does not mean that it is impossible for two correlated variables to have a cause-and-effect relationship. Rather, it means that we

STUDENT NO.	IQ X	GRADE POINT AVERAGE Y	X SCORE SQUARED X^2	Y SCORE SQUARED Y^2	X TIMES Y XY
1	110	1.0	12,100	1.00	110.0
2	112	1.6	12,544	2.56	179.2
3	118	1.2	13,924	1.44	141.6
4	119	2.1	14,161	4.41	249.9
5	122	2.6	14,884	6.76	317.2
6	125	1.8	15,625	3.24	225.0
7	127	2.6	16,124	6.76	330.2
8	130	2.0	16,900	4.00	260.0
9	132	3.2	17,424	10.24	422.4
10	134	2.6	17,956	6.76	348.4
11	136	3.0	18,496	9.00	408.0
12	138	3.6	19,044	12.96	496.8
Total	1503	27.3	189,187	69.13	3488.7

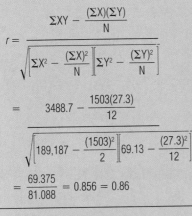

$$r = \frac{\Sigma XY - \frac{(\Sigma X)(\Sigma Y)}{N}}{\sqrt{\left[\Sigma X^2 - \frac{(\Sigma X)^2}{N}\right]\left[\Sigma Y^2 - \frac{(\Sigma Y)^2}{N}\right]}}$$

$$= \frac{3488.7 - \frac{1503(27.3)}{12}}{\sqrt{\left[189,187 - \frac{(1503)^2}{2}\right]\left[69.13 - \frac{(27.3)^2}{12}\right]}}$$

$$= \frac{69.375}{81.088} = 0.856 = 0.86$$

Adapted from Pagano, 1981.

cannot *conclude*, solely on the basis of correlation, that a causal link exists. To gain greater confidence that a cause-and-effect relationship exists, an experiment must be performed (see Chapter 1).

Often, two correlated measures are related as a result of the influence of a third variable. For example, we might observe that the more hours students devote to studying, the better their grades. Although it is tempting to conclude that more studying produces (causes) better grades, it is possible (indeed, it is probable) that grades and the amount of study time are both related to the amount of motivation or interest a student has.

The difference between cause-and-effect data and data that reveal a relationship of unknown origin is one that should not be forgotten. Because we rarely run experiments in daily life,

the information on which we act is largely correlational. This should make us more humble and more tentative in the confidence with which we make pronouncements about human behavior.

Coefficient of correlation *A statistical index ranging from −1.00 to + 1.00 that indicates the direction and degree of correlation.*
Perfect positive relationship *A mathematical relationship in which the correlation between two measures is + 1.00.*
Perfect negative relationship *A mathematical relationship in which the correlation between two measures is −1.00.*
Percent of variance *A portion of the total amount of variation in a group of scores.*
Causation *The act of causing some effect.*

APPENDIX IN REVIEW

What are descriptive statistics?

- Descriptive statistics organize and summarize numbers.
- Graphical statistics, such as histograms and frequency polygons, are used to represent numbers pictorially.

How are statistics used to identify an average score?

- Measures of central tendency define the "typical score" in a group of scores.
- The mean is found by adding all the scores in a group and then dividing by the total number of scores.
- The median is found by arranging a group of scores from the highest to the lowest and selecting the middle score.
- The mode is the score that occurs most frequently in a group of scores.

What statistics do psychologists use to measure how much scores differ from one another?

- Measures of variability provide a number that shows how much scores vary.
- The range is the difference between the highest score and the lowest score in a group of scores.
- The standard deviation shows how much, on average, all the scores in a group differ from the mean.
- To change an original score into a standard score (or z-score), you must subtract the mean from the score and divide the result by the standard deviation.
- Standard scores (z-scores) tell, in standard deviation units, how far above or below the mean a score is. This allows meaningful comparisons between scores from different groups.
- Scores that form a normal curve are easy to interpret because the properties of the normal curve are well known.

What are inferential statistics?

- Inferential statistics are used to make decisions, to generalize from samples, and to draw conclusions.
- Most studies in psychology are based on samples. Findings from representative samples are assumed to also apply to entire populations.

- In psychology experiments, differences in the average performance of groups could occur purely by chance. Tests of statistical significance tell us if the observed differences between groups are common or rare. If a difference is large enough to be improbable, it suggests that the results did not occur by chance alone.

How are correlations used in psychology?

- Pairs of scores that vary together in an orderly fashion are said to be correlated.
- The relationship between two variables or measures can be positive or negative.
- Correlation coefficients tell how strongly two groups of scores are related.
- Correlation alone does not demonstrate cause-and-effect links between variables or measures.

PSYCHOLOGY ON THE NET

- **Statistics to Use** If you enter a series of numbers, this site will calculate basic descriptive statistics and more advanced inferential statistics. http:www.physics.csbsju.edu/stats/

INTERACTIVE LEARNING

- *PsychNow!* 1c. Research methods.

Glossary

Ablation Surgical removal of tissue.

Absolute threshold The minimum amount of physical energy necessary to produce a sensation.

Accommodation (perceptual) Changes in the shape of the lens of the eye that serve to focus objects at varying distances.

Accommodation (Piaget) The modification of existing mental patterns to fit new demands.

Acculturative stress Stress caused by the many changes and adaptations required when a person moves to a foreign culture.

Acetylcholine The neurotransmitter released by neurons to activate muscles.

Achieved role A role that is assumed voluntarily.

Achievement motivation A need for success or the attainment of excellence.

Acquisition The period in conditioning during which a response is reinforced.

Action component That part of an attitude consisting of how one tends to act toward the object of the attitude.

Action potential The nerve impulse, which is a rapid change in electrical charge across the cell membrane.

Activation As reflected in facial expressions, the degree of arousal experienced by the person making the expression.

Activation-synthesis hypothesis Theory that relates dream content to motor commands in the brain, which are made but not carried out during sleep.

Active euthanasia Deliberately inducing death.

Activity theory Theory of aging stating that the best adjustment to aging occurs for individuals who remain active mentally, socially, and physically.

Actor In making attributions, the person whose behavior is being interpreted.

Acuity That aspect of visual perception having to do with the sharpness or resolution of images.

Acupuncture The Chinese medical art of relieving pain and treating illness by inserting thin needles at various points on the body.

Acute stress disorder Psychological disturbance lasting up to 1 month following stresses, such as natural disasters or military combat, that would produce anxiety in anyone who experienced them.

Adaptation level An internal or mental "average" or "medium" point that is used to judge amounts.

Adaptive behaviors (emotion) Actions that aid humans and animals in their attempts to survive and adapt to changing conditions.

Adaptive behaviors (retardation) Basic skills and actions considered necessary for self-care and for dealing successfully with the environment.

Addiction Development of physical dependence on a drug such that craving and physical discomfort (withdrawal symptoms) occur in its absence.

Adjustment disorder Emotional disturbance caused by stressors within the range of common experience; stress is ongoing and produces anxiety and physical symptoms.

Adolescence The socially defined period between childhood and adulthood.

Adrenal glands Endocrine glands whose hormones arouse the body, regulate salt balance, adjust the body to stress, and affect sexual functioning.

Adrenaline A hormone produced by the adrenal glands that tends, in general, to arouse the body.

Affect Pertaining to emotion or feelings.

Affectional needs One's emotional needs in general but, especially, needs for love, attention, and affection.

Affective psychosis A general term for any major mood disorder that includes psychotic symptoms.

Afterimage A visual sensation that persists after a stimulus is removed.

Ageism Discrimination or prejudice based on a person's age.

Aggression Any action carried out with the intent of harming another person.

Aggression cues Stimuli or signals that are associated with aggression and tend to elicit it.

Agnosia A disturbance in the ability to perceive the meaning of stimuli, such as words, objects, or pictures.

Agoraphobia (without panic) People fear that something extremely embarrassing will happen to them if they leave the house or enter unfamiliar situations.

Alarm reaction First stage of the G.A.S., during which bodily resources are mobilized to cope with a stressor.

Alcohol Common name for ethyl alcohol, the intoxicating element in fermented and distilled liquors.

All-or-nothing thinking Classifying objects or events as absolutely right or wrong, good or bad, acceptable or unacceptable, and so forth.

Altered state of consciousness A condition of awareness distinctly different in quality or pattern from waking consciousness.

Alzheimer's disease An age-related disease characterized by memory loss, mental confusion, and in its later stages, a nearly total loss of mental abilities.

Ambiguous stimuli Patterns that allow more than one perceptual organization.

Ambivalence Mixed positive and negative feelings or simultaneous attraction and repulsion.

Ambivalent attachment An emotional bond marked by conflicting feelings of affection, anger, and emotional turmoil.

American Sign Language A language system of hand gestures used by deaf and hearing-impaired people.

Ames room An intentionally distorted room that interrupts perceptual constancies.

Amnesia Loss of memory (partial or complete) for past events and, especially, loss of memory for one's identity.

Amniocentesis Testing of the amniotic fluid from a pregnant woman's womb to identify fetal sex and to detect genetic defects in the fetus.

Amphetamine psychosis A severe disruption of psychological functioning caused by abuse of amphetamines.

Amphetamines A class of synthetic drugs having stimulant effects on the nervous system.

Anagrams test A test of creativity in which subjects try to make as many new words as possible from the letters in a given word.

Anal stage In Freud's theory, the psychosexual stage corresponding roughly to the period of toilet training (age 1 to 3) and characterized by a preoccupation with the process of elimination.

Androgen Any of a number of male sex hormones, especially testosterone.

Androgen insensitivity An inherited disorder in which male embryos fail to develop male genitals because of an unresponsiveness to testosterone.

Androgenital syndrome An inherited disorder that causes the adrenal glands to produce excess androgens, sometimes masculinizing developing females before birth.

Androgyny The presence of both "masculine" and "feminine" traits in a single person (as masculinity and femininity are traditionally defined within one's culture).

Animal model In research, an animal whose behavior is used to discover principles that may apply to human behavior.

Anorexia nervosa Active self-starvation or a sustained loss of appetite that has psychological origins.

Anosmia Loss or impairment of the sense of smell.

Antecedents Events that precede a response.

Anterograde amnesia Loss of the ability to form or retrieve memories for events that occur after an injury or trauma.

Anthropomorphic fallacy The error of attributing human thoughts, feelings, or motives to animals.

Antidepressant A mood-elevating drug.

Antipsychotic A drug that, in addition to having tranquilizing effects, also tends to reduce hallucinations and delusional thinking.

Antisocial personality A person who seems to lack a conscience, is emotionally shallow, impulsive, selfish, and tends to manipulate others; also referred to as a sociopath or psychopath.

Anxiety Apprehension, dread, or uneasiness similar to fear but based on an unclear threat.

Anxiety disorder A disorder characterized by disruptive feelings of fear, apprehension, or anxiety or by distortions in behavior that are anxiety related.

Anxiety reduction hypothesis An explanation of the self-defeating nature of many avoidance responses that emphasizes the immediate reinforcing effects of relief from anxiety.

Aphasia A speech disturbance resulting from damage to language areas on the temporal lobes of the brain.

Apparent distance hypothesis An explanation of the moon illusion stating that the horizon seems more distant than the night sky because there are more depth cues near the horizon.

Applied psychology The use of psychological principles and research methods to solve practical problems.

Applied research Scientific study undertaken to solve immediate practical problems.

Approach-approach conflict A condition in which a person or animal must choose between two positive, or desirable, alternatives.

Approach-avoidance conflict An unpleasant condition in which a person or animal is simultaneously attracted to and repelled by the same goal.

Aptitude A capacity for learning certain abilities.

Aptitude test A test that rates a person's potential to learn skills required by various occupations.

Archetype A universal idea, image, or pattern, found in the collective unconscious.

Architectural psychology Study of the effects buildings have on behavior and the design of buildings using behavioral principles.

Arousal The overall level of excitation or activation in a person or animal.

Arousal theory A theory of motivation that assumes people prefer to maintain "ideal," or comfortable, levels of arousal.

Artificial insemination Medically engineered impregnation.

Artificial intelligence Any artificial system (often a computer program) that is capable of human-like problem solving or skilled responding.

Ascribed role A role that is assigned to a person; a role one has no choice about playing.

Assertiveness training Instruction in how to be self-assertive.

Assessment Evaluation or measurement.

Assessment center A program set up within an organization to conduct in-depth evaluations of job candidates.

Assimilation In Piaget's theory, the application of existing mental patterns to new situations (that is, the new situation is assimilated to existing mental schemes).

Association cortex All areas of the cerebral cortex that are not specifically sensory or motor in function.

Astigmatism Defects in the cornea, lens, or eye that cause some areas of vision to be out of focus.

Astrology False system based on the belief that human behavior is influenced by the position of stars and planets.

Attention Orienting toward or focusing on some stimulus.

Attentional overload A stressful condition caused when sensory stimulation, information, and social contacts make excessive demands on attention.

Attention-deficit hyperactivity disorder A behavioral problem characterized by short attention span and restless movement.

Attitude A learned tendency to respond to people, objects, or institutions in a positive or negative way.

Attitude scale A collection of attitude statements with which respondents indicate agreement or disagreement.

Attribution The process of making inferences about the causes of one's own behavior and that of others. In emotion, the process of attributing perceived arousal to a particular source.

Auditory area Sites on the temporal lobes where auditory information registers.

Auditory ossicles The three small bones that link the eardrum to the inner ear.

Authenticity In Carl Rogers's terms, the ability of a therapist to be genuine and honest regarding his or her feelings.

Authoritarian parents Parents who enforce rigid rules and demand strict obedience to authority.

Authoritarian personality A personality pattern characterized by rigidity, inhibition, prejudice, and an excessive concern with power, authority, and obedience.

Authoritative parents Parents who supply firm and consistent guidance combined with love and affection.

Autism A severe disorder of childhood involving mutism, sensory spin-outs, sensory blocking, tantrums, unresponsiveness to others, and other difficulties.

Autokinetic effect The apparent movement of a stationary pinpoint of light displayed in a darkened room.

Autonomic nervous system The neural system that connects the brain with the internal organs and glands.

Autonomy A freedom from dependence on external authority or the opinions of others.

Aversion therapy Suppression of an undesirable response by associating it with aversive (painful or uncomfortable) stimuli.

Aversive stimulus Any stimulus that produces discomfort or displeasure.

Avoidance learning Learning that occurs when making a particular response delays or prevents the onset of a painful or unpleasant stimulus.

Avoidance-avoidance conflict An unpleasant condition requiring a choice between two negative, or mutually undesirable, alternatives.

Avoidant attachment An emotional bond marked by a tendency to resist commitment to others.

Axon A thin fiber that conducts information away from the cell body of a neuron.

Babbling The repetition by infants of meaningless language sounds (including both vowel and consonant sounds).

Bait shyness An unwillingness or hesitation on the part of animals to eat a particular food; often caused by the presence of a taste aversion.

Barbiturate One of a large group of sedative drugs.

Barnum effect The tendency to consider a personal description accurate if it is stated in very general terms.

Base rate The basic rate at which an event occurs over time; the basic probability of an event.

Baseline A record of the initial frequency of a target behavior.

Basic (or "pure") research Scientific study undertaken without concern for immediate practical application.

Basic needs The first four levels of needs in Maslow's hierarchy; lower needs tend to be more potent than higher needs.

Basic research Scientific inquiry done to advance basic knowledge, not to solve a practical problem.

Basic suggestion effect The tendency of hypnotized people to carry out suggested actions as if they were involuntary.

Behavior modification The application of learning principles to change human behavior, especially maladaptive behavior.

Behavior therapy The use of learning principles to make constructive changes in behavior.

Behavioral assessment Recording the frequency of various behaviors.

Behavioral genetics The study of inherited behavioral traits and tendencies.

Behavioral medicine The study of behavioral factors associated with physical illness and its treatment.

Behavioral personality theory Any model of personality that emphasizes observable behavior, stimuli and responses, and the impact of learning.

Behavioral risk factors Behaviors that increase the chances of disease or injury or that shorten life expectancy.

Behavioral setting A smaller area within an environment whose use is well defined, such as a bus depot, waiting room, or lounge.

Behaviorism The study of overt, observable behavior.

Bem Sex Role Inventory (BSRI) A list of 60 personal traits including "masculine," "feminine," and "neutral" traits; used to rate one's degree of androgyny.

Bereavement Period of emotional adjustment that follows the death of a loved one.

Beta-endorphin A natural chemical produced by the pituitary gland that is similar in structure and pain-killing effect to opiate drugs such as morphine.

Biased sample A sample that does not accurately reflect the population from which it was drawn.

Bibliotherapy Use of books to impart helpful information, either alone or as an adjunct to other forms of therapy.

Binocular depth cues Depth cues that function only when both eyes are used.

Biochemical abnormality A disturbance of the body's chemical systems, especially in brain chemicals or neurotransmitters.

Biodata Detailed biographical information about a job applicant.

Biofeedback Information about bodily activities that aids voluntary regulation of bodily states.

Biological aging Physiological changes that accompany increasing age and alter a variety of physical and psychological functions.

Biological biasing effect Hypothesized effect that prenatal exposure to male or female hormones has on development of the body, nervous system, and later behavior patterns.

Biological constraints Biological limits on what an animal or person can easily learn.

Biological determinism Belief that behavior is controlled by biological processes, such as heredity or evolution.

Biological predisposition The presumed biological readiness of humans to learn certain skills, such as how to use language.

Biological rhythm Any cycle of biological activity, such as sleep and waking cycles or changes in body temperature.

Biopsychologist A psychologist who studies the relationship between behavior and biological processes, especially activity in the nervous system.

Biopsychology The study of biological processes as they relate to behavior.

Bipolar disorders Emotional disorders involving both depression and extremely elevated or manic moods and behavior.

Bipolar I disorder A mood disorder in which a person has episodes of mania and also periods of deep depression.

Bipolar II disorder A mood disorder in which a person is mostly depressed (sad, despondent, guilt ridden) but has also had one or more mildly manic episodes.

Birth injury Any injury or damage that occurs to an infant during delivery.

Birthing room A room designed to minimize the medical aspects of giving birth.

Bisexual A person romantically and erotically attracted to both men and women.

Blind spot A portion of the retina lacking visual receptors (the point where the optic nerve leaves the eye).

Bottom-up processing Organizing perceptions by beginning with low-level features.

Brain dominance The language-producing cerebral hemisphere.

Brainstem The lowest portions of the brain, including the cerebellum, medulla, and reticular formation.

Brainstorming Method of creative thinking that separates the production and evaluation of ideas.

Brainwashing Engineered or forced attitude change involving a captive audience.

Branching program A computer program that gives learners corrective information and exercises based on the nature of their errors.

Brand image The image that consumers have of various products, especially with regard to their personal or emotional meanings.

Brief reactive psychosis A sudden, brief psychotic break that follows an extremely stressful event.

Brightness The intensity of light reflected from or emanating from a surface.

Brightness constancy The apparent (or relative) brightness of various objects remains the same as long as each object is illuminated by the same amount of light.

Broca's area A language area in the brain related to grammar and pronunciation.

Bulimia nervosa Excessive eating (gorging) usually followed by self-induced vomiting and/or taking laxatives.

Burnout A job-related condition of mental, physical, and emotional exhaustion.

Caffeine A natural drug with stimulant properties; found in coffee and tea and added to artificial beverages and medicines.

Caffeinism Excessive consumption of caffeine, leading to dependence and a variety of physical and psychological complaints.

Camouflage Designs that break up figure-ground organization, making objects more difficult to see.

Cannabis sativa The hemp plant, from whose leaves and flowers marijuana and hashish are derived.

Cannon-Bard theory According to this theory, emotional feelings and bodily arousal occur simultaneously, and both begin with activity in the thalamus.

Cardinal trait A personality trait so basic or powerful that all or most of a person's activities spring from existence of the trait.

Career center A counseling facility that offers testing, career guidance, and information on various careers.

Career development One's entire career path, from choosing an initial vocation through retirement.

Caregiving styles Identifiable patterns of parental caretaking and interaction with children.

Caretaker speech An exaggerated pattern of speech used by adults for talking to infants.

Case study An intensive investigation of the behavior of a single person.

Castration Surgical removal of the testicles. Castration differs from sterilization, a procedure (such as vasectomy or tubal ligation) that merely makes a man or woman infertile.

Cataplexy A sudden temporary paralysis of the muscles.

Catatonic episode Period of extreme stupor, immobility, and unresponsiveness.

Catatonic schizophrenia Schizophrenia marked by stupor, rigidity, unresponsiveness, posturing, mutism, and, sometimes, agitated, purposeless behavior.

Causation The act of causing some effect.

Central nervous system The brain and spinal cord.

Central traits The core traits that characterize an individual personality.

Cerebellum A cauliflower-shaped projection at the base of the brain that controls posture and coordination.

Cerebral cortex The layer of tissue that forms the outer layer and surface of the cerebrum; the cerebral cortex is responsible for basic sensory and motor functions, as well as higher mental processes in humans.

Cerebral hemispheres The right and left halves of the cerebrum.

Cerebrum The two large hemispheres that cover the upper part of the brain.

Character Personal characteristics that have been judged or evaluated; a person's desirable or undesirable qualities.

Chemical senses Senses, such as smell and taste, that respond to chemical molecules.

Chemotherapy Use of psychoactive drugs to treat mental or emotional disturbances.

Chorionic villus sampling Testing of a small piece of the placenta early in pregnancy to detect genetic defects in the fetus.

Chromosomes Thread-like structures ("colored bodies") in the nucleus of each cell that are made up of DNA, which carries the genes. Normal human cells have 23 pairs of chromosomes (46 total).

Chronological age A person's age in years.

Circadian rhythms Cyclical changes in bodily function and arousal that vary on a schedule approximating one 24-hour day.

Clairvoyance The purported ability to perceive events at a distance or through physical barriers.

Classical conditioning A basic form of learning in which existing reflex responses come to be elicited by new stimuli (also known as respondent conditioning).

Client-centered therapy A nondirective therapy based on drawing insights from conscious thoughts and feelings; emphasizes accepting one's true self.

Climacteric A time in late middle age when males experience a significant change in health, vigor, or appearance.

Clinging A problem in which a child literally clings to a parent or refuses to leave the parent's side.

Clinical psychologist A specialist who treats or does research on psychological problems.

Clinical study An intensive investigation of the behavior of a single person, especially one suffering from some injury, disease, or disorder.

Cloning The production of an entire organism using the DNA from a single cell.

Closure Gestalt term for the perceptual tendency to complete figures by "closing" or ignoring small gaps.

Cocaine A crystalline drug derived from coca leaves; used as a central nervous system stimulant and local anesthetic.

Cochlea The snail-shaped organ that makes up the inner ear.

Coefficient of correlation A statistical index ranging from −1.00 to +1.00 that indicates the direction and degree of correlation.

Coercive power Social power based on the ability to punish others.

Cognition The process of thinking, knowing, or mentally processing information.

Cognitive behavior therapy The use of learning principles to change maladaptive thoughts, beliefs, and feelings that underlie emotional and behavioral problems.

Cognitive behaviorism An approach that combines behavioral principles with cognition (perception, thinking, anticipation) to explain behavior.

Cognitive dissonance An uncomfortable clash between self-image, thoughts, beliefs, attitudes, or perceptions and one's behavior.

Cognitive learning Higher level learning involving thinking, knowing, understanding, and anticipation.

Cognitive map A mental image of an area (building, city, country) that guides movement from one location to another.

Cognitive psychology The study of human thinking, knowing, understanding, and information processing.

Cognitive therapy The use of learning principles and other methods to change maladaptive thoughts, beliefs, and feelings.

Collective unconscious A mental storehouse for unconscious ideas and images shared by all humans.

Color blindness A total inability to perceive colors.

Color weakness An inability to fully distinguish some colors from others.

Colostrum The first milk produced by a woman for a few days after giving birth. Colostrum is rich in antibodies to disease.

Commitment In a relationship, the degree to which you feel bound to another person.

Common traits Personality traits that are shared by most members of a particular culture.

Communicator In persuasion, the person presenting arguments or information.

Community health campaign A community-wide education program that provides information about factors that affect health and what to do about them.

Community mental health center A facility offering a wide range of mental health services, such as prevention, counseling, consultation, and crisis intervention.

Community psychology Use of community resources to promote mental health and treat or prevent mental health problems.

Companionate love Intimacy and commitment without passion.

Comparative psychology The study and comparison of the behavior of different species, especially animals.

Compensation Counteracting a real or imagined weakness by emphasizing desirable traits or by seeking to excel in other areas.

Competence As a factor in interpersonal attraction, the degree of general ability or proficiency a person displays.

Compliance Bending to the requests of a person who has little or no authority or other form of social power.

Compulsion An act an individual feels driven to repeat, often against his or her will.

Computer simulations Computer programs that mimic some aspect of human thinking, decision making, or problem solving.

Computer-assisted instruction (CAI) Learning aided by computer-presented information and exercises.

Concentrative meditation Mental exercise based on focusing attention on a single target of contemplation.

Concept A generalized idea representing a class of related objects or events.

Concept formation The process of classifying information into meaningful categories by direct experience, rule learning, or exposure to prototypes (idealized models).

Conceptual rule A formal rule by which one may decide if an object or event is an example of a particular concept.

Concrete operational stage Period of cognitive development during which children become able to use the concepts of time, space, volume, and number, but in ways that remain simplified and concrete.

Condensation Combining several people, objects, or events into a single dream image.

Conditional statement A statement that contains a qualification, often of the *if-then* form.

Conditioned aversion A learned dislike or conditioned negative emotional response to some stimulus.

Conditioned emotional response An emotional response that has been linked to a previously nonemotional stimulus by classical conditioning.

Conditioned response A reflex response linked to a new stimulus through learning.

Conditioned stimulus A previously neutral stimulus that acquires the capacity to evoke a response by being paired with an unconditioned stimulus.

Conditioning chamber An apparatus designed for the study of operant conditioning in animals; a Skinner box.

Conditions of worth Internal standards used to judge the value of one's thoughts, actions, feelings, or experiences.

Conduction deafness Poor transfer of sounds from the eardrum to the inner ear.

Cones Visual receptors for colors and daylight visual acuity.

Conflict A stressful condition that occurs when a person must choose between incompatible or contradictory alternatives.

Conformity Bringing one's behavior into agreement or harmony with norms or with the behavior of others in a group.

Confrontation In existential therapy, the process of confronting clients with their own values and with the need to take responsibility for the quality of their existence.

Congenital problems Problems or defects that originate during prenatal development.

Conjunctive concept A concept defined by the presence of two or more specific features. (For example, to qualify as an example of the concept, an object must be both red *and* triangular.)

Connector neuron A nerve cell that serves as a link between two others.

Connotative meaning The subjective, personal, or emotional meaning of a word or concept.

Conscience In Freudian theory, the part of the superego that causes guilt when its standards are not met.

Conscious Region of the mind that includes all mental contents (thoughts, images, feelings, memories, and so on) a person is aware of at any given moment.

Consciousness A person's experience of mental awareness, including current sensations, perceptions, memories, and feelings.

Consensus The degree to which people respond alike. In making attributions, consensus implies that responses are externally caused.

Consequences Effects that follow a response.

Consequences test A test of creativity based on listing the consequences that would follow a basic change in the world.

Conservation In Piaget's theory, mastery of the concept that the volume of matter remains unchanged (is conserved) even when the shape or appearance of objects changes.

Consistency When making attributions, noticing that a behavior changes very little on different occasions.

Consolidation Process by which relatively permanent memories are formed in the brain.

Constructive processing Reorganizing memories on the basis of logic, inference, or the addition of new information.

Consumer behavior All of the actions involved in deciding to spend, selecting a brand, shopping, making the purchase, and evaluating a product in use.

Consumer psychology Specialty area that focuses on understanding consumer behavior and applying psychology to advertising, marketing, product testing, and the like.

Consumerism Formal attempts to enhance consumer knowledge, rights, and welfare.

Consummate love A loving relationship that combines passion, commitment, and intimacy.

Contact comfort A pleasant and reassuring feeling human and animal infants get from touching or clinging to something soft and warm, usually the mother.

Context Information surrounding a stimulus that gives meaning to the stimulus; with regard to behavior, the social situation, behavioral setting, or other surrounding circumstances in which an action takes place.

Continuous reinforcement A schedule of reinforcement in which every correct response is followed by a reinforcer.

Control (experimental) Eliminating, identifying, or equalizing all factors in an experiment that could affect the outcome.

Control (human factors) Any knob, handle, button, lever, or other device used to alter the activity of a machine.

Control (stress) With regard to stress, the ability to exert some influence over one's circumstances.

Control group In an experiment, subjects exposed to all conditions *except* the independent variable.

Control questions In a polygraph exam, questions that almost always provoke anxiety, thus providing a baseline of emotional responsiveness.

Conventional moral reasoning Moral thinking based on a desire to please others or to follow accepted rules and values.

Convergence The simultaneous turning inward of the two eyes as they focus on nearby objects.

Convergent thought Thinking directed toward discovery of a single established correct answer; conventional thinking.

Conversion disorder A symptom or disability that appears to be physical but that actually results from anxiety, stress, or emotional conflict.

Cooing Spontaneous repetition of vowel sounds by infants.

Coping statements Reassuring, self-enhancing statements that are used to stop self-critical thinking.

Corpus callosum The large bundle of fibers connecting the right and left cerebral hemispheres.

Correlation An orderly relationship between two events, measures, or variables.

Correlational study A nonexperimental study designed to measure the degree of relationship (if any) between two or more events, measures, or variables.

Corticalization An increase in the relative size of the cerebral cortex.

Counseling psychologist A specialist who treats milder emotional and behavioral disturbances.

Counselor An adviser who helps people solve problems with marriage, career, schoolwork, or the like.

Counterirritation Using mild pain to block more intense or long-lasting pain.

Courtesy bias The tendency to give "polite" answers so as not to hurt an interviewer's feelings.

Covert behavior A response that is internal or hidden from view.

Covert reinforcement Using positive imagery to reinforce desired behavior.

Covert sensitization Use of aversive imagery to reduce the occurrence of an undesired response.

Cranial nerve One of 12 major nerves that leave the brain without passing through the spinal cord.

Created image A mental image that has been assembled or invented rather than simply remembered.

Cretinism Stunted growth and mental retardation caused by an insufficient supply of thyroid hormone.

Critical incidents Situations that arise in a job, with which a competent worker must be able to cope.

Critical period During development, a period of increased sensitivity to environmental influences. Also, a time during which certain events must take place for normal development to occur.

Critical situations Situations during childhood that are capable of leaving a lasting imprint on personality.

Critical thinking An ability to evaluate, compare, analyze, critique, and synthesize information.

Cross-cultural psychologist A psychologist who studies the ways in which culture affects human behavior.

Crowding A subjective feeling of being overstimulated by a loss of privacy or by the nearness of others (especially when social contact with them is unavoidable).

Cryonic suspension Freezing the body or head at death in hopes that future revival will become possible.

Crystalized abilities Abilities that a person has intentionally mastered; accumulated knowledge and skills.

CT scan Computed tomography scan; a computer-enhanced X-ray image of the brain.

Cue External stimuli or signs that guide responses, especially those that signal the likely presence or absence of reinforcement.

Cult A group that professes great devotion to some person, idea, or thing.

Cultural psychologist A psychologist who studies the ways in which culture affects human behavior.

Cultural relativity Perceptions and judgments made relative to the values of one's culture.

Cultural values The values attached to various objects and activities by people in a given culture.

Culture An ongoing pattern of life, characterizing a society at a particular stage in its development or at a given point in history.

Culture-fair test A test (such as an intelligence test) designed to minimize the importance of skills and knowledge that may be more common in some cultures than in others.

Curare A drug that competes with acetylcholine, causing paralysis.

Curiosity drive A hypothesized drive assumed to underlie a wide range of investigative and stimulus-seeking behaviors.

Curve of forgetting A graph that shows the amount of memorized information remembered after varying lengths of time.

Curvilinear relationship A relationship that forms a curved line when graphed.

Cyclothymic disorder Moderate manic and depressive behavior that persists for 2 years or more.

Dark adaptation The process by which the eye adapts to low illumination and becomes more light sensitive, principally by a shift to rod vision.

Data Observed facts or evidence (*data:* plural; *datum:* singular).

Data reduction system Any system that selects, analyzes, or condenses information.

Daydream A vivid waking fantasy.

Declarative memory That part of long-term memory containing factual information.

Deductive thought Thought that applies a general set of rules to specific situations; for example, using the laws of gravity to predict the behavior of a single falling object.

Deep lesioning Use of an electrode (electrified wire) to destroy small areas deep within the brain.

Deep sleep Stage 4 sleep; the deepest form of normal sleep.

Defense mechanisms Habitual and often unconscious psychological strategies used to avoid or reduce anxiety.

Deinstitutionalization Reduced use of full-time commitment to mental institutions to treat mental disorders.

Delayed speech Speech that is developmentally delayed; that is, speech that begins well after the normal age for language development has passed.

Delta waves Large, slow brain waves that occur in deeper sleep (stage 3 and stage 4).

Delusion A false belief held against all contrary evidence.

Delusional disorder A psychosis marked by severe delusions of grandeur, jealousy, persecution, or similar preoccupations.

Demonology In medieval Europe, the study of demons and the treatment of people "possessed" by demons.

Dendrites Fibers projecting from nerve cells that receive information from other neurons and carry it to the cell body.

Denial Protecting oneself from an unpleasant reality by refusing to perceive it or believe it.

Denotative meaning The exact, dictionary definition of a word or concept; its objective meaning.

Density The number of people in a given space or, inversely, the amount of space available to each person.

Dependent variable In an experiment, the condition (usually a behavior) that reflects the effects of the independent variable.

Depressant A substance that decreases activity in the body and nervous system.

Depression A state of deep despondency marked by apathy, emotional negativity, and behavioral inhibition.

Depressive disorders Emotional disorders primarily involving sadness, despondency, and depression.

Deprivation In development, the loss or withholding of normal stimulation, nutrition, comfort, love, and so forth; a condition of lacking.

Deprivation dwarfism Stunted growth caused by isolation, rejection, or general deprivation.

Depth cues Perceptual features that impart information about distance and three-dimensional space.

Depth perception The ability to see three-dimensional space and to accurately estimate distances.

Desensitization Reducing fear or anxiety by repeatedly exposing a person to emotional stimuli while the person is deeply relaxed.

Determinism The doctrine that all behavior has prior causes.

Detoxification To remove poison or the effects of poison; in the treatment of alcoholism, the withdrawal of the patient from alcohol.

Developmental level An individual's current state of physical, emotional, and intellectual development.

Developmental milestone A significant turning point or marker in personal development.

Developmental psychologist A psychologist who studies the course of human growth and development.

Developmental psychology The study of progressive changes in behavior and abilities from conception to death.

Developmental task Any skill that must be mastered, or personal change that must take place, for optimal development at a particular life stage.

Deviant communication Patterns of communication that cause guilt, anxiety, confusion, anger, conflict, and emotional turmoil.

Deviation IQ An IQ obtained statistically from a person's relative standing in his or her age group.

Diet The types and amounts of food and drink regularly consumed over a period of time.

Difference threshold The smallest change in stimulus intensity that can be detected by an observer.

Digit-span test A test of attention and short-term memory in which a string of digits is recalled.

Diminished capacity Impaired mental competence to control actions or know right from wrong.

Direct instruction Presentation of factual information by lecture, demonstration, and rote practice.

Direct observation (personality) Any observation of a person's behavior in a natural or prearranged situation undertaken to form an impression of his or her personality.

Discounting Downgrading internal explanations of behavior when a person's actions appear to have strong external causes.

Discovery learning Learning based on insight or understanding rather than on mechanical application of rules.

Discrimination Treating members of various social groups differently in circumstances where their rights or treatment should be identical.

Discriminative stimuli Stimuli that precede rewarded and non-rewarded responses in operant conditioning and that come to exert some control over whether the response is made.

Disease-prone personality A personality style associated with poor health; marked by persistent negative emotions, including anxiety, depression, and hostility.

Disengagement theory of aging States that it is normal and desirable for the aged to withdraw from roles they held earlier.

Dishabituation A reversal of habituation.

Disinhibition The removal of inhibition, resulting in the acting out of behavior that normally would be restrained.

Disjunctive concept A concept defined by the presence of at least one of several possible features. (For example, to qualify an object must be either blue *or* circular.)

Disorganized schizophrenia Schizophrenia marked by incoherence, disorganized behavior, bizarre thinking, and flat or grossly inappropriate emotions.

Displaced aggression Redirecting aggression to a target other than the actual source of one's frustration.

Display Any dial, screen, light, or other device used to provide information about a machine's activity to a human operator.

Dissection Separation of tissues into their parts.

Dissociative amnesia Loss of memory (partial or complete) for past events and, especially, loss of memory for one's personal identity.

Dissociative disorder Temporary amnesia, multiple personality, or depersonalization.

Dissociative fugue Fleeing to escape extreme emotional conflict, anxiety, or threat.

Dissociative identity disorder The presence of two or more distinct personalities or personal identities (multiple personality).

Distinctiveness As a basis for making causal attributions, noticing that a behavior occurs only under a specific (distinct) set of circumstances.

Distractors False items included with a correct item to form a test of recognition memory (for example, the wrong answers on a multiple-choice test).

Disuse Theory that memory traces weaken when memories are not periodically used or retrieved.

Divergent thought Thinking that produces many ideas or alternatives; a major element in original or creative thought.

Divided attention Allotting mental space or effort to various tasks or parts of a task.

DNA Deoxyribonucleic acid; a twisted, ladder-like molecular structure containing the chemical code for genetic information.

Dogmatism An unwarranted positiveness or certainty in matters of belief or opinion.

Dominant gene A gene whose influence will be expressed each time the gene is present.

Door-in-the-face effect The tendency for a person who has refused a major request to subsequently be more likely to comply with a minor request.

Dopamine An important transmitter substance found in the brain, especially in the limbic system, an area associated with emotional response.

Double approach-avoidance conflict An unpleasant state in which one is simultaneously attracted to and repelled by each of two alternatives.

Double standard Applying different standards for judging the appropriateness of male and female sexual behavior.

Double-blind experiment A test in which neither subjects nor experimenters know which subjects are in the experimental group.

Down syndrome A genetic disorder caused by the presence of an extra chromosome; results in mental retardation.

Dream symbols Images in dreams that serve as visible signs of hidden ideas, desires, impulses, emotions, relationships, and so forth.

Drill and practice A basic computer-assisted learning format, typically consisting of questions and answers.

Drive The psychological expression of a motive; for example, hunger, thirst, or a drive for success.

Drug interaction A combined effect of two drugs that exceeds the addition of one drug's effects to the other.

Drug tolerance A reduction in the body's response to a drug.

Dyslexia An inability to read with understanding, often caused by a tendency to misread letters (by seeing their mirror images, for instance).

Dyspareunia Genital pain before, during, or after sexual intercourse.

Dysthymic disorder A moderate level of depression that has persisted for 2 years or more but has not included periods of severe depression.

Early childhood education program Programs that provide stimulating intellectual experiences, typically for disadvantaged preschoolers.

Easy child A child who is temperamentally relaxed and agreeable.

Echo A brief continuation of sensory activity in the auditory system after a sound is heard.

Echolalia A compulsion, sometimes observed in autistic children, to repeat everything that is said.

Eclectic Selected from many sources.

Educational psychology The study of learning, teaching, and related topics.

Educational simulations Computer programs that simulate real-world settings or situations to promote learning.

Effective parents Parents who supply firm and consistent guidance combined with love and affection.

Effector cells Cells in muscles and glands specialized for the production of responses.

Ego In Freudian theory, the executive part of personality that directs rational, realistic behavior.

Ego ideal In Freudian theory, the part of the superego representing ideal behavior; a source of pride when its standards are met.

Egocentric thought Thought that is self-centered and fails to consider the viewpoints of others.

Eidetic imagery The ability to retain a "projected" mental image long enough to use it as a source of information.

Ejaculation The release of sperm and seminal fluid by the male at the time of orgasm.

Elaborative rehearsal Rehearsal that links new information with existing memories and knowledge.

Electra conflict Freudian concept referring to a girl's sexual attraction to her father and resultant feelings of rivalry with her mother.

Electrical stimulation of the brain (ESB) Direct electrical stimulation and action of brain tissue.

Electroconvulsive therapy (ECT) A medical treatment for severe depression, consisting of an electric shock passed directly through the brain, which produces a convulsion.

Electrode Any wire, needle, or metal plate used to electrically stimulate nerve tissue or to record its activity.

Electroencephalograph (EEG) A device designed to detect, amplify, and record electrical activity in the brain.

Electromagnetic spectrum The full range of electrical and magnetic wavelengths, including X-rays, radio waves, light waves, and so forth.

Emblems Gestures that have widely understood meanings within a particular culture.

Emotion A state characterized by physiological arousal, subjective feelings, changes in facial expression, and adaptive behaviors.

Emotion-focused coping Managing or controlling one's emotional reaction to a stressful or threatening situation.

Emotional appraisal Evaluating the personal meaning of a situation; specific emotions are assumed to result from various appraisals, such as an appraisal of threat leading to anxiety.

Emotional attachment A close emotional bond that infants form with their parents, caregivers, or others.

Emotional bonding An especially close emotional bond between infants and their parents, caregivers, or others (another term for attachment).

Emotional component One's feelings toward the object of an attitude.

Emotional expression Any behavior that gives an outward sign of emotion, especially those signs that communicate emotional states to others.

Emotional feelings The private, subjective experience of having an emotion.

Emotional tone The underlying emotional state an individual is experiencing at any given moment.

Empathy A capacity for taking another's point of view; the ability to feel what another is feeling.

Empirical evidence Facts or information gained by direct observation or experience.

Empty love A relationship based almost entirely on commitment.

Encoding Changing information into a form that allows it to be stored in memory and manipulated in thought.

Encoding failure Failure to store sufficient information to form a useful memory.

Encopresis A lack of bowel control; "soiling."

Encounter group A group experience based on intensely honest expressions of feelings and reactions of participants to one another.

Endocrine system Glands whose secretions pass directly into the bloodstream or lymph system.

Endogenous depression Depression that appears to be produced from within (perhaps by chemical imbalances in the brain), rather than as a reaction to life events.

Endorphins A class of chemicals produced by the pituitary gland that are similar in structure and pain-killing effect to opiate drugs such as morphine.

Energizers Mood-elevating drugs.

Engineering psychology A specialty concerned with the design of machines and work environments so that they are compatible with human perceptual and physical capacities.

Engram Hypothesized physical changes that take place in the brain as it stores information; a memory trace.

Enkephalins Opiate-like brain chemicals that regulate reactions to pain and stress.

Enriched environment An environment deliberately made more novel, complex, and perceptually stimulating.

Enrichment In development, any attempt to make a child's environment more novel, complex, and perceptually or intellectually stimulating.

Enuresis An inability to control urination, particularly with regard to bed-wetting.

Environment ("nurture") The sum total of all external conditions affecting development.

Environmental assessment Measurement and analysis of the effects an environment has on the behavior of people within that environment.

Environmental psychology The formal study of how environments affect behavior.

Episodic drive A drive that occurs in distinct episodes associated with particular conditions (for example, pain avoidance, sexual motivation).

Episodic memory A subpart of declarative memory that records personal experiences that are linked with specific times and places.

Equal-status contact Social interaction that occurs on an equal footing, without obvious differences in power or status.

Ergotism A pattern of psychotic-like symptoms that accompanies poisoning by ergot fungus.

Erogenous zone Any body area that produces pleasurable sensations.

Eros Freud's name for the "life instincts" postulated by his theory.

Escape Reducing discomfort by leaving frustrating situations or by psychologically withdrawing from them.

Escape learning Learning to make a response in order to end an aversive (painful or uncomfortable) stimulus.

Establishment phase The period during which a person enters a career and builds competence in it.

Estrogen Any of a number of female sex hormones.

Estrus Changes in the reproductive organs and sexual drives of animals that create a desire for mating; particularly used to refer to females in heat.

Ethnocentrism Placing one's own group or race at the center—that is, tending to reject all other groups but one's own.

Ethologist A person who studies the natural behavior patterns of animals.

Eugenics Selective breeding for desirable characteristics.

Evolutionary psychology Study of the evolutionary origins of human behavior patterns.

Excitement General emotional arousal associated with activation of the autonomic nervous system.

Excitement phase The first phase of sexual response, indicated by initial signs of sexual arousal.

Exhibitionism Deriving sexual pleasure from displaying the genitals (usually), to an unwilling viewer ("flashing").

Existential therapy An insight therapy that focuses on the problems of existence, such as death, meaning, choice, and responsibility; emphasizes making courageous life choices.

Exorcism In medieval Europe, the practice of expelling or driving off an "evil spirit," especially one residing in the body of a person who is "possessed."

Expectancy An anticipation concerning future events or relationships.

Experiment A formal trial undertaken to confirm or disconfirm a fact or principle.

Experimental group In a controlled experiment, the group of subjects exposed to the independent variable or experimental manipulation.

Experimental psychologist One who scientifically studies human and animal behavior.

Experimental self-observation Wilhelm Wundt's technique of combining trained introspection with objective measurement.

Experimental subjects Humans or animals whose behavior is investigated in an experiment.

Experimenter effect Changes in subjects' behavior caused by the unintended influence of an experimenter's actions.

Expert power Social power derived from possession of knowledge or expertise.

Expert systems Computer programs designed to respond as a human expert would; programs based on the knowledge and rules that underlie human expertise in specific topics.

Expert witness A person recognized by a court of law as qualified to give expert testimony on a specific topic.

Explicit memory A memory that a person is aware of having; a memory that is consciously retrieved.

Exploration drive Drive to investigate unfamiliar areas of the environment.

Exploration phase The period during which career alternatives are explored.

Expressive behavior Behavior that expresses or communicates emotion.

External cause A cause of behavior that is assumed to lie outside a person.

External eating cue Any external stimulus that tends to encourage hunger or to elicit eating.

External frustration A negative emotional state caused by events or conditions that hinder satisfaction of a motive or that block progress toward a goal.

Extinction A gradual decrease in the frequency of a non-reinforced response.

Extracellular thirst Thirst caused by a reduction in the volume of fluids found between body cells.

Extraneous variable In an experiment, any condition prevented from influencing the outcome.

Extrasensory perception The purported ability to perceive events in ways that cannot be explained by known capacities of the sensory organs.

Extrinsic motivation Motivation based on obvious external rewards, obligations, or similar factors.

Extrovert A person whose attention is directed outward; a bold, sociable, outgoing person.

Eye movement desensitization A reduction in fear or anxiety that occurs when a person holds upsetting thoughts in mind while rapidly moving the eyes from side to side.

Facial agnosia An inability to recognize familiar faces.

Facial blend A facial gesture that mixes parts of two or more basic facial expressions.

Facial feedback hypothesis Explanation that says facial expressions generate feelings that help define what emotion a person is feeling.

Fact memory That part of long-term memory containing factual information (declarative memory).

Factor analysis A statistical technique used to correlate multiple measurements. Measurements that form "clusters" of correlations are assumed to reflect some general underlying factor.

Fallacy of positive instances The tendency to remember or notice information that fits one's expectations, while forgetting discrepancies.

False positive An erroneous sense of recognition.

Familial retardation Mild mental retardation associated with homes that are intellectually, nutritionally, and emotionally impoverished.

Family system The family as an entire unit, including all its members, their relationships, and their typical patterns of behavior.

Family therapy Technique in which all family members participate, both individually and as a group, to change destructive relationships and communication patterns.

Fantasy A product of the imagination determined mainly by one's motives or feelings. Fantasy may be used as an escape mechanism.

Fantasy stage Stage of career exploration in which persons imagine themselves filling unlikely roles.

Fatuous love A relationship based on commitment and passion that lacks intimacy.

Feature detector A sensory system highly attuned to a specific stimulus pattern.

Feedback Information on the effects a response has had that is returned to the person performing the response (also known as knowledge of results).

Feeding system Areas on each side of the hypothalamus that initiate eating when stimulated.

Feeling of knowing The ability to predict beforehand whether one will be able to remember something.

Female orgasmic disorder An inability to reach orgasm during intercourse.

Female sexual arousal disorder A lack of physical arousal to sexual stimulation.

Fetal alcohol syndrome A pattern of birth complications and bodily defects in infants caused by consumption of alcohol by the mother during pregnancy.

Fetal damage A congenital problem; that is, damage or injury that occurs to the fetus during prenatal development.

Fetishism Gaining sexual gratification from inanimate objects; especially, an inability to achieve sexual arousal without the object.

Field experiment An experiment conducted in a natural setting.

Figure-ground organization A basic perceptual organization in which part of a stimulus appears to stand out as an object (figure) against a less prominent background (ground).

Five-factor model A model proposing that the five most universal dimensions of personality are extroversion, agreeableness, conscientiousness, neuroticism, and openness to experience.

Fixation (cognition) The tendency to repeat wrong solutions or faulty responses, especially as a result of becoming blind to alternatives.

Fixation (Freudian) In Freudian theory, lasting conflicts developed during a particular psychosexual stage as a result of frustration or over-indulgence.

Fixed action pattern (FAP) An instinctual chain of movements found in almost all members of a species.

Fixed interval schedule A pattern in which a reinforcer is given only when a correct response is made after a set amount of time has passed since the last reinforced response. Responses made before the time interval has ended are not reinforced.

Fixed ratio schedule A pattern in which a set number of correct responses must be made to get a reinforcer. For example, a reinforcer is given for every four correct responses.

Flashbulb memories Memories created at times of high emotion that seem especially vivid.

Flat affect An extreme lack of emotion.

Flextime A work schedule that allows flexible starting and quitting times, centered around a core work period.

Fluency In tests of creativity, fluency refers to the total number of solutions produced.

Fluid abilities Innate abilities based on perceptual, motor, or intellectual speed and flexibility; abilities that are not based on prior intentional learning.

Foot-in-the-door effect The tendency for a person who has first complied with a small request to be more likely later to fulfill a larger request.

Forcible rape Sexual intercourse carried out against the victim's will, under the threat of force.

Forebrain The highest brain areas, including the hypothalamus, thalamus, corpus callosum, and cerebrum.

Formal operations stage Period of cognitive development marked by a capacity for abstract, theoretical, and hypothetical thinking.

Fovea A small depression at the center of the retina containing only cones and providing the greatest sharpness of vision.

Frame of reference A mental or emotional perspective used for evaluating events.

Framing In thought, the terms in which a problem is stated or the way that it is structured.

Fraternal twins Twins conceived from two separate eggs. Fraternal twins are no more alike genetically than other siblings.

Free association In psychoanalysis, the technique of having a client say anything that comes to mind, regardless of how embarrassing or unimportant it may seem.

Free choice The ability to freely make choices that are not controlled by genetics, learning, or unconscious forces.

Free will The doctrine that human beings are capable of freely making choices.

Free-floating anxiety Anxiety that is very general and pervasive.

Frequency theory Holds that, in hearing, the cochlea converts tones up to about 4,000 hertz into nerve impulses that match the frequency of each tone.

Frontal lobes Areas at the top front of the cerebral cortex that include sites associated with the control of movement, the processing of smell, and higher mental functions.

Frontal lobotomy The destruction of brain tissue in frontal areas of the brain.

Frotteurism Sexually touching or rubbing against a nonconsenting person.

Frustration An internal emotional state resulting from interference with satisfaction of a motive or blocking of goal-directed behavior.

Frustration-aggression hypothesis Hypothesis stating that frustration tends to lead to aggression.

Fugue Taking flight to escape extreme emotional conflict, anxiety, or threat.

Fully functioning person Carl Rogers's term for people living in harmony with their deepest feelings, impulses, and intuitions.

Functional fixedness A rigidity in problem solving caused by an inability to see new uses for familiar objects.

Functional MRI An MRI scan that records brain activity.

Functional psychosis A psychosis of unknown origin or one presumed to be caused by psychological factors.

Functional solution A detailed, practical, and workable solution.

Functionalism School of psychology concerned with how behavior and mental abilities help people adapt to their environments.

Fundamental attributional error The tendency to attribute the behavior of others to internal causes (personality, likes, and so forth).

Galvanic skin response (GSR) A change in the electrical resistance (or inversely, the conductance) of the skin, due to activity in the sweat glands associated with arousal or anxiety.

Gate control theory Proposes that pain messages pass through neural "gates" in the spinal cord.

Gender Psychological and social characteristics associated with being male or female; defined especially by one's gender identity and learned gender roles.

Gender bias A tendency for researchers to base conclusions solely on subjects of one sex (usually males).

Gender identity One's personal, private sense of maleness or femaleness.

Gender role socialization The process of learning behaviors considered appropriate for one's sex in a given culture.

Gender role stereotypes Oversimplified and widely held beliefs about the basic characteristics of men and women.

Gender roles Separate patterns of traits, mannerisms, interests, and behaviors that are regarded as "male" and "female" by one's culture.

General adaptation syndrome (G.A.S.) A series of bodily reactions to prolonged stress, occurring in three stages: alarm, resistance, and exhaustion.

General intelligence test A test that measures a wide variety of mental abilities.

General negativism A tendency to respond negatively to almost all situations or social interactions.

General paresis A disease that occurs when syphilis attacks the brain; can cause an organic psychosis.

General solution A solution that states the requirements for success, but not in enough detail for further action.

Generalization Transfer of a learned response from one stimulus situation to similar situations.

Generalized anxiety disorder The person is in a chronic state of tension and worries about work, relationships, ability, or impending disaster.

Generalized reinforcer A secondary reinforcer that has become independent of direct association with primary reinforcers.

Genes Specific areas on a strand of DNA that carry hereditary information affecting various personal characteristics.

Genetic abnormality Any abnormality in the genes, including missing genes, extra genes, or defective genes.

Genetic sex Sex as indicated by the presence of *XX* (female) or *XY* (male) chromosomes.

Genital sex Sex as indicated by the presence of male or female genitals.

Genital stage In Freud's theory, the culmination of personality development, marked, among other things, by the attainment of mature adult sexuality.

Gerontologist One who scientifically studies aging and its effects.

Gestalt A German word meaning form, pattern, or whole.

Gestalt psychology The school of psychology emphasizing the study of thinking, learning, and perception in whole units, not by analysis into parts.

Gestalt therapy An approach that focuses on immediate experience and awareness to help clients rebuild thinking, feeling, and acting into connected wholes; emphasizes the integration of fragmented experiences.

Giantism Excessive bodily growth caused by too much growth hormone.

Giftedness Either the possession of a high IQ or special talents or aptitudes.

Goal The target or objective of a motivated and directed chain of behaviors.

Gonadal sex Sex as indicated by the presence of ovaries (female) or testes (male).

Gonads The primary sex glands—the testes in males and ovaries in females.

Grammar A set of rules for combining language units into meaningful speech or writing.

Graphology False system based on the belief that handwriting can reveal personality traits.

Grasping reflex A neonatal reflex consisting of grasping objects placed in the palms.

Gray matter Areas in the nervous system that have a grayish color due to a high concentration of nerve cell bodies.

Grief An intense emotional state that follows the death of a lover, friend, or relative.

Group cohesiveness The degree of attraction among group members or their degree of commitment to remaining in the group.

Group intelligence test Any intelligence test that can be administered to a group of people with minimal supervision.

Group prejudice Prejudice held out of conformity to group views.

Group sanctions Rewards and punishments (such as approval or disapproval) administered by groups to enforce a degree of conformity among members.

Group structure The network of roles, communication pathways, and power in a group.

Group therapy Psychotherapy conducted with a group of people.

Groupthink A compulsion by members of decision-making groups to maintain agreement, even at the cost of critical thinking.

Growth needs In Maslow's hierarchy, the higher level needs associated with self-actualization (needs that contribute to personal growth and full development of personal potential).

Growth spurt An often dramatic acceleration in physical growth that coincides with puberty.

Guided imagery Intentional visualization of images that are calming, relaxing, or beneficial in other ways.

Gustation The sense of taste.

Habit A deeply ingrained, learned pattern of behavior.

Habituation A decrease in perceptual response to a repeated stimulus.

Hair cells Receptor cells within the cochlea that transduce vibrations into nerve impulses.

Halfway house A community-based facility for individuals making the transition from an institution (mental hospital, prison, and so forth) to independent living.

Hallucination An imaginary sensation—such as seeing, hearing, or smelling something that does not exist in the external world.

Hallucinogen Any substance that alters or distorts sensory impressions.

Halo effect The tendency of an interviewer to extend a favorable or unfavorable impression to unrelated aspects of an individual's personality.

Handedness A preference for the right or left hand in most activities.

Hardy personality A personality style associated with superior stress resistance.

Hassle Any distressing, day-to-day annoyance; also called a microstressor.

Health psychology Study of the ways in which psychological principles can be used to maintain and promote health.

Heredity ("nature") The transmission of physical and psychological characteristics from parents to offspring through genes.

Hermaphroditism The condition of having genitals suggestive of both sexes; ambiguous genital sexuality.

Hertz One cycle (or vibration) per second.

Heterosexism The belief that heterosexuality is better or more natural than homosexuality.

Heterosexual A person romantically and erotically attracted to members of the opposite sex.

Heuristic Any strategy or technique that aids problem solving, especially by limiting the number of possible solutions to be tried.

Hidden observer A detached part of the hypnotized person's awareness that silently observes events.

Hierarchy A rank-ordered series of higher and lower amounts, levels, degrees, or steps.

Hierarchy of needs A rank ordering of needs based on their presumed strength or potency.

High self-monitors People who try to adapt their public image to the demands of various situations by managing the impression they make on others.

Higher order conditioning Classical conditioning in which a conditioned stimulus is used to reinforce further learning; that is, a CS is used as if it were a US.

Hippocampus A structure in the brain associated with the regulation of emotions and the transfer of information from short-term memory to long-term memory.

Homeostasis A steady state of bodily equilibrium normally maintained automatically by various physiological mechanisms.

Homogamy Marriage of two people who are similar to one another.

Homophobia A powerful fear of homosexuality.

Homosexual A person romantically and erotically attracted to same-sex people.

Honesty test A paper-and-pencil test designed to detect attitudes, beliefs, and behavior patterns that predispose a person to engage in dishonest behavior.

Hormonal sex Sex as indicated by a preponderance of estrogens (female) or androgens (male) in the body.

Hormone A glandular secretion that affects bodily functions or behavior.

Hospice A medical facility or program dedicated to providing optimal care for persons who are dying.

Hospitalism A pattern of deep depression observed in institutionalized infants, marked by weeping and sadness and a lack of normal responsiveness to other humans.

Hue Classification of colors into basic categories of red, orange, yellow, green, blue, indigo, and violet.

Human genome The entire set of human genes.

Human growth sequence The general pattern of physical development from conception to death.

Human immunodeficiency virus (HIV) The sexually transmitted virus that disables the immune system and causes AIDS.

Human nature Those traits, qualities, potentials, and behavior patterns most characteristic of the human species.

Humanism An approach to psychology that focuses on human experience, problems, potentials, and ideals.

Hydrocephaly A buildup of cerebrospinal fluid within brain cavities.

Hyperactivity A behavioral state characterized by short attention span, restless movement, and impaired learning capacity.

Hyperopia Difficulty in focusing nearby objects (farsightedness).

Hypersomnia Extreme daytime sleepiness.

Hyperthyroidism Faster metabolism and excitability caused by an overactive thyroid gland.

Hypnic jerk A reflex muscle twitch throughout the body that often occurs as one is falling asleep.

Hypnogogic images Vivid mental images that may occur just as one enters stage 1 sleep; although somewhat dream-like, the images are usually not associated with REMs.

Hypnosis An altered state of consciousness characterized by narrowed attention and increased suggestibility.

Hypnotic susceptibility scale Any test designed to assess an individual's capacity for becoming hypnotized.

Hypoactive sexual desire A persistent loss of sexual motivation.

Hypochondriac A person who is excessively preoccupied with minor bodily problems or who complains about illnesses that appear to be imaginary.

Hypochondriasis A preoccupation with minor bodily problems and the presence of illnesses that appear to be imaginary.

Hypoglycemia Below-normal blood sugar level.

Hypopituitary dwarfism Shortness and smallness caused by too little growth hormone.

Hypothalamus A small area at the base of the brain that regulates many aspects of motivation and emotion, especially hunger, thirst, and sexual behavior.

Hypothesis The predicted outcome of an experiment or an educated guess about the relationship between variables.

Hypothetical possibilities Suppositions, guesses, or projections.

Hypothyroidism Slower metabolism and sluggishness caused by an underactive thyroid gland.

Hysteria Wild emotional excitability sometimes associated with the development of apparent physical disabilities (numbness, blindness, and the like) without known physical cause.

Icon A mental image or representation.

Id According to Freud, the most primitive part of personality, which remains unconscious, supplies energy to other parts of the psyche, and demands immediate gratification.

Ideal self An idealized image of oneself (the person one would like to be).

Identical twins Twins who develop from the same egg and who, therefore, have identical genes.

Identification Incorporating the goals and values of another person into one's own behavior; feeling emotionally connected to a person and wanting to be like him or her.

Illogical thought Thought that is intuitive, invalid, or haphazard.

Illusion A misleading or distorted perception.

Illusory figure An implied shape that is not actually bounded by an edge or an outline.

Illustrators Gestures used while speaking to illustrate what one is saying.

Image Most often, a mental representation that has picture-like qualities; an icon.

Imaginary audience The group of people a person imagines is watching (or will watch) his or her actions.

Imitation An attempt to match one's own behavior to another person's behavior.

Immune system System that mobilizes bodily defenses (such as white blood cells) against invading microbes and other disease agents.

Implicit memory A memory that a person does not know exists; a memory that is retrieved unconsciously.

Impossible figure A stimulus pattern that cannot be organized into a stable perception.

Impotence An outdated term for male erectile disorder.

Imprinting A rapid and relatively permanent type of learning that occurs during a limited time period early in life.

In vitro fertilization Fertilization of an ovum outside a woman's body.

In-basket test A testing procedure that simulates the individual decision-making challenges that executives face.

Incentive value The value a goal holds for a person or animal above and beyond the goal's ability to fill a need.

Incest Sexual contact with a close relative or family member.

Incongruence State that exists when there is a discrepancy between one's experiences and self-image or between one's self-image and ideal self.

Incongruent person A person who has an inaccurate self-image or a person whose self-image differs greatly from the ideal self.

Independent variable In an experiment, the condition being investigated as a possible cause of some change in behavior. The values that this variable takes do not depend on any other condition; they are chosen by the experimenter.

Individual intelligence test A test of intelligence designed for administration to a single individual by a trained specialist.

Individual traits Personality traits that comprise a person's unique individual qualities.

Individuating information Information that helps define a person as an individual, rather than as a member of a group or social category.

Inductive thought A type of thinking in which a general rule or principle is inferred from a series of specific examples; for instance, inferring the laws of gravity by observing many falling objects.

Industrial-organizational psychology The psychology of work and organizations, especially with respect to personnel selection, human relations, and management.

Infatuation Passionate attraction to another person in the absence of intimacy and commitment.

Information bits Meaningful units of information, such as numbers, letters, words, or phrases.

Information chunks Information bits grouped into larger units.

Innate behavior Inborn, unlearned behavior.

Insanity Legally, a mental disability shown by an inability to manage one's affairs or to be aware of the consequences of one's actions.

Insecure-ambivalent attachment An anxious emotional bond marked by a desire to be with a parent or caregiver and resistance to being reunited.

Insecure-avoidant attachment An anxious emotional bond marked by a tendency to avoid reunion with a parent or caregiver.

Insight A sudden mental reorganization of a problem that causes the solution to seem self-evident.

Insomnia Difficulty in getting to sleep or staying asleep.

Instinctive drift The tendency of learned responses to shift toward innate response patterns.

Instructional games Educational computer programs designed to resemble games in order to motivate learning.

Instrumental behavior Behavior directed toward the achievement of some goal; behavior that is instrumental in producing some effect.

Intelligence An overall capacity to think rationally, act purposefully, and deal effectively with the environment.

Intelligence quotient (IQ) An index of intelligence defined as a person's mental age divided by his or her chronological age and multiplied by 100.

Interference The tendency for new memories to impair retrieval of older memories, and the reverse.

Internal cause A cause of behavior that is assumed to lie within a person—for instance, a need, preference, or personality trait.

Internal representation Any image, concept, precept, symbol, or process used to mentally represent information during thought.

Internet A connection of networks that enables computers to communicate with one another, usually through the telephone system.

Interpersonal attraction Social attraction to another person.

Interview (personality) A face-to-face meeting held for the purpose of gaining information about an individual's personal history, personality traits, current psychological state, and so forth.

Intimacy The presence of affection, sharing, communication, and mutual support in a relationship.

Intimate distance The most private space immediately surrounding the body (about 18 inches from the skin).

Intracellular thirst Thirst triggered when fluid is drawn out of cells because of an increased concentration of salts and minerals outside the cell.

Intracranial stimulation Direct electrical stimulation and activation of brain tissue.

Intrauterine environment The physical and chemical environment within the uterus during prenatal development.

Intrinsic motivation Motivation that comes from personal enjoyment of an activity, rather than from external rewards.

Introspection To look within; to examine one's own thoughts, feelings, or sensations.

Introvert A person whose attention is focused inward; a shy, reserved, self-centered person.

Intuitive thought Quick, impulsive thinking that makes little or no use of formal reasoning and logic.

Inverted U function A curve, roughly in the shape of an upside-down U, that relates the quality of performance to levels of arousal.

Ion An electrically charged molecule.

Ion channels Channels through the axon membrane.

Iris Colored circular muscle of the eye that opens and closes to admit more or less light into the eye.

Irrelevant questions In a polygraph exam, neutral, nonthreatening, or nonemotional questions.

Ishihara test A test for color blindness and color weakness.

James-Lange theory According to this theory, emotional feelings follow bodily arousal and come from awareness of such arousal.

Jigsaw classroom A method of reducing prejudice in which each student receives a different part of a body of information needed to complete a project or prepare for a test.

Job analysis A detailed description of the skills, knowledge, and activities required by a particular job.

Job enrichment A deliberate attempt to make a job more personally rewarding, interesting, or intrinsically motivating.

Job satisfaction The degree to which a person is comfortable with or satisfied with his or her work.

Just noticeable difference The amount of increase or decrease in a stimulus that can be reliably detected as a change in amount, value, or intensity.

Justification In cognitive dissonance theory, the degree to which one's actions are justified by rewards or other circumstances.

Just-world beliefs Belief that people generally get what they deserve.

Keyword method As an aid to memory, using a familiar word or image to link two items.

Kinesics Study of the meaning of body movements, posture, hand gestures, and facial expressions, commonly called body language.

Kinesthetic imagery Images created by produced, remembered, or imagined muscular sensations.

Kinesthetic senses The senses of body movement and positioning.

Knowledge of results During learning, feedback or information provided about the correctness of responses or other aspects of performance.

Language A collection of words or symbols and rules for combining them that allows them to be used for thinking and communication.

Large-group awareness training Any of a number of programs (many of them commercialized) that claim to increase self-awareness and facilitate constructive personal change.

Latency (Freudian) According to Freud, a period in childhood when psychosexual development is more or less interrupted.

Latency (response) The amount of time that passes between the presentation of a stimulus and the occurrence of a response.

Latent dream content The hidden or symbolic meaning of a dream, as revealed by dream interpretation and analysis.

Latent learning Learning that occurs without obvious reinforcement and that remains unexpressed until reinforcement is provided.

Later career phase The concluding career phase prior to retirement; marked by high status and respect arising from long experience.

Lateralization Specialization in the abilities of the brain hemispheres.

Law of effect Responses that lead to desirable effects are repeated; those that produce undesirable results are not.

Leaderless group discussion A test of leadership that simulates group decision making and problem solving.

Learned helplessness A learned inability to overcome obstacles or to avoid punishment. A learned state of passivity and inaction in the face of aversive stimuli.

Learning Any relatively permanent change in behavior that can be attributed to experience but not to fatigue, malnutrition, injury, and so forth.

Learning disability Any substantial problem with reading, math, or writing.

Learning psychologist A psychologist who studies how learning occurs.

Learning theorist A psychologist interested in the ways that learning shapes and explains personality.

Legitimate power Social power based on a person's position as an agent of an accepted social order.

Lesbianism Female homosexuality.

Lexigram A geometric shape used as a symbol for a word.

Libido In Freudian theory, the force, primarily pleasure oriented, that energizes the subparts of personality.

Life change units (LCUs) Numerical values assigned to each life event on the Social Readjustment Rating Scale and used to predict the likelihood of illness.

Life expectancy The average number of years a person of a given sex, race, and nationality can expect to live.

Life stages Widely recognized periods of life corresponding to various ages and broad phases of development.

Light sleep Stage 1 sleep, marked by small, irregular brain waves and some alpha waves.

Liking A relationship based on intimacy but lacking passion and commitment.

Limbic system A system of interconnected structures in the forebrain that are closely associated with emotional response.

Limen A threshold or a limit.

Linear relationship A relationship that forms a straight line when graphed.

Lithium carbonate A drug used to lessen mood swings in people suffering from some types of affective disorders.

Living will A written declaration stating that a person prefers not to have his or her life artificially prolonged in the event of a terminal illness.

Lobes (cerebral cortex) Areas on the cortex bordered by major fissures or associated with particular functions.

Localization of function The principle stating that sensations are determined by the area of the brain that is activated.

Lock and key theory The theory of olfaction that holds that odors are related to the shapes of chemical molecules.

Logical thought Drawing conclusions on the basis of formal principles of reasoning.

Logotherapy A form of existential therapy that emphasizes the need to find and maintain meaning in one's life.

Long-term memory (LTM) The memory system used for relatively permanent storage of meaningful information.

Looking chamber An experimental apparatus used to test infant perception by presenting visual stimuli and observing infant responses.

Loudness The intensity of a sound; determined by the amplitude of sound waves.

Low self-monitor A person who seeks to faithfully express who she or he is, regardless of the situation.

Low-ball technique A strategy in which commitment is gained first to reasonable or desirable terms, which are then made less reasonable or desirable.

Lucid dream A dream in which the dreamer feels awake and capable of normal thought and action.

M'Naghten rule A rule in English common law for judging sanity and legal responsibility.

Maintenance rehearsal Silently repeating or mentally reviewing information to hold it in short-term memory.

Major depressive disorder A mood disorder in which the person has suffered one or more intense episodes of depression.

Major mood disorders Disorders marked by lasting extremes of mood or emotion and often accompanied by psychotic symptoms.

Major tranquilizers (antipsychotics) Drugs that, in addition to having tranquilizing effects, also tend to reduce hallucinations and delusional thinking.

Maladaptive behavior Behavior that makes it more difficult for a person to adapt to his or her environment and meet the demands of day-to-day life.

Male erectile disorder An inability to maintain an erection for sexual intercourse.

Male orgasmic disorder An inability to reach orgasm during intercourse.

Management by objectives A management technique in which employees are given specific goals to meet in their work.

Mandala A circular design representing balance, unity, and completion.

Manic Extremely excited, hyperactive, or irritable.

Manifest dream content The surface, "visible" content of a dream; dream images as they are remembered by the dreamer.

Manipulation drive Drive to investigate objects by touching and handling them.

Mantra A word or sound used as the focus of attention in concentrative meditation.

Marijuana The leaves and flowers of the hemp plant, *Cannabis sativa.*

Marketing research A type of public opinion polling used to assess consumer views of products, services, and advertising.

Masochism Deriving sexual arousal or pleasure from having pain inflicted during the sex act.

Mass media Collectively, all media that reach very large audiences (magazines, for instance, are a medium of mass communication).

Massed practice A practice schedule in which studying continues for long periods, without interruption.

Mastery training Reinforcement of responses that lead to mastery of a threat or control over one's environment.

Masturbation Production of sexual pleasure or orgasm by manipulation of the genitals other than by intercourse.

Maternal influences The aggregate of all psychological effects mothers have on their children.

Maternity blues A brief and relatively mild state of depression often experienced by mothers 2 or 3 days after giving birth.

Maturation The physical growth and development of the body and nervous system.

Maximum life span The biologically determined maximum number of years humans could live under optimal conditions.

Mean worldview Viewing the world and other people as dangerous and threatening.

Means-ends analysis An analysis of how to reduce the difference between the present state of affairs and a desired goal.

Mechanical solution A problem solution achieved by trial and error or by a fixed procedure based on learned rules.

Medicated birth The common practice in Western medicine of giving painkilling drugs during labor and birth.

Meditation A mental technique for quieting the mind and body.

Medulla The enlarged stalk at the base of the brain that connects to the spinal cord and controls vital life functions.

Melatonin A hormone produced by the pineal gland in response to cycles of light and dark.

Memory The mental system for receiving, storing, organizing, altering, and recovering information.

Memory cue Any stimulus associated with a particular memory. The presence of such cues usually enhances memory retrieval.

Memory decay The fading or weakening of memories assumed to occur when memory traces become weaker.

Memory structure The pattern of associations among bits of information stored in memory.

Memory traces Hypothesized physical changes that take place in the brain as it stores information; engrams.

Menarche The onset of menstruation; a woman's first menstrual period.

Menopause An end to regular monthly menstrual periods.

Mental age The average mental ability displayed by people of a given age.

Mental disorder A significant impairment in psychological functioning.

Mental hospitalization Confinement to a protected environment that provides various forms of therapy for mental, emotional, and behavioral problems.

Mental retardation The presence of a developmental disability, a formal IQ score below 70, or a significant impairment of adaptive behavior.

Mental rotation The ability to change the position of an image in mental space in order to examine it from a new perspective.

Mesmerize To hypnotize.

Metabolic disorder Any disorder in metabolism (the rate of energy production and use in the body).

Metabolic rate The rate at which energy is consumed by bodily activity.

Meta-needs In Maslow's hierarchy, those needs above and beyond the ordinary; needs associated with impulses for self-actualization.

Microcephaly A disorder in which the head and brain are abnormally small.

Micro-electrode An electrode small enough to record the activity of a single neuron.

Micromovements Tiny, nearly imperceptible movements associated with changes in muscular tension and activity.

Microsleep A momentary shift in brain-wave patterns to those of sleep.

Midbrain The area of the brain consisting of structures linking the forebrain and the brainstem.

Midcareer phase A stable central career phase marked by high competence and full status.

Mild punishment Punishment that has a relatively weak effect, especially punishment that only temporarily slows responding.

Minimal brain dysfunction (MBD) A hypothesized explanation for hyperactivity, involving a lag in brain development or low-level damage to the brain.

Minnesota Multiphasic Personality Inventory-2 (MMPI-2) The latest version of one of the best-known and most widely used objective personality questionnaires.

Minor tranquilizers Drugs (such as Valium) that produce relaxation or reduce anxiety.

Mirror technique Observing another person re-enact one's own behavior, like a character in a play; designed to help people to see themselves more clearly.

Misdirected letter technique A way of measuring attitudes toward a group; letters addressed to the group are sent to households and the number forwarded is counted.

MMPI-2 profile A graphic representation of an individual's scores on each of the primary scales of the MMPI-2.

Mnemonic A memory system or aid.

Mock jury A group that realistically simulates a courtroom jury.

Model (learning) A person (either live or filmed) who serves as an example for observational learning or vicarious conditioning.

Model (scientific) In research, an animal whose behavior is used to derive principles that may apply to human behavior.

Modeling Any process in which information is imparted by example, before direct practice is allowed.

Monocular depth cues Depth cues that can be sensed with one eye.

Mood A low-intensity, long-lasting emotional state.

Mood disorder A major disturbance in mood or emotion, such as depression or mania.

Moon illusion The apparent change in size that occurs as the moon moves from the horizon (large moon) to overhead (small moon).

Moral anxiety Apprehension felt when one's thoughts, impulses, or actions conflict with standards enforced by the superego.

Moral development The development of values, beliefs, and thinking abilities that act as a guide regarding what is acceptable behavior.

Moro reflex Neonatal reflex evoked by sudden loss of support or the sounding of a loud noise; in response, the arms are extended and then brought toward each other.

Morphemes The smallest meaningful units in a language, such as syllables or words.

Motivation Mechanisms within an organism that initiate, sustain, and direct activities.

Motor cortex An area on the top of the brain directly associated with control of voluntary movements.

Motor neuron A nerve cell that carries motor commands from the central nervous system to muscles and glands.

Motor program A mental plan or model that guides skilled movement.

Motor skill A series of actions molded into a smooth and efficient performance.

MRI scan Magnetic resonance imaging; a computer-enhanced three-dimensional representation of the brain or body, based on the body's response to a magnetic field.

Müller-Lyer illusion A stimulus consisting of two parallel lines tipped with inward or outward pointing Vs. Although they are of equal length, one of the lines appears longer than the other.

Multiculturalism Giving equal status, recognition, and acceptance to different ethnic, racial, and cultural groups.

Multiple approach-avoidance conflict Being simultaneously attracted to and repelled by each of several alternatives.

Multiple aptitude test Test that measures two or more aptitudes.

Multiple personality A form of dissociative disorder in which a person develops two or more distinct personalities.

Muscular imagery Any mental representation based on produced, remembered, or imagined muscular sensations; for instance, the images produced when one imagines hammering a nail.

Muscular responses Visible movement of the muscles or unseen changes in their tension, which create kinesthetic sensations.

Mutual absorption With regard to romantic love, the almost exclusive attention lovers give to one another.

Mutual interdependence A condition in which two or more people must depend on one another to meet each person's needs or goals.

Myelin A fatty layer coating some axons that increases the rate at which nerve impulses travel along the axon.

Myoclonus Restless spasms of the leg muscles that disturb sleep.

Myopia A visual defect that makes it difficult to focus distant objects (nearsightedness).

Narcolepsy A serious sleep disturbance in which the individual suffers uncontrollable sleep attacks.

Natural clinical test An accident or other natural event that provides psychological data.

Natural design Human factors engineering that makes use of perceptual signals that are understood by people without any need to learn them.

Natural selection Darwin's theory that evolution favors those plants and animals best suited to their living conditions.

Natural setting The environment in which an organism typically lives.

Naturalistic observation Observation and recording of naturally occurring behavior that is not manipulated experimentally.

Near-death experience A pattern of experiences that may occur when a person is clinically dead and then resuscitated.

Need An internal deficiency that may energize behavior.

Need for achievement (nAch) The desire to excel or meet some internalized standard of excellence.

Need for power The desire to have social impact and control over others.

Need to affiliate The desire to associate with other people.

Negative after-potential A drop in electrical charge below the resting potential.

Negative attention seeking A pattern, seen especially in children, in which misbehavior is used to gain attention.

Negative instance In concept learning, an object or event that does not belong to the concept class.

Negative reinforcement Occurs when a response is followed with an end to discomfort or with the removal of a negative state of affairs.

Negative relationship A relationship in which increases in one measure correspond to decreases in the other.

Negative self-statements Self-critical thoughts that increase anxiety and lower performance.

Negative transfer Mastery of one task conflicts with learning or performing another.

Neglect Ignoring one side of vision or of the body after damage to a brain hemisphere.

Neo-Freudian A personality theorist who accepts the broad features of Freud's theory but has revised the theory to fit his or her own concepts.

Neonate A newborn infant during the first weeks following birth.

Nerve A bundle of neuron fibers supported by connective tissue; nerves can be seen with the unaided eye; neuron fibers are microscopic projections from single cells.

Nerve deafness Deafness caused by damage to the hair cells or auditory nerve.

Network model A model of memory that views it as an organized system of linked information.

Neurilemma A layer of living cells that encases the axons of many neurons.

Neurons Individual nerve cells.

Neuropeptides Brain chemicals that regulate the activity of neurons, thereby influencing memory, emotion, pain, hunger, and other behavior.

Neurosis An outdated term once used to refer, as a group, to anxiety disorders, somatoform disorders, dissociative disorders, and some forms of depression.

Neurotic anxiety Apprehension felt when the ego must struggle to maintain control over id impulses.

Neurotransmitter Any of a number of chemical substances secreted by neurons that alter activity in other neurons.

Neutral stimulus A stimulus that fails to elicit a response.

Nicotine A potent stimulant drug found primarily in tobacco; nicotine is a known carcinogen.

Night blindness A visual defect in which daylight vision is normal, but blindness occurs under conditions of low illumination.

Night terror A very frightening NREM sleep episode.

Nightmare An upsetting dream.

Nocturnal orgasm An orgasm that occurs spontaneously during sleep or dreaming.

Noise pollution Stressful and intrusive noise; usually artificially generated by machinery but also including noises made by animals and humans.

Nonhomeostatic drive A drive that is relatively independent of physical deprivation cycles or bodily need states.

Nonlove An absence of intimacy, passion, and commitment in a relationship.

Non-reinforcement Withholding reinforcement after selected responses (in other words, extinction training).

Nonsense syllables Invented three-letter words used to test learning and memory.

Noradrenaline A hormone produced by the adrenal glands that tends to arouse the body; noradrenaline is associated with anger.

Norm (social) An accepted (but often unspoken) standard of conduct for appropriate behavior.

Norm (testing) An average score for a designated group of people.

Normal curve A bell-shaped curve with a large number of scores in the middle, tapering to very few extremely high and low scores.

NREM sleep Non–rapid eye movement sleep characteristic of stages 2, 3, and 4, and largely dream-free.

Nystagmus Any involuntary vibration, oscillation, or movement of the eye.

Obedience Conformity to the demands of an authority.

Object In making attributions, the aim, motive, or target of an action.

Object permanence Concept, gained in infancy, that objects continue to exist even when they are hidden from view.

Objective test A test that gives the same score when different people correct it.

Observation Directly gathering data by recording facts or events.

Observational learning Learning achieved by watching and imitating the actions of another or noting the consequences of those actions.

Observer bias The tendency of an observer to distort observations or perceptions to match his or her expectations.

Observer effect Changes in a person's behavior brought about by an awareness of being observed.

Obsession Recurring irrational or disturbing thoughts or mental images a person cannot prevent.

Obsessive-compulsive disorder An extreme, unavoidable preoccupation with certain thoughts and compulsive performance of certain behaviors.

Occipital lobes Portion at the back of the cerebral cortex that includes areas where vision registers in the brain.

Oedipus conflict Freudian concept referring to a boy's sexual attraction to his mother and his feelings of rivalry with his father.

Olfaction The sense of smell.

Olfactory area Sites on the frontal lobes where information on smell registers.

Open teaching Instruction based on active teacher-student discussion.

Open-ended interview An interview in which people are allowed to freely state their views.

Operant conditioning Learning based on the consequences of responding.

Operant extinction The weakening or disappearance of a non-reinforced operant response.

Operant reinforcer Any event that reliably increases the probability or frequency of responses it follows.

Operant shaping Gradually molding responses by rewarding ever-closer approximations to a final desired pattern.

Operant stimulus discrimination The tendency to make a response when stimuli previously associated with reward are present and to withhold the response when stimuli associated with non-reward are present.

Operant stimulus generalization The tendency to respond to stimuli similar to those present when an operant response was acquired.

Operational definition Defining a scientific concept by stating the specific actions or procedures used to measure it. For example, "hunger" might be defined as "the number of hours of food deprivation."

Opponent-process theory (motivation) States that strong emotions tend to be followed by an opposite emotional state; also, the strength of both emotional states changes over time.

Opponent-process theory (sensation) The theory of color vision stating that three coding systems (red or green, yellow or blue, black or white) are used by the visual system to analyze color information.

Oral stage In Freud's theory, the period early in life when infants are preoccupied with the mouth as a source of pleasure and means of expression.

Organ of Corti Center part of the cochlea, containing hair cells, canals, and membranes.

Organic mental disorder A mental or emotional problem caused by malfunction of the brain.

Organic psychosis A psychosis caused by a known brain injury or disease.

Organismic valuing Placing value on an experience on the basis of how one responds to it as an entire organism; judgment made directly on the basis of one's perceptions and feelings.

Organizational psychology A field that focuses on the psychology of work and on behavior within organizations.

Orgasm A climax and release of sexual excitement.

Orientation response The pattern of changes occurring throughout the body that prepares an organism to receive information from a particular stimulus.

Originality In tests of creativity, originality refers to the degree of novelty or unusualness of the solutions produced.

Otolith organs Vestibular structures sensitive to movement, acceleration, and gravity.

Oval window A membrane on the cochlea connected to the third auditory ossicle.

Overdisclosure Self-disclosure that exceeds what is appropriate for a particular relationship or social situation.

Overeating Eating in excess of one's daily caloric needs.

Overgeneralization Blowing a single event out of proportion by extending it to a large number of unrelated situations.

Overlearning Study or learning that continues after initial mastery of skills or information.

Overly permissive parents Parents who give their children little guidance, allow them too much freedom, or do not require the child to take responsibility for his or her actions.

Overprotection Excessively guarding and shielding a child from possible stresses.

Overt behavior An action or response that is directly observable.

Ovulation The release of an ovum (egg cell) by the ovaries; ova combine with sperm cells to begin the growth of an embryo.

Pain disorder Pain that has no identifiable physical cause and appears to be of psychological origin.

Palmistry False system that claims to reveal personality traits and to predict the future by "reading" lines on the palms of the hands.

Panic disorder (with agoraphobia) The person is in a chronic state of anxiety and also has brief moments of sudden, intense, unexpected panic. In addition, the person fears that these panic attacks will occur in public places or unfamiliar situations.

Panic disorder (without agoraphobia) The person is in a chronic state of anxiety and also has brief moments of sudden, intense, unexpected panic.

Paranoid psychosis A delusional disorder centered especially on delusions of persecution.

Paranoid schizophrenia Schizophrenia marked by a preoccupation with delusions or by frequent auditory hallucinations related to a single theme, especially grandeur or persecution.

Paraphilias Compulsive or destructive deviations in sexual preferences or behavior.

Paraprofessional An individual who works in a near-professional capacity under the supervision of a more highly trained person.

Parapsychology The study of extranormal psychological events, such as extrasensory perception.

Parascience A system that resembles science but is not truly scientific.

Parasympathetic rebound Excess activity in the parasympathetic nervous system following a period of intense emotion.

Parasympathetic system A branch of the autonomic system responsible for quieting the body and conserving energy.

Parental responsiveness Caregiving that is based on sensitivity to a child's feelings, needs, rhythms, and signals.

Parietal lobes Area at the top of the brain that includes sites where bodily sensations register in the brain.

Part learning Separately studying subparts of a larger body of information (such as sections of a textbook chapter).

Partial hospitalization Treatment in which patients spend only part of their time at the hospital.

Partial reinforcement A pattern in which only a portion of responses are reinforced (also called intermittent reinforcement).

Partial reinforcement effect Greater resistance to extinction is found in responses acquired on a schedule of partial reinforcement.

Participative management An approach to management that allows employees at all levels to participate in decision making.

Passion The presence of heightened arousal in one's emotional response to another person.

Passive compliance Passively bending to unreasonable demands or circumstances.

Passive euthanasia Allowing death to occur without trying to prevent it or encourage it.

Paternal influences The aggregate of all psychological effects fathers have on their children.

Peak experiences Temporary moments of self-actualization, marked by feelings of ecstasy, harmony, and deep meaning.

Peak performance A performance during which physical, mental, and emotional states are harmonious and optimal.

Pedophilia Sex with children, or child molesting.

Peer counselor A nonprofessional person who has learned basic counseling skills.

Peer group A group of people who share similar social status.

Perception The mental process of organizing sensations into meaningful patterns.

Perceptual category A pre-existing class, type, or grouping.

Perceptual defense Resistance to perceiving threatening or disturbing stimuli.

Perceptual expectancy (or set) A readiness to perceive in a particular manner, induced by strong expectations.

Perceptual features Important elements of a stimulus pattern, such as lines, shapes, edges, spots, and colors.

Perceptual habits Established patterns of perceptual organization and attention.

Perceptual hypothesis An initial guess regarding the correct way to organize (perceive) a stimulus pattern.

Perceptual stimulation Varied, patterned, and meaningful sensory input.

Performance intelligence Intelligence measured by solving puzzles, assembling objects, completing pictures, and other nonverbal tasks.

Peripheral nervous system All parts of the nervous system lying outside the brain and spinal cord.

Peripheral vision Vision at the periphery (edges) of the visual field.

Persistence As a response to frustration, persistence refers to repeated, more vigorous efforts and more variable responding.

Persona The "mask" or public self presented to others.

Personal distance The distance maintained when interacting with close friends (about 18 inches to 4 feet from the body).

Personal frustration A negative emotional state caused by personal characteristics that hinder satisfaction of a motive or that block progress toward a goal.

Personal interview Formal or informal questioning of job applicants to learn their qualifications and to gain an impression of their personalities.

Personal prejudice Prejudicial attitudes held toward people who are perceived as a direct threat to one's own interests.

Personal space An area immediately surrounding the body that is regarded as private and subject to personal control.

Personal unconscious A mental storehouse for a single individual's unconscious thoughts.

Personality An individual's unique and relatively unchanging psychological characteristics and behavior patterns.

Personality disintegration A shattering of the coordination among thoughts, actions, and emotions normally found in personality.

Personality disorder A deeply ingrained, unhealthy, maladaptive personality pattern.

Personality psychologist A psychologist who studies personality traits and dynamics.

Personality questionnaire A paper-and-pencil test consisting of questions designed to reveal various aspects of the respondent's personality.

Personality theory An interrelated system of concepts and principles used to understand and explain personality.

Personality trait A behavioral characteristic displayed in most situations.

Personality type A style of personality defined by a group of related traits.

Personnel psychology Branch of industrial-organizational psychology concerned with testing, selection, placement, and promotion of employees.

Persuasion A deliberate attempt to change attitudes or beliefs with information and arguments.

PET scan Positron emission tomography; a computer-generated image of brain activity, based on glucose consumption in the brain.

Phallic stage In Freud's theory, the psychosexual stage (roughly age 3 to 6) when a person is preoccupied with the genitals as a source of pleasure.

Phenylketonuria A genetic disease that allows phenylpyruvic acid to accumulate in the body.

Pheromone An airborne chemical signal.

Philosophy The study of knowledge, reality, and human nature.

Phobia An intense and unrealistic fear of some object or situation.

Phobic disorder A type of anxiety disorder in which irrational fears (phobias) are focused on specific objects, activities, or situations.

Phonemes The basic sounds of a language that can be joined into syllables and words.

Phosphene A visual sensation caused by mechanical excitation of the retina.

Photon One quantum of light energy.

Photoreceptor Sensory receptors sensitive to light and specialized for the transduction of light stimuli into neural impulses.

Phototherapy A treatment for seasonal affective disorder that involves exposure to bright, full-spectrum light.

Phrenology False and antiquated system based on the belief that personality traits are revealed by the shape of the skull.

Physical attractiveness A person's degree of physical beauty, as defined by his or her culture.

Physical dependence Physical addiction, as indicated by the presence of drug tolerance and withdrawal symptoms.

Physical environments Natural settings, such as forests and beaches, as well as environments built by humans, such as buildings, ships, and cities.

Physical proximity As a factor in interpersonal attraction, one's actual physical nearness to others in terms of housing, work, school, and so forth.

Physiological changes in emotion Changes in bodily activities (especially involuntary responses) that accompany emotional states.

Physiological nystagmus An involuntary tremor of the eye.

Physiological psychologist A psychologist who studies the relationship between the nervous system and behavior.

Pica A craving for unnatural foods or substances such as chalk, ashes, and the like.

Pictorial depth cues Features found in paintings, drawings, and photographs that impart information about space, depth, and distance.

Pineal gland Gland in the brain that helps regulate body rhythms and sleep cycles.

Pitch Higher or lower tones; related to the frequency of sound waves.

Pituitary gland The "master gland" at the base of the brain whose hormones influence the output of other endocrine glands.

Place theory Theory of hearing that higher and lower frequency tones are detected at specific locations in the cochlea.

Placebo A substance that resembles a drug but has no chemical effect.

Placebo effect Changes in behavior due to expectations that a drug (or other treatment) will have some effect.

Plasticity The brain's capacity for revising its organization.

Plateau phase The second phase of sexual response, during which physical arousal is further heightened.

Pleasure principle The principle under which the id operates, consisting of a desire for immediate satisfaction of wishes, desires, or needs.

Polygenic characteristics Personal characteristics that are influenced by a combination of genes.

Polygraph A device for recording several physiological activities, typically including heart rate, blood pressure, respiration, and galvanic skin response; commonly called a "lie detector."

Population An entire group of animals or people belonging to a particular category (for example, all college students or all married women).

Positive instance In concept learning, an object or event that belongs to the concept class.

Positive reinforcement Occurs when a response is followed with a reward or other positive event.

Positive relationship A relationship in which increases in one measure correspond to increases in the other.

Positive self-regard Thinking of oneself as a good, lovable, worthwhile person.

Positive transfer Mastery of one task aids learning or performing another.

Positron emission tomography An image of brain activity based on glucose consumption.

Possible self A collection of thoughts, beliefs, feelings, and images concerning a self one could become.

Post-traumatic stress disorder Psychological disturbance lasting more than 1 month following stresses, such as natural disasters or military combat, that would produce anxiety in anyone who experienced them.

Postconventional moral reasoning Moral thinking based on carefully examined and self-chosen moral principles.

Postpartum depression A mild to moderately severe depression that begins within 3 months following childbirth.

Power assertion The use of physical punishment or coercion to enforce child discipline.

Preadaptation Gradual matching of sleep-waking cycles to a new time schedule before an anticipated major change in circadian rhythms.

Precognition The purported ability to accurately predict future events.

Preconscious An area of the mind that contains information not currently in consciousness but that can be voluntarily brought to awareness.

Preconventional moral reasoning Moral thinking based on the consequences of one's choices or actions (punishment, reward, or an exchange of favors).

Prefrontal lobotomy An antiquated surgery in which portions of the frontal lobes were destroyed or disconnected from other brain areas.

Prejudice A negative attitude or prejudgment held against members of a particular group of people.

Premack principle Any high-frequency response can be used to reinforce a low-frequency response.

Premature ejaculation Ejaculation that consistently occurs before the man and his partner want it to occur.

Premature puberty The development of sexual maturity in childhood.

Preoperational stage Period of intellectual development during which children begin to use language and think symbolically, yet remain intuitive and egocentric in their thought.

Prepared childbirth Techniques to manage discomfort and facilitate birth with a minimum of painkilling drugs.

Prepared childbirth training System for preparing women and their partners for childbirth.

Prepared fear theory Holds that people and animals are prepared by evolution to readily learn fears of certain stimuli.

Presbyopia Farsightedness caused by a loss of elasticity in the lens due to aging.

Pressure A stressful condition that occurs when a person must respond at, or near, maximum capacity for long periods.

Primary appraisal The first step in coping with a threatening situation, consisting of deciding if the situation is indeed a threat.

Primary auditory area Main area on the temporal lobes where hearing registers.

Primary emotions According to Plutchik, the most basic emotions are fear, surprise, sadness, disgust, anger, anticipation, joy, and acceptance.

Primary motives Innate motives based on biological needs.

Primary reinforcers Unlearned reinforcers; usually those that satisfy physiological needs.

Primary sexual characteristics Gender as defined by the genitals and internal reproductive organs.

Primary visual area Main area of the cerebral cortex that processes visual information.

Primate A member of the family of mammals including humans, apes, and monkeys.

Priming Activating implicit (hidden) memories by providing partial information that is linked with them.

Principle of motor primacy Principle that motor, muscular, and physical development must precede the learning of certain skills.

Proactive interference The tendency for old memories to interfere with the retrieval of newer memories.

Proactive maternal involvement Sensitive caregiving in which a mother actively provides her child with educational experiences.

Problem-focused coping Directly managing or remedying a stressful or threatening situation.

Procedural memory That part of long-term memory made up of conditioned responses and learned skills.

Productivity The capacity of language for generating new ideas and possibilities.

Programmed instruction Any learning format that presents information in small amounts, gives immediate practice, and provides continuous feedback to learners.

Progressive relaxation A method for producing deep relaxation of all parts of the body.

Projection Attributing one's own feelings, shortcomings, or unacceptable impulses to others.

Projective tests Psychological tests making use of ambiguous or unstructured stimuli. Subjects are presumed to project their own thoughts and impulses onto these stimuli.

Prosocial behavior Behavior toward others that is helpful, constructive, or altruistic.

Prototype An ideal, or model, used as a prime example of a particular concept.

Proxemics Systematic study of the human use of space, particularly interpersonal space in various social settings.

Pseudo-memories False memories that a person believes are real or accurate.

Pseudo-psychology Any false and unscientific system of beliefs and practices that is offered as an explanation of behavior.

Psi phenomena Events that seem to lie outside the realm of accepted scientific laws.

Psyche The mind, mental life, and personality as a whole.

Psychiatric social worker A professional who applies social science principles to help patients in clinics and hospitals.

Psychiatrist A medical doctor who specializes in treating mental disorders.

Psychoactive drug A substance capable of altering attention, memory, judgment, time sense, self-control, mood, or perception.

Psychoanalysis A Freudian approach to psychotherapy emphasizing the exploration of unconscious conflicts.

Psychoanalyst A mental health professional (usually a medical doctor) trained to practice psychoanalysis.

Psychoanalytic theory Freudian theory of personality that emphasizes unconscious forces and internal conflicts in its explanations of behavior.

Psychobiology A viewpoint that seeks to explain behavior through biological processes, such as activity in the brain and nervous system, genetics, the endocrine system, and evolution.

Psychodrama A therapy in which clients act out personal conflicts and feelings in the presence of others, who play supporting roles.

Psychodynamic theory Any theory of behavior that emphasizes internal conflicts, motives, and unconscious forces.

Psychokinesis The purported ability to mentally alter or influence objects or events.

Psycholinguist A specialist in the psychology of language and language development.

Psychological androgyny The presence of both "masculine" and "feminine" traits in a single person (as masculinity and femininity are defined within one's culture).

Psychological dependence Drug dependence that is based primarily on emotional or psychological needs.

Psychological efficiency Maintenance of good morale, labor relations, employee satisfaction, and similar aspects of work behavior.

Psychological situation A situation as it is perceived and interpreted by an individual, not as it exists objectively.

Psychological trauma A psychological injury or shock, such as that caused by violence, abuse, neglect, or separation.

Psychologist An individual highly trained in the methods, factual knowledge, and theories of psychology.

Psychology The scientific study of human and animal behavior.

Psychometrics Mental measurement or testing.

Psychoneuroimmunology Study of the links among behavior, disease, and the immune system.

Psychopath An individual who appears to make no distinctions between right and wrong and who feels no guilt about destructive or antisocial behavior.

Psychopathology The scientific study of mental, emotional, and behavioral disorders; also, abnormal or maladaptive behavior.

Psychophysics The study of the relationship between physical stimuli and the sensations they evoke in a human observer.

Psychosexual stages In Freud's theory of personality development, the oral, anal, phallic, and genital stages, during which various personality traits are formed.

Psychosis A severe psychological disorder characterized by a retreat from reality, hallucinations and delusions, disturbed emotions, and social withdrawal.

Psychosocial dilemma A conflict, between personal impulses and the social world, that affects development.

Psychosomatic disorder Illness in which psychological factors contribute to bodily damage or to damaging changes in bodily functioning.

Psychosurgery Any surgical alteration of the brain designed to bring about desirable behavioral or emotional changes.

Psychotherapist Anyone who does psychological therapy. People who call themselves psychotherapists are not always psychologists.

Psychotherapy Any form of psychological treatment for behavioral or emotional problems.

Psychotic disorder A severe psychological disorder characterized by a retreat from reality, by hallucinations and delusions, and by social withdrawal.

Puberty The biologically defined period during which a person matures sexually and becomes capable of reproduction.

Public distance Distance at which formal interactions, such as giving a speech, occur (about 12 feet or more from the body).

Punisher Any event that decreases the probability or frequency of responses it follows.

Punishment Occurs when a response is followed with pain or an otherwise negative event or when a response is followed with the removal of a positive reinforcer (response cost).

Pupil The dark spot at the front of the eye through which light passes.

Quality circle A discussion group in which employees voluntarily seek to solve business problems.

Racism Racial prejudice that has become institutionalized (that is, it is reflected in government policy, schools, and so forth) and that is enforced by the existing social power structure.

Random assignment The use of chance (for example, flipping a coin) to assign subjects to experimental and control groups.

Random search strategy Trying possible solutions to a problem in a more or less random order.

Rapid eye movements (REMs) Swift eye movements during sleep.

Rapid smoking Forced cigarette smoking designed to make smoking aversive and unappealing.

Rating scale A list of various personality traits or aspects of behavior on which a person is rated, during or after observation of the person's behavior.

Rational-emotive behavior therapy (REBT) An approach that attempts to change or remove irrational beliefs that cause emotional problems.

Rationalization Justifying one's own behavior by giving reasonable and "rational" but false reasons for it.

Reaction formation Preventing dangerous or threatening impulses from being expressed by exaggerating opposite behavior.

Reactive depression A serious depression that appears to be a reaction to some identifiable event.

Readiness Sufficient maturation for rapid acquisition of a skill.

Realistic stage Stage of career exploration in which career options are narrowed and more specific plans are made.

Reality principle The principle by which the ego functions, involving delaying action (or pleasure) until it is appropriate.

Reality testing Obtaining additional information to check on the accuracy of perceptions.

Recall To supply or reproduce memorized information with a minimum of external cues.

Receptive meditation Meditation in which attention is widened to include an awareness of one's total subjective experience.

Receptor sites Areas on the surface of neurons and other cells that are sensitive to neurotransmitters or hormones.

Recessive gene A gene whose influence will be expressed only when it is paired with a second recessive gene (it cannot be expressed when paired with a dominant gene).

Reciprocal inhibition Principle that one emotional state can block another, such as joy preventing fear, or anxiety inhibiting pleasure.

Reciprocity A reciprocal interchange or return in kind.

Recitation As a memory aid, repeating aloud information one wishes to retain.

Recoding Reorganizing or otherwise transforming information to facilitate storage in memory.

Recognition Memory in which previously learned material is correctly identified as that which was seen before.

Redintegration The process of reconstructing an entire complex memory after observing or remembering only a part of it.

Reference group Any group that an individual identifies with and uses as a standard for social comparison.

Referent power Social power gained when one is used as a point of reference by others.

Referred pain Pain that is felt in one part of body but comes from another part.

Reflection In client-centered therapy, the process of rephrasing or repeating thoughts and feelings so that clients become aware of what they are saying about themselves.

Reflex An innate, automatic response to a stimulus; for example, an eye blink, knee jerk, or dilation of the pupil.

Reflex arc The simplest behavior pattern, involving only three neurons; leads from a stimulus to an automatic response, such as an eye blink or knee jerk.

Refractory period A short time period after orgasm during which males are unable to again reach orgasm.

Refreezing In brainwashing, the process of rewarding and strengthening new attitudes and beliefs.

Refusal skills training Training that teaches youngsters how to resist influences to begin smoking (can also be applied to other drugs, such as alcohol or cocaine).

Regression Any return to an earlier, more infantile behavior pattern.

Rehearsal Silently repeating or mentally reviewing information to hold it in short-term memory or aid its long-term storage.

Reinforcement Any event that brings about learning or increases the probability that a particular response will occur.

Reinforcement value The subjective value a person attaches to a particular activity or reinforcer.

Relational concept A concept defined by the relationship between features of an object or between an object and its surroundings (for example, "greater than," "lopsided").

Relaxation response The pattern of physiological changes that occurs in the body at times of relaxation.

Relearning Learning again something that was previously learned. Used to measure one's memory of prior learning.

Relevant questions In a polygraph exam, questions to which only a guilty person should react.

Reliability The ability of a test to yield the same score, or nearly the same score, each time it is given to the same person.

REM behavior disorder A failure of normal muscle paralysis, leading to violent actions during REM sleep.

REM rebound The occurrence of extra amounts of rapid eye movement sleep in a person who has been deprived of REM sleep.

REM sleep Sleep marked by rapid eye movements, a return to stage 1 EEG patterns; usually associated with dreaming.

Replicate To reproduce or repeat.

Representative sample A small, randomly selected part of a larger population that accurately reflects characteristics of the whole population.

Representativeness heuristic A tendency to select wrong answers because they seem to match pre-existing mental categories.

Repression Unconsciously pushing out or barring from awareness unwanted memories.

Research method A systematic approach to answering scientific questions.

Resistance Blocking that occurs in psycho-analysis during free association; topics the client resists thinking or talking about.

Resolution (grief) With respect to grief, an acceptance of loss and the need for building a new life.

Resolution (sexual) The fourth phase of sexual response, involving a return to lower levels of sexual tension and arousal.

Respondent conditioning Another term for classical conditioning.

Respondent reinforcement In classical conditioning, reinforcement that occurs when the unconditioned stimulus closely follows the conditioned stimulus.

Response Any muscular action, glandular activity, or other identifiable behavior.

Response chaining The assembly of a series of responses into a chain of actions leading to reinforcement.

Response cost Punishment that occurs when a response leads to the removal of a positive reinforcer.

Response cost Removal of a positive reinforcer after a response is made.

Response-contingent Applying reinforcement, punishment, or other consequences only when a certain response is made.

REST Restricted environmental stimulation therapy.

Resting potential The electrical charge that exists between the inside and outside of a neuron at rest.

Retardation Mental capacity significantly below average; traditionally defined as an IQ score below 70.

Reticular activating system (RAS) A part of the reticular formation that activates the cerebral cortex.

Reticular formation A network of fibers within the medulla associated with attention, alertness, and activation of higher brain areas.

Retina The light-sensitive layer of cells at the back of the eye.

Retinal Part of the chemical compound that makes up rhodopsin (also known as retinene).

Retinal disparity Small discrepancies in the images falling on each retina caused by separation of the eyes.

Retrieval Recovering information from memory.

Retroactive interference The tendency for new memories to interfere with the retrieval of old memories.

Retrograde amnesia Loss of memory for events that preceded a head injury or other amnesia-causing event.

Reversibility of thought Recognition that relationships involving equality or identity can be reversed (for example, if A = B, then B = A).

Reversible figure A stimulus pattern that allows perceivers to reverse figure-ground organization.

Reward Anything that produces pleasure or satisfaction; a positive reinforcer.

Reward power Social power based on the capacity to reward a person for acting as desired.

Rhodopsin The photosensitive pigment in the rods.

Rods Visual receptors that are responsive to dim light but produce only black-and-white sensations.

Role conflict An upsetting condition that exists when a person tries to occupy two or more roles that make conflicting demands on behavior.

Role model A person who serves as a positive example of desirable behavior.

Role-playing The dramatic enactment or re-enactment of significant life events.

Sadism Deriving erotic satisfaction by the infliction of pain on another; more broadly, love of cruelty.

Sample A subset or portion of a population.

Satiety system Areas on the bottom middle of the hypothalamus that terminate eating.

Saturation That quality of colors related to their being very pure, from a narrow area of the spectrum, or free from mixture with other colors.

Savings score The amount of time saved (expressed as a percentage) when relearning information.

Scapegoating Selecting a person or group of people to take the blame for conditions not of their making; habitual redirection of aggression toward some person or group.

Schedule of reinforcement A rule or plan for determining which responses will be reinforced.

Schizophrenia A psychosis characterized by delusions, hallucinations, apathy, and a "split" between thought and emotion.

Schizotypal personality A nonpsychotic personality disorder involving withdrawal, social isolation, and odd behavior, but no break with reality.

Science A body of knowledge gained through systematic observation and experimentation.

Scientific Conducted strictly according to the principles of evidence used in the natural sciences.

Scientific management (Theory X) An approach to managing employees that emphasizes work efficiency.

Scientific method Testing the truth of a proposition by careful measurement and controlled observation.

Scientific observation Orderly observation designed to answer questions about the world.

Scientist-practitioner model Training of clinical psychologists to do both research and therapy.

Seasonal affective disorder Depression that occurs during fall and winter; presumably related to decreased exposure to sunlight.

Secondary appraisal Deciding how to cope with a threat or challenge.

Secondary elaboration Making a dream more logical and complete while remembering it.

Secondary motives Motives based on learned psychological needs.

Secondary reinforcer A learned reinforcer; often one that gains reinforcing properties by association with a primary reinforcer.

Secondary sexual characteristics Sexual features other than the genitals and reproductive organs—such as the breasts, body shape, and facial hair.

Secondary traits Personality traits that are inconsistent or relatively superficial.

Secure attachment A stable and positive emotional bond.

Sedative A substance that calms, tranquilizes, or induces sleep by depressing activity in the nervous system.

Selective attention Voluntarily focusing on a selected portion of sensory input, most likely by re-routing messages within the brain.

Selective combination In problem solving, the ability to connect seemingly unrelated items of information.

Selective comparison The ability to relate a present problem to similar problems solved in the past or to prior experience.

Selective encoding The mental ability to select relevant information while ignoring useless or distracting information.

Selective perception Perceiving only certain stimuli among a larger array of possibilities.

Self A continuously evolving conception of one's personal identity.

Self archetype An unconscious image representing unity, wholeness, completion, and balance.

Self-actualization The ongoing process of fully developing one's personal potential.

Self-assertion A direct, honest expression of feelings and desires.

Self-awareness Consciousness of oneself as a person.

Self-concept Personal perception of one's own personality traits; a collection of beliefs, ideas, and feelings about one's own identity.

Self-disclosure The process of revealing private thoughts, feelings, and personal history to others.

Self-esteem Regarding oneself as a worthwhile person; a positive evaluation of oneself.

Self-evaluation Positive and negative feelings held toward oneself.

Self-fulfilling prophecy A prediction that prompts people to act in ways that make the prediction come true.

Self-handicapping Arranging to perform under conditions that usually lower performance, so as to have an excuse available for a poor showing.

Self-help group A group of people who share a particular type of problem and provide mutual support to one another.

Self-hypnosis A state of hypnosis attained without the aid of a hypnotist; autosuggestion.

Self-image Total subjective perception of one's body and personality (another term for self-concept).

Self-instruction Use of silent questions and instructions to structure learning.

Self-monitoring Regulation and control of the image one displays to others in public.

Self-recording Self-management based on keeping records of response frequencies.

Self-regulated learning Active, self-guided learning.

Self-reinforcement Praising or rewarding oneself for having made a particular response (such as completing a school assignment).

Self-selection feeding Free choice concerning the foods eaten.

Self-testing Answering self-administered questions.

Semantic differential A measure of connotative meaning obtained by rating words or concepts on several dimensions.

Semantic memory A subpart of declarative memory that records impersonal knowledge about the world.

Semantics The study of meanings in language.

Semicircular canals Fluid-filled vestibular canals; the sensory organs for balance.

Senile dementia Serious mental impairment in old age, caused by physical deterioration of the brain.

Sensate focus Form of therapy that directs a couple's attention to natural sensations of sexual pleasure.

Sensation The immediate response in the brain caused by excitation of a sensory organ.

Sensation and perception psychologist A psychologist with expert knowledge on the sense organs and the processes involved in perception.

Sensation seeking A personality characteristic of people who prefer high levels of stimulation.

Sensitivity group A group experience designed to increase self-awareness and sensitivity to others.

Sensorimotor stage Stage of intellectual development during which sensory input and motor responses become coordinated.

Sensory adaptation A decrease in sensory response to an unchanging stimulus.

Sensory analysis The capacity of sensory systems to separate incoming information into important elements.

Sensory coding Various codes used by the sense organs to transmit information to the brain.

Sensory conflict theory Attributes motion sickness to mismatched information from vision, the vestibular system, and kinesthesis.

Sensory deprivation Any major reduction in the amount or variety of sensory stimulation.

Sensory gating Alteration of incoming sensory messages in the spinal cord, before they reach the brain.

Sensory memory The first stage of memory, which holds an explicit and literal record of incoming information for 2 seconds or less.

Sensory neuron A nerve cell that carries information from the senses toward the central nervous system.

Separation anxiety Distress displayed by infants when they are separated from their parents or principal caregivers.

Serial position effect The tendency for the greatest number of memory errors to occur in the middle portion of an ordered list.

Set A predisposition to respond in a certain way.

Set point A theoretical proportion of body fat that tends to be maintained by changes in hunger and eating.

Setting In making attributions, the social and/or physical environment in which an action occurs.

Severe punishment Intense punishment; by definition, punishment capable of suppressing a response for long periods.

Sex drive The strength of one's motivation to engage in sexual behavior.

Sexism Institutionalized prejudice against members of either sex, based solely on their gender.

Sex-linked trait Traits other than gender that are influenced by genes carried on an *X* or a *Y* chromosome.

Sexual and gender identity disorders Any of a wide range of difficulties with sexual identity, deviant sexual behavior, or sexual adjustment.

Sexual aversion Fear, anxiety, or disgust about engaging in sex.

Sexual disorder Any of a wide range of difficulties with sexual identity, sexual behavior, or sexual adjustment.

Sexual masochism Deriving sexual pleasure from having pain inflicted during the sex act.

Sexual orientation One's degree of emotional and erotic attraction to members of the same sex, opposite sex, or both sexes.

Sexual sadism Gaining sexual pleasure by inflicting pain during the sex act.

Sexual script An unspoken mental plan that defines a "plot," dialogue, and actions expected to take place in a sexual encounter.

Sexually transmitted disease A disease that is typically passed from one person to the next by intimate physical contact; a venereal disease.

Shape constancy The perceived shape of objects is unaltered by changes in the shape of their images on the retina.

Shaping Gradually molding responses to a final desired pattern.

Short-term dynamic therapy Modern psychodynamic therapy designed to produce insights within a shorter time than traditional psychoanalysis.

Short-term memory (STM) The memory system used to hold small amounts of information for relatively brief periods.

Shyness A tendency to avoid others, plus uneasiness and strain when socializing.

Sibling rivalry Competition among brothers and sisters for attention, dominance, status within the family, and so forth.

Signal In early language development, any behavior, such as touching, vocalizing, gazing, or smiling, that allows nonverbal interaction and turn-taking between parent and child.

Similarity In interpersonal attraction, the extent to which two people are alike in background, age, interests, attitudes, beliefs, and so forth.

Single-blind experiment An arrangement in which subjects remain unaware of whether they are in the experimental group or the control group.

Single-word stage In language development, the period during which a child first begins to use single words.

Situational context The social situation, behavioral setting, or general circumstances in which an action takes place.

Situational demands Unstated expectations that define desirable or appropriate behavior in various settings and social situations.

Situational determinants External conditions that strongly influence behavior.

Situational test Simulating real-life conditions so that a person's reactions may be directly observed.

Size constancy The perceived size of objects remains unchanged despite changes in the size of the images they cast on the retina.

Size-distance invariance The strict relationship that exists between the distance an object lies from the eyes and the size of its image.

Skin receptors Sensory organs for touch, pressure, pain, cold, and warmth.

Skin senses The senses of touch, pressure, pain, heat, and cold.

Sleep apnea Repeated interruption of breathing during sleep.

Sleep deprivation Being deprived of desired or needed amounts of sleep.

Sleep patterns The order and duration of daily sleep and waking periods.

Sleep spindles Distinctive bursts of brain-wave activity that indicate a person is asleep.

Sleep stages Various levels of sleep depth identified by brain-wave patterns and behavioral changes.

Sleep-deprivation psychosis A major disruption of mental and emotional functioning brought about by lack of sleep.

Sleeptalking Speaking while asleep.

Slow-to-warm-up child A child who is temperamentally restrained, unexpressive, or shy.

Social comparison Making judgments about ourselves through comparison with others.

Social development The development of self-awareness, attachment to caregivers, and relationships with other children and adults.

Social distance Distance at which impersonal interaction takes place (about 4 to 12 feet from the body).

Social distance scale An attitude measure that asks people to rate the degree to which they would be willing to have contact with a member of another group.

Social environment An environment defined by a group of people and their activities or interrelationships (such as a parade, revival meeting, or sports event).

Social exchange Any exchange between two people of attention, information, affection, favors, or the like.

Social exchange theory Theory stating that rewards must exceed costs for relationships to endure.

Social influence Changes in a person's behavior induced by the presence or actions of others.

Social learning theory An approach that combines learning principles with cognitive processes (perception, thinking, anticipation), plus the effects of observational learning, to explain behavior.

Social markers Visible or tangible signs that indicate a person's social status or role.

Social motives Learned motives acquired as part of growing up in a particular society or culture.

Social nonconformity Failure to conform to societal norms or the usual minimum standards for social conduct.

Social phobia An intense, irrational fear of being observed, evaluated, embarrassed, or humiliated by others in social situations, such as eating, writing, blushing, or speaking in public.

Social power The capacity to control, alter, or influence the behavior of another person.

Social psychology The study of human social behavior (behavior that is influenced by one's relationship with others).

Social Readjustment Rating Scale (SRRS) A scale that rates the impact of various life events on the likelihood of illness.

Social referencing Observing others in social situations to obtain information or guidance.

Social reinforcement Praise, attention, approval, and/or affection from others.

Social role Expected behavior patterns associated with particular social positions (such as daughter, worker, or student).

Social stereotypes Oversimplified images of the traits of individuals who belong to a particular social group.

Social support Close, positive relationships with other people.

Social trap A social situation that tends to provide immediate rewards for actions that will have undesired effects in the long run.

Socialization The process of learning to live in a particular culture by adopting socially acceptable values and behavior.

Sociobiology Theory that social behavior evolved in ways that maximize fitness for survival of the species.

Sociopath Another name for the psychopath or antisocial personality.

Soma The main body of a neuron or other cell.

Somatic pain Pain from the skin, muscles, joints, and tendons.

Somatic system The system of nerves linking the spinal cord with the body and sense organs.

Somatic therapy Any bodily therapy, such as drug therapy, electroconvulsive therapy, or psychosurgery.

Somatization disorder Afflicted people have numerous physical complaints. Typically, they have consulted many doctors, but no organic cause for their distress can be identified.

Somatoform disorder The presence of physical symptoms that mimic disease or injury for which there is no identifiable physical cause.

Somatoform pain Pain that has no identifiable physical cause and appears to be of psychological origin.

Somatosensory area The part of the parietal lobes that serves as a receiving area for bodily sensations.

Somesthetic sense Pertaining to sensations produced by the skin, muscles, joints, viscera, and organs of balance.

Somnambulist One who sleepwalks.

Sound wave A cyclic compression of air molecules.

Source traits Basic underlying traits of personality; each source trait is reflected in a larger number of surface traits.

Space adaptation syndrome Motion sickness caused by weightlessness.

Spaced practice A practice schedule that alternates study periods with brief rests. (Massed practice, in comparison, continues for long periods, without interruption.)

Spatial neglect A tendency to ignore the left or right side of one's body and the left or right side of visual space after damage to one of the brain hemispheres.

Special aptitude test Test to predict a person's likelihood of succeeding in a particular area of work or skill.

Species-specific behavior Behavior patterns that occur with little variation in almost all members of a species.

Species-typical behavior Behavior patterns that are typical of a species but not automatic.

Specific phobia An intense, irrational fear of specific objects, activities, or situations.

Spinal nerve One of 62 major nerves that channel sensory and motor information in and out of the spinal cord.

Split-brain operation A surgical technique in which the corpus callosum is cut, functionally disconnecting the two cerebral hemispheres.

Spontaneous recovery The reappearance of a learned response after its apparent extinction.

Spontaneous remission The disappearance of a psychological disturbance without the aid of therapy.

Sports psychology Study of the psychological and behavioral dimensions of sports performance.

SQ4R method A reading method based on these steps: survey, question, read, recite, relate, and review.

Squeeze technique Method for inhibiting ejaculation by compressing the tip of the penis.

Stage ESP The simulation of ESP for the purpose of entertainment.

Stage hypnosis Use of hypnosis to entertain; often, merely a simulation of hypnosis.

Stage of exhaustion Third stage of the G.A.S., at which time the body's resources are exhausted and serious health consequences occur.

Stage of resistance Second stage of the G.A.S., during which bodily adjustments to stress stabilize but at a high physical cost.

Staining Chemically treating tissues to make their details more visible.

Stanford-Binet Intelligence Scale A widely used individual test of intelligence; a direct descendant of Alfred Binet's first intelligence test.

State-dependent learning Memory influenced by one's bodily state at the time of learning and at the time of retrieval. Improved memory occurs when the bodily states match.

Statistical abnormality Abnormality defined on the basis of an extreme score on some measure or dimension, such as IQ or anxiety.

Statistical significance Experimental results that would rarely occur by chance alone.

Status An individual's position in a group or social structure, especially with respect to power, privilege, importance, and so forth.

Status inequalities Differences in the power, prestige, or privileges of two or more people or groups.

Stereocilia Bristle-like structures on hair cells.

Stereoscopic vision Perception of space and depth caused chiefly by the fact that the eyes receive different images.

Stereotype An inaccurate, rigid, and oversimplified image of members of a social group, especially an outgroup.

Stereotyped response A rigid, repetitive, and unproductive response made mechanically and without regard for its appropriateness.

Stimulant A substance that produces a temporary increase of activity in the body and nervous system.

Stimulation deafness Deafness resulting from damage caused by exposure to excessively loud sounds.

Stimulus Any physical energy sensed by an organism.

Stimulus control The tendency of stimuli present when an operant response is acquired to subsequently control when and where the response is made.

Stimulus discrimination The learned ability to detect differences in stimuli, often produced by reinforcing responses to one stimulus but not another.

Stimulus generalization The tendency to respond to stimuli similar to, but not identical to, a conditioned stimulus.

Stimulus motives Innate needs for stimulation and information.

Stress The condition that occurs when a challenge or a threat forces a person to adjust or adapt to the environment.

Stress inoculation Use of positive coping statements to control fear and anxiety.

Stress management The application of behavioral strategies to reduce stress and improve coping skills.

Stress reaction The physical response to stress, consisting mainly of bodily changes related to autonomic nervous system arousal.

Stressor A specific condition or event in the environment that challenges or threatens a person.

Stroboscopic movement Illusion of movement in which an object is shown in a rapidly changing series of positions.

Structuralism The school of thought in psychology concerned with analyzing sensations and personal experience into basic elements.

Structured interview An interview that follows a prearranged plan, usually defined by asking a series of planned questions.

Stuttering Chronic hesitation or stumbling in speech.

Subcortex All brain structures below the cerebral cortex.

Subjective discomfort Personal, private feelings of discomfort or unhappiness.

Subjective experience Reality as it is perceived and interpreted, not as it exists objectively; personal, private, nonobjective experience.

Sublimation Working off frustrated desires or unacceptable impulses in substitute activities that are constructive or accepted by society.

Subliminal perception Perception of a stimulus presented below the threshold for conscious recognition.

Substance related disorder Abuse of or dependence on a mood- or behavior-altering drug.

Successive approximations A series of steps that change behavior to a desired response pattern.

Sucking reflex Rhythmic sucking movements elicited by touching the neonate's mouth.

Sudden infant death syndrome The sudden, unexplained death of an apparently healthy infant.

Superego In Freudian theory, an internalization of parental values and societal standards.

Superordinate goal A goal that exceeds or overrides all others; a goal that renders other goals relatively less important.

Superstitious behavior In conditioning, a behavior repeated because it seems to produce reinforcement, even though it is actually unnecessary.

Support group A group formed to provide emotional support for its members through discussion of shared stresses and concerns.

Suppression A conscious effort to not think of something or to keep it from awareness.

Surface traits The visible or observable traits of one's personality.

Surrogate mother A substitute mother (often an inanimate dummy in animal research).

Survey method The use of public polling techniques to answer psychological questions.

Syllogism A format for analyzing logical arguments.

Symbolic prejudice Prejudice that is expressed in disguised fashion.

Symbolization In Carl Rogers's theory, the process of admitting an experience to awareness.

Sympathetic system A branch of the autonomic system responsible for arousing and activating the body at times of stress.

Synapse The microscopic space, between an axon terminal and another neuron, over which neurotransmitters pass.

Synesthesia Experiencing one sense in terms normally associated with another sense; for example, "seeing" sounds as colors.

Syntax Rules for ordering words when forming sentences.

Systematic desensitization A guided reduction in fear, anxiety, or aversion.

Tardive dyskinesia A neurological disorder associated with excessive use of major tranquilizers.

Target behaviors Actions or other behaviors (such as speech) that a behavior therapist seeks to modify.

Task centering Focusing on the task at hand, rather than on one's own feelings or needs.

Taste aversion An active dislike for a particular food; frequently created when the food is associated with illness or discomfort.

Taste bud The receptor organ for taste.

Telegraphic speech In language development, the formation of simple two-word sentences that "telegraph" (communicate) a simple idea.

Telepathy The purported ability to directly know another person's thoughts.

Temperament The physical foundation of personality, including emotional and perceptual sensitivity, energy levels, and typical mood.

Temporal lobes Areas on each side of the cerebral cortex that include the sites where hearing registers in the brain.

Temporary threshold shift A temporary decrease in sensitivity to sound.

Tentative stage Stage of career exploration in which planning becomes more realistic, although still broad.

Terminal decline An abrupt decline in measured intelligence about 5 years before death.

Territorial behavior Any behavior that tends to define a space as one's own or that protects it from intruders.

Territorial markers Objects and other signals whose placement indicates to others the "ownership" of a particular area.

Test anxiety High levels of arousal and worry that seriously impair test performance.

Test battery A group of tests and interviews given to the same individual.

Test standardization Establishing standards for administering a test and interpreting scores.

Testosterone Male sex hormone, secreted mainly by the testes and responsible for the development of male sexual characteristics.

Thalamus A structure at the center of the brain that relays sensory information to the cerebral cortex.

Thanatologist A specialist who studies emotional and behavioral reactions to death and dying.

Thanatos The death instinct postulated by Freud.

THC Tetrahydrocannabinol, the main active chemical in marijuana.

Thematic Apperception Test (TAT) A projective test consisting of 20 different scenes and life situations about which respondents make up stories.

Theory A system designed to interrelate concepts and facts in a way that summarizes existing data and predicts future observations.

Theory Y A management style that emphasizes human relations at work and that views people as industrious, responsible, and interested in challenging work.

Therapy placebo effect Improvement caused not by the actual process of therapy but by a client's expectation that therapy will help.

Thought stopping Use of aversive stimuli to interrupt or prevent upsetting thoughts.

Threat An event or situation perceived as potentially harmful to one's well-being.

Thyroid gland Endocrine gland whose hormones help regulate metabolism (the production and expenditure of energy within the body).

Time out Removing a person from a situation in which rewards for maladaptive behavior are available, in order to produce extinction; also, the withholding of social reinforcers (attention, approval) when undesirable responses are made.

Tinnitus A ringing or buzzing sensation in the ears not caused by an external stimulus.

Tip-of-the-tongue state The experience of feeling that a memory is available, while being unable to retrieve it.

Token economy A therapeutic program in which desirable behaviors are reinforced with tokens that can be exchanged for goods, services, activities, and privileges.

Token reinforcer A tangible secondary reinforcer such as money, gold stars, or poker chips.

Tokens Symbolic rewards, or secondary reinforcers (such as plastic chips, gold stars, or points), that can be exchanged for real reinforcers.

Top-down processing Applying higher level knowledge to rapidly organize sensory information into a meaningful perception.

Tragedy of the commons A social trap in which individuals, each acting in his or her immediate self-interest, overuse a scarce group resource.

Trait profile A graphic representation of the ratings obtained by an individual (or sometimes a group) on each of several personality traits.

Trait theorist A psychologist who is interested in classifying, analyzing, and interrelating traits, and in discovering their origins, to understand and explain personality.

Traits (personality) Relatively permanent and enduring qualities of behavior that a person displays in most situations.

Trait-situation interaction Variations in behavior that occur when the expression of a trait is influenced by settings or circumstances.

Transducer A device that converts energy from one system into energy in another.

Transference In psychoanalysis, the tendency of a client to transfer to the therapist feelings that correspond to those the client had for important persons in his or her past.

Transformation In Piaget's theory, the mental ability to change the shape or form of a substance (such as clay or water) and to perceive that its volume remains the same.

Transformation rules Rules by which a simple declarative sentence may be changed to other voices or forms (past tense, passive voice, and so forth).

Transition period Time span during which a person leaves an existing life pattern behind and moves into a new pattern.

Transvestic fetishism Achieving sexual arousal by wearing clothing of the opposite sex.

Trepanning In modern usage, any surgical procedure in which a hole is bored in the skull; historically, the chipping or boring of holes in the skull to "treat" mental disturbance.

Triangular theory of love Theory that love is composed of three elements: intimacy, passion, and commitment; different types of love are defined by the presence or absence of each element.

Trichromatic theory The theory of color vision based on the assumption that there are three types of cones, with peak sensitivity to red, green, or blue.

Tryptophan A sleep-promoting amino acid.

Tunnel vision Vision restricted to the center of the visual field.

Turn-taking In early language development, the tendency of parent and child to alternate in the sending and receiving of signals or messages.

Two-factor learning Learning that involves both classical conditioning and operant conditioning.

Tympanic membrane The eardrum.

Type A personality A personality type with an elevated risk of heart disease; characterized by time urgency, anger, and hostility.

Type B personality All personality types other than Type A; a low-cardiac-risk personality.

Unconditional positive regard Unshakable love and approval given without qualification.

Unconditioned response An innate reflex response elicited by an unconditioned stimulus.

Unconditioned stimulus A stimulus innately capable of eliciting a response.

Unconscious Region of the mind that is beyond awareness, especially impulses and desires not directly known to a person.

Undifferentiated schizophrenia Schizophrenia lacking the specific features of catatonic, disorganized, or paranoid types.

Unfreezing In brainwashing, a loosening of convictions about former values, attitudes, and beliefs.

Unipolar disorder A mood disorder in which a person experiences extended periods of deep depression but has no history of ever having been manic.

Unstructured interview An interview in which conversation is informal and topics are taken up freely as they arise.

Unusual uses test A test of creativity in which subjects try to think of new uses for a common object.

Vacillation Wavering in intention or feelings.

Vaginismus Muscle spasms of the vagina that prevent intercourse or cause pain.

Validity The ability of a test to measure what it purports to measure.

Validity scales Scales that tell whether test scores should be invalidated for lying, inconsistency, or "faking good."

Variable Any condition that changes or can be made to change; a measure, event, or state that may vary.

Variable interval schedule A schedule in which a reinforcer is given for the first correct response made after a varied amount of time has passed (measured from the previous reinforced response). Responses made before the time interval has ended are not reinforced.

Variable ratio schedule A pattern in which a varied number of correct responses must be made to get a reinforcer. For example, a reinforcer is given after three to seven correct responses; the actual number changes randomly.

Verbal intelligence Intelligence measured by answering questions involving vocabulary, general information, arithmetic, and other language- or symbol-oriented tasks.

Vestibular senses The senses of balance, body position, and acceleration.

Vicarious classical conditioning Classical conditioning brought about by observing another person react to a particular stimulus.

Vicarious desensitization A reduction in fear or anxiety that takes place vicariously ("secondhand") when a client watches models perform the feared behavior.

Virilism The development of male sexual characteristics in a female.

Visceral pain Pain originating in the internal organs.

Visible spectrum That portion of the electromagnetic spectrum to which the eyes are sensitive.

Visual acuity The clarity or sharpness of visual perception.

Visual cliff An apparatus that looks like the edge of an elevated platform or cliff; used to test for depth perception in infants and baby animals.

Visual pigment A chemical found in the rods and cones that is sensitive to light.

Visually directed reaching Coordinated, visually guided reaching for a particular object.

Vocational counselor A counseling psychologist who helps people match their interests, talents, and goals with available careers.

Vocational interest test A paper-and-pencil test that assesses a person's interests and matches them to interests found among successful workers in various occupations.

Volume transmission The spread of neuropeptides into groups of neurons, affecting their behavior.

Vomeronasal organ A sensory organ sensitive to pheromones.

Voyeurism Deriving sexual pleasure from viewing the genitals of others, usually without their knowledge or permission (peeping).

Waiting-list control group A group of people who receive no treatment in experiments designed to test the effectiveness of psychotherapy.

Waking consciousness A state of normal, alert awareness.

Warning system Pain based on large nerve fibers; warns that bodily damage may be occurring.

Weapons effect The observation that weapons serve as strong cues for aggressive behavior; also, the tendency for eyewitnesses to focus almost entirely on an assailant's weapon.

Weber's law States that the just noticeable difference is a constant proportion of the original stimulus intensity; actually applies most accurately to stimuli in the mid-range of intensities.

Wechsler Adult Intelligence Scale, Third Edition (WAIS-III) A widely used adult intelligence test that rates both verbal and performance intelligence.

Wechsler Intelligence Scale for Children, Third Edition (WISC-III) A widely used intelligence test for children that rates both verbal and performance intelligence.

Weight cycling Repeated swings between losing and gaining weight.

Wellness A positive state of good health; more than the absence of disease.

Wernicke's area An area of the brain related to language comprehension.

White matter Portions of the nervous system that appear white because of the presence of myelin.

Whole learning Studying an entire package of information (such as a complete poem) at once.

Wish fulfillment Freudian belief that the content of many dreams reflects unfulfilled desires that cannot be consciously expressed.

Withdrawal of love Withholding affection to enforce child discipline.

Withdrawal symptoms Physical illness and discomfort that accompany the withdrawal of an addictive drug.

Work efficiency Maximum output (productivity) at lowest cost.

Working memory Another name for short-term memory, especially as it is used for thinking and problem solving.

X chromosome The female chromosome contributed by the mother; produces a female when paired with another X chromosome, and a male when paired with a Y chromosome.

Y chromosome The male chromosome contributed by the father; produces a male when paired with an X chromosome. Fathers may give either an X or a Y chromosome to their offspring.

Yerkes-Dodson law A qualification of the inverted U function that states the relationships among arousal, task complexity, and performance.

Zener cards A deck of 25 cards bearing various symbols and used in early parapsychological research.

A nation's shame: Fatal child abuse and neglect in the United States. (1995). United States Advisory Board on Child Abuse and Neglect, United States Department of Health and Human Services.

Abbey, A., McAuslan, P., & Ross, L. T. (1998). Sexual assault perpetration by college men. *Journal of Social & Clinical Psychology, 17*(2), 167–195.

Abbott, A., & Concar, D. (1992). A trip into the unknown. *New Scientist,* Aug., 30–34.

Abe, K., Amatomi, M., & Oda, N. (1984). Sleepwalking and recurrent sleeptalking in children of childhood sleepwalkers. *American Journal of Psychiatry, 141,* 800–801.

Abelson, R. P. (1988). Conviction. *American Psychologist, 43*(4), 267–275.

Abi-Dargham, A., et al. (1998). Increased striatal dopamine transmission in schizophrenia. *American Journal of Psychiatry, 155*(6), 761–767.

Abrahamson, D. J., Barlow, D. H., & Abrahamson, L. S. (1989). Differential effects of performance demand and distraction on sexually functional and dysfunctional males. *Journal of Abnormal Psychology, 98*(3), 241–247.

Abrams, A. (1983, January 7). Honda Ohio plant transplants Japan methods, harmony. *Los Angeles Times,* pp. IV1–IV2.

Abrams, R. (1997). *Electroconvulsive therapy.* New York: Oxford University Press.

Abramson, R. (1993, January 8). EPA officially links passive smoke, cancer. *Los Angeles Times,* p. A27.

Ackerman, M. D., & Carey, M. P. (1995). Psychology's role in the assessment of erectile dysfunction. *Journal of Consulting & Clinical Psychology, 63*(6), 862–876.

Ackerson, J., et al. (1998). Cognitive bibliotherapy for mild and moderate adolescent depressive symptomatology. *Journal of Consulting & Clinical Psychology, 66*(4), 685–690.

Adams, J. (1988). *Conceptual blockbusting.* New York: Norton.

Adams, R. J., & Corage, M. L. (1998). Human newborn color vison. *Journal of Experimental Child Psychology, 68*(1), 22–34.

Adelmann, P. K., & Zajonc, R. B. (1989). Facial efference and the experience of emotion. *Annual Review of Psychology, 40,* 249–280.

Ader, R., & Cohen, N. (1993). Psychoneuroimmunology: Conditioning and stress. *Annual Review of Psychology, 44,* 53–85.

Adler, T. (1992, December). Are hormone's benefits real—or a tall tale? *APA Monitor,* 42, 43.

Adolph, K. E. (1997). Learning in the development of infant locomotion. *Monographs of the Society for Research in Child Development, 62*(3), 1–140.

Adorno, T. W., Frenkel-Brunswik, E., Levinson, D. J., & Sanford, R. N. (1950). *The authoritarian personality.* New York: Harper.

Aggleton, J. P., & Waskett, L. (1999). The ability of odours to serve as state-dependent cues for real-world memories. *British Journal of Psychology, 90*(1), 1–7.

Aging with Dignity. (1998). *Five wishes.* Tallahassee, FL: Aging with Dignity.

Agnati, L. F., Bjelke, B., & Fuxe, K. (1992). Volume transmission in the brain. *American Scientist, 80,* 362–373.

Ahissar, M. (1999). Perceptual learning. *Current Directions in Psychological Science, 8*(4), 124–128.

Ahles, T. A., Blanchard, E. B., & Leventhal, H. (1983). Cognitive control of pain: Attention to the sensory aspects of the cold pressor stimulus. *Cognitive Therapy and Research, 7,* 159–178.

Ainsworth, M. D. (1989). Attachments beyond infancy. *American Psychologist, 44*(4), 709–716.

Akerstedt, T. (1990). Psychological and psychophysiological effects of shift work. *Scandinavian Journal of Work, Environment & Health, 16*(Suppl. 1), 67–73.

Akerstedt, T., Hume, K., Minors, D., & Waterhouse, J. (1993). Regulation of sleep and naps on an irregular schedule. *Sleep, 16*(8), 736–743.

Alarcon, R. D. (1995). Culture and psychiatric diagnosis: Impact on DSM-IV and ICD-10. *Psychiatric Clinics of North America, 18*(3), 449–465.

Albert, E. M. (1963). The roles of women: Question of values. In Farber & Wilson (Eds.), *The potential of women.* New York: McGraw-Hill.

Alberti, R., & Emmons, M. (1995). *Your perfect right.* San Luis Obispo, CA: Impact.

Alberto, P. A. & Troutman, A. C. (1998). *Applied behavior analysis for teachers.* Englewood Cliffs, NJ: Prentice Hall.

Alcock, J. E. (1990). *Science and supernature: A critical appraisal of parapsychology.* Buffalo, NY: Prometheus.

Alden, L. E., & Wallace, S. T. (1995). Social phobia and social appraisal in successful and unsuccessful social interactions. *Behaviour Research & Therapy, 33*(5), 497–505.

Alfeld-Liro, C., & Sigelman, C. K. (1998). Sex differences in self-concept and symptoms of depression during the transition to college. *Journal of Youth & Adolescence, 27*(2), 219–244.

Alicke, M. D., & Doherty, K. (1992). Social disagreement and conformity. *Journal of Social Behavior & Personality, 7*(1), 125–137.

Alicke, M. D., Yurak, T. J., & Vredenburg, D. S. (1996). Using personal attitudes to judge others. *Journal of Research in Personality, 30*(1), 103–119.

Allen, B. (1979). Winged victory of "Gossamer Albatross." *National Geographic, 156,* 642–651.

Allen, M., Mabry, E., & McKelton, D. (1998). Impact of juror attitudes about the death penalty on juror evaluations of guilt and punishment: A meta-analysis. *Law & Human Behavior, 22*(6), 715–731.

Allgeier, A. R., & Allgeier, E. R. (1995). *Sexual interactions.* Lexington, MA: Heath.

Alloy, L. B., & Clements, C. M. (1998). Hopelessness theory of depression. *Cognitive Therapy & Research, 22*(4), 303–335.

Alloy, L. B., Peterson, C., Abramson, L. Y., & Seligman, M. E. (1984). Attributional style and the generality of learned helplessness. *Journal of Personality & Social Psychology, 46,* 681–687.

Allport, G. W. (1958). *The nature of prejudice.* Garden City, NY: Anchor Books, Doubleday.

Allport, G. W. (1961). *Pattern and growth in personality.* New York: Holt, Rinehart, and Winston.

Alsaker, F. D. (1992). Pubertal timing, overweight, and psychological adjustment. *Journal of Early Adolescence, 12*(4), 396–419.

Alsaker, F. D. (1995). Is puberty a critical period for socialization? *Journal of Adolescence, 18*(4), 427–444.

Althof, S. E., & Seftel, A. D. (1995). The evaluation and management of erectile dysfunction. *Psychiatric Clinics of North America, 18*(1), 171–192.

Alvarado, N. (1994). Empirical validity of the Thematic Apperception Test. *Journal of Personality Assessment, 63*(1), 59–79.

Alvino, J., & the Editors of *Gifted Children Monthly.* (1996). *Parents' guide to raising a gifted child.* New York: Ballantine.

Amabile, T. M. (1983). *The social psychology of creativity.* New York: Springer-Verlag.

Amar, P. B. (1993). Biofeedback and applied psychophysiology at the crossroads. *Biofeedback & Self-Regulation, 18*(4), 201–209.

Anastasi, A. (1996). *Psychological tests.* Englewood Cliffs, NJ: Prentice Hall.

Anastasi, A., & Urbina, S. (1996). *Psychological tests.* Englewood Cliffs, NJ: Prentice Hall.

Andersen, S. M., Klatzky, R. L., & Murray, J. (1990). Traits and social stereotypes: Efficiency differences in social processing. *Journal of Personality & Social Psychology, 59*(2), 192–201.

Anderson, B. L., Kiecolt-Glaser, J. K., & Glaser, R. (1994). A biobehavioral model of cancer stress and disease course. *American Psychologist, 49*(5), 389–404.

Anderson, C. A. (1989). Temperature and aggression. *Psychological Bulletin, 106,* 74–96.

Anderson, C. A., Anderson, K. B., & Deuser, W. E. (1996). Examining an affective aggression framework. *Personality & Social Psychology Bulletin, 22*(4), 366–376.

Anderson, C. A., Bushman, B. J., & Groom, R. W. (1997). Hot years and serious and deadly assault. *Journal of Personality and Social Psychology, 73*(6), 1213–1223.

Anderson, J. R. (1990). *Cognitive psychology.* New York: Freeman.

Anderson, J. R. (1993). Problem solving and learning. *American Psychologist, 48*(1), 35–44.

Anderson, J. R., Reder, L. M., & Lebiere, C. (1996). Working memory: Activation limitations on retrieval. *Cognitive Psychology, 30*(3), 221–256.

Anderson, K. J. (1990). Arousal and the inverted-U hypothesis. *Psychological Bulletin, 107*(1), 96–100.

Anderson, R. H., Anderson, K., Flemming, D. E., & Kinghorn, E. (1984). A multidimensional test of the attributional reformulation of learned helplessness. *Bulletin of the Psychonomic Society, 22,* 211–213.

Annett, M., & Manning, M. (1990). Arithmetic and laterality. *Neuropsychologia, 28*(1), 61–69.

Anshel, M. H. (1995a). An examination of self-regulatory cognitive-behavioural strategies of Australian elite and non-elite competitive male swimmers. *Australian Psychologist, 30*(2), 78–83.

Anshel, M. H. (1995b). Effect of chronic aerobic exercise and progressive relaxation on motor performance and affect following acute stress. *Behavioral Medicine, 21*(4), 186–196.

Anthony, W. A., Cohen, M., & Kennard, W. (1990). Understanding the current facts and principles of mental health systems planning. *American Psychologist, 45*(11), 1249–1252.

APA. (1998). *APA directory (draft).* American Psychological Association Research Office. Washington, DC: APA.

Archer, J. (1996). Sex differences in social behavior. *American Psychologist, 51*(9), 909–917.

Arena, J. G., Bruno, G. M., Hannah, S. L., & Meador, K. J. (1995). A comparison of frontal electromyographic biofeedback training, trapezius electromyographic biofeedback training, and progressive muscle relaxation therapy in the treatment of tension headache. *Headache, 35*(7), 411–419.

Arendt, J. (1994). Clinical perspectives for melatonin and its agonists. *Biological Psychiatry, 35*(1), 1–2.

Arendt, R., Singer, L., Angelopoulos, J., Bass-Busdiecker, O., & Mascia, J. (1998). Sensorimotor development in cocaine-exposed infants. *Infant Behavior & Development, 21*(4), 627–640.

Arnett, J. J. (1998). Learning to stand alone: The contemporary American transition to adulthood in cultural and historical context. *Human Development, 41*(5–6), 295–315.

Arnett, J. J. (1999). Adolescent storm and stress, reconsidered. *American Psychologist, 54*(3), 317–326.

Aron, A., & Westbay, L. (1996). Dimensions of the prototype of love. *Journal of Personality & Social Psychology, 70*(3), 535–551.

Aronoff, J., Barclay, A. M., & Stevenson, L. A. (1988). The recognition of threatening facial stimuli. *Journal of Personality & Social Psychology, 54*(4), 647–655.

Aronson, E. (1969). Some antecedents of interpersonal attraction. In W. J. Arnold & D. Levine (Eds.), *Nebraska Symposium on Motivation.* Lincoln: University of Nebraska Press.

Aronson, E. (1992). *The Social Animal.* San Francisco: W. H. Freeman.

Arthur, W. Jr., & Graziano, W. G. (1996). The five-factor model, conscientiousness, and driving accident involvement. *Journal of Personality, 64*(3), 593–618.

Ary, D. V., Duncan, T. E., Biglan, A., Metzler, C. W., et al. (1999). *Journal of Abnormal Child Psychology, 27*(2), 141–150.

Asch, S. E. (1956). Studies of independence and conformity: A minority of one against a unanimous majority. *Psychological Monographs, 70*(416).

Asendorpf, J. B. (1996). Self-awareness and other-awareness. II: Mirror self-recognition, social contingency awareness, and synchronic imitation. *Developmental Psychology, 32*(2), 313–321.

Asendorpf, J. B., & Wilpers, S. (1998). Personality effects on social relationships. *Journal of Personality and Social Psychology, 74*(6), 1531–1544.

Ash, D. W., & Holding, D. H. (1990). Backward versus forward chaining in the acquisition of a keyboard skill. *Human Factors, 32*(2), 139–146.

Ashton, W. A., & Fuehrer, A. (1993). Effects of gender and gender role identification of participant and type of social support resource on support seeking. *Sex Roles, 28*(7–8), 461–476.

Aslin, R. N., & Smith, L. B. (1988). Perceptual development. *Annual Review of Psychology, 39,* 435–473.

Assanand, S., Pinel, J. P. J., & Lehman, D. R. (1998). Personal theories of hunger and eating. *Journal of Applied Social Psychology, 28*(11), 998–1015.

Aston-Jones, G., & Druhan, J. (1999). Breaking the chain of addiction. *Nature, 400*(6742), 317, 319.

Athenasiou, R., Shaver, P., & Tavris, C. (1970). Sex. *Psychology Today, 4*(2), 37–52.

Attenburrow, M. E. J., Cowen, P. J., & Sharpley, A. L. (1996). Low dose melatonin improves sleep in healthy middle-aged subjects. *Psychopharmacology, 126*(2), 179–181.

Ayers, L., Beaton, S., & Hunt, H. (1999). The significance of transpersonal experiences, emotional conflict, and cognitive abilities in creativity. *Empirical Studies of the Arts, 17*(1), 73–82.

Ayllon, T. (1963). Intensive treatment of psychotic behavior by stimulus satiation and food reinforcement. *Behavior Research and Therapy, 1,* 53–61.

Ayllon, T., & Azrin, N. H. (1965). The measurement and reinforcement of behavior of psychotics. *Journal of the Experimental Analysis of Behavior, 8,* 357–383.

Azrin, N. H., Hutchinson, R. R., & McLaughlin, R. (1965). The opportunity for aggression as an operant reinforcer during aversive stimulation. *Journal of Experimental Analysis of Behavior, 8,* 171–180.

Bachman, J. G., & Johnson, L. D. (1979). The freshmen. *Psychology Today, 13,* 78–87.

Baddeley, A. (1990). *Human memory.* Needham Heights, MA: Allyn and Bacon.

Baddeley, A. (1996). *Your memory: A user's guide.* North Pomfret: Trafalgar Square.

Baer, J. M. (1993). *Creativity and divergent thinking.* Hillsdale, NJ: Erlbaum.

Bagley, C., & Tremblay, P. (1998). On the prevalence of homosexuality and bisexuality, in a random community survey of 750 men aged 18 to 27. *Journal of Homosexuality, 36*(2), 1–18.

Bahrick, H. P. (1984). Semantic memory content in permastore: Fifty years of memory for Spanish learned in school. *Journal of Experimental Psychology: General, 113*(1), 1–37.

Bahrick, H. P., Hall, L. K., & Berger, S. A. (1996). Accuracy and distortion in memory for high school grades. *Psychological Science, 7*(5), 265–271.

Bahrke, M. S., Yesalis, C. E., & Brower, K. J. (1998). Anabolic-androgenic steroid abuse and performance-enhancing drugs among adolescents. *Child & Adolescent Psychiatric Clinics of North America, 7*(4), 821–838.

Bailey, J. M., & Pillard, R. C. (1991). A genetic study of male sexual orientation. *Archives of General Psychiatry, 48*(12), 1089–1096.

Bailey, J. M., Pillard, R. C., Neale, M. C., & Agyei, Y. (1993). Heritable factors influence sexual orientation in women. *Archives of General Psychiatry, 50*(3), 217–223.

Bailey, M. B., & Bailey, R. E. (1993, November). "Misbehavior": A case history. *American Psychologist,* 1157–1158.

Baillargeon, R. (1991). Reasoning about the height and location of a hidden object in 4.5- and 6.5-month-old infants. *Cognition, 38*(1), 13–42.

Baillargeon, R., & DeVos, J. (1992). Object permanence in young infants: Further evidence. *Child Development, 62*(6), 1227–1246.

Baillargeon, R., De Vos, J., & Graber, M. (1989). Location memory in 8-month-old infants in a non-serach AB task. *Cognitive Development, 4,* 345–367.

Baisden, R. H. (1995). Therapeutic uses for neural grafts: Progress slowed but not abandoned. *Behavioral & Brain Sciences, 18*(1), 47–48, 90–107.

Bajracharya, S. M., Sarvela, P. D., & Isberner, F. R. (1995). A retrospective study of first sexual intercourse experiences among undergraduates. *Journal of American College Health, 43*(4), 169–177.

Baker, L. A., & Daniels, D. (1990). Nonshared environmental influences and personality differences in adult twins. *Journal of Personality & Social Psychology, 58*(1), 103–110.

Baker, R. C., & Kirschenbaum, D. S. (1998). Weight control during the holidays. *Health Psychology, 17*(4), 367–370.

Bakich, I. (1995). Hypnosis in the treatment of sexual desire disorders. *Australian Journal of Clinical & Experimental Hypnosis, 23*(1), 70–77.

Bakker, F. C., Boschker, M. S. J., & Chung, T. (1996). Changes in muscular activity while imagining weight lifting using stimulus or response propositions. *Journal of Sport & Exercise Psychology, 18*(3), 313–324.

Balch, W. R., & Lewis, B. S. (1996). Music-dependent memory. *Journal of Experimental Psychology: Learning, Memory, & Cognition, 22*(6), 1354–1363.

Balk, D. E., et al. (1998). TAT results in a longitudinal study of bereaved college students. *Death Studies, 22*(1), 3–21.

Ball, G. G., & Grinker, J. A. (1981). Overeating and obesity. In S. J. Mule (Ed.), *Behavior in excess* (pp. 194–220). New York: Free Press.

Ballard, C., & Davies, R. (1996). Postnatal depression in fathers. *International Review of Psychiatry, 8*(1), 65–71.

Ballard, M. E., & West, J. R. (1996). Mortal Kombat™: The effects of violent videogame play on males' hostility and cardiovascular responding. *Journal of Applied Social Psychology, 26*(8), 717–730.

Baltes, B. B., Briggs, T. E., Huff, J. W., Wright, J. A., & Neuman, G. A. (1999). Flexible and compressed workweek schedules. *Journal of Applied Psychology, 84*(4), 496–513.

Banaji, M. R., & Prentice, D. A. (1994). The self in social contexts. *Annual Review of Psychology, 45,* 297–332.

Bandura, A. (1971). *Social learning theory.* New York: General Learning Press.

Bandura, A. (1973). *Aggression: A social learning analysis.* Englewood Cliffs, NJ: Prentice-Hall.

Bandura, A. (1986). *Social foundations of thought and action: A social cognitive theory.* Englewood Cliffs, NJ: Prentice-Hall.

Bandura, A., Blanchard, E. B., & Ritter, B. (1969). Relative efficacy of desensitization and modeling approaches for inducing behavioral, affective, and attitudinal changes. *Journal of Personality & Social Psychology, 13*(3), 173–199.

Bandura, A., & Rosenthal, T. L. (1966). Vicarious classical conditioning as a function of arousal level. *Journal of Personality & Social Psychology, 3,* 54–62.

Bandura, A., Ross, D., & Ross, S. A. (1963). Vicarious reinforcement and imitative learning. *Journal of Abnormal and Social Psychology, 67,* 601–607.

Bandura, A., & Walters, R. (1959). *Adolescent aggression.* New York: Ronald.

Bandura, A., & Walters, R. (1963a). Aggression. In H. W. Stevenson (Ed.), *Child psychology.* Chicago: University of Chicago Press.

Bandura, A., & Walters, R. (1963b). *Social learning and personality development.* New York: Holt.

Bank, S. P., & Kahn, M. D. (1982). *The sibling bond.* New York: Basic Books.

Banks, A., & Gartrell, N. K. (1995). Hormones and sexual orientation: A questionable link. *Journal of Homosexuality, 28*(3–4), 247–268.

Banks, T., & Dabbs, J. M. Jr. (1996). Salivary testosterone and cortisol in delinquent and violent urban subculture. *Journal of Social Psychology, 136*(1), 49–56.

Baranek, G. T. (1999). Autism during infancy. *Journal of Autism & Developmental Disorders, 29*(3), 213–224.

Barber, T. X. (1970). *Suggested ("hypnotic") behavior: The trance paradigm versus an alternative paradigm.* Harding, MA: Medfield Foundation, Report No. 103.

Bard, C., Fleury, M., & Goulet, C. (1994). Relationship between perceptual strategies and response adequacy in sport situations. *International Journal of Sport Psychology, 25*(3), 266–281.

Barker, E. A. (1993). Evaluating graphology. *Skeptical Inquirer, 17,* 312–315.

Barnet, A. B., & Barnet, R. J. (1998). *The youngest minds.* New York: Touchstone.

Barnett, W. S. (1995). Long-term effects of early childhood programs on cognitive and school outcomes. *The Future of Children, 5,* 25–51.

Baron, J. (1993). Why teach thinking? *Applied Psychology: An International Review, 42*(3), 191–214.

Baron, J., & Jurney, J. (1993). Norms against voting for coerced reform. *Journal of Personality & Social Psychology, 64*(3), 347–355.

Baron, R. A. (1983). "Sweet smell of success"? The impact of pleasant artificial scents on evaluations of job applicants. *Journal of Applied Psychology, 68,* 709–713.

Baron, R. A., & Byrne, D. (1997). *Social psychology.* Boston: Allyn & Bacon.

Baron, R. A., & Richardson, D. R. (1994). *Human aggression.* New York: Plenum.

Barowsky, E. I., Moskowitz, J., & Zweig, J. B. (1990). Biofeedback for disorders of initiating and maintaining sleep. *Annals of the New York Academy of Sciences, 602,* 97–103.

Barrett, D. (1993). The "committee of sleep": A study of dream incubation for problem solving. *Dreaming, 3*(2), 115–122.

Barrett, R. J. (1985). Behavioral approaches to individual differences in substance abuse. In M. Galizio & S. A. Maisto (Eds.), *Determinants of substance abuse treatment: Biological, psychological, and environmental factors.* New York: Plenum.

Barron, F. (1958). The psychology of imagination. *Scientific American, 199*(3), 150–170.

Barsalou, L. W. (1992). *Cognitive psychology.* Hillsdale, NJ: Lawrence Erlbaum.

Barsky, S. H., Roth, M. D., Kleerup, E. C., et al. (1998). Histopathologic and molecular alterations in bronchial epithelium in habitual smokers of marijuana, cocaine, and/or tobacco. *Journal of the National Cancer Institute, 90*(16), 1198–1205.

Bartlett, J. C., & Searcy, J. (1993). Inversion and configuration of faces. *Cognitive Psychology, 25*(3), 281–316.

Bartoshuk, L. M., Duffy, V. B., & Miller, I. J. (1994). PTC/PROP taste: Anatomy, psychophysics, and sex effects. *Physiology & Behavior, 56*(6), 1165–1171.

Bartz, W. (1990). The basics of critical thought. Personal communication.

Batejat, D. M., & Lagarde, D. P. (1999). Naps and modafinil as countermeasures for the effects of sleep deprivation on cognitive performance. *Aviation, Space, & Environmental Medicine, 70*(5), 493–498.

Bath, H. (1996). Everyday discipline or control with care. *Journal of Child & Youth Care, 10*(2), 23–32.

Batson, C. D. (1990). How social an animal? The human capacity for caring. *American Psychologist, 45*(3), 336–346.

Batson, C. D., et al. (1997). Is empathy-induced helping due to self-other merging? *Journal of Personality & Social Psychology, 73*(3), 495–509.

Bauer, P. J. (1996). What do infants recall of their lives? *American Psychologist, 51*(4), 29–41.

Bauer, W. D., & Twentyman, C. T. (1985). Abusing, neglectful, and comparison mothers' response to child-related and non–child-related stressors. *Journal of Consulting and Clinical Psychology, 53,* 335–343.

Baum, A., & Davis, G. E. (1980). Reducing the stress of high-density living: An architectural intervention. *Journal of Personality & Social Psychology, 38,* 471–481.

Baum, A., & Fleming, I. (1993). Implications of psychological research on stress and technological accidents. *American Psychologist, 48*(6), 665–672.

Baum, A., & Posluszny, D. M. (1999). Health psychology. *Annual Review of Psychology, 50,* 137–163.

Baum, A., & Valins, S. (Eds.). (1977). *Human response to crowding: Studies of the effects of residential group size.* Hillsdale, NJ: Erlbaum.

Baum, A., & Valins, S. (1979). Architectural mediation of residential density and control: Crowding and the regulation of social contact. *Advances in Experimental and Social Psychology, 12,* 131–175.

Baumeister, A. A. (1987). Mental retardation: Some conceptions and dilemmas. *American Psychologist, 42*(2), 796–800.

Baumeister, R. F. (1994). Self-esteem. *Encyclopedia of human behavior, Vol. 4.* San Diego, CA: Academic.

Baumrind, D. (1991). The influence of parenting style on adolescent competence and substance use. *Journal of Early Adolescence, 11*(1), 56–95.

Beach, F. A. (1975). Behavioral endocrinology: An emerging discipline. *American Scientist, 63,* 178–187.

Beauchamp, P. H., Halliwell, W. R., Fournier, J. F., & Koestner, R. (1996). Effects of cognitive-behavioral psychological skills training on the motivation, preparation, and putting performance of novice golfers. *Sport Psychologist, 10*(2), 157–170.

Bech, P., Munk-Jensen, N., Obel, E. B., Ulrich, L. G., et al. (1998). Combined versus sequential hormonal replacement therapy. *Psychotherapy & Psychosomatics, 67*(4–5), 259–265.

Beck, A. T. (1985). Cognitive therapy of depression: New perspectives. In P. Clayton (Ed.), *Depression.* New York: Raven.

Beck, A. T. (1991). Cognitive therapy. *American Psychologist, 46*(4), 368–375.

Beck, A. T., Brown, C., Berchick, R. J., Stewart, B. L., et al. (1990). Relationship between hopelessness and ultimate suicide. *American Journal of Psychiatry, 147*(2), 190–195.

Beck, A. T., & Greenberg, R. L. (1974). *Coping with depression.* Institute for Rational Living.

Beck, J. G. (1995). Hypoactive sexual desire disorder: An overview. *Journal of Consulting & Clinical Psychology, 63*(6), 919–927.

Becker, J. T., & Morris, R. G. (1999). Working memory(s). *Brain & Cognition, 41*(1), 1–8.

Beebe, B., Gerstman, L., Carson, B., Dolins, M., Zigman, A., Rosenweig, H., Faughey, K., & Korman, M. (1982). Rhythmic communication in the mother-infant dyad. In M. Davis (Ed.), *Interaction rhythms, periodicity in communicative behavior.* New York: Human Sciences Press.

Beeman, M. J., & Chiarello, C. (1998). Complementary right- and left-hemisphere language comprehension. *Current Directions in Psychological Science, 7*(1), 2–8.

Begg, I. M., Needham, D. R., & Bookbinder, M. (1993). Do backward messages unconsciously affect listeners? No. *Canadian Journal of Experimental Psychology, 47*(1), 1–14.

Beilin, H. (1992). Piaget's enduring contribution to developmental psychology. *Developmental Psychology, 28*(2), 191–204.

Beljan, J. R., Rosenblatt, L. S., Hetherington, N. W., Layman, J., Flaim, S. E. T., Dale, G. T., & Holley, D. C. (1972). *Human performance in the aviation environment.* NASA Contract No. 2-6657, Pt. Ia, 253–259.

Bell, A. P., Weinberg, M. S., & Hammersmith, S. K. (1981). *Sexual preference.* Indiana University Press.

Bellani, M. L., Furlani, F., Gnecchi, M., & Pezzotta, P. (1996). Burnout and related factors among HIV/AIDS health care workers. *AIDS Care, 8*(2), 207–221.

Bellisle, F. (1999). Glutamate and the UMAMI taste. *Neuroscience & Biobehavioral Reviews, 23*(3), 423–438.

Belloc, N. B. (1973). Relationship of physical health practices and mortality. *Preventive Medicine, 2,* 67–81.

Belloc, N. B., & Breslow, L. (1972). Relationship of physical health status and healthy practices. *Preventive Medicine, 1,* 409–421.

Belsky, J. (1996). Parent, infant, and social-contextual antecedents of father-son attachment security. *Developmental Psychology, 32*(5), 905–913.

Belsky, J., Gilstrap, B., & Rovine, M. (1984). The Pennsylvania infant and family development project, I: Stability and change in mother-infant and father-infant interactions in a family setting at one, three, and nine months. *Child Development, 55,* 692–705.

Bem, S. L. (1975a). Sex-role adaptability: One consequence of psychological androgyny. *Journal of Personality & Social Psychology, 31,* 634–643.

Bem, S. L. (1975b, September). Androgyny vs. the tight little lives of fluffy women and chesty men. *Psychology Today,* 58–62.

Bem, S. L. (1981). Gender schema theory. A cognitive account of sex typing. *Psychological Review, 88,* 354–364.

Benbow, C. P. (1986). Physiological correlates of extreme intellectual precocity. *Neuropsychologia, 24*(5), 719–725.

Beneke, W. M., & Harris, M. B. (1972). Teaching self-control of study behavior. *Behavior Research and Therapy, 10,* 35–41.

Benloucif, S., Bennett, E. L., & Rosenzweig, M. R. (1995). Norephinephrine and neural plasticity: The effects of xylamine on experience-induced changes in brain weight, memory, and behavior. *Neurobiology of Learning & Memory, 63*(1), 33–42.

Benoit, S. C., & Thomas, R. L. (1992). The influence of expectancy in subliminal perception experiments. *Journal of General Psychology, 119*(4), 335–341.

Ben-Shakhar, G., Bar-Hillel, M., Bilu, Y., Ben-Abba, E., & Flug, A. (1986). Can graphology predict occupational success? Two empirical studies and some methodological ruminations. *Journal of Applied Psychology, 71*(4), 645–653.

Ben-Shakhar, G., & Dolev, K. (1996). Psychophysiological detection through the guilty knowledge technique: Effect of mental countermeasures. *Journal of Applied Psychology, 81*(3), 273–281.

Benson, H. (1975). *The relaxation response.* New York: Morrow.

Benson, H. (1977). Systematic hypertension and the relaxation response. *The New England Journal of Medicine, 296,* 1152–1156.

Benton, A. L. (1980, February). The neuropsychology of facial recognition. *American Psychologist, 35,* 176–186.

Berenbaum, S. A., & Snyder, E. (1995). Early hormonal influences on childhood sex-typed activity and playmate preferences. *Developmental Psychology, 31*(1), 31–42.

Bergin, A. E. (1991). Values and religious issues in psychotherapy and mental health. *American Psychologist, 46,* (4), 394–403.

Berkowitz, L. (1968). The frustration-aggression hypothesis revisited. In L. Berkowitz (Ed.), *Roots of aggression: A re-examination of the frustration-aggression hypothesis.* New York: Atherton.

Berkowitz, L. (1984). Some effects of thoughts on anti- and prosocial influences of media events: A cognitive-neoassociation analysis. *Psychological Bulletin, 95,* 410–427.

Berkowitz, L. (1988). Frustrations, appraisals, and aversively stimulated aggression. *Aggressive Behavior, 14*(1), 3–11.

Berkowitz, L. (1990). On the formation and regulation of anger and aggression. *American Psychologist, 45*(4), 494–503.

Berlyne, D. (1966). Curiosity and exploration. *Science, 153,* 25–33.

Berman, S. L., Kurtines, W. M., Silverman, W. K., & Serafini, L. T. (1996). The impact of exposure to crime and violence on urban youth. *American Journal of Orthopsychiatry, 66*(3), 329–336.

Bernat, J. A., Calhoun, K. S., & Stolp, S. (1998). Sexually aggressive men's responses to a date rape analogue. *Journal of Sex Research, 35*(4), 41–348.

Berne, E. (1964). *Games people play.* New York: Grove.

Bernstein, H. J., et al., (1998). Patient attitudes about ECT after treatment. *Psychiatric Annals, 28*(9), 524–527.

Bernthal, P. R., & Insko, C. A. (1993). Cohesiveness without groupthink: The interactive effects of social and task cohesion. *Group & Organization Management, 18*(1), 66–87.

Berry, J. W. (1990). The psychology of acculturation. In R. A. Dienstbier & J. J. Berman (Eds.), *Nebraska Symposium on Motivation 1989: Cross-cultural perspectives, 37.* Lincoln: University of Nebraska Press.

Bersheid, E. (1994). Interpersonal relations. *Annual Review of Psychology, 45,* 79–129.

Bersheid, E., & Walster, E. (1974). A little bit about love. In T. L. Huston (Ed.), *Foundations of interpersonal attraction.* New York: Academic.

Bersoff, D. M. (1999). Why good people sometimes do bad things: Motivated reasoning and unethical behavior. *Personality & Social Psychology Bulletin, 25*(1), 28–39.

Bertsch, G. J. (1976). Punishment of consummatory and instrumental behavior: A review. *Psychological Record, 26,* 13–31.

Best, J. B. (1999). *Cognitive psychology.* Pacific Grove, CA: Brooks/Cole.

Betancur, C., Velez, A., Cabanieu, G., le Moal, M., et al. (1990). Association between left-handedness and allergy: A reappraisal. *Neuropsychologia, 28*(2), 223–227.

Bettelheim, B. (1960). *The informed heart.* New York: Free Press.

Beyerstein, B. (1985). The myth of alpha consciousness. *Skeptical Inquirer, 10,* 42–59.

Beyerstein, B. L. (1990). Brainscams: Neuromythologies of the New Age. *International Journal of Mental Health, 19*(3), 27–36.

Beyerstein, B. L., & Beyerstein, D. F. (1992). *The write stuff: Evaluations of graphology.* Buffalo, NY: Prometheus.

Bialystok, E. (1999). Cognitive complexity and attentional control in the bilingual mind. *Child Development, 70*(3), 636–644.

Bickman, L. (1974, April). Clothes make the person. *Psychology Today,*

Bierley, C., McSweeney, F. K., & Vannieuwerk, R. (1985). Classical conditioning of preferences for stimuli. *Journal of Consumer Research, 12,* 316–323.

Biglan, A., Ary, D., Yudelson, H., & Duncan, T. E. (1996). Experimental evaluation of a modular approach to mobilizing antitobacco influences of peers and parents. *American Journal of Community Psychology, 24*(3), 311–339.

Bigler, E. D., Johnson, S. C., Anderson, C. V., & Blatter, D. D. (1996). Traumatic brain injury and memory: The role of hippocampal atrophy. *Neuropsychology, 10*(3), 333–342.

Binder, V. (1976). Behavior modification: Operant approaches to therapy. In V. Binder, A. Binder, & B. Rimland (Eds.), *Modern therapies.* Englewood Cliffs, NJ: Prentice-Hall.

Binks, P.G., Waters, W. F., & Hurry, M. (1999). Short-term total sleep deprivations does not selectively impair higher cortical functioning. *Sleep, 22*(3), 328–334.

Biondi, M., & Zannino, L. (1997). Psychological stress, neuroimmunomodulation, and susceptibility to infectious diseases in animals and man. *Psychotherapy & Psychosomatics, 66*(1), 3–26.

Birch, J., & McKeever, L. M. (1993). Survey of the accuracy of new pseudoisochromatic plates. *Ophthalmic & Physiological Optics, 13*(1), 35–40.

Birren, J. E., & Fisher, L. M. (1995a). Aging and speed of behavior *Annual Review of Psychology, 46,* 329–353.

Birren, J. E., & Fisher, L. M. (1995b). Rules and reason in the forced retirement of commercial airline pilots at age 60. *Ergonomics, 38*(3), 518–525.

Blackmore, S. (1989). What do we really think? A survey of parapsychologists and sceptics. *Journal of the Society for Psychical Research, 55*(814), 251–262.

Blackmore, S. (1991a). Lucid dreaming. *Skeptical Inquirer, 15,* 362–370.

Blackmore, S. (1991b). Near-death experiences: In or out of the body? *Skeptical Inquirer, 16,* 34–45.

Blackmore, S. (1993). *Dying to live.* Buffalo, NY: Prometheus.

Blackmore, S. (1995). What's in the box? An ESP test with Chris Robinson. *Journal of the Society for Psychical Research, 60*(840), 322–324.

Blackwell, R. T., Galassi, J. P., Galassi, M. D., & Watson, T. E. (1985). Are cognitive assessments equal? A comparison of think aloud and thought listing. *Cognitive Therapy and Research, 9,* 399–413.

Blanchard, E. B., Eisele, G., Vollmer, A., & Payne, A. (1996). Controlled evaluation of thermal biofeedback in treatment of elevated blood pressure in unmedicated mild hypertension. *Biofeedback & Self Regulation, 21*(2), 167–190.

Blanck, P. D., Bellack, A. S., Rosnow, R. L., et al. (1992). Scientific rewards and conflicts of ethical choices in human subjects research. *American Psychologist, 47*(7), 959–965.

Blane, H. T. (1988). Prevention issues with children of alcoholics. *British Journal of Addiction, 83*(7), 793–798.

Blaske, D. M. (1984). Occupational sex-typing by kindergarten and fourth-grade children. *Psychological Reports, 54,* 795–801.

Blaustein, A. R. (1983). The situation of sociobiology. *Science, 220,* 188–189.

Block, J. (1979, September). *Socialization influence of personality development in males and females.* American Psychological Association Master Lecture presented at theconvention of the American Psychological Association, New York City.

Bloom, B. (1985). *Developing talent in young people.* New York: Ballantine.

Bloom, J. W. (1998). The ethical practice of Web-Counseling. *British Journal of Guidance & Counseling, 26*(1), 53–59.

Bloom, K., Russell, A., & Wassenberg, K. (1987). Turn taking affects the quality of infant vocalizations. *Journal of Child Language, 14*(2), 211–227.

Bloomfield, H. H., Nordfors, M., & McWilliams, P. (1997). *Hypericum and depression.* Los Angeles: Prelude Press.

Blumberg, M. S., & Wasserman, E. A. (1995). Animal mind and the argument from design. *American Psychologist, 50*(3), 133–144.

Boergers, J., Spirito, A., & Donaldson, D. (1998). Reasons for adolescent suicide attempts. *Journal of the American Academy of Child & Adolescent Psychiatry, 37*(12), 1287–1293.

Bohan, J. S. (1990). Social constructionism and contextual history: An expanded approach to the history of psychology. *Teaching of Psychology, 17*(2), 82–89.

Bohannon, J. N., & Stanowicz, L. B. (1988). The issue of negative evidence: Adult responses to children's language errors. *Developmental Psychology, 24*(5), 684–689.

Bohart, A. C., & Tallman, K. (1996). The active client: Therapy as self-help. *Journal of Humanistic Psychology, 36*(3), 7–30.

Bohart, W. (1995). The person-centered therapies. In A. S. Gurman & S. B. Messer (Eds.), *Essential psychotherapies.* New York: Guilford.

Boivin, D. B., Czeisler, C. A., & Waterhouse, J. W. (1997). Complex interaction of the sleep-wake cycle and circadian phase modulates mood in healthy subjects. *Archives of General Psychiatry, 54*(2), 145.

Bolles, R. C. (1979). *Learning theory.* New York: Holt, Rinehart & Winston.

Bonanno, G. A., Keltner, D., Holen, A., & Horowitz, M. J. (1995). When avoiding unpleasant emotions might not be such a bad thing. *Journal of Personality & Social Psychology, 69*(5), 975–989.

Bond, R., & Smith, P. B. (1996). Culture and conformity: A meta-analysis of studies using Asch's (1952b, 1956) line judgment task. *Psychological Bulletin, 119*(1), 111–137.

Bond, T., & Wooten, V. (1996). The etiology and management of insomnia. *Virginia Medical Quarterly, 123*(4), 254–255.

Bongard, S., al'Absi, M., & Lovallo, W. R. (1998). Interactive effects of trait hostility and anger expression on cardiovascular reactivity in young men. *International Journal of Psychophysiology, 28*(2), 181–191.

Book, H. E., & Luborsky, L. (1998). *Brief psychodynamic psychotherapy.* Washington, DC: American Psychological Association.

Booker, J. M., & Hellekson, C. J. (1992). Prevalence of seasonal affective disorder in Alaska. *American Journal of Psychiatry, 149*(9), 1176–1182.

Borlongan, C. V., Sanberg, P. R., & Freeman, T. B. (1999). Neural transplantation for neurodegenerative disorders. *Lancet, 353*(Suppl. 1), S29–30.

Borman, W. C., Hanson, M. A., & Hedge, J. W. (1997). Personnel psychology. *Annual Review of Psychology, 48,* 299–337.

Bornstein, M. H. (1989). Sensitive periods in development: Structural characteristics and causal interpretations. *Psychological Bulletin, 105*(2), 179–197.

Bornstein, M. H. (1995). Parenting infants. In M. H. Bornstein (Ed.), *Handbook of parenting.* Mahwah, NJ: Erlbaum.

Bornstein, M. H., Haynes, O. M., Azuma, H., Galperín, C., et al. (1998). A cross-national study of self-evaluations and attributions in parenting. *Developmental Psychology, 34,* 662–676.

Bornstein, R. F. 1996. Sex differences in dependent personality disorder prevalence rates. *Clinical Psychology: Science & Practice, 3*(1), 1–12.

Borod, J. C., Cicero, B. A., Obler, L. K., et al. (1998). Right hemisphere emotional perception. *Neuropsychology, 12*(3), 446–458.

Borrie, R. A. (1990–1991). The use of restricted environmental stimulation therapy in treating addictive behaviors. *International Journal of the Addictions, 25*(7A–8A), 995–1015.

Borrie, R. A., & Suedfeld, P. (1980). Restricted environmental stimulation therapy in a weight reduction program. *Journal of Behavioral Medicine, 3,* 147–161.

Bosse, R., Aldwin, C. M., Levenson, M. R., & Workman-Daniels, K. (1991). How stressful is retirement? *Journal of Gerontology, 46*(1), 9–14.

Botella, C., et al. (1998). Virtual reality treatment of claustrophobia. *Behaviour Research & Therapy, 36*(2), 239–246.

Botvin, G. J., et al. (1997). School-based drug abuse prevention with inner-city minority youth. *Journal of Child & Adolescent Substance Abuse, 6*(1), 5–19.

Botvin, G. J., Schinke, S., & Orlandi, M. A. (1995). School-based health promotion: Substance abuse and sexual behavior. *Applied & Preventive Psychology, 4*(3), 167–184.

Bouchard, T. J., Lykken, D. T., McGue, M., Segal, N. L., & Tellegen, A. (1990). Sources of human psychological differences: The Minnesota study of twins reared apart. *Science, 250,* 223–228.

Bouchard, T. J. Jr. (1983). Twins—Nature's twice-told tale. In *Yearbook of science and the future* (pp. 66–81). Chicago: Encyclopedia Britannica.

Boutros, N. N., & Bowers, M. B. Jr. (1996). Chronic substance-induced psychotic disorders. *Journal of Neuropsychiatry & Clinical Neurosciences, 8*(3), 262–269.

Bower, B. (1990, November 17). Gone but not forgotten. *Science News, 138,* 312–314.

Bower, G. H. (1973, October). How to . . . uh . . . remember. *Psychology Today*, 63–70.

Bower, G. H. (1981). Mood and memory. *American Psychologist, 36*, 129–148.

Bower, G. H., & Springston, F. (1970). Pauses as recoding points in letter series. *Journal of Experimental Psychology, 83*, 421–430.

Bower, G. H., Wagner, A. D., Newman, S. E., & Randle, J. D. (1996). Does recoding interfering material improve recall? *Journal of Experimental Psychology: Learning, Memory, & Cognition, 22*(1), 240–245.

Bowers, K. S., & Farvolden, P. (1996). Revisiting a century-old Freudian slip—From suggestion disavowed to the truth repressed. *Psychological Bulletin, 119*(3), 355–380.

Bowers, K. S., & Woody, E. Z. (1996). Hypnotic amnesia and the paradox of intentional forgetting. *Journal of Abnormal Psychology, 105*(3), 381–390.

Bowling, A. C., & Mackenzie, B. D. (1996). The relationship between speed of information processing and cognitive ability. *Personality & Individual Differences, 20*(6), 775–800.

Boyatzis, C. J., Matillo, G. M., & Nesbitt, K. M. (1995). Effects of "The Mighty Morphin Power Rangers" on children's aggression with peers. *Child Study Journal, 25*(1), 45–55.

Boysen, S. T., & Berntson, G. G. (1989). Numerical competence in a chimpanzee (*Pan troglodytes*). *Journal of Comparative Psychology, 103*(1), 23–31.

Boysen, S. T., Berntson, G. G., Shreyer, T. A., & Hannan, M. B. (1995). Indicating acts during counting by a chimpanzee (*Pan troglodytes*). *Journal of Comparative Psychology, 109*(1), 47–51.

Bradley, R. H., Caldwell, B. M., Rock, S. L., Ramey, C. T., et al. (1989). Home environment and cognitive development in the first 3 years of life: A collaborative study involving six sites and three ethnic groups in North America. *Developmental Psychology, 25*(2), 217–235.

Braffman, W., & Kirsch, I. (1999). Imaginative suggestibility and hypnotizability. *Journal of Personality & Social Psychology, 77*(3), 578–587.

Brannon, L. (1996). *Gender*. Boston: Allyn & Bacon.

Bransford, J., & Stein, B. S. (1984). *The IDEAL problem solver*. New York: Freeman.

Bransford, J., Sherwood, R., Vye, N., & Rieser, J. (1986). Teaching thinking and problem solving. *American Psychologist, 41*(10), 1078–1089.

Bransford, J. D., & McCarrell, N. S. (1977). A sketch of cognitive approach to comprehension: Some thoughts about understanding what it means to comprehend. In P. N. Johnson-Laird & P. C. Wason (Eds.), *Thinking: Readings in cognitive science*. Cambridge: Cambridge University Press.

Braun, A. R., Balkin, T. J., & Herscovitch, P. (1998). Dissociated pattern of activity in visual cortices and their projections during human rapid eye movement sleep. *Science, 279*(5347), 91–95.

Braungart, J. M., Plomin, R., DeFries, J. C., & Fulker, D. W. (1992). Genetic influence on tester-rated infant temperament as assessed by Bayley's Infant Behavior Record. *Developmental Psychology, 28*(1), 40–47.

Brawman-Mintzer, O., & Lydiard, R. B. (1996). Generalized anxiety disorder: Issues in epidemiology. *Journal of Clinical Psychiatry, 57*(Suppl. 7), 3–8.

Brebner, J. (1998). Happiness and personality. *Personality & Individual Differences, 25*(2), 279–296.

Breedlove, S. M. (1994). Sexual differentiation of the human nervous system. *Annual Review of Psychology, 45*, 389–418.

Breedlove, S. M., Cooke, B. M., & Jordan, C. L. (1999). The orthodox view of brain sexual differentiation. *Brain, Behavior & Evolution, 54*(1), 8–14.

Breland, K., & Breland, M. (1961). The misbehavior of organisms. *American Psychologist, 16*, 681–684.

Brenner, V., & Fox, R. A. (1998). Parental discipline and behavior problems in young children. *Journal of Genetic Psychology, 159*(2), 251–256.

Bresler, D. E., & Trubo, R. (1979). *Free yourself from pain*. New York: Simon & Schuster.

Breslow, L., & Enstrom, J. E. (1980). Persistence of health habits and their relationship to mortality. *Preventive Medicine, 9*, 469–483.

Bressi, C., Albonetti, S., & Razzoli, E. (1998). "Communication deviance" and schizophrenia. *New Trends in Experimental & Clinical Psychiatry, 14*(1), 33–39.

Brewer, J. S. (1981). Duration of intromission and female orgasm rates. *Medical Aspects of Human Sexuality, 15*(4), 70–71.

Brewer, K. R., & Wann, D. L. (1998). Observational learning effectiveness as a function of model characteristics. *Social Behavior & Personality, 26*(1), 1–10.

Brewer, M. B., & Kramer, R. K. (1985). The psychology of intergroup attitudes and behavior. *Annual Review of Psychology, 36*, 219–243.

Bridges, K. M. B. (1932). Emotional development in early infancy. *Child Development, 3*, 324–334.

Brigham, J. C., & Wasserman, A. W. (1999). The impact of race, racial attitude, and gender on reactions to the criminal trial of O. J. Simpson. *Journal of Applied Social Psychology, 29*(7), 1333–1370.

Brim, O. G., Baltes, P. B., Bumpass, L. L., Cleary, P. D., et al. (1999). *National survey of midlife development in the United States (MIDUS), 1995–1996*. Ann Arbor, MI: DataStat, Inc./Boston, MA: Harvard Medical School, Dept. of Health Care Policy.

"Bringing Up Baby." (1999, January–February). *Sierra*, 17.

Britton, B. K., & Tesser, A. (1991). Effects of time-management practices on college grades. *Journal of Educational Psychology, 83*(3), 405–410.

Brockhaus, A., & Elger, C. E. (1990). Hypalgesic efficacy of acupuncture on experimental pain in man: Comparison of laser acupuncture and needle acupuncture. *Pain, 43*(2), 181–185.

Brody, N. (1992). *Intelligence*. San Diego, CA: Academic Press.

Brooks-Gunn, J., & Warren, M. P. (1988). The psychological significance of secondary sexual characteristics in nine- to eleven-year-old girls. *Child Development, 59*(4), 1061–1069.

Broughton, W. A., & Broughton, R. J. (1994). Psychosocial impact of narcolepsy. *Sleep, 17*(8, Suppl.), S45–S49.

Brown, A. M. (1990). Development of visual sensitivity to light and color vision in human infants: A critical review. *Vision Research, 30*(8), 1159–1188.

Brown, B. (1980). Perspectives on social stress. In H. Selye (Ed.), *Selye's guide to stress research, Vol. 1*. New York: Van Nostrand Reinhold.

Brown, B. B., & Bentley, D. L. (1993). Residential burglars judge risk. *Journal of Environmental Psychology, 13*(1), 51–61.

Brown, B. R. Jr., Baranowski, M. D., Kulig, J. W., & Stephenson, J. N. (1996). Searching for the Magic Johnson effect: AIDS, adolescents, and celebrity disclosure. *Adolescence, 31*(122), 253–264.

Brown, G. M. (1994). Light, melatonin and the sleep-wake cycle. *Journal of Psychiatry & Neuroscience, 19*(5), 345–353.

Brown, R., & McNeill, D. (1966). The "tip of the tongue" phenomenon. *Journal of Verbal Learning and Verbal Behavior, 5*, 325–337.

Brown, R. L., Leonard, T., Saunders, L. A., & Papasouiotis, O. (1997). A two-item screening test for alcohol and other drug problems. *Journal of Family Practice, 44*(2), 151–160.

Brown, R. T. (1991). Helping students confront and deal with stress and procrastination. *Journal of College Student Psychotherapy, 6*(2), 87–102.

Brown, S. A., Goldman, M. S., & Christiansen, B. A. (1985). Do alcohol expectancies mediate drinking patterns of adults? *Journal of Consulting and Clinical Psychology, 53*(4), 512–519.

Brown, T. D., Dane, F. C., & Durham, M. D. (1998). Perception of race and ethnicity. *Journal of Social Behavior & Personality, 13*(2), 295–306.

Brown, V., Tumeo, M., Larey, T. S., & Paulus, P. B. (1998). Modeling cognitive interactions during group brainstorming. *Small Group Research, 29*(4), 495–526.

Browne, B. A. (1998). Gender stereotypes in advertising on children's television in the 1990s. *Journal of Advertising, 27*(1), 83–96.

Brownell, K. D., Greenwood, M. R. C., Stellar, E., & Shrager, E. E. (1986). The effects of repeated cycles of weight loss and regain in rats. *Physiology and Behavior, 38*, 459–464.

Brownell, K. D., & Rodin, J. (1994). The dieting maelstrom. *American Psychologist, 49*, 781–791.

Brownlee, S. (1997, January 13). The senses. *U.S. News & World Report*, 51–59.

Bruch, M. A., Berko, E. H., & Haase, R. F. (1998). Shyness, masculine ideology, physical attractiveness, and emotional inexpressiveness. *Journal of Counseling Psychology, 45*,(1), 84–97.

Bruer, J. T. (1999). *The myth of the first three years*. New York: Free Press.

Brugger, P., Landis, T., & Regard, M. (1990). A "sheep-goat" effect in repetition avoidance: Extrasensory perception as an effect of subjective probability? *British Journal of Psychology, 81*(4), 455–468.

Bruner, J. (1983). *Child's talk*. New York: Norton.

Bruner, J. S. (1968). *Toward a theory of instruction*. New York: Norton.

Bruner, J. S., & Postman, L. (1949). On the perception of incongruity: A paradigm. *Journal of Personality, 18*, 206–223.

Bryan, J. H., & Test, M. A. (1967). Models and helping. Naturalistic studies in aiding behavior. *Journal of Personality & Social Psychology, 6*, 400–407.

Bryan, J. H., & Walbek, N. H. (1970). Preaching and practicing generosity: Children's actions and reactions. *Child Development, 41*, 329–353.

Bryant, D. M., & Maxwell, K. L. (1999). The environment and mental retardation. *International Review of Psychiatry, 11*(1) 56–67.

Buch, K., & Spangler, R. (1990). The effects of quality circles on performance and promotions. *Human Relations, 43*(6), 573–582.

Buchanan, R. W., et al. (1998). Positive and negative symptom response to clozapine in schizophrenic patients. *American Journal of Psychiatry, 155*(6), 751–760.

Buchwald, A. (1965, June 20). Psyching out. *The Washington Post*,

Buck, L. A. (1990). Abnormality, normality and health. *Psychotherapy, 27*(2), 187–194.

Buckelew, S. P., et al. (1998). Biofeedback/relaxation training and exercise interventions for fibromyalgia. *Arthritis Care & Research, 11*(3), 196–209.

Buckhout, R. (1974). Eyewitness testimony. *Scientific American, 231*, 23–31.

Budiansky, S. (1998). *If a lion could talk: Animal intelligence and the evolution of consciousness*. New York: Free Press.

Budney, A. J., Novy, P. L., & Hughes, J. R. (1999). Marijuana withdrawal among adults seeking treatment for marijuana dependence. *Addiction, 94*(9), 1311–1322.

Bugental, J. F. T., & Sterling, M. M. (1995). Existential-humanistic psychotherapy: New perspectives. In A. S. Gurman & S. B. Messer (Eds.), *Essential Psychotherapies*. New York: Guilford.

Bunge, M. (1984). What is pseudoscience? *Skeptical Inquirer, 9*, 36–46.

Burgess, C. A., & Kirsch, I. (1999). Expectancy information as a moderator of the effects of hypnosis on memory. *Contemporary Hypnosis, 16*(1), 22–31.

Burgner, D., & Hewstone, M. (1993). Young children's causal attributions for success and failure. *British Journal of Developmental Psychology, 11*(2), 125–129.

Burka, J. B., & L. M. Yuen. (1990). *Procrastination: Why you do it; what to do about it*. Cambridge, MA: Perseus Books.

Burnham, D. K., & Harris, M. (1992). Effects of real gender and labeled gender on adults' perceptions of infants. *Journal of Genetic Psychology, 153*(2), 165183.

Burns, D. D., & Persons, J. (1982). Hope and hopelessness: A cognitive approach. In L. E. Abt & I. R. Stuart (Eds.), *The newer therapies: A sourcebook*. New York: Van Nostrand Reinhold.

Burtt, H. E. (1941). An experimental study of early childhood memory: Final report. *Journal of General Psychology, 58*, 435–439.

Bushman, B. J., & Cooper, H. M. (1990). Effects of alcohol on human aggression. *Psychological Bulletin, 107*(3), 341–354.

Bushman, B. J., & Geen, R. G. (1990). Role of cognitive-emotional mediators and individual differences in the effects of media violence on aggression. *Journal of Personality & Social Psychology, 58*(1), 156–163.

Bushnell, L. W., Sai, F., & Mullin, L. T. (1989). Neonatal recognition of the mother's face. *British Journal of Developmental Psychology, 7*(1), 3–15.

Buss, A. H. (1980). *Self-consciousness and social anxiety*. San Francisco: Freeman.

Buss, A. H. (1986). A theory of shyness. In W. H. Jones, J. M. Cheek & S.R. Briggs (Eds.), *Shyness: Perspectives on research and treatment*. New York: Plenum.

Buss, D. M. (1985). Human mate selection. *American Scientist, 73*, 47–51.

Buss, D. M. (1994). *The evolution of desire*. New York: Basic.

Buss, D. M. (1995). Psychological sex differences. *American Psychologist, 50*(3), 164–168.

Buss, D. M., Larsen, R. J., Western, D., & Semmelroth, J. (1992). Sex differences in jealousy. *Psychological Science, 3*, 251–255.

Butler, R. (1954). Curiosity in monkeys. *Scientific American, 190*(18), 70–75.

Butler, R., & Harlow, H. F. (1954). Persistence of visual exploration in monkeys. *Journal of Comparative Physiological Psychology, 47*, 258–263.

Buyer, L. S. (1988). Creative problem solving: A comparison of performance under different instructions. *Journal of Creative Behavior, 22*(1), 55–61.

Byrd, K. R. (1994). The narrative reconstructions of incest survivors. *American Psychologist, 49*(5), 439–440.

Byrnes, J. P., Miller, D. C., & Schafer, W. D. (1999). Gender differences in risk taking: A meta-analysis. *Psychological Bulletin, 125*(3), 367–383.

Cabanac, M., & Duclaux, P. (1970). Obesity: Absence of satiety aversion to sucrose. *Science, 168*, 496–497.

Cahill, S. P., Carrigan, M. H., & Frueh, B. C. (1999). Does EMDR work? And if so, why? *Journal of Anxiety Disorders, 13*(1–2), 5–33.

Caldera, Y. M., Huston, A. C. & O'Brien, M. (1989). Social interactions and play patterns of parents and toddlers with feminine, masculine, and neutral toys. *Child Development, 60*(1), 70–76.

Calhoun, J. B. (1962). A "behavioral sink." In E. L. Bliss (Ed.), *Roots of behavior*. New York: Harper & Row.

Calle, E. E., Thun, M. J., Petrelli, J. M., Rodriguez, C., & Heath, C. W. (1999). Body-mass index and mortality in a prospective cohort of U.S. adults. *New England Journal of Medicine, 341*(15), 1097–1105.

Calvert, S. L., & Cocking, R. R. (1992). Health promotion through mass media. *Journal of Applied Developmental Psychology, 13*(2), 143–149.

Camatta, C. D., & Nagoshi, C. T. (1995). Stress, depression, irrational beliefs, and alcohol use and problems in a college student sample. *Alcoholism: Clinical & Experimental Research, 19*(1), 142–146.

Cameron, L. D., & Nicholls, G. (1998). Expression of stressful experiences through writing. *Health Psychology, 17*(1), 84–92.

Campbell, F. A., & Ramey, C. T. (1994). Effect of early intervention on intellectual and academic achievement. *Child Development, 65*, 684–698.

Campbell, J. B., & Hawley, C. W. (1982). Study habits and Eysenck's theory of extraversion-introversion. *Journal of Research in Personality, 16*, 139–146.

Campfield, L. A., Smith, F. J., Rosenbaum, M., & Hirsch, J. (1996). Human eating: Evidence for a physiological basis using a modified paradigm. *Neuroscience & Biobehavioral Reviews, 20*(1), 133–137.

Campion, M. A., & McClelland, C. L. (1993). Follow-up and extension of interdisciplinary costs and benefits of enlarged jobs. *Journal of Applied Psychology, 78*(3), 339–351.

Campion, M. A., Palmer, D. K., & Campion, J. E. (1998). Structuring employment interviews to improve reliability, validity and users' reactions. *Current Directions in Psychological Science, 7*(3), 77–82.

Campos, A., & Perez, M. J. (1997). Mnemonic images and associated pair recall. *Journal of Mental Imagery, 21*(3–4), 73–82.

Campos, J. J., Hiatt, S., Ramsay, D., Henderson, C., & Svejda, M. (1978). The emergence of fear on the visual cliff. In M. Lewis & L. A. Rosenblum (Eds.), *The development of affect* (pp. 149–182). New York: Plenum Press.

Camras, L. A., Sullivan, J., & Michel, G. (1993). Do infants express discrete emotions? *Journal of Nonverbal Behavior, 17*(3), 171–186.

Canivez, G. L., & Watkins, M. W. (1998). Long-term stability of the Wechsler Intelligence Scale for Children—Third Edition. *Psychological Assessment, 10*(3), 285–291.

Canli, T., Desmond, J. E., Zhao, Z., Glover, G., et al. (1998). Hemispheric asymmetry for emotional stimuli detected with fMRI. *Neuroreport, 9*(14) 3233–3239.

Cann, A., Holt, K., & Calhoun, L. G. (1999). The roles of humor and sense of humor in responses to stressors. *Humor: International Journal of Humor Research, 12*(2), 177–193.

Cannon, T. D. (1998). Neurodevelopmental influences in the genesis and epigenesis of schizophrenia. *Applied & Preventive Psychology, 7*(1), 47–62.

Cannon, T. D., et al. (1998). The genetic epidemiology of schizophrenia in a Finnish twin cohort. *Archives of General Psychiatry, 55*(1), 67–74.

Cannon, W. B. (1932). *The wisdom of the body*. New York: Norton.

Cannon, W. B. (1934). Hunger and thirst. In C. Murchinson (Ed.), *Handbook of general experimental psychology*. Worcester, MA: Clark University Press.

Cannon, W. B., & Washburn, A. L. (1912). An exploration of hunger. *American Journal of Physiology, 29*, 441–454.

Caplan, N., Choy, M. H., & Whitmore, J. K. (1992, February). Indochinese refugee families and academic achievement. *Scientific American,* 36–42.

Caplan, P. J. (1995). *They say you're crazy*. Reading, MA: Addison-Wesley.

Caplan, P. J., MacPherson, G. M., & Tobin, P. (1985). Do sex-related differences in spatial abilities exist? A multilevel critique with new data. *American Psychologist, 40*, 786–799.

Capner, M., & Caltabiano, M. L. (1993). Factors affecting the progression towards burnout. *Psychological Reports, 73*(2), 555–561.

Capron, C., & Duyme, M. (1992). Assessment of effects of socio-economic status on IQ in a full cross-fostering study. *Nature, 340*, 552–554.

Carducci, B. J., & Stein, N. D. (1988, April). *The personal and situational pervasiveness of shyness in college students: A nine-year comparison*. Paper presented at the meeting of the Southeastern Psychological Association, New Orleans.

Carey, A. R., & McLean, E. A. (1997, January 6). What's on your mind? *USA Today*, p. 1.

Carey, J. C., Stanley, D. A., & Biggers, J. (1988). Peak alert time and rapport between residence hall roommates. *Journal of College Student Development, 29*(3), 239–243.

Carli, L. L., Ganley, R., & Pierce-Otay, A. (1991). Similarity and satisfaction in roommate relationships. *Personality & Social Psychology Bulletin, 17*(4), 419–426.

Carlson, C. L., Pelhan, W. E., Milich, R., & Dixon, J. (1992). Single and combined effects of methylphenidate and behavior therapy on the classroom performance of children with attention-deficit hyperactivity disorder. *Journal of Abnormal Child Psychology, 20*(2), 213–232.

Carlson, J. G., et al. (1998). Eye movement desensitization and reprocessing (EDMR) treatment for combat-related posttraumatic stress disorder. *Journal of Traumatic Stress, 11*(1), 3–24.

Carlson, J. G., Chemtob, C. M., Rusnak, K., & Hedlund, N. L. (1996). *Psychotherapy, 33*(1), 104–113.

Carlson, J. M. (1986). *Prime time law enforcement*. New York: Praeger.

Carlson, M., Marcus-Hewhall, A., & Miller, N. (1990). Effects of situational aggression cues: A quantitative review. *Journal of Personality & Social Psychology, 58*(4), 622–633.

Carlson, N. R. (1994). *Physiology of behavior* (5th ed.). Boston: Allyn & Bacon.

Carlson, N. R. (1998). *Physiology of behavior* (6th ed.). Boston: Allyn & Bacon.

Carman, R., & Adams, W. R. (1985). *Study skills: A student's guide for survival*. New York: Wiley.

Carnegie Corporation of New York. (1994). *Starting points: Meeting the needs of our youngest children*. New York: Carnegie Corporation.

Carney, R. N., & Levin, J. R. (1998). Do mnemonic memories fade as time goes by? *Contemporary Educational Psychology, 23*(3), 276–297.

Carney, R. N., Levin, J. R., & Stackhouse, T. L. (1997). The face-name mnemonic strategy from a different perspective. *Contemporary Educational Psychology, 22*(3), 399–412.

Carroll, J. M., & Russell, J. A. (1996). Do facial expressions signal specific emotions? Judging emotion from the face in context. *Journal of Personality & Social Psychology, 70*(2), 205–218.

Carson, R. C., Butcher, J. N., & Mineka, S. (1996) *Abnormal psychology and modern life*. New York: HarperCollins.

Carson, R. C., Butcher, J. N., & Mineka, S. (1997). *Abnormal psychology and modern life*. Reading, MA: Addison-Wesley.

Carter, R. (1998). *Mapping the mind*. Berkeley: University of California Press.

Carter, W. E. (Ed.). (1980). *Cannabis in Costa Rica: A study of chronic marihuana use*. Philadelphia: Institute for the Study of Human Issues.

Cartwright, R., & Lamberg, L. (1992). *Crisis dreaming*. New York: HarperCollins.

Caspi, A., & Herbener, E. S. (1990). Continuity and change: Associative marriage and the consistency of personality in adulthood. *Journal of Personality & Social Psychology, 58*(2), 250–258.

Casto, S. D., DeFries, J. C., & Fulker, D. W. (1995). Multivariate genetic analysis of Wechsler Intelligence Scale for Children—Revised (WISC—R) factors. *Behavior Genetics, 25*(1), 25–32.

Catalano, R., Novaco, R., & McConnell, W. (1997). A model of the net effect of job loss on violence. *Journal of Personality & Social Psychology, 72*(6), 1440–1447.

Cattell, R. B. (1965). *The scientific analysis of personality.* Baltimore: Penguin.

Cattell, R. B. (1973, July). Personality pinned down. *Psychology Today,* 40–46.

Cautela, J. R., & Bennett, A. K. (1981). Covert conditioning. In R. J. Corsini (Ed.), *Handbook of innovative psychotherapies* (pp. 189–204). New York: Wiley.

Cautela, J. R., & Kearney, A. J. (1986). *The covert conditioning handbook.* New York: Springer.

Cavalli-Sforza, L. L. (1991, November). Genes, peoples, and languages. *Scientific American,* 104–110.

Ceci, S. J. (1991). How much does schooling influence general intelligence and its cognitive components? *Developmental Psychology, 27*(5), 703–722.

Cecil, H., Evans, R. J., & Stanley, M. A. (1996). Perceived believability among adolescents of health warning labels on cigarette packs. *Journal of Applied Social Psychology, 26*(6), 502–519.

Chabris, C. F., Steele, K. M., Bella, S. D., et al. (1999). Prelude or requiem for the "Mozart effect"? *Nature, 400*(6747), 826–828.

Chakos, M. H., Alvir, J. M. J., Woerner, M., & Koreen, A. (1996). Incidence and correlates of tardive dyskinesia in first episode of schizophrenia. *Archives of General Psychiatry, 53*(4), 313–319.

Chamberlin, J., & Rogers, J. A. (1990). Planning a community-based mental health system. *American Psychologist, 45*(11), 1241–1244.

Chan, G. C., Hinds, T. R., Impey, S., & Storm, D. R. (1998). Hippocampal neurotoxicity of Delta-sup-9-tetrahydrocannabinol. *Journal of Neuroscience, 18*(14), 5322–5332.

Chan, R. W., Raboy, B., & Patterson, C. J. (1998). Psychosocial adjustment among children conceived via donor insemination by lesbian and heterosexual mothers. *Child Development, 69*(2), 443–457.

Chapanis, A., & Lindenbaum, L. E. (1959). A reaction time study of four control-display linkages. *Human Factors, 1,* 1–7.

Charren, P., & Sandler, M. W. (1983). *Changing channels.* Reading, MA: Addison-Wesley.

Chartrand, T. L., & Bargh, J. A. (1999). The chameleon effect: The perception-behavior link and social interaction. *Journal of Personality & Social Psychology, 76*(6), 893–910.

Chastain, G., & Thurber, S. (1989). The SQ3R study technique enhances comprehension of an introductory psychology textbook. *Reading Improvement, 26*(1), 94.

Cheadle, A., Psaty, B. M., Diehr, P., Koepsell, T., et al. (1992–1993). An empirical exploration of a conceptual model for community-based health-promotion. *International Quarterly of Community Health Education, 13*(4), 329–363.

Check, J. V. P., & Malamuth, N. M. (1983). Sex role stereotyping and reactions to depictions of stranger versus acquaintance rape. *Journal of Personality & Social Psychology, 45,* 344–356.

Cheek, J., & Buss, A. H. (1979). Scales of shyness, sociability and self-esteem and correlations among them. Unpublished research, University of Texas. (Cited in Buss, 1980.)

Chen, Z., Lawson, R. B., Gordon, L. R., & McIntosh, B. (1996). Groupthink: Deciding with the leader and the devil. *Psychological Record, 46*(4), 581–590.

Cheng, H., Cao, Y., & Olson, L. (1996). Spinal cord repair in adult paraplegic rats: Partial restoration of hind limb function. *Science, 273*(5274), 510.

Chess, S., & Thomas, A. (1986). *Know your child.* New York: Basic.

Chess, S., Thomas, A., & Birch, H. G. (1976). *Your child is a person: A psychological approach to parenthood without guilt.* New York: Penguin.

Chiras, D. D. (1991). *Human biology.* St. Paul, MN: West.

Chisholm, K., Carter, M. C., Ames, E. W., & Morison, S. J. (1995). Attachment security and indiscriminately friendly behavior in children adopted from Romanian orphanages. *Development & Psychopathology, 7*(2), 283–294.

Chollar, S. (1989, April). Dreamchasers. *Psychology Today,* 60–61.

Chomsky, N. (1975). *Reflections on language.* New York: Pantheon.

Chomsky, N. (1986). *Knowledge of language.* New York: Praeger.

Christensen, A., & Jacobson, N. S. (1994). Who (or what) can do psychotherapy. *Psychological Science, 5*(1), 8–14.

Christensen, D. (1999). Mind over matter. *Science News, 156,* 142–143.

Christian, A. G., & McDonald, J. L. (1987). Smokeless tobacco country: From nicotine dependency to oral problems and cancer. *Aviation, Space, & Environmental Medicine, 58*(2), 97–104.

Christiansen, B. A., Smith, G. T., Roehling, P. V., & Goldman, M. S. (1989). Using alcohol expectancies to predict adolescent drinking behavior after one year. *Journal of Consulting & Clinical Psychology, 57*(1), 93–99.

Christianson, S., Saisa, J., & Silfvenius, H. (1995). The right hemisphere recognises the bad guys. *Cognition & Emotion, 9*(4), 309–324.

Chua, P., & Fujino, D. C. (1999). Negotiating new Asian-American masculinities: Attitudes and gender expectations. *Journal of Men's Studies, 7*(3), 391–413.

Cialdini, R. B., Eisenberg, N., & Green, B. L., et al. (1998). Undermining the undermining effect of reward on sustained interest. *Journal of Applied Social Psychology, 28*(3), 249–263.

Cialdini, R. B., Petty, R. E., & Cacippo, T. J. (1981). Attitude and attitude change. *Annual Review of Psychology, 32,* 357–404.

Cialdini, R. B., Reno, R. R., & Kallgren, C. A. (1990). A focus theory of normative conduct: Recycling the concept of norms to reduce littering in public places. *Journal of Personality & Social Psychology, 58*(6), 1015–1026.

Cialdini, R. B., Vincent, J. E., Lewis, S. K., Catalan, J., Wheeler, D., & Darby, B. L. (1975). A reciprocal concessions procedure for inducing compliance. The door-in-the-face technique. *Journal of Personality & Social Psychology, 21,* 206–215.

Cinciripini, P. M., Wetter, D. W., & McClure, J. B. (1997). Scheduled reduced smoking. *Addictive Behaviors, 22*(6), 759–767.

Clair, J. M., Karp, D. A., & Yoels, W. C. (1994). *Experiencing the life cycle.* Springfield, IL: Charles C Thomas.

Clark, J. L., & Hill, O. W. (1994). Academic procrastination among African-American college students. *Psychological Reports, 75*(2), 931–936.

Clark, K. B. (1965). *Dark ghetto.* New York: Harper & Row.

Clark, M. S., & Reis, H. T. (1988). Interpersonal processes in close relationships. *Annual Review of Psychology, 39,* 609–672.

Clark, M. S., & Williamson, G. M. (1989). Moods and social judgments. In H. Wagner & A. Manstead (Eds.), *Handbook of social psychophysiology.* New York: Wiley.

Clark, R., Anderson, N. B., Clark, V. R., & Williams, D. R. (1999). Racism as a stressor for African Americans. *American Psychologist, 54*(10), 805–816.

Clark, R., Hyde, J. S., Essex, M. J., & Klein, M. H. (1997). Length of maternity leave and quality of mother-infant interactions. *Child Development, 68*(2), 364–383.

Clark, R. D. (1990). The impact of AIDS on gender differences in willingness to engage in casual sex. *Journal of Applied Social Psychology, 20*(9, Pt 2), 771–782.

Clauss, C. S. (1998). Language: The unspoken variable in psychotherapy practice. *Psychotherapy, 35*(2), 188–196.

Clearwater, Y. (1985, July). A human place in outer space. *Psychology Today,* 34–43.

Click, P., Zion, C., & Nelson, C. (1988). What mediates sex discrimination in hiring decisions? *Journal of Personality & Social Psychology, 55*(2), 178–186.

Cline, V. B., Croft, R. G., & Courrier, S. (1972). Desensitization of children to television violence. *Journal of Personality & Social Psychology, 27,* 360–365.

Clore, G. L. (1976). Interpersonal attraction: An overview. In *Contemporary topics in social psychology.* Morristown, NJ: General Learning Press.

Cohen, D. J., & Bennett, S. (1997). Why can't most people draw what they see? *Journal of Experimental Psychology: Human Perception and Performance, 23*(3), 609–621.

Cohen, J. E. (1995). *How many people can the earth support?* New York: Norton.

Cohen, N. L., Waltzman, S. B., & Fisher, S. G. (1993). A prospective, randomized study of cochlear implants. *New England Journal of Medicine, 328*(4), 233–237.

Cohen, S., Evans, G. W., Krantz, D. S., & Stokols, D. (1981). Cardiovascular and behavioral effects of community noise. *American Scientist, 69,* 528–535.

Cohen, S., & Lichtenstein, E. (1990). Partner behaviors that support quitting smoking. *Journal of Consulting & Clinical Psychology, 58*(3), 304–309.

Cohen, S., et al. (1998). Types of stressors that increase susceptibility to the common cold in healthy adults. *Health Psychology, 17*(3), 214–223.

Cohen, S., Tyrrell, D. A., & Smith, A. P. (1993). Negative life events, perceived stress, negative affect, and susceptibility to the common cold. *Journal of Personality and Social Psychology, 64*(1), 131–140.

Cole, D. E., Protinsky, H. O., & Cross, L. H. (1992). An empirical investigation of adolescent suicidal ideation. *Adolescence, 27*(108), 813–818.

Cole, J. (1995). *Pride and a daily marathon.* Cambridge, MA: MIT Press.

Cole, P. H. (1998). Affective process in psychotherapy: A *Gestalt* therapist's view. *Gestalt Journal, 21*(1), 49–72.

Colin, A. K., & Moore, K., & West, A. N. (1996). Creativity, oversensitivity, and rate of habituation. *EDRA: Environmental Design Research Association, 20*(4), 423–427.

Collins, A. M., & Quillian, M. R. (1969). Retrieval time from semantic memory. *Journal of Verbal Learning and Verbal Behavior, 8,* 240–247.

Collins, R. L. (1996). For better or worse: The impact of upward social comparison on self-evaluations. *Psychological Bulletin, 119*(1), 51–69.

Collins, W. A., & Gunnar, M. R. (1990). Social and personality development. *Annual Review of Psychology, 41,* 387–416.

Comperatore, C. A., Lieberman, H. R., Kirby, A. W., & Adams, B. (1996). Melatonin efficacy in aviation missions requiring rapid deployment and night operations. *Aviation, Space, & Environmental Medicine, 67*(6), 520–524.

Condon, W. S., & Sander, L. W. (1974) Synchrony demonstrated between movements of the neonate and adult speech. *Child Development, 45*(2), 456–462.

Coni, N., Davison, W., & Webster, S. (1984). *Ageing.* Oxford: Oxford University Press.

Conlan, R. (1999). Introduction. In R. Conlan (Ed.), *States of mind.* New York: Wiley.

Considine, R. V., Sinha, M. K., Heiman, M. L., Kriauciunas, A., et al. (1996). Serum immunoreactive-leptin concentrations in normal-weight and obese humans. *New England Journal of Medicine, 334*(5), 292–295.

Consumer Reports. (1995, November). Mental health: Does therapy help? 734–739.

Conway, M. A., Cohen, G., & Stanhope, N. (1992). Very long-term memory for knowledge acquired at school and university. *Applied Cognitive Psychology, 6*(6), 467–482.

Conyne, R. K., & Clack, R. J. (1981). *Environmental assessment and design.* New York: Praeger.

Cooper, G. D., Adams, H. B., & Scott, J. C. (1988). Studies in REST: I. Reduced environmental stimulation therapy (REST) and reduced alcohol consumption. *Journal of Substance Abuse Treatment, 5*(2), 61–68.

Cooper, J., Bennett, E. A., & Sukel, H. L. (1996). Complex scientific testimony: How do jurors make decisions? *Law & Human Behavior, 20*(4), 379–394.

Cooper, J., & Fazio, R. H. (1984). A new look at dissonance theory. *Advances in Experimental Social Psychology, 17,* 226–229.

Cooper, R. P., Abraham, J., Berman, S., & Staska, M. (1997). The development of infants' preference for motherese. *Infant Behavior and Development, 20*(4), 477–488.

Coopersmith, S. (1968). Studies in self-esteem. *Scientific American, 218,* 96–106.

Corballis, M. C. (1999). The gestural origins of language. *American Scientist, 87,* 138–145.

Cordova, D. I., & Lepper, M. R. (1996). Intrinsic motivation and the process of learning. *Journal of Educational Psychology, 88*(4), 715–730.

Coren, S. (1992). *The left-hander syndrome.* New York: Free Press.

Coren, S. (1996), *Sleep thieves.* New York: Free Press.

Coren, S., & Aks, D. J. (1990). Moon illusion in pictures: A multimechanism approach. *Journal of Experimental Psychology: Human Perception & Performance, 16*(2), 365–380.

Coren, S., & Halpern, D. F. (1991). Left-handedness: A marker for decreased survival fitness. *Psychological Bulletin, 109*(1), 90–106.

Coren, S., Ward, L. M., & Enns, J. T. (1994). *Sensation and perception.* Ft. Worth, TX: Harcourt Brace.

Corey, M. S., & Corey, G. (1996). *Groups: Process and practice.* Pacific Grove, CA: Brooks/Cole.

Cormier, J. F., & Thelen, M. H. (1998). Professional skepticism of multiple personality disorder. *Professional Psychology: Research and Practice, 29*(2), 163–167.

Cornsweet, T. N. (1970). *Visual perception.* New York: Academic.

Corrigan, P. W. (1997). Behavior therapy empowers persons with severe mental illness. *Behavior Modification, 21*(1), 45–61.

Corrigan, P. W., & Penn, D. L. (1999). Lessons from social psychology on discrediting psychiatric stigma. *American Psychologist, 54*(9), 765–776.

Corteen, R. S., & Williams, T. M. (1986). Television and reading skills. In T. M. Williams (Ed.), *The impact of television: A natural experiment in three communities.* Orlando, FL: Academic.

Costa, P. T., & McCrae, R. R. (1992). Multiple uses for longitudinal personality data. *European Journal of Personality, 6*(2), 85–102.

Costello, T. W., & Costello, J. T. (1992). *Abnormal psychology.* New York: HarperCollins.

Cote, S. (1999). Affect and performance in organizational settings. *Current Directions in Psychological Science, 8*(2), 65–68.

Coulton, C. J., Korbin, J. E., & Su, M. (1996). Measuring neighborhood context for young children in an urban area. *American Journal of Community Psychology, 24*(1), 5–32.

Coursey, R. D., Ward-Alexander, L., & Katz, B. (1990). Cost-effectiveness of providing insurance benefits for posthospital psychiatric halfway house stays. *American Psychologist, 45*(10), 1118–1126.

Courtois, C. A. (1999). *Recollections of sexual abuse.* New York: Norton Professional Books.

Covell, K., Grusec, J. E., & King, G. (1995). The intergenerational transmission of maternal discipline and standards for behavior. *Social Development, 4*(1), 32–43.

Cover, J. D. (1995). The effects of social contact on prejudice. *Journal of Social Psychology, 135*(3), 403–405.

Cowles, J. T. (1937). Food tokens as incentives for learning by chimpanzees. *Comparative Psychology,* Monograph, *14*(5,71).

Cox, W. E. (1994). Exceptional evidence of ESP by a reputed sensitive. *Journal of the Society for Psychical Research, 60*(836), 16–28.

Coye, R. W., & Belohlav, J. A. (1995). An exploratory analysis of employee participation. *Group & Organization Management, 20*(1), 4–17.

Coyne, J. C., & Downey, G. (1991). Social factors and psychopathology. *Annual Review of Psychology, 42,* 401–425.

Craig, T. Y., & Kelly, J. R. (1999). Group cohesiveness and creative performance. *Group Dynamics, 3*(4), 243–256.

Craik, F. I. M. (1970). The fate of primary items in free recall. *Journal of Verbal Learning and Verbal Behavior, 9,* 143–148.

Crandall, C. S., Preisler, J. J., & Aussprung, J. (1992). Measuring life event stress in the lives of college students: The Undergraduate Stress Questionnaire (USQ). *Journal of Behavioral Medicine, 15*(6), 627–662.

Cravatt, B. F., Prospero-Garcia, O., Siuzdak, G., Gilula, N. B., et al. (1995). Chemical characterization of a family of brain lipids that induce sleep. *Science, 268*(5216), 1506–1509.

Crawford, C. B. (1994a). Effects of sex and sex roles on avoidance of same- and opposite-sex touch. *Perceptual & Motor Skills, 79*(1, Pt 1), 107–112.

Crawford, C. B. (1994b). Effects of sex and sex roles on same-sex touch. *Perceptual & Motor Skills, 78*(2), 391–394.

Crawley, S. B., & Sherrod, K. B. (1984). Parent-infant play during the first year of life. *Infant Behavior & Development, 7,* 65–75.

Cregler, L.L., & Mark, H. (1985). Medical complications of cocaine abuse. *New England Journal of Medicine, 315*(23), 1495–1500.

Crencavage, L. M., & Norcross, J. C. (1990). Where are the commonalities among the therapeutic common factors? *Professional Psychology: Research & Practice, 21*(5), 372–378.

Crick, F., & Mitchison, G. (1995). REM sleep and neural nets. *Behavioural Brain Research, 69*(1–2), 147–155.

Cromdal, J. (1999). Childhood bilingualism and metalinguistic skills. *Applied Psycholinguistics, 20*(1), 1–20.

Cronbach, L. (1990). *Essentials of psychological testing.* Reading, PA: Addison-Wesley.

Crooks, R., & Baur, K. (1999). *Our sexuality.* Pacific Grove, CA: Brooks/Cole.

Cross, J. G., & Guyer, M. J. (1980). *Social traps.* Ann Arbor: University of Michigan Press.

Crowe, L. C., & George, W. H. (1989). Alcohol and human sexuality: Review and integration. *Psychological Bulletin, 105*(3), 374–386.

Csikszentmihalyi, M. (1997). *Creativity.* New York: HarperCollins.

Csikszentmihalyi, M. (1999). If we are so rich, why aren't we happy? *American Psychologist, 54*(10), 821–827.

Cuijpers, P. (1997). Bibliotherapy in unipolar depression: A meta-analysis. *Journal of Behavior Therapy & Experimental Psychiatry, 28*(2), 139–147.

Culertson, F. M. (1997). Depression and gender. *American Psychologist, 52*(1), 25–31.

Cull, W. L., Shaughnessy, J. J., & Zechmeister, E. B. (1996). Expanding understanding of the expanding-pattern-of-retrieval mnemonic. *Journal of Experimental Psychology: Applied, 2*(4) 365–378.

Cumming, E., & Henry, W. E. (1961). *Growing old: The process of disengagement.* New York: Basic.

Cumming, S., Hay, P., Lee, T., & Sachdev, P. (1995). Neuropsychological outcome from psychosurgery for obsessive-compulsive disorder. *Australian & New Zealand Journal of Psychiatry, 29*(2), 293–298.

Cummins, D. D. (1995). *The other side of psychology.* New York: St. Martins.

Cutler, W. B. (1999). Human sex-attractant hormones: Discovery, research, development, and application in sex therapy. *Psychiatric Annals, 29*(1), 54–59.

Cutler, W. B., Friedmann, E., & McCoy, N. L. (1998). Pheromonal influences on sociosexual behavior in men. *Archives of Sexual Behavior, 27*(1), 1–13.

Cutting, J. E. (1987). Rigidity in cinema seen from the front row, side aisle. *Journal of Experimental Psychology: Human Perception and Performance, 13*(3), 323–334.

Cytowic, R. E. (1993). *The man who tasted shapes.* Putnam's Sons.

Czeisler, C. A., Kronauer, R. E., Allan, J. S., et al., (1989). Bright light induction of strong (Type O) resetting of the human circadian pacemaker. *Science, 244,* 1328–1333.

Czeisler, C. A., Richardson, G. S., Zimmerman, J. C., Moore-Ede, M. C., & Weitzman, E. D. (1981). Entrainment of human circadian rhythms by light-dark cycles: A reassessment. *Photochemistry, Photobiology, 34,* 239–247.

Dabbs, J. M. Jr., Hargrove, M. F., & Heusel, C. (1996). Testosterone differences among college fraternities. *Personality & Individual Differences, 20*(2), 157–161.

Dacey, J. S. (1989). *Fundamentals of creative thinking.* Lexington, MA: Lexington.

Darley, J. M., & Latane, B. (1968). Bystander intervention in emergencies: Diffusion of responsibility. *Journal of Personality & Social Psychology, 8,* 377–383.

Darling, C. A., Davidson, J. K., & Passarello, L. C. (1992). The mystique of first intercourse among college youth: The role of partners, contraceptive practices, and psychological reactions. *Journal of Youth & Adolescence, 21*(1), 97–117.

Darwin, C. (1872). *The expression of emotion in man and animals.* Chicago: University of Chicago Press.

Darwin, M., & Wowk, B. (1992). Cryonics: Reaching for tomorrow. *Skeptic, 1*(2), 32–43.

DasGupta, B. (1992). Perceived control and examination stress. *Psychology: A Journal of Human Behavior, 29*(1), 31–34.

Davanloo, H. (1995). Intensive short-term dynamic psychotherapy. *International Journal of Short-Term Psychotherapy, 10*(3–4), 121–155.

David, H., Borgeat, F., & Saucier, J. (1990). The relation between tachystoscopic pictures and neurotic postpartum depression. *Pre- & Peri-Natal Psychology Journal, 4*(3), 219–227.

Davies, M. F. (1993). Dogmatism and the persistence of discredited beliefs. *Personality & Social Psychology Bulletin, 19*(6), 692–699.

Davis, J. H. (1989). Psychology and law: The last 15 years. *Journal of Applied Social Psychology, 19*(3, Pt. 1), 199–230.

Davis, J. R., Vanderploeg, J. M., Santy, P. A., Jennings, R. T., et al. (1988). Space motion sickness during 24 flights of the Space Shuttle. *Aviation, Space, & Environmental Medicine, 59*(12), 1185–1189.

Davis, M. H., & Harvey, J. C. (1992). Declines in major league batting performance as a function of game pressure. *Journal of Applied Social Psychology, 22*(9), 714–735.

Davis, M. J., & Bibace, R. (1999). Dating couples and their relationships: Intimacy and contraceptive use. *Adolescence, 34*(133), 1–7.

Dawson, M. E. (1990). Where does the truth lie? A review of the polygraph test: Lies, truth, and science. *Psychophysiology, 27*(1), 120–121.

De Benedittis, G., Lorenzetti, A., & Pieri, A. (1990). The role of stressful life events in the onset of chronic primary headache. *Pain, 40(1),* 65–75.

De Bono, E. (1992). *Serious creativity.* New York: HarperCollins.

De Haan, E. H. F., Heywood, C. A., Young, A. W., Edelstyn, N., et al. (1995). Ettlinger revisited: The relation between agnosia and sensory impairment. *Journal of Neurology, Neurosurgery & Psychiatry, 58*(3), 350–356.

De Jong, T., & van Joolingen, W. R. (1998). Scientific discovery learning with computer simulations of conceptual domains. *Review of Educational Research, 68*(2), 179–201.

De las Fuentes, C., & Vasquez, M. J. T. (1999). Immigrant adolescent girls of color. In N. G. Johnson, M. C. Roberts, & J. Worell (Eds.), *Beyond appearance.* Washington, DC: APA.

De Luccie, M. F., & Davis, A. J. (1991). Father-child relationships from the preschool years through mid-adolescence. *Journal of Genetic Psychology, 152*(2), 225–238.

De Raad, B. (1998). Five big, Big Five issues. *European Psychologist, 3*(2), 113–124.

De Roiste, A., & Bushnell, I. W. R. (1996). Tactile stimulation: Short- and long-term benefits for pre-term infants. *British Journal of Developmental Psychology, 14,* 41–53.

Dean-Church, L., & Gilroy, F. D. (1993). Relation of sex-role orientation to life satisfaction in a healthy elderly sample. *Journal of Social Behavior & Personality, 8*(1), 133–140.

Deary, I. J., & Stough, C. (1996). Intelligence and inspection time. *American Psychologist, 51*(6), 599–608.

Deaux, K., Dane, F., & Wrightsman, L. S. (1993). *Social psychology in the '90s.* Monterey: Brooks/Cole.

Deaux, K., & Emswiller, T. (1974). Explanation of successful performance on sex-linked tasks: What is skill for the male is luck for the female. *Journal of Personality & Social Psychology, 29,* 80–85.

DeBell, C. S., & Harless, D. K. (1992). B. F. Skinner: Myth and misperception. *Teaching of Psychology, 19*(2), 68–73.

Deese, J., & Hulse, S. J. (1967). *The psychology of learning* (3rd ed.)). New York: McGraw-Hill.

Deffenbacher, J. L., & Suinn, R. M. (1988). Systematic desensitization and the reduction of anxiety. *Counseling Psychologist, 16*(1), 9–30.

Degirmencioglu, S. M., Urberg, K. A., Tolson, J. M., & Richard, P. (1998). Adolescent friendship networks. *Merrill-Palmer Quarterly, 44*(3), 313–337.

DeGood, D. E. (1975). Cognitive factors in vascular stress responses. *Psychophysiology, 12,* 399–401.

Degreef, G., Ashtari, M., Bogerts, B., et al. (1992). Volumes of ventricular system subdivisions measured from magnetic resonance images in first-episode schizophrenic patients. *Archives of General Psychiatry, 49*(7), 531–537.

DeGroot, G. (1994, June). Psychologists explain Barney's power. *APA Monitor,* p. 4.

DeKlyen, M., Biernbaum, M. A., Spelz, M. L., & Greenberg, M. T. (1998). *Developmental Psychology, 34*(2), 264–275.

Delgado, B. M., & Ford, L. (1998). Parental perceptions of child development among low-income Mexican American families. *Journal of Child & Family Studies, 7*(4), 469–481.

Demyttenaere, K., Lenaerts, H., Nijs, P., & Van Assche, F. A. (1995). Individual coping style and psychological attitudes during pregnancy predict depression levels during pregnancy and during postpartum. *Acta Psychiatrica Scandinavica, 91*(2), 95–102.

DeNeve, K. M., & Cooper, H. (1998). The happy personality. *Psychological Bulletin, 124*(2), 197–229.

Denmark, F. L. (1994). Engendering psychology. *American Psychologist, 49*(4), 329–334.

Denning, P. J. (1988). Blindness in designing intelligent systems. *American Scientist, 76,* 118–120.

Deregowski, J. B. (1972, November). Pictorial perception and culture. *Scientific American,* 82–88.

Dermer, A. (1998). Breastfeeding and women's health. *Journal of Women's Health, 7*(4), 427–433.

Derzon, J. H., & Lipsey, M. W. (1999). A synthesis of the relationship of marijuana use with delinquent and problem behaviors. *School Psychology International, 20*(1), 57–68.

Desimone, R., & Duncan, J. (1995). Neural mechanisms of selective visual attention. *Annual Review of Neuroscience, 18,* 193–222.

DeSpelder, L. A., & Strickland, A. L. (1995). *The last dance.* Mountain View, CA: Mayfield.

Deutsch, M. (1993). Educating for a peaceful world. *American Psychologist, 48*(5), 510–517.

Devilly, G. J., Spence, S. H., & Rapee, R. M. (1998). Statistical and reliable change with eye movement desensitization and reprocessing. *Behavior Therapy, 29*(3) 435–455.

Devine, D. P., & Spanos, N. P. (1990). Effectiveness of maximally different cognitive strategies and expectancy in attenuation of reported pain. *Journal of Personality & Social Psychology, 58*(4), 672–678.

Devine, P. G. (1990). Stereotypes and prejudice: Their automatic and controlled components. *Journal of Personality & Social Psychology, 56*(1), 5–18.

Devine, P. G., Monteith, M. J., Zuerink, J. R., & Elliot, A. J. (1991). Prejudice with and without compunction. *Journal of Personality & Social Psychology, 60*(6), 817–830.

Devlin, B., Daniels, M., & Roeder, K. (1997). The heritability of IQ. *Nature, 388*(6641), 468–471.

Devoto, A., Lucidi, F., Violani, C., & Bertini, M. (1999). Effects of different sleep reductions on daytime sleepiness. *Sleep, 22*(3), 336–343.

Dewhurst, S. A., & Conway, M. A. (1994). Pictures, images, and recollective experience. *Journal of Experimental Psychology: Learning, Memory, and Cognition, 20,* 1088–1098.

Diamond, L. M. (1998). Development of sexual orientation among adolescent and young adult women. *Developmental Psychology, 34*(5), 1085–1095.

Dickinson, D. J., & O'Connell, D. Q. (1990). Effect of quality and quantity of study on student grades. *Journal of Educational Research, 83*(4), 227–231.

Diefenbach, D. L. (1997). Portrayal of mental illness on prime-time television. *Journal of Community Psychology, 25*(3), 289–302.

Diekstra, R. F., & Garnefski, N. (1995). On the nature, magnitude, and causality of suicidal behaviors: An international perspective. *Suicide & Life-Threatening Behavior, 25*(1), 36–57.

Diener, E., Sapyta, J. J., & Suh, E. (1998). Subjective well-being is essential to well-being. *Psychological Inquiry, 9,* 33–37.

Diener, E., Suh, E. M., Lucas, R. E., & Smith, H. L. (1999). Subjective well-being: Three decades of progress. *Psychological Bulletin, 125*(2), 276–302.

Dies, R. R. (1995). Group psychotherpies. In A. S. Gurman & S. B. Messer, *Essential psychotherapies.* New York: Guilford.

Dieter, J. N. I., & Emory, E. K. (1997). Supplemental stimulation of premature infants. *Journal of Pediatric Psychology, 22*(3), 281–295.

Dietz, T. L. (1998). An examination of violence and gender role portrayals in video games. *Sex Roles, 38*(5–6), 425–442.

Digman, J. M. (1990). Personality structure: Emergence of the five-factor model. *Annual Review of Psychology, 41,* 417–440.

Dignon, A. M. (1996). Acceptability of a computer-administered psychiatric interview. *Computers in Human Behavior, 12*(2), 177–191.

Dillard, J. P. (1991). The current status of research on sequential-request compliance techniques. *Personality & Social Psychology Bulletin, 17*(3), 283–288.

Diller, L. H. (1998). *Running on ritalin.* New York: Bantam.

Dinkmeyer, D. Sr., McKay, G. D., & Dinkmeyer, D. Jr. (1997). *The parent's handbook.* Circle Pines, MN: American Guidance Service.

Dobelle, W. H. (2000). Artificial vision for the blind by connecting a television camera to the visual cortex. *American Society of Artificial Internal Organs, 46,* 3–9.

Dobratz, M. C. (1995). Analysis of variables that impact psychological adaptation in home hospice patients. *Hospice Journal, 10*(1), 75–88.

Docherty, N. M., et al. (1998). Communication disturbances and family psychiatric history in parents of schizophrenic patients. *Journal of Nervous & Mental Disease, 186*(12), 761–768.

Doctor, R. M., & Doctor, J. N. (1994). Stress. In *Encyclopedia of human behavior, Vol. 4* (pp. 311–323). San Diego, CA: Academic.

Doidge, N. (1997). Empirical evidence for the efficacy of *psychoanalytic* psychotherapies and psychoanalysis. *Psychoanalytic Inquiry, Suppl.,* 102–150.

Dollard, J., et al. (1939). *Frustration and aggression.* New Haven: Yale University Press.

Dollard, J., & Miller, N. E. (1950). *Personality and psychotherapy: An analysis in terms of learning, thinking and culture.* New York: McGraw-Hill.

Domhoff, G. W. (1999). Drawing theoretical implications from descriptive empirical findings on dream content. *Dreaming: Journal of the Association for the Study of Dreams, 9*(2–3), 201–210.

Domingo, R. A., & Goldstein-Alpern, N. (1999). "What dis?" and other toddler-initiated, expressive language-learning strategies. *Infant-Toddler Intervention, 9*(1), 39–60.

Donnerstein, E. I., & Linz, D. G. (1986, December). The question of pornography. *Psychology Today,* 56–59.

Donohue, H. E. F. (1968). *Where should you touch?* New York: Hearst.

Dooling, D. J., & Lachman, R. (1971). Effects of comprehension on retention of prose. *Journal of Experimental Psychology, 88,* 216–222.

Dorfman, J., Shames, J., & Kihlstrom, J. F. (1996). Intuition, incubation, & insight. In G. Underwood (Ed.), *Implicit cognition.* New York: Oxford University Press.

Dosher, B. A., & Ma, J. (1998). Output loss or rehearsal loop? *Journal of Experimental Psychology: Learning, Memory, & Cognition, 24*(2), 316–335.

Doty, R. M., Peterson, B. E., & Winter, D. G. (1991). *Journal of Personality & Social Psychology, 61*(4), 629–640.

Douvan, E. (1997). Erik Erikson: Critical times, critical theory. *Child Psychiatry & Human Development, 28*(1), 15–21.

Dovidio, J. F. (1984). Helping behavior and altruism: An empirical and conceptual overview. In L. Berkowitz (Ed.), *Advances in experimental social psychology, Vol. 17.* New York: Academic.

Dovido, J. F., Allen, J. L., & Schroeder, D. A. (1990). Specificity of empathy-induced helping: Evidence for altruistic motivation. *Journal of Personality & Social Psychology, 59*(2), 249–260.

Dovidio, J. F., & Gaertner, S. L. (1999). Reducing prejudice: Combating intergroup biases. *Current Directions in Psychological Science, 8*(4), 101–105.

Dragoi, V., & Staddon, J. E. R. (1999). The dynamics of operant conditioning. *Psychological Review, 106*(1), 20–61.

Dretzke, Beverly J., & Levin, Joel R. (1996). Assessing students' application and transfer of a mnemonic strategy. *Contemporary Educational Psychology, 21*(1), 83–93.

Drexler, L. P., Ahrens, A. H., & Haaga, D. A. (1995). The affective consequences of self-handicapping. *Journal of Social Behavior & Personality, 10*(4), 861–870.

Drigotas, S. M., Rusbult, C. E., Wieselquist, J., & Whitton, S. W. (1999). Close partner as sculptor of the ideal self: Behavioral affirmation and the Michelangelo phenomenon. *Journal of Personality & Social Psychology, 77*(2), 293–323.

Druckman, D., & Bjork, R. A. (1994). Learning, remembering, believing: Enhancing human performance. Washington, DC: National Academy Press.

DSM-IV: Diagnostic and statistical manual of mental disorders (4th ed.). (1994). Washington, DC: American Psychiatric Association.

Dubbert, P M. (1995). Behavioral (life-style) modification in the prevention and treatment of hypertension. *Clinical Psychology Review, 15*(3), 187–216.

Dubow, E. F., Huesmann, L. R., & Eron, L. D. (1987). Childhood correlates of adult ego development. *Child Development, 58*(3), 859–869.

Dugas, M. J., et al. (1998). Worry themes in primary GAD, secondary GAD, and other anxiety disorders. *Journal of Anxiety Disorders, 12*(3), 253–261.

Duncker, K. (1945). On problem solving. *Psychological Monographs, 58*(270).

Dunham, I. Shimizu, N., & Chissoe, S. (1999). The DNA sequence of human chromosome 22. *Nature, 402*(6761), 489.

Durham, M. D., & Dane, F. C. (1999). Juror knowledge of eyewitness behavior. *Journal of Social Behavior & Personality, 14*(2), 299–308.

Durso, F. T., Rea, C. B., & Dayton, T. (1994). Graph-theoretic confirmation of restructuring during insight. *Psychological Science, 5*(2), 94–98.

Dusek, J. B. (1996). *Adolescent development and behavior.* Englewood Cliffs, NJ: Prentice Hall.

Dutton, D. G., & Aron, A. P. (1974). Some evidence for heightened sexual attraction under conditions of high anxiety. *Journal of Personality & Social Psychology, 30*, 510–517.

Dwyer, W. O., Leeming, F. C., Cobern, M. K., Porter, B. E., et al. (1993). Critical review of behavioral interventions to preserve the environment. *Environment and Behavior, 25*(3), 275–321.

Dyer, F. J. (1993). Clinical presentation of the lead-poisoned child on mental ability tests. *Journal of Clinical Psychology, 49*(1), 94–101.

Dywan, J., & Bowers, K. S. (1983). The use of hypnosis to enhance recall. *Science, 222*, 184–185.

Eagly, A. H., & Chaiken, S. (1992). *The psychology of attitudes.* San Diego, CA: Harcourt Brace Jovanovich.

Eastman, C. I., Stewart, K. T., Mahoney, M. P., Liu, L., et al. (1994). Dark goggles and bright light improve circadian rhythm adaptation to night-shift work. *Sleep, 17*(6), 535–543.

Ebbinghaus, H. (1913). *Memory: A contribution to experimental psychology* (H. A. Ruger & C. E. Bussenius, Trans.). New York: New York Teacher's College, Columbia University. (Original work published 1885)

Eberhardt, B. J., & Muchinsky, P. M. (1982). An empirical investigation of the factor stability of Owens' biographical questionnaire. *Journal of Applied Psychology, 67*, 138–145.

Eccles, J. S., Midgley, C., Wigfield, A., Buchanan, C. M., Reuman, K. D., Flanagan, C., & Mac Iver, D. (1993). Development during adolescence. *American Psychologist, 48*, 90–101.

Eckensberger, L. H., & Zimba, R. F. (1997). The development of moral judgment. In P. Dasen & T. S. Saraswathi (Eds.), *Handbook of cross-cultural psychology, Vol. 3, Developmental psychology.* Boston: Allyn & Bacon.

Eckerman, D. A. (1999). Scheduling reinforcement about once a day. *Behavioural Processes, 45*(1–3), 101–114.

Edwards, D. J. A. (1998). Types of case study work. *Journal of Humanistic Psychology, 38*(3), 36–70.

Egeland, B., Jacobvitz, D., & Sroufe, L. A. (1988). Breaking the cycle of abuse. *Child Development, 59*(4), 1080–1088.

Eich, E. (1995). Mood as a mediator of place dependent memory. *Journal of Experimental Psychology: General, 124*(3), 293-308.

Eich, E., Rachman, S., & Lopatka, C. (1990). Affect, pain, and autobiographical memory. *Journal of Abnormal Psychology, 99*(2) 174–178.

Eichorn, D. H., Hunt, J. V., & Honzik, M. P. (1981). Experience, personality, and IQ: Adolescence to middle age. In D. H. Eichorn, J. A. Clausen, N. Haan, M. P. Honzik, & P. H. Mussen (Eds.), *Present and past in middle life.* New York: Academic.

Eimas, P. D., Quinn, P. C., & Cowan, P. (1994). Development of exclusivity in perceptually based categories of young infants. *Journal of Experimental Child Psychology, 58*(3), 418–431.

Einspieler, C., Widder, J., Holzer, A., & Kenner, T. (1988). The predictive value of behavioural risk factors for sudden infant death. *Early Human Development, 18*(2–3), 101–109.

Eisenberg, N. (1991). Meta-analytic contributions to the literature on prosocial behavior. *Personality & Social Psychology Bulletin, 17*(3), 273–282.

Eisenberg, N., & Miller, P. A. (1987). The relation of empathy to prosocial and related behaviors. *Psychological Bulletin, 101*(1), 91–119.

Ekman, P. (1986). *Telling Lies.* New York: Berkley.

Ekman, P. (1993). Facial expression and emotion. *American Psychologist, 48(4)*, 384–392.

Ekman, P., Friesen, W. V., & Bear, J. (1984, May). The international language of gestures. *Psychology Today,* 64–69.

Ekman, P., Levenson, R. W., & Friesen, W. V. (1983). Autonomic nervous system activity distinguishes among emotions. *Science, 221*, 1208–1210.

Ekman, P., & O'Sullivan, M. (1991). Who can catch a liar? *American Psychologist, 46*(9), 913–920.

Ekman, P., & Rosenberg, E. (1997). *What the face reveals.* New York: Oxford University Press.

Eliot, L. (1999). *What's going on in there?* New York: Bantam

Elkind, D. (1981). *The hurried child.* Reading, MA: Addison-Wesley.

Elkind, D. (1984). *All grown up & no place to go.* Reading, MA: Addison-Wesley.

Elkind, D. (1995). *Ties that stress.* Cambridge, MA: Harvard University Press.

Elkins, D. B., et al. (1998). Relaying the message of safer sex. *Health Education Research, 13*(3), 357–370.

Elliott, M., Browne, K., & Kilcoyne, J. (1995). Child sexual abuse prevention: What offenders tell us. *Child Abuse & Neglect, 19*(5), 579–594.

Ellis, A. (1973, February). The no cop-out therapy. *Psychology Today, 7*, 56–60, 62.

Ellis, A. (1979). The practice of rational-emotive therapy. In A. Ellis & J. Whiteley (Eds.), *Theoretical and empirical foundations of rational-emotive therapy.* Monterey, CA: Brooks/Cole.

Ellis, A. (1987). A sadly neglected cognitive component in depression. *Cognitive Therapy & Research, 11*(1), 121-145.

Ellis, A. (1993). Reflections on rational-emotive therapy. *Journal of Consulting & Clinical Psychology, 61*(2), 199–201.

Ellis, A. (1995). Changing rational-emotive therapy (RET) to rational emotive behavior therapy (REBT). *Journal of Rational-Emotive & Cognitive Behavior Therapy, 13*(2), 85–89.

Ellis, H. C., & Hunt, R. R. (1983). *Fundamentals of human memory and cognition.* Dubuque, IA: William C Brown.

Ellis, H. C., & Hunt, R. R. (1992). *Fundamentals of cognitive psychology.* Madison, WI: Brown & Benchmark.

Elovainio, M., Kivimaeki, M., Steen, N., & Kalliomaeki-Levanto, T. (2000). Organizational and individual factors affecting mental health and job satisfaction. *Journal of Occupational Health Psychology, 5*(4), 269–277.

Emmons, K. M., et al. (1998). Predictors of smoking among U.S. college students. *American Journal of Public Health, 88*(1), 104–107.

Endler, N. S., & Persad, E. (in press). *Electroconvulsive therapy.* Hans Huber.

Engel, G. (1977, November). Emotional stress and sudden death. *Psychology Today,* 144.

Engler, J., & Goleman, D. (1992). *The consumer's guide to psychotherapy.* New York: Simon & Schuster.

Enns, J. T., & Coren, S. (1995). The box alignment illusion. *Perception & Psychophysics, 57*(8), 1163–1174.

Enright, J. T. (1996). Sequential stereopsis: A simple demonstration. *Vision Research, 36*(2), 307–312.

Eppley, K. R., Abrams, A. I., & Shear, J. (1989). Differential effects of relaxation techniques on trait anxiety: A meta-analysis. *Journal of Clinical Psychology, 45*(6), 957–974.

Epstein, R., Langa, R. P., & Skinner, B. F. (1981). "Self-awareness" in the pigeon. *Science, 212*, 695–696.

Epstein, R. S., Fullerton, C. S., & Ursano, R. J. (1998). Posttraumatic stress disorder following an air disaster. *American Journal of Psychiatry, 155*(7), 934–938.

Erdelyi, M. H., & Appelbaum, A. G., (1973). Cognitive masking: The disruptive effect of an emotional stimulus upon the perception of contiguous neutral items. *Bulletin of the Psychonomic Society, 1*, 59–61.

Ericsson, K. A., & Charness, N. (1994). Expert performance. *American Psychologist, 49*(8), 725–747.

Ericsson, K. A., & Chase, W. G. (1982). Exceptional memory. *American Scientist, 70*, 607–615.

Erikson, E. H. (1963). *Childhood and society.* New York: Norton.

Erk, R. R. (1995). The conundrum of attention deficit disorder. *Journal of Mental Health Counseling, 17*(2), 131–145.

Erlich, P. R., & Erlich, A. H. (1990). The population explosion. *Amicus Journal,* 18–29.

Ernst, E. (1994). Is acupuncture effective for pain control? *Journal of Pain & Symptom Management, 9*(2), 72–74.

Eron, L. D. (1986). Interventions to mitigate the psychological effects of media violence on aggressive behavior. *Journal of Social Issues, 42*(3), 155–169.

Eron, L. D. (1987). The development of aggressive behavior from the perspective of a developing behaviorism. *American Psychologist, 42,* 435–442.

Eronen, S., & Nurmi, J. (1999). Life events, predisposing cognitive strategies and well-being. *European Journal of Personality, 13*(2), 129–148.

Ertel, S. (1998). Astro-quiz: Can astrologers pick politicians from painters? *Correlation, 17,* 3–8.

Espy, K. A., Kaufmann, P. M., & Glisky, M. L. (1999). Neuropsychological function in toddlers exposed to cocaine in utero: A preliminary study. *Developmental Neuropsychology, 15*(3), 447–460.

Esser, J. K. (1998). Alive and well after 25 years: A review of groupthink research. *Organizational Behavior & Human Decision Processes, 73*(2–3), 116–141.

Esterling, B. A., L'Abate, L., Murray, E. J., & Pennebaker, J. W. (1999). Empirical foundations for writing in prevention and psychotherapy: Mental and physical health outcomes. *Clinical Psychology Review, 19*(1), 79–96.

Ethical principles of psychologists and code of conduct (1992). *American Psychologist, 47*(12), 1597–1611.

Evans, G. W., Bullinger, M., & Hygge, S. (1998). Chronic noise exposure and physiological response. *Psychological Science, 9*(1) 75–77.

Evans, G. W., & Lepore, S. J. (1993). Household crowding and social support. *Journal of Personality & Social Psychology, 65*(2), 308–316.

Evans, G. W., Lepore, S. J., & Schroeder, A. (1996). The role of interior design elements in human responses to crowding. *Journal of Personality & Social Psychology, 70*(1), 41–46.

Evans, S. (1993, January 25). Keeping cool when the baby won't stop crying. *Los Angeles Times,* p. E-2.

Everard, K. M. (1999). The relationship between reasons for activity and older adult well-being. *Journal of Applied Gerontology, 18*(3), 325–340.

Everson, C. A. (1998). Physiological consequences of sleep deprivation. *Journal of Musculoskeletal Pain, 6*(3), 93-101.

Everson, S. A., Goldberg, D. E., & Salonen, J. T. (1996). Hopelessness and risk of mortality and incidence of myocardial infarction and cancer. *Psychosomatic Medicine, 58*(2), 113.

Eyer, Diane E. (1994). Mother-infant bonding: A scientific fiction. *Human Nature, 5*(1), 69-94.

Eysenck, H. J. (1967, June). New ways in psychotherapy. *Psychology Today,* 40.

Eysenck, H. J. (Ed.). (1981). *A model for personality.* New York: Springer-Verlag.

Eysenck, H. J. (1994). The outcome problem in psychotherapy: What have we learned? *Behaviour Research & Therapy, 32*(5), 477–495.

Eysenck, M. W., & Keane, M. T. (1995). *Cognitive psychology.* Hove, East Sussex, UK: Erlbaum.

Fabes, R. A., Carlo, G., Kupanoff, K., & Laible, D. (1999). Early adolescence and prosocial/moral behavior. *Journal of Early Adolescence, 19*(1), 5–16.

Faigel, H. C., Sznajderman, S., Tishby, O., et al. (1995). Attention deficit disorder during adolescence: A review. *Journal of Adolescent Health, 16*(3), 174–184.

Fairclough, S. H., & Graham, R. (1999). Impairment of driving performance caused by sleep deprivation or alcohol. *Human Factors, 41*(1), 118–128.

Faith, M. S., Wong, F. Y., & Carpenter, K. M. (1995). Group sensitivity training: Update, meta-analysis, and recommendations. *Journal of Counseling Psychology, 42*(3), 390–399.

Famularo, R., Kinscherff, R., & Fenton, T. (1992). Psychiatric diagnoses of abusive mothers. *Journal of Nervous & Mental Disease, 180*(10), 658–661.

Fantz, R. L. (1961, May). The origin of form perception. *Scientific American,* 71.

Farah, M. J. (1988). Is visual imagery really visual? Overlooked evidence from neuropsychology. *Psychological Review, 95*(3), 307–317.

Farah, M. J., Weisberg, L. L., Monheit, M. A., & Peronnet, F. (1989). Brain activity underlying mental imagery. *Journal of Cognitive Neuroscience, 1*(4), 302–316.

Farquhar, J. W., et al., (1997). Short- and long-term outcomes of a health promotion program in a small rural community. *American Journal of Health Promotion, 11*(6), 411–414.

Farquhar, J. W., Fortmann, S. P., Maccoby, N., Wood, P. D., et al. (1984). The Stanford Five City Project: An overview. In J. D. Matarazzo, S. M. Weiss, J. A. Herd, N. E. Miller, & S. M. Weiss (Eds.), *Behavioral health: A handbook of health enhancement and disease prevention.* New York: Wiley.

Farrimond, T. (1990). Effect of alcohol on visual constancy values and possible relation to driving performance. *Perceptual & Motor Skills, 70*(1), 291–295.

Farthing, G. W. (1992). The psychology of consciousness. Englewood Cliffs, NJ: Prentice Hall.

Farver, J. M., et al. (1997). Toy stories: Aggression in children's narratives in the United States, Sweden, Germany, and Indonesia. *Journal of Cross-Cultural Psychology, 28*(4) 393–420.

Fava, G. A., et al. (1998). Prevention of recurrent depression with cognitive behavioral therapy. *Archives of General Psychiatry, 55*(9), 816–820.

Feingold, A. (1990). Gender differences in effects of physical attractiveness on romantic attraction. *Journal of Personality & Social Psychology, 59*(5), 981–993.

Feingold, A. (1992a). Gender differences in mate selection preferences. *Psychological Bulletin, 111,* 304–341.

Feingold, A. (1992b). Good-looking people are not what we think. *Psychological Bulletin, 111*(2), 304-341.

Feldhusen, J. F. (1995). Creativity: A knowledge base, metacognitive skills, and personality factors. *Journal of Creative Behavior, 29*(4), 255–268.

Feldhusen, J. F., & Goh, B. E. (1995). Assessing and accessing creativity: An integrative review of theory, research, and development. *Creativity Research Journal, 8*(3), 231–247.

Feldman, R., Greenbaum, C. W., & Yirmiya, N. (1999). Mother-infant affect synchrony as an antecedent of the emergence of self-control. *Developmental Psychology, 35*(1), 223–231.

Feldman, R., Weller, A., Leckman, J. F., Kuint, J., & Eidelman, A. I. (1999). The nature of the mother's tie to her infant. *Journal of Child Psychology & Psychiatry & Allied Disciplines, 40*(6), 929–939.

Feldman, R. S., & Meyer, J. (1996). *Fundamentals of neuropsychopharmacology.* Sunderland, MA: Sinauer Associates.

Felmlee, D. H. (1998). "Be careful what you wish for . . .": A quantitative and qualitative investigation of "fatal attractions." *Personal Relationships, 5*(3), 235–253.

Felsenfeld, S. (1996). Progress and needs in the genetics of stuttering. *Journal of Fluency Disorders, 21*(2), 77–103.

Fenton, G. W. (1998). Neurosurgery for mental disorder. *Irish Journal of Psychological Medicine, 15*(2), 45–48.

Fernald, A. (1989). Intonation and communicative intent in mothers' speech to infants: Is the melody the message? *Child Development, 60*(6)1497–1510.

Fernald, A., & Mazzie, C. (1991). Prosody and focus in speech to infants and adults. *Developmental Psychology, 27*(2), 209–221.

Fernandez, E., & Turk, D. C. (1989). The utility of cognitive coping strategies for altering pain perception. *Pain, 38*(2), 123–135.

Ferrari, J. R. (1991). Self-handicapping by procrastinators: Protecting self-esteem, social-esteem, or both? *Journal of Research in Personality, 25*(3), 245–261.

Ferrari, J. R. (1992). Procrastinators and perfect behavior. *Journal of Research in Personality, 26*(1), 75–84.

Ferster, C. B., Nurnberger, J. I., & Levitt, E. B. (1962). The control of eating. *Journal of Mathematics, 1,* 87-109.

Festinger, L. (1954). A theory of social comparison processes. *Human Relations, 7,* 117–140.

Festinger, L. (1957). *A theory of cognitive dissonance.* Stanford, CA: Stanford University Press.

Festinger, L., & Carlsmith, J. M. (1959). Cognitive consequences of forced compliance. *Journal of Abnormal and Social Psychology, 58,* 203–210.

Festinger, L., Schachter, S., & Back, K. (1950). *Social pressures in informal groups: A study of a housing project.* New York: Harper.

Fetsch, R. J., Schultz, C. J., & Wahler, J. J. (1999). A preliminary evaluation of the Colorado rethink parenting and anger management program. *Child Abuse & Neglect, 23*(4), 353–360.

Feuerstein, M., Labbé, E. E., & Kuczmierczyk, A. R. (1986). *Health psychology: A psychobiological perspective.* New York: Plenum.

Feuerstein, R., Hoffman, M. B., Rand, Y., & Jensen, M. R. (1986). Learning to learn: Mediated learning experiences and instrumental enrichment. *Special Services in the Schools, 3*(1–2), 49–82.

Field, T. M. (1998). Touch therapy effects on development. *International Journal of Behavioral Development, 22*(4), 779–797.

Finke, R. (1990). *Creative imagery.* Hillsdale, NJ: Erlbaum.

Finkelhor, D., & Dziuba-Leatherman, J. (1994). Victimization of children. *American Psychologist, 49*(3), 173–183.

Finkelson, L., & Oswalt, R. (1995). College date rape: Incidence and reporting. *Psychological Reports, 77*(2), 526.

Finkelstein, P., Wenegrat, B., & Yalom, I. (1982). Large group awareness training. *Annual Review of Psychology, 33,* 515–539.

Finkenauer, C., Luminet, O., Gisle, L., et al. (1998). Flashbulb memories and the underlying mechanisms of their formation. *Memory & Cognition, 26*(3), 516–531.

Firth, U. (1993, June). Autism. *Scientific American,* 108–114.

Fisher, C. B., & Fyrberg, D. (1994). Participant partners. *American Psychologist, 49*(5), 417–427.

Fisher, K. (1984, December). Berkeley study finds stress is value-laden. *APA Monitor, 26,* 30.

Fisher, R. P., & Geiselman, R. E. (1987). Enhancing eyewitness memory with the cognitive interview. In M. M. Gruneberg, P. E. Morris, & R. N. Sykes (Eds.), *Practical aspects of memory: Current research and issues.* Chinchester, UK: Wiley.

Fisher, S. (1973). *The female orgasm.* New York: Basic.

Fiske, S. T. (1993a). Social cognition and social perception. *Annual Review of Psychology, 44,* 155–194.

Fiske, S. T., (1993b). Controlling other people. *American Psychologist, 48*(6), 621–628.

Flannery, D. J., Rowe, D. C., & Gulley, B. L. (1993). Impact of pubertal status, timing, and age on adolescent sexual experience and delinquency. *Journal of Adolescent Research, 8*(1), 21–40.

Flannery, R. B., & Wieman, D. (1989). Social support, life stress, and psychological distress: An empirical assessment. *Journal of Clinical Psychology, 45*(6), 867–872.

Flashman, L. A., Andreasen, N. C., Flaum, M., & Swayze, V. W. II. (1997). Intelligence and regional brain volumes in normal controls. *Intelligence, 25*(3), 149–160.

Flavell, J. H. (1992). Cognitive development: Past, present, and future. *Developmental Psychology, 28*(6), 998–1005.

Flavell, J. H. (1999). Cognitive development: Children's knowledge about the mind. *Annual Review of Psychology, 50,* 21–45.

Fleming, J. (1974, January). Field report: The state of the apes. *Psychology Today,* 46.

Flynn, J. R. (1987). Massive IQ gains in 14 nations: What IQ tests really measure. *Psychological Bulletin, 101*(2), 171–191.

Flynn, J. R. (1990). Massive IQ gains on the Scottish WISC: Evidence against Brand et al.'s hypothesis. *Irish Journal of Psychology, 11*(1), 41–51.

Flynn, K. J., & Fitzgibbon, M. (1998). Body images and obesity risk among black females: A review of the literature. *Annals of Behavioral Medicine, 20*(1), 13–24.

Foa, E. B., Franklin, M. E., Perry, K. J., & Herbert, J. D. (1996). Cognitive biases in generalized social phobia. *Journal of Abnormal Psychology, 105*(3), 433–439.

Fobair, P. (1997). Cancer support groups and group therapies. *Journal of Psychosocial Oncology, 15*(3–4), 123–147.

Fochtmann, L. J. (1995). Intractable sneezing as a conversion symptom. *Psychosomatics, 36*(2), 103–112.

Fones, C. S. L., et al. (1998). Social phobia: An update. *Harvard Review of Psychiatry, 5*(5), 247–259.

Fontana, A., Rosenheck, R., & Brett, E. (1992). War zone traumas and posttraumatic stress disorder symptomatology. *Journal of Nervous & Mental Disease, 180*(12), 748–755.

Fontenelle, D. H. (1989). *How to live with your children.* Tucson, AZ: Fisher Books.

Foos, P., & Clark, M. C. (1984). *Human learning, 2*(3).

Ford, C. V. (1995). Dimensions of somatization and hypochondriasis. *Neurologic Clinics, 13*(2), 241–253.

Ford, G. G., Gallagher, S. H., Lacy, B. A., Bridwell, A. M., & Goodwin, F. (1999). Repositioning the home plate umpire to provide enhanced perceptual cues and more accurate ball-strike judgments. *Journal of Sport Behavior, 22*(1), 28–44.

Foreyt, J. P. (1987a). Behavioral medicine. In *Review of behavior therapy: Theory and practice, Vol. II.* New York: Guilford.

Foreyt, J. P. (1987b). The addictive disorders. In G. T. Wilson, C. M. Franks, P. C. Kendall, & J. P. Foreyt. *Review of behavior therapy: Theory and practice, Vol. II.* New York: Guilford.

Foss, R. D. (1986). Using social psychology to increase altruistic behavior: Will it help? In M. J. Saks & L. Saxe (Eds.), *Advances in applied social psychology, Vol. 3.* Hillsdale, NJ: Erlbaum.

Foster, C. A., et al. (1998). Arousal and attraction. *Journal of Personality & Social Psychology, 74*(1), 86–101.

Foster, G., & Ysseldyke, J. (1976). Expectancy and halo effects as a result of artificially induced teacher bias. *Contemporary Educational Psychology, 1,* 37–45.

Foulds, J., Stapleton, J., Swettenham, J., & Bell, N. (1996). Cognitive performance effects of subcutaneous nicotine in smokers and never-smokers. *Psychopharmacology, 127*(1), 31–38.

Fouts, R., Fouts, D., & Schoenfeld, D. (1984). Sign language conversational interaction between chimpanzees. *Sign Language Studies, 42,* 1–12.

Fowers, B. J., & Richardson, F. C. (1996). Why is multiculturalism good? *American Psychologist, 51*(6), 609–621.

Fowles, D. C. (1992). Schizophrenia: Diathesis-stress revisited. *Annual Review of Psychology, 43,* 303–336.

Foxhall, K. (1999, September). State legislatures address key issues for psychology. *APA Monitor,* p. 22.

Foxhall, K. (2000, January). Suddenly, a big impact on criminal justice. APA Monitor, pp. 36–37.

Foxx, R. M. (1998). A comprehensive treatment program for inpatient adolescents. *Behavioral Interventions, 13*(1), 67–77.

Franche, R., & Dobson, K. S. (1992). Self-criticism and interpersonal dependency as vulnerability factors to depression. *Cognitive Therapy & Research, 16*(4), 419–435.

Francis, W. S. (1999). Analogical transfer of problem solutions within and between languages in Spanish-English bilinguals. *Journal of Memory & Language, 40*(3), 301–329.

Frankenburg, W. K., & Dodds, J. B. (1967). The Denver Developmental Screening Test. *Journal of Pediatrics, 1,* 181–191.

Frankl, V. (1955). *The doctor and the soul.* New York: Knopf.

Franklin, N., & Tversky, B. (1990). Searching imagined environments. *Journal of Experimental Psychology: General, 119*(1), 63–76.

Franzoi, S. L. (1996). *Social psychology.* Dubuque, IA: Brown & Benchmark.

Frazier, J. A., Giedd, J. N., Hamburger, S. D., & Albus, K. E. (1996). Brain anatomic magnetic resonance imaging in childhood-onset schizophrenia. *Archives of General Psychiatry, 53*(7), 617–624.

Frederick, C. J. (1987) Psychic trauma in victims of crime and terrorism. In G. R. VandenBos & B. K. Bryant (Eds.), *Cataclysms, crises, and catastrophes: Psychology in action.* Washington, DC: American Psychological Association.

Fredrickson, B. L., Roberts, T., Noll, S. M., et al. (1998). That swimsuit becomes you. *Journal of Personality & Social Psychology, 75*(1), 269–284.

Freedman, J. L. (1984). Effect of television violence on aggressiveness. *Psychological Bulletin, 96,* 227–246.

Freedman, J. L., & Fraser, S. C. (1966). Compliance without pressure: The foot-in-the-door technique. *Journal of Personality & Social Psychology, 4,* 195–202.

Freeman, A., & Reinecke, M. A. (1995). Cognitive therapy. In A. S. Gurman & S. B. Messer, *Essential psychotherapies.* New York: Guilford.

Freeman, J. (1995). Recent studies of giftedness in children. *Journal of Child Psychology & Psychiatry & Allied Disciplines, 36*(4), 531–547.

Freeman, W. J. (1991, February). The physiology of perception. *Scientific American,* 78–85.

Freize, I. H. (1987). The female victim. In G. R. VandenBos & B. K. Bryant (Eds.), *Cataclysms, crises, and catastrophes: Psychology in action.* Washington, DC: American Psychological Association.

French, C. C., Fowler, M., McCarthy, K., & Peers, D. (1991). A test of the Barnum effect. *Skeptical Inquirer, 15*(4), 66–72.

Freud, S. (1900). *The interpretation of dreams.* London: Hogarth.

Freud, S. (1949). *An outline of psychoanalysis.* New York: Norton.

Fried, P. A., O'Connell, C. M., & Walkinson, B. (1992). 60- and 72-month follow-up of children prenatally exposed to marijuana, cigarettes, and alcohol. *Journal of Developmental & Behavioral Pediatrics, 13*(6), 383–391.

Friedman, M., & Rosenman, R. (1983). *Type A behavior and your heart.* New York: Knopf.

Friedman, R. C., et al. (1998). Private psychotherapy patients of psychiatrist psychoanalysts. *American Journal of Psychiatry, 155,* 1772–1774.

Frieske, D. A., & Park, D. C. (1999). Memory for news in young and old adults. *Psychology & Aging, 14*(1), 90–98.

Frieze, I. H., Olson, J. E., & Good, D. C. (1990). Perceived and actual discrimination in the salaries of male and female managers. *Journal of Applied Social Psychology, 20*(1), 46–67.

Frone, M. R., & Yardley, J. K. (1996). Workplace family-supportive programmes. *Journal of Occupational & Organizational Psychology, 69*(4), 351–366.

Fuligni, A. J. (1998). Authority, autonomy, and parent-adolescent conflict and cohesion: A study of adolescents from Mexican, Chinese, Filipino, and European backgrounds. *Developmental Psychology, 34*(4), 782–792.

Fuller, B. (1969). *Utopia or oblivion: The prospects for humanity.* New York: Bantam Matrix.

Fuller, T. D., Edwards, J. N., Vorakitphokatorn, S., & Sermsri, S. (1996). Chronic stress and psychological well-being: Evidence from Thailand on household crowding. *Social Science & Medicine, 42*(2), 265–280.

Furumoto, L., & Scarborough, E. (1986). Placing women in the history of psychology. *American Psychologist, 41,* 35–42.

Gabrieli, J. D. E. (1998). Cognitive neuroscience of human memory. *Annual Review of Psychology, 49,* 87–115.

Gaertner, S. L., Mann, J. A., Dovido, J. E., et al. (1990). How does cooperation reduce intergroup bias? *Journal of Personality & Social Psychology, 59*(4), 692–704.

Gagnon, J. H. (1977). *Human sexualities.* Glenview, IL: Scott, Foresman.

Galanter, E. (1962). Contemporary psychophysics. In *New directions in psychology, Vol. I* (pp. 87–156). New York: Holt, Rinehart & Winston.

Galanti, G. (1993). Cult conversion, deprogramming, and the triune brain. *Cultic Studies Journal, 10*(1), 45–52.

Galati, D., Scherer, K. R., & Ricci-Bitti, P. E. (1997). Voluntary facial expression of emotion: Comparing congenitally blind with normally sighted encoders. *Journal of Personality & Social Psychology, 73*(6), 1363–1379.

Gallup, G. H. Jr., & Newport, F. (1991). Belief in paranormal phenomena among adult Americans. *Skeptical Inquirer, 15,* 137–146.

Galston, A. W., & Slayman, C. L. (1983). Plant sensitivity and sensation. In G. O. Abell & B. Singer (Eds.), *Science and the paranormal* (pp. 40–55). New York: Scribner's.

Gambrill, E. (1992). Self-help books. *Skeptical Inquirer, 16,* 389–399.

Ganellen, R. J. (1996). Comparing the diagnostic efficiency of the MMPI, MCMI-II, and Rorschach. *Journal of Personality Assessment, 67*(2), 219–243.

Gannon, L. (1993). Menopausal symptoms as consequences of dysrhythmia. *Journal of Behavioral Medicine, 16*(4), 387–402.

Garcia, J., Hankins, W. G., & Rusiniak, K. W. (1974). Behavioral regulation of the milieu interne in man and rat. *Science, 185,* 824–831.

Garcia, L. T. (1998). Perceptions of resistance to unwanted sexual advances. *Journal of Psychology & Human Sexuality, 10*(1), 43–52.

Gardner, H. (1993). *Frames of mind.* New York: Basic.

Gardner, M. (1993). The false memory syndrome. *Skeptical Inquirer, 17(4),* 370–375.

Gardner, R. A., & Gardner, B. T. (1989). *Teaching sign language to chimpanzees.* Albany: State University of New York Press.

Gardner, R. M., & Bokenkamp, E. D. (1996). The role of sensory and nonsensory factors in body size estimations of eating disorders subjects. *Journal of Clinical Psychology, 52(1),* 3–15.

Garland, A. F., & Zigler, E. (1993). Adolescent suicide prevention. *American Psychologist, 48(2),* 169–182.

Garland, A. F., & Zigler, E. (1999). Emotional and behavioral problems among highly intellectually gifted youth. *Roeper Review, 22(1),* 41–44.

Garnets, L., & Kimmel, D. (1991). Lesbian and gay male dimensions in the psychological study of human diversity. In *Psychological perspectives on human diversity in America.* Washington, DC: American Psychological Association.

Garza-Trevino, E. (1994). Neurobiological factors in aggressive behavior. *Hospital & Community Psychiatry, 45(7),* 690–699.

Gaston, L., et al. (1998). Alliance, technique, and their interactions in predicting outcome of behavioral, cognitive, and brief dynamic therapy. *Psychotherapy Research, 8(2),* 190–209.

Gates, A. I. (1958). Recitation as a factor in memorizing. In J. Deese (Ed.), *The psychology of learning.* New York: McGraw-Hill.

Gatz, M. (1990). Interpreting behavioral genetic results. *Journal of Counseling & Development, 68,* 601–605.

Gatz, M., & Pearson, C. G. (1988). Agesim revised and the provision of psychological services. *American Psychologist, 43(3),* 184–188.

Gauthier, J., Cote, G., & French, D. (1994). The role of home practice in the thermal biofeedback treatment of migraine headache. *Journal of Consulting & Clinical Psychology, 62(1),* 180–184.

Gazzaniga, M. S. (1970). *The bisected brain.* New York: Plenum.

Gazzaniga, M. S. (1995). On neural circuits and cognition. *Neural Computation, 7(1),* 1–12.

Geehr, J. L., Burke, M. J., & Sulzer, J. L. (1995). Quality circles: The effects of varying degrees of voluntary participation on employee attitudes and program efficacy. *Educational & Psychological Measurement, 55(1),* 124–134.

Geiger, M. A. (1991) Changing multiple-choice answers: Do students accurately perceive their performance? *Journal of Experimental Education, 59(3),* 250–257.

Geiselman, R. E., Fisher, R. P., MacKinnon, D. P., & Holland, H. L. (1986). Eyewitness memory enhancement with the cognitive interview. *American Journal of Psychology, 99,* 385–401.

Genesee, F. (1994). Bilingualism. In V. S. Ramachandram (Ed.), *Encyclopedia of human behavior, Vol. 1.* San Diego, CA: Academic.

Gersh, R. D. (1982, June 20). Learning when not to shoot. *Santa Barbara News Press,*

Gershon, E. S., et al. (1998). Closing in on genes for manic-depressive illness and schizophrenia. *Neuropsychopharmacology, 18(4),* 233–242.

Gerwood, J. B. (1998). The legacy of Viktor Frankl. *Psychological Reports, 82(2),* 673–674.

Geschwind, N. (1979). Specializations of the human brain. *Scientific American, 241,* 180–199.

Gewirtz, J. C., & Davis, M. (1998). Application of Pavlovian higher-order conditioning to the analysis of the neural substrates of fear conditioning. *Neuropharmacology, 37(4–5),* 453–459.

Gibson, B., & Werner, C. M. (1994). The airport as a behavior setting: The role of legibility in communicating the setting program. *Journal of Personality and Social Psychology, 66,* 1049–1060.

Gibson, E. J., & Walk, R. D. (1960). The "visual cliff." *Scientific American, 202(4),* 67–71.

Gibson, H. B., & Heap, M. (1991). *Hypnosis in therapy.* Hillsdale, NJ: Erlbaum.

Gierl, M. J., & Rogers, W. T. (1996). A confirmatory factor analysis of the Test Anxiety Inventory using Canadian high school students. *Educational & Psychological Measurement, 56(2),* 315–324.

Gifford, R. (1987). *Environmental psychology.* Boston: Allyn & Bacon.

Gilbert, A. N., & Wysocki, C. J. (1987, October). The smell survey results. *National Geographic,* 514–524.

Gilbert, D. G., Gilbert, B. O., & Schultz, V. L. (1998). Withdrawal symptoms: Individual differences and similarities across addictive behaviors. *Personality & Individual Differences, 24(3),* 351–356.

Gilbert, D. G., Stunkard, M. E., Jensen, R. A., & Detwiler, F. R. J. (1996). Effects of exam stress on mood, cortisol, and immune functioning. *Personality & Individual Differences, 21(2),* 235–246.

Gilbert, S. (1996, May 1). Estrogen patch appears to lift severe depression in new mothers. *The New York Times,* p. B-9.

Gilchrist, H., Povey, R., Dickinson, A., & Povey, R. (1995). The Sensation Seeking Scale: Its use in a study of the characteristics of people choosing "adventure holidays." *Personality & Individual Differences, 19(4),* 513–516.

Gill, S. T. (1991). Carrying the war into the never-never land of psi. *Skeptical Inquirer, 15(1),* 269–273.

Gillam, B. (1980). Geometrical illusions. *American Psychologist, 242,* 102–111.

Gillberg, M., & Akerstedt, T. (1998). Sleep loss performance: No "safe" duration of a monotonous task. *Physiology & Behavior, 64(5),* 599–604.

Gilligan, C. (1982). *In a different voice.* Cambridge, MA: Harvard University Press.

Gilligan, C., & Attanucci, J. (1988). Two moral orientations: Gender differences and similarities. *Merrill-Palmer Quarterly, 34(3),* 223–237.

Gilmore, D. C., & Ferris, G. R. (1989). The effects of applicant impression management tactics on interviewer judgments. *Journal of Management, 15(4),* 557–564.

Giniger, S., Dispenzieri, A., & Eisenberg, J. (1983). Age, experience, and performance on speed and skill jobs in an applied setting. *Journal of Applied Psychology, 68,* 469–475.

Ginott, H. G. (1965). *Between parent and child: New solutions to old problems.* New York: Macmillan.

Ginzberg, E. (1984). Career development. In D. Brown & L. Brooks (Eds.), *Career choice and development.* San Francisco: Josey-Bass.

Girodo, M. (1978). *Shy? (You don't have to be!).* New York: Pocket Books.

Gladue, B. A. (1987). Psychobiological contributions. In L. Diamant (Ed.), *Male and female homosexuality: Psychological approaches.* Washington, DC: Hemisphere.

Glass, A. L., Holyoak, K. J., & Santa, J. L. (1979). *Cognition.* Reading, MA: Addison-Wesley.

Glik, D. C., Kronenfeld, J. J., & Jackson, N. K. (1996). Predictors of well role performance behaviors. *American Journal of Health Behavior, 20(4),* 218–228.

Glisky, M. L., Williams, J. M., & Kihlstrom, J. F. (1996). Internal and external mental imagery perspectives and performance on two tasks. *Journal of Sport Behavior, 19(1),* 3–18.

Gloaguen, V., et al. (1998). A meta-analysis of the effects of cognitive therapy in depressed patients. *Journal of Affective Disorders, 49(1)* 59–72.

Globus, G. (1987). *Dream life, wake life: The human condition through dreams.* Albany: State University of New York Press.

Gluhoski, V. L. (1995). A cognitive perspective on bereavement: Mechanism and treatment. *Journal of Cognitive Psychotherapy, 9(2),* 75–84.

Gobet, F., & Simon, H. A. (1996). Recall of random and distorted chess positions: Implications for the theory of expertise. *Memory & Cognition, 24(4),* 493–503.

Goel, V., & Grafman, J. (1995). Are the frontal lobes implicated in "planning" functions? Interpreting data from the Tower of Hanoi. *Neuropsychologia, 33(5),* 623–642.

Goff, B. G., & Goddard, H. W. (1999). Terminal core values associated with adolescent problem behaviors. *Adolescence, 34(133),* 47–60.

Goin, R. P. (1998). Nocturnal enuresis in children. *Child: Care, Health, and Development, 24(4),* 277–278.

Gold, P. E. (1987). Sweet memories. *American Scientist, 75,* 151–155.

Goldberg, L. R. (1993). The structure of phenotypic personality traits. *American Psychologist, 48(1),* 26–34.

Goldfried, M. R., Greenberg, L. S., & Marmar, C. (1990). Individual psychotherapy: Process and outcome. *Annual Review of Psychology, 41,* 659–688.

Goldiamond, I. (1971). Self-control procedures in personal behavior problems. In M. S. Gazzaniga & E. P. Lovejoy (Eds.), *Good reading in psychology.* Englewood Cliffs, NJ: Prentice-Hall.

Golding, J., Rogers, I. S., & Emmett, P. M. (1997). Association between breast feeding, child development and behaviour. *Early Human Development, 49*(Suppl.), S175–S184.

Goldman, H. H. (1998). Deinstitutionalization and community care. *Harvard Review of Psychiatry, 6(4),* 219–222.

Goldstein, E. (1997). False memory syndrome. *American Journal of Family Therapy, 25(4),* 307–317.

Goldstein, E. B. (1999). *Sensation and perception.* Belmont, CA: Wadsworth.

Goldstein, I. L., & Gilliam, P. (1990). Training system issues in the year 2000. *American Psychologist, 45(2),* 134–143.

Goldstein, M. J. (1985). *The UCLA family project.* Paper presented at NIMH High-Risk Consortium, San Francisco. Cited by Mirsky & Duncan, 1986.

Goldstone, R. L. (1998). Perceptual learning. *Annual Review of Psychology, 49,* 585–612.

Goleman, D. (1982, March). Staying up: The rebellion against sleep's gentle tyranny. *Psychology Today,* pp. 24–35.

Goleman, D. (1995). *Emotional intelligence.* New York: Bantam.

Golinkoff, R. M., & Hirsh-Pasek, K. (1999). *How babies talk.* New York: Dutton.

Golombok, S., Cook, R., Bish, A., & Murray, C. (1995). Families created by the new reproductive technologies: Quality of parenting and social and emotional development of the children. *Child Development, 66(2),* 285–298.

Golombok, S. & Tasker, F. (1996). Do parents influence the sexual orientation of their children? *Developmental Psychology, 32(1),* 3–11.

Gomberg, E. L. (1993). Women and alcohol: Use and abuse. *Journal of Nervous and Mental Disease, 18(4),* 211–219.

Gondola, J. C., & Tuckman, B. W. (1982). Psychological mood state in "average" marathon runners. *Perceptual and Motor Skills, 55,* 1295–1300.

Gonzalez, M. A., Campos, A., & Perez, M. J. (1997). Mental imagery and creative thinking. *Journal of Psychology, 131(4),* 357–364.

Good, M. (1995). A comparison of the effects of jaw relaxation and music on postoperative pain. *Nursing Research, 44(1),* 52–57.

Goodall, J. (1990). *Through a window: My thirty years with the chimpanzees of the Gombe.* Boston: Houghton Mifflin.

Goode, E. (1996). Gender and courtship entitlement: Responses to personal ads. *Sex Roles, 34*(3–4), 141–169.

Goodman, G. (1984). SASHA tapes: Expanding options for help-intended communication. In D. Larson (Ed.), *Teaching psychological skills.* Monterey, CA: Brooks/Cole.

Goodman-Delahunty, J. Greene, E., & Hsiao, W. (1998). Construing motive in videotaped killings: The role of jurors' attitudes toward the death penalty. *Law & Human Behavior, 22*(3), 257–271.

Goodwin, D. W. (1995). Alcohol amnesia. *Addiction, 90*(3), 315–317.

Gopnik, A., Meltzoff, A. N., & Kuhl, P. K. (1999). *The scientist in the crib.* New York: William Morrow.

Gordon, T. (1970). *P.E.T. parent effectiveness training: A tested new way to raise children.* New York: Peter H. Wyden.

Gorman, J. M. (1996). The essential guide to mental health. New York: St. Martin's Griffin.

Gotlib, D. A. (1997, Summer). St. John's wort. *Smooth Sailing—Newsletter of the Depression & Related Affective Disorders Association,* pp. 6–7.

Gottesman, I. I. (1991). *Schizophrenia genesis: The origins of madness.*

Gottfried, A. W., & Gottfried, A. E. (1994). *Gifted IQ.* New York: Plenum.

Gottlieb, G. (1998). Normally occurring environmental and behavioral influences on gene activity: From central dogma to probabilistic epigenesis. *Psychological Review, 105*(4), 792–802.

Gottman, J. (1994). *Why marriages succeed or fail.* New York: Simon & Schuster.

Gottman, J. M., & Krokoff, L. J. (1989). Marital interaction and satisfaction: A longitudinal view. *Journal of Consulting & Clinical Psychology, 57*(1), 47–52.

Gould, D., & Udry, E. (1994). Psychological skills for enhancing performance: Arousal regulation strategies. *Medicine & Science in Sports & Exercise, 26*(4), 478–485.

Gould, E., Beylin, A., Tanapat, P., Reeves, A., & Shors, T. J. (1999). Learning enhances adult neurogenesis in the hippocampal formation. *Nature Neuroscience, 2*(3), 260–265.

Gould, E., Reeves, A.J., & Gross, C. G. (1999). Neurogenesis in the neocortex of adult primates. *Science, 286*(5439), 548.

Gould, M. S., et al. (1998). Psychopathology associated with suicidal ideation and attempts among children and adolescents. *Journal of the American Academy of Child & Adolescent Psychiatry, 37*(9), 915–923.

Gould, R. (1975, February). Growth toward self-tolerance. *Psychology Today,*

Gould, S. J. (1976). Biological potential vs. biological determinism. *Natural History, 85*(5).

Grack, C., & Richman, C. L. (1996). Reducing general and specific heterosexism through cooperative contact. *Journal of Psychology & Human Sexuality, 8*(4), 59–68.

Graeff, T. R. (1996). Image congruence effects on product evaluations: The role of self-monitoring and public/private consumption. *Psychology & Marketing, 13*(5), 481–499.

Graffin, N. F., Ray, W. J., & Lundy, R. (1995). EEG concomitants of hypnosis and hypnotic susceptibility. *Journal of Abnormal Psychology, 104*(1), 123–131.

Graham, S. (1992). Most of the subjects were white and middle class. *American Psychologist, 47,* 629–639.

Grant, B. F., & Dawson, D. A. (1997). Age at onset of alcohol use and its association with DSM-IV alcohol abuse and dependence. *Journal of Substance Abuse, 9,* 103.

Graziano, W. G., Jensen-Campbell, L. A., & Sullivan-Logan, G. (1998). Temperament, activity, and expectations for later personality development. *Journal of Personality & Social Psychology, 74*(5), 1266–1277.

Graziottin, A. (1998). The biological basis of female sexuality. *International Clinical Psychopharmacology, 13*(Suppl. 6), S15–S22.

Greene, A. S., & Saxe, L. (1990). *Tall tales told to teachers.* Unpublished manuscript. Brandeis University.

Greene, D., & Lepper, M. R. (1974, September). How to turn play into work. *Psychology Today,* 49.

Greenfield, P. M. (1997). You can't take it with you: Why ability assessments don't cross cultures. *American Psychologist, 52*(10), 1115–1124.

Greenfield, P. M., & Savage-Rumbaugh, E. S. (1993). Comparing communicative competence in child and chimp: The pragmatics of repetition. *Journal of Child Language, 20*(1), 1–26.

Greenglass, E. R., Burke, R. J., & Konarski, R. (1998). Components of burnout, resources, and gender-related differences. *Journal of Applied Social Psychology, 28*(12), 1088–1106.

Greenwald, A. G., Spangenberg, E. R., Pratkanis, A. R., & Eskenazi, J. (1991). Double-blind tests of subliminal self-help audiotapes. *Psychological Science, 2*(2), 119–122.

Gregory, R. L. (1990). *Eye and brain: The psychology of seeing.* Princeton, NJ: Princeton University Press.

Grenier, G., & Byers, E. S. (1995). Rapid ejaculation: A review of conceptual, etiological, and treatment issues. *Archives of Sexual Behavior, 24*(4), 447–472.

Griffin, D. R. (1992). *Animal minds.* Chicago: University of Chicago Press.

Grobstein, P., & Chow, K. L. (1975). Perceptive field development and individual experience. *Science, 190,* 352–358.

Grolnick, W. S., Cosgrove, T. J., & Bridges, L. J. (1996). Age-graded change in the initiative of positive affect. *Infant Behavior & Development, 19*(1), 153–157.

Groth-Marnat, G., & Schumaker, J. (1995). Psychologists in disease prevention and health promotion: A review of the cost effectiveness literature. *Psychology: A Journal of Human Behavior, 32*(1), 1–10.

Groth-Marnat, G., & Summers, R. (1998). Altered beliefs, attitudes, and behaviors following near-death experiences. *Journal of Humanistic Psychology, 38*(3), 110–125.

Gruder, C. L., Mermelstein, R. J., Kirkendol, S., et al. (1993). Effects of social support and relapse prevention training as adjuncts to a televised smoking-cessation intervention. *Journal of Consulting & Clinical Psychology, 61*(1), 113–120.

Gruner, C. R., & Tighe, M. R. (1995). Semantic differential measurements of connotations of verbal terms and their doublespeak facsimiles in sentence contexts. *Psychological Reports, 77*(3,Pt 1), 778.

Gump, B. B., & Kulik, J. A. (1997). Stress, affiliation, and emotional contagion. *Journal of Personality & Social Psychology, 72*(2), 305–319.

Gur, R. E., et al. (1998). A follow-up magnetic resonance imaging study of schizophrenia. *Archives of General Psychiatry, 55*(2), 145–152.

Gushin, V. I., et al. (1998). Subject's perceptions of the crew interaction dynamics under prolonged isolation. *Aviation, Space, & Environmental Medicine, 69*(6), 556–561.

Gustavson, C. R., & Garcia, J. (1974, May). Pulling a gag on the wily coyote. *Psychology Today,* 68–72.

Gustavsson, J. P., et al. (1997). Stability and predictive ability of personality traits across 9 years. *Personality & Individual Differences, 22*(6), 783–791.

Gutek, B. A. (1981, August). Experiences of sexual harassment: Results from a representative survey. Paper presented at symposium of the annual convention, American Psychological Association, Los Angeles.

Guterl, F. (1997, May). Celestial mechanics. *Discover,* pp. 91–93.

Haas, L. J., Benedict, J. G., & Kobos, J. C. (1996). Psychotherapy by telephone: Risks and benefits for psychologists and consumers. *Professional Psychology: Research & Practice, 27*(2), 154–160.

Haber, R. N. (1969). Eidetic images; with biographical sketches. *Scientific American, 220*(12), 36–44.

Haber, R. N. (1970, May). How we remember what we see. *Scientific American,* 104–112.

Hadwin, A. F., Kirby, J. R., & Woodhouse, R. A. (1999). Individual differences in notetaking, summarization and learning from lectures. *Alberta Journal of Educational Research, 45*(1), 1–17.

Haier, R. J., Siegel, B. V., Nuechterlein, K. H., Hazlett, et al. (1988). Cortical glucose metabolic rate correlates of abstract reasoning and attention studied with positron emission tomography. *Intelligence, 12,* 199–217.

Hall, B. A. (1996a). The psychiatric model: A critical analysis. *Advances in Nursing Science, 18*(3), 16–26.

Hall, C. (1966a). *The meaning of dreams.* New York: McGraw-Hill.

Hall, C. (1974a). What people dream about. In R. L. Woods & H. B. Greenhouse (Eds.), *The new world of dreams: An anthology.* New York: Macmillan.

Hall, C., Domhoff, G. W., Blick, K. A., & Weesner, K. E. (1982). The dreams of college men and women in 1950 and 1980: A comparison of dream contents and sex differences. *Sleep, 5*(2), 188–194.

Hall, E. T. (1966b). *The hidden dimension.* Garden City, NY: Doubleday.

Hall, E. T. (1974b). *Handbook for proxemic research.* Washington, DC: Social Anthropology and Visual Communication.

Hall, J. A. (1996b). Touch, status, and gender at professional meetings. *Journal of Nonverbal Behavior, 20*(1), 23–44.

Hall, R. C. W., Platt, D. E., & Hall, R. C. W. (1999). Suicide risk assessment. *Psychosomatics, 40*(1), 18–27.

Halonen, J. S. (1986). *Teaching critical thinking in psychology.* Milwaukee, WI: Alverno Productions.

Hamer, D. & Copeland, P. (1998). *Living with our genes.* New York: Anchor.

Hamer, D. H., Hu, S., Magnuson, V. L., Hu, N., & Pattatucci, A. M. (1993). A linkage between DNA markers on the X chromosome and male sexual orientation. *Science, 16:261*(5119), 291–292.

Hamill, J. A. (1995). Dexterity and sexuality: Is there a relationship? *Journal of Homosexuality, 28*(3–4), 375–396.

Hamilton, V. L., & Sanders, J. (1995). Crimes of obedience and conformity in the workplace. *Journal of Social Issues, 51*(3), 67–88.

Hammer, D. (1997). Discovery learning and discovery teaching. *Cognition & Instruction, 15*(4), 485–529.

Hammer, J. C., Fisher, J. D., Fitzgerald, P., & Fisher, W. A. (1996). When two heads aren't better than one: AIDS risk behavior in college-age couples. *Journal of Applied Social Psychology, 26*(5), 375–397.

Hammer, L. B., Grigsby, T. D., & Woods, S. (1998). The conflicting demands of work, family, and school among students at an urban university. *Journal of Psychology, 132*(2), 220–226.

Hancock, L. (1996). Mother's little helper. *Newsweek, 127*(12), 51–57.

Haney, C., Hurtado, A., & Vega, L. (1994). "Modern" death qualification: New data on its biasing effects. *Law & Human Behavior, 18*(6), 619–633.

Haney, M., Ward, A. S., Comer, S. D., Foltin, R. W., & Fischman, M. W. (1999). Abstinence symptoms following oral THC administration to humans. *Psychopharmacology, 141*(4), 385–394.

Hannon, K. (1996, May 13). Upset? Try cybertherapy. *U.S. News and World Report*, pp. 81–83.

Hansel, C. E. M. (1980). *ESP and parapsychology: A critical reevaluation*. Buffalo, NY: Prometheus.

Hansen, C. H. & Hansen, R. D. (1990). Rock music videos and antisocial behavior. *Basic and Applied Social Psychology, 11*(4), 357–369.

Hardin, G. (1968). The tragedy of the commons. *Science, 162*, 1243–1248.

Hardin, G. (1985). *Filters against folly*. New York: Viking.

Harding, R. W., et al. (1998). Road rage and the epidemiology of violence. *Studies on Crime & Crime Prevention, 7*(2), 221–238.

Hare, R. D. (1996). Psychopathy: A clinical construct whose time has come. *Criminal Justice and Behavior, 23*, 25–54.

Hare-Mustin, R. T., & Marecek, J. (1988). The meaning of difference. *American Psychologist, 43*(6), 455–464.

Harlow, H. F., & Harlow, M. K. (1962). Social deprivation in monkeys. *Scientific American, 207*, 136–146.

Harm, D. L., Parker, D. E., Reschke, M. F., & Skinner, N. C. (1998). Relationship between selected orientation rest frame, circular vection and space motion sickness. *Brain Research Bulletin, 47*(5), 497–501.

Harma, M., Laitinen, J., Partinen, M., & Suvanto, S. (1994). The effect of four-day round trip flights over 10 time zones on the circadian variation of salivary melatonin and cortisol in airline flight attendants. *Ergonomics, 37*(9), 1479–1489.

Harris, B. (1996). Hormonal aspects of postnatal depression. *International Review of Psychiatry, 8*(1), 27–36.

Harris, D. A. (1999, June). *Driving while black*. American Civil Liberties Union Special Report.

Harris, J. A., Rushton, J. P., Hampson, E., & Jackson, D. N. (1996). Salivary testosterone and self-report aggressive and pro-social personality characteristics in men and women. *Aggressive Behavior, 22*(5), 321–331.

Harris, J. R., & Liebert, R. M. (1991). *The child*. Englewood Cliffs, NJ: Prentice Hall.

Harris, L. J. (1993a). Do left-handers die sooner than right-handers? *Psychological Bulletin, 114*(2), 203–234.

Harris, L. J. (1993b). "Left-handedness and life span": Reply to Halpern and Coren. *Psychological Bulletin, 114*(2), 242–247.

Harrison, G. P., & Katz, D. L. (1987). Letter. *The Lancet, 1*, 863.

Harrison, L. F., & Williams, T. M. (1986). Television and cognitive development. In T. M. Williams (Ed.), *The impact of television: A natural experiment in three communities*. Orlando, FL: Academic.

Harsch, N., & Neisser, U. (1989, November). *Substantial and irreversible errors in flashbulb memories of the* Challenger *explosion*. Poster presented at the meeting of the Psychonomic Society, Atlanta, GA.

Hart, B., & Risley, T. R. (1999). *The social world of children learning to talk*. Baltimore, MD: Paul H. Brookes.

Hartgrove-Freile, J. (1990). *Organizations, communication, and culture*. St. Paul, MN: West.

Hartung, C. M., & Widiger, T. A. (1998). Gender differences in the diagnosis of mental disorders. *Psychological Bulletin, 123*(3), 260–278.

Harvey, C. A., Curson, D. A., Pantelis, C., & Taylor, J. (1996). Four behavioural syndromes of schizophrenia. *British Journal of Psychiatry, 168*(5), 562–570.

Harvil, L. M., & Davis, G. (1997). Medical students' reasons for changing answers on multiple-choice tests. *Academic Medicine, 72*(10, Suppl. 1), S97–S99.

Hatfield, E., Greenberger, D., Traupmann, J., & Lambert, P. (1982). Equity and sexual satisfaction in recently married couples. *Journal of Sex Research, 18*, 18–32.

Hatfield, E., & Sprecher, S. (1995). Men's and women's preferences in marital partners in the United States, Russia, and Japan. *Journal of Cross-Cultural Psychology, 26*(6), 728–750.

Hathaway, S. R., & McKinley, J. C. (1989). *MMPI-2: Manual for administration and scoring*. Minneapolis: University of Minnesota Press.

Hauri, P., & Linde, S. (1990). *No more sleepless nights*. New York: Wiley.

Havighurst, R. J. (1961). Successful aging. *Gerontologist, 1*, 8–13.

Hawkins, D. B., & Gruber, J. J. (1982). Little league baseball and players' self-esteem. *Perceptual and Motor Skills, 55*, 1335–1340.

Hawkins, M. J., Gray, C., & Hawkins, W. E. (1995). Gender difference of reported safer sex behaviors within a random sample of college students. *Psychological Reports, 77*(3, Pt 1), 963–968.

Hay, I., Ashman, A. F., & Van Kraayenoord, C. E. (1998). Educational characteristics of students with high or low self-concept. *Psychology in the Schools, 35*(4), 391–400.

Hayes, C. (1951). *The ape in our house*. New York: Harper & Row.

Hayne, H., & Rovee-Collier, C. (1995). The organization of reactivated memory in infancy. *Child Development, 66*(3), 893–906.

Hearold, S. L. (1987). Meta-analysis of the effects of television on social behavior. In G. Comstock (Ed.), *Public communication and behavior: Vol. 1*. New York: Academic.

Heath, L., & Gilbert, K. (1996). Mass media and fear of crime. *American Behavioral Scientist, 39*(4), 379–386.

Hebb, D. O. (1966). *A textbook of psychology*. Philadelphia: Saunders.

Hebl, M. R., & Heatherton, T. F. (1998). The stigma of obesity in women: The difference is black and white. *Personality & Social Psychology Bulletin, 24*(4), 417–426.

Hecht, M. L., Marston, P. J., & Larkey, L. K. (1994). Love ways and relationship quality in heterosexual relationships. *Journal of Social & Personal Relationships, 11*(1), 25–43.

Heckhausen, J. (1987). Balancing for weaknesses and challenging developmental potential. *Developmental Psychology, 23*(6), 762–770.

Heermann, J. A., Jones, L. C., & Wikoff, R. L. (1994). Measurement of parent behavior during interactions with their infants. *Infant Behavior & Development, 17*(3), 311–321.

Heiby, E. M. (1983). Assessment of frequency of self-reinforcement. *Journal of Personality & Social Psychology, 44*, 1304–1307.

Heimann, M., & Meltzoff, A. N. (1996). Deferred imitation in 9- and 14-month-old infants. *British Journal of Developmental Psychology, 14*, 55–64.

Heine, S. J., & Lehman, D. R. (1999). Culture, self-discrepancies, and self-satisfaction. *Personality & Social Psychology Bulletin, 25*(8), 915–925.

Heinrich, R. K., Corbine, J. L., & Thomas, K. R. (1990). Counseling Native Americans. *Journal of Counseling and Development, 69*, 128–133.

Heinrichs, R. W. (1993). Schizophrenia and the brain. *American Psychologist, 48*(3), 221–233.

Heinze, H. J., Hinrichs, H., Scholz, M., Burchert, W., & Mangun, G. R. (1998). Neural mechanisms of global and local processing. *Journal of Cognitive Neuroscience, 10*(4), 485–498.

Held, R. (1971). Plasticity in sensory-motor systems. In *Contemporary psychology*. San Francisco: Freeman.

Heller, J. (1961). *Catch 22*. New York: Simon & Schuster.

Hellerstein, D. J., et al. (1998). A randomized prospective study comparing supportive and dynamic therapies. *Journal of Psychotherapy Practice & Research, 7*(4), 261–271.

Hellige, J. B. (1990). Hemispheric asymmetry. *Annual Review of Psychology, 41*, 55–60.

Hellige, J. B. (1993). *Hemispheric asymmetry*. Cambridge, MA: Harvard University Press.

Hellriegel, D., Slocum, J. W., & Woodman, R. W. (1995). *Organizational behavior*. St. Paul, MN: West.

Helms, J. E. (1992). Why is there no study of cultural equivalence in standardized ability testing? *American Psychologist, 47*(9), 1083–1101.

Helson, H. (1964). *Adaptation-level theory*. New York: Harper & Row.

Helwig, A. A. (1998). Gender-role stereotyping: Testing theory with a longitudinal sample. *Sex Roles, 38*(5–6), 403–423.

Henderson, L. (1997). Mean MMPI profile of referrals to a shyness clinic. *Psychological Reports, 80*(2) 695–702.

Henderson, N. D. (1982). Human behavior genetics. *Annual Review of Psychology, 33*, 403–440.

Hendin, H. (1995). Assisted suicide, euthanasia, and suicide prevention. *Suicide & Life-Threatening Behavior, 25*(1), 193–204.

Hendrick, S. S., & Hendrick, C. (1993). Lovers as friends. *Journal of Social & Personal Relationships, 10*(3), 459–466.

Henningfield, J. E., & Heishman, S. J. (1995). The addictive role of nicotine in tobacco use. *Psychopharmacology, 117*(1), 11–13.

Hepburn, D. A., Deary, I. J., & MacLeod, K. M. (1996). Adrenaline and psychometric mood factors: A controlled case study of two patients with bilateral adrenalectomy. *EDRA: Environmental Design Research Association, 20*(4), 451–455.

Hepper, P.G., McCartney, G. R., & Shannon, E. A. (1998). Lateralised behaviour in first trimester human foetuses. *Neuropsychologia, 36*(6), 531–534.

Herbert. T. B., & Cohen, S. (1993). Depression and immunity. *Psychological Bulletin, 113*(3), 472–486.

Hernstein, R., & Murray, C. (1994). *The bell curve*. New York: Free Press.

Herrnstein, R. J. (1979). Acquisition, generalization, and discrimination reversal of a natural concept. *Journal of Experimental Psychology: Animal Behavior Processes, 5*, 116–129.

Hershey, J. M., Kopplin, D. A., & Cornell, J. E. (1991). Doctors of psychology: Their career experiences and attitudes toward degree and training. *Professional Psychology: Research & Practice, 22*(5), 351–356.

Herzog, A. R., Franks, M. M., Markus, H. R., & Holmberg, D. (1998). Activities and well-being in older age. *Psychology & Aging, 13*(2), 179–185.

Herzog, H. A. (1990). Discussing animal rights and animal research in the classroom. *Teaching of Psychology, 17*(2), 90–94.

Hess, E. H. (1959). Imprinting. *Science, 130*, 133–141.

Hess, E. H. (1975a). *The tell-tale eye: How your eyes reveal hidden thoughts and emotions*. New York: Van Nostrand Reinhold.

Hess, E. H. (1975b, November). The role of pupil size in communication. *Scientific American*, 110–119.

Heussenstamm, F. K. (1971). Bumper stickers and the cops. *Transaction, 8,* 32-33.

Higbee, K. L. (1997). Novices, apprentices, and mnemonists: Acquiring expertise with the phonetic mnemonic. *Applied Cognitive Psychology, 11*(2), 147–161.

Higbee, K. L., Clawson, C., DeLano, L., & Campbell, S. (1990). Using the link mnemonic to remember errands. *Psychological Record, 40*(3), 429–436.

Higgins, A.W., Schueler, M.G., & Willard, H. F. (1999). Chromosome engineering. *Chromosoma, 108*(4), 256–265.

Hilgard, E. R. (1968). *The experience of hypnosis.* New York: Harcourt Brace Jovanovich.

Hilgard, E. R. (1977). *Divided consciousness.* New York: Wiley.

Hilgard, E. R. (1978). Hypnosis and pain. In R. A. Sternbach (Ed.), *The psychology of pain.* New York: Raven.

Hill, L. (1990). Effort and reward in college: A replication of some puzzling findings. *Journal of Social Behavior & Personality, 5(4),* 151–161.

Hill, P. (1993). Recent advances in selected aspects of adolescent development. *Journal of Child Psychology & Psychiatry & Allied Disciplines, 34*(1), 69–99.

Hilts, P. J. (1995). *Memory's ghost.* New York: Simon & Schuster.

Hine, D. W., & Gifford, R. (1996). Individual restraint and group efficiency in commons dilemmas. *Journal of Applied Social Psychology, 26*(11), 993–1009.

Hirshberg, L. M., & Svejda, M. (1990). When infants look to their parents. *Child Development, 61*(4), 1175–1186.

Hirt, M., & Pithers, W. (1991). Selective attention and levels of coding in schizophrenia. *British Journal of Clinical Psychology, 30*(2), 139–149.

Hite, S. (1976). *The Hite report.* New York: Macmillan.

Hixon, M. D. (1998). Ape language research: A review and behavioral perspective. *Analysis of Verbal Behavior, 15,* 17–39.

Hobson, J. A. (1999). Order from chaos. In R. Conlan (Ed.), *States of mind.* New York: Wiley.

Hobson, J. A., Pace-Schott, E. F., Stickgold, R., & Kahn, D. (1998). *Current Opinion in Neurobiology, 8*(2), 239–244.

Hochstenbach, J., Mulder, T., van Limbeek, J., Donders, R., & Schoonderwaldt, H. (1998). Cognitive decline following stroke. *Journal of Clinical & Experimental Neuropsychology, 20*(4), 503–517.

Hodapp, R. M. (1994). Mental retardation. *Encyclopedia of human behavior, Vol 3* (pp. 175–185).

Hodgson, R., & Miller, P. (1982). *Selfwatching.* New York: Facts on File.

Hoff, K. E., & DuPaul, G. J. (1998). Reducing disruptive behavior in general education classrooms: The use of self-management strategies. *School Psychology Review, 27*(2), 290–303.

Hoffman, D. D. (1999). *Visual intelligence.* New York: Norton.

Hogben, D., & Lawson, M. J. (1992). Superiority of the keyword method for backward recall in vocabulary acquisition. *Psychological Reports, 71*(3, Pt 1), 880–882.

Hogben, M. (1998). Factors moderating the effect of televised aggression on viewer behavior. *Communication Research, 25*(2), 220–247.

Holden, C. (1980, November). Twins reunited. *Science 80,* 55–59.

Holden, G. W., Coleman, S. M., & Schmidt, K. L. (1995). Why do 3-year-old children get spanked. *Merrill-Palmer Quarterly, 41*(4), 431–452.

Holland, J. L. (1997). *Making vocational choices.* Odessa, FL: Psychological Assessment Resources.

Holmes, D. S. (1984). Meditation and somatic arousal reduction: A review of the experimental evidence. *American Psychologist, 39*(1), 1–10.

Holmes, D. S., Curtright, C. A., McCaul, K. D., & Thissen, D. (1980). Biorhythms: Their utility for predicting postoperative recuperative time, death, and athletic performance. *Journal of Applied Psychology, 65,* 233–236.

Holmes, D. S., Solomon, S., Cappo, B. M., & Greenberg, J. L. (1983). Effects of transcendental meditation versus resting on physiological and subjective arousal. *Journal of Personality & Social Psychology, 44,* 1245–1252.

Holmes, T., & Masuda, M. (1972, April). Psychosomatic syndrome. *Psychology Today,* 71.

Holstein, M. (1997). Reflections on death and dying. *Academic Medicine, 72*(10), 848–855.

Holtzman, W. (1997). Community psychology and full-service schools in different cultures. *American Psychologist, 52*(4), 381–389.

Holtzworth-Munroe, A., & Hutchinson, G. (1993). Attributing negative intent to wife behavior. *Journal of Abnormal Psychology, 102*(2), 206–211.

Honorton, C., & Bem, D. J. (1994). Does psi exist? *Psychological Bulletin, 115*(1), 4–18.

Hopson, J. L. (1986, June). The unraveling of insomnia. *Psychology Today,* 43–49.

Horgan, J. (1995, November). Get smart, take a test: A long-term rise in IQ scores baffles intelligence experts. *Scientific American,* 2–14.

Horn, J. C. (1987, July). Bigger pay for better work. *Psychology Today,* 54–57.

Horn, J. M., Loehlin, J. C., & Willerman, L. (1979). Intellectual resemblance among adoptive and biological relatives: The Texas adoption project. *Behavior Genetics, 9,* 177–207.

Horne, J. A., & Reyner, L. A. (1996). Counteracting driver sleepiness: Effects of napping, caffeine, and placebo. *Psychophysiology, 33*(3), 306–309.

Horvath, A. 0., & Goheen, M. D. (1990). Factors mediating the success of defiance- and compliance-based interventions. *Journal of Counseling Psychology, 37*(4), 363–371.

Horwitz, W. A., Kestenbaum, C., Person, E., & Jarvik, L. (1965). Identical twin "Idiot savants" calendar calculators. *The American Journal of Psychiatry, 121,* 1075–1079.

Hosch, H. M., & Cooper, D. S. (1982). Victimization as a determinant of eyewitness accuracy. *Journal of Applied Psychology, 67,* 649–652.

Hough, L. M., & Oswald, F. L. (2000). Personnel selection. *Annual Review of Psychology, 51,* 631–664.

Howard, A., Pion, G. M., Gottfredson, G. D., Flattau, P. E., et al. (1986a). The changing face of American psychology. *American Psychologist, 41,* 1311–1327.

Howard, J. L., & Ferris, G. R. (1996). The employment interview context. *Journal of Applied Social Psychology, 26*(2), 112–136.

Howard, K. I., Kopta, S. M., Krause, M. S., & Orlinsky, D. E. (1986b). The dose-effect relationship in psychotherapy. *American Psychologist, 41,* 159–164.

Howell, W. C. (1993). Engineering psychology in a changing world. *Annual Review of Psychology, 44,* 231–263.

Howes, C. (1997). Children's experiences in center-based child care as a function of teacher background and adult:child ratio. *Merrill-Palmer Quarterly, 43*(3), 404–425.

Howitt, D., Craven, G., Iveson, C., Kremer, J., McCabe, J., & Rolph, T. (1977). The misdirected letter. *British Journal of Social and Clinical Psychology, 16,* 285–286.

Hsia, Y., & Graham, C. H. (1997). Color blindness. In A. Byrne, D. R. Hilbert, et al., (Eds), *Readings on color, Vol. 2: The science of color.* Cambridge, MA: MIT Press.

Hsiung, P. (1990). Expansion of field of view via wide angle imaging. Unpublished document.

Hu, S., Pattatucci, A. M., Patterson, C., Li. L., et al. (1995). Linkage between sexual orientation and chromosome Xq28 in males but not in females. *Nature Genetics 11*(3), 248–256.

Hubble, M.A., Duncan, B. L., & Miller, S. D. (Eds.). (1999). *The heart and soul of change: What works in therapy.* Washington, DC: American Psychological Association.

Hubel, D. H. (1979a). The visual cortex of normal and deprived monkeys. *American Scientist, 67,* 532–543.

Hubel, D. H. (1979b, September). The brain. *Scientific American, 241* 45–53.

Huebner, R. (1998). Hemispheric differences in global/local processing revealed by same-different judgements. *Visual Cognition, 5*(4), 457–478.

Huesmann, L. R. (1986). Psychological processes promoting the relation between exposure to media violence and aggressive behavior by the viewer. *Journal of Social Issues, 42*(3), 125–139.

Huesmann, L. R., & Eron, L. D. (1986). The development of aggression in American children as a consequence of television violence viewing. In L. R. Huesmann & L. D. Eron (Eds.), *Television and the aggressive child: A cross-national comparison.* Hillsdale, NJ: Erlbaum.

Huesmann, L. R., Eron, L., Klein, L., Brice, P., & Fischer, P. (1983). Mitigating the imitation of aggressive behaviors by changing children's attitudes about media violence. *Journal of Personality & Social Psychology, 44,* 899–910.

Huesmann, L. R., Moise, J. F., & Podolski, C. (1997). The effects of media violence on the development of antisocial behavior. In D. M. Stoff, et al.(Eds.), *Handbook of antisocial behavior.*

Hugdahl, K., & Karker, A. C. (1981). Biological vs. experimental factors in phobic conditioning. *Behavior Research and Therapy, 19,* 109–115.

Hughes, J. N., & Hasbrouck, J. E. (1996). Television violence: Implications for violence prevention. *School Psychology Review, 25*(2), 134–151.

Hughes, J. R., Oliveto, A. H., Liguori, A., Carpenter, J., & Howard, T. (1998). Endorsement of DSM-IV dependence criteria among caffeine users. *Drug & Alcohol Dependence, 52*(2), 99–107.

Humphries, S. A., Johnson, M. H., & Long, N. R. (1996). An investigation of the gate control theory of pain using the experimental pain stimulus of potassium iontophoresis. *Perception & Psychophysics, 58*(5), 693–703.

Hunt E. (1995). The role of intelligence in modern society. *American Scientist, 83,* 356–368.

Hunter, E. (1998). Adolescent attraction to cults. *Adolescence, 33*(131), 709–714.

Hurlbert, D. F., & Apt, C. (1995). The coital alignment technique and directed masturbation: A comparative study on female orgasm. *Journal of Sex & Marital Therapy, 21*(1), 21–29.

Hyde, J. S. (1996). *Understanding human sexuality.* New York: McGraw-Hill.

Hyde, J. S., Klein, M. H., Essex, M. J., & Clark, R. (1995). Maternity leave and women's mental health. *Psychology of Women Quarterly, 19*(2), 257–285.

Hyman, R. (1989). *The elusive quarry: A scientific appraisal of psychical research.* Buffalo, NY: Prometheus.

Hyman, R. (1996a). Evaluation of the military's twenty-year program on psychic spying. *Skeptical Inquirer, 20*(2), 21–23.

Hyman, R. (1996b). The evidence for psychic functioning: Claims vs. reality. *Skeptical Inquirer, 20*(2), 24–26.

Hyman, S. (1999a). Protecting patients, preserving progress: Ethics in mental health illness research. *Academic Medicine, 74*(3), 258–259.

Hyman, S. (1999b). Susceptibility and "second hits." In R. Conlan (Ed.), *States of mind.* New York: Wiley.

Hyson, M. G., Hirsh-Pasek, K., Rescorla, L., Cone, J., et al. (1991). Ingredients of parental "pressure" in early childhood. *Journal of Applied Developmental Psychology, 12*(3), 347–365.

Iacono, W. G., & Lykken, D. T. (1997). The validity of the lie detector. *Journal of Applied Psychology, 82*(3), 426–433.

Ickes, W. (1993). Traditional gender roles: Do they make, then break, our relationships? *Journal of Social Issues, 49*(3), 71–86.

Immelman, A. (1998). The political personalities of 1996 U.S. presidential candidates Bill Clinton and Bob Dole. *Leadership Quarterly, 9*(3), 335–366.

Institute of Medicine. (1990). *Broadening the base of treatment for alcohol problems.* Washington, DC: National Academy Press.

Isaac, R. J., & Armat, V. C. (1990). *Madness in the streets: How psychiatry & the law abandoned the mentally ill.* New York: Free Press.

Isaak, M. I., & Just, A. (1995). Constraints on thinking in insight and invention. In R. J. Sternberg & J. E. Davidson (Eds.), *The nature of insight.* Cambridge, MA: MIT Press.

Isabella, R. A. (1993). Origins of attachment. *Child Development, 64*(2), 605–621.

Isabella, R. A., & Belsky, J. (1991). Interactional synchrony and the origins of infant-mother attachment. *Child Development, 62,* 373–384.

Isenberg, P. L., & Schatzberg, A. F. (1976). Psychoanalytic contribution to a theory of depression. In J. O. Cole, A. F. Schatzberg, & S. H. Frazier (Eds.), *Depression: Biology, psychodynamics, and treatment.* New York: Plenum.

Isser, N. (1991). Why cultic groups develop and flourish. *Cultic Studies Journal, 8*(2), 104–121.

Ito, T. A., Miller, N., & Pollock, V. E. (1996). Alcohol and aggression. *Psychological Bulletin, 120*(1), 60–82.

Iverson, J. M., & Goldin-Meadow, S. (1998). Why people gesture when they speak. *Nature, 396,* 228.

Ivey, A. E., & Galvin, M. (1984). Microcounseling: A metamodel for counseling, therapy, business, and medical interviews. In D. Larson (Ed.), *Teaching psychological skills.* Monterey, CA: Brooks/Cole.

Izard, C. E. (1977). *Human emotions.* New York: Plenum.

Izard, C. E. (1990). Facial expressions and the regulation of emotions. *Journal of Personality & Social Psychology, 58*(3), 487–498.

Izard, C. E., Fantauzzo, C. A., Castle, J. M., Haynes, O. M., Rayias, M. F., & Putnam, P. H. (1995). The ontogeny and significance of infants' facial expressions in the first 9 months of life. *Developmental Psychology, 31*(6), 997–1013.

Jack, S. J., & Ronan, K. R. (1998). Sensation seeking among high- and low-risk sports participants. *Personality & Individual Differences, 25*(6), 1063–1083.

Jackson, B. (1973, September 22). Our prisons are criminal. *New York Times Magazine,* pp. 54, 57.

Jackson, R. J. (1994). A multimodal method for assessing and treating airsickness. *International Journal of Aviation Psychology, 4*(1), 85–96.

Jackson, S. E. (1983). Participation in decision making as a strategy for reducing job-related strain. *Journal of Applied Psychology, 68,* 3–19.

Jackson, T., Towson, S., & Narduzzi. (1997). Predictors of shyness. *Social Behavior & Personality, 25*(2), 149–154.

Jacobsen, P. B., Bovbjerg, D. H., Schwartz, M. D., et al. (1993). Formation of food aversions in cancer patients receiving repeated infusions of chemotherapy. *Behavior Research & Therapy, 31*(8), 739–748.

Jacobson, S. W. (1998). Specificity of neurobehavioral outcomes associated with prenatal alcohol exposure. *Alcoholism: Clinical & Experimental Research, 22*(2), 313–320.

Jaeger, J. J., Lockwood, A. H., Van Valin, R. D. Jr., Kemmerer, D. L., et al. (1998). Sex differences in brain regions activated by grammatical and reading tasks. *Neuroreport: An International Journal for the Rapid Communication of Research in Neuroscience, 9*(12), 2803–2807.

Jackaclac, P., Riekkinen, M., Sirvioe, J., Koivisto, E., et al. (1999). Guanfacine, but not clonidine, improves planning and working memory performance in humans. *Neuropsychopharmacology, 20*(5), 460–470.

Jahn, R. G. (1982). The persistent paradox of psychic phenomena. *Proceedings of the IEEE, 70*(2), 136–166.

Jang, K. L., & Livesley, W. J. (1998). Support for a hierarchical model of personality. *Journal of Personality and Social Psychology, 74*(6), 1556–1565.

Janis, I. L. (1989). *Crucial decisions.* New York: Free Press.

Janis, I. L., & Mann, L. (1965). Effectiveness of emotional role-playing in modifying smoking habits and attitudes. *Journal of Experimental Research in Personality, 1,* 84–90.

Janis, I. L., & Wheeler, D. (1978). Thinking clearly about career choices. *Psychology Today, 11,* 66–78.

Janofsky, J. S., Dunn, M. H., Roskes, E. J., & Briskin, J. K. (1996). Insanity defense pleas in Baltimore city: An analysis of outcome. *American Journal of Psychiatry, 153*(11), 1464–1468.

Janowiak, J. J., & Hackman, R. (1994). Meditation and college students' self-actualization and rated stress. *Psychological Reports, 75*(2), 1007–1010.

Janus, S. S., & Janus, C. L. (1993). *The Janus report.* New York: Wiley.

Jarvik, M. E. (1995). "The scientific case that nicotine is addictive": Comment. *Psychopharmacology, 117*(1), 18–20.

Jellinik, E. M. (1960). *The disease concept of alcoholism.* New Haven: Hill House.

Jenkins, J. G., & Dallenbach, K. M. (1924). Oblivescence during sleep and waking. *American Journal of Psychology, 35,* 605–612.

Jennings, L., & Skovholt, T. M. (1999). The cognitive, emotional, and relational characteristics of master therapists. *Journal of Counseling Psychology, 46*(1), 3–11.

Jerabek, I., & Standing, L. (1992). Imagined test situations produce contextual memory enhancement. *Perceptual & Motor Skills, 75*(2), 400.

Jewell, L. N. (1989). *Psychology and effective behavior.* St. Paul, MN: West.

Jewell, L. N. (1990). *Contemporary industrial/organizational psychology.* St. Paul, MN: West.

Johnson, B. T. (1991). Insights about attitudes: Meta-analytic perspectives. *Personality & Social Psychology Bulletin, 17*(3), 289–299.

Johnson, J. G., & Sherman, M. F. (1997). Daily hassles mediate the relationship between major life events and psychiatric symptomatology. *Journal of Social & Clinical Psychology, 16*(4), 389–404.

Johnson, K. E., & Mervis, C. B. (1997). Effects of varying levels of expertise on the basic level of categorization. *Journal of Experimental Psychology: General, 126*(3), 248–277.

Johnson, M. H. (1999). Cortical plasticity in normal and abnormal cognitive development: Evidence and working hypotheses. *Development & Psychopathology, 11*(3), 419–437.

Johnson, M. H., Breakwell, G., Douglas, W., & Humphries, S. (1998). The effects of imagery and sensory detection distractors on different measures of pain. *British Journal of Psychology, 37*(2), 141–154.

Johnson, M. K., & Hasher, L. (1987). Human learning and memory. *Annual Review of Psychology, 38,* 631–668.

Johnson, N. G., & Roberts, M. C. (1999). Passage on the wild river of adolescence. In N. G. Johnson, M. C. Roberts, & J. Worell (Eds.), *Beyond Appearance.* Washington, DC: APA.

Johnson, S. M., & White, G. (1971). Self-observation as an agent of behavioral change. *Behavior Therapy, 2,* 488–497.

Johnson, S. P., & Nanez, J. E. (1995). Young infants' perception of object unity in two-dimensional displays. *Infant Behavior & Development, 18*(2), 133–143.

Johnsrude, I. S, Owen, A. M., Zhao, W. V., & White, N. M. (1999). Conditioned preference in humans. *Learning & Motivation, 30*(3), 250–264.

Johnston, W. A., & Dark, V. J. (1986). Selective attention. *Annual Review of Psychology, 37,* 43–75.

Jokerst, M. D., Gatto, M., Fazio, R., Stern, R. M., & Koch, K. L. (1999). Slow deep breathing prevents the development of tachygastria and symptoms of motion sickness. *Aviation, Space, & Environmental Medicine, 70*(12), 1189–1192.

Jones, E. E., & Nisbett, R. E. (1971). The actor and observer: Divergent perceptions of the causes of behavior. In E. E. Jones, D. E. Kanouse, H. H. Kelley, R. E. Nisbett, S. Valins, & B. Weiner (Eds.), *Attribution: Perceiving the causes of behavior.* Morristown, NJ: General Learning Press.

Jones, L., & Petruzzi, D. C. (1995). Test anxiety: A review of theory and current treatment. *Journal of College Student Psychotherapy, 10*(1), 3–15.

Jones, L. V., & Appelbaum, M. L. (1989). Psychometric methods. *Annual Review of Psychology, 40,* 23–43.

Jones, M. E., Russell, R. L., & Bryant, F. B. (1998). The structure of rape attitudes for men and woman. *Journal of Research in Personality, 32*(3), 331–350.

Jones, M. K., & Menzies, R. G. (1998). Danger ideation reduction therapy (DIRT) for obsessive-compulsive washers. *Behaviour Research & Therapy, 36*(10), 959–970.

Jones, R. T., Corbin, S. K., Sheehy, L., & Bruce, S. (1995). Substance refusal: More than "just say no." *Journal of Child & Adolescent Substance Abuse, 4*(2), 1–26.

Jones, S. S., Collins, K., & Hong, H. W. (1991). An audience effect on smile production in 10-month-old infants. *Psychological Science, 2,* 45–49.

Joseph, R. (1999). Environmental influences on neural plasticity, the limbic system, emotional development and attachment. *Child Psychiatry & Human Development, 29*(3), 189–208.

Jourard, S. M. (1963). *Personal adjustment.* New York: Macmillan.

Jourard, S. M. (1966). An exploratory study of body-accessibility. *British Journal of Social and Clinical Psychology, 5,* 221–231.

Jourard, S. M. (1974). *Healthy personality.* New York: Macmillan.

Jouvet, M. (1999). The paradox of sleep. Boston: MIT Press.

Joy, L. A., Kimball, M. M., & Zabrack, M. L. (1986). Television and aggressive behavior. In T. M. Williams (Ed.), *The impact of television: A natural experiment involving three towns.* New York: Academic.

Julesz, B. (1971). *Foundations of cyclopean perception.* Chicago: University of Chicago Press.

Julesz, B. (1975). Experiments in the visual perception of texture. *Scientific American, 232,* 34–43.

Julien, R. M. (1998). *A primer of drug action.* San Francisco: Freeman.

Jurma, W. E., & Powell, M. L. (1994). Perceived gender roles of managers and effective conflict management. *Psychological Reports, 74*(1), 104–106.

Jussim, L., & Eccles, J. S. (1992). Teacher expectations. *Journal of Personality & Social Psychology, 63*(6), 947–961.

Juster, H. R., Heimberg, R. G., Frost, R. O., & Holt, C. S. (1996). Social phobia and perfectionism. *Personality & Individual Differences, 21*(3), 403–410.

Kagan, J. (1971). *Change and continuity in infancy.* New York: Wiley.

Kagan, J. (1989). Temperamental contributions to social behavior. *American Psychologist, 44*(4), 668–674.

Kagan, J. (1991). The theoretical utility of constructs for self. *Developmental Review, 11*(3), 244–250.

Kagan, J. (1999). Born to be shy? In R. Conlan (Ed.), *States of mind.* New York: Wiley.

Kahneman, D., Slovic, P., & Tversky, A. (1982). *Judgment under uncertainty: Heuristics and biases.* Cambridge: Cambridge University Press.

Kahneman, D., & Tversky, A. (1972). Subjective probability: A judgment of representativeness. *Cognitive Psychology, 3,* 430–454.

Kahneman, D., & Tversky, A. (1973). On the psychology of prediction. *Psychological Review, 80,* 237–251.

Kaitz, M., Zvi, H., Levy, M., Berger, A., et al. (1995). The uniqueness of mother–own-infant interactions. *Infant Behavior & Development, 18*(2), 247–252.

Kakigi, R., Matsuda, Y., & Kuroda, Y. (1993). Effects of movement-related cortical activities on pain-related somatosensory evoked potentials. *Acta Neurologica Scandinavica, 88*(5), 376–380.

Kalal, D. M. (1999). Critical thinking in clinical practice: Pseudoscience, fad psychology, and the behavioral therapist. *The Behavior Therapist, 22*(4), 81–84.

Kamin, L. J. (1981). *The intelligence controversy.* New York: Wiley.

Kamin, L. J. (1985, October). Genes and behavior: The missing link. *Psychology Today,* 76–78.

Kamiya, J. (1968). Conscious control of brain waves. *Psychology Today 1,* 57–66.

Kamphaus, R. W. (1993). *Clinical assessment of children's intelligence.* Needham Heights, MA: Allyn and Bacon.

Kandel, E. (1999). Of learning, memory, and genetic switches. In R. Conlan (Ed.), *States of mind.* New York: Wiley.

Kaplan, E. B. (1997). Women's perceptions of adolescent experience. *Adolescence, 32*(127), 715–734.

Kaplan, E. H. (1997). Telepsychotherapy. *Journal of Psychotherapy Practice & Research, 6*(3), 227–237.

Kaplan, H. S. (1974). *The new sex therapy.* New York: Brunner/Mazel.

Kaplan, P. S. (1998). *The human odyssey.* Pacific Grove, CA: Brooks/Cole.

Kaplan, P. S., Goldstein, M. H., Huckeby, E. R., & Cooper, R. P. (1995). Habituation, sensitization, and infants' responses to motherese speech. *Developmental Psychobiology, 28*(1), 45–57.

Kaplan, P. S., & Stein, J. (1984). *Psychology of adjustment.* Belmont, CA: Wadsworth.

Kapleau, P. (1966). *The three pillars of Zen.* New York: Harper & Row.

Karlberg, L., Krakau, I., & Unden, A. (1998). Type A behavior intervention in primary health care reduces hostility and time pressure. *Social Science & Medicine, 46*(3), 397–402.

Karon, B. P., & Widener, A. (1998). Repressed memories: The real story. *Professional Psychology: Research & Practice, 29*(5), 482–487.

Karon, B. P., & Widener, A. J. (1997). Repressed memories and World War II: Lest we forget! *Professional Psychology: Research & Practice, 28*(4), 338–340.

Kasamatsu, A., & Hirai, T. (1966). An electroencephalographic study of Zen meditation (Zazen). *Folia Psychiatria et Neurologia Japonica, 20,* 315–336.

Kasper, M. E., Rogers, R., & Adams, P. A. (1996). Dangerousness and command hallucinations. *Bulletin of the American Academy of Psychiatry & the Law, 24*(2), 219–224.

Kasser, T., & Ryan, R. M. (1993). A dark side of the American dream: Correlates of financial success as a central life aspiration. *Journal of Personality & Social Psychology, 65*(2), 410–422.

Kasser, T., & Ryan, R. M. (1996). Further examining the American dream: Differential correlates of intrinsic and extrinsic goals. *Personality & Social Psychology Bulletin, 22*(3), 280–287.

Kassin, S. M., Ellsworth, P. C., & Smith, V. L. (1989). The "general acceptance" of psychological research on eyewitness testimony: A survey of the experts. *American Psychologist, 44,* 1089–1098.

Kastenbaum, R., & Aisenberg R. (1972). *The psychology of death.* New York: Springer.

Katz, M. R. (1993). *Computer-assisted career decision making.* Educational Testing Service.

Kaufman, A. S. (2000). Intelligence tests and school psychology: Predicting the future by studying the past. *Psychology in the Schools, 37*(1), 7–16.

Kaufman, L., & Kaufman, J. H. (2000. Explaining the moon illusion. *Proceedings of the National Academy of Sciences, 97*(1), 500–505.

Kazdin, A. E. (1975). *Behavior modification in applied settings.* Homewood, IL: Dorsey Press.

Kebbell, M. R., & Milne, R. (1998). Police officers' perceptions of eyewitness performance in forensic investigations. *Journal of Social Psychology, 138*(3), 323–330.

Kebbell, M. R., & Wagstaff, G. F. (1998). Hypnotic interviewing: The best way to interview eyewitnesses? *Behavioral Sciences & the Law, 16*(1), 115–129.

Keefe, F. J. (1982). Behavioral assessment and treatment of chronic pain: Current status and future directions. *Journal of Consulting and Clinical Psychology, 50,* 896–911.

Kellehear, A. (1993). Culture, biology, and the near-death experience. *Journal of Nervous & Mental Disease, 181*(3), 148–156.

Keller, M. C., & Young, R. K. (1996). Mate assortment in dating and married couples. *Personality & Individual Differences, 21*(2), 217–221.

Kellermann, A. L., Rivara, F. P., Rushforth, N. B., Banton, J. G., et al. (1993). Gun ownership as a risk factor for homicide in the home. *New England Journal of Medicine, 329*(15), 1084–1091.

Kelley, H. H. (1950). The warm-cold variable in first impressions of persons. *Journal of Personality, 18,* 431–439.

Kelley, H. H. (1967). Attribution in social psychology. *Nebraska Symposium on Motivation, 15,* 192–238.

Kellner, C. H. (1998). ECT in the media. *Psychiatric Annals, 28*(9), 528–529.

Kelly, A. D., & Kanas, N. (1993). Communication between space crews and ground personnel. *Aviation, Space, & Environmental Medicine, 64*(9, Sect. 1), 795–800.

Kelly, G. F. (1996). Using meditative techniques in psychotherapy. *Journal of Humanistic Psychology, 36*(3), 49–66.

Kelly, I. W. (1998). Why astrology doesn't work. *Psychological Reports, 82,* 527–546.

Kelly, I. W. (1999, November–December). "Debunking the debunkers": A response to an astrologer's debunking of skeptics. *Skeptical Inquirer,* 37–43.

Kelly, I. W., & Saklofske, D. H. (1994). Psychology and pseudoscience. *Encyclopedia of human behavior, 3,* 611–618.

Kelly, T. H., Foltin, R. W., Emurian, C. S., & Fischman, M. W. (1990). Multidimensional behavioral effects of marijuana. *Progress in Neuropsychopharmacology & Biological Psychiatry, 14*(6), 885–902.

Kelman, H. C., & Hamilton, V. L. (1989). *Crimes of obedience.* New Haven, CT: Yale University Press.

Kemp, M. (1998). Why is learning American Sign Language a challenge? *Accident Analysis & Prevention, 143*(3), 255–259.

Kempermann, G., & Gage, F. H. (1999). Experienced-dependent regulation of adult hippocampal neurogenesis. *Hippocampus, 9*(3), 321–332.

Kempton, W., Darley, J. M., & Stern, P. C. (1992). Psychological research for the new energy problems. *American Psychologist, 47*(10), 1213–1232.

Kenen, R. H., & Smith, A. C. (1995). Genetic counseling for the next 25 years. *Journal of Genetic Counseling, 4*(2), 115–124.

Kennedy, J. M. (1983). What can we learn about pictures from the blind? *American Scientist, 71,* 19–26.

Kennedy, P. R., & Bakay, R. A. (1998). Restoration of neural output from a paralyzed patient by a direct brain connection. *Neuroreport, 9*(8), 1707–1711.

Kenneth, M., Carpenter, K. M., & Hasin, D. S. (1998). Reasons for drinking alcohol. *Psychology of Addictive Behaviors, 12*(3), 168–184.

Kenrick, D. T., & MacFarlane, S. W. (1986). Ambient temperature and horn honking: A field study of the heat/aggression relationship. *Environment and Behavior, 18*(2), 179–191.

Kessen, W., & Cahan, E. D. (1986). A century of psychology: From subject to object to agent. *American Scientist, 74,* 640–649.

Kessler, R. C. (1997). The effects of stressful life events on depression. *Annual Review of Psychology, 48,* 191–214.

Kessler, R. C., Sonnega, A., & Nelson, C. B. (1995). Posttraumatic stress disorder in the National Comorbidity Survey. *Archives of General Psychiatry, 52*(12), 1048.

Kety, S. S. (1979, September). Disorders of the human brain. *Scientific American, 241,* 202–214.

Kiecolt-Glaser, J. K., & Glaser, R. (1992). Psychoneuroimmunology: Can psychological interventions modulate immunity? *Journal of Consulting & Clinical Psychology, 60*(4), 569–575.

Kiewra, K. A., DuBois, N. F., Christian, D., McShane, A., et al. (1991). Note-taking functions and techniques. *Journal of Educational Psychology, 83*(2), 240–245.

Kiewra, K. A., Mayer, R. E., DuBois, N. F., Christensen, M., et al. (1997). Effects of advance organizers and repeated presentations on students' learning. *Journal of Experimental Education, 65*(2) 147–159.

Kihlstrom, J. F. (1985). Hypnosis. *Annual Review of Psychology 36,* 385–418.

Kihlstrom, J. F. (1997). Convergence in understanding hypnosis? Perhaps, but perhaps not quite so fast. *International Journal of Clinical & Experimental Hypnosis, 45*(3), 324–332.

Killen, J. D., & Fortmann, S. P. (1997). Craving is associated with smoking relapse. *Experimental and Clinical Psychopharmacology, 5*(2), 137–142.

Killen, J. D., et al. (1997). Prospective study of risk factors for the initiation of cigarette smoking. *Journal of Consulting & Clinical Psychology, 65*(6), 1011–1016.

Kim, A., Martin, D., & Martin, M. (1989). Effects of personality on marital satisfaction. *Family Therapy, 16*(3), 243–248.

Kim, J., Singer, R. N., & Radlo, S. J. (1996). Degree of cognitive demands in psychomotor tasks and the effects of the five-step strategy on achievement. *Human Performance, 9*(2), 155–169.

Kimball, M. M. (1986). Television and sex-role attitudes. In T. M. Williams (Ed.), *The impact of television: A natural experiment in three communities.* Orlando, FL: Academic.

Kimble, G. A. (1989). Psychology from the standpoint of a generalist. *American Psychologist, 44*(3), 491–499.

Kimmel, A. J. (1998). In defense of deception. *American Psychologist, 53*(7), 803–805.

Kimmel, D. C. (1988). Ageism, psychology, and public policy. *American Psychologist, 43*(3), 175–178.

Kimmel, D. C. (1990). *Adulthood and aging.* New York: Wiley & Sons.

King, A. (1992). Comparison of self-questioning, summarizing, and notetaking-review as strategies for learning from lectures. *American Educational Research Journal, 29*(2), 303–323.

King, A. (1995). Cognitive strategies for learning from direct teaching. In E. Wood, V. Woloshyn, & T. Willoughby (Eds.), *Cognitive strategy instruction for middle and high schools,* Brookline, Cambridge, MA.

King, H. E. (1961). Psychological effects of excitation in the limbic system. In D. E. Sheer (Ed.), *Electrical stimulation of the brain.* Austin: University of Texas Press.

King, K. B. (1997). Psychologic and social aspects of cardiovascular disease. *Annals of Behavioral Medicine, 19*(3), 264–270.

King, L., & Napa, C. (1998). What makes a life good? *Journal of Personality and Social Psychology, 75*(1), 156–165.

King, L. A., & Broyles, S. (1997). Wishes, gender, personality, and well-being. *Journal of Personality, 65,* 50–75.

King, L. A., Richards, J. H., & Stemmerich, E. (1998). Daily goals, life goals, and worst fears. *Journal of Personality, 66*(5), 713–744.

Kinsey, A., Pomeroy, W., & Martin, C. (1948). *Sexual behavior in the human male.* Philadelphia: Saunders.

Kinsey, A., Pomeroy, W., & Martin, C. (1953). *Sexual behavior in the human female.* Philadelphia: Saunders.

Kipnis, D. (1987). Psychology and behavioral technology. *American Psychologist, 42,* 30–36.

Kipper, D. A. (1992). The effect of two kinds of role playing on self-evaluation of improved assertiveness. *Journal of Clinical Psychology, 48*(2), 246–250.

Kirk, M. A. (1995). Menopause: A developmental stage, not a deficiency disease. *Psychotherapy, 32*(2), 233–241.

Kirsch, I., & Lynn, S. J. (1995). The altered state of hypnosis. *American Psychologist, 50*(10), 846–858.

Kirsch, I., & Lynn, S. J. (1999). Automaticity in clinical psychology. *American Psychologist, 54*(7), 504–515.

Kirsch, I., Montgomery, G., & Sapirstein, G. (1995). Hypnosis as an adjunct to cognitive behavioral psychotherapy: A meta-analysis. *Journal of Consulting and Clinical Psychology, 63,* 214–220.

Kirsch, I., & Sapirstein, G. (1998). Listening to Prozac but hearing placebo: A meta-analysis of antidepressant medication. *Prevention & Treatment, 1,* np.

Kirsh, S. J. (1998). Seeing the world through Mortal Kombat–colored glasses. *Childhood: A Global Journal of Child Research, 5*(2), 177–184.

Kisilevsky, B. S., & Low, J. A. (1998). Human fetal behavior. *Developmental Review, 18*(1), 1–29.

Kistler, A., Mariauzouls, C., & von Berlepsch, K. (1998). Fingertip temperature as an indicator for sympathetic responses. *International Journal of Psychophysiology, 29*(1), 35–41.

Kitayama, S., Markus, H. R., Matsumoto, H., & Norasakkunkit, V. (1997). Individual and collective processes in the construction of the self. *Journal of Personality & Social Psychology, 72*(6), 1245–1267.

Kitcher, P. (1985). *Vaulting ambition: Sociobiology and the quest for human nature.* Cambridge, MA: MIT Press.

Klaus, M. H., & Kennell, J. H. (1982). *Parent-infant bonding.* St. Louis: Mosby.

Klaus, M. H., Kennell, J. H., & Klaus, . (1995). *Bonding.* Reading, MA: Addison-Wesley.

Klausmeir, H. J., & Goodwin, W. (1975). *Learning and human abilities.* New York: Harper & Row.

Klebanoff, M. A., Levine, R. J., DerSimonian, R., Clemens, J. D., & Wilkins, D. G. (1999). Maternal serum paraxanthine, a caffeine metabolite, and the risk of spontaneous abortion. *New England Journal of Medicine, 341*(22), 1639–1644.

Klein, G., Wolf, S., Militello, L., & Zsambok, C. (1995). Characteristics of skilled option generation in chess. *Organizational Behavior & Human Decision Processes, 62*(1), 63–69.

Klein, S. B., Loftus, J., & Kihlstrom, J. F. (1996). Self-knowledge of an amnesic patient. *Journal of Experimental Psychology: General, 125*(3), 250–260.

Kleinke, C. L. (1986). *Meeting and understanding people.* New York: Freeman.

Kleinke, C. L., Peterson, T. R., & Rutledge, T. R. (1998). Effects of self-generated facial expressions on mood. *Journal of Personality and Social Psychology, 74*(1), 272–279.

Kleinknecht, R. A. (1986). *The anxious self: Diagnosis and treatment of fears and phobias.* New York: Human Sciences Press.

Kleinplatz, P. J. (1996). The erotic encounter. *Journal of Humanistic Psychology, 36*(3), 105–123.

Klinger, E. (1990). *Daydreaming.* Los Angeles: J. P. Tarcher.

Klintsova, A. Y., & Greenough, W. T. (1999). Synaptic plasticity in cortical systems. *Current Opinion in Neurobiology, 9*(2), 203–208.

Klonoff-Cohen, H. S., Edelstein, S. L., Lefkowitz, E. S., Srinivasan, I. P., et al. (1995). The effect of passive smoking and tobacco exposure through breast milk on sudden infant death syndrome. *Journal of the American Medical Association, 273*(10), 795–798.

Knesper, D. J., Belcher, B. E., & Cross, J. G. (1989). A market analysis comparing the practices of psychiatrists and psychologists. *Archives of General Psychiatry, 46*(4), 305–314.

Knowles, J. (1995, February). HIV/STI update. *Insider,* 2.

Knox, D. (1984). *Human sexuality.* St. Paul, MN: West.

Knutson, J. (1995). Psychological characteristics of maltreated children. *Annual Review of Psychology, 46,* 401–431.

Koenig, S. M. (1996). Central sleep apnea. *Virginia Medical Quarterly, 123*(4), 247–250.

Koepke, J. E., & Bigelow, A. E. (1997). Observations of newborn suckling behavior. *Infant Behavior & Development, 20*(1), 93–98.

Kohlberg, L. (1969). The cognitive-developmental approach to socialization. In A. Goslin (Ed.), *Handbook of socialization theory and research.* Chicago: Rand McNally.

Kohlberg, L. (1981a). *Essays on moral development. Vol. I. The philosophy of moral development.* San Francisco: Harper.

Kohlberg, L. (1981b). *The meaning and measurement of moral development.* Worcester, MA: Clark University Press.

Kohler, I. (1962). Experiments with goggles. *Scientific American,* Offprint No. 465, 62–72.

Kohler, W. (1925). *The mentality of apes.* New York: Harcourt Brace Jovanovich.

Kohn, A. (1987, September). Art for art's sake. *Psychology Today,* 52–57.

Kohn, A. (1988, March 21). Shock therapy makes a comeback. *Los Angeles Times,* p. II, 5.

Kolb, B. (1999). Synaptic plasticity and the organization of behaviour after early and late brain injury. *Canadian Journal of Experimental Psychology, 53*(1), 62–75.

Kolb, B., & Whishaw, I. Q. (1998). Brain plasticity and behavior. *Annual Review of Psychology, 49,* 43–64.

Kolbe, L. J., Collins, J., & Cortese, P. (1997). Building the capacity of schools to improve the health of the nation. *American Psychologist, 52*(3), 256–265.

Konner, M. (1991). *Childhood.* Boston: Little, Brown.

Koocher, G. P. (1977). Bathroom behavior and human dignity. *Journal of Personality and Social Psychology, 35,* 120–121.

Kopta, M. S., Lueger, R. J., Saunders, S. M., & Howard, K. I. (1999). Individual psycho-therapy outcome and process research. *Annual Review of Psychology, 50,* 441–469.

Kopta, S. M., et al. (1999). Individual psychotherapy outcome and process research. *Annual Review of Psychology, 50,* 441–469.

Korte, C., & Milgram, S. (1970). Acquaintance networks between racial groups. *Journal of Personality & Social Psychology, 15,* 101–108.

Koss, M. P. (1993). Rape. *American Psychologist, 48*(10), 1062–1069.

Koss, M., Gidycz, C. A., & Wisniewski, N. (1987). The scope of rape: Incidence and prevalence of sexual aggression and victimization in a national sample of higher education students. *Journal of Consulting and Clinical Psychology, 55*(2), 162–170.

Kosslyn, S. M. (1983). *Ghosts in the mind's machine.* New York: Norton.

Kosslyn, S. M. (1985, May). Stalking the mental image. *Psychology Today,* 23–28.

Kosslyn, S. M. (1990). Mental imagery. In D. N. Osherson, S. M. Kosslyn, & J. M. Hollerbach (Eds.), *Visual cognition and action.* Cambridge, MA: MIT Press.

Kosslyn, S. M., Ball, T. M., & Reiser, B. J. (1978). Visual images preserve metric spatial information: Evidence from studies of image scanning. *Journal of Experimental Psychology: Human Perception and Performance, 4,* 47–60.

Kosslyn, S. M., Seger, C., Pani, J. R., & Hillger, L. A. (1990). When is imagery used in everyday life? A diary study. *Journal of Mental Imagery, 14*(3–4), 131–152.

Kosslyn, S. M., Thompson, W. L., & Alpert, N. N. (1995). Topographical representation of mental images in primary visual cortex. *Nature, 378*(6556), 496.

Kotkin, M., Daviet, C., & Gurin, J. (1996). The Consumer Reports mental health survey. *American Psychologist, 51*(10), 1080–1082.

Kottler, J. A., & Brown, R. W. (1999). *Introduction to therapeutic counseling.* Monterey, CA: Brooks/Cole.

Kozlowski, L. T., Goldberg, M. E., Yost, B. A., White, J., et al. (1998). Smokers' misperceptions of light and ultra-light cigarettes may keep them smoking. *American Journal of Preventive Medicine, 15*(1), 9–16.

Kozulin, A. (1999). Cognitive learning in younger and older immigrant students. *School Psychology International, 20*(2), 177–190.

Krakow, B., Kellner, R., Pathak, D., & Lambert, L. (1996). Long term reduction of nightmares with imagery rehearsal treatment. *Behavioural & Cognitive Psychotherapy, 24*(2), 135–148.

Krakow, B., & Neidhardt, J. (1992). *Conquering bad dreams and nightmares.* Berkley Books.

Krantz, L. (1995). *Jobs rated almanac.* New York: Wiley.

Kratofil, P. H., Baberg, H. T., & Dimsdale, J. E. (1996). Self-mutilation and severe self-injurious behavior associated with amphetamine psychosis. *General Hospital Psychiatry, 18*(2), 117–120.

Kring, A. M., & Gordon, A. H. (1998). Sex differences in emotion. *Journal of Personality & Social Psychology, 74*(3), 686–703.

Krivascka, J. J., Savin-Williams, R. C., & Slater, B. R. (1992, November 8). *Background paper for the resolution on lesbian, gay, and bisexual youths in the schools.*

Kroon, M. B., Van Kreveld, D., & Rabbie, J. M. (1992). Group versus individual decision making: Effects of accountability and gender on groupthink. *Small Group Research, 23*(4), 427–458.

Kropp, P., et al. (1997) Behavioral treatment in migraine. *Functional Neurology, 12*(1), 17–24.

Krosnick, J. A. (1999). Survey research. *Annual Review of Psychology, 50,* 537–567.

Krosnick, J. A., Betz, A. L., Jussim, L. J., & Lynn, A. R. (1992). Subliminal conditioning of attitudes. *Personality & Social Psychology Bulletin, 18*(2), 152–162.

Krueger, J., Ham, J. J., & Linford, K. M. (1996). Perceptions of behavioral consistency: Are people aware of the actor-observer effect? *Psychological Science, 7*(5), 259–264.

Kruger, J., & Dunning, D. (1999). Unskilled and unaware of it: How difficulties in recognizing one's own incompetence lead to inflated self-assessments. *Journal of Personality & Social Psychology, 77*(6), 1121–1134.

Kruger, L., & Liebeskind, J. C. (Eds.). (1984). *Advances in pain research and therapy.* New York: Raven Press.

Kübler-Ross, E. (1975). *Death: The final stage of growth.* Englewood Cliffs, NJ: Prentice-Hall.

Kubovy, M., & Holcombe, A. O. (1998). *On the lawfulness of grouping by proximity. Cognitive Psychology, 35*(1), 71–98.

Kunkel, M. A. (1993). A teaching demonstration involving perceived lunar size. *Teaching of Psychology, 20*(3), 178–180.

Kunzendorf, R. G. (1989). After-images of eidetic images: A developmental study. *Journal of Mental Imagery, 13*(1), 55–62.

Kusseling, F. S., Shapiro, M. F., Greenberg, J. M., & Wenger, N. S. (1996). Understanding why heterosexual adults do not practice safer sex: A comparison of two samples. *AIDS Education & Prevention, 8*(3), 247–257.

La Berge, S. P. (1981, January). Lucid dreaming: Directing the action as it happens. *Psychology Today,* 48–57.

La Berge, S. P. (1985). *Lucid dreaming.* Los Angeles: Tarcher.

Laan, E., Everaerd, W., van Bellen, G., & Hanewald, G. J. F. P. (1994). Women's sexual and emotional responses to male- and female-produced erotica. *Archives of Sexual Behavior, 23*(2), 153–169.

Laan, E., Everaerd, W., van der Velde, J., & Geer, J. H. (1995). Determinants of subjective experience of sexual arousal in women. *Psychophysiology, 32*(5), 444–451.

Labov, W. (1973). The boundaries of words and their meanings. In C. J. N. Bailey & R. W. Shuy (Eds.), *New ways of analyzing variation in English.* Washington, DC: Georgetown University Press.

Lacayo, A. (1995). Neurologic and psychiatric complications of cocaine abuse. *Neuropsychiatry, Neuropsychology, & Behavioral Neurology, 8*(1), 53–60.

Lachman, M. E., & Weaver, S. L. (1998). The sense of control as a moderator of social class differences in health and well-being. *Journal of Personality & Social Psychology, 74*(3), 763–773.

Lackner, J. R., & DiZio, P. (1993). Multisensory, cognitive, and motor influences on human spatial orientation in weightlessness. *Journal of Vestibular Research, 3*(3), 361–372.

Lacks, P., & Morin, C. M. (1992). Recent advances in the assessment and treatment of insomnia. *Journal of Clinical and Consulting Psychology, 60*(4), 586–594.

Lahtinen, V., Lonka, K., & Lindbloom-Ylaenne, S. (1997). Spontaneous study strategies and the quality of knowledge construction. *British Journal of Educational Psychology, 67*(1), 13–24.

Lal, S. K. L., et al. (1998). Effect of feedback signal and psychological characteristics on blood pressure self-manipulation capability. *Psychophysiology, 35*(4), 405–412.

Lamb, M. R., & Yund, E. W. (1996). Spatial frequency and attention. *Perception & Psychophysics, 58*(3), 363–373.

Lambert, M. J. (1999). Are differential treatment effects inflated by researcher therapy allegiance? *Clinical Psychology: Science & Practice, 6*(1), 127–130.

Lambert, M. J., & Cattani-Thompson, K. (1996). Current findings regarding the effectiveness of counseling. *Journal of Counseling & Development, 74*(6), 601–608.

Lambert, W. E. (1987). The effects of bilingual and bicultural experiences on children's attitudes and social perspectives. In P. Homel, M. Palij, & D. Aaronson (Eds.), *Childhood bilingualism.* Hillsdale, NJ: Erlbaum.

Lamme, V. A. F. (1995). The neurophysiology of figure-ground segregation in primary visual cortex. *Journal of Neuroscience, 15*(2), 1605–1615.

Lance, C. E., LaPointe, J. A., & Stewart, A. M. (1994). A test of the context dependency of three causal models of halo rater error. *Journal of Applied Psychology, 79*(3), 332–340.

Landers, S. (1986, December). Judge reiterates I.Q. test ban. *APA Monitor,* p. 18.

Landers, S. (1989, January). In U.S., mental disorders affect 15 percent of adults. *APA Monitor,* p. 16.

Landy, F. J., Shankster, L. J., & Kohler, S. S. (1994). Personnel selection and placement. *Annual Review of Psychology, 45,* 261–296.

Langer, E. J., & Abelson, R. P. (1974). A patient by any other name: Clinician group difference in labeling bias. *Journal of Consulting and Clinical Psychology, 42*(1), 4–9.

Langer, E. J., & Piper, A. I. (1987). Prevention of mindblindness. *Journal of Personality & Social Psychology, 53,* 280–287.

Lantz, J. (1998). Dream reflection in logotherapy. *Journal of Contemporary Psychotherapy, 28*(1) 81–89.

Lanzetta, J. T., & Englis, B. G. (1989). Expectations of cooperation and competition and their effects on observers' vicarious emotional responses. *Journal of Personality & Social Psychology, 56*(4), 543–554.

Larner, A. J., Moss, J., Rossi, M. L., & Anderson, M. (1994). Congenital insensitivity to pain. *Journal of Neurology, Neurosurgery & Psychiatry, 57*(8), 973–974.

Larsen, R. J., & Kasimatis, M. (1990). Individual differences in entrainment of mood to the weekly calendar. *Journal of Personality & Social Psychology, 58*(1), 164–171.

Larson, C. A., & Carey, K. B. (1998). Caffeine. *Professional Psychology: Research & Practice, 29*(4), 373–376.

Larson, D. E. (Ed.). (1990). *Mayo Clinic family healthbook.* New York: Morrow.

Larson, M. E., Houlihan, D., & Goernert, P. N. (1995). Effects of informational feedback on aluminum can recycling. *Behavioral Interventions, 10*(2), 111–117.

Latane, L., Nida, S. A., & Wilson, D. W. (1981). The effects of group size on helping behavior. In J. P. Rushton & R. M. Sorrentino (Eds.), *Altruism and helping behavior: Social, personality and developmental perspectives.* Hillsdale, NJ: Erlbaum.

Lattal, K. A., Reilly, M. P., & Kohn, J. P. (1998). Response persistence under ratio and interval reinforcement schedules. *Journal of the Experimental Analysis of Behavior, 70*(2), 165–183.

Lattanzi-Licht, M., & Connor, S. (1995). Care of the dying: The hospice approach. In H. Wass & R. A. Neimeyer (Eds.), *Dying: Facing the facts.* Washington, DC: Taylor & Francis.

Latty-Mann, H., & Davis, K. E. (1996). Attachment theory and partner choice. *Journal of Social & Personal Relationships, 13*(1), 5–23.

Laumann, E., Michael, R., Michaels, S., & Gagnon, J. (1994). *The social organization of sexuality.* Chicago: University of Chicago Press.

Laursen, B., Coy, K. C., & Collins, W. A. (1998). Resonsidering changes in parent-child conflict across adolesence. *Child Development, 69,* 817–832.

Lavallee, A. C. (1999). Capuchin (*Cebus apella*) tool use in a captive naturalistic environment. *International Journal of Primatology, 20*(3), 399–414.

Lavelli, M., & Poli, M. (1998). Early mother-infant interaction during breast- and bottle-feeding. *Infant Behavior & Development, 21*(4), 667–683.

Lawler, K. A., Kline, K. A., Harriman, H. L., & Kelly, K. M. (1999). Stress and illness. In: V. J. Derlega, et al. (Eds.), *Personality: Contemporary theory and research.* Chicago: Nelson-Hall.

Lawrence, B., Myerson, J., & Hale, S. (1998). Differential decline of verbal and visuospatial processing speed across the adult life span. *Aging, Neuropsychology, & Cognition, 5*(2), 129–146.

Lay, C., & Verkuyten, M. (1999). Ethnic identity and its relation to personal self-esteem. *Journal of Social Psychology, 139*(3), 288–299.

Lazarus, A. H. (1964). The treatment of chronic frigidity by systematic desensitization. In H. J. Eysenck (Ed.), *Experiments in behavior therapy.* New York: Pergamon.

Lazarus, R. S. (1981, July). Little hassles can be hazardous to health. *Psychology Today,* 12–14.

Lazarus, R. S. (1991a). Progress on a cognitive-motivational-relational theory of emotion. *American Psychologist, 46*(8), 819–834.

Lazarus, R. S. (1991b). Cognition and motivation in emotion. *American Psychologist, 46*(4), 352–367.

Lazarus, R. S. (1993). From psychological stress to the emotions: A history of changing outlooks. *Annual Review of Psychology, 44,* 1–21.

Lazarus, R. S., DeLongis, A., Folkman, S., & Gruen, R. (1985). Stress and adaptational outcomes. *American Psychologist, 40,* 770–779.

Lazgrove, S., et al. (1998). An open trial for EMDR as treatment for chronic PTSD. *American Journal of Orthopsychiatry, 68*(4), 601–608.

Lea, S. E. G., & Kiley-Worthington, M. (1996). Can animals think? In V. Bruce (Ed.), *Unsolved mysteries of the mind: Tutorial essays in cognition.* Hove, East Sussex: Erlbaum (UK), Taylor & Francis.

Leavens, D. A., & Hopkins, W. D. (1998). Intentional communication by chimpanzees. *Developmental Psychology, 34*(5), 813–822.

Lecomte, D., & Fornes, P. (1998). Suicide among youth and young adults, 15 through 24 years of age. *Journal of Forensic Sciences, 43*(5), 964–968.

LeDoux, J. (1996). *The emotional brain: The mysterious underpinnings of emotional life.* New York: Simon & Schuster.

LeDoux, J. (1998). Fear and the brain: Where have we been, and where are we going? *Biological Psychiatry, 44*(12), 1229–1238.

LeDoux, J. (1999). The power of emotions. In R. Conlan (Ed.), *States of mind*. New York: Wiley.

Lee, C. C. (1991a). Cultural dynamics. In C. C. Lee & B. L. Richardson (Eds.), *Multicultural issues in counseling*. Alexandria, VA: American Association for Counseling and Development.

Lee, C. C. (1991b). New approaches to diversity. In C. C. Lee & B. L. Richardson (Eds.), *Multicultural issues in counseling*. Alexandria, VA: American Association for Counseling and Development.

Lee, C. C., & Richardson, B. L. (1991). Promise and pitfalls of multicultural counseling. In C. C. Lee & B. L. Richardson (Eds.), *Multicultural issues in counseling*. Alexandria, VA: American Association for Counseling and Development.

Lee, M., Zimbardo, P. G., & Bertholf, M. (1977, November). Shy murderers. *Psychology Today*,

Lee, R. T., & Ashforth, B. E. (1990). On the meaning of Maslach's three dimensions of burnout. *Journal of Applied Psychology, 75*(6), 743–747.

Lee, T. D., & Carnahan, H. (1990). When to provide knowledge of results during motor learning: Scheduling effects. *Human Performance, 3*(2), 87–105.

Leeming, F. C. (1997). Commitment to study as a technique to improve exam performance. *Journal of College Student Development, 38*(5), 499–507.

Leenaars, A. A. (1995). Suicide. In H. Wass & R. A. Neimeyer (Eds.), *Dying*. Washington, DC: Taylor & Francis.

Leeper, R. W. (1935). A study of a neglected portion of the field of learning: The development of sensory organization. *Pedagogical Seminary and Journal of Genetic Psychology, 46*, 41–75.

Lefcourt, H. M., & Thomas, S. (1998). Humor and stress revisited. In W. Ruch, et al. (Eds.), *The sense of humor*. Berlin: Walter De Gruyter.

Lefkowitz, M., Blake, R. R., & Mouton, J. S. (1955). Status factors in pedestrian violation of traffic signals. *Journal of Abnormal and Social Psychology, 51*, 704–706.

Legerstee, M., Anderson, D., & Schaffer, A. (1998). Five- and eight-month-old infants recognize their faces and voices as familiar and social stimuli. *Child Development, 69*(1), 37–50.

Leibel, R. L., Rosenbaum, M., & Hirsch, J. (1995). Changes in energy expenditure resulting from altered body weight. *New England Journal of Medicine, 332*(10), 621–628.

Lemley, B. (1986, June 22). I'm not a nerd. *Parade Magazine*, pp. 8–9.

Lenzenweger, M. F., Cornblatt, B. A., & Putnick, M. (1991). Schizotypy and sustained attention. *Journal of Abnormal Psychology, 100*(1), 84–89.

Lenzenweger, M. F., & Gottesman, I. I. (1994). Schizophrenia. In V. S. Ramachandran (Ed.), *Encyclopedia of human behavior*. San Diego, CA: Academic.

Leonard, C. M. (1997). Language and the prefrontal cortex. In: N. A. Krasnegor, G. R. Lyon, et al. (Eds). *Development of the prefrontal cortex: Evolution, neurobiology, and behavior*. Baltimore: Paul H. Brookes.

Leor, J., Poole, W. K., & Kloner, R. A. (1996). Sudden cardiac death triggered by earthquake. *New England Journal of Medicine, 334*(7), 413.

Lepore, S. J., Evans, G. W., & Schneider, M. L. (1992). Role of control and social support in explaining the stress of hassles and crowding. *Environment & Behavior, 24*(6), 795–811.

Lepper, M. R., Keavney, M., & Drake, M. (1996). Intrinsic motivation and extrinsic rewards. *Review of Educational Research, 66*(1), 5–32.

Lerner, R. M., & von Eye, A. (1992). Sociobiology and human development: Arguments and evidence. *Human Development, 35*(1), 12–33.

Leslie, K., & Ogilvie, R. (1996). Vestibular dreams: The effect of rocking on dream mentation. Dreaming: *Journal of the Association for the Study of Dreams, 6*(1), 1–16.

Lester, B. M., LaGasse, L. L., & Seifer, R. (1998). Cocaine exposure and children: The meaning of subtle effects. *Science, 282*(5389), 633–634.

Lester, D. (1990). Biorhythms and the timing of death. *Skeptical Inquirer, 14*(4), 410–411.

Lett, J. (1990). A field guide to critical thinking. *Skeptical Inquirer, 14*, 153–160.

Lettvin, J. Y. (1961). Two remarks on the visual system of the frog. In W. Rosenblith (Ed.), *Sensory communication*. Cambridge, MA: MIT Press.

Leutwyler, K. (1996). Paying attention. *Scientific American, 275*(2), 12–14.

Levant, R. F. (1996). The new psychology of men. *Professional Psychology: Research & Practice, 27*(3), 259–265.

LeVay, S. (1993). *The sexual brain*. Cambridge, MA: MIT Press.

Leventhal, E. A., Leventhal, H., Shacham, S., & Easterling, D. V. (1989). Active coping reduces reports of pain from childbirth. *Journal of Consulting & Clinical Psychology, 57*(3), 365–371.

Levesque, M. F., & Neuman, T. (1999). Human trials to begin. *Spinal Cord Society Newsletter, 246*, 3–4.

Levi, A. M. (1998). Are defendants guilty if they were chosen in a lineup? *Law & Human Behavior, 22*(4), 389–407.

Levine, J. M., & Moreland, R. L. (1990). Progress in small group research. *Annual Review of Psychology, 41*, 485–634.

Levine, M., Toro, P. A., & Perkins, D. V., (1993). Social and community interventions. *Annual Review of Psychology, 44*, 525–558.

Levine, R. (1998). *A geography of time*. New York: Basic.

Levinger, G. (1986). Editor's page. *Journal of Social Issues, 42*(3).

Levinson, D. J. (1986). A conception of adult development. *American Psychologist, 41*(1), 3–13.

Levinson, D. J., & Levinson, J. D. (1996). *The seasons of a woman's life*. New York: Knopf.

Levis, D. J. (1989). The case for a return to a two-factor theory of avoidance: The failure of non-fear interpretations. In S. B. Klein & R. R. Mower (Eds.), *Contemporary learning theories*. Hillsdale, NJ: Erlbaum.

Levy, D. A. (1989). Social support and the media: Analysis of responses by radio psychology talk show hosts. *Professional Psychology: Research & Practice, 20*(2), 73–78.

Levy, J., & Reid, M. (1976). Cerebral organization. *Science*, 337–339.

Lewis, M. (1995). Self-conscious emotions. *American Scientist, 83*, 68–78.

Lewis, M., & Brooks-Gunn, J. (1979). *Social cognition and the acquisition of self*. New York: Plenum.

Lewis, P. S., Goodman, S. H., & Fandt, P. M. (1995). *Management*. St Paul, MN: West.

Lewy, A. J., et al. (1998). Morning vs evening light treatment of patients with winter depression. *Archives of General Psychiatry, 55*(10), 890–896

Lichtenstein, E. (1982). The smoking problem: A behavioral perspective. *Journal of Consulting and Clinical Psychology, 50*, 804–819.

Lidderdale, J. M., & Walsh, J. J. (1998). The effects of social support on cardiovascular reactivity and perinatal outcome. *Psychology & Health, 13*(6), 1061–1070.

Light, P. (1997). Computers for learning. *Journal of Child Psychology & Psychiatry & Allied Disciplines, 38*(5), 497–504.

Lightsey, O. R. Jr. (1996). What leads to wellness? The role of psychological resources in well-being. *Counseling Psychologist, 24*(4), 589–759.

Lilienfeld, S. (1998). Pseudoscience in contemporary clinical psychology. *Clinical Psychologist, 51*(4), 3–9.

Lilienfeld, S. O. (1999, September–October). Projective measures of personality and psychopathology. *Skeptical Inquirer*, 32–39.

Lilly, J. C. (1972). *The center of the cyclone*. New York: Julian Press.

Linde, K., et al. (1996). St. John's wort for depression. *British Medical Journal, 313*, 253–258.

Lindemann, B. (1996).Taste reception. *Physiological Reviews, 76*(3), 719–748.

Lindsay, D. S. (1998). Depolarizing views on recovered memory experiences. In: S. J Lynn, K. M. McConkey, et al. (Eds.) *Truth in memory*. New York: Guilford Press.

Lindsay, E. W., Mize, J., & Pettit, G. S. (1997). Differential pay patterns of mothers and fathers of sons and daughters. *Sex Roles, 37*(9–10), 643–661.

Lindstrom, T. C. (1995). Anxiety and adaptation in bereavement. *Anxiety, Stress & Coping: An International Journal, 8*(3), 251–261.

Linton, M. (1979, July). I remember it well. *Psychology Today*, 81–86.

Lipman, J. J., Miller, B. E., Mays, K. S., Miller, M. N., et al. (1990). Peak B-endorphin concentration in cerebrospinal fluid: Reduced in chronic pain patients and increased during the placebo response. *Psychopharmacology, 102*(1), 112–116.

Lipschitz, D. S., Kaplan, M. L., Sorkenn, J., & Chorney, P. (1996). Childhood abuse, adult assault, and dissociation. *Comprehensive Psychiatry, 37*(4), 261–266.

Lipsey, M. W., & Wilson, D. B. (1993). The efficacy of psychological, educational, and behavioral treatment. *American Psychologist, 48*(12), 1181–1209.

Liu, X., Matochik, J. A., Cadet, J., et al. (1998). Smaller volume of prefrontal lobe in polysubstance abusers. *Neuropsychopharmacology, 18*(4), 243–252.

Lobo, L. L., & Tufik, S. (1997). Effects of alcohol on sleep parameters of sleep-deprived healthy volunteers. *Sleep, 20*(1), 52–59.

Loeber, R., & Hay, D. (1997). Key issues in the development of aggression and violence from childhood to early adulthood. *Annual Review of Psychology, 48*, 371–410.

Loehlin, J. C., McCrae, R. R., Costa, P. T., & John, O. (1998). Heritabilities of common and measure-specific components of the Big Five personality factors. *Journal of Research in Personality, 32*(4), 431–453.

Loftus, E. (1979, November). Words that could save your life. *Psychology Today, 102*, 105–106.

Loftus, E. (1980). *Memory*. Reading MA: Addison-Wesley.

Loftus, E. (1993a). Psychologists in the eyewitness world. *American Psychologist, 48*(5), 550–552.

Loftus, E. (1993b). The reality of repressed memories. *American Psychologist, 48*(5), 518–537.

Loftus, E., & Ketcham, K. (1991). *Witness for the defense*. New York: St. Martin's Press.

Loftus, E., & Loftus, G. (1980). On the permanence of stored information in the human brain. *American Psychologist, 35*, 409–420.

Loftus, E., & Palmer, J. C. (1974). Reconstruction of automobile destruction: An example of interaction between language and memory. *Journal of Verbal Learning and Verbal Behavior, 13*, 585–589.

Loftus, E. F. (1994). The repressed memory controversy. *American Psychologist, 49*(5), 443-444.

Loftus, G. R., & Mackworth, N. H. (1978). Cognitive determinants of fixation location during picture viewing. *Journal of Experimental Psychology: Human Perception and Performance, 4*, 565–572.

Lohr, J. M., Tolin, D. F., & Lilienfeld, S. O. (1998). Efficacy of eye movement desensitization and reprocessing. *Behavior Therapy, 29*(1), 123–156.

Long, D. M. (1991). Fifteen years of transcutaneous electrical stimulation for pain control. *Stereotactic & Functional Neurosurgery, 56*(1), 2–19.

Long, E. C., & Andrews, D. W. (1990). Perspective taking as a predictor of marital adjustment. *Journal of Personality & Social Psychology, 59*(1), 126–131.

Long, G. M. (1994). Exercises for training vision and dynamic visual acuity among college students. *Perceptual & Motor Skills, 78*(3, Pt 1), 1049–1050.

Long, V. 0. (1989). Relation of masculinity to self-esteem and self-acceptance in male professionals, college students, and clients. *Journal of Counseling Psychology, 36*(1), 84–87.

Loo, R., & Thorpe, K. (1998). Attitudes toward women's roles in society. *Sex Roles, 39*(11–12), 903–912.

Lopez, R. (1997). The practical impact of current research and issues in intelligence test interpretation and use for multicultural populations. *School Psychology Review, 26*(2), 249–254.

López, S. R., & Guarnaccia, P. J. J. (2000). Cultural psychopathology. *Annual Review of Psychology, 51*, 571–598.

Lore, R. K., & Schultz, L. A. (1993). Control of human aggression. *American Psychologist, 48(1)*, 16–25.

Lorenz, K. (1937). Imprinting. *Auk, 54*, 245–273.

Lorenz, K. (1962). *King Solomon's ring.* New York: Time.

Lorenz, K. (1966). *On aggression.* (M. Kerr-Wilson, Trans.). New York: Harcourt Brace Jovanovich.

Lorenz, K. (1974). *The eight deadly sins of civilized man.* (M. Kerr-Wilson, Trans.). New York: Harcourt Brace Jovanovich.

Lovaas, O., & Simmons, J. (1969). Manipulation of self-destruction in three retarded children. *Journal of Applied Behavior Analysis, 2*, 143–157.

Low, K. G., & Feissner, J. M. (1998). Seasonal affective disorder in college students: Prevalence and latitude. *Journal of American College Health, 47*(3), 135–137.

Lubinski, D. (2000). Scientific and social significance of assessing individual differences

Luborsky, L., et al. (1997). The psychotherapist matters. *Clinical Psychology: Science & Practice, 4*(1), 53–65.

Lucas, F., & Sclafani, A. (1990). Hyperphagia in rats produced by a mixture of fat and sugar. *Physiology & Behavior, 47*(1), 51–55.

Luce, G. G. (1965). *Current research on sleep and dreams.* Health Service Publication, No. 1389. U.S. Department of Health, Education, and Welfare.

Luckie, W. R., & Smethurst, W. (1998). *Study power.* Cambridge, MA: Brookline.

Ludwig, T. D., Gray, T. W., & Rowell, A. (1998). Increasing recycling in academic buildings. *Journal of Applied Behavior Analysis, 31*(4), 683–686.

Luiselli, J. K. (1994). Behavioral medicine. *Encyclopedia of human behavior, Vol. 1*, 359–363.

Lumsden, C., & Wilson, E. O. (1983). *Promethean fire.* Cambridge, MA: Harvard University Press.

Luria, A. R. (1968). *The mind of a mnemonist.* New York: Basic.

Luster, T., & Dubow, E. (1992). Home environment and maternal intelligence as predictors of verbal intelligence. *Merrill-Palmer Quarterly, 38(2)*, 151–175.

Luszcz, M. A., & Bryan, J. (1999). Toward understanding age-related memory loss in late adulthood. *Gerontology, 45*(1), 2–9.

Luxem, M., & Christophersen, E. (1994). Behavioral toilet training in early childhood: Research, practice, and implications. *Journal of Developmental & Behavioral Pediatrics, 15*(5), 370–378.

Lykken, D. T. (1995). *The antisocial personalities.* Hillsdale, NJ: Erlbaum.

Lykken, D. T. (1998). *A tremor in the blood: Uses and abuses of the lie detector.* New York: Plenum.

Lykken, D. T., McGue, M., Tellegen, A., & Bouchar, T. J. (1992). Emergenesis. *American Psychologist, 47*, 1565–1567.

Lyons, P., & Rittner, B. (1998). The construction of the crack babies phenomenon as a social problem. *American Journal of Orthopsychiatry, 68*(2), 313–320.

Lyubomirsky, S., & Tucker, K. L. (1998). Implications of individual differences in subjective happiness for perceiving, interpreting, and thinking about life events. *Motivation & Emotion, 22*(2), 155–186.

Lyznicki, J. M., Doege, T. C., Davis, R. M., & Williams, M. A. (1998). Sleepiness, driving, and motor vehicle crashes. *Journal of the American Medical Association, 279*(23), 1908–1913.

Maas, J. (1999). *Power sleep.* New York: Harper-Collins.

Mabry, J. H. (1998). Something for the future. *Analysis of Verbal Behavior, 15*, 129–130.

Maccoby, E. E. (1990). Gender and relationships: A developmental account. *American Psychologist, 45*(4), 513–520.

Maccoby, E. E., & Jacklin, C. N. (1974). *The psychology of sex differences.* Stanford, CA: Stanford University Press.

MacCoun, R. J. (1993). Drugs and the law: A psychological analysis of drug prohibition. *Psychological Bulletin, 113*(3), 497–512.

MacHovec, F. (1994). Near-death experiences: Psychotherapeutic aspects. *Psychotherapy in Private Practice, 13*(3), 99–105.

Mack, J. E. (1986). Adolescent suicide: An architectural model. In G. L. Klerman (Ed.), *Suicide and depression among adolescents and young adults.* Washington, DC: American Psychiatric Press.

Mackey, M. C. (1995). Women's evaluation of their childbirth performance. *Maternal-Child Nursing Journal, 23*(2), 57–72.

Macy, P. (1990, November). Research with animals and the new zeitgeist. *American Psychologist,* 1269.

Maddi, S. R., Kahn, S., & Maddi, K. L. (1998). The effectiveness of hardiness training. *Consulting Psychology Journal: Practice & Research, 50*(2), 78–86.

Madigan, S., & O'Hara, R. (1992). Short-term memory at the turn of the century. *American Psychologist, 47(2)*, 170–174.

Madon, S., Jussim, L., & Eccles, J. (1997). In search of the powerful self-fulfilling prophecy.

Madsen, C. H. Jr., Becher, W. C., Thomas, D. R., Koser, L., & Plager, E. (1968). An analysis of the reinforcing function of "sit down" commands. In R. K. Parker (Ed.), *Readings in educational psychology.* Boston: Allyn & Bacon.

Magee, W. J., Eaton, W. W., & Wittchen, H. (1996). Agoraphobia, simple phobia, and social phobia in the national comorbidity survey. *Archives of General Psychiatry, 53*(2), 159–168.

Magid, K. (1988). *High risk: Children without a conscience.* New York: Bantam.

Maguire, E. A., Frackowiak, R. S. J., & Frith, C. D. (1997). Recalling routes around London: Activation of the hippocampus in taxi drivers. *Journal of Neuroscience, 17*(8), 7103.

Maier, N. R. F. (1949). *Frustration.* New York: McGraw-Hill.

Major, B., Schmidlin, A. M., & Williams, L. (1990). *Journal of Personality & Social Psychology, 58*(4), 634–643.rMalamuth, N. M., & Donnerstein, E. (1982). The effects of aggressive-pornographic mass media stimuli. *Advances in Experimental Social Psychology, 15*, 103–136.

Malinosky-Rummell, R., & Hansen, D. R. (1993). Long-term consequences of childhood physical abuse. *Psychological Bulletin, 114*(1), 68–79.

Malnic, B., Hirono, J., & Buck, L. B. (1999). Combinatorial receptor codes for odors. *Cell, 96*(5), 713.

Maloney, A. (1999). Preference ratings of images representing archetypal themes. *Journal of Analytical Psychology, 44*(1) 101–116.

Man tells how rod ran through head. (1981, September 24). *Los Angeles Times,* p. A3.

Mandler, J. M., & McDonough, L. (1998). On developing a knowledge base in infancy. *Developmental Psychology, 34*(6), 1274–1288.

Mangun, G. R. (1995). Neural mechanisms of visual selective attention. *Psychophysiology, 32*(1), 4–18.

Manschreck, T. C. (1996). Delusional disorder: The recognition and management of paranoia. *Journal of Clinical Psychiatry, 57*(3, Suppl.), 32–38.

Mansouri, A., & Adityanjee. (1995). Delusion of pregnancy in males: A case report and literature review. *Psychopathology, 28*(6), 307–311.

Mantyla, T. (1986). Optimizing cue effectiveness: Recall of 600 incidentally learned words. *Journal of Experimental Psychology: Learning, Memory, and Cognition, 12*(1), 66–71.

Margolin, G., & Gordis, E. B. (2000). The effects of family and community violence on children. *Annual Review of Psychology, 51*, 445–479.

Marion, S. L., Shayka, J. J., & Marcus, S. C. (1996). A short computer interview for obtaining psychiatric diagnoses. *Psychiatric Services, 47*(3), 293–297.

Markovits, H., & Nantel, G. (1989). The belief-bas effect in the production and evaluation of logical conclusions. *Memory and Cognition, 17*, 11–17.

Marks, D. F. (1990). Comprehensive commentary, insightful criticism. *Skeptical Inquirer, 14*(3), 413–418.

Marks, D. F., & Kammann, R. (1979). *The psychology of the psychic.* Buffalo, NY: Prometheus.

Markson, E. W. (1995). To be or not to be: Assisted suicide revisited. *Omega: Journal of Death & Dying, 31*(3), 221–235.

Markus, H., & Kitayama, S. (1991). Culture and the self: Implications for cognition, emotion, and motivation. *Psychological Bulletin, 98*, 224–253.

Markus, H., Kitayama, S., & VandenBos, G. R. (1996). The mutual interactions of culture and emotion. *Psychiatric Services, 47*(3), 225–226.

Markus, H., & Nurius, P. (1986). Possible selves. *American Psychologist, 41*, 954–969.

Markus, H. R., & Kitayama, S. (1998). The cultural psychology of personality. *Journal of Cross-Cultural Psychology, 29*(1), 63–87.

Marlatt, G. A., Baer, J. S., Dononovan, D. M., & Kivlahan, D. R. (1988). Addictive behaviors: Etiology and treatment. *Annual Review of Psychology, 39*, 223–252.

Marlatt, G. A., & Gordon, J. R. (Eds.). (1985). *Relapse prevention: Maintenance strategies in the treatment of addictive behaviors.* New York: Guilford.

Marmor, J. (Ed.) (1980). *Homosexual behavior: A modern reappraisal.* New York: Basic.

Marques, P., Bradley, J., Shappee, J., & Marques, C. (1982). *Bienestar: Health, well-being and lifestyle choices for Pinal County.* Project West Pinal, University of Arizona Health Sciences Center.

Marrs, R. W. (1995). A meta-analysis of bibliotherapy studies. *American Journal of Community Psychology, 23*(6), 843–870.

Marsella, A. J. (1998). Urbanization, mental health, and social deviancy. *American Psychologist, 53*(6), 624–634.

Marston, P. J., et al. (1998). The subjective experience of intimacy, passion, and commitment in heterosexual loving relationships. *Personal Relationships, 5*(1) 15–30.

Martens, R., & Trachet, T. (1998). *Making sense of astrology.* Amherst, MA: Prometheus.

Martin, K. A., Moritz, S. E., & Hall, C. R. (1999). Imagery use in sport. *Sport Psychologist, 13*(3), 245–268.

Martin, M. A. (1985). Students' applications of self-questioning study techniques: An investigation of their efficacy. *Reading Psychology, 6*(1–2), 69–83.

Martin, P. Y., & Benton, D. (1999). The influence of a glucose drink on a demanding working memory task. *Physiology & Behavior, 67*(1), 69–74.

Martin, S. (1995, January). Field's status unaltered by the influx of women. *APA Monitor,* p. 9.

Marx, B. P., Gross, A. M., & Adams, H. E. (1999). The effect of alcohol on the responses of sexually coercive and noncoercive men to an experimental rape analogue. *Sexual Abuse: Journal of Research & Treatment, 11*(2), 131–145.

Marx, J. A., Gyorky, Z. K., Royalty, G. M., & Stern, T. E. (1992). Use of self-help books in psychotherapy. *Professional Psychology: Research & Practice, 23*(4), 300–305.

Maslach, C. (1982). *Burnout: The cost of caring.* Englewood Cliffs, NJ: Prentice-Hall.

Maslow, A. H. (1954). *Motivation and personality.* New York: Harper.

Maslow, A. H. (1967). Self-actualization and beyond. In J. F. T. Bugental (Ed.), *Challenges of humanistic psychology.* New York: McGraw-Hill.

Maslow, A. H. (1968). *Toward a psychology of being.* New York: Van Nostrand.

Maslow, A. H. (1969). *The psychology of science.* Chicago: Henry Regnery.

Maslow, A. H. (1970). *Motivation and personality.* New York: Harper & Row.

Maslow, A. H. (1971). *The farther reaches of human nature.* New York: Viking.

Masse, L. C., & Tremblay, R. E. (1997). Behavior of boys in kindergarten and the onset of substance use during adolescence. *Archives of General Psychiatry, 54*(1), 62.

Masters, W. H., & Johnson, V. E. (1966). *Human sexual response.* Boston: Little, Brown.

Masters, W. H., & Johnson, V. E. (1970). *The pleasure bond: A new look at sexuality and commitment.* Boston: Little, Brown.

Matheny, K. B., Brack, G. L., McCarthy, C. J., & Penick, J. M. (1996). The effectiveness of cognitively-based approaches in treating stress-related symptoms. *Psychotherapy, 33*(2), 305–320.

Matias, R., & Cohn, J. F. (1993). Are max-specified infant facial expressions during face-to-face interaction consistent with differential emotions theory? *Developmental Psychology, 29*(3), 524–531.

Matossian, M. K. (1982). Ergot and the Salem witchcraft affair. *American Scientist, 70,* 355–357.

Matson, J. L., Sevin, J. A., Fridley D., & Love, S. R. (1990). Increasing spontaneous language in three autistic children. *Journal of Applied Behavior Analysis, 23*(2), 223–227.

Matsuda, L. A., Lolait, S. J., Brownstein, M. J., Young, A. C., & Bonner, T. I. (1990). Structure of a cannabinoid receptor and functional expression of the cloned cDNA. *Nature, 346*(6284), 561–564.

Matthews, D. B. (1990). A comparison of burnout in selected occupational fields. *Career Development Quarterly, 38*(3), 230–239.

Mattson, S. N., Riley, E. P., Gramling, L., et al. (1998). Neuropsychological comparison of alcohol-exposed children with or without physical features of fetal alcohol syndrome. *Neuropsychology, 12*(1), 146–153.

Mauer, M. H., Burnett, K. F., Ouellette, E. A., Ironson, G. H., et al., (1999). Medical hypnosis and orthopedic hand surgery. *International Journal of Clinical & Experimental Hypnosis, 47*(2), 144–161.

Maupin, E. W. (1965). Individual differences in response to a Zen meditation exercise. *Journal of Consulting Psychology, 29,* 139–145.

Mauthner, N. S. (1999). "Feeling low and feeling really bad about feeling low": Women's experiences of motherhood and postpartum depression. *Canadian Psychology, 40*(2), 143–161.

May, M. (1996). Resistance: Friend or foe? *American Journal of Psychotherapy, 50*(1), 32–44.

Mayer, J. D., & Hanson, E. (1995). Mood-congruent judgment over time. *Personality & Social Psychology Bulletin, 21*(3) 237–244.

Mayer, R. E. (1995). *Thinking, problem solving, and cognition.* New York: Freeman.

McAfee, T., et al. (1998). The role of tobacco intervention in population-based health care. *American Journal of Preventive Medicine, 14*(3S), 46–52.

McBride, W. J., Murphy, J. M., & Ikemoto, S. (1999). Localization of brain reinforcement mechanisms. *Behavioural Brain Research, 101*(2), 129–152.

McCabe, M. P. (1992). A program for the treatment of inhibited sexual desire in males. *Psychotherapy, 29*(2), 288–296.

McCann, S. L., & Stewin, L. L. (1988). Worry, anxiety, and preferred length of sleep. *Journal of Genetic Psychology, 149*(3), 413–418.

McCardel, J., & Murray, E. J. (1974). Nonspecific factors in weekend encounter groups. *Journal of Consulting Psychology, 42,* 337–345.

McCarley, R. W. (1998). Dreams: Disguise of forbidden wishes or transparent reflections of a distinct brain state? In R. M. Bilder, F. F. LeFever, et al. (Eds.), *Neuroscience of the mind on the centennial of Freud's Project for a Scientific Psychology.* New York: New York Academy of Sciences.

McCarthy, B. W. (1995). Bridges to sexual desire. *Journal of Sex Education & Therapy, 21*(2), 132–141.

McCartney, K., Bernieri, F., & Harris, M. J. (1990). Growing up and growing apart: A developmental meta-analysis of twin studies. *Psychological Bulletin, 107*(2), 226–237.

McCarty, R. (1998, November). Making the case for animal research. *APA Monitor,* p. 18.

McCaul, K. D., & Malott, J. M. (1984). Distraction and coping with pain. *Psychological Bulletin, 95,* 516–533.

McCleary, R., Chew, K. S., Hellsten, J. J., & Flynn-Bransford, M. (1991). Age- and sex-specific cycles in United States suicides, 1973 to 1985. *American Journal of Public Health, 81*(11), 1494–1497.

McClelland, D. C. (1961). *The achieving society.* New York: Van Nostrand.

McClelland, D. C. (1965). Achievement and entrepreneurship. *Journal of Personality & Social Psychology, 1,* 389–393.

McClelland, D. C. (1973). Testing for competence rather than "intelligence." *American Psychologist, 28,* 1–14.

McClelland, D. C. (1975). *Power: The inner experience.* New York: Irvington.

McClelland, D. C. (1994). The knowledge-testing-educational complex strikes back. *American Psychologist, 49*(1), 66–69.

McClelland, D. C., & Cheriff, A. D. (1997). The immunoenhancing effects of humor on secretory IgA and resistance to respiratory infections. *Psychology & Health, 12*(3), 329–344.

McClelland, D. C., & Pilon, D. A. (1983). Sources of adult motives in patterns of parent behavior in early childhood. *Journal of Personality & Social Psychology, 44,* 564–574.

McClelland, L., & Cook, S. W. (1980). Promoting energy conservation in master-metered apartments through group financial incentives. *Journal of Applied and Social Psychology, 10,* 20–31.

McCormick, J., & Kalb, C. (1998, June 15). Dying for a drink. *Newsweek,* pp. 30–34.

McCrae, R. R. (1987). Creativity, divergent thinking, and openness to experience. *Journal of Personality & Social Psychology, 52*(6), 1258–1265.

McCrae, R. R., & Costa, P. T. (1990). *Personality in adulthood.* New York: Guilford.

McCrae, R. R., & Costa, P. T. (1997). Personality trait structure as a human universal. *American Psychologist, 52*(5), 509–516.

McCrae, R. R., Costa, P. T., de Lima, M. P., Simdes, A., et al. (1999). Age differences in personality across the adult life span: Parallels in five cultures. *Developmental Psychology, 35*(2), 466–477.

McDaniel, M. A., & Schlager, M. S. (1990). Discovery learning and transfer of problem-solving skills. *Cognition & Instruction, 7*(2), 129–159.

McDonald, S. M. (1989). Sex bias in the representation of male and female characters in children's picture books. *Journal of Genetic Psychology, 150*(4), 389–401.

McEachin, J. J., Smith, T., & Lovaas, O. I. (1993). Long-term outcome for children with autism who received early intensive behavioral treatment. *American Journal of Mental Retardation, 97*(4), 359–372.

McGaugh, J. L. (1983). Hormonal influences on memory. *Annual Review of Psychology, 34,* 297–323.

McGee, M. G., & Snyder, M. (1975). Attribution and behavior: Two field studies. *Journal of Personality & Social Psychology, 32,* 185–190.

McGinnies, E. (1949). Emotionality and perceptual defense. *Psychological Review, 56,* 244–251.

McGinnis, J. M., & Foege, W. H. (1993). Actual causes of death in the United States. *Journal of the American Medical Association, 270*(18), 2207–2212.

McGregor, D. (1960). *The human side of enterprise.* New York: McGraw-Hill.

McGregor, I., & Little, B. R. (1998). Personal projects, happiness, and meaning. *Journal of Personality and Social Psychology, 74*(2), 494–512.

McIntosh, D. N. (1996). Facial feedback hypotheses. *Motivation & Emotion, 20*(2), 121–147.

McIntosh, W. D., Harlow, T. F., & Martin, L. L. (1995). Linkers and nonlinkers: Goal beliefs as a moderator of the effects of everyday hassles on rumination, depression, and physical complaints. *Journal of Applied Social Psychology, 25*(14), 1231–1244.

McKean, K. (1984, May). The fine art of reading voters' minds. *Discover,* pp. 66–69.

McKean, K. (1985, April). Of two minds: Selling the right brain. *Discover,* pp. 30–40.

McKean, K. J. (1994). Using multiple risk factors to assess the behavioral, cognitive, and affective effects of learned helplessness. *Journal of Psychology, 128*(2), 177–183.

McKellar, P. (1995). Creative imagination: Hypnagogia and surrealism. *Journal of Mental Imagery, 19*(1–2), 33–42.

McKenna, K. Y., A. & Bargh, J. A. (1998). Coming out in the age of the Internet: Identity "demarginalization" through virtual group participation. *Journal of Personality & Social Psychology, 75*(3), 681–694.

McKenna, M. W., & Ossoff, E. P. (1998). Age differences in children's comprehension of a popular television program. *Child Study Journal, 28*(1), 52–68.

McKenzie-Mohr, D., & Oskamp, S. (1995). Psychology and sustainability. *Journal of Social Issues, 51*(4), 1–14.

McKim, W. A. (1997). *Drugs and behavior.* Upper Saddle River, NJ: Prentice Hall.

McKinzie, S. J., Williamson, D. A., & Cubic, B. A. (1993). Stable and reactive body image distortions in bulimia nervosa. *Behavior Therapy, 24*(2), 195–207.

McKnight, J. D., & Glass, D. C. (1995). Perceptions of control, burnout, and depressive symptomatology. *Journal of Consulting & Clinical Psychology, 63*(3), 490–494.

McLauglin, S., & Margolskee, R. F. (1994). The sense of taste. *American Scientist, 82*, 538–545.

McLennan, J. (1992). "University blues": Depression among tertiary students during an academic year. *British Journal of Guidance & Counselling, 20*(2), 186–192.

McLoyd, V. (1998). Socioeconomic disadvantage and child development. *American Psychologist, 53*(2), 185–204.

McManus, I. C., Sik, G., Cole, D. R., Muellon, A. F., et al. (1988). The development of handedness in children. *British Journal of Developmental Psychology, 6*(3), 257–273.

McMullan, W. E., & Stocking, J. R. (1978). Conceptualizing creativity in three dimensions. *Journal of Creative Behavior, 12*, 161–167.

McMurdo, M. E., & Gaskell, A. (1991). Dark adaptation and falls in the elderly. *Gerontology, 37*(4), 221–224.

McRoberts, C., Burlingame, G. M., & Hoag, M. J. (1998). Comparative efficacy of individual and group psychotherapy. *Group Dynamics, 2*(2), 101–117.

Mead, M. (1935). *Sex and temperament in three primitive societies.* New York: Morrow.

Medin, D. L., & Ross, B. H. (1992). *Cognitive psychology.* Fort Worth, TX: Harcourt Brace Jovanovich.

Mednick, M. T. (1989). On the politics of psychological constructs: Stop the bandwagon, I want to get off. *American Psychologist, 44*(8), 1118–1123.

Mehren, E. (1994, April 8). Study finds most child care lacking. *Los Angeles Times,* p. E-5.

Meichenbaum, D., Henshaw, D., & Himel, N. (1982). Coping with stress as a problem-solving process. In H. W. Krohne & L. Laux (Eds.), *Achievement, stress, and anxiety.* New York: Hemisphere.

Meier, R. P. (1991). Language acquisition by deaf children. *American Scientist, 79*(1), 60–70.

Meleshko, K. G., & Alden, L. E. (1993). Anxiety and self-disclosure. *Journal of Personality & Social Psychology, 64*(6), 1000–1009.

Melton, G. B. (1989). Public policy and private prejudice. *American Psychologist, 44*(6), 933–940.

Meltzoff, A. N., & Moore, M. K. (1983). Newborn infants imitate adult facial gestures. *Child Development, 54*, 702–709.

Meltzoff, J. (1998). *Critical thinking about research.* Washington, DC: American Psychological Association.

Melzack, R. (1974). Shutting the gate on pain. In *Science Year: The World Book science annual.* Palo Alto, CA: Field.

Melzack, R. (1984). The myth of painless childbirth. *Pain, 19*, 321–337.

Melzack, R. (1993). Pain: Past, present and future. *Canadian Journal of Experimental Psychology, 47*(4), 615–629.

Melzack, R., & Wall, P. D. (1996). *The challenge of pain.* Harmondworth, UK: Penguin.

Mendolia, M., Moore, J., & Tesser, A. (1996). Dispositional and situational determinants of repression. *Journal of Personality & Social Psychology, 70*(4), 856–867.

Menzel, C. R. (1999). Unprompted recall and reporting of hidden objects by a chimpanzee (*Pan troglodytes*) after extended delays. *Journal of Comparative Psychology, 113*(4), 426–434.

Menzel, P., Eisert, S., Mann, C. C., & Kennedy, P. (1994). *Material world: A global family portrait.* Sierra Club Books.

Menzies, R. G., & Clarke, J. C. (1993). A comparison of *in vivo* and vicarious exposure in the treatment of childhood water phobia. *Behaviour Research and Therapy, 31*(1), 9–15.

Mercer, J. G., Beck, B., Burlet, A., et al. (1998). Leptin (ob) mRNA and hypothalamic NPY in food-deprived/refed Syrian hamsters. *Physiology & Behavior, 64*(2), 191–195.

Merckelbach, H., & Muris, P. (1997). The etiology of childhood spider phobia. *Behaviour Research & Therapy, 35*(11), 1031–1034.

Merenda, P. F. (1996). BASC: Behavior assessment system for children. *Measurement & Evaluation in Counseling & Development, 28*(4), 229–232.

Merikle, P. M., & Skanes, H. E. (1992). Subliminal self-help audiotapes: A search for placebo effects. *Journal of Applied Psychology, 77*(5), 772–776.

Mermelstein, R. (1986). Social support and smoking cessation and maintenance. *Journal of Consulting & Clinical Psychology, 54*(4), 447–453.

Merritt, J. M., Stickgold, R., Pace-Schott, E., Williams, J., et al. (1994). Emotion profiles in the dreams of men and women. *Consciousness & Cognition, 3*(1), 46–60.

Mesquita, B., & Frijda, N. H. (1992). Cultural variations in emotions. *Psychological Bulletin, 112*(2), 179–204.

Messick, D. M., & Mackie, D. M. (1989). Intergroup relations. *Annual Review of Psychology, 40*, 45–81.

Messick, D. M., Wilke, H., Brewer, M., Kramer, R. M., Zemke, P. E., & Lui, L. (1983). Individual adaptations and structural change as solutions to social dilemmas. *Journal of Personality & Social Psychology, 44*, 294–309.

Metcalfe, J. (1986). Premonitions of insight predict impending error. *Journal of Experimental Psychology: Learning, Memory, and Cognition, 12*, 623–634.

Metzner, R. (1998). Hallucinogenic drugs and plants in psychotherapy and shamanism. *Journal of Psychoactive Drugs, 30*(4), 333–341.

Meyer, A. J., Nash, J. D., McAlister, A. L., Maccoby, N., & Farquhar, J. W. (1980). Skills training in a cardiovascular health education campaign. *Journal of Consulting and Clinical Psychology, 48*, 129–142.

Meyer, I. H. (1995). Minority stress and mental health in gay men. *Journal of Health & Social Behavior, 36*(1), 38–56.

Meyer, R. G., & Youngjohn, J. R. (1991). Effects of feedback and validity expectancy on responses in a lie detector interview. *Forensic Reports, 4(3),* 235–244.

Meyer-Bahlburg, H. F. L., Ehrhardt, A. A., Rosen, L. R., Gruen, R. S., et al. (1995). Prenatal estrogens and the development of homosexual orientation. *Developmental Psychology, 31*(1), 12–21.

Meyer-Bisch, C. (1996). Epidemiological evaluation of hearing damage related to strongly amplified music (personal cassette players, discotheques, rock concerts). *Audiology, 35*(3), 121–142.

Michalko, M. (1998). *Cracking creativity.* Berkeley, CA: Ten Speed Press.

Michel, D. E., & Chesky, K. S. (1995). A survey of music therapists using music for pain relief. *Arts in Psychotherapy, 22*(1), 49–51.

Michotte, A. (1963). *The perception of causality.* New York: Methuen/Basic.

Mickelson, K. D., Kessler, R. C., & Shaver, P. R. (1997). Adult attachment in a nationally representative sample. *Journal of Personality & Social Psychology, 73*(5), 1092–1106.

Middlemist, R. D., Knowles, E. S., & Matter, C. F. (1976). Personal space invasions in the lavatory: Suggestive evidence for arousal. *Journal of Personality and Social Psychology, 33*, 541–546.

Mielke, H. W. (1999). Lead in the inner cities. *American Scientist, 87*, 62–73.

Mikulincer, M., & Nachshon, O. (1991). Attachment styles and patterns of self-disclosure. *Journal of Personality & Social Psychology, 61*(2), 321–331.

Milgram, S. (1963). Behavioral study of obedience. *Journal of Abnormal and Social Psychology, 67*, 371–378.

Milgram, S. (1965). Some conditions of obedience and disobedience to authority. *Human Relations, 18,* 57–76.

Milgram, S. (1967, May). The small-world problem. *Psychology Today,* 61–67.

Milgram, S. (1970). The experience of living in the cities: A psychological analysis. *Science, 167,* 1461–1468.

Milgram, S. (1974). *Obedience to authority: An experimental view.* New York: Harper & Row.

Milgram, S., Bickman, L., & Berkowitz, L. (1969). Note on the drawing power of crowds of different size. *Journal of Personality & Social Psychology, 13,* 79–82.

Miller, A. H. (1998). Neuroendocrine and immune system interactions in stress and depression. *Psychiatric Clinics of North America, 21*(2), 443–463.

Miller, D. T., Turnbull, W., & McFarland, C. (1988). Particularistic and universalistic evaluation in the social comparison process. *Journal of Personality & Social Psychology, 55*(6), 908–917.

Miller, G. (1956). The magical number seven, plus or minus two: Some limits on our capacity for processing information. *Psychological Review, 63,* 81–87.

Miller, G. A. (1999). On knowing a word. *Annual Review of Psychology, 50,* 1–19.

Miller, L. C. (1990). Intimacy and liking: Mutual influence and the role of unique relationships. *Journal of Personality & Social Psychology, 59*(1), 50–60.

Miller, L. K. (1976). The design of better communities through the application of behavioral principles. In W. E. Craighead, A. E. Kazdin, & M. J. Mahone (Eds.), *Behavior modification: Principles, issues, and applications.* Boston: Houghton-Mifflin.

Miller, M. A., & Rahe, R. H. (1997). Life changes scaling for the 1990s. *Journal of Psychosomatic Research, 43*(3), 279–292.

Miller, N. E. (1944). Experimental studies of conflict. In J. McV. Hunt (Ed.), *Personality and the behavior disorders, Vol. I* (pp. 431–465). New York: Ronald Press.

Miller, N. E., & Bugelski, R. (1970). The influence of frustration imposed by the in-group on attitudes expressed toward out-groups. In R. I. Evans & R. M. Rozelle (Eds.), *Social psychology in life.* Boston: Allyn & Bacon.

Miller, T. Q., Smith, T. W., Turner, C. W., & Guijarro, M. L. (1996). Meta-analytic review of research on hostility and physical health. *Psychological Bulletin, 119*(2), 322348.

Miller, T. Q., Turner, C. W., Tindale, R. S., Posavac, E. J., et al. (1991). Reasons for the trend toward null findings in research on Type A behavior. *Psychological Bulletin, 110(3),* 469–485.

Miller, W. C. (1999). Fitness and fatness in relation to health. *Journal of Social Issues, 55*(2), 207–219.

Miller-Jones, D. (1989). Culture and testing. *American Psychologist, 44*(2), 360–366.

Millon, T. (1981) *Disorders of personality: DSM-III: Axis II.* New York: Wiley.

Milner, B. (1965). Memory disturbance after bilateral hippocampal lesions. In P. Milner, & S. Glickman (Eds.), *Cognitive processes and the brain* (pp. 97-111). Princeton, NJ: Van Nostrand.

Milton, J., & Wiseman, R. (1997). *Guidelines for extrasensory perception research.* Hertfordshire, England, UK: University of Hertfordshire Press.

Milton, J., & Wiseman, R. (1999a). Does psi exist? Lack of replication of an anomalous process of information transfer. *Psychological Bulletin, 125*(4), 387–391.

Milton, J., & Wiseman, R. (1999b). A meta-analysis of mass-media tests of extrasensory perception. *British Journal of Psychology, 90*(2), 235–240.

Milunsky, A. (1992). *Heredity and your family's health.* Boston: Houghton Mifflin.

Mineka, S., & Hamida, S. B. (1998). Observational and nonconscious learning. In W. T. O'Donohue, et al. (Eds.), *Learning and behavior therapy.* Boston: Allyn & Bacon

Miranda, J. (1992). Dysfunctional thinking is activated by stressful life events. *Cognitive Therapy & Research, 16*(4), 473–483.

Mirsky, A. F., & Duncan, C. C. (1986). Etiology and expression of schizophrenia. *Annual Review of Psychology, 37,* 291–319.

Mischel, W. (1968). *Personality and assessment.* New York: Wiley.

Mischel, W. (1973). Toward a cognitive social learning reconceptualization of personality. *Psychological Review, 80,* 252–283.

Mischel, W., & Shoda, Y. (1998). Reconciling processing dynamics and personality dispositions. *Annual Review of Psychology, 49,* 229–258.

Mitchell, C. W. (1995). Effects of subliminally presented auditory suggestions of itching on scratching behavior. *Perceptual & Motor Skills, 80*(1), 87–96.

Mitchell, D. (1987, February). Firewalking cults: Nothing but hot air. *Laser,* pp. 7–8.

Mitchell, D. B. (1989). How many memory systems? Evidence from aging. *Journal of Experimental Psychology: Learning, Memory, and Cognition, 15*(1), 31–49.

Mogg, K., Bradley, B. P., Hyare, H., & Lee, S. (1998). Selective attention to food-related stimuli in hunger. *Behaviour Research & Therapy, 36*(2), 227–237.

Mohanty, S., Pati, N. C., & Kumar, R. (1998). Effects of token economy on the rate of envelope making in the persons with mental retardation. *Social Science International, 14*(1-2), 84–97.

Mombaerts, P. (1999). Molecular biology of odorant receptors in vertebrates. *Annual Review of Neuroscience, 22,* 487–509.

Monahan, J. (1992). Mental disorder and violent behavior. *American Psychologist, 47*(4), 511–521.

Money, J. (1987). Sin, sickness, or status? *American Psychologist, 42*(4), 384–399.

Money, J., & Mathews, D. (1982). Prenatal exposure to virilizing progestins: An adult follow-up study of twelve women. *Archives of Sexual Behavior, 11,* 73–83.

Monfort, M., Martin, S. A., & Frederickson, W. (1990). Information-processing differences and laterality of students from different colleges and disciplines. *Perceptual & Motor Skills, 70*(1), 163–172.

Monmaney, T. (1987, September). Are we led by the nose? *Discover,* pp. 48–56.

Montague, J. (1996). Counseling families from diverse cultures: A nondeficit approach. *Journal of Multicultural Counseling & Development, 24*(1), 37–41.

Montgomery, G. (1989, March). The mind in motion. *Discover,* pp. 58–68.

Monti-Bloch, L., Jennings-White, C., Dolberg, D. S., & Berliner, D. L. (1994). The human vomeronasal system. *Psychoneuroendocrinology, 19*(5–7), 673–686.

Moody, R. (1975). *Life after life.* Covinda, GA: Mockingbird.

Moon, Y., & Nass, C. (1998). Are computers scapegoats? Attributions of responsibility in human-computer interaction. *International Journal of Human-Computer Studies, 49*(1), 79.

Moore, T. E. (1992). Subliminal perception: Facts and fallacies. *Skeptical Inquirer, 16,* 273–281.

Moore, T. E. (1995). Subliminal self-help auditory tapes: An empirical test of perceptual consequences. *Canadian Journal of Behavioural Science, 27*(1), 9–20.

Moore-Ede, M. C., Sulzman, F. M., & Fuller, C. A. (1982). *The clocks that time us.* Cambridge, MA: Harvard University Press.

Moos, R. H., & Swindle, R. W. (1990). Stressful life circumstances: Concepts and measures. *Stress Medicine, 6*(3), 171–178.

Morelli, G. A., Rogoff, B., Oppenheim, D., & Goldsmith, D. (1992). Cultural variation in infants' sleeping arrangements. *Developmental Psychology, 28*(4), 604–613.

Moreno, J. L. (1953). *Who shall survive?* New York: Beacon.

Morgan, J. D. (1995). Living our dying and our grieving: Historical and cultural attitudes. In H. Wass & R. A. Neimeyer (Eds.), *Dying: Facing the facts.* Washington, DC: Taylor & Francis.

Morgan, M. J., Hole, G. J., & Glennerster, A. (1990). Biases and sensitivities in geometrical illusions. *Vision Research, 30*(11), 1793–1810.

Morgenstern, J., Labouvie, E., McCrady, B. S., et al. (1997). Affiliation with Alcoholics Anonymous after treatment. *Journal of Consulting & Clinical Psychology, 65*(5), 768–777.

Moriarty, T. (1975, April). A nation of willing victims. *Psychology Today,* 43–50.

Moritz, A. P., & Zamchech, N. (1946). Sudden and unexpected deaths of young soldiers. *American Medical Association Archives of Pathology, 42,* 459–494.

Morrill, A. C., et al. (1996). Safer sex. *Journal of Consulting and Clinical Psychology, 64*(4), 819–828.

Moser, D. (1965, May 7). The nightmare of life with Billy. *Life.*

Mosher, D. L., & MacIan, P. (1994). College men and women respond to X-rated videos intended for male or female audiences: Gender and sexual scripts. *Journal of Sex Research, 31*(2), 99–113.

Moss, K. (1989). Performing the light-switch task in lucid dreams: A case study. *Journal of Mental Imagery, 13*(2), 135–137.

Mshelia, A. Y., & Lapidus, L. B. (1990). Depth picture perception in relation to cognitive style and training in non-Western children. *Journal of Cross-Cultural Psychology, 21*(4), 414–433.

Mueller, R., Behen, M. E., Rothermel, R. D., Muzik, O., et al. (1999). Brain organization for language in children, adolescents, and adults with left hemisphere lesion: A PET study. *Progress in Neuro-Psychopharmacology & Biological Psychiatry, 23*(4), 657668.

Mullen, P. E., Martin, J. L., Anderson, J. C., & Romans, S. E. (1996). The long-term impact of the physical, emotional, and sexual abuse of children: A community study. *Child Abuse & Neglect, 20*(1), 7–21.

Mullington, J., & Broughton, R. (1993). Scheduled naps in the management of daytime sleepiness in narcolepsy-cataplexy. *Sleep, 16*(5) 444–456.

Muris, P., & Merckelbach, H. (1999). Traumatic memories, eye movements, phobia, and panic. *Journal of Anxiety Disorders, 13*(1–2), 209–223.

Murphy, L. B., & Moriarty, A. E. (1976). *Vulnerability, coping and growth.* New Haven, CT: Yale University Press.

Murray, C. B., & Warden, M. R. (1992). Implications of self-handicapping strategies for academic achievement. *Journal of Social Psychology, 132*(1), 23–37.

Murray, F. S. (1980). Estimation of performance levels by students in introductory psychology. *Teaching of Psychology, 7,* 61–62.

Murray, J. B. (1995). Evidence for acupuncture's analgesic effectiveness and proposals for the physiological mechanisms involved. *Journal of Psychology, 129*(4), 443–461.

Murray, S. H., Touyz, S. W., & Beumont, P. J. V. (1996). Awareness and perceived influence of body ideals in the media: A comparison of eating disorder patients and the general community. *Eating Disorders: The Journal of Treatment & Prevention, 4*(1), 33–46.

Murray, S. L., & Holmes, J. G. (1993). Seeing virtues in faults. *Journal of Personality & Social Psychology, 65*(4), 707–722.

Murray, S. L., Holmes, J. G., & Griffin, D. W. (1996). The self-fulfilling nature of positive illusions in romantic relationships. *Journal of Personality & Social Psychology, 71*(6), 1155–1180.

Murrell, J., Farlow, M., Ghetti, B., & Benson, M. D. (1991). A mutation in the amyloid precursor protein associated with hereditary Alzheimer's disease. *Science, 254*(5028), 97–98.

Murstein, B. I., & Fontaine, P. A. (1993). The public's knowledge about psychologists and other mental health professionals. *American Psychologist, 48*(7), 839–845.

Mussen, P. H., Conger, J. J., Kagan, J., & Geiwitz, J. (1979). *Psychological development: A life span approach.* New York: Harper & Row.

Myers, M. M., Fifer, W. P., Schacffer, L., Sahni, R., et al. (1998). Effects of sleeping position and time after feeding on the organization of sleep/wake states in prematurely born infants. *Sleep, 21*(4), 343–349.

Nagel, K. L., & Jones, K. H. (1992a). Sociological factors in the development of eating disorders. *Adolescence, 27*(105), 107–113.

Nagel, K. L., & Jones, K. H. (1992b). Predisposition factors in anorexia nervosa. *Adolescence, 27*(106), 381–386.

Nagy, Z., Esiri, M. M., Jobst, K. A., & Morris, J. H. (1996). Clustering of pathological features in Alzheimer's disease. *Dementia, 7*(3), 121–127.

Naitoh, P., Kelly, T. L., & Englund, C. E. (1989). *Health effects of sleep deprivation.* U.S. Naval Health Research Center Report, No. 89-46.

Naka, M. (1998). The variables affecting the reliability of eyewitness testimony. *Japanese Journal of Psychonomic Science, 16*(2), 100–106.

Nanninga, R. (1997). The Astrotest: A tough match for astrologers. *Correlation, 15,* 14–20.

Nantais, K. M., & Schellenberg, E. G. (1999). The Mozart effect: An artifact of preference. *Psychological Science, 10*(4), 370–373.

Naranjo, C. (1970). Present-centeredness: Technique, prescription, and ideal. In J. Fagan & I. L. Shepherd (Eds), *What is Gestalt therapy?* New York: Harper & Row.

Narby, D. J., Cutler, B. L., & Moran, G. (1993). A meta-analysis of the association between authoritarians and jurors' perceptions of defendant culpability. *Journal of Applied Psychology, 78,* 34–42.

Nardi, P. M. (1992). "Seamless souls": An introduction to men's friendships. In P. M. Nardi (Ed.), *Men's friendships.* Newbury Park, CA: Sage.

Natale, V., & Cicogna, P. (1996). Circadian regulation of subjective alertness in morning and evening types. *EDRA: Environmental Design Research Association, 20*(4), 491–497.

Nathan, P. E., & Langenbucher, J. W. (1999). Psychopathology. *Annual Review of Psychology, 50,* 79–107.

Nathans, J., Thomas, P., Piantandia, R. L., Eddy, T. B., Shows, D. S., & Hogness, D. S. (1986). Molecular genetics of inherited variations in human color vision. *Science, 232,* 203–210.

National Institute of Child Health and Human Development (1999). The NICHD study of early child care.

National television violence study. (1995–96). Studio City, CA: Mediascope.

Navarro, M. (1995, December 9) Drug sold abroad by prescription becomes widely abused in U.S. *New York Times,* pp. 1, 9.

Naveh-Benjamin, M. (1990) The acquisition and retention of knowledge: Exploring mutual benefits to memory research and the educational setting. *Applied Cognitive Psychology, 4*(4), 295–320.

Neath, I. (1998). *Human memory.* Pacific Grove, CA: Brooks/Cole.

Needles, D. J., & Abramson, L. Y. (1990). Positive life events, attributional style, and hopelessness: Testing a model of recovery from depression. *Journal of Abnormal Psychology, 99*(2), 156–165.

Neff, F. (1990). Delivering sport psychology services to a professional sport organization. *Sport Psychologist, 4*(4), 378–385.

Neidert, G. P., & Linder, D. E. (1990). Avoiding social traps. *Social Behaviour, 5*(4), 261–284.

Neisser, U. (1997). Rising scores on intelligence tests. *American Scientist, 85,* 440–447.

Neisser, U., Boodoo, G., Bouchard, T. J., et al, (1996). Intelligence: Knowns and unknowns. *American Psychologist, 51*(2), 77–101.

Nelson, C. A. (1999a). How important are the first 3 years of life? *Applied Developmental* Science, 3(4), 235–238.

Nelson, C. A. (1999b). Neural plasticity and human development. *Current Directions in Psychological Science, 8*(2), 42–45.

Nelson, J. R., Smith, D. J., & Dodd, J. (1990). The moral reasoning of juvenile delinquents. *Journal of Abnormal Child Psychology, 18*(3), 231–239.

Nelson, T. O. (1987). Predictive accuracy of the feeling of knowing across different tasks and across different subject populations and individuals. In M. M. Grunegerg, P. E. Morris, & R. N. Sykes (Eds.), *Practical aspects of memory: Current research and issues.* Chinchester, UK: Wiley.

Nesca, M., & Koulack, D. (1994). Recognition memory, sleep and circadian rhythms. *Canadian Journal of Experimental Psychology, 48*(3), 359–379.

Neter, E., & Ben-Shakhar, G. (1989). The predictive validity of graphological inferences: A meta-analytic approach. *Personality and Individual Differences, 10*(7), 737–745.

Neubert, M. J. (1998). The value of feedback and goal setting over goal setting alone and potential moderators of this effect: A meta-analysis. *Human Performance, 11*(4), 321–335.

Neufeld, R. W. (1970). The effect of experimentally altered cognitive appraisal on pain tolerance. *Psychonomic Science, 20*(2), 106–107.

Neugarten, B. (1971, December). Grow old along with me! The best is yet to be. *Psychology Today,* p. 45.

Neuman, G. A., & Baydoun, R. (1998). An empirical examination of overt and covert integrity tests. *Journal of Business & Psychology, 13*(1), 65–79.

Nevin, J. A., & Fuld, K. (1993). On armament traps and how to get out of them. *Behavior & Social Issues, 3*(1–2), 63–74.

Newell, A., & Simon, H. A. (1972). *Human problem solving.* Englewood Cliffs, NJ: Prentice-Hall.

Newman, B. M., & Newman, P. R. (1987). The impact of high school on social development. *Adolescence, 22*(87), 525–534.

Newman, P. R. (1982). The peer group. In B. B. Wolman, G. Stricker, S. J. Ellman, P. Keith-Spiegel, & D. S. Palermo (Eds.), *Handbook of developmental psychology.* Englewood Cliffs, NJ: Prentice-Hall.

Newman, R. (1994, August). Electronic therapy raises issues, risks. *APA Monitor,* p. 25.

Nicholas, J. M., & Penwell, L. W. (1995). A proposed profile of the effective leader in human space-flight based on findings from analog environments. *Aviation, Space, & Environmental Medicine, 66*(1), 63–72.

Nickelson, D. W. (1998). Telehealth and the evolving health care system. *Professional Psychology: Research & Practice, 29*(6), 527–535.

Nickerson, R. S., & Adams, M. J. (1979). Long-term memory for a common object. *Cognitive Psychology, 11,* 287–307.

Nielsen, D. M., & Metha, A. (1994). Parental behavior and adolescent self-esteem in clinical and nonclinical samples. *Adolescence, 29*(115), 525–542.

Nijstad, B. A., Stroebe, W., & Lodewijkx, H. F. M. (1999). Persistence of brainstorming groups: How do people know when to stop? *Journal of Experimental Social Psychology, 35*(2), 165–185.

Nikles, C. D., Brecht, D. L., Klinger, E., & Bursell, A. L. (1998). *Journal of Personality & Social Psychology, 75*(1), 242–255.

Nist, S. L., Sharman, S. J., & Holschuh, J. L. (1996). The effects of rereading, self-selected strategy use, and rehearsal on the immediate and delayed understanding of text. *Reading Psychology, 17*(2), 137–157.

Nixon, M. (1990). Professional training in psychology. *American Psychologist, 45*(11), 1257–1262.

Njeri, I. (1991, January 13). Beyond the melting pot. *Los Angeles Times,* pp. E-1, E-8.

Noble, K. D., Subotnik, R. F., & Arnold, K. D. (1996). A new model for adult female talent development. In K. D. Arnold, K. D: Noble, & R. F. Subotnik (Eds.), *Remarkable women.* Cresskill, NJ: Hampton Press.

Noble, P. (1997). Violence in psychiatric in-patients. *International Review of Psychiatry, 9*(2–3), 207–216.

Noel, J. G., Forsyth, D. R., & Kelley, K. N. (1987). Improving the performance of failing students by overcoming their self-serving attributional biases. *Basic and Applied Social Psychology, 8*(1–2), 151–162.

Noice, H., & Noice, T. (1999). Long-term retention of theatrical roles. *Memory, 7*(3), 357–382.

Noller, P., & Ruzzene, M. (1991). Communication in marriage. In G. J. O. Fletcher & F. D. Fincham (Eds.), *Cognition and close relationships.* Hillsdale, NJ: Erlbaum.

Nori, G. (1998). Glucagon and the control of meal size. In G. P. Smith, G. P. et al. (Eds.), *Satiation: From gut to brain.* New York: Oxford University Press.

Norlander, T., Anonymous, & Archer, T. (1998). Effects of flotation rest on creative problem solving and originality. *Journal of Environmental Psychology, 18*(4), 399–408.

Norlander, T., Bergman, H., & Archer, T. (1999). Primary process in competitive archery performance: Effects of flotation REST. *Journal of Applied Sport Psychology, 11*(2), 194–209.

Norman, A. D., Ramsay, S. G., Martray, C. R., & Roberts, J. L. (1999). Relationship between levels of giftedness and psychosocial adjustment. *Roeper Review, 22*(1), 5–9.

Norman, D. A. (1994) *Things that make us smart.* Menlo Park, CA: Addison-Wesley.

Normann, R. A., Maynard, E. M., Rousche, P. J., & Warren, D. J. (1999). A neural interface for a cortical vision prosthesis. *Vision Research, 39*(15), 2577–2587.

Norris, R. M., & Weinman, J. A. (1996). Psychological change following a long sail training voyage. *Personality & Individual Differences, 21*(2), 189–194.

North, C. S. (1987). *Welcome silence.* New York: Simon & Schuster.

Nurmi, J. (1992). Age differences in adult life goals, and their temporal extension. *International Journal of Behavioral Development, 80*(4), 487–508.

Nurnberger, J. I., & Zimmerman, J. (1970). Applied analysis of human behaviors: An alternative to conventional motivational inferences and unconscious determination in therapeutic programming. *Behavior Therapy, 1,* 59–69.

Nyberg, L., & Tulving, E. (1996). Classifying human long-term memory: Evidence from converging dissociations. *European Journal of Cognitive Psychology, 8*(2), 163–183.

Oatley, K., & Jenkins, J. M. (1992). Human emotions: Function and dysfunction. In M. R. Rosenzweig & L. W. Porter (Eds.), *Annual Review of Psychology, 45,* 55–85.

O'Brien, R. M., Figlerski, R. W., Howard, S. R., & Caggiano, J. (1981, August). The effects of multi-year, guaranteed contracts on the performance of pitchers in major league baseball. Paper presented at the annual meeting of the American Psychological Association, Los Angeles.

Oehman, A., & Soares, J. J. (1993). On the automatic nature of phobic fear. *Journal of Abnormal Psychology, 102*(1), 121–132.

Oehman, A., & Soares, J. J. F. (1998). Emotional conditioning to masked stimuli. *Journal of Experimental Psychology: General, 127*(1), 69–82.

Ofosu, H. B., Lafreniere, K. D., & Senn, C. Y. (1998). Body image perception among women of African descent: A normative context? *Feminism & Psychology, 8*(3), 303–323.

Ohayon, M. M., Guilleminault, C., & Priest, R. G. (1999). Night terrors, sleepwalking, and confusional arousals in the general population. *Journal of Clinical Psychiatry, 60*(4), 268–276.

Ohzawa, I., DeAngelis, G. C., & Freeman, R. D. (1990). Stereoscopic depth discrimination in the visual cortex: Neurons ideally suited as disparity detectors. *Science, 249*(4972), 1037–1041.

Olander, F. (1990). Consumer psychology: Not necessarily a manipulative science. *Applied Psychology: An International Review, 39*(1), 105–126.

Olds, M. E., & Fobes, J. L. (1981). The central basis of motivation: Intracranial self-stimulation studies. *Annual Review of Psychology, 32,* 523–574.

O'Leary, K. D., Barling, J., Arias, I., Rosenbaum, A., et al. (1989). Prevalence and stability of physical aggression between spouses: A longitudinal analysis. *Journal of Consulting & Clinical Psychology, 57*(2), 263–268.

Oliver, J. E. (1993). Intergenerational transmission of child abuse. *American Journal of Psychiatry, 150*(9), 1315–1324.

Oliver, M. B., & Hyde, J. S. (1993). Gender differences in sexuality. *Psychological Bulletin, 114*(1), 29–51.

Oliwenstein, L. (1993, May). The gene with two faces. *Discover,* p. 26.

Ollendick, T. H., & King, N. J. (1991). Origins of childhood fears. *Behaviour Research & Therapy, 29*(2), 117–123.

Olson, J. M., & Zanna, M. P. (1993). Attitudes and attitude change. In L. W. Porter & M. R. Rosenzweig (Eds.), *Annual Review of Psychology, 44,* 117–154.

Olson, R. L.– & Roberts, M. W. (1987). Alternative treatments for sibling aggression. *Behavior Therapy, 18*(3), 243–250.

Olson, S. L., Bates, J. E., & Kaskie, B. (1992). Caregiver-infant interaction antecedents of children's school-age cognitive ability. *Merrill-Palmer Quarterly, 38*(3), 309–330.

Ones, D., Viswesvaran, C., & Schmidt, F. L. (1993). Comprehensive meta-analysis of integrity test validities. *Journal of Applied Psychology, 78*(4), 679–703.

Orleans, C. T., Gruman, J., & Hollendonner, J. K. (1999). Rating our progress in population health promotion: Report card on six behaviors. *American Journal of Health Promotion 14*(2), 75–82.

Orlick, T. D. (1975). The sports environment: A capacity to enhance—a capacity to destroy. In B. S. Rushall (Ed.), *The status of psychomotor learning and sport psychology research.* Dartmouth, Nova Scotia: Sport Science Associates.

Orlock, C. (1993). *Inner time.* New York: Birch Lane Press.

Ornstein, R. (1997). *The right mind.* San Diego, CA: Harcourt Brace.

Ornstein, R., & Ehrlich, P. (1989). *New world new mind.* New York: Simon & Schuster.

Orlick, T. D. (1975). The sports environment: A capacity to enhance—a capacity to destroy. In B. S. Rushall (Ed.), *The status of psychomotor learning and sport psychology research.* Dartmouth, Nova Scotia: Sport Science Associates.

Orlock, C. (1993). *Inner time.* New York: Birch Lane Press.

Ornstein, R. (1997). *The right mind.* San Diego, CA: Harcourt Brace.

Ornstein, R., & Ehrlich, P. (1989). *New world new mind.* New York: Simon & Schuster.

Ornstein, S., & Isabella, L. (1990). Age vs. stage models of career attitudes of women: A partial replication and extension. *Journal of Vocational Behavior, 36,* 1–19.

Osgood, C. E. (1952). The nature and measurement of meaning. *Psychological Bulletin, 49,* 197–237.

Oskamp, S. (1995a). Applying social psychology to avoid ecological disaster. *Journal of Social Issues, 51*(4), 217–239.

Oskamp, S. (1995b). Resouce conservation and recycling: Behavior and policy. *Journal of Social Issues, 51*(4), 157–177.

Ost, L. (1996). One-session group treatment of spider phobia. *Behaviour Research & Therapy, 34*(9), 707–715.

O'Sullivan, J. J., & Quevillon, R. P. (1992). 40 years later: Is the Boulder model still alive? *American Psychologist, 47*(1), 67–70.

Outline for cultural formulation and glossary of culture-bound syndromes. (1994). *DSM-IV: Diagnostic and statistical manual of mental disorders* (4th ed.). Washington, DC: American Psychiatric Association.

Overmier, J. B., & LoLordo, V. M. (1998). Learned helplessness. In W. T. O'Donohue, et al. (Eds.) *Learning and behavior therapy.* Boston: Allyn & Bacon.

Owen, J. D. (1976). Flextime: Some problems and solutions. *Industrial and Labor Relations Review, 29,* 152–160.

Oyama, T., & Ichikawa, S. (1990). Some experimental studies on imagery in Japan. *Journal of Mental Imagery, 14*(3–4), 185–195.

Pagano, R. R. (1981). *Understanding statistics.* St. Paul, MN: West.

Palfai, T., & Jankiewicz, H. (1991). *Drugs and human behavior.* Dubuque, IA: Wm. C. Brown.

Palinkas, L. A., Suedfeld, P., & Steel, G. D. (1995). Psychological functioning among members of a small polar expedition. *Aviation and Space Environmental Medicine, 66,* 943–950.

Palkovitz, R. J., & Lore, R. K. (1980). Note taking and note review: Why students fail questions based on lecture material. *Teaching of Psychology, 7,* 159–160.

Palm, K., & Gibson, P. (1998). Recovered memories of childhood sexual abuse: Clinicians' practices and beliefs. *Professional Psychology: Research & Practice, 29*(3), 257–261.

Palmer, S. E. (1992). Common region: A new principle of perceptual grouping. *Cognitive Psychology, 24*(3), 436–447.

Pandey, S. (1999). Role of perceived control in coping with crowding. *Psychological Studies, 44*(3), 86–91.

Papa, F. J., Aldrich, D., & Schumacker, R. E. (1999). The effects of immediate online feedback upon diagnostic performance. *Academic Medicine, 74*(Suppl. 10), S16–S18.

Papps, F., Walker, M., Trimboli, A., & Trimboli, C. (1995). Parental discipline in Anglo, Greek, Lebanese, and Vietnamese cultures. *Journal of Cross-Cultural Psychology, 26*(1), 49–64.

Park, D. C., Smith, A. D., & Cavanaugh, J. C. (1990). Metamemories of memory researchers. *Memory & Cognition, 18*(3), 321–327.

Parke, R. D. (1995). Fathers and families. In M. H. Bornstein (Ed.), *Handbook of parenting, Vol. 3.* Mahwah, NJ: Erlbaum.

Parkes, C. M. (1979). *Grief: The painful reaction to the loss of a loved one.* Monograph, University of California, San Diego.

Parks, C. A. (1998). Lesbian parenthood: A review of the literature. *American Journal of Orthopsychiatry, 68*(3), 376–389.

Parrott, A. C. (1999). Does cigarette smoking cause stress? *American Psychologist, 54*(10), 817–820.

Parsons, L. M., Fox, P. T., Downs, J. H., Glass, T., et al. (1995). Use of implicit motor imagery for visual shape discrimination as revealed by PET. *Nature, 375*(6526), 54–58.

Partonen, T. (1997). Medical use of melatonin. *Psychiatria Fennica, 28,* 135–144.

Passman, R. H. (1987). Attachments to inanimate objects: Are children who have security blankets insecure? *Journal of Consulting and Clinical Psychology, 55*(6), 825–830.

Patrick, C. J., Bradley, M. M., & Lang, P. J. (1993). Emotion in the criminal psychopath: Startle reflex modulation. *Journal of Abnormal Psychology, 102*(1), 82–92.

Patrick, C. J., & Iacono, W. G. (1989). Psychopathy, threat, and polygraph test accuracy. *Journal of Applied Psychology, 74*(2), 347–355.

Patten, B. M. (1990). The history of memory arts. *Neurology, 40*(2), 346–352.

Patterson, C. H. (1989). Foundations for a systematic eclectic psychotherapy. *Psychotherapy, 26*(4), 427–435.

Patterson, C. J. (1995). Sexual orientation and human development: An overview. *Developmental Psychology, 31*(1), 3–11.

Paulhus, D. L. (1998). Interpersonal and intrapsychic adaptiveness of trait self-enhancement. *Journal of Personality and Social Psychology, 74*(5), 1197–1208.

Pavlov, I. P. (1927). *Conditioned reflexes* (G. V. Anrep, Trans.). New York: Dover.

Pavot, W., & Diener, E. (1993). Review of the Satisfaction with Life Scale. *Psychological Assessments, 5*(2), 164–172.

Peeters, M. C. W., Buunk, B. P., & Schaufeli, W. B. (1995). A micro-analysis exploration of the cognitive appraisal of daily stressful events at work. *Anxiety, Stress & Coping: An International Journal, 8*(2), 127–139.

Peisner-Feinberg, E., & Burchinal, M. (in press). Concurrent relations between child care quality and child outcomes: The study of cost, quality, and outcomes in child care center. *Merrill-Palmer Quarterly.*

Peisner-Feinberg, E. S., & Burchinal, M. R. (1997). Relations between preschool children's child-care experiences and concurrent development. *Merrill-Palmer Quarterly, 43*(3), 451–477.

Pelton, T. (1983). The shootists. *Science 83, 4*(4), 84–86.

Pence, G. E. (1998). *Who's afraid of human cloning?* Lanham, MD: Rowman and Littlefield.

Pendergast, M. (1995). *Victims of memory: Incest accusations and shattered lives.* Hinesburg, VT: Upper Access.

Penfield, W. (1957, April 27). Brain's record of past a continuous movie film. *Science News Letter,* p. 265.

Penfield, W. (1958). *The excitable cortex in conscious man.* Springfield, IL: Charles C Thomas.

Pennebaker, James W., & Francis, Martha E. (1996). Cognitive, emotional, and language processes in disclosure. *Cognition & Emotion, 10*(6), 601–626.

Pennisi, E. (1992, February 15). Valentine bind. *Science News, 141* 110–111.

Pepler, D. J., & Craig, W. M. (1995). A peek behind the fence: Naturalistic observations of aggressive children with remote audiovisual recording. *Developmental Psychology, 31*(4), 548–553.

Pepler, D. J., Craig, W. M., & Roberts, W. L. (1998). Observations of aggressive and nonaggressive children on the school playground. *Merrill-Palmer Quarterly, 44*(1), 55–76.

Perin, C. T. (1943). A quantitative investigation of the delay of reinforcement gradient. *Journal of Experimental Psychology, 32,* 37–51.

Perkins, D. (1995). *Outsmarting IQ: The emerging science of learnable intelligence.* New York: Free Press.

Perkins, D. N., & Grotzer, T. A. (1997). Teaching intelligence. *American Psychologist, 52*(10), 1125–1133.

Perkins, K. A. (1993). Weight gain following smoking cessation. *Journal of Consulting & Clinical Psychology, 61*(5), 768–777.

Perkins, K. A. (1995). Individual variability in responses to nicotine. *Behavior Genetics, 25*(2), 119–132.

Perlman, D., & Cozby, P. C. (1983). *Social psychology.* New York: Holt, Rinehart & Winston.

Perls, F. (1969). *Gestalt therapy verbatim.* Lafayette, CA: Real People.

Perry, C., Orne, M. T., London, R. W., & Orne, E. C. (1996). Rethinking per se exclusions of hypnotically elicited recall as legal testimony. *International Journal of Clinical & Experimental Hypnosis, 44*(1), 66–81.

Perry, D. G., Perry, L. C., & Weiss, R. J. (1989). Sex differences in the consequences that children anticipate for aggression. *Developmental Psychology, 25*(2), 312–319.

Perugini, E. M., Kirsch, I., Allen, S. T., et al., (1998). Surreptitious observation of responses to hypnotically suggested hallucinations. *International Journal of Clinical & Experimental Hypnosis, 46*(2), 191–203.

Peters, L., Clark, D., & Carroll, F. (1998). Are computerized interviews equivalent to human interviewers? *Psychological Medicine, 28*(4), 893–901.

Peters, W. A. (1971). *A class divided.* Garden City, NY: Doubleday.

Petersen, A. C., Kennedy, R. E., & Sullivan, P. (1991). Coping with adolescence. In M. E. Colten & S. Gore (Eds.), *Adolescent stress.* New York: Aldine de Gruyter.

Petersen, S. E., Fox, P. T., Posner, M. I., Mintun, M., et al. (1988). Positron emission tomographic studies of the cortical anatomy of single-word processing. *Nature, 331*(6157), 585–589.

Peterson, B. E., & Klohnen, E. C. (1995). Realization of generativity in two samples of women at midlife. *Psychology & Aging, 10*(1), 20–29.

Peterson, J. (1995, March). How are psychologists perceived by the public? *APA Monitor,* p. 31.

Peterson, L. R., & Peterson, M. J. (1959). Short-term retention of individual verbal items. *Journal of Experimental Psychology, 58,* 193–198.

Peterson, P. L. (1979). Direct instruction: Effective for what and for whom? *Educational Leadership, 37,* 46–48.

Peterson, S. E. (1992). The cognitive functions of underlining as a study technique. *Reading Research & Instruction, 31*(2), 49–56.

Petri, H. (1996). *Motivation.* Pacific Grove, CA: Brooks/Cole.

Petrie, T. A., & Diehl, N. S. (1995). Sport psychology in the profession of psychology. *Professional Psychology: Research & Practice, 26*(3), 288–291.

Pettigrew, T. F. (1998). Intergroup contact theory. *Annual Review of Psychology, 49,* 65–85.

Pettit, G. S., Brown, E. G., Mize, J., & Lindsey, E. (1998). Mothers' and fathers' socializing behaviors in three contexts. *Merrill-Palmer Quarterly, 44*(2), 173–193.

Petty, R. E., Wegener, D. T., & Fabrigar, L. R. (1997). Attitudes and attitude change. *Annual Review of Psychology, 48,* 609–647.

Pfiffner, L. J., & McBurnett, K. (1997). Social skills training with parent generalization. *Journal of Consulting & Clinical Psychology, 65*(5), 749–757.

Phillips, D. P., & Wills, J. S. (1987). A drop in suicides around major national holidays. *Suicide and Life-Threatening Behavior, 17,* 1–12.

Phillips, J. L. (1969). *Origins of intellect: Piaget's theory.* San Francisco: Freeman.

Piaget, J. (1951). *The psychology of intelligence.* New York: Norton.

Piaget, J. (1952). *The origins of intelligence in children.* New York: International University Press.

Piccione, C., Hilgard, E. R., & Zimbardo, P. G. (1989). On the degree of stability of measured hypnotizability over a 25-year period. *Journal of Personality & Social Psychology, 56*(2), 289–295.

Pierce, J. P. (1991). Progress and problems in international public health efforts to reduce tobacco usage. *Annual Review of Public Health, 12,* 383–400.

Pierrel, R., & Sherman, J. G. (1963, February). Train your pet the Barnabus way. *Brown Alumni Monthly,*

Pike, J. L., et al., (1997). Chronic life stress alters sympathetic, neuroendocrine, and immune responsivity over an acute psychological stressor in humans. *Psychosomatic Medicine, 59*(4), 447–459.

Piliavin, I. M., Rodin, J., & Piliavin, J. A. (1969). Good samaritanism: An underground phenomenon? *Journal of Personality & Social Psychology, 13,* 289–299.

Pilkington, N. W., & D'Augelli, A. R. (1995). Victimization of lesbian, gay, and bisexual youth in community settings. *Journal of Community Psychology, 23*(1), 34–56.

Pillow, D. R., Zautra, A. J., & Sandler, I. (1996). Major life events and minor stressors: Identifying mediational links in the stress process. *Journal of Personality & Social Psychology, 70*(2), 381–394.

Pines, A. M. (1998). A prospective study of personality and gender differences in romantic attraction. *Personality & Individual Differences, 25*(1), 147–157.

Pinsof, W. M., Wynne, L. C., & Hambright, A. B. (1996). The outcomes of couple and family therapy. *Psychotherapy, 33*(2), 321–331.

Pisacreta, R. (1998). Superstitious behavior and response stereotypy prevent the emergence of efficient rule-governed behavior in humans. *Psychological Record, 48*(2), 251–274.

Pittman, T., & Heller, J. F. (1987). Social motivation. *Annual Review of Psychology, 38,* 461–489.

Piven, J., Arndt, S., & Palmer, P. (1995). An MRI study of brain size in autism. *American Journal of Psychiatry, 152*(8), 1145.

Pliner, P., Eng, A., & Krishnan, K. (1995). The effects of fear and hunger on food neophobia in humans. *Appetite, 25*(1), 77–87.

Pliner, P., & Haddock, G. (1996). Perfectionism in weight-concerned and -unconcerned women. *International Journal of Eating Disorders, 19*(4), 381–389.

Plomin, R., & Rende, R. (1991). Human behavioral genetics. *Annual Review of Psychology, 42,* 161–190.

Plug, C., & Ross, H. E. (1994). The natural moon illusion: A multifactor angular account. *Perception, 23*(3), 321–333.

Plutchik, R. (1980). *Emotion.* New York: Harper & Row.

Plutchik, R. (1990). Emotions in psychotherapy: A psychoevolutionary perspective. In R. Plutchik & H. Kellerman (Eds.), *Emotion.* San Diego, CA: Academic Press.

Plutchik, R. (1994). *The psychology and biology of emotion.* New York: HarperCollins.

Pogatchnik, S. (1990, January 26). Kids' TV gets more violent, study finds. *Los Angeles Times,* pp. F1, F27.

Polce-Lynch, M., Myers, B. J., Kilmartin, C. T., Forssmann-Falck, R., & Kliewer, W. (1998). Gender and age patterns in emotional expression, body image, and self-esteem. *Sex Roles, 38*(11–12), 1025–1048.

Pollard, P. (1995). Pornography and sexual aggression. *Current Psychology: Developmental, Learning, Personality, Social, 14*(3), 200–221.

Pollner, M. (1998). The effects of interviewer gender in mental health interviews. *Journal of Nervous & Mental Disease, 186*(6), 369–373.

Pollock, V. E., Briere, J., Schneider, L., Knop, J., et al. (1990). Childhood antecedents of antisocial behavior. *American Journal of Psychiatry, 147*(10), 1290–1293.

Poothullil, J. M. (1999). Maintenance of weight loss using taste and smell sensations. *Journal of Women's Health, 8*(1), 109–113.

Pope, H. G., Gruber, A. J., & Yurgelun-Todd, D. (1995). The residual neuropsychological effects of cannabis. *Drug & Alcohol Dependence, 38*(1), 25–34.

Pope, H. G., & Yurgelun-Todd, D. (1996). The residual cognitive effects of heavy marijuana use in college students. *Journal of the American Medical Association, 275*(7), 521–527.

Porac, C., Friesen, I. C., Barnes, M. P., & Gruppuso, V. (1998). Illness and accidental injury in young and older adult left- and right-handers: Implications for genetic theories of hand preference. *Developmental Neuropsychology, 14*(1), 157–172.

Port, R. L., & Seybold, K. S. (1995). Hippocampal synaptic plasticity as a biological substrate underlying episodic psychosis. *Biological Psychiatry, 37*(5), 318–324.

Posner, M. I., & Levitin, D. J. (1999). Imaging the future. In R. L. Solso (Ed.), *Mind and brain sciences in the 21st century.* Cambridge, MA: MIT Press.

Potashkin, B. D., & Beckles, N. (1990). Relative efficacy of Ritalin and biofeedback treatments in the management of hyperactivity. *Biofeedback & Self-Regulation, 15*(4), 305–315.

Potkay, C. R., & Allen, B. P. (1986). *Personality: Theory, research, and applications.* Monterey, CA: Brooks/Cole.

Poulin, J., & Walter, C. (1993). Social worker burnout. *Social Work Research & Abstracts, 29*(4), 5–11.

Poulton, R. G., & Andrews, G. (1996). Change in danger cognitions in agoraphobia and social phobia during treatment. *Behaviour Research & Therapy, 34*(5–6), 413–421.

Powell, A. L., & Thelen, M. H. (1996). Emotions and cognitions associated with bingeing and weight control behavior in bulimia. *Journal of Psychosomatic Research, 40*(3), 317–328.

Pratkanis, A. R. (1992). The Cargo-cult science of subliminal persuasion. *Skeptical Inquirer, 16,* 260–272.

Preiser, R. (1997, May). Personal space. *Discover,* pp. 94–95.

Premack, A. J., & Premack, D. (1972, October). Teaching language to an ape. *Scientific American,* 92–99.

Premack, D. (1983). Animal cognition. *Annual Review of Psychology, 34,* 351–362.

Premack, D., & Premack, A. J. (1983). *The mind of an ape.* New York: Norton.

Prentice, D. A., & Miller, D. T. (1993). Pluralistic ignorance of alcohol use on campus. *Journal of Personality and Social Psychology, 64*(2), 243–256.

Pressley, M. (1987). Are key-word method effects limited to slow presentation rates? An empirically based reply to Hall and Fuson (1986). *Journal of Educational Psychology, 79*(3), 333–335.

Pressley, M., Symons, S., McDaniel, M. A., Snyder, B., et al. (1988). Elaborative interrogation facilitates acquisition of confusing facts. *Journal of Educational Psychology, 80*(3), 268–278.

Pressman, J. D. (1998). *Last resort: Psycho-surgery and the limits of medicine.* New York: Cambridge University Press.

Pritchard, R. M. (1961). A collimator stabilizing system. *Quarterly Journal of Experimental Psychology, 13,* 181–183.

Proite, R., Dannells, M., & Benton, S. L. (1993). Gender, sex-role stereotypes, and the attribution of responsibility for date and acquaintance rape. *Journal of College Student Development, 34*(6), 411–417.

Puca, R. M., & Schmalt, H. (1999). Task enjoyment: A mediator between achievement motives and performance. *Motivation & Emotion, 23*(1), 15–29.

Pursch, J. A. (1983, June 12). Cocaine can give you the business. *Los Angeles Times,* p. VII 12.

Quinn, P. C., & Bhatt, R. S. (1998). Visual pop-out in young infants. *Infant Behavior & Development, 21*(2), 273–288.

Quitkin, F. M. (1999). Placebos, drug effects, and study design: A clinician's guide. *American Journal of Psychiatry, 156*(6), 829–836.

Raag, T., & Rackliff, C. L. (1998). Preschoolers' awareness of social expectations of gender: Relationships to toy choices. *Sex Roles, 38*(9–10), 685–700.

Rabasca, L. (1999, September). High marks for psychologists who prescribe. *APA Monitor,* p. 21.

Rader, P. E., & Hicks, R. A. (1987, April). Jet lag desynchronization and self-assessment of business related performance. Paper presented at the Western Psychological Association meeting in Long Beach, CA.

Radetsky, P. (1992, January). Straight sex and AIDS vaccines. *Discover,* pp. 52–53.

Rafaeli, A., & Klimoski, R. J. (1983). Predicting sales success through handwriting analysis: An evaluation of the effects of training and handwriting sample content. *Journal of Applied Psychology, 68,* 212–217.

Rahe, R. H. (1972). Subjects' recent life changes and their near-future illness reports. *Annals of Clinical Research, 4,* 250–265.

Raison, C. L., Klein, H. M., & Steckler, M. (1999). The moon and madness reconsidered.

Ramachandran, V. S. (1992a). Filling in gaps in perception. *Current directions in psychological science 1*(6), 199–205.

Ramachandran, V. S. (1992b, May). Blind spots. *Scientific American,* 86–91.

Ramachandran, V. S. (1995). 2-D or not 2-D—that is the question. In R. Gregory, J. Harris, P. Heard, & D. Rose (Eds.), *The artful eye.* Oxford: Oxford University Press.

Ramanaiah, N. V., Detwiler, F. R. J., & Byravan, A. (1995). Sex-role orientation and satisfaction with life. *Psychological Reports, 77*(3, Pt 2), 1260–1262.

Ramirez-Valles, J., Zimmerman, M. A., & Newcomb, M. D. (1998). Sexual risk behavior among youth. *Journal of Health & Social Behavior, 39*(3), 237–253.

Ramsey, P. H., Ramsey, P. P., & Barnes, M. J. (1987). Effects of student confidence and item difficulty on test score gains due to answer changing. *Teaching of Psychology, 14*(4), 206–209.

Randi, J. (1980). *Flim-flam!* New York: Lippincott & Crowell.

Randi, J. (1983). Science and the chimera. In G. O. Abell & B. Singer (Eds.), *Science and the paranormal.* New York: Scribner's.

Rando, T. A. (1995). Grief and mourning: Accommodating to loss. In H. Wass & R. A. Neimeyer (Eds.), *Dying: Facing the facts.* Washington, DC: Taylor & Francis.

Rauscher, F. H., & Shaw, G. L. (1998). Key components of the Mozart effect. *Perceptual & Motor Skills, 86*(3, Pt 1), 835–841.

Raven, B. H. (1974). The analysis of power and power preference. In J. T. Tebeschi (Ed.), *Prospectus on social power.* Chicago: Aldine.

Raymond, C. (1991). Pioneering research challenges accepted notions concerning the cognitive abilities of infants. *Chronicle of Higher Education, 23,* A5–7.

Read, J. (1995). Female sexual dysfunction. *International Review of Psychiatry, 7*(2), 175–182.

Reed, J. D., & Bruce, D. (1982). Longitudinal tracking of difficult memory retrievals. *Cognitive Psychology, 14,* 280–300.

Reed, S. K. (1996). *Cognition: Theory and applications* (3rd ed.). Pacific Grove, CA: Brooks/Cole.

Regan, P. C. (1998). Of lust and love. *Personal Relationships, 5*(2), 139–157.

Regeser López, S., & Guarnaccia, P. J. J. (2000). Cultural psychopathology: Uncovering the social world of mental illness. *Annual Review of Psychology, 51,* 571–598.

Reid, H. M., & Fine, G. A. (1992). Self-disclosure in men's friendships. In P. M. Nardi (Ed.), *Men's friendships.* Newbury Park, CA: Sage.

Reif, L. V., Patton, M. J., & Gold, P. B. (1995). Bereavement, stress, and social support in members of a self-help group. *Journal of Community Psychology, 23*(4), 292–306.

Reiff, S., Katkin, E. S., & Friedman, R. (1999). Classical conditioning of the human blood pressure response. *International Journal of Psychophysiology, 34*(2), 135–145.

Reifman, A. S., Larrick, R. P., & Fein, S. (1991). Temper and temperature on the diamond: The heat-aggression relationship in major league baseball. *Personality & Social Psychology Bulletin, 17*(5), 580–585.

Reisner, A. D. (1996). Repressed memories: True and false. *Psychological Record, 46*(4), 563–579.

Reiss, M., Tymnik, G., Koegler, P., Koegler, W., & Reiss, G. (1999). Laterality of hand, foot, eye, and ear in twins. *Laterality, 4*(3), 287–297.

Reiterman, T. (1993, April 23). Parallel roads led to Jonestown, Waco. *Los Angeles Times,* p. A-24.

Remland, M. S., Jones, T. S., & Brinkman, H. (1991). Proxemic and haptic behavior in three European countries. *Journal of Nonverbal Behavior, 15*(4), 215–232.

Renner, M. J., & Mackin, R. S. (1998). A life stress instrument for classroom use. *Teaching of Psychology, 25*(1), 46–48.

Rennie, J. (1994, June). Grading the gene tests. *Scientific American,* 88–97.

Renwick, P. A., & Lawler, E. E. (1979). What you really want from your job. *Psychology Today, 11*(12), 53–65.

Renzulli, J. S. (1999). What is this thing called giftedness, and how do we develop it? *Journal for the Education of the Gifted, 23*(1), 3–54.

Repacholi, B. M. (1998). Infant's use of attentional cues to identify the referent of another person's emotional expression. *Developmental Psychology, 34,* 1017–1025.

Reppucci, N. D., Woolard, J. L., & Fried, C. S. (1999). Social, community, and preventive interventions. *Annual Review of Psychology, 50,* 387–418.

Rescorla, R. A. (1987). A Pavlovian analysis of goal-directed behavior. *American Psychologist, 42,* 119–126.

Research versus animal rights: Is there a middle ground? (1989). A. Newman, *American Scientist, 77,* 135–137.

Reynolds, S., Stiles, W. B., Barkham, M., & Shapiro, D. A. (1996). Acceleration of changes in session impact during contrasting time-limited psychotherapies. *Journal of Consulting & Clinical Psychology, 64*(3), 577–586.

Reznick, J. S., & Goldfield, B. A. (1992). Rapid change in lexical development in comprehension and production. *Developmental Psychology, 28*(3), 406–413.

Rhine, J. B. (1953). *New world of the mind.* New York: Sloane.

Rhine, J. B. (1974). Security versus deception in parapsychology. *Journal of Parapsychology, 38,* 99–121.

Rhodewalt, F. (1994). Conceptions of ability, achievement goals, and individual differences in self-handicapping behavior. *Journal of Personality, 62*(1), 67–85.

Ricci, L. C., & Wellman, M. W. (1990). Monamines: Biochemical markers of suicide? *Journal of Clinical Psychology, 46*(1), 106–116.

Rice, K. M., Blanchard, E. B., & Purcell, M. (1993). Biofeedback treatments of generalized anxiety disorder. *Biofeedback & Self-Regulation, 18*(2), 93–105.

Rice, M. E. (1997). Violent offender research and implications for the criminal justice system. *American Psychologist, 52*(4), 414–423.

Richards, L., Rollerson, B., & Phillips, J. (1991). Perceptions of submissiveness: Implications for victimization. *Journal of Psychology, 125*(4), 407–411.

Richelle, M. N. (1995). *B. F. Skinner: A reappraisal.* Hillsdale, NJ: Erlbaum.

Ricketts, M. S., & Galloway, R. E. (1984). Effects of three different one-hour single-session treatments for test anxiety. *Psychological Reports, 54,* 113–119.

Rideout, B. E., Dougherty, S., & Wernert, L. (1998). Effect of music on spatial performance: A test of generality. *Perceptual & Motor Skills, 86*(2), 512–514.

Rideout, B. E., & Taylor, J. (1997). Enhanced spatial performance following 10 minutes exposure to music: A replication. *Perceptual & Motor Skills, 85*(1), 112–114.

Rieber, R. W. (1999). Hypnosis, false memory and multiple personality. *History of Psychiatry, 10*(37, Pt 1), 3–11.

Riefer, D. M., Keveri, M. K., & Kramer, D. L. (1995). Name that tune: Eliciting the tip-of-the-tongue experience using auditory stimuli. *Psychological Reports, 77*(3, Pt 2), 1379–1390.

Rieke, M. L., & Guastello, S. J. (1995, June). Unresolved issues in honesty and integrity testing. *American Psychologist,* 458–459.

Rind, B., Tromovitch, P., & Bauserman, R. (1998). A meta-analytic examination of assumed properties of child sexual abuse using college students. *Psychological Bulletin, 124*(1), 22–53.

Ring, K. (1980). *Life at death.* New York: Coward, McCann & Geoghegan.

Ritchie, R. J., & Moses, J. L. (1983). Assessment center correlates of women's advancement into middle management: A 7-year longitudinal analysis. *Journal of Applied Psychology, 68,* 227–231.

Ritter, J. (1998, October 15). Uniforms changing the culture of the nation's classrooms. *USA Today,* pp. 1A, 2A.

Roan, S. (1992, September 1). Forever set in your ways at 30? *Los Angeles Times,* pp. E1, E2.

Roan, S. (1993, February 2). Growth-drug debate: What is too short? *Los Angeles Times,* pp. E1, E8.

Roberts, R. (1989). Passenger fear of flying: Behavioural treatment with extensive *in-vivo* exposure and group support. *Aviation, Space, & Environmental Medicine, 60*(4), 342–348.

Roberts, R. E., Phinney, J. S., Masse, L. C., Chen, Y. R., et al. (1999). The structure of ethnic identity of young adolescents from diverse ethnocultural groups. *Journal of Early Adolescence, 19*(3), 301–322.

Roberts, S. M. (1995). Applicability of the goodness-of-fit hypothesis to coping with daily hassles. *Psychological Reports, 77*(3, Pt 1), 943–954.

Robertson, T. S., & Kassarjian, H. H. (Eds.). (1991). *Handbook of consumer behavior.* Engelwood Cliffs, NJ: Prentice-Hall.

Robins, L. N. (1998). The intimate connection between antisocial personality and substance abuse. *Social Psychiatry & Psychiatric Epidemiology, 33*(8), 393–399.

Robins, R. W., Gosling, S. D., & Craik, K. H. (1998). Psychological science at the crossroads. *American Scientist, 86,* 310–313.

Robins, R. W., Gosling, S. D., & Craik, K. H. (1999). An empirical analysis of trends in psychology. *American Psychologist, 54*(2), 117–128.

Robinson, A., & Clinkenbeard, P. R. (1998). Giftedness. *Annual Review of Psychology, 49,* 117–139.

Robinson, B., Frye, E. M., & Bradley, L. J. (1997). Cult affiliation and disaffiliation. *Counseling & Values, 41*(2), 166–173.

Robinson, D. L. (1999). The "IQ" factor: Implications for intelligence theory and measurement. *Personality & Individual Differences, 27*(4), 715–735.

Robinson-Riegler, B., & McDaniel, M. (1994). Further constraints on the bizarreness effect: Elaboration at encoding. *Memory & Cognition, 22*(6), 702–712.

Robson, P. (1984). Prewalking locomotor movements and their use in predicting standing and walking. *Child Care, Health & Development, 10,* 317–330.

Rodin, J. (1981). Current status of the internal-external hypothesis for obesity: What went wrong? *American Psychologist, 36,* 361–372.

Roediger, H. L. (1990). Implicit memory. *American Psychologist, 45*(9), 1043–1056.

Roediger, H. L., & McDermott, K. B. (1995). Creating false memories: Remembering words not presented on lists. *Journal of Experimental Psychology: Learning, Memory, and Cognition, 21*(4), 803–814.

Rogers, C. R. (1959). A theory of therapy, personality, and interpersonal relationships, as developed in the client-centered framework. In S. Koch (Ed.), *Psychology: A study of a science, Vol. 3.* New York: McGraw-Hill.

Rogers, C. R. (1961). *On becoming a person: A therapist's view of psychotherapy.* Boston: Houghton Mifflin.

Rogers, C. R. (1980). *A way of being.* Boston: Houghton Mifflin.

Rogers, J. M. (1971, September). Drug abuse—Just what the doctor ordered. *Psychology Today,* 16–24.

Rogers, J. R. (1990). Female suicide. *Journal of Counseling & Development, 69*(6), 37–38.

Rogerson, J. (1997). Canine fears and phobias: A regimen for treatment without recourse to drugs. *Applied Animal Behaviour Science, 52*(3–4), 291–297.

Rogler, L. H., Cortes, D. E., & Malgady, R. G. (1991). Acculturation and mental health status among Hispanics. *American Psychologist, 46*(6), 585–597.

Rohsenow, D. J., & Smith, R. E. (1982). Irrational beliefs as predictors of negative affective states. *Motivation and Emotion, 6,* 299–301.

Roizen, M. F. (1999). *Real age.* New York: Harper-Collins.

Rolling, B. L., & Belsky, J. (1992). The contribution of mother-child and father-child relationships to the quality of sibling interaction: A longitudinal study. *Child Development, 63*(5), 1209–1222.

Rollman, G. B. (1998). Culture and pain. In S. S. Kazarian, et al., (Eds.), *Cultural clinical psychology*. New York: Oxford University Press.

Ronen, T., & Wozner, Y. (1995). A self-control intervention package for the treatment of primary nocturnal enuresis. *Child & Family Behavior Therapy, 17*(1), 1–20.

Rorer, L. G., & Widiger, T. A. (1983). Personality structure and assessment. *Annual Review of Psychology, 34,* 431–463.

Rosch, E. (1977). Classification of real-world objects: Origins and representations in cognition. In P. N. Johnson-Laird & P. C. Wason (Eds.), *Thinking: Reading in cognitive science.* Cambridge: Cambridge University Press.

Rose, K. J. (1984). How animals think. *Science Digest, 89,* 59–61.

Rose, R. J. (1995). Genes and human behavior. *Annual Review of Psychology, 46,* 625–654.

Rosenbaum, J. F., Biederman, J., Gersten, M., D. R., et al. (1989). Behavioral inhibition in children of parents with panic disorder and agoraphobia: A controlled study. *Annual Progress in Child Psychiatry & Child Development,* 294–315.

Rosenbaum, J. F., Biederman, J., Hirshfeld, D. R., Bolduc, E. A., et al. (1991). Further evidence of an association between behavioral inhibition and anxiety disorders. *Journal of Psychiatric Research, 25*(1–2), 49–65.

Rosenbaum, M. B. (1979). The changing body image of the adolescent girl. In M. Sugar (Ed.), *Female adolescent development.* New York: Brunner/Mazel.

Rosenberg, L. B. (1994, July). The effect of interocular distance upon depth perception when using stereoscopic displays to perform work within virtual and telepresent environments. USAF AMRL Technical Report (Wright-Patterson), AL/CF-TR-1994-0052. 30 pp.

Rosenblith, J. F. (1992). *In the beginning.* Newbury Park, CA: Sage.

Rosenfeld, P., Giacalone, R. A., & Tedeschi, J. T. (1983). Cognitive dissonance vs. impression management. *Journal of Social Psychology, 120,* 203–211.

Rosenhan, D. L. (1973). On being sane in insane places. *Science, 179,* 250–258.

Rosenman, R. H., Brand, R. J., Jenkins, C. D., Friedman, M., Straus, R., & Wurm, M. (1975). Coronary heart disease in the Western Collaborative Group Study: Final follow-up experience of 8 1/2 years. *Journal of the American Medical Association, 233,* 872–877.

Rosenstiel, T. (1991, March 25). Americans praise media but still back censorship, postwar poll says. *Los Angeles Times,* p. A9.

Rosenthal, D., & Quinn, O. W. (1977). Quadruplet hallucinations: Phenotypic variations of a schizophrenic genotype. *Archives of General Psychiatry, 34*(7), 817–827.

Rosenthal, D. A., Smith, A. M. A., & de Visser, R. (1999). Personal and social factors influencing age at first sexual intercourse. *Archives of Sexual Behavior, 28*(4), 319–333.

Rosenthal, N. E. (1993). *Winter blues: Seasonal affective disorder.* New York: Guilford Press.

Rosenthal, R. (1965). *Clever Hans: A case study of scientific method. Introduction to Clever Hans: (The horse of Mr. Von Osten).* O. Pfungst. New York: Holt, Rinehart & Winston.

Rosenthal, R. (1973, September). The Pygmalion effect lives. *Psychology Today,* 56–63.

Rosenthal R. (1994). Science and ethics in conducting, analyzing, and reporting psychological research. *Psychological Science, 5,* 127–134

Rosenthal, T. L. (1993). To soothe the savage breast. *Behavior Research & Therapy, 31*(5), 439–462.

Rosenthal, T. L., & Rosenthal, R. (1980). *The vicious cycle of stress reaction.* Memphis, TN: Stress Management Clinic, Department of Psychiatry, University of Tennessee College of Medicine.

Rosenthal, T. L., & Steffek, B. D. (1991). Modeling methods. In F. H. Kanfer & A. P. Goldstein (Eds.), *Helping people change.* Elmsford, NY: Pergamon.

Rosenzweig, M. R. (1999). Continuity and change in the development of psychology around the world. *American Psychologist, 54*(4), 252–259.

Ross, D. C., Jaffe, J., Collins, R. L., Page, W., & Robinette, D. (1999). Handedness in the NAS/NRC Twin Study. *Laterality, 4*(3), 257–264.

Ross, J. (1976, March). The resources of binocular perception. *Scientific American,* 80–86.

Ross, M., Karniol, R., & Rothstein, M. (1976). Reward contingency and intrinsic motivation in children. *Journal of Personality & Social Psychology, 33,* 442–447.

Roth, W. T., Breivik, G., Jorgensen, P. E., & Hofmann. (1996). Activation in novice and expert parachutists while jumping. *Psychophysiology, 33*(1), 63–72.

Rothbaum, B. O., Hodges, L., & Kooper, R. (1997). Virtual reality and tactile augmentation in the treatment of spider phobia. *Journal of Psychotherapy Practice & Research, 6*(3), 219–226.

Rothbaum, B. O., Hodges, L. F., Kooper, R., Opdyke, D., et al. (1995). Effectiveness of computer-generated (virtual reality) graded exposure in the treatment of acrophobia. *American Journal of Psychiatry, 152*(4), 626–628.

Rothbaum, B. O., Hodges, L., Watson, B. A., Kessler, G. D., et al. (1996). Virtual reality exposure therapy in the treatment of fear of flying: A case report. *Behaviour Research & Therapy, 34*(5–6), 477–481.

Rotter, J. B., & Hochreich, D. J. (1975). *Personality.* Glenview, IL: Scott, Foresman.

Rowe, D. C., Chassin, L., Presson, C., & Sherman, S. J. (1996). Parental smoking and the "epidemic" spread of cigarette smoking. *Journal of Applied Social Psychology, 26*(5), 437–454.

Rowe, J. W., & Kahn, R. L. (1998). *Successful aging.* New York: Dell.

Rubenstein, C. (1983, July). The modern art of courtly love. *Psychology Today.*

Rubenstein, C., & Tavris, C. (1987). Special survey results: 2600 women reveal the secrets of intimacy. *Redbook, 159,* 147–149.

Rubin, D. C. (1985, September). The subtle deceiver: Recalling our past. *Psychology Today,* 38–46.

Rubin, D. C., & Schulkind, M. D. (1997). Distribution of important and word-cued autobiographical memories in 20-, 35-, and 70-year-old-adults. *Psychology and Aging, 12*(3), 524–535.

Rubin, J. (1990). Drugs for treating behavior problems: How safe are they? *American Psychologist, 45*(8), 985–986.

Rubin, K. H. (1998). Social and emotional development from a cultural perspective. *Developmental Psychology, 34*(4), 611–615.

Rubin, V., & Comitas, L. (Eds.). (1975). *Ganja in Jamaica.* The Hague: Mouton.

Rubin, Z. (1970a, December). Jokers wild in the lab. *Psychology Today,*

Rubin, Z. (1970b). Measurement of romantic love. *Journal of Personality & Social Psychology, 16,* 265–273.

Rubin, Z. (1973). *Liking and loving: An invitation to social psychology.* New York: Holt.

Rubin, Z. (1975). Disclosing oneself to a stranger: Reciprocity and its limits. *Journal of Experimental and Social Psychology, 11,* 233–260.

Rumbaugh, D. M., Hopkins, W. D., Washburn, D. A., & Savage-Rumbaugh, E. S. (1989). Lana chimpanzee learns to count by "numath": A summary of a videotaped experimental report. *Psychological Record, 39*(4), 459–470.

Runco, M. A., & Chand, I. (1995). Cognition and creativity. *Educational Psychology Review, 7*(3), 243–268.

Ruscio, J., Whitney, D. M., & Amabile, T. M. (1998). Looking inside the fishbowl of creativity. *Creativity Research Journal, 11*(3), 243–263.

Rushton, J. P. (1995). Sex and race differences in cranial capacity from international labour office data. *Intelligence, 19*(3), 281–294.

Russell, T. G., Rowe, W., & Smouse, A. D. (1991). Subliminal self-help tapes and academic achievement: An evaluation. *Journal of Counseling and Development, 69,* 359–362.

Russo, M. B., et al. (1998). Conversion disorder presenting as multiple sclerosis. *Military Medicine, 163*(10), 709–710.

Russo, N. F. (1990). Forging research priorities for women's mental health. *American Psychologist, 45*(3), 368–373.

Rutledge, T., & Linden, W. (1998). To eat or not to eat: Affective and physiological mechanisms in the stress-eating relationship. *Journal of Behavioral Medicine, 21*(3), 221–240.

Rutter, M. (1995). Maternal deprivation. In M. H. Bornstein (Ed.), *Handbook of parenting, Vol. 4.* Mahwah, NJ: Erlbaum.

Ryan, R. M, & Deci, E. L. (2000). Self-determination theory and the facilitation of intrinsic motivation, social development, and well-being. *American Psychologist, 55*(1), 68–78.

Ryba, N. J. P. (1999). Pheromone reception: A complex map of activation in the brain. *Current Biology, 9*(13), R472–R474.

Rye, D. B. (1999). Tracking neural pathways with MRI. *Trends in Neurosciences, 22*(9), 373–374.

Ryff, C. D. (1995). Psychological well-being in adult life. *Current Directions in Psychological Science, 4*(4), 99–104.

Ryff, C. D., & Keyes, C. L. (1995). The structure of psychological well-being revisited. *Journal of Personality & Social Psychology, 69*(4), 719–727.

Saariluoma, P. (1994). Location coding in chess. *Quarterly Journal of Experimental Psychology: Human Experimental Psychology, 47A*(3), 607–630.

Sacks, O. (1990). *Seeing voices.* New York: Harper Perennial.

Sadato, N., Pascual-Leone, A., & Hallett, M. (1996). Activation of the primary visual cortex by Braille reading in blind subjects. *Nature, 380*(6574), 526.

Sadker, M., & Sadker, D. (1994). Failing at fairness: How America's schools cheat girls. New York: Scribner's.

Sadowski, C., & Kelley, M. L. (1993). Social problem solving in suicidal adolescents. *Journal of Consulting and Clinical Psychology, 61*(1), 121–127.

Saegert, S., Swap, W., & Zajonc, R. B. (1973). Exposure, context, and interpersonal attraction. *Journal of Personality & Social Psychology, 25,* 234–242.

Sagan, C., & Turco, R. (1990, February 4). Too many weapons in the world. *Parade,* pp. 10–13.

Sagi, A. (1990). Attachment theory and research from a cross-cultural perspective. *Human Development, 33*(1), 10–22.

Sagvolden, T., & Sergeant, J. A. (1998). Attention deficit/hyperactivity disorder: From brain dysfunctions to behaviour. *Behavioural Brain Research, 94*(1), 1–10.

Sahelian, R. (1998). *5-HTP.* Wakefield, RI: Moyer Bell.

Sales, B. D., & Hafemeister, T. L. (1985). Law and psychology. In E. M. Altmeir& M. E. Meyer (Eds.), *Applied specialties in psychology.* New York: Random House.

Salive, M. E., Guralnik, J. M., & Glynn, R. J. (1993). Left-handedness and mortality. *American Journal of Public Health, 83*(2), 265–267.

Salmela, J. H. (1974). An information processing approach to volleyball. *C.V.A. Technical Journal, 1,* 49–62.

Salmela, J. H. (1975). Psycho-motor task demands of artistic gymnastics. In J. H. Salmela (Ed.), *The advanced study of gymnastics: A textbook.* Sundby.

Salovey, P., & Mayer, J. (1997). *Emotional development and emotional intelligence.* New York: Basic.

Salovey, P., & Singer, J. A. (1989). Mood congruency effects in recall of childhood versus recent memories. *Journal of Social Behavior & Personality, 4*(2), 99–120.

Salthouse, T. A., & Maurer, T. J. (1996). Aging, job performance, and career development. In J. E. Birren, et al. (Eds.), *Handbook of the psychology of aging.* San Diego, CA: Academic Press.

Sampson, E. E. (1993). Identity politics. *American Psychologist, 48*(12), 1219–1230.

Sanders, P., & Rosenfield, M. (1998). Counselling at a distance. *British Journal of Guidance & Counselling, 26*(1), 5–10.

Sansone, R. A., Sansone, L. A., & Righter, E. L. (1998). Panic disorder. *Journal of Women's Health, 7*(8), 983–989.

Santrock, J., Minnett, A., & Campbell, B. (1994). *The authoritative guide to self-help books.* New York: Guilford.

Santrock, J. W. (1995). *Adolescence.* Madison, WI: Brown & Benchmark.

Santy, P. A., Holland, A. W., Looper, L., & Marcondes-North, R. (1993). Multicultural factors in the space environment. *Aviation, Space, & Environmental Medicine, 64*(3), 196–200.

Sapp, M. (1997). Theories of hypnosis. *Australian Journal of Clinical Hypnotherapy & Hypnosis, 18*(2), 43–53.

Sarason, I. G. (1981). Test anxiety, stress, and social support. *Journal of Personality, 49,* 101–114.

Saucier, G., & Goldberg, L. R. (1998). What is beyond the Big Five? *Journal of Personality, 66*(4), 495–524.

Saudino, K. J., et al. (1997). Can personality explain genetic influences on life events? *Journal of Personality & Social Psychology, 72*(1), 196–206.

Saunders, T., Driskell, J. E., Johnston, J. H., & Salas, E. (1996). The effect of stress inoculation training on anxiety and performance. *Journal of Occupational Health Psychology, 1*(2), 170–186.

Savage-Rumbaugh, E. S., Murphy, J., Sevcik, R. A., Brakke, K. E., et al. (1993). Language comprehension in ape and child. *Monographs of the Society for Research in Child Development, 58*(3–4), v–221.

Savage-Rumbaugh, S., & Lewin, R. (1996). *Kanzi.* New York: Wiley.

Savage-Rumbaugh, S., Sevcik, R. A., Brakke, K. E., Rumbaugh, D. M., et al. (1990). Symbols: Their communicative use, comprehension, and combination by bonobos (*Pan paniscus*). *Advances in Infancy Research, 6,* 221–278.

Savant syndrome. (1995). *Education & Training in Mental Retardation & Developmental Disabilities, 30*(3), 243–253.

Sawyer, R. G., & Smith, N. G. (1996). A survey of situational factors at first intercourse among college students. *American Journal of Health Behavior, 20*(4), 208–217.

Saxe, L. (1991). Lying. *American Psychologist, 46*(4), 409–415.

Saxe, L. (1994). Detection of deception: Polygraph and integrity tests. *Current Directions in Psychological Science, 3*(3), 69–73.

Saxe, L., Dougherty, D., & Cross, T. (1985). The validity of polygraph testing. *American Psychologist, 40,* 355–366.

Scarr, S. (1998). American child care today. *American Psychologist, 53*(2), 95–108.

Schachter, S. (1951). Communication, deviation, and rejection. *Journal of Abnormal and Social Psychology, 46,* 190–207.

Schachter, S. (1959). *Psychology of affiliation.* Stanford, CA: Stanford University Press.

Schachter, S., & Wheeler, L. (1962). Epinephrine, chlorpromazine and amusement. *Journal of Abnormal and Social Psychology, 65,* 121–128.

Schacter, D. L. (1996). *Searching for memory.* New York: Basic.

Schacter, D. L. (1999). The seven sins of memory. *American Psychologist, 54*(3), 194–201.

Schacter, D. L., Norman, K. A., & Koutstaal, W. (1998). The cognitive neuroscience of constructive memory. *Annual Review of Psychology, 49,* 289–318.

Schafer, M., & Crichlow, S. (1996). Antecedents of groupthink: A quantitative study. *Journal of Conflict Resolution, 40*(3), 415–435.

Schafer, W. D. (1999). Methods, plainly speaking: An overview of meta-analysis. *Measurement & Evaluation in Counseling & Development, 32*(1), 43–61.

Schaie, K. W. (1988). Ageism in psychological research. *American Psychologist, 43*(3), 179–183.

Schaie, K. W. (1994). The course of adult intellectual development. *American Psychologist, 49*(4), 304–313.

Schaller, S. (1991). *A man without words.* New York: Summit.

Scheck, M. M., Schaeffer, J. A., & Gillette, C. (1998). Brief psychological intervention with traumatized young women. *Journal of Traumatic Stress, 11*(1), 25–44.

Schein, E. H., Hill, W. F., Lubin, A., & Williams, H. L. (1957). Distinguishing characteristics of collaborators and resistors among American prisoners of war. *Journal of Abnormal and Social Psychology, 55,* 197–201.

Schein, E. H., Schneier, I., & Barker, C. H. (1961). *Coercive persuasion.* New York: Norton.

Schick, T., & Vaughn, L. (1995). How to think about weird things: Critical thinking for a new age. Mountain View, CA: Mayfield.

Schlosberg, H. (1954). Three dimensions of emotion. *Psychological Review, 61,* 81–88.

Schmidt, F. L., & Hunter, J. E. (1998). The validity and utility of selection methods in personnel psychology. *Psychological Bulletin, 124*(2), 262–274.

Schmidt, F. L., Ones, D. S., & Hunter, J. E. (1992). Personnel selection. *Annual Review of Psychology, 43,* 627–670.

Schmidt, L. A., & Fox, N. A. (1995). Individual differences in young adults' shyness and sociability. *Personality & Individual Differences, 19*(4), 455–462.

Schmitt, D. P., & Buss, D. M. (1996). Strategic self-promotion and competitor derogation. *Journal of Personality & Social Psychology, 70*(6), 1185–1204.

Schneider, C. (1987). *Children's television: The art, the business, and how it works.* Chicago: NTC Business Books.

Schneider, H. G., & Shugar, G. J. (1990). Audience and feedback effects in computer learning. *Computers in Human Behavior, 6*(4), 315–321.

Schoggen, P. (1989). *Behavior settings.* Stanford, CA: Stanford University Press.

Schooler, C., Flora, J. A., & Farquhar, J. W. (1993). Moving toward synergy: Media supplementation in the Stanford Five-City Project. *Communication Research, 20*(4), 587–610.

Schotte, D. E., Cools, J., & McNally, R. J. (1990). Film-induced negative affect triggers overeating in restrained eaters. *Journal of Abnormal Psychology, 99*(3), 317–320.

Schouten, S. A. (1994). An overview of quantitatively evaluated studies with mediums and psychics. *Journal of the American Society for Psychical Research, 88*(3), 221–254.

Schredl, M. (1995). Creativity and dream recall. *Journal of Creative Behavior, 29*(1), 16–24.

Schreiber, E. H., & Schreiber, D. E. (1999). Use of hypnosis with witnesses of vehicular homicide. *Contemporary Hypnosis, 16*(1), 40–44.

Schreiber, F. R. (1973). *Sybil.* Chicago: Regency.

Schroeder, J. E. (1995). Self-concept, social anxiety, and interpersonal perception skills. *Personality & Individual Differences, 19*(6), 955–958.

Schroots, J. J. F. (1996). Theoretical developments in the psychology of aging. *Gerontologist, 36*(6), 742–748

Schuerger, J. M., & Witt, A. C. (1989). The temporal stability of individually tested intelligence. *Journal of Clinical Psychology, 45*(2), 294–302.

Schulz, R. (1978). *The psychology of death, dying and bereavement.* Reading, MA: Addison-Wesley.

Schulz, R., & Heckhausen, J. (1996). A life span model of successful aging. *American Psychologist, 51*(7), 702–714.

Schunk, D. H. (1990). Goal setting and self-efficacy during self-regulated learning. *Educational Psychologist, 25*(1), 71–86.

Schwartz, B., & Robbins, S. J. (1995). *Psychology of learning & behavior.* New York: Norton.

Schwartz, L. L. (1991). The historical dimension of cultic techniques of persuasion and control. *Cultic Studies Journal, 8*(1), 37–45.

Schweickert, R. (1993). A multinomial processing tree model for degradation and redintegration in immediate recall. *Memory & Cognition, 21*(2), 168–175.

Sclafani, A., & Springer, D. (1976). Dietary obesity in adult rats: Similarities to hypothalamic and human obesity syndromes. *Psychology and Behavior, 17,* 461–471.

Scopesi, A., Zanobini, M., & Carossino, P. (1997). Childbirth in different cultures: Psychophysical reactions of women delivering in US, German, French, and Italian hospitals. *Journal of Reproductive & Infant Psychology, 15*(1), 9–30.

Scott, J. (1996). New chapter for the fat controller. *Nature, 379*(6561), 113–114.

Scott, J. P., & Ginsburg, B. E. (1994). The Seville statement on violence revisited. *American Psychologist, 49*(10), 849–850.

Scott, L., & O'Hara, M. W. (1993). Self-discrepancies in clinically anxious and depressed university students. *Journal of Abnormal Psychology, 102*(2), 282–287.

Scott, N. E., & Borodovsky, L. G. (1990). Effective use of cultural role taking. *Professional Psychology: Research & Practice, 21*(3), 167–170.

Scroppo, J. C., Drob, S. L., Weinberger, J. L., & Eagle, P. (1998). Identifying dissociative identity disorder: A self-report and projective study. *Journal of Abnormal Psychology, 107*(2), 272–284.

Seal, D. W., & Palmer-Seal, D. A. (1996). Barriers to condom use and safer sex talk among college dating couples. *Journal of Community & Applied Social Psychology, 6*(1), 15–33.

Sears, R. R., Maccoby, E. E., & Levin, H. (1957). *Patterns of child rearing.* Evanston, IL: Row, Peterson.

Segall, M. H., Lonner, W. J., & Berry, J. W. (1998). Cross-cultural psychology as a scholarly discipline. *American Psychologist, 53*(10), 1101–1110.

Segerstrom, S. C., et al., (1998). Optimism is associated with mood, coping and immune change in response to stress. *Journal of Personality & Social Psychology, 74*(6), 1646–1655.

Segraves, R. T., & Segraves, K. B. (1995). Human sexuality and aging. *Journal of Sex Education & Therapy, 21*(2), 88–102.

Seligman, M. E. P. (1972a). For helplessness: Can we immunize the weak? In *Readings in psychology today* (2nd ed.). Del Mar, CA: CRM.

Seligman, M. E. P. (1972b). Phobias and preparedness. In M. E. P. Seligman & J. L. Hager (Eds.), *Biological boundaries of learning.* New York: Appleton-Century-Crofts.

Seligman, M. E. P. (1989). *Helplessness.* New York: Freeman.

Seligman, M. E. P. (1994). *What you can change and what you can't.* New York: Knopf.

Seligman, M. E. P. (1995). The effectiveness of psychotherapy. *American Psychologist, 50*(12), 965–974.

Seligman, M. E. P. (1998). Why therapy works. *APA Monitor, 29*(12), 2.

Selye, H. (1956, 1976). *The stress of life.* New York: Knopf.

Senden, M. V. (1960). *Space and sight* (P. Heath, Trans.). Glencoe, IL: Free Press.

Serbin, L. A., & O'Leary, K. D. (1975, December). How nursery schools teach girls to shut up. *Psychology Today,* 57–58, 102–103.

Serdula, M. K., Mokdad, A. H., Williamson, D. F., Galuska, D. A., et al. (1999). Prevalence of attempting weight loss and strategies for controlling weight. *Journal of the American Medical Association, 282*(14), 1353–1358.

Seto, M. C., & Kuban, M. (1996). Criterion-related validity of a phallometric test for paraphilic rape and sadism. *Behaviour Research & Therapy, 34*(2), 175–183.

Seybolt, D. C., & Wagner, M. K. (1997). Self-reinforcement, gender-role, and sex of participant in prediction of life satisfaction. *Psychological Reports, 81*(2), 519–522.

Shaffer, D. R. (1999). *Developmental psychology.* Pacific Grove, CA: Brooks/Cole.

Shaffer, J. B., & Galinsky, M. D. (1989). *Models of group therapy.* Englewood Cliffs, NJ: Prentice Hall.

Shafir, E. (1993). Choosing versus rejecting: Why some options are both better and worse than others. *Memory and Cognition, 21,* 546–556.

Shapiro, F. (1995). *Eye movement desensitization and reprocessing.* New York: Guilford.

Shapiro, J. P., & Bowermaster, D. (1994, April 25). The case of Dr. Kevorkian obscures critical issues—and dangers. *US News & World Report,* online edition.

Sharma, T., et al. (1998). Brain changes in schizophrenia. *British Journal of Psychiatry, 173,* 132–138.

Shatz, M. (1986). Students' guessing strategies: Do they work? *Psychological Reports, 57*(3), 1167–1168.

Shaver, P. R., & Hazen, C. (1993). Adult romantic attachment. In D. Perlman & W. H. Jones (Eds.), *Advances in personal relationships, 4.* London: Kingsley.

Shaw, G. L. (1999). Keeping Mozart in mind. San Diego, CA: Academic.

Shaw, J. S. (1996). Increases in eyewitness confidence resulting from postevent questioning. *Journal of Experimental Psychology: Applied, 2*(2), 126–146.

Shaywitz, S. E., & Gore, J. C. (1995). Sex differences in functional organization of the brain for language. *Nature, 373*(6515), 607.

Sheehan, P. W., Statham, D. (1989). Hypnosis, the timing of its introduction, and acceptance of misleading information. *Journal of Abnormal Psychology, 98*(2), 170–176.

Sheehy, G. (1995). *New passages.* New York: Random House.

Sheehy, M., & Cournos, F. (1992). What is mental illness? In F. I. Kass, J. M. Oldham, & H. Pardes (Eds.), *The Columbia University College of Physicians and Surgeons Complete Home Guide to Mental Health.* New York: Sharpe Communications/Henry Holt.

Sheeran, P., Abraham, C., & Orbell, S. (1999). Psychosocial correlates of heterosexual condom use: A meta-analysis. *Psychological Bulletin, 125*(1), 90–132.

Sheldon, K. M, & Elliot, A. J. (1999). Goal striving, need satisfaction, and longitudinal well-being. *Journal of Personality and Social Psychology, 76,*(3), 482–497.

Sheldon, K. M., Ryan, R. M., Rawsthorne, L. J., & Ilardi, B. (1997). Trait self and true self: Cross-role variation in the Big-Five personality traits and its relations with psychological authenticity and subjective well-being. *Journal of Personality & Social Psychology, 73*(6), 1380–1393.

Shepard, R. N. (1975). Form, formation, and transformation of internal representations. In R. L. Solso (Ed.), *Information processing and cognition: The Loyola Symposium.* Hillsdale, NJ: Erlbaum.

Sherif, M., Harvey, O. J., White, B. J., Hood, W. R., & Sherif, C. W. (1961). *Intergroup conflict and cooperation: The Robbers Cave experiment.* University of Oklahoma, Institute of Group Relations.

Shermer, M. (1992). A skeptical look at cryonic suspension. *Skeptic, 1*(2), 50–51.

Shields, P. L., & Rovee-Collier, C. (1992). Long-term memory for context-speciflc category information at six months. *Child Development, 63*(2), 245–259.

Shires, A., & Miller, D. (1998). A preliminary study comparing psychological factors associated with erectile dysfunction in heterosexual and homosexual men. *Sexual & Marital Therapy, 13*(1), 37–49.

Shneidman, E. (1987a, March). At the point of no return. *Psychology Today,* 54–58.

Shneidman, E. S. (1987b). Psychological approaches to suicide. In G. R. VandenBos & B. K. Bryant (Eds.), *Cataclysms, crises, and catastrophes: Psychology in action.* Washington, DC: American Psychological Association.

Shogren, E. (1994, August 18). Treatment against their will. *Los Angeles Times,* pp. A1, A14, A15.

Shore, L. A. (1990). Skepticism in light of scientific literacy. *Skeptical Inquirer, 15,* 3–4.

Short, R. H., & Hess, G. C. (1995). Fetal alcohol syndrome: Characteristics and remedial implications. *Developmental Disabilities Bulletin, 23*(1), 12–29.

Shrum, L. J., Lowrey, T. M., & McCarty, J. A. (1995). Applying social and traditional marketing principles to the reduction of household waste. *American Behavioral Scientist, 38*(4), 646–657.

Shulman, G. I. (1974). Race, sex and violence: A laboratory test of the sexual threat of the black male hypothesis. *American Journal of Sociology, 79,* 1260–1277.

Shurkin, J. N. (1992). *Terman's kids.* Boston: Little, Brown.

Shweder, R. A. (1999). Why cultural psychology? *Ethos, 27*(1), 62–73.

Siau, K. L. (1996). Group creativity and technology. *Journal of Creative Behavior, 29*(3), 201–216.

Sieber, J. E., & Saks, M. J. (1989). A census of subject pool characteristics and policies. *American Psychologist, 44*(7), 1053–1061.

Siegel, J. M., Nienhuis, R., Fahringer, H. M., et al. (1991). Neuronal activity in narcolepsy: Identification of cataplexy related cells in the medial medulla. *Science, 252*(5010), 1315–1318.

Siegelman, M. (1987). Kinsey and others: Empirical input. In L. Diamant (Ed.), *Male and female homosexuality: Psychological approaches.* Washington, DC: Hemisphere.

Siegler, R. S. (1989). Mechanisms of cognitive development. *Annual Review of Psychology, 40,* 353–379.

Sigman, M. (1995). Current research findings on childhood autism. *Canadian Journal of Psychiatry, 40*(6), 289–294.

Silva, C. E., & Kirsch, I. (1992). Interpretive sets, expectancy, fantasy proneness, and dissociation as predictors of hypnotic response. *Journal of Personality & Social Psychology, 63*(5), 847–856.

Silver, E., Cirincione, C., & Steadman, H. J. (1994). Demythologizing inaccurate perceptions of the insanity defense. *Law & Human Behavior, 18*(1), 63–70.

Silverman, K., Evans, S. M., Strain, E. C., & Griffiths, R. R. (1992). Withdrawal syndrome after the double-blind cessation of caffeine consumption. *New England Journal of Medicine, 327*(16), 1109–1114.

Silverman, L. K. (1998). Through the lens of giftedness. *Roeper Review, 20*(3) 204–210.

Silverstein, B. (1989). Enemy images. *American Psychologist, 44*(6), 903–913.

Simon, A. (1998). Aggression in a prison setting as a function of lunar phases.

Simon, L. (1998). *Genuine reality: A life of William James.* Ft. Worth, TX: Harcourt-Brace.

Simons, D. J., & Levin, D. T. (1998). Failure to detect changes to people during a real-world interaction. *Psychonomic Bulletin & Review, 5*(4), 644–649.

Simonton, D. K. (1988). Age and outstanding achievement: What do we know after a century of research? *Psychological Bulletin, 104*(2), 251–267.

Simpson, D. D., Joe, G. W., Fletcher, B. W., Hubbard, R. L, & Anglin, M. D. (1999). A national evaluation of treatment outcomes for cocaine dependence. *Archives of General Psychiatry, 57*(6), 507–514.

Simpson, J. A. (1990). Influence of attachment styles on romantic relationships. *Journal of Personality & Social Psychology, 59*(5), 971–980.

Singer, J. L. (1974). Daydreaming and the stream of thought. *American Scientist, 62,* 417–425.

Singer, L. T., Arendt, R., Fagan, J., Minnes, S., et al. (1999). Neonatal visual information processing in cocaine-exposed and non-exposed infants. *Infant Behavior & Development, 22*(l), 1–15.

Singer, M. T. (1979, January). Coming out of the cults. *Psychology Today,* 72–82.

Singer, M. T., & Addis, M. E. (1992). Cults, coercion, and contumely. *Cultic Studies Journal, 9*(2), 163–189.

Singh, N. N., McKay, J. D., & Singh, A. N. (1998). Culture and mental health: Nonverbal communication. *Journal of Child & Family Studies, 7*(4), 403–409.

Sirkin, M. I. (1990). Cult involvement: A systems approach to assessment and treatment. *Psychotherapy, 27*(1), 116–123.

Sison, C. E., Alpert, M., Fudge, R., & Stern, R. M. (1996). Constricted expressiveness and psychophysiological reactivity in schizophrenia. *Journal of Nervous & Mental Disease, 184*(10), 589–597.

Skeels, H. M. (1966). Adult status of children with contrasting early life experiences. *Monograph of the Society for Research in Child Development, 31*(3).

Skinner, B. F. (1938). *The behavior of organisms.* Englewood Cliffs, NJ: Prentice-Hall.

Skinner, B. F. (1971). *Beyond freedom and dignity.* New York: Bantam.

Skinner, B. F. (1990). Can psychology be a science of mind? *American Psvchologist, 45*(11), 1206–1210.

Skipton, L. H. (1997). The many faces of character. *Consulting Psychology Journal: Practice & Research, 49*(4), 235–245.

Skoog, I. (1996). Sex and Swedish 85-year-olds. *British Journal of Clinical Psychology, 334*(17), 1140–1141.

Skrandies, W., Reik, P., & Kunze, C. (1999). Topography of evoked brain activity during mental arithmetic and language tasks: Sex differences. *Neuropsychologia, 37*(4), 421–430.

Skuy, M., Mentis, M., Durbach, F., & Cockcroft, K. (1995). Crosscultural comparison of effects of instrumental enrichment on children in a South African mining town. *School Psychology International, 16*(3), 265–282.

Slaby, A. E., Garfinkel, B. D., & Garfinkel, L. F. (1994). *No one say my pain.* New York: Norton.

Slater, A., Mattock, A., Brown, E., & Bremner, J. G. (1991). Form perception at birth: Cohen and Younger (1984) revisited. *Journal of Experimental Child Psychology, 51*(3), 395–406.

Sledge, W. H., Tebes, J., Rakfeldt, J., & Davidson, L. (1996). Day hospital/crisis respite care versus inpatient care: I. Clinical outcomes. *American Journal of Psychiatry, 153*(8), 1065–1073.

Sleek, S. (1995, November). Online therapy services raise ethical questions. *APA Monitor,* p. 9.

Sleek, S. (1998, November). How are psychologists portrayed on screen? *APA Monitor,* p. 11.

Slot, L. A. B., & Colpaert, F. C. (1999). Recall rendered dependent on an opiate state. *Behavioral Neuroscience, 113*(2), 337–344.

Slotkin, T. A. (1998). Fetal nicotine or cocaine exposure: which one is worse?

Smit, R. (1999). Results of the Knegt follow-up test. *Correlation, 17,* 5–7.

Smith, A., Sturgess, W., & Gallagher, J. (1999). Effects of a low dose of caffeine given in different drinks on mood and performance. *Human Psychopharmacology Clinical & Experimental, 14*(7), 473–482.

Smith, A., & Sugar, O. (1975). Development of above normal language and intelligence 21 years after left hemispherectomy. *Neurology, 25,* 813–818.

Smith, A. P., Clark, R., & Gallagher, J. (1999). Breakfast cereal and caffeinated coffee: Effects on working memory, attention, mood and cardiovascular function. *Physiology & Behavior, 67*(1), 9–17.

Smith, C. (1995). Sleep states and memory processes. *Behavioural Brain Research, 69*(1–2), 137–145.

Smith, C., Carey, S., & Wiser, M. (1985). On differentiation: A case study of the development of the concepts of size, weight, and density. *Cognition, 21*(3), 177–237.

Smith, E. E. (1989). Concepts and induction. In M. I. Posner (Ed.), *Foundations of cognitive science,* Cambridge, MA: MIT Press.

Smith, J. C. (1986, September). Meditation, biofeedback, and the relaxation controversy: A cognitive-behavioral perspective. *American Psychologist,* 1007–1009.

Smith, K. H., & Rogers, M. (1994). Effectiveness of subliminal messages in television commercials: Two experiments. *Journal of Applied Psychology, 79*(6), 866–874.

Smith, R. W., & Kounios, J. (1996). Sudden insight: All-or-none processing revealed by speed-accuracy decomposition. *Journal of Experimental Psychology: Learning, Memory, & Cognition, 22*(6), 1443–1462.

Smith, S. M, McIntosh, W. D., & Bazzini, D. G. (1999). Are the beautiful good in Hollywood? *Basic & Applied Social Psychology, 21*(1), 69–80.

Smith, T. W. (1990, February). *Adult sexual behavior in 1989: Number of partners, frequency, and risk.* Paper presented to the American Association for the Advancement of Science, New Orleans.

Smith, V. L., Kassin, S. M., & Ellsworth, P. C. (1989). Eyewitness accuracy and confidence: Within- versus between-subjects correlations. *Journal of Applied Psychology, 74*(2), 356–359.

Smith, W. P., Compton, W. C., & West, W. B. (1995). Meditation as an adjunct to a happiness enhancement program. *Journal of Clinical Psychology, 51*(2), 269–273.

Smyth, M. M., & Waller, A. (1998). Movement imagery in rock climbing. *Applied Cognitive Psychology, 12*(2), 145–157.

Snow, C. P. (1961, February). Either-or. *Progressive,* p. 24.

Snowden, P. L., & Christian, L. G. (1999). Parenting the young gifted child: Supportive behaviors. *Roeper Review, 21*(3), 215–221.

Snowdon, C. T. (1983). Ethology, comparative psychology, and animal behavior. *Annual Review of Psychology, 34,* 63–94.

Snyder, M. (1987). *Public appearances and private realities.* New York: Freeman.

Snyder, M., & Harkness, A. R. (1984). *Ef(p): The impact of personality on choice of situation.* Paper presented at the annual meeting of the Midwestern Psychological Association, Chicago.

Snyder, M., & Smith, D. (1985). *Self-monitoring and depression: Precipitating events and coping strategies.* Paper presented at the annual meeting of the Midwestern Psychological Association, Chicago.

Snyderman, M., & Rothman, S. (1987). Survey of expert opinion on intelligence and aptitude testing. *American Psychologist, 42*(2), 137–144.

Sobel, E., Shine, D., DiPietro, D., & Rabinowitz, M. (1996). Condom use among HIV/infected patients in South Bronx, New York. *AIDS, 10*(2), 235–236.

Solomon, R. C., & Wynne, L. C. (1953). Traumatic avoidance learning: Acquisition in normal dogs. *Psychological Monographs, 67*(4, Whole No. 354).

Solomon, R. L. (1980, August). The opponent-process theory of acquired motivation. *American Psychologist,* 691–721.

Solowij, N., Michie, P. T., & Fox, A. M. (1995). Differential impairments of selective attention due to frequency and duration of cannabis use. *Biological Psychiatry, 37*(10), 731–739.

Somberg, D. R., Stone, G., & Claiborn, C. D. (1993). Informed consent: Therapist's beliefs and practices. *Professional Psychology: Research & Practice, 24*(2), 153–159.

Spangenberg, J. J., & Lategan, T. P. (1993). Coping, androgyny, and attributional style. *South African Journal of Psychology, 23*(4), 195–203.

Spence, J. T. (1984). Masculinity, femininity, and gender-related traits. In B. A. Maker & W. B. Maker (Eds.), *Progress in experimental personality research: Normal personality processes, Vol. 13.* New York: Academic.

Sperry, R. W. (1968). Hemisphere deconnection and unity in conscious awareness. *American Psychologist, 23,* 723–733.

Sperry, R. W. (1995). The riddle of consciousness and the changing scientific worldview. *Journal of Humanistic Psychology, 35*(2), 7–33.

Spiegel, D. (1986). Dissociation, double binds, and posttraumatic stress in multiple personality disorder. In B. G. Braun (Ed.), *Treatment of multiple personality disorder.* Washington, DC: American Psychiatric Press.

Spiegler, M. D., & Guevremont, D. C. (1998). *Contemporary behavior therapy.* Pacific Grove, CA: Brooks/Cole.

Spitz, R. A. (1945). Hospitalism: An inquiry into the genesis of psychiatric conditions in early childhood. In *The psychoanalytic study of the child, Vol. 1.* (pp. 53–74). New York: International University Press.

Sprafka, J. M., Folsom, A. R., Burke, G. L., et al. (1990). Type A behavior and its association with cardiovascular disease prevalence in blacks and whites: The Minnesota Heart Survey. *Journal of Behavioral Medicine, 13*(1), 1–13.

Sprecher, S. (1998). Insiders' perspectives on reasons for attraction to a close other. *Social Psychology Quarterly, 61*(4), 287–300.

Sprecher, S., & Hatfield, E. (1996). Premarital sexual standards among U.S. college students. *Archives of Sexual Behavior, 25*(3), 261–288.

Springer, S. P., & Deutsch, G. (1998). *Left brain, right brain.* New York: Freeman.

Squire, L. R., Knowlton, B., & Musen, G. (1993). The structure and organization of memory. *Annual Review of Psychology, 44,* 453–495.

Squire, L. R., & Zola-Morgan, S. (1988). Memory: Brain systems and behavior. *Trends in Neurosciences, 11*(4), 170–175.

Staats, P., Hekmat, H., & Staats, A. (1998). Suggestion/placebo effects on pain: Negative as well as positive. *Journal of Pain & Symptom Management, 15*(4), 235–243

Stacy, A. W., Galaif, E. R., Sussman, S., & Dent, C. W. (1996). Self-generated drug outcomes in high-risk adolescents. *Psychology of Addictive Behaviors, 10*(1), 18–27.

Stalheim-Smith, A., & Fitch, G. K. (1993). *Understanding human anatomy and physiology.* St. Paul, MN: West.

Stamm, B. H. (1998). Clinical applications of telehealth in mental health care. *Professional Psychology: Research & Practice, 29*(6), 536–542.

Stanovich, K. E. (1998). *How to think straight about psychology,* 5th ed. New York: Longman.

Staples, S. L. (1996). Human response to environmental noise. *American Psychologist, 51*(2), 143–150.

Staum, M. J., & Brotons, M. (1992). The influence of auditory subliminals on behavior. *Journal of Music Therapy, 29*(3), 130–185.

Staw, B. M., Sutton, R. I., & Pelled, L. H. (1994). Employee positive emotion and favorable outcomes at the workplace. *Organization Science, 5*(1), 51–71.

Steblay, N. M. (1987). Helping behavior in rural and urban environments: A meta-analysis. *Psychological Bulletin, 102*(3), 346–356.

Steblay, N. M. (1992). A meta-analytic review of the weapon focus effect. *Law and Human Behavior, 16,* 413–424.

Steele, C. M. (1997). A threat in the air. *American Psychologist, 52*(6), 613–629.

Steele, C. M., & Josephs, R. A. (1990). Alcohol myopia. *American Psychologist, 45*(8), 921–933.

Steele, K. M., Bass, K. E., & Crook, M.D. (1999). The mystery of the Mozart effect: Failure to replicate. *Psychological Science, 10*(4), 366–369.

Steele, K. M., Brown, J. D., & Stoecker, J. A. (1999). Failure to confirm the Rauscher and Shaw description of recovery of the Mozart effect. *Perceptual & Motor Skills, 88*(3, Pt 1), 843–848.

Steen, R. G. (1996). *DNA and destiny: nature and nurture in human behavior.* New York: Plenum.

Stefanis, C., Dornbush, R. L., & Fink, M. (1977). *Hashish: A study of long-term use.* New York: Raven.

Stein, M., Miller, A. H., & Trestman, R. L. (1990). Depression and the immune system. In R. Ader, N. Cohen, & D. L. Felten (Eds.), *Psychoneuroimmunology II.* New York: Academic Press.

Stein, M. I. (1974). *Stimulating creativity, Vol. 1.* New York: Academic.

Steinbacher, R., & Gilroy, F. (1990). Sex selection technology: A prediction of its use and effect. *Journal of Psychology, 124*(3), 283–288.

Steinberg, L. D., Catalano, R., & Dooley, P. (1981). Economic antecedents of child abuse and neglect. *Child Development, 52,* 975–985.

Steinhausen, H., & Spohr, H. (1998). Long-term outcome of children with fetal alcohol syndrome. *Alcoholism: Clinical & Experimental Research, 22*(2), 334–338.

Stenberg, G., & Hagekull, B. (1997). Social referencing and mood modification in 1-year-olds. *Infant Behavior and Development, 20*(2), 209–217.

Stephan, W., Berscheid, E., & Walster, E. (1971). Sexual arousal and heterosexual perception. *Journal of Personality & Social Psychology, 20*(1), 93–101.

Stephens, K., Kiger, L., Karnes, F. A., & Whorton, J. E. (1999). Use of nonverbal measures of intelligence in identification of culturally diverse gifted students in rural areas. *Perceptual & Motor Skills, 88*(3, Pt 1), 793–796.

Steriade, M., & McCarley, R. W. (1990). Brainstem control of wakefulness and sleep. New York: Plenum.

Sterman, M. B. (1996). Physiological origins and functional correlates of EEG rhythmic activities: Implications for self-regulation. *Biofeedback & Self Regulation, 21*(1), 3–33.

Stern, D. (1982). Some interactive functions of rhythm changes between mother and infant. In M. Davis (Ed.), *Interaction rhythms, periodicity in communicative behavior.* New York: Human Sciences Press.

Stern, R. M., Hu, S., Anderson, R. B., Leibowitz, H. W., et al. (1990). The effects of fixation and restricted visual field on vection-induced motion sickness. *Aviation, Space, & Environmental Medicine, 61*(8), 712–715.

Stern, R. M., & Koch, K. L. (1996). Motion sickness and differential susceptibility. *Current Directions in Psychological Science, 5*(4), 115–120.

Sternbach, H. (1998). Age-associated testosterone decline in men: Clinical issues for psychiatry. *American Journal of Psychiatry, 155*(10), 1310–1318.

Sternberg, R. J. (1988). *The triangle of love.* New York: Basic.

Sternberg, R. J. (1995). Love as a story. *Journal of Social & Personal Relationships, 12*(4), 541–546.

Sternberg, R. J. (1996). *Successful intelligence.* New York: Simon & Schuster.

Sternberg, R. J., & Barnes, M. (1986). Real and ideal others in romantic relationships: Is four a crowd? *Journal of Personality & Social Psychology, 49,* 1586–1608.

Sternberg, R. J., & Davidson, J. D. (1982, June). The mind of the puzzler. *Psychology Today,*

Sternberg, R. J., & Grajek, S. (1984). The nature of love. *Journal of Personality & Social Psychology, 47,* 312–329.

Sternberg, R. J., & Lubart, T. I. (1995). *Defying the crowd.* New York: Free Press.

Sternberg, W. F., Bailin, D., Grant, M., & Gracely, R. H. (1998). Competition alters the perception of noxious stimuli in male and female athletes. *Pain, 76*(1–2), 231–238.

Stewart, A. J., & Ostrove, J. M. (1998). Women's personality in middle age. *American Psychologist, 53*(11), 1185–1194.

Stewart, A. J., & Vandewater, E. A. (1999). "If I had it to do over again . . .": Midlife review, midcourse corrections, and women's well-being in midlife. *Journal of Personality & Social Psychology, 76*(2), 270–283.

Stewart, J. V. (1996). *Astrology: What's really in the stars.* Amherst, NY: Prometheus.

Stiles, W. B., et al. (1998). Relations of the alliance with psychotherapy outcome. *Journal of Consulting & Clinical Psychology, 66*(5), 791–802.

Stiles, W. B., Shapiro, D. A., & Elliott, R. (1986). Are all psychotherapies equivalent? *American Psychologist, 41,* 165–180.

Stockhorst, U., Klosterhalfen, S., & Steingrueber, H. (1998). Conditioned nausea and further side-effects in cancer chemotherapy. *Journal of Psychophysiology, 12*(Suppl. 1), 14–33.

Stokols, D. (1995). The paradox of environmental psychology. *American Psychologist, 50*(10), 821–837.

Stolerman, I. P., & Jarvis, M. J. (1995) The scientific case that nicotine is addictive. *Psychopharmacology, 117*(1), 2–10.

Stone, J., Perry, Z. W., & Darley, J. M. (1997). "White men can't jump." *Basic and Applied Social Psychology, 19*(3), 291–306.

Stoney, S., & Wild, M. (1998). Motivation and interface design: Maximising learning opportunities. *Journal of Computer Assisted Learning, 14*(1), 40–50.

Storck, L. E. (1997). Cultural psychotherapy. *Group, 21*(4), 331–349.

Strack, F., Martin, L. L., & Stepper, S. (1988). Inhibiting and facilitating conditions of facial expressions: A non-obtrusive test of the facial feedback hypothesis. *Journal of Personality & Social Psychology, 54,* 768–777.

Strange, J. R. (1965). *Abnormal psychology.* New York: McGraw-Hill.

Straus, M. A., & Mouradian, V. E. (1998). Impulsive corporal punishment by mothers and antisocial behavior and impulsiveness of children. *Behavioral Sciences & the Law, 16*(3), 353–374.

Streissguth, A. P., Treder, R. P., Barr, H. M., Shepard, T. H., Bleyer, W. A., Sampson, P. D., & Martin, D. C. (1987). Aspirin and acetaminophen use by pregnant women and subsequent child IQ and attention decrements. *Teratology, 35*(2), 211–219.

Strickler, E. M., & Verbalis, J. G. (1988, May–June). Hormones and behavior: The biology of thirst and sodium appetite. *American Scientist,* 261–267.

Strier, F. (1999). Whither trial consulting? Issues and projections. *Law & Human Behavior, 23*(1), 93–115.

Stroeher, S. K. (1994). Sixteen kindergartners' gender-related views of careers. *Elementary School Journal, 95*(1), 95–103.

Strong, B., & DeVault, C. (1994). *Understanding our sexuality.* St. Paul, MN: West.

Strongman, K. T. (1996). *The psychology of emotion.* New York: Wiley.

Strupp, H. H. (1989). Psychotherapy: Can the practitioner learn from the researcher? *American Psychologist, 44*(4), 717–724.

Stunkard, A. J., Sorenson, T. I. A., Hanis, C., Teasdale, T., et al. (1986). An adoption study of human obesity. *New England Journal of Medicine, 314,* 193–198.

Sturges, J. W., & Sturges, L. V. (1998). In vivo *systematic desensitization* in a single-session treatment of an 11-year-old girl's elevator phobia. *Child & Family Behavior Therapy, 20*(4), 55–62.

Sue, D., & Sue, D. W. (1991). Counseling strategies for Chinese Americans. In C. C. Lee & B. L. Richardson (Eds.), *Multicultural issues in counseling.* Alexandria, VA: American Association for Counseling and Development.

Sue, D., Sue, D. W., & Sue, S. (1996). *Understanding abnormal behavior.* Boston: Houghton Mifflin.

Sue, D. W., & Sue, D. (1990). *Counseling the culturally different: Theory and practice.* New York: Wiley.

Sue, S. (1998). In search of cultural competence in psychotherapy and counseling. *American Psychologist, 53*(4), 440–448.

Suedfeld, P. (1980). *Restricted environmental stimulation: Research and clinical applications.* New York: Wiley-Interscience.

Suedfeld, P., & Borrie, R. A. (1999). Health and therapeutic applications of chamber and flotation restricted environmental stimulation therapy (REST). *Psychology & Health, 14*(3), 545–566.

Suedfeld, P., & Piedrahita, L. E. (1984). Intimations of mortality: Integrative simplification as a precursor of death. *Journal of Personality and Social Psychology, 47,* 848–852.

Suedfeld, P., & Steel, G. D. (2000). The environmental psychology of capsule habitats. *Annual Review of Psychol, 51,* 227–253.

Sugihara, Y., & Warner, J. A. (1999). Endorsements by Mexican-Americans of the Bem Sex-Role Inventory: Cross-ethnic comparison. *Psychological Reports, 85*(1), 201–211.

Suinn, R. M. (1970). *Fundamentals of behavior pathology.* New York: Wiley.

Suinn, R. M. (1975). *Fundamentals of behavior pathology* (2nd ed.). New York: Wiley.

Suinn, R. M. (1999, March). Scaling the summit: Valuing ethnicity. *APA Monitor,* p. 2.

Sullivan, M. J., Johnson, P. I., Kjelberg, B. J., Williams, J., et al. (1998). Community leadership opportunities for psychologists. *Professional Psychology: Research and Practice, 29*(4), 328–331.

Suls, J. (1989). Self-awareness and self-identity in adolescence. In J. Worell & F. Danner (Eds.), *The adolescent as decision-maker.* New York: Academic.

Suls, J., & Swain, A. (1994). Type A-Type B personalities. *Encyclopedia of human behavior, Vol. 4* (pp. 427–436). San Diego, CA: Academic.

Sumerlin, J. R. (1997). Self-actualization and hope. *Journal of Social Behavior & Personality, 12*(4), 1101–1110.

Sumerlin, J. R., & Bundrick, C. M. (1996). Brief Index of Self-Actualization: A measure of Maslow's model. *Journal of Social Behavior & Personality, 11*(2), 253–271.

Susman-Stillman, A., Kalkose, M., Egeland, B., & Waldman, I. (1996). Infant temperament and maternal sensitivity as predictors of attachment security. *Infant Behavior & Development, 19*(1), 33–47.

Swan, G. E., & Denk, C. E. (1987). Dynamic models for the maintenance of smoking cessation: Event history analysis of late relapse. *Journal of Behavioral Medicine, 10*(6), 527–554.

Swanson, H. L. (1999). What develops in working memory? A life span perspective. *Developmental Psychology, 35*(4), 986–1000.

Swanson, M. W., Streissguth, A. P., Sampson, P. D., & Carmichael-Olson, H. (1999). Prenatal cocaine and neuromotor outcome at four months: Effect of duration of exposure. *Journal of Developmental & Behavioral Pediatrics, 20*(5), 325–334.

Swart, L. C., & Morgan, C. L. (1992). Effects of subliminal backward-recorded messages on attitudes. *Perceptual & Motor Skills, 75*(3, Pt 2), 1107–1113.

Swartz, C. M. (1993). ECT or programmed seizures? *American Journal of Psychiatry, 150*(8), 1274–1275.

Swayze, V. W. (1995). Frontal leukotomy and related psychosurgical procedures in the era before antipsychotics (1935–1954): A historical overview. *American Journal of Psychiatry, 152*(4), 505–515.

Swets, J., Bjork, R. A., Cook, T. D., Davison, G. C., et al. (1988). *Enhancing human performance: Issues, theories, and techniques.* Washington, DC: National Academy Press of the United States National Research Council.

Swim, J. K., & Sanna, L. J. (1996). He's skilled, she's lucky: A meta-analysis of observers' attributions for women's and men's successes and failures. *Personality & Social Psychology Bulletin, 22*(5), 507–519.

Symons, C. S., & Johnson, B. T. (1997). The self-reference effect in memory: A meta-analysis. *Psychological Bulletin, 121*(3), 371–394.

Szasz, T. S. (1966, June 12). Mental illness is a myth. *New York Times Magazine.*

Szasz, T. S. (1983). *Thomas Szasz: Primary values and major contentions.* Buffalo, NY: Prometheus.

Szasz, T. S. (1987). *Insanity: The idea and its consequences.* New York: Wiley.

Taeuber, C. M. (1993). *Sixty-five plus in America.* Washington, DC: United States Bureau of Census.

Takei, N., Sham, P., O'Callaghan, E., Murray, G. K., et al. (1994). Prenatal exposure to influenza and the development of schizophrenia. *American Journal of Psychiatry, 151*(1), 117–119.

Takooshian, H., Haber, S., & Lucido, D. J. (1977, February). Who wouldn't help a lost child? You, maybe. *Psychology Today,* 67.

Talley, P. F., Strupp, H. H., & Morey, L. C. (1990). Matchmaking in psychotherapy: Patient-therapist dimensions and their impact on outcome. *Journal of Consulting & Clinical Psychology, 58*(2), 182–188.

Tallis, F. (1996). Compulsive washing in the absence of phobic and illness anxiety. *Behaviour Research & Therapy, 34*(4), 361–362.

Tamis-LeMonvda, C. S., & Bornstein, M. H. (1994). Specificity in mother-toddler language-play relations across the second year. *Developmental Psychology, 30*(2), 283–292.

Tang, S., & Hall, V. C. (1995). The overjustification effect: A meta-analysis. *Applied Cognitive Psychology, 9*(5), 365–404.

Tannenbaum, S. I., & Yukl, G. (1992). Training and development in work organizations. *Annual Review of Psychology, 43,* 399–441.

Tanner, J. M. (1973, September). Growing up. *Scientific American,* 34–43.

Tardif, T. Z., & Sternberg, R. J. (1988). What do we know about creativity? In R. J. Sternberg (Ed.), *The nature of creativity.* Cambridge University Press.

Tart, C. T. (1986). Consciousness, altered states, and worlds of experience. *Journal of Transpersonal Psychology, 18*(2), 159–170.

Tavris, C. (1992). *The mismeasure of woman.* New York: Touchstone/Simon & Schuster.

Taylor, S. E. (1990). Health psychology. *American Psychologist, 45*(1), 40–50.

Taylor, S. E., Kemeny, M. E., Reed, G. M., Bower, J. E., & Gruenewald, T. L. (2000). Psychological resources, positive illusions, and health. *American Psychologist, 55*(1), 99–109.

Taylor, T. E. (1983, March 17). Learning studies of higher cognitive levels in short-term sensory isolation environment. Paper delivered at First International Conference on REST and Self-regulation, Denver, Colorado.

Tedeschi, J. T., Lindskold, S., & Rosenfeld, P. (1985). *Introduction to social psychology.* St. Paul: West Publishing.

Teen sex: Not for love. (1989, May). *Psychology Today,* 10.

Tellegen, A. & Waller, N. G. (2000). Exploring personality through test construction: development of the Multidimensional Personality Questionnaire. In S. R. Briggs & J. M. Cheek (Eds.), *Personality measures: Development and evaluation.* Greenwich, CT: JAI.

Tenenbaum, G., Bar-Eli, M., & Eyal, N. (1996). Imagery orientation and vividness: Their effect on a motor skill performance. *Journal of Sport Behavior, 19*(1), 32–49.

Teng, E., & Squire, L. R. (1999). Memory for places learned long ago is intact after hippocampal damage. *Nature, 400*(6745), 675–677.

Teplin, L. A., Abram, K. M., & McClelland, . (1994). Does psychiatric disorder predict violent crime among released jail detainees? *American Psychologist, 49*(4), 335–342.

Ter Riet, G., de Craen, A. J. M., de Boer, A., & Kessels, A.G. H. (1998). Is placebo analgesia mediated by endogenous opioids? A systematic review. *Pain, 76*(3), 273–275.

Terborg, J. R. (1998). Health psychology in the United States. *Applied Psychology: An International Review, 47*(2), 199–217.

Terman, L. M., & Merrill, M. A. (1937; revised, 1960). *Stanford-Binet Intelligence Scale.* Boston: Houghton Mifflin.

Terman, L. M., & Oden, M. (1959). *The gifted group in mid-life. Vol. 5, Genetic studies of genius.* Stanford, CA: Stanford University Press.

Terry, D. J., & Hogg, M. A. (1996). Group norms and the attitude-behavior relationship. *Personality & Social Psychology Bulletin, 22*(8), 776–793.

Teti, D. M. (1996). And baby makes four: Predictors of attachment security among preschool-age firstborns during the transition to siblinghood. *Child Development, 67*(2), 579–596.

Thase, M. E., & Kupfer, D. L. (1996). Recent developments in the pharmacotherapy of mood disorders. *Journal of Consulting & Clinical Psychology, 64*(4), 646–659.

Thatcher, R. W., Walker, R. A., & Giudice, S. (1987). Human cerebral hemispheres develop at different rates and ages. *Science, 236,* 1110–1113.

Thayer, S. (1988, March). Close encounters. *Psychology Today,* 31–36.

Thelen, E. (1995). Motor development. *American Psychologist, 50*(2), 79–95.

They'd kill for $1 million. (1991, July 1). *Los Angeles Times,* p. A8.

Thibodeau, R., & Aronson, E. (1992). Taking a closer look: Reasserting the role of self-concept in dissonance theory. *Personality and Social Psychology Bulletin, 18*(5), 591–602.

Thies, C. F., & Register, C. A. (1993). Decriminalization of marijuana and the demand for alcohol, marijuana and cocaine. *Social Science Journal, 30*(4), 385–399.

Thoman, E. B., Davis, D. H., Graham, S., Scholz, J. P., et al. (1988). Infants at risk for sudden infant death syndrome (SIDS): Differential prediction for three siblings of SIDS infants. *Journal of Behavioral Medicine, 11*(6), 565–583.

Thomas, T. N. (1995). Acculturative stress in the adjustment of immigrant families. *Journal of Social Distress & the Homeless, 4*(2), 131–142.

Thompson, C. P., Cowan, T. M., & Frieman, J. (1993). *Memory search by a menorist.* Hillsdale, NJ: Lawrence Erlbaum.

Thompson, R. F. (1991). Are memory traces localized or distributed? *Neuropsychologia, 29*(6), 571–582.

Thornburg, H. D. (1984). *Introduction to educational psychology.* St. Paul, MN: West.

Thorson, J. A., & Powell, F. C. (1990). Meanings of death and intrinsic religiosity. *Journal of Clinical Psychology, 46*(4), 379–391.

Tice, D. M., & Baumeister, R. F. (1997). Longitudinal study of procrastination, performance, stress, and health: The costs and benefits of dawdling. *Psychological Science, 8*(6), 454–458.

Tidwell, M. O., Reis, H. T., & Shaver, P. R. (1996). Attachment, attractiveness, and social interaction. *Journal of Personality & Social Psychology, 71*(4), 729–745.

Tierny, J. (1987, September–October). Stitches: Good news; Better health liked to sin, sloth. *Hippocrates,* pp. 30–35.

Tiffany, S. T., Martin, E. M., & Baker, T. B. (1986). Treatments for cigarette smoking: An evaluation of the contributions of aversion and counseling procedures. *Behavior Research & Therapy, 24*(4), 437–452.

Tijerino, R. (1998). Civil spaces: A critical perspective of defensible space. *Journal of Architectural & Planning Research, 15*(4), 321–337.

Till, B. D., & Priluck, R. L. (2000). Stimulus generalization in classical conditioning: An initial investigation and extension. *Psychology & Marketing, 17*(1), 55–72.

Timm, P. R., & Peterson, B. D. (1993). *People at work.* St. Paul, MN: West.

Timmerman, I. G. H., Emmelkamp, P. M. G., & Sanderman, R. (1998). The effects of a stress-management training program in individuals at risk in the community at large. *Behaviour Research & Therapy, 36*(9), 863–875.

Tolman, E. C., & Honzik, C. H. (1930). Introduction and removal of reward and maze performance in rats. *University of California Publications in Psychology, 4,* 257–275.

Tolman, E. C., Ritchie, B. F., & Kalish, D. (1946). Studies in spatial learning: II. Place learning versus response learning. *Journal of Experimental Psychology, 36,* 221–229.

Tomes, H. (1998, December). Diversity: Psychology's life depends on it. *APA Monitor,* p. 28.

Tomlinson-Keasey, C., & Little, T. D. (1990). Predicting educational attainment, occupational achievement, intellectual skill, and personal adjustment among gifted men and women. *Journal of Educational Psychology, 82*(3), 442–455.

Toneatto, T., Sobell, L. C., Sobell, M. B., & Rubel, E. (1999). Natural recovery from cocaine dependence. *Psychology of Addictive Behaviors, 13*(4), 259–268.

Torrance, M., Thomas, Glyn, V., & Robinson, E. J. (1991). Strategies for answering examination essay questions: Is it helpful to write a plan? *British Journal of Educational Psychology, 61*(1), 46–54.

Torrey, E. F. (1988). *Surviving schizophrenia: A family manual.* New York: Harper & Row.

Torrey, E. F. (1996). *Out of the shadows.* New York: John Wiley & Sons.

Townsend, J. M., & Wasserman, T. (1998). Sexual attractiveness. *Evolution & Human Behavior, 19*(3), 171–191.

Trappey, C. (1996). A meta-analysis of consumer choice and subliminal advertising. *Psychology & Marketing, 13*(5), 517–530.

Trehub, S. E., Unyk, A. M., & Trainor, L. J. (1993a). Adults identify infant-directed music across cultures. *Infant Behavior & Development, 16*(2), 193–211.

Trehub, S. E., Unyk, A. M., & Trainor, L. J. (1993b). Maternal singing in cross-cultural perspective. *Infant Behavior & Development, 16*(3), 285–295.

Troll, L. E., & Skaff, M. M. (1997). Perceived continuity of self in very old age. *Psychology & Aging, 12*(1), 162–169.

Truax, S. R. (1983). Active search, mediation, and the manipulation of cue dimensions: Emotion attribution in the false feedback paradigm. *Motivation and Emotion, 7,* 41–60.

Truchlicka, M., McLaughlin, T. F., & Swain, J. C. (1998). Effects of token reinforcement and response cost on the accuracy of spelling performance with middle-school special education students with behavior disorders. *Behavioral Interventions, 13*(1), 1–10.

Truman, D. M., Tokar, D. M., & Fischer, A. R. (1996). Dimensions of masculinity: Relations to date rape supportive attitudes and sexual aggression in dating situations. *Journal of Counseling & Development, 74*(6), 555–562.

Trut, L. N. (1999). Early canid domestication. *American Scientist, 87,* 160–169.

Tryon, R. C. (1929). The genetics of learning ability in rats. *University of California Publications in Psychology, 4,* 71–89.

Tsai, C., Hoerr, S. L., & Song, W. O. (1998). Dieting behavior of Asian college women attending a US university. *Journal of American College Health, 46*(4), 163–168.

Tse, L. (1999). Finding a place to be: Ethnic identity exploration of Asian Americans. *Adolescence, 34*(133), 121–138.

Tucker, P., & Aron, A. (1993). Passionate love and marital satisfaction at key transition points in the family life cycle. *Journal of Social & Clinical Psychology, 12*(2), 135–147.

Tulley, M., & Chiu, L. H. (1995). Student teachers and classroom discipline. *Journal of Educational Research, 88*(3), 164–171.

Tulving, E. (1989). Remembering and knowing the past. *American Scientist, 77*(4), 361–367.

Turco, R. P., Toon, O. B., Ackerman, T. P., Pollack, J. B., & Sagan, C. (1983). Nuclear winter: Global consequences of multiple nuclear explosions. *Science, 222*(1), 283–292.

Turkheimer, E. (1998). Heritability and biological explanation. *Psychological Review, 105*(4), 782–791.

Turkheimer, E., & Parry, C. D. H. (1992). Why the gap? *American Psychologist, 47*(5), 646–655.

Turkington, C. (1986, August). Pot and the immune system. *APA Monitor*, p. 22.

Turkington, C. (1992, December). Ruling opens door—a crack—to IQ testing some black kids. *APA Monitor*, pp. 28–29.

Turnbull, C. M. (1961). Some observations regarding the experiences and behavior of the Bambuti Pygmies. *American Journal of Psychology, 74*, 304–308.

Turner, S. J. M. (1997). The use of the reflective team in a psychodrama therapy group. *International Journal of Action Methods, 50*(1), 17–26.

Turner, S. L., Hamilton, H., Jacobs, M., et al. (1997). The influence of fashion magazines on the body image satisfaction of college women. *Adolescence, 32*(127), 603–614.

Turton, M. D., O'Shea, D., Gunn, I., Beak, S. A., et al. (1996). A role for glucagon-like peptide-1 in the central regulation of feeding. *Nature, 379*(6560), 69–74.

Turvey, M. T. (1996). Dynamic touch. *American Psychologist, 51*(11), 1134–1152.

Tutkun, H., Yargic, L. I., & Sar, V. (1995). Dissociative identity disorder. *Dissociation: Progress in the Dissociative Disorders, 8*(1), 3–9.

Tversky, A., & Kahneman, D. (1981). The framing of decisions and the psychology of choice. *Science, 211*, 453–458.

Tversky, A., & Kahneman, D. (1982). Judgments of and by representativeness. In D. Kahneman, P. Slovic, & A. Tversky (Eds.), *Judgment under uncertainty: Heuristics and biases.* Cambridge: Cambridge University Press.

Tye-Murray, N., Spencer, L., & Woodworth, G. G. (1995). Acquisition of speech by children who have prolonged cochlear implant experience. *Journal of Speech & Hearing Research, 38*(2), 327–337.

Tyler, L. E. (1992). Counseling psychology: Why? *Professional Psychology: Research & Practice. 23*(5), 342–344.

Tzeng, M. (1992). The effects of socioeconomic heterogamy and changes on marital dissolution for first marriages. *Journal of Marriage and Family, 54*, 609–619.

Tzeng, O. J., & Wang, W. S. (1983). The first two r's. *American Scientist, 71*(3), 238–243.

Tzuriel, D., & Alfassi, M. (1994). Cognitive and motivational modifiability as a function of the Instrumental Enrichment (IE) program. *Special Services in the Schools, 8*(2), 91–128.

Udry, J. R., & Morris, N. M. (1977). Human sexual behavior at different stages of the menstrual cycle. *Journal of Reproduction and Fertility, 51*, 419.

Ulett, G. A. (1992). 3000 years of acupuncture: From metaphysics to neurophysiology. *Integrative Psychiatry, 8*(2), 91–100.

Ulrich, R. E., Stachnik, T. J., & Stainton, N. R. (1963). Student acceptance of generalized personality interpretations. *Psychological Reports, 131*, 831–834.

Underwood, B. J. (1957). Interference and forgetting. *Psychological Review, 64*, 49–60.

UNESCO. (1990). The Seville statement on violence. *American Psychologist, 45*(10), 1167–1168.

United Nations Population Fund. (1993). *Population issues: Briefing kit.* New York: Author.

Valery, J. H., O'Connor, P., & Jennings, S. (1997). The nature and amount of support college-age adolescents request and receive from parents. *Adolescence, 32*(126), 323–338.

Valins, S. (1966). Cognitive effects of false heart-rate feedback. *Journal of Personality & Social Psychology, 4*, 400–408.

Valins, S. (1967). Emotionality and information concerning internal reactions. *Journal of Personality & Social Psychology, 6*, 458–463.

Van der Hart, O., Lierens, R., & Goodwin, J. (1996). Jeanne Fery: A sixteenth-century case of dissociative identity disorder. *Journal of Psychohistory, 24*(1), 18–35.

Van Goozen, S. H. M., Cohen-Kettenis, P. T., Gooren, L. J. G., & Frijda, N. H. (1995). Gender differences in behaviour: Activating effects of cross-sex hormones. *Psychoneuroendocrinology, 20*(4), 343–363.

Van Lawick-Goodall, J. (1971). *In the shadow of man.* New York: Houghton Mifflin.

Van Maanen, J., & Schein, E. H. (1977). Career development. In J. R. Hackman & J. L. Suttle (Eds.), *Improving life at work.* Santa Monica, CA: Goodyear.

Van Rooij, J. J. F. (1994). Introversion-extraversion: Astrology versus psychology. *Personality & Individual Differences, 16*(6), 985–988.

Van Wyk, P. H., & Geist, C. S. (1995). Biology of bisexuality: Critique and observations. *Journal of Homosexuality, 28*(3–4), 357–373.

VandenBos, G. R., & Bryant, B. K. (1987). Preface. In G. R. VandenBos & B. K. Bryant (Eds.), *Cataclysms, crises, and catastrophes: Psychology in action.* Washington, DC: American Psychological Association.

Vane, J. R., & Guarnaccia, V. J. (1989). Personality theory and personality assessment measures: How helpful to the clinician? *Journal of Clinical Psychology, 45*(1), 5–19.

Vasquez, M. J. T., & de las Fuentes, C. (1999). American-born Asian, African, Latina, and American Indian adolescent girls: Challenges and strengths. In N. G. Johnson, M. C. Roberts, & J. Worell (Eds.), *Beyond appearance.* Washington, DC: APA.

Velakoulis, D., & Pantelis, C. (1996). What have we learned from functional imaging studies in schizophrenia? *Australian & New Zealand Journal of Psychiatry, 30*(2), 195–209.

Ventura, J., Nuechterlein, K. H., Lukow, D., & Hardesty, J. P. (1989). A prospective study of stressful life events and schizophrenic relapse. *Journal of Abnormal Psychology, 98*(4), 407–411.

Verkuyten, M., & Lay, C. (1998). Ethnic minority identity and psychological well-being: The mediating role of collective self-esteem. *Journal of Applied Social Psychology, 28*(21), 1969–1986.

Vernoy, M. W. (1989). Simultaneous adaptation to size, distance, and curvature underwater. *Human Factors, 31*(1), 77–85.

Vertosick, F. T. (1997, October). Lobotomy's back. *Discover*, pp. 66–71.

Viegener, B. J., Perri, M. G., Nezu, A. M., et al. (1990). Effects of an intermittent, low-fat, low-calorie diet in the behavioral treatment of obesity. *Behavior Therapy, 21*(4), 499–509.

Visalberghi, E., Fragaszy, D. M., & Savage-Rumbaugh, S. (1995). Performance in a tool-using task by common chimpanzees (*Pan troglodytes*), bonobos (*Pan paniscus*), an orangutan (*Pongo pygmaeus*), and capuchin monkeys (*Cebus apella*). *Journal of Comparative Psychology, 109*(1), 52–60.

Vogler, R. E., & Bartz, W. R. (1982). *The better way to drink.* New York: Simon and Schuster.

Vogler, R. E., & Bartz, W. R. (1992). *Teenagers and alcohol.* Philadelphia: Charles Press.

Vogler, R. E., Weissbach, T. A., Compton, J. V., & Martin, G. T. (1977). Integrated behavior change techniques for problem drinkers in the community. *Journal of Consulting and Clinical Psychology, 45*, 267–279.

Vokey, J. R., & Read, J. D. (1985). Subliminal messages: Between the Devil and the media. *American Psychologist, 40*(11), 1231–1239.

Volkmann, J., Schnitzler, A., Witte, O. W., & Freund, H. J. (1998). Handedness and asymmetry of hand representation in human motor cortex. *Journal of Neurophysiology, 79*(4), 2149–2154.

Volkow, N. D., Gillespie, H., Mullani, N., & Tancredi, L. (1996). Brain glucose metabolism in chronic marijuana users at baseline and during marijuana intoxication. *Psychiatry Research: Neuroimaging, 67*(1), 29–38.

Volpicelli, J. R., Ulm, R. R., Altenor, A., & Seligman, M. E. P. (1983). Learned mastery in the rat. *Learning and Motivation, 14*, 204–222.

Von Baumgarten, R., Benson, A., Berthoz, A., Brandt, T., et al. (1984). Spatial orientation in weightlessness and readaptation to earth's gravity. *Science, 225*, 205–225.

Vygotsky, L. S. (1962). *Thought and language.* Cambridge, MA: MIT Press.

Vygotsky, L. S. (1978). Mind in society. In M. Cole, V. John-Steiner, S. S. Scribner, & E. Souberman (Eds.), *The development of higher mental processes.* Cambridge, MA: Harvard University Press.

Wadden, T. A., Vogt, R. A., Foster, G. D., & Anderson, D. A. (1998). Exercise and the maintenance of weight loss. *Journal of Consulting and Clinical Psychology, 66*(2), 429–433.

Wagaman, J. R., Miltenberger, R. G., & Woods, D. (1995). Long-term follow-up of a behavioral treatment for stuttering in children. *Journal of Applied Behavior Analysis, 28*(2), 233–234.

Waid, W. M., & Orne, M. T. (1982). The physiological detection of deception. *American Scientist, 70*, 402–409.

Wakefield, J. C. (1992). The concept of mental disorder. *American Psychologist, 47*(3), 373–388.

Wakeling, A. (1996). Epidemiology of anorexia nervosa. *Psychiatry Research, 62*(1), 3–9.

Waldenstroem, U. (1999). Experience of labor and birth in 1111 women. *Journal of Psychosomatic Research, 47*(5), 471–482.

Waldvogel, J. A. (1990). The bird's eye view. *American Scientist, 78*(4), 342–353.

Walker, I., & Crogan, M. (1998). Academic performance, prejudice, and the Jigsaw classroom. *Journal of Community & Applied Social Psychology, 8*(6), 381–393.

Wallach, M. A. (1985). Creativity testing and giftedness. In F. D. Horowitz & M. O'Brien (Eds.), *The gifted and talented: Developmental perspectives* (pp. 99–123). Washington, DC: American Psychological Association.

Wallach, M. A., & Kogan, N. (1965). *Modes of thinking in young children.* New York: Holt.

Waller, N. G. (1999). Evaluating the structure of personality. In C. R. Cloninger (Ed.), *Personality and psychopathology.* Washington, DC: American Psychiatric Association.

Walsh, J., & Uestuen, T. B. (1999). Prevalence and health consequences of insomnia. *Sleep, 22*(Suppl. 3), S427–S436.

Walsh, J. K., & Scweitzer, P. K. (1999). Ten-year trends in the pharmacological treatment of insomnia. *Sleep, 22*(3), 371–375.

Walsh, M. F., & Flynn, T. J. (1995). A 54-month evaluation of a popular very low calorie diet program. *Journal of Family Practice, 41*(3), 231–236.

Walsh, R. (1984). An evolutionary model of meditation research. In D. H. Shapiro & R. N. Walsh (Eds.), *Meditation: Classic and contemporary perspectives.* New York: Aldine.

Walster, E. (1971). Passionate love. In B. I. Murstein (Ed.), *Theories of attraction and love.* New York: Springer.

Walster, E., & Walster, G. W. (1978). *A new look at love.* Reading, MA: Addison-Wesley.

Walton, C. E., Bower, M. L., & Bower, T. G. (1992). Recognition of familiar faces by newborns. *Infant Behavior & Development, 15*(2), 265–269.

Wampold, B. E., et al. (1997). A meta-analysis of outcome studies comparing bona fide psychotherapies. *Psychological Bulletin, 122*(3), 203–215.

Ward, C., & Rana-Deuba, A. (1999). Acculturation and adaptation revisited. *Journal of Cross-Cultural Psychology, 30*(4), 422–442.

Ward, C. A. (1989). The cross-cultural study of altered states of consciousness and mental health. In C. A. Ward (Ed.), *Altered states of consciousness and mental health.* Newbury Park, CA: Sage.

Ward, E., & Ogden, J. (1994). Experiencing vaginismus: Sufferers' beliefs about causes and effects. *Sexual & Marital Therapy, 9*(1), 33–45.

Ward, P. B., Catts, S. V., Fox, A. M., Michie, P. T., et al. (1991). Auditory selective attention and event-related potentials in schizophrenia. *British Journal of Psychiatry, 158*, 534–539.

Wark, G. R., & Krebs, D. L. (1996). Gender and dilemma differences in real-life moral judgment. *Developmental Psychology, 32*(2), 220–230.

Warrington, E. K., & McCarthy, R. A. (1995). Multiple meaning systems in the brain: A case for visual semantics. *Neuropsychologia, 32*(12), 1465–1473.

Warwick-Evans, L. A., Symons, N., Fitch, T., & Burrows, L. (1998). Evaluating sensory conflict and postural instability. Theories of motion sickness. *Brain Research Bulletin, 47*(5), 465–469.

Watson, D. L., deBortali-Tregerthan, G., & Frank, J. (1984). *Social psychology: Science and application.* Glenview, IL: Scott, Foresman.

Watson, D. L., & Tharp, R. G. (1996). *Self-directed behavior: Self-modification for personal adjustment,* 4th ed. Monterey, CA: Brooks/Cole.

Watson, J. B. (1913). Psychology as the behaviorist views it. *Psychological Review, 20,* 158–177.

Watson, J. B. (1994). Psychology as the behaviorist views it. *Psychological Review, 101*(2), 248–253.

Weaver, C. A. (1993). Do you need a "flash" to form a flashbulb memory? *Journal of Experimental Psychology: General, 122*(1), 39–46.

Weaver, C. N., & Matthews, M. D. (1987). What white males want from their jobs: Ten years later. *Personnel, 4*(9), 62–65.

Weaver, M. T., et al., (1998). Health risk influence on medical care costs and utilization among 2,898 municipal employees. *American Journal of Preventive Medicine, 15*(3), 250–253.

Webb, N. M., & Farivar, S. (1994). Promoting helping behavior in cooperative small groups in middle school mathematics. *American Educational Research Journal, 31*(2), 369–395.

Webb, W. B. (1994). Sleep as a biological rhythm: A historical view. *Sleep, 17*(2), 188–194.

Wechsler, H., Molnar, B.E., Davenport, A. E., & Baer, J. S. (1999). College alcohol use: A full or empty glass? *Journal of American College Health, 47*(6), 247–252.

Weekley, J. A., & Jones, C. (1997). Video-based situational testing. *Personnel Psychology, 50*(1), 25–49.

Weems, C. F. (1998). The evaluation of heart rate biofeedback using a multi-element design. *Journal of Behavior Therapy & Experimental Psychiatry, 29*(2), 157–162.

Weinberg, R. A. (1989). Intelligence and IQ. *American Psychologist, 44*(2), 98–104.

Weinberger, M., Hiner, S. L., & Tierney, W. M. (1987). In support of hassles as a measure of stress in predicting health outcomes. *Journal of Behavioral Medicine, 10*(1), 19–31.

Weiner, I. B. (1996). Some observations on the validity of the Rorschach Inkblot Method. *Psychological Assessment, 8*(2), 206–213.

Weiner, I. B. (1997). Current status of the Rorschach Inkblot Method. *Journal of Personality Assessment, 68*(1), 5–19.

Weintraub, M. I. (1983). *Hysterical conversion reactions.* New York: SP Medical & Scientific Books.

Weintraub, S., Powell, D. H., & Whitla, D. K. (1994). Successful cognitive aging. *Journal of Geriatric Psychiatry, 27*(1), 15–34.

Weisburd, D. E. (1990). Planning a community-based mental health system: Perspective of a family member. *American Psychologist, 45*(11), 1245–1248.

Weisenberg, R. W. (1986). *Creativity.* New York: W. H. Freeman.

Weisfeld, G. E., & Beresford, J. M. (1982). Erectness of posture as an indicator of dominance or success in humans. *Motivation and Emotion, 6*, 113–131.

Weiss, B., Dodge, K. A., Bates, J. E., & Pettit, G. S. (1992). Some consequences of early harsh discipline. *Child Development, 63*(6), 1321–1335.

Weiss, J. (1990, March). Unconscious mental functioning. *Scientific American,* 103–109.

Weiss, J. M. (1972). Psychological factors in stress and disease. *Scientific American, 26,* 104–113.

Weiss, R. (1990). Shadows of thoughts revealed. *Science News, 138*(19), 297.

Weiten, W. (1998). Pressure, major life events, and psychological symptoms. *Journal of Social Behavior & Personality, 13*(1), 51–68.

Weller, L., & Weller, A. (1995). Menstrual synchrony. *Psychoneuroendocrinology, 20*(4), 377–383.

Wells, G. L. (1993). What do we know about eyewitness identification? *American Psychologist, 48*(5), 553–571.

Wells, G. L., Small, M., Penrod, S., Malpass, et al. (1999). Eyewitness identification procedures: Recommendations for lineups and photospreads. *Law & Human Behavior, 22*(6), 603–647.

Wells, N. (1994). Perceived control over pain: Relation to distress and disability. *Research in Nursing & Health, 17*(4), 295–302.

Welte, J. W., Barnes, G. M., Hoffman, J. H., & Dintcheff, B.A. (1999). Trends in adolescent alcohol and other substance use. *Substance Use & Misuse, 34*(10), 1427–1449.

Werner, C. M., & Makela, E. (1998). Motivations and behaviors that support recycling. *Journal of Environmental Psychology, 18*(4), 373–386.

Wertheimer, M. (1959). *Productive thinking.* New York: Harper & Row.

West, L. J. (1993). A psychiatric overview of cult-related phenomena. *Journal of the American Academy of Psychoanalysis, 21*(1), 1–19.

West, T. G. (1991). *In the mind's eye.* Buffalo, NY: Prometheus.

Westen, D. (1998). The scientific legacy of Sigmund Freud: Toward a psychodynamically informed psychological science. *Psychological Bulletin, 124*(3), 333–371.

Wexler, M., Kosslyn, S. M., & Berthoz, A. (1998). Motor processes in mental rotation. *Cognition, 68*(1), 77–94.

Wexler, M. N. (1995). Expanding the groupthink explanation to the study of contemporary cults. *Cultic Studies Journal, 12*(1), 49–71.

Whatley, M. A., Webster, J. M., Smith, R. H., & Rhodes, A. (1999). The effect of a favor on public and private compliance. *Basic & Applied Social Psychology, 21*(3), 251–259.

Wheeler, L., & Miyake, K. (1992). Social comparison in everyday life. *Journal of Personality & Social Psychology, 62*(5), 760–773.

Wheeler, R. J., & Frank, M. A. (1988). Identification of stress buffers. *Behavioral Medicine, 14*(2), 78–89.

White, B. L., & Watts, J. C. (1973). *Experience and environment, Vol. I.* Englewood Cliffs, NJ: Prentice-Hall.

White, S. D., & DeBlassie, R. R. (1992). Adolescent sexual behavior. *Adolescence, 27*(105), 183–191.

Whitehead, W. E. (1992). Behavioral medicine approaches to gastrointestinal disorders. *Journal of Consulting and Clinical Psychology, 60*(4), 605–612.

Whitley, B. E. (1993). Reliability and aspects of the construct validity of Sternberg's Triangular Love Scale. *Journal of Social & Personal Relationships, 10*(3), 475–480.

Whitley, B. E. (1999). Right-wing authoritarianism, social dominance orientation, and prejudice. *Journal of Personality & Social Psychology, 77*(l), 126–134.

Whittal, M. L., Agras, W. S., & Gould, R. A. (1999). Bulimia nervosa: A meta-analysis of psychosocial and pharmacological treatments. *Behavior Therapy, 30*(1), 117–135.

Wichstrom, L. (1995). Social, psychological and physical correlates of eating problems. *Psychological Medicine, 25*(3), 567–579.

Wickett, J. C., Vernon, P. A., & Lee, D. H. (1995). In vivo brain size, head perimeter, and intelligence in a sample of healthy adult females. *Personality & Individual Differences, 16*(6), 831–838.

Widiger, T. A., & Sankis, L. M. (2000). Adult psychopathology. *Annual Review of Psychology, 51,* 377–404.

Widiger, T. A., & Trull, T. J. (1991). Diagnosis and clinical assessment. In M. R. Rosenzweig & L. W. Porter (Eds.), *Annual Review of Psychology, 42,* 109–133.

Wiederman, M. W. (1999). Volunteer bias in sexuality research using college student participants. *Journal of Sex Research, 36*(1), 59–66.

Wieneke, G. H., Janssen, P., & Brutten, G. J. (1995). Variance of central timing of voiced and voiceless periods among stutterers and nonstutterers. *Journal of Fluency Disorders, 20*(2), 171–189.

Wilder, D. A., Simon, A. F., & Faith, M. (1996). Enhancing the impact of counterstereotypic information. *Journal of Personality & Social Psychology, 71*(2), 276–287.

Wilding, J., & Valentine, E. (1994a). Memory champions. *British Journal of Psychology, 85*(2), 231–244.

Wilding, J., & Valentine, E. (1994b). Mnemonic wizardry with the telephone directory: But stories are another story. *British Journal of Psychology, 85*(4), 501–509.

Wilhelm, J. L. (1976). *The search for superman.* New York: Simon & Schuster.

Wilkinson, D., & Daoud, J. (1998). The stigma and the enigma of ECT. *International Journal of Geriatric Psychiatry, 13*(12), 833–835.

Wilkinson, G., Piccinelli, M., Roberts, S., Micciolo, R., & Fry, J. (1997). Lunar cycle and consultations for anxiety and depression in general practice. *International Journal of Social Psychiatry, 43*(1), 29–34.

Wilkinson, R. B. (1997). Interactions between self and external reinforcement in predicting depressive symptoms. *Behaviour Research & Therapy, 35*(4), 281–289.

Williams, B. A. (1984, November 30). U.S. approves implants to aid the totally deaf. *Santa Barbara News Press,* p. C6.

Williams, C. L., & Berry, J. W. (1991). Primary prevention of acculturative stress among refugees. *American Psychologist, 46*(6), 632–641.

Williams, D. G., & Morris, G. (1996). Crying, weeping or tearfulness in British and Israeli adults. *British Journal of Psychology, 87*(3), 479–505.

Williams, J. M. (1995). Applied sport psychology: Goals, issues, and challenges. *Journal of Applied Sport Psychology, 7*(1), 81–91.

Williams, K., & Umberson, D. (1999). Medical technology and childbirth. *Sex Roles, 41*(3–4), 147–168.

Williams, L. J. (1995). Peripheral target recognition and visual field narrowing in aviators and non-aviators. *International Journal of Aviation Psychology, 5*(2), 215–232.

Williams, R. (1989). The trusting heart: Great news about Type A behavior. New York: Random House.

Williams, R. L. (1975). The Bitch-100: A culture-specific test. *Journal of Afro-American Issues, 3,* 103–116.

Williams, R. L., et al. (1964). Sleep patterns in young adults: An EEG study. *Electroencephalography and Clinical Neurophysiology,* 376–381.

Williams, R. L., & Long, J. D. (1991). *Toward a self-managed life style.* Boston: Houghton Mifflin.

Williams, W. M., & Ceci, S. J. (1997). Are Americans becoming more or less alike? *American Psychologist, 52*(11), 1226–1235.

Williamson, A. M., & Sanderson, J. W. (1986). Changing the speed of shift rotations: A field study. *Ergonomics, 29*(9), 1085–1095.

Willinger, M., Hoffman, H. J., & Hartford, R. B. (1994). Infant sleep position and risk for sudden infant death syndrome. *Pediatrics, 93*(5), 814–819.

Willoughby, T., Wood, E., Desmarais, S., Sims, S., & Kalra, M. (1997). Mechanisms that facilitate the effectiveness of elaboration strategies. *Journal of Educational Psychology, 89*(4), 682–685.

Wilson, E. O. (1975, October 12). Human decency is animal. *New York Times Magazine,* .

Wilson, F. L. (1995). The effects of age, gender, and ethnic/cultural background on moral reasoning. *Journal of Social Behavior & Personality, 10*(1), 67–78.

Wilson, G. T. (1987). Chemical aversion conditioning as a treatment for alcoholism: A re-analysis. *Behaviour Research and Therapy, 25*(6), 503–516.

Wilson, R. R. (1986). *Don't panic: Taking control of anxiety attacks.* New York: Harper & Row.

Wilson, T. L., & Brown, T. L. (1997). Reexamination of the effect of Mozart's music on spatial-task performance. *Journal of Psychology, 131*(4), 365–370.

Wilson, W. H. (1989). Reassessment of state hospital patients diagnosed with schizophrenia. *Journal of Neuropsychiatry & Clinical Neurosciences, 1*(4), 394–397.

Winzelberg, A. J., & Luskin, F. M. (1999). The effect of a meditation training in stress levels in secondary school teachers. *Stress Medicine, 15*(2), 69–77.

Wise, J. (1982, September). A gentle deterrent to vandalism. *Psychology Today,* 31–38.

Wise, R. A., & Rompre, P. P. (1989). Brain dopamine and reward. *Annual Review of Psychology, 40,* 191–225.

Wisniewski, A. B. (1998). Sexually-dimorphic patterns of cortical asymmetry, and the role for sex steroid hormones in determining cortical patterns of lateralization. *Psychoneuroendocrinology, 23*(5), 519–547.

Witelson, S. F. (1991). Neural sexual mosaicism: Sexual differentiation of the human temporo-parietal region for functional asymmetry. *Psychoneuroendocrinology, 16*(1–3), 131–153.

Withers, N. W., Pulvirenti, L., Koob, G. F., & Gillin, J. C. (1995). Cocaine abuse and dependence. *Journal of Clinical Psychopharmacology, 15*(1), 63–78.

Witherspoon, W. (1994, July 28). Disorder consumed her life. *Los Angeles Times,* p. C1.

Witt, S. D. (1997). Parental influences on children's socialization to gender roles. *Adolescence, 32*(126), 253–259.

Woehr, D. J., & Cavell, T. A. (1993). Self-report measures of ability, effort, and nonacademic activity as predictors of introductory psychology test scores. *Teaching of Psychology, 20*(3), 156–160.

Wolcott, J. H., McNeekin, R. R., Burgin, R. E., & Yanowitch, R. E. (1977). Correlation of general aviation accidents with the biorhythm theory. *Human Factors, 19,* 283–293.

Wolfe, J. B. (1936). Effectiveness of token rewards for chimpanzees. *Comparative Psychology Monographs, 12*(5), Whole No. 60.

Wolitzky, D. L. (1995). The theory and practice of traditional psychoanalytic psychotherapy. In A. S. Gurman & S. B. Messer, *Essential psychotherapies.* New York: Guilford.

Wolpe, J. (1974). *The practice of behavior therapy* (2nd ed.). New York: Pergamon.

Wolpe, J., & Plaud, J. J. (1997). Pavlov's contributions to behavior therapy. *American Psychologist, 52*(9), 966–972.

Wolpin, M., Marston, A., Randolph, C., & Clothier, A. (1992). Individual difference correlates of reported lucid dreaming frequency and control. *Journal of Mental Imagery, 16*(3–4), 231–236.

Wolraich, M. L., Wilson, D. B., & White, J. W. (1995). The effect of sugar on behavior or cognition in children. *Journal of the American Medical Association, 274*(20), 1617–1621.

Wolters, C. A. (1998). Self-regulated learning and college students' regulation of motivation. *Journal of Educational Psychology, 90*(2), 224–235.

Wong, C. Y., Sommer, R., & Cook, E. J. (1992). The soft classroom 17 years later. *Journal of Environmental Psychology, 12*(4), 337–343.

Wong, J. L., & Whitaker, D. J. (1993). Depressive mood states and their cognitive and personality correlates in college students. *Journal of Clinical Psychology, 49*(5), 615–621.

Woo, E. (1995, January 20). Teaching that goes beyond IQ. *Los Angeles Times,* pp. A-1, A-22, A-23.

Wood, E., & Willoughby, T. (1995). Cognitive strategies for test-taking. In E. Wood, V. Woloshyn, & T. Willoughby (Eds.), *Cognitive strategy instruction for middle and high schools,* Brookline, Cambridge, MA.

Wood, J. M., & Bootzin, R. R. (1990). The prevalence of nightmares and their independence from anxiety. *Journal of Abnormal Psychology, 99*(1), 64–68.

Wood, J. M., Bootzin, R. R., Kihlstrom, J. F., & Schacter, D. L. (1992). Implicit and explicit memory for verbal information presented during sleep. *Psychological Science, 3*(4), 236–239.

Wood, N. L., & Cowan, N. (1995). The cocktail party phenomenon revisited. *Journal of Experimental Psychology: General, 124*(3), 243–262.

Woods, B. T. (1998). Is schizophrenia a progressive neurodevelopmental disorder? *American Journal of Psychiatry, 155,* 1661–1670.

Woods, D. W., Miltenberger, R. G., & Lumley, V. A. (1996). A simplified habit reversal treatment for pica-related chewing. *Journal of Behavior Therapy & Experimental Psychiatry, 27*(3), 257–262.

Woods, S. C., Schwartz, M. W, Baskin, D. G., & Seeley, R J. (2000). Food intake and the regulation of body weight. *Annual Review of Psychology, 51,* 255–277.

Woods, S. C., Seeley, R. J., & Porte, D. (1998). Signals that regulate food intake and energy homeostasis. *Science, 280*(5368), 1378–1383.

Woodward, J., & Goodstein, D. (1996). Conduct, misconduct and the structure of science. *American Scientist, (84),* 479–490.

Woody, S. R. (1996). Effects of focus of attention on anxiety levels and social performance of individuals with social phobia. *Journal of Abnormal Psychology, 105*(1), 61–69.

Work in America. (1973). Special Task Force, Department of Health, Education and Welfare. Cambridge, MA: MIT Press.

Worthen, J. B., & Marshall, P. H. (1996). Intralist and extralist sources of distinctiveness and the bizarreness effect. *American Journal of Psychology, 109*(2), 239–263.

Worthen, J. B., & Wade, C. E. (1999). Direction of travel and visiting team athletic performance: Support for a circadian dysrhythmia hypothesis. *Journal of Sport Behavior, 22*(2), 279–287.

Wright, D. B. (1993). Recall of the Hillsborough disaster over time: Systematic biases of "flash-bulb" memories. *Applied Cognitive Psychology, 7*(2), 129–138.

Wright, T. A., & Cropanzano, R. (2000). Psychological well-being and job satisfaction as predictors of job performance. *Journal of Occupational Health Psychology, 5*(1), 84–94.

Wulf, G., Shea, C. H., & Matschiner, S. (1998). Frequent feedback enhances complex motor skill learning. *Journal of Motor Behavior, 30*(2), 180–192.

Wyatt, J. W., Posey, A., Welker, W., & Seamonds, C. (1984). Natural levels of similarities between identical twins and between unrelated people. *The Skeptical Inquirer, 9,* 62–66.

Yadama, G. N., & Drake, B. (1995). Confirmatory factor analysis of the Maslach Burnout Inventory. *Social Work Research, 19*(3), 184–192.

Yalom, I. D. (1980). *Existential psychotherapy.* New York: Basic.

Yank, G. R., Bentley, K. J., & Hargrove, D. S. (1993). The vulnerability-stress model of schizophrenia. *American Journal of Orthopsychiatry, 63*(1), 55–69.

Yardley, L. (1992). Motion sickness and perception. *British Journal of Psychology, 83*(4), 449–471.

Yarmey, A. D., Yarmey, M. J., & Yarmey, A. L. (1996). Accuracy of eyewitness identification in showups and lineups. *Law & Human Behavior, 20*(4), 459–477.

Yontef, G. M. (1995). Gestalt therapy. In A. S. Gurman & S. B. Messer, *Essential psychotherapies.* New York: Guilford.

Yoshida, M. (1993). Three-dimensional electrophysiological atlas created by computer mapping of clinical responses elicited on stimulation of human subcortical structures. *Stereotactic & Functional Neurosurgery, 60*(1–3), 127–134.

Young, R. L. (1994). The "intelligence" of calendrical calculators. *American Journal on Mental Retardation, 99*(2), 186–200.

Yuille, J. C., & Tollestrup, P. A. (1990). Some effects of alcohol on eyewitness memory. *Journal of Applied Psychology, 75*(3), 268–273.

Zametkin, A. J. (1995). Attention-deficit disorder: Born to be hyperactive? *Journal of the American Medical Association, 273*(23), 1871–1874.

Zayas, L. H., Torres, L. R., Malcolm, J., & DesRosiers, F. S. (1996). Clinicians' definitions of ethnically sensitive therapy. *Professional Psychology: Research & Practice, 27*(1), 78–82.

Zeidner, M. (1995). Adaptive coping with test situations: A review of the literature. *Educational Psychologist, 30*(3), 123–133.

Zelezny, L. C. (1999). Educational interventions that improve environmental behaviors: A meta-analysis. *Journal of Environmental Education, 31*(1), 5–14.

Zelkowitz, P., & Milet, T. H. (1995). Screening for postpartum depression in a community sample. *Canadian Journal of Psychiatry, 40*(2), 80–86.

Zellner, D. A., Harner, D. E., & Adler, R. L. (1989). Effects of eating abnormalities and gender on perceptions of desirable body shape. *Journal of Abnormal Psychology, 98*(1), 93–96.

Zentall, T. R. (1999). Animal cognition: The bridge between animal learning and human cognition. *Psychological Science, 10*(3), 206–208.

Zetlin, A., & Murtaugh, M. (1990). Whatever happened to those with borderline IQs? *American Journal on Mental Retardation, 94*(5), 463–469.

Zgodzinski, D. (1996, February). Cybertherapy. *Internet World,* pp. 50–53.

Zhang, A. Y., & Snowden, L. R. (1999). Ethnic characteristics of mental disorders in five U.S. communities. *Cultural Diversity and Ethnic Minority Psychology, 5*(2), 134–146.

Zigler, E. (1995). Can we "cure" mild mental retardation among individuals in the lower socioeconomic stratum? *American Journal of Public Health, 85*(3), 302–304.

Zigler, E., & Muenchow, S. (1992). *Head Start: The inside story of America's most successful educational experience.* New York: Basic.

Zigler, E., & Styfco, S. J. (1994). Head start. *American Psychologist, 49*(2), 127–132.

Zigler, E. F., & Gilman, E. D. (1998). Day care and early childhood settings. *Child & Adolescent Psychiatric Clinics of North America, 7*(3), 483–498.

Zimbardo, P. G., Haney, C., & Banks, W. C. (1973, April 8). A pirandellian prison. *New York Times Magazine,*

Zimbardo, P. G., Pilkonis, P. A., & Norwood, R. M. (1978). The social disease called shyness. In *Annual editions, personality and adjustment 78/79.* Guilford, CT: Dushkin.

Zimmerman, B. J. (1996a). Enhancing student academic and health functioning: A self-regulatory perspective. *School Psychology Quarterly, 11*(1), 47–66.

Zimmerman, J. D. (1996b). A prosocial media strategy. *American Journal of Orthopsychiatry, 66*(3), 354–362.

Zimmerman, S., & Zimmerman, A. M. (1990). Genetic effects of marijuana. *International Journal of Addictions, 25*(1A), 19–33.

Zinbarg, R. E., Barlow, D. H., Brown, T. A., & Hertz, R. M. (1992). Cognitive-behavioral approaches to the nature and treatment of anxiety disorders. *Annual Review of Psychology, 43,* 235–267.

Zohar, D. (1998). An additive model of test anxiety: Role of exam-specific expectations.

Zucker, A. (1995). Rights and the dying. In H. Wass & R. A. Neimeyer (Eds.), *Dying: Facing the facts.* Washington, DC: Taylor & Francis.

Zuckerman, M. (1990). The psychophysiology of sensation seeking. *Journal of Personality, 58*(1), 313–345.

Zuckerman, M. (1996). Item revisions in the Sensation Seeking Scale Form V (SSS-V). *EDRA: Environmental Design Research Association, 20*(4), 515.

Zuckerman, M., Eysenck, S., & Eysenck, H. J. (1978). Sensation seeking in England and America: Cross-cultural, age, and sex comparisons. *Journal of Consulting and Clinical Psychology, 46,* 139–149.

Zuckerman, M., Kieffer, S. C., & Knee, C. R. (1998). Consequences of self-handicapping. *Journal of Personality & Social Psychology, 74*(6), 1619–1628.

Zuwerink, J. R., Devine, P. G., Monteith, M. J., & Cook, D. A. (1996). Prejudice toward blacks: With and without compunction? *Basic & Applied Social Psychology, 18*(2), 131–150.

Subject Index

Dreams, *(continued)*
 and memories, 245
 need for, 240, 245
 nightmares, 242–243
 problem-solving in, 268
 theories of, 245–246
 using, 267–268
Drives, 404–405, 414–417, 496
Drugs
 and cultural values, 269–270
 dependence, 241, 254
 designer, 255
 effects on dreaming, 245, 267
 comparison chart, 252–253
 and fetal development, 87–88
 pharmacotherapy, 620–621
 psychoactive, 251–265, 269–271
 substance abuse disorders, 558, 560
 use patterns, 254
Drug abuse, 251–259, 260–263, 264–265, 269–271,
  558, 560
Drug addiction, 254, 419
Drug interaction, 261
DSM-IV, 557–559, 561
Dual memory, 313
Duncker, K., 355, 358
Dwarfism, 72
 deprivation, 112–113
Dynamic therapy, 601, 618
Dyslexia, 134
Dyspareunia, 472
Dysthymic disorder, 582–583

Ear, structure of, 180–181
Eating disorders, 411–413
 in children, 133–134
Ebbinghaus, H., 324–325
Educational psychology, 9, 18, 20, A17–A18
EEG (electroencephalograph), 4, 58
 in biofeedback, 539
 and hypnotism, 247
 and sleep stages, 238, 239, 242, 243
Ego, 489–491,570
Eidetic imagery (photographic memory), 322–323
Ekman, P., 433, 435
Electra complex, 492
Electrical stimulation of the brain (ESB), 58, 166,
  286–287, 314–315
Electroconvulsive shock, and memory, 330
Electroconvulsive therapy (ECT), 621
Electrode, 58, 79
Electronic databases,
 Infotrac, xlvii
 PsycINFO, xlvii
 psychology study center, xlvi
 Psych sites, xlvii
Electronic media, xlvi-xlviii
Elkind, D., 139, 140
Elliot, J., 677
Ellis, A., 614
Emotion, 156–157, 425–437, 440–442
 appraisal, 436–437
 and arousal, 427–430
 basic, 93, 431
 contemporary model, 436–437
 cultural differences in, 431–432
 development of, 93–94
 expression, 425, 428, 430–433, 435–436
 in infants, 93–94, 431
 and the limbic system, 70
 and the nervous system, 56
 and perception, 168, 222, 227
 physiological changes, 425, 426–430
 primary, 425–426
 theories of, 419–420, 434–437

Emotional intelligence, 437
Empiricism, 3–4
Encounter groups, 616
Endocrine system (glandular), 71–74
Endorphins, 37, 54, 190
Engineering psychology, 18, 204
Engrams, 331
Enkephalins, 54
Environment
 and development, 84, 87, 488
 enriched, 113–115
 and intelligence, 114–115, 388–389, 391–392,
  396–397
 and schizophrenia, 578–579
Environmental psychology, 18, A9–A16, A26–A28
 crowding, A10–A12, A14–A15
 noise pollution, A12–A13
 problem solving, A14–A16
 toxic environments, A13–A14
Episodic memory, 318
Erectile disorder, 470–471
Ergotism, 599
Erickson, E., 13, 126–129, 146
ESB, see Electrical stimulation of the brain
Escape learning, 296–297
Ethics of psychological research, 46–48
Eugenics, 121, 390
Euthanasia, 160
Evolutionary psychology, 647–648
Exhibitionism, 462
Existential theory of anxiety, 570
Existential therapy, 602–603, 618
Experimental group, 35–36
Experimental method, 28–30, 31, 34–38, 42
Experimental psychologist (research psychologist),
  13, 18, 20
Experimenter influence (effect), 38
Extinction, 278–279, 285, 304, 610–613
 effects of punishment on, 295
Extraneous variables, 35–36
Extrasensory perception (ESP), 228–231
Extrinsic motives, 424
Extroversion, 482, 484, 493
Eye, structure of, 169–174
 and emotional expression, 428
 eye movement desensitization, 610
Eyewitness testimony, 225–226, 315–316, 320, 326
Eysenck, H. J., 484, 601

Facial agnosia, 68
Facial feedback hypothesis, 435–436
Fact memory, 317–318
Fallacy of positive instances, 25
Familial retardation, 388–389
Family therapy, 615–616, 618
Fantasy,
 and creativity, 362
 as a defense mechanism, 530
Fantz, R., 90–91
Farsightedness (hyperopia), 170–171
Fear, 70, 280–281, 306–307, 425, 427–429, 434,
  436–437
Feedback (in learning), 288–290, 303, 333, 538–539,
  A16, A22
Female sexual arousal disorder, 471
Festinger, L., 642
Fetal alcohol syndrome, 88
Feuerstein, R., 392
Field experiment, 36–37
Figure-ground organization, 202
Five-factor model of personality, 486
Fixation, 357–358, 491
Fixed action pattern (FAP), 306
Fixed interval (FI) reinforcement, 291, 292
Fixed ratio (FR) reinforcement, 291

Flat affect, 572
Flexitime, A7
Forebrain, 68, 69–70
Forensic psychologist, 18
Forgetting, 311, 312, 313–314, 324–330
Fouts, D. and R., 354
Fovea, 170, 173
Fragile-X syndrome, 390
Frankl, V., 603
Free association, Freudian, 600
Free will, 13, 603
Frequency distribution, B3
Freud, S., 12–13, 245–246, 266, 456, 461, 489–492,
  495, 497, 530, 531–532, 569–570, 600–601,
  602, B4
Friedman, M., 504
Frontal lobe, 39, 65, 66
Frontal lobotomy, 621–622
Frustration, 518, 525–527, 547–548
 and aggression hypothesis, 681–682
 coping with, 547–548
 reactions to, 526–527
 sources of, 525–526
Fugue, 568
Functional fixedness, 357–358
Functional psychotic disorders, 573, 574–582
Functionalism, 9, 13

Galvanic skin response (GSR), 429
Gardner, B. and A. Gardner, 353
Gardner, H., 394
Gating,sensory, 190–191
Geller, U., 228, 230–231
Gender
 androgyny, 452–454
 anxiety disorders, 565
 bias, 41, 556
 and brain lateralization, 67
 cultural differences, 450–451
 depression, 584
 development, 446–450
 dimensions of, 448
 disorders, 558, 562
 and emotion, 432
 friendship, 644–645
 and happiness, 157
 identity, 446, 450, 497–498
 and IQ, 384–385
 loving and liking, 645–646
 mate preference, 642–644, 647–648
 menopause vs climacteric, 147
 midlife transitions, 146
 moral reasoning, 142–143
 personal space, 637–638
 psychology of, 6, 18
 psychosocial differences, 449–450
 and rape, 465
 risk taking, 36–37
 roles, 450–452, 497–498
 role socialization, 450, 451–452
 role stereotypes, 451, 465
 sexual harassment, 41
 social learning, 497–498
 study of, 6
 and touching, 636
 women in psychology, 12
General adaptation syndrome (G.A.S.), 541–542
Generalization, 279, 292–293, 607, 613
Genes, 85–86
Genetics, 120–122
 behavioral, 391, 487–488, 579
 counseling, 120–121
 engineering, 121–122
 and sexual orientation, 458
Genital stage, 492

Genius, 386–387
Gerontology, 149–150
Gestalt psychology, 11, 13, 203–206
Gestalt therapy, 603–604, 618
Giantism, 71
Gilligan, C., 142–143
Ginott, H., 117
Glandular system (endocrine), 71–74
Glove anesthesia, 569, 570
Goals, 404–405
   superordinate, 678–680
Goleman, D., 437
Goodall, J., 31
Gordon, T., 117–118
Gould, R., 145–146
Graphical statistics, B2–B3
Graphology, 23–24
Graphs, 33–34
Gregory, R., 200, 219
Grief, (see bereavement)
Group(s), 634–636, 649–650
   conflict, 675–680
   conformity, 140–141, 649–650
   cults, 671–673
   membership, 140–141, 351, 634–635, 666
   membership and attitudes, 666
   norms, 635–636
   peer, 140–141
   prejudice, 674, 675–680
   reference, 668
   sanctions, 650
   status, 635
Group therapy, 598, 615–617, 627
   encounter, 616
   family therapy, 615–616, 618
   group awareness training, 616–617
   psychodrama, 615, 618
   sensitivity, 616
Groupthink, 650
Growth hormone, 71, 72
Growth sequence, human, 86

Habits, breaking bad, 250, 303–304
Habituation, 221, 227
Hall, C., 245, 266
Hallucinations, 572
   and illusions, 218
   during sleep deprivation, 234, 263
Hallucinogen, 263
Halo effect, 504, 642, A4
Hand dominance, 74–77
Happiness, 156–158, 541
Hardin, G., 660
Harlow, H. F., 97–98
Health, 518–550
Health psychology, 18, 518–522
Hearing, 179–183
   absolute thresholds, 167, 182
   artificial, 181
   loss, 181–183
   stimulus for, 179
   and temporal lobe, 66
   theories of, 181
Helping (prosocial behavior), 684, 685–688
Helping a troubled person, 618–620
Helplessness, learned, 532–534, 584, 681, A13
Hemispheres of the brain, 61–64, 74–77
   specialization, 62–64, 67–68, 74–77
Heredity,
   and development, 84–87, 119–122, 487–488
   and homosexuality, 458
   and intelligence, 390–392
   and personality, 487–488
   and schizophrenia, 579
   and sociobiology, 691–692

Hermaphroditism, 448–449, 450
Hess, E., 428
Heuristics, 356, 367
Hierarchy, constructing, 625
   use in desensitization, 607–609
Hindbrain, 68–69
Hippocampus, and memory, 70, 79, 331
History of psychology, 8–16
HIV, 466–469
Hobson, A., 246
Holmes, T., 535, 536
Homeostasis, 406, 415
Homogamy, 644
Homophobia, 459
Homosexuality, 458–459
Honesty tests, 508
Hormones, 71–73
   growth, 71, 72
   sex, 71, 73, 448–449, 455–456, 458
   and the sex drive, 414
   sleep, 238
Horney, K., 493
Hospice, 159
Hospitalization, 584–586, 587
Hostility, 541
Hubel, D., 173, 189
Human factors engineering, 204
Humanistic psychology, 13–15
Humanistic-existential theory of anxiety, 570
Humanistic theory of personality, 483, 499–502, 503
Humanistic therapies, 602–604
Hunger, 334, 406–413
   causes, 406–409
   cultural factors in, 410
   and the hypothalamus, 407–408
   and taste, 410–411
Hydrocephaly, 389
Hyperactivity in children, (ADHD), 134, 135
Hyperopia (farsightedness), 170–171
Hypnogogic images, 250
Hypnotism, 247–249
   and memory, 248, 316, 335
Hypochondria, 537, 569
Hypoglycemia, 407, 681
Hypothalamus, 69, 72
   and hunger, 407–408
Hypothesis, 28–29, 30
Hysteria, 600

Id, 489–491, 570
Identity disorders, 568
Illusions, perceptual, 218–219
Images,
   eidetic, 321–323
   guided, 546
   kinesthetic, 347
   and thought, 344, 345–347
   3–D, 346
Imitation, (see modeling)
Immune system, 542
Implicit memory, 321
Impotence in males, 470–471
Imprinting, 95–96
Independent variable, 35–36
Industrial psychology, 9, 18, 20, A2–A8
Infant
   attachment, 96–97, 99, 131
   cognition, 108, 111
   day care, 97
   depth perception, 207
   effects of deprivation and enrichment, 112–115
   emotion, 93–94, 131
   intelligence, 90
   maturation, 91–92
   motor development, 92–93

Infant, (continued)
   parental influence, 96, 99–102
   prelanguage communication, 103–105
   reflexes, 89–90
   self-awareness, 94
   sensory stimulation, 114–115
   sleep, 237, 243–244
   social development, 94–95, 97
   social referencing, 94–95
   sudden infant death syndrome, 243–244
   temperament, 87
   vision, 90–91
Inferential statistics, B7
Innate behavior, 306, 307
Insanity defense, 562, 591–592
Insight therapy, 598, 600–604, 615–617
Insomnia, 240–242
Instinctive drift, 307
Instincts, 306–307, 680–681
Instrumental learning, (See operant conditioning)
Intellectualization, 530
Intelligence, 378–400
   and achievement, 385–386
   and aging, 149–150
   artificial, 289, 359–360
   in childhood, 107–112, 113–115
   and creativity, 364
   definition of, 379
   distribution of, 384
   environmental factors in, 114–115, 388–389, 391–392, 396–397
   genius and gifted, 386–387
   hereditary factors in, 390–392
   in infants, 90
   mental retardation, 378, 388–390
   multiple, 394
   and the nervous system, 393, 394
   pluralistic testing, 394–400
   and poverty, 113
   sex differences in, 384–385
   teaching, 392
   twin studies, 391
   variations in, 384–386
Intelligence tests, 379, 380–384, 394, 396–400
   aptitude, 379, 380
   and cultural bias, 396–397
   Dove Test, 396
   evaluating, 396–398
   group tests, 384
   reliability, 380
   SOMPA, 399–400
   Stanford-Binet, 380–383, 385
   validity of, 380
   Wechsler, 383, 384, 385
Intergroup conflict, 675–680
Internet, xlvi-xlvii
Interpersonal attraction, 642–648
   romantic love, 435, 440–442, 645–647
   social exchange theory, 645
Interviews, 504, 667–668, A3–A4
   cognitive, 335
   computer, 504
Intrinsic motives, 423–424
Introspection, 8
Introversion, 482, 484, 493
Intuition, 366–367
Inverted-U function, 416, 417
IQ, 378, 380–388, 391–394, 396–400
   and achievement, 385–386
   and creativity, 364
   and environment, 388–389, 391–392, 396–397
   and race, 396–397
Iris, 170, 171
Ishihara test (for color blindness), 177
Izard, C., 93, 94, 435

James, W., 9, 202, 434, 436
James-Lange theory (of emotion), 434
Janis, I., 650, 669, A8
Jet lag, 418–419
Jigsaw classrooms, 679
Job
    analysis, A3
    burnout, 524
    choice, 143–144
    communication, A23–A25
    efficiency, A6
    enrichment, A8
    interviews, A3–A4
    management A5–A7
    satisfaction, A7
    stressful, 523
Johnson, V., 460, 461, 462, 470, 471, 473
Jourard, S., 226, 475–476
Jung, C., 13, 481–482, 493–494
Jury,
    behavior, 225, A18–A19
    death-qualified, A20
    selection, A19–A20
Just noticeable difference (JND), 167–168

Kagan, J., 91, 396
Kahneman, D., 366–367
Kamin, L., 397
Kaplan, H., 472
Keating, J., A2
Kennel, J., 131
Kinesics (body language), 432–433
Kinesthetic imagery, 347
Kinesthetic sense, 186–188
Kinsey, A., 455, 464
Klaus, M., 131
Knowledge, of results, 288–289, 333
Kohlberg, L., 141–143
Kohler, W., 372
Kosslyn, S., 322, 345, 347
Kübler-Ross, 153

Lange, C., 434, 436
Language, 63–64, 66, 76, 344, 350–354
    American Sign Language, 352
    bilingualism, 351
    development, 103–106
    use by animals, 353–354
    structure of, 351–353
    and social status, 105
    and thought, 350–354
Large group awareness training, 616
Latanæ, B., 686
Latent learning, 298, 299
Lateralization of the brain, 61–64, 67–68, 74–77
Law and psychology, 562, 591–592, A18–A20
Law of effect, 282
Lazarus, R., 524, 537
Learned helplessness, 532–534, 584, 681, A13
Learned motives, 405, 419–422
    opponent-process theory, 174–175, 419–420
Learning, 275–307
    aids, 288, 289–290
    biological constraints, 306–307
    cognitive, 298–299
    definition of, 275
    discovery, 298–299
    disorders, 134
    effects of feedback on, 288–290, 333, 538–539
    escape and avoidance, 296–297
    forced teaching, 387
    latent, 298, 299
    maturation and, 91–93
    motor, A22

Learning, (continued)
    noise, effects of, A12–A13
    observational, 300–302
    perceptual, 214–219
    recitation and, 333
    review and, 334
    sleep, 235
    self-regulated, 304–305
    state dependent, 326–327
    study of, 4–5, 18
    transfer of training, 328–329
    whole versus part, 333
Learning theory, 495–498, 503
Lens of the eye, 170, 171
Lesbianism, 459
Lesioning, 58
Levinson, D., 146
Lie detection, 37, 429–430
    behavioral, 433
    polygraph, 37, 429–430
    life change and illness, 535–538
Lilly, J., 234
Limbic system, 70
Linear perspective, 211
LISAN study method, xliii
Living will, 159–160
Lobes, of the cerebral cortex, 64–66
Lobotomy, 39, 621–622
Localization of function, 166–167
Loftus, E., 315, 339, A2
Loftus, G., 221
Logical reasoning, 366–367
Logotherapy, 603
Long-term memory, 312–313, 314–318, 324–325, 327, 331
Lorenz, K., 95–96, 681
Love, romantic, 435, 440–442, 645–647
Lucid dream, 268

Major mood disorders, 583–584
Marijuana, 252–253, 263–265
Maslow, A., 13–14, 226, 422–423, 499–500, 503
Massed practice, 334
Masters, W., 460, 461, 462, 470, 471, 473
Masturbation, 457–458
Maternal influence (on development), 96, 99–102, 131
Mate selection, 644, 647–648
Maturation, and learning, 91–92
McCarley, 246
McClelland, D., 398, 421
McConnell, J., 671
MDMA ("ecstasy"), 255
Mean (statistical), 133
Median, B4
Medical psychologist, 18
Medical therapies, 620–622
Meditation, 545, 548–550
Medulla, 66, 68, 69
Melatonin, 72–73, 419
Meltzoff, A., 90
Melzack, R., 190, 193
Memory, 311–340
    chemical studies of, 330–331, 332
    constructive processing, 315–316
    declarative, 317–318
    and dream sleep, 245
    drug effects on, 330–331
    dual, 313
    episodic, 318
    exceptional, 321–324
    fact, 317–318
    false memory syndrome, 338–340
    flashbulb, 329–330
    formation, 314–318, 330–332

Memory, (continued)
    and hypnotism, 248, 316
    imagery in, 321–323, 336
    implicit, 321
    improving, 323–324, 330–331, 333–338
    interference, 327–328
    and the limbic system, 70
    long term, 312–313, 314–318, 324–325, 327, 331
    measurement of, 319–321
    network model of, 316–317
    priming, 321
    recoding, 314
    recovered, 338–340
    redintegrative, 317
    rehearsal, 333
    semantic, 318
    sensory, 312
    serial position effect, 320, 333
    short term memory (STM), 312, 313–314, 324–325, 327, 331
    skill (procedural), 317–318
    stages of, 311–313
    traces, 325, 331
    types, 318
Menopause, 147, 448
Mental disorders, 558–559
Mental retardation, 378, 388–390
Mercer, J., 399–400
Mesmer, F., 247
Meta analysis, 36–37
Meta needs, 422
Microcephaly, 389
Microsleep, 236
Midbrain, 68, 69
Midlife crisis, 146
Milgram, S., 47, 634, 652–654, A12
Miller, G., 314
Miller, N., 496, 497
Minnesota Multiphasic Personality Inventory-2 (MMPI-2), 506–507
M'Naghten rule, 591
Mnemonics, xliii–xliv, 323, 336–338
Mode, B4
Modeling (observational learning), 300–302, 498, 683, A22
Mood disorders, 558, 560, 582–584
    major, 583–584
Moon illusion, 213, 214
Moore, K., 90
Moral development, 141–143
Moreno, J. L., 615
Moriarty, T., 656
Motion parallax, 212–213
Motion sickness, 194–196
Motivation, 404–424
    arousal theory, 415–416
    definition, 404
    intrinsic and extrinsic, 423–424
    model of, 404–405
    types of, 405
Motives,
    hierarchy of, 422–423
    intrinsic and extrinsic, 423–424
    learned, 405, 419–422
    perception and, 221–222, 227
    primary, 405, 406–409, 413–414
    secondary, 405, 419–422
    social, 420–422
    stimulus, 405, 415–417
    types of, 405
Motor cortex, 66, 80
Motor development, 92–93
Motor skills learning, A22
Mozart effect, 115
MRI,
    functional, 59

Pleasure centers, 286–287
Plutchik, R., 425–426
Polls, public opinion, 40–41
Polygraphs, 37, 429–430
Ponzo illusion, 214
Population growth, A10–A12
Pornography, 683
Positive correlation, 32–34
Positive psychology, xxxi
Positive reinforcement, 610, 612
Positron emission tomography (PET), 59–60, 62, 563, 580–581
Postpartum depression, 131–132
Post-traumatic stress disorders, 568
Poverty, 113
   and language development, 105
Precognition, 228
Prefrontal lobotomy, 39, 621–622
Prejudice, 674–680
   combating, 678–680, 688–690
Premack, D., 303, 353
Premack principle, 303
Premature ejaculation, 472
Prenatal development, 86, 87–88, 448–449
Prepared childbirth, 130–131
Presbyopia, 171
Primary emotions, 425–426
Primary motives, 405, 406–409, 413–414
Primary reinforcement, 286–287
Problem solving, 344, 355–358, 359, 368–371
   approaches, 355–358
   and brainstorming, 370–371
   in animals, 372–374
   creative, 361–367, 368–371
   difficulties in, 358, 366–367, 368–370
   and dreams, 268, 362
   using images, 345–347
   insight in, 356–357
   and intuition, 366–367
   tests of, 363
Procedural memory, 317–318
Procrastination, xliv
Professional help, how to find, 625–628
Programmed instruction, 289
Projection, 530, 531
Projective tests, 508–509
Prosocial behavior, 684, 685–688
Prototypes, 348–349
Proxemics, 636–637
Pseudopatient research, 556–557
Pseudo-psychologies, 23–25
Psi phenomena, (see psychic phenomena)
Psychiatric labels, 556–557
Psychiatric social worker, 19
Psychiatrist, 17, 19, 626
Psychic phenomena (psi phenomena), 44, 228–231
Psychoactive drugs, 251–265, 269–271
Psychoanalysis, 12, 19, 600–601, 618
Psychoanalysts, 17, 19
Psychoanalytic psychology, 12–13, 15
Psychoanalytic theory of personality, 489–492, 503
Psychodrama, 615, 618
Psychodynamic,
   theory of anxiety, 569–570
   theory of dreams, 245–246
   theory of personality, 12–13, 14, 15, 483, 489–494, 503
   therapy, 600–601
Psychokinesis, 228, 230
Psychologist, 17–20, 626
   media, 604
Psychological disorders, 554–593
   anxiety disorders, 558, 560, 564–571
   and bias, 555–556
   causes, 561–562
   civil rights, 592–593

Psychological disorders, (continued)
   classifying, 557–562
   defining, 554–556
   features, 556, 557
   levels of functioning, 556, 557
   medical model, 592
   personality disorders, 558, 560, 562–563
   psychosis, 572–573, 583
   sexual disorders, 561
   and violence, 578
Psychological research, 4–6, 19, 28–48
   and ethics, 46–48
Psychology
   animals in the study of, 6, 31–32, 47–48
   careers in, 18, 19–20
   defined, 2
   goals of, 6–8
   history of, 8–16
   and the law, 562, 591–592
   as a science, 4
   women in, 12
Psychometrics, 7
Psychopathology, 554–593
   classifying, 557–562
   defining, 554–556
   and violence, 578
Psychophysics, 167–169
Psychosexual stages, 491–492
Psychosis, see psychotic disorders
Psychotic disorders, 558, 572–582, 583, 584–587
   affective, 583–584
   characteristics of, 572–573
   delusional disorders, 574–575
   functional, 573, 574–582
   organic, 573–574
   major mood disorders, 583–584
   paranoid, 574–575, 576
   schizophrenia, 575–582, 587
   treatment, 584–587
Psychosocial dilemmas, 126–129
Psychosomatic disorders, 535–542
Psychosurgery, 621–622
Psychotherapy, 584, 597–630
   bibliotherapy, 627
   comparison of approaches, 597–598, 617–618
   cybertherapy, 604–605
   defined, 597
   effectiveness, 617
   history, 598–600
   media, 604
   telephone, 604
Puberty, 73, 86, 138
Punishment, 286, 294–297, 623–624
   and aggression, 297
   in behavior therapy, 611
   effects of, 296–297
Pupil, 170, 171

Questionnaires, personality, 506–608

Racism, 674, 688–690
Rape, 465–466, 683
Rating scales, 505
Rational-emotive therapy, 614–615, 618
Rationalization, 530, 531
Reaction formation, 530
Reactive depression, 583
Readiness, principle of, 92–93
Reality testing, 226, 227
Recall, memory, 319–320, 334–335
Reciprocal inhibition, 607
Recoding, memory, 314
Recognition, memory, 320
Recovered memory, 338–340

Redintegration, memory, 317
Reflex, 57, 276, 277, 280
   arc, 57
   in infants, 89–90
Regression, 530, 531
Rehearsal, memory, 314, 333
Reinforcement, 275, 278, 282–292, 296, 298, 303, 304, 496–497, 610–613
   covert, 624
   delayed, 284
   negative, 285–286
   partial, 290–292
   response contingent, 283–284
   secondary, 287–288
   social, 288
   value, 496
Relative motion, 212–213
Relative size, 211
Relaxation, 545–546
   exercises to achieve, 548–550, 624–625
   and insomnia, 242
   response, 549
   and sensory deprivation, 250
Relearning, memory, 321
Reliability, of tests, 380, 506
REM behavior disorder, 240, 241
REM (rapid-eye-movement) sleep, 239–240, 242–243, 244–246, 266–268
REM rebound effect, 245
Remission, spontaneous, 601
Representative sample, 40–41
Repression, 12, 329, 530
Research, 19–20, 28–48
   and ethics, 46–48
   methods, 4–6, 28–48, 229–230
   report, 30
Resistance, Freudian, 600
Response chains, 284, 304
Retardation, mental, 378, 388–390
Reticular activating system, 69
Reticular formation (RF), 69
Retina, 170, 171, 172, 173, 174, 189
Retinal disparity, 208–209
Rhine, J. B., 229
Risperdal, 620–621
Ritalin, 134
Rods, 171–174, 178, 189
Rogers, C., 13, 499, 500–501, 502, 570, 602
Role(s),
   and behavior, 634–635
   conflict, 634
   confusion, 128
   gender, 451–452
   group, 634–635
Rorschach Inkblot Test, 508, 509
Rosenhan, D., 556–557
Rosenman, R., 540
Rotter, J., 496
Rubin, Z., 646

Sample (representative), 40–41, B7
Savant syndrome, 378
Scapegoating, 527, 674
Scatter diagram, B7–B8
Schachter, S., 434, 436
Schachter's cognitive theory of emotion, 443
Schizophrenia, 568, 575–582, 587
   catatonic, 575, 576–577
   causes, 578–582
   disorganized, 575, 576
   paranoid, 576, 577
   pharmacotherapy, 620–621
   stress-vulnerability model, 582
   undifferentiated, 576, 578
Schizotypal personality, 576

Index of Names

Bertholf, M., 510
Berthoz, A., 346
Bertsch, G.J., 295
Best, J.B., 313
Bettelheim, B., 532
Beumont, P.J.V., 412
Beyerstein, B.L., 24, 539
Bhatt, R.S., 166
Bibace, R., 469
Bickman, L., 635
Bigelow, A.E., 89
Biglan, A., 521
Bigler, E.D., 70
Binder, V., 613
Binet, A., 380, 401
Binks, P.G., 236
Biondi, M., 542
Birch, J., 133, 177
Birren, J.E., 148, 151
Bjork, R.A., 45, 248, 249, 422, 549
Blackmore, S., 154, 230
Blackwell, R.T., 505
Blakemore, C., 215
Blake, W., 227
Blanchard, E.B., 539
Blanck, P.D., 47
Blane, H.T., 261
Blaustein, A.R., 692
Block, J., 451
Bloomfield, H.H., 621
Bloom, J., 105
Bloom, J.W., 421, 605
Blumberg, M.S., 31
Boergers, J., 589
Bohan, J.S., 12
Bohannon, J.N., 105
Bohart, A.C., 602
Boivin, D.B., 426
Bokenkamp, E.D., 412
Bolger, R., 334
Bolles, R.C., 283
Bonanno, G.A., 155
Bond, R., 650
Bongard, S., 540
Booker, J.M., 585
Book, H.E., 601
Bootzin, R.R., 242
Borlongan, C.V., 79
Borman, W.C., 697, 698, 699
Bornstein, M.H., 87, 102, 105
Bornstein, R.E., 556
Borod, J.C., 63
Borodovsky, L.G., 629
Borrie, R.A., 250, 251
Boschker, M.S.J., 347
Bosse, R., 152
Bottela, C., 609
Botvin, G.J., 521
Bouchard, T.J., 391, 488
Boutros, N.N., 560
Bower, G.H., 91, 314, 325, 327, 336
Bowermaster, D., 160
Bowers, K.S., 248, 316, 329, 560
Bowling, A.C., 394
Boyatzis, C.J., 302
Bradley, R.H., 114, 672
Bransford, J., 110
Bransford, J.D., 349
Braun, A.R., 239
Braungart, J.M., 87
Brawman-Mintzer, O., 565
Breedlove, S.M., 448, 449, 450, 451
Brenner, V., 297
Bresler, D.E., 192
Breslow, L., 520
Bressi, C., 579

Brewer, J.S., 461
Brewer, M.B., 676
Bridges, K.M.B., 93, 94
Brigham, J.C., 714
Brinkman, H., 637
Brody, N., 383, 385, 392
Brooks-Gunn, J., 94, 138
Brothers, J., 45
Brotons, M., 421
Broughton, R.J., 243
Broughton, W.A., 243
Brower, K.J., 73
Brown, B., 269
Brown, B.B., 704
Brown, B.R., 467
Brown, G.M., 419
Brown, J.D., 114
Brown, R., 319, 419
Brown, R.L., 90, 614
Brown, R.T., 201
Brown, S.A., 254
Brown, T.D., 618, 677
Brown, T.L., 114
Browne, B.A., 452, 463
Brownell, K.D., 410, 440
Brownlee, S., 186
Bruce, D., 334
Bruch, M.A., 432
Brugger, P., 229
Bruner, J., 90
Bruner, J.S., 106, 224
Bryan, J.H., 36, 300, 332, 687
Bryant, B., 20
Bryant, D.M., 389, 465
Buch, K., 701
Buchanan, R.W., 620
Buck, L.A., 183, 598
Buckelew, S.P., 539
Buckhout, R., 225
Budney, A.J., 264
Bugelski, R., 674
Bullinger, M., 706
Bundrick, C.M., 499
Burchinal, M., 97
Burgess, C.A., 248, 316
Burgner, D., 640
Burke, E.R., 524
Burlingame, G.M., 615
Burnham, D.K., 450
Burns, D.D., 613
Burtt, H.E., 320
Bushman, B.J., 681
Buss, A.H., 450, 511, 642
Buss, D.M., 647, 648
Butcher, J.N., 554, 563, 579
Butler, R., 415
Buunk, B.P., 526
Byers, E.S., 472
Byravan, A., 453
Byrd, K.R., 340
Byrnes, J.P., 37, 634, 649, 689

Cabanac, M., 410
Cahill, S.P., 610
Caldera, Y.M., 452
Calhoun, J.B., 465, 547, 705
Calhoun, P., 344
Calkins, M., 12
Calle, E.E., 518
Calley, W., 652
Calment, J., 149
Caltabiano, M.L., 524
Calvert, S.L., 521
Camatta, C.D., 534
Cameron, L.D., 546
Campbell, F.A., 114, 392

Campbell, J.B., 484, 627
Campfield, L.A., 407
Campion, M.A., 698, 702
Campos, A., 207, 336, 347
Camras, L.A., 93
Canivez, G.L., 382
Canli, T., 427
Cann, A., 547
Cannon, I., 148
Cannon, T.D., 406, 578, 579
Cannon, W.B., 407, 434, 436
Cao, Y., 56
Caplan, N., 449, 450
Caplan, P.J., 556
Capner, M., 524
Capron, C., 392
Carducci, B.J., 511
Carey, A.R., 257
Carey, J.C., 418, 470
Carli, L.L., 644
Carlsmith, J.M., 670
Carlson, C.L., 53, 65, 70, 72
Carlson, J.G., 179, 187
Carlson, J.M., 682, 683
Carlson, M., 134
Carnahan, 289
Carney, R.N., 336, 337
Carpenter, K., 412
Carpenter, K.M., 261, 616
Carrigan, M.H., 610
Carroll, J.M., 431, 504
Carroll, L., 322, 347
Carson, R.C., 554, 563, 579
Carter, R., 51, 58, 64
Carter, W.E., 264
Cartwright, R., 245, 246, 266, 267, 268
Caspi, A., 644
Casto, S.D., 391
Catalano, R., 527
Cattani-Thompson, K., 617
Cattell, R.B., 397, 485, 486
Cautela, J.R., 605, 623, 624
Cavalli-Sforza, L.L., 689
Cecil, H., 258
Ceci, S.J., 397
Chabris, C.F., 114
Chaiken, S., 669
Chakos, M.H., 620
Challinor, M.E.
Chamberlin, J., 586
Chan, G.C., 265
Chan, R.W., 458
Charness, N., 422
Charren, P., 683
Chartrand, T.L., 433
Chase, R., 323, 591
Cheadle, A., 521
Check, J., 465
Cheek, J., 511
Cheng, H., 56
Chen, Z., 650
Cheriff, A.D., 547
Chesky, 192
Chess, S., 87, 100, 133
Chiarello, C., 64
Chiras, D.D., 188
Chisholm, K., 113
Chissoe, 120
Chiu, L.H., 297
Chollar, S., 245
Chomsky, N., 104
Chow, K.L., 216
Christensen, A., 79
Christensen, D., 626, 627
Christian, A.G., 392
Christiansen, B.A., 269

Kempermann, G., 78
Kempton, W., 708
Kennard, M., 586
Kennedy, J.F., 329
Kennedy, J.M., 205, 650
Kennedy, P., 79
Kennedy, P.R., 206
Kenneth, M., 261
Kenrick, D., 3
Kessler, R.C., 568, 584, 646
Ketcham, K., 315
Kety, S.S., 573, 599
Keveri, M.K., 319
Kevorkian, J., 160
Keyes, C.L., 147
Kiecolt-Glaser, J.K., 542
Kieffer, S.C., 639
Kihlstrom, J.F., 40, 248, 347
Kilcoyne, J., 463
Killen, J.D., 257
Kim, A., 644
Kim, J., 717
Kimball, M.M., 301
Kimble, G.A., 3
Kimmel, A.J., 46, 126, 458, 459
Kimmel, D.C., 459, 460
King, A., 281
King, K.B., 116
King, L.A., 70, 157
King, M.L., 329
King, R., 651
Kinsey, A., 455
Kipnis, D., 7
Kirby, J.R., 333
Kirk, M.A., 147, 722
Kirschenbaum, D.S., 439
Kirsch, I., 37, 38, 247, 248, 316
Kisilevsky, B.S., 87
Kitayama, S., 102, 432, 483
Kitcher, P., 692
Klatzky, R.L., 675
Klebanoff, M.A., 257
Klein, G., 40, 45
Kleinke, C.L., 436, 717
Kleinknecht, R.A., 427
Kleinplatz, P.J., 473
Klimoski, R.J., 24
Klintsova, A.Y., 332
Klohnen, E.C., 129
Kloner, R.A., 429
Klonoff-Cohen, H.S., 243
Knee, C.R., 639
Knesper, D.J., 620
Knowles, J., 467
Knox, D., 473
Knutson, J., 136
Kobos, J.C., 604
Koenig, S.M., 243
Koepke, J.E., 89
Kohlberg, L., 141, 162
Kohler, L., 216
Kohn, A., 424, 621
Kolb, B., 78, 79, 332
Kolbe, L.J., 519, 520
Konarski, R., 524
Konner, M., 99
Koocher, G.P., 46
Kooper, R., 609
Kopplin, D.A., 17
Kopta, S.M., 618, 620
Koresh, D., 672
Korte, C., 634
Kosslyn, S.M., 322, 345, 346, 347
Koss, M., 465, 466
Kotkin, M., 617
Kottler, J.A., 614, 618

Koulack, D., 330
Koutstaal, W., 316
Kozulin, A., 392
Krakau, I., 540
Krakow, B., 243
Kramer, D.L., 319
Kramer, R.K., 676
Kratofil, P.H., 254
Krebs, D.L., 143
Kring, A.M., 432
Krishnan, K., 410
Krivacska, J.J., 459
Krokoff, L.J., 473
Kroon, M.B., 650
Kropp, P., 539
Krosnick, J.A., 40, 41, 168
Krueger, J., 640
Kruger, J., 192, 483
Kruger, L., 190
Kuban, M., 683
Kübler-Ross, E., 153
Kubovy, M., 203
Kuhl, P.K., 88, 90, 91, 104, 109, 112
Kumar, R., 612
Kunze, C., 67
Kunzendorf, R.G., 322
Kupfer, D.L., 621
Kusseling, F.S., 468

Laan, E., 455, 456
La Berge, S., 268
Labov, W., 348
Lacayo, A., 256
Lachman, M.E., 313, 534
Lackner, J.R., 194
Lacks, P., 242
Ladd-Franklin, C., 12
Lafreniere, K.D., 413
Lagarde, D.P., 237
Lal, S.K.L., 539
Lamaze, F., 130
Lamb, M.R., 220
Lambert, M.J., 245, 246, 266, 267, 617
Lambert, W.E., 689
Lamme, V.A.F., 202
Lampley, B.W., 121
Lance, C.E., 504
Landers, S., 400, 565, 582
Landis, T., 229
Landy, F.J., 698, 699
Lange, C., 434, 436
Langenbucher, J.W., 556, 558
Langer, E.J., 224
Lantz, J., 603
Lanzetta, J.T., 690
Lapidus, L.B., 213
LaPointe, J.A., 504
Larner, A.J., 188
Larrick, R.P., 682
Larsen, R.J., 426
Larson, C.A., 257
Larson, D.E., 472, 574, 710
Lashley, K., 331
Latan, L., 7, 686
Lategan, T.P., 453
Lattal, K.A., 292
Lattanzi-Licht, M., 159
Latty-Mann, H., 646
Laumann, E., 455, 456, 458, 464
Laursen, B., 140
Lavallee, A.C., 31
Lawler, K.A., 143, 519
Lawrence, B., 383
Lawson, M.J., 337
Lay, C., 140, 483
Lazarus, A.H., 523

Lazarus, R.S., 524, 525, 530, 537, 608
Lebiere, C., 312
Lecomte, D., 589
LeDoux, J., 70, 427, 491
Lee, C.C., 61, 289
Lee, M., 510
Lee, R.T., 630
Lee, T.D., 629
Leenaars, A.A., 589
Leeper, R.W., 223
Lefcourt, H.M., 547
Lefkowitz, M., 648
Lehman, D.R., 439, 483
Leibel, R.L., 410
Leikind, B., 44
Lemley, B., 382
Lensenweger, M.F., 575, 579, 580
Leonard, C.M., 67
Leor, J., 429
Lepore, S.J., 706
Lepper, M.R., 290, 424
Lerner, R.M., 691, 692
Leslie, K., 268
Lett, J., 37
Lettvin, J., 166
Leutwyler, K., 134
Levant, R.F., 452
LeVay, S., 458
Leventhal, E.A., 192
Levesque, M.F., 56
Levin, D., 326
Levin, J.R., 336, 337
Levine, J.M., 627, 635
Levine, M., 622
Levine, R., 703
Levinson, D.J., 146
Levitin, D.J., 78
Levy, W.J., 229
Lewis, M., 94, 95
Lewis, P.S., 701, 702
Lewy, A.J., 585
Liberman, R.P., 612
Lichtenstein, E., 259
Lidderdale, J.M., 132
Liebert, R.M., 92
Liebeskind, 192
Liebeskind, J.C., 190
Lierens, R., 599
Light, 289
Lightsey, O.R., 521
Lilienfeld, S., 44, 610
Lillienfeld, S.O., 509
Lincoln, A., 485
Linde, K., 241, 418, 621
Lindemann, B., 185
Lindenberger, 149–151
Linder, D.E., 660
Lindsay, E.W., 100, 340
Linford, K.M., 640
Linton, D., 91
Linton, M., 329
Linz, D., 683
Lipman, J.J., 190
Lipschitz, D.S., 568
Lipsey, M.W., 269, 617
Lissner, 410
Little, B., 157, 158, 386
Liu, X., 66
Lobo, L.L., 244
Loeber, R., 683
Loewi, O., 267
Loftus, E., 40, 225, 311, 315, 339, 340
Loftus, G., 221, 315
Lohr, J.M., 610
LoLordo, V.M., 532
Long, D.M., 453

Long, E.C., 173, 190
Long, G.M., 474
Long, J.D., 305, 605
Lonner, W.J., 15, 689
López, S.R., 400, 562
Lorenz, K., 95, 96, 681
Lore, R.K., 681
Lovaas, I., 135
Lovaas, O., 611
Lovallo, W.R., 540
Low, K.G., 87, 585
Lubart, T.I., 424
Luborsky, L., 601, 627
Lucas, F., 409
Luccina, L., 186
Ludwig, T.D., 710
Luiselli, J.K., 518
Lumley, V.A., 134
Lumsden, C., 692
Lundy, R., 247
Luria, A., 323
Luskin, F.M., 549
Luster, T., 114
Luszcz, M.A., 332
Luxem, M., 92, 93
Lydiard, R.B., 565
Lykken, D.T., 429, 430, 488, 563
Lynn, S.J., 37, 247, 248
Lyubonirsky, S., 541
Lyznicki, J.M., 236

Maas, J., 236
Mabry, J.H., 289, 714
Maccoby, E.E., 451
MacCoun, R.J., 269, 270
MacFarlane, S., 3
MacHovec, F., 154
Mack, J.E., 589
Mackenzie, B.D., 394
Mackey, M.C., 131
Mackie, D.M., 689
Mackin, R.S., 544
Mackworth, N., 221
Maclan, P., 455
MacLeod, K.M., 425
Macy, P., 47
Maddi, K.L., 540
Maddi, S.R., 541
Madigan, S., 12
Madon, S., 38
Madsen, C.H., 611
Magee, W.J., 566, 567
Magid, K., 563
Magritta, R., 250
Maguire, E.A., 70
Mahadevan, R., 323
Maier, N.R.E., 547
Ma, J., 325
Major, B., 636
Makela, E., 710
Malamuth, N.M., 465, 683
Malgady, R.G., 538
Malinosky-Rummell, R., 136
Malnic, B., 183
Maloney, A., 494
Malott, J.M., 193
Mandler, J.M., 90
Mann, L., 669
Manning, M., 77
Manschreck, T.C., 574
Mansouri, A., 572
Mantyla, T., 333
Marcus-Newhall, A., 682
Marcus, S.C., 504
Marecek, J., 449
Margolin, G., 684

Margolskee, R.F., 184
Marion, S.L., 504
Marks, D.F., 228, 229, 231
Markus, H., 102, 432, 483, 502
Marlatt, G.A., 254, 269, 440
Marmor, J., 459, 616
Marrs, R.W., 627
Marsella, A.J., 704
Marshall, P.H., 336
Martens, R., 24
Martin, L.L., 436
Martin, M.A., 716
Martin, P.Y., 644
Martin, S., 12, 334, 534
Marx, B.P., 465
Marx, J.A., 627
Maslach, C., 524
Maslow, A.H., 13, 14, 226, 422, 423, 499, 500, 503
Masse, L.C., 269
Masters, W.H., 460–462, 470, 471
Masuda, M., 535
Matheny, K.B., 546
Mathews, D., 449
Mathews, M.D., 701
Matias, R., 93
Matillo, G.M., 302
Matossian, M.K., 599
Matson, J.L., 283
Matsuda, L.A., 263
Matthews, D.B., 524
Mattock, A., 201
Mattson, S.N., 88
Mauer, M.H., 248
Maupin, E.W., 549
Maurer, T.J., 151
Mauthner, N.S., 131
Maxwell, K.L., 389
Mayer, J.D., 9
Mayer, R.E., 350, 437
Mazzie, C., 106
McAuslan, P., 465
McBride, W.J., 287
McCabe, M.P., 471
McCann, S.L., 237
McCardel, K., 617
McCarley, R.W., 238, 246
McCarrell, N.S., 349
McCarthy, K., 68, 473
McCartney, G.R., 76
McCartney, K., 86, 488
McCarty, R., 6
McCaul, K.D., 193
McCleary, R., 588
McClelland, D.C., 386, 398, 420, 421, 497, 547, 578, 702
McClelland, L., 710
McConnell, W., 527
McCormick, J., 261
McCoy, N.L., 184
McCrae, R.R., 481, 486, 487
McDaniel, M.A., 299, 336
McDermott, K.B., 316
McDonald, C., 258
McDonald, S.M., 452
McDonough, L., 90
McEachen, J.J., 135
McFarland, C., 642
McGaugh, J.L., 330
McGee, M.G., 638
McGinnies, E., 168
McGinnis, J.M., 518, 519, 520
McGregor, D., 157, 700
McGregor, I., 158
McIntosh, W.D., 436, 534, 642
McKay, G., 117, 118, 629
McKean, K., 41, 532

McKeever, L.M., 177
McKelton, D., 714
McKenna, K.Y.A., 650
McKensie-Mohr, D., 707
McKim, W.A., 255, 259, 260
McKinley, J.C., 507
McKinzie, S.J., 412
McKnight, J.D., 524
McLaren, W., 258
McLauglin, S., 184, 612
McLennan, J., 534
McLoyd, V., 113
McLuhan, M., 666
McMahon, K., 202
McManus, I.C., 76
McMurdo, M.E., 178
McNally, R.J., 409
McNeill, D., 319
McRoberts, C., 615
McWilliams, P., 621
Mead, M., 450
Medin, D.L., 320
Mednick, M.T., 143
Mehren, E., 97
Meichenbaum, D., 685
Meleshko, K.G., 644
Melnick, M.T., 39
Melton, G.B., 459
Meltzoff, A.N., 88, 90, 91
Meltzoff, J., 30, 33, 104, 109, 112
Melzack, R., 190, 192, 193
Mendolia, M., 329
Menzies, R.G., 608, 613
Mercer, J.G., 408
Merckelbach, H., 281, 610
Merenda, P.F., 505
Merikle, P.M., 169, 421
Mermelstein, R., 606
Merrill, M.A., 382, 385
Merritt, J.M., 245
Mervis, C.B., 348
Mesmer, F., 247
Mesquita, B., 427
Messick, D.M., 660, 689
Meyer, I.H., 254, 430, 459
Meyer, R.G., 459, 521
Meyer-Bahlburg, H.F.L., 458
Meyer-Bisch, C., 183
Meyers, T., 244
Meyer, T., 609
Michailko, M., 344, 386
Michelangelo, 344
Michel, D.E., 93, 192
Michie, P.T., 264
Michotte, A., 204
Mickelson, K.D., 646
Middlemist, R.D., 46
Mielke, H.W., 573
Mikulincer, M., 644, 646
Milet, T.H., 132
Milgram, S., 47, 634, 652–654, 706
Milk, H., 591
Miller, A.H., 37, 186
Miller, D.T., 284, 350, 439, 642
Miller, G., 471, 497
Miller, G.A., 528, 542
Miller, L.C., 567
Miller, L.K., 636, 644
Miller, M., 535
Miller, N., 408, 496
Miller, N.E., 674, 681
Miller, S.D., 627
Miller, T.Q., 682, 687
Miller, W.C., 540
Miller-Jones, D., 397
Millon, T., 562

Peters, L., 504, 677
Peterson, B.E., 129, 675
Peterson, B.R., 712
Peterson, J., 333, 436
Peterson, P.L., 17
Peterson, S.E., 314
Petrie, T.A., 717
Petri, H., 404
Petruzzi, D.C., 417
Pettigrew, T.F., 680
Pettit, G.S., 100
Petty, R.E., 667, 669, 670
Phillips, D.P., 109
Phillips, J.L., 588, 656
Piaget, J., 107–108, 110
Picard, 722
Piccione, C., 248
Piedrahita, L.E., 383
Pierce, J.P., 259
Pierce-Otay, A., 644
Pike, J.L., 542
Piliavin, I.M. & J.A., 687
Pillard, R.C., 458
Pillow, D.R., 537
Pilon, D.A., 497
Pinel, P., 439, 600
Pines, A.M., 648
Pinsof, W.M., 616
Pisacreta, R., 284
Pithers, W., 575
Pittman, T., 424
Piven, J., 135
Platt, D.E. & R.C., 588
Plaud, J.J., 607
Pliner, P., 410, 412
Plomin, R., 391, 579
Plug, C., 213
Plutchik, R., 425, 426
Podolski, C., 302
Pogatchnik, S., 301
Polce-Lynch, M., 432
Pollard, P., 683
Pollner, M., 504
Pollock, V.E., 563, 681
Poole, W.K., 429
Pope, H.G., 264
Porac, C., 76
Porte, D., 408
Posluszny, D.M., 518, 545
Posner, M.I., 78
Postman, L., 224
Potashkin, B.D., 539
Potkay, C.R., 481, 482
Poulin, J., 524
Poulton, R.G., 571
Powell, A.L., 152, 412, 453
Pratkanis, A.R., 168
Preiser, R., 720, 721
Preisler, J.J., 536
Prentice, D.A., 636, 642
Pressley, M., 334, 337
Pressman, J.D., 622
Priluck, 279
Proite, R., 465
Proust, M., 603
Puca, R.M., 420
Pursch, J.A., 256

Quevillon, R.P., 17
Quillian, K.A., 316, 317
Quinlan, K.A., 159, 160, 260
Quinn, P.C., 111, 166
Quitkin, F.M., 37

Raag, T., 452
Rabasca, L., 19

Raboy, B., 458
Rackliff, C.L., 452
Rader, P.E., 418
Radetsky, P., 468
Rafaeli, A., 24
Rahe, R., 535, 536
Raison, C.L., 45
Ramachandran, V.S., 172, 212
Ramanaiah, N.V., 453
Ramey, C.T., 114, 392
Ramirez-Valles, J., 466, 468
Ramona, G., 339
Ramona, H., 339
Rana-Deuba, A., 538
Randi, J., 228, 230, 231
Rando, T.A., 155
Rank, O., 13, 493
Raskin, R., 446
Raven, B.H., 651
Raymond, C., 111
Ray, W.J., 247
Razzoli, E., 579
Read, D., 168
Read, J., 470, 471, 472
Reagan, R., 574, 580, 650
Reder, L.M., 312
Reed, J.D., 220
Reed, S.K., 333, 334
Reeves, A., 79
Regan, P.C., 645
Regard, M., 229
Register, C.A., 270
Reid, H.M., 645
Reif, L.V., 155
Reiff, S., 280
Reifman, A.S., 682
Reik, P., 67
Reinecke, M.A., 613
Reiser, B., 322
Reis, H.T., 441, 647
Reisner, A.D., 340
Reiss, M., 76
Reiterman, T., 672
Remland, M.S., 637
Rende, R., 391, 579
Renner, M.J., 544
Reno, R.R., 636
Renwick, P.A., 143
Repacholi, B.M., 95
Reppucci, N.D., 136, 270, 465, 468, 521
Rescorla, R.A., 278
Reyner, L.A., 236
Reynolds, S., 601
Rhine, J.B., 228, 229
Ricci-Bitti, P.E., 431
Ricci, L.C., 584
Rice, K.M., 563
Rice, M.E., 578
Richards, L., 157, 656
Richards, R., 446
Richardson, F.C., 688
Richelle, M.N., 11
Richman, C.L., 678
Rideout, B.E., 114
Rieber, R.W., 568
Riefer, D.M., 319
Rieke, M.L., 508
Righter, E.L., 565
Ring, K., 154
Risley, T.R., 105, 115
Ritchie, R.J., 699
Roan, S., 72, 487
Robbins, R., 278, 292, 296
Robertson, T.S., 669
Roberts, R., 31, 138, 140
Roberts, R.E., 537

Roberts, S.M., 611
Roberts, S.M., 608
Robins, R.W., 14
Robinson, A., 387, 394
Robinson, B., 394, 672
Robinson, C., 230
Robinson-Riegler, B., 336
Rodewalt, F., 639
Rodin, J., 409, 410
Roeder, K., 391
Roediger, H.L., 316, 320
Rogers, C., 13, 499, 500–502, 570, 602–603
Rogers, C.R., 98, 168, 269, 417, 572
Rogers, J.M., 586
Rogers, J.R., 588
Rogerson, J., 281
Rogler, L.H., 538
Rohsenow, D.J., 614
Roizen, M.F., 149
Rokeach, M., 675
Rollerson, B., 656
Rolling, B.L., 133
Rollman, G.B., 414
Rompre, P.P., 70
Ronen, T., 133
Roos, 454
Rorer, L.G., 487
Rorschach, H., 508
Rosch, E., 348
Rose, K.J., 390, 392
Rose, R.J., 487, 488
Rosenbaum, M.B., 410, 569
Rosenberg, I.B., 209, 431
Rosenblith, J.F., 88
Rosenfeld, P., 671
Rosenhan, D., 556
Rosenman, R., 540
Rosenstiel, T.B., 40
Rosenthal, N.E., 546
Rosenthal, R., 38
Rosenthal, T.L., 29, 300, 464, 585, 606, 608
Rosenzweig, M.R., 17, 113
Ross, D.C., 209, 213
Ross, J., 424, 465
Ross, M., 320
Rothbaum, B.O., 609
Rothman, S., 379
Rotter, J.B., 496
Rovee-Collier, C., 92, 111
Rowe, J.W., 149, 301
Rowe, W., 421
Rowell, A., 710
Rubenstein, C., 464
Rubin, D., 318
Rubin, V., 264
Rubin, Z., 646
Ruscio, J., 424
Rushton, J.P., 61
Russell, T., 421
Russell, T.G., 431, 465
Russo, M.B., 569
Rutledge, T., 436
Rutter, M., 87
Ruzzene, M., 640
Ryan, R.M., 420, 423, 424
Ryba, N.J.P., 184
Rye, D.B., 60
Ryff, C.D., 147, 158

Sadker, M. & D., 498
Sadowski, C., 589
Saegert, S., 642
Sagan, C., 678
Sagi, A., 96
Saklofske, D.H., 3
Saks, M.J., 40

Credits

age Works; **569:** © Myrleen Ferguson / Photo-Edit; **572:** © David Young-Wolff / PhotoEdit; **573:** © Joe Sohm / The Image Works; **574:** © Dirck Halstead / Liaison Agency; **576:** © Barbara J. Feigles / Stock Boston; **577:** left, © Grunnitus / Monkmeyer; right, © Bruce Ely / Liaison Agency; **578:** © Sygma; **580:** © Derek Bayes / Courtesy Guttmann-Maclay Life Picture Service; **581:** left, © Dennis Brack / Black Star; center, © Duke University Hospital; right, © The Brookhaven Institute; **584:** © Dennis Coon; **585:** © Dan McCoy / Rainbow; **586:** top, © Peter Southwick / Stock Boston; bottom, © David M. Grossman

Chapter 18 596: top, © Will & Deni McIntyre / Photo Researchers; bottom left, © D. Greco / The Image Works; bottom right, © Larry F. Hidges, Thomas C. Meyer, Rob Kooper; **598 :** © Danielle Pellegrini / Photo Researchers; **599:** left, © Demon from "The Temptation of St. Anthony," by Martin Schonganer. Treasury of Fantastic and Mythological Creatures by Richard Huber. Dover, 1981; top right, © Mary Evans Picture Library / Photo Researchers; bottom right, © CORBIS / Bettmann; **600:** © Archive / Photo Researchers; **602:** Courtesy of Dr. Natalie Rogers; **604:** © D. Greco/ The Image Works; **607:** © Curt Gunther / Camera 5; **608:** © Teresa Zabula / Uniphoto; **609:** top, Courtesy of Dr. Albert Bandura; bottom left, Larry F. Hidges, Thomas C. Meyer, Rob Kooper; bot-

tom right, © Georgia Tech Telephoto; **616:** © Joel Gordon; **619:** © Gilles Mingasson / Liaison Agency; **621:** © Will & Deni McIntyre / Photo Researchers

Chapter 19 633: top, © Joel Gordon; bottom right, © AP / Wide World Photos; bottom middle, © Joe Sohm / The Image Works; bottom left, © Anthony Wood / Stock Boston; **635:** © Bonnie Kamin / PhotoEdit; **637:** © Spencer Grant / PhotoEdit; **638:** © AP / Wide World Photos; **640:** © Esbin-Anderson / The Image Works; **641:** © Mark Richards / PhotoEdit; **642:** © Jeff Greenberg / Rainbow; **643:** © Joe Sohm / The Image Works; **644:** © Frank Siteman / Stock Boston; **645:** © David Young-Wolff / PhotoEdit; **648:** © Anthony Wood / Stock Boston; **649:** © Juneart 1983, The Image Bank; **651:** © Bill Swersey / Liaison Agency; **652:** © From the film "Obedience," by Stanley Milgram, The Pennsylvania State University, Audio Visual Services; **654:** © Billy E. Barnes / PhotoEdit; **656:** © Michael Newman / PhotoEdit

Chapter 20 664: top, © David Young-Wolff / PhotoEdit; bottom right, © Sotographs / Liaison Agency; bottom left, © Joel Gordon; **666:** © Sotographs / Liaison Agency; **668:** left, © Ulrike Welsch / PhotoEdit; right, © Joel Gordon; **671:** © Mark Antman / The Image Works; **672:** © Dallas Morning News / Liaison Agency; **673:** © Spencer Grant; **675:** © Vic Bider / PhotoEdit; **676:** © David Young-Wolff / PhotoEdit; **677:** © AP /

Wide World Photos; **678:** © Mary Kate Denny / PhotoEdit; **679:** © Charles Gupton / Stock Boston; **681:** © Dennis Brack / Black Star; **682:** © Robert Ginn / PhotoEdit; **685:** © The Photo Works / Photo Researchers; **686:** © Joel Gordon

Appendix A A-1: bottom left, © Richard Pasley / Stock Boston; bottom right , © Charles Gupton / Stock Boston; top, David Hanover Photography; **A-3:** Photograph courtesy of the General Electric Company; **A-4:** © David Young-Wolff / PhotoEdit; **A-5:** © Lawrence Migdale / Stock Boston; **A-6:** © David Young-Wolff / PhotoEdit; **A-9:** © F. Pedrick / The Image Works; **A-10:** © Joel Gordon; **A-11:** © Laura Dwight / CORBIS; **A-12:** © Peter Finger / Stock Boston; **A-13:** top right, © UNEP / Photog / The Image Works; bottom left, © Jeff Greenberg / Photo Researchers; top left, © Martin Jones, Ecoscene / CORBIS; **A-15:** bottom, © 1994 Peter Ginter / Peter Menzel / MATERIAL WORLD, © 1994 Peter Ginter / MATERIAL WORLD; top, © 1994 Peter Ginter / Peter Menzel / MATERIAL WORLD, © 1994 Peter Ginter / MATERIAL WORLD; **A-16:** © Cleo / PhotoEdit; **A-17:** © Charles Gupton / Stock Boston; **A-18:** © Tim Street-Porter / Esto; **A-19:** © Pool / Liaison Agency; **A-20:** right, © Richard Pasley / Stock Boston; left, © Tony Savion / The Image Works; **A-21:** © Bonnie Kamin / PhotoEdit;

Appendix B B-1: © Dennis Coon.

TO THE OWNER OF THIS BOOK:

I hope that you have found *Introduction to Psychology: Gateways to Mind and Behavior,* **Ninth Edition,** useful. So that this book can be improved in a future edition, would you take the time to complete this sheet and return it? Thank you.

School and address: _____

_____

Department: _____

Instructor's name: _____

1. What I like most about this book is: _____

_____

_____

2. What I like least about this book is: _____

_____

_____

3. My general reaction to this book is: _____

_____

_____

4. The name of the course in which I used this book is: _____

_____

5. Were all of the chapters of the book assigned for you to read?_____

   If not, which ones weren't? _____

6. In the space below, or on a separate sheet of paper, please write specific suggestions for improving this book and anything else you'd care to share about your experience in using this book.

_____

_____

_____

_____

_____

OPTIONAL:

Your name: ______________________________ Date: ________________

May we quote you, either in promotion for ***Introduction to Psychology: Gateways to Mind and Behavior,* Ninth Edition,** or in future publishing ventures?

Yes: __________ No: __________

Sincerely yours,

Dennis Coon

FOLD HERE

NO POSTAGE
NECESSARY
IF MAILED
IN THE
UNITED STATES

BUSINESS REPLY MAIL

FIRST CLASS PERMIT NO. 358 PACIFIC GROVE, CA

POSTAGE WILL BE PAID BY ADDRESSEE

ATTN: Lisa Gebo, Executive Editor

BROOKS/COLE/THOMSON LEARNING
511 FOREST LODGE ROAD
PACIFIC GROVE, CA 93950-9968

FOLD HERE